Key to map pages

Urban area mapping

Birmingham	202-203
Bournemouth	191
Bradford & Leeds	214-215
Bristol	196
Cardiff & Newport	195
Coventry	204
Derby & Nottingham	206-207
Edinburgh	217
Glasgow	218-219
Greater Manchester	212-213
Leeds & Bradford	214-215
Leicester	205
Liverpool	210-211
London	198-201
Manchester	212-213
Merseyside	210-211
Milton Keynes	197
Newcastle upon Tyne	216
Newport & Cardiff	195
Nottingham & Derby	206-207
Plymouth	190
Portsmouth & Southampton	192-193
Sheffield	209
Southampton & Portsmouth	192-193
Stoke-on-Trent	208
Swansea	194
West Midlands	202-203

54-55 Road mapping

Birmingham — Urban area maps

● Oxford — City and town centre plans

● LONDON — Central London map

City and town centre plans

Aberdeen	227
Bath	227
Belfast	188
Birmingham	228
Blackpool	228
Bournemouth	229
Bradford	229
Brighton	230
Bristol	230
Cambridge	231
Canterbury	231
Cardiff	232
Carlisle	232
Cheltenham	233
Chester	233
Coventry	234
Derby	234
Dover	235
Dublin	189
Dundee	235
Durham	236
Eastbourne	236
Edinburgh	237
Exeter	237
Folkestone	238
Glasgow	238
Gloucester	239
Guildford	239
Harrogate	240
Hastings	240
Hereford	241
Inverness	241
Kingston upon Hull	242
Leeds	242
Leicester	243
Lincoln	243
Liverpool	244
Manchester	244
Middlesbrough	245
Milton Keynes	245
Newcastle upon Tyne	246
Norwich	246
Nottingham	247
Oxford	247
Plymouth	248
Portsmouth	248
Reading	249
Salisbury	249
Sheffield	250
Southampton	250
Stoke-on-Trent	251
Stratford-upon-Avon	251
Sunderland	252
Swansea	252
Swindon	253
Torquay	253
Watford	254
Weston-super-Mare	254
Winchester	255
Windsor	255
Worcester	256
York	256

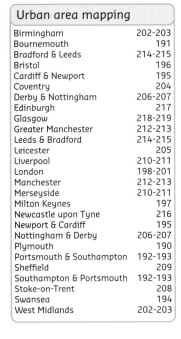

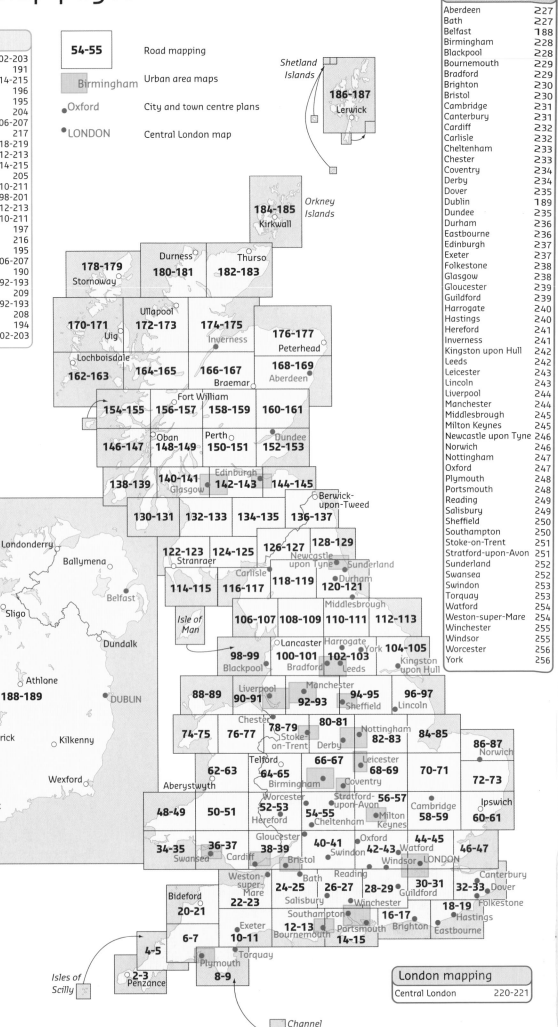

London mapping

Central London — 220-221

Road Atlas of Britain

Contents

Information	ii-xiii
Key to map symbols	ii-iii
Route planning maps	iv-ix
Restricted motorway junctions	x-xi
Motorway services information	xii-xiii

Road mapping	**2-189**
England, Wales & Southern Scotland (3.2 miles to 1 inch)	2-161
Northern Scotland (4.2 miles to 1 inch)	162-187
Ireland (25 miles to 1 inch)	188-189

Urban area mapping	**190-219**
Plymouth	190
Bournemouth	191
Southampton & Portsmouth	192-193
Swansea	194
Cardiff & Newport	195
Bristol	196
Milton Keynes	197
London	198-201
West Midlands	202-203
Coventry	204
Leicester	205
Derby & Nottingham	206-207
Stoke-on-Trent	208
Sheffield	209
Merseyside	210-211
Greater Manchester	212-213
Leeds & Bradford	214-215
Newcastle upon Tyne	216
Edinburgh	217
Glasgow	218-219

London mapping	**220-226**
Central London (5 inches to 1 mile)	220-221
Index to London street names	222-226

City and town centre plans	**227-256**
Aberdeen	227	Kingston upon Hull	242
Bath	227	Leeds	242
Birmingham	228	Leicester	243
Blackpool	228	Lincoln	243
Bournemouth	229	Liverpool	244
Bradford	229	Manchester	244
Brighton	230	Middlesbrough	245
Bristol	230	Milton Keynes	245
Cambridge	231	Newcastle upon Tyne	246
Canterbury	231	Norwich	246
Cardiff	232	Nottingham	247
Carlisle	232	Oxford	247
Cheltenham	233	Plymouth	248
Chester	233	Portsmouth	248
Coventry	234	Reading	249
Derby	234	Salisbury	249
Dover	235	Sheffield	250
Dundee	235	Southampton	250
Durham	236	Stoke-on-Trent	251
Eastbourne	236	Stratford-upon-Avon	251
Edinburgh	237	Sunderland	252
Exeter	237	Swansea	252
Folkestone	238	Swindon	253
Glasgow	238	Torquay	253
Gloucester	239	Watford	254
Guildford	239	Weston-super-Mare	254
Harrogate	240	Winchester	255
Hastings	240	Windsor	255
Hereford	241	Worcester	256
Inverness	241	York	256

Index to Britain	**257-291**
Index to Ireland	**292**
Distance chart	293

Published by Collins
An imprint of HarperCollins*Publishers*
77-85 Fulham Palace Road, Hammersmith, London W6 8JB

www.collins.co.uk

Copyright © HarperCollins*Publishers* Ltd 2005

Collins® is a registered trademark of HarperCollins*Publishers* Limited

Mapping generated from Collins Bartholomew digital databases

The grid on this map is the National Grid taken from the Ordnance Survey map with the permission of the Controller of Her Majesty's Stationery Office.

Printed in Italy

MDE

e-mail: roadcheck@harpercollins.co.uk

Key to map symbols

Route planning maps — Pages iv-ix

M25	Motorway	Road proposed or under construction		National boundary	
4 — 5	Motorway junction with full / limited access	Gradient / Toll		River	
Fleet / Killington Lake	Motorway service area	Tunnel		Canal	
A82	Primary route with dual / single carriageway	Car ferry route		National / Forest park	
A894	'A' road with dual / single carriageway	Bristol	Airport	886	Summit height in metres
	'B' road	International boundary		Channel Tunnel	

Road maps — Pages 2-189

M5	Motorway	Roundabout		Hythe	Seaside destination
M6Toll	Toll motorway	4	Road distance in miles between markers		National boundary
8 — 9	Motorway junction with full / limited access		Road tunnel	KENT	County / Unitary Authority boundary and name
Maidstone / Birch / Sarn	Motorway service area with off road / full / limited access		Steep hill (arrows point downhill)		National Park boundary
A556	Primary route with dual / single carriageway	Toll	Level crossing / Toll		Forest / Regional Park boundary
Peterhead	Primary route destination	St. Malo 8hrs(10hrs)	Car ferry route with journey times; daytime and (night-time)		Woodland
	Primary route destinations are places of major traffic importance linked by the primary route network. They are shown on a green background on direction signs.		Railway line / station / tunnel	Danger Zone	Military range
A30	'A' road dual / single carriageway	South Downs Way	National Trail / Long Distance Route	468 · 941 ▲	Spot / Summit height (in metres)
B1403	'B' road dual / single carriageway	✈	Airport with scheduled services		Lake / Dam / River / Waterfall
	Minor road	Ⓗ	Heliport		Canal / Dry canal / Canal tunnel
	Road with restricted access	Ⓟ	Park and Ride site (operates at least 5 days a week)		Beach
	Roads with passing places		Built up area		Lighthouse
	Road proposed or under construction	□ □ □	Settlement	SEE PAGE 206	Area covered by urban area map
24	Multi-level junction (occasionally with junction number)				

0	490	985	1640	2295	2950	feet
water 0	150	300	500	700	900	metres

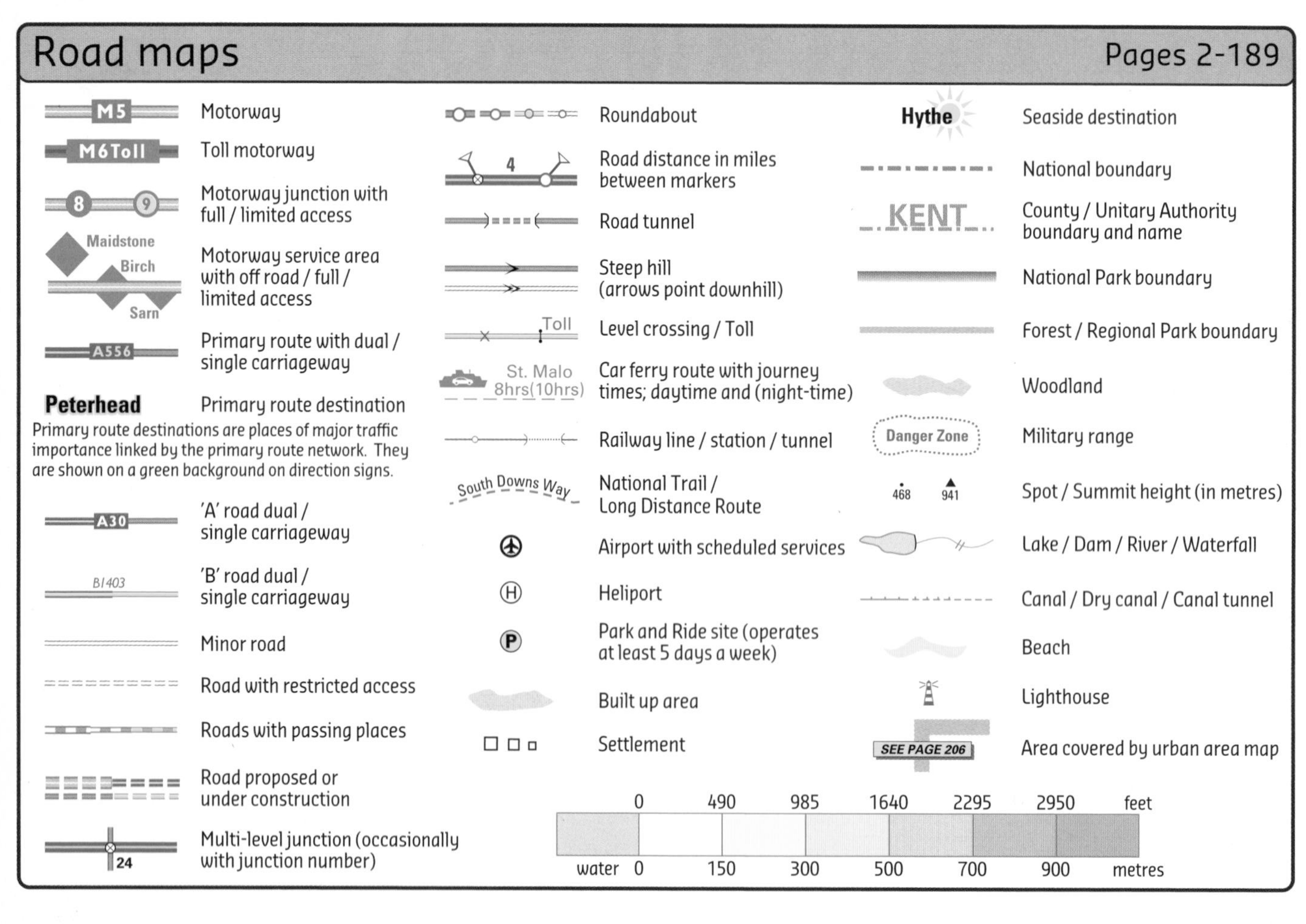

Tourist information

A selection of tourist detail is shown on the mapping. It is advisable to check with the local tourist information centre regarding opening times and facilities available.

ℹ	Tourist information centre (open all year)	✠	Ecclesiastical building		Preserved railway
ⓘ	Tourist information centre (open seasonally)	⚽	Football club (Major British club)		Racecourse
m	Ancient monument	❋	Garden		Spotlight Nature Reserve
	Aquarium	⛳	Golf course		Theme park
✕ 1643	Battlefield	🏛	Historic house		University
▲	Camp site / Caravan site	£	Major shopping centre / Outlet village		Wildlife park / Zoo
	Castle	🏆	Major sports venue	★	Other interesting feature
	Country park	🏁	Motor racing circuit	(NT)	National Trust property
		🏛	Museum / Art gallery	(NTS)	National Trust for Scotland property
			Nature reserve		

Urban area maps

Pages 190-219

12 13	Motorway junctions with full access
14 15	Motorway junctions with limited access
LEICESTER SERVICES	Motorway service area
M6 Toll	Toll motorway
A316	Primary route with dual / single carriageway
A4054	'A' road with dual / single carriageway
B7078	'B' road with dual / single carriageway
	Minor road with dual / single carriageway

≡≡≡ ∷∷∙∙∙∙	Road proposed or under construction
	Road tunnel
○ ○ ○ ○	Roundabout
T	Toll
→	One way street
✕	Level crossing
P	Park and Ride site (operates at least 5 days a week)
Dublin 8hrs	Car ferry with destination
	Airport with scheduled services
	Railway line / Railway tunnel

⇌ •	Railway station / Light rail station
⊖ Ⓢ	Underground station
	Congestion Charging Zone
	Public building
362 ▲	Spot height in metres
	Built up area
	National Park
	Woodland / Park
BRISTOL	County / Unitary Authority boundary and name
SEE PAGE 231	Area covered by town plan

Central London map

Pages 220-221

A4	Primary route with dual / single carriageway
A302	'A' road with dual / single carriageway
B240	'B' road
	Other road
→ •	One way street / Access restriction
	Street market / Pedestrian street
∷∷∷∷∷-----	Track / Path
	Congestion charging zone
P	Car park
----⊖----	Pedestrian ferry with landing stage

⇌ ⇌	Main / Other national railway station
⊖	London Underground station
⬯	Bus or coach station
i	Tourist information centre
🎥 🎦	Cinema / Theatre
⊠	Major hotel
⌐USA	Embassy
WC	Public toilet
+ ☾	Church / Mosque
✡ ■Mormon	Synagogue / Other place of worship

▪POL Fire Sta ■PO	Police station / Fire station / Post office
	Leisure and tourism
	Shopping
	Administration and law
	Health and welfare
	Education
	Industry and commerce
	Park / Garden / Sports ground
	Borough boundary
	Postal district boundary

City and town centre plans

Pages 227-256

	Motorway
	Primary route with dual / single carriageway
	'A' road with dual / single carriageway
	'B' road with dual / single carriageway
	Other road with dual / single carriageway
	Restricted access street
	Pedestrian street

	Path / Footbridge
←	One way street
P	Car park
P	Park and Ride site (operates at least 5 days a week)
⇌	Railway line / station
⑧	Glasgow Subway station
Ⓜ	Metro station
•	Light rail station

+	Ecclesiastical building
🄸 i	Tourist information centre (open all year / seasonally)
	Tourist building
	Important building
	Higher Education building
	Hospital
✝	Cemetery
	Recreational area / Open space

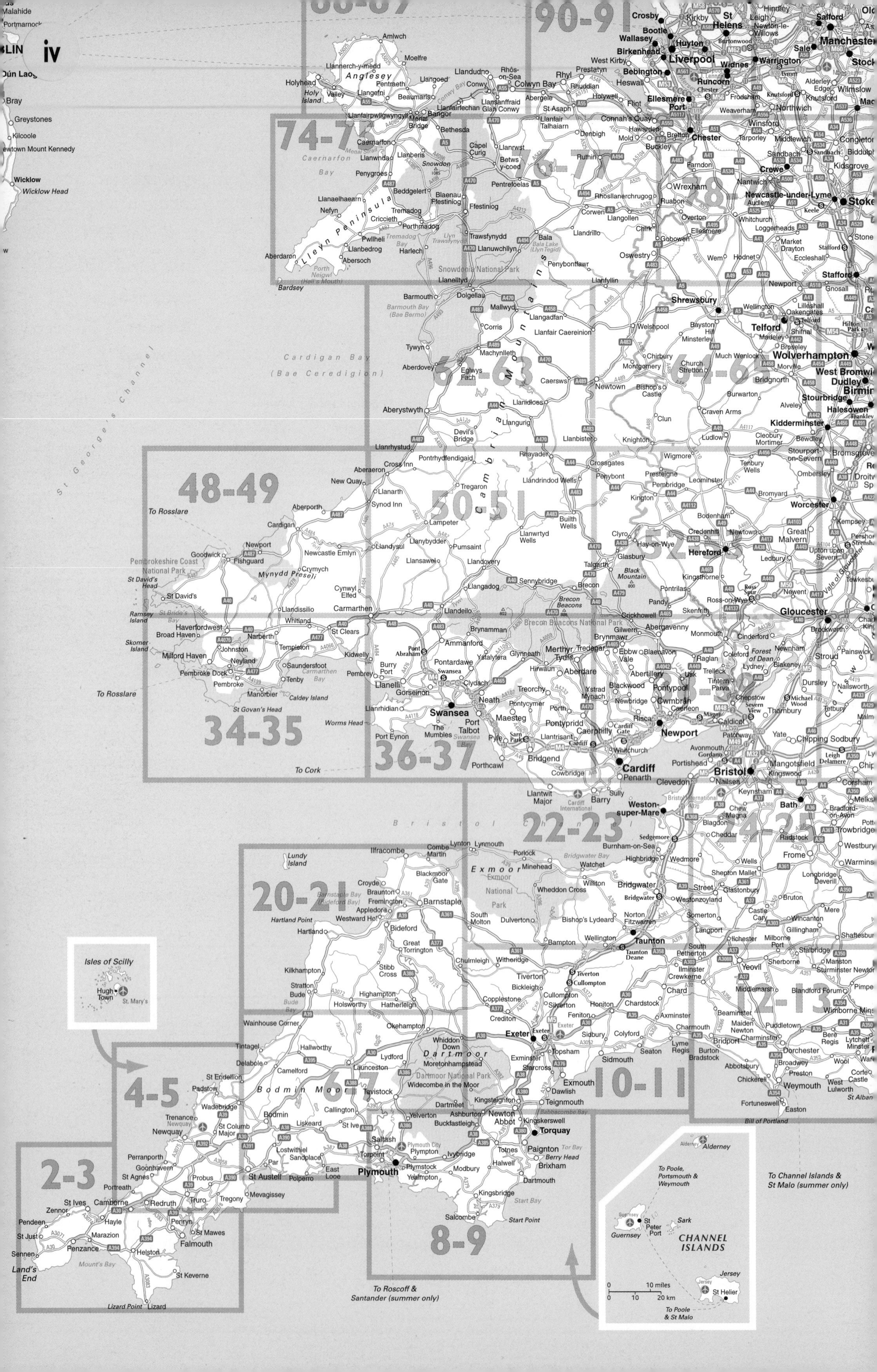
90-91
74-75
76-77
78-79
62-63
64-65
48-49
50-51
52-53
34-35
36-37
38-39
22-23
24-25
20-21
12-13
10-11
6-7
4-5
2-3
8-9
Isles of Scilly
Hugh Town
St. Mary's
CHANNEL ISLANDS
Alderney
Guernsey
St Peter Port
Sark
Jersey
St Helier
To Poole, Portsmouth & Weymouth
To Poole & St Malo
To Channel Islands & St Malo (summer only)
To Roscoff & Santander (summer only)
To Rosslare
To Cork
Cardigan Bay
(Bae Ceredigion)
St George's Channel
Bristol Channel
Anglesey
Holy Island
Lleyn Peninsula
Snowdonia National Park
Cambrian Mountains
Pembrokeshire Coast National Park
Brecon Beacons National Park
Exmoor National Park
Dartmoor National Park
Bodmin Moor
Lundy Island
Land's End
Lizard Point
Bill of Portland
Liverpool
Manchester
Chester
Wrexham
Shrewsbury
Telford
Wolverhampton
Hereford
Worcester
Gloucester
Swansea
Cardiff
Newport
Bristol
Bath
Taunton
Exeter
Torquay
Plymouth
Falmouth
Penzance
Weymouth
Aberystwyth
Carmarthen
Bangor
Holyhead
0 10 miles
0 10 20 km

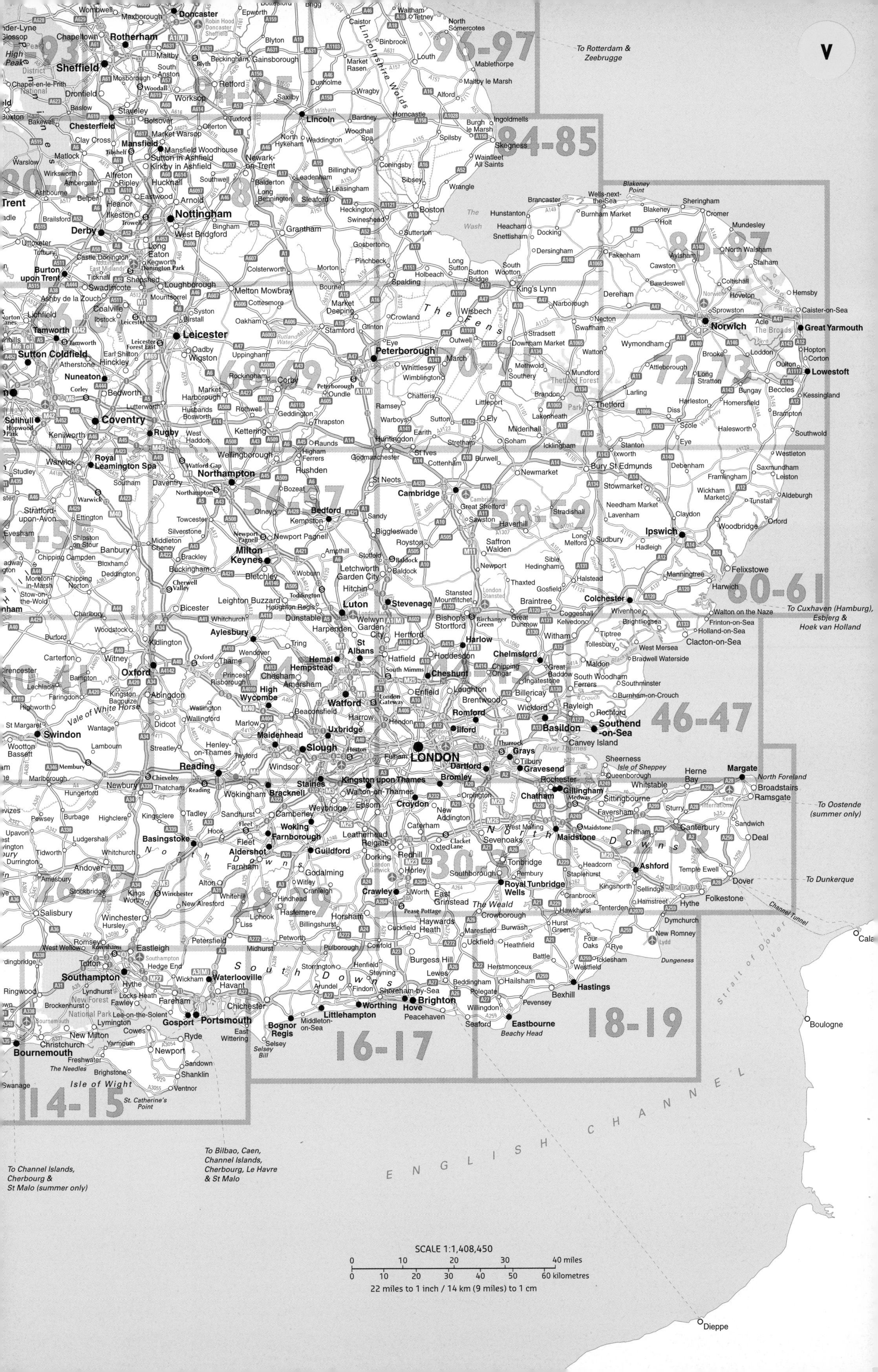
V
96-97
94-95
84-85
86-87
80-81
66-67
68-69
70-71
72-73
54-55
56-57
58-59
60-61
40-41
42-43
44-45
46-47
26-27
28-29
30-31
32-33
14-15
16-17
18-19
To Rotterdam & Zeebrugge
To Cuxhaven (Hamburg), Esbjerg & Hoek van Holland
To Oostende (summer only)
To Dunkerque
To Channel Islands, Cherbourg & St Malo (summer only)
To Bilbao, Caen, Channel Islands, Cherbourg, Le Havre & St Malo
ENGLISH CHANNEL
Strait of Dover
Channel Tunnel
Calais
Boulogne
Dieppe
The Wash
The Fens
The Broads
North Downs
South Downs
The Weald
Lincolnshire Wolds
Vale of White Horse
Isle of Wight
Isle of Sheppey
Peak District National Park
New Forest National Park
Thetford Forest Park
LONDON
Sheffield
Doncaster
Rotherham
Lincoln
Nottingham
Derby
Leicester
Coventry
Peterborough
Northampton
Cambridge
Norwich
Great Yarmouth
Lowestoft
Ipswich
Colchester
Luton
Oxford
Reading
Swindon
Southampton
Portsmouth
Brighton
Bournemouth
Southend-on-Sea
Chelmsford
Maidstone
Canterbury
Dover
Margate
Hastings
Eastbourne
SCALE 1:1,408,450
0 10 20 30 40 miles
0 10 20 30 40 50 60 kilometres
22 miles to 1 inch / 14 km (9 miles) to 1 cm

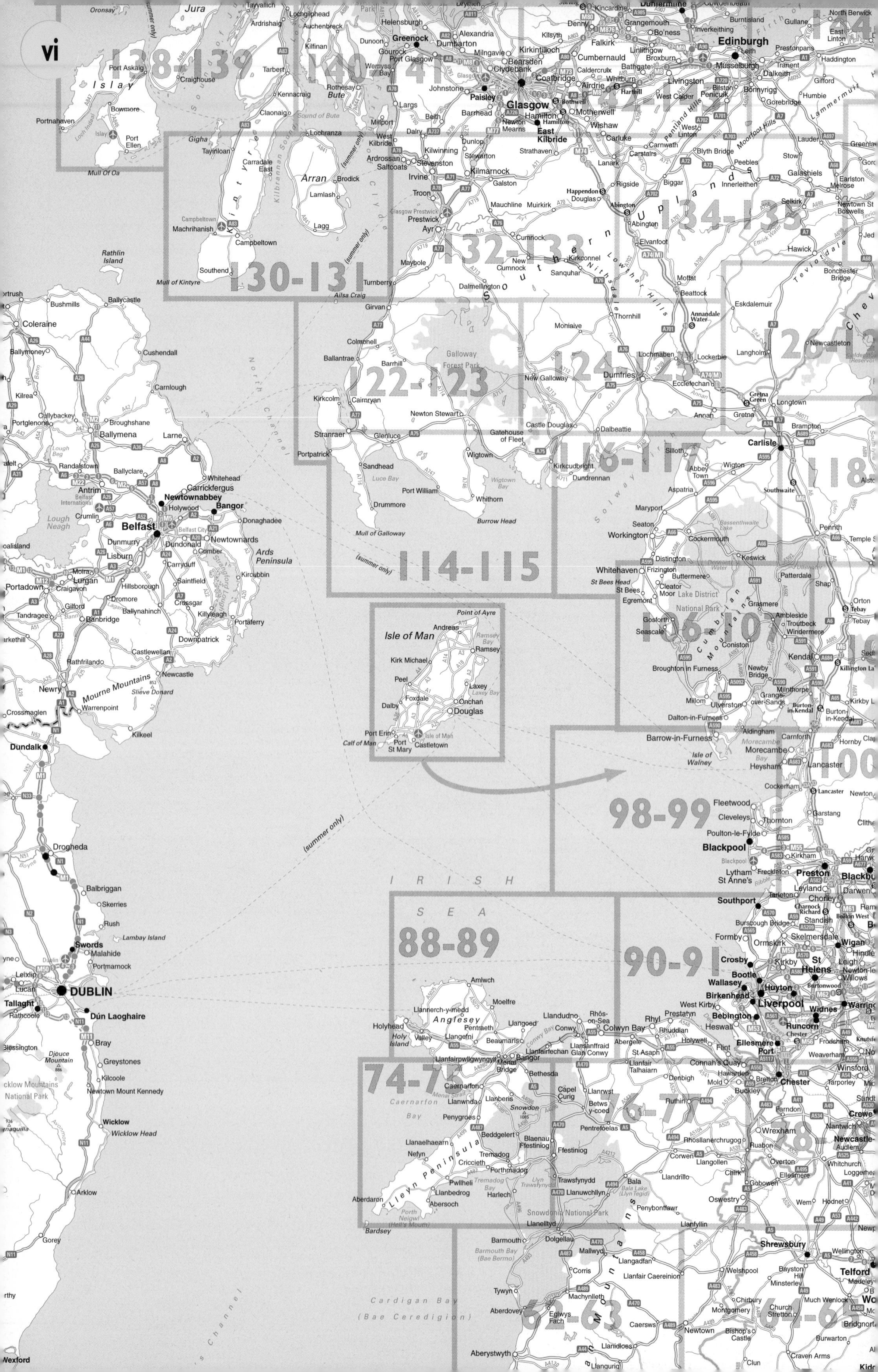
138-139
140-141
142-143
130-131
132-133
134-135
122-123
124-125
126-127
114-115
116-117
118
106-107
98-99
100
88-89
90-91
74-75
76-77
78
62-63
64-65
Jura
Islay
Port Askaig
Craighouse
Bowmore
Portnahaven
Port Ellen
Mull of Oa
Tarbert
Kennacraig
Claonaig
Gigha
Tayinloan
Carradale East
Kintyre
Campbeltown
Machrihanish
Southend
Mull of Kintyre
Arran
Brodick
Lamlash
Lagg
Lochranza
Ailsa Craig
Rathlin Island
Lochgilphead
Ardrishaig
Auchenbreck
Kilfinan
Dunoon
Rothesay
Bute
Sound of Bute
Largs
Millport
Helensburgh
Greenock
Gourock
Port Glasgow
Dumbarton
Alexandria
Milngavie
Bearsden
Clydebank
Johnstone
Paisley
Glasgow
Barrhead
Newton Mearns
East Kilbride
Hamilton
Motherwell
Wishaw
Airdrie
Coatbridge
Kirkintilloch
Cumbernauld
Kilsyth
Denny
Falkirk
Grangemouth
Bo'ness
Linlithgow
Bathgate
Broxburn
Livingston
West Calder
Whitburn
Harthill
Edinburgh
Leith
Musselburgh
Dalkeith
Bonnyrigg
Gorebridge
Penicuik
Bilston
Prestonpans
Tranent
Haddington
Gifford
Humbie
North Berwick
Gullane
East Linton
Dunfermline
Inverkeithing
Burntisland
Kincardine
Pentland Hills
Moorfoot Hills
Lammermuir Hills
West Linton
Carnwath
Carstairs
Lanark
Carluke
Strathaven
Blyth Bridge
Peebles
Innerleithen
Galashiels
Stow
Lauder
Earlston
Melrose
Selkirk
Newtown St Boswells
Hawick
Jedburgh
Teviotdale
Ettrick Water
Bonchester Bridge
Kilwinning
Stewarton
Dunlop
West Kilbride
Ardrossan
Saltcoats
Stevenston
Irvine
Kilmarnock
Galston
Troon
Prestwick
Ayr
Mauchline
Muirkirk
Douglas
Happendon
Abington
Rigside
Biggar
Cumnock
New Cumnock
Kirkconnel
Sanquhar
Maybole
Turnberry
Dalmellington
Girvan
Southern Uplands
Lowther Hills
Nithsdale
Elvanfoot
Moffat
Beattock
Thornhill
Moniaive
Annandale Water
Lockerbie
Lochmaben
Dumfries
Ecclefechan
Annan
Gretna
Gretna Green
Longtown
Langholm
Eskdalemuir
Newcastleton
Cheviot Hills
Colmonell
Ballantrae
Barrhill
Galloway Forest Park
Kirkcolm
Cairnryan
Stranraer
Portpatrick
Glenluce
Newton Stewart
New Galloway
Castle Douglas
Dalbeattie
Gatehouse of Fleet
Kirkcudbright
Dundrennan
Wigtown
Wigtown Bay
Whithorn
Burrow Head
Sandhead
Luce Bay
Port William
Drummore
Mull of Galloway
North Channel
Solway Firth
Silloth
Abbey Town
Wigton
Carlisle
Brampton
Aspatria
Maryport
Seaton
Workington
Cockermouth
Keswick
Penrith
Whitehaven
Frizington
Distington
Cleator Moor
St Bees Head
St Bees
Egremont
Buttermere
Patterdale
Grasmere
Ambleside
Troutbeck
Windermere
Lake District National Park
Cumbrian Mountains
Gosforth
Seascale
Coniston
Kendal
Broughton in Furness
Newby Bridge
Ulverston
Millom
Dalton-in-Furness
Grange-over-Sands
Milnthorpe
Burton-in-Kendal
Barrow-in-Furness
Isle of Walney
Morecambe
Morecambe Bay
Heysham
Lancaster
Carnforth
Cockerham
Garstang
Fleetwood
Cleveleys
Thornton
Poulton-le-Fylde
Blackpool
Kirkham
Lytham St Anne's
Freckleton
Preston
Blackburn
Leyland
Chorley
Darwen
Isle of Man
Point of Ayre
Andreas
Ramsey
Ramsey Bay
Kirk Michael
Peel
Laxey
Laxey Bay
Foxdale
Dalby
Onchan
Douglas
Port Erin
Calf of Man
Port St Mary
Castletown
IRISH SEA
(summer only)
Coleraine
Bushmills
Ballycastle
Ballymoney
Cushendall
Carnlough
Kilrea
Cullybackey
Portglenone
Ballymena
Broughshane
Larne
Lough Beg
Randalstown
Ballyclare
Whitehead
Carrickfergus
Antrim
Newtownabbey
Holywood
Bangor
Donaghadee
Crumlin
Lough Neagh
Belfast
Dunmurry
Dundonald
Newtownards
Lisburn
Comber
Ards Peninsula
Carryduff
Kircubbin
Moira
Lurgan
Portadown
Craigavon
Hillsborough
Saintfield
Strangford Lough
Gilford
Dromore
Crossgar
Tandragee
Ballynahinch
Killyleagh
Portaferry
Banbridge
Downpatrick
Castlewellan
Rathfriland
Newcastle
Newry
Mourne Mountains
Slieve Donard
Warrenpoint
Crossmaglen
Kilkeel
Dundalk
Drogheda
Balbriggan
Skerries
Rush
Lambay Island
Swords
Malahide
Portmarnock
Leixlip
Lucan
DUBLIN
Tallaght
Rathcoole
Dún Laoghaire
Bray
Blessington
Djouce Mountain
Greystones
Kilcoole
Wicklow Mountains National Park
Newtown Mount Kennedy
Wicklow
Wicklow Head
Arklow
Gorey
Wexford
Amlwch
Moelfre
Llannerch-y-medd
Anglesey
Holyhead
Holy Island
Valley
Llangefni
Pentraeth
Beaumaris
Llangoed
Llanfairpwllgwyngyll
Menai Bridge
Bangor
Llandudno
Rhôs-on-Sea
Colwyn Bay
Conwy
Conwy Bay
Llanfairfechan
Llansanffraid Glan Conwy
Abergele
Rhyl
Prestatyn
Rhuddlan
St Asaph
Holywell
Flint
Caernarfon
Caernarfon Bay
Llanberis
Llanwnda
Snowdon
Bethesda
Capel Curig
Betws-y-coed
Llanrwst
Penygroes
Beddgelert
Blaenau Ffestiniog
Ffestiniog
Llanaelhaearn
Nefyn
Lleyn Peninsula
Tremadog
Porthmadog
Criccieth
Pwllheli
Llanbedrog
Abersoch
Aberdaron
Porth Neigwl (Hell's Mouth)
Bardsey
Tremadog Bay
Harlech
Trawsfynydd
Llyn Trawsfynydd
Llanuwchllyn
Bala
Bala Lake (Llyn Tegid)
Snowdonia National Park
Llanelltyd
Dolgellau
Barmouth
Barmouth Bay (Bae Bermo)
Mallwyd
Corris
Tywyn
Aberdovey
Machynlleth
Cardigan Bay (Bae Ceredigion)
Eglwys Fach
Cambrian Mountains
Aberystwyth
Llanidloes
Llangurig
Caersws
Newtown
Llanfair Caereinion
Llangadfan
Welshpool
Montgomery
Chirbury
Bishop's Castle
Clun
Church Stretton
Much Wenlock
Craven Arms
Burwarton
Bridgnorth
Shrewsbury
Telford
Wellington
Bayston Hill
Minsterley
Llanfyllin
Penybontfawr
Llandrillo
Corwen
Llangollen
Ruthin
Denbigh
Llanfair Talhaiarn
Pentrefoelas
Rhosllanerchrugog
Chirk
Ruabon
Wrexham
Gobowen
Oswestry
Overton
Ellesmere
Whitchurch
Wem
Hodnet
Mold
Buckley
Hawarden
Bretton
Connah's Quay
Chester
Ellesmere Port
Frodsham
Runcorn
Widnes
Warrington
Farndon
Tarporley
Winsford
Nantwich
Crewe
Audlem
Newcastle-under-Lyme
Southport
Formby
Ormskirk
Skelmersdale
Crosby
Bootle
Kirkby
St Helens
Wallasey
Birkenhead
Liverpool
Huyton
West Kirby
Bebington
Heswall
Wigan
Haslingden
Standish
Leigh
Newton-le-Willows
Burscough Bridge
Tarleton
Heswall

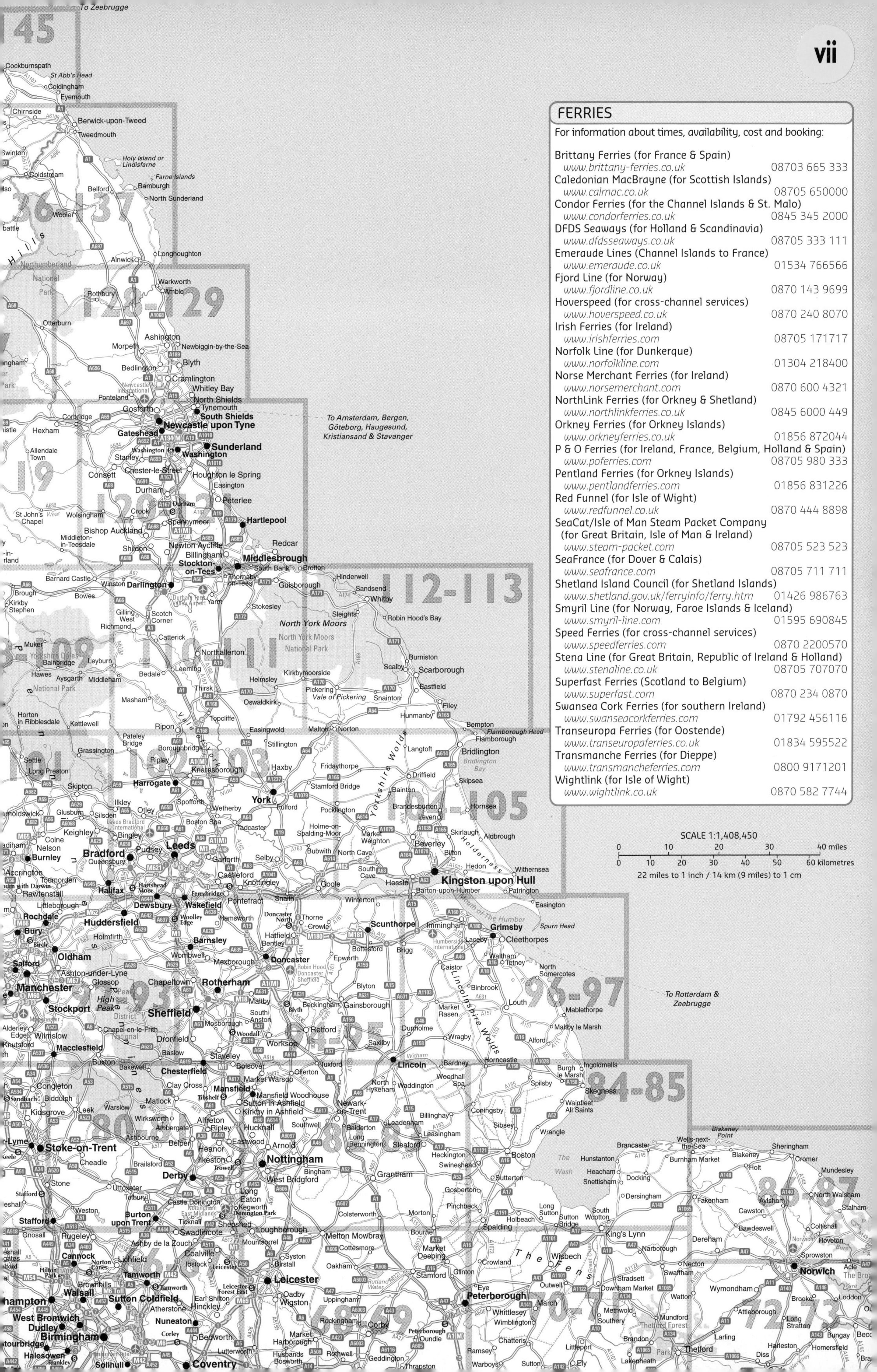

FERRIES

For information about times, availability, cost and booking:

Brittany Ferries (for France & Spain)
www.brittany-ferries.co.uk — 08703 665 333

Caledonian MacBrayne (for Scottish Islands)
www.calmac.co.uk — 08705 650000

Condor Ferries (for the Channel Islands & St. Malo)
www.condorferries.co.uk — 0845 345 2000

DFDS Seaways (for Holland & Scandinavia)
www.dfdsseaways.co.uk — 08705 333 111

Emeraude Lines (Channel Islands to France)
www.emeraude.co.uk — 01534 766566

Fjord Line (for Norway)
www.fjordline.co.uk — 0870 143 9699

Hoverspeed (for cross-channel services)
www.hoverspeed.co.uk — 0870 240 8070

Irish Ferries (for Ireland)
www.irishferries.com — 08705 171717

Norfolk Line (for Dunkerque)
www.norfolkline.com — 01304 218400

Norse Merchant Ferries (for Ireland)
www.norsemerchant.com — 0870 600 4321

NorthLink Ferries (for Orkney & Shetland)
www.northlinkferries.co.uk — 0845 6000 449

Orkney Ferries (for Orkney Islands)
www.orkneyferries.co.uk — 01856 872044

P & O Ferries (for Ireland, France, Belgium, Holland & Spain)
www.poferries.com — 08705 980 333

Pentland Ferries (for Orkney Islands)
www.pentlandferries.com — 01856 831226

Red Funnel (for Isle of Wight)
www.redfunnel.co.uk — 0870 444 8898

SeaCat/Isle of Man Steam Packet Company
(for Great Britain, Isle of Man & Ireland)
www.steam-packet.com — 08705 523 523

SeaFrance (for Dover & Calais)
www.seafrance.com — 08705 711 711

Shetland Island Council (for Shetland Islands)
www.shetland.gov.uk/ferryinfo/ferry.htm — 01426 986763

Smyril Line (for Norway, Faroe Islands & Iceland)
www.smyril-line.com — 01595 690845

Speed Ferries (for cross-channel services)
www.speedferries.com — 0870 2200570

Stena Line (for Great Britain, Republic of Ireland & Holland)
www.stenaline.co.uk — 08705 707070

Superfast Ferries (Scotland to Belgium)
www.superfast.com — 0870 234 0870

Swansea Cork Ferries (for southern Ireland)
www.swanseacorkferries.com — 01792 456116

Transeuropa Ferries (for Oostende)
www.transeuropaferries.com — 01834 595522

Transmanche Ferries (for Dieppe)
www.transmancheferries.com — 0800 9171201

Wightlink (for Isle of Wight)
www.wightlink.co.uk — 0870 582 7744

SCALE 1:1,408,450

22 miles to 1 inch / 14 km (9 miles) to 1 cm

178-179

180-181

Butt of Lewis
Port Nis
Barvas
Carloway
Great Bernera
Mlabhig
Garrynahine
Stornoway
Loch a'Tuath
Tolsta Head
Portnaguran
Lewis
Scarp
Loch Langavat
Kebock Head
North Harris

Cape Wrath
Durness
Strathy Point
Dounreay
Kinlochbervie
Strathy
Bettyhill
Tongue
Ben Hope
927
Strath Halladale
Forsinard
Scourie
Laxford Bridge
Altnaharra
Kinbrace
Point of Stoer
Unapool
Sutherland
North West Highlands
Lochinver
Ledmore
Elphin
Summer Isles
Invercassley
Lairg
Pittentrail
Brora
Golspie
An Teallach
Ullapool
Bonar Bridge
Dornoch
Ardgay
Dornoch Firth
Tain
Hill of Fearn
Balintore

WESTERN ISLES
Tarbert
Scalpay
Shiant Islands
Rubha Reidh
Gairloch
Loch Maree
South Harris
Leverburgh
Rodel
Northton
Pabbay
Berneray
Rubha Hunish
An Teallach
1062
Aultbea
Poolewe
Easter Ross
Garve
Dingwall
Strathpeffer
Conon Bridge
Black Isle
Fortrose
Rosemarkie
Nairn
Ardersier
Alness
Invergordon
Cromarty

170-171
North Uist
Lochmaddy
Monach Islands
Benbecula
Loch Snizort
Uig
The Storr
Rona
Loch Snizort
172-173
Liathach
1054
Kinlochewe
Torridon
Achnasheen
Wester Ross
Shieldaig
Loch Monar
Muir of Ord
Beauly
Beauly Firth
Inverness
174-175

South Uist
Skye
Borve
Portree
Raasay
Dunvegan
Bracadale
Sconser
Scalpay
Stromeferry
Lochcarron
Glen Cannich
Cannich
Drumnadrochit
Dores
Loch Ness
Glen Affric
Glen Albyn (Glen Mor)
Tomatin
Grantown-on-Dulnain Br
Sligachan
Cuillin Hills
Bla Bheinn
928
Broadford
Kyle of Lochalsh
Kyleakin
Dornie
166-167
Monadhliath Mountains
Aviemore
Kincraig
Lochboisdale
Soay
Elgol
Loch Eishort
Ardvasar
Knoydart
164-165
Loch Quoich
Glen Garry
Fort Augustus
Invergarry
Foyers
Invermoriston
Kingussie
Newtonmore
Cairngorm

Barra
Vatersay
Castlebay
162-163
Rum
Canna
Mallaig
Morar
Loch Morar
Loch Arkaig
Loch Lochy
Loch Laggan
Laggan
Ben
Pabaigh
Mingulay
Eriskay
Eigg
Arisaig
Glenfinnan
Spean Bridge
Roybridge
Glen Spean
Dalwhinnie

ATLANTIC OCEAN
Muck
Sound of Arisaig
154-155
Fort William
Ben Nevis
1344
Loch Treig
Rannoch Station
Rannoch Moor
Loch Garry
Glen Garry
158
Kinloch Rannoch
Blair Atholl
Spittal
Coll
Kilchoan
Tobermory
Salen
Strontian
156-157
Loch Shiel
Kinlochleven
Ballachulish
Glen Coe
1150
Bidean nam Bian
Appin
Rannoch
Loch Rannoch
Grandtully
Aberfeldy
Kenmore
Pitlochry

Tiree
Tiree
Salen
Lochaline
Ben Lawers
1214
Tyndrum
Killin
Bridge of Orchy
Glen Orchy
Loch Lyon

Ulva
Mull
Ben More
966
Craignure
Taynuilt
Oban
Dalmally
Crianlarich
Lochearnhead
Comrie
Crieff

Pennyghael
148-14
Loch Awe
Loch Lomond & The Trossachs National Park
Strathyre
Fionnphort
Iona
150-15
Kilmelford
Inveraray
Argyll
Ben Lomond
Aberfoyle
Callander
Doune
Dunblane
Dollar

146-147
Scarba
Luing
Kilmartin
Arrochar
Lochgoilhead
Garelochhead
Queen Elizabeth Forest Park
Stirling
Alloa
Kincardine

Colonsay
Scalasaig
Oronsay
Jura
Tayvallich
Lochgilphead
Ardrishaig
Argyll Forest Park
Helensburgh
Drymen
Stirling

138-139
Islay
Port Askaig
Craighouse
Tarbert
Kilfinan
140-141
Dunoon
Gourock
Port Glasgow
Wemyss Bay
Rothesay
Bute
Greenock
Dumbarton
Alexandria
Milngavie
Bearsden
Clydebank
Kilsyth
Kirkintilloch
Cumbernauld
Falkirk

Bowmore
Kennacraig
Claonaig
Sound of Bute
Largs
Millport
West Kilbride
Johnstone
Paisley
Glasgow
Barrhead
Newton Mearns
Coatbridge
Airdrie
Whitburn
Bathgate
Portnahaven
Port Ellen
Lochranza
Dalry
Beith
Hamilton
East Kilbride
Motherwell
Wishaw
Mull Of Oa
Gigha
Tayinloan
Arran
Brodick
Lamlash
Dunlop
Stewarton
Kilwinning
Ardrossan
Saltcoats
Irvine
Kilmarnock
Galston
Newton
Carluke
Lanark
Rigside

Carradale East
Lagg
Troon
132-133
Happendon
Douglas
Campbeltown
Machrihanish
130-131
Southend
Mull of Kintyre
Ailsa Craig
Girvan
Glasgow Prestwick
Prestwick
Ayr
Maybole
Turnberry
New Cumnock
Cumnock
Kirkconnel
Sanquhar

Inishtrahull Sound
Malin Head
Rathlin Island
Dalmellington
Mochaive
Thornhill
Carndonagh
Inishowen
Portrush
Bushmills
Ballycastle
Southern Uplands
Barrhill
Galloway Forest Park
124
Moville
Buncrana
Lough Swilly
Portstewart
Cushendall
Colmonell
Ballantrae
Dumfries
New Galloway
Lough Foyle
Eglinton
City of Derry
Coleraine
Ballymoney
Garvagh
Limavady
Londonderry

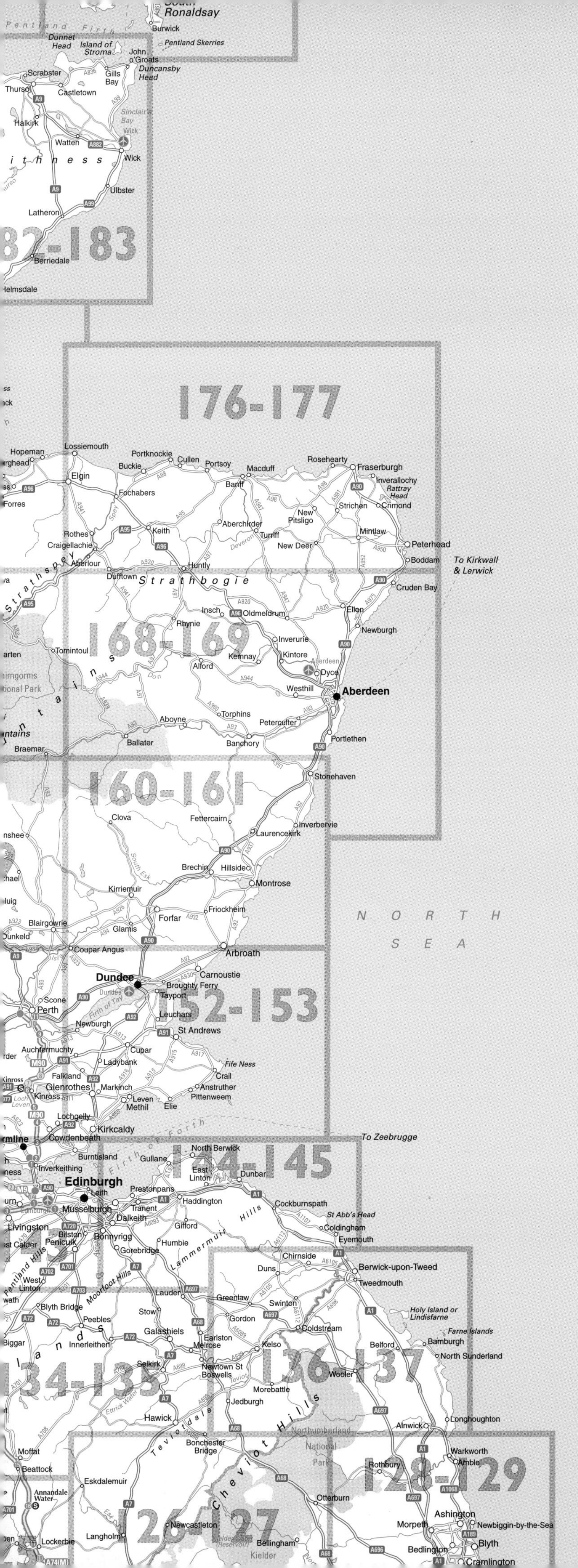

South Ronaldsay
Burwick
Pentland Firth
Pentland Skerries
Dunnet Head
Island of Stroma
John o'Groats
Duncansby Head
Scrabster
Thurso
Gills Bay
Castletown
Sinclair's Bay
Halkirk
Watten
Wick
Caithness
Ulbster
Latheron
182-183
Berriedale
Helmsdale
176-177
Hopeman
Lossiemouth
Portknockie
Cullen
Portsoy
Buckie
Macduff
Rosehearty
Fraserburgh
Elgin
Banff
Inverallochy
Rattray Head
Fochabers
Crimond
Forres
Strichen
New Pitsligo
Aberchirder
Mintlaw
Rothes
Keith
Turriff
Craigellachie
New Deer
Peterhead
Aberlour
Boddam
Huntly
Dufftown
Strathbogie
Strathspey
To Kirkwall & Lerwick
Cruden Bay
168-169
Insch
Oldmeldrum
Ellon
Rhynie
Newburgh
Tomintoul
Inverurie
Kintore
Kemnay
Alford
Dyce
Cairngorms National Park
Westhill
Aberdeen
Torphins
Aboyne
Peterculter
Ballater
Banchory
Braemar
Portlethen
Stonehaven
160-161
Clova
Fettercairn
Inverbervie
Laurencekirk
Brechin
Hillside
Montrose
Kirriemuir
Blairgowrie
Frockheim
Forfar
Glamis
Dunkeld
Coupar Angus
Arbroath
NORTH SEA
Dundee
Carnoustie
Broughty Ferry
Tayport
Scone
Perth
Firth of Tay
152-153
Leuchars
Newburgh
St Andrews
Auchtermuchty
Cupar
Ladybank
Fife Ness
Crail
Falkland
Kinross
Glenrothes
Markinch
Anstruther
Pittenweem
Loch Leven
Leven
Methil
Elie
Lochgelly
Kirkcaldy
Cowdenbeath
Dunfermline
To Zeebrugge
Firth of Forth
Burntisland
Gullane
North Berwick
144-145
Inverkeithing
East Linton
Dunbar
Edinburgh
Leith
Prestonpans
Tranent
Haddington
Musselburgh
Dalkeith
Cockburnspath
St Abb's Head
Livingston
Bonnyrigg
Gifford
Coldingham
Eyemouth
Lammermuir Hills
Penicuik
Humbie
Gorebridge
Chirnside
Pentland Hills
West Linton
Moorfoot Hills
Duns
Berwick-upon-Tweed
Tweedmouth
Lauder
Greenlaw
Swinton
Blyth Bridge
Stow
Holy Island or Lindisfarne
Peebles
Gordon
Coldstream
Farne Islands
Biggar
Innerleithen
Galashiels
Earlston
Bamburgh
Melrose
Kelso
Belford
North Sunderland
Selkirk
Newtown St Boswells
134-135
136-137
Wooler
Morebattle
Jedburgh
Hawick
Teviotdale
Cheviot Hills
Longhoughton
Alnwick
Northumberland National Park
Moffat
Bonchester Bridge
Warkworth
Amble
Beattock
Rothbury
128-129
Eskdalemuir
Annandale Water
Otterburn
Ashington
Newcastleton
126-127
Morpeth
Newbiggin-by-the-Sea
Langholm
Lockerbie
Bellingham
Kielder
Blyth
Bedlington
Cramlington

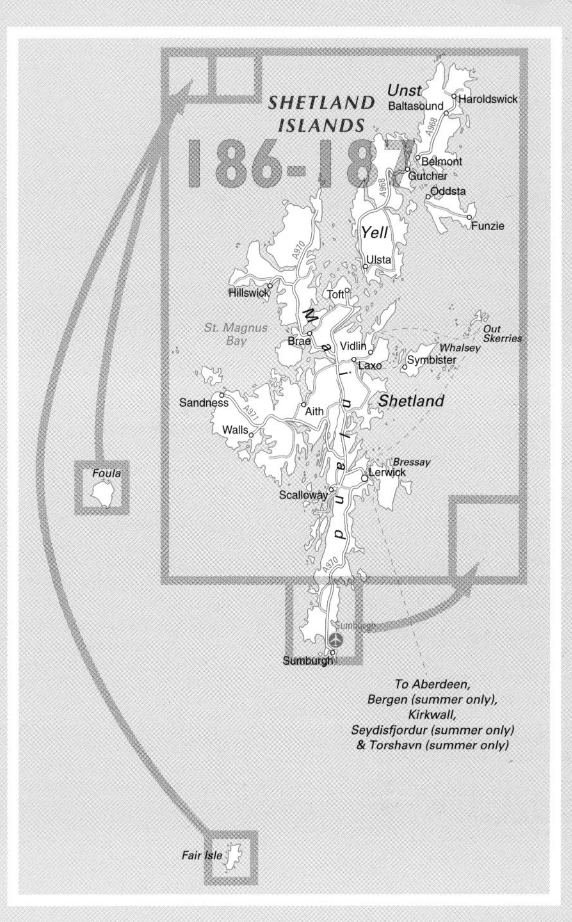

SHETLAND ISLANDS
186-187
Unst
Baltasound
Haroldswick
Belmont
Gutcher
Oddsta
Yell
Funzie
Ulsta
Hillswick
Toft
St. Magnus Bay
Mainland
Out Skerries
Whalsey
Brae
Vidlin
Symbister
Laxo
Sandness
Aith
Shetland
Walls
Bressay
Lerwick
Foula
Scalloway
Sumburgh
To Aberdeen, Bergen (summer only), Kirkwall, Seydisfjordur (summer only) & Torshavn (summer only)
Fair Isle

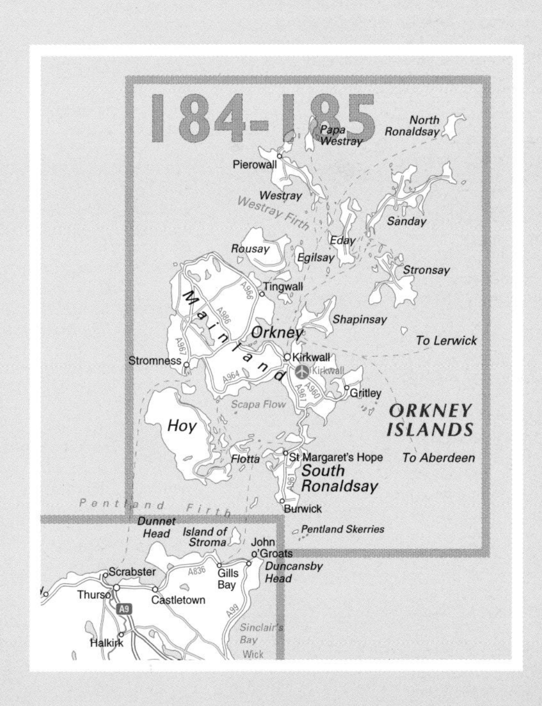

184-185
Papa Westray
North Ronaldsay
Pierowall
Westray
Westray Firth
Sanday
Rousay
Eday
Egilsay
Stronsay
Tingwall
Mainland
Shapinsay
Orkney
To Lerwick
Stromness
Kirkwall
Gritley
Scapa Flow
ORKNEY ISLANDS
Hoy
Flotta
St Margaret's Hope
To Aberdeen
South Ronaldsay
Burwick
Pentland Firth
Pentland Skerries
Dunnet Head
Island of Stroma
John o'Groats
Duncansby Head
Scrabster
Thurso
Gills Bay
Castletown
Halkirk
Sinclair's Bay
Wick

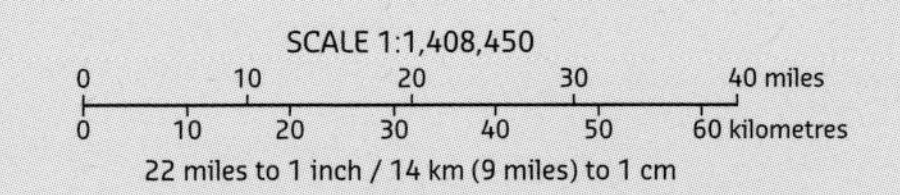

SCALE 1:1,408,450
0 10 20 30 40 miles
0 10 20 30 40 50 60 kilometres
22 miles to 1 inch / 14 km (9 miles) to 1 cm

Restricted motorway junctions are shown on the mapping as: 9

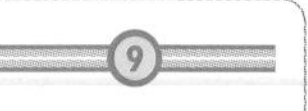

A1(M) LONDON TO NEWCASTLE
②
Northbound : No access
Southbound : No exit
③
Southbound : No access
⑤
Northbound : No exit
Southbound : No access
: No exit
44
Northbound : No exit to M1 westbound
Junction of A1(M), A1 & A63
Northbound : Access only from A1
Southbound : Exit only to A1
Dishforth
Southbound : No access from A168 Eastbound
57
Northbound : No access
: Exit only to A66(M) Northbound
Southbound : Access only from A66(M) Southbound
: No exit
65
Northbound : No access from A1
Southbound : No exit to A1

A3(M) PORTSMOUTH
①
Northbound : No exit
Southbound : No access
④
Northbound : No access
Southbound : No exit

A38(M) BIRMINGHAM
Victoria Road
Northbound : No exit
Southbound : No access

A48(M) CARDIFF
Junction with M4
Westbound : No access from M4 ㉙ Eastbound
Eastbound : No exit to M4 ㉙ Westbound
29A
Westbound : No exit to A48 Eastbound
Eastbound : No access from A48 Westbound

A57(M) MANCHESTER
Brook Street
Westbound : No exit
Eastbound : No access

A58(M) LEEDS
Westgate
Southbound : No access
Woodhouse Lane
Westbound : No exit

A64(M) LEEDS
Claypit Lane
Eastbound : No access

A66(M) DARLINGTON
Junction with A1(M)
Northbound : No access from A1(M) Southbound
: No exit
Southbound : No access
: No exit to A1(M) Northbound

A74(M) LOCKERBIE
⑱
Northbound : No access
Southbound : No exit

A167(M) NEWCASTLE
Campden Street
Northbound : No exit
Southbound : No access
: No exit

M1 LONDON TO LEEDS
②
Northbound : No exit
Southbound : No access
④
Northbound : No exit
Southbound : No access
6A
Northbound : Access only from M25 ㉑
: No exit
Southbound : No access
: Exit only to M25 ㉑
⑦
Northbound : Access only from M10
: No exit
Southbound : No access
: Exit only to M10

⑰
Northbound : No access
: Exit only to M45
Southbound : Access only from M45
: No exit
⑲
Northbound : Exit only to M6
Southbound : Access only from M6
21A
Northbound : No access
Southbound : No exit
23A
Northbound : No access from A453
Southbound : No exit to A453
24A
Northbound : No exit
Southbound : No access
35A
Northbound : No access
Southbound : No exit
43
Northbound : No access
: Exit only to M621
Southbound : No exit
: Access only from M621
48
Northbound : No exit to A1 Southbound
: Access only from A1 Northbound
Southbound : Exit only to A1 Southbound
: No access

M2 ROCHESTER TO CANTERBURY
①
Westbound : No exit to A2 Eastbound
Eastbound : No access from A2 Westbound

M3 LONDON TO WINCHESTER
⑧
Westbound : No access
Eastbound : No exit
⑩
Northbound : No access
Southbound : No exit
⑬
Southbound : No exit to A335 Eastbound
: No access
⑭
Westbound : No access
Eastbound : No exit

M4 LONDON TO SWANSEA
①
Westbound : No access from A4 Eastbound
Eastbound : No exit to A4 Westbound
②
Westbound : No access from A4 Eastbound
: No exit to A4 Eastbound
Eastbound : No access from A4 Westbound
: No exit to A4 Westbound
㉑
Westbound : No access from M48 Eastbound
Eastbound : No exit to M48 Westbound
㉓
Westbound : No exit to M48 Eastbound
Eastbound : No access from M48 Westbound
㉕
Westbound : No access
Eastbound : No exit
25A
Westbound : No access
Eastbound : No exit
㉙
Westbound : No access
: Exit only to A48(M)
Eastbound : Access only from A48(M) Eastbound
: No exit
⑱
Westbound : No access
㊴
Westbound : No exit
Eastbound : No access
: No exit
㊶
Westbound : No exit
Eastbound : No access
㊷
Westbound : No exit to A48
Eastbound : No access from A48

M5 BIRMINGHAM TO EXETER
⑩
Northbound : No exit
Southbound : No access
11A
Northbound : No access from A417 Eastbound
Southbound : No exit to A417 Westbound

M6 COVENTRY TO CARLISLE
Junction with M1
Northbound : No access from M1 ⑲ Southbound
Southbound : No exit to M1 ⑲ Northbound
3A
Northbound : No access from M6 Toll
Southbound : No exit to M6 Toll
④
Northbound : No exit to M42 Northbound
: No access from M42 Southbound
Southbound : No exit to M42
: No access from M42 Southbound
4A
Northbound : No access from M42 ⑧ Northbound
: No exit
Southbound : No access
: Exit only to M42 ⑧
⑤
Northbound : No access
Southbound : No exit
10A
Northbound : No access
: Exit only to M54
Southbound : Access only from M54
: No exit
11A
Northbound : No exit to M6 Toll
Southbound : No access from M6 Toll
㉔
Northbound : No exit
Southbound : No access
㉕
Northbound : No access
Southbound : No exit
㉚
Northbound : Access only from M61 Northbound
: No exit
Southbound : No access
: Exit only to M61 Southbound
31A
Northbound : No access
Southbound : No exit

M6 Toll BIRMINGHAM
T1
Northbound : Exit only to M42
: Access only from A4097
Southbound : No exit
: Access only from M42 Southbound
T2
Northbound : No exit
: No access
Southbound : No access
T5
Northbound : No exit
Southbound : No access
T7
Northbound : No access
Southbound : No exit
T8
Northbound : No access
Southbound : No exit

M8 EDINBURGH TO GLASGOW
⑧
Westbound : No access from M73 ② Southbound
: No access from A8 Eastbound
: No access from A89 Eastbound
Eastbound : No access from A89 Westbound
: No exit to M73 ② Northbound
⑨
Westbound : No exit
Eastbound : No access
⑬
Westbound : Access only from M80
Eastbound : Exit only to M80
⑭
Westbound : No exit
Eastbound : No access
⑯
Westbound : No access
Eastbound : No exit
⑰
Eastbound : Access only from A82, not central Glasgow
: Exit only to A82, not central Glasgow
⑱
Westbound : No access
Eastbound : No access
⑲
Westbound : Access only from A814 Eastbound
Eastbound : Exit only to A814 Westbound, not central Glasgow

⑳
Westbound : No access
Eastbound : No exit
㉑
Westbound : No exit
Eastbound : No access
㉒
Westbound : No access
: Exit only to M77 Southbound
Eastbound : Access only from M77 Northbound
: No exit
㉓
Westbound : No access
Eastbound : No exit
㉕
Westbound : No access from A739 Northbound
: No exit to A739 Southbound
Eastbound : No access from A739 Northbound
: No exit to A739 Southbound
25A
Eastbound : No exit
Westbound : No access
㉘
Westbound : No access
Eastbound : No exit
28A
Westbound : No access
Eastbound : No exit

M9 EDINBURGH TO STIRLING
1A
Westbound : No access
Eastbound : No exit
②
Westbound : No exit
Eastbound : No access
③
Westbound : No access
Eastbound : No exit
⑥
Westbound : No exit
Eastbound : No access
⑧
Westbound : No access
Eastbound : No exit

M10 ST ALBANS
Junction with M1
Northbound : No access
: Exit only to M1 ⑦ Northbound
Southbound : Access only from M1 ⑦ Southbound
: No exit

M11 LONDON TO CAMBRIDGE
④
Northbound : No access from A1400 Westbound
: No exit
Southbound : No access
: No exit to A1400 Eastbound
⑤
Northbound : No access
Southbound : No exit
8A
Northbound : No access
Southbound : No exit
⑨
Northbound : No access
Southbound : No exit
⑬
Northbound : No access
Southbound : No exit
⑭
Northbound : No access from A428 Eastbound
: No exit to A428 Westbound
: No exit to A1307
Southbound : No access from A428 Eastbound
: No access from A1307
: No exit

M20 LONDON TO FOLKESTONE
②
Westbound : No exit
Eastbound : No access
③
Westbound : No access
: Exit only to M26 Westbound
Eastbound : Access only from M26 Eastbound
: No exit
11A
Westbound : No exit
Eastbound : No access

M23 LONDON TO CRAWLEY
⑦
Northbound : No exit to A23 Southbound
Southbound : No access from A23 Northbound

(10A)
Southbound : No access from *B2036*
Northbound : No exit to *B2036*

M25 LONDON ORBITAL MOTORWAY
(1B)
Clockwise : No access
Anticlockwise : No exit
(5)
Clockwise : No exit to M26 Eastbound
Anticlockwise : No access from M26 Westbound
Spur of M25 (5)
Clockwise : No access from M26 Westbound
Anticlockwise : No exit to M26 Eastbound
(19)
Clockwise : No access
Anticlockwise : No exit
(21)
Clockwise : No access from M1 (6A)
Northbound
: No exit to M1 (6A) Southbound
Anticlockwise : No access from M1 (6A)
Northbound
: No exit to M1 (6A) Southbound
(31)
Clockwise : No exit
Anticlockwise : No access

M26 SEVENOAKS
Junction with M25 (5)
Westbound : No exit to M25 Anticlockwise
: No exit to M25 spur
Eastbound : No access from M25 Clockwise
: No access from M25 spur
Junction with M20
Westbound : No access from M20 (3)
Eastbound
Eastbound : No exit to M20 (3) Westbound

M27 SOUTHAMPTON TO PORTSMOUTH
(4) West
Westbound : No exit
Eastbound : No access
(4) East
Westbound : No access
Eastbound : No exit
(10)
Westbound : No access
Eastbound : No exit
(12) West
Westbound : No access
Eastbound : No exit
(12) East
Westbound : No access from A3
Eastbound : No exit

M40 LONDON TO BIRMINGHAM
(3)
Westbound : No access
Eastbound : No exit
(7)
Eastbound : No exit
(8)
Northbound : No access
Southbound : No exit
(13)
Northbound : No access
Southbound : No exit
(14)
Northbound : No exit
Southbound : No access
(16)
Northbound : No exit
Southbound : No access

M42 BIRMINGHAM
(1)
Northbound : No exit
Southbound : No access
(7)
Northbound : No access
: Exit only to M6 Northbound
Southbound : No access from M6 Northbound
(7A)
Northbound : No access
: Exit only to M6 Eastbound
Southbound : No access
: No exit
(8)
Northbound : Access only from M6 Southbound
: No exit
Southbound : Access only from M6 Southbound
: Exit only to M6 Northbound

M45 COVENTRY
Junction with M1
Westbound : No access from M1 (17)
Southbound
Eastbound : No exit to M1 (17) Northbound
Junction with A45
Westbound : No exit
Eastbound : No access

M48 CHEPSTOW
M4
Westbound : No exit to M4 Eastbound
Eastbound : No access from M4 Westbound

M49 BRISTOL
(18A)
Northbound : No access from M5 Southbound
Southbound : No access from M5 Northbound

M53 BIRKENHEAD TO CHESTER
(11)
Northbound : No access from M56 (15)
Eastbound
: No exit to M56 (15) Westbound
Southbound : No access from M56 (15)
Eastbound
: No exit to M56 (15) Westbound

M54 WOLVERHAMPTON TO TELFORD
Junction with M6
Westbound : No access from M6 (10A)
Southbound
Eastbound : No exit to M6 (10A) Northbound

M56 STOCKPORT TO CHESTER
(1)
Westbound : No access from M60 Eastbound
: No access from A34 Northbound
Eastbound : No exit to M60 Westbound
: No exit to A34 Southbound
(2)
Westbound : No access
Eastbound : No exit
(3)
Westbound : No exit
Eastbound : No access
(4)
Westbound : No access
Eastbound : No exit
(7)
Westbound : No access
Eastbound : No exit
(8)
Westbound : No exit
Eastbound : No access
(9)
Westbound : No exit to M6 Southbound
Eastbound : No access from M6 Northbound
(15)
Westbound : No access
Eastbound : No exit

M57 LIVERPOOL
(3)
Northbound : No exit
Southbound : No access
(5)
Northbound : Access only from A580 Westbound
: No exit
Southbound : No access
: Exit only to A580 Eastbound

M58 LIVERPOOL TO WIGAN
(1)
Westbound : No access
Eastbound : No exit

M60 MANCHESTER
(2)
Westbound : No exit
Eastbound : No access
(3)
Westbound : No access from M56 (1)
: No access from A34 Southbound
: No exit to A34 Northbound
Eastbound : No access from A34 Southbound
: No exit to M56 (1)
: No exit to A34 Northbound
(4)
Westbound : No access
Eastbound : No exit to M56

(5)
Westbound : No access from A5103 Southbound
: No exit to A5103 Southbound
Eastbound : No access from A5103 Northbound
: No exit to A5103 Northbound
(14)
Westbound : No access from A580
: No exit to A580 Eastbound
Eastbound : No access from A580 Westbound
: No exit to A580
(16)
Westbound : No access
Eastbound : No exit
(20)
Westbound : No access
Eastbound : No exit
(22)
Westbound : No access
(25)
Westbound : No access
(26)
Eastbound : No access
: No exit
(27)
Westbound : No exit
Eastbound : No access

M61 MANCHESTER TO PRESTON
(2)
Northbound : No access from A580 Eastbound
: No access from A666
Southbound : No exit to A580 Westbound
(3)
Northbound : No access from A580 Eastbound
: No access from A666
Southbound : No exit to A580 Westbound
Junction with M6
Northbound : No exit to M6 (30) Southbound
Southbound : No access from M6 (30)
Northbound

M62 LIVERPOOL TO HULL
(23)
Westbound : No exit
Eastbound : No access

M65 BURNLEY
(9)
Westbound : No access
Eastbound : No access
(11)
Westbound : No access
Eastbound : No exit

M66 MANCHESTER TO EDENFIELD
(1)
Northbound : No access
Southbound : No exit
Junction with A56
Northbound : Exit only to A56 Northbound
Southbound : Access only from A56 Southbound

M67 MANCHESTER
(1)
Westbound : No exit
Eastbound : No access
(2)
Westbound : No access
Eastbound : No exit

M69 COVENTRY TO LEICESTER
(2)
Northbound : No exit
Southbound : No access

M73 GLASGOW
(1)
Northbound : No access from A721 Eastbound
Southbound : No exit to A721 Eastbound
(2)
Northbound : No access from M8 (8)
Eastbound
Southbound : No exit to M8 (8) Westbound
(3)
Northbound : No exit to A80 Southbound
Southbound : No access from A80 Northbound

M74 GLASGOW
(2)
Westbound : No access
Eastbound : No exit
(3)
Westbound : No exit
Eastbound : No access

(7)
Northbound : No exit
Southbound : No access
(9)
Northbound : No access
: No exit
Southbound : No access
(10)
(11)
Northbound : No exit
Southbound : No access
(12)
Northbound : Access only from A70 Northbound
Southbound : Exit only to A70 Southbound

M77 GLASGOW
Junction with M8
Northbound : No exit to M8 (22) Westbound
Southbound : No access from M8 (22)
Eastbound
(4)
Northbound : No exit
Southbound : No access
Junction with A77
Northbound : No access from A77 Southbound
Southbound : No exit to A77 Northbound

M80 STIRLING
(3)
Southbound : No access
(5)
Northbound : No exit
: No access from M876
Southbound : No exit
: No exit to M876

M90 EDINBURGH TO PERTH
(2A)
Northbound : No access
Southbound : No exit
(7)
Northbound : No exit
Southbound : No access
(8)
Northbound : No access
Southbound : No exit
(10)
Northbound : No access from A912
: No exit to A912 Southbound
Southbound : No access from A912 Northbound
: No exit to A912

M180 SCUNTHORPE
(1)
Westbound : No exit
Eastbound : No access

M606 BRADFORD
Straithgate Lane
Northbound : No access

M621 LEEDS
(2A)
Northbound : No exit
Southbound : No access
(4)
Southbound : No access
(5)
Northbound : No access
Southbound : No exit
(6)
Northbound : No exit
Southbound : No access

M876 FALKIRK
Junction with M80
Westbound : No exit to M80 (5) Northbound
Eastbound : No access from M80 (5)
Southbound
Junction with M9
Westbound : No access
Eastbound : No exit
(2)
Northbound : No access
Southbound : No exit

Motorway services information

xii

For further information on motorway services providers:

Moto   www.moto-way.com

RoadChef   www.roadchef.com

Welcome Break   www.welcomebreak.co.uk

Motorway	Junction	Service Provider	Service Name
A1(M)	1	Welcome Break	South Mimms
	10	Extra	Baldock
	17	Extra	Peterborough
	34	Moto	Blyth
	61	RoadChef	Durham
	64	Moto	Washington
A74(M)	16	RoadChef	Annandale Water
	22	Welcome Break	Gretna Green
M1	2–4	Welcome Break	London Gateway
	11–12	Moto	Toddington
	14–15	Welcome Break	Newport Pagnell
	15A	RoadChef	Northampton
	16–17	RoadChef	Watford Gap
	21–21A	Welcome Break	Leicester Forest East
	22	Moto	Leicester
	23A	Moto	Donington Park
	25–26	Moto	Trowell
	28–29	RoadChef	Tibshelf
	30–31	Welcome Break	Woodall
	38–39	Moto	Woolley Edge
M2	4–5	Moto	Medway
M3	4A–5	Welcome Break	Fleet
	8–9	RoadChef	Winchester
M4	3	Moto	Heston
	11–12	Moto	Reading
	13	Moto	Chieveley
	14–15	Welcome Break	Membury
	17–18	Moto	Leigh Delamere
	23A	First Motorway	Magor
	30	Travel Rest	Cardiff Gate
	33	Moto	Cardiff West
	36	Welcome Break	Sarn Park
	47	Moto	Swansea
	49	RoadChef	Pont Abraham
M5	3–4	Moto	Frankley
	8	RoadChef	Strensham (South)
	8	RoadChef	Strensham (North)
	13–14	Welcome Break	Michael Wood
	19	Welcome Break	Gordano
	21–22	RoadChef	Sedgemoor (South)
	21–22	Welcome Break	Sedgemoor (North)
	24	Moto	Bridgwater
	25–26	RoadChef	Taunton Deane
	27	Moto	Tiverton
	28	Extra	Cullompton
	29–30	Moto	Exeter

On-site Services: Fuel   Disabled facilities   Food

£ Service shops   *i* Information   Accommodation

£ Other shops   Conference facilities   Showers

xiii

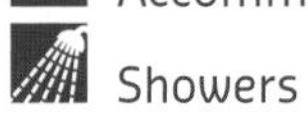

All motorway service areas must provide fuel, free toilets and free short term parking 24 hours a day

Motorway	Junction	Service Provider	Service Name	On-site Services
M6	3–4	Welcome Break	Corley	
	10–11	Moto	Hilton Park	
	14–15	RoadChef	Stafford (South)	
	14–15	Moto	Stafford (North)	
	15–16	Welcome Break	Keele	
	16–17	RoadChef	Sandbach	
	18–19	Moto	Knutsford	
	20	Moto	Lymm	
	27–28	Welcome Break	Charnock Richard	
	32–33	Moto	Lancaster	
	35A–36	Moto	Burton-in-Kendal (North)	
	36–37	RoadChef	Killington Lake (South)	
	38–39	Westmorland	Tebay	
	41–42	Moto	Southwaite	
M6 Toll	T6–T7	RoadChef	Norton Canes	
M8	4–5	BP	Harthill	
M9	9	Moto	Stirling	
M11	8	Welcome Break	Birchanger Green	
M18	5	Moto	Doncaster North	
M20	8	RoadChef	Maidstone	
M23	11	Moto	Pease Pottage	
M25	5–6	RoadChef	Clacket Lane	
	23	Welcome Break	South Mimms	
	30	Moto	Thurrock	
M27	3–4	RoadChef	Rownhams	
M40	8	Welcome Break	Oxford	
	10	Moto	Cherwell Valley	
	12–13	Welcome Break	Warwick	
M42	2	Welcome Break	Hopwood Park	
	10	Moto	Tamworth	
M48	1	Moto	Severn View	
M50	4	Welcome Break	Ross Spur	
M54	4	Welcome Break	Telford	
M56	14	RoadChef	Chester	
M61	6–7	First Motorway	Bolton West	
M62	7–9	Welcome Break	Burtonwood	
	18–19	Moto	Birch	
	25–26	Welcome Break	Hartshead Moor	
	33	Moto	Ferrybridge	
M65	4	Extra	Blackburn with Darwen	
M74	4–5	RoadChef	Bothwell (South)	
	5–6	RoadChef	Hamilton (North)	
	11–12	Cairn Lodge	Happendon	
	12–13	Welcome Break	Abington	
M90	6	Moto	Kinross Sevices	

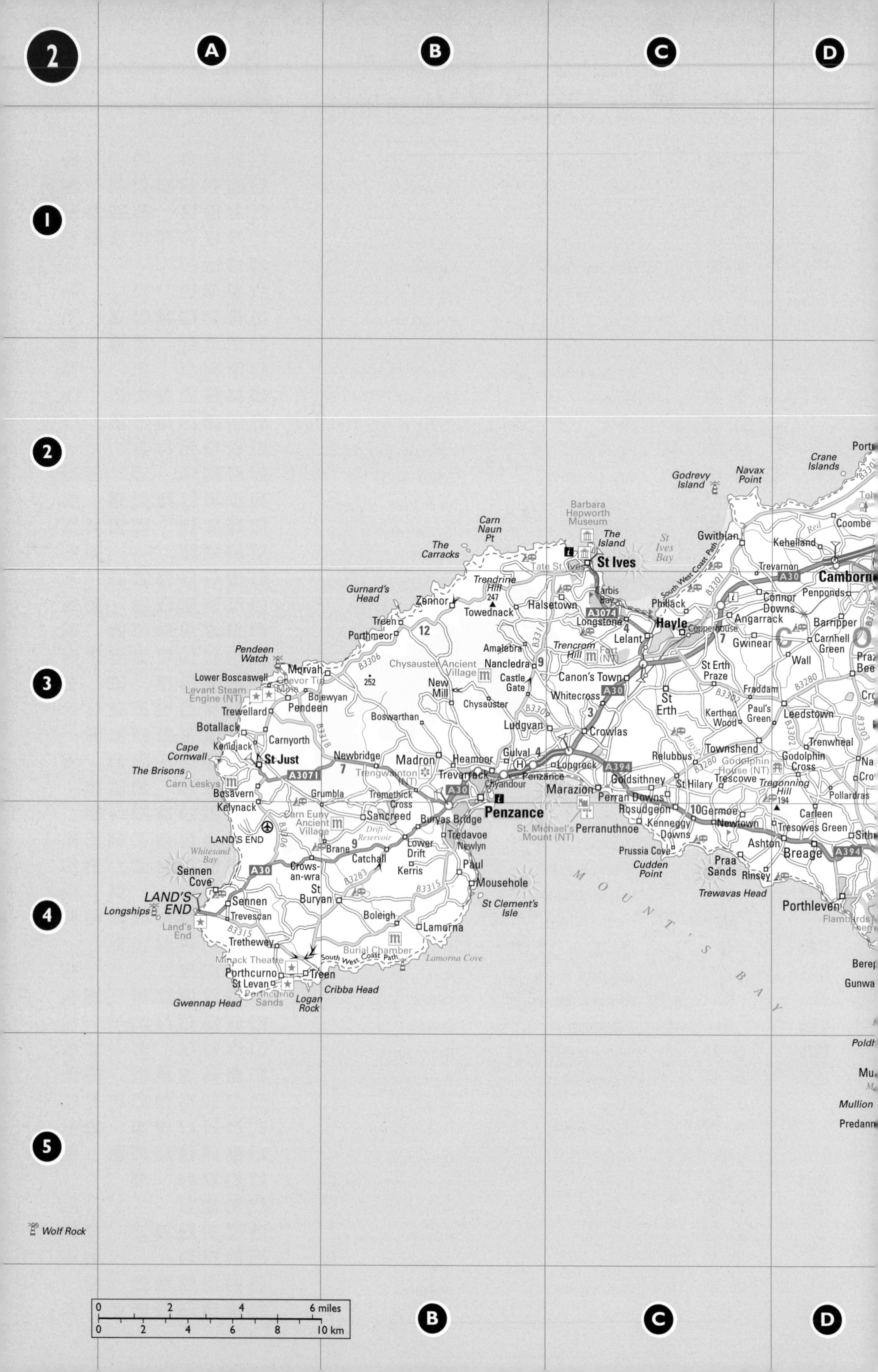
A
B
C
D
1
2
3
4
5
Godrevy Island
Navax Point
Crane Islands
Barbara Hepworth Museum
The Island
St Ives Bay
Carn Naun Pt
The Carracks
Tate St. Ives
St Ives
Gwithian
Kehelland
Coombe
Trevarnon
A30
Camborne
Gurnard's Head
Zennor
Trendrine Hill
247
Towednack
Halsetown
Carbis Bay
A3074
Phillack
Connor Downs
Penponds
South West Coast Path
B3301
Longstone
Hayle
Angarrack
Barripper
Treen
Porthmeor
12
Lelant
Copperhouse
Gwinear
Carnhell Green
Amalebra
Trencrom Hill
Fort (NT)
7
Pendeen Watch
Morvah
Chysauster Ancient Village
Nancledra
St Erth Praze
Wall
Lower Boscaswell
Geevor Tin Mine
B3306
252
Castle Gate
Canon's Town
Levant Steam Engine (NT)
Bojewyan
Pendeen
New Mill
Chysauster
Whitecross
St Erth
Fraddam
B3280
Trewellard
Boswarthan
B3309
Kerthen Wood
Paul's Green
Leedstown
Botallack
Ludgvan
Crowlas
Kenidjack
Carnyorth
B3318
Trenwheal
Cape Cornwall
St Just
Newbridge
Madron
Heamoor
Gulval
Longrock
Relubbus
Townshend
Godolphin House (NT)
Godolphin Cross
The Brisons
A3071
Trengwainton (NT)
Trevarrack
Penzance
A394
Goldsithney
St Hilary
Trescowe
Tregonning Hill
194
Pollardras
Carn Leskys
Bosavern
Grumbla
Tremethick Cross
A30
Chyandour
Marazion
Perran Downs
Kelynack
Carn Euny Ancient Village
Sancreed
Buryas Bridge
Penzance
Rosudgeon
10
Germoe
Carleen
Drift Reservoir
Tredavoe
St. Michael's Mount (NT)
Perranuthnoe
Kenneggy Downs
Newtown
Tresowes Green
LAND'S END
Brane
Lower Drift
Newlyn
Whitesand Bay
Catchall
Prussia Cove
Ashton
Breage
Sennen Cove
Crows-an-wra
Kerris
Paul
Cudden Point
Praa Sands
Rinsey
A394
St Buryan
B3283
B3315
Mousehole
Trewavas Head
LAND'S END
Sennen
St Clement's Isle
Porthleven
Longships
Trevescan
MOUNT'S BAY
Land's End
B3315
Boleigh
Lamorna
Trethewey
Burial Chamber
Minack Theatre
South West Coast Path
Lamorna Cove
Porthcurno
Treen
St Levan
Cribba Head
Porthcurno Sands
Gwennap Head
Logan Rock
Wolf Rock
0
2
4
6 miles
0
2
4
6
8
10 km
B
C
D

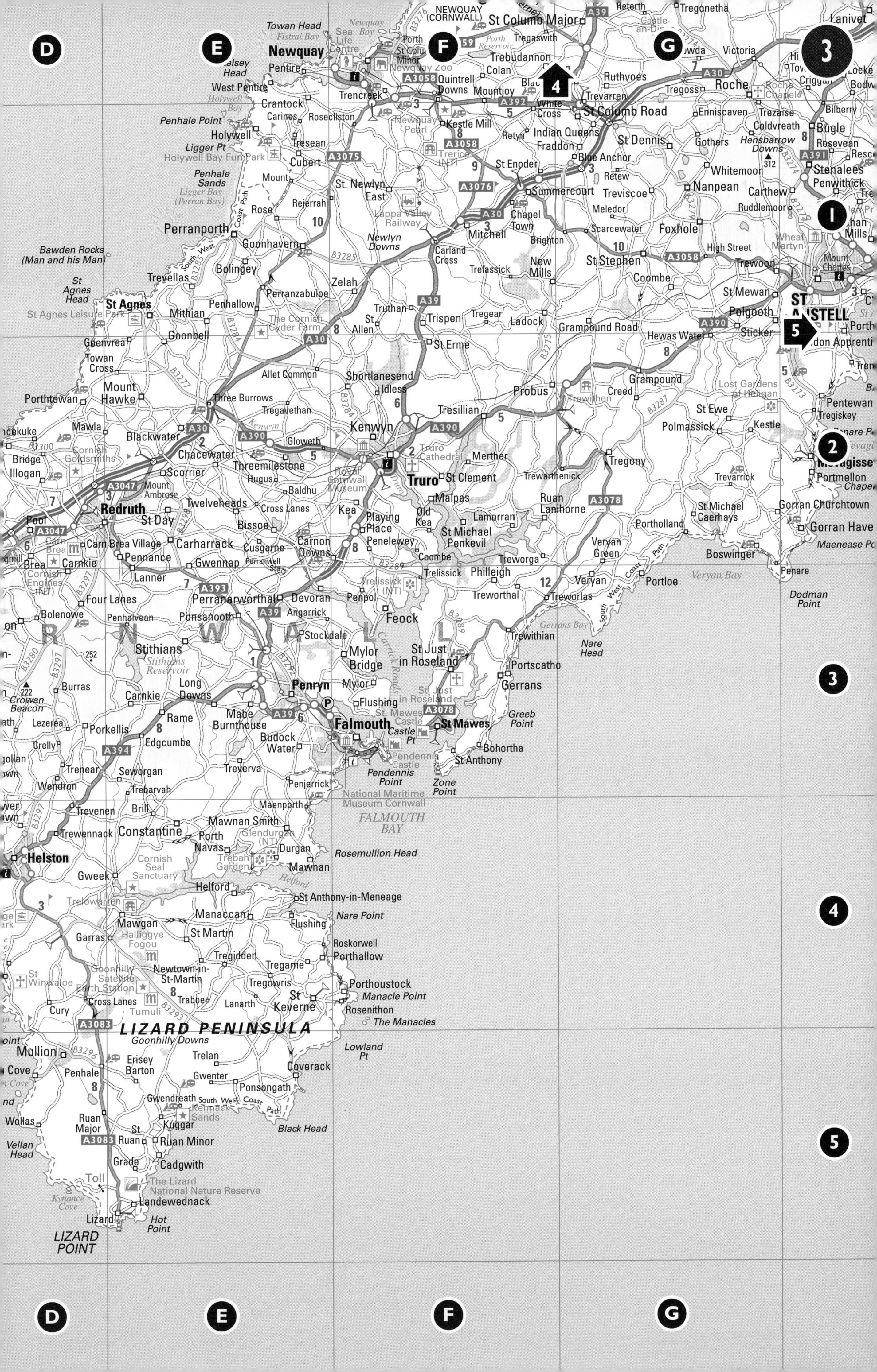

D
E
F
G
3
4
5
1
2
Newquay
Towan Head
Fistral Bay
Newquay Bay
Sea Life Centre
Porth
Porth Reservoir
Newquay Zoo
Pentire
West Pentire
Holywell Bay
Crantock
Carines
Rosecliston
Trencreek
Quintrell Downs
Penhale Point
Ligger Pt
Holywell
Holywell Bay Fun Park
Tresean
Cubert
Newquay Pearl
Kestle Mill
Trerice (NT)
Penhale Sands
Ligger Bay (Perran Bay)
Mount
Rose
Rejerrah
St. Newlyn East
Lappa Valley Railway
Newlyn Downs
Perranporth
Bawden Rocks (Man and his Man)
Goonhavern
Bolingey
Trevellas
St Agnes Head
St Agnes
St Agnes Leisure Park
Mithian
Penhallow
Perranzabuloe
The Cornish Cyder Farm
Zelah
Truthan
St Allen
Goonbell
Goonvrea
Towan Cross
Mount Hawke
Porthtowan
Allet Common
Shortlanesend
Idless
Three Burrows
Tregavethan
Mawla
Blackwater
Kenwyn
Gloweth
Chacewater
Threemilestone
Scorrier
Mount Ambrose
Hugus
Baldhu
Cornish Goldsmiths
Bridge
Illogan
Redruth
St Day
Twelveheads
Cross Lanes
Pool
Carn Brea
Carn Brea Village
Pennance
Carharrack
Bissoe
Cusgarne
Carnon Downs
Brea
Carnkie
Cornish Engines (NT)
Gwennap
Perranwell Sta
Lanner
Four Lanes
Perranarworthal
Devoran
Bolenowe
Penhalvean
Ponsanooth
Angarrick
Stockdale
Stithians
Stithians Reservoir
Crowan Beacon
Burras
Long Downs
Carnkie
Rame
Mabe Burnthouse
Lezerea
Porkellis
Edgcumbe
Crelly
Trenear
Seworgan
Trebarvah
Wendron
Trevenen
Brill
Constantine
Trewennack
Helston
Gweek
Cornish Seal Sanctuary
Trelowarren
Mawgan
Garras
Halliggye Fogou
Manaccan
St Martin
Tregidden
Newtown-in-St-Martin
Goonhilly Satellite Earth Station
St Winwaloe
Cross Lanes
Cury
Traboe
Tumuli
Lanarth
Tregowris
Tregarne
St Keverne
LIZARD PENINSULA
Goonhilly Downs
Mullion
Cove
Trelan
Erisey Barton
Penhale
Gwenter
Ponsongath
Coverack
Gwendreath
South West Coast Path
Kennack Sands
Kuggar
Ruan Major
Ruan Minor
St Ruan
Wollas
Vellan Head
Grade
Cadgwith
Toll
The Lizard National Nature Reserve
Kynance Cove
Landewednack
Lizard
Hot Point
LIZARD POINT
Black Head
Lowland Pt
The Manacles
Manacle Point
Rosenithon
Porthoustock
Porthallow
Roskorwell
Flushing
Nare Point
St Anthony-in-Meneage
Helford
Mawnan
Durgan
Trebah Garden
Glendurgan (NT)
Porth Navas
Mawnan Smith
Maenporth
Rosemullion Head
FALMOUTH BAY
National Maritime Museum Cornwall
Penjerrick
Treverva
Budock Water
Penryn
Falmouth
Pendennis Castle
Pendennis Point
Flushing
Mylor
Mylor Bridge
Carrick Roads
Feock
Penpol
Trelissick (NT)
Playing Place
Penelewey
Kea
Old Kea
Coombe
Truro
Truro Cathedral
Royal Cornwall Museum
Malpas
St Clement
Lamorran
St Michael Penkevil
Trelissick
Philleigh
Treworga
Treworthal
St Just in Roseland
St Just in Roseland
St Mawes
St Mawes Castle
Castle Pt
St Anthony
Bohortha
Zone Point
Gerrans
Portscatho
Greeb Point
Trewithian
Gerrans Bay
Nare Head
Treworlas
Veryan
Veryan Green
Portloe
Veryan Bay
Portholland
Boswinger
St Michael Caerhays
Gorran Churchtown
Gorran Haven
Maenease Point
Penare
Dodman Point
Trevarrick
Portmellon
Mevagissey
Pentewan
Tregiskey
Lost Gardens of Heligan
St Ewe
Polmassick
Kestle
Trewarthenick
Tregony
Ruan Lanihorne
Creed
Grampound
Trewithen
Probus
Tresillian
Merther
Trispen
St Erme
Tregear
Ladock
Grampound Road
Hewas Water
Sticker
Polgooth
St Mewan
ST AUSTELL
Trewoon
High Street
Coombe
Mount Charles
Wheal Martyn
St Stephen
New Mills
Trelassick
Carland Cross
Mitchell
Brighton
Scarcewater
Foxhole
Chapel Town
Summercourt
Meledor
Treviscoe
Nanpean
Carthew
Ruddlemoor
Retew
St Enoder
Blue Anchor
Fraddon
Indian Queens
St Dennis
Gothers
Hensbarrow Downs
Whitemoor
Stenalees
Penwithick
Bugle
Rosevean
Bilberry
Enniscaven
Trezaise
Coldvreath
Roche
Tregoss
Ruthvoes
Trevarren
St Columb Road
White Cross
Retyn
Mountjoy
Colan
Trebudannon
Tregaswith
St Columb Major
NEWQUAY (CORNWALL)
Reterth
Tregonetha
Victoria
Roche Chapel
Lanivet
Criggan
Bodwen
Lockengate
Pentewan
Retyn
A30
A39
A3058
A392
A3075
A3076
A390
A3047
A393
A394
A3078
A3083
A391
B3285
B3284
B3277
B3300
B3297
B3298
B3280
B3292
B3289
B3287
B3275
B3273
B3274
B3279
B3296
B3293
B3276
B3266

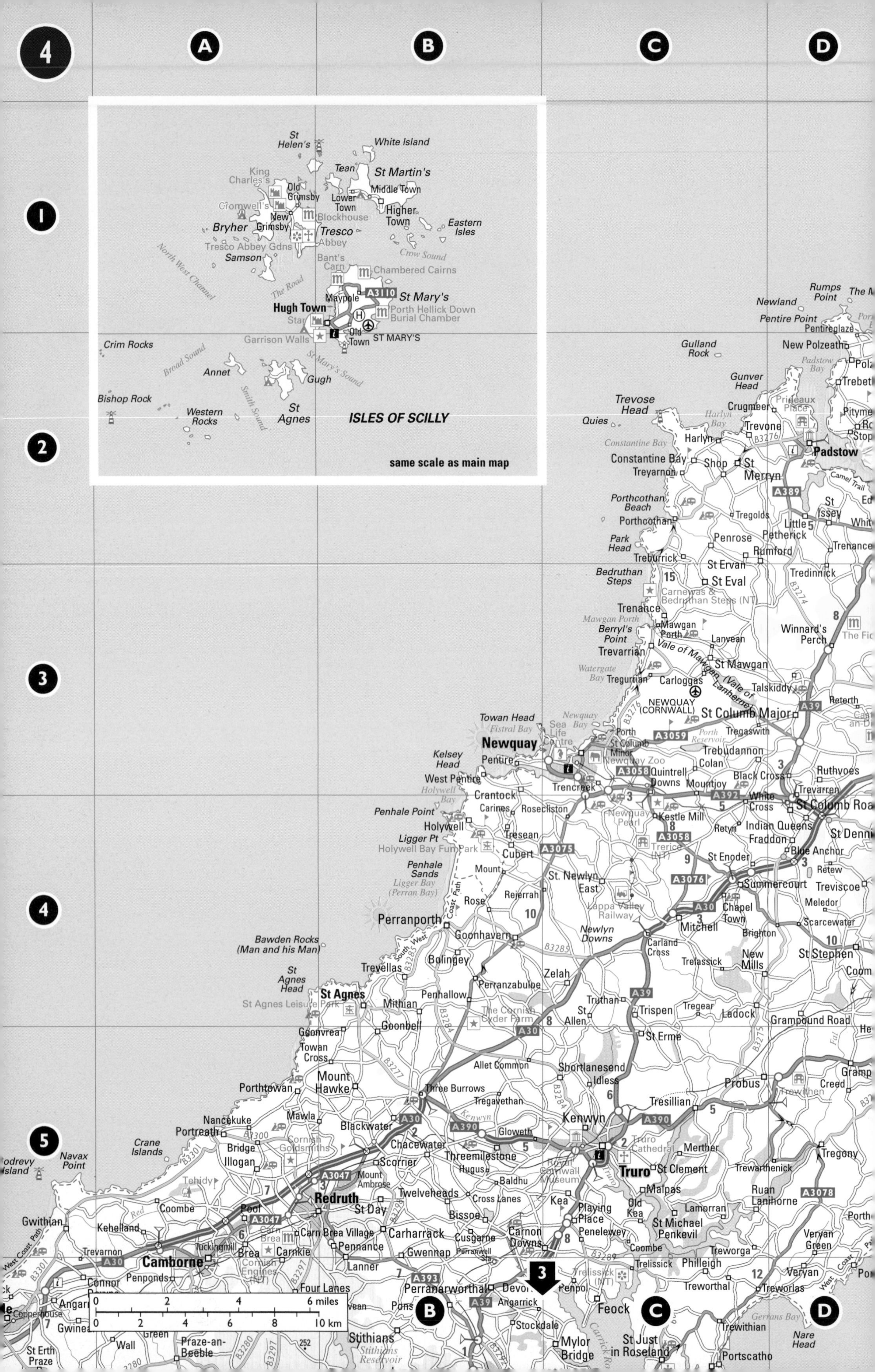

4
A
B
C
D
1
2
3
4
5
St Helen's
White Island
Tean
St Martin's
King Charles's
Old Grimsby
Lower Town
Middle Town
Cromwell's
New Grimsby
Blockhouse
Higher Town
Eastern Isles
Bryher
Tresco
Tresco Abbey Gdns
Abbey
Samson
North West Channel
Crow Sound
Bant's Carn
Chambered Cairns
The Road
A3110
St Mary's
Maypole
Hugh Town
Porth Hellick Down Burial Chamber
Star
Old Town
ST MARY'S
Crim Rocks
Garrison Walls
Broad Sound
Annet
St Mary's Sound
Gugh
Bishop Rock
Smith Sound
Western Rocks
St Agnes
ISLES OF SCILLY
same scale as main map
Rumps Point
The M
Newland
Pentire Point
Pentireglaze
New Polzeath
Gulland Rock
Padstow Bay
Gunver Head
Prideaux Place
Trevose Head
Harlyn Bay
Crugmeer
Quies
Trevone
Constantine Bay
Harlyn
B3276
Constantine Bay
Shop
St Merryn
Padstow
Treyarnon
Camel Trail
A389
Porthcothan Beach
St Issey
Porthcothan
Tregolds
Little Petherick
Park Head
Penrose
Rumford
Trenance
Treburrick
St Ervan
Tredinnick
Bedruthan Steps
15
St Eval
Carnewas & Bedruthan Steps (NT)
B3274
Trenance
8
Mawgan Porth
Berryl's Point
Mawgan Porth
Lanvean
Winnard's Perch
Trevarrian
Vale of Mawgan (Vale of Lanherne)
St Mawgan
Watergate Bay
Tregurrian
Carloggas
Talskiddy
NEWQUAY (CORNWALL)
St Columb Major
Reterth
A39
Towan Head
Fistral Bay
Newquay Bay
Sea Life Centre
Porth
A3059
Porth Reservoir
Tregaswith
Newquay
St Columb Minor
Trebudannon
Kelsey Head
Pentire
Newquay Zoo
Colan
West Pentire
A3058
Quintrell Downs
Mountjoy
Black Cross
Ruthvoes
Holywell Bay
Trencreek
3
A392
White Cross
Trevarren
Crantock
St Columb Road
Carines
Rosecliston
Newquay Pearl
5
Penhale Point
Kestle Mill
Retyn
Indian Queens
Holywell
8
A3058
Fraddon
St Dennis
Ligger Pt
Tresean
Trerice (NT)
Holywell Bay Fun Park
A3075
St Enoder
Blue Anchor
Penhale Sands
Cubert
9
Retew
Mount
St. Newlyn East
A3076
Summercourt
Treviscoe
Ligger Bay (Perran Bay)
Coast Path
Rejerrah
Lappa Valley Railway
Meledor
Rose
A30
Chapel Town
Perranporth
10
Mitchell
Scarcewater
Goonhavern
Newlyn Downs
Brighton
Carland Cross
10
Bawden Rocks (Man and his Man)
South West
B3285
B3285
New Mills
St Stephen
Bolingey
Trelassick
Coom
Trevellas
Zelah
St Agnes Head
Perranzabuloe
Truthan
A39
St Agnes
Penhallow
Tregear
St Agnes Leisure Park
Mithian
The Cornish Cyder Farm
Trispen
Ladock
St Allen
Grampound Road
B3284
8
Goonvrea
Goonbell
A30
St Erme
B3275
Towan Cross
B3277
Allet Common
Shortlanesend
Grampound
Mount Hawke
Idless
Probus
Porthtowan
Three Burrows
Creed
6
Trewithen
Tregavethan
Tresillian
5
Mawla
Kenwyn
Kenwyn
Nancekuke
Blackwater
A30
A390
A390
Portreath
B3300
Cornish Goldsmiths
2
Gloweth
Crane Islands
Bridge
Chacewater
5
Truro Cathedral
Merther
Tregony
Navax Point
Illogan
Scorrier
Threemilestone
Royal Cornwall Museum
Godrevy Island
B3301
Tehidy
A3047
Mount Ambrose
Hugus
Baldhu
Truro
St Clement
Trewarthenick
7
Redruth
Twelveheads
Malpas
Ruan Lanihorne
A3078
Coombe
Pool
Cross Lanes
Kea
Gwithian
St Day
Playing Place
Old Kea
Lamorran
Kehelland
A3047
Carn Brea
Carn Brea Village
Bissoe
St Michael Penkevil
Porth
Carharrack
Cusgarne
Carnon Downs
Penelewey
Veryan Green
Tuckingmill
6
Pennance
8
West Coast Path
Trevarnon
Brea
Carnkie
Gwennap
Perranwell Sta
Coombe
Treworga
A30
Camborne
Cornish Engines (NT)
Lanner
B3289
Trelissick
Philleigh
B3330
B3297
7
A393
Trelissick (NT)
12
Veryan
Connor Downs
Penponds
Four Lanes
Perranarworthal
Devoran
Penpol
Treworthal
Treworlas
Angarrack
Copperhouse
Pons
A39
Angarrick
3
Feock
Gerrans Bay
Gwinear
Green
Stithians
Stockdale
Trewithian
Nare Head
St Erth Praze
Wall
Praze-an-Beeble
B3280
B3297
252
Stithians Reservoir
1
Mylor Bridge
Carrick Roads
St Just in Roseland
Portscatho
0
2
4
6 miles
0
2
4
6
8
10 km

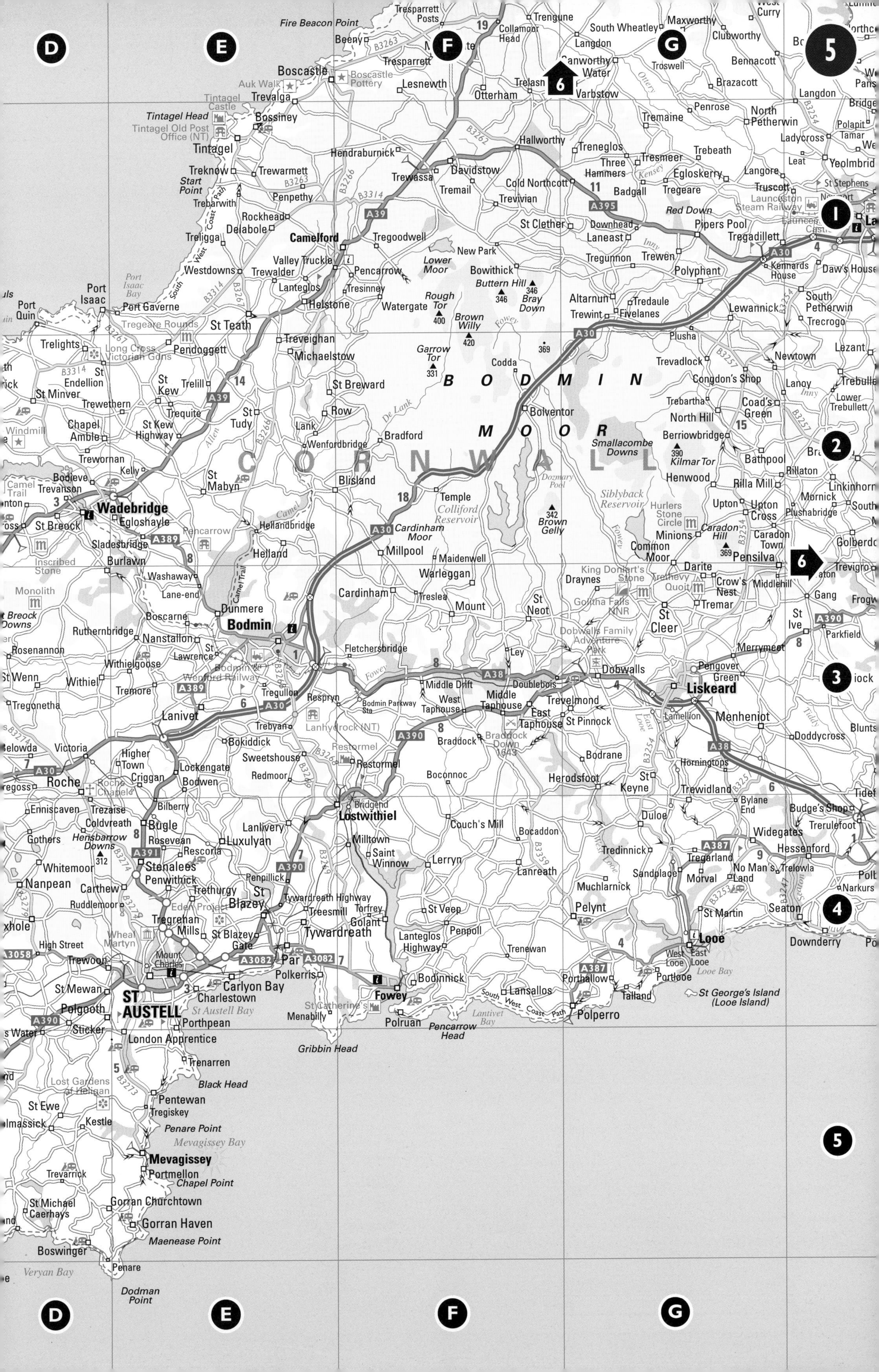

D
E
F
G
5
6
Fire Beacon Point
Tresparrett Posts
Trengune
South Wheatley
Maxworthy
Clubworthy
Collamoor Head
Langdon
Beeny
B3263
Tresparrett
Canworthy Water
Bennacott
Boscastle
Boscastle Pottery
Lesnewth
Otterham
Trelash
Warbstow
Troswell
Brazacott
Auk Walk
Tintagel Castle
Trevalga
Penrose
North Petherwin
Langdon
Bridge
Tintagel Head
Tintagel Old Post Office (NT)
Bossiney
Tremaine
Polapit Tamar
B3262
B3254
Hallworthy
Ladycross
Tintagel
Hendraburnick
Treneglos
Trebeath
Three Hammers
Tresmeer
Leat
Yeolmbridge
Treknow
Trewarmett
Davidstow
Egloskerry
Langore
Start Point
B3263
Trewassa
Cold Northcott
Tregeare
Truscott
St Stephens
Trebarwith
Penpethy
B3314
Tremail
11
Badgall
Launceston Steam Railway
Trevivian
A395
Red Down
Rockhead
A39
St Clether
Downhead
Pipers Pool
Delabole
Camelford
Tregoodwell
Laneast
Tregadillett
Launceston Castle
Treligga
New Park
Inny
Valley Truckle
Lower Moor
Bowithick
Tregunnon
Trewen
A30
Westdowns
Trewalder
Pencarrow
Polyphant
Kennards House
Daw's House
Port Isaac Bay
Buttern Hill
346
Lanteglos
Tresinney
Rough Tor
400
346 Bray Down
Altarnun
Tredaule
South Petherwin
Port Isaac
South West Coast Path
B3314
Helstone
Watergate
Trewint
Fivelanes
Lewannick
Trecrogo
Port Quin
Port Gaverne
Brown Willy
420
Tregeare Rounds
St Teath
Plusha
Treveighan
369
Lezant
Trelights
Long Cross Victorian Gdns
Pendoggett
Garrow Tor
331
Codda
Newtown
Michaelstow
Trevadlock
B3257
St Endellion
Congdon's Shop
Lanoy
Trebullett
St Kew
Trelill
14
St Breward
B O D M I N
Trebartha
Lower Trebullett
St Minver
A39
Coad's Green
Trewethern
Trequite
Row
Bolventor
North Hill
Windmill
Chapel Amble
St Kew Highway
St Tudy
De Lank
Lank
15
M O O R
Smallacombe Downs
Berriowbridge
390
Kilmar Tor
2
Allen
Wenfordbridge
Bradford
B3266
C O R N W A L L
Bathpool
Trewornan
Kelly
Dozmary Pool
Rillaton
Bodieve
St Mabyn
Blisland
Henwood
Camel Trail
Trevanson
Temple
Sibleyback Reservoir
Rilla Mill
Linkinhorne
Mornick
3
Wadebridge
18
Colliford Reservoir
Upton
Upton Cross
Hurlers Stone Circle
Plushabridge
South
St Breock
Egloshayle
Pencarrow
Hellandbridge
Cardinham Moor
342 Brown Gelly
Minions
Caradon Hill
369
Caradon Town
Sladesbridge
A389
A30
Helland
Common Moor
Golberdon
Inscribed Stone
Burlawn
8
Millpool
Maidenwell
Fowey
Pensilva
Washaway
Warleggan
King Doniert's Stone
Darite
Trevigro
Monolith
Camel Trail
Lane-end
Cardinham
Treslea
Draynes
Trethevy Quoit
Crow's Nest
Middlehill
Gang
St Breock Downs
Dunmere
Mount
St Neot
Golitha Falls NNR
Tremar
Frogwell
Boscarne
Bodmin
St Cleer
St Ive
A390
Parkfield
Ruthernbridge
Nanstallon
1
Dobwalls Family Adventure Park
Ley
Rosenannon
St Lawrence
Fletchersbridge
Merrymeet
8
Withielgoose
Bodmin & Wenford Railway
8
Pengover Green
St Wenn
Withiel
Tremore
A389
A38
Middle Drift
Doublebois
Dobwalls
4
Liskeard
3
Tregullon
Respryn
Bodmin Parkway Sta
West Taphouse
Middle Taphouse
Trevelmond
Tregonetha
6
A30
East Taphouse
St Pinnock
Lamellion
Menheniot
Lanivet
Trebyan
Lanhydrock (NT)
A390
8
East Looe
Tiddy
Blunts
Belowda
Victoria
Higher Town
Bokiddick
Braddock
Braddock Down 1643
Doddycross
B3274
Restormel
Sweetshouse
Bodrane
A38
A30
Lockengate
Restormel
B3254
7
Roche
Criggan
Redmoor
Boconnoc
Herodsfoot
St Keyne
Horningtops
Roche Chapel
Bodwen
B3268
B3252
6
Tideford
Bilberry
Bridgend
Trewidland
Bylane End
Enniscaven
Trezaise
Lostwithiel
Budge's Shop
Coldvreath
Bugle
Lanlivery
Couch's Mill
Duloe
Trerulefoot
Gothers
Hensbarrow Downs
312
Roseveah
Luxulyan
Milltown
Bocaddon
Widegates
8
A391
Rescorla
7
Saint Winnow
B3359
Tredinnick
A387
Hessenford
Whitemoor
Stenalees
Penwithick
Lerryn
Tregarland
9
B3274
A390
West Looe River
Sandplace
Morval
No Man's Land
Trelowia
Polbathic
Nanpean
Carthew
Penpillick
Lanreath
Narkurs
Trethurgy
St Blazey
Tywardreath Highway
Muchlarnick
Seaton
B3279
Ruddlemoor
Eden Project
Treesmill
Torfrey
St Veep
Pelynt
B3253
4
Tregrehan Mills
Golant
St Martin
Wheal Martyn
St Blazey Gate
Tywardreath
Lanteglos Highway
Penpoll
Looe
Downderry
High Street
Trenewan
4
Trewoon
A3082
Par
A3082
7
West Looe
East Looe
A3058
Mount Charles
Looe Bay
Polkerris
A387
St Mewan
3
Carlyon Bay
Bodinnick
Lansallos
Porthallow
Portlooe
St George's Island (Looe Island)
Charlestown
Fowey
Talland
St Austell
St Austell Bay
St Catherine's
South West Coast Path
Polgooth
Porthpean
Menabilly
Polruan
Lantivet Bay
Polperro
A390
Pencarrow Head
Sticker
London Apprentice
Gribbin Head
5
Trenarren
B3273
Lost Gardens of Heligan
Black Head
Pentewan
St Ewe
Tregiskey
Kestle
Penare Point
Mevagissey Bay
5
Mevagissey
Portmellon
Trevarrick
Chapel Point
St Michael Caerhays
Gorran Churchtown
Gorran Haven
Maenease Point
Boswinger
Penare
Veryan Bay
Dodman Point
D
E
F
G

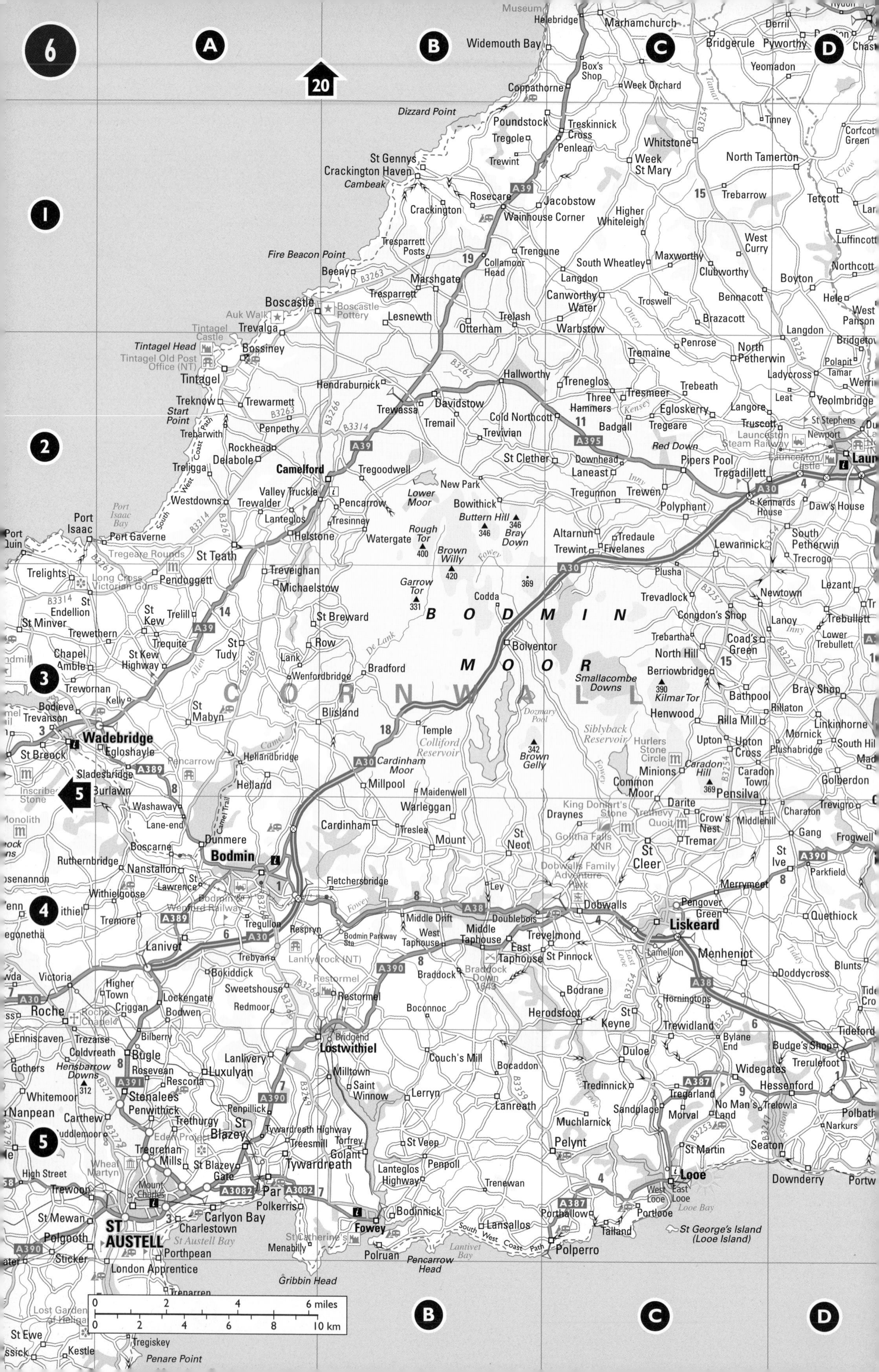
A
B
C
D
20
1
2
3
4
5
Museum
Helebridge
Marhamchurch
Derril
Bridgerule
Pyworthy
Widemouth Bay
Box's Shop
Yeomadon
Coppathorne
Week Orchard
Tamar
Dizzard Point
Poundstock
Treskinnick Cross
Tinney
Corfcott Green
Tregole
Penlean
Whitstone
Trewint
B3254
North Tamerton
St Gennys
Crackington Haven
Week St Mary
Cambeak
Claw
A39
Rosecare
Jacobstow
15
Trebarrow
Tetcott
Crackington
Wainhouse Corner
Higher Whiteleigh
Luffincott
Trengune
West Curry
Tresparrett Posts
Fire Beacon Point
19
Collamoor Head
South Wheatley
Maxworthy
Northcott
Beeny
B3263
Clubworthy
Langdon
Boyton
Marshgate
Tresparrett
Canworthy Water
Troswell
Bennacott
Hele
Boscastle
Boscastle Pottery
Auk Walk
Lesnewth
Trelash
Brazacott
West Panson
Trevalga
Tintagel Castle
Otterham
Warbstow
Ottery
Langdon
Tintagel Head
Bossiney
Penrose
Bridgetown
Tintagel Old Post Office (NT)
Tremaine
North Petherwin
B3254
Polapit Tamar
Tintagel
B3262
Hallworthy
Ladycross
Hendraburnick
Treneglos
Trebeath
Werrington
Treknow
Trewarmett
Davidstow
Three Hammers
Tresmeer
Leat
Yeolmbridge
Start Point
B3263
B3266
Trewassa
Kensey
Egloskerry
Langore
Tremail
Cold Northcott
St Stephens
Trebarwith
Penpethy
B3314
11
Badgall
Tregeare
Truscott
Newport
Coast Path
Rockhead
A39
Trevivian
A395
Red Down
Launceston Steam Railway
Delabole
St Clether
Downhead
Pipers Pool
Launceston Castle
Tregoodwell
Laneast
Tregadillett
Treligga
Camelford
Inny
Lower Moor
New Park
A30
South West
Valley Truckle
Tregunnon
Trewen
4
Port Isaac Bay
Westdowns
Trewalder
Pencarrow
Bowithick
Polyphant
Kennards House
Daw's House
Port Isaac
Lanteglos
Tresinney
Rough Tor
Buttern Hill
346
346
Bray Down
Port Quin
Port Gaverne
B3314
B3267
Helstone
Watergate
400
Altarnun
Tredaule
South Petherwin
Tregeare Rounds
St Teath
Brown Willy
Trewint
Fivelanes
Lewannick
Trecrogo
420
Fowey
Trelights
Long Cross Victorian Gdns
Treveighan
Pendoggett
A30
Plusha
B3267
Garrow Tor
369
Lezant
B3314
St Endellion
Michaelstow
Codda
B3257
Newtown
331
Trevadlock
St Minver
Trelill
St Kew
14
St Breward
B O D M I N
Congdon's Shop
Lanoy
Trebullett
Trewethern
Trequite
A39
Inny
Lower Trebullett
St Tudy
Row
Bolventor
Trebartha
Coad's Green
B3257
Chapel Amble
St Kew Highway
De Lank
Lank
M O O R
North Hill
15
Bradford
Berriowbridge
Smallacombe Downs
Allen
Wenfordbridge
390
Kilmar Tor
Trewornan
Kelly
C O R N W A L L
Bathpool
Bray Shop
Bodieve
St Mabyn
Blisland
Dozmary Pool
Henwood
Rillaton
Trevanson
3
Wadebridge
18
Temple
Rilla Mill
Linkinhorne
Egloshayle
Colliford Reservoir
Siblyback Reservoir
Hurlers Stone Circle
Upton
Upton Cross
Camel
St Breock
Pencarrow
Hellandbridge
342
South Hill
A389
A30
Cardinham Moor
Brown Gelly
Minions
Caradon Hill
Plushabridge
B3254
Mornick
Sladesbridge
Caradon Town
Golberdon
Inscribed Stone
5
Burlawn
8
Helland
Millpool
Common Moor
369
Pensilva
Maidenwell
Darite
Trevigro
Washaway
Camel Trail
Warleggan
Draynes
King Doniert's Stone
Trethevy Quoit
Crow's Nest
Charaton
Middlehill
Lane-end
Cardinham
Treslea
St Neot
Golitha Falls NNR
Gang
Dunmere
Mount
St Cleer
Tremar
St Ive
Frogwell
Boscarne
Bodmin
A390
Ruthernbridge
Nanstallon
Dobwalls Family Adventure Park
Parkfield
St Lawrence
Fletchersbridge
Ley
8
Merrymeet
Withielgoose
Bodmin & Wenford Railway
1
B3268
8
Dobwalls
Pengover Green
Withiel
Fowey
Middle Drift
A38
Doublebois
Quethiock
Tremore
A389
Tregullon
Respryn
Middle Taphouse
Trevelmond
4
Liskeard
6
A30
Bodmin Parkway Sta
West Taphouse
East Taphouse
Lamellion
Menheniot
Lanivet
Trebyan
St Pinnock
East Looe
Tideford
Lanhydrock (NT)
A390
8
Braddock
Braddock Down 1643
Victoria
Bokiddick
Higher Town
Restormel
Doddycross
Blunts
Sweetshouse
B3268
Bodrane
B3254
Lockengate
Restormel
A38
A30
Redmoor
Criggan
Boconnoc
Roche
Roche Chapel
Bodwen
B3269
Horningtops
Herodsfoot
St Keyne
Trezaise
Enniscaven
Bilberry
Bridgend
Trewidland
B3252
6
Tideford
Coldvreath
Bugle
Lostwithiel
Bylane End
Budge's Shop
Lanlivery
Duloe
Gothers
Hensbarrow Downs
8
Rosevean
Couch's Mill
Bocaddon
Trerulefoot
Luxulyan
Milltown
Widegates
312
Rescorla
A391
Saint Winnow
Tredinnick
A387
Hessenford
Whitemoor
Stenalees
A390
B3269
B3359
7
West Looe
Tregarland
9
Lerryn
Lanreath
Nanpean
Penwithick
Penpillick
Sandplace
Morval
No Man's Land
Trelowla
Polbathic
Carthew
Trethurgy
Tywardreath Highway
Muchlarnick
Narkurs
Eden Project
St Blazey
Treesmill
Torfrey
St Veep
Pelynt
B3253
B3247
Seaton
Tregrehan Mills
Wheal Martyn
Golant
St Martin
St Blazey Gate
Tywardreath
Penpoll
Lanteglos Highway
Looe
High Street
Trewoon
Mount Charles
A3082
Par
A3082
7
Trenewan
4
Downderry
Portwrinkle
East Looe
A387
Bodinnick
Looe Bay
St Mewan
Carlyon Bay
Polkerris
West Looe
Porthallow
ST AUSTELL
Charlestown
Fowey
Lansallos
Portlooe
St George's Island (Looe Island)
Polgooth
St Austell Bay
St Catherine's
Talland
A390
Menabilly
Lantivet Bay
South West Coast Path
Polperro
Sticker
Porthpean
Polruan
Pencarrow Head
London Apprentice
Gribbin Head
Trenarren
Lost Gardens of Heligan
0
2
4
6 miles
0
2
4
6
8
10 km
B
C
D
St Ewe
Tregiskey
Kestle
Penare Point

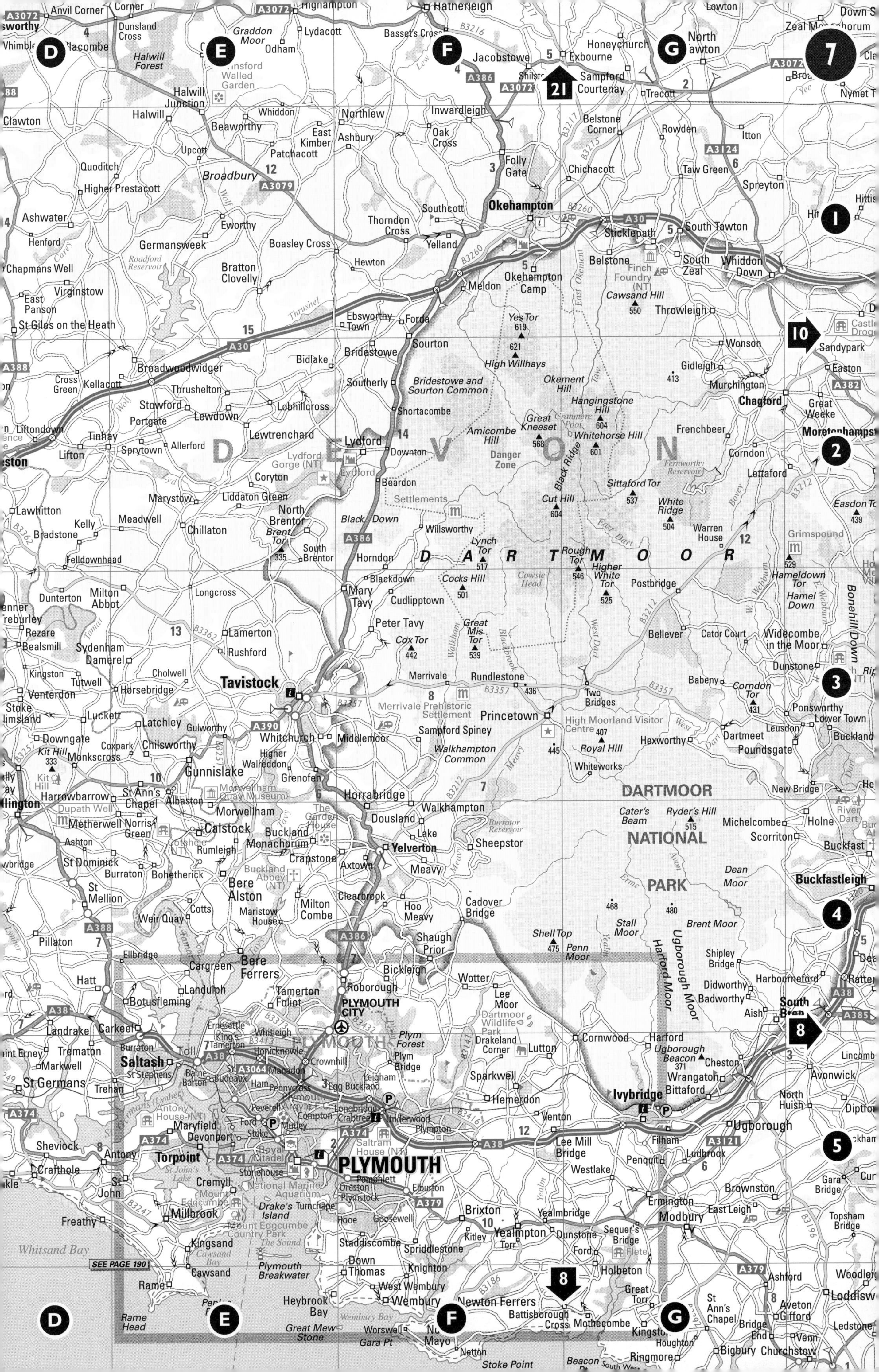

7
21
10
8
8
DEVON
DARTMOOR
DARTMOOR NATIONAL PARK
Anvil Corner
Dunsland Cross
Graddon Moor
Highampton
Hatherleigh
Lydacott
Odham
Basset's Cross
Jacobstowe
Exbourne
Honeychurch
North Tawton
Sampford Courtenay
Halwill Forest
Halwill Junction
Halwill
Whiddon
Beaworthy
Northlew
Inwardleigh
East Kimber
Ashbury
Oak Cross
Folly Gate
Belstone Corner
Rowden
Itton
Trecott
Clawton
Upcott
Patchacott
Quoditch
Higher Prestacott
Broadbury
Chichacott
Taw Green
Spreyton
Ashwater
Southcott
Okehampton
Eworthy
Thorndon Cross
Sticklepath
South Tawton
Henford
Germansweek
Roadford Reservoir
Boasley Cross
Yelland
Belstone
South Zeal
Whiddon Down
Chapmans Well
Bratton Clovelly
Hewton
Okehampton Camp
Finch Foundry (NT)
Cawsand Hill
Virginstow
Meldon
Throwleigh
East Panson
Thrushel
St Giles on the Heath
Ebsworthy Town
Forda
Yes Tor
High Willhays
Sourton
Wonson
Sandypark
Easton
Bidlake
Bridestowe
Gidleigh
Murchington
Chagford
Broadwoodwidger
Cross Green
Kellacott
Southerly
Bridestowe and Sourton Common
Okement Hill
Thrushelton
Stowford
Lobhillcross
Shortacombe
Hangingstone Hill
Great Weeke
Portgate
Lewdown
Cranmere Pool
Moretonhampstead
Liftondown
Tinhay
Lewtrenchard
Great Kneeset
Amicombe Hill
Whitehorse Hill
Frenchbeer
Lifton
Sprytown
Allerford
Lydford
Downton
Lydford Gorge (NT)
Danger Zone
Black Ridge
Fernworthy Reservoir
Corndon
Lettaford
Coryton
Beardon
Settlements
Sittaford Tor
Lawhitton
Marystow
Liddaton Green
North Brentor
Cut Hill
White Ridge
Easdon Tor
Kelly
Meadwell
Black Down
Willsworthy
Warren House
Grimspound
Bradstone
Chillaton
Brent Tor
South Brentor
Lynch Tor
Rough Tor
Higher White Tor
Felldownhead
Horndon
Blackdown
Cocks Hill
Cowsic Head
Postbridge
Hameldown Tor
Hamel Down
Milton Abbot
Longcross
Mary Tavy
Dunterton
Cudlipptown
Bonehill Down
Rezare
Peter Tavy
Great Mis Tor
Lamerton
Rushford
Cox Tor
Bellever
Cator Court
Widecombe in the Moor
Sydenham Damerel
Bealsmill
Kingston
Cholwell
Tutwell
Horsebridge
Tavistock
Merrivale
Rundlestone
Dunstone
Babeny
Corndon Tor
Two Bridges
Venterdon
Stoke Climsland
Luckett
Latchley
Merrivale Prehistoric Settlement
Princetown
Ponsworthy
Lower Town
High Moorland Visitor Centre
Gulworthy
Whitchurch
Middlemoor
Sampford Spiney
Dartmeet
Leusdon
Downgate
Coxpark
Chilsworthy
Higher Walreddon
Walkhampton Common
Royal Hill
Hexworthy
Poundsgate
Buckland
Kit Hill
Monkscross
Gunnislake
Grenofen
Whiteworks
Harrowbarrow
St Ann's Chapel
Morwellham Quay Museum
Horrabridge
New Bridge
Dupath Well
Albaston
The Garden House
Morwellham
Walkhampton
Cater's Beam
Ryder's Hill
Metherwell
Norris Green
Calstock
Dousland
Burrator Reservoir
Michelcombe
Holne
River Dart
Ashton
Cotehele (NT)
Buckland Monachorum
Lake
Sheepstor
Scorriton
Rumleigh
Yelverton
Buckfast
St Dominick
Crapstone
Axtown
Meavy
Dean Moor
Burraton
Bohetherick
Buckland Abbey (NT)
Buckfastleigh
St Mellion
Bere Alston
Erme
Clearbrook
Cadover Bridge
Cotts
Milton Combe
Hoo Meavy
Maristow House
Weir Quay
Stall Moor
Brent Moor
Shell Top
Penn Moor
Harford Moor
Ugborough Moor
Pillaton
Shaugh Prior
Shipley Bridge
Ellbridge
Bere Ferrers
Cargreen
Bickleigh
Wotter
Harbourneford
Rattery
Hatt
Landulph
Roborough
Lee Moor
Dartmoor Wildlife Park
Didworthy
Badworthy
Tamerton Foliot
Botusfleming
PLYMOUTH CITY
South Brent
Aish
Landrake
Carkeel
Ernesettle
King's Tamerton
Whitleigh
PLYMOUTH
Plym Forest
Drakeland Corner
Lutton
Cornwood
Harford
Burraton
Saltash
Trematon
Honicknowle
Crownhill
Plym Bridge
Ugborough Beacon
Cheston
St Erney
Markwell
St Stephens
Barne Barton
Bude
Mannamead
Egg Buckland
Leigham
Sparkwell
Wrangaton
Avonwick
St Germans
Trehan
Ham
Pennycross
Plymouth Argyle F.C.
Longbridge
Crabtree
Hemerdon
Ivybridge
Bittaford
North Huish
Antony House (NT)
Peverell
Compton
Underwood
Plympton
Venton
Diptford
Maryfield
Ford
Stoke
Mutley
Ugborough
Devonport
Royal Citadel
Saltram House (NT)
Lee Mill Bridge
Filham
Sheviock
Antony
Torpoint
St John's Lake
Stonehouse
Westlake
Penquit
Ludbrook
Crafthole
St John
Cremyll
Mount Edgcumbe
National Marine Aquarium
Pomphlett
Oreston
Plymstock
Elburton
Ermington
Brownston
Gara Bridge
Millbrook
Drake's Island
Turnchapel
Hooe
Goosewell
Brixton
Yealmbridge
Modbury
East Leigh
Topsham Bridge
Freathy
Mount Edgcumbe Country Park
Staddiscombe
Kitley
Yealmpton
Torr
Dunstone
Sequer's Bridge
Flete
Kingsand
Cawsand Bay
The Sound
Spriddlestone
Ford
Whitsand Bay
SEE PAGE 190
Cawsand
Plymouth Breakwater
Down Thomas
Knighton
Holbeton
Ashford
Woodleigh
Loddiswell
Rame
West Wembury
Great Torr
Heybrook Bay
Wembury
Newton Ferrers
Battisborough Cross
Mothecombe
St Ann's Chapel
Aveton Gifford
Rame Head
Wembury Bay
Great Mew Stone
Worswell
Noss Mayo
Gara Pt
Kingston
Houghton
Bridge End
Venn
Ledstone
Netton
Ringmore
Bigbury
Churchstow
Stoke Point
Beacon Point
A3072
A386
A30
A3079
A388
A384
B3260
B3216
B3217
B3215
A3124
A382
B3212
B3357
A390
B3362
B3257
A3064
B3413
B3373
B3432
A374
A38
A385
A379
A3121
B3416
B3247
B3186
B3213
B3196

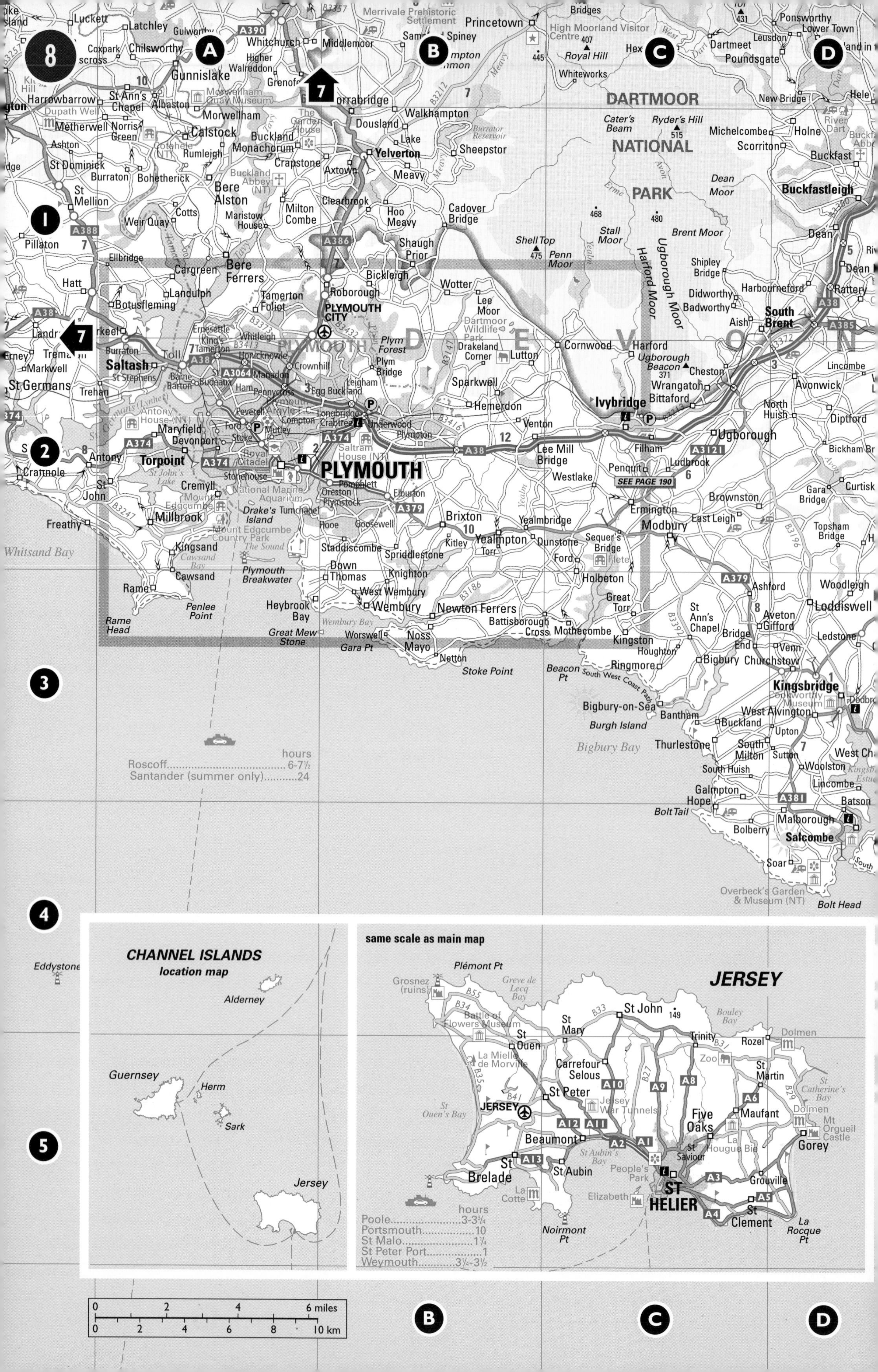

8
A
B
C
D
1
2
3
4
5
7
Luckett
Latchley
Gulworthy
A390
Whitchurch
Middlemoor
B3357
Merrivale Prehistoric Settlement
Princetown
Bridges
High Moorland Visitor Centre
407
Royal Hill
445
Hex
Dartmeet
Poundsgate
Ponsworthy
Lower Town
Leusdon
Coxpark
Chilsworthy
Gunnislake
Higher Walreddon
Sampford Spiney
Whiteworks
Harrowbarrow
St Ann's Chapel
Albaston
Morwellham Quay Museum
Grenofen
Horrabridge
Metherwell
Norris Green
Morwellham
Calstock
Dupath Well
Dousland
Walkhampton
B3212
Burrator Reservoir
DARTMOOR
NATIONAL
PARK
Cater's Beam
Ryder's Hill
515
Michelcombe
Holne
New Bridge
Hele
River Dart
Ashton
Cotehele (NT)
Rumleigh
Buckland Monachorum
The Garden House
Lake
Yelverton
Sheepstor
Scorriton
Buckfast
St Dominick
Crapstone
Axtown
Meavy
Burraton
Bohetherick
Buckland Abbey (NT)
Dean Moor
Buckfastleigh
St Mellion
Bere Alston
Milton Combe
Clearbrook
Hoo Meavy
Cadover Bridge
468
480
Brent Moor
Erme
Avon
Weir Quay
Cotts
Maristow House
A388
Pillaton
Shaugh Prior
Stall Moor
Shell Top
475
Penn Moor
Yealm
Harford Moor
Ugborough Moor
Dean
A386
Ellbridge
Cargreen
Bere Ferrers
Shipley Bridge
Hatt
Landulph
Tamerton Foliot
Bickleigh
Roborough
Wotter
Lee Moor
Didworthy
Badworthy
Harbourneford
Rattery
Botusfleming
PLYMOUTH CITY
Dartmoor Wildlife Park
Aish
South Brent
A385
A38
Landrake
Tremateon
Burraton
Saltash
Ernesettle
King's Tamerton
Whitleigh
B3373
B3413
B3432
Plym Forest
Drakeland Corner
Lutton
Cornwood
Harford
Ugborough Beacon
371
Cheston
Lincombe
Markwell
St Stephens
Toll
Honicknowle
Crownhill
Plym Bridge
St Budeaux
A3064
Manadon
Barne Barton
Leigham
St Germans
Trehan
Ham
Pennycross
Egg Buckland
Sparkwell
Wrangaton
Bittaford
Avonwick
Antony House (NT)
Peverell
Mutley
Longbridge
Crabtree
Underwood
Plympton
Hemerdon
Ivybridge
North Huish
Diptford
Maryfield
Devonport
Ford
Stoke
Compton
B3416
Venton
A374
Saltram House (NT)
Lee Mill Bridge
Filham
Ugborough
Bickham Br
Antony
Torpoint
Royal Citadel
PLYMOUTH
A38
A3121
Ludbrook
Crafthole
St John's Lake
Stonehouse
Pomphlett
Westlake
Penquit
SEE PAGE 190
Curtisk
St John
Cremyll
National Marine Aquarium
Oreston
Plymstock
Elburton
A379
Ermington
Brownston
Gara Bridge
Freathy
B3247
Mount Edgcumbe
Millbrook
Drake's Island
Turnchapel
Hooe
Goosewell
Brixton
Yealmbridge
Modbury
East Leigh
Topsham Bridge
Whitsand Bay
Mount Edgcumbe Country Park
Kitley
Yealmpton
Dunstone
Sequer's Bridge
Kingsand
Cawsand Bay
The Sound
Staddiscombe
Spriddlestone
Torr
Flete
B3196
Cawsand
Plymouth Breakwater
Down Thomas
Knighton
B3186
Holbeton
Ashford
Woodleigh
Rame
West Wembury
Great Torr
Loddiswell
Penlee Point
Heybrook Bay
Wembury
Newton Ferrers
Battisborough Cross
Mothecombe
St Ann's Chapel
B3392
Aveton Gifford
Rame Head
Wembury Bay
Kingston
Bridge End
Ledstone
Great Mew Stone
Worswell
Noss Mayo
Houghton
Venn
Gara Pt
Netton
Ringmore
Bigbury
Churchstow
Stoke Point
Beacon Pt
South West Coast Path
Kingsbridge
Cookworthy Museum
Dodbrooke
Bigbury-on-Sea
Bantham
West Alvington
Burgh Island
Buckland
Upton
Bigbury Bay
Thurlestone
South Milton
Sutton
West Charleton
hours
Roscoff........................6-7½
Santander (summer only)..........24
South Huish
Woolston
Lincombe
Galmpton
Hope
A381
Batson
Bolt Tail
Malborough
Bolberry
Salcombe
Soar
Overbeck's Garden & Museum (NT)
Bolt Head
Eddystone
CHANNEL ISLANDS
location map
Alderney
Guernsey
Herm
Sark
Jersey
same scale as main map
JERSEY
Plémont Pt
Grosnez (ruins)
Greve de Lecq Bay
B55
B34
Battle of Flowers Museum
St John
149
St Mary
B33
Bouley Bay
Trinity
Rozel
Dolmen
St Ouen
La Mielle de Morville
Carrefour Selous
B27
Zoo
St Martin
St Catherine's Bay
B35
A10
A9
A8
B29
St Ouen's Bay
B41
St Peter
Jersey War Tunnels
A6
Dolmen
Mt Orgueil Castle
JERSEY
Five Oaks
Maufant
A12
A11
La Hougue Bie
Gorey
Beaumont
A2
A1
St Saviour
St Brelade
A13
St Aubin's Bay
St Aubin
People's Park
A3
Grouville
La Cotte
Elizabeth
ST HELIER
A5
A4
St Clement
hours
Poole........................3-3¾
Portsmouth..................10
St Malo........................1¼
St Peter Port..................1
Weymouth...........3¼-3½
Noirmont Pt
La Rocque Pt
0 2 4 6 miles
0 2 4 6 8 10 km

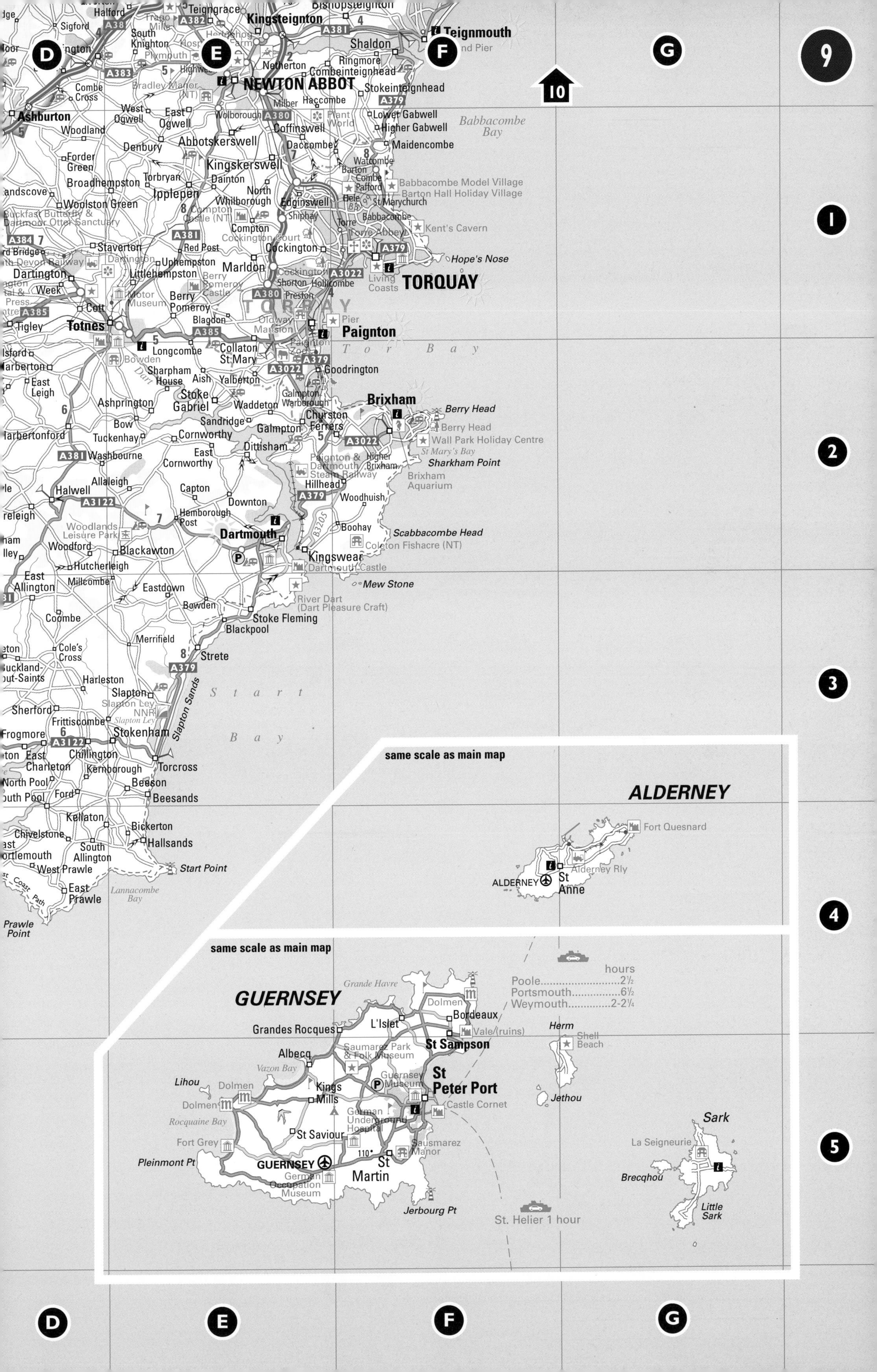

Teignmouth
Kingsteignton
Shaldon
NEWTON ABBOT
Ashburton
Babbacombe Bay
Kingskerswell
Ipplepen
Babbacombe Model Village
Barton Hall Holiday Village
Kent's Cavern
Hope's Nose
TORQUAY
TORBAY
Paignton
Tor Bay
Totnes
Dartington
Brixham
Berry Head
Wall Park Holiday Centre
Sharkham Point
Brixham Aquarium
Scabbacombe Head
Coleton Fishacre (NT)
Dartmouth
Kingswear
Dartmouth Castle
Mew Stone
River Dart (Dart Pleasure Craft)
Stoke Fleming
Strete
Start Bay
Slapton Sands
Torcross
Start Point
Prawle Point
same scale as main map
ALDERNEY
Fort Quesnard
Alderney Rly
St Anne
GUERNSEY
Grande Havre
L'Islet
Bordeaux
St Sampson
St Peter Port
Castle Cornet
St Martin
Jerbourg Pt
Pleinmont Pt
Lihou
Rocquaine Bay
Vazon Bay
Herm
Shell Beach
Jethou
Sark
La Seigneurie
Brecqhou
Little Sark
hours
Poole........2½
Portsmouth........6½
Weymouth........2-2¼
St. Helier 1 hour

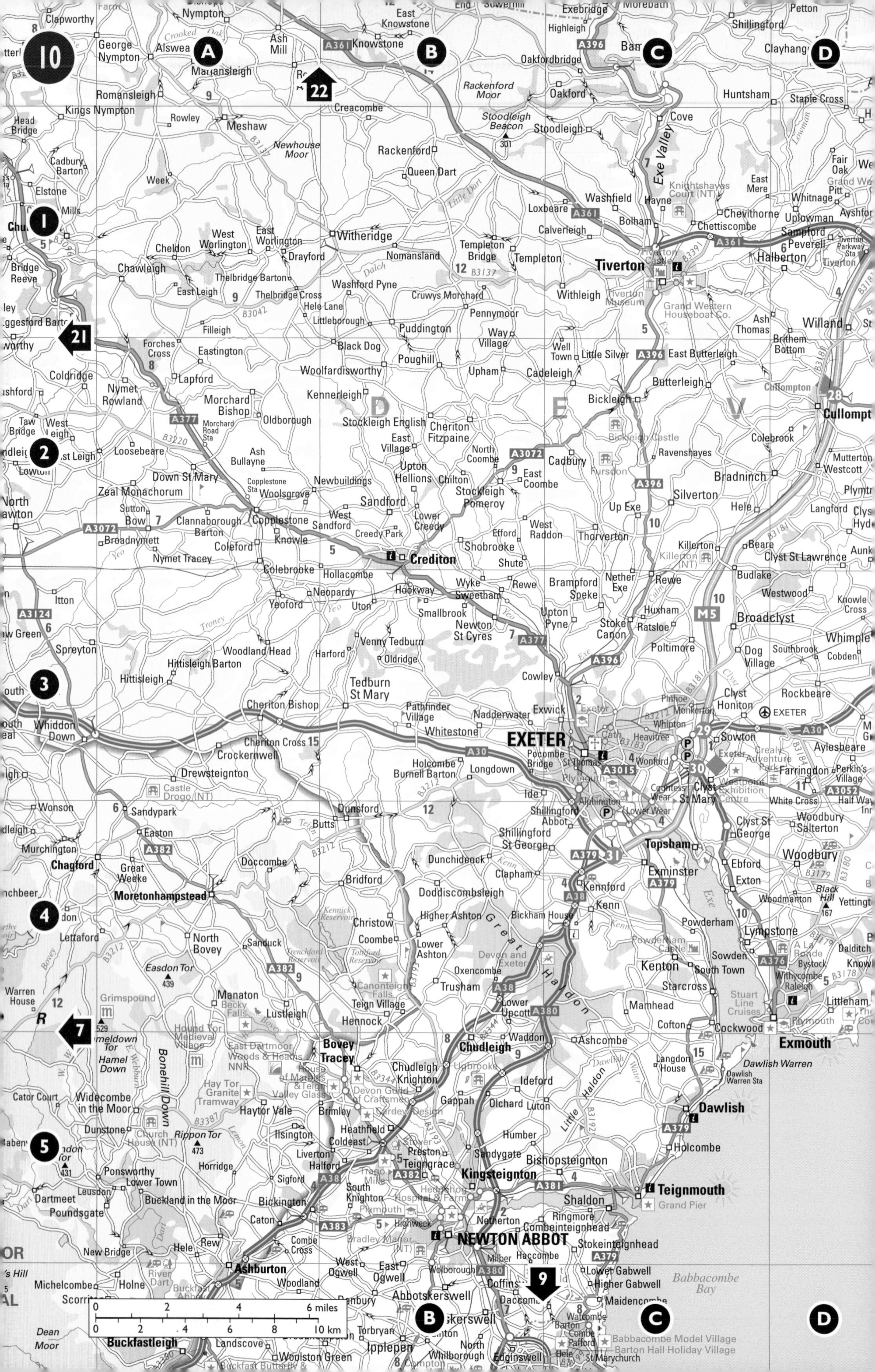
10
A
B
C
D
1
2
3
4
5
22
21
28
7
9
Clapworthy
Nympton
East Knowstone
Exebridge
Morebath
Petton
Shillingford
George Nympton
Alswear
Ash Mill
Knowstone
Highleigh
Oakfordbridge
Clayhanger
Mariansleigh
Rackenford Moor
Oakford
Romansleigh
Creacombe
Kings Nympton
Rowley
Meshaw
Stoodleigh Beacon
301
Stoodleigh
Cove
Huntsham
Staple Cross
Head Bridge
Newhouse Moor
Rackenford
Cadbury Barton
Queen Dart
Exe Valley
Fair Oak
Week
Knightshayes Court (NT)
East Mere
Elstone
Little Dart
Loxbeare
Washfield
Hayne
Whitnage
Mills
Bolham
Chevithorne
Uplowman
Chettiscombe
Sampford Peverell
Tiverton Parkway Sta
West Worlington
East Worlington
Witheridge
Templeton Bridge
Calverleigh
Cheldon
Drayford
Nomansland
Templeton
Tiverton
Halberton
Bridge Reeve
Chawleigh
Thelbridge Barton
Dalch
Tiverton Castle
East Leigh
Washford Pyne
Thelbridge Cross
Cruwys Morchard
Withleigh
Tiverton Museum
Grand Western Houseboat Co.
Hele Lane
Pennymoor
Littleborough
Ash Thomas
Willand
Eggesford Barton
Filleigh
Puddington
Way Village
Brithem Bottom
Forches Cross
Eastington
Black Dog
Well Town
Little Silver
East Butterleigh
Poughill
Coldridge
Lapford
Woolfardisworthy
Upham
Cadeleigh
Butterleigh
Nymet Rowland
Morchard Bishop
Kennerleigh
Bickleigh
Cullompton
Taw Bridge
West Leigh
Oldborough
Stockleigh English
Cheriton Fitzpaine
D
E
V
Morchard Road Sta
East Village
Bickleigh Castle
Colebrook
Ravenshayes
Looseheare
Ash Bullayne
North Coombe
Cadbury
Mutterton
Westcott
Upton Hellions
Fursdon
Down St Mary
Chilton
East Coombe
Bradninch
Lowton
Copplestone Sta
Newbuildings
Stockleigh Pomeroy
Silverton
Plymtree
Zeal Monachorum
Woolsgrove
North Tawton
Sandford
Up Exe
Hele
Langford
Sutton
Bow
Clannaborough Barton
Copplestone
West Sandford
Lower Creedy
West Raddon
Thorverton
Broadnymett
Knowle
Creedy Park
Efford
Killerton
Beare
Nymet Tracey
Coleford
Crediton
Shobrooke
Killerton (NT)
Clyst St Lawrence
Yeo
Shute
Colebrooke
Hollacombe
Wyke
Rewe
Brampford Speke
Nether Exe
Budlake
Itton
Neopardy
Hookway
Sweetham
Westwood
Knowle Cross
Yeoford
Uton
Smallbrook
Upton Pyne
Huxham
Broadclyst
Newton St Cyres
Stoke Canon
Ratsloe
Whimple
Spreyton
Venny Tedburn
Poltimore
Troney
Woodland Head
Harford
Dog Village
Southbrook
Cobden
Hittisleigh Barton
Oldridge
Hittisleigh
Tedburn St Mary
Cowley
Clyst Honiton
Rockbeare
Cheriton Bishop
Pathfinder Village
Nadderwater
Exwick
Pinhoe
Monkerton
Whipton
EXETER
Whiddon Down
Whitestone
Heavitree
Sowton
Cheriton Cross
EXETER
Aylesbeare
Crockernwell
Pocombe Bridge
St Thomas
Wonford
Exeter Crealy Adventure Park
Holcombe Burnell Barton
Longdown
Farringdon
Perkin's Village
Drewsteignton
Westpoint Exhibition Centre
Castle Drogo (NT)
Ide
Countess Wear
Clyst St Mary
Alphington
Shillingford Abbot
Lower Wear
White Cross
Half Way Inn
Wonson
Sandypark
Dunsford
Butts
Clyst St George
Woodbury Salterton
Shillingford St George
Easton
Topsham
Woodbury
Murchington
Dunchideock
Doccombe
Chagford
Clapham
Exminster
Ebford
Great Weeke
Bridford
Kennford
Exton
Kenn
Doddiscombsleigh
Moretonhampstead
Black Hill
167
Woodmanton
Yettington
Kennick Reservoir
Bickham House
Higher Ashton
Powderham
Lympstone
Christow
Lettaford
Coombe
Powderham Castle
North Bovey
Lower Ashton
Sanduck
Devon and Exeter
Dalditch
Kenton
Sowden
Trenchford Reservoir
Tottiford Reservoir
South Town
Easdon Tor
439
Oxencombe
Great Haldon
Bystock
Withycombe Raleigh
Trusham
Starcross
Canonteign Falls
Warren House
Manaton
Lower Upcott
Mamhead
Littleham
Grimspound
Becky Falls
Teign Village
Stuart Line Cruises
Lustleigh
529
Hennock
Cofton
Cockwood
Exmouth
Hound Tor Medieval Village
Waddon
Ashcombe
East Dartmoor Woods & Heaths NNR
Bovey Tracey
Chudleigh
Langdon House
Dawlish Warren
Hamel Down
Chudleigh Knighton
Ugbrooke
House of Marbles & Teign Valley Glass
Dawlish Warren Sta
Hay Tor Granite Tramway
Devon Guild of Craftsmen
Ideford
Cator Court
Widecombe in the Moor
Haytor Vale
Gappah
Olchard
Luton
Little Haldon
Dawlish
Bonehill Down
Brimley
Dunstone
Church House (NT)
Rippon Tor
473
Heathfield
Ilsington
Humber
Coldeast
Stover
Holcombe
Liverton
Preston
Sandygate
Bishopsteignton
Horridge
Halford
Teigngrace
Ponsworthy
Lower Town
Sigford
Kingsteignton
Leusdon
South Knighton
Shaldon
Teignmouth
Dartmeet
Grand Pier
Buckland in the Moor
Bickington
Ringmore
Poundsgate
Highweek
Netherton
Combeinteignhead
Caton
Bradley Manor (NT)
Combe Cross
NEWTON ABBOT
New Bridge
Hele
Rew
Milber
Haccombe
Stokeinteignhead
West Ogwell
East Ogwell
Ashburton
Wolborough
Coffinswell
Lower Gabwell
Higher Gabwell
Babbacombe Bay
Michelcombe
Holne
River Dart
Woodland
Abbotskerswell
Daccombe
Maidencombe
Scorriton
Watcombe
Barton
Combe
Pafford
Babbacombe Model Village
Barton Hall Holiday Village
Dean Moor
Buckfastleigh
Landscove
Torbryan
Ipplepen
North Whilborough
Edginswell
Woolston Green
Compton
Hele
St Marychurch
0
2
4
6 miles
0
2
4
6
8
10 km
A361
A396
A3072
A377
A3124
A30
A3015
A3052
A379
A382
A38
A380
A376
A381
A383
M5
B3137
B3042
B3220
B3212
B3193
B3344
B3387
B3391
B3181
B3183
B3184
B3179
B3180
B3178
B3192

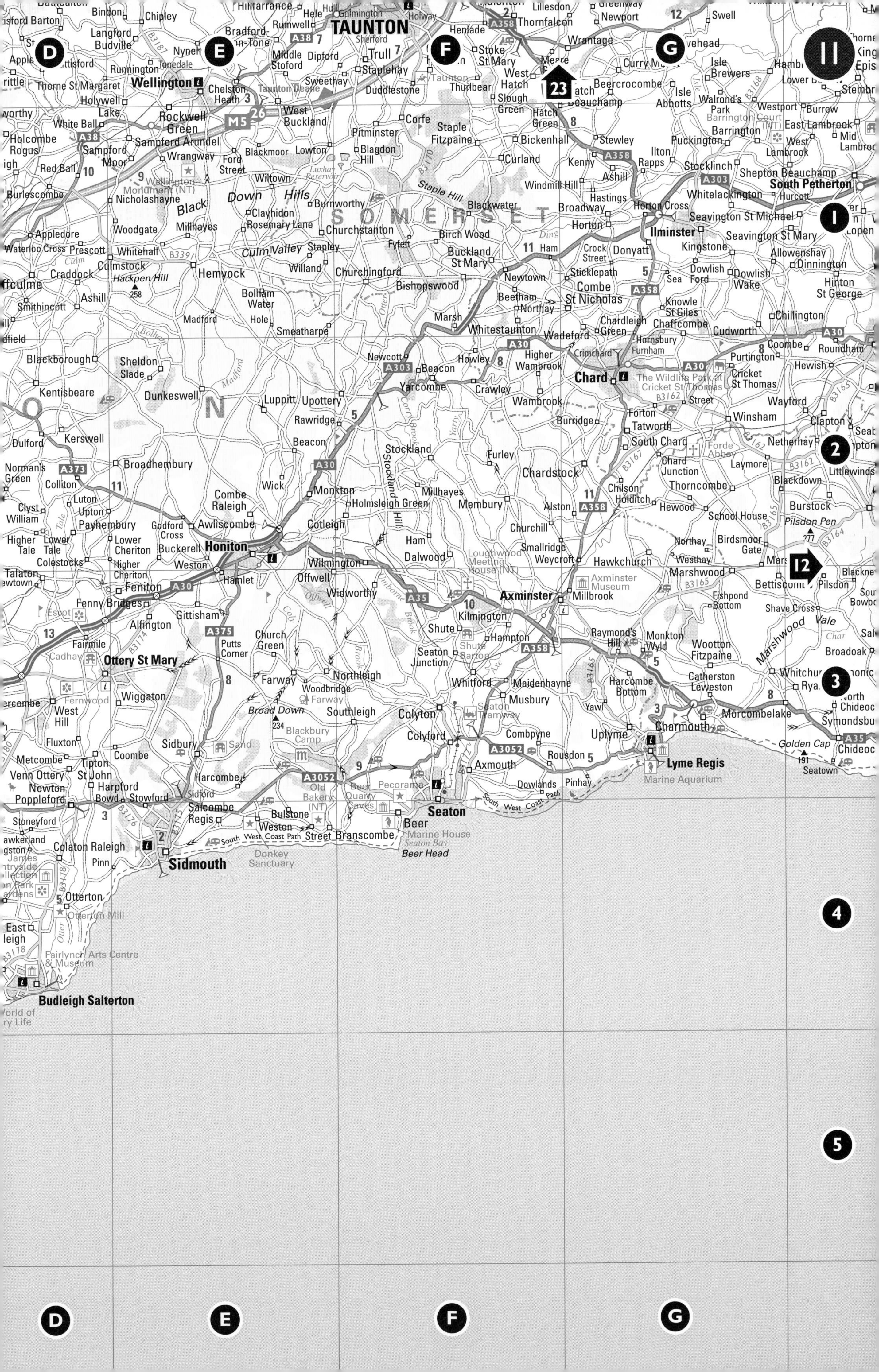

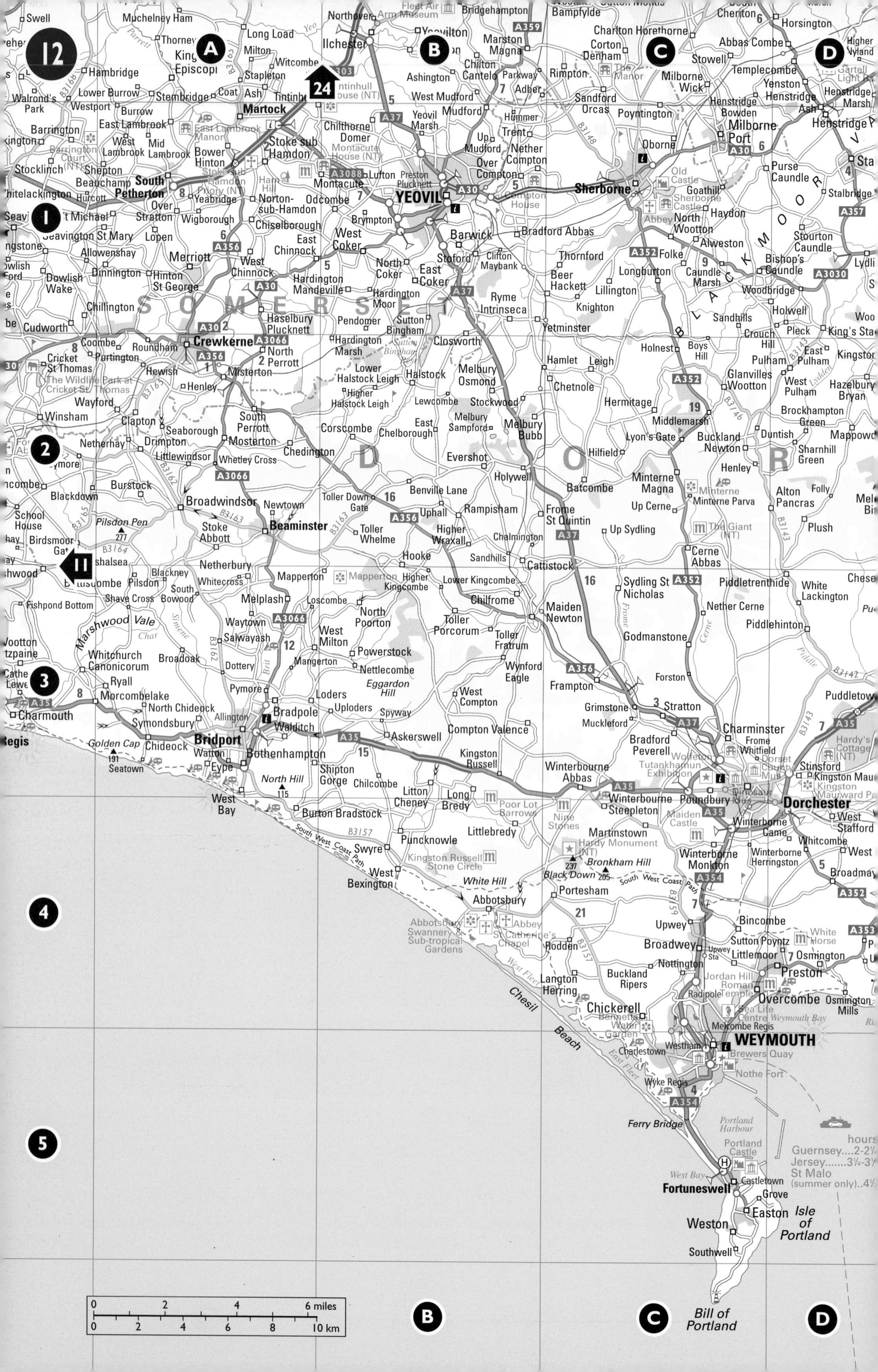

12
A
B
C
D
1
2
3
4
5
24
11
SOMERSET
DORSET
BLACKMOOR VALE
Swell
Muchelney Ham
Long Load
Northover
Ilchester
Yeovilton
Bridgehampton
Bampfylde
Charlton Horethorne
Cheriton
Horsington
Thorney
Kingsbury Episcopi
Milton
Witcombe
Stapleton
Martock
Coat
Ash
Tintinhull House (NT)
Ashington
Marston Magna
Chilton Cantelo
Corton Denham
The Manor
Stowell
Abbas Combe
Templecombe
Higher Nyland
Gartell Light Rly
Hambridge
Lower Burrow
Stembridge
Burrow
Walrond's Park
Westport
West Mudford
Parkway
Adber
Rimpton
Sandford Orcas
Milborne Wick
Yenston
Henstridge
Henstridge Marsh
Henstridge Bowden
Henstridge Ash
Barrington
East Lambrock
East Lambrock Manor
West Lambrock
Mid Lambrock
Barrington Court (NT)
Stoke sub Hamdon
Chilthorne Domer
Yeovil Marsh
Mudford
Hummer
Trent
Poyntington
Oborne
Milborne Port
Stocklinch
Shepton Beauchamp
Bower Hinton
Stoke sub Hamdon Priory (NT)
Ham Hill
Montacute House (NT)
Montacute
Lufton
Preston Plucknett
Up Mudford
Over Compton
Nether Compton
Compton House
Sherborne
Old Castle
Sherborne Castle
Purse Caundle
Stalbridge
Whitelackington
Hurcott
South Petherton
Over Stratton
Yeabridge
Norton-sub-Hamdon
Odcombe
YEOVIL
Goathill
Haydon
Seavington St Michael
Seavington St Mary
Lopen
Wigborough
Chiselborough
Brympton
West Coker
East Chinnock
Barwick
Bradford Abbas
Abbey
North Wootton
Alweston
Stourton Caundle
Bishop's Caundle
Ilminster
Allowenshay
Merriott
West Chinnock
Hinton St George
Dinnington
Dowlish Wake
Stoford
Clifton Maybank
Thornford
Beer Hackett
Longburton
Folke
Caundle Marsh
Lydlinch
Chillington
Hardington Mandeville
North Coker
East Coker
Hardington Moor
Ryme Intrinseca
Lillington
Knighton
Woodbridge
Holwell
Sandhills
Cudworth
Haselbury Plucknett
Pendomer
Sutton Bingham
Yetminster
Crouch Hill
Pleck
King's Stag
Coombe
Roundham
Crewkerne
North Perrott
Hardington Marsh
Closworth
Holnest
Boys Hill
East Pulham
Pulham
Kingston
Cricket St Thomas
Purtington
The Wildlife Park at Cricket St Thomas
Hewish
Misterton
Lower Halstock Leigh
Halstock
Higher Halstock Leigh
Melbury Osmond
Hamlet
Leigh
Chetnole
Glanvilles Wootton
West Pulham
Hazelbury Bryan
Henley
Wayford
Lewcombe
Stockwood
Melbury Bubb
Hermitage
Winsham
Clapton
South Perrott
Seaborough
Corscombe
East Chelborough
Melbury Sampford
Middlemarsh
Brockhampton Green
Netherhay
Drimpton
Mosterton
Lyon's Gate
Buckland Newton
Duntish
Mappowder
Littlewindsor
Whetley Cross
Chedington
Evershot
Hilfield
Sharnhill Green
Blackdown
Burstock
Holywell
Batcombe
Minterne Magna
Minterne Parva
Henley
Alton Pancras
Folly
School House
Broadwindsor
Newtown
Toller Down Gate
Benville Lane
Uphall
Rampisham
Frome St Quintin
Up Cerne
Pilsdon Pen
Stoke Abbott
Beaminster
Toller Whelme
Higher Wraxall
Chalmington
Up Sydling
The Giant (NT)
Plush
Birdsmoor Gate
Hooke
Sandhills
Cattistock
Cerne Abbas
Blackney
Netherbury
Mapperton
Higher Kingcombe
Lower Kingcombe
Sydling St Nicholas
Piddletrenthide
White Lackington
Pilsdon
Whitecross
South Bowood
Shave Cross
Melplash
Loscombe
Chilfrome
Maiden Newton
Nether Cerne
Fishpond Bottom
Marshwood Vale
Waytown
North Poorton
Toller Porcorum
Toller Fratrum
Frome
Piddlehinton
Salwayash
West Milton
Powerstock
Godmanstone
Whitchurch Canonicorum
Broadoak
Dottery
Mangerton
Nettlecombe
Eggardon Hill
Wynford Eagle
Forston
Ryall
Pymore
Loders
West Compton
Frampton
Charmouth
Morcombelake
North Chideock
Allington
Bradpole
Uploders
Spyway
Grimstone
Stratton
Puddletown
Symondsbury
Walditch
Askerswell
Compton Valence
Muckleford
Charminster
Frome Whitfield
Golden Cap
Chideock
Bridport
Watton
Bothenhampton
Kingston Russell
Bradford Peverell
Wolfeton
Hardy's Cottage (NT)
Stinsford
Seatown
Eype
Shipton Gorge
Chilcombe
Winterbourne Abbas
Tutankhamun Exhibition
Dorset County Mus
Kingston Maurward
North Hill
Litton Cheney
Long Bredy
Poor Lot Barrows
Nine Stones
Winterbourne Steepleton
Poundbury
Dinosaur Mus
Dorchester
West Bay
Burton Bradstock
Maiden Castle
Winterborne Came
West Stafford
Whitcombe
Littlebredy
Martinstown
Hardy Monument (NT)
Puncknowle
Swyre
Kingston Russell Stone Circle
Bronkham Hill
Black Down
Winterborne Monkton
Winterborne Herringston
West Knighton
Broadmayne
West Bexington
White Hill
South West Coast Path
Portesham
Abbotsbury
Abbotsbury Swannery & Sub-tropical Gardens
Abbey
St Catherine's Chapel
Bincombe
Upwey
Broadwey
Sutton Poyntz
White Horse
Rodden
Littlemoor
Osmington
Nottington
Preston
Langton Herring
Buckland Ripers
Jordan Hill Roman Temple
Radipole
Overcombe
Osmington Mills
Weymouth Bay
West Fleet
Chesil Beach
Chickerell
Bennetts Water Gardens
Sea Life Centre
Melcombe Regis
WEYMOUTH
Charlestown
Westham
Brewers Quay
Nothe Fort
East Fleet
Wyke Regis
Ferry Bridge
Portland Harbour
Portland Castle
West Bay
Castletown
Fortuneswell
Grove
Easton
Isle of Portland
Weston
Southwell
Bill of Portland
hours
Guernsey....2-2¼
Jersey.......3¼-3
St Malo
(summer only)..4¼
A30
A37
A303
A3088
A356
A359
A352
A357
A3030
A3066
A35
A354
A353
B3168
B3165
B3162
B3163
B3164
B3157
B3159
B3143
B3146
B3148
B3142
B3151
0
2
4
6 miles
0
2
4
6
8
10 km

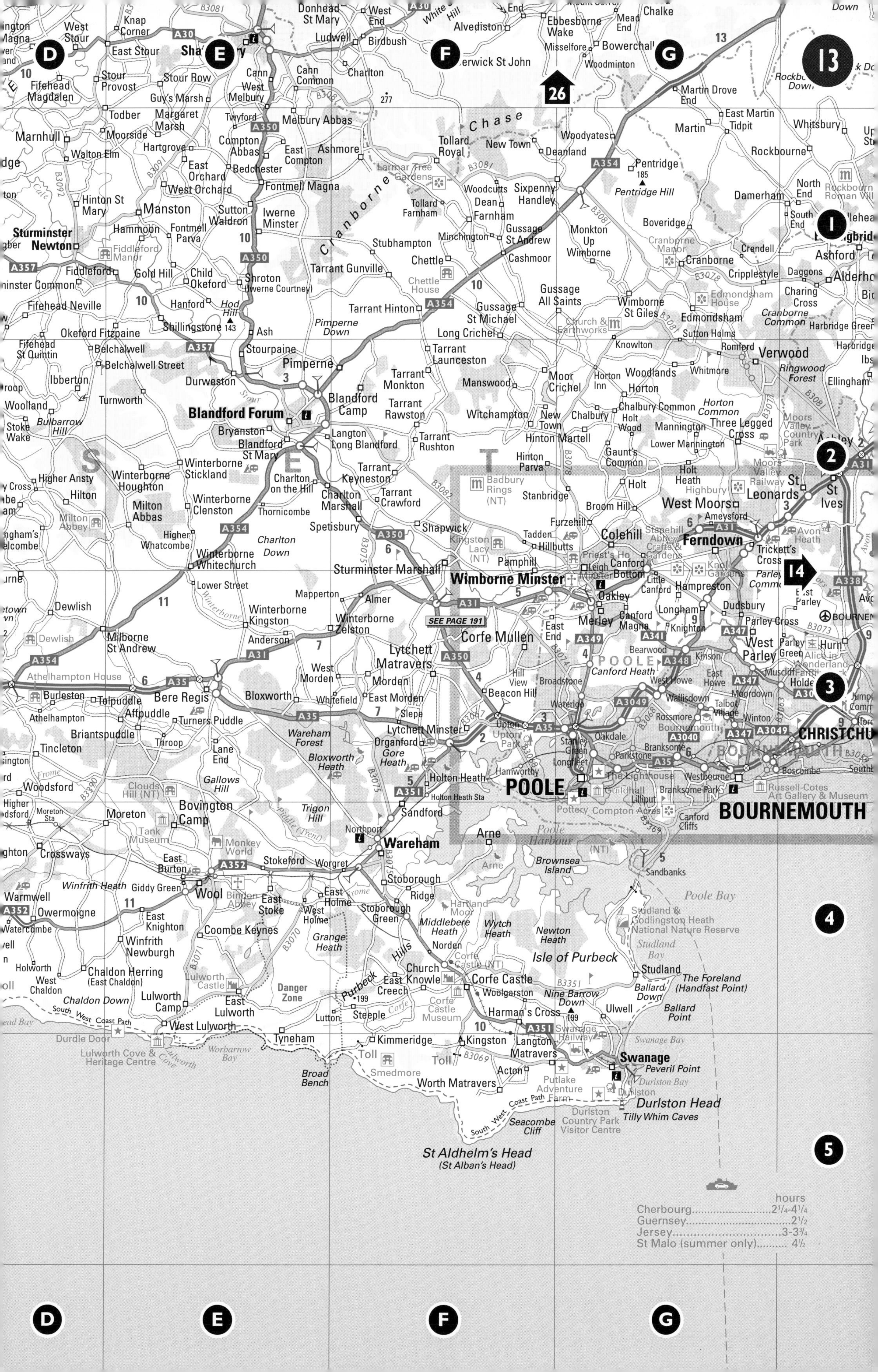

13
D
E
F
G
26
14
SEE PAGE 191
1
2
3
4
5
Donhead St Mary
West End
Chalke
Ebbesborne Wake
Mead End
Knap Corner
West Stour
East Stour
Alvediston
Ludwell
Birdbush
Misselfore
Bowerchalke
Woodminton
Stour Row
Stour Provost
Fifehead Magdalen
Cann
Cann Common
West Melbury
Charlton
Martin Drove End
Todber
Margaret Marsh
Guy's Marsh
Twyford
Melbury Abbas
Chase
East Martin
Tidpit
Martin
Whitsbury
Marnhull
Moorside
Walton Elm
Hartgrove
Compton Abbas
East Compton
Ashmore
Tollard Royal
New Town
Woodyates
Deanland
Pentridge
Pentridge Hill
Rockbourne
Larmer Tree Gardens
East Orchard
Bedchester
West Orchard
Fontmell Magna
Cranborne
Woodcutts
Sixpenny Handley
Dean
Tollard Farnham
Farnham
Damerham
North End
South End
Hinton St Mary
Manston
Sutton Waldron
Iwerne Minster
Monkton Up Wimborne
Boveridge
Sturminster Newton
Hammoon
Fontmell Parva
Fiddleford Manor
Stubhampton
Minchington
Gussage St Andrew
Cranborne Manor
Crendell
Ashford
Chettle
Cashmoor
Cranborne
Fiddleford
Gold Hill
Child Okeford
Shroton (Iwerne Courtney)
Tarrant Gunville
Chettle House
Cripplestyle
Daggons
Alderholt
Gussage All Saints
Charing Cross
Edmondsham House
Fifehead Neville
Hanford
Hod Hill
Tarrant Hinton
Gussage St Michael
Wimborne St Giles
Edmondsham
Cranborne Common
Harbridge Green
Shillingstone
Ash
Pimperne Down
Church & Earthworks
Okeford Fitzpaine
Long Crichel
Sutton Holms
Fifehead St Quintin
Belchalwell
Stourpaine
Tarrant Launceston
Knowlton
Romford
Verwood
Harbridge
Belchalwell Street
Pimperne
Ringwood Forest
Ibberton
Durweston
Tarrant Monkton
Manswood
Moor Crichel
Horton Inn
Woodlands
Whitmore
Ellingham
Turnworth
Blandford Camp
Horton
Woolland
Blandford Forum
Tarrant Rawston
Witchampton
New Town
Chalbury
Chalbury Common
Horton Common
Moors Valley Country Park
Bulbarrow Hill
Bryanston
Langton Long Blandford
Holt Wood
Mannington
Three Legged Cross
Stoke Wake
Blandford St Mary
Tarrant Rushton
Hinton Martell
Lower Mannington
Gaunt's Common
Winterborne Stickland
Hinton Parva
Moors Valley Railway
Higher Ansty
Winterborne Houghton
Charlton on the Hill
Tarrant Keyneston
Badbury Rings (NT)
Holt
Holt Heath
Highbury
St Leonards
St Ives
Hilton
Charlton Marshall
Tarrant Crawford
Stanbridge
West Moors
Milton Abbas
Winterborne Clenston
Thornicombe
Broom Hill
Amesyford
Milton Abbey
Furzehill
Spetisbury
Shapwick
Stapehill Abbey Crafts & Gardens
Colehill
Ferndown
Avon Heath
Higher Whatcombe
Tadden
Kingston Lacy (NT)
Hillbutts
Charlton Down
Trickett's Cross
Winterborne Whitechurch
Pamphill
Priest's Ho
Canford Bottom
Knoll Gardens
Sturminster Marshall
Leigh
Little Canford
Parley Common
East Parley
Lower Street
Wimborne Minster
Hampreston
Dewlish
Mapperton
Almer
Oakley
Longham
Dudsbury
Bournemouth
Winterborne Kingston
Winterborne Zelston
Merley
Canford Magna
Knighton
Parley Cross
Milborne St Andrew
Anderson
Lytchett Matravers
Corfe Mullen
East End
Bearwood
West Parley
Parley Green
Hurn
Alice in Wonderland
Athelhampton House
Poole
Canford Heath
Kinson
East Howe
Muscliff
Holdenhurst
Burleston
Tolpuddle
Bere Regis
Bloxworth
West Morden
Morden
Hill View
Broadstone
West Howe
Wallisdown
Moordown
Athelhampton
Affpuddle
Turners Puddle
Whitefield
East Morden
Beacon Hill
Talbot Village
Winton
Briantspuddle
Slepe
Waterloo
Rossmore
Christchurch
Tincleton
Throop
Wareham Forest
Lytchett Minster
Upton
Upton Park
Stanley Green
Oakdale
Bournemouth
Lane End
Organford
Gore Heath
Bloxworth Heath
Longfleet
Parkstone
Branksome
Gallows Hill
Holton Heath
Hamworthy
The Lighthouse
Westbourne
Boscombe
Southbourne
Woodsford
Clouds Hill (NT)
Holton Heath Sta
POOLE
Guildhall
Branksome Park
Russell-Cotes Art Gallery & Museum
Moreton Sta
Moreton
Bovington Camp
Trigon Hill
Sandford
Lilliput
Pottery
Compton Acres
Canford Cliffs
BOURNEMOUTH
Tank Museum
Northport
Arne
Poole Harbour
Crossways
Monkey World
Piddle (Trent)
Wareham
East Burton
Stokeford
Worgret
Brownsea Island
Sandbanks
Winfrith Heath
Giddy Green
Wool
Bindon Abbey
East Stoke
Stoborough
Ridge
Poole Bay
Warmwell
East Holme
West Holme
Stoborough Green
Hartland Moor
Studland & Godlingston Heath National Nature Reserve
Owermoigne
East Knighton
Middlebere Heath
Wytch Heath
Newton Heath
Watercombe
Coombe Keynes
Grange Heath
Hills
Norden
Studland Bay
Winfrith Newburgh
Corfe Castle (NT)
Isle of Purbeck
Holworth
Chaldon Herring (East Chaldon)
Lulworth Castle
Danger Zone
Church Knowle
Corfe Castle
Studland
The Foreland (Handfast Point)
West Chaldon
Purbeck
East Creech
Woolgarston
Ballard Down
Chaldon Down
Lulworth Camp
East Lulworth
Corfe Castle Museum
Nine Barrow Down
Ulwell
Ballard Point
South West Coast Path
Lutton
Steeple
Harman's Cross
Durdle Door
West Lulworth
Tyneham
Kimmeridge
Kingston
Swanage Railway
Swanage Bay
Lulworth Cove & Heritage Centre
Worbarrow Bay
Toll
Langton Matravers
Swanage
Broad Bench
Smedmore
Acton
Peveril Point
Worth Matravers
Putlake Adventure Farm
Durlston Bay
Durlston
Durlston Head
Tilly Whim Caves
Seacombe Cliff
Durlston Country Park Visitor Centre
St Aldhelm's Head (St Alban's Head)
hours
Cherbourg 2¼-4¼
Guernsey 2½
Jersey 3-3¾
St Malo (summer only) 4½

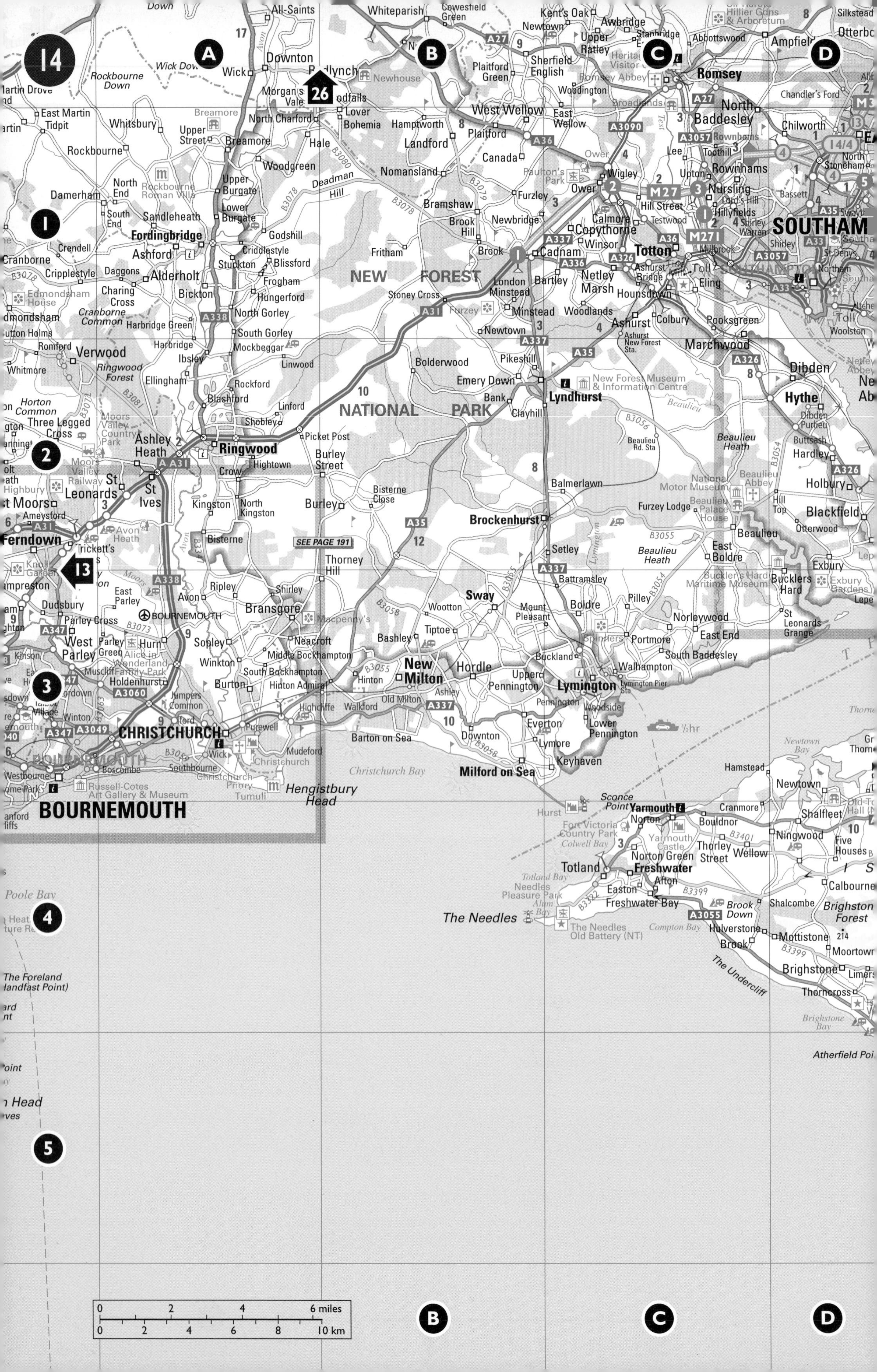

14
A
B
C
D
1
2
3
4
5
26
13
Rockbourne Down
Wick Down
Downton
All-Saints
Redlynch
Whiteparish
Cowesfield Green
Kent's Oak
Awbridge
Hillier Gdns & Arboretum
Silkstead
Newtown
Stanbridge
Abbottswood
Ampfield
Upper Ratley
Sherfield English
Plaitford Green
Romsey
Romsey Abbey
Woodington
Broadlands
Chandler's Ford
North Baddesley
Chilworth
East Martin
Tidpit
Whitsbury
Breamore
Upper Street
North Charford
Morgan's Vale
Woodfalls
Lover
Bohemia
Hamptworth
Landford
Plaitford
West Wellow
East Wellow
Rownhams
Toothill
Lee
Upton
Nursling
North Stoneham
Rockbourne
Damerham
North End
Rockbourne Roman Villa
Upper Burgate
Lower Burgate
Woodgreen
Hale
Deadman Hill
Nomansland
Canada
Paulton's Park
Ower
Wigley
Furzley
Bramshaw
Brook Hill
Newbridge
Hill Street
Testwood
Calmore
Copythorne
Winsor
Hillyfields
Shirley Warren
Bassett
SOUTHAMPTON
South End
Sandleheath
Fordingbridge
Ashford
Crendell
Cranborne
Cripplestyle
Daggons
Alderholt
Criddlestyle
Stuckton
Blissford
Godshill
Frogham
Hungerford
Bickton
Charing Cross
Cranborne Common
Edmondsham House
Edmondsham
Harbridge Green
North Gorley
South Gorley
Fritham
NEW FOREST
Brook
Cadnam
Netley Marsh
Totton
Ashurst Bridge
Eling
Millbrook
Northam
Southampton F.C.
London Minstead
Minstead
Bartley
Woodlands
Hounsdown
Ashurst
Colbury
Pooksgreen
Marchwood
Woolston
Stoney Cross
Furzey
Newtown
Ashurst New Forest Sta.
Sutton Holms
Romford
Verwood
Ringwood Forest
Harbridge
Ibsley
Mockbeggar
Linwood
Bolderwood
Pikeshill
Emery Down
Bank
Lyndhurst
New Forest Museum & Information Centre
Dibden
Dibden Purlieu
Hythe
Whitmore
Ellingham
Rockford
Blashford
Linford
Shobley
NATIONAL PARK
Clayhill
Beaulieu
Beaulieu Rd. Sta
Horton Common
Three Legged Cross
Moors Valley Country Park
Ashley Heath
Ringwood
Picket Post
Burley Street
Hightown
Beaulieu Heath
Buttsash
Hardley
Holbury
Moors Valley Railway
St Leonards
St Ives
Crow
Kingston
North Kingston
Bisterne Close
Burley
Balmerlawn
National Motor Museum
Beaulieu Abbey
Beaulieu Palace House
Furzey Lodge
Hill Top
Blackfield
Otterwood
Brockenhurst
Ameysford
Ferndown
Avon Heath
Tricketts Cross
Bisterne
SEE PAGE 191
Thorney Hill
Setley
East Boldre
Exbury
Exbury Gardens
Bucklers Hard
Buckler's Hard Maritime Museum
Beaulieu Heath
Ripley
Shirley
Bransgore
Macpenny's
Avon
East Parley
Parley Cross
Dudsbury
BOURNEMOUTH
Wootton
Sway
Mount Pleasant
Battramsley
Boldre
Pilley
Norleywood
St Leonards Grange
East End
West Parley
Parley Green
Hurn
Sopley
Neacroft
Middle Bockhampton
Bashley
Tiptoe
Portmore
South Baddesley
Alice in Wonderland Family Park
Winkton
South Bockhampton
Hinton
New Milton
Hordle
Buckland
Walhampton
Lymington
Lymington Pier Sta
Holdenhurst
Burton
Hinton Admiral
Upper Pennington
Pennington
Jumpers Common
Highcliffe
Walkford
Old Milton
Ashley
Woodside
Lower Pennington
Winton
CHRISTCHURCH
Purewell
Mudeford
Barton on Sea
Downton
Everton
Lymore
Keyhaven
Milford on Sea
Wick
Christchurch
Christchurch Priory
Tumuli
Hengistbury Head
Christchurch Bay
Boscombe
Southbourne
Westbourne
Russell-Cotes Art Gallery & Museum
BOURNEMOUTH
Hurst
Sconce Point
Yarmouth
Norton
Fort Victoria Country Park
Colwell Bay
Yarmouth Castle
Norton Green
Freshwater
Thorley Street
Wellow
Bouldnor
Cranmore
Hamstead
Newtown Bay
Newtown
Shalfleet
Ningwood
Five Houses
Totland
Totland Bay
Needles Pleasure Park
Alum Bay
Easton
Freshwater Bay
Afton
Brook Down
Shalcombe
Calbourne
Brighstone Forest
The Needles
The Needles Old Battery (NT)
Compton Bay
Hulverstone
Brook
Mottistone
Moortown
Brighstone
Thorncross
Brighstone Bay
The Undercliff
Atherfield Point
Poole Bay
The Foreland (Handfast Point)
½hr
0 2 4 6 miles
0 2 4 6 8 10 km
A27
A36
A3090
A3057
M27
M271
A337
A336
A326
A35
A33
A31
A338
A347
A3060
A3049
A3055
B3078
B3080
B3079
B3081
B3072
B3056
B3055
B3054
B3058
B3073
B3347
B3059
B3063
B3401
B3399
B3322

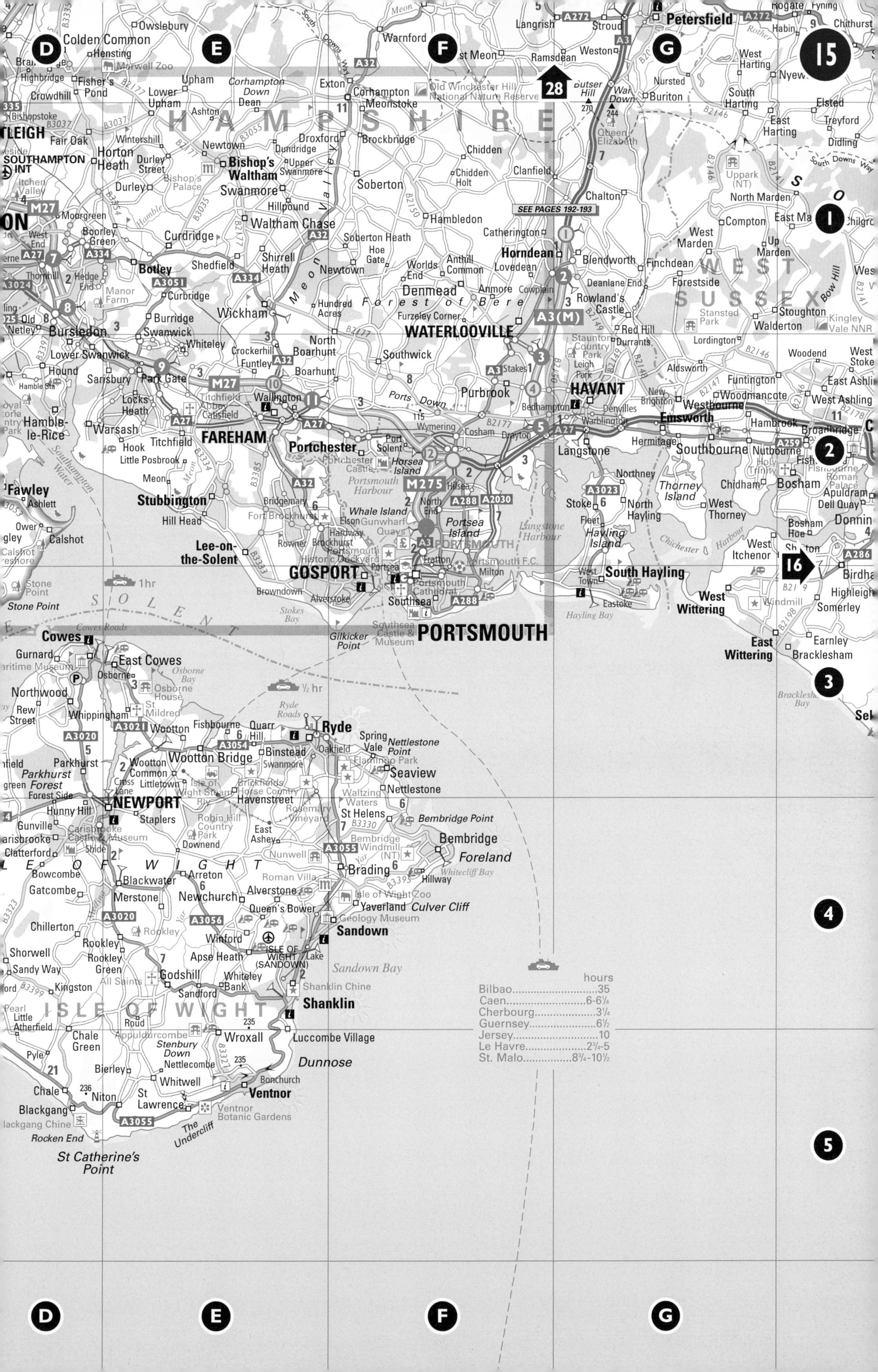
15
D
E
F
G
1
2
3
4
5
28
16
SEE PAGES 192-193
HAMPSHIRE
WEST SUSSEX
ISLE OF WIGHT
SOLENT
Colden Common
Owslebury
Warnford
Langrish
Stroud
Petersfield
Rogate
Fyning
Chithurst
Hensting
Marwell Zoo
Highbridge
Fisher's Pond
Crowdhill
Upham
Lower Upham
Corhampton Down
Dean
Exton
Corhampton
Meonstoke
Old Winchester Hill National Nature Reserve
Ramsdean
Weston
Butser Hill
War Down
Queen Elizabeth
Nurstead
Buriton
West Harting
South Harting
East Harting
Elsted
Treyford
Didling
Habin
Nyewood
Bishopstoke
Fair Oak
Wintershill
Ashton
Newtown
Droxford
Dundridge
Upper Swanmore
Brockbridge
Chidden
Chidden Holt
Clanfield
Horton Heath
Durley Street
Durley
Bishop's Waltham
Bishop's Palace
Swanmore
Hillpound
Soberton
Uppark (NT)
North Marden
Chalton
SOUTHAMPTON INT
Itchen Valley
M27
Moorgreen
West End
Boorley Green
Curdridge
Waltham Chase
Hambledon
Catherington
Compton
East Marden
West Marden
Up Marden
Soberton Heath
Hoe Gate
Worlds End
Anthill Common
Horndean
Lovedean
Blendworth
Finchdean
Forestside
Botley
Shedfield
Shirrell Heath
Newtown
Denmead
Forest of Bere
Deanlane End
Hedge End
Thornhill
Manor Farm
Curbridge
Hundred Acres
Furzeley Corner
Cowplain
Rowland's Castle
Stansted Park
Stoughton
Kingley Vale NNR
Walderton
Old Netley
Bursledon
Burridge
Swanwick
Wickham
North Boarhunt
WATERLOOVILLE
A3(M)
Red Hill
Durrants
Lordington
Whiteley
Lower Swanwick
Crockerhill
Funtley
Southwick
Staunton Country Park
Leigh Park
Aldsworth
Woodend
West Stoke
Hound
Sarisbury
Park Gate
Boarhunt
Purbrook
Stakes
HAVANT
Funtington
East Ashling
West Ashling
Hamble Sta
Titchfield Abbey
Catisfield
Wallington
Ports Down
Bedhampton
Denvilles
New Brighton
Westbourne
Woodmancote
Hamble-le-Rice
Locks Heath
Warsash
FAREHAM
A27
Wymering
Cosham
Drayton
Warblington
Emsworth
Hambrook
Broadbridge
Hook
Little Posbrook
Titchfield
Portchester
Portchester Castle
Port Solent
Horsea Island
Langstone
Hermitage
Southbourne
Nutbourne
Fishbourne
Southampton Water
Meon
Portsmouth Harbour
M275
Hilsea
Northney
Holy Trinity
Bosham
Chidham
Fishbourne Roman Palace
Apuldram
Dell Quay
Fawley
Ashlett
Stubbington
Bridgemary
Fort Brockhurst
Whale Island
North End
A288
A2030
Portsea Island
Thorney Island
Stoke
North Hayling
West Thorney
Hill Head
Elson
Gunwharf Quays
Langstone Harbour
Fleet
Hayling Island
Bosham Hoe
Donnington
Owers
Calshot
Lee-on-the-Solent
Hardway
Brockhurst
Rowner
Historic Dockyard
PORTSMOUTH
Chichester Harbour
West Itchenor
Shipton Green
Fratton
Portsmouth F.C.
GOSPORT
Portsea
Milton
West Town
South Hayling
Birdham
Highleigh
Stone Point
1hr
Browndown
Alverstoke
Portsmouth Cathedral
Southsea
Eastoke
West Wittering
Windmill
Somerley
Hayling Bay
Stokes Bay
Southsea Castle & Museum
Cowes Roads
Cowes
Gilkicker Point
East Wittering
Earnley
Bracklesham
Bracklesham Bay
Gurnard
Maritime Museum
East Cowes
Osborne
Osborne Bay
Osborne House
Northwood
½ hr
Rew Street
Whippingham
St Mildred's
Ryde Roads
A3021
A3020
Wootton
Fishbourne
Quarr Hill
Ryde
Spring Vale
Nettlestone Point
Oakfield
Binstead
Swanmore
Parkhurst
Parkhurst Forest
Wootton Bridge
Wootton Common
Isle of Wight Steam Rly
Flamingo Park
Seaview
Cross Lane
Littletown
Brickfields Horse Country
Nettlestone
Forest Side
Hunny Hill
NEWPORT
Havenstreet
Waltzing Waters
St Helens
Gunville
Staplers
Robin Hill Country Park
Rosemary Vineyard
Bembridge Point
Carisbrooke
Carisbrooke Castle & Museum
East Ashey
Downend
Bembridge
Bembridge Windmill (NT)
Clatterford
Shide
Nunwell
A3055
Foreland
Bowcombe
Arreton
Roman Villa
Brading
Whitecliff Bay
Gatcombe
Blackwater
Hillway
Merstone
Newchurch
Alverstone
Isle of Wight Zoo
Queen's Bower
Yaverland
Culver Cliff
Geology Museum
Chillerton
A3056
Rookley
Sandown
Shorwell
Winford
Apse Heath
ISLE OF WIGHT (SANDOWN)
Lake
Sandown Bay
Sandy Way
Rookley Green
All Saints
Godshill
Whiteley Bank
Kingston
Sandford
Shanklin Chine
Shanklin
Little Atherfield
Roud
Appuldurcombe
Wroxall
Luccombe Village
Chale Green
Stenbury Down
Nettlecombe
Dunnose
Pyle
Bierley
Whitwell
Bonchurch
Chale
Niton
St Lawrence
Ventnor
Blackgang
Blackgang Chine
Ventnor Botanic Gardens
The Undercliff
Rocken End
St Catherine's Point
hours
Bilbao.............................35
Caen..........................6-6¼
Cherbourg...................3¼
Guernsey......................6½
Jersey............................10
Le Havre....................2¾-5
St. Malo..............8¾-10½

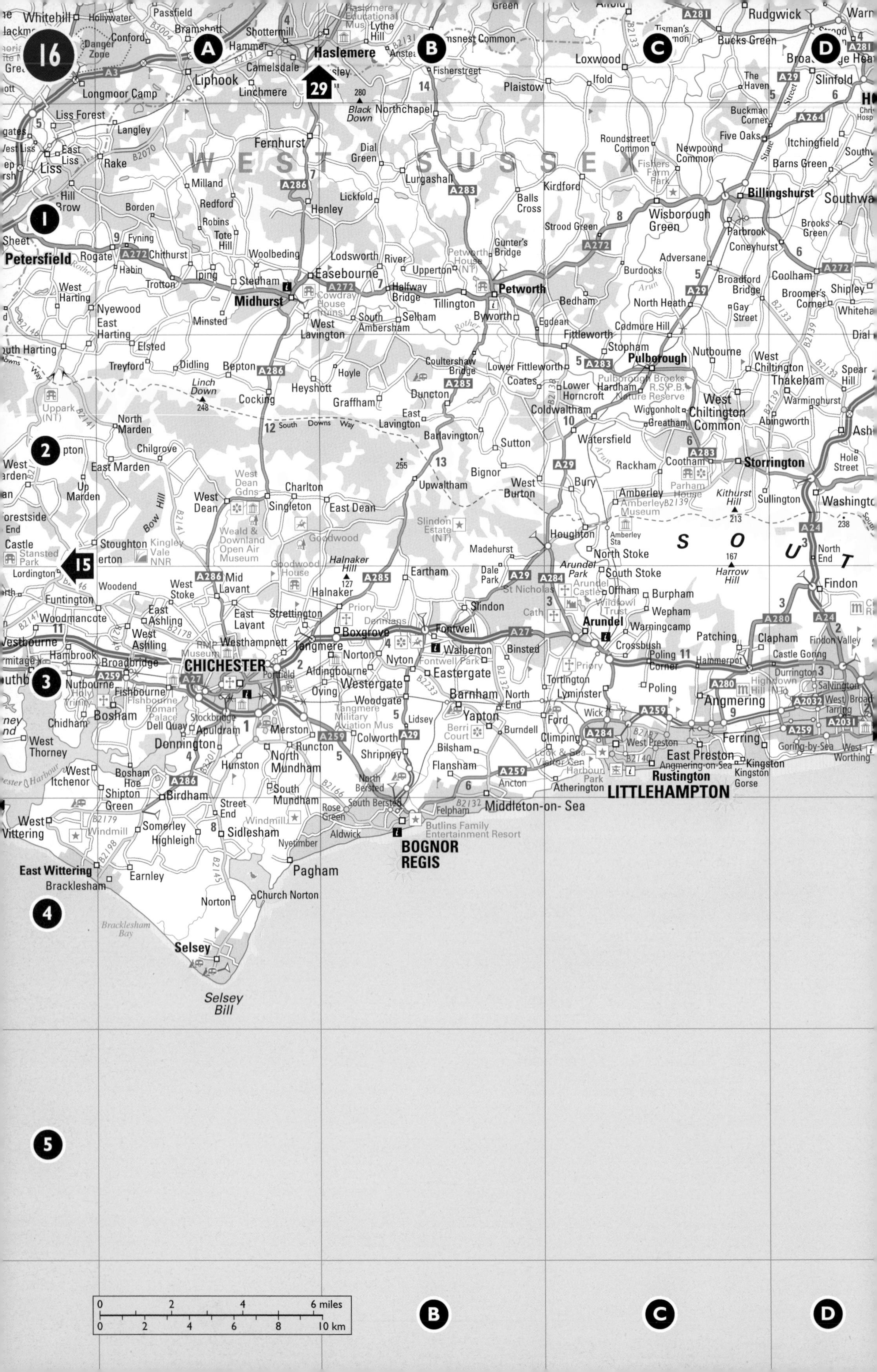
WEST SUSSEX
Haslemere
Petersfield
Midhurst
Petworth
Billingshurst
Pulborough
Storrington
Arundel
CHICHESTER
BOGNOR REGIS
LITTLEHAMPTON
Rustington
Selsey
Selsey Bill
East Wittering
Bracklesham
Pagham
Liphook
Liss
Fernhurst
Easebourne
Rogate
Singleton
Westbourne
Bosham
Angmering
Findon
Washington
Rudgwick
Loxwood
Wisborough Green
Slinfold
29
15
A B C D
1 2 3 4 5
0 2 4 6 miles
0 2 4 6 8 10 km

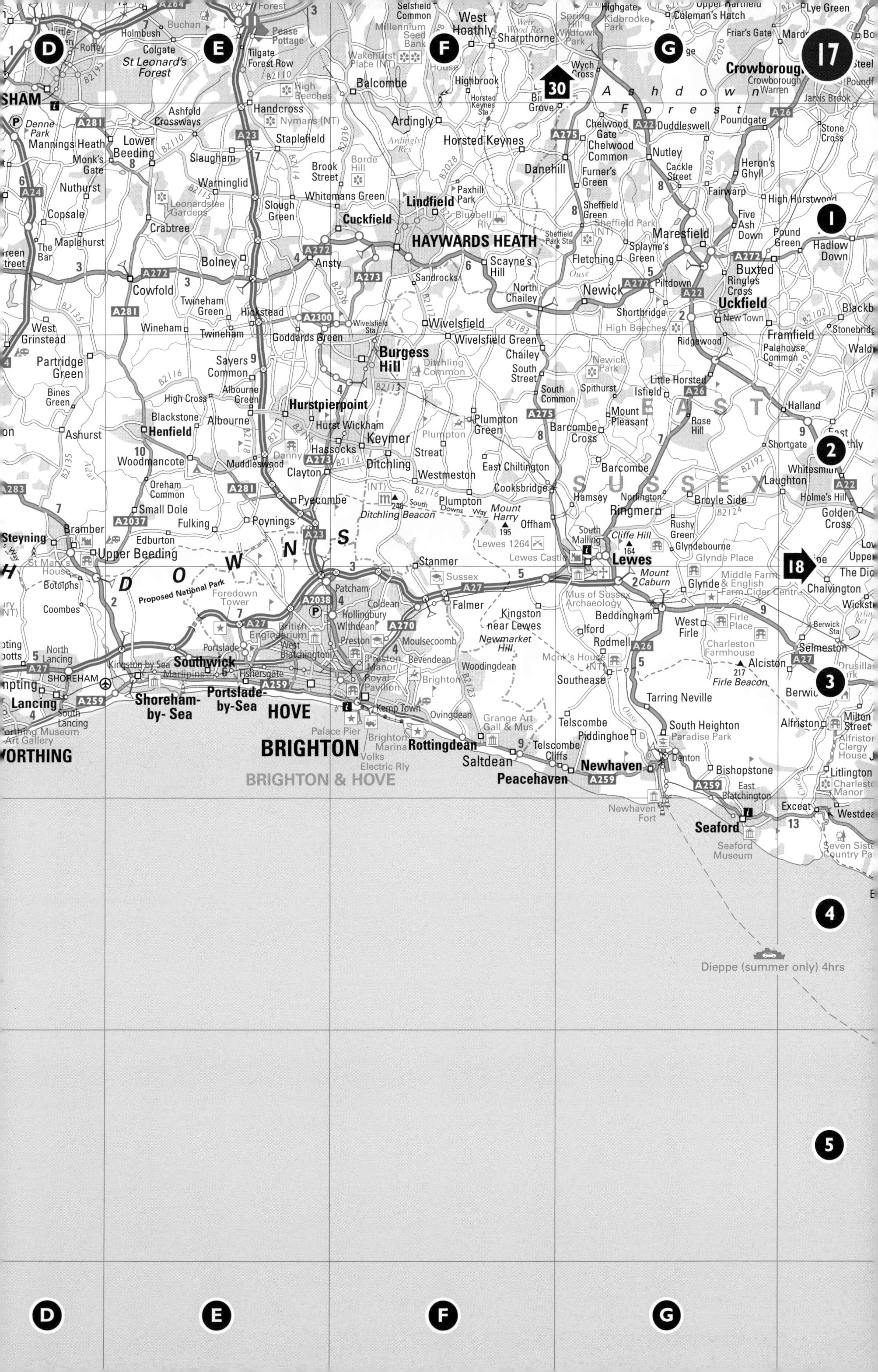
17
D
E
F
G
Horsham
Roffey
Holmbush
Colgate
Buchan
St Leonard's Forest
Pease Pottage
Tilgate Forest Row
Selsfield Common
Millennium Seed Bank
Wakehurst Place (NT)
West Hoathly
Sharpthorne
Weir Wood Res
Highbrook
Balcombe
High Beeches
Handcross
Nymans (NT)
Ashfold Crossways
Denne Park
Mannings Heath
Lower Beeding
Monk's Gate
Staplefield
Slaugham
Ardingly
Ardingly Res
Horsted Keynes
Horsted Keynes Sta
Birch Grove
Wych Cross
30
Spring Hill Wildfowl Park
Highgate
Kidbrooke Park
Coleman's Hatch
Friar's Gate
Lye Green
Crowborough
Crowborough Warren
Jarvis Brook
Ashdown Forest
Chelwood Gate
Chelwood Common
Duddleswell
Poundgate
Stone Cross
Nutley
Cackle Street
Heron's Ghyll
Danehill
Furner's Green
Fairwarp
High Hurstwood
Nuthurst
Warninglid
Leonardslee Gardens
Brook Street
Borde Hill
Whitemans Green
Lindfield
Paxhill Park
Bluebell Rly
Copsale
Slough Green
Cuckfield
Crabtree
Maplehurst
The Bar
Bolney
Ansty
HAYWARDS HEATH
Sheffield Park Sta
Sheffield Green
Sheffield Park (NT)
Maresfield
Five Ash Down
Pound Green
Hadlow Down
Scayne's Hill
Splayne's Green
Fletching
Buxted
Ringles Cross
Uckfield
New Town
Cowfold
Twineham Green
Sandrocks
North Chailey
Newick
Piltdown
Shortbridge
High Beeches
Framfield
Stonebridge
Blackboys
West Grinstead
Wineham
Twineham
Hickstead
Goddards Green
Wivelsfield Sta
Wivelsfield
Wivelsfield Green
Ridgewood
Palehouse Common
Partridge Green
Sayers Common
Burgess Hill
Ditchling Common
Chailey
South Street
Newick Park
Little Horsted
Isfield
Bines Green
High Cross
Albourne Green
Hurstpierpoint
Plumpton Green
South Common
Spithurst
Mount Pleasant
Halland
Blackstone
Albourne
Henfield
Hurst Wickham
Plumpton
Barcombe Cross
Rose Hill
East Hoathly
Ashurst
Hassocks
Danny
Keymer
Streat
Shortgate
Woodmancote
Muddleswood
Ditchling
Clayton
Westmeston
East Chiltington
Barcombe
Whitesmith
Laughton
Oreham Common
Cooksbridge
EAST SUSSEX
Hamsey
Norlington
Broyle Side
Holme's Hill
Small Dole
Pyecombe
Ditchling Beacon
South Downs Way
Plumpton
Mount Harry
Offham
Ringmer
Rushy Green
Golden Cross
Fulking
Poynings
Steyning
Bramber
Edburton
South Malling
Cliffe Hill
Glyndebourne
Upper Beeding
SOUTH DOWNS
Lewes 1264
Lewes Castle
Lewes
Glynde Place
St Mary's House
Botolphs
Stanmer
Sussex
Mount Caburn
Middle Farm & English Farm Cider Centre
Glynde
18
Chalvington
The Dicker
Proposed National Park
Foredown Tower
Patcham
Coldean
Falmer
Mus of Sussex Archaeology
Beddingham
Coombes
Hollingbury
Withdean
Kingston near Lewes
Firle Place
West Firle
Wickst
Berwick Sta
Arlington Res
British Engineerium
Preston
Moulsecoomb
Newmarket Hill
Iford
Rodmell
Charleston Farmhouse
Selmeston
North Lancing
Portslade
West Blatchington
Preston Manor
Bevendean
Monk's House (NT)
Alciston
Kingston by Sea
Southwick
Woodingdean
Southease
Firle Beacon
Berwick
SHOREHAM
Marlipins
Fishersgate
Royal Pavilion
Brighton
Lancing
Shoreham-by-Sea
Portslade-by-Sea
HOVE
Kemp Town
Ovingdean
Tarring Neville
Milton Street
South Lancing
Grange Art Gall & Mus
Telscombe
South Heighton
Paradise Park
Alfriston
Alfriston Clergy House
Worthing Museum & Art Gallery
WORTHING
Palace Pier
BRIGHTON
Brighton Marina
Volks Electric Rly
Rottingdean
Saltdean
Telscombe Cliffs
Piddinghoe
Newhaven
Denton
Bishopstone
Litlington
Charleston Manor
Peacehaven
East Blatchington
BRIGHTON & HOVE
Newhaven Fort
Exceat
Westdean
Seaford
Seaford Museum
Seven Sisters Country Park
Dieppe (summer only) 4hrs
1
2
3
4
5

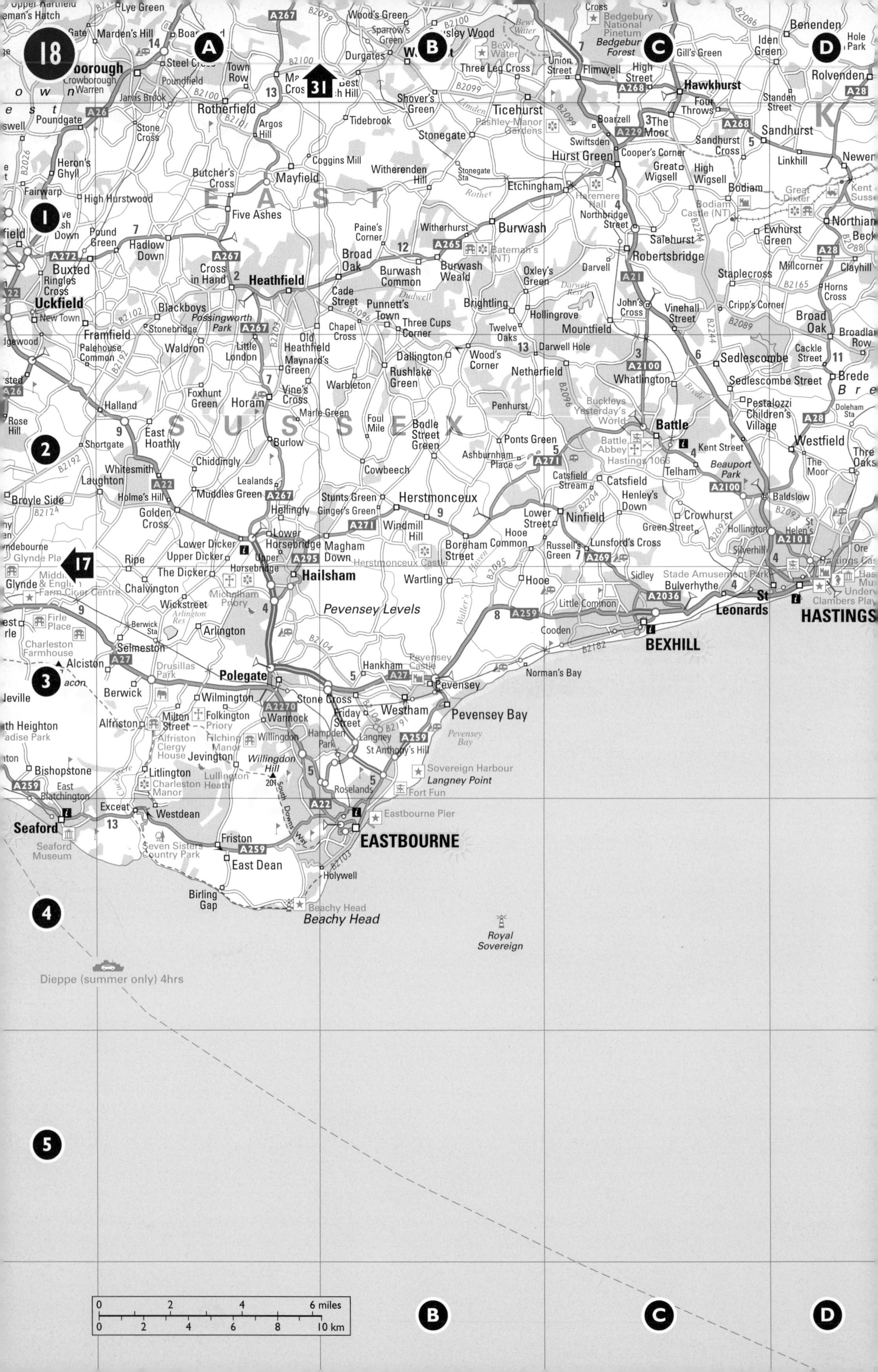

18
A
B
C
D
1
2
3
4
5
31
17
EAST SUSSEX
Lye Green
Marden's Hill
Boarshead
Steel Cross
Crowborough Warren
Poundfield
Jarvis Brook
Town Row
Rotherfield
Poundgate
Stone Cross
Heron's Ghyll
Fairwarp
High Hurstwood
Butcher's Cross
Mayfield
Argos Hill
Five Ashes
Pound Green
Hadlow Down
Buxted
Ringles Cross
Uckfield
New Town
Framfield
Palehouse Common
Blackboys
Stonebridge
Possingworth Park
Waldron
Little London
Cross in Hand
Heathfield
Halland
East Hoathly
Foxhunt Green
Horam
Vine's Cross
Old Heathfield
Maynard's Green
Shortgate
Whitesmith
Laughton
Chiddingly
Lealands
Muddles Green
Holme's Hill
Golden Cross
Broyle Side
Lower Dicker
Upper Dicker
The Dicker
Ripe
Chalvington
Wickstreet
Arlington
Arlington Res
Michelham Priory
Hellingly
Lower Horsebridge
Upper Horsebridge
Hailsham
Magham Down
Pevensey Levels
Glynde Place
Glynde
Middle Farm & English Cider Centre
Firle Place
Charleston Farmhouse
Selmeston
Berwick Sta
Alciston
Berwick
Drusillas Park
Polegate
Wilmington
Milton Street
Folkington
Alfriston
Alfriston Clergy House
Filching Manor
Jevington
Willingdon
Wannock
Willingdon Hill
Lullington Heath
Litlington
Charleston Manor
Bishopstone
East Blatchington
Seaford
Seaford Museum
Exceat
Westdean
Seven Sisters Country Park
Friston
East Dean
Birling Gap
Beachy Head
Holywell
EASTBOURNE
Eastbourne Pier
Roselands
Hampden Park
Langney
St Anthony's Hill
Stone Cross
Friday Street
Westham
Pevensey
Pevensey Bay
Sovereign Harbour
Langney Point
Fort Fun
Hankham
Pevensey Castle
Royal Sovereign
Dieppe (summer only) 4hrs
Wood's Green
Sparrow's Green
Durgates
Wadhurst
Bewl Water
Three Leg Cross
Best Beech Hill
Mark Cross
Shover's Green
Tidebrook
Ticehurst
Pashley Manor Gardens
Stonegate
Coggins Mill
Witherenden Hill
Stonegate Sta
Etchingham
Rother
Burwash
Witherhurst
Paine's Corner
Broad Oak
Burwash Common
Burwash Weald
Bateman's (NT)
Cade Street
Punnett's Town
Three Cups Corner
Chapel Cross
Dallington
Rushlake Green
Warbleton
Marle Green
Foul Mile
Bodle Street Green
Cowbeech
Stunts Green
Ginger's Green
Herstmonceux
Windmill Hill
Herstmonceux Castle
Boreham Street
Wartling
Brightling
Oxley's Green
Hollingrove
Twelve Oaks
Mountfield
Wood's Corner
Darwell Hole
Netherfield
Penhurst
Ponts Green
Ashburnham Place
Buckleys Yesterday's World
Battle
Battle Abbey
Hastings 1066
Catsfield
Catsfield Stream
Henley's Down
Lower Street
Ninfield
Hooe Common
Russell's Green
Lunsford's Cross
Hooe
Sidley
Little Common
Cooden
BEXHILL
Norman's Bay
Bulverhythe
Stade Amusement Park
St Leonards
HASTINGS
Clambers Play
Bedgebury National Pinetum
Bedgebury Forest
Union Street
Flimwell
High Street
Hawkhurst
Gill's Green
Four Throws
The Moor
Boarzell
Swiftsden
Hurst Green
Cooper's Corner
Great Wigsell
High Wigsell
Sandhurst Cross
Sandhurst
Haremere Hall
Northbridge Street
Salehurst
Robertsbridge
Darvell
Bodiam
Bodiam Castle (NT)
Ewhurst Green
John's Cross
Vinehall Street
Whatlington
Sedlescombe
Sedlescombe Street
Pestalozzi Children's Village
Kent Street
Beauport Park
Telham
Crowhurst
Green Street
Hollington
Silverhill
Baldslow
St Helen's
Staplecross
Cripp's Corner
Broad Oak
Cackle Street
Brede
Westfield
Three Oaks
The Moor
Doleham Sta
Benenden
Iden Green
Hole Park
Rolvenden
Standen Street
Linkhill
Great Dixter
Northiam
Millcorner
Clayhill
Horns Cross
Broadland Row
A267
A26
A272
A22
A265
A21
A268
A229
A2100
A271
A295
A27
A2270
A259
A2036
A269
A2101
A28
B2100
B2099
B2026
B2102
B2192
B2124
B2096
B2203
B2104
B2191
B2095
B2204
B2182
B2092
B2089
B2165
B2244
B2086
B2088
B2093
B2103
0 2 4 6 miles
0 2 4 6 8 10 km

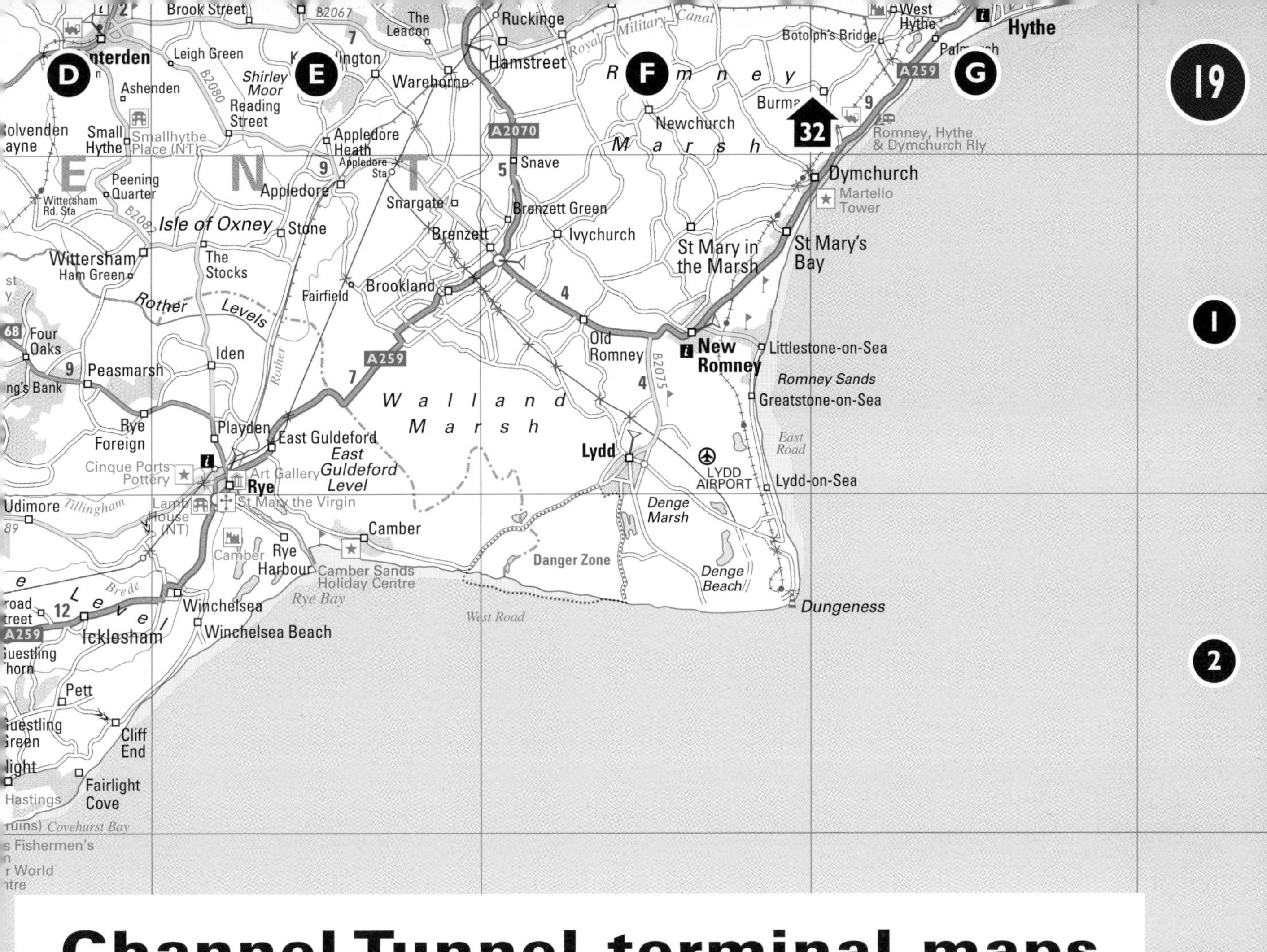

Channel Tunnel terminal maps

Eurotunnel: Access from the UK

FOLKESTONE TERMINAL

France

8 Eurotunnel's shuttle train enters tunnel

Arrivals

1 The shuttle train exits tunnel and loops round terminal to stop at platform

2 Vehicles disembark from the shuttle train and join exit road via overbridges

3 Vehicles follow exit road to M20/A20

7 Vehicles board the shuttle train

6 Vehicles drive onto platform via overbridges

5 Vehicle allocation zone

4 UK and French frontier controls and security

3 Passenger Terminal Building

2 Check-In

1 Leave M20/A20 at junction 11a

Departures

Cars Coaches Motor cycles

Arrivals only

Freight

M20/A20

ASHFORD LONDON — Terminal — Tunnel to France
A20 — DOVER
A261 — Access to Terminal — A259
FOLKESTONE

Arrivals
▭▭▭ Passenger vehicles
▭▭▭ Freight

Departures
▭▭▭ Passenger vehicles
▭▭▭ Freight

Eurotunnel: Access from France

Arrivals

1 The shuttle train exits tunnel and loops round terminal to stop at platform

UK

8 Eurotunnel's shuttle train enters tunnel

CALAIS/COQUELLES TERMINAL

2 Vehicles disembark from the shuttle train and join exit road via overbridges

3 Vehicles follow exit road to A16

CALAIS
RN1 — A16
Tunnel to UK
Terminal — Access to Terminal — DUNKIRK BELGIUM
BOULOGNE AMIENS ROUEN — A26 — PARIS
RN43

7 Vehicles board the shuttle train

6 Vehicles drive onto platforms via overbridges

5 Vehicle allocation zone

4 French and UK frontier controls and security

3 Passenger Terminal Building

2 Check-In

Arrivals only

Cars Coaches Motor cycles

1 Leave A16 at junction 13

Departures

A16

Freight

Arrivals
▭▭▭ Passenger vehicles
▭▭▭ Freight

Departures
▭▭▭ Passenger vehicles
▭▭▭ Freight

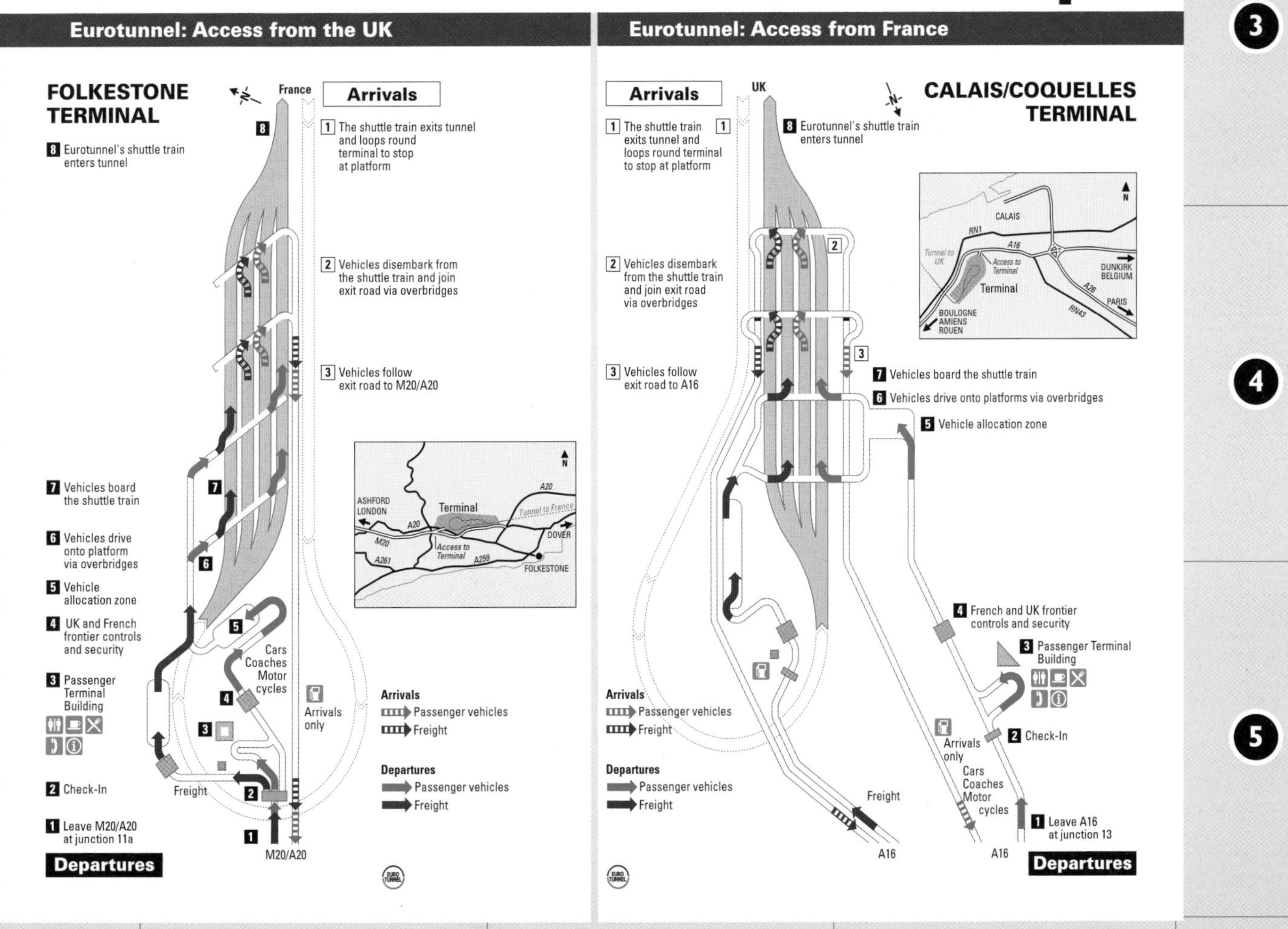

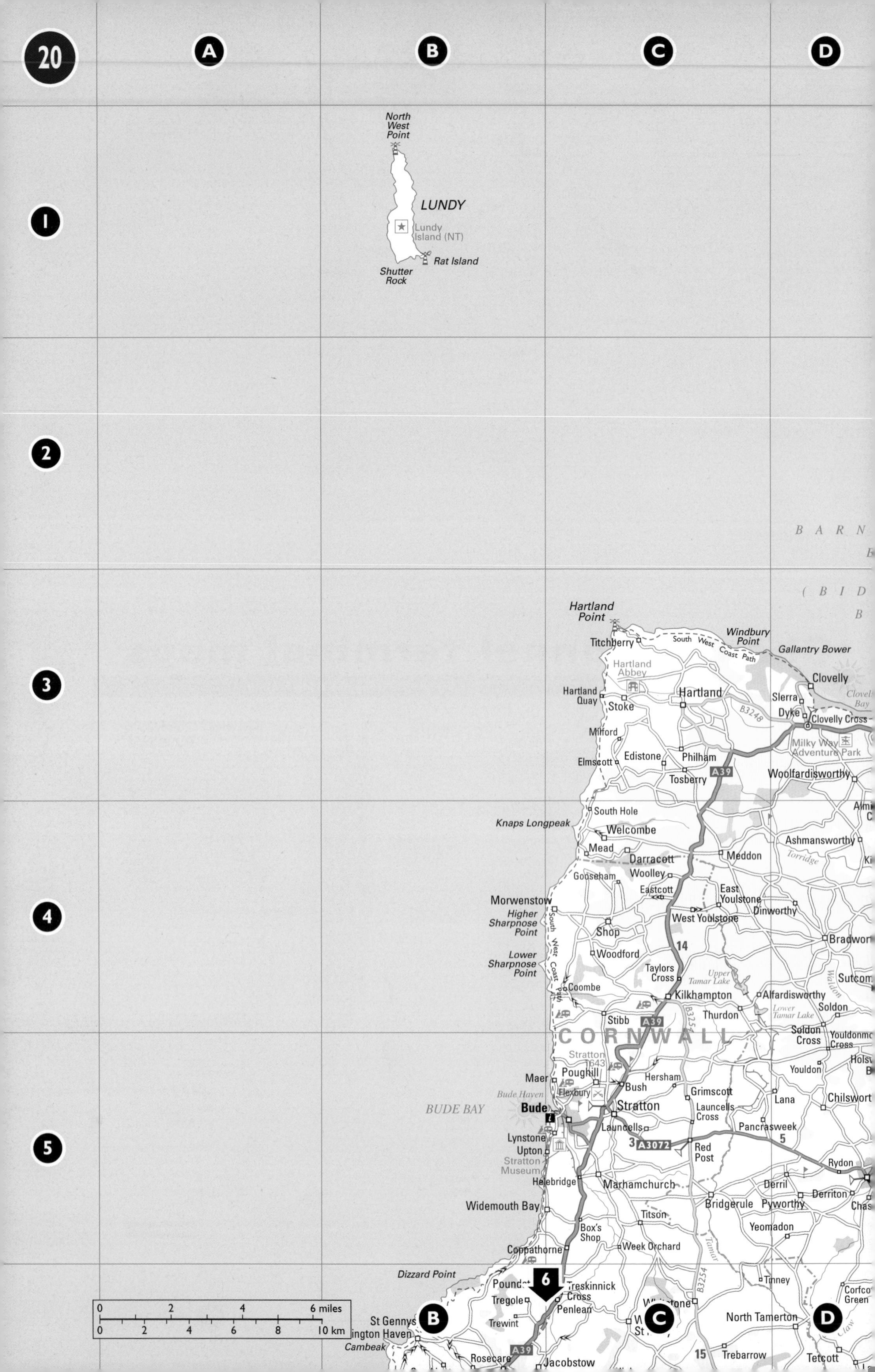

20

A   B   C   D

1

North
West
Point

LUNDY

★ Lundy
Island (NT)

☩ Rat Island

*Shutter
Rock*

2

B A R N

(B I D

B

3

Hartland
Point

Windbury
Point

Titchberry

South West Coast Path

Gallantry Bower

Clovelly

Hartland
Abbey

Hartland

Sierra
Dyke

Clovelly
Bay

Hartland
Quay

Stoke

B3248

Clovelly Cross

Milford

Milky Way
Adventure Park

Elmscott

Edistone

Philham

A39

Woolfardisworthy

Tosberry

Almi
C

South Hole

Knaps Longpeak

Welcombe

Ashmansworthy

Mead

Darracott

Meddon

Torridge

Ki

4

Morwenstow

Gooseham

Woolley

Eastcott

East
Youlstone

*Higher
Sharpnose
Point*

Shop

West Youlstone

Dinworthy

Bradwor

Woodford

*Upper
Tamar Lake*

14

Sutcom

*Lower
Sharpnose
Point*

Taylors
Cross

South West Coast Path

Coombe

Kilkhampton

Alfardisworthy

*Lower
Tamar Lake*

Soldon

Stibb

A39

Thurdon

B3235

Soldon
Cross

Youldonmo
Cross

C O R N W A L L

Youldon

Hols

Stratton
1643

Maer

Poughill

Hersham

Youldon

B

Bush

Grimscott

Lana

Chilswort

Flexbury

Bude Haven

Bude

Stratton

Launcells
Cross

Pancrasweek

BUDE BAY

ℹ

Lynstone

Launcells

3 A3072

Red
Post

5

Rydon

5

Upton

Marhamchurch

Derril

Derriton

Chas

Stratton
Museum

Helebridge

Bridgerule

Pyworthy

Widemouth Bay

Titson

Yeomadon

Dizzard Point

Box's
Shop

Week Orchard

Tamar

Tinney

Coppathorne

B3254

Corfco
Green

Pound

6

Treskinnick
Cross

Tregole

W   C

North Tamerton

D

St Gennys

B

Penlean

W
St

Trewint

ington Haven

Cambeak

A39

15

Trebarrow

Tetcott

Rosecare

Jacobstow

0   2   4   6 miles
0 2 4 6 8 10 km

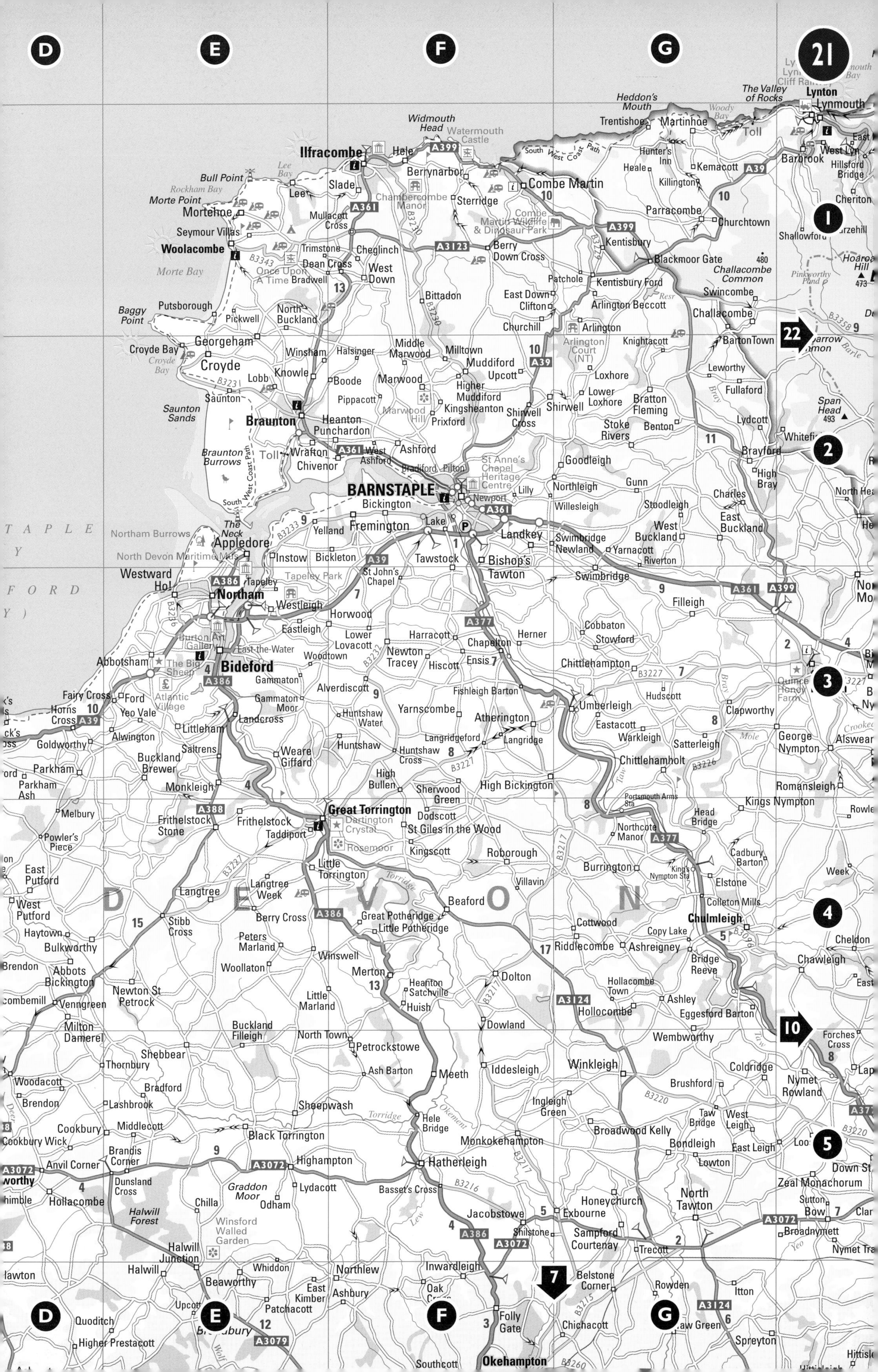

21
D
E
F
G
Heddon's Mouth
Trentishoe
Martinhoe
Woody Bay
Lynton
Lynmouth
The Valley of Rocks
Toll
Barbrook
West Lyn
Hillsford Bridge
Cheriton
Widmouth Head
Watermouth Castle
Ilfracombe
Hele
Lee Bay
Bull Point
Rockham Bay
Morte Point
Mortehoe
Lee
Slade
Berrynarbor
Chambercombe Manor
Sterridge
Combe Martin
South West Coast Path
Hunter's Inn
Heale
Kemacott
Killington
Parracombe
Churchtown
Mullacott Cross
Combe Martin Wildlife & Dinosaur Park
Kentisbury
Seymour Villas
Woolacombe
Trimstone
Cheglinch
Berry Down Cross
Blackmoor Gate
Challacombe Common
Morte Bay
Once Upon A Time
Dean Cross
West Down
Bradwell
Patchole
Kentisbury Ford
Pinkworthy Pond
Swincombe
Bittadon
East Down
Clifton
Arlington Beccott
Challacombe
Putsborough
Baggy Point
Pickwell
North Buckland
Churchill
Arlington
Arlington Court (NT)
Knightacott
Barton Town
Croyde Bay
Georgeham
Croyde
Winsham
Halsinger
Middle Marwood
Milltown
Muddiford
Upcott
Loxhore
Lower Loxhore
Leworthy
Fullaford
Lobb
Knowle
Boode
Marwood
Higher Muddiford
Kingsheanton
Shirwell Cross
Shirwell
Bratton Fleming
Saunton
Pippacott
Marwood Hill
Prixford
Saunton Sands
Braunton
Heanton Punchardon
Stoke Rivers
Benton
Lydcott
Span Head
Braunton Burrows
Toll
Wrafton
Chivenor
West Ashford
Ashford
Bradiford
Pilton
St Anne's Chapel Heritage Centre
Goodleigh
Brayford
High Bray
West Coast Path
BARNSTAPLE
Newport
Lilly
Northleigh
Gunn
Charles
North Heasley
The Neck
Bickington
Willesleigh
Stoodleigh
East Buckland
Northam Burrows
Appledore
Yelland
Fremington
Lake
Landkey
Swimbridge Newland
West Buckland
North Devon Maritime Mus.
Instow
Bickleton
Tawstock
Bishop's Tawton
Yarnacott
Riverton
Westward Ho!
Northam
Tapeley
Tapeley Park
St John's Chapel
Swimbridge
Westleigh
Filleigh
Horwood
Cobbaton
Eastleigh
Lower Lovacott
Harracott
Herner
Stowford
Burton Art Gallery
East-the-Water
Newton Tracey
Chapelton
Abbotsham
The Big Sheep
Bideford
Woodtown
Hiscott
Ensis
Chittlehampton
Quince Honey Farm
Gammaton
Alverdiscott
Fishleigh Barton
Umberleigh
Hudscott
Fairy Cross
Ford
Atlantic Village
Gammaton Moor
Yarnscombe
Clapworthy
Horns Cross
Yeo Vale
Landcross
Huntshaw Water
Atherington
Eastacott
George Nympton
Alswear
Littleham
Alwington
Langridgeford
Langridge
Warkleigh
Satterleigh
Goldworthy
Saltrens
Weare Giffard
Huntshaw
Huntshaw Cross
Chittlehamholt
Parkham
Buckland Brewer
Romansleigh
Parkham Ash
Monkleigh
High Bullen
Sherwood Green
High Bickington
Portsmouth Arms Sta
Kings Nympton
Melbury
Frithelstock Stone
Frithelstock
Great Torrington
Dartington Crystal
Dodscott
Head Bridge
Taddiport
St Giles in the Wood
Northcote Manor
Powler's Piece
Rosemoor
Kingscott
Roborough
Cadbury Barton
East Putford
Little Torrington
Burrington
King's Nympton Sta
Week
Langtree
Langtree Week
Villavin
Elstone
West Putford
DEVON
Beaford
Colleton Mills
Stibb Cross
Berry Cross
Great Potheridge
Little Potheridge
Chulmleigh
Haytown
Cottwood
Copy Lake
Cheldon
Bulkworthy
Peters Marland
Riddlecombe
Ashreigney
Bridge Reeve
Chawleigh
Brendon
Abbots Bickington
Woollaton
Winswell
Merton
Dolton
Newton St Petrock
Heanton Satchville
Hollacombe Town
Venngreen
Little Marland
Huish
Ashley
Milton Damerel
Hollocombe
Eggesford Barton
Buckland Filleigh
North Town
Dowland
Forches Cross
Shebbear
Petrockstowe
Wembworthy
Thornbury
Ash Barton
Meeth
Iddesleigh
Winkleigh
Coldridge
Woodacott
Bradford
Nymet Rowland
Brendon
Lashbrook
Sheepwash
Brushford
Ingleigh Green
Hele Bridge
Taw Bridge
West Leigh
Cookbury
Middlecott
Black Torrington
Broadwood Kelly
Cookbury Wick
Brandis Corner
Monkokehampton
Bondleigh
East Leigh
Anvil Corner
Highampton
Hatherleigh
Lowton
Down St
Dunsland Cross
Lydacott
Basset's Cross
Zeal Monachorum
Hollacombe
Graddon Moor
Odham
North Tawton
Chilla
Honeychurch
Halwill Forest
Jacobstowe
Exbourne
Sutton
Bow
Winsford Walled Garden
Shilstone
Sampford Courtenay
Broadnymett
Halwill Junction
Trecott
Nymet Tracey
Halwill
Whiddon
Northlew
Inwardleigh
Belstone Corner
Rowden
Beaworthy
East Kimber
Ashbury
Oak Cross
Itton
Upcott
Patchacott
Folly Gate
Chichacott
Quoditch
Spreyton
Higher Prestacott
Okehampton
Southcott
Hittisleigh
A399
A361
A3123
A39
A386
A377
A388
A3124
A3072
A3079
B3343
B3231
B3233
B3230
B3229
B3232
B3227
B3226
B3217
B3220
B3216
B3215
B3260
B3236
B3358
Torridge
Okement
Taw
Mole
Bray
Lew
Yeo
22
10
7

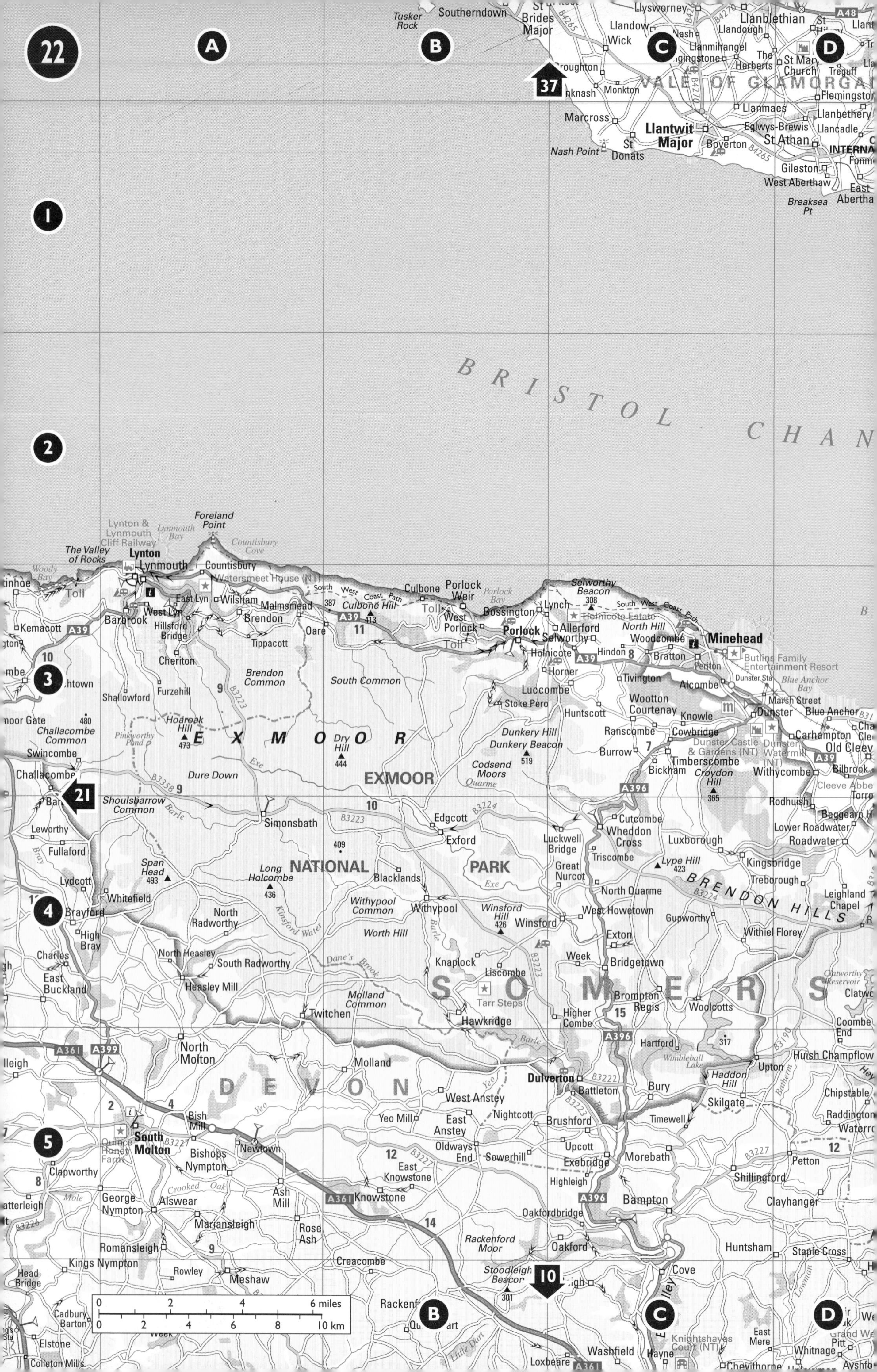
A
B
C
D
1
2
3
4
5
Tusker Rock
Southerndown
St Brides Major
Llysworney
Llanblethian
Llandow
Wick
Nash
Llanmihangel
Llandough
St Mary Church
The Herberts
Treguff
Flemingston
A48
37
Monkton
VALE OF GLAMORGAN
Llanmaes
Llanbethery
Marcross
Llantwit Major
Eglwys-Brewis
Llancadle
St Athan
Nash Point
St Donats
Boverton
Gileston
West Aberthaw
East Aberthaw
Breaksea Pt
B4265
B4270
BRISTOL CHAN
Foreland Point
Lynton & Lynmouth Cliff Railway
Lynmouth Bay
Countisbury Cove
The Valley of Rocks
Woody Bay
Lynton
Lynmouth
Countisbury
Watersmeet House (NT)
Toll
Kemacott
A39
Barbrook
West Lyn
East Lyn
Wilsham
Malmsmead
Brendon
Oare
Hillsford Bridge
Tippacott
Cheriton
South West Coast Path
387
Culbone Hill
413
Culbone
Porlock Weir
Porlock Bay
West Porlock
Bossington
Porlock
Selworthy Beacon
308
Lynch
Holnicote Estate
Allerford
North Hill
Selworthy
Holnicote
Horner
Hindon
Woodcombe
Minehead
Bratton
Periton
Butlins Family Entertainment Resort
Dunster Sta
Blue Anchor Bay
Alcombe
Tivington
Brendon Common
South Common
Shallowford
Furzehill
B3223
Challacombe Common
480
Hoaroak Hill
473
Pinkworthy Pond
EXMOOR
Dry Hill
444
Swincombe
Challacombe
Dure Down
Exe
B3358
Luccombe
Stoke Pero
Huntscott
Wootton Courtenay
Knowle
Marsh Street
Dunster
Blue Anchor
Dunkery Hill
Dunkery Beacon
519
Ranscombe
Cowbridge
Carhampton
Dunster Castle & Gardens (NT)
Dunster Watermill (NT)
Burrow
Timberscombe
Old Cleeve
Codsend Moors
Quarme
Bickham
Croydon Hill
365
Withycombe
Bilbrook
Cleeve Abbey
21
Shoulsbarrow Common
Barle
Simonsbath
Edgcott
B3224
A396
Rodhuish
Cutcombe
Wheddon Cross
Leworthy
Fullaford
Lydcott
Span Head
493
Long Holcombe
436
409
NATIONAL
Blacklands
Exford
Luckwell Bridge
PARK
Great Nurcot
Triscombe
Luxborough
Lype Hill
423
Kingsbridge
Treborough
Lower Roadwater
Roadwater
BRENDON HILLS
Leighland Chapel
Whitefield
Brayford
High Bray
North Radworthy
Withypool Common
Withypool
Kinsford Water
Worth Hill
Winsford Hill
426
Winsford
North Quarme
West Howetown
Gupworthy
Withiel Florey
Exton
Charles
East Buckland
North Heasley
South Radworthy
Heasley Mill
Dane's Brook
Knaplock
Liscombe
Week
Bridgetown
SOMERS
Tarr Steps
Brompton Regis
Woolcotts
Clatworthy Reservoir
Molland Common
Twitchen
Hawkridge
Higher Combe
Hartford
317
Coombe End
Wimbleball Lake
A361
A399
North Molton
Molland
DEVON
Yeo
Dulverton
B3222
Battleton
Bury
Haddon Hill
Upton
Huish Champflower
West Anstey
Skilgate
Chipstable
Bish Mill
Nightcott
Brushford
Timewell
Raddington
Yeo Mill
East Anstey
South Molton
Quince Honey Farm
B3227
Newtown
Oldways End
Sowerhill
Upcott
Exebridge
Morebath
Petton
Bishops Nympton
East Knowstone
Highleigh
Shillingford
Clapworthy
Crooked Oak
Ash Mill
Knowstone
Bampton
Clayhanger
George Nympton
Alswear
Mole
Oakfordbridge
Mariansleigh
Rose Ash
Rackenford Moor
Oakford
Huntsham
Romansleigh
Staple Cross
Kings Nympton
Rowley
Creacombe
Stoodleigh Beacon
301
Cove
Head Bridge
Meshaw
10
Rackenford
Cadbury Barton
Elstone
Colleton Mills
Little Dart
Loxbeare
Washfield
Hayne
Knightshayes Court (NT)
East Mere
Whitnage
Chevithorne
Lowman
0 2 4 6 miles
0 2 4 6 8 10 km

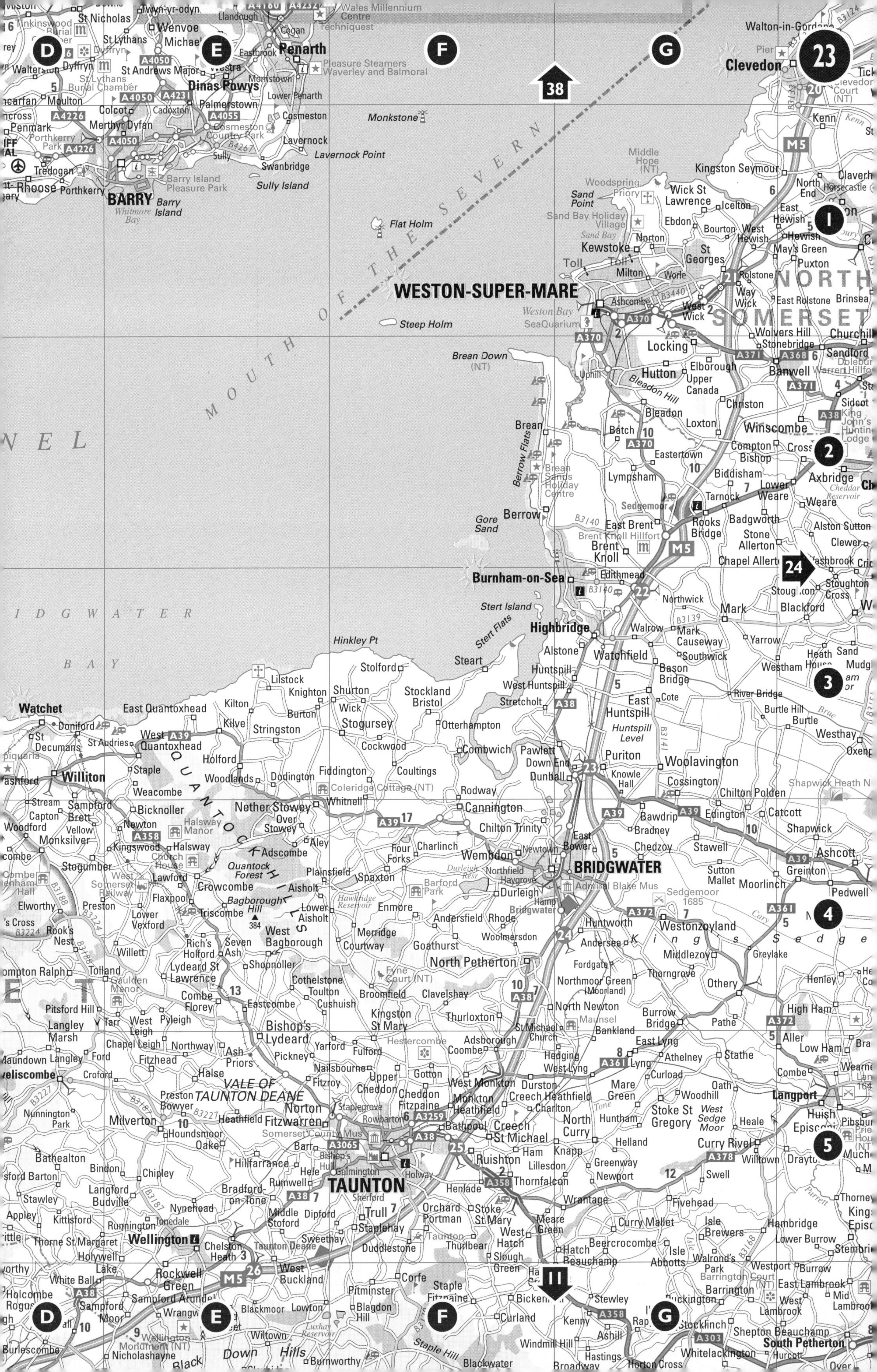
23
D
E
F
G
38
24
11
I
2
3
4
5
St Nicholas
Wenvoe
Tinkinswood Burial Chamber
St Lythans
Michaelston
Dyffryn
Walterston
St Andrews Major
Wales Millennium Centre
Techniquest
Cogan
Penarth
Pleasure Steamers Waverley and Balmoral
Eastbrook
Llandough
Dinas Powys
Westra
Morristown
Lower Penarth
Moulton
St Lythans Burial Chamber
Colcot
Merthyr Dyfan
Cadoxton
Palmerstown
Cosmeston
Cosmeston Country Park
Lavernock
Lavernock Point
Monkstone
Penmark
Porthkerry Park
Sully
Swanbridge
Sully Island
Tredogan
Rhoose
Porthkerry
BARRY
Barry Island
Barry Island Pleasure Park
Whitmore Bay
Flat Holm
Steep Holm
MOUTH OF THE SEVERN
WESTON-SUPER-MARE
Weston Bay
SeaQuarium
Walton-in-Gordano
Pier
Clevedon
Clevedon Court (NT)
Kenn
Middle Hope (NT)
Kingston Seymour
Woodspring Priory
Sand Point
Sand Bay Holiday Village
Sand Bay
Wick St Lawrence
Icelton
Ebdon
Bourton
West Hewish
East Hewish
Hewish
North End
Horsecastle
Claverham
May's Green
Puxton
Norton
Kewstoke
Toll
Milton
Worle
St Georges
Rolstone
Way Wick
East Rolstone
Brinsea
NORTH SOMERSET
Ashcombe
West Wick
Wolvers Hill
Stonebridge
Churchill
Sandford
Dolebury
Locking
Banwell
Hutton
Elborough
Upper Canada
Bleadon Hill
Uphill
Brean Down (NT)
Christon
Sidcot
King John's Hunting Lodge
Bleadon
Loxton
Winscombe
Brean
Batch
Compton Bishop
Cross
Axbridge
Cheddar Reservoir
Eastertown
Berrow Flats
Brean Sands Holiday Centre
Lympsham
Biddisham
Lower Weare
Weare
Tarnock
Sedgemoor
Rooks Bridge
Badgworth
Alston Sutton
Clewer
Gore Sand
Berrow
East Brent
Brent Knoll Hillfort
Brent Knoll
Stone Allerton
Chapel Allerton
Ashbrook
Burnham-on-Sea
Edithmead
Stoughton
Stoughton Cross
Blackford
Northwick
Stert Island
Stert Flats
Highbridge
Mark
Walrow
Mark Causeway
Yarrow
Southwick
Heath House
Sand
Mudgley
Westham
Watchfield
Alstone
Bason Bridge
Hinkley Pt
Stolford
Steart
Huntspill
West Huntspill
Stretcholt
East Huntspill
Huntspill Level
Cote
River Bridge
Burtle Hill
Burtle
Westhay
Lilstock
Knighton
Shurton
Stockland Bristol
Kilton
Burton
Wick
Stogursey
Otterhampton
Watchet
East Quantoxhead
Kilve
Stringston
Doniford
St Decumans
St Audries
West Quantoxhead
QUANTOCK HILLS
Holford
Cockwood
Combwich
Pawlett
Down End
Dunball
Puriton
Woolavington
Knowle Hall
Cossington
Shapwick Heath
Williton
Staple
Woodlands
Dodington
Fiddington
Coultings
Rodway
Coleridge Cottage (NT)
Chilton Polden
Weacombe
Stream
Capton
Sampford Brett
Bicknoller
Nether Stowey
Over Stowey
Whitnell
Cannington
Bawdrip
Bradney
Edington
Catcott
Shapwick
Woodford
Vellow
Newton
Halsway Manor
Chilton Trinity
Monksilver
Kingswood
Halsway
Aley
Four Forks
Charlinch
Chedzoy
Stawell
Ashcott
Adscombe
Wembdon
Newtown
East Bower
BRIDGWATER
Greinton
Stogumber
Church House
Quantock Forest
Plainsfield
Spaxton
Durleigh Resr
Northfield
Hamp
Admiral Blake Mus
Sutton Mallet
Moorlinch
Pedwell
West Somerset Railway
Lawford
Crowcombe
Aisholt
Hawkridge Reservoir
Barford Park
Haygrove
Durleigh
Sedgemoor 1685
Combe Sydenham Hall
Elworthy
Preston
Flaxpool
Bagborough Hill
384
Lower Aisholt
Enmore
Bridgwater
Triscombe
Andersfield
Rhode
Huntworth
Westonzoyland
King's Sedgemoor
Lower Vexford
West Bagborough
Merridge
Woolmersdon
Andersea
Greylake
Rook's Nest
Rich's Holford
Seven Ash
Courtway
Goathurst
Middlezoy
Willett
Fordgate
Lydeard St Lawrence
Shopnoller
North Petherton
Thorngrove
Othery
Tolland
Northmoor Green (Moorland)
Gaulden Manor
Cothelstone
Toulton
Fyne Court (NT)
Henley
Combe Florey
Eastcombe
Cushuish
Broomfield
Clavelshay
North Newton
Maunsel
Burrow Bridge
High Ham
Pitsford Hill
Kingston St Mary
Thurloxton
St Michael Church
Bankland
Pathe
Langley Marsh
Tarr
West Leigh
Pyleigh
Bishop's Lydeard
Adsborough
Coombe
Aller
Chapel Leigh
Northway
Ash Priors
Hestercombe
East Lyng
Low Ham
Yarford
Fulford
Hedging
West Lyng
Lyng
Athelney
Stathe
Fitzhead
Pickney
Langley
Ford
Nailsbourne
Curload
Combe
Wearne
Croford
Halse
Fitzroy
Upper Cheddon
Gotton
West Monkton
Durston
Mare Green
Oath
Langport
Preston Bowyer
VALE OF TAUNTON DEANE
Cheddon Fitzpaine
Monkton Heathfield
Creech Heathfield
Woodhill
Nunnington Park
Norton Fitzwarren
Staplegrove
Charlton
Stoke St Gregory
West Sedge Moor
Huish Episcopi
Milverton
Heathfield
Rowbarton
Bathpool
Creech St Michael
North Curry
Hunham
Heale
Houndsmoor
Oake
Somerset County Mus
Barr
Helland
Curry Rivel
Bathealton
Bindon
Hillfarrance
Bishop's Hull
Ruishton
Ham
Knapp
Willtown
Drayton
Much
Chipley
Hele
Galmington
Holway
Lillesdon
Greenway
Newport
Swell
Langford Budville
Bradford-on-Tone
Rumwell
TAUNTON
Henlade
Thornfalcon
Sherford
Wrantage
Stawley
Nynehead
Middle Stoford
Dipford
Trull
Orchard Portman
Stoke St Mary
Fivehead
Appley
Kittisford
Tonedale
Runnington
Staplehay
Taunton
West Hatch
Meare Green
Curry Mallet
Isle Brewers
Hambridge
Thorne St Margaret
Wellington
Chelston Heath
Taunton Deane
Sweethay
Thurlbear
Hatch Beauchamp
Beercrocombe
Lower Burrow
Holywell Lake
Duddlestone
Slough Green
Isle Abbotts
Walrond's Park
Westport
Burrow
Rockwell Green
West Buckland
Barrington Court (NT)
East Lambrook
White Ball
Corfe
Staple Fitzpaine
Barrington
West Lambrook
Holcombe Rogus
Sampford Arundel
Pitminster
Bickenhall
Stewley
Puckington
Sampford Moor
Wrangway
Blagdon Hill
Lowton
Curland
Kenny
Stocklinch
Shepton Beauchamp
Blackmoor
Luxhay Reservoir
Ashill
South Petherton
Wellington Monument (NT)
Wiltown
Windmill Hill
Whitelackington
Burlescombe
Nicholashayne
Black Down Hills
Staple Hill
Hastings
Hurcott
Burnworthy
Blackwater
Broadway
Horton Cross
M5
A38
A39
A358
A361
A370
A371
A372
A368
A378
A303
A3259
A3065
A4050
A4226
A4231
A4055
B4267
B3140
B3139
B3141
B3440
B3133
B3124
B3224
B3188
B3227
B3187
B3168
B3170

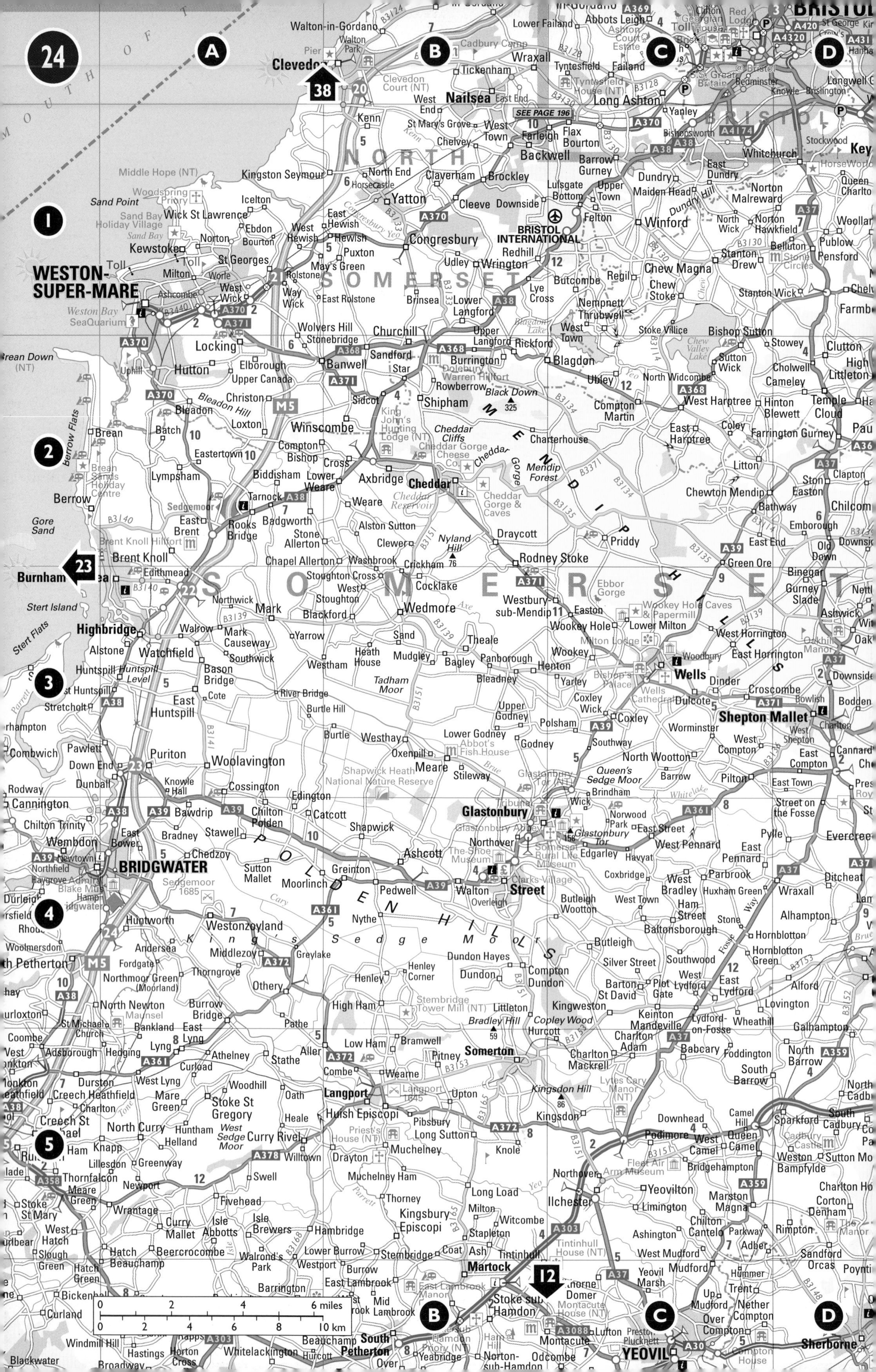
A
B
C
D
MOUTH OF THE
Walton-in-Gordano
Walton Park
Pier
Clevedon
38
20
Clevedon Court (NT)
Cadbury Camp
Lower Failand
Abbots Leigh
Ashton Court Estate
A369
Clifton
Georgian House
Red Lodge
BRISTOL
Wraxall
Tickenham
Tyntesfield
Failand
Tyntesfield House (NT)
S.S. Great Britain
Bedminster
Knowle
Brislington
Longwell Green
West End
Nailsea
East End
Long Ashton
Yanley
St Mary's Grove
West Town
SEE PAGE 196
Kenn
Chelvey
Farleigh
Flax Bourton
Bishopsworth
A4174
Whitchurch
Stockwood
Keynsham
Backwell
Barrow Gurney
Dundry
East Dundry
NORTH
Middle Hope (NT)
Kingston Seymour
North End
Horsecastle
Claverham
Brockley
Lulsgate Bottom
Upper Town
Maiden Head
Dundry Hill
Norton Malreward
Queen Charlton
Sand Point
Woodspring Priory
Icelton
Yatton
Cleeve
Downside
Felton
Winford
North Wick
Norton Hawkfield
Woollard
Sand Bay Holiday Village
Sand Bay
Wick St Lawrence
Ebdon
Bourton
East Hewish
West Hewish
Hewish
Congresbury Yeo
Congresbury
BRISTOL INTERNATIONAL
Belluton
Publow
Kewstoke
Norton
Puxton
Redhill
Stanton Drew
Stone Circles
Pensford
Toll
Milton
Worle
St Georges
May's Green
Rolstone
SOMERSET
Udley
Wrington
Chew Magna
Regil
WESTON-SUPER-MARE
Ashcombe
West Wick
Way Wick
East Rolstone
Brinsea
Lower Langford
Lye Cross
Butcombe
Chew Stoke
Stanton Wick
Weston Bay SeaQuarium
A370
A371
Nempnett Thrubwell
Blagdon Lake
West Town
Stoke Villice
Bishop Sutton
Chew Valley Lake
Wolvers Hill
Stonebridge
Churchill
Upper Langford
Rickford
Stowey
Clutton
Brean Down (NT)
Uphill
Locking
Hutton
Elborough
Upper Canada
Banwell
Sandford
Star
A368
Burrington
Dolebury Warren Hillfort
Blagdon
Sutton Wick
Cholwell
High Littleton
Cameley
Christon
Bleadon Hill
Bleadon
Sidcot
Rowberrow
Black Down
325
Ubley
North Widcombe
Hinton Blewett
Temple Cloud
M5
Shipham
King John's Hunting Lodge (NT)
Compton Martin
West Harptree
Berrow Flats
Brean
Batch
Loxton
Winscombe
Cheddar Cliffs
Cheddar Gorge
Cheese Co.
Charterhouse
East Harptree
Coley
Farrington Gurney
Paulton
Eastertown
Compton Bishop
Cross
MENDIP HILLS
Mendip Forest
Litton
Clapton
Brean Sands Holiday Centre
Lympsham
Biddisham
Lower Weare
Axbridge
Cheddar
Cheddar Reservoir
Cheddar Gorge & Caves
Chewton Mendip
Ston Easton
Chilcompton
Berrow
Tarnock
Weare
Bathway
Emborough
Gore Sand
Sedgemoor
East Brent
Rooks Bridge
Badgworth
Alston Sutton
Stone Allerton
Clewer
Nyland Hill
Draycott
Priddy
East End
Old Down
Downside
Brent Knoll Hillfort
Brent Knoll
Chapel Allerton
Washbrook
Crickham
Rodney Stoke
Green Ore
Binegar
Burnham-on-Sea
23
Edithmead
Stoughton Cross
West Stoughton
Cocklake
Ebbor Gorge
Gurney Slade
Stert Island
22
Northwick
Mark
Blackford
Wedmore
Westbury-sub-Mendip
Easton
Wookey Hole Caves & Papermill
Ashwick
Stert Flats
Highbridge
Walrow
Mark Causeway
Yarrow
Sand
Theale
Wookey Hole
Lower Milton
West Horrington
Oakhill Manor
Alstone
Watchfield
Southwick
Heath House
Mudgley
Bagley
Panborough
Wookey
Milton Lodge
Woodbury
East Horrington
Huntspill
Huntspill Level
Bason Bridge
Westham
Tadham Moor
Bleadney
Henton
Yarley
Bishop's Palace
Wells
Wells Cathedral
Dinder
Downside
East Huntspill
Cote
River Bridge
Upper Godney
Coxley Wick
Dulcote
Croscombe
Bowlish
Stretcholt
Burtle Hill
Coxley
Polsham
Shepton Mallet
Charlton
Bodden
Combwich
Pawlett
Burtle
Westhay
Lower Godney
Abbot's Fish House
Godney
Southway
Worminster
West Shepton
West Compton
Cannard's Grave
Down End
Puriton
Woolavington
Oxenpill
Meare
North Wootton
East Compton
Shapwick Heath National Nature Reserve
Stileway
Glastonbury Tor (NT)
Queen's Sedge Moor
Barrow
Rodway
Dunball
Knowle Hall
Cossington
Edington
Brindham
Pilton
East Town
Cannington
Bawdrip
Chilton Polden
Catcott
Glastonbury
Tribunal
Wick
Norwood Park
Whitelake
Street on the Fosse
Chilton Trinity
East Bower
Bradney
Stawell
Shapwick
Glastonbury Abbey
East Street
West Pennard
Pylle
Evercreech
Wembdon
Newtown
Chedzoy
Ashcott
Northover
The Shoe Museum
Somerset Rural Life Museum
Glastonbury Tor
156
Edgarley
Havyatt
East Pennard
Northfield
BRIDGWATER
Sutton Mallet
Greinton
Moorlinch
Coxbridge
Parbrook
Ditcheat
Haygrove
Admiral Blake Museum
Sedgemoor 1685
Pedwell
Walton
Street
Clarks Village
West Bradley
Huxham Green
Wraxall
Durleigh
Hamp
POLDEN HILLS
Overleigh
Butleigh Wootton
West Town
Ham Street
Fosse Way
Alhampton
Huntworth
Westonzoyland
Nythe
Baltonsborough
Stone
Hornblotton
KING'S SEDGE MOORS
Andersea
Middlezoy
Greylake
Dundon Hayes
Butleigh
Silver Street
Southwood
Hornblotton Green
Woolmersdon
North Petherton
Fordgate
Thorngrove
A372
Henley Corner
Henley
Dundon
Compton Dundon
Barton St David
Plot Gate
West Lydford
East Lydford
Alford
Northmoor Green (Moorland)
Othery
Stembridge Tower Mill (NT)
Littleton
Kingweston
Lovington
North Newton
Maunsel
Burrow Bridge
High Ham
Bradley Hill
59
Copley Wood
Hurcott
Keinton Mandeville
Lydford-on-Fosse
Wheathill
Galhampton
St Michael Church
Bankland
East Lyng
Pathe
Aller
Low Ham
Bramwell
Pitney
Somerton
Charlton Adam
Charlton Mackrell
Babcary
Foddington
North Barrow
Coombe
Adsborough
Hedging
Lyng
Athelney
Stathe
South Barrow
West Monkton
Curload
Combe
Wearne
Lytes Cary Manor (NT)
Durston
West Lyng
Woodhill
Langport
Langport 1645
Upton
Kingsdon Hill
86
North Cadbury
Creech Heathfield
Mare Green
Oath
Stoke St Gregory
Huish Episcopi
Kingsdon
Camel Hill
South Cadbury
Creech St Michael
Charlton
North Curry
Huntham
Heale
Pibsbury
Downhead
Sparkford
Helland
West Sedge Moor
Curry Rivel
Priest's House (NT)
Long Sutton
Podimore
West Camel
Queen Camel
Cadbury Castle
Ham
Knapp
Willtown
Muchelney
Knole
Weston Bampfylde
Sutton Montis
Ruishton
Lillesdon
Greenway
A378
Drayton
Fleet Air Arm Museum
Bridgehampton
Thornfalcon
Swell
Muchelney Ham
Northover
Yeovilton
Charlton Horethorne
Meare Green
Newport
Long Load
Ilchester
Limington
Marston Magna
Corton Denham
Stoke St Mary
Wrantage
Fivehead
Thorney
Milton
Kingsbury Episcopi
Witcombe
Chilton Cantelo
Parkway
Adber
Rimpton
West Hatch
Curry Mallet
Isle Abbotts
Isle Brewers
Hambridge
Stapleton
Ashington
The Manor
Slough Green
Hatch Beauchamp
Beercrocombe
Walrond's Park
Lower Burrow
Stembridge
Coat
Ash
Tintinhull
Tintinhull House (NT)
West Mudford
Mudford
Sandford Orcas
Hatch Green
Westport
Burrow
Martock
Yeovil Marsh
Hummer
Poyntington
Bickenhall
Barrington
East Lambrook
East Lambrook Manor
Stoke sub Hamdon
Thorne
Domer
Montacute House (NT)
Trent
Up Mudford
Nether Compton
Over Compton
Curland
Mid Lambrook
Sherborne
Windmill Hill
Hastings
Horton Cross
Whitelackington
Beauchamp
Hurcott
South Petherton
Stoke sub Hamdon Priory (NT)
Ham Hill
Norton-sub-Hamdon
Montacute
Odcombe
Lufton
Preston Plucknett
YEOVIL
Compton House
Blackwater
Broadway
Over
Yeabridge
0 2 4 6 miles
0 2 4 6 8 10 km
12

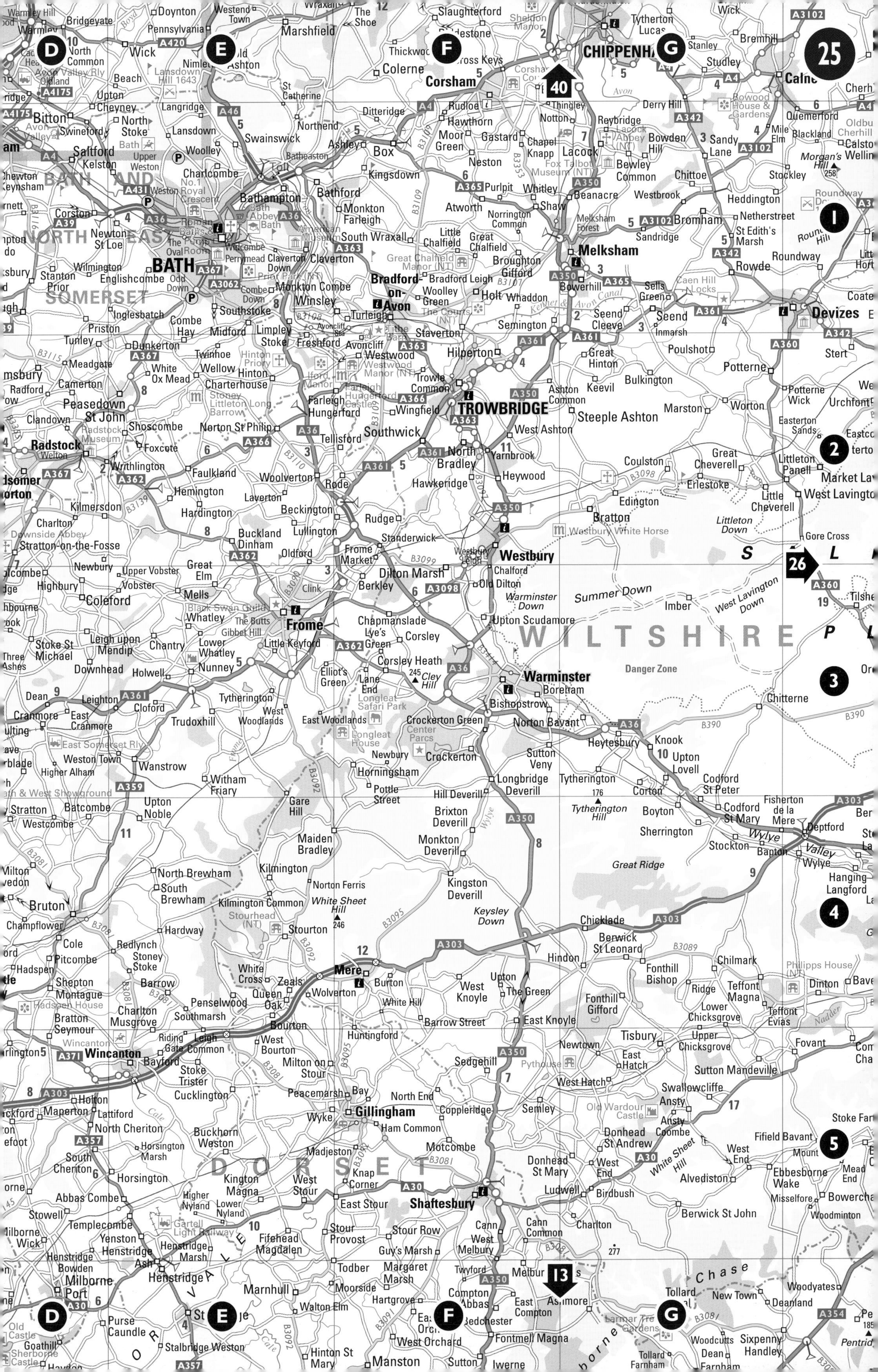

D
E
F
G
Warmley Hill
Warmley
Doynton
Westend Town
Marshfield
The Shoe
Slaughterford
Sheldon Manor
Tytherton Lucas
Wick
A3102
North Common
Bridgeyate
Pennsylvania
Wick
A420
Nimlet
Thickwood
Cross Keys
Colerne
Corsham
CHIPPENHAM
Stanley
Bremhill
Studley
Calne
Avon Valley Rly
Oldland
Beach
Lansdown Hill 1643
St Catherine
Upton Cheyney
Bitton
Swineford
North Stoke
Langridge
Lansdown
A46
Swainswick
Northend
Ditteridge
Ashley
Box
Rudloe
Hawthorn
Moor Green
Gastard
Thingley
Notton
Chapel Knapp
Reybridge
Lacock Abbey (NT)
Lacock
Fox Talbot Museum (NT)
Bowden Hill
Bewley Common
Derry Hill
Bowood House & Gardens
Sandy Lane
Quemerford
Mile Elm
Blackland
Oldbury
Cherhill
Calstone Wellington
Morgan's Hill
258
Saltford
Kelston
Upper Weston
Woolley
Charlcombe
Batheaston
Kingsdown
Neston
Chittoe
Stockley
BATH AND NORTH EAST SOMERSET
Corston
Newton St Loe
No.1 Royal Crescent
Weston
Bathampton
Bathford
Monkton Farleigh
Purlpit
Atworth
Whitley
Shaw
Beanacre
Melksham Forest
Westbrook
Heddington
Roundway
Netherstreet
Bromham
Sandridge
St Edith's Marsh
Roundway Hill
Bath Abbey
Roman Baths & Pump Room
The Oval
Widcombe
Perrymead
American Museum
South Wraxall
Little Chalfield
Great Chalfield
Great Chalfield Manor (NT)
Norrington Common
Broughton Gifford
Melksham
Rowde
BATH
Wilmington
Englishcombe
Stanton Prior
Odd Down
Claverton
Claverton Down
Prior Park (NT)
Combe Down
Monkton Combe
Winsley
Bradford-on-Avon
Bradford Leigh
Woolley Green
The Courts (NT)
Holt
Whaddon
Bowerhill
Kennet & Avon Canal
Sells Green
Caen Hill Locks
Seend
Seend Cleeve
Devizes
Coate
Inglesbatch
Priston
Combe Hay
Southstoke
Midford
Limpley Stoke
Freshford
Avoncliff
Turleigh
Staverton
Semington
Inmarsh
Poulshot
Stert
Tunley
Dunkerton
Meadgate
Camerton
Twinhoe
Wellow
Hinton Priory
Westwood
Westwood Manor (NT)
Iford Manor
Hilperton
Great Hinton
Keevil
Bulkington
Potterne
White Ox Mead
Radford
Peasedown St John
Charterhouse Hinton
Stoney Littleton Long Barrow
Farleigh Hungerford
Farleigh Hungerford Castle
Trowle Common
Wingfield
TROWBRIDGE
Ashton Common
Steeple Ashton
Marston
Worton
Potterne Wick
Urchfont
Clandown
Radstock
Radstock Museum
Welton
Shoscombe
Foxcote
Norton St Philip
Tellisford
Southwick
West Ashton
Easterton Sands
Writhlington
Faulkland
Hemington
Woolverton
Rode
North Bradley
Yarnbrook
Coulston
Great Cheverell
Littleton Panell
Market Lavington
West Lavington
Heywood
Hawkeridge
Erlestoke
Little Cheverell
Edington
Kilmersdon
Laverton
Beckington
Hardington
Charlton
Downside Abbey
Stratton-on-the-Fosse
Buckland Dinham
Lullington
Rudge
Standerwick
Bratton
Westbury White Horse
Littleton Down
Gore Cross
Newbury
Great Elm
Upper Vobster
Vobster
Oldford
Frome Market
Westbury Leigh
Westbury
Chalford
Dilton Marsh
Old Dilton
Berkley
Clink
Highbury
Coleford
Mells
Black Swan Guild
Whatley
The Butts
Gibbet Hill
Frome
Warminster Down
Summer Down
Imber
West Lavington Down
Tilshead
WILTSHIRE
Chapmanslade
Lye's Green
Corsley
Upton Scudamore
Stoke St Michael
Three Ashes
Leigh upon Mendip
Chantry
Lower Whatley
Little Keyford
Nunney
Downhead
Holwell
Corsley Heath
Cley Hill
245
Elliot's Green
Lane End
Longleat Safari Park
Warminster
Boreham
Bishopstrow
Danger Zone
Chitterne
Dean
Leighton
Cloford
Cranmore
East Cranmore
Tytherington
West Woodlands
East Woodlands
Crockerton Green
Center Parcs
Longleat House
Norton Bavant
Heytesbury
Knook
Trudoxhill
East Somerset Rly
Weston Town
Higher Alham
Wanstrow
Witham Friary
Newbury
Crockerton
Horningsham
Sutton Veny
Upton Lovell
Codford St Peter
Codford St Mary
Fisherton de la Mere
Deptford
Bath & West Showground
Stratton
Westcombe
Batcombe
Upton Noble
Gare Hill
Pottle Street
Hill Deverill
Longbridge Deverill
Tytherington
Tytherington Hill
176
Corton
Boyton
Sherrington
Stockton
Bapton
Wylye
Wylye Valley
Brixton Deverill
Monkton Deverill
Maiden Bradley
Great Ridge
Hanging Langford
North Brewham
South Brewham
Kilmington
Norton Ferris
Kingston Deverill
Bruton
Champflower
White Sheet Hill
246
Kilmington Common
Stourhead (NT)
Stourton
Keysley Down
Chicklade
Berwick St Leonard
Cole
Pitcombe
Redlynch
Stoney Stoke
Hardway
Hindon
Fonthill Bishop
Chilmark
Philipps House
Dinton
Hadspen
Shepton Montague
Barrow
White Cross
Zeals
Mere
Burton
Queen Oak
Wolverton
West Knoyle
Upton
The Green
Fonthill Gifford
Ridge
Teffont Magna
Teffont Evias
Lower Chicksgrove
Hadspen House
Charlton Musgrove
Penselwood
Southmarsh
White Hill
Barrow Street
East Knoyle
Tisbury
Bratton Seymour
Wincanton
Riding Gate
Leigh Common
Bourton
West Bourton
Huntingford
Newtown
East Hatch
Upper Chicksgrove
Fovant
Bayford
Stoke Trister
Milton on Stour
Sedgehill
Pythouse
Sutton Mandeville
West Hatch
Swallowcliffe
Cucklington
Holton
Maperton
Lattiford
North Cheriton
Peacemarsh
Bay
North End
Gillingham
Wyke
Ham Common
Coppleridge
Semley
Old Wardour Castle
Ansty
Ansty Coombe
Stoke Farthing
Buckhorn Weston
Horsington Marsh
South Cheriton
Horsington
Madjeston
Motcombe
Donhead St Andrew
Donhead St Mary
West End
White Sheet Hill
Fifield Bavant
Mount
West End
Ebbesborne Wake
Alvediston
DORSET
Kington Magna
West Stour
Knap Corner
Shaftesbury
Ludwell
Birdbush
Misselfore
Bowerchalke
Woodminton
Abbas Combe
Higher Nyland
Lower Nyland
East Stour
Stowell
Templecombe
Gartell Light Railway
Stour Provost
Stour Row
Cann
Cann Common
Charlton
Berwick St John
Milborne Wick
Yenston
Henstridge
Henstridge Marsh
Fifehead Magdalen
Guy's Marsh
West Melbury
277
Henstridge Bowden
Henstridge Ash
Henstridge
Milborne Port
Todber
Margaret Marsh
Marnhull
Moorside
Twyford
Melbury
Compton Abbas
Ashmore
Chase
Tollard Royal
New Town
Woodyates
Deanland
Old Castle
Sherborne Castle
Goathill
Purse Caundle
Stalbridge Weston
Walton Elm
Hartgrove
East Orchard
East Compton
Bedchester
Larmer Tree Gardens
Woodcutts
Dean
Sixpenny Handley
West Orchard
Fontmell Magna
Hinton St Mary
Manston
Sutton
Iwerne
Tollard Farnham
Farnham
Pentridge
A4175
A4
A431
A36
A39
A367
A3062
A363
A365
A350
A3102
A342
A361
A360
A366
A362
A3098
A359
A371
A303
A357
A30
A354
B3109
B3353
B3107
B3108
B3115
B3110
B3139
B3099
B3090
B3098
B3414
B390
B3092
B3095
B3089
B3081
B3091
40
26
13
1
2
3
4
5

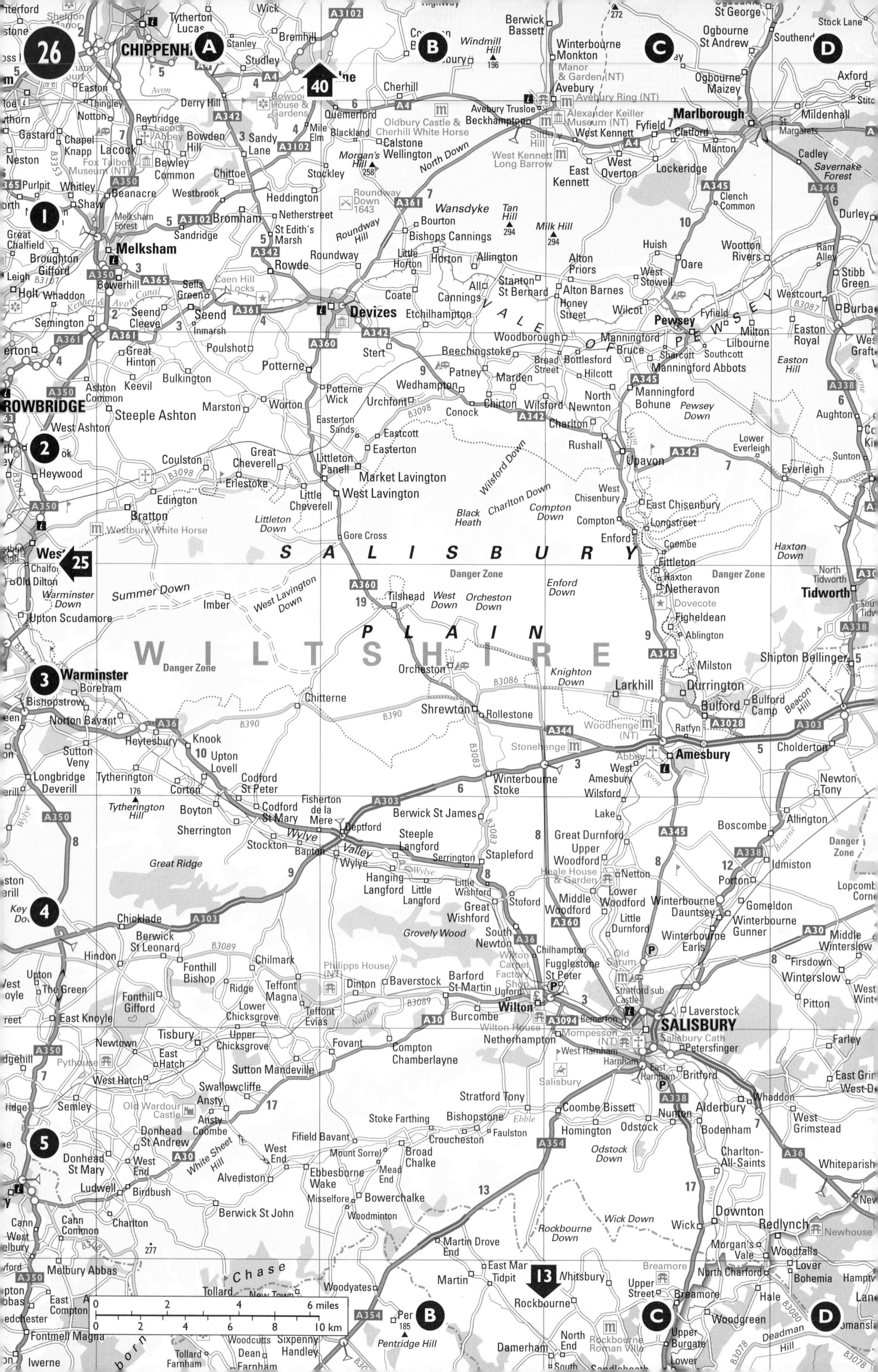
26
40
25
13
A
B
C
D
1
2
3
4
5
CHIPPENHAM
Tytherton Lucas
Stanley
Studley
Bremhill
Berwick Bassett
Winterbourne Monkton
Windmill Hill
Ogbourne St George
Ogbourne St Andrew
Ogbourne Maizey
Southend
Stock Lane
Axford
Easton
Thingley
Notton
Derry Hill
Reybridge
Lacock Abbey (NT)
Bowden Hill
Sandy Lane
Bowood House & Gardens
Cherhill
Quemerford
Mile Elm
Blackland
Oldbury Castle & Cherhill White Horse
Calstone Wellington
Avebury Trusloe
Beckhampton
Avebury
Manor & Garden (NT)
Avebury Ring (NT)
Alexander Keiller Museum (NT)
Silbury Hill
West Kennett
West Kennett Long Barrow
East Kennett
West Overton
Fyfield
Lockeridge
Marlborough
Clatford
Manton
Mildenhall
St Margarets
Cadley
Savernake Forest
Gastard
Chapel Knapp
Lacock
Fox Talbot Museum (NT)
Bewley Common
Chittoe
Neston
Purlpit
Whitley
Shaw
Beanacre
Westbrook
Heddington
Stockley
Morgan's Hill
Roundway Down 1643
North Down
Wansdyke
Tan Hill
Milk Hill
Clench Common
Durley
Melksham Forest
Bromham
Sandridge
Netherstreet
St Edith's Marsh
Roundway Hill
Bourton
Bishops Cannings
Great Chalfield
Melksham
Broughton Gifford
Roundway
Rowde
Little Horton
Horton
Allington
Alton Priors
Huish
Wootton Rivers
Ram Alley
Oare
Leigh
Holt
Whaddon
Bowerhill
Sells Green
Caen Hill Locks
Kennet & Avon Canal
Seend Cleeve
Seend
Inmarsh
Semington
Devizes
Coate
All Cannings
Etchilhampton
Stanton St Bernard
Alton Barnes
Honey Street
Wilcot
West Stowell
Pewsey
Fyfield
Stibb Green
Westcourt
Burbage
VALE OF PEWSEY
Great Hinton
Poulshot
Potterne
Stert
Woodborough
Beechingstoke
Broad Street
Bottlesford
Manningford Bruce
Sharcott
Southcott
Milton Lilbourne
Easton Royal
Manningford Abbots
Easton Hill
Ashton Common
Keevil
Bulkington
Patney
Marden
Hilcott
TROWBRIDGE
Steeple Ashton
Marston
Worton
Potterne Wick
Urchfont
Wedhampton
Chirton
Wilsford
North Newton
Manningford Bohune
Pewsey Down
Aughton
West Ashton
Easterton Sands
Eastcott
Easterton
Conock
Charlton
Rushall
Upavon
Lower Everleigh
Everleigh
Sunton
Heywood
Coulston
Great Cheverell
Erlestoke
Edington
Littleton Panell
Market Lavington
West Lavington
Little Cheverell
Wilsford Down
Charlton Down
Black Heath
Compton Down
West Chisenbury
East Chisenbury
Compton
Longstreet
Enford
Coombe
Fittleton
Haxton
Netheravon
Bratton
Westbury White Horse
Littleton Down
Gore Cross
SALISBURY PLAIN
WILTSHIRE
Danger Zone
Haxton Down
North Tidworth
Tidworth
Old Dilton
Warminster Down
Summer Down
Imber
West Lavington Down
Tilshead
West Down
Orcheston Down
Enford Down
Dovecote
Figheldean
Ablington
Upton Scudamore
Milston
Shipton Bellinger
Warminster
Boreham
Bishopstrow
Norton Bavant
Chitterne
Orcheston
Knighton Down
Larkhill
Durrington
Bulford
Bulford Camp
Beacon Hill
Ratfyn
Shrewton
Rollestone
Woodhenge (NT)
Stonehenge
Heytesbury
Knook
Upton Lovell
Sutton Veny
Amesbury
Abbey
West Amesbury
Cholderton
Newton Tony
Longbridge Deverill
Tytherington
Tytherington Hill
Corton
Codford St Peter
Codford St Mary
Boyton
Sherrington
Fisherton de la Mere
Deptford
Winterbourne Stoke
Berwick St James
Steeple Langford
Wilsford
Lake
Boscombe
Allington
Stockton
Wylye Valley
Bapton
Wylye
Great Ridge
Hanging Langford
Little Langford
Serrington
Stapleford
Great Durnford
Upper Woodford
Heale House & Garden
Netton
Idmiston
Porton
Little Wishford
Great Wishford
Stoford
Middle Woodford
Lower Woodford
Winterbourne Dauntsey
Gomeldon
Winterbourne Gunner
Little Durnford
Lopcombe Corner
Key Down
Chicklade
Grovely Wood
South Newton
Berwick St Leonard
Hindon
Chilmark
Fonthill Bishop
Philipps House (NT)
Chilhampton
Old Sarum
Winterbourne Earls
Middle Winterslow
Firsdown
Winterslow
Upton
The Green
West Knoyle
East Knoyle
Fonthill Gifford
Ridge
Teffont Magna
Lower Chicksgrove
Teffont Evias
Dinton
Baverstock
Barford St Martin
Wilton Carpet Factory Shop
Fugglestone St Peter
Ugford
Wilton
Burcombe
Bemerton
Stratford sub Castle
Laverstock
Pitton
SALISBURY
Salisbury Cath
Wilton House
Netherhampton
Mompesson (NT)
Petersfinger
Farley
Tisbury
Upper Chicksgrove
Newtown
East Hatch
Pythouse
West Hatch
Fovant
Compton Chamberlayne
Sutton Mandeville
West Harnham
Harnham
East Harnham
Britford
Salisbury
East Grimstead
West Dean
Swallowcliffe
Ansty
Old Wardour Castle
Semley
Stratford Tony
Coombe Bissett
Homington
Odstock
Nunton
Alderbury
Whaddon
West Grimstead
Bodenham
Donhead St Andrew
Ansty Coombe
Stoke Farthing
Bishopstone
Faulston
Fifield Bavant
Croucheston
Odstock Down
White Sheet Hill
West End
Mount Sorrel
Broad Chalke
Charlton-All-Saints
Whiteparish
Donhead St Mary
Alvediston
Ebbesborne Wake
Mead End
Misselfore
Bowerchalke
Woodminton
Ludwell
Birdbush
Berwick St John
Downton
Wick
Redlynch
Newhouse
Wick Down
Rockbourne Down
Cann
Cann Common
Charlton
West Melbury
Martin Drove End
Morgan's Vale
Woodfalls
Melbury Abbas
Chase
East Martin
Tidpit
Breamore
Lover
Bohemia
Hamptworth
North Charford
Tollard Royal
New Town
Woodyates
Martin
Whitsbury
Upper Street
Breamore
Hale
East Compton
Pentridge
Pentridge Hill
Rockbourne
Woodgreen
Fontmell Magna
Woodcutts
Dean
Sixpenny Handley
Tollard Farnham
Farnham
Damerham
North End
Rockbourne Roman Villa
Upper Burgate
Deadman Hill
Iwerne
0 2 4 6 miles
0 2 4 6 8 10 km
A4
A342
A3102
A350
A365
A361
A360
A345
A346
A338
A36
A344
A303
A3028
A30
A3094
A354
B3098
B3086
B390
B3083
B3089
B3087
B3107
B3353
B3078
B3080
Avon
Nadder
Ebble
Bourne
Wylye
Kennet & Avon Canal

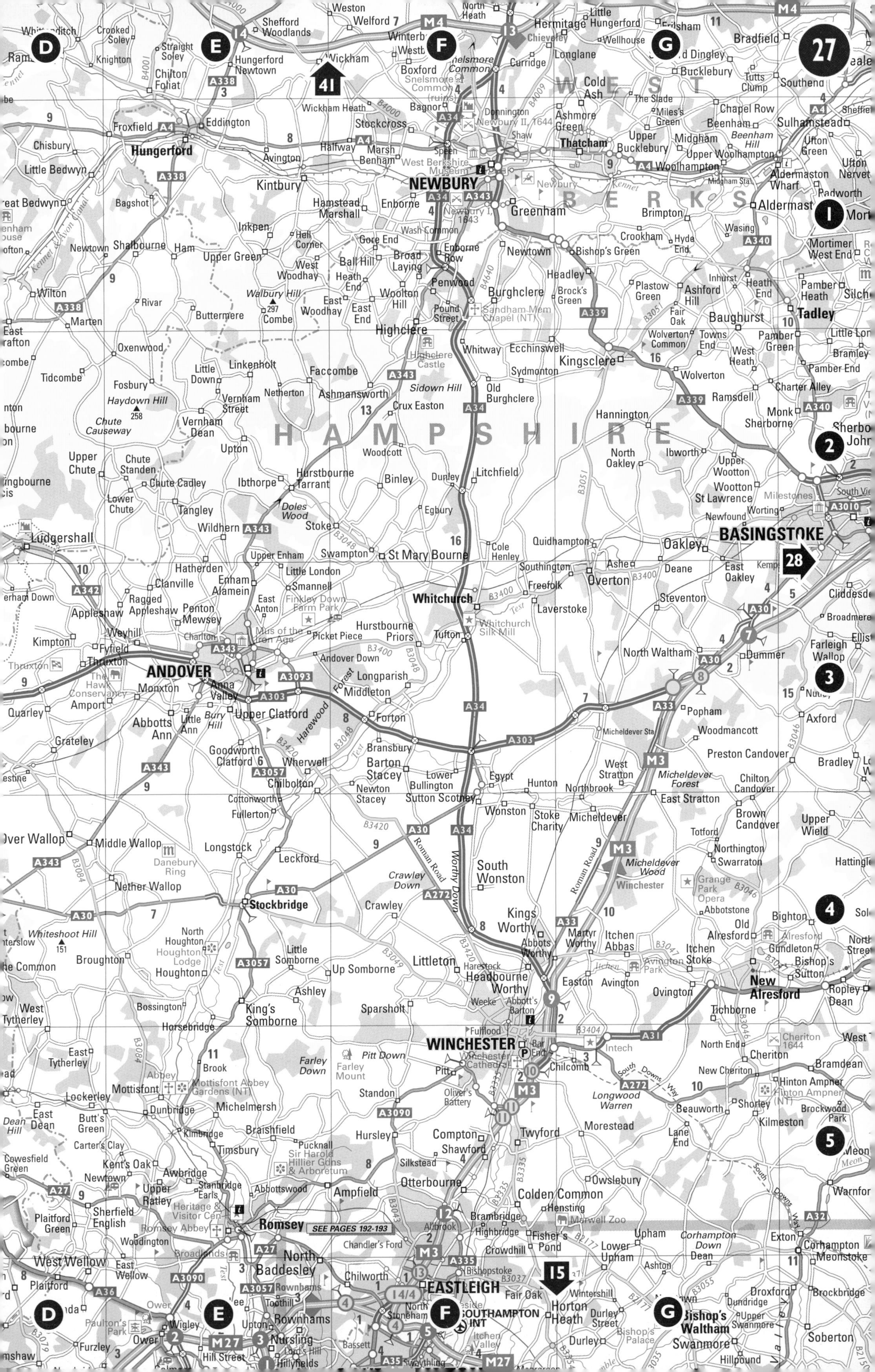

27
41
28
15
D
E
F
G
I
2
3
4
5
M4
Weston
Welford
Winterbourne
North Heath
Hermitage
Little Hungerford
Frilsham
Whitley Ditch
Crooked Soley
Shefford Woodlands
Straight Soley
Chieveley
Wellhouse
Bradfield
Ramsbury
Knighton
Wickham
Westbrook
Snelsmore Common
Curridge
Longlane
Dingley
Hungerford Newtown
Chilton Foliat
Boxford
Snelsmore Common (ruins)
Cold Ash
Bucklebury
Tutts Clump
Southend
WEST
BERKS
Bagnor
Donnington
Newbury II, 1644
Ashmore Green
The Slade
Miles's Green
Chapel Row
Wickham Heath
Stockcross
Eddington
Froxfield
Hungerford
Beenham
Sulhamstead
Beenham Hill
Ufton Green
Shaw
Thatcham
Upper Bucklebury
Midgham
Chisbury
Halfway
Marsh Benham
Speen
Avington
Upper Woolhampton
Woolhampton
Ufton Nervet
Little Bedwyn
West Berkshire Museum
Midgham Sta
Aldermaston Wharf
Kintbury
NEWBURY
Newbury
Kennet
Padworth
Great Bedwyn
Bagshot
Hamstead Marshall
Enborne
Newbury I, 1643
Greenham
Brimpton
Aldermaston
Mortimer
Wash Common
Inkpen
Hell Corner
Crookham
Wasing
Hyde End
Mortimer West End
Newtown
Shalbourne
Ham
Upper Green
Gore End
Enborne Row
Newtown
Bishop's Green
Kennet and Avon Canal
Ball Hill
Broad Laying
West Woodhay
Heath End
Headley
Brock's Green
Plastow Green
Inhurst
Ashford Hill
Heath End
Pamber Heath
Silchester
Wilton
Rivar
Walbury Hill
297
East Woodhay
Woolton Hill
Penwood
Burghclere
Fair Oak
Baughurst
Tadley
Marten
Buttermere
Combe
East End
Pound Street
Sandham Mem Chapel (NT)
Wolverton Common
Towns End
Pamber Green
Little London
East Grafton
Highclere
Highclere Castle
Whitway
Ecchinswell
Kingsclere
West Heath
Bramley
Oxenwood
Linkenholt
Little Down
Sydmonton
Wolverton
Pamber End
Tidcombe
Fosbury
Faccombe
Netherton
Vernham Street
Old Burghclere
Charter Alley
Haydown Hill
258
Chute Causeway
Ashmansworth
Crux Easton
Sidown Hill
Ramsdell
Vernham Dean
Hannington
Monk Sherborne
Sherborne St John
HAMPSHIRE
Upton
Woodcott
North Oakley
Ibworth
Upper Chute
Chute Standen
Hurstbourne Tarrant
Binley
Dunley
Litchfield
Upper Wootton
Ludgershall
Chute Cadley
Ibthorpe
Lower Chute
Tangley
Doles Wood
Egbury
Wootton St Lawrence
Milestones
Worting
Newfound
BASINGSTOKE
Wildhern
Stoke
Quidhampton
Oakley
Upper Enham
Swampton
St Mary Bourne
Cole Henley
Hatherden
Little London
Southington
Ashe
Deane
East Oakley
Kempshott
Cliddesden
Clanville
Enham Alamein
Smannell
Freefolk
Overton
Ragged Appleshaw
Penton Mewsey
East Anton
Finkley Down Farm Park
Whitchurch
Laverstoke
Steventon
Appleshaw
Weyhill
Charlton
Mus of the Iron Age
Picket Piece
Hurstbourne Priors
Whitchurch Silk Mill
Broadmere
Kimpton
Fyfield
Tufton
Farleigh Wallop
Ellisfield
Thruxton
Andover Down
North Waltham
Dummer
ANDOVER
The Hawk Conservancy
Monxton
Anna Valley
Longparish
Harewood Forest
Middleton
Quarley
Amport
Upper Clatford
Forton
Popham
Nuthley
Axford
Abbotts Ann
Little Ann
Bury Hill
Woodmancott
Grateley
Goodworth Clatford
Bransbury
Micheldever Sta
Preston Candover
Bradley
Wherwell
Barton Stacey
West Stratton
Chilton Candover
Chilbolton
Lower Bullington
Micheldever Forest
Cottonworth
Newton Stacey
Sutton Scotney
Egypt
Hunton
Northbrook
East Stratton
Fullerton
Wonston
Stoke Charity
Micheldever
Brown Candover
Over Wallop
Middle Wallop
Longstock
Upper Wield
Danebury Ring
Leckford
Roman Road
Worthy Down
Totford
Northington
Swarraton
Nether Wallop
Crawley Down
South Wonston
Micheldever Wood
Winchester
Grange Park Opera
Stockbridge
Crawley
Abbotstone
Bighton
Whiteshoot Hill
151
North Houghton
Houghton Lodge
Kings Worthy
Abbots Worthy
Martyr Worthy
Itchen Abbas
Itchen Stoke
Old Alresford
Alresford
Gundleton
Bishop's Sutton
Broughton
Little Somborne
Littleton
Harestock
Headbourne Worthy
Avington Park
New Alresford
Houghton
Up Somborne
Easton
Avington
Ovington
Ropley Dean
West Tytherley
Bossington
King's Somborne
Ashley
Sparsholt
Weeke
Abbott's Barton
Tichborne
Horsebridge
Fulflood
WINCHESTER
Bar End
Intech
Cheriton 1644
North End
Cheriton
East Tytherley
Brook
Pitt Down
Farley Down
Farley Mount
Winchester Cathedral
Chilcomb
South Downs Way
Bramdean
Abbey
Mottisfont
Mottisfont Abbey Gardens (NT)
Pitt
Oliver's Battery
New Cheriton
Hinton Ampner
Hinton Ampner (NT)
Longwood Warren
Lockerley
Standon
Shorley
Brockwood Park
East Dean
Dunbridge
Michelmersh
Beauworth
Kilmeston
Butt's Green
Braishfield
Hursley
Compton
Twyford
Morestead
Lane End
Carter's Clay
Kimbridge
Timsbury
Pucknall
Sir Harold Hillier Gdns & Arboretum
Shawford
Kent's Oak
Cowesfield Green
Silkstead
Meon
Newtown
Awbridge
Owslebury
Upper Ratley
Stanbridge Earls
Abbottswood
Ampfield
Otterbourne
Colden Common
Warnford
Sherfield English
Heritage & Visitor Cen
Hensting
Plaitford Green
Romsey
Romsey Abbey
SEE PAGES 192-193
Brambridge
Highbridge
Marwell Zoo
Woodington
Allbrook
Chandler's Ford
Fisher's Pond
Upham
Corhampton Down
Exton
Corhampton
Meonstoke
Broadlands
North Baddesley
Crowdhill
Lower Upham
Dean
West Wellow
East Wellow
Chilworth
Bishopstoke
Ashton
Plaitford
Rownhams
Toothill
EASTLEIGH
Fair Oak
Wintershill
Droxford
Dundridge
Brockbridge
Ower
Paulton's Park
North Stoneham
SOUTHAMPTON INT
Horton Heath
Durley Street
Bishop's Palace
Bishop's Waltham
Upper Swanmore
Wigley
Upton
Nursling
Itchen Valley
Durley
Swanmore
Soberton
Furzley
Hill Street
Lord's Hill
Hillyfields
Bassett
Hill Pound
Whitenap
A4
A34
A338
A343
A339
A340
A342
A303
A3093
A3057
A30
A272
A33
A31
A3090
A27
A36
A335
A35
A32
A3010
M3
M27
B4000
B4001
B4009
B4640
B3051
B3048
B3400
B3420
B3084
B3049
B3046
B3047
B3404
B3335
B3043
B3037
B3354
B2177
B3035
B3055
B3079
B2150

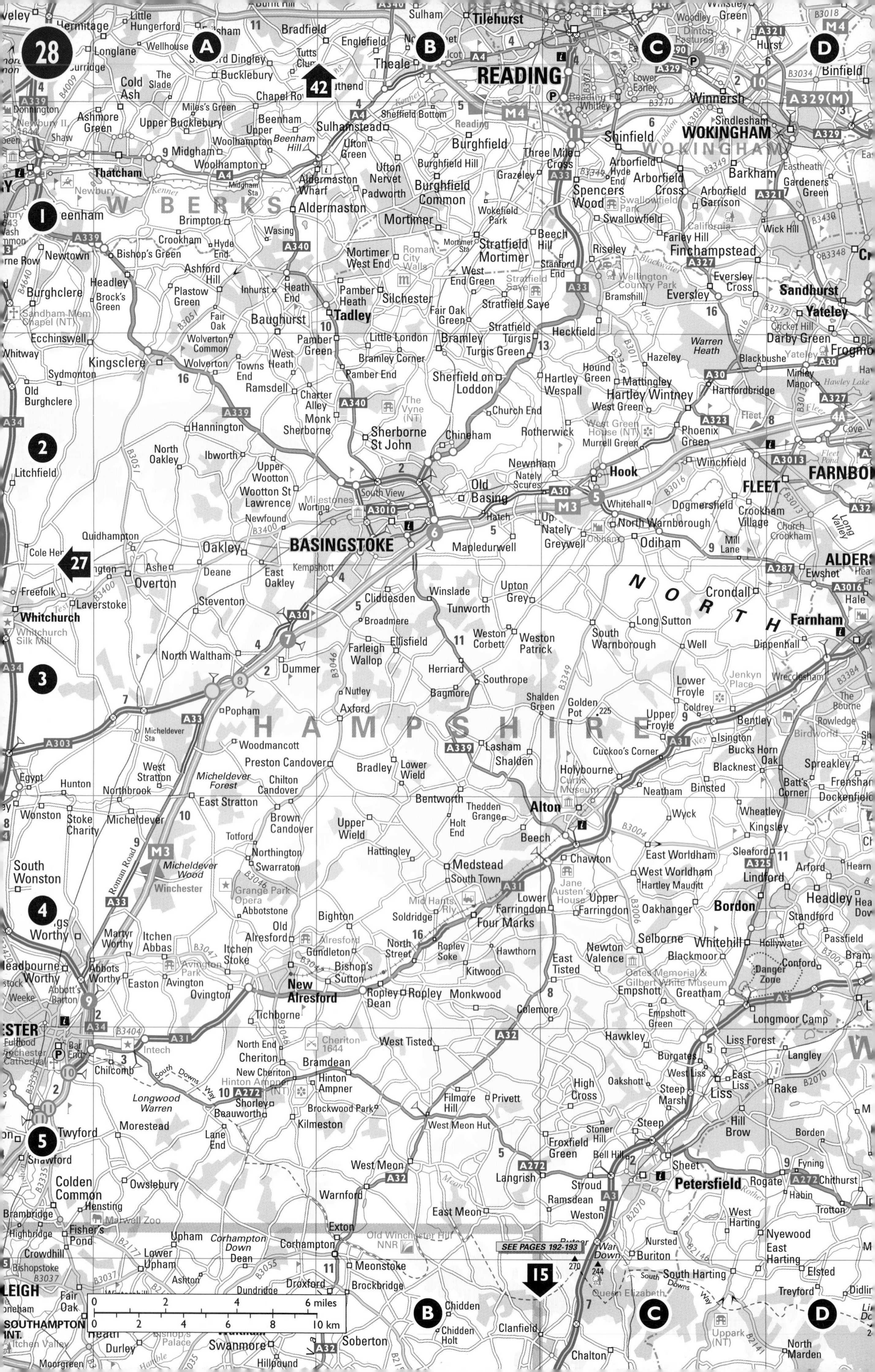

28
A
B
C
D
42
27
15
SEE PAGES 192-193
1
2
3
4
5
READING
BASINGSTOKE
WOKINGHAM
W BERKS
HAMPSHIRE
NORTH
Hermitage
Little Hungerford
Bradfield
Englefield
Sulham
Tilehurst
Woodley
Theale
Longlane
Wellhouse
Stanford Dingley
Bucklebury
The Slade
Cold Ash
Chapel Row
Ashmore Green
Upper Bucklebury
Miles's Green
Donnington
Newbury
Shaw
Thatcham
Midgham
Woolhampton
Beenham
Upper Woolhampton
Beenham Hill
Sulhamstead
Sheffield Bottom
Ufton Green
Ufton Nervet
Burghfield
Burghfield Hill
Burghfield Common
Padworth
Aldermaston Wharf
Aldermaston
Mortimer
Brimpton
Wasing
Crookham
Hyde End
Newtown
Bishop's Green
Ashford Hill
Headley
Burghclere
Brock's Green
Plastow Green
Inhurst
Heath End
Pamber Heath
Silchester
Tadley
Baughurst
Fair Oak
Sandham Mem Chapel (NT)
Ecchinswell
Whitway
Kingsclere
Sydmonton
Old Burghclere
Wolverton Common
Wolverton
Towns End
West Heath
Ramsdell
Pamber Green
Little London
Bramley Corner
Pamber End
Charter Alley
Monk Sherborne
The Vyne (NT)
Sherborne St John
Chineham
Hannington
North Oakley
Ibworth
Upper Wootton
Wootton St Lawrence
Newfound
Worting
South View
Litchfield
Quidhampton
Oakley
Deane
East Oakley
Kempshott
Cole Henley
Ashe
Overton
Freefolk
Laverstoke
Whitchurch
Whitchurch Silk Mill
Steventon
North Waltham
Dummer
Cliddesden
Broadmere
Farleigh Wallop
Ellisfield
Popham
Micheldever Sta
West Stratton
Woodmancott
Preston Candover
Chilton Candover
Micheldever Forest
Egypt
Hunton
Northbrook
Wonston
Stoke Charity
Micheldever
East Stratton
Brown Candover
South Wonston
Roman Road
Micheldever Wood
Winchester
Totford
Northington
Swarraton
Grange Park Opera
Abbotstone
Old Alresford
Martyr Worthy
Itchen Abbas
Headbourne Worthy
Abbots Worthy
Abbott's Barton
Easton
Avington
Avington Park
Itchen Stoke
Ovington
Gundleton
New Alresford
Bishop's Sutton
Tichborne
Cheriton 1644
Cheriton
North End
New Cheriton
Hinton Ampner (NT)
Hinton Ampner
Bramdean
Intech
Chilcomb
Bar End
Winchester Cathedral
South Downs Way
Longwood Warren
Shorley
Beauworth
Brockwood Park
Kilmeston
Twyford
Morestead
Lane End
Shawford
Colden Common
Owslebury
Brambridge
Hensting
Marwell Zoo
Highbridge
Fisher's Pond
Crowdhill
Bishopstoke
Upham
Lower Upham
Corhampton Down
Dean
Ashton
Corhampton
Exton
Old Winchester Hill NNR
Meonstoke
Brockbridge
Droxford
Dundridge
Fair Oak
SOUTHAMPTON INT.
Itchen Valley
Durley
Swanmore
Hillpound
Moorgreen
Soberton
Chidden
Chidden Holt
Clanfield
Chalton
Bishop's Waltham
Hamble
Woolhampton
Shinfield
Three Mile Cross
Grazeley
Spencers Wood
Arborfield
Arborfield Cross
Arborfield Garrison
Swallowfield
Swallowfield Park
Wokefield Park
Stratfield Mortimer
Mortimer Sta
Mortimer West End
Roman City Walls
Beech Hill
Riseley
West End Green
Stanford End
Stratfield Saye
Farley Hill
Finchampstead
Eversley
Eversley Cross
Bramshill
Wellington Country Park
Fair Oak Green
Stratfield Turgis
Turgis Green
Bramley
Heckfield
Sherfield on Loddon
Hartley Wespall
Hound Green
Mattingley
Hazeley
Hartley Wintney
West Green
West Green House (NT)
Murrell Green
Church End
Rotherwick
Newnham
Nately Scures
Hook
Old Basing
Hatch
Up Nately
Greywell
Odiham
North Warnborough
Whitehall
Dogmersfield
Winchfield
Phoenix Green
Hartfordbridge
Warren Heath
Blackbushe
Yateley
Darby Green
Cricket Hill
Sandhurst
Frogmore
Minley Manor
Hawley Lake
Fleet
FLEET
Crookham Village
Church Crookham
FARNBOROUGH
Cove
Fleet Pond
Long Valley
ALDERSHOT
Mill Lane
Crondall
Ewshot
Hale
Farnham
Dippenhall
Wrecclesham
The Bourne
Rowledge
Birdworld
Mapledurwell
Winslade
Tunworth
Upton Grey
Long Sutton
South Warnborough
Well
Lower Froyle
Jenkyn Place
Coldrey
Upper Froyle
Bentley
Isington
Bucks Horn Oak
Spreakley
Frensham
Batt's Corner
Dockenfield
Weston Corbett
Weston Patrick
Herriard
Southrope
Bagmore
Nutley
Axford
Shalden Green
Golden Pot
225
Lasham
Shalden
Bradley
Lower Wield
Upper Wield
Bentworth
Thedden Grange
Holt End
Hattingley
Medstead
South Town
Mid Hants Rly
Soldridge
Bighton
Four Marks
Lower Farringdon
Upper Farringdon
Jane Austen's House
Chawton
Beech
Alton
Holybourne
Curtis Museum
Cuckoo's Corner
Neatham
Binsted
Blacknest
Wyck
Wheatley
Kingsley
East Worldham
West Worldham
Hartley Mauditt
Sleaford
Lindford
Arford
Headley
Oakhanger
Bordon
Standford
Whitehill
Hollywater
Passfield
Selborne
Blackmoor
Conford
Danger Zone
Newton Valence
Oates Memorial & Gilbert White Museum
Empshott
Empshott Green
Greatham
Longmoor Camp
East Tisted
Hawthorn
Ropley Soke
Kitwood
North Street
Ropley
Ropley Dean
Monkwood
Colemore
West Tisted
Hawkley
Liss Forest
Langley
Burgates
West Liss
East Liss
Liss
Rake
Oakshott
High Cross
Steep Marsh
Steep
Hill Brow
Borden
Filmore Hill
Privett
West Meon Hut
Stoner Hill
Froxfield Green
Bell Hill
Sheet
Petersfield
Rogate
Fyning
Chithurst
Habin
Trotton
Langrish
Stroud
Ramsdean
Weston
West Meon
Warnford
East Meon
West Harting
Nyewood
East Harting
Elsted
Nursted
Buriton
War Down
Butser Hill
270
244
Queen Elizabeth
South Harting
Treyford
Didling
Uppark (NT)
North Marden
Winnersh
Sindlesham
Binfield
Hurst
Dinton Pastures
Lower Earley
Whitley
Barkham
Eastheath
Gardeners Green
Wick Hill
California
Crowthorne
M4
M3
A4
A30
A31
A32
A33
A34
A303
A339
A340
A327
A329
A329(M)
A321
A323
A325
A287
A3016
A3013
A3010
A272
A3
0
2
4
6 miles
0
2
4
6
8
10 km

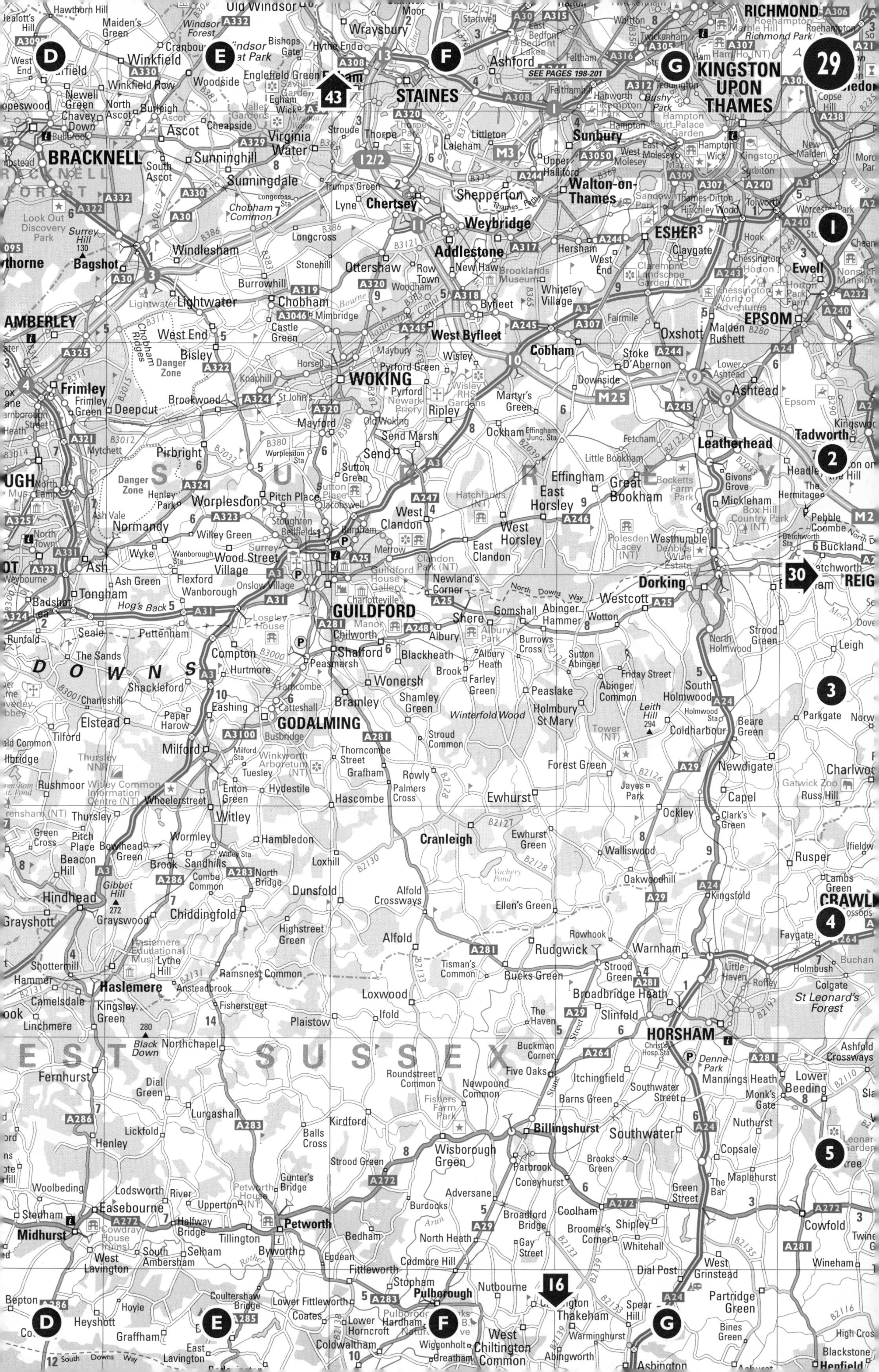
29
SEE PAGES 198-201
43
30
16
RICHMOND
KINGSTON UPON THAMES
STAINES
Ashford
Wraysbury
Old Windsor
Windsor Great Park
Winkfield
Ascot
Sunninghill
Sunningdale
Virginia Water
Egham
Thorpe
Laleham
Sunbury
Hampton Court Palace & Garden
Shepperton
Walton-on-Thames
Chertsey
Weybridge
Addlestone
ESHER
Claygate
Ewell
EPSOM
Ashtead
Leatherhead
Tadworth
BRACKNELL
Bagshot
Windlesham
Lightwater
Chobham
Ottershaw
West Byfleet
Byfleet
Cobham
Oxshott
Stoke D'Abernon
WOKING
Pyrford
Ripley
Frimley
Deepcut
Bisley
Pirbright
Worplesdon
Send
Ockham
Effingham
East Horsley
West Horsley
Great Bookham
West Clandon
East Clandon
Mickleham
Dorking
Westcott
GUILDFORD
Shere
Gomshall
Abinger Hammer
Albury
Chilworth
Shalford
Wonersh
Bramley
GODALMING
Compton
Puttenham
Elstead
Milford
Witley
Hambledon
Dunsfold
Cranleigh
Ewhurst
Holmbury St Mary
Leith Hill
Coldharbour
Newdigate
Capel
Ockley
Rudgwick
Warnham
Slinfold
HORSHAM
Alfold
Loxwood
Chiddingfold
Hindhead
Grayshott
Haslemere
Fernhurst
Midhurst
Easebourne
Petworth
Wisborough Green
Billingshurst
Southwater
Pulborough
Storrington
Thakeham
West Chiltington
Cowfold
West Grinstead
Partridge Green
Henfield
CRAWLEY
Faygate
Rusper
S U R R E Y
WEST SUSSEX
DOWNS
M25
M3
A3
A24
A29
A272
A281
A283
A286

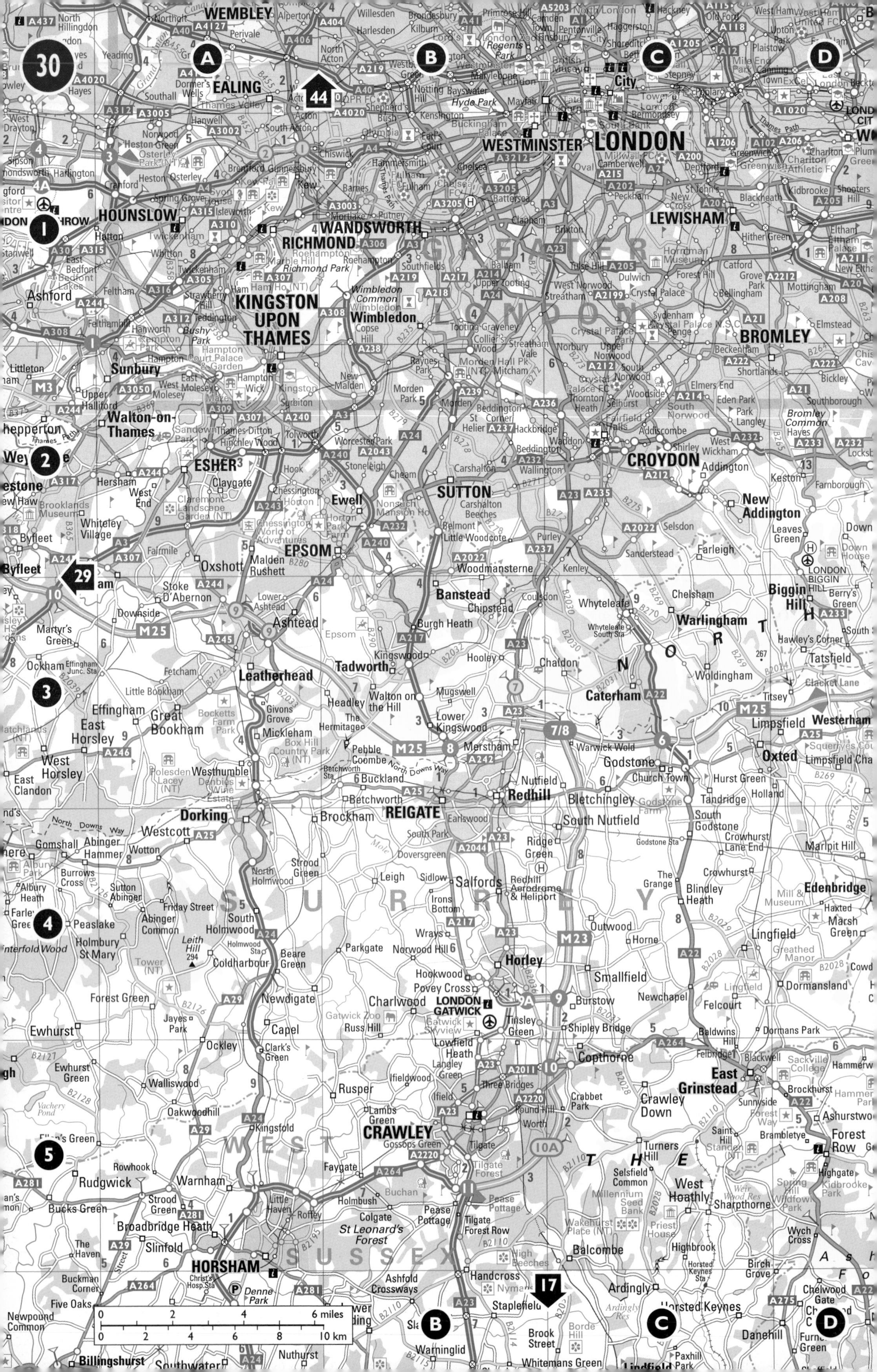

30
44
29
17
A
B
C
D
WEMBLEY
EALING
LONDON
WESTMINSTER
City
HOUNSLOW
RICHMOND
WANDSWORTH
LEWISHAM
GREATER LONDON
KINGSTON UPON THAMES
Wimbledon
BROMLEY
CROYDON
SUTTON
ESHER
Ewell
EPSOM
Sunbury
Walton-on-Thames
Shepperton
Ashford
Oxshott
Banstead
Ashtead
Leatherhead
Tadworth
Caterham
Warlingham
Biggin Hill
New Addington
Westerham
Oxted
Godstone
Redhill
REIGATE
Dorking
Bletchingley
South Nutfield
Edenbridge
Lingfield
Horley
LONDON GATWICK
CRAWLEY
East Grinstead
Forest Row
West Hoathly
Balcombe
Ardingly
Horsted Keynes
HORSHAM
Rudgwick
Warnham
Ewhurst
Capel
Newdigate
Effingham
East Horsley
West Horsley
Great Bookham
Ockham
Byfleet
SURREY
WEST SUSSEX
NORTH DOWNS
M25
M23
M3
Billingshurst
Southwater
Nuthurst
Handcross
Warninglid
Copthorne
Crawley Down
Turners Hill
Dormansland
0 2 4 6 miles
0 2 4 6 8 10 km

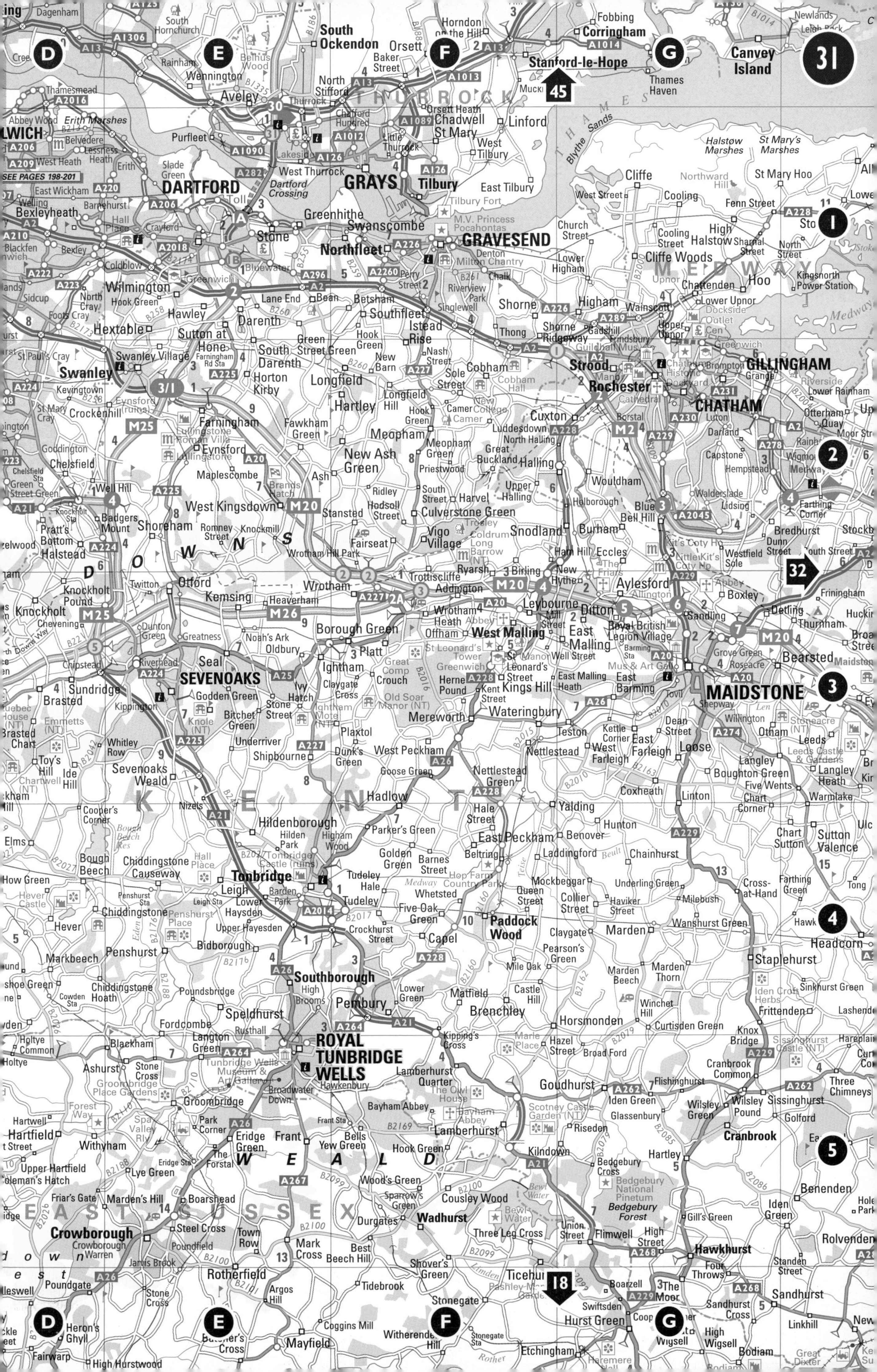

31
D
E
F
G
Dagenham
South Hornchurch
Rainham
Wennington
Belhus Wood
Aveley
South Ockendon
Orsett
Horndon on the Hill
Fobbing
Corringham
Stanford-le-Hope
45
Canvey Island
Newlands
Baker Street
North Stifford
Thurrock
THURROCK
Chafford Hundred
Orsett Heath
Chadwell St Mary
Linford
West Tilbury
Thames Haven
Thamesmead
Erith Marshes
Abbey Wood
Belvedere
Lessness Heath
West Heath
Erith
Purfleet
Lakeside
Little Thurrock
GRAYS
Tilbury
West Thurrock
Slade Green
DARTFORD
Dartford Crossing
East Tilbury
Tilbury Fort
SEE PAGES 198-201
East Wickham
Welling
Barnehurst
Bexleyheath
Hall Place
Crayford
Bexley
Blackfen
Coldblow
Stone
Greenhithe
Swanscombe
Northfleet
M.V. Princess Pocahontas
GRAVESEND
Denton
Milton Chantry
Bluewater
Greenwich
Wilmington
Hook Green
Sidcup
North Cray
Foots Cray
Hawley
Lane End
Bean
Betsham
Southfleet
Perry Street
Riverview Park
Singlewell
Chalk
Shorne
Higham
Lower Higham
Church Street
West Street
Cliffe
Northward Hill
Cooling
Cooling Street
High Halstow
Halstow Marshes
St Mary's Marshes
St Mary Hoo
Fenn Street
Sharnal Street
North Street
Cliffe Woods
MEDWAY
Chattenden
Hoo
Kingsnorth Power Station
Upnor
Lower Upnor
Wainscott
Upper Upnor
Frindsbury
Gadshill
Dockside Outlet Cen
Hextable
Darenth
Sutton at Hone
Farningham Rd Sta
South Darenth
Green Street Green
Hook Green
Istead Rise
Nash Street
Thong
Shorne Ridgeway
Guildhall Mus
Strood
Rochester
Chatham Historic Dockyard
Brompton
GILLINGHAM
Grange
Riverside
Lower Rainham
St Paul's Cray
Swanley Village
Swanley
Horton Kirby
New Barn
Longfield
Sole Street
Cobham
Cobham Hall
Manor
Cathedral
CHATHAM
Kevingtown
St Mary Cray
Crockenhill
Eynsford
Hartley
Longfield Hill
Hook Green
Camer
New College
Cuxton
Luddesdown
Borstal
Luton
Otterham Quay
Farningham
Lullingstone Roman Villa
Lullingstone
Fawkham Green
Meopham
Meopham Green
Great Buckland
North Halling
Halling
Darland
Capstone
Hempstead
Wigmore
Goddington
Chelsfield
Well Hill
Eynsford
Maplescombe
New Ash Green
Ash
Priestwood
Upper Halling
Wouldham
Walderslade
Lidsing
Farthing Corner
Brands Hatch
Ridley
South Street
Harvel
Holborough
Blue Bell Hill
West Kingsdown
Hodsoll Street
Culverstone Green
Trosley
Snodland
Burham
Bredhurst
Knockholt Sta
Badgers Mount
Pratt's Bottom
Halstead
Shoreham
Romney Street
Knockmill
Stansted
Vigo Village
Coldrum Long Barrow
Kit's Coty Ho
Little Kit's Coty Ho
Westfield Sole
Dunn Street
DOWNS
Fairseat
Wrotham Hill Park
Ham Hill
Eccles
The Friars
Ryarsh
Birling
New Hythe
Aylesford
Boxley
32
Knockholt Pound
Twitton
Otford
Kemsing
Wrotham
Trottiscliffe
Addington
Allington
Detling
Thurnham
Knockholt
Chevening
Heaverham
Wrotham Heath
Abbey
Leybourne
Ditton
Sandling
North Downs Way
Dunton Green
Greatness
Noah's Ark
Oldbury
Borough Green
Offham
West Malling
Mill Street
East Malling
Royal British Legion Village
Barming Sta
Grove Green
Bearsted
Roseacre
Chipstead
Riverhead
Seal
SEVENOAKS
Platt
Ightham
Great Comp
St Leonard's Tower
Greenwich
St Leonard's Street
Manor
Well Street
Mus & Art Gall
Brasted
Sundridge
Kippington
Godden Green
Ivy Hatch
Claygate Cross
Crouch
Herne Pound
Kent Street
Kings Hill
East Malling Heath
East Barming
MAIDSTONE
Shepway
Emmetts
Bitchet Green
Stone Street
Ightham Mote
Old Soar Manor
Mereworth
Wateringbury
Tovil
Dean Street
Willington
Otham
Brasted Chart
Knole
Plaxtol
Teston
Kettle Corner
West Farleigh
East Farleigh
Loose
Leeds
Leeds Castle & Gardens
Whitley Row
Underriver
Shipbourne
Dunk's Green
West Peckham
Nettlestead
Toy's Hill
Ide Hill
Chartwell
Sevenoaks Weald
Goose Green
Nettlestead Green
Langley
Boughton Green
Langley Heath
Five Wents
Coxheath
Linton
Chart Corner
Warmlake
KENT
Cooper's Corner
Nizels
Hadlow
Hale Street
Yalding
Hunton
Hildenborough
Hilden Park
Higham Wood
Parker's Green
East Peckham
Benover
Chart Sutton
Sutton Valence
Bough Beech
Chiddingstone Causeway
Hall Place
Tonbridge Castle (ruins)
Golden Green
Barnes Street
Beltring
Laddingford
Chainhurst
How Green
Tonbridge
Leigh
Tudeley Hale
Hop Farm Country Park
Mockbeggar
Underling Green
Cross-at-Hand
Farthing Green
Hever Castle
Penshurst Sta
Leigh Sta
Lower Haysden
Barden Park
Tudeley
Whetsted
Queen Street
Collier Street
Haviker Street
Milebush
Tong
Chiddingstone
Penshurst Place
Five Oak Green
Paddock Wood
Wanshurst Green
Hever
Upper Hayesden
Crockhurst Street
Capel
Claygate
Marden
Hawk
Headcorn
Markbeech
Penshurst
Bidborough
Southborough
Pearson's Green
Staplehurst
Mile Oak
Marden Beech
Marden Thorn
Chiddingstone Hoath
Cowden Sta
Poundsbridge
High Brooms
Lower Green
Pembury
Matfield
Castle Hill
Iden Croft Herbs
Sinkhurst Green
Speldhurst
Brenchley
Winchet Hill
Frittenden
Fordcombe
Rusthall
Kipping's Cross
Horsmonden
Curtisden Green
Knox Bridge
Holtye Common
Blackham
Langton Green
ROYAL TUNBRIDGE WELLS
Marle Place
Hazel Street
Broad Ford
Sissinghurst Castle (NT)
Holtye
Ashurst
Stone Cross
Tunbridge Wells Museum & Art Gallery
Lamberhurst Quarter
The Owl House
Cranbrook Common
Three Chimneys
Groombridge Place Gardens
Broadwater Down
Hawkenbury
Goudhurst
Flishinghurst
Iden Green
Wisley Pound
Sissinghurst
Groombridge
Bayham Abbey
Scotney Castle Garden (NT)
Glassenbury
Wilsley Green
Golford
Hartwell
Forest Way
Park Corner
Frant Sta
Bells Yew Green
Lamberhurst
Riseden
Cranbrook
Hartfield
Withyham
Spa Valley Rly
Eridge Green
Frant
Hook Green
Kilndown
Hartley
Eridge Sta
The Forstal
WEALD
Bedgebury Cross
Upper Hartfield
Coleman's Hatch
Lye Green
Wood's Green
Sparrow's Green
Bedgebury National Pinetum
Bedgebury Forest
Benenden
Friar's Gate
Marden's Hill
Boarshead
Cousley Wood
Bewl Water
Iden Green
EAST SUSSEX
Steel Cross
Durgates
Wadhurst
Three Leg Cross
Union Street
Flimwell
Gill's Green
High Street
Crowborough
Crowborough Warren
Poundfield
Town Row
Mark Cross
Best Beech Hill
Hawkhurst
Rolvenden
Jarvis Brook
Rotherfield
Shover's Green
Ticehurst
Pashley Manor Gardens
Four Throws
Standen Street
Poundgate
Stone Cross
Argos Hill
Tidebrook
18
Boarzell
The Moor
Sandhurst Cross
Sandhurst
Stonegate
Swiftsden
Hurst Green
Linkhill
Heron's Ghyll
Butcher's Cross
Coggins Mill
Witherenden Hill
Stonegate Sta
Wigsell
High Wigsell
Fairwarp
High Hurstwood
Mayfield
Etchingham
Bodiam
Great Dixter
Rother
Ashdown Forest
M25
M26
M20
M2
A2
A13
A20
A21
A25
A26
A225
A227
A228
A229
A264
A267
A268

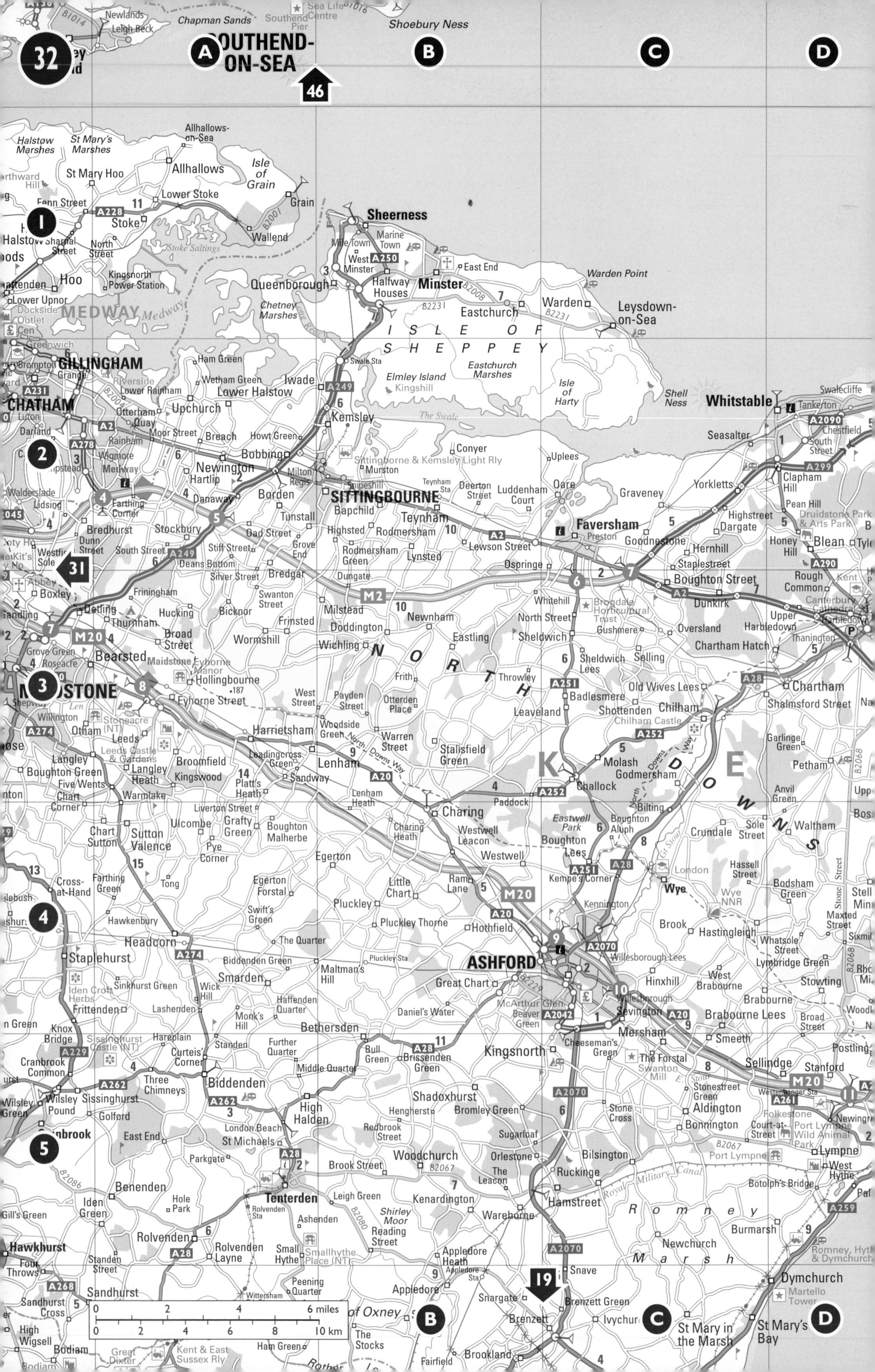

32
A
B
C
D
46
31
19
SOUTHEND-ON-SEA
Chapman Sands
Southend Pier
Sea Life Centre
Shoebury Ness
Newlands
Leigh Beck
B1014
B1016
Halstow Marshes
St Mary's Marshes
Allhallows-on-Sea
Allhallows
St Mary Hoo
Isle of Grain
Grain
Fenn Street
Lower Stoke
Stoke
A228
Halstow
Sharnal Street
North Street
Wallend
Stoke Saltings
B2001
Hoo
Kingsnorth Power Station
Lower Upnor
Dockside Outlet Cen
MEDWAY
Medway
Greenwich
Brompton
GILLINGHAM
Grange
Riverside
CHATHAM
A231
Luton
Darland
Lower Rainham
Otterham Quay
Rainham
Wigmore
Medway
Walderslade
Lidsing
A278
A2
Sheerness
Mile Town
Marine Town
West Minster
A250
Queenborough
Halfway Houses
Minster
East End
B2008
Warden Point
Warden
Eastchurch
B2231
Leysdown-on-Sea
Chetney Marshes
Long Reach
ISLE OF SHEPPEY
Swale Sta
Elmley Island
Kingshill
Eastchurch Marshes
Isle of Harty
Shell Ness
The Swale
Whitstable
Tankerton
Swalecliffe
A2090
Chestfield
South Street
Seasalter
Ham Green
Wetham Green
Iwade
Lower Halstow
A249
Upchurch
Moor Street
Breach
Howt Green
Bobbing
Kemsley
Conyer
Uplees
Newington
Hartlip
Milton Regis
Sittingbourne & Kemsley Light Rly
Murston
Snipeshill
SITTINGBOURNE
Teynham Sta
Deerton Street
Luddenham Court
Oare
Graveney
Yorkletts
Clapham Hill
A299
Farthing Corner
Danaway
Borden
Bapchild
Teynham
Faversham
Preston
Goodnestone
Highstreet
Dargate
Pean Hill
Druidstone Park & Arts Park
Bredhurst
Stockbury
Tunstall
Highsted
Rodmersham
Lewson Street
Hernhill
Honey Hill
Blean
Dunn Street
South Street
Oad Street
Stiff Street
Grove End
Rodmersham Green
Lynsted
Ospringe
Staplestreet
A290
Westfield Sole
Deans Bottom
Silver Street
Bredgar
Dungate
Boughton Street
Rough Common
Kent
Boxley
M2
Dunkirk
Canterbury Cathedral
Harbledown
Abbey
Detling
Friningham
Swanton Street
Milstead
Newnham
Whitehill
Brogdale Horticultural Trust
Upper Harbledown
Sandling
Thurnham
Hucking
Bicknor
Frinsted
North Street
Gushmere
Oversland
Thanington
M20
Broad Street
Wormshill
Doddington
Eastling
Sheldwich
Chartham Hatch
Grove Green
Bearsted
Roseacre
Maidstone
Eyhorne Manor
Wichling
NORTH
Sheldwich Lees
Selling
MAIDSTONE
Hollingbourne
Frith
Throwley
A251
Old Wives Lees
A28
Chartham
Shepway
Eyhorne Street
West Street
Payden Street
Badlesmere
Shalmsford Street
Willington
Stoneacre (NT)
Otterden Place
Leaveland
Shottenden
Chilham
A274
Otham
Harrietsham
Woodside Green
Chilham Castle
Leeds
Leeds Castle & Gardens
Warren Street
North Downs Way
A252
Garlinge Green
Langley
Broomfield
Leadingcross Green
Lenham
Stalisfield Green
Molash
Godmersham
Petham
Boughton Green
Langley Heath
Kingswood
Platt's Heath
Sandway
A20
DOWNS
Five Wents
Chart Corner
Warmlake
Lenham Heath
Paddock
Challock
Anvil Green
Liverton Street
Charing
Bilting
Chart Sutton
Sutton Valence
Ulcombe
Grafty Green
Boughton Malherbe
Charing Heath
Westwell Leacon
Eastwell Park
Boughton Aluph
Crundale
Sole Street
Waltham
Pye Corner
Egerton
Westwell
Boughton Lees
Hassell Street
Cross-at-Hand
Farthing Green
Tong
Egerton Forstal
Little Chart
Ram Lane
Kempe's Corner
London
Wye
Bodsham Green
Stone Street
Hawkenbury
Swift's Green
Pluckley
Pluckley Thorne
Hothfield
Kennington
Wye NNR
Brook
Hastingleigh
Maxted Street
Headcorn
The Quarter
ASHFORD
A2070
Willesborough Lees
Whatsole Street
Lymbridge Green
B2068
Staplehurst
Biddenden Green
Pluckley Sta
Maltman's Hill
Great Chart
Hinxhill
West Brabourne
Stowting
Sinkhurst Green
Smarden
Wick Hill
Iden Croft Herbs
Lashenden
Haffenden Quarter
Daniel's Water
McArthur Glen
Beaver Green
A2042
Willesborough
Sevington
Brabourne
Brabourne Lees
Broad Street
Frittenden
Monk's Hill
Bethersden
Mersham
Smeeth
Knox Bridge
Hareplain
Standen
Further Quarter
Bull Green
Brissenden Green
Kingsnorth
Cheeseman's Green
The Forstal
Swanton Mill
Postling
A229
Sissinghurst Castle (NT)
Curteis' Corner
Middle Quarter
Sellindge
Stanford
Cranbrook Common
A262
Three Chimneys
Biddenden
Shadoxhurst
Stonestreet Green
Westenhanger Sta
Wisley Pound
Sissinghurst
Hengherst
Bromley Green
Stone Cross
Aldington
Golford
High Halden
Redbrook Street
Sugarloaf
Bonnington
Court-at-Street
Folkestone
Port Lympne Wild Animal Park
Newingreen
Cranbrook
East End
London Beach
St Michaels
Woodchurch
Orlestone
Bilsington
B2067
Port Lympne
Lympne
Parkgate
Brook Street
The Leacon
Ruckinge
West Hythe
B2086
Benenden
Royal Military Canal
Bodsham
Tenterden
Leigh Green
Kenardington
Hamstreet
Romney
Bolotph's Bridge
Iden Green
Hole Park
Rolvenden Sta
B2080
Shirley Moor
Warehorne
A259
Gill's Green
Ashenden
Reading Street
Burmarsh
Hawkhurst
Rolvenden
Rolvenden Layne
Small Hythe
Smallhythe Place (NT)
Appledore Heath
Newchurch
Romney, Hythe & Dymchurch
Marsh
Standen Street
Four Throws
A268
Appledore Sta
Snave
Dymchurch
Sandhurst
Wittersham
Peening Quarter
Appledore
Martello Tower
Sandhurst Cross
Isle of Oxney
Snargate
Brenzett Green
High Wigsell
The Stocks
Brenzett
Ivychurch
St Mary in the Marsh
St Mary's Bay
Bodiam
Great Dixter
Kent & East Sussex Rly
Ham Green
Fairfield
Brookland
Rother
0 2 4 6 miles
0 2 4 6 8 10 km

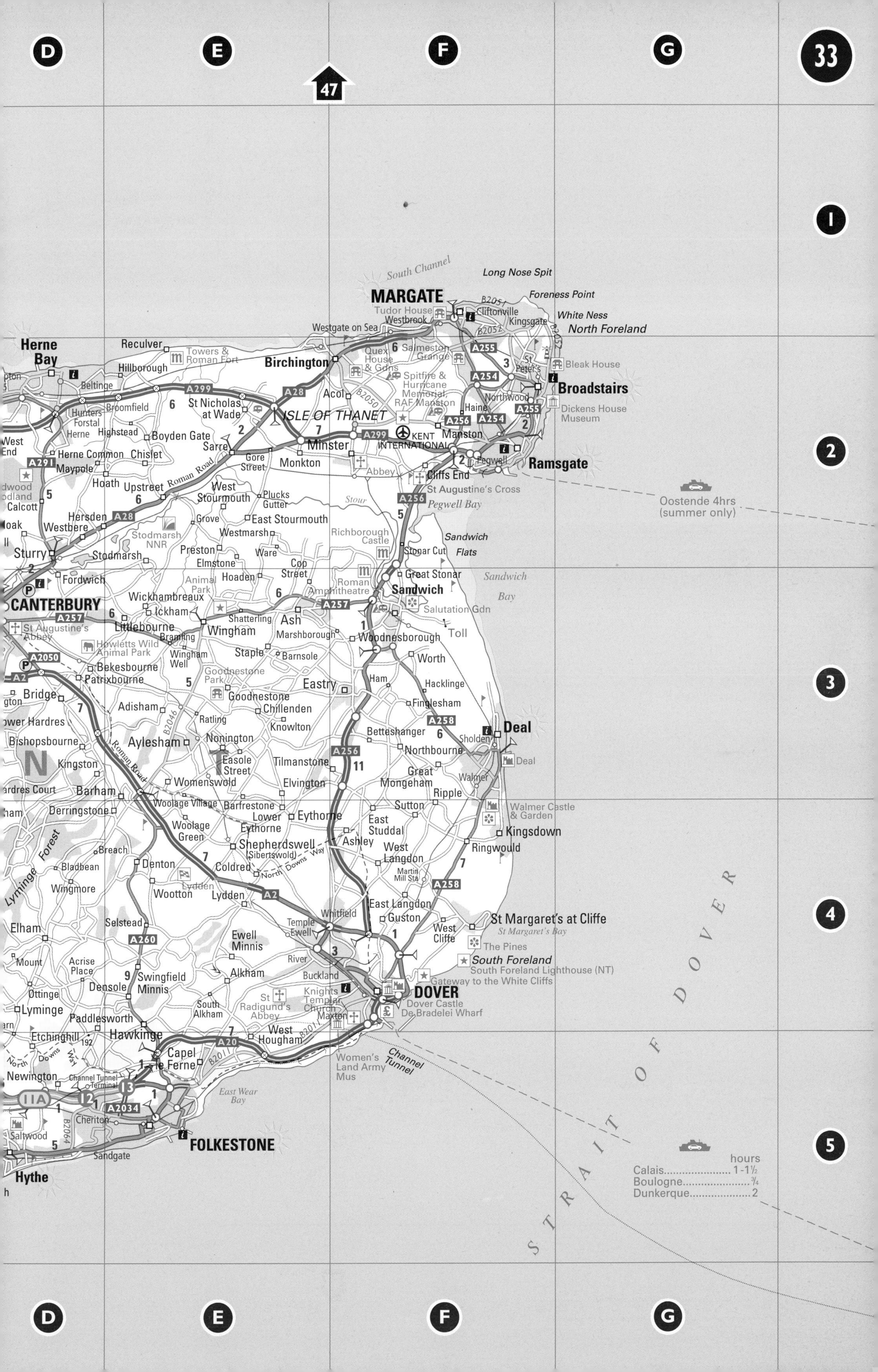
D
E
F
G
47
1
2
3
4
5
South Channel
Long Nose Spit
MARGATE
Foreness Point
Tudor House
Westbrook
Cliftonville
White Ness
Kingsgate
North Foreland
Westgate on Sea
B2051
B2052
Herne Bay
Reculver
Towers & Roman Fort
Hillborough
Birchington
Quex House & Gdns
Salmeston Grange
A255
Bleak House
St Peter's
Broadstairs
Beltinge
A299
A28
Acol
Spitfire & Hurricane Memorial, RAF Manston
A254
Northwood
Dickens House Museum
Hunters Forstal
Broomfield
St Nicholas at Wade
ISLE OF THANET
Haine
Herne
Highstead
Boyden Gate
Sarre
Minster
KENT INTERNATIONAL
Manston
A256
West End
Herne Common
Chislet
Gore Street
Monkton
Abbey
Pegwell
Ramsgate
A291
Maypole
Hoath
Upstreet
Roman Road
West Stourmouth
Plucks Gutter
Cliffs End
St Augustine's Cross
Calcott
Hersden
Westbere
Grove
East Stourmouth
Stour
Pegwell Bay
Oostende 4hrs (summer only)
Stodmarsh NNR
Westmarsh
Richborough Castle
Sandwich
Flats
Sturry
Stodmarsh
Preston
Ware
Stonar Cut
Elmstone
Cop Street
Great Stonar
Sandwich Bay
Fordwich
Animal Park
Hoaden
Roman Amphitheatre
Wickhambreaux
CANTERBURY
A257
Ickham
Shatterling
Ash
Salutation Gdn
Littlebourne
Wingham
Marshborough
Toll
St Augustine's Abbey
Bramling
Woodnesborough
Howletts Wild Animal Park
Wingham Well
Staple
Barnsole
Worth
A2050
Bekesbourne
Goodnestone Park
A2
Patrixbourne
Ham
Eastry
Hacklinge
Bridge
Goodnestone
Adisham
Chillenden
Finglesham
Lower Hardres
Ratling
Knowlton
A258
Deal
Bishopsbourne
B2046
Nonington
Betteshanger
Aylesham
Sholden
Roman Road
Easole Street
Tilmanstone
Northbourne
Kingston
Womenswold
Elvington
Great Mongeham
Walmer
Barham
Ripple
Derringstone
Woolage Village
Barfrestone
Sutton
Walmer Castle & Garden
Lower Eythorne
Eythorne
East Studdal
Kingsdown
Woolage Green
Lyminge Forest
Shepherdswell (Sibertswold)
Ashley
West Langdon
Ringwould
Breach
North Downs Way
Bladbean
Denton
Coldred
Martin Mill Sta
Wingmore
Lydden
Wootton
East Langdon
Whitfield
Elham
Selstead
Guston
St Margaret's at Cliffe
St Margaret's Bay
Temple Ewell
West Cliffe
A260
Ewell Minnis
The Pines
Mount
Acrise Place
River
South Foreland
Swingfield Minnis
Alkham
South Foreland Lighthouse (NT)
Densole
Buckland
Gateway to the White Cliffs
Ottinge
South Alkham
St Radigund's Abbey
Knights Templar Church
DOVER
Lyminge
Dover Castle
Paddlesworth
Maxton
De Bradelei Wharf
Hawkinge
Etchinghill
West Hougham
B2011
A20
Capel le Ferne
North Downs Way
Women's Land Army Mus
Channel Tunnel
Newington
Channel Tunnel Terminal
East Wear Bay
A2034
Cheriton
B2064
Saltwood
FOLKESTONE
Sandgate
Hythe
STRAIT OF DOVER
hours
Calais.......................1-1½
Boulogne........................¾
Dunkerque.....................2

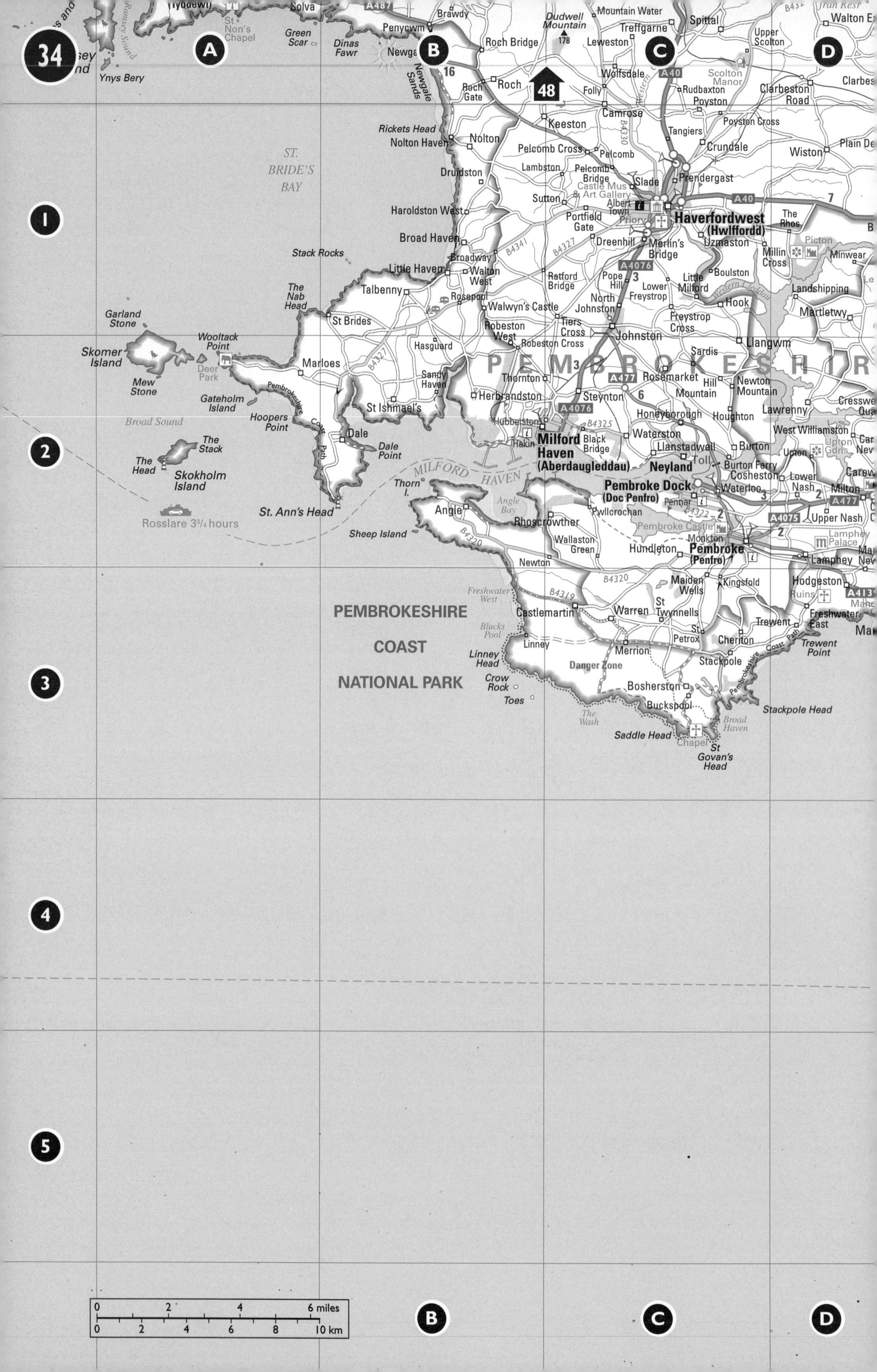

34
A
B
C
D
Ynys Bery
Ramsey Sound
St Non's Chapel
Solva
Green Scar
Dinas Fawr
A487
Brawdy
Penycwm
Newgale Sands
Roch Bridge
Dudwell Mountain
178
Mountain Water
Treffgarne
Leweston
Spittal
Upper Scolton
Walton East
Scolton Manor
Wolfsdale
A40
Roch Gate
Roch
48
Folly
Rudbaxton
Clarbeston
Clarbeston Road
Poyston
Camrose
B4330
Keeston
Tangiers
Poyston Cross
Rickets Head
Nolton Haven
Nolton
Crundale
Pelcomb Cross
Pelcomb
Wiston
ST. BRIDE'S BAY
Druidston
Lambston
Pelcomb Bridge
Castle Mus & Art Gallery
Slade
Prendergast
Sutton
Albert Town
Priory
Haverfordwest (Hwlffordd)
The Rhos
Haroldston West
Portfield Gate
Broad Haven
B4341
B4327
Dreenhill
Merlin's Bridge
Uzmaston
Picton
Millin Cross
Minwear
Stack Rocks
Broadway
Little Haven
Walton West
A4076
Ratford Bridge
Pope Hill
Boulston
Talbenny
Rosepool
Lower Freystrop
Little Milford
Landshipping
The Nab Head
Western Cleddau
North Johnston
Hook
Garland Stone
Walwyn's Castle
Martletwy
St Brides
Robeston West
Tiers Cross
Freystrop Cross
Johnston
Skomer Island
Wooltack Point
Deer Park
Hasguard
Robeston Cross
Sardis
Llangwm
Marloes
PEMBROKESHIRE
Thornton
A477
Rosemarket
Hill Mountain
Newton Mountain
Mew Stone
Sandy Haven
Herbrandston
Steynton
Gateholm Island
St Ishmael's
Lawrenny
Cresswell Quay
Pembrokeshire Coast Path
Broad Sound
Hoopers Point
Hubberston
Hakin
Honeyborough
Houghton
West Williamston
Upton
The Stack
Dale
Waterston
Milford Haven (Aberdaugleddau)
B4325
Black Bridge
Llanstadwell
Burton
Upton Gdns
Dale Point
The Head
Skokholm Island
MILFORD HAVEN
Neyland
Burton Ferry
Cosheston
Lower Nash
Carew
Thorn I.
Pembroke Dock (Doc Penfro)
Pennar
Waterloo
Milton
St. Ann's Head
Angle
Angle Bay
Pwllcrochan
B4322
A477
Rosslare 3¾ hours
Sheep Island
Rhoscrowther
Pembroke Castle
A4075
Upper Nash
Lamphey Palace
B4320
Wallaston Green
Hundleton
Monkton
Pembroke (Penfro)
Newton
Lamphey
Freshwater West
Maiden Wells
Kingsfold
Hodgeston
Ruins
B4319
PEMBROKESHIRE COAST NATIONAL PARK
Castlemartin
Warren
St Twynnells
Freshwater East
Blucks Pool
Trewent
St Petrox
Linney
Cheriton
Trewent Point
Merrion
Linney Head
Danger Zone
Stackpole
Crow Rock
Toes
Bosherston
Stackpole Head
The Wash
Buckspool
Broad Haven
Saddle Head
Chapel
St Govan's Head
1
2
3
4
5
0 2 4 6 miles
0 2 4 6 8 10 km

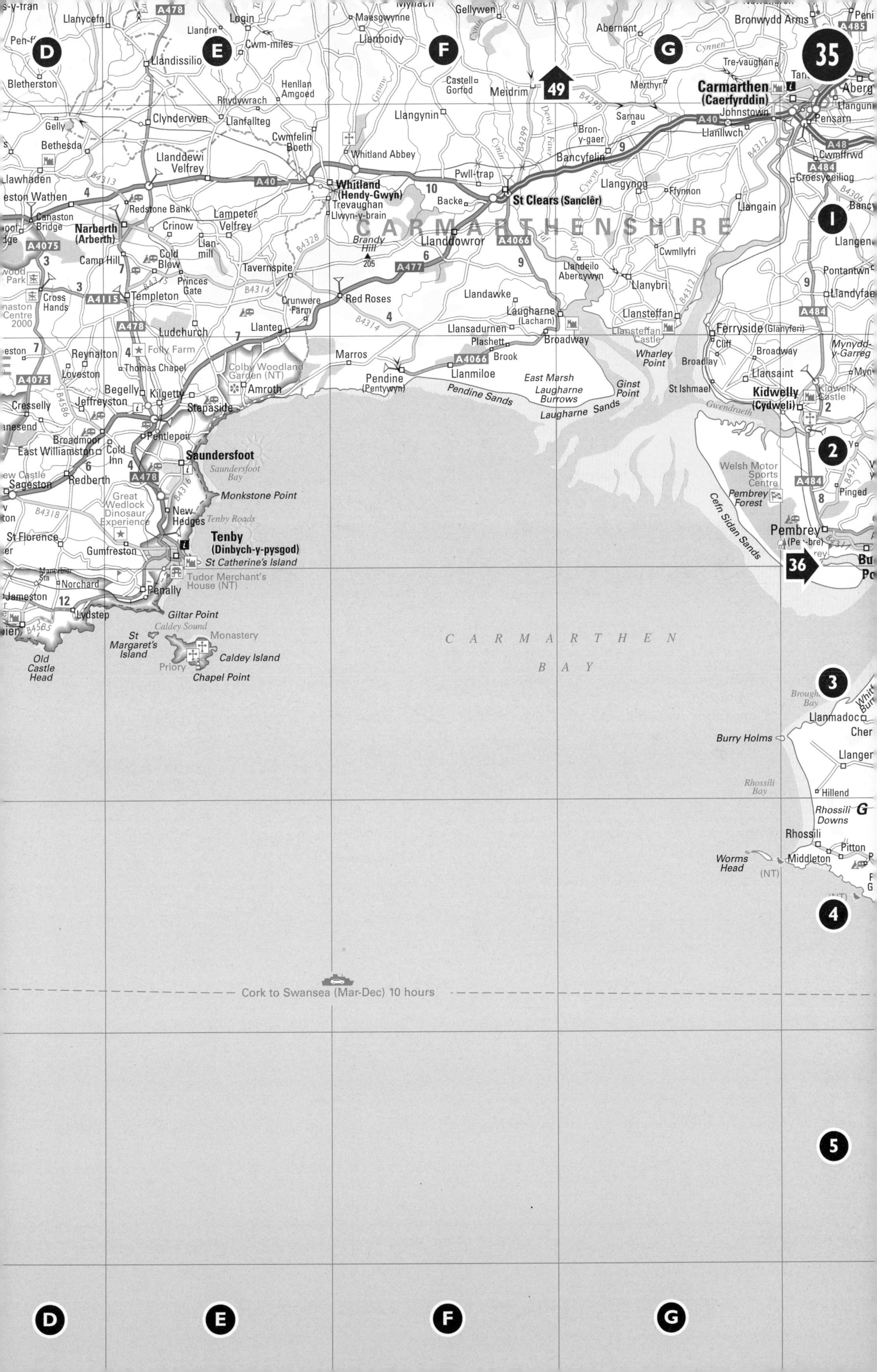

35
49
36
D
E
F
G
1
2
3
4
5
Llanycefn
Login
Llandre
Cwm-miles
Maesgwynne
Llanboidy
Gellywen
Abernant
Bronwydd Arms
A485
A478
Llandissilio
Bletherston
Henllan Amgoed
Castell Gorfod
Meidrim
Merthyr
Tre-vaughan
Carmarthen
(Caerfyrddin)
Johnstown
Sarnau
Pensarn
Rhydywrach
Clynderwen
Llanfallteg
Gelly
Llangynin
Bethesda
Cwmfelin Boeth
Bron-y-gaer
Llanllwch
A40
A48
Cwmffrwd
Whitland Abbey
Bancyfelin
A484
Croesyceiliog
Llanddewi Velfrey
Llawhaden
Pwll-trap
Llangynog
Ffynnon
Whitland
(Hendy-Gwyn)
Trevaughan
Llwyn-y-brain
Backe
St Clears (Sanclêr)
Llangain
Canaston Bridge
Redstone Bank
Narberth
(Arberth)
Lampeter Velfrey
Crinow
Llan-mill
CARMARTHENSHIRE
Brandy Hill
205
Llanddowror
A4066
A4075
Camp Hill
Cold Blow
Princes Gate
Tavernspite
A477
Llandeilo Abercywyn
Cwmllyfri
Llanybri
Pontantwn
Llandyfaelog
Cross Hands
A4115
Templeton
A478
Crunwere Farm
Red Roses
Llandawke
Laugharne
(Lacharn)
Llansteffan
Llansteffan Castle
Ferryside (Glanyfferi)
Cliff
Ludchurch
Llanteg
Llansadurnen
Plashett
Broadway
Mynydd-y-Garreg
Reynalton
Folly Farm
Thomas Chapel
Colby Woodland Garden (NT)
Marros
A4066
Brook
Wharley Point
Broadlay
Broadway
Loveston
Amroth
Pendine
(Pentywyn)
Llanmiloe
East Marsh
Laugharne Burrows
Ginst Point
St Ishmael
Llansaint
Kidwelly
(Cydweli)
Kidwelly Castle
Begelly
Kilgetty
Cresselly
Jeffreyston
Stepaside
Pendine Sands
Laugharne Sands
Gwendraeth
Pentlepoir
Broadmoor
East Williamston
Cold Inn
Saundersfoot
Saundersfoot Bay
Welsh Motor Sports Centre
Pembrey Forest
Pinged
Sageston
Redberth
A478
Monkstone Point
Great Wedlock Dinosaur Experience
New Hedges
Tenby Roads
Cefn Sidan Sands
Pembrey
St Florence
Gumfreston
Tenby
(Dinbych-y-pysgod)
St Catherine's Island
Tudor Merchant's House (NT)
Norchard
Jameston
Penally
Lydstep
Giltar Point
Caldey Sound
Monastery
St Margaret's Island
Caldey Island
Priory
Chapel Point
Old Castle Head
CARMARTHEN BAY
Llanmadoc
Burry Holms
Llangennith
Rhossili Bay
Hillend
Rhossili Downs
Rhossili
Pitton
Worms Head
Middleton
(NT)
Cork to Swansea (Mar-Dec) 10 hours

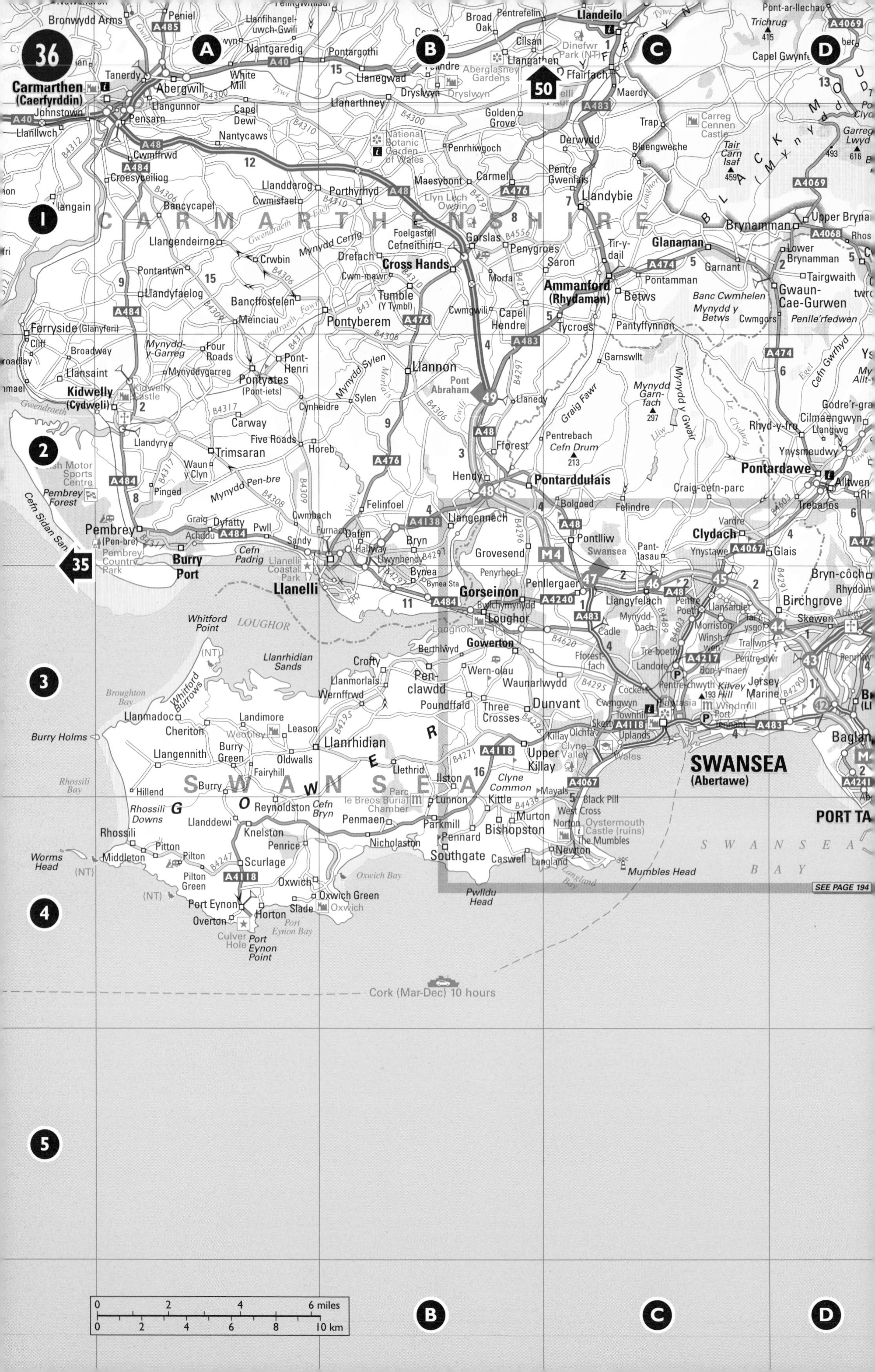

A
B
C
D
1
2
3
4
5
Carmarthen
(Caerfyrddin)
Bronwydd Arms
Peniel
Llanfihangel-
uwch-Gwili
Nantgaredig
Pontargothi
Broad
Oak
Pentrefelin
Llandeilo
Pont-ar-llechau
Trichrug
Tanerdy
Abergwili
White
Mill
Llanegwad
Felindre
Aberglasney
Gardens
Llangathen
Dinefwr
Park (NT)
Ffairfach
Capel Gwynfe
Johnstown
Llanllwch
Llangunnor
Pensarn
Capel
Dewi
Llanarthney
Dryslwyn
Golden
Grove
Maerdy
Trap
Carreg
Cennen
Castle
Tair
Carn
Isaf
Garreg
Lwyd
Nantycaws
National
Botanic
Garden
of Wales
Penrhiwgoch
Derwydd
Blaengweche
Cwmffrwd
Croesyceiliog
Llangain
Llanddarog
Porthyrhyd
Maesybont
Carmel
Pentre
Gwenlais
Llandybie
Bancycapel
Cwmisfael
Llyn Llech
Owain
CARMARTHENSHIRE
BLACK MOUNTAIN
Upper Brynamman
Brynamman
Llangendeirne
Foelgastell
Cefneithin
Gorslas
Penygroes
Tir-y-
dail
Glanaman
Lower
Brynamman
Crwbin
Drefach
Cross Hands
Saron
Garnant
Pontantwn
Cwm-mawr
Morfa
Ammanford
(Rhydaman)
Pontamman
Betws
Gwaun-
Cae-Gurwen
Tairgwaith
Llandyfaelog
Bancffosfelen
Tumble
(Y Tymbl)
Cwmgwili
Capel
Hendre
Banc Cwmhelen
Mynydd y
Betws
Cwmgors
Penlle'rfedwen
Ferryside (Glanyferi)
Meinciau
Pontyberem
Tycroes
Pantyffynnon
Cliff
Broadway
Mynydd-
y-Garreg
Four
Roads
Pont-
Henri
Garnswllt
Llansaint
Mynyddygarreg
Pontyates
(Pont-iets)
Llannon
Pont
Abraham
Mynydd
Garn-
fach
Mynydd y Gwair
Cefn Gwrhyd
Kidwelly
(Cydweli)
Kidwelly
Castle
Cynheidre
Sylen
Mynydd Sylen
Llanedy
Graig Fawr
Godre'r-graig
Cilmaengwyn
Llangiwg
Carway
Pentrebach
Cefn Drum
Rhyd-y-fro
Llandyry
Five Roads
Trimsaran
Horeb
Fforest
Ynysmeudwy
Motor
Sports
Centre
Pembrey
Forest
Waun
y Clyn
Mynydd Pen-bre
Hendy
Pontarddulais
Pontardawe
Alltwen
Pinged
Felinfoel
Bolgoed
Felindre
Craig-cefn-parc
Trebanos
Cefn Sidan San
Pembrey
(Pen-bre)
Pembrey
Country
Park
Graig
Dyfatty
Achddu
Pwll
Cwmbach
Sandy
Furnace
Dafen
Llangennech
Pontlliw
Vardre
Clydach
Burry
Port
Cefn
Padrig
Llanelli
Coastal
Park
Halfway
Llwynhendy
Bryn
Grovesend
Swansea
Pant-
lasau
Ynystawe
Glais
Bryn-côch
Rhyddings
Llanelli
Bynea
Bynea Sta
Penyrheol
Gorseinon
Bwlchymynydd
Penllergaer
Llangyfelach
Pentre
Poeth
Llansamlet
Birchgrove
Skewen
Whitford
Point
LOUGHOR
Loughor
Mynydd-
bach
Morriston
Tai'r
ysgol
Cadle
Winsh-
wen
Trallwn
Berthlwyd
Gowerton
Fforest-
fach
Tre-boeth
Landore
Bon-y-maen
Pentre-dwr
Llanrhidian
Sands
Crofty
Wern-olau
Waunarlwydd
Whitford
Burrows
(NT)
Broughton
Bay
Llanmorlais
Pen-
clawdd
Wernffrwd
Poundffald
Three
Crosses
Dunvant
Cockett
Pentre-chwyth
Kilvey
Hill
Jersey
Marine
Llanmadoc
Landimore
Cheriton
Leason
Weobley
Cwmgwyn
Townhill
Plantasia
Windmill
Port
Tennant
Burry Holms
Burry
Green
Llangennith
Oldwalls
Llanrhidian
Sketty
Uplands
Killay
Olchfa
Clyne
Valley
Baglan
Fairyhill
Llethrid
Upper
Killay
Wales
SWANSEA
(Abertawe)
Rhossili
Bay
Hillend
Burry
SWANSEA
GOWER
Ilston
Clyne
Common
Mayals
Black Pill
West Cross
Rhossili
Downs
Llanddewi
Reynoldston
Cefn
Bryn
Parc
le Breos Burial
Chamber
Lunnon
Kittle
Murton
Bishopston
Norton
Oystermouth
Castle (ruins)
The Mumbles
PORT TA
Rhossili
Knelston
Penmaen
Parkmill
Pennard
Worms
Head
Middleton
Pitton
Pilton
Penrice
Nicholaston
Southgate
Caswell
Newton
Langland
Mumbles Head
SWANSEA BAY
Pilton
Green
Scurlage
Oxwich
Oxwich Bay
Langland Bay
(NT)
Port Eynon
Oxwich Green
Slade
Oxwich
Pwlldu
Head
SEE PAGE 194
Overton
Horton
Port
Eynon Bay
Culver
Hole
Port
Eynon
Point
Cork (Mar-Dec) 10 hours
M4
A40
A48
A484
A485
A476
A483
A4069
A4068
A474
A4138
A4240
A4067
A4118
A4217
A4241
B4300
B4310
B4312
B4306
B4317
B4309
B4308
B4297
B4556
B4296
B4295
B4620
B4489
B4603
B4290
B4271
B4436
B4247
B4291
B4295
35
50
0 2 4 6 miles
0 2 4 6 8 10 km

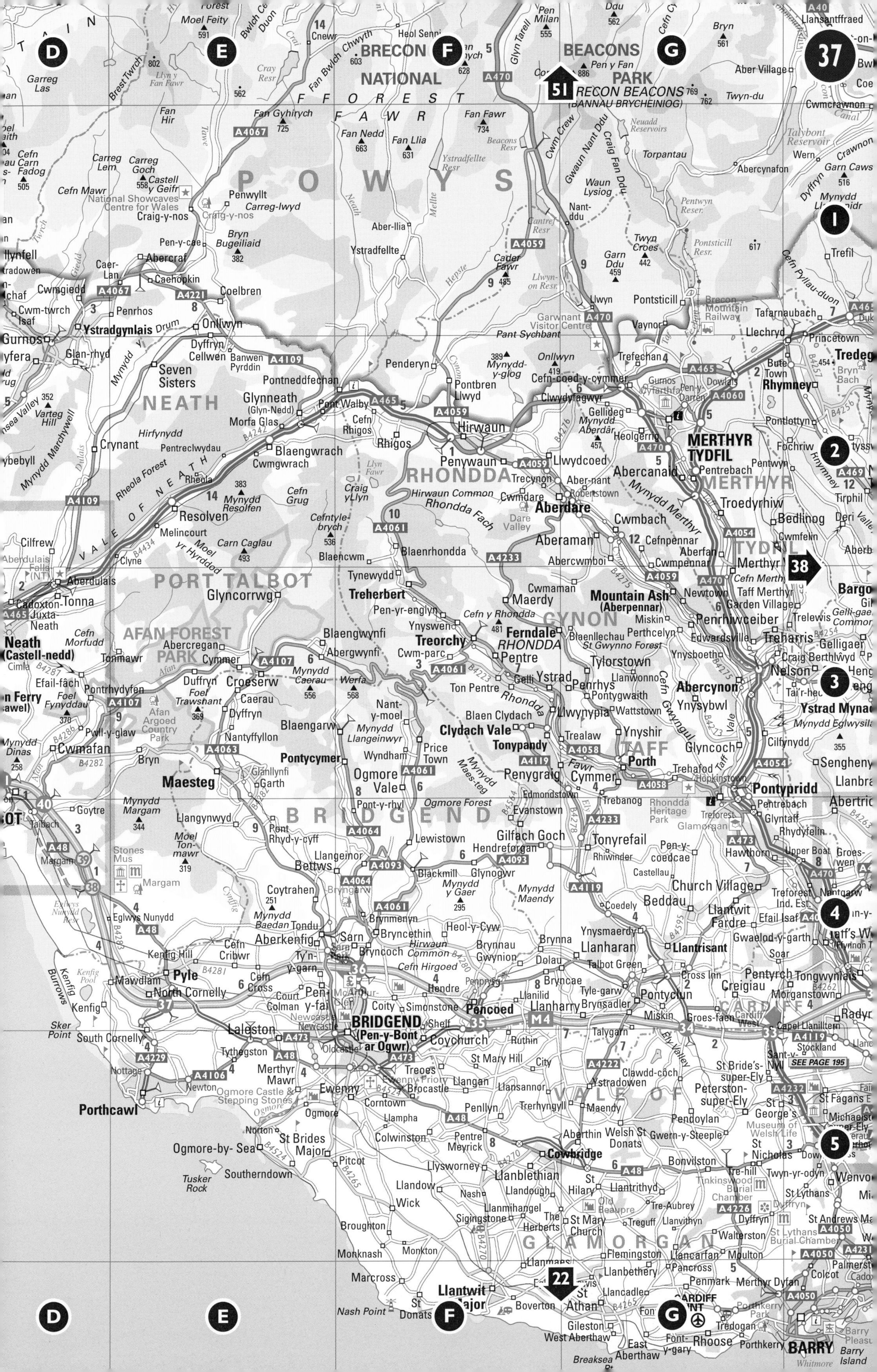

37
51
38
22
D
E
F
G
D
E
F
G
1
2
3
4
5
BRECON
NATIONAL
BEACONS
PARK
BRECON BEACONS
(BANNAU BRYCHEINIOG)
FOREST
FAWR
POWYS
NEATH
PORT TALBOT
RHONDDA
CYNON
TAFF
MERTHYR
TYDFIL
BRIDGEND
VALE OF
GLAMORGAN
CARDIFF
VALE OF NEATH
AFAN FOREST PARK
Moel Feity
591
Garreg Las
Heol Senni
Cray Resr
Llyn y Fan Fawr
Fan Gyhirych
725
Fan Nedd
663
Fan Llia
631
Fan Fawr
734
Beacons Resr
Ystradfellte Resr
Pen Milan
555
Pen y Fan
886
Bryn
561
Aber Village
Twyn-du
762
769
Cwmcrawnon
Talybont Reservoir
Neuadd Reservoirs
Torpantau
Abercynafon
Garn Caws
516
Wern
Crawnon
Fan Hir
Carreg Lem
Carreg Goch
Castell y Geifr
558
Cefn Carn Fadog
505
Cefn Mawr
National Showcaves Centre for Wales
Craig-y-nos
Penwyllt
Carreg-lwyd
Bryn Bugeiliaid
382
Pen-y-cae
Abercraf
Caer-Lan
Caehopkin
Coelbren
Cwmgiedd
Cwm-twrch Isaf
Penrhos
Ystradgynlais
Onllwyn
Gurnos
Glan-rhyd
Dyffryn Cellwen
Banwen Pyrddin
Seven Sisters
Pontneddfechan
Glynneath
(Glyn-Nedd)
Morfa Glas
Pont Walby
Aber-llia
Ystradfellte
Cader Fawr
485
Cantref Resr
Nant-ddu
Llwyn-on Resr
Garn Ddu
459
Twyn Croes
442
Pentwyn Reser
Pontsticill Resr
617
Trefil
Llwyn
Pontsticill
Brecon Mountain Railway
Tafarnaubach
Llechryd
Princetown
Tredegar
Garwnant Visitor Centre
Pant Sychbant
Vaynor
Penderyn
Mynydd-y-glog
389
Onllwyn
419
Cefn-coed-y-cymmer
Trefechan
Gurnos
Cyfarthfa
Pen-y-Darren
Dowlais
Bute Town
Rhymney
Pontbren Llwyd
Clwydyfagwyr
Hirwaun
Cefn Rhigos
Rhigos
Penywaun
Gellideg
Mynydd Aberdâr
457
Heolgerrig
MERTHYR TYDFIL
Pentrebach
Abercanaid
Pontlottyn
Fochriw
Pentwyn
Troedyrhiw
Bedlinog
Tirphil
Deri
Cwmfelin
Aberfan
Merthyr Vale
Taff Merthyr Garden Village
Cwmpennar
Cefnpennar
Cwmbach
Mynydd Merthyr
Llwydcoed
Aber-nant
Robertstown
Aberdare
Trecynon
Cwmdare
Dare Valley
Aberaman
Abercwmboi
Hirwaun Common
Rhondda Fach
Llyn Fawr
Craig y Llyn
Cefn Grug
Cefntyle-brych
536
Blaencwm
Blaenrhondda
Tynewydd
Treherbert
Pen-yr-englyn
Ynyswen
Treorchy
Cwm-parc
Cefn y Rhondda
481
Maerdy
Cwmaman
Ferndale
Mountain Ash
(Aberpennar)
Miskin
Penrhiwceiber
Blaenllechau
Perthcelyn
St Gwynno Forest
Edwardsville
Treharris
Trelewis
Bargoed
Gelligaer
Nelson
Ystrad Mynach
Mynydd Eglwysilan
355
Cilfynydd
Senghenydd
Llanbradach
Abertridwr
Ynysboeth
Abercynon
Ynysybwl
Tylorstown
Llanwonno
Penrhys
Pontygwaith
Wattstown
Ynyshir
Porth
Trealaw
Glyncoch
Trehafod
Hopkinstown
Pontypridd
Pentrebach
Glyntaff
Rhydyfelin
Upper Boat
Groes-wen
Hawthorn
Treforest Ind. Est.
Nantgarw
Efail Isaf
Taff's Well
Gwaelod-y-garth
Pentyrch
Tongwynlais
Creigiau
Morganstown
Radyr
Rhondda Heritage Park
Treforest
Glamorgan
Ystrad
Gelli
Ton Pentre
Pentre
Rhondda
Llwynypia
Blaen Clydach
Clydach Vale
Tonypandy
Penygraig
Cymmer
Trebanog
Edmondstown
Evanstown
Tonyrefail
Gilfach Goch
Hendreforgan
Glynogwr
Rhiwinder
Pen-y-coedcae
Castellau
Church Village
Beddau
Llantwit Fardre
Llantrisant
Ynysmaerdy
Llanharan
Talbot Green
Brynna
Cross Inn
Pontyclun
Miskin
Groes-faen
Cardiff West
Llanharry
Brynsadler
Tyle-garw
Llanilid
Bryncae
Dolau
Brynnau Gwynion
Mynydd Maendy
Coedely
Mynydd y Gaer
295
Heol-y-Cyw
Blackmill
Lewistown
Ogmore Forest
Ogmore Vale
Wyndham
Price Town
Nant-y-moel
Mynydd Llangeinwyr
Mynydd Maes-teg
Pont-y-rhyl
Blaengarw
Pontycymer
Werfa
568
Mynydd Caerau
556
Abergwynfi
Blaengwynfi
Cymmer
Abercregan
Croeserw
Caerau
Duffryn
Foel Trawsnant
369
Dyffryn
Nantyffyllon
Afan Argoed Country Park
Maesteg
Garth
Llangynwyd
Moel Ton-mawr
319
Pont Rhyd-y-cyff
Llangeinor
Bettws
Coytrahen
251
Mynydd Baedan
Tondu
Bryngarw
Brynmenyn
Bryncethin
Sarn
Aberkenfig
Bryncoch
Hirwaun Common
Cefn Hirgoed
Hendre
Penprysg
Pencoed
Coity
Simonstone
Shelf
BRIDGEND
(Pen-y-Bont ar Ogwr)
Coychurch
Ruthin
Talygarn
St Mary Hill
Llangan
Treoes
Ewenny Priory
Brocastle
Ewenny
Corntown
Ogmore
Ogmore Castle & Stepping Stones
Merthyr Mawr
Tythegston
Laleston
Newcastle
Court Colman
Cefn Cross
Pen-y-fai
Ty'n-y-garn
Cefn Cribwr
Kenfig Hill
Pyle
North Cornelly
Mawdlam
Kenfig Pool
Kenfig Burrows
Kenfig
Sker Point
South Cornelly
Nottage
Newton
Porthcawl
Eglwys Nunydd Resr
Eglwys Nunydd
Margam
Stones Mus
Mynydd Margam
344
Goytre
Taibach
Cwmafan
Bryn
Pwll-y-glaw
Foel Fynyddau
370
Pontrhydyfen
Efail-fâch
Tonmawr
Cefn Morfudd
Neath
(Castell-nedd)
Cimla
Cadoxton-Juxta-Neath
Tonna
Aberdulais
Aberdulais Falls (NT)
Cilfrew
Clyne
Melincourt
Resolven
Moel yr Hyrddod
Carn Caglau
493
Mynydd Resolfen
383
Rheola
Rheola Forest
Blaengwrach
Cwmgwrach
Pentreclwydau
Hirfynydd
Crynant
Mynydd Marchywell
Varteg Hill
352
Glyncorrwg
Mynydd Dinas
258
Ystradowen
Clawdd-coch
Llansannor
Trerhyngyll
Maendy
Welsh St Donats
Aberthin
Cowbridge
Penllyn
Pentre Meyrick
Llanblethian
Llandough
Llysworney
Nash
Llanmihangel
Sigingstone
The Herberts
St Mary Church
Old Beaupre
St Hilary
Llantrithyd
Tre-Aubrey
Treguff
Llanvithyn
Llancarfan
Flemingston
Moulton
Walterston
Llanbethery
Pancross
Penmark
Llancadle
Merthyr Dyfan
Colcot
Palmerstown
Porthkerry Park
Porthkerry
Tredogan
Rhoose
Font-y-gary
East Aberthaw
West Aberthaw
Gileston
Breaksea
St Athan
Boverton
Llantwit Major
St Donats
Nash Point
Marcross
Monknash
Monkton
Broughton
Wick
Llandow
Colwinston
Llampha
Pitcot
St Brides Major
Ogmore-by-Sea
Southerndown
Tusker Rock
Norton
Peterston-super-Ely
St Bride's-super-Ely
Pendoylan
Gwern-y-Steeple
Bonvilston
St Nicholas
Dyffryn
St Lythans
St Lythans Burial Chamber
Tinkinswood Burial Chamber
Twyn-yr-odyn
Wenvoe
St Georges
Museum of Welsh Life
St Fagans
Michaelston-super-Ely
Capel Llaniltern
Stockland
Sant-y-Nyll
SEE PAGE 195
St Andrews Major
BARRY
Barry Island
Whitmore
CARDIFF
A40
A470
A4067
A4221
A4109
A465
A4059
A4061
A4233
A4058
A4119
A4054
A4060
A469
A4107
A4063
A4064
A4093
A48
A473
A4106
A4229
A4222
A4226
A4050
A4232
A4231
M4
B4242
B4434
B4287
B4286
B4282
B4281
B4283
B4524
B4265
B4270
B4280
B4223
B4564
B4278
B4275
B4273
B4595
B4262
B4254
B4256
B4257

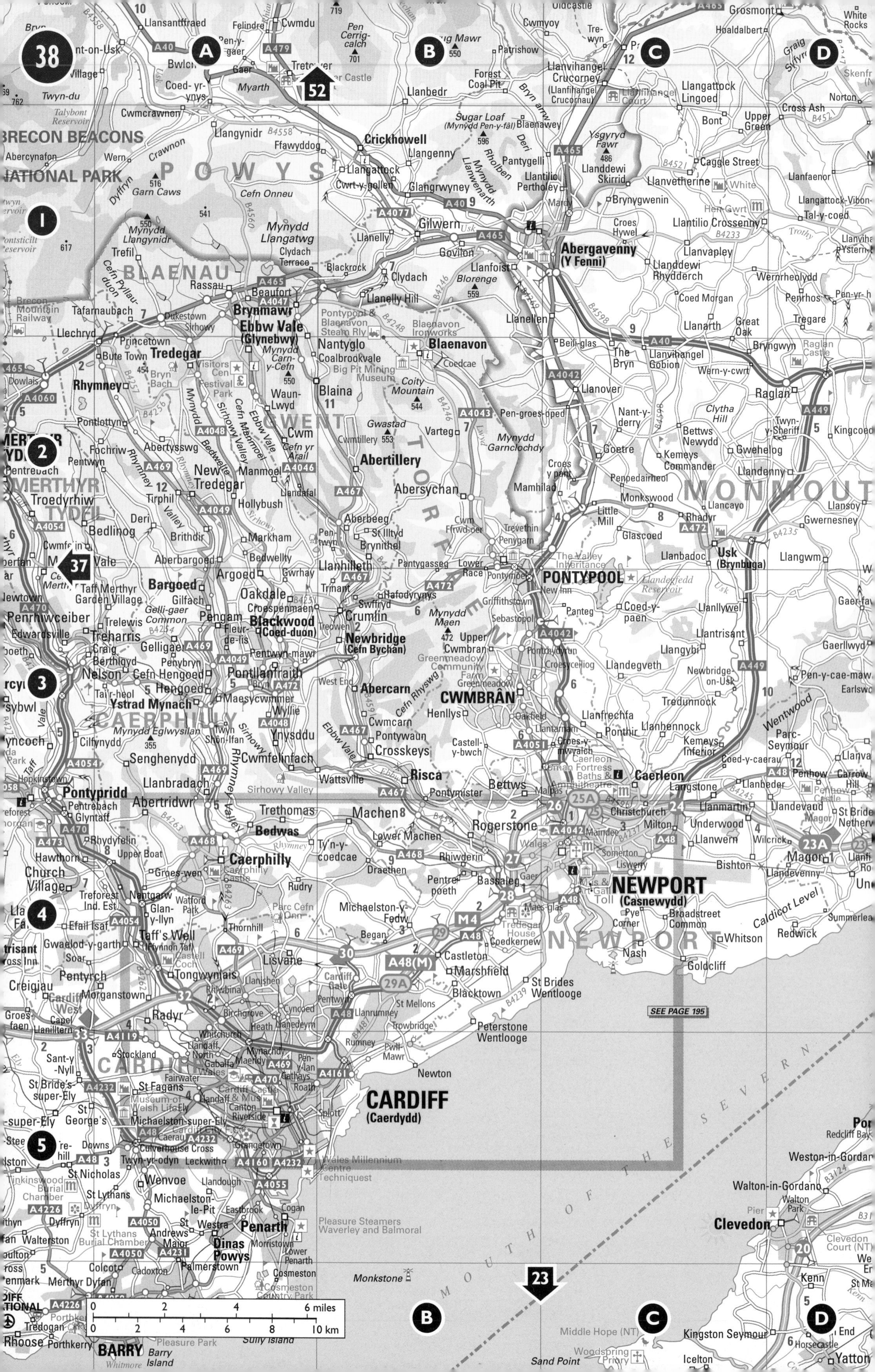

A
B
C
D
1
2
3
4
5
52
37
23
BRECON BEACONS
NATIONAL PARK
POWYS
BLAENAU
GWENT
TORFAEN
MERTHYR TYDFIL
CAERPHILLY
MONMOUTHSHIRE
NEWPORT
CARDIFF
Llansantffraed
Bwlch
Cwmdu
Tretower
Crickhowell
Llangattock
Gilwern
Govilon
Abergavenny
(Y Fenni)
Llanvihangel Crucorney
Grosmont
Sugar Loaf
Blorenge
Llanfoist
Brynmawr
Ebbw Vale
(Glynebwy)
Tredegar
Rhymney
Nantyglo
Blaina
Blaenavon
Big Pit Mining Museum
Pontypool & Blaenavon Steam Rly
Abertillery
Abersychan
Llanover
Raglan
Usk
(Brynbuga)
PONTYPOOL
Llandegfedd Reservoir
CWMBRÂN
Caerleon
Roman Fortress Baths & Amphitheatre
NEWPORT
(Casnewydd)
Magor
Caldicot Level
Risca
Crosskeys
Newbridge
(Cefn Bychan)
Abercarn
Blackwood
(Coed-duon)
Oakdale
Bargoed
New Tredegar
Merthyr Tydfil
Troedyrhiw
Treharris
Nelson
Ystrad Mynach
Senghenydd
Pontypridd
Llanbradach
Caerphilly
Caerphilly Castle
Bedwas
Machen
Rogerstone
Bassaleg
Tredegar House
Castleton
Marshfield
St Brides Wentlooge
Peterstone Wentlooge
Taff's Well
(Ffynnon Taf)
Castell Coch
Tongwynlais
Radyr
Llandaff
Whitchurch
Lisvane
Rumney
St Mellons
CARDIFF
(Caerdydd)
Cardiff Castle
Museum of Welsh Life
Wales Millennium Centre
Techniquest
Penarth
Dinas Powys
Barry
Barry Island
Sully Island
Wenvoe
St Nicholas
Tinkinswood Burial Chamber
St Lythans Burial Chamber
Dyffryn
Cosmeston Country Park
Pleasure Steamers Waverley and Balmoral
Monkstone
MOUTH OF THE SEVERN
Middle Hope (NT)
Woodspring Priory
Sand Point
Kingston Seymour
Clevedon
Clevedon Court (NT)
Walton-in-Gordano
Weston-in-Gordano
Yatton
Goldcliff
Nash
Whitson
Redwick
SEE PAGE 195
0 2 4 6 miles
0 2 4 6 8 10 km

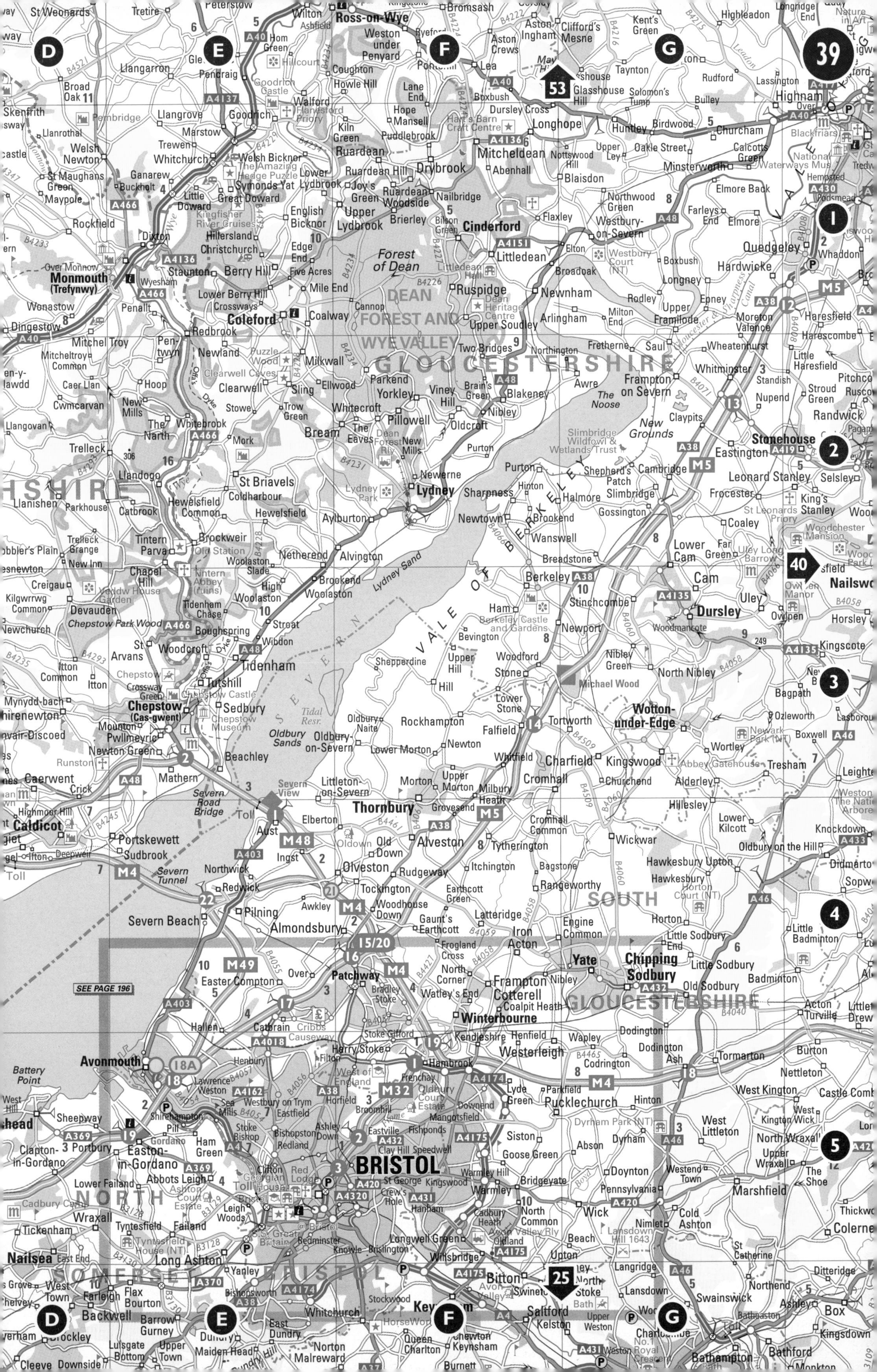
39
D
E
F
G
St Weonards
Tretire
Peterstow
Wilton
Ross-on-Wye
Bromsash
Aston Ingham
Clifford's Mesne
Kent's Green
Highleadon
Weston under Penyard
Ryeford
Hom Green
Hillcourt
Pontshill
Lea
Aston Crews
53
Glasshouse Hill
Taynton
Rudford
Lassington
Highnam
Over
Llangarron
Pencraig
Coughton
Howle Hill
Lane End
Goodrich Castle
Walford
Flanesford Priory
Broad Oak
Skenfrith
Pembridge
Llangrove
Goodrich
Hope Mansell
Boxbush
Dursley Cross
Longhope
Huntley
Solomon's Tump
Bulley
Birdwood
Churcham
Llanrothal
Welsh Newton
Marstow
Kiln Green
Puddlebrook
Hart's Barn Craft Centre
Trewen
Whitchurch
Welsh Bicknor
The Amazing Hedge Puzzle
Ruardean
Drybrook
Mitcheldean
Nottswood Hill
Upper Ley
Oakle Street
Calcotts Green
Blackfriars
National Waterways Mus
St Maughans Green
Ganarew
Symonds Yat
Lower Lydbrook
Ruardean Hill
Joy's Green
Ruardean Woodside
Abenhall
Blaisdon
Minsterworth
Buckholt
Maypole
Little Doward
Great Doward
Upper Lydbrook
Nailbridge
Elmore Back
Hempsted
Rockfield
Kingfisher River Cruises
Hillersland
English Bicknor
Brierley
Bilson Green
Cinderford
Flaxley
Northwood Green
Westbury-on-Severn
Farleys End
Elmore
Podsmead
Dixton
Christchurch
Edge End
Forest of Dean
Littledean
Elton
Westbury Court (NT)
Quedgeley
Whaddon
Monmouth (Trefynwy)
Over Monnow
Staunton
Berry Hill
Five Acres
Littledean Hall
Broadoak
Boxbush
Hardwicke
Longney
Wyesham
Mile End
Ruspidge
Newnham
Rodley
Epney
Wonastow
Penallt
Lower Berry Hill
Crossways
Coleford
Coalway
Cannop
DEAN FOREST AND WYE VALLEY
Dean Heritage Centre
Upper Soudley
Arlingham
Milton End
Upper Framilode
Moreton Valence
Haresfield
Dingestow
Redbrook
Harescombe
Mitchel Troy
Pen-twyn
Two Bridges
Northington
Fretherne
Saul
Wheatenhurst
Mitcheltroy Common
Newland
Puzzle Wood
Milkwall
GLOUCESTERSHIRE
Little Haresfield
Clearwell Caves
Whitminster
Standish
Caer Llan
Hoop
Clearwell
Sling
Ellwood
Parkend
Yorkley
Viney Hill
Brain's Green
Blakeney
Awre
Frampton on Severn
Stroud Green
Cwmcarvan
New Mills
Offa's Dyke
Stowe
Trow Green
Whitecroft
Pillowell
Nibley
The Noose
Nupend
Randwick
Llangovan
The Narth
Whitebrook
Bream
The Eaves
Dean Forest Rly
New Mills
Oldcroft
Claypits
New Grounds
Stonehouse
Trelleck
Mork
Purton
Slimbridge Wildfowl & Wetlands Trust
Eastington
Llandogo
St Briavels
Coldharbour
Newerne
Purton
Shepherd's Patch
Cambridge
Leonard Stanley
Selsley
Llanishen
Parkhouse
Hewelsfield Common
Hewelsfield
Lydney Park
Lydney
Sharpness
Hinton
Halmore
Slimbridge
Frocester
King's Stanley
Catbrook
Aylburton
Newtown
Brookend
Gossington
St Leonards Priory
Coaley
Trelleck Grange
Tintern Parva
Brockweir
Old Station
Alvington
Wanswell
Lower Cam
Far Green
Uley Long Barrow
Woodchester Mansion
New Inn
Chapel Hill
Tintern Abbey (ruins)
Woolaston Slade
Netherend
Lydney Sand
Breadstone
40
Creigau
Yellow House Garden
High Woolaston
Brookend
Woolaston
Berkeley
Cam
Kilgwrrwg Common
Devauden
Tidenham Chase
Stinchcombe
Dursley
Uley
Owlpen Manor
Nailsworth
Chepstow Park Wood
Boughspring
Streat
Wibdon
Ham
Berkeley Castle and Gardens
Newport
Woodmancote
Owlpen
Horsley
St Arvans
Woodcroft
Tidenham
SEVERN
VALE OF BERKELEY
Bevington
Woodford
Nibley Green
Kingscote
Itton Common
Itton
Chepstow Crossway Green
Shepperdine
Upper Hill
Stone
North Nibley
Michael Wood
Mynydd-bach
Tutshill
Chepstow Castle
Hill
Lower Stone
Bagpath
Chepstow (Cas-gwent)
Sedbury
Chepstow Museum
Tidal Resr.
Oldbury Naite
Rockhampton
Falfield
Tortworth
Wotton-under-Edge
Ozleworth
Mounton
Pwllmeyric
Oldbury Sands
Oldbury-on-Severn
Newton
Newark Park (NT)
Boxwell
Newton Green
Beachley
Lower Morton
Whitfield
Charfield
Kingswood
Wortley
Abbey Gatehouse
Tresham
Runston
Mathern
Littleton-on-Severn
Morton
Upper Morton
Milbury Heath
Cromhall
Churchend
Alderley
Leighterton
Caerwent
Crick
Severn Road Bridge
Severn View
Thornbury
Gravesend
Hillesley
Lower Kilcott
Highmoor Hill
Caldicot
Toll
Aust
Elberton
Cromhall Common
Knockdown
Portskewett
Sudbrook
Oldown
Old Down
Alveston
Tytherington
Wickwar
Hawkesbury Upton
Oldbury on the Hill
Didmarton
Deepweir
Ingst
Northwick
Olveston
Rudgeway
Itchington
Bagstone
Hawkesbury
Horton Court (NT)
Severn Tunnel
Redwick
Tockington
Rangeworthy
SOUTH
Awkley
Woodhouse Down
Earthcott Green
Pilning
Gaunt's Earthcott
Latteridge
Horton
Engine Common
Little Sodbury End
Little Badminton
Severn Beach
Almondsbury
Frogland Cross
Iron Acton
Yate
Chipping Sodbury
Little Sodbury
SEE PAGE 196
Easter Compton
Over
Patchway
Bradley Stoke
North Corner
Watley's End
Frampton Cotterell
Nibley
Coalpit Heath
Old Sodbury
Badminton
GLOUCESTERSHIRE
Acton Turville
Hallen
Catbrain
Cribbs Causeway
Winterbourne
Stoke Gifford
Kendleshire
Henfield
Wapley
Dodington
Westerleigh
Dodington Ash
Tormarton
Burton
Battery Point
Avonmouth
Henbury
Harry Stoke
Filton
Hambrook
Codrington
Nettleton
Lawrence Weston
West of England
Frenchay
Oldbury Court Estate
Lyde Green
Parkfield
Pucklechurch
Hinton
West Kington
Castle Combe
Sheepway
Sea Mills
Westbury on Trym
Horfield
Broomhill
Downend
Mangotsfield
Dyrham Park (NT)
West Littleton
West Kington Wick
Shirehampton
Pill
Eastfield
Stoke Bishop
Ashley Down
Eastville
Fishponds
Siston
Abson
Dyrham
North Wraxall
Portbury
Clapton-in-Gordano
Easton-in-Gordano
Gordano
Ham Green
Bishopston
Redland
Clay Hill
Speedwell
Goose Green
Upper Wraxall
Abbots Leigh
Clifton
Red Lodge
BRISTOL
St George
Kingswood
Warmley Hill
Doynton
Westend Town
The Shoe
Lower Failand
Ashton Court Estate
Georgian House
Crew's Hole
Warmley
Bridgeyate
Pennsylvania
Marshfield
NORTH
Cadbury Camp
Leigh Woods
Toll
Hanham
Cadbury Heath
North Common
Wick
Nimlet
Cold Ashton
Wraxall
Tyntesfield
Failand
SS Great Britain
Bristol
Redminster
Longwell Green
Avon Valley Rly
Oldland
Lansdown Hill 1643
Colerne
Tickenham
Tyntesfield House (NT)
Knowle
Brislington
Beach
St Catherine
Nailsea
East End
Long Ashton
Willsbridge
Upton
Langridge
Ditteridge
SOMERSET
Yanley
BRISTOL
Bitton
Swineford
Avon Valley
North Stoke
Lansdown
Northend
Grove
West Town
Flax Bourton
Bishopsworth
Stockwood
Keynsham
25
Saltford
Bath
Swainswick
Ashley
Box
Chelvey
Farleigh
Backwell
Barrow Gurney
Whitchurch
HorseWorld
Kelston
Upper Weston
Batheaston
Kingsdown
Brockley
Dundry
East Dundry
Queen Charlton
Chewton Keynsham
Charlcombe
No.1 Royal Crescent
Weston
Bathampton
Bathford
Lulsgate Bottom
Upper Town
Maiden Head
Norton Malreward
Burnett
Cleeve
Downside
M4
M5
M48
M49
M32
A40
A48
A466
A4136
A4137
A4151
A38
A403
A4018
A369
A370
A420
A4320
A431
A4174
A4175
A432
A46
A4135
A419
A430
A433
B4228
B4226
B4234
B4058
B4059
B4060
B4061
B4509
B4465
B4040
B4055
B4056
B4057
B4054
B3128
B3129
B3130
B4231
B4293
B4245
B4235

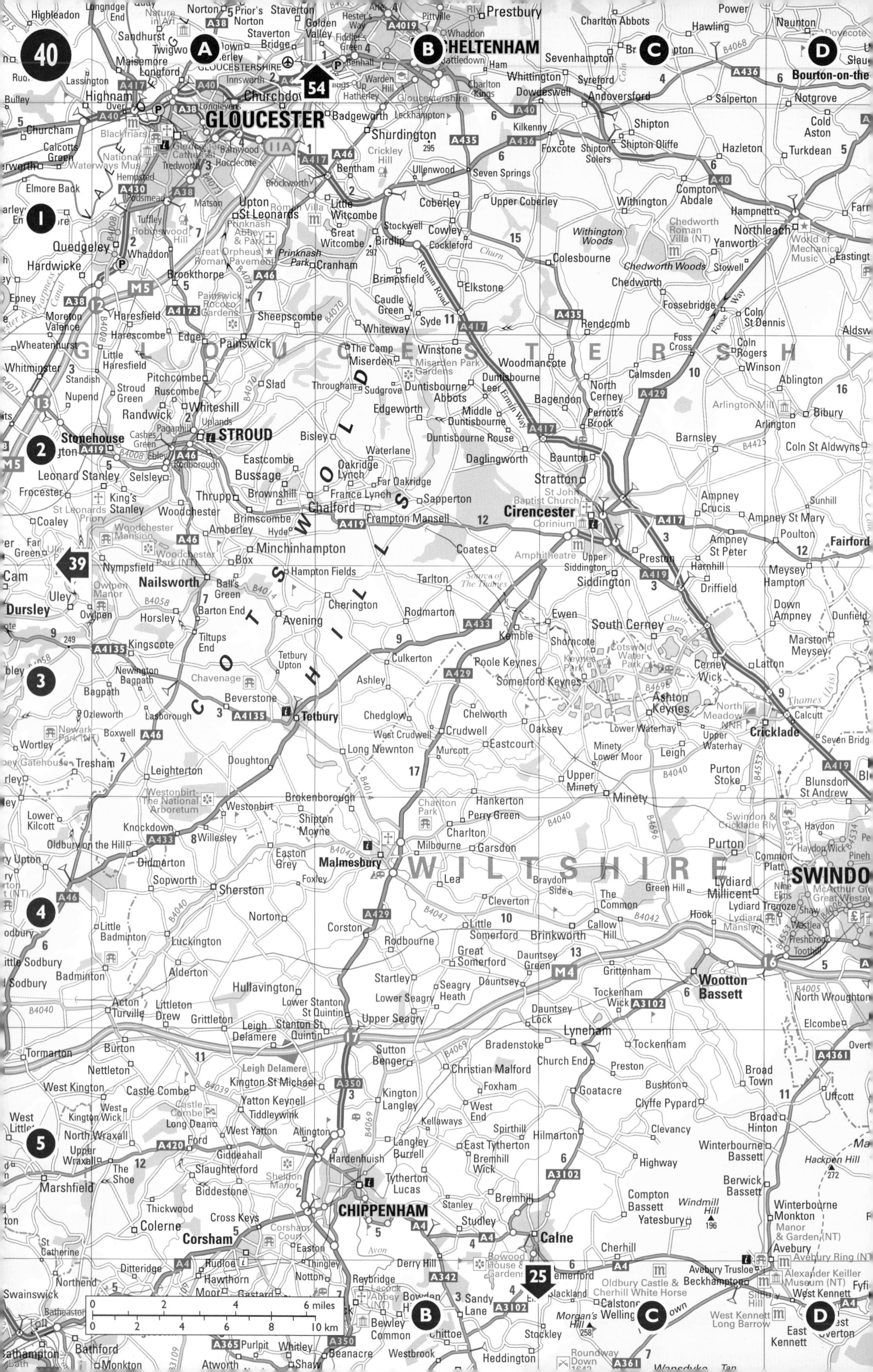

40
A
B
C
D
54
39
25
1
2
3
4
5
Highleadon
Sandhurst
Twigworth
Maisemore
Longford
Norton
Prior's Norton
Staverton
Staverton Bridge
Golden Valley
Down Hatherley
GLOUCESTERSHIRE
Innsworth
Churchdown
Prestbury
Pittville
Whaddon
CHELTENHAM
Battledown
Ham
Charlton Kings
Leckhampton
Charlton Abbots
Hawling
Power
Naunton
Dovecote
Brockhampton
Sevenhampton
Whittington
Syreford
Dowdeswell
Andoversford
Salperton
Notgrove
Bourton-on-the
Cold Aston
Turkdean
Lassington
Highnam
Over
Bulley
Churcham
Calcotts Green
Elmore Back
GLOUCESTER
Blackfriars
Gloucester Cathedral
National Waterways Mus
Hempsted
Tredworth
Barnwood
Hucclecote
Podsmead
Matson
Badgeworth
Shurdington
Crickley Hill
Bentham
Brockworth
Upton St Leonards
Kilkenny
Foxcote
Shipton Solers
Shipton
Shipton Oliffe
Hazleton
Seven Springs
Ullenwood
Coberley
Upper Coberley
Cowley
Cockleford
Withington
Compton Abdale
Hampnett
Northleach
Farmington
Yanworth
Chedworth Roman Villa (NT)
Withington Woods
Chedworth Woods
Stowell
World of Mechanical Music
Eastington
Colesbourne
Chedworth
Fossebridge
Coln St Dennis
Little Witcombe
Great Witcombe
Birdlip
Prinknash Abbey & Park
Prinknash Park
Great Orpheus Roman Pavement
Cranham
Quedgeley
Whaddon
Tuffley
Robinswood Hill
Hardwicke
Brookthorpe
Brimpsfield
Elkstone
Caudle Green
Syde
Whiteway
Rendcomb
Epney
Moreton Valence
Haresfield
Harescombe
Edge
Painswick
Painswick Rococo Garden
Sheepscombe
The Camp
Miserden
Winstone
Misarden Park Gardens
Woodmancote
Foss Cross
Coln Rogers
Winson
Aldsworth
Wheatenhurst
Whitminster
Little Haresfield
Standish
Nupend
Stroud Green
Pitchcombe
Ruscombe
Slad
Throughham
Sudgrove
Duntisbourne Abbots
Duntisbourne Leer
Middle Duntisbourne
Duntisbourne Rouse
Ermin Way
Roman Road
Fosse Way
North Cerney
Calmsden
Bagendon
Perrott's Brook
Ablington
Arlington Mill
Arlington
Bibury
Randwick
Whiteshill
Uplands
Paganhill
Cashes Green
STROUD
Stonehouse
Ebley
Rodborough
Leonard Stanley
Selsley
Frocester
King's Stanley
St Leonards Priory
Coaley
Woodchester
Woodchester Mansion
Woodchester Park (NT)
Eastcombe
Bussage
Brownshill
Thrupp
Brimscombe
Amberley
Hyde
Chalford
France Lynch
Oakridge Lynch
Far Oakridge
Waterlane
Bisley
Edgeworth
Sapperton
Frampton Mansell
Daglingworth
Baunton
Stratton
St John Baptist Church
Cirencester
Corinium
Amphitheatre
Barnsley
Coln St Aldwyns
Ampney Crucis
Ampney St Mary
Ampney St Peter
Sunhill
Poulton
Fairford
Minchinhampton
Box
Nympsfield
Nailsworth
Owlpen Manor
Owlpen
Uley
Cam
Dursley
Far Green
Hampton Fields
Ball's Green
Barton End
Horsley
Cherington
Avening
Tarlton
Rodmarton
Coates
Source of The Thames
Upper Siddington
Siddington
Preston
Harnhill
Driffield
Meysey Hampton
Down Ampney
Dunfield
Kingscote
Tiltups End
Tetbury Upton
Culkerton
Kemble
Ewen
South Cerney
Shorncote
Cotswold Water Park
Keynes Park
Cerney Wick
Latton
Marston Meysey
Newington Bagpath
Bagpath
Chavenage
Beverstone
Lasborough
Ozleworth
Newark Park (NT)
Wortley
Boxwell
Tetbury
Ashley
Poole Keynes
Somerford Keynes
Ashton Keynes
Chedglow
Chelworth
Crudwell
West Crudwell
Oaksey
Lower Waterhay
Upper Waterhay
North Meadow NNR
Cricklade
Calcutt
Seven Bridges
Thames (Isis)
Tresham
Gatehouse
Leighterton
Doughton
Long Newnton
Murcott
Eastcourt
Minety Lower Moor
Leigh
Purton Stoke
Blunsdon St Andrew
Upper Minety
Minety
Westonbirt - The National Arboretum
Westonbirt
Brokenborough
Charlton Park
Hankerton
Perry Green
Lower Kilcott
Knockdown
Willesley
Shipton Moyne
Charlton
Swindon & Cricklade Rly
Haydon
Haydon Wick
Oldbury on the Hill
Didmarton
Easton Grey
Malmesbury
Milbourne
Garsdon
Purton
Sopworth
Sherston
Foxley
Lea
WILTSHIRE
GLOUCESTERSHIRE
COTSWOLD HILLS
Braydon Side
The Common
Green Hill
Lydiard Millicent
Common Platt
SWINDON
McArthur Glen
Great Western
Nine Elms
Shaw
Lydiard Tregoze
Lydiard Mansion
Westlea
Freshbrook
Toothill
Cleverton
Little Somerford
Brinkworth
Callow Hill
Hook
Little Badminton
Norton
Corston
Rodbourne
Luckington
Great Somerford
Dauntsey Green
Grittenham
Wootton Bassett
Little Sodbury
Badminton
Alderton
Startley
Seagry Heath
Dauntsey
Tockenham Wick
North Wroughton
Acton Turville
Littleton Drew
Hullavington
Lower Stanton St Quintin
Lower Seagry
Upper Seagry
Dauntsey Lock
Grittleton
Leigh Delamere
Stanton St Quintin
Lyneham
Elcombe
Tormarton
Burton
Nettleton
Sutton Benger
Bradenstoke
Tockenham
Church End
Preston
Overtown
West Kington
Castle Combe
Kington St Michael
Christian Malford
Foxham
Bushton
Broad Town
Yatton Keynell
Tiddleywink
Kington Langley
Goatacre
Clyffe Pypard
Uffcott
West Littleton
Kington West
Long Dean
West Yatton
Allington
Kellaways
West End
Spirthill
Hilmarton
Clevancy
Broad Hinton
North Wraxall
Upper Wraxall
Ford
Giddeahall
Hardenhuish
Langley Burrell
East Tytherton
Bremhill Wick
Highway
Winterbourne Bassett
Hackpen Hill
Marshfield
The Shoe
Slaughterford
Sheldon Manor
Tytherton Lucas
Berwick Bassett
Biddestone
Thickwood
Colerne
Cross Keys
CHIPPENHAM
Stanley
Bremhill
Compton Bassett
Windmill Hill
Yatesbury
Winterbourne Monkton
Manor & Garden (NT)
Corsham
Corsham Court
Easton
Studley
Calne
Cherhill
Avebury
Avebury Ring (NT)
St Catherine
Ditteridge
Rudloe
Hawthorn
Thingley
Notton
Derry Hill
Bowood House & Gardens
Quemerford
Oldbury Castle & Cherhill White Horse
Avebury Trusloe
Beckhampton
Alexander Keiller Museum (NT)
West Kennett
Fyfield
Northend
Swainswick
Batheaston
Box
Gastard
Lacock
Lacock Abbey (NT)
Reybridge
Bowden Hill
Sandy Lane
Blackland
Calstone Wellington
Morgan's Hill
Silbury Hill
West Kennett Long Barrow
East Kennett
West Overton
Bathampton
Bathford
Monkton
Purlpit
Whitley
Shaw
Atworth
Bewley Common
Chittoe
Westbrook
Beanacre
Stockley
Heddington
Roundway Down
Wansdyke
Dovecote
0 2 4 6 miles
0 2 4 6 8 10 km
M4
M5
A38
A40
A417
A419
A429
A433
A435
A436
A46
A4135
A4173
A430
A4019
A420
A350
A342
A3102
A4
A365
A361
A4361
B4008
B4070
B4014
B4058
B4040
B4042
B4069
B4039
B4425
B4696
B4553
B4534
B4005
B4068
B4073
B4006
11A
12
13
16
17
295
297
249
258
272
196

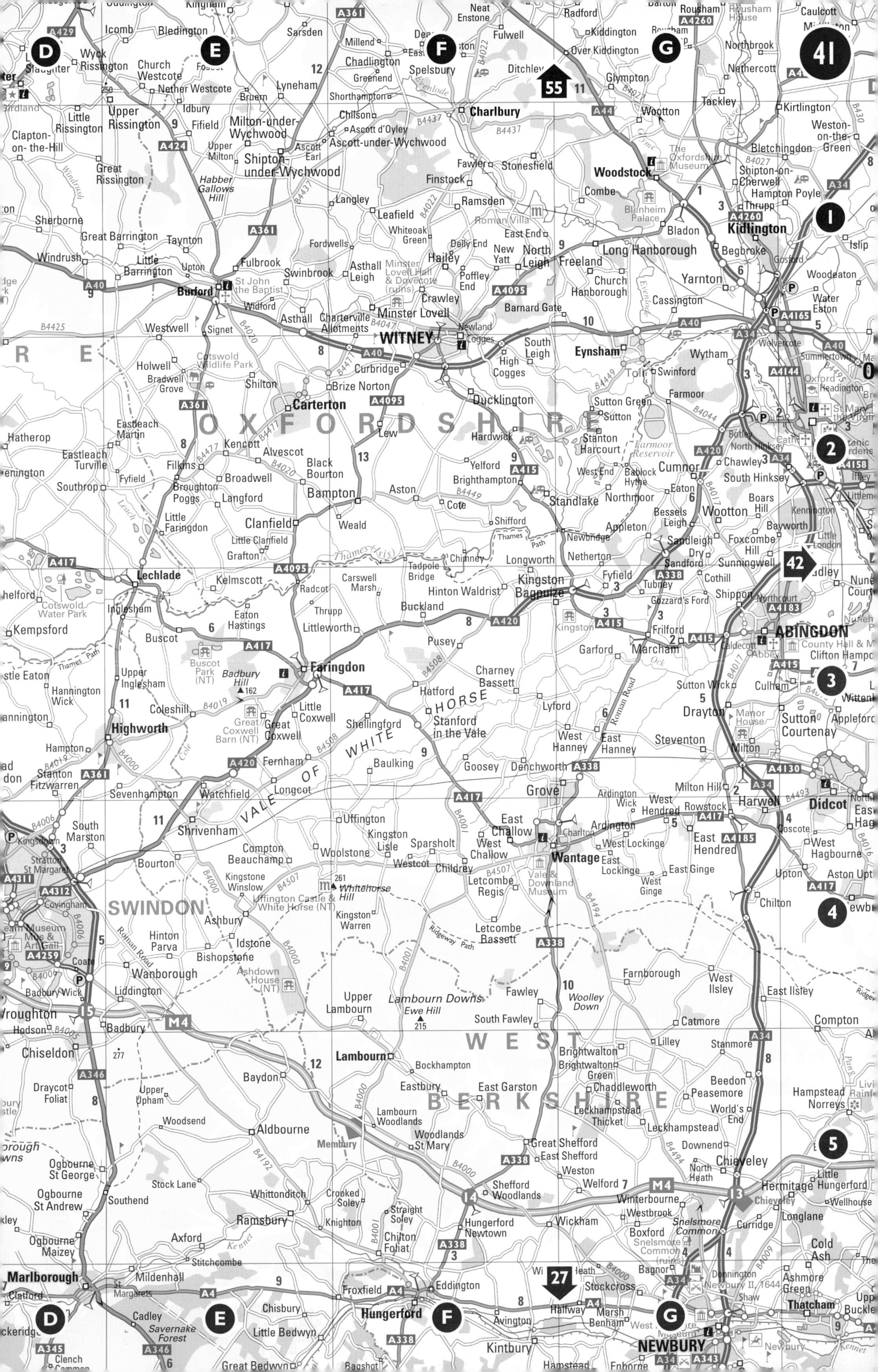
41
D
E
F
G
55
Icomb
Bledington
Kingham
Sarsden
Neat Enstone
Radford
Kiddington
Over Kiddington
Rousham
Caulcott
A429
A361
A4260
Wyck Rissington
Church Westcote
Nether Westcote
Millend
Chadlington
Greenend
Spelsbury
Fulwell
Ditchley
Glympton
Northbrook
Nethercott
Lyneham
Shorthampton
Charlbury
B4437
Tackley
Kirtlington
Little Rissington
Upper Rissington
Idbury
Fifield
Bruern
Milton-under-Wychwood
Chilson
Ascott d'Oyley
Ascott-under-Wychwood
Wootton
Weston-on-the-Green
Clapton-on-the-Hill
A424
Upper Milton
Ascott Earl
Shipton-under-Wychwood
Fawler
Stonesfield
Woodstock
The Oxfordshire Museum
Bletchingdon
Great Rissington
Habber Gallows Hill
Finstock
Shipton-on-Cherwell
Hampton Poyle
A34
Combe
Langley
Leafield
Ramsden
Blenheim Palace
Thrupp
Sherborne
Roman Villa
A4260
Kidlington
Great Barrington
Taynton
A361
Whiteoak Green
East End
Bladon
Long Hanborough
Islip
Fordwells
Delly End
New Yatt
North Leigh
Freeland
Begbroke
Windrush
Little Barrington
Fulbrook
Asthall Leigh
Minster Lovell Hall & Dovecote (ruins)
Hailey
Poffley End
Church Hanborough
Yarnton
Woodeaton
Upton
Swinbrook
A40
Burford
St John the Baptist
Crawley
A4095
Water Eaton
Widford
Asthall
Charterville Allotments
Minster Lovell
Barnard Gate
Cassington
B4425
Westwell
Signet
B4047
Newland
WITNEY
Cogges
Eynsham
Wolvercote
A4165
A40
Holwell
Cotswold Wildlife Park
Curbridge
South Leigh
High Cogges
Wytham
Summertown
Bradwell Grove
Shilton
Brize Norton
Toll
Swinford
A4144
Oxford
Headington
A361
Carterton
A4095
Ducklington
Farmoor
OXFORDSHIRE
Sutton Green
Sutton
Botley
North Hinksey
Hatherop
Eastleach Martin
Lew
Hardwick
Stanton Harcourt
Farmoor Reservoir
Kencott
Alvescot
Eastleach Turville
Filkins
Black Bourton
Yelford
West End
Bablock Hythe
Cumnor
Chawley
South Hinksey
A420
Fyfield
Broadwell
Brighthampton
A415
Southrop
Broughton Poggs
Langford
Bampton
Aston
Cote
Standlake
Northmoor
Eaton
Boars Hill
Kennington
Bessels Leigh
Little Faringdon
Clanfield
Weald
Shifford
Appleton
Wootton
Bayworth
Little Clanfield
Thames Path
Newbridge
Sandleigh
Foxcombe Hill
Grafton
Chimney
Longworth
Netherton
Dry Sandford
Sunningwell
42
A417
A4095
Lechlade
Kelmscott
Radcot
Carswell Marsh
Tadpole Bridge
Kingston Bagpuize
Fyfield
Tubney
A338
Cothill
Hinton Waldrist
Shippon
Cotswold Water Park
Inglesham
Eaton Hastings
Thrupp
Buckland
Gozzard'sFord
Northcourt
A4183
Kempsford
Buscot
Littleworth
A420
Kingston
A415
Frilford
ABINGDON
Pusey
A417
Garford
Marcham
Caldecott
County Hall & Museum
Abbey
Clifton Hampden
Buscot Park (NT)
Badbury Hill
Faringdon
Charney Bassett
A415
Upper Inglesham
Hannington Wick
Hatford
Culham
Sutton Wick
HORSE
Little Coxwell
Coleshill
B4019
Lyford
Drayton
Manor House
Sutton Courtenay
Appleford
Highworth
Great Coxwell Barn (NT)
Great Coxwell
Shellingford
Stanford in the Vale
WHITE
West Hanney
East Hanney
Steventon
Roman Road
Hampton
Fernham
Baulking
OF
Goosey
Denchworth
A338
Milton
Stanton Fitzwarren
A361
A420
VALE
B4508
A4130
Sevenhampton
Watchfield
Longcot
Grove
Ardington Wick
Milton Hill
Harwell
Didcot
A417
West Hendred
Rowstock
A34
B4493
Shrivenham
Uffington
East Challow
Charlton
Ardington
A417
South Marston
Kingston Lisle
Sparsholt
West Challow
West Lockinge
East Hendred
Coscote
West Hagbourne
Kingsdown
Stratton St Margaret
Compton Beauchamp
Woolstone
Wantage
East Lockinge
A4185
Bourton
Westcot
Childrey
Letcombe Regis
Vale & Downland Museum
East Ginge
West Ginge
Upton
Aston Upthorpe
A4311
A4312
Covingham
SWINDON
Kingstone Winslow
Whitehorse Hill
Uffington Castle & White Horse (NT)
B4507
A417
Chilton
Museum & Art Gallery
Ashbury
Kingston Warren
Ridgeway Path
Letcombe Bassett
Hinton Parva
Idstone
A338
A4259
Coate
Bishopstone
Wanborough
Ashdown House (NT)
Farnborough
West Ilsley
East Ilsley
Badbury Wick
Liddington
Upper Lambourn
Lambourn Downs
Ewe Hill
Fawley
Woolley Down
Wroughton
Hodson
Badbury
M4
South Fawley
Catmore
Compton
WEST
Lilley
Stanmore
Chiseldon
Lambourn
Bockhampton
Brightwalton
Brightwalton Green
A346
Draycot Foliat
Upper Upham
Baydon
Eastbury
East Garston
Chaddleworth
BERKSHIRE
Beedon
Pease more
Hampstead Norreys
Lambourn Woodlands
Leckhampstead Thicket
World's End
Woodsend
Aldbourne
Leckhampstead
Membury
Woodlands St Mary
Great Shefford
Downend
East Shefford
Chieveley
Ogbourne St George
Weston
North Heath
Stock Lane
Shefford Woodlands
Welford
M4
Little Hungerford
Ogbourne St Andrew
Southend
Whittonditch
Crooked Soley
Straight Soley
Winterbourne
Hermitage
Chieveley
Wellhouse
Westbrook
Snelsmore Common
Curridge
Longlane
Ramsbury
Knighton
Hungerford Newtown
Wickham
Boxford
Snelsmore Common (ruins)
Ogbourne Maizey
Axford
Chilton Foliat
A338
Cold Ash
Stitchcombe
Bagnor
Donnington
Newbury II, 1644
Ashmore Green
Marlborough
Mildenhall
St Margarets
A4
Eddington
Froxfield
27
Stockcross
Shaw
Thatcham
Clatford
Chisbury
Hungerford
Avington
Halfway
Marsh Benham
West
Cadley
Savernake Forest
Little Bedwyn
Kintbury
NEWBURY
Newbury
A345
A346
A338
A34
A343
Clench Common
Great Bedwyn
Bagshot
Hamstead
Enborne

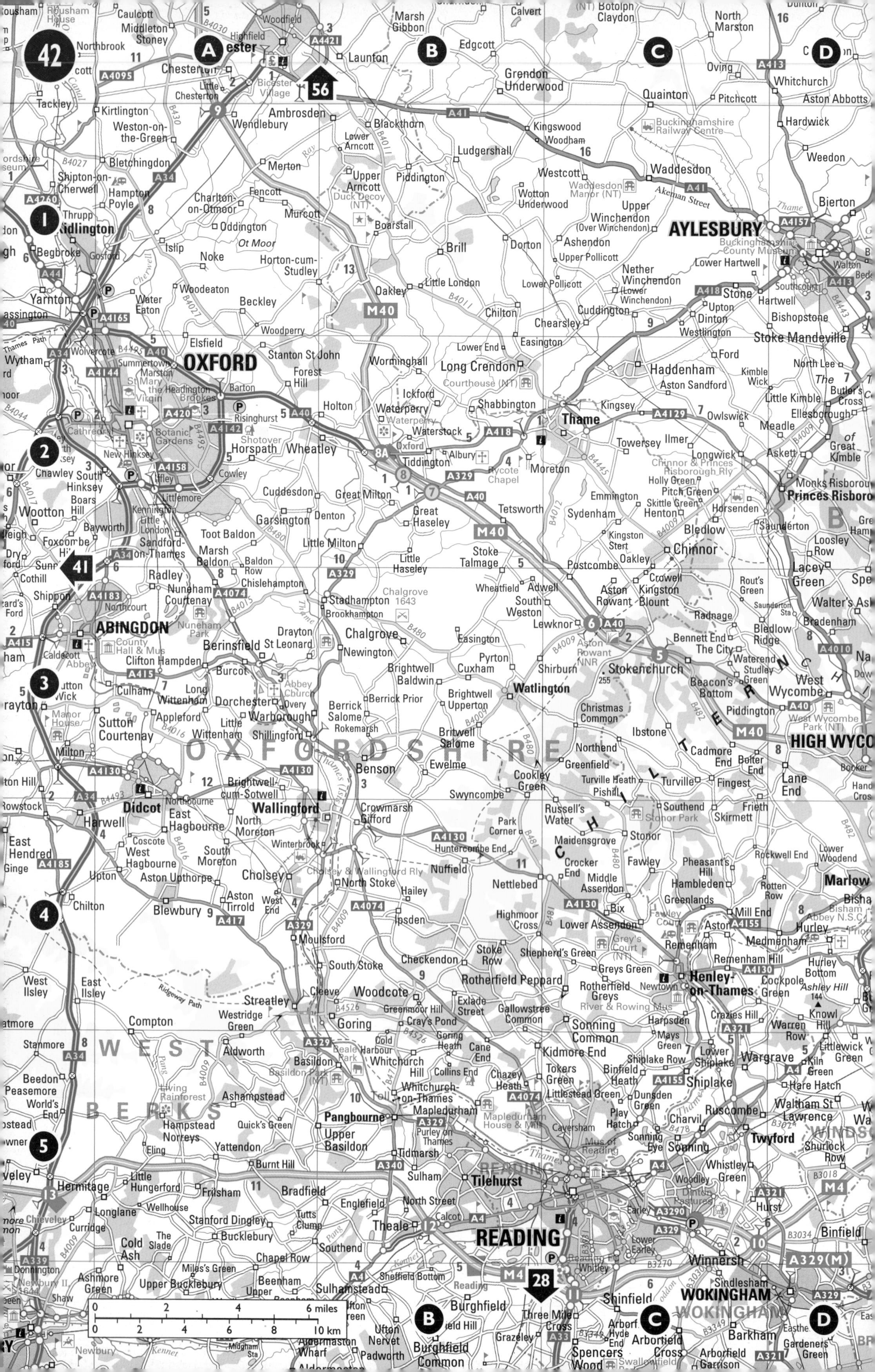
42
A
B
C
D
1
2
3
4
5
56
41
28
OXFORD
AYLESBURY
ABINGDON
READING
WOKINGHAM
HIGH WYCO
OXFORDSHIRE
WEST BERKS
CHILTERN
Rousham House
Caulcott
Middleton Stoney
Northbrook
Tackley
Kirtlington
Weston-on-the-Green
Bletchingdon
Shipton-on-Cherwell
Hampton Poyle
Thrupp
Kidlington
Begbroke
Gosford
Yarnton
Wytham
Wolvercote
Summertown
Marston
Headington
Botley
Cumnor
North Hinksey
South Hinksey
Chawley
Wootton
Boars Hill
Bayworth
Foxcombe Hill
Sunningwell
Kennington
Littlemore
Cowley
Iffley
Sandford-on-Thames
Radley
Nuneham Courtenay
Marsh Baldon
Toot Baldon
Baldon Row
Chislehampton
Culham
Sutton Courtenay
Appleford
Long Wittenham
Little Wittenham
Clifton Hampden
Burcot
Dorchester
Warborough
Shillingford
Berinsfield
Drayton St Leonard
Milton
Didcot
Northbourne
East Hagbourne
West Hagbourne
Harwell
East Hendred
Ginge
Upton
Chilton
Blewbury
Aston Tirrold
Aston Upthorpe
South Moreton
North Moreton
Cholsey
Wallingford
Crowmarsh Gifford
Benson
Brightwell-cum-Sotwell
Moulsford
South Stoke
North Stoke
Streatley
Goring
Woodcote
Checkendon
Ipsden
Nuffield
Nettlebed
Highmoor Cross
Stoke Row
Rotherfield Peppard
Rotherfield Greys
Sonning Common
Kidmore End
Caversham
Henley-on-Thames
Remenham
Shiplake
Wargrave
Twyford
Sonning
Woodley
Earley
Winnersh
Tilehurst
Theale
Pangbourne
Whitchurch-on-Thames
Mapledurham
Purley on Thames
Upper Basildon
Basildon
Compton
West Ilsley
East Ilsley
Aldworth
Ashampstead
Hampstead Norreys
Yattendon
Hermitage
Chieveley
Frilsham
Bradfield
Bucklebury
Southend
Burghfield
Burghfield Common
Spencers Wood
Shinfield
Arborfield
Three Mile Cross
Grazeley
Sulhamstead
Bicester
Chesterton
Wendlebury
Ambrosden
Merton
Blackthorn
Launton
Marsh Gibbon
Edgcott
Grendon Underwood
Calvert
Botolph Claydon
North Marston
Oving
Whitchurch
Aston Abbotts
Quainton
Pitchcott
Hardwick
Weedon
Kingswood
Woodham
Waddesdon
Westcott
Wotton Underwood
Ludgershall
Piddington
Upper Arncott
Lower Arncott
Boarstall
Brill
Dorton
Ashendon
Upper Winchendon
Nether Winchendon
Cuddington
Chearsley
Long Crendon
Shabbington
Ickford
Worminghall
Waterperry
Waterstock
Tiddington
Thame
Moreton
Towersey
Haddenham
Stone
Hartwell
Bishopstone
Stoke Mandeville
Bierton
Dinton
Kingsey
Aston Sandford
Owlswick
Longwick
Ilmer
Princes Risborough
Monks Risborough
Bledlow
Chinnor
Kingston Blount
Aston Rowant
Lewknor
Postcombe
Tetsworth
Stokenchurch
Watlington
Christmas Common
Ibstone
Turville
Fingest
Stonor
Hambleden
Medmenham
Hurley
Marlow
Wheatley
Holton
Forest Hill
Stanton St John
Elsfield
Beckley
Woodeaton
Noke
Islip
Oddington
Charlton-on-Otmoor
Murcott
Horton-cum-Studley
Oakley
Horspath
Garsington
Cuddesdon
Denton
Great Milton
Little Milton
Great Haseley
Little Haseley
Stadhampton
Chalgrove
Newington
Brightwell Baldwin
Cuxham
Pyrton
Shirburn
Berrick Salome
Ewelme
Britwell Salome
Swyncombe
Cookley Green
Russell's Water
Maidensgrove
Pishill
Northend
Wokingham
Binfield
Hurst
Ruscombe
Lower Earley
Barkham
Finchampstead
Calcot
Sulham
Tidmarsh
Englefield
Upper Bucklebury
Cold Ash
Curridge
Beedon
Stanmore
Pasemore
World's End

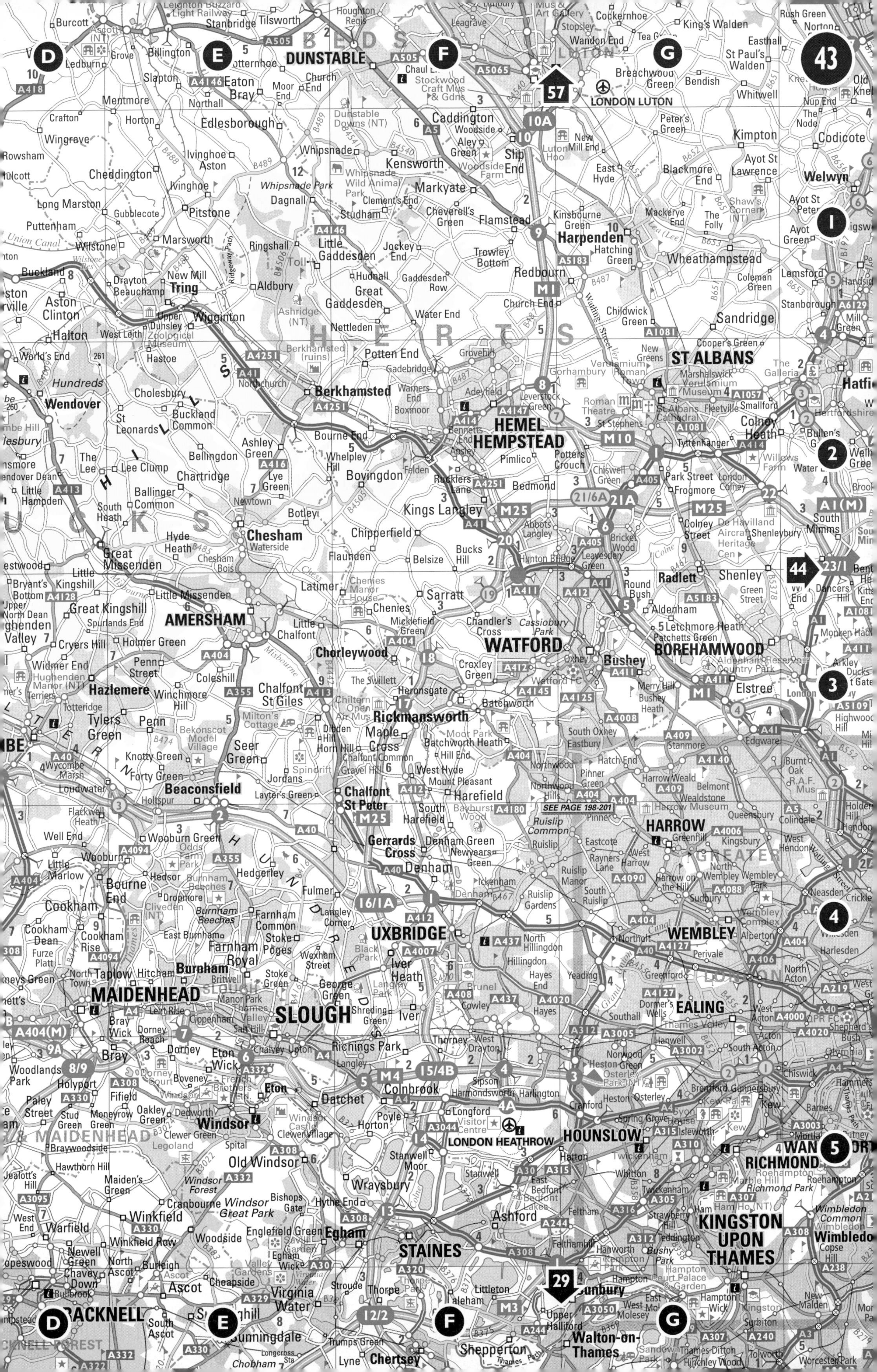

43
57
44
29
D
E
F
G
1
2
3
4
5
BEDS
HERTS
BUCKS
CHILTERN HILLS
BURNHAM BEECHES
GREATER LONDON
DUNSTABLE
LUTON
LONDON LUTON
Leighton Buzzard Light Railway
Burcott
Ascott (NT)
Stanbridge
Tilsworth
Houghton Regis
Leagrave
Stopsley
Cockernhoe
King's Walden
Rush Green
Norton
Ledburn
Grove
Billington
Totternhoe
Wandon End
Tea Green
Easthall
St Paul's Walden
Slapton
Eaton Bray
Moor End
Church End
Chaul End
Stockwood Craft Mus & Gdns
Breachwood Green
Bendish
Whitwell
Mentmore
Northall
Nup End
Crafton
Horton
Edlesborough
Dunstable Downs (NT)
Caddington
Woodside
Aley Green
Slip End
Luton Hoo
New Mill End
Peter's Green
Kimpton
Codicote
Wingrave
Rowsham
Mulcott
Cheddington
Ivinghoe Aston
Whipsnade
Kensworth
Woodside Farm
East Hyde
Blackmore End
Ayot St Lawrence
Welwyn
Ivinghoe
Whipsnade Park
Whipsnade Wild Animal Park
Markyate
Long Marston
Dagnall
Clement's End
Studham
Cheverell's Green
Flamstead
Kinsbourne Green
Mackerye End
The Folly
Shaw's Corner (NT)
Ayot St Peter
Ayot Green
Puttenham
Gubblecote
Pitstone
Marsworth
Harpenden
Hatching Green
Wheathampstead
Union Canal
Wilstone
Ringshall
Little Gaddesden
Jockey End
Trowley Bottom
Lemsford
Buckland
Drayton Beauchamp
New Mill
Tring
Aldbury
Toll
Hudnall
Gaddesden Row
Redbourn
Coleman Green
Aston Clinton
Great Gaddesden
Church End
Stanborough
Halton
West Leith
Upper Dunsley
Wigginton
Zoological Museum
Ashridge (NT)
Nettleden
Water End
Childwick Green
Sandridge
Mill Green
World's End
Hastoe
Berkhamsted (ruins)
Potten End
Gadebridge
Grovehill
New Greens
Verulamium Roman Town
ST ALBANS
Cooper's Green
The Galleria
Hundreds
Northchurch
Gorhambury
Marshalswick
Verulamium Museum
Hatfield
Wendover
Cholesbury
Berkhamsted
Warners End
Boxmoor
Adeyfield
Leverstock Green
Roman Theatre
St Albans Cathedral
Fleetville
Smallford
Hertfordshire
St Leonards
Buckland Common
HEMEL HEMPSTEAD
St Stephens
Colney Heath
Bullen's Green
Ashley Green
Bourne End
Bennetts End
Apsley
Pimlico
Potters Crouch
Tyttenhanger
Bellingdon
Whelpley Hill
Felden
Chiswell Green
Willows Farm
Welham Green
The Lee
Lee Clump
Chartridge
Lye Green
Bovingdon
Rucklers Lane
Bedmond
Park Street
London Colney
Water End
Little Hampden
Ballinger Common
Newtown
Kings Langley
Frogmore
South Heath
Botley
Abbots Langley
Bricket Wood
Colney Street
De Havilland Aircraft Heritage Cen
Shenleybury
South Mimms
Hyde Heath
Chesham
Waterside
Chipperfield
Great Missenden
Chesham Bois
Flaunden
Belsize
Bucks Hill
Hunton Bridge
Leavesden Green
Radlett
Shenley
Little Kingshill
Latimer
Chenies Manor House
Sarratt
Round Bush
Green Street
Dancers Hill
Bryant's Bottom
Little Missenden
Chenies
Aldenham
Great Kingshill
Spurlands End
AMERSHAM
Mickiefield Green
Chandler's Cross
Cassiobury Park
Letchmore Heath
Patchetts Green
Monken Hadley
Little Chalfont
Chorleywood
WATFORD
BOREHAMWOOD
Holmer Green
Cryers Hill
Penn Street
Coleshill
Croxley Green
Bushey
Aldenham Reservoir Country Park
Arkley
Widmer End
Hughenden Manor (NT)
Hazlemere
Winchmore Hill
Chalfont St Giles
The Swillett
Heronsgate
Watford FC
Merry Hill
Bushey Heath
Elstree
Totteridge
Tylers Green
Penn
Milton's Cottage
Chiltern Open Air Mus
Rickmansworth
Batchworth
South Oxhey
Eastbury
Highwood Hill
Bekonscot Model Village
Seer Green
Dibden
Maple Cross
Moor Park
Batchworth Heath
Stanmore
Edgware
Knotty Green
Horn Hill
Chalfont Common
Hill End
Hatch End
Burnt Oak
Wycombe Marsh
Forty Green
Spindrift
Gravel Hill
West Hyde
Mount Pleasant
Northwood
Pinner Green
Harrow Weald
Belmont
R.A.F. Mus
Loudwater
Beaconsfield
Jordans
Layter's Green
Chalfont St Peter
Harefield
Northwood Hills
Wealdstone
Holtspur
South Harefield
Bayhurst Wood
SEE PAGE 198-201
Harrow Museum
Queensbury
Colindale
Flackwell Heath
Ruislip Common
Pinner
HARROW
Well End
Wooburn Green
Gerrards Cross
Denham Green
Newyears Green
Greenhill
Kingsbury
West Hendon
Little Marlow
Wooburn
Odds Farm Park
Hedgerley
Ruislip
Eastcote
Rayners Lane
West Harrow
North Wembley
Wembley Park
Bourne End
Hedsor
Denham
Ruislip Manor
Harrow on the Hill
Cookham
Dropmore
Fulmer
Ickenham
South Ruislip
Sudbury
Neasden
Cricklewood
Cliveden (NT)
Farnham Common
Langley Corner
Ruislip Gardens
Wembley Complex
Cookham Dean
East Burnham
Stoke Poges
UXBRIDGE
Northolt
WEMBLEY
Alperton
Cookham Rise
Farnham Royal
Wexham Street
Black Park
North Hillingdon
Canal
Willesden
Harlesden
Furze Platt
Hillingdon
Perivale
Taplow
Hitcham
Burnham
Britwell
Stoke Green
Iver Heath
Hayes End
Yeading
Greenford
North Acton
Maidenhead
North Town
Langley Park
Brunel
Grand Union Canal
Dormer's Wells
EALING
West Acton
George Green
Cowley
Hayes
Southall
Manor Park
Shredding Green
Thames Valley
QPR FC
Shepherd's Bush
Bray Wick
Lent Rise
Cippenham
Salt Hill
SLOUGH
Iver
Thorney
West Drayton
Hanwell
Acton
South Acton
Dorney Reach
Dorney
Chalvey
Upton
Richings Park
Norwood Green
Heston Green
Osterley Park (NT)
Olympia
Bray
Woodlands Park
Eton Wick
Langley
Sipson
Chiswick
Dorney Court
Boveney
Colnbrook
Harmondsworth
Harlington
Heston
Osterley
Brentford
Gunnersbury
Hammersmith
Holyport
Fifield
Windsor
French Brothers Ltd
Eton
Datchet
Cranford
Spring Grove
Syon House
Kew
Barnes
Paley Street
Oakley Green
Dedworth
Poyle
Longford
Isleworth
Stud Green
Moneyrow Green
Windsor Castle
Clewer Village
Horton
Visitor Centre
LONDON HEATHROW
HOUNSLOW
Putney
Windsor & Maidenhead
Braywoodside
Clewer Green
Legoland
Spital
Stanwell Moor
Hatton
Twickenham
WANDSWORTH
RICHMOND
Roehampton
Hawthorn Hill
Old Windsor
Stanwell
East Bedfont
Bedfont Lakes
Whitton
Marble Hill
Richmond Park
Jealott's Hill
Maiden's Green
Windsor Forest
Wraysbury
Feltham
Ham
Ham Ho (NT)
Wimbledon Common
Cranbourne
Windsor Great Park
Bishops Gate
Hythe End
Ashford
Strawberry Hill
KINGSTON UPON THAMES
Wimbledon
West End
Warfield
Winkfield
Englefield Green
Egham
Teddington
Copse Hill
Winkfield Row
Woodside
Savill Garden
STAINES
Hanworth
Kempton Park
Bushy Park
Newell Green
North Ascot
Egham Wick
Valley Gardens
Virginia Water
Feltham Hill
Hampton Court Palace & Garden
New Malden
Popeswood
Chavey Down
Burleigh
Ascot
Cheapside
Stroude
Thorpe
Thorpe Park
Littleton
Sunbury
Hampton
Hampton Wick
Kingston
Bullbrook
BRACKNELL
Sunninghill
South Ascot
Sunningdale
Trumps Green
Laleham
Upper Halliford
West Molesey
East Molesey
Surbiton
Easthampstead
Bracknell Forest
Chobham
Longcross
Lyne
Chertsey
Shepperton
Walton-on-Thames
Sandown Park
Thames Ditton
Hinchley Wood
Tolworth
Worcester Park
Thames Path
M1
M3
M4
M10
M25
A1(M)
A5
A41
A404(M)
10A
21/6A
21A
16/1A
15/4B
12/2
23/1
8/9
9A

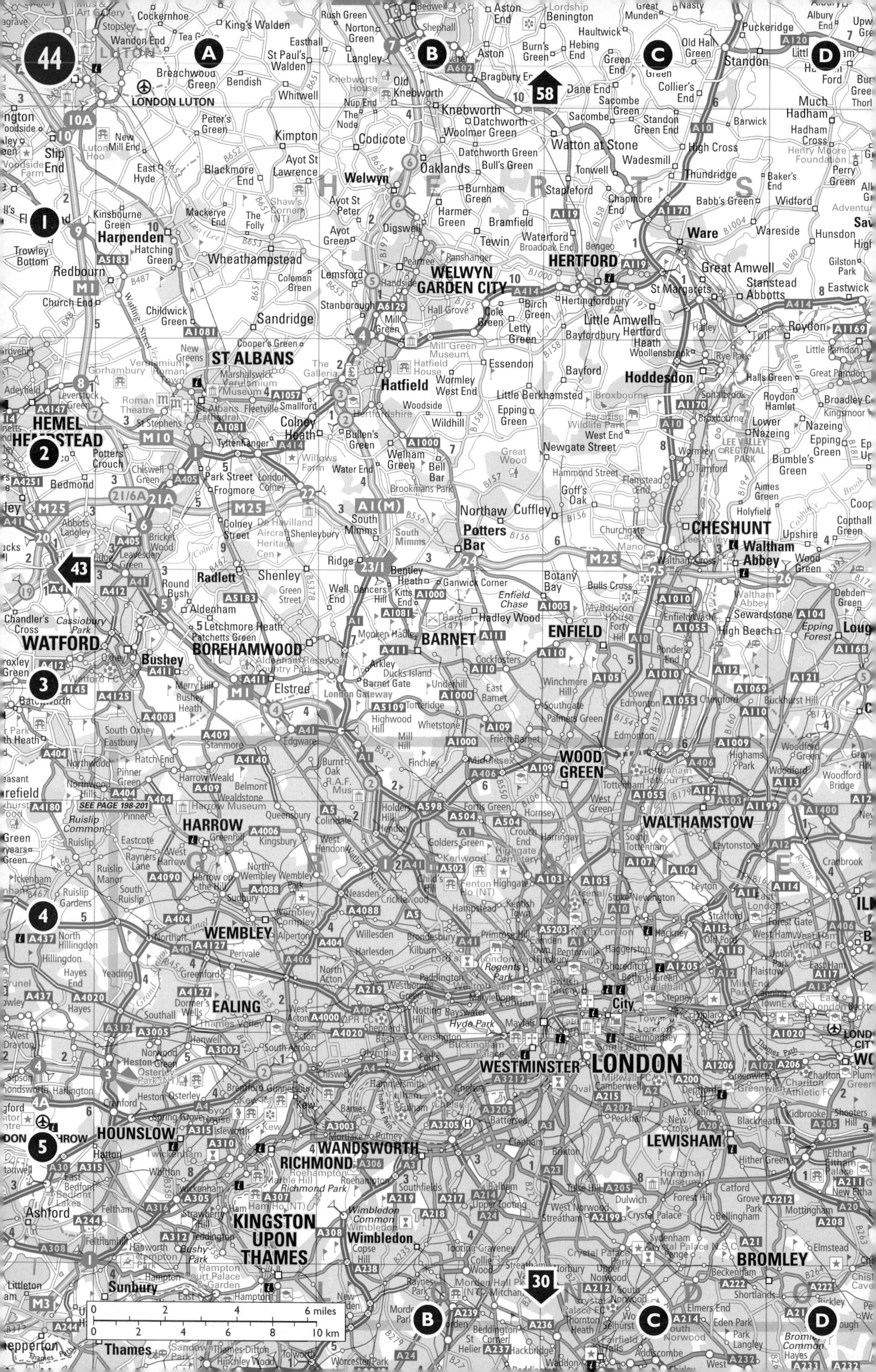

44
A
B
C
D
58
43
30
SEE PAGE 198-201
LUTON
LONDON LUTON
Cockernhoe
Stopsley
Wandon End
Tea Green
King's Walden
Breachwood Green
Bendish
Rush Green
Norton Green
Easthall
St Paul's Walden
Langley
Whitwell
Bedwell
Shephall
Aston End
Aston
Lordship
Benington
Great Munden
Hebing End
Burn's Green
Haultwick
Old Hall Green
Puckeridge
Standon
Albury End
Hadham Ford
Much Hadham
Hadham Cross
Henry Moore Foundation
Perry Green
Knebworth
Knebworth House
Old Knebworth
Bragbury End
Dane End
Sacombe
Sacombe Green
Standon Green End
Collier's End
Barwick
High Cross
Thundridge
Baker's End
Widford
Babb's Green
Wadesmill
Tonwell
Chapmore End
Watton at Stone
Datchworth
Datchworth Green
Bull's Green
Woolmer Green
Codicote
Kimpton
Peter's Green
New Mill End
Slip End
Luton Hoo
Woodside Farm
East Hyde
Blackmore End
Ayot St Lawrence
Welwyn
Oaklands
Ayot St Peter
Ayot Green
Shaw's Corner (NT)
Mackerye End
The Folly
Kinsbourne Green
Harpenden
Hatching Green
Wheathampstead
Trowley Bottom
Redbourn
Coleman Green
Digswell
Harmer Green
Burnham Green
Bramfield
Tewin
Stapleford
Waterford
Broadoak End
Bengeo
HERTFORD
Ware
Wareside
Hunsdon
Great Amwell
Gilston Park
Stanstead Abbotts
Eastwick
St Margarets
Roydon
Little Amwell
Hertingfordbury
Hertford Heath
Bayfordbury
Woollensbrook
Rye Park
Little Parndon
Great Parndon
Halls Green
Hoddesdon
Roydon Hamlet
Broadley Common
Nazeing
Lower Nazeing
Kingsmoor
Epping Green
Spitalbrook
Broxbourne
LEE VALLEY REGIONAL PARK
Bumble's Green
Turnford
Wormley
Aimes Green
Holyfield
Cheshunt
Upshire
Copthall Green
Waltham Abbey
Wood Green
Waltham Cross
Debden Green
Sewardstone
High Beach
Epping Forest
Loughton
Welwyn Garden City
Panshanger
Peartree
Handside
Lemsford
Stanborough
Hall Grove
Cole Green
Birch Green
Letty Green
Mill Green
Mill Green Museum
Hatfield
Hatfield House
Essendon
Wormley West End
Bayford
Little Berkhamsted
Epping Green
Paradise Wildlife Park
West End
Newgate Street
Great Wood
Hammond Street
Flamstead End
Goff's Oak
Churchgate
Northaw
Cuffley
Potters Bar
Botany Bay
Bulls Cross
Enfield Chase
Myddelton House
Forty Hill
Enfield Wash
Waltham Abbey
Enfield
Ponders End
Hadley Wood
Barnet
Cockfosters
Winchmore Hill
Lower Edmonton
Edmonton
Chingford
Buckhurst Hill
East Barnet
Southgate
Palmers Green
Friern Barnet
Woodford Green
Woodford
Woodford Bridge
Highams Park
Sandridge
Childwick Green
Church End
New Greens
Cooper's Green
ST ALBANS
Gorhambury
Verulamium Roman Town
Marshalswick
Verulamium Museum
Roman Theatre
St Albans Cathedral
Fleetville
Smallford
St Stephens
Tyttenhanger
Colney Heath
Welham Green
Bell Bar
Brookmans Park
Water End
Bullen's Green
Wildhill
Woodside
Hertfordshire
The Galleria
Leverstock Green
Adeyfield
HEMEL HEMPSTEAD
Potters Crouch
Bedmond
Chiswell Green
Park Street
Frogmore
London Colney
Willows Farm
Abbots Langley
Bricket Wood
Leavesden Green
Colney Street
De Havilland Aircraft Heritage Cen
Shenleybury
South Mimms
Ridge
Radlett
Shenley
Green Street
Round Bush
Aldenham
Letchmore Heath
Patchetts Green
Well End
Dancers Hill
Bentley Heath
Kitts End
Ganwick Corner
Monken Hadley
Arkley
Ducks Island
Barnet Gate
Underhill
London Gateway
Chandler's Cross
Cassiobury Park
WATFORD
Croxley Green
Oxhey
Watford FC
Bushey
Merry Hill
Bushey Heath
Borehamwood
Aldenham Reservoir Country Park
Elstree
Batchworth
South Oxhey
Eastbury
Northwood
Hatch End
Stanmore
Edgware
Totteridge
Highwood Hill
Mill Hill
Whetstone
Burnt Oak
R.A.F. Mus
Finchley
Middlesex
Wood Green
Tottenham
Tottenham Hotspur FC
West Green
Walthamstow
Pinner
Pinner Green
Harrow Weald
Belmont
Wealdstone
Harrow Museum
Northwood Hills
Ruislip Common
Ruislip
Harefield
Eastcote
HARROW
Greenhill
Kenton
Queensbury
Kingsbury
Colindale
Hendon
West Hendon
Golders Green
Fortis Green
Hornsey
Crouch End
Harringay
Highgate
Highgate Cemetery
South Tottenham
Leytonstone
Leyton
Cranbrook
Rayners Lane
West Harrow
Ruislip Manor
South Ruislip
Ruislip Gardens
Ickenham
Harrow on the Hill
North Wembley
Wembley Park
Sudbury
Wembley Complex
Neasden
Cricklewood
Child's Hill
Kenwood
Fenton Ho (NT)
Hampstead
Kentish Town
Arsenal FC
Stoke Newington
Hackney
Stratford
Forest Gate
West Ham
West Ham United FC
Upton Park
East Ham
Plaistow
WEMBLEY
Alperton
Northolt
North Hillingdon
Hillingdon
Hayes End
Hayes
Yeading
Perivale
Greenford
Willesden
Harlesden
Brondesbury
Kilburn
Primrose Hill
Camden Town
Pentonville
Finsbury
Haggerston
Shoreditch
Bethnal Green
Lord's
London Zoo
Regents Park
North Acton
Westbourne Green
Paddington
Marylebone
British Museum
City
Guildhall
Stepney
Mile End
Poplar
Canning Town
ExCel London
EALING
Dormer's Wells
Southall
Thames Valley
Hanwell
West Acton
Acton
South Acton
QPR FC
Shepherd's Bush
Notting Hill
Bayswater
Kensington
Hyde Park
Mayfair
Buckingham Palace
Westminster
LONDON
Tower of London
Bermondsey
South Bank
LONDON CITY
West Drayton
Norwood Green
Heston
Osterley Park (NT)
Harlington
Cranford
Osterley
Brentford
Gunnersbury
Kew
Chiswick
Olympia
Earl's Court
Hammersmith
Fulham
Chelsea
Chelsea FC
Battersea
Barnes
Mortlake
Putney
Camberwell
Millwall FC
Oval
Peckham
Deptford
Greenwich
Charlton
Charlton Athletic FC
Kidbrooke
Shooters Hill
Blackheath
New Cross
St John's
LEWISHAM
Hither Green
Eltham
Eltham Palace
New Eltham
HOUNSLOW
Spring Grove
Syon House
Isleworth
Heathrow
Hatton
Twickenham
Whitton
Richmond
Richmond Park
Roehampton
WANDSWORTH
Clapham
Brixton
Southfields
Balham
Upper Tooting
Tulse Hill
Dulwich
Horniman Museum
Forest Hill
Catford
Grove Park
Mottingham
Bellingham
East Bedfont
Bedfont Lakes
Ashford
Feltham
Hanworth
Strawberry Hill
Teddington
Ham
Ham Ho (NT)
Marble Hill
KINGSTON UPON THAMES
Wimbledon Common
Wimbledon
Copse Hill
Tooting Graveney
Collier's Wood
West Norwood
Streatham
Crystal Palace
Sydenham
Crystal Palace N.S.C.
Penge
Beckenham
BROMLEY
Elmstead
Shortlands
Bickley
Feltham Hill
Bushy Park
Hampton Court Palace & Garden
Hampton
Sunbury
Littleton
Morden Hall Park (NT)
Mitcham
Norbury
Upper Norwood
South Norwood
Crystal Palace FC
Thornton Heath
Selhurst
Elmers End
Eden Park
Park Langley
Bromley Common
Hayes
Morden
Beddington Corner
St Helier
Hackbridge
Addiscombe
Fairfield Halls
Thames Ditton
Hinchley Wood
Sandown Park
Tolworth
Worcester Park
Shepperton
Thames
Thames Path
0 2 4 6 miles
0 2 4 6 8 10 km

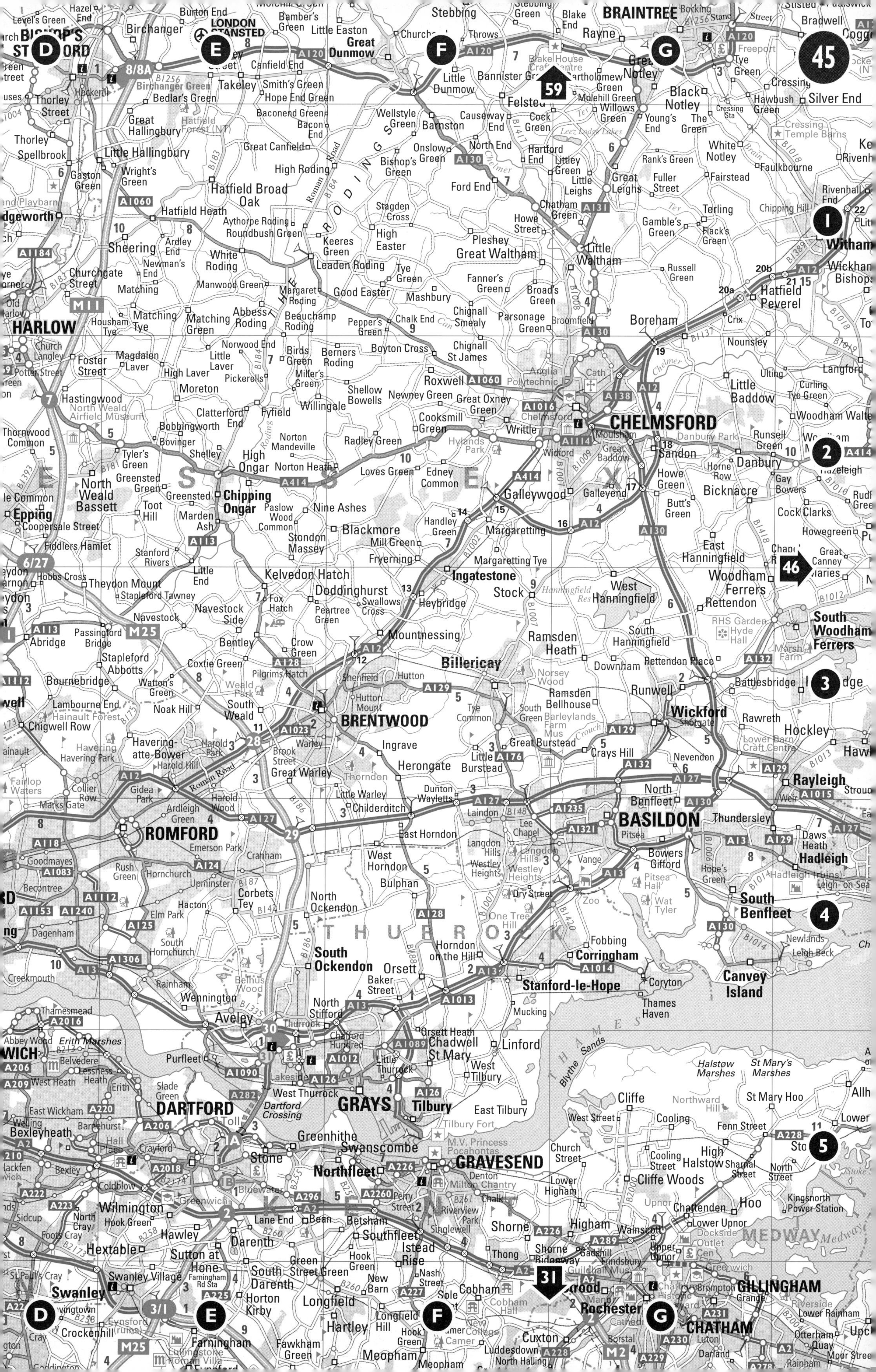

45
46
59
31
BISHOP'S STORTFORD
LONDON STANSTED
Great Dunmow
Stebbing
BRAINTREE
Rayne
Great Notley
Bradwell
Silver End
Cressing
Black Notley
Witham
Hatfield Peverel
Boreham
Felsted
Takeley
Hatfield Broad Oak
Little Hallingbury
Sheering
HARLOW
Matching Tye
High Roding
Leaden Roding
Great Waltham
Little Waltham
Pleshey
Writtle
CHELMSFORD
Great Baddow
Danbury
Sandon
Galleywood
Margaretting
Ingatestone
Chipping Ongar
North Weald Bassett
Epping
Theydon Mount
Kelvedon Hatch
Doddinghurst
Mountnessing
Billericay
Stock
West Hanningfield
South Woodham Ferrers
Woodham Ferrers
Wickford
Runwell
Battlesbridge
Hockley
Rayleigh
BRENTWOOD
Shenfield
Ingrave
Herongate
Abridge
Chigwell Row
Havering-atte-Bower
Harold Wood
ROMFORD
Hornchurch
Upminster
Rainham
Dagenham
BASILDON
Laindon
Pitsea
Thundersley
Hadleigh
South Benfleet
Canvey Island
Leigh-on-Sea
Corringham
Stanford-le-Hope
Coryton
Thames Haven
Orsett
South Ockendon
Aveley
Purfleet
GRAYS
Tilbury
Chadwell St Mary
East Tilbury
DARTFORD
Dartford Crossing
Greenhithe
Swanscombe
Northfleet
GRAVESEND
Stone
Wilmington
Hextable
Swanley
Farningham
Longfield
Hartley
Meopham
Cobham
Shorne
Higham
Cliffe
Cliffe Woods
High Halstow
Hoo
Strood
Rochester
CHATHAM
GILLINGHAM
Cuxton
MEDWAY
THURROCK
ESSEX
KENT
THAMES
M11
M25
M2
A12
A127
A13
A130
A120
A414
A128
A2
D
E
F
G
1
2
3
4
5

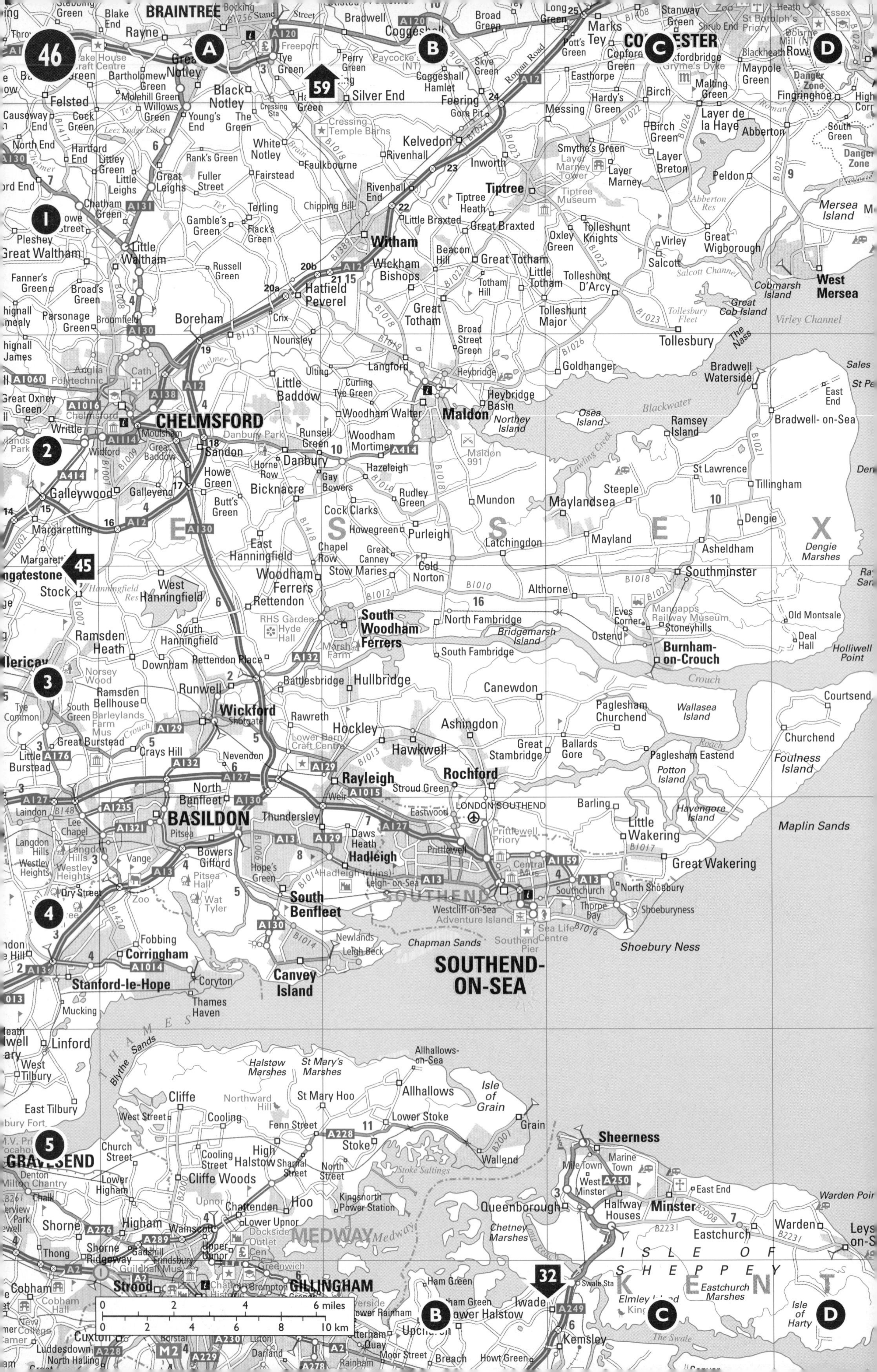
46
A
B
C
D
59
45
32
1
2
3
4
5
BRAINTREE
Bocking
Rayne
Great Notley
Black Notley
Felsted
Bradwell
Coggeshall
Coggeshall Hamlet
Perry Green
Silver End
Cressing Temple Barns
Feering
Kelvedon
Rivenhall
Faulkbourne
Marks Tey
COLCHESTER
Copford Green
Stanway Green
Easthorpe
Messing
Birch
Birch Green
Layer Breton
Layer de la Haye
Abberton
Fingringhoe
Peldon
Mersea Island
West Mersea
Tiptree
Tiptree Heath
Inworth
Layer Marney
Tolleshunt Knights
Tolleshunt D'Arcy
Tolleshunt Major
Salcott
Virley
Great Wigborough
Tollesbury
Goldhanger
Great Totham
Little Totham
Great Braxted
Little Braxted
Witham
Wickham Bishops
Hatfield Peverel
Boreham
Terling
White Notley
Fairstead
Great Leighs
Little Leighs
Great Waltham
Little Waltham
Pleshey
Broomfield
CHELMSFORD
Writtle
Widford
Galleywood
Margaretting
Ingatestone
Stock
Great Baddow
Sandon
Danbury
Little Baddow
Ulting
Langford
Heybridge
Heybridge Basin
Maldon
Northey Island
Osea Island
Blackwater
Bradwell Waterside
Bradwell-on-Sea
Ramsey Island
St Lawrence
Tillingham
Steeple
Maylandsea
Mayland
Dengie
Asheldham
Dengie Marshes
Southminster
Althorne
Latchingdon
Mundon
Purleigh
Cold Norton
Stow Maries
Woodham Walter
Woodham Mortimer
Hazeleigh
Bicknacre
East Hanningfield
West Hanningfield
South Hanningfield
Woodham Ferrers
Rettendon
South Woodham Ferrers
North Fambridge
South Fambridge
Burnham-on-Crouch
Mangapps Railway Museum
Ostend
Old Montsale
Holliwell Point
Crouch
Canewdon
Hullbridge
Battlesbridge
Wickford
Runwell
Ramsden Heath
Billericay
Great Burstead
Crays Hill
Rawreth
Hockley
Hawkwell
Ashingdon
Rayleigh
Rochford
Great Stambridge
Ballards Gore
Paglesham Churchend
Paglesham Eastend
Wallasea Island
Potton Island
Foulness Island
Courtsend
Churchend
Havengore Island
Maplin Sands
Barling
Little Wakering
Great Wakering
North Shoebury
Shoeburyness
Shoebury Ness
LONDON SOUTHEND
Eastwood
Prittlewell
SOUTHEND-ON-SEA
Southchurch
Westcliff-on-Sea
Leigh-on-Sea
Hadleigh
Thundersley
South Benfleet
Canvey Island
Chapman Sands
BASILDON
Pitsea
Vange
Bowers Gifford
Laindon
Langdon Hills
Corringham
Fobbing
Stanford-le-Hope
Coryton
Thames Haven
Mucking
Linford
West Tilbury
East Tilbury
GRAVESEND
THAMES
Cliffe
Cooling
Halstow Marshes
St Mary's Marshes
St Mary Hoo
Allhallows-on-Sea
Allhallows
Isle of Grain
Grain
Lower Stoke
Stoke
High Halstow
Cliffe Woods
Hoo
Chattenden
Kingsnorth Power Station
MEDWAY
Higham
Shorne
Strood
GILLINGHAM
Chatham
Rainham
Upchurch
Iwade
Kemsley
Sheerness
Queenborough
Minster
Eastchurch
Warden
ISLE OF SHEPPEY
KENT
The Swale
ESSEX
0 2 4 6 miles
0 2 4 6 8 10 km

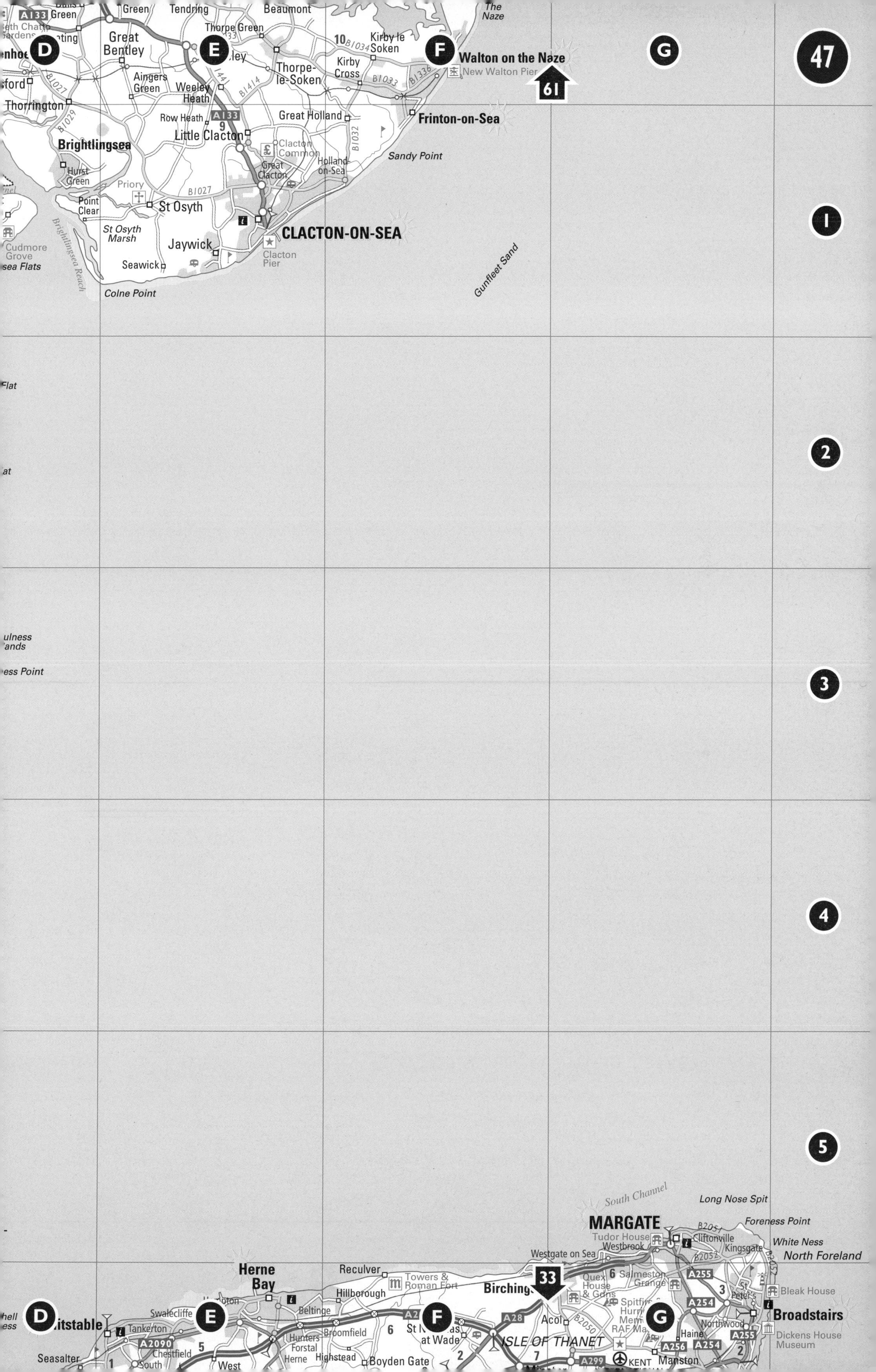

D | **E** | **F** Walton on the Naze | **G** | **47**

Green Tendring Beaumont

The Naze

Thorpe Green

Green 10 B1034 Kirby le Soken

Great Bentley E ley Kirby Cross

th Cha ardens ting Aingers Green Thorpe-le-Soken B1414 F Walton on the Naze

New Walton Pier

nhoe Weeley Heath B1033 B1336

Thorrington ford Row Heath A133 Great Holland **61**

9 Frinton-on-Sea

B1027 Little Clacton

Brightlingsea Clacton Common B1032 Sandy Point

Priory Great Clacton Holland-on-Sea

Point Clear B1027 St Osyth

Hurst Green

Cudmore Grove St Osyth Marsh CLACTON-ON-SEA **I**

sea Flats Jaywick Clacton Pier

Seawick

Colne Point

Brightlingsea Reach Gunfleet Sand

Flat

at **2**

ulness ands

ess Point **3**

4

5

South Channel Long Nose Spit

Foreness Point

MARGATE White Ness

Tudor House Westbrook Cliftonville North Foreland

Westgate on Sea Kingsgate

Reculver B2051 B2052

Herne Bay Towers & Roman Fort Birchings **33** Quex House & Gdns Salmeston Grange A255 Bleak House

Hillborough St Peter's

Beltinge Spitfire Humr Mem A254

D itstable **E** Hunters Forstal **F** St N las at Wade A28 Acol B2050 RAF Ma **G** Haine Northwood A255 **Broadstairs**

Swalecliffe Broomfield 6 ISLE OF THANET KENT Manston Dickens House Museum

hell ness Tankerton A2090 Chestfield 5 Highstead 7 2 A256 A254 2

Seasalter South West Herne Boyden Gate A299

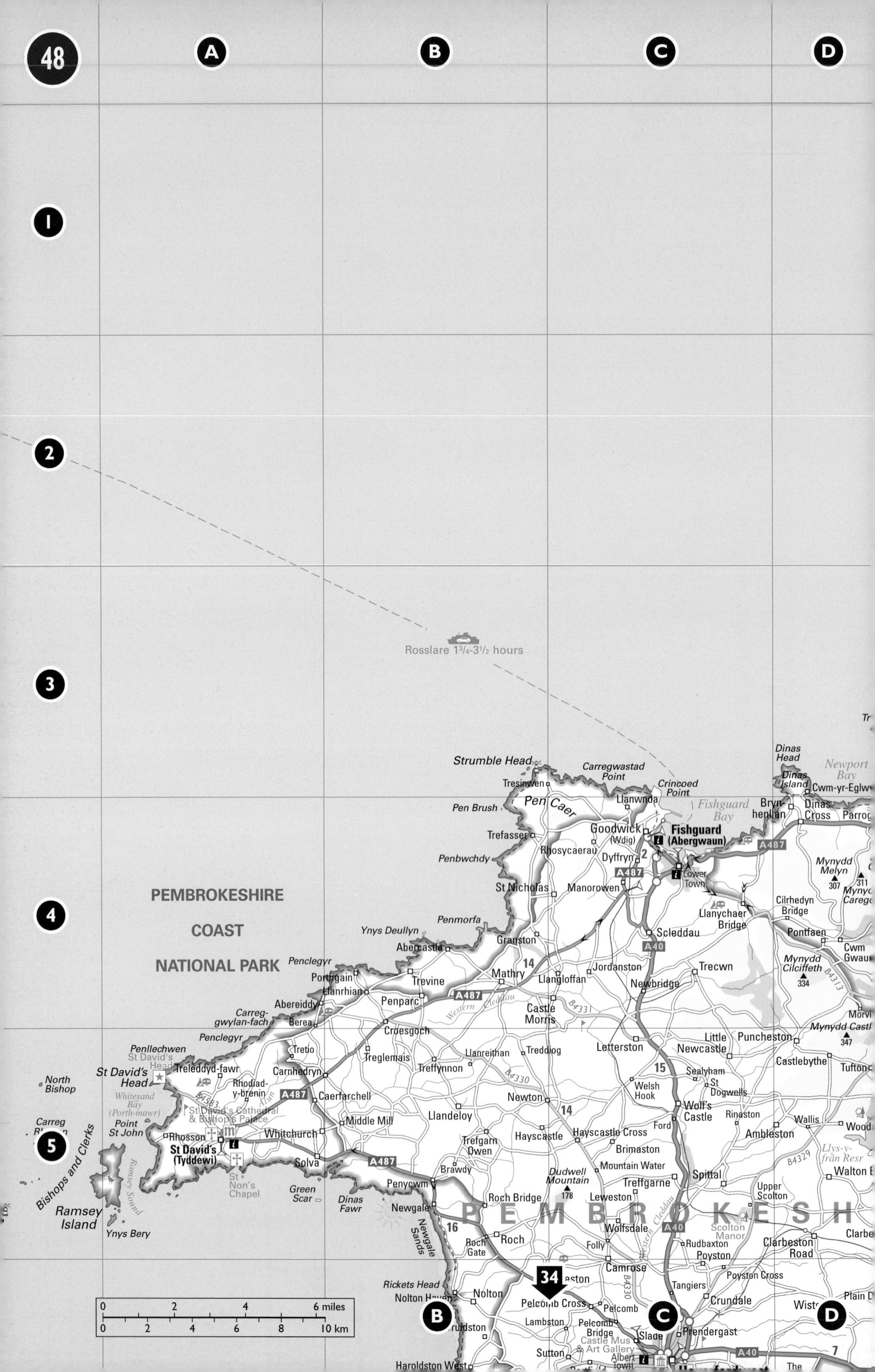
A
B
C
D
1
2
3
4
5
Rosslare 1¾-3½ hours
PEMBROKESHIRE
COAST
NATIONAL PARK
Strumble Head
Carregwastad Point
Crincoed Point
Dinas Head
Newport Bay
Dinas Island
Cwm-yr-Eglwys
Tresinwen
Pen Caer
Pen Brush
Llanwnda
Fishguard Bay
Goodwick (Wdig)
Fishguard (Abergwaun)
Bryn-henllan
Dinas Cross
Parrog
Trefasser
Rhosycaerau
Dyffryn
Penbwchdy
Lower Town
Mynydd Melyn
307
311
St Nicholas
Manorowen
A487
Llanychaer Bridge
Cilrhedyn Bridge
Penmorfa
Ynys Deullyn
Granston
Scleddau
A40
Pontfaen
Abercastle
Cwm Gwaun
Penclegyr
Porthgain
Trevine
Mathry
Llangloffan
Jordanston
Trecwn
Mynydd Cilciffeth
334
Llanrhian
Penparc
Newbridge
B4313
Abereiddy
Castle Morris
B4331
Western Cleddau
Carreg-gwylan-fach
Berea
Croesgoch
Morvil
Mynydd Castlebythe
347
Penclegyr
Little Newcastle
Puncheston
Pencllechwen
St David's Head
Tretio
Llanreithan
Treddiog
Letterston
Castlebythe
St David's Head
Treleddyd-fawr
Treglemais
Treffynnon
15
Sealyham
North Bishop
Rhodiad-y-brenin
Carnhedryn
B4330
Welsh Hook
St Dogwells
Whitesand Bay (Porth-mawr)
B4583
Caerfarchell
Newton
Wolf's Castle
St David's Cathedral & Bishop's Palace
14
Rinaston
Wallis
Carreg
Point St John
Middle Mill
Llandeloy
Ford
Ambleston
Rhosson
Whitchurch
Hayscastle Cross
St David's (Tyddewi)
Hayscastle
Brimaston
Llys-y-frân Resr
Bishops and Clerks
Solva
Trefgarn Owen
B4329
Ramsey Sound
A487
Mountain Water
Spittal
Walton East
St Non's Chapel
Brawdy
Dudwell Mountain
Treffgarne
Green Scar
Dinas Fawr
Penycwm
178
Upper Scolton
Roch Bridge
Leweston
Ramsey Island
Newgale
PEMBROKESH
Newgale Sands
16
Wolfsdale
Scolton Manor
Ynys Bery
Roch Gate
Roch
A40
Rudbaxton
Clarbeston Road
Folly
Poyston
Camrose
Rickets Head
Poyston Cross
34
Tangiers
Nolton Haven
Nolton
B4330
Crundale
Pelcomb Cross
Pelcomb
Wiston
Plain Dealings
Lambston
Pelcomb Bridge
Prendergast
Castle Museum & Art Gallery
Slade
Sutton
A40
Albert Town
7
Haroldston West
The
0 2 4 6 miles
0 2 4 6 8 10 km

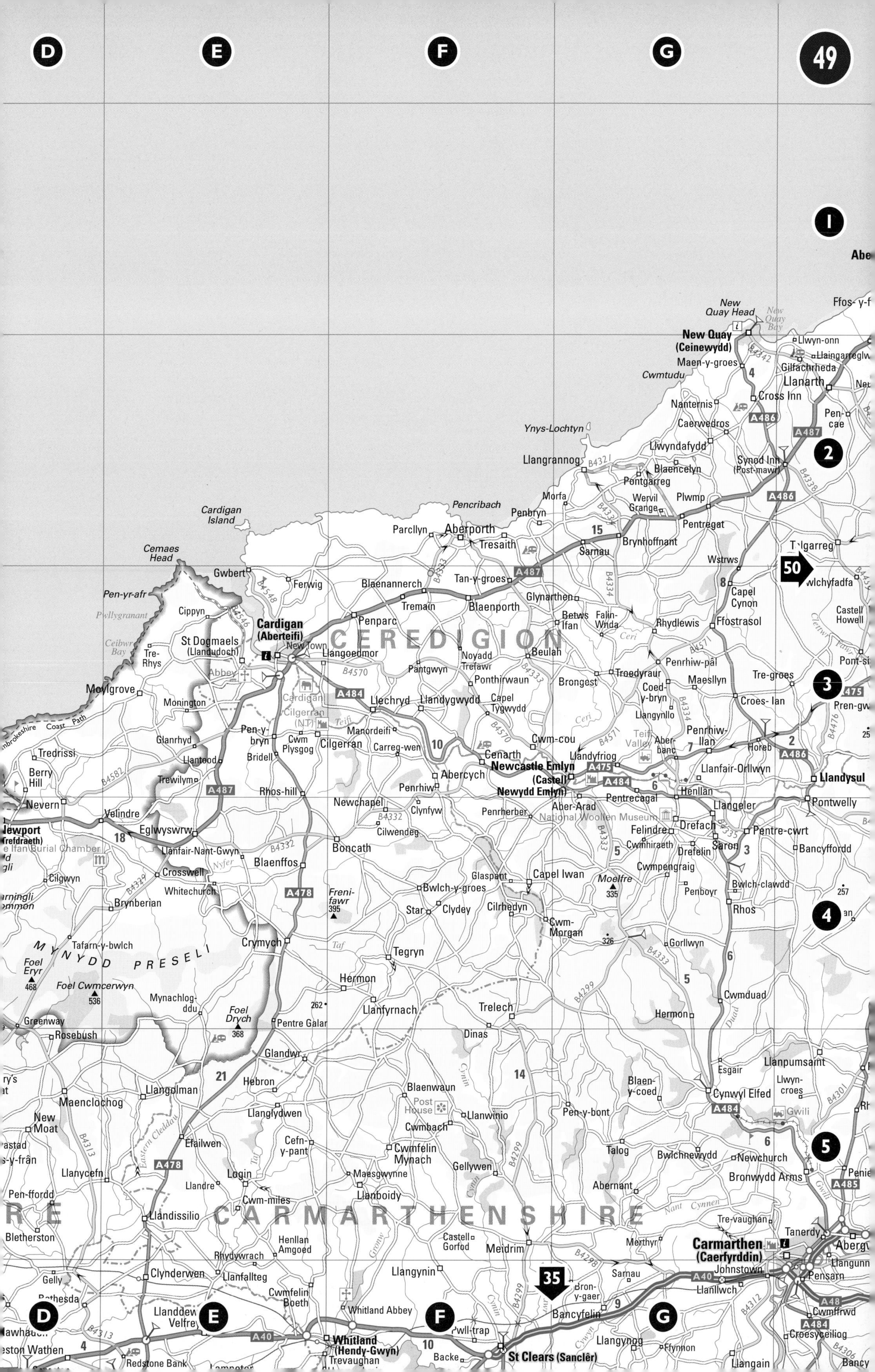

49
D
E
F
G
I
New Quay Head
New Quay Bay
New Quay (Ceinewydd)
Llwyn-onn
Maen-y-groes
Gilfachrheda
Llanarth
Cwmtudu
Cross Inn
Nanternis
A486
Pen-cae
Caerwedros
A487
Ynys-Lochtyn
Llwyndafydd
2
Llangrannog
B4321
Blaencelyn
Synod Inn (Post-mawr)
Pontgarreg
Morfa
Plwmp
Wervil Grange
Pencribach
Penbryn
Pentregat
Cardigan Island
Parcllyn
Aberporth
Tresaith
15
Brynhoffnant
Sarnau
Talgarreg
Cemaes Head
Gwbert
Wstrws
50
Ferwig
Blaenannerch
Tan-y-groes
A487
B4548
B4334
8
Capel Cynon
Pen-yr-afr
Glynarthen
Pwllygranant
Cippyn
Tremain
Blaenporth
Castell Howell
Penparc
Betws Ifan
Falin-Wnda
Rhydlewis
Ffostrasol
Cardigan (Aberteifi)
CEREDIGION
Ceibwr Bay
St Dogmaels (Llandudoch)
New Town
Ceri
Tre-Rhys
Llangoedmor
Noyadd Trefawr
Beulah
Penrhiw-pâl
Abbey
Pantgwyn
B4570
Troedyraur
Tre-groes
Moylgrove
Ponthirwaun
Brongest
Maesllyn
3
Cardigan
A484
Coed-y-bryn
Monington
Llechryd
Llandygwydd
Capel Tygwydd
Croes-lan
Cilgerran (NT)
Teifi
Llangynllo
Pembrokeshire Coast Path
Glanrhyd
Pen-y-bryn
Cwm Plysgog
Cilgerran
Manordeifi
Cwm-cou
Penrhiw-llan
Horeb
2
Tredrissi
Llantood
Bridell
Carreg-wen
10
Cenarth
Teifi Valley
Aber-banc
7
A486
Berry Hill
B4582
Trewilym
Newcastle Emlyn
Llandyfriog
A475
Llanfair-Orllwyn
Llandysul
A487
Rhos-hill
Abercych
(Castell
A484
6
Nevern
Penrhiw
Newydd Emlyn)
Pentrecagal
Henllan
Newchapel
Clynfyw
Aber-Arad
Llangeler
Pontwelly
Velindre
B4332
Penrherber
National Woollen Museum
Eglwyswrw
Felindre
Drefach
Pentre-cwrt
18
Cilwendeg
Cwmhiraeth
Saron
Bancyffordd
Llanfair-Nant-Gwyn
B4332
Boncath
B4333
5
Drefelin
3
Nyfer
Blaenffos
Cwmpengraig
Crosswell
Glaspant
Capel Iwan
Moelfre 335
Bwlch-clawdd
Cilgwyn
257
B4329
Whitechurch
A478
Bwlch-y-groes
Penboyr
Freni-fawr 395
Brynberian
Star
Clydey
Cilrhedyn
Rhos
4
Cwm-Morgan
326
Crymych
Gorllwyn
Tafarn-y-bwlch
Taf
Tegryn
MYNYDD PRESELI
6
Foel Eryr 468
B4333
Foel Cwmcerwyn 536
Hermon
5
Mynachlog-ddu
Foel Drych 368
262
Llanfyrnach
Trelech
B4299
Cwmduad
Greenway
Pentre Galar
Hermon
Rosebush
Dinas
Duad
Glandwr
Esgair
Llanpumsaint
Hebron
21
14
Cynin
Blaen-y-coed
Llwyn-croes
Maenclochog
Llangolman
Blaenwaun
Cynwyl Elfed
Post House
B4301
New Moat
Llanglydwen
Llanwinio
Pen-y-bont
A484
Gwili
Cwmbach
Cefn-y-pant
Cwmfelin Mynach
6
B4313
Efailwen
Talog
5
Eastern Cleddau
Bwlchnewydd
Newchurch
A478
Gellywen
B4299
Llanycefn
Login
Maesgwynne
Bronwydd Arms
A485
Pen-ffordd
Llandre
Abernant
Cwm-miles
Llanboidy
CARMARTHENSHIRE
Nant Cynnen
Llandissilio
Tre-vaughan
Tanerdy
Bletherston
Henllan Amgoed
Castell Gorfod
Meidrim
Merthyr
Carmarthen (Caerfyrddin)
Rhydywrach
Clynderwen
Llangynin
B4298
Sarnau
Johnstown
Pensarn
Llanfallteg
Gelly
Cwmfelin Boeth
35
Bron-y-gaer
A40
Llanllwch
Whitland Abbey
Llanddewi Velfrey
9
B4312
Bancyfelin
Cwmffrwd
A484
B4313
A40
Pwll-trap
Croesyceiliog
Whitland (Hendy-Gwyn)
10
Llangynog
Ffynnon
4
Trevaughan
St Clears (Sancler)
Redstone Bank
Backe
Llangain

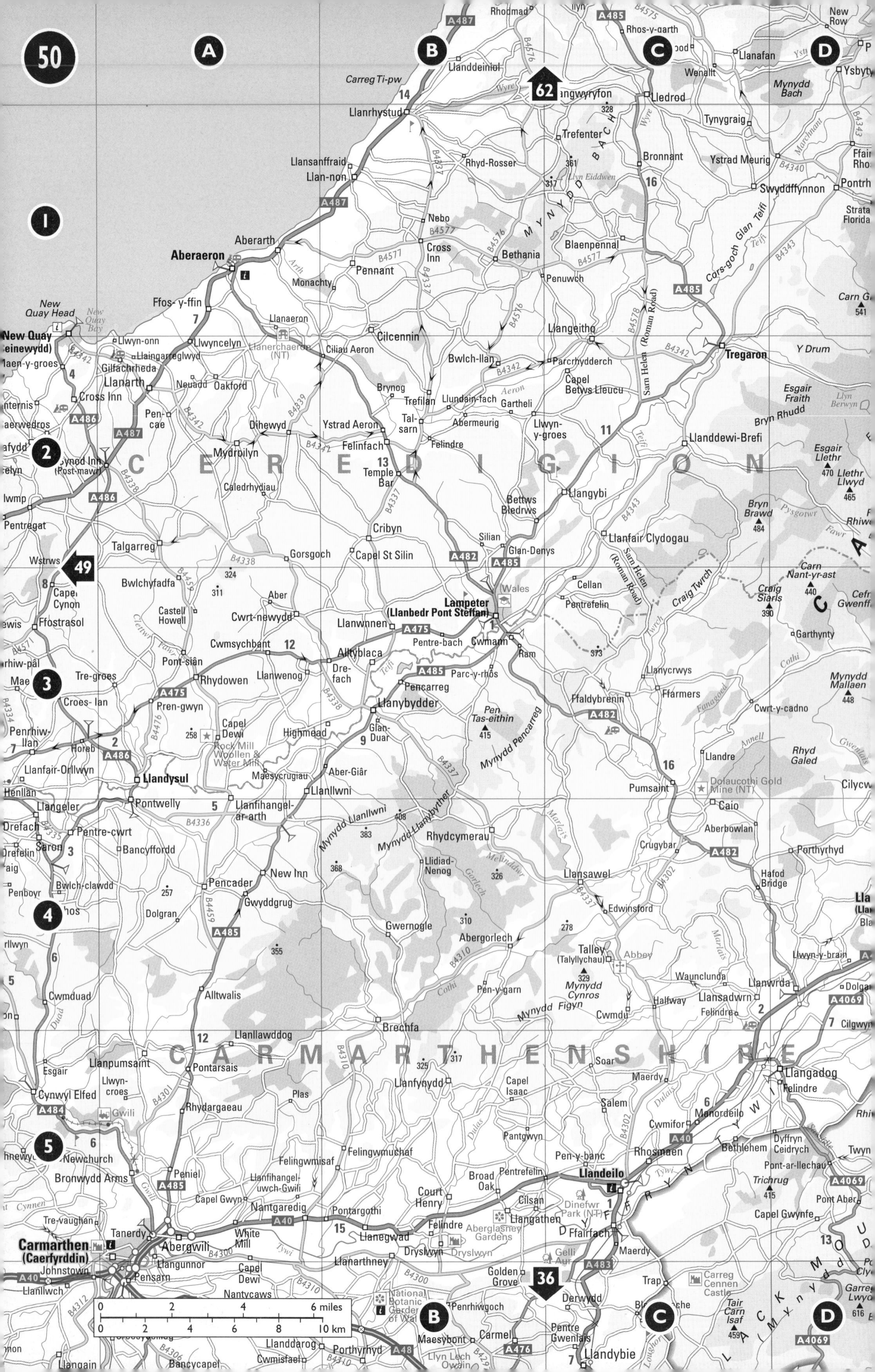
A
B
C
D
1
2
3
4
5
62
49
36
CEREDIGION
CARMARTHENSHIRE
Carreg Ti-pw
Llanddeiniol
Llanrhystud
Llansanffraid
Llan-non
Rhyd-Rosser
Trefenter
Lledrod
Bronnant
Ystrad Meurig
Swyddffynnon
Llanafan
Wenallt
Tynygraig
Mynydd Bach
Ysbyty
Rhos-y-garth
New Row
Strata Florida
Pontrhydfendigaid
Llyn Eiddwen
Nebo
Cross Inn
Aberarth
Aberaeron
Pennant
Monachty
Bethania
Blaenpennal
Penuwch
Cors-goch Glan Teifi
Carn Gron
Ffos-y-ffin
Llanaeron
Llanerchaeron (NT)
Cilcennin
Ciliau Aeron
Llangeitho
Tregaron
Y Drum
New Quay Head
New Quay Bay
New Quay (Ceinewydd)
Llwyn-onn
Llaingarreglwyd
Gilfachrheda
Llanarth
Llwyncelyn
Neuadd
Oakford
Cross Inn
Bwlch-llan
Parcrhydderch
Capel Betws Lleucu
Sarn Helen (Roman Road)
Brynog
Trefilan
Llundain-fach
Gartheli
Talsarn
Abermeurig
Llwyn-y-groes
Esgair Fraith
Llyn Berwyn
Bryn Rhudd
Pen-cae
Dihewyd
Ystrad Aeron
Felinfach
Felindre
Llanddewi-Brefi
Synod Inn (Post-mawr)
Mydroilyn
Temple Bar
Esgair Llethr
Llethr Llwyd
Caledrhydiau
Bettws Bledrws
Llangybi
Bryn Brawd
Pentregat
Talgarreg
Cribyn
Llanfair Clydogau
Wstrws
Gorsgoch
Capel St Silin
Silian
Glan-Denys
Bwlchyfadfa
Carn Nant-yr-ast
Capel Cynon
Castell Howell
Aber
Cwrt-newydd
Llanwnnen
Lampeter (Llanbedr Pont Steffan)
Cellan
Pentrefelin
Craig Twrch
Craig Siarls
Ffostrasol
Cwmsychbant
Pentre-bach
Cwmann
Garthynty
Pont-siân
Alltyblaca
Ram
Rhydowen
Llanwenog
Drefach
Parc-y-rhos
Llanycrwys
Mynydd Mallaen
Tre-groes
Pencarreg
Ffaldybrenin
Ffarmers
Croes-lan
Pren-gwyn
Llanybydder
Cwrt-y-cadno
Penrhiw-llan
Capel Dewi
Highmead
Pen Tas-eithin
Mynydd Pencarreg
Horeb
Glan-Duar
Rock Mill Woollen & Water Mill
Llandre
Rhyd Galed
Llanfair-Orllwyn
Llandysul
Maesycrugiau
Aber-Giâr
Dolaucothi Gold Mine (NT)
Pumsaint
Henllan
Llanllwni
Caio
Llangeler
Pontwelly
Llanfihangel-ar-arth
Mynydd Llanllwni
Mynydd Llanybyther
Rhydcymerau
Aberbowlan
Pentre-cwrt
Saron
Bancyffordd
Crugybar
Porthyrhyd
Llidiad-Nenog
Penboyr
Bwlch-clawdd
Pencader
New Inn
Llansawel
Hafod Bridge
Dolgran
Gwyddgrug
Edwinsford
Gwernogle
Abergorlech
Talley (Talyllychau)
Abbey
Llwyn-y-brain
Mynydd Cynros
Waunclunda
Llanwrda
Pen-y-garn
Alltwalis
Cwmduad
Mynydd Figyn
Halfway
Llansadwrn
Felindre
Cwmdu
Cilgwyn
Brechfa
Llanllawddog
Pontarsais
Soar
Llanpumsaint
Esgair
Llanfynydd
Capel Isaac
Maerdy
Llangadog
Felindre
Llwyn-croes
Cynwyl Elfed
Plas
Rhydargaeau
Salem
Manordeilo
Cwmifor
Gwili
Dyffryn Ceidrych
Bethlehem
Rhosmaen
Newchurch
Felingwmuchaf
Felingwmisaf
Pantgwyn
Pen-y-banc
Pont-ar-llechau
Bronwydd Arms
Peniel
Llanfihangel-uwch-Gwili
Broad Oak
Pentrefelin
Llandeilo
Trichrug
Capel Gwyn
Nantgaredig
Court Henry
Cilsan
Dinefwr Park (NT)
Pont Aber
Capel Gwynfe
Tre-vaughan
Pontargothi
Llangathen
Tanerdy
Felindre
Aberglasney Gardens
Ffairfach
Carmarthen (Caerfyrddin)
Abergwili
White Mill
Llanegwad
Dryslwyn
Gelli Aur
Maerdy
Johnstown
Llangunnor
Llanarthney
Golden Grove
Trap
Carreg Cennen Castle
Llanllwch
Pensarn
Capel Dewi
Nantycaws
National Botanic Garden of Wales
Penrhiwgoch
Derwydd
Tair Carn Isaf
Garreg Lwyd
Maesybont
Carmel
Pentre Gwenlais
Llanddarog
Porthyrhyd
Llandybie
Llyn Llech Owain
Cwmisfael
Bancycapel
Llangain
Black Mountain
Mynydd Du
Cothi
Teifi
Tywi
Aeron
Wyre
Arth
Gwili
Duad
Cynnen
Dulas
Marlais
0 2 4 6 miles
0 2 4 6 8 10 km

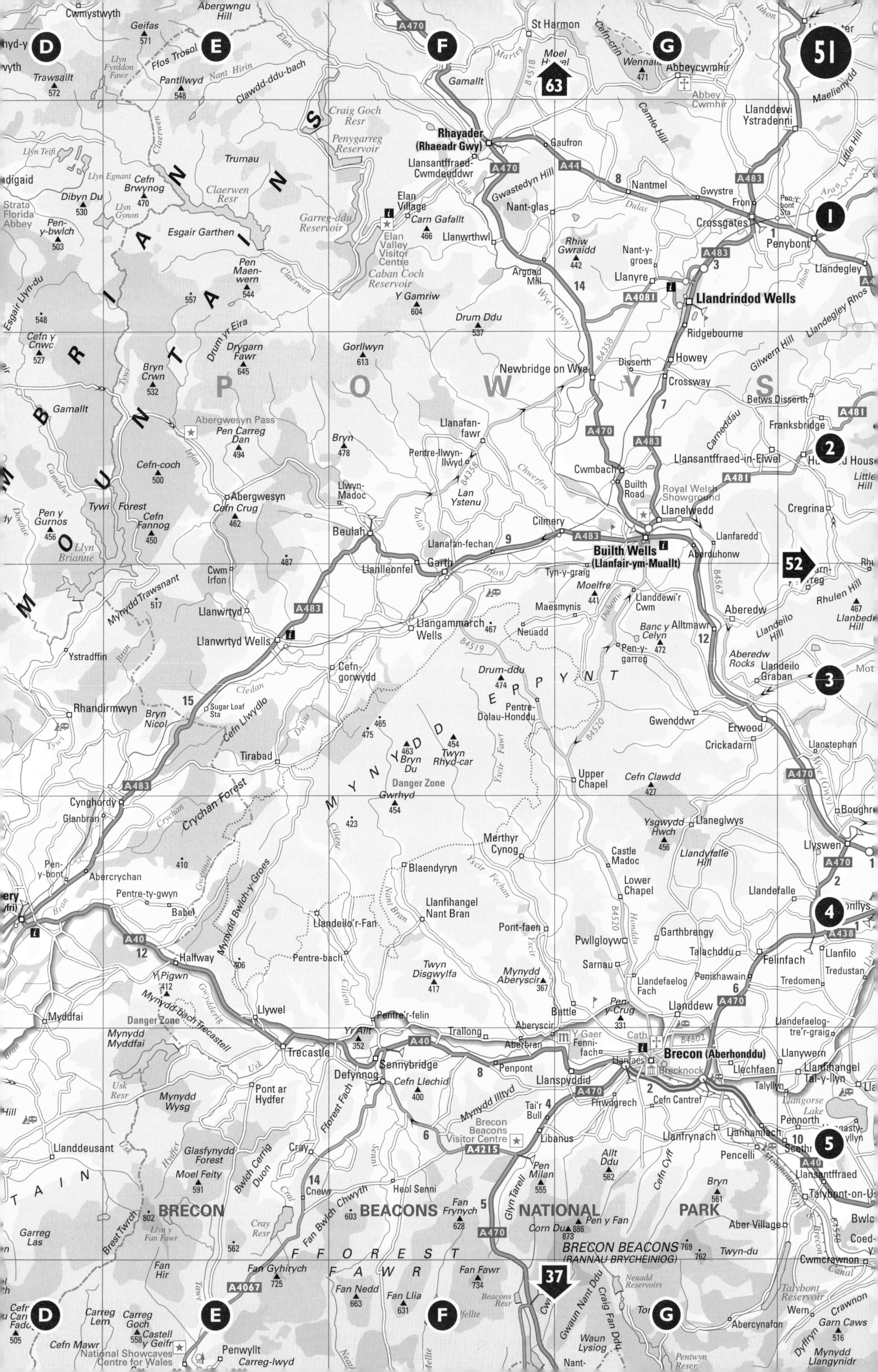
51
52
63
37
D
E
F
G
I
2
3
4
5
Cwmystwyth
Abergwngu Hill
Geifas
571
Ffos Trosol
Elan
St Harmon
A470
Gamallt
Marteg
B4518
Moel Hywel
Cefn-crin
Wennallt
471
Abbeycwmhir
Abbey Cwmhir
Trawsallt
572
Llyn Fyrddon Fawr
Pantllwyd
548
Nant Hirin
Clawdd-ddu-bach
Craig Goch Resr
Rhayader
(Rhaeadr Gwy)
Gaufron
Camlo Hill
Llanddewi Ystradenni
Maelienydd
Llyn Teifi
Claerwen
Trumau
Penygarreg Reservoir
Llansantffraed-Cwmdeuddwr
A44
A483
Little Hill
Llyn Egnant
Cefn Brwynog
470
Claerwen Resr
Gwastedyn Hill
8
Nantmel
Gwystre
Strata Florida Abbey
Dibyn Du
530
Llyn Gynon
Elan Village
Garreg-ddu Reservoir
Dulas
Nant-glas
Fron
Pen-y-bont Sta
Arrow
Pen-y-bwlch
503
Esgair Garthen
Carn Gafallt
466
Llanwrthwl
Crossgates
1
Penybont
Elan Valley Visitor Centre
Rhiw Gwraidd
442
Nant-y-groes
Llandegley
Pen Maen-wern
544
Caban Coch Reservoir
Argoed Mill
14
Llanyre
3
Esgair Llyn-du
557
Y Gamriw
604
A4081
Llandrindod Wells
548
Wye (Gwy)
Ithon
Llandegley Rhos
Drum Ddu
537
Ridgebourne
Cefn y Cnwc
527
Drum yr Eira
Drygarn Fawr
645
Gorllwyn
613
B4358
Disserth
Howey
Gilwern Hill
Bryn Crwn
532
Newbridge on Wye
Crossway
Betws Disserth
P
O
W
Y
S
C
A
M
B
R
I
A
N
M
O
U
N
T
A
I
N
S
Gamallt
Tywi
Abergwesyn Pass
Pen Carreg Dan
494
Bryn
478
Llanafan-fawr
7
A470
Carneddau
Franksbridge
A481
Pentre-llwyn-llwyd
Llansantffraed-in-Elwel
Cefn-coch
500
Irfon
Chwefru
Cwmbach
Builth Road
Lan Ystenu
Llwyn-Madoc
Royal Welsh Showground
Cregrina
Camddwr
Abergwesyn
Cefn Crug
462
Tywi
Forest
Cefn Fannog
450
Pen y Gurnos
456
Doethie
Llyn Brianne
Beulah
Cilmery
Llanelwedd
Llanafan-fechan
9
Builth Wells
(Llanfair-ym-Muallt)
Llanfaredd
Aberduhonw
487
Llanlleonfel
Garth
B4567
Cwm Irfon
Tyn-y-graig
Moelfre
441
Llanddewi'r Cwm
Rhulen Hill
467
Llanbedr Hill
Mynydd Trawsnant
517
Llanwrtyd
A483
Llangammarch Wells
467
Maesmynis
Neuadd
Duhonw
Aberedw
Alltmawr
12
Llandeilo Hill
Llanwrtyd Wells
B4519
Banc y Celyn
472
Pen-y-garreg
Aberedw Rocks
Ystradffin
Bran
Cefn-gorwydd
Drum-ddu
474
E
P
P
Y
N
T
Llandeilo Graban
15
Cledan
Sugar Loaf Sta
Rhandirmwyn
Bryn Nicol
Cefn Llwydlo
Dulas
465
475
Pentre-Dolau-Honddu
Gwenddwr
Erwood
463
Bryn Du
454
Twyn Rhyd-car
Yscir Fawr
B4520
Crickadarn
Llanstephan
Tirabad
Upper Chapel
Cefn Clawdd
427
A483
M
Y
N
Y
D
D
Danger Zone
Gwrhyd
454
Boughrood
Cynghordy
Crychan Forest
Crychan
Glanbran
423
Ysgwydd Hwch
456
Llaneglwys
Cilieni
Merthyr Cynog
Castle Madoc
Llandyfalle Hill
Llyswen
A470
Pen-y-bont
Abercrychan
410
Gwennol
Mynydd Bwlch-y-Groes
Blaendyryn
Yscir Fechan
Lower Chapel
Pentre-ty-gwyn
Babel
Llanfihangel Nant Bran
Nant Bran
Llandefalle
Llandeilo'r-Fan
Pont-faen
B4520
Honddu
Garthbrengy
Pwllgloyw
A438
A40
12
Halfway
406
Pentre-bach
Sarnau
Talachddu
Felinfach
Llanfilo
Tredustan
Y Pigwn
412
Twyn Disgwylfa
417
Mynydd Aberyscir
367
Penishawain
Llandefaelog Fach
6
Tredomen
Mynydd-bach Trecastell
Gwydderig
Danger Zone
Myddfai
Llywel
Pentre'r-felin
Pen-y-Crug
331
Battle
Llanddew
A470
Llandefaelog-tre'r-graig
Mynydd Myddfai
Yr Allt
352
Trallong
Aberyscir
Aberbran
Y Gaer
Fenni-fach
Cath
B4602
Trecastle
A40
Brecon (Aberhonddu)
Llanywern
Sennybridge
Penpont
Llanfaes
Brecknock
Llechfaen
Llanfihangel Tal-y-llyn
Usk
8
Llanspyddid
Usk Resr
Pont ar Hydfer
Defynnog
Cefn Llechid
400
A470
2
Talyllyn
Mynydd Wysg
Fforest Fach
Mynydd Illtyd
Tai'r Bull
4
Ffrwdgrech
Cefn Cantref
Llangorse Lake
Pennorth
Brecon Beacons Visitor Centre
Libanus
Llanfrynach
Llanhamlach
10
Llanddeusant
Glasfynydd Forest
6
Cray
A4215
Pen Milan
555
Allt Ddu
562
Cefn Cyff
Pencelli
Scethrog
Hydfer
Senni
Moel Feity
591
Bwlch Cerrig Duon
14
Cnewr
Heol Senni
A40
Llansantffraed
Bryn
561
Talybont-on-Usk
Craig
A I N
802
Llyn y Fan Fawr
BRECON
Fan Bwlch Chwyth
603
BEACONS
Fan Frynych
628
5
Glyn Tarell
NATIONAL
Corn Du
873
886
Pen y Fan
PARK
Aber Village
Bwlch
Garreg Las
Brest Twrch
Cray Resr
562
A470
BRECON BEACONS
(BANNAU BRYCHEINIOG)
769
762
Twyn-du
Coed-
Cwmcrawnon
F F O R E S T
F A W R
Fan Hir
Tawe
A4067
Fan Gyhirych
725
Fan Fawr
734
Beacons Resr
Gwaun Nant Ddu
Craig Fan Ddu
Neuadd Reservoirs
Canal
Talybont Reservoir
Crawnon
Cefn Carn Fadog
505
Carreg Lem
Carreg Goch
558
Castell y Geifr
Fan Nedd
663
Fan Llia
631
Nedd Fechan
Wern
Abercynafon
Garn Caws
516
Dyffryn Crawnon
Mynydd Llangynidr
Cefn Mawr
National Showcaves Centre for Wales
Penwyllt
Carreg-lwyd
Waun Lysiog
Pentwyn Resr
Nant-

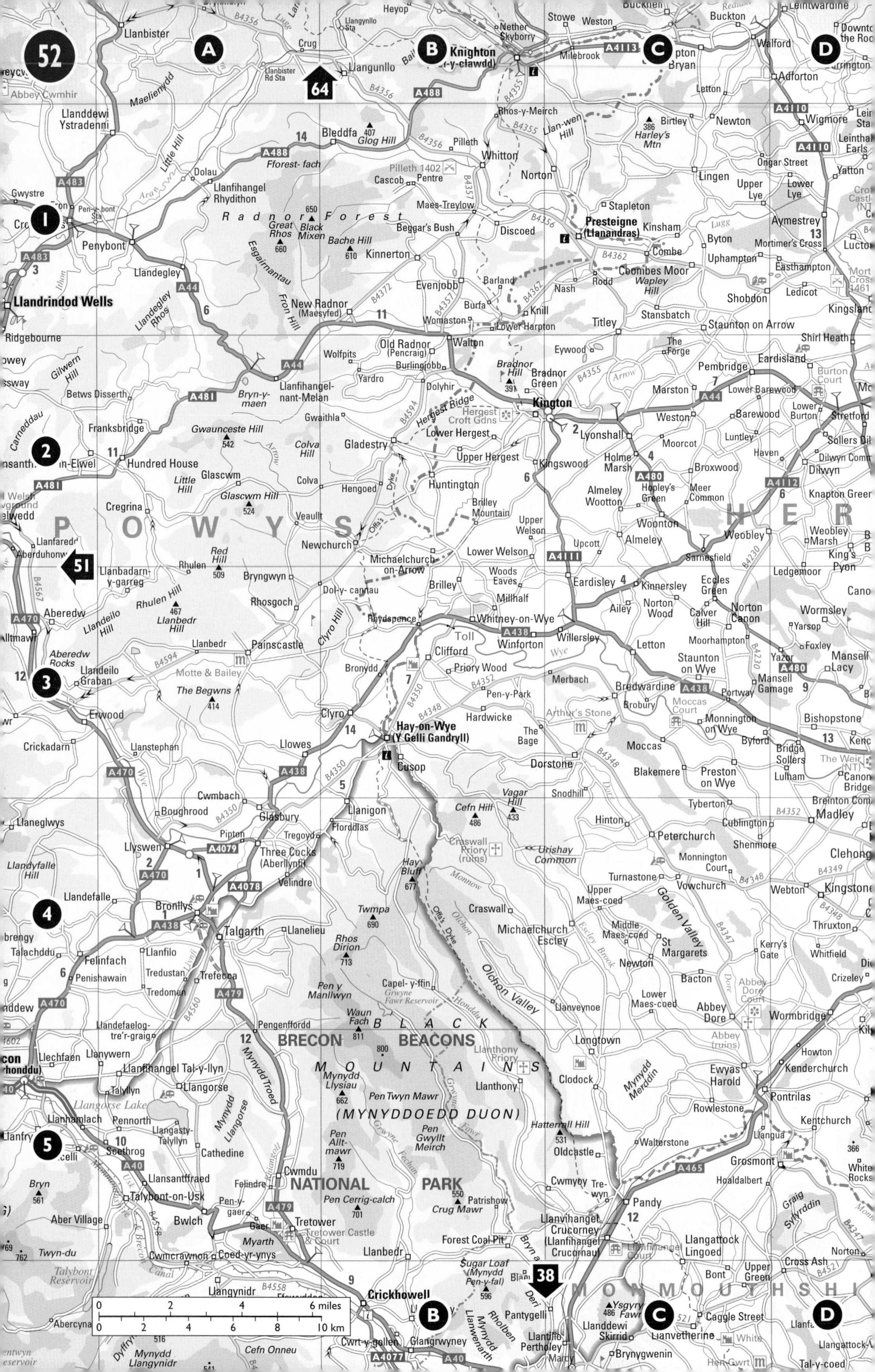

52
A
B
C
D
64
51
38
Llanbister
Crug
Llangunllo
Heyop
Knighton (Tref-y-clawdd)
Nether Skyborry
Stowe
Weston
Milebrook
Bucknell
Buckton
Brampton Bryan
Leintwardine
Walford
Adforton
Letton
Abbey Cwmhir
Maelienydd
Llanddewi Ystradenni
Little Hill
Bleddfa
Glog Hill
Pilleth
Rhos-y-Meirch
Llan-wen Hill
Whitton
Norton
Harley's Mtn
Birtley
Newton
Wigmore
Lingen
Upper Lye
Lower Lye
Ongar Street
Yatton
Fforest- fach
Dolau
Llanfihangel Rhydithon
Pilleth 1402
Cascob
Pentre
Maes-Treylow
Stapleton
Presteigne (Llanandras)
Kinsham
Byton
Aymestrey
Gwystre
Pen-y-bont Sta
Penybont
Radnor Forest
Great Rhos
Black Mixen
Bache Hill
Beggar's Bush
Discoed
Combe
Uphampton
Mortimer's Cross
Lucton
Llandrindod Wells
Llandegley
Esgairnantau
Fron Hill
Kinnerton
Evenjobb
Barland
Coombes Moor
Wapley Hill
Nash
Rodd
Easthampton
Ledicot
Shobdon
Kingsland
Ridgebourne
Llandegley Rhos
New Radnor (Maesyfed)
Burfa
Womaston
Knill
Lower Harpton
Titley
Stansbatch
Staunton on Arrow
Shirl Heath
Old Radnor (Pencraig)
Walton
Wolfpits
Burlingjobb
Yardro
Eywood
The Forge
Pembridge
Eardisland
Burton Court
Gilwern Hill
Betws Disserth
Bryn-y-maen
Llanfihangel-nant-Melan
Dolyhir
Bradnor Hill
Bradnor Green
Marston
Lower Barewood
Kington
Hergest Ridge
Hergest Croft Gdns
Gwaithla
Lyonshall
Weston
Barewood
Lower Burton
Stretford
Carneddau
Franksbridge
Gwaunceste Hill
Colva Hill
Gladestry
Lower Hergest
Upper Hergest
Moorcot
Luntley
Sollers Dilwyn
Hundred House
Little Hill
Glascwm
Colva
Hengoed
Huntington
Kingswood
Holme Marsh
Broxwood
Haven
Dilwyn
Glascwm Hill
Cregrina
Veault
Brilley Mountain
Upper Welson
Almeley Wootton
Hopley's Green
Meer Common
Knapton Green
POWYS
HEREFORDSHIRE
Llanfaredd
Aberduhonw
Newchurch
Offa's Dyke
Woonton
Almeley
Weobley
Weobley Marsh
Red Hill
Rhulen
Bryngwyn
Michaelchurch-on-Arrow
Lower Welson
Upcott
Sarnesfield
King's Pyon
Llanbadarn-y-garreg
Rhulen Hill
Woods Eaves
Brilley
Eardisley
Kinnersley
Eccles Green
Ledgemoor
Aberedw
Llandeilo Hill
Llanbedr Hill
Rhosgoch
Dol-y-cannau
Millhalf
Norton Wood
Ailey
Calver Hill
Norton Canon
Wormsley
Rhydspence
Whitney-on-Wye
Toll
Willersley
Winforton
Moorhampton
Yarsop
Foxley
Aberedw Rocks
Llanbedr
Painscastle
Clyro Hill
Clifford
Letton
Staunton on Wye
Yazor
Mansell Lacy
Llandeilo Graban
Motte & Bailey
Bronydd
Priory Wood
Merbach
Bredwardine
Mansell Gamage
Portway
The Begwns
Pen-y-Park
Hardwicke
Brobury
Moccas Court
Erwood
Clyro
Arthur's Stone
Monnington on Wye
Bishopstone
Crickadarn
Llanstephan
Llowes
Hay-on-Wye (Y Gelli Gandryll)
Cusop
The Bage
Dorstone
Moccas
Byford
Bridge Sollers
Blakemere
Preston on Wye
The Weir (NT)
Lulham
Canon Bridge
Cwmbach
Snodhill
Tyberton
Breinton Common
Boughrood
Llanigon
Cefn Hill
Vagar Hill
Hinton
Cublington
Madley
Llaneglwys
Glasbury
Pipton
Fforddlas
Tregoyd
Peterchurch
Shenmore
Llyswen
Three Cocks (Aberllynfi)
Craswall Priory (ruins)
Urishay Common
Monnington Court
Clehonger
Llandyfalle Hill
Hay Bluff
Turnastone
Vowchurch
Webton
Kingstone
Velindre
Llandefalle
Bronllys
Craswall
Upper Maes-coed
Golden Valley
Thruxton
Twmpa
Talgarth
Llanelieu
Michaelchurch Escley
Middle Maes-coed
St Margarets
Kerry's Gate
Talachddu
Felinfach
Llanfilo
Rhos Dirion
Escley Brook
Newton
Whitfield
Penishawain
Tredustan
Trefecca
Olchon Valley
Bacton
Crizeley
Tredomen
Capel-y-ffin
Pen y Manllwyn
Grwyne Fawr Reservoir
Llanveynoe
Lower Maes-coed
Abbey Dore Court
Abbey Dore
Wormbridge
Llandefaelog-tre'r-graig
Pengenffordd
Waun Fach
BLACK MOUNTAINS
BRECON BEACONS
Llanthony Priory
Longtown
Abbey (ruins)
Howton
Llechfaen
Llanywern
Llanfihangel Tal-y-llyn
Mynydd Troed
Mynydd Llysiau
Llanthony
Clodock
Mynydd Merddin
Ewyas Harold
Kenderchurch
Talyllyn
Llangorse
Pen Twyn Mawr
(MYNYDDOEDD DUON)
Pontrilas
Llangorse Lake
Llanhamlach
Pennorth
Llangasty-Talyllyn
Mynydd Llangorse
Pen Gwyllt Meirch
Hatterrall Hill
Rowlestone
Kentchurch
Llanfrynach
Scethrog
Cathedine
Pen Allt-mawr
Oldcastle
Walterstone
Llangua
Grosmont
White Rocks
Bryn
Llansantffraed
Cwmdu
Felindre
NATIONAL PARK
Cwmyoy
Tre-wyn
Hoaldalbert
Talybont-on-Usk
Pen-y-gaer
Pen Cerrig-calch
Crug Mawr
Patrishow
Pandy
Graig Syfyrddin
Aber Village
Bwlch
Gaer
Tretower
Tretower Castle & Court
Myarth
Llanvihangel Crucorney (Llanfihangel Crucornau)
Llanfihangel Court
Llangattock Lingoed
Twyn-du
Cwmcrawnon
Coed-yr-ynys
Forest Coal Pit
Bryn arw
Llanbedr
Talybont Reservoir
Sugar Loaf (Mynydd Pen-y-fal)
Blaen
Bont
Upper Green
Cross Ash
Norton
Talybont Canal
Llangynidr
Crickhowell
Deri
MONMOUTHSHIRE
Ysgyryd Fawr
Caggle Street
Llanfair
Abercynafon
Mynydd Llangynidr
Cefn Onneu
Cwrt-y-gollen
Glangrwyney
Mynydd Llanwenarth
Rholben
Pantygelli
Llantilio Pertholey
Llanddewi Skirrid
Llanvetherine
White Castle
Brynygwenin
Llangattock-Vibon-Avel
Tal-y-coed
Hen Gwrt
Mardy
0 2 4 6 miles
0 2 4 6 8 10 km

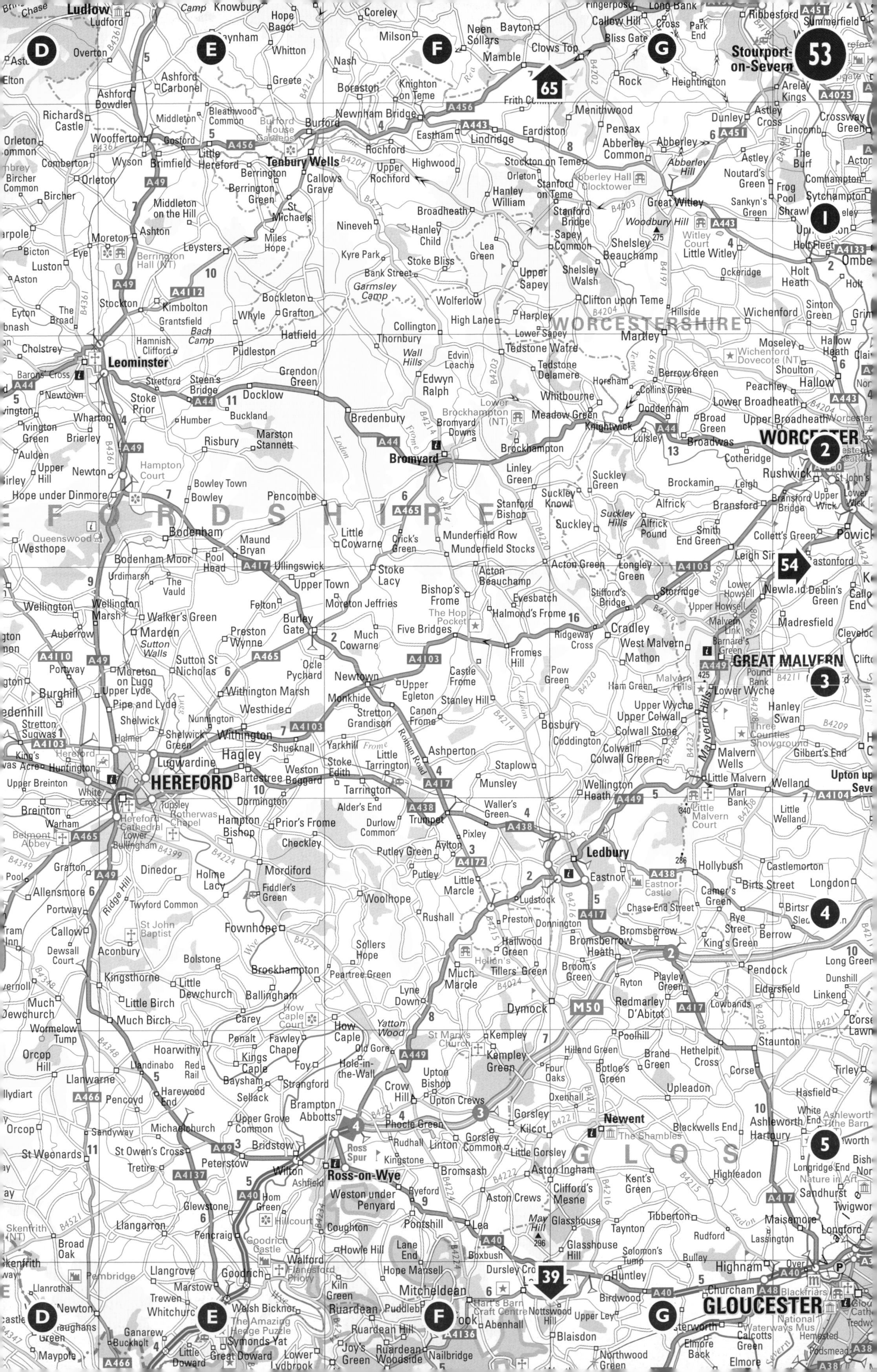

Ludlow
Ludford
Knowbury
Hope Bagot
Coreley
Long Bank
Callow Hill
Bliss Gate
Ribbesford
Stourport-on-Severn
53
D
E
F
G
Overton
Whitton
Milson
Neen Sollars
Bayton
Clows Top
Mamble
Rock
Park End
Heightington
Areley Kings
Ashford Carbonel
Greete
Nash
Boraston
Knighton on Teme
65
Frith Common
Menithwood
Astley Cross
Crossway Green
Ashford Bowdler
Richards Castle
Middleton
Bleathwood Common
Burford House Gardens
Burford
Newnham Bridge
Eastham
Lindridge
Eardiston
Pensax
Abberley Common
Abberley
Dunley
Lincomb
Orleton Common
Woofferton
Gosford
Little Hereford
Tenbury Wells
Rochford
Upper Rochford
Highwood
Stockton on Teme
Orleton
Abberley Hall Clocktower
Abberley Hill
Astley
The Burf
Comberton
Wyson
Brimfield
Berrington
Callows Grave
Hanley William
Stanford on Teme
Noutard's Green
Comhampton
Bircher Common
Orleton
Berrington Green
St Michaels
Broadheath
Stanford Bridge
Great Witley
Sankyn's Green
Frog Pool
Sytchampton
Bircher
Middleton on the Hill
Nineveh
Hanley Child
Sapey Common
Woodbury Hill
Witley Court
Little Witley
Shrawley
I
Moreton
Ashton
Leysters
Miles Hope
Kyre Park
Lea Green
Shelsley Beauchamp
Holt Fleet
Ombersley
Bicton
Eye
Berrington Hall (NT)
Stoke Bliss
Upper Sapey
Shelsley Walsh
Ockeridge
Holt Heath
Luston
Aston
Bank Street
Garmsley Camp
Wolferlow
Clifton upon Teme
Hillside
Wichenford
Sinton Green
Eyton
The Broad
Stockton
Kimbolton
Bockleton
Grafton
Whyle
High Lane
Harpley
Grantsfield
Bach Camp
Collington
Lower Sapey
WORCESTERSHIRE
Martley
Hamnish Clifford
Hatfield
Thornbury
Wall Hills
Edvin Loach
Tedstone Wafre
Moseley
Wichenford Dovecote (NT)
Hallow Heath
Cholstrey
Leominster
Pudleston
Tedstone Delamere
Horsham
Shoulton
Barons' Cross
Stretford
Steen's Bridge
Grendon Green
Edwyn Ralph
Berrow Green
Hallow
Newtown
Stoke Prior
Docklow
Whitbourne
Collins Green
Peachley
Ivington
Buckland
Lower Brockhampton (NT)
Meadow Green
Doddenham
Lower Broadheath
Wharton
Ivington Green
Humber
Bredenbury
Bromyard Downs
Knightwick
Broad Green
Upper Broadheath
Brierley
Marston Stannett
Lulsley
Aulden
Risbury
Bromyard
Brockhampton
Broadwas
WORCESTER
Hampton Court
Cotheridge
Upper Hill
Newton
Linley Green
Suckley Green
Rushwick
Hope under Dinmore
Bowley Town
Bowley
Pencombe
Suckley Knowl
Brockamin
Leigh
St John's
Alfrick
Bransford
Bransford Bridge
Upper Wick
Lower Wick
Stanford Bishop
Suckley
Suckley Hills
Alfrick Pound
Smith End Green
Collett's Green
Powick
Queenswood
Westhope
Bodenham
Maund Bryan
Little Cowarne
Crick's Green
Munderfield Row
Munderfield Stocks
Leigh Sinton
Callow End
Bodenham Moor
Pool Head
Ullingswick
Stoke Lacy
Acton Green
Longley Green
Newland
Deblin's Green
54
Stanford
Urdimarsh
The Vauld
Upper Town
Bishop's Frome
Acton Beauchamp
Stifford's Bridge
Storridge
Lower Howsell
Upper Howsell
Evesbatch
Wellington
Wellington Marsh
Walker's Green
Felton
Moreton Jeffries
The Hop Pocket
Halmond's Frome
Madresfield
Auberrow
Marden
Sutton Walls
Preston Wynne
Burley Gate
Much Cowarne
Five Bridges
Ridgeway Cross
Cradley
Malvern Link
Barnard's Green
Cleveload
Portway
Moreton on Lugg
Sutton St Nicholas
Ocle Pychard
Newtown
Fromes Hill
West Malvern
Mathon
GREAT MALVERN
Burghill
Upper Lyde
Withington Marsh
Upper Egleton
Castle Frome
Pow Green
Ham Green
Malvern Hills
Pound Bank
Lower Wyche
Edenhill
Pipe and Lyde
Westhide
Monkhide
Stretton Grandison
Canon Frome
Stanley Hill
Upper Wyche
Upper Colwall
Hanley Swan
Stretton Sugwas
Shelwick
Nunnington
Bosbury
Colwall Stone
Three Counties Showground
King's Acre
Huntington
Holmer
Shelwick Green
Withington
Shucknall
Yarkhill
Little Tarrington
Coddington
Colwall
Colwall Green
Malvern Wells
Gilbert's End
Hagley
Lugwardine
Weston Beggard
Stoke Edith
Ashperton
Staplow
Little Malvern
Welland
Upton upon Severn
HEREFORD
Bartestree
Tarrington
Munsley
Wellington Heath
Marl Bank
Upper Breinton
White Cross
Tupsley
Rotherwas Chapel
Dormington
Alder's End
Trumpet
Waller's Green
Little Malvern Court
Little Welland
Breinton
Warham
Hereford Cathedral
Hampton Bishop
Prior's Frome
Durlow Common
Pixley
Belmont Abbey
Lower Bullingham
Checkley
Putley Green
Aylton
Ledbury
Hollybush
Castlemorton
Grafton
Dinedor
Mordiford
Little Marcle
Putley
Eastnor
Eastnor Castle
Birts Street
Longdon
Pool
Allensmore
Holme Lacy
Fiddler's Green
Woolhope
Ludstock
Chase End Street
Camer's Green
Portway
Twyford Common
Preston
Donnington
Rye Street
Birtsmorton
Callow
Ridge Hill
St John Baptist
Fownhope
Rushall
Bromsberrow
Berrow
Dewsall Court
Aconbury
Sollers Hope
Hallwood Green
Bromsberrow Heath
King's Green
Long Green
Bolstone
Hellen's
Tillers' Green
Broom's Green
Pendock
Dunshill
Kingsthorne
Little Dewchurch
Brockhampton
Peartree Green
Much Marcle
Ryton
Playley Green
Eldersfield
Linkend
Much Dewchurch
Little Birch
Ballingham
Lyne Down
Dymock
M50
Redmarley D'Abitot
Lowbands
Corse Lawn
Wormelow Tump
Much Birch
Carey
How Caple Court
How Caple
Yatton Wood
Kempley
Poolhill
Orcop Hill
Hoarwithy
Penalt
Kings Caple
Fawley Chapel
Old Gore
St Mary's Church
Kempley Green
Hillend Green
Brand Green
Hethelpit Cross
Staunton
Llanwarne
Llandinabo
Red Rail
Baysham
Foy
Hole-in-the-Wall
Upton Bishop
Four Oaks
Botloe's Green
Corse
Tirley
Llydiart
Pencoyd
Harewood End
Sellack
Strangford
Crow Hill
Upton Crews
Oxenhall
Upleadon
Hasfield
Orcop
Sandyway
Michaelchurch
Upper Grove Common
Brampton Abbotts
Phocle Green
Gorsley
Kilcot
Newent
The Shambles
Blackwells End
Ashleworth
Ashleworth Tithe Barn
Hartpury
St Weonards
St Owen's Cross
Bridstow
Ross Spur
Rudhall
Linton
Gorsley Common
Little Gorsley
GLOS
Tretire
Peterstow
Wilton
Kingstone
Aston Ingham
Ross-on-Wye
Ashfield
Bromsash
Kent's Green
Highleadon
Longridge End
Nature in Art
Glewstone
Hom Green
Weston under Penyard
Ryeford
Aston Crews
Clifford's Mesne
Sandhurst
Twigworth
Skenfrith
Llangarron
Pencraig
Hillcourt
Coughton
Pontshill
Lea
May Hill
Glasshouse
Taynton
Tibberton
Maisemore
Longford
Broad Oak
Goodrich Castle
Howle Hill
Lane End
Boxbush
Glasshouse Hill
Rudford
Lassington
Walford
Solomon's Tump
Bulley
Highnam
Over
Pembridge
Llangrove
Goodrich
Flanesford Priory
Hope Mansell
Dursley Cross
39
Huntley
Llanrothal
Marstow
Kiln Green
Mitcheldean
Churcham
Blackfriars
Newton
Trewen
Welsh Bicknor
Ruardean
Puddlebrook
Hart's Barn Craft Centre
Nottswood Hill
Birdwood
GLOUCESTER
Whitchurch
The Amazing Hedge Puzzle
Drybrook
Abenhall
Upper Ley
Waterways Museum
Ganarew
Buckholt
Symonds Yat
Ruardean Hill
Blaisdon
Elmore Back
Calcotts Green
Hempsted
Maypole
Little Doward
Great Doward
Lower Lydbrook
Joy's Green
Ruardean Woodside
Nailbridge
Northwood Green
Elmore

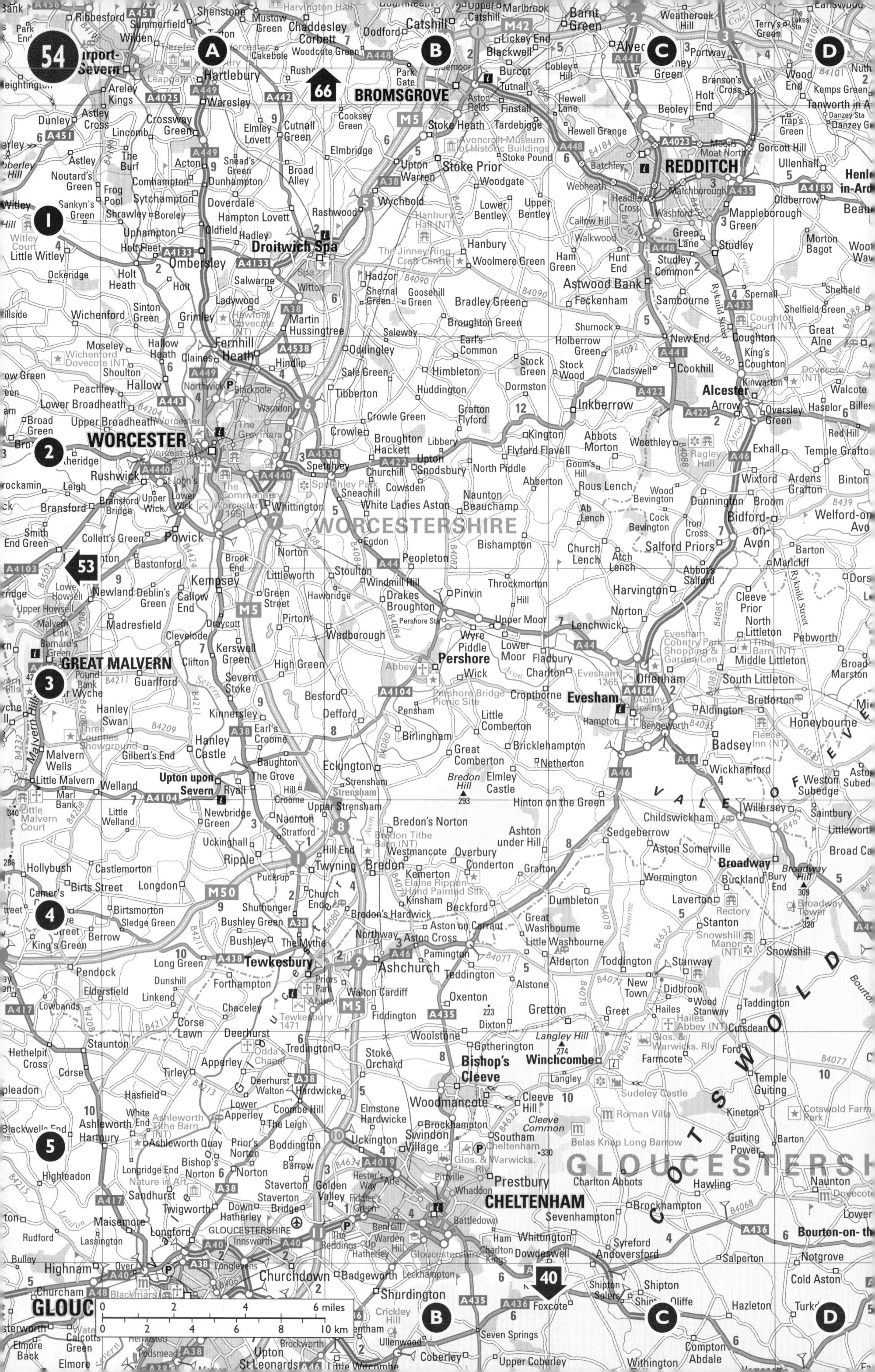
54
A
B
C
D
66
53
40
1
2
3
4
5
Stourport-on-Severn
Ribbesford
Summerfield
Wilden
Shenstone
Mustow Green
Chaddesley Corbett
Woodcote Green
Dodford
Catshill
Upper Catshill
Marlbrook
Lickey End
Barnt Green
Blackwell
Burcot
Alvechurch
Weatheroak Hill
Portway
Hartlebury
Areley Kings
Waresley
Bromsgrove
Stoke Heath
Astley Cross
Dunley
Crossway Green
Elmley Lovett
Cutnall Green
Cooksey Green
Elmbridge
Stoke Prior
Upton Warren
Tardebigge
Hewell Grange
Avoncroft Museum of Historic Buildings
Stoke Pound
Batchley
Redditch
Webheath
Matchborough
Headless Cross
Astley
Noutard's Green
The Burf
Acton
Snead's Green
Broad Alley
Woodgate
Lower Bentley
Upper Bentley
Callow Hill
Walkwood
Washford
Mapplebrough Green
Frog Pool
Sytchampton
Dunhampton
Doverdale
Hampton Lovett
Rashwood
Wychbold
Hanbury Hall (NT)
Hanbury
Hunt End
Studley
Shrawley
Boreley
Uphampton
Oldfield
Hadley
Droitwich Spa
The Jinney Ring Craft Centre
Woolmere Green
Ham Green
Studley Common
Holt Heath
Ombersley
Holt Fleet
Little Witley
Witley Court
Ockeridge
Salwarpe
Witton
Hadzor
Sherrnal Green
Goosehill Green
Astwood Bank
Feckenham
Sambourne
Spernall
Wichenford
Sinton Green
Ladywood
Grimley
Hawford Dovecote (NT)
Martin Hussingtree
Bradley Green
Broughton Green
Coughton
Coughton Court (NT)
Great Alne
Shelfield Green
Saleway
Shurnock
New End
Moseley
Hallow Heath
Fernhill Heath
Claines
Hindlip
Oddingley
Earl's Common
Holberrow Green
Stock Wood
Cookhill
King's Coughton
Wichenford Dovecote (NT)
Shoulton
Hallow
Sale Green
Himbleton
Stock Green
Cladswell
Kinwarton
Tibberton
Huddington
Dormston
Inkberrow
Alcester
Arrow
Oversley Green
Walcote
Haselor
Peachley
Lower Broadheath
Upper Broadheath
Northwick
Blackpole
Warndon
The Greyfriars
Crowle
Crowle Green
Grafton Flyford
Kington
Abbots Morton
Weethley
Ragley Hall
Broad Green
Worcester
Broughton Hackett
Libbery
Flyford Flavell
Exhall
Temple Grafton
Rushwick
Spetchley
Spetchley Park
Upton Snodsbury
Churchill
Sneachill
Cowsden
North Piddle
Goom's Hill
Abberton
Rous Lench
Wood Bevington
Wixford
Ardens Grafton
Binton
Leigh
Bransford
Bransford Bridge
Upper Wick
Lower Wick
St John's
The Commandery
Worcester 1651
Whittington
White Ladies Aston
Naunton Beauchamp
Ab Lench
Cock Bevington
Iron Cross
Dunnington
Broom
Bidford-on-Avon
Welford-on-Avon
Collett's Green
Smith End Green
Powick
Worcestershire
Egdon
Bishampton
Church Lench
Atch Lench
Salford Priors
Abbot's Salford
Barton
Marlcliff
Bastonford
Brook End
Norton
Peopleton
Stoulton
Windmill Hill
Littleworth
Kempsey
Callow End
Newland
Deblin's Green
Lower Howsell
Upper Howsell
Green Street
Hawbridge
Drakes Broughton
Pershore Sta
Pinvin
Throckmorton
Hill
Harvington
Cleeve Prior
North Littleton
Norton
Upper Moor
Lenchwick
Madresfield
Draycott
Pirton
Wadborough
Wyre Piddle
Lower Moor
Fladbury
Evesham Country Park Shopping & Garden Cen
Middle Littleton
Pebworth
Malvern Link
Barnard's Green
Great Malvern
Cleevelode
Clifton
Kerswell Green
High Green
Abbey
Pershore
Wick
Charlton
Evesham 1265
Offenham
South Littleton
Broad Marston
Pound Bank
Upper Wyche
Guarlford
Severn Stoke
Besford
Pershore Bridge Picnic Site
Cropthorne
Evesham
Abbey ruins
Bretforton
Hanley Swan
Kinnersley
Earl's Croome
Defford
Pensham
Little Comberton
Hampton
Bengeworth
Aldington
Honeybourne
Three Counties Showground
Malvern Wells
Gilbert's End
Hanley Castle
Birlingham
Great Comberton
Bricklehampton
Netherton
Badsey
Fleece Inn (NT)
Baughton
Eckington
Strensham
Wickhamford
Little Malvern
Welland
Upton upon Severn
Ryall
The Grove
Hill Croome
Bredon Hill 293
Elmley Castle
Weston Subedge
Vale of Evesham
Little Malvern Court
Marl Bank
Little Welland
Newbridge Green
Naunton
Upper Strensham
Bredon's Norton
Bredon Tithe Barn (NT)
Hinton on the Green
Childswickham
Willersey
Saintbury
Uckinghall
Stratford
Ashton under Hill
Sedgeberrow
Aston Somerville
Hollybush
Castlemorton
Ripple
Hill End
Twyning
Westmancote
Bredon
Overbury
Conderton
Grafton
Broadway
Buckland
Bury End
Broadway Hill 309
Birts Street
Longdon
Puckrup
Kemerton
Elaine Rippon Hand Painted Silk
Wormington
Camer's Green
Birtsmorton
Sledge Green
Church End
Shuthonger
Kinsham
Beckford
Dumbleton
Laverton
Rectory
Broadway Tower
Bushley Green
Bredon's Hardwick
Aston on Carrant
Great Washbourne
Little Washbourne
Stanton
Snowshill Manor (NT)
Snowshill
Berrow
King's Green
Bushley
The Mythe
Northway
Aston Cross
Pamington
Teddington
Alderton
Toddington
Stanway
Long Green
Tewkesbury
Ashchurch
Alstone
New Town
Didbrook
Wood Stanway
Pendock
Dunshill
Forthampton
Priors Park
Walton Cardiff
Eldersfield
Linkend
Chaceley
Fiddington
Oxenton
Gretton
Greet
Hailes
Hailes Abbey (NT)
Taddington
Cutsdean
Corse Lawn
Tewkesbury 1471
Dixton
Lowbands
Staunton
Deerhurst
Odda's Chapel
Woolstone
Gotherington
Langley Hill 274
Glos. & Warwicks. Rly
Ford
Hethelpit Cross
Corse
Apperley
Tredington
Stoke Orchard
Bishop's Cleeve
Winchcombe
Farmcote
Tirley
Deerhurst Walton
Hardwicke
Langley
Sudeley Castle
Temple Guiting
Hasfield
Lower Apperley
Coombe Hill
Woodmancote
Cleeve Hill
Roman Villa
Kineton
Cotswold Farm Park
Ashleworth Tithe Barn
Ashleworth
Hartpury
The Leigh
Elmstone Hardwicke
Cleeve Common
Blackwells End
Ashleworth Quay
Prior's Norton
Boddington
Uckington
Brockhampton
Swindon Village
Southam
Cheltenham
Belas Knap Long Barrow
Guiting Power
Barton
Gloucestershire
Cotswold
Highleadon
Longridge End
Nature in Art
Bishop's Norton
Norton
Barrow
Staverton
Golden Valley
Hester's Way
Arle
Pittville
Prestbury
Charlton Abbots
Hawling
Naunton
Sandhurst
Twigworth
Staverton Bridge
Fiddler's Green
Whaddon
Cheltenham
Brockhampton
Maisemore
Down Hatherley
Gloucestershire Innsworth
Benhall
Warden Hill
Up Hatherley
The Reddings
Battledown
Sevenhampton
Bourton-on-the-Water
Rudford
Lassington
Longford
Ham
Whittington
Syreford
Andoversford
Salperton
Notgrove
Highnam
Over
Longlevens
Churchdown
Badgeworth
Leckhampton
Charlton Kings
Dowdeswell
Churcham
Blackfriars
Shurdington
Shipton Solers
Shipton
Shipton Oliffe
Hazleton
Cold Aston
Turkdean
Gloucester
Crickley Hill
Foxcote
Seven Springs
Walls
Calcotts Green
Elmore Back
Elmore
Podsmead
Upton St Leonards
Brockworth
Ullenwood
Coberley
Upper Coberley
Withington
Compton Abdale
Little Witcombe
Cole
Terry's Green
The Lakes Sta
Wood End
Kemps Green
Tanworth in Arden
Danzey Sta
Trap's Green
Gorcott Hill
Ullenhall
Henley-in-Arden
Oldberrow
Morton Bagot
Shelfield
Red Hill
Holt End
Beoley
Branson's Cross
Hewell Lane
Cobley Hill
Aston Fields
Finstall
Park Gate
Rushock
Tutnall
Green Lane
0 2 4 6 miles
0 2 4 6 8 10 km

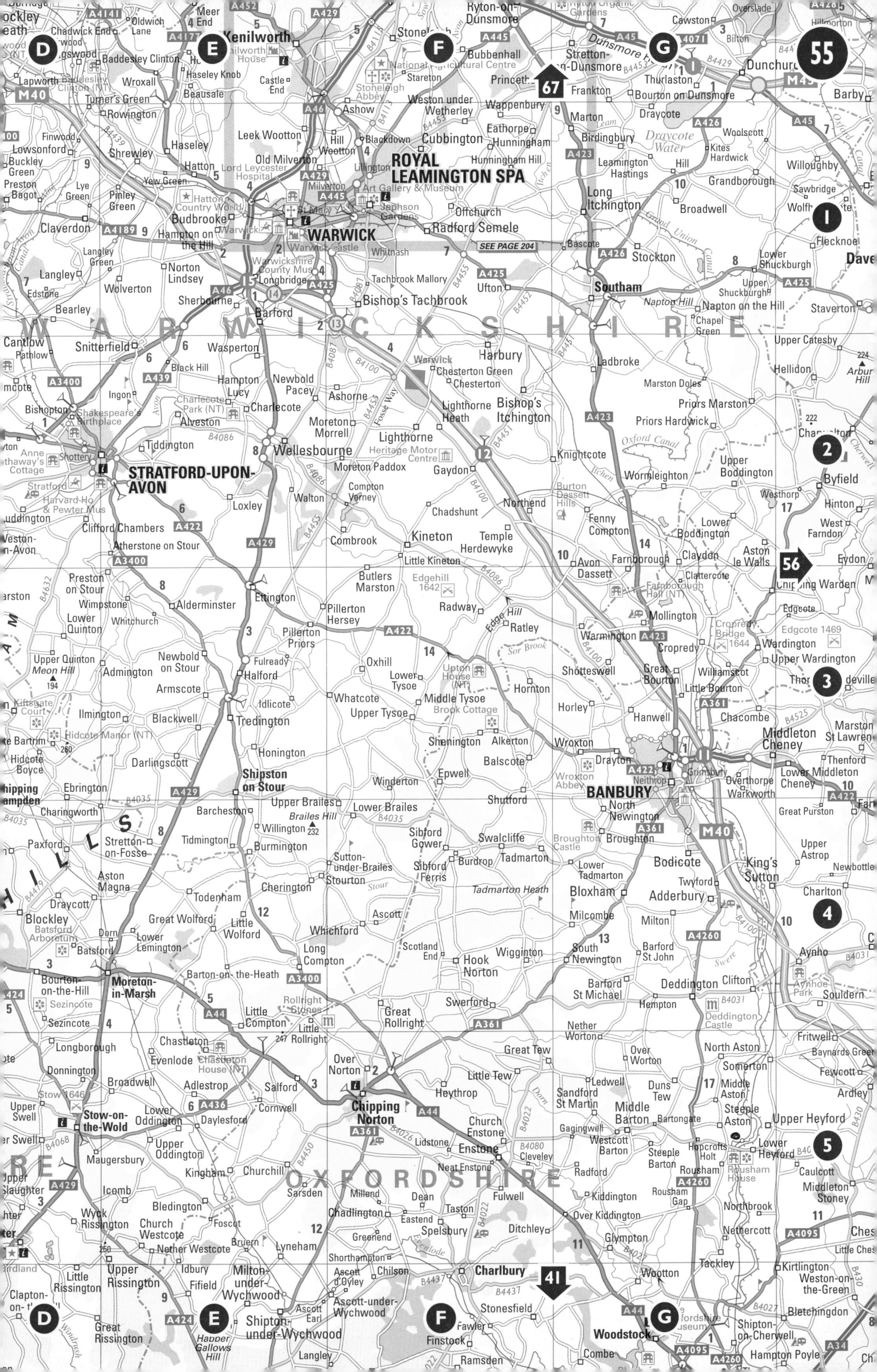
55
Kenilworth
Kenilworth House
Meer End
Oldwich Lane
Chadwick End
Baddesley Clinton
Lapworth
Haseley Knob
Beausale
Wroxall
Turner's Green
Rowington
Finwood
Lowsonford
Shrewley
Haseley
Hatton
Buckley Green
Preston Bagot
Lye Green
Pinley Green
Yew Green
Hatton Country World
Budbrooke
Claverdon
Hampton on the Hill
Langley Green
Langley
Norton Lindsey
Wolverton
Edstone
Bearley
Sherbourne
Barford
Snitterfield
Cantlow
Pathlow
Wasperton
Black Hill
Ingon
Hampton Lucy
Charlecote Park (NT)
Charlecote
Alveston
Bishopton
Shakespeare's Birthplace
Tiddington
Anne Hathaway's Cottage
Shottery
STRATFORD-UPON-AVON
Stratford
Harvard Ho & Pewter Mus
Clifford Chambers
Atherstone on Stour
Loxley
Wellesbourne
Newbold Pacey
Ashorne
Moreton Morrell
Moreton Paddox
Lighthorne
Heritage Motor Centre
Gaydon
Compton Verney
Walton
Combrook
Kineton
Little Kineton
Chadshunt
Northend
Temple Herdewyke
Butlers Marston
Edgehill 1642
Radway
Edge Hill
Ratley
Pillerton Hersey
Pillerton Priors
Ettington
Alderminster
Preston on Stour
Wimpstone
Whitchurch
Lower Quinton
Upper Quinton
Meon Hill 194
Admington
Newbold on Stour
Armscote
Fulready
Halford
Idlicote
Tredington
Oxhill
Lower Tysoe
Upton House (NT)
Middle Tysoe
Whatcote
Upper Tysoe
Brook Cottage
Hornton
Ilmington
Blackwell
Hidcote Manor (NT)
Hidcote Boyce
Darlingscott
Honington
Shenington
Alkerton
Balscote
Shipston on Stour
Ebrington
Chipping Campden
Charingworth
Barcheston
Winderton
Epwell
Upper Brailes
Brailes Hill 232
Lower Brailes
Willington
Shutford
Paxford
Stretton-on-Fosse
Tidmington
Burmington
Sibford Gower
Swalcliffe
Burdrop
Tadmarton
Sibford Ferris
Sutton-under-Brailes
Stourton
Cherington
Aston Magna
Todenham
Tadmarton Heath
Draycott
Blockley
Batsford Arboretum
Batsford
Great Wolford
Little Wolford
Lower Lemington
Whichford
Ascott
Long Compton
Scotland End
Hook Norton
Wiggington
Bourton-on-the-Hill
Sezincote
Moreton-in-Marsh
Barton-on-the-Heath
Rollright Stones
Little Compton
Little Rollright
Great Rollright
Swerford
Longborough
Donnington
Chastleton
Evenlode
Chastleton House (NT)
Adlestrop
Salford
Over Norton
Chipping Norton
Broadwell
Stow-on-the-Wold
Upper Swell
Lower Swell
Lower Oddington
Daylesford
Upper Oddington
Cornwell
Maugersbury
Kingham
Churchill
Sarsden
Upper Slaughter
Icomb
Bledington
Wyck Rissington
Church Westcote
Foscot
Nether Westcote
Bruern
Lyneham
Little Rissington
Upper Rissington
Idbury
Fifield
Milton-under-Wychwood
Clapton-on-the-Hill
Great Rissington
Shipton-under-Wychwood
Happer Gallows Hill
Ascott Earl
Ascott-under-Wychwood
Ascott d'Oyley
Chilson
Shorthampton
Langley
Millend
Chadlington
Dean
Eastend
Taston
Spelsbury
Greenend
Charlbury
Finstock
Fawler
Stonesfield
Ramsden
Lidstone
Enstone
Neat Enstone
Church Enstone
Heythrop
Little Tew
Great Tew
Cleveley
Fulwell
Ditchley
OXFORDSHIRE
WARWICKSHIRE
Stoneleigh
Stoneleigh Abbey
Stareton
National Agricultural Centre
Castle End
Ashow
Leek Wootton
Hill Wootton
Blackdown
Old Milverton
Lord Leycester Hospital
Milverton
Lillington
Cubbington
ROYAL LEAMINGTON SPA
Art Gallery & Museum
Jephson Gardens
WARWICK
Warwick Castle
Whitnash
Warwickshire County Mus
Longbridge
Tachbrook Mallory
Bishop's Tachbrook
Warwick
Chesterton Green
Chesterton
Lighthorne Heath
Harbury
Bishop's Itchington
Ryton-on-Dunsmore
Bubbenhall
Weston under Wetherley
Wappenbury
Eathorpe
Hunningham
Hunningham Hill
Princethorpe
67
Offchurch
Radford Semele
SEE PAGE 204
Ufton
Stretton-on-Dunsmore
Frankton
Marton
Birdingbury
Leamington Hastings
Long Itchington
Bascote
Stockton
Southam
Ladbroke
Knightcote
Burton Dassett Hills
Fenny Compton
Avon Dassett
Farnborough
Farnborough Hall (NT)
Mollington
Warmington
Shotteswell
Hanwell
Horley
Wroxton
Wroxton Abbey
Drayton
BANBURY
Neithrop
Grimsbury
North Newington
Broughton
Broughton Castle
Lower Tadmarton
Bloxham
Milcombe
South Newington
Barford St Michael
Nether Worton
Over Worton
Ledwell
Sandford St Martin
Duns Tew
Middle Barton
Gagingwell
Westcott Barton
Steeple Barton
Radford
Kiddington
Over Kiddington
Glympton
Wootton
Woodstock
Combe
Cawston
Overslade
Hillmorton
Bilton
Dunsmore Heath
Thurlaston
Dunchurch
Bourton on Dunsmore
Draycote
Draycote Water
Kites Hardwick
Woolscott
Hill
Grandborough
Broadwell
Barby
Willoughby
Sawbridge
Wolfhampcote
Flecknoe
Lower Shuckburgh
Upper Shuckburgh
Napton Hill
Napton on the Hill
Chapel Green
Staverton
Upper Catesby
Hellidon
Arbury Hill 224
Marston Doles
Priors Marston
Priors Hardwick
Oxford Canal
Charwelton
Upper Boddington
Wormleighton
Byfield
Westhorp
Hinton
West Farndon
Lower Boddington
Claydon
Aston le Walls
Eydon
56
Clattercote
Chipping Warden
Edgcote
Cropredy Bridge 1644
Edgcote 1469
Wardington
Upper Wardington
Cropredy
Great Bourton
Williamscot
Little Bourton
Thorpe Mandeville
Chacombe
Middleton Cheney
Marston St Lawrence
Thenford
Lower Middleton Cheney
Overthorpe
Warkworth
Great Purston
Upper Astrop
King's Sutton
Newbottle
Bodicote
Twyford
Adderbury
Charlton
Milton
Barford St John
Aynho
Aynhoe Park
Souldern
Deddington
Deddington Castle
Clifton
Hempton
Fritwell
Baynards Green
North Aston
Somerton
Fewcott
Middle Aston
Ardley
Steeple Aston
Upper Heyford
Hopcrofts Holt
Lower Heyford
Rousham
Rousham House
Caulcott
Rousham Gap
Middleton Stoney
Northbrook
Nethercott
Tackley
Kirtlington
Weston-on-the-Green
Bletchingdon
Shipton-on-Cherwell
Hampton Poyle
41
D
E
F
G
I
2
3
4
5
M40
M45
A46
A45
A445
A452
A429
A4177
A4141
A4189
A4071
A426
A423
A425
A439
A3400
A422
A361
A4260
A44
A436
A424
A4095
A34
B4455
B4100
B4086
B4087
B4035
B4450
B4026
B4022
B4027
B4437
B4031
B4525
B4632
B4068
B4080
B4451
B4452
B4453
B4439
B4429
B4479

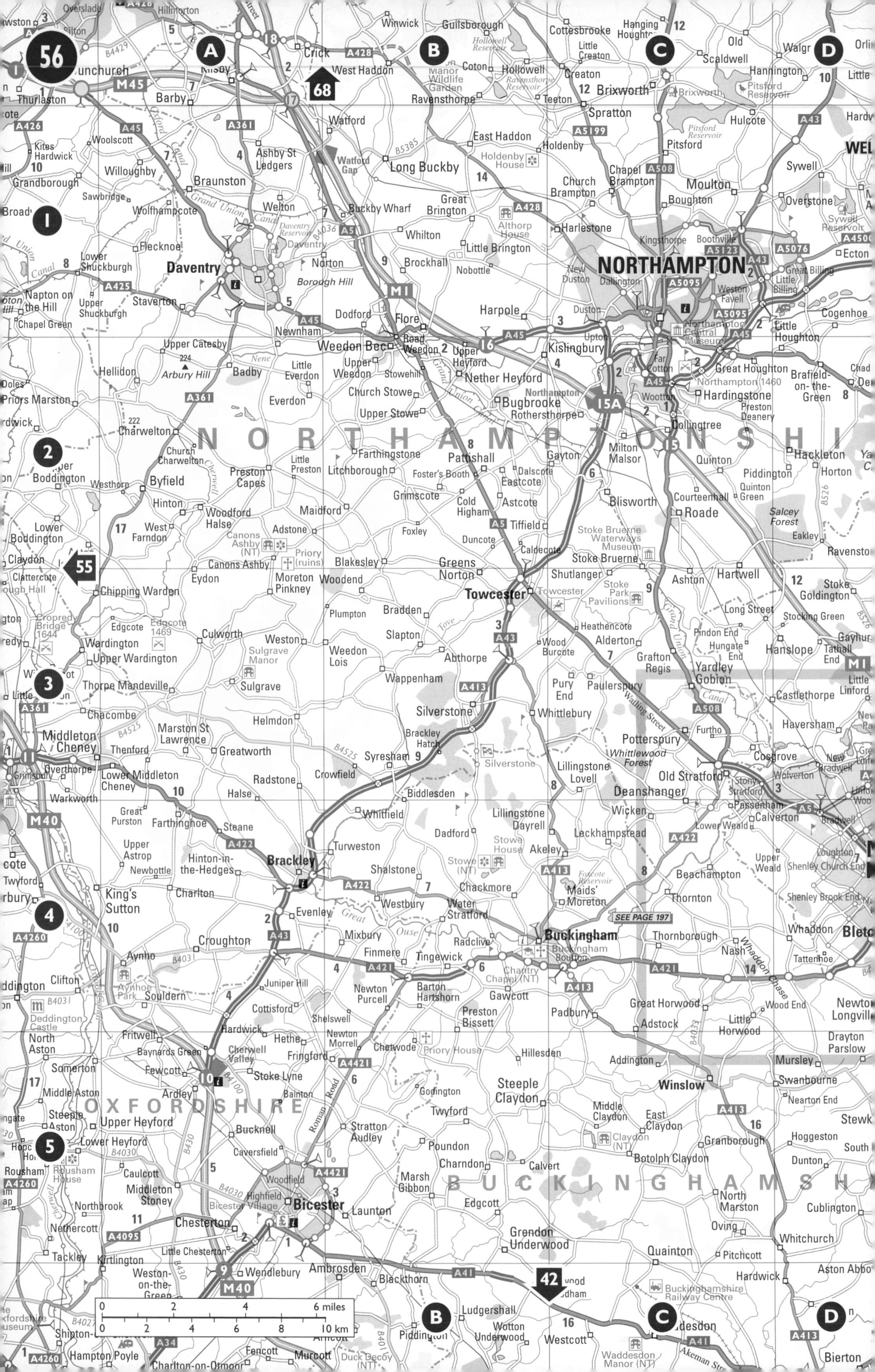

56
A
B
C
D
68
Overslade
Hillmorton
Winwick
Guilsborough
Hollowell Reservoir
Cottesbrooke
Hanging Houghton
12
Old
Walgrave
Crick
West Haddon
A428
Little Creaton
Scaldwell
Dunchurch
M45
Kilsby
Barby
Manor Wildlife Garden
Coton
Hollowell
Ravensthorpe Reservoir
Creaton
Hannington
Thurlaston
Ravensthorpe
Teeton
Brixworth
Pitsford Reservoir
A426
A45
Oxford Canal
A361
Watford
Spratton
A5199
Hulcote
A43
Woolscott
Kites Hardwick
Ashby St Ledgers
East Haddon
Holdenby
Pitsford
10
Watford Gap
B5385
Long Buckby
Holdenby House
Willoughby
Grandborough
Braunston
14
Chapel Brampton
A508
Church Brampton
Sywell
Moulton
Sawbridge
Grand Union Canal
Welton
Broadwell
I
Wolfhampcote
Buckby Wharf
Great Brington
Althorp House
A428
Boughton
Overstone
Sywell Reservoir
Daventry Reservoir
Daventry
B4036
A5
Whilton
Harlestone
Kingsthorpe
Boothville
Flecknoe
Little Brington
A5123
A5076
Ecton
Lower Shuckburgh
Daventry
Norton
Brockhall
Nobottle
NORTHAMPTON
Great Billing
Borough Hill
New Duston
Dallington
A5095
Little Billing
Napton on the Hill
A425
Upper Shuckburgh
Staverton
M1
Weston Favell
Dodford
Flore
Harpole
Duston
A5095
Cogenhoe
Chapel Green
Newnham
Northampton Central Museum
Little Houghton
Upper Catesby
Weedon Bec
Road Weedon
Upper Heyford
16
Upton
Kislingbury
224
Arbury Hill
Nene
Little Everdon
Upper Weedon
Stowehill
Nether Heyford
Far Cotton
Great Houghton
Brafield-on-the-Green
Hellidon
Badby
Grand Union Canal
Northampton 1460
Hardingstone
Priors Marston
A361
Everdon
Church Stowe
Bugbrooke
Northampton
15A
Wootton
Preston Deanery
222
Upper Stowe
Rothersthorpe
Collingtree
Charwelton
NORTHAMPTONSHIRE
Church Charwelton
8
Pattishall
Milton Malsor
Gayton
Quinton
Hackleton
Upper Boddington
Little Preston
Farthingstone
Foster's Booth
Dalscote
Piddington
Horton
Westhorp
Byfield
Preston Capes
Litchborough
Eastcote
Quinton Green
Cherwell
Grimscote
Cold Higham
Blisworth
Courteenhall
Hinton
Astcote
Roade
Salcey Forest
B526
Lower Boddington
Woodford Halse
Maidford
Tiffield
17
West Farndon
Adstone
Stoke Bruerne Waterways Museum
Foxley
Duncote
Eakley
Canons Ashby (NT)
Caldecote
Ravenstone
Claydon
55
Priory (ruins)
Blakesley
Greens Norton
Stoke Bruerne
Canons Ashby
Shutlanger
Eydon
Moreton Pinkney
Woodend
Ashton
Hartwell
Clattercote
Stoke Park Pavilions
12
Stoke Goldington
Chipping Warden
Towcester
Plumpton
Bradden
Long Street
Stocking Green
Cropredy Bridge 1644
Edgcote 1469
Edgcote
Culworth
Slapton
Heathencote
Pindon End
Gayhurst
Wardington
Weston
Tove
Alderton
Hungate End
Hanslope
Tathall End
Upper Wardington
Sulgrave Manor
Weedon Lois
Abthorpe
A43
Wood Burcote
Grafton Regis
Yardley Gobion
Thorpe Mandeville
Wappenham
Sulgrave
Pury End
Paulerspury
Little Linford
A361
Castlethorpe
Chacombe
A413
Silverstone
Watling Street
A508
Whittlebury
Helmdon
Furtho
Haversham
Middleton Cheney
B4525
Marston St Lawrence
Brackley Hatch
Potterspury
Thenford
Greatworth
B4525
Syresham
Silverstone
Whittlewood Forest
Lillingstone Lovell
Cosgrove
Grimsbury
Overthorpe
Lower Middleton Cheney
Crowfield
Old Stratford
New Bradwell
Radstone
Deanshanger
Stony Stratford
Wolverton
10
Halse
Biddlesden
Passenham
Warkworth
Wicken
A5
Calverton
Bradwell
M40
Great Purston
Whitfield
Lillingstone Dayrell
Farthinghoe
Steane
Dadford
Leckhampstead
Lower Weald
Turweston
Stowe House
Upper Astrop
A422
Hinton-in-the-Hedges
Akeley
Upper Weald
Loughton
Brackley
Stowe (NT)
A413
Newbottle
Shalstone
Foxcote Reservoir
Beachampton
Shenley Church End
Twyford
A422
Chackmore
King's Sutton
Charlton
Westbury
Maids' Moreton
Thornton
Water Stratford
Shenley Brook End
Evenley
SEE PAGE 197
A4260
Great Ouse
Whaddon
Mixbury
Buckingham
Thornborough
Croughton
A43
Radclive
Buckingham
Nash
Aynho
Finmere
Tingewick
Tattenhoe
B4031
Chantry Chapel (NT)
Bourton
A421
14
Whaddon Chase
Aynhoe Park
Juniper Hill
Barton Hartshorn
A421
Deddington
Clifton
Newton Purcell
Gawcott
A413
Great Horwood
Newton Longville
Souldern
B4031
Preston Bissett
Padbury
Deddington Castle
Cottisford
Shelswell
Little Horwood
Wood End
Adstock
B4033
Drayton Parslow
North Aston
Fritwell
Hardwick
Newton Morrell
Baynards Green
Hethe
Chetwode
Priory House
Hillesden
Mursley
Cherwell Valley
Somerton
Fewcott
Fringford
A4421
Addington
Swanbourne
Stoke Lyne
B4100
Winslow
Middle Aston
Ardley
Bainton
Roman Road
Godington
Steeple Claydon
Nearton End
OXFORDSHIRE
Middle Claydon
Steeple Aston
Upper Heyford
Twyford
East Claydon
A413
Stewkley
Bucknell
Stratton Audley
Granborough
Hoggeston
Lower Heyford
B4030
Claydon (NT)
Poundon
Rousham
Rousham House
Caversfield
Botolph Claydon
Dunton
Caulcott
Woodfield
A4421
Charndon
Calvert
Middleton Stoney
B4030
Highfield
Marsh Gibbon
BUCKINGHAMSHIRE
Cublington
A4260
Northbrook
Bicester Village
Bicester
Launton
North Marston
Edgcott
Nethercott
Chesterton
Oving
Grendon Underwood
Whitchurch
A4095
Little Chesterton
Tackley
Kirtlington
A41
Quainton
Pitchcott
Weston-on-the-Green
Wendlebury
Ambrosden
Blackthorn
42
Hardwick
Aston Abbotts
M40
Buckinghamshire Railway Centre
Ludgershall
Piddington
Wotton Underwood
Westcott
Waddesdon
Waddesdon Manor (NT)
Shipton-on-Cherwell
Hampton Poyle
Fencott
Murcott
Duck Decoy (NT)
Charlton-on-Otmoor
Akeman Street
A34
A4260
A413
Bierton
0 2 4 6 miles
0 2 4 6 8 10 km

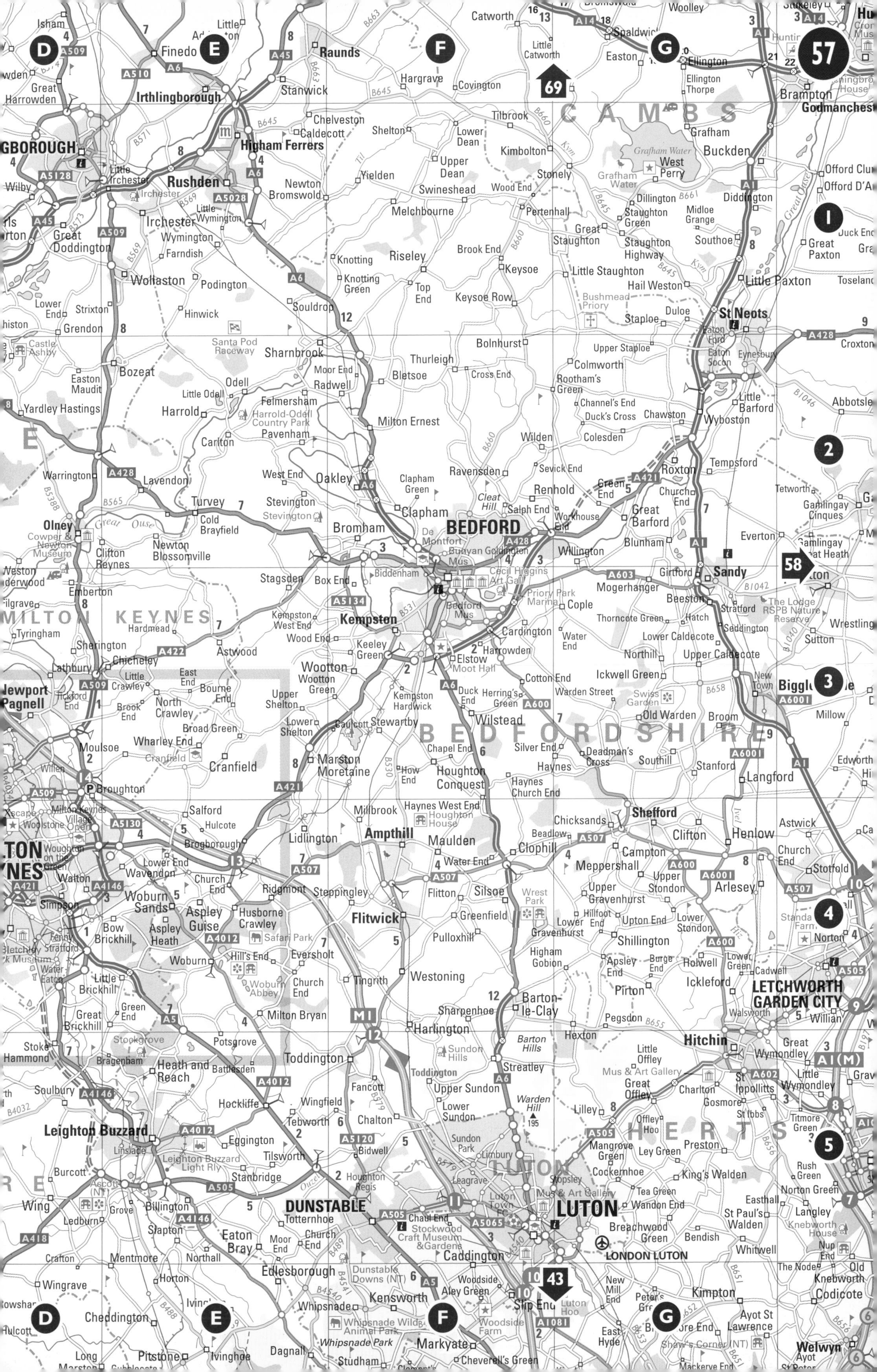

57
69
58
43
CAMBS
BEDFORDSHIRE
MILTON KEYNES
HERTS
Isham
Finedon
Raunds
Catworth
Little Catworth
Spaldwick
Easton
Ellington
Ellington Thorpe
Woolley
Brampton
Godmanchester
Irthlingborough
Stanwick
Hargrave
Covington
Great Harrowden
Wellingborough
Chelveston
Caldecott
Higham Ferrers
Shelton
Lower Dean
Tilbrook
Kimbolton
Grafham
Grafham Water
West Perry
Buckden
Rushden
Little Irchester
Irchester
Newton Bromswold
Yielden
Upper Dean
Swineshead
Stonely
Wood End
Dillington
Staughton Green
Midloe Grange
Diddington
Offord Cluny
Offord D'Arcy
Wilby
Little Wymington
Wymington
Great Doddington
Farndish
Melchbourne
Pertenhall
Great Staughton
Staughton Highway
Southoe
Great Paxton
Duck End
Wollaston
Podington
Knotting
Knotting Green
Riseley
Top End
Brook End
Keysoe
Keysoe Row
Little Staughton
Hail Weston
Little Paxton
Toseland
Lower End
Strixton
Grendon
Hinwick
Souldrop
Bushmead Priory
Stapload
Duloe
St Neots
Eaton Ford
Eaton Socon
Eynesbury
Croxton
Castle Ashby
Santa Pod Raceway
Sharnbrook
Bolnhurst
Upper Staploe
Thurleigh
Colmworth
Easton Maudit
Bozeat
Moor End
Radwell
Bletsoe
Cross End
Rootham's Green
Little Odell
Odell
Felmersham
Channel's End
Duck's Cross
Chawston
Little Barford
Wyboston
Abbotsley
Yardley Hastings
Harrold
Harrold-Odell Country Park
Pavenham
Milton Ernest
Carlton
Wilden
Colesden
Warrington
Lavendon
West End
Oakley
Clapham Green
Ravensden
Sevick End
Roxton
Tempsford
Olney
Turvey
Cold Brayfield
Stevington
Clapham
Cleat Hill
Salph End
Renhold
Green End
Workhouse End
Church End
Great Barford
Tetworth
Gamlingay Cinques
Cowper & Newton Museum
Clifton Reynes
Newton Blossomville
Bromham
BEDFORD
De Montfort
Bunyan Goldington Mus
Blunham
Everton
Gamlingay Great Heath
Weston Underwood
Emberton
Stagsden
Box End
Biddenham
Cecil Higgins Art Gall
Willington
Girtford
Sandy
Olney
Filgrave
Kempston West End
Kempston
Bedford Mus
Priory Park Marina
Mogerhanger
Cople
Beeston
Stratford
The Lodge RSPB Nature Reserve
Tyringham
Hardmead
Astwood
Wood End
Cardington
Thorncote Green
Hatch
Seddington
Wrestlingworth
Sherington
Keeley Green
Harrowden
Water End
Lower Caldecote
Sutton
Chicheley
Lathbury
Wootton
Elstow
Moot Hall
Northill
Upper Caldecote
Newport Pagnell
Little Crawley
East End
Bourne End
Wootton Green
Upper Shelton
Kempston Hardwick
Cotton End
Duck End
Herring's Green
Warden Street
Ickwell Green
Swiss Garden
New Town
Biggleswade
Tickford End
Brook End
North Crawley
Lower Shelton
Caulcott
Stewartby
Wilstead
Old Warden
Broom
Millow
Broad Green
Wharley End
Moulsoe
Cranfield
Marston Moretaine
Chapel End
Silver End
Deadman's Cross
Haynes
Southill
Stanford
Edworth
Willen
Broughton
How End
Houghton Conquest
Haynes Church End
Langford
Milton Keynes Village
Salford
Hulcote
Millbrook
Haynes West End
Houghton House
Shefford
Chicksands
Woolstone
Lidlington
Ampthill
Maulden
Beadlow
Clophill
Clifton
Henlow
Astwick
Campton
Wavendon
Lower End
Brogborough
Water End
Meppershall
Church End
Stotfold
Walton
Church End
Ridgmont
Steppingley
Flitton
Silsoe
Wrest Park
Upper Stondon
Upper Gravenhurst
Arlesey
Simpson
Woburn Sands
Aspley Guise
Husborne Crawley
Flitwick
Greenfield
Hillfoot End
Lower Gravenhurst
Upton End
Lower Stondon
Standalone Farm
Norton
Bow Brickhill
Aspley Heath
Safari Park
Pulloxhill
Shillington
Fenny Stratford
Bletchley
Hill's End
Woburn
Eversholt
Higham Gobion
Apsley End
Burge End
Holwell
Lower Green
Cadwell
Water Eaton
Woburn Abbey
Church End
Tingrith
Westoning
Pirton
Ickleford
LETCHWORTH GARDEN CITY
Little Brickhill
Green End
Great Brickhill
Milton Bryan
Barton-le-Clay
Sharpenhoe
Pegsdon
Walsworth
William
Stockgrove
Potsgrove
Harlington
Hexton
Barton Hills
Hitchin
Great Wymondley
Stoke Hammond
Bragenham
Heath and Reach
Battlesden
Toddington
Sundon Hills
Streatley
Little Offley
Mus & Art Gallery
Little Wymondley
Soulbury
Fancott
Upper Sundon
Great Offley
Charlton
St Ippollitts
Gosmore
Hockliffe
Wingfield
Lower Sundon
Warden Hill
Lilley
Offley Hoo
St Ibbs
Titmore Green
Leighton Buzzard
Tebworth
Chalton
Eggington
Bidwell
Sundon Park
Limbury
Stopsley
Mangrove Green
Ley Green
Preston
Linslade
Leighton Buzzard Light Rly
Tilsworth
Leagrave
LUTON
Cockernhoe
King's Walden
Rush Green
Burcott
Ascott (NT)
Stanbridge
Houghton Regis
Mus & Art Gallery
Tea Green
Norton Green
Wing
Grove
Billington
DUNSTABLE
Totternhoe
Chaul End
Stockwood Craft Museum & Gardens
Luton Town FC
Wandon End
Breachwood Green
Eastall
Langley
St Paul's Walden
Knebworth House
Ledburn
Slapton
Eaton Bray
Moor End
Church End
Caddington
LONDON LUTON
Bendish
Whitwell
Nup End
Crafton
Mentmore
Northall
Edlesborough
Dunstable Downs (NT)
Woodside
Aley Green
The Node
Old Knebworth
Wingrave
Horton
Whipsnade
Kensworth
Slip End
Luton Hoo
New Mill End
Peter's Green
Kimpton
Codicote
Cheddington
Ivinghoe Aston
Whipsnade Wild Animal Park
Woodside Farm
Ayot St Lawrence
Shaw's Corner (NT)
East Hyde
Welwyn
Whipsnade Park
Markyate
Long Marston
Pitstone
Ivinghoe
Dagnall
Studham
Cheverell's Green
Ayot St Peter
A1
A14
A6
A45
A509
A510
A5128
A5028
A428
A421
A603
A5134
A422
A600
A6001
A507
A5130
A4146
A4012
A5120
A505
A5065
A1081
A418
A5
A1(M)
M1
B645
B663
B660
B661
B571
B569
B573
B5388
B565
B531
B530
B1042
B1040
B1046
B658
B655
B4032
B579
B489
B4540
B4541
B488
B651
B656
B652
B653

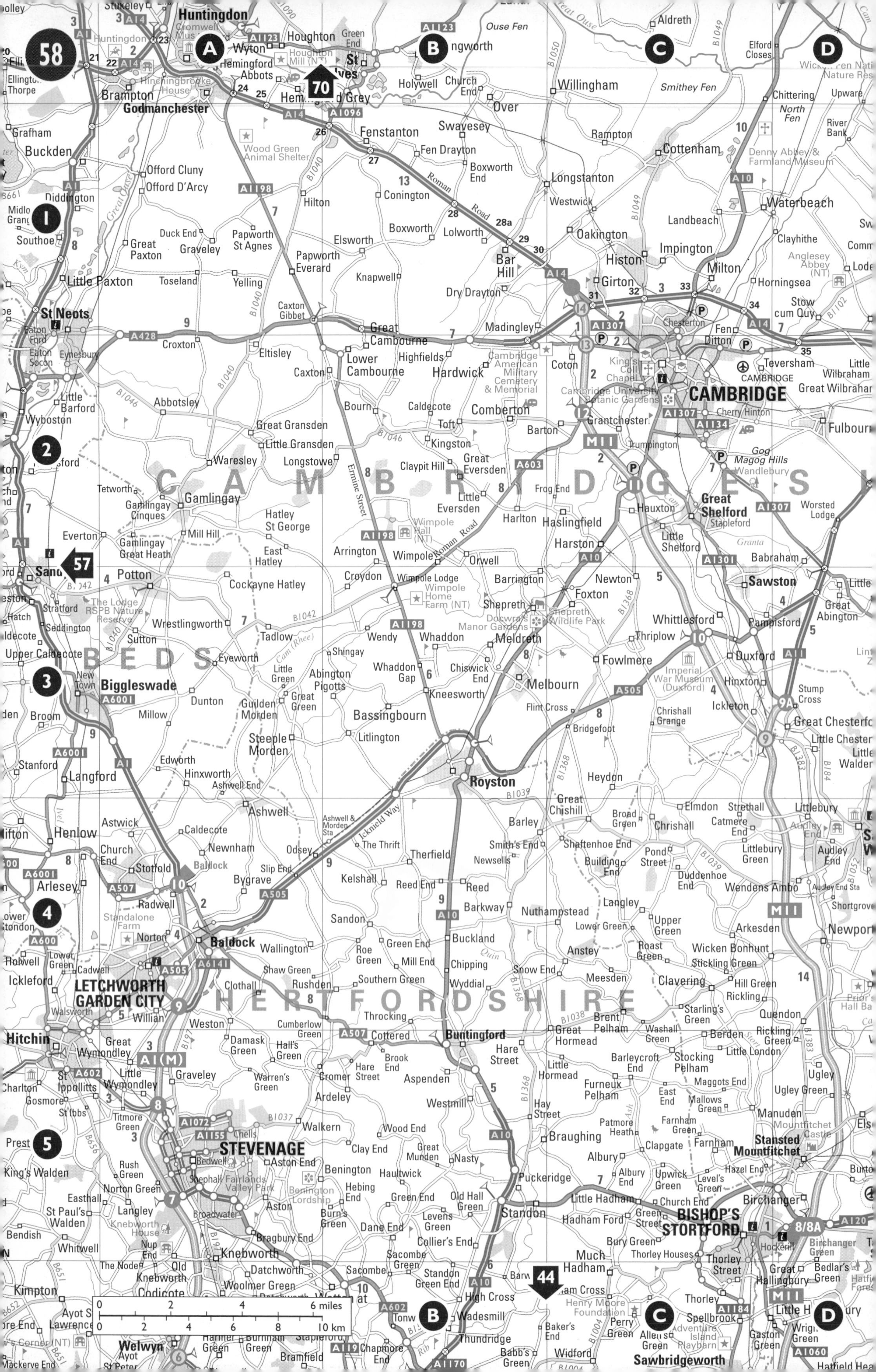

58
A
B
C
D
70
57
44
1
2
3
4
5
Huntingdon
Cromwell Mus
Hinchingbrooke House
Brampton
Godmanchester
Wyton
Houghton
Hemingford Abbots
Hemingford Grey
St Ives
Holywell
Church End
Over
Willingham
Aldreth
Ouse Fen
Smithey Fen
Elford Closes
Wicken Fen Nature Reserve
Chittering
North Fen
Upware
River Bank
Denny Abbey & Farmland Museum
Ellington Thorpe
Grafham
Buckden
Offord Cluny
Offord D'Arcy
Diddington
Midloe Grange
Southoe
Wood Green Animal Shelter
Fenstanton
Fen Drayton
Swavesey
Boxworth End
Rampton
Cottenham
Longstanton
Westwick
Hilton
Conington
Roman Road
Waterbeach
Landbeach
Great Paxton
Duck End
Graveley
Papworth St Agnes
Papworth Everard
Elsworth
Boxworth
Lolworth
Oakington
Impington
Histon
Clayhithe
Anglesey Abbey (NT)
Lode
Milton
Horningsea
Little Paxton
Toseland
Yelling
Knapwell
Bar Hill
Dry Drayton
Girton
Stow cum Quy
St Neots
Eaton Ford
Eaton Socon
Eynesbury
Caxton Gibbet
Great Cambourne
Madingley
Chesterton
Fen Ditton
Teversham
Little Wilbraham
Great Wilbraham
Croxton
Eltisley
Caxton
Lower Cambourne
Highfields
Hardwick
Cambridge American Military Cemetery & Memorial
Coton
King's Coll Chapel
CAMBRIDGE
Cambridge University Botanic Gardens
Cherry Hinton
Fulbourn
Little Barford
Abbotsley
Wyboston
Bourn
Caldecote
Comberton
Toft
Barton
Grantchester
Trumpington
Great Gransden
Little Gransden
Kingston
Gog Magog Hills
Wandlebury
Longstowe
Waresley
Claypit Hill
Great Eversden
Little Eversden
Frog End
CAMBRIDGESHIRE
Tetworth
Gamlingay
Gamlingay Cinques
Gamlingay Great Heath
Hatley St George
East Hatley
Mill Hill
Everton
Ermine Street
Wimpole Hall (NT)
Harlton
Haslingfield
Hauxton
Great Shelford
Stapleford
Worsted Lodge
Little Shelford
Harston
Babraham
Sawston
Arrington
Wimpole
Orwell
Sandy
Potton
Cockayne Hatley
Croydon
Wimpole Lodge
Wimpole Home Farm (NT)
Barrington
Newton
Foxton
Shepreth
Shepreth Wildlife Park
Docwra's Manor Gardens
Little Abington
Great Abington
Pampisford
Whittlesford
Thriplow
The Lodge RSPB Nature Reserve
Stratford
Seddington
Wrestlingworth
Tadlow
Wendy
Whaddon
Meldreth
Sutton
Eyeworth
Shingay
Fowlmere
Duxford
Imperial War Museum (Duxford)
Hatch
Upper Caldecote
BEDS
Little Green
Abington Pigotts
Whaddon Gap
Chiswick End
Melbourn
Hinxton
Ickleton
Stump Cross
New Town
Biggleswade
Dunton
Guilden Morden
Great Green
Kneesworth
Flint Cross
Chrishall Grange
Bridgefoot
Great Chesterford
Broom
Millow
Bassingbourn
Steeple Morden
Litlington
Little Chesterford
Little Walden
Stanford
Langford
Edworth
Hinxworth
Ashwell End
Royston
Heydon
Ashwell
Ashwell & Morden Sta
Icknield Way
Great Chishill
Elmdon
Strethall
Littlebury
Barley
Broad Green
Chrishall
Catmere End
Audley End
Henlow
Astwick
Caldecote
Newnham
Odsey
The Thrift
Smith's End
Shaftenhoe End
Littlebury Green
Church End
Stotfold
Baldock
Therfield
Newsells
Building End
Pond Street
Duddenhoe End
Audley End Sta
Arlesey
Slip End
Bygrave
Kelshall
Reed End
Reed
Wendens Ambo
Radwell
Barkway
Nuthampstead
Langley
Shortgrove
Standalone Farm
Norton
Sandon
Lower Green
Upper Green
Arkesden
Newport
Roe Green
Green End
Buckland
Anstey
Roast Green
Wicken Bonhunt
Holwell
Lower Green
Cadwell
Wallington
Shaw Green
Mill End
Chipping
Snow End
Stickling Green
Ickleford
LETCHWORTH GARDEN CITY
Clothall
Rushden
Southern Green
Wyddial
Meesden
Clavering
Hill Green
Rickling
Walsworth
William
HERTFORDSHIRE
Throcking
Starling's Green
Quendon
Hitchin
Weston
Cumberlow Green
Cottered
Buntingford
Great Hormead
Brent Pelham
Washall Green
Berden
Rickling Green
Great Wymondley
Damask Green
Hall's Green
Hare Street
Little London
Little Wymondley
Graveley
Brook End
Hare Street
Little Hormead
Barleycroft End
Stocking Pelham
Ugley
Charlton
St Ippollitts
Gosmore
Warren's Green
Cromer
Aspenden
Furneux Pelham
Maggots End
St Ibbs
Titmore Green
Ardeley
Westmill
East End
Mallows Green
Ugley Green
Walkern
Hay Street
Manuden
Prest
STEVENAGE
Chells
Wood End
Patmore Heath
Farnham Green
Stansted Mountfitchet
Mountfitchet Castle
Bedwell
Aston End
Clay End
Great Munden
Braughing
Clapgate
Farnham
Rush Green
Shephall
Fairlands Valley Park
Benington
Nasty
Albury
King's Walden
Norton Green
Benington Lordship
Haultwick
Puckeridge
Albury End
Upwick Green
Level's Green
Hazel End
Easthall
Hebing End
Little Hadham
Church End
Birchanger
St Paul's Walden
Langley
Aston
Green End
Old Hall Green
Standon
Hadham Ford
Green Street
BISHOP'S STORTFORD
Knebworth House
Broadwater
Burn's Green
Levens Green
Bendish
Dane End
Bury Green
Birchanger Green
Nup End
Bragbury End
Collier's End
Thorley Houses
Whitwell
Knebworth
Sacombe Green
Much Hadham
Thorley Street
Great Hallingbury
Bedlar's Green
The Node
Old Knebworth
Datchworth
Sacombe
Standon Green End
Barwick
Kimpton
Codicote
Woolmer Green
Watton at Stone
High Cross
Henry Moore Foundation
Thorley
Ayot St Lawrence
Wadesmill
Perry Green
Spellbrook
Little Hallingbury
Tonwell
Allens Green
Adventure Island Playbarn
Wrights Green
Baker's End
Gaston Green
Welwyn
Ayot St Peter
Harmer Green
Burnham Green
Stapleford
Chapmore End
Thundridge
Babb's Green
Widford
Sawbridgeworth
Hatfield Heath
Bramfield
0
2
4
6 miles
0
2
4
6
8
10 km
A1
A14
A123
A1123
A1096
A1198
A428
A10
A1307
A1134
M11
A603
A1301
A505
A6001
A507
A600
A6141
A1(M)
A602
A1072
A1155
A120
A1184
A1060
A119
A1170
A11

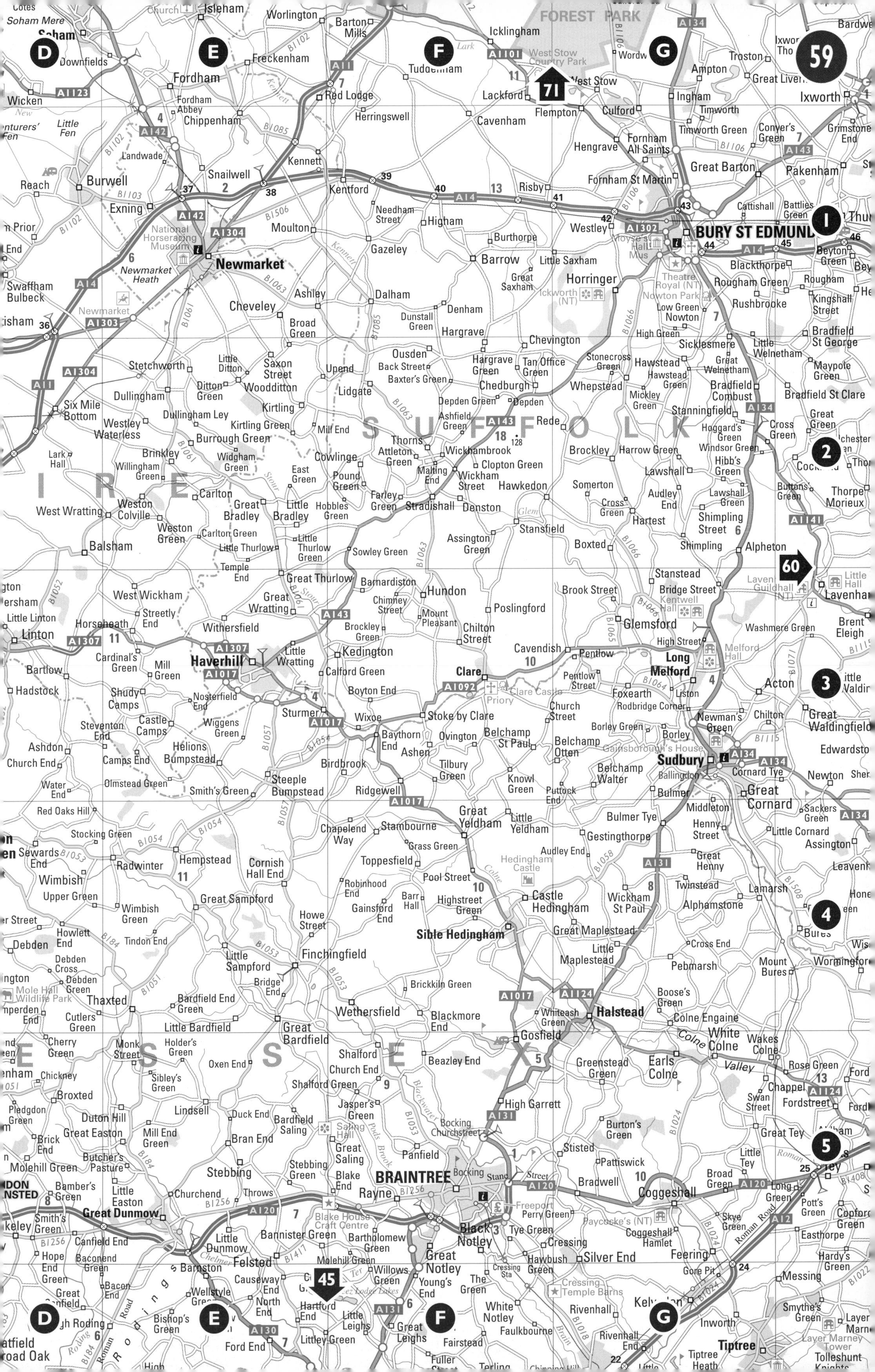
59
FOREST PARK
Soham Mere
Soham
Isleham
Worlington
Barton Mills
Icklingham
West Stow Country Park
Wordwell
Bardwell
Ixworth Thorpe
Downfields
Freckenham
Tuddenham
West Stow
Troston
Ampton
Great Livermere
Ixworth
Wicken
Fordham
Red Lodge
Lackford
Flempton
Culford
Ingham
Timworth
Fordham Abbey
Chippenham
Herringswell
Cavenham
Hengrave
Fornham All Saints
Timworth Green
Conyer's Green
Grimstone End
Little Fen
Landwade
Kennett
Great Barton
Pakenham
Burwell
Snailwell
Kentford
Risby
Fornham St Martin
Reach
Exning
Needham Street
Higham
Cattishall
Battlies Green
National Horseracing Museum
Moulton
Westley
BURY ST EDMUNDS
Newmarket
Gazeley
Barrow
Burthorpe
Little Saxham
Moyse's Hall Mus
Beyton Green
Newmarket Heath
Ashley
Dalham
Great Saxham
Horringer
Theatre Royal (NT)
Nowton Park
Blackthorpe
Rougham Green
Rougham
Swaffham Bulbeck
Cheveley
Broad Green
Dunstall Green
Denham
Ickworth (NT)
Low Green
Nowton
Rushbrooke
Kingshall Street
Bradfield St George
Hargrave
High Green
Chevington
Sicklesmere
Little Whelnetham
Great Whelnetham
Stetchworth
Little Ditton
Saxon Street
Upend
Ousden
Back Street
Hargrave Green
Tan Office Green
Stonecross Green
Hawstead
Hawstead Green
Maypole Green
Ditton Green
Woodditton
Lidgate
Baxter's Green
Chedburgh
Whepstead
Bradfield Combust
Bradfield St Clare
Six Mile Bottom
Dullingham
Kirtling
Depden Green
Depden
Mickley Green
Stanningfield
Dullingham Ley
Ashfield Green
Great Green
Westley Waterless
Kirtling Green
Mill End
SUFFOLK
Rede
Hoggard's Green
Cross Green
Burrough Green
Thorns
Windsor Green
Brinkley
Lark Hall
Willingham Green
Widgham Green
Cowlinge
Attleton Green
Wickhambrook
Clopton Green
Brockley
Harrow Green
Hibb's Green
East Green
Pound Green
Malting End
Wickham Street
Hawkedon
Lawshall
Cockfield
Carlton
Somerton
Audley End
Lawshall Green
Buttons' Green
Thorpe Morieux
Great Bradley
Little Bradley
Hobbles Green
Farley Green
Stradishall
Denston
Cross Green
Hartest
Shimpling Street
West Wratting
Weston Colville
Weston Green
Carlton Green
Little Thurlow
Little Thurlow Green
Sowley Green
Assington Green
Stansfield
Boxted
Shimpling
Alpheton
Balsham
Temple End
Great Thurlow
Barnardiston
Hundon
Stanstead
Bridge Street
Kentwell Hall
60
Little Hall
Lavenham
West Wickham
Chimney Street
Poslingford
Brook Street
Linton
Streetly End
Horseheath
Great Wratting
Withersfield
Brockley Green
Mount Pleasant
Chilton Street
Glemsford
Washmere Green
Brent Eleigh
Little Linton
Bartlow
Cardinal's Green
Mill Green
Haverhill
Little Wratting
Kedington
Cavendish
Pentlow
Long Melford
High Street
Melford Hall
Hadstock
Shudy Camps
Nosterfield End
Calford Green
Boyton End
Clare
Clare Castle
Priory
Pentlow Street
Foxearth
Liston
Acton
Little Waldingfield
Steventon End
Castle Camps
Wiggens Green
Sturmer
Wixoe
Stoke by Clare
Church Street
Rodbridge Corner
Newman's Green
Chilton
Great Waldingfield
Ashdon
Helions Bumpstead
Baythorn End
Ashen
Ovington
Belchamp St Paul
Borley Green
Borley
Edwardstone
Church End
Camps End
Birdbrook
Tilbury Green
Belchamp Otten
Gainsborough's House
Sudbury
Cornard Tye
Newton
Water End
Olmstead Green
Smith's Green
Steeple Bumpstead
Ridgewell
Knowl Green
Belchamp Walter
Ballingdon
Bulmer
Great Cornard
Puttock End
Red Oaks Hill
Great Yeldham
Little Yeldham
Bulmer Tye
Middleton
Sackers Green
Stocking Green
Chapelend Way
Stambourne
Henny Street
Little Cornard
Sewards End
Hempstead
Grass Green
Gestingthorpe
Assington
Radwinter
Cornish Hall End
Toppesfield
Audley End
Great Henny
Wimbish
Hedingham Castle
Leavenheath
Upper Green
Pool Street
Wickham St Paul
Twinstead
Lamarsh
Robinhood End
Barr Hall
Castle Hedingham
Great Sampford
Highstreet Green
Alphamstone
Wimbish Green
Gainsford End
Howe Street
Sible Hedingham
Great Maplestead
Bures
Howlett End
Tindon End
Little Maplestead
Cross End
Debden
Finchingfield
Mount Bures
Wormingford
Debden Cross
Little Sampford
Pebmarsh
Debden Green
Mole Hall Wildlife Park
Bridge End
Brickkiln Green
Boose's Green
Thaxted
Bardfield End Green
Wethersfield
Whiteash Green
Halstead
Colne Engaine
Cutlers Green
Blackmore End
White Colne
Wakes Colne
Cherry Green
Little Bardfield
Great Bardfield
Gosfield
Colne Valley
Monk Street
Holder's Green
Shalford
ESSEX
Earls Colne
Rose Green
Oxen End
Beazley End
Greenstead Green
Chickney
Sibley's Green
Church End
Chappel
Broxted
Shalford Green
Jasper's Green
Swan Street
Fordstreet
Pledgdon Green
Duton Hill
Lindsell
High Garrett
Burton's Green
Great Tey
Duck End
Bardfield Saling
Saling Hall
Bocking Churchstreet
Brick End
Great Easton
Mill End Green
Bran End
Great Saling
Panfield
Stisted
Little Tey
Molehill Green
Butcher's Pasture
Stebbing Green
Pattiswick
Stebbing
Blake End
BRAINTREE
Bocking
Stanway
Broad Green
Bamber's Green
Little Easton
Churchend
Throws
Rayne
Bradwell
Coggeshall
Long Green
Great Dunmow
Blake House Craft Centre
Freeport
Perry Green
Pott's Green
Smith's Green
Canfield End
Bannister Green
Bartholomew Green
Black Notley
Tye Green
Paycocke's (NT)
Coggeshall Hamlet
Skye Green
Copford Green
Little Dunmow
Cressing
Easthorpe
Hope End Green
Baconend Green
Molehill Green
Great Notley
Hawbush Green
Silver End
Feering
Hardy's Green
Barnston
Felsted
Willows Green
Cressing Sta
Gore Pit
Messing
Great Canfield
Bacon End
Causeway End
Young's End
The Green
Cressing Temple Barns
Wellstyle Green
North End
Hartford End
Kelvedon
Smythe's Green
Layer Marney
Layer Marney Tower
White Notley
Rivenhall
High Roding
Bishop's Green
Little Leighs
Great Leighs
Faulkbourne
Inworth
Rivenhall End
Tiptree
Hatfield Broad Oak
Ford End
Littley Green
Fairstead
Tiptree Heath
Tolleshunt Knights
Roman Road
45
71

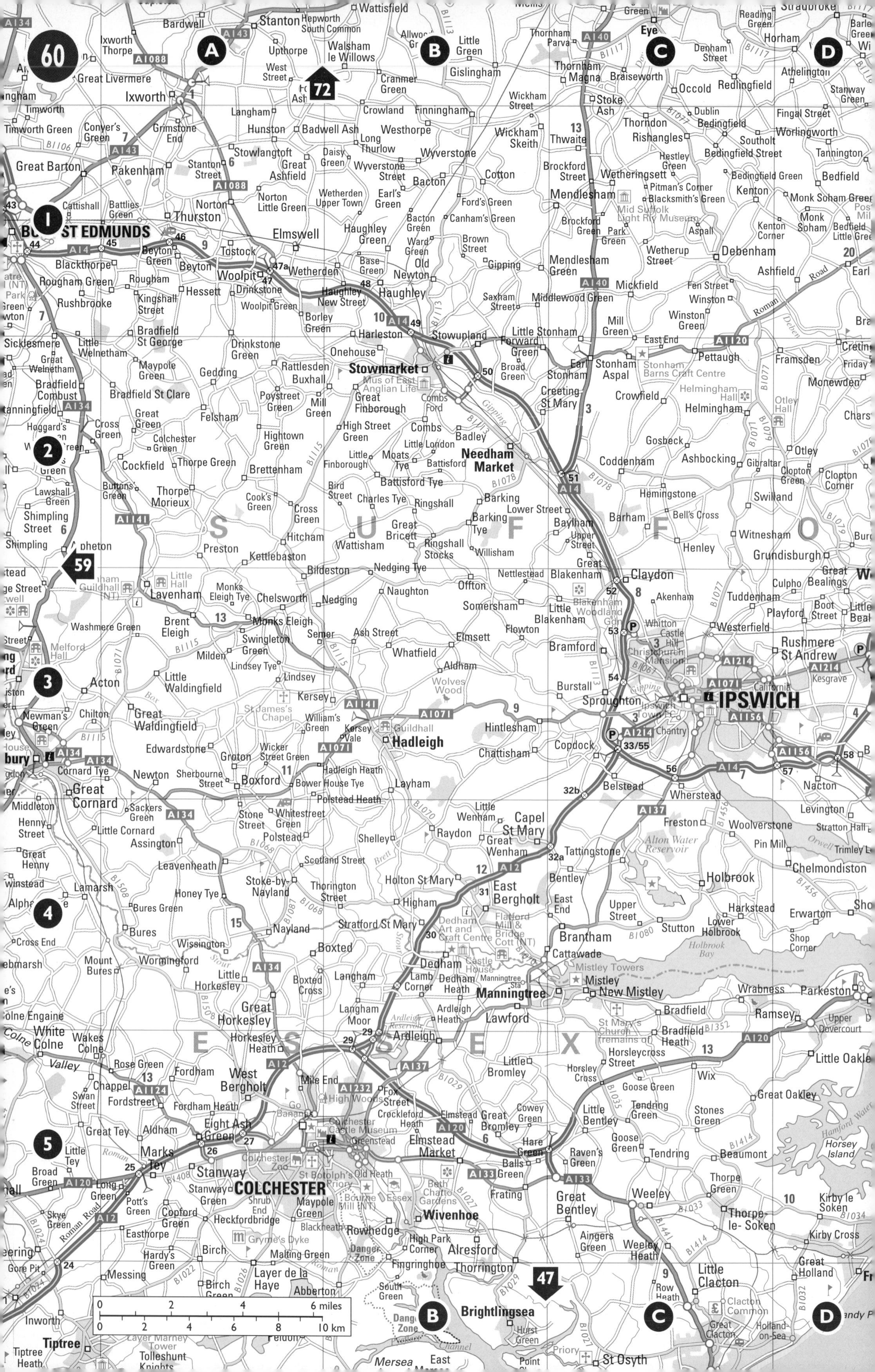
60
A
B
C
D
72
59
47
1
2
3
4
5
Bardwell
Stanton
Hepworth South Common
Wattisfield
Ixworth Thorpe
Upthorpe
Walsham le Willows
Little Green
Thornham Parva
Eye
Reading Green
Stradbroke
Horham
Denham Street
Great Livermere
West Street
Cranmer Green
Gislingham
Thornham Magna
Braiseworth
Athelington
Ixworth
Langham
Crowland
Finningham
Wickham Street
Stoke Ash
Occold
Redlingfield
Stanway Green
Timworth
Hunston
Badwell Ash
Long Thurlow
Westhorpe
Wickham Skeith
Thwaite
Thorndon
Dublin
Bedingfield
Fingal Street
Timworth Green
Conyer's Green
Grimstone End
Stowlangtoft
Daisy Green
Wyverstone
Rishangles
Southolt
Worlingworth
Great Barton
Pakenham
Stanton Street
Great Ashfield
Wyverstone Street
Cotton
Brockford Street
Hestley Green
Bedingfield Street
Tannington
Bacton
Wetheringsett
Bedingfield Green
Bedfield
Norton Little Green
Wetherden Upper Town
Earl's Green
Mendlesham
Pitman's Corner
Kenton
Cattishall
Battlies Green
Norton
Thurston
Ford's Green
Blacksmith's Green
Monk Soham Green
Bacton Green
Canham's Green
Mid Suffolk Light Rly Museum
Brockford Green
Park Green
Aspall
Monk Soham
Kenton Corner
Bedfield Little Green
BURY ST EDMUNDS
Elmswell
Haughley Green
Brown Street
Wetherup Street
Debenham
Beyton Green
Tostock
Ward Green
Blackthorpe
Beyton
Base Green
Old Newton
Gipping
Mendlesham Green
Ashfield
Rougham Green
Rougham
Woolpit
Wetherden
Haughley New Street
Fen Street
Winston
Hessett
Drinkstone
Haughley
Saxham Street
Middlewood Green
Mickfield
Rushbrooke
Kingshall Street
Woolpit Green
Borley Green
Mill Green
Winston Green
Bradfield St George
Harleston
Stowupland
Little Stonham
East End
Pettaugh
Sicklesmere
Little Welnetham
Drinkstone Green
Onehouse
Forward Green
Earl Stonham
Stonham Aspal
Framsden
Great Welnetham
Maypole Green
Gedding
Rattlesden
Stowmarket
Broad Green
Stonham Barns Craft Centre
Bradfield Combust
Buxhall
Mus of East Anglian Life
Combs Ford
Creeting St Mary
Crowfield
Helmingham Hall
Monewden
Bradfield St Clare
Poystreet Green
Great Finborough
Helmingham
Otley Hall
Great Green
Felsham
Mill Green
Hoggard's Green
Cross Green
High Street Green
Combs
Badley
Colchester Green
Hightown Green
Little London
Gosbeck
Little Finborough
Moats Tye
Needham Market
Coddenham
Ashbocking
Gibraltar
Otley
Cockfield
Thorpe Green
Brettenham
Battisford
Clopton Green
Clopton Corner
Battisford Tye
Buttons Green
Thorpe Morieux
Bird Street
Charles Tye
Ringshall
Barking
Hemingstone
Swilland
Lawshall Green
Cook's Green
Lower Street
Cross Green
Barking Tye
Baylham
Barham
Bell's Cross
Shimpling Street
S
U
F
F
O
Great Bricett
Upper Street
Witnesham
Hitcham
Wattisham
Shimpling
Alpheton
Preston
Ringshall Stocks
Willisham
Great Blakenham
Henley
Grundisburgh
Kettlebaston
Nedging Tye
Bildeston
Nettlestead
Claydon
Great Bealings
Little Hall
Monks Eleigh Tye
Chelsworth
Offton
Akenham
Culpho
Lavenham
Nedging
Naughton
Somersham
Blakenham Woodland Gdn
Tuddenham
Boot Street
Playford
Brent Eleigh
Monks Eleigh
Little Blakenham
Whitton
Westerfield
Washmere Green
Swingleton Green
Semer
Ash Street
Elmsett
Flowton
Castle Hill
Rushmere St Andrew
Melford Hall
Milden
Whatfield
Bramford
Christchurch Mansion
Lindsey Tye
Aldham
Acton
Little Waldingfield
Lindsey
Wolves Wood
Burstall
Kesgrave
Kersey
IPSWICH
California
Newman's Green
Chilton
Great Waldingfield
St James's Chapel
William's Green
Sproughton
Ipswich Town FC
Hintlesham
Kersey Vale
Guildhall
Hadleigh
Chantry
Edwardstone
Wicker Street Green
Copdock
Chattisham
Groton
Cornard Tye
Newton
Sherbourne Street
Boxford
Hadleigh Heath
Belstead
Bower House Tye
Layham
Wherstead
Nacton
Great Cornard
Sackers Green
Polstead Heath
Middleton
Stone Street
Whitestreet Green
Little Wenham
Capel St Mary
Freston
Levington
Henny Street
Little Cornard
Assington
Polstead
Shelley
Raydon
Great Wenham
Woolverstone
Stratton Hall
Great Henny
Leavenheath
Scotland Street
Tattingstone
Alton Water Reservoir
Pin Mill
Trimley
Chelmondiston
Twinstead
Lamarsh
Stoke-by-Nayland
Thorington Street
Holton St Mary
Bentley
Holbrook
Alphamstone
Honey Tye
Higham
East Bergholt
East End
Upper Street
Harkstead
Erwarton
Bures Green
Nayland
Stratford St Mary
Dedham Art and Craft Centre
Flatford Mill & Bridge Cott (NT)
Lower Holbrook
Stutton
Shotley
Bures
Wissington
Boxted
Brantham
Holbrook Bay
Shop Corner
Cross End
Cattawade
Mount Bures
Wormingford
Little Horkesley
Boxted Cross
Langham
Dedham
Castle House
Mistley Towers
Lamb Corner
Dedham Heath
Manningtree
Mistley
New Mistley
Wrabness
Parkeston
Great Horkesley
Langham Moor
Ardleigh Reservoir
Ardleigh Heath
Lawford
Bradfield
Ramsey
Upper Dovercourt
Colne Engaine
St Mary's Church (remains of)
White Colne
Wakes Colne
Horkesley Heath
Ardleigh
Bradfield Heath
E
S
S
E
X
Horsleycross Street
Little Oakley
Valley
Rose Green
Fordham
West Bergholt
Little Bromley
Horsley Cross
Wix
Chappel
Mile End
Fox Street
Goose Green
Great Oakley
Swan Street
Fordstreet
High Woods
Fordham Heath
Crockleford Heath
Elmstead
Great Bromley
Cowey Green
Little Bentley
Tendring Green
Stones Green
Great Tey
Aldham
Eight Ash Green
Colchester Castle Museum
Greenstead
Elmstead Market
Hare Green
Goose Green
Hamford Water
Horsey Island
Little Tey
Marks Tey
Stanway
Colchester Zoo
Old Heath
Balls Green
Raven's Green
Tendring
Beaumont
Broad Green
Long Green
St Botolph's Priory
Beth Chatto Gardens
Frating
Thorpe Green
Pott's Green
Copford Green
Stanway Green
COLCHESTER
Shrub End
Maypole Green
Bourne Mill (NT)
Essex
Wivenhoe
Great Bentley
Weeley
Kirby le Soken
Skye Green
Heckfordbridge
Blackheath
Rowhedge
Thorpe-le-Soken
Easthorpe
Gryme's Dyke
High Park Corner
Aingers Green
Kirby Cross
Birch
Malting Green
Danger Zone
Alresford
Weeley Heath
Hardy's Green
Great Holland
Gore Pit
Messing
Layer de la Haye
Fingringhoe
Thorrington
Little Clacton
Birch Green
Abberton
South Green
Row Heath
Brightlingsea
Clacton Common
Inworth
Holland-on-Sea
Great Clacton
Tiptree
Layer Marney Tower
Peldon
Hurst Green
Tiptree Heath
Tolleshunt Knights
Mersea
East Mersea
Priory
St Osyth
Point
0 2 4 6 miles
0 2 4 6 8 10 km
A134
A143
A1088
A14
A140
A1120
A1141
A1071
A1214
A1156
A137
A12
A120
A1124
A232
A133
B1106
B1115
B1113
B1078
B1077
B1079
B1071
B1067
B1070
B1068
B1087
B1508
B1080
B1035
B1029
B1027
B1033
B1441
B1414
B1032
B1034
B1352
B1456
B1022
B1026
B1024
B1408
B1021
B1117
B1070
Gipping
Deben
Orwell
Stour
Brett
Colne
Roman Road
Channel

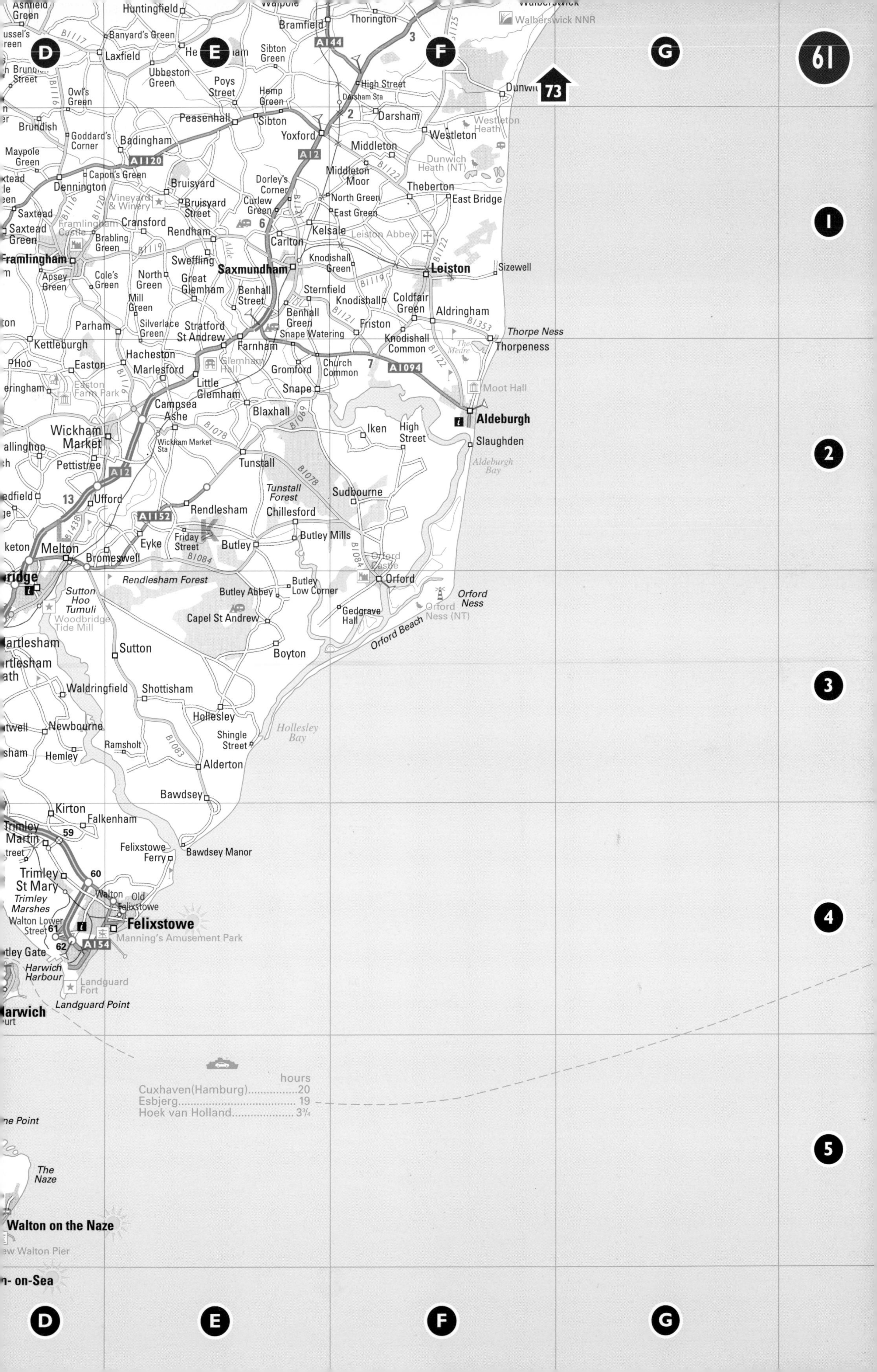
D
E
F
G
73
Walberswick NNR
Huntingfield
Bramfield
Thorington
Banyard's Green
Laxfield
Sibton Green
Ubbeston Green
Poys Street
Hemp Green
High Street
Darsham Sta
Darsham
Owl's Green
Brundish
Peasenhall
Sibton
Yoxford
Westleton
Westleton Heath
Goddard's Corner
Badingham
Middleton
Maypole Green
Dunwich Heath (NT)
Capon's Green
Dennington
Bruisyard
Dorley's Corner
Middleton Moor
Theberton
Vineyard & Winery
Bruisyard Street
Curlew Green
North Green
East Bridge
Saxtead
Framlingham Castle
Cransford
East Green
Saxtead Green
Brabling Green
Rendham
Kelsale
Leiston Abbey
Carlton
Framlingham
Sweffling
Knodishall Green
Leiston
Sizewell
Apsey Green
Cole's Green
North Green
Great Glemham
Saxmundham
Benhall Street
Sternfield
Knodishall
Coldfair Green
Aldringham
Mill Green
Benhall Green
Parham
Silverlace Green
Stratford St Andrew
Snape Watering
Friston
Knodishall Common
Thorpe Ness
Thorpeness
Kettleburgh
Farnham
The Meare
Hoo
Easton
Hacheston
Marlesford
Glemham Hall
Gromford
Church Common
Easton Farm Park
Little Glemham
Snape
Moot Hall
Campsea Ashe
Blaxhall
Aldeburgh
Wickham Market
Wickham Market Sta
Iken
High Street
Slaughden
Pettistree
Tunstall
Aldeburgh Bay
Tunstall Forest
Sudbourne
Ufford
Rendlesham
Chillesford
Eyke
Friday Street
Butley
Butley Mills
Melton
Bromeswell
Orford Castle
Orford
Rendlesham Forest
Butley Low Corner
Sutton Hoo Tumuli
Butley Abbey
Orford Ness
Woodbridge Tide Mill
Capel St Andrew
Gedgrave Hall
Orford Ness (NT)
Orford Beach
Sutton
Boyton
Waldringfield
Shottisham
Hollesley
Newbourne
Shingle Street
Hollesley Bay
Ramsholt
Hemley
Alderton
Bawdsey
Kirton
Falkenham
Trimley Martin
Felixstowe Ferry
Bawdsey Manor
Trimley St Mary
Trimley Marshes
Walton
Old Felixstowe
Walton Lower Street
Felixstowe
Manning's Amusement Park
Harwich Harbour
Landguard Fort
Landguard Point
Harwich
hours
Cuxhaven(Hamburg)....................20
Esbjerg....................19
Hoek van Holland....................3¾
The Naze
Walton on the Naze
A144
A12
A1120
A1094
A1152
A154
A14
B1117
B1116
B1120
B1119
B1121
B1122
B1125
B1353
B1069
B1078
B1084
B1083
B1438
1
2
3
4
5

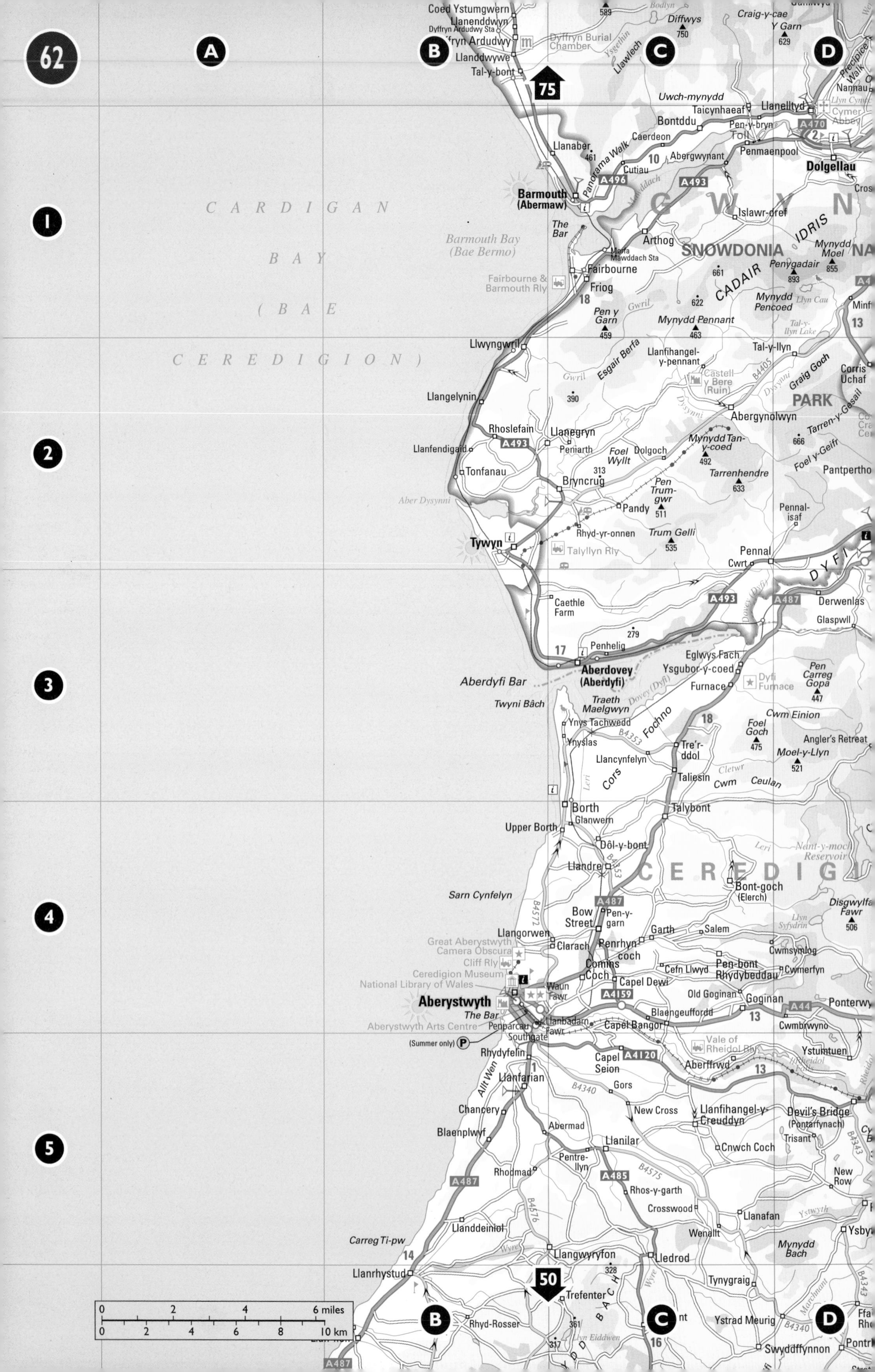
CARDIGAN BAY (BAE CEREDIGION)
Coed Ystumgwern
Llanenddwyn
Dyffryn Ardudwy Sta
Dyffryn Ardudwy
Dyffryn Burial Chamber
Llanddwywe
Tal-y-bont
75
Ysgethin
Llawlech
Bodlyn
589
Diffwys
750
Craig-y-cae
Y Garn
629
Uwch-mynydd
Taicynhaeaf
Llanelltyd
Cymer Abbey
Nannau
Llyn Cynwch
Precipice Walk
Bontddu
Pen-y-bryn
Toll
A470
Caerdeon
Llanaber
461
Panorama Walk
10
Abergwynant
Penmaenpool
Dolgellau
Cutiau
A496
A493
Mawddach
Barmouth (Abermaw)
Islawr-dref
GWYNEDD
The Bar
Barmouth Bay (Bae Bermo)
Arthog
Morfa Mawddach Sta
SNOWDONIA
CADAIR IDRIS
Mynydd Moel
855
Penygadair
893
Fairbourne
Fairbourne & Barmouth Rly
Friog
661
622
18
Gwril
Mynydd Pencoed
Llyn Cau
Tal-y-llyn Lake
Pen y Garn
459
Mynydd Pennant
463
13
Llwyngwril
Esgair Berfa
Llanfihangel-y-pennant
Tal-y-llyn
Castell y Bere (Ruin)
B4405
Dysynni
Craig Goch
Corris Uchaf
Llangelynin
390
PARK
Abergynolwyn
Tarren-y-Gesail
Rhoslefain
A493
Llanegryn
Peniarth
Mynydd Tan-y-coed
492
666
Llanfendigaid
Foel Wyllt
Dolgoch
Foel y Geifr
Tonfanau
313
Tarrenhendre
633
Pantperthog
Bryncrug
Pen Trum-gwr
511
Aber Dysynni
Pandy
Pennal-isaf
Rhyd-yr-onnen
Trum Gelli
535
Tywyn
Talyllyn Rly
Pennal
Cwrt
DYFI
A493
A487
Derwenlas
Caethle Farm
Glaspwll
279
17
Penhelig
Eglwys Fach
Aberdovey (Aberdyfi)
Ysgubor-y-coed
Pen Carreg Gopa
447
Aberdyfi Bar
Dovey (Dyfi)
Dyfi Furnace
Furnace
Twyni Bâch
Traeth Maelgwyn
Fochno
18
Cwm Einion
Ynys Tachwedd
B4353
Foel Goch
475
Angler's Retreat
Ynyslas
Tre'r-ddol
Moel-y-Llyn
521
Llancynfelyn
Cors
Cletwr
Taliesin
Cwm
Ceulan
Leri
Borth
Talybont
Glanwern
Upper Borth
Nant-y-moch Reservoir
Dôl-y-bont
Llandre
CEREDIGION
Bont-goch (Elerch)
Sarn Cynfelyn
A487
Disgwylfa Fawr
506
B4572
Bow Street
Pen-y-garn
Llyn Syfydrin
Llangorwen
Garth
Salem
Great Aberystwyth Camera Obscura
Clarach
Penrhyn-coch
Cwmsymlog
Cliff Rly
Comins Coch
Cefn Llwyd
Pen-bont Rhydybeddau
Cwmerfyn
Ceredigion Museum
National Library of Wales
Waun Fawr
Capel Dewi
A4159
Old Goginan
Goginan
Ponterwyd
Aberystwyth
The Bar
Llanbadarn Fawr
Blaengeuffordd
13
A44
Aberystwyth Arts Centre
Penparcau
Capel Bangor
Cwmbrwyno
(Summer only)
Southgate
Vale of Rheidol Rly
Ystumtuen
Rhydyfelin
Capel Seion
A4120
Aberffrwd
Rheidol
13
Allt Wen
Llanfarian
Gors
B4340
Chancery
New Cross
Llanfihangel-y-Creuddyn
Devil's Bridge (Pontarfynach)
Abermad
Blaenplwyf
Llanilar
Trisant
B4343
Cnwch Coch
Pentre-llyn
Rhodmad
A485
B4575
New Row
A487
Rhos-y-garth
B4576
Crosswood
Llanafan
Ystwyth
Llanddeiniol
Wenallt
Mynydd Bach
Carreg Ti-pw
Wyre
Llangwyryfon
Lledrod
14
328
Llanrhystud
50
Tynygraig
Trefenter
BACH
Marchnant
B4343
361
Ystrad Meurig
B4340
Rhyd-Rosser
Llyn Eiddwen
317
16
Swyddffynnon
A487
0 2 4 6 miles
0 2 4 6 8 10 km
A B C D
1 2 3 4 5

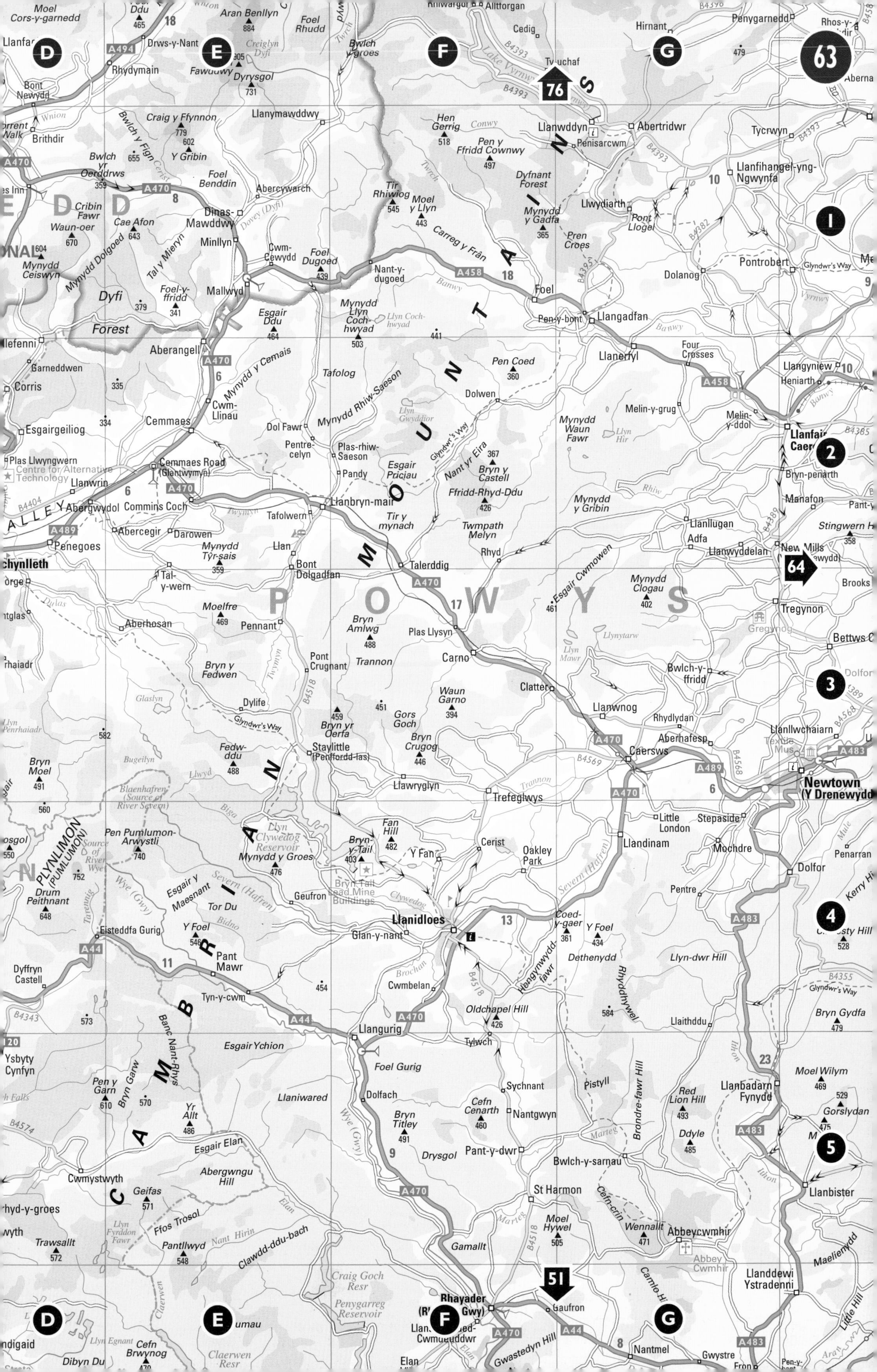

63
D
E
F
G
I
2
3
4
5
76
64
51
Moel Cors-y-garnedd
Ddu
465
18
Aran Benllyn
884
Foel Rhudd
Bwlch y Groes
Rhiwargor
Allt-forgan
Cedig
B4393
Lake Vyrnwy
Tyuchaf
Hirnant
Penygarneddl
479
Rhos-y-llir
Aberna
Llanfar
A494
Drws-y-Nant
Creiglyn Dyfi
305
Fawddwy
Dyrysgol
731
Rhydymain
Bont Newydd
Wnion
Brithdir
Craig y Ffynnon
779
602
Y Gribin
Bwlch y Fign
655
Llanymawddwy
Hen Gerrig
518
Conwy
Pen y Ffridd Cownwy
497
Llanwddyn
Penisarcwm
Abertridwr
B4393
Tycrwyn
Llanfihangel-yng-Ngwynfa
10
A470
Bwlch yr Oerddrws
359
A470
8
Foel Benddin
Abercywarch
Cribin Fawr
Cae Afon
643
Waun-oer
670
Dinas-Mawddwy
Minllyn
Dovey (Dyfi)
Tir Rhiwiog
545
Moel y Llyn
443
Carreg y Frân
Dyfnant Forest
Mynydd y Gadfa
365
Pren Croes
Llwydiarth
Pont Llogel
B4382
Dolanog
Pontrobert
Glyndŵr's Way
Vyrnwy
604
Mynydd Ceiswyn
Mynydd Dolgoed
Tal y Mieryn
Foel-y-ffridd
341
Mallwyd
Cwm-Cewydd
Foel Dugoed
439
Nant-y-dugoed
A458
18
Banwy
Foel
B4395
Pen-y-bont
Llangadfan
Dyfi
Forest
379
Esgair Ddu
464
Mynydd Llyn Coch-hwyad
503
Llyn Coch-hwyad
441
Banwy
Llanerfyl
Four Crosses
A458
Llangyniew
10
Heniarth
lefenni
Garneddwen
Corris
335
Aberangell
A470
6
Mynydd y Cemais
Cwm-Llinau
Tafolog
Mynydd Rhiw-Saeson
Llyn Gwyddior
Pen Coed
360
Dolwen
Melin-y-grug
Melin-y-ddol
Llanfair Caereinion
B4385
334
Esgairgeiliog
Cemmaes
Dol Fawr
Pentre-celyn
Plas-rhiw-Saeson
Glyndŵr's Way
Mynydd Waun Fawr
Llyn Hir
Plas Llwyngwern
Centre for Alternative Technology
Cemmaes Road (Glantwymyn)
A470
Llanwrin
6
Pandy
Esgair Priciau
Nant yr Eira
367
Bryn y Castell
Ffridd-Rhyd-Ddu
426
Rhiw
Bryn-penarth
Manafon
Pant-y
B4404
Abergwydol
Commins Coch
Twymyn
Llanbryn-mair
Tafolwern
Tir y mynach
Mynydd y Gribin
Llanllugan
Adfa
B4389
Stingwern H
358
A489
Abercegir
Darowen
Penegoes
Mynydd Tŷr-sais
359
Llan
Bont Dolgadfan
Talerddig
Twmpath Melyn
Rhyd
Esgair Cwmowen
Llanwyddelan
New Mills
chynlleth
Tal-y-wern
A470
Mynydd Clogau
402
Brooks
Dulas
Moelfre
469
P O W Y S
17
461
Tregynon
Gregynog
Aberhosan
Pennant
Bryn Amlwg
488
Plas Llysyn
Carno
Llyn Mawr
Llynytarw
Bettws C
rhaiadr
Bryn y Fedwen
Pont Crugnant
Trannon
Twymyn
Clatter
Bwlch-y-ffridd
Dolfor
Glaslyn
Dylife
B4518
459
451
Waun Garno
394
Gors Goch
Llanwnog
Rhydlydan
Glyndŵr's Way
Bryn yr Oerfa
Bryn Crugog
446
Aberhafesp
Llanllwchaiarn
582
Fedw-ddu
488
Staylittle (Penffordd-las)
A470
Caersws
B4569
Textile Mus
A483
Bryn Moel
491
Bugeilyn
Llwyd
Llawryglyn
Trannon
A489
B4568
6
Newtown (Y Drenewydd)
Blaenhafren (Source of River Severn)
Biga
Trefeglwys
A470
560
PLYNLIMON (PUMLUMON)
Pen Pumlumon-Arwystli
740
Llyn Clywedog Reservoir
Mynydd y Groes
476
Fan Hill
482
Bryn-y-Tail
403
Y Fan
Cerist
Oakley Park
Little London
Stepaside
Llandinam
Mochdre
Penarran
Mule
550
Source of River Wye
752
Esgair y Maesnant
Severn (Hafren)
Bryn Tail Lead Mine Buildings
Geufron
Clywedog
Severn (Hafren)
Dolfor
Drum Peithnant
648
Wye (Gwy)
Tor Du
Pentre
Kerry Hi
Tarenig
Eisteddfa Gurig
Y Foel
546
Bidno
Llanidloes
Glan-y-nant
13
Coed-y-gaer
361
Y Foel
434
A483
Kerry Hill
528
A44
Dyffryn Castell
11
Pant Mawr
Brochan
Hengynwydd-fawr
Dethenydd
Rhyddhywel
Llyn-dwr Hill
B4355
Glyndŵr's Way
454
Cwmbelan
B4518
Tyn-y-cwm
B4343
573
Banc Nant-Rhys
A44
A470
Oldchapel Hill
426
584
Llaithddu
Bryn Gydfa
479
120
Llangurig
Tylwch
Ithon
Ysbyty Cynfyn
Esgair Ychion
23
Foel Gurig
Moel Wilym
469
Pen y Garn
610
Bryn Garw
570
Llaniwared
Dolfach
Sychnant
Pistyll
Brondre-fawr Hill
Red Lion Hill
493
Llanbadarn Fynydd
529
Gorslydan
475
Cefn Cenarth
460
Nantgwyn
B4574
Yr Allt
486
Bryn Titley
491
Wye (Gwy)
A483
Ddyle
485
Drysgol
Pant-y-dwr
Marteg
9
Esgair Elan
Bwlch-y-sarnau
Ithon
Cwmystwyth
Abergwngu Hill
A470
Geifas
571
St Harmon
Cefn-crin
Llanbister
rhyd-y-groes
Ffos Trosol
Llyn Fyrddon Fawr
Elan
Marteg
Moel Hywel
505
B4518
Wennallt
471
Abbeycwmhir
Nant Hirin
Trawsallt
572
Pantllwyd
548
Clawdd-ddu-bach
Gamallt
Abbey Cwmhir
Maelienydd
Craig Goch Resr
Camlo Hill
Llanddewi Ystradenni
Claerwen
Penygarreg Reservoir
Rhayader (Rhaeadr Gwy)
Gaufron
Little Hill
umau
Llyn Egnant
Cefn Brwynog
Llansantffraed-Cwmdeuddwr
A470
A44
Gwastedyn Hill
8
Nantmel
Gwystre
A483
ndigaid
Dibyn Du
Claerwen Resr
Elan
Fron
C A M B R I A N
M O U N T A I N S

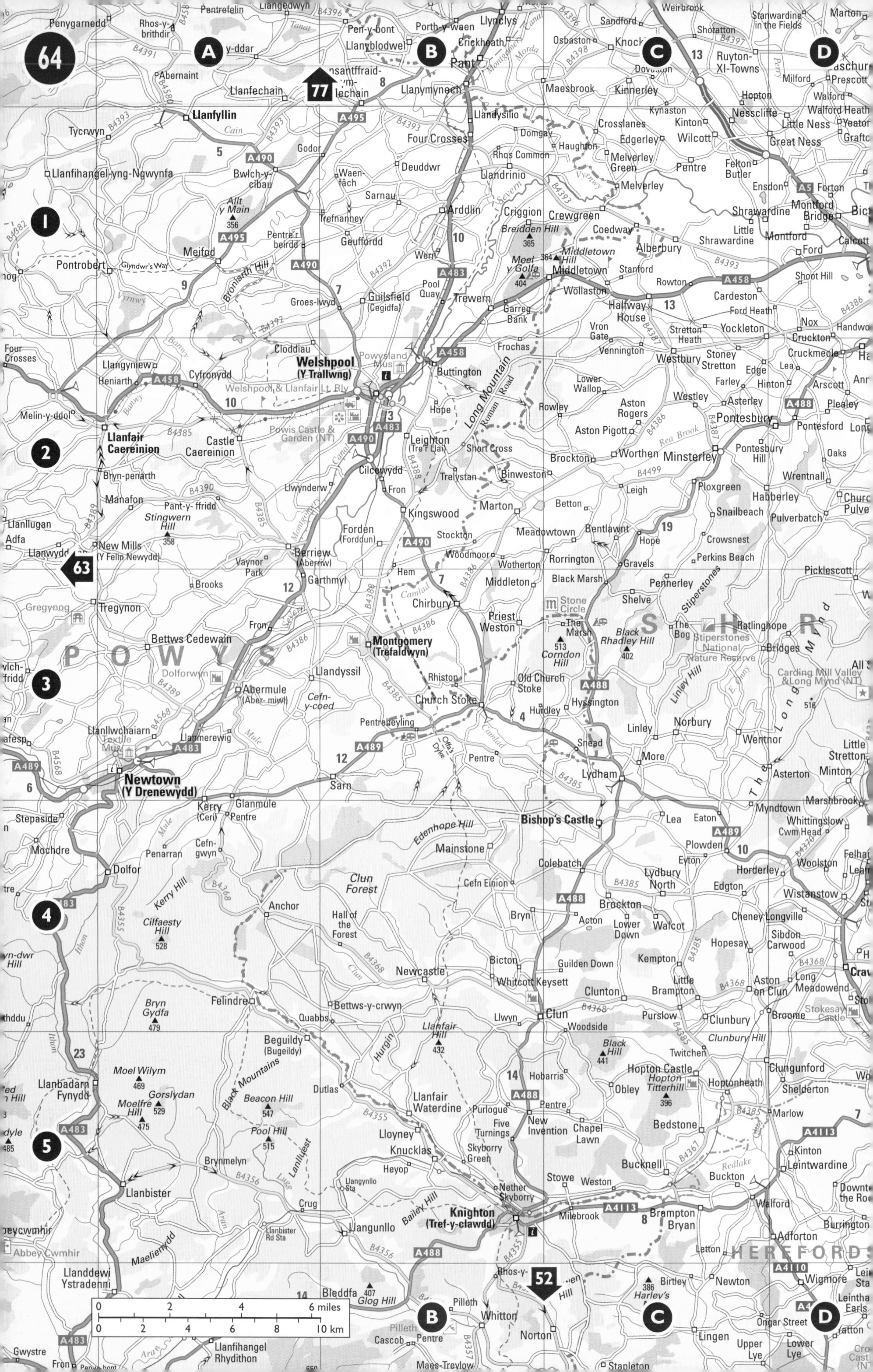
64
A
B
C
D
77
63
52
1
2
3
4
5
Penygarnedd
Pentrefelin
Llangedwyn
Rhos-y-brithdir
Pen-y-bont
Llanyblodwel
Porth-y-waen
Llynclys
Crickheath
Pant
Sandford
Osbaston
Knockin
Weirbrook
Shotatton
Stanwardine in the Fields
Marton
Ruyton-XI-Towns
Abernaint
Llanfechain
Llanymynech
Maesbrook
Kinnerley
Dovaston
Milford
Prescott
Llanfyllin
Llandysilio
Kynaston
Hopton
Walford
Walford Heath
Nesscliffe
Tycrwyn
Four Crosses
Domgay
Crosslanes
Kinton
Little Ness
Edgerley
Wilcott
Great Ness
Godor
Haughton
Rhos Common
Melverley Green
Pentre
Felton Butler
Llanfihangel-yng-Ngwynfa
Bwlch-y-cibau
Deuddwr
Llandrinio
Melverley
Ensdon
Forton
Wæn-fâch
Sarnau
Allt y Main
356
Trefnanney
Arddlin
Criggion
Crewgreen
Shrawardine
Montford Bridge
Little Shrawardine
Montford
Pentre'r beirdd
Geufford
Breidden Hill
365
Coedway
Alberbury
Ford
Calcott
Meifod
Pontrobert
Glyndwr's Way
Wern
Moel y Golfa
404
Middletown Hill
364
Middletown
Stanford
Rowton
Shoot Hill
Broniarth Hill
Pool Quay
Trewern
Wollaston
Halfway House
Cardeston
Groes-lwyd
Guilsfield (Cegidfa)
Garreg Bank
Ford Heath
Nox
Vron Gate
Stretton Heath
Yockleton
Cruckton
Four Crosses
Cloddiau
Frochas
Vennington
Westbury
Stoney Stretton
Cruckmeole
Llangyniew
Powysland Mus
Welshpool (Y Trallwng)
Buttington
Lea
Edge
Heniarth
Cyfronydd
Farley
Hinton
Arscott
Welshpool & Llanfair Lt Rly
Lower Wallop
Hope
Long Mountain
Roman Road
Rowley
Aston Rogers
Westley
Asterley
Plealey
Melin-y-ddol
Llanfair Caereinion
Castle Caereinion
Powis Castle & Garden (NT)
Leighton (Tre'r Llai)
Aston Pigott
Pontesbury
Pontesford
Short Cross
Rea Brook
Bryn-penarth
Cilcewydd
Trelystan
Brockton
Worthen
Minsterley
Pontesbury Hill
Oaks
Binweston
Fron
Llwynderw
Leigh
Wrentnall
Manafon
Pant-y-ffridd
Plox Green
Stingwern Hill
358
Kingswood
Marton
Betton
Habberley
Snailbeach
Llanllugan
Forden (Forddun)
Stockton
Meadowtown
Bentlawnt
Hope
Crowsnest
Pulverbatch
Adfa
New Mills (Y Felin Newydd)
Llanwydd
Berriew (Aberriw)
Woodmoor
Wotherton
Rorrington
Perkins Beach
Vaynor Park
Hem
Gravels
Picklescott
Brooks
Garthmyl
Middleton
Black Marsh
Pennerley
Stiperstones
Gregynog
Tregynon
Chirbury
Stone Circle
Shelve
Fron
Priest Weston
The Marsh
The Bog
Ratlinghope
Bettws Cedewain
POWYS
SHR
Montgomery (Trefaldwyn)
Black Rhadley Hill
402
Stiperstones National Nature Reserve
Bridges
Corndon Hill
513
Dolforwyn
Llandyssil
Rhiston
Old Church Stoke
Carding Mill Valley & Long Mynd (NT)
Abermule (Aber-miwl)
Cefn-y-coed
Church Stoke
Hyssington
Linley Hill
516
Hurdley
Linley
Norbury
Llanllwchaiarn
Llanmerewig
Textile Mus
Pentrebeyling
Offa's Dyke
Snead
Wentnor
Little Stretton
Pentre
More
Lydham
Asterton
Minton
Newtown (Y Drenewydd)
Sarn
The Long Mynd
Stepaside
Kerry (Ceri)
Glanmule
Pentre
Bishop's Castle
Lea
Eaton
Myndtown
Marshbrook
Whittingslow
Cwm Head
Mochdre
Cefn-gwyn
Penarran
Edenhope Hill
Mainstone
Plowden
Eyton
Horderley
Woolston
Dolfor
Colebatch
Lydbury North
Clun Forest
Cefn Einion
Edgton
Wistanstow
Kerry Hill
Anchor
Brockton
Hall of the Forest
Bryn
Acton
Lower Down
Walcot
Cheney Longville
Cilfaesty Hill
528
Sibdon Carwood
Hopesay
Kempton
Newcastle
Bicton
Guilden Down
Whitcott Keysett
Little Brampton
Aston on Clun
Long Meadowend
Felindre
Bettws-y-crwyn
Bryn Gydfa
479
Llwyn
Clun
Clunton
Purslow
Clunbury
Broome
Stokesay Castle
Quabbs
Woodside
Llanfair Hill
432
Beguildy (Bugeildy)
Black Hill
441
Twitchen
Clunbury Hill
Hurgin
Moel Wilym
469
Hobarris
Hopton Castle
Hopton Titterhill
396
Hoptonheath
Clungunford
Llanbadarn Fynydd
Black Mountains
Obley
Shelderton
Dutlas
Llanfair Waterdine
Gorslydan
Beacon Hill
547
Moelfre Hill
529
475
Purlogue
Pentre
New Invention
Chapel Lawn
Bedstone
Marlow
Five Turnings
Kinton
Leintwardine
Lloyney
Pool Hill
515
Knucklas
Skyborry Green
Bucknell
Llanlluest
Brynmelyn
Heyop
Llangynllo Sta
Stowe
Weston
Buckton
Redlake
Llanbister
Nether Skyborry
Walford
Downton on the Rock
Crug
Bailey Hill
Knighton (Tref-y-clawdd)
Milebrook
Brampton Bryan
Abbey Cwmhir
Llanbister Rd Sta
Llangunllo
Burrington
Adforton
Maelienydd
Letton
HEREFORDS
Llanddewi Ystradenni
Rhos-y-
Birtley
Newton
Wigmore
Bleddfa
407
Glog Hill
386
Harley's Hill
Pilleth
Whitton
Ongar Street
Norton
Lingen
Pilleth
Cascob
Pentre
Upper Lye
Lower Lye
Llanfihangel Rhydithon
Maes-Treylow
Stapleton
Gwystre
Fron
0 2 4 6 miles
0 2 4 6 8 10 km
A495
A490
A483
A458
A5
A488
A489
A4113
A4110
B4393
B4392
B4385
B4386
B4388
B4390
B4389
B4568
B4355
B4356
B4368
B4367
B4357
B4398
B4396
B4397
B4387
B4499
B4399

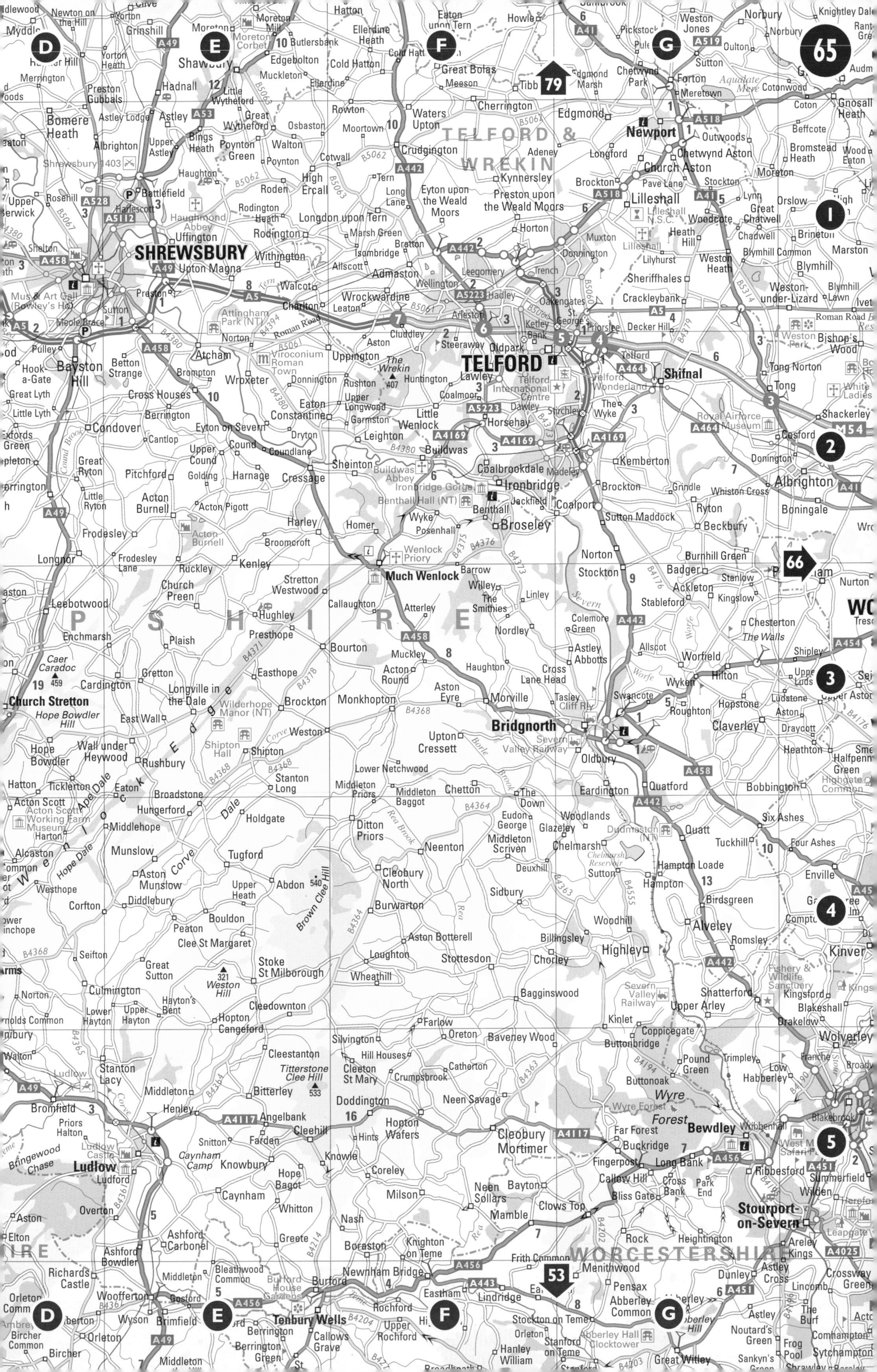
65
79
66
53
D
E
F
G
D
E
F
G
I
2
3
4
5
TELFORD & WREKIN
SHROPSHIRE
WORCESTERSHIRE
Wenlock Edge
SHREWSBURY
TELFORD
Newport
Lilleshall
Shifnal
Much Wenlock
Bridgnorth
Ironbridge
Broseley
Albrighton
Church Stretton
Ludlow
Cleobury Mortimer
Bewdley
Stourport-on-Severn
Tenbury Wells
Kinver
Wolverley
Highley
Alveley
Shawbury
Bayston Hill
Condover
Wellington
Oakengates
Dawley
Madeley
Coalbrookdale
Coalport
Cressage
Buildwas
Wroxeter
Atcham
Upton Magna
High Ercall
Crudgington
Edgmond
Tibberton
Donnington
Hadley
Lawley
Horsehay
Leighton
Kenley
Harley
Church Preen
Hughley
Bourton
Monkhopton
Morville
Worfield
Claverley
Quatt
Eardington
Oldbury
Quatford
Chelmarsh
Billingsley
Chorley
Stottesdon
Burwarton
Cleobury North
Ditton Priors
Neenton
Abdon
Tugford
Munslow
Diddlebury
Culmington
Stanton Lacy
Bromfield
Ludford
Caynham
Clee Hill
Cleehill
Hopton Wafers
Doddington
Farlow
Oreton
Kinlet
Upper Arley
Shatterford
Far Forest
Buckridge
Callow Hill
Rock
Heightington
Areley Kings
Astley
Dunley
Abberley
Pensax
Lindridge
Eastham
Rochford
Burford
Newnham Bridge
Knighton on Teme
Boraston
Nash
Milson
Coreley
Knowle
Hope Bagot
Whitton
Greete
Ashford Carbonel
Ashford Bowdler
Richards Castle
Brimfield
Middleton
Orleton
Woofferton
Wyre Forest
Brown Clee Hill
Titterstone Clee Hill
Caer Caradoc
The Wrekin
Hope Bowdler Hill
Viroconium Roman Town
Attingham Park (NT)
Benthall Hall (NT)
Wenlock Priory
Buildwas Abbey
Ironbridge Gorge
Wilderhope Manor (NT)
Shipton Hall
Dudmaston (NT)
Severn Valley Railway
Telford International Centre
Telford Wonderland
Royal Airforce Museum
Weston Park
West Midland Safari Park
Kinver
A5
A41
A49
A53
A442
A454
A456
A458
A464
A518
A4117
A4169
A5223
M54
Severn
Teme
Corve
Rea Brook
Worfe

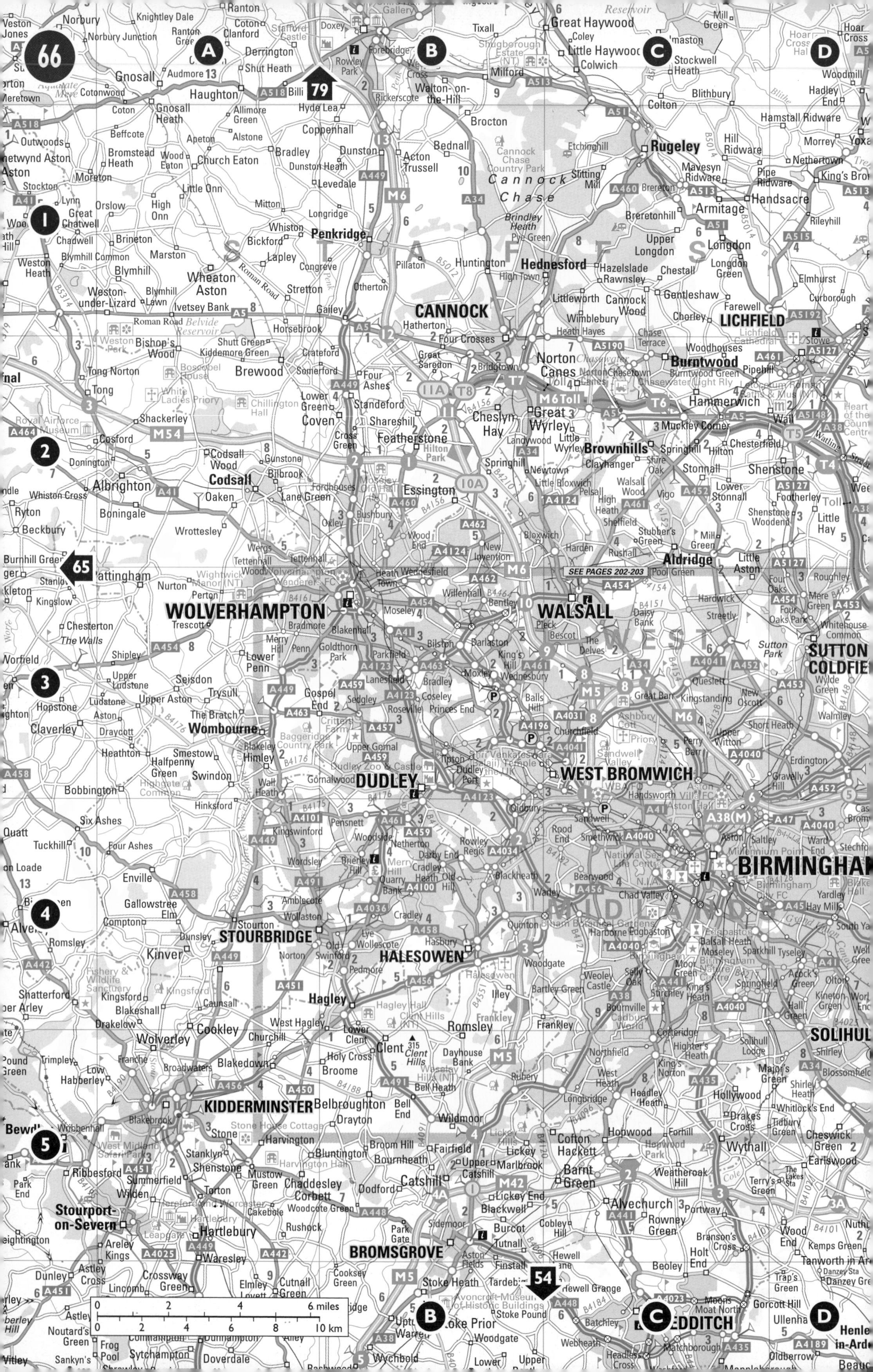

66
A
B
C
D
79
Norbury
Norbury Junction
Knightley Dale
Ranton
Coton Clanford
Derrington
Shut Heath
Doxey
Forebridge
Rowley Park
Tixall
Great Haywood
Little Haywood
Colwich
Shugborough Estate (NT)
Milford
Walton-on-the-Hill
Stockwell Heath
Blithbury
Colton
Hoar Cross
Woodmill
Hadley End
Gnosall
Audmore
Gnosall Heath
Haughton
Billi
Hyde Lea
Rickerscote
Cotonwood
Coton
Beffcote
Allimore Green
Apeton
Alstone
Coppenhall
Brocton
Bednall
Cannock Chase Country Park
Cannock Chase
Etchinghill
Rugeley
Hamstall Ridware
Hill Ridware
Morrey
Yoxall
Nethertown
King's Bromley
Mavesyn Ridware
Pipe Ridware
Outwoods
Bromstead Heath
Wood Eaton
Church Eaton
Bradley
Dunston
Dunston Heath
Acton Trussell
Levedale
Slitting Mill
Brereton
Armitage
Handsacre
Rileyhill
Moreton
Stockton
Little Onn
High Onn
Orslow
Great Chatwell
Mitton
Longridge
Whiston
Bickford
Penkridge
Brindley Heath
Pye Green
Breretonhill
Upper Longdon
Longdon
Longdon Green
Chadwell
Brineton
Marston
Blymhill Common
Blymhill
Weston Heath
Lapley
Congreve
Pillaton
Huntington
Hednesford
Hazelslade
Rawnsley
Chestall
Elmhurst
Curborough
Wheaton Aston
Weston-under-Lizard
Blymhill Lawn
Ivetsey Bank
Roman Road
Stretton
Otherton
High Town
Littleworth
Cannock Wood
Gentleshaw
Farewell
Gailey
CANNOCK
Hatherton
Wimblebury
Heath Hayes
Chorley
LICHFIELD
Lichfield Cathedral
Stowe
Belvide Reservoir
Weston Park
Bishop's Wood
Horsebrook
Shutt Green
Kiddemore Green
Crateford
Four Crosses
Great Saredon
Chase Terrace
Woodhouses
Burntwood
Burntwood Green
Pipehill
Chasewater Light Rly
Tong Norton
Tong
Boscobel House
Brewood
Somerford
Four Ashes
Bridgtown
Norton Canes
Chasetown
White Ladies Priory
Chillington Hall
Lower Green
Standeford
Cheslyn Hay
Great Wyrley
Hammerwich
Wall
Royal Airforce Museum
Shackerley
Coven
Shareshill
Muckley Corner
Cosford
M54
Cross Green
Featherstone
Hilton Park
Landywood
Little Wyrley
Brownhills
Springhill
Hilton
Chesterfield
Codsall Wood
Gunstone
Bilbrook
Codsall
Donington
Albrighton
Whiston Cross
Boningale
Oaken
Moseley Old Hall (NT)
Fordhouses
Lane Green
Essington
Springhill
Newtown
Clayhanger
Shire Oak
Stonnall
Lower Stonnall
Shenstone
Little Bloxwich
Pelsall
Walsall Wood
Vigo
Fotherley
Ryton
Beckbury
Wrottesley
Oxley
Bushbury
Wood End
High Heath
Shelfield
Stubber's Green
Shenstone Woodend
Little Hay
Bloxwich
New Invention
Harden
Rushall
Mill Green
Aldridge
Little Aston
Burnhill Green
65
Pattingham
Tettenhall Wood
Tettenhall
Wergs
Wightwick Manor (NT)
Wolverhampton Wanderers FC
Heath Town
Wednesfield
Willenhall
Bentley
SEE PAGES 202-203
Pool Green
Roughley
Four Oaks
Mere Green
Four Oaks Park
Kingslow
Nurton
Perton
WOLVERHAMPTON
Trescott
Moseley
Bradmore
Blakenhall
WALSALL
Daisy Bank
Pleck
Bescot
Hardwick
Streetly
Whitehouse Common
Chesterton
The Walls
Merry Hill
Penn
Goldthorn Park
Parkfield
Bilston
Darlaston
King's Hill
The Delves
WEST
Sutton Park
SUTTON COLDFIELD
Worfield
Shipley
Lower Penn
Upper Ludstone
Seisdon
Trysull
Lanesfield
Bradley
Moxley
Wednesbury
Queslett
Wylde Green
Ludstone
Hopstone
Upper Aston
Gospel End
Sedgley
Coseley
Roseville
Princes End
Balls Hill
Great Barr
Kingstanding
New Oscott
Aston
Claverley
Draycott
The Bratch
Wombourne
Crittens Farm
Baggeridge Country Park
Upper Gornal
Churchfield
Ashbury Cott
Priory
Perry Barr
Upper Witton
Short Heath
Walmley
Heathton
Smestow
Halfpenny Green
Swindon
Blakeley
Himley
Dudley Zoo & Castle
Tipton
Sri Venkateswara (Balaji) Temple of the UK
Dudley Port
WEST BROMWICH
Sandwell Valley
Erdington
Gravelly Hill
Bobbington
Highgate Common
Gornalwood
Wall Heath
DUDLEY
WBA FC
Handsworth
Aston Villa FC
Aston Hall
Hinksford
Kingswinford
Pensnett
Oldbury
Sandwell
Rood End
Smethwick
Saltley
Ward End
Stechford
Six Ashes
Quatt
Tuckhill
Four Ashes
Wordsley
Woodside
Netherton
Brierley Hill
Merry Hill
Darby End
Cradley Heath
Old Hill
Rowley Regis
Blackheath
National Sea Life Centre
N.I.A.
Millennium Point
BIRMINGHAM
Birmingham City FC
Blake Hall
Yardley
Hay Mills
Enville
Gallowstree Elm
Compton
Amblecote
Wollaston
Quarry Bank
Cradley
Bearwood
Warley
Chad Valley
MIDLANDS
South Yardley
Stourton
Dunsley
STOURBRIDGE
Kinver
Norton
Oldswinford
Lye
Wollescote
Hasbury
HALESOWEN
Quinton
Birmingham Botanical Gardens
Harborne
Edgbaston
Balsall Heath
Moseley
Sparkhill
Tyseley
Romsley
Pedmore
Woodgate
Weoley Castle
Selly Oak
Moor Green
Birmingham Nature Centre
King's Heath
Springfield
Acock's Green
Olton
Kineton Green
Shatterford
Kingsford
Fishery & Wildlife Sanctuary
Caunsall
Blakeshall
Hagley
Hagley Hall
Clent Hills (NT)
Illey
Bartley Green
Stirchley
Bournville
Cadbury World
Hall Green
Drakelow
Cookley
Wolverley
Churchill
West Hagley
Lower Clent
Clent
Romsley
Frankley
Cotteridge
Highter's Heath
Solihull Lodge
SOLIHULL
Shirley
Pound Green
Trimpley
Low Habberley
Franche
Broadwaters
Blakedown
Holy Cross
Broome
Dayhouse Bank
Rubery
Northfield
West Heath
King's Norton
Major's Green
Blossomfield
Shirley Heath
Hollywood
Headley Heath
Longbridge
Whitlock's End
Drakes Cross
Tidbury Green
KIDDERMINSTER
Belbroughton
Bell End
Bell Heath
Wildmoor
Blakebrook
Drayton
Stone House Cottage
Bewdley
Wribbenhall
West Midland Safari Park
Stone
Harvington
Lickey Hills
Cofton Hackett
Hopwood
Forhill
Hopwood Park
Wythall
Cheswick Green
Earlswood
Stanklyn
Bluntington
Broom Hill
Fairfield
Bournheath
Lickey
Marlbrook
Barnt Green
Weatheroak Hill
Terry's Green
Park End
Ribbesford
Summerfield
Shenstone
Mustow Green
Chaddesley Corbett
Harvington Hall
Dodford
Catshill
Upper Catshill
The Lakes Sta
Stourport-on-Severn
Wilden
Torton
Hereford and Worcester
Cakebole
Woodcote Green
Lickey End
Alvechurch
Portway
Blackwell
Burcot
Cobley Hill
Rowney Green
Branson's Cross
Wood End
Nuthurst
Kemps Green
Leighton
Areley Kings
Leapgate
Hartlebury
Rushock
Park Gate
Sidemoor
Tutnall
Holt End
Tanworth in Arden
Danzey Sta
Danzey Green
Waresley
BROMSGROVE
Aston Fields
Finstall
Hewell Lane
Beoley
Dunley
Astley Cross
Crossway Green
Elmley Lovett
Cutnall Green
Cooksey Green
Stoke Heath
Tardebigge
Hewell Grange
Trap's Green
Lincomb
Avoncroft Museum of Historic Buildings
Moons Moat North
Gorcott Hill
Ullenhall
Henley-in-Arden
Stoke Pound
Batchley
REDDITCH
Astley
Noutard's Green
Frog Pool
Sankyn's Green
Sytchampton
Dunhampton
Doverdale
Upton Warren
Stoke Prior
Woodgate
Webheath
Headless Cross
Matchborough
Oldberrow
Wychbold
Upper
Lower
0 2 4 6 miles
0 2 4 6 8 10 km
54
M6
M6 Toll
M5
M42
M54
A38(M)

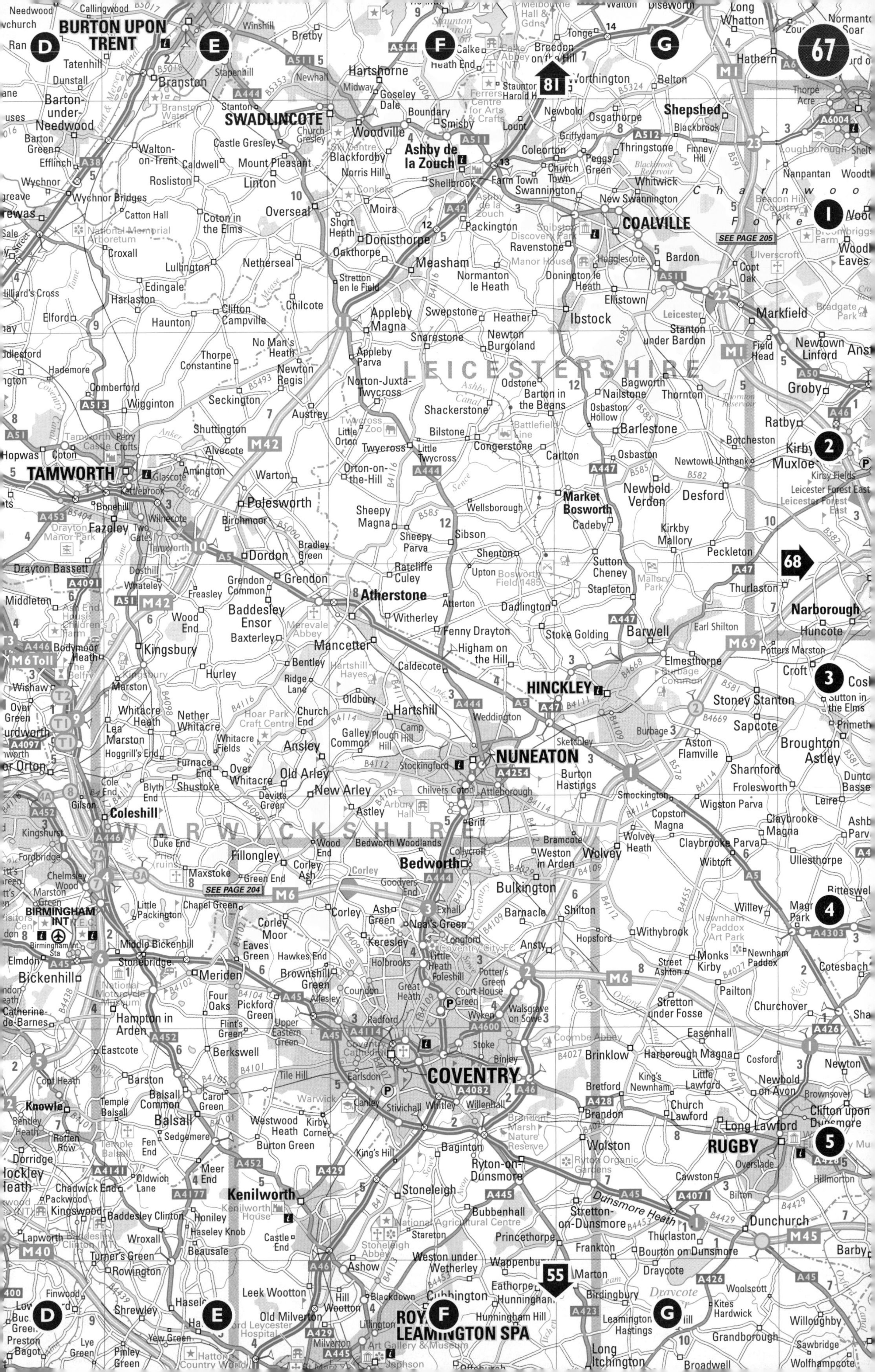
BURTON UPON TRENT
Branston
Stapenhill
Winshill
Bretby
Tatenhill
Dunstall
Barton-under-Needwood
Barton Green
Efflinch
Wychnor
Wychnor Bridges
Catton Hall
National Memorial Arboretum
Croxall
Alrewas
Fradley
Stanton
SWADLINCOTE
Church Gresley
Castle Gresley
Walton-on-Trent
Caldwell
Mount Pleasant
Rosliston
Linton
Overseal
Coton in the Elms
Lullington
Netherseal
Edingale
Harlaston
Elford
Clifton Campville
Haunton
Chilcote
No Man's Heath
Thorpe Constantine
Newton Regis
Seckington
Hademore
Comberford
Wigginton
Shuttington
Alvecote
Amington
TAMWORTH
Tamworth Castle
Perry Crofts
Glascote
Kettlebrook
Bonehill
Wilnecote
Fazeley
Two Gates
Drayton Manor Park
Drayton Bassett
Dosthill
Whateley
Middleton
Hopwas
Coton
Polesworth
Birchmoor
Warton
Dordon
Bradley Green
Grendon
Grendon Common
Freasley
Baddesley Ensor
Baxterley
Wood End
Kingsbury
Hurley
Marston
Whitacre Heath
Nether Whitacre
Lea Marston
Hoggrill's End
Whitacre Fields
Furnace End
Over Whitacre
Shustoke
Blyth End
Coleshill
Gilson
Kingshurst
Fordbridge
Chelmsley Wood
Marston Green
BIRMINGHAM INT
Elmdon
Bickenhill
Catherine-de-Barnes
Middle Bickenhill
Stonebridge
Meriden
National Motorcycle Museum
Hampton in Arden
Eastcote
Barston
Knowle
Bentley Heath
Rotten Row
Temple Balsall
Balsall Common
Balsall
Carol Green
Fen End
Sedgemere
Dorridge
Hockley Heath
Chadwick End
Packwood
Kingswood
Baddesley Clinton
Oldwich Lane
Meer End
Honiley
Haseley Knob
Wroxall
Beausale
Lapworth
Turner's Green
Rowington
Finwood
Shrewley
Haseley
Yew Green
Pinley Green
Lye Green
Preston Bagot
Hatton Country World
Duke End
Priory (ruins)
Maxstoke
Little Packington
Chapel Green
Fillongley
Corley Ash
Green End
Corley
Corley Moor
Eaves Green
Hawkes End
Brownshill Green
Four Oaks
Pickford Green
Allesley
Flint's Green
Upper Eastern Green
Berkswell
Tile Hill
Westwood Heath
Kirby Corner
Burton Green
Kenilworth
Kenilworth House
Castle End
Leek Wootton
Old Milverton
Ashow
Hill Wootton
Blackdown
Lillington
ROYAL LEAMINGTON SPA
Milverton
Art Gallery & Museum
Cubbington
Weston under Wetherley
Stoneleigh Abbey
Stareton
National Agricultural Centre
Stoneleigh
King's Hill
Baginton
Ryton-on-Dunsmore
Bubbenhall
Princethorpe
Wappenbury
Eathorpe
Hunningham
Hunningham Hill
Marton
Frankton
Stretton-on-Dunsmore
Dunsmore Heath
Birdingbury
Leamington Hastings
Long Itchington
Draycote
Draycote Water
Bourton on Dunsmore
Thurlaston
Dunchurch
Grandborough
Sawbridge
Woolscott
Kites Hardwick
Willoughby
Broadwell
Barby
Wolfhampcote
COVENTRY
Coventry Cathedral
Earlsdon
Canley
Stivichall
Whitley
Willenhall
Binley
Stoke
Wyken
Walsgrave on Sowe
Court House Green
Potter's Green
Great Heath
Foleshill
Little Heath
Holbrooks
Longford
Coventry City FC
Keresley
Coundon
Radford
Ash Green
Neal's Green
Exhall
Goodyers End
Bedworth
Bedworth Woodlands
Collycroft
Bulkington
Barnacle
Shilton
Ansty
Hopsford
Withybrook
Coombe Abbey
Brinklow
Brandon
Brandon Marsh Nature Reserve
Wolston
Ryton Organic Gardens
Bretford
King's Newnham
Church Lawford
Little Lawford
Harborough Magna
Easenhall
Long Lawford
RUGBY
Overslade
Bilton
Cawston
Hillmorton
Newbold on Avon
Brownsover
Clifton upon Dunsmore
Cosford
Newton
Churchover
Stretton under Fosse
Street Ashton
Monks Kirby
Pailton
Newnham Paddox
Cotesbach
Willey
Magna Park
Bitteswell
Ullesthorpe
Claybrooke Parva
Claybrooke Magna
Wibtoft
Wolvey
Wolvey Heath
Weston in Arden
Bramcote
Copston Magna
Smockington
Burton Hastings
Wigston Parva
Frolesworth
Sharnford
Leire
Broughton Astley
Sapcote
Stoney Stanton
Sutton in the Elms
Croft
Potters Marston
Elmesthorpe
Burbage
Aston Flamville
Sketchley
NUNEATON
Attleborough
Chilvers Coton
Stockingford
Griff
Arbury Hall
Astley
Galley Common
Plough Hill
Camp Hill
Hartshill
Ansley
Old Arley
New Arley
Devitts Green
Church End
Hoar Park Craft Centre
Oldbury
Hartshill Hayes
Ridge Lane
Bentley
Mancetter
Caldecote
Weddington
Atherstone
Merevale Abbey
Witherley
Atterton
Fenny Drayton
Higham on the Hill
Ratcliffe Culey
Sheepy Parva
Sheepy Magna
Sibson
Upton
Shenton
Bosworth Field 1485
Dadlington
Stoke Golding
Stapleton
Sutton Cheney
Cadeby
Market Bosworth
Wellsborough
Carlton
Congerstone
Bilstone
Shackerstone
Barton in the Beans
Odstone
Twycross
Twycross Zoo
Little Orton
Little Twycross
Orton-on-the-Hill
Norton-Juxta-Twycross
Appleby Parva
Appleby Magna
Austrey
Snarestone
Swepstone
Newton Burgoland
Heather
Ibstock
Ellistown
Hugglescote
Donington le Heath
Manor House
Ravenstone
Normanton le Heath
Measham
Packington
Stretton en le Field
Oakthorpe
Donisthorpe
Short Heath
Moira
Conkers
Norris Hill
Blackfordby
Woodville
Ashby de la Zouch
Shellbrook
Smisby
Boundary
Goseley Dale
Midway
Hartshorne
Newhall
Calke
Calke Abbey
Heath End
Staunton Harold
Lount
Breedon on the Hill
Tonge
Worthington
Newbold
Griffydam
Osgathorpe
Coleorton
Peggs Green
Thringstone
Whitwick
Farm Town
Swannington
New Swannington
COALVILLE
Snibston Discovery Park
Bardon
Belton
Shepshed
Blackbrook
Finney Hill
Long Whatton
Hathern
Diseworth
Loughborough
Thorpe Acre
Nanpantan
Beacon Hill Country Park
Charnwood Forest
Ulverscroft
Copt Oak
Markfield
Stanton under Bardon
Field Head
Newtown Linford
Groby
Ratby
Kirby Muxloe
Kirby Fields
Leicester Forest East
Botcheston
Newtown Unthank
Desford
Newbold Verdon
Osbaston
Barlestone
Nailstone
Osbaston Hollow
Bagworth
Thornton
Thornton Reservoir
Kirkby Mallory
Peckleton
Mallory Park
Earl Shilton
Barwell
Thurlaston
Narborough
Huncote
HINCKLEY
LEICESTERSHIRE
WARWICKSHIRE
SEE PAGE 204
SEE PAGE 205
81
68
55

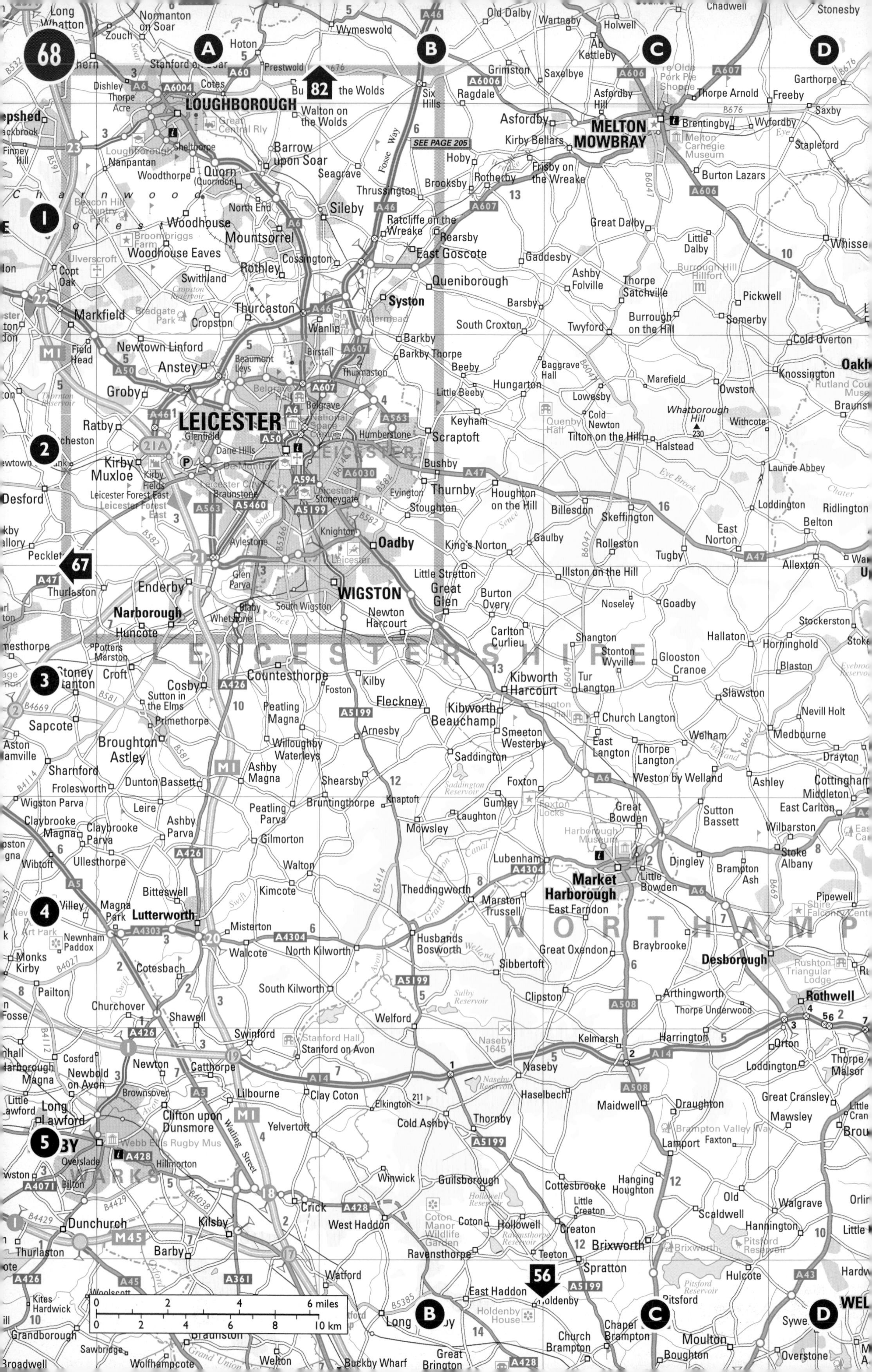

68
A
B
C
D
82
67
56
SEE PAGE 205
Long Whatton
Normanton on Soar
Zouch
Hoton
Wymeswold
Old Dalby
Wartnaby
Holwell
Chadwell
Stonesby
Stanford on Soar
Prestwold
Ab Kettleby
Dishley
Thorpe Acre
Cotes
LOUGHBOROUGH
Burton on the Wolds
Walton on the Wolds
Six Hills
Ragdale
Grimston
Saxelbye
Asfordby Hill
Ye Olde Pork Pie Shoppe
Thorpe Arnold
Freeby
Garthorpe
Saxby
Shepshed
Great Central Rly
Asfordby
MELTON MOWBRAY
Brentingby
Wyfordby
Kirby Bellars
Melton Carnegie Museum
Stapleford
Loughborough
Nanpantan
Barrow upon Soar
Fosse Way
Hoby
Frisby on the Wreake
Rotherby
Shelthorpe
Woodthorpe
Quorn (Quorndon)
Seagrave
Brooksby
Burton Lazars
Thrussington
Charnwood Forest
Beacon Hill Country Park
North End
Sileby
Ratcliffe on the Wreake
Rearsby
Woodhouse
Mountsorrel
Broombriggs Farm
Woodhouse Eaves
Great Dalby
Little Dalby
Whissendine
East Goscote
Gaddesby
Ulverscroft
Copt Oak
Rothley
Cossington
Queniborough
Ashby Folville
Burrough Hill Hillfort
Swithland
Cropston Reservoir
Thorpe Satchville
Pickwell
Markfield
Bradgate Park
Cropston
Thurcaston
Syston
Barsby
Burrough on the Hill
Somerby
Watermead
Wanlip
South Croxton
Twyford
Field Head
Newtown Linford
Birstall
Barkby
Cold Overton
Barkby Thorpe
Anstey
Beaumont Leys
Thurmaston
Beeby
Baggrave Hall
Knossington
Oakham
Marefield
Groby
Belgrave
Hungarton
Lowesby
Owston
Little Beeby
Rutland County Museum
Braunston
Thornton Reservoir
LEICESTER
National Space Centre
Keyham
Whatborough Hill
Withcote
Ratby
Glenfield
Humberstone
Quenby Hall
Cold Newton
Kirby Muxloe
Dane Hills
Scraptoft
Tilton on the Hill
Halstead
Kirby Fields
De Montfort
Bushby
Launde Abbey
Leicester Forest East
Leicester City FC
Braunstone
Thurnby
Evington
Houghton on the Hill
Desford
Stoneygate
Eye Brook
Stoughton
Billesdon
Skeffington
Loddington
Ridlington
Chater
Knighton
Aylestone
Oadby
Sence
Gaulby
Rolleston
East Norton
Belton
King's Norton
Tugby
Allexton
Peckleton
Thurlaston
Glen Parva
Enderby
Little Stretton
Great Glen
Illston on the Hill
WIGSTON
South Wigston
Blaby
Burton Overy
Noseley
Goadby
Narborough
Newton Harcourt
Whetstone
Huncote
Carlton Curlieu
Stockerston
Shangton
Hallaton
Stoke Dry
Horninghold
LEICESTERSHIRE
Potters Marston
Stonton Wyville
Glooston
Cranoe
Blaston
Eyebrook Reservoir
Stoney Stanton
Croft
Countesthorpe
Kilby
Foston
Kibworth Harcourt
Tur Langton
Slawston
Cosby
Sutton in the Elms
Peatling Magna
Fleckney
Kibworth Beauchamp
Langton Hall
Church Langton
Nevill Holt
Sapcote
Primethorpe
Arnesby
Smeeton Westerby
Welham
Medbourne
Broughton Astley
Willoughby Waterleys
Saddington
East Langton
Thorpe Langton
Aston Flamville
Drayton
Sharnford
Ashby Magna
Saddington Reservoir
Weston by Welland
Ashley
Cottingham
Frolesworth
Dunton Bassett
Shearsby
Foxton
Middleton
Knaptoft
Foxton Locks
Wigston Parva
Leire
Peatling Parva
Bruntingthorpe
Gumley
Great Bowden
Sutton Bassett
East Carlton
Claybrooke Magna
Claybrooke Parva
Ashby Parva
Laughton
Mowsley
Harborough Museum
Wilbarston
Gilmorton
Ullesthorpe
Wibtoft
Walton
Lubenham
Dingley
Stoke Albany
Brampton Ash
Market Harborough
Little Bowden
Theddingworth
Bitteswell
Kimcote
Marston Trussell
East Farndon
Pipewell
Shire Falconry Centre
Willey
Magna Park
Lutterworth
Newnham Paddox
Misterton
Husbands Bosworth
NORTHAMPTONSHIRE
Monks Kirby
Walcote
North Kilworth
Great Oxendon
Braybrooke
Desborough
Cotesbach
Sibbertoft
Rushton Triangular Lodge
Pailton
Clipston
South Kilworth
Sulby Reservoir
Arthingworth
Churchover
Rothwell
Shawell
Welford
Thorpe Underwood
Stanford Hall
Naseby 1645
Kelmarsh
Harrington
Orton
Swinford
Stanford on Avon
Cosford
Newton
Catthorpe
Naseby
Loddington
Thorpe Malsor
Newbold on Avon
Naseby Reservoir
Harborough Magna
Brownsover
Lilbourne
Clay Coton
Elkington
Haselbech
Maidwell
Draughton
Great Cransley
Little Lawford
Long Lawford
Clifton upon Dunsmore
Cold Ashby
Thornby
Mawsley
Watling Street
Yelvertoft
Brampton Valley Way
RUGBY
Webb Ellis Rugby Mus
Lamport
Faxton
Overslade
Hillmorton
Winwick
Guilsborough
Cottesbrooke
Hanging Houghton
Old
Walgrave
Bilton
Hollowell Reservoir
Little Creaton
Scaldwell
Dunchurch
Crick
Kilsby
West Haddon
Coton Manor Wildlife Garden
Coton
Hollowell
Creaton
Ravensthorpe Reservoir
Hannington
Pitsford Reservoir
Thurlaston
Barby
Ravensthorpe
Teeton
Brixworth
Spratton
Hulcote
Watford
Pitsford
Kites Hardwick
Woolscott
East Haddon
Holdenby
Holdenby House
Long Buckby
Chapel Brampton
Church Brampton
Moulton
Sywell
Grandborough
Braunston
Boughton
Overstone
Sawbridge
Wolfhampcote
Welton
Buckby Wharf
Great Brington
Broadwell
0 2 4 6 miles
0 2 4 6 8 10 km
M1
M45
A6
A46
A60
A6004
A6006
A606
A607
A47
A50
A594
A5199
A563
A5460
A6030
A426
A4303
A4304
A5
A14
A508
A43
A45
A361
A428
A4071
A427
B676
B6047
B5366
B582
B581
B4114
B4669
B4027
B4112
B4429
B4038
B5385
B5414
B664
B669
B591
B532

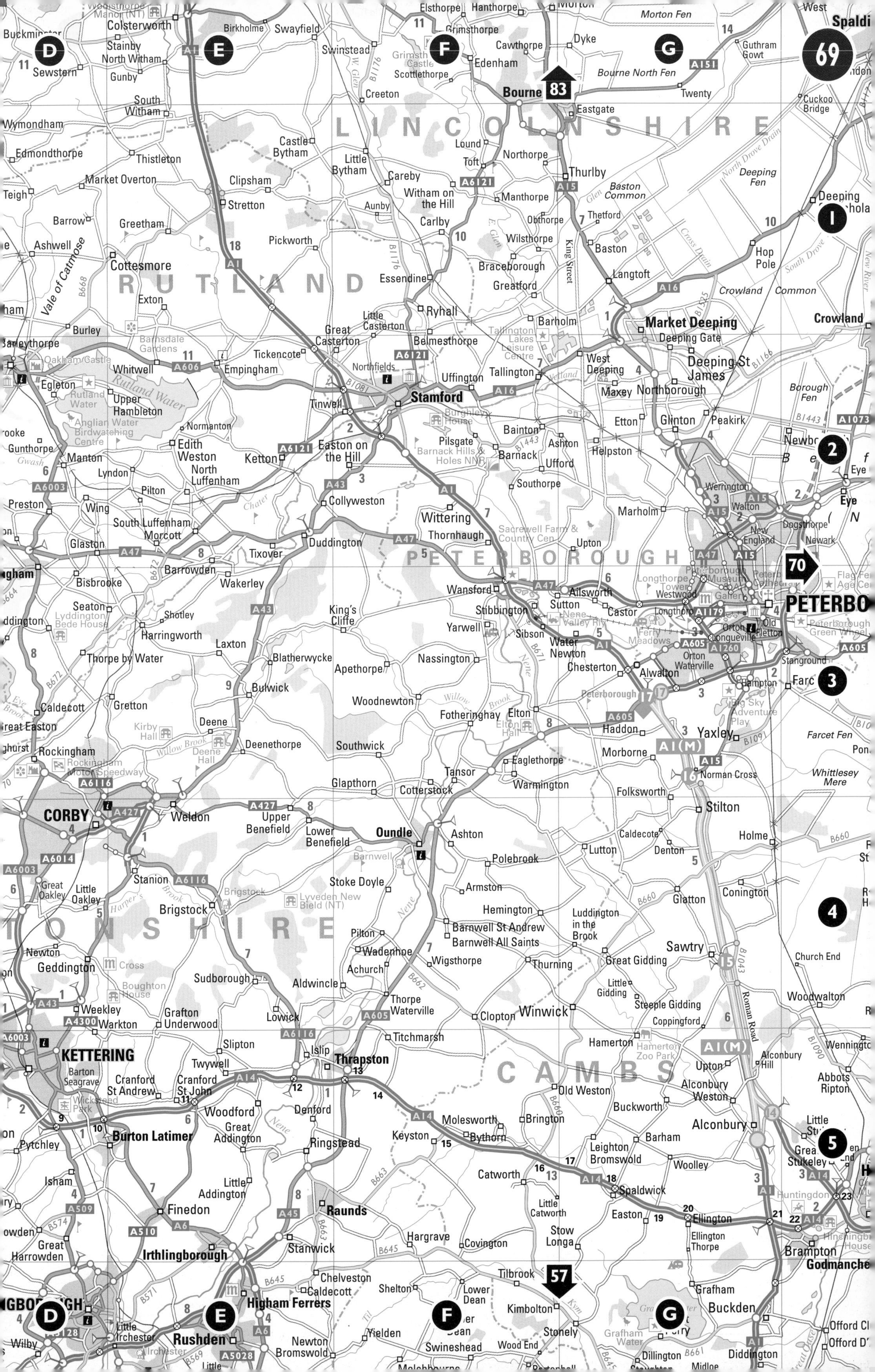

69
D
E
F
G
83
Buckminster
Colsterworth
Stainby
North Witham
Gunby
Sewstern
Birkholme
Swayfield
Swinstead
Elsthorpe
Hanthorpe
Grimsthorpe
Grimsthorpe Castle
Scottlethorpe
Cawthorpe
Edenham
Dyke
Morton Fen
Bourne North Fen
Guthram Gowt
Twenty
Cuckoo Bridge
Spaldi
West
Bourne
Eastgate
Creeton
South Witham
Wymondham
Edmondthorpe
Thistleton
Castle Bytham
Little Bytham
LINCOLNSHIRE
Lound
Toft
Northorpe
Thurlby
Deeping Fen
Baston Common
Market Overton
Clipsham
Stretton
Careby
Witham on the Hill
Manthorpe
Teigh
Barrow
Greetham
Aunby
Carlby
Obthorpe
Thetford
Deeping St Nicholas
Ashwell
Cottesmore
Pickworth
Wilsthorpe
Braceborough
Baston
Hop Pole
Vale of Catmose
RUTLAND
Exton
Essendine
Greatford
King Street
Langtoft
Crowland
Common
Crowland
Burley
Barnsdale Gardens
Ryhall
Little Casterton
Great Casterton
Barholm
Tallington Lakes Leisure Centre
Market Deeping
Deeping Gate
Barleythorpe
Oakham
Oakham Castle
Whitwell
Tickencote
Empingham
Belmesthorpe
Northfields
Uffington
Tallington
West Deeping
Deeping St James
Egleton
Rutland Water
Upper Hambleton
Anglian Water Birdwatching Centre
Tinwell
Stamford
Burghley House
Maxey
Northborough
Borough Fen
Normanton
Bainton
Etton
Glinton
Peakirk
Gunthorpe
Manton
Edith Weston
North Luffenham
Ketton
Easton on the Hill
Pilsgate
Barnack Hills & Holes NNR
Barnack
Ashton
Ufford
Helpston
Newborough
Eye
Lyndon
Pilton
Southorpe
Werrington
Walton
Eye
Preston
Wing
South Luffenham
Morcott
Collyweston
Wittering
Thornhaugh
Sacrewell Farm & Country Centre
Marholm
Dogsthorpe
Newark
Glaston
Duddington
Tixover
Barrowden
Upton
New England
PETERBOROUGH
70
Bisbrooke
Wakerley
Wansford
Ailsworth
Longthorpe Tower
Peterborough Museum
Peterborough Cathedral
Flag Fen Age Centre
Seaton
Lyddington Bede House
Shotley
King's Cliffe
Stibbington
Sutton
Castor
Westwood
Gallery
PETERBOROUGH
Harringworth
Laxton
Yarwell
Sibson
Nene Valley Rly
Ferry Meadows
Orton Longueville
Old Fletton
Peterborough Green Wheel
Thorpe by Water
Blatherwycke
Apethorpe
Nassington
Water Newton
Chesterton
Orton Waterville
Alwalton
Stanground
Farcet
Caldecott
Bulwick
Woodnewton
Fotheringhay
Elton
Elton Hall
Peterborough
Hampton
Big Sky Adventure Play
Gretton
Kirby Hall
Deene
Deene Hall
Deenethorpe
Southwick
Haddon
Yaxley
Farcet Fen
Great Easton
Rockingham
Rockingham Motor Speedway
Eaglethorpe
Morborne
Norman Cross
Whittlesey Mere
Tansor
Glapthorn
Cotterstock
Warmington
Folksworth
CORBY
Weldon
Upper Benefield
Lower Benefield
Oundle
Ashton
Stilton
Barnwell
Caldecote
Lutton
Denton
Holme
Polebrook
Stanion
Great Oakley
Little Oakley
Brigstock
Lyveden New Bield (NT)
Stoke Doyle
Armston
Glatton
Conington
Hemington
Luddington in the Brook
Barnwell St Andrew
Barnwell All Saints
Sawtry
NORTHAMPTONSHIRE
Pilton
Wadenhoe
Achurch
Wigsthorpe
Thurning
Great Gidding
Church End
Newton
Geddington
Cross
Boughton House
Sudborough
Aldwincle
Thorpe Waterville
Little Gidding
Steeple Gidding
Woodwalton
Weekley
Warkton
Grafton Underwood
Lowick
Clopton
Winwick
Coppingford
Roman Road
KETTERING
Barton Seagrave
Slipton
Islip
Titchmarsh
Thrapston
Hamerton
Hamerton Zoo Park
Alconbury Hill
Wennington
Twywell
Cranford St Andrew
Cranford St John
CAMBS
Upton
Alconbury Weston
Abbots Ripton
Wicksteed Park
Woodford
Great Addington
Denford
Molesworth
Bythorn
Old Weston
Brington
Buckworth
Alconbury
Little Stukeley
Great Stukeley
Pytchley
Burton Latimer
Ringstead
Keyston
Leighton Bromswold
Barham
Woolley
Isham
Little Addington
Catworth
Spaldwick
Huntingdon
Finedon
Raunds
Little Catworth
Easton
Ellington
Ellington Thorpe
Great Harrowden
Irthlingborough
Stanwick
Hargrave
Covington
Stow Longa
Brampton
Hinchingbrooke House
Godmanchester
Chelveston
Caldecott
Shelton
Lower Dean
Tilbrook
57
Grafham
Higham Ferrers
Kimbolton
Buckden
Wilby
Little Irchester
Rushden
Newton Bromswold
Yielden
Swineshead
Wood End
Stonely
Grafham Water
Dillington
Diddington
Offord Cluny
Offord D'Arcy

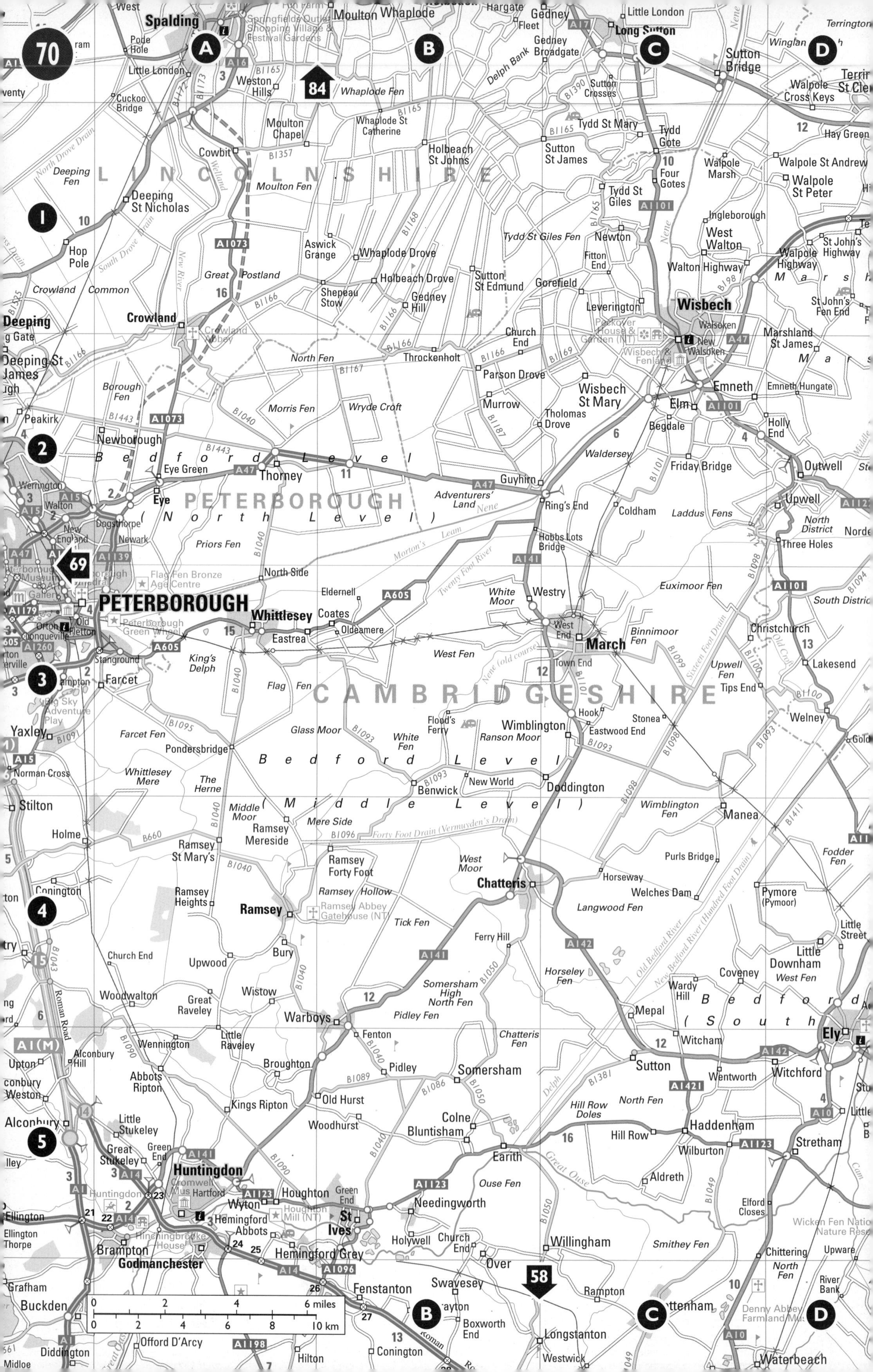

70
Spalding
Moulton
Whaplode
Gedney
Long Sutton
Sutton Bridge
84
LINCOLNSHIRE
Deeping St Nicholas
Crowland
Whaplode Drove
Holbeach Drove
Tydd St Giles
Wisbech
Wisbech St Mary
Parson Drove
Thorney
Eye
PETERBOROUGH (North Level)
Bedford Level
69
PETERBOROUGH
Whittlesey
March
Guyhirn
Outwell
Upwell
CAMBRIDGESHIRE
Yaxley
Stilton
Ramsey
Chatteris
Manea
Doddington
Benwick
Bedford Level (Middle Level)
Warboys
Somersham
Huntingdon
St Ives
Ely
Sutton
Haddenham
Earith
Willingham
Swavesey
Godmanchester
Brampton
Buckden
Cottenham
Waterbeach
Longstanton
58
0 2 4 6 miles
0 2 4 6 8 10 km

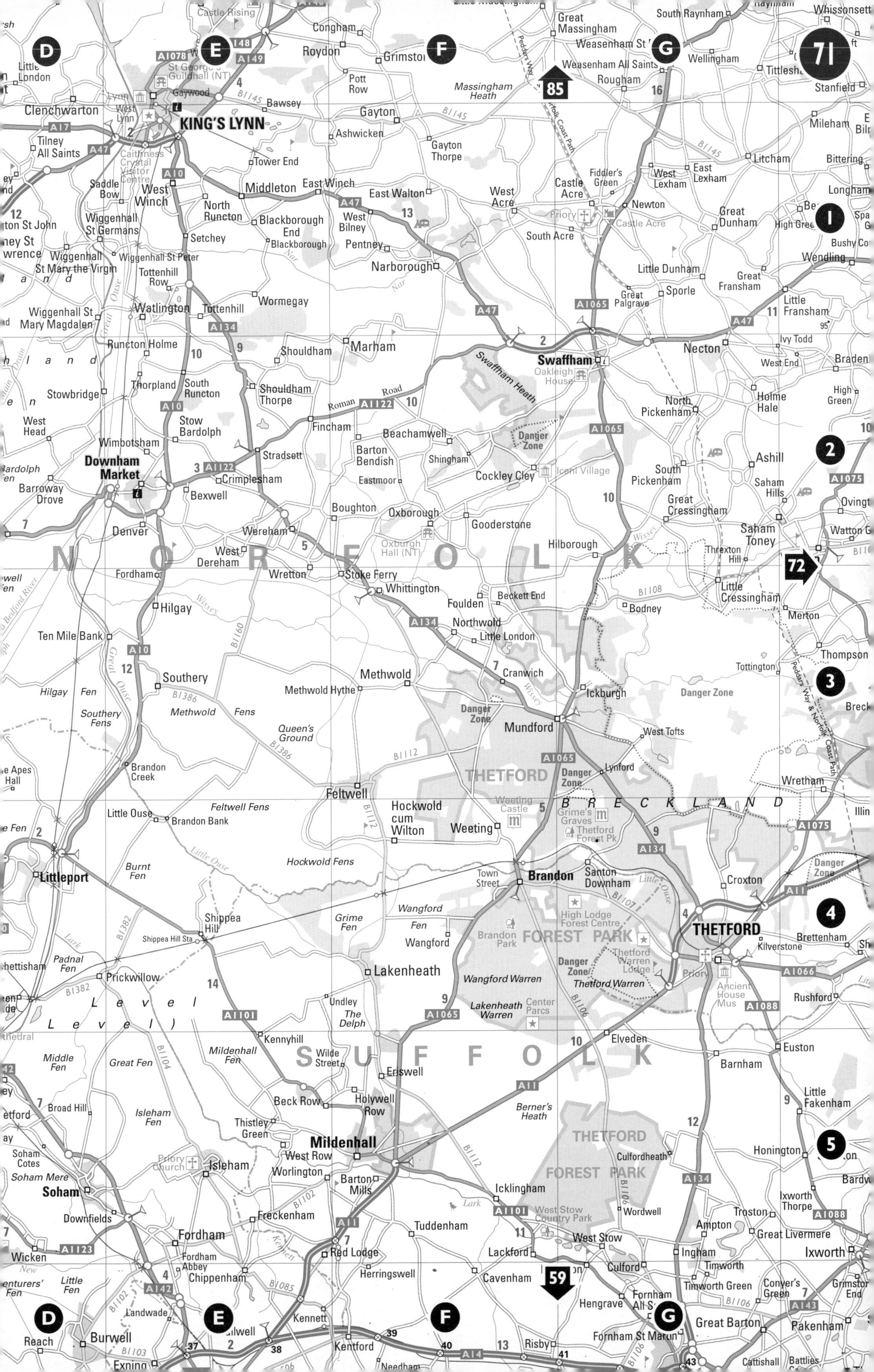
71
D
E
F
G
Castle Rising
Congham
Roydon
Grimston
Great Massingham
Weasenham St Peter
Weasenham All Saints
South Raynham
Wellingham
Whissonsett
Tittleshall
Stanfield
85
Little London
Clenchwarton
St George's Guildhall (NT)
Gaywood
Lynn
West Lynn
KING'S LYNN
Bawsey
Pott Row
Gayton
Massingham Heath
Rougham
Mileham
Tilney All Saints
Caithness Crystal Visitor Centre
Ashwicken
Gayton Thorpe
Tower End
Litcham
Bittering
Saddle Bow
West Winch
Middleton
East Winch
East Walton
West Acre
Castle Acre
Fiddler's Green
West Lexham
East Lexham
Longham
North Runcton
Blackborough End
Blackborough
West Bilney
Pentney
Narborough
Newton
Priory
Castle Acre
South Acre
Great Dunham
High Green
Wiggenhall St Germans
Wiggenhall St Peter
Wiggenhall St Mary the Virgin
Setchey
Tottenhill Row
Tottenhill
Wormegay
Watlington
Little Dunham
Great Palgrave
Sporle
Great Fransham
Little Fransham
Wendling
Bushy Common
Wiggenhall St Mary Magdalen
Runcton Holme
Shouldham
Marham
Swaffham Heath
Swaffham
Oakleigh House
Necton
Ivy Todd
West End
Bradenham
Stowbridge
Thorpland
South Runcton
Shouldham Thorpe
Roman Road
North Pickenham
Holme Hale
High Green
West Head
Stow Bardolph
Fincham
Beachamwell
Danger Zone
Wimbotsham
Downham Market
Stradsett
Barton Bendish
Shingham
Cockley Cley
Iceni Village
South Pickenham
Ashill
Saham Hills
Bardolph Fen
Barroway Drove
Crimplesham
Bexwell
Eastmoor
Great Cressingham
Denver
Boughton
Oxborough
Gooderstone
Saham Toney
Watton
Wereham
Oxburgh Hall (NT)
Hilborough
Threxton Hill
72
N O R F O L K
West Dereham
Fordham
Wretton
Stoke Ferry
Whittington
Beckett End
Foulden
Bodney
Little Cressingham
Merton
Hilgay
Ten Mile Bank
Northwold
Little London
Thompson
Tottington
Cranwich
Southery
Hilgay Fen
Methwold Hythe
Methwold
Ickburgh
Danger Zone
Southery Fens
Methwold Fens
Queen's Ground
Mundford
West Tofts
Pedders Way & Norfolk Coast Path
Brandon Creek
Lynford
Wretham
THETFORD
Feltwell
Hockwold cum Wilton
Weeting Castle
Weeting
B R E C K L A N D
Grime's Graves
Thetford Forest Pk
Little Ouse
Brandon Bank
Feltwell Fens
Littleport
Burnt Fen
Hockwold Fens
Town Street
Brandon
Santon Downham
Croxton
Danger Zone
Shippea Hill
Shippea Hill Sta
Grime Fen
Wangford Fen
Wangford
High Lodge Forest Centre
Brandon Park
FOREST PARK
THETFORD
Brettenham
Kilverstone
Padnal Fen
Prickwillow
Lakenheath
Thetford Warren Lodge
Wangford Warren
Thetford Warren
Ancient House Mus
Rushford
L e v e l
Undley
The Delph
Lakenheath Warren
Center Parcs
Kennyhill
Mildenhall Fen
Wilde Street
S U F F O L K
Elveden
Euston
Middle Fen
Great Fen
Eriswell
Barnham
Broad Hill
Isleham Fen
Beck Row
Holywell Row
Berner's Heath
Little Fakenham
Thistley Green
Mildenhall
THETFORD FOREST PARK
Soham Cotes
Soham Mere
West Row
Priory Church
Isleham
Worlington
Culfordheath
Honington
Soham
Barton Mills
Icklingham
Ixworth Thorpe
Downfields
Freckenham
West Stow Country Park
Wordwell
Troston
Ampton
Great Livermere
Fordham
Tuddenham
West Stow
Ingham
Ixworth
Wicken
Fordham Abbey
Red Lodge
Lackford
Culford
Timworth
Chippenham
Herringswell
Cavenham
Timworth Green
Conyer's Green
Little Fen
Hengrave
Fornham All Saints
59
Kennett
Great Barton
Pakenham
Landwade
Burwell
Reach
Kentford
Risby
Fornham St Martin
Exning
Needham
Cattishall
Battlies

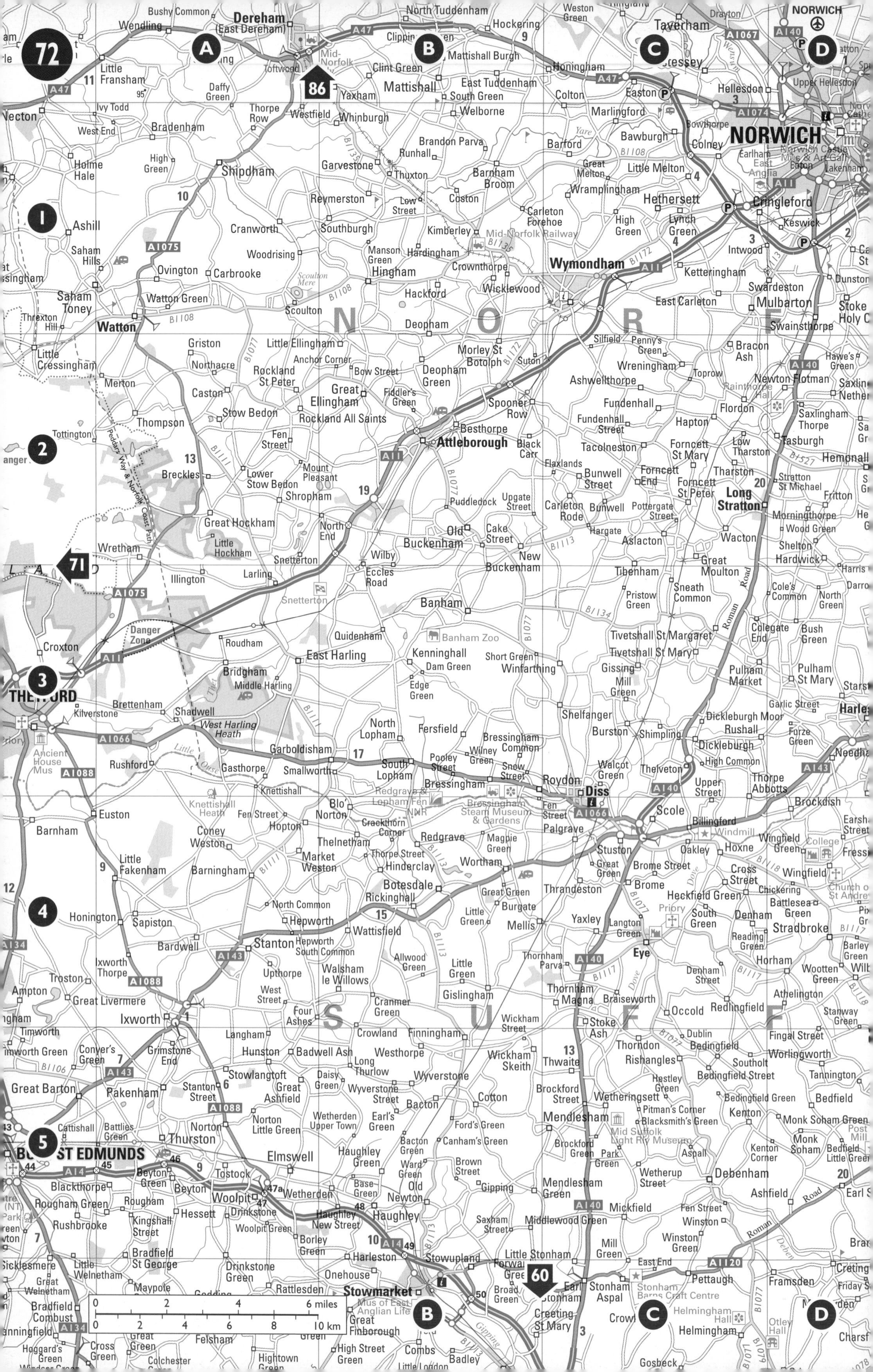

72
A
B
C
D
NORWICH
Bushy Common
Dereham (East Dereham)
North Tuddenham
Hockering
Weston Green
Taverham
Drayton
Wendling
Toftwood
Mid-Norfolk
86
Clippings Green
Mattishall Burgh
Honingham
A47
A1067
A140
Little Fransham
Daffy Green
Clint Green
Mattishall
East Tuddenham
South Green
Colton
Easton
Costessey
Hellesdon
Upper Hellesdon
Necton
Ivy Todd
Thorpe Row
Westfield
Yaxham
Whinburgh
Welborne
Marlingford
Bowthorpe
Bawburgh
Colney
NORWICH
Norwich Castle Mus & Art Gall
West End
Bradenham
Brandon Parva
Runhall
Barford
B1108
Earlham
East Anglia
Eaton
Lakenham
Holme Hale
High Green
Shipdham
Garvestone
Thuxton
Barnham Broom
Great Melton
Little Melton
Wramplingham
10
Reymerston
Low Street
Coston
Carleton Forehoe
Hethersett
Cringleford
Keswick
Ashill
Cranworth
Southburgh
Kimberley
Mid-Norfolk Railway
High Green
Lynch Green
Saham Hills
A1075
Woodrising
Manson Green
Hardingham
Crownthorpe
Intwood
Ovington
Carbrooke
Scoulton Mere
Hingham
Wymondham
A11
Ketteringham
Swardeston
Saham Toney
Watton Green
Hackford
Wicklewood
Mulbarton
Threxton Hill
Watton
B1108
Scoulton
East Carleton
Stoke Holy Cross
Deopham
Swainsthorpe
N
O
R
Little Cressingham
Griston
Little Ellingham
Morley St Botolph
Silfield
Penny's Green
Bracon Ash
Northacre
Anchor Corner
Suton
Wreningham
Rockland St Peter
Bow Street
Deopham Green
Toprow
Newton Flotman
Caston
Great Ellingham
Fiddler's Green
Ashwellthorpe
Rainthorpe Hall
Merton
Stow Bedon
Rockland All Saints
Spooner Row
Fundenhall
Flordon
Saxlingham Thorpe
Thompson
Fundenhall Street
Hapton
Tottington
Fen Street
Besthorpe
Attleborough
Black Carr
Tacolneston
Forncett St Mary
Low Tharston
Tasburgh
Danger
Pedders Way & Norfolk Coast Path
Mount Pleasant
Flaxlands
Bunwell Street
Forncett End
Forncett St Peter
Tharston
Hempnall
13
Breckles
Lower Stow Bedon
Shropham
19
Stratton St Michael
Long Stratton
20
Fritton
Puddledock
Upgate Street
Carleton Rode
Bunwell
Pottergate Street
Morningthorpe
Great Hockham
North End
Old Buckenham
Cake Street
Hargate
Aslacton
Wacton
Wood Green
Little Hockham
Shelton
Wretham
Wilby
New Buckenham
Hardwick
71
Snetterton
Eccles Road
Tibenham
Great Moulton
Illington
Larling
Pristow Green
Sneath Common
Cole's Common
North Green
A1075
Banham
Danger Zone
Quidenham
Banham Zoo
Tivetshall St Margaret
Roman Road
Colegate End
Bush Green
Croxton
Roudham
Tivetshall St Mary
Kenninghall
Short Green
Winfarthing
East Harling
Gissing
Pulham Market
Pulham St Mary
Dam Green
Bridgham
Middle Harling
Edge Green
Mill Green
Garlic Street
3
THETFORD
Brettenham
Kilverstone
Shadwell
West Harling Heath
North Lopham
Fersfield
Shelfanger
Dickleburgh Moor
Burston
Shimpling
Rushall
Dickleburgh
Forze Green
Harleston
Ancient House Mus
A1066
Little Ouse
Garboldisham
17
South Lopham
Bressingham Common
Wilney Green
Walcot Green
High Common
Needham
Rushford
Gasthorpe
Smallworth
Pooley Street
Snow Street
Roydon
Diss
Thelveton
Upper Street
Thorpe Abbotts
A1088
Knettishall
Bressingham
Redgrave & Lopham Fen NNR
Bressingham Steam Museum & Gardens
A143
A1066
Knettishall Heath
Fen Street
Blo' Norton
Fen Street
Scole
Brockdish
Euston
Hopton
Crackthorn Corner
Palgrave
Billingford
Windmill
Barnham
Coney Weston
Thelnetham
Redgrave
Magpie Green
Stuston
Oakley
Hoxne
Wingfield Green
College
Market Weston
Thorpe Street
Wortham
Great Green
Brome Street
Little Fakenham
Barningham
Hinderclay
Cross Street
Wingfield
Botesdale
Great Green
Thrandeston
Brome
Chickering
Rickinghall
Burgate
Heckfield Green
Battlesea Green
North Common
Little Green
Priory
Honington
Sapiston
Hepworth
15
Mellis
Yaxley
Langton Green
South Green
Denham
Stradbroke
Wattisfield
Eye
Reading Green
Barley Green
Bardwell
Stanton
Hepworth South Common
Allwood Green
Thornham Parva
Horham
Ixworth Thorpe
Upthorpe
Walsham le Willows
Little Green
Denham Street
Wootten Green
Troston
A1088
Athelington
Ampton
Great Livermere
West Street
Cranmer Green
Gislingham
Thornham Magna
Braiseworth
Occold
Redlingfield
Stanway Green
Ixworth
1
Four Ashes
S
U
F
Wickham Street
Stoke Ash
Timworth
Langham
Crowland
Finningham
Dublin
Fingal Street
Timworth Green
Conyer's Green
Grimstone End
Hunston
Badwell Ash
Westhorpe
Thorndon
Bedingfield
Worlingworth
B1106
Long Thurlow
Wickham Skeith
13
Thwaite
Rishangles
Southolt
Stowlangtoft
Daisy Green
Wyverstone
Hestley Green
Bedingfield Street
Tannington
Great Barton
Pakenham
Stanton Street
Great Ashfield
Wyverstone Street
Cotton
Brockford Street
Wetheringsett
Bedingfield Green
Bedfield
Bacton
Pitman's Corner
Kenton
A1088
Norton Little Green
Wetherden Upper Town
Earl's Green
Mendlesham
Blacksmith's Green
Monk Soham Green
Cattishall
Battlies Green
Norton
Ford's Green
Mid Suffolk Light Rly Museum
Monk Soham
5
BURY ST EDMUNDS
Thurston
Bacton Green
Canham's Green
Brockford Green
Park Green
Aspall
Kenton Corner
Bedfield Little Green
A14
Elmswell
Haughley Green
Brown Street
Wetherup Street
Debenham
20
Beyton Green
Tostock
Ward Green
Blackthorpe
Beyton
Woolpit
Wetherden
Base Green
Old Newton
Gipping
Mendlesham Green
Ashfield
Earl Soham
Rougham Green
Rougham
Drinkstone
Haughley New Street
Haughley
A140
Mickfield
Fen Street
Rushbrooke
Kingshall Street
Hessett
Woolpit Green
Borley Green
Saxham Street
Middlewood Green
Winston
Bradfield St George
Harleston
Stowupland
Little Stonham
Mill Green
Winston Green
Little Welnetham
Great Welnetham
Drinkstone Green
Onehouse
Forward Green
East End
A1120
Pettaugh
Cretingham
Maypole Green
Rattlesden
Stowmarket
60
Earl Stonham
Stonham Aspal
Stonham Barns Craft Centre
Framsden
Bradfield Combust
Mus of East Anglian Life
Broad Green
Crowfield
Helmingham Hall
Otley Hall
Great Finborough
Creeting St Mary
Helmingham
Felsham
High Street Green
Combs
Badley
Gosbeck
Hoggard's Green
Cross Green
Colchester Green
Hightown Green
Little London
0 2 4 6 miles
0 2 4 6 8 10 km

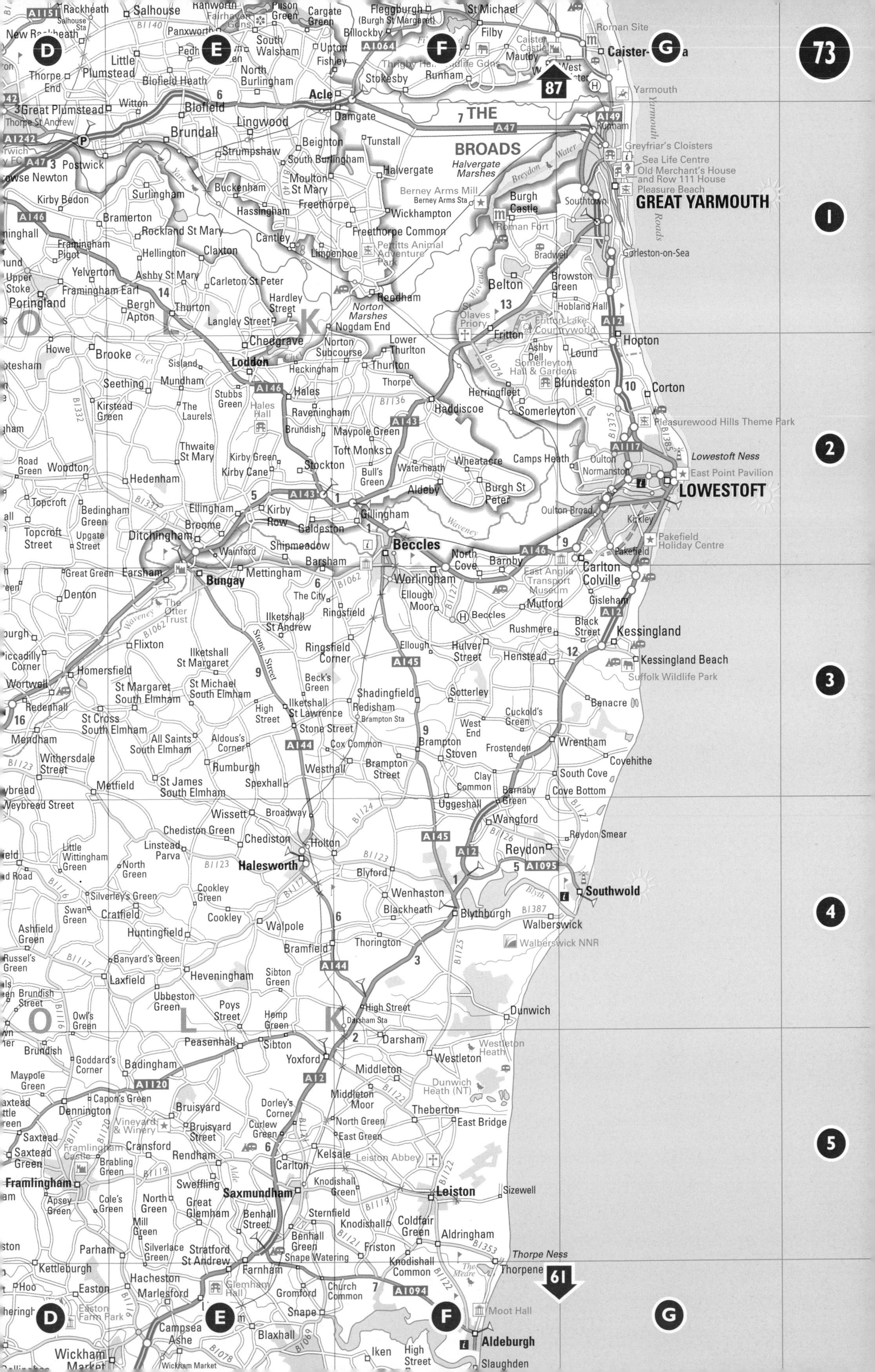
D
E
F
G
87
A1151
Rackheath
Salhouse
Salhouse Sta
Ranworth
Pilson Green
Cargate Green
Fleggburgh (Burgh St Margaret)
St Michael
Roman Site
New Rackheath
B1140
Panxworth
Billockby
Filby
Caister-on-Sea
South Walsham
Upton
A1064
Mautby
West Caister
Little Plumstead
Thorpe End
Blofield Heath
North Burlingham
Fishley
Stokesby
Thrigby Hall Wildlife Gdns
Runham
Yarmouth
Great Plumstead
Witton
Blofield
Acle
Damgate
THE BROADS
Thorpe St Andrew
A47
A149
Runham
Lingwood
Brundall
Beighton
Tunstall
A1242
Strumpshaw
South Burlingham
Greyfriar's Cloisters
Sea Life Centre
Old Merchant's House and Row 111 House
Pleasure Beach
Postwick
Moulton St Mary
Halvergate
Halvergate Marshes
Breydon Water
Trowse Newton
Buckenham
Berney Arms Mill
Berney Arms Sta
Burgh Castle
Southtown
GREAT YARMOUTH
Kirby Bedon
Surlingham
Freethorpe
Hassingham
Wickhampton
A146
Bramerton
Roman Fort
Rockland St Mary
Cantley
Freethorpe Common
Framingham Pigot
Hellington
Claxton
Limpenhoe
Pettitts Animal Adventure Park
Bradwell
Gorleston-on-Sea
Yelverton
Ashby St Mary
Carleton St Peter
Browston Green
Upper Stoke
Framingham Earl
Poringland
Bergh Apton
Thurton
Hardley Street
Reedham
Belton
Norton Marshes
Hobland Hall
Langley Street
St Olaves Priory
Fritton Lake Countryworld
Nogdam End
Fritton
A12
Hopton
Howe
Brooke
Chedgrave
Norton Subcourse
Lower Thurlton
Ashby Dell
Lound
Sisland
Loddon
Thurlton
Somerleyton Hall & Gardens
Heckingham
Seething
Mundham
Thorpe
Blundeston
Corton
Kirstead Green
Stubbs Green
Hales Hall
Hales
Herringfleet
The Laurels
Raveningham
Haddiscoe
Somerleyton
B1136
Brundish
Maypole Green
A143
Pleasurewood Hills Theme Park
Thwaite St Mary
Toft Monks
Kirby Green
Wheatacre
Camps Heath
Lowestoft Ness
Road Green
Woodton
Oulton
Kirby Cane
Stockton
Bull's Green
Waterheath
Burgh St Peter
Normanston
East Point Pavilion
Hedenham
LOWESTOFT
Aldeby
Topcroft
Bedingham Green
Ellingham
Kirby Row
Gillingham
Oulton Broad
Topcroft Street
Upgate Street
Broome
Geldeston
Kirkley
Ditchingham
Beccles
Pakefield Holiday Centre
Wainford
Shipmeadow
North Cove
Barnby
A146
Pakefield
Great Green
Earsham
Bungay
Mettingham
Barsham
East Anglia Transport Museum
Carlton Colville
Worlingham
Denton
The City
Ellough Moor
Mutford
Gisleham
The Otter Trust
Ringsfield
Beccles
Ilketshall St Andrew
Black Street
Flixton
Stone Street
Rushmere
Kessingland
Piccadilly Corner
Ilketshall St Margaret
Ringsfield Corner
Ellough
Hulver Street
Henstead
Homersfield
A145
Kessingland Beach
Suffolk Wildlife Park
Wortwell
St Margaret South Elmham
St Michael South Elmham
Beck's Green
Redenhall
Ilketshall St Lawrence
Shadingfield
Sotterley
Benacre
St Cross South Elmham
High Street
Redisham
Brampton Sta
Cuckold's Green
Mendham
All Saints South Elmham
Aldous's Corner
Stone Street
West End
Wrentham
A144
Cox Common
Brampton
Frostenden
Withersdale Street
Rumburgh
Brampton Street
Stoven
Covehithe
Westhall
Metfield
St James South Elmham
Spexhall
Clay Common
South Cove
Weybread Street
Barnaby Green
Cove Bottom
Wissett
Broadway
Uggeshall
Wangford
B1124
Reydon Smear
Chediston Green
Linstead Parva
Chediston
Holton
Little Wittingham Green
Reydon
North Green
Halesworth
B1123
Blyford
A1095
Southwold
Silverley's Green
Cookley Green
Wenhaston
Swan Green
Cratfield
Blackheath
Blythburgh
Walberswick
Ashfield Green
Cookley
Walpole
Huntingfield
Walberswick NNR
Bramfield
Thorington
Russel's Green
Banyard's Green
Laxfield
Heveningham
Sibton Green
Brundish Street
Ubbeston Green
Poys Street
High Street
Owl's Green
Hemp Green
Darsham Sta
Dunwich
Brundish
Peasenhall
Sibton
Darsham
Westleton Heath
Goddard's Corner
Badingham
Yoxford
Westleton
Maypole Green
A1120
Middleton
Dunwich Heath (NT)
Capon's Green
Middleton Moor
Dennington
Bruisyard
Dorley's Corner
Theberton
Vineyard & Winery
Bruisyard Street
Curlew Green
North Green
East Bridge
Saxtead
Framlingham Castle
Cransford
East Green
Saxtead Green
Brabling Green
Rendham
Carlton
Kelsale
Leiston Abbey
Framlingham
Sweffling
Knodishall Green
Saxmundham
Leiston
Sizewell
Apsey Green
Cole's Green
North Green
Great Glemham
Benhall Street
Sternfield
Knodishall
Coldfair Green
Mill Green
Benhall Green
Aldringham
Parham
Silverlace Green
Stratford St Andrew
Friston
Snape Watering
Thorpe Ness
Knodishall Common
Kettleburgh
Farnham
The Meare
Thorpeness
Hoo
Easton
Hacheston
Glemham Hall
Church Common
Gromford
A1094
61
Marlesford
Easton Farm Park
Snape
Moot Hall
Campsea Ashe
Blaxhall
Aldeburgh
Wickham Market
Iken
High Street
Slaughden
1
2
3
4
5

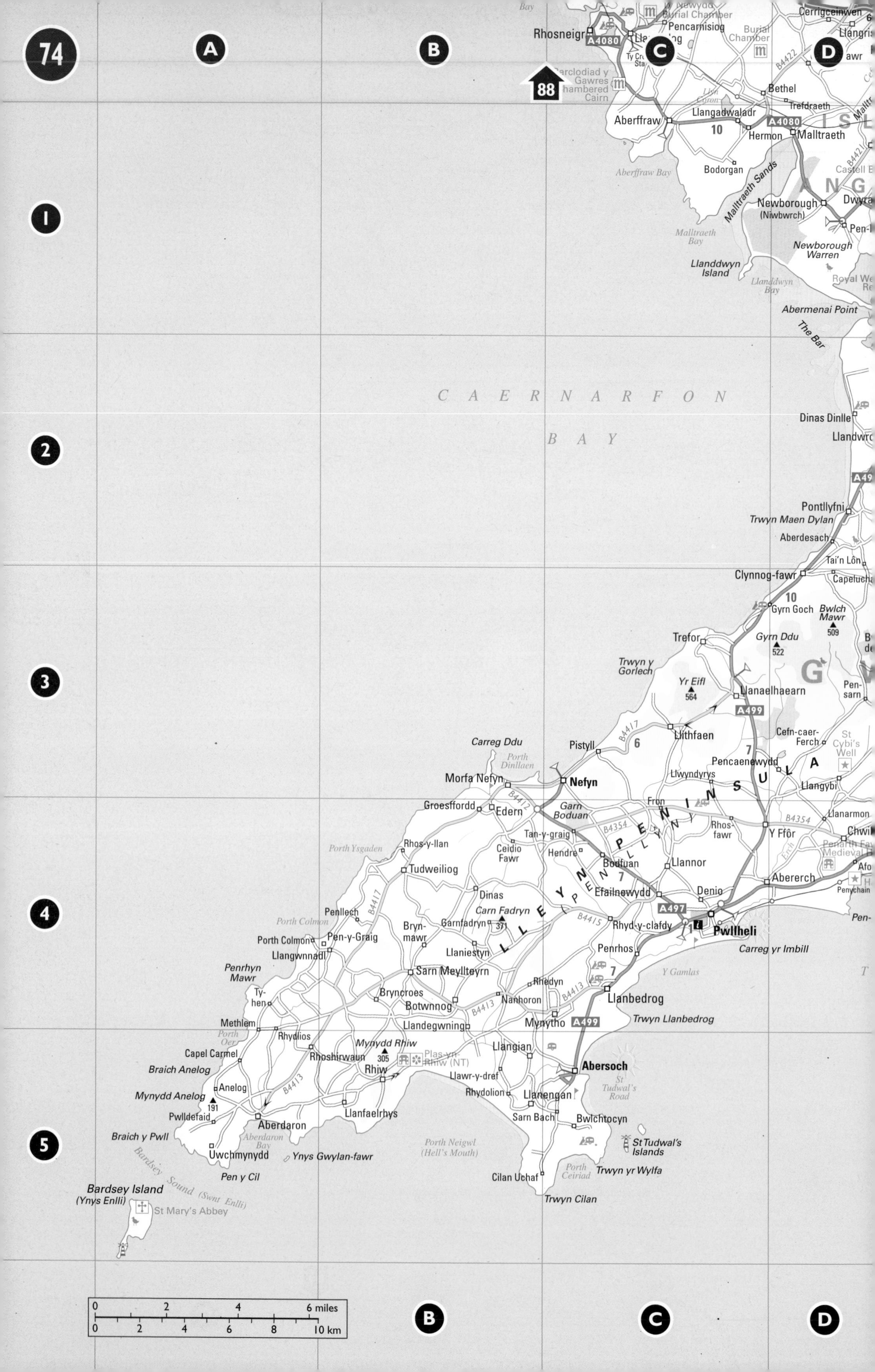

A
B
C
D
1
2
3
4
5
88
Rhosneigr
A4080
Pencarnisiog
Burial Chamber
Barclodiad y Gawres Chambered Cairn
Bethel
Trefdraeth
Aberffraw
Llangadwaladr
10
Hermon
Malltraeth
B4422
Bodorgan
Aberffraw Bay
Malltraeth Sands
Newborough
(Niwbwrch)
Newborough Warren
Malltraeth Bay
Llanddwyn Island
Llanddwyn Bay
Abermenai Point
The Bar
C A E R N A R F O N
B A Y
Dinas Dinlle
Pontllyfni
Trwyn Maen Dylan
Aberdesach
Clynnog-fawr
Gyrn Goch
Bwlch Mawr
509
Trefor
Gyrn Ddu
522
Trwyn y Gorlech
Yr Eifl
564
Llanaelhaearn
A499
B4417
Llithfaen
Cefn-caer-Ferch
St Cybi's Well
Carreg Ddu
Pistyll
6
Porth Dinllaen
Pencaenewydd
Morfa Nefyn
Nefyn
Llwyndyrys
Llangybi
Groesffordd
Edern
Garn Boduan
Fron
B4354
Llanarmon
Porth Ysgaden
Tan-y-graig
Rhos-fawr
Y Ffôr
Rhos-y-llan
Ceidio Fawr
Hendre
Tudweiliog
Bodfuan
Llannor
Abererch
Penychain
Dinas
Efailnewydd
Denio
A497
Penllech
Carn Fadryn
371
Porth Colmon
Garnfadryn
Bryn-mawr
B4415
Rhyd-y-clafdy
Pwllheli
Porth Colmon
Pen-y-Graig
Llangwnnadl
Llaniestyn
Penrhos
Carreg yr Imbill
LLEYN PENINSULA
(PEN LLŶN)
Penrhyn Mawr
Sarn Meyllteyrn
7
Y Gamlas
Ty-hen
Bryncroes
Rhedyn
Botwnnog
Nanhoron
Llanbedrog
Methlem
B4413
Porth Oer
Rhydlios
Llandegwning
Mynytho
Trwyn Llanbedrog
Capel Carmel
Mynydd Rhiw
305
Llangian
Braich Anelog
Rhoshirwaun
Plas-yn-Rhiw (NT)
Rhiw
Abersoch
Anelog
Llawr-y-dref
St Tudwal's Road
Mynydd Anelog
191
Rhydolion
Llanengan
Pwlldefaid
Llanfaelrhys
Aberdaron
Sarn Bach
Bwlchtocyn
Braich y Pwll
Aberdaron Bay
Porth Neigwl
(Hell's Mouth)
St Tudwal's Islands
Uwchmynydd
Ynys Gwylan-fawr
Bardsey Sound (Swnt Enlli)
Pen y Cil
Cilan Uchaf
Porth Ceiriad
Trwyn yr Wylfa
Trwyn Cilan
Bardsey Island
(Ynys Enlli)
St Mary's Abbey
0 2 4 6 miles
0 2 4 6 8 10 km

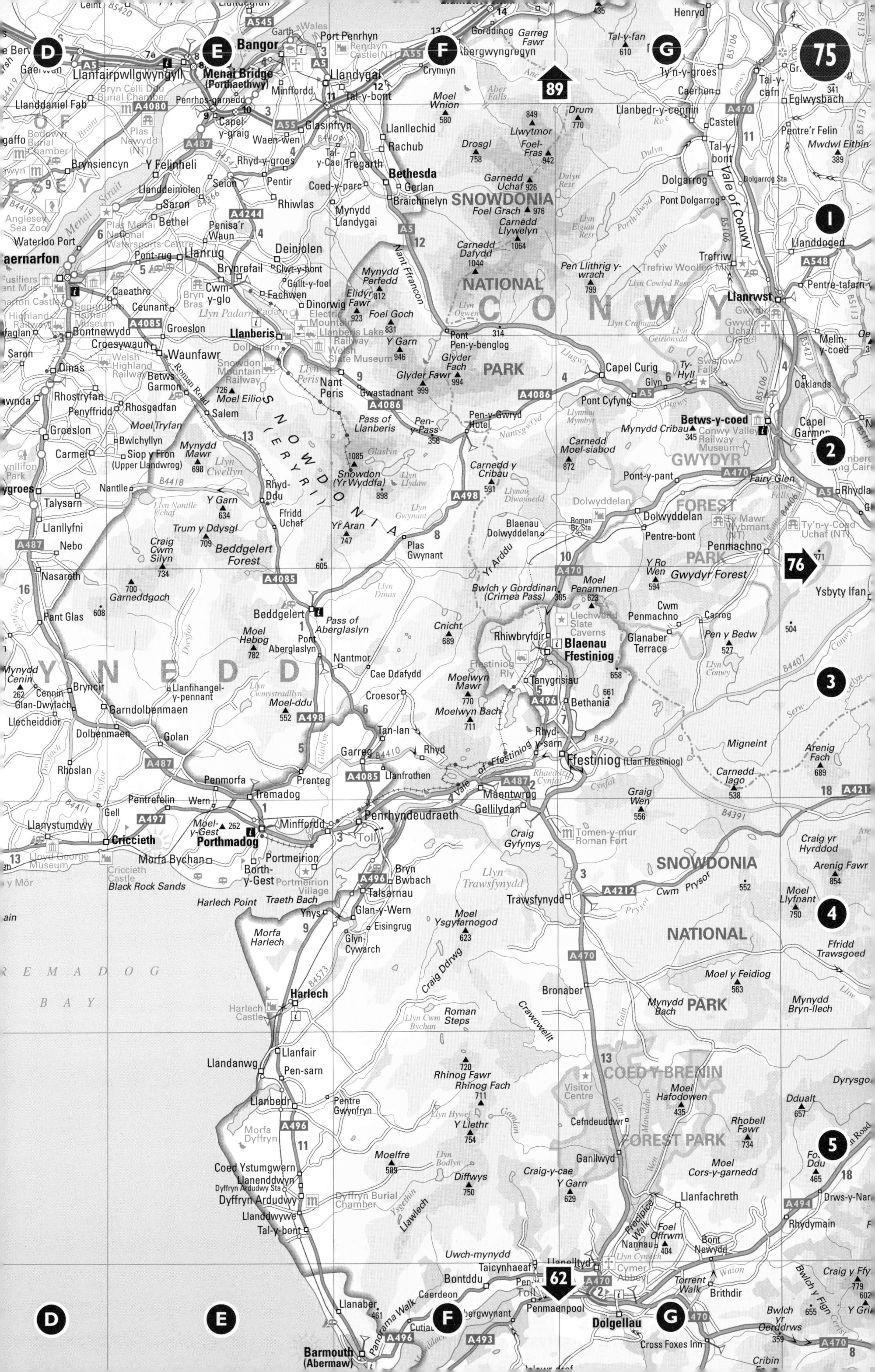
Bangor
Menai Bridge (Porthaethwy)
Llanfairpwllgwyngyll
Port Penrhyn
Penrhyn Castle (NT)
Llandygai
Tal-y-bont
Abergwyngregyn
Crymlyn
Gorddinog
Garreg Fawr
Tal-y-fan
Henryd
Ty'n-y-groes
Caerhun
Llanbedr-y-cennin
Castell
Tal-y-bont
Dolgarrog
Pont Dolgarrog
Vale of Conwy
Tal-y-cafn
Eglwysbach
Pentre'r Felin
Mwdwl Eithin
Llanddoged
Trefriw
Trefriw Woollen Mill
Llanrwst
Pentre-tafarn-y-fedw
Gwydir Uchaf Chapel
Melin-y-coed
Oaklands
Capel Garmon
Betws-y-coed
Conwy Valley Railway Museum
Mynydd Cribau
GWYDYR FOREST PARK
Fairy Glen
Conwy Falls
Rhydlanfair
Ty Mawr Wybrnant (NT)
Ty'n-y-Coed Uchaf (NT)
Penmachno
Gwydyr Forest
Ysbyty Ifan
Llanddaniel Fab
Bryn Celli Ddu Burial Chamber
Penrhos-garnedd
Capel-y-graig
Glasinfryn
Waen-wen
Minffordd
Llanllechid
Rachub
Bethesda
Gerlan
Tregarth
Coed-y-parc
Braichmelyn
Mynydd Llandygai
Rhiwlas
Pentir
Rhyd-y-groes
Y Felinheli
Brynsiencyn
Llanddeiniolen
Saron
Bethel
Seion
Penisa'r Waun
Plas Menai National Watersports Centre
Anglesey Sea Zoo
Waterloo Port
Caernarfon
Pont-rug
Llanrug
Brynrefail
Deiniolen
Clwt-y-bont
Gallt-y-foel
Fachwen
Dinorwig
Cwm-y-glo
Caeathro
Ceunant
Segontium Roman Museum
Bontnewydd
Groeslon
Waunfawr
Croesywaun
Llanberis
Dolbadarn
Llyn Padarn
Electric Mountain
Llanberis Lake Railway
Welsh Slate Museum
Snowdon Mountain Railway
Welsh Highland Railway
Betws Garmon
Moel Eilio
Dinas
Rhostryfan
Penyffridd
Rhosgadfan
Moel Tryfan
Salem
Groeslon
Bwlchyllyn
Carmel
Siop y Fron (Upper Llandwrog)
Mynydd Mawr
Llyn Cwellyn
Nantlle
Llyn Nantlle Uchaf
Talysarn
Llanllyfni
Nebo
Y Garn
Rhyd-Ddu
Ffridd Uchaf
Trum y Ddysgl
Craig Cwm Silyn
Beddgelert Forest
Nasareth
Garneddgoch
Pant Glas
Mynydd Cenin
Cennin
Bryncir
Glan-Dwyfach
Llecheiddior
Garndolbenmaen
Dolbenmaen
Golan
Rhoslan
Llanfihangel-y-pennant
GWYNEDD
SNOWDONIA NATIONAL PARK
CONWY
Moel Wnion
Aber Falls
Drum
Llwytmor
Foel-Fras
Drosgl
Garnedd Uchaf
Foel Grach
Carnedd Llywelyn
Carnedd Dafydd
Pen Llithrig y-wrach
Nant Ffrancon
Mynydd Perfedd
Elidyr Fawr
Foel Goch
Y Garn
Llyn Ogwen
Pont Pen-y-benglog
Glyder Fach
Glyder Fawr
Capel Curig
Ty-Hyll
Swallow Falls
Glyn
Pont Cyfyng
Llynnau Mymbyr
Carnedd Moel-siabod
Nant Peris
Gwastadnant
Pass of Llanberis
Pen-y-Pass
Pen-y-Gwryd Hotel
Llyn Peris
SNOWDONIA (ERYRI)
Glaslyn
Snowdon (Yr Wyddfa)
Llyn Llydaw
Carnedd y Cribau
Llyn Gwynant
Yr Aran
Plas Gwynant
Yr Arddu
Bwlch y Gorddinan (Crimea Pass)
Pont-y-pant
Dolwyddelan
Blaenau Dolwyddelan
Pentre-bont
Moel Penamnen
Y Ro Wen
Cwm Penmachno
Carrog
Llechwedd Slate Caverns
Rhiwbryfdir
Blaenau Ffestiniog
Glanaber Terrace
Pen y Bedw
Llyn Conwy
Llyn Dinas
Beddgelert
Pass of Aberglaslyn
Pont Aberglaslyn
Moel Hebog
Nantmor
Cae Ddafydd
Cnicht
Ffestiniog Rly
Tanygrisiau
Bethania
Moelwyn Mawr
Moelwyn Bach
Croesor
Llyn Cwmystradllyn
Moel-ddu
Tan-lan
Rhyd
Garreg
Llanfrothen
Rhyd-y-sarn
Ffestiniog (Llan Ffestiniog)
Migneint
Arenig Fach
Carnedd Iago
Vale of Ffestiniog
Maentwrog
Rhaeadr Cynfal
Gellilydan
Graig Wen
Penmorfa
Prenteg
Tremadog
Pentrefelin
Wern
Moel-y-Gest
Porthmadog
Minffordd
Penrhyndeudraeth
Toll
Llanystumdwy
Lloyd George Museum
Criccieth
Criccieth Castle
Morfa Bychan
Black Rock Sands
Borth-y-Gest
Portmeirion
Portmeirion Village
Craig Gyfynys
Tomen-y-mur Roman Fort
Craig yr Hyrddod
Arenig Fawr
Moel Llyfnant
Ffridd Trawsgoed
Bryn Bwbach
Talsarnau
Glan-y-Wern
Eisingrug
Ynys
Glyn-Cywarch
Harlech Point
Traeth Bach
Morfa Harlech
TREMADOG BAY
Llyn Trawsfynydd
Trawsfynydd
Cwm Prysor
Moel Ysgyfarnogod
Craig Ddrwg
Bronaber
Moel y Feidiog
Mynydd Bach
Mynydd Bryn-llech
Harlech
Harlech Castle
Roman Steps
Llyn Cwm Bychan
Crawcwellt
Llanfair
Llandanwg
Pen-sarn
Llanbedr
Pentre Gwynfryn
Rhinog Fawr
Rhinog Fach
Llyn Hywel
Y Llethr
COED Y BRENIN FOREST PARK
Visitor Centre
Moel Hafodowen
Cefndeuddwr
Dyrysgol
Dduallt
Rhobell Fawr
Morfa Dyffryn
Moelfre
Llyn Bodlyn
Diffwys
Craig-y-cae
Y Garn
Ganllwyd
Moel Cors-y-garnedd
Foel Ddu
Coed Ystumgwern
Llanenddwyn
Dyffryn Ardudwy Sta
Dyffryn Ardudwy
Dyffryn Burial Chamber
Llanddwywe
Tal-y-bont
Llawlech
Llanfachreth
Drws-y-Nant
Rhydymain
Precipice Walk
Foel Offrwm
Nannau
Llyn Cynwch
Bont Newydd
Uwch-mynydd
Taicynhaeaf
Llanelltyd
Cymer Abbey
Bontddu
Caerdeon
Penmaenpool
Torrent Walk
Brithdir
Craig y Ffynnon
Bwlch y Fign
Bwlch yr Oerddrws
Llanaber
Panorama Walk
Cutiau
Abergwynant
Dolgellau
Cross Foxes Inn
Cribin
Barmouth (Abermaw)
89
76
62

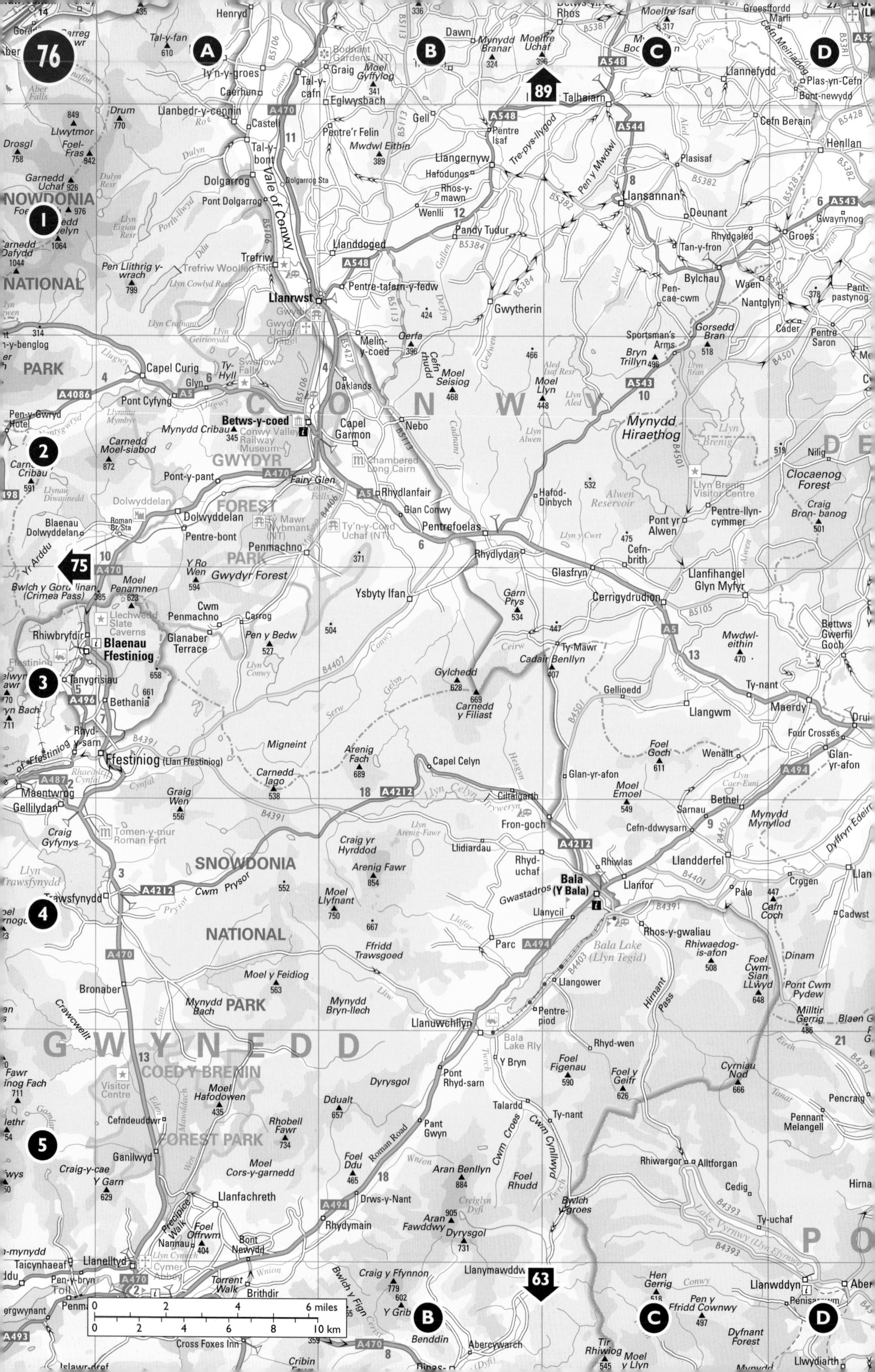

76
A
B
C
D
89
75
63
Henryd
Tal-y-fan
610
Ty'n-y-groes
Caerhun
Bodnant Gardens (NT)
Graig
Moel Gyffylog
341
Tal-y-cafn
Eglwysbach
Dawn
Mynydd Branar
324
Moelfre Uchaf
396
Rhos
Moelfre Isaf
317
Groesffordd Marli
Cefn Meiriadog
Llannefydd
Plas-yn-Cefn
Bont-newydd
Talhaiarn
Aber Falls
Drum
770
849
Llwytmor
Foel-Fras
942
Drosgl
758
Garnedd Uchaf
926
Dulyn Resr
SNOWDONIA
NATIONAL
PARK
976
1064
Carnedd Dafydd
1044
Llanbedr-y-cennin
Castell
Tal-y-bont
Dolgarrog
Dolgarrog Sta
Pont Dolgarrog
Vale of Conwy
Gell
Pentre'r Felin
Mwdwl Eithin
389
Pentre Isaf
Tre-pys-llygod
Llangernyw
Hafodunos
Rhos-y-mawn
Wenlli
Pen y Mwdwl
Llansannan
Plasisaf
Cefn Berain
Henllan
Deunant
Gwaynynog
Rhydgaled
Tan-y-fron
Groes
Bylchau
Waen
Pen-cae-cwm
Nantglyn
Pant-pastynog
Cader
Pentre Saron
Llyn Eigiau Resr
Porth-llwyd
Trefriw
Trefriw Woollen Mill
Llyn Cowlyd Resr
Pen Llithrig y-wrach
799
Llanddoged
Pandy Tudur
B5384
Llanrwst
Gwydir
Gwydir Uchaf Chapel
Pentre-tafarn-y-fedw
424
Gwytherin
314
Llyn Crafnant
Llyn Geirionydd
Capel Curig
Ty-Hyll
Swallow Falls
Glyn
Pont Cyfyng
Melin-y-coed
Oerfa
396
Cefn rhudd
Moel Seisiog
468
466
Aled Isaf Resr
Moel Llyn
448
Llyn Aled
Sportsman's Arms
Bryn Trillyn
496
Gorsedd Bran
518
Llyn Bran
Oaklands
CONWY
Pen-y-Gwryd Hotel
Carnedd Moel-siabod
872
Mynydd Cribau
345
Betws-y-coed
Conwy Valley Railway Museum
Capel Garmon
Nebo
Chambered Long Cairn
GWYDYR
FOREST
PARK
Pont-y-pant
Fairy Glen
Conwy Falls
Rhydlanfair
Glan Conwy
Pentrefoelas
Mynydd Hiraethog
Llyn Brenig
Llyn Brenig Visitor Centre
519
Nilig
Clocaenog Forest
Carnedd Cribau
591
Llynau Diwaunedd
Dolwyddelan
Blaenau Dolwyddelan
Roman Br. Sta
Pentre-bont
Ty Mawr Wybrnant (NT)
Ty'n-y-Coed Uchaf (NT)
Penmachno
371
Hafod-Dinbych
532
Alwen Reservoir
Pentre-llyn-cymmer
Pont yr Alwen
Craig Bron-banog
501
Llyn y Cwrt
475
Cefn-brith
Rhydlydan
Glasfryn
Llanfihangel Glyn Myfyr
Yr Arddu
Bwlch y Gorddinan (Crimea Pass)
385
Moel Penamnen
623
Y Ro Wen
594
Gwydyr Forest
Ysbyty Ifan
Garn Prys
534
Cerrigydrudion
Cwm Penmachno
Carrog
Llechwedd Slate Caverns
Rhiwbryfdir
Blaenau Ffestiniog
Glanaber Terrace
504
Pen y Bedw
527
447
Ty-Mawr
Cadair Benllyn
407
Mwdwl-eithin
470
Bettws Gwerful Goch
Tanygrisiau
658
661
Bethania
Llyn Conwy
B4407
Gylchedd
628
669
Carnedd y Filiast
Gellioedd
Ty-nant
Llangwm
Maerdy
Rhyd-y-sarn
Ffestiniog (Llan Ffestiniog)
Migneint
Arenig Fach
689
Capel Celyn
Foel Goch
611
Four Crosses
Wenallt
Glan-yr-afon
Maentwrog
Gellilydan
Carnedd Iago
538
Graig Wen
556
A4212
Llyn Celyn
Ciltalgarth
Glan-yr-afon
Moel Emoel
549
Llyn Caer-Euni
Bethel
Sarnau
Mynydd Mynyllod
Craig Gyfynys
Tomen-y-mur Roman Fort
Craig yr Hyrddod
Llyn Arenig-Fawr
Arenig Fawr
854
Fron-goch
Llidiardau
Rhyd-uchaf
Rhiwlas
Cefn-ddwysarn
Llandderfel
Llyn Trawsfynydd
Trawsfynydd
Cwm Prysor
SNOWDONIA
NATIONAL
552
Moel Llyfnant
750
667
Gwastadros
Bala (Y Bala)
Llanfor
Pale
447
Crogen
Cefn Coch
Cadwst
Llanycil
Rhos-y-gwaliau
Ffridd Trawsgoed
Parc
Bala Lake (Llyn Tegid)
Rhiwaedog-is-afon
508
Dinam
Bronaber
Moel y Feidiog
563
Llangower
Hirnant Pass
Foel Cwm-Sian Llwyd
648
Pont Cwm Pydew
Crawcwellt
Mynydd Bach
PARK
Mynydd Bryn-llech
Pentre-piod
Milltir Gerrig
486
GWYNEDD
Llanuwchllyn
Bala Lake Rly
Rhyd-wen
COED Y BRENIN
Visitor Centre
Moel Hafodowen
435
Dyrysgol
Pont Rhyd-sarn
Y Bryn
Foel Figenau
590
Foel y Geifr
626
Cyrniau Nod
666
Cefndeuddwr
Dduallt
657
Rhobell Fawr
734
Roman Road
Pant Gwyn
Talardd
Ty-nant
Cwm Croes
Cwm Cynllwyd
Pencraig
Pennant Melangell
FOREST PARK
Ganllwyd
Craig-y-cae
Y Garn
629
Moel Cors-y-garnedd
Foel Ddu
465
Aran Benllyn
884
Foel Rhudd
Rhiwargor
Alltforgan
Cedig
Llanfachreth
Drws-y-Nant
Creiglyn Dyfi
Aran Fawddwy
905
Dyrysgol
731
Bwlch y groes
Lake Vyrnwy (Llyn Efyrnwy)
Ty-uchaf
Precipice Walk
Foel Offrwm
404
Nannau
Bont Newydd
Rhydymain
Llanelltyd
Taicynhaeaf
Cymer Abbey
Llyn Cynwch
Pen-y-bryn
Torrent Walk
Brithdir
Craig y Ffynnon
779
602
Y Grib
Bwlch y Fign
Llanymawddwy
Hen Gerrig
518
Pen y Ffridd Cownwy
497
Dyfnant Forest
Llanwddyn
Abertridwr
Penisarcwm
0 2 4 6 miles
0 2 4 6 8 10 km
Cross Foxes Inn
Benddin
Abercywarch
Tir Rhiwiog
545
Moel y Llyn
Llwydiarth

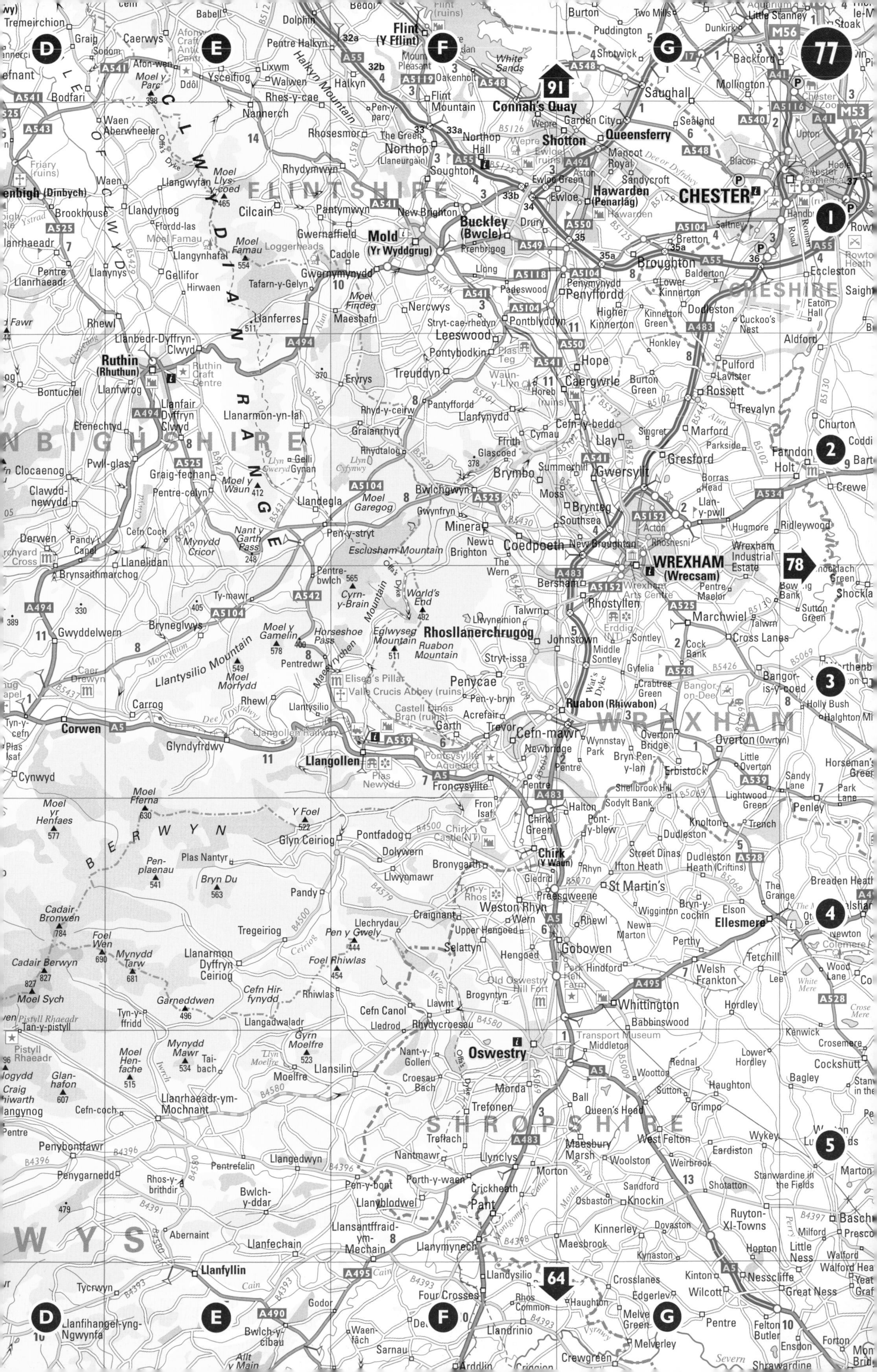
77
D
E
F
G
I
2
3
4
5
91
78
64
Tremeirchion
Babell
Caerwys
Afonwen
Ysceifiog
Dolphin
Pentre Halkyn
Flint (Y Fflint)
Halkyn Mountain
Halkyn
Oakenholt
Flint Mountain
Connah's Quay
White Sands
Burton
Puddington
Shotwick
Two Mills
Little Stanney
Dunkirk
Backford
Mollington
Saughall
Chester Zoo
Garden City
Sealand
Upton
Queensferry
Shotton
Wepre
Mancot Royal
Sandycroft
Dee or Dyfrdwy
Blacon
Hoole
Chester Cathedral
CHESTER
Hawarden (Penarlâg)
Ewloe
Ewloe Green
Aston
Northop
Northop Hall
Soughton
The Green
Rhosesmor
Pen-y-parc
Nannerch
Rhes-y-cae
Lixwm
Walwen
Ddôl
Moel y Parc
398
Graig
Sodom
Bodfari
Waen
Aberwheeler
Offa's Dyke
Friary (ruins)
Denbigh (Dinbych)
Brookhouse
Llangwyfan
Moel Llys-y-coed
465
FLINTSHIRE
Rhydymwyn
Pantymwyn
Cilcain
Llandyrnog
Ffordd-las
Moel Famau
554
Loggerheads
Llangynhafal
Gellifor
Hirwaen
Tafarn-y-Gelyn
Gwernaffield
Mold (Yr Wyddgrug)
Cadole
Gwernymynydd
New Brighton
Buckley (Bwcle)
Prenbrigog
Drury
Saltney
Bretton
Broughton
Balderton
Eccleston
Lower Kinnerton
Penymynydd
Penyffordd
Higher Kinnerton
Kinnerton Green
Dodleston
Cuckoo's Nest
Eaton Hall
CHESHIRE
Pentre Llanrhaeadr
Llanynys
Rhewl
Moel Findeg
Maeshafn
Nercwys
Llong
Padeswood
Stryt-cae-rhedyn
Pontblyddyn
Leeswood
Pontybodkin
Plas Teg
Llanferres
511
Llanbedr-Dyffryn-Clwyd
Ruthin (Ruthun)
Ruthin Craft Centre
Llanfwrog
Bontuchel
370
Eryrys
Treuddyn
Hope
Caergwrle
Horeb (ruins)
Waun-y-Llyn
Burton Green
Honkley
Pulford
Lavister
Rossett
Trevalyn
Aldford
Churton
Farndon
Holt
Coddington
Llanfair Dyffryn Clwyd
Efenechtyd
Llanarmon-yn-Ial
Rhyd-y-ceirw
Pantyffordd
Llanfynydd
Cefn-y-bedd
Llay
Singret
Marford
Parkside
Gresford
Gwersyllt
Summerhill
Ffrith
Cymau
Glascoed
378
Brymbo
Moss
Brynteg
Southsea
Borras Head
Llan-y-pwll
Crewe
DENBIGHSHIRE
CLWYDIAN RANGE
VALE OF CLWYD
Clocaenog
Pwll-glas
Graig-fechan
Gelli Gynan
Llyn Gweryd
Llyn Cyfynwy
Rhydtalog
Clawdd-newydd
Pentre-celyn
Moel y Waun
412
Llandegla
Moel Garegog
Bwlchgwyn
Gwynfryn
Minera
Coedpoeth
New Brighton
New Broughton
Acton
Rhosnesni
WREXHAM (Wrecsam)
Wrexham Industrial Estate
Hugmore
Ridleywood
Derwen
Pandy'r Capel
Cefn Coch
Mynydd Cricor
Nant y Garth Pass
248
Pen-y-stryt
Esclusham Mountain
Llanelidan
Brynsaithmarchog
Pentre-bwlch
565
Cyrn-y-Brain
World's End
482
The Wern
Bersham
Rhostyllen
Wrexham Arts Centre
Pentre Maelor
Bowling Bank
Sutton Green
Shocklach
330
405
Ty-mawr
389
Gwyddelwern
Bryneglwys
Moel y Gamelin
578
Horseshoe Pass
Eglwyseg Mountain
511
Ruabon Mountain
Rhosllanerchrugog
Llwyneinion
Talwrn
Erddig (NT)
Johnstown
Marchwiel
Sontley
Middle Sontley
Cross Lanes
Cock Bank
Llantysilio Mountain
549
Moel Morfydd
Pentredwr
Caer Drewyn
Eliseg's Pillar
Valle Crucis Abbey (ruins)
Stryt-issa
Penycae
Pen-y-bryn
Gyfelia
Crabtree Green
Bangor-on-Dee
Bangor-is-y-coed
Holly Bush
Halghton Mill
Carrog
Rhewl
Llantysilio
Castell Dinas Bran (ruins)
Acrefair
Trevor
Ruabon (Rhiwabon)
Wat's Dyke
WREXHAM
Corwen
Glyndyfrdwy
Llangollen Railway
Garth
Cefn-mawr
Newbridge
Wynnstay Park
Overton Bridge
Bryn Pen-y-lan
Overton (Owrtyn)
Little Overton
Erbistock
Horseman's Green
Cynwyd
Llangollen
Plas Newydd
Pontcysyllte Aqueduct
Froncysyllte
Pentre
Shellbrook Hill
Sandy Lane
Park Lane
Lightwood Green
Penley
Moel yr Henfaes
577
Moel Fferna
630
Y Foel
522
BERWYN
Glyn Ceiriog
Pontfadog
Fron Isaf
Chirk Castle (NT)
Chirk Green
Halton
Sodylt Bank
Pont-y-blew
Knolton
Trench
Dudleston
Plas Nantyr
Pen-plaenau
541
Bryn Du
563
Dolywern
Llwynmawr
Bronygarth
Chirk (Y Waun)
Gledrid
Rhyn
Street Dinas
Ifton Heath
St Martin's
Dudleston Heath (Criftins)
Breaden Heath
Pandy
Tyn-y-Rhos
Preesgweene
Weston Rhyn
Wern
Wigginton
Bryn-y-cochin
Elson
The Grange
Ellesmere
Cadair Bronwen
784
Foel Wen
690
Tregeiriog
Llechrydau
Pen y Gwely
444
Craignant
Upper Hengoed
Rhewl
New Marton
Perthy
Newton
Colemere
Cadair Berwyn
827
Mynydd Tarw
681
Llanarmon Dyffryn Ceiriog
Foel Rhiwlas
454
Selattyn
Hengoed
Gobowen
Hindford
Tetchill
Welsh Frankton
Lee
Wood Lane
White Mere
Moel Sych
Garneddwen
496
Cefn Hir-fynydd
Rhiwlas
Old Oswestry Hill Fort
Park Hall Farm
Brogyntyn
Llawnt
Whittington
Hordley
Crose Mere
Pistyll Rhaeadr
Tan-y-pistyll
Tyn-y-ffridd
Llangadwaladr
Cefn Canol
Lledrod
Rhydycroesau
Babbinswood
Transport Museum
Middleton
Kenwick
Crosemere
Moel Hen-fache
515
Mynydd Mawr
534
Tai-bach
Llyn Moelfre
Gyrn Moelfre
523
Llansilin
Nant-y-Gollen
Oswestry
Lower Hordley
Rednal
Cockshutt
Glan-hafon
607
Moelfre
Croesau Bach
Morda
Wootton
Haughton
Bagley
Llanrhaeadr-ym-Mochnant
Cefn-coch
Trefonen
Ball
Queen's Head
Sutton
Grimpo
SHROPSHIRE
Penybontfawr
Treflach
Maesbury Marsh
West Felton
Wykey
Eardiston
Marton
Pentrefelin
Llangedwyn
Nantmawr
Llynclys
Woolston
Weirbrook
Stanwardine in the Fields
Penygarnedd
Rhos-y-brithdir
Pen-y-bont
Porth-y-waen
Crickheath
Morton
Sandford
Knockin
Shotatton
Ruyton-XI-Towns
Baschurch
Prescott
479
Bwlch-y-ddar
Llanyblodwel
Pant
Osbaston
Montgomery Canal
Kinnerley
Dovaston
Milford
Little Ness
Hopton
Abernaint
Llansantffraid-ym-Mechain
Llanfechain
Llanymynech
Maesbrook
Kynaston
Walford
Walford Heath
Llanfyllin
Llandysilio
Crosslanes
Kinton
Nesscliffe
Great Ness
Tycrwyn
Four Crosses
Rhos Common
Haughton
Edgerley
Wilcott
Melverley Green
Pentre
Melverley
Felton Butler
Godor
Llanfihangel-yng-Ngwynfa
Bwlch-y-cibau
Waen-fâch
Llandrinio
Crewgreen
Sarnau
Ensdon
Forton
Severn
Shrawardine
Allt y Main
Arddlin
Criggion
Montford Bridge
POWYS

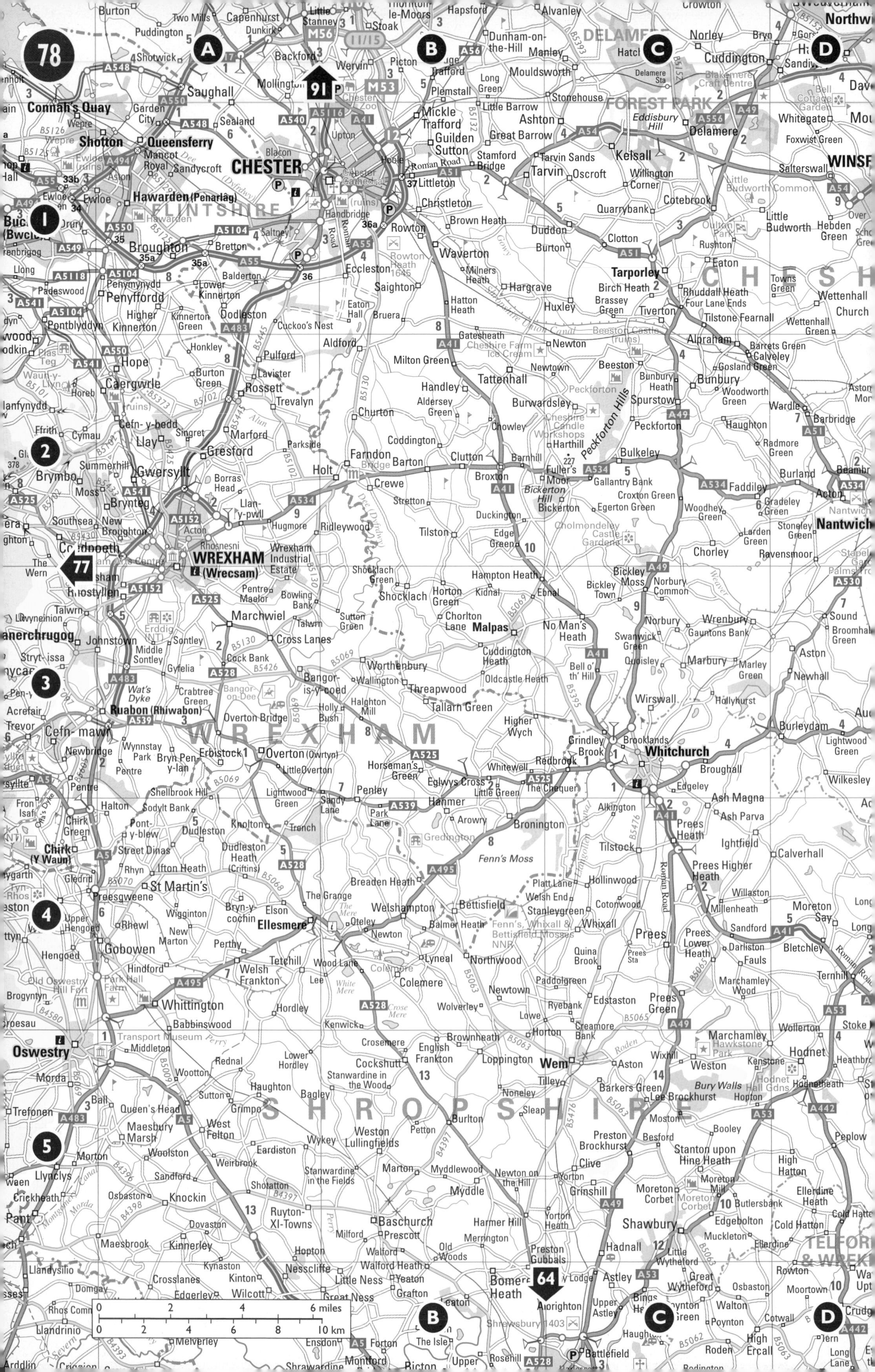
78
A
B
C
D
91
M56
M53
64
77
1
2
3
4
5
Burton
Puddington
Two Mills
Capenhurst
Dunkirk
Little Stanney
Stoak
Thornton-le-Moors
Hapsford
Alvanley
Norley
Bryn
Northwich
Shotwick
Backford
Wervin
Picton
Dunham-on-the-Hill
Manley
Hatch
Cuddington
Sandiway
Saughall
Mollington
Trafford
Mouldsworth
Delamere Sta
Blakemere Craft Centre
Davenham
Connah's Quay
Garden City
Sealand
Chester Zoo
Plemstall
Long Green
Stonehouse
FOREST PARK
Whitegate
Shotton
Queensferry
Mickle Trafford
Little Barrow
Ashton
Eddisbury Hill
Delamere
Foxwist Green
Mancot Royal
Sandycroft
Blacon
Upton
Guilden Sutton
Great Barrow
Tarvin Sands
Kelsall
WINSFORD
Ewloe
CHESTER
Hoole
Roman Road
Stamford Bridge
Tarvin
Oscroft
Willington Corner
Salterswall
Hawarden (Penarlâg)
FLINTSHIRE
Chester Cathedral
Littleton
Little Budworth Common
Buckley (Bwcle)
Drury
Handbridge
Christleton
Quarrybank
Cotebrook
Saltney
Rowton
Brown Heath
Little Budworth
Hebden Green
Broughton
Bretton
Waverton
Duddon
Burton
Clotton
Oulton Park
Rushton
Llong
Balderton
Eccleston
Rowton Heath 1645
Milners Heath
Tarporley
Eaton
CHESHIRE
Padeswood
Penymynydd
Penyffordd
Lower Kinnerton
Saighton
Hargrave
Birch Heath
Rhuddall Heath
Four Lane Ends
Towns Green
Wettenhall
Pontblyddyn
Higher Kinnerton
Kinnerton Green
Dodleston
Eaton Hall
Bruera
Hatton Heath
Huxley
Brassey Green
Tiverton
Tilstone Fearnall
Church Minshull
Cuckoo's Nest
Gatesheath
Cheshire Farm Ice Cream
Newton
Beeston Castle (ruins)
Alpraham
Barrets Green
Calveley
Hope
Aldford
Honkley
Pulford
Milton Green
Beeston
Gosland Green
Caergwrle
Burton Green
Lavister
Rossett
Tattenhall
Newtown
Bunbury Heath
Bunbury
Woodworth Green
Trevalyn
Handley
Burwardsley
Peckforton
Spurstow
Peckforton Hills
Wardle
Barbridge
Ffrith
Cymau
Cefn-y-bedd
Churton
Aldersey Green
Cheshire Candle Workshops
Chowley
Haughton
Llay
Singret
Marford
Parkside
Coddington
Harthill
Radmore Green
Brymbo
Summerhill
Gwersyllt
Gresford
Farndon
Barton
Clutton
Barnhill
Fuller's Moor
Bulkeley
Burland
Moss
Borras Head
Holt
Crewe
Broxton
Gallantry Bank
Faddiley
Acton
Brynteg
Llan-y-pwll
Stretton
Bickerton Hill
Bickerton
Croxton Green
Egerton Green
Woodhey Green
Gradeley Green
Nantwich
Southsea
New Broughton
Hugmore
Ridleywood
Duckington
Cholmondeley Castle Gardens
Stoneley Green
Coedpoeth
Acton
Rhosnesni
WREXHAM
(Wrecsam)
Wrexham Industrial Estate
Tilston
Edge Green
Larden Green
The Wern
Rhostyllen
Shocklach Green
Hampton Heath
Chorley
Ravensmoor
Pentre Maelor
Bowling Bank
Shocklach
Horton Green
Kidnal
Ebnal
Bickley Moss
Bickley Town
Norbury Common
Talwrn
Marchwiel
Sutton Green
Chorlton Lane
Malpas
No Man's Heath
Norbury
Wrenbury
Sound
Broomhall Green
Johnstown
Erddig (NT)
Sontley
Cross Lanes
Swanwick Green
Gauntons Bank
Middle Sontley
Cock Bank
Cuddington Heath
Quoisley
Marbury
Aston
Marley Green
Newhall
Gyfelia
Worthenbury
Bangor-is-y-coed
Wallington
Threapwood
Oldcastle Heath
Bell o' th' Hill
Crabtree Green
Bangor-on-Dee
Halghton Mill
Tallarn Green
Wirswall
Hollyhurst
Acrefair
Wat's Dyke
Ruabon (Rhiwabon)
Overton Bridge
Holly Bush
Higher Wych
Burleydam
Trevor
Cefn-mawr
WREXHAM
Grindley Brook
Brooklands
Whitchurch
Lightwood Green
Newbridge
Wynnstay Park
Bryn Pen-y-lan
Erbistock
Overton (Owrtyn)
Horseman's Green
Whitewell
Redbrook
Broughall
Wilkesley
Pentre
Little Overton
Eglwys Cross
Little Green
The Chequer
Edgeley
Shellbrook Hill
Lightwood Green
Penley
Hanmer
Alkington
Ash Magna
Halton
Sodylt Bank
Sandy Lane
Park Lane
Arowry
Bronington
Ash Parva
Chirk Green
Pont-y-blew
Dudleston
Knolton
Trench
Gredington
Tilstock
Prees Heath
Ightfield
Chirk (Y Waun)
Street Dinas
Dudleston Heath (Criftins)
Fenn's Moss
Calverhall
Rhyn
Ifton Heath
St Martin's
Breaden Heath
Plett Lane
Hollinwood
Prees Higher Heath
Preesgweene
Welsh End
Willaston
Millenheath
Bryn-y-cochin
Elson
The Grange
The Mere
Welshampton
Bettisfield
Stanleygreen
Cotonwood
Moreton Say
Upper Hengoed
Rhewl
Wigginton
Ellesmere
Oteley
Balmer Heath
Fenn's, Whixall & Bettisfield Mosses NNR
Whixall
Prees
Prees Lower Heath
Sandford
New Marton
Newton
Darliston
Bletchley
Hengoed
Gobowen
Perthy
Lyneal
Quina Brook
Prees Sta
Fauls
Tetchill
Wood Lane
Northwood
Hindford
Welsh Frankton
Lee
Colemere
Marchamley Wood
Ternhill
Old Oswestry Hill Fort
Park Hall Farm
White Mere
Newtown
Paddolgreen
Brogyntyn
Whittington
Hordley
Crose Mere
Wolverley
Edstaston
Prees Green
Babbinswood
Kenwick
Lowe
Ryebank
Creamore Bank
Wollerton
Stoke
Oswestry
Transport Museum
Middleton
Crosemere
Brownheath
Horton
Marchamley
Hawkstone Park
Hodnet
Heathbrook
Morda
Wootton
Rednal
Lower Hordley
Cockshutt
English Frankton
Loppington
Wem
Aston
Wixhill
Weston
Kenstone
Haughton
Stanwardine in the Wood
Tilley
Bury Walls
Hodnet Hall Gdns
Hodnetheath
Ball
Sutton
Bagley
Noneley
Barkers Green
Lee Brockhurst
Hopton
Trefonen
Queen's Head
Grimpo
SHROPSHIRE
Burlton
Sleap
Moston
Maesbury Marsh
West Felton
Weston Lullingfields
Petton
Preston Brockhurst
Besford
Booley
Peplow
Morton
Woolston
Eardiston
Wykey
Stanton upon Hine Heath
High Hatton
Llynclys
Sandford
Weirbrook
Stanwardine in the Fields
Marton
Myddlewood
Newton on the Hill
Clive
Yorton
Crickheath
Osbaston
Shotatton
Myddle
Grinshill
Moreton Mill
Moreton Corbet
Ellerdine Heath
Knockin
Ruyton-XI-Towns
Yorton Heath
Butlersbank
Pant
Dovaston
Baschurch
Harmer Hill
Shawbury
Edgebolton
Cold Hatton
Maesbrook
Kinnerley
Prescott
Milford
Merrington
Muckleton
Ellerdine
TELFORD & WREKIN
Hopton
Walford
Old Woods
Preston Gubbals
Hadnall
Little Wytheford
Llandysilio
Kynaston
Nesscliffe
Walford Heath
Crosslanes
Kinton
Little Ness
Yeaton
Bomere Heath
Lodge
Astley
Great Wytheford
Rowton
Osbaston
Moortown
Domgay
Edgerley
Wilcott
Great Ness
Grafton
Albrighton
Upper Astley
Walton
Rhos Common
Llandrinio
Shrewsbury 1403
Poynton
Cotwall
Crudgington
High Ercall
Melverley
Ensdon
Forton
The Isle
Battlefield
Roden
Long Lane
Arddlin
Shrawardine
Montford
Upper
Rosehill
Rodington
0
2
4
6 miles
0
2
4
6
8
10 km

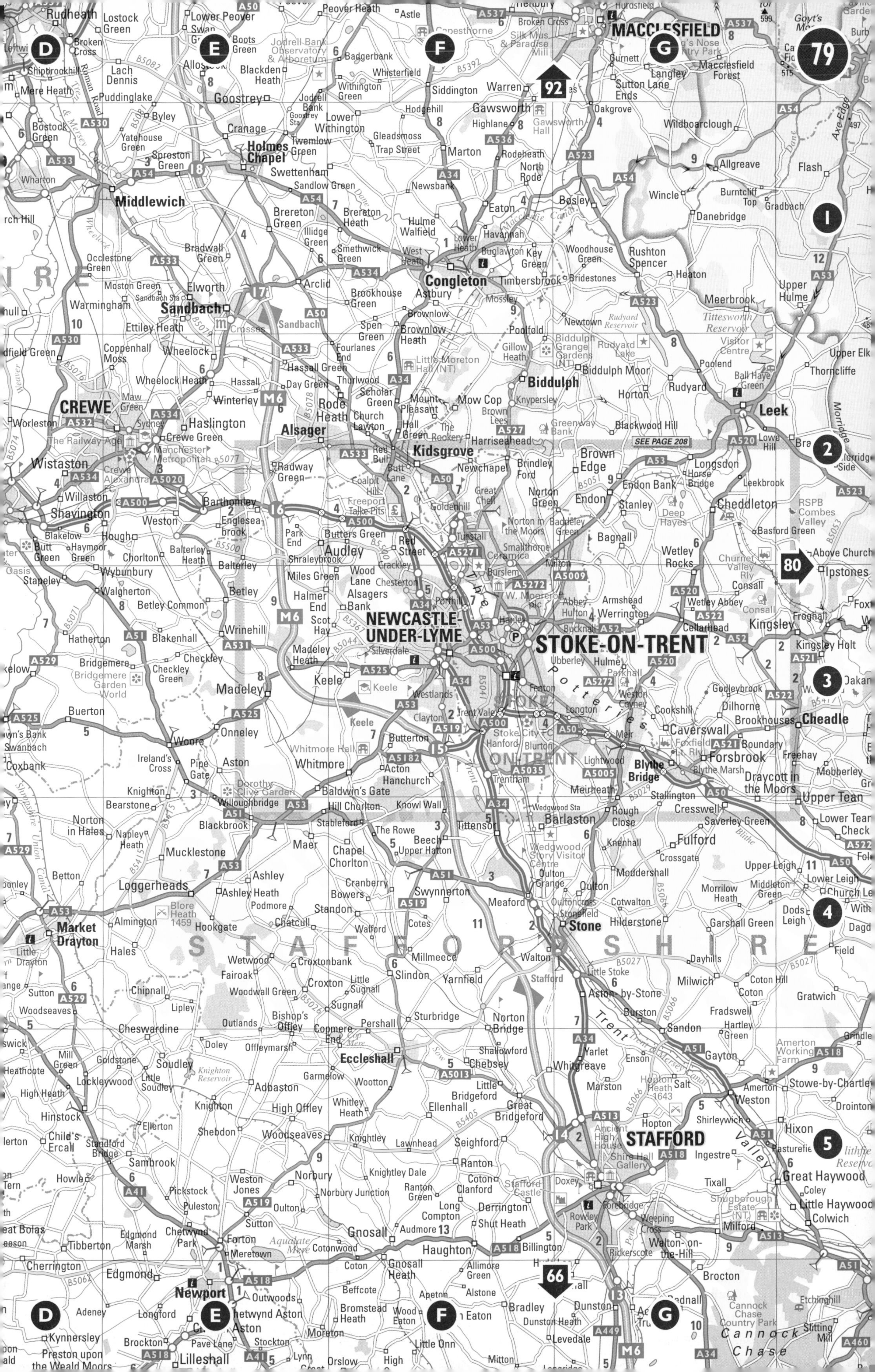
79
92
SEE PAGE 208
80
66
D
E
F
G
I
2
3
4
5
Rudheath
Lostock Green
Lower Peover
Peover Heath
Astle
Capesthorne
Broken Cross
Silk Mus. & Paradise Mill
MACCLESFIELD
Hurdsfield
Macclesfield Forest
Broken Cross
Shipbrookhill
Lach Dennis
Allostock
Boots Green
Jodrell Bank Observatory & Arboretum
Badgerbank
Whisterfield
Withington Green
Siddington
Warren
Gurnett
Langley
Sutton Lane Ends
Mere Heath
Puddinglake
Goostrey
Byley
Cranage
Jodrell Bank
Lower Withington
Hodgehill
Gawsworth
Gawsworth Hall
Highlane
Oakgrove
Wildboarclough
Bostock Green
Yatehouse Green
Holmes Chapel
Twemlow Green
Gleadsmoss
Trap Street
Marton
Rodeheath
North Rode
Allgreave
Flash
Wharton
Spreston Green
Swettenham
Sandlow Green
Newsbank
Wincle
Burntcliff Top
Gradbach
Middlewich
Brereton Green
Brereton Heath
Illidge Green
Hulme Walfield
Eaton
Havannah
Bosley
Danebridge
Occlestone Green
Bradwall Green
Smethwick Green
West Heath
Lower Heath
Buglawton
Key Green
Woodhouse Green
Rushton Spencer
Heaton
Moston Green
Elworth
Arclid
Congleton
Astbury
Timbersbrook
Bridestones
Upper Hulme
Warmingham
Sandbach
Brookhouse Green
Mossley
Meerbrook
Tittesworth Reservoir
Crosses
Brownlow
Newtown
Rudyard Reservoir
Ettiley Heath
Spen Green
Brownlow Heath
Poolfold
Biddulph Grange Gardens (NT)
Rudyard Lake
Visitor Centre
Upper Elk
Coppenhall Moss
Wheelock
Fourlanes End
Hassall Green
Little Moreton Hall (NT)
Gillow Heath
Biddulph Moor
Poolend
Thorncliffe
Wheelock Heath
Hassall
Day Green
Thurlwood
Scholar Green
Biddulph
Horton
Rudyard
Ball Haye Green
Maw Green
Winterley
Rode Heath
Mount Pleasant
Mow Cop
Knypersley
Leek
CREWE
Sydney
Haslington
Alsager
Church Lawton
Brown Lees
Worleston
Crewe Green
The Railway Age
Manchester Metropolitan
Hall Green
The Rookery
Harriseahead
Greenway Bank
Blackwood Hill
Lowe Hill
Wistaston
Crewe Alexandra
Radway Green
Red Bull
Kidsgrove
Brindley Ford
Brown Edge
Longsdon
Horse Bridge
Willaston
Butt Lane
Newchapel
Endon Bank
Leekbrook
Shavington
Barthomley
Coalpit Hill
Great Chell
Norton Green
Endon
Stanley
Cheddleton
RSPB Coombes Valley
Blakelow
Weston
Englesea-brook
Freeport Talke Pits
Goldenhill
Deep Hayes
Basford Green
Butt Green
Haymoor Green
Hough
Park End
Butters Green
Red Street
Tunstall
Norton in the Moors
Baddeley Green
Bagnall
Chorlton
Balterley Heath
Audley
Smallthorne
Ceramica
Wetley Rocks
Above Church
Oasis
Wybunbury
Balterley
Shraleybrook
Crackley
Burslem
Milton
Churnet Valley Rly
Ipstones
Stapeley
Miles Green
Wood Lane
Chesterton
Consall
Walgherton
Betley
Alsagers Bank
Porthill
W. Moorcroft plc
Abbey Hulton
Armshead
Wetley Abbey
Betley Common
Halmer End
NEWCASTLE-UNDER-LYME
Hanley
Werrington
Froghall
Scot Hay
Bucknall
Cellarhead
Kingsley
Hatherton
Blakenhall
Wrinehill
Madeley Heath
Silverdale
STOKE-ON-TRENT
Kingsley Holt
Bridgemere
Checkley
Ubberley
Hulme
Parkhall
Bridgemere Garden World
Checkley Green
Keele
Westlands
Fenton
Weston Coyney
Godleybrook
Madeley
Dilhorne
Buerton
Onneley
Clayton
Trent Vale
Longton
Cookshill
Brookhouses
Cheadle
Caverswall
Woore
Whitmore Hall
Butterton
Stoke City FC
Hanford
Blurton
Meir
Foxfield Lt. Rly
Boundary
Coxbank
Ireland's Cross
Pipe Gate
Aston
Whitmore
Lightwood
Blythe Bridge
Forsbrook
Freehay
Acton
Hanchurch
Trentham
Blythe Marsh
Mobberley
Knighton
Dorothy Clive Garden
Baldwin's Gate
Draycott in the Moors
Bearstone
Willoughbridge
Hill Chorlton
Knowl Wall
Wedgwood Sta
Meirheath
Stallington
Upper Tean
Norton in Hales
Blackbrook
Stableford
Tittensor
Barlaston
Rough Close
Cresswell
Saverley Green
Lower Tean
Napley Heath
The Rowe
Beech
Wedgwood Story Visitor Centre
Knenhall
Fulford
Mucklestone
Maer
Chapel Chorlton
Upper Hatton
Crossgate
Moddershall
Upper Leigh
Lower Leigh
Church Leigh
Betton
Ashley
Cranberry
Swynnerton
Oulton Grange
Oulton
Morrilow Heath
Middleton Green
Loggerheads
Ashley Heath
Bowers
Meaford
Oultoncross
Cotwalton
Podmore
Blore Heath 1459
Standon
Stonefield
Stone
Hilderstone
Dods Leigh
Market Drayton
Almington
Hookgate
Chatcull
Cotes
Garshall Green
Walford
STAFFORDSHIRE
Hales
Little Drayton
Millmeece
Walton
Stafford
Dayhills
Field
Wetwood
Croxtonbank
Slindon
Little Stoke
Fairoak
Yarnfield
Milwich
Coton Hill
Croxton
Little Sugnall
Coton
Gratwich
Sutton
Chipnall
Woodwall Green
Aston-by-Stone
Sugnall
Woodseaves
Lipley
Bishop's Offley
Sturbridge
Burston
Fradswell
Outlands
Pershall
Norton Bridge
Sandon
Hartley Green
Cheswardine
Copmere End
Doley
Offleymarsh
Shallowford
Mill Green
Goldstone
Soudley
Knighton Reservoir
Eccleshall
Chebsey
Yarlet
Enson
Gayton
Amerton Working Farm
Heathcote
Little Soudley
Lockleywood
Garmelow
Wootton
Whitgreave
Hopton Heath 1643
Salt
Stowe-by-Chartley
Adbaston
Little Bridgeford
Marston
Amerton
High Heath
Whitley Heath
Weston
Drointon
Hinstock
Knighton
High Offley
Ellenhall
Great Bridgeford
Hopton
Shirleywich
Child's Ercall
Ellerton
Shebdon
Woodseaves
Knightley
Lawnhead
Seighford
Ancient High House
STAFFORD
Hixon
Stanford Bridge
Sambrook
Norbury
Ranton
Shire Hall Gallery
Ingestre
Pasturefields
Howle
Weston Jones
Knightley Dale
Coton Clanford
Stafford Castle
Doxey
Tixall
Great Haywood
Tern
Pickstock
Norbury Junction
Ranton Green
Coley
Puleston
Oulton
Long Compton
Derrington
Shugborough Estate (NT)
Little Haywood
Colwich
Chetwynd Park
Sutton
Shut Heath
Rowley Park
Forebridge
Weeping Cross
Milford
Great Bolas
Edgmond Marsh
Forton
Aqualate Mere
Gnosall
Audmore
Tibberton
Meretown
Cotonwood
Haughton
Billington
Walton-on-the-Hill
Rickerscote
Cherrington
Edgmond
Coton
Gnosall Heath
Allimore Green
Brocton
Newport
Outwoods
Beffcote
Apeton
Alstone
Dunston
Radnall
Cannock Chase Country Park
Etchinghill
Adeney
Longford
Chetwynd Aston
Bromstead Heath
Wood Eaton
Eaton
Bradley
Dunston Heath
Kynnersley
Brockton
Church Aston
Pave Lane
Stockton
Moreton
Little Onn
Levedale
Cannock Chase
Slitting Mill
Preston upon the Weald Moors
Lilleshall
Lynn
Orslow
High
Mitton
A50
A537
A530
A533
A54
A34
A536
A523
A532
A5020
A534
A500
A50
A527
A53
A5271
A5272
A5009
A520
A522
A52
A51
A531
A529
A525
A519
A5182
A5035
A5005
A521
A5013
A513
A518
A41
A449
A460
A5077
B5082
B5081
B5392
B5078
B5077
B5500
B5071
B5074
B5076
B5415
B5026
B5405
B5062
B5027
B5066
B5029
B5051
B5053
B5044
B5367
B5041
B5417
M6
Trent & Mersey Canal
Roman Road
Shropshire Union Canal
River Trent
Macclesfield Canal
Dane
Wheelock
Weaver
Trent Valley
Potteries
Sow
Blithe
Morridge
Axe Edge
Cheshire
Valley
12
10
9
8
7
6
5
4
3
2
1
11
13
14
15
16
17
18
497
515
599

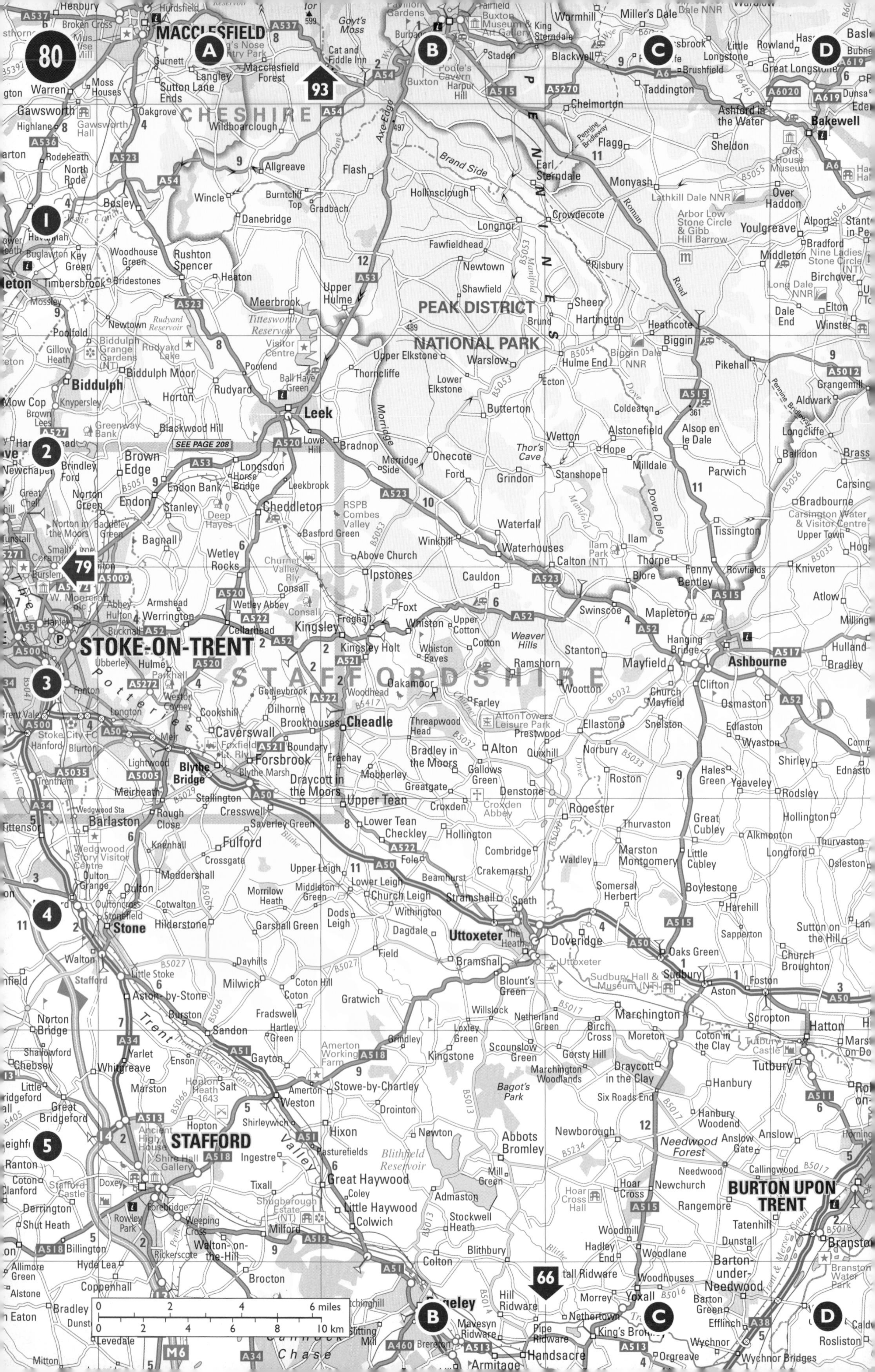

80
A
B
C
D
93
79
66
SEE PAGE 208
MACCLESFIELD
Henbury
Broken Cross
Hurdsfield
Langley
Macclesfield Forest
Cat and Fiddle Inn
Goyt's Moss
Pavilion Gardens
Buxton Museum & King Art Gallery
Buxton
Burbage
Staden
Poole's Cavern
Harpur Hill
Wormhill
Miller's Dale
Blackwell
Sterndale
Taddington
Little Longstone
Rowland
Great Longstone
Brushfield
Ashford in the Water
Bakewell
Old House Museum
Sheldon
Gawsworth
Gawsworth Hall
Warren
Moss Houses
Sutton Lane Ends
Gurnett
Oakgrove
CHESHIRE
Wildboarclough
Highlane
Rodeheath
North Rode
Allgreave
Flash
Brand Side
Axe Edge
Chelmorton
Flagg
Earl Sterndale
Monyash
Lathkill Dale NNR
Over Haddon
Wincle
Burntcliff Top
Gradbach
Hollinsclough
Bosley
Danebridge
Longnor
Crowdecote
Arbor Low Stone Circle & Gibb Hill Barrow
Youlgreave
Alport
Bradford
Middleton
Nine Ladies Stone Circle (NT)
Fawfieldhead
Newtown
Pilsbury
Birchover
Havannah
Buglawton
Key Green
Woodhouse Green
Rushton Spencer
Heaton
Timbersbrook
Bridestones
Congleton
Shawfield
Upper Hulme
PEAK DISTRICT NATIONAL PARK
Sheen
Hartington
Brund
Long Dale NNR
Elton
Dale End
Winster
Mossley
Meerbrook
Tittesworth Reservoir
Visitor Centre
Rudyard Reservoir
Newtown
Poolfold
Biddulph Grange Gardens (NT)
Rudyard Lake
Gillow Heath
Heathcote
Biggin
Biggin Dale NNR
Hulme End
Warslow
Upper Elkstone
Thorncliffe
Pikehall
Grangemill
Biddulph
Biddulph Moor
Poolend
Ball Haye Green
Lower Elkstone
Ecton
Mow Cop
Knypersley
Horton
Rudyard
Leek
Butterton
Coldeaton
Aldwark
Brown Lees
Greenway Bank
Blackwood Hill
Lowe Hill
Bradnop
Morridge
Alstonefield
Alsop en le Dale
Longcliffe
Harriseahead
Newchapel
Brindley Ford
Brown Edge
Longsdon
Horse Bridge
Endon Bank
Endon
Morridge Side
Onecote
Wetton
Thor's Cave
Hope
Milldale
Parwich
Ballidon
Brassington
Great Chell
Norton Green
Stanley
Leekbrook
Cheddleton
Ford
Grindon
Stanshope
Carsington
Bradbourne
Carsington Water & Visitor Centre
Norton in the Moors
Baddeley Green
Deep Hayes
RSPB Coombes Valley
Basford Green
Dove Dale
Tunstall
Smallthorne
Bagnall
Waterfall
Winkhill
Ilam
Tissington
Upper Town
Hognaston
Burslem
Wetley Rocks
Churnet Valley Rly
Above Church
Waterhouses
Ilam Park
Calton (NT)
Thorpe
Fenny Bentley
Rowfields
Kniveton
Milton
W. Moorcroft plc
Abbey Hulton
Consall
Ipstones
Cauldon
Blore
Armshead
Wetley Abbey
Foxt
Swinscoe
Mapleton
Atlow
Hanley
Werrington
Bucknall
Cellarhead
Kingsley
Froghall
Whiston
Upper Cotton
Weaver Hills
Hanging Bridge
Ashbourne
Hulland
Bradley
STOKE-ON-TRENT
Kingsley Holt
Whiston Eaves
Cotton
Stanton
Mayfield
Ubberley
Hulme
Parkhall
Potteries
STAFFORDSHIRE
Ramshorn
Wootton
Church Mayfield
Clifton
Osmaston
Fenton
Godleybrook
Oakamoor
Woodhead
Farley
Alton Towers Leisure Park
Ellastone
Snelston
Edlaston
Wyaston
Trent Vale
Longton
Weston Coyney
Cookshill
Dilhorne
Brookhouses
Cheadle
Threapwood Head
Prestwood
Stoke City FC
Hanford
Blurton
Meir
Caverswall
Foxfield Lt. Rly
Boundary
Bradley in the Moors
Alton
Quixhill
Norbury
Roston
Shirley
Ednaston
Lightwood
Blythe Bridge
Forsbrook
Freehay
Gallows Green
Trentham
Blythe Marsh
Draycott in the Moors
Mobberley
Greatgate
Denstone
Hales Green
Yeaveley
Rodsley
Meirheath
Stallington
Upper Tean
Croxden
Croxden Abbey
Rocester
Wedgwood Sta
Rough Close
Cresswell
Saverley Green
Lower Tean
Checkley
Hollington
Thurvaston
Great Cubley
Alkmonton
Tittensor
Barlaston
Wedgwood Story Visitor Centre
Fulford
Crossgate
Cambridge
Crakemarsh
Marston Montgomery
Little Cubley
Longford
Osleston
Knenhall
Moddershall
Fole
Upper Leigh
Lower Leigh
Beamhurst
Waldley
Somersal Herbert
Boylestone
Oulton Grange
Oulton
Morrilow Heath
Middleton Green
Church Leigh
Stramshall
Spath
Harehill
Oultoncross
Stonefield
Stone
Cotwalton
Hilderstone
Garshall Green
Dods Leigh
Withington
Dagdale
Uttoxeter
The Heath
Doveridge
Sapperton
Sutton on the Hill
Oaks Green
Church Broughton
Walton
Dayhills
Field
Bramshall
Uttoxeter
Sudbury
Sudbury Hall & Museum (NT)
Aston
Foston
Little Stoke
Stafford
Milwich
Coton Hill
Coton
Blount's Green
Aston-by-Stone
Gratwich
Willslock
Netherland Green
Marchington
Scropton
Hatton
Norton Bridge
Burston
Fradswell
Loxley Green
Moreton
Coton in the Clay
Tutbury
Tutbury Castle
Shallowford
Sandon
Hartley Green
Grindley
Kingstone
Scounslow Green
Gorsty Hill
Birch Cross
Chebsey
Yarlet
Whitgreave
Trent
Enson
Gayton
Amerton Working Farm
Marchington Woodlands
Draycott in the Clay
Bagot's Park
Hanbury
Little Bridgeford
Great Bridgeford
Marston
Hopton Heath 1643
Salt
Amerton
Stowe-by-Chartley
Weston
Six Roads End
Hanbury Woodend
Drointon
Hopton
Shirleywich
Hixon
Newton
Abbots Bromley
Newborough
Anslow
Needwood Forest
Anslow Gate
Ranton
STAFFORD
Ancient High House
Shire Hall Gallery
Ingestre
Pasturefields
Blithfield Reservoir
Mill Green
Hoar Cross
Newchurch
Callingwood
Needwood
Coton Clanford
Stafford Castle
Doxey
Tixall
Great Haywood
Coley
Little Haywood
Shugborough Estate (NT)
Admaston
Hoar Cross Hall
BURTON UPON TRENT
Derrington
Forebridge
Rowley Park
Weeping Cross
Colwich
Stockwell Heath
Rangemore
Tatenhill
Shut Heath
Billington
Milford
Walton-on-the-Hill
Rickerscote
Blithbury
Woodmill
Hadley End
Woodlane
Dunstall
Branston
Branston Water Park
Hyde Lea
Brocton
Colton
Barton-under-Needwood
Allimore Green
Coppenhall
Alstone
Hill Ridware
Yoxall
Woodhouses
Morrey
Barton Green
Bradley
Dunston
Rugeley
Nethertown
Efflinch
Levedale
Slitting Mill
Mavesyn Ridware
Pipe Ridware
King's Bromley
Wychnor
Rosliston
Cannock Chase
Brereton
Handsacre
Orgreave
Wychnor Bridges
Mitton
Armitage
Trent & Mersey Canal
Roman Road
Pennine Bridleway
0 2 4 6 miles
0 2 4 6 8 10 km

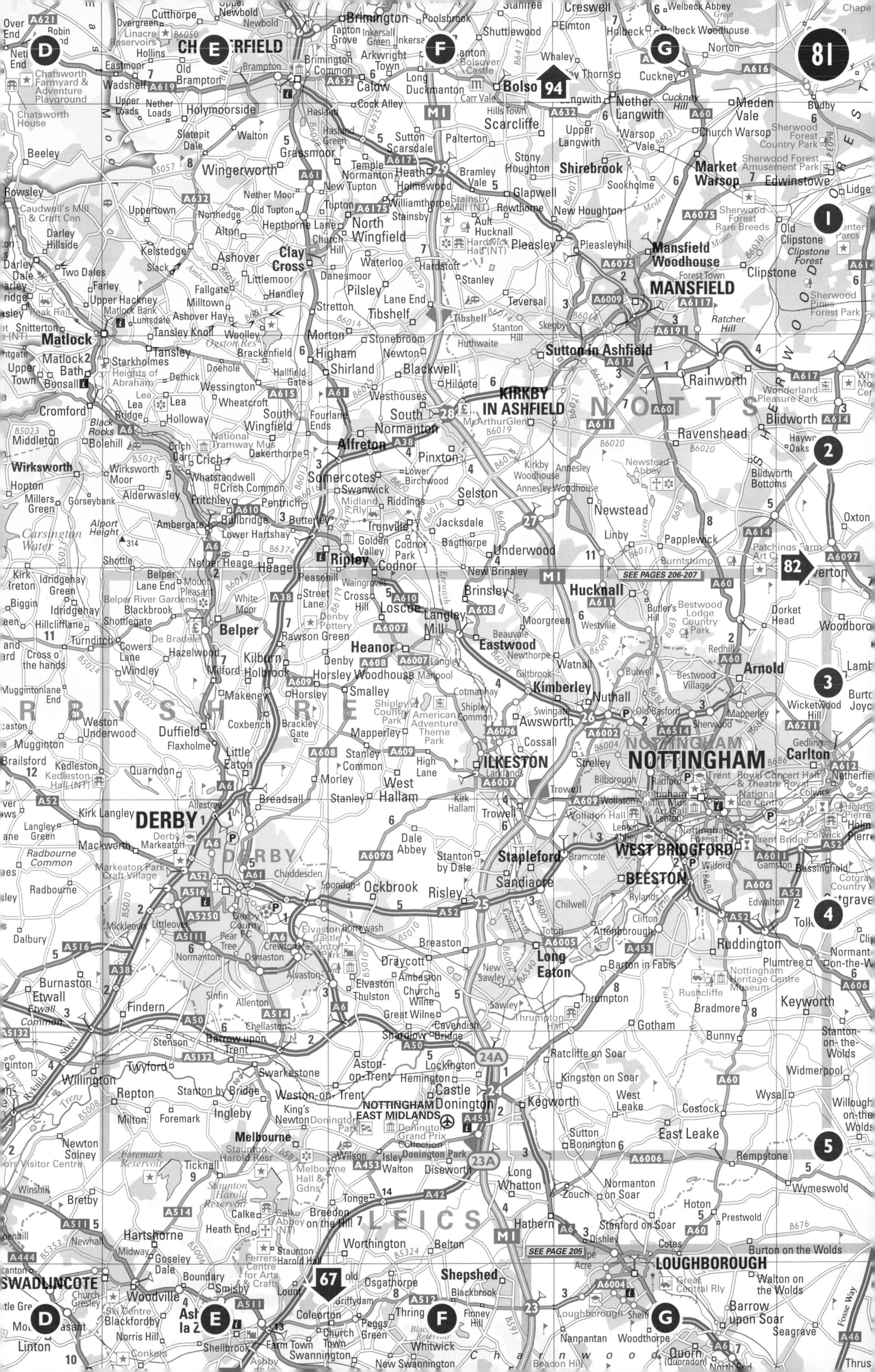

81
CHESTERFIELD
Brimington
Poolsbrook
Staveley
Creswell
Welbeck Abbey
Elmton
Holbeck
Welbeck Woodhouse
Norton
Cutthorpe
Newbold
Overgreen
Linacre Reservoirs
Old Brampton
Brampton
Wadshelf
Eastmoor
Chatsworth Farmyard & Adventure Playground
Chatsworth House
Holymoorside
Walton
Calow
Long Duckmanton
Arkwright Town
Bolsover Castle
Bolsover
94
Whaley Thorns
Cuckney
Nether Langwith
Upper Langwith
Scarcliffe
Palterton
Sutton Scarsdale
Hasland
Grassmoor
Temple Normanton
Heath
Holmewood
Bramley Vale
Glapwell
Stony Houghton
Shirebrook
Sookholme
Market Warsop
Meden Vale
Church Warsop
Warsop Vale
Budby
Sherwood Forest Country Park
Sherwood Forest Amusement Park
Edwinstowe
Wingerworth
Beeley
Rowsley
Caudwell's Mill & Craft Cen
Darley Hillside
Darley Dale
Two Dales
Uppertown
Northedge
Alton
Kelstedge
Ashover
Clay Cross
North Wingfield
Tupton
Williamthorpe
Stainsby
Stainsby Mill (NT)
Ault Hucknall
Hardwick Hall (NT)
Rowthorne
Pleasley
Pleasleyhill
New Houghton
Mansfield Woodhouse
MANSFIELD
Clipstone
Sherwood Forest Rare Breeds
Clipstone Forest
Old Clipstone
Sherwood Pines Forest Park
Farley
Upper Hackney
Matlock Bank
Matlock
Matlock Bath
Snitterton
Tansley
Starkholmes
Heights of Abraham
Lumsdale
Ashover Hay
Milltown
Fallgate
Littlemoor
Handley
Danesmoor
Pilsley
Waterloo
Hardstoft
Stanley
Teversal
Tibshelf
Lane End
Stretton
Morton
Higham
Shirland
Stonebroom
Newton
Blackwell
Hilcote
Huthwaite
Stanton Hill
Skegby
Sutton in Ashfield
Forest Town
Ratcher Hill
Rainworth
Blidworth
Ravenshead
KIRKBY IN ASHFIELD
McArthurGlen
NOTTS
Wonderland Pleasure Park
Tansley Knoll
Woolley
Ogston Res
Brackenfield
Dethick
Lea
Holloway
Wessington
Wheatcroft
South Wingfield
Westhouses
South Normanton
Fourlane Ends
Alfreton
Pinxton
Kirkby Woodhouse
Annesley
Annesley Woodhouse
Newstead Abbey
Newstead
Blidworth Bottoms
Haywood Oaks
Upper Town
Bonsall
Cromford
Lea Bridge
Black Rocks
Bolehill
Middleton
Wirksworth
Hopton
Millers Green
Gorseybank
Wirksworth Moor
Crich
National Tramway Mus
Whatstandwell
Crich Common
Alderwasley
Fritchley
Bullbridge
Ambergate
Lower Hartshay
Butterley
Pentrich
Somercotes
Swanwick
Lower Birchwood
Riddings
Midland Rly
Ironville
Jacksdale
Selston
Underwood
Bagthorpe
Codnor Park
Golden Valley
Ripley
Codnor
Linby
Papplewick
Burntstump
Patchings Farm Art Centre
Oxton
82
Calverton
Carsington Water
Alport Height
Shottle
Nether Heage
Heage
Kirk Ireton
Idridgehay
Biggin
Hillcliffelane
Belper
Belper Lane End
Belper River Gardens
Mount Pleasant
Blackbrook
Shottlegate
White Moor
Cowers Lane
Turnditch
Windley
Hazelwood
Milford
Kilburn
Holbrook
Street Lane
Denby Pottery
Rawson Green
Denby
Heanor
Loscoe
Langley Mill
Eastwood
Brinsley
New Brinsley
Moorgreen
Beauvale
Newthorpe
Hucknall
Westville
Butler's Hill
Bestwood Lodge Country Park
Dorket Head
Woodborough
Redhill
Arnold
Watnall
Kimberley
Nuthall
Bulwell
Bestwood Village
Giltbrook
Cross o' the hands
Muggintonlane End
Weston Underwood
Mugginton
DERBYSHIRE
Duffield
Flaxholme
Makeney
Coxbench
Horsley
Horsley Woodhouse
Smalley
Shipley Country Park
American Adventure Theme Park
Marlpool
Cotmanhay
Shipley Common
Swingate
Awsworth
Cossall
ILKESTON
Larklands
Strelley
Bilborough
Old Basford
Sherwood
Mapperley
Wicketwood Hill
Gedling
Carlton
NOTTINGHAM
Radford
Royal Concert Hall & Theatre Royal
National Ice Centre
Netherfield
Colwick
Brailsford
Kedleston
Kedleston Hall (NT)
Quarndon
Little Eaton
Brackley Gate
Mapperley
Stanley Common
Morley
Stanley
West Hallam
High Lane
Kirk Hallam
Trowell
Wollaton
Wollaton Hall
Nottingham Castle Mus & Art Gall
Lenton
Lenton Abbey
Nottingham Forest FC
Trent Bridge
Kirk Langley
Langley Green
DERBY
Allestree
Breadsall
Derby Markeaton
Mackworth
Radbourne Common
Radbourne
Markeaton Park Craft Village
Chaddesden
Spondon
Ockbrook
Dale Abbey
Stanton by Dale
Risley
Stapleford
Sandiacre
Bramcote
WEST BRIDGFORD
Wilford
BEESTON
Chilwell
Gamston
Bassingfield
Edwalton
Tollerton
Cotgrave
Mickleover
Littleover
Derby County FC
Pear Tree
Normanton
Osmaston
Crewton
Alvaston
Elvaston Castle Country Park
Borrowash
Breaston
Draycott
Long Eaton
Toton
Attenborough
Clifton
Rylands
Ruddington
Plumtree
Normanton-on-the-Wolds
Dalbury
Burnaston
Etwall
Etwall Common
Findern
Sinfin
Allenton
Chellaston
Ambaston
Elvaston
Thulston
Church Wilne
Great Wilne
New Sawley
Sawley
Thrumpton
Thrumpton Hall
Barton in Fabis
Nottingham Heritage Centre Museum
Rushcliffe
Bradmore
Keyworth
Gotham
Bunny
Stenson
Barrow upon Trent
Shardlow
Cavendish Bridge
Twyford
Swarkestone
Aston-on-Trent
Lockington
Hemington
Castle Donington
Ratcliffe on Soar
Kingston on Soar
West Leake
Stanton-on-the-Wolds
Widmerpool
Willington
Repton
Stanton by Bridge
Ingleby
Weston-on-Trent
King's Newton
Donington Park
NOTTINGHAM EAST MIDLANDS
Donington Grand Prix Collection
Kegworth
Costock
Wysall
Willoughby-on-the-Wolds
Milton
Foremark
Newton Solney
Melbourne
Staunton Harold Resr
Foremark Reservoir
Wilson
Isley Walton
Diseworth
Sutton Bonington
East Leake
Rempstone
Bretby
Ticknall
Staunton Harold Reservoir
Melbourne Hall & Gdns
Tonge
Long Whatton
Zouch
Normanton on Soar
Hoton
Wymeswold
Prestwold
Winshill
Newhall
Hartshorne
Calke
Calke Abbey (NT)
Heath End
Breedon on the Hill
Worthington
Belton
LEICS
Hathern
Stanford on Soar
Dishley
Cotes
Burton on the Wolds
Midway
Goseley Dale
Boundary
Smisby
Staunton Harold Hall
Ferrers Centre for Arts & Crafts
Osgathorpe
Shepshed
Blackbrook
Acre
LOUGHBOROUGH
Great Central Rly
Walton on the Wolds
SWADLINCOTE
Church Gresley
Woodville
Ski Centre
Blackfordby
Norris Hill
Conkers
Ashby de la Zouch
Shellbrook
Lount
Griffydam
Coleorton
67
Thringstone
Peggs Green
Finney Hill
Blackbrook Reservoir
Whitwick
New Swannington
Swannington
Farm Town
Church Town
Charnwood
Loughborough
Nanpantan
Woodthorpe
Quorn (Quorndon)
Barrow upon Soar
Seagrave
Fosse Way
Linton
SEE PAGES 206-207
SEE PAGE 205
M1
A38
A6
A52
A60
A61
A50
A42
A453
A610
A608
A617
A632
A619
A616
A614

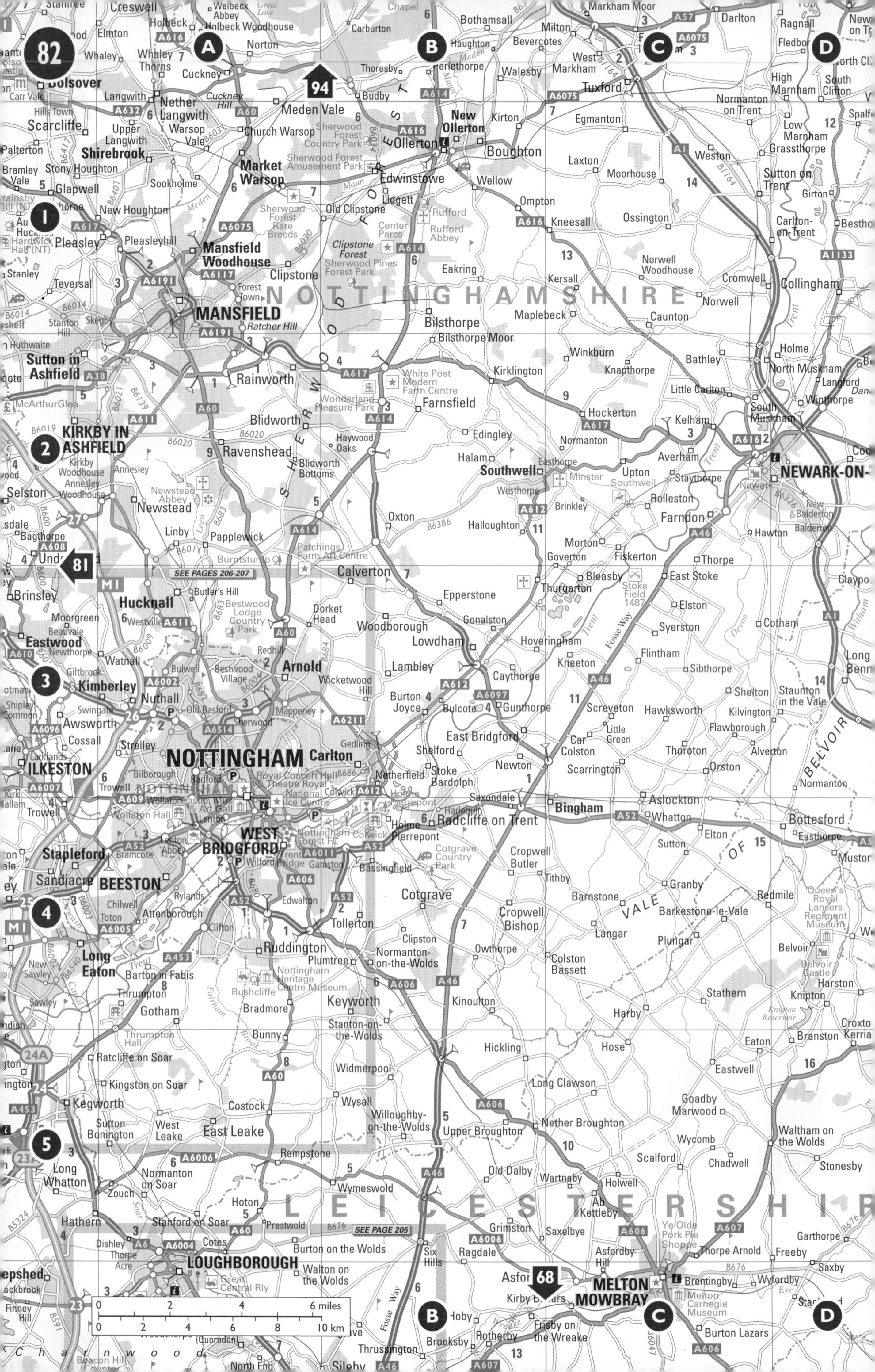
82
94
81
68
A
B
C
D
1
2
3
4
5
SEE PAGES 206-207
SEE PAGE 205
NOTTINGHAMSHIRE
LEICESTERSHIRE
SHERWOOD FOREST
VALE OF BELVOIR
Charnwood
Creswell
Welbeck Abbey
Holbeck
Holbeck Woodhouse
Elmton
Whaley
Whaley Thorns
Norton
Carburton
Bothamsall
Markham Moor
Milton
Darlton
Ragnall
Bolsover
Cuckney
Haughton
Bevercotes
West Markham
Fledborough
High Marnham
South Clifton
Thoresby
Perlethorpe
Walesby
Tuxford
Normanton on Trent
Langwith
Nether Langwith
Cuckney Hill
Meden Vale
Budby
Carr Vale
Hills Town
Scarcliffe
Upper Langwith
Warsop
Warsop Vale
Church Warsop
Sherwood Forest Country Park
New Ollerton
Ollerton
Kirton
Boughton
Egmanton
Low Marnham
Grassthorpe
Palterton
Shirebrook
Bramley Vale
Stony Houghton
Market Warsop
Sherwood Forest Amusement Park
Edwinstowe
Wellow
Laxton
Moorhouse
Weston
Sutton on Trent
Glapwell
Sookholme
Old Clipstone
Lidgett
Ompton
Ossington
Girton
New Houghton
Sherwood Forest Rare Breeds
Rufford
Rufford Abbey
Center Parcs
Kneesall
Carlton-on-Trent
Pleasley
Pleasleyhill
Mansfield Woodhouse
Clipstone Forest
Sherwood Pines Forest Park
Eakring
Norwell Woodhouse
Stanley
Teversal
Clipstone
Forest Town
Kersall
Cromwell
Collingham
Norwell
MANSFIELD
Ratcher Hill
Maplebeck
Caunton
Stanton Hill
Skegby
Bilsthorpe
Bilsthorpe Moor
Huthwaite
Sutton in Ashfield
Winkburn
Holme
Rainworth
White Post Modern Farm Centre
Kirklington
Knapthorpe
Bathley
North Muskham
Langford
McArthurGlen
Wonderland Pleasure Park
Farnsfield
Little Carlton
South Muskham
Winthorpe
Hockerton
Kelham
KIRKBY IN ASHFIELD
Bildworth
Edingley
Normanton
Kirkby Woodhouse
Annesley
Annesley Woodhouse
Ravenshead
Haywood Oaks
Bildworth Bottoms
Halam
Southwell
Easthorpe
Minster
Upton
Averham
Staythorpe
NEWARK-ON-TRENT
Newark
Selston
Newstead Abbey
Newstead
Westhorpe
Brinkley
Rolleston
Farndon
New Balderton
Balderton
Bagthorpe
Underwood
Linby
Papplewick
Oxton
Halloughton
Morton
Hawton
Fiskerton
Thorpe
Brinsley
Burntstump
Patchings Farm Art Centre
Calverton
Goverton
Bleasby
East Stoke
Butler's Hill
Hucknall
Bestwood Lodge Country Park
Epperstone
Thurgarton
Stoke Field 1487
Elston
Moorgreen
Beauvale
Westville
Dorket Head
Woodborough
Gonalston
Syerston
Cotham
Eastwood
Newthorpe
Lowdham
Hoveringham
Fosse Way
Watnall
Redhill
Flintham
Giltbrook
Kimberley
Bulwell
Bestwood Village
Arnold
Lambley
Kneeton
Sibthorpe
Long Bennington
Wicketwood Hill
Caythorpe
Nuthall
Burton Joyce
Shelton
Staunton in the Vale
Shipley Common
Swingate
Awsworth
Old Basford
Sherwood
Mapperley
Bulcote
Gunthorpe
Screveton
Hawksworth
Kilvington
Cossall
Strelley
Gedling
East Bridgford
Little Green
Flawborough
Larklands
ILKESTON
NOTTINGHAM
Carlton
Shelford
Car Colston
Thoroton
Alverton
Bilborough
Radford
Royal Concert Hall & Theatre Royal
Netherfield
Stoke Bardolph
Newton
Scarrington
Orston
Trowell
Colwick
National Ice Centre
Holme Pierrepont
Saxondale
Normanton
Wollaton
Castle Mus & Art Gall
Wollaton Hall
Lenton
Harlequin
Bingham
Aslockton
Whatton
Bottesford
Radcliffe on Trent
WEST BRIDGFORD
Nottingham Forest FC
Lenton Abbey
Holme Pierrepont
Elton
Easthorpe
Stapleford
Bramcote
Trent Bridge
Wilford
Gamston
Cotgrave Country Park
Cropwell Butler
Sutton
Muston
Sandiacre
BEESTON
Bassingfield
Tithby
Granby
Redmile
Chilwell
Rylands
Edwalton
Cotgrave
Barnstone
Barkestone-le-Vale
Queen's Royal Lancers Regiment Museum
Toton
Attenborough
Clifton
Tollerton
Cropwell Bishop
Langar
Plungar
Long Eaton
Clipston
Normanton-on-the-Wolds
Owthorpe
Colston Bassett
Belvoir
Belvoir Castle
New Sawley
Ruddington
Plumtree
Barton in Fabis
Nottingham Heritage Centre Museum
Harston
Thrumpton
Rushcliffe
Keyworth
Stathern
Knipton
Sawley
Gotham
Bradmore
Stanton-on-the-Wolds
Kinoulton
Knipton Reservoir
Harby
Croxton Kerrial
Thrumpton Hall
Bunny
Branston
Eaton
Hickling
Hose
Ratcliffe on Soar
Widmerpool
Eastwell
Kingston on Soar
Long Clawson
Kegworth
Costock
Wysall
Goadby Marwood
Willoughby-on-the-Wolds
Sutton Bonington
West Leake
East Leake
Upper Broughton
Nether Broughton
Waltham on the Wolds
Wycomb
Scalford
Chadwell
Rempstone
Stonesby
Long Whatton
Normanton on Soar
Old Dalby
Wartnaby
Holwell
Zouch
Wymeswold
Hoton
Ab Kettleby
Hathern
Stanford on Soar
Prestwold
Grimston
Saxelbye
Ye Olde Pork Pie Shoppe
Garthorpe
Dishley
Thorpe Acre
Cotes
Burton on the Wolds
Six Hills
Ragdale
Asfordby Hill
Thorpe Arnold
Freeby
LOUGHBOROUGH
Walton on the Wolds
Great Central Rly
Asfordby
MELTON MOWBRAY
Brentingby
Wyfordby
Saxby
Shepshed
Kirby Bellars
Melton Carnegie Museum
Stapleford
Finney Hill
Hoby
Frisby on the Wreake
Brooksby
Rotherby
Burton Lazars
Thrussington
Quorndon
Beacon Hill
North End
Sileby
0 2 4 6 miles
0 2 4 6 8 10 km

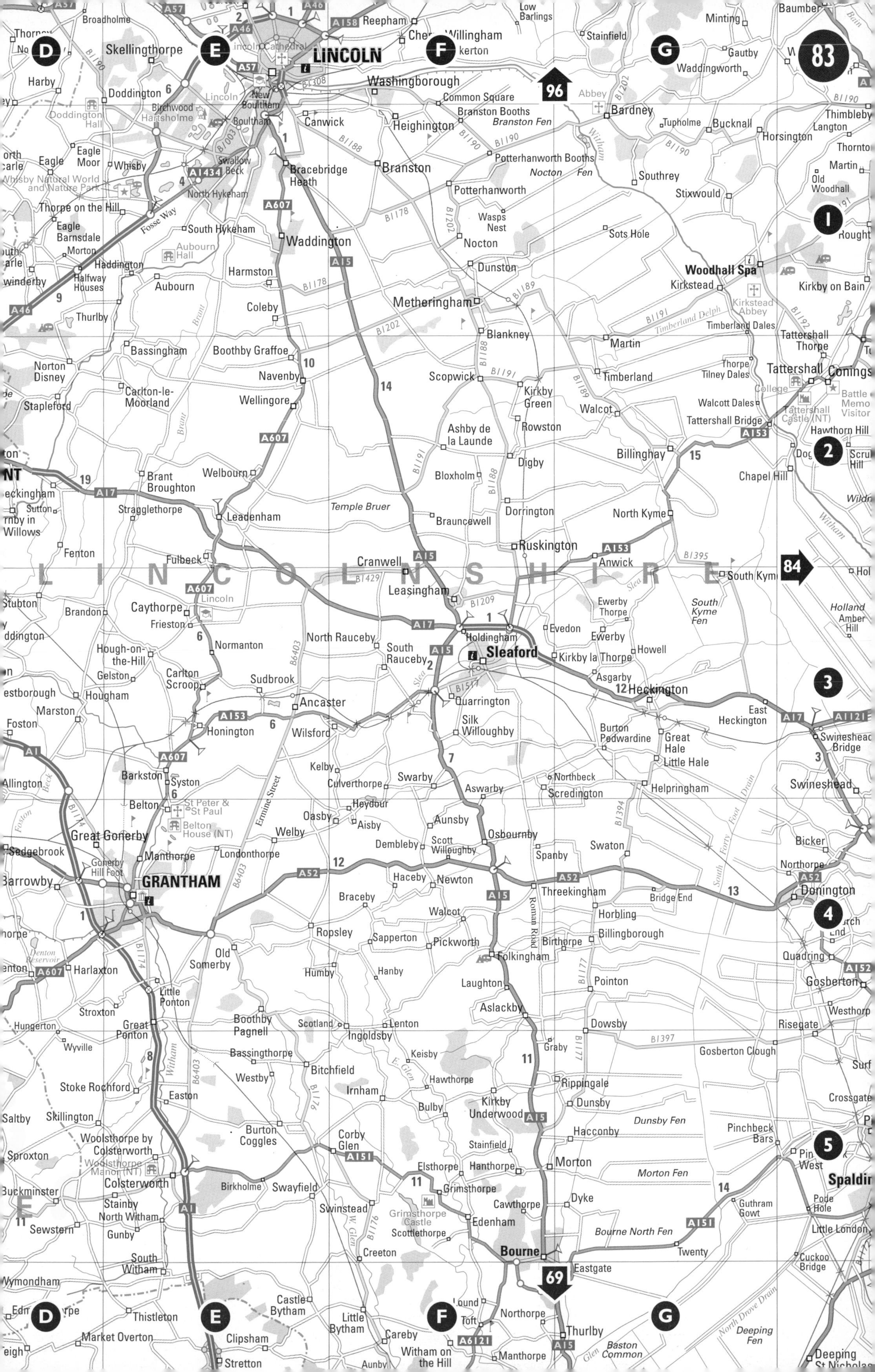

83
LINCOLN
Skellingthorpe
Washingborough
Heighington
Branston
Bracebridge Heath
Waddington
Metheringham
Woodhall Spa
Kirkstead
Martin
Timberland
Tattershall
Coningsby
Billinghay
North Kyme
Ruskington
Cranwell
Leasingham
Sleaford
Heckington
LINCOLNSHIRE
Ancaster
Caythorpe
Leadenham
Navenby
Wellingore
Welbourn
Brant Broughton
Bassingham
Great Gonerby
GRANTHAM
Barrowby
Harlaxton
Colsterworth
Corby Glen
Bourne
Folkingham
Billingborough
Donington
Swineshead
Morton
Thurlby
Castle Bytham
Little Bytham
Clipsham
Stretton
96
84
69

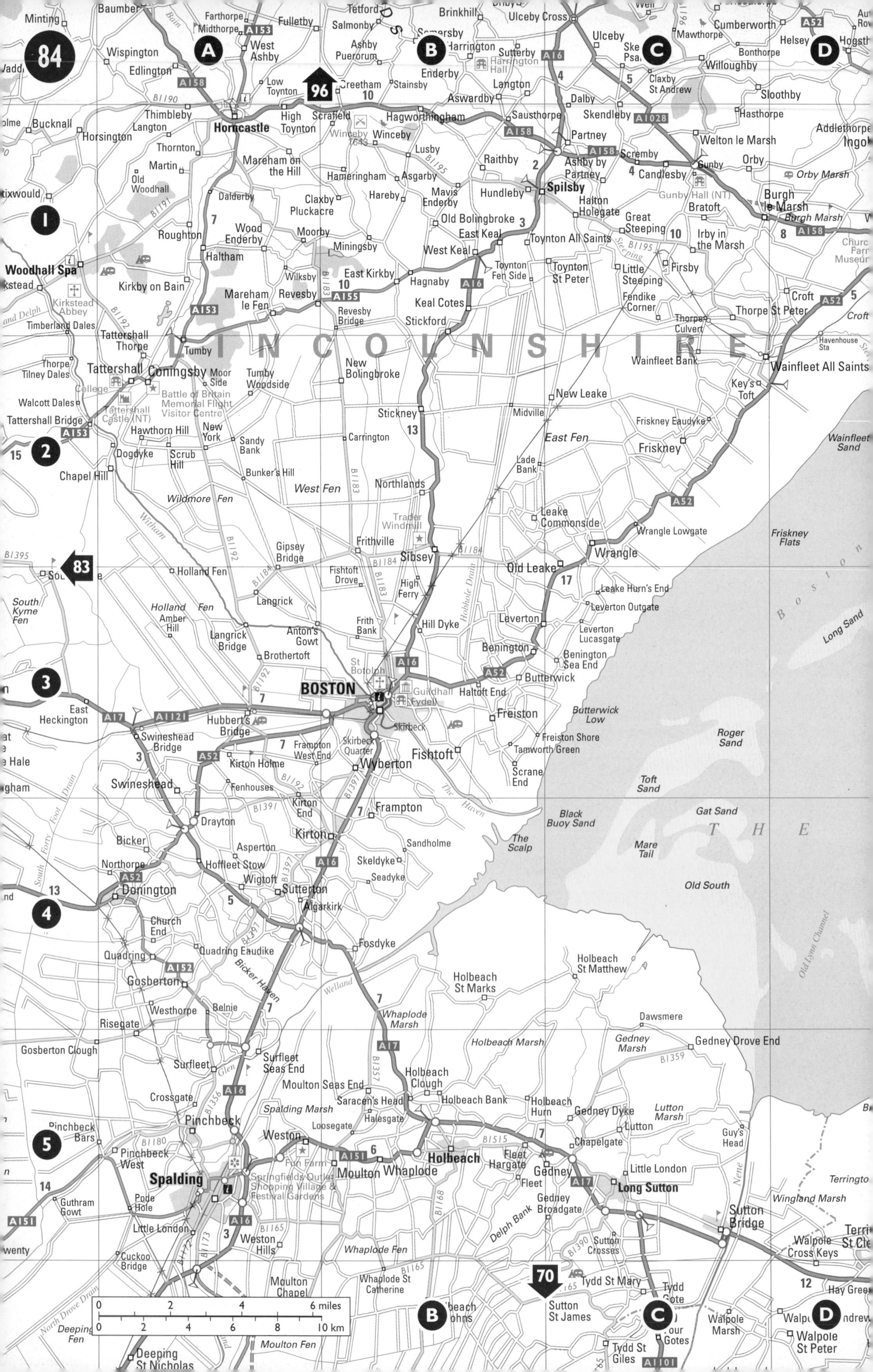
A
B
C
D
1
2
3
4
5
96
83
70
LINCOLNSHIRE
Minting
Baumber
Farthorpe
Midthorpe
A153
Fulletby
Tetford
Salmonby
Brinkhill
Ulceby Cross
Ulceby
Cumberworth
Mawthorpe
A52
Helsey
Hogsthorpe
Wispington
West Ashby
Ashby Puerorum
Somersby
Harrington
Sutterby
Harrington Hall
A16
Skendleby Psalter
Bonthorpe
Willoughby
Edlington
A158
Low Toynton
Creetham
Stainsby
Enderby
Langton
Claxby St Andrew
Sloothby
Thimbleby
Langton
Horncastle
High Toynton
Scrafield
Hagworthingham
Aswardby
Sausthorpe
Dalby
Skendleby
Hasthorpe
Bucknall
Horsington
Thornton
Mareham on the Hill
Winceby
Lusby
Raithby
Partney
Ashby by Partney
Scremby
Candlesby
Gunby
Welton le Marsh
Orby
Addlethorpe
Ingoldmells
Martin
Old Woodhall
Hameringham
Asgarby
Mavis Enderby
Hundleby
Spilsby
Gunby Hall (NT)
Orby Marsh
Burgh le Marsh
Burgh Marsh
Stixwould
Dalderby
Claxby Pluckacre
Hareby
Old Bolingbroke
Halton Holegate
Bratoft
Great Steeping
Irby in the Marsh
Roughton
Wood Enderby
Moorby
East Keal
West Keal
Toynton All Saints
Miningsby
Haltham
Woodhall Spa
Kirkstead
Kirkby on Bain
Wilksby
East Kirkby
Hagnaby
Toynton Fen Side
Toynton St Peter
Little Steeping
Firsby
Kirkstead Abbey
Mareham le Fen
Revesby
A155
Keal Cotes
Fendike Corner
Croft
Timberland Dales
Revesby Bridge
Stickford
Thorpe St Peter
Tattershall Thorpe
Tumby
Thorpe Culvert
Havenhouse Sta
Thorpe Tilney Dales
Tattershall
Coningsby
Moor Side
Tumby Woodside
New Bolingbroke
Wainfleet Bank
Wainfleet All Saints
College
Battle of Britain Memorial Flight Visitor Centre
Key's Toft
Walcott Dales
Tattershall Castle (NT)
New Leake
Stickney
Midville
Tattershall Bridge
Hawthorn Hill
New York
Sandy Bank
Carrington
East Fen
Friskney Eaudyke
Wainfleet Sand
Dogdyke
Scrub Hill
Friskney
Chapel Hill
Bunker's Hill
Lade Bank
Wildmore Fen
West Fen
Northlands
Witham
Trader Windmill
Leake Commonside
Friskney Flats
Frithville
Wrangle Lowgate
Gipsey Bridge
Sibsey
Wrangle
B1395
Holland Fen
Fishtoft Drove
Old Leake
High Ferry
Leake Hurn's End
South Kyme Fen
Langrick
Leverton Outgate
Holland Fen
Amber Hill
Frith Bank
Hill Dyke
Leverton
Leverton Lucasgate
Long Sand
Langrick Bridge
Anton's Gowt
Benington
Brothertoft
Benington Sea End
St Botolph
A16
A52
Butterwick
BOSTON
Guildhall
Fydell
Haltoft End
East Heckington
A17
A1121
Hubbert's Bridge
Freiston
Butterwick Low
Swineshead Bridge
Skirbeck
Roger Sand
Frampton West End
Skirbeck Quarter
Freiston Shore
Kirton Holme
Wyberton
Fishtoft
Tamworth Green
Swineshead
Fenhouses
Scrane End
Toft Sand
Kirton End
Frampton
The Haven
Drayton
Black Buoy Sand
Gat Sand
Bicker
Asperton
Kirton
Sandholme
The Scalp
Mare Tail
Northorpe
Hoffleet Stow
Skeldyke
Wigtoft
Seadyke
Donington
Sutterton
Old South
Algarkirk
Church End
Quadring
Quadring Eaudike
Fosdyke
Holbeach St Matthew
A152
Gosberton
Bicker Haven
Welland
Holbeach St Marks
Westhorpe
Belnie
Whaplode Marsh
Dawsmere
Risegate
Holbeach Marsh
Gedney Marsh
Gedney Drove End
Gosberton Clough
Surfleet
Surfleet Seas End
Holbeach Clough
Moulton Seas End
Crossgate
Saracen's Head
Holbeach Bank
Holbeach Hurn
Spalding Marsh
Halesgate
Gedney Dyke
Lutton Marsh
Pinchbeck
Pinchbeck Bars
Loosegate
Lutton
Guy's Head
Weston
Chapelgate
Pinchbeck West
Fun Farm
A151
Fleet Hargate
Moulton
Whaplode
Holbeach
Gedney
Little London
Spalding
Springfields Outlet Shopping Village & Festival Gardens
Fleet
Long Sutton
Terrington
Guthram Gowt
Pode Hole
Gedney Broadgate
Wingland Marsh
Sutton Bridge
Little London
Delph Bank
Sutton Crosses
Walpole Cross Keys
Weston Hills
Cuckoo Bridge
Whaplode Fen
Tydd St Mary
Hay Green
Moulton Chapel
Whaplode St Catherine
Tydd Gote
Sutton St James
Four Gotes
Walpole Marsh
Walpole St Peter
Deeping Fen
Moulton Fen
Tydd St Giles
Deeping St Nicholas
A1101
Nene
Old Lynn Channel
0 2 4 6 miles
0 2 4 6 8 10 km

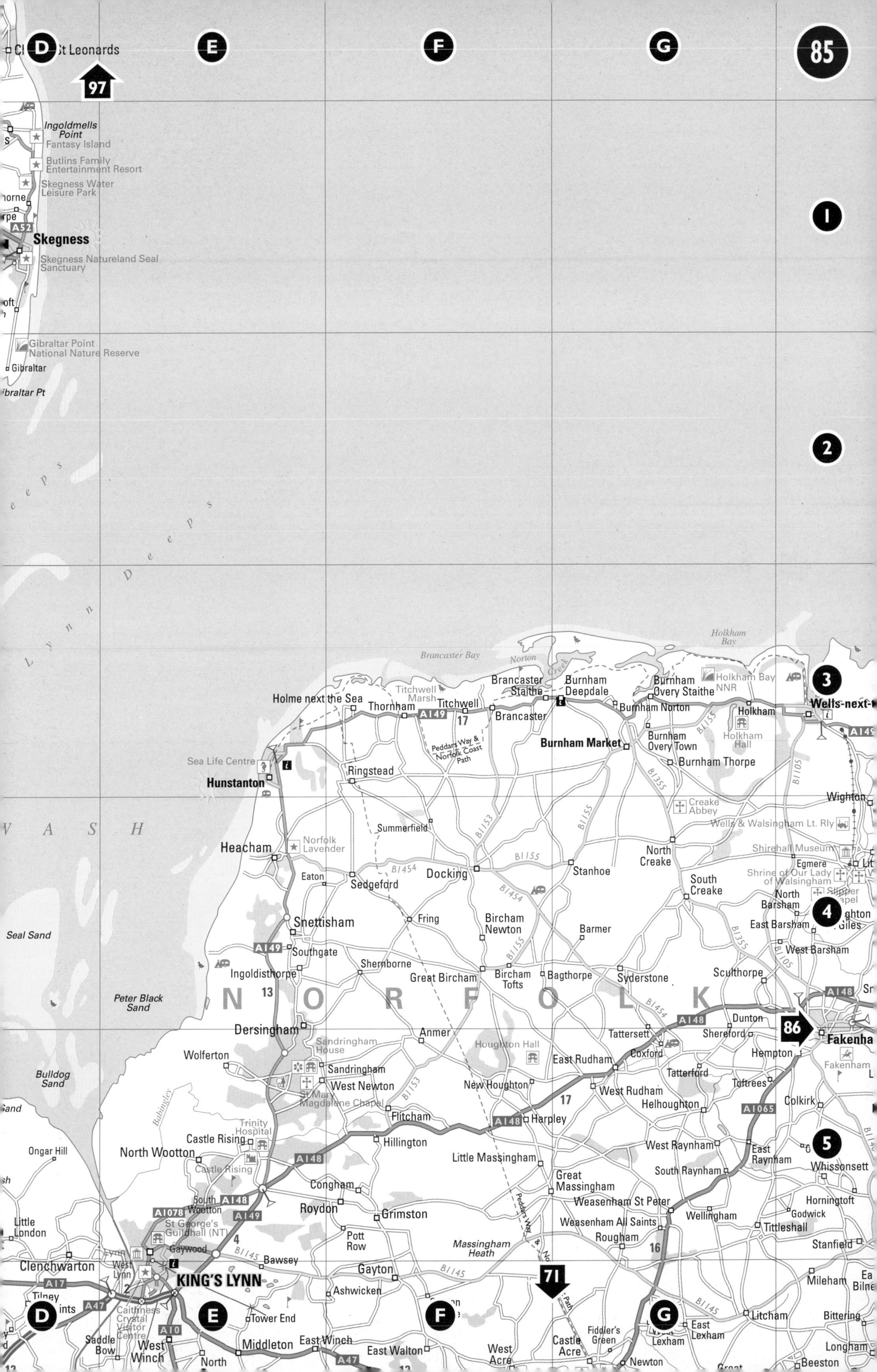
St Leonards
97
Ingoldmells Point
Fantasy Island
Butlins Family Entertainment Resort
Skegness Water Leisure Park
Skegness
Skegness Natureland Seal Sanctuary
Gibraltar Point National Nature Reserve
Gibraltar
Lynn Deeps
WASH
Seal Sand
Peter Black Sand
Bulldog Sand
Ongar Hill
Little London
Clenchwarton
Tilney
West Lynn
KING'S LYNN
Gaywood
St George's Guildhall (NT)
South Wootton
North Wootton
Castle Rising
Trinity Hospital
Wolferton
Dersingham
Sandringham House
Sandringham
West Newton
St Mary Magdalene Chapel
Ingoldisthorpe
Southgate
Snettisham
Heacham
Norfolk Lavender
Hunstanton
Sea Life Centre
Holme next the Sea
Thornham
Titchwell Marsh
Titchwell
Brancaster Bay
Brancaster
Brancaster Staithe
Norton Creek
Burnham Deepdale
Burnham Overy Staithe
Burnham Norton
Burnham Market
Burnham Overy Town
Burnham Thorpe
Holkham Bay
Holkham Bay NNR
Holkham
Holkham Hall
Wells-next-
Wighton
Wells & Walsingham Lt. Rly
Shirehall Museum
Egmere
Shrine of Our Lady of Walsingham
Slipper Chapel
North Barsham
East Barsham
West Barsham
Creake Abbey
North Creake
South Creake
Ringstead
Peddars Way & Norfolk Coast Path
Summerfield
Eaton
Sedgeford
Docking
Stanhoe
Fring
Bircham Newton
Barmer
Shernborne
Great Bircham
Bircham Tofts
Bagthorpe
Syderstone
Sculthorpe
NORFOLK
Anmer
Houghton Hall
Tattersett
Coxford
East Rudham
Dunton
Shereford
86
Fakenham
Hempton
Fakenham
Tatterford
Toftrees
West Rudham
New Houghton
Helhoughton
Colkirk
Harpley
Flitcham
Hillington
Little Massingham
West Raynham
East Raynham
South Raynham
Whissonsett
Great Massingham
Weasenham St Peter
Weasenham All Saints
Wellingham
Horningtoft
Godwick
Tittleshall
Rougham
Stanfield
Massingham Heath
Congham
Roydon
Grimston
Pott Row
Bawsey
Gayton
Ashwicken
Tower End
Middleton
East Winch
East Walton
West Acre
Castle Acre
Fiddler's Green
Newton
West Lexham
East Lexham
Litcham
Mileham
Bittering
Longham
Beeston
Caithness Crystal Visitor Centre
Saddle Bow
West Winch
North
71
A149
A148
A1065
A1078
A17
A47
A10
A52
B1155
B1153
B1454
B1355
B1105
B1145
17
16
13
4
2

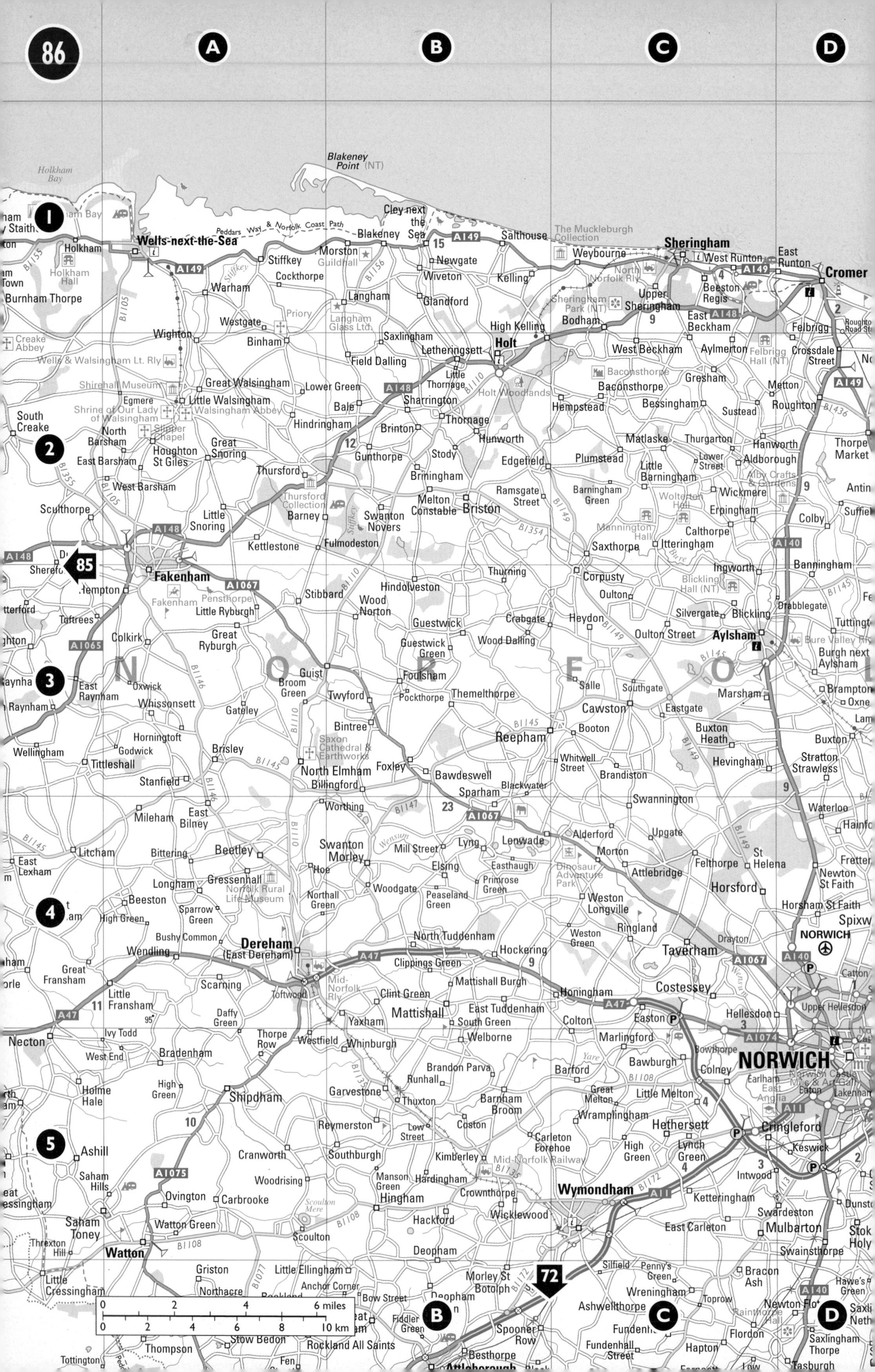
86
A
B
C
D
Blakeney Point (NT)
Holkham Bay
Peddars Way & Norfolk Coast Path
Wells-next-the-Sea
Holkham
Holkham Hall
Burnham Thorpe
Creake Abbey
Wells & Walsingham Lt. Rly
Stiffkey
Warham
Wighton
Westgate
Priory
Binham
Morston
Guildhall
Cockthorpe
Blakeney
Cley next the Sea
Newgate
Wiveton
Glandford
Langham
Langham Glass Ltd.
Saxlingham
Field Dalling
Letheringsett
Salthouse
Kelling
The Muckleburgh Collection
Weybourne
High Kelling
Holt
Little Thornage
Holt Woodlands
Thornage
Sharrington
Brinton
Hunworth
Sheringham
West Runton
East Runton
Cromer
North Norfolk Rly
Upper Sheringham
Sheringham Park (NT)
Bodham
Beeston Regis
East Beckham
West Beckham
Aylmerton
Felbrigg
Felbrigg Hall (NT)
Crossdale Street
Roughton
Metton
Baconsthorpe
Gresham
Hempstead
Bessingham
Sustead
Shirehall Museum
Egmere
Great Walsingham
Little Walsingham
Walsingham Abbey
Shrine of Our Lady of Walsingham
Slipper Chapel
South Creake
North Barsham
East Barsham
Houghton St Giles
Great Snoring
Thursford
Thursford Collection
West Barsham
Sculthorpe
Little Snoring
Lower Green
Bale
Hindringham
Gunthorpe
Stody
Briningham
Melton Constable
Briston
Barney
Swanton Novers
Fulmodeston
Kettlestone
Edgefield
Ramsgate Street
Plumstead
Barningham Green
Matlaske
Little Barningham
Thurgarton
Lower Street
Hanworth
Aldborough
Alby Crafts & Gardens
Wickmere
Wolterton Hall
Erpingham
Mannington Hall
Calthorpe
Thorpe Market
Antingham
Suffield
Colby
Saxthorpe
Itteringham
Corpusty
Thurning
Ingworth
Banningham
Blickling Hall (NT)
Oulton
Silvergate
Blickling
Drabblegate
Heydon
Oulton Street
Aylsham
Bure Valley Rly
Tuttington
Burgh next Aylsham
Fakenham
Pensthorpe
Hempton
Little Ryburgh
Great Ryburgh
Toftrees
Colkirk
Stibbard
Wood Norton
Hindolveston
Guestwick
Guestwick Green
Crabgate
Wood Dalling
Foulsham
East Raynham
Oxwick
Whissonsett
Guist
Broom Green
Twyford
Pockthorpe
Themelthorpe
Salle
Southgate
Marsham
Brampton
Oxnead
Gateley
Bintree
Cawston
Eastgate
Booton
Reepham
Buxton Heath
Buxton
Horningtoft
Godwick
Wellingham
Tittleshall
Brisley
Saxon Cathedral & Earthworks
North Elmham
Foxley
Bawdeswell
Whitwell Street
Brandiston
Hevingham
Stratton Strawless
Stanfield
Billingford
Sparham
Blackwater
Swannington
Mileham
East Bilney
Worthing
Waterloo
Hainford
Litcham
East Lexham
Bittering
Beetley
Swanton Morley
Mill Street
Lyng
Lenwade
Alderford
Upgate
Hoe
Elsing
Easthaugh
Morton
Felthorpe
St Helena
Frettenham
Gressenhall
Norfolk Rural Life Museum
Longham
Primrose Green
Dinosaur Adventure Park
Attlebridge
Newton St Faith
Beeston
Sparrow Green
High Green
Northall Green
Woodgate
Peaseland Green
Weston Longville
Horsford
Horsham St Faith
Spixworth
Bushy Common
Dereham (East Dereham)
North Tuddenham
Ringland
Weston Green
Drayton
NORWICH
Wendling
Great Fransham
Little Fransham
Hockering
Taverham
Catton
Scarning
Toftwood
Mid-Norfolk Rly
Clippings Green
Mattishall Burgh
Honingham
Costessey
Old Catton
Upper Hellesdon
Hellesdon
Daffy Green
Clint Green
Mattishall
East Tuddenham
South Green
Colton
Easton
Necton
Ivy Todd
Yaxham
Welborne
Marlingford
West End
Bradenham
Thorpe Row
Westfield
Whinburgh
Bowthorpe
Brandon Parva
Barford
Bawburgh
Colney
Earlham
University of East Anglia
Norwich Castle Museum & Art Gallery
Eaton
Lakenham
Holme Hale
High Green
Shipdham
Garvestone
Runhall
Thuxton
Barnham Broom
Great Melton
Little Melton
Wramplingham
Hethersett
Cringleford
Reymerston
Low Street
Coston
Carleton Forehoe
Ashill
Cranworth
Southburgh
Kimberley
Mid-Norfolk Railway
High Green
Lynch Green
Keswick
Saham Hills
Woodrising
Manson Green
Hardingham
Intwood
Ovington
Carbrooke
Scoulton Mere
Hingham
Crownthorpe
Wymondham
Ketteringham
Saham Toney
Watton Green
Hackford
Wicklewood
Swardeston
Mulbarton
Threxton Hill
Watton
Scoulton
East Carleton
Swainsthorpe
Deopham
Little Cressingham
Griston
Little Ellingham
Morley St Botolph
Silfield
Penny's Green
Bracon Ash
Hawe's Green
Northacre
Anchor Corner
Wreningham
Toprow
Bow Street
Deopham Green
Ashwellthorpe
Newton Flotman
Fiddler Green
Fundenhall
Rainthorpe Hall
Flordon
Saxlingham Nethergate
Saxlingham Thorpe
Stow Bedon
Spooner Row
Fundenhall Street
Hapton
Thompson
Rockland All Saints
Besthorpe
Tottington
Attleborough
Tasburgh
N
O
R
F
O
L
85
72
0 2 4 6 miles
0 2 4 6 8 10 km

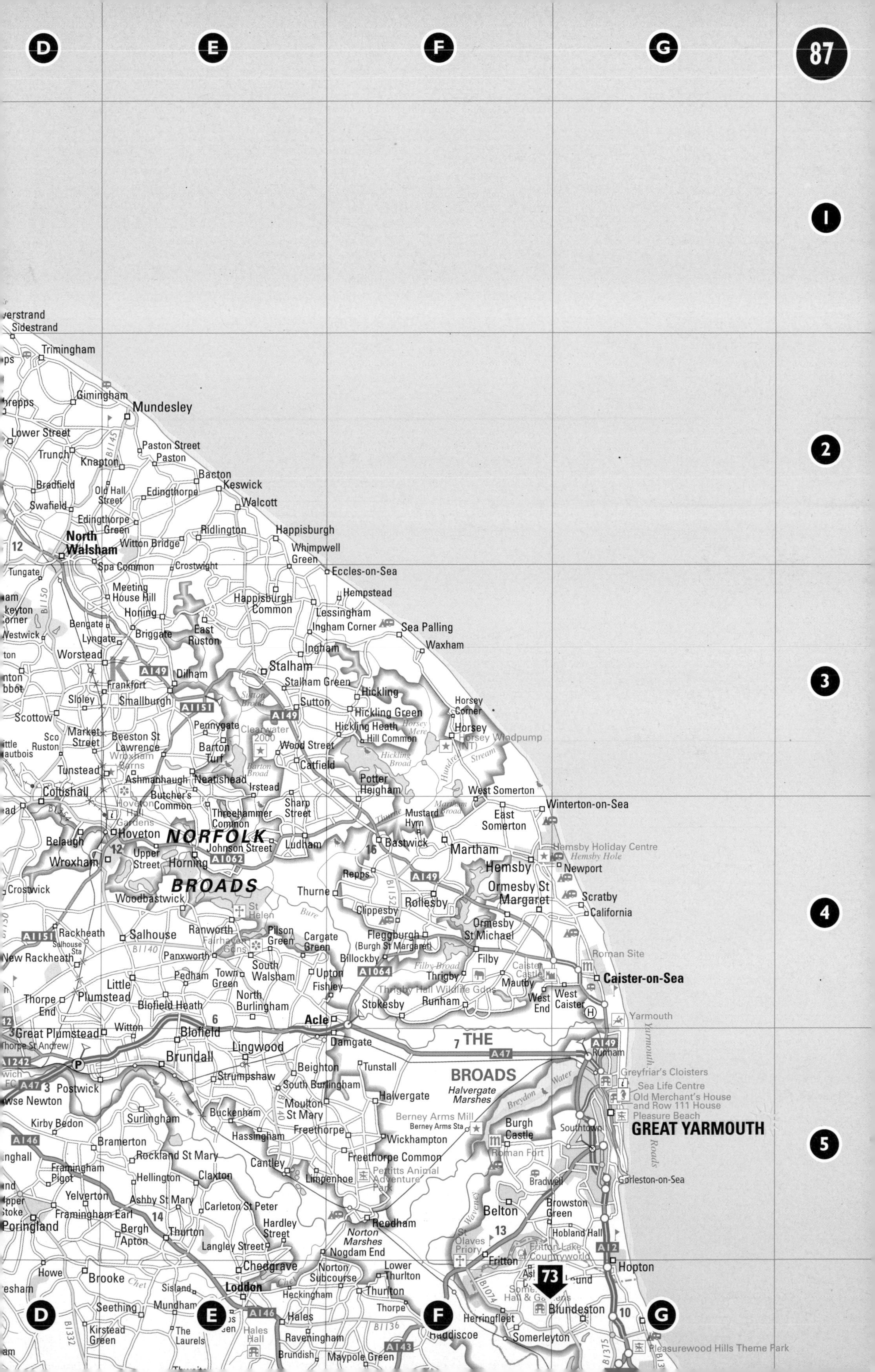
D
E
F
G
1
2
3
4
5
Sidestrand
Trimingham
Gimingham
Mundesley
Lower Street
Trunch
Knapton
Paston Street
Paston
Bacton
Keswick
Bradfield
Old Hall Street
Edingthorpe
Walcott
Swafield
Edingthorpe Green
Ridlington
Happisburgh
North Walsham
Witton Bridge
Whimpwell Green
Tungate
Spa Common
Crostwight
Eccles-on-Sea
Meeting House Hill
Happisburgh Common
Hempstead
Honing
Lessingham
Bengate
East Ruston
Ingham Corner
Sea Palling
Westwick
Lyngate
Briggate
Waxham
Worstead
Ingham
Stalham
A149
Dilham
Frankfort
Stalham Green
Sloley
Smallburgh
A1151
Sutton
Hickling
Horsey Corner
Scottow
Sutton Broad
A149
Hickling Green
Pennygate
Clearwater 2000
Hickling Heath
Horsey Mere
Horsey
Market Street
Beeston St Lawrence
Hill Common
Horsey Windpump
Ruston
Barton Turf
Wood Street
(NT)
Wroxham Barns
Hickling Broad
Tunstead
Catfield
Barton Broad
Hundred Stream
Ashmanhaugh
Neatishead
Potter Heigham
Coltishall
Irstead
West Somerton
Butcher's Common
Winterton-on-Sea
Hoveton Hall Gardens
Sharp Street
Threehammer Common
Mustard Hyrn
Martham Broad
East Somerton
Thurne
Hoveton
NORFOLK
Ludham
Bastwick
Hemsby Holiday Centre
Belaugh
Johnson Street
Martham
Hemsby Hole
12
Upper Street
A1062
16
Hemsby
Newport
Wroxham
Horning
Repps
A149
Crostwick
BROADS
Ormesby St Margaret
Thurne
B1152
Rollesby
Scratby
Woodbastwick
California
St Helen
Clippesby
Ormesby St Michael
Bure
A1151
Rackheath
Salhouse
Ranworth
Pilson Green
Cargate Green
Fleggburgh
Salhouse Sta
Fairhaven Gdns
(Burgh St Margaret)
B1140
Billockby
Roman Site
New Rackheath
Panxworth
Filby
Filby Broad
Caister Castle
South Walsham
Upton
A1064
Thrigby
Caister-on-Sea
Little Plumstead
Pedham
Town Green
Fishley
Thrigby Hall Wildlife Gdns
Mautby
Thorpe End
North Burlingham
West Caister
Blofield Heath
Stokesby
Runham
West End
6
Yarmouth
Acle
Great Plumstead
Witton
Blofield
Thorpe St Andrew
Damgate
7
THE
A149
Runham
A1242
Lingwood
A47
P
Brundall
Tunstall
BROADS
Greyfriar's Cloisters
Beighton
Strumpshaw
A47
3
Postwick
South Burlingham
Halvergate Marshes
Sea Life Centre
Breydon Water
Old Merchant's House and Row 111 House
Halvergate
Moulton St Mary
Yare
Buckenham
Pleasure Beach
Surlingham
Berney Arms Mill
Burgh Castle
Southtown
GREAT YARMOUTH
Kirby Bedon
Freethorpe
Berney Arms Sta
Hassingham
Yarmouth Roads
A146
Bramerton
Wickhampton
Rockland St Mary
Roman Fort
Freethorpe Common
Cantley
Framingham Pigot
Pettitts Animal Adventure Park
Bradwell
Hellington
Claxton
Limpenhoe
Gorleston-on-Sea
Yelverton
Waveney
Ashby St Mary
Browston Green
Carleton St Peter
Belton
Framingham Earl
14
Hardley Street
Reedham
Poringland
Bergh Apton
Thurton
Norton Marshes
13
Hobland Hall
St Olaves Priory
Langley Street
Fritton Lake Countryworld
A12
Nogdam End
Howe
Chedgrave
Norton Subcourse
Lower Thurlton
Fritton
Hopton
Brooke
Chet
73
Sisland
Loddon
Thurlton
Lound
Heckingham
Somerleyton Hall & Gardens
Seething
Mundham
B1074
Blundeston
A146
Thorpe
10
Hales
Herringfleet
B1332
Kirstead Green
The Laurels
Hales Hall
Raveningham
B1136
Haddiscoe
Somerleyton
B1375
Brundish
Maypole Green
A143
Pleasurewood Hills Theme Park

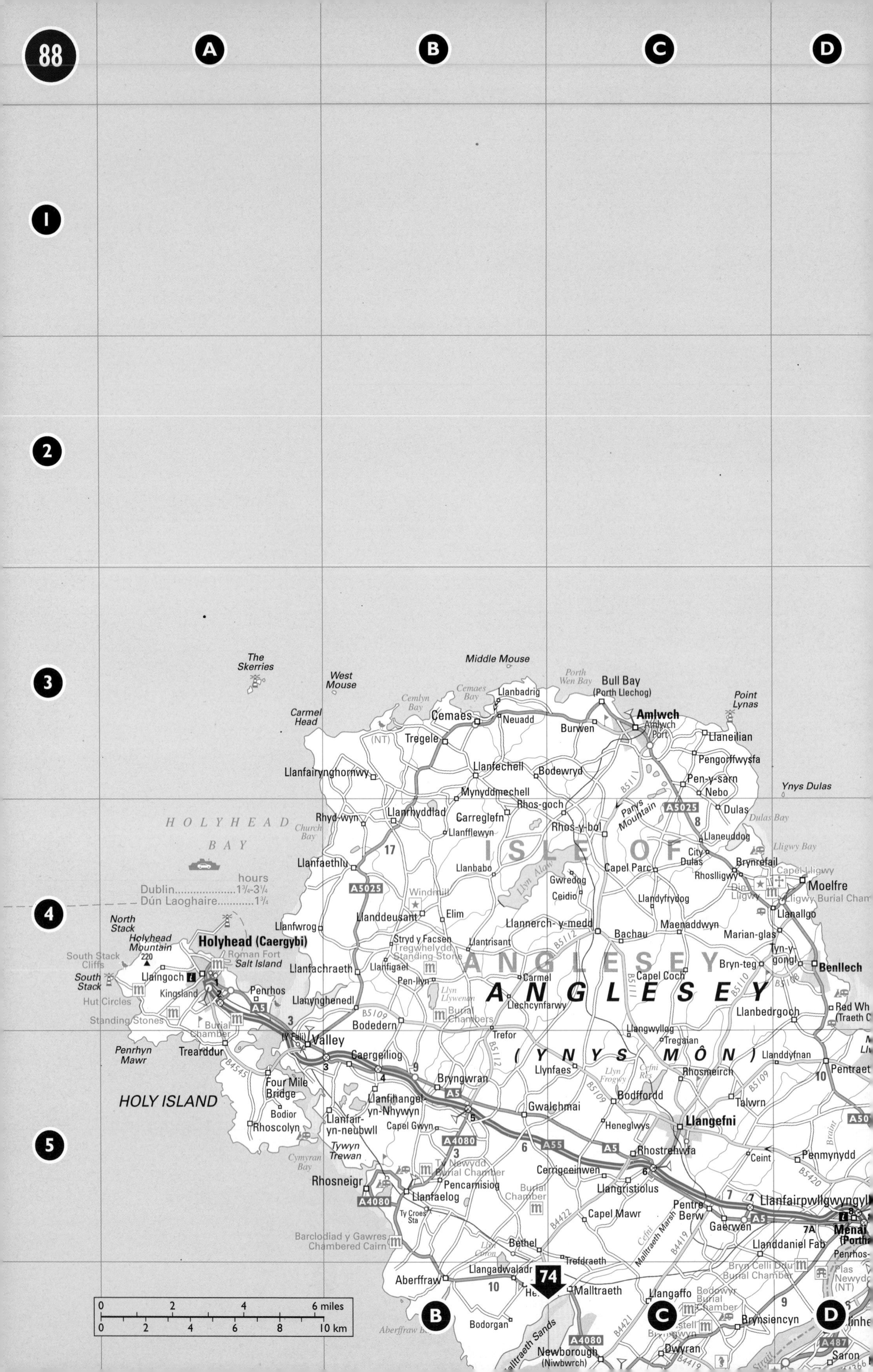
A
B
C
D
1
2
3
4
5
The Skerries
West Mouse
Middle Mouse
Carmel Head
Cemlyn Bay
Cemaes Bay
Porth Wen Bay
Bull Bay (Porth Llechog)
Point Lynas
Amlwch
Amlwch Port
Llanbadrig
Cemaes
Neuadd
Burwen
Llaneilian
Tregele
(NT)
Llanfairynghornwy
Llanfechell
Bodewryd
Pengorffwysfa
Pen-y-sarn
Nebo
Ynys Dulas
Mynyddmechell
Rhos-goch
Parys Mountain
Dulas
Dulas Bay
HOLYHEAD BAY
Church Bay
Rhyd-wyn
Llanrhyddlad
Carreglefn
Llanfflewyn
Rhos-y-bol
Llaneuddog
Lligwy Bay
ISLE OF ANGLESEY
ANGLESEY
(YNYS MÔN)
City Dulas
Brynrefail
Llanfaethlu
Llanbabo
Llyn Alaw
Capel Parc
Rhoslligwy
Capel Lligwy
hours
Dublin....................1¾-3¼
Dún Laoghaire............1¾
Windmill
Gwredog
Ceidio
Llandyfrydog
Din Lligwy
Moelfre
Lligwy Burial Cham
North Stack
Llanddeusant
Elim
Llannerch-y-medd
Maenaddwyn
Llanallgo
Holyhead Mountain
220
Holyhead (Caergybi)
Llanfwrog
Stryd y Facsen
Tregwhelydd Standing Stone
Llantrisant
Bachau
Marian-glas
South Stack Cliffs
Roman Fort
Salt Island
Tyn-y-gongl
Bryn-teg
Benllech
South Stack
Llaingoch
Llanfachraeth
Llanfigael
Carmel
Capel Coch
Kingsland
Penrhos
Pen-llyn
Llyn Llywenan
Red Wh
(Traeth C
Hut Circles
Llanynghenedl
Llechcynfarwy
Llanbedrgoch
Standing Stones
Burial Chamber
Bodedern
Burial Chambers
Trefor
Llangwyllog
Tregaian
Penrhyn Mawr
Trearddur
(Y Fali)
Valley
Caergeiliog
Llynfaes
Llyn Frogwy
Cefni Res
Rhosmeirch
Llanddyfnan
Pentraet
Four Mile Bridge
Bryngwran
Bodffordd
Talwrn
HOLY ISLAND
Llanfihangel-yn-Nhywyn
Gwalchmai
Bodior
Llanfair-yn-neubwll
Capel Gwyn
Heneglwys
Llangefni
Rhoscolyn
Tywyn Trewan
Rhostrehwfa
Ceint
Penmynydd
Cymyran Bay
Ty Newydd Burial Chamber
Cerrigceinwen
Rhosneigr
Pencarnisiog
Llangristiolus
Llanfairpwllgwyngyll
Llanfaelog
Burial Chamber
Pentre Berw
Ty Croes Sta
Capel Mawr
Malltraeth Marsh
Gaerwen
Menai
(Porthae
Barclodiad y Gawres Chambered Cairn
Bethel
Llanddaniel Fab
Penrhos-
Llyn Coron
Trefdraeth
Bryn Celli Ddu Burial Chamber
Plas Newydd (NT)
Aberffraw
Llangadwaladr
74
Malltraeth
Llangaffo
Bodowyr Burial Chamber
Brynsiencyn
Bodorgan
Malltraeth Sands
Newborough (Niwbwrch)
Dwyran
Saron
Aberffraw Bay
0 2 4 6 miles
0 2 4 6 8 10 km
A5
A55
A5025
A4080
A487
B5109
B5111
B5112
B5110
B4545
B4422
B4419
B4421
B5420
B5108

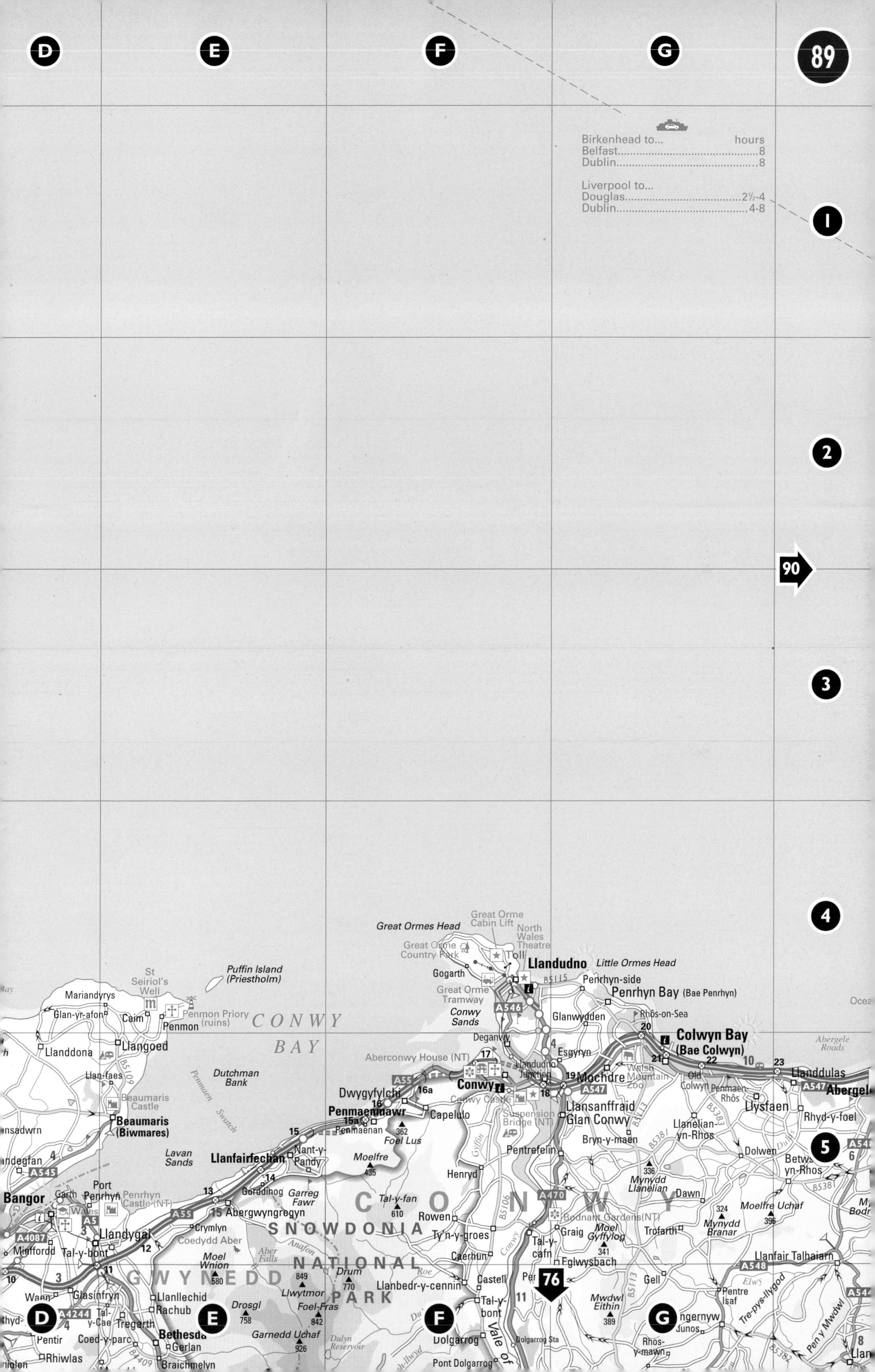

Birkenhead to...   hours
Belfast..8
Dublin..8

Liverpool to...
Douglas......................................2½-4
Dublin..4-8

I

2

90

3

4

Great Orme
Great Ormes Head   Cabin Lift
North
Wales
Theatre
Great Orme
Country Park   Toll
Gogarth   **Llandudno**
Great Orme   Little Ormes Head
Tramway   B5115
Conwy   Penrhyn-side
Sands   Penrhyn Bay (Bae Penrhyn)
A546   Glanwydden
Deganwy   Rhôs-on-Sea
Aberconwy House (NT)   17   Llandudno   20
Junction   **Colwyn Bay**
St Seiriol's   Esgyryn   (Bae Colwyn)
Well   Penmon Priory   C O N W Y   4   21   Abergele
Mariandyrys   (ruins)   A55   19 Mochdre   22   10   23   Roads
Glan-yr-afon   Caim   B A Y   A547   Welsh   Old   A547   Llanddulas
Penmon   Dwygyfylchi   16a   **Conwy**   18   Mountain   Colwyn   Abergel
Llanddona   Llangoed   Dutchman   **Penmaenmawr**   Conwy Castle   Llansanffraid   Zoo   Penmaen   Llysfaen
Llan-faes   Bank   15a   Suspension   Glan Conwy   Rhôs   Rhyd-y-foel
B5109   Penmaen   Capelulo   Bridge (NT)   Bryn-y-maen   Llanelian-
Beaumaris   Pennal   362   yn-Rhos   Dolwen
Castle   15   Foel Lus   Pentrefelin   B5383   Betws
Beaumaris   Lavan   Moelfre   Henryd   336   yn-Rhos
(Biwmares)   Sands   **Llanfairfechan**   435   C O N W Y   Mynydd   Dawn
A545   14   Tal-y-fan   Llanelian   Moelfre Uchaf
Nant-y-   610   Mynydd   324   396
ndegfan   Port   Pandy   Rowen   Graig   Moel   Trofarth   Branar
Bangor   Penrhyn   13   Gorddinog   Garreg   S N O W D O N I A   Gyffylog   Llanfair Talhaiarn
Penrhyn   Fawr   Ty'n-y-groes   Bodnant Gardens(NT)   341
Castle (NT)   A55   15   Abergwyngregyn   Caerhun   Eglwysbach   A548
Llandygai   Crymlyn   N A T I O N A L   Per   **76**   Gell   Elwy
Mynffordd   Coedydd Aber   Tal-y-   cafn   Pentre
A4087   Tal-y-bont   Moel   Aber   Anafon   11   Isaf
Wion   Falls   Llanbedr-y-cennin   Castell   Mwdwl   Tre-pys-llygod
Waun   580   P A R K   Roe   Tal-y-   Eithin
Glasinfryn   849   Drum   bont   389   Pen y Mwdwl
Llanllechid   770   B5113
Rachub   Drosgl   Llwytmor   ngernyw   Junos   Llan
G W Y N E D D   758   Foel-Fras
Tal-   942   D   E   F   G   Bodr
y-Cae Tregarth   Garnedd Uchaf   Dolgarrog   Rhos-
Pentir   Coed-y-parc   926   Dulyn   Dolgarrog Sta   y-mawn
Rhiwlas   **Bethesda**   Reservoir
Gerlan   Dolgarrog
Braichmelyn   B409   Pont Dolgarrog

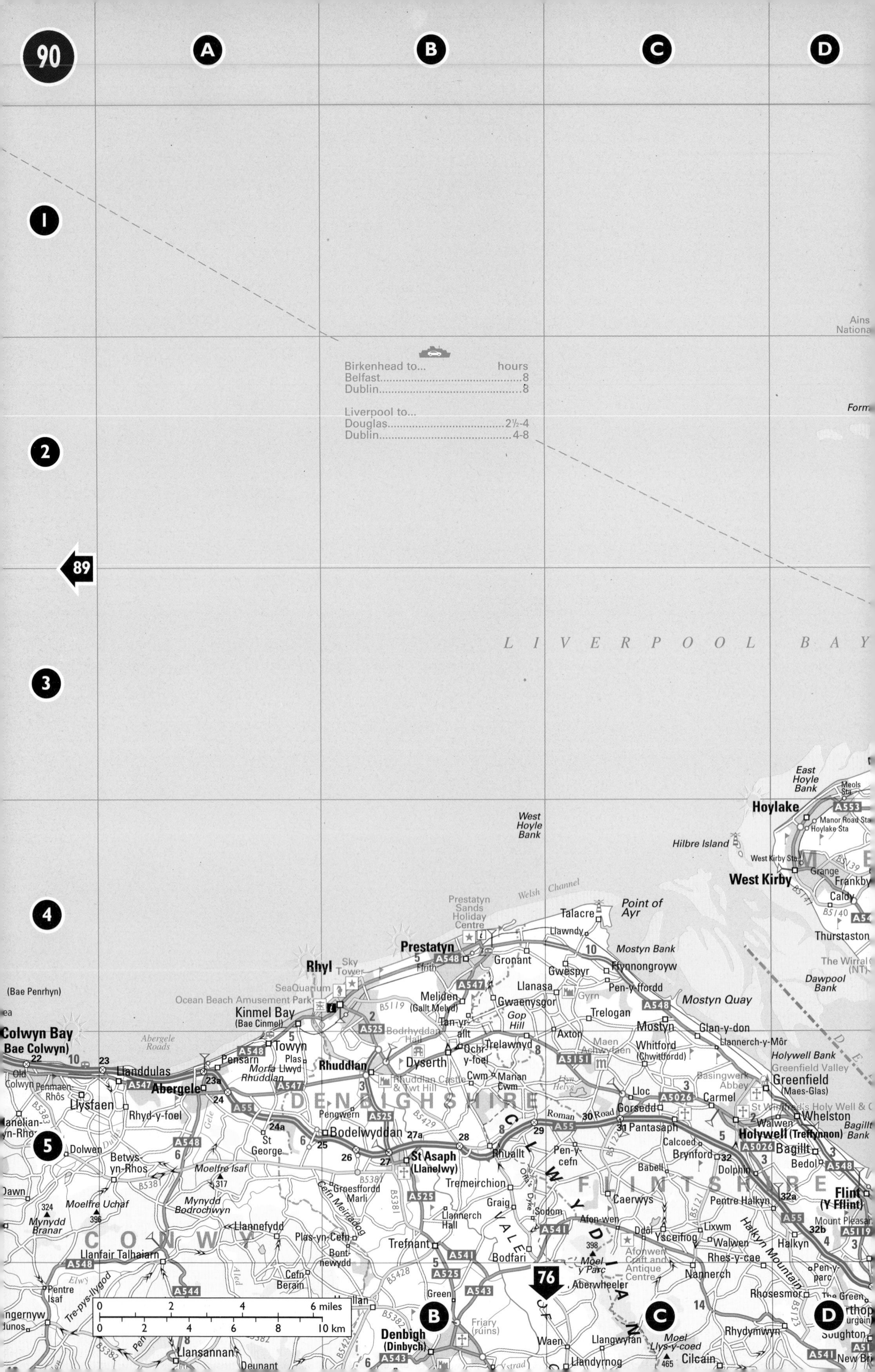

A   B   C   D

1

2

89

3

4

5

Birkenhead to...   **hours**
Belfast.........................8
Dublin.........................8

Liverpool to...
Douglas....................2½–4
Dublin......................4–8

L I V E R P O O L   B A Y

Ains
National

Form

West
Hoyle
Bank

East
Hoyle
Bank

Meols
Sta

Hoylake
Manor Road Sta
Hoylake Sta

A553

Hilbre Island

West Kirby Sta

Grange
Frankby

Caldy

B5140

A54

West Kirby

Thurstaston

The Wirral
(NT)

Dawpool
Bank

Welsh Channel

Point of
Ayr

Talacre

Llawndy

Mostyn Bank

Prestatyn
Sands
Holiday
Centre

Prestatyn

A548

Gronant

10

Ffynnongroyw

Mostyn Quay

Rhyl
Sky
Tower

Ffrith

A547

Gwespyr

Pen-y-ffordd

SeaQuarium

Meliden
(Gallt Melyd)

Llanasa

Gyrn

Trelogan

A548

Ocean Beach Amusement Park

Gwaenysgor

Kinmel Bay
(Bae Cinmel)

B5119

Tan-yr-
allt

Gop
Hill

Axton

Maen
Achwyfaen

Mostyn

Glan-y-don

Llannerch-y-Môr

(Bae Penrhyn)

A525

Bodrhyddan
Hall

Ochr-
y-foel

Trelawnyd

Whitford
(Chwitffordd)

Holywell Bank

Greenfield Valley

ea

Colwyn Bay
Bae Colwyn

Abergele
Roads

Towyn

Rhuddlan

Dyserth

Cwm

Marian
Cwm

Hwn
Helyg

Basingwerk
Abbey

Greenfield
(Maes-Glas)

22   10   23

A548

Pensarn

Morfa
Rhuddlan

Plas
Llwyd

Lloc

A5026

Carmel

St Winifred's Holy Well & C

Old
Colwyn

Penmaen-
Rhôs

Llanddulas

Rhuddlan Castle
& Twt Hill

D E N B I G H S H I R E

Roman

30

Road

Gorsedd

Walwen

Whelston

Bagillt

anelian-
yn-Rho

A547

Abergele

23a

B5429

29

A55

31

Pantasaph

Calcoed

5

Holywell (Treffynnon)

Bank

Bagillt

Llysfaen

24

A55

Pengwern

A525

Rhuallt

Pen-y-
cefn

Brynford

32

A5026

3

Bedol

Rhyd-y-foel

24a

Bodelwyddan

27a

28

Dolphin

Babell

F L I N T S H I R E

A548

Dolwen

Betws
yn-Rhos

6

St
George

25

26

27

St Asaph
(Llanelwy)

Tremeirchion

Graig

Ola's
Dyke

Sodom

Caerwys

B5121

Pentre Halkyn

32a

Flint
(Y Fflint)

Dawn

324
Mynydd
Branar

Moelfre Isaf
317

Greesffordd
Marli

B538

B525

Llannerch
Hall

Afon-wen

398

Lixwm

Walwen

Halkyn

A55

32b

A5119

396

Moelfre Uchaf

Mynydd
Bodrochwyn

Cefn Meiriadog

B5381

Llandyrnog

C L W Y D   V A L E

Afonwen
Craft and
Antique
Centre

Ysceifiog

Rhes-y-cae

Pen-y-
parc

C O L W Y

Llanfair Talhaiarn

Llannefydd

Plas-yn-Cefn

Bont-
newydd

Trefnant

A541

Bodfari

76

Moel
y Parc

Aberwheeler

Nannerch

Halkyn Mountain

Rhosesmor

The Green

urgain

rthop

Pentre
Isaf

A544

Cefn
Berain

A525

B5428

Green

A543

Rhydymwyn

A541

New Br

ngernyw

Elwy

Tre-pys-llygod

5

Llan

B5382

Waen

Llangwyfan

Moel
Llys-y-coed

14

Soughton

unos

0   2   4   6 miles

0   2   4   6   8   10 km

B   **Denbigh**
(Dinbych)

Friary
(ruins)

Deunant

Llansannan

B5382

Pen

A543

Ystrad

Llandyrnog

C   465

Moel

Rhydymwyn

D   A541

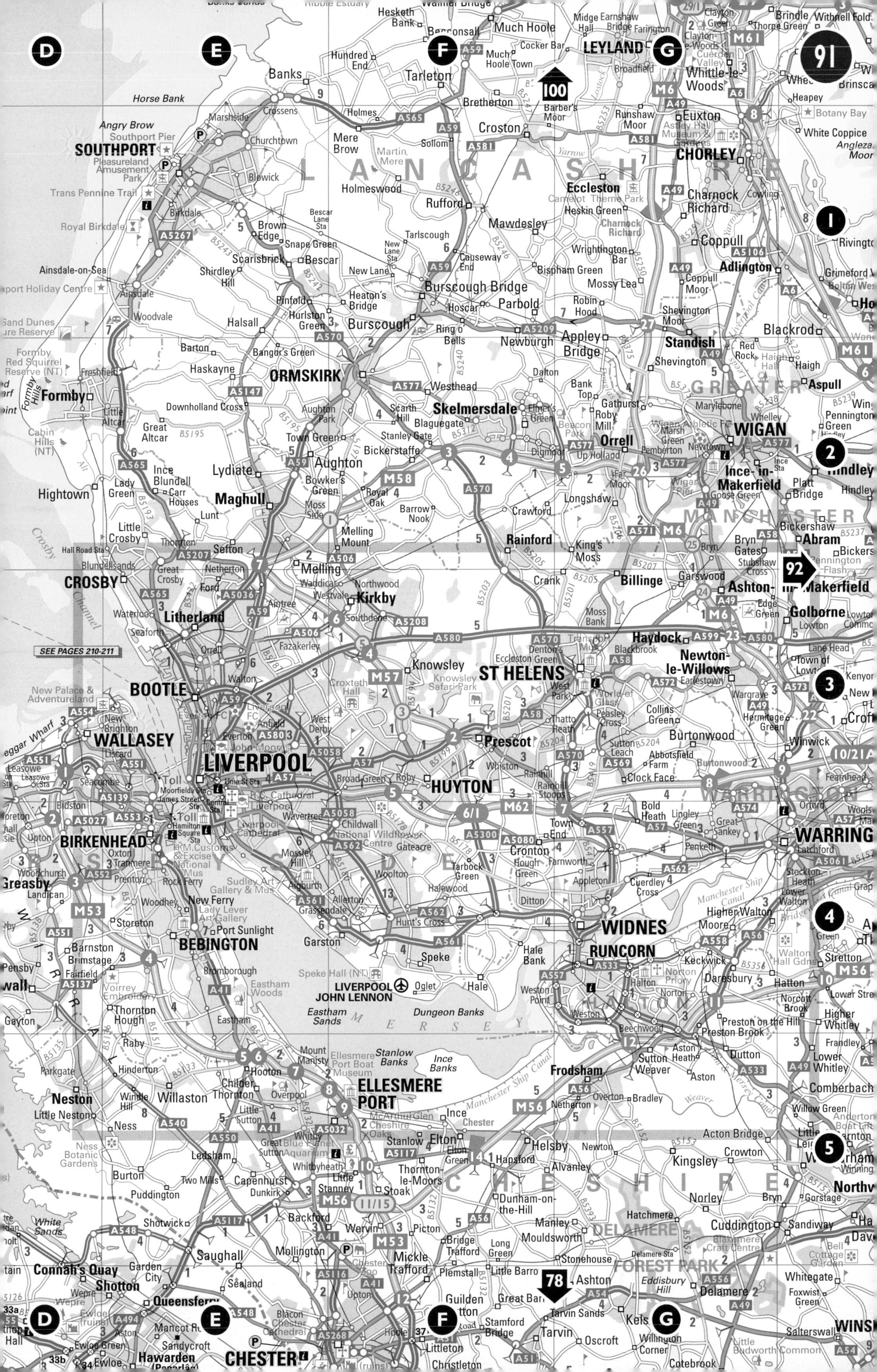

91
D
E
F
G
100
LEYLAND
Much Hoole
Tarleton
Banks
Horse Bank
Angry Brow
Southport Pier
SOUTHPORT
Pleasureland Amusement Park
Trans Pennine Trail
Royal Birkdale
Ainsdale-on-Sea
Southport Holiday Centre
Sand Dunes Nature Reserve
Formby Red Squirrel Reserve (NT)
Formby
Cabin Hills (NT)
Hightown
LANCASHIRE
Crossens
Churchtown
Marshside
Blowick
Birkdale
Ainsdale
Woodvale
Freshfield
Little Altcar
Great Altcar
Holmes
Mere Brow
Martin Mere
Holmeswood
Rufford
Croston
Bretherton
Eccleston
Camelot Theme Park
Heskin Green
Charnock Richard
Coppull
Adlington
CHORLEY
Euxton
Whittle-le-Woods
Wrightington Bar
Bispham Green
Mawdesley
Scarisbrick
Bescar
Burscough Bridge
Burscough
Parbold
Appley Bridge
Newburgh
Standish
Shevington
ORMSKIRK
Halsall
Barton
Haskayne
Downholland Cross
Aughton
Skelmersdale
Westhead
Bickerstaffe
Orrell
WIGAN
Ince-in-Makerfield
Hindley
Abram
Lydiate
Maghull
Ince Blundell
Lunt
Sefton
Thornton
Little Crosby
CROSBY
Great Crosby
Litherland
Melling
Kirkby
Rainford
Billinge
Ashton-in-Makerfield
Golborne
Haydock
Newton-le-Willows
ST HELENS
Knowsley
Knowsley Safari Park
Prescot
HUYTON
Rainhill
BOOTLE
WALLASEY
LIVERPOOL
BIRKENHEAD
Seacombe
Greasby
Bebington
BEBINGTON
Port Sunlight
Lady Lever Art Gallery
Garston
Speke
Speke Hall (NT)
LIVERPOOL JOHN LENNON
Hale
Hale Bank
WIDNES
RUNCORN
Halton
Frodsham
Helsby
Daresbury
WARRINGTON
Burtonwood
Penketh
Great Sankey
Cronton
Ditton
Eastham
Eastham Sands
Dungeon Banks
MERSEY
Ince Banks
Stanlow Banks
ELLESMERE PORT
Neston
Little Neston
Ness
Ness Botanic Gardens
Parkgate
Heswall
Willaston
Burton
Puddington
Capenhurst
Saughall
Mollington
Connah's Quay
Shotton
Queensferry
Hawarden
CHESTER
Chester Zoo
Upton
Guilden Sutton
Tarvin
Kelsall
Ashton
Delamere
DELAMERE FOREST PARK
Manley
Mouldsworth
Alvanley
Kingsley
Norley
Cuddington
Sandiway
Weaverham
Acton Bridge
CHESHIRE
WIRRAL
GREATER MANCHESTER
MERSEYSIDE
HALTON
SEE PAGES 210-211
78
92
M6
M58
M57
M62
M53
M56
M61
A59
A580
A565
A570
A577
A49
A56
A41
A5117
A540
A550

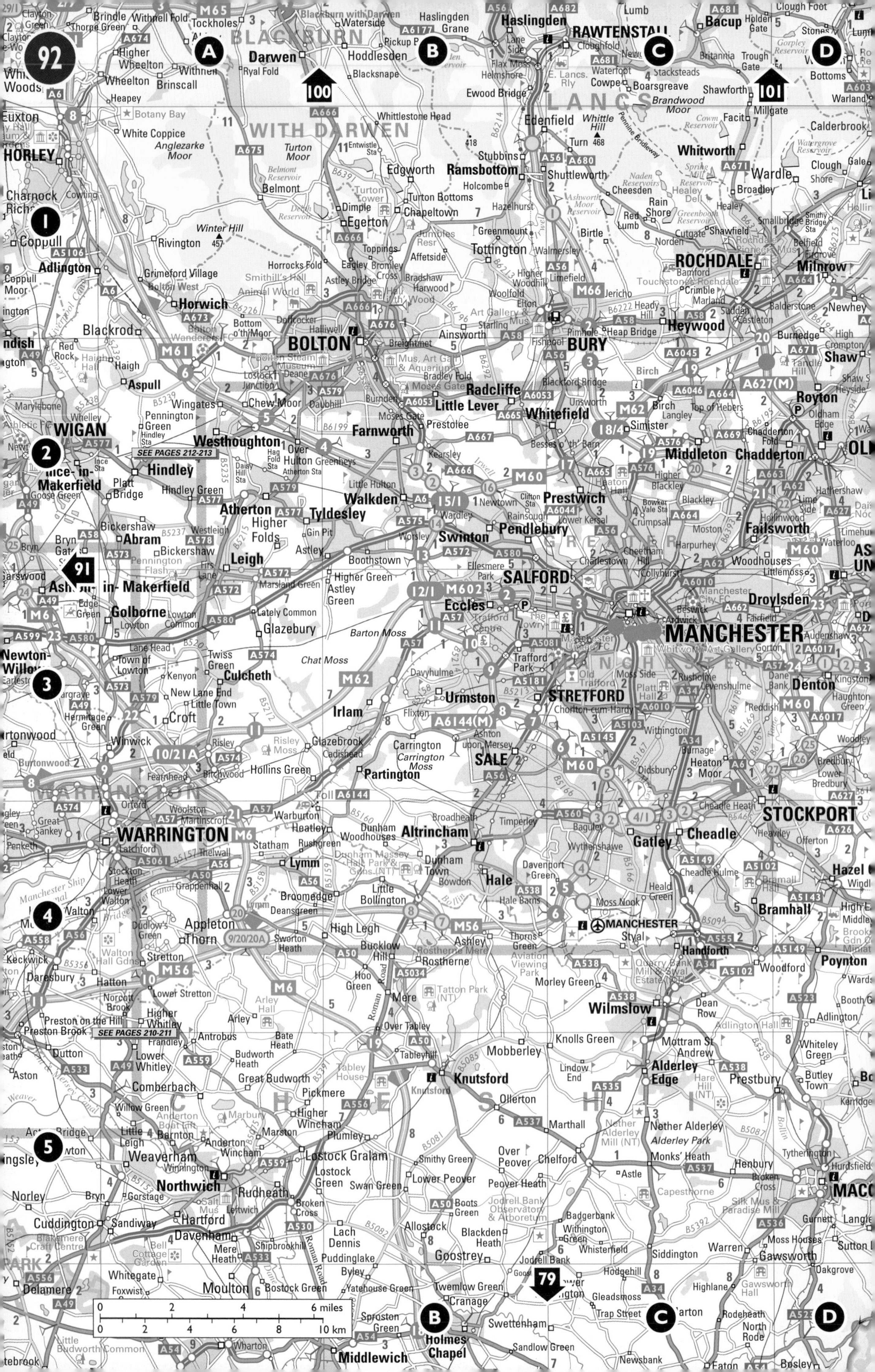
A
B
C
D
1
2
3
4
5
100
101
91
79
SEE PAGES 212-213
SEE PAGES 210-211
0 2 4 6 miles
0 2 4 6 8 10 km
Clayton Green
Brindle
Withnell Fold
Tockholes
M65
Blackburn with Darwen
BLACKBURN
Waterside
Haslingden Grane
Haslingden
A56
A682
RAWTENSTALL
Lumb
A681
Bacup
Holden Gate
Clough Foot
Thorpe Green
A674
Higher Wheelton
Withnell
Darwen
Ryal Fold
Hoddlesden
Pickup Bank
A6177
Lane Side
Cloughfold
Flax Moss
Helmshore
A681
Waterfoot
Cowpe
Newchurch
Stacksteads
Boarsgreave
Brandwood Moor
Britannia
Trough Gate
Gorpley Reservoir
Bottoms
A6033
Warland
Wheelton
Brinscall
Blacksnape
Ewood Bridge
E. Lancs. Rly
LANCS
Shawforth
Millgate
Whittle Woods
Heapey
Botany Bay
A6
Euxton
A666
WITH DARWEN
Whittlestone Head
Edenfield
Whittle Hill
468
Pennine Bridleway
Cowm Reservoir
Facit
Calderbrook
Watergrove Reservoir
White Coppice
Anglezarke Moor
CHORLEY
A675
Turton Moor
Entwistle Sta
B6214
418
Turn
Stubbins
A56
A680
Whitworth
A671
Clough
Shore
Gale
Belmont Reservoir
Belmont
B6391
Edgworth
Ramsbottom
Shuttleworth
Naden Reservoirs
Spring Mill Reservoir
Healey Dell
Wardle
Broadley
Charnock Richard
Cowling
Turton Tower
Turton Bottoms
Dimple
Chapeltown
Holcombe
Cheesden
Ashworth Moor Reservoir
Rain Shore
Greenbooth Reservoir
Healey
Smallbridge
Smithy Bridge Sta
Delph Reservoir
Egerton
Hazelhurst
Red Lumb
Coppull
A5106
Winter Hill
457
Rivington
A666
Jumbles Resr
Greenmount
Birtle
Norden
Cutgate
Shawfield
Rochdale Pioneers Mus
Belfield
Firgrove
Toppings
Affetside
Tottington
Walmersley
ROCHDALE
Milnrow
Adlington
Horrocks Fold
Eagley
Bromley Cross
Bamford
Coppull Moor
Grimeford Village
Bolton West
Smithill's Hall
Astley Bridge
Bradshaw
Harwood
Higher Woodhill
Limefield
Touchstones Rochdale
A664
Animal World
Hall i' th' Wood
Woolfold
M66
Jericho
Crimble
Marland
Balderstone
Newhey
Horwich
A673
B6226
Bottom o' th' Moor
Doffcocker
A666
A676
Art Gallery & Mus
Elton
B6222
Heady Hill
A58
Heywood
Sudden
Castleton
Blackrod
Bolton Wanderers FC
Halliwell
Starling
Ainsworth
Fishpool
Pimhole
Heap Bridge
Burnedge
High Crompton
Standish
Red Rock
Haigh Hall
Haigh
M61
BOLTON
Breightmet
BURY
A58
A6045
A671
Shaw
A49
Bolton Steam Museum
Mus, Art Gall & Aquarium
B6292
Birch
Tandle Hill
Aspull
Lostock Junction
Deane
Bradley Fold
Moses Gate
Radcliffe
Blackford Bridge
A627(M)
Shaw Side
Heyside
Marylebone
B5239
Chew Moor
A676
A579
A6053
Unsworth
A6046
A664
Royton
Whelley
Wingates
Daubhill
Burnden
Little Lever
A6053
M62
Birch
Langley
Top of Hebers
Oldham Edge
WIGAN
Pennington Green
Hindley Sta
Moses Gate
Prestolee
Whitefield
A665
Simister
A669
Chadderton Fold
OLDHAM
Westhoughton
B6199
Farnworth
A667
Besses o' th' Barn
18/4
A576
Ince Sta
A577
Hag Fold Sta
Over Hulton
Greenheys
Kearsley
Irwell
Middleton
Chadderton
Ince-in-Makerfield
Hindley
Daisy Hill Sta
Atherton Sta
A666
M60
A665
Heaton Hall
Higher Blackley
A663
Hathershaw
B5235
Little Hulton
Clifton Sta
Prestwich
A62
Lime Side
Platt Bridge
Hindley Green
A579
Walkden
15/1
Newtown
A6044
Bowker Vale Sta
Blackley
Hollinwood
Goose Green
A577
Atherton
Higher Folds
A577
Tyldesley
Wardley
Rainsough
Lower Kersal
Crumpsall
A664
A627
Failsworth
Bickershaw
Westleigh
Gin Pit
A575
Swinton
Pendlebury
A56
Moston
Bryn
Abram
B5237
A578
Astley
Worsley
GREATER
Harpurhey
Waterloo
Bryn Gates
A58
Bickershaw
A573
Pennington Flash
Leigh
Boothstown
A572
A580
Cheetham Hill
Charlestown
A62
Woodhouses
M60
Ashton-in-Makerfield
Firs Lane
A572
Ellesmere Park
SALFORD
Collyhurst
Littlemoss
Garswood
Marsland Green
Higher Green
Astley Green
M602
A6010
Manchester City FC
Edge Green
A49
A572
12/1
Eccles
Droylsden
Golborne
M6
Lowton Common
Lately Common
A57
Trafford Centre
The Lowry
Beswick
Ardwick
A662
Fairfield
Lowton
A580
Glazebury
Barton Moss
Audenshaw
A599
A580
MANCHESTER
Manchester United FC
A5081
Whitworth Art Gallery
Gorton
A6017
Newton-le-Willows
Lane Head
Twiss Green
A574
Chat Moss
A57
Davyhulme
Trafford Park
Old Trafford
MANCHESTER
Moss Side
Rusholme
Levenshulme
A57
Denton
Dane Bank
Kingston
Earlestown
Town of Lowton
Kenyon
Culcheth
A5181
Urmston
STRETFORD
Platt Hall
Haughton Green
Hargrave
A49
A573
New Lane End
Little Town
M62
B5213
Chorlton-cum-Hardy
A6010
A34
Reddish
M60
A6017
Hermitage Green
A579
Croft
B5212
Irlam
Flixton
A6144(M)
Withington
Burtonwood
Winwick
Risley
Risley Moss
Glazebrook
Cadishead
Carrington
Carrington Moss
Ashton upon Mersey
A5145
A5103
Burnage
Woodley
10/21A
A574
Birchwood
Hollins Green
Partington
SALE
M60
Didsbury
Heaton Moor
Bredbury
Lower Bredbury
Fearnhead
A56
WARRINGTON
Toll
A6144
Orford
Woolston
Martinscroft
A57
Warburton
B5160
Broadheath
Timperley
A560
4/1
Cheadle Heath
STOCKPORT
A627
A626
Great Sankey
A574
A57
Heatley
Dunham Woodhouses
Altrincham
Baguley
Gatley
Cheadle
Heaviley
Offerton
Penketh
WARRINGTON
M6
Latchford
A5061
B5157
Thelwall
A56
Statham
Rushgreen
Lymm
Dunham Massey Hall, Park & Gdns (NT)
Dunham Town
Bowdon
Wythenshawe
A5149
Cheadle Hulme
A5102
Bramhall
Hazel Grove
Stockton Heath
Lower Walton
A50
Grappenhall
B5158
B5159
A56
Little Bollington
Hale
Davenport Green
A538
Heald Green
A5143
Manchester Ship Canal
Bridgewater Canal
Walton
Broomedge
Deansgreen
Hale Barns
Bollin
Moss Nook
B5094
High Lane
Middlewood
Moore
A558
A56
Dudlow's Green
Appleton Thorn
9/20/20A
Swinton Heath
High Legh
M56
Ashley
Thorns Green
MANCHESTER
Styal
Handforth
A555
A5149
Poynton
Keckwick
Walton Hall Gdns
Stretton
M56
A50
Bucklow Hill
Rostherne Mere
Rostherne
Aviation Viewing Park
A538
Quarry Bank Mill & Styal Estate (NT)
A34
A5102
Woodford
Daresbury
B5356
Hatton
M6
Hoo Green
A5034
Tatton Park (NT)
Morley Green
Norcott Brook
Lower Stretton
Arley Hall
Roman Road
Mere
A538
Wilmslow
Dean Row
A523
Booth Green
Preston on the Hill
Preston Brook
Higher Whitley
Frandley
Arley
Antrobus
Bate Heath
Over Tabley
A50
Knolls Green
Mottram St Andrew
Adlington Hall
Adlington
Dutton
A533
Lower Whitley
A49
A559
Budworth Heath
Tabley House
Tableyhill
B5085
Mobberley
Lindow End
Alderley Edge
A538
B5358
Whiteley Green
Aston
Comberbach
Great Budworth
Knutsford
Hare Hill (NT)
Prestbury
Butley Town
Weaver
Pickmere
A556
Ollerton
A535
Kerridge
Willow Green
Anderton Boat Lift
Marbury
CHESHIRE
Higher Wincham
A537
Marthall
Nether Alderley Mill (NT)
Nether Alderley
Alderley Park
B5087
Bollin
Acton Bridge
Little Leigh
Barnton
Anderton
Wincham
Marston
Plumley
B5081
Tytherington
Kingsley
Crowton
Weaverham
Winnington
A559
Lostock Gralam
Smithy Green
Over Peover
Chelford
Monks' Heath
A537
Henbury
Hurdsfield
Norley
Bryn
Gorstage
Northwich
Salt Mus
Rudheath
Lostock Green
Swan Green
Lower Peover
Peover Heath
Astle
Capesthorne
Broken Cross
MACCLESFIELD
Cuddington
Sandiway
Hartford
Leftwich
Broken Cross
A50
Boots Green
Jodrell Bank Observatory & Arboretum
Badgerbank
Silk Mus & Paradise Mill
A536
Gurnett
Langley
Blakemere Craft Centre
Davenham
Shipbrookhill
A530
Lach Dennis
Allostock
Blackden Heath
Withington Green
Whisterfield
B5392
Moss Houses
Sutton
Bell Cottage Garden
Mere Heath
A533
B5082
Puddinglake
Goostrey
Jodrell Bank
Siddington
Warren
Gawsworth
A556
Whitegate
Foxwist
Moulton
Bostock Green
Byley
Yatehouse Green
Twemlow Green
Lower Withington
Hodgehill
Gleadsmoss
A34
Highlane
Gawsworth Hall
Oakgrove
Delamere
A49
Cranage
Trap Street
Marton
Rodeheath
North Rode
A523
Little Budworth Common
Sproston Green
A54
Holmes Chapel
Swettenham
Sandlow Green
A54
Wharton
Middlewich
Newsbank
Eaton
Bosley

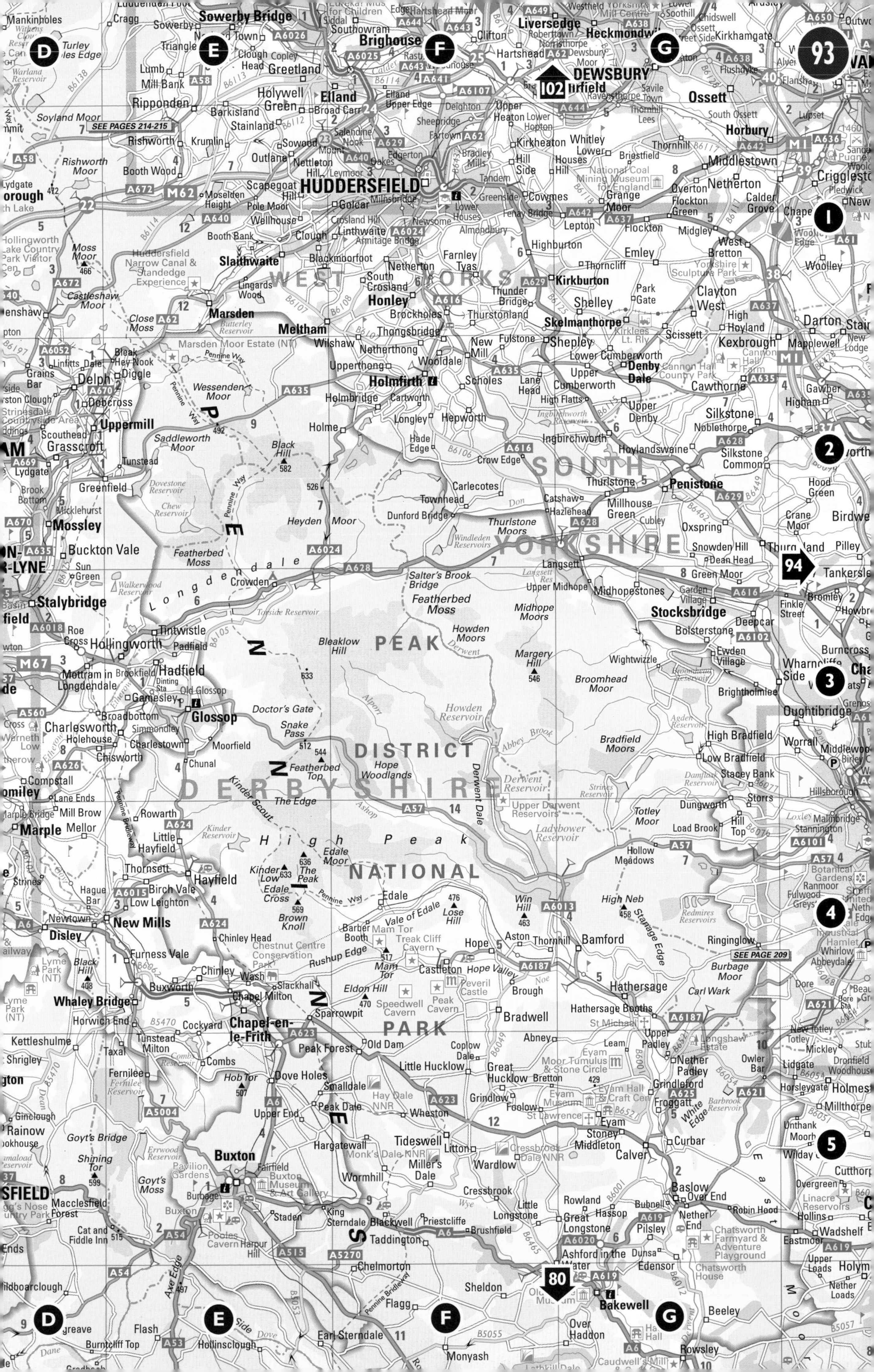
93
Sowerby Bridge
Brighouse
Liversedge
Heckmondwike
DEWSBURY
102
Mankinholes
Turley Holes Edge
Cragg
Sowerby
Triangle
Norland Town
Clough Head
Copley
Greetland
Lumb
Mill Bank
Ripponden
Holywell Green
Elland
Barkisland
Stainland
Soyland Moor
SEE PAGES 214-215
Rishworth
Krumlin
Rishworth Moor
Booth Wood
Outlane
Salendine Nook
Sowood
Nettleton Hill
Leymoor
Oakes
Edgerton
Scapegoat Hill
HUDDERSFIELD
Golcar
Milnsbridge
Moselden Height
Pole Moor
Wellhouse
Crosland Hill
Linthwaite
Armitage Bridge
Booth Bank
Clough
Slaithwaite
Blackmoorfoot
Netherton
South Crosland
Honley
Brockholes
Thongsbridge
Netherthong
Wilshaw
Meltham
Marsden
Close Moss
Castleshaw Moor
Moss Moor
Huddersfield Narrow Canal & Standedge Experience
Lingards Wood
Marsden Moor Estate (NT)
Butterley Reservoir
Pennine Way
Bleak Hey Nook
Diggle
Delph
Dobcross
Uppermill
Grasscroft
Scouthead
Lydgate
Greenfield
Mossley
Buckton Vale
Stalybridge
Tintwistle
Hollingworth
Padfield
Hadfield
Mottram in Longdendale
Glossop
Old Glossop
Gamesley
Broadbottom
Charlesworth
Simmondley
Charlestown
Chisworth
Holehouse
Compstall
Marple
Mellor
Mill Brow
Rowarth
Little Hayfield
Hayfield
Thornsett
Birch Vale
Low Leighton
Hague Bar
New Mills
Newtown
Disley
Furness Vale
Chinley Head
Chinley
Buxworth
Whaley Bridge
Horwich End
Chapel Milton
Chapel-en-le-Frith
Tunstead Milton
Combs
Kettleshulme
Taxal
Fernilee
Fernilee Reservoir
Errwood Reservoir
Goyt's Bridge
Goyt's Moss
Shining Tor
Buxton
Fairfield
Burbage
Poole's Cavern
Harpur Hill
King Sterndale
Staden
Cat and Fiddle Inn
Axe Edge
Macclesfield Forest
Flash
Hollinsclough
Earl Sterndale
Flagg
Monyash
Chelmorton
Taddington
Blackwell
Priestcliffe
Brushfield
Sheldon
Wormhill
Hargatewall
Peak Dale
Smalldale
Dove Holes
Upper End
Peak Forest
Old Dam
Sparrowpit
Slackhall
Wash
Hob Tor
Tideswell
Miller's Dale
Litton
Wardlow
Cressbrook
Little Longstone
Great Longstone
Ashford in the Water
Bakewell
Over Haddon
Rowsley
Beeley
Edensor
Chatsworth House
Pilsley
Baslow
Calver
Curbar
Froggatt
Stoney Middleton
Eyam
Foolow
Grindlow
Great Hucklow
Bretton
Little Hucklow
Wheston
Bradwell
Abney
Brough
Hope
Castleton
Peveril Castle
Speedwell Cavern
Peak Cavern
Treak Cliff Cavern
Mam Tor
Rushup Edge
Barber Booth
Edale
Edale Moor
Kinder Low
The Peak
Kinder Scout
Brown Knoll
Lose Hill
Win Hill
Aston
Thornhill
Bamford
Hathersage
Hathersage Booths
Upper Padley
Nether Padley
Grindleford
Stanage Edge
High Neb
Ladybower Reservoir
Derwent Reservoir
Upper Derwent Reservoirs
Howden Reservoir
Howden Moors
Margery Hill
Broomhead Moor
Bradfield Moors
High Bradfield
Low Bradfield
Dungworth
Storrs
Stacey Bank
Worrall
Oughtibridge
Wharncliffe Side
Brightholmlee
Ewden Village
Stocksbridge
Deepcar
Bolsterstone
Midhopestones
Upper Midhope
Langsett
Midhope Moors
Salter's Brook Bridge
Featherbed Moss
Bleaklow Hill
Doctor's Gate
Snake Pass
Featherbed Top
Hope Woodlands
Crowden
Longdendale
Torside Reservoir
Black Hill
Heyden Moor
Saddleworth Moor
Wessenden Moor
Holme
Holmbridge
Holmfirth
Upperthong
Cartworth
Hade Edge
Longley
Hepworth
Scholes
Wooldale
New Mill
Fulstone
Thurstonland
Thunder Bridge
Farnley Tyas
Almondbury
Kirkburton
Highburton
Shelley
Skelmanthorpe
Shepley
Lower Cumberworth
Upper Cumberworth
Denby Dale
Upper Denby
Ingbirchworth
Hoylandswaine
Penistone
Thurlstone
Millhouse Green
Oxspring
Crow Edge
Carlecotes
Townhead
Dunford Bridge
Thurlstone Moors
Windleden Reservoirs
Kirkheaton
Lepton
Flockton
Grange Moor
Emley
Clayton West
Scissett
High Hoyland
Kexbrough
Darton
Cawthorne
Silkstone
Silkstone Common
Hood Green
Crane Moor
Thurgoland
Green Moor
Tankersley
Ossett
Horbury
Middlestown
Netherton
Crigglestone
Woolley
Yorkshire Sculpture Park
National Coal Mining Museum for England
WEST YORKS
SOUTH YORKSHIRE
DERBYSHIRE
PEAK DISTRICT NATIONAL PARK
High Peak
PENNINE
94
SEE PAGE 209
80

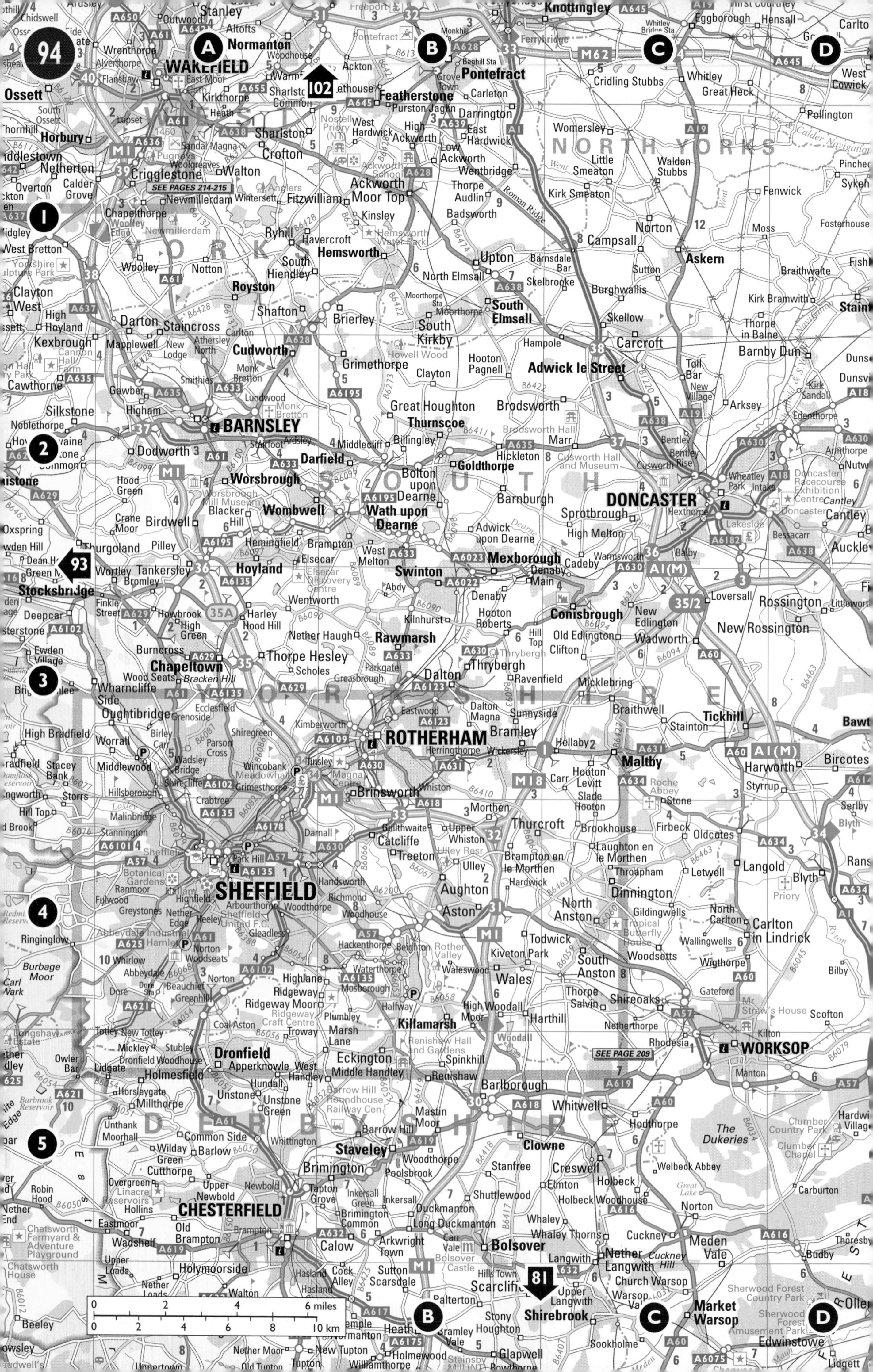

94
A
B
C
D
WAKEFIELD
Normanton
Stanley
Outwood
Altofts
Ossett
Horbury
Crigglestone
Netherton
Walton
Sharlston
Crofton
102
Featherstone
Pontefract
Knottingley
Ferrybridge
Eggborough
Hensall
Whitley
Cridling Stubbs
Great Heck
West Cowick
Pollington
M62
Darrington
East Hardwick
Ackworth Moor Top
Wentbridge
Thorpe Audlin
Womersley
Little Smeaton
Walden Stubbs
Kirk Smeaton
NORTH YORKS
Fenwick
Norton
Campsall
Askern
Moss
Badsworth
Upton
Hemsworth
South Hiendley
Royston
Fitzwilliam
Kinsley
Ryhill
Havercroft
North Elmsall
South Elmsall
Skelbrooke
Burghwallis
Sutton
Kirk Bramwith
Skellow
Carcroft
Thorpe in Balne
Barnby Dun
Adwick le Street
Hampole
Hooton Pagnell
Brierley
Grimethorpe
South Kirkby
Shafton
Cudworth
Darton
Staincross
Clayton West
High Hoyland
Kexbrough
Mapplewell
Cawthorne
Silkstone
Dodworth
BARNSLEY
Worsbrough
Darfield
Great Houghton
Thurnscoe
Goldthorpe
Bolton upon Dearne
Brodsworth
Hickleton
Marr
Barnburgh
Sprotbrough
DONCASTER
Bentley
Arksey
Edenthorpe
Armthorpe
Cantley
Bessacarr
Wombwell
Wath upon Dearne
Mexborough
Conisbrough
Swinton
Hoyland
Birdwell
Pilley
Thurgoland
93
Stocksbridge
Deepcar
Tankersley
Chapeltown
Wentworth
Rawmarsh
Thorpe Hesley
Rossington
New Rossington
Edlington
Wadworth
Loversall
Dalton
Thrybergh
Ravenfield
Micklebring
Braithwell
Tickhill
Stainton
ROTHERHAM
Bramley
Maltby
Harworth
Bircotes
Wickersley
Hellaby
Brinsworth
Whiston
Grenoside
Ecclesfield
Oughtibridge
Worrall
Middlewood
High Bradfield
Hillsborough
SHEFFIELD
Handsworth
Catcliffe
Treeton
Aughton
Aston
Thurcroft
Dinnington
North Anston
South Anston
Todwick
Kiveton Park
Wales
Harthill
Shireoaks
Thorpe Salvin
Carlton in Lindrick
Langold
Blyth
Oldcotes
WORKSOP
Killamarsh
Eckington
Dronfield
Holmesfield
Unstone
Staveley
Barlborough
Whitwell
Clowne
Creswell
Brimington
CHESTERFIELD
Old Brampton
Bolsover
Calow
Cuckney
Meden Vale
Market Warsop
Shirebrook
Edwinstowe
Langwith
81
Scarcliffe
Heath
Glapwell
The Dukeries
Clumber Country Park
Welbeck Abbey
Carburton
Norton
DERBYSHIRE
SEE PAGES 214-215
SEE PAGE 209
Burbage Moor
Ringinglow
Holymoorside
Walton
Beeley
0 2 4 6 miles
0 2 4 6 8 10 km

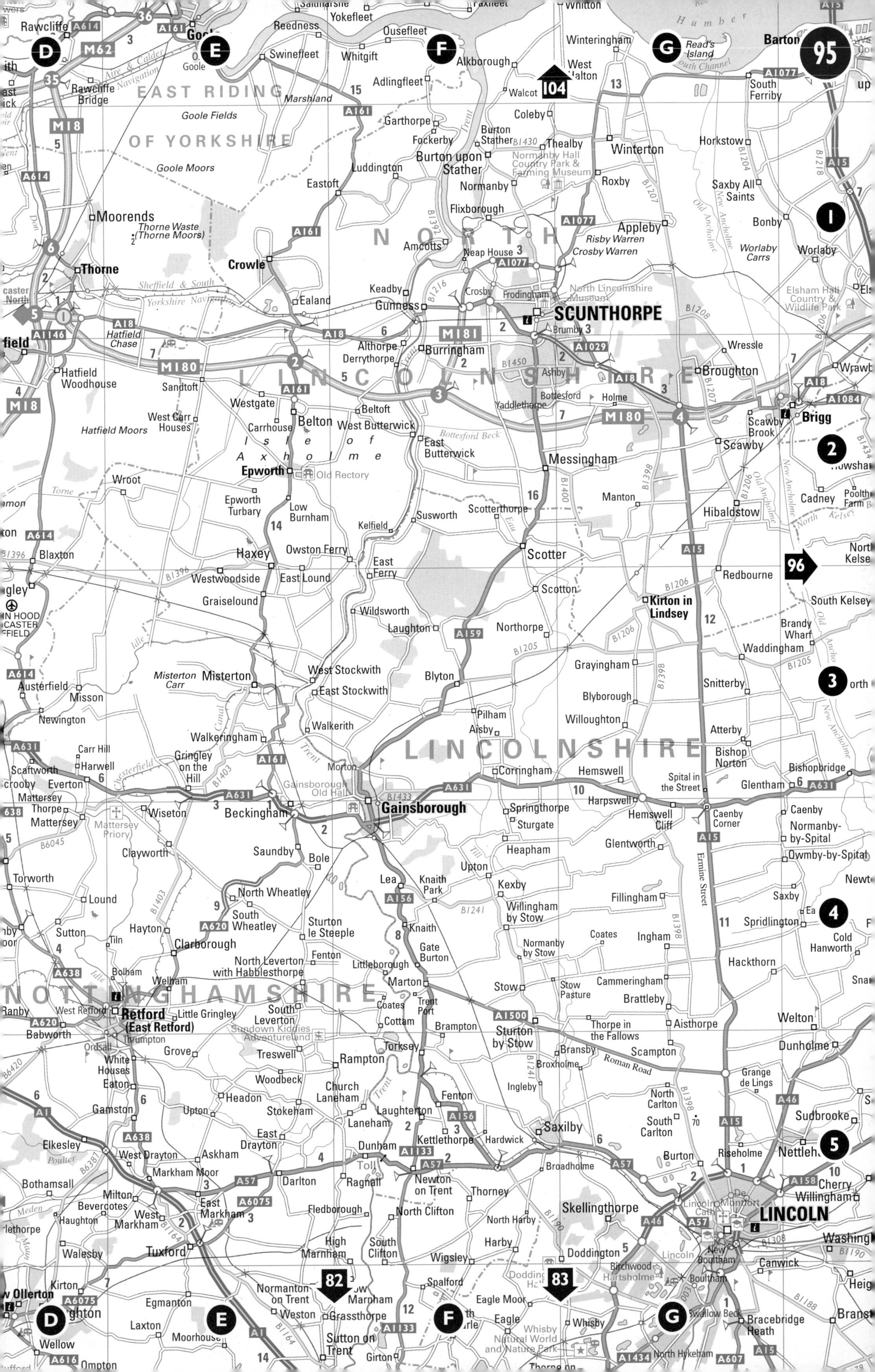
95
Rawcliffe
A614
36
A161
Goole
Reedness
Yokefleet
Ousefleet
M62
Swinefleet
Whitgift
Alkborough
Winteringham
Humber
Read's Island
South Channel
Barton
West Halton
104
Walcot
Adlingfleet
Rawcliffe Bridge
EAST RIDING
OF YORKSHIRE
Marshland
15
Aire & Calder Navigation
Goole Fields
Goole Moors
M18
Garthorpe
Fockerby
Burton upon Stather
Burton Stather
Thealby
Normanby Hall Country Park & Farming Museum
Winterton
Roxby
Coleby
South Ferriby
A1077
Horkstow
Saxby All Saints
Bonby
Worlaby
Worlaby Carrs
Luddington
Eastoft
Normanby
Flixborough
Appleby
Risby Warren
Crosby Warren
Moorends
Thorne Waste (Thorne Moors)
Thorne
Crowle
Amcotts
Neap House
NORTH
LINCOLNSHIRE
Sheffield & South Yorkshire Navigation
Eland
Keadby
Gunness
Crosby
Frodingham
North Lincolnshire Museum
SCUNTHORPE
Brumby
Elsham Hall Country & Wildlife Park
A18
Hatfield Chase
M180
M181
Althorpe
Derrythorpe
Burringham
Ashby
A1029
Wressle
Broughton
Hatfield Woodhouse
Sandtoft
Westgate
Belton
Beltoft
West Butterwick
Bottesford
Yaddlethorpe
Holme
Scawby Brook
Brigg
Scawby
A1084
West Carr Houses
Carrhouse
Hatfield Moors
Isle of Axholme
East Butterwick
Bottesford Beck
Messingham
Epworth
Old Rectory
Wroot
Epworth Turbary
Low Burnham
Manton
Hibaldstow
Cadney
Kelfield
Susworth
Scotterthorpe
Blaxton
Haxey
Owston Ferry
East Ferry
Scotter
Redbourne
96
Westwoodside
East Lound
Graiselound
Scotton
Kirton in Lindsey
South Kelsey
Wildsworth
Laughton
Northorpe
Brandy Wharf
Waddingham
Misterton Carr
Misterton
West Stockwith
East Stockwith
Blyton
Grayingham
Snitterby
Austerfield
Misson
Newington
Blyborough
Willoughton
Walkerith
Pilham
Aisby
Atterby
Walkeringham
LINCOLNSHIRE
Bishop Norton
Carr Hill
Harwell
Gringley on the Hill
Morton
Corringham
Hemswell
Bishopbridge
Scaftworth
Everton
Mattersey
Gainsborough Old Hall
Spital in the Street
Glentham
Thorpe
Mattersey Priory
Wiseton
Beckingham
Gainsborough
Springthorpe
Harpswell
Hemswell Cliff
Caenby Corner
Caenby
Normanby-by-Spital
Sturgate
Clayworth
Saundby
Bole
Heapham
Glentworth
Owmby-by-Spital
Torworth
Upton
Lea
Knaith Park
Ermine Street
Lound
North Wheatley
Kexby
Willingham by Stow
Fillingham
Saxby
South Wheatley
Sturton le Steeple
Knaith
Spridlington
Sutton
Hayton
Clarborough
Gate Burton
Normanby by Stow
Coates
Ingham
Cold Hanworth
Fenton
North Leverton with Habblesthorpe
Littleborough
Hackthorn
Bolham
Welham
Marton
Stow
Stow Pasture
Cammeringham
NOTTINGHAMSHIRE
Little Gringley
West Retford
Retford (East Retford)
South Leverton
Coates
Trent Port
Cottam
Brattleby
Thorpe in the Fallows
Aisthorpe
Welton
Babworth
Thrumpton
Sundown Kiddies Adventureland
Brampton
Sturton by Stow
Ordsall
Grove
Treswell
Torksey
Bransby
Scampton
Dunholme
White Houses
Rampton
Broxholme
Roman Road
Eaton
Woodbeck
Church Laneham
Ingleby
Grange de Lings
Headon
North Carlton
South Carlton
Gamston
Upton
Stokeham
Laughterton
Fenton
Sudbrooke
Laneham
Saxilby
East Drayton
Elkesley
Kettlethorpe
Hardwick
Riseholme
Nettleham
Askham
West Drayton
Dunham
Toll
Burton
Markham Moor
Newton on Trent
Broadholme
Bothamsall
Darlton
Ragnall
Thorney
Cherry Willingham
Milton
Beverotes
West Markham
East Markham
Fledborough
North Clifton
Skellingthorpe
Lincoln
Monfort
LINCOLN
Haughton
North Harby
Harby
Washingborough
Walesby
Tuxford
High Marnham
South Clifton
Wigsley
Doddington
New Boultham
Canwick
Birchwood
Hartsholme
Boultham
Kirton
Normanton on Trent
82
Low Marnham
Spalford
Doddington Hall
83
Eagle Moor
New Ollerton
Egmanton
Weston
Grassthorpe
Eagle
Whisby
Whisby Natural World and Nature Park
Swallow Beck
Bracebridge Heath
Laxton
Moorhouse
Sutton on Trent
North Hykeham
Wellow
Ompton
Girton
A1
A15
A46
A57
A156
A159
A161
A620
A631
A638
A1133
A1500
A6075
B1398
B1400

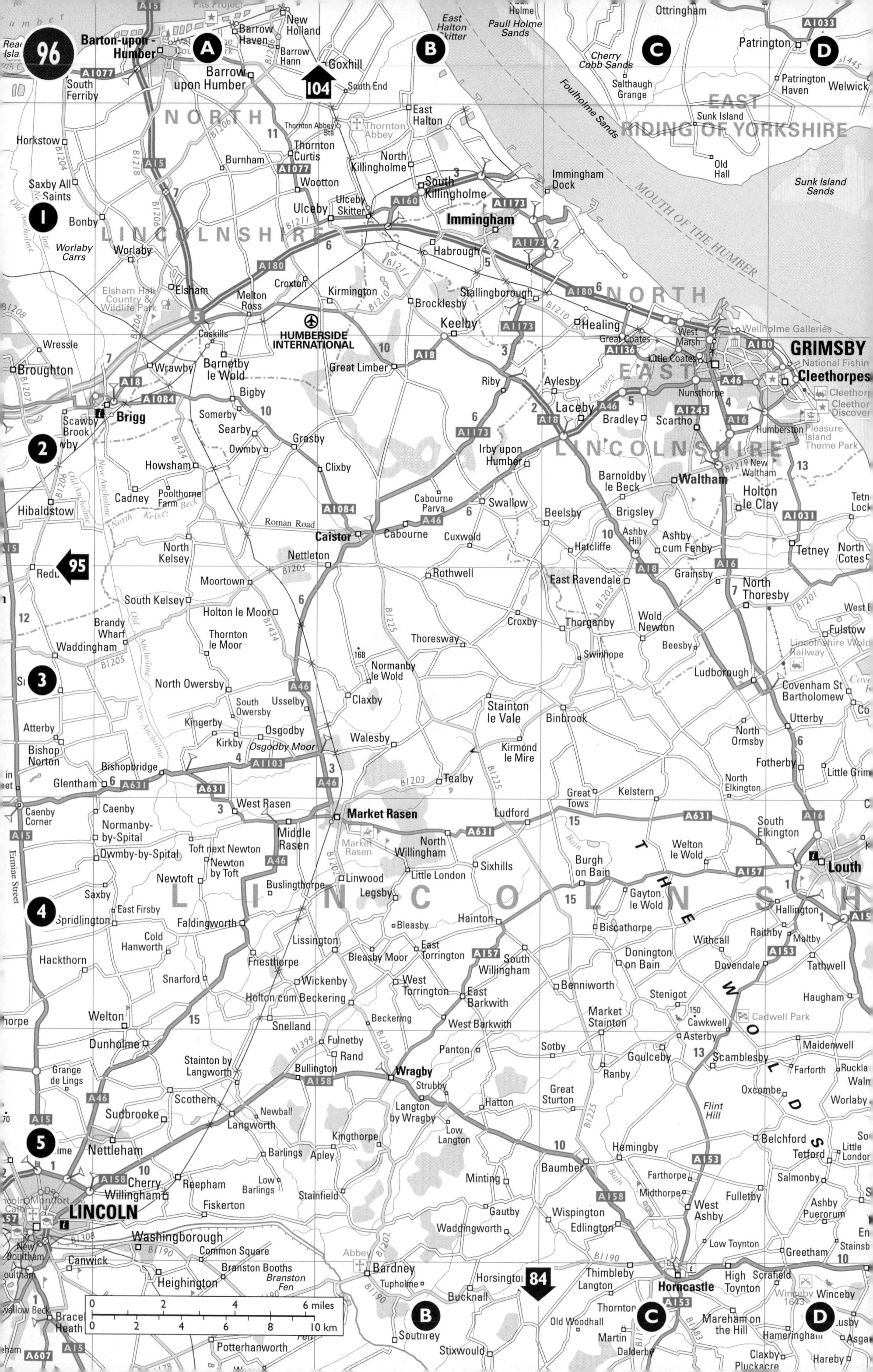
96
A
B
C
D
104
95
84
Barton-upon-Humber
Barrow Haven
New Holland
Barrow Haven
Goxhill
South End
East Halton Skitter
Paull Holme Sands
Ottringham
Cherry Cobb Sands
Salthaugh Grange
Patrington
Patrington Haven
Welwick
Foulholme Sands
EAST RIDING OF YORKSHIRE
Sunk Island
Old Hall
Sunk Island Sands
MOUTH OF THE HUMBER
South Ferriby
Barrow upon Humber
NORTH
East Halton
Thornton Abbey Sta
Thornton Abbey
Thornton Curtis
North Killingholme
Horkstow
Burnham
Wootton
South Killingholme
Immingham Dock
Saxby All Saints
Ulceby
Ulceby Skitter
Immingham
Bonby
LINCOLNSHIRE
Worlaby Carrs
Worlaby
Habrough
Elsham Hall Country & Wildlife Park
Elsham
Croxton
Melton Ross
Kirmington
Brocklesby
Stallingborough
NORTH
HUMBERSIDE INTERNATIONAL
Keelby
Healing
Great Coates
West Marsh
Wellholme Galleries
GRIMSBY
Wressle
Broughton
Coskills
Wrawby
Barnetby le Wold
Great Limber
Riby
Aylesby
Little Coates
EAST
National Fishing
Cleethorpes
Brigg
Bigby
Laceby
Bradley
Scartho
Nunsthorpe
Humberston
Pleasure Island Theme Park
Scawby Brook
Somerby
Searby
Grasby
Irby upon Humber
LINCOLNSHIRE
Owmby
Howsham
Clixby
Barnoldby le Beck
Waltham
New Waltham
Holton le Clay
Cadney
Poolthorne Farm
Cabourne Parva
Swallow
Beelsby
Brigsley
Hibaldstow
Roman Road
Caistor
Cabourne
Cuxwold
Ashby Hill
Ashby cum Fenby
Hatcliffe
Tetney
North Cotes
North Kelsey
Nettleton
Rothwell
East Ravendale
Grainsby
Tetney Lock
Moortown
North Thoresby
South Kelsey
Holton le Moor
Croxby
Thorganby
Wold Newton
Brandy Wharf
Thornton le Moor
Thoresway
Swinhope
Beesby
Fulstow
Waddingham
Normanby le Wold
Lincolnshire Wolds Railway
Ludborough
North Owersby
South Owersby
Usselby
Claxby
Stainton le Vale
Binbrook
Covenham St Bartholomew
Atterby
Kingerby
Osgodby
Walesby
Kirmond le Mire
Utterby
North Ormsby
Bishop Norton
Kirkby
Osgodby Moor
Fotherby
Bishopbridge
Glentham
Tealby
North Elkington
Little Grimsby
Caenby
Caenby Corner
West Rasen
Market Rasen
Ludford
Great Tows
Kelstern
Normanby-by-Spital
Middle Rasen
Market Rasen
North Willingham
South Elkington
Ermine Street
Owmby-by-Spital
Toft next Newton
Newton by Toft
Welton le Wold
Newtoft
Linwood
Little London
Sixhills
Burgh on Bain
Louth
Buslingthorpe
Legsby
Gayton le Wold
Saxby
East Firsby
Spridlington
Faldingworth
Hainton
Hallington
LINCOLNSHIRE
Cold Hanworth
Bleasby
Biscathorpe
Withcall
Raithby
Maltby
Hackthorn
Lissington
East Torrington
South Willingham
Donington on Bain
Dovendale
Tathwell
Friesthorpe
Bleasby Moor
Snarford
Wickenby
West Torrington
Benniworth
THE WOLDS
Holton cum Beckering
East Barkwith
Stenigot
Haugham
Welton
Beckering
West Barkwith
Market Stainton
Cawkwell
Cadwell Park
Snelland
Asterby
Dunholme
Fulnetby
Rand
Panton
Sotby
Maidenwell
Goulceby
Scamblesby
Grange de Lings
Stainton by Langworth
Bullington
Wragby
Ranby
Farforth
Strubby
Great Sturton
Scothern
Hatton
Oxcombe
Worlaby
Newball
Langton by Wragby
Flint Hill
Sudbrooke
Langworth
Low Langton
Nettleham
Kingthorpe
Hemingby
Belchford
Little London
Tetford
Barlings
Apley
Baumber
Cherry Willingham
Low Barlings
Minting
Farthorpe
Salmonby
Reepham
Stainfield
Midthorpe
Fulletby
LINCOLN
Fiskerton
Gautby
Wispington
West Ashby
Ashby Puerorum
Waddingworth
Edlington
Washingborough
Low Toynton
Common Square
Abbey
Greetham
New Boultham
Canwick
Branston Booths
Branston Fen
Bardney
Thimbleby
Langton
High Toynton
Scrafield
Heighington
Tupholme
Horsington
Horncastle
Winceby
Bracebridge Heath
Bucknall
Old Woodhall
Thornton
Mareham on the Hill
Hameringham
Southrey
Martin
Dalderby
Stixwould
Potterhanworth
Claxby
Pluckacre
Hareby
0 2 4 6 miles
0 2 4 6 8 10 km

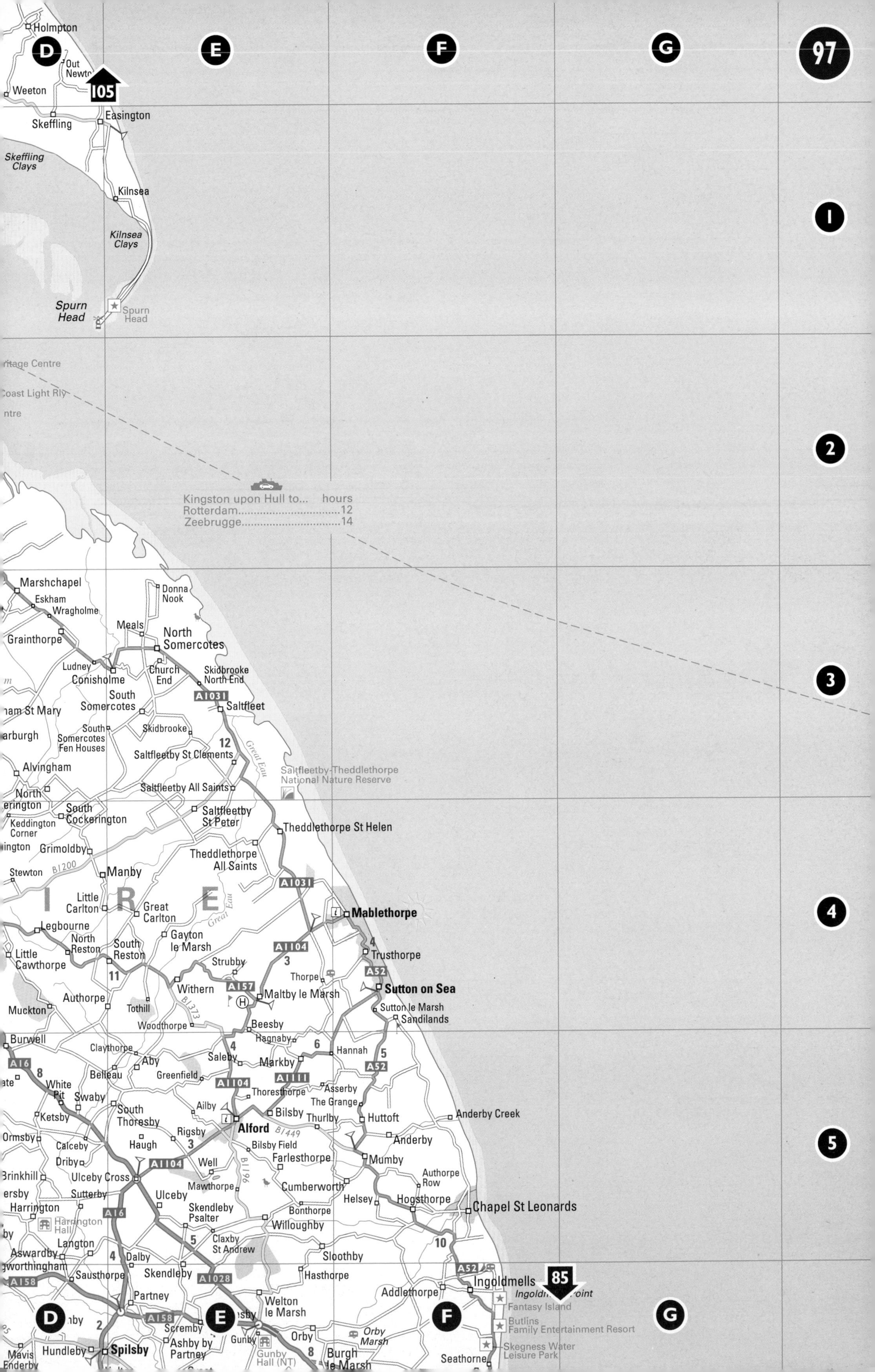

Holmpton

Out Newton

Weeton

105

Easington

Skeffling

Skeffling Clays

Kilnsea

Kilnsea Clays

Spurn Head

★ Spurn Head

I

ritage Centre

Coast Light Rly

ntre

2

🚗 Kingston upon Hull to... hours
Rotterdam.................................12
Zeebrugge..............................14

Marshchapel

Eskham

Wragholme

Donna Nook

Meals

North Somercotes

Grainthorpe

Ludney

Conisholme

Church End

Skidbrooke North End

3

am St Mary

South Somercotes

A1031

Saltfleet

arburgh

South Somercotes Fen Houses

Skidbrooke

12

Saltfleetby St Clements

Alvingham

Great Eau

North erington

South Cockerington

Saltfleetby All Saints

Saltfleetby-Theddlethorpe National Nature Reserve

Keddington Corner

Saltfleetby St Peter

Theddlethorpe St Helen

ington

Grimoldby

Stewton B1200

Manby

Theddlethorpe All Saints

I R E E

A1031

4

Little Carlton

Great Carlton

Great Eau

Legbourne

Gayton le Marsh

ℹ **Mablethorpe**

North Reston

South Reston

Strubby

A1104

A52

Little Cawthorpe

11

Authorpe

Tothill

Withern

A157

Thorpe

3

4

Trusthorpe

Maltby le Marsh

Sutton on Sea

Muckton

Ⓗ

Woodthorpe

Beesby

Sutton le Marsh

Sandilands

Burwell

Claythorpe

Hagnaby

6

Hannah

A16

8

Aby

Saleby

Markby

5

A52

White Pit

Belleau

Greenfield

A1104

A1111

Asserby

Swaby

Thoresthorpe

The Grange

Huttoft

Anderby Creek

Ketsby

South Thoresby

Ailby

Bilsby

Thurlby

Ormsby

Rigsby

ℹ **Alford**

B1449

Anderby

Calceby

Haugh

3

Well

Bilsby Field

Mumby

Authorpe Row

Driby

A1104

Mawthorpe

Farlesthorpe

Cumberworth

Helsey

Hogsthorpe

Chapel St Leonards

Brinkhill

Ulceby Cross

Ulceby

Skendleby Psalter

Bonthorpe

ersby

Harrington

A16

Claxby St Andrew

Willoughby

Langton

5

Sloothby

10

Aswardby

4

Dalby

Skendleby

A1028

Hasthorpe

A52

Ingoldmells

85

Ingold Point

worthingham

A158

Sausthorpe

Partney

Welton le Marsh

Addlethorpe

Fantasy Island

Butlins Family Entertainment Resort

by

2

A158

Scremby

Spilsby

Ashby by Partney

Gunby

Orby

Orby Marsh

Skegness Water Leisure Park

Mavis Enderby

Hundleby

Gunby Hall (NT)

8

Burgh le Marsh

Seathorne

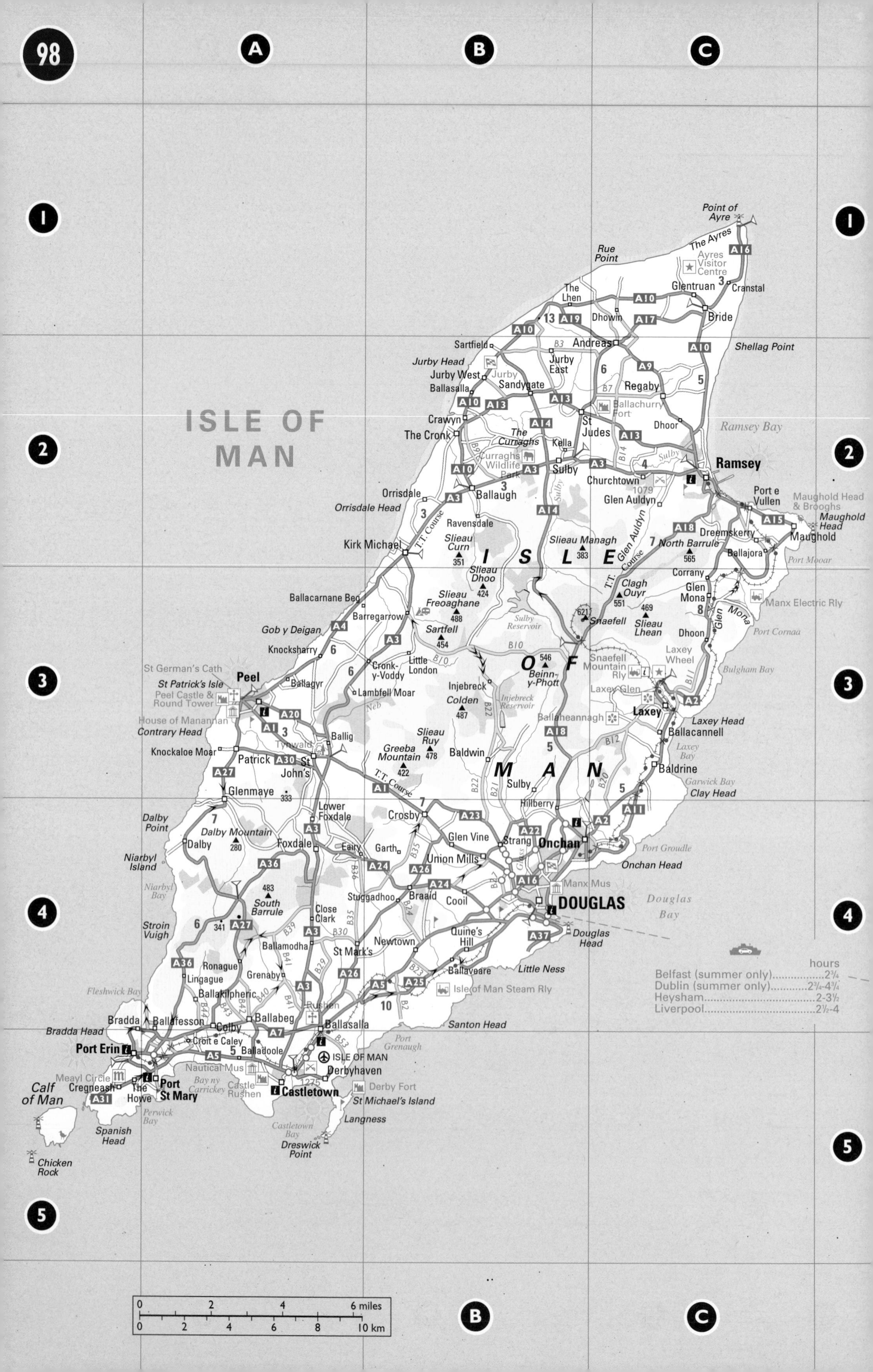
98
A
B
C
1
2
3
4
5
ISLE OF MAN
Point of Ayre
The Ayres
Ayres Visitor Centre
Rue Point
The Lhen
Glentruan
Cranstal
Dhowin
Bride
Andreas
Sartfield
Jurby Head
Jurby West
Jurby
Jurby East
Sandygate
Ballasalla
Shellag Point
Regaby
Ballachurry Fort
Crawyn
The Cronk
The Curraghs
Kella
St Judes
Dhoor
Ramsey Bay
Curraghs Wildlife Park
Sulby
Churchtown
Ramsey
Orrisdale
Orrisdale Head
Ballaugh
Glen Auldyn
Port e Vullen
Maughold Head & Brooghs
Maughold Head
Maughold
Ravensdale
Slieau Curn
351
Kirk Michael
T.T. Course
Slieau Managh
383
North Barrule
565
Dreemskerry
Ballajora
Port Mooar
Corrany
Slieau Dhoo
424
ISLE OF MAN
Glen Mona
Clagh Ouyr
551
469
Slieau Lhean
Ballacarnane Beg
Slieau Freoaghane
488
Barregarrow
Sulby Reservoir
621
Snaefell
Manx Electric Rly
Gob y Deigan
Sartfell
454
Dhoon
Port Cornaa
Knocksharry
Little London
546
Beinn-y-Phott
Laxey Wheel
St German's Cath
Peel
St Patrick's Isle
Peel Castle & Round Tower
Ballagyr
Cronk-y-Voddy
Snaefell Mountain Rly
Bulgham Bay
Lambfell Moar
Injebreck
Colden
487
Injebreck Reservoir
Laxey Glen
Laxey
House of Manannan
Contrary Head
Ballig
Ballaheannagh
Laxey Head
Ballacannell
Tynwald
Slieau Ruy
478
Greeba Mountain
422
Knockaloe Moar
Patrick
St John's
Baldwin
Laxey Bay
Baldrine
Sulby
Garwick Bay
Clay Head
Glenmaye
333
Lower Foxdale
Crosby
Hillberry
Dalby Point
Dalby Mountain
280
Dalby
Foxdale
Fairy
Garth
Glen Vine
Strang
Onchan
Port Groudle
Niarbyl Island
Union Mills
Onchan Head
Niarbyl Bay
483
South Barrule
Stuggadhoo
Braaid
Cooil
Manx Mus
DOUGLAS
Douglas Bay
Stroin Vuigh
341
Close Clark
Quine's Hill
Douglas Head
Ballamodha
St Mark's
Newtown
Ronague
Lingague
Grenaby
Ballaveare
Little Ness
Fleshwick Bay
Ballakilpheric
Rushen
Isle of Man Steam Rly
Bradda
Ballafesson
Ballabeg
Colby
Ballasalla
Santon Head
Bradda Head
Croit e Caley
Balladoole
Port Grenaugh
Port Erin
Nautical Mus
ISLE OF MAN
Derbyhaven
Calf of Man
Meayl Circle
Cregneash
The Howe
Port St Mary
Bay ny Carrickey
Castle Rushen
Castletown
Derby Fort
St Michael's Island
Perwick Bay
Spanish Head
Castletown Bay
Langness
Dreswick Point
Chicken Rock
hours
Belfast (summer only)........2¾
Dublin (summer only)........2¼-4¾
Heysham........2-3½
Liverpool........2½-4
0 2 4 6 miles
0 2 4 6 8 10 km

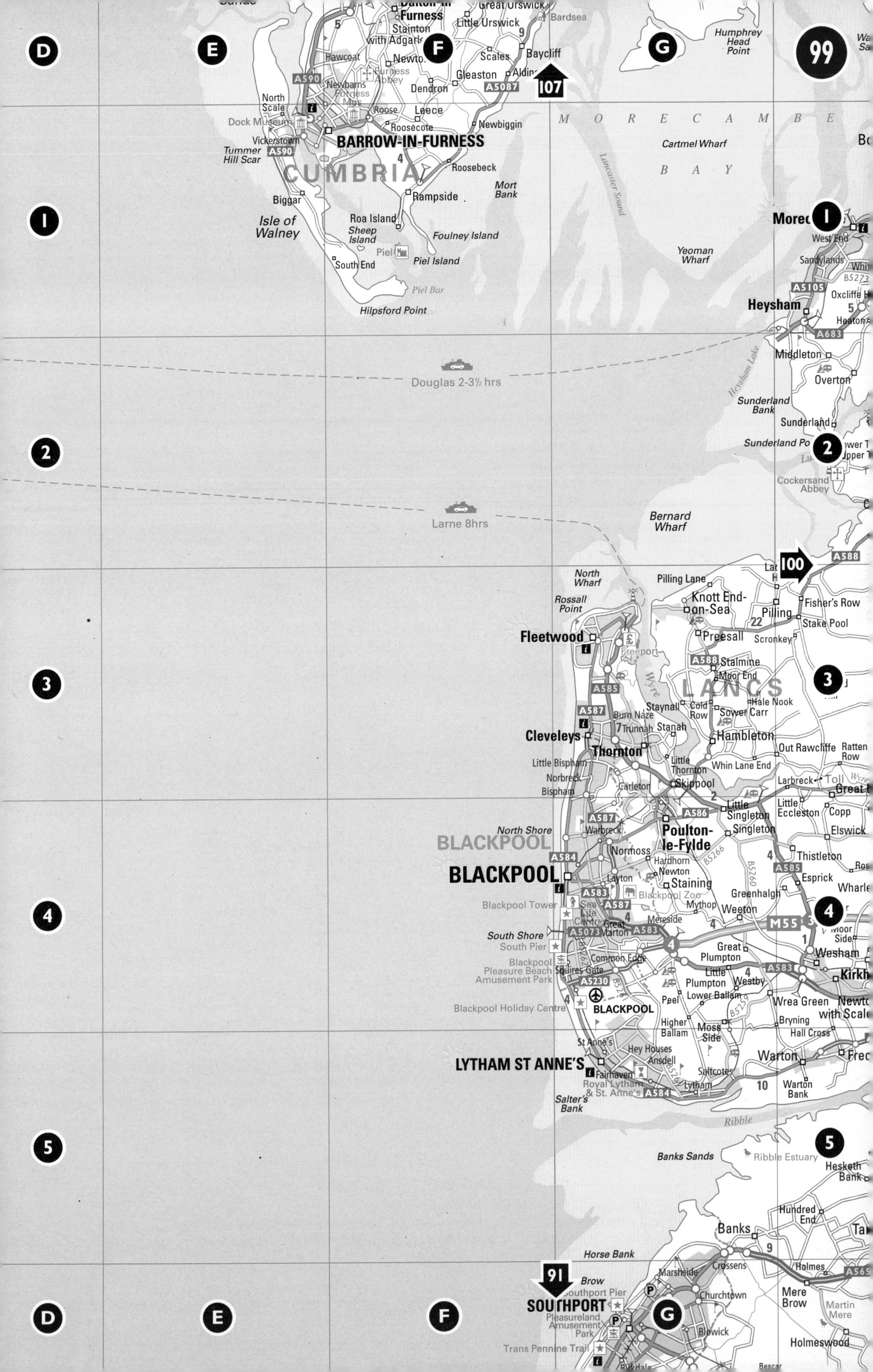

Dalton-in-**Furness**

Great Urswick
Little Urswick   9
Bardsea

Hawcoat
Stainton
with Adgarley

Newto.
Scales
Baycliff

Furness
Abbey
Gleaston
Aldin
Dendron
107

North
Scale
Roose
Leece
Newbiggin

Dock Museum
Roosecote

BARROW-IN-FURNESS

Newbarns
Furness
Mus

CUMBRIA   4

Tummer
Hill Scar
A590

Vickerstown
Rampside
Mort
Bank

M O R E C A M B E

Cartmel Wharf

B A Y

Biggar

Roa Island
Sheep
Island

Roosebeck

Yeoman
Wharf

*Isle of
Walney*

Foulney Island

Piel
South End
Piel Island

*Sunderland
Bank*

Morec
West End
Sandylands
Whi
Oxcliffe
5
Heato

Heysham

A5105
B5273

Middleton

Overton

Piel Bar

Hilpsford Point

Sunderland Po
wer T
pper

Cockersand
Abbey

Douglas 2-3½ hrs

Heysham Lake

*Bernard
Wharf*

Larne 8hrs

North
Wharf

Pilling Lane
La
100
A588

*Rossall
Point*

Knott End-
on-Sea
Pilling
Fisher's Row

Preesall
22
Stake
Pool
Scronkey

Fleetwood
Freeport
A588   Stalmine
Moor End

LANCS

3

Staynall
Cold
Row
Hale Nook
Sower Carr

Burn Naze
7 Trunnah Stanah
Hambleton

Cleveleys
Little
Thornton
Whin Lane End
Out Rawcliffe
Ratten
Row

Thornton

Little Bispham
Skippool
Larbreck
Toll
Great

Norbreck
Carleton
2
Little
Singleton
Little
Eccleston
Copp

Bispham
A586
Singleton
Elswick

BLACKPOOL
A587
Warbreck

**Poulton-
le-Fylde**

North Shore
Normoss

BLACKPOOL
A584
Hardhorn
Newton
Thistleton

Layton
Staining
Esprick
Wharle

Blackpool Tower
Se
Life
A583
Blackpool Zoo
Mythop
Greenhalgh
A585

South Shore
South Pier
A587
Mereside
Weeton
M55

Blackpool
Pleasure Beach
Amusement Park
Squires Gate
A5073
Great
Marton
A583
4
Moor
Side

Common Edge
Great
Plumpton
Wesham

Blackpool Holiday Centre
A5230
Peel
Little
Plumpton
Lower Ballam
Westby
Wrea Green
Kirkh
Newto
with Scale

BLACKPOOL
Higher
Ballam
Moss
Side
Bryning
Hall Cross

LYTHAM ST ANNE'S
St Anne's
Hey Houses
Ansdell
Warton
Fre

Fairhaven
Lytham
Warton
Bank
Royal Lytham
& St. Annes
A584
10

Salter's
Bank

Ribble

Banks Sands
Ribble Estuary
Hesketh
Bank

Horse Bank

Hundred
End
Ta

Banks

91
Brow
Southport Pier
Crossens
Holmes
A56

SOUTHPORT
Pleasureland
Amusement
Park
Marshside
Churchtown
Mere
Brow

Blowick
Holmeswood
Martin
Mere

Trans Pennine Trail

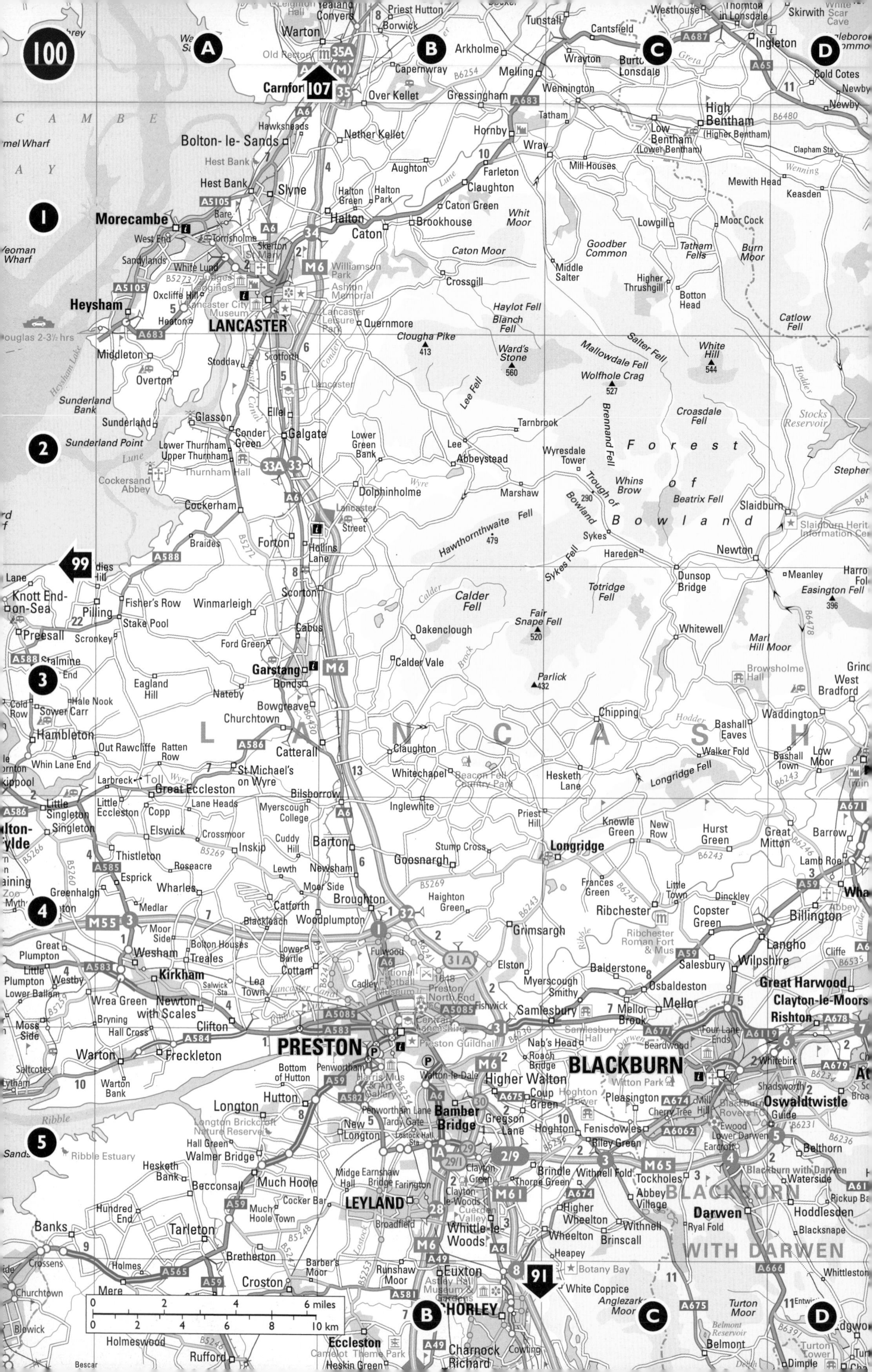

100
A
B
C
D
Warton
Priest Hutton
Borwick
Yealand Conyers
Old Rectory
35A
Carnforth
107
35
Capernwray
Over Kellet
Arkholme
Melling
Gressingham
Tunstall
Cantsfield
Wrayton
Burton in Lonsdale
Westhouse
Thornton in Lonsdale
Ingleton
Skirwith
Cold Cotes
Newby
Wennington
Tatham
High Bentham
(Higher Bentham)
Low Bentham
(Lower Bentham)
Clapham Sta
Hornby
Wray
Farleton
Claughton
Mill Houses
Caton Green
Caton
Brookhouse
Halton
Halton Green
Halton Park
Aughton
Nether Kellet
Hawksheads
Bolton- le- Sands
Hest Bank
Slyne
Morecambe
Bare
Torrisholme
West End
Skerton
Sandylands
White Lund
Heysham
Oxcliffe Hill
Heaton
LANCASTER
Lancaster City Museum
Williamson Park
Ashton Memorial
Lancaster Leisure Park
Quernmore
Crossgill
Caton Moor
Whit Moor
Goodber Common
Middle Salter
Lowgill
Tatham Fells
Burn Moor
Moor Cock
Mewith Head
Keasden
Higher Thrushgill
Botton Head
Haylot Fell
Blanch Fell
Clougha Pike
413
Ward's Stone
560
Mallowdale Fell
Salter Fell
Wolfhole Crag
527
White Hill
544
Catlow Fell
Middleton
Overton
Stodday
Scotforth
Sunderland Bank
Sunderland
Sunderland Point
Glasson
Conder Green
Lower Thurnham
Upper Thurnham
Thurnham Hall
Cockersand Abbey
Ellel
Galgate
33A
33
Lower Green Bank
Lee Fell
Tarnbrook
Lee
Abbeystead
Wyresdale Tower
Brennand Fell
Forest of Bowland
Croasdale Fell
Stocks Reservoir
Dolphinholme
Marshaw
Trough of Bowland
290
Whins Brow
Beatrix Fell
Slaidburn
Cockerham
Forton
Street
Hollins Lane
Braides
Hawthornthwaite Fell
479
Sykes
Hareden
Newton
Dunsop Bridge
Meanley
Easington Fell
396
99
Knott End-on-Sea
Pilling
Fisher's Row
Stake Pool
Winmarleigh
Scorton
Preesall
Scronkey
Cabus
Calder Fell
Sykes Fell
Totridge Fell
Fair Snape Fell
520
Oakenclough
Whitewell
Marl Hill Moor
Stalmine
Ford Green
Garstang
Bonds
Calder Vale
Parlick
432
Browsholme Hall
West Bradford
Eagland Hill
Nateby
Hale Nook
Sower Carr
Bowgreave
Churchtown
Chipping
Waddington
Bashall Eaves
Hambleton
Out Rawcliffe
Ratten Row
Catterall
Claughton
Walker Fold
Bashall Town
Low Moor
Whin Lane End
St Michael's on Wyre
Whitechapel
Beacon Fell Country Park
Hesketh Lane
Longridge Fell
Larbreck
Great Eccleston
Bilsborrow
Little Singleton
Singleton
Little Eccleston
Copp
Lane Heads
Myerscough College
Inglewhite
Priest Hill
Knowle Green
New Row
Hurst Green
Great Mitton
Barrow
Elswick
Crossmoor
Inskip
Cuddy Hill
Barton
Stump Cross
Longridge
Lamb Roe
Thistleton
Roseacre
Lewth
Newsham
Goosnargh
Esprick
Wharles
Moor Side
Frances Green
Little Town
Dinckley
Greenhalgh
Medlar
Catforth
Broughton
Haighton Green
Ribchester
Copster Green
Billington
Blackleach
Woodplumpton
Grimsargh
Ribchester Roman Fort & Mus
Langho
Moor Side
Bolton Houses
Great Plumpton
Wesham
Treales
Lower Bartle
Cottam
Fulwood
Elston
Balderstone
Salesbury
Wilpshire
Clitheroe
Little Plumpton
Westby
Kirkham
Salwick Sta
Lea Town
Cadley
National Football Museum
Preston North End FC
Myerscough Smithy
Osbaldeston
Great Harwood
Lower Ballam
Wrea Green
Newton with Scales
Mellor
Mellor Brook
Samlesbury
Clayton-le-Moors
Bryning
Hall Cross
Moss Side
Clifton
Fishwick
Rishton
Samlesbury Hall
Four Lane Ends
Warton
Freckleton
PRESTON
Preston Guildhall
Nab's Head
Roach Bridge
BLACKBURN
Beardwood
Whitebirk
Saltcotes
Warton Bank
Bottom of Hutton
Penwortham
Harris Mus & Art Gallery
Walton-le-Dale
Higher Walton
Witton Park
Shadsworth
Hutton
Coup Green
Hoghton Tower
Pleasington
Cherry Tree
Mill Hill
Blackburn Rovers FC
Oswaldtwistle
Guide
Longton
Longton Brickcroft Nature Reserve
New Longton
Penwortham Lane
Tardy Gate
Bamber Bridge
Gregson Lane
Hoghton
Feniscowles
Ewood
Lower Darwen
Earcroft
Belthorn
Hall Green
Walmer Bridge
Ribble Estuary
Lostock Hall Sta
Riley Green
Hesketh Bank
Much Hoole
Midge Hall
Earnshaw Bridge
Farington
Clayton Green
Thorpe Green
Brindle
Withnell Fold
Tockholes
Blackburn with Darwen
Waterside
Becconsall
Clayton-le-Woods
Higher Wheelton
Abbey Village
BLACKBURN WITH DARWEN
Pickup Bank
Hundred End
Much Hoole Town
Cocker Bar
LEYLAND
Cuerden Valley
Darwen
Hoddlesden
Broadfield
Whittle-le-Woods
Withnell
Ryal Fold
Banks
Tarleton
Wheelton
Brinscall
Blacksnape
Heapey
Crossens
Holmes
Bretherton
Barber's Moor
Botany Bay
Whittlestone
Churchtown
Mere
Croston
Runshaw Moor
Euxton
Astley Hall Museum & Gardens
91
White Coppice
Anglezarke Moor
Turton Moor
Entwistle
Birkdale
CHORLEY
Belmont Reservoir
Holmeswood
Eccleston
Camelot Theme Park
Charnock Richard
Cowling
Belmont
Turton Tower
Dimple
Rufford
Heskin Green
Bescar
0 2 4 6 miles
0 2 4 6 8 10 km
M6
M55
M61
M65
A6
A65
A683
A687
A588
A586
A585
A583
A584
A5105
A5085
A59
A582
A581
A565
A49
A675
A674
A677
A678
A679
A666
A6062
A6119
A671
A671
B6254
B6480
B6478
B6243
B6245
B6269
B5269
B5266
B5260
B5259
B5248
B5247
B5253
B5246
B6430
B5272
B5273
B6241
B6242
B6230
B6258
B6256
B6231
B6236
B6391
B6535
B6246
M
Lune
Wyre
Wenning
Greta
Hodder
Ribble
Calder
Darwen
Brock
Conder
Lostock
Lancaster Canal
Douglas 2-3½ hrs
Heysham Lake
MORECAMBE BAY
LANCASHIRE

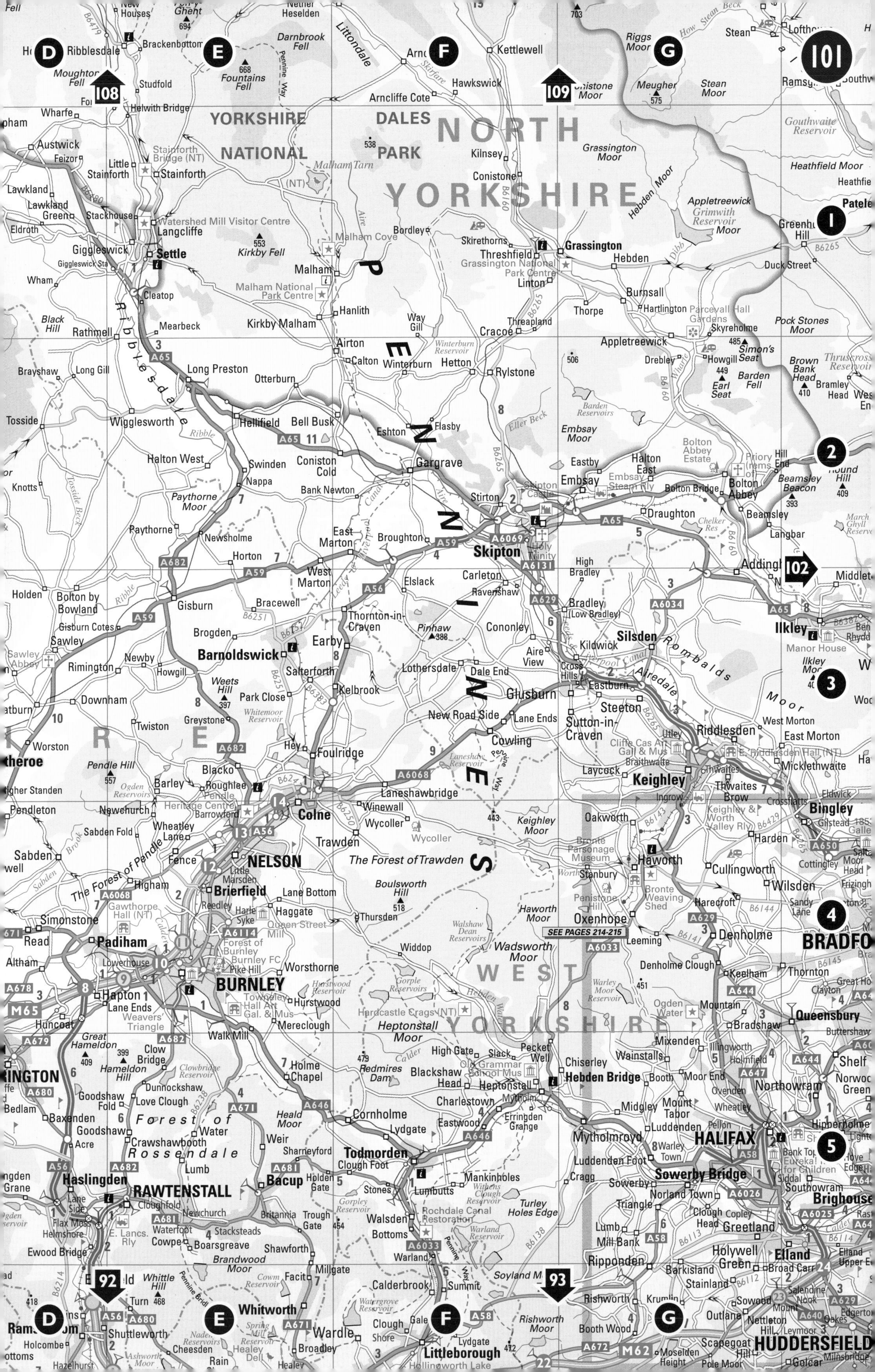
101
108
109
102
92
93
D
E
F
G
1
2
3
4
5
YORKSHIRE DALES NATIONAL PARK
NORTH YORKSHIRE
PENNINES
WEST YORKSHIRE
SEE PAGES 214-215
Ribblesdale
Moughton Fell
Brackenbottom
Studfold
Horton in Ribblesdale
Helwith Bridge
Wharfe
Austwick
Feizor
Little Stainforth
Stainforth
Stainforth Bridge (NT)
Lawkland
Lawkland Green
Stackhouse
Eldroth
Watershed Mill Visitor Centre
Langcliffe
Giggleswick
Settle
Wham
Cleatop
Black Hill
Rathmell
Mearbeck
Long Preston
Brayshaw
Long Gill
Tosside
Wigglesworth
Hellifield
Halton West
Knotts
Paythorne Moor
Paythorne
Newsholme
Horton
Gisburn
Holden
Bolton by Bowland
Gisburn Cotes
Sawley
Sawley Abbey
Rimington
Newsby
Howgill
Downham
Twiston
Worston
Pendle Hill
Pendleton
Sabden Fold
Sabden
Higham
Simonstone
Read
Padiham
Altham
Hapton
Huncoat
Great Hameldon
Hameldon Hill
Clow Bridge
Dunnockshaw
Goodshaw Fold
Love Clough
Baxenden
Goodshaw
Acre
Crawshawbooth
Forest of Rossendale
Haslingden
RAWTENSTALL
Cloughfold
Newchurch
Waterfoot
Cowpe
Stacksteads
Boarsgreave
Brandwood Moor
Helmshore
Ewood Bridge
Lumb
Bacup
Britannia
Weir
Sharneyford
Shawforth
Facit
Whitworth
Millgate
Wardle
Broadley
Healey Dell
Shuttleworth
Cheesden
Turn
Whittle Hill
Edenfield
Ramsbottom
Holcombe
Fountains Fell
Darnbrook Fell
Littondale
Pennine Way
Arncliffe
Arncliffe Cote
Kettlewell
Hawkswick
Skirfare
Kilnsey
Conistone
Malham Tarn
Malham Cove
Malham
Malham National Park Centre
Kirkby Fell
Kirkby Malham
Hanlith
Airton
Calton
Winterburn
Winterburn Reservoir
Hetton
Otterburn
Bell Busk
Eshton
Flasby
Gargrave
Coniston Cold
Swinden
Nappa
Bank Newton
East Marton
West Marton
Broughton
Bracewell
Brogden
Barnoldswick
Salterforth
Earby
Thornton-in-Craven
Elslack
Kelbrook
Weets Hill
Park Close
Whitemoor Reservoir
Greystone
Foulridge
Blacko
Roughlee
Barley
Newchurch
Barrowford
Colne
NELSON
Brierfield
Reedley
Burnley
Worsthorne
Hurstwood
Mereclough
Walk Mill
Towneley Hall Art Gall & Mus
Weavers' Triangle
Holme Chapel
Cornholme
Lydgate
Todmorden
Walsden
Calderbrook
Summit
Littleborough
Clough Foot
Stones
Mankinholes
Lumbutts
Laneshawbridge
Winewall
Wycoller
Trawden
The Forest of Trawden
Boulsworth Hill
Thursden
Widdop
Gorple Reservoirs
Hardcastle Crags (NT)
Heptonstall Moor
Heptonstall
Blackshaw Head
Charlestown
Eastwood
Hebden Bridge
Mytholmroyd
Pecket Well
Chiserley
Wadsworth Moor
Walshaw Dean Reservoirs
Haworth Moor
Keighley Moor
Cowling
Lane Ends
Glusburn
Sutton-in-Craven
New Road Side
Cononley
Carleton
Lothersdale
Dale End
Pinhaw
Skipton
Stirton
Rylstone
Cracoe
Threapland
Linton
Threshfield
Grassington
Hebden
Burnsall
Thorpe
Hartlington
Appletreewick
Skyreholme
Parcevall Hall Gardens
Simon's Seat
Howgill
Drebley
Barden Fell
Earl Seat
Embsay
Embsay Moor
Eastby
Halton East
Bolton Abbey
Bolton Bridge
Beamsley
Beamsley Beacon
Draughton
Langbar
Addingham
Ilkley
Manor House
Ilkley Moor
Rombalds Moor
Silsden
Kildwick
Cross Hills
Eastburn
Steeton
Airedale
Riddlesden
East Morton
West Morton
Keighley
Utley
Laycock
Oakworth
Haworth
Stanbury
Bronte Parsonage Museum
Oxenhope
Leeming
Cullingworth
Wilsden
Harecroft
Denholme
Denholme Clough
Bingley
Harden
Cottingley
BRADFORD
Thornton
Queensbury
Mixenden
Halifax
Sowerby Bridge
Luddenden
Luddenden Foot
Cragg
Norland Town
Triangle
Ripponden
Greetland
Elland
Brighouse
Holywell Green
Stainland
Barkisland
Rishworth
Rishworth Moor
Krumlin
Outlane
HUDDERSFIELD
Scapegoat Hill
Booth Wood
Soyland Moor
Turley Holes Edge
Riggs Moor
Meugher
Stean Moor
Stean
Grassington Moor
Hebden Moor
Appletreewick Moor
Grimwith Reservoir
Greenhow Hill
Duck Street
Pock Stones Moor
Brown Bank Head
Bramley Head
Heathfield Moor
Gouthwaite Reservoir
Ramsgill
Lofthouse
Pateley Bridge
M65
M62
A65
A59
A56
A682
A6068
A629
A6131
A6069
A6034
A646
A671
A681
A680
A6033
A58
A644
A647
A629
A6026
A672

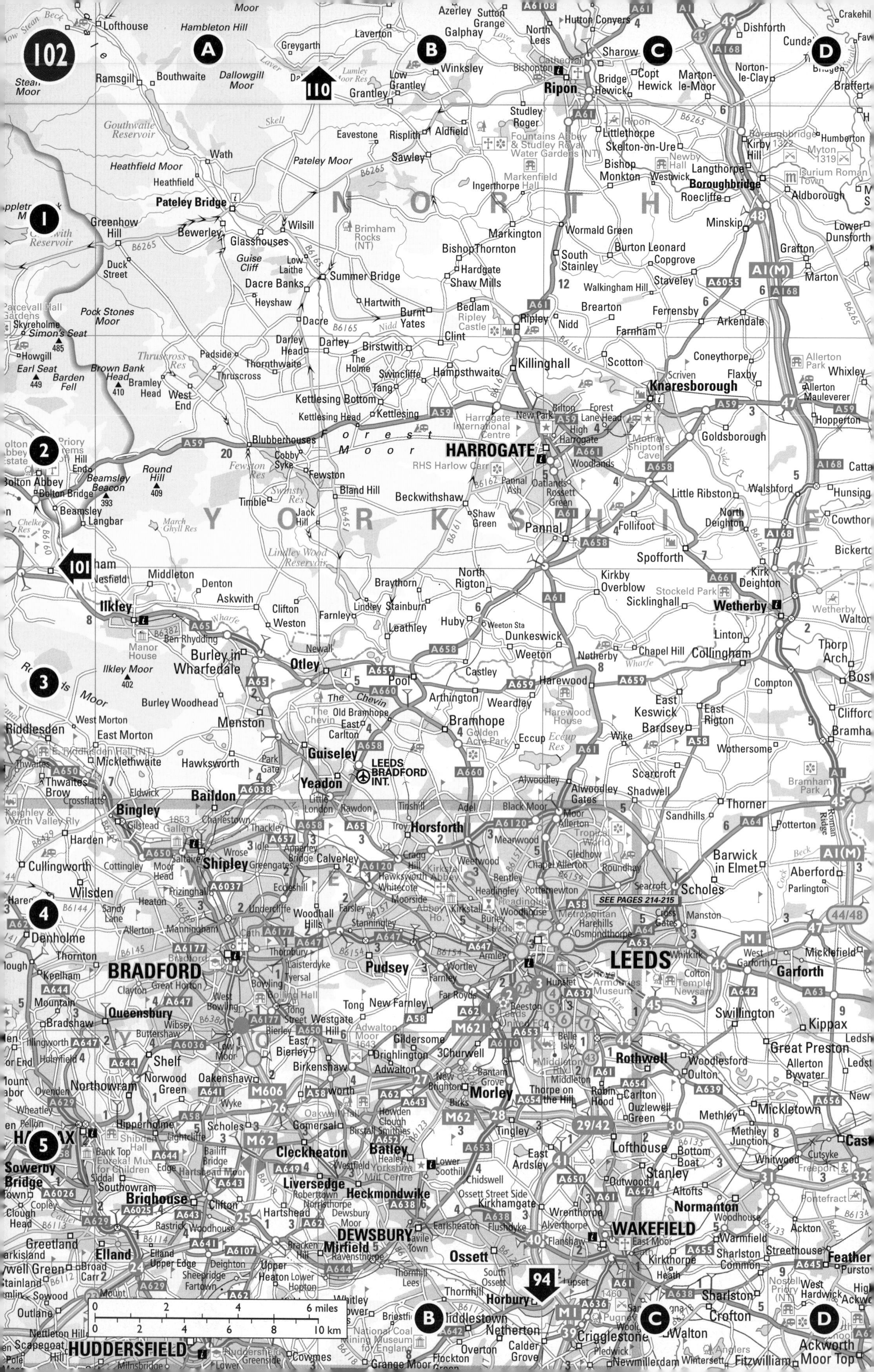
A
B
C
D
1
2
3
4
5
110
101
94
NORTH YORKSHIRE
WEST YORKSHIRE
SEE PAGES 214-215
Lofthouse
Hambleton Hill
Ramsgill
Bouthwaite
Dallowgill Moor
Greygarth
Laverton
Azerley
Sutton Grange
Galphay
Winksley
Low Grantley
Grantley
North Lees
Hutton Conyers
Sharow
Copt Hewick
Bridge Hewick
Ripon
Bishopton
Cathedral
Dishforth
Cundall
Norton-le-Clay
Marton-le-Moor
Stean Moor
Gouthwaite Reservoir
Eavestone
Risplith
Aldfield
Studley Roger
Fountains Abbey & Studley Royal Water Gardens (NT)
Littlethorpe
Skelton-on-Ure
Newby Hall
Kirby Hill
Humberton
Myton
Boroughbridge
Langthorpe
Aldborough
Roecliffe
Wath
Heathfield Moor
Heathfield
Pateley Moor
Sawley
Markenfield Hall
Ingerthorpe
Bishop Monkton
Westwick
Pateley Bridge
Greenhow Hill
Bewerley
Wilsill
Glasshouses
Brimham Rocks (NT)
Markington
Wormald Green
Minskip
Lower Dunsforth
Bishop Thornton
South Stainley
Burton Leonard
Copgrove
Grafton
Duck Street
Guise Cliff
Low Laithe
Summer Bridge
Dacre Banks
Hardgate
Shaw Mills
Walkingham Hill
Staveley
Marton
Heyshaw
Hartwith
Burnt Yates
Bedlam
Ripley Castle
Ripley
Brearton
Ferrensby
Arkendale
Pock Stones Moor
Skyreholme
Simon's Seat
Howgill
Earl Seat
Barden Fell
Brown Bank Head
Dacre
Darley Head
Darley
Birstwith
Clint
Nidd
Farnham
Coneythorpe
Allerton Park
Whixley
Padside
Thruscross Res
Thruscross
Thornthwaite
The Holme
Swincliffe
Tang
Hampsthwaite
Killinghall
Scotton
Scriven
Flaxby
Knaresborough
Allerton Mauleverer
Bramley Head
West End
Kettlesing Bottom
Kettlesing Head
Kettlesing
Harrogate International Centre
New Park
Bilton
Forest Lane Head
High Harrogate
Goldsborough
Hopperton
Priory Rems
Hill End
Bolton Abbey
Bolton Bridge
Beamsley Beacon
Beamsley
Blubberhouses
Forest Moor
HARROGATE
RHS Harlow Carr
Woodlands
Mother Shipton's Cave
Round Hill
Cobby Syke
Fewston Res
Fewston
Bland Hill
Swinsty Res
Pannal Ash
Oatlands
Rossett Green
Beckwithshaw
Little Ribston
Walshford
Hunsingore
Langbar
Timble
Jack Hill
Shaw Green
March Ghyll Res
Pannal
Follifoot
North Deighton
Cowthorpe
Lindley Wood Reservoir
Spofforth
Bickerton
Middleton
Denton
Askwith
Braythorn
North Rigton
Kirkby Overblow
Kirk Deighton
Stockeld Park
Ilkley
Clifton
Weston
Farnley
Lindley
Stainburn
Huby
Weeton Sta
Sicklinghall
Wetherby
Walton
Ben Rhydding
Manor House
Burley in Wharfedale
Newall
Otley
Leathley
Dunkeswick
Weeton
Netherby
Chapel Hill
Linton
Collingham
Thorp Arch
Ilkley Moor
The Chevin
Pool
Castley
Arthington
Weardley
Harewood
Harewood House
Compton
Boston Spa
East Keswick
Bardsey
East Rigton
Clifford
Bramham
Burley Woodhead
West Morton
East Morton
Riddlesden
East Riddlesden Hall (NT)
Micklethwaite
Thwaites
Thwaites Brow
Menston
Hawksworth
Old Bramhope
East Carlton
Bramhope
Golden Acre Park
Eccup
Eccup Res
Wike
Wothersome
Guiseley
Park Gate
Yeadon
LEEDS BRADFORD INT.
Alwoodley
Alwoodley Gates
Scarcroft
Shadwell
Bramham Park
Eldwick
Crossflats
Bingley
Gilstead
Baildon
Charlestown
Little London
Rawdon
Tinshill
Adel
Black Moor
Moor Allerton
Sandhills
Thorner
Keighley & Worth Valley Rly
Harden
1853 Gallery
Saltaire
Thackley
Idle
Apperley Bridge
Calverley
Troy
Horsforth
Meanwood
Tropical World
Potterton
Roman Ridge
Cullingworth
Cottingley
Wrose
Moor Head
Shipley
Greengates
Cragg Hill
Hawksworth
Kirkstall
Weetwood
Chapel Allerton
Gledhow
Roundhay
Barwick in Elmet
Aberford
Parlington
Wilsden
Frizinghall
Eccleshill
Whitecote
Moorside
Kirkstall Abbey
Bentley
Headingley
Potternewton
Seacroft
Scholes
Heaton
Sandy Lane
Undercliffe
Farsley
Woodhall Hills
Stanningley
Abbey Ho.
Burley
Woodhouse
Metropolitan
Harehills
Osmondthorpe
Cross Gates
Manston
Denholme
Allerton
Manningham
Thornbury
Armley
Whitkirk
Thornton
Laisterdyke
Pudsey
Wortley
LEEDS
Colton
Micklefield
Keelham
BRADFORD
Great Horton
Clayton
Tyersal
Bowling
Farnley
Hunslet
Royal Armouries Museum
Temple Newsam
West Garforth
Garforth
Mountain
Queensbury
West Bowling
Tong
New Farnley
Far Royds
Beeston
Leeds United F.C.
Swillington
Kippax
Bradshaw
Buttershaw
Wibsey
Tong Street
Westgate Hill
Bierley
Adwalton Moor 1643
Gildersome
Belle Isle
Illingworth
Holmfield
Shelf
Low Moor
East Bierley
Drighlington
Churwell
Middleton Rly
Rothwell
Woodlesford
Oulton
Great Preston
Allerton Bywater
Ledsham
Northowram
Norwood Green
Oakenshaw
Birkenshaw
Adwalton
Bantam Grove
Middleton
Ovenden
Hunsworth
New Brighton
Birks
Morley
Thorpe on the Hill
Robin Hood
Carlton
Oulton
Wheatley
Wyke
Oakwell Hall
Howden Clough
Tingley
Oulzewell Green
Methley
Mickletown
Pellon
HALIFAX
Hipperholme
Scholes
Gomersal
Birstall Smithies
Lofthouse
Methley Junction
Bank Top
Lightcliffe
Shibden Hall
Bailiff Bridge
Cleckheaton
Batley
Healey
East Ardsley
Bottom Boat
Whitwood
Cutsyke
Castleford
Sowerby Bridge
Eureka! Museum for Children
Edge
Hartshead Moor
Westfield
Yorkshire Mill Centre
Lower Soothill
Stanley
Outwood
Freeport
Siddal
Southowram
Liversedge
Robertown
Chidswell
Altofts
Pontefract
Copley
Brighouse
Clifton
Norristhorpe
Heckmondwike
Ossett Street Side
Kirkhamgate
Wrenthorpe
Normanton
Clough Head
Rastrick
Woodhouse
Hartshead
Dewsbury Moor
Earlsheaton
Flushdyke
Alverthorpe
WAKEFIELD
Woodhouse
Ackton
Greetland
Elland
Upper Edge
Deighton
Mirfield
DEWSBURY
Ravensthorpe
Savile Town
Ossett
Flanshaw
East Moor
Warmfield
Sharlston Common
Streethouse
Featherstone
Stainland
Broad Carr
Sheepridge
Fartown
Upper Heaton
Lower Hopton
Thornhill Lees
South Ossett
Kirkthorpe
Heath
Nostell Priory (NT)
West Hardwick
Ackworth
Sowood
Outlane
Netherton Hill
Scapegoat Hill
HUDDERSFIELD
Whitley Lower
Briestfield
Thornhill
Horbury
Middlestown
National Coal Mining Museum for England
Netherton
Calder Grove
Overton
Flockton
Grange Moor
Crigglestone
Pugneys
Sharlston
Crofton
Walton
Newmillerdam
Wintersett
Fitzwilliam
Ackworth Moor Top
Cowmes
Milnsbridge
Lower Greenside
0 2 4 6 miles
0 2 4 6 8 10 km

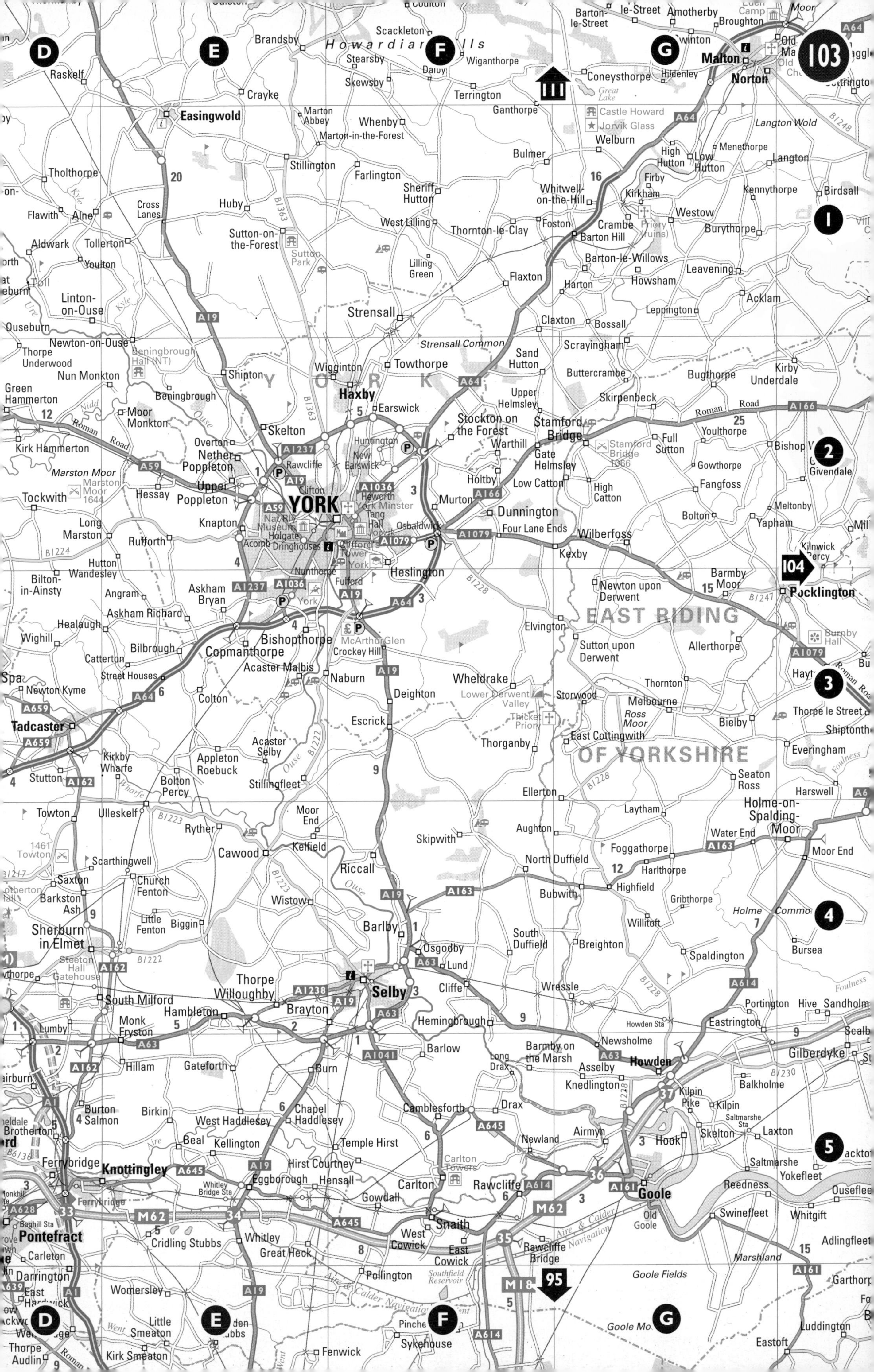

103
D
E
F
G
Brandsby
Howardian Hills
Scackleton
Stearsby
Skewsby
Dalby
Wiganthorpe
Terrington
Ganthorpe
Coneysthorpe
Castle Howard
Jorvik Glass
Welburn
Great Lake
Barton-le-Street
Amotherby
Broughton
Swinton
Hildenley
Malton
Norton
Old Malton
Langton Wold
Menethorpe
Langton
High Hutton
Low Hutton
Firby
Kirkham
Kennythorpe
Birdsall
Raskelf
Easingwold
Crayke
Marton Abbey
Whenby
Marton-in-the-Forest
Stillington
Farlington
Sheriff Hutton
Bulmer
Whitwell-on-the-Hill
Tholthorpe
Flawith
Alne
Cross Lanes
Huby
Sutton-on-the-Forest
Sutton Park
West Lilling
Lilling Green
Thornton-le-Clay
Foston
Crambe
Barton Hill
Priory (ruins)
Westow
Burythorpe
Aldwark
Tollerton
Youlton
Barton-le-Willows
Leavening
Flaxton
Harton
Howsham
Acklam
Linton-on-Ouse
Strensall
Claxton
Bossall
Leppington
Ouseburn
Newton-on-Ouse
Thorpe Underwood
Beningbrough Hall (NT)
Strensall Common
Sand Hutton
Scrayingham
Nun Monkton
Shipton
Wigginton
Towthorpe
Buttercrambe
Bugthorpe
Kirby Underdale
Green Hammerton
Beningbrough
YORK
Haxby
Upper Helmsley
Skirpenbeck
Moor Monkton
Earswick
Stockton on the Forest
Stamford Bridge
Roman Road
Kirk Hammerton
Skelton
Overton
Huntington
Warthill
Stamford Bridge 1066
Full Sutton
Youlthorpe
Bishop Wilton
Nether Poppleton
Rawcliffe
New Earswick
Gate Helmsley
Gowthorpe
Givendale
Marston Moor
Marston Moor 1644
Upper Poppleton
Holtby
Low Catton
High Catton
Fangfoss
Tockwith
Hessay
Clifton
Heworth
York Minster
Murton
Dunnington
Meltonby
Bolton
Yapham
Long Marston
Knapton
Nat Rly Museum
Holgate
Tang Hall
Jorvik
Osbaldwick
Four Lane Ends
Wilberfoss
Kexby
Kilnwick Percy
Rufforth
Acomb
Dringhouses
Clifford's Tower
104
Pocklington
Hutton Wandesley
York
Heslington
Barmby Moor
Bilton-in-Ainsty
Nunthorpe
Fulford
Newton upon Derwent
Angram
Askham Bryan
EAST RIDING OF YORKSHIRE
Askham Richard
Elvington
Burnby Hall
Healaugh
Bishopthorpe
McArthurGlen
Wighill
Bilbrough
Copmanthorpe
Crockey Hill
Sutton upon Derwent
Allerthorpe
Catterton
Acaster Malbis
Street Houses
Naburn
Wheldrake
Thornton
Hayton
Newton Kyme
Lower Derwent Valley
Storwood
Melbourne
Deighton
Thicket Priory
Ross Moor
Thorpe le Street
Tadcaster
Colton
Escrick
Bielby
Shiptonthorpe
East Cottingwith
Acaster Selby
Thorganby
Everingham
Kirkby Wharfe
Appleton Roebuck
Stutton
Bolton Percy
Stillingfleet
Seaton Ross
Ellerton
Harswell
Towton
Ulleskelf
Ryther
Moor End
Laytham
Holme-on-Spalding-Moor
Aughton
Water End
Towton 1461
Cawood
Kelfield
Skipwith
Foggathorpe
Scarthingwell
North Duffield
Harlthorpe
Saxton
Church Fenton
Riccall
Highfield
Barkston Ash
Wistow
Bubwith
Gribthorpe
Holme Common
Little Fenton
Biggin
Willitoft
Sherburn in Elmet
Barlby
South Duffield
Breighton
Bursea
Steeton Hall
Gatehouse
Osgodby
Spaldington
Lund
Thorpe Willoughby
Selby
Cliffe
Wressle
Foulness
South Milford
Portington
Hive
Sandholme
Hambleton
Brayton
Hemingbrough
Howden Sta
Eastrington
Monk Fryston
Barmby on the Marsh
Newsholme
Gilberdyke
Lumby
Barlow
Long Drax
Asselby
Howden
Hillam
Gateforth
Burn
Knedlington
Balkholme
Kilpin Pike
Kilpin
Burton Salmon
Birkin
Chapel Haddlesey
Camblesforth
Drax
Brotherton
West Haddlesey
Saltmarshe Sta
Beal
Kellington
Temple Hirst
Airmyn
Hook
Skelton
Laxton
Newland
Ferrybridge
Knottingley
Hirst Courtney
Carlton Towers
Saltmarshe
Yokefleet
Whitley Bridge Sta
Eggborough
Hensall
Carlton
Rawcliffe
Goole
Reedness
Ouseflee
Gowdall
Old Goole
Swinefleet
Whitgift
Baghill Sta
Pontefract
Cridling Stubbs
Whitley
Snaith
West Cowick
East Cowick
Aire & Calder Navigation
Rawcliffe Bridge
Adlingfleet
Carleton
Great Heck
Marshland
Darrington
Pollington
Southfield Reservoir
Goole Fields
Garthorpe
East Hardwick
Womersley
95
Little Smeaton
Pinchbeck
Goole Moor
Went
Luddington
Thorpe Audlin
Kirk Smeaton
Fenwick
Sykehouse
Eastoft
A19
A64
A1237
A59
A1036
A1079
A166
A659
A162
A63
A1041
A645
A1238
A163
A614
A161
A628
A639
A1
M62
M18
B1363
B1224
B1228
B1222
B1223
B1217
B1230
B1247
B1248
B1136

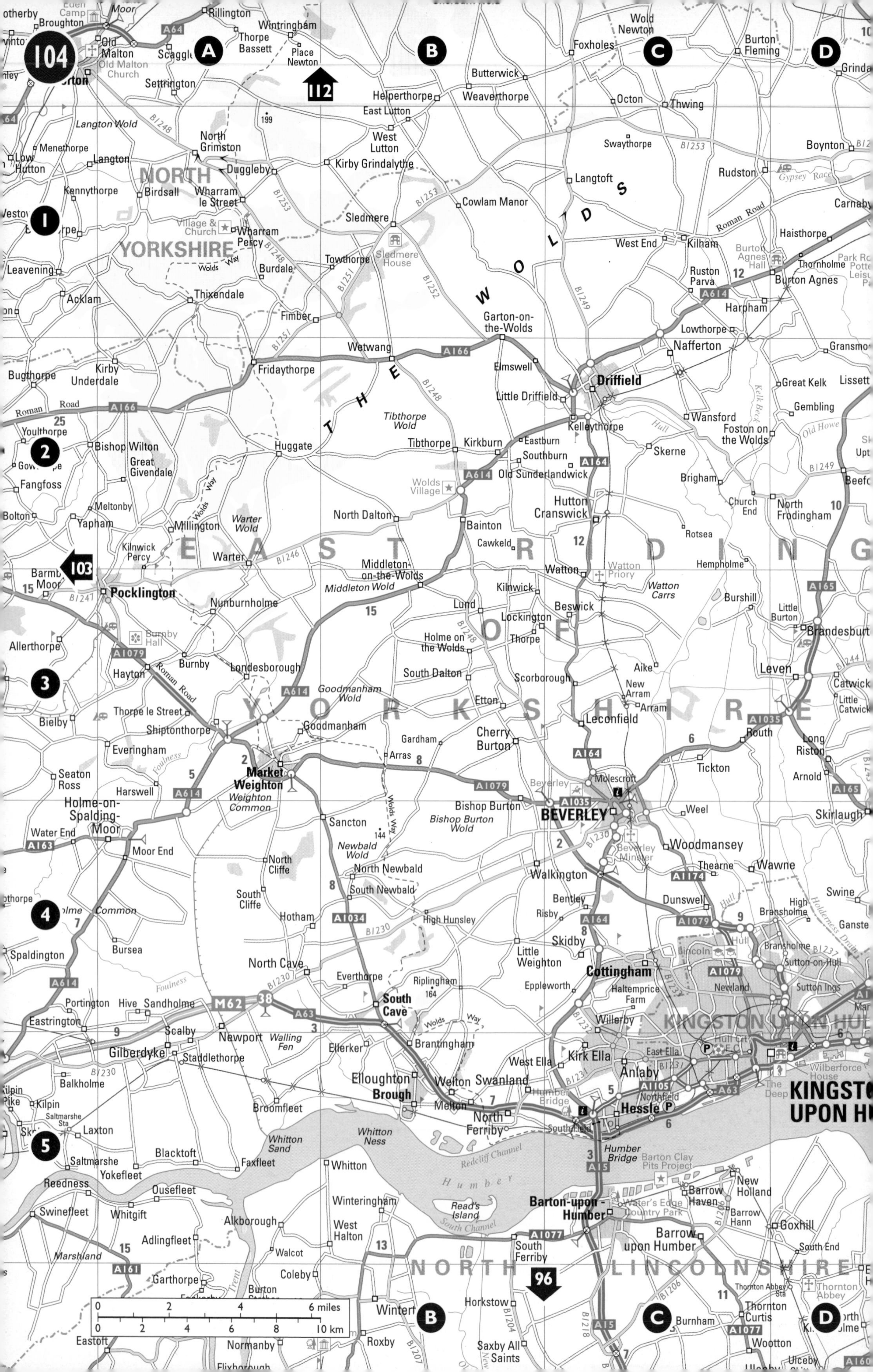

104
A
B
C
D
112
1
2
3
4
5
103
96
Broughton
Malton
Old Malton
Old Malton Church
Rillington
Scagglethorpe
Thorpe Bassett
Wintringham
Place Newton
Settrington
Langton Wold
B1248
Menethorpe
Langton
Low Hutton
North Grimston
Duggleby
Kennythorpe
Birdsall
NORTH
YORKSHIRE
Wharram le Street
Village & Church
Wharram Percy
Leavening
Burdale
Acklam
Thixendale
Wolds Way
199
Helperthorpe
East Lutton
West Lutton
Kirby Grindalythe
Butterwick
Weaverthorpe
Foxholes
Wold Newton
Burton Fleming
Grindale
Octon
Thwing
Swaythorpe
B1253
Boynton
Rudston
Gypsey Race
Langtoft
Cowlam Manor
Sledmere
Sledmere House
B1252
B1251
Towthorpe
Fimber
THE WOLDS
West End
Kilham
Roman Road
Haisthorpe
Carnaby
Burton Agnes Hall
Thornholme
Ruston Parva
Burton Agnes
A614
Harpham
Lowthorpe
Nafferton
Gransmoor
Garton-on-the-Wolds
B1249
Wetwang
A166
Fridaythorpe
Kirby Underdale
Bugthorpe
Elmswell
Driffield
Little Driffield
Great Kelk
Lissett
Gembling
Kelk Beck
Wansford
Foston on the Wolds
Old Howe
Kelleythorpe
Hull
Skerne
Eastburn
Southburn
A164
Old Sunderlandwick
Tibthorpe Wold
Tibthorpe
Kirkburn
Roman Road
Youlthorpe
Bishop Wilton
Great Givendale
Huggate
Fangfoss
Meltonby
Yapham
Bolton
Millington
Warter Wold
Wolds Village
North Dalton
Bainton
Cawkeld
Hutton Cranswick
Brigham
Church End
North Frodingham
Rotsea
Beeford
EAST RIDING
OF
YORKSHIRE
Kilnwick Percy
Warter
B1246
Middleton-on-the-Wolds
Middleton Wold
Watton
Watton Priory
Watton Carrs
Hempholme
Pocklington
B1247
Barmby Moor
Nunburnholme
Kilnwick
Lockington
Beswick
Burshill
Little Burton
Brandesburton
A165
Burnby Hall
Burnby
Allerthorpe
A1079
Hayton
Londesborough
Holme on the Wolds
Thorpe
South Dalton
Aike
Leven
Scorborough
New Arram
Arram
Catwick
Little Catwick
A1035
Goodmanham Wold
Etton
Leconfield
Thorpe le Street
Bielby
Shiptonthorpe
Goodmanham
Cherry Burton
Gardham
Arras
Routh
Long Riston
Everingham
Foulness
Seaton Ross
Market Weighton
Weighton Common
Harswell
Holme-on-Spalding-Moor
Water End
A163
Moor End
Sancton
Bishop Burton
Bishop Burton Wold
Beverley
BEVERLEY
Molescroft
Tickton
Arnold
Weel
Skirlaugh
Newbald Wold
North Cliffe
North Newbald
South Newbald
South Cliffe
Hotham
A1034
B1230
High Hunsley
Walkington
Beverley Minster
Woodmansey
Thearne
Wawne
A1174
Swine
Bentley
Risby
Dunswell
Holme Common
Spaldington
Bursea
North Cave
Everthorpe
Riplingham
Little Weighton
Skidby
Cottingham
Eppleworth
Haltemprice Farm
Willerby
Lincoln
Newland
Bransholme
High Bransholme
Sutton-on-Hull
Sutton Ings
Holderness Drain
Portington
Hive
Sandholme
M62
A63
Eastrington
Scalby
Newport
Walling Fen
South Cave
Wolds Way
Ellerker
Brantingham
KINGSTON UPON HULL
Gilberdyke
Staddlethorpe
Balkholme
West Ella
Kirk Ella
East Ella
Anlaby
Hull City F.C.
Wilberforce House
The Deep
KINGSTON UPON HULL
Kilpin Pike
Kilpin
Saltmarshe Sta
Laxton
Broomfleet
Elloughton
Brough
Welton
Swanland
Melton
Humber Bridge
North Ferriby
A105
Hessle
Saltmarshe
Blacktoft
Faxfleet
Whitton Sand
Whitton Ness
Southfield
Humber Bridge
A15
Barton Clay Pits Project
Redcliff Channel
Yokefleet
Reedness
Ousefleet
Whitton
Humber
New Holland
Swinefleet
Whitgift
Winteringham
Read's Island
South Channel
Barton-upon-Humber
Water's Edge Country Park
Barrow Haven
Barrow Hann
Goxhill
Alkborough
West Halton
A1077
Barrow upon Humber
Adlingfleet
South Ferriby
South End
Marshland
A161
Walcot
NORTH LINCOLNSHIRE
Garthorpe
Trent
Coleby
Burton upon Stather
Thornton Abbey Sta
Thornton Abbey
Horkstow
Thornton Curtis
0 2 4 6 miles
0 2 4 6 8 10 km
Winterton
Burnham
Eastoft
Normanby
Roxby
B1207
B1204
Saxby All Saints
B1218
B1206
Wootton
Ulceby

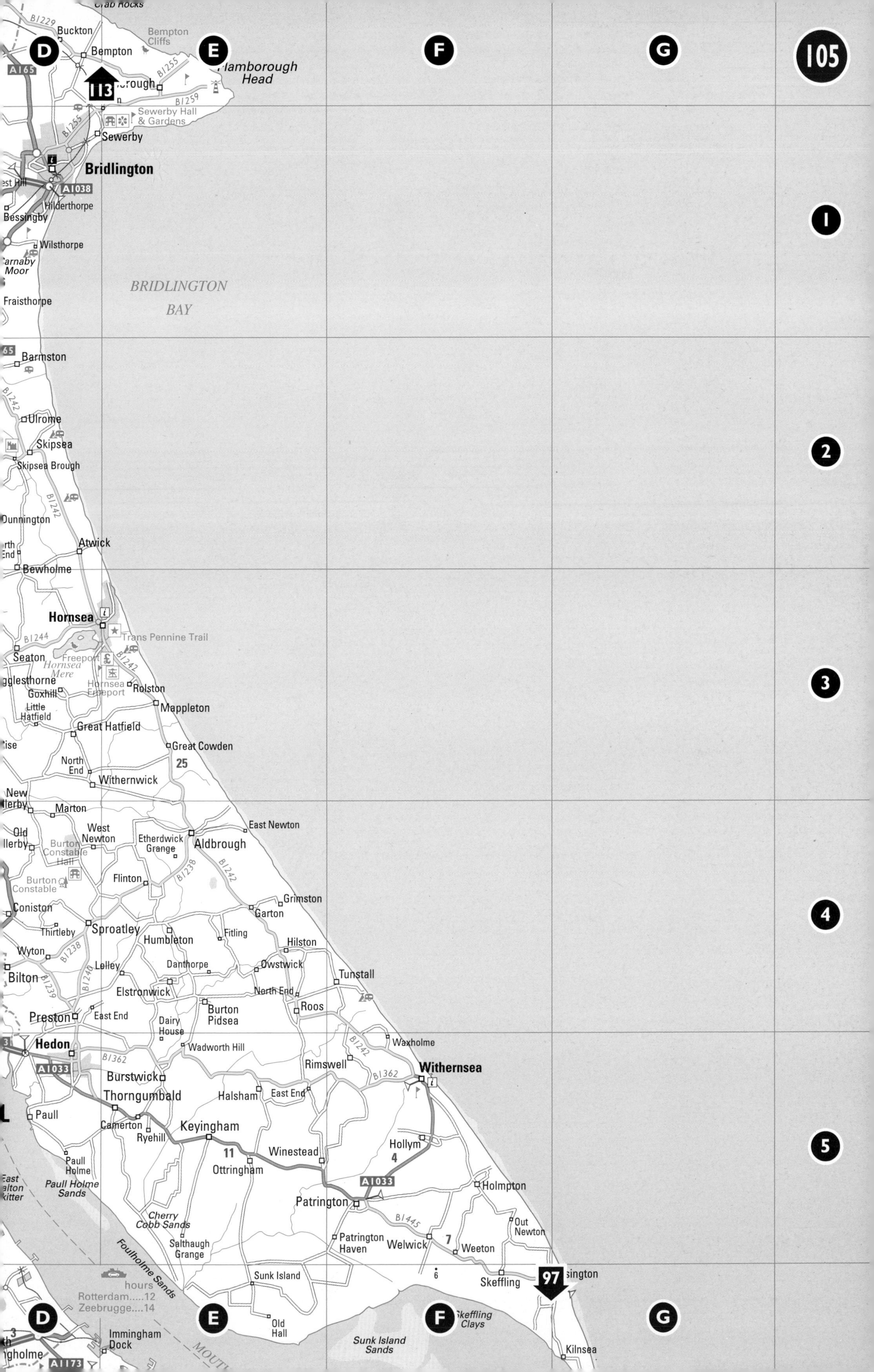

Crab Rocks

B1229
Buckton
Bempton
Bempton
Cliffs
Flamborough
Head
113
Sewerby Hall
& Gardens
B1255
B1259
Sewerby
Bridlington
A1038
West Hill
Hilderthorpe
Bessingby
Wilsthorpe
Carnaby
Moor
Fraisthorpe

BRIDLINGTON
BAY

65
Barmston

B1242
Ulrome
Skipsea
Skipsea Brough

B1242
Dunnington

North
End
Atwick
Bewholme

Hornsea
Trans Pennine Trail
B1244
Seaton
Hornsea
Mere
Freeport
Egglesthorne
Hornsea
Freeport
Goxhill
Rolston
Little
Hatfield
Mappleton
Great Hatfield

Great Cowden
North
End
25
Withernwick
New
Ellerby
Marton
West
Newton
East Newton
Old
Ellerby
Etherdwick
Grange
Aldbrough
Burton
Constable
Hall
B1238
B1242
Burton
Constable
Flinton

Coniston
Grimston
Thirtleby
Sproatley
Garton

Wyton
Humbleton
Fitling
Hilston
B1238
B1240
Lelley
Danthorpe
Owstwick
Bilton
Elstronwick
North End
Roos
Tunstall
B1239
Preston
East End
Burton
Pidsea
Dairy
House
Wadworth Hill
Waxholme
Hedon
B1362
B1242
Rimswell
Withernsea
A1033
Burstwick
B1362
Thorngumbald
Halsham
East End
Paull
Camerton
Keyingham
Hollym

Ryehill
11
Winestead
4
Ottringham
Paull
Holme
A1033
Holmpton
East
Halton
Skitter
Paull Holme
Sands
Patrington
Out
Newton
Cherry
Cobb Sands
Salthaugh
Grange
Patrington
Haven
Welwick
7
Weeton
B1445
Foulholme Sands
hours
Rotterdam.....12
Zeebrugge.....14
Sunk Island
6
Skeffling
97
sington

Immingham
Dock
Old
Hall
Skeffling
Clays
Kilnsea
A1173
Sunk Island
Sands
MOUTH

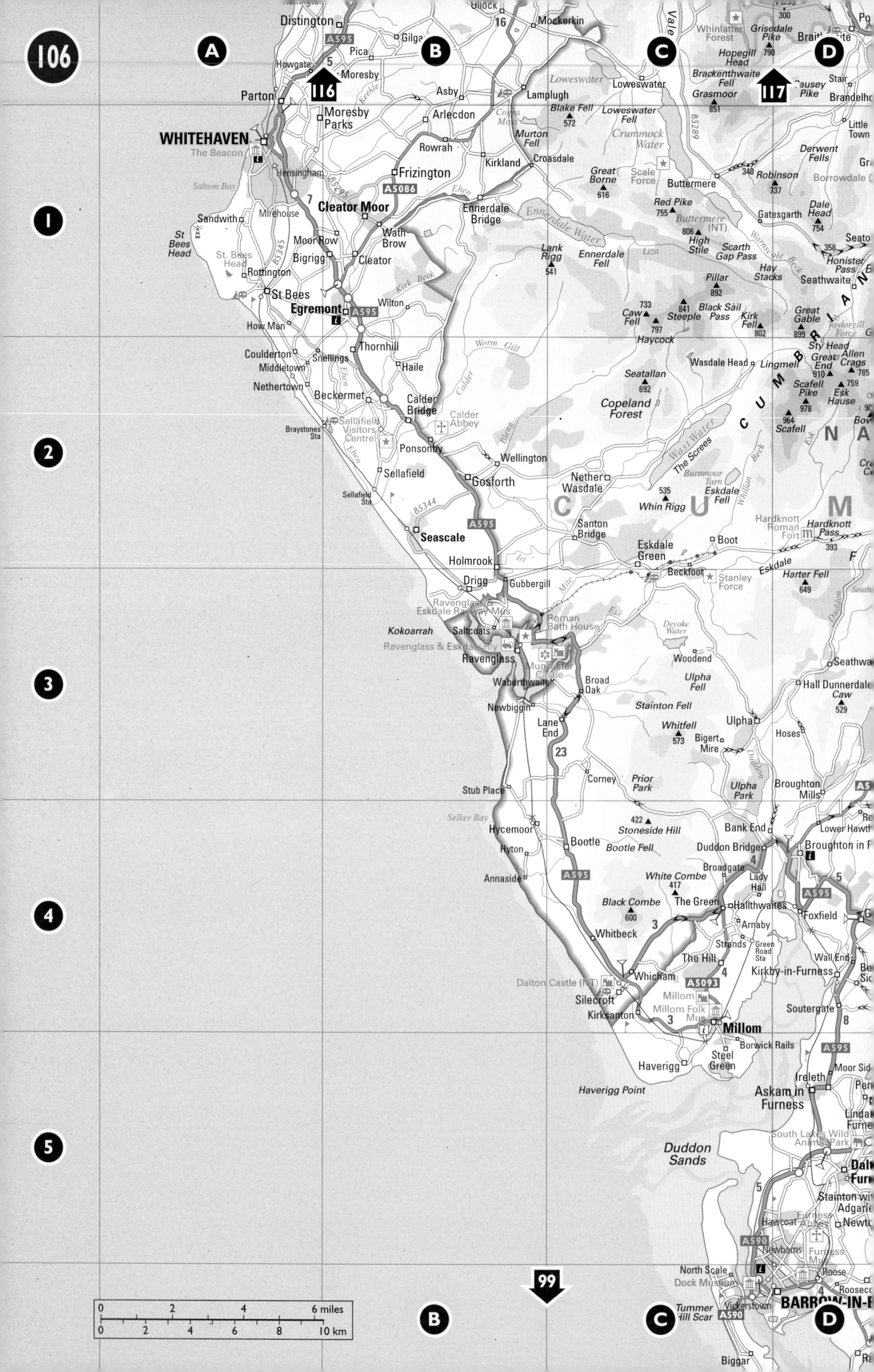
A
B
C
D
1
2
3
4
5
116
117
99
Distington
Gilgarran
Pica
Howgate
Moresby
Parton
Moresby Parks
Asby
Arlecdon
Mockerkin
Lamplugh
Loweswater
Loweswater
Whinlatter Forest
Grisedale Pike
790
Hopegill Head
Brackenthwaite Fell
Grasmoor
851
Causey Pike
Braithwaite
Stair
Brandelhow
Little Town
WHITEHAVEN
The Beacon
Hensingham
Rowrah
Frizington
Kirkland
Croasdale
Blake Fell
572
Loweswater Fell
Crummock Water
Murton Fell
Cogra Moss
Scale Force
Buttermere
Derwent Fells
Robinson
737
Borrowdale
Great Borne
616
Saltom Bay
Cleator Moor
A5086
A595
B5295
Ennerdale Bridge
Ennerdale Water
Red Pike
755
Buttermere (NT)
806
High Stile
Gatesgarth
Dale Head
754
Sandwith
Mirehouse
St Bees Head
St. Bees Head
Moor Row
Bigrigg
Cleator
Wath Brow
Rottington
St Bees
Lank Rigg
541
Ennerdale Fell
Liza
Scarth Gap Pass
Hay Stacks
Honister Pass
358
Seathwaite
B5345
Egremont
Wilton
Kirk Beck
Pillar
892
Caw Fell
733
797
Haycock
841
Steeple
Black Sail Pass
Kirk Fell
802
Great Gable
899
Taylorgill Force
How Man
Coulderton
Snellings
Middletown
Nethertown
Thornhill
Haile
Worm Gill
Wasdale Head
Lingmell
Sty Head
Great End
910
Allen Crags
785
Seatallan
692
Scafell Pike
978
759
Esk Hause
Beckermet
Calder Bridge
Calder Abbey
Copeland Forest
964
Scafell
Braystones Sta
Sellafield Visitors Centre
Ponsonby
Wellington
Bleng
Wast Water
The Screes
CUMBRIA
Sellafield
Sellafield Sta
Gosforth
Nether Wasdale
Burnmoor Tarn
Eskdale Fell
535
Whin Rigg
B5344
Seascale
Santon Bridge
Hardknott Roman Fort
Hardknott Pass
393
Holmrook
Irt
Eskdale Green
Boot
Drigg
Gubbergill
Beckfoot
Stanley Force
Eskdale
Harter Fell
649
Ravenglass & Eskdale Railway Mus
Mite
Esk
Roman Bath House
Devoke Water
Kokoarrah
Saltcoats
Ravenglass & Eskdale Rly
Ravenglass
Muncaster Castle
Woodend
Waberthwaite
Broad Oak
Ulpha Fell
Seathwaite
Hall Dunnerdale
Caw
529
Newbiggin
Stainton Fell
Lane End
Whitfell
573
Bigert Mire
Ulpha
Hoses
23
Corney
Prior Park
Duddon
Ulpha Park
Broughton Mills
Stub Place
Selker Bay
Hycemoor
422
Stoneside Hill
Bank End
Lower Hawthwaite
Bootle
Bootle Fell
Duddon Bridge
Broughton in Furness
Hyton
A595
Broadgate
Annaside
White Combe
417
Lady Hall
The Green
Black Combe
600
Hallthwaites
Foxfield
Arnaby
Whitbeck
Strands
Green Road Sta
Wall End
The Hill
Whicham
Kirkby-in-Furness
Dalton Castle (NT)
A5093
Silecroft
Millom
Millom Folk Mus
Soutergate
Kirksanton
Millom
Borwick Rails
Haverigg
Steel Green
Moor Side
Ireleth
Haverigg Point
Askam in Furness
Duddon Sands
South Lakes Wild Animal Park
Dalton-in-Furness
Stainton with Adgarley
Hawcoat
Furness Abbey
A590
Newbarns
Furness Mus
North Scale
Dock Museum
Roose
Roosecote
Tummer Hill Scar
Vickerstown
BARROW-IN-FURNESS
Biggar
0
2
4
6 miles
0
2
4
6
8
10 km

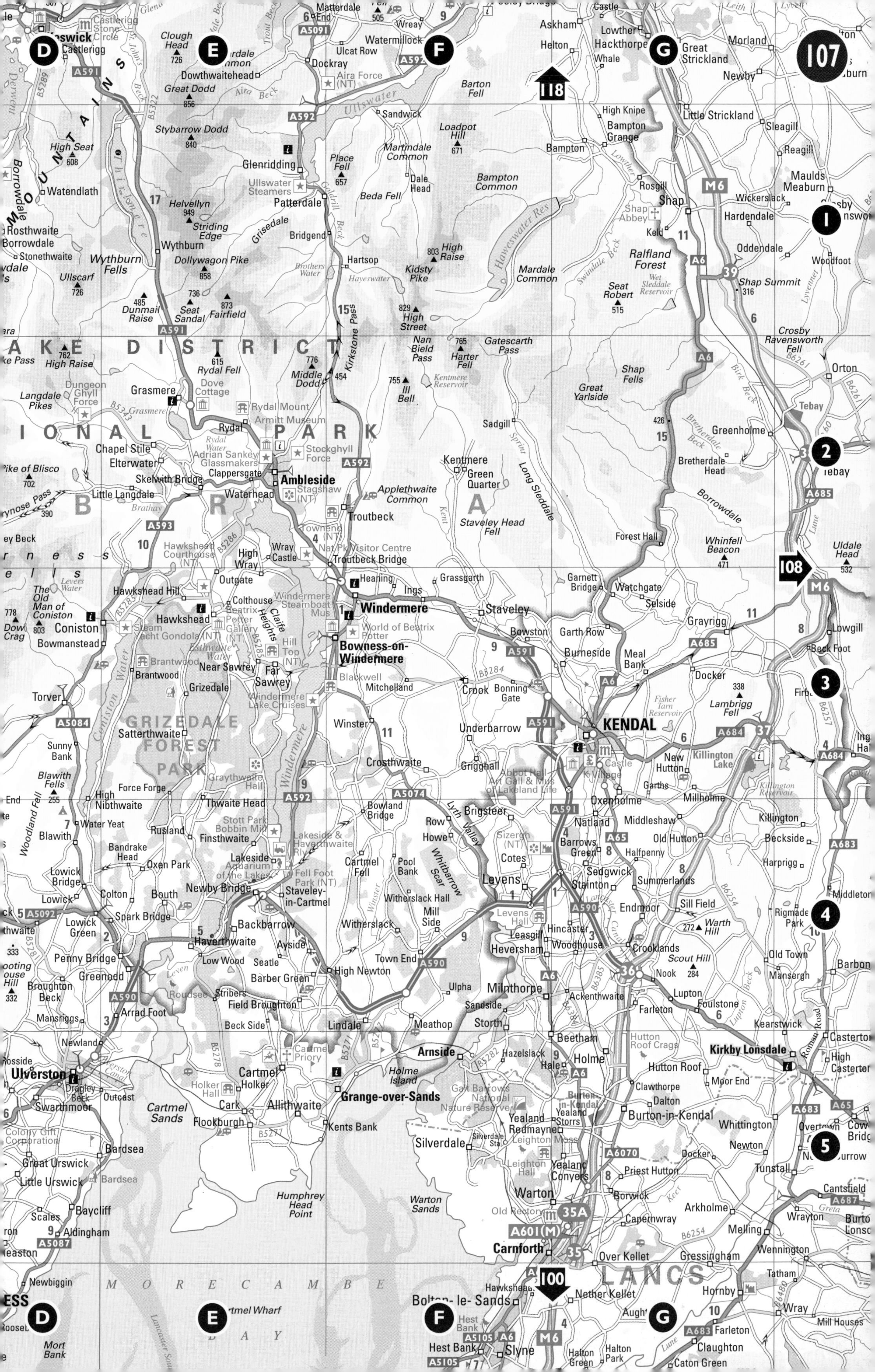
107
D
E
F
G
118
108
100
LAKE DISTRICT NATIONAL PARK
GRIZEDALE FOREST PARK
MORECAMBE BAY
LANCS
Keswick
Castlerigg
Castlerigg Stone Circle
Clough Head
726
Dowthwaitehead
Great Dodd
856
Stybarrow Dodd
840
High Seat
608
Watendlath
Borrowdale
Rosthwaite
Stonethwaite
Ullscarf
726
Wythburn Fells
Wythburn
Thirlmere
Helvellyn
949
Striding Edge
Dollywagon Pike
858
Grisedale
Seat Sandal
736
Fairfield
873
Dunmail Raise
485
High Raise
762
Langdale Pikes
Dungeon Ghyll Force
Grasmere
Dove Cottage
Rydal Fell
615
Rydal
Rydal Mount
Armitt Museum
Rydal Water
Chapel Stile
Elterwater
Adrian Sankey Glassmakers
Clappersgate
Skelwith Bridge
Ambleside
Stockghyll Force
Stagshaw (NT)
Pike of Blisco
702
Little Langdale
Waterhead
Brathay
Wrynose Pass
390
Hawkshead Courthouse (NT)
High Wray
Wray Castle
Townend (NT)
Troutbeck
Troutbeck Bridge
Nat Pk Visitor Centre
Hawkshead Hill
Outgate
Colthouse
Windermere Steamboat Mus
Hawkshead
Beatrix Potter Gallery (NT)
Claife Heights
Windermere
Heaning
Ings
Coniston
Old Man of Coniston
803
Dow Crag
778
Bowmanstead
Steam Yacht Gondola (NT)
Esthwaite Water
Brantwood
Near Sawrey
Far Sawrey
Hill Top (NT)
Bowness-on-Windermere
World of Beatrix Potter
Blackwell
Mitchelland
Grizedale
Windermere Lake Cruises
Torver
Coniston Water
Satterthwaite
Sunny Bank
Blawith Fells
255
Woodland Fell
High Nibthwaite
Water Yeat
Blawith
Force Forge
Graythwaite Hall
Thwaite Head
Rusland
Stott Park Bobbin Mill
Finsthwaite
Bandrake Head
Oxen Park
Lakeside
Aquarium of the Lakes
Lakeside & Haverthwaite Rly
Lowick Bridge
Colton
Bouth
Newby Bridge
Fell Foot Park (NT)
Staveley-in-Cartmel
Lowick
Lowick Green
Spark Bridge
Backbarrow
Haverthwaite
Ayside
Penny Bridge
Greenodd
Low Wood
Seatle
Barber Green
Broughton Beck
Roudsea
Stribers
Field Broughton
Arrad Foot
Mansriggs
Newland
Beck Side
Ulverston
Ulverston Canal
Dragley Beck
Outcast
Swarthmoor
Cartmel
Cartmel Priory
Holker Hall
Holker
Cark
Allithwaite
Flookburgh
Cartmel Sands
Grange-over-Sands
Kents Bank
Humphrey Head Point
Colony Gift Corporation
Bardsea
Great Urswick
Little Urswick
Scales
Baycliff
Aldingham
Newbiggin
Cartmel Wharf
Mort Bank
Matterdale End
Wreay
Watermillock
Ulcat Row
Dockray
Aira Force (NT)
Ullswater
Sandwick
Glenridding
Ullswater Steamers
Patterdale
Place Fell
657
Martindale Common
Loadpot Hill
671
Beda Fell
Dale Head
Bampton Common
Bridgend
Goldrill Beck
Hartsop
Brothers Water
Hayeswater
High Raise
803
Kidsty Pike
Haweswater Res
High Street
829
Kirkstone Pass
Middle Dodd
776
454
Ill Bell
755
Nan Bield Pass
Harter Fell
765
Kentmere Reservoir
Gatescarth Pass
Mardale Common
Applethwaite Common
Kentmere
Green Quarter
Sadgill
Long Sleddale
Staveley Head Fell
Grassgarth
Staveley
Bowston
Crook
Bonning Gate
Winster
Crosthwaite
Underbarrow
Grigghall
Bowland Bridge
Row
Howe
Lyth Valley
Brigsteer
Whitbarrow Scar
Cartmel Fell
Pool Bank
Witherslack Hall
Mill Side
Witherslack
Town End
High Newton
Ulpha
Lindale
Meathop
Arnside
Holme Island
Sandside
Storth
Levens
Levens Hall
Leasgill
Heversham
Milnthorpe
Sizergh (NT)
Cotes
Askham
Helton
Lowther
Hackthorpe
Whale
Barton Fell
High Knipe
Bampton Grange
Bampton
Rosgill
Shap
Shap Abbey
Keld
Ralfland Forest
Wet Sleddale Reservoir
Seat Robert
515
Swindale Beck
Shap Fells
Great Yarlside
Forest Hall
Garnett Bridge
Watchgate
Selside
Garth Row
Burneside
Meal Bank
Grayrigg
Docker
Fisher Tarn Reservoir
Lambrigg Fell
338
KENDAL
Castle
K Village
Abbot Hall Art Gall & Mus of Lakeland Life
New Hutton
Killington Lake
Garths
Millholme
Oxenholme
Natland
Middleshaw
Old Hutton
Barrows Green
Halfpenny
Sedgwick
Stainton
Summerlands
Endmoor
Sill Field
Warth Hill
272
Hincaster
Woodhouse
Crooklands
Scout Hill
284
Nook
Lancaster Canal
Ackenthwaite
Lupton
Farleton
Foulstone
Beetham
Hazelslack
Hale
Holme
Hutton Roof Crags
Hutton Roof
Clawthorpe
Dalton
Burton-in-Kendal
Gait Barrows National Nature Reserve
Yealand Redmayne
Yealand Storrs
Leighton Moss
Silverdale
Silverdale Sta
Leighton Hall
Yealand Conyers
Priest Hutton
Borwick
Warton
Warton Sands
Old Rectory
Capernwray
Carnforth
Over Kellet
Nether Kellet
Hawkshead
Bolton-le-Sands
Hest Bank
Slyne
Aughton
Halton Green
Halton Park
Great Strickland
Morland
Newby
Little Strickland
Sleagill
Reagill
Maulds Meaburn
Wickerslack
Hardendale
Oddendale
Woodfoot
Shap Summit
316
Crosby Ravensworth Fell
Orton
Tebay
Birk Beck
Greenholme
Bretherdale Head
Borrowdale
Whinfell Beacon
471
Uldale Head
532
Lowgill
Beck Foot
Killington Reservoir
Killington
Beckside
Harprigg
Middleton
Rigmaden Park
Old Town
Mansergh
Barbon
Kearstwick
Kirkby Lonsdale
Roman Road
Casterton
High Casterton
Moor End
Whittington
Overtown
Newton
Docker
Tunstall
Cantsfield
Arkholme
Wrayton
Melling
Wennington
Gressingham
Tatham
Hornby
Wray
Mill Houses
Farleton
Claughton
Caton Green
M6
A6
A65
A591
A592
A593
A590
A5074
A5084
A5092
A5087
A684
A685
A683
A687
A6070
A601(M)
A5105
A5091
B5289
B5322
B5343
B5285
B5286
B5284
B5278
B5277
B5271
B5282
B6254
B6257
B6261
B6385
B6480
35A
35
36
37
38
39

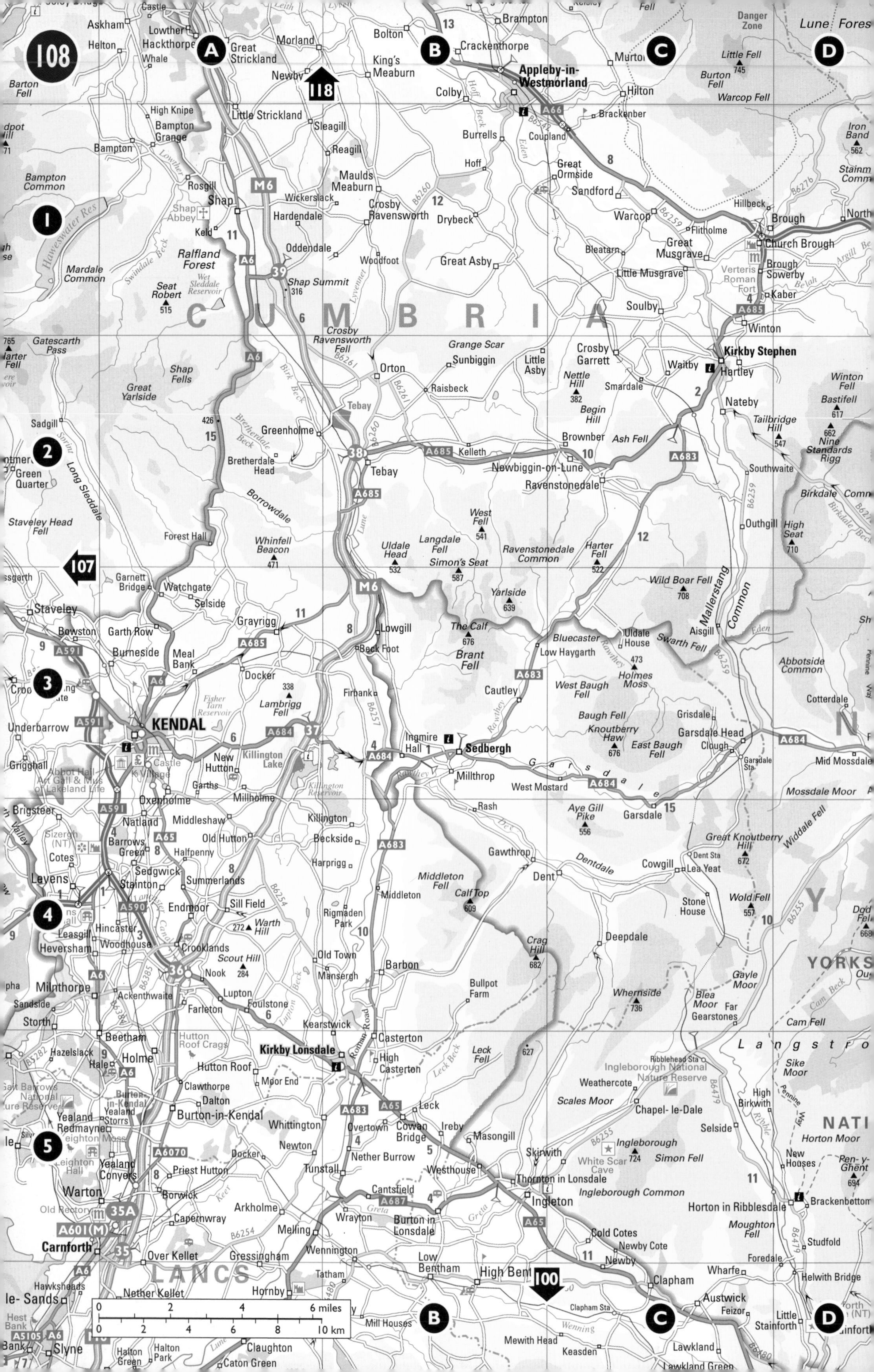

A
B
C
D
118
107
100
C U M B R I A
LANCS
YORKS
Askham
Helton
Lowther
Hackthorpe
Whale
Barton Fell
Great Strickland
Morland
Bolton
Brampton
Crackenthorpe
Appleby-in-Westmorland
Murton
Danger Zone
Lune Forest
Little Fell
745
Burton Fell
Warcop Fell
Newby
King's Meaburn
Colby
Hilton
Brackenber
Coupland
Burrells
Hoff
Great Ormside
Sandford
Warcop
Flitholme
Hillbeck
Brough
Church Brough
Brough Sowerby
Verteris Roman Fort
Kaber
Winton
Kirkby Stephen
Hartley
High Knipe
Bampton Grange
Bampton
Little Strickland
Sleagill
Reagill
Maulds Meaburn
Wickerslack
Crosby Ravensworth
Hardendale
Drybeck
Bampton Common
Haweswater Res
Rosgill
Shap
Shap Abbey
Keld
Ralfland Forest
Mardale Common
Swindale Beck
Seat Robert
515
Wet Sleddale Reservoir
Oddendale
Woodfoot
Great Asby
Shap Summit
316
Great Musgrave
Bleatarn
Little Musgrave
Soulby
Crosby Ravensworth Fell
Gatescarth Pass
Orton
Grange Scar
Sunbiggin
Little Asby
Crosby Garrett
Waitby
Smardale
Nettle Hill
382
Begin Hill
Raisbeck
Shap Fells
Great Yarlside
Sadgill
426
Tebay
Greenholme
Bretherdale Beck
Bretherdale Head
Kelleth
Brownber
Ash Fell
Newbiggin-on-Lune
Ravenstonedale
Nateby
Tailbridge Hill
547
Winton Fell
Bastifell
617
Nine Standards Rigg
662
Southwaite
Birkdale Common
Green Quarter
Long Sleddale
Staveley Head Fell
Borrowdale
Forest Hall
Whinfell Beacon
471
Uldale Head
532
Langdale Fell
West Fell
541
Simon's Seat
587
Ravenstonedale Common
Harter Fell
522
Outhgill
High Seat
710
Wild Boar Fell
708
Mallerstang Common
Garnett Bridge
Watchgate
Selside
Staveley
Bowston
Garth Row
Grayrigg
Lowgill
Yarlside
639
The Calf
676
Brant Fell
Bluecaster
Low Haygarth
Uldale House
Swarth Fell
Aisgill
Burneside
Meal Bank
Beck Foot
473
Holmes Moss
Abbotside Common
Docker
338
Lambrigg Fell
Fisher Tarn Reservoir
Firbank
Cautley
West Baugh Fell
Baugh Fell
Grisdale
Cotterdale
Underbarrow
KENDAL
New Hutton
Killington Lake
Ingmire Hall
Sedbergh
Knoutberry Haw
676
East Baugh Fell
Garsdale Head
Clough
Garsdale Sta
Mid Mossdale
Grigghall
Abbot Hall Art Gall & Mus of Lakeland Life
Castle
K Village
Garths
Killington Reservoir
Millthrop
West Mostard
Garsdale
Mossdale Moor
Brigsteer
Oxenholme
Millholme
Rash
Aye Gill Pike
556
Sizergh (NT)
Natland
Middleshaw
Killington
Barrows Green
Old Hutton
Beckside
Great Knoutberry Hill
672
Widdale Fell
Cotes
Halfpenny
Harprigg
Gawthrop
Dent
Dentdale
Cowgill
Dent Sta
Lea Yeat
Levens
Sedgwick
Stainton
Summerlands
Middleton Fell
Middleton
Calf Top
609
Stone House
Wold Fell
557
Endmoor
Sill Field
Rigmaden Park
Leasgill
Hincaster
Warth Hill
272
Heversham
Woodhouse
Crooklands
Old Town
Mansergh
Crag Hill
682
Deepdale
Scout Hill
284
Nook
Barbon
Milnthorpe
Ackenthwaite
Lupton
Farleton
Foulstone
Bullpot Farm
Whernside
736
Blea Moor
Far Gearstones
Gayle Moor
Sandside
Storth
Kearstwick
Cam Fell
Beetham
Hutton Roof Crags
Casterton
Kirkby Lonsdale
High Casterton
Leck Fell
627
Langstro
Hazelslack
Hale
Holme
Hutton Roof
Moor End
Ribblehead Sta
Ingleborough National Nature Reserve
Sike Moor
Clawthorpe
Dalton
Weathercote
Scales Moor
High Birkwith
Burton-in-Kendal
Leck
Chapel- le-Dale
Selside
NATI
Yealand Redmayne
Yealand Storrs
Whittington
Overtown
Cowan Bridge
Ireby
Masongill
Ingleborough
724
Simon Fell
Horton Moor
Leighton Hall
Yealand Conyers
Newton
Docker
Nether Burrow
Skirwith
White Scar Cave
New Houses
Pen-y-Ghent
694
Priest Hutton
Tunstall
Westhouse
Thornton in Lonsdale
Ingleborough Common
Warton
Borwick
Cantsfield
Ingleton
Horton in Ribblesdale
Brackenbottom
Old Rectory
Arkholme
Wrayton
Burton in Lonsdale
Moughton Fell
Carnforth
Capernwray
Melling
Cold Cotes
Newby Cote
Studfold
Over Kellet
Gressingham
Wennington
Low Bentham
High Bentham
Newby
Foredale
Wharfe
Helwith Bridge
Hawksheads
Nether Kellet
Tatham
Hornby
Clapham
Austwick
Feizor
Little Stainforth
Clapham Sta
Mill Houses
Mewith Head
Keasden
Lawkland
Lawkland Green
Slyne
Halton Green
Halton Park
Claughton
Caton Green
Bank
Wenning
Greta
Keer
Lune
Rawthey
Dee
Eden
Lyvennet
Birk Beck
Lupton Beck
Leck Beck
Cam Beck
Ribble
Pennine Way
M6
A6
A66
A685
A683
A684
A591
A65
A590
A6070
A687
A601(M)
A5105
B6260
B6261
B6259
B6276
B6542
B6257
B6254
B6385
B6384
B5282
B6255
B6479
B6480
13
38
39
37
36
35
35A
0 2 4 6 miles
0 2 4 6 8 10 km

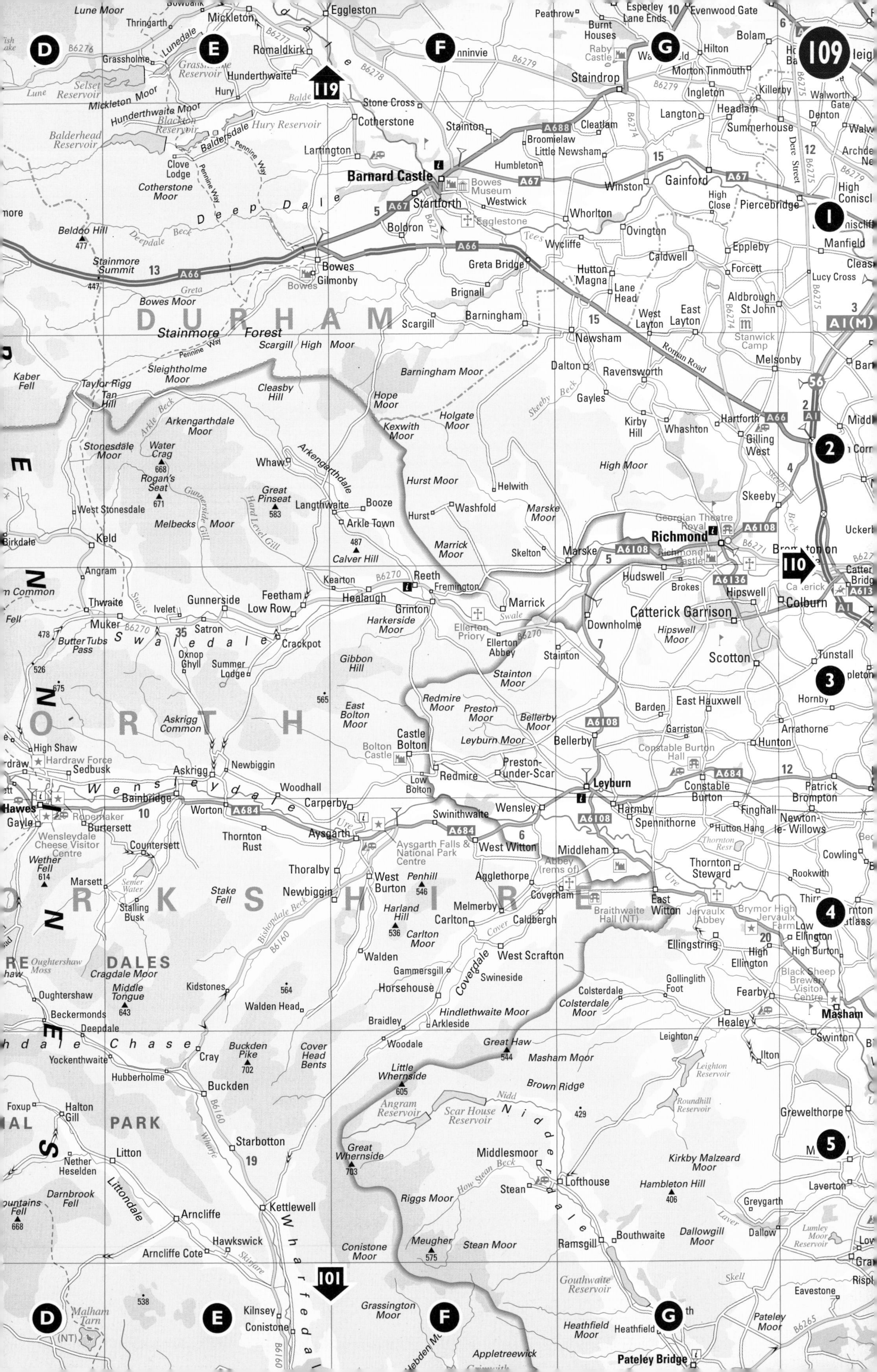
109
119
101
110
D
E
F
G
1
2
3
4
5
Lune Moor
Thringarth
Mickleton
Eggleston
Peathrow
Burnt Houses
Esperley Lane Ends
Evenwood Gate
Bolam
Lunedale
Grassholme
Grassholme Reservoir
Romaldkirk
Hunderthwaite
Selset Reservoir
Lune
Hury
Mickleton Moor
Hunderthwaite Moor
Blackton Reservoir
Balderhead Reservoir
Baldersdale
Hury Reservoir
Balder
Stone Cross
Cotherstone
Lartington
Clove Lodge
Cotherstone Moor
Pennine Way
Deep Dale
Raby Castle
Staindrop
Hilton
Morton Tinmouth
Ingleton
Killerby
Headlam
Walworth Gate
Denton
Langton
Summerhouse
Cleatlam
Broomielaw
Little Newsham
Stainton
Humbleton
Barnard Castle
Bowes Museum
Startforth
Westwick
Boldron
Egglestone
Winston
Gainford
High Close
Piercebridge
Whorlton
Ovington
Wycliffe
Tees
Manfield
Eppleby
Caldwell
Forcett
Cleasby
Lucy Cross
Greta Bridge
Hutton Magna
Lane Head
Aldbrough St John
West Layton
East Layton
Stanwick Camp
Dere Street
High Coniscliffe
Beldoo Hill
477
Deepdale
Beck
Stainmore Summit
447
Bowes
Gilmonby
Greta
Bowes Moor
DURHAM
Stainmore Forest
Scargill High Moor
Scargill
Brignall
Barningham
Newsham
Dalton
Ravensworth
Melsonby
Kaber Fell
Taylor Rigg
Tan Hill
Sleightholme Moor
Cleasby Hill
Barningham Moor
Hope Moor
Holgate Moor
Kexwith Moor
Roman Road
Gayles
Skeeby Beck
Kirby Hill
Whashton
Hartforth
Gilling West
Arkengarthdale Moor
Arkle Beck
Stonesdale Moor
Water Crag
668
Rogan's Seat
671
Whaw
Arkengarthdale
Great Pinseat
583
Langthwaite
Booze
Arkle Town
Hurst Moor
Helwith
High Moor
Skeeby
Washfold
Hurst
Marske Moor
West Stonesdale
Melbecks Moor
Gunnerside Gill
Hard Level Gill
Keld
Birkdale
487
Calver Hill
Marrick Moor
Skelton
Marske
Georgian Theatre Royal
Richmond
Richmond Castle
Hudswell
Brokes
Hipswell
Colburn
Catterick
Catterick Garrison
Angram
Kearton
Reeth
Fremington
Thwaite
Gunnerside
Feetham
Low Row
Healaugh
Grinton
Marrick
Muker
Ivelet
Satron
Swaledale
Crackpot
Harkerside Moor
Swale
Ellerton Priory
Ellerton Abbey
Downholme
Hipswell Moor
Tunstall
Scotton
Butter Tubs Pass
Oxnop Ghyll
Summer Lodge
Gibbon Hill
Stainton
Stainton Moor
478
526
675
565
East Bolton Moor
Redmire Moor
Preston Moor
Bellerby Moor
Barden
East Hauxwell
Hornby
Askrigg Common
NORTH
Castle Bolton
Bolton Castle
Leyburn Moor
Bellerby
Garriston
Arrathorne
Hunton
Constable Burton Hall
High Shaw
Hardraw Force
Hardraw
Sedbusk
Askrigg
Newbiggin
Preston-under-Scar
Redmire
Low Bolton
Leyburn
Constable Burton
Patrick Brompton
Wensleydale
Bainbridge
Woodhall
Carperby
Wensley
Harmby
Finghall
Newton-le-Willows
Hawes
Gayle
Ropemaker
Burtersett
Worton
Swinithwaite
Spennithorne
Hutton Hang
Thornton Rust
Aysgarth
Ure
Wensleydale Cheese Visitor Centre
Countersett
Aysgarth Falls & National Park Centre
West Witton
Middleham
Thornton Resr
Thornton Steward
Cowling
Wether Fell
614
Thoralby
Abbey (rems of)
Rookwith
Marsett
Semer Water
West Burton
Penhill
546
Agglethorpe
Stake Fell
Newbiggin
Coverham
East Witton
Jervaulx Abbey
Brymor High Jervaulx Farm
Low Ellington
YORKSHIRE
Stalling Busk
Bishopdale Beck
Harland Hill
536
Melmerby
Carlton
Carlton Moor
Caldbergh
Braithwaite Hall (NT)
Cover
Ellingstring
High Ellington
High Burton
DALES
Oughtershaw Moss
Cragdale Moor
B6160
Walden
West Scrafton
Coverdale
Gammersgill
Swineside
Golinglith Foot
Black Sheep Brewery Visitor Centre
Middle Tongue
643
Kidstones
564
Horsehouse
Colsterdale
Colsterdale Moor
Fearby
Masham
Oughtershaw
Walden Head
Hindlethwaite Moor
Beckermonds
Braidley
Arkleside
Healey
Deepdale
Langstrothdale Chase
Buckden Pike
702
Cover Head Bents
Woodale
Great Haw
544
Masham Moor
Leighton
Swinton
Ilton
Yockenthwaite
Cray
Little Whernside
605
Leighton Reservoir
Hubberholme
Buckden
Brown Ridge
Nidd
Foxup
Halton Gill
PARK
Angram Reservoir
Scar House Reservoir
Nidderdale
429
Roundhill Reservoir
Grewelthorpe
Wharfe
Starbotton
Great Whernside
703
Middlesmoor
How Stean Beck
Kirkby Malzeard Moor
Nether Heselden
Litton
Littondale
19
Stean
Lofthouse
Hambleton Hill
406
Laverton
Darnbrook Fell
Fountains Fell
668
Arncliffe
Kettlewell
Riggs Moor
Greygarth
Laver
Lumley Moor Reservoir
Dallow
Hawkswick
Arncliffe Cote
Skirfare
Conistone Moor
Meugher
575
Stean Moor
Ramsgill
Bouthwaite
Dallowgill Moor
Wharfedale
Gouthwaite Reservoir
Skell
Eavestone
538
Malham Tarn
(NT)
Kilnsey
Conistone
Grassington Moor
Hebden Moor
Heathfield Moor
Heathfield
Pateley Bridge
Pateley Moor
Appletreewick
B6265
A66
A67
A688
A6108
A6136
A684
A1
A1(M)
B6276
B6277
B6278
B6279
B6274
B6275
B6271
B6270
B6160
13
5
15
35
10
6
7
12
20
56

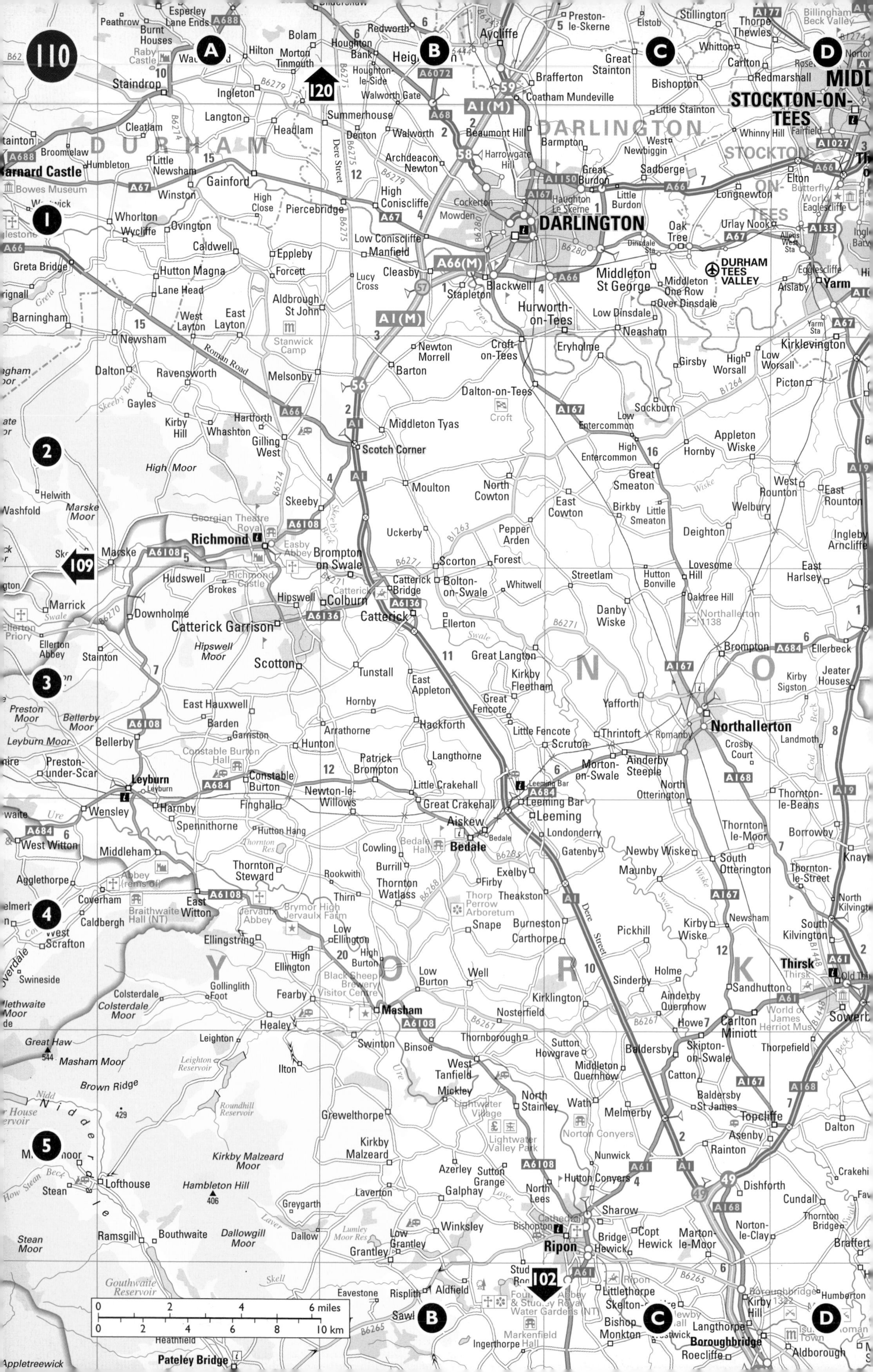
110
A
B
C
D
1
2
3
4
5
120
109
102
DURHAM
DARLINGTON
STOCKTON-ON-TEES
NORTH
YORK
Staindrop
Esperley Lane Ends
Peathrow
Burnt Houses
Raby Castle
Hilton
Bolam
Morton Tinmouth
Redworth
Houghton Bank
Houghton-le-Side
Walworth Gate
Heighington
Aycliffe
Preston-le-Skerne
Elstob
Great Stainton
Bishopton
Stillington
Whitton
Thorpe Thewles
Carlton
Redmarshall
Billingham Beck Valley
Ingleton
Langton
Headlam
Summerhouse
Denton
Walworth
Archdeacon Newton
Brafferton
Coatham Mundeville
Beaumont Hill
Harrowgate Hill
Barmpton
Little Stainton
West Newbiggin
Sadberge
Whinny Hill
Fairfield
Cleatlam
Broomielaw
Barnard Castle
Humbleton
Little Newsham
Gainford
Winston
Bowes Museum
High Close
Piercebridge
High Coniscliffe
Cockerton
Mowden
Haughton le Skerne
Great Burdon
Little Burdon
Longnewton
Elton
Butterfly World
Eaglescliffe
Whorlton
Wycliffe
Ovington
Caldwell
Eppleby
Forcett
Low Coniscliffe
Manfield
Cleasby
Lucy Cross
Blackwell
Stapleton
Oak Tree
Urlay Nook
Allens West
Dinsdale Sta
Middleton St George
Middleton One Row
Over Dinsdale
DURHAM TEES VALLEY
Egglescliffe
Aislaby
Yarm
Greta Bridge
Hutton Magna
Lane Head
Aldbrough St John
Hurworth-on-Tees
Low Dinsdale
Neasham
Barningham
West Layton
East Layton
Newsham
Stanwick Camp
Newton Morrell
Croft-on-Tees
Eryholme
Girsby
High Worsall
Low Worsall
Kirklevington
Picton
Yarm Sta
Dalton
Ravensworth
Roman Road
Melsonby
Barton
Dalton-on-Tees
Croft
Sockburn
Gayles
Kirby Hill
Whashton
Hartforth
Gilling West
Middleton Tyas
Scotch Corner
Low Entercommon
High Entercommon
Appleton Wiske
Hornby
High Moor
Helwith
Marske Moor
Washfold
Moulton
North Cowton
Great Smeaton
East Cowton
Birkby
Little Smeaton
West Rounton
East Rounton
Welbury
Skeeby
Georgian Theatre Royal
Richmond
Easby Abbey
Brompton on Swale
Uckerby
Scorton
Pepper Arden
Deighton
Ingleby Arncliffe
Marske
Hudswell
Richmond Castle
Brokes
Catterick Bridge
Bolton-on-Swale
Forest
Whitwell
Streetlam
Hutton Bonville
Lovesome Hill
East Harlsey
Marrick
Downholme
Hipswell
Colburn
Catterick
Ellerton
Danby Wiske
Oaktree Hill
Northallerton
Ellerton Priory
Ellerton Abbey
Stainton
Catterick Garrison
Hipswell Moor
Scotton
Great Langton
Brompton
Ellerbeck
Preston Moor
Bellerby Moor
Tunstall
East Appleton
Kirby Fleetham
Yafforth
Kirby Sigston
Jeater Houses
East Hauxwell
Hornby
Great Fencote
Barden
Garriston
Arrathorne
Hackforth
Leyburn Moor
Bellerby
Hunton
Little Fencote
Thrintoft
Romanby
Landmoth
Crosby Court
Constable Burton Hall
Scruton
Morton-on-Swale
Ainderby Steeple
Preston-under-Scar
Patrick Brompton
Langthorne
North Otterington
Leyburn
Constable Burton
Newton-le-Willows
Little Crakehall
Leeming Bar
Thornton-le-Beans
Wensley
Harmby
Finghall
Great Crakehall
Leeming
Aiskew
Londonderry
West Witton
Spennithorne
Hutton Hang
Thornton Res
Bedale Hall
Bedale
Gatenby
Newby Wiske
Thornton-le-Moor
Borrowby
Middleham
Cowling
Burrill
Exelby
Maunby
South Otterington
Thornton-le-Street
Agglethorpe
Abbey (rems of)
Thornton Steward
Rookwith
Thornton Watlass
Firby
Coverham
Braithwaite Hall (NT)
East Witton
Thirn
Thorp Perrow Arboretum
Theakston
North Kilvington
Caldbergh
West Scrafton
Jervaulx Abbey
Brymor High Jervaulx Farm
Snape
Burneston
Newsham
South Kilvington
Ellingstring
Low Ellington
Carthorpe
Pickhill
Kirby Wiske
Swineside
High Ellington
High Burton
Black Sheep Brewery Visitor Centre
Low Burton
Well
Sinderby
Holme
Thirsk
Sandhutton
Gollinglith Foot
Colsterdale
Colsterdale Moor
Fearby
Masham
Kirklington
Ainderby Quernhow
Howe
Carlton Miniott
World of James Herriot Mus
Sowerby
Healey
Nosterfield
Leighton
Great Haw
Masham Moor
Swinton
Binsoe
Thornborough
Sutton Howgrave
Baldersby
Skipton-on-Swale
Thorpefield
Leighton Reservoir
Ilton
West Tanfield
Middleton Quernhow
Catton
Brown Ridge
Mickley
North Stainley
Wath
Melmerby
Baldersby St James
Topcliffe
Dalton
Roundhill Reservoir
Grewelthorpe
Lightwater Village
Lightwater Valley Park
Norton Conyers
Asenby
Rainton
Kirkby Malzeard Moor
Kirkby Malzeard
Nunwick
Azerley
Sutton Grange
Hutton Conyers
Dishforth
Lofthouse
Stean
Hambleton Hill
Laverton
Galphay
North Lees
Sharow
Cundall
Norton-le-Clay
Thornton Bridge
Greygarth
Winksley
Bishopton
Cathedral
Ripon
Bridge Hewick
Copt Hewick
Marton-le-Moor
Stean Moor
Ramsgill
Bouthwaite
Dallowgill Moor
Dallow
Lumley Moor Res
Low Grantley
Grantley
Brafferton
Gouthwaite Reservoir
Stud Farm
Littlethorpe
Skelton-on-Ure
Boroughbridge
Humberton
Kirby Hill
Eavestone
Risplith
Aldfield
Fountains Abbey & Studley Royal Water Gardens (NT)
Bishop Monkton
Langthorpe
Sawley
Markenfield Hall
Ingerthorpe
Westwick
Roecliffe
Aldborough
Heathfield
Pateley Bridge
Appletreewick
Dere Street
Swale
Ure
Tees
Greta
Nidderdale
Wiske
Skell
Laver
Cod Beck
A1(M)
A1
A66
A66(M)
A67
A68
A167
A6108
A6136
A684
A61
A168
A19
A1027
A135
A177
A688
A6072
A1150
B6275
B6279
B6274
B6280
B6271
B6270
B6263
B6285
B6267
B6265
B1264
B1263
B1448
0 2 4 6 miles
0 2 4 6 8 10 km

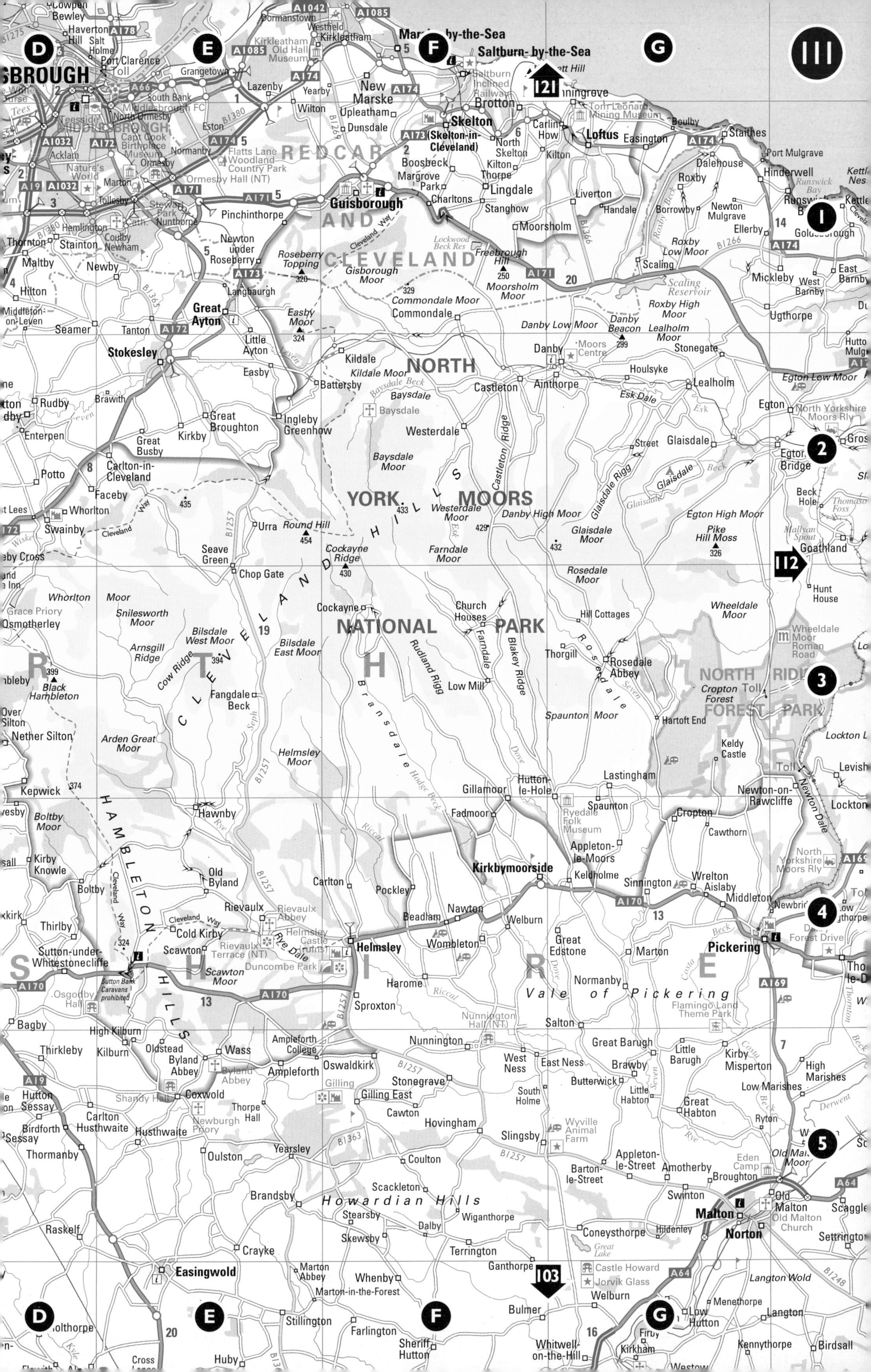
D
E
F
G
Marske-by-the-Sea
Saltburn-by-the-Sea
121
Coatham
Bewley
Haverton Hill
Salt Holme
Port Clarence
Dormanstown
Westfield
Kirkleatham
Kirkleatham Old Hall Museum
Grangetown
Lazenby
Yearby
New Marske
Wilton
Upleatham
Dunsdale
Saltburn Inclined Railway
Brotton
Skelton
(Skelton-in-Cleveland)
Carlin How
Loftus
Easington
Tom Leonard Mining Museum
Boulby
Staithes
Port Mulgrave
Hinderwell
Runswick Bay
Dalehouse
Roxby
Newton Mulgrave
Ellerby
Goldsborough
Kettleness
MIDDLESBROUGH
Middlesbrough FC
North Ormesby
South Bank
Teesside
Eston
Capt Cook Birthplace Museum
Normanby
Flatts Lane Woodland Country Park
Ormesby
Ormesby Hall (NT)
Acklam
Nature's World
Marton
Tollesby
Stewart Park
Nunthorpe
Hemlington
Coulby Newham
Stainton
Thornton
Maltby
Newby
Hilton
Middleton-on-Leven
Seamer
Tanton
REDCAR AND CLEVELAND
Boosbeck
Margrove Park
Charltons
North Skelton
Kilton Thorpe
Kilton
Lingdale
Stanghow
Liverton
Handale
Moorsholm
Guisborough
Pinchinthorpe
Newton under Roseberry
Roseberry Topping
320
Gisborough Moor
329
Lockwood Beck Res
Freebrough Hill
250
Moorsholm Moor
Commondale Moor
Commondale
Cleveland Way
Scaling
Scaling Reservoir
Roxby High Moor
Borrowby
Roxby Low Moor
Mickleby
West Barnby
East Barnby
Ugthorpe
Great Ayton
Little Ayton
Langbaurgh
Easby Moor
324
Stokesley
Easby
Kildale
Kildale Moor
Battersby
Baysdale Beck
Baysdale
Danby Low Moor
Danby Beacon
299
Lealholm Moor
Danby
Moors Centre
Castleton
Ainthorpe
Houlsyke
Lealholm
Stonegate
Egton Low Moor
Egton
North Yorkshire Moors Rly
Grosmont
NORTH
YORK MOORS
NATIONAL PARK
Rudby
Hutton Rudby
Enterpen
Brawith
Great Broughton
Kirkby
Great Busby
Ingleby Greenhow
Westerdale
Esk Dale
Glaisdale
Street
Egton Bridge
Potto
Carlton-in-Cleveland
Faceby
Whorlton
Swainby
Baysdale Moor
Castleton Ridge
Glaisdale Rigg
Beck Hole
Thomason Foss
Mallyan Spout
Goathland
112
CLEVELAND HILLS
435
433
Westerdale Moor
429
Danby High Moor
Egton High Moor
Pike Hill Moss
326
Urra
Round Hill
454
Glaisdale Moor
432
Ingleby Cross
Seave Green
Chop Gate
Cockayne Ridge
430
Farndale Moor
Rosedale Moor
Hunt House
Whorlton Moor
Mount Grace Priory
Osmotherley
Snilesworth Moor
Bilsdale West Moor
Arnsgill Ridge
Cockayne
Church Houses
Hill Cottages
Wheeldale Moor
Wheeldale Moor Roman Road
19
Bilsdale East Moor
Rudland Rigg
Farndale
Blakey Ridge
Thorgill
Rosedale Abbey
Rosedale
Black Hambleton
399
394
Cow Ridge
Fangdale Beck
Low Mill
Bransdale
NORTH RIDING FOREST PARK
Cropton Forest
Toll
Spaunton Moor
Hartoft End
Over Silton
Nether Silton
Arden Great Moor
Helmsley Moor
Keldy Castle
Lockton
Levisham
Kepwick
374
HAMBLETON HILLS
Hawnby
Gillamoor
Hutton-le-Hole
Lastingham
Newton-on-Rawcliffe
Newton Dale
Boltby Moor
Fadmoor
Ryedale Folk Museum
Spaunton
Cropton
Cawthorn
Kirby Knowle
Old Byland
Appleton-le-Moors
Kirkbymoorside
Keldholme
Sinnington
Wrelton
Aislaby
Middleton
North Yorkshire Moors Rly
Boltby
Carlton
Pockley
Rievaulx
Rievaulx Abbey
Nawton
Beadlam
Welburn
Newbridge
Thirlby
Cleveland Way
Cold Kirby
Helmsley Castle (ruins)
Rievaulx Terrace (NT)
Rye Dale
Helmsley
Wombleton
Great Edstone
Marton
Pickering
Forest Drive
Sutton-under-Whitestonecliffe
Scawton
324
Duncombe Park
Scawton Moor
Sutton Bank Caravans prohibited
Harome
Normanby
Vale of Pickering
Osgodby Hall
Sproxton
Flamingo Land Theme Park
Thornton-le-Dale
Bagby
High Kilburn
Nunnington Hall (NT)
Salton
Thirlkleby
Kilburn
Oldstead
Wass
Ampleforth College
Oswaldkirk
Nunnington
Great Barugh
Little Barugh
Kirby Misperton
High Marishes
Byland Abbey
Ampleforth
Gilling
Stonegrave
West Ness
East Ness
Brawby
Butterwick
Low Marishes
Hutton Sessay
Shandy Hall
Coxwold
Gilling East
South Holme
Little Habton
Great Habton
Ryton
Carlton Husthwaite
Thorpe Hall
Newburgh Priory
Cawton
Hovingham
Wyville Animal Farm
Birdforth
Sessay
Husthwaite
Slingsby
Thormanby
Oulston
Yearsley
Coulton
Barton-le-Street
Appleton-le-Street
Amotherby
Eden Camp
Broughton
Old Malton
Scackleton
Brandsby
Howardian Hills
Swinton
Malton
Old Malton Church
Scagglethorpe
Raskelf
Stearsby
Wiganthorpe
Dalby
Coneysthorpe
Hildenley
Norton
Settrington
Skewsby
Great Lake
Crayke
Terrington
Easingwold
Marton Abbey
Whenby
Ganthorpe
Castle Howard
Jorvik Glass
103
Langton Wold
Welburn
Menethorpe
Marton-in-the-Forest
Bulmer
Low Hutton
Langton
Tholthorpe
Stillington
Farlington
Firby
Sheriff Hutton
Whitwell-on-the-Hill
Kirkham
Kennythorpe
Birdsall
Huby
Cross
Westow
Kyle
20
16
Derwent
Rye
Seph
Dove
Riccal
Costa Beck
Leven
Esk
Seven
Tees
A1042
A1085
A178
A66
A174
A1032
A172
A19
A171
A173
A170
A169
A64
A1
B1257
B1365
B1380
B1266
B1366
B1363
B1248
B1269

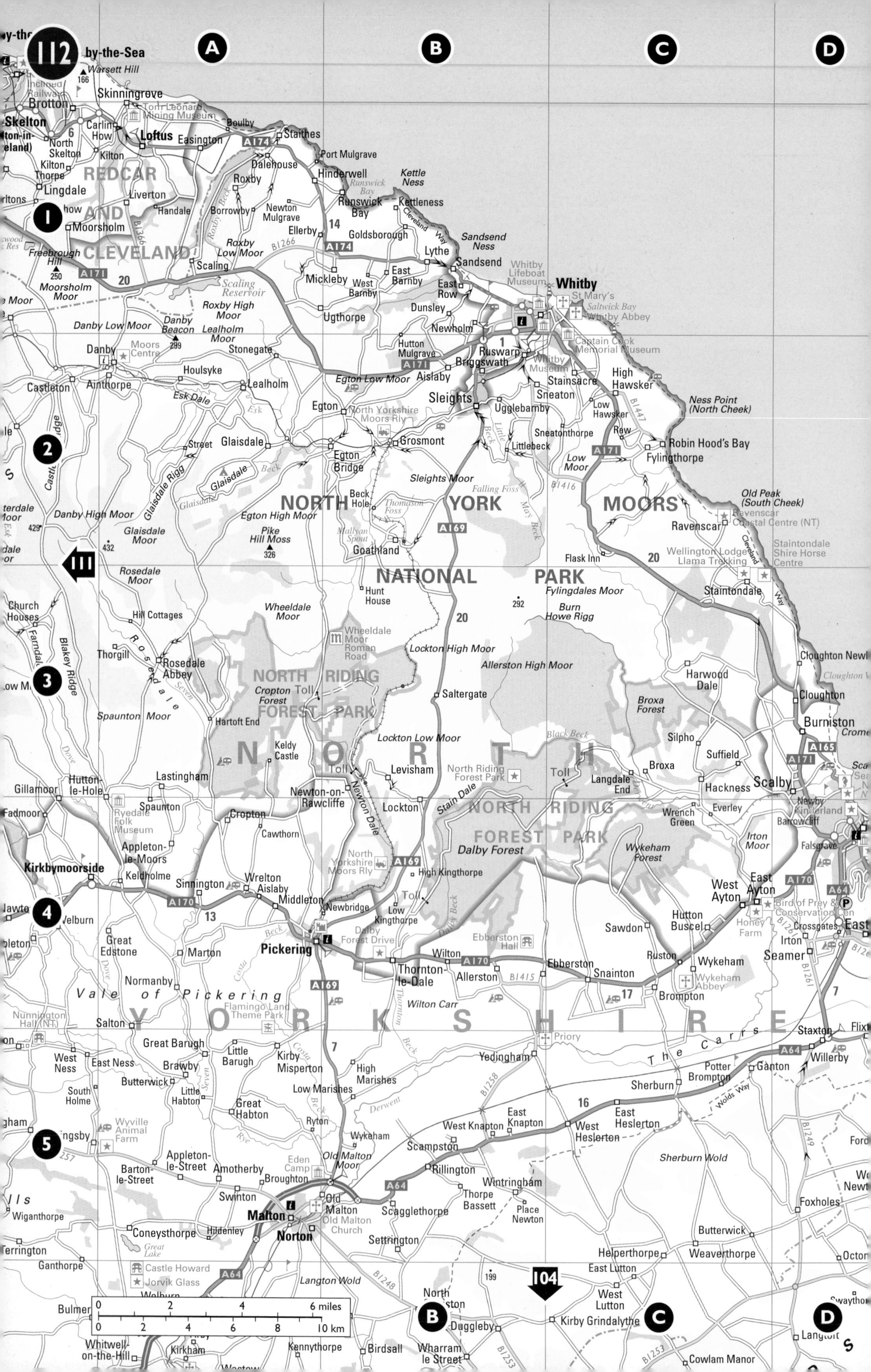

A
B
C
D
by-the-Sea
Warsett Hill
166
Skinningrove
Tom Leonard Mining Museum
Brotton
Skelton
Carlin How
Loftus
Easington
Boulby
Staithes
A174
North Skelton
Kilton
Kilton Thorpe
Lingdale
REDCAR AND CLEVELAND
Liverton
Handale
Moorsholm
Freebrough Hill
250
A171
20
Moorsholm Moor
Port Mulgrave
Dalehouse
Hinderwell
Kettle Ness
Runswick Bay
Roxby
Borrowby
Newton Mulgrave
Ellerby
14
Goldsborough
Kettleness
Cleveland Way
Sandsend Ness
Roxby Low Moor
B1266
Scaling
Lythe
Sandsend
Mickleby
West Barnby
East Barnby
East Row
Whitby Lifeboat Museum
Whitby
St Mary's
Saltwick Bay
Whitby Abbey
Scaling Reservoir
Roxby High Moor
Danby Beacon
299
Lealholm Moor
Danby Low Moor
Ugthorpe
Dunsley
Newholm
Captain Cook Memorial Museum
Danby
Moors Centre
Stonegate
Hutton Mulgrave
Ruswarp
1
Briggswath
Whitby Museum
Houlsyke
Castleton
Ainthorpe
Lealholm
Egton Low Moor
Aislaby
Stainsacre
High Hawsker
Esk Dale
Esk
Sleights
Sneaton
Ness Point (North Cheek)
Egton
North Yorkshire Moors Rly
Ugglebarnby
Low Hawsker
B1447
Street
Glaisdale
Grosmont
Sneatonthorpe
Raw
Robin Hood's Bay
Castleton Rigg
Egton Bridge
Littlebeck
Little Beck
Low Moor
Fylingthorpe
Glaisdale Rigg
Glaisdale
Beck
Sleights Moor
Falling Foss
B1416
Beck Hole
Thomason Foss
NORTH YORK MOORS
Old Peak (South Cheek)
Danby High Moor
Egton High Moor
Ravenscar
Ravenscar Coastal Centre (NT)
429
Glaisdale Moor
Mallyan Spout
A169
May Beck
Pike Hill Moss
326
432
Goathland
Flask Inn
20
Wellington Lodge Llama Trekking
Staintondale Shire Horse Centre
111
Rosedale Moor
NATIONAL PARK
Hunt House
Fylingdales Moor
Staintondale
Church Houses
Wheeldale Moor
292
Burn Howe Rigg
Hill Cottages
20
Farndale
Blakey Ridge
Wheeldale Moor Roman Road
Thorgill
Rosedale
Lockton High Moor
Cloughton Newl
Rosedale Abbey
Allerston High Moor
Seven
Harwood Dale
NORTH RIDING
Cropton Forest
Toll
Saltergate
Cloughton
FOREST PARK
Broxa Forest
Spaunton Moor
Burniston
Hartoft End
Black Beck
Silpho
A165
Lockton Low Moor
Keldy Castle
N O R T H
Suffield
A171
Dove
Toll
Broxa
Levisham
North Riding Forest Park
Toll
Langdale End
Lastingham
Hutton-le-Hole
Newton-on-Rawcliffe
Stain Dale
Hackness
Scalby
Gillamoor
Lockton
Ryedale Folk Museum
Spaunton
Newton Dale
NORTH RIDING
Wrench Green
Everley
Newby
Fadmoor
Cropton
Barrowcliff
Cawthorn
FOREST PARK
Irton Moor
Appleton-le-Moors
Dalby Forest
Wykeham Forest
Falsgrave
North Yorkshire Moors Rly
Kirkbymoorside
A169
High Kingthorpe
Keldholme
A170
Wrelton
Sinnington
East Ayton
West Ayton
Aislaby
A170
Middleton
Toll
Velburn
13
Newbridge
Low Kingthorpe
Bird of Prey & Conservation Cen
Hutton Buscel
Sawdon
Honey Farm
Crossgates
Great Edstone
Dalby Forest Drive
Ebberston Hall
Irton
Marton
Pickering
Wilton
Ruston
Seamer
Thornton-le-Dale
A170
Ebberston
Wykeham
Normanby
Allerston
B1415
Snainton
Wykeham Abbey
B1261
A169
Brompton
17
Vale of Pickering
Wilton Carr
Flamingo Land Theme Park
7
Nunnington Hall (NT)
Salton
Y O R K S H I R E
Staxton
Priory
Great Barugh
Little Barugh
The Carrs
West Ness
East Ness
Kirby Misperton
7
Yedingham
Willerby
Brawby
High Marishes
Potter Brompton
Ganton
A64
Butterwick
Sherburn
South Holme
Little Habton
Low Marishes
Wolds Way
Great Habton
Derwent
B1258
16
East Knapton
East Heslerton
Ryton
West Knapton
West Heslerton
Wyville Animal Farm
Wykeham
B1249
Rye
Scampston
Eden Camp
Old Malton Moor
Sherburn Wold
Appleton-le-Street
Barton-le-Street
Amotherby
Broughton
Rillington
A64
Wintringham
Swinton
Old Malton
Thorpe Bassett
Place Newton
Foxholes
Wiganthorpe
Malton
Scagglethorpe
Old Malton Church
Coneysthorpe
Hildenley
Norton
Butterwick
Settrington
Great Lake
Helperthorpe
Weaverthorpe
Terrington
Castle Howard
Ganthorpe
Jorvik Glass
A64
B1248
East Lutton
Langton Wold
199
104
West Lutton
North Grimston
Bulmer
0 2 4 6 miles
0 2 4 6 8 10 km
Kirby Grindalythe
Duggleby
Whitwell-on-the-Hill
Kirkham
Kennythorpe
Birdsall
Wharram le Street
B1253
B1253
Cowlam Manor

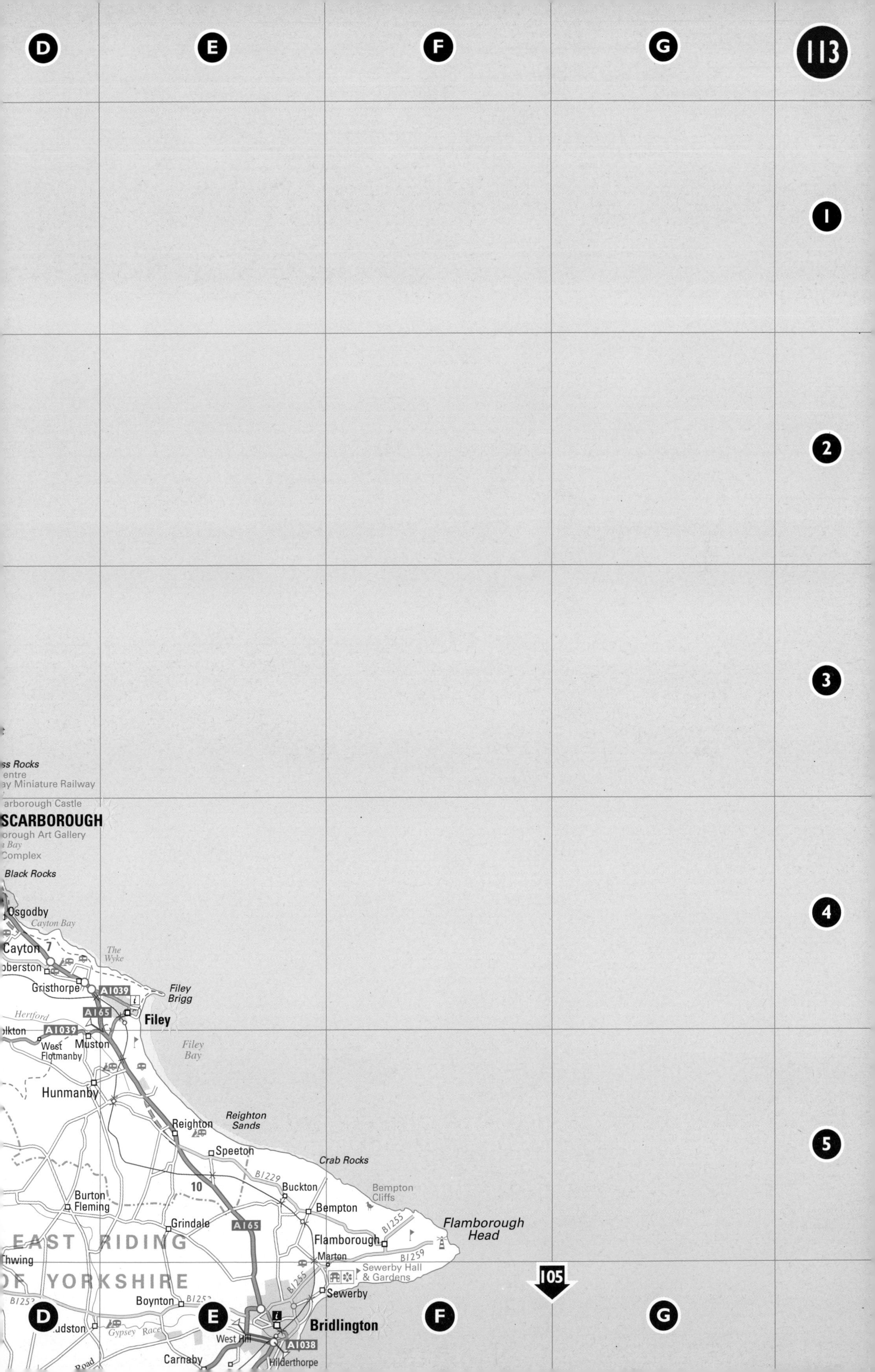

ss Rocks
ay Miniature Railway
arborough Castle

SCARBOROUGH
orough Art Gallery
a Bay
Complex

Black Rocks

Osgodby
Cayton Bay

Cayton 7
The Wyke
oberston
Gristhorpe
A1039
Filey Brigg
Hertford
A165
olkton
A1039
Filey

West Muston
Flotmanby
Filey Bay

Hunmanby

Reighton
Reighton Sands

Speeton
Crab Rocks

Burton
Fleming
10
B1229
Buckton
Bempton Cliffs

Grindale
Bempton
B1255

A165
Flamborough
B1259
Flamborough Head

EAST RIDING
Marton
B1259
Sewerby Hall
& Gardens

Thwing

OF YORKSHIRE
Sewerby

B1252
Boynton
B1252

105

udston
Gypsey Race

West Hill
Bridlington

Carnaby
A1038

Hilderthorpe

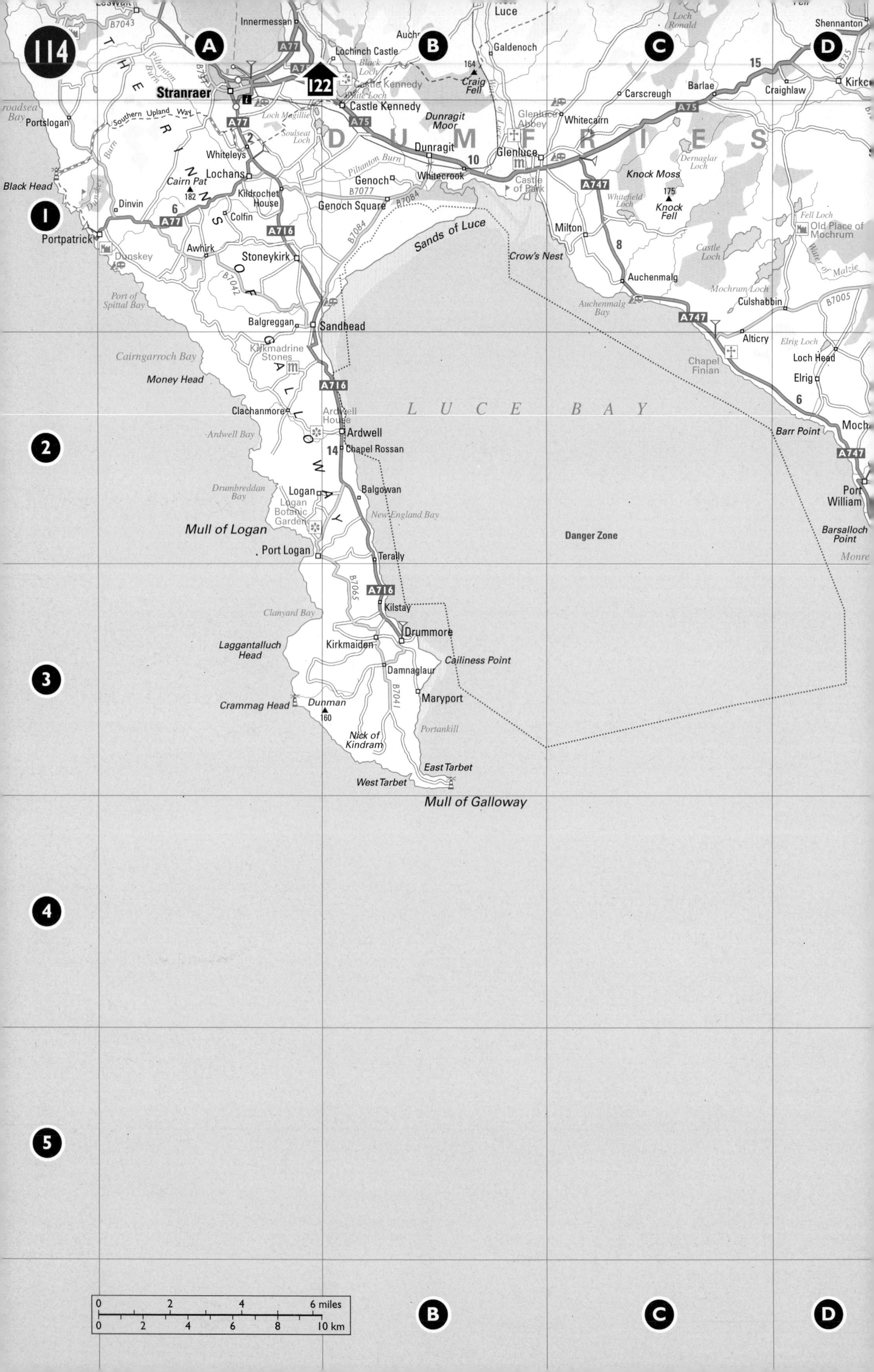

Stranraer
Portpatrick
Portslogan
Black Head
Dinvin
Lochans
Whiteleys
Cairn Pat
182
Kildrochet House
Colfin
Awhirk
Dunskey
Stoneykirk
Port of Spittal Bay
Balgreggan
Sandhead
Kirkmadrine Stones
Cairngarroch Bay
Money Head
Clachanmore
Ardwell House
Ardwell
Ardwell Bay
Chapel Rossan
Drumbreddan Bay
Logan
Logan Botanic Garden
Balgowan
Mull of Logan
Port Logan
New England Bay
Terally
Kilstay
Clanyard Bay
Drummore
Laggantalluch Head
Kirkmaiden
Cailiness Point
Damnaglaur
Maryport
Crammag Head
Dunman
160
Portankill
Nick of Kindram
East Tarbet
West Tarbet
Mull of Galloway
Innermessan
Lochinch Castle
Black Loch
Castle Kennedy
White Loch
Loch Magillie
Soulseat Loch
Dunragit Moor
Dunragit
Pilltanton Burn
Genoch
Genoch Square
Whitecrook
Galdenoch
Craig Fell
164
Luce
Glenluce Abbey
Glenluce
Castle of Park
Sands of Luce
Crow's Nest
LUCE BAY
Danger Zone
Carscreugh
Whitecairn
Barlae
Craighlaw
Shennanton
Kirkcowan
Loch Ronald
Dernaglar Loch
Knock Moss
Knock Fell
175
Whitefield Loch
Milton
Auchenmalg
Auchenmalg Bay
Castle Loch
Mochrum Loch
Culshabbin
Fell Loch
Old Place of Mochrum
Water of Malzie
Alticry
Elrig Loch
Loch Head
Elrig
Chapel Finian
Barr Point
Port William
Barsalloch Point
Monreith
Southern Upland Way
THE RINNS OF GALLOWAY
DUMFRIES
A77
A75
A716
A747
B7043
B737
B7077
B7084
B7042
B7065
B7041
B7005
B735
122
A
B
C
D
1
2
3
4
5
0 2 4 6 miles
0 2 4 6 8 10 km

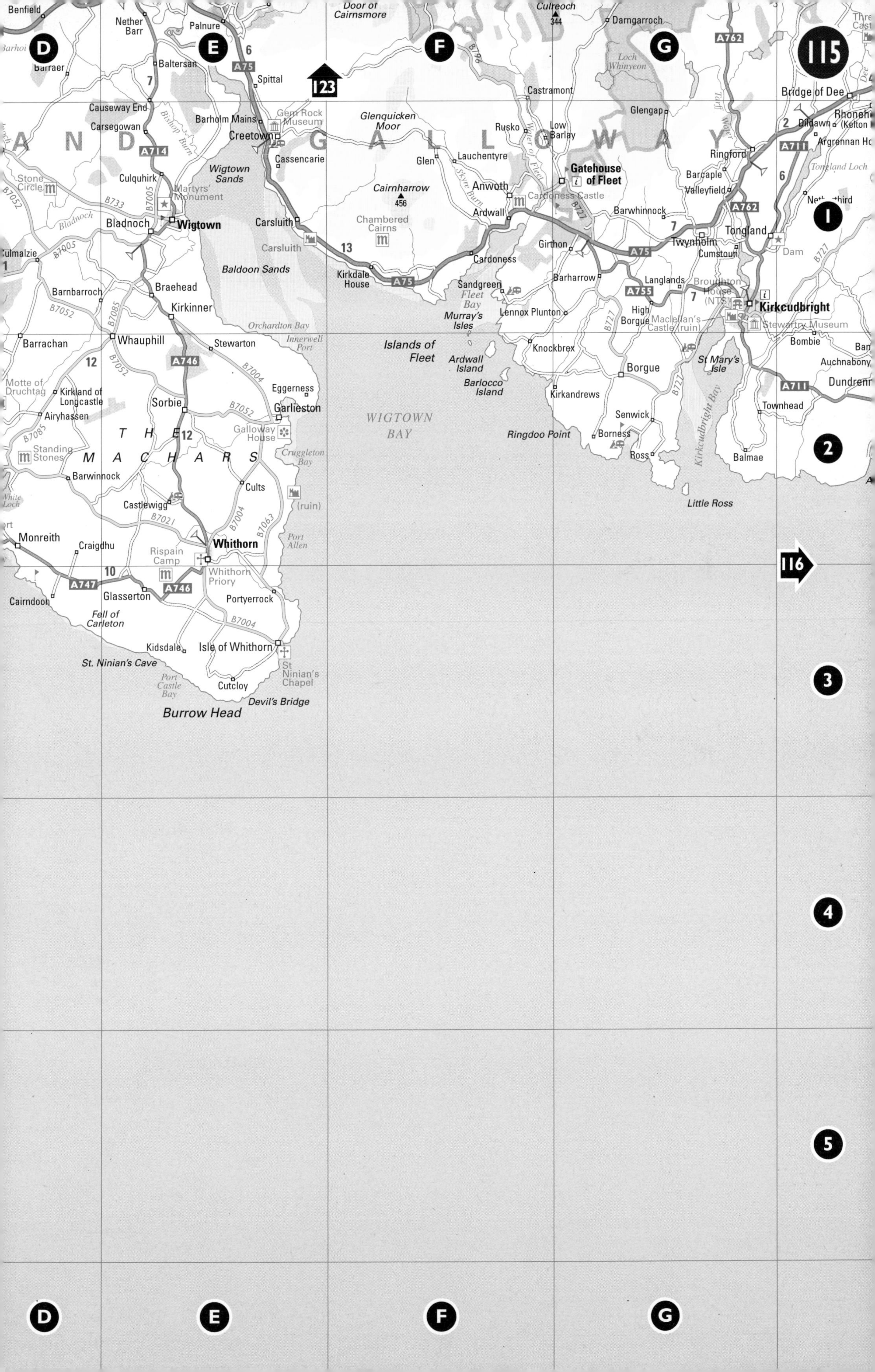
Benfield
Nether Barr
Palnure
Door of Cairnsmore
Culreoch
344
Darngarroch
A762
D
E
F
G
Barraer
Baltersan
6
A75
Spittal
123
B796
Loch Whinyeon
Castramont
Bridge of Dee
Rhonehouse
Causeway End
Carsegowan
7
Bishop Burn
Barholm Mains
Gem Rock Museum
Creetown
Glenquicken Moor
Rusko
Low Barlay
Glengap
Tarff Water
2
Dildawn
(Kelton)
A N D
G A L L O W A Y
A714
A711
Argrennan House
Ringford
Cassencarie
Glen
Lauchentyre
Water of Fleet
Gatehouse of Fleet
Stone Circle
Culquhirk
Wigtown Sands
Barcaple
Tongland Loch
Valleyfield
6
B7052
B7005
Martyrs' Monument
Cairnharrow
456
Anwoth
Skyre Burn
Cardoness Castle
B727
Nether Third
B733
Bladnoch
Chambered Cairns
Ardwall
Barwhinnock
A762
1
Bladnoch
Wigtown
Carsluith
7
Tongland
Culmalzie
B7005
Carsluith
13
Girthon
Twynholm
Dam
Cumstoun
A75
B727
Baldoon Sands
Cardoness
Braehead
Kirkdale House
A75
Barharrow
Langlands
Broughton House (NTS)
Barnbarroch
Sandgreen
Fleet Bay
A755
7
B7052
B7085
Kirkinner
Lennox Plunton
High Borgue
Maclellan's Castle (ruin)
Kirkcudbright
Murray's Isles
B727
Stewartry Museum
Orchardton Bay
Whauphill
Innerwell Port
Barrachan
Stewarton
Islands of Fleet
Knockbrex
Bombie
12
St Mary's Isle
Ardwall Island
Auchnabony
B7052
B7004
Borgue
A746
Dundrennan
Motte of Druchtag
Kirkland of Longcastle
Eggerness
Barlocco Island
A711
Sorbie
Garlieston
Kirkandrews
B727
Airyhassen
B7052
Kirkcudbright Bay
Townhead
WIGTOWN BAY
T H E
12
Galloway House
Senwick
B7085
Ringdoo Point
Borness
Standing Stones
M A C H A R S
Cruggleton Bay
2
Ross
Balmae
Barwinnock
Cults
(ruin)
White Loch
Castlewigg
B7004
Little Ross
B7021
B7063
Monreith
Port Allen
Craigdhu
Whithorn
Rispain Camp
116
10
Whithorn Priory
A747
A746
Glasserton
Cairndoon
Portyerrock
Fell of Carleton
B7004
Kidsdale
Isle of Whithorn
St. Ninian's Cave
St Ninian's Chapel
3
Port Castle Bay
Cutcloy
Devil's Bridge
Burrow Head
4
5
D
E
F
G

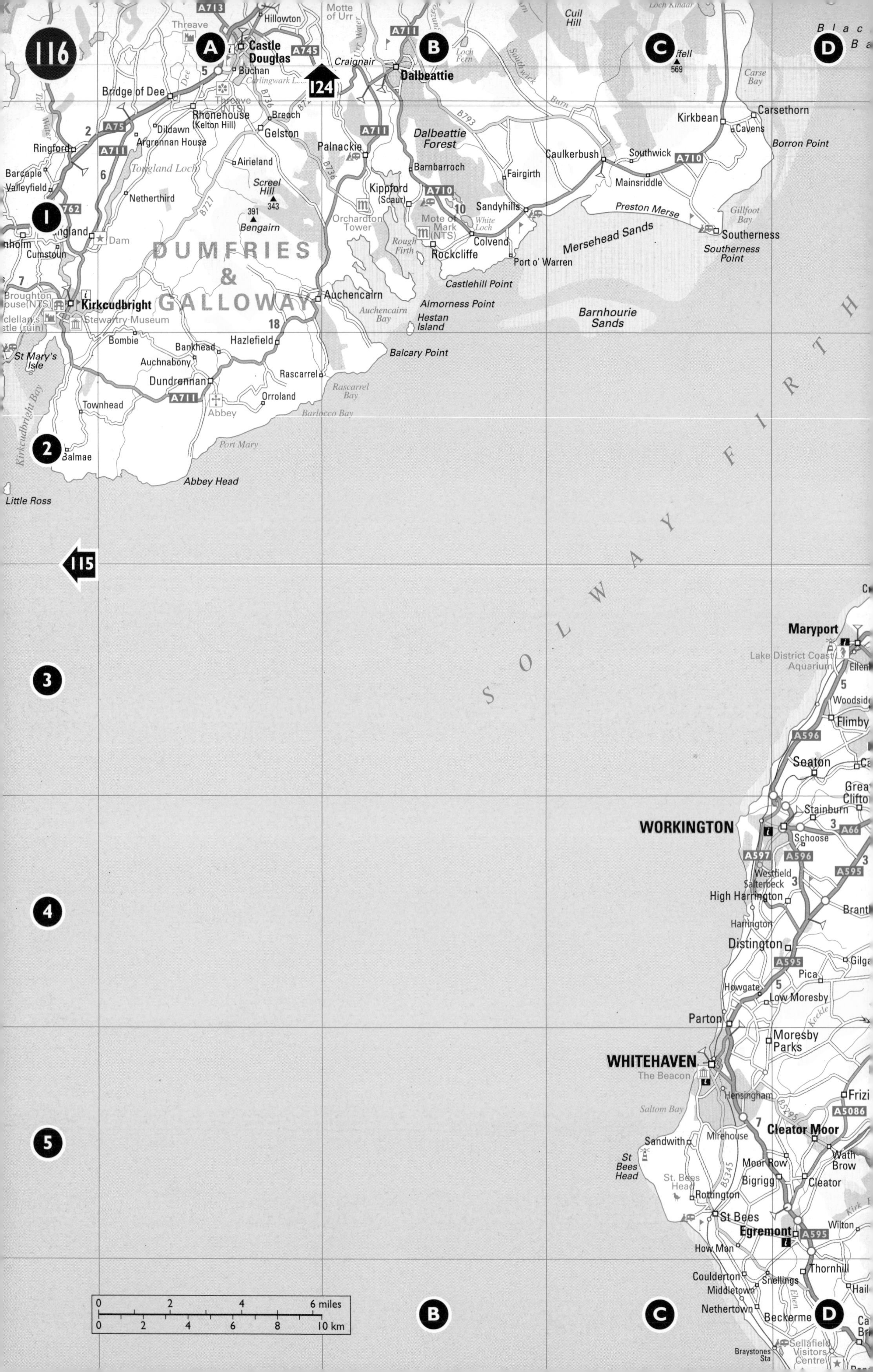

A713
Hillowton
Motte of Urr
Threave
Castle Douglas
A745
Buchan
Carlingwark L.
Craignair
A711
Dalbeattie
Loch Fern
Southwick Burn
Cuil Hill
Loch Kindar
569
Carse Bay
Blac
Ba
124
Bridge of Dee
Dee
Tarff Water
Threave (NTS)
B736
Rhonehouse (Kelton Hill)
Breoch
Gelston
A75
Dildawn
Argrennan House
Ringford
A711
Barcaple
Valleyfield
762
Tongland Loch
Netherthird
Airieland
Palnackie
B736
A711
Dalbeattie Forest
B793
Barnbarroch
Kipppford (Scaur)
A710
Fairgirth
Caulkerbush
Southwick
A710
Mainsriddle
Kirkbean
Carsethorn
Cavens
Borron Point
Screel Hill
343
391
Bengairn
B727
Orchardton Tower
Mote of Mark (NTS)
White Loch
Sandyhills
Rough Firth
Rockcliffe
Colvend
Port o' Warren
Preston Merse
Mersehead Sands
Gillfoot Bay
Southerness
Southerness Point
Dam
Cumstoun
DUMFRIES & GALLOWAY
Castlehill Point
Broughton House (NTS)
Kirkcudbright
Stewartry Museum
Auchencairn
Auchencairn Bay
Almorness Point
Hestan Island
Barnhourie Sands
18
Bombie
Bankhead
Hazlefield
St Mary's Isle
Auchnabony
Dundrennan
Rascarrel
Balcary Point
Rascarrel Bay
A711
Townhead
Abbey
Orroland
Barlocco Bay
Kirkcudbright Bay
Balmae
Port Mary
Abbey Head
Little Ross
115
SOLWAY FIRTH
Maryport
Lake District Coast Aquarium
Ellen
Woodside
Flimby
A596
Seaton
Great Clifton
Stainburn
WORKINGTON
Schoose
A66
A597
A596
A595
Westfield
Salterbeck
High Harrington
Harrington
Distington
A595
Gilga
Pica
Howgate
Low Moresby
Parton
Keekle
Moresby Parks
WHITEHAVEN
The Beacon
Hensingham
B5295
Frizi
A5086
Saltom Bay
Mirehouse
Cleator Moor
Sandwith
St Bees Head
St. Bees Head
B5345
Moor Row
Wath Brow
Bigrigg
Cleator
Rottington
St Bees
Egremont
A595
Wilton
How Man
Thornhill
Coulderton
Middletown
Snellings
Ehen
Nethertown
Beckerme
Braystones Sta
Sellafield Visitors Centre
0 2 4 6 miles
0 2 4 6 8 10 km
A B C D
1 2 3 4 5

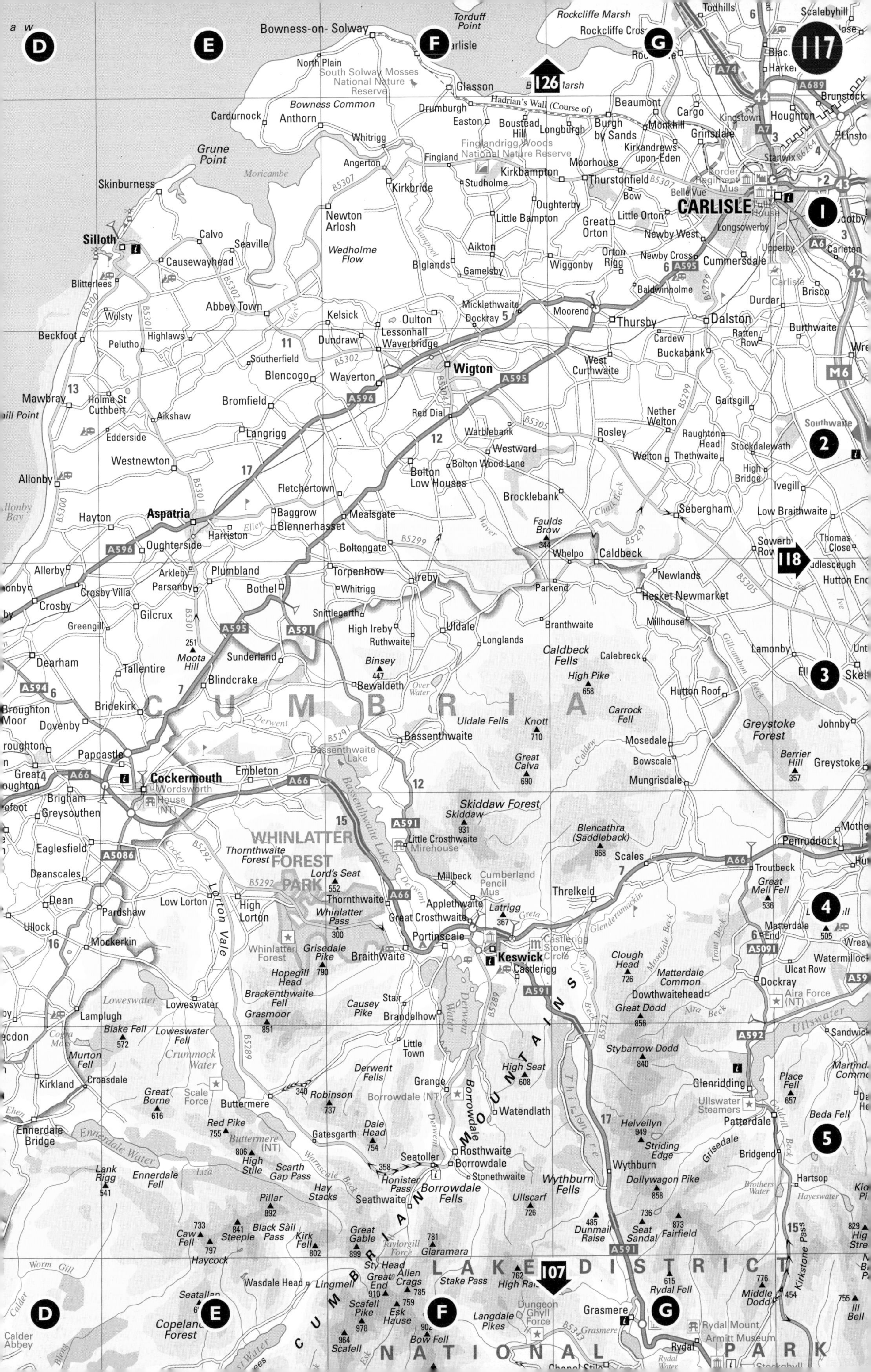

Bowness-on-Solway
Torduff Point
Rockcliffe Marsh
Rockcliffe Cross
Todhills
Scalebyhill
North Plain
South Solway Mosses National Nature Reserve
Glasson
126
Hadrian's Wall (Course of)
Beaumont
Cargo
Brunstock
Houghton
Kingstown
Cardurnock
Anthorn
Bowness Common
Drumburgh
Easton
Boustead Hill
Longburgh
Burgh by Sands
Monkhill
Grinsdale
Kirkandrews-upon-Eden
Whitrigg
Finglandrigg Woods National Nature Reserve
Fingland
Grune Point
Moricambe
Angerton
Kirkbampton
Moorhouse
Stanwix
Border Regiment Mus
Skinburness
Kirkbride
Studholme
Thurstonfield
Belle Vue
Bow
CARLISLE
Tullie House
Newton Arlosh
Oughterby
Little Bampton
Great Orton
Little Orton
Longsowerby
Newby West
Upperby
Carleton
Silloth
Calvo
Seaville
Causewayhead
Wedholme Flow
Wampool
Biglands
Aikton
Gamelsby
Wiggonby
Orton Rigg
Newby Cross
Cummersdale
Blitterlees
Abbey Town
Baldwinholme
Carlisle
Brisco
Durdar
Wolsty
Kelsick
Oulton
Micklethwaite
Dockray
Moorend
Thursby
Dalston
Beckfoot
Highlaws
Pelutho
Lessonhall
Waverbridge
Dundraw
Cardew
Ratten Row
Burthwaite
Buckabank
Southerfield
Wigton
West Curthwaite
Blencogo
Waverton
M6
Mawbray
Holme St Cuthbert
Bromfield
Red Dial
Gaitsgill
Aikshaw
Nether Welton
Southwaite
Edderside
Langrigg
Warblebank
Rosley
Raughton Head
Stockdalewath
Westnewton
Westward
Welton
Thethwaite
Bolton Wood Lane
Allonby
Bolton Low Houses
High Bridge
Ivegill
Fletchertown
Brocklebank
Chalk Beck
Sebergham
Low Braithwaite
Allonby Bay
Hayton
Aspatria
Baggrow
Mealsgate
Blennerhasset
Harriston
Ellen
Faulds Brow
344
Oughterside
Boltongate
Whelpo
Caldbeck
Sowerby Row
Thomas Close
118
Allerby
Arkleby
Plumbland
Torpenhow
Ireby
Parkend
Newlands
Hutton End
Crosby Villa
Parsonby
Bothel
Whitrigg
Hesket Newmarket
Crosby
Gilcrux
Snittlegarth
Greengill
High Ireby
Uldale
Branthwaite
Millhouse
Ruthwaite
Longlands
Moota Hill
251
Sunderland
Caldbeck Fells
Calebreck
Lamonby
Dearham
Binsey
447
High Pike
658
Tallentire
Blindcrake
Bewaldeth
Over Water
Hutton Roof
Bridekirk
CUMBRIA
Broughton Moor
Dovenby
Derwent
Carrock Fell
Greystoke Forest
Johnby
Uldale Fells
Knott
710
Bassenthwaite
Mosedale
Papcastle
Bassenthwaite Lake
Great Calva
690
Bowscale
Berrier Hill
357
Greystoke
Cockermouth
Wordsworth House (NT)
Embleton
Mungrisdale
Brigham
Greysouthen
Skiddaw Forest
Skiddaw
931
Eaglesfield
WHINLATTER FOREST PARK
Little Crosthwaite
Mirehouse
Blencathra (Saddleback)
868
Penruddock
Thornthwaite Forest
Scales
Troutbeck
Deanscales
Lord's Seat
552
Millbeck
Cumberland Pencil Mus
Threlkeld
Great Mell Fell
536
Dean
Low Lorton
High Lorton
Lorton Vale
Thornthwaite
Applethwaite
Latrigg
367
Pardshaw
Whinlatter Pass
300
Great Crosthwaite
Greta
Glenderamackin
Matterdale End
505
Ullock
Mockerkin
Portinscale
Keswick
Castlerigg Stone Circle
Whinlatter Forest
Grisedale Pike
790
Braithwaite
Castlerigg
Clough Head
726
Matterdale Common
Watermillock
Ulcat Row
Dockray
Hopegill Head
Brackenthwaite Fell
Aira Force (NT)
Loweswater
Lamplugh
Causey Pike
Stair
Brandelhow
Derwent Water
Dowthwaitehead
Grasmoor
851
Great Dodd
856
Blake Fell
572
Loweswater Fell
Ullswater
Sandwick
Crummock Water
Little Town
Stybarrow Dodd
840
Murton Fell
Derwent Fells
High Seat
608
Martindale Common
Kirkland
Croasdale
Grange
Borrowdale
Glenridding
Place Fell
657
Great Borne
616
Scale Force
Buttermere
Robinson
737
Borrowdale (NT)
Watendlath
Ullswater Steamers
Beda Fell
Ennerdale Bridge
Red Pike
755
Buttermere (NT)
Dale Head
754
Helvellyn
949
Patterdale
Gatesgarth
Striding Edge
Ennerdale Water
806
High Stile
Seatoller
Rosthwaite
Borrowdale
Wythburn
Bridgend
Lank Rigg
541
Ennerdale Fell
Scarth Gap Pass
Honister Pass
Stonethwaite
Wythburn Fells
Dollywagon Pike
858
Hartsop
Hay Stacks
Seathwaite
Borrowdale Fells
Brothers Water
Hayeswater
Pillar
892
Ullscarf
726
736
Seat Sandal
873
Fairfield
Caw Fell
733
841
Steeple
797
Black Sail Pass
Kirk Fell
802
Great Gable
899
Taylorgill Force
781
Glaramara
485
Dunmail Raise
829
Haycock
Worm Gill
Sty Head
Great End
910
Allen Crags
785
LAKE DISTRICT
762
High Raise
107
Stake Pass
615
Rydal Fell
776
Middle Dodd
454
Kirkstone Pass
755
Ill Bell
Wasdale Head
Lingmell
Seatallan
Scafell Pike
978
759
Esk Hause
902
Bow Fell
Dungeon Ghyll Force
Langdale Pikes
Grasmere
Rydal Mount
Armitt Museum
Copeland Forest
Calder Abbey
964
Scafell
CUMBRIAN MOUNTAINS
NATIONAL PARK
Rydal
Rydal Water
A74
A689
A7
B6264
A6
A595
B5299
B5307
B5300
B5302
B5301
A596
B5304
B5305
A594
A591
B5291
A66
A5086
B5292
B5289
B5322
A5091
A592
B5343
A59

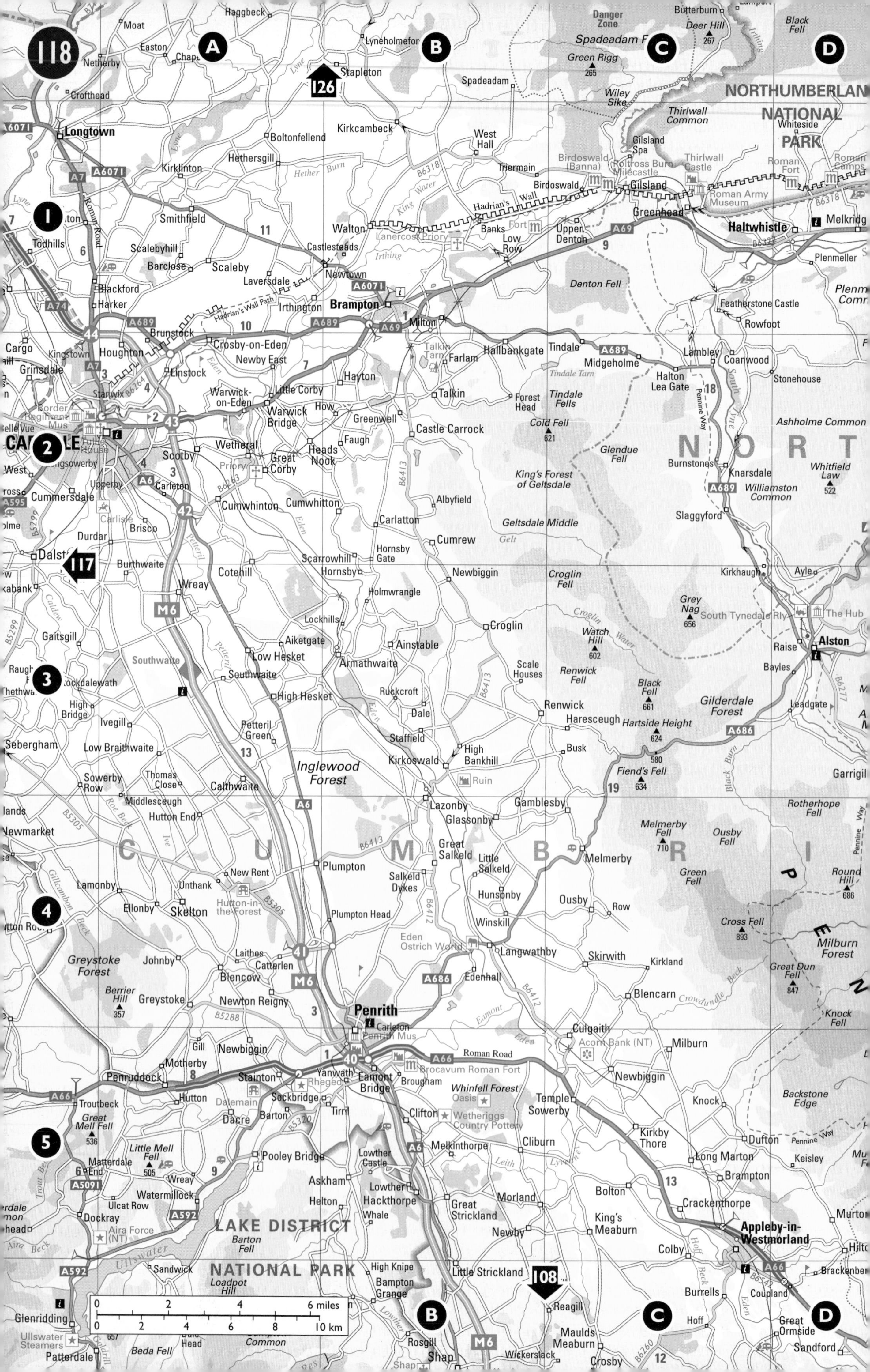
A
B
C
D
1
2
3
4
5
126
117
108
Haggbeck
Moat
Easton
Chapel
Netherby
Crofthead
Lyneholmeford
Stapleton
Danger Zone
Spadeadam Forest
Butterburn
Deer Hill 267
Black Fell
Green Rigg 265
Spadeadam
Wiley Sike
NORTHUMBERLAND NATIONAL PARK
Thirlwall Common
Whiteside
Longtown
Boltonfellend
Kirkcambeck
West Hall
Gilsland Spa
Birdoswald (Banna)
Poltross Burn Milecastle
Thirlwall Castle
Roman Fort
Roman Camps
Hethersgill
Hether Burn
Kirklinton
Triermain
Birdoswald
Gilsland
Roman Army Museum
Greenhead
Haltwhistle
Melkridge
Smithfield
Hadrian's Wall
Walton
Banks
Lanercost Priory
Low Row
Upper Denton
Todhills
Castlesteads
Irthing
Plenmeller
Scalebyhill
Barclose
Scaleby
Newtown
Laversdale
Denton Fell
Blackford
Harker
Hadrian's Wall Path
Irthington
Brampton
Milton
Featherstone Castle
Rowfoot
Brunstock
Crosby-on-Eden
Newby East
Talkin Tarn
Farlam
Hallbankgate
Tindale
Midgeholme
Lambley
Coanwood
Cargo
Kingstown
Houghton
Linstock
Hayton
Tindale Tarn
Halton Lea Gate
Stonehouse
Grinsdale
Stanwix
Little Corby
Warwick-on-Eden
Warwick Bridge
Talkin
Forest Head
Tindale Fells
Pennine Way
South Tyne
Border Regiment Mus
How
Greenwell
Castle Carrock
Cold Fell 621
Ashholme Common
Belle Vue
CARLISLE
Tullie House
Wetheral
Scotby
Great Corby
Heads Nook
Faugh
Glendue Fell
Burnstones
Harraby
Botcherby
Upperby
Carleton
Priory
King's Forest of Geltsdale
Knarsdale
Whitfield Law 522
Williamston Common
Cummersdale
Cumwhinton
Cumwhitton
Albyfield
Slaggyford
Carlisle
Brisco
Carlatton
Geltsdale Middle
Durdar
Cumrew
Gelt
Dalston
Burthwaite
Scarrowhill
Hornsby Gate
Hornsby
Cotehill
Newbiggin
Croglin Fell
Kirkhaugh
Ayle
Wreay
Holmwrangle
Caldew
Grey Nag 656
South Tynedale Rly
The Hub
Gaitsgill
Lockhills
Croglin
Watch Hill 602
Croglin Water
Alston
Southwaite
Aiketgate
Low Hesket
Ainstable
Armathwaite
Raise
Rockdalewath
Scale Houses
Renwick Fell
Bayles
High Bridge
High Hesket
Ruckcroft
Black Fell 661
Gilderdale Forest
Leadgate
Ivegill
Dale
Renwick
Haresceugh
Hartside Height 624
Petteril Green
Staffield
Sebergham
Low Braithwaite
High Bankhill
Busk
580
Inglewood Forest
Kirkoswald
Ruin
Fiend's Fell 634
Black Burn
Garrigill
Sowerby Row
Thomas Close
Calthwaite
Middlesceugh
Hutton End
Lazonby
Glassonby
Gamblesby
Rotherhope Fell
Newmarket
Roe Beck
Great Salkeld
Melmerby Fell 710
Ousby Fell
CUMBRIA
NORTH PENNINES
Plumpton
Little Salkeld
Melmerby
Round Hill 686
Lamonby
New Rent
Unthank
Salkeld Dykes
Green Fell
Hutton-in-the-Forest
Hunsonby
Ousby
Row
Ellonby
Skelton
Plumpton Head
Winskill
Cross Fell 893
Gillcambon Beck
Eden Ostrich World
Langwathby
Milburn Forest
Greystoke Forest
Johnby
Laithes
Catterlen
Skirwith
Kirkland
Great Dun Fell 847
Blencow
Edenhall
Berrier Hill 357
Greystoke
Newton Reigny
Blencarn
Crowdundle Beck
Penrith
Eamont
Knock Fell
Carleton
Penrith Mus
Culgaith
Acorn Bank (NT)
Milburn
Gill
Newbiggin
Roman Road
Motherby
Brocavum Roman Fort
Penruddock
Stainton
Yanwath
Rheged
Eamont Bridge
Brougham
Newbiggin
Troutbeck
Hutton
Whinfell Forest
Oasis
Temple Sowerby
Knock
Backstone Edge
Great Mell Fell 536
Dalemain
Sockbridge
Barton
Tirril
Dacre
Clifton
Wetheriggs Country Pottery
Kirkby Thore
Dufton
Little Mell Fell 505
Melkinthorpe
Cliburn
Long Marton
Keisley
Matterdale End
Pooley Bridge
Lowther Castle
Leith
Lyvennet
Brampton
Wreay
Askham
Watermillock
Lowther
Bolton
Ulcat Row
Helton
Hackthorpe
Great Strickland
Morland
Crackenthorpe
Dockray
LAKE DISTRICT NATIONAL PARK
Whale
King's Meaburn
Appleby-in-Westmorland
Aira Force (NT)
Barton Fell
Newby
Aira Beck
Colby
Hoff Beck
Ullswater
Sandwick
High Knipe
Little Strickland
Brackenber
Loadpot Hill
Bampton
Bampton Grange
Burrells
Coupland
Reagill
Glenridding
Hoff
Great Ormside
Rosgill
Maulds Meaburn
Ullswater Steamers
Wickerslack
Sandford
Patterdale
Beda Fell
Shap
Crosby
Goldrill Beck
0 2 4 6 miles
0 2 4 6 8 10 km
A6071
A7
A74
A689
A69
B6318
B6264
A595
B5299
M6
A6
B6413
B6412
A686
B5305
B5288
A66
A5091
A592
B5320
B6263
B6277
B6260
B6542
44
43
42
41
40

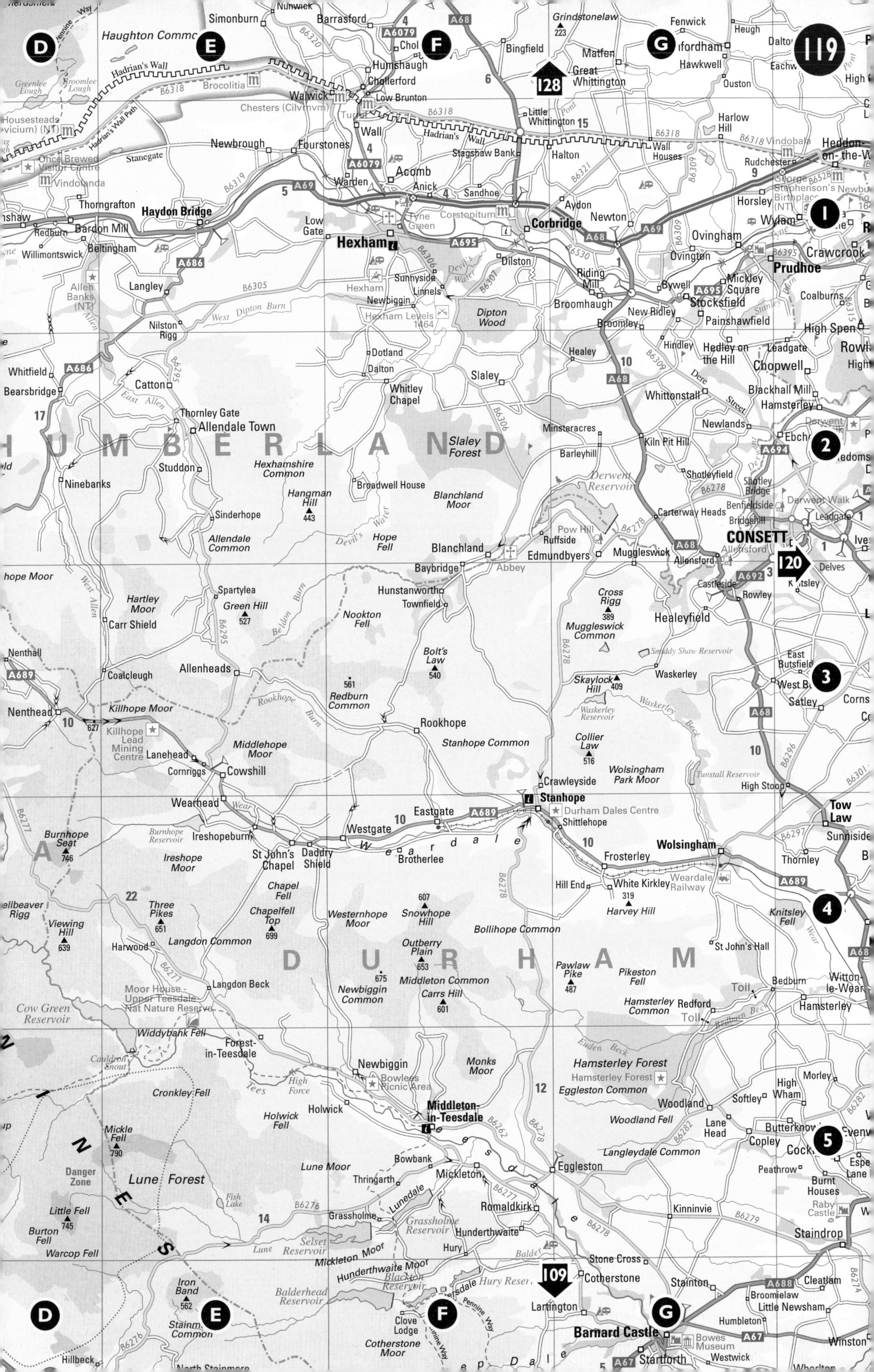
119
D
E
F
G
I
2
3
4
5
128
120
109
Haughton Common
Simonburn
Nunwick
Barrasford
A6079
Chollerton
Humshaugh
Chollerford
Walwick
Chesters (Cilurnum)
Low Brunton
Brocolitia
Hadrian's Wall
Hadrian's Wall Path
Greenlee Lough
Broomlee Lough
Housesteads (Vercovicium) (NT)
Once Brewed Visitor Centre
Vindolanda
Stanegate
Newbrough
Fourstones
Wall
Warden
Acomb
Anick
Sandhoe
Stagshaw Bank
Grindstonelaw
223
Bingfield
Matfen
Great Whittington
Fenwick
Ingoe
Heugh
Dalton
Hawkwell
Ouston
Eachwick
High Callerton
Little Whittington
Halton
Wall Houses
Harlow Hill
Vindobala
Rudchester
Heddon-on-the-Wall
George Stephenson's Birthplace (NT)
Horsley
Wylam
Ovingham
Ovington
Crawcrook
Prudhoe
Mickley Square
Bywell
Stocksfield
New Ridley
Painshawfield
Coalburns
Stanley Burn
High Spen
Rowlands Gill
Leadgate
Chopwell
Hedley on the Hill
Hindley
Blackhall Mill
Hamsterley
Newlands
Ebchester
Derwent
Medomsley
Shotley Bridge
Benfieldside
Derwent Walk
Bridgehill
CONSETT
Allensford
Delves
Knitsley
Castleside
Rowley
Healeyfield
Thorngrafton
Haydon Bridge
Bardon Mill
Redburn
Willimontswick
Beltingham
Allen Banks (NT)
Langley
A686
Low Gate
Hexham
Tyne Green
Corstopitum
Corbridge
Aydon
Newton
Dilston
Riding Mill
Broomhaugh
Broomley
Sunnyside
Linnels
Newbiggin
Hexham Levels
1464
Dipton Wood
West Dipton Burn
Devil's Water
Nilston Rigg
Whitfield
Bearsbridge
Catton
East Allen
Dotland
Dalton
Whitley Chapel
Slaley
Healey
Whittonstall
Dere Street
Minsteracres
Barleyhill
Kiln Pit Hill
Shotleyfield
Carterway Heads
Derwent Reservoir
Slaley Forest
NORTHUMBERLAND
Thornley Gate
Allendale Town
Studdon
Ninebanks
Hexhamshire Common
Hangman Hill
443
Broadwell House
Blanchland Moor
Sinderhope
Allendale Common
Devil's Water
Hope Fell
Blanchland
Abbey
Pow Hill
Ruffside
Edmundbyers
Muggleswick
Baybridge
Hunstanworth
Townfield
Cross Rigg
389
Muggleswick Common
Smiddy Shaw Reservoir
hope Moor
West Allen
Hartley Moor
Carr Shield
Spartylea
Green Hill
527
Beldon Burn
Nookton Fell
Nenthall
A689
Coalcleugh
Allenheads
561
Redburn Common
Bolt's Law
540
Skaylock Hill
409
Waskerley
Waskerley Reservoir
Waskerley Beck
East Butsfield
West Butsfield
Satley
Cornsay
Nenthead
Killhope Moor
627
Killhope Lead Mining Centre
Lanehead
Cornriggs
Cowshill
Middlehope Moor
Rookhope Burn
Rookhope
Stanhope Common
Collier Law
516
Wolsingham Park Moor
Tunstall Reservoir
High Stoop
Crawleyside
Stanhope
Durham Dales Centre
Shittlehope
Tow Law
Sunniside
Wearhead
Wear
Burnhope Reservoir
Burnhope Seat
746
Ireshopeburn
Ireshope Moor
St John's Chapel
Daddry Shield
Westgate
Eastgate
Brotherlee
Weardale
Frosterley
Wolsingham
Hill End
White Kirkley
Weardale Railway
Harvey Hill
319
Thornley
Knitsley Fell
Bellbeaver Rigg
Viewing Hill
639
Three Pikes
651
Chapel Fell
Chapelfell Top
699
Westernhope Moor
Snowhope Hill
607
Bollihope Common
St John's Hall
Harwood
Langdon Common
Outberry Plain
653
DURHAM
Pawlaw Pike
487
Pikeston Fell
Witton-le-Wear
Bedburn
Langdon Beck
Moor House - Upper Teesdale Nat Nature Reserve
675
Newbiggin Common
Middleton Common
Carrs Hill
601
Hamsterley Common
Redford
Toll
Hamsterley
Cow Green Reservoir
Widdybank Fell
Forest-in-Teesdale
Cauldron Snout
Eudon Beck
Hamsterley Forest
Eggleston Common
Newbiggin
Bowlees Picnic Area
Monks Moor
High Force
Tees
Cronkley Fell
Holwick
Holwick Fell
Middleton-in-Teesdale
Woodland
Woodland Fell
Softley
High Wham
Morley
Lane Head
Copley
Butterknowle
Cockfield
Evenwood
Langleydale Common
Peathrow
Esperley Lane
Mickle Fell
790
Danger Zone
Lune Forest
Lune Moor
Bowbank
Thringarth
Mickleton
Lunedale
Eggleston
Fish Lake
Little Fell
745
Burton Fell
Warcop Fell
PENNINES
Grassholme
Grassholme Reservoir
Romaldkirk
Kinninvie
Burnt Houses
Raby Castle
Staindrop
Hunderthwaite
Selset Reservoir
Lune
Hury
Balder
Mickleton Moor
Hunderthwaite Moor
Blackton Reservoir
Hury Reservoir
Stone Cross
Cotherstone
Stainton
Cleatlam
Iron Band
562
Balderhead Reservoir
Baldersdale
Pennine Way
Lartington
Broomielaw
Little Newsham
Stainmore Common
Clove Lodge
Cotherstone Moor
Barnard Castle
Bowes Museum
Humbleton
Westwick
Startforth
Winston
Hillbeck
North Stainmore
Deepdale
Whorlton

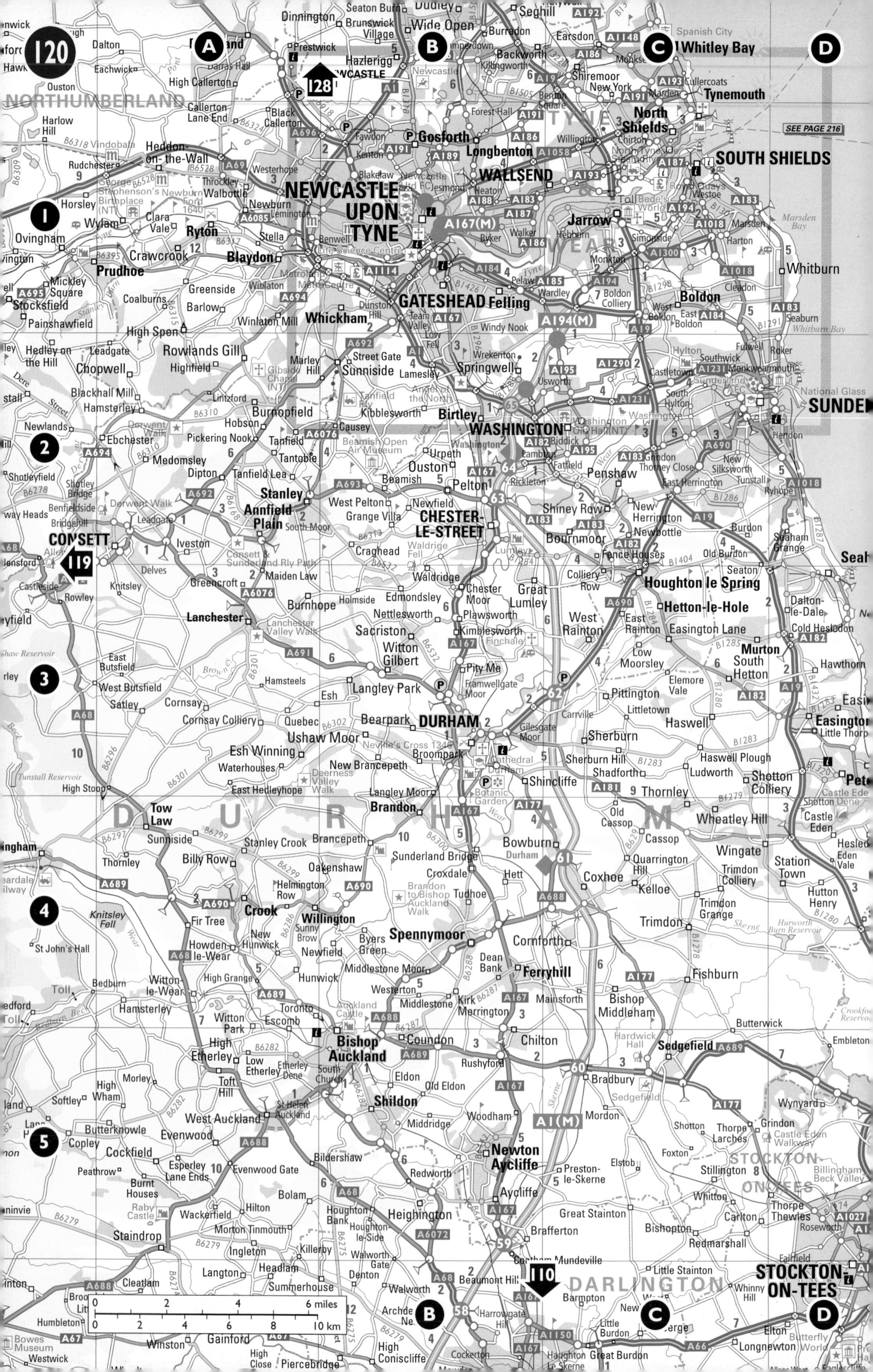

120
A
B
C
D
1
2
3
4
5
NORTHUMBERLAND
DURHAM
TYNE & WEAR
DARLINGTON
STOCKTON-ON-TEES
SEE PAGE 216
128
119
110
Dinnington
Seaton Burn
Brunswick Village
Wide Open
Seghill
Earsdon
Spanish City
Whitley Bay
Prestwick
Hazlerigg
Burradon
Backworth
Killingworth
Shiremoor
New York
Cullercoats
Tynemouth
Dalton
Eachwick
High Callerton
Darras Hall
Ouston
Callerton Lane End
Black Callerton
Forest Hall
Benton Square
North Shields
Harlow Hill
Vindobala
Heddon-on-the-Wall
Gosforth
Longbenton
Willington
Chirton
SOUTH SHIELDS
Rudchester
Westerhope
Fawdon
Kenton
WALLSEND
Throckley
Walbottle
Blakelaw
Jesmond
Heaton
Newburn Ford 1640
NEWCASTLE UPON TYNE
George Stephenson's Birthplace (NT)
Horsley
Newburn
Lemington
Byker
Walker
Jarrow
Hebburn
Bede's World
Westoe
Marsden
Marsden Bay
Wylam
Clara Vale
Ryton
Stella
Benwell
Life Science Centre
Simonside
Harton
Ovingham
Crawcrook
Blaydon
Metroland
MetroCentre
Monkton
Whitburn
Prudhoe
Mickley Square
Winlaton
Pelaw
Wardley
Boldon Colliery
Cleadon
Stocksfield
Greenside
Coalburns
Dunston Hill
GATESHEAD
Felling
Boldon
Barlow
Winlaton Mill
Whickham
Team Valley
West Boldon
East Boldon
Painshawfield
High Spen
Low Fell
Windy Nook
Seaburn
Whitburn Bay
Hedley on the Hill
Leadgate
Rowlands Gill
Highfield
Gibside Chapel (NT)
Marley Hill
Street Gate
Sunniside
Lamesley
Wrekenton
Springwell
Usworth
Hylton
Castletown
Southwick
Fulwell
Roker
Monkwearmouth
Chopwell
Blackhall Mill
Hamsterley
Lintzford
Tanfield Rly
Kibblesworth
Angel of the North
Birtley
WASHINGTON
South Hylton
Sunderland AFC
National Glass
SUNDERLAND
Newlands
Ebchester
Derwent Walk
Hobson
Burnopfield
Causey
Pickering Nook
Tanfield
Beamish Open Air Museum
Washington Old Hall (NT)
Biddick
Lambton
Hendon
Medomsley
Dipton
Tantobie
Urpeth
Ouston
Grindon
Thorney Close
New Silksworth
Shotleyfield
Shotley Bridge
Tanfield Lea
Beamish
Pelton
Rickleton
Fatfield
Penshaw
Tunstall
Ryhope
Benfieldside
Bridgehill
Stanley
West Pelton
Newfield
Shiney Row
East Herrington
Annfield Plain
Grange Villa
CHESTER-LE-STREET
New Herrington
Newbottle
Burdon
Seaham Grange
CONSETT
South Moor
Iveston
Craghead
Waldridge Fell
Lumley
Bournmoor
Fence Houses
Old Burdon
Allensford
Delves
Consett & Sunderland Rly Path
Colliery Row
Seaton
Houghton le Spring
Seaham
Castleside
Knitsley
Greencroft
Maiden Law
Waldridge
Chester Moor
Great Lumley
Rowley
Burnhope
Holmside
Edmondsley
Hetton-le-Hole
Dalton-le-Dale
Lanchester
Nettlesworth
Plawsworth
West Rainton
East Rainton
Easington Lane
Cold Hesledon
Lanchester Valley Walk
Sacriston
Kimblesworth
Finchale
Low Moorsley
Murton
Hawthorn
East Butsfield
Witton Gilbert
South Hetton
West Butsfield
Hamsteels
Pity Me
Framwellgate Moor
Elemore Vale
Satley
Cornsay
Esh
Langley Park
Pittington
Easington
Little Thorpe
Cornsay Colliery
Quebec
Bearpark
DURHAM
Carrville
Littletown
Haswell
Ushaw Moor
Neville's Cross 1346
Gilesgate Moor
Sherburn
Esh Winning
Broompark
Cathedral
Sherburn Hill
Haswell Plough
Waterhouses
New Brancepeth
Shadforth
Ludworth
Shotton Colliery
Tunstall Reservoir
Deerness Valley Walk
Shincliffe
High Stoop
East Hedleyhope
Langley Moor
Botanic Garden
Thornley
Castle Eden
Tow Law
Brandon
Old Cassop
Wheatley Hill
Sunniside
Stanley Crook
Brancepeth
Bowburn
Cassop
Wingate
Station Town
Thornley
Billy Row
Oakenshaw
Sunderland Bridge
Croxdale
Quarrington Hill
Hett
Coxhoe
Trimdon Colliery
Helmington Row
Brandon to Bishop Auckland Walk
Tudhoe
Kelloe
Hutton Henry
Knitsley Fell
Crook
Willington
Fir Tree
Sunny Brow
Trimdon Grange
Trimdon
St John's Hall
New Hunwick
Byers Green
Spennymoor
Cornforth
Howden-le-Wear
Newfield
Dean Bank
Hurworth Burn Reservoir
Ferryhill
High Grange
Hunwick
Middlestone Moor
Fishburn
Bedburn
Witton-le-Wear
Westerton
Middlestone
Kirk Merrington
Mainsforth
Bishop Middleham
Hamsterley
Toronto
Escomb
Auckland Castle
Witton Park
Coundon
Butterwick
High Etherley
Bishop Auckland
Chilton
Hardwick Hall
Sedgefield
Embleton
Low Etherley
Etherley Dene
South Church
Rushyford
Bradbury
Morley
High Wham
Toft Hill
Eldon
Old Eldon
Softley
Shildon
St Helen Auckland
West Auckland
Woodham
Mordon
Wynyard
Middridge
Butterknowle
Evenwood
Grindon
Thorpe Larches
Shotton
Castle Eden Walkway
Copley
Cockfield
Newton Aycliffe
Elstob
Foxton
Bildershaw
Peathrow
Esperley Lane Ends
Evenwood Gate
Redworth
Preston-le-Skerne
Stillington
Billingham Beck Valley
Burnt Houses
Bolam
Aycliffe
Whitton
Raby Castle
Wackerfield
Hilton
Houghton Bank
Heighington
Great Stainton
Thorpe Thewles
Morton Tinmouth
Houghton-le-Side
Brafferton
Carlton
Bishopton
Roseworth
Staindrop
Killerby
Redmarshall
Ingleton
Walworth Gate
Coatham Mundeville
Fairfield
Langton
Headlam
Denton
Little Stainton
Cleatham
Summerhouse
Walworth
Beaumont Hill
Whinny Hill
Archdeacon Newton
Harrowgate Hill
Barmpton
Little Burdon
Elton
Humbleton
Bowes Museum
Westwick
Winston
Gainford
High Close
Piercebridge
High Coniscliffe
Cockerton
Haughton le Skerne
Great Burdon
Longnewton
Butterfly World
0
2
4
6 miles
8
10 km

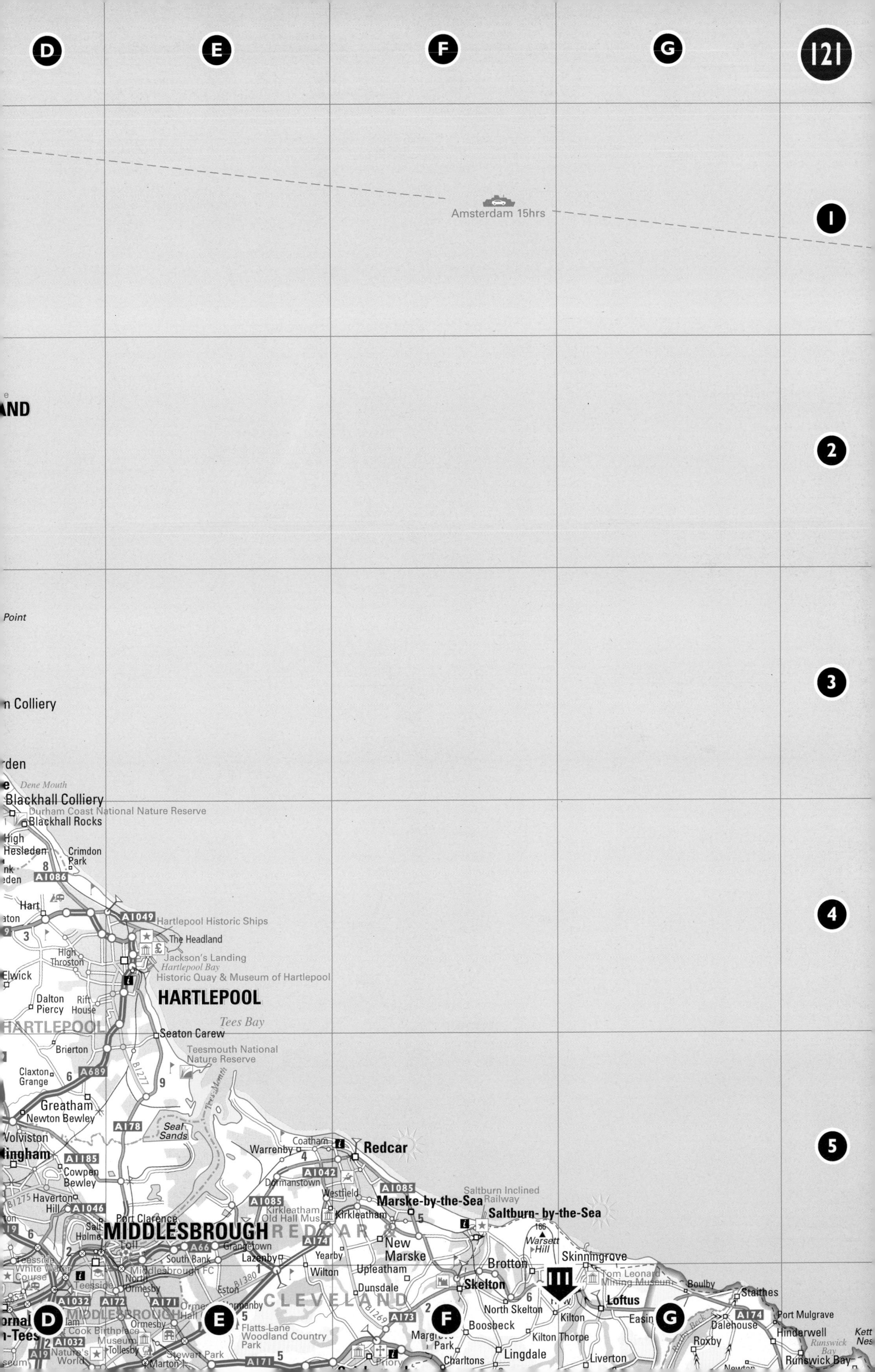

121
D
E
F
G
1
2
3
4
5
Amsterdam 15hrs
Point
Dene Mouth
Blackhall Colliery
Durham Coast National Nature Reserve
Blackhall Rocks
High Hesleden
Crimdon Park
A1086
Hart
A1049
Hartlepool Historic Ships
The Headland
High Throston
Jackson's Landing
Hartlepool Bay
Historic Quay & Museum of Hartlepool
Elwick
Dalton Piercy
Rift House
HARTLEPOOL
Tees Bay
Seaton Carew
Brierton
Teesmouth National Nature Reserve
Claxton Grange
A689
B1277
Greatham
Newton Bewley
Tees Mouth
A178
Seal Sands
Wolviston
A1185
Cowpen Bewley
Coatham
Redcar
Warrenby
A1042
Dormanstown
A1085
Saltburn Inclined Railway
Haverton Hill
A1046
A1085
Westfield
Marske-by-the-Sea
Kirkleatham Old Hall Museum
Kirkleatham
Saltburn-by-the-Sea
Port Clarence
MIDDLESBROUGH
REDCAR
Salt Holme
A66
Grangetown
A174
New Marske
Warsett Hill
South Bank
Lazenby
Yearby
Skinningrove
Teesside White Water Course
Middlesbrough FC
Wilton
Upleatham
Brotton
Tom Leonard Mining Museum
Teesside
North Ormesby
B1380
Eston
Dunsdale
Skelton
Boulby
Staithes
CLEVELAND
A1032
A172
A171
Normanby
North Skelton
Loftus
MIDDLESBROUGH
Ormesby Hall
B1269
A173
Kilton
Easington
A174
Port Mulgrave
Ormesby
Flatts Lane Woodland Country Park
Boosbeck
Dalehouse
Hinderwell
Captain Cook Birthplace Museum
Margrove Park
Kilton Thorpe
Roxby
Runswick Bay
A1032
Tollesby
Nature's World
Stewart Park
Marton
A171
Priory
Charltons
Lingdale
Liverton
Runswick Bay
Kettle Ness

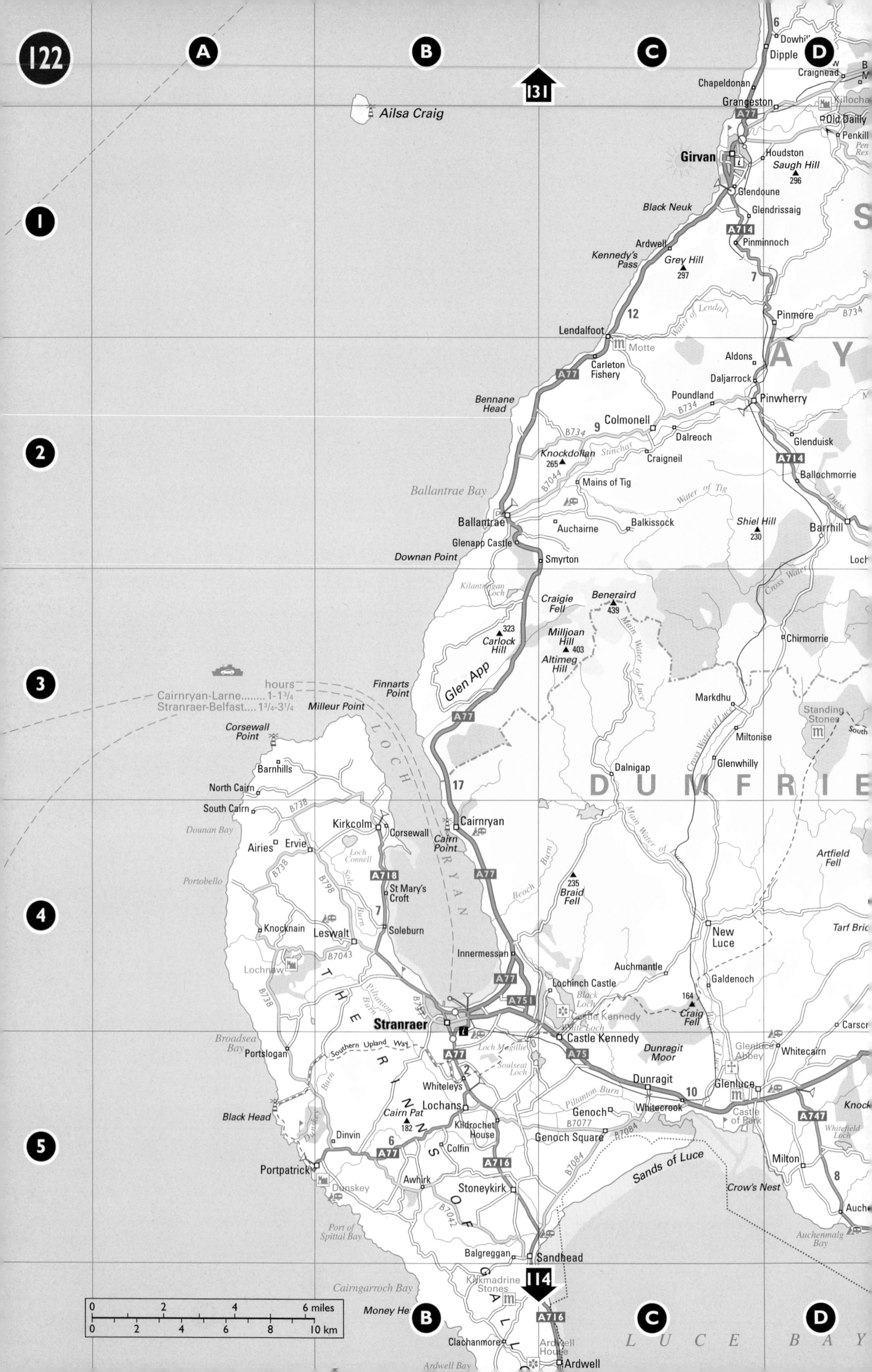
Ailsa Craig
131
Girvan
Dipple
Dowhill
Craignead
Chapeldonan
Grangeston
Killochan
Old Dailly
Penkill
Houdston
Saugh Hill
296
Glendoune
Black Neuk
Glendrissaig
Ardwell
Pinminnoch
Kennedy's Pass
Grey Hill
297
Water of Lendal
Pinmore
B734
Lendalfoot
Motte
Aldons
Carleton Fishery
Daljarrock
Poundland
Pinwherry
Bennane Head
Colmonell
Dalreoch
Glenduisk
Knockdolian
265
Stinchar
Craigneil
Ballochmorrie
Mains of Tig
Water of Tig
Ballantrae Bay
Ballantrae
Auchairne
Balkissock
Shiel Hill
230
Barrhill
Glenapp Castle
Downan Point
Smyrton
Kilantringan Loch
Cross Water
Craigie Fell
Beneraird
439
Carlock Hill
323
Milljoan Hill
403
Altimeg Hill
Main Water of Luce
Chirmorrie
Glen App
Cairnryan-Larne....... 1-1¾ hours
Stranraer-Belfast.... 1¾-3¼
Finnarts Point
Milleur Point
Markdhu
Standing Stones
Corsewall Point
Cross Water of Luce
Miltonise
Glenwhilly
Barnhills
Loch Ryan
Dalnigap
North Cairn
DUMFRIES
South Cairn
B738
Cairnryan
Kirkcolm
Corsewall
Dounan Bay
Cairn Point
Airies
Ervie
Loch Connell
Artfield Fell
Portobello
A718
St Mary's Croft
Beoch Burn
235
Braid Fell
Sole Burn
B798
Knocknain
Leswalt
Soleburn
New Luce
Tarf Bridge
Innermessan
B7043
Auchmantle
Lochnaw
THE RINNS OF GALLOWAY
Lochinch Castle
Galdenoch
Black Loch
164
Craig Fell
Piltanton Burn
A751
Stranraer
Castle Kennedy
White Loch
Broadsea Bay
Portslogan
Southern Upland Way
Loch Magillie
Dunragit Moor
A75
Glenluce Abbey
Whitecairn
Soulseat Loch
Dunragit
Whiteleys
Lochans
Glenluce
Black Head
Whitecrook
Genoch
Castle of Park
A747
Cairn Pat
182
Kildrochet House
B7077
Whitefield Loch
Dinvin
Genoch Square
B7084
Colfin
Milton
Portpatrick
A716
Sands of Luce
Crow's Nest
Dunskey
Awhirk
Stoneykirk
B7042
Port of Spittal Bay
Auchenmalg Bay
Balgreggan
Sandhead
Cairngarroch Bay
Kirkmadrine Stones
114
Money Head
0 2 4 6 miles
0 2 4 6 8 10 km
Clachanmore
Ardwell House
LUCE BAY
Ardwell Bay
Ardwell
A77
A714
AYRSHIRE
A B C D
1 2 3 4 5

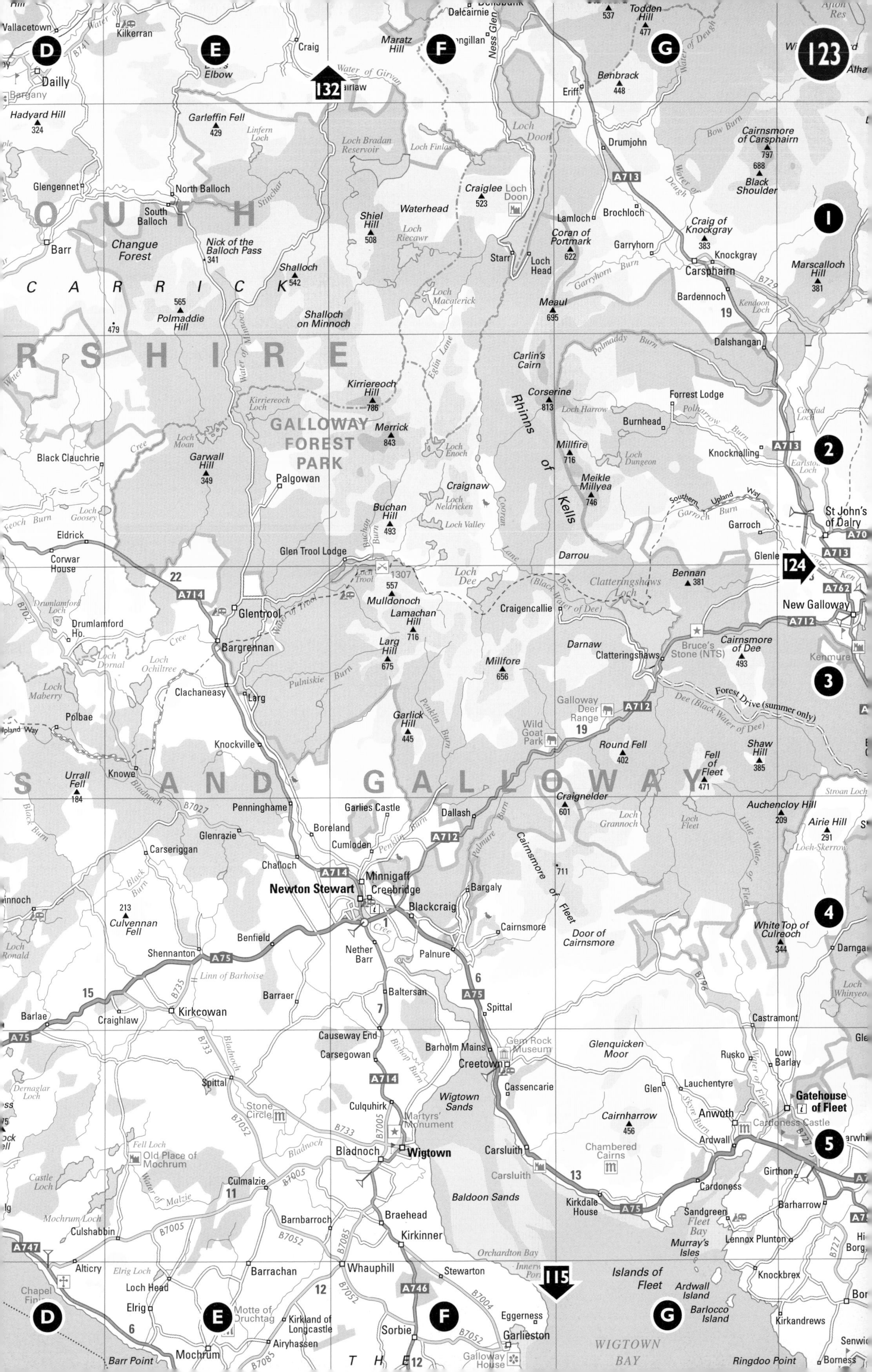
123
D
E
F
G
Vallacetown
Kilkerran
Craig
Dalcairnie
Maratz Hill
Ness Glen
Todden Hill
477
537
Afton Res
Dailly
Bargany
B741
Water of Girvan
132
Benbrack
448
Eriff
Water of Deugh
Hadyard Hill
324
Garleffin Fell
429
Linfern Loch
Loch Bradan Reservoir
Loch Finlas
Loch Doon
Drumjohn
Bow Burn
Cairnsmore of Carsphairn
797
688
Black Shoulder
Glengennet
North Balloch
South Balloch
Stinchar
Craiglee
523
Loch Doon
A713
Water of Deugh
I
SOUTH
Barr
Changue Forest
Nick of the Balloch Pass
341
Shiel Hill
508
Waterhead
Loch Riecawr
Lamloch
Brochloch
Coran of Portmark
622
Craig of Knockgray
383
Knockgray
Garryhorn
Starr
Loch Head
Garryhorn Burn
Carsphairn
Marscalloch Hill
381
CARRICK
Shalloch
542
565
Polmaddie Hill
479
Loch Macaterick
Shalloch on Minnoch
Water of Minnoch
Meaul
695
Bardennoch
B729
Kendoon Loch
19
Dalshangan
RSHIRE
Polmaddy Burn
Carlin's Cairn
Kirriereoch Hill
786
Kirriereoch Loch
Eglin Lane
Corserine
813
Rhinns of Kells
Loch Harrow
Forrest Lodge
Polharrow Burn
Carsfad Loch
GALLOWAY FOREST PARK
Merrick
843
Loch Moan
Cree
Garwall Hill
349
Loch Enoch
Burnhead
Millfire
716
Loch Dungeon
A713
Knocknalling
Earlstoun Loch
2
Black Clauchrie
Palgowan
Craignaw
Meikle Millyea
746
Loch Neldricken
Loch Valley
Cooran Lane
Southern Upland Way
Garroch Burn
Garroch
St John's of Dalry
Loch Goosey
Feoch Burn
Eldrick
Buchan Hill
493
Buchan Burn
Glen Trool Lodge
Darrou
A70
A713
Glenlee
124
Water of Ken
Corwar House
22
Loch Trool
1307
557
Mulldonoch
Loch Dee
Dee (Black Water of Dee)
Clatteringshaws Loch
Bennan
381
A762
A714
Glentrool
Water of Trool
Lamachan Hill
716
Craigencallie
New Galloway
A712
Drumlamford Loch
B7027
Drumlamford Ho.
Bargrennan
Cree
Larg Hill
675
Darnaw
Clatteringshaws
Bruce's Stone (NTS)
Cairnsmore of Dee
493
Kenmure
Loch Dornal
Loch Ochiltree
Millfore
656
3
Loch Maberry
Clachaneasy
Larg
Pulniskie Burn
Penkiln Burn
Galloway Deer Range
19
A712
Forest Drive (summer only)
Dee (Black Water of Dee)
Polbae
Upland Way
Garlick Hill
445
Wild Goat Park
Round Fell
402
Shaw Hill
385
Knockville
Fell of Fleet
471
Urrall Fell
184
Knowe
SAND GALLOWAY
Stroan Loch
Bladnoch
B7027
Penninghame
Garlies Castle
Dallash
Craignelder
601
Auchencloy Hill
209
Black Burn
Glenrazie
Boreland
Penkiln Burn
Palnure Burn
Loch Grannoch
Loch Fleet
Airie Hill
291
Carseriggan
Cumloden
A712
Cairnsmore of Fleet
Loch Skerrow
Little Water of Fleet
Challoch
A714
Minnigaff
Newton Stewart
Creebridge
Bargaly
711
Black Burn
Blackcraig
4
213
Culvennan Fell
Benfield
1
Cree
Cairnsmore
Door of Cairnsmore
White Top of Culreoch
344
Loch Ronald
Shennanton
A75
Nether Barr
Palnure
Darnga
Linn of Barhoise
B735
6
Loch Whinyeo
15
Barraer
Baltersan
A75
B796
Barlae
Craighlaw
Kirkcowan
7
Spittal
Castramont
A75
B733
Bladnoch
Causeway End
Bishop Burn
Barholm Mains
Gem Rock Museum
Glenquicken Moor
Rusko
Water of Fleet
Low Barlay
Carsegowan
Creetown
Dernaglar Loch
Spittal
A714
Cassencarie
Glen
Lauchentyre
Gatehouse of Fleet
Stone Circle
Culquhirk
Wigtown Sands
Cairnharrow
456
Skyre Burn
Anwoth
B7052
B7005
Martyrs' Monument
B733
Cardoness Castle
Fell Loch
Old Place of Mochrum
Bladnoch
Bladnoch
Wigtown
Carsluith
Chambered Cairns
Ardwall
B727
5
Water of Malzie
Castle Loch
Culmalzie
B7005
Carsluith
13
Girthon
11
Baldoon Sands
Cardoness
Kirkdale House
A75
Mochrum Loch
Braehead
Sandgreen
Barharrow
Barnbarroch
Fleet Bay
Culshabbin
B7005
B7052
B7085
Kirkinner
Lennox Plunton
A747
Orchardton Bay
Murray's Isles
B727
Alticry
Elrig Loch
Barrachan
Whauphill
Stewarton
Innerwell Port
115
Islands of Fleet
Knockbrex
Chapel Finian
Loch Head
12
A746
Ardwall Island
Elrig
B7052
Motte of Druchtag
B7004
Barlocco Island
Kirkandrews
6
Kirkland of Longcastle
Eggerness
Sorbie
Garlieston
B7052
Airyhassen
Mochrum
Barr Point
B7085
THE
12
Galloway House
WIGTOWN BAY
Ringdoo Point
Borness

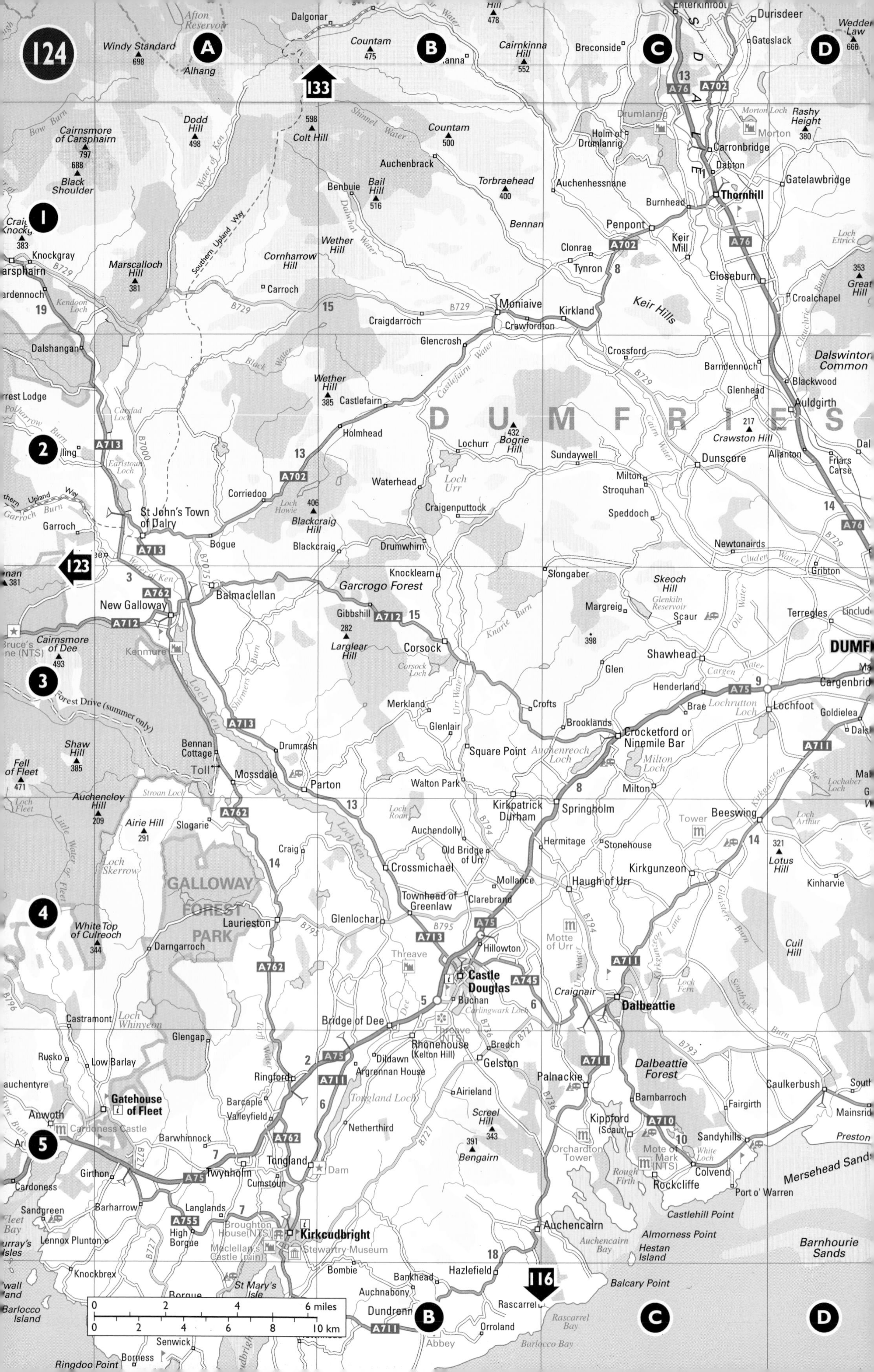
A
B
C
D
1
2
3
4
5
133
123
116
Afton Reservoir
Windy Standard 698
Alhang
Dalgonar
Countam 475
Cairnkinna Hill 552
Breconside
Enterkinfoot
Durisdeer
Gateslack
Wedder Law 666
13
A76
A702
Drumlanrig
Morton Loch
Rashy Height 380
Morton
Holm of Drumlanrig
Carronbridge
Dabton
Gatelawbridge
Thornhill
Cairnsmore of Carsphairn 797
688
Black Shoulder
Dodd Hill 498
Water of Ken
598
Colt Hill
Shinnel Water
Countam 500
Auchenbrack
Bail Hill 516
Benbuie
Torbraehead 400
Auchenhessnane
Burnhead
Penpont
Keir Mill
Bennan
Craig Knocky 383
Knockgray
Carsphairn
B729
Marscalloch Hill 381
Southern Upland Way
Wether Hill
Cornharrow Hill
Dalwhat Water
Clonrae
Tynron
A702
8
Closeburn
Loch Ettrick
353
Great Hill
Carroch
Dalwhat Water
Moniaive
Kirkland
Crawfordton
Keir Hills
Croalchapel
Kendoon Loch
Dardennoch
19
15
Craigdarroch
Glencrosh
Crossford
Barndennoch
Dalswinton Common
Blackwood
Dalshangan
Black Water
Wether Hill 385
Castlefairn
Castlefairn Water
B729
Glenhead
Auldgirth
Forrest Lodge
Polharrow Burn
Carsfad Loch
Holmhead
DUMFRIES
432
Bogrie Hill
217
Crawston Hill
Lochurr
Cairn Water
Dunscore
Allanton
Friars Carse
A713
B7000
13
Earlstoun Loch
Sundaywell
Milton
Stroquhan
A702
Waterhead
Loch Urr
Corriedoo
Loch Howie
406
Blackcraig Hill
Craigenputtock
Speddoch
14
A76
Southern Upland Way
Garroch Burn
Garroch
St John's Town of Dalry
Bogue
Blackcraig
Drumwhirn
Newtonairds
B729
Cluden Water
Gribton
Knocklearn
Slongaber
Skeoch Hill
Water of Ken
3
B7075
Balmaclellan
Garcrogo Forest
Glenkiln Reservoir
A762
Margreig
Old Water
New Galloway
Gibbshill
A712
15
Scaur
Terregles
Lincluden
A712
Cairnsmore of Dee 493
282
Larglear Hill
Knarie Burn
398
Kenmure
Corsock
Corsock Loch
Shawhead
DUMFRIES
Glen
Urr Water
Cargen Water
Henderland
A75
9
Cargenbridge
Forest Drive (summer only)
Loch Ken
Shirmers Burn
Merkland
Crofts
Brae
Lochrutton Loch
Lochfoot
Goldielea
Glenlair
Brooklands
Crocketford or Ninemile Bar
Shaw Hill 385
A713
Bennan Cottage
Drumrash
Square Point
Auchenreoch Loch
Milton Loch
A711
Fell of Fleet 471
Toll
Mossdale
Parton
Walton Park
8
Milton
Kirkgunzeon Lane
Lochaber Loch
Stroan Loch
Auchencloy Hill 209
Loch Fleet
13
Loch Roan
Kirkpatrick Durham
Springholm
Tower
Beeswing
Loch Arthur
Airie Hill 291
Slogarie
A762
Loch Ken
Auchendolly
B794
Hermitage
Stonehouse
14
321
Lotus Hill
Little Water of Fleet
Loch Skerrow
GALLOWAY FOREST PARK
Craig
14
Old Bridge of Urr
Crossmichael
Mollance
Haugh of Urr
Kirkgunzeon
Kinharvie
Townhead of Greenlaw
Clarebrand
B794
Glaisters Burn
White Top of Culreoch 344
Laurieston
Glenlochar
B795
A75
Motte of Urr
Darngarroch
B795
A713
Threave
Hillowton
Urr Water
A711
Cuil Hill
A762
Castle Douglas
A745
Loch Fern
Southwick
B796
Castramont
Loch Whinyeon
Bridge of Dee
5
Buchan
Carlingwark Loch
6
Craignair
Dalbeattie
Glengap
Tarff Water
Threave (NTS)
B736
B727
Rhonehouse (Kelton Hill)
Breoch
Gelston
B793
Rusko
Low Barlay
2
A75
Dildawn
A711
Dalbeattie Forest
Ringford
A711
Argrennan House
Palnackie
Caulkerbush
Southerness
Auchentyre
Gatehouse of Fleet
Barcaple
Valleyfield
6
Tongland Loch
Airieland
Barnbarroch
Fairgirth
Mainsriddle
Anworth
Cardoness Castle
Netherthird
Screel Hill 343
B736
Kipford (Scaur)
A710
10
Sandyhills
Preston
Barwhinnock
A762
391
Bengairn
Orchardton Tower
Mote of Mark (NTS)
White Loch
Mersehead Sands
B727
7
Tongland
Dam
Rough Firth
Colvend
Girthon
A75
Twynholm
Cumstoun
Rockcliffe
Port o' Warren
Cardoness
Sandgreen
Barharrow
Langlands
7
Castlehill Point
Fleet Bay
A755
High Borgue
Broughton House (NTS)
Kirkcudbright
Auchencairn
Almorness Point
Barnhourie Sands
Murray's Isles
Lennox Plunton
B727
Maclellan's Castle (ruin)
Stewartry Museum
Auchencairn Bay
Hestan Island
18
Knockbrex
Bombie
Bankhead
Hazlefield
Balcary Point
Borgue
St Mary's Isle
Auchnabony
Rascarrel
Barlocco Island
Dundrennan
Rascarrel Bay
A711
Abbey
Orroland
Barlocco Bay
Senwick
Borness
Ringdoo Point
0 2 4 6 miles
0 2 4 6 8 10 km

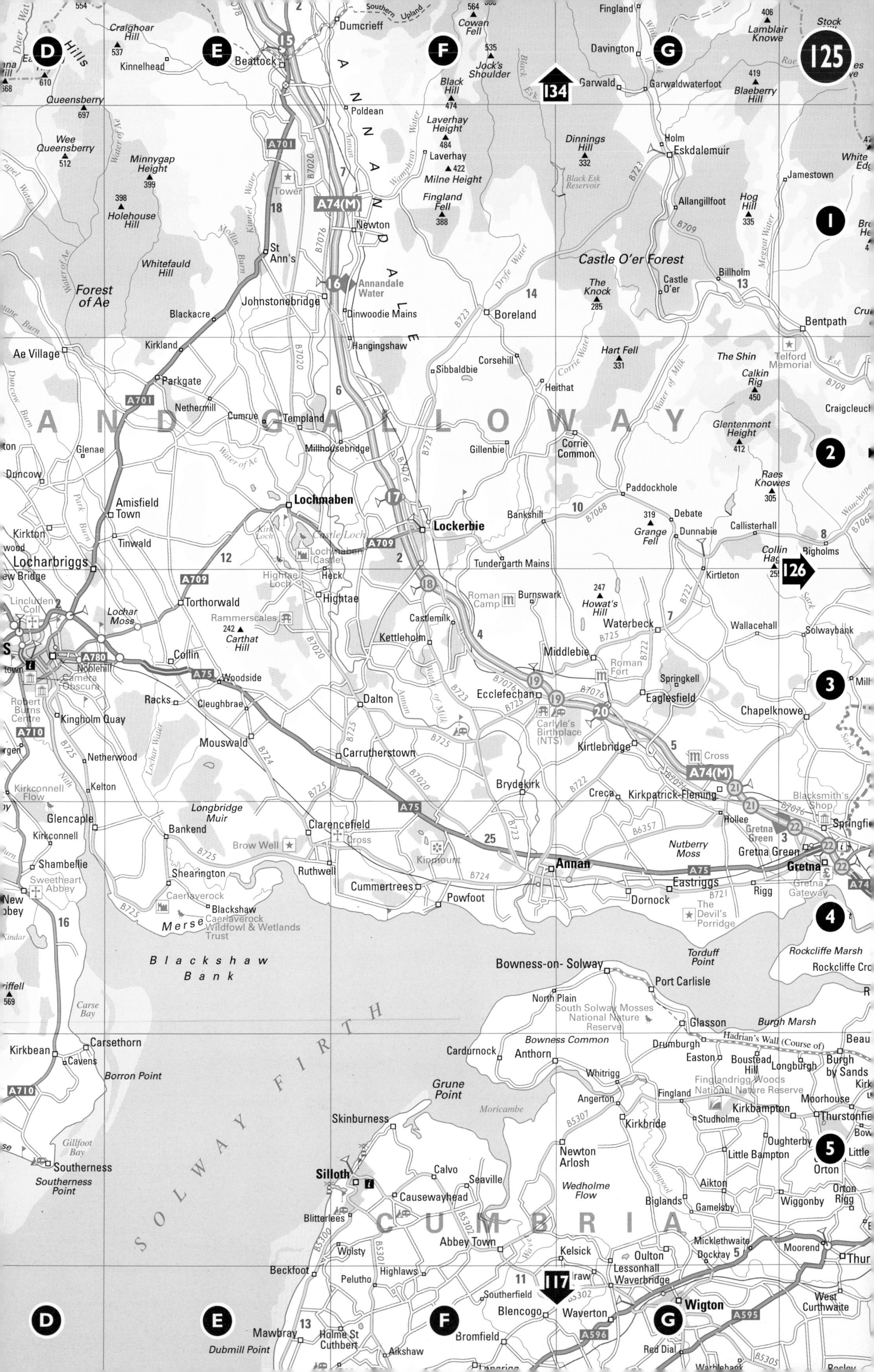

125
D
E
F
G
Southern Upland
Craighoar Hill
537
Kinnelhead
Beattock
Dumcrieff
Cowan Fell
564
Jock's Shoulder
535
Fingland
Davington
406
Lamblair Knowe
Stock
Hills
610
Queensberry
697
Wee Queensberry
512
Minnygap Height
399
398
Holehouse Hill
Whitefauld Hill
Forest of Ae
Water of Ae
Blackacre
Johnstonebridge
St Ann's
Kinnel Water
Mollin Burn
A701
B7020
B7076
Tower
18
A74(M)
7
15
Poldean
ANNANDALE
Newton
16
Annandale Water
Dinwoodie Mains
Hangingshaw
Black Hill
474
Laverhay Height
484
Laverhay
422
Milne Height
Fingland Fell
388
Wamphray Water
Black Esk
134
Garwald
Garwaldwaterfoot
419
Blaeberry Hill
Dinnings Hill
332
Black Esk Reservoir
Holm
Eskdalemuir
B723
B709
Allangillfoot
Hog Hill
335
Jamestown
White Edge
Meggat Water
I
Castle O'er Forest
The Knock
285
Castle O'er
Billholm
13
Bentpath
Dryfe Water
14
Boreland
Ae Village
Kirkland
Parkgate
A701
Nethermill
Cumrue
Templand
6
Sibbaldbie
Corsehill
Corrie Water
Heithat
Hart Fell
331
Water of Milk
The Shin
Telford Memorial
Calkin Rig
450
Esk
B709
Craigcleuch
DUMFRIES AND GALLOWAY
Glenae
Duncow
Millhousebridge
Gillenbie
Corrie Common
Glentenmont Height
412
2
Water of Ae
Park Burn
Amisfield Town
Kirkton
Tinwald
Lochmaben
Castle Loch
Lochmaben (Castle)
17
Lockerbie
A709
Bankshill
10
B7068
Paddockhole
319
Grange Fell
Debate
Dunnabie
Raes Knowes
305
Callisterhall
8
Bigholms
Collin Hag
126
Locharbriggs
12
A709
Hightae Loch
Heck
Hightae
Tundergarth Mains
Kirtleton
B722
Lincluden Coll
Torthorwald
Rammerscales
242
Carthat Hill
Roman Camp
Burnswark
247
Howat's Hill
Waterbeck
Wallacehall
Solwaybank
Lochar Moss
Collin
Castlemilk
Kettleholm
4
Middlebie
Roman Fort
B725
A780
Noblehill
A75
Woodside
Camera Obscura
Robert Burns Centre
A710
Kingholm Quay
Racks
Cleughbrae
Lochar Water
Dalton
Ecclefechan
19
20
B7076
Carlyle's Birthplace (NTS)
Springkell
Eaglesfield
3
Chapelknowe
Sark
Mouswald
B724
Carrutherstown
Kirtlebridge
5
Cross
A74(M)
21
Netherwood
B725
Nith
Kirkconnell Flow
Kelton
Longbridge Muir
Brydekirk
Creca
Kirkpatrick-Fleming
Blacksmith's Shop
Springfield
Glencaple
Kirkconnell
Bankend
Clarencefield
Cross
Brow Well
25
Kinmount
B723
B6357
Hollee
Nutberry Moss
Gretna Green
22
Shambellie
Sweetheart Abbey
New Abbey
Shearington
B725
Ruthwell
Cummertrees
Powfoot
B724
Annan
A75
Eastriggs
Dornock
Rigg
B721
Gretna
Gretna Gateway
A74
Caerlaverock
Blackshaw
Caerlaverock Wildfowl & Wetlands Trust
Merse
The Devil's Porridge
16
Kindar
Criffell
569
Blackshaw Bank
Torduff Point
Rockcliffe Marsh
Rockcliffe Cross
Bowness-on-Solway
Port Carlisle
North Plain
South Solway Mosses National Nature Reserve
Glasson
Burgh Marsh
Carse Bay
SOLWAY FIRTH
Kirkbean
Carsethorn
Cavens
Borron Point
A710
Cardurnock
Anthorn
Bowness Common
Drumburgh
Hadrian's Wall (Course of)
Easton
Boustead Hill
Longburgh
Burgh by Sands
Whitrigg
Finglandrigg Woods National Nature Reserve
Fingland
Grune Point
Moricambe
Angerton
Kirkbampton
Moorhouse
Thurstonfield
Skinburness
B5307
Kirkbride
Studholme
Oughterby
Newton Arlosh
Little Bampton
Gillfoot Bay
Southerness
Southerness Point
Silloth
Calvo
Seaville
Causewayhead
Wedholme Flow
Aikton
Wampool
Orton
Orton Rigg
Wiggonby
Biglands
Gamelsby
CUMBRIA
Blitterlees
B5302
B5300
Wolsty
B5301
Abbey Town
Kelsick
Oulton
Lessonhall
Waverbridge
Micklethwaite
Dockray
Moorend
Beckfoot
Pelutho
Highlaws
11
117
Southerfield
Wigton
A595
West Curthwaite
Blencogo
Waverton
A596
13
Mawbray
Holme St Cuthbert
Dubmill Point
Bromfield
Aikshaw
Red Dial
B5305

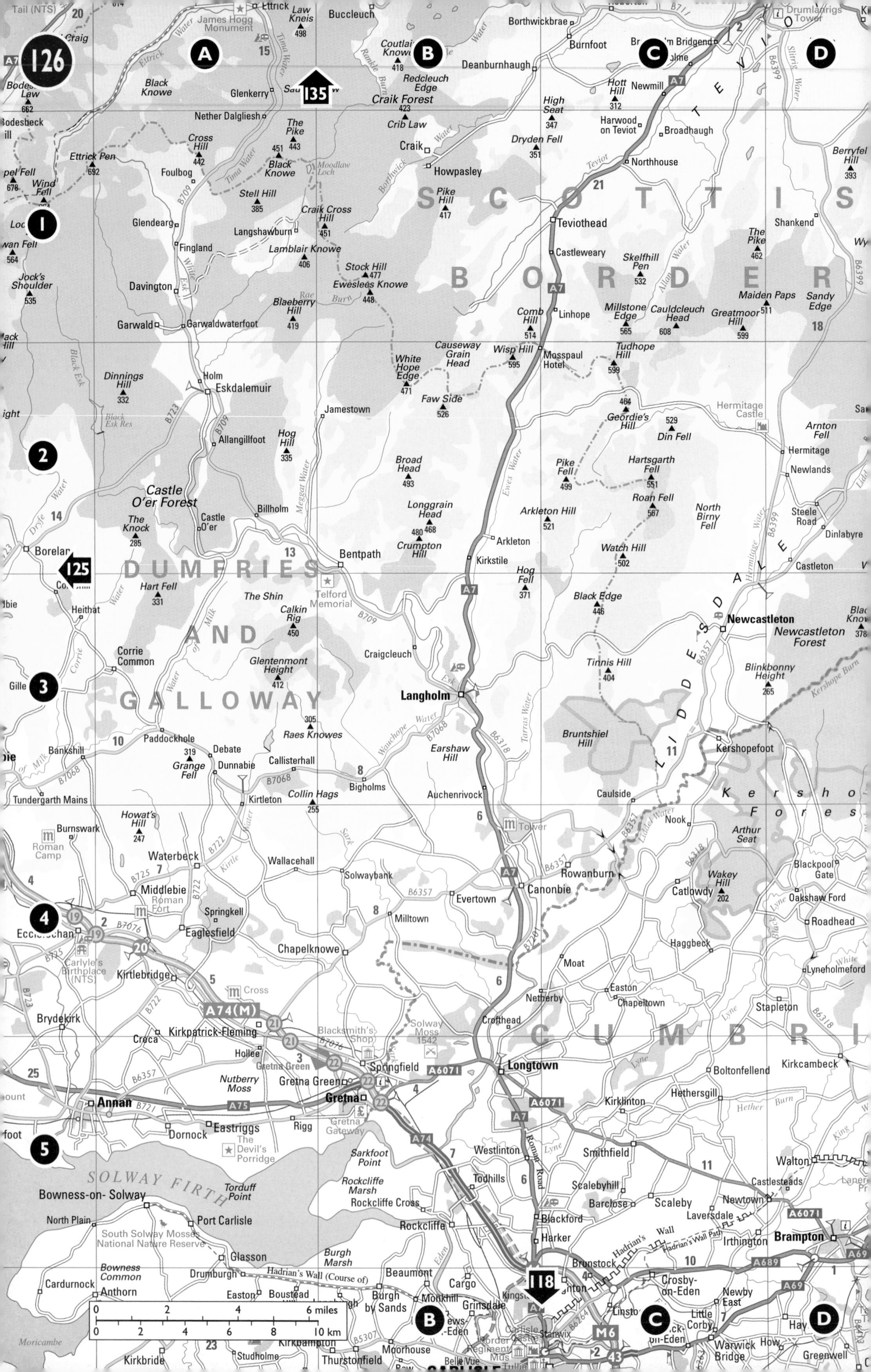

126
A
B
C
D
135
125
118
1
2
3
4
5
Ettrick
James Hogg Monument
Law Kneis 498
Buccleuch
Borthwickbrae
Burnfoot
Drumlanrig's Tower
Coutlair Knowe 418
Redcleuch Edge
Craik Forest 423
Crib Law
Deanburnhaugh
Hott Hill 312
Newmill
Black Knowe
Glenkerry
Nether Dalgliesh
The Pike 443
Craik
Howpasley
High Seat 347
Dryden Fell 351
Harwood on Teviot
Broadhaugh
Northhouse
Berryfel Hill 393
Bodesbeck Law 662
Ettrick Pen 692
Cross Hill 442
Black Knowe 451
Moodlaw Loch
Foulbog
Wind Fell
Stell Hill 385
Craik Cross Hill 451
Pike Hill 417
SCOTTISH BORDERS
Teviothead
Castleweary
Shankend
The Pike 462
Glendearg
Langshawburn
Fingland
Lamblair Knowe 406
Stock Hill 477
Ewesless Knowe 448
Skelfhill Pen 532
Jock's Shoulder 535
Davington
Blaeberry Hill 419
Comb Hill 514
Linhope
Millstone Edge 565
Cauldcleuch Head 608
Greatmoor Hill 599
Maiden Paps 511
Sandy Edge
Garwald
Garwaldwaterfoot
Causeway Grain Head
Wisp Hill 595
Mosspaul Hotel
Tudhope Hill 599
White Hope Edge 471
Faw Side 526
Dinnings Hill 332
Holm
Eskdalemuir
Black Esk Res
Jamestown
Geordie's Hill
529 Din Fell
Hermitage Castle
Arnton Fell
Hermitage
Allangillfoot
Hog Hill 335
Broad Head 493
Pike Fell 499
Hartsgarth Fell 551
Newlands
Castle O'er Forest
Castle O'er
Billholm
Longrain Head 468
Arkleton Hill 521
Roan Fell 567
North Birny Fell
Steele Road
Dinlabyre
The Knock 285
Arkleton
Kirkstile
Crumpton Hill
Watch Hill 502
Castleton
Borelan
Bentpath
DUMFRIES AND GALLOWAY
Telford Memorial
Hart Fell 331
Hog Fell 371
Black Edge 446
Heithat
The Shin
Calkin Rig 450
Newcastleton
Newcastleton Forest
Corrie Common
Glentenmont Height 412
Craigcleuch
Tinnis Hill 404
Blinkbonny Height 265
Gille
Langholm
Paddockhole
Raes Knowes
Earshaw Hill
Bruntshiel Hill
LIDDESDALE
Kershopefoot
Bankshill
Grange Fell
Debate
Dunnabie
Callisterhall
Bigholms
Auchenrivock
Caulside
Kershope Forest
Tundergarth Mains
Kirtleton
Collin Hags 255
Howat's Hill 247
Burnswark
Roman Camp
Tower
Nook
Arthur Seat
Waterbeck
Wallacehall
Solwaybank
Rowanburn
Blackpool Gate
Middlebie
Roman Fort
Evertown
Canonbie
Catlowdy
Wakey Hill 202
Oakshaw Ford
Ecclefechan
Springkell
Milltown
Roadhead
Eaglesfield
Carlyle's Birthplace (NTS)
Chapelknowe
Haggbeck
Moat
Kirtlebridge
Cross
Easton
Netherby
Chapeltown
Lyneholmeford
Brydekirk
Solway Moss 1542
Crofthead
Stapleton
Kirkpatrick-Fleming
Creca
Blacksmith's Shop
CUMBRIA
Hollee
Gretna Green
Springfield
Longtown
Kirkcambeck
Nutberry Moss
Boltonfellend
Annan
Gretna
Kirklinton
Hethersgill
Eastriggs
Dornock
Rigg
Gretna Gateway
The Devil's Porridge
Sarkfoot Point
Westlinton
Smithfield
Walton
SOLWAY FIRTH
Torduff Point
Rockcliffe Marsh
Todhills
Roman Road
Scalebyhill
Castlesteads
Bowness-on-Solway
Rockcliffe Cross
Barclose
Scaleby
Newtown
Port Carlisle
Laversdale
North Plain
South Solway Mosses National Nature Reserve
Rockcliffe
Blackford
Hadrian's Wall
Hadrian's Wall Path
Irthington
Brampton
Harker
Glasson
Burgh Marsh
Brunstock
Bowness Common
Drumburgh
Hadrian's Wall (Course of)
Beaumont
Cargo
Crosby-on-Eden
Newby East
Cardurnock
Anthorn
Easton
Boustead
Burgh by Sands
Monkhill
Grinsdale
Linstock
Little Corby
Warwick Bridge
Hayton
Border Regiment Mus
Stanwix
Kirkbampton
Moorhouse
Thurstonfield
Studholme
Kirkbride
How
Greenwell
Moricambe
0 2 4 6 miles
0 2 4 6 8 10 km
A7
A74(M)
A75
A6071
A74
A689
A69
M6
B709
B723
B7068
B6357
B6318
B6399
B722
B725
B7076
B721
B6264
B5307

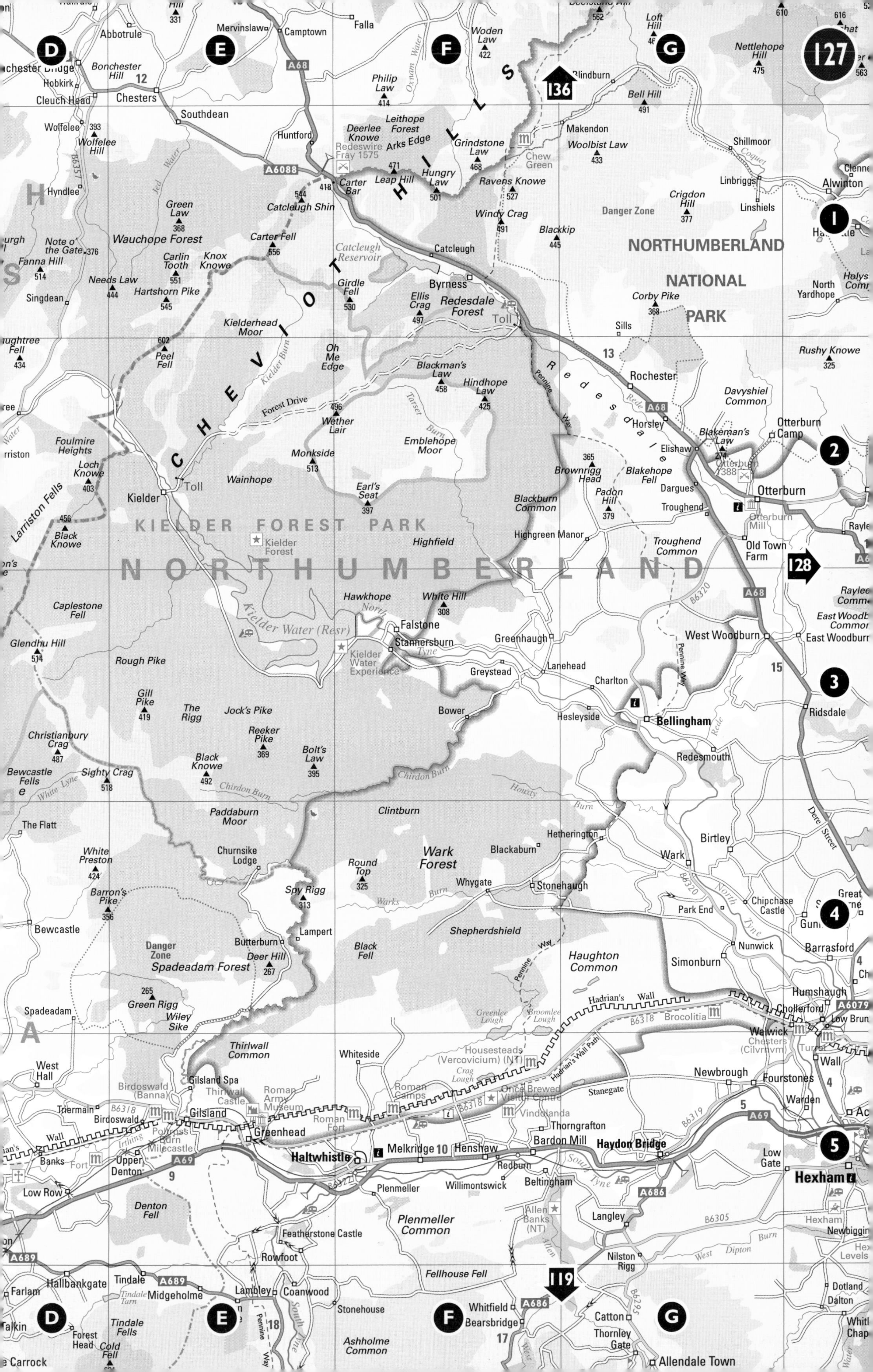
D
E
F
G
Abbotrule
Mervinslaw
Camptown
Falla
Woden Law
422
Loft Hill
Nettlehope Hill
475
Bonchester Bridge
Bonchester Hill
12
Hobkirk
Cleuch Head
Chesters
Southdean
A68
Philip Law
414
Blindburn
136
Bell Hill
491
Wolfelee
393
Wolfelee Hill
B6357
Hyndlee
Huntford
Leithope Forest
Deerlee Knowe
Redeswire Fray 1575
Arks Edge
Grindstone Law
468
Makendon
Woolbist Law
433
Chew Green
Shillmoor
Coquet
A6088
471
Leap Hill
Hungry Law
501
Carter Bar
418
544
Catcleugh Shin
Ravens Knowe
527
Linbriggs
Linshiels
Alwinton
Jed Water
Green Law
368
Wauchope Forest
Note o' the Gate
376
Fanna Hill
514
Carter Fell
556
Carlin Tooth
551
Knox Knowe
Needs Law
444
Hartshorn Pike
545
Singdean
Windy Crag
491
Blackkip
445
Crigdon Hill
377
Danger Zone
NORTHUMBERLAND NATIONAL PARK
Catcleugh Reservoir
Catcleugh
Byrness
Girdle Fell
530
Ellis Crag
497
Redesdale Forest
Toll
North Yardhope
Corby Pike
368
Sills
Kielderhead Moor
602
Peel Fell
Oh Me Edge
Blackman's Law
458
Hindhope Law
425
13
Rochester
Rushy Knowe
325
Davyshiel Common
CHEVIOT HILLS
Kielder Burn
Forest Drive
496
Wether Lair
Tarset Burn
Emblehope Moor
Pennine Way
Redesdale
Rede
A68
Horsley
Elishaw
Blakeman's Law
274
Otterburn Camp
Otterburn
388
2
Foulmire Heights
Loch Knowe
403
Larriston Fells
Kielder
Toll
Wainhope
Monkside
513
Earl's Seat
397
365
Brownrigg Head
Blakehope Fell
Padon Hill
379
Dargues
Blackburn Common
Troughend
Otterburn Mill
456
Black Knowe
KIELDER FOREST PARK
Kielder Forest
Highfield
Highgreen Manor
Troughend Common
Old Town Farm
128
NORTHUMBERLAND
Caplestone Fell
Hawkhope
White Hill
308
B6320
A68
Kielder Water (Resr)
North
Falstone
Stannersburn
Tyne
Kielder Water Experience
Greenhaugh
West Woodburn
East Woodburn
Glendhu Hill
514
Rough Pike
Greystead
Lanehead
Charlton
15
3
Gill Pike
419
The Rigg
Jock's Pike
Bower
Hesleyside
Bellingham
Ridsdale
Christianbury Crag
487
Reeker Pike
369
Bolt's Law
395
Black Knowe
492
Redesmouth
Bewcastle Fells
Sighty Crag
518
White Lyne
Chirdon Burn
Houxty Burn
The Flatt
Paddaburn Moor
Clintburn
Dere Street
White Preston
424
Churnsike Lodge
Wark Forest
Blackaburn
Hetherington
Birtley
Wark
Round Top
325
Barron's Pike
356
Spy Rigg
313
Whygate
Stonehaugh
Warks Burn
North Tyne
Chipchase Castle
Park End
4
Bewcastle
Lampert
Shepherdshield
Nunwick
Simonburn
Barrasford
Danger Zone
Butterburn
Deer Hill
267
Spadeadam Forest
Black Fell
Haughton Common
265
Green Rigg
Wiley Sike
Humshaugh
Chollerford
A6079
Spadeadam
Hadrian's Wall
Greenlee Lough
Broomlee Lough
B6318
Brocolitia
Walwick
Chesters (Cilurnum)
Thirlwall Common
Whiteside
Housesteads (Vercovicium) (NT)
Crag Lough
Hadrian's Wall Path
West Hall
Gilsland Spa
Roman Army Museum
Roman Camps
Once Brewed Visitor Centre
Stanegate
Newbrough
Fourstones
Wall
Birdoswald (Banna)
Thirlwall Castle
Warden
Triermain
B6318
Birdoswald
Gilsland
Roman Fort
Vindolanda
5
Greenhead
Thorngrafton
A69
Wall
Irthing
Poltross Burn Milecastle
Banks
Bardon Mill
Haydon Bridge
Upper Denton
Haltwhistle
Melkridge
10
Henshaw
B6319
Low Gate
Fort
A69
Redburn
9
B6322
Plenmeller
Willimontswick
Beltingham
South Tyne
Hexham
Low Row
A686
Denton Fell
Allen Banks (NT)
Langley
B6305
Plenmeller Common
Featherstone Castle
Rowfoot
Nilston Rigg
West Dipton Burn
A689
Fellhouse Fell
119
Farlam
Hallbankgate
Tindale
A689
Midgeholme
Tindale Tarn
Lambley
Coanwood
South Tyne
Whitfield
A686
B6295
Dotland
Dalton
Stonehouse
Bearsbridge
Catton
Falkin
Forest Head
Tindale Fells
Pennine Way
18
17
Thornley Gate
Cold Fell
Ashholme Common
Carrock
Allendale Town

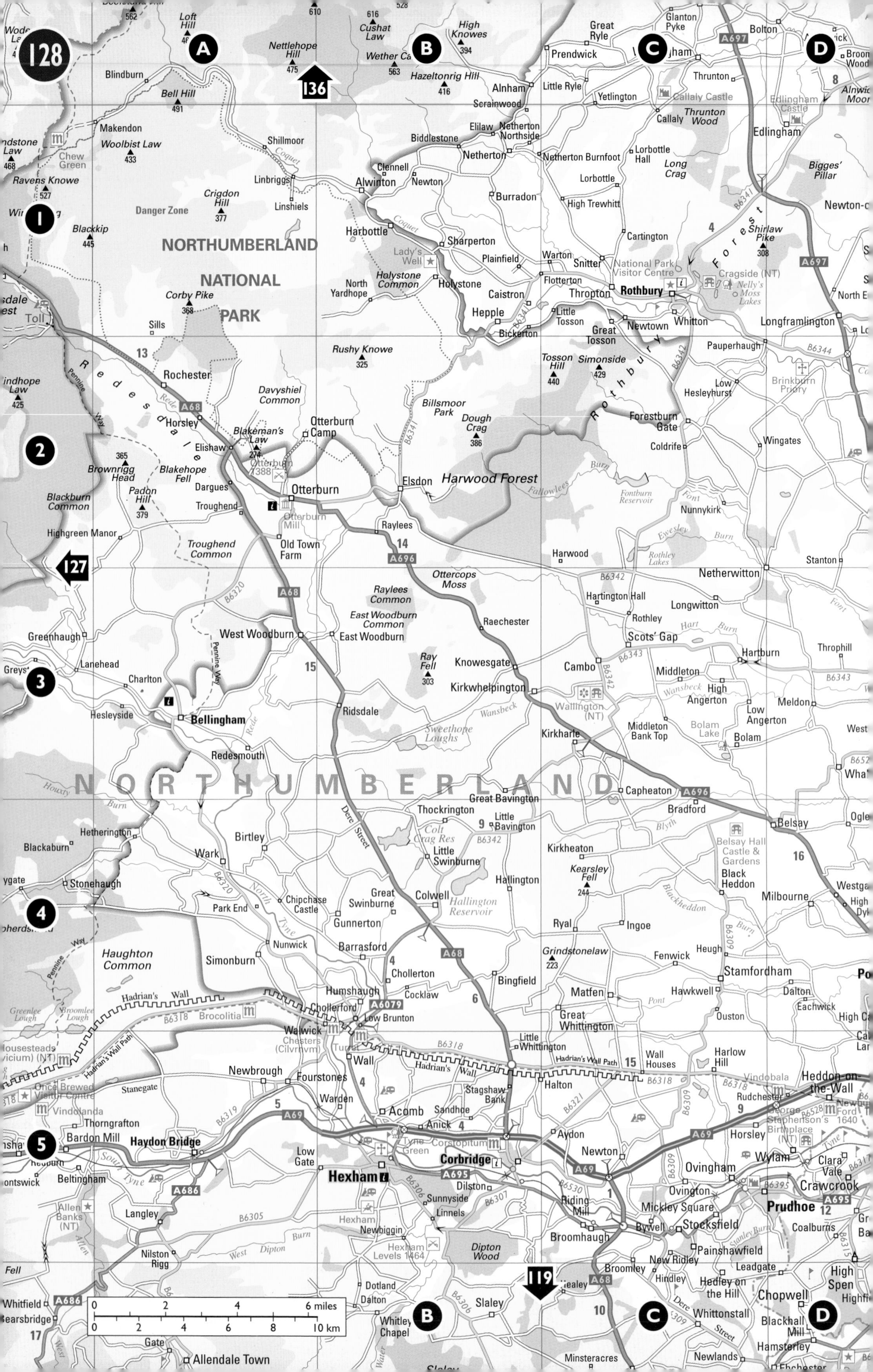
A
B
C
D
136
Loft Hill
Nettlehope Hill
475
Cushat Law
616
610
562
Wether Cairn
563
High Knowes
394
Great Ryle
Glanton Pyke
Bolton
A697
Prendwick
Blindburn
Bell Hill
491
Hazeltonrig Hill
416
Alnham
Little Ryle
Thrunton
Yetlington
Callaly Castle
Callaly
Thrunton Wood
Edlingham Castle
Edlingham
Alnwick Moor
Scrainwood
Elilaw
Netherton Northside
Makendon
Woolbist Law
433
Shillmoor
Coquet
Biddlestone
Netherton
Netherton Burnfoot
Lorbottle Hall
Long Crag
Lorbottle
Chew Green
Sandstone Law
468
Ravens Knowe
527
Linbriggs
Clennell
Alwinton
Newton
Burradon
High Trewhitt
Bigges' Pillar
Newton-on-the-Moor
B6341
Crigdon Hill
377
Danger Zone
Linshiels
Harbottle
Sharperton
Cartington
Shirlaw Pike
308
Forest
1
Blackkip
445
NORTHUMBERLAND NATIONAL PARK
Lady's Well
Holystone Common
Holystone
Plainfield
Warton
Snitter
National Park Visitor Centre
Cragside (NT)
Nelly's Moss Lakes
A697
North Yardhope
Flotterton
Thropton
Rothbury
Caistron
Hepple
Little Tosson
Bickerton
Great Tosson
Newtown
Whitton
Longframlington
Corby Pike
368
Sills
Toll
Rushy Knowe
325
Tosson Hill
440
Simonside
429
Rothbury
Pauperhaugh
B6344
Brinkburn Priory
B6342
13
Rochester
Redesdale
Pennine Way
Windhope Law
425
Davyshiel Common
Low Hesleyhurst
Billsmoor Park
A68
Horsley
Otterburn Camp
Dough Crag
386
Forestburn Gate
Coldrife
Wingates
Elishaw
Blakeman's Law
274
2
365
Brownrigg Head
Blakehope Fell
Otterburn 1388
Padon Hill
379
Dargues
Otterburn
Elsdon
Harwood Forest
Blackburn Common
Troughend
Otterburn Mill
Fallowlees
Fontburn Reservoir
Font
Nunnykirk
Highgreen Manor
Raylees
Troughend Common
Old Town Farm
14
A696
Ewesley
Burn
Harwood
Rothley Lakes
Stanton
127
Ottercops Moss
B6342
Netherwitton
A68
B6320
Raylees Common
Hartington Hall
Longwitton
Rothley
East Woodburn Common
West Woodburn
East Woodburn
Raechester
Scots' Gap
Hart Burn
Greenhaugh
Ray Fell
303
Knowesgate
Cambo
B6343
Hartburn
Throphill
Lanehead
15
3
Charlton
Kirkwhelpington
Middleton
B6343
Wansbeck
High Angerton
Wallington (NT)
Meldon
Low Angerton
Hesleyside
Bellingham
Ridsdale
Sweethope Loughs
Middleton Bank Top
Bolam Lake
Bolam
Kirkharle
Redesmouth
NORTHUMBERLAND
Capheaton
A696
Great Bavington
Thockrington
Little Bavington
9
Bradford
Belsay
Colt Crag Res
B6342
Blyth
Belsay Hall Castle & Gardens
Hetherington
Birtley
Little Swinburne
Kirkheaton
Kearsley Fell
244
Black Heddon
16
Wark
Dere Street
Blackaburn
Stonehaugh
B6320
North Tyne
Chipchase Castle
Great Swinburne
Colwell
Hallington
Hallington Reservoir
Milbourne
Park End
4
Gunnerton
Ryal
Ingoe
Blackheddon
B6309
Nunwick
Barrasford
A68
Grindstonelaw
223
Fenwick
Heugh
Haughton Common
Simonburn
4
Chollerton
Bingfield
Stamfordham
Humshaugh
Cocklaw
A6079
Matfen
Hawkwell
Dalton
Hadrian's Wall
Chollerford
6
Pont
Eachwick
Brocolitia
B6318
Low Brunton
Great Whittington
Ouston
Walwick
Chesters (Cilurnvm)
Turret
Little Whittington
Greenlee Lough
Broomlee Lough
Housesteads (Vercovicium) (NT)
Hadrian's Wall Path
Wall
B6318
Harlow Hill
Hadrian's Wall
Hadrian's Wall Path
15
Wall Houses
B6318
Vindobala
Heddon-on-the-Wall
Newbrough
Fourstones
Stagshaw Bank
Halton
Once Brewed Visitor Centre
Stanegate
Warden
Rudchester
4
5
B6321
B6318
9
Vindolanda
Acomb
Sandhoe
George Stephenson's Birthplace (NT)
Newburn Ford 1640
B6319
A69
Thorngrafton
Anick
4
A69
Bardon Mill
Haydon Bridge
Tyne Green
Corstopitum
Aydon
Horsley
5
Low Gate
Corbridge
Newton
Wylam
Clara Vale
Hexham
A695
A69
Ovingham
Crawcrook
South Tyne
B6306
Dilston
B6530
B6309
Ovington
Beltingham
A686
Sunnyside
B6307
Riding Mill
1
Mickley Square
Prudhoe
12
A695
Allen Banks (NT)
Linnels
Langley
B6305
Hexham
Bywell
Stocksfield
Coalburns
Newbiggin
Hexham Levels 1464
Dipton Wood
Broomhaugh
West Dipton Burn
Nilston Rigg
Painshawfield
New Ridley
Allen
119
Broomley
Leadgate
Healey
A68
Hindley
Hedley on the Hill
High Spen
Dotland
Whitfield
A686
Dalton
Slaley
Chopwell
10
Bearsbridge
B6306
Dere Street
Whittonstall
Blackhall Mill
B
C
D
Whitley Chapel
17
Hamsterley
0 2 4 6 miles
0 2 4 6 8 10 km
Gate
Allendale Town
Minsteracres
Newlands

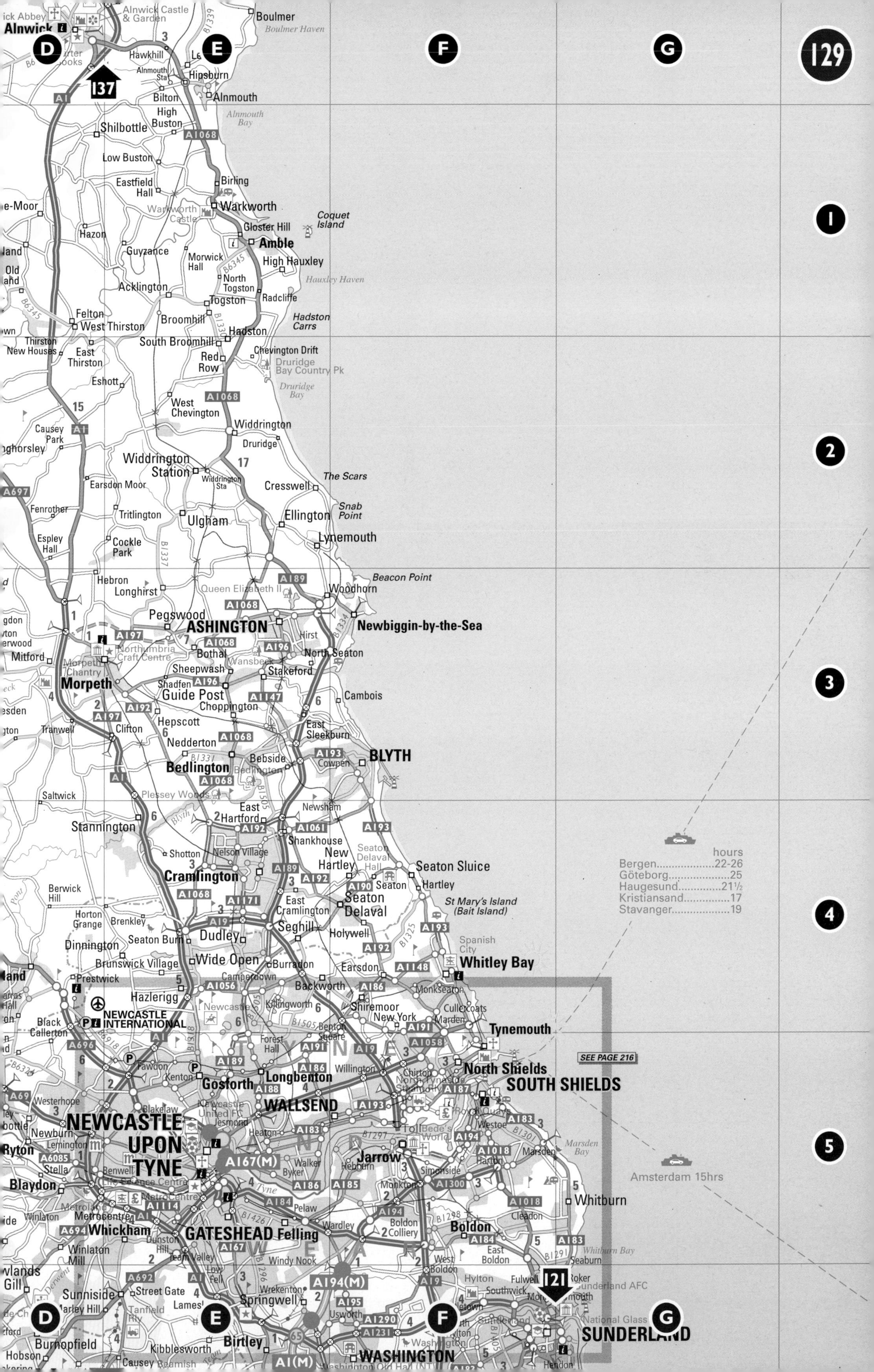
D
E
F
G
1
2
3
4
5
137
121
SEE PAGE 216
Alnwick
Alnwick Castle & Garden
Boulmer
Boulmer Haven
Hawkhill
Alnmouth Sta
Hipsburn
Bilton
Alnmouth
Alnmouth Bay
High Buston
Shilbottle
Low Buston
Birling
Eastfield Hall
Warkworth
Warkworth Castle
Coquet Island
Gloster Hill
Amble
Hazon
Guyzance
Morwick Hall
High Hauxley
Hauxley Haven
North Togston
Acklington
Togston
Radcliffe
Felton
West Thirston
Broomhill
Hadston Carrs
Hadston
South Broomhill
Thirston New Houses
East Thirston
Chevington Drift
Druridge Bay Country Pk
Red Row
Eshott
Druridge Bay
West Chevington
Widdrington
Causey Park
Druridge
Widdrington Station
Widdrington Sta
The Scars
Earsdon Moor
Cresswell
Fenrother
Tritlington
Snab Point
Ellington
Ulgham
Espley Hall
Cockle Park
Lynemouth
Beacon Point
Hebron
Longhirst
Queen Elizabeth II
Woodhorn
Pegswood
ASHINGTON
Newbiggin-by-the-Sea
Hirst
Northumbria Craft Centre
Bothal
North Seaton
Mitford
Morpeth Chantry
Wansbeck
Sheepwash
Stakeford
Morpeth
Shadfen
Guide Post
Cambois
Choppington
Tranwell
Clifton
Hepscott
East Sleekburn
Nedderton
Bebside
BLYTH
Cowpen
Bedlington
Saltwick
Plessey Woods
East Hartford
Newsham
Stannington
Shankhouse
Seaton Delaval Hall
Shotton
Nelson Village
New Hartley
Seaton Sluice
Cramlington
Seaton
Hartley
Berwick Hill
East Cramlington
Seaton Delaval
St Mary's Island (Bait Island)
Horton Grange
Brenkley
Dudley
Seghill
Holywell
Seaton Burn
Spanish City
Dinnington
Wide Open
Burradon
Earsdon
Whitley Bay
Brunswick Village
Camperdown
Prestwick
Backworth
Monkseaton
Hazlerigg
Killingworth
Cullercoats
NEWCASTLE INTERNATIONAL
Shiremoor
Black Callerton
New York
Marden
Tynemouth
Benton Square
Forest Hall
Fawdon
Willington
Kenton
North Shields
Gosforth
Longbenton
SOUTH SHIELDS
Chirton
North Tyneside Steam Rly
WALLSEND
Westerhope
Blakelaw
Newcastle United FC
Jesmond
Westoe
NEWCASTLE UPON TYNE
Newburn
Heaton
Bede's World
Lemington
Ryton
Walker
Jarrow
Harton
Marsden
Marsden Bay
Hebburn
Byker
Stella
Benwell
Simonside
Blaydon
Life Science Centre
Monkton
Whitburn
Metroland
MetroCentre
Pelaw
Cleadon
Winlaton
Metrocentre
Boldon Colliery
Wardley
Boldon
Whickham
GATESHEAD
Felling
East Boldon
Winlaton Mill
Dunston Hill
Windy Nook
Whitburn Bay
Seaburn
Team Valley
West Boldon
Low Fell
Hylton
Fulwell
Roker
Sunderland AFC
Wrekenton
Southwick
Monkwearmouth
Sunniside
Street Gate
Springwell
Lamesley
Usworth
Marley Hill
Tanfield Rly
National Glass
SUNDERLAND
Burnopfield
Birtley
Washington
Kibblesworth
WASHINGTON
Hobson
Causey
Beamish
Hendon
hours
Bergen....................22-26
Göteborg.......................25
Haugesund...............21½
Kristiansand...............17
Stavanger...................19
Amsterdam 15hrs
A1
A1068
A189
A197
A196
A192
A1147
A193
A1061
A19
A171
A1056
A191
A1058
A187
A186
A188
A183
A194
A1018
A167(M)
A185
A1300
A184
A1114
A694
A167
A692
A194(M)
A195
A1290
A1231
A1(M)
A696
A69
A6085
A697
A1148
A1171
B1339
B6345
B1330
B1337
B1334
B1331
B1505
B1325
B1318
B1297
B1301
B1426
B1296
B1298
B1291
B1405

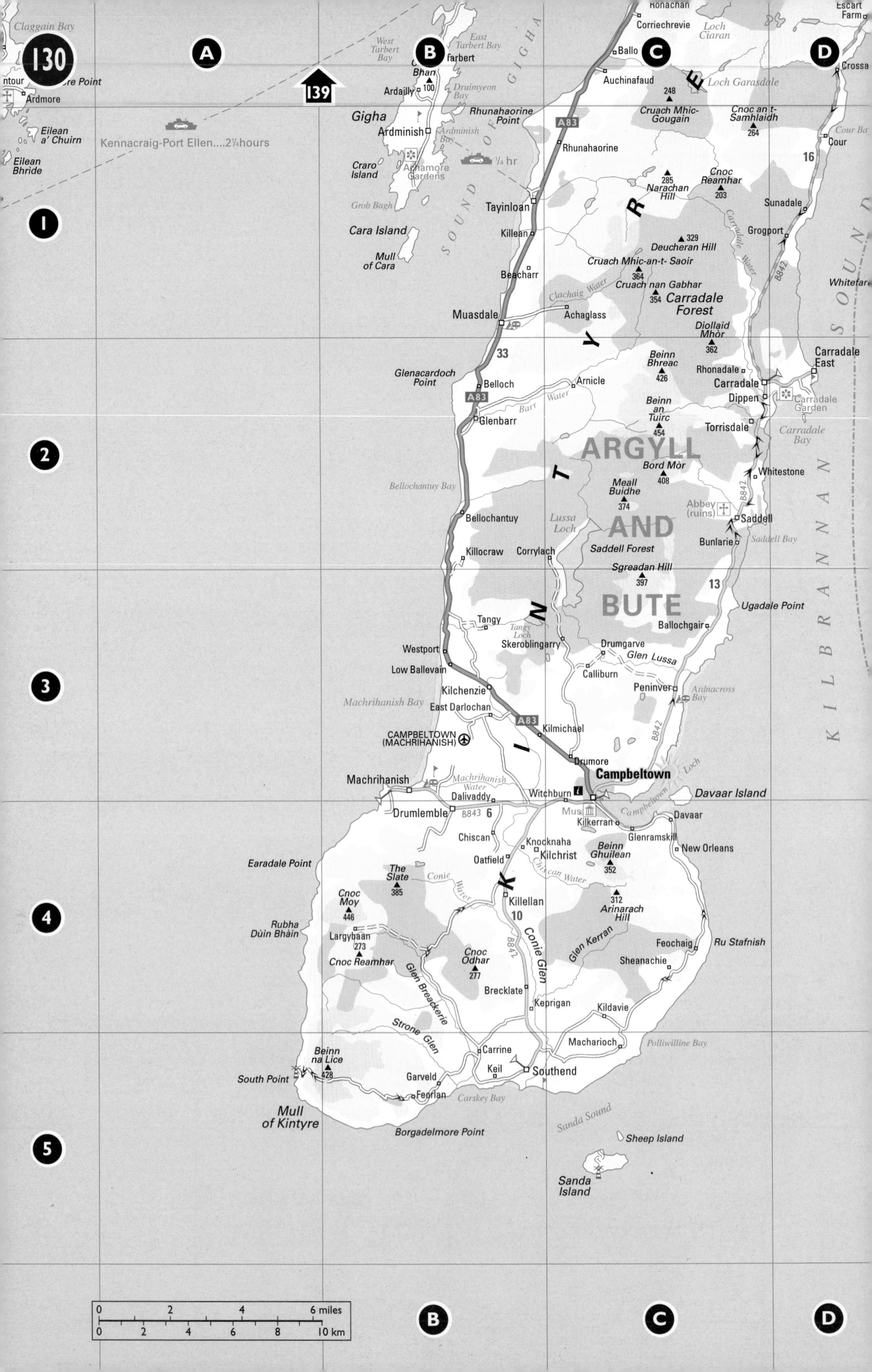
139
Claggain Bay
Ardmore
Eilean a' Chuirn
Eilean Bhride
Kennacraig-Port Ellen....2¼hours
West Tarbert Bay
East Tarbert Bay
Tarbert
Ardailly
Druimyeon Bay
Gigha
Ardminish
Ardminish Bay
Craro Island
Achamore Gardens
¼ hr
Grob Bagh
Cara Island
Mull of Cara
SOUND OF GIGHA
Rhunahaorine Point
Rhunahaorine
Tayinloan
Killean
Beacharr
Muasdale
Achaglass
Clachaig Water
Glenacardoch Point
Belloch
Glenbarr
Barr Water
Arnicle
Bellochantuy Bay
Bellochantuy
Killocraw
Corrylach
Lussa Loch
Tangy
Tangy Loch
Skeroblingarry
Westport
Low Ballevain
Kilchenzie
Machrihanish Bay
East Darlochan
CAMPBELTOWN (MACHRIHANISH)
Kilmichael
Drumore
Campbeltown
Campbeltown Loch
Machrihanish
Machrihanish Water
Dalivaddy
Witchburn
Drumlemble
B843
Mus
Kilkerran
Davaar Island
Davaar
Glenramskill
New Orleans
Chiscan
Knocknaha
Kilchrist
Oatfield
Chiscan Water
Beinn Ghuilean
352
Earadale Point
The Slate
385
Conie Water
Cnoc Moy
446
Killellan
312
Arinarach Hill
Rubha Dùin Bhàin
Largybaan
273
Cnoc Reamhar
Glen Breackerie
Cnoc Odhar
277
B842
Conie Glen
Glen Kerran
Feochaig
Ru Stafnish
Sheanachie
Brecklate
Kepригan
Kildavie
Strone Glen
Carrine
Macharioch
Polliwilline Bay
Beinn na Lice
428
South Point
Keil
Southend
Garveld
Feorlan
Carskey Bay
Mull of Kintyre
Borgadelmore Point
Sanda Sound
Sheep Island
Sanda Island
Ronachan
Corriechrevie
Loch Ciaran
Ballo
Auchinafaud
Loch Garasdale
248
Cruach Mhic-Gougain
A83
Escart Farm
Crossa
Cnoc an t-Samhlaidh
264
Cour Bay
Cour
285
Narachan Hill
Cnoc Reamhar
203
Sunadale
Grogport
Carradale Water
329
Deucheran Hill
Cruach Mhic-an-t-Saoir
364
Cruach nan Gabhar
354
Carradale Forest
B842
Whitefarland
Diollaid Mhòr
362
Beinn Bhreac
426
Carradale East
Rhonadale
Carradale
Dippen
Carradale Garden
Beinn an Tuirc
454
Torrisdale
Carradale Bay
KINTYRE
ARGYLL AND BUTE
Bord Mòr
408
Whitestone
Meall Buidhe
374
Abbey (ruins)
Saddell
Bunlarie
Saddell Bay
Saddell Forest
Sgreadan Hill
397
KILBRANNAN SOUND
Ugadale Point
Ballochgair
Drumgarve
Glen Lussa
Calliburn
Peninver
Ardnacross Bay
33
16
13
6
10
0 2 4 6 miles
0 2 4 6 8 10 km
A B C D
1 2 3 4 5

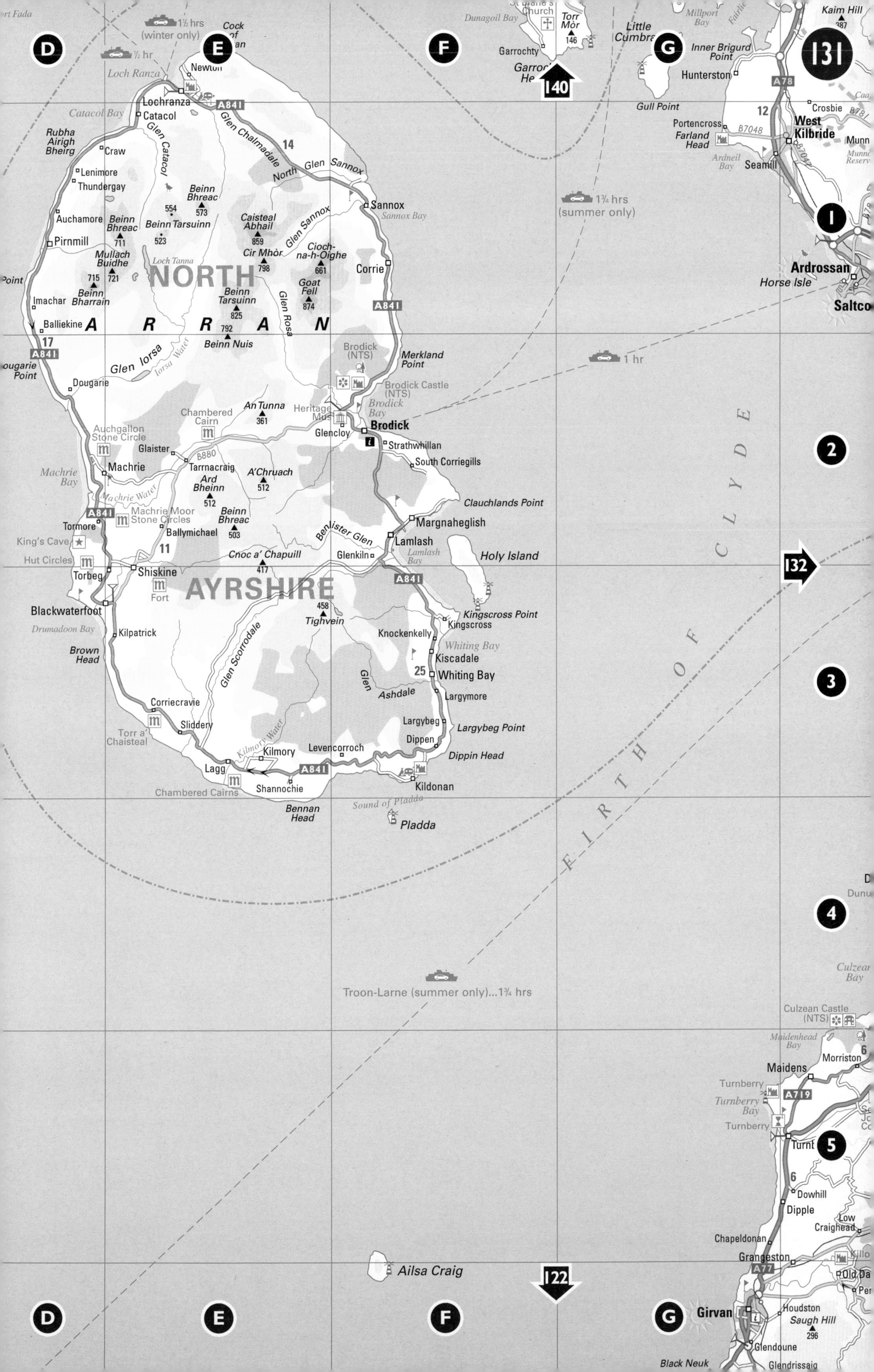
NORTH
ARRAN
AYRSHIRE
FIRTH OF CLYDE
Lochranza
Catacol
Catacol Bay
Loch Ranza
Newton
Cock of Arran
1½ hrs (winter only)
½ hr
Rubha Airigh Bheirg
Craw
Lenimore
Thundergay
Auchamore
Pirnmill
Imachar
Balliekine
Dougarie Point
Dougarie
Glen Catacol
Glen Chalmadale
North Glen Sannox
Glen Sannox
Sannox
Sannox Bay
Corrie
Beinn Bhreac 711
Beinn Tarsuinn 523
Beinn Bhreac 573
Caisteal Abhail 859
Cir Mhòr 798
Cioch-na-h-Oighe 661
Goat Fell 874
Mullach Buidhe 721
Beinn Bharrain 715
Loch Tanna
Beinn Tarsuinn 825
Beinn Nuis 792
Glen Rosa
Glen Iorsa
Iorsa Water
Brodick (NTS)
Merkland Point
Brodick Castle (NTS)
Brodick Bay
Brodick
Heritage Mus
Glencloy
Strathwhillan
South Corriegills
Clauchlands Point
Margnaheglish
Lamlash
Lamlash Bay
Holy Island
Kingscross Point
Kingscross
Chambered Cairn
An Tunna 361
Auchgallon Stone Circle
Glaister
Machrie
Machrie Bay
Machrie Water
Tarrnacraig
Ard Bheinn 512
A'Chruach 512
Beinn Bhreac 503
Machrie Moor Stone Circles
Ballymichael
Tormore
King's Cave
Hut Circles
Torbeg
Shiskine
Fort
Cnoc a' Chapuill 417
Benlister Glen
Glenkiln
Blackwaterfoot
Drumadoon Bay
Kilpatrick
Brown Head
Tighvein 458
Glen Scorrodale
Knockenkelly
Whiting Bay
Kiscadale
Largymore
Glen Ashdale
Largybeg
Largybeg Point
Dippen
Dippin Head
Corriecravie
Sliddery
Torr a' Chaisteal
Kilmory Water
Kilmory
Levencorroch
Lagg
Shannochie
Chambered Cairns
Bennan Head
Kildonan
Sound of Pladda
Pladda
A841
B880
Dunagoil Bay
Garrochty
Torr Mòr 146
Little Cumbrae
Millport Bay
Fairlie
Inner Brigurd Point
Hunterston
Kaim Hill 387
Gull Point
Portencross
Farland Head
Crosbie
West Kilbride
Ardneil Bay
Seamill
B7048
A78
1¾ hrs (summer only)
1 hr
Ardrossan
Horse Isle
Troon-Larne (summer only)...1¾ hrs
Culzean Bay
Culzean Castle (NTS)
Maidenhead Bay
Maidens
Morriston
Turnberry
Turnberry Bay
A719
Chapeldonan
Grangeston
A77
Houston
Saugh Hill 296
Girvan
Glendoune
Glendrissaig
Black Neuk
Ailsa Craig
D
E
F
G
1
2
3
4
5
140
132
122

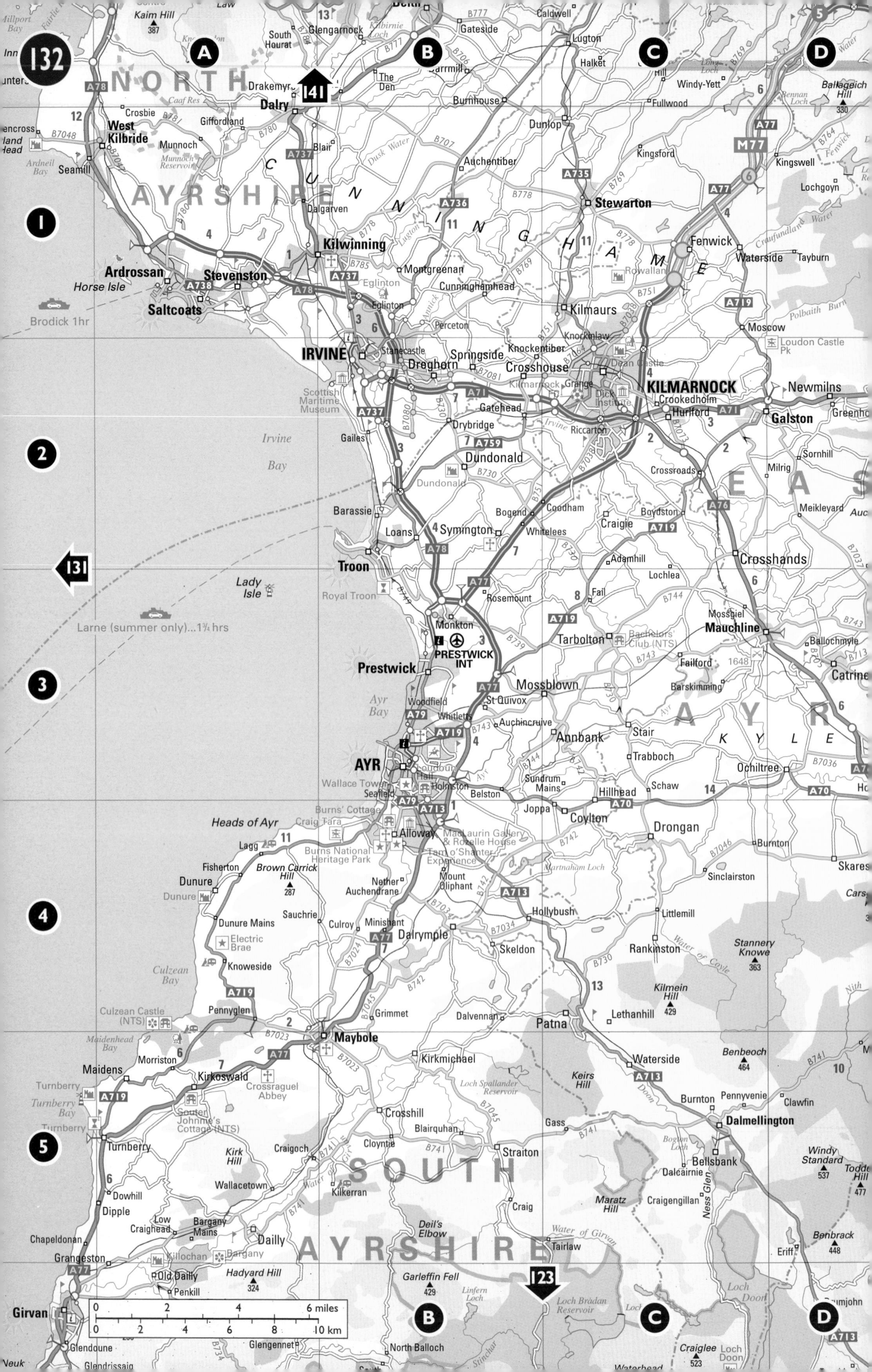
A
B
C
D
1
2
3
4
5
141
131
123
NORTH AYRSHIRE
CUNNINGHAME
EAST AYRSHIRE
KYLE
SOUTH AYRSHIRE
Kaim Hill
387
Glengarnock
Kilbirnie Loch
South Hourat
Gateside
Caldwell
Lugton
Halket
Windy-Yett
Fullwood
Ballageich Hill
330
Drakemyre
Dalry
The Den
Barrmill
Burnhouse
Crosbie
West Kilbride
Fairlie
Seamill
Ardneil Bay
Portencross
Hunterston
Giffordland
Munnoch
Munnoch Reservoir
Caaf Res
Blair
Dusk Water
Dunlop
Kingsford
Kingswell
Lochgoyn
Auchentiber
Stewarton
Dalgarven
Kilwinning
Montgreenan
Fenwick
Waterside
Tayburn
Craufurdland Water
Ardrossan
Horse Isle
Stevenston
Saltcoats
Brodick 1hr
Eglinton
Cunninghamhead
Rowallan
Kilmaurs
Moscow
Polbaith Burn
Perceton
Knockentiber
Knockinlaw
Loudon Castle Pk
IRVINE
Stanecastle
Dreghorn
Springside
Crosshouse
Grange
Dean Castle
KILMARNOCK
Newmilns
Scottish Maritime Museum
Dick Institute
Crookedholm
Hurlford
Galston
Gatehead
Drybridge
Riccarton
Irvine Bay
Gailes
Dundonald
Crossroads
Sornhill
Milrig
Barassie
Bogend
Coodham
Whitelees
Boydston
Craigie
Meikleyard
Loans
Symington
Troon
Adamhill
Lochlea
Crosshands
Royal Troon
Lady Isle
Rosemount
Fail
Larne (summer only)...1¾ hrs
Monkton
Mossgiel
Mauchline
Ballochmyle
PRESTWICK INT
Tarbolton
Bachelors' Club (NTS)
Failford
1648
Prestwick
Mossblown
Barskimming
Catrine
Ayr Bay
Woodfield
St Quivox
Whitletts
Auchincruive
Annbank
Stair
AYR
Trabboch
Ochiltree
Wallace Tower
Seafield
Loudoun Hall
Holmston
Sundrum Mains
Belston
Hillhead
Schaw
Joppa
Coylton
Burns' Cottage
Heads of Ayr
Craig Tara
Alloway
MacLaurin Gallery & Rozelle House
Tam o'Shanter Experience
Drongan
Burnton
Lagg
Burns National Heritage Park
Martnaham Loch
Sinclairston
Skares
Fisherton
Brown Carrick Hill
287
Nether Auchendrane
Mount Oliphant
Dunure
Sauchrie
Hollybush
Littlemill
Dunure Mains
Culroy
Minishant
Dalrymple
Skeldon
Rankinston
Stannery Knowe
363
Electric Brae
Water of Coyle
Culzean Bay
Knoweside
Kilmein Hill
429
Culzean Castle (NTS)
Pennyglen
Grimmet
Dalvennan
Patna
Lethanhill
Maidenhead Bay
Maybole
Kirkmichael
Waterside
Benbeoch
464
Maidens
Morriston
Kirkoswald
Crossraguel Abbey
Loch Spallander Reservoir
Keirs Hill
Turnberry
Turnberry Bay
Souter Johnnie's Cottage (NTS)
Crosshill
Burnton
Pennyvenie
Clawfin
Dalmellington
Blairquhan
Gass
Bogton Loch
Cloyntie
Craigoch
Kirk Hill
Straiton
Bellsbank
Windy Standard
537
Dalcairnie
Dowhill
Wallacetown
Kilkerran
Craig
Maratz Hill
Craigengillan
Ness Glen
Dipple
Low Craighead
Bargany Mains
Deil's Elbow
Water of Girvan
Chapeldonan
Dailly
Tairlaw
Benbrack
448
Eriff
Grangeston
Killochan
Bargany
Hadyard Hill
324
Old Dailly
Penkill
Garleffin Fell
429
Linfern Loch
Loch Bradan Reservoir
Loch Doon
Girvan
Glendoune
Glengennet
North Balloch
Craiglee
523
Loch Doon
0 2 4 6 miles
0 2 4 6 8 10 km

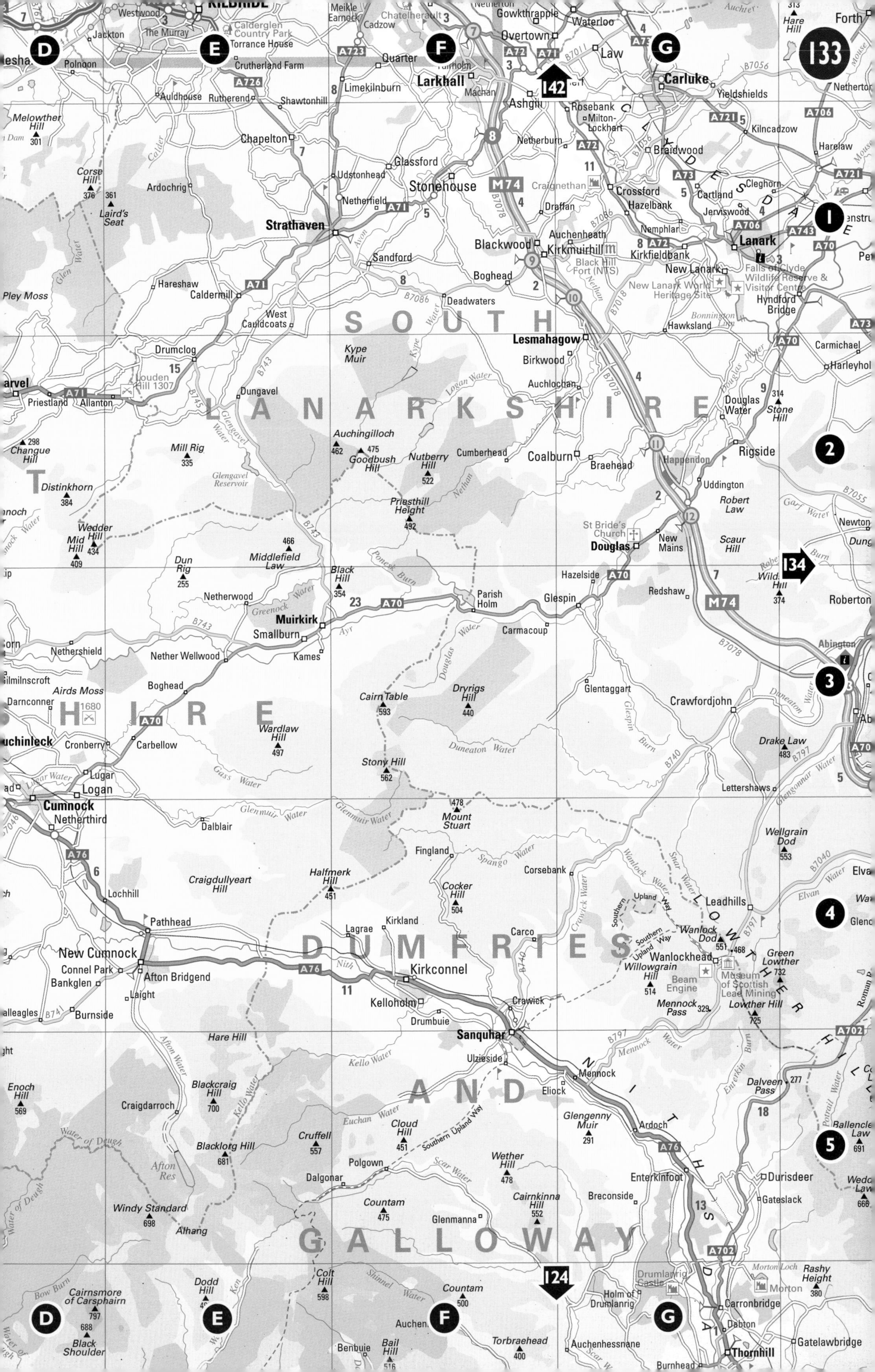

133
Forth
142
134
124
D
E
F
G
I
2
3
4
5
SOUTH LANARKSHIRE
DUMFRIES AND GALLOWAY
NITHSDALE
CLYDESDALE
LOWTHER HILLS
Westwood
Jackton
The Murray
Calderglen Country Park
Torrance House
Polnoon
Crutherland Farm
Auldhouse
Rutherend
Shawtonhill
Meikle Earnock
Chatelherault
Cadzow
Quarter
Limekilnburn
Larkhall
Machan
Ashgill
Gowkthrapple
Overtown
Waterloo
Law
Carluke
Yieldshields
Netherton
Kilncadzow
Harelaw
Rosebank
Milton-Lockhart
Netherburn
Braidwood
Melowther Hill 301
Corse Hill 376
361 Laird's Seat
Ardochrig
Chapelton
Glassford
Udstonhead
Stonehouse
Craignethan
Crossford
Hazelbank
Cartland
Cleghorn
Jerviswood
Lanark
Netherfield
Strathaven
Draffan
Auchenheath
Nemphlar
Sandford
Blackwood
Kirkmuirhill
Kirkfieldbank
Black Hill Fort (NTS)
New Lanark
Falls of Clyde Wildlife Reserve & Visitor Centre
New Lanark World Heritage Site
Hyndford Bridge
Bonnington Linn
Hareshaw
Caldermill
Boghead
Deadwaters
West Cauldcoats
Pley Moss
Kype Muir
Lesmahagow
Birkwood
Hawksland
Carmichael
Harleyhol
Drumclog
Louden Hill 1307
Auchlochan
Darvel
Priestland
Allanton
Dungavel
Douglas Water
314 Stone Hill
Auchingilloch 462
475 Goodbush Hill
Nutberry Hill 522
Cumberhead
Coalburn
Braehead
Happendon
Rigside
298 Changue Hill
Mill Rig 335
Glengavel Reservoir
Uddington
Distinkhorn 384
Priesthill Height 492
Robert Law
Newton
Wedder Hill 434
Mid Hill 409
466 Middlefield Law
St Bride's Church
Douglas
New Mains
Scaur Hill
Dun Rig 255
Black Hill 354
Hazelside
Redshaw
Wild Hill 374
Roberton
Netherwood
Muirkirk
Smallburn
Parish Holm
Glespin
Carmacoup
Abington
Nethershield
Nether Wellwood
Kames
Airds Moss
Darnconner
Boghead
Cairn Table 593
Dryrigs Hill 440
Glentaggart
Crawfordjohn
Auchinleck
Cronberry
Carbellow
Wardlaw Hill 497
Drake Law 483
Stony Hill 562
Lugar
Logan
Cumnock
Netherthird
Lettershaws
Dalblair
478 Mount Stuart
Wellgrain Dod 553
Fingland
Corsebank
Craigdullyeart Hill
Halfmerk Hill 451
Cocker Hill 504
Lochhill
Leadhills
Pathhead
Lagrae
Kirkland
Carco
Wanlock Dod 551
468
New Cumnock
Connel Park
Bankglen
Afton Bridgend
Laight
Burnside
Kirkconnel
Kelloholm
Drumbuie
Wanlockhead
Willowgrain Hill 514
Beam Engine
Museum of Scottish Lead Mining
Green Lowther 732
Mennock Pass 329
Lowther Hill 725
Crawick
Sanquhar
Hare Hill
Ulzieside
Mennock
Eliock
Dalveen Pass 277
Enoch Hill 569
Craigdarroch
Blackcraig Hill 700
Cloud Hill 451
Cruffell 557
Glengenny Muir 291
Ardoch
Ballencleuch Law 691
Blacklorg Hill 681
Afton Res
Polgown
Dalgonar
Wether Hill 478
Enterkinfoot
Durisdeer
Gateslack
Windy Standard 698
Alhang
Countam 475
Glenmanna
Cairnkinna Hill 552
Breconside
Wedder Law 666
Dodd Hill
Cairnsmore of Carsphairn 797
688 Black Shoulder
Colt Hill 598
Countam 500
Drumlanrig Castle
Holm of Drumlanrig
Morton Loch
Morton
Rashy Height 380
Carronbridge
Dabton
Auchen
Torbraehead 400
Bail Hill 516
Benbuie
Auchenhessnane
Thornhill
Gatelawbridge
Burnhead
Southern Upland Way
M74
A71
A70
A76
A72
A73
A723
A726
A721
A706
A743
A702
B7078
B7086
B743
B745
B740
B797
B7040
B7055
B741

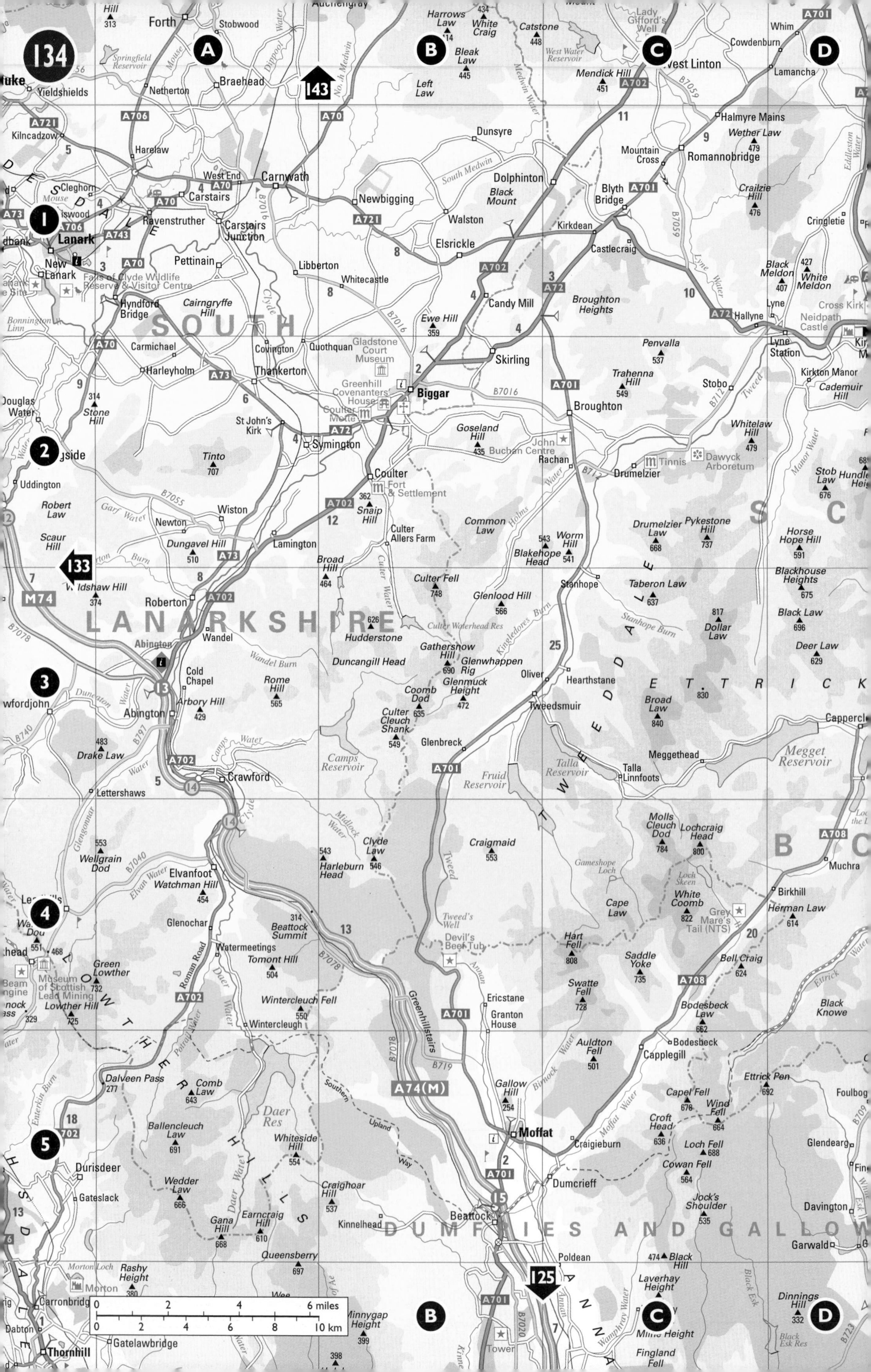
134
A
B
C
D
1
2
3
4
5
143
133
125
Forth
Stobwood
Springfield Reservoir
Braehead
Netherton
Yieldshields
Kilncadzow
Harelaw
A721
A706
A70
A72
A73
A743
A702
A701
A708
A74(M)
M74
B7016
B7055
B7078
B7059
B7040
B740
B797
B712
B719
B7020
B709
B723
Cleghorn
Carstairs
West End
Carnwath
Newbigging
Ravenstruther
Carstairs Junction
Lanark
New Lanark
Pettinain
Libberton
Whitecastle
Falls of Clyde Wildlife Reserve & Visitor Centre
Hyndford Bridge
Cairngryffe Hill
Bonnington Linn
Carmichael
Covington
Quothquan
Harleyholm
Thankerton
Gladstone Court Museum
Greenhill Covenanters' House
Coulter Motte
Biggar
St John's Kirk
Symington
Coulter
Fort & Settlement
Snaip Hill
Stone Hill
Douglas Water
Uddington
Tinto
Robert Law
Scaur Hill
Newton
Wiston
Dungavel Hill
Lamington
Culter Allers Farm
Wildshaw Hill
Roberton
SOUTH LANARKSHIRE
Wandel
Abington
Cold Chapel
Arbory Hill
Rome Hill
Hudderstone
Duncangill Head
Broad Hill
Culter Fell
Culter Waterhead Res
Gathersnow Hill
Glenwhappen Rig
Glenmuck Height
Coomb Dod
Culter Cleuch Shank
Glenbreck
Camps Reservoir
Crawford
Drake Law
Lettershaws
Wellgrain Dod
Elvanfoot
Watchman Hill
Glenochar
Harleburn Head
Clyde Law
Beattock Summit
Watermeetings
Green Lowther
Tomont Hill
Museum of Scottish Lead Mining
Lowther Hill
Wintercleuch Fell
Wintercleugh
Roman Road
Dalveen Pass
Comb Law
Ballencleuch Law
Daer Res
Whiteside Hill
Southern Upland Way
Wedder Law
Gana Hill
Earncraig Hill
Craighoar Hill
Kinnelhead
Queensberry
Durisdeer
Gateslack
Morton Loch
Morton
Rashy Height
Carronbridge
Dabton
Thornhill
Gatelawbridge
Minnygap Height
Harrows Law
White Craig
Catstone
Bleak Law
Left Law
Lady Gifford's Well
West Water Reservoir
Mendick Hill
West Linton
Whim
Cowdenburn
Lamancha
Halmyre Mains
Dunsyre
Wether Law
Mountain Cross
Romannobridge
Dolphinton
South Medwin
Black Mount
Blyth Bridge
Crailzie Hill
Walston
Elsrickle
Kirkdean
Castlecraig
Cringletie
Black Meldon
White Meldon
Candy Mill
Broughton Heights
Hallyne
Lyne
Cross Kirk
Neidpath Castle
Ewe Hill
Skirling
Penvalla
Lyne Station
Trahenna Hill
Stobo
Kirkton Manor
Cademuir Hill
Broughton
Goseland Hill
John Buchan Centre
Whitelaw Hill
Rachan
Tinnis
Dawyck Arboretum
Drumelzier
Stob Law
Common Law
Drumelzier Law
Pykestone Hill
Horse Hope Hill
Blakehope Head
Worm Hill
Stanhope
Taberon Law
Blackhouse Heights
Glenlood Hill
Dollar Law
Black Law
Deer Law
Kingledores Burn
Stanhope Burn
Oliver
Hearthstane
Tweedsmuir
Broad Law
Capperclei
Megget Reservoir
Meggethead
Talla Reservoir
Talla Linnfoots
Fruid Reservoir
TWEEDDALE
ETTRICK
Molls Cleuch Dod
Lochcraig Head
Craigmaid
Gameshope Loch
Loch Skeen
Muchra
Birkhill
Cape Law
White Coomb
Grey Mare's Tail (NTS)
Herman Law
Tweed's Well
Devil's Beef Tub
Hart Fell
Saddle Yoke
Bell Craig
Swatte Fell
Ericstane
Granton House
Black Knowe
Bodesbeck Law
Greenhillstairs
Auldton Fell
Bodesbeck
Capplegill
Ettrick Pen
Gallow Hill
Capel Fell
Wind Fell
Foulbog
Moffat
Craigieburn
Croft Head
Glendearg
Loch Fell
Cowan Fell
Dumcrieff
Jock's Shoulder
Davington
Beattock
DUMFRIES AND GALLOWAY
Poldean
Black Hill
Garwald
Laverhay Height
Black Esk
Dinnings Hill
Black Esk Res
Wamphray Water
Mine Height
Tower
Finglang Fell
0 2 4 6 miles
0 2 4 6 8 10 km

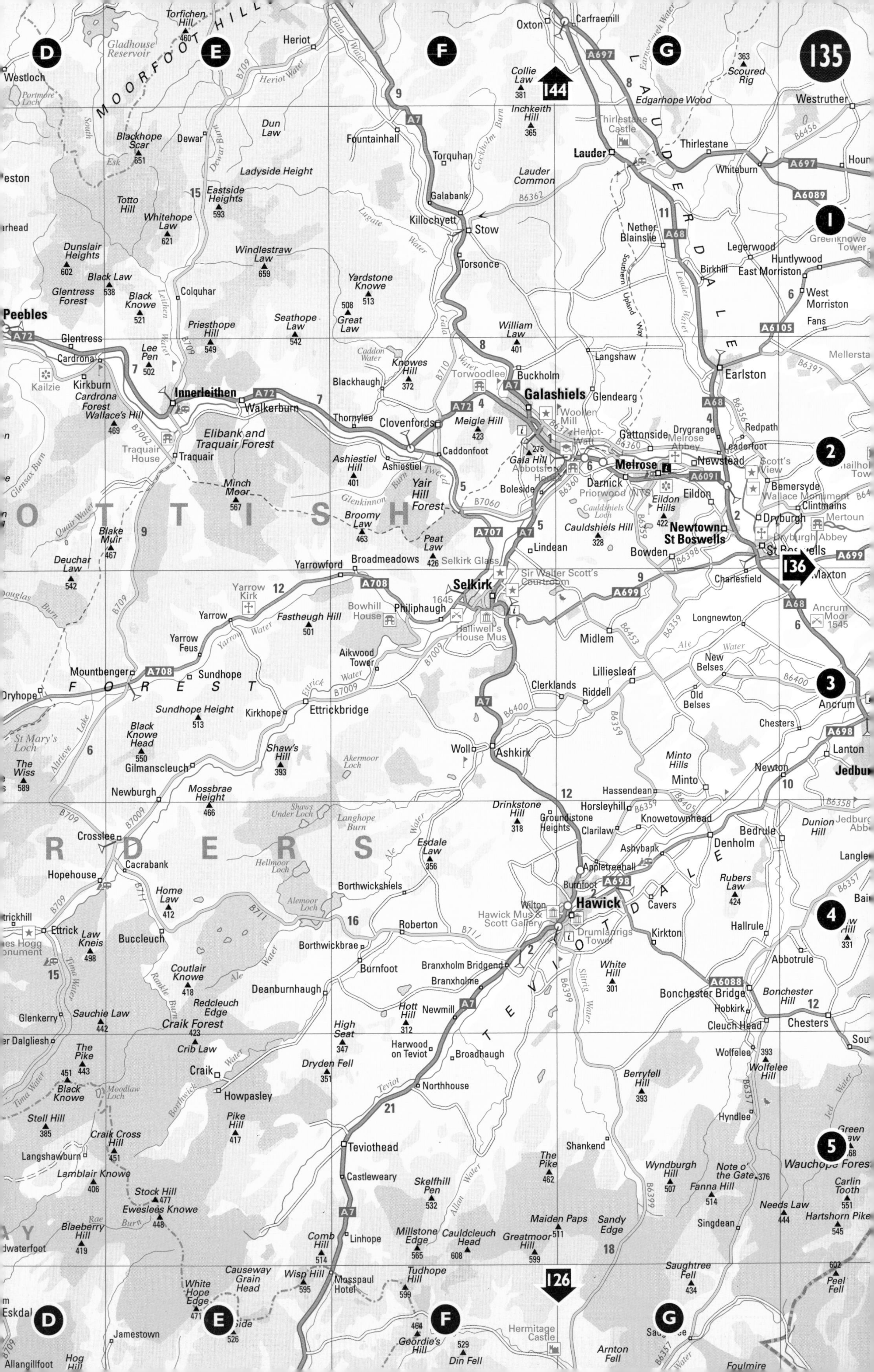

135
144
136
126
D
E
F
G
1
2
3
4
5
Peebles
Innerleithen
Galashiels
Melrose
Selkirk
Hawick
Lauder
Stow
Earlston
Newtown St Boswells
Jedburgh
Walkerburn
Clovenfords
Yarrowford
Ettrickbridge
Ashkirk
Denholm
Teviothead
Mosspaul Hotel
Westruther
Thirlestane
Legerwood
Dryburgh
St Boswells
Maxton
Ancrum
Lilliesleaf
Midlem
Bowden
Buccleuch
Craik
Roberton
Ettrick
Traquair
Heriot
Fountainhall
MOORFOOT HILLS
LAUDERDALE
TEVIOTDALE
SCOTTISH BORDERS
Elibank and Traquair Forest
Yair Hill Forest
Craik Forest
Wauchope Forest

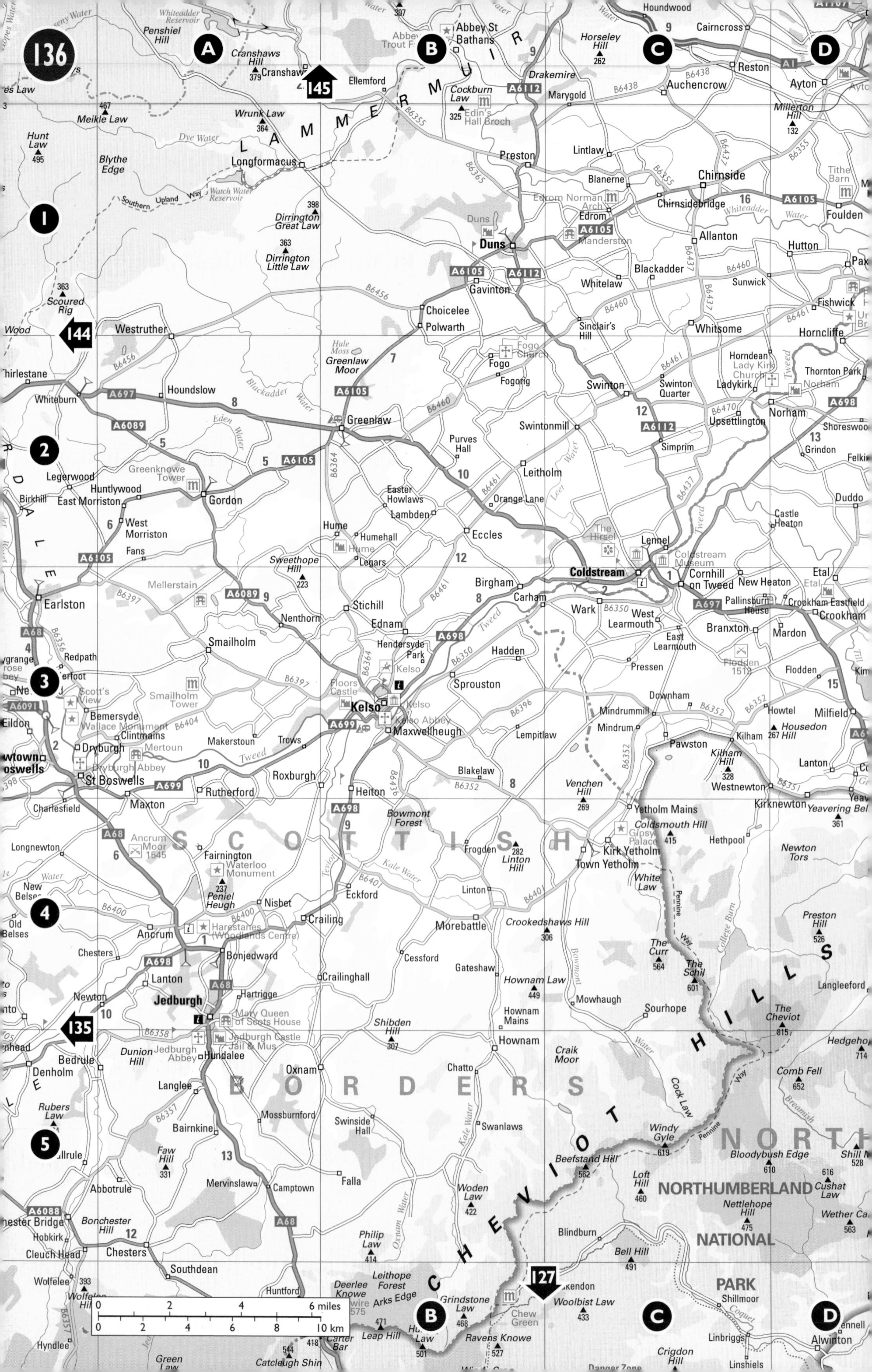

136
A
B
C
D
145
144
135
127
Whiteadder Reservoir
Penshiel Hill
Cranshaws Hill
379
Cranshaws
Abbey St Bathans
Ellemford
Houndwood
Cairncross
Horseley Hill
262
Reston
Ayton
Drakemire
Auchencrow
Marygold
Cockburn Law
325
Edin's Hall Broch
Millerton Hill
132
Meikle Law
467
Wrunk Law
364
LAMMERMUIR
Hunt Law
495
Blythe Edge
Dye Water
Longformacus
Preston
Lintlaw
Blanerne
Chirnside
Tithe Barn
Southern Upland Way
Watch Water Reservoir
Edrom Norman Arch
Chirnsidebridge
Foulden
Edrom
Manderston
Allanton
Whiteadder Water
Duns
Hutton
Dirrington Great Law
398
Dirrington Little Law
363
Blackadder
Paxton
Gavinton
Whitelaw
Sunwick
Scoured Rig
363
Choicelee
Polwarth
Sinclair's Hill
Whitsome
Fishwick
Horncliffe
Westruther
Hule Moss
Greenlaw Moor
Fogo
Fogo Church
Fogorig
Horndean
Lady Kirk Church
Ladykirk
Thornton Park
Norham
Thirlestane
Whiteburn
Houndslow
Swinton
Swinton Quarter
Upsettlington
Shoreswood
Greenlaw
Swintonmill
Simprim
Grindon
Legerwood
Greenknowe Tower
Gordon
Purves Hall
Leitholm
Leet Water
Felkington
Birkhill
Huntlywood
East Morriston
West Morriston
Easter Howlaws
Lambden
Orange Lane
Duddo
Castle Heaton
Hume
Humehall
Eccles
The Hirsel
Lennel
Coldstream Museum
Fans
Legars
Sweethope Hill
223
Coldstream
Cornhill on Tweed
Etal
Mellerstain
Earlston
Birgham
Carham
Wark
West Learmouth
New Heaton
Pallinsburn House
Crookham Eastfield
Crookham
Stichill
Ednam
Nenthorn
Smailholm
Hendersyde Park
Kelso
Hadden
East Learmouth
Branxton
Mardon
Redpath
Pressen
Flodden 1513
Flodden
Floors Castle
Sprouston
Smailholm Tower
Scott's View
Bemersyde
Wallace Monument
Clintmains
Kelso Abbey
Maxwellheugh
Downham
Mindrummill
Mindrum
Howtel
Milfield
Housedon Hill
Eildon
Lempitlaw
Pawston
Kilham
267
Dryburgh
Mertoun
Makerstoun
Trows
Dryburgh Abbey
Newtown St Boswells
St Boswells
Roxburgh
Kilham Hill
328
Lanton
Blakelaw
Rutherford
Heiton
Venchen Hill
269
Westnewton
Kirknewton
Yeavering Bell
361
Charlesfield
Maxton
Bowmont Forest
Yetholm Mains
Coldsmouth Hill
415
Ancrum Moor 1545
Gipsy Palace
Hethpool
SCOTTISH
Frogden
282
Linton Hill
Kirk Yetholm
Town Yetholm
Newton Tors
Longnewton
Fairnington
Waterloo Monument
Kale Water
White Law
Pennine Way
New Belses
Eckford
Linton
Old Belses
237
Peniel Heugh
Nisbet
Harestanes (Woodlands Centre)
Crailing
Morebattle
Crookedshaws Hill
306
Preston Hill
526
Ancrum
Chesters
Bonjedward
Cessford
The Curr
564
Gateshaw
The Schil
601
Langleeford
Lanton
Crailinghall
Hownam Law
449
Newton
Hartrigge
Mowhaugh
Jedburgh
Mary Queen of Scots House
Hownam Mains
Sourhope
The Cheviot
815
Jedburgh Castle Jail & Mus
Shibden Hill
307
Hownam
Hedgehope
714
Dunion Hill
Jedburgh Abbey
Hundalee
Craik Moor
Bedrule
Denholm
Oxnam
Chatto
Comb Fell
652
BORDERS
Langlee
Cock Law
CHEVIOT HILLS
Rubers Law
Mossburnford
Swinside Hall
Kale Water
Swanlaws
Bairnkine
Windy Gyle
619
NORTH
Faw Hill
331
Beefstand Hill
562
Bloodybush Edge
610
Shill Moor
528
Falla
Loft Hill
460
616
Cushat Law
Abbotrule
Mervinslaw
Camptown
Woden Law
422
NORTHUMBERLAND
Bonchester Bridge
Bonchester Hill
Nettlehope Hill
475
Wether Cairn
563
Hobkirk
Philip Law
414
Oxnam Water
Blindburn
NATIONAL
Cleuch Head
Chesters
Bell Hill
491
Southdean
PARK
Wolfelee
393
Wolfelee Hill
Huntford
Deerlee Knowe
Leithope Forest
Arks Edge
Grindstone Law
468
Buckenden
Woolbist Law
433
Shillmoor
Coquet
575
471
Leap Hill
Hungry Law
501
Carter Bar
418
Chew Green
Ravens Knowe
527
Linbriggs
Alwinton
Hyndlee
Green Law
544
Catcleugh Shin
Crigdon Hill
Linshiels
Danger Zone
0 2 4 6 miles
0 2 4 6 8 10 km

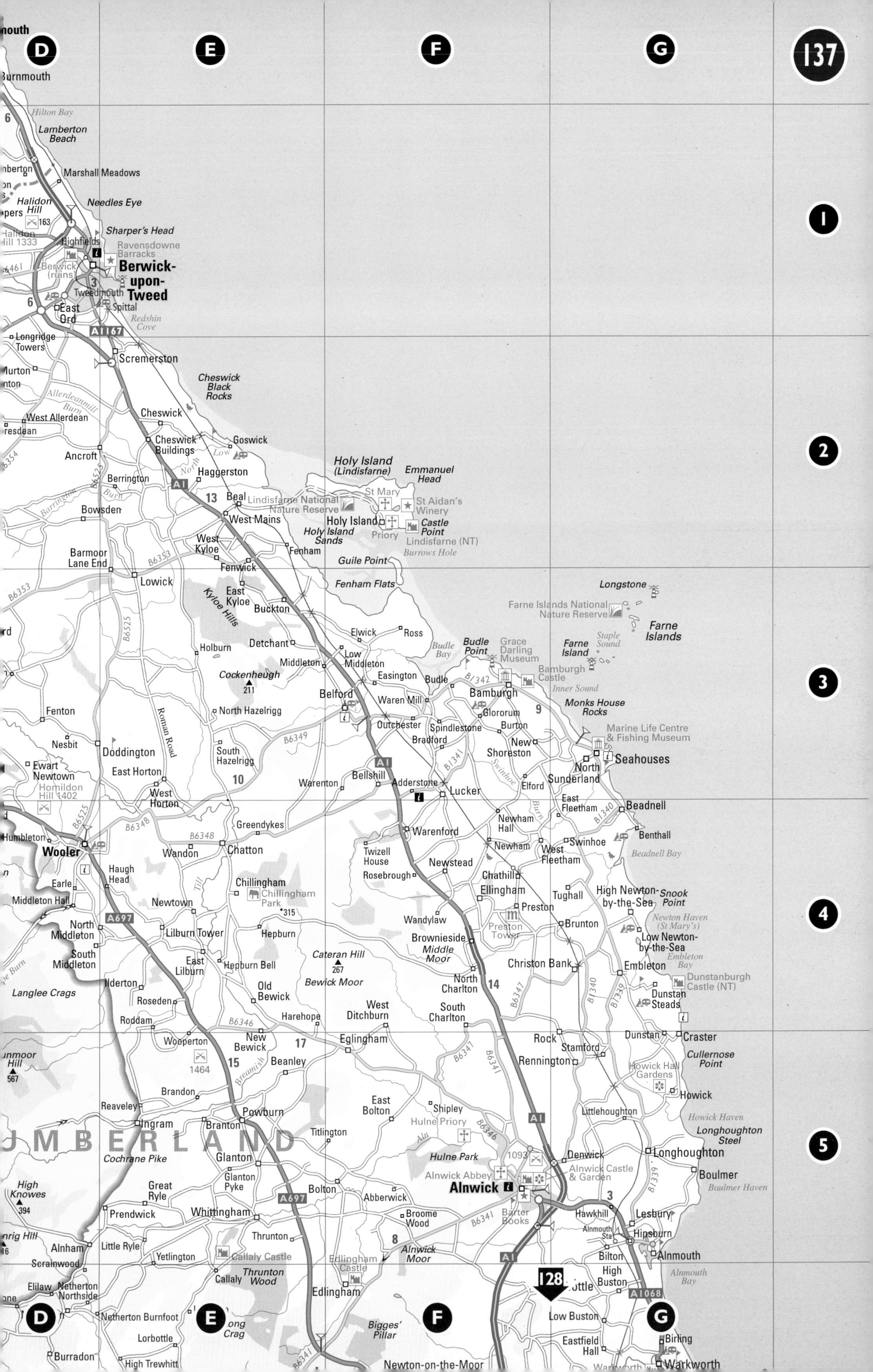
D
E
F
G
Burnmouth
Hilton Bay
Lamberton Beach
Marshall Meadows
Needles Eye
Halidon Hill
163
Sharper's Head
Highfields
Ravensdowne Barracks
Berwick-upon-Tweed
Berwick (ruins)
Tweedmouth
Spittal
East Ord
Redshin Cove
A1167
Longridge Towers
Scremerston
Cheswick Black Rocks
Allerdean Mill Burn
West Allerdean
Cheswick
Cheswick Buildings
Goswick
Ancroft
Holy Island (Lindisfarne)
Emmanuel Head
Berrington
Haggerston
Low
North
A1
13
Beal
Lindisfarne National Nature Reserve
St Mary
St Aidan's Winery
Bowsden
Barrington Burn
West Mains
Holy Island
Castle Point
Holy Island Sands
Priory
Lindisfarne (NT)
Burrows Hole
Barmoor Lane End
West Kyloe
Fenham
B6353
Guile Point
Fenwick
Lowick
Fenham Flats
Longstone
East Kyloe
Kyloe Hills
Farne Islands National Nature Reserve
Buckton
B6525
Elwick
Ross
Farne Islands
Staple Sound
Holburn
Detchant
Budle Bay
Budle Point
Grace Darling Museum
Farne Island
Low Middleton
Middleton
Cockenheugh
211
Easington
Budle
B1342
Bamburgh Castle
Inner Sound
Belford
Waren Mill
Bamburgh
Monks House Rocks
Fenton
North Hazelrigg
Glororum
9
Outchester
Spindlestone
Burton
Marine Life Centre & Fishing Museum
Roman Road
B6349
Bradford
Nesbit
Doddington
South Hazelrigg
New
Seahouses
Shoreston
Ewart
Newtown
A1
B1341
North Sunderland
Swinhoe Burn
East Horton
10
Bellshill
Warenton
Adderstone
Homildon Hill 1402
Elford
Lucker
West Horton
East Fleetham
Beadnell
B1340
Newham Hall
B6348
Greendykes
Humbleton
Warenford
Benthall
Wooler
Wandon
Chatton
Twizell House
Newham
West Fleetham
Swinhoe
Beadnell Bay
Haugh Head
Rosebrough
Newstead
Earle
Chillingham
Chillingham Park
Chathill
Till
Ellingham
Tughall
High Newton-by-the-Sea
Snook Point
Middleton Hall
Newtown
315
Preston
Newton Haven (St Mary's)
A697
Wandylaw
Preston Tower
Brunton
North Middleton
Lilburn Tower
Hepburn
Brownieside
Low Newton-by-the-Sea
Middle Moor
Embleton Bay
South Middleton
Cateran Hill
Christon Bank
East Lilburn
Hepburn Bell
267
Embleton
Dunstanburgh Castle (NT)
Langlee Crags
Ilderton
Bewick Moor
North Charlton
14
B6347
B1340
B1339
Dunstan Steads
Old Bewick
Roseden
West Ditchburn
South Charlton
Roddam
Harehope
B6346
Dunstan
Craster
New Bewick
17
Eglingham
Rock
Wooperton
Cullernose Point
Hill
567
Stamford
B6341
1464
15
Beanley
Rennington
Howick Hall Gardens
Breamish
Brandon
Howick
East Bolton
Reaveley
Shipley
Littlehoughton
Powburn
A1
Howick Haven
Ingram
Branton
Titlington
Hulne Priory
Longhoughton Steel
NORTHUMBERLAND
Aln
1093
Denwick
Longhoughton
Cochrane Pike
Glanton
Hulne Park
Alnwick Castle & Garden
B1339
Boulmer
Alnwick Abbey
High Knowes
Glanton Pyke
Great Ryle
Bolton
Alnwick
Boulmer Haven
394
A697
Abberwick
3
Prendwick
Whittingham
Broome Wood
Barter Books
Lesbury
Hawkhill
Alnmouth Sta
Hipsburn
Thrunton
B6341
Alnham
Little Ryle
8
Alnwick Moor
A1
Bilton
Alnmouth
Scrainwood
Yetlington
Callaly Castle
Edlingham Castle
High Buston
Alnmouth Bay
Callaly
Thrunton Wood
128
Elilaw
Netherton Northside
Edlingham
A1068
Netherton Burnfoot
Long Crag
Biggers' Pillar
Low Buston
Lorbottle
Birling
Eastfield Hall
Burradon
High Trewhitt
B6341
Newton-on-the-Moor
Warkworth
2
3
4
5

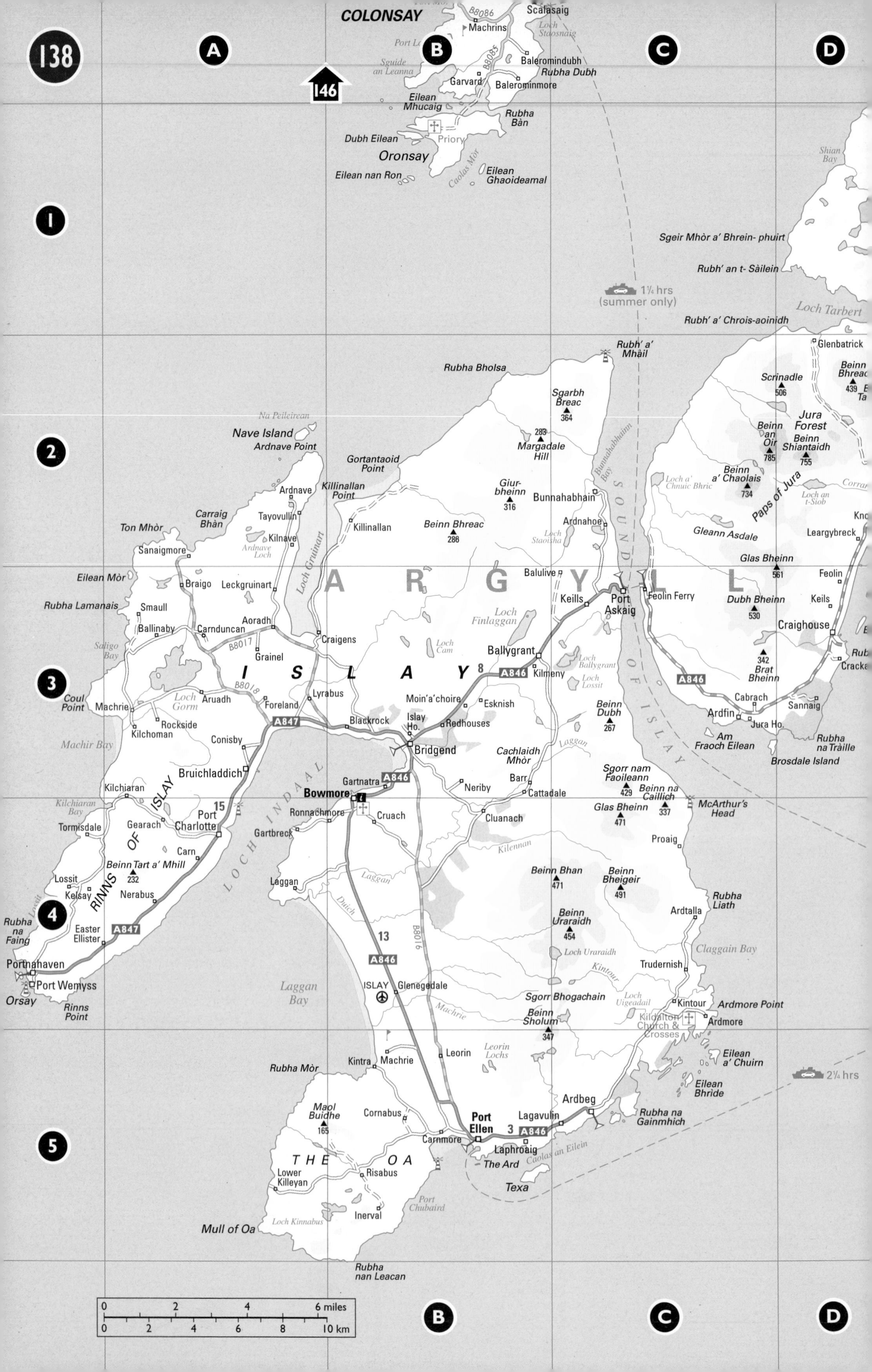

COLONSAY
Scalasaig
Machrins
Balerominmore
Baleromindubh
Rubha Dubh
Garvard
Eilean Mhucaig
Rubha Bàn
Dubh Eilean
Priory
Oronsay
Eilean nan Ron
Eilean Ghaoideamal
146
Sgeir Mhòr a' Bhrein- phuirt
Rubh' an t- Sàilein
1¼ hrs (summer only)
Loch Tarbert
Rubh' a' Chrois-aoinidh
Rubh' a' Mhàil
Rubha Bholsa
Glenbatrick
Scrinadle 506
Sgarbh Breac 364
Jura Forest
Beinn an Oir 785
Beinn Shiantaidh 755
Nave Island
Ardnave Point
Margadale Hill 283
Gortantaoid Point
Killinallan Point
Giur-bheinn 316
Bunnahabhain
Beinn a' Chaolais 734
Paps of Jura
Ardnave
Carraig Bhàn
Tayovullin
Killinallan
Beinn Bhreac 286
Ardnahoe
Gleann Asdale
Leargybreck
Ton Mhòr
Kilnave
Loch Gruinart
Sanaigmore
Glas Bheinn 561
Eilean Mòr
Braigo
Leckgruinart
Balulive
Feolin
A R G Y L L
Keills
Port Askaig
Feolin Ferry
Dubh Bheinn 530
Keils
Rubha Lamanais
Smaull
Aoradh
Loch Finlaggan
Craighouse
Ballinaby
Carnduncan
Craigens
Ballygrant
Saligo Bay
B8017
Grainel
Kilmeny
342 Brat Bheinn
I S L A Y
A846
Coul Point
Machrie
Loch Gorm
Aruadh
B8018
Foreland
Lyrabus
Moin'a'choire
Esknish
Beinn Dubh 267
Cabrach
Sannaig
Ardfin
Jura Ho.
Rockside
Kilchoman
A847
Blackrock
Islay Ho.
Redhouses
Am Fraoch Eilean
Rubha na Tràille
Machir Bay
Conisby
Bridgend
Cachlaidh Mhòr
Brosdale Island
SOUND OF ISLAY
Bruichladdich
Gartnatra
Barr
Sgorr nam Faoileann 429
Kilchiaran
Bowmore
Neriby
Cattadale
Beinn na Caillich 337
McArthur's Head
Kilchiaran Bay
15
Port Charlotte
Ronnachmore
Cruach
Cluanach
Glas Bheinn 471
Tormisdale
Gearach
RINNS OF ISLAY
Gartbreck
LOCH INDAAL
Proaig
Carn
Beinn Tart a' Mhill 232
Kilennan
Lossit
Kelsay
Nerabus
Laggan
Beinn Bhan 471
Beinn Bheigeir 491
Rubha Liath
Ardtalla
Rubha na Faing
Easter Ellister
13
B8016
Beinn Uraraidh 454
Loch Uraraidh
Claggain Bay
Portnahaven
Port Wemyss
Orsay
Rinns Point
Laggan Bay
ISLAY
Glenegedale
Trudernish
Kintour
Sgorr Bhogachain
Loch Uigeadail
Ardmore Point
Beinn Sholum 347
Kildalton Church & Crosses
Ardmore
Leorin
Leorin Lochs
Eilean a' Chuirn
2¼ hrs
Rubha Mòr
Kintra
Machrie
Eilean Bhride
Ardbeg
Maol Buidhe 165
Cornabus
Port Ellen
Lagavulin
Rubha na Gainmhich
3
Carnmore
Laphroaig
THE OA
Lower Killeyan
Risabus
The Ard
Caolas an Eilein
Texa
Inerval
Port Chubaird
Mull of Oa
Loch Kinnabus
Rubha nan Leacan
0 2 4 6 miles
0 2 4 6 8 10 km

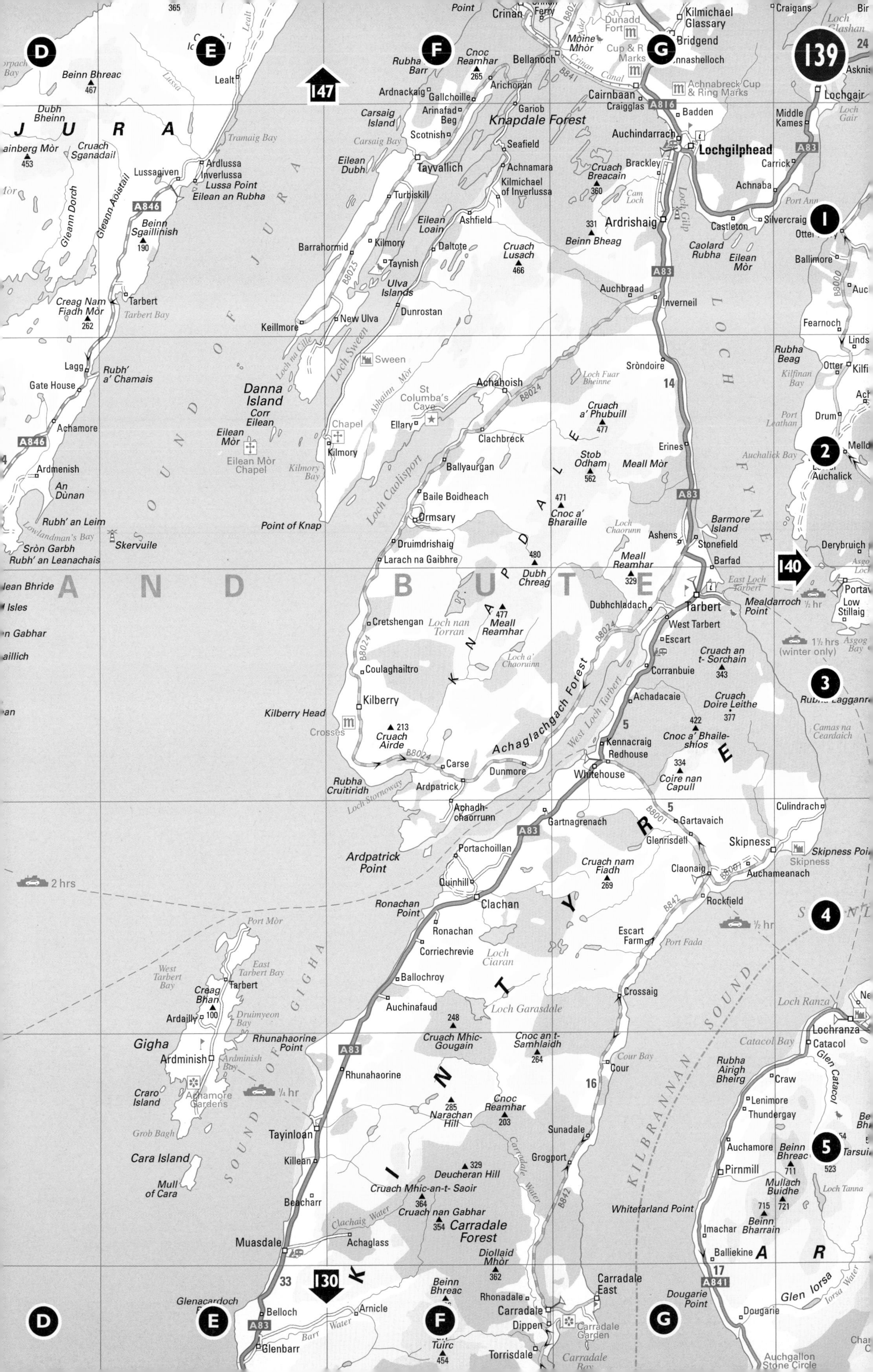

139
147
140
130
D
E
F
G
1
2
3
4
5
365
Crinan
Crinan Ferry
Dunadd Fort
Kilmichael Glassary
Craigans
Moine Mhor
Cup & R Marks
Bridgend
Rubha Barr
Cnoc Reamhar
265
Bellanoch
Crinan Canal
Beinn Bhreac
467
Lealt
Lussa
Ardnackaig
Gallchoille
Arichonan
Achnabreck Cup & Ring Marks
Lochgair
Cairnbaan
Craigglas
A816
Badden
Carsaig Island
Arinafad Beg
Gariob
Knapdale Forest
Middle Kames
Loch Gair
Dubh Bheinn
JURA
Tramaig Bay
Carsaig Bay
Scotnish
Auchindarrach
Seafield
Lochgilphead
A83
Cruach Sganadail
Ardlussa
Inverlussa
Lussa Point
Eilean an Rubha
Lussagiven
Eilean Dubh
Tayvallich
Achnamara
Kilmichael of Inverlussa
Cruach Breacan
360
Brackley
Carrick
Achnaba
453
Gleann Dorch
Gleann Aoistail
A846
Beinn Sgaillinish
190
Turbiskill
Cam Loch
Port Ann
Silvercraig
Castleton
Ardrishaig
Loch Gilp
331
Beinn Bheag
Eilean Loain
Ashfield
Barrahormid
Kilmory
Daltote
Cruach Lusach
466
Caolard Rubha
Eilean Mòr
Ballimore
Taynish
B8025
Ulva Islands
Auchbraad
Creag Nam Fiadh Mòr
262
Tarbert
Tarbert Bay
New Ulva
Dunrostan
Inverneil
Keillmore
Fearnoch
Loch na Cille
Loch Sween
Sween
Lagg
Rubh' a' Chamais
Gate House
Srondoire
Loch Fuar Bheinne
14
Rubha Beag
Kilfinan Bay
Otter
Danna Island
Corr Eilean
St Columba's Cave
Achahoish
B8024
Abhainn Mòr
Cruach a' Phubuill
477
Port Leathan
Drum
Achamore
Chapel
Ellary
Eilean Mòr
Eilean Mòr Chapel
Clachbreck
Erines
Auchalick Bay
Auchalick
Ardmenish
Kilmory Bay
Ballyaurgan
Stob Odham
562
Meall Mòr
An Dùnan
Loch Caolisport
Baile Boidheach
471
Cnoc a' Bharaille
Rubh' an Leim
Lowlandman's Bay
Skervuile
Point of Knap
Ormsary
Loch Chaorunn
Barmore Island
Ashens
Stonefield
Sròn Garbh
Rubh' an Leanachais
Druimdrishaig
Larach na Gaibhre
480
Dubh Chreag
Meall Reamhar
329
Barfad
Derybruich
ARGYLL AND BUTE
East Loch Tarbert
Portavadie
Dubhchladach
Tarbert
Mealdarroch Point
½ hr
Low Stillaig
Isles
Cretshengan
Loch nan Torran
477
Meall Reamhar
West Tarbert
Escart
1½ hrs (winter only)
Asgog Bay
Cruach an t- Sorchain
343
Coulaghailtro
Loch a' Chaoruinn
Corranbuie
Achaglachgach Forest
Achadacaie
Kilberry
Cruach Doire Leithe
377
Kilberry Head
Crosses
213
Cruach Airde
West Loch Tarbert
422
Cnoc a' Bhaile-shios
Camas na Ceardaich
Kennacraig
Redhouse
Carse
Dunmore
334
Coire nan Capull
Rubha Cruitiridh
Loch Stornoway
Ardpatrick
Whitehouse
Achadh-chaorrunn
Gartnagrenach
B8001
Gartavaich
Culindrach
KNAPDALE
KINTYRE
Ardpatrick Point
Portachoillan
Glenrisdell
Skipness
Skipness Point
Cruach nam Fiadh
269
Claonaig
Auchameanach
B8001
2 hrs
Quinhill
Clachan
Rockfield
Ronachan Point
Ronachan
B842
Escart Farm
Port Fada
Port Mòr
Corriechrevie
Loch Ciaran
West Tarbert Bay
East Tarbert Bay
Ballochroy
Creag Bhan
100
Tarbert
Crossaig
Loch Ranza
Ardailly
Druimyeon Bay
Auchinafaud
248
Loch Garasdale
Lochranza
Gigha
Rhunahaorine Point
Cruach Mhic-Gougain
Cnoc an t-Samhlaidh
264
Catacol Bay
Catacol
Ardminish
Ardminish Bay
A83
Cour Bay
Cour
Rubha Airigh Bheirg
Glen Catacol
Craw
Rhunahaorine
16
Craro Island
Achamore Gardens
¼ hr
285
Narachan Hill
Cnoc Reamhar
203
Lenimore
Thundergay
SOUND OF GIGHA
Tayinloan
Sunadale
Grob Bagh
KILBRANNAN SOUND
Auchamore
Beinn Bhreac
711
Tarsuinn
523
Cara Island
Killean
Grogport
Carradale Water
329
Deucheran Hill
Pirnmill
Mull of Cara
Cruach Mhic-an-t- Saoir
Mullach Buidhe
Loch Tanna
Beacharr
B842
364
Whitefarland Point
715
721
Cruach nan Gabhar
354
Carradale Forest
Beinn Bharrain
Clachaig Water
Imachar
Muasdale
Achaglass
Diollaid Mhòr
362
Balliekine
ARRAN
33
Carradale East
17
A841
Glen Iorsa
Iorsa Water
Beinn Bhreac
Rhonadale
Glenacardoch
Belloch
Arnicle
Carradale
Dougarie Point
Dougarie
Dippen
Carradale Garden
Barr Water
Glenbarr
Tuirc
454
Torrisdale
Carradale Bay
Auchgallon Stone Circle

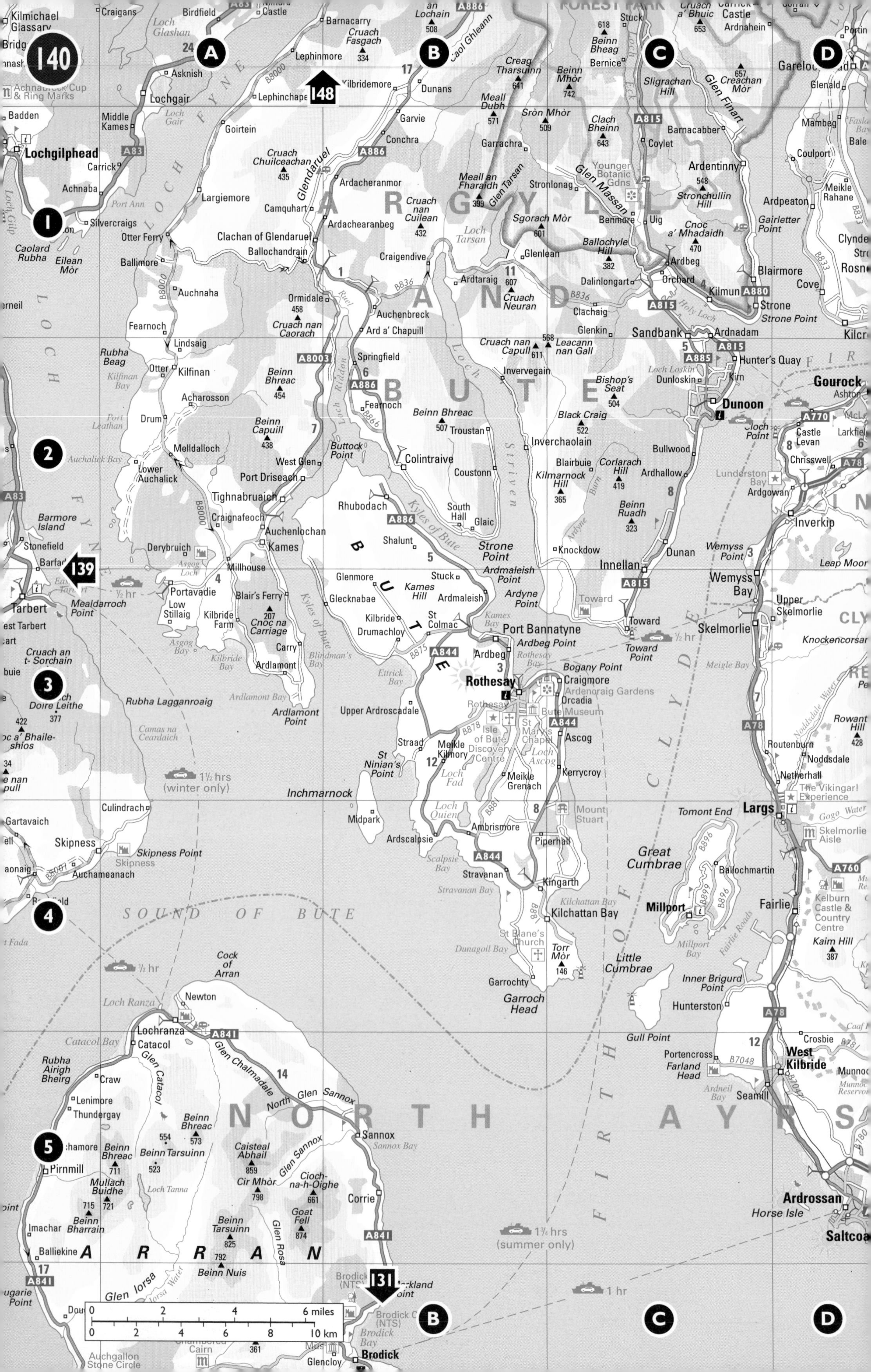

140
A
B
C
D
148
139
131
Kilmichael Glassary
Craigans
Birdfield
Loch Glashan
Asknish
Lochgair
Loch Gair
Middle Kames
Badden
Lochgilphead
Carrick
Achnaba
Achnabreck Cup & Ring Marks
Silvercraigs
Caolard Rubha
Eilean Mòr
Loch Gilp
Port Ann
Otter Ferry
Ballimore
Largiemore
Goirtein
Lephinchapel
Lephinmore
Barnacarry
Cruach Fasgach
334
Kilbridemore
Dunans
Caol Ghleann
Garvie
Conchra
Glendaruel
Cruach Chuilceachan
435
Ardacheranmor
Camquhart
Ardachearanbeg
Clachan of Glendaruel
Ballochandrain
Cruach nan Cuilean
432
Craigendive
Ormidale
458
Cruach nan Caorach
Auchenbreck
Ard a' Chapuill
Springfield
Fearnoch
Colintraive
Auchnaha
Fearnoch
Lindsaig
Rubha Beag
Kilfinan Bay
Otter
Kilfinan
Acharosson
Drum
Port Leathan
Melldalloch
Lower Auchalick
Auchalick Bay
Beinn Bhreac
454
Beinn Capuill
438
Buttock Point
West Glen
Port Driseach
Tighnabruaich
Craignafeoch
Auchenlochan
Kames
Derybruich
Millhouse
Portavadie
Low Stillaig
Kilbride Farm
Blair's Ferry
Cnoc na Carriage
207
Asgog Bay
Kilbride Bay
Ardlamont
Ardlamont Bay
Ardlamont Point
Carry
Kyles of Bute
Rhubodach
Shalunt
Glenmore
Kames Hill
Stuck
Ardmaleish
Ardmaleish Point
Glecknabae
Kilbride
Drumachloy
St Colmac
Port Bannatyne
Kames Bay
Ardbeg
Ardbeg Point
Rothesay Bay
Rothesay
Bogany Point
Craigmore
Ardencraig Gardens
Orcadia
Bute Museum
Ascog
Isle of Bute Discovery Centre
St Mary's Chapel
Loch Ascog
Kerrycroy
Upper Ardroscadale
Straad
Meikle Kilmory
Loch Fad
Meikle Grenach
St Ninian's Point
Inchmarnock
Midpark
Loch Quien
Ambrismore
Mount Stuart
Ardscalpsie
Scalpsie Bay
Piperhall
Stravanan
Stravanan Bay
Kingarth
Kilchattan Bay
St Blane's Church
Dunagoil Bay
Torr Mòr
146
Garrochty
Garroch Head
Ettrick Bay
Blindman's Bay
Loch Striven
Troustan
Beinn Bhreac
507
Coustonn
South Hall
Glaic
Strone Point
Ardyne Point
Toward
Toward Point
Innellan
Dunan
Knockdow
Inverchaolain
Blairbuie
Kilmarnock Hill
365
Corlarach Hill
419
Beinn Ruadh
323
Black Craig
522
Bishop's Seat
504
Invervegain
Cruach nan Capull
611
Leacann nan Gall
568
Glenkin
Clachaig
Ardtaraig
Cruach Neuran
607
Loch Tarsan
Glenlean
Sgorach Mòr
601
Stronlonag
Glen Tarsan
Meall an Fharaidh
399
Garrachra
Meall Dubh
571
Creag Tharsuinn
641
Beinn Mhòr
742
Sròn Mhòr
509
Clach Bheinn
643
Beinn Bheag
618
Bernice
Stuck
Loch Eck
Glen Massan
Younger Botanic Gdns
Benmore
Uig
Ballochyle Hill
382
Ardbeg
Dalinlongart
Orchard
Kilmun
Holy Loch
Sandbank
Ardnadam
Hunter's Quay
Kirn
Loch Loskin
Dunloskin
Dunoon
Bullwood
Ardhallow
Sligrachan Hill
Glen Finart
Coylet
Barnacabber
Ardentinny
Stronchullin Hill
548
Cnoc a' Mhadaidh
470
Creachan Mòr
657
Cruach a' Bhuic
653
Ardnahein
Blairmore
Strone
Strone Point
Gareloch
Glenald
Mambeg
Coulport
Meikle Rahane
Ardpeaton
Gairletter Point
Clynder
Rosneath
Cove
Kilcreggan
Gourock
Ashton
Cloch Point
Castle Levan
Lunderston Bay
Ardgowan
Chrisswell
Inverkip
Wemyss Point
Wemyss Bay
Leap Moor
Upper Skelmorlie
Skelmorlie
Knockencorsan
Meigle Bay
Rowant Hill
428
Routenburn
Noddsdale
Netherhall
The Vikingar! Experience
Largs
Skelmorlie Aisle
Tomont End
Great Cumbrae
Ballochmartin
Millport
Millport Bay
Fairlie Roads
Fairlie
Kelburn Castle & Country Centre
Kaim Hill
387
Little Cumbrae
Inner Brigurd Point
Hunterston
Gull Point
Portencross
Farland Head
Ardneil Bay
Seamill
West Kilbride
Crosbie
Munnoch
Ardrossan
Horse Isle
Saltcoats
FIRTH OF CLYDE
ARGYLL AND BUTE
NORTH AYRSHIRE
ARRAN
BUTE
LOCH FYNE
SOUND OF BUTE
Barmore Island
Stonefield
Barfad
Tarbert
East Tarbert
Mealdarroch Point
West Tarbert
Cruach an t-Sorchain
Doire Leithe
377
422
Rubha Lagganroaig
Camas na Ceardaich
1½ hrs (winter only)
½ hr
Culindrach
Gartavaich
Skipness
Skipness Point
Auchameanach
Cock of Arran
Loch Ranza
Newton
Lochranza
Catacol
Catacol Bay
Rubha Airigh Bheirg
Craw
Lenimore
Thundergay
Glen Catacol
Glen Chalmadale
North Glen Sannox
Sannox
Sannox Bay
Glen Sannox
Beinn Bhreac
573
554
Beinn Tarsuinn
523
Beinn Bhreac
711
Pirnmill
Mullach Buidhe
721
715
Beinn Bharrain
Loch Tanna
Caisteal Abhail
859
Cir Mhòr
798
Cioch-na-h-Oighe
661
Goat Fell
874
Corrie
Beinn Tarsuinn
825
Glen Rosa
792
Beinn Nuis
Imachar
Balliekine
Glen Iorsa
Brodick Bay
Brodick
Glencloy
Auchgallon Stone Circle
361
1¾ hrs (summer only)
1 hr
0 2 4 6 miles
0 2 4 6 8 10 km
A83
A886
A8003
A844
A815
A885
A880
A770
A78
A760
A841
B8000
B836
B866
B875
B878
B881
B896
B899
B833
B7048

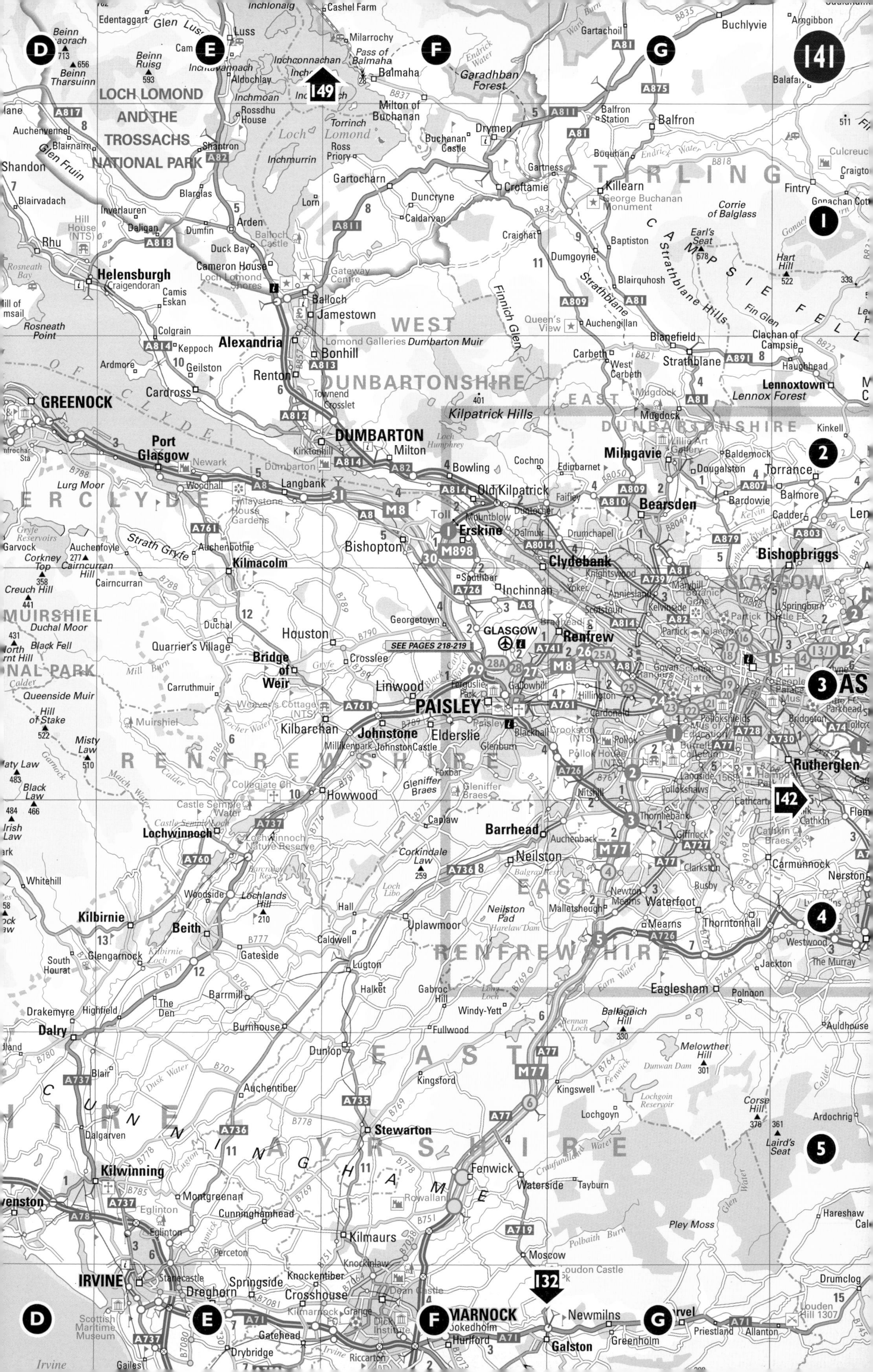
D
E
F
G
LOCH LOMOND AND THE TROSSACHS NATIONAL PARK
Loch Lomond
149
Luss
Balmaha
Milton of Buchanan
Drymen
Garadhban Forest
Buchlyvie
Balfron
Killearn
Fintry
STIRLING
CAMPSIE FELLS
Strathblane Hills
Strathblane
Blanefield
Lennoxtown
Lennox Forest
Croftamie
Gartocharn
Arden
Helensburgh
Rhu
Shandon
Balloch
Jamestown
Alexandria
Bonhill
Renton
Cardross
WEST DUNBARTONSHIRE
DUMBARTON
Milton
Kilpatrick Hills
EAST DUNBARTONSHIRE
Milngavie
Bearsden
Torrance
Bishopbriggs
GREENOCK
Port Glasgow
Langbank
Bowling
Old Kilpatrick
Erskine
Bishopton
Clydebank
Renfrew
GLASGOW
SEE PAGES 218-219
Rutherglen
142
Kilmacolm
Houston
Bridge of Weir
Linwood
PAISLEY
Johnstone
Elderslie
Kilbarchan
Howwood
Lochwinnoch
Barrhead
Neilston
Newton Mearns
Waterfoot
Busby
Thorntonhall
Eaglesham
Carmunnock
EAST RENFREWSHIRE
RENFREWSHIRE
MUIRSHIEL
Kilbirnie
Beith
Dalry
Uplawmoor
Lugton
Dunlop
Stewarton
Fenwick
Kilmaurs
Kilwinning
CUNNINGHAME
NORTH AYRSHIRE
EAST AYRSHIRE
Cunninghamhead
IRVINE
Dreghorn
Springside
Crosshouse
KILMARNOCK
Hurlford
Galston
Newmilns
Darvel
Priestland
Moscow
132
Eglinton
Scottish Maritime Museum

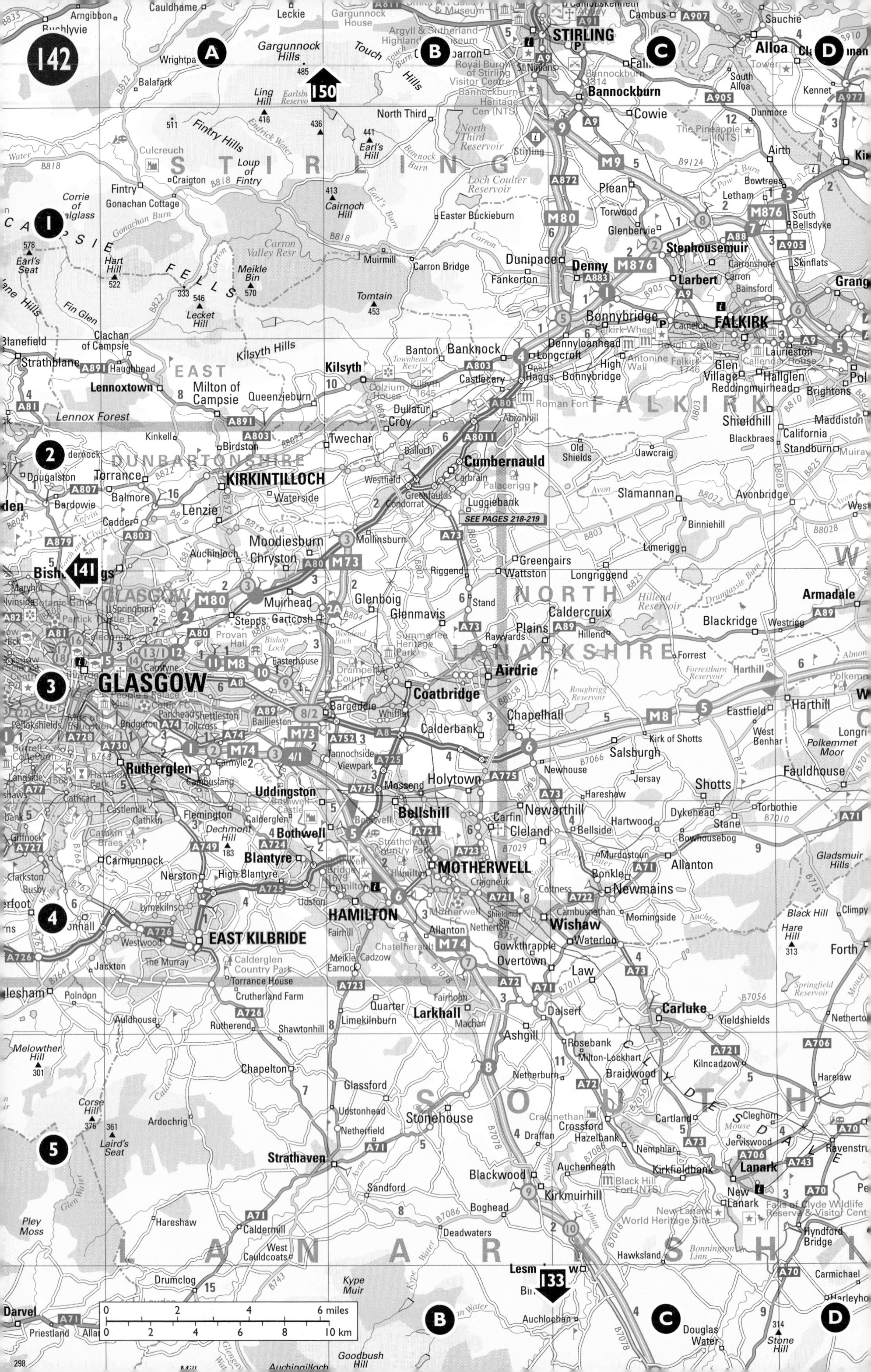
STIRLING
Bannockburn
Alloa
Cowie
Plean
Airth
Stenhousemuir
Larbert
Denny
Dunipace
Bonnybridge
FALKIRK
Grangemouth
Laurieston
Polmont
Kilsyth
Banknock
Longcroft
Haggs
Castlecary
Croy
Dullatur
Cumbernauld
KIRKINTILLOCH
Lenzie
Torrance
Milton of Campsie
Lennoxtown
Strathblane
Blanefield
Fintry
Campsie Fells
Kilsyth Hills
Gargunnock Hills
Touch Hills
Fintry Hills
Carron Valley Resr
Loch Coulter Reservoir
Slamannan
Avonbridge
Limerigg
Greengairs
Wattston
Caldercruix
Plains
Airdrie
Coatbridge
Glenboig
Glenmavis
Moodiesburn
Chryston
Muirhead
Stepps
Gartcosh
Bishopbriggs
GLASGOW
Rutherglen
Cambuslang
Uddingston
Bothwell
Blantyre
Bellshill
Holytown
MOTHERWELL
HAMILTON
EAST KILBRIDE
Wishaw
Newmains
Cleland
Newarthill
Shotts
Harthill
Armadale
Blackridge
Salsburgh
Fauldhouse
Carluke
Larkhall
Stonehouse
Strathaven
Lanark
New Lanark
Law
Overtown
Blackwood
Kirkmuirhill
Lesmahagow
Douglas Water
Darvel
STIRLING
EAST DUNBARTONSHIRE
NORTH LANARKSHIRE
FALKIRK
SOUTH LANARKSHIRE
SEE PAGES 218-219
150
141
133
0 2 4 6 miles
0 2 4 6 8 10 km

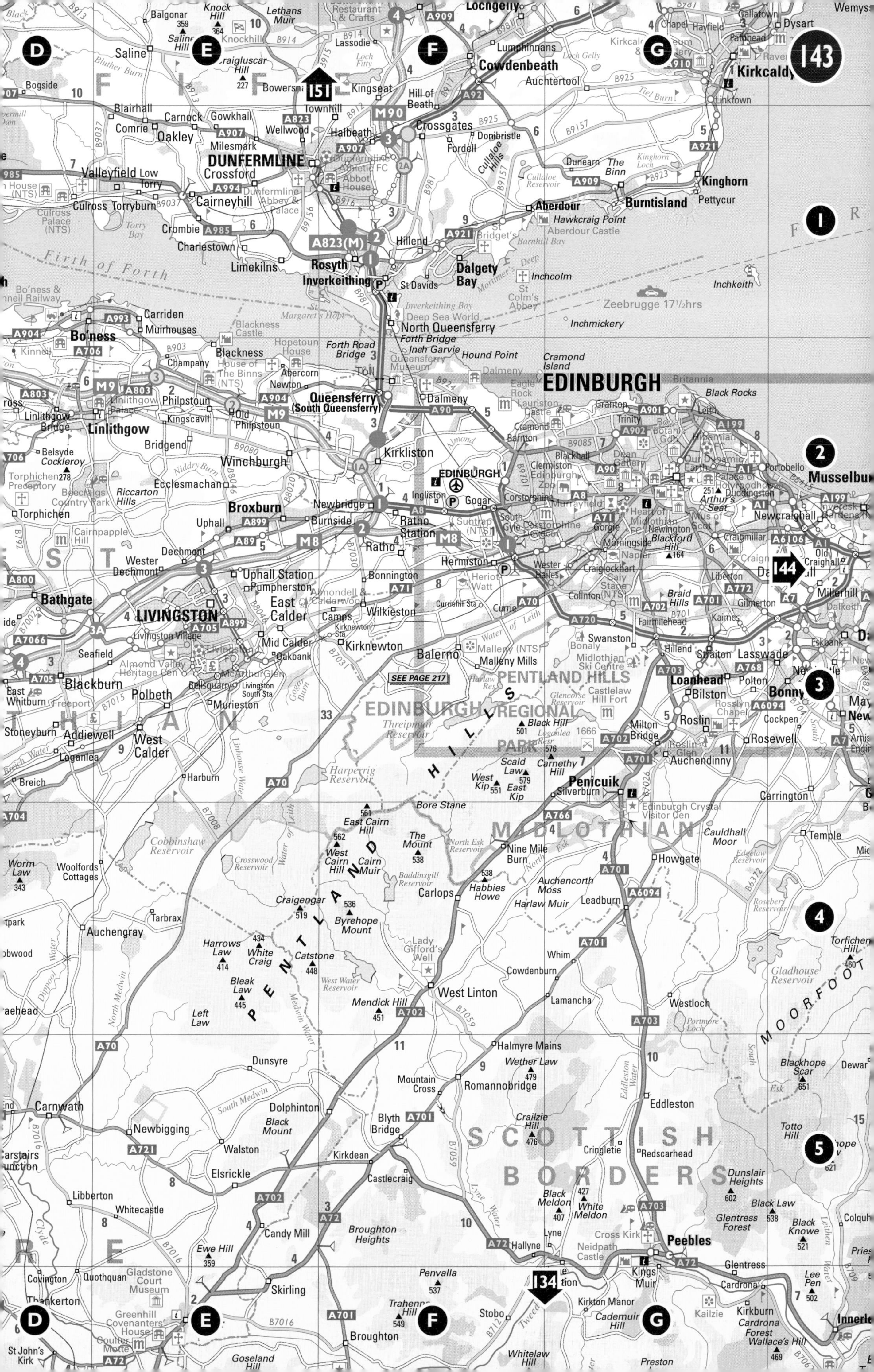
143
151
144
134
SEE PAGE 217
D
E
F
G
D
E
F
G
1
2
3
4
5
FIFE
WEST LOTHIAN
MIDLOTHIAN
SCOTTISH BORDERS
EDINBURGH
PENTLAND HILLS
PENTLAND HILLS REGIONAL PARK
MOORFOOT
Firth of Forth
Balgonar
Saline
Saline Hill
Knock Hill
Knockhill
Lethans Muir
Lassodie
Lochgelly
Lumphinnans
Cowdenbeath
Auchtertool
Kirkcaldy
Dysart
Gallatown
Pathhead
Chapel
Hayfield
Linktown
Wemyss
Bogside
Blairhall
Comrie
Carnock
Gowkhall
Oakley
Craigluscar Hill
Bowershall
Kingseat
Hill of Beath
Townhill
Wellwood
Halbeath
Crossgates
Donibristle
Fordell
Cullaloe Hills
Cullaloe Reservoir
Milesmark
DUNFERMLINE
Crossford
Dunfermline Athletic FC
Abbot House
Dunfermline Abbey & Palace
Valleyfield
Low Torry
Culross
Torryburn
Culross Palace (NTS)
Cairneyhill
Crombie
Torry Bay
Charlestown
Limekilns
Rosyth
Inverkeithing
Hillend
St Bridget's
Dalgety Bay
St Davids
Aberdour
Hawkcraig Point
Aberdour Castle
Barnhill Bay
Burntisland
Pettycur
Kinghorn
Dunearn
The Binn
Kinghorn Loch
Inchcolm
St Colm's Abbey
Mortimer's Deep
Inchkeith
Inchmickery
Zeebrugge 17½hrs
Cramond Island
Inverkeithing Bay
Deep Sea World
North Queensferry
Forth Bridge
Inch Garvie
Hound Point
Forth Road Bridge
Toll
Queensferry Museum
Dalmeny
Queensferry (South Queensferry)
Newton
Abercorn
Hopetoun House
Blackness
Blackness Castle
St Margaret's Hope
Bo'ness
Bo'ness & Kinneil Railway
Carriden
Muirhouses
Kinneil
Champany
House of The Binns (NTS)
Philpstoun
Old Philpstoun
Linlithgow
Linlithgow Palace
Linlithgow Bridge
Kingscavil
Bridgend
Winchburgh
Kirkliston
Belsyde
Cockleroy
Torphichen Preceptory
Beecraigs Country Park
Riccarton Hills
Torphichen
Ecclesmachan
Broxburn
Newbridge
Burnside
Uphall
Cairnpapple Hill
Dechmont
Wester Dechmont
Ratho
Ratho Station
Bathgate
LIVINGSTON
Livingston Village
Uphall Station
Pumpherston
East Calder
Almondell & Calderwood
Camps
Wilkieston
Bonnington
Mid Calder
Oakbank
Kirknewton
Seafield
Almond Valley Heritage Cen
Blackburn
Polbeth
East Whitburn
Freeport
Bellsquarry
Livingston South Sta
Murieston
Stoneyburn
Addiewell
West Calder
Loganlea
Breich
Harburn
Eagle Rock
Lauriston Castle
Cramond
Barnton
Granton
Trinity
Leith
Britannia
Black Rocks
Royal Botanic Gdn
Dean Gallery
Clermiston
Edinburgh Zoo
Blackhall
EDINBURGH
Ingliston
Gogar
Corstorphine
Murrayfield
South Gyle
Suntrap (NTS)
Hermiston
Heriot Watt
Currie
Currie Hill Sta
Balerno
Malleny (NTS)
Malleny Mills
Wester Hailes
Sighthill
Morningside
Napier
Blackford Hill
Craiglockhart
Colinton
Caiy Stane (NTS)
Braid Hills
Fairmilehead
Swanston
Bonaly
Midlothian Ski Centre
Castlelaw Hill Fort
Our Dynamic Earth
Palace of Holyroodhouse
Arthur's Seat
Duddingston
Newington
Craigmillar
Liberton
Gilmerton
Kaimes
Portobello
Musselburgh
Newcraighall
Old Craighall
Dalkeith
Millerhill
Eskbank
Lasswade
Hillend
Straiton
Loanhead
Bilston
Polton
Bonnyrigg
Roslin
Rosslyn Chapel
Roslin Glen
Cockpen
Rosewell
Auchendinny
Milton Bridge
Penicuik
Silverburn
Edinburgh Crystal Visitor Cen
Carrington
Temple
Threipmuir Reservoir
Harlaw Res
Glencorse Reservoir
Black Hill
Loganlea Resr
Carnethy Hill
Scald Law
West Kip
East Kip
Harperrig Reservoir
Bore Stane
East Cairn Hill
West Cairn Hill
Cairn Muir
The Mount
North Esk Reservoir
Nine Mile Burn
Baddinsgill Reservoir
Carlops
Habbies Howe
Auchencorth Moss
Harlaw Muir
Leadburn
Howgate
Cauldhall Moor
Edgelaw Reservoir
Rosebery Reservoir
Craigengar
Byrehope Mount
Cobbinshaw Reservoir
Crosswood Reservoir
Worm Law
Woolfords Cottages
Tarbrax
Auchengray
Harrows Law
White Craig
Catstone
Bleak Law
Left Law
West Water Reservoir
Mendick Hill
Lady Gifford's Well
West Linton
Whim
Cowdenburn
Lamancha
Westloch
Portmore Loch
Gladhouse Reservoir
Torfichen Hill
Halmyre Mains
Wether Law
Romannobridge
Mountain Cross
Blackhope Scar
Eddleston
Dunsyre
Carnwath
Newbigging
Dolphinton
Black Mount
Walston
Blyth Bridge
Kirkdean
Castlecraig
Elsrickle
Crailzie Hill
Cringletie
Redscarhead
Totto Hill
Carstairs Junction
Libberton
Whitecastle
Black Meldon
White Meldon
Dunslair Heights
Black Law
Glentress Forest
Black Knowe
Candy Mill
Broughton Heights
Hallyne
Lyne
Cross Kirk
Neidpath Castle
Peebles
Kings Muir
Glentress
Cardrona
Lee Pen
Kirkburn
Cardrona Forest
Wallace's Hill
Innerleithen
Ewe Hill
Covington
Quothquan
Gladstone Court Museum
Thankerton
Greenhill Covenanters' House
Coulter Motte
St John's Kirk
Skirling
Penvalla
Trahenna Hill
Broughton
Stobo
Kirkton Manor
Cademuir Hill
Kailzie
Whitelaw Hill
Goseland Hill
Preston
Tweed
A70
A71
A72
A90
A701
A702
A703
A720
A721
A8
M8
M9
M90
A823(M)
A92
A921
A985
A994
A907
A909
A904
A706
A803
A899
A89
A705
A7066
A6094
A6106
A766
A768
A772
A199
A1
A7
A901
A902
A993
A800
A704
A800
A823
A910
B914
B925
B9157
B923
B981
B9156
B916
B9037
B903
B9080
B8020
B8046
B7030
B7031
B7015
B7008
B7059
B7016
B7026
B6372
B9085
B701
B924
B792
B712
B709
B7002

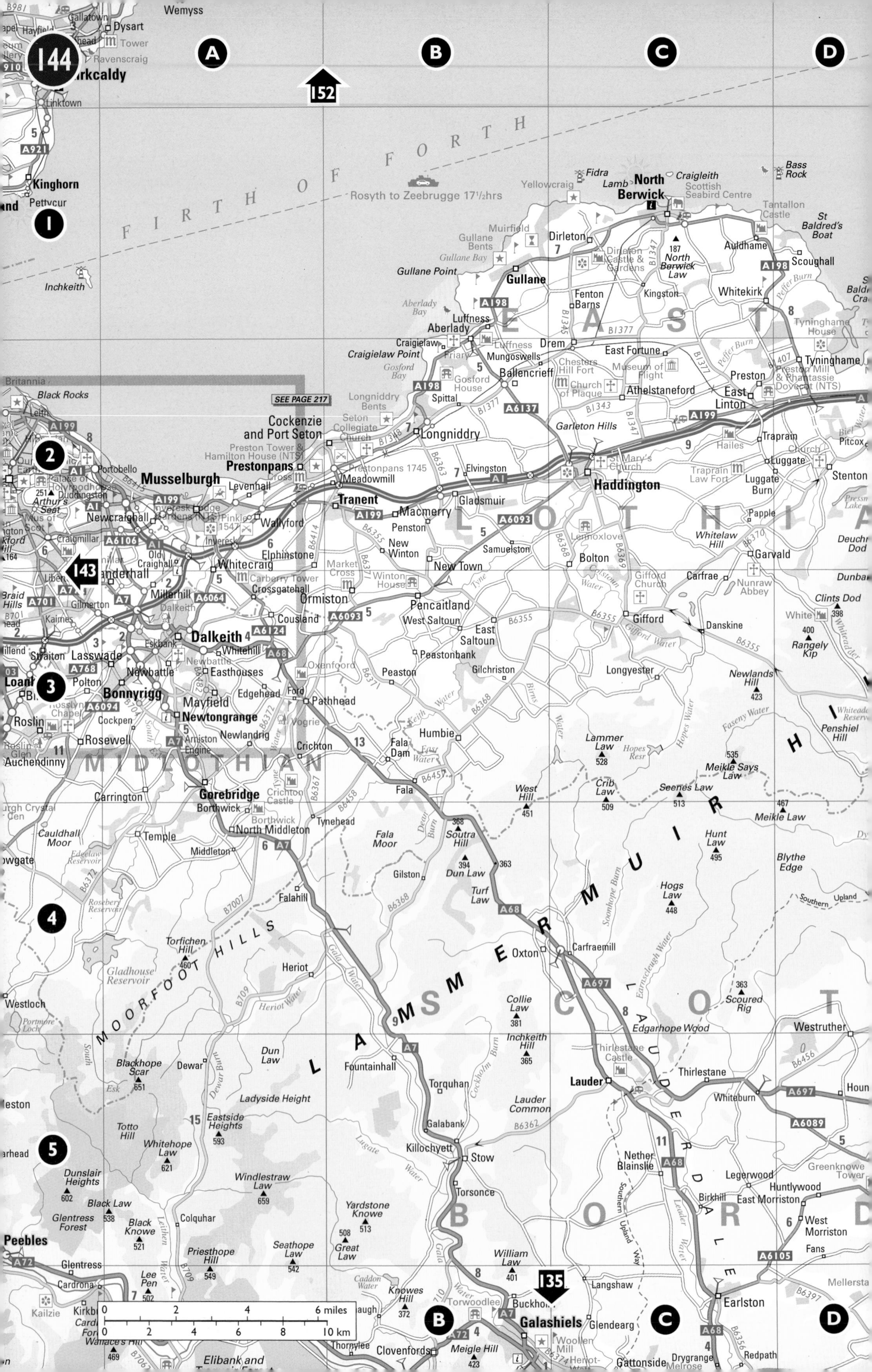

144
A
B
C
D
152
Wemyss
Dysart
Tower
Ravenscraig
Kirkcaldy
Linktown
A921
Kinghorn
Pettycur
1
Inchkeith
FIRTH OF FORTH
Rosyth to Zeebrugge 17½hrs
Fidra
Lamb
Yellowcraig
North Berwick
Craigleith
Scottish Seabird Centre
Bass Rock
Tantallon Castle
St Baldred's Boat
Muirfield
Gullane Bents
Gullane Bay
Gullane Point
Dirleton
Dirleton Castle & Gardens
187
North Berwick Law
Auldhame
Scoughall
A198
Gullane
Fenton Barns
Kingston
Whitekirk
Peffer Burn
Aberlady Bay
Luffness
Aberlady
Craigielaw
Craigielaw Point
Luffness
Mungoswells
Drem
East Fortune
Museum of Flight
Tyninghame House
Tyninghame
Gosford Bay
Gosford House
Ballencrieff
Chesters Hill Fort
Church of Plaque
Athelstaneford
Preston
Preston Mill & Phantassie Dovecot (NTS)
East Linton
Spittal
A6137
B1343
Garleton Hills
A199
Britannia
Black Rocks
SEE PAGE 217
Longniddry Bents
Seton Collegiate Church
Cockenzie and Port Seton
Longniddry
Preston Tower & Hamilton House (NTS)
Prestonpans
Prestonpans 1745
Meadowmill
Hailes
Traprain
Luggate
Traprain Law Fort
Luggate Burn
St Mary's Church
Haddington
Stenton
Pitcox
2
Leith
Portobello
Palace of Holyroodhouse
Duddingston
Arthur's Seat
Musselburgh
Levenhall
Elvingston
Tranent
Gladsmuir
Macmerry
Penston
Newcraighall
Inveresk Lodge Gardens (NTS)
Pinkie 1547
Wallyford
Inveresk
Craigmillar
A6106
Elphinstone
New Winton
Samuelston
A6093
Lennoxlove
Papple
Whitelaw Hill
Garvald
Deuchrie Dod
143
Liberton
Gilmerton
Old Craighall
Whitecraig
Carberry Tower
Crossgatehall
Market Cross
Winton House
New Town
Bolton
Gifford Church
Carfrae
Nunraw Abbey
Dunbar
Braid Hills
Kaimes
Millerhill
Dalkeith
A6064
Ormiston
Pencaitland
West Saltoun
East Saltoun
Gifford
Danskine
Clints Dod
398
White
400
Rangely Kip
Straiton
Lasswade
Eskbank
Whitehill
A6124
A68
Newbattle
Easthouses
Peastonbank
Gilchriston
Gifford Water
Longyester
Loanhead
3
Polton
Bonnyrigg
Mayfield
Newtongrange
Edgehead
Oxenfoord
Ford
Pathhead
Peaston
Newlands Hill
423
Roslin
Rosslyn Chapel
A6094
Cockpen
Arniston Engine
Newlandrig
Vogrie
Humbie
Fala Dam
Penshiel Hill
Rosewell
Auchendinny
Crichton
Lammer Law
528
Hopes Resr
Meikle Says Law
535
MIDLOTHIAN
Gorebridge
Borthwick
Carrington
Crichton Castle
Fala
Crib Law
509
Seenes Law
513
West Hill
451
467
Meikle Law
Tynehead
368
Soutra Hill
Borthwick
North Middleton
Temple
Cauldhall Moor
Fala Moor
Hunt Law
495
Middleton
394
Dun Law
363
Blythe Edge
4
Gilston
Turf Law
Hogs Law
448
Falahill
Rosebery Reservoir
Southern Upland
Torfichen Hill
460
Heriot
Carfraemill
Oxton
LAMMERMUIR HILLS
Gladhouse Reservoir
MOORFOOT HILLS
Westloch
A697
363
Scoured Rig
Collie Law
381
Edgarhope Wood
Westruther
Portmore Loch
Inchkeith Hill
365
Thirlestane Castle
Blackhope Scar
651
Dewar
Dun Law
Fountainhall
Lauder
Thirlestane
Whiteburn
Torquhan
Lauder Common
Ladyside Height
Eastside Heights
593
Totto Hill
Whitehope Law
621
5
Galabank
Killochyett
Stow
Nether Blainslie
Legerwood
Greenknowe Tower
Dunslair Heights
602
Windlestraw Law
659
Torsonce
Hunltywood
Birkhill
East Morriston
Black Law
538
Glentress Forest
Black Knowe
521
Colquhar
Yardstone Knowe
513
508 Great Law
West Morriston
Peebles
A72
Glentress
Priesthope Hill
549
Seathope Law
542
William Law
401
Fans
Cardrona
Lee Pen
502
135
Langshaw
Mellerstain
Kailzie
Knowes Hill
372
Buckholm
Galashiels
Glendearg
Earlston
Torwoodlee
Clovenfords
Meigle Hill
423
Wallace's Hill
469
Elibank and
Thornylee
Woollen Mill
Gattonside
Melrose
Drygrange
Redpath
0 2 4 6 miles
0 2 4 6 8 10 km

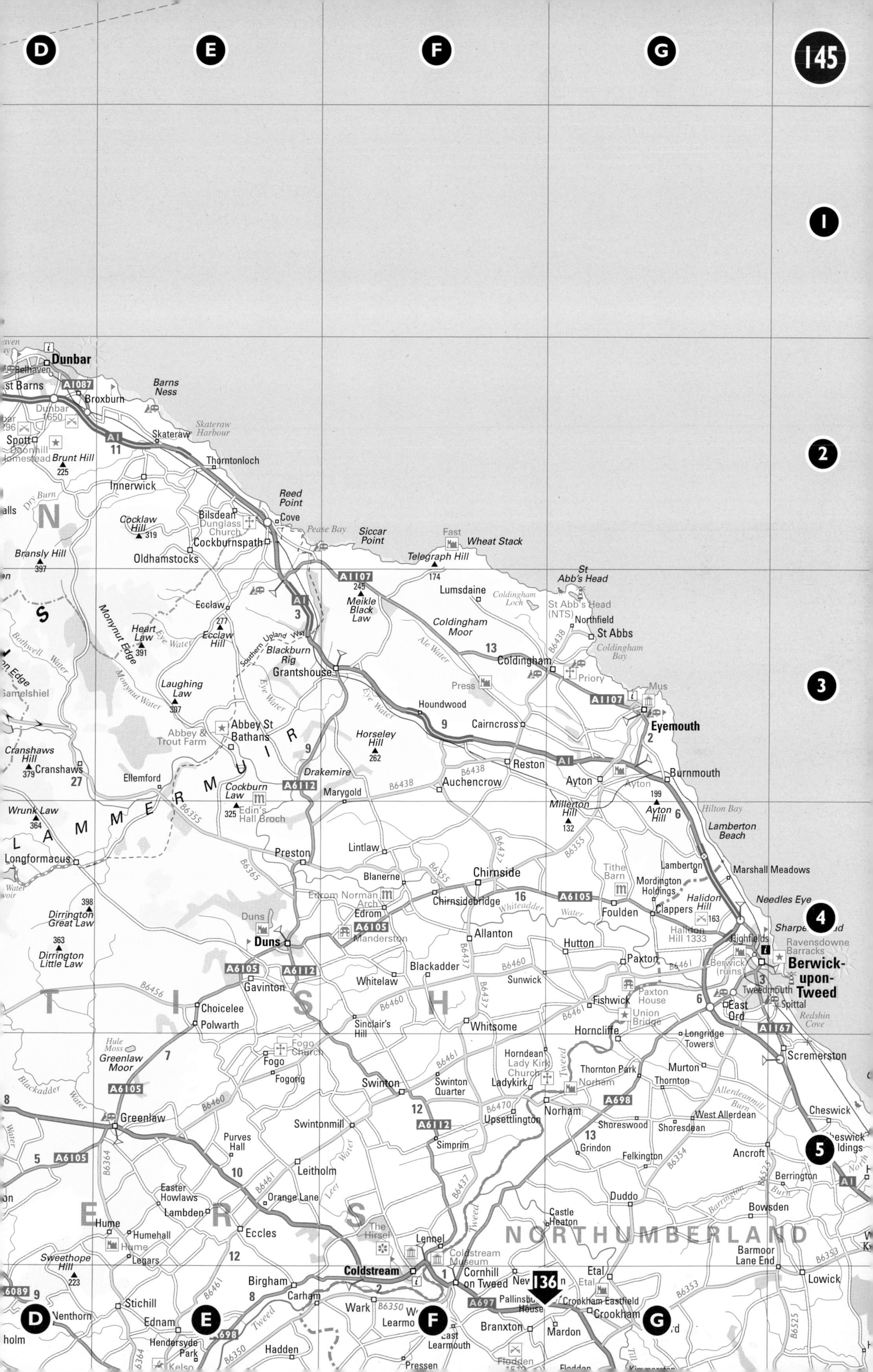

145
D
E
F
G
1
2
3
4
5
Dunbar
Belhaven
Broxburn
A1087
Barns Ness
Dunbar 1650
Skateraw Harbour
Skateraw
Spott
Brunt Hill
225
A1
11
Thorntonloch
Innerwick
Reed Point
Cove
Bilsdean
Dunglass Church
Cocklaw Hill
319
Cockburnspath
Pease Bay
Siccar Point
Fast
Wheat Stack
Telegraph Hill
174
Oldhamstocks
Bransly Hill
397
A1107
245
Meikle Black Law
Lumsdaine
Coldingham Loch
St Abb's Head
St Abb's Head (NTS)
Northfield
St Abbs
Coldingham Bay
Ecclaw
277
Ecclaw Hill
3
Monynut Edge
Heart Law
391
Eye Water
Southern Upland Way
Blackburn Rig
Grantshouse
Coldingham Moor
Ale Water
13
Coldingham
Priory
B6438
Bothwell Water
Monynut Water
Laughing Law
307
Press
Houndwood
Mus
Eyemouth
Abbey St Bathans
Abbey & Trout Farm
Horseley Hill
262
9
Cairncross
2
Cranshaws Hill
379
Cranshaws
27
Drakemire
Reston
Burnmouth
Ellemford
Auchencrow
Ayton
Cockburn Law
325
Edin's Hall Broch
A6112
Marygold
199
Ayton Hill
6
Millerton Hill
132
Hilton Bay
Lamberton Beach
Wrunk Law
364
LAMMERMUIR
B6355
B6365
B6437
Longformacus
Preston
Lintlaw
Tithe Barn
Lamberton
Marshall Meadows
Chirnside
Blanerne
Mordington Holdings
Edrom Norman Arch
Edrom
Chirnsidebridge
16
Whiteadder Water
A6105
Foulden
Clappers
Halidon Hill
163
Needles Eye
398
Dirrington Great Law
Duns
Manderston
Allanton
Halidon Hill 1333
Sharpe's Head
Ravensdowne Barracks
363
Dirrington Little Law
Hutton
Paxton
Berwick (ruins)
Berwick-upon-Tweed
Blackadder
B6460
Sunwick
B6461
Tweedmouth
Spittal
Gavinton
Whitelaw
Paxton House
Fishwick
East Ord
Redshin Cove
B6456
Choicelee
Polwarth
Sinclair's Hill
Whitsome
Union Bridge
Horncliffe
Longridge Towers
A1167
Hule Moss
Greenlaw Moor
7
Fogo Church
Fogo
Fogorig
Horndean
Lady Kirk Church
Ladykirk
Thornton Park
Murton
Scremerston
Blackadder Water
Swinton
Swinton Quarter
Norham
Thornton
Allerdean Mill Burn
A6105
Greenlaw
B6470
Upsettlington
A698
Cheswick
12
Shoreswood
Shoresdean
West Allerdean
Swintonmill
Purves Hall
13
Grindon
Felkington
B6354
Ancroft
Cheswick Buildings
5
A6105
Simprim
B6364
Leitholm
10
Berrington
Easter Howlaws
Orange Lane
Leet Water
Duddo
Bowsden
Hume
Lambden
Eccles
The Hirsel
Lennel
Castle Heaton
NORTHUMBERLAND
Humehall
Sweethope Hill
223
Legars
Coldstream
Coldstream Museum
Cornhill on Tweed
Etal
Barmoor Lane End
Lowick
B6353
6089
Birgham
Carham
Wark
Crookham Eastfield
Crookham
Stichill
B6350
A697
Pallinsburn House
136
Nenthorn
Ednam
Learmouth
East Learmouth
Branxton
Mardon
B6525
Hendersyde Park
Kelso
Hadden
Pressen
Flodden
Tweed

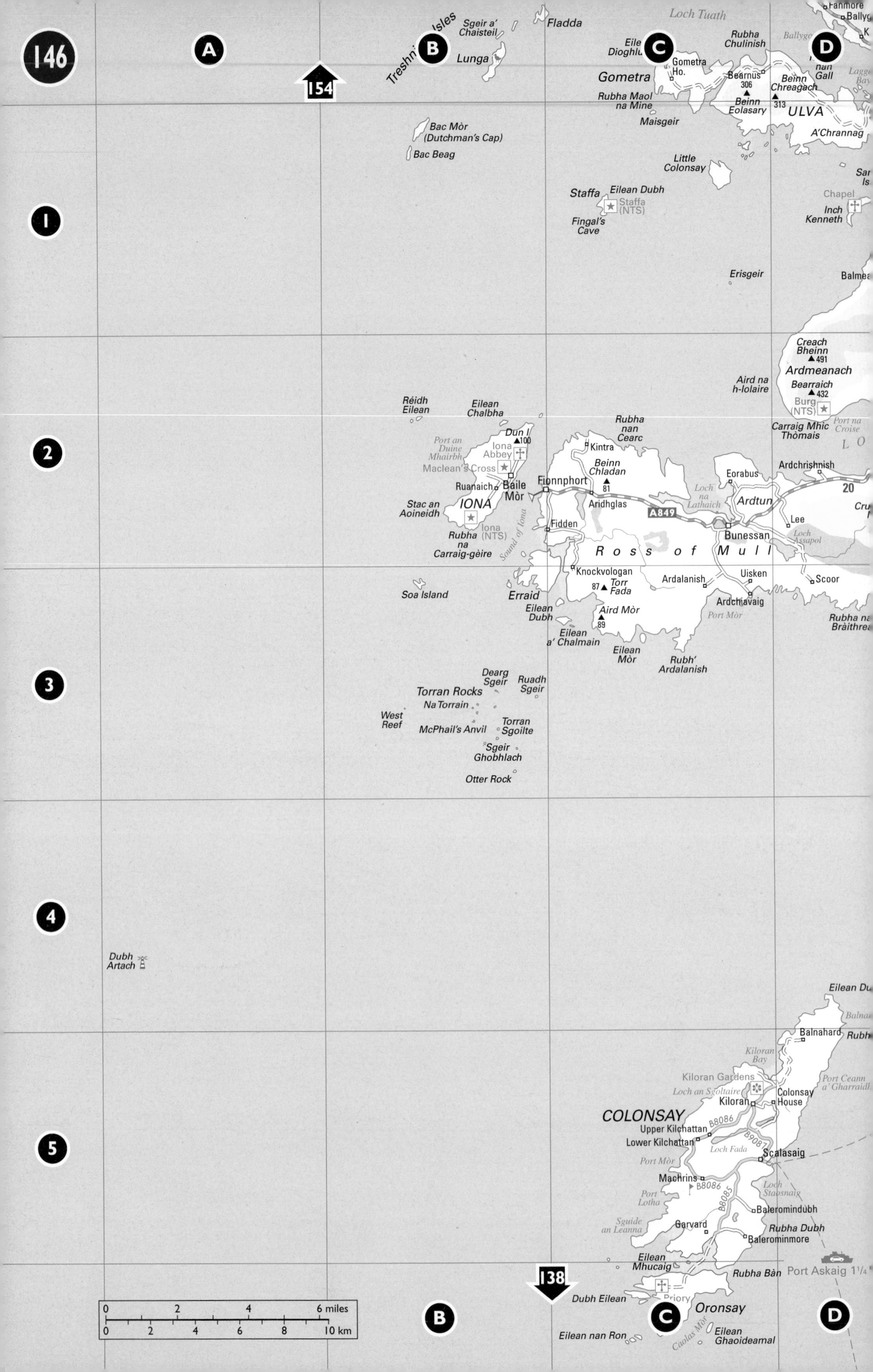
Treshnish Isles
Sgeir a' Chaisteil
Lunga
Fladda
Loch Tuath
Gometra
Gometra Ho.
Rubha Chulinish
Rubha Maol na Mine
Maisgeir
Beinn Eolasary
Beinn Chreagach
ULVA
A'Chrannag
Bac Mòr (Dutchman's Cap)
Bac Beag
Little Colonsay
Staffa
Eilean Dubh
Staffa (NTS)
Fingal's Cave
Inch Kenneth
Chapel
Erisgeir
Creach Bheinn
Ardmeanach
Bearraich
Burg (NTS)
Aird na h-Iolaire
Carraig Mhic Thòmais
Réidh Eilean
Eilean Chalbha
Dun I
Iona Abbey
Maclean's Cross
Port an Duine Mhairbh
Baile Mòr
Ruanaich
Stac an Aoineidh
IONA
Iona (NTS)
Rubha na Carraig-gèire
Sound of Iona
Rubha nan Cearc
Kintra
Beinn Chladan
Fionnphort
Aridhglas
A849
Fidden
Ross of Mull
Eorabus
Ardtun
Loch na Lathaich
Bunessan
Lee
Loch Assapol
Ardchrishnish
Knockvologan
Torr Fada
Ardalanish
Uisken
Scoor
Ardchiavaig
Port Mòr
Erraid
Soa Island
Eilean Dubh
Aird Mòr
Eilean a' Chalmain
Eilean Mòr
Rubh' Ardalanish
Rubha nam Bràithrean
Torran Rocks
Na Torrain
Dearg Sgeir
Ruadh Sgeir
West Reef
McPhail's Anvil
Torran Sgoilte
Sgeir Ghobhlach
Otter Rock
Dubh Artach
COLONSAY
Balnahard
Kiloran Bay
Kiloran Gardens
Loch an Sgoltaire
Kiloran
Colonsay House
Port Ceann a' Gharraidh
Upper Kilchattan
Lower Kilchattan
B8086
B8087
Loch Fada
Scalasaig
Port Mòr
Machrins
Port Lotha
Loch Staosnaig
B8085
Balerominhdubh
Sguide an Leanna
Garvard
Rubha Dubh
Balerominmore
Eilean Mhucaig
Rubha Bàn
Port Askaig 1¼
Priory
Dubh Eilean
Oronsay
Eilean nan Ron
Caolas Mòr
Eilean Ghaoideamal
0 2 4 6 miles
0 2 4 6 8 10 km

154
138

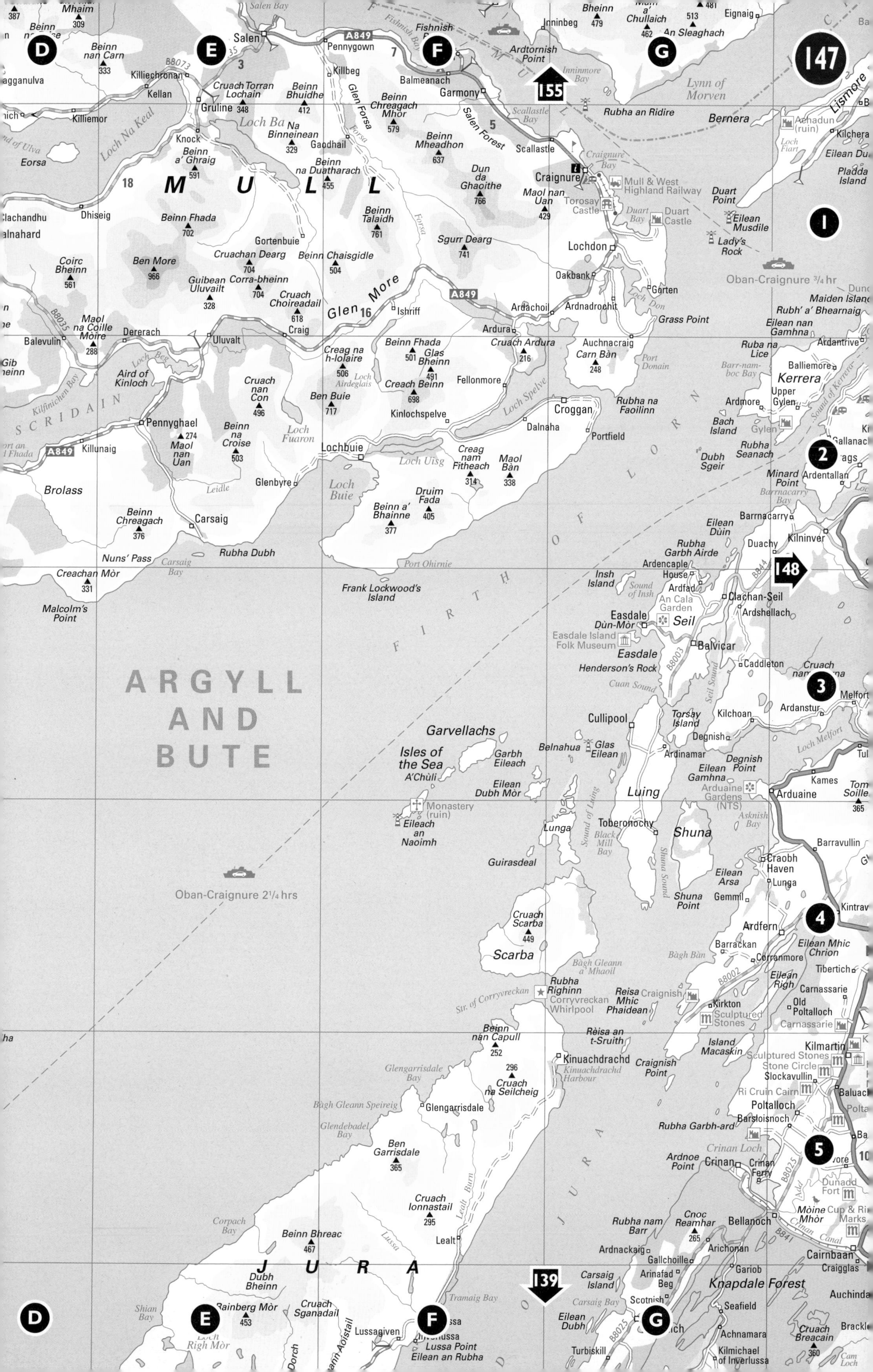
D
E
F
G
Salen
Salen Bay
Mhaim
309
387
Beinn nan Carn
333
Killiechronan
Kellan
Gruline
B8073
Cruach Torran Lochain
348
Pennygown
A849
Killbeg
Fishnish Bay
Fishnish
Balmeanach
Garmony
Beinn Bhuidhe
412
Glen Forsa
Beinn Chreagach Mhòr
579
Salen Forest
Ardtornish Point
Inninbeg
Inninmore Bay
155
Bheinn
479
Chullaich
462
An Sleaghach
513
Eignaig
Lynn of Morven
Rubha an Ridire
Bernera
Lismore
Achadun (ruin)
Loch Fiart
Kilchera
Eilean Dubh
Pladda Island
Killiemor
Loch Na Keal
Knock
Loch Ba
Na Binneinean
329
Gaodhail
Beinn Mheadhon
637
Scallastle Bay
Scallastle
Craignure
Craignure Bay
Mull & West Highland Railway
Torosay Castle
Duart Bay
Duart Castle
Duart Point
Eilean Musdile
Lady's Rock
I
Eorsa
Sound of Ulva
Beinn a' Ghraig
591
Beinn na Duatharach
455
MULL
18
Dun da Ghaoithe
766
Maol nan Uan
429
Clachandhu
Dhiseig
Beinn Fhada
702
Beinn Talaidh
761
Gortenbuie
Sgurr Dearg
741
Lochdon
Oban-Craignure 3/4 hr
Coirc Bheinn
561
Ben More
966
Cruachan Dearg
704
Beinn Chaisgidle
504
Oakbank
Gorten
Guibean Uluvailt
328
Corra-bheinn
704
Cruach Choireadail
618
Glen More
16
Ishriff
A849
Ardachoil
Ardnadrochit
Loch Don
Grass Point
Dun
Maiden Island
Rubh' a' Bhearnaig
Eilean nan Gamhna
Ardantrive
B8035
Maol na Coille Mòire
288
Dererach
Uluvalt
Craig
Balevulin
Creag na h-Iolaire
506
Beinn Fhada
501
Glas Bheinn
491
Ardura
Cruach Ardura
216
Auchnacraig
Carn Bàn
248
Port Donain
Ruba na Lice
Balliemore
Barr-nam-boc Bay
Kerrera
Upper Gylen
Gylen
Ardmore
Bach Island
Loch Beg
Aird of Kinloch
Gib
Kilfinichen Bay
Cruach nan Con
496
Loch Airdeglais
Creach Beinn
698
Fellonmore
Ben Buie
717
Kinlochspelve
Loch Spelve
Croggan
Rubha na Faoilinn
SCRIDAIN
Pennyghael
274
Maol nan Uan
Beinn na Croise
503
Loch Fuaron
Lochbuie
Loch Uisg
Dalnaha
Portfield
Rubha Seanach
Gallanach
A849
Killunaig
Creag nam Fitheach
314
Maol Bàn
338
Dubh Sgeir
2
Minard Point
Ardentallan
Barnacarry Bay
Brolass
Leidle
Glenbyre
Loch Buie
Druim Fada
405
Beinn a' Bhainne
377
Beinn Chreagach
376
Carsaig
Barnacarry
Eilean Dùin
Kilninver
Duachy
Rubha Garbh Airde
Nuns' Pass
Rubha Dubh
Carsaig Bay
Port Ohirnie
148
Creachan Mòr
331
Ardencaple House
Insh Island
Sound of Insh
Ardfad
Frank Lockwood's Island
B844
Malcolm's Point
An Cala Garden
Clachan-Seil
Ardshellach
FIRTH OF LORN
Eascdale
Dùn-Mòr
Seil
Easdale Island Folk Museum
Easdale
Balvicar
B8003
Henderson's Rock
Caddleton
Cruach
ARGYLL AND BUTE
Cuan Sound
Seil Sound
3
Melfort
Ardanstur
Cullipool
Torsay Island
Kilchoan
Degnish
Loch Melfort
Garvellachs
Isles of the Sea
Garbh Eileach
A' Chùli
Belnahua
Glas Eilean
Ardinamar
Degnish Point
Eilean Dubh Mòr
Eilean Gamhna
Arduaine Gardens (NTS)
Arduaine
Kames
Luing
Monastery (ruin)
Eileach an Naoimh
Lunga
Sound of Luing
Toberonochy
Black Mill Bay
Shuna
Asknish Bay
365
Barravullin
Guirasdeal
Shuna Sound
Craobh Haven
Lunga
Eilean Arsa
Oban-Craignure 2 1/4 hrs
Shuna Point
Gemmil
4
Kintraw
Cruach Scarba
449
Ardfern
Eilean Mhic Chrion
Barrackan
Corranmore
Bàgh Bàn
Scarba
Bàgh Gleann a' Mhaoil
Tibertich
B8002
Eilean Righ
Carnassarie
Rubha Righinn
Corryvreckan Whirlpool
Reisa Mhic Phaidean
Craignish
Str. of Corryvreckan
Kirkton
Sculptured Stones
Old Poltalloch
Carnassarie
Beinn nan Capull
252
Rèisa an t-Sruith
Island Macaskin
Kilmartin
296
Cruach na Seilcheig
Kinuachdrachd
Kinuachdrachd Harbour
Glengarrisdale Bay
Craignish Point
Sculptured Stones
Stone Circle
Slockavullin
Ri Cruin Cairn
Baluach
Bàgh Gleann Speireig
Glengarrisdale
Poltalloch
Barsloisnoch
Glendebadel Bay
Rubha Garbh-ard
Ben Garrisdale
365
Crinan Loch
5
Ardnoe Point
Crinan
Crinan Ferry
B8025
Dunadd Fort
Cruach Ionnastail
295
Corpach Bay
Lealt Burn
Mòine Mhòr
Cup & Ring Marks
Beinn Bhreac
467
Lussa
Lealt
Rubha nam Barr
Cnoc Reamhar
265
Bellanoch
B841
Crinan Canal
Ardnackaig
Arichonan
Cairnbaan
Gallchoille
Craigglas
JURA
139
Dubh Bheinn
Carsaig Island
Arinafad Beg
Gariob
Knapdale Forest
Auchindarroch
Tramaig Bay
Carsaig Bay
Scotnish
Seafield
Brackley
Shian Bay
Rainberg Mòr
453
Cruach Sganadail
Eilean Dubh
Achnamara
Cruach Breacain
360
Lussagiven
Lussa Point
Eilean an Rubha
B8025
Turbiskill
Kilmichael of Inverlussa
Loch Righ Mòr
Dorch
Cam Loch
Tom Soille

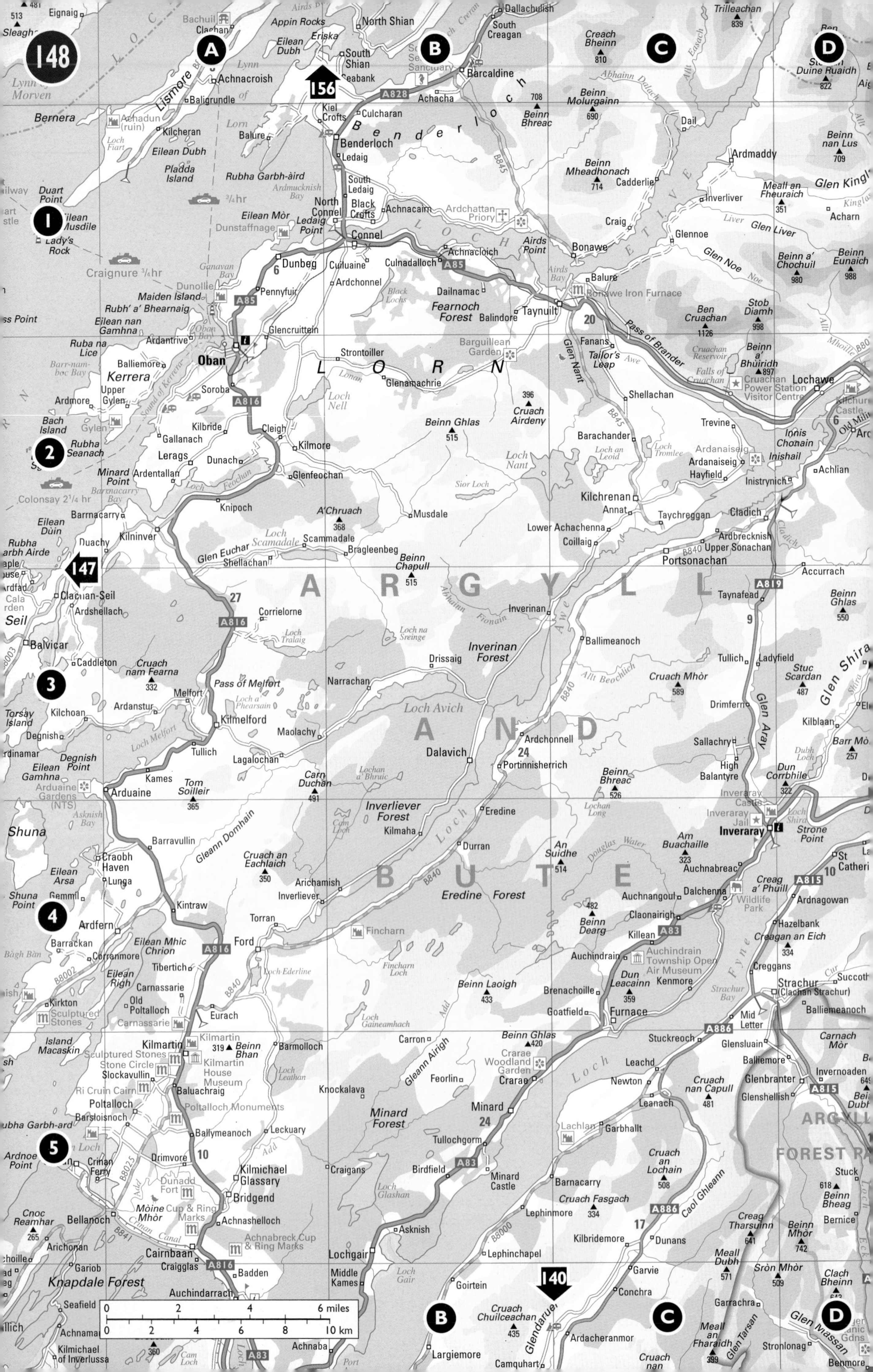

148
A
B
C
D
156
Eignaig
Sleagh
Lynn of Morven
Bachuil
Clachan
Lismore
Achnacroish
Baligrundle
Bernera
Achadun (ruin)
Kilcheran
Eilean Dubh
Pladda Island
Loch Fiart
Lynn of Lorn
Appin Rocks
Eriska
Eilean Dubh
North Shian
South Shian
Seabank
Sea Life Sanctuary
Dallachulish
South Creagan
Barcaldine
A828
Achacha
Kiel Crofts
Culcharan
Benderloch
Ledaig
Balure
Rubha Garbh-àird
Ardmucknish Bay
South Ledaig
North Connel
Black Crofts
Achnacairn
Ardchattan Priory
Ledaig Point
Connel
Creach Bheinn
810
Beinn Molurgainn
690
708
Beinn Bhreac
Beinn Mheadhonach
714
Cadderlie
Abhainn Dalach
Allt Easach
Dail
Trilleachan
839
Ben Starav
Stob Duine Ruaidh
822
Beinn nan Lus
709
Ardmaddy
Meall an Fheuraich
351
Glen Kinglass
Inverliver
Acharn
Glen Liver
Glennoe
Glen Noe
Beinn a' Chochuil
980
Beinn Eunaich
988
Craig
Bonawe
Loch Etive
Airds Point
Airds Bay
Balure
Bonawe Iron Furnace
B845
Duart Point
Eilean Musdile
Lady's Rock
1
¾hr
Eilean Mòr
Dunstaffnage
Craignure ¾hr
Ganavan Bay
Dunollie
Maiden Island
Rubh' a' Bhearnaig
Eilean nan Gamhna
Dunbeg
Pennyfuir
A85
Culuaine
Ardchonnel
Culnadalloch
Achnacloich
Black Lochs
Dailnamac
Fearnoch Forest
Balindore
Taynuilt
20
Pass of Brander
Ben Cruachan
1126
Stob Diamh
998
Beinn a' Bhùiridh
897
Cruachan Reservoir
Falls of Cruachan
Cruachan Power Station Visitor Centre
Lochawe
Kilchurn Castle
Ruba na Lice
Ardantrive
Oban Bay
Oban
Glencruitten
Strontoiller
L O R N
Glenamachrie
Loch Nell
Barguillean Garden
Fanans
Tailor's Leap
Glen Nant
Shellachan
Balliemore
Barr-nam-boc Bay
Kerrera
Sound of Kerrera
Upper Gylen
Ardmore
Gylen
Soroba
A816
Bach Island
2
Rubha Seanach
Kilbride
Gallanach
Lerags
Dunach
Cleigh
Kilmore
Glenfeochan
396
Cruach Airdeny
Beinn Ghlas
515
B845
Barachander
Loch an Leoid
Loch Tromlee
Loch Nant
Sior Loch
Trevine
Ardanaiseig
Hayfield
Innis Chonain
Inishail
Achlian
Inistrynich
Minard Point
Ardentallan
Loch Feochan
Barranacarry Bay
Colonsay 2¼ hr
Knipoch
A'Chruach
368
Musdale
Kilchrenan
Annat
Taychreggan
Cladich
Eilean Dùin
Barnacarry
Rubha Garbh Airde
Duachy
Kilninver
Loch Scamadale
Scammadale
Bragleenbeg
Glen Euchar
Shellachan
Beinn Chapull
515
Lower Achachenna
Coillaig
Ardbrecknish
Upper Sonachan
B840
Portsonachan
Accurrach
147
Ardfad
Clachan-Seil
Ardshellach
Seil
27
A R G Y L L
Corrielorne
A816
Loch Tralaig
Abhainn Fionain
Inverinan
Loch na Sreinge
A819
Taynafead
Beinn Ghlas
550
9
Balvicar
Caddleton
3
Cruach nam Fearna
332
Ballimeanoch
Drissaig
Inverinan Forest
Allt Beochlich
Tullich
Ladyfield
Cruach Mhòr
589
Stuc Scardan
487
Glen Shira
Torsay Island
Kilchoan
Ardanstur
Pass of Melfort
Melfort
Loch a' Phearsain
Narrachan
Kilmelford
Degnish
Loch Melfort
Loch Avich
A N D
Maolachy
Dalavich
Ardchonnell
24
Portinnisherrich
Drimfern
Glen Aray
Kilblaan
Sallachry
Barr Mòr
257
Dubh Loch
High Balantyre
Dun Corrbhile
322
Eilean Gamhna
Degnish Point
Tullich
Lagalochan
Arduaine Gardens (NTS)
Arduaine
Kames
Tom Soilleir
365
Carn Duchan
491
Lochan a' Bhruic
Beinn Bhreac
526
Lochan Long
Inveraray Castle
Inveraray Jail
Inveraray
Loch Shira
Strone Point
Shuna
Asknish Bay
Barravullin
Gleann Domhain
Inverliever Forest
Cam Loch
Kilmaha
Eredine
Loch Awe
Durran
An Suidhe
514
Douglas Water
Am Buachaille
323
Auchnabreac
St Catherines
10
Craobh Haven
Lunga
Eilean Arsa
Cruach an Eachlaich
350
Arichamish
Inverliever
B840
B U T E
Eredine Forest
Auchnangoul
Dalchenna
Wildlife Park
Creag a' Phuill
A815
Ardnagowan
Shuna Point
Gemmil
4
Ardfern
Kintraw
Torran
Fincharn
482
Beinn Dearg
Claonairigh
Killean
A83
Hazelbank
Creagan an Eich
334
Bàgh Bàn
Barrackan
Corranmore
Eilean Mhic Chrion
A816
Ford
Fincharn Loch
Auchindrain
Auchindrain Township Open Air Museum
Kenmore
Fyne
Creggans
Tibertich
Eilean Righ
Carnassarie
Loch Ederline
B840
B8002
Beinn Laoigh
433
Brenachoille
Dun Leacainn
359
Strachur Bay
Strachur (Clachan Strachur)
Succoth
Kirkton
Sculptured Stones
Old Poltalloch
Carnassarie
Eurach
Loch Gaineamhach
Add
Goatfield
Furnace
Mid Letter
Balliemeanoch
Island Macaskin
Kilmartin
319
Beinn Bhan
Barmolloch
Carron
Beinn Ghlas
420
Crarae Woodland Garden
Stuckreoch
A886
Glensluain
Carnach Mòr
Sculptured Stones
Stone Circle
Slockavullin
Kilmartin House Museum
Loch Leathan
Gleann Airigh
Feorlin
Crarae
Leachd
Newton
Loch Fyne
Balliemore
Inveroaden
Ri Cruin Cairn
Baluachraig
Knockalava
Cruach nan Capull
481
Glenbranter
Glenshellish
A815
Poltalloch
Poltalloch Monuments
Minard Forest
Minard
Leanach
Barsloisnoch
Leckuary
24
Lachlan
Garbhalt
ARGYLL FOREST PARK
5
Ardnoe Point
Crinan Loch
Crinan Ferry
Ballymeanoch
Drimvore
10
Tullochgorm
Cruach an Lochain
508
Stuck
Kilmichael Glassary
Craigans
Birdfield
A83
Minard Castle
Barnacarry
618
Beinn Bheag
Dunadd Fort
B8025
Bridgend
Loch Glashan
Cruach Fasgach
334
Caol Ghleann
Bernice
Cnoc Reamhar
265
Bellanoch
Mòine Mhòr
Cup & Ring Marks
Achnashelloch
Lephinmore
A886
17
Creag Tharsuinn
641
Beinn Mhòr
742
Arichonan
B841
Crinan Canal
Achnabreck Cup & Ring Marks
Asknish
Kilbridemore
Dunans
Cairnbaan
Lochgair
Lephinchapel
B8000
Meall Dubh
571
Sròn Mhòr
509
Clach Bheinn
Gariob
Craigglas
A816
Badden
Middle Kames
Loch Gair
Garvie
Knapdale Forest
Auchindarrach
Goirtein
140
Conchra
Seafield
Achnamara
Kilmichael of Inverlussa
360
Cam Loch
Achnaba
Cruach Chuilceachan
435
Glendaruel
Ardacheranmor
Garrachra
Meall an Fharaidh
399
Glen Tarsan
Glen Massan
Stronlonag
Benmore
Camquhart
Largiemore
0 2 4 6 miles
0 2 4 6 8 10 km

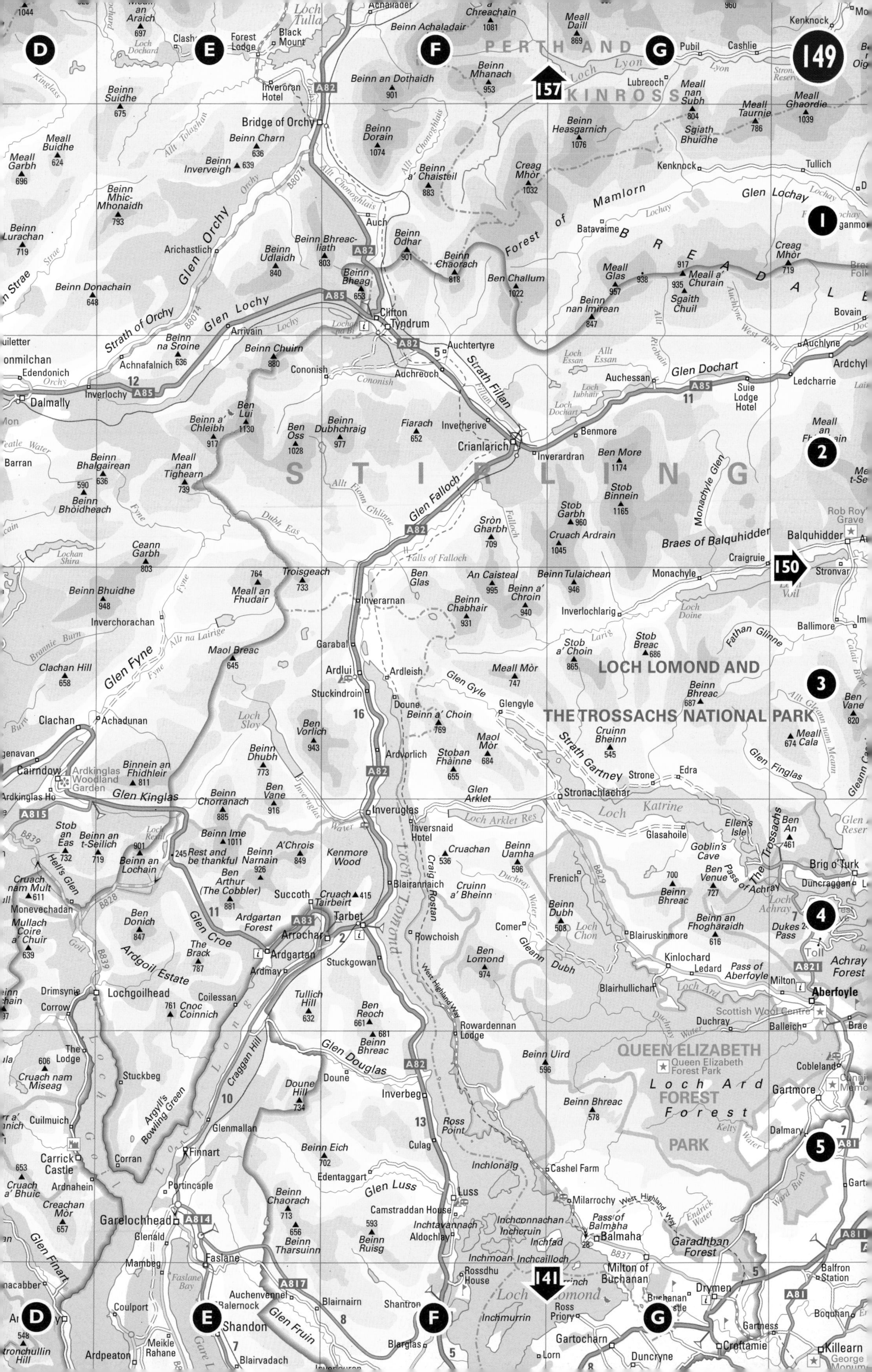
149
D
E
F
G
I
2
3
4
5
157
150
141
PERTH AND KINROSS
BREADALBANE
STIRLING
LOCH LOMOND AND THE TROSSACHS NATIONAL PARK
QUEEN ELIZABETH FOREST PARK
Loch Ard Forest
Loch Tulla
Black Mount
Forest Lodge
Clashgour
Loch Dochard
Meall an Araich 697
Achallader
Beinn Achaladair
Beinn a' Chreachain 1081
Meall Daill 869
Pubil
Cashlie
Kenknock
Loch Lyon
Lubreoch
Meall nan Subh 804
Meall Taurnie 786
Meall Ghaordie 1039
Beinn an Dothaidh 901
Beinn Mhanach 953
Inveroran Hotel
Beinn Suidhe 675
Bridge of Orchy
Beinn Charn 636
Beinn Inverveigh 639
Beinn Dorain 1074
Beinn a' Chaisteil 883
Allt Chonoghlais
Beinn Heasgarnich 1076
Sgiath Bhuidhe
Creag Mhòr 1032
Tullich
Meall Buidhe 624
Meall Garbh 696
Allt Tolaghan
B8074
A82
Beinn Mhic-Mhonaidh 793
Glen Orchy
Auch
Forest of Mamlorn
Batavaime
Glen Lochay
Beinn Lurachan 719
Arichastlich
Beinn Udlaidh 840
Beinn Bhreac-liath 803
Beinn Odhar 901
Beinn Chaorach 818
Ben Challum 1022
Meall Glas 957
938
917
Meall a' Churain
935
Sgiath Chuil
Beinn nan Imirean 847
Creag Mhòr 719
Beinn Donachain 648
Beinn Bheag 653
Clifton
Tyndrum
Strath of Orchy
Glen Lochy
A85
Arrivain
Lochan nam Bi
Bovain
Auchlyne
Ardchyle
Ledcharrie
Beinn na Sroine 636
Achnafalnich
Beinn Chuirn 880
Cononish
Auchtertyre
Auchreoch
Strath Fillan
Loch Essan
Allt Essan
Auchessan
Glen Dochart
Suie Lodge Hotel
Loch Iubhair
Loch Dochart
Edendonich
Dalmally
Inverlochy
12
11
Beinn a' Chleibh 917
Ben Lui 1130
Ben Oss 1028
Beinn Dubhchraig 977
Fiarach 652
Inverherive
Crianlarich
Benmore
Inverardran
Ben More 1174
Stob Binnein 1165
Meall an Fhiodhain
Monachyle Glen
Barran
Beinn Bhalgairean 636
590
Meall nan Tighearn 739
Beinn Bhòidheach
Allt Fionn Ghlinne
Glen Falloch
Stob Garbh 960
Cruach Ardrain 1045
Sròn Gharbh 709
Braes of Balquhidder
Rob Roy's Grave
Balquhidder
Craigruie
Monachyle
Stronvar
Loch Voil
Ceann Garbh 803
Lochan Shira
Dubh Eas
Falls of Falloch
Troisgeach 733
764
Meall an Fhudair
Ben Glas
An Caisteal 995
Beinn Tulaichean 946
Beinn a' Chroin 940
Beinn Chabhair 931
Inverarnan
Inverlochlarig
Loch Doine
Ballimore
Beinn Bhuidhe 948
Inverchorachan
Allt na Lairige
Brannie Burn
Maol Breac 645
Garabal
Stob a' Choin 865
Stob Breac 686
Fathan Glinne
Clachan Hill 658
Glen Fyne
Ardlui
Ardleish
Meall Mòr 747
Stuckindroin
Glen Gyle
Glengyle
Beinn Bhreac 687
Ben Vane 820
Clachan
Achadunan
Loch Sloy
Ben Vorlich 943
16
Doune
Beinn a' Choin 769
Strath Gartney
Cruinn Bheinn 545
Meall Cala 674
Glen Finglas
Cairndow
Ardkinglas Woodland Garden
Binnein an Fhidhleir 811
Beinn Dubhchraig
Beinn Dubh 773
Ardvorlich
Stoban Fhàinne 655
Maol Mòr 684
Strone
Edra
Glen Kinglas
Ardkinglas Ho
A815
Beinn Chorranach 885
Ben Vane 916
Inveruglas
Glen Arklet
Stronachlachar
Loch Arklet Res
Loch Katrine
Ellen's Isle
The Trossachs
Ben An 461
Stob an Eas 732
Beinn an t-Seilich 719
901
Beinn an Lochain
Beinn Ime 1011
Rest and be thankful
245
A'Chrois 849
Beinn Narnain 926
Kenmore Wood
Inversnaid Hotel
Cruachan 536
Beinn Uamha 596
Glasahoile
Goblin's Cave
Ben Venue 727
Pass of Achray
Brig o' Turk
Duncraggan
Loch Achray
Hell's Glen
Cruach nam Mult 611
Ben Arthur (The Cobbler) 881
Succoth
Cruach Tairbeirt 415
Blairannaich
Craig Rostan
Cruinn a' Bheinn
Frenich
Beinn Bhreac 700
Monevechadan
B828
Ben Donich 847
Glen Croe
Ardgartan Forest
A83
Arrochar
Tarbet
Beinn Dubh 508
Loch Chon
Beinn an Fhogharaidh 616
Dukes Pass
Mullach Coire a' Chuir 639
The Brack 787
Ardgartan
Rowchoish
Comer
Ben Lomond 974
Gleann Dubh
Blairuskinmore
Kinlochard
Ledard
Pass of Aberfoyle
Achray Forest
A821
Ardgoil Estate
Ardmay
Stuckgowan
Loch Lomond
West Highland Way
Milton
Aberfoyle
Loch Ard
Blairhullichan
Drimsynie
Lochgoilhead
Corrow
761 Cnoc Coinnich
Coilessan
Tullich Hill 632
Ben Reoch 661
681
Rowardennan Lodge
Scottish Wool Centre
Duchray
Balleich
The Lodge
606
Cruach nam Miseag
Stuckbeg
Craggan Hill
Beinn Bhreac
Glen Douglas
Beinn Uird 596
Queen Elizabeth Forest Park
Cobleland
Gartmore
Argyll's Bowling Green
10
Doune Hill 734
Inverbeg
Beinn Bhreac 578
Kelty Water
Cuilmuich
Glenmallan
13
Ross Point
Dalmary
A81
Carrick Castle
Finnart
Corran
Beinn Eich 702
Culag
Inchlonaig
Cashel Farm
653
Cruach a' Bhuic
Ardnahein
Portincaple
Edentaggart
Glen Luss
Luss
Milarrochy
Pass of Balmaha
West Highland Way
Endrick Water
Creachan Mòr 657
Beinn Chaorach 713
656
Camstraddan House
593
Beinn Ruisg
Inchtavannach
Aldochlay
Inchconnachan
Inchcruin
Inchfad
28
Balmaha
Garadhban Forest
Garelochhead
A814
Glenald
Beinn Tharsuinn
Glen Finart
Mambeg
Faslane
Faslane Bay
Inchmoan
Inchcailloch
B837
Milton of Buchanan
Balfron Station
Rossdhu House
Inchmurrin
Drymen
Buchanan Castle
Coulport
Auchenvennel
Balernock
A817
Blairnairn
Glen Fruin
8
Shantron
Loch Lomond
Ross Priory
Boquhan
Gartness
Ardentinny
548
Stronchullin Hill
Shandon
Meikle Rahane
Ardpeaton
7
Blairvadach
Blarglas
Gartocharn
Lorn
Duncryne
Croftamie
Killearn

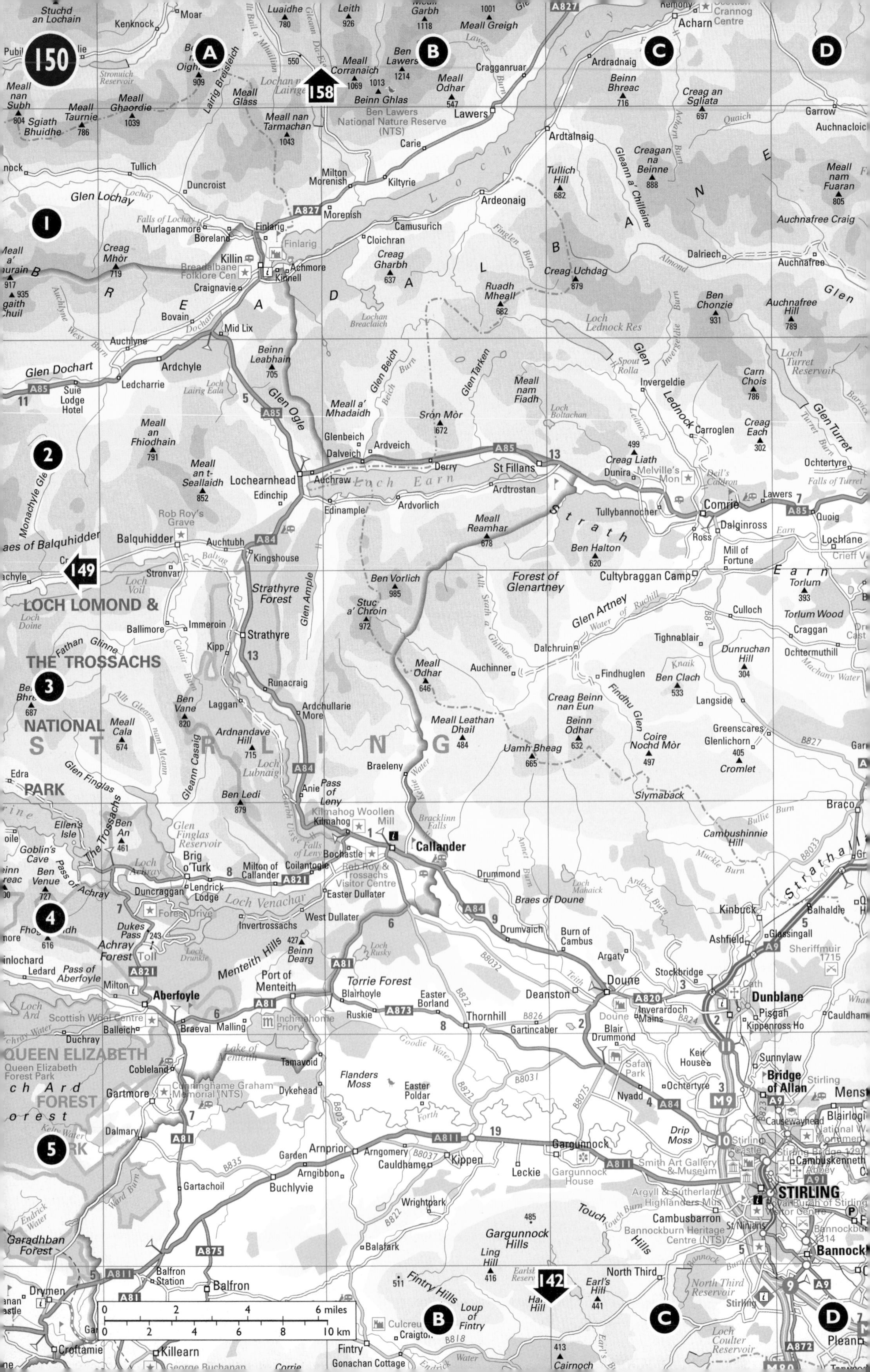
150
A
B
C
D
158
149
142
1
2
3
4
5
Stuchd an Lochain
Kenknock
Moar
Luaidhe 780
Leith 926
Meall Garbh 1118
Meall Greigh
1001
A827
Kenmore
Scottish Crannog Centre
Acharn
Stronuich Reservoir
Meall Oighe 909
Lairig Breisleich
550
Meall Corranaich 1069
Ben Lawers 1214
1013
Cragganruar
Ardradnaig
Meall nan Subh 804
Meall Taurnie 786
Meall Ghaordie 1039
Meall Glass
Lochan na Lairige
Beinn Ghlas
Meall Odhar 547
Beinn Bhreac 716
Creag an Sgliata 697
Garrow
Auchnacloich
Sgiath Bhuidhe
Meall nan Tarmachan 1043
Ben Lawers National Nature Reserve (NTS)
Lawers
Quaich
Carie
Ardtalnaig
Creagan na Beinne 888
Gleann a' Chilleine
Acharn Burn
Tullich
Tullich Hill 682
Meall nam Fuaran 805
Duncroist
Milton Morenish
Kiltyrie
Glen Lochay
Lochay
Morenish
Loch Tay
Ardeonaig
Auchnafree Craig
Falls of Lochay
Murlaganmore
Boreland
Finlarig
Camusurich
Cloichran
Killin
Breadalbane Folklore Cen
Achmore
Kinnell
Craignavie
Creag Mhòr 719
Creag Gharbh 637
Finglen Burn
Dalriech
Auchnafree
Almond
Creag Uchdag 879
Ruadh Mheall 682
Glen
Bovain
Dochart
Mid Lix
Auchlyne
Lochan Breaclaich
Ben Chonzie 931
Auchnafree Hill 789
Loch Lednock Res
Beinn Leabhain 705
Glen Dochart
Ardchyle
Ledcharrie
A85
11
Suie Lodge Hotel
Loch Lairig Eala
Glen Ogle
Glen Beich
Beich Burn
Glen Tarken
Spout Rolla
Invergeldie
Loch Turret Reservoir
Carn Chois 786
Meall nam Fiadh
Loch Boltachan
Glen Lednock
Carroglen
Creag Each 302
Glen Turret
Meall an Fhiodhain 791
Meall a' Mhadaidh
Sròn Mòr 672
Glenbeich
Ardveich
Dalveich
Derry
St Fillans
13
499
Creag Liath
Dunira
Melville's Mon
Deil's Cauldron
Ochtertyre
Falls of Turret
Meall an t-Seallaidh 852
Lochearnhead
Auchraw
Loch Earn
Ardtrostan
Edinchip
Edinample
Ardvorlich
Tullybannocher
Comrie
Lawers
Dalginross
Quoig
Monachyle Glen
Rob Roy's Grave
Balquhidder
Braes of Balquhidder
Auchtubh
A84
Kingshouse
Meall Reamhar 678
Strath Earn
Ross
Lochlane
Ben Halton 620
Mill of Fortune
Stronvar
Balvag
Loch Voil
Ben Vorlich 985
Forest of Glenartney
Cultybraggan Camp
Torlum 393
LOCH LOMOND &
Loch Doine
Strathyre Forest
Glen Ample
Stuc a' Chroin 972
Glen Artney
Water of Ruchill
Culloch
Torlum Wood
Ballimore
Immeroin
Strathyre
B827
Craggan
Fathan Glinne
Kipp
Tighnablair
Ochtermuthill
Dalchruin
Dunruchan Hill 304
THE TROSSACHS
Calair Burn
Auchinner
Meall Odhar 646
Findhuglen
Knaik
Ben Clach 533
Machany Water
Runacraig
Ardchullarie More
Laggan
Ben Vane 820
Meall Cala 674
NATIONAL
Creag Beinn nan Eun
Findhu Glen
Langside
Meall Leathan Dhail 484
Beinn Odhar 632
Coire Nochd Mòr 497
Greenscares
Glenlichorn
405
Cromlet
Ardnandave Hill 715
Uamh Bheag 665
STIRLING
Loch Lubnaig
Glen Finglas
Gleann Casaig
PARK
Edra
Braeleny
Keltie Water
Pass of Leny
Anie
Slymaback
Braco
Ben Ledi 879
Bullie Burn
The Trossachs
Ben An 461
Ellen's Isle
Glen Finglas Reservoir
Kilmahog Woollen Mill
Kilmahog
Bracklinn Falls
Callander
Cambushinnie Hill
Goblin's Cave
Ben Venue 727
Loch Achray
Pass of Achray
Brig o'Turk
Milton of Callander
Coilantogle
Falls of Leny
Bochastle
Rob Roy & Trossachs Visitor Centre
Drummond
Muckle Burn
B8033
Strathallan
A821
Duncraggan
Lendrick Lodge
Loch Venachar
Easter Dullater
Loch Mahaick
Braes of Doune
Ardoch Burn
Kinbuck
Balhaldie
7
Forest Drive
Dukes Pass
243
Invertrossachs
West Dullater
Drumvaich
Burn of Cambus
Ashfield
Glassingall
Achray Forest
Toll
Loch Drunkie
Menteith Hills
427
Beinn Dearg
Loch Rusky
B8032
Argaty
Sheriffmuir 1715
Loch Ard
Ledard
Pass of Aberfoyle
Milton
Aberfoyle
Port of Menteith
A81
Torrie Forest
Blairhoyle
Easter Borland
Deanston
Doune
Stockbridge
Cath
Dunblane
A9
Scottish Wool Centre
Balleich
Braeval
Malling
Inchmahome Priory
Ruskie
A873
B822
Thornhill
B826
Gartincaber
A820
Inverardoch Mains
Doune Castle
B824
Pisgah
Kippenross Ho
Cauldhame
QUEEN ELIZABETH
Queen Elizabeth Forest Park
Duchray
Lake of Menteith
Goodie Water
Blair Drummond
Safari Park
Keir House
Sunnylaw
Cobleland
Tamavoid
Flanders Moss
Easter Poldar
B8031
B8075
Ochtertyre
Nyadd
Bridge of Allan
Gartmore
Cunninghame Graham Memorial (NTS)
Dykehead
M9
FOREST
Dalmary
Kelty Water
Forth
B8034
Drip Moss
Stirling
Causewayhead
National Wallace Monument
A811
19
Garden
Arnprior
Arngomery
B8037
Kippen
Gargunnock
Leckie
Gargunnock House
Smith Art Gallery & Museum
Stirling Castle
Cambuskenneth Abbey
B835
Arngibbon
Cauldhame
Gartachoil
Buchlyvie
Argyll & Sutherland Highlanders Mus
STIRLING
Royal Burgh of Stirling Visitor Centre
Ward Burn
Endrick Water
Wrightpark
Touch Hills
Touch Burn
Cambusbarron
Bannockburn Heritage Centre (NTS)
St Ninians
485
Bannockburn 1314
Garadhban Forest
A875
Balafark
Gargunnock Hills
Ling Hill 416
Bannock
North Third
North Third Reservoir
Drymen
Balfron Station
Balfron
511
Fintry Hills
Loup of Fintry
Earlsburn Reservoir
Hart Hill
Earl's Hill 441
Stirling
0
2
4
6 miles
0
2
4
6
8
10 km
Culcreuch
Craigton
B818
Fintry
Loch Coulter Reservoir
A872
Plean
Croftamie
Killearn
Gonachan Cottage
Endrick Water
413
Cairnoch

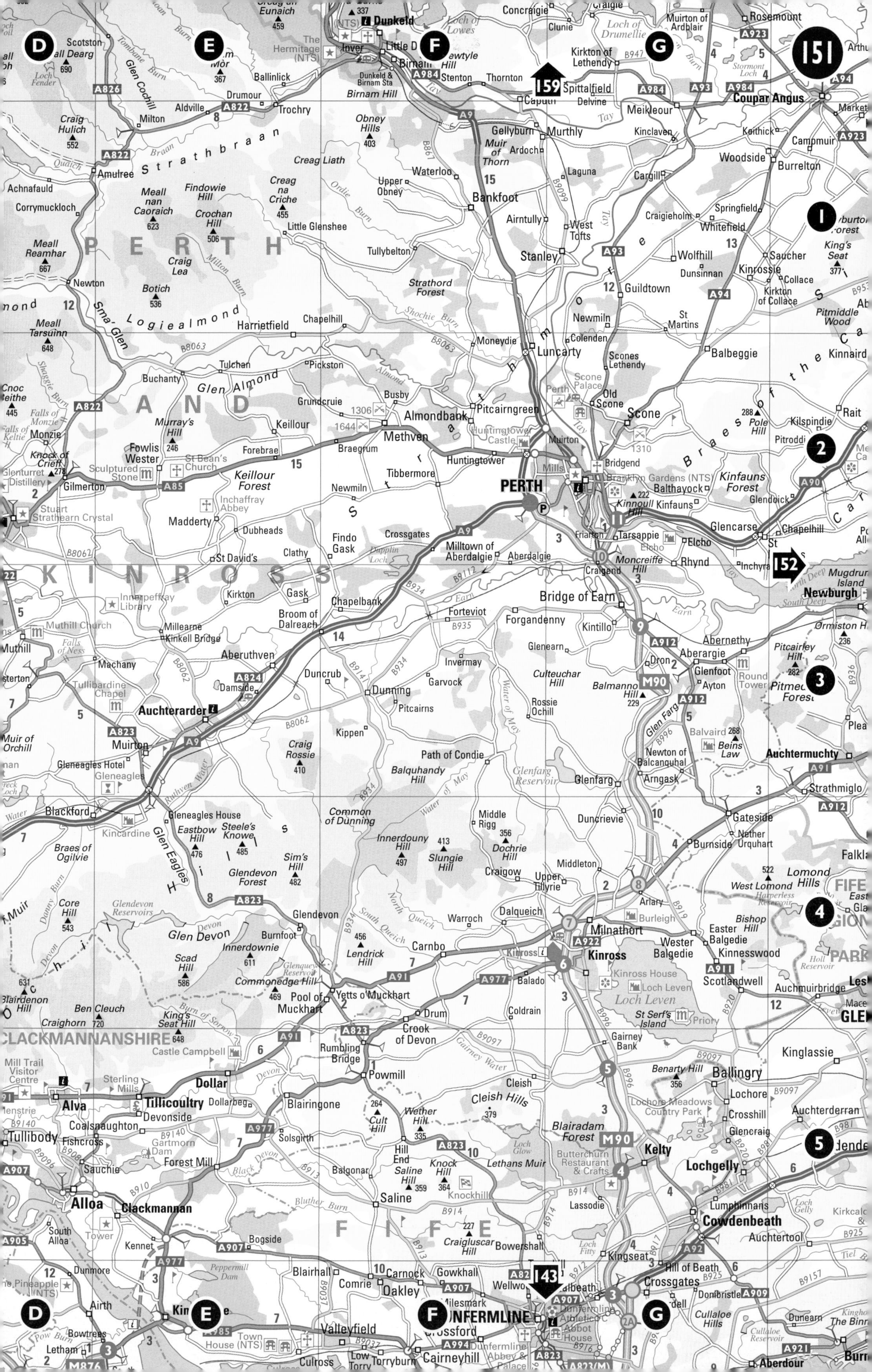

151
159
152
143
D
E
F
G
I
2
3
4
5
PERTH AND KINROSS
CLACKMANNANSHIRE
FIFE
Dunkeld
Birnam
Little Dunkeld
Inver
The Hermitage (NTS)
Dunkeld & Birnam Sta
Birnam Hill
Loch of Lowes
Hawtyle Hill
Stenton
Thornton
Concraigie
Clunie
Loch of Drumellie
Muirton of Ardblair
Rosemount
Kirkton of Lethendy
Spittalfield
Caputh
Delvine
Meikleour
Coupar Angus
Stormont Loch
Keithick
Campmuir
Kinclaven
Woodside
Burrelton
Cargill
Murthly
Gellyburn
Muir of Thorn
Ardoch
Laguna
Waterloo
Upper Obney
Obney Hills
403
Bankfoot
Airntully
West Tofts
Stanley
Craigieholm
Springfield
Whitefield
Wolfhill
Dunsinnan
Saucher
Kinrossie
Collace
Kirkton of Collace
King's Seat
377
Pitmiddle Wood
Kinnaird
Guildtown
St Martins
Balbeggie
Newmiln
Colenden
Scones Lethendy
Luncarty
Moneydie
Strathord Forest
Tullybelton
Little Glenshee
Creag Liath
Creag na Criche
455
Scotston
Meall Dearg
690
Loch Fender
Glen Cochill
Ballinlick
Drumour
Trochry
Aldville
Milton
Craig Hulich
552
Strathbraan
Amulree
Achnafauld
Corrymuckloch
Meall nan Caoraich
623
Findowie Hill
Crochan Hill
506
Meall Reamhar
667
Craig Lea
Botich
536
Newton
Sma' Glen
Logiealmond
Meall Tarsuinn
648
Harrietfield
Chapelhill
Tulchan
Pickston
Buchanty
Glen Almond
Grundcruie
Busby
Almondbank
Pitcairngreen
Huntingtower Castle
Scone Palace
Old Scone
Scone
Pole Hill
288
Rait
Kilspindie
Pitroddie
Glendoick
Kinfauns Forest
Balthayock
Kinfauns
Kinnoull Hill
222
Glencarse
Chapelhill
St Madoes
Inchyra
Mugdrum Island
Newburgh
Cnoc Beithe
445
Falls of Monzie
Monzie
Knock of Crieff
278
Glenturret Distillery
Gilmerton
Stuart Strathearn Crystal
Murray's Hill
246
Keillour
Methven
Fowlis Wester
St Bean's Church
Sculptured Stone
Forebrae
Braegrum
Huntingtower
Keillour Forest
Tibbermore
Muirton
Bridgend
Branklyn Gardens (NTS)
PERTH
Inchaffray Abbey
Madderty
Dubheads
Newmiln
Findo Gask
Crossgates
Friarton
Tarsappie
Elcho
Rhynd
Moncreiffe Hill
Craigend
Dupplin Loch
Milltown of Aberdalgie
Aberdalgie
St David's
Clathy
Kirkton
Gask
Innerpeffray Library
Chapelbank
Broom of Dalreach
Forteviot
Forgandenny
Bridge of Earn
Kintillo
Abernethy
Ormiston
236
Pitcairley Hill
282
Pitmedden Forest
Aberargie
Glenfoot
Ayton
Round Tower
Dron
Muthill Church
Muthill
Falls of Ness
Millearne
Kinkell Bridge
Aberuthven
Machany
Tullibardine Chapel
Damside
Auchterarder
Duncrub
Dunning
Invermay
Garvock
Glenearn
Culteuchar Hill
Balmanno Hill
229
Rossie Ochill
Pitcairns
Kippen
Craig Rossie
410
Glen Farg
Balvaird
Beins Law
268
Newton of Balcanquhal
Arngask
Glenfarg
Glenfarg Reservoir
Path of Condie
Balquhandy Hill
Auchtermuchty
Strathmiglo
Gateside
Muir of Orchill
Muirton
Gleneagles Hotel
Gleneagles
Blackford
Kincardine
Gleneagles House
Ruthven Water
Glen Eagles
Eastbow Hill
476
Steele's Knowe
485
Braes of Ogilvie
Common of Dunning
Middle Rigg
356
Dochrie Hill
Innerdouny Hill
497
413
Slungie Hill
Duncrievie
Burnside
Nether Urquhart
Sim's Hill
482
Glendevon Forest
Ochil Hills
Craigow
Middleton
Upper Tillyrie
Lomond Hills
522
West Lomond
Harperleas Reservoir
Arlary
Burleigh
Bishop Hill
Easter Balgedie
Wester Balgedie
Kinnesswood
Core Hill
543
Glendevon Reservoirs
Glen Devon
Glendevon
Burnfoot
Warroch
Dalqueich
Milnathort
Kinross
Kinross House
Loch Leven
Scotlandwell
Auchmuirbridge
Holl Reservoir
Innerdownie
611
Scad Hill
586
456
Lendrick Hill
Carnbo
Balado
Commonedge Hill
469
Glenquey Reservoir
Pool of Muckhart
Yetts o' Muckhart
Drum
Coldrain
St Serf's Island
Priory
Blairdenon Hill
631
Ben Cleuch
720
Craighorn
King's Seat Hill
648
Burn of Sorrow
Castle Campbell
Crook of Devon
Rumbling Bridge
Gairney Water
Gairney Bank
Kinglassie
Mill Trail Visitor Centre
Sterling Mills
Dollar
Powmill
Cleish
Benarty Hill
356
Ballingry
Lochore
Lochore Meadows Country Park
Crosshill
Auchterderran
Alva
Tillicoultry
Dollarbeg
Devonside
Blairingone
264
Cult Hill
Wether Hill
335
Cleish Hills
379
Blairadam Forest
Glencraig
Menstrie
Coalsnaughton
Tullibody
Fishcross
Gartmorn Dam
Solsgirth
Hill End
Loch Glow
Lethans Muir
Kelty
Lochgelly
Forest Mill
Sauchie
Black Devon
Balgonar
Saline Hill
359
Knock Hill
364
Knockhill
Butterchurn Restaurant & Crafts
Alloa
Clackmannan
Bluther Burn
Saline
Lassodie
Lumphinnans
Lochgelly Loch
Kirkcaldy
Cowdenbeath
South Alloa
Tower
Kennet
Bogside
227
Craigluscar Hill
Bowershall
Loch Fitty
Auchtertool
Tiel Burn
Dunmore
Pineapple (NTS)
Peppermill Dam
Blairhall
Comrie
Carnock
Oakley
Gowkhall
Wellwood
Kingseat
Hill of Beath
Crossgates
Donibristle
Airth
Kincardine
Milesmark
DUNFERMLINE
Dunfermline Athletic FC
Abbot House
Halbeath
Cullaloe Hills
Cullaloe Reservoir
Dunearn
The Binn
Letham
Bowtrees
Pow Burn
Town House (NTS)
Valleyfield
Crossford
Dunfermline Abbey & Palace
Cairneyhill
Torryburn
Low Torry
Culross
Aberdour
Burntisland
A9
A822
A826
A984
A93
A923
A94
A85
A824
A823
A912
M90
A91
A977
A922
A911
A907
A905
A876
A985
A994
A92
A909
A921
A823(M)
B8063
B8062
B934
B935
B9112
B9141
B867
B9099
B947
B953
B996
B919
B920
B9097
B913
B914
B910
B9140
B908
B9096
B9037
B912
B925
B981
B9157
B917

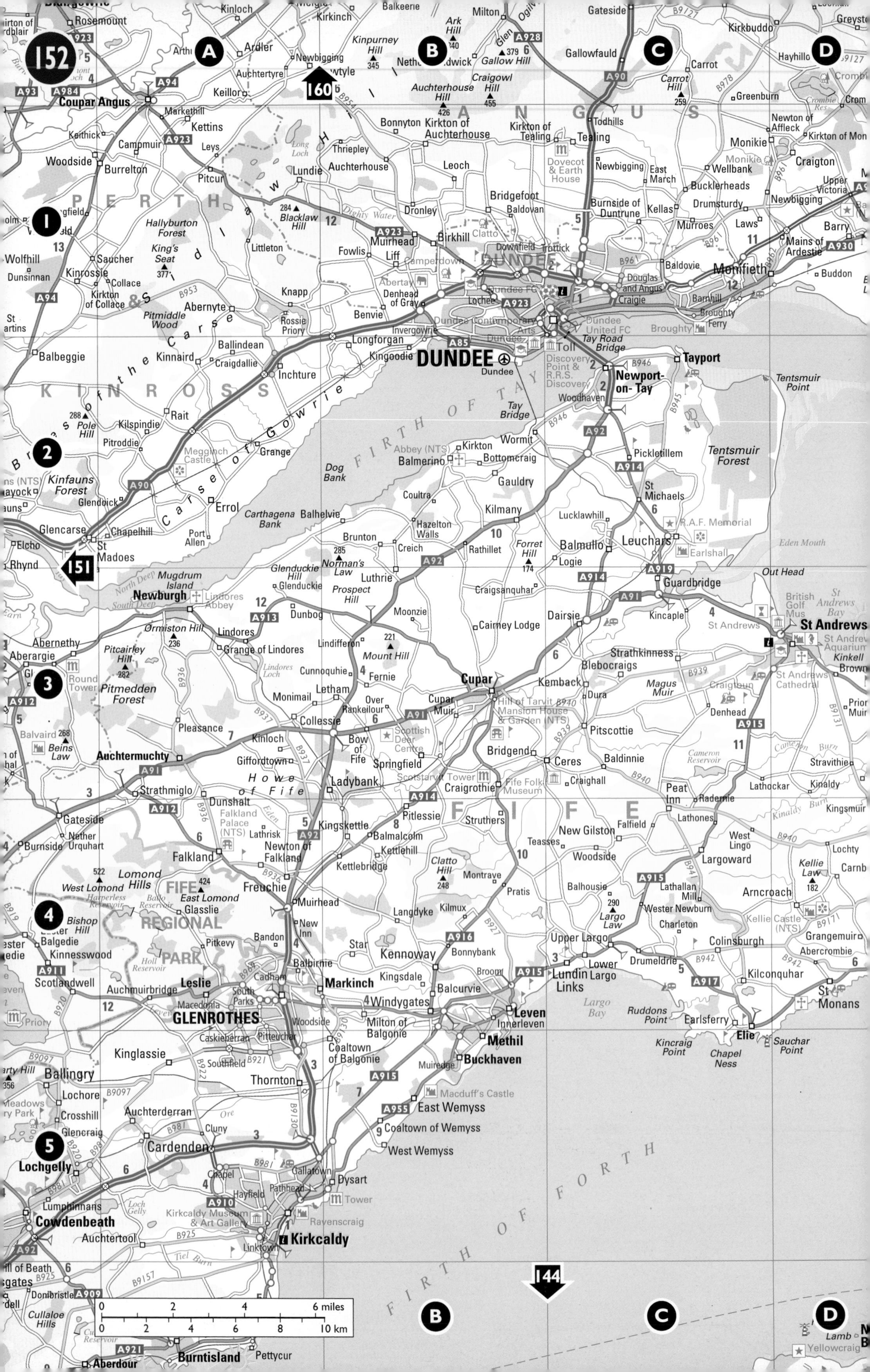
A
B
C
D
160
151
144
1
2
3
4
5
Rosemount
Kinloch
Kirkinch
Balkeerie
Milton
Gateside
Kirkbuddo
Ardler
Newbigging
Ark Hill
Kinpurney Hill
345
379
Gallow Hill
Gallowfauld
Carrot
Hayhillo
Coupar Angus
Keillor
Auchtertyre
Auchterhouse Hill
426
Craigowl Hill
455
Carrot Hill
259
Greenburn
Markethill
Kettins
Bonnyton
Kirkton of Auchterhouse
Kirkton of Tealing
Tealing
Todhills
Newton of Affleck
Kirkton of Monikie
Keithick
Campmuir
Leys
Thrieplev
Monikie
Craigton
Woodside
Burrelton
Pitcur
Lundie
Auchterhouse
Leoch
Dovecot & Earth House
Newbigging
East March
Wellbank
Bucklerheads
Upper Victoria
PERTH
ANGUS
Bridgefoot
Baldovan
Burnside of Duntrune
Kellas
Drumsturdy
Newbigging
Hallyburton Forest
Blacklaw Hill
284
Dronley
Murroes
Laws
Barry
King's Seat
377
Littleton
Muirhead
Birkhill
Clatto
Downfield
Trottick
Mains of Ardestie
Wolfhill
Dunsinnan
Saucher
Kinrossie
Collace
Kirkton of Collace
Fowlis
Liff
Camperdown
DUNDEE
Baldovie
Monifieth
Buddon
Abertay
Denhead of Gray
Dundee FC
Douglas and Angus
Craigie
Barnhill
Broughty Ferry
Knapp
Abernyte
Pitmiddle Wood
Benvie
Lochee
Dundee Contemporary Arts
Dundee United FC
Broughty
Rossie Priory
Invergowrie
Balbeggie
Ballindean
Kinnaird
Craigdallie
Longforgan
Kingoodie
DUNDEE
Dundee
Toll
Tay Road Bridge
Discovery Point & R.R.S. Discovery
Tayport
Newport-on-Tay
Inchture
Tentsmuir Point
KINROSS
Woodhaven
Pole Hill
288
Kilspindie
Rait
Tay Bridge
Pitroddie
Megginch Castle
Grange
Carse of Gowrie
FIRTH OF TAY
Abbey (NTS)
Kirkton
Balmerino
Bottomcraig
Wormit
Pickletillem
Tentsmuir Forest
Kinfauns Forest
Glendoick
Dog Bank
Gauldry
Coultra
St Michaels
Errol
Carthagena Bank
Balhelvie
Kilmany
Lucklawhill
R.A.F. Memorial
Glencarse
Chapelhill
Port Allen
Hazelton Walls
Brunton
Creich
Rathillet
Forret Hill
174
Balmullo
Leuchars
Earlshall
Elcho
St Madoes
Rhynd
Norman's Law
285
Logie
Eden Mouth
Mugdrum Island
Glenduckie Hill
Glenduckie
Luthrie
Prospect Hill
Craigsanquhar
Guardbridge
Out Head
Newburgh
Lindores Abbey
Dunbog
Moonzie
Cairney Lodge
Dairsie
Kincaple
British Golf Mus
St Andrews Bay
St Andrews
Ormiston Hill
236
Lindores
Grange of Lindores
Lindifferon
Mount Hill
221
Strathkinness
Abernethy
Aberargie
Pitcairlie Hill
282
Round Tower
Pitmedden Forest
Lindores Loch
Cunnoquhie
Fernie
Cupar
Kemback
Blebocraigs
Magus Muir
St Andrews Aquarium
Kinkell
St Andrews Cathedral
Letham
Monimail
Over Rankeilour
Cupar Muir
Hill of Tarvit Mansion House & Garden (NTS)
Dura
Denhead
Craigtoun
Collessie
Scottish Deer Centre
Pitscottie
Balvaird
268
Beins Law
Pleasance
Kinloch
Bow of Fife
Bridgend
Ceres
Baldinnie
Cameron Reservoir
Auchtermuchty
Giffordtown
Springfield
Stravithie
Howe of Fife
Ladybank
Scotstarvit Tower
Craigrothie
Fife Folk Museum
Craighall
Peat Inn
Lathockar
Kinaldy
Strathmiglo
Dunshalt
Falkland Palace (NTS)
Lathrisk
Kingskettle
Pitlessie
Struthers
FIFE
Radernie
Kingsmuir
Gateside
Nether Urquhart
Burnside
Newton of Falkland
Balmalcolm
Kettlehill
Teasses
New Gilston
Falfield
Lathones
West Lingo
Lochty
Falkland
Kettlebridge
Clatto Hill
248
Montrave
Woodside
Largoward
Kellie Law
182
Carnbee
West Lomond
522
Lomond Hills
424
East Lomond
FIFE REGIONAL PARK
Freuchie
Pratis
Balhousie
Lathallan Mill
Arncroach
Glasslie
Muirhead
Langdyke
Kilmux
290
Largo Law
Wester Newburn
Charleton
Kellie Castle (NTS)
Bishop Hill
Balgedie
New Inn
Bandon
Star
Kennoway
Bonnybank
Upper Largo
Colinsburgh
Grangemuir
Abercrombie
Kinnesswood
Pitkevy
Holl Reservoir
Balbirnie
Broom
Lower Largo
Drumeldrie
Scotlandwell
Auchmuirbridge
Leslie
Cadham
Markinch
Kingsdale
Balcurvie
Lundin Links
Kilconquhar
St Monans
Macedonia
South Parks
Windygates
Leven
Innerleven
Largo Bay
Ruddons Point
Earlsferry
Elie
GLENROTHES
Woodside
Milton of Balgonie
Methil
Saucharr Point
Caskieberran
Pitteuchar
Coaltown of Balgonie
Kincraig Point
Chapel Ness
Kinglassie
Southfield
Muiredge
Buckhaven
Ballingry
Thornton
Lochore
Macduff's Castle
Crosshill
Auchterderran
East Wemyss
Glencraig
Cluny
Coaltown of Wemyss
Lochgelly
Cardenden
West Wemyss
FIRTH OF FORTH
Chapel
Gallatown
Dysart
Lumphinnans
Hayfield
Pathhead
Tower
Cowdenbeath
Kirkcaldy Museum & Art Gallery
Ravenscraig
Auchtertool
Linktown
Kirkcaldy
Donibristle
Cullaloe Hills
Aberdour
Burntisland
Pettycur
Lamb
Yellowcraig
0 2 4 6 miles
0 2 4 6 8 10 km

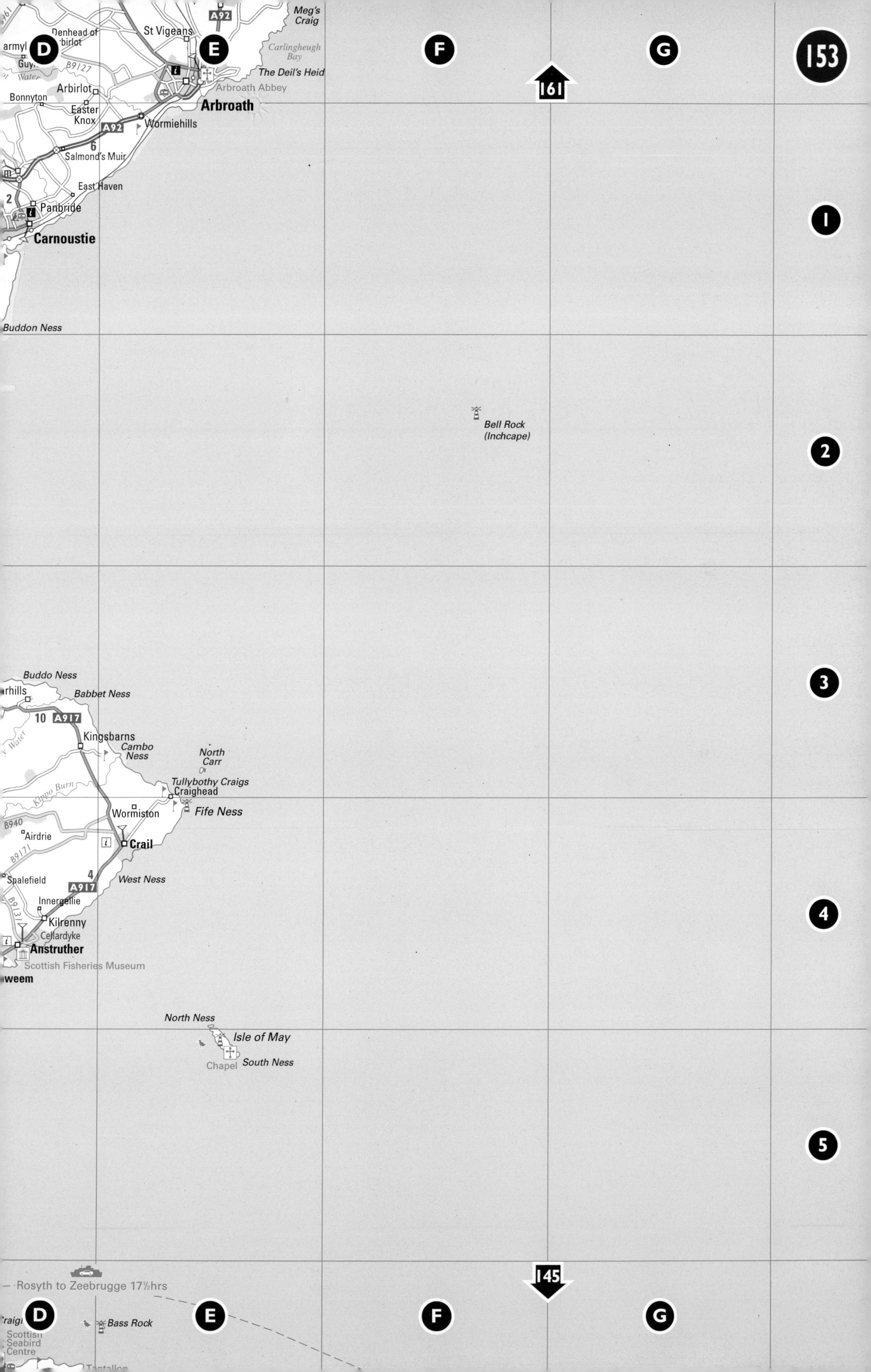

D

Denhead of
birlot

armyl
Guy

B9127

Arbirlot

Bonnyton

Easter
Knox

A92

6

Salmond's Muir

m

East Haven

2

Panbride

Carnoustie

Buddon Ness

St Vigeans

A92

E

Arbroath Abbey

Arbroath

Wormiehills

Meg's
Craig

Carlingheugh
Bay

The Deil's Heid

F

G

161

I

Bell Rock
(Inchcape)

2

Buddo Ness

rhills

Babbet Ness

10 A917

Kingsbarns

Cambo
Ness

Kingo Burn

Wormiston

B940

Airdrie

i

Crail

B9171

Spalefield

4

A917

West Ness

B9131

Innergellie

Kilrenny

Cellardyke

i

Anstruther

Scottish Fisheries Museum

weem

North
Carr

Tullybothy Craigs
Craighead

Fife Ness

3

4

North Ness

Isle of May

Chapel

South Ness

5

Rosyth to Zeebrugge 17½hrs

145

D

raig

Bass Rock

E

F

G

Scottish
Seabird
Centre

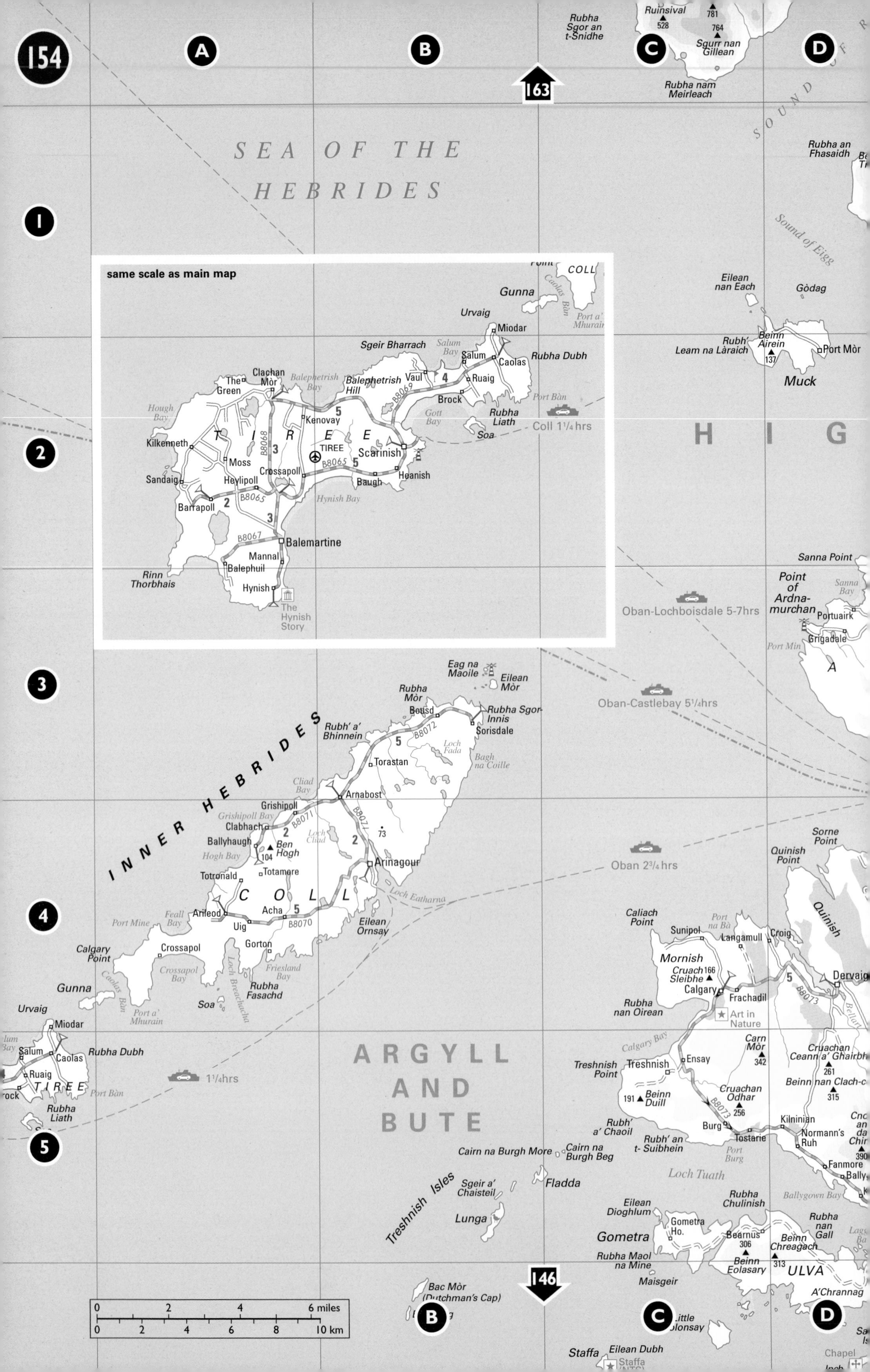
A
B
C
D
1
2
3
4
5
163
146
SEA OF THE HEBRIDES
same scale as main map
TIREE
COLL
Gunna
Urvaig
Miodar
Caolas
Salum
Salum Bay
Sgeir Bharrach
Rubha Dubh
Ruaig
Vaul
Balephetrish Hill
Balephetrish Bay
Clachan Mòr
The Green
Hough Bay
Kilkenneth
Moss
Kenovay
Sandaig
Heylipoll
Crossapoll
Barrapoll
Scarinish
Heanish
Baugh
Brock
Gott Bay
Rubha Liath
Soa
Port Bàn
Coll 1¼hrs
Hynish Bay
Balemartine
Mannal
Balephuil
Hynish
The Hynish Story
Rinn Thorbhais
Caolas Bàn
Port a' Mhurain
B8068
B8065
B8067
B8069
Ruinsival
528
781
764
Sgurr nan Gillean
Rubha Sgor an t-Snidhe
Rubha nam Meirleach
SOUND OF
Rubha an Fhasaidh
Sound of Eigg
Eilean nan Each
Gòdag
Rubh' Leam na Làraich
Beinn Airein
137
Port Mòr
Muck
H I G
Sanna Point
Point of Ardnamurchan
Sanna Bay
Portuairk
Grigadale
Port Min
Oban-Lochboisdale 5-7hrs
Oban-Castlebay 5¼hrs
Oban 2¾hrs
Eag na Maoile
Eilean Mòr
Rubha Mòr
Bousd
Rubha Sgor-Innis
Sorisdale
Rubh' a' Bhinnein
Torastan
Loch Fada
Bagh na Coille
INNER HEBRIDES
Cliad Bay
Arnabost
Grishipoll
Grishipoll Bay
Clabhach
Loch Cliad
Ballyhaugh
Ben Hogh
104
73
Hogh Bay
Totronald
Totamore
Arinagour
Loch Eatharna
Arileod
Acha
Uig
Gorton
Eilean Ornsay
Feall Bay
Port Mine
Calgary Point
Crossapol
Crossapol Bay
Friesland Bay
Loch Breachacha
Rubha Fasachd
Soa
B8070
B8071
B8072
1¼hrs
Caliach Point
Sunipol
Port na Bà
Langamull
Croig
Quinish
Quinish Point
Sorne Point
Mornish
Cruach Sleibhe
166
Calgary
Frachadil
Dervaig
Art in Nature
Rubha nan Oirean
Calgary Bay
Carn Mòr
342
Treshnish Point
Treshnish
Ensay
Cruachan Ceann a' Ghairbh
261
Beinn nan Clach-c
315
191
Beinn Duill
Cruachan Odhar
256
Rubh' a' Chaoil
Burg
Tostarie
Kilninian
Normann's Ruh
Rubh' an t- Suibhein
Port Burg
Loch Tuath
Fanmore
Bally
Ballygown Bay
B8073
Cairn na Burgh More
Cairn na Burgh Beg
Fladda
Treshnish Isles
Sgeir a' Chaisteil
Lunga
Eilean Dioghlum
Rubha Chulinish
Gometra
Gometra Ho.
Bearnus
306
Beinn Eolasary
313
Beinn Chreagach
Rubha nan Gall
ULVA
A'Chrannag
Rubha Maol na Mine
Maisgeir
Bac Mòr (Dutchman's Cap)
Little Colonsay
Staffa
Eilean Dubh
Chapel
ARGYLL AND BUTE
0 2 4 6 miles
0 2 4 6 8 10 km

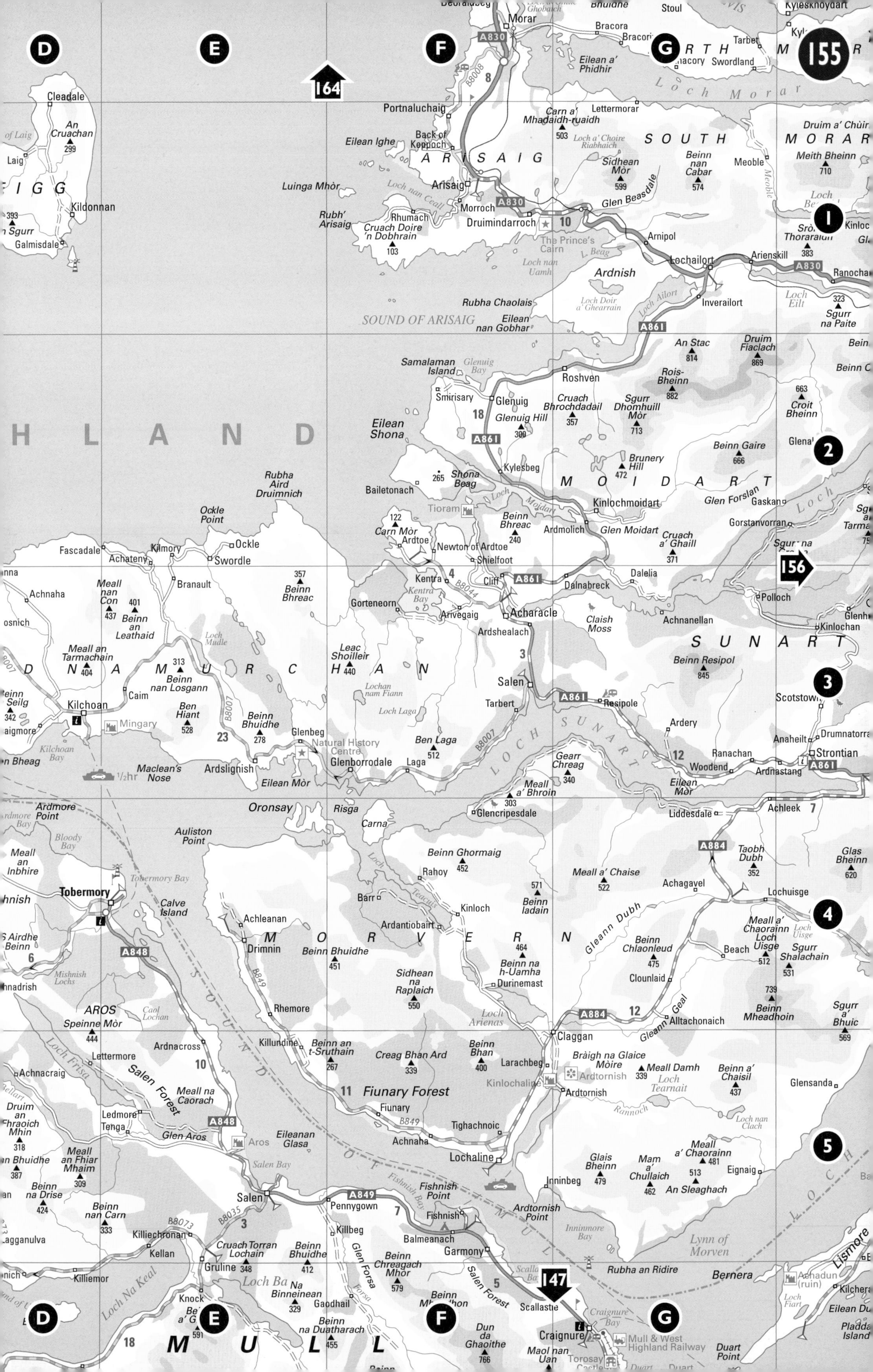

155
D
E
F
G
164
156
147
1
2
3
4
5
Morar
A830
Bracora
Bracorina
Tarbet
Swordland
Stoul
Eilean a' Phìdhir
Loch Morar
Cleadale
An Cruachan
299
Laig
EIGG
Kildonnan
393
Galmisdale
Portnaluchaig
Eilean Ighe
Back of Keppoch
ARISAIG
Arisaig
Luinga Mhòr
Loch nan Ceall
Rubh' Arisaig
Rhumach
Cruach Doire 'n Dobhrain
103
Morroch
Druimindarroch
The Prince's Cairn
Loch nan Uamh
Carn a' Mhadaidh-ruaidh
503
Lettermorar
Loch a' Choire Riabhaich
SOUTH MORAR
Sidhean Mòr
599
Beinn nan Cabar
574
Meoble
Druim a' Chùirn
Meith Bheinn
710
Glen Beasdale
Arnipol
Lochailort
Arienskill
Thorarainn
383
Ardnish
Inverailort
Loch Eilt
Sgurr na Paite
323
Rubha Chaolais
Eilean nan Gobhar
SOUND OF ARISAIG
Loch Doir a' Ghearrain
Loch Ailort
A861
An Stac
814
Druim Fiaclach
869
Samalaman Island
Glenuig Bay
Smirisary
Roshven
Rois-Bheinn
882
Glenuig
Glenuig Hill
300
Cruach Bhrochdadail
357
Sgurr Dhomhuill Mòr
713
663
Croit Bheinn
Eilean Shona
HIGHLAND
Beinn Gaire
666
Kylesbeg
Brunery Hill
472
Shona Beag
265
MOIDART
Baileтonach
Loch Moidart
Kinlochmoidart
Glen Forslan
Gaskan
Tioram
Beinn Bhreac
240
Ardmolich
Glen Moidart
Gorstanvorran
Cruach a' Ghaill
371
Rubha Aird Druimnich
Ockle Point
Ockle
122
Carn Mòr
Ardtoe
Newton of Ardtoe
Shielfoot
Fascadale
Achateny
Kilmory
Swordle
Branault
357
Beinn Bhreac
Kentra
Kentra Bay
B8044
Cliff
Dalnabreck
Dalelia
Polloch
Achnaha
Meall nan Con
437
401
Beinn an Leathaid
Gorteneorn
Arivegaig
Acharacle
Ardshealach
Claish Moss
Achnanellan
Kinlochan
Loch Mudle
Meall an Tarmachain
404
ARDNAMURCHAN
313
Beinn nan Losgann
Leac Shoilleir
440
Lochan nam Fiann
SUNART
Beinn Resipol
845
Salen
Tarbert
Resipole
Scotstown
Loch Laga
Kilchoan
Caim
Mingary
Ben Hiant
528
Beinn Bhuidhe
278
Glenbeg
Natural History Centre
Ben Laga
512
Loch Sunart
Ardery
Anaheilt
Drumnatorran
Strontian
Kilchoan Bay
Maclean's Nose
½hr
Ardslignish
23
Eilean Mòr
Glenborrodale
Laga
Gearr Chreag
340
Meall a' Bhroin
303
Ranachan
Woodend
Ardnastang
Eilean Mòr
Glencripesdale
Liddesdale
Achleek
Ardmore Point
Oronsay
Risga
Carna
Auliston Point
Bloody Bay
A884
Taobh Dubh
352
Glas Bheinn
620
Tobermory
Tobermory Bay
Beinn Ghormaig
452
Rahoy
Meall a' Chaise
522
571
Beinn Iadain
Achagavel
Lochuisge
Calve Island
Barr
Loch Teacuis
Kinloch
Gleann Dubh
Meall a' Chaorainn
Loch Uisge
A848
Achleanan
Drimnin
MORVERN
Ardantiobairt
Beinn Chlaonleud
475
Beach
512
Sgurr Shalachain
531
Mishnish Lochs
Beinn Bhuidhe
451
Sidhean na Raplaich
550
464
Beinn na h-Uamha
Durinemast
Clounlaid
739
Beinn Mheadhoin
Sgurr a' Bhuic
569
AROS
Caol Lochan
Speinne Mòr
444
Rhemore
B849
Loch Arienas
A884
Gleann Geal
Alltachonaich
Lettermore
Ardnacross
Killundine
Beinn an t-Sruthain
267
Claggan
Bràigh na Glaice Mòire
339
Meall Damh
Beinn a' Chaisil
437
Achnacraig
Loch Frisa
Salen Forest
Creag Bhan Ard
339
Beinn Bhan
400
Larachbeg
Kinlochaline
Ardtornish
Loch Teàrnait
Glensanda
Meall na Caorach
Finnary Forest
Fiunary
Rannoch
Loch nan Clach
Ledmore
Tenga
Glen Aros
Aros
Eileanan Glasa
Tighachnoic
Achnaha
Lochaline
Glais Bheinn
479
Meall a' Chaorainn
481
Mam a' Chullaich
462
513
An Sleaghach
Eignaig
Salen Bay
Sound of Mull
Salen
A849
Pennygown
Fishnish Bay
Fishnish Point
Fishnish
Inninbeg
Ardtornish Point
Loch Linnhe
Beinn nan Carn
333
Beinn na Drise
424
B8073
B8035
Killiechronan
Kellan
Cruach Torran Lochain
348
Beinn Bhuidhe
412
Killbeg
Glen Forsa
Balmeanach
Beinn Chreagach Mhor
579
Garmony
Inninmore Bay
Lynn of Morven
Lismore
Killiemor
Gruline
Loch Ba
Na Binneinean
329
Salen Forest
Rubha an Ridire
Bernera
Achadun (ruin)
Kilcheran
Loch Na Keal
Knock
Gaodhail
Scallastle
Craignure Bay
Loch Fiart
Eilean Dubh
MULL
591
Beinn na Duatharach
455
Dun da Ghaoithe
766
Craignure
Mull & West Highland Railway
Maol nan Uan
Torosay Castle
Duart Point
Pladda Island
Lagganulva
Glen Aros
Tobermory
Mishnish
Druim an Fhraoich Mhin
318
Meall an Fhiar Mhaim
309
Meall an Inbhire

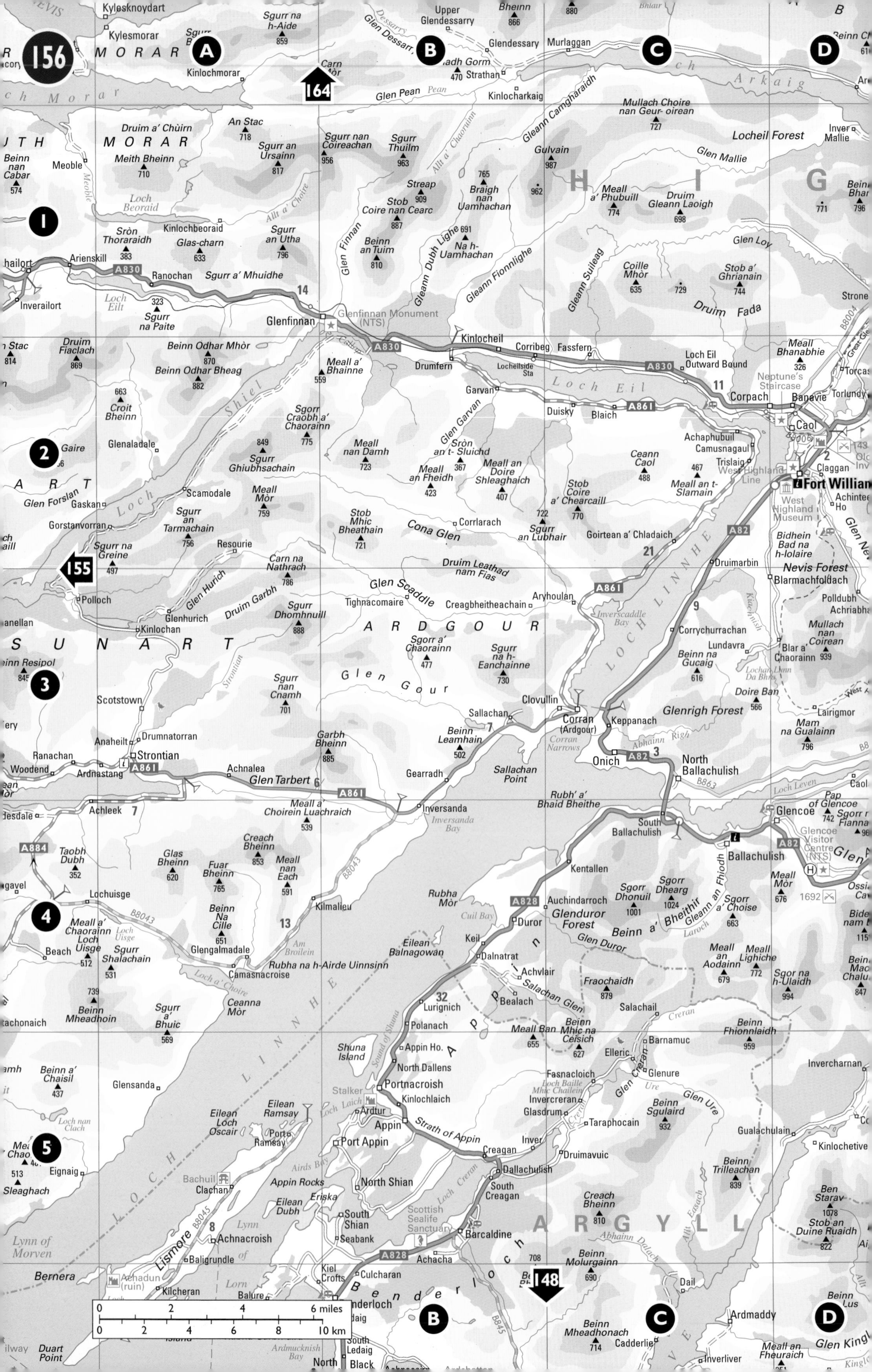

A
B
C
D
Kylesknoydart
Kylesmorar
MORAR
Kinlochmorar
Sgurr na h-Aide
859
164
Carn Mòr
Upper Glendessarry
Glen Dessarry
Glendessary
Strathan
470
Murlaggan
Bheinn
866
880
Loch Arkaig
Kinlocharkaig
Glen Pean
Loch Morar
Druim a' Chùirn
An Stac
718
Sgurr an Ursainn
817
Sgurr nan Coireachan
956
Sgurr Thuilm
963
Meith Bheinn
710
Meoble
Beinn nan Cabar
574
Loch Beoraid
Kinlochbeoraid
Gleann Camgharaidh
Mullach Choire nan Geur-oirean
727
Locheil Forest
Inver Mallie
Glen Mallie
Gulvain
987
962
765
Braigh nan Uamhachan
Streap
909
Stob Coire nan Cearc
887
Meall a' Phubuill
774
Druim Gleann Laoigh
698
771
796
1
Sròn Thoraraidh
383
Glas-charn
633
Sgurr an Utha
796
Beinn an Tuim
810
Glen Finnan
Gleann Dubh Lighe
691
Na h-Uamhachan
Gleann Fionnlighe
Gleann Suileag
Coille Mhòr
635
729
Stob a' Ghrianain
744
Glen Loy
Druim Fada
Strone
Arienskill
A830
Ranochan
Sgurr a' Mhuidhe
14
Loch Eilt
Inverailort
323
Sgurr na Paite
Glenfinnan
Glenfinnan Monument (NTS)
Kinlocheil
Corribeg
Fassfern
Loch Eil Outward Bound
Meall Bhanabhie
326
B8004
Druim Fiaclach
869
Beinn Odhar Mhòr
870
Beinn Odhar Bheag
882
Meall a' Bhainne
559
Drumfern
Lochailside Sta
Loch Eil
A861
11
Corpach
Banavie
Neptune's Staircase
Torlundy
663
Croit Bheinn
Loch Shiel
Sgorr Craobh a' Chaorainn
775
Garvan
Duisky
Blaich
Caol
2
Gaire
Glenaladale
849
Sgurr Ghiubhsachain
Meall nan Damh
723
Glen Garvan
Sròn an t-Sluichd
367
Meall an Fheidh
423
Meall an Doire Shleaghaich
407
Achaphubuil
Camusnagaul
Trislaig
West Highland Line
Ceann Caol
488
467
Meall an t-Slamain
Claggan
Fort William
West Highland Museum
Achintee
Glen Forslan
Gaskan
Scamodale
Meall Mòr
759
Stob Coire a' Chearcaill
770
Gorstanvorran
Sgurr an Tarmachain
756
Stob Mhic Bheathain
721
Corrlarach
Cona Glen
722
Sgurr an Lubhair
Goirtean a' Chladaich
A82
Bidhein Bad na h-Iolaire
155
Sgurr na Greine
497
Resourie
Carn na Nathrach
786
Druim Leathad nam Fias
21
Druimarbin
Nevis Forest
Blarmachfoldach
Polloch
Glen Hurich
Druim Garbh
Glen Scaddle
Tighnacomaire
Creagbheitheachain
Aryhoulan
Inverscaddle Bay
9
Polldubh
Achriabhach
Glenhurich
Kinlochan
Sgurr Dhomhnuill
888
ARDGOUR
Loch Linnhe
Corrychurrachan
Mullach nan Coirean
939
SUNART
Sgorr a' Chaorainn
477
Sgurr na h-Eanchainne
730
Lundavra
Beinn na Gucaig
616
Blar a' Chaorainn
Beinn Resipol
845
3
Glen Gour
Sgurr nan Cnamh
701
Doire Ban
566
Scotstown
Clovullin
Sallachan
Corran (Ardgour)
Keppanach
Glenrigh Forest
Lairigmor
Corran Narrows
Mam na Gualainn
796
Anaheilt
Drumnatorran
Strontian
Garbh Bheinn
885
Beinn Leamhain
502
7
Onich
3
North Ballachulish
Ranachan
Woodend
Ardnastang
Achnalea
Glen Tarbert
6
Gearradh
Sallachan Point
B863
Loch Leven
Pap of Glencoe
742
Achleek
7
Meall a' Choirein Luachraich
539
Inversanda
Inversanda Bay
Rubh' a' Bhaid Bheithe
South Ballachulish
Glencoe
Glencoe Visitor Centre (NTS)
A884
Taobh Dubh
352
Glas Bheinn
620
Fuar Bheinn
765
Creach Bheinn
853
Meall nan Each
591
B8043
Ballachulish
Kentallen
Meall Mòr
676
1692
Lochuisge
Rubha Mòr
A828
Auchindarroch
Sgorr Dhonuil
1001
Sgorr Dhearg
1024
Sgorr a' Choise
663
4
Meall a' Chaorainn
Loch Uisge
Beinn Na Cille
651
13
Kilmalieu
Cuil Bay
Duror
Glenduror Forest
Beinn a' Bheithir
Gleann an Fhiodh
Glen Duror
Beach
512
Sgurr Shalachain
531
Glengalmadale
Am Broilein
Eilean Balnagowan
Keil
Dalnatrat
Meall an Aodainn
679
Meall Lighiche
772
Sgor na h-Ulaidh
994
847
Camasnacroise
Rubha na h-Airde Uinnsinn
Achvlair
Salachan Glen
Fraochaidh
879
Loch a' Choire
739
Beinn Mheadhoin
Ceanna Mòr
Sgurr a' Bhuic
569
32
Lurignich
Bealach
Salachail
Creran
Polanach
Meall Ban
655
Beinn Mhic na Ceisich
627
Beinn Fhionnlaidh
959
Shuna Island
Sound of Shuna
Appin Ho.
Elleric
Barnamuc
North Dallens
Invercharnan
Beinn a' Chaisil
437
Glensanda
Portnacroish
Stalker
Kinlochlaich
Fasnacloich
Loch Baile Mhic Chailein
Invercreran
Glasdrum
Glenure
Glen Ure
Beinn Sgulaird
932
Eilean Loch Oscair
Eilean Ramsay
Port Ramsay
Loch Laich
Ardtur
Appin
Strath of Appin
Taraphocain
Gualachulain
5
Port Appin
Inver
Creagan
Druimavuic
Kinlochetive
Eignaig
513
Sleaghach
Bachuil
Clachan
Airds Bay
Appin Rocks
Eriska
North Shian
Dallachulish
South Creagan
Beinn Trilleachan
839
Ben Starav
1078
Stob an Duine Ruaidh
822
Eilean Dubh
South Shian
Seabank
Scottish Sealife Sanctuary
Loch Creran
Creach Bheinn
810
ARGYLL
Abhainn Dalach
Allt Easach
Lynn of Morven
Lismore
B8045
8
Achnacroish
Lynn of Lorn
Baligrundle
A828
Achacha
Barcaldine
708
Beinn Molurgainn
690
Bernera
Achadun (ruin)
Kilcheran
Balure
Kiel Crofts
Culcharan
148
Benderloch
Dail
Beinn Lus
0 2 4 6 miles
0 2 4 6 8 10 km
B
C
D
Ardmaddy
B845
Beinn Mheadhonach
714
Cadderlie
Duart Point
Ardmucknish Bay
South Ledaig
North
Black
Inverliver
Meall an Fheuraich
Glen Kinglass

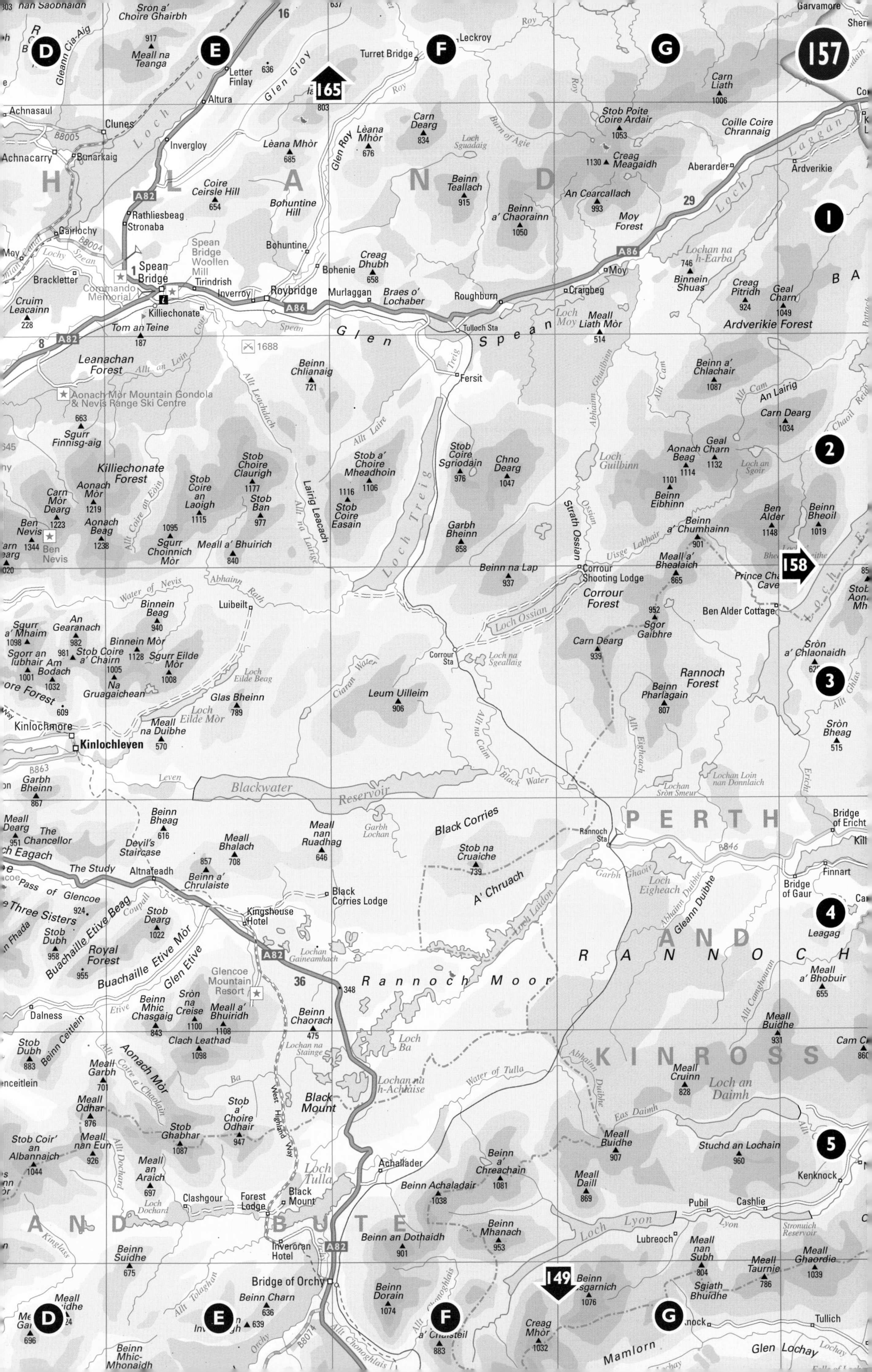
Sron a' Choire Ghairbh
16
Garvamore
Leckroy
Turret Bridge
Roy
165
917
Meall na Teanga
Gleann Cia-Aig
Letter Finlay
636
Altura
Glen Gloy
803
Achnasaul
Clunes
B8005
Loch Lochy
Achnacarry
Bunarkaig
Invergloy
Lèana Mhòr
685
Glen Roy
Lèana Mhòr
676
Carn Dearg
834
Loch Sguadaig
Burn of Agie
Stob Poite Coire Ardair
1053
1130
Creag Meagaidh
Carn Liath
1006
Coille Coire Chrannaig
Loch Laggan
Aberarder
Ardverikie
H
L
A
N
D
A82
Coire Ceirsle Hill
654
Bohuntine Hill
Beinn Teallach
915
Beinn a' Chaorainn
1050
An Cearcallach
993
Moy Forest
29
Rathliesbeag
Stronaba
Gairlochy
B8004
Spean Bridge Woollen Mill
Bohuntine
Creag Dhubh
658
Bohenie
A86
Moy
Lochan na h-Earba
746
Binnein Shuas
Creag Pitridh
924
Geal Charn
1049
BA
Moy
Brackletter
Commando Memorial
Spean Bridge
Tirindrish
Inverroy
Roybridge
Murlaggan
Braes o' Lochaber
Roughburn
Craigbeg
Cruim Leacainn
228
Killiechonate
A86
Tom an Teine
187
Spean
Glen Spean
Tulloch Sta
Loch Moy
Meall Liath Mòr
514
Ardverikie Forest
8
A82
1688
Leanachan Forest
Allt an Loin
Beinn Chlianaig
721
Treig
Fersit
Beinn a' Chlachair
1087
Allt Cam
An Lairig
Aonach Mòr Mountain Gondola & Nevis Range Ski Centre
663
Sgurr Finnisg-aig
Allt Leachdach
Allt Laire
Abhainn Ghuilbinn
Carn Dearg
1034
Killiechonate Forest
Stob Choire Claurigh
1177
Stob a' Choire Mheadhoin
1106
Stob Coire Sgriodain
976
Chno Dearg
1047
Loch Guilbinn
Aonach Beag
1114
Geal Charn
1132
Loch an Sgoir
Carn Mòr Dearg
1223
Aonach Mòr
1219
Stob Coire an Laoigh
1115
Stob Ban
977
1116
Stob Coire Easain
Lairig Leacach
Allt na Lairige
Loch Treig
1101
Beinn Eibhinn
Strath Ossian
Ossian
Ben Alder
1148
Beinn Bheoil
1019
Ben Nevis
1344
Ben Nevis
Aonach Beag
1238
Allt Coire an Eoin
1095
Sgurr Choinnich Mòr
Meall a' Bhuirich
840
Garbh Bheinn
858
Beinn a' Chumhainn
901
Uisge Labhair
Meall a' Bhealaich
865
158
Beinn na Lap
937
Corrour Shooting Lodge
Corrour Forest
Prince Charlie's Cave
Water of Nevis
Abhainn Rath
Luibeilt
Binnein Beag
940
Sgurr a' Mhaim
1098
An Gearanach
982
Loch Ossian
952
Sgor Gaibhre
Ben Alder Cottage
981
Stob Coire a' Chairn
Binnein Mòr
1128
Sgurr Eilde Mòr
1008
Corrour Sta
Loch na Sgeallaig
Carn Dearg
939
Sròn a' Chlaonaidh
Sgorr an Iubhair
1001
Am Bodach
1032
1005
Na Gruagaichean
Loch Eilde Beag
Ciaran Water
Rannoch Forest
Mamore Forest
Leum Uilleim
906
Beinn Pharlagain
807
Allt Ghlas
609
Glas Bheinn
789
Loch Eilde Mòr
Allt na Caim
Sròn Bheag
515
Kinlochmore
Kinlochleven
Meall na Duibhe
570
Allt Eigheach
B863
Garbh Bheinn
867
Leven
Blackwater Reservoir
Black Water
Lochan Sròn Smeur
Lochan Loin nan Donnlaich
Ericht
Meall Dearg
951
The Chancellor
Beinn Bheag
616
Devil's Staircase
Meall nan Ruadhag
646
Garbh Lochan
Black Corries
Rannoch Sta
PERTH
Bridge of Ericht
Kill
Loch Eagach
Meall Bhalach
708
Stob na Cruaiche
739
B846
The Study
Altnafeadh
857
Beinn a' Chrulaiste
Garbh Ghaoir
Loch Eigheach
Finnart
Bridge of Gaur
Pass of Glencoe
Black Corries Lodge
A' Chruach
Abhainn Duibhe
Gleann Duibhe
Three Sisters
924
Coupall
Kingshouse Hotel
Loch Laidon
4
Leagag
Stob Dubh
958
Buachaille Etive Beag
Stob Dearg
1022
Lochan Gaineamhach
AND
RANNOCH
Royal Forest
955
Buachaille Etive Mòr
A82
Glen Etive
Glencoe Mountain Resort
36
348
Rannoch Moor
Allt Camghouran
Meall a' Bhobuir
655
Dalness
Etive
Beinn Mhic Chasgaig
843
Sròn na Creise
1100
Meall a' Bhuiridh
1108
Beinn Chaorach
475
Meall Buidhe
931
Stob Dubh
883
Beinn Ceitlein
Clach Leathad
1098
Lochan na Stainge
Loch Ba
Abhainn Duibhe
KINROSS
Aonach Mòr
Meall Garbh
701
Allt Coire a' Chaolain
Ba
West Highland Way
Lochan na h-Achlaise
Water of Tulla
Meall Cruinn
828
Loch an Daimh
Meall Odhar
876
Stob a' Choire Odhair
947
Black Mount
Eas Daimh
Stob Coir' an Albannaich
1044
Meall nan Eun
926
Stob Ghabhar
1087
Meall Buidhe
907
Beinn a' Chreachain
1081
Stuchd an Lochain
960
5
Meall an Araich
697
Allt Dochard
Loch Tulla
Achallader
Beinn Achaladair
1038
Meall Daill
869
Kenknock
Clashgour
Loch Dochard
Forest Lodge
Black Mount
Pubil
Cashlie
AND
BUTE
Loch Lyon
Lyon
Lubreoch
Stronuich Reservoir
Kinglass
Beinn Suidhe
675
Inveroran Hotel
A82
Orchy
Beinn an Dothaidh
901
Beinn Mhanach
953
Meall nan Subh
804
Meall Taurnie
786
Meall Ghaordie
1039
Allt Tolaghan
Bridge of Orchy
Beinn Dorain
1074
149
Beinn Heasgarnich
1076
Sgiath Bhuidhe
696
Beinn Charn
636
639
Allt Chonoghlais
B8074
Creag Mhor
1032
Tullich
Mamlorn
Glen Lochay
Beinn Mhic-Mhonaidh

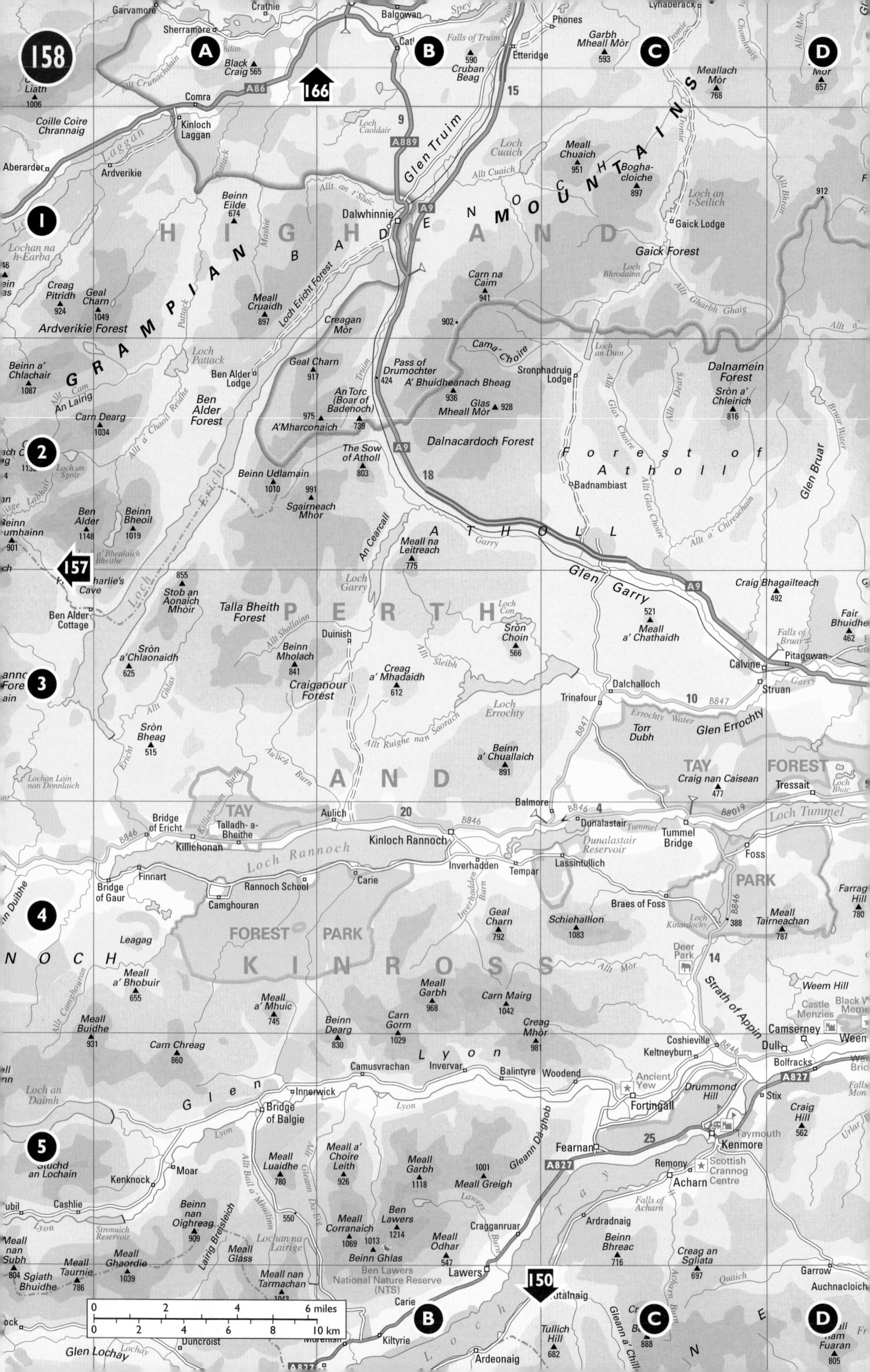

158
A
B
C
D
166
157
150
1
2
3
4
5
Garvamore
Crathie
Balgowan
Spey
Lynaberack
Sherramore
Phones
Cat
Falls of Truim
Garbh Mheall Mòr
593
Black Craig
565
590
Cruban Beag
Etteridge
Meallach Mòr
768
857
Liath
1006
A86
Comra
15
Coille Coire Chrannaig
Kinloch Laggan
Laggan
9
Loch Caoldair
A889
Glen Truim
Loch Cuaich
Meall Chuaich
951
Bogha-cloiche
897
Aberarder
Ardverikie
Pattack
Allt Cuaich
Allt an t-Sluic
Loch an t-Seilich
912
Beinn Eilde
674
Dalwhinnie
A9
Gaick Lodge
Gaick Forest
Lochan na h-Earba
HIGHLAND
GRAMPIAN
MOUNTAINS
BADENOCH
Creag Pitridh
924
Geal Charn
1049
Meall Cruaidh
897
Loch Ericht Forest
Carn na Caim
941
Loch Bhrodainn
Allt Gharbh Ghaig
Ardverikie Forest
Creagan Mòr
902
Cama' Choire
Loch an Duin
Loch Pattack
Beinn a' Chlachair
1087
An Lairig
Ben Alder Lodge
Geal Charn
917
Pass of Drumochter
424
A' Bhuidheanach Bheag
Sronphadruig Lodge
Dalnamein Forest
Ben Alder Forest
An Torc (Boar of Badenoch)
975
739
A'Mharconaich
936
Glas Mheall Mòr
928
Sròn a' Chleirich
816
Carn Dearg
1034
Dalnacardoch Forest
The Sow of Atholl
803
Forest of Atholl
Glen Bruar
Loch an Sgoir
Beinn Udlamain
1010
991
Sgairneach Mhòr
18
Badnambiast
Allt Glas Choire
Ben Alder
1148
Beinn Bheoil
1019
ATHOLL
Meall na Leitreach
775
An Cearcall
Garry
Allt a' Chireachain
Prince Charlie's Cave
855
Stob an Aonaich Mhòir
Loch Garry
Glen Garry
A9
Craig Bhagailteach
492
Ben Alder Cottage
Talla Bheith Forest
PERTH
Loch Con
521
Meall a' Chathaidh
Fair Bhuidhe
462
Falls of Bruar
Duinish
Sròn Choin
566
Calvine
Pitagowan
Sròn a'Chlaonaidh
625
Beinn Mholach
841
Creag a' Mhadaidh
612
Allt Sleibh
Dalchalloch
Struan
Craiganour Forest
Trinafour
10
B847
Loch Errochty
Errochty Water
Glen Errochty
Torr Dubh
Sròn Bheag
515
Allt Ruighe nan Saorach
Beinn a' Chuallaich
891
TAY
FOREST
Craig nan Caisean
477
Tressait
Loch Bhac
Lochan Loin nan Donnlaich
AND
Balmore
Aulich Burn
B846
4
B8019
Loch Tummel
Bridge of Ericht
TAY
Talladh-a-Bheithe
Aulich
20
Dunalastair
Tummel Bridge
Killichonan
Kinloch Rannoch
Dunalastair Reservoir
Loch Rannoch
Inverhadden
Tempar
Lassintullich
Foss
Finnart
Bridge of Gaur
Rannoch School
Carie
PARK
Camghouran
Braes of Foss
Farrag Hill
780
Geal Charn
792
Schiehallion
1083
Loch Kinardochy
388
Meall Tairneachan
787
FOREST PARK
Leagag
KINROSS
Deer Park
14
Meall a' Bhobuir
655
Allt Mòr
Meall Garbh
968
Carn Mairg
1042
Strath of Appin
Weem Hill
Castle Menzies
Meall a' Mhuic
745
Meall Buidhe
931
Beinn Dearg
830
Carn Gorm
1029
Creag Mhòr
981
Camserney
Coshieville
Dull
Cam Chreag
860
Lyon
Keltneyburn
Bolfracks
Camusvrachan
Invervar
Balintyre
Woodend
Ancient Yew
A827
Drummond Hill
Stix
Glen
Innerwick
Fortingall
Craig Hill
562
Loch an Daimh
Bridge of Balgie
Taymouth
25
Fearnan
Kenmore
Meall a' Choire Leith
926
Meall Luaidhe
780
Meall Garbh
1118
1001
Meall Greigh
Gleann Da-ghob
Remony
Scottish Crannog Centre
Stuchd an Lochain
Kenknock
Moar
Acharn
Cashlie
Beinn nan Oighreag
909
550
Ben Lawers
1214
Cragganruar
Falls of Acharn
Ardradnaig
Stronuich Reservoir
Lochan na Lairige
Meall Corranaich
1069
1013
Meall Odhar
547
Beinn Bhreac
716
Creag an Sgliata
697
Meall nan Subh
804
Meall Taurnie
786
Meall Ghaordie
1039
Meall Glass
Beinn Ghlas
Lawers
Garrow
Sgiath Bhuidhe
Meall nan Tarmachan
Ben Lawers National Nature Reserve (NTS)
Quaich
Auchnacloich
Carie
0 2 4 6 miles
0 2 4 6 8 10 km
Kiltyrie
Glen Lochay
Duncroist
Tullich Hill
682
888
Ardeonaig
Meall nam Fuaran
805
Loch

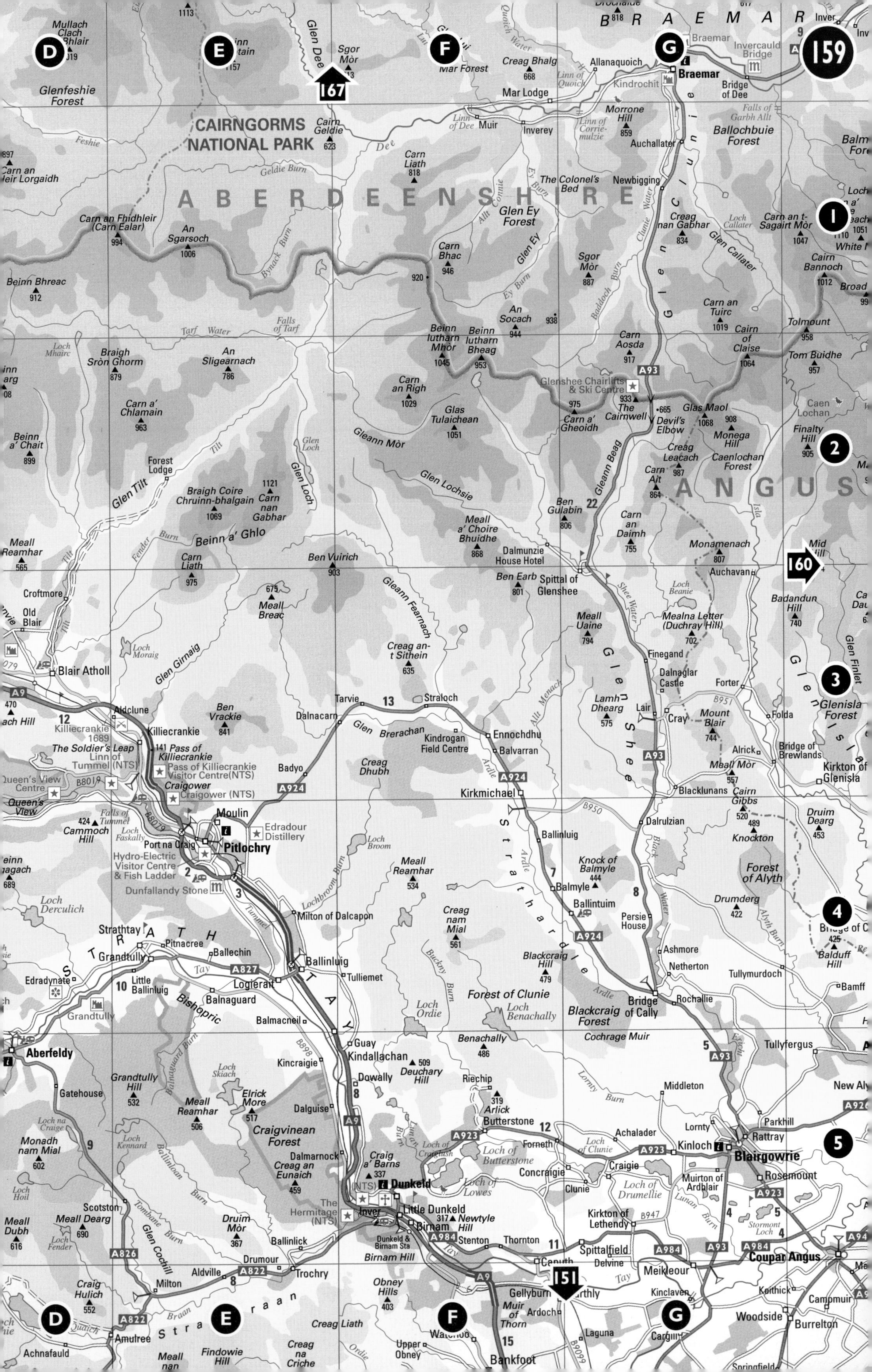

159
167
160
151
D
E
F
G
I
2
3
4
5
B R A E M A R
Braemar
Invercauld Bridge
Bridge of Dee
Mullach Clach a' Bhlair
Glenfeshie Forest
Glen Dee
Sgor Mòr
Mar Forest
Creag Bhalg 668
Allanaquoich
Linn of Quoich
Kindrochit
Mar Lodge
Falls of Garbh Allt
Ballochbuie Forest
CAIRNGORMS NATIONAL PARK
Cairn Geldie 623
Feshie
Dee
Linn of Dee
Muir
Inverey
Linn of Corriemulzie
Morrone Hill 859
Auchallater
Geldie Burn
Carn Liath 818
A B E R D E E N S H I R E
Carn an Fhidhleir (Carn Ealar) 994
An Sgarsoch 1006
Bynack Burn
Allt Connie
The Colonel's Bed
Glen Ey Forest
Glen Ey
Newbigging
Clunie Water
Glen Clunie
Creag nan Gabhar 834
Loch Callater
Glen Callater
Carn an t-Sagairt Mòr 1047
Cairn Bannoch 1012
Carn Bhac 946
Sgor Mòr 887
Baddoch Burn
920
Beinn Bhreac 912
Ey Burn
An Socach 944
938
Carn an Tuirc 1019
Cairn of Claise 1064
Tolmount 958
Tom Buidhe 957
Falls of Tarf
Tarf Water
Loch Mhairc
Braigh Sròn Ghorm 879
An Sligearnach 786
Beinn Iutharn Mhòr 1045
Beinn Iutharn Bheag 953
Carn Aosda 917
A93
Glenshee Chairlifts & Ski Centre
Carn an Righ 1029
933 The Cairnwell
975
Carn a' Gheoidh
665
Devil's Elbow
Glas Maol 1068
908
Monega Hill
Caenlochan Forest
Caen Lochan
Finalty Hill 905
Carn a' Chlamain 963
Glas Tulaichean 1051
Gleann Mòr
Glen Loch
Creag Leacach 987
Carn Aligh 864
A N G U S
Beinn a' Chait 899
Forest Lodge
Tilt
Glen Tilt
Braigh Coire Chruinn-bhalgain 1069
1121 Carn nan Gabhar
Glen Lochsie
Gleann Beag
Ben Gulabin 806
22
Carn an Daimh 755
Isla
Beinn a' Ghlo
Fender Burn
Meall a' Choire Bhuidhe 868
Dalmunzie House Hotel
Monamenach 807
Meall Reamhar 565
Carn Liath 975
Ben Vuirich 903
Auchavan
Ben Earb 801
Spittal of Glenshee
Croftmore
675
Meall Breac
Gleann Fearnach
Loch Beanie
Badandun Hill 740
Old Blair
Meall Uaine 794
Shee Water
Mealna Letter (Duchray Hill) 702
Loch Moraig
Creag an-t Sithein 635
Glen Girnaig
Glen Shee
Finegand
Glen Finlet
Blair Atholl
Dalnaglar Castle
Forter
Glen Isla
A9
470
12
Aldclune
Killiecrankie 1689
Tarvie
13
Straloch
Allt Menach
Lamh Dhearg 575
Lair
Cray
B951
Mount Blair 744
Glenisla Forest
Folda
Killiecrankie
Ben Vrackie 841
Dalnacarn
Glen Brerachan
Kindrogan Field Centre
Ennochdhu
Alrick
Bridge of Brewlands
The Soldier's Leap
Linn of Tummel (NTS)
141 Pass of Killiecrankie
Pass of Killiecrankie Visitor Centre(NTS)
Balvarran
Ardle
A93
Meall Mòr 557
Kirkton of Glenisla
Queen's View Centre
B8019
Craigower
Craigower (NTS)
Badyo
Creag Dhubh
A924
Kirkmichael
Blacklunans
Cairn Gibbs
Queen's View
Falls of Tummel
B8079
Moulin
Edradour Distillery
B950
Dalrulzian
520
489
Druim Dearg 453
424
Cammoch Hill
Loch Faskally
Port na Craig
Pitlochry
Loch Broom
Ballinluig
Knockton
Hydro-Electric Visitor Centre & Fish Ladder
2
Meall Reamhar 534
Strathardle
Knock of Balmyle 444
Forest of Alyth
Dunfallandy Stone
3
Lochbroom Burn
7
Balmyle
Black Water
Loch Derculich
Tummel
Milton of Dalcapon
Creag nam Mial 561
Ballintuim
Persie House
8
Drumderg 422
Alyth Burn
Strathtay
S T R A T H
Pitnacree
Ballechin
Grandtully
A924
Ashmore
Bridge of Cally
425
Balduff Hill
Tay
A827
Ballinluig
Buckny Burn
Blackcraig Hill 479
Netherton
Edradynate
10
Little Ballinluig
Logierait
Tulliemet
Tullymurdoch
Bamff
Balnaguard
Bishopric
Loch Ordie
Forest of Clunie
Loch Benachally
Blackcraig Forest
Rochallie
Grandtully
Balmacneil
T A Y
Benachally 486
Cochrage Muir
Aberfeldy
B898
Guay
Kindallachan
509 Deuchary Hill
5
A93
Tullyfergus
Balnaguard Burn
Loch Skiach
Kincraigie
Dowally
Riechip
Lornty Burn
Gatehouse
Grandtully Hill 532
Meall Reamhar 506
Elrick More 517
Dalguise
8
319 Arlick
Middleton
New Alyth
Loch na Craige
Craigvinean Forest
A9
Butterstone
12
Achalader
Lornty
Parkhill
Rattray
Monadh nam Mial 602
9
Loch Kennard
Ballinloan Burn
Dalmarnock
Craig a' Barns
Lunan Burn
Loch of Craiglush
A923
Loch of Butterstone
Forneth
Loch of Clunie
A923
Kinloch
Blairgowrie
Creag an Eunaich 459
337
Dunkeld
Concraigie
Craigie
Muirton of Ardblair
Rosemount
Loch Hoil
Loch of Lowes
Clunie
Loch of Drumellie
A923
The Hermitage (NTS)
Inver
Little Dunkeld
317 Newtyle Hill
Kirkton of Lethendy
B947
Lunan Burn
4
5
Stormont Loch
Scotston
Meall Dearg 690
Druim Mòr 367
Tombane Burn
Birnam
Dunkeld & Birnam Sta
A984
Stenton
Thornton
11
Spittalfield
A984
A93
A984
Coupar Angus
Meall Dubh 616
Loch Fender
Ballinlick
Birnam Hill
Caputh
Delvine
A826
Glen Cochill
Drumour
A822
Trochry
Aldville
Tay
Meikleour
8
Milton
Gellyburn
Murthly
Kinclaven
Keithick
Campmuir
Craig Hulich 552
Obney Hills 403
Muir of Thorn
Ardoch
Woodside
Burrelton
A822
Quaich
Braan
S t r a t h b r a a n
Creag Liath
Laguna
Amulree
Creag na Criche
Upper Obney
15
Cargill
Achnafauld
Findowie Hill
Meall nan
Ordie
Bankfoot
B9099
Springfield

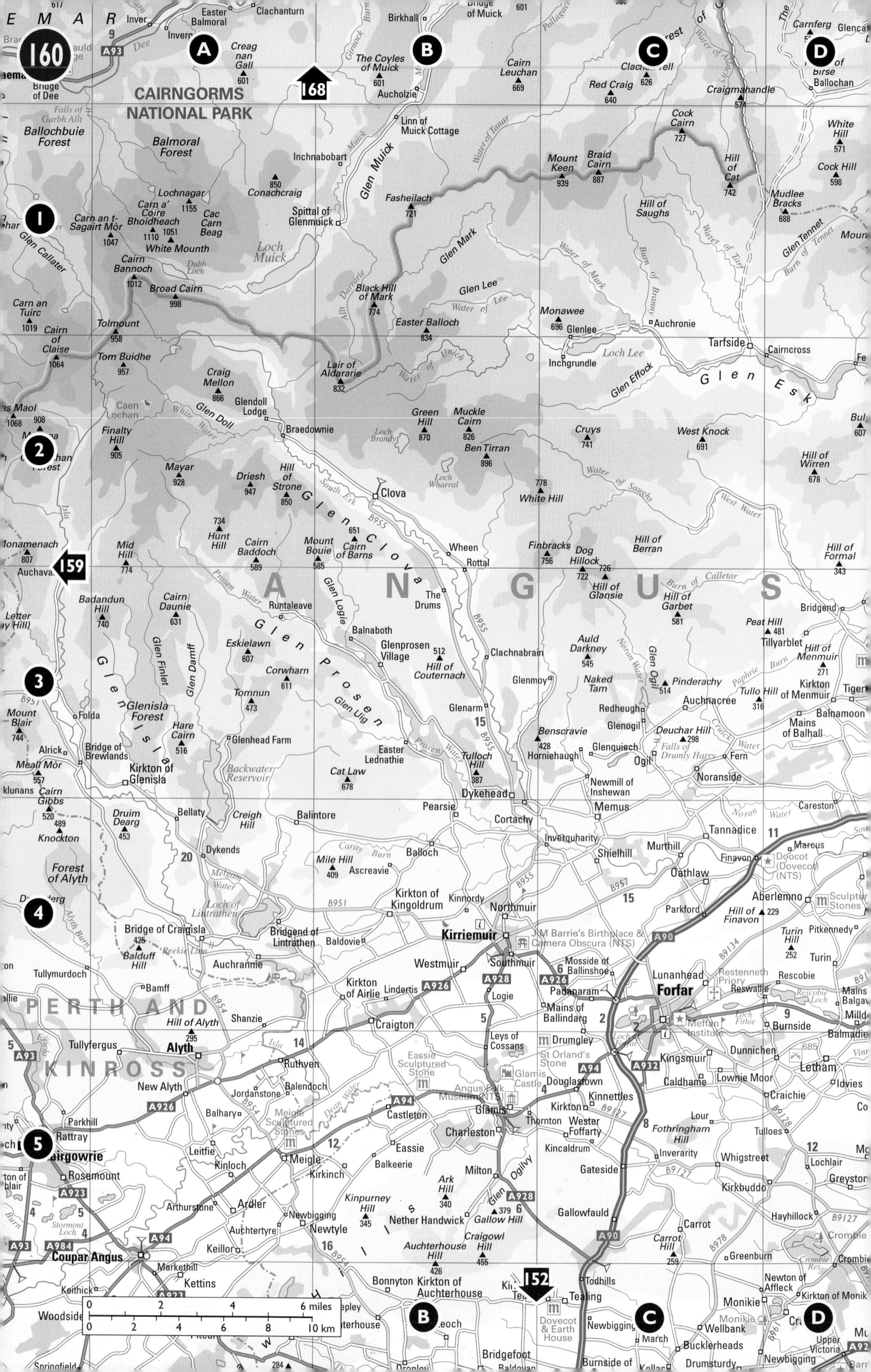

160
168
159
152
A
B
C
D
1
2
3
4
5
CAIRNGORMS
NATIONAL PARK
Ballochbuie
Forest
Balmoral
Forest
Easter
Balmoral
Clachanturn
Inver
Invercauld
Bridge
of Dee
Falls of
Garbh Allt
Creag
nan
Gall
601
Birkhall
Bridge
of Muick
The Coyles
of Muick
601
Aucholzie
Linn of
Muick Cottage
Inchnabobart
Cairn
Leuchan
669
Red Craig
640
Clachan Yell
626
Craigmahandle
574
Carnferg
Hill of
Birse
Ballochan
White
Hill
571
Cock Hill
598
Cock
Cairn
727
Mount
Keen
939
Braid
Cairn
887
Hill
of
Cat
742
Mudlee
Bracks
688
Hill of
Saughs
Glen Tennet
Lochnagar
1155
Conachcraig
850
Carn a'
Coire
Bhoidheach
1110
1051
Carn an t-
Sagairt Mòr
1047
Cac
Carn
Beag
White Mounth
Spittal of
Glenmuick
Glen Muick
Loch
Muick
Dubh
Loch
Fasheilach
721
Glen Mark
Glen Lee
Water of Mark
Water of Lee
Water of Tarf
Water of Tanar
Glen Callater
Cairn
Bannoch
1012
Broad Cairn
998
Carn an
Tuirc
1019
Cairn
of
Claise
1064
Tolmount
958
Tom Buidhe
957
Black Hill
of Mark
774
Easter Balloch
834
Monawee
696
Glenlee
Auchronie
Inchgrundle
Loch Lee
Glen Effock
Tarfside
Cairncross
Glen Esk
Lair of
Aldararie
832
Craig
Mellon
866
Glendoll
Lodge
Glen Doll
White Water
Caen
Lochan
Braedownie
Green
Hill
870
Muckle
Cairn
826
Ben Tirran
896
Loch
Brandy
Loch
Wharral
Cruys
741
West Knock
691
Hill of
Wirren
678
Water of Saughs
West Water
Finalty
Hill
905
Mayar
928
Driesh
947
Hill
of
Strone
850
Clova
South Esk
B955
Glen Clova
Cairn
of Barns
651
Mount
Bouie
585
778
White Hill
Wheen
Rottal
Finbracks
756
Dog
Hillock
722
726
Hill of
Berran
Hill of
Formal
343
734
Hunt
Hill
Cairn
Baddoch
589
Mid
Hill
774
Monamenach
807
Auchavan
ANGUS
Prosen Water
Runtaleave
Glen Logie
The
Drums
Hill of
Glansie
Burn of Calletar
Hill of
Garbet
581
Bridgend
Peat Hill
481
Tillyarblet
Hill of
Menmuir
271
Badandun
Hill
740
Cairn
Daunie
631
Eskielawn
607
Glen Prosen
Balnaboth
Glenprosen
Village
512
Hill of
Couternach
Clachnabrain
Auld
Darkney
545
Noran Water
Glen Ogil
Pinderachy
514
Paphrie Burn
Kirkton
of Menmuir
Tullo Hill
316
Balnamoon
Mains
of Balhall
Glen Finlet
Glen Damff
Glenisla
Glenisla
Forest
Corwharn
611
Tomnun
473
Glen Uig
Glenmoy
Naked
Tam
Auchnacree
Redheugh
Glenogil
Glenarm
15
Benscravie
428
Horniehaugh
Glenquiech
Ogil
Deuchar Hill
298
Falls of
Drumly Harry
Cruick Water
Fern
Noranside
Mount
Blair
744
B951
Folda
Alrick
Meall Mòr
557
Bridge of
Brewlands
Kirkton of
Glenisla
Hare
Cairn
516
Glenhead Farm
Backwater
Reservoir
Easter
Lednathie
Cat Law
678
Tulloch
Hill
387
Newmill of
Inshewan
Dykehead
Cortachy
Memus
Careston
Cairn
Gibbs
520
489
Knockton
Druim
Dearg
453
Bellaty
Creigh
Hill
Balintore
Pearsie
Inverquharity
Tannadice
11
Marcus
Finavon
Doocot
(Dovecot)
(NTS)
Forest
of Alyth
20
Dykends
Carity Burn
Balloch
Mile Hill
409
Ascreavie
Shielhill
Murthill
Oathlaw
Aberlemno
Sculptured
Stones
Melgam Water
B957
15
Parkford
Hill of
Finavon
229
Alyth Burn
Loch of
Lintrathen
B951
Kirkton of
Kingoldrum
Kinnordy
Northmuir
B955
Turin
Hill
252
Pitkennedy
Bridge of Craigisla
425
Balduff
Hill
Reekie Linn
Bridgend of
Lintrathen
Baldovie
Kirriemuir
JM Barrie's Birthplace &
Camera Obscura (NTS)
A90
B9134
Turin
Tullymurdoch
Auchrannie
Westmuir
Southmuir
Mosside of
Ballinshoe
6
Lunanhead
Restenneth
Priory
Rescobie
Bamff
A926
A928
A926
Padanaram
Forfar
Reswallie
Rescobie
Loch
Mains
Balgav
PERTH AND
KINROSS
B954
Kirkton
of Airlie
Lindertis
Logie
Mains of
Ballindarg
2
Loch
Fithie
9
Shanzie
Craigton
5
Meffan
Institute
Burnside
Balmadie
Hill of Alyth
295
Leys of
Cossans
Drumgley
Loch of
Forfar
Dunnichen
685
A93
Tullyfergus
Alyth
14
Ruthven
Eassie
Sculptured
Stone
St Orland's
Stone
A94
A932
Kingsmuir
Letham
Isla
Balendoch
Glamis
Castle
Douglastown
Caldhame
Lownie Moor
Idvies
New Alyth
Jordanstone
A94
Angus Folk
Museum (NTS)
4
Kinnettles
Craichie
A926
B954
Balhary
Meigle
Sculptured
Stones
Dean Water
Castleton
Glamis
Kirkton
B9127
Parkhill
Rattray
Leitfie
12
Eassie
Charleston
Thornton
Wester
Foffarty
8
Lour
Fothringham
Hill
Tulloes
B9128
Blairgowrie
Kinloch
Meigle
Kirkinch
Balkeerie
Milton
Glen Ogilvy
Kincaldrum
Gateside
Inverarity
Whigstreet
12
Lochlair
Greystone
Rosemount
A923
Ark
Hill
340
Kirkbuddo
Arthurstone
Ardler
Newbigging
Kinpurney
Hill
345
Sidlaw Hills
Nether Handwick
379
Gallow Hill
A928
6
Gallowfauld
Hayhillock
B9127
Stormont
Loch
Auchtertyre
Newtyle
Carrot
Crombie
A93
A984
Coupar Angus
A94
Keillor
16
Auchterhouse
Hill
426
Craigowl
Hill
455
A90
Carrot
Hill
259
B978
Greenburn
Crombie
Res.
Markethill
B954
Kettins
A923
Keithick
Bonnyton
Kirkton of
Auchterhouse
Todhills
Tealing
Newton of
Affleck
Monikie
Kirkton of Monikie
Woodside
Leoch
Dovecot
& Earth
House
Newbigging
March
Wellbank
Monikie
B961
Upper
Victoria
Bridgefoot
Buckler heads
Burnside of
Drumsturdy
Newbigging
Springfield
284
0 2 4 6 miles
0 2 4 6 8 10 km

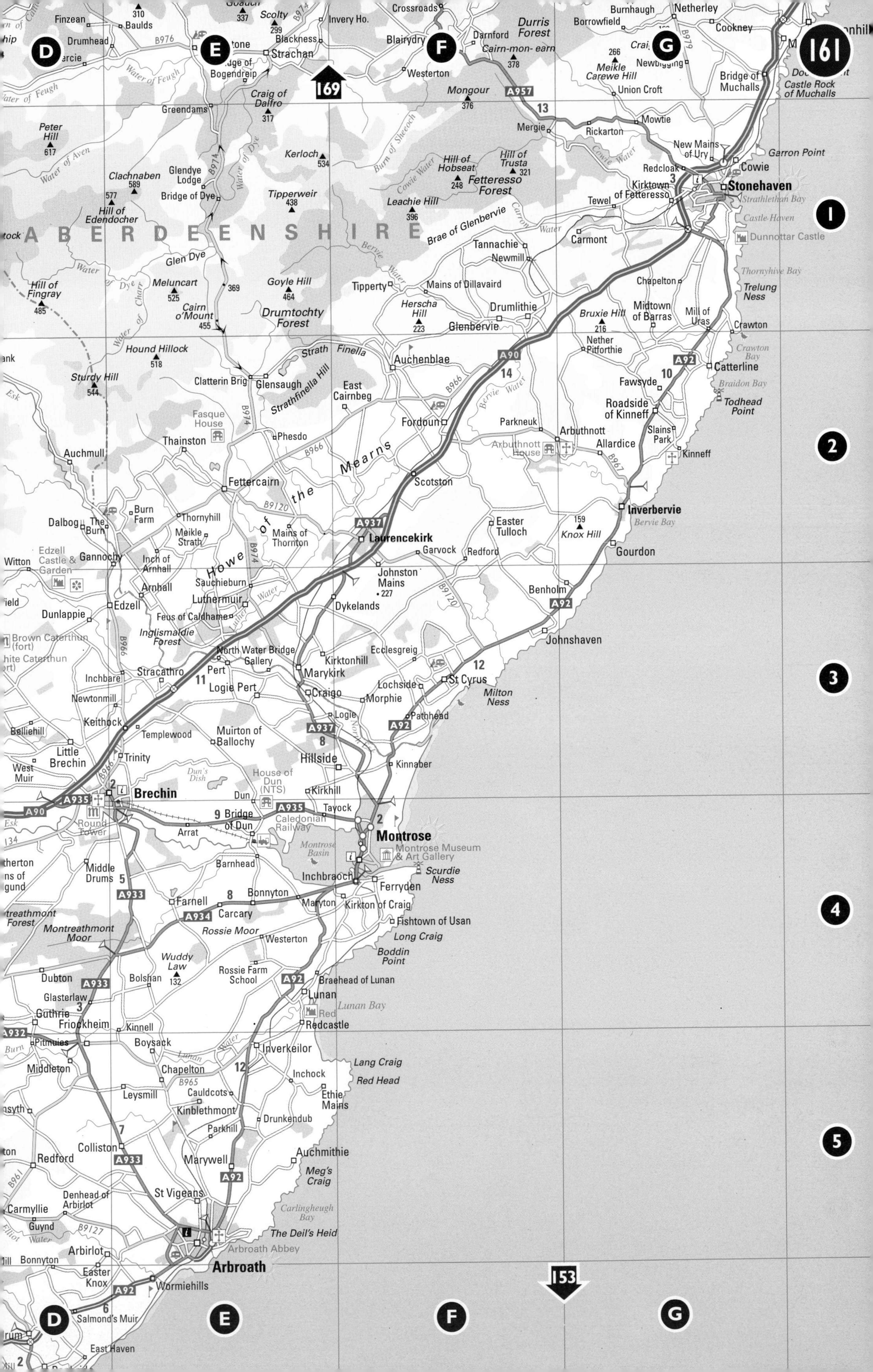
ABERDEENSHIRE
D
E
F
G
169
153
1
2
3
4
5
Finzean
Baulds
310
337
Scolty
299
Invery Ho.
Crossroads
Burnhaugh
Netherley
Borrowfield
Cookney
Drumhead
Strachan
Blackness
Blairydry
Darnford
Durris Forest
Cairn-mon- earn
378
266
Meikle Carewe Hill
Newbigging
Bridge of Muchalls
Castle Rock of Muchalls
Bridge of Bogendreip
Water of Feugh
Westerton
Union Croft
Craig of Dalfro
317
Mongour
376
A957
13
Greendams
Mergie
Rickarton
Mowtie
Peter Hill
617
Water of Aven
Kerloch
534
Burn of Sheeoch
Hill of Hobseat
248
Hill of Trusta
321
Fetteresso Forest
Cowie Water
New Mains of Ury
Garron Point
Cowie
Redcloak
Stonehaven
Strathlethan Bay
Kirktown of Fetteresso
Tewel
Clachnaben
589
Glendye Lodge
Bridge of Dye
577
Hill of Edendocher
Tipperweir
438
Leachie Hill
396
Castle Haven
Dunnottar Castle
Brae of Glenbervie
Carron Water
Carmont
Tannachie
Newmill
Glen Dye
Water of Dye
Hill of Fingray
485
Meluncart
525
369
Goyle Hill
464
Tipperty
Mains of Dillavaird
Chapelton
Thornyhive Bay
Trelung Ness
Cairn o'Mount
455
Drumtochty Forest
Herscha Hill
223
Drumlithie
Glenbervie
Bruxie Hill
216
Midtown of Barras
Mill of Uras
Crawton
Crawton Bay
Nether Pitforthie
Hound Hillock
518
Strath Finella
Auchenblae
A90
14
A92
Catterline
Braidon Bay
Todhead Point
Sturdy Hill
544
Clatterin Brig
Glensaugh
Strathfinella Hill
East Cairnbeg
B966
Fawsyde
10
Roadside of Kinneff
Fordoun
Bervie Water
Parkneuk
Arbuthnott
Arbuthnott House
Allardice
Slains Park
Kinneff
Fasque House
B974
Thainston
Phesdo
Auchmull
Scotston
B967
Fettercairn
Howe of the Mearns
B9120
Inverbervie
Bervie Bay
Burn Farm
Thornyhill
Dalbog
The Burn
Meikle Strath
Mains of Thornton
A937
Laurencekirk
Easter Tulloch
159
Knox Hill
Garvock
Redford
Gourdon
Witton
Edzell Castle & Garden
Gannochy
Inch of Arnhall
Arnhall
Johnston Mains
227
Sauchieburn
Luthermuir
Dykelands
Benholm
Edzell
Dunlappie
Feus of Caldhame
Luther Water
Johnshaven
Brown Caterthun (fort)
White Caterthun
Inglismaldie Forest
North Water Bridge
Gallery
Ecclesgreig
Kirktonhill
B966
Inchbare
Stracathro
Pert
11
Marykirk
12
St Cyrus
Logie Pert
Lochside
Craigo
Morphie
Milton Ness
Newtonmill
Keithock
Templewood
Logie
Pathhead
Belliehill
Muirton of Ballochy
8
Little Brechin
Trinity
Hillside
Kinnaber
West Muir
Dun's Dish
House of Dun (NTS)
Dun
Kirkhill
A935
Brechin
Tayock
2
Round Tower
9
Bridge of Dun
Caledonian Railway
Montrose
Arrat
Montrose Basin
Montrose Museum & Art Gallery
Scurdie Ness
Middle Drums
5
Barnhead
Inchbraoch
Ferryden
A933
Farnell
Bonnyton
Maryton
Kirkton of Craig
Montreathmont Forest
A934
Carcary
Fishtown of Usan
Montreathmont Moor
Rossie Moor
Westerton
Long Craig
Boddin Point
Wuddy Law
132
Rossie Farm School
Dubton
Bolshan
Braehead of Lunan
Glasterlaw
Lunan
Lunan Bay
Guthrie
Friockheim
Red Castle
Redcastle
A932
Kinnell
Pitmuies
Boysack
Lunan Water
Inverkeilor
Middleton
Chapelton
Inchock
Lang Craig
Red Head
B965
Leysmill
Cauldcots
Ethie Mains
Kinblethmont
Drunkendub
Parkhill
7
Colliston
Auchmithie
Redford
Marywell
Meg's Craig
Denhead of Arbirlot
St Vigeans
Carmyllie
Carlingheugh Bay
Guynd
B9127
Elliot Water
The Deil's Heid
Arbirlot
Arbroath Abbey
Bonnyton
Arbroath
Easter Knox
Wormiehills
6
Salmond's Muir
East Haven

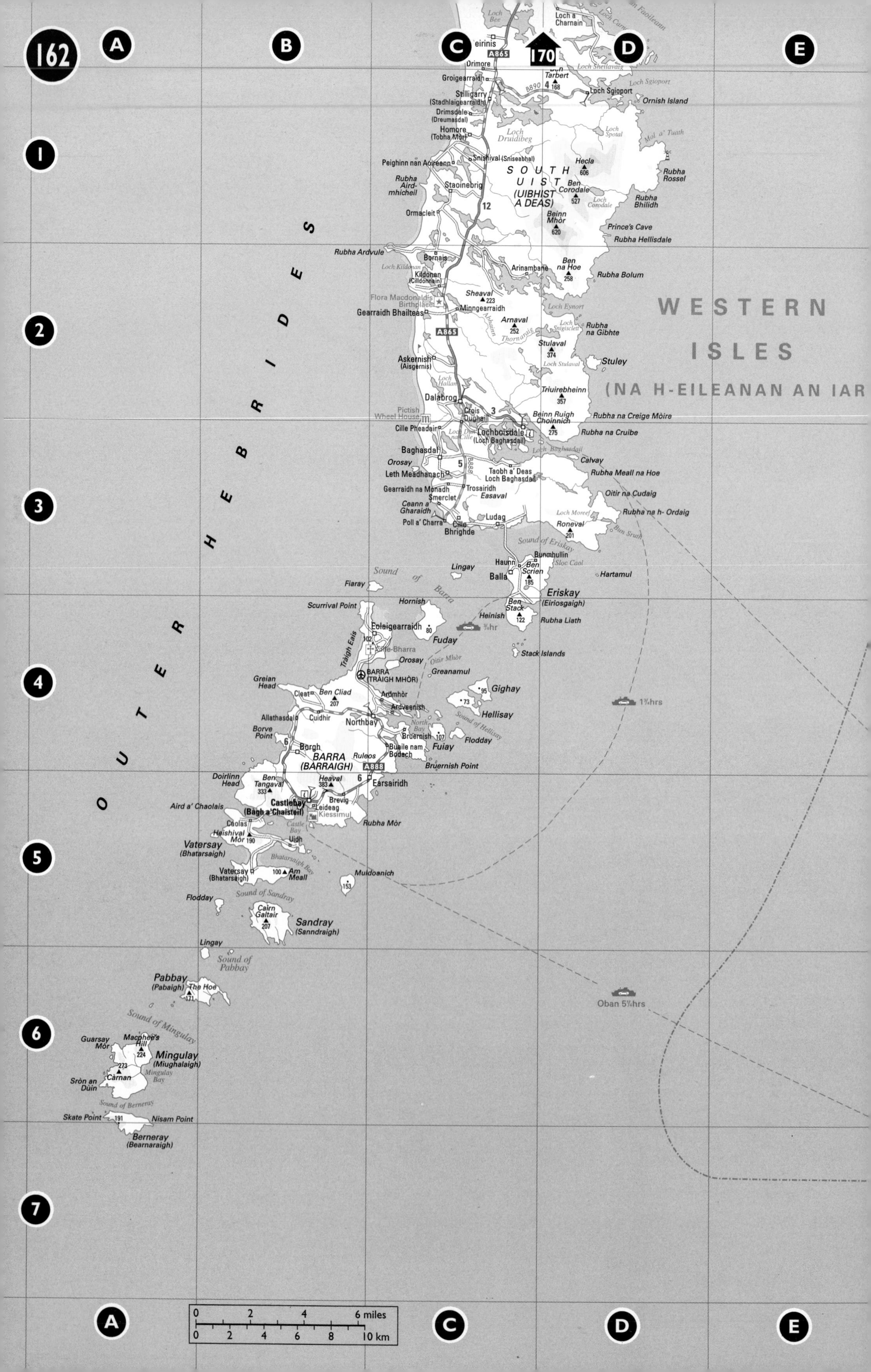

A **B** **C** **D** **E**

1

2

3

4

5

6

7

WESTERN

ISLES

(NA H-EILEANAN AN IAR

OUTER HEBRIDES

SOUTH UIST (UIBHIST A DEAS)

BARRA (TRÀIGH MHÒR)

BARRA (BARRAIGH)

Castlebay (Bàgh a'Chaisteil)

Vatersay (Bhatarsaigh)

Sandray (Sanndraigh)

Pabbay (Pabaigh)

Mingulay (Miughalaigh)

Berneray (Bearnaraigh)

Ceirinis
Drimore
Groigearraidh
Tarbert
Loch Sgioport
Ornish Island
Stilligarry (Stadhlaigearraidh)
Drimsdale (Dreumasdal)
Homore (Tobha Mòr)
Loch Druidibeg
Loch Spotal
Peighinn nan Aoireann
Snishival (Sniseabhal)
Rubha Aird-mhicheil
Staoinebrig
Rubha Rossel
Ben Corodale 527
Hecla 606
Rubha Bhilidh
Loch Corodale
Ormacleit
Prince's Cave
Rubha Hellisdale
12
Rubha Ardvule
Bornais
Arinambane
Ben na Hoe 258
Rubha Bolum
Loch Kildonan
Kildonan (Cildonnain)
Flora Macdonald's Birthplace
Sheaval 223
Gearraidh Bhailteas
Minngearraidh
Arnaval 252
Rubha na Gibhte
Loch Eynort
Askernish (Aisgernis)
Loch Hallan
Stulaval 374
Stuley
Loch Stulaval
Dalabrog
Triuirebheinn 357
Pictish Wheel House
Crois Dùghaill
3
Beinn Ruigh Choinnich 275
Rubha na Creige Mòire
Cille Pheadair
Lochboisdale (Loch Baghasdail)
Rubha na Cruibe
Baghasdal
Calvay
Orosay
5
Taobh a' Deas Loch Baghasdal
Rubha Meall na Hoe
Leth Meadhanach
Trosairidh
Oitir na Cudaig
Gearraidh na Monadh
Smerclet
Easaval
Loch Moreef
Rubha na h-Ordaig
Ceann a' Gharaidh
Ludag
Roneval 201
Poll a' Charra
Cille Bhrighde
Sound of Eriskay
Bunmhullin
Lingay
Haunn
Balla
Ben Scrien 185
Hartamul
Fiaray
Sound of Barra
Eriskay (Eiriosgaigh)
Hornish
Ben Stack 122
Rubha Liath
Scurrival Point
Eolaigearraidh
80
Heinish
¾hr
Traigh Eais
Kille-Bharra
Fuday
Stack Islands
Orosay
Oitir Mhòr
102
Greanamul
Greian Head
BARRA (TRÀIGH MHÒR)
95
Gighay
Cleat
Ben Cliad 207
Ardmhòr
73
Hellisay
Allathasdale
Cuidhir
Ardveenish
North Bay
Sound of Hellisay
1¾hrs
Borve Point
Northbay
Bruernish 107
Floddday
Fuiay
6
Borgh
Buaile nam Bodach
Bruernish Point
Ruleos
Earsairidh
A888
Doirlinn Head
Ben Tangaval 333
Heaval 383
6
Aird a' Chaolais
Brevig
Castlebay (Bàgh a'Chaisteil)
Leideag
Kiessimul
Rubha Mòr
Caolas
Heishival Mòr 190
Uidh
Vatersay (Bhatarsaigh)
Bhatarsaigh Bay
Muldoanich
Vatersay (Bhatarsaigh)
Am Meall 100
153
Floddday
Sound of Sandray
Cairn Galtair 207
Sandray (Sanndraigh)
Lingay
Sound of Pabbay
Pabbay (Pabaigh)
The Hoe 171
Oban 5¾hrs
Sound of Mingulay
Guarsay Mòr
Macphee's Hill 224
Mingulay (Miughalaigh)
Sròn an Dùin
Càrnan 273
Mingulay Bay
Sound of Berneray
Skate Point
Nisam Point 191
Berneray (Bearnaraigh)

A865
B890
4 168
A865
B888
A888

170

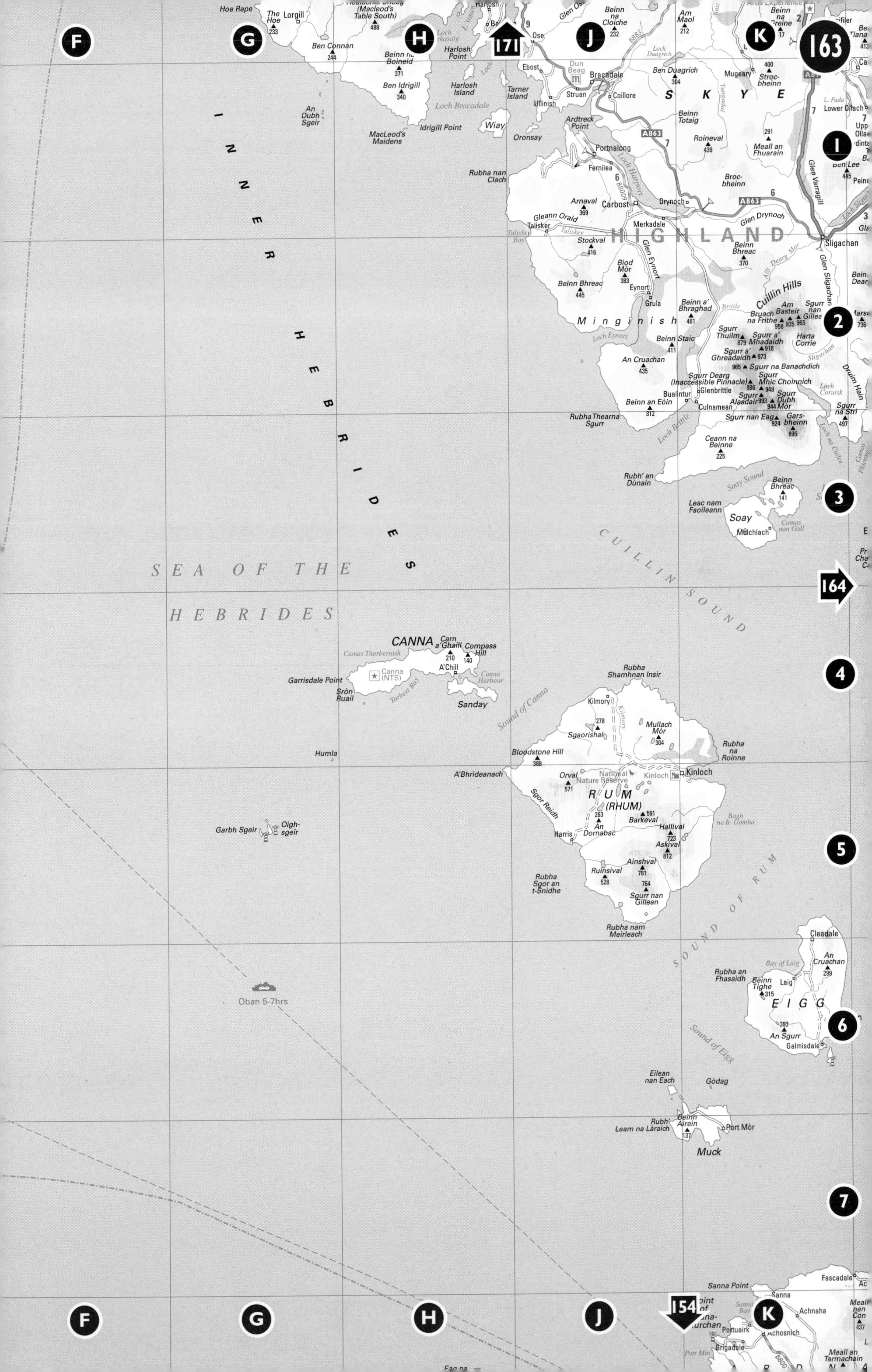
163
171
164
154
SEA OF THE HEBRIDES
INNER HEBRIDES
SKYE
HIGHLAND
Minginish
Cuillin Hills
CULLIN SOUND
SOUND OF RUM
Sound of Canna
Sound of Eigg
CANNA
Sanday
RUM (RHUM)
National Nature Reserve
Kinloch
Soay
EIGG
Muck
Hoe Rape
The Hoe
Lorgill
Ben Connan
Beinn na Boineid
Ben Idrigill
Harlosh Point
Harlosh Island
Tarner Island
Loch Bracadale
Idrigill Point
MacLeod's Maidens
An Dubh Sgeir
Wiay
Oronsay
Rubha nan Clach
Ose
Ebost
Dun Beag
Bracadale
Struan
Coillore
Ullinish
Ardtreck Point
Portnalong
Fernilea
Loch Harport
Carbost
Arnaval
Drynoch
Merkadale
Gleann Oraid
Talisker
Talisker Bay
Stockval
Glen Eynort
Biod Mòr
Beinn Bhreac
Eynort
Grula
Beinn a' Bhraghad
Beinn Staic
An Cruachan
Loch Eynort
Sgurr Dearg (Inaccessible Pinnacle)
Glenbrittle
Bualintur
Beinn an Eòin
Culnamean
Rubha Thearna Sgurr
Loch Brittle
Ceann na Beinne
Rubh' an Dùnain
Soay Sound
Leac nam Faoileann
Mòlchlach
Camas nan Gall
Beinn na Cloiche
Am Maol
Ben Duagrich
Mugeary
Stroc-bheinn
Beinn Totaig
Roineval
Meall an Fhuarain
Broc-bheinn
Glen Drynoch
Glen Varragill
Ben Lee
Lower Ollach
Sligachan
Glen Sligachan
Beinn Bhreac
Sgurr nan Gillean
Am Basteir
Bruach na Frithe
Harta Corrie
Sgurr Thuilm
Sgurr a' Mhadaidh
Sgurr a' Ghreadaidh
Sgurr na Banachdich
Sgurr Mhic Choinnich
Sgurr Alasdair
Sgurr Dubh Mòr
Sgurr nan Eag
Gars-bheinn
Loch Coruisk
Druim Hain
Sgurr na Stri
Loch na Cuilce
Carn a' Ghaill
Compass Hill
A'Chill
Camas Tharbernish
Canna Harbour
Canna (NTS)
Garrisdale Point
Sròn Ruail
Tarbert Bay
Humla
Garbh Sgeir
Oigh-sgeir
Oban 5-7hrs
Rubha Shamhnan Insir
Kilmory
Sgaorishal
Mullach Mòr
Bloodstone Hill
Rubha na Roinne
A'Bhrìdeanach
Orval
Sgor Reidh
An Dornabac
Barkeval
Harris
Hallival
Askival
Bagh na h-Uamha
Ainshval
Ruinsival
Rubha Sgor an t-Snìdhe
Sgurr nan Gillean
Rubha nam Meirleach
Cleadale
An Cruachan
Bay of Laig
Laig
Rubha an Fhasaidh
Beinn Tighe
An Sgurr
Galmisdale
Eilean nan Each
Gòdag
Rubh' Leam na Làraich
Beinn Airein
Port Mòr
Sanna Point
Sanna
Sanna Bay
Achnaha
Achosnich
Portuairk
Brigadale
Port Min
Fascadale
Meall an Tarmachain
A863
B885
B8009
A87
F
G
H
J
K
I
2
3
4
5
6
7

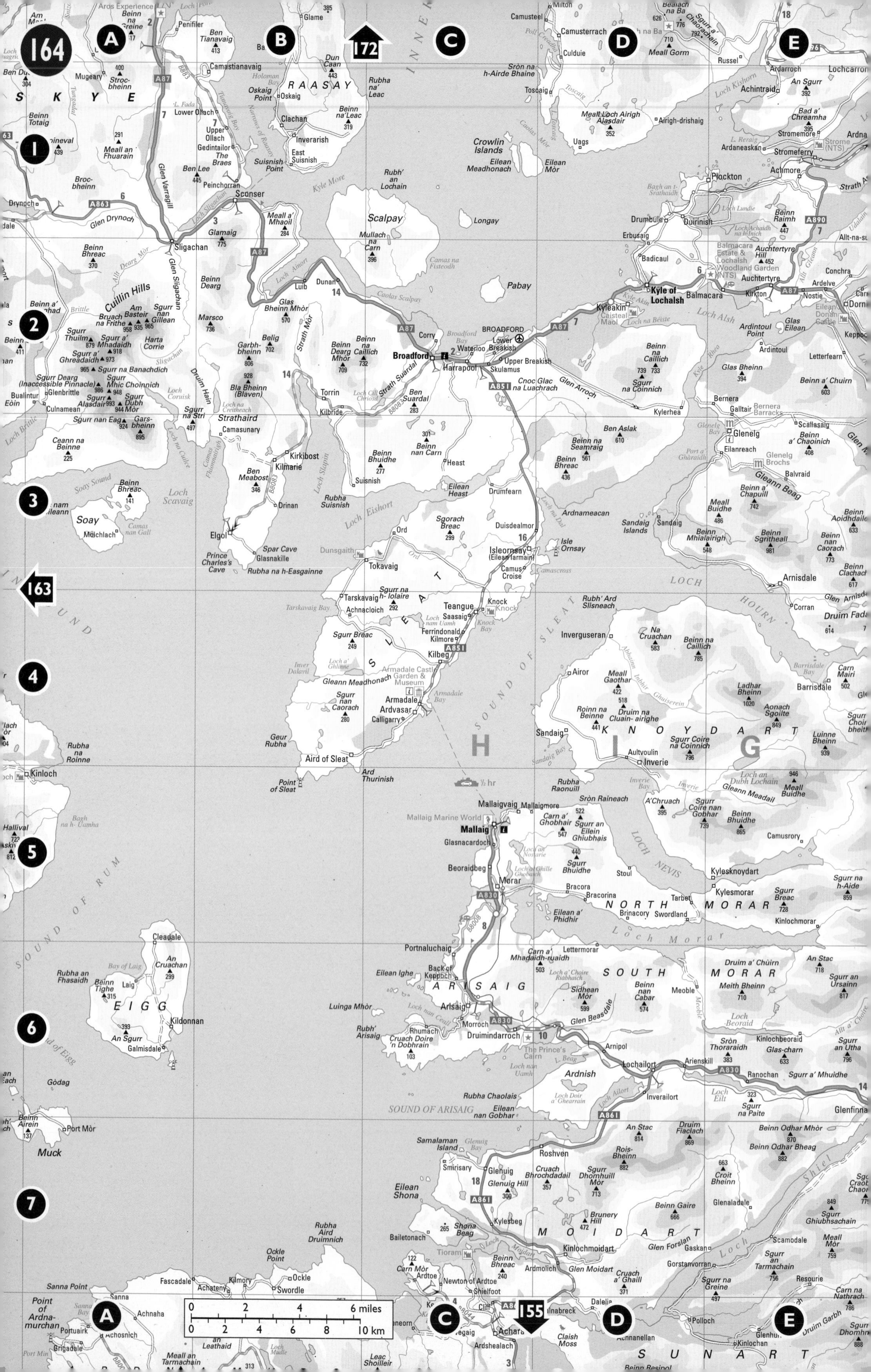

164
A
B
C
D
E
172
163
155
1
2
3
4
5
6
7
SKYE
RAASAY
Scalpay
Pabay
Longay
Crowlin Islands
Soay
EIGG
Muck
SLEAT
KNOYDART
NORTH MORAR
SOUTH MORAR
ARISAIG
MOIDART
SUNART
Cuillin Hills
Sligachan
Sconser
Glen Varragill
Glen Drynoch
Drynoch
Portree
Penifiler
Ben Tianavaig
Camastianavaig
Mugeary
Beinn Totaig
Meall an Fhuarain
Lower Ollach
Upper Ollach
Gedintailor
The Braes
Ben Lee
Peinchorran
Glamaig
Meall a' Mhaoil
Beinn Dearg
Marsco
Glen Sligachan
Beinn Bhreac
Am Basteir
Sgurr nan Gillean
Bruach na Frithe
Harta Corrie
Sgurr Thuilm
Sgurr a' Mhadaidh
Sgurr a' Ghreadaidh
Sgurr na Banachdich
Sgurr Dearg (Inaccessible Pinnacle)
Sgurr Mhic Choinnich
Sgurr Alasdair
Sgurr Dubh Mòr
Sgurr nan Eag
Gars-bheinn
Glenbrittle
Culnamean
Ceann na Beinne
Loch Coruisk
Druim Hain
Sgurr na Stri
Camasunary
Strathaird
Bla Bheinn (Blaven)
Garbh-bheinn
Belig
Glas Bheinn Mhòr
Strath Mòr
Loch Scavaig
Soay Sound
Beinn Bhreac
Mòichlach
Elgol
Ben Meabost
Kilmarie
Kirkibost
Drinan
Glasnakille
Spar Cave
Prince Charles's Cave
Rubha na h-Easgainne
Loch Slapin
Torrin
Kilbride
Beinn Dearg Mhòr
Beinn na Caillich
Ben Suardal
Strath Suardal
Broadford
Harrapool
Waterloo
Corry
Lower Breakish
Upper Breakish
Skulamus
Luib
Dunan
Loch Ainort
Caolas Scalpay
Mullach na Carn
Camas na Fisteodh
Beinn nan Carn
Beinn Bhuidhe
Heast
Suisnish
Rubha Suisnish
Loch Eishort
Eilean Heast
Drumfearn
Duisdealmor
Isleornsay (Eilean Iarmain)
Isle Ornsay
Camus Croise
Camascross
Sgorach Breac
Ord
Dunsgaith
Tokavaig
Tarskavaig
Achnacloich
Sgurr na h-Iolaire
Teangue
Saasaig
Knock
Ferrindonald
Kilmore
Kilbeg
Sgurr Breac
Gleann Meadhonach
Armadale Castle Garden & Museum
Armadale
Ardvasar
Calligarry
Sgurr nan Caorach
Geur Rubha
Aird of Sleat
Point of Sleat
Ard Thurinish
Sound of Sleat
Glame
Dun Caan
Oskaig
Oskaig Point
Holoman Bay
Rubha na' Leac
Beinn na'Leac
Clachan
Inverarish
East Suisnish
Suisnish Point
Narrows of Raasay
Kyle More
Rubh' an Lochain
Eilean Meadhonach
Eilean Mòr
Camusteel
Camusterrach
Culduie
Sròn na h-Airde Bhaine
Toscaig
Meall Loch Airigh Alasdair
Airigh-drishaig
Uags
Meall Gorm
Russel
Ardarroch
Achintraid
Loch Kishorn
An Sgurr
Lochcarron
Bad a' Chreamha
Stromemore
Ardaneaskan
Strome (NTS)
Stromeferry
Achmore
Plockton
Duirinish
Drumbuie
Erbusaig
Badicaul
Beinn Raimh
Auchtertyre Hill
Balmacara Estate & Lochalsh Woodland Garden (NTS)
Auchtertyre
Kyle of Lochalsh
Kyleakin
Caisteal Maol
Balmacara
Kirkton
Nostie
Ardelve
Conchra
Eilean Donan Castle
Dornie
Loch Alsh
Ardintoul Point
Ardintoul
Glas Eilean
Letterfearn
Beinn na Caillich
Sgurr na Coinnich
Cnoc Glac na Luachrach
Glen Arroch
Kylerhea
Glas Bheinn
Beinn a' Chuirn
Bernera
Galltair
Bernera Barracks
Glenelg
Glenelg Bay
Eilanreach
Glenelg Brochs
Scallasaig
Beinn a' Chaoinich
Balvraid
Gleann Beag
Ben Aslak
Beinn na Seamraig
Beinn Bhreac
Ardnameacan
Sandaig Islands
Sandaig
Meall Buidhe
Beinn a' Chapuill
Beinn Mhialairigh
Beinn Sgritheall
Beinn nan Caorach
Beinn Aoidhdailean
Arnisdale
Corran
Beinn Clachach
Loch Hourn
Druim Fada
Rubh' Ard Slisneach
Inverguseran
Na Cruachan
Beinn na Caillich
Barrisdale Bay
Barrisdale
Carn Mairi
Airor
Meall Gaothar
Druim na Cluain-airighe
Ladhar Bheinn
Aonach Sgoilte
Roinn na Beinne
Sandaig
Sgurr Coire na Coinnich
Aultvoulin
Inverie
Inverie Bay
Luinne Bheinn
Loch an Dubh Lochain
Gleann Meadail
Meall Buidhe
Rubha Raonuill
Sròn Raineach
A'Chruach
Sgurr Coire nan Gobhar
Beinn Bhuidhe
Camusrory
Mallaigvaig
Mallaigmore
Mallaig Marine World
Mallaig
Glasnacardoch
Carn a' Ghobhair
Sgurr an Eilein Ghiubhais
Sgurr Bhuidhe
Stoul
Loch Nevis
Kylesknoydart
Kylesmorar
Beoraidbeg
Morar
Bracora
Bracorina
Brinacory
Swordland
Tarbet
Sgurr Breac
Kinlochmorar
Sgurr na h-Aide
Eilean a' Phidhir
Loch Morar
Portnaluchaig
Lettermorar
Carn a' Mhadaidh-ruaidh
Druim a' Chùirn
An Stac
Meith Bheinn
Sgurr an Ursainn
Eilean Ighe
Back of Keppoch
Arisaig
Sidhean Mòr
Beinn nan Cabar
Meoble
Loch Beoraid
Luinga Mhòr
Rubh' Arisaig
Rhumach
Cruach Doire 'n Dobhrain
Morroch
Druimindarroch
The Prince's Cairn
Loch nan Uamh
Glen Beasdale
Arnipol
Sròn Thoraraidh
Kinlochbeoraid
Glas-charn
Sgurr an Utha
Lochailort
Arienskill
Ranochan
Sgurr a' Mhuidhe
Ardnish
Inverailort
Loch Eilt
Sgurr na Paite
Glenfinnan
Rubha Chaolais
Eilean nan Gobhar
Sound of Arisaig
Loch Ailort
An Stac
Druim Fiaclach
Beinn Odhar Mhòr
Beinn Odhar Bheag
Samalaman Island
Glenuig Bay
Roshven
Rois-Bheinn
Smirisary
Glenuig
Glenuig Hill
Cruach Bhrochdadail
Sgurr Dhomhnuill Mòr
Croit Bheinn
Eilean Shona
Brunery Hill
Beinn Gaire
Glenaladale
Loch Shiel
Shona Beag
Bailetonach
Tioram
Beinn Bhreac
Kylesbeg
Kinlochmoidart
Glen Forslan
Gaskan
Scamodale
Gorstanvorran
Meall Mòr
Carn Mòr
Ardtoe
Newton of Ardtoe
Shielfoot
Ardmolich
Glen Moidart
Cruach a' Ghaill
Sgurr an Tarmachain
Resourie
Sgurr na Greine
Carn na Nathrach
Acharacle
Ardshealach
Dalelia
Claish Moss
Acharacle
Polloch
Glenhurich
Kinlochan
Druim Garbh
Rubha Aird Druimnich
Ockle Point
Ockle
Swordle
Kilmory
Achateny
Fascadale
Sanna Point
Sanna
Achnaha
Point of Ardnamurchan
Portuairk
Achosnich
Brigadale
Meall an Tarmachain
Leac Shoilleir
Sound of Rum
Cleadale
Bay of Laig
An Cruachan
Rubha an Fhasaidh
Beinn Tighe
Laig
Kildonnan
An Sgurr
Galmisdale
Gòdag
Beinn Airein
Port Mòr
Kinloch
Hallival
Rubha na Roinne
Bagh na h-Uamha
A87
A863
A851
A890
A830
A861
B883
B8083
B8008
0 2 4 6 miles
0 2 4 6 8 10 km
½ hr

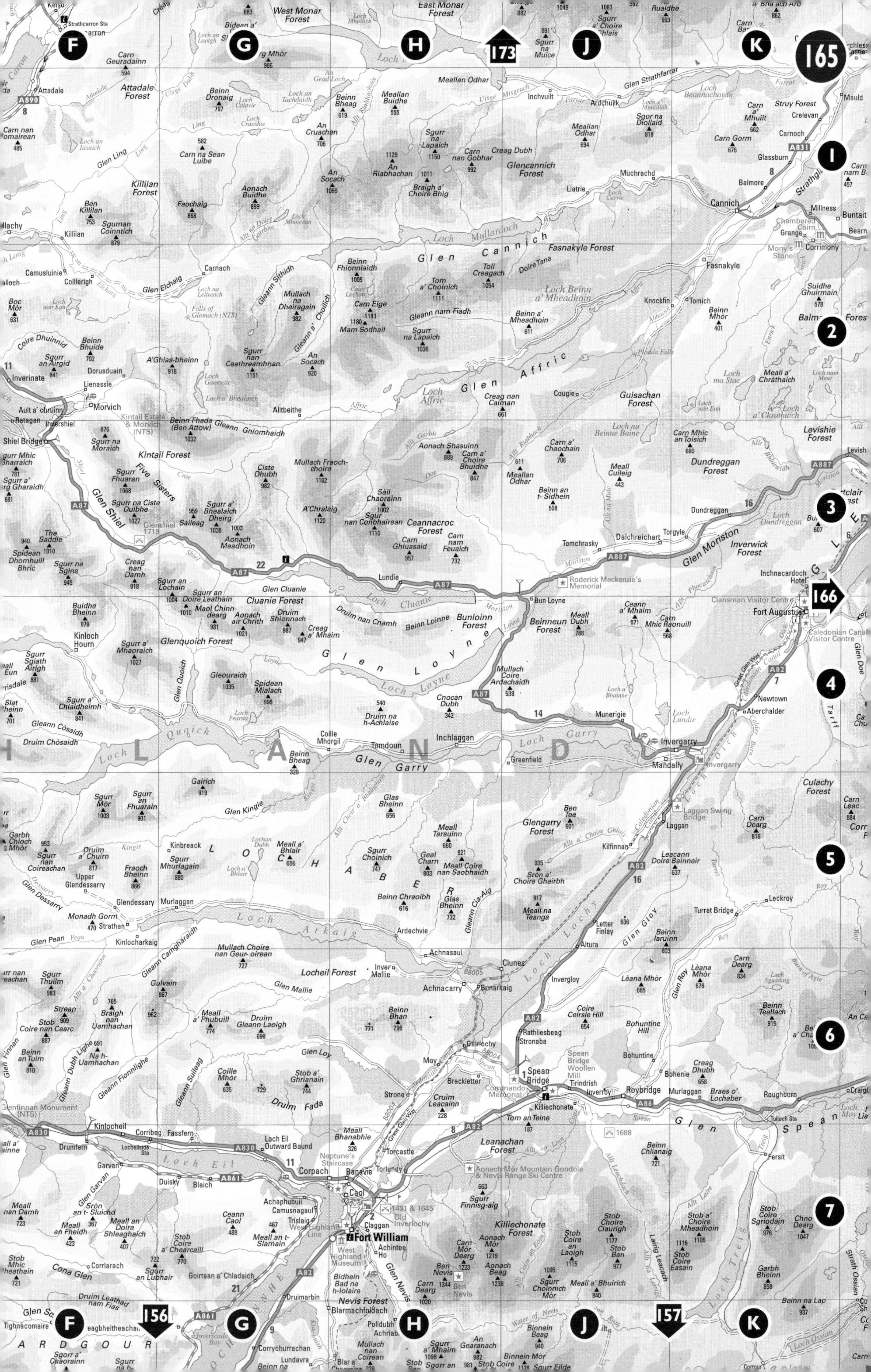
165
F
G
H
J
K
173
166
156
157
I
2
3
4
5
6
7
West Monar Forest
East Monar Forest
Loch Monar
Strathcarron Sta
Carn Geuradainn
594
Attadale
Attadale Forest
A890
Beinn Dronaig
797
Loch Calavie
Loch an Tachdaidh
An Gead Loch
Beinn Bheag
619
Meallan Buidhe
555
Meallan Odhar
Glen Strathfarrar
Inchvuilt
Ardchuilk
Loch Beannacharan
Struy Forest
Mauld
Erchless Castle
Crelevan
Carn a' Mhuilt
662
Carnoch
Sgor na Diollaid
818
Meallan Odhar
694
Carn Gorm
676
Glassburn
A831
Carn nan Gobhar
992
Creag Dubh
Sgurr na Lapaich
1150
An Cruachan
706
An Riabhachan
1129
Braigh a' Choire Bhig
1011
An Socach
1069
Glencannich Forest
Muchrachd
Liatrie
Loch Carrie
Cannich
Balmore
Strathglass
Millness
Buntait
Chambered Cairn
Grange
Corrimony
Mony's Stone
Carn nan Oumairean
485
Loch an Iasaich
Glen Ling
Carn na Sean Luibe
582
Killilan Forest
Faochaig
868
Aonach Buidhe
899
Ben Killilan
753
Sguman Coinntich
879
Killilan
Loch Mullardoch
Glen Cannich
Fasnakyle Forest
Fasnakyle
Beinn Fhionnlaidh
1005
Toll Creagach
1054
Tom a' Choinich
1111
Doire Tana
Loch Beinn a' Mheadhoin
Camusluinie
Coillerigh
Carnach
Glen Elchaig
Gleann Sithidh
Mullach na Dheiragain
982
Carn Eige
1183
Mam Sodhail
1180
Gleann nam Fiadh
Sgurr na Lapaich
1036
Beinn a' Mheadhoin
611
Knockfin
Tomich
Beinn Mhòr
401
Suidhe Ghuirmain
578
Boc Mòr
631
Falls of Glomach (NTS)
Loch Lochrach
Beinn Bhuide
702
Dorusduain
A' Ghlas-bheinn
918
Sgurr nan Ceathreamhnan
1151
An Socach
920
Plodda Falls
Loch ma Stac
Meall a' Chràthaich
Sgurr an Airgid
841
Inverinate
Lienassie
Morvich
Loch Gaorsaic
Loch a' Bhealaich
Glen Affric
Loch Affric
Cougie
Guisachan Forest
Ault a' chruinn
Ratagan
Invershiel
Kintail Estate & Morvich (NTS)
Beinn Fhada (Ben Attow)
1032
Gleann Gniomhaidh
Alltbeithe
Creag nan Caiman
661
Loch na Beinne Baine
Carn Mhic an Toisich
680
Levishie Forest
Shiel Bridge
876
Sgurr na Moraich
Kintail Forest
Five Sisters
Aonach Shasuinn
889
Carn a' Choire Bhuidhe
847
Carn a' Chaochain
706
Meallan Odhar
611
Meall Cuileig
443
Dundreggan Forest
Levish
A887
Sgurr Fhuaran
1068
Ciste Dhubh
982
Mullach Fraoch-choire
1102
Beinn an t- Sidhein
508
Glen Shiel
A87
Sgurr na Ciste Duibhe
1027
Glenshiel 1719
Saileag
959
Sgurr a' Bhealaich Dheirg
1038
Aonach Meadhoin
1003
Sàil Chaorainn
1002
A' Chralaig
1120
Sgurr nan Conbhairean
1110
Ceannacroc Forest
Carn Ghluasaid
957
Carn nam Feuaich
732
Tomchrasky
Dalchreichart
Torgyle
Dundreggan
Loch Dundreggan
Glen Moriston
Inverwick Forest
The Saddle
1010
Spidean Dhomhuill Bhric
940
Sgurr na Sgine
945
Creag nan Damh
918
Sgurr an Lochain
1004
Sgurr an Doire Leathain
1010
Glen Cluanie
Lundie
Loch Cluanie
Roderick Mackenzie's Memorial
Inchnacardoch Hotel
Clansman Visitor Centre
Fort Augustus
Caledonian Canal Visitor Centre
Bun Loyne
Buidhe Bheinn
879
Maol Chinn-dearg
981
Aonach air Chrith
1021
Cluanie Forest
Druim Shionnach
987
Creag a' Mhaim
947
Druim nan Cnamh
Beinn Loinne
Bunloinn Forest
Beinneun Forest
Meall Dubh
788
Ceann a' Mhaim
671
Carn Mhic Raonuill
568
Kinloch Hourn
Sgurr a' Mhaoraich
1027
Glenquoich Forest
Glen Loyne
Loch Loyne
Mullach Coire Ardachaidh
539
Gleouraich
1035
Spidean Mialach
996
Glen Quoich
Loch Fearna
Cnocan Dubh
342
Druim na h-Achlaise
540
Muneragie
Loch Lundie
Great Glen Way
Caledonian Canal
A82
Newtown
Aberchalder
Glen Doe
Sgurr Sgiath Airigh
881
Sgurr a' Chlaidheimh
841
Gleann Còsaidh
Druim Chòsaidh
Loch Quoich
Coille Mhorgil
Tomdoun
Inchlaggan
Loch Garry
Invergarry
Mandally
Greenfield
Beinn Bheag
329
Glen Garry
Gairich
919
Glen Kingie
Sgurr Mòr
1003
Sgurr an Fhuarain
901
Glas Bheinn
656
Ben Tee
901
Glengarry Forest
Laggan Swing Bridge
Laggan
Culachy Forest
Carn Dearg
816
Garbh Chioch Mhòr
953
Sgurr nan Coireachan
Druim a' Chuirn
817
Fraoch Bheinn
866
Upper Glendessarry
Kinbreack
Sgurr Mhurlagain
880
Meall a' Bhlair
656
Sgurr Choinich
747
Meall Tarsuinn
660
Geal Charn
803
Meall Coire nan Saobhaidh
821
Srón a' Choire Ghairbh
935
Kilfinnan
Leacann Doire Bainneir
637
Glen Dessarry
Glendessary
Murlaggan
Monadh Gorm
470
Strathan
Beinn Chraoibh
616
Glas Bheinn
732
Meall na Teanga
917
Letter Finlay
Glen Gloy
Turret Bridge
Leckroy
Glen Pean
Kinlocharkaig
Loch Arkaig
Ardechvie
Achnasaul
Altura
Beinn Iaruinn
803
Glen Roy
Carn Dearg
834
Lèana Mhòr
676
Mullach Choire nan Geur-oirean
727
Locheil Forest
Inver Mallie
Clunes
Glen Mallie
Achnacarry
Bunarkaig
B8005
Invergloy
Lèana Mhòr
685
Sgurr Thuilm
963
Gulvain
987
Braigh nan Uamhachan
765
Streap
909
Stob Coire nan Cearc
887
Meall a' Phubuill
774
Druim Gleann Laoigh
698
Beinn Bhan
796
Coire Ceirsle Hill
654
Bohuntine Hill
Beinn Teallach
915
Glen Finnan
Beinn an Tuim
810
Gleann Dubh Lighe
Na h-Uamhachan
691
Gleann Fionnlighe
Glen Loy
Rathliesbeag
Stronaba
Gairlochy
B8004
Spean Bridge
Spean Bridge Woollen Mill
Tirindrish
Bohuntine
Creag Dhubh
658
Coille Mhòr
635
Stob a' Ghrianain
744
Druim Fada
Moy
Brackletter
Commando Memorial
Inverroy
Roybridge
Murlaggan
Braes o' Lochaber
Roughburn
Glenfinnan Monument (NTS)
Kinlocheil
A830
Corribeg
Fassfern
Strone
Cruim Leacainn
228
Killiechonate
Tom an Teine
187
A86
Tulloch Sta
Glen Spean
Drumfern
Lochailside Sta
Loch Eil
Loch Eil Outward Bound
Meall Bhanabhie
326
Torcastle
Leanachan Forest
1688
Beinn Chlianaig
721
Fersit
Garvan
A861
Corpach
Banavie
Neptune's Staircase
Tomonie
Aonach Mòr Mountain Gondola & Nevis Range Ski Centre
Glen Garvan
Duisky
Blaich
Caol
Achaphubuil
Camusnagaul
1431 & 1645
Old Inverlochy
Sgurr Finnisg-aig
663
Meall nan Damh
723
Srón an t- Sluichd
Meall an Fheidh
423
Meall an Doire Shleaghaich
407
Ceann Caol
488
Trislaig
West Highland Line
Meall an t- Slamain
467
Claggan
Fort William
West Highland Museum
Achintee
Killiechonate Forest
Aonach Mòr
1219
Carn Mòr Dearg
1223
Stob Coire Claurigh
1177
Stob Coire an Laoigh
1115
Stob Ban
977
Stob a' Choire Mheadhoin
1106
Stob Coire Easain
1116
Stob Coire Sgriodain
976
Chno Dearg
1047
Stob Choire a' Chearcaill
770
Sgurr an Lubhair
722
Corrlarach
Cona Glen
Goirtean a' Chladaich
Ben Nevis
1344
Aonach Beag
1238
Carn Dearg
1020
Sgurr Choinnich Mòr
1095
Meall a' Bhuiridh
840
Lairig Leacach
Loch Treig
Garbh Bheinn
858
Strath Ossian
Stob Mhic Mhartuin
721
Druim Leathad nam Fias
Druimarbin
Bidhein Bad na h-Iolaire
Nevis Forest
Glen Nevis
Blarmachfoldach
Beinn na Lap
937
Glen Scaddle
Tighnacomaire
A861
Inverscadale Bay
Corrychurrachan
Polldubh
Achriabhach
Water of Nevis
Binnein Beag
940
Loch Ossian
Corrour
Ardgour
Sgorr a' Chaorainn
Lundavra
Mullach nan Coirean
Sgurr a' Mhaim
1098
An Gearanach
982
Binnein Mòr
Stob Coire
Sgurr Eilde
Glen Sgurr
Sgorr an

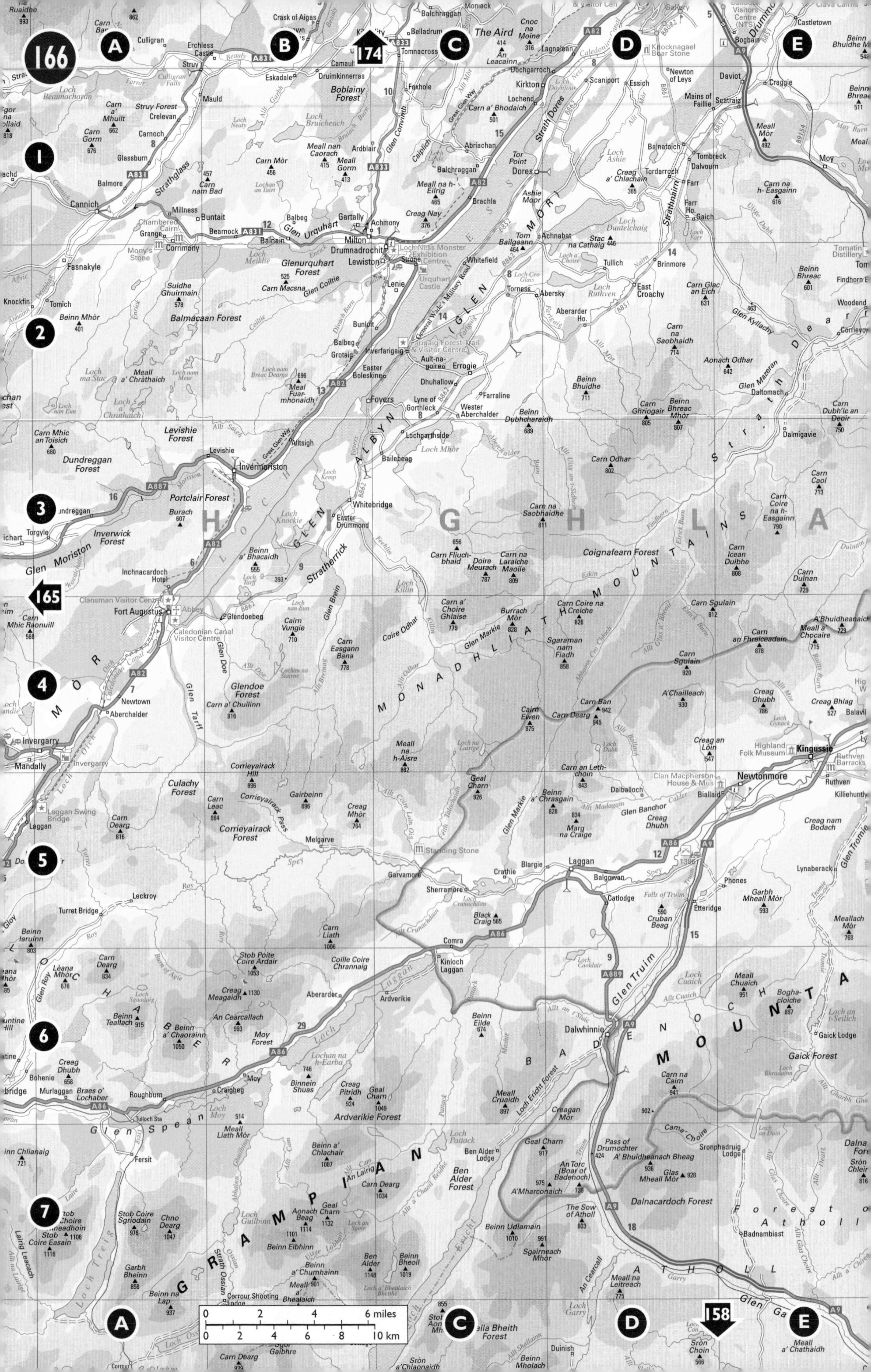

166
A
B
C
D
E
174
165
158
1
2
3
4
5
6
7
Culligran
Erchless Castle
Struy
Crask of Aigas
Kiltarlity
Belladrum
Balchraggan
Moniack
The Aird
Cnoc na Moine
316
414
An Leacainn
Lagnalean
Knocknagael Boar Stone
Castletown
Bogbain
Clava Cairns
Loch Beannacharan
Struy Forest
Crelevan
Carn a' Mhuilt
662
Carnoch
Carn Gorm
676
Glassburn
Mauld
Eskadale
Camault
Druimkinnerras
Tomnacross
Boblainy Forest
Foxhole
Dochgarroch
Kirkton
Lochend
Scaniport
Essich
Newton of Leys
Daviot
Craggie
Mains of Faillie
Scatraig
Carn a' Bhodaich
501
Strath Dores
Loch Bruicheach
Meall nan Caorach
415
Ardblair
Glen Convinth
Meall Gorm
413
Carn Mòr
456
Caiplich
Abriachan
Balchraggan
Tor Point
Dores
Loch Ashie
Creag a' Chlachain
365
Balnafoich
Tombreck
Tordarroch
Dalvourn
Farr
Meall Mòr
492
Moy
Carn na h-Easgainn
616
Cannich
Balmore
Strathglass
Carn nam Bad
457
Millness
Buntait
Chambered Cairn
Grange
Corrimony
Mony's Stone
Bearnock
Balbeg
Balnain
Glen Urquhart
Gartally
Achmony
Milton
Drumnadrochit
Loch Ness Monster Exhibition Centre
Lewiston
Strone
Urquhart Castle
Lenie
Meall na h-Eilrig
465
Creag Nay
376
Brachla
Ashie Moor
Tom Bailgeann
464
Achnabat
Stac na Cathaig
446
Loch Duntelchaig
Strathnairn
Gaich
Farr Ho.
Tomatin Distillery
Fasnakyle
Glenurquhart Forest
Carn Macsna
525
Glen Coiltie
Whitefield
Loch Ceo Glais
Tullich
Brinmore
Loch Ruthven
East Croachy
Beinn Bhreac
601
Findhorn Bridge
Woodend
Knockfin
Tomich
Suidhe Ghuirmain
578
Balmacaan Forest
Beinn Mhòr
401
Torness
Abersky
Aberarder Ho.
Carn Glac an Eich
631
Glen Kyllachy
Carn na Saobhaidh
714
General Wade's Military Road
Great Glen Way
Bunloit
Balbeg
Grotaig
Inverfarigaig
Farigaig Forest Trail & Visitor Centre
Ault-na-goire
Errogie
Aonach Odhar
642
Glen Mazeran
Daltomach
Loch ma Stac
Meall a' Chràthaich
Meall Fuar-mhonaidh
696
Easter Boleskine
Dhuhallow
Foyers
Lyne of Gorthleck
Wester Aberchalder
Farraline
Beinn Bhuidhe
711
Carn Ghriogair
805
Beinn Bhreac Mhòr
807
Carn Dubh'Ic an Deoir
750
Loch a' Chrathaich
Beinn Dubhcharaidh
689
Carn Mhic an Toisich
680
Levishie Forest
Dundreggan Forest
Levishie
Alltsigh
Lochgarthside
Loch Mhòr
Bailebeag
Dalmigavie
Invermoriston
Carn Odhar
802
Carn Caol
713
A887
A82
A831
A833
A86
A889
A9
B862
B851
B8082
Portclair Forest
Burach
607
Dundreggan
Torgyle
Whitebridge
Easter Drummond
Carn na Saobhaidhe
811
Carn Coire na h-Easgainn
790
HIGHLAND
Inverwick Forest
Glen Moriston
Beinn a' Bhacaidh
555
Stratherrick
Carn Fliuch-bhaid
656
Doire Meurach
787
Carn na Laraiche Maoile
809
Coignafearn Forest
Carn Icean Duibhe
808
Carn Dulnan
729
Inchnacardoch Hotel
Loch Killin
Clansman Visitor Centre
Fort Augustus
Abbey
Glendoebeg
Caledonian Canal Visitor Centre
Cairn Vungie
710
Carn a' Choire Ghlaise
779
Burrach Mòr
828
Carn Coire na Creiche
826
Carn Sgulain
812
A'Bhuidheanaich
729
Carn Mhic Raonuill
568
Glen Brein
Coire Odhar
Glen Markie
Sgaraman nam Fiadh
858
Carn an Fhreiceadain
878
Meall a' Chocaire
715
Carn Easgann Bana
778
Carn Sgulain
920
MONADHLIATH MOUNTAINS
Glen Doe
Glendoe Forest
Carn a' Chuilinn
816
Newtown
Aberchalder
Glen Tarff
A'Chailleach
930
Creag Dhubh
786
Creag Bhlag
527
Balavil
Carn Ban
942
Carn Dearg
945
Cairn Ewen
875
Invergarry
Mandally
Meall na h-Aisre
862
Creag an Loin
547
Highland Folk Museum
Kingussie
Ruthven Barracks
Ruthven
Corrieyairack Hill
896
Gairbeinn
896
Geal Charn
926
Carn an Leth-choin
843
Clan Macpherson House & Mus
Newtonmore
Biallaid
Dalballoch
Killiehuntly
Culachy Forest
Carn Leac
884
Corrieyairack Pass
Corrieyairack Forest
Creag Mhòr
764
Beinn a' Chrasgain
828
834
Marg na Craige
Glen Banchor
Creag Dhubh
Creag nam Bodach
Laggan Swing Bridge
Laggan
Carn Dearg
816
Melgarve
Standing Stone
Blargie
Laggan
Crathie
Balgowan
Lynaberack
Glen Tromie
Garvamore
Sherramore
Catlodge
Falls of Truim
Phones
Etteridge
Garbh Mheall Mòr
593
Leckroy
Turret Bridge
Black Craig
565
Cruban Beag
590
Meallach Mòr
768
Beinn Iaruinn
803
Carn Liath
1006
Comra
Kinloch Laggan
Stob Poite Coire Ardair
1053
Coille Coire Chrannaig
Carn Dearg
834
Glen Roy
Glen Truim
Loch Cuaich
Meall Chuaich
951
Bogha-cloiche
897
Creag Meagaidh
1130
Aberarder
Ardverikie
An Cearcallach
993
Beinn Eilde
674
Dalwhinnie
Beinn Teallach
915
Beinn a' Chaorainn
1050
Moy Forest
Gaick Lodge
Gaick Forest
BADENOCH
MOUNTAINS
Creag Dhubh
658
Bohenie
Murlaggan
Braes o' Lochaber
Roughburn
Craigbeg
Moy
Binnein Shuas
746
Lochan na h-Earba
Creag Pitridh
924
Geal Charn
1049
Ardverikie Forest
Meall Cruaidh
897
Loch Ericht Forest
Creagan Mor
Carn na Caim
941
902
Glen Spean
Tulloch Sta
Loch Moy
514
Meall Liath Mòr
Fersit
Beinn a' Chlachair
1087
Loch Pattack
Ben Alder Lodge
Ben Alder Forest
Geal Charn
917
Pass of Drumochter
A' Bhuidheanach Bheag
936
Glas Mheall Mòr
928
Sronphadruig Lodge
An Lairig
Carn Dearg
1034
An Torc (Boar of Badenoch)
739
975
A'Mharconaich
Dalnacardoch Forest
Forest of Atholl
Stob Coire Sgriodain
976
Chno Dearg
1047
Aonach Beag
1114
Geal Charn
1132
Beinn Eibhinn
1101
Loch Gulbinn
Beinn Udlamain
1010
The Sow of Atholl
803
Badnambiast
Stob Coire Easain
1116
1106
Garbh Bheinn
858
Beinn a' Chumhainn
901
Ben Alder
1148
Beinn Bheoil
1019
991
Sgairneach Mhòr
Meall na Leitreach
775
ATHOLL
GRAMPIAN
Strath Ossian
Meall a' Bhealaich
Beinn na Lap
937
Corrour Shooting Lodge
Loch Ossian
855
Talla Bheith Forest
Loch Garry
Glen Garry
Sròn a' Chlaonaidh
Duinish
Beinn Mholach
Meall a' Chathaidh
Carn Dearg
939
Corrour
Loch Treig
Lairig Leacach
0
2
4
6 miles
0
2
4
6
8
10 km

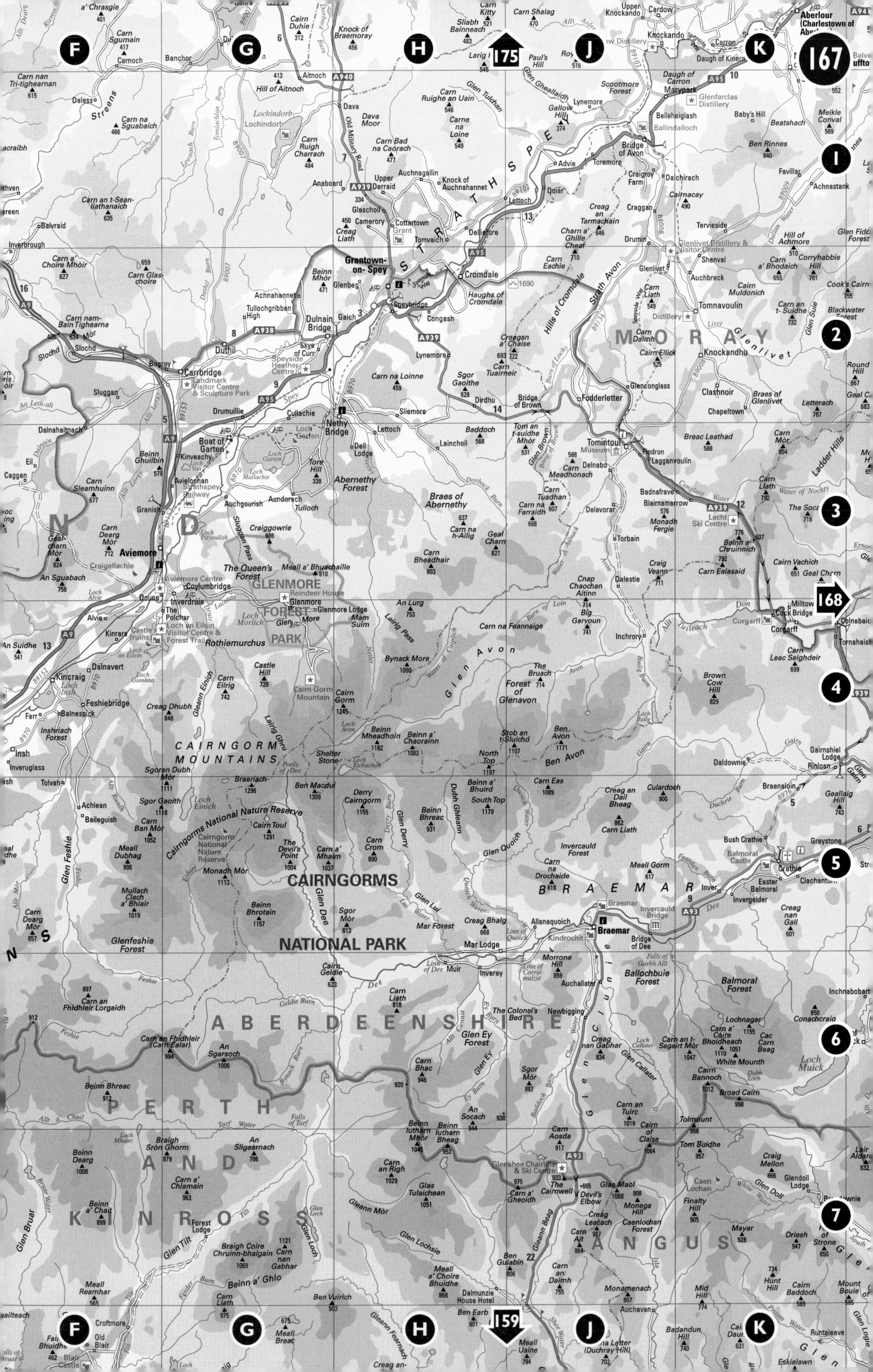
167
175
168
159
F
G
H
J
K
I
2
3
4
5
6
7
Aberlour (Charlestown of Aberlour)
Knock of Braemoray
Carn Kitty
Sliabh Bainneach
Carn Shalag
Upper Knockando
Cardow
Knockando
Carron
Daugh of Kinermony
a' Chrasgie
Carn Sgumain
Carnoch
Banchor
Carn Duhie
Aitnoch
Hill of Aitnoch
Larig Hill
Paul's Hill
Glen Gheallaidh
Scootmore Forest
Daugh of Carron
Marypark
Glenfarclas Distillery
Carn nan Tri-tighearnan
Dalees
Streens
Carn na Sguabaich
Lochindorb
Dava
Dava Moor
Old Military Road
Carn Ruighe an Uain
Glen Tulchan
Carne na Loine
Gallow Hill
Lynemore
Belleheiglash
Ballindalloch
Baby's Hill
Meikle Conval
Beatshach
Ben Rinnes
Carn Ruigh Charrach
Carn Bad na Caorach
Auchnagallin
Knock of Auchnahannet
Upper Derraid
Anaboard
Bridge of Avon
Advie
Toremore
Craigroy Farm
Dalchirach
Favillar
Achnastank
Findhorn
Carn an t-Sean-liathanaich
Balvraid
Glaschoil
Camerory
Creag Liath
Cottartown
Grant
Tomvaich
S T R A T H S P E Y
Lettoch
Dellefure
Creag an Tarmachain
Craggan
Cairnacay
Tervieside
Hill of Achmore
Glen Fiddich Forest
Inverbrough
Carn a' Choire Mhòir
Carn Glas-choire
Grantown-on-Spey
Beinn Mhòr
Glenbeg
Speyside Way
Cromdale
Haughs of Cromdale
Charn a' Ghille Chear
Drumin
Glenlivet Distillery & Visitor Centre
Glenlivet
Shenval
Carn a' Bhodaich
Corryhabbie Hill
Cook's Cairn
Carn Eachie
Hills of Cromdale
Strath Avon
Carn Liath
Auchbreck
Cairn Muldonich
Tomnavoulin
Carn an t-Suidhe
Blackwater Forest
Achnahannet
Tullochgribban High
Dulnain Bridge
Gaich
Speybridge
Congash
Distillery
Carn nam-Bain Tighearna
Slochd
Carn Mòr
Duthil
Skye of Curr
Speyside Heather Centre
Creagan a' Chaise
Carn Tuairneir
M O R A Y
Carn Daimh
Cairn Ellick
Knockandhu
Glenlivet
Round Hill
Carrbridge
Landmark Visitor Centre & Sculpture Park
Bogroy
Sluggan
Carn na Loinne
Sgor Gaoithe
Dirdhu
Bridge of Brown
Fodderletter
Glenconglass
Clashnoir
Braes of Glenlivet
Chapeltown
An Leth-allt
Dalnahaitnach
Drumuillie
Cullachie
Nethy Bridge
Lettoch
Sliemore
Lainchoil
Baddoch
Tom an t-suidhe Mhòr
Glen Brown
Tomintoul
Museum
Findron
Lagganvoulin
Breac Leathad
Letterach
Carn Mòr
Ladder Hills
Boat of Garten
Loch Garten
Kinveachy
Beinn Ghuilbin
Avielochan
Strathspey Railway
Loch Mallachie
Tore Hill
Dell Lodge
Abernethy Forest
Carn Meadhonach
Delnabo
Carn Sleamhuinn
Auchgeurish
Aundorach
Tulloch
Braes of Abernethy
Carn Tuadhan
Carn na Farraidh
Badnafrave
Blairnamarrow
Monadh Fergie
Conglass Water
Carn Liath
Water of Nochty
The Socach
Granish
Aviemore
Carn Dearg Mòr
Craiggowrie
Sluggan Pass
Carn na h-Ailig
Geal Charn
Delavorar
Torbain
Lecht Ski Centre
Beinn a' Chruinnich
Craigellachie
An Sguabach
The Queen's Forest
Meall a' Bhuachaille
GLENMORE FOREST PARK
Carn Bheadhair
Water of Ailnack
Dalestie
Craig Veann
Carn Ealasaid
Cairn Vachich
Geal Charn
Aviemore Centre
Coylumbridge
Doune
Inverdruie
Reindeer House
Glenmore
Glenmore Lodge
An Lurg
Cnap Chaochan Aitinn
Big Garvoun
Milltown
Cock Bridge
Corgarff
Alvie
The Polchar
Loch an Eilein Visitor Centre & Forest Trail
Loch Morlich
Rothiemurchus
Mam Suim
Lairig Pass
Carn na Feannaige
Inchrory
Kinrara
An Suidhe
Castle (ruins)
Dalnavert
Kincraig
Loch Insh
Feshiebridge
Castle Hill
Cairn Gorm Mountain
Bynack More
Water of Caiplich
Glen Avon
The Bruach
Forest of Glenavon
Carn Leac Saighdeir
Tornahaish
Brown Cow Hill
Carn Eilrig
Creag Dhubh
Gleann Einich
Balnespick
Farr
Inshriach Forest
Insh
Inveruglass
Lairig Ghru
Cairn Gorm
Loch Avon
Beinn Mheadhoin
Beinn a' Chaorainn
Stob an t-Sluichd
Ben Avon
Loch Builg
Gairnshiel Lodge
Daldownie
Rinloan
CAIRNGORM MOUNTAINS
Shelter Stone
Pools of Dee
North Top
Carn Eas
Sgoran Dubh Mòr
Braeriach
Ben Macdui
Derry Cairngorm
Beinn a' Bhuird
South Top
Creag an Dail Bheag
Culardoch
Braenaloin
Geallaig Hill
Tolvah
Achlean
Baileguish
Sgor Gaoith
Loch Einich
Cairngorms National Nature Reserve
Cairn Toul
Beinn Bhreac
Dubh Ghleann
Carn Liath
Carn Ban Mòr
The Devil's Point
Carn a' Mhaim
Carn Crom
Glen Derry
Glen Quoich
Invercauld Forest
Bush Crathie
Greystone
Balmoral Castle
Crathie
Meall Dubhag
Monadh Mòr
Glen Feshie
Mullach Clach a' Bhlair
CAIRNGORMS
Glen Dee
Glen Lui
Carn na Drochaide
B R A E M A R
Meall Gorm
Inver
Easter Balmoral
Clachanturn
Invergelder
Beinn Bhrotain
Sgor Mòr
Mar Forest
Creag Bhalg
Linn of Quoich
Allanaquoich
Kindrochit
Braemar
Invercauld Bridge
Bridge of Dee
Creag nan Gall
Carn Dearg Mòr
Glenfeshie Forest
NATIONAL PARK
Mar Lodge
Linn of Dee
Muir
Inverey
Morrone Hill
Falls of Garbh Allt
Ballochbuie Forest
Balmoral Forest
Cairn Geldie
Carn Liath
Auchallater
Inchnabobart
Carn an Fhidhleir Lorgaidh
Geldie Burn
The Colonel's Bed
Newbigging
Lochnagar
Conachcraig
A B E R D E E N S H I R E
Carn an Fhidhleir (Carn Ealar)
An Sgarsoch
Glen Ey Forest
Creag nan Gabhar
Glen Callater
Loch Callater
Carn an t-Sagairt Mòr
Carn a' Coire Bhoidheach
Cac Carn Beag
White Mounth
Loch Muick
Beinn Bhreac
P E R T H
Carn Bhac
Sgor Mòr
Glen Clunie
Carn Bannoch
Dubh Loch
Broad Cairn
Allt a' Chuil
Tarf Water
Falls of Tarf
An Socach
Carn an Tuirc
Cairn of Claise
Tolmount
Braigh Sròn Ghorm
An Sligearnach
A N D
Beinn Iutharn Mhor
Beinn Iutharn Bheag
Carn Aosda
Tom Buidhe
Lair Aldararie
Beinn Dearg
Carn a' Chlamain
Carn an Righ
Glenshee Chairlift & Ski Centre
The Cairnwell
Glas Maol
Devil's Elbow
Monega Hill
Creag Leacach
Caenlochan Forest
Caen Lochan
Craig Mellon
Glendoll Lodge
Glen Doll
Carn a' Gheoidh
Glas Tulaichean
K I N R O S S
Beinn a' Chait
Gleann Mòr
Glen Loch
Forest Lodge
Glen Tilt
Glen Lochsie
Finalty Hill
Mayar
Driesh
Glen Bruar
Braigh Coire Chruinn-bhalgain
Carn nan Gabhar
Gleann Beag
Carn Alt
A N G U S
Ben Gulabin
Meall a' Choire Bhuidhe
Carn an Daimh
Monamenach
Beinn a' Ghlo
Meall Reamhar
Carn Liath
Ben Vuirich
Dalmunzie House Hotel
Ben Earb
Auchavan
Mid Hill
Hunt Hill
Cairn Baddoch
Mount Bouie
Croftmore
Old Blair
Meall Breac
Gleann Fearnach
Meall Uaine
Shee Water
Badandun Hill
Runtaleave
Glen Loyne
Cairn Daunie
Eskielawn
Mona Letter (Duchray Hill)
Blair Castle
Creag an-

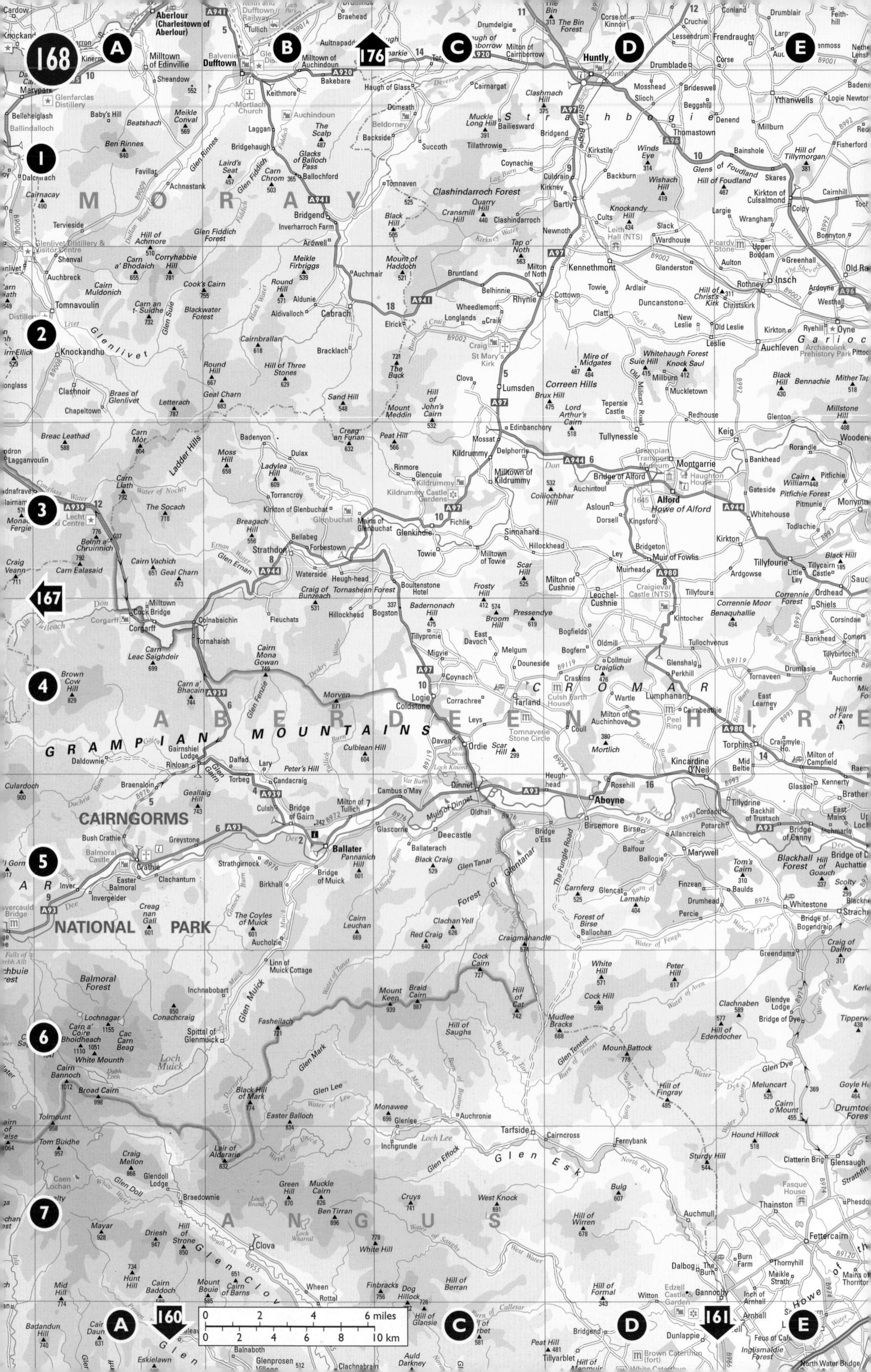

168
176
167
160
161
A
B
C
D
E
1
2
3
4
5
6
7
M O R A Y
A B E R D E E N S H I R E
C R O M A R
A N G U S
S t r a t h b o g i e
GRAMPIAN MOUNTAINS
CAIRNGORMS
NATIONAL PARK
Aberlour (Charlestown of Aberlour)
Milltown of Edinvillie
Dufftown
Balvenie
Milltown of Auchindoun
Bakebare
Haugh of Glass
Huntly
Drumblade
Frendraught
Conland
Cruchie
Lessendrum
Drumblair
Corse
Forgue
Milton of Cairnborrow
Drumdelgie
Braehead
Tullich
Keithmore
Mortlach Church
Auchindoun
Dumeath
Beldorney
Backside
Succoth
Cairnargat
Clashmach Hill
375
Muckle Long Hill
391
Bailiesward
Bridgend
Kirkstile
Tillathrowie
Coynachie
Clashindarroch Forest
Quarry Hill
440
Cransmill Hill
Clashindarroch
Culdrain
Kirkney
Gartly
Backburn
Winds Eye
314
Wishach Hill
419
Mosshead
Slioch
Brideswell
Beggshill
Denend
Thomastown
Ythanwells
Logie Newton
Millburn
Bainshole
Glens of Foudland
Hill of Foudland
467
Skares
Hill of Tillymorgan
381
Fisherford
Kirkton of Culsalmond
Colpy
Cairnhill
Largie
Wrangham
Bonnyton
Upper Boddam
Aulton
Greenhall
Insch
Old Rayne
Rothney
Ardoyne
Westhall
Oyne
Picardy Stone
Leith Hall (NTS)
Knockandy Hill
434
Slack
Wardhouse
Glanderston
Kennethmont
Cults
Newnoth
Tap o' Noth
563
Milton of Noth
Rhynie
Cottown
Towie
Ardlair
Duncanston
Hill of Christ's Kirk
311
Christskirk
Clatt
New Leslie
Old Leslie
Leslie
Kirkton
Ryehill
Auchleven
Garioch
Archaeolink Prehistory Park
Premnay
Whitehaugh Forest
Suie Hill
415
Knock Saul
412
Millburn
Muckletown
Mire of Midgates
487
484
Correen Hills
Brux Hill
475
Lord Arthur's Cairn
518
Tepersie Castle
Old Military Road
Redhouse
Keig
Tullynessle
Black Hill
430
Bennachie
Mither Tap
518
Millstone Hill
408
Glenton
Rorandle
Wooden
Bankhead
Cairn William
448
Pitfichie
Pitfichie Forest
Pitmunie
Monymusk
Gateside
Whitehouse
Todlachie
Grampian Transport Museum
Montgarrie
Bridge of Alford
Haughton House
Alford
Howe of Alford
Auchintoul
Asloun
Dorsell
Kingsford
1645
Coiliochbhar Hill
532
Don
Kildrummy
Mossat
Delphorrie
Milltown of Kildrummy
Edinbanchory
Lumsden
Clova
Craig
St Mary's Kirk
Longlands
Craik
Wheedlemont
Bruntland
Belhinnie
Mount of Haddoch
521
Black Hill
505
Tomnaven
525
Ballochford
Bridgend
Inverharroch Farm
Ardwell
Auchmair
Cabrach
Aldunie
Aldivalloch
Elrick
Bracklach
Meikle Firbriggs
539
Round Hill
571
Cairnbrallan
618
Hill of Three Stones
629
The Buck
721
Sand Hill
548
Hill of John's Cairn
532
Mount Meddin
Creag an Funan
632
Peat Hill
566
Rinmore
Glencuie
Kildrummy Castle Gardens
Kildrummy
Fichlie
Glenkindie
Sinnahard
Hillockhead
Ley
Muir of Fowlis
Muirhead
Bridgeton
Craigievar Castle (NTS)
Leochel-Cushnie
Milton of Cushnie
Scar Hill
525
Tillyfour
Kintocher
Tillyfourie
Little Ley
Black Hill
Tillycairn Castle
185
Corrennie Moor
Corrennie Forest
Benaquhallie
494
Ordhead
Shiels
Corsindae
Bankhead
Comers
Tillybirloch
Tullochvenus
Bogfields
Oldmill
Bogfern
Collmuir
Craiglich
476
Glenshalg
Perkhill
Drumlasie
Tornaveen
Auchorrie
East Learney
Hill of Fare
471
Lumphanan
Cairnbeathie
Peel Ring
Craskins
Cruls Earth House
Tarland
Wartle
Milton of Auchinhove
Coull
Tomnaverie Stone Circle
Mortlich
380
Torphins
Craigmyle Ho.
Milton of Campfield
Mid Beltie
Kincardine O'Neil
Kennerty
Glassel
Brathens
Rosehill
Aboyne
Heugh-head
Dinnet
Oldhall
Muir of Dinnet
Cambus o'May
Ordie
Davan
Loch Davan
Loch Kinord
Scar Hill
299
Leys
Corrachree
Coynach
Logie Coldstone
Migvie
Tillypronie
Badernonach Hill
475
Frosty Hill
412
574
Broom Hill
Pressendye
619
East Davoch
Melgum
Douneside
Milltown of Towie
Towie
Boultenstone Hotel
Bogston
337
Tornashean Forest
Heugh-head
Hillockhead
Craig of Bunzeach
531
Waterside
Strathdon
Forbestown
Bellabeg
Mains of Glenbuchat
Glenbuchat
Kirkton of Glenbuchat
Torrancroy
Ladylea Hill
609
Dulax
Badenyon
Moss Hill
658
Breagach Hill
556
Glen Ernan
Carn Vachich
651
Geal Charn
673
Carn Ealasaid
792
Beinn a' Chruinnich
776
Lecht Ski Centre
The Socach
718
Carn Liath
792
Carn Mòr
804
Ladder Hills
Breac Leathad
588
Lagganvoulin
Craig Veann
711
Milltown
Cock Bridge
Corgarff
Colnabaichin
Tornahaish
Fleuchats
Carn Leac Saighdeir
699
Cairn Mona Gowan
749
Brown Cow Hill
829
Carn a' Bhacain
744
Morven
871
Culblean Hill
604
Peter's Hill
Gairnshiel Lodge
Rinloan
Dalfad
Lary
Candacraig
Torbeg
Daldownie
Culardoch
900
Braenaloin
Geallaig Hill
743
Culsh
Bridge of Gairn
Milton of Tullich
Ballater
Pannanich Hill
601
Bridge of Muick
Birkhall
Glascorrie
Ballaterach
Deecastle
Black Craig
529
Glen Tanar
Forest of Glentanar
Bridge o'Ess
The Fungle Road
Birsemore
Birse
Allancreich
Balfour
Ballogie
Marywell
Potarch
Cordach
Tillydrine
Backhill of Trustach
Bridge of Canny
Inchmarlo
Blackhall Forest
Hill of Goauch
337
Bridge of Dee
Auchattie
Tom's Cairn
310
Baulds
Finzean
Drumhead
Percie
Whitestone
Scolty
299
Strachan
Bridge of Bogendreip
Craig of Dalfro
317
Greendams
Carnferg
525
Glencat
Lamahip
404
Forest of Birse
Ballochan
Water of Feugh
Bush Crathie
Greystone
Balmoral Castle
Crathie
Easter Balmoral
Clachanturn
Strathgirnock
Inver
Invergelder
Creag nan Gall
601
The Coyles of Muick
601
Aucholzie
Cairn Leuchan
669
Clachan Yell
626
Red Craig
640
Craigmahandle
574
Linn of Muick Cottage
Cock Cairn
727
Hill of Cat
742
White Hill
571
Peter Hill
617
Cock Hill
598
Clachnaben
589
Glendye Lodge
Bridge of Dye
Hill of Edendocher
577
Balmoral Forest
Lochnagar
1155
Carn a' Coire Bhoidheach
1110
Cac Carn Beag
1051
White Mounth
Loch Muick
Dubh Loch
Conachcraig
850
Spittal of Glenmuick
Inchnabobart
Glen Muick
Fasheilach
721
Mount Keen
939
Braid Cairn
887
Hill of Saughs
Mudlee Bracks
688
Glen Tennet
Mount Battock
778
Hill of Fingray
485
Glen Dye
Meluncart
525
Cairn o'Mount
455
Goyle Hill
464
Drumtochty Forest
Cairn Bannoch
1012
Broad Cairn
998
Black Hill of Mark
774
Glen Mark
Glen Lee
Easter Balloch
834
Monawee
696
Glenlee
Auchronie
Tarfside
Cairncross
Fernybank
Hound Hillock
518
Clatterin Brig
Glensaugh
Sturdy Hill
544
Tolmount
958
Tom Buidhe
957
Lair of Aldararie
832
Inchgrundle
Loch Lee
Glen Effock
Glen Esk
North Esk
Craig Mellon
866
Glendoll Lodge
Glen Doll
Braedownie
Green Hill
870
Muckle Cairn
826
Ben Tirran
896
Loch Brandy
Loch Wharral
Cruys
741
West Knock
691
Bulg
607
Hill of Wirren
678
Fasque House
Thainston
Phesdo
Auchmull
Fettercairn
Mayar
928
Driesh
947
Hill of Strone
850
Glen Clova
Clova
South Esk
White Hill
778
Water of Saughs
West Water
Burn Farm
Thornyhill
Dalbog
The Burn
Meikle Strath
Mains of Thornton
Howe of the Mearns
Hunt Hill
734
Carn Baddoch
Mount Boule
585
Cairn of Barns
651
Wheen
Rottal
Finbracks
756
Dog Hillock
726
Hill of Berran
Hill of Formal
343
Witton
Edzell Castle & Garden
Gannochy
Inch of Arnhall
Arnhall
Mid Hill
774
Badandun Hill
740
Cairn Daunie
631
Hill of Glansie
Hill of Corbet
581
Peat Hill
481
Tillyarblet
Bridgend
Brown Caterthun (fort)
Dunlappie
Inglismaldie Forest
Feus of Caldhame
North Water Bridge
Balnaboth
Glenprosen Village
Clachnabrain
Auld Darkney
Eskielawn
Glen Prosen
Benrinnes
Glenfarclas Distillery
Marypark
Knockando
Cardow
Belleheiglash
Ballindalloch
Baby's Hill
Beatshach
Ben Rinnes
840
Meikle Conval
569
Sheandow
552
Laird's Seat
457
Carn Chrom
503
Glacks of Balloch Pass
The Scalp
487
Laggan
Bridgehaugh
Glen Rinnes
Glen Fiddich
Favillar
Achnastank
Dalnachrach
Cairnacay
490
Tervieside
Hill of Achmore
Glen Fiddich Forest
Glenlivet Distillery & Visitor Centre
Shenval
Auchbreck
Corryhabbie Hill
781
Carn a' Bhodaich
655
Cairn Muldonich
Cook's Cairn
755
Tomnavoulin
Carn an t-Suidhe
732
Blackwater Forest
Glen Suie
Black Water
Glenlivet
Knockandhu
Round Hill
667
Clashnoir
Braes of Glenlivet
Chapeltown
Letterach
787
Geal Charn
683
A941
A920
A97
A96
A944
A980
A939
A93
B9002
B976
B993
B9119
B9094
B974
B955
B9008
B9009
B9014
B992
B9001
B9120
B966
B972
0
2
4
6 miles
8
10 km

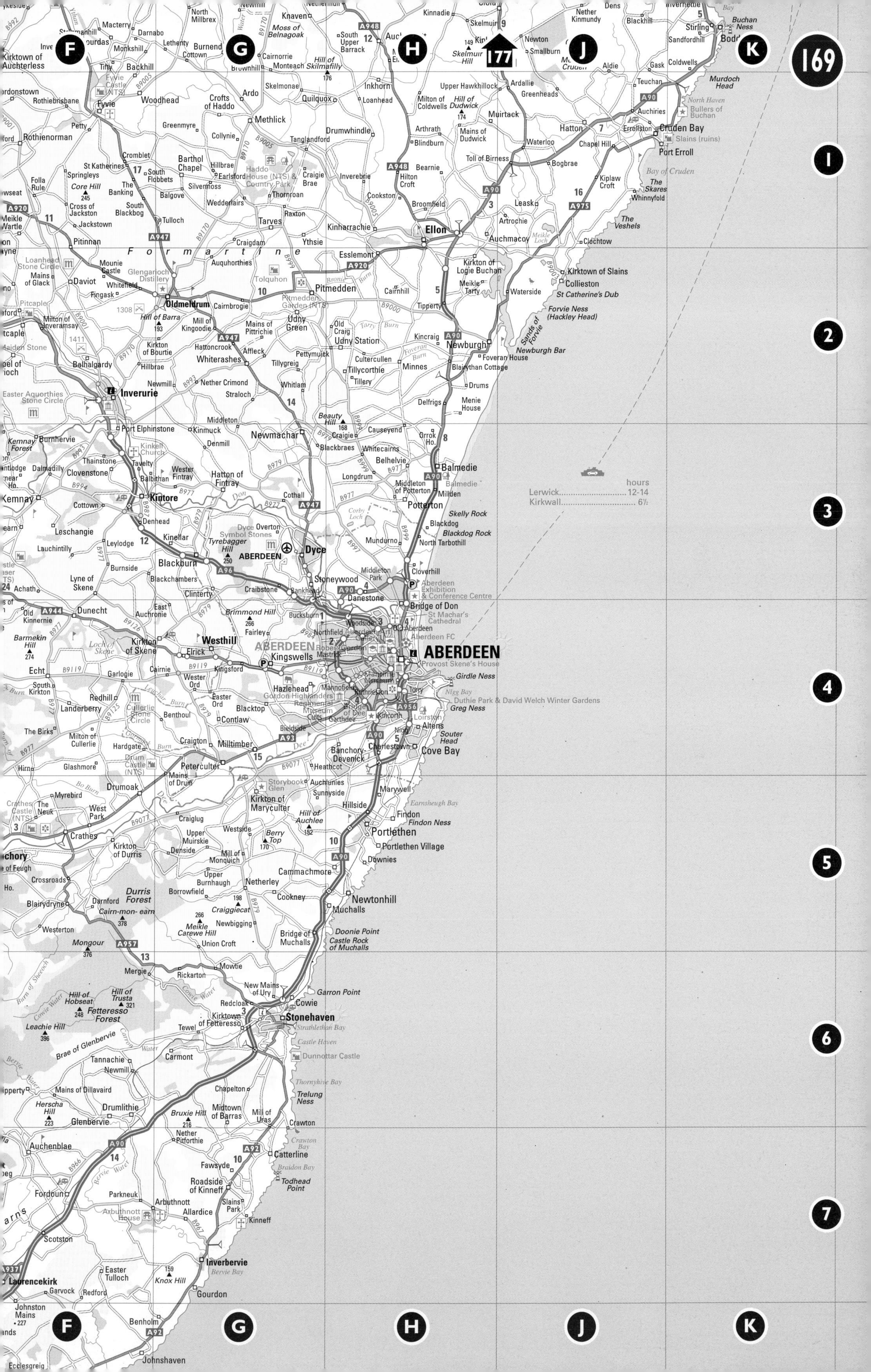

169
F
G
H
J
K
177
North Millbrex
Knaven
Kinnadie
Skelmuir
Nether Kinmundy
Dens
Blackhill
Stirling
Buchan Ness
Macterry
Darnabo
Moss of Belnagoak
South Upper Barrack
A948
Kirktown of Auchterless
Monkshill
Lethenty
Burnend
Cottown
Cairnorrie
Monteach
Hill of Skilmafilly
Skelmuir Hill
Newton
Smallburn
Sandfordhill
Coldwells
Backhill
Fyvie Castle (NTS)
Brownhill
Aldie
Gask
Teuchan
Murdoch Head
Fyvie
Woodhead
Crofts of Haddo
Ardo
Skelmonae
Quilquox
Inkhorn
Loanhead
Upper Hawkhillock
Milton of Coldwells
Hill of Dudwick
Ardallie
Greenheads
North Haven
Bullers of Buchan
Auchiries
Rothiebrisbane
Petty
Methlick
Greenmyre
Collynie
Tanglandford
Drumwhindle
Arthrath
Blindburn
Mains of Dudwick
Muirtack
Hatton
Erroliston
Cruden Bay
Slains (ruins)
Port Erroll
Rothienorman
Cromblet
St Katherines
Springleys
Core Hill
Cross of Jackston
Jackstown
South Flobbets
The Banking
South Blackbog
Balgove
Barthol Chapel
Hillbrae
Earlsford
Haddo House (NTS) & Country Park
Silvermoss
Wedderlairs
Thornroan
Craigie Brae
Inverebrie
Hilton Croft
Bearnie
Cookston
Broomfield
Waterloo
Chapel Hill
Toll of Birness
Bogbrae
Kiplaw Croft
Bay of Cruden
The Skares
Whinnyfold
Leask
Artrochie
Auchmacoy
The Veshels
Clochtow
Folla Rule
A920
Meikle Wartle
Tulloch
A947
Tarves
Raxton
Kinharrachie
Ellon
Pitinnan
Craigdam
Ythsie
Formartine
Esslemont
Kirkton of Logie Buchan
Meikle Tarty
Kirktown of Slains
Collieston
St Catherine's Dub
Waterside
Loanhead Stone Circle
Mains of Glack
Mounie Castle
Auquhorthies
Glengarioch Distillery
Daviot
Whitefield
Fingask
Tolquhon
Pitmedden
Pitmedden Garden (NTS)
Cairnhill
Tipperty
Forvie Ness (Hackley Head)
Sands of Forvie
Oldmeldrum
Cairnbrogie
Hill of Barra
Milton of Inveramsay
Mill of Kingoodie
Mains of Pittrichie
Udny Green
Old Craig
Udny Station
Kincraig
Newburgh
Newburgh Bar
Foveran House
Pitcaple
Maiden Stone
Kirkton of Bourtie
Hattoncrook
Affleck
Whiterashes
Pettymuick
Cultercullen
Tillygreig
Tillycorthie
Tillery
Minnes
Blairythan Cottage
Drums
Balhalgardy
Hillbrae
Newmill
Nether Crimond
Straloch
Whitlam
Inverurie
Easter Aquorthies Stone Circle
Menie House
Delfrigs
Middleton
Beauty Hill
Port Elphinstone
Kinmuck
Newmachar
Denmill
Craigie
Causeyend
Orrok Ho.
Blackbraes
Whitecairns
Belhelvie
Kemnay Forest
Burnhervie
Kinkell Church
Thainstone
Tavelty
Dalmadilly
Wester Fintray
Balbithan
Hatton of Fintray
Longdrum
Balmedie
Clovenstone
Middleton of Potterton
Milldens
Kintore
Cothall
Potterton
Lerwick
Kirkwall
hours
12-14
Kemnay
Cottown
Denhead
Skelly Rock
Blackdog
Blackdog Rock
Leschangie
Dyce
Overton
Symbol Stones
Tyrebagger Hill
Kinellar
Leylodge
Mundurno
North Tarbothill
Lauchintilly
ABERDEEN
Blackburn
Burnside
Stoneywood
Middleton Park
Cloverhill
Aberdeen Exhibition & Conference Centre
Lyne of Skene
Blackchambers
Clinterty
Craibstone
Bankhead
Danestone
Bridge of Don
Achath
East Auchronie
Dunecht
A944
Old Kinnernie
Brimmond Hill
Bucksburn
St Machar's Cathedral
Aberdeen FC
Old Aberdeen
Fairley
Woodside
Northfield
Barmekin Hill
Loch of Skene
Kirkton of Skene
Westhill
Elrick
Robert Gordon
Mastrick
Provost Skene's House
Girdle Ness
Echt
Garlogie
Cairnie
Kingswells
Kingsford
Wester Ord
South Kirkton
Redhill
Hazlehead
Gordon Highlanders Regimental Museum
Mannofield
Ruthrieston
Torry
Nigg Bay
Duthie Park & David Welch Winter Gardens
Greg Ness
Landerberry
Cullerlie Stone Circle
Benthoul
Easter Ord
Blacktop
Contlaw
Kincorth
Cults
Garthdee
Bridge of Dee
Loirston
Altens
The Birks
Milton of Cullerlie
Hardgate
Craigton
Milltimber
Bieldside
Nigg
Charlestown
Souter Head
Cove Bay
Drum Castle (NTS)
Glashmore
Hirn
Peterculter
Banchory-Devenick
Heathcot
Mains of Drum
Storybook Glen
Auchlunies
Sunnyside
Marywell
Drumoak
Crathes Castle (NTS)
Myrebird
The Neuk
West Park
Kirkton of Maryculter
Hillside
Earnsheugh Bay
Findon
Findon Ness
Craiglug
Hill of Auchlee
Crathes
Upper Muirskie
Westside
Berry Top
Portlethen
Portlethen Village
Kirkton of Durris
Denside
Mill of Monquich
Downies
Upper Burnhaugh
Cammachmore
Netherley
Crossroads
Borrowfield
Cookney
Newtonhill
Durris Forest
Blairydryne
Darnford
Cairn-mon-earn
Craiggiecat
Muchalls
Meikle Carewe Hill
Newbigging
Doonie Point
Westerton
Castle Rock of Muchalls
Mongour
A957
Union Croft
Bridge of Muchalls
Mergie
Mowtie
Rickarton
Hill of Trusta
Hill of Hobseat
Fetteresso Forest
New Mains of Ury
Garron Point
Cowie
Redcloak
Kirktown of Fetteresso
Stonehaven
Strathlethan Bay
Leachie Hill
Tewel
Castle Haven
Brae of Glenbervie
Carmont
Dunnottar Castle
Tannachie
Newmill
Thornyhive Bay
Mains of Dillavaird
Chapelton
Trelung Ness
Herscha Hill
Drumlithie
Bruxie Hill
Midtown of Barras
Mill of Uras
Glenbervie
Crawton
Nether Pitforthie
Crawton Bay
Auchenblae
A90
Catterline
Braidon Bay
Fawsyde
Todhead Point
Fordoun
Roadside of Kinneff
Parkneuk
Arbuthnott
Arbuthnott House
Allardice
Slains Park
Kinneff
Scotston
Inverbervie
Bervie Bay
Easter Tulloch
Knox Hill
Laurencekirk
Garvock
Redford
Gourdon
Johnston Mains
Benholm
A92
Johnshaven
Ecclesgreig

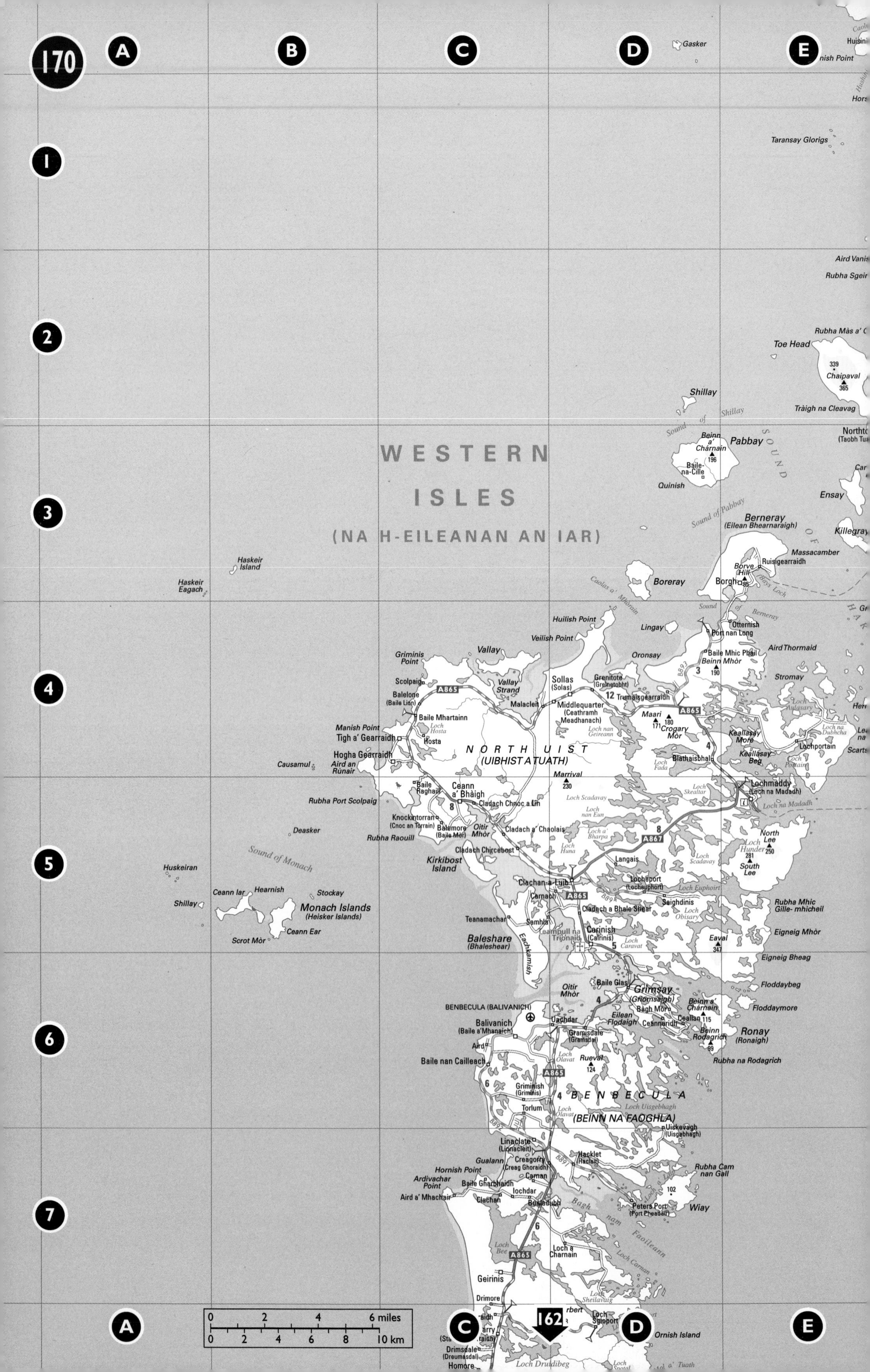
A
B
C
D
E
1
2
3
4
5
6
7
WESTERN
ISLES
(NA H-EILEANAN AN IAR)
Gasker
Huisinis
Hushinish Point
Taransay Glorigs
Aird Vanish
Rubha Sgeir
Toe Head
339
Chaipaval
365
Tràigh na Cleavag
Shillay
Sound of Shillay
Beinn a' Chàrnain
196
Pabbay
Baile-na-Cille
Quinish
SOUND OF HARRIS
Northton
(Taobh Tuath)
Ensay
Killegray
Sound of Pabbay
Berneray
(Eilean Bhearnaraigh)
Massacamber
Ruisigearraidh
Borve Hill
85
Borgh
Bays Loch
Boreray
Caolas a' Mhòrain
Haskeir Island
Haskeir Eagach
Sound of Berneray
Otternish
Port nan Long
Lingay
Huilish Point
Veilish Point
Oronsay
Baile Mhic Phail
Beinn Mhòr
190
Aird Thormaid
Stromay
Vallay
Griminis Point
Scolpaig
Vallay Strand
Sollas
(Solas)
Grenitote
(Greinetobht)
Trumaisgearraidh
Balelone
(Baile Lìon)
A865
Malaclete
Middlequarter
(Ceathramh Meadhanach)
Maari
171
180
Crogary Mòr
Loch Aulasary
Baile Mhartainn
Loch Hosta
Hosta
Loch nan Geireann
Keallasay Mòre
Keallasay Beg
Loch na Dubhcha
Lochportain
Manish Point
Tigh a' Gearraidh
NORTH UIST
(UIBHIST A TUATH)
Blathaisbhal
Loch Fada
Loch Portain
Hogha Gearraidh
Aird an Rùnair
Causamul
Marrival
230
Lochmaddy
(Loch na Madadh)
Baile Raghaill
Ceann a' Bhàigh
Cladach Chnoc a Lin
Loch Scadavay
Loch Skealtar
Loch na Madadh
Rubha Port Scolpaig
Knockintorran
(Cnoc an Torrain)
Balemore
(Baile Mòr)
Oitir Mhòr
Cladach a' Chaolais
Loch a' Bharpa
A867
North Lee
250
Loch Hunder
281
South Lee
Deasker
Rubha Raouill
Cladach Chircebost
Loch Huna
Langais
Loch Scadavay
Sound of Monach
Kirkibost Island
Huskeiran
Clachan-a-Luib
Locheport
(Locheuphort)
Loch Euphoirt
Ceann Iar
Hearnish
Stockay
Shillay
Monach Islands
(Heisker Islands)
Carnach
Cladach a Bhale Shear
Saighdinis
Loch Obisary
Rubha Mhic Gille-mhicheil
Ceann Ear
Scrot Mòr
Teanamachar
Sàmhla
Teampull na Trionaid
Carinish
(Cairinis)
Loch Caravat
Eaval
347
Eigneig Mhòr
Baleshare
(Bhaleshear)
Eachkamish
Eigneig Bheag
Baile Glas
Grimsay
(Griomsaigh)
Floddaybeg
Oitir Mhòr
Beinn a' Chàrnain
115
Floddaymore
BENBECULA (BALIVANICH)
Bàgh Mòr
Eilean Flodaigh
Ceallan
Ceann a' Ruidh
Uachdar
Balivanich
(Baile a'Mhanaich)
Gramisdale
(Gramsdal)
Beinn Rodagrich
89
Ronay
(Ronaigh)
Aird
Loch Olavat
Rueval
124
Rubha na Rodagrich
Baile nan Cailleach
Griminish
(Griminis)
BENBECULA
(BEINN NA FAOGHLA)
Loch Uisgebhagh
Loch Olavat
Torlum
Uiskevagh
(Uisgebhagh)
B892
Linaclate
(Lionacleit)
Hacklet
(Haclait)
B891
Gualann
Creagorry
(Creag Ghoraidh)
Rubha Cam nan Gall
Hornish Point
Ardivachar Point
Caman
Baile Gharbhaidh
Iochdar
102
Aird a' Mhachair
Clachan
Buaile Dubh
Loch a' Laip
Peters Port
(Port Pheadair)
Wiay
Bagh nam Faoileann
Loch Bee
Loch a Charnain
Loch Carnan
Geirinis
Loch Sheilavaig
Drimore
Loch Sgioport
Ornish Island
Drimsdale
(Dreumasdal)
Homore
Loch Druidibeg
0
2
4
6 miles
0
2
4
6
8
10 km
162

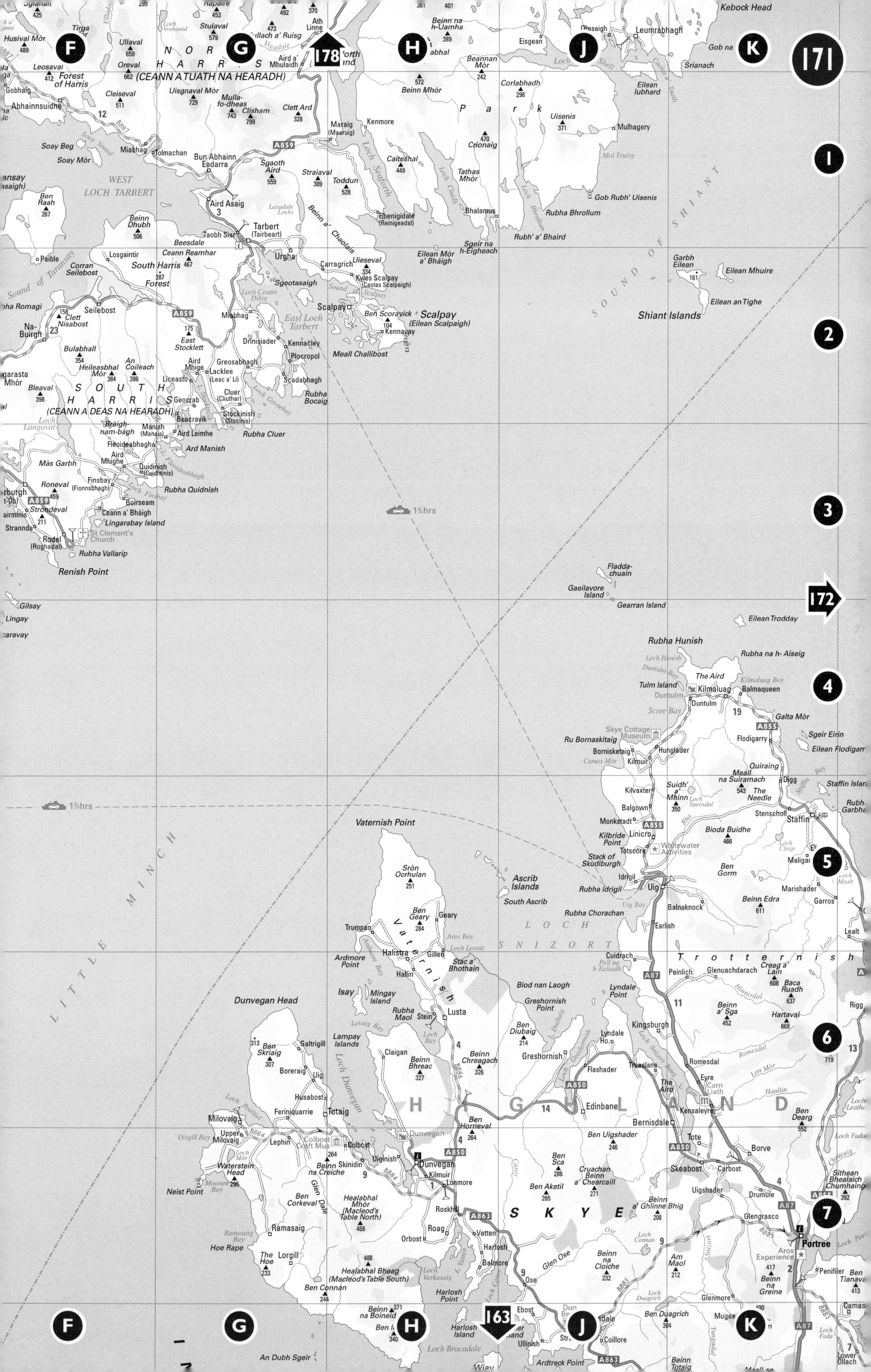
F
G
H
J
K
I
2
3
4
5
6
7
178
172
163
Husival Mòr
Tirga Mòr
Ullaval
NORTH HARRIS
(CEANN A TUATH NA HEARADH)
Stulaval
Ath Linne
Beinn na h-Uamha
Eisgean
Orasaigh
Leumrabhagh
Kebock Head
Gob na
Srianach
Leosaval
Forest of Harris
Oreval
Aird a' Mhulaidh
Beannan Mòr
Corlabhadh
Loch Shell
Caolas a' Tuath
Eilean Iubhard
Beinn Mhòr
Gobhaig
Abhainnsuidhe
Cleiseval
Uisgnaval Mòr
Mulla-fo-dheas
Clisham
Clett Ard
Park
Uisenis
Mulhagery
Maraig (Maaruig)
Kenmore
Soay Beg
Soay Mòr
Soay Sound
Miabhag
Tolmachan
A859
B887
Bun Abhainn Eadarra
Sgaoth Aird
Caiteshal
Crionaig
Mol Truisg
Loch Seaforth
Loch Claidh
WEST LOCH TARBERT
Straiaval
Toddun
Tathas Mhòr
Ben Raah
Aird Asaig
Laxadale Lochs
Rhenigidale (Reinigeadal)
Bhalamus
Gob Rubh' Uisenis
Rubha Bhrollum
Loch Bhrollum
Beinn Dhubh
Tarbert (Tairbeart)
Taobh Siar
Beinn a' Chaolais
Rubh' a' Bhaird
Sgeir na h-Eigheach
Paible
Losgaintir
Beesdale
Ceann Reamhar
South Harris Forest
Urgha
Eilean Mòr a' Bhàigh
Carragrich
Uieseval
Garbh Eilean
Eilean Mhuire
Sound of Taransay
Corran Seilebost
Sgeotasaigh
Kyles Scalpay (Caolas Scalpaigh)
SOUND OF SHIANT
Loch Ceann Dibig
Scalpay Sound
Eilean an Tighe
Shiant Islands
Seilebost
Clett Nisabost
Na-Buirgh
Miabhag
East Loch Tarbert
Scalpay
Ben Scoravick
Scalpay (Eilean Scalpaigh)
Kennavay
Drinisiader
Kennacley
East Stocklett
Plocropol
Meall Challibost
Bulabhall
Heileasbhal Mòr
An Coileach
Aird Mhige
Greosabhagh
Lacklee (Leac a' Li)
Liceasto
Scadabhagh
Cluer (Cluithar)
Geocrab
Rubha Bocaig
Bleaval
SOUTH HARRIS
(CEANN A DEAS NA HEARADH)
Stockinish (Stocinis)
Beacravik
Loch Grosebay
Loch Langavat
Bràigh-nam-bàgh
Manish (Manais)
Aird Leimhe
Rubha Cluer
Fleoideabhagh
Ard Manish
Màs Garbh
Aird Mhighe
Quidinish (Cuidhtinis)
L. Fleoideabhagh
Roneval
Finsbay (Fionnsbhagh)
Loch Finsbay
Rubha Quidnish
Boirseam
Strondeval
Ceann a' Bhàigh
Lingarabay Island
Strannda
Rodel (Roghadal)
St Clement's Church
Rubha Vallarip
Renish Point
1¾hrs
Fladda-chuain
Gaeilavore Island
Gearran Island
Eilean Trodday
Gilsay
Lingay
Rubha Hunish
Rubha na h-Aiseig
Loch Hunish
Duntulm Bay
The Aird
Kilmaluag Bay
Tulm Island
Kilmaluag
Balmaqueen
Duntulm
Score Bay
Galta Mòr
Skye Cottage Museum
A855
Sgeir Eirin
Ru Bornaskitaig
Borniesketaig
Hungladder
Flodigarry
Eilean Flodigarry
Camas Mòr
Kilmuir
Quiraing
Meall na Suiramach
Digg
Staffin Bay
Staffin Island
Kilvaxter
Suidh' a' Mhinn
The Needle
Balgown
Loch Sneosdal
Stenscholl
Staffin
Monkstadt
Vaternish Point
Kilbride Point
Linicro
Biodha Buidhe
Loch Cleap
Totscore
Whitewater Activities
Maligar
Stack of Skudiburgh
Sròn Ocrhulan
Ascrib Islands
Idrigil
Ben Gorm
Rubha Idrigil
Uig
Marishader
South Ascrib
Uig Bay
Balnaknock
Beinn Edra
Garros
Ben Geary
Geary
Rubha Chorachan
LITTLE MINCH
Trumpan
LOCH SNIZORT
Earlish
Vaternish
Aros Bay
Loch Losait
Halistra
Gillen
Cuidrach
Trotternish
Ardmore Point
Stac a' Bhothain
Poll na h-Ealaidh
Peinlich
Glenuachdarach
Creag a' Lain
Hallin
Baca Ruadh
Isay
Mingay Island
Biod nan Laogh
Lyndale Point
Dunvegan Head
Rubha Maol
Lusta
Greshornish Point
Beinn a' Sga
Hartaval
Stein
Ben Diubaig
Loch Dubaig
Lyndale Ho.
Kingsburgh
Lampay Islands
Loch Bay
Ben Skriaig
Galtrigill
Claigan
Beinn Chreagach
Greshornish
Romesdal
Boreraig
Beinn Bhreac
Loch Dunvegan
Treaslane
Flashader
Eyre
Carn Liath
Uig
Husabost
Loch Greshornish
The Aird
Loch Pooltiel
HIGHLAND
Milovaig
Feriniquarrie
Totaig
Edinbane
Kensaleyre
Ben Dearg
Upper Milovaig
B884
Lephin
Dunvegan
Ben Horneval
Bernisdale
Oisgill Bay
Colbost Croft Mus
Colbost
Ben Uigshader
Tote
Borve
Loch Mòr
Waterstein Head
Beinn na Creiche
Skinidin
Uiginish
A850
Ben Sca
Skeabost
Carbost
Sithean Bhealaich Chumhaing
Mooneen Bay
Dunvegan
Kilmuir
Lonmore
Cruachan Beinn a' Chearcaill
Neist Point
Ben Corkeval
Glen Dale
Healabhal Mhòr (Macleod's Table North)
Ben Aketil
Uigshader
Drumuie
Roskhill
A863
SKYE
Beinn a' Ghlinne Bhig
Glengrasco
Ramasaig
Roag
Loch Connan
Portree
Ramasaig Bay
Orbost
Vatten
Hoe Rape
Harlosh
Glen Ose
Am Maol
Aros Experience
Penifiler
The Hoe
Lorgill
Healabhal Bheag (Macleod's Table South)
Loch Varkasaig
Balmore
Beinn na Cloiche
Beinn na Greine
Ben Tianavaig
Ose
Ben Connan
Harlosh Point
Loch Duagrich
Glenmore
Camas
Beinn na Boineid
Ben Duagrich
Mugeary
Harlosh Island
Ebost
Coillore
Loch Fada
An Dubh Sgeir
Loch Bracadale
Ullinish
Ardtreck Point
Beinn Totaig
Lower Ollach
Wiay
B885
A87
B883
B886

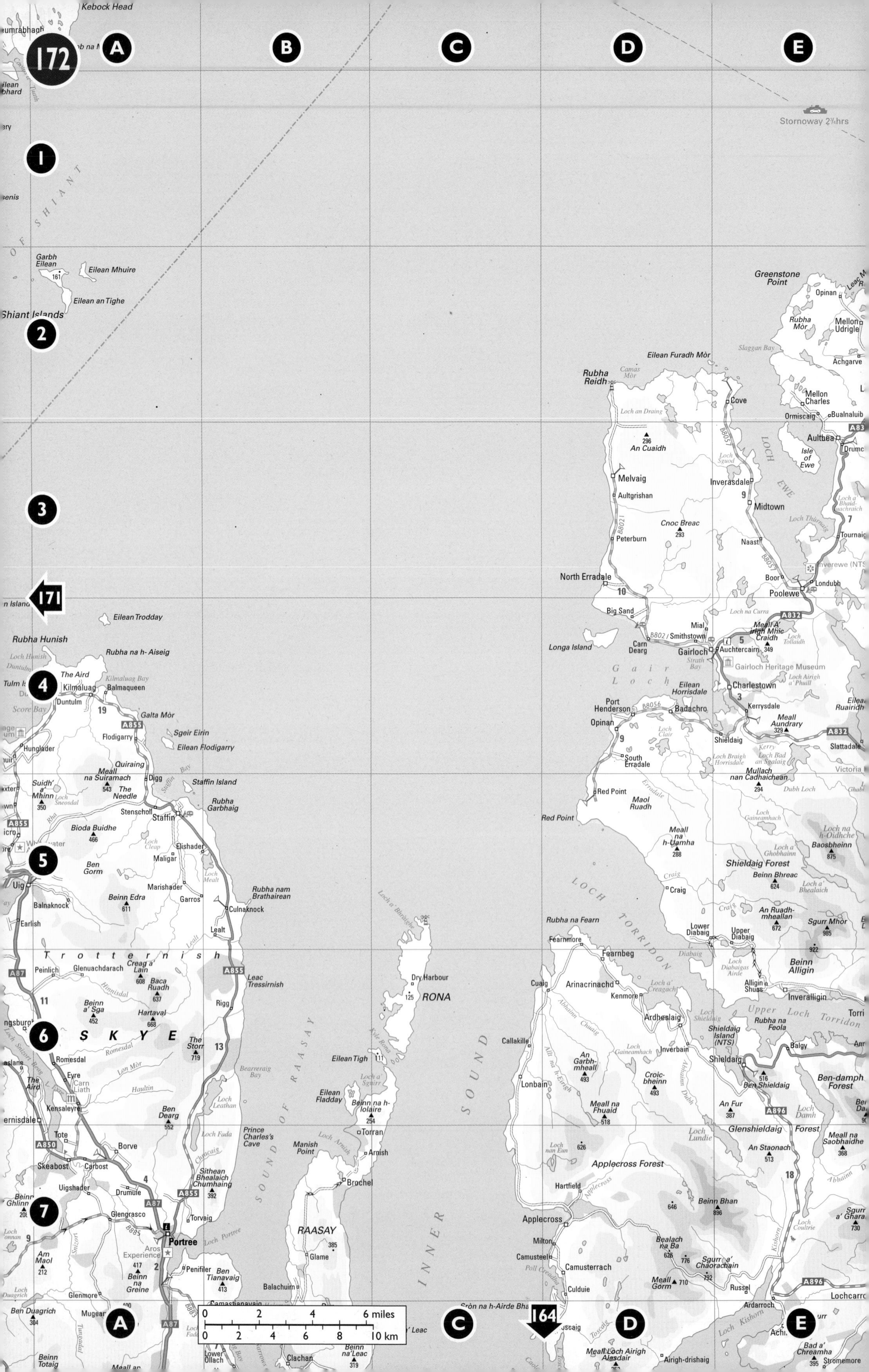
172
A
B
C
D
E
1
2
3
4
5
6
7
171
164
Kebock Head
Stornoway 2¾hrs
Garbh Eilean
161
Eilean Mhuire
Eilean an Tighe
Shiant Islands
Greenstone Point
Opinan
Rubha Mòr
Mellon Udrigle
Slaggan Bay
Achgarve
Eilean Furadh Mòr
Rubha Reidh
Camas Mòr
Cove
Mellon Charles
Ormiscaig
Bualnaluib
Loch an Draing
296
An Cuaidh
B8057
Aultbea
Isle of Ewe
LOCH EWE
Melvaig
Aultgrishan
Inverasdale
Midtown
B8021
Peterburn
Cnoc Breac
293
Naast
Loch Thùrnaig
Tournaig
Inverewe (NTS)
North Erradale
10
Boor
Londubh
Poolewe
Big Sand
Loch na Curra
A832
Mial
Meall A' Ghiubhais
Craidh
349
Longa Island
Carn Dearg
B8021 Smithstown
Gairloch
Auchtercairn
Strath Bay
Gairloch Heritage Museum
Gair Loch
Eilean Horrisdale
Charlestown
Loch Airigh a' Phuill
Port Henderson
B8056
Badachro
Opinan
Kerrysdale
Meall Aundrary
329
Shieldaig
Slattadale
Loch Clair
South Erradale
Loch Bad an Sgalaig
Mullach nan Cadhaichean
294
Victoria Falls
Red Point
Dubh Loch
Maol Ruadh
Red Point
Loch Gaineamhach
Meall na h-Uamha
288
Loch na h-Oidhche
Baosbheinn
875
Shieldaig Forest
Beinn Bhreac
624
Loch a' Bhealaich
LOCH TORRIDON
Craig
An Ruadh-mheallan
672
Sgurr Mhòr
985
Rubha na Fearn
Lower Diabaig
Upper Diabaig
Fearnmore
Fearnbeg
922
Beinn Alligin
Cuaig
Arinacrinachd
Kenmore
Alligin Shuas
Inveralligin
Upper Loch Torridon
Ardheslaig
Rubha na Feola
Shieldaig Island (NTS)
Callakille
An Garbh-mheall
493
Loch Gaineamhach
Inverbain
Balgy
Shieldaig
516
Ben Shieldaig
Ben-damph Forest
Lonbain
Croic-bheinn
493
Meall na Fhuaid
518
An Fur
387
A896
Glenshieldaig Forest
Meall na Saobhaidhe
368
Loch Lundie
626
An Staonach
513
Applecross Forest
18
Hartfield
646
Beinn Bhan
896
Applecross
Milton
Bealach na Bà
626
776
Sgurr a' Chaorachain
792
Camusteel
Camusterrach
Culduie
Meall Gorm
710
Russel
A896
Lochcarron
Ardarroch
Loch Kishorn
Achintraid
Bad a' Chreamha
395
Stromemore
Airigh-drishaig
Meall Loch Airigh Alasdair
Sròn na h-Àirde Bhaige
Eilean Trodday
Rubha Hunish
Rubha na h- Aiseig
Loch Hunish
Duntulm
The Aird
Kilmaluag Bay
Kilmaluag
Balmaqueen
Duntulm
19
Galta Mòr
Score Bay
A855
Sgeir Eirin
Flodigarry
Eilean Flodigarry
Hunglader
Quiraing
Meall na Suiramach
543
Digg
Staffin Bay
Staffin Island
Suidh' a' Mhinn
350
The Needle
Rubha Garbhaig
Loch Sneosdal
Stenscholl
Staffin
A855
Bioda Buidhe
466
Loch Cleap
Ellishader
Maligar
Ben Gorm
Loch Mealt
Uig
Marishader
Rubha nam Brathairean
Balnaknock
Beinn Edra
611
Garros
Culnaknock
Earlish
Lealt
Trotternish
A87
Peinlich
Glenuachdarach
Creag a' Lain
608
Baca Ruadh
637
A855
Leac Tressirnish
Hinnisdal
Beinn a' Sga
452
Hartaval
668
Rigg
11
Kingsburgh
SKYE
The Storr
719
13
Romesdal
Romesdal
Bearreraig Bay
Eyre
Carn Liath
Lon Mòr
The Aird
Haultin
Loch Leathan
Kensaleyre
Ben Dearg
552
Tote
Loch Fada
Prince Charles's Cave
A850
Borve
Skeabost
Carbost
Sithean Bhealaich Chumhaing
392
4
A855
Uigshader
Drumuie
A87
Glengrasco
Torvaig
B885
Portree
Loch Portree
Am Maol
212
Aros Experience
417
Beinn na Greine
2
Penifiler
Ben Tianavaig
413
Glenmore
Ben Duagrich
304
Mugeary
Camastianavaig
Beinn Totaig
Lower Ollach
SOUND OF RAASAY
Loch a' Bhràighe
Dry Harbour
125
RONA
Kyle Rona
Eilean Tigh
111
Eilean Fladday
Beinn na h-Iolaire
254
Torran
Manish Point
Loch Arnish
Arnish
Brochel
RAASAY
385
Glame
Balachuirn
Clachan
Beinn na' Leac
319
INNER SOUND
0 2 4 6 miles
0 2 4 6 8 10 km

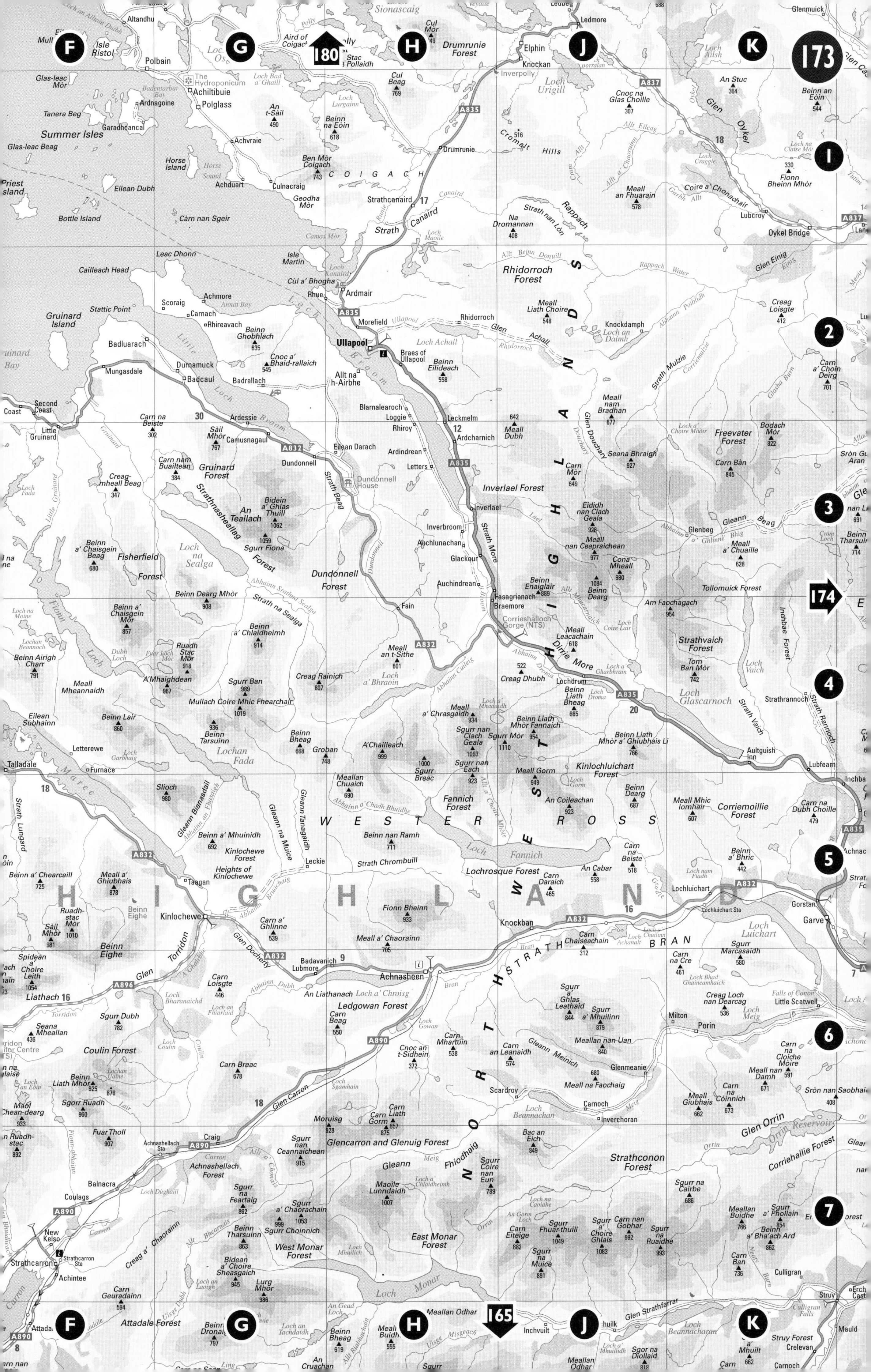
F
G
H
J
K
180
174
165
1
2
3
4
5
6
7
Isle Ristol
Altandhu
Polbain
Aird of Coigach
Stac Pollaidh
Cul Mòr
849
Drumrunie Forest
Elphin
Knockan
Ledmore
Loch Ailsh
Glenmuick
Glas-leac Mòr
The Hydroponicum
Achiltibuie
Polglass
Ardnagoine
Tanera Beg
Garadheancal
Summer Isles
Glas-leac Beag
Cul Beag
769
An t-Sàil
490
Beinn na Eòin
618
Inverpolly
Loch Urigill
A835
A837
Cnoc na Glas Choille
307
An Stuc
364
Beinn an Eòin
544
Glen Oykel
18
Cromalt Hills
516
Drumrunie
Achvraie
Horse Island
Eilean Dubh
Priest Island
Achduart
Culnacraig
Ben Mòr Coigach
743
COIGACH
Geodha Mòr
Strathcanaird
17
Strath Canaird
Meall an Fhuarain
578
Fionn Bheinn Mhòr
330
Coire a' Chonachair
Lubcroy
Oykel Bridge
Bottle Island
Càrn nan Sgeir
Na Dromannan
408
Strath nan Lòn
Rappach
Leac Dhonn
Isle Martin
Cailleach Head
Rhidorroch Forest
Glen Einig
Cùl a' Bhogha
Rhue
Ardmair
Scoraig
Achmore
Carnach
Rhireavach
Stattic Point
Gruinard Island
Badluarach
Beinn Ghobhlach
635
Cnoc a' Bhaid-rallaich
545
A835
Morefield
Rhidorroch
Glen Achall
Meall Liath Choire
548
Knockdamph
Creag Loisgte
412
Ullapool
Braes of Ullapool
Loch Achall
Beinn Eilideach
558
Strath Mulzie
Carn a' Choin Deirg
701
Mungasdale
Durnamuck
Badcaul
Little Loch Broom
Badrallach
Allt na h-Airbhe
Second Coast
Coast
Little Gruinard
Carn na Beiste
302
30
Ardessie
Sàil Mhòr
767
Camusnagaul
A832
Blarnalearoch
Loggie
Rhiroy
Leckmelm
12
Ardcharnich
642
Meall Dubh
Meall nam Bradhan
677
Glen Douchary
Freevater Forest
Bodach Mòr
822
Eilean Darach
Dundonnell
Ardindrean
Letters
Carn nam Buailtean
384
Gruinard Forest
Creag-mheall Beag
347
Strathnasheallag Forest
Dundonnell House
Strath Beag
Carn Mòr
649
Seana Bhraigh
927
Carn Bàn
845
Inverlael Forest
Inverlael
An Teallach
Bidein a' Ghlas Thuill
1062
1059
Sgurr Fiona
Inverbroom
Auchlunachan
Eididh nan Clach Geala
928
Meall nan Ceapraichean
977
Glenbeg
Gleann Beag
Meall a' Chuaille
628
Beinn Tharsuinn
714
691
Beinn a' Chaisgein Beag
680
Fisherfield Forest
Loch na Sealga
Dundonnell Forest
Strath More
Glackour
Cona Mheall
980
Auchindrean
1084
Beinn Dearg
Beinn Enaiglair
889
Tollomuick Forest
Beinn Dearg Mhòr
908
Fasagrianach
Braemore
Fain
Am Faochagach
954
Strath na Sealga
Beinn a' Chaisgein Mòr
857
Beinn a' Chlaidheimh
914
Corrieshalloch Gorge (NTS)
Meall Leacachain
618
Strathvaich Forest
Inchbae Forest
Beinn Airigh Charr
791
Ruadh Stac Mòr
918
Meall an t-Sithe
601
A832
Dirrie More
Tom Ban Mòr
742
Loch Vaich
A'Mhaighdean
967
Sgurr Ban
989
Creag Rainich
807
Loch a' Bhraoin
522
Creag Dhubh
Lochdrum
Meall Mheannaidh
Mullach Coire Mhic Fhearchair
1019
Meall a' Chrasgaidh
934
Beinn Liath Bheag
665
A835
20
Loch Glascarnoch
Strathrannoch
Strath Rannoch
Strath Vaich
Eilean Subhainn
Beinn Lair
860
936
Beinn Tarsuinn
Beinn Bheag
668
Groban
748
A'Chailleach
999
Sgurr nan Clach Geala
1093
Sgurr Mòr
1110
Beinn Liath Mhòr Fannaich
954
Beinn Liath Mhòr a' Ghiubhais Li
766
Aultguish Inn
Letterewe
Lochan Fada
1000
Sgurr Breac
Sgurr nan Each
923
Meall Gorm
949
Kinlochluichart Forest
Lubfearn
Talladale
Furnace
Slioch
980
Meallan Chuaich
690
Fannich Forest
Beinn Dearg
687
18
Loch Maree
Gleann Bianasdail
Gleann na Muice
Gleann Tanagaidh
WESTER ROSS
An Coileachan
923
Meall Mhic Iomhair
607
Corriemoillie Forest
Carn na Dubh Choille
479
A835
Strath Lungard
Beinn a' Mhuinidh
692
Kinlochewe Forest
Heights of Kinlochewe
Beinn nan Ramh
711
Loch Fannich
Carn na Beiste
518
Beinn a' Bhric
442
Achnac
Beinn a' Chearcaill
725
Meall a' Ghiubhais
878
A832
Leckie
Strath Chrombuill
Lochrosque Forest
Carn Daraich
465
An Cabar
558
Lochluichart
A832
Gorstan
Garve
HIGHLAND
Taagan
Ruadh-stac Mòr
1010
Sàil Mhòr
981
Beinn Eighe
Kinlochewe
Carn a' Ghlinne
539
Fionn Bheinn
933
Knockban
16
A832
Loch Luichart
Glen Docherty
Glen Torridon
Meall a' Chaorainn
705
Carn Chaiseachain
312
STRATH BRAN
Carn na Cre
461
Sgurr Marcasaidh
580
Spidean a' Choire Leith
1054
A896
Liathach 16
A832
Badavanich
9
Lubmore
Achnasheen
Carn Loisgte
446
An Liathanach
Loch a' Chroisg
Ledgowan Forest
Sgurr a' Ghlas Leathaid
844
Sgurr a' Mhuilinn
879
Creag Loch nan Dearcag
536
Falls of Conon
Little Scatwell
Milton
Porin
Seana Mheallan
436
Sgurr Dubh
782
Carn Beag
550
Carn Mhartuin
538
Meallan nan Uan
840
Coulin Forest
Carn Breac
678
A890
Cnoc an t-Sidhein
372
Carn an Leanaidh
574
Gleann Meinich
Glenmeanie
Carn na Cloiche Mòire
591
Liath Mhòr
925
876
680
Meall na Faochaig
Meall nan Damh
671
Sgorr Ruadh
960
Glen Carron
18
Scardroy
Carnoch
Meall Giubhais
662
Carn na Còinnich
673
Sròn nan Saobhaidhe
408
Maol Chean-dearg
933
Moruisg
928
Carn Gorm
875
Carn Liath
857
Loch Beannachan
Inverchoran
Glen Orrin
Orrin Reservoir
Fuar Tholl
907
Craig
A890
Achnashellach Sta
Sgurr nan Ceannaichean
915
Glencarron and Glenuig Forest
Bac an Eich
849
Strathconon Forest
Corriehallie Forest
Achnashellach Forest
Gleann Fhiodhaig
Sgurr Coire nan Eun
789
Balnacra
Coulags
Maoile Lunndaidh
1007
NORTH STRATH
Sgurr na Feartaig
862
Sgurr a' Chaorachain
1053
999
Sgurr Choinnich
Sgurr na Cairbe
686
Meallan Buidhe
766
Sgurr a' Phollain
854
A890
New Kelso
Creag a' Chaorainn
Beinn Tharsuinn
863
West Monar Forest
East Monar Forest
Carn Eiteige
882
Sgurr Fhuar-thuill
1049
Sgurr a' Choire Ghlais
1083
Carn nan Gobhar
992
Sgurr na Ruaidhe
993
Beinn a' Bha'ach Ard
862
Strathcarron
Strathcarron Sta
Achintee
Bidean a' Choire Sheasgaich
945
Lurg Mhòr
986
Sgurr na Muice
891
Carn Ban
736
Culligran
Loch Monar
Carn Geuradainn
594
Struy
Attadale
Attadale Forest
Beinn Dronaig
797
Beinn Bheag
619
Meallan Odhar
Inchvuilt
Glen Strathfarrar
Loch Beannacharan
Mauld
Struy Forest
Crelevan
A890
8
662
Carnoch

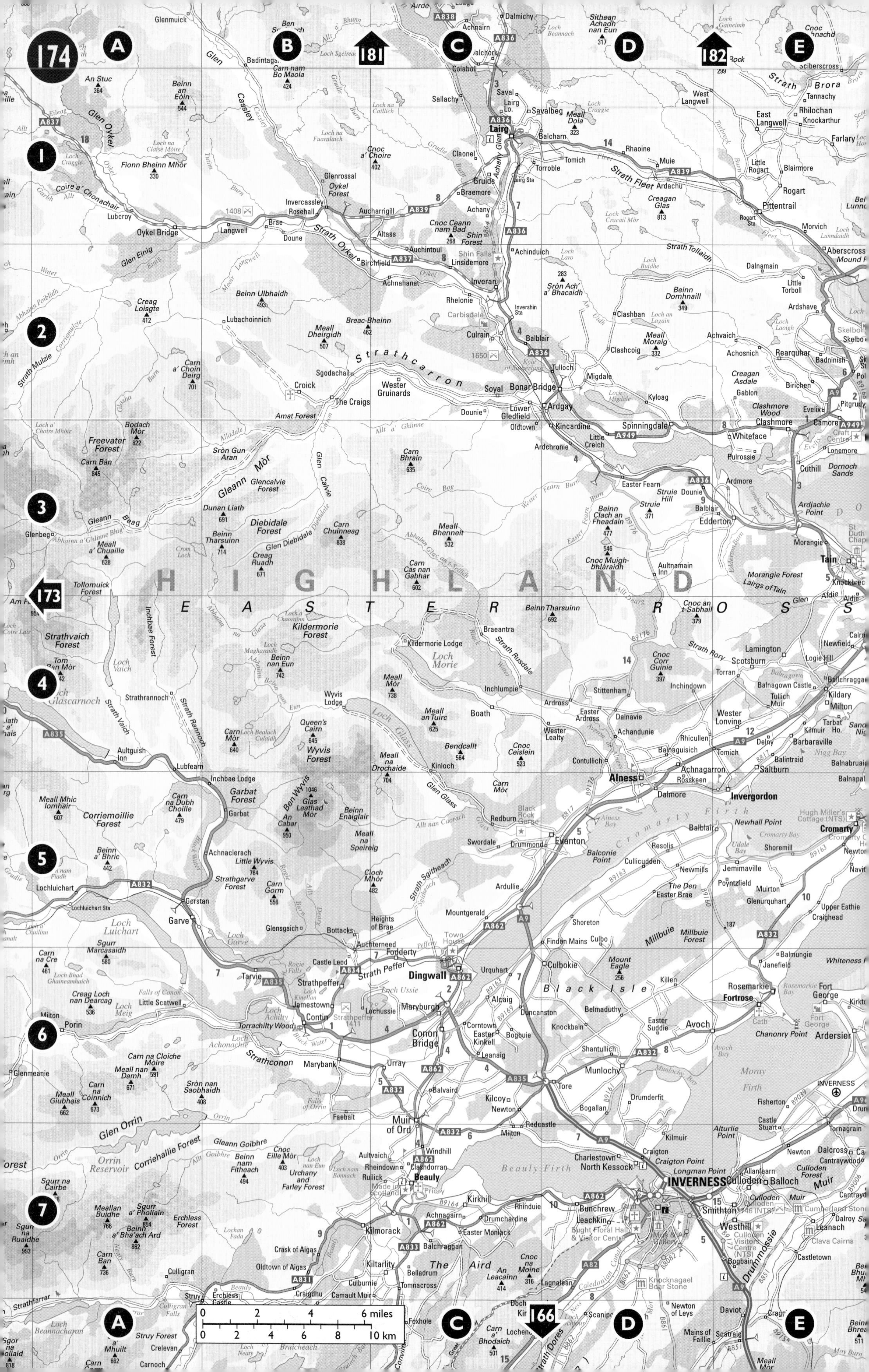
A
B
C
D
E
181
182
173
166
1
2
3
4
5
6
7
Glenmuick
An Stuc
364
Beinn an Eòin
544
Glen Oykel
Glen Cassley
Badintagairt
Carn nam Bo Maola
424
Loch Sgeireach
Achnairn
Dalmichy
A838
A836
Colaboll
Sallachy
Saval
Lairg
Savalbeg
Meall Dola
323
Sithean Achadh nan Eun
317
Loch Beannach
Loch Craggie
Balcharn
Achany Glen
Claonel
Gruids
Braemore
Achany
Torroble
Tomich
Rhaoine
Muie
Strath Fleet
Ardachu
A839
Creagan Glas
813
West Langwell
East Langwell
Knockarthur
Rhilochan
Tannachy
Strath Brora
Sciberscross
Cnoc Achadh
Farlary
Little Rogart
Blairmore
Rogart
Pittentrail
Rogart Sta
Morvich
Loch Lunndaidh
Aberscross
Mound
A837
Loch Craggie
Fionn Bheinn Mhòr
330
Loch na Claise Mòire
Loch na Fuaralaich
Cnoc a' Choire
402
Loch na Caillich
Glenrossal
Oykel Forest
Coire a' Chonachair
Lubcroy
Oykel Bridge
Langwell
1408
Invercassley
Rosehall
Brae
Doune
Aucharrigill
Altass
Cnoc Ceann nam Bad
268
Shin Forest
Strath Oykel
Glen Einig
Auchintoul
Birchfield
Linsidemore
Shin Falls
Achinduich
Loch Laro
Strath Tollaidh
Dalnamain
Achnahanat
Inveran
Rhelonie
Carbisdale
Invershin Sta
283
Sròn Ach' a' Bhacaidh
Loch Buidhe
Beinn Domhnaill
349
Little Torboll
Ardshave
Beinn Ulbhaidh
493
Creag Loisgte
412
Lubachoinnich
Breac-Bheinn
462
Meall Dheirgidh
507
Culrain
Balblair
Clashban
Loch an Lagain
Meall Moraig
332
Clashcoig
Achvaich
Achosnich
Rearquhar
Badninish
Skelbo
Strath Mulzie
Carn a' Choin Deirg
701
Sgodachail
Strathcarron
Croick
Wester Gruinards
The Craigs
Amat Forest
Soyal
Bonar Bridge
Tulloch
Migdale
Kyle of Sutherland
Loch Migdale
Kyloag
Creagan Asdale
Gablon
Birichen
Dounie
Lower Gledfield
Ardgay
Oldtown
Kincardine
Spinningdale
Clashmore Wood
Clashmore
Evelix
Camore
Pitgrudy
A949
A9
Whiteface
Pulrossie
Little Creich
Ardchronie
Craft Centre
Lonemore
Dornoch Sands
Loch a' Choire Mhòir
Bodach Mòr
822
Freevater Forest
Carn Bàn
845
Alladale
Sròn Gun Aran
Gleann Mòr
Glencalvie Forest
Glen Calvie
Carn Bhrain
635
Coire Bog
Wester Fearn Burn
Easter Fearn
Struie Hill
Dounie
Struie
371
Balblair
Edderton
Ardmore
Cuthill
Ardjachie Point
Glenbeg
Gleann Beag
Dunan Liath
691
Diebidale Forest
Carn Chuinneag
838
Glen Diebidale
Meall Bhenneit
532
Beinn Clach an Fheadain
477
546
Cnoc Muigh-bhlàraidh
Morangie
Tain
Meall a' Chuaille
628
Beinn Tharsuinn
714
Creag Ruadh
671
Carn Cas nan Gabhar
602
Aultnamain Inn
Morangie Forest
Lairgs of Tain
Tollomuick Forest
HIGHLAND
EASTER ROSS
Beinn Tharsuinn
692
Cnoc an t-Sabhail
379
Glen Aldie
Knockbreck
Aldie
Strathvaich Forest
Tom Ban Mòr
Inchbae Forest
Loch Vaich
Kildermorie Forest
Beinn nan Eun
742
Kildermorie Lodge
Loch Morie
Braeantra
Strath Rusdale
Cnoc Corr Guinie
397
Strath Rory
Lamington
Scotsburn
Newfield
Logie Hill
Ballchraggan
Kildary
Milton
Strathrannoch
Strath Vaich
Wyvis Lodge
Meall Mòr
738
Loch Glass
Meall an Tuirc
625
Inchlumpie
Boath
Stittenham
Ardross
Easter Ardross
Dalnavie
Achandunie
Inchindown
Torran
Balnagown Castle
Tulloch Muir
Western Lonvine
Tarbat Ho.
Kilmuir
Barbaraville
Nigg Bay
Delny
Balintraid
Saltburn
Invergordon
Loch Glascarnoch
A835
Aultguish Inn
Strath Rannoch
Carn Mòr
640
Queen's Cairn
645
Wyvis Forest
Bendcallt
564
Meall na Drochaide
704
Kinloch
Wester Lealty
Cnoc Ceislein
523
Contullich
Alness
Rhicullen
Balnaguisich
Achnagarron
Rosskeen
Dalmore
Tomich
Lubfearn
Inchbae Lodge
Garbat Forest
Garbat
Carn na Dubh Choille
479
Ben Wyvis
1046
Glas Leathad Mòr
An Cabar
950
Beinn Enaiglair
Glen Glass
Carn Mòr
Redburn
Black Rock Gorge
Allt nan Caorach
Evanton
Swordale
Drummond
Balconie Point
Cromarty Firth
Balblair
Newhall Point
Hugh Miller's Cottage (NTS)
Cromarty
Resolis
Udale Bay
Shoremill
Cullicudden
Newmills
Jemimaville
Poyntzfield
B9163
Meall Mhic Iomhair
607
Corriemoillie Forest
Beinn a' Bhric
442
Achnaclerach
Little Wyvis
764
Meall na Speireig
Strathgarve Forest
Carn Gorm
556
Cloch Mhòr
482
Strath Sgitheach
Ardullie
The Den
Easter Brae
Muirton
Glenurquhart
Upper Eathie
Craighead
Lochluichart
A832
Lochluichart Sta
Gorstan
Garve
Loch Luichart
Sgurr Marcasaidh
580
Carn na Cre
461
Glensgaich
Bottacks
Heights of Brae
Mountgerald
A862
Shoreton
Findon Mains
Culbo
Millbuie
Millbuie Forest
Mount Eagle
256
Balmungie
Janefield
Whiteness Head
Loch Garve
Achterneed
Fodderty
Strath Peffer
Castle Leod
A834
Dingwall
Town House
Urquhart
Culbokie
Black Isle
Killen
Rosemarkie
Fortrose
Fort George
Tarvie
Strathpeffer
Loch Ussie
Jamestown
Contin
Lochussie
Maryburgh
Alcaig
Duncanston
Belmaduthy
Easter Suddie
Avoch
Chanonry Point
Ardersier
Creag Loch nan Dearcag
536
Loch Meig
Little Scatwell
Falls of Conon
Milton
Porin
Torrachilty Wood
Loch Achilty
Achonachie
Conon Bridge
Corntown
Easter Kinkell
Bogbuie
Knockbain
Shantullich
Leanaig
Munlochy
Strathconon
Marybank
Urray
Carn na Cloiche Mòire
591
Meall nan Damh
671
Sròn nan Saobhaidh
408
Glenmeanie
Carn na Coinnich
673
Meall Giubhais
662
Glen Orrin
Falls of Orrin
Faebait
Balvaird
Kilcoy
Newton
Tore
Drumderfit
Bogallan
Moray Firth
INVERNESS
Fisherton
Castle Stuart
Alturlie Point
Tornagrain
Muir of Ord
Redcastle
Milton
Kilmuir
Craigton
Craigton Point
Longman Point
Orrin Reservoir
Corriehallie Forest
Gleann Goibhre
Beinn nam Fitheach
494
Cnoc Eille Mòr
403
Urchany and Farley Forest
Aultvaich
Rheindown
Windhill
Clashdorran
Ruilick
Beauly
Priory
Beauly Firth
Charlestown
North Kessock
Culloden
Balloch
Allanfearn
Dalcross
Cantraywood
Culloden Forest
Newton
Sgurr na Cairbe
Meallan Buidhe
766
Sgurr a' Phollain
854
Beinn a' Bha'ach Ard
862
Erchless Forest
Sgurr na Ruaidhe
993
Carn Ban
736
Kilmorack
Kirkhill
Achnagairn
Drumchardine
Rhindiue
Bunchrew
Leachkin
Easter Moniack
Balchraggan
A833
Bught Floral Hall & Visitor Centre
Mus & Art Gallery
Smithton
Westhill
Culloden Visitors Centre (NTS)
Cumberland Stone
Leanach
Clava Cairns
Dalroy
Castletown
Crask of Aigas
Oldtown of Aigas
Kiltarlity
Belladrum
The Aird
An Leacainn
414
Cnoc na Moine
316
Lagnalean
Caledonian Canal
Knocknagael Boar Stone
Bogbain
Drummossie
Culligran
Struy
Erchless Castle
A831
Craigdhu
Culburnie
Tomnacross
Camault Muir
Newton of Leys
Daviot
Strathfarrar
Culligran Falls
0 2 4 6 miles
0 2 4 6 8 10 km
Foxhole
Loch Beannacharan
Struy Forest
Crelevan
Carnoch
a' Mhuilt
662
Bruicheach
Carn a' Bhodaich
501
Lochend
Strath Dores
Scaniport
Mains of Faillie
Scatraig
Cragie
B9006
B9176
B9177
B851
Moy Burn

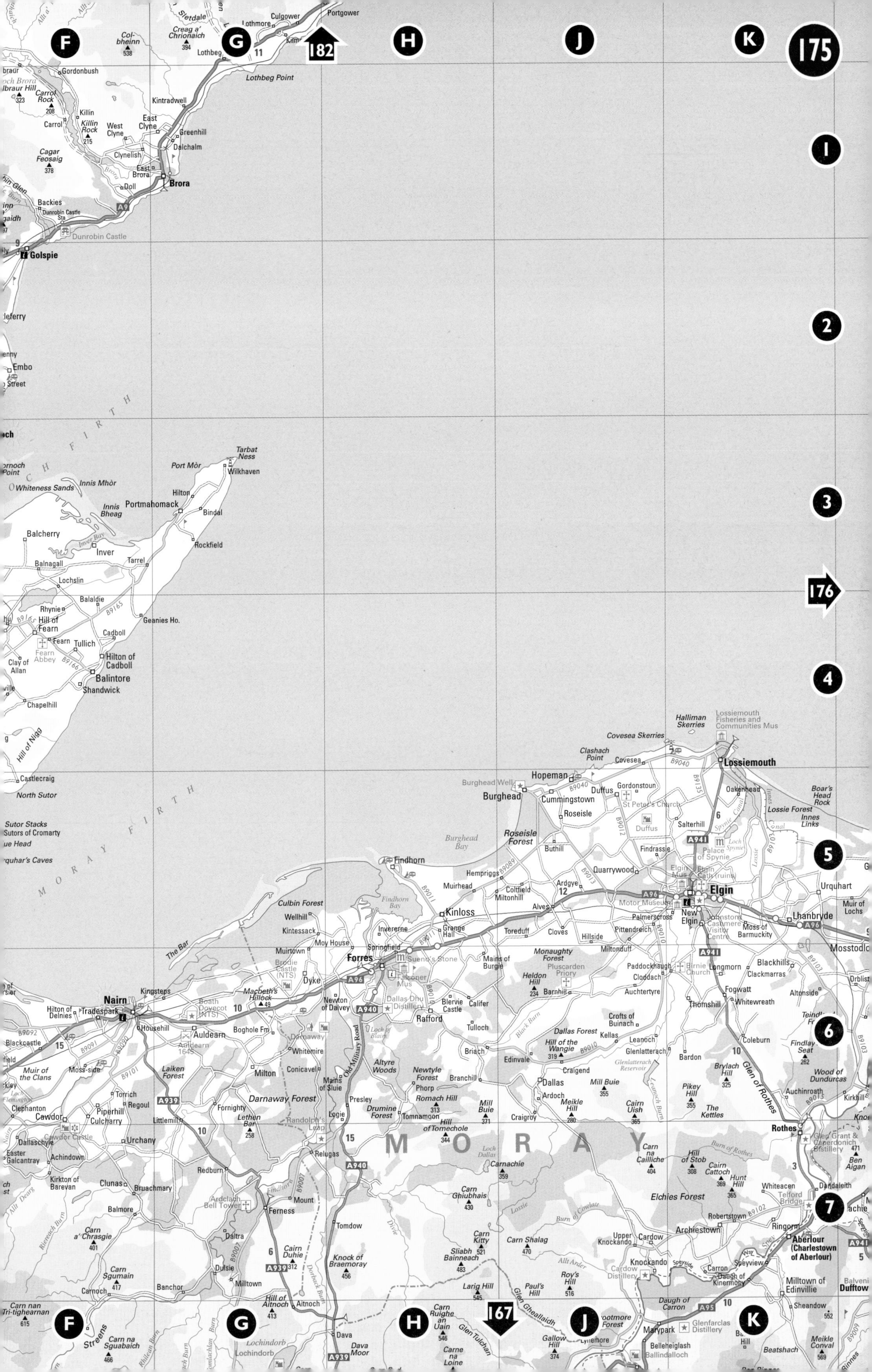

175
F
G
H
J
K
182
176
167
1
2
3
4
5
6
7
Sletdale
Culgower
Portgower
Lothmore
Col-bheinn
538
Creag a' Chrionaich
394
Lothbeg
11
Lothbeg Point
Gordonbush
Carrol Rock
208
Killin
Carrol
Killin Rock
215
West Clyne
East Clyne
Kintradwell
Greenhill
Dalchalm
Cagar Feosaig
378
Clynelish
East Brora
Brora
Doll
Backies
Dunrobin Castle Sta
A9
Dunrobin Castle
9
Golspie
Embo
Street
FIRTH
Port Mòr
Tarbat Ness
Wilkhaven
Whiteness Sands
Innis Mhòr
Hilton
Innis Bheag
Portmahomack
Bindal
Balcherry
Inver Bay
Inver
Rockfield
Tarrel
Balnagall
Lochslin
Balaldie
Rhynie
Hill of Fearn
B9165
Geanies Ho.
Fearn
Fearn Abbey
Tullich
Cadboll
Clay of Allan
B9166
Hilton of Cadboll
Balintore
Shandwick
Chapelhill
Hill of Nigg
Castlecraig
North Sutor
Sutor Stacks
Sutors of Cromarty
MORAY FIRTH
Halliman Skerries
Lossiemouth Fisheries and Communities Mus
Covesea Skerries
Clashach Point
Covesea
B9040
Lossiemouth
Burghead Well
Hopeman
Burghead
Duffus
Gordonstoun
Cummingstown
St Peter's Church
Oakenhead
Boar's Head Rock
Lossie Forest
Innes Links
Roseisle
Duffus
Salterhill
Roseisle Forest
Burghead Bay
Buthill
A941
Findrassie
Palace of Spynie
Findhorn
Hempriggs
Quarrywood
Muirhead
Coltfield
Miltonhill
Ardgye
12
Elgin
Urquhart
Findhorn Bay
Culbin Forest
Kinloss
Alves
A96
Motor Museum
Wellhill
Palmerscross
New Elgin
Lhanbryde
Muir of Lochs
Kintessack
Invererne
Grange Hall
Toreduff
Cloves
Hillside
Pittendreich
Moss of Barmuckity
Moy House
Springfield
Miltonduff
Mosstodloch
The Bar
Muirtown
Forres
Sueno's Stone
Mains of Burgie
Monaughty Forest
Brodie Castle (NTS)
Falconer Mus
Pluscarden Priory
Paddockhaugh
Birnie Church
Longmorn
Blackhills
Clackmarras
Dyke
Heldon Hill
234
Barnhill
Cloddach
Auchtertyre
Fogwatt
Orbliston
Kingsteps
Macbeth's Hillock
49
Newton of Dalvey
Dallas Dhu Distillery
Blervie Castle
Califer
Whitewreath
Thomshill
Altonside
Nairn
Hilton of Delnies
Tradespark
Boath Dovecot (NTS)
10
A940
Rafford
Crofts of Buinach
Househill
Boghole Fm
Darnaway
Tulloch
Kellas
Blackcastle
15
Auldearn
Auldearn 1645
Whitemire
Loch of Blairs
Dallas Forest
Leanoch
Coleburn
Findlay Seat
262
B9091
Briach
Hill of Wangie
319
Glenlatterach
Bardon
Muir of the Clans
Moss-side
B9101
Laiken Forest
Milton
Conicavel
Altyre Woods
Newtyle Forest
Edinvale
Craigend
Glenlatterach Reservoir
Brylach Hill
325
Wood of Dunduras
Torrich
Mains of Sluie
Branchill
Dallas
Mill Buie
355
Pikey Hill
355
Glen of Rothes
Auchinroath
Regoul
Darnaway Forest
Presley
Phorp
Ardoch
Kirkhill
Clephanton
Piperhill
A939
Fornighty
Drumine Forest
Romach Hill
313
Meikle Hill
280
Cairn Uish
365
The Kettles
Cawdor
Culcharry
Littlemill
Lethen Bar
258
Logie
Tomnamoon
Mill Buie
371
Craigroy
Rothes
Cawdor Castle
Randolph's Leap
Hill of Tomechole
344
Glen Grant & Caperdonich Distillery
Dallaschyle
Urchany
MORAY
Loch Dallas
Carn na Cailliche
404
Hill of Stob
308
Cairn Catroch
369
Burn of Rothes
Ben Aigan
471
Easter Galcantray
Achindown
Relugas
Carnachie
359
Hunt Hill
365
Whiteacen
Dandaleith
Kirkton of Barevan
Redburn
Carn Ghiubhais
430
Elchies Forest
Telford Bridge
Clunas
Bruachmary
Ardclach Bell Tower
Mount
Tomdow
Robertstown
B9102
Archiestown
Ringorm
Balmore
Ferness
Burn of Cowlatt
Aberlour (Charlestown of Aberlour)
Carn a' Chrasgie
401
Daltra
Cairn Duhie
312
Knock of Braemoray
456
Carn Kitty
521
Carn Shalag
470
Upper Knockando
Cardow
Speyview
Sliabh Bainneach
483
Knockando
Carron
Carn Sgumain
417
Dulsie
Roy's Hill
516
Cardow Distillery
Daugh of Kinermony
Milltown of Edinvillie
Dufftown
Carnoch
Banchor
Milltown
Larig Hill
545
Paul's Hill
Glen Gheallaidh
Daugh of Carron
A95
Sheandow
552
Carn nan Tri-tighearnan
615
Hill of Aitnoch
413
Aitnoch
Carn Ruighe an Uain
546
Glen Tulchan
Scootmore Forest
Glenfarclas Distillery
Marypark
Streens
Carn na Sguabaich
466
Lochindorb
Dava
Dava Moor
Carne na Loine
Gallow Hill
374
Belleheiglash
Ballindalloch
Beatshach
Meikle Conval
569
A939

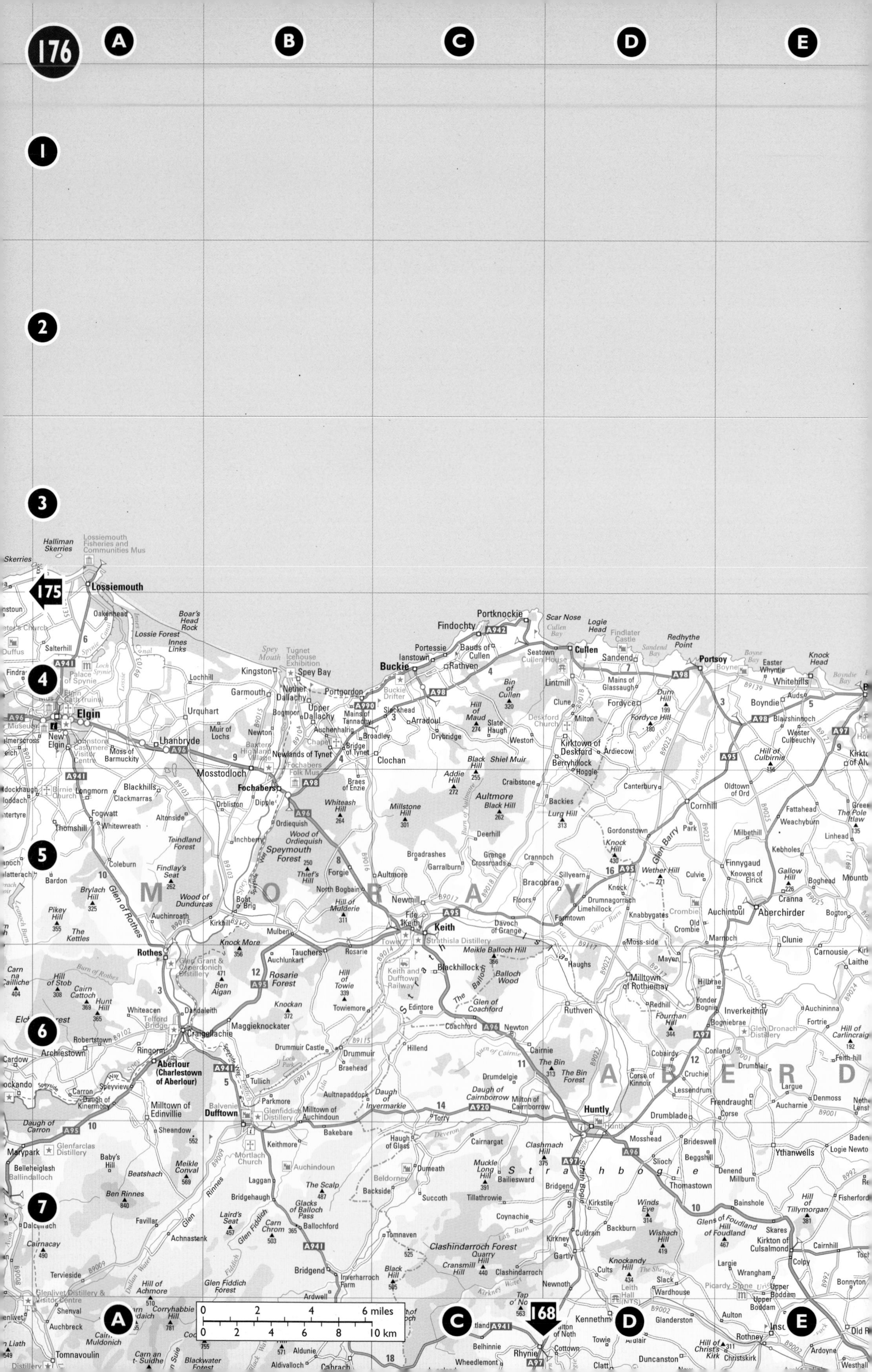

176
A
B
C
D
E
1
2
3
4
5
6
7
175
168
Halliman Skerries
Skerries
Lossiemouth Fisheries and Communities Mus
Lossiemouth
Oakenhead
Boar's Head Rock
Lossie Forest
Innes Links
Spey Mouth
Tugnet Icehouse Exhibition
Spey Bay
Salterhill
Duffus
Kingston
Garmouth
Lochhill
Elgin
Palace of Spynie
Elgin Cath (ruins)
Urquhart
Lhanbryde
Muir of Lochs
Newton
Nether Dallachy
Upper Dallachy
Bogmoor
Portgordon
Buckie
Buckie Drifter
Findochty
Portknockie
Ianstown
Portessie
Bauds of Cullen
Rathven
Scar Nose
Cullen Bay
Logie Head
Findlater Castle
Sandend Bay
Redhythe Point
Seatown
Cullen House
Cullen
Sandend
Portsoy
Boyne
Boyne Bay
Knock Head
Easter Whyntie
Whitehills
Boyndie Bay
Boyndie
Auds
Blairshinnoch
Wester Culbeuchly
Mains of Glassaugh
Fordyce
Durn Hill
Fordyce Hill
Lintmill
Clune
Milton
Deskford Church
Kirktown of Deskford
Ardiecow
Berryhillock
Hoggie
Bin of Cullen
Hill of Maud
Slate Haugh
Weston
Arradoul
Drybridge
Slackhead
Mains of Tannachy
Auchenhalrig
Broadley
Bridge of Tynet
Newlands of Tynet
Clochan
Baxters Highland Village
Fochabers Folk Mus
Fochabers
Mosstodloch
Moss of Barmuckity
New Elgin
Johnstons Cashmere Visitor Centre
Birnie Church
Longmorn
Blackhills
Clackmarras
Orbliston
Dipple
Braes of Enzie
Whiteash Hill
Black Hill
Addie Hill
Shiel Muir
Craibstone
Aultmore
Millstone Hill
Canterbury
Backies
Lurg Hill
Cornhill
Hill of Culbirnie
Oldtown of Ord
Fogwatt
Whitewreath
Thomshill
Altonside
Ordiequish
Inchberry
Wood of Ordiequish
Speymouth Forest
Thief's Hill
Teindland Forest
Coleburn
Findlay's Seat
Glen of Rothes
Brylach Hill
Pikey Hill
The Kettles
Bardon
Deerhill
Broadrashes
Garralburn
Grange Crossroads
Crannoch
Gordonstown
Knock Hill
Glen Barry
Park
Milbethill
Fattahead
Weachyburn
Linhead
Kebholes
Finnygaud
Knowes of Elrick
Gallow Hill
Boghead
Cranna
Aberchirder
Auchintoul
Wether Hill
Culvie
Forgie
Aultmore
North Bogbain
Hill of Mulderie
Newmill
Fife Keith
Keith
Strathisla Distillery
Davoch of Grange
Bracobrae
Floors
Sillyearn
Drumnagorrach
Limehillock
Farmtown
Knock
Knabbygates
Crombie
Old Crombie
Marnoch
Clunie
Carnousie
Moss-side
Mayen
Milltown of Rothiemay
Hillbrae
MORAY
Boat o' Brig
Wood of Dundurcas
Auchinroath
Kirkhill
Mulben
Knock More
Rothes
Glen Grant & Caperdonich Distillery
Ben Aigan
Tauchers
Auchlunkart
Rosarie
Rosarie Forest
Hill of Towie
Towiemore
Keith and Dufftown Railway
Blackhillock
Meikle Balloch Hill
Balloch Wood
Haughs
Glen of Coachford
The Balloch
Edintore
Coachford
Newton
Ruthven
Redhill
Fourman Hill
Yonder Bognie
Inverkeithny
Bogniebrae
Glen Dronach Distillery
Auchininna
Fortrie
Hill of Carlincraig
Cairn na Cailliche
Hill of Stob
Cairn Cattoch
Hunt Hill
Burn of Rothes
Knockan
Dandaleith
Maggieknockater
Craigellachie
Telford Bridge
Whiteacen
Elchies Forest
Archiestown
Robertstown
Ringorm
Aberlour (Charlestown of Aberlour)
Drummuir Castle
Drummuir
Hillend
Braehead
Cairnie
The Bin
The Bin Forest
Cobairdy
Conland
Drumblair
Corse of Kinnoir
Cruchie
Lessendrum
Largue
ABERD
Cardow
Knockando
Speyview
Carron
Daugh of Kinermony
Milltown of Edinvillie
Balvenie
Dufftown
Tullich
Parkmore
Glenfiddich Distillery
Milltown of Auchindoun
Aultnapaddock
Daugh of Invermarkie
Drumdelgie
Daugh of Cairnborrow
Milton of Cairnborrow
Torry
Huntly
Drumblade
Frendraught
Corse
Auchernie
Denmoss
Daugh of Carron
Sheandow
Marypark
Glenfarclas Distillery
Baby's Hill
Belleheiglash
Ballindalloch
Meikle Conval
Beatshach
Keithmore
Mortlach Church
Bakebare
Haugh of Glass
Cairnargat
Clashmach Hill
Deveron
Mosshead
Brideswell
Beggshill
Sliochd
Thomastown
Denend
Millbrum
Ythanwells
Logie Newton
Auchindoun
Laggan
Dumeath
Beldorney
Backside
The Scalp
Glacks of Balloch Pass
Muckle Long Hill
Bailiesward
Bridgend
Strathbogie
Strath Bogie
Ben Rinnes
Favillar
Achnastank
Dalcorrach
Cairnacay
Tervieside
Laird's Seat
Glen Fiddich
Carn Chrom
Bridgehaugh
Ballochford
Succoth
Tillathrowie
Coynachie
Kirkstile
Winds Eye
Backburn
Wishach Hill
Bainshole
Hill of Tillymorgan
Glens of Foudland
Hill of Foudland
Skares
Kirkton of Culsalmond
Cairnhill
Tomnaven
Clashindarroch Forest
Quarry Hill
Cransmill Hill
Clashindarroch
Kirkney
Gartly
Cuildrain
Knockandy Hill
The Shevock
Largie
Wrangham
Colpy
Glenlivet Distillery & Visitor Centre
Hill of Achmore
Corryhabbie Hill
Glen Fiddich Forest
Bridgend
Inverharroch Farm
Black Hill
Ardwell
Tap o' Noth
Newnoth
Cults
Slack
Leith Hall (NTS)
Wardhouse
Picardy Stone
Upper Boddam
Bonnyton
Kennethmont
Glanderston
Aulton
Rothney
Insch
Shenval
Auchbreck
Cairn Muldonich
Carn an t-Suidhe
Blackwater Forest
Tomnavoulin
Aldunie
Aldivalloch
Cabrach
Belhinnie
Wheedlemont
Rhynie
Cottown
Towie
Ardlair
Clatt
Duncanston
Hill of Christ's Kirk
Christskirk
Ardoyne
Westhall
A96
A941
A98
A990
A942
A95
A97
A920
B9015
B9103
B9104
B9016
B9017
B9018
B9022
B9023
B9025
B9139
B9121
B9117
B9014
B9115
B9102
B9009
B9008
B9001
B9002
B9024
0 2 4 6 miles
0 2 4 6 8 10 km

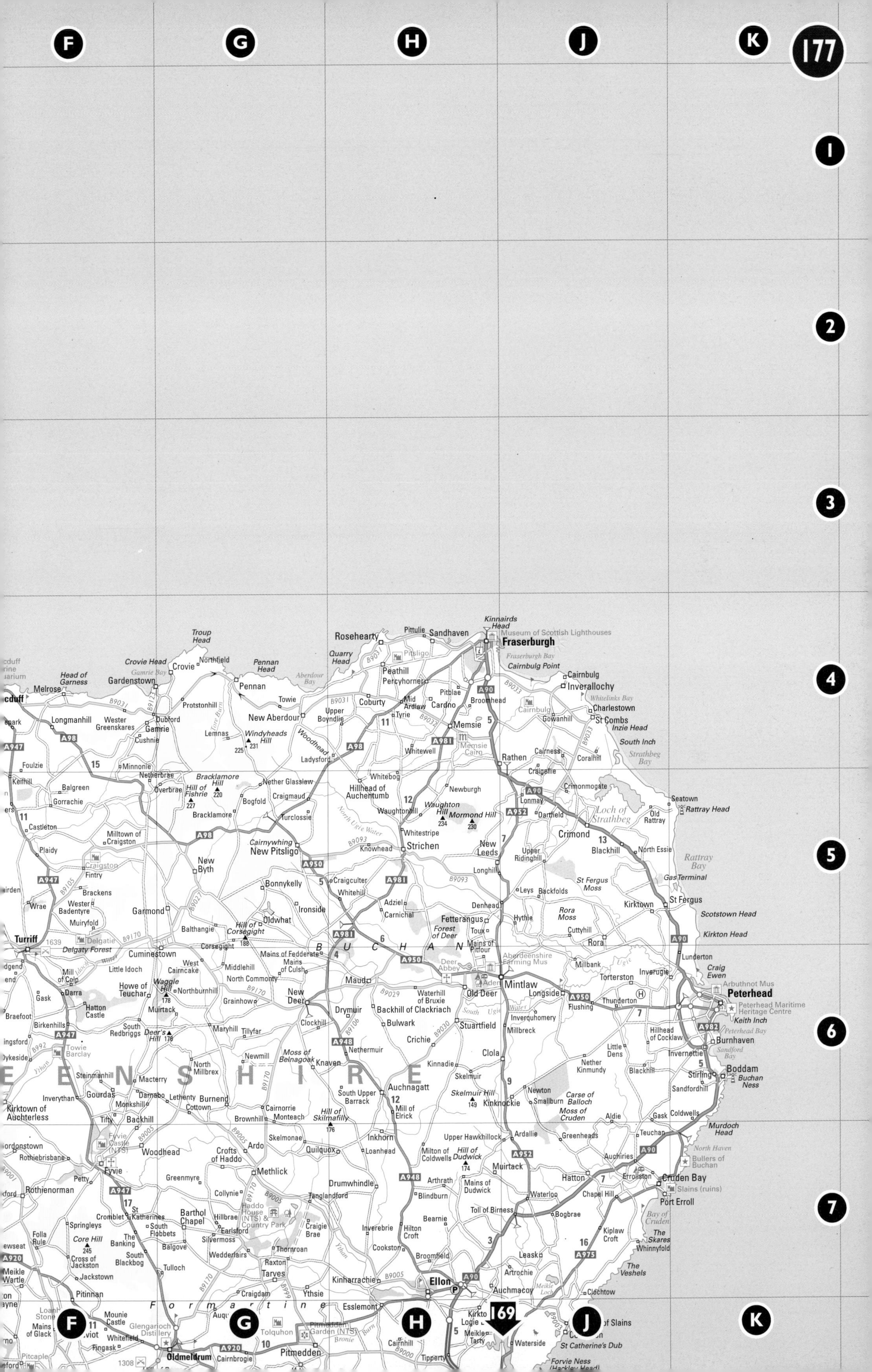

F
G
H
J
K
1
2
3
4
5
6
7
Kinnairds Head
Museum of Scottish Lighthouses
Fraserburgh
Fraserburgh Bay
Cairnbulg Point
Pittulie
Sandhaven
Rosehearty
Quarry Head
Pitsligo
Peathill
Percyhorner
Troup Head
Crovie Head
Crovie
Northfield
Pennan Head
Pennan
Aberdour Bay
Gamrie Bay
Gardenstown
Head of Garness
Melrose
Macduff
Longmanhill
Western Greenskares
Dubford
Gamrie
Cushnie
Protstonhill
Towie
New Aberdour
Upper Boyndlie
Coburty
Mid Ardlaw
Tyrie
Cardno
Pitblae
Broomhead
Memsie
Memsie Cairn
Whitewell
Ladysford
Woodhead
Lemnas
Windyheads Hill
231
225
Minnonie
Netherbrae
Overbrae
Bracklamore Hill
220
Hill of Fishrie
227
Bracklamore
Bogfold
Nether Glasslaw
Craigmaud
Turclossie
Whitebog
Hillhead of Auchentumb
Newburgh
Waughtonhill
Waughton Hill
234
Mormond Hill
230
Whitestripe
Strichen
Knowhead
Cairnywhing
New Pitsligo
New Byth
Foulzie
Keilhill
Balgreen
Gorrachie
Castleton
Milltown of Craigston
Plaidy
Craigston
Fintry
Brackens
Wester Badentyre
Wrae
Muiryfold
Turriff
1639
Delgatie
Delgaty Forest
Garmond
Balthangie
Cuminestown
Bonnykelly
Ironside
Oldwhat
Hill of Corsegight
188
Corsegight
Craigculter
Whitehill
Adziel
Carnichal
Fetterangus
Forest of Deer
Toux
Mains of Pitfour
Longhill
Denhead
Inverallochy
Cairnbulg
Whitelinks Bay
Charlestown
St Combs
Inzie Head
South Inch
Strathbeg Bay
Gowanhill
Rathen
Cairness
Corahill
Craigellie
Crimonmogate
Lonmay
Dartfield
Loch of Strathbeg
Old Rattray
Seatown
Rattray Head
Crimond
Blackhill
North Essie
Rattray Bay
Gas Terminal
New Leeds
Upper Ridinghill
Leys
Backfolds
St Fergus Moss
Rora Moss
Hythie
Cuttyhill
Rora
Kirktown
St Fergus
Scotstown Head
Kirkton Head
Lunderton
Craig Ewen
Arbuthnot Mus
Aberdeenshire Farming Mus
Deer Abbey
Millbank
Torterston
Inverugie
Mintlaw
Longside
Flushing
Thunderton
Peterhead
Peterhead Maritime Heritage Centre
Keith Inch
Peterhead Bay
Burnhaven
Sandford Bay
Hillhead of Cocklaw
Little Dens
Invernettie
Nether Kinmundy
Blackhill
Stirling
Boddam
Buchan Ness
Sandfordhill
B U C H A N
Mains of Fedderate
Mains of Culsh
Middlehill
North Commonty
Waggle Hill
178
Northburnhill
Little Idoch
Caircake
West
Mill of Colp
Darra
Howe of Teuchar
Gask
Hatton Castle
Braefoot
Birkenhills
Muirtack
Grainhow
New Deer
Maud
Waterhill of Bruxie
Old Deer
Clockhill
Drymuir
Backhill of Clackriach
Bulwark
Crichie
Stuartfield
Inverquhomery
Millbreck
South
Redbriggs
Deer's Hill
178
Maryhill
Tillyfar
Towie Barclay
Nethermuir
Moss of Belnagoak
Knaven
Newmill
North Millbrex
Steinmanhill
Macterry
Darnabo
Lethenty
Burnend
Cottown
Gourdas
Monkshill
Inverythan
Kirktown of Auchterless
Tifty
Backhill
Fyvie Castle (NTS)
Woodhead
Fyvie
Crofts of Haddo
Ardo
Brownhill
Cairnorrie
Monteach
Hill of Skilmafilly
176
South Upper Barrack
Auchnagatt
Mill of Elrick
Kinnadie
Skelmuir
Skelmuir Hill
149
Clola
Kinknockie
Newton
Smallburn
Carse of Balloch
Moss of Cruden
Aldie
Gask
Coldwells
Murdoch Head
Teuchan
Greenheads
Ardallie
Upper Hawkhillock
Skelmonae
Quilquox
Inkhorn
Loanhead
Milton of Coldwells
Hill of Dudwick
174
Muirtack
Mains of Dudwick
Auchiries
Hatton
Errolston
Cruden Bay
North Haven
Bullers of Buchan
Slains (ruins)
Port Erroll
Chapel Hill
Waterloo
Bogbrae
Toll of Birness
Arthrath
Blindburn
Drumwhindle
Tanglandford
Methlick
Greenmyre
Collynie
Haddo House (NTS) & Country Park
Barthol Chapel
Hillbrae
Earlsford
Silvermoss
Craigie Brae
Inverebrie
Bearnie
Hilton Croft
Kiplaw Croft
Bay of Cruden
The Skares
Whinnyfold
The Veshels
Leask
Artrochie
Auchmacoy
Meikle Loch
Clochtow
Ellon
Broomfield
Cookston
Thornroan
Raxton
Tarves
Wedderlairs
Balgove
Tulloch
Kinharrachie
Ythsie
Craigdam
F o r m a r t i n e
Esslemont
Kirkton
Logie
Meikle Tarty
Waterside
St Catherine's Dub
Forvie Ness (Hackley Head)
169
Tipperty
Cairnhill
Pitmedden Garden (NTS)
Pitmedden
Tolquhon
Cairnbrogie
Oldmeldrum
Glengarioch Distillery
Whiteford
Fingask
Mounie Castle
Mains of Glack
Loanhead Stone
Pitinnan
Jackstown
South Blackbog
The Banking
Core Hill
245
Cross of Jackston
Folla Rule
Springleys
Cromblet
St Katherines
South Flobbets
Rothienorman
Petty
Rothiebrisbane
Gordonstown
Meikle Wartle
Pitcaple
1308
A90
A98
A947
A981
A952
A950
A948
A982
A975
A920
B9031
B9033
B9032
B9093
B9029
B9030
B9170
B9105
B9005
B9000
B9003
B992
B9001

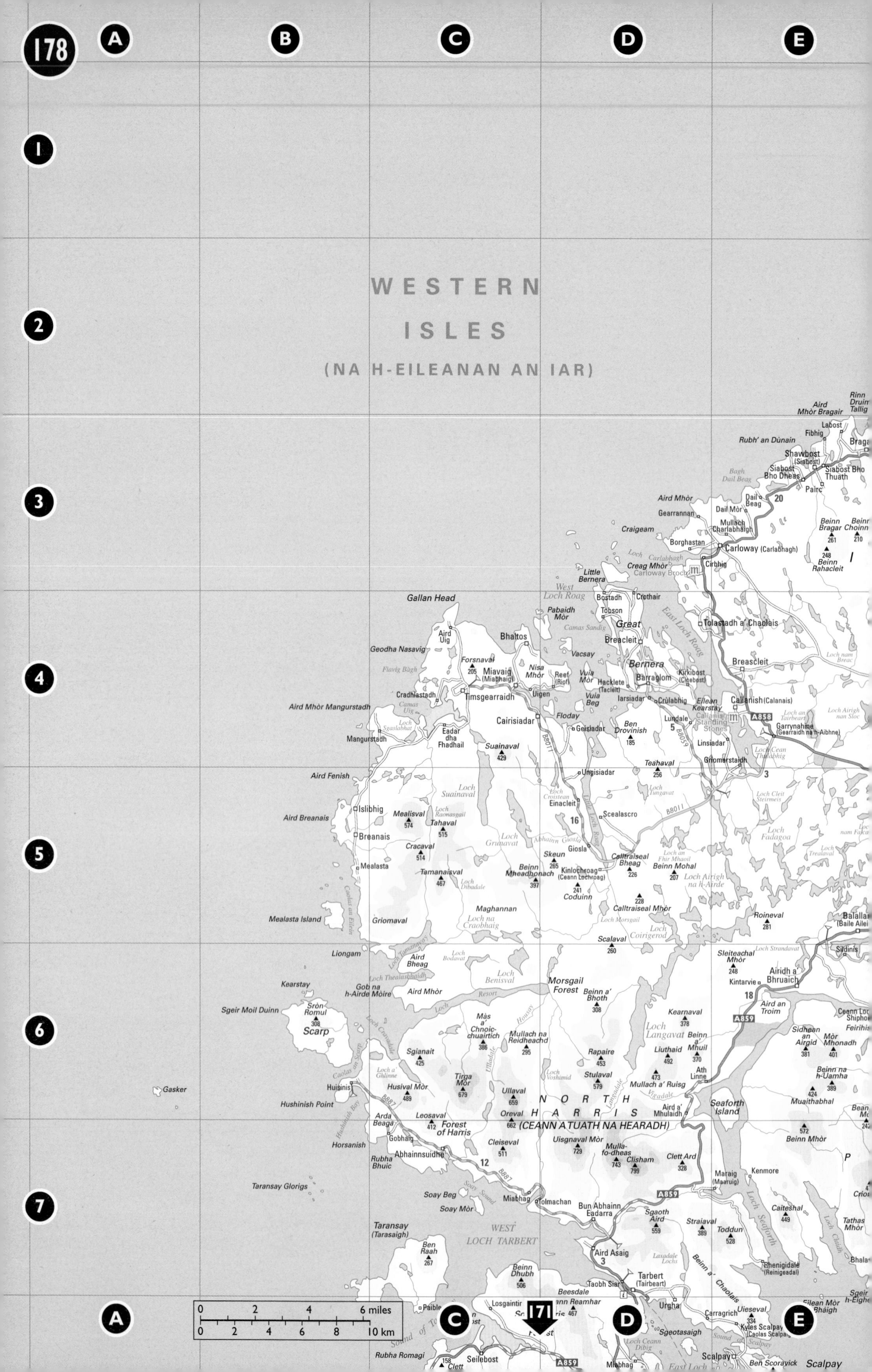

A B C D E

1

W E S T E R N

I S L E S

(NA H-EILEANAN AN IAR)

2

Rinn Druim Taillg
Àird Mhòr Bragair
Labost
Rubh' an Dùnain   Fibhig
Shawbost   Braga
(Siabost)
Siabost   Siabost Bho
Bho Dheas   Thuath
Bàgh   Pairc
Dail Beag   20
Àird Mhòr   Dail Beag
Gearrannan   Dail Mòr   Beinn   Beinn
Mullach   Bragar   Choinn
Craigeam   Charlabhaigh   261   210
Borghastan   Carloway (Carlabhagh)   248
Beinn   I
Cirbhig   Rahacleit

3

Little   Creag Mhòr
Bernera   Carloway Broch
Gallan Head   West   Bostadh   Crothair
Loch Roag   Pabaidh   Tobson
Mòr   Great   Tolastadh a Chaolais
Àird   Breaclet
Uig   Bhaltos   Loch nam
Geodha Nasavig   Vacsay   Breac
Forsnaval   Nisa   Bernera   Breasclet
Flavig Bàgh   205   Mhòr   Reef   Vula   Kirkibost
Miavaig   (Rìof)   Mòr   (Ciabost)   A858
(Miabhaigh)   Hacklete   Callanish (Calanais)
Àird Mhòr Mangurstadh   Cradhlastadh   Timsgearraidh   (Tacleit)   Crùlabhig   Loch Airigh
Camas   Uigen   Iarsiadar   Eilean   Garrynahine   nan Sloc
Uig   Kearstay   (Gearraidh na h-Aibhne)
Loch   Cairisiadar   Floday   Callanish
Sgealabhat   Eadar   Geisiadar   Standing   3
Mangurstadh   dha   Ben   5   Stones   Loch Cean
Fhadhail   Suainaval   Drovinish   Lundale   Thuabhig
Àird Fenish   429   185   Linsiadar
Loch   Griomarstaidh
Suainaval   Teahaval
Loch   Ungisiadar   256
Aird Breanais   Ramasgail   Loch   B8011   Loch Cleit
Islibhig   Mealisval   Tahaval   Loch Croistean   Tungavat   Steirness
574   515   Einacleit   Scealascro   Loch
Breanais   Cracaval   Loch   16   Fadagoa
514   Grimavat   Skeun   Giosla   Calltraiseal   Loch an
Mealasta   Tamanaisval   265   Bheag   Fhir Mhaoil   Loch
467   Loch   Kinlochroag   Beinn   Roineval   Trealaval
Dibadale   (Ceann Lochroag)   Mheadhonach   (Ceann Lochroag)   Mohal   Loch Airigh
Mealasta Island   Griomaval   397   241   207   na h-Àirde
Maghannan   Coduinn   281   Sildinis
Loch na   228   Calltraiseal Mhòr   Balalla
Craobhaig   Loch Morsgail   (Baile Ailei
Liongam   Loch   Scalaval   Loch
Àird   Bodavat   260   Coirigerod   Sleiteachal
Bheag   Mhòr   Loch Strandavat
Kearstay   Loch   248   Airidh a
Gob na   Benisval   Kintarvie   Bhruaich
Sgeir Moil Duinn   h-Àirde Mòire   Àird Mhòr   Morsgail   18   Àird an
Sròn   Resort   Forest   Beinn a'   A859   Troim
Romul   Bhoth   Ceann Loc
308   Màs a'   308   Kearnaval   Shipho
Scarp   Chnoic-   378   Sidhean   Feirihis
Sgianait   chuairtich   Mullach na   Beinn   an   Mòr
Gasker   425   386   Reidheachd   Loch   Liuthaid   Mhuil   Airgid   Mhonadh
295   Langavat   492   370   381   401
Rapaire   Beinn na
Huisinis   Tirga   453   473   Ath   h-Uamha
Hushinish Point   Mòr   Stulaval   Linne   424   389
679   579   Mullach a' Ruisg
Ullaval   572   Beann
Mò

6

Arda   Husival Mòr   659   N O R T H   Mc
Beaga   489   Aird a'   Muaithabhal   242
Leosaval   Oreval   H A R R I S   Mhulaidh   Seaforth
Gobhaig   412   662   Island   Beinn Mòr
Abhainnsuidhe   Forest   (CEANN A TUATH NA HEARADH)
Rubha   of Harris   Cleiseval   Uisgnaval Mòr   Maraig   Kenmore
Bhuic   511   729   Mullá-   (Maaruig)   Crìo
12   fo-dheas   Clett Ard
Horsanish   743   Clisham   328   Caitesha
Taransay Glorigs   799   449   Tathas
A859   Mhòr
Soay Beg   Miabhag   Bun Abhainn   Sgaoth
Taransay   Tolmachan   Eadarra   Àird   Straiaval   Bhala
(Tarasaigh)   Soay Mòr   559   389
W E S T   Toddun
Ben   528
Raah   L O C H   T A R B E R T   Rhenigidale
267   Àird Asaig   (Reinigeadal)
3   Beinn a'   Sgeir
Beinn   Chaolais   h-Eighe
Dhubh   Tarbert   Eilean Mòr
506   (Tairbeart)   Bhàigh
Beesdale   t   Uieseval
Taobh Siar   334   Bhala
eann Reamhar   Urgha   Kyles Scalpay
Paible   ris   467   Carragrich   (Caolas Scalpay
Losgaintir   171   Loch Ceann   Uieseval
0   2   4   6 miles   A859   Dibig   Scalpay   Scalpay
Rubha Romagi   158   Seilebost   Miabhag   Ben Scoravick
0 2 4 6 8 10 km   Clett   Sgeotasaigh   East Loch

A   C   D   E

7

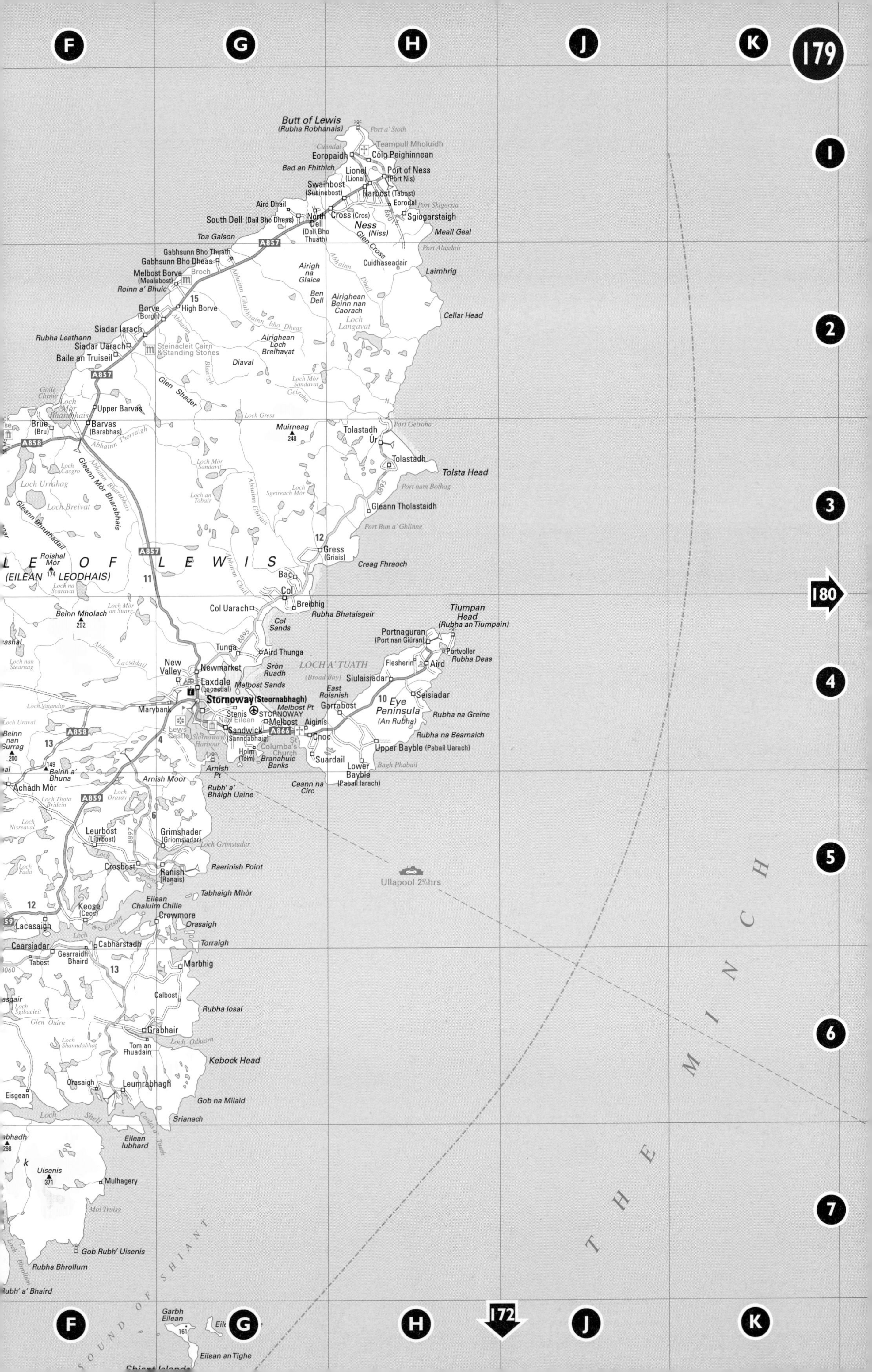
179
F
G
H
J
K
1
2
3
4
5
6
7
180
172
Butt of Lewis
(Rubha Robhanais)
Port a' Stoth
Teampull Mholuidh
Eoropaidh
Còig Peighinnean
Bad an Fhithich
Lionel
(Lional)
Port of Ness
(Port Nis)
Swainbost
(Suainebost)
Habost (Tabost)
Eorodal
Port Skigersta
Aird Dhail
Sgiogarstaigh
South Dell (Dail Bho Dheas)
North Dell
(Dail Bho Thuath)
Cross (Cros)
Ness
(Niss)
Meall Geal
Toa Galson
Port Alasdair
Gabhsunn Bho Thuath
Gabhsunn Bho Dheas
Cuidhaseadair
Melbost Borve
(Mealabost)
Roinn a' Bhuic
Laimhrig
Airigh na Glaice
Ben Dell
Airighean Beinn nan Caorach
Borve
(Borgh)
High Borve
Cellar Head
Loch Langavat
Siadar Iarach
Rubha Leathann
Siadar Uarach
Steinacleit Cairn & Standing Stones
Airighean Loch Breihavat
Baile an Truiseil
Diaval
Glen Shader
Loch Mòr Sandavat
Upper Barvas
Brue
(Bru)
Barvas
(Barabhas)
Loch Gress
Muirneag
248
Tolastadh Ùr
Port Geiraha
Tolastadh
Tolsta Head
Port nam Bothag
Loch Urrahag
Loch Breivat
Gleann Mòr Bharabhais
Gleann Tholastaidh
Port Bun a' Ghlinne
Gress
(Griais)
Creag Fhraoch
ISLE OF LEWIS
(EILEAN LEODHAIS)
Roishal Mòr
174
Bac
Col
Breibhig
Col Uarach
Rubha Bhataisgeir
Beinn Mholach
292
Col Sands
Tiumpan Head
(Rubha an Tiumpain)
Portnaguran
(Port nan Giùran)
Portvoller
Tunga
Aird Thunga
Rubha Deas
New Valley
Newmarket
Sròn Ruadh
LOCH A' TUATH
(Broad Bay)
Flesherin
Aird
Laxdale
(Lacasdal)
Melbost Sands
Siulaisiadar
Stornoway (Steornabhagh)
East Roinish
Melbost Pt
Marybank
Stenis
STORNOWAY
Garrabost
Eye Peninsula
(An Rubha)
Seisiadar
Rubha na Greine
Melbost
Aiginis
Lews Castle
Sandwick
(Sanndabhaig)
Cnoc
Rubha na Bearnaich
Upper Bayble (Pabail Uarach)
St Columba's Church
Holm
(Tolm)
Branahuie Banks
Suardail
Lower Bayble
(Pabail Iarach)
Bagh Phabail
Arnish Pt
Ceann na Circ
Arnish Moor
Rubh' a' Bhàigh Uaine
Achadh Mòr
Leurbost
(Liurbost)
Grimshader
(Griomsiadar)
Loch Grimsiadar
Raerinish Point
Crosbost
Ranish
(Ranais)
Ullapool 2¾hrs
Tabhaigh Mhòr
Eilean Chaluim Chille
Keose
(Ceos)
Crowmore
Orasaigh
Lacasaigh
Torraigh
Cearsiadar
Gearraidh Bhaird
Cabharstadh
Marbhig
Calbost
Rubha Iosal
Grabhair
Tom an Fhuadain
Kebock Head
Orasaigh
Leumrabhagh
Gob na Milaid
Eisgean
Srianach
Eilean Iubhard
Uisenis
371
Mulhagery
Mol Truisg
Gob Rubh' Uisenis
Rubha Bhrollum
Rubh' a' Bhaird
SOUND OF SHIANT
Garbh Eilean
161
Eilean an Tighe
THE MINCH
A857
A858
A859
A866
B895
B897

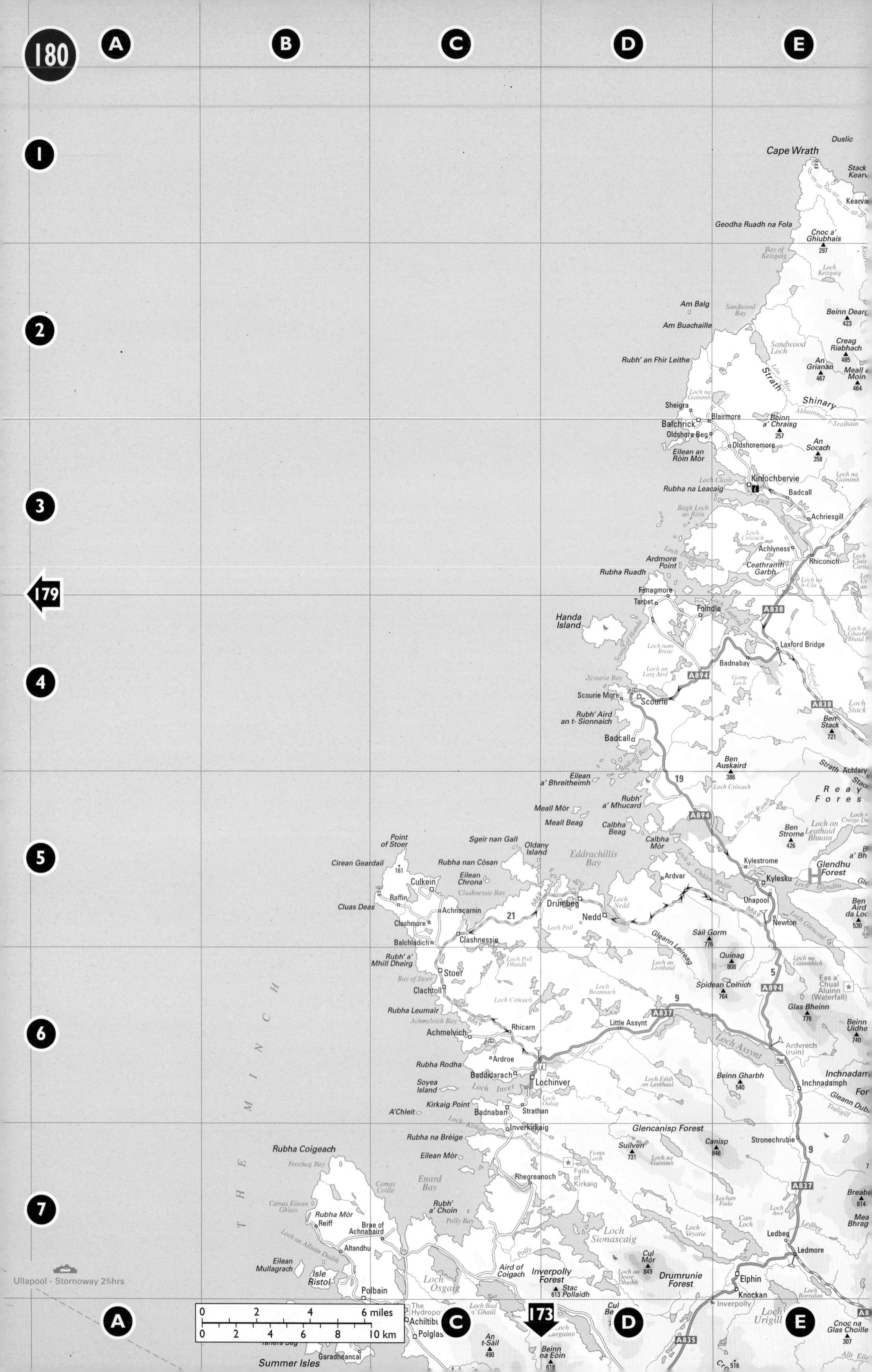
180
A
B
C
D
E
1
2
3
4
5
6
7
179
173
Duslic
Cape Wrath
Stack Kearv
Kearva
Geodha Ruadh na Fola
Cnoc a' Ghiubhais
297
Bay of Keisgaig
Loch Keisgaig
Am Balg
Sandwood Bay
Am Buachaille
Beinn Dearg
423
Sandwood Loch
Creag Riabhach
485
Rubh' an Fhir Leithe
An Grianan
467
Meall Moin
464
Strath
Shinary
Loch na Gainimh
Sheigra
Blairmore
Balchrick
Beinn a' Chraisg
257
Oldshore Beg
Oldshoremore
An Socach
358
Eilean an Ròin Mòr
Loch Clash
Kinlochbervie
Loch na Gainimh
Rubha na Leacaig
Badcall
B801
Bàgh Loch an Ròin
Achriesgill
Loch Crocach
Achlyness
Loch Dùghaill
Ardmore Point
Ceathramh Garbh
Rhiconich
Rubha Ruadh
Loch na h-Ula
Fanagmore
Tarbet
Foindle
Loch Laxford
A838
Handa Island
Sound of Handa
Loch nam Breac
Laxford Bridge
Loch an Laig Aird
Badnabay
Scourie Bay
A894
Gorm Loch
Scourie More
Scourie
A838
Loch Stack
Rubh' Aird an t- Sionnaich
Ben Stack
721
Badcall
Badcall Bay
Ben Auskaird
386
Strath
Achfary
Eilean a' Bhreitheimh
19
Loch Crocach
Reay Forest
Rubh' a' Mhucard
A894
Meall Mòr
Allt nan Ramh
Meall Beag
Calbha Beag
Loch an Leathaid Bhuain
Ben Strome
426
Point of Stoer
Sgeir nan Gall
Calbha Mòr
Oldany Island
Eddrachillis Bay
Glendhu Forest
Cirean Geardail
161
Rubha nan Còsan
Kylestrome
Eilean Chrona
Ardvar
Kylesku
Culkein
Clashnessie Bay
Loch a' Chàirn Bhàin
Loch Glendhu
Raffin
Drumbeg
Unapool
Cluas Deas
Achnacarnin
B869
Loch Nedd
Nedd
Newton
Clashmore
21
Loch Poll
Loch Glencoul
Balchladich
Clashnessie
Gleann Leireag
Sàil Gorm
776
Loch na Gainmhich
Rubh' a' Mhill Dheirg
Loch Poll Dhaidh
Quinag
808
Stoer
Loch an Leothaid
Bay of Stoer
5
Eas a' Chual Aluinn (Waterfall)
Clachtoll
Loch Beannach
Spidean Coinich
764
A894
Loch Crocach
9
Glas Bheinn
776
Rubha Leumair
A837
Achmelvich Bay
B869
Little Assynt
Beinn Uidhe
740
Achmelvich
Rhicarn
Loch Assynt
Ardvreck (ruin)
Inver
Ardroe
Rubha Rodha
Baddidarach
Inchnadamph
Loch Fèith an Leothaid
Lochinver
Beinn Gharbh
540
Inchnadamph
Soyea Island
Loch Inver
Gleann Dubh
Loch Culag
Kirkaig Point
Badnaban
Strathan
A'Chleit
Loch Kirkaig
Glencanisp Forest
Inverkirkaig
Canisp
846
Stronechrubie
Rubha na Brèige
Suilven
731
Fionn Loch
Loch na Gainimh
9
Rubha Coígeach
Eilean Mòr
Falls of Kirkaig
Feochag Bay
Enard Bay
Rhegreanoch
A837
Camas Coille
Breabag
814
Rubh' a' Choin
Lochan Fada
Cam Loch
Cam Loch
Camas Eilean Ghlais
Rubha Mòr
Reiff
Polly Bay
Loch Awe
Brae of Achnahaird
Loch Sionascaig
Loch Veyatie
Ledbeg
Ledbeg
Loch an Alltain Duibh
Altandhu
Polly
Cul Mòr
849
Ledmore
Eilean Mullagrach
Isle Ristol
Aird of Coigach
Inverpolly Forest
Loch an Doire Dhuibh
Drumrunie Forest
Elphin
Ullapool - Stornoway 2¾hrs
Loch Osgaig
Stac Pollaidh
613
Knockan
Loch Borralan
Polbain
Inverpolly
Loch Bad a' Ghaill
Loch Urigill
Achiltibuie
Polglass
An t-Sàil
490
Loch Lurgainn
A835
Cnoc na Glas Choille
307
Tanera Beg
Beinn na Eòin
618
Garadheancal
Summer Isles
516
0 2 4 6 miles
0 2 4 6 8 10 km
THE MINCH

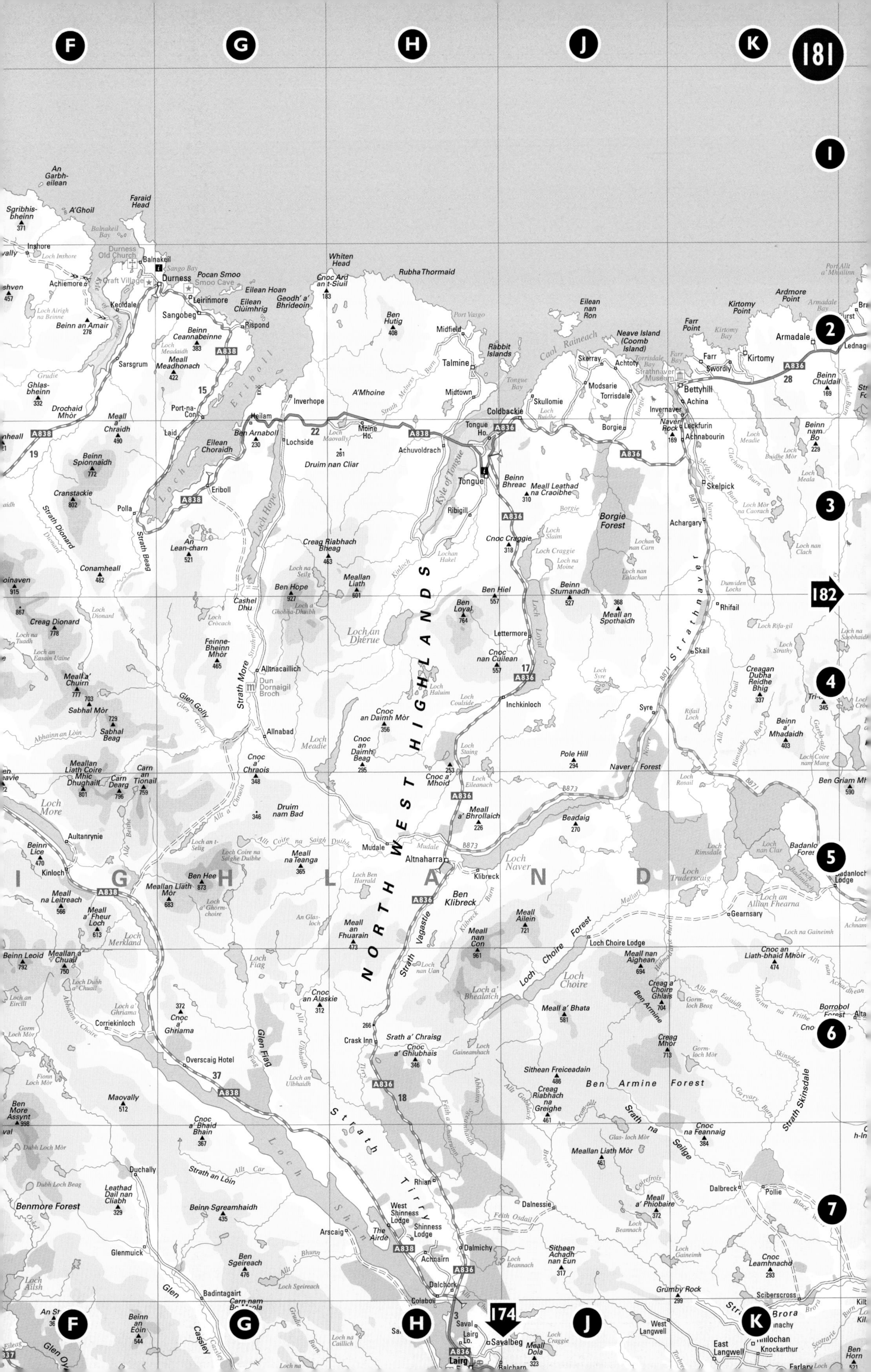
F
G
H
J
K
An Garbh-eilean
Faraid Head
Sgribhis-bheinn 371
A'Gheoil
Balnakeil Bay
Inshore
Loch Inshore
Durness Old Church
Balnakeil
Sango Bay
Craft Village
Durness
Pocan Smoo
Smoo Cave
Achiemore
Leirinmore
Eilean Hoan
Eilean Clùimhrig
Geodh' a' Bhrideoin
Whiten Head
Cnoc Ard an t-Siuil 183
Rubha Thormaid
Keoldale
Kyle of Durness
Loch Airigh na Beinne
Beinn an Amair 278
Sangobeg
Rispond
Beinn Ceannabeinne 383
Loch Meadaidh
Meall Meadhonach 422
A838
Ben Hutig 408
Port Vasgo
Midfield
Rabbit Islands
Eilean nan Ron
Caol Raineach
Neave Island (Coomb Island)
Farr Point
Kirtomy Point
Ardmore Point
Armadale Bay
Armadale
Kirkomy Bay
Torrisdale Bay
Farr Bay
Skerray
Achtoty
Strathnaver Museum
Farr
Swordly
Kirtomy
A836
28
Lednag
Talmine
Tongue Bay
Modsarie
Torrisdale
Bettyhill
Achina
Beinn Chuldail 169
Sarsgrum
Grudie
Glas-bheinn 332
15
Loch Eriboll
Port-na-Con
Inverhope
A'Mhoine
Strath Melness
Midtown
Skullomie
Loch Buidhe
Coldbackie
Invernaver
Naver Rock 169
Leckfurin
Achnabourin
Drochaid Mhòr
Meall a' Chraidh 490
Laid
Heilam
22
Ben Arnaboll 230
Lochside
Moine Ho.
Loch Maovally
261
A838
Achuvoldrach
Tongue Ho.
Borgie
Beinn nam Bo 229
Loch Meadie
Loch Buidhe Mòr
19
Eilean Choraidh
Druim nan Cliar
Beinn Spionnaidh 772
Eriboll
Tongue
Beinn Bhreac
Meall Leathad na Craoibhe 310
Skelpick
Loch Meala
Cranstackie 802
Polla
Ribigill
Kyle of Tongue
Borgie
Borgie Forest
Loch Mòr na Caoraich
Achargary
Strath Dionard
Strath Beag
Loch Hope
An Lean-charn 521
Creag Riabhach Bheag 463
Cnoc Craggie 318
Loch Slaim
Loch Craggie
Lochan nan Carn
Loch nan Clach
Conamheall 482
Loch na Seilg
Meallan Liath 601
Kinloch
Lochan Hakel
Loch na Moine
Loch nan Ealachan
Dunviden Lochs
Foinaven 915
Ben Hope 927
Cashel Dhu
Loch a' Ghobha-Dhuibh
Ben Hiel 557
Beinn Stumanadh 527
368
Meall an Spothaidh
Rhifail
182
867
Loch Dionard
Creag Dionard 778
Loch Crocach
Loch an Dherue
Ben Loyal 764
Lettermore
Loch Loyal
Loch Rifa-gil
Loch na Tuadh
Loch an Easain Uaine
Feinne-Bheinn Mhòr 465
Cnoc nan Cùilean 557
Skail
Loch Strathy
Meall a' Chuirn 777
703
Sabhal Mòr
729
Sabhal Beag
Strath More
Altnacaillich
Dun Dornaigil Broch
Glen Golly
Loch Haluim
Loch Coulside
17
A836
Inchkinloch
Loch Syre
Strathnaver
B871
Creagan Dubha Reidhe Bhig 337
Tri-a 345
Syre
Rifail Loch
Beinn a' Mhadaidh 403
Abhainn an Loin
Allnabad
Cnoc an Daimh Mòr 356
Loch Meadie
Cnoc an Daimh Beag 295
NORTH WEST HIGHLANDS
Loch Staing
253
Cnoc a' Mhoid
Pole Hill 294
Naver Forest
Loch Coire nam Mang
Ben Griam Mh 590
Meallan Liath Coire Mhic Dhughaill 801
Carn Dearg 796
Carn an Tionail 759
Cnoc a' Chraois 348
Loch Eileanach
B873
Loch Rosail
B871
Loch More
Allt a' Chraois
346
Druim nam Bad
Meall a' Bhrollaich 226
Beadaig 270
Aultanrynie
Loch an t-Seilg
Allt Coire na Saigh Duibhe
Mudale
B873
Loch Rimsdale
Loch nan Clar
Badanloch Forest
5
Beinn Lice 470
Loch Coire na Saighe Duibhe
Meall na Teanga 365
Altnaharra
Loch Naver
Loch Truderscaig
Kinloch
Ben Hee 873
Loch Ben Harrald
Klibreck
Badanloch Lodge
HIGHLAND
A838
Meallan Liath Mòr 683
Loch a' Ghorm-choire
A836
Ben Klibreck
Mallart
Loch an Alltan Fhearna
Meall na Leitreach 566
Meall a' Fheur Loch 613
An Glas-loch
Meall an Fhuarain 473
Meall nan Con 961
Meall Ailein 721
Loch Choire Forest
Gearnsary
Loch Merkland
Loch na Gaineimh
Beinn Leoid 792
Meallan a' Chuail 750
Loch Fiag
Strath Vagastie
Loch nan Uan
Loch Choire Lodge
Meall nan Aighean 694
Cnoc an Liath-bhaid Mhòir 474
Loch Dubh a' Chuail
Loch Choire
Loch a' Bhealaich
Creag a' Choire Ghlais 704
Ben Armine
Gorm-loch Beag
Allt an Ealaidh
Loch an Eircill
Loch a' Ghriama
372
Cnoc a' Ghriama
Cnoc an Alaskie 312
Meall a' Bhata 581
Borrobol Forest
Corriekinloch
Glen Fiag
266
Crask Inn
Srath a' Chraisg
Creag Mhòr 713
Cnoc a' Ghiubhais 346
Loch Gaineamhach
Gorm-loch Mòr
Fionn Loch Mòr
Overscaig Hotel
37
Loch an Ulbhaidh
Sithean Freiceadain 486
Ben Armine Forest
Strath Skinsdale
A838
A836
18
Ben More Assynt 998
Maovally 512
Cnoc a' Bhaid Bhain 367
Strath Tirry
Creag Riabhach na Greighe 461
Strath na Seilge
Cnoc na Feannaig 384
Dubh Loch Mòr
Loch Shin
Meallan Liath Mòr 461
Duchally
Strath an Loin
Allt Car
Rhian
Dalbreck
Pollie
7
Dubh Loch Beag
Leathad Dail nan Cliabh 329
Benmore Forest
Beinn Sgreamhaidh 435
West Shinness Lodge
Shinness Lodge
Dalnessie
Feith Osdail
Meall a' Phiobaire 372
Loch Beannach
Arscaig
The Airde
A838
Dalmichy
Glenmuick
Ben Sgeireach 476
Achnairn
Loch Beannach
Sithean Achadh nan Eun 317
Loch Gaineimh
Cnoc Leamhnachd 293
A836
Loch Ailsh
Glen Cassley
Badintagairt
Loch Sgeireach
Dalchork
Grumby Rock 299
Sciberscross
Carn nam Bo Maola
Colaboll
174
An Stac 36
Beinn an Eoin 544
Saval
Lairg Lo.
Savalbeg
Meall Dola 323
Loch Craggie
West Langwell
East Langwell
Brora
Knockarthur
Ben Horn 521
Loch na Caillich
A836
Lairg
Balcharn
Farlary
2
3
4
6

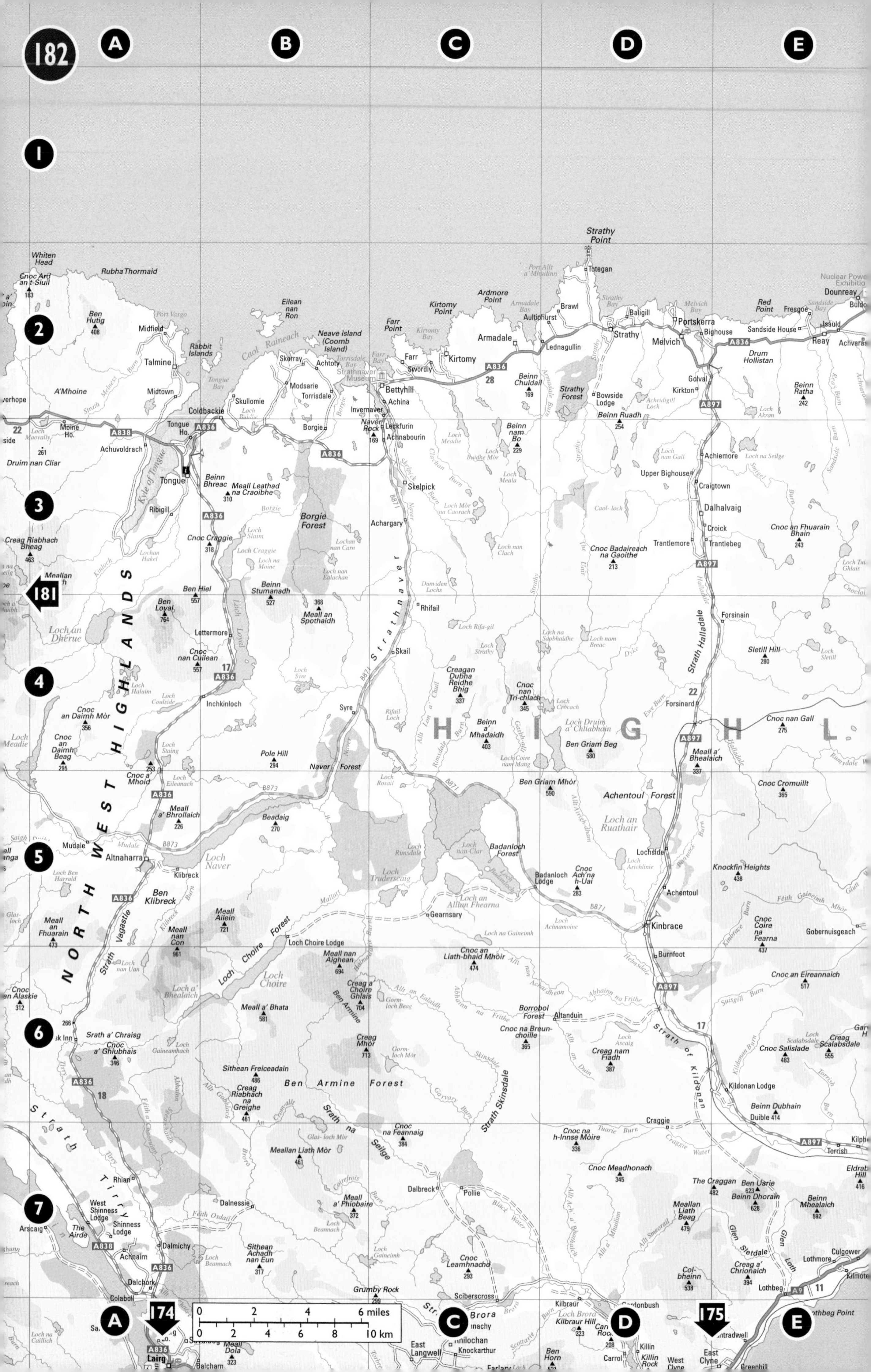
182
A
B
C
D
E
1
2
3
4
5
6
7
Strathy Point
Whiten Head
Rubha Thormaid
Cnoc Ard an t-Siuil
Ben Hutig
Midfield
Port Vasgo
Rabbit Islands
Talmine
Eilean nan Ron
Caol Raineach
Neave Island (Coomb Island)
Skerray
Achtoty
Modsarie
Torrisdale
Farr Point
Kirtomy Point
Farr
Swordly
Kirtomy
Ardmore Point
Armadale
Totegan
Brawl
Aultiphurst
Lednagullin
Baligill
Strathy
Melvich
Portskerra
Bighouse
Red Point
Fresgoe
Sandside House
Isauld
Reay
Achvarasdal
Dounreay
Nuclear Power Exhibition
Drum Hollistan
A'Mhoine
Midtown
Skullomie
Coldbackie
Tongue Ho.
Moine Ho.
Achuvoldrach
Druim nan Cliar
Kyle of Tongue
Tongue
Ribigill
Strathnaver Museum
Bettyhill
Achina
Invernaver
Naver Rock
Leckfurin
Achnabourin
Borgie
Beinn Chuldail
Strathy Forest
Bowside Lodge
Beinn Ruadh
Golval
Kirkton
Beinn Ratha
Beinn nam Bo
Beinn Bhreac
Meall Leathad na Craoibhe
Skelpick
Achiemore
Upper Bighouse
Craigtown
Dalhalvaig
Croick
Trantlemore
Trantlebeg
Borgie Forest
Achargary
Cnoc Craggie
Creag Riabhach Bheag
Cnoc Badaireach na Gaoithe
Cnoc an Fhuarain Bhain
Ben Hiel
Beinn Stumanadh
Meall an Spothaidh
Rhifail
Ben Loyal
Loch Loyal
Loch an Dherue
Lettermore
Cnoc nan Cuilean
Strathnaver
Strath Halladale
Forsinain
Sletill Hill
Skail
Creagan Dubha Reidhe Bhig
Cnoc nan Tri-chlach
Inchkinloch
Cnoc an Daimh Mòr
Cnoc an Daimh Beag
Syre
Forsinard
Cnoc nan Gall
Beinn a' Mhadaidh
Loch Druim a' Chliabhain
Ben Griam Beg
Meall a' Bhealaich
Pole Hill
Naver Forest
Cnoc a' Mhoid
HIGHLAND
NORTH WEST HIGHLANDS
Ben Griam Mhòr
Achentoul Forest
Cnoc Cromuillt
Meall a' Bhrollaich
Beadaig
Loch an Ruathair
Mudale
Altnaharra
Loch Naver
Klibreck
Lochside
Knockfin Heights
Badanloch Forest
Badanloch Lodge
Cnoc Ach'na h-Uai
Loch Truderscaig
Ben Klibreck
Achentoul
Meall an Fhuarain
Meall Ailein
Meall nan Con
Loch Choire Forest
Gearnsary
Kinbrace
Cnoc Coire na Fearna
Gobernuisgeach
Loch Choire Lodge
Meall nan Aighean
Cnoc an Liath-bhaid Mhòir
Burnfoot
Cnoc an Eireannaich
Strath Vagastie
Loch Choire
Creag a' Choire Ghlais
Ben Armine
Cnoc Alaskie
Meall a' Bhata
Borrobol Forest
Altanduin
Cnoc na Breun-choille
Strath of Kildonan
Strath a' Chraisg
Cnoc a' Ghiubhais
Creag Mhòr
Creag nam Fiadh
Cnoc Salislade
Creag Scalabsdale
Sithean Freiceadain
Ben Armine Forest
Kildonan Lodge
Creag Riabhach na Greighe
Strath Skinsdale
Beinn Dubhain
Duible
Strath Tirry
Strath na Seilge
Cnoc na Feannaig
Cnoc na h-Innse Mòire
Craggie
Torrish
Meallan Liath Mòr
Cnoc Meadhonach
Rhian
Dalbreck
Pollie
The Craggan
Ben Uarie
Beinn Dhorain
Eldrable Hill
West Shinness Lodge
Shinness Lodge
Dalnessie
Meall a' Phiobaire
Meallan Liath Beag
Beinn Mhealaich
Arscaig
The Airde
Dalmichy
Achnairn
Sithean Achadh nan Eun
Cnoc Leamhnachd
Glen Sletdale
Glen Loth
Creag a' Chrionaich
Col-bheinn
Lothmore
Culgower
Kilmote
Dalchork
Lothbeg
Grumby Rock
Sciberscross
Kilbraur
Gordonbush
Colaboll
Loch Brora
Kilbraur Hill
Lothbeg Point
Strath Brora
Meall Dola
Lairg
Balcharn
East Langwell
Knockarthur
Killin
Killin Rock
Carrol
West Clyne
East Clyne
Greenhill
Ben Horn
Farlary
174
175
181
A836
A838
A897
A9
B871
B873
0 2 4 6 miles
0 2 4 6 8 10 km

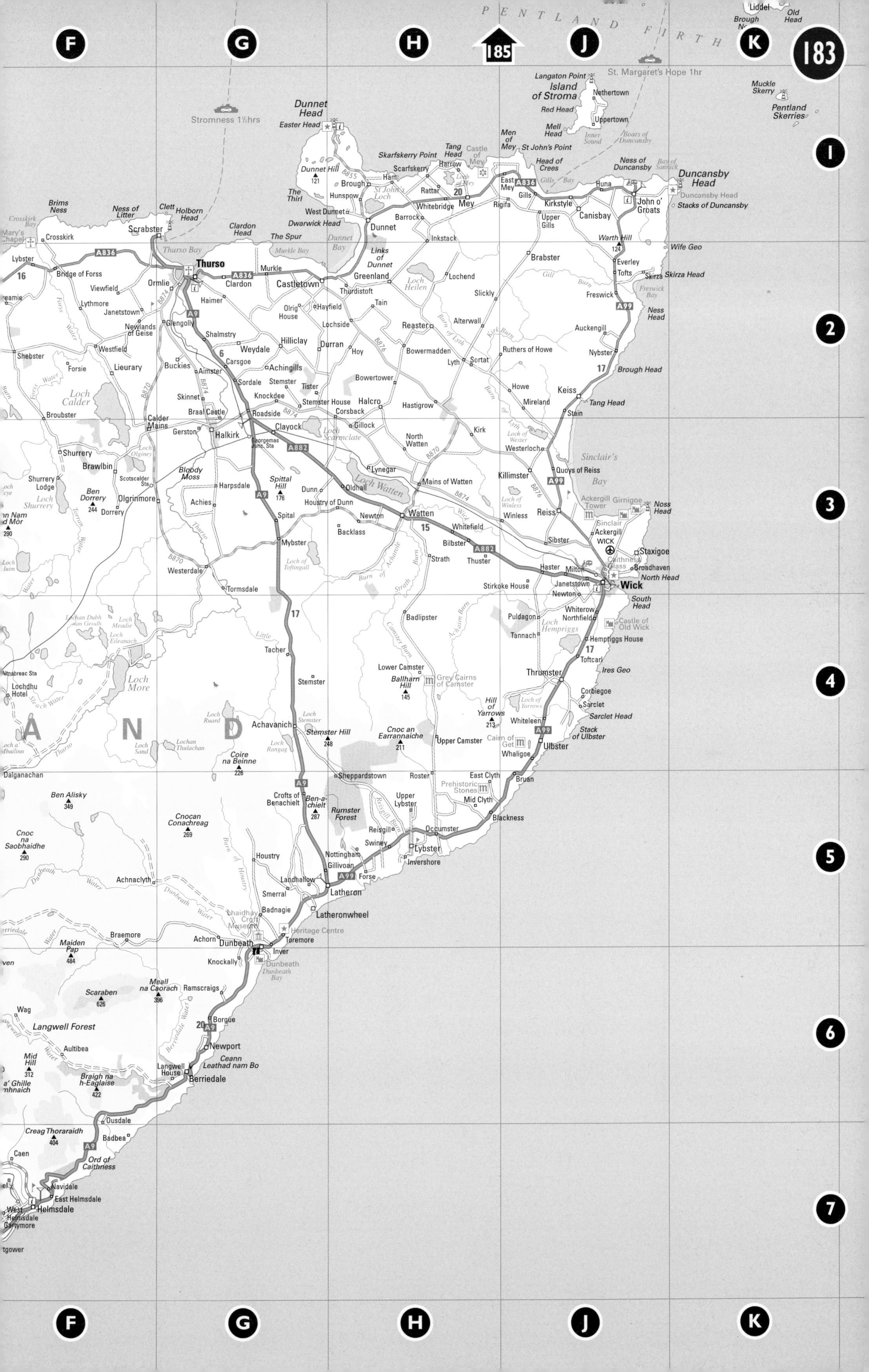
F
G
H
185
J
K
PENTLAND FIRTH
Liddel
Old Head
Brough Ness
Langaton Point
Island of Stroma
Nethertown
Red Head
Mell Head
Uppertown
Inner Sound
Boars of Duncansby
St. Margaret's Hope 1hr
Muckle Skerry
Pentland Skerries
Stromness 1½hrs
Dunnet Head
Easter Head
Dunnet Hill
121
Men of Mey
St John's Point
Tang Head
Castle of Mey
Skarfskerry Point
Scarfskerry
Harrow
Head of Crees
Ness of Duncansby
Bay of Sannick
Duncansby Head
Gills Bay
Ham
Brough
The Thirl
Hunspow
St John's Loch
Rattar
Loch of Mey
East Mey
A836
Gills
Huna
Whitebridge
20
Mey
Rigifa
Kirkstyle
John o' Groats
Duncansby Head
Stacks of Duncansby
Canisbay
West Dunnet
Barrock
Upper Gills
Brims Ness
Ness of Litter
Clett
Holborn Head
Clardon Head
Crosskirk Bay
Mary's Chapel
Crosskirk
Scrabster
Dunwick Head
The Spur
Dunnet
Dunnet Bay
Inkstack
Warth Hill
124
Wife Geo
Thurso Bay
Murkle Bay
Links of Dunnet
Brabster
Lybster
A836
Thurso
Murkle
Everley
16
Bridge of Forss
Ormlie
Clardon
Castletown
Greenland
Loch Heilen
Lochend
Tofts
Skirza
Skirza Head
Viewfield
Thurdistoft
Gill Burn
Freswick Bay
Freswick
Lythmore
B874
Haimer
Slickly
Janetstown
Olrig House
Hayfield
Tain
A99
Ness Head
Glengolly
Lochside
Alterwall
Newlands of Geise
Shalmstry
Reaster
Auckengill
Forss Water
Burn of Lyth
Kirk Burn
Weydale
Hilliclay
Durran
B876
Westfield
Hoy
Bowermadden
Ruthers of Howe
Nybster
Shebster
Carsgoe
Achingills
Lyth
Sortat
Buckies
Lieurary
17
Brough Head
Forsie
Aimster
Bowertower
Sordale
Stemster
Tister
Howe
Keiss
Loch Calder
Skinnet
Knockdee
B870
Halcro
Mireland
Tang Head
Braal Castle
Stemster House
Hastigrow
Broubster
Calder Mains
Roadside
B874
Corsback
Stain
Gerston
Clayock
Gillock
Kirk
Halkirk
Loch Scarmclate
North Watten
Loch of Wester
Shurrery
Georgemas Junc. Sta
A882
Westerloch
Sinclair's Bay
Loch Olginey
Brawlbin
Lynegar
B870
Quoys of Reiss
Scotscalder Sta
Bloody Moss
Loch Watten
Mains of Watten
Killimster
A99
Shurrery Lodge
Harpsdale
Spittal Hill
176
Dunn
Oldhall
B874
B876
Ben Dorrery
244
Olgrinmore
Loch of Winless
Ackergill Tower
Girnigoe
Noss Head
Loch Shurrery
Dorrery
Achies
A9
Houstry of Dunn
Watten
Reiss
Winless
Spital
Newton
Whitefield
Sinclair
Ackergill
WICK
Backlass
15
Sibster
Staxigoe
Bilbster
A882
Mybster
Strath
Thuster
Caithness Glass
Broadhaven
Loch of Toftingall
Burn of Acharole
Haster
Milton
North Head
Westerdale
Stirkoke House
Janetstown
Wick
Tormsdale
Strath Burn
Newton
South Head
17
Badlipster
Achairn Burn
Whiterow
Puldagon
Northfield
Castle of Old Wick
Lochan Dubh nan Geodh
Loch Meadie
Loch Hempriggs
Loch Eileanach
Little
Tannach
Hempriggs House
Tacher
Camster Burn
17
Toftcarl
Ires Geo
Lower Camster
Altnabreac Sta
Loch More
Stemster
Ballharn Hill
145
Grey Cairns of Camster
Thrumster
Lochdhu Hotel
Corbiegoe
Sleach Water
Sarclet
Hill of Yarrows
213
Loch of Yarrows
Sarclet Head
Loch Ruard
Loch Stemster
Whiteleen
Stack of Ulbster
A N D
Achavanich
Stemster Hill
248
Cnoc an Earrannaiche
211
A99
Cairn of Get
Upper Camster
Ulbster
Whaligoe
Loch Sand
Lochan Thulachan
Loch Rangag
Coire na Beinne
226
Dalganachan
Sheppardstown
Roster
East Clyth
Bruan
A9
Ben Alisky
349
Crofts of Benachielt
Ben-a-chielt
287
Rumster Forest
Upper Lybster
Prehistoric Stones
Mid Clyth
Blackness
Cnocan Conachreag
269
Reisgill Burn
Reisgill
Occumster
Cnoc na Saobhaidhe
290
Swiney
Lybster
Houstry
Nottingham
Inverhore
Gillivoan
A99
Landhallow
Forse
Achnaclyth
Dunbeath Water
Burn of Houstry
Smerral
Latheron
Badnagie
Latheronwheel
Laidhay Croft Museum
Heritage Centre
Braemore
Achorn
Toremore
Maiden Pap
484
Dunbeath
Inver
Knockally
Dunbeath Bay
Meall na Caorach
396
Scaraben
626
Ramscraigs
Wag
Langwell Forest
Borgue
20
A9
Berriedale Water
Newport
Aultibea
Mid Hill
312
Ceann Leathad nam Bo
Langwell House
Berriedale
Braigh na h-Eaglaise
422
Ousdale
Creag Thoraraidh
404
Badbea
A9
Caen
Ord of Caithness
Navidale
West Helmsdale
East Helmsdale
Helmsdale
Gartymore
1
2
3
4
5
6
7
F
G
H
J
K

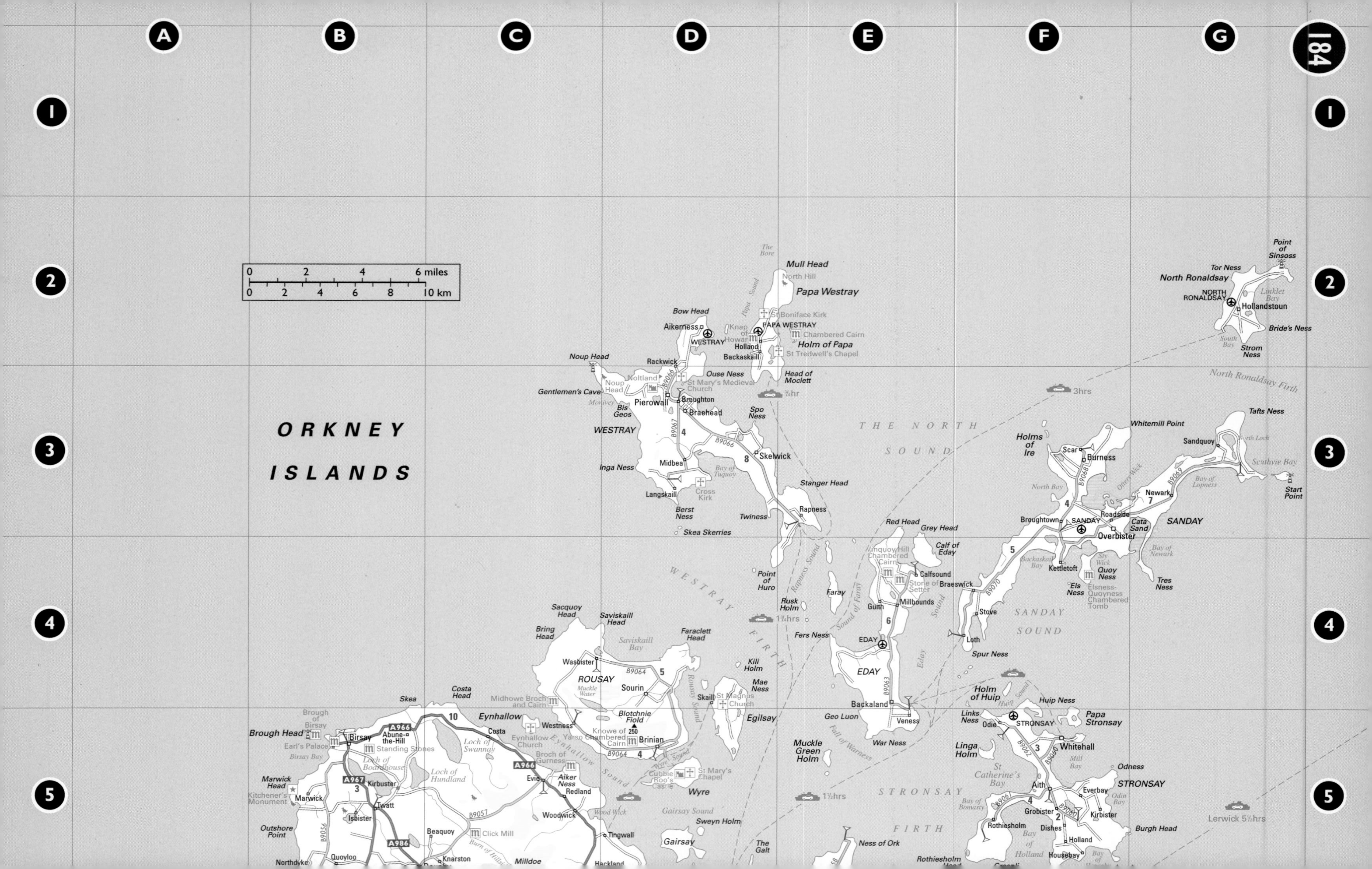
ORKNEY ISLANDS
0 2 4 6 miles
0 2 4 6 8 10 km
A
B
C
D
E
F
G
1
2
3
4
5
North Ronaldsay
Point of Sinsoss
Tor Ness
NORTH RONALDSAY
Hollandstoun
Linklet Bay
Bride's Ness
South Bay
Strom Ness
North Ronaldsay Firth
3hrs
Mull Head
North Hill
The Bore
Papa Westray
Papa Sound
St Boniface Kirk
PAPA WESTRAY
Knap of Howar
Chambered Cairn
Holm of Papa
Holland
Backaskaill
St Tredwell's Chapel
Head of Moclett
¾hr
Bow Head
Aikerness
WESTRAY
Noup Head
Rackwick
Noltland
Ouse Ness
St Mary's Medieval Church
Gentlemen's Cave
Noup Head
Bis Geos
Pierowall
Broughton
Braehead
Spo Ness
WESTRAY
B9066
B9067
Skelwick
Inga Ness
Midbea
Bay of Tuquoy
Cross Kirk
Langskaill
Stanger Head
Rapness
Berst Ness
Twiness
Skea Skerries
THE NORTH SOUND
Holms of Ire
Scar
Burness
Whitemill Point
Tafts Ness
Sandquoy
North Loch
Scuthvie Bay
Start Point
Bay of Lopness
B9069
B9068
North Bay
Otter Wick
Newark
Broughtown
SANDAY
Roadside
Overbister
Cata Sand
SANDAY
Red Head
Grey Head
Calf of Eday
Vinquoy Hill Chambered Cairn
Calfsound
Stone of Setter
Braeswick
Backaskail Bay
Kettletoft
Sty Wick
Quoy Ness
Bay of Newark
Els Ness
Elsness-Quoyness Chambered Tomb
Tres Ness
B9070
Stove
Loth
Spur Ness
SANDAY SOUND
Point of Huro
Rusk Holm
Rapness Sound
Faray
Sound of Faray
Guth
Millbounds
Calf Sound
1¼hrs
Fers Ness
EDAY
EDAY
Eday Sound
WESTRAY FIRTH
Sacquoy Head
Saviskaill Head
Bring Head
Saviskaill Bay
Faraclett Head
Wasbister
B9064
ROUSAY
Muckle Water
Sourin
Rousay Sound
Kili Holm
Mae Ness
Skaill
St Magnus Church
Egilsay
Backaland
B9063
Veness
Geo Luon
War Ness
Fall of Warness
Muckle Green Holm
Holm of Huip
Huip Ness
Links Ness
Odie
STRONSAY
Papa Stronsay
Whitehall
Linga Holm
B9062
St Catherine's Bay
Mill Bay
Odness
Aith
STRONSAY
Everbay
Odin Bay
Bay of Bomasty
B9061
Grobister
B9060
Kirbister
Rothiesholm
Dishes
Holland
Burgh Head
Bay of Holland
Housebay
Lerwick 5½hrs
STRONSAY FIRTH
1½hrs
Ness of Ork
Rothiesholm Head
Skea
Costa Head
Eynhallow
Midhowe Broch and Cairn
Westness
Blotchnie Fiold
250
Knowe of Yarso Chambered Cairn
Brinian
Brough of Birsay
Brough Head
Earl's Palace
Birsay
A966
Abune-the-Hill
Costa
Loch of Swannay
Eynhallow Church
Eynhallow Sound
Broch of Gurness
Wyre Sound
St Mary's Chapel
Cubbie Roo's Castle
Wyre
Birsay Bay
Standing Stones
Loch of Boardhouse
Loch of Hundland
A966
Evie
Aiker Ness
Redland
Marwick Head
Kitchener's Monument
Marwick
A967
Kirbuster
Twatt
Isbister
B9056
B9057
Click Mill
Woodwick
Wood Wick
Gairsay Sound
Sweyn Holm
Outshore Point
Beaquoy
Tingwall
Gairsay
The Galt
A986
Quoyloo
Northdyke
Knarston
Burn of Hillside
Milldoe
Hackland

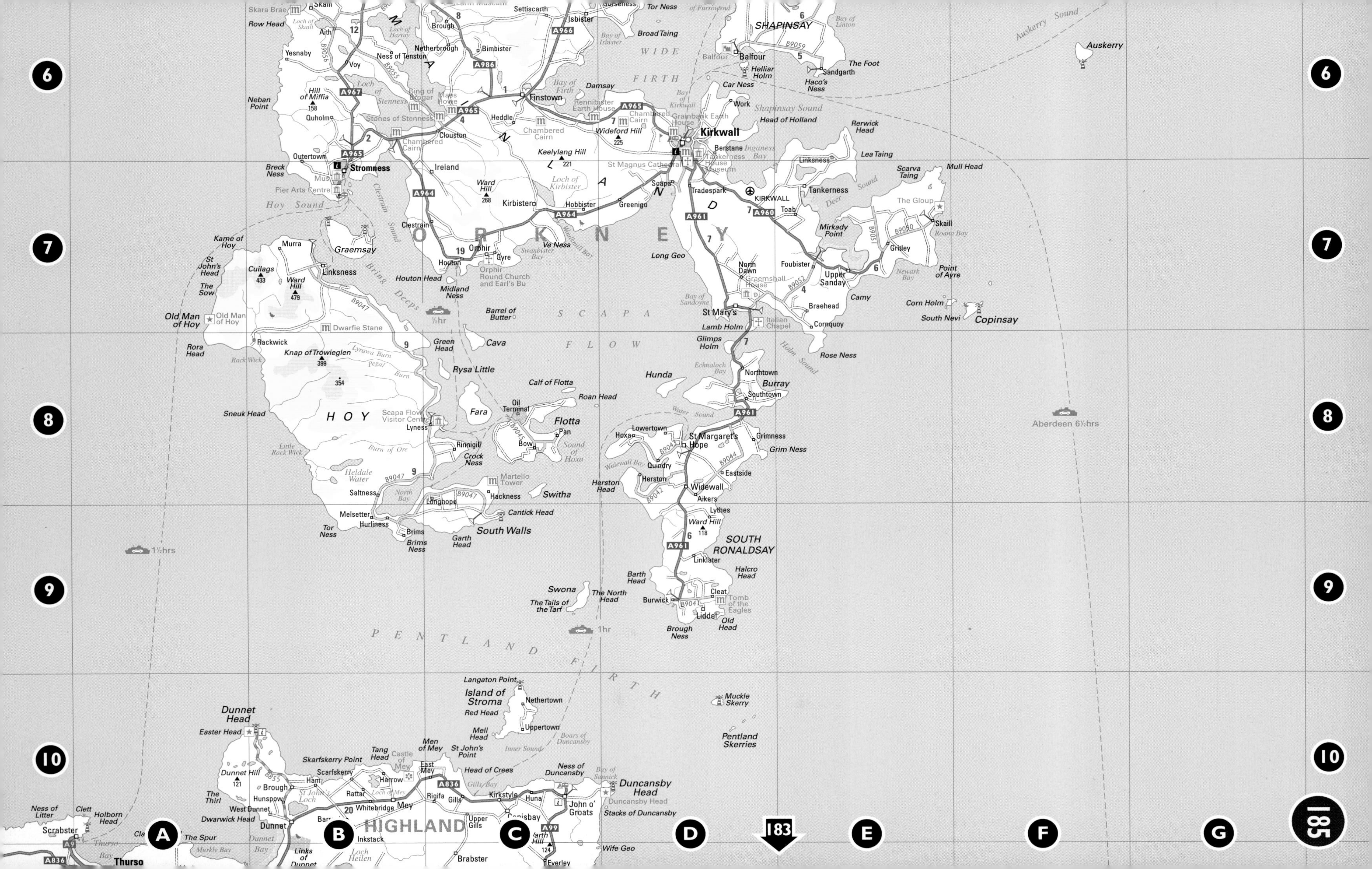
185
ORKNEY
Kirkwall
Stromness
Finstown
St Mary's
St Margaret's Hope
HOY
SHAPINSAY
SOUTH RONALDSAY
Burray
Flotta
Fara
Cava
Graemsay
Hunda
Swona
Switha
South Walls
Copinsay
Auskerry
Island of Stroma
Pentland Skerries
Muckle Skerry
Dunnet Head
Duncansby Head
John o' Groats
Thurso
Scrabster
HIGHLAND
PENTLAND FIRTH
SCAPA FLOW
WIDE FIRTH
Hoy Sound
Clestrain Sound
Bring Deeps
Holm Sound
Water Sound
Shapinsay Sound
Deer Sound
Auskerry Sound
Inner Sound
Old Man of Hoy
Skara Brae
Stones of Stenness
Ring of Brogar
Maes Howe
St Magnus Cathedral
Italian Chapel
Tomb of the Eagles
Scapa Flow Visitor Centre
Pier Arts Centre
Dwarfie Stane
Martello Tower
Orphir Round Church and Earl's Bu
Aberdeen 6½hrs
1½hrs
1hr
½hr
A965
A964
A961
A960
A966
A967
A986
A836
A99
A9
B9047
B9045
B9044
B9043
B9042
B9041
B9050
B9051
B9052
B9055
B9056
B9059
B855
183
A
B
C
D
E
F
G
6
7
8
9
10

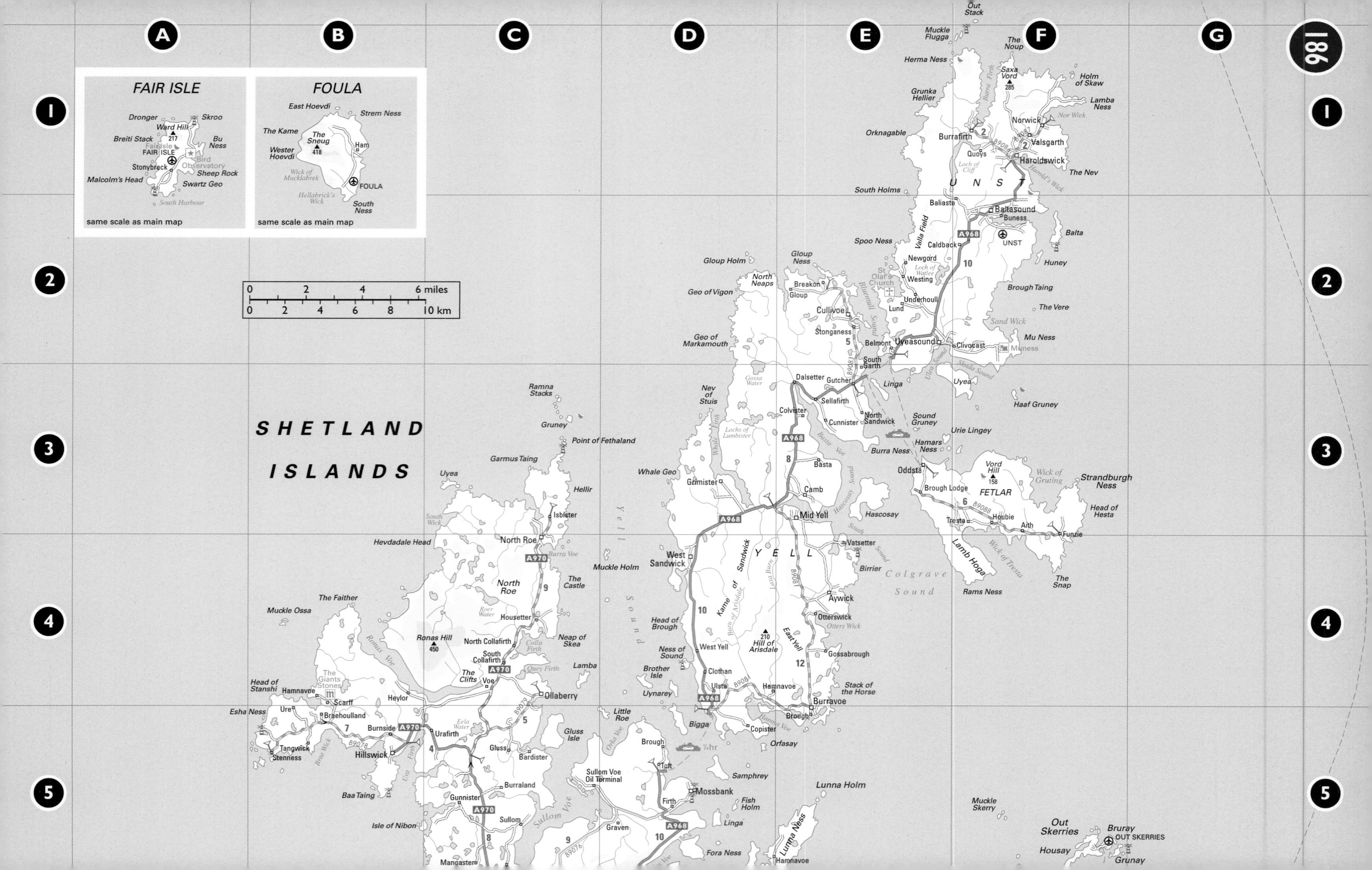
SHETLAND ISLANDS
FAIR ISLE
Dronger
Skroo
Ward Hill
217
Breiti Stack
Bu Ness
Fair Isle
FAIR ISLE
Bird Observatory
Stonybreck
Sheep Rock
Malcolm's Head
Swartz Geo
South Harbour
same scale as main map
FOULA
East Hoevdi
Strem Ness
The Kame
The Sneug
418
Ham
Wester Hoevdi
Wick of Mucklabrek
FOULA
Hellabrick's Wick
South Ness
same scale as main map
0 2 4 6 miles
0 2 4 6 8 10 km
Out Stack
Muckle Flugga
Herma Ness
The Noup
Saxa Vord
285
Holm of Skaw
Grunka Hellier
Lamba Ness
Burra Firth
Norwick
Nor Wick
Orknagable
Burrafirth
Valsgarth
Quoys
Haroldswick
Loch of Cliff
The Nev
Harold's Wick
South Holms
UNST
Baliasta
Baltasound
Buness
Balta
Valla Field
UNST
Spoo Ness
Caldback
Gloup Holm
Gloup Ness
Newgord
Huney
Loch of Watlee
Westing
St Olaf's Church
North Neaps
Breakon
Geo of Vigon
Gloup
Brough Taing
Underhoull
Bluemull Sound
Lund
Cullivoe
The Vere
Sand Wick
Stonganess
Geo of Markamouth
Mu Ness
Belmont
Uyeasound
Clivocast
Muness
South Garth
Uyea Sound
Skuda Sound
Dalsetter
Gutcher
Linga
Gossa Water
Uyea
Ramna Stacks
Nev of Stuis
Sellafirth
Haaf Gruney
Colvister
North Sandwick
Cunnister
Sound Gruney
Lochs of Lumbister
Urie Lingey
Gruney
Whale Firth
Basta Voe
Point of Fethaland
Hamars Ness
Burra Ness
Garmus Taing
Basta
Oddsta
Vord Hill
158
Wick of Gruting
Whale Geo
Uyea
Strandburgh Ness
Gremister
Camb
Brough Lodge
FETLAR
Hellir
Hascosay Sound
South Wick
Hascosay
Head of Hesta
Isbister
Mid Yell
B9088
Houbie
Tresta
Aith
Funzie
Yell Sound
Hevdadale Head
North Roe
South Sound
Vatsetter
Burra Voe
West Sandwick
YELL
Sandwick
Kame of Sandwick
Laxa Burn
B9081
Lamb Hoga
Birrier
Wick of Tresta
Colgrave Sound
Muckle Holm
North Roe
The Castle
Rams Ness
The Snap
The Faither
Aywick
Muckle Ossa
Roer Water
Housetter
Head of Brough
Otterswick
Otters Wick
Burn of Arisdale
Ronas Hill
450
Neap of Skea
210
Hill of Arisdale
East Yell
Ronas Voe
North Collafirth
West Yell
Colla Firth
Ness of Sound
Gossabrough
South Collafirth
Lamba
Brother Isle
Clothan
The Clifts
Voe
Quey Firth
The Giants Stones
Head of Stanshi
Hamnavoe
Stack of the Horse
Ulsta
Hamnavoe
Heylor
Ollaberry
Uynarey
Burravoe
Scarff
Esha Ness
Ure
Braehoulland
Little Roe
Bigga
Brough
Eela Water
Burnside
Urafirth
Hamna Voe
Gluss Isle
Copister
Orfasay
Tangwick
Orka Voe
Brough
¼hr
Brae Wick
Hillswick
Gluss
Stenness
Bardister
Ura Firth
Toft
Samphrey
Sullom Voe Oil Terminal
Burraland
Lunna Holm
Mossbank
Baa Taing
Gunnister
Firth
Fish Holm
Muckle Skerry
Out Skerries
Bruray
Isle of Nibon
Sullom
Sullom Voe
OUT SKERRIES
Linga
Graven
Lunna Ness
Housay
Fora Ness
Grunay
Mangaster
Hamnavoe
A968
A970
B9081
B9082
B9083
B9084
B9088
B9076
B9078
B9079

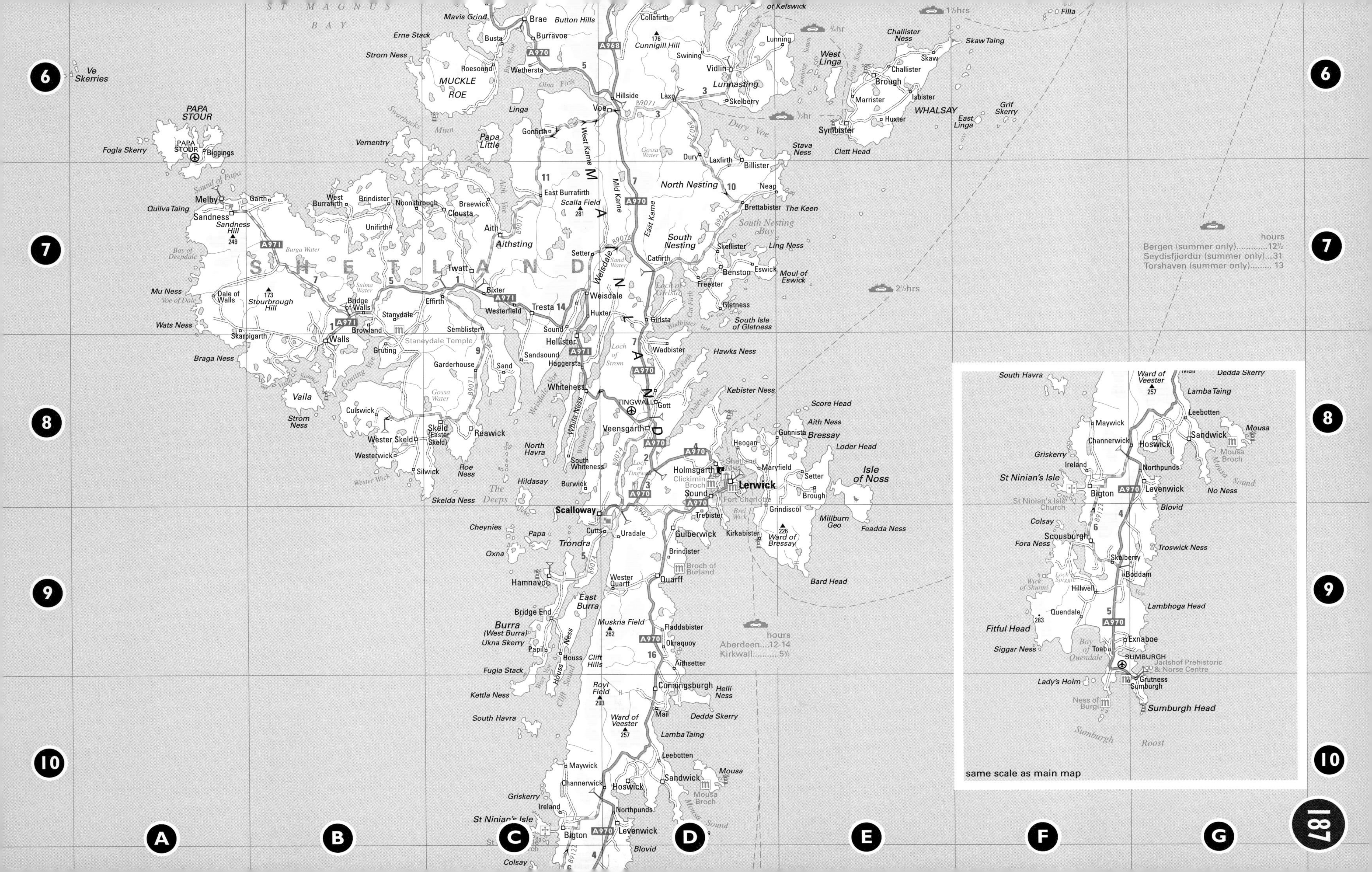
ST MAGNUS
BAY
SHETLAND
Ve Skerries
PAPA STOUR
Fogla Skerry
Biggings
Mavis Grind
Erne Stack
Strom Ness
Brae
Button Hills
Busta
Burravoe
Wethersta
Roesound
MUCKLE ROE
Linga
Vementry
Papa Little
Gonfirth
West Kame
Mid Kame
East Kame
Collafirth
Cunnigill Hill
Hillside
Voe
Swining
Vidlin
Lunning
Lunnasting
Laxo
Skelberry
Dury Voe
Dury
Laxfirth
Billister
West Linga
Challister Ness
Skaw Taing
Skaw
Challister
Brough
Marrister
Isbister
WHALSAY
Huxter
Symbister
Clett Head
Stava Ness
Grif Skerry
East Linga
Filla
Melby
Sandness
Sandness Hill
Quilva Taing
Bay of Deepdale
Garth
West Burrafirth
Brindister
Noonsbrough
Braewick
Clousta
Unifirth
Aith
Aithsting
East Burrafirth
Scalla Field
North Nesting
Neap
Brettabister
The Keen
South Nesting Bay
South Nesting
Catfirth
Skellister
Ling Ness
Benston
Eswick
Moul of Eswick
Freester
Gletness
South Isle of Gletness
Mu Ness
Dale of Walls
Stourbrough Hill
Wats Ness
Skarpigarth
Bridge of Walls
Walls
Browland
Stanydale
Staneydale Temple
Twatt
Effirth
Bixter
Westerfield
Tresta
Setter
Weisdale
Huxter
Sound
Semblister
Gruting
Gruting Voe
Braga Ness
Vaila
Strom Ness
Garderhouse
Sand
Sandsound
Hellister
Haggersta
Whiteness
Girlsta
Wadbister
Hawks Ness
Kebister Ness
Culswick
Wester Skeld
Skeld (Easter Skeld)
Reawick
Westerwick
Silwick
Roe Ness
Wester Wick
Skelda Ness
The Deeps
North Havra
Hildasay
White Ness
South Whiteness
Burwick
TINGWALL
Gott
Veensgarth
Holmsgarth
Clickimin Broch
Shetland Mus.
Lerwick
Sound
Fort Charlotte
Heogan
Gunnista
Bressay
Aith Ness
Score Head
Loder Head
Maryfield
Setter
Brough
Isle of Noss
Grindiscol
Millburn Geo
Feadda Ness
Ward of Bressay
Kirkabister
Bard Head
Scalloway
Cheynies
Papa
Oxna
Trondra
Cutts
Uradale
Trebister
Gulberwick
Brindister
Broch of Burland
Hamnavoe
Western Quarff
Quarff
East Burra
Bridge End
Burra (West Burra)
Ukna Skerry
Papil
Houss
Muskna Field
Fladdabister
Okraquoy
Aithsetter
Clift Hills
Fugla Stack
Kettla Ness
Royl Field
Cunningsburgh
Helli Ness
South Havra
Ward of Veester
Mail
Dedda Skerry
Lamba Taing
Leebotten
Sandwick
Mousa
Mousa Broch
Mousa Sound
Maywick
Channerwick
Hoswick
Griskerry
Ireland
Northpunds
St Ninian's Isle
Bigton
Levenwick
Blovid
Colsay
hours
Bergen (summer only)............12½
Seydisfjordur (summer only)...31
Torshaven (summer only)......... 13
2½hrs
hours
Aberdeen....12-14
Kirkwall...........5½
South Havra
Ward of Veester
Dedda Skerry
Lamba Taing
Leebotten
Maywick
Channerwick
Hoswick
Sandwick
Mousa
Mousa Broch
Mousa Sound
Griskerry
Ireland
Northpunds
St Ninian's Isle
St Ninian's Isle Church
Bigton
Levenwick
No Ness
Blovid
Colsay
Scousburgh
Fora Ness
Troswick Ness
Skelberry
Boddam
Wick of Shunni
Loch of Spiggie
Hillwell
Lambhoga Head
Quendale
Fitful Head
Bay of Quendale
Toab
Exnaboe
Siggar Ness
SUMBURGH
Jarlshof Prehistoric & Norse Centre
Grutness
Sumburgh
Lady's Holm
Ness of Burgi
Sumburgh Head
Sumburgh Roost
same scale as main map
A
B
C
D
E
F
G
6
7
8
9
10

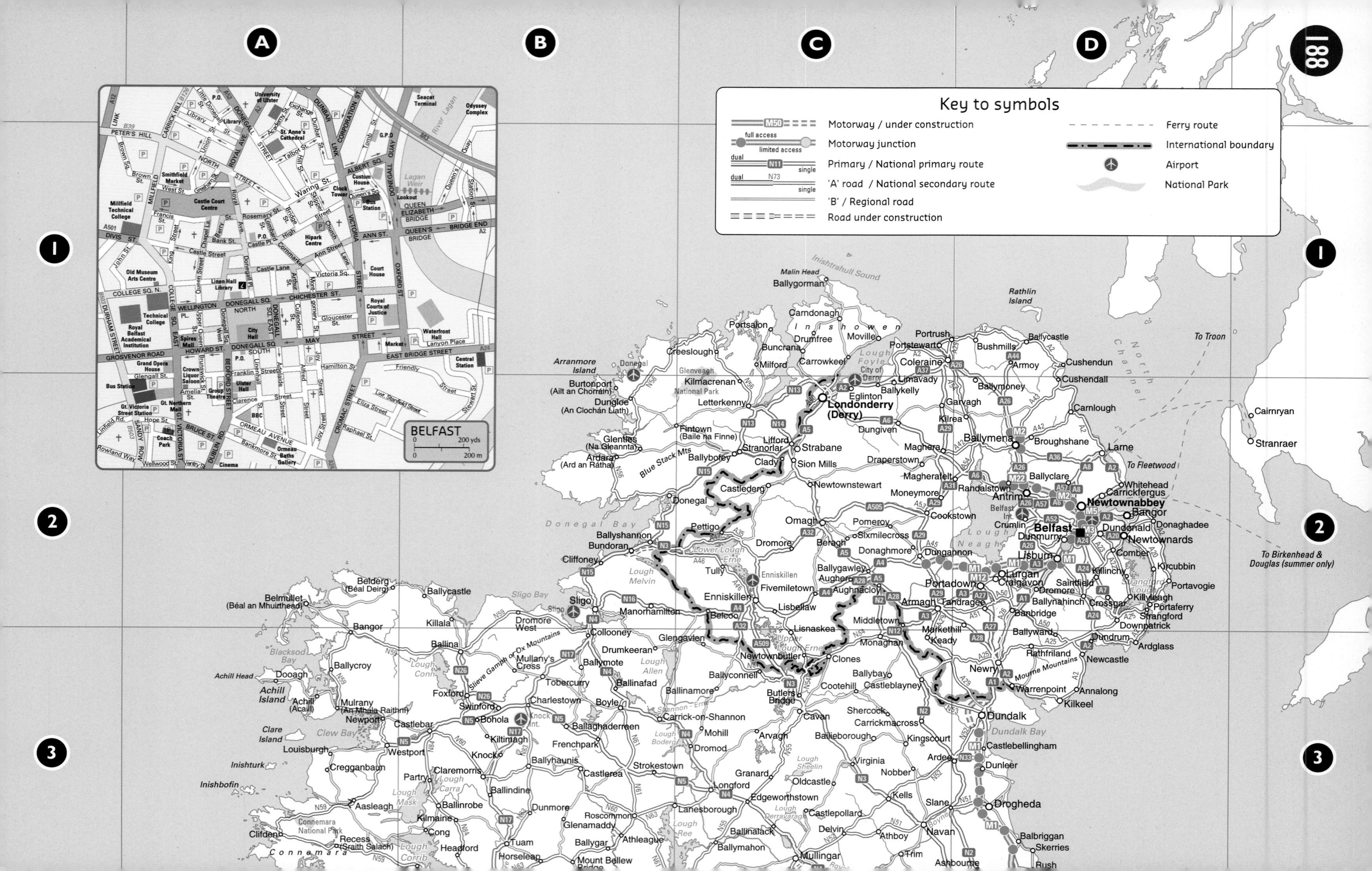

Key to symbols

M50 full access	Motorway / under construction
limited access	Motorway junction
N11 dual single	Primary / National primary route
N73 dual single	'A' road / National secondary route
	'B' / Regional road
	Road under construction

Ferry route
International boundary
Airport
National Park

North Channel

Cairnryan
Stranraer
To Troon
To Birkenhead & Douglas (summer only)
To Fleetwood

BELFAST

Belfast

Londonderry (Derry)

Donegal Bay
Sligo Bay
Clew Bay
Blacksod Bay

Rathlin Island
Arranmore Island
Achill Island (Acaill)
Clare Island
Inishturk
Inishbofin
Achill Head
Malin Head

Connemara National Park
Glenveagh National Park

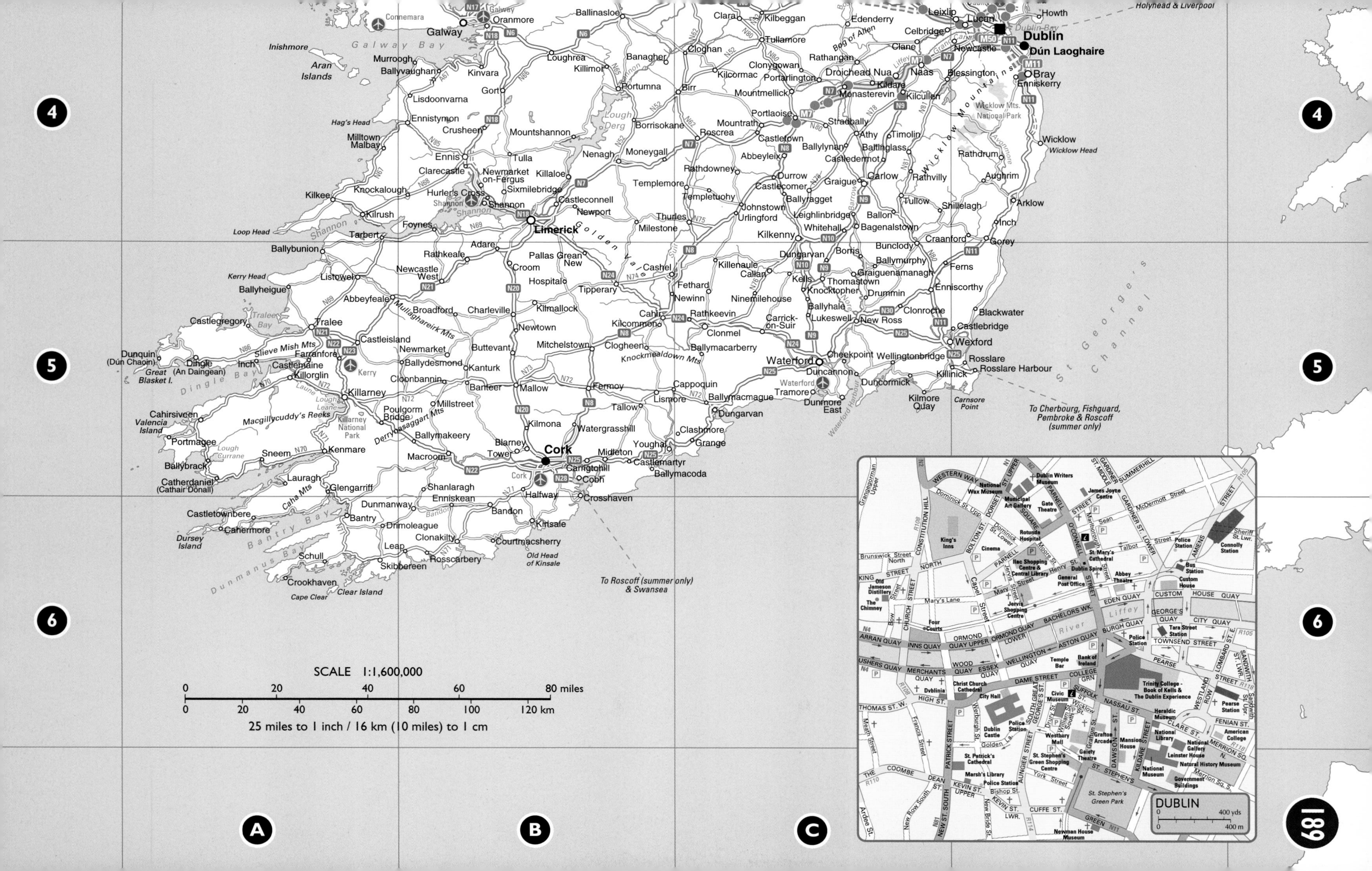

189
4
5
6
A
B
C
Dublin
Dún Laoghaire
Howth
Bray
Enniskerry
Leixlip
Lucan
Celbridge
Clane
Newcastle
Naas
Blessington
Kildare
Kilcullen
Droichead Nua
Rathangan
Monasterevin
Portarlington
Edenderry
Bog of Allen
Kilbeggan
Tullamore
Clara
Clonygowan
Kilcormac
Mountmellick
Portlaoise
Stradbally
Athy
Timolin
Baltinglass
Castledermot
Carlow
Mountrath
Castletown
Abbeylelix
Ballylynan
Durrow
Castlecomer
Ballyragget
Graigue
Leighlinbridge
Bagenalstown
Whitehall
Kilkenny
Johnstown
Urlingford
Thurles
Milestone
Templemore
Templetuohy
Rathdowney
Roscrea
Borrisokane
Moneygall
Nenagh
Birr
Banagher
Cloghan
Portumna
Lough Derg
Mountshannon
Tulla
Ennis
Clarecastle
Newmarket on-Fergus
Killaloe
Sixmilebridge
Castleconnell
Newport
Hurler's Cross
Shannon
Limerick
Golden Vale
Pallas Grean New
Cashel
Tipperary
Croom
Hospital
Adare
Rathkeale
Foynes
Tarbert
Kilrush
Kilkee
Knockalough
Loop Head
Ballybunion
Kerry Head
Ballyheigue
Listowel
Newcastle West
Abbeyfeale
Mullaghareirk Mts
Broadford
Charleville
Kilmallock
Newtown
Buttevant
Mitchelstown
Kilcommon
Cahir
Rathkeevin
Clonmel
Carrick-on-Suir
Fethard
Killenaule
Callan
Kells
Newinn
Ninemilehouse
Knocktopher
Thomastown
Graiguenamanagh
Borris
Dungarvan
Ballyhale
Lukeswell
New Ross
Drummin
Clonroche
Enniscorthy
Ferns
Ballymurphy
Bunclody
Craanford
Gorey
Inch
Arklow
Aughrim
Rathdrum
Tullow
Shillelagh
Ballon
Rathvilly
Wicklow
Wicklow Head
Wicklow Mountains
Wicklow Mts. National Park
Blackwater
Castlebridge
Wexford
Rosslare
Rosslare Harbour
Killinick
Carnsore Point
Kilmore Quay
Wellingtonbridge
Duncormick
Cheekpoint
Duncannon
Waterford
Tramore
Dunmore East
Waterford Harbour
Ballymacarbery
Knockmealdown Mts
Clogheen
Cappoquin
Lismore
Ballymacmague
Dungarvan
Clashmore
Grange
Youghal
Castlemartyr
Ballymacoda
Midleton
Carrigtohill
Cobh
Crosshaven
Fermoy
Tallow
Watergrasshill
Kilmona
Mallow
Banteer
Kanturk
Ballydesmond
Newmarket
Castleisland
Tralee
Tralee Bay
Castlegregory
Slieve Mish Mts
Farranfore
Kerry
Castlemaine
Killorglin
Inch
Dingle (An Daingean)
Dingle Bay
Dunquin (Dún Chaoin)
Great Blasket I.
Killarney
Killarney National Park
Lough Leane
Cloonbannin
Millstreet
Poulgorm Bridge
Derrynasaggart Mts
Ballymakeery
Macroom
Blarney
Tower
Cork
Kenmare
Macgillycuddy's Reeks
Cahirsiveen
Valencia Island
Portmagee
Lough Currane
Sneem
Ballybrack
Catherdaniel (Cathair Dónall)
Lauragh
Caha Mts
Glengarriff
Castletownbere
Cahermore
Dursey Island
Bantry Bay
Bantry
Dunmanway
Drimoleague
Shanlaragh
Enniskean
Bandon
Halfway
Kinsale
Old Head of Kinsale
Courtmacsherry
Clonakilty
Leap
Rosscarbery
Skibbereen
Schull
Crookhaven
Clear Island
Cape Clear
Dunmanus Bay
Galway
Galway Bay
Oranmore
Connemara
Inishmore
Aran Islands
Murrough
Ballyvaughan
Kinvara
Gort
Loughrea
Ballinasloe
Killimor
Lisdoonvarna
Ennistymon
Crusheen
Hag's Head
Milltown Malbay
St George's Channel
Holyhead & Liverpool
To Cherbourg, Fishguard, Pembroke & Roscoff (summer only)
To Roscoff (summer only) & Swansea
SCALE 1:1,600,000
0 20 40 60 80 miles
0 20 40 60 80 100 120 km
25 miles to 1 inch / 16 km (10 miles) to 1 cm
DUBLIN
0 400 yds
0 400 m
O'CONNELL STREET
Dublin Writers Museum
National Wax Museum
Municipal Art Gallery
Gate Theatre
James Joyce Centre
Rotunda Hospital
King's Inns
St. Mary's Cathedral
Dublin Spire
General Post Office
Abbey Theatre
Ilac Shopping Centre & Central Library
Jervis Shopping Centre
Connolly Station
Bus Station
Custom House
Police Station
Tara Street Station
Four Courts
Old Jameson Distillery
The Chimney
River Liffey
Temple Bar
Bank of Ireland
Trinity College - Book of Kells & The Dublin Experience
Christ Church Cathedral
Dvblinia
City Hall
Civic Museum
Dublin Castle
Westbury Mall
Grafton Arcade
Mansion House
Heraldic Museum
National Library
National Gallery
Leinster House
Natural History Museum
National Museum
Government Buildings
American College
Pearse Station
St. Patrick's Cathedral
Marsh's Library
St. Stephen's Green Shopping Centre
Gaiety Theatre
St. Stephen's Green Park
Newman House Museum

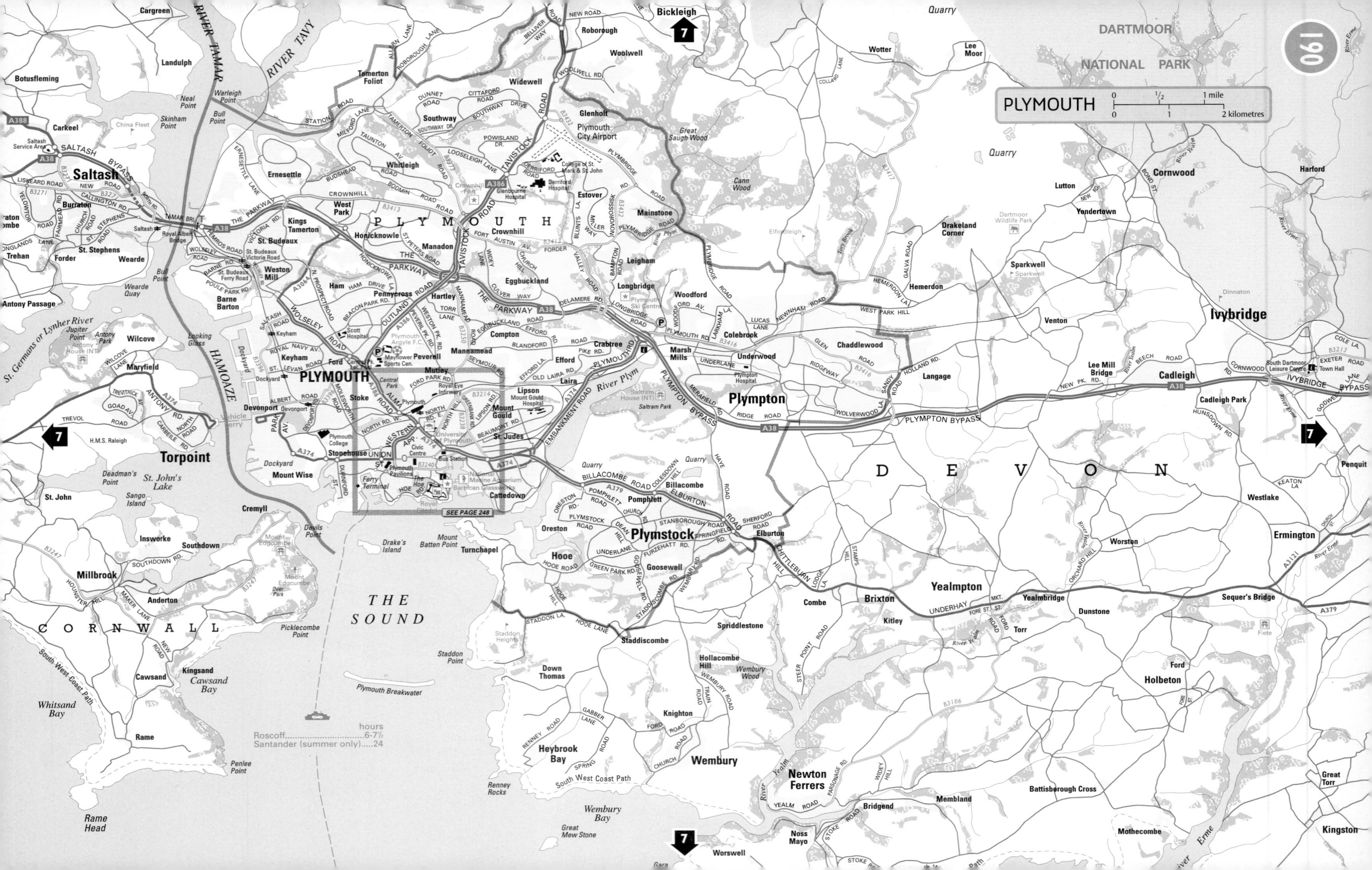
PLYMOUTH
0
1/2
1 mile
0
1
2 kilometres
DARTMOOR
NATIONAL PARK
DEVON
CORNWALL
THE SOUND
PLYMOUTH
Plymouth
Plympton
Plymstock
Saltash
Torpoint
Ivybridge
Yealmpton
Wembury
Newton Ferrers
Noss Mayo
Bickleigh
Roborough
Woolwell
Widewell
Glenholt
Plymouth City Airport
Tamerton Foliot
Southway
Whitleigh
Estover
Crownhill
Mainstone
Leigham
Eggbuckland
Honicknowle
Manadon
Kings Tamerton
St. Budeaux
West Park
Ernesette
Weston Mill
Ham
Pennycross
Hartley
Peverell
Mutley
Mannamead
Compton
Efford
Laira
Lipson
Mount Gould
St. Judes
Cattedown
Stoke
Keyham
Ford
Devonport
Stonehouse
Mount Wise
Longbridge
Woodford
Marsh Mills
Crabtree
Colebrook
Underwood
Chaddlewood
Langage
Oreston
Hooe
Pomphlett
Billacombe
Elburton
Goosewell
Turnchapel
Staddiscombe
Down Thomas
Heybrook Bay
Knighton
Hollacombe Hill
Spriddlestone
Combe
Brixton
Kitley
Yealmbridge
Dunstone
Torr
Worston
Westlake
Ermington
Sequer's Bridge
Holbeton
Ford
Mothecombe
Membland
Battisborough Cross
Bridgend
Worswell
Great Torr
Kingston
Harford
Cornwood
Lutton
Yondertown
Sparkwell
Drakeland Corner
Hemerdon
Venton
Lee Mill Bridge
Cadleigh
Cadleigh Park
Penquit
Lee Moor
Wotter
Quarry
Dinnaton
Cargreen
Landulph
Botusfleming
Carkeel
Burraton
St. Stephens
Wearde
Forder
Trehan
Antony Passage
Wilcove
Maryfield
Barne Barton
Millbrook
Anderton
Insworke
Southdown
Kingsand
Cawsand
Rame
Cremyll
St. John
Cawsand Bay
Whitsand Bay
Rame Head
Penlee Point
Picklecombe Point
Drake's Island
Mount Batten Point
Staddon Point
Renney Rocks
Wembury Bay
Great Mew Stone
Plymouth Breakwater
South West Coast Path
River Tamar
River Tavy
Hamoaze
River Plym
River Yealm
River Erme
St. Germans or Lynher River
St. John's Lake
Saltram House (NT)
Saltram Park
SEE PAGE 248
hours
Roscoff....................6-7½
Santander (summer only).....24
A38
A374
A386
A379
A3121
A388
PLYMPTON BYPASS
THE PARKWAY
TAVISTOCK ROAD
EMBANKMENT ROAD
7

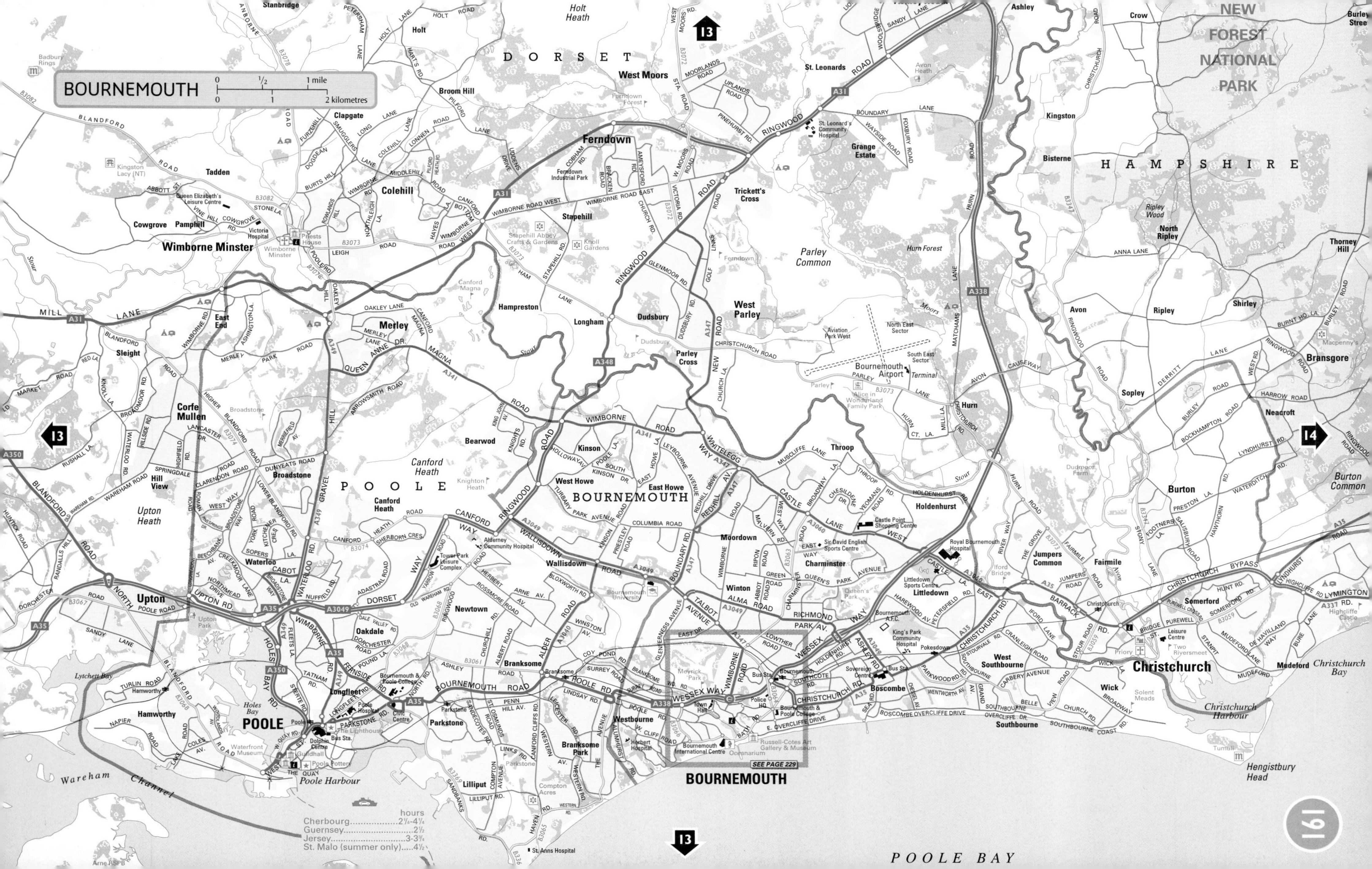

BOURNEMOUTH
0 1/2 1 mile
0 1 2 kilometres
DORSET
HAMPSHIRE
NEW FOREST NATIONAL PARK
POOLE
BOURNEMOUTH
Christchurch
Wimborne Minster
Ferndown
West Moors
St. Leonards
Colehill
Corfe Mullen
Upton
Hamworthy
Parkstone
Branksome
Westbourne
Boscombe
Southbourne
Wick
Mudeford
Highcliffe
Hurn
Bournemouth Airport
Kinson
Throop
Holdenhurst
Burton
Bransgore
Sopley
Ripley
Avon
Kingston
Bisterne
Holt Heath
Holt
Broom Hill
Clapgate
Tadden
Cowgrove
Pamphill
Merley
Hampreston
Longham
Dudsbury
West Parley
Parley Common
Stapehill
Trickett's Cross
Canford Heath
Broadstone
Bearwod
Wallisdown
Moordown
Charminster
Winton
Newtown
Oakdale
Longfleet
Lilliput
Poole Harbour
Holes Bay
Christchurch Harbour
Christchurch Bay
Hengistbury Head
POOLE BAY
Wareham Channel
SEE PAGE 229
13
14
hours
Cherbourg.................2¼-4¼
Guernsey.......................2½
Jersey..........................3-3¾
St. Malo (summer only).....4½
191

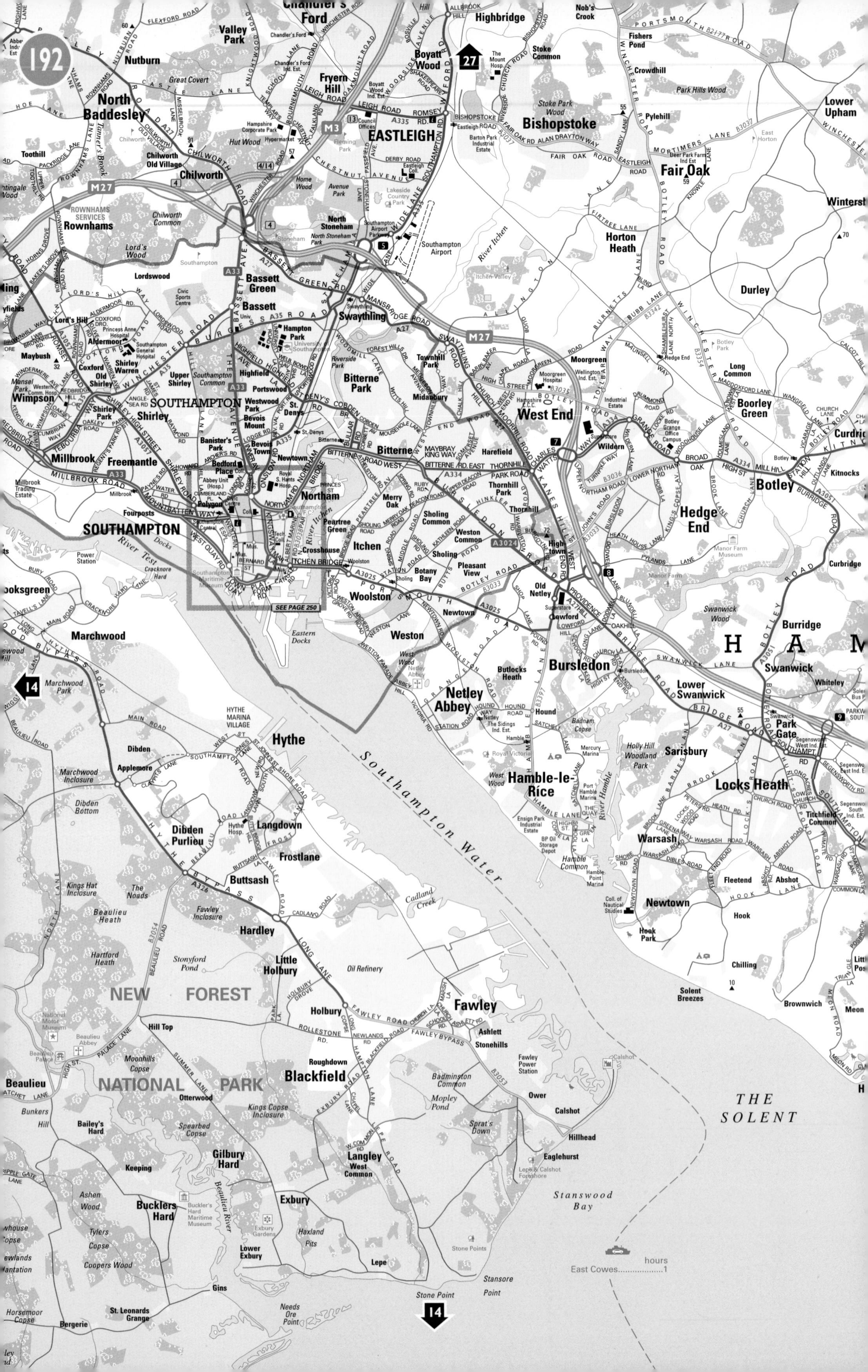
Chandler's Ford
Valley Park
Nutburn
North Baddesley
Hiltingbury
Fryern Hill
Boyatt Wood
Highbridge
Nob's Crook
Fishers Pond
Stoke Common
Crowdhill
Bishopstoke
Lower Upham
EASTLEIGH
Pylehill
Toothill
Chilworth Old Village
Chilworth
Fair Oak
Rownhams
Rownhams Services
Chilworth Common
North Stoneham
Southampton Airport
Horton Heath
Lord's Wood
Lordswood
Bassett Green
Bassett
Durley
Lord's Hill
Aldermoor
Swaythling
Hampton Park
Maybush
Shirley Warren
Upper Shirley
Southampton Common
Highfield
Townhill Park
Bitterne Park
Moorgreen
Long Common
Boorley Green
Coxford
Old Shirley
Portswood
Midanbury
West End
Wimpson
Shirley
SOUTHAMPTON
Westwood Park
Bevois Mount
St. Denys
Wildern
Shirley Park
Banister's Park
Bevois Town
Bitterne
Harefield
Curdridge
Millbrook
Freemantle
Bedford Place
Newtown
Northam
Thornhill Park
Thornhill
Botley
Kitnocks
Polygon
Merry Oak
Sholing Common
Hedge End
Fourposts
SOUTHAMPTON
Peartree Green
Weston Common
Itchen
Crosshouse
Sholing
Botany Bay
Peartree View
Hightown
Manor Farm Museum
Curbridge
Power Station
River Test
Docks
Cracknore Hard
Itchen Bridge
Woolston
Old Netley
Lowford
Swanwick Wood
Burridge
Marchwood
Weston
Eastern Docks
Newtown
Bursledon
HAMPSHIRE
Swanwick
Whiteley
Marchwood Park
West Wood
Butlocks Heath
Netley Abbey
Lower Swanwick
Hound
Park Gate
Hythe Marina Village
Hythe
Holly Hill Woodland Park
Sarisbury
Dibden
Applemore
Southampton Water
Hamble-le-Rice
Locks Heath
Marchwood Inclosure
Dibden Bottom
Titchfield Common
Dibden Purlieu
Langdown
Warsash
Frostlane
Buttsash
Fleetend
Abshot
Kings Hat Inclosure
The Noads
Newtown
Beaulieu Heath
Fawley Inclosure
Hook
Hardley
Cadland Creek
Hook Park
Hartford Heath
Stonyford Pond
Little Holbury
Oil Refinery
Chilling
NEW FOREST
Solent Breezes
Holbury
Fawley
Brownwich
Meon
Hill Top
Ashlett
Stonehills
Moonhills Copse
Roughdown
Fawley Power Station
Beaulieu
NATIONAL PARK
Blackfield
Badminton Common
Otterwood
Mopley Pond
Ower
THE SOLENT
Bunkers Hill
Kings Copse Inclosure
Calshot
Bailey's Hard
Spearbed Copse
Sprat's Down
Hillhead
Gilbury Hard
Langley
West Common
Eaglehurst
Keeping
Stanswood Bay
Ashen Wood
Bucklers Hard
Exbury
Tylers Copse
Haxland Pits
Coopers Wood
Lower Exbury
Lepe
Stone Points
East Cowes hours 1
Gins
Stansore Point
Stone Point
St. Leonards Grange
Needs Ore Point
Horsemoor Copse
Bergerie
SEE PAGE 250
27
14
14

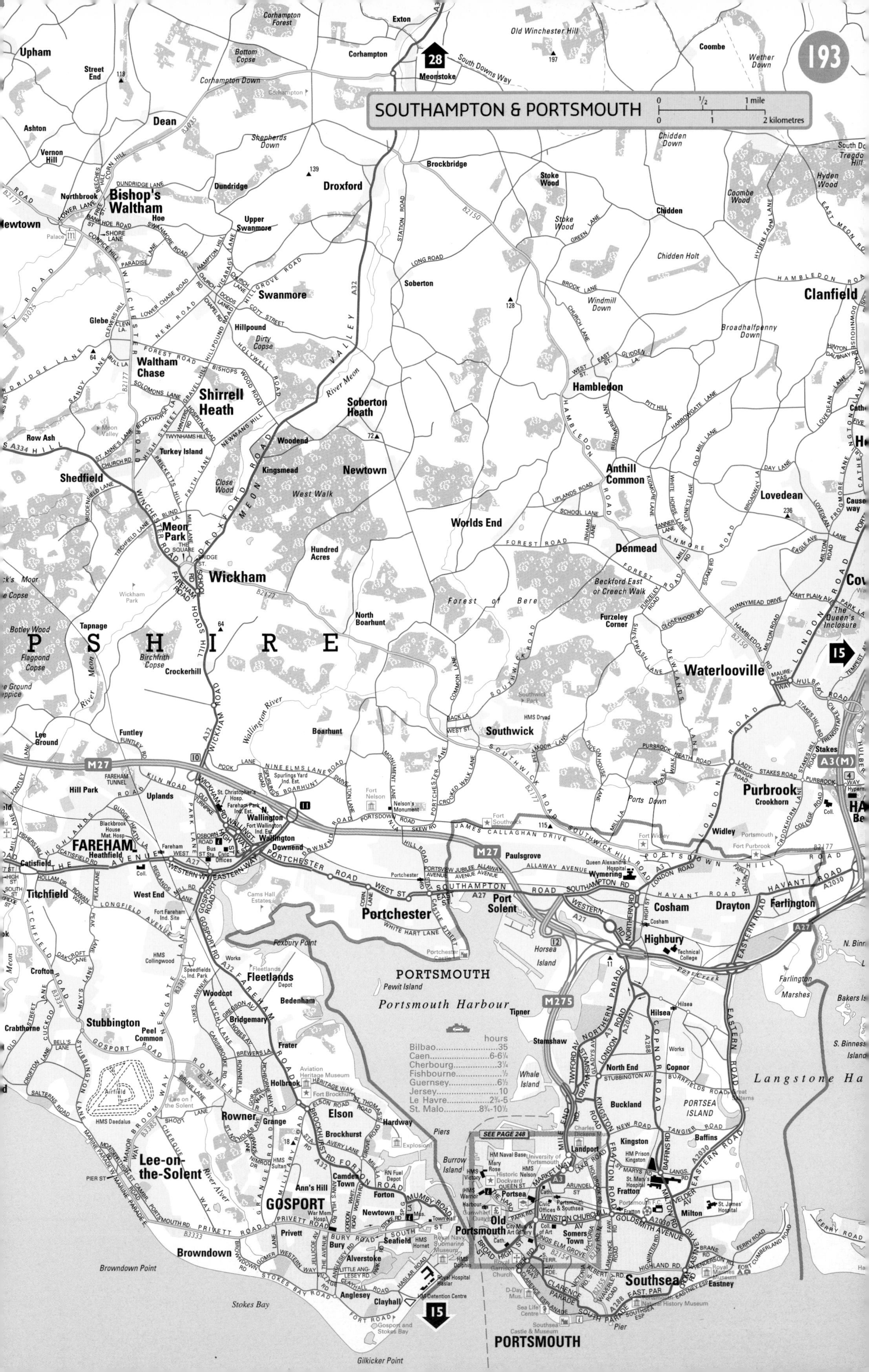
193
SOUTHAMPTON & PORTSMOUTH
0 1/2 1 mile
0 1 2 kilometres
Upham
Street End
Corhampton Forest
Exton
Old Winchester Hill
Coombe
Wether Down
Bottom Copse
Corhampton
28
Meonstoke
South Downs Way
Corhampton Down
Ashton
Dean
Shepherds Down
Chidden Down
Vernon Hill
Brockbridge
Dundridge
Droxford
Stoke Wood
Coombe Wood
Hyden Wood
Northbrook
Bishop's Waltham
Hoe
Newtown
Upper Swanmore
Chidden
Chidden Holt
Soberton
Swanmore
Windmill Down
Clanfield
Glebe
Hillpound
Dirty Copse
Broadhalfpenny Down
Waltham Chase
Shirrell Heath
River Meon
Soberton Heath
Hambledon
Row Ash
Woodend
Turkey Island
Kingsmead
Newtown
Anthill Common
Shedfield
Close Wood
West Walk
Lovedean
Meon Park
Worlds End
Wickham
Hundred Acres
Denmead
Beckford East or Creech Walk
Forest of Bere
North Boarhunt
Furzeley Corner
Tapnage
Botley Wood
P S H I R E
Birchfrith Copse
Crockerhill
Waterlooville
15
Flagpond Copse
Wallington River
Lee Ground
Funtley
Boarhunt
Southwick
HMS Dryad
M27
Hill Park
Uplands
Fareham Tunnel
Ports Down
Purbrook
Crookhorn
Widley
Fort Nelson
Nelson's Monument
Fort Southwick
Fort Widley
Fort Purbrook
FAREHAM
Heathfield
Catisfield
Paulsgrove
Wymering
Titchfield
West End
Portchester
Port Solent
Cosham
Drayton
Farlington
Highbury
Horsea Island
Foxbury Point
Fleetlands
PORTSMOUTH
Pewit Island
Portsmouth Harbour
Crofton
Woodcot
Bedenham
Bridgemary
Tipner
M275
Farlington Marshes
Stubbington
Peel Common
Crabthorne
Frater
Stamshaw
Hilsea
Bilbao 35
Caen 6-6¾
Cherbourg 3¼
Fishbourne ½
Guernsey 6½
Jersey 10
Le Havre 2¾-5
St. Malo 8¾-10½
hours
Whale Island
North End
Copnor
Langstone Harbour
Holbrook
Elson
Buckland
Portsea Island
HMS Daedalus
Rowner
Grange
Hardway
Kingston
Baffins
Brockhurst
SEE PAGE 248
Landport
Lee-on-the-Solent
Camden Town
Burrow Island
Portsea
Fratton
Ann's Hill
Forton
Milton
GOSPORT
Newtown
Old Portsmouth
Somers Town
Privett
Seafield
Browndown
Bury
Alverstoke
Southsea
Eastney
Browndown Point
Anglesey
Clayhall
Stokes Bay
15
PORTSMOUTH
Gilkicker Point

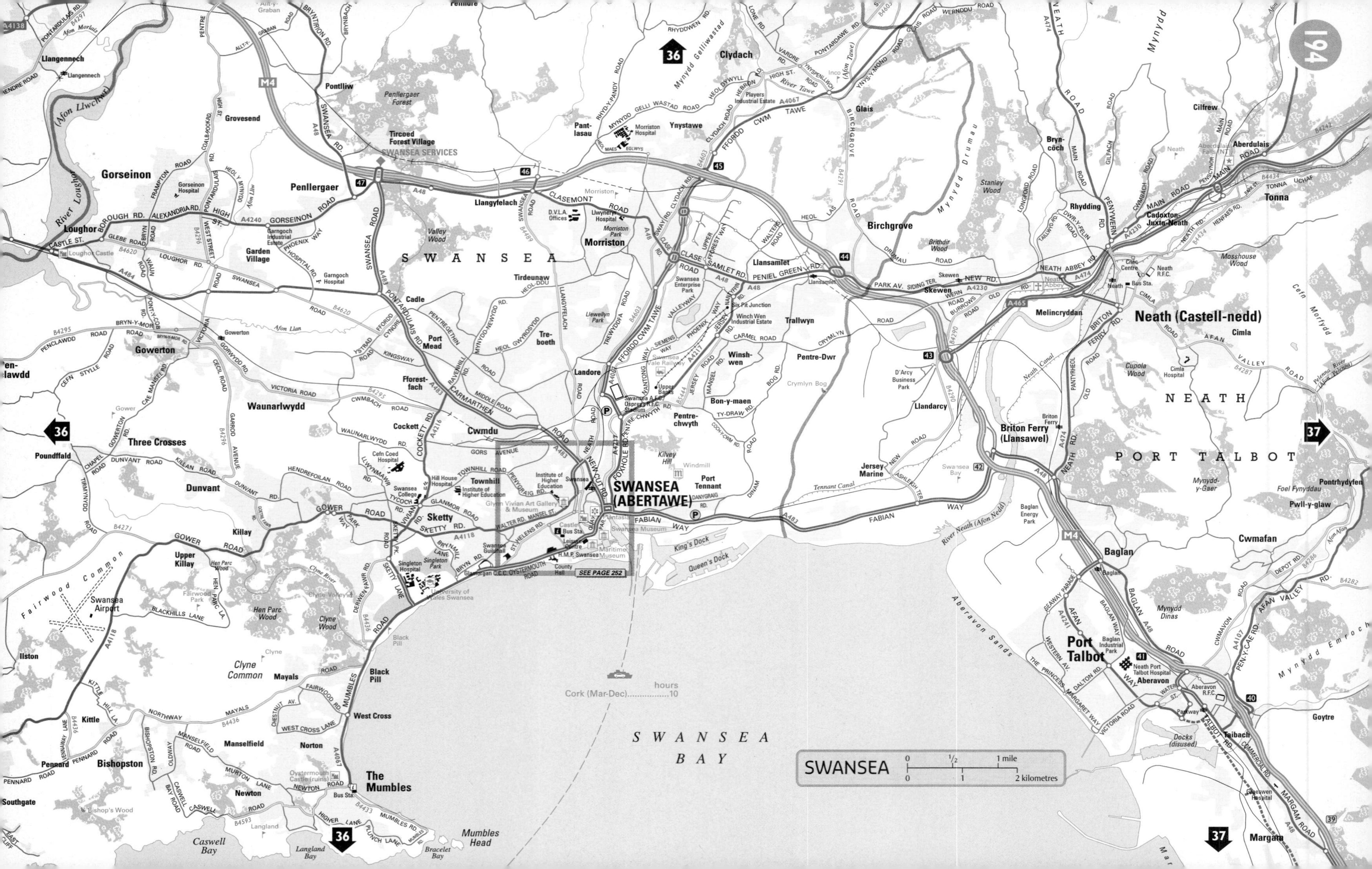
SWANSEA
0 1/2 1 mile
0 1 2 kilometres
SWANSEA (ABERTAWE)
SEE PAGE 252
SWANSEA BAY
Cork (Mar-Dec)................10 hours
S W A N S E A
N E A T H
P O R T T A L B O T
Neath (Castell-nedd)
Port Talbot
Gorseinon
Loughor
Llangennech
Pontlliw
Penllergaer
Grovesend
Garden Village
Gowerton
Waunarlwydd
Three Crosses
Poundffald
Dunvant
Killay
Upper Killay
Swansea Airport
Fairwood Common
Ilston
Kittle
Pennard
Bishopston
Southgate
Caswell Bay
Langland Bay
Bracelet Bay
Mumbles Head
The Mumbles
Newton
Mansselfield
Norton
West Cross
Black Pill
Mayals
Clyne Common
Clyne Wood
Hen Parc Wood
Sketty
Townhill
Cwmdu
Cockett
Fforest-fach
Port Mead
Cadle
Tirdeunaw
Tre-boeth
Landore
Morriston
Llangyfelach
Pant-lasau
Ynystawe
Clydach
Glais
Birchgrove
Llansamlet
Trallwyn
Pentre-Dwr
Winsh-wen
Bon-y-maen
Pentre-chwyth
Port Tennant
Jersey Marine
Llandarcy
Skewen
Briton Ferry (Llansawel)
Melincryddan
Bryn-côch
Rhydding
Cadoxton-Juxta-Neath
Cilfrew
Aberdulais
Tonna
Cimla
Baglan
Aberavon
Cwmafan
Taibach
Margam
Goytre
Pwll-y-glaw
Pontrhydyfen
Swansea Bay
Aberavon Sands
King's Dock
Queen's Dock
Tircoed Forest Village
SWANSEA SERVICES
Penllergaer Forest
Valley Wood
M4
36
37

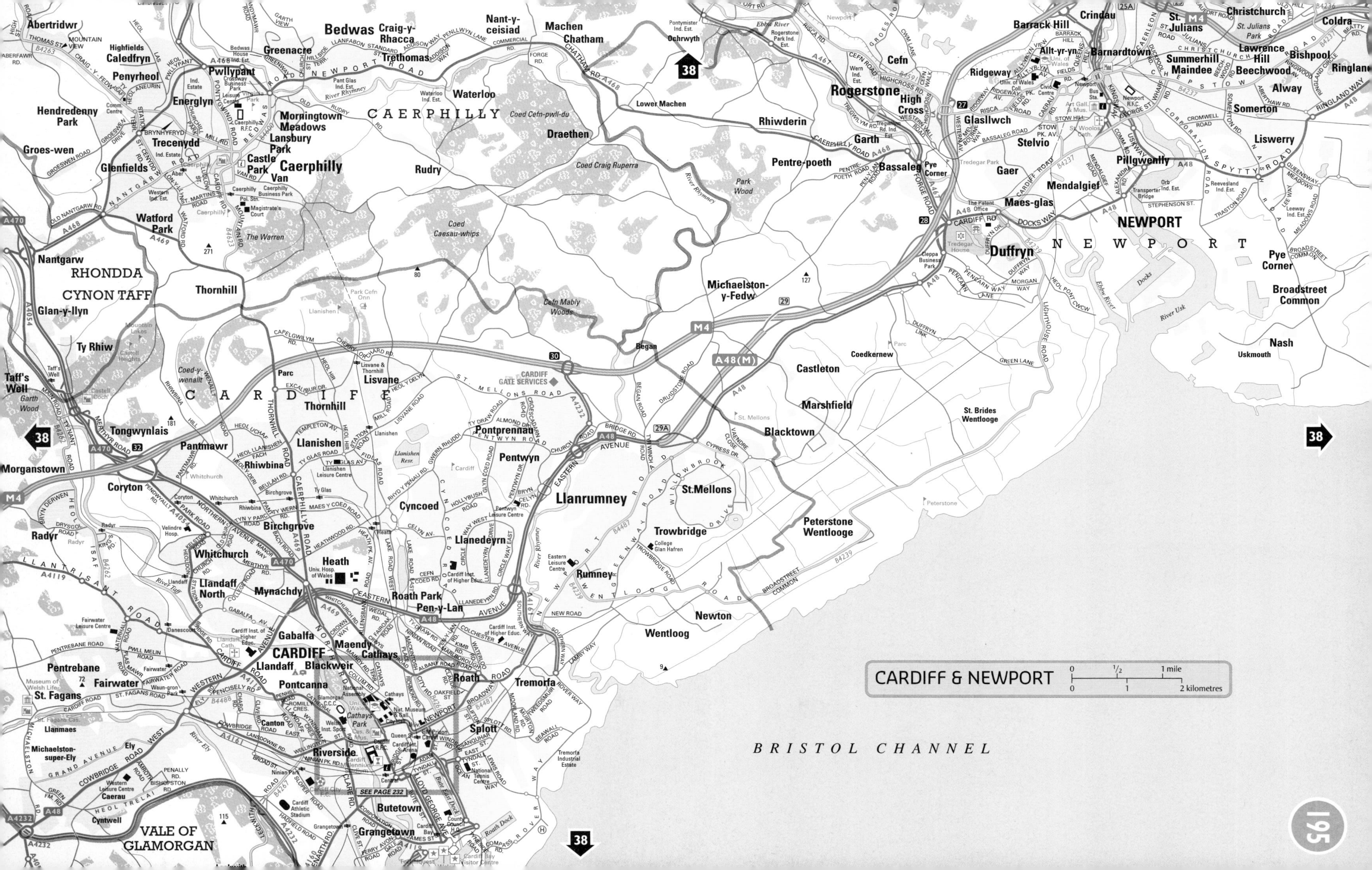
CARDIFF & NEWPORT
0 ½ 1 mile
0 1 2 kilometres
BRISTOL CHANNEL
NEWPORT
CARDIFF
CAERPHILLY
RHONDDA CYNON TAFF
VALE OF GLAMORGAN
SEE PAGE 232
38
195
Abertridwr
Caerphilly
Bedwas
Machen
Chatham
Rogerstone
Bassaleg
Duffryn
Newport
Crindau
Christchurch
St. Julians
Coldra
Lisvery
Pillgwenlly
Pye Corner
Broadstreet Common
Nash
Uskmouth
Castleton
Marshfield
St. Brides Wentlooge
Peterstone Wentlooge
Michaelston-y-Fedw
Lisvane
Thornhill
Llanishen
Pontprennau
Pentwyn
Llanrumney
St.Mellons
Trowbridge
Rumney
Newton
Wentloog
Cyncoed
Llanedeyrn
Heath
Birchgrove
Rhiwbina
Whitchurch
Llandaff North
Llandaff
Gabalfa
Roath Park
Pen-y-Lan
Cathays
Roath
Tremorfa
Splott
Butetown
Grangetown
Riverside
Canton
Pontcanna
Fairwater
Pentrebane
St. Fagans
Radyr
Coryton
Tongwynlais
Taff's Well
Nantgarw
Morganstown
Ely
Caerau
Cyntwell
Michaelston-super-Ely

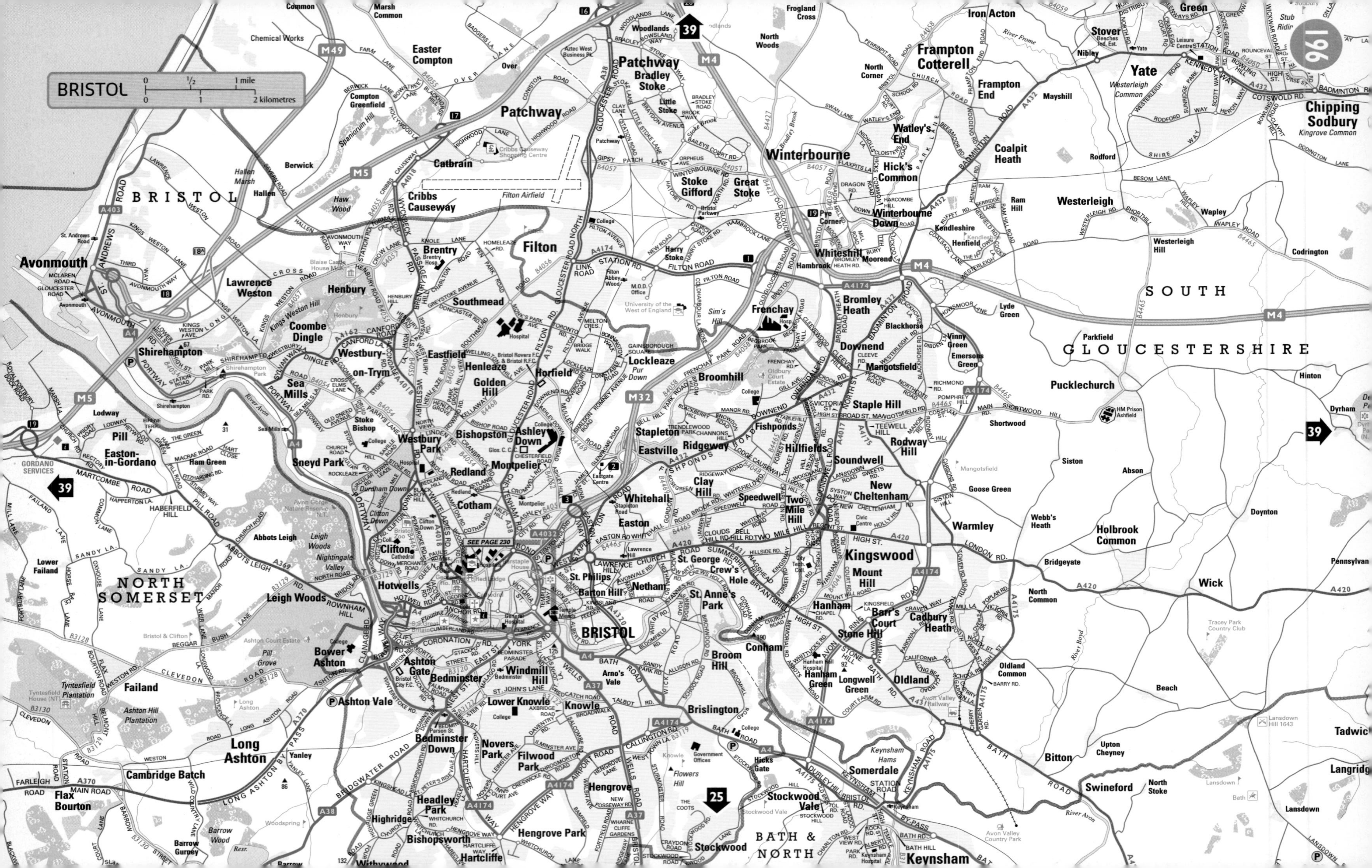
BRISTOL
0 ½ 1 mile
0 1 2 kilometres
SEE PAGE 230
39
25
SOUTH GLOUCESTERSHIRE
NORTH SOMERSET
BATH & NORTH
BRISTOL
Avonmouth
Shirehampton
Lawrence Weston
Henbury
Coombe Dingle
Sea Mills
Westbury-on-Trym
Stoke Bishop
Sneyd Park
Westbury Park
Bishopston
Redland
Cotham
Clifton
Hotwells
Leigh Woods
Abbots Leigh
Pill
Easton-in-Gordano
Lodway
Ham Green
Patchway
Bradley Stoke
Filton
Brentry
Southmead
Henleaze
Golden Hill
Horfield
Ashley Down
Montpelier
Lockleaze
Stapleton
Eastville
Fishponds
Frenchay
Broomhill
Winterbourne
Stoke Gifford
Great Stoke
Frampton Cotterell
Yate
Chipping Sodbury
Downend
Staple Hill
Mangotsfield
Kingswood
Hanham
Oldland
Keynsham
Warmley
Wick
Pucklechurch
Brislington
Knowle
Bedminster
Ashton Gate
Ashton Vale
Long Ashton
Failand
Flax Bourton
Cambridge Batch
Hengrove
Hengrove Park
Bishopsworth
Hartcliffe
Stockwood
Whitchurch
Easton
St. Philips
St. George
Whitehall
Cribbs Causeway
Catbrain
Filton Airfield
Hallen
Berwick
Easter Compton
Over

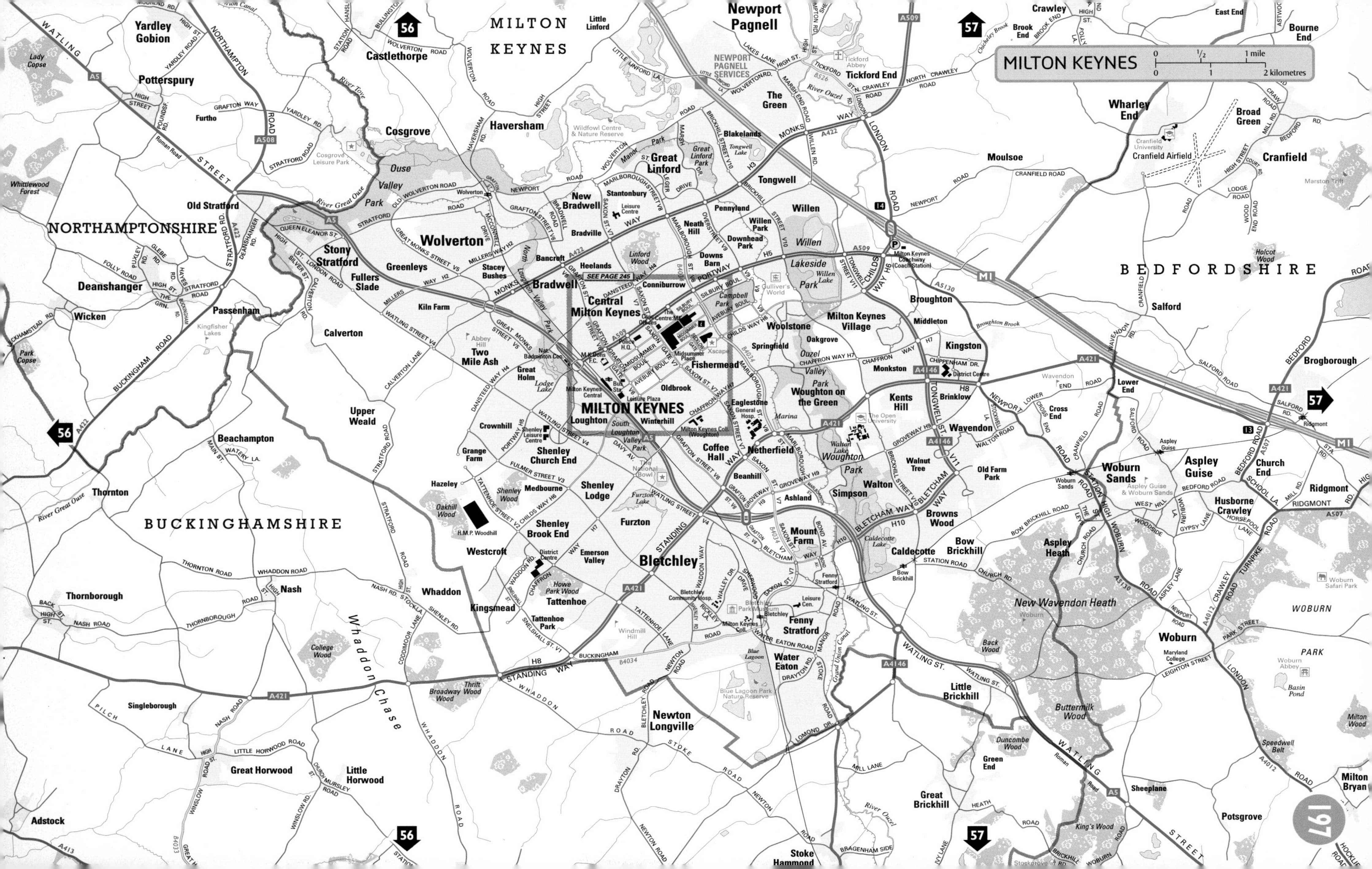
MILTON KEYNES
0 1/2 1 mile
0 1 2 kilometres
MILTON KEYNES
NORTHAMPTONSHIRE
BEDFORDSHIRE
BUCKINGHAMSHIRE
Newport Pagnell
Tickford End
The Green
Tongwell
Willen
Great Linford
New Bradwell
Wolverton
Stony Stratford
Old Stratford
Cosgrove
Haversham
Castlethorpe
Yardley Gobion
Potterspury
Furtho
Deanshanger
Passenham
Wicken
Calverton
Upper Weald
Beachampton
Thornton
Nash
Thornborough
Great Horwood
Little Horwood
Singleborough
Adstock
Whaddon
Whaddon Chase
Kingsmead
Westcroft
Tattenhoe
Emerson Valley
Furzton
Bletchley
Fenny Stratford
Water Eaton
Newton Longville
Stoke Hammond
Great Brickhill
Little Brickhill
Bow Brickhill
Caldecotte
Walton
Kents Hill
Wavendon
Woburn Sands
Aspley Guise
Aspley Heath
Woburn
Husborne Crawley
Ridgmont
Brogborough
Salford
Moulsoe
Cranfield
Cranfield Airfield
Broad Green
Wharley End
Crawley
Brook End
Bourne End
East End
Milton Bryan
Potsgrove
Sheeplane
New Wavendon Heath
Central Milton Keynes
SEE PAGE 245
Bradwell
Heelands
Conniburrow
Fishermead
Oldbrook
Woolstone
Milton Keynes Village
Broughton
Kingston
Monkston
Woughton on the Green
Netherfield
Coffee Hall
Simpson
Shenley Church End
Shenley Lodge
Shenley Brook End
Two Mile Ash
Great Holm
Loughton
Crownhill
Greenleys
Kiln Farm
Fullers Slade
Stacey Bushes
M1
A5
A421
A422
A509
56
57
197

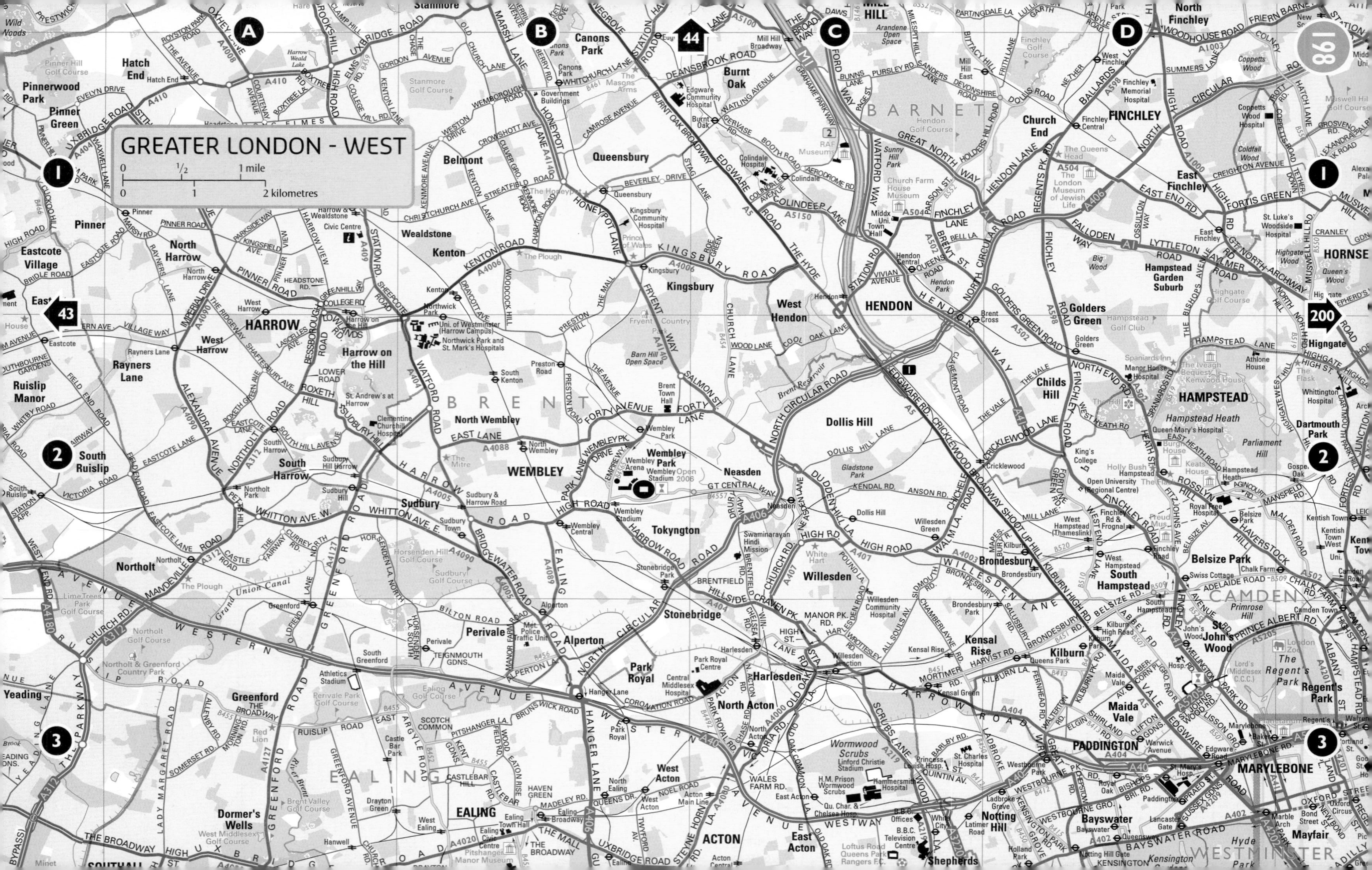
GREATER LONDON - WEST
0 1/2 1 mile
0 1 2 kilometres
A
B
C
D
1
2
3
44
43
200
BARNET
BRENT
EALING
CAMDEN
WESTMINSTER
HARROW
WEMBLEY
HENDON
HAMPSTEAD
FINCHLEY
PADDINGTON
MARYLEBONE
EALING
ACTON
Hatch End
Pinnerwood Park
Pinner Green
Pinner
Eastcote Village
North Harrow
West Harrow
Rayners Lane
Ruislip Manor
South Ruislip
Northolt
Yeading
Greenford
Dormer's Wells
Canons Park
Burnt Oak
Queensbury
Belmont
Wealdstone
Kenton
Kingsbury
West Hendon
Harrow on the Hill
North Wembley
South Harrow
Sudbury
Wembley Park
Neasden
Tokyngton
Dollis Hill
Willesden
Stonebridge
Harlesden
Park Royal
North Acton
West Acton
East Acton
Alperton
Perivale
Kensal Rise
Kilburn
Brondesbury
Childs Hill
Golders Green
Hampstead Garden Suburb
East Finchley
North Finchley
Church End
Belsize Park
South Hampstead
St John's Wood
Maida Vale
Bayswater
Notting Hill
Shepherds
Regent's Park
Mayfair
Dartmouth Park
Highgate
HORNSE
Wormwood Scrubs
Hampstead Heath
Parliament Hill
Primrose Hill
The Regent's Park
Grand Union Canal
Brent Reservoir
River Brent
Stanmore Golf Course
Hendon Golf Course
Horsenden Hill Golf Course
Sudbury Golf Course
Ealing Golf Course
Perivale Park Golf Course
Brent Valley Golf Course
West Middlesex Golf Course
Northolt Golf Course
Lime Trees Park Golf Course
Pinner Hill Golf Course
Finchley Golf Course
Hampstead Golf Club
Highgate Golf Course
RAF Museums
Wembley Stadium
Wembley Arena
Northwick Park and St. Mark's Hospitals
Central Middlesex Hospital
Edgware Community Hospital
Colindale Hospital
Royal Free Hospital
Hammersmith Hospital
Loftus Road Queens Park Rangers F.C.
B.B.C. Television Centre
Lord's Middlesex C.C.C.
London Zoo
Uni. of Westminster (Harrow Campus)
NORTH CIRCULAR ROAD
WESTERN AVENUE
EDGWARE ROAD
WATFORD WAY
HARROW ROAD
UXBRIDGE ROAD
KINGSBURY ROAD
KENTON ROAD
FINCHLEY ROAD
HENDON WAY
WESTWAY
GREENFORD ROAD
FORTY AVENUE
HIGH ROAD
ALEXANDRA AVENUE
WATFORD ROAD
HONEYPOT LANE
GREAT NORTH WAY
BAYSWATER ROAD

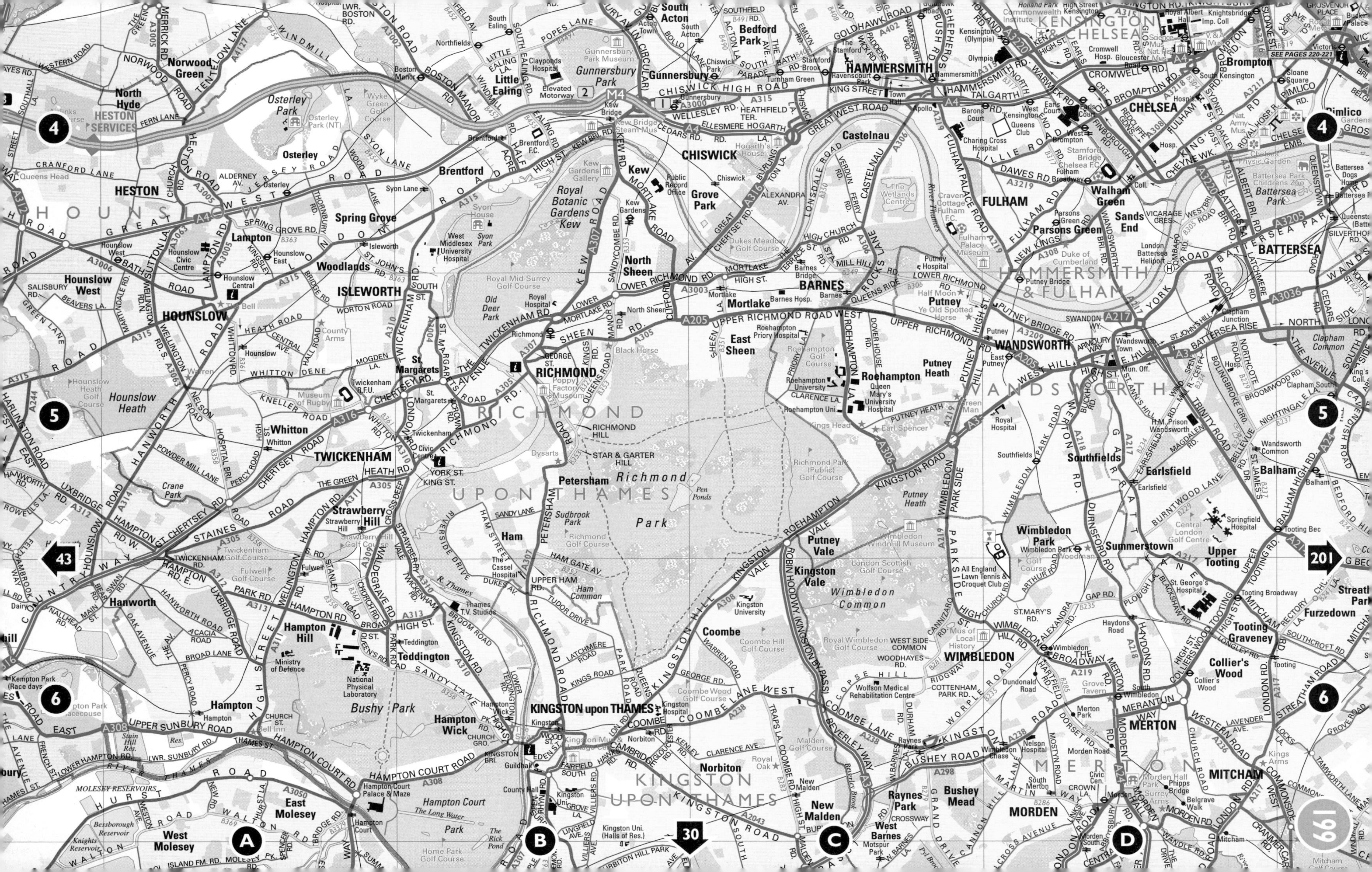

KENSINGTON & CHELSEA
HAMMERSMITH & FULHAM
WANDSWORTH
RICHMOND UPON THAMES
KINGSTON UPON THAMES
MERTON
HOUNSLOW
SEE PAGES 220-221
Pimlico
Chelsea
Brompton
Battersea
Fulham
Walham Green
Sands End
Parsons Green
Hammersmith
Bedford Park
South Acton
Gunnersbury
Gunnersbury Park
Chiswick
Grove Park
Castelnau
Barnes
Mortlake
East Sheen
Putney
Putney Heath
Roehampton
Wandsworth
Southfields
Earlsfield
Balham
Summerstown
Upper Tooting
Tooting Graveney
Furzedown
Collier's Wood
Mitcham
Merton
Morden
Wimbledon
Wimbledon Park
Wimbledon Common
Putney Vale
Kingston Vale
Coombe
Norbiton
New Malden
Raynes Park
Bushey Mead
West Barnes
Kingston upon Thames
Richmond Park
Richmond
North Sheen
Kew
Royal Botanic Gardens Kew
Petersham
Ham
Old Deer Park
Brentford
Little Ealing
Osterley
Osterley Park
Norwood Green
North Hyde
Heston
Spring Grove
Lampton
Isleworth
Woodlands
Hounslow
Hounslow West
Hounslow Heath
St Margarets
Twickenham
Whitton
Strawberry Hill
Teddington
Hampton Hill
Hampton
Hampton Wick
Bushy Park
Hampton Court Park
Hanworth
Crane Park
East Molesey
West Molesey
201
43
30

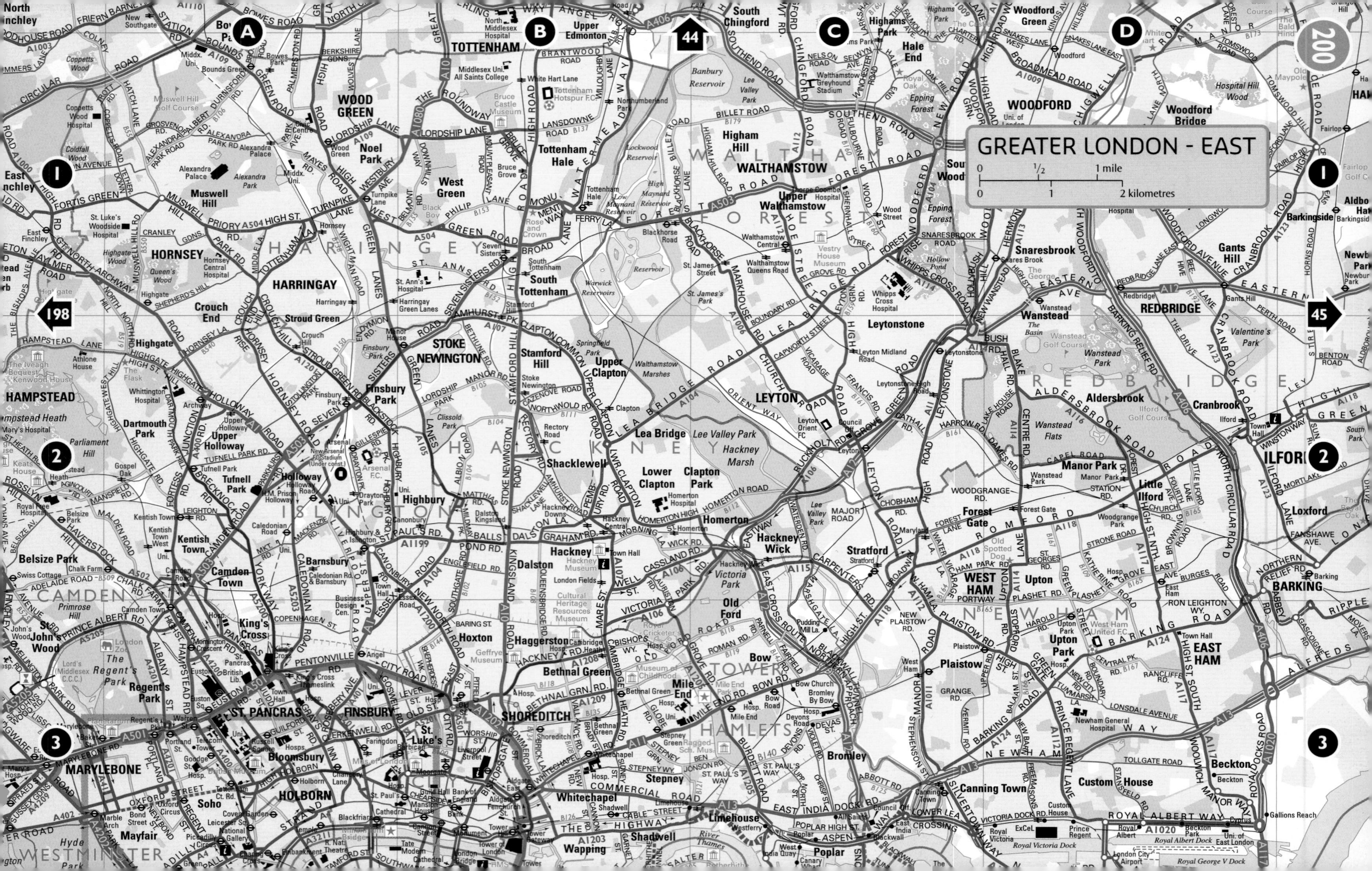

GREATER LONDON - EAST
0
1/2
1 mile
0
1
2 kilometres
44
45
198
A
B
C
D
1
2
3
North Finchley
East Finchley
HAMPSTEAD
Highgate
Crouch End
HORNSEY
Muswell Hill
WOOD GREEN
Noel Park
HARRINGAY
Stroud Green
TOTTENHAM
Upper Edmonton
Tottenham Hale
West Green
South Tottenham
STOKE NEWINGTON
Stamford Hill
Upper Clapton
Finsbury Park
Highbury
Holloway
Upper Holloway
Tufnell Park
Dartmouth Park
Kentish Town
Camden Town
Belsize Park
Barnsbury
King's Cross
ST. PANCRAS
FINSBURY
St. Luke's
Bloomsbury
HOLBORN
MARYLEBONE
Soho
Mayfair
Regent's Park
Dalston
Hackney
Shacklewell
Lower Clapton
Clapton Park
Homerton
Hackney Wick
Lea Bridge
Lee Valley Park
Hackney Marsh
Haggerston
Hoxton
SHOREDITCH
Bethnal Green
Whitechapel
Stepney
Wapping
Shadwell
Limehouse
Poplar
Bromley
Bow
Mile End
Old Ford
Stratford
LEYTON
Leytonstone
WALTHAMSTOW
Upper Walthamstow
Higham Hill
South Chingford
Highams Park
Hale End
WOODFORD
Woodford Green
Woodford Bridge
Snaresbrook
Wanstead
Aldersbrook
Wanstead Flats
Forest Gate
Manor Park
Little Ilford
WEST HAM
Upton
Upton Park
Plaistow
Canning Town
Custom House
Beckton
EAST HAM
BARKING
ILFORD
Loxford
Cranbrook
Gants Hill
REDBRIDGE
Barkingside
Aldborough Hatch
HARINGEY
HACKNEY
ISLINGTON
CAMDEN
WALTHAM FOREST
REDBRIDGE
NEWHAM
TOWER HAMLETS
WESTMINSTER
Banbury Reservoir
Walthamstow Marshes
Royal Victoria Dock
Royal Albert Dock
Royal George V Dock
River Thames

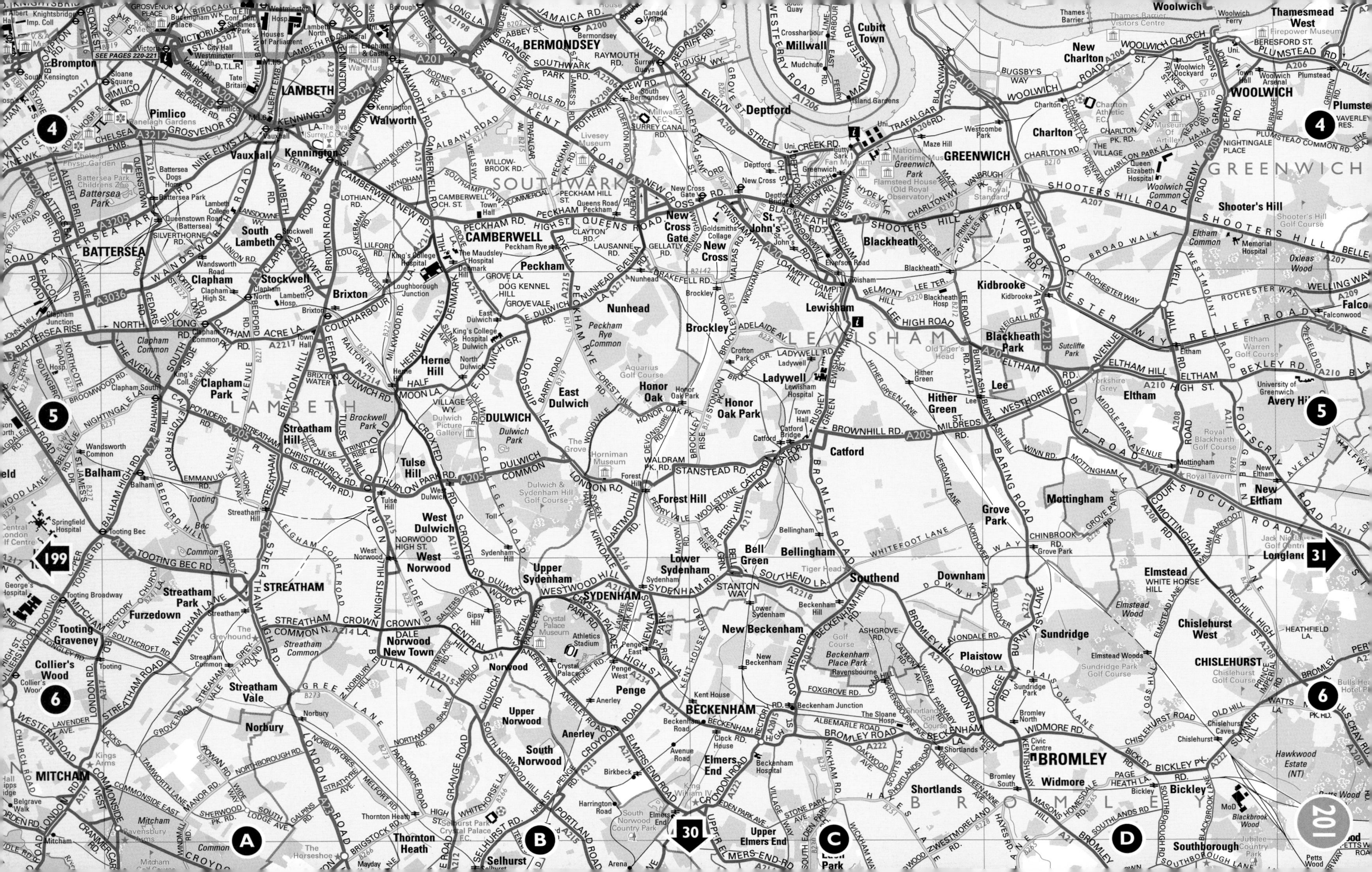

201
SEE PAGES 220-221
199
31
30
4
5
6
A
B
C
D
Brompton
Pimlico
LAMBETH
Walworth
BERMONDSEY
Deptford
Millwall
Cubitt Town
Woolwich
Thamesmead West
New Charlton
WOOLWICH
Plumstead
Charlton
GREENWICH
Vauxhall
Kennington
SOUTHWARK
CAMBERWELL
Peckham
New Cross Gate
New Cross
St. John's
Blackheath
Kidbrooke
Shooter's Hill
BATTERSEA
South Lambeth
Stockwell
Clapham
Brixton
Nunhead
Brockley
Lewisham
LEWISHAM
Blackheath Park
Eltham
Clapham Park
LAMBETH
Herne Hill
East Dulwich
Honor Oak
Ladywell
Honor Oak Park
Hither Green
Lee
Avery Hill
Streatham Hill
DULWICH
Catford
Balham
Tulse Hill
West Dulwich
Forest Hill
Grove Park
Mottingham
New Eltham
West Norwood
Upper Sydenham
Lower Sydenham
Bell Green
Bellingham
Southend
Downham
Elmstead
Longlands
STREATHAM
Streatham Park
Furzedown
SYDENHAM
Tooting Graveney
Norwood New Town
Norwood
New Beckenham
Sundridge
Plaistow
Chislehurst West
CHISLEHURST
Collier's Wood
Streatham Vale
Penge
BECKENHAM
Norbury
Upper Norwood
Anerley
MITCHAM
South Norwood
Elmers End
Shortlands
BROMLEY
Widmore
Bickley
Thornton Heath
Selhurst
Upper Elmers End
Southborough

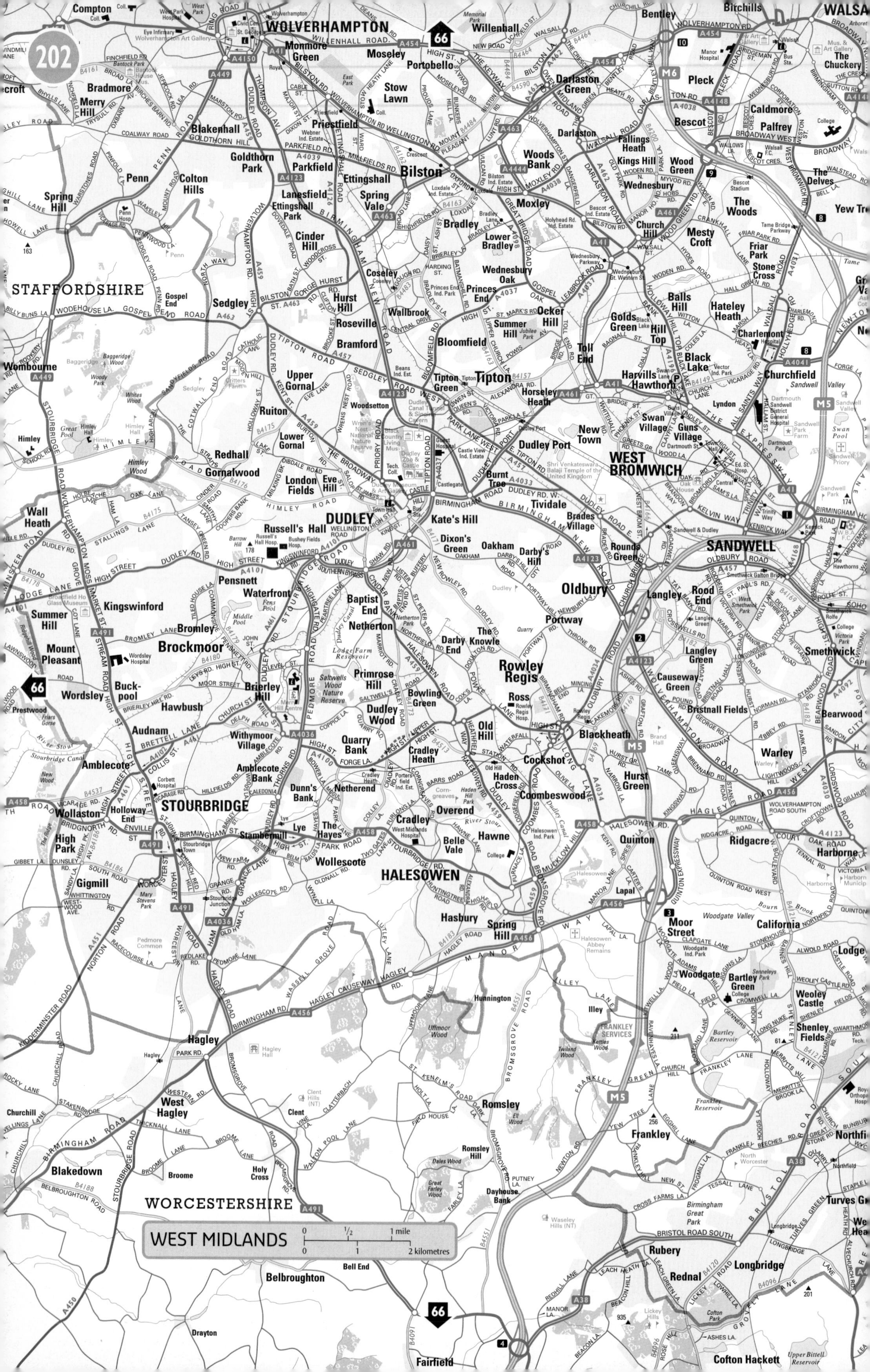
WOLVERHAMPTON
Compton
Bentley
Birchills
WALSALL
Willenhall
Monmore Green
Moseley
Portobello
Bradmore
Merry Hill
Stow Lawn
Priestfield
Darlaston Green
Pleck
Caldmore
Palfrey
Bescot
Blakenhall
Goldthorn Park
Parkfield
Bilston
Darlaston
Fallings Heath
Kings Hill
Woods Bank
Wood Green
Penn
Colton Hills
Ettingshall
Spring Hill
Lanesfield
Ettingshall Park
Spring Vale
Wednesbury
Moxley
The Delves
The Woods
Yew Tree
Bradley
Lower Bradley
Cinder Hill
Church Hill
Mesty Croft
Friar Park
Stone Cross
Coseley
Wednesbury Oak
STAFFORDSHIRE
Gospel End
Sedgley
Hurst Hill
Princes End
Balls Hill
Hateley Heath
Wallbrook
Ocker Hill
Golds Green
Hill Top
Roseville
Summer Hill
Bramford
Bloomfield
Toll End
Charlemont
Black Lake
Wombourne
Upper Gornal
Tipton Green
Tipton
Harvills Hawthorn
Churchfield
Horseley Heath
Lyndon
Woodsetton
Ruiton
Swan Village
Guns Village
Himley
Lower Gornal
New Town
Dudley Port
WEST BROMWICH
Redhall
Gornalwood
Himley Wood
London Fields
Eve Hill
Burnt Tree
Tividale
Wall Heath
DUDLEY
Russell's Hall
Kate's Hill
Brades Village
Dixon's Green
Oakham
Darby's Hill
Rounds Green
SANDWELL
Pensnett
Waterfront
Baptist End
Oldbury
Langley
Rood End
Summer Hill
Kingswinford
Netherton
Portway
Mount Pleasant
Bromley
Brockmoor
Darby End
The Knowle
Langley Green
Smethwick
Rowley Regis
Primrose Hill
Causeway Green
Wordsley
Buckpool
Brierley Hill
Bowling Green
Ross
Bristnall Fields
Bearwood
Prestwood
Hawbush
Dudley Wood
Audnam
Old Hill
Blackheath
Withymoor Village
Quarry Bank
Cradley Heath
Cockshot
Warley
Amblecote
Amblecote Bank
Haden Cross
Hurst Green
Dunn's Bank
Netherend
Coombeswood
Wollaston
STOURBRIDGE
Holloway End
Overend
High Park
Lye
The Hayes
Cradley
Stambermill
Hawne
Quinton
Ridgacre
Harborne
Belle Vale
Wollescote
HALESOWEN
Gigmill
Lapal
Moor Street
California
Hasbury
Spring Hill
Lodge Hill
Woodgate
Bartley Green
Weoley Castle
Hunnington
Illey
FRANKLEY SERVICES
Shenley Fields
Hagley
West Hagley
Churchill
Romsley
Clent
Frankley
Northfield
Blakedown
Broome
Holy Cross
Romsley Hill
Dayhouse Bank
WORCESTERSHIRE
Turves Green
WEST MIDLANDS
0 ½ 1 mile
0 1 2 kilometres
Rubery
Rednal
Longbridge
Bell End
Belbroughton
Drayton
Fairfield
Cofton Hackett
66
M5
M6
A449
A41
A454
A4123
A459
A461
A491
A456
A458
A38

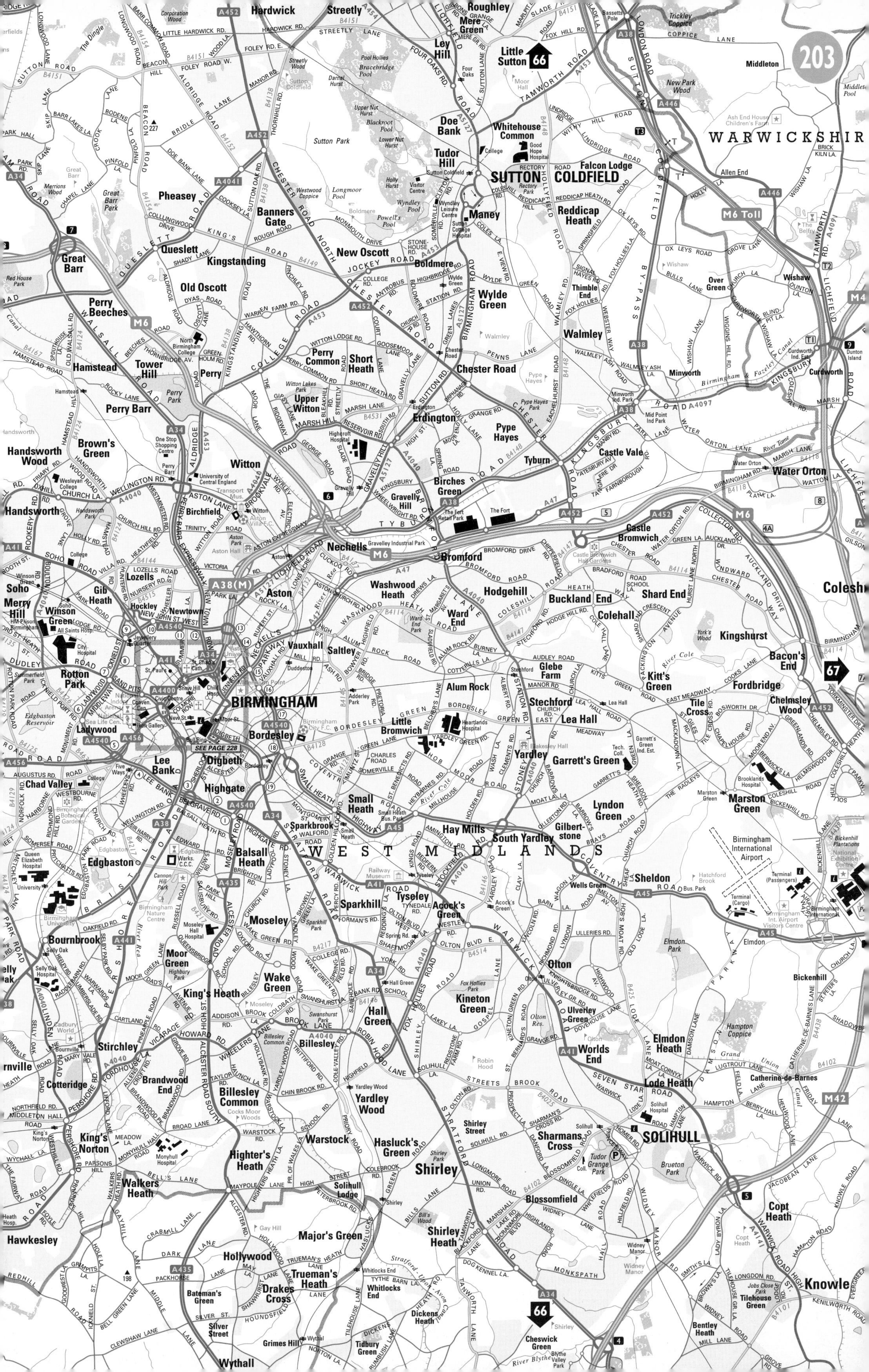
203
Hardwick
Streetly
Roughley
Mere Green
Ley Hill
Little Sutton
66
Middleton
Doe Bank
Whitehouse Common
Tudor Hill
Sutton Park
WARWICKSHIRE
SUTTON COLDFIELD
Falcon Lodge
Pheasey
Banners Gate
Maney
Reddicap Heath
M6 Toll
Great Barr
Queslett
Kingstanding
New Oscott
Boldmere
Old Oscott
Over Green
Wishaw
Perry Beeches
Wylde Green
Thimble End
Walmley
Hamstead
Tower Hill
Perry
Perry Common
Short Heath
Chester Road
Minworth
Curdworth
Perry Barr
Upper Witton
Erdington
Pype Hayes
Brown's Green
Handsworth Wood
Witton
Tyburn
Castle Vale
Water Orton
Birchfield
Birches Green
Gravelly Hill
Handsworth
Castle Bromwich
Nechells
Bromford
Lozells
Washwood Heath
Hodgehill
Buckland End
Shard End
Coleshill
Soho
Gib Heath
Aston
Newtown
Ward End
Colehall
Kingshurst
Merry Hill
Winson Green
Hockley
Vauxhall
Saltley
Glebe Farm
Kitt's Green
Bacon's End
Rotton Park
Alum Rock
Stechford
Fordbridge
67
BIRMINGHAM
Tile Cross
Chelmsley Wood
Ladywood
Little Bromwich
Lea Hall
Bordesley
Yardley
Garrett's Green
Lee Bank
Digbeth
Highgate
Chad Valley
Small Heath
Lyndon Green
Marston Green
Sparkbrook
Hay Mills
South Yardley
Gilbertstone
Edgbaston
Balsall Heath
WEST MIDLANDS
Birmingham International Airport
Sheldon
Wells Green
Sparkhill
Tyseley
Acock's Green
Bournbrook
Moseley
Elmdon
Moor Green
Wake Green
Olton
Bickenhill
King's Heath
Kineton Green
Ulverley Green
Hall Green
Stirchley
Billesley
Elmdon Heath
Worlds End
Hampton Coppice
Catherine-de-Barnes
Cotteridge
Brandwood End
Lode Heath
Billesley Common
Yardley Wood
Shirley Street
M42
King's Norton
Warstock
Sharmans Cross
SOLIHULL
Hasluck's Green
Highter's Heath
Shirley
Walkers Heath
Solihull Lodge
Blossomfield
Copt Heath
Hawkesley
Major's Green
Shirley Heath
Hollywood
Trueman's Heath
Knowle
Drakes Cross
Whitlocks End
Bateman's Green
Tilehouse Green
Dickens Heath
Silver Street
Cheswick Green
Bentley Heath
Grimes Hill
Tidbury Green
Wythall
SEE PAGE 228

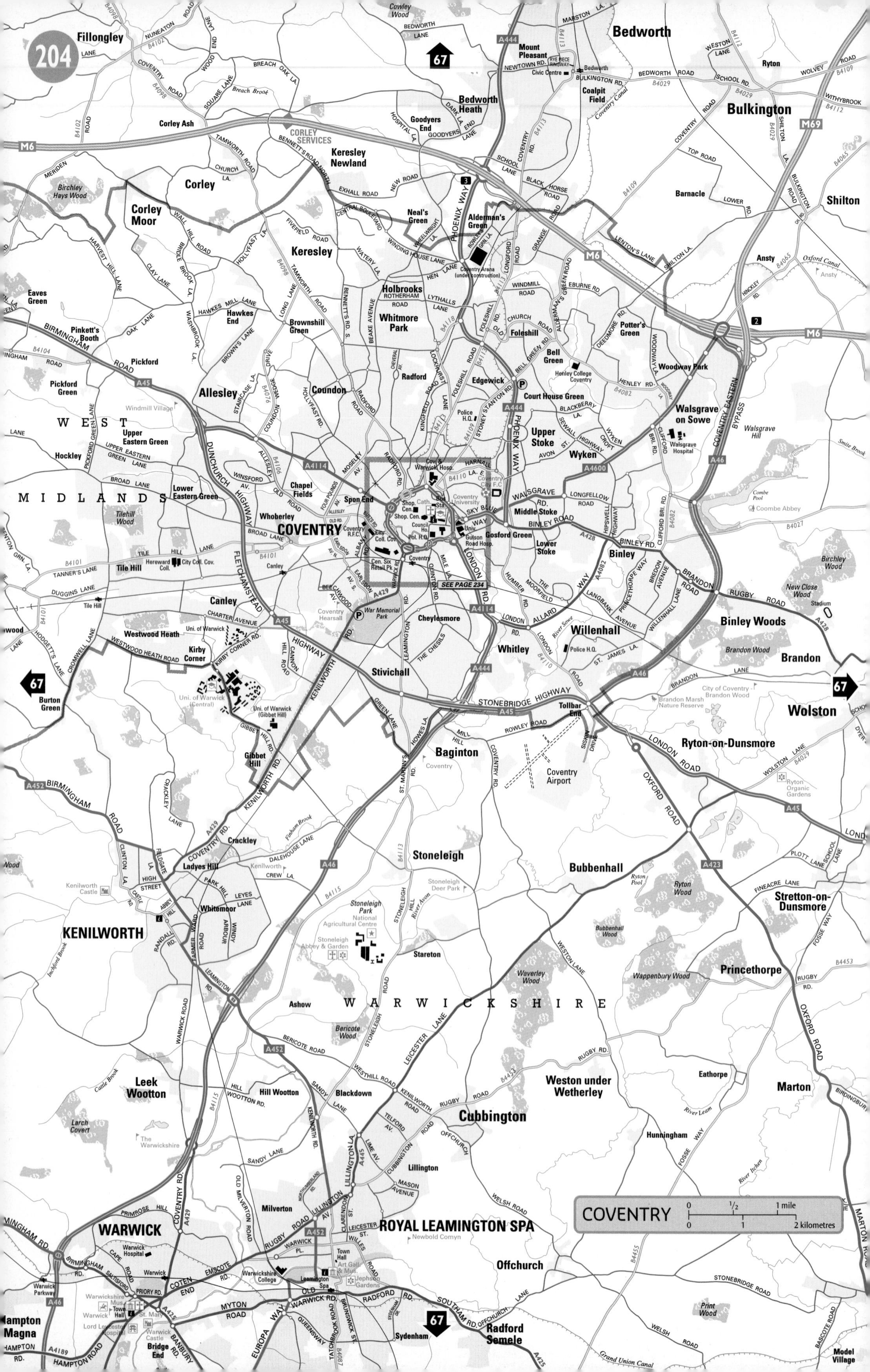
Fillongley
Cowley Wood
67
Bedworth
Mount Pleasant
Ryton
Bulkington
Corley Ash
M6
CORLEY SERVICES
Keresley Newland
Goodyers End
Bedworth Heath
Coalpit Field
Corley
Corley Moor
Birchley Hays Wood
Neal's Green
Alderman's Green
Barnacle
Shilton
Keresley
Holbrooks
Whitmore Park
Coventry Arena (under construction)
Ansty
Eaves Green
Hawkes End
Brownshill Green
Foleshill
Potter's Green
Pinkett's Booth
Pickford
Radford
Bell Green
Woodway Park
Pickford Green
Allesley
Coundon
Edgewick
Henley College Coventry
Court House Green
Walsgrave on Sowe
Windmill Village
WEST MIDLANDS
Upper Eastern Green
Upper Stoke
Walsgrave Hill
Walsgrave Hospital
Hockley
Wyken
Lower Eastern Green
Chapel Fields
Spon End
Coventry City F.C.
Coventry University
Middle Stoke
Combe Pool
Coombe Abbey
Tilehill Wood
Whoberley
COVENTRY
Gosford Green
Lower Stoke
Binley
Tile Hill
Canley
Birchley Wood
New Close Wood
Stadium
SEE PAGE 234
Canley
Cheylesmore
War Memorial Park
Willenhall
Binley Woods
Westwood Heath
Uni. of Warwick
Kirby Corner
Whitley
Police H.Q.
Brandon Wood
Brandon
Stivichall
Uni. of Warwick (Central)
Uni. of Warwick (Gibbet Hill)
Burton Green
Tollbar End
City of Coventry Brandon Wood
Brandon Marsh Nature Reserve
Wolston
Baginton
Ryton-on-Dunsmore
Gibbet Hill
Coventry Airport
Ryton Organic Gardens
Crackley
Ladyes Hill
Kenilworth Castle
Stoneleigh
Bubbenhall
Ryton Pool
Ryton Wood
Stretton-on-Dunsmore
Whitemoor
Stoneleigh Deer Park
Stoneleigh Park National Agricultural Centre
Stoneleigh Abbey & Garden
KENILWORTH
Bubbenhall Wood
Stareton
Waverley Wood
Wappenbury Wood
Princethorpe
Ashow
WARWICKSHIRE
Bericote Wood
Leek Wootton
Weston under Wetherley
Eathorpe
Marton
Hill Wootton
Blackdown
Cubbington
Larch Covert
The Warwickshire
Hunningham
Lillington
Milverton
WARWICK
ROYAL LEAMINGTON SPA
Newbold Comyn
Warwick Hospital
Offchurch
Warwickshire College
Leamington Spa
Jephson Gardens
Warwick Parkway
Warwick Castle
Lord Leycester Hospital
Bridge End
Sydenham
Radford Semele
Print Wood
Hampton Magna
Model Village
Grand Union Canal
COVENTRY
0 1/2 1 mile
0 1 2 kilometres

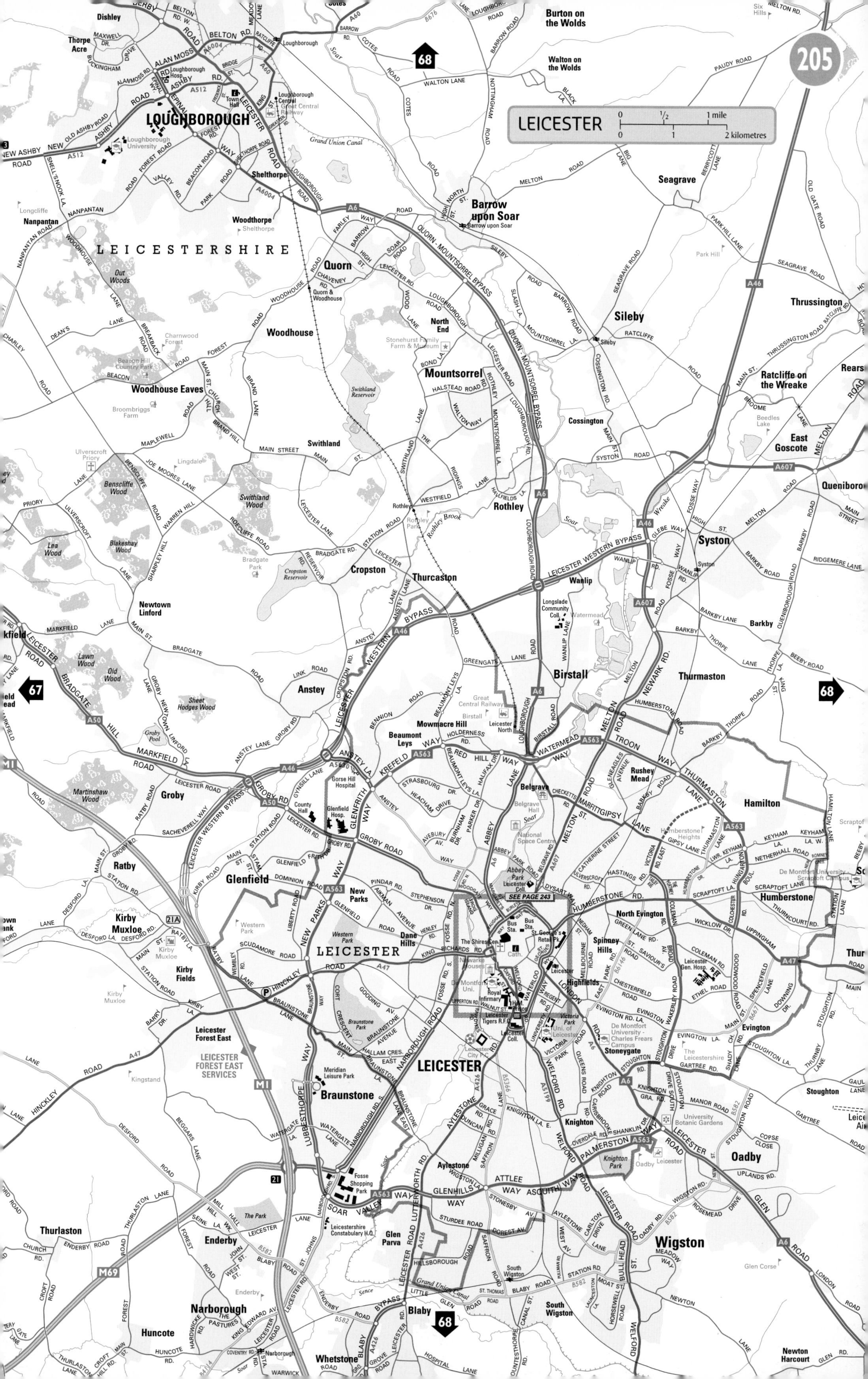
LEICESTER
0 1/2 1 mile
0 1 2 kilometres
68
67
68
68
LEICESTERSHIRE
LOUGHBOROUGH
Loughborough University
Loughborough
Loughborough Central
Great Central Railway
Grand Union Canal
Dishley
Thorpe Acre
Shelthorpe
Nanpantan
Longcliffe
Woodthorpe
Burton on the Wolds
Walton on the Wolds
Seagrave
Barrow upon Soar
Quorn
Quorn & Woodhouse
Woodhouse
Out Woods
Charnwood Forest
Beacon Hill Country Park
Woodhouse Eaves
Broombriggs Farm
North End
Stonehurst Family Farm & Museum
Mountsorrel
Swithland Reservoir
Swithland
Swithland Wood
Ulverscroft Priory
Lingdale
Bensliffe Wood
Blakeshay Wood
Lea Wood
Rothley
Rothley Park
Rothley Brook
Sileby
Cossington
Thrussington
Ratcliffe on the Wreake
East Goscote
Queniborough
Park Hill
Beedles Lake
Syston
Cropston
Cropston Reservoir
Bradgate Park
Thurcaston
Wanlip
Longslade Community Coll.
Watermead
Newtown Linford
Lawn Wood
Old Wood
Sheet Hedges Wood
Anstey
Birstall
Thurmaston
Barkby
Great Central Railway
Leicester North
Mowmacre Hill
Beaumont Leys
Rushey Mead
Groby
Groby Pool
Martinshaw Wood
Gorse Hill Hospital
County Hall
Glenfield Hosp.
Belgrave
Belgrave Hall
National Space Centre
Humberstone Heights
Hamilton
Scraptoft
Ratby
Glenfield
Abbey Park
Leicester Coll.
SEE PAGE 243
New Parks
North Evington
Humberstone
De Montfort University - Scraptoft Campus
Kirby Muxloe
Western Park
Dane Hills
Bus Sta.
The Shires Cen.
Cath.
St George's Retail Pk.
Spinney Hills
LEICESTER
Newarke Houses
De Montfort Uni.
Royal Infirmary
Leicester Gen. Hosp.
Highfields
Kirby Fields
Leicester Tigers R.F.C.
Victoria Park
Uni. of Leicester
Leicester Coll.
Leicester City F.C.
Braunstone Park
De Montfort University - Charles Frears Campus
Stoneygate
Evington
The Leicestershire
Stoughton
Leicester Forest East
LEICESTER FOREST EAST SERVICES
Kingstand
Meridian Leisure Park
Braunstone
LEICESTER
Knighton
University Botanic Gardens
Knighton Park
Oadby
Leicester
Aylestone
Fosse Shopping Park
The Park
Leicestershire Constabulary H.Q.
Glen Parva
Thurlaston
Enderby
Wigston
Glen Corse
South Wigston
Enderby
Narborough
Huncote
Blaby
Whetstone
Newton Harcourt
M1
M69
A6
A46
A47
A50
A563
A607
A512
A6004
A60
A426
A5199
A594
B582
B5366
B667
B676
21
21A
LEICESTER WESTERN BYPASS
QUORN - MOUNTSORREL BYPASS

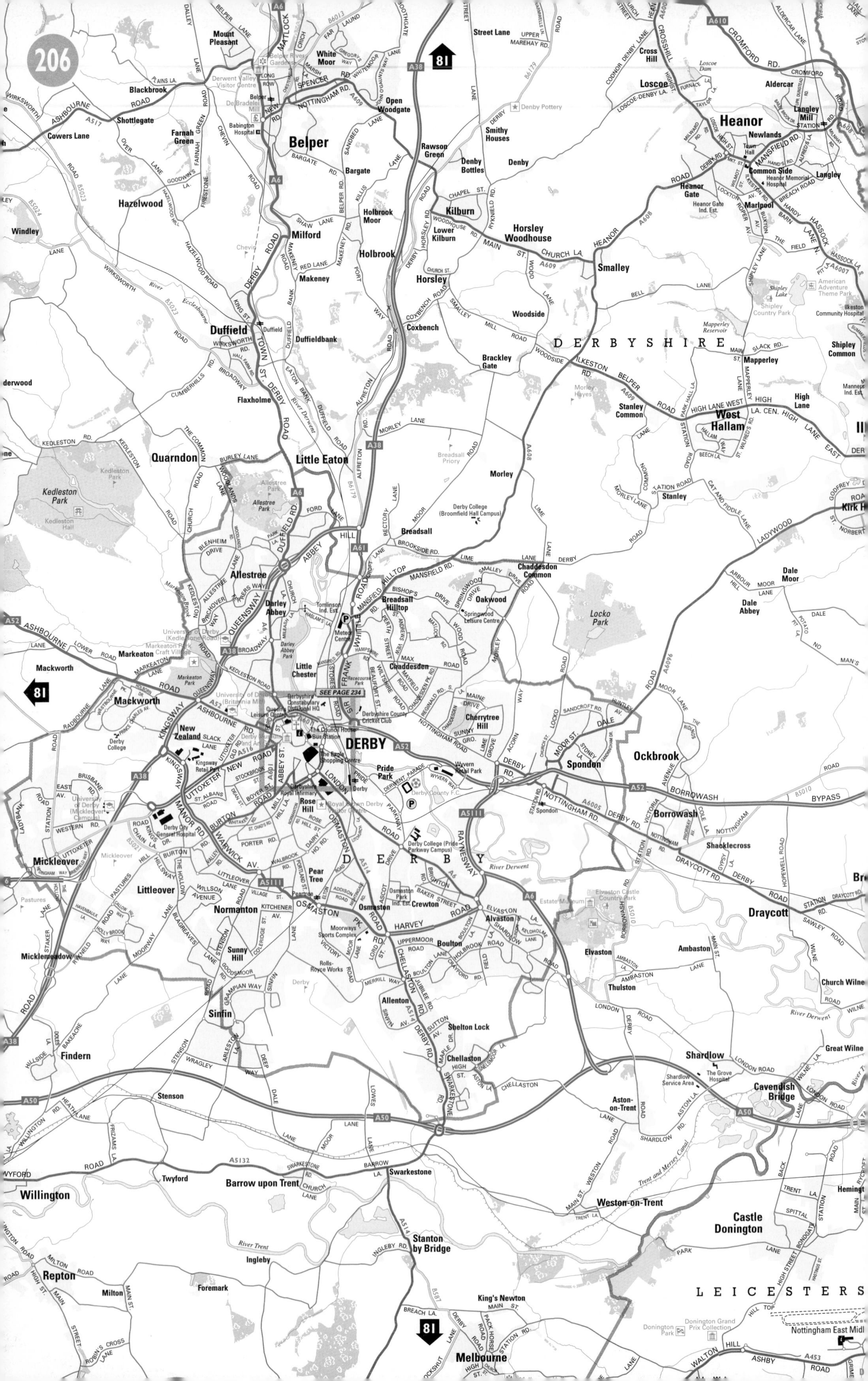
81
Mount Pleasant
Belper River Gardens
Derwent Valley Visitor Centre
White Moor
Open Woodgate
Street Lane
Blackbrook
Shottlegate
Cowers Lane
Farnah Green
Babington Hospital
Belper
Bargate
Rawson Green
Denby Pottery
Smithy Houses
Denby Bottles
Denby
Cross Hill
Loscoe
Aldercar
Heanor
Langley Mill
Newlands
Common Side
Heanor Memorial Hospital
Langley
Heanor Gate
Heanor Gate Ind. Est.
Marlpool
Hazelwood
Windley
Milford
Holbrook Moor
Holbrook
Kilburn
Lower Kilburn
Horsley Woodhouse
Smalley
Makeney
Horsley
Duffield
Duffieldbank
Coxbench
Woodside
Shipley Lake
Shipley Country Park
American Adventure Theme Park
Ilkeston Community Hospital
Mapperley Reservoir
DERBYSHIRE
Mapperley
Shipley Common
Brackley Gate
Flaxholme
Morley Hayes
Stanley Common
West Hallam
High Lane
Quarndon
Little Eaton
Breadsall Priory
Morley
Stanley
Kedleston Park
Kedleston Hall
Allestree Park
Derby College (Broomfield Hall Campus)
Breadsall
Allestree
Chaddesden Common
Dale Moor
Darley Abbey
Breadsall Hilltop
Oakwood
Springwood Leisure Centre
Locko Park
Dale Abbey
Tomlinson Ind. Est.
Meteor Centre
Markeaton Park Craft Village
Markeaton
Mackworth
Little Chester
Chaddesden
Darley Abbey Park
Racecourse Park
Markeaton Park
SEE PAGE 234
Derbyshire County Cricket Club
Cherrytree Hill
Mackworth
Derby College
New Zealand
DERBY
Kingsway Retail Park
The Council House
Bus Station
The Eagle Shopping Centre
Pride Park
Wyvern Retail Park
Derby County F.C.
Spondon
Ockbrook
Borrowash
Rose Hill
Royal Derby Hospital
Derby City General Hospital
Mickleover
Littleover
Pear Tree
DERBY
Derby College (Pride Parkway Campus)
River Derwent
Shacklecross
Draycott
Normanton
Osmaston
Osmaston Park Ind. Est.
Crewton
Alvaston
Elvaston Castle Country Park
Estate Museum
Moorways Sports Complex
Boulton
Elvaston
Ambaston
Micklemeadow
Sunny Hill
Rolls-Royce Works
Thulston
Church Wilne
Allenton
Sinfin
Shelton Lock
Findern
Chellaston
Shardlow
Great Wilne
Shardlow Service Area
The Grove Hospital
Cavendish Bridge
Stenson
Aston-on-Trent
Twyford
Barrow upon Trent
Swarkestone
Willington
Weston-on-Trent
Trent and Mersey Canal
Castle Donington
Hemington
Stanton by Bridge
River Trent
Ingleby
Repton
Milton
Foremark
King's Newton
LEICESTERSHIRE
Donington Park
Donington Grand Prix Collection
Nottingham East Midlands
Melbourne
81

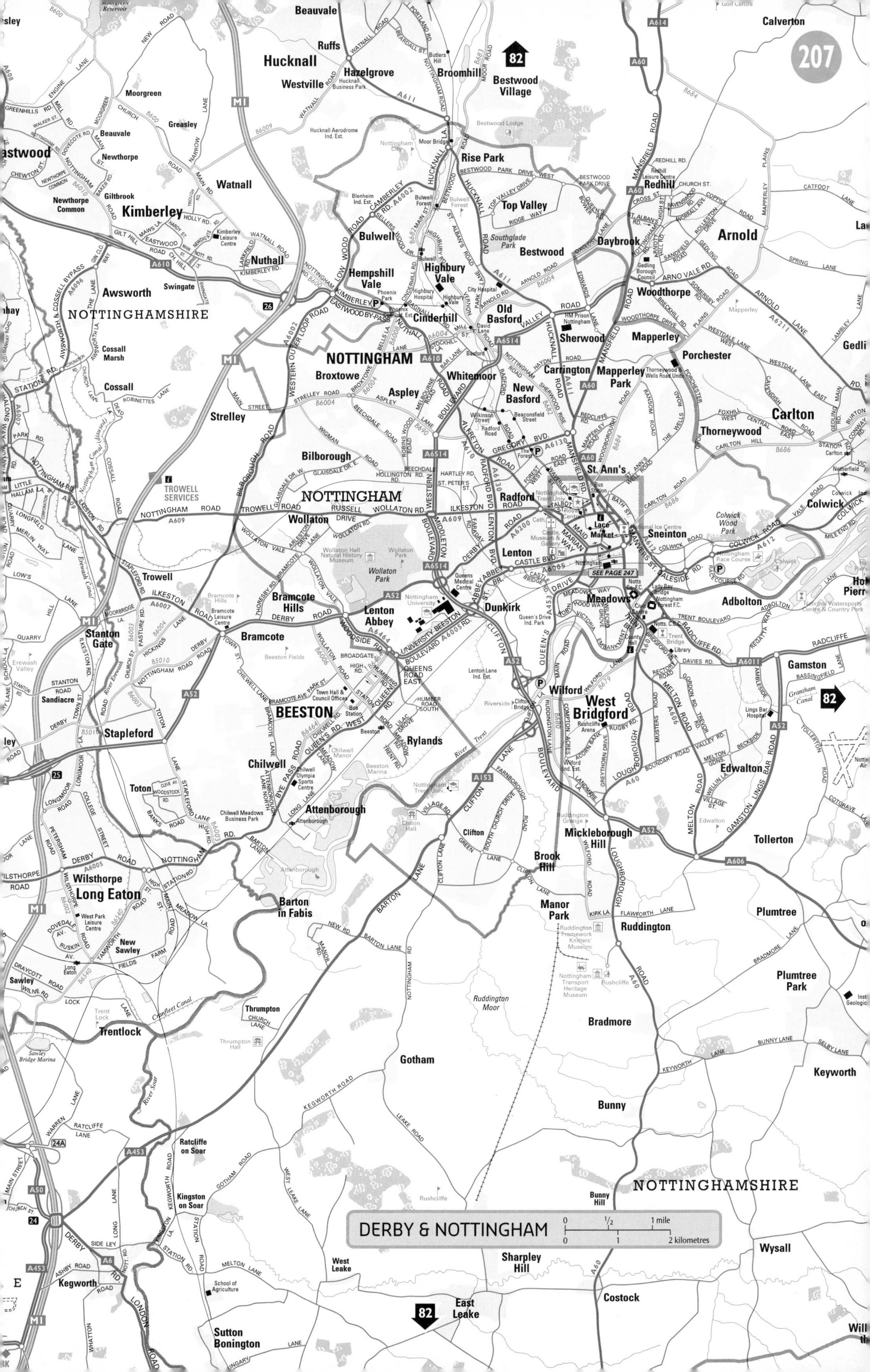
DERBY & NOTTINGHAM
0
1/2
1 mile
0
1
2 kilometres
NOTTINGHAMSHIRE
NOTTINGHAM
SEE PAGE 247
82
Beauvale
Ruffs
Hucknall
Hazelgrove
Westville
Broomhill
Bestwood Village
Calverton
Moorgreen
Greasley
Eastwood
Newthorpe
Giltbrook
Newthorpe Common
Kimberley
Watnall
Nuthall
Awsworth
Swingate
Rise Park
Top Valley
Bestwood
Redhill
Arnold
Daybrook
Bulwell
Hempshill Vale
Highbury Vale
Cinderhill
Old Basford
Woodthorpe
Sherwood
Mapperley
Porchester
Carrington
Mapperley Park
New Basford
Whitemoor
Broxtowe
Aspley
Strelley
Cossall Marsh
Cossall
Bilborough
Carlton
Thorneywood
St. Ann's
Radford
Colwick
Colwick Wood Park
Sneinton
Lenton
Wollaton
Wollaton Park
Lace Market
Trowell
TROWELL SERVICES
Bramcote Hills
Lenton Abbey
Dunkirk
Meadows
Adbolton
Stanton Gate
Bramcote
Gamston
Wilford
West Bridgford
BEESTON
Rylands
Stapleford
Sandiacre
Chilwell
Toton
Attenborough
Edwalton
Clifton
Mickleborough Hill
Tollerton
Brook Hill
Wilsthorpe
Long Eaton
Barton in Fabis
New Sawley
Manor Park
Ruddington
Plumtree
Plumtree Park
Sawley
Thrumpton
Trentlock
Bradmore
Gotham
Keyworth
Bunny
Ratcliffe on Soar
Kingston on Soar
Bunny Hill
Wysall
Sharpley Hill
West Leake
Kegworth
East Leake
Costock
Sutton Bonington
Ruddington Moor
River Trent
River Soar
River Erewash
Erewash Canal
Nottingham Canal (disused)
Cranfleet Canal
Grantham Canal
M1
A52
A60
A610
A6514
A453
A606
A614
A611
A609
A6005
A612
A6011
A6002
A6096
A6007
A50
A6
A153
A6130
A6200
B6004
B6010
B600
B6009
B684
B686
B679
B680
B6003
B6464
B6540
B6002
B5010
26
25
24A
24

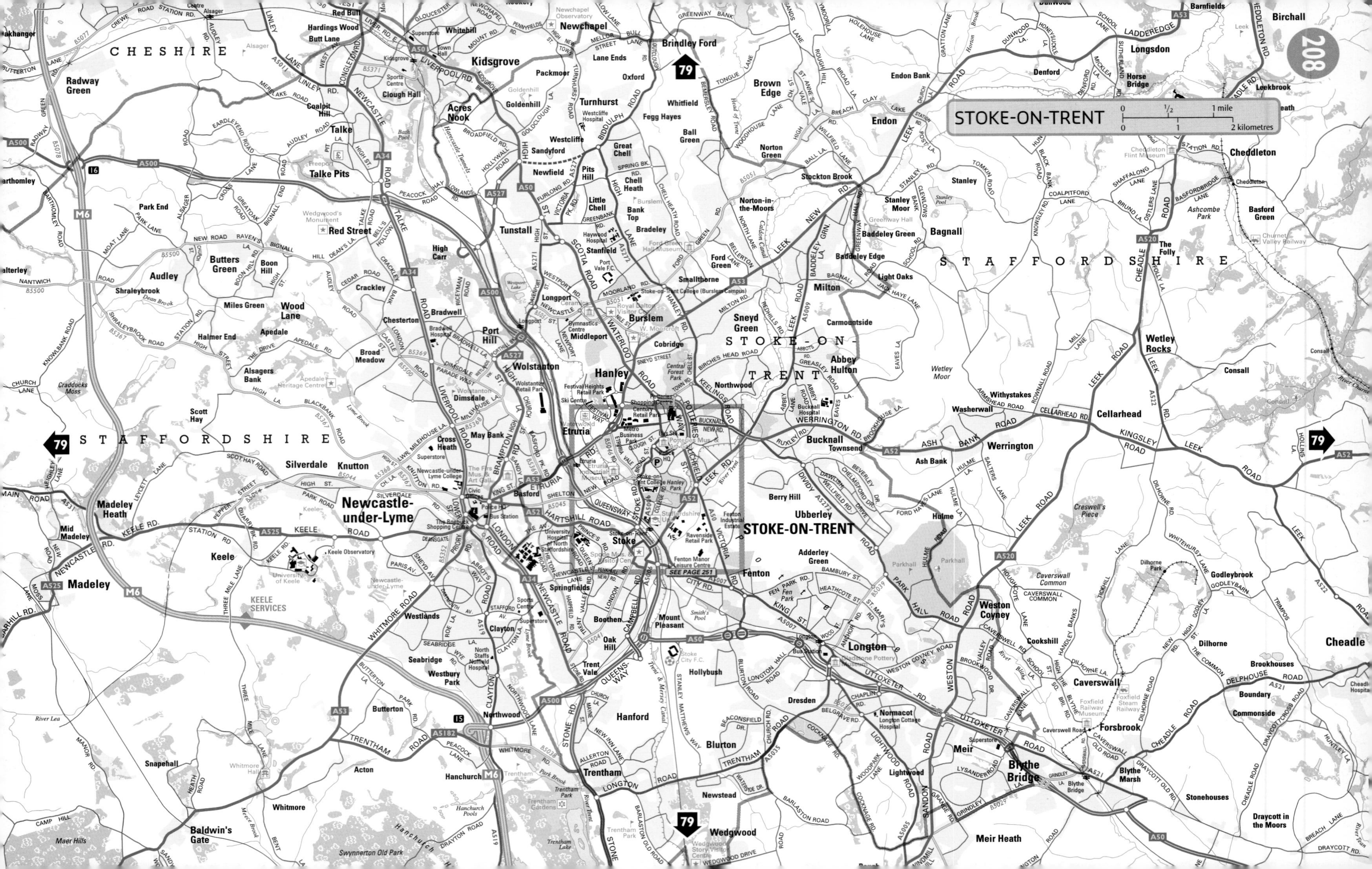
STOKE-ON-TRENT
0 ½ 1 mile
0 1 2 kilometres
CHESHIRE
STAFFORDSHIRE
STAFFORDSHIRE
STOKE-ON-TRENT
STOKE-ON-TRENT
SEE PAGE 251
79
Newcastle-under-Lyme
Hanley
Burslem
Tunstall
Stoke
Longton
Fenton
Etruria
Kidsgrove
Endon
Cheddleton
Cheadle
Meir
Meir Heath
Blythe Bridge
Trentham
Wedgwood
Keele
Madeley
Madeley Heath
Mid Madeley
Audley
Talke
Talke Pits
Werrington
Bucknall
Milton
Abbey Hulton
Smallthorne
Norton-in-the-Moors
Brown Edge
Stockton Brook
Baddeley Green
Wolstanton
Port Hill
Silverdale
Knutton
Chesterton
Clayton
Hanford
Blurton
Dresden
Caverswall
Cellarhead
Wetley Rocks
Consall
Longsdon
Birchall
Dilhorne
Draycott in the Moors
Whitmore
Baldwin's Gate
Acton
Hanchurch
Butterton
Westbury Park
Seabridge
Westlands
Trent Vale
Basford
Cobridge
Sneyd Green
Northwood
Ubberley
Berry Hill
Adderley Green
Weston Coyney
Washerwall
Ash Bank
Hulme
Sandyford
Goldenhill
Packmoor
Newchapel
Whitehill
Butt Lane
Hardings Wood
Red Bull
Radway Green
Wood Lane
Miles Green
Halmer End
Alsagers Bank
Scot Hay
Red Street
Butters Green
Boon Hill
Crackley
Bradwell
Middleport
Longport
Dimsdale
May Bank
Cross Heath
Springfields
Boothen
Oak Hill
Mount Pleasant
Hollybush
Normacot
Lightwood
Forsbrook
Godleybrook
Boundary
Commonside
Brookhouses
Stonehouses
Blythe Marsh
Newstead
Snapehall
Bagnall
Stanley
Stanley Moor
Light Oaks
Carmountside
Withystakes
Ball Green
Fegg Hayes
Whitfield
Brindley Ford
Turnhurst
Oxford
Lane Ends
Great Chell
Chell Heath
Little Chell
Bank Top
Bradeley
Pitts Hill
Newfield
Westcliffe
Stanfield
Ford Green
Norton Green
Endon Bank
Denford
Horse Bridge
Basford Green
The Folly
Acres Nook
Clough Hall
Coalpit Hill
High Carr
Park End
Shraleybrook
Apedale
Broad Meadow
Cookshill
Parkhall
Creswell's Piece
Caverswall Common
Townsend
KEELE SERVICES
Swynnerton Old Park
Maer Hills

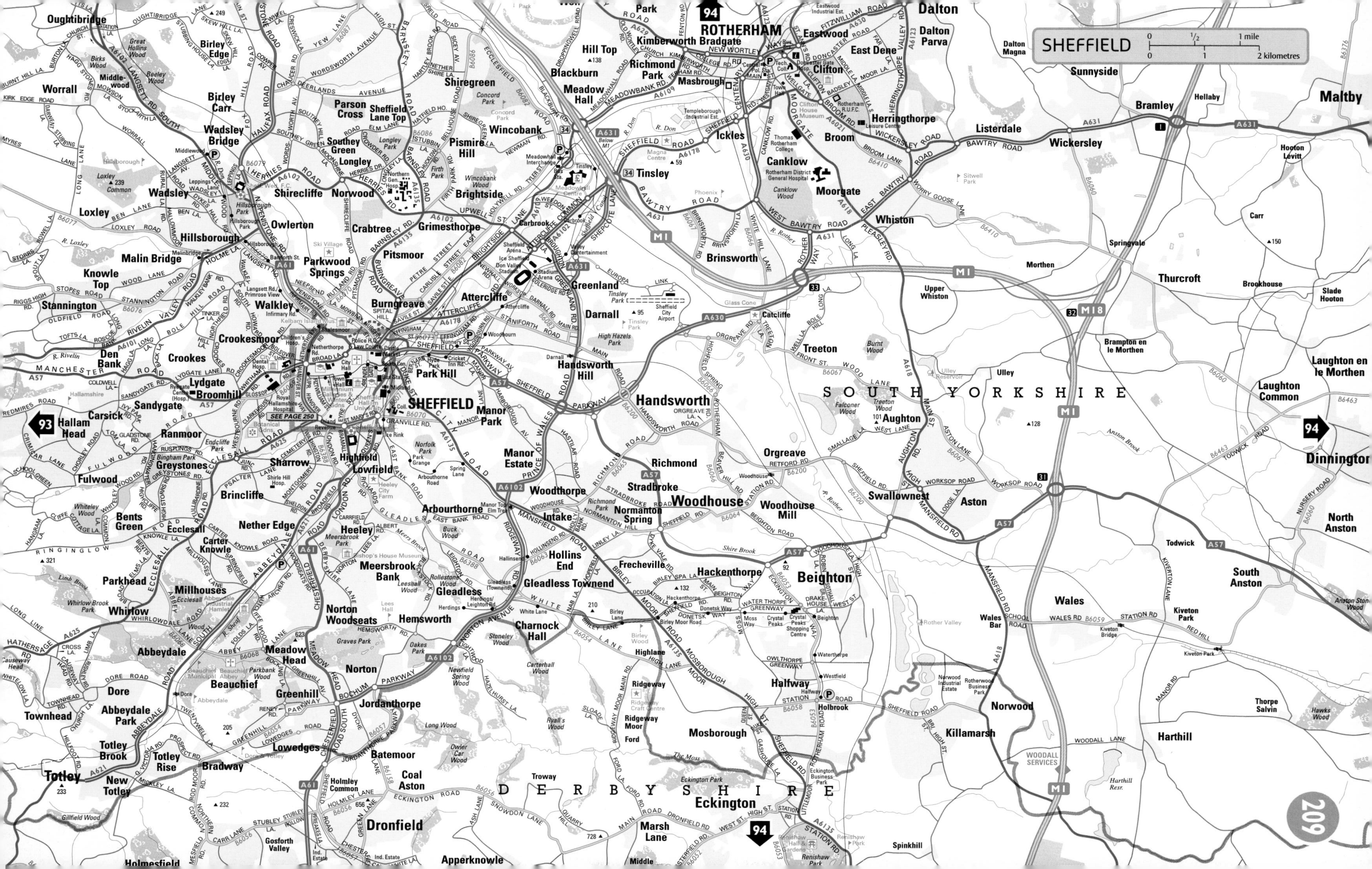
SHEFFIELD
0 ½ 1 mile
0 1 2 kilometres
SOUTH YORKSHIRE
DERBYSHIRE
94
93
SEE PAGE 250
ROTHERHAM
SHEFFIELD
Oughtibridge
Worrall
Birley Edge
Birley Carr
Wadsley Bridge
Wadsley
Loxley
Hillsborough
Owlerton
Malin Bridge
Knowle Top
Stannington
Walkley
Crookesmoor
Crookes
Den Bank
Lydgate
Broomhill
Sandygate
Carsick
Hallam Head
Ranmoor
Sharrow
Greystones
Fulwood
Bents Green
Ecclesall
Brincliffe
Nether Edge
Carter Knowle
Parkhead
Millhouses
Whirlow
Abbeydale
Beauchief
Dore
Townhead
Abbeydale Park
Totley Brook
Totley Rise
Totley
New Totley
Bradway
Greenhill
Meadow Head
Lowedges
Norton Woodseats
Norton
Jordanthorpe
Batemoor
Coal Aston
Dronfield
Apperknowle
Heeley
Meersbrook Bank
Gleadless
Hemsworth
Lowfield
Highfield
Arbourthorne
Manor Estate
Manor Park
Park Hill
Intake
Woodthorpe
Gleadless Townend
Hollins End
Charnock Hall
Frecheville
Hackenthorpe
Beighton
Halfway
Holbrook
Mosborough
Eckington
Marsh Lane
Ridgeway
Ridgeway Moor
Ford
Highlane
Troway
Woodhouse
Woodhouse Mill
Normanton Spring
Stradbroke
Richmond
Orgreave
Handsworth
Handsworth Hill
Darnall
Greenland
Attercliffe
Carbrook
Tinsley
Brinsworth
Burngreave
Pitsmoor
Grimesthorpe
Brightside
Crabtree
Parkwood Springs
Shirecliffe
Norwood
Longley
Southey Green
Parson Cross
Sheffield Lane Top
Shiregreen
Wincobank
Pismire Hill
Blackburn
Meadow Hall
Hill Top
Kimberworth
Bradgate
Richmond Park
Masbrough
Ickles
Canklow
Moorgate
Broom
Clifton
Eastwood
East Dene
Herringthorpe
Dalton
Dalton Parva
Dalton Magna
Sunnyside
Listerdale
Wickersley
Bramley
Hellaby
Maltby
Hooton Levitt
Carr
Springvale
Morthen
Thurcroft
Brookhouse
Slade Hooton
Whiston
Upper Whiston
Catcliffe
Treeton
Ulley
Brampton en le Morthen
Laughton en le Morthen
Laughton Common
Dinnington
North Anston
South Anston
Todwick
Aughton
Swallownest
Aston
Wales
Wales Bar
Kiveton Park
Harthill
Norwood
Killamarsh
Thorpe Salvin
Spinkhill
WOODALL SERVICES
Sheffield City Airport
Rotherham District General Hospital
Northern Gen. Hosp.
Royal Hallamshire Hospital
Meadowhall Interchange
Ski Village
Sheffield Arena
Don Valley Stadium
M1
M18
A57
A61
A631
A6102
A6135
A618
A630

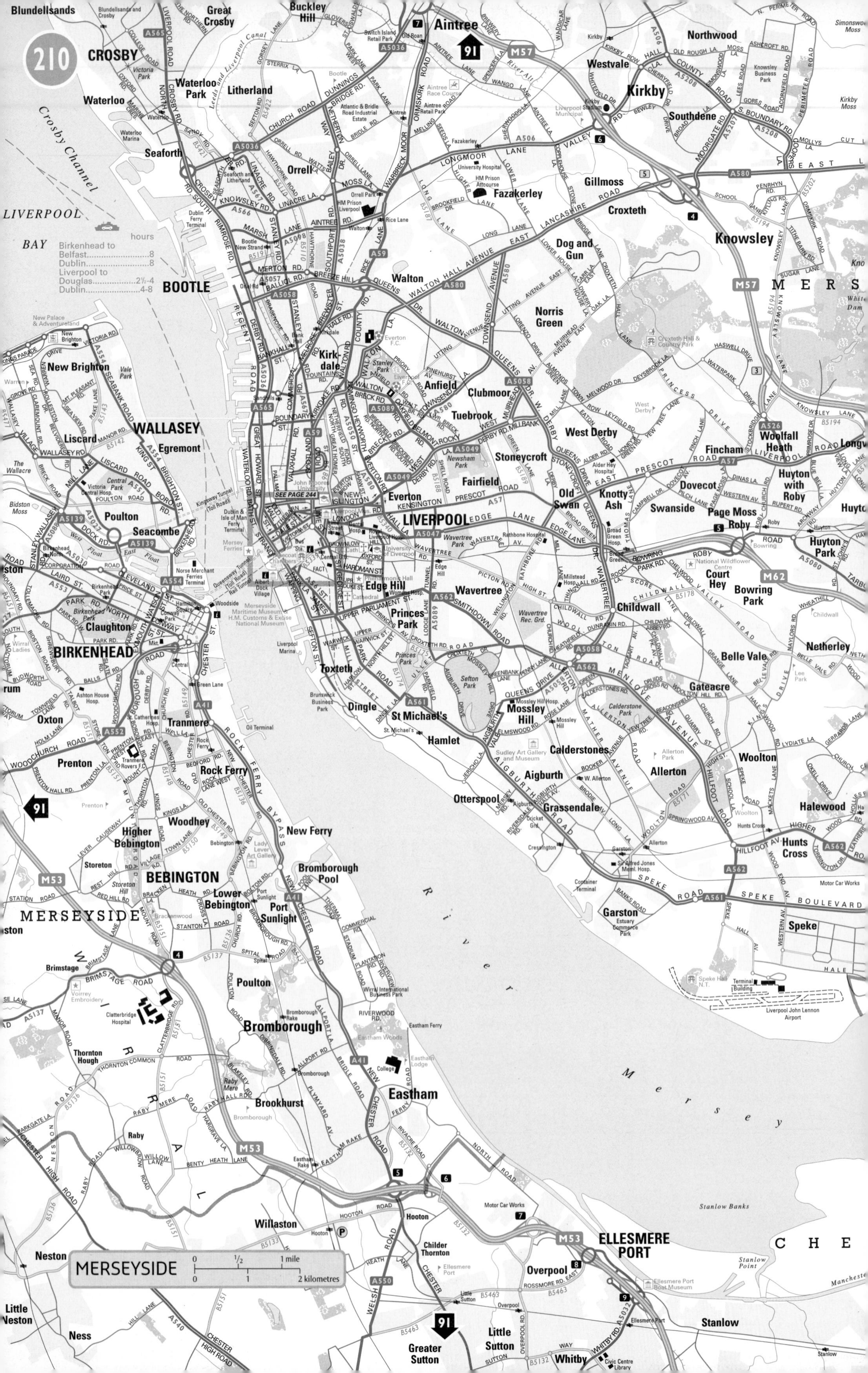
MERSEYSIDE
0 ½ 1 mile
0 1 2 kilometres
Birkenhead to
Belfast 8
Dublin 8
Liverpool to
Douglas 2½-4
Dublin 4-8
hours
SEE PAGE 244
LIVERPOOL BAY
Crosby Channel
River Mersey
WIRRAL
MERSEYSIDE
Blundellsands
CROSBY
Great Crosby
Waterloo
Waterloo Park
Litherland
Seaforth
Orrell
Buckley Hill
Aintree
Northwood
Westvale
Kirkby
Southdene
Gillmoss
Croxteth
Fazakerley
Knowsley
BOOTLE
Walton
Dog and Gun
Norris Green
Kirkdale
Anfield
Clubmoor
Tuebrook
West Derby
Stoneycroft
Fairfield
Everton
LIVERPOOL
Old Swan
Knotty Ash
Dovecot
Swanside
Page Moss
Roby
Fincham
Woolfall Heath
Huyton with Roby
Huyton Park
Court Hey
Bowring Park
Edge Hill
Wavertree
Childwall
Princes Park
Toxteth
Dingle
St Michael's
Hamlet
Mossley Hill
Calderstones
Aigburth
Allerton
Grassendale
Otterspool
Belle Vale
Netherley
Gateacre
Woolton
Halewood
Hunts Cross
Garston
Speke
Liverpool John Lennon Airport
New Brighton
WALLASEY
Liscard
Egremont
Poulton
Seacombe
Claughton
BIRKENHEAD
Oxton
Tranmere
Prenton
Rock Ferry
Woodhey
Higher Bebington
New Ferry
Bromborough Pool
Storeton
BEBINGTON
Lower Bebington
Port Sunlight
Brimstage
Poulton
Bromborough
Thornton Hough
Brookhurst
Eastham
Raby
Willaston
Hooton
Childer Thornton
Neston
Little Neston
Ness
ELLESMERE PORT
Overpool
Stanlow
Little Sutton
Greater Sutton
Whitby
Stanlow Banks
M57
M62
M53
A41
A580
A5058
91

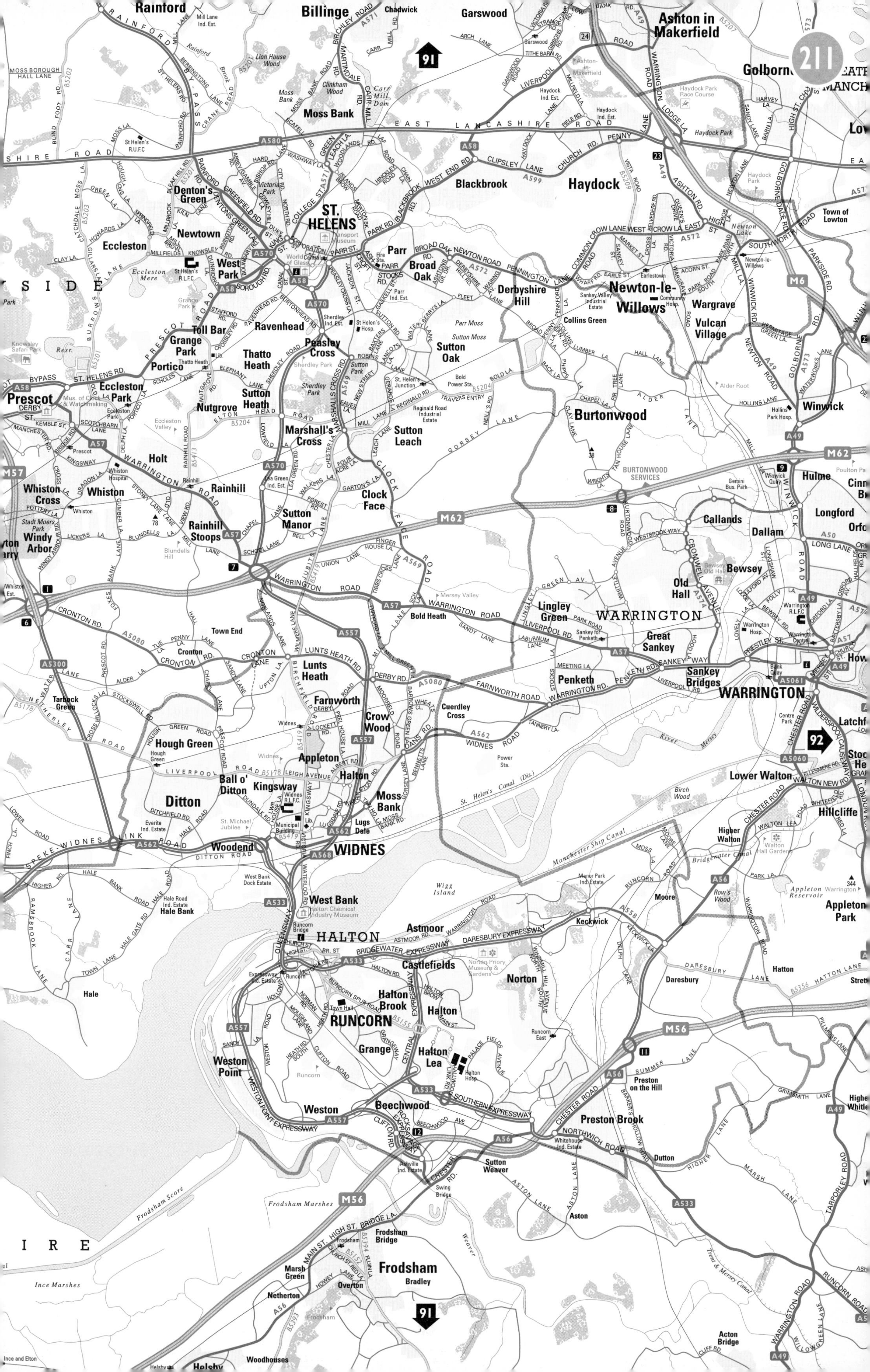
Rainford
Billinge
Chadwick
Garswood
Ashton in Makerfield
Golborne
Mill Lane Ind. Est.
Lion House Wood
Moss Bank
Clinkham Wood
Carr Mill Dam
Haydock Park Race Course
Haydock Park
91
EAST LANCASHIRE ROAD
Moss Bank
Moss Borough Hall Lane
St Helen's R.U.F.C.
Blackbrook
Haydock
Town of Lowton
Denton's Green
Newtown
Eccleston
ST. HELENS
Transport Museum
Parr
Broad Oak
Derbyshire Hill
Newton-le-Willows
Wargrave
Vulcan Village
Newton Lake
Newton-le-Willows
Eccleston Mere
West Park
World of Glass
Collins Green
Sankey Valley Industrial Estate
Earlestown
SIDE
Toll Bar
Ravenhead
Grange Park
Portico
Thatto Heath
Sutton Heath
Peasley Cross
Sherdley Park
Sutton Park
Sutton Oak
Parr Moss
Sutton Moss
Bold Power Sta.
Knowsley Safari Park
Prescot
Eccleston Park
Mus. of Clock & Watchmaking
Nutgrove
Marshall's Cross
Sutton Leach
Reginald Road Industrial Estate
Burtonwood
Alder Root
Winwick
Hollins Park Hosp.
Holt
Rainhill
Whiston Cross
Whiston
Whiston Hospital
Clock Face
Sutton Manor
Rainhill Stoops
BURTONWOOD SERVICES
Hulme
Winwick Quay
Gemini Bus. Park
Longford
Callands
Dallam
Stadt Moers Park
Windy Arbor
Blundells Hill
M62
M57
M6
Bewsey
Old Hall
Lingley Green
WARRINGTON
Warrington R.L.F.C.
Warrington Hosp.
Mersey Valley
Bold Heath
Town End
Cronton
Lunts Heath
Great Sankey
Sankey for Penketh
Penketh
Sankey Bridges
WARRINGTON
Tarbock Green
Farnworth
Crow Wood
Cuerdley Cross
Centre Park
92
Hough Green
Appleton
Halton
Widnes
River Mersey
Power Sta.
Lower Walton
Ditton
Ball o' Ditton
Kingsway
Widnes R.U.F.C.
Moss Bank
Lugs Dale
Birch Wood
Hillcliffe
Higher Walton
Walton Hall Gardens
St. Helen's Canal (Dis.)
Everite Ind. Estate
St. Michael Jubilee
Municipal Building
Woodend
WIDNES
Manchester Ship Canal
Bridgewater Canal
West Bank Dock Estate
Hale Road Ind. Estate
Hale Bank
West Bank
Halton Chemical Industry Museum
Wigg Island
Manor Park Ind. Estate
Moore
Row's Wood
Appleton Reservoir
Appleton Park
HALTON
Astmoor
Keckwick
Runcorn Bridge
Castlefields
Norton Priory Museum & Gardens
Norton
Daresbury
Hatton
Hale
Halton Brook
Halton
RUNCORN
Town Hall
Runcorn East
Grange
Halton Lea
Halton Hosp.
M56
Preston on the Hill
Weston Point
Runcorn
Weston
Beechwood
Preston Brook
Dutton
Whitehouse Ind. Estate
Sutton Weaver
Astmoor Ind. Estate
Swing Bridge
Aston
Frodsham Marshes
Frodsham Score
Frodsham Bridge
IRE
Marsh Green
Frodsham
Bradley
Overton
Ince Marshes
Netherton
Trent & Mersey Canal
Acton Bridge
Woodhouses
Helsby
Ince and Elton
91

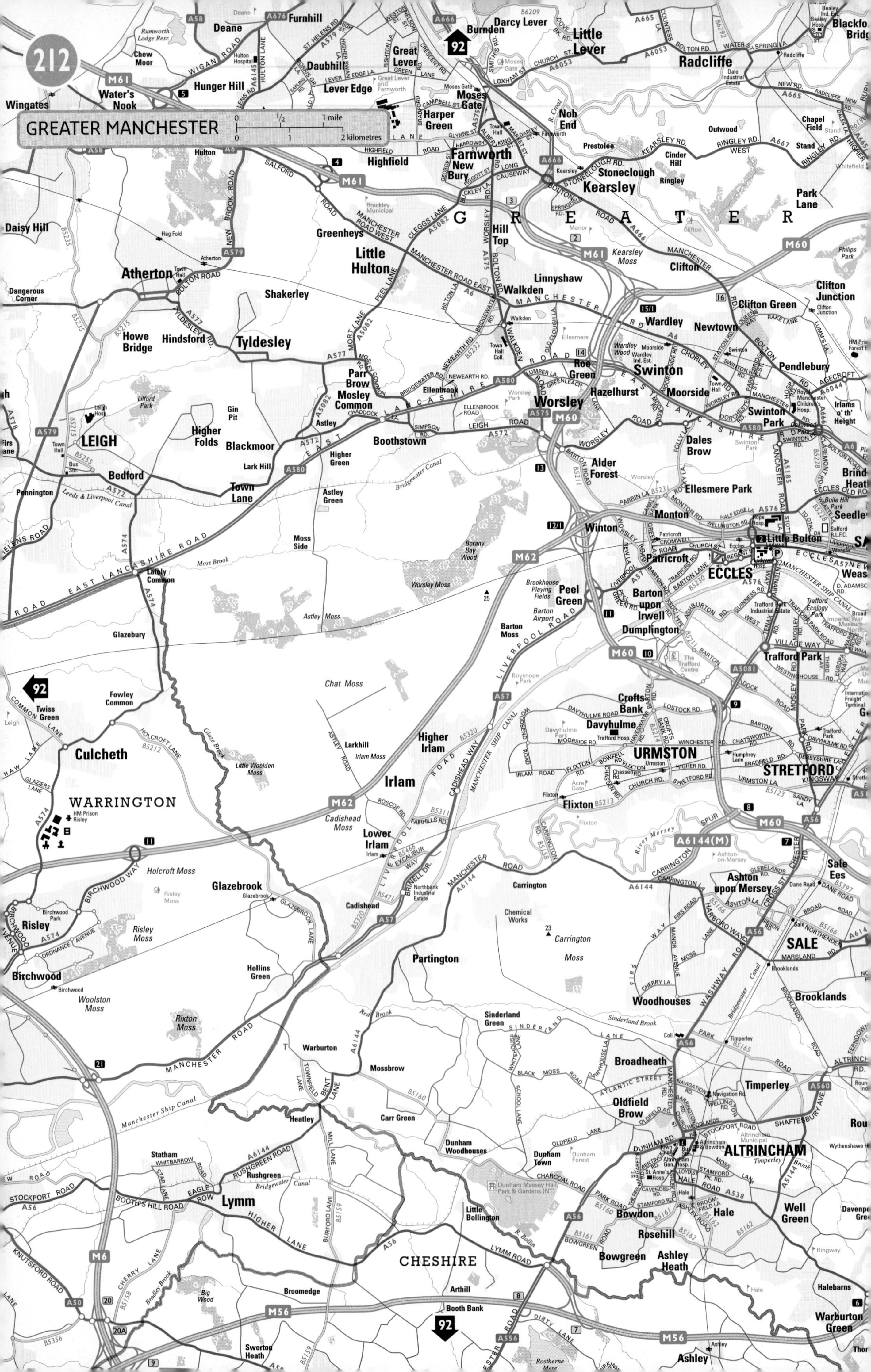
212
GREATER MANCHESTER
0 ½ 1 mile
0 1 2 kilometres
G R E A T E R
CHESHIRE
WARRINGTON
92
Deane
Furnhill
Burnden
Darcy Lever
Little Lever
Radcliffe
Rumworth Lodge Resr.
Chew Moor
Hunger Hill
Daubhill
Great Lever
Lever Edge
Moses Gate
Water's Nook
Wingates
Harper Green
Nob End
Farnworth
New Bury
Highfield
Hulton
Prestolee
Stoneclough
Kearsley
Cinder Hill
Ringley
Outwood
Chapel Field
Stand
Park Lane
Daisy Hill
Greenheys
Little Hulton
Hill Top
Kearsley Moss
Clifton
Atherton
Dangerous Corner
Shakerley
Walkden
Linnyshaw
Wardley
Newtown
Clifton Green
Clifton Junction
Howe Bridge
Hindsford
Tyldesley
Roe Green
Swinton
Pendlebury
Parr Brow
Mosley Common
Ellenbrook
Worsley
Hazelhurst
Moorside
Swinton Park
Irlams o' th' Height
LEIGH
Gin Pit
Higher Folds
Blackmoor
Astley
Boothstown
Dales Brow
Lark Hill
Higher Green
Alder Forest
Bedford
Town Lane
Pennington
Ellesmere Park
Astley Green
Bridgewater Canal
Leeds & Liverpool Canal
Monton
Seedley
Winton
Little Bolton
Moss Side
Botany Bay Wood
Patricroft
ECCLES
Lately Common
Moss Brook
Worsley Moss
Peel Green
Barton upon Irwell
Astley Moss
Barton Moss
Dumplington
Glazebury
Trafford Park
Chat Moss
Crofts Bank
Davyhulme
Fowley Common
Twiss Green
Culcheth
Higher Irlam
Larkhill
Irlam Moss
URMSTON
STRETFORD
Little Woolden Moss
Irlam
Flixton
Cadishead Moss
Lower Irlam
Holcroft Moss
Glazebrook
Ashton upon Mersey
Carrington
Risley Moss
Risley
Cadishead
Chemical Works
Carrington Moss
Birchwood
Hollins Green
Partington
SALE
Woolston Moss
Woodhouses
Brooklands
Rixton Moss
Sinderland Green
Warburton
Broadheath
Mossbrow
Timperley
Oldfield Brow
Heatley
Carr Green
Manchester Ship Canal
Statham
Dunham Woodhouses
Dunham Town
ALTRINCHAM
Rushgreen
Lymm
Little Bollington
Bowdon
Hale
Well Green
Rosehill
Bowgreen
Ashley Heath
Broomedge
Arthill
Big Wood
Booth Bank
Halebarns
Warburton Green
Swarton Heath
Ashley
M61
M60
M62
M6
M56
A6144(M)
River Mersey

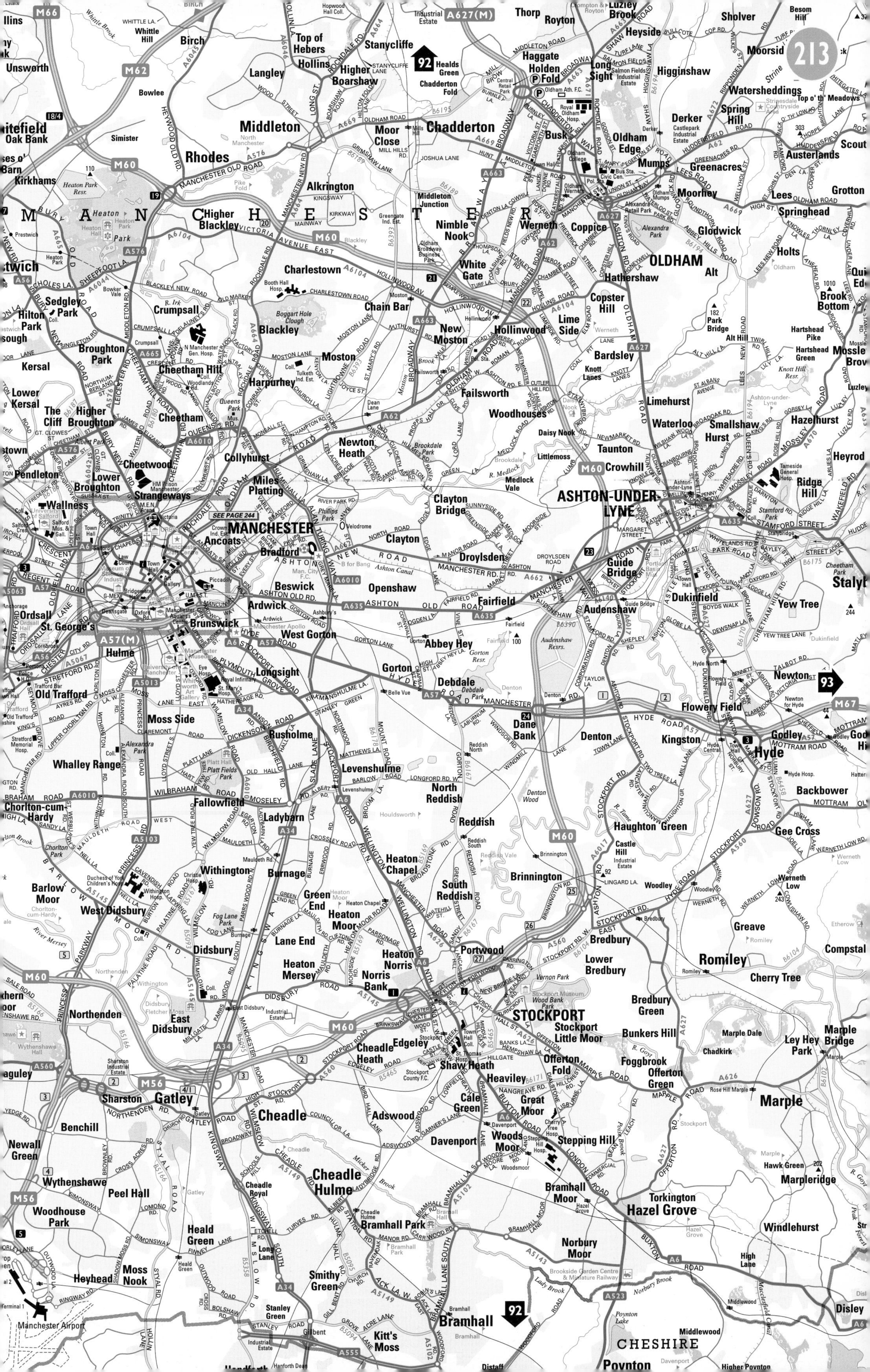

213
MANCHESTER
Middleton
Chadderton
Royton
Thorp
Sholver
Moorsid
Heyside
Haggate
Holden Fold
Long Sight
Higginshaw
Watersheddings
Spring Hill
Derker
Busk
Oldham Edge
Mumps
Greenacres
Austerlands
Scouthead
Moorhey
Lees
Grotton
Springhead
Glodwick
Holts
OLDHAM
Alt
Hathershaw
Werneth
Coppice
Rhodes
Alkrington
Langley
Top of Hebers
Hollins
Stanycliffe
Higher Boarshaw
Moor Close
Heaton Park
Higher Blackley
Nimble Nook
White Gate
Charlestown
Chain Bar
Blackley
Crumpsall
Sedgley Park
Hilton Park
Broughton Park
Kersal
Lower Kersal
The Cliff
Higher Broughton
Cheetham Hill
Cheetham
Harpurhey
Moston
New Moston
Hollinwood
Lime Side
Copster Hill
Bardsley
Failsworth
Woodhouses
Daisy Nook
Limehurst
Waterloo
Smallshaw
Hurst
Hazelhurst
Heyrod
Ridge Hill
Taunton
Crowhill
ASHTON-UNDER-LYNE
Newton Heath
Collyhurst
Miles Platting
Cheetwood
Lower Broughton
Pendleton
Strangeways
Wallness
Ancoats
Bradford
Clayton
Clayton Bridge
Droylsden
Guide Bridge
Dukinfield
Stalybridge
Yew Tree
Openshaw
Beswick
Fairfield
Audenshaw
Ardwick
West Gorton
Abbey Hey
Ordsall
St. George's
Hulme
Brunswick
Longsight
Gorton
Debdale
Old Trafford
Moss Side
Rusholme
Dane Bank
Denton
Kingston
Flowery Field
Newton
Hyde
Godley
Whalley Range
Levenshulme
North Reddish
Backbower
Chorlton-cum-Hardy
Fallowfield
Ladybarn
Reddish
Haughton Green
Gee Cross
Castle Hill
Withington
Burnage
Heaton Chapel
South Reddish
Brinnington
Woodley
Werneth Low
Barlow Moor
West Didsbury
Green End
Heaton Moor
Greave
Lane End
Bredbury
Lower Bredbury
Romiley
Compstall
Didsbury
Heaton Mersey
Heaton Norris
Norris Bank
Portwood
Cherry Tree
Northenden
East Didsbury
STOCKPORT
Stockport Little Moor
Bredbury Green
Bunkers Hill
Marple Bridge
Ley Hey Park
Cheadle Heath
Edgeley
Shaw Heath
Offerton Fold
Foggbrook
Offerton Green
Marple
Sharston
Gatley
Cheadle
Heaviley
Cale Green
Great Moor
Adswood
Davenport
Woods Moor
Stepping Hill
Benchill
Newall Green
Wythenshawe
Peel Hall
Cheadle Hulme
Woodhouse Park
Heald Green
Bramhall Park
Bramhall Moor
Torkington
Hazel Grove
Marpleridge
Windlehurst
Norbury Moor
Heyhead
Moss Nook
Smithy Green
Stanley Green
Kitt's Moss
Bramhall
High Lane
Disley
Manchester Airport
CHESHIRE
Poynton
Higher Poynton
Middlewood
SEE PAGE 244

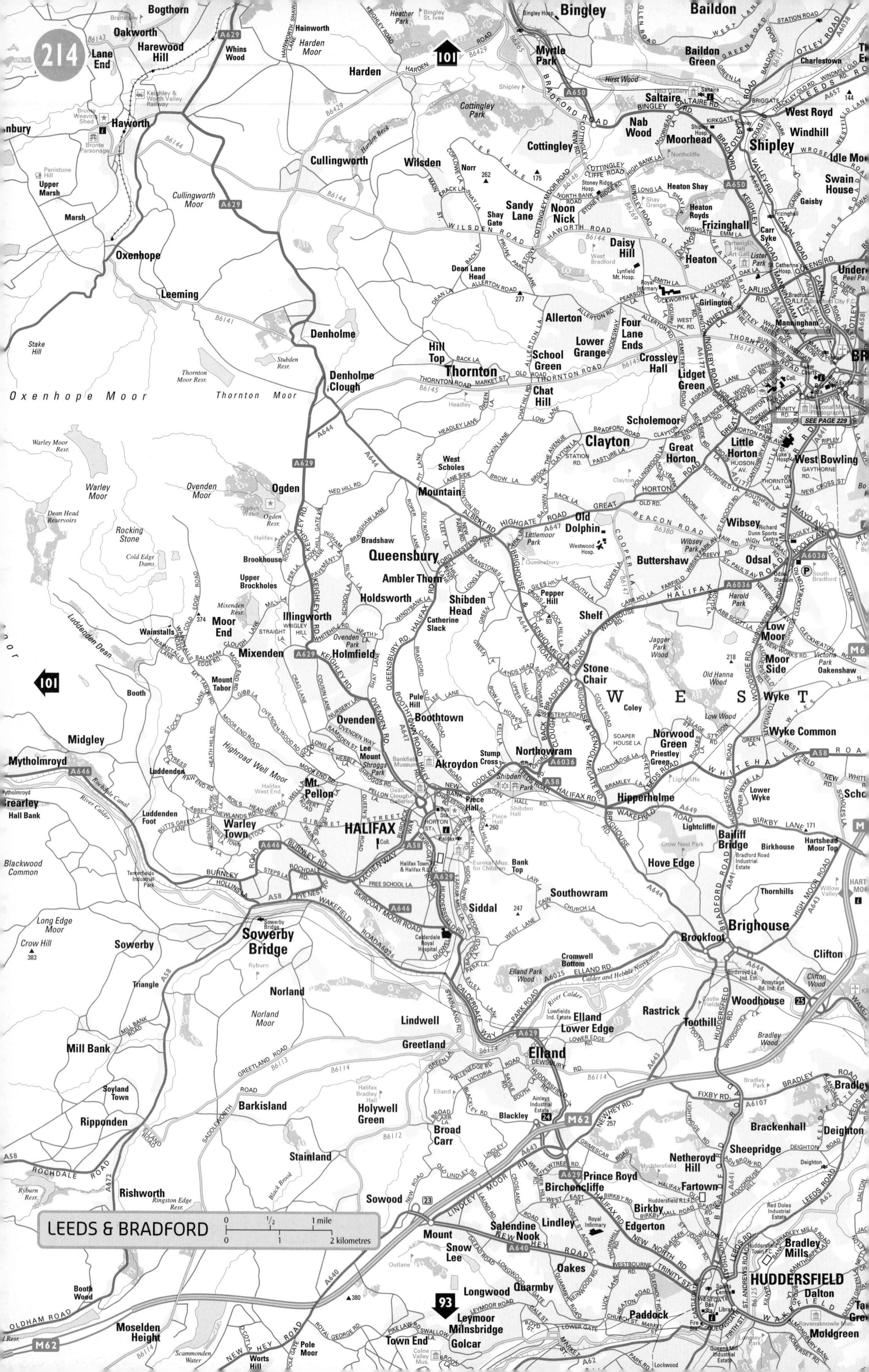
LEEDS & BRADFORD
0 1/2 1 mile
0 1 2 kilometres
SEE PAGE 229
101
93
Bogthorn
Oakworth
Harewood Hill
Lane End
Whins Wood
Hainworth
Harden Moor
Harden
Heather Park
Bingley
Baildon
Baildon Green
Charlestown
Myrtle Park
Hirst Wood
Saltaire
Nab Wood
Moorhead
Shipley
West Royd
Windhill
Idle Moor
Swain House
Gaisby
Haworth
Cottingley Park
Cottingley
Cullingworth
Wilsden
Norr
Upper Marsh
Marsh
Cullingworth Moor
Sandy Lane
Shay Gate
Noon Nick
Heaton Shay
Heaton Royds
Frizinghall
Carr Syke
Daisy Hill
Heaton
Lister Park
Manningham
Oxenhope
Leeming
Dean Lane Head
Girlington
Allerton
Four Lane Ends
Denholme
Stake Hill
Hill Top
Thornton
School Green
Lower Grange
Crossley Hall
Lidget Green
Denholme Clough
Chat Hill
Oxenhope Moor
Thornton Moor
Thornton Moor Resr.
Scholemoor
Clayton
Great Horton
Little Horton
West Bowling
Warley Moor Resr.
Warley Moor
Ovenden Moor
Ogden
West Scholes
Mountain
Dean Head Reservoirs
Rocking Stone
Cold Edge Dams
Brookhouse
Bradshaw
Queensbury
Old Dolphin
Littlemoor Park
Wibsey
Buttershaw
Odsal
Upper Brockholes
Ambler Thorn
Holdsworth
Shibden Head
Pepper Hill
Shelf
Harold Park
Moor End
Illingworth
Catherine Slack
Low Moor
Wainstalls
Mixenden
Holmfield
Jagger Park Wood
Moor Side
Oakenshaw
Mount Tabor
Booth
Stone Chair
Old Hanna Wood
WEST
Wyke
Pule Hill
Boothtown
Coley
Low Wood
Ovenden
Norwood Green
Wyke Common
Midgley
Mytholmroyd
Northowram
Priestley Green
Luddenden
Lee Mount
Akroydon
Stump Cross
Shibden Park
Mt. Pellon
Hipperholme
Lower Wyke
Luddenden Foot
Hall Bank
Piece Hall
HALIFAX
Lightcliffe
Bailiff Bridge
Birkhouse
Hartshead Moor Top
Warley Town
Bank Top
Hove Edge
Blackwood Common
Southowram
Thornhills
Long Edge Moor
Crow Hill
Sowerby
Sowerby Bridge
Siddal
Brighouse
Brookfoot
Clifton
Cromwell Bottom
Norland
Norland Moor
Triangle
Elland Park Wood
Rastrick
Woodhouse
Lindwell
Elland
Lower Edge
Toothill
Greetland
Mill Bank
Barkisland
Holywell Green
Blackley
Bradley
Soyland Town
Ripponden
Broad Carr
Brackenhall
Deighton
Stainland
Netheroyd Hill
Sheepridge
Prince Royd
Birchencliffe
Fartown
Rishworth
Sowood
Birkby
Edgerton
Mount
Salendine Nook
Lindley
Bradley Mills
Snow Lee
Oakes
HUDDERSFIELD
Dalton
Booth Wood
Longwood
Quarmby
Paddock
Moselden Height
Leymoor
Milnsbridge
Moldgreen
Town End
Golcar
Pole Moor
Worts Hill

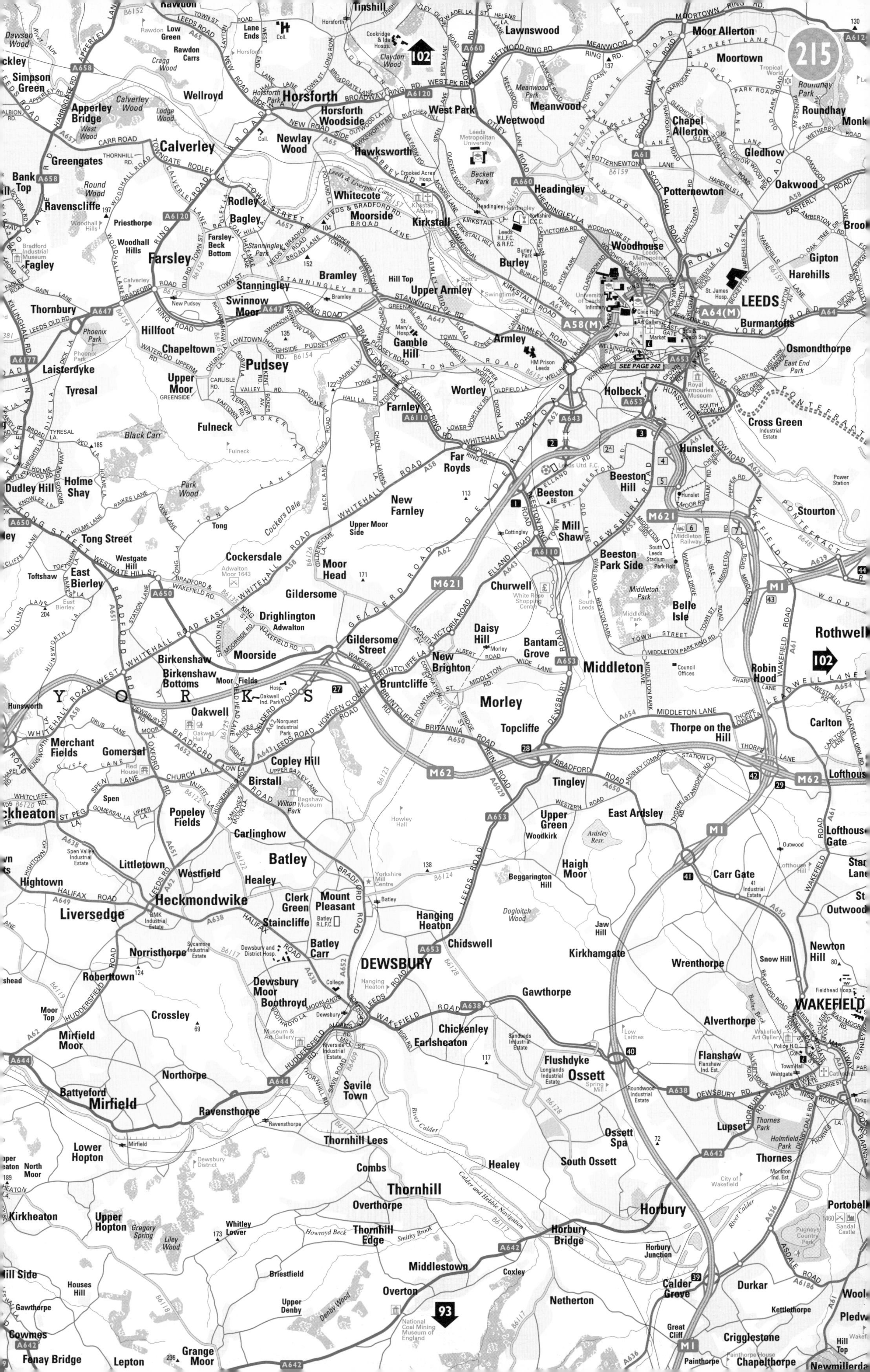
215
Rawdon
Tinshill
Lawnswood
Moor Allerton
Moortown
Dawson Wood
Low Green
Lane Ends
Cookridge & Ida Hosps.
Claydon Wood
102
Rawdon Carrs
Cragg Wood
Horsforth
Simpson Green
Wellroyd
Horsforth Woodside
West Park
Meanwood Park
Meanwood
Weetwood
Chapel Allerton
Roundhay Park
Roundhay
Apperley Bridge
Calverley Wood
Lodge Wood
West Wood
Newlay Wood
Hawksworth
Leeds Metropolitan University
Beckett Park
Gledhow
Oakwood
Greengates
Calverley
Potternewton
Headingley
Bank Top
Round Wood
Rodley
Whitecote
Kirkstall Abbey
Ravenscliffe
Priesthorpe
Bagley
Moorside
Kirkstall
Yorkshire C.C.C.
Leeds R.L.F.C. & R.F.C.
Woodhouse
Gipton
Harehills
Woodhall Hills
Farsley-Beck Bottom
Stanningley Park
Burley
Bradford Industrial Museum
Fagley
Farsley
Stanningley
Bramley
Hill Top
Upper Armley
St. James Hosp.
LEEDS
Thornbury
Swinnow Moor
Civic Hall
Art Gallery
Burmantofts
Hillfoot
Phoenix Park
Chapeltown
St. Mary's Hosp.
Gamble Hill
Armley
HM Prison Leeds
Osmondthorpe
East End Park
Laisterdyke
Pudsey
Upper Moor
SEE PAGE 242
Holbeck
Royal Armouries Museum
Tyresal
Wortley
Farnley
Cross Green Industrial Estate
Fulneck
Black Carr
Hunslet
Beeston Hill
Far Royds
Leeds Utd. F.C.
Holme Shay
Dudley Hill
Park Wood
New Farnley
Beeston
Power Station
Mill Shaw
Stourton
Tong
Cockers Dale
Upper Moor Side
Middleton Railway
Tong Street
Cockersdale
Moor Head
Beeston Park Side
South Leeds Stadium
Park Holt
Westgate Hill
Adwalton Moor 1643
East Bierley
Toftshaw
Gildersome
Churwell
White Rose Shopping Centre
Middleton Park
Belle Isle
Drighlington
Adwalton
Daisy Hill
Bantam Grove
Rothwell
Gildersome Street
Birkenshaw
Birkenshaw Bottoms
Moorside
New Brighton
Middleton
Council Offices
Robin Hood
Bruntcliffe
Morley
Hunsworth
YORKS
Oakwell
Oakwell Ind. Park
Norquest Industrial Park
Topcliffe
Thorpe on the Hill
Carlton
Merchant Fields
Gomersal
Red House
Copley Hill
Birstall
Lofthouse
Tingley
Spen
Bagshaw Museum
Wilton Park
East Ardsley
Cleckheaton
Popeley Fields
Upper Green
Woodkirk
Ardsley Resr.
Lofthouse Gate
Carlinghow
Howley Hall
Batley
Spen Valley Industrial Estate
Littletown
Westfield
Haigh Moor
Carr Gate
41 Industrial Estate
Stanley
Hightown
Healey
Yorkshire Mill Centre
Beggarington Hill
Outwood
Heckmondwike
Clerk Green
Mount Pleasant
Liversedge
BMK Industrial Estate
Staincliffe
Batley R.L.F.C.
Dogloitch Wood
Hanging Heaton
Jaw Hill
Norristhorpe
Sycamore Industrial Estate
Dewsbury and District Hosp.
Batley Carr
Chidswell
Kirkhamgate
Wrenthorpe
Newton Hill
Snow Hill
DEWSBURY
Roberttown
Dewsbury Moor
Boothroyd
Gawthorpe
Fieldhead Hosp.
WAKEFIELD
Moor Top
Crossley
Alverthorpe
Mirfield Moor
Museum & Art Gallery
Chickenley
Earlsheaton
Wakefield Art Gallery
Riverside Industrial Estate
Sandbeds Industrial Estate
Low Laithes
Flanshaw
Flanshaw Ind. Est.
Flushdyke
Longlands Industrial Estate
Ossett
Northorpe
Savile Town
Roundwood Industrial Estate
Battyeford
Mirfield
Ravensthorpe
Lupset
Thornes Park
Holmfield Park
Ossett Spa
Lower Hopton
Thornhill Lees
Thornes
North Moor
Dewsbury District
Healey
South Ossett
Combs
City of Wakefield
Thornhill
Overthorpe
Horbury
Kirkheaton
Upper Hopton
Gregory Spring
Whitley Lower
Thornhill Edge
Horbury Bridge
Portobello
Pugneys Country Park
Sandal Castle
Liley Wood
Horbury Junction
Middlestown
Briestfield
Coxley
Houses Hill
Overton
Calder Grove
Durkar
Gawthorpe
Upper Denby
Denby Wood
Netherton
93
National Coal Mining Museum of England
Kettlethorpe
Great Cliff
Crigglestone
Fenay Bridge
Lepton
Grange Moor
Painthorpe
Chapelthorpe
Newmillerdam
Hill Top
River Calder
Calder and Hebble Navigation
Smithy Brook
Howroyd Beck
Leeds & Liverpool Canal
M62
M621
M1
A58(M)
A64(M)
A61
A62
A643
A653
A650
A651
A652
A638
A644
A642
A6110
A6120
A660
A65
A647
A657
A658
A654
A639
A636
A6186

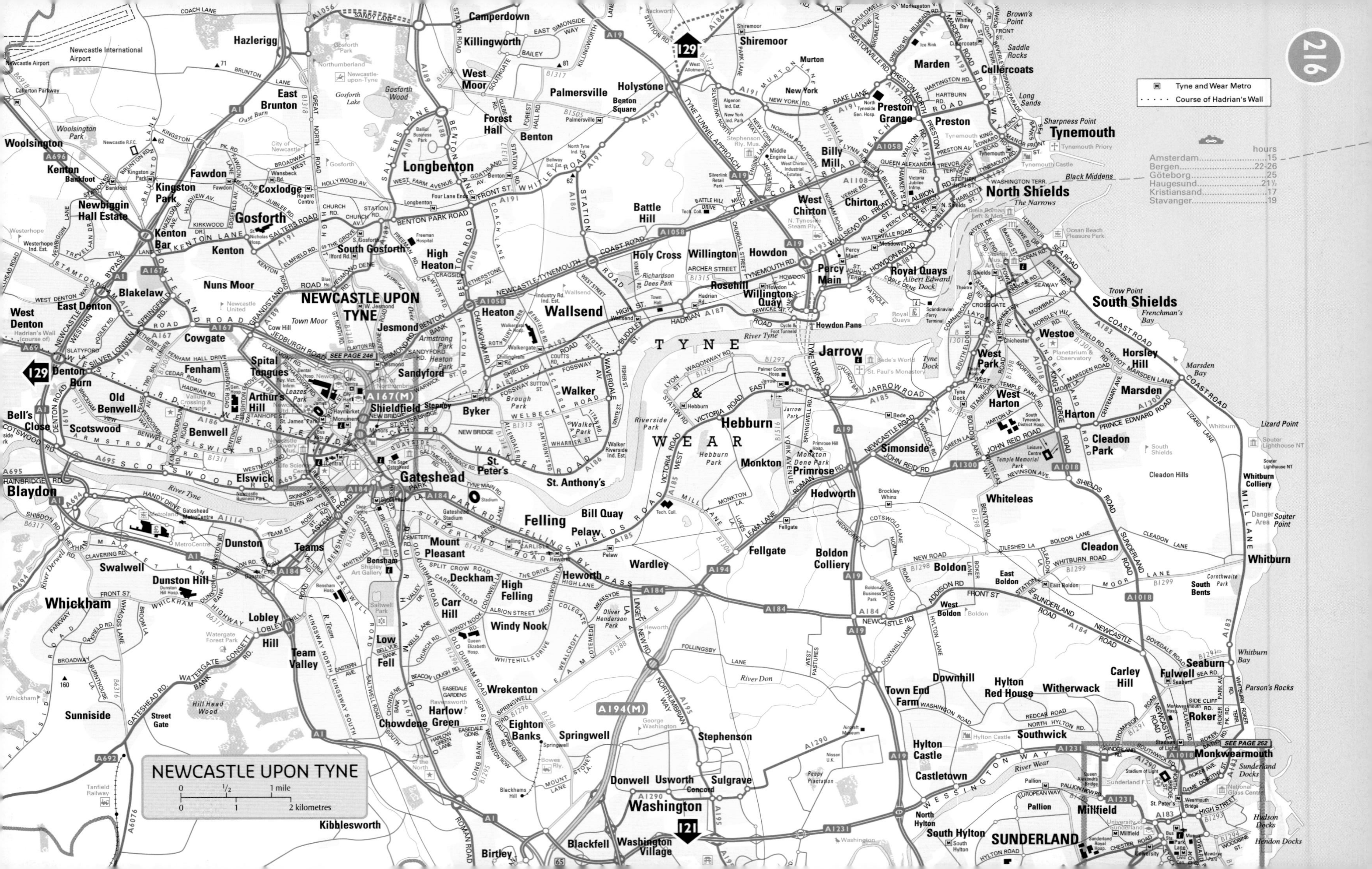
Tyne and Wear Metro
Course of Hadrian's Wall
hours
Amsterdam 15
Bergen 22-26
Göteborg 25
Haugesund 21½
Kristiansand 17
Stavanger 19
NEWCASTLE UPON TYNE
0 1/2 1 mile
0 1 2 kilometres
SEE PAGE 246
SEE PAGE 252
Newcastle International Airport
Hazlerigg
Camperdown
Killingworth
West Moor
Palmersville
Holystone
Benton Square
Shiremoor
Murton
New York
Marden
Cullercoats
Preston Grange
Preston
Tynemouth
North Shields
Billy Mill
West Chirton
Chirton
Percy Main
Royal Quays
Howdon
Willington
Holy Cross
Battle Hill
Rosehill
Willington Quay
Howdon Pans
Forest Hall
Benton
Longbenton
East Brunton
Woolsington
Kenton
Fawdon
Kingston Park
Coxlodge
Gosforth
South Gosforth
Newbiggin Hall Estate
Kenton Bar
High Heaton
Heaton
Wallsend
Nuns Moor
NEWCASTLE UPON TYNE
Jesmond
Sandyford
Blakelaw
East Denton
West Denton
Cowgate
Spital Tongues
Fenham
Arthur's Hill
Shieldfield
Byker
Walker
Denton Burn
Old Benwell
Benwell
Bell's Close
Scotswood
Elswick
Gateshead
St. Peter's
St. Anthony's
Blaydon
Felling
Bill Quay
Pelaw
Dunston
Teams
Mount Pleasant
Deckham
High Felling
Heworth
Wardley
Swalwell
Dunston Hill
Whickham
Lobley Hill
Team Valley
Low Fell
Carr Hill
Windy Nook
Wrekenton
Harlow Green
Chowdene
Eighton Banks
Springwell
Sunniside
Street Gate
Kibblesworth
Birtley
Blackfell
Washington Village
Washington
Donwell
Usworth
Concord
Sulgrave
Stephenson
South Shields
Westoe
Horsley Hill
Marsden
West Park
West Harton
Harton
Cleadon Park
Jarrow
Hebburn
Monkton
Primrose
Simonside
Hedworth
Fellgate
Boldon Colliery
Whiteleas
Cleadon
Boldon
East Boldon
West Boldon
Whitburn
Whitburn Colliery
South Bents
Seaburn
Fulwell
Roker
Monkwearmouth
Carley Hill
Witherwack
Hylton Red House
Downhill
Town End Farm
Southwick
Hylton Castle
Castletown
North Hylton
South Hylton
Pallion
Millfield
SUNDERLAND
TYNE & WEAR
River Tyne
River Wear
River Don
A1
A19
A184
A194(M)
A167(M)
A1058
A1018
A1231
A1290
A195
121
129

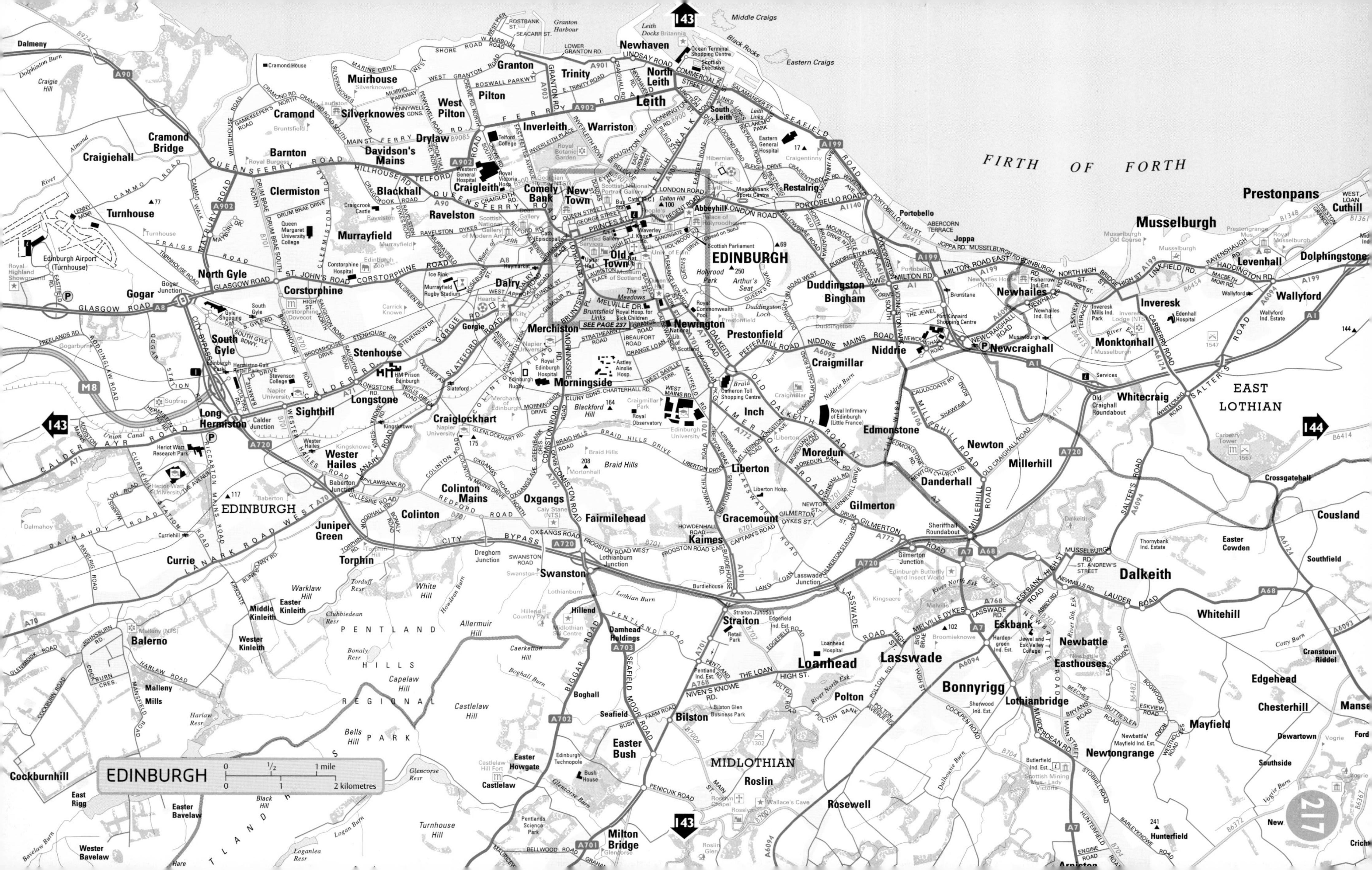

EDINBURGH
0 1/2 1 mile
0 1 2 kilometres
217
143
144
FIRTH OF FORTH
EAST LOTHIAN
MIDLOTHIAN
PENTLAND HILLS REGIONAL PARK
SEE PAGE 237
EDINBURGH
Leith
Newhaven
Granton
Trinity
North Leith
Muirhouse
Pilton
West Pilton
Silverknowes
Cramond
Cramond Bridge
Craigiehall
Barnton
Davidson's Mains
Drylaw
Inverleith
Warriston
Clermiston
Blackhall
Craigleith
Comely Bank
New Town
Old Town
Turnhouse
Ravelston
Murrayfield
Edinburgh Airport (Turnhouse)
North Gyle
Corstorphine
Gogar
Dalry
South Gyle
Stenhouse
Gorgie
Merchiston
Newington
Prestonfield
Duddingston
Bingham
Restalrig
Abbeyhill
Portobello
Joppa
Musselburgh
Prestonpans
Cuthill
Levenhall
Dolphingstone
Wallyford
Inveresk
Newhailes
Monktonhall
Newcraighall
Niddrie
Craigmillar
Whitecraig
Sighthill
Longstone
Long Hermiston
Craiglockhart
Morningside
Inch
Edmonstone
Newton
Millerhill
Wester Hailes
Colinton Mains
Oxgangs
Fairmilehead
Liberton
Moredun
Danderhall
Gilmerton
Gracemount
Kaimes
Colinton
Juniper Green
Currie
Torphin
Swanston
Balerno
Malleny Mills
Hillend
Damhead Holdings
Straiton
Loanhead
Lasswade
Bonnyrigg
Lothianbridge
Eskbank
Dalkeith
Newbattle
Easthouses
Newtongrange
Mayfield
Edgehead
Chesterhill
Whitehill
Cousland
Crossgatehall
Easter Cowden
Southfield
Cranstoun Riddel
Polton
Bilston
Roslin
Rosewell
Seafield
Easter Bush
Boghall
Easter Howgate
Castlelaw
Milton Bridge
Middle Kinleith
Easter Kinleith
Wester Kinleith
Cockburnhill
East Rigg
Easter Bavelaw
Wester Bavelaw
Dalmeny
Dewartown
Southside
New
Braid Hills
Blackford Hill
Arthur's Seat
Holyrood Park
Middle Craigs
Eastern Craigs
Black Rocks

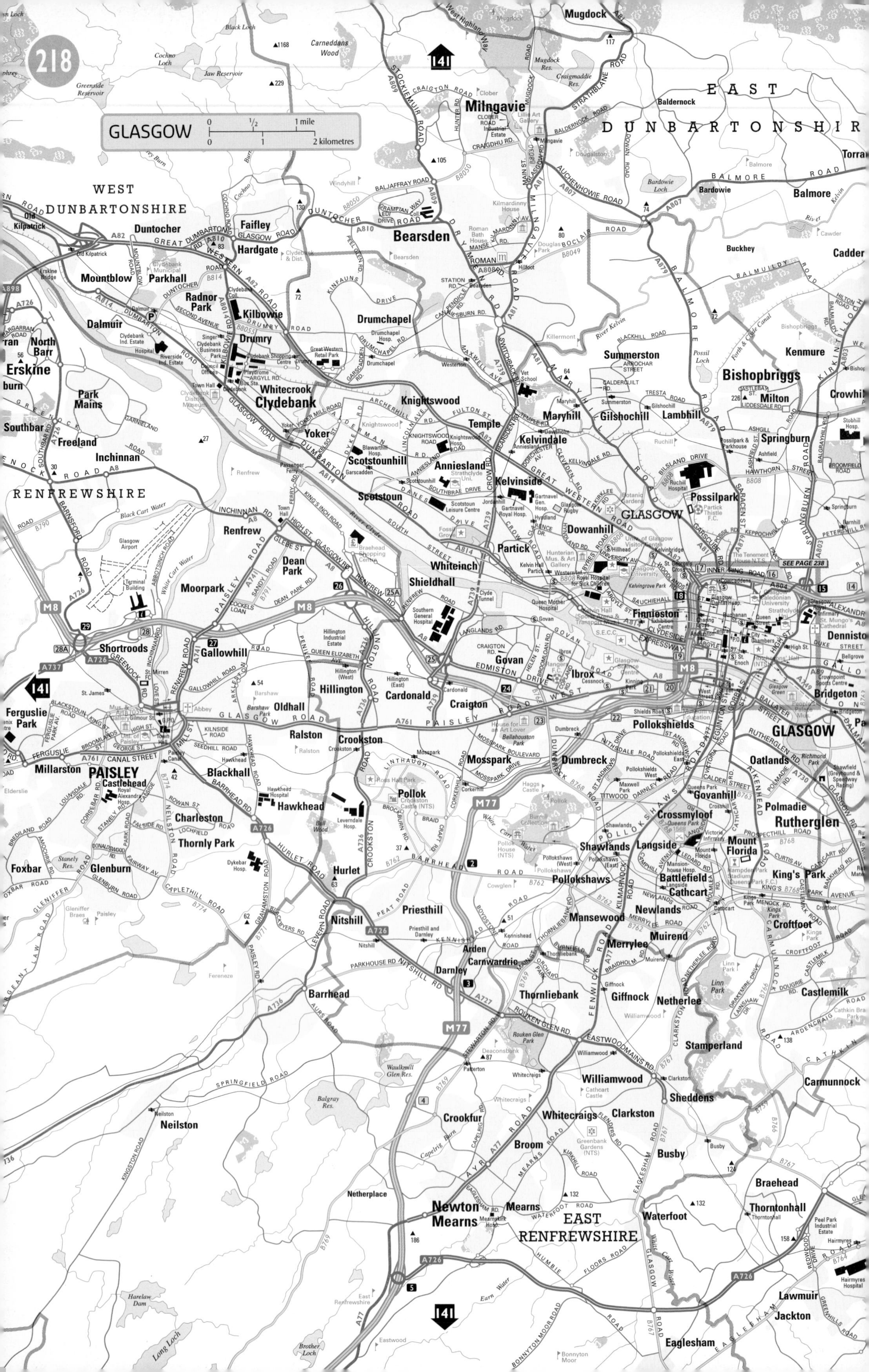
GLASGOW
0 1/2 1 mile
0 1 2 kilometres
141
141
141
SEE PAGE 238
Mugdock
Mugdock Res.
Craigmaddie Res.
West Highland Way
Milngavie
Baldernock
EAST
DUNBARTONSHIRE
Torrance
Bardowie Loch
Bardowie
Balmore
BALMORE ROAD
River Kelvin
Buckhey
Cadder
Carnedans Wood
Black Loch
Cochno Loch
Jaw Reservoir
Greenside Reservoir
WEST
DUNBARTONSHIRE
Old Kilpatrick
Duntocher
Faifley
Hardgate
Bearsden
Mountblow
Parkhall
Radnor Park
Kilbowie
Dalmuir
Drumry
Drumchapel
North Barr
Erskine
Park Mains
Clydebank
Whitecrook
Southbar
Freeland
Inchinnan
Yoker
Knightswood
Temple
Anniesland
Scotstounhill
Scotstoun
Maryhill
Kelvindale
Kelvinside
Gilshochill
Lambhill
Summerston
Possilpark
Bishopbriggs
Kenmure
Milton
Springburn
Crowhill
RENFREWSHIRE
Renfrew
Glasgow Airport
Moorpark
Dean Park
Shieldhall
Whiteinch
Partick
Dowanhill
GLASGOW
Finnieston
Dennistoun
Bridgeton
Shortroods
Gallowhill
Ferguslie Park
Millarston
PAISLEY
Castlehead
Oldhall
Ralston
Hillington
Cardonald
Crookston
Craigton
Govan
Ibrox
Pollokshields
Mosspark
Dumbreck
Pollok
Blackhall
Hawkhead
Charleston
Thornly Park
Foxbar
Glenburn
Hurlet
Nitshill
Priesthill
Govanhill
Crossmyloof
Shawlands
Langside
Pollokshaws
Battlefield
Cathcart
Mount Florida
Oatlands
Polmadie
Rutherglen
King's Park
Croftfoot
Newlands
Mansewood
Merrylee
Muirend
Arden
Carnwadric
Darnley
Thornliebank
Giffnock
Netherlee
Castlemilk
Linn Park
Barrhead
Rouken Glen Park
Stamperland
Williamwood
Carmunnock
Sheddens
Clarkston
Whitecraigs
Crookfur
Broom
Busby
Neilston
Netherplace
Newton Mearns
Mearns
EAST RENFREWSHIRE
Waterfoot
Braehead
Thorntonhall
Lawmuir
Jackton
Eaglesham
Harelaw Dam
Long Loch
Brother Loch
Waulkmill Glen Res.
Balgray Res.
M8
M77
A726
A736
A737
A8
A82
A81
A739
A814
A803
A77
A727
A761
GREAT WESTERN ROAD
DUMBARTON ROAD
PAISLEY ROAD WEST
BARRHEAD ROAD
SPRINGFIELD ROAD
KINGSTON ROAD
AYR ROAD
EASTWOODMAINS RD.
ROUKEN GLEN RD.
CLYDESIDE EXPRESSWAY
River Clyde
White Cart Water

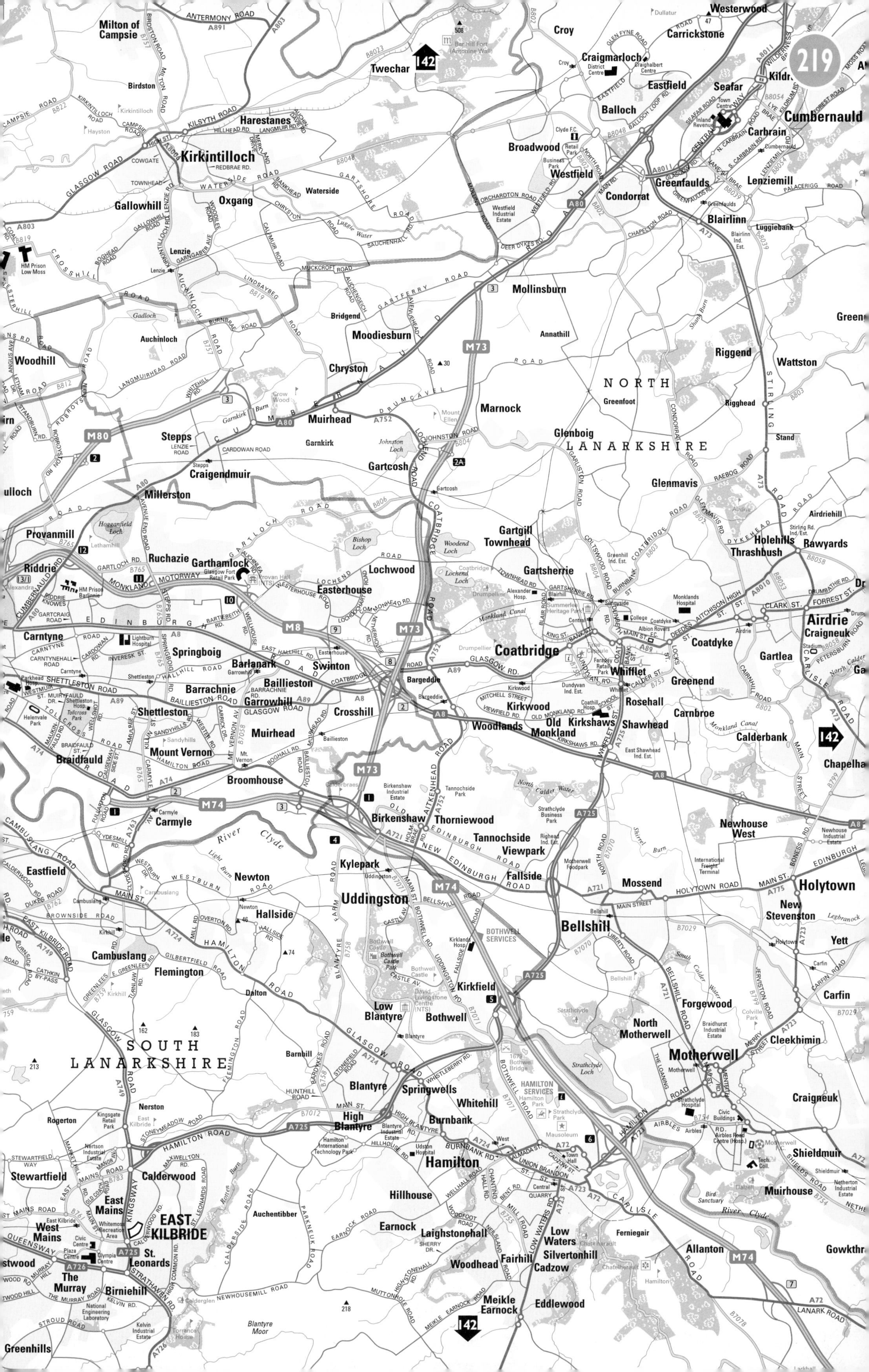
Milton of Campsie
Birdston
Twechar
Croy
Westerwood
Carrickstone
Craigmarloch
Eastfield
Seafar
Kildrum
Cumbernauld
Balloch
Harestanes
Kirkintilloch
Broadwood
Westfield
Carbrain
Greenfaulds
Lenziemill
Condorrat
Waterside
Oxgang
Gallowhill
Blairlinn
Luggiebank
Lenzie
HM Prison Low Moss
Mollinsburn
Gadloch
Auchinloch
Bridgend
Moodiesburn
Annathill
Riggend
Wattston
Woodhill
Chryston
NORTH
LANARKSHIRE
Greenfoot
Rigghead
Marnock
Muirhead
Garnkirk
Stepps
Craigendmuir
Glenboig
Stand
Gartcosh
Glenmavis
Millerston
Airdriehill
Provanmill
Gartgill
Townhead
Holehills
Rawyards
Thrashbush
Ruchazie
Garthamlock
Lochwood
Gartsherrie
Riddrie
Easterhouse
Airdrie
Craigneuk
Carntyne
Springboig
Coatbridge
Coatdyke
Gartlea
Barlanark
Swinton
Whifflet
Greenend
Barrachnie
Baillieston
Garrowhill
Bargeddie
Rosehall
Shettleston
Crosshill
Kirkwood
Old Monkland
Kirkshaws
Shawhead
Carnbroe
Muirhead
Woodlands
Calderbank
Mount Vernon
Braidfauld
Broomhouse
Chapelhall
Carmyle
Birkenshaw
Thorniewood
Tannochside
Viewpark
Newhouse
West
River Clyde
Eastfield
Newton
Kylepark
Fallside
Mossend
Holytown
Uddingston
New Stevenston
Hallside
Bellshill
Yett
Cambuslang
Flemington
Kirkfield
Carfin
Dalton
Forgewood
Low Blantyre
Bothwell
North Motherwell
SOUTH
LANARKSHIRE
Cleekhimin
Motherwell
Barnhill
Blantyre
Springwells
Whitehill
Craigneuk
Nerston
Rogerton
High Blantyre
Burnbank
Shieldmuir
Stewartfield
Calderwood
Hamilton
Muirhouse
East Mains
Hillhouse
Auchentibber
Earnock
Ferniegair
West Mains
EAST KILBRIDE
Laighstonehall
Low Waters
Allanton
St. Leonards
Silvertonhill
Gowkthrapple
Woodhead
Fairhill
Cadzow
The Murray
Birniehill
Meikle Earnock
Eddlewood
Blantyre Moor
Greenhills
M73
M80
M8
M74
A80
A8
A725
A721
A724
A749
A726
A73
A72
142

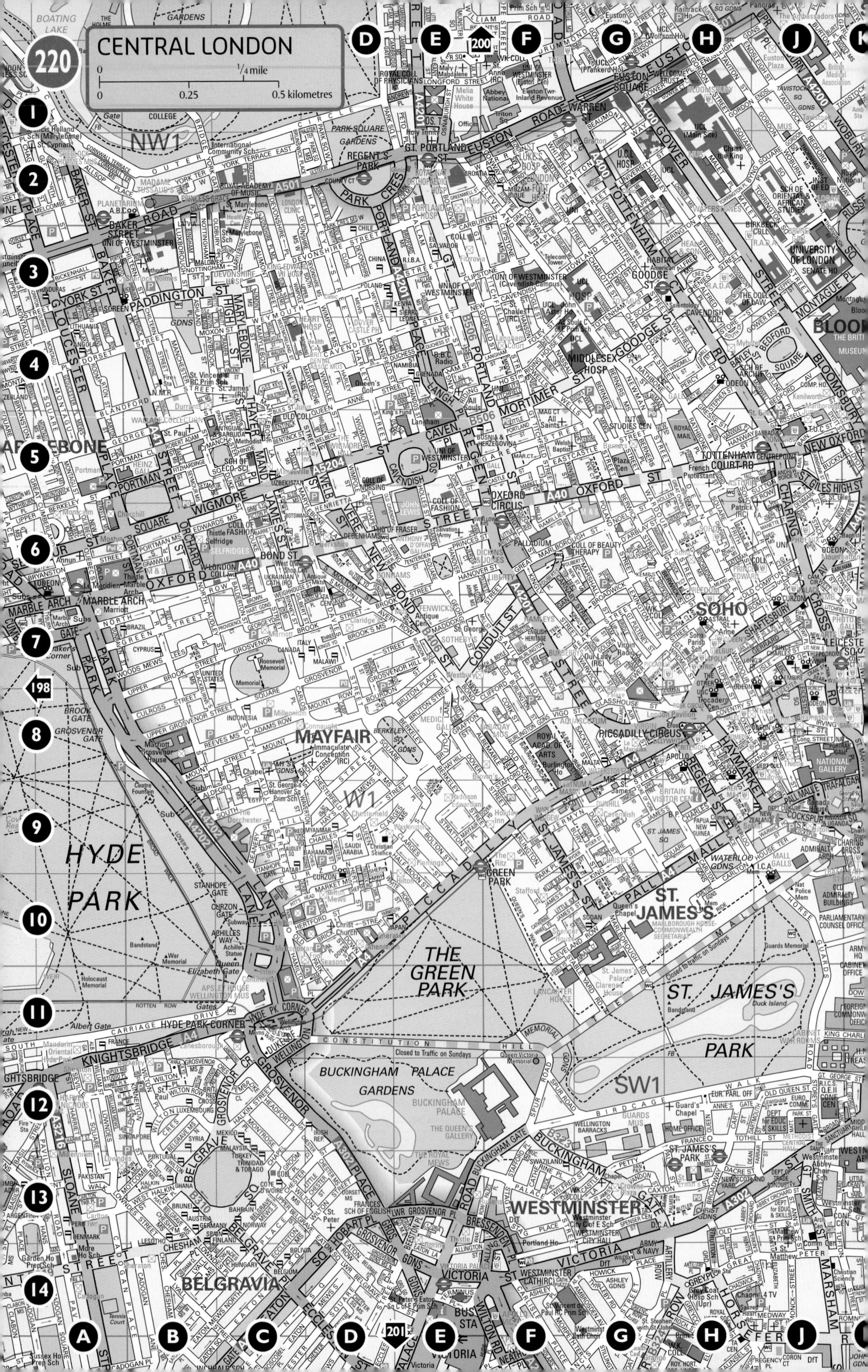
220
CENTRAL LONDON
1/4 mile
0 0.25 0.5 kilometres
200
198
201
D E F G H J K
A B C D E F G H J
1 2 3 4 5 6 7 8 9 10 11 12 13 14
NW1
REGENT'S PARK
BAKER STREET
MARYLEBONE
EUSTON SQUARE
WARREN ST
GT. PORTLAND ST
GOODGE ST
TOTTENHAM COURT RD
OXFORD CIRCUS
BOND ST
MARBLE ARCH
SOHO
MAYFAIR
W1
PICCADILLY CIRCUS
GREEN PARK
HYDE PARK
THE GREEN PARK
ST. JAMES'S PARK
ST. JAMES'S
HYDE PARK CORNER
KNIGHTSBRIDGE
BELGRAVIA
BUCKINGHAM PALACE GARDENS
BUCKINGHAM PALACE
WESTMINSTER
VICTORIA
SW1
UNIVERSITY OF LONDON SENATE HO
OXFORD ST
PICCADILLY
REGENT ST
BAKER ST
PARK LANE
EUSTON ROAD
MARYLEBONE ROAD
WIGMORE ST
VICTORIA ST
GROSVENOR PL
BUCKINGHAM GATE
BIRDCAGE WALK
CONSTITUTION HILL
PALL MALL
HAYMARKET
CHARING CROSS RD
SHAFTESBURY AV
NATIONAL GALLERY

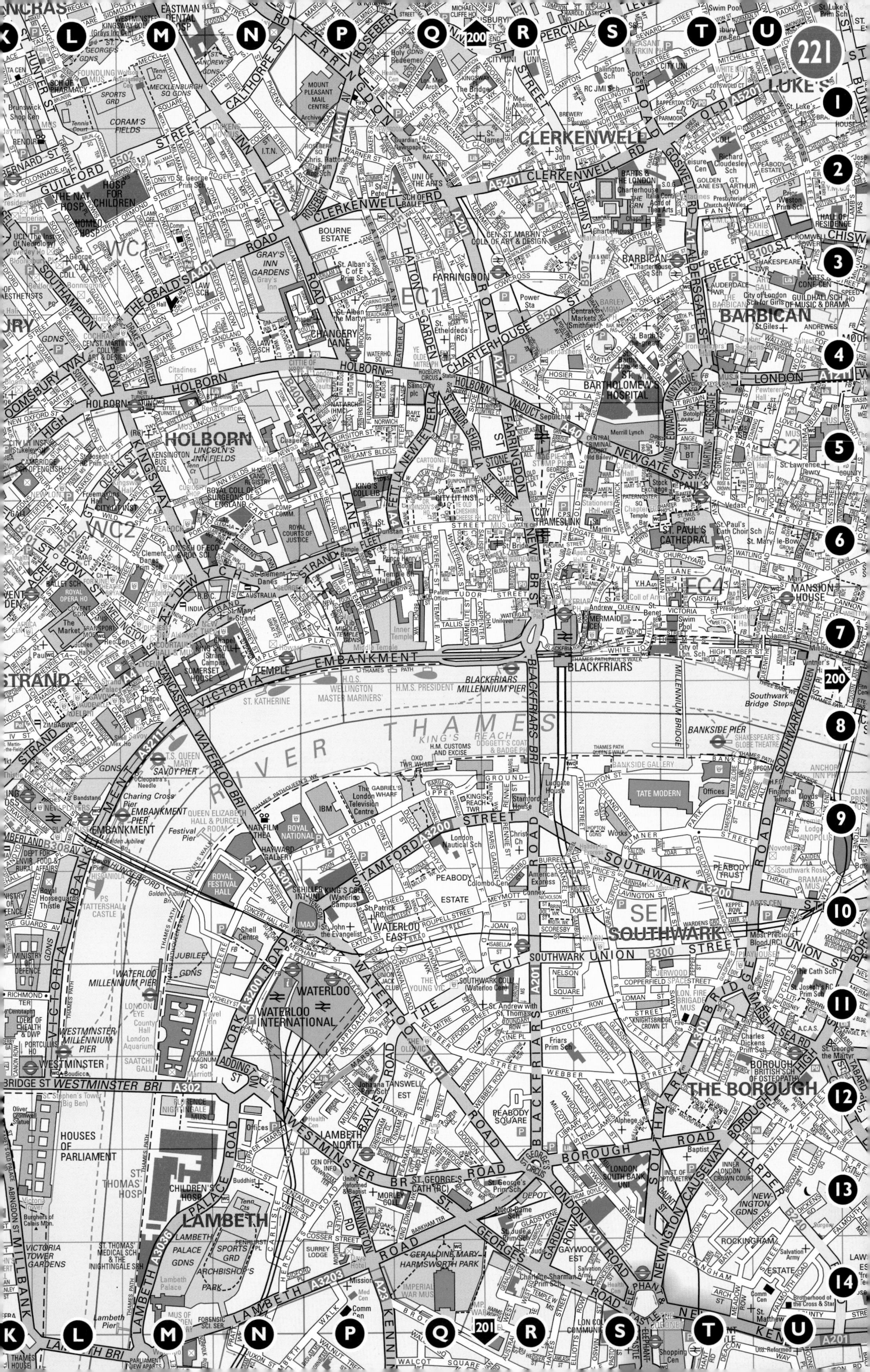
221
CLERKENWELL
BARBICAN
HOLBORN
EC1
EC2
EC4
WC1
WC2
SE1
SOUTHWARK
THE BOROUGH
LAMBETH
STRAND
RIVER THAMES
KING'S REACH
BLACKFRIARS
WATERLOO
WATERLOO INTERNATIONAL
FARRINGDON
CHANCERY LANE
MANSION HOUSE
WESTMINSTER
EMBANKMENT
TEMPLE
HOUSES OF PARLIAMENT
ST. BARTHOLOMEW'S HOSPITAL
ST. PAUL'S CATHEDRAL
TATE MODERN
ROYAL FESTIVAL HALL
ROYAL NATIONAL THEATRE
IMAX
CORAM'S FIELDS
GRAY'S INN GARDENS
LINCOLN'S INN FIELDS
ROYAL COURTS OF JUSTICE
SOMERSET HOUSE
ST. THOMAS' HOSP
GERALDINE MARY HARMSWORTH PARK
IMPERIAL WAR MUS
VICTORIA TOWER GARDENS
ARCHBISHOP'S PARK
LAMBETH PALACE GDNS
PEABODY ESTATE
JUBILEE GDNS
MILLENNIUM BRIDGE
BANKSIDE PIER
WATERLOO MILLENNIUM PIER
WESTMINSTER MILLENNIUM PIER
BLACKFRIARS MILLENNIUM PIER
HOLBORN
FLEET ST
NEWGATE ST
CHEAPSIDE
VICTORIA EMBANKMENT
WATERLOO BRI
BLACKFRIARS BRI
SOUTHWARK BRI
SOUTHWARK ST
STAMFORD ST
THE CUT
WESTMINSTER BRI
BOROUGH RD
ST. GEORGE'S RD
LAMBETH RD
KENNINGTON RD
NEWINGTON CAUSEWAY
LONDON RD
CLERKENWELL RD
CHARTERHOUSE ST
FARRINGDON RD
GRAY'S INN RD
THEOBALD'S RD
KINGSWAY
ALDWYCH
ALDERSGATE ST
GOSWELL RD

General abbreviations

All	Alley	Circ	Circus	Flds	Fields	Ms	Mews	St	Street
App	Approach	Clo	Close	Gdn/Gdns	Garden/Gardens	N	North	St.	Saint
Arc	Arcade	Cor	Corner	Grd	Ground	Par	Parade	Ter	Terrace
Av/Ave	Avenue	Cres	Crescent	Grn	Green	Pas	Passage	Twr	Tower
Bdy	Broadway	Ct	Court	Gro	Grove	Pk	Park	W	West
Bldgs	Buildings	Ctyd	Courtyard	Ho	House	Pl	Place	Wf	Wharf
Br/Bri	Bridge	Dr	Drive	La	Lane	Rd	Road	Wk	Walk
Cen	Central, Centre	E	East	Lo	Lodge	Ri	Rise	Yd	Yard
Ch	Church	Embk	Embankment	Mans	Mansions	S	South		
Chyd	Churchyard	Est	Estate	Mkt/Mkts	Market/Markets	Sq	Square		

Post town abbreviations

Bark.	Barking	Edg.	Edgware	Ilf.	Ilford	Nthlt.	Northolt	Th.Hth.	Thornton Heath
Beck.	Beckenham	Enf.	Enfield	Islw.	Isleworth	Pnr.	Pinner	Twick.	Twickenham
Brent.	Brentford	Felt.	Feltham	Kings.T.	Kingston upon Thames	Rich.	Richmond	Uxb.	Uxbridge
Brom.	Bromley	Grnf.	Greenford	Mitch.	Mitcham	Ruis.	Ruislip	Walt.	Walton-on-Thames
Chig.	Chigwell	Har.	Harrow	Mord.	Morden	Stan.	Stanmore	W.Mol.	West Molesey
Chis.	Chislehurst	Hmptn.	Hampton	N.Mal.	New Malden	Sthl.	Southall	Wdf.Grn.	Woodford Green
E.Mol.	East Molesey	Houns.	Hounslow			Tedd.	Teddington	Wem.	Wembley

A

Abbeville Rd SW4 **201** A5
Abbey Orchard St SW1 **220** J13
Abbey Rd NW6; NW8 **198** D3
Abbey Rd, Bark. IG11 **200** D2
Abbey St SE1 **201** B4
Abbott Rd E14 **200** C3
Abercorn Pl NW8 **198** D3
Abingdon St SW1 **221** K13
Acacia Rd, Hmptn. TW12 **199** A6
Academy Rd SE18 **201** D4
Achilles Way W1 **220** C10
Acre La SW2 **201** A5
Acton La NW10 **198** C3
Acton La W3; W4 **199** C4
Adam & Eve Ct W1 **220** G5
Adams Row W1 **220** C8
Adam St WC2 **221** L8
Addington St SE1 **221** N12
Addle Hill EC4 **221** S7
Addle St EC2 **221** U4
Adelaide Av SE4 **201** C5
Adelaide Rd NW3 **198** D2
Adelaide St WC2 **221** K8
Adeline Pl WC1 **220** J4
Adelphi Ter WC2 **221** L8
Aerodrome Rd NW4; NW9 **198** C1
Agar St WC2 **221** K8
Agdon St EC1 **221** R1
Agincourt Rd NW3 **198** D2
Air St W1 **220** G8
Akerman Rd SW9 **201** A4
Alaska St SE1 **221** P10
Albany W1 **220** F8
Albany Ctyd W1 **220** G8
Albany Rd SE5 **201** B4
Albany St NW1 **200** A3
Albemarle Rd, Beck. BR3 **201** C6
Albemarle St W1 **220** E8
Albemarle Way EC1 **221** R2
Albert Br Rd SW11 **199** D4
Albert Embk SE1 **201** A4
Albert Gate SW1 **220** A11
Albert Rd E16 **200** D3
Albert Rd N22 **200** A1
Albion Pl EC1 **221** R3
Albion Rd N16 **200** B2
Albion Way EC1 **221** T4
Aldburgh Ms W1 **220** C5
Aldermanbury EC2 **221** U5
Aldermanbury Sq EC2 **221** U4
Alderney Av, Houns. TW5 **199** A4
Aldersbrook Rd E11; E12 **200** D2
Aldersgate St EC1 **221** T5
Alford St W1 **220** B9
Aldwych WC2 **221** M7
Alexandra Av W4 **199** C4
Alexandra Av, Har. HA2 **198** A2
Alexandra Pk Rd N10; N22 **200** A1
Alexandra Rd SW19 **199** D6
Alfred Ms W1 **220** H3
Alfred Pl WC1 **220** H3
Allenby Rd, Sthl. UB1 **198** A3
Allington St SW1 **220** F14
Allsop Pl NW1 **220** A2
All Souls Av NW10 **198** C3
All Souls Pl W1 **220** E4
Alperton La, Grnf. UB6; Wem. HA0 **198** B3
Ambassador's Ct SW1 **220** G10
Ambrosden Av SW1 **220** G14
Amen Cor EC4 **221** S6
Amen Ct EC4 **221** S5
America St SE1 **221** T10
Amhurst Pk N16 **200** B2
Amhurst Rd N16 **200** B2
Anchor Yd EC1 **221** U1
Andrew Borde St WC2 **220** J5
Andrewes Ho EC2 **221** U4
Andrews Crosse WC2 **221** P6
Anerley Hill SE19 **201** B6
Anerley Rd SE19; SE20 **201** B6
Angel Ct SW1 **220** G10
Angel St EC1 **221** T5
Ann's Cl SW1 **220** A12
Anson Rd NW2 **198** C2
Apothecary St EC4 **221** R6
Apple Tree Yd SW1 **220** G9
Apsley Way W1 **220** C11
Aquinas St SE1 **221** Q10
Archer St W1 **220** H7
Arches, The WC2 **221** L9
Archibald Ms W1 **220** C8
Arch St SE1 **221** T14
Archway Rd N6; N19 **198** D1
Argyle Rd W13; Grnf. UB6 **198** B3
Argyll St W1 **220** F6
Arlington St SW1 **220** F9
Armoury Way SW18 **199** D5
Arne St WC2 **221** L6
Arneway St SW1 **220** J14
Arthur Rd SW19 **199** D6
Artillery Pl SW1 **220** H14
Artillery Row SW1 **220** H14
Arundel Gt Ct WC2 **221** N7
Arundel St WC2 **221** N7
Ashentree Ct EC4 **221** Q6
Ashgrove Rd, Brom. BR1 **201** C6
Ashland Pl W1 **220** B3
Ashley Gdns SW1 **220** G14
Ashley Pl SW1 **220** F14
Askew Rd W12 **198** C3
Aspen Way E14 **200** C3
Audley Sq W1 **220** C9
Ave Maria La EC4 **221** S6
Avenue, The SW4 **201** A5
Avenue, The W4 **199** C4
Avenue, The, Hmptn. TW12 **199** A6
Avenue, The (Hatch End), Pnr. HA5 **198** A1
Avenue, The, Ilf. IG1, IG4 **200** D1
Avenue, The, Twick. TW1 **199** B5
Avenue, The, Wem. HA9 **198** B2
Avenue Rd NW8 **198** D2
Avery Row W1 **220** D7
Avondale Rd, Brom. BR1 **201** C6
Avonmouth St SE1 **221** T13
Avon Pl SE1 **221** U12
Aybrook St W1 **220** B4
Aylesbury St EC1 **221** R2
Aylmer Rd N2 **198** D1
Ayres St SE1 **221** U11

B

Babmaes St SW1 **220** G8
Back Hill EC1 **221** P2
Bainbridge St WC1 **220** J5
Baird St EC1 **221** U1
Baker's Ms W1 **220** B5
Baker's Row EC1 **221** P2
Baker St NW1 **220** A2
Baker St W1 **220** A3
Balaam St E13 **200** D3
Balderton St W1 **220** C6
Baldwin's Gdns EC1 **221** P3
Balfour Ms W1 **220** C9
Balfour Pl W1 **220** C8
Balham High Rd SW12; SW17 **201** A5
Balham Hill SW12 **201** A5
Ballards La N3; N12 **198** D1
Balls Pond Rd N1 **200** B2
Baltic St E EC1 **221** T2
Baltic St W EC1 **221** T2
Banbury Ct WC2 **221** K7
Bank End SE1 **221** U9
Bankside SE1 **221** T8
Banner St EC1 **221** U2
Barbican, The EC2 **221** T3
Barbon Cl WC1 **221** M3
Barge Ho St SE1 **221** Q9
Baring Rd SE12 **201** D5
Baring St N1 **200** B3
Barkham Ter SE1 **221** Q13
Barking Rd E6; E13; E16 **200** C3
Barlby Rd W10 **198** C3
Barley Mow Pas EC1 **221** S4
Barlow Pl W1 **220** E8
Barnard's Inn EC1 **221** Q5
Barnes High St SW13 **199** C4
Barons Pl SE1 **221** Q12
Barrett St W1 **220** C6
Barry Rd SE22 **201** B5
Barter St WC1 **221** L4
Bartholomew Cl EC1 **221** T4
Bartholomew Pl EC1 **221** T4
Bartholomew Sq EC1 **221** U1
Bartlett Ct EC4 **221** Q5
Bartletts Pas EC4 **221** Q5
Barton St SW1 **220** K13
Bastwick St EC1 **221** T1
Bateman's Bldgs W1 **220** H6
Bateman St W1 **220** H6
Bath Ct EC1 **221** P2
Bath Rd W4 **199** C4
Bath Ter SE1 **221** T14
Battersea Br Rd SW11 **199** D4
Battersea Pk Rd SW8; SW11 **199** D4
Battersea Ri SW11 **199** D5
Bayley St WC1 **220** H4
Baylis Rd SE1 **221** P12
Bayswater Rd W2 **198** D3
Beak St W1 **220** G7
Bear All EC4 **221** R5
Bear Gdns SE1 **221** T9
Bear La SE1 **221** S9
Bear St WC2 **220** J7
Beauchamp St EC1 **221** P4
Beaumont Ms W1 **220** C3
Beaumont Pl W1 **220** G1
Beaumont St W1 **220** C3
Beckenham Hill Rd SE6; Beck. BR3 **201** C6
Beckenham La, Brom. BR2 **201** C6
Beckenham Rd, Beck. BR3 **201** C6
Bedford Av WC1 **220** J4
Bedfordbury WC2 **221** K7
Bedford Ct WC2 **221** K8
Bedford Hill SW12; SW16 **201** A5
Bedford Pl WC1 **221** K3
Bedford Rd SW4 **201** A5
Bedford Row WC1 **221** N3
Bedford Sq WC1 **220** J4
Bedford St WC2 **221** K7
Bedford Way WC1 **220** J2
Beech St EC2 **221** T3
Beehive La, Ilf. IG1, IG4 **200** D1
Beeston Pl SW1 **220** E14
Belgrave Ms N SW1 **220** B12
Belgrave Ms S SW1 **220** C13
Belgrave Ms W SW1 **220** B13
Belgrave Pl SW1 **220** C13
Belgrave Rd SW1 **201** A4
Belgrave Sq SW1 **220** B13
Belgrave Yd SW1 **220** D14
Belleville Rd SW11 **199** D5
Bellevue Rd SW17 **199** D5
Bell Grn SE26 **201** C5
Bell La NW4 **198** C1
Bell Wf La EC4 **221** U7
Bell Yd WC2 **221** P5
Belmont Hill SE13 **201** C5
Belmont Rd N15 **200** B1
Belsize Rd NW6 **198** D3
Belvedere Bldgs SE1 **221** S12
Belvedere Pl SE1 **221** S12
Belvedere Rd SE1 **221** N11
Benjamin St EC1 **221** R3
Ben Jonson Rd E1 **200** C3
Bennet's Hill EC4 **221** S7
Bennett St SW1 **220** F9
Bennetts Yd SW1 **220** J14
Bentinck Ms W1 **220** C5
Bentinck St W1 **220** C5
Beresford St SE18 **201** D4
Berkeley Ms W1 **220** A5
Berkeley Sq W1 **220** E8
Berkeley St W1 **220** E8
Berkshire Gdns N13 **200** A1
Bernard St WC1 **221** K2
Berners Ms W1 **220** G4
Berners Pl W1 **220** G5
Berners St W1 **220** G4
Berry St EC1 **221** S1
Berwick St W1 **220** H6
Bessborough Rd, Har. HA1 **198** A2
Bethnal Grn Rd E1; E2 **200** B3
Bethune Rd N16 **200** B2
Betterton St WC2 **221** K6
Beulah Hill SE19 **201** A6
Beverley Dr, Edg. HA8 **198** B1
Beverley Way (Kingston Bypass) SW20 **199** C6
Bexley Rd SE9 **201** D5
Bickenhall St W1 **220** A3
Bickley Pk Rd, Brom. BR1 **201** D6
Bickley Rd, Brom. BR1 **201** D6
Billet Rd E17 **200** B1
Bilton Rd, Grnf. UB6 **198** B3
Bingham Pl W1 **220** B3
Binney St W1 **220** C7
Birdcage Wk SW1 **220** G12
Bird St W1 **220** C6
Bishops Av, The N2 **198** D2
Bishops Br Rd W2 **198** D3
Bishop's Ct EC4 **221** R5
Bishop's Ct WC2 **221** P5
Bishopsgate EC2 **200** B3
Bishops Way E2 **200** B3
Bittacy Hill NW7 **198** C1
Bittern St SE1 **221** T12
Blackbrook La, Brom. BR1, BR2 **201** D6
Blackburne's Ms W1 **220** B7
Blackfriars Br EC4 **221** R7
Blackfriars Br SE1 **221** R7
Blackfriars Ct EC4 **221** R7
Black Friars La EC4 **221** R7
Blackfriars Pas EC4 **221** R7
Blackfriars Rd SE1 **221** R12
Blackheath Rd SE10 **201** C4
Blackhorse La E17 **200** B1
Blackshaw Rd SW17 **199** D6
Blackstock Rd N4; N5 **200** A2
Blackwall La SE10 **201** C4
Blackwall Tunnel E14 **200** C3
Blake Hall Rd E11 **200** D2
Blandford St W1 **220** A5
Bleeding Heart Yd EC1 **221** Q4
Blenheim St W1 **220** D6
Bloomfield Pl W1 **220** E7
Bloomsbury Ct WC1 **221** L4
Bloomsbury Pl WC1 **221** L3
Bloomsbury Sq WC1 **221** L4
Bloomsbury St WC1 **220** J4
Bloomsbury Way WC1 **221** K5
Blore Ct W1 **220** H6
Blue Ball Yd SW1 **220** F10
Bolingbroke Gro SW11 **199** D5
Bollo La W3; W4 **199** B4
Bolsover St W1 **220** E2
Bolt Ct EC4 **221** Q6
Bolton St W1 **220** E9
Book Ms WC2 **220** J6
Booth Rd NW9 **198** C1
Booth's Pl W1 **220** G4
Borough High St SE1 **221** T12
Borough Rd SE1 **221** R13
Borough Sq SE1 **221** T12
Boston Manor Rd, Brent. TW8 **199** B4
Boston Rd W7 **199** A4
Boswell Ct WC1 **221** L3
Boswell St WC1 **221** L3
Boundary Rd E13 **200** D3
Boundary Rd E17 **200** C2
Boundary Row SE1 **221** R11
Bounds Grn Rd N11; N22 **200** A1
Bourchier St W1 **220** H7
Bourdon Pl W1 **220** E7
Bourdon St W1 **220** E7
Bourlet Cl W1 **220** F4
Bourne Est EC1 **221** P3
Bouverie St EC4 **221** Q6
Bow Chyd EC4 **221** U6
Bowland Yd SW1 **220** A12
Bow La EC4 **221** U6
Bowling Grn La EC1 **221** Q1
Bow Rd E3 **200** C3
Bow St WC2 **221** L6
Boxtree La, Har. HA3 **198** A1
Boxtree Rd, Har. HA3 **198** A1
Boyce St SE1 **221** N10
Boyfield St SE1 **221** S12
Boyle St W1 **220** F7
Brackley St EC1 **221** T3
Brad St SE1 **221** Q10
Brady St E1 **200** B3
Brantwood Rd N17 **200** B1
Bread St EC4 **221** U6
Bream's Bldgs EC4 **221** P5
Brecknock Rd N7; N19 **200** A2
Brentfield NW10 **198** C2
Brentfield Rd NW10 **198** C2
Brent St NW4 **198** C1
Bressenden Pl SW1 **220** E13
Brewer's Grn SW1 **220** H13
Brewers Hall Gdns EC2 **221** U4
Brewer St W1 **220** G7
Brewery Sq EC1 **221** S1
Brewhouse Yd EC1 **221** S1
Brick Ct EC4 **221** P6
Brick La E1; E2 **200** B3
Brick St W1 **220** D10
Bride Ct EC4 **221** R6
Bride La EC4 **221** R6
Bridewell Pl EC4 **221** R6
Bridford Ms W1 **220** E3
Bridge La NW11 **198** D1
Bridge Rd, E.Mol. KT8 **199** A6
Bridge Rd, Houns. TW3; Islw. TW7 **199** A5
Bridge St SW1 **221** K12
Bridgewater Rd, Wem. HA0 **198** B2
Bridgewater Sq EC2 **221** T3
Bridgewater St EC2 **221** T3
Bridle La W1 **220** G7
Brinton Wk SE1 **221** R10
Briset St EC1 **221** R3
Britton St EC1 **221** R2
Brixton Hill SW2 **201** A5
Brixton Rd SW9 **201** A4
Brixton Water La SW2 **201** A5
Broadbent St W1 **220** D7
Broad Ct WC2 **221** L6
Broad La N15 **200** B1
Broad La, Hmptn. TW12 **199** A6
Broadmead Rd, Wdf.Grn. IG8 **200** D1
Broad Sanctuary SW1 **220** J12
Broadstone Pl W1 **220** B4
Broad Wk SE3 **201** D4
Broad Wk W1 **220** B9
Broadwall SE1 **221** Q9
Broadway E15 **200** C2
Broadway SW1 **220** H13
Broadway, The SW19 **199** D6
Broadway, The W5 **198** B3
Broadway, The, Grnf. UB6 **198** A3
Broadway, The, Sthl. UB1 **198** A3
Broadwick St W1 **220** G7
Broad Yd EC1 **221** R2
Brockham St SE1 **221** U13
Brockley Gro SE4 **201** C5
Brockley Ri SE23 **201** C5
Brockley Rd SE4 **201** C5
Broken Wf EC4 **221** T7
Bromley Common, Brom. BR2 **201** D6
Bromley Hill, Brom. BR1 **201** C6
Bromley Pl W1 **220** F3
Bromley Rd SE6; Brom. BR1 **201** C5
Bromley Rd, Beck. BR3; Brom. BR2 **201** C6
Brompton Rd SW1; SW3; SW7 **199** D4
Brondesbury Pk NW2; NW6 **198** C2
Brondesbury Rd NW6 **198** D3
Brook Dr SE11 **221** Q14
Brooke's Ct EC1 **221** P3
Brookes Mkt EC1 **221** Q3
Brooke St EC1 **221** P4
Brook Gate W1 **220** A8
Brookmill Rd SE8 **201** C4
Brook's Ms W1 **220** D7
Brook St W1 **220** C7
Broom Rd, Tedd. TW11 **199** B6
Broomwood Rd SW11 **199** D5
Brown Hart Gdns W1 **220** C7
Brownhill Rd SE6 **201** C5
Browning Ms W1 **220** D4
Browning Rd E12 **200** D2
Brownlow Ms WC1 **221** N2
Brownlow Rd N11 **200** A1
Brownlow St WC1 **221** N4
Bruce Gro N17 **200** B1
Brunswick Ms W1 **220** A5
Brunswick Pl NW1 **220** C1
Brunswick Rd W5 **198** B3
Brunswick Shop Cen WC1 **221** K1
Brunswick Sq WC1 **221** L2
Bruton La W1 **220** E8
Bruton Pl W1 **220** E8
Bruton St W1 **220** E8
Brydges Pl WC2 **221** K8
Buckhold Rd SW18 **199** D5
Buckingham Arc WC2 **221** L8
Buckingham Gate SW1 **220** F12
Buckingham Ms SW1 **220** F13
Buckingham Pl SW1 **220** F13
Buckingham St WC2 **221** L8
Buckley St SE1 **221** P10
Bucknall St WC2 **220** J5
Bugsby's Way SE7; SE10 **201** D4
Bull Inn Ct WC2 **221** L8
Bulstrode Pl W1 **220** C4
Bulstrode St W1 **220** C5
Bunns La NW7 **198** C1
Burdett Rd E3; E14 **200** C3
Burdett St SE1 **221** P13
Burges Rd E6 **200** D2
Burgon St EC4 **221** S6
Burleigh St WC2 **221** M7
Burlington Arc W1 **220** F8
Burlington Gdns W1 **220** F8
Burlington La W4 **199** C4
Burlington Rd, N.Mal. KT3 **199** C6
Burnt Ash Hill SE12 **201** D5
Burnt Ash La, Brom. BR1 **201** D6
Burnt Ash Rd SE12 **201** C5
Burnt Oak Bdy, Edg. HA8 **198** B1
Burntwood La SW17 **199** D5
Burrage Rd SE18 **201** D4
Burrell St SE1 **221** R9
Burrows Ms SE1 **221** R11
Bury Pl WC1 **221** K4
Bury St SW1 **220** F9
Bushey Rd SW20 **199** C6
Bush Rd E11 **200** D2
Butler Pl SW1 **220** H13
Byng Pl WC1 **220** H2
Bywell Pl W1 **220** F4

C

Cable St E1 **200** B3
Cadogan La SW1 **220** B14
Cadogan Pl SW1 **220** A13
Cadogan Sq SW1 **220** A14
Cahill St EC1 **221** U2
Caleb St SE1 **221** T11
Caledonian Rd N1; N7 **200** A2
Calmont Rd, Brom. BR1 **201** C6
Calthorpe St WC1 **221** N1
Camberwell Ch St SE5 **201** B4
Camberwell New Rd SE5 **201** A4
Camberwell Rd SE5 **201** B4
Cambridge Circ WC2 **220** J6
Cambridge Heath Rd E1; E2 **200** B3
Camden High St NW1 **200** A3
Camden Rd N7; NW1 **200** A2
Camrose Av, Edg. HA8 **198** B1
Candover St W1 **220** F4
Cannizaro Rd SW19 **199** C6
Cannon St EC4 **221** T6
Cannon St Rd E1 **200** B3
Canonbury Rd N1 **200** A2
Canon Row SW1 **221** K12
Canvey St SE1 **221** S9
Capel Rd E7; E12 **200** D2
Capener's Cl SW1 **220** B12
Capper St WC1 **220** G2
Capworth St E10 **200** C2
Carburton St W1 **220** E3
Carey La EC2 **221** T5
Carey St WC2 **221** N6
Carlisle La SE1 **221** N14
Carlisle Pl SW1 **220** F14
Carlisle St W1 **220** H6
Carlos Pl W1 **220** C8
Carlton Gdns SW1 **220** H10
Carlton Ho Ter SW1 **220** H10
Carlton St SW1 **220** H8
Carlton Twr Pl SW1 **220** A13
Carmelite St EC4 **221** Q7
Carnaby St W1 **220** F6
Carpenters Rd E15 **200** C2
Carpenter St W1 **220** D8
Carrington St W1 **220** D10
Carr Rd, Nthlt. UB5 **198** A2
Carteret St SW1 **220** H12
Carter La EC4 **221** S6
Carthusian St EC1 **221** T3
Carting La WC2 **221** L8
Carton St W1 **220** A5
Cassland Rd E9 **200** B2
Castelnau SW13 **199** C4
Castlebar Hill W5 **198** B3
Castlebar Rd W5 **198** B3
Castle Baynard St EC4 **221** S7
Castle La SW1 **220** G13
Castle Yd SE1 **221** S9
Catford Hill SE6 **201** C5
Catford Rd SE6 **201** C5
Cathall Rd E11 **200** C2
Cathedral Piazza SW1 **220** F14
Catherine Griffiths Ct EC1 **221** Q1
Catherine Pl SW1 **220** F13
Catherine St WC2 **221** M7
Catherine Wheel Yd SW1 **220** F10
Catton St WC1 **221** M4
Cavendish Ms N W1 **220** E3
Cavendish Ms S W1 **220** E4
Cavendish Pl W1 **220** E5
Cavendish Rd SW12 **201** A5
Cavendish Sq W1 **220** E5
Caxton St SW1 **220** G13
Cazenove Rd N16 **200** B2
Cecil Ct WC2 **220** J8
Cedars Rd SW4 **201** A5
Cedars Rd W4 **199** B4
Centaur St SE1 **221** N13
Central Av, Houns. TW3 **199** A5
Central Hill SE19 **201** B6
Central Mkts EC1 **221** S4
Central Pk Rd E6 **200** D3
Centrepoint WC1 **220** J5
Centre Rd E7; E11 **200** D2
Chadwick St SW1 **220** J14
Chalk Fm Rd NW1 **200** A2
Chamberlayne Rd NW10 **198** C3
Chancel St SE1 **221** R9
Chancery La WC2 **221** P5
Chandos Pl WC2 **221** K8
Chandos St W1 **220** E4
Chapel Pl W1 **220** D6
Chapel St SW1 **220** C13
Chaplin Cl SE1 **221** Q11
Chapone Pl W1 **220** H6
Chapter Ho Ct EC4 **221** T6
Charing Cross SW1 **220** K9
Charing Cross Rd WC2 **220** J5
Charles II St SW1 **220** H9
Charles St W1 **220** D9

Charles Townsend Ho EC1 221 R1
Charlotte Ms W1 220 G3
Charlotte Pl W1 220 G4
Charlotte St W1 220 G3
Charlton Ch La SE7 201 D4
Charlton Pk La SE7 201 D4
Charlton Pk Rd SE7 201 D4
Charlton Rd SE3; SE7 201 D4
Charlton Rd, Har. HA3 198 B1
Charlton Way SE3 201 C4
Charterhouse Bldgs EC1 221 S2
Charterhouse Ms EC1 221 S3
Charterhouse Sq EC1 221 S3
Charterhouse St EC1 221 Q4
Charter Rd, The, Wdf.Grn. IG8 200 C1
Chase, The, Stan. HA7 198 B1
Chase Rd NW10; W3 198 C3
Cheapside EC2 221 U6
Chelsea Embk SW3 201 A4
Chenies Ms WC1 220 H2
Chenies St WC1 220 H3
Chepstow Rd W2 198 D3
Chequer St EC1 221 U2
Cherry Tree Wk EC1 221 U2
Chertsey Rd, Twick. TW1, TW2 199 A5
Chesham Cl SW1 220 B14
Chesham Ms SW1 220 B13
Chesham Pl SW1 220 B14
Chesham St SW1 220 B14
Cheshire Ct EC4 221 Q6
Chester Cl SW1 220 C12
Chesterfield Gdns W1 220 D9
Chesterfield Hill W1 220 D8
Chesterfield St W1 220 D9
Chester Ms SW1 220 D13
Chester Sq Ms SW1 220 D14
Chester St SW1 220 C13
Cheyne Wk SW10 199 D4
Chichele Rd NW2 198 C2
Chicheley St SE1 221 N11
Chichester Rents WC2 221 P5
Chigwell Rd, E18; Wdf.Grn. IG8 200 D1
Chiltern St W1 220 B3
Chinbrook Rd SE12 201 D5
Ching Ct WC2 220 K6
Chingford Rd E4; E17 200 C1
Chislehurst Rd, Brom. BR1; Chis. BR7 201 D6
Chiswell St EC1 221 U3
Chiswick High Rd W4; Brent. TW8 199 B4
Chiswick La W4 199 C4
Chitty St W1 220 G3
Chobham Rd E15 200 C2
Chrisp St E14 200 C3
Christchurch Av, Har. HA3 198 B1
Christ Ch Pas EC1 221 S5
Christchurch Rd SW2 201 A5
Church Entry EC4 221 S6
Church Gro, Kings.T. KT1 199 B6
Church La E11 200 C2
Church La NW9 198 C1
Church La SW17 201 A6
Church Pl SW1 220 G8
Church Rd E10 200 C2
Church Rd NW10 198 C2
Church Rd SE19 201 B6
Church Rd SW13 199 C4
Church Rd SW19 199 C6
Church Rd W7 198 A3
Church Rd (Heston), Houns. TW5 199 A4
Church Rd, Mitch. CR4 199 D6
Church St, Hmptn. TW12 199 A6
City Rd EC1 200 A3
Clapham Common N Side SW4 201 A5
Clapham Common S Side SW4 201 A5
Clapham Pk Rd SW4 201 A5
Clapham Rd SW9 201 A4
Clapton Common E5 200 B2
Clare Mkt WC2 221 M6
Claremont Rd NW2 198 C2
Clarence Av, N.Mal. KT3 199 C6
Clarence La SW15 199 C5
Clarence Ter NW1 220 A1
Clarges Ms W1 220 D9
Clarges St W1 220 E9
Clarke's Ms W1 220 C3
Clay St W1 220 A4
Clayton Rd SE15 201 B4
Clement's Inn WC2 221 N6
Clement's Inn Pas WC2 221 N6
Clennam St SE1 221 U11
Clerkenwell Cl EC1 221 Q1
Clerkenwell Grn EC1 221 Q2
Clerkenwell Rd EC1 221 P2
Cleveland Ms W1 220 F3
Cleveland Pl SW1 220 G9
Cleveland Row SW1 220 F10
Cleveland St W1 220 F2
Clifford Av SW14 199 B5
Clifford's Inn Pas EC4 221 P6
Clifford St W1 220 F8
Clifton Gdns W9 198 D3
Clink St SE1 221 U9
Clipstone Ms W1 220 F2
Clipstone St W1 220 E3
Cloak La EC4 221 U7
Cloth Ct EC1 221 S4
Cloth Fair EC1 221 S4
Cloth St EC1 221 T3
Coach & Horses Yd W1 220 E7
Cock La EC1 221 R4
Cockpit Steps SW1 220 J12
Cockpit Yd WC1 221 N3
Cockspur Ct SW1 220 J9
Cockspur St SW1 220 J9
Coin St SE1 221 P9
Coldbath Sq EC1 221 P1
Coldharbour La SE5; SW9 201 A5
Cole St SE1 221 U12
Coley St WC1 221 N2
Colindale Av NW9 198 C1
Colindeep La NW4; NW9 198 C1
College Hill EC4 221 U7
College Hill Rd, Har. HA3 198 A1
College Ms SW1 221 K13
College Rd SE19; SE21 201 B5
College Rd, Brom. BR1 201 D6
College Rd, Har. HA1 198 A1
College St EC4 221 U7
Collinson St SE1 221 T12
Collinson Wk SE1 221 T12
Colnbrook St SE1 221 R14
Colney Hatch La N10; N11 198 D1
Colombo St SE1 221 R10
Colonnade WC1 221 K2
Colville Pl W1 220 G4
Commercial Rd E1; E14 200 B3
Commercial St E1 200 B3
Commercial Way SE15 201 B4
Commonside E, Mitch. CR4 201 A6
Commonside W, Mitch. CR4 199 D6
Compton Pas EC1 221 S1
Compton Pl WC1 221 K1
Compton St EC1 221 R1
Concert Hall App SE1 221 N10
Conduit Ct WC2 221 K7
Conduit St W1 220 E7
Coningham Rd W12 198 C3
Connaught Rd E16 200 D3
Cons St SE1 221 Q11
Constitution Hill SW1 220 D11
Conway Ms W1 220 F2
Conway St W1 220 F2
Cool Oak La NW9 198 C2
Coombe La SW20 199 C6
Coombe La W, Kings.T. KT2 199 B6
Coombe Rd, Kings.T. KT2 199 B6
Coombe Rd, N.Mal. KT3 199 C6
Cooper Cl SE1 221 Q12
Copenhagen St N1 200 A3
Copperfield St SE1 221 S11
Coppetts Rd N10 200 A1
Copse Hill SW20 199 C6
Coptic St WC1 220 K4
Coral St SE1 221 Q12
Coram St WC1 220 K2
Cork St W1 220 F8
Cork St Ms W1 220 F8
Corner Ho St WC2 221 K9
Cornwall Rd SE1 221 P9
Cornwall Ter NW1 220 A2
Cornwall Ter Ms NW1 220 A2
Coronation Rd NW10 198 B3
Corporation Row EC1 221 Q1
Cosmo Pl WC1 221 L3
Cosser St SE1 221 P13
Cotswold Ct EC1 221 T1
Cottenham Pk Rd SW20 199 C6
Cottesloe Ms SE1 221 Q13
County St SE1 221 U14
Courtenay Av, Har. HA3 198 A1
Court Rd SE9 201 D5
Covent Gdn WC2 221 L7
Coventry St W1 220 H8
Cowcross St EC1 221 R3
Cowley St SW1 220 K13
Crab Hill, Beck. BR3 201 C6
Craigs Ct SW1 220 K9
Cramer St W1 220 C4
Cranbourn All WC2 220 J7
Cranbourn St WC2 220 J7
Cranbrook Rd, Ilf. IG1, IG2, IG6 200 D1
Crane Ct EC4 221 Q6
Cranfield Row SE1 221 Q13
Cranley Gdns N10 200 A1
Cranmer Rd, Mitch. CR4 199 D6
Craven Pk NW10 198 C3
Craven Pas WC2 221 K9
Craven St WC2 221 K9
Crawford Pas EC1 221 P2
Creed La EC4 221 S6
Creek Rd SE8; SE10 201 C4
Creighton Av N2; N10 198 D1
Crescent Row EC1 221 T2
Cricklewood Bdy NW2 198 C2
Cricklewood La NW2 198 D2
Cripplegate St EC2 221 T3
Cromwell Rd SW5; SW7 199 D4
Cromwell Twr EC2 221 U3
Cross Deep, Twick. TW1 199 A5
Cross Keys Cl W1 220 C4
Cross Keys Sq EC1 221 T4
Crossway SW20 199 C6
Crouch End Hill N8 200 A2
Crouch Hill N4; N8 200 A1
Crown Ct EC2 221 U6
Crown Ct WC2 221 L6
Crown Dale SE19 201 B6
Crown La SW16 201 A6
Crown La, Mord. SM4 199 D6
Crown Office Row EC4 221 P7
Crown Pas SW1 220 G10
Crown Rd, Twick. TW1 199 B5
Crowshott Av, Stan. HA7 198 B1
Croxted Rd SE21; SE24 201 B5
Croydon Rd SE20 201 B6
Croydon Rd, Beck. BR3 201 C6
Crystal Palace Par SE19 201 B6
Crystal Palace Pk Rd SE26 201 B6
Cubitts Yd WC2 221 L7
Culross St W1 220 B8
Culver Gro, Stan. HA7 198 B1
Currey Rd, Grnf. UB6 198 A2
Cursitor St EC4 221 P5
Curzon Gate W1 220 C10
Curzon Sq W1 220 C10
Curzon St W1 220 C10
Cut, The SE1 221 Q11
Cypress Pl W1 220 G2
Cyrus St EC1 221 S1

D

Dacre St SW1 220 H13
Dallington St EC1 221 S1
Dalston La E8 200 B2
Dames Rd E7 200 D2
Dane St WC1 221 M4
Dansey Pl W1 220 H7
D'Arblay St W1 220 G6
Dartmouth Pk Hill N19; NW5 200 A2
Dartmouth Rd SE23; SE26 201 B5
Dartmouth St SW1 220 H12
Davidge St SE1 221 R12
David Ms W1 220 A3
Davies Ms W1 220 D7
Davies St W1 220 D7
Dawes Rd SW6 199 D4
Dean Bradley St SW1 221 K14
Deanery Ms W1 220 C9
Deanery St W1 220 C9
Dean Farrar St SW1 220 H13
Deansbrook Rd, Edg. HA8 198 B1
Deans Ct EC4 221 S6
Deans La, Edg. HA8 198 C1
Deans Ms W1 220 E5
Dean Stanley St SW1 221 K14
Dean St W1 220 H5
Dean's Yd SW1 220 J13
Dean Trench St SW1 221 K14
Defoe Ho EC2 221 U3
Denman St W1 220 H8
Denmark Hill SE5 201 B5
Denmark Pl WC2 220 J5
Denmark St WC2 220 J6
Deptford Ch St SE8 201 C4
Derby Gate SW1 221 K11
Derby St W1 220 C10
Dering St W1 220 D6
Devas St E3 200 C3
Devereux Ct WC2 221 P6
Devonshire Cl W1 220 D3
Devonshire Ms N W1 220 D3
Devonshire Ms S W1 220 D3
Devonshire Ms W W1 220 D2
Devonshire Pl W1 220 C2
Devonshire Pl Ms W1 220 C2
Devonshire Rd NW7 198 C1
Devonshire Rd SE23 201 B5
Devonshire Row Ms W1 220 E2
Devonshire St W1 220 C3
Devons Rd E3 200 C3
De Walden St W1 220 C4
Diadem Ct W1 220 H6
Dickens Sq SE1 221 U13
Disney Pl SE1 221 U11
Disney St SE1 221 U11
Distaff La EC4 221 T7
Doby Ct EC4 221 U7
Dodson St SE1 221 Q12
Dog Kennel Hill SE22 201 B5
Dolben St SE1 221 R10
Dollis Hill La NW2 198 C2
Dollis Rd N3; NW7 198 D1
Dombey St WC1 221 M3
Domingo St EC1 221 T1
Doon St SE1 221 P10
Dorrington St EC1 221 P3
Dorrit St SE1 221 U11
Dorset Bldgs EC4 221 R6
Dorset Ms SW1 220 D13
Dorset Ri EC4 221 R6
Dorset Rd SW19 199 D6
Dorset St W1 220 A4
Doughty Ms WC1 221 M2
Doughty St WC1 221 M1
Dover Ho Rd SW15 199 C5
Dover St W1 220 E8
Dover Yd W1 220 F9
Downham Way, Brom. BR1 201 C6
Downhills Way N17 200 B1
Downing St SW1 220 K11
Down St W1 220 D10
Down St Ms W1 220 D10
Doyce St SE1 221 T11
Drakefell Rd SE4; SE14 201 B5
Drake St WC1 221 M4
Draycott Av, Har. HA3 198 B1
Drayton Grn Rd W13 198 B3
Drayton Pk N5 200 A2
Drive, The, Ilf. IG1 200 D2
Drummond St NW1 220 F1
Drury La WC2 221 L6
Drury Way NW10 198 C2
Dryden St WC2 221 L6
Duchess Ms W1 220 E4
Duchess St W1 220 E4
Duchy St SE1 221 Q9
Duck La W1 220 H6
Dudden Hill La NW10 198 C2
Dufferin St EC1 221 U2
Dufour's Pl W1 220 G6
Duke of Wellington Pl SW1 220 C11
Duke of York St SW1 220 G9
Dukes Av, Rich. TW10; Kings.T. KT2 199 B6
Duke's Ms W1 220 C5
Duke St SW1 220 G9
Duke St W1 220 C5
Duke's Yd W1 220 C7
Dulwich Common SE21; SE22 201 B5
Dulwich Rd SE24 201 A5
Dulwich Village SE21 201 B5
Dulwich Wd Pk SE19 201 B6
Duncannon St WC2 221 K8
Dunns Pas WC1 221 L5
Dunraven St W1 220 A7
Dunstable Ms W1 220 C3
Dunton Rd SE1 201 B4
Duplex Ride SW1 220 A12
Durham Ho St WC2 221 L8
Durham Rd SW20 199 C6
Durnsford Rd N11 200 A1
Durnsford Rd SW19 199 D5
Durweston Ms W1 220 A3
Durweston St W1 220 A3
Dyer's Bldgs EC1 221 P4
Dyott St WC1 220 K5

E

Eagle Ct EC1 221 R3
Eagle Pl SW1 220 G8
Eagle St WC1 221 M4
Ealing Grn W5 198 B3
Ealing Rd, Brent. TW8 199 B4
Ealing Rd, Wem. HA0 198 B2
Earlham St WC2 220 J6
Earls Ct Rd SW5; W8 199 D4
Earlsfield Rd SW18 199 D5
Earnshaw St WC2 220 J5
Easley's Ms W1 220 C5
East Av E12 200 D2
Eastcastle St W1 220 F5
Eastcote La, Har. HA2 198 A2
Eastcote La, Nthlt. UB5 198 A2
East Cross Route E3 200 C2
East Dulwich Gro SE22 201 B5
East Dulwich Rd SE15; SE22 201 B5
East End Rd N2; N3 198 D1
Eastern Av E11; Ilf. IG2, IG4 200 D1
East Ferry Rd E14 201 C4
East Harding St EC4 221 Q5
East Heath Rd NW3 198 D2
East Hill SW18 199 D5
East India Dock Rd E14 200 C3
East La, Wem. HA0 198 B2
East Pas EC1 221 S3
East Poultry Av EC1 221 R4
East Rd N1 200 B3
East St SE17 201 B4
Eastway E9; E10; E15 200 C2
Eaton La SW1 220 E14
Eaton Pl SW1 220 B14
Eaton Ri W5 198 B3
Eaton Row SW1 220 D14
Eaton Sq SW1 220 D13
Eccleston Ms SW1 220 C14
Eccleston St SW1 220 D14
Eden Pk Av, Beck. BR3 201 C6
Eden St, Kings.T. KT1 199 B6
Edgware Rd NW2 198 C2
Edgware Rd NW9 198 C1
Edgware Rd W2 198 D3
Edwards Ms W1 220 B6
Effra Rd SW2 201 A5
Elder Rd SE27 201 B6
Elephant & Castle SE1 221 S14
Elgin Av W9 198 D3
Elizabeth Ct SW1 220 J14
Ellesmere Rd W4 199 C4
Elm Ct EC4 221 P7
Elmers End Rd, SE20; Beck. BR3 201 B6
Elms Rd, Har. HA3 198 A1
Elmstead La, Chis. BR7 201 D6
Elm St WC1 221 N2
Eltham High St SE9 201 D5
Eltham Hill SE9 201 D5
Eltham Rd SE9; SE12 201 D5
Ely Ct EC1 221 Q4
Ely Pl EC1 221 Q4
Embankment Pl WC2 221 L9
Emerald St WC1 221 M3
Emerson St SE1 221 T9
Emery Hill St SW1 220 G14
Emery St SE1 221 Q13
Emlyn Rd W12 199 C4
Emmanuel Rd SW12 201 A5
Empire Way, Wem. HA9 198 B2
Endell St WC2 220 K5
Endsleigh Gdns WC1 220 H1
Endsleigh Pl WC1 220 J1
Endsleigh St WC1 220 H1
Endymion Rd N4 200 A2
Englefield Rd N1 200 B2
Errol St EC1 221 U2
Essex Ct EC4 221 P6
Essex Rd N1 200 A3
Essex St WC2 221 P7
Euston Rd NW1 220 E2
Euston St NW1 220 G1
Euston Twr NW1 220 F1
Evelina Rd SE15 201 B4
Evelyn St SE8 201 C4
Evelyn Yd W1 220 H5
Ewer St SE1 221 T10
Excel Ct WC2 220 J8
Exchange Ct WC2 221 L8
Exeter St WC2 221 L7
Exmouth Mkt EC1 221 P1
Exton St SE1 221 P10
Eyre St Hill EC1 221 P2

F

Fairfield Rd E3 200 C3
Fairfield S, Kings.T. KT1 199 B6
Falconberg Ct W1 220 J5
Falconberg Ms W1 220 H5
Falcon Cl SE1 221 S9
Falcon Ct EC4 221 P6
Falcon Rd SW11 199 D4
Falloden Way NW11 198 D1
Falmouth Rd SE1 221 U13
Fann St EC1 221 T2
Fann St EC2 221 T2
Fareham St W1 220 H5
Farm St W1 220 D8
Farnaby Rd, Brom. BR1, BR2 201 C6
Farnham Pl SE1 221 S10
Farringdon La EC1 221 Q2
Farringdon Rd EC1 221 P1
Farringdon St EC4 221 R5
Faulkner's All EC1 221 R3
Fentiman Rd SW8 201 A4
Fernhead Rd W9 198 D3
Fern La, Houns. TW5 199 A4
Ferry La N17 200 B1
Ferry Rd SW13 199 C4
Fetter La EC4 221 Q6
Field Ct WC1 221 N4
Finborough Rd SW10; SW17 199 D4
Finchley La NW4 198 C1
Finchley Rd NW2; NW3; NW8; NW11 198 D2
Fisher St WC1 221 L4
Fitzhardinge St W1 220 B5
Fitzjohns Av NW3 198 D2
Fitzmaurice Pl W1 220 E9
Fitzroy Ct W1 220 G2
Fitzroy Ms W1 220 F2
Fitzroy Sq W1 220 F2
Fitzroy St W1 220 F2
Flaxman Ct W1 220 H6
Fleet St EC4 221 P6
Flitcroft St WC2 220 J5
Floral St WC2 221 K7
Foley St W1 220 F4
Footscray Rd SE9 201 D5
Forest Dr E12 200 D2
Forest Hill Rd SE22; SE23 201 B5
Forest La E7; E15 200 C2
Fore St EC2 221 U4
Fore St N9; N18 200 B1
Forest Ri E17 200 C1
Forest Rd E17 200 B1
Fortess Rd NW5 200 A2
Fortis Grn N2; N10 198 D1
Fortune Grn Rd NW6 198 D2
Fortune St EC1 221 U2
Forty Av, Wem. HA9 198 B2
Forty La, Wem. HA9 198 B2
Forum Magnum Sq SE1 221 M11
Foster La EC2 221 T5
Foubert's Pl W1 220 F6
Foundry Ms NW1 220 G1
Fountain Ct EC4 221 P7
Fourth Av E12 200 D2
Fox & Knot St EC1 221 S3
Foxgrove Rd, Beck. BR3 201 C6
Frances St SE18 201 D4
Francis Rd E10 200 C2
Frazier St SE1 221 P12
Frederic Ms SW1 220 A12
Freemasons Rd E16 200 D3
Friars Cl SE1 221 S10
Friar St EC4 221 S6
Friary Ct SW1 220 G10
Friday St EC4 221 T6
Frith La NW7 198 D1
Frith St W1 220 H6
Fryent Way NW9 198 B1
Fulbourne Rd E17 200 C1
Fulham Palace Rd SW6; W6 199 C4
Fulham Rd SW3; SW10 199 D4
Fulham Rd SW6 199 D4
Fulwood Pl WC1 221 N4
Furnival St EC4 221 P5

G

Gabriel's Wf SE1 221 P9
Gage St WC1 221 L3
Galen Pl WC1 221 L4
Galpins Rd, Th.Hth. CR7 201 A6
Gambia St SE1 221 S10
Ganton St W1 220 F7
Gap Rd SW19 199 D6
Garbutt Pl W1 220 C3
Garden Ct EC4 221 P7
Garden Row SE1 221 R14
Gardners La EC4 221 T7
Garlick Hill EC4 221 U7
Garnet St E1 200 B3
Garrad's Rd SW16 201 A5
Garratt La SW17; SW18 199 D5
Garrett St EC1 221 U1
Garrick St WC2 220 K7
Gate St WC2 221 M5
Gaunt St SE1 221 S13
Gayfere St SW1 220 K14
Gaywood Est SE1 221 S14
Gaywood St SE1 221 S14
Gees Ct W1 220 C6
Gee St EC1 221 T1
Gellatly Rd SE14 201 B4
George Ct WC2 221 L8
George Rd, Kings.T. KT2 199 B6
George St W1 220 A5
George St, Rich. TW9 199 B5
George Yd W1 220 C7
Geraldine St SE11 221 R14
Gerrard Pl W1 220 J7
Gerrard St W1 220 H7
Gerridge St SE1 221 Q12
Gervase Rd, Edg. HA8 198 C1
Gilbert Pl WC1 221 K4
Gilbert St W1 220 C6
Gildea St W1 220 E4
Gillespie Rd N5 200 A2
Giltspur St EC1 221 S5
Gipsy Hill SE19 201 B6
Gipsy Rd SE27 201 B6
Gladstone St SE1 221 R13
Glasshill St SE1 221 S11
Glasshouse St W1 220 G8
Glasshouse Yd EC1 221 T2
Glentworth St NW1 220 A2
Globe Rd E1; E2 200 B3
Globe St SE1 221 U13
Globe Yd W1 220 D6
Gloucester Pl W1 220 A3
Gloucester Pl Ms W1 220 A4
Gloucester Rd SW7 199 D4
Gloucester Rd, Kings.T. KT1 199 B6
Goddard Rd, Beck. BR3 201 B6
Godliman St EC4 221 T6
Goffers Rd SE3 201 C4
Golden Jubilee Br SE1 221 M10
Golden Jubilee Br WC2 221 M9
Golden La EC1 221 T2
Golden La Est EC1 221 T2
Golden Sq W1 220 G7
Golders Grn Rd NW11 198 D1
Goldhawk Rd W6; W12 199 C4
Goldsmith St EC2 221 U5
Goodge Pl W1 220 G4
Goodge St W1 220 G4
Goodwins Ct WC2 220 K7
Gordon Av, Stan. HA7 198 A1
Gordon Sq WC1 220 J2
Gordon St WC1 220 H1
Gosfield St W1 220 F3
Goslett Yd WC2 220 J6
Goswell Rd EC1 221 T2
Gough Sq EC4 221 Q5
Gough St WC1 221 N1
Gower Ct WC1 220 H1
Gower Ms WC1 220 H4
Gower Pl WC1 220 G1
Gower St WC1 220 G1
Grafton Ms W1 220 F2
Grafton St W1 220 E8
Grafton Way W1 220 F2
Grafton Way WC1 220 F2
Grahame Pk Way NW7; NW9 198 C1
Graham Rd E8 200 B2
Granby Pl SE1 221 P12
Grand Av EC1 221 S3
Grand Dep Rd SE18 201 D4
Grand Dr SW20 199 C6
Grange Ct WC2 221 N6
Grange Rd E13 200 C3
Grange Rd SE1 201 B4
Grange Rd SE19; SE25; Th.Hth. CR7 201 B6
Grantham Pl W1 220 D10
Granville Pl W1 220 B6
Grape St WC2 221 K5
Gray's Inn WC1 221 N3
Gray's Inn Pl WC1 221 N4
Gray's Inn Rd WC1 200 A3
Gray's Inn Sq WC1 221 P3
Gray St SE1 221 Q12
Gray's Yd W1 220 C6
Great Arthur Ho EC1 221 T2
Great Cambridge Rd N9; N17; N18; Enf. EN1; Wal.Cr. EN8 200 B1
Great Castle St W1 220 E5
Great Cen Way NW10; Wem. HA9 198 C2
Great Chapel St W1 220 H5
Great Chertsey Rd W4 199 C4
Great Chertsey Rd (Whitton), Felt. TW13 199 A5
Great Coll St SW1 220 K13
Great Dover St SE1 221 U12
Great George St SW1 220 J12
Great Guildford St SE1 221 T9
Great James St WC1 221 M2
Great Marlborough St W1 220 F6
Great New St EC4 221 Q5
Great N Rd N2 198 D1
Great N Way NW4 198 C1
Great Ormond St WC1 221 L3
Great Peter St SW1 220 H14
Great Portland St W1 220 E3
Great Pulteney St W1 220 G7
Great Queen St WC2 221 L6
Great Russell St WC1 220 J5
Great St. Thomas Apostle EC4 221 U7
Great Scotland Yd SW1 220 K10
Great Smith St SW1 220 J13
Great Suffolk St SE1 221 S10
Great Sutton St EC1 221 S2
Great Titchfield St W1 220 F5
Great Trinity La EC4 221 U7
Great Turnstile WC1 221 N4
Great Western Rd W2; W9; W11 198 D3
Great W Rd W4; W6 199 C4
Great W Rd, Brent. TW8; Houns. TW5; Islw. TW7 199 A4
Great Windmill St W1 220 H7
Greek Ct W1 220 J6
Greek St W1 220 J6
Greek Yd WC2 220 K7
Green, The, Sthl. UB2 199 A4
Green, The, Twick. TW2 199 A5
Green Arbour Ct EC1 221 R5
Greencoat Row SW1 220 G14
Greenford Av W7 198 A3
Greenford Rd, Grnf. UB6; Sthl. UB1 198 A3
Greengate St E13 200 D3
Greenham Cl SE1 221 P12
Greenhill's Rents EC1 221 S3
Greenhill Way, Har. HA1 198 A1
Green La SE9; Chis. BR7 201 D5
Green La SW16 201 A6
Green Las N4; N8; N15; N16 200 A1
Green's Ct W1 220 H7
Green St E7; E13 200 D2
Green St W1 220 A7
Greenwell St W1 220 E2
Greenwich High Rd SE10 201 C4
Greenwich S St SE10 201 C4
Greet St SE1 221 Q10
Grenville St WC1 221 L2
Gresham St EC2 221 T5
Gresse St W1 220 H4
Greville St EC1 221 Q4
Greycoat Pl SW1 220 H14
Greycoat St SW1 220 H14
Greyfriars Pas EC1 221 S5
Greyhound La SW16 201 A6
Greystoke Pl EC4 221 P5
Grindal St SE1 221 P12
Groom Pl SW1 220 C13
Grosvenor Cres SW1 220 C12
Grosvenor Cres Ms SW1 220 B12
Grosvenor Gdns SW1 220 D13
Grosvenor Gdns Ms E SW1 220 E13
Grosvenor Gdns Ms N SW1 220 D14
Grosvenor Gdns Ms S SW1 220 E14
Grosvenor Gate W1 220 A8
Grosvenor Hill W1 220 D7

Grosvenor Pl SW1 220 C12
Grosvenor Rd N10 200 A1
Grosvenor Rd SW1 201 A4
Grosvenor Sq W1 220 C7
Grosvenor St W1 220 D7
Grotto Pas W1 220 C3
Grove End Rd NW8 198 D3
Grove Grn Rd E11 200 C2
Groveland Ct EC4 221 U6
Grove La SE5 201 B4
Grove La, Kings.T. KT1 199 B6
Grove Pk Rd SE9 201 D5
Grove Rd E3 200 C3
Grove Rd E17 200 C1
Grove Rd, Mitch. CR4 201 A6
Grove St SE8 201 C4
Grove Vale SE22 201 B5
Guilford Pl WC1 221 M2
Guilford St WC1 221 L2
Gunnersbury Av W3; W4; W5 198 B3
Gunnersbury La W3 199 B4
Gunpowder Sq EC4 221 Q5
Gutter La EC2 221 U5

H

Hackney Rd E2 200 B3
Ha-Ha Rd SE18 201 D4
Hale End Rd E4; E17; Wdf.Grn. IG8 200 C1
Half Acre, Brent. TW8 199 B4
Half Moon Ct EC1 221 T4
Half Moon La SE24 201 B5
Half Moon St W1 220 E9
Halkin Arc SW1 220 B13
Halkin Ms SW1 220 B13
Halkin Pl SW1 220 B13
Halkin St SW1 220 C12
Hallam Ms W1 220 E3
Hallam St W1 220 E2
Hall Rd, Islw. TW7 199 A5
Ham Gate Av, Rich. TW10 199 B5
Hamilton Ms W1 220 D11
Hamilton Pl W1 220 C10
Hammersmith Gro W6 199 C4
Hammersmith Rd W6; W14 199 C4
Ham Pk Rd E7; E15 200 C2
Hampstead La N6; NW3 198 D2
Hampstead Rd NW1 200 A3
Hampton Ct Rd, E.Mol. KT8; Hmptn. TW12; Kings.T. KT1 199 A6
Hampton Rd, Hmptn. TW12 199 A6
Hampton Rd, Twick. TW2 199 A5
Hampton Rd E, Felt. TW13 199 A6
Hampton Rd W, Felt. TW13 199 A5
Ham St, Rich. TW10 199 B5
Ham Yd W1 220 H7
Hand Ct WC1 221 N4
Handel St WC1 221 K1
Hanger La W5 198 B3
Hanging Sword All EC4 221 Q6
Hanover Pl WC2 221 L6
Hanover Sq W1 220 E6
Hanover St W1 220 E6
Hanson St W1 220 F3
Hans Pl SW1 220 A13
Hans St SW1 220 A14
Hanway Pl W1 220 H5
Hanway St W1 220 H5
Hanworth Rd, Hmptn. TW12 199 A6
Hanworth Rd, Houns. TW3, TW4 199 A5
Hare Ct EC4 221 P6
Hare Pl EC4 221 Q6
Harewood Pl W1 220 E6
Harlesden Rd NW10 198 C3
Harley Pl W1 220 D4
Harley St W1 220 D4
Harmsworth Ms SE11 221 R14
Harold Rd E13 200 D3
Harold Rd SE19 201 B6
Harp All EC4 221 R5
Harper Rd SE1 221 T13
Harpur Ms WC1 221 M3
Harpur St WC1 221 M3
Harriet St SW1 220 A12
Harriet Wk SW1 220 A12
Harrow Rd E11 200 C2
Harrow Rd NW10; W9; W10 198 C3
Harrow Rd, Wem. HA0 198 B2
Harrow Rd (Tokyngton), Wem. HA9 198 B2
Harrow Vw, Har. HA2, HA3 198 A1
Hartfield Rd SW19 199 D6
Harvist Rd NW6 198 C3
Hat & Mitre Ct EC1 221 S2
Hatfields SE1 221 Q9
Hatton Gdn EC1 221 Q3
Hatton Pl EC1 221 Q2
Hatton Wall EC1 221 P3
Haunch of Venison Yd W1 220 D6
Haven Grn W5 198 B3
Haverstock Hill NW3 198 D2
Hawks Rd, Kings.T. KT1 199 B6
Haydons Rd SW19 199 D6
Hayes La, Beck. BR3 201 C6
Hayes Rd, Brom. BR2 201 D6
Hay Hill W1 220 E8
Haymarket SW1 220 H8
Haymarket Arc SW1 220 H8
Hayne St EC1 221 S3
Hay's Ms W1 220 D8
Hayward's Pl EC1 221 R2
Headfort Pl SW1 220 C12
Headstone Rd, Har. HA1 198 A1
Heathcote St WC1 221 M1
Heathfield Ter W4 199 C4
Heath Rd, Houns. TW3 199 A5
Heath Rd, Twick. TW1, TW2 199 A5
Heath St NW3 198 D2
Heddon St W1 220 F7
Helmet Row EC1 221 U1
Hendon La N3 198 D1
Hendon Way NW2; NW4 198 C1
Henrietta Ms WC1 221 L1
Henrietta Pl W1 220 D6
Henrietta St WC2 221 L7
Herbal Hill EC1 221 Q2
Herbert Cres SW1 220 A13
Herbrand St WC1 221 K1
Hercules Rd SE1 221 N14
Hermitage Rd SE19 201 B6
Hermit Rd E16 200 C3
Hermon Hill E11; E18 200 D1
Herne Hill SE24 201 B5
Hertford Pl W1 220 F2
Hertford St W1 220 D9
Heston Rd, Houns. TW5 199 A4
Higham Hill Rd E17 200 C1
Highbury Gro N5 200 A2
Highbury Pk N5 200 A2
Highgate High St N6 200 A2
Highgate Hill N6; N19 200 A2
Highgate Rd NW5 200 A2
Highgate W Hill N6 200 A2
High Holborn WC1 221 L5
High Rd E18; Wdf.Grn. IG8 200 C1
High Rd N2; N12; N20 198 D1
High Rd N15 200 B1
High Rd N22 200 A1
High Rd NW10 198 C2
High Rd, Har. HA3 198 A1
High Rd, Wem. HA0 198 B2
High Rd Leyton E10; E15 200 C2
High Rd Leytonstone E11; E15 200 C2
High St E11 200 D1
High St E13 200 D3
High St E15 200 C3
High St N8 200 A1
High St NW10 198 C3
High St SE20 201 B6
High St SE25 201 B6
High St W3 198 B3
High St, Beck. BR3 201 C6
High St, Brent. TW8 199 B4
High St, Brom. BR1 201 D6
High St, Chis. BR7 201 D6
High St, Hmptn. TW12 199 A6
High St (Hampton Wick), Kings.T. KT1 199 B6
High St, N.Mal. KT3 199 C6
High St, Sthl. UB1 198 A3
High St, Tedd. TW11 199 B6
High St, Th.Hth. CR7 201 B6
High St (Whitton), Twick. TW2 199 A5
High St Colliers Wd SW19 199 D6
High St N E6; E12 200 D2
High St S E6 200 D3
High St Wimbledon SW19 199 C6
High Timber St EC4 221 T7
Highway, The E1; E14 200 B3
Hillreach SE18 201 D4
Hillside NW10 198 C3
Hills Pl W1 220 F6
Hill St W1 220 C9
Hind Ct EC4 221 Q6
Hinde St W1 220 C5
Hither Grn La SE13 201 C5
Hobart Pl SW1 220 D13
Hoe St E17 200 C1
Hogarth La W4 199 C4
Holborn EC1 221 P4
Holborn Circ EC1 221 Q4
Holborn Pl WC1 221 M4
Holborn Viaduct EC1 221 Q4
Holders Hill Rd NW4; NW7 198 C1
Holland Pk Av W11 199 C4
Holland Rd W14 199 D4
Holland St SE1 221 S9
Hollen St W1 220 H5
Holles St W1 220 E5
Holloway Rd N7; N19 200 A2
Hollybush Hill E11 200 C1
Holmes Ter SE1 221 P11
Holsworthy Sq WC1 221 N2
Homerton High St E9 200 B2
Homerton Rd E9 200 C2
Homesdale Rd, Brom. BR1, BR2 201 D6
Honduras St EC1 221 T1
Honey La EC2 221 U6
Honeypot La NW9; Stan. HA7 198 B1
Honor Oak Pk SE23 201 B5
Hood Ct EC4 221 Q6
Hop Gdns WC2 220 K8
Hopkins St W1 220 G6
Hopton Gdns SE1 221 S9
Hopton St SE1 221 S9
Hornfair Rd SE7 201 D4
Horn La W3 198 C3
Hornsey La N6; N19 200 A2
Hornsey Ri N19 200 A2
Hornsey Rd N7; N19 200 A2
Horse & Dolphin Yd W1 220 J7
Horseferry Rd SW1 220 H14
Horse Guards Av SW1 221 K10
Horse Guards Rd SW1 220 J10
Horsemongers Ms SE1 221 U12
Horsenden La N, Grnf. UB6 198 A2
Horsenden La S, Grnf. UB6 198 B3
Horse Ride SW1 220 G10
Hosier La EC1 221 R4
Hospital Br Rd, Twick. TW2 199 A5
Houghton St WC2 221 N6
Howberry Rd, Edg. HA8; Stan. HA7 198 B1
Howick Pl SW1 220 G14
Howland Ms E W1 220 G3
Howland St W1 220 F3
Huggin Ct EC4 221 U7
Huggin Hill EC4 221 U7
Hulme Pl SE1 221 U12
Hungerford Br SE1 221 L9
Hungerford Br WC2 221 L9
Hungerford La WC2 221 K9
Hunter St WC1 221 L1
Huntley St WC1 220 G2
Hunt's Ct WC2 220 J8
Hurst La, E.Mol. KT8 199 A6
Hurst Rd, E.Mol. KT8; W.Mol. KT8 199 A6
Hutton St EC4 221 Q6
Hyde, The NW9 198 C1
Hyde Pk Cor W1 220 C11
Hyde Vale SE10 201 C4

I

Ilderton Rd SE15; SE16 201 B4
Ilford La, Ilf. IG1 200 D2
Imperial Dr, Har. HA2 198 A2
India Pl WC2 221 M7
Ingestre Pl W1 220 G6
Inigo Pl WC2 221 K7
Inner Temple La EC4 221 P6
Invicta Plaza SE1 221 R9
Ireland Yd EC4 221 S6
Ironmonger Pas EC1 221 U1
Irving St WC2 220 J8
Isabella St SE1 221 R10
Ivybridge La WC2 221 L8

J

Jacob's Well Ms W1 220 C5
Jamaica Rd SE1; SE16 201 B4
James St W1 220 C5
James St WC2 221 L7
Jermyn St SW1 220 F9
Jerningham Rd SE14 201 C4
Jersey Rd, Houns. TW5; Islw. TW7 199 A4
Jerusalem Pas EC1 221 R2
Jervis Ct W1 220 E6
Joan St SE1 221 R10
Jockey's Flds WC1 221 N3
Johanna St SE1 221 P12
John Adam St WC2 221 L8
John Carpenter St EC4 221 R7
John Princes St W1 220 E5
John Ruskin St SE5 201 A4
John's Ms WC1 221 N2
John St WC1 221 N2
John Wilson St SE18 201 D4
Jones St W1 220 D8
Judd St WC1 200 A3
Junction Rd N19 200 A2

K

Katherine Rd E6; E7 200 D2
Kean St WC2 221 M6
Keeley St WC2 221 M6
Kell St SE1 221 S13
Kemble St WC2 221 M6
Kemp's Ct W1 220 G6
Kendall Pl W1 220 B4
Kendal Rd NW10 198 C2
Kenley Rd, Kings.T. KT1 199 B6
Kenmore Av, Har. HA3 198 B1
Kenmore Rd, Har. HA3 198 B1
Kennet Wf La EC4 221 U7
Kennington La SE11 201 A4
Kennington Pk Rd SE11 201 A4
Kennington Rd SE1 221 P13
Kennington Rd SE11 221 P14
Kenrick Pl W1 220 B3
Kensington Ch St W8 198 D3
Kensington High St W8; W14 199 D4
Kensington Pk Rd W11 198 D3
Kensington Rd SW7; W8 199 D4
Kent Gdns W13 198 B3
Kent Ho Rd SE26; Beck. BR3 201 B6
Kentish Way, Brom. BR1 201 D6
Kenton La (Belmont), Har. HA3 198 B1
Kenton La (Harrow Weald), Har. HA3 198 A1
Kenton Rd, Har. HA3 198 B1
Kenton St WC1 221 K1
Keppel Row SE1 221 T10
Keppel St WC1 220 J3
Kew Br Rd, Brent. TW8 199 B4
Kew Rd, Rich. TW9 199 B4
Keyworth St SE1 221 S13
Kidbrooke Pk Rd SE3 201 D4
Kilburn High Rd NW6 198 D2
Kilburn La W9; W10 198 D3
Kilburn Pk Rd NW6 198 D3
King Charles St SW1 220 J11
King Edward St EC1 221 T5
King Edward Wk SE1 221 Q13
Kinghorn St EC1 221 T4
King James Ct SE1 221 S12
King James St SE1 221 S12
Kingly Ct W1 220 F7
Kingly St W1 220 F6
King's Av SW4; SW12 201 A5
Kings Bench St SE1 221 S11
Kings Bench Wk EC4 221 Q6
Kingsbury Rd NW9 198 B1
Kingscote St EC4 221 R7
Kingsfield Av, Har. HA2 198 A1
Kingsland Rd E2; E8 200 B2
Kingsley Rd, Houns. TW3 199 A4
King's Ms WC1 221 N2
Kings Pl SE1 221 T12
King's Reach Twr SE1 221 Q9
King's Rd SW1; SW3; SW6; SW10 199 D4
Kings Rd, Kings.T. KT2 199 B6
Kings Rd, Rich. TW10 199 B5
Kingston Hill, Kings.T. KT2 199 B6
Kingston Rd SW15 199 C5
Kingston Rd SW20 199 C6
Kingston Rd, Kings.T. KT1; N.Mal. KT3 199 B6
Kingston Rd, Tedd. TW11 199 B6
Kingston Vale SW15 199 C6
King St EC2 221 U6
King St SW1 220 G10
King St W6 199 C4
King St WC2 221 K7
King St, Twick. TW1 199 B5
Kingsway WC2 221 M5
Kingsway Pl EC1 221 Q1
Kinnerton Pl N SW1 220 A12
Kinnerton Pl S SW1 220 A12
Kinnerton St SW1 220 B12
Kinnerton Yd SW1 220 A12
Kirby St EC1 221 Q3
Kirkdale SE26 201 B5
Kirkman Pl W1 220 H4
Kirk St WC1 221 M2
Kneller Rd, Twick. TW2 199 A5
Knightrider St EC4 221 T7
Knightsbridge SW1 220 A12
Knights Hill SE27 201 A6

L

Ladbroke Gro W10; W11 198 D3
Lady Margaret Rd, Sthl. UB1 198 A3
Ladywell Rd SE13 201 C5
Lake Ho Rd E11 200 D2
Lambeth Hill EC4 221 T7
Lambeth Palace Rd SE1 221 M14
Lambeth Rd SE1 221 N14
Lambeth Rd SE11 221 N14
Lambs Conduit Pas WC1 221 M3
Lamb's Conduit St WC1 221 M2
Lamp Office Ct WC1 221 M2
Lampton Rd, Houns. TW3 199 A5
Lancashire Ct W1 220 E7
Lancaster Pl WC2 221 M7
Lancaster St SE1 221 S12
Lanesborough Pl SW1 220 C11
Langham Pl W1 220 E4
Langham St W1 220 E4
Langley Ct WC2 221 K7
Langley St WC2 221 K6
Lansdowne Rd N17 200 B1
Lansdowne Row W1 220 E9
Lansdowne Ter WC1 221 L2
Lansdowne Way SW8 201 A4
Lant St SE1 221 T11
Larden Rd W3 199 C4
Larkshall Rd E4 200 C1
Lascelles Av, Har. HA1 198 A2
Latchmere Rd SW11 199 D4
Latchmere Rd, Kings.T. KT2 199 B6
Lauderdale Twr EC2 221 T3
Launcelot St SE1 221 P12
Lauriston Rd E9 200 B2
Lausanne Rd SE15 201 B4
Lavender Av, Mitch. CR4 199 D6
Lavington St SE1 221 S10
Lawrence La EC2 221 U6
Lawrie Pk Rd SE26 201 B6
Laxton Pl NW1 220 E1
Laystall St EC1 221 P2
Laytons Bldgs SE1 221 U11
Lea Br Rd E5; E10; E17 200 B2
Leake St SE1 221 N11
Leather La EC1 221 Q4
Lee High Rd SE12; SE13 201 C5
Lee Rd SE3 201 C5
Lees Pl W1 220 B7
Lee Ter SE3; SE13 201 C5
Leicester Ct WC2 220 J7
Leicester Pl WC2 220 J7
Leicester Sq WC2 220 J8
Leicester St WC2 220 J7
Leigham Ct Rd SW16 201 A5
Leigh Hunt St SE1 221 T11
Leigh Pl EC1 221 P3
Leigh St WC1 220 K1
Leighton Rd NW5 200 A2
Leopards Ct EC1 221 P3
Leo Yd EC1 221 S2
Lever St EC1 200 B3
Lewisham High St SE13 201 C5
Lewisham Rd SE13 201 C4
Lewisham St SW1 220 J12
Lewisham Way SE4; SE14 201 C4
Lexington St W1 220 G6
Leyton Grn Rd E10 200 C1
Library St SE1 221 R12
Lilford Rd SE5 201 A4
Lillie Rd SW6 199 C4
Lily Pl EC1 221 Q3
Limeburner La EC4 221 R6
Limeharbour E14 201 C4
Lincoln's Inn WC2 221 N5
Lincoln's Inn Flds WC2 221 M5
Lindsey St EC1 221 S3
Lingfield Av, Kings.T. KT1 199 B6
Links Av, Mord. SM4 199 D6
Lisle St WC2 220 J7
Lisson Gro NW1; NW8 198 D3
Litchfield St WC2 220 J7
Little Albany St NW1 220 E1
Little Argyll St W1 220 F6
Little Britain EC1 221 T5
Little Chester St SW1 220 C13
Little Coll St SW1 221 K13
Little Dean's Yd SW1 220 K13
Little Dorrit Ct SE1 221 U11
Little Ealing La W5 199 B4
Little Essex St WC2 221 P7
Little George St SW1 220 K12
Little Heath SE7 201 D4
Little Ilford La E12 200 D2
Little Marlborough St W1 220 F6
Little Newport St WC2 220 J7
Little New St EC4 221 Q5
Little Portland St W1 220 F5
Little Russell St WC1 220 K4
Little St. James's St SW1 220 F10
Little Sanctuary SW1 220 J12
Little Smith St SW1 220 J13
Little Titchfield St W1 220 F4
Little Trinity La EC4 221 U7
Little Turnstile WC1 221 M5
Liverpool Rd N1; N7 200 A2
Livonia St W1 220 G6
Loampit Hill SE13 201 C4
Loampit Vale SE13 201 C4
Locks La, Mitch. CR4 201 A6
Logs Hill, Brom. BR1; Chis. BR7 201 D6
Loman St SE1 221 S11
Lombard La EC4 221 Q6
Lombard Rd SW11 199 D4
London La, Brom. BR1 201 C6
London Pav, The W1 220 H8
London Rd SE1 221 R13
London Rd SE23 201 B5
London Rd SW16 201 A6
London Rd, Brent. TW8; Houns. TW3; Islw. TW7 199 A4
London Rd, Brom. BR1 201 C6
London Rd, Kings.T. KT2 199 B6
London Rd, Mitch. CR4 199 D6
London Rd, Twick. TW1 199 B5
London Silver Vaults WC2 221 P4
London Trocadero, The W1 220 H8
London Wall EC2 221 U4
Long Acre WC2 220 K7
Longford St NW1 220 E1
Long La EC1 221 S3
Long La SE1 201 B4
Longley Rd SW17 199 D6
Long Rd SW4 201 A5
Long's Ct WC2 220 H7
Longwood Gdns, Ilf. IG5 200 D1
Long Yd WC1 221 M2
Lonsdale Av E6 200 D3
Lord N St SW1 220 K14
Lordship La N17; N22 200 A1
Lordship La SE22 201 B5
Lordship Pk N16 200 B2
Lothian Rd SW9 201 A4
Loughborough Rd SW9 201 A4
Love La EC2 221 U5
Lover's Wk W1 220 B9
Lower Belgrave St SW1 220 D14
Lower Boston Rd W7 199 A4
Lower Clapton Rd E5 200 B2
Lower Grosvenor Pl SW1 220 D13
Lower James St W1 220 G7
Lower John St W1 220 G7
Lower Lea Crossing E14; E16 200 C3
Lower Marsh SE1 221 P12
Lower Mortlake Rd, Rich. TW9 199 B5
Lower Richmond Rd SW14; Rich. TW9 199 B5
Lower Richmond Rd SW15 199 C5
Lower Rd SE16 201 B4
Lower Rd, Har. HA2 198 A2
Lower Sunbury Rd, Hmptn. TW12 199 A6
Lower Teddington Rd, Kings.T. KT1 199 B6
Lowlands Rd, Har. HA1 198 A2
Lowndes Cl SW1 220 C14
Lowndes Ct W1 220 F6
Lowndes Pl SW1 220 B14
Lowndes Sq SW1 220 A12
Lowndes St SW1 220 A13
Ludgate Bdy EC4 221 R6
Ludgate Circ EC4 221 R6
Ludgate Hill EC4 221 R6
Ludgate Sq EC4 221 S6
Ludlow St EC1 221 T1
Lumley Ct WC2 221 L8
Lumley St W1 220 C6
Luxborough St W1 220 B3
Lyall Ms SW1 220 B14
Lyall Ms W SW1 220 B14
Lyall St SW1 220 B14
Lygon Pl SW1 220 D14
Lyttleton Rd N8 198 D1

M

McAuley Cl SE1 221 P13
Macclesfield St W1 220 J7
McCoid Way SE1 221 T12
Macfarren Pl NW1 220 C2
Mackenzie Rd N7 200 A2
Macklin St WC2 221 L5
Mac's Pl EC4 221 P5
Maddox St W1 220 E7
Madeley Rd W5 198 B3
Magdalen Rd SW18 199 D5
Magpie All EC4 221 Q6
Maida Vale W9 198 D3
Maiden La SE1 221 U9
Maiden La WC2 221 L8
Maidstone Bldgs Ms SE1 221 U10
Major Rd E15 200 C2
Malden Rd NW5 198 D2
Malet Pl WC1 220 H2
Malet St WC1 220 H2
Mall, The SW1 220 G11
Mall, The W5 198 B3
Mall, The, Har. HA3 198 B1
Malpas Rd SE4 201 C5
Malta St EC1 221 S1
Maltravers St WC2 221 N7
Manchester Ms W1 220 B4
Manchester Rd E14 201 C4
Manchester Sq W1 220 B5
Manchester St W1 220 B4
Mandeville Pl W1 220 C5
Mandeville Rd, Nthlt. UB5 198 A2
Manette St W1 220 J6
Manor Fm Rd, Wem. HA0 198 B3
Manor Pk Rd NW10 198 C3
Manor Rd E16 200 C3
Manor Rd N16 200 B2
Manor Rd, Chig. IG7 200 D1
Manor Rd, Mitch. CR4 201 A6
Manor Rd, Rich. TW9 199 B5
Mansfield Ms W1 220 D4
Mansfield Rd NW3 198 D2
Mansfield St W1 220 D4
Mapesbury Rd NW2 198 D2
Maple Pl W1 220 G2
Maple St W1 220 F3
Marble Arch W1 220 A7
Marchmont St WC1 220 K1
Mare St E8 200 B3
Margaret Ct W1 220 F5
Margaret St W1 220 E5
Marigold All SE1 221 R8
Market Ct W1 220 F5
Market Ms W1 220 D10
Market Pl W1 220 F5
Market Rd N7 200 A2
Markhouse Rd E17 200 C1
Marlborough Ct W1 220 F6
Marlborough Rd SW1 220 G10
Marshall St W1 220 G6
Marshalsea Rd SE1 221 U11
Marsham St SW1 220 J14
Marshgate La E15 200 C2
Marsh Rd, Pnr. HA5 198 A1
Marsh Wall E14 201 C4
Martindale Rd, Houns. TW4 199 A5
Martin Way SW20; Mord. SM4 199 D6
Marlett Ct WC2 221 L6
Marylebone High St W1 220 C3
Marylebone La W1 220 D6
Marylebone Ms W1 220 D4
Marylebone Pas W1 220 G5
Marylebone Rd NW1 198 D3
Marylebone St W1 220 C4
Masons Arms Ms W1 220 E6
Masons Hill, Brom. BR1 201 D6
Mason's Yd SW1 220 G9
Matthew Parker St SW1 220 J12
Matthews Yd WC2 221 K6
Matthias Rd N16 200 B2
Mayes Rd N22 200 A1
Mayfair Pl W1 220 E9
Mayow Rd SE23; SE26 201 B5
Mays Ct WC2 220 K8
Maze Hill SE3; SE10 201 C4
Meadow Row SE1 221 T14
Mead Row SE1 221 P13
Meard St W1 220 H6
Mecklenburgh Pl WC1 221 M1
Mecklenburgh Sq WC1 221 M1
Mecklenburgh St WC1 221 M1
Medway St SW1 220 J14
Melbourne Pl WC2 221 N7
Melcombe St NW1 220 A2
Melfort Rd, Th.Hth. CR7 201 A6
Memel Ct EC1 221 T2
Memel St EC1 221 T2
Mepham St SE1 221 N10
Merantun Way SW19 199 D6
Mercer St WC2 220 K6
Merrick Rd, Sthl. UB2 199 A4
Merrick Sq SE1 221 U13
Merton Rd SW18 199 D5
Merton Rd SW19 199 D6
Meymott St SE1 221 R10
Middle La N8 200 A1
Middle Pk Av SE9 201 D5
Middlesex Pas EC1 221 S4
Middle St EC1 221 T3
Middle Temple EC4 221 P7
Middle Temple La EC4 221 P6
Middleton Pl W1 220 F4
Midford Pl W1 220 G2
Milcote St SE1 221 R12
Mildmay Pk N1 200 B2
Mile End Rd E1; E3 200 C3
Milford La WC2 221 N7
Milk St EC2 221 U6
Milkwood Rd SE24 201 A5
Millbank SW1 221 K14
Millennium Br EC4 221 T7
Millennium Br SE1 221 T7
Miller Wk SE1 221 Q10
Mill Hill Rd SW13 199 C4
Mill La NW6 198 D2
Millman Ms WC1 221 M2
Millman St WC1 221 M2
Mill St W1 220 E7
Milroy Wk SE1 221 R9
Mint St SE1 221 T11
Mitcham La SW16 201 A6
Mitcham Rd SW17 199 D6
Mitchell St EC1 221 T1
Mitre Ct EC2 221 U5
Mitre Ct EC4 221 Q6
Mitre Rd SE1 221 Q11
Mogden La, Islw. TW7 199 A5
Monck St SW1 220 J14
Monkwell Sq EC2 221 U4
Monmouth St WC2 220 K6
Montague Pl WC1 220 J3
Montague St EC1 221 T4
Montague St WC1 220 K3
Montagu Mans W1 220 A3
Montagu Ms N W1 220 A4
Montagu Ms S W1 220 A5
Montagu Ms W W1 220 A5
Montagu Row W1 220 A4
Montagu Sq W1 220 A4
Montagu St W1 220 A5
Montreal Pl WC2 221 M7
Montrose Pl SW1 220 C12
Monument Way N17 200 B1
Moor St W1 220 J6
Morden Hall Rd, Mord. SM4 199 D6
Morden Rd SW19 199 D6

Morden Rd, Mitch. CR4 199 D6
Morley St SE1 221 Q13
Morning La E9 200 B2
Mornington Rd, Grnf. UB6 198 A3
Morpeth Ter SW1 220 F14
Mortimer Mkt WC1 220 G2
Mortimer Rd NW10 198 C3
Mortimer St W1 220 F5
Mortlake High St SW14 199 C4
Mortlake Rd, Rich. TW9 199 B4
Morton Pl SE1 221 P14
Morwell St WC1 220 J4
Mostyn Rd SW19 199 D6
Motcomb St SW1 220 A13
Mottingham La SE9; SE12 201 D5
Mottingham Rd SE9 201 D5
Mount Pleasant WC1 221 N2
Mount Pleasant Rd N17 200 B1
Mount Row W1 220 D8
Mount St W1 220 C8
Moxon St W1 220 B4
Mumford Ct EC2 221 U5
Murphy St SE1 221 P12
Museum St WC1 220 K4
Muswell Hill N10 200 A1
Muswell Hill Rd N6; N10 200 A1

N

Nag's Head Ct EC1 221 T2
Nassau St W1 220 F4
Neal St WC2 220 K6
Neal's Yd WC2 220 K6
Neasden La NW10 198 C2
Nelson Rd E4 200 C1
Nelson Rd, Houns. TW3, TW4; Twick. TW2 199 A5
Nelson Sq SE1 221 R11
Nether St N3; N12 198 D1
New Barn St E13 200 D3
New Bond St W1 220 D6
New Br St EC4 221 R6
Newburgh St W1 220 F6
New Burlington Ms W1 220 F7
New Burlington Pl W1 220 F7
New Burlington St W1 220 F7
Newbury St EC1 221 T4
Newcastle Cl EC4 221 R5
Newcastle Row EC1 221 Q1
New Cavendish St W1 220 E3
New Change EC4 221 T6
New City Rd E13 200 D3
New Compton St WC2 220 J6
New Ct EC4 221 P7
New Cross Rd SE14 201 B4
New Fetter La EC4 221 Q5
Newgate St EC1 221 S5
New Globe Wk SE1 221 T9
Newham Way E6; E16 200 D3
Newington Causeway SE1 221 S14
New Inn Pas WC2 221 N6
New Kent Rd SE1 221 T14
New Kings Rd SW6 199 D4
Newlands Pk SE26 201 B6
Newman Pas W1 220 G4
Newman's Row WC2 221 N4
Newman St W1 220 G4
Newman Yd W1 220 G5
Newnham Ter SE1 221 P13
New N Rd N1 200 B2
New N St WC1 221 M3
New Oxford St WC1 220 J5
New Plaistow Rd E15 200 C3
Newport Ct WC2 220 J7
Newport Pl WC2 220 J7
New Quebec St W1 220 A6
New Rd E1 200 B3
New Rd, W.Mol. KT8 199 A6
New Row WC2 220 K7
New Sq WC2 221 N5
New St Sq EC4 221 Q5
Newton St WC2 221 L5
New Turnstile WC1 221 M4
New Wanstead E11 200 C2
Nicholson St SE1 221 R10
Nightingale La SW4; SW12 199 D5
Nightingale Pl SE18 201 D4
Nine Elms La SW8 201 A4
Noble St EC2 221 T5
Noel Rd W3 198 B3
Noel St W1 220 G6
Norbury Cres SW16 201 A6
Norbury Hill SW16 201 A6
Norris St SW1 220 H8
North Acton Rd NW10 198 C3
Northampton Rd EC1 221 Q1
North Audley St W1 220 B6
Northborough Rd SW16 201 A6
Northburgh St EC1 221 S1
Northcote Rd SW11 199 D5
North Cres WC1 220 H3
North End Rd NW11 198 D2
North End Rd SW6; W14 199 D4
Northern Relief Rd, Bark. IG11 200 D2
Northfield Av W5; W13 198 B3
North Hill N6 200 A1
Northington St WC1 221 M2
North Ms WC1 221 N2
Northolt Rd, Har. HA2 198 A2
Northover, Brom. BR1 201 C5
North Rd N6 200 A1
North Row W1 220 A7
North St SW4 201 A5
Northumberland Av WC2 220 K9
Northumberland St WC2 221 K9
Northwold Rd E5; N16 200 B2
Northwood Rd, Th.Hth. CR7 201 B6
North Woolwich Rd E16 200 D3
Norwich St EC4 221 P5
Norwood High St SE27 201 B5
Norwood Rd SE24; SE27 201 A5
Norwood Rd, Sthl. UB2 199 A4
Nottingham Ct WC2 221 K6
Nottingham Pl W1 220 B2
Nottingham St W1 220 B3
Nottingham Ter NW1 220 B2
Notting Hill Gate W11 198 D3
Nunhead La SE15 201 B5

O

Oak Av, Hmptn. TW12 199 A6
Oakey La SE1 221 P13
Oak Hill, Wdf.Grn. IG8 200 C1
Oakley St SW3 199 D4
Oakwood Av, Beck. BR3 201 C6
Oat La EC2 221 T5
Odhams Wk WC2 221 L6
Ogle St W1 220 F3
Old Bailey EC4 221 S6
Old Barrack Yd SW1 220 B11
Old Bond St W1 220 F8
Old Brewers Yd WC2 221 K6
Old Brompton Rd SW5; SW7 199 D4
Old Bldgs WC2 221 P5
Old Burlington St W1 220 F7
Oldbury Pl W1 220 C3
Old Cavendish St W1 220 D5
Old Compton St W1 220 H7
Oldfield La N, Grnf. UB6 198 A3
Old Fish St Hill EC4 221 T7
Old Fleet La EC4 221 R5
Old Ford Rd E2; E3 200 B3
Old Gloucester St WC1 221 L3
Old Hill, Chis. BR7 201 D6
Old Kent Rd SE1; SE15 201 B4
Old N St WC1 221 M3
Old Oak Common La NW10; W3 198 C3
Old Oak La NW10 198 C3
Old Oak Rd W3 198 C3
Old Palace Yd SW1 221 K13
Old Pk La W1 220 C10
Old Pye St SW1 220 H13
Old Quebec St W1 220 A6
Old Queen St SW1 220 J12
Old Seacoal La EC4 221 R5
Old Sq WC2 221 N5
Old St EC1 221 T1
Old Town SW4 201 A5
O'Meara St SE1 221 U10
Onslow St EC1 221 Q2
Ontario St SE1 221 S14
Orange St WC2 220 H8
Orange Yd W1 220 J6
Orchard St W1 220 B6
Orde Hall St WC1 221 M2
Ormond Cl WC1 221 L3
Ormond Ms WC1 221 L2
Ormond Yd SW1 220 G9
Osnaburgh St NW1 220 E2
Osnaburgh Ter NW1 220 E1
Ossington Bldgs W1 220 B3
Ossulton Way N2 198 D1
Outer Circle NW1 220 B2
Oxendon St SW1 220 H8
Oxford Circ Av W1 220 F6
Oxford St W1 220 G5
Oxo Twr Wf SE1 221 Q8

P

Paddenswick Rd W6 199 C4
Paddington St W1 220 B3
Pageantmaster Ct EC4 221 R6
Page Heath La, Brom. BR1 201 D6
Page St NW7 198 C1
Palace Pl SW1 220 F13
Palace St SW1 220 F13
Pall Mall SW1 220 G10
Pall Mall E SW1 220 J9
Palmerston Rd N22 200 A1
Palmer St SW1 220 H12
Pancras La EC4 221 U6
Pancras Rd NW1 200 A3
Panton St SW1 220 H8
Panyer All EC4 221 T6
Parchmore Rd, Th.Hth. CR7 201 B6
Pardon St EC1 221 S1
Paris Gdn SE1 221 R9
Parish La SE20 201 B6
Park Av N22 200 A1
Park Cres W1 220 D2
Park Cres Ms E W1 220 E2
Park Cres Ms W W1 220 D3
Parker Ms WC2 221 L5
Parker St WC2 221 L5
Parkhurst Rd N7 200 A2
Park La W1 220 C10
Park La, Wem. HA9 198 B2
Park Pl SW1 220 F10
Park Rd N8 200 A1
Park Rd NW1; NW8 198 D3
Park Rd, Hmptn. TW12 199 A6
Park Rd (Hampton Wick), Kings.T. KT1 199 B6
Park Rd, Kings.T. KT2 199 B6
Park Rd, Tedd. TW11 199 A6
Park Royal Rd NW10; W3 198 C3
Parkside SW19 199 C5
Parkside Way, Har. HA2 198 A1
Park Sq E NW1 220 D1
Park Sq Ms NW1 220 D2
Park Sq W NW1 220 D1
Park St SE1 221 T9
Park St W1 220 B7
Parliament Sq SW1 220 K12
Parliament St SW1 221 K12
Parmoor Ct EC1 221 T1
Parnell Rd E3 200 C3
Parson St NW4 198 C1
Passing All EC1 221 S2
Paternoster Row EC4 221 T6
Paternoster Sq EC4 221 S6
Paul's Wk EC4 221 S7
Pavilion Rd SW1 220 A14
Pavilion St SW1 220 A14
Peabody Dws WC1 220 K1
Peabody Est EC1 221 U2
Peabody Est SE1 221 Q10
Peabody Sq SE1 221 R12
Peabody Trust SE1 221 T10
Pearman St SE1 221 Q13
Pear Pl SE1 221 P11
Pear Tree Ct EC1 221 Q2
Pear Tree St EC1 221 S1
Peckham High St SE15 201 B4
Peckham Hill St SE15 201 B4
Peckham Pk Rd SE15 201 B4
Peckham Rd SE5; SE15 201 B4
Peckham Rye SE15; SE22 201 B5
Pemberton Row EC4 221 Q5
Pembroke Cl SW1 220 C12
Pembury Rd E5 200 B2
Penge Rd SE20; SE25 201 B6
Penhurst Pl SE1 221 N14
Penrhyn Rd, Kings.T. KT1 199 B6
Pentonville Rd N1 200 A3
Pepper St SE1 221 T11
Percival St EC1 221 R1
Percy Ms W1 220 H4
Percy Pas W1 220 G4
Percy Rd, Hmptn. TW12 199 A6
Percy Rd, Twick. TW2 199 A5
Percy St W1 220 H4
Perkin's Rents SW1 220 H13
Perkins Sq SE1 221 U9
Perry Hill SE6 201 C5
Perry Ri SE23 201 C5
Perrys Pl W1 220 H5
Perry Vale SE23 201 B5
Perth Rd, Ilf. IG2 200 D1
Petersham Rd, Rich. TW10 199 B5
Peters Hill EC4 221 T7
Peter's La EC1 221 S3
Peter St W1 220 G7
Peto Pl NW1 220 E1
Petts Hill, Nthlt. UB5 198 A2
Petty France SW1 220 G13
Philip La N15 200 B1
Phipp's Ms SW1 220 E14
Phoenix Pl WC1 221 N1
Phoenix St WC2 220 J6
Piccadilly W1 220 E10
Piccadilly Arc SW1 220 F9
Piccadilly Circ W1 220 H8
Piccadilly Pl W1 220 G8
Pickering Pl SW1 220 G10
Pickwick St SE1 221 T12
Picton Pl W1 220 C6
Pilgrim St EC4 221 R6
Pimlico Rd SW1 201 A4
Pineapple Ct SW1 220 F13
Pine St EC1 221 P1
Pinner Rd, Har. HA1 198 A1
Pinner Rd, Pnr. HA5 198 A1
Pinner Vw, Har. HA1, HA2 198 A1
Pitfield St N1 200 B3
Pitshanger La W5 198 B3
Pitt's Head Ms W1 220 C10
Plaistow La, Brom. BR1 201 D6
Plaistow Rd E13; E15 200 C3
Plashet Gro E6 200 D2
Plashet Rd E13 200 D3
Playhouse Yd EC4 221 R6
Plaza Shop Cen, The W1 220 G5
Pleydell Ct EC4 221 Q6
Pleydell St EC4 221 Q6
Plough La SW17; SW19 199 D6
Plough Pl EC4 221 Q5
Plough Way SE16 201 B4
Plumstead Common Rd SE18 201 D4
Plumstead Rd SE18 201 D4
Plumtree Ct EC4 221 Q5
Pocock St SE1 221 R11
Poland St W1 220 G6
Pollen St W1 220 E6
Pomeroy St SE14 201 B4
Pontypool Pl SE1 221 R11
Pooles Bldgs EC1 221 P2
Popes La W5 199 B4
Poplar High St E14 200 C3
Poppins Ct EC4 221 R6
Porter St SE1 221 U9
Porter St W1 220 A3
Portland Ms W1 220 G6
Portland Pl W1 220 E4
Portland Rd SE25 201 B6
Portman Cl W1 220 A5
Portman Ms S W1 220 B6
Portman Sq W1 220 A5
Portman St W1 220 B6
Portpool La EC1 221 P3
Portsmouth St WC2 221 M6
Portugal St WC2 221 M6
Pound La NW10 198 C2
Powder Mill La, Twick. TW2 199 A5
Powis Pl WC1 221 L2
Poynders Rd SW4 201 A5
Praed St W2 198 D3
Preston Hill, Har. HA3 198 B2
Preston Rd, Har. HA3; Wem. HA9 198 B2
Prestons Rd E14 201 C4
Price's St SE1 221 S10
Priest Ct EC2 221 T5
Primrose Hill EC4 221 Q6
Prince Albert Rd NW1; NW8 198 D3
Prince Imperial Rd, Chis. BR7 201 D6
Prince of Wales Rd SE3 201 C4
Prince Regent La E13; E16 200 D3
Prince's Arc SW1 220 G9
Princes Pl SW1 220 G9
Princess St SE1 221 S14
Princes St W1 220 E6
Princeton St WC1 221 M3
Printers Inn Ct EC4 221 P5
Printer St EC4 221 Q5
Priory La SW15 199 C5
Priory Rd N8 200 A1
Procter St WC1 221 M4
Providence Ct W1 220 C7
Prudent Pas EC2 221 U5
Puddle Dock EC4 221 S7
Pump Ct EC4 221 P6
Pursley Rd NW7 198 C1
Putney Br Rd SW15; SW18 199 D5
Putney Heath SW15 199 C5
Putney High St SW15 199 C5
Putney Hill SW15 199 C5

Q

Quadrant Arc W1 220 G8
Quality Ct WC2 221 P5
Quebec Ms W1 220 A6
Queen Anne Av, Brom. BR2 201 C6
Queen Anne Ms W1 220 E4
Queen Anne's Gate SW1 220 H12
Queen Anne St W1 220 D5
Queenhithe EC4 221 U7
Queensbridge Rd E2; E8 200 B2
Queens Dr W3; W5 198 B3
Queen's Head Pas EC4 221 T5
Queen Sq WC1 221 L2
Queen Sq Pl WC1 221 L2
Queens Ride SW13; SW15 199 C5
Queens Rd NW4 198 C1
Queens Rd SE14; SE15 201 B4
Queens Rd, Kings.T. KT2 199 B6
Queens Rd, Rich. TW10 199 B5
Queen's Rd, Tedd. TW11 199 A6
Queenstown Rd SW8 201 A4
Queen St EC4 221 U7
Queen St W1 220 D9
Queen St Pl EC4 221 U8
Queen's Wk SE1 221 M10
Queen's Wk SW1 220 F10
Queens Yd WC1 220 G2
Queen Victoria St EC4 221 S7
Quilp St SE1 221 T11

R

Railton Rd SE24 201 A5
Ramillies Pl W1 220 F6
Ramillies St W1 220 F6
Rancliffe Rd E6 200 D3
Rathbone Pl W1 220 H5
Rathbone St W1 220 G4
Ravensbourne Av, Beck. BR3; Brom. BR2 201 C6
Raymond Bldgs WC1 221 N3
Raymouth Rd SE16 201 B4
Rayners La, Har. HA2; Pnr. HA5 198 A1
Ray St EC1 221 Q2
Ray St Br EC1 221 Q2
Rectory La SW17 201 A6
Rectory Rd N16 200 B2
Rectory Rd, Beck. BR3 201 C6
Redbridge La E, Ilf. IG4 200 D1
Redcliffe Gdns SW5; SW10 199 D4
Redcross Way SE1 221 U11
Red Hill, Chis. BR7 201 D6
Red Lion Ct EC4 221 Q5
Red Lion Sq WC1 221 M4
Red Lion St WC1 221 M3
Red Lion Yd W1 220 C9
Red Pl W1 220 B7
Redriff Rd SE16 201 B4
Reeves Ms W1 220 B8
Regent Pl W1 220 G7
Regents Pk Rd N3 198 D1
Regent St SW1 220 H8
Regent St W1 220 E5
Regnart Bldgs NW1 220 G1
Remnant St WC2 221 M5
Rennie St SE1 221 R9
Repository Rd SE18 201 D4
Rex Pl W1 220 C8
Richardson's Ms W1 220 F2
Richbell Pl WC1 221 M3
Richmond Bldgs W1 220 H6
Richmond Hill, Rich. TW10 199 B5
Richmond Ms W1 220 H6
Richmond Rd, Kings.T. KT2 199 B6
Richmond Rd, Twick. TW1 199 B5
Richmond Ter SW1 221 K11
Ridgeway, The (North Harrow), Har. HA2 198 A1
Ridgmount Gdns WC1 220 H2
Ridgmount Pl WC1 220 H3
Ridgmount St WC1 220 H3
Ridgway SW19 199 C6
Riding Ho St W1 220 F4
Risborough St SE1 221 S11
Rising Sun Ct EC1 221 S4
Riverside Dr, Rich. TW10 199 B5
Robert Adam St W1 220 B5
Roberts Ms SW1 220 B14
Robert's Pl EC1 221 Q1
Robert St WC2 221 L8
Robin Hood Way (Kingston Bypass) SW15; SW20 199 C5
Rochester St SW1 220 H14
Rochester Way SE3; SE9 201 D5
Rochester Way Relief Rd SE3; SE9 201 D4
Rockingham Est SE1 221 T14
Rockingham St SE1 221 T14
Rocks La SW13 199 C5
Rodmarton St W1 220 A4
Rodney Rd SE17 201 B4
Roe Grn NW9 198 C1
Roehampton La SW15 199 C5
Roehampton Vale SW15 199 C5
Roger St WC1 221 N2
Rolls Bldgs EC4 221 P5
Rolls Pas EC4 221 P5
Rolls Rd SE1 201 B4
Roman Rd E2; E3 200 C3
Romford Rd E7; E15 200 C2
Romilly St W1 220 H7
Romney Ms W1 220 B3
Romney St SW1 220 J14
Ron Leighton Way E6 200 D3
Roscoe St EC1 221 U2
Rose All SE1 221 U9
Rose & Crown Ct EC2 221 T5
Rose & Crown Yd SW1 220 G9
Rosebery Av EC1 221 P2
Rosebery Sq EC1 221 P2
Rose St EC4 221 S5
Rose St WC2 221 K7
Rosoman Pl EC1 221 Q1
Rosslyn Hill NW3 198 D2
Rotary St SE1 221 R13
Rotherham Wk SE1 221 R10
Rotherhithe New Rd SE16 201 B4
Rotherhithe Tunnel E1 200 B3
Rotten Row SW1 220 B11
Roundway, The N17 200 B1
Roupell St SE1 221 Q10
Rowan Rd SW16 201 A6
Roxeth Grn Av, Har. HA2 198 A2
Roxeth Hill, Har. HA2 198 A2
Royal Albert Way E16 200 D3
Royal Arc W1 220 F8
Royal Docks Rd E6 200 D3
Royal Hosp Rd SW3 199 D4
Royal Ms, The SW1 220 E13
Royal Opera Arc SW1 220 H9
Royal St SE1 221 N13
Royalty Ms W1 220 H6
Royston Pk Rd, Pnr. HA5 198 A1
Ruckholt Rd E10 200 C2
Rugby St WC1 221 M2
Ruislip Rd E W7; W13; Grnf. UB6 198 A3
Rupert Ct W1 220 H7
Rupert St W1 220 H7
Rushey Grn SE6 201 C5
Rushworth St SE1 221 S11
Russell Ct SW1 220 G10
Russell Sq WC1 220 K2
Russell St WC2 221 L7
Russia Ct EC2 221 U5
Russia Row EC2 221 U6
Rutland Pl EC1 221 T2
Ryder Ct SW1 220 G9
Ryder St SW1 220 G9
Ryder Yd SW1 220 G9
Rye La SE15 201 B4

S

Sackville St W1 220 G8
Saddle Yd W1 220 D9
Saffron Hill EC1 221 Q2
Saffron St EC1 221 Q3
St. Albans Ct EC2 221 U5
St. Albans St SW1 220 H8
St. Alphage Gdns EC2 221 U4
St. Andrew's Hill EC4 221 S7
St. Andrews Pl NW1 220 E1
St. Andrew St EC4 221 Q4
St. Anne's Ct W1 220 H6
St. Ann's Hill SW18 199 D5
St. Ann's La SW1 220 J13
St. Ann's Rd N15 200 B1
St. Ann's St SW1 220 J13
St. Anselm's Pl W1 220 D6
St. Brides Av EC4 221 R6
St. Bride's Pas EC4 221 R6
St. Bride St EC4 221 R5
St. Christopher's Pl W1 220 C5
St. Clement's La WC2 221 N6
St. Cross St EC1 221 Q3
St. Ermin's Hill SW1 220 H13
St. Georges Circ SE1 221 R13
St. Georges Ct EC4 221 R5
St. Georges Ms SE1 221 Q13
St. Georges Rd E7 200 D2
St. Georges Rd SE1 221 Q13
St. George St W1 220 E6
St. Giles High St WC2 220 J5
St. Giles Pas WC2 220 J6
St. James's Ct SW1 220 G13
St. James's Dr SW12; SW17 199 D5
St. James's Mkt SW1 220 H8
St. James's Palace SW1 220 G11
St. James's Pk SW1 220 H11
St. James's Pl SW1 220 F10
St. James's Rd SE1; SE16 201 B4
St. James's Sq SW1 220 G9
St. James's St SW1 220 F9
St. James's Wk EC1 221 R1
St. John's Hill SW11 199 D5
St. John's La EC1 221 R2
St. John's Path EC1 221 R2
St. John's Pl EC1 221 R2
St. John's Rd, Islw. TW7 199 A4
St. John's Sq EC1 221 R2
St. John St EC1 221 S2
St. John's Wd Rd NW8 198 D3
St. Luke's Cl EC1 221 U1
St. Margaret's Ct SE1 221 U10
St. Margarets Rd, Twick. TW1 199 B5
St. Margaret's St SW1 221 K12
St. Martin's La WC2 220 K7
St. Martin's-le-Grand EC1 221 T5
St. Martin's Ms WC2 220 K8
St. Martin's Pl WC2 220 K8
St. Martin's St WC2 220 J8
St. Mary's Rd SW19 199 D6
St. Mary's Rd W5 199 B4
St. Matthew St SW1 220 H14
St. Mildreds Rd SE12 201 C5
St. Paul's Chyd EC4 221 S6
St. Paul's Rd N1 200 A2
St. Paul's Way E3; E14 200 C3
St. Quintin Av W10 198 C3
St. Vincent St W1 220 C4
Salisbury Ct EC4 221 R6
Salisbury Sq EC4 221 Q6
Salmon St NW9 198 B2
Salter Rd SE16 201 B4
Salters Hill SE19 201 B6
Salusbury Rd NW6 198 D3
Sanctuary, The SW1 220 J12
Sanctuary St SE1 221 U12
Sandell St SE1 221 P11
Sanders La NW7 198 C1
Sandland St WC1 221 N4
Sandycombe Rd, Rich. TW9 199 B5
Sandy La, Kings.T. KT1; Tedd. TW11 199 B6
Sandy La, Rich. TW10 199 B5
Sanford St SE14 201 C4
Sans Wk EC1 221 Q1
Sapperton Ct EC1 221 T1
Sardinia St WC2 221 M6
Savile Row W1 220 F7
Savoy Bldgs WC2 221 M8
Savoy Ct WC2 221 L8
Savoy Hill WC2 221 M8
Savoy Pl WC2 221 L8
Savoy Row WC2 221 M7
Savoy St WC2 221 M7
Savoy Way WC2 221 M8
Sawyer St SE1 221 T11
Scala St W1 220 G3
Scoresby St SE1 221 R10
Scotch Common W13 198 B3
Scotland Pl SW1 221 K9
Scotswood St EC1 221 Q1
Scotts La, Brom. BR2 201 C6
Scovell Cres SE1 221 T12
Scovell Rd SE1 221 T12
Scrubs La NW10; W10 198 C3
Secker St SE1 221 P10
Sedley Pl W1 220 D6
Sekforde St EC1 221 R2
Selwyn Av E4 200 C1
Serjeants Inn EC4 221 Q6
Serle St WC2 221 N5
Sermon La EC4 221 T6
Seven Sisters Rd N4; N7; N15 200 A2
Seville St SW1 220 A12
Seward St EC1 221 S1
Seymour Ms W1 220 B5
Shacklewell La E8 200 B2
Shaftesbury Av W1 220 H7
Shaftesbury Av WC2 220 H7
Shaftesbury Av, Har. HA2 198 A2
Shakespeare Twr EC2 221 U3
Shavers Pl SW1 220 H8
Sheen La SW14 199 C5
Sheen Rd, Rich. TW9 199 B5
Sheepcote Rd, Har. HA1 198 A1
Sheffield St WC2 221 M6
Shelton St WC2 220 K6
Shepherdess Wk N1 200 B3
Shepherd Mkt W1 220 D9
Shepherds Bush Rd W6 199 C4
Shepherds Hill N6 200 A1
Shepherd's Pl W1 220 B7
Shepherd St W1 220 D10
Sheraton St W1 220 H6
Sherlock Ms W1 220 B3
Shernhall St E17 200 C1
Sherwood Pk Rd, Mitch. CR4 201 A6
Sherwood St W1 220 G7
Shirland Rd W9 198 D3
Shoe La EC4 221 Q5
Shooters Hill Rd SE3; SE10; SE18 201 C4
Shoot Up Hill NW2 198 D2
Shortlands Rd, Brom. BR2 201 C6
Shorts Gdns WC2 220 K6
Short St SE1 221 Q11
Shropshire Pl WC1 220 G2
Sicilian Av WC1 221 L4
Sidcup Rd SE9; SE12 201 D5
Siddons La NW1 220 A2
Sidford Pl SE1 221 N14
Sidmouth Rd NW2 198 C2
Sidney St E1 200 B3
Silex St SE1 221 S12
Silk St EC2 221 U3
Silver Pl W1 220 G7
Silverthorne Rd SW8 201 A4
Silvertown Way E16 200 C3
Silvester St SE1 221 U12
Skinners La EC4 221 U7
Slingsby Pl WC2 220 K7
Sloane St SW1 220 A13
Smart's Pl WC2 221 L5
Smithfield St EC1 221 R4
Smith's Ct W1 220 G7
Smith Sq SW1 220 K14
Smokehouse Yd EC1 221 S3
Snakes La E, Wdf.Grn. IG8 200 D1
Snakes La W, Wdf.Grn. IG8 200 D1
Snaresbrook Rd E11 200 C1
Snow Hill EC1 221 R4
Snow Hill Ct EC1 221 S5
Soho Sq W1 220 H5
Soho St W1 220 H5
Somerset Rd, Sthl. UB1 198 A3
Southampton Bldgs WC2 221 P5
Southampton Pl WC1 221 L4
Southampton Row WC1 221 L3
Southampton St WC2 221 L7
Southampton Way SE5 201 B4
South Audley St W1 220 C8
Southborough Rd, Brom. BR1 201 D6
South Circular Rd SW2 201 A5
South Cres WC1 220 H4
Southcroft Rd SW16; SW17 201 A6

South Croxted Rd SE21 201 B5
South Ealing Rd W5 199 B4
Southend La SE6; SE26 201 C6
Southend Rd E4; E17; E18 200 C1
Southend Rd, Beck. BR3 201 C6
Southfield Rd W4 199 C4
Southgate Rd N1 200 B3
South Hill Av, Har. HA1, HA2 198 A2
South Lambeth Rd SW8 201 A4
Southlands Rd, Brom. BR1, BR2 201 D6
South La, N.Mal. KT3 199 C6
South Lo Av, Mitch. CR4 201 A6
South Molton La W1 220 D6
South Molton St W1 220 D6
South Norwood Hill SE25 201 B6
Southover, Brom. BR1 201 D6
South Par W4 199 C4
South Rd, Sthl. UB1 199 A4
South Sq WC1 221 P4
South St W1 220 C9
South St, Islw. TW7 199 B5
Southwark Br EC4 221 U9
Southwark Br SE1 221 U9
Southwark Br Rd SE1 221 S13
Southwark Pk Rd SE16 201 B4
Southwark St SE1 221 S9
South Woodford to Barking Relief Rd E11; E12; E18; Bark. IG11; Ilf. IG1 200 D1
Southwood La, 200 A2
Spafield St EC1 221 P1
Spa Hill SE19 201 B6
Spaniards Rd NW3 198 D2
Spanish Pl W1 220 C5
Spencer Pk SW18 199 D5
Spenser St SW1 220 G13
Spring Gdns SW1 220 J9
Spring Gro Rd, Houns. TW3; Islw. TW7 199 A4
Spring Ms W1 220 A3
Spur Rd SE1 221 P11
Spur Rd SW1 220 F12
Stable Yd SW1 220 F11
Stable Yd Rd SW1 220 F10
Stacey St WC2 220 J6
Stafford Pl SW1 220 F13
Stafford St W1 220 F9
Stag La NW9 198 B1
Stag Pl SW1 220 F13
Staines Rd, Twick. TW2 199 A5
Staining La EC2 221 U5
Stamford Hill N16 200 B2
Stamford St SE1 221 P10
Stanhope Gate W1 220 C9
Stanhope Row W1 220 D10
Stanley Rd, Tedd. TW11; Twick. TW2 199 A6
Stansfeld Rd E6 200 D3
Stanstead Rd SE6; SE23 201 B5
Stanton Way SE26 201 C6
Staple Inn WC1 221 P4
Staple Inn Bldgs WC1 221 P4
Star & Garter Hill, Rich. TW10 199 B5
Star Yd WC2 221 P5
Station App SE1 221 N10
Station Rd E12 200 D2
Station Rd NW4 198 C1
Station Rd NW10 198 C3
Station Rd SW13 199 C4
Station Rd, Edg. HA8 198 B1
Station Rd, Har. HA1 198 A1
Stedham Pl WC1 220 K5
Stephen Ms W1 220 H4
Stephenson St E16 200 C3
Stephenson Way NW1 220 G1
Stephen St W1 220 H4
Stepney Grn E1 200 B3
Stepney Way E1 200 B3
Stew La EC4 221 T7
Steyne Rd W3 198 B3
Stockwell Rd SW9 201 A4
Stoke Newington Rd N16 200 B2
Stondon Pk SE23 201 C5
Stone Bldgs WC2 221 N4
Stonecutter St EC4 221 R5
Stone Pk Av, Beck. BR3 201 C6
Stones End St SE1 221 T12
Stopford Rd E13 200 D3
Store St WC1 220 H4
Storey's Gate SW1 220 J12
Strand WC2 221 K8
Strand La WC2 221 N7
Stratford Pl W1 220 D6
Strathyre Av SW16 201 A6
Stratton St W1 220 E9
Strawberry Vale, Twick. TW1 199 B5
Streatfield Rd, Har. HA3 198 B1
Streatham Common N SW16 201 A6
Streatham High Rd SW16 201 A5
Streatham Hill SW2 201 A5
Streatham Pl SW2 201 A5
Streatham Rd, Mitch. CR4 201 A6
Streatham St WC1 220 J5
Streatham Vale SW16 201 A6
Strone Rd E7; E12 200 D2
Stroud Grn Rd N4 200 A2
Strutton Grd SW1 220 H13
Studio Pl SW1 220 A12
Stukeley St WC2 221 L5
Sturge St SE1 221 T11
Sudbury Hill, Har. HA1 198 A2
Sudrey St SE1 221 T12
Suffolk Pl SW1 220 J9
Suffolk St SW1 220 J9
Summer Hill, Chis. BR7 201 D6
Summers La N12 198 D1
Summer St EC1 221 P2
Sumner St SE1 221 S9
Sunray Av SE24 201 B5
Surbiton Rd, Kings.T. KT1 199 B6
Surrey Canal Rd SE14; SE15 201 B4
Surrey Lo SE1 221 P14
Surrey Quays Rd SE16 201 B4
Surrey Row SE1 221 R11
Surrey St WC2 221 N7
Sussex Gdns W2 198 D3
Sutton La EC1 221 S2
Sutton La, Houns. TW3 199 A5
Sutton Row W1 220 J5
Sutton's Way EC1 221 U2
Sutton Wk SE1 221 N10
Swallow Pas W1 220 E6
Swallow Pl W1 220 E6
Swallow St W1 220 G8
Swandon Way SW18 199 D5
Swan Rd (Hanworth), Felt. TW13 199 A6
Swan St SE1 221 U13
Swiss Ct W1 220 J8
Sycamore St EC1 221 T2
Sydenham Hill SE23; SE26 201 B5
Sydenham Rd SE26 201 B6
Sydney St SW3 199 D4
Syon La, Islw. TW7 199 A4

T

Talgarth Rd W6; W14 199 C4
Tallis St EC4 221 Q7
Tamworth La, Mitch. CR4 201 A6
Tanswell Est SE1 221 Q12
Tanswell St SE1 221 P12
Tarn St SE1 221 T14
Tavistock Pl WC1 220 J1
Tavistock Sq WC1 220 J1
Tavistock St WC2 221 L7
Taviton St WC1 220 H1
Teignmouth Gdns, Grnf. UB6 198 B3
Temple Av EC4 221 Q7
Temple La EC4 221 Q6
Temple Pl WC2 221 N7
Temple W Ms SE11 221 R14
Tenison Ct W1 220 F7
Tenison Way SE1 221 P10
Tennison Rd SE25 201 B6
Tentelow La, Sthl. UB2 199 A4
Tenterden St W1 220 E6
Terminus Pl SW1 220 E14
Terrace, The SW13 199 C4
Tetherdown N10 200 A1
Thavies Inn EC1 221 Q5
Thayer St W1 220 C4
Theed St SE1 221 P10
Theobald's Rd WC1 221 M3
Thicket Rd SE20 201 B6
Thirleby Rd SW1 220 G14
Thomas Doyle St SE1 221 R13
Thornbury Rd, Islw. TW7 199 A4
Thornhaugh Ms WC1 220 J2
Thornhaugh St WC1 220 J3
Thornton Av SW2 201 A5
Thornton Pl W1 220 A3
Thrale St SE1 221 U10
Three Barrels Wk EC4 221 U7
Three Cups Yd WC1 221 N4
Three Kings Yd W1 220 D7
Thurlow Pk Rd SE21 201 A5
Tilney Ct EC1 221 U1
Tilney St W1 220 C9
Timber St EC1 221 T1
Tiverton St SE1 221 T14
Tollgate Rd E16 200 D3
Tollington Pk N4 200 A2
Tolmers Sq NW1 220 G1
Tomswood Hill, Ilf. IG6 200 D1
Tomswood Rd, Chig. IG7 200 D1
Took's Ct EC4 221 P5
Tooting Bec Rd SW16; SW17 201 A5
Tooting High St SW17 199 D6
Topham St EC1 221 P1
Torrington Pl WC1 220 G3
Torrington Sq WC1 220 J2
Tothill St SW1 220 H12
Tottenham Ct Rd W1 220 G2
Tottenham La N8 200 A1
Tottenham Ms W1 220 G3
Tottenham St W1 220 G4
Toulmin St SE1 221 T12
Tower Br Rd SE1 201 B4
Tower Ct WC2 220 K6
Tower Royal EC4 221 U7
Tower St WC2 220 J6
Trafalgar Av SE15 201 B4
Trafalgar Rd SE10 201 C4
Trafalgar Sq SW1 220 J9
Trafalgar Sq WC2 220 J9
Traps La, N.Mal. KT3 199 C6
Trebeck St W1 220 D9
Treveris St SE1 221 R10
Triangle, The EC1 221 S1
Trig La EC4 221 T7
Trinity Ch Sq SE1 221 U13
Trinity Ri SW2 201 A5
Trinity Rd SW17; SW18 199 D5
Trinity St SE1 221 U12
Trio Pl SE1 221 U12
Triton Sq NW1 220 F1
Trott Rd N10 198 D1
Trump St EC2 221 U6
Trundle St SE1 221 T11
Trundleys Rd SE8 201 B4
Tudor Dr, Kings.T. KT2 199 B6
Tudor St EC4 221 Q7
Tufnell Pk Rd N7; N19 200 A2
Tufton St SW1 220 J13
Tulse Hill SW2 201 A5
Tunmarsh La E13 200 D3
Turk's Head Yd EC1 221 R3
Turnagain La EC4 221 R5
Turnmill St EC1 221 Q2
Turnpike La N8 200 A1
Tweezer's All WC2 221 P7
Twickenham Rd (Hanworth), Felt. TW13 199 A5
Twickenham Rd, Islw. TW7 199 B5
Twickenham Rd, Rich. TW9 199 B5
Twickenham Rd, Tedd. TW11 199 B6
Twyford Av W3 198 B3
Twyford Pl WC2 221 M5
Tyburn Way W1 220 A7
Tyler's Ct W1 220 H6

U

Ufford St SE1 221 Q11
Ulster Pl NW1 220 D2
Ulster Ter NW1 220 D1
Union Jack Club SE1 221 P11
Union Rd SW4; SW8 201 A4
Union St SE1 221 S10
University St WC1 220 G2
Upper Belgrave St SW1 220 C13
Upper Brook St W1 220 B8
Upper Clapton Rd E5 200 B2
Upper Elmers End Rd, Beck. BR3 201 C6
Upper Grosvenor St W1 220 B8
Upper Grd SE1 221 P9
Upper Ham Rd, Rich. TW10 199 B6
Upper James St W1 220 G7
Upper John St W1 220 G7
Upper Marsh SE1 221 N13
Upper N St E14 200 C3
Upper Richmond Rd SW15 199 C5
Upper Richmond Rd W SW14; Rich. TW10 199 C5
Upper Rd E13 200 D2
Upper St. Martin's La WC2 220 K7
Upper St N1 200 A3
Upper Sunbury Rd, Hmptn. TW12 199 A6
Upper Thames St EC4 221 S7
Upper Tooting Rd SW17 199 D6
Upper Tulse Hill SW2 201 A5
Upper Wimpole St W1 220 D3
Upton La E7 200 D2
Uxbridge Rd W3; W5 198 B3
Uxbridge Rd W12 198 C3
Uxbridge Rd, Hmptn. TW12 199 A6
Uxbridge Rd, Har. HA3; Pnr. HA5; Stan. HA7 198 A1
Uxbridge Rd, Sthl. UB1 198 A3

V

Vale, The NW11 198 C2
Vale, The W3 198 C3
Valentine Pl SE1 221 R11
Valentine Row SE1 221 R12
Vallance Rd E1; E2 200 B3
Valley Rd, Brom. BR2 201 C6
Vanbrugh Pk SE3 201 C4
Vandon Pas SW1 220 G13
Vandon St SW1 220 G13
Vauxhall Br Rd SW1 201 A4
Verdant La SE6 201 C5
Verdun Rd SW13 199 C4
Vere St W1 220 D6
Vernon Pl WC1 221 L4
Verulam Bldgs WC1 221 N3
Verulam St WC1 221 P3
Vicarage Cres SW11 199 D4
Vicarage La E15 200 C2
Vicarage Rd E10 200 C2
Victoria Dock Rd E16 200 D3
Victoria Embk EC4 221 M8
Victoria Embk SW1 221 L11
Victoria Embk WC2 221 M8
Victoria Pk Rd E9 200 B3
Victoria Rd NW10; W3 198 C3
Victoria Sq SW1 220 E13
Victoria St SW1 220 F14
Vigo St W1 220 F8
Village, The SE7 201 D4
Village Way SE21 201 B5
Village Way, Beck. BR3 201 C6
Village Way, Pnr. HA5 198 A2
Villiers Rd, Kings.T. KT1 199 B6
Villiers St WC2 221 K8
Vine Hill EC1 221 P2
Vine St W1 220 G8
Vine St Br EC1 221 Q2
Vine Yd SE1 221 U11
Vineyard Wk EC1 221 P1
Vintners Ct EC4 221 U7
Violet Rd E3 200 C3
Virgil St SE1 221 N13
Viscount St EC1 221 T2
Vivian Av NW4 198 C1

W

Waithman St EC4 221 R6
Wakefield St WC1 221 L1
Waldegrave Rd, Tedd. TW11; Twick. TW1 199 A5
Waldram Pk Rd SE23 201 B5
Wales Fm Rd W3 198 C3
Walkers Ct W1 220 H7
Wallis All SE1 221 U11
Wallside EC2 221 U4
Walm La NW2 198 C2
Walterton Rd W9 198 D3
Walton Rd, E.Mol. KT8; Walt. KT12; W.Mol. KT8 199 A6
Walworth Rd SE1; SE17 201 B4
Wandle Rd, Mord. SM4 199 D6
Wandsworth Br Rd SW6 199 D4
Wandsworth High St SW18 199 D5
Wandsworth Rd SW8 201 A5
Wapping High St E1 200 B3
Wardens Gro SE1 221 T10
Wardour Ms W1 220 G6
Wardour St W1 220 H7
Wardrobe Ter EC4 221 S6
Warner St EC1 221 P2
Warner Yd EC1 221 P2
Warren Av, Brom. BR1 201 C6
Warren Ms W1 220 F2
Warren Rd, Kings.T. KT2 199 C6
Warren St W1 220 E2
Warwick Ct WC1 221 N4
Warwick Ho St SW1 220 J9
Warwick La EC4 221 S6
Warwick Pas EC4 221 S5
Warwick Rd W14 199 D4
Warwick Row SW1 220 E13
Warwick Sq EC4 221 S5
Warwick St W1 220 G7
Warwick Yd EC1 221 U2
Waterden Rd E15 200 C2
Watergate EC4 221 R7
Watergate Wk WC2 221 L9
Waterhouse Sq EC1 221 P4
Water La E15 200 C2
Waterloo Br SE1 221 M8
Waterloo Br WC2 221 M8
Waterloo Pl SW1 220 H9
Waterloo Rd SE1 221 P11
Watermead Way N17 200 B1
Water St WC2 221 N7
Watford Way NW4; NW7 198 C1
Watling Av, Edg. HA8 198 C1
Watling Ct EC4 221 U6
Watling St EC4 221 T6
Watts La, Chis. BR7 201 D6
Waverton St W1 220 C9
Webber Row SE1 221 Q13
Webber St SE1 221 Q11
Wedgwood Ms W1 220 J6
Weigall Rd SE12 201 D5
Weighhouse St W1 220 C6
Welbeck St W1 220 D5
Welbeck Way W1 220 D5
Well Ct EC4 221 U6
Weller St SE1 221 T11
Wellesley Rd W4 199 B4
Well Hall Rd SE9 201 D4
Wellington Rd NW8 198 D3
Wellington Rd, Hmptn. TW12 199 A6
Wellington Rd N, Houns. TW4 199 A5
Wellington Rd S, Houns. TW4 199 A5
Wellington St SE18 201 D4
Wellington St WC2 221 L7
Wells Ms W1 220 G4
Wells St W1 220 F4
Well St E9 200 B2
Wells Way SE5 201 B4
Wembley Pk Dr, Wem. HA9 198 B2
Wemborough Rd, Stan. HA7 198 B1
Wesley St W1 220 C4
West Barnes La SW20; N.Mal. KT3 199 C6
Westbourne Gro W2; W11 198 D3
Westbourne Pk Rd W2; W11 198 D3
Westbridge Rd SW11 199 D4
Westbury Av N22 200 A1
West Cen St WC1 221 K5
West End La NW6 198 D2
Western Av W3; W5; Grnf. UB6; Nthlt. UB5; Ruis. HA4; Uxb. UB9, UB10 198 B3
Western Rd SW19; Mitch. CR4 199 D6
Westferry Rd E14 201 C4
West Grn Rd N15 200 A1
West Halkin St SW1 220 B13
West Ham La E15 200 C2
West Harding St EC4 221 Q5
West Heath Rd NW3 198 D2
West Hill SW15; SW18 199 D5
Westhorne Av SE9; SE12 201 D5
Westminster Br SE1 221 L12
Westminster Br SW1 221 L12
Westminster Br Rd SE1 221 N12
Westmoreland St W1 220 C4
Westmount Rd SE9 201 D4
Weston Av, W.Mol. KT8 199 A6
Weston Dr, Stan. HA7 198 B1
West One Shop Cen W1 220 C6
West Poultry Av EC1 221 R4
West Side Common SW19 199 C6
West Smithfield EC1 221 R4
West Sq SE11 221 R14
West St WC2 220 J6
Westway W2; W9; W10; W12 198 C3
Westwood Hill SE26 201 B6
Weymouth Ms W1 220 D3
Weymouth St W1 220 C4
Wheatley St W1 220 C4
Whetstone Pk WC2 221 M5
Whichcote St SE1 221 P10
Whipps Cross Rd E11 200 C1
Whitchurch La, Edg. HA8 198 B1
Whitcomb St WC2 220 J8
Whitechapel Rd E1 200 B3
Whitecross St EC1 221 U1
Whitefoot La, Brom. BR1 201 C5
Whitefriars St EC4 221 Q6
Whitehall SW1 220 K9
Whitehall Ct SW1 221 K10
Whitehall Gdns SW1 221 K10
Whitehall Pl SW1 221 K10
White Hart St EC4 221 S5
White Horse All EC1 221 R3
White Horse Hill, Chis. BR7 201 D6
Whitehorse La SE25 201 B6
White Horse Ms SE1 221 Q13
White Horse St W1 220 D10
White Lion Hill EC4 221 S7
Whitfield Pl W1 220 F2
Whitfield St W1 220 H4
Whittlesey St SE1 221 P10
Whitton Av E, Grnf. UB6 198 A2
Whitton Av W, Grnf. UB6; Nthlt. UB5 198 A2
Whitton Dene, Houns. TW3; Islw. TW7 199 A5
Whitton Rd, Houns. TW3 199 A5
Whitton Rd, Twick. TW1 199 A5
Wickham Rd SE4 201 C5
Wickham Rd, Beck. BR3 201 C6
Wickham Way, Beck. BR3 201 C6
Wick Rd E9 200 B2
Wide Way, Mitch. CR4 201 A6
Widmore Rd, Brom. BR1 201 D6
Wightman Rd N4; N8 200 A1
Wigmore Pl W1 220 D5
Wigmore St W1 220 B6
Wilcox Pl SW1 220 G14
Wild Ct WC2 221 M5
Wild St WC2 221 L6
Wilfred St SW1 220 F13
Willesden La NW2; NW6 198 C2
William Barefoot Dr SE9 201 D6
William IV St WC2 220 K8
William Ms SW1 220 A12
William St SW1 220 A12
Willoughby La N17 200 B1
Willoughby St WC1 220 K4
Willowbrook Rd SE15 201 B4
Wilton Cres SW1 220 B12
Wilton Ms SW1 220 C13
Wilton Pl SW1 220 B12
Wilton Rd SW1 220 E14
Wilton Row SW1 220 B12
Wilton St SW1 220 D13
Wilton Ter SW1 220 B13
Wimbledon Hill Rd SW19 199 C6
Wimbledon Pk Rd SW18; SW19 199 D5
Wimbledon Pk Side SW19 199 C5
Wimpole Ms W1 220 D3
Wimpole St W1 220 D5
Winchelsea Rd NW10 198 C3
Winchester Rd E4 200 C1
Winchester St W3 199 C4
Windmill La, Islw. TW7; Sthl. UB2 199 A4
Windmill Rd SW18 199 D5
Windmill Rd W5; Brent. TW8 199 B4
Windmill St W1 220 H4
Windmill Wk SE1 221 Q10
Windsor Pl SW1 220 G14
Wine Office Ct EC4 221 Q5
Winnett St W1 220 H7
Winn Rd SE12 201 D5
Winsley St W1 220 F5
Winston Way, Ilf. IG1 200 D2
Woburn Pl WC1 220 J1
Woburn Sq WC1 220 J2
Woodbridge St EC1 221 R1
Woodcock Hill, Har. HA3 198 B1
Woodfield Rd W5 198 B3
Woodford Av, Ilf. IG2, IG4; Wdf.Grn. IG8 200 D1
Woodford New Rd E17; E18; Wdf.Grn. IG8 200 C1
Woodford Rd E18 200 D1
Woodgrange Rd E7 200 C2
Woodhayes Rd SW19 199 C6
Wood La NW9 198 C2
Wood La W12 198 C3
Wood La, Islw. TW7 199 A4
Woods Ms W1 220 A7
Woodstock Ms W1 220 C4
Woodstock St W1 220 D6
Wood St E17 200 C1
Wood St EC2 221 U6
Wood St, Kings.T. KT1 199 B6
Wood Vale SE23 201 B5
Woolf Ms WC1 220 J1
Woolstone Rd SE23 201 C5
Woolwich Ch St SE18 201 D4
Woolwich High St SE18 201 D4
Woolwich Manor Way E6; E16 200 D3
Woolwich Rd SE7 201 D4
Wootton St SE1 221 Q11
Worple Rd SW19; SW20 199 C6
Worship St EC2 200 B3
Worton Rd, Islw. TW7 199 A5
Wren St WC1 221 N1
Wrottesley Rd NW10 198 C3
Wybert St NW1 220 E1
Wyndham Rd SE5 201 A4

Y

Yarmouth Pl W1 220 D10
York Br NW1 220 B1
York Bldgs WC2 221 L8
York Gate NW1 220 B2
York Pl WC2 221 L8
York Rd SE1 221 N11
York Rd SW11; SW18 199 D5
Yorkshire Grey Yd WC1 221 M4
York St W1 220 A3
York St, Twick. TW1 199 B5
York Ter E NW1 220 C2
York Ter W NW1 220 B2
York Way N1; N7 200 A2
Young's Bldgs EC1 221 U1

Z

Zoar St SE1 221 T9

Tourist Information Centre: 23 Union Street
Tel: 01224 288828

Albert Quay	C3
Albert Street	B2
Albury Road	C2
Albyn Place	C1
Argyll Place	B1
Ashgrove Road	A1
Ashgrove Road West	A1
Ash-hill Drive	A1
Ashley Road	C1
Back Hilton Road	A1
Baker Street	B2
Beach Boulevard	A3
Bedford Place	A2
Bedford Road	A2
Beechgrove Terrace	B1
Belgrave Terrace	B1
Berryden Road	A2
Blaikie's Quay	C3
Bon-Accord Street	C2
Bonnymuir Place	B1
Bridge Street	B2
Brighton Place	C1
Cairncry Road	A1
Canal Road	A2
Carden Place	C1
Carlton Place	C1
Cattofield Place	A1
Causewayend	A2
Chapel Street	B2
Claremont Street	C1
Clifton Road	A1
College Bounds	A2
College Street	C3
Commerce Street	B3
Commercial Quay	C3
Constitution Street	B3
Cornhill Drive	A1
Cornhill Road	A1
Cornhill Terrace	A1
Cotton Street	B3
Cromwell Road	C1
Crown Street	C2
Desswood Place	C1
Devonshire Road	C1
Elmbank Terrace	A2
Esslemont Avenue	B2
Ferryhill Road	C2
Fonthill Road	C2
Forest Road	C1
Forest Avenue	C1
Fountainhall Road	B1
Froghall Terrace	A2
Gallowgate	B3
George Street	A2
Gillespie Crescent	A1
Gladstone Place	C1
Golf Road	A3
Gordondale Road	B1
Great Southern Road	C2
Great Western Road	C1
Guild Street	C3
Hamilton Place	B1
Hardgate	C2
Hilton Drive	A1
Hilton Street	A1
Holburn Road	C2
Holburn Street	C2

Holland Street	A2
Hutcheon Street	B2
Justice Mill Lane	C2
King's Crescent	A3
King Street	A3
Langstane Place	C2
Leadside Road	B2
Leslie Terrace	A2
Linksfield Road	A3
Loch Street	B2
Maberly Street	B2
Market Street	B3
Menzies Road	C3
Merkland Road East	B3
Mid Stocket Road	B1
Mile-end Avenue	B1
Miller Street	B3
Mount Street	B2
Nelson Street	B3
North Esplanade East	C3
North Esplanade West	C3
Orchard Street	A2
Osborne Place	C1
Palmerston Road	C3
Park Road	A3
Park Street	B3
Pittodrie Place	A3
Pittodrie Street	A3
Powis Place	A2
Powis Terrace	A2
Queens Road	C1
Queens Terrace	C1
Regent Quay	B3
Rosehill Crescent	A1
Rosehill Drive	A1
Rosemount Place	B1
Rose Street	B2
Rubislaw Terrace	C2
St. Swithin Street	C1
Schoolhill	B2
Seaforth Road	A3
Sinclair Road	B2
Skene Square	B2
Skene Street	B2
South Esplanade West	C3
Spital	A3
Springbank Terrace	C2
Spring Gardens	B2
Stanley Street	C1
Sumnybank Road	A2
Sunnyside Road	A2
Union Glen	C2
Union Grove	C1
Union Street	C2
Urquhart Road	B3
Victoria Bridge	C3
Victoria Road	C3
Walker Road	C3
Waterloo Quay	B3
Waverley Place	C1
Well Place	C3
Westburn Drive	A1
Westburn Road	B1
West North Street	B3
Whitehall Place	B1
Whitehall Road	B1
Willowbank Road	C2

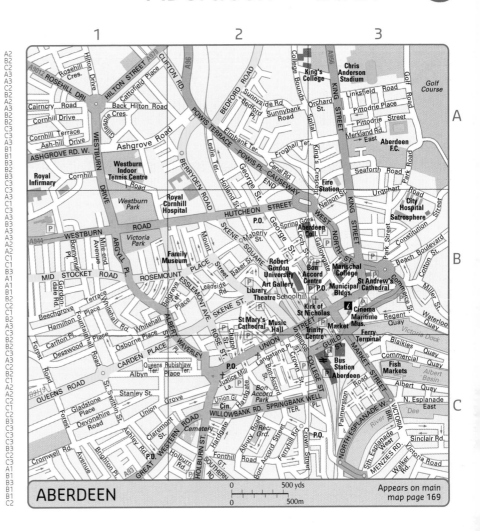

ABERDEEN

| 0 | 500 yds |
| 0 | 500m |

Appears on main
map page 169

Tourist Information Centre: Abbey Chambers, Abbey Churchyard
Tel: 0906 711 2000 (Premium Rate)

Ambury	C1
Archway Street	C3
Argyle Street	B2
Avon Street	B1
Barton Street	B1
Bath Street	B2
Bathwick Hill	A3
Beau Street	B2
Bennett Street	A1
Bridge Street	B2
Broad Quay	C1
Broad Street	A2
Broadway	C3
Brock Street	A1
Chapel Row	B1
Charles Street	B1
Charlotte Street	A1
Cheap Street	B2
Claverton Street	C2
Corn Street	C1
Daniel Street	A3
Darlington Street	A3
Dorchester Street	C2
Edward Street	A3
Excelsior Street	C3
Ferry Lane	B3
Gay Street	A1
George Street	A1
Grand Parade	B2
Great Pulteney Street	A3
Green Park Road	B1
Green Street	A2
Grove Street	A2
Henrietta Gardens	A3
Henrietta Mews	A3
Henrietta Road	A2
Henrietta Street	A2
Henry Street	B2
High Street	B2
Holloway	C1
James Street West	B1
John Street	A1
Kingsmead East	B1
Lansdown Road	A2
Laura Place	A2
Lime Grove	B3
Lime Grove Gardens	B3
Lower Borough Walls	B2
Lower Bristol Road	C1
Magdalen Avenue	C1
Manvers Street	C2
Milk Street	B1
Milsom Street	A2
Monmouth Place	A1
Monmouth Street	B1
Newark Street	C2
New Bond Street	B2
New King Street	B1
New Orchard Street	B2
New Street	B1
North Parade	B2
North Parade Road	B3
Old King Street	A1
Orange Grove	B2
Paragon	A2
Pierrepont Street	B2
Pulteney Crescent	C3

Pulteney Mews	A3
Pulteney Road	B3
Queen Street	B1
Quiet Street	A1
Rossiter Road	C2
St. James's Parade	B1
St. John's Road	A2
St. Marks Road	C2
Sawclose	B1
Southgate Street	C2
Spring Crescent	C3
Stall Street	B2
Sutton Street	A3
Sydney Place	A3
The Circus	A1
Union Street	B2
Upper Borough Walls	B1
Walcot Street	B1
Wells Road	C1
Westgate Buildings	B1
Westgate Street	B1
Wood Street	A1
York Street	B2

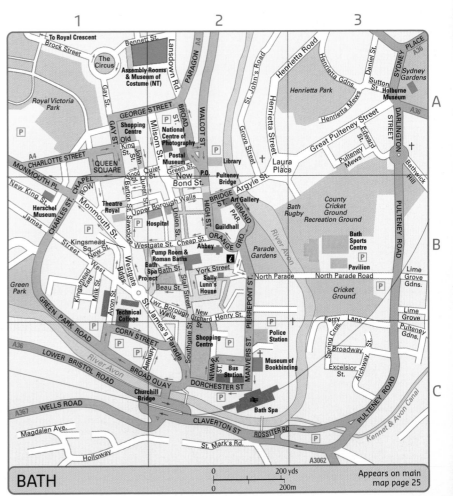

BATH

| 0 | 200 yds |
| 0 | 200m |

Appears on main
map page 25

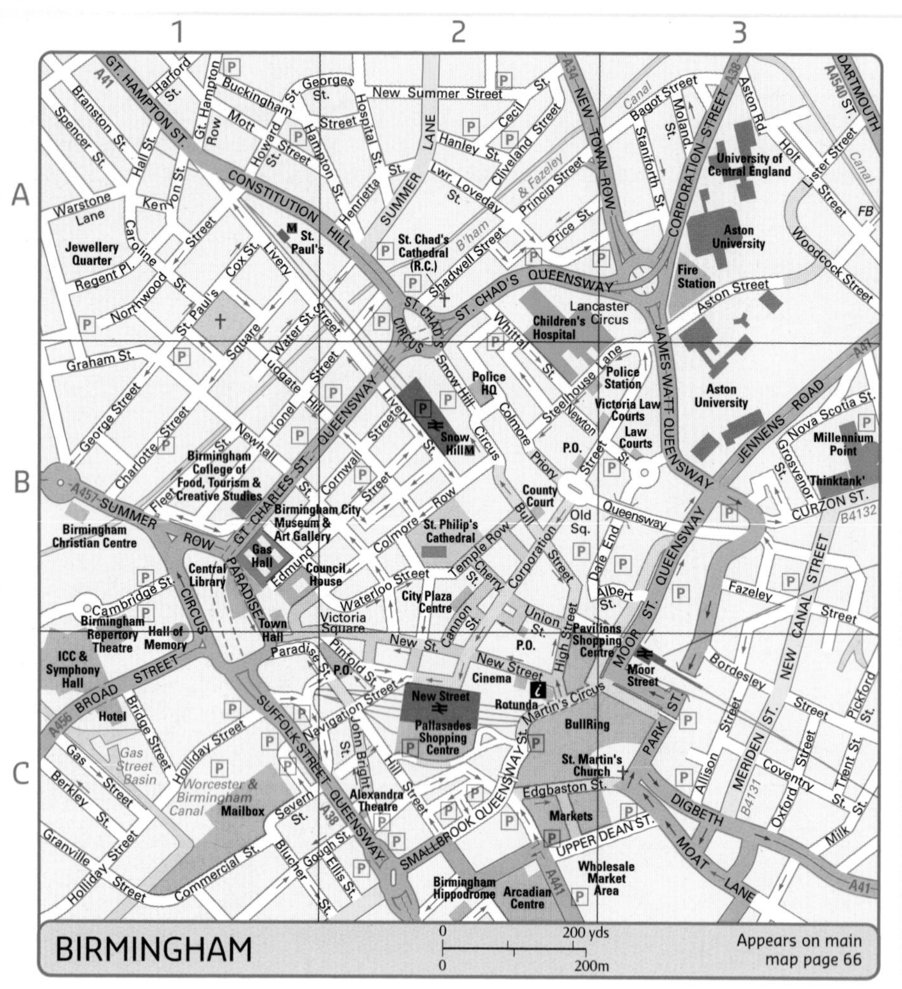

BIRMINGHAM

0 200 yds
0 200m

Appears on main map page 66

Tourist Information Centre: The Rotunda, Tourism & Ticket Shop, 150 New Street   Tel: 0121 202 5099

Albert Street	B3	Masshouse Circus	B3
Allison Street	C3	Meriden Street	C3
Aston Road	A3	Milk Street	C3
Aston Street	A3	Moat Lane	C3
Bagot Street	A3	Moor Street Queensway	C3
Berkley Street	C1	Moland Street	A3
Blucher Street	C1	Mott Street	A1
Bordesley Street	C3	Navigation Street	C1
Branston Street	A1	New Canal Street	C3
Bridge Street	C1	New Street	A2
Broad Street	C1	New Summer Street	A2
Buckingham Street	A1	New Town Row	A3
Bull Street	B2	Newhall Street	B1
Cambridge Street	B1	Newton Street	B2
Cannon Street	C2	Northwood Street	A1
Caroline Street	A1	Nova Scotia Street	B3
Cecil Street	A2	Oxford Street	C3
Charlotte Street	B1	Paradise Circus	B1
Cherry Street	B2	Paradise Street	C1
Cliveland Street	A2	Park Street	C3
Colmore Circus	B2	Pickford Street	C3
Colmore Row	B2	Pinfold Street	C2
Commercial Street	C1	Price Street	A2
Constitution Hill	A1	Princip Street	A2
Cornwall Street	B2	Priory Queensway	B2
Corporation Street	B2/A3	Queensway	B2
Coventry Street	C3	Regent Place	A1
Cox Street	A1	St. Chad's Circus	A2
Curzon Street	B3	St. Chad's Queensway	A2
Dale End	B2	St. Georges Street	A1
Dartmouth Street	A3	St. Martin's Circus	C2
Digbeth	C3	St. Paul's Square	A1
Edgbaston Street	C2	Severn Street	C1
Edmund Street	B1	Shadwell Street	A2
Ellis Street	C2	Smallbrook Queensway	C2
Fazeley Street	B3	Snow Hill	B2
Fleet Street	B1	Spencer Street	A1
Gas Street	C1	Staniforth Street	A3
George Street	B1	Steelhouse Lane	B2
Gough Street	C1	Suffolk Street Queensway	C1
Graham Street	B1	Summer Lane	A2
Granville Street	C1	Summer Row	B1
Great Charles Street	B1	Temple Row	B2
Queensway		Trent Street	A3
Great Hampton Row	A1	Union Street	B2
Great Hampton Street	A1	Upper Dean Street	C2
Grosvenor Street	B3	Victoria Square	B2
Hall Street	A1	Warstone Lane	A1
Hampton Street	A1	Waterloo Street	B2
Hanley Street	A2	Water Street	B1
Harford Street	A1	Whittal Street	A2
Henrietta Street	A2	Woodcock Street	A3
High Street	C2		
Hill Street	C2		
Holliday Street	C1		
Holt Street	A3		
Hospital Street	A2		
Howard Street	A1		
James Watt Queensway	A3		
Jennens Road	B3		
John Bright Street	C2		
Kenyon Street	A1		
Lionel Street	B1		
Lister Street	A3		
Livery Street	A1/B2		
Lower Loveday Street	A2		
Ludgate Hill	B1		

BLACKPOOL

0 300 yds
0 300m

Appears on main map page 99

Tourist Information Centre: 1 Clifton Street   Tel: 01253 478222

Abingdon Street	B1	Market Street	B1
Adelaide Street	B1	Mather Street	A3
Albert Road	C1	Mere Road	B3
Ascot Road	A3	Milbourne Street	B2
Ashburton Road	A1	Mount Street	A1
Ashton Road	C2	New Bonny Street	C1
Bank Hey Street	B1	Newcastle Avenue	B3
Banks Street	A1	Newton Drive	B3
Beech Avenue	B3	Oxford Road	B2
Birchway Avenue	A3	Palatine Road	C2
Bonny Street	C1	Park Road	C2
Boothley Road	A2	Peter Street	B2
Breck Road	C3	Pleasant Street	A1
Bryan Road	B3	Portland Road	C3
Buchanan Street	B2	Princess Parade	B1
Butler Street	A2	Promenade	A1/C1
Caunce Street	B2/A3	Queens Square	B1
Cecil Street	A2	Queen Street	B1
Central Drive	C1	Rathlyn Avenue	A3
Chapel Street	C1	Reads Avenue	C2
Charles Street	B2	Regent Road	B2
Charnley Road	C1	Ribble Road	C2
Church Street	B2	Ripon Road	C2
Clifford Road	A1	St. Albans Road	C3
Clifton Street	B1	Salisbury Road	C3
Clinton Avenue	C2	Seasiders Way	C1
Cocker Square	A1	Selbourne Road	A2
Cocker Street	A1	Somerset Avenue	C3
Coleridge Road	A2	South King Street	B2
Collingwood Avenue	A3	Stirling Road	A2
Cookson Street	B2	Talbot Road	B1/A2
Coopers Way	A2	Talbot Square	B1
Coronation Street	C1	Topping Street	B1
Corporation Street	B1	Victory Road	A2
Cumberland Avenue	C3	Wayman Road	B3
Deansgate	B1	Westmorland Avenue	C3
Devonshire Road	A2	West Park Drive	B3
Devonshire Square	B3	Whitegate Drive	B3/C3
Dickson Road	A1	Woodland Grove	C3
Egerton Road	A1	Woolman Road	C2
Elizabeth Street	A2	Yates Street	A1
Exchange Street	A1		
Forest Gate	B3		
Gainsborough Road	C2		
George Street	B2/A2		
Gloucester Avenue	C3		
Gorse Road	C3		
Gorton Street	A2		
Granville Road	B2		
Grosvenor Street	B2		
High Street	A1		
Hollywood Avenue	B3		
Hornby Road	C1		
Hounds Hill	C1		
King Street	B1		
Knowsley Avenue	C3		
Larbreck Avenue	A3		
Laycock Gate	A3		
Layton Road	A3		
Leamington Road	B2		
Leicester Road	B2		
Lincoln Road	B2		
Liverpool Road	B2		
London Road	A3		
Lord Street	A1		
Manchester Road	A3		
Manor Road	C3		

Tourist Information Centre: Westover Road
Tel: 0906 802 0234 (Premium Rate)

Ascham Road	A3	Wessex Way	B1/A3
Avenue Road	B1	West Cliff Promenade	C1
Bath Road	C2	West Cliff Road	C1
Beechey Road	A3	West Hill Road	C1
Bennett Road	A3	West Overcliff Drive	C1
Bourne Avenue	B1	West Promenade	C1
Bradley Road	B2	Westover Road	C2
Branksome Wood Road	B1	Wimborne Road	B2
Cavendish Road	A2		
Central Drive	A1		
Charminster Road	A2		
Christchurch Road	B3		
Cotlands	B3		
Dean Park Road	B2		
Dunbar Road	A2		
Durley Chine Road	C1		
Durley Chine Road South	C1		
Durley Road	C1		
East Avenue	A1		
East Overcliff Drive	C3		
Elgin Road	A1		
Exeter Road	C2		
Gervis Place	C2		
Gervis Road	C3		
Grove Road	C3		
Hinton Road	C2		
Holdenhurst Road	B3		
Knyveton Road	B3		
Lansdowne Road	A2		
Leven Avenue	A1		
Little Forest Road	A1		
Lowther Road	A3		
Madeira Road	B2		
Malmesbury Park Road	A3		
Manor Road	A3		
Methuen Road	A3		
Meyrick Road	B3		
Milton Road	A2		
Old Christchurch Road	B2		
Ophir Road	A3		
Oxford Road	B3		
Pier Approach	C2		
Poole Hill	C1		
Portchester Road	A3		
Priory Road	C1		
Queen's Road	B1		
Richmond Hill	B2		
Russell Cotes Road	C2		
St. Augustin's Road	A2		
St. Anthony's Road	A2		
St. Leonard's Road	A3		
St. Michael's Road	C1		
St. Pauls' Road	B3		
St. Peter's Road	B2		
St. Stephen's Road	B1		
St. Swithun's Road	B3		
St. Swithun's Road South	B3		
St. Valerie Road	A2		
St. Winifred's Road	A2		
Stewart Road	A3		
Surrey Road	B1		
The Lansdowne	B3		
The Square	B2		
The Triangle	B1		
Tregonwell Road	C1		
Undercliff Drive	C3		
Wellington Road	A2		

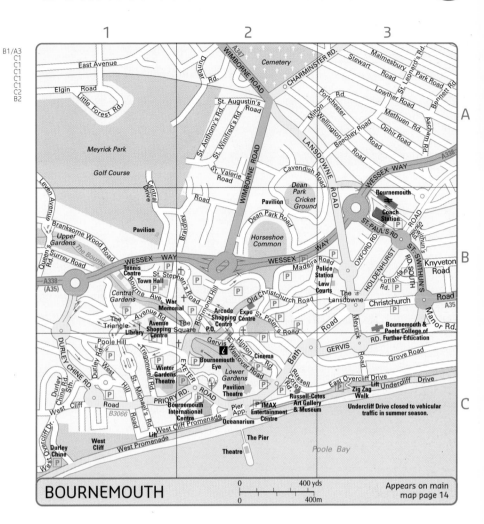

BOURNEMOUTH

Appears on main map page 14

Tourist Information Centre: City Hall, Centenary Square
Tel: 01274 753678

Akam Road	A1	Leeds Road	B3
Ann Place	C1	Little Horton Lane	C1
Ashgrove	C1	Lumb Lane	A1
Balme Street	A2	Manchester Road	C2
Bank Street	B2	Manningham Lane	A1
Baptist Place	A1	Mannville Terrace	C1
Barkerend Road	A3	Manor Row	A2
Barry Street	B1	Melbourne Place	C1
Bolling Road	C3	Midland Road	A2
Bolton Road	A3	Moody Street	C3
Brearton Street	A1	Morley Street	C1
Bridge Street	B2	Neal Street	C1
Britannia Street	C2	Nelson Street	C2
Broadway	B2	North Parade	A2
Burnett Street	B3	North Street	A3
Caledonia Street	C2	North Wing	A3
Canal Road	A2	Nuttall Road	A3
Captain Street	A3	Otley Road	A3
Carlton Street	B1	Paradise Street	A1
Carter Street	C3	Park Road	C2
Chain Street	A1	Prince's Way	B2
Channing Way	B2	Prospect Street	C3
Charles Street	B2	Radwell Drive	C1
Cheapside	B2	Rawson Road	A1
Chester Street	C1	Rebecca Street	A1
Churchbank	B3	Rouse Fold	C3
Claremont	C1	Russell Street	C1
Croft Street	C2	Salem Street	A2
Currer Street	B3	Sawrey Place	C1
Darfield Street	A1	Sedgwick Close	A1
Darley Street	A2	Sharpe Street	C2
Drake Street	B2	Shipley Airedale Road	A3
Drewton Road	A1	Simes Street	A1
Dryden Street	C3	Snowden Street	A1
Duke Street	A2	Sunbridge Road	A1
Dyson Street	A1	Sylhet Close	A1
East Parade	B3	Ternhill Grove	C2
Edmund Street	C1	Tetley Street	B1
Edward Street	C3	Thornton Road	B1
Eldon Place	A1	Trafalgar Street	A1
Fairfax Street	C3	Trinity Road	C1
Filey Street	B3	Tumbling Hill Street	B1
Fitzwilliam Street	C3	Valley Road	A2
Fountain Street	A1	Vaughan Street	A1
George Street	B3	Vicar Lane	B3
Godwin Street	B2	Vincent Street	B1
Gracechurch Street	A1	Wakefield Road	C3
Grafton Street	C1	Wapping Road	A3
Grattan Road	B1	Water Lane	B1
Great Horton Road	C1	Westgate	A1
Grove Terrace	C1	Wigan Street	B1
Guy Street	C3		
Hall Ings	B2		
Hall Lane	C3		
Hallfield Road	A1		
Hamm Strasse	A2		
Hammerton Street	B3		
Hanover Square	A1		
Harris Street	B3		
Heap Lane	A3		
Houghton Place	A1		
Howard Street	C1		
Hustlergate	B2		
Ivegate	B2		
James Street	B2		
John Street	B1		
Kirkgate	B2		

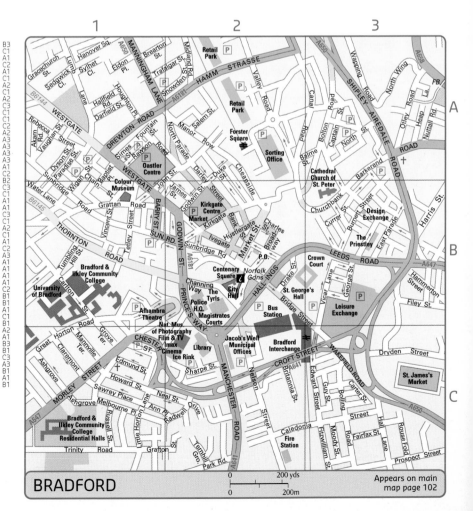

BRADFORD

Appears on main map page 102

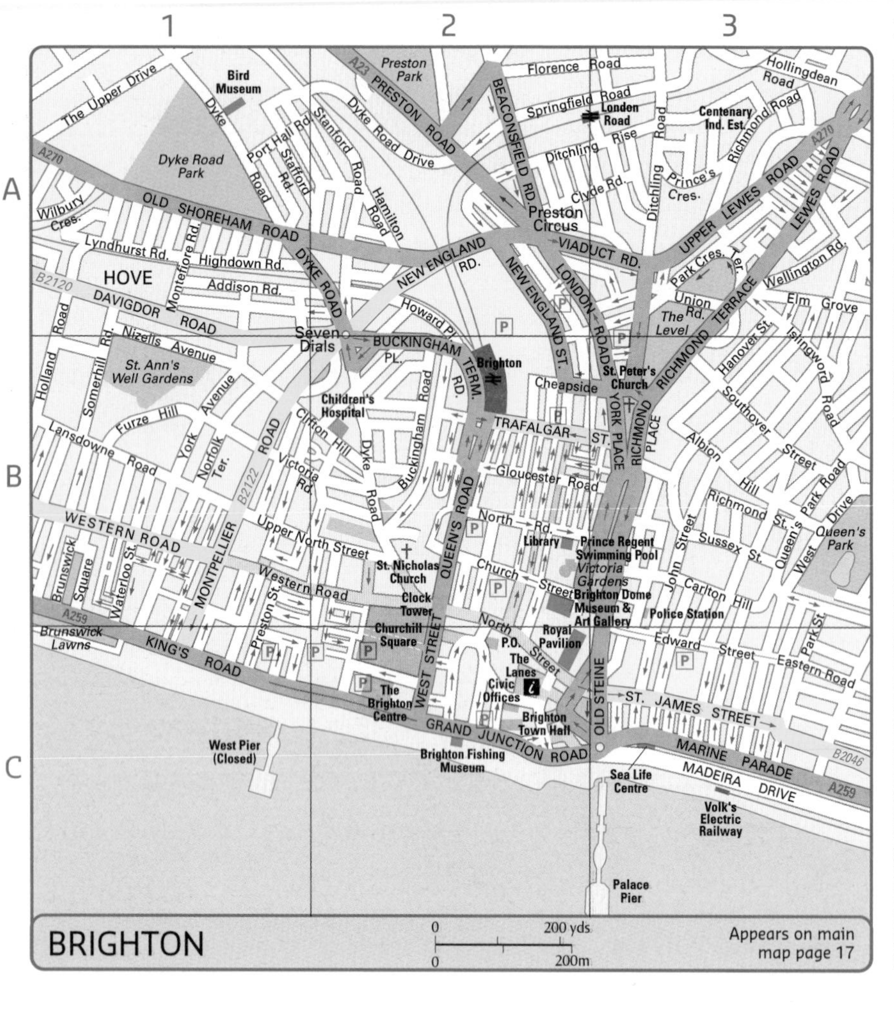

BRIGHTON

Appears on main map page 17

0 — 200 yds
0 — 200m

Tourist Information Centre: 10 Bartholomew Square
Tel: 0906 711 2255 (Premium Rate)

Addison Road	A1
Albion Hill	B3
Beaconsfield Road	A2
Brunswick Square	B1
Buckingham Place	A2
Buckingham Road	B2
Carlton Hill	B3
Cheapside	B2
Church Street	B2
Churchill Square	C2
Clifton Hill	B1
Clyde Road	A2
Davigdor Road	A1
Ditchling Rise	A2
Ditchling Road	A3
Dyke Road	B2
Dyke Road Drive	A2
Eastern Road	C3
Edward Street	C3
Elm Grove	A3
Florence Road	A2
Freshfield Road	C3
Furze Hill	B1
Gloucester Road	B2
Grand Junction Road	C2
Hamilton Road	A2
Hanover Street	B3
Highdown Road	A1
Holland Road	B1
Hollingdean Road	A3
Howard Place	A2
Islingword Road	A3
John Street	B3
King's Road	C1
Lansdowne Road	B1
Lewes Road	A3
London Road	A2
Lyndhurst Road	A1
Madeira Drive	C3
Marine Parade	C3
Montefiore Road	A1
Montpelier Road	B1
New England Road	A2
New England Street	A2
Nizells Avenue	A1
Norfolk Terrace	B1
North Road	B2
North Street	B2
Old Shoreham Road	A1
Old Steine	C3
Park Crescent Terrace	A3
Park Street	B3
Port Hall Road	A1
Preston Circus	A2
Preston Road	A2
Preston Street	C1
Prince's Crescent	A3
Queen's Park Road	B3
Queen's Road	B2
Richmond Place	B3
Richmond Road	A3
Richmond Street	B3
Richmond Terrace	A3
St. James's Street	C3
Somerhill Road	B1
Southover Street	B3
Springfield Road	A2

Stafford Road	A1
Stanford Road	A2
Sussex Street	B3
Terminus Road	B2
The Lanes	C2
The Upper Drive	A1
Trafalgar Street	B2
Union Road	A3
Upper Lewes Road	A3
Upper North Street	B1
Viaduct Road	A2
Victoria Road	B1
Waterloo Street	B1
Wellington Road	A3
West Drive	B3
West Street	C2
Western Road	B1
Wilbury Crescent	A1
York Avenue	B1
York Place	B3

BRISTOL

Appears on main map page 39

0 — 200 yds
0 — 200m

Tourist Information Centre: The Annexe, Wildscreen Walk,
Harbourside Tel: 0906 711 2191 (Premium Rate)

Alfred Hill	A1
Anchor Road	C1
Avon Street	B3
Baldwin Street	B1
Bath Road	C3
Bond Street	A2
Bridge Street	B2
Bristol Bridge	B2
Broadmead	A2
Broad Quay	B1
Broad Street	B2
Broad Weir	A3
Canon's Road	C1
Canon's Way	C1
Castle Street	B3
Charles Street	A2
Cheese Lane	B3
Christmas Steps	A1
Church Lane	B3
College Green	B1
Colston Avenue	B1
Colston Street	B1
Corn Street	B1
Countership	B2
Dale Street	A3
Eugene Street	A1
Fairfax Street	A2
Frogmore Street	B1
Harbour Way	C1
High Street	B2
Horfield Road	A1
Houlton Street	A3
John Street	B2
King Street	B1
Lewins Mead	A1
Lower Castle Street	A3
Lower Maudlin Street	A2
Marlborough Street	A2
Marsh Street	B1
Merchant Street	A2
Nelson Street	B1
Newfoundland Street	A3
Newgate	B2
New Street	A3
North Street	A2
Old Bread Street	B3
Old Market Street	B3
Park Row	B1
Park Street	B1
Passage Street	B3
Penn Street	A3
Perry Road	B1
Pipe Lane	B1
Portwall Lane	C2
Prewett Street	C2
Prince Street	C1
Prince Street Bridge	C1
Queen Charlotte Street	B2
Queen Square	C2
Queen Street	B3
Redcliff Backs	C2
Redcliffe Bridge	C2
Redcliffe Parade	C2
Redcliff Hill	C2
Redcliff Mead Lane	C3
Redcliff Street	B2
Redcross Street	A3

River Street	A3
Rupert Street	A1
St. Michael's Hill	A1
St. Nicholas Street	B2
St. Thomas Street	B2
Small Street	B1
Somerset Street	C3
Southwell Street	A1
Station Approach Road	C3
Straight Street	B3
Surrey Street	A3
Temple Back	B3
Temple Gate	C3
Temple Street	B2
Temple Way	C3
Terrell Street	A1
The Grove	C1
The Haymarket	A2
The Horsefair	A2
Thomas Lane	B2
Trenchard Street	B1
Tyndall Avenue	A1
Union Street	A2
Unity Street	B1
Unity Street	B3
Upper Maudlin Street	A1
Victoria Street	B2
Wapping Road	C1
Water Lane	B3
Wellington Road	A3
Welsh Back	B2
Wilder Street	A2
Wine Street	B2

Cambridge   Canterbury

Tourist Information Centre: Wheeler Street
Tel: 0870 225 4900

Adam and Eve Street	B3	Tennis Court Road	B2
Alpha Road	A2	Trinity Street	B2
Aylestone Road	A3	Trumpington Road	C2
Barton Road	C1	Trumpington Street	C2
Bateman Street	C2	Union Road	C2
Belvoir Road	A3	Victoria Avenue	A2
Brookside	C2	Victoria Road	A2
Burleigh Street	B3	West Road	B1
Carlyle Road	A2		
Castle Street	A1		
Chesterton Lane	A2		
Chesterton Road	A2		
Clarendon Road	B3		
De Freville Avenue	A3		
Devonshire Road	C3		
Downing Street	B2		
East Road	B3		
Eden Street	B3		
Elizabeth Way	A3		
Emmanuel Road	B2		
Fen Causeway, The	C1		
Glisson Road	C3		
Gonville Place	C3		
Granchester Street	C1		
Grange Road	B1		
Gresham Road	C3		
Hamilton Road	A3		
Harvey Road	C3		
Hills Road	C3		
Humberstone Road	A3		
Huntingdon Road	A1		
Jesus Lane	B2		
King's Parade	B2		
King Street	B2		
Lensfield Road	C2		
Madingley Road	A1		
Magdalene Bridge Street	A2		
Maids Causeway	B3		
Market Street	B2		
Mawson Road	C3		
Millington Road	C1		
Mill Road	C3		
Montague Road	A3		
Newmarket Road	B3		
Newnham Road	C1		
Norfolk Street	B3		
Panton Street	C2		
Parker Street	B2		
Park Parade	A2		
Parkside	B3		
Park Terrace	B2		
Pembroke Street	B2		
Queen's Road	B1		
Regent Street	B2		
Regent Terrace	B2		
St. Andrew's Street	B2		
St. Barnabas Road	C3		
St. John's Street	B2		
St. Matthew's Street	B3		
St. Paul's Road	C3		
Searce Street	A1		
Sidgwick Avenue	C1		
Sidney Street	B2		
Silver Street	C1		
Station Road	C3		
Storey's Way	A1		
Tenison Road	C3		

CAMBRIDGE

| 0 | | 400 yds |
| 0 | | 400m |

Appears on main map page 58

Tourist Information Centre: 12/13 Sun Street, The Buttermarket
Tel: 01227 378100

Best Lane	B2	Whitehall Gardens	B1
Borough Northgate	A2	Whitehall Road	B1
Broad Street	A3	Wincheap	C1
Burgate	B2	York Road	C1
Castle Row	C1		
Castle Street	C1		
College Road	A3		
Cossington Road	C3		
Craddock Road	A3		
Dover Street	B3		
Edgar Road	A3		
Ersham Road	C3		
Forty Acres Road	A1		
Gordon Road	C1		
Havelock Street	A3		
Hawk's Lane	B2		
High Street	B2		
Ivy Lane	B3		
King Street	A2		
Kirby's Lane	A1		
Lansdown Road	C2		
Longport	B3		
Lower Bridge Street	B3		
Lower Chantry Lane	B3		
Marlowe Avenue	C2		
Martyrs' Field Road	C1		
Mead Way	B1		
Military Road	A3		
Monastery Street	B3		
New Dover Road	C3		
North Holmes Road	A3		
North Lane	A1		
Nunnery Fields	C3		
Oaten Hill	C3		
Old Dover Road	C3		
Orchard Street	A1		
Oxford Road	C2		
Palace Street	B2		
Pin Hill	C1		
Pound Lane	A1		
Puckle Lane	C3		
Rheims Way	B1		
Rhodaus Town	C2		
Roper Road	A1		
Rose Lane	B2		
St. Dunstan's Street	A1		
St. George's Lane	B2		
St. George's Place	B3		
St. George's Street	B2		
St. Gregory's Road	A3		
St. Margarets Street	B2		
St. Peter's Lane	A2		
St. Peter's Place	B1		
St. Peter's Street	A1		
St. Radigund's Street	A2		
St. Stephen's Road	A2		
Simmonds Road	C1		
Station Road East	C1		
Station Road-West	A1		
Stour Street	B1		
The Causeway	A2		
The Friar's	B2		
Tourtel Road	A3		
Tudor Road	C1		
Union Street	A3		
Upper Bridge Street	C2		
Watling Street	B2		

CANTERBURY

| 0 | | 200 yds |
| 0 | | 200m |

Appears on main map page 32

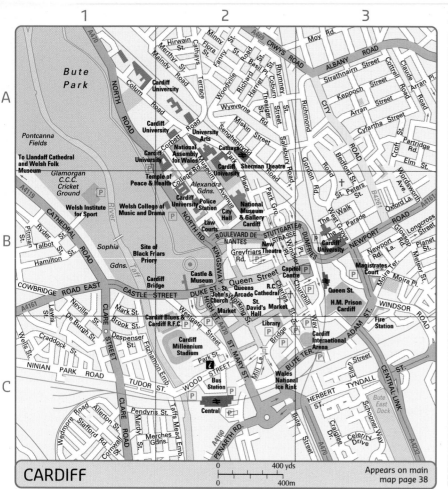

CARDIFF

Tourist Information Centre: Cardiff Visitor Centre, 16 Wood St
Tel: 029 2022 7281

Adam Street	C3	Moy Road	A3	
Albany Road	A3	Museum Avenue	A2	
Allerton Street	C1	Neville Street	B1	
Arran Place	A3	Newport Road	B3	
Arran Street	A3	Newport Road Lane	B3	
Basil Place	A2	Ninian Park Road	C1	
Bedford Street	A3	North Road	A1	
Boulevard de Nantes	B2	Oxford Lane	B3	
Bridge Street	C2	Park Grove	B2	
Brook Street	C1	Park Place	A2	
Bute Street	C2	Park Street	C2	
Bute Terrace	C2	Partridge Road	A3	
Castle Street	B1	Penarth Road	C2	
Cathays Terrace	A2	Pendyris Street	C1	
Cathedral Road	B1	Pitman Street	B1	
Celerity Drive	C3	Planet Street	B3	
Central Link	C3	Queen Street	B2	
Charles Street	B2	Rhymney Street	A2	
Churchill Way	B2	Richard Street	A2	
City Road	A3	Richmond Road	A3	
Clare Road	C1	Ryder Street	B1	
Clare Street	B1	St. Mary Street	C2	
Claude Road	A3	St. Peters Street	B3	
Coburn Street	A2	Salisbury Road	A2	
College Road	B2	Schooner Way	C3	
Colum Road	A1	Senghennydd Road	A2	
Corbett Road	A2	Stafford Road	C1	
Cornwall Street	C1	Strathnairn Street	A3	
Cottrell Road	A3	Stuttgarter Strasse	B2	
Cowbridge Road East	B1	Taffs Mead Embankment	C2	
Craddock Street	C1	Talbot Street	B1	
Craiglee Drive	C3	Thesiger Street	A2	
Croft Street	A3	The Parade	B3	
Crwys Road	A2	The Walk	A3	
Cyfartha Street	A3	Tudor Street	C1	
De Burgh Street	B1	Tyndall Street	C3	
Despenser Street	C1	Wedmore Road	C1	
Duke Street	B2	Wells Street	C1	
Dumfries Place	B3	West Grove	B3	
Ellen Street	C3	Westgate Street	B2	
Elm Street	A3	Windsor Place	B2	
Fanny Street	A2	Windsor Road	B3	
Fitzhamon Embankment	C1	Wood Street	C2	
Flora Street	A2	Woodville Road	A2	
Glossop Road	B3	Wordsworth Avenue	A3	
Gordon Road	A3	Working Street	B2	
Greyfriars Road	B2	Wyeverne Road	A2	
Hamilton Street	B1			
Harriet Street	A2			
Herbert Street	C3			
High Street	B2			
Hirwain Street	A2			
Keppoch Street	A3			
Kingsway	B2			
Lewis Street	B1			
Longcross Street	B3			
Maindy Road	A1			
Mardy Street	C1			
Mark Street	B1			
Merches Gardens	C1			
Merthyr Street	A2			
Meteor Street	B3			
Mill Lane	C2			
Minny Street	A2			
Miskin Street	A2			
Moira Place	B3			
Moira Terrace	B3			

Appears on main map page 38

CARLISLE

Tourist Information Centre: Old Town Hall, Green Market
Tel: 01228 625600

Abbey Street	B2	Lindon Street	C3
Aglionby Street	B3	Lismore Place	B3
Albion Street	C3	Lismore Street	B3
Alexander Street	C3	London Road	C3
Alfred Street	B3	Lonsdale	B2
Ashley Street	B1	Lorne Crescent	C2
Bank Street	B2	Lorne Street	C2
Bassenthwaite Street	C1	Lowther Street	B2
Bedford Road	C1	Marlborough Gardens	A2
Botchergate	C2	Mary Street	B2
Brampton Road	A2	Metcalfe Street	C2
Bridge Lane	B1	Milbourne Street	B2
Bridge Street	B1	Morton Street	B1
Broad Street	B3	Myddleton Street	B3
Brook Street	C3	Nelson Street	C1
Brunswick Street	B3	Norfolk Road	C1
Byron Street	B1	Norfolk Street	C1
Caldcotes	B1	Peel Street	B1
Carlton Gardens	A2	Petteril Street	B3
Castle Street	B2	Port Road	B1
Castle Way	B2	Portland Place	C3
Cavendish Terrace	A2	Rickergate	B2
Cecil Street	B3	Rigg Street	B1
Charlotte Street	C2	River Street	B3
Chatsworth Square	B3	Robert Street	C2
Chiswick Street	B3	Rome Street	C2
Church Lane	A2	Rydal Street	C3
Church Road	A2	St. George's Crescent	A2
Church Street	B1	St. James Road	C1
Clifton Street	C1	St. Nicholas Street	C3
Close Street	C2	Scawfell Road	C1
Collingwood Street	C2	Scotch Street	B2
Colville Street	C1	Scotland Road	A2
Crown Street	C2	Shaddongate	B1
Currock Road	C2	Silloth Street	B1
Currock Street	C2	Skiddaw Road	C1
Dale Street	C2	Spencer Street	B3
Denton Street	C1	Stanhope Road	B1
Dunmail Drive	C1	Strand Road	B3
East Dale Street	C2	Sybil Street	C3
East Norfolk Street	C2	Tait Street	C2
Eden Bridge	A2	Talbot Road	C1
Edward Street	C2	Trafalgar Street	C2
Elm Street	C2	Viaduct Estate Road	B2
English Street	B2	Victoria Place	B3
Etterby Street	A2	Victoria Viaduct	C2
Finkle Street	B2	Warwick Road	B3
Fisher Street	B2	Warwick Square	B3
Fusehill Street	C3	Water Street	C2
Georgian Way	B2	Weardale Road	C1
Goschen Road	C1	West Tower Street	B2
Graham Street	C2	West Walls	B2
Granville Road	B1	Westmorland Street	C2
Greta Avenue	C1	Wigton Road	B1
Grey Street	C3	Willow Holme Road	A1
Hardwicke Circus	A2		
Hart Street	B3		
Hartington Place	B3		
Howard Place	B3		
Infirmary Street	B1		
James Street	B1		
John Street	B1		
Junction Street	B1		
Kendal Street	B1		
King Street	C3		
Lancaster Street	C3		
Lime Street	C2		

Appears on main map page 118

Cheltenham

Tourist Information Centre: 77 The Promenade
Tel: 01242 522878

Albany Road	C1
Albert Road	A3
Albion Street	B2
All Saints Road	B3
Andover Road	C1
Arle Avenue	A1
Ashford Road	C1
Bath Parade	B2
Bath Road	C2
Bayshill Road	B1
Berkeley Street	B2
Brunswick Street	A2
Carlton Street	B3
Central Cross Drive	B1
Christchurch Road	B1
Churchill Drive	C3
Clarence Street	A2
College Lawn	C2
College Road	C2
Douro Road	B1
Dunnally Street	A2
Eldon Road	B3
Evesham Road	A3
Fairview Road	B3
Folly Lane	A2
Gloucester Road	B1
Grafton Road	C1
Hale's Road	C3
Hanover Street	A2
Hayward's Road	C3
Henrietta Street	B2
Hewlett Road	B3
High Street	A2
Honeybourne Way	A1
Hudson Street	A2
Imperial Square	B2
Keynsham Road	C2
King Alfred Way	C3
King's Road	B3
Lansdown Crescent	C1
Lansdown Road	C1
London Road	C3
Lypiatt Road	C1
Malvern Road	B1
Market Street	A1
Marle Hill Parade	A2
Marle Hill Road	A2
Millbrook Street	A1
Montpellier Spa Road	B2
Montpellier Street	C1
Montpellier Terrace	C1
Montpellier Walk	C1
New Street	A2
North Place	B2
North Street	B2
Old Bath Road	C3
Oriel Road	B2
Overton Road	B1
Painswick Road	C1
Parabola Road	B1
Park Place	C1
Park Street	A1
Pittville Circus	A3
Pittville Circus Road	B3
Pittville Lawn	A3
Portland Street	B2
Prestbury Road	A3
Princes Road	C1
Priory Street	C3
Promenade	B2
Rodney Road	B2
Rosehill Street	B3
Royal Well Road	B2
St. George's Place	B2
St. George's Road	B1
St. James Street	B2
St. Johns Avenue	B2
St. Margaret's Road	A2
St. Paul's Road	A2
St. Paul's Street North	A2
St. Paul's Street South	A2
St. Stephen's Road	C1
Sandford Road	C2
Sherborne Street	B3
Southgate Drive	C3
Strickland Road	C3
Suffolk Place	C1
Suffolk Road	C1
Sun Street	A1
Swindon Road	A1
Sydenham Road	B3
Sydenham Villas Road	C3
Tewkesbury Road	A1
Thirlestaine Road	C2
Tivoli Road	C1
Townsend Street	A1
Vittoria Walk	C2
Wellington Road	A3
West Drive	A3
Western Road	B1
Whaddon Road	A3
Winchcombe Street	B2
Windsor Road	A3

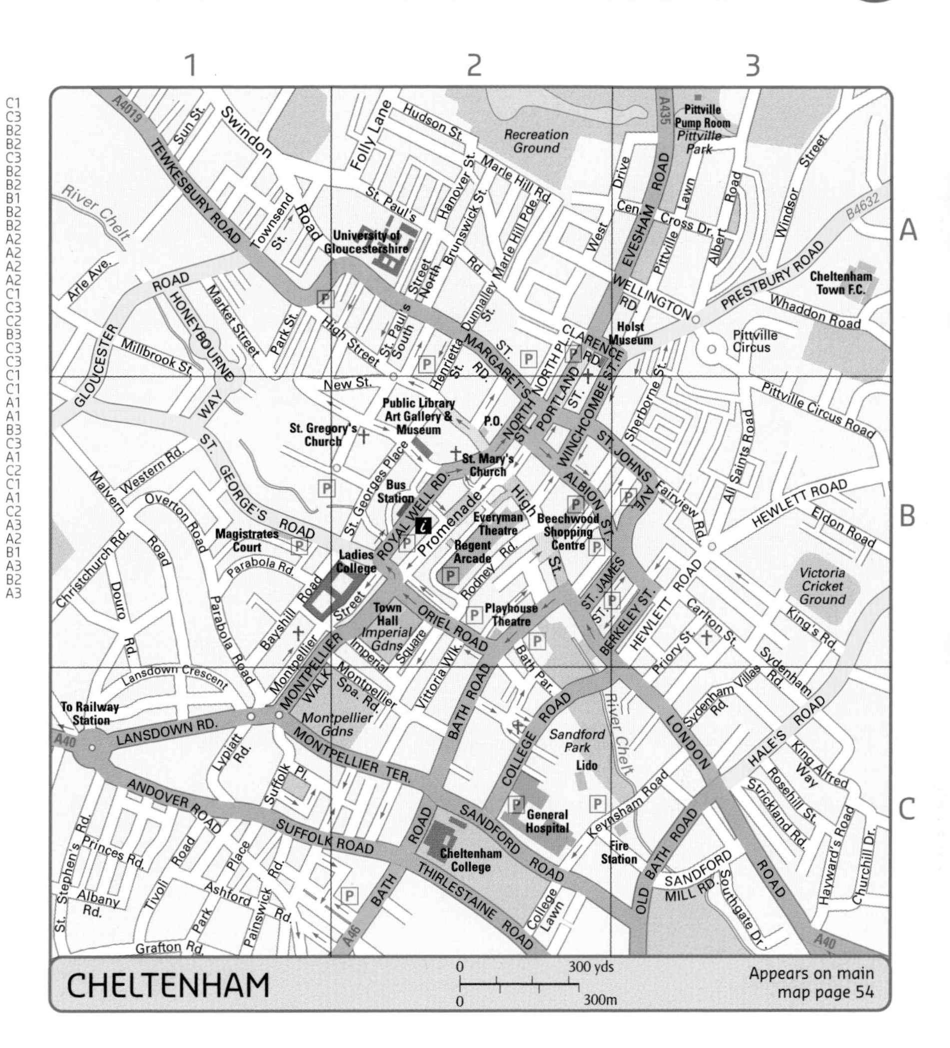

CHELTENHAM

0   300 yds
0   300m

Appears on main
map page 54

Chester

Tourist Information Centre: Town Hall, Northgate Street
Tel: 01244 402111

Bath Street	B3
Bedward Row	B1
Black Diamond Street	A2
Black Friars	C1
Bold Square	B2
Boughton	B3
Bouverie Street	A1
Bridge Street	B2
Brook Street	A2
Canal Street	A1
Castle Drive	C1
Charles Street	A2
Cheyney Road	A1
Chichester Street	A1
City Road	B3
City Walls Road	B1
Commonhall Street	B1
Cornwall Street	A2
Crewe Street	A3
Cuppin Street	C1
Dee Hills Park	B3
Dee Lane	B3
Deva Terrace	B3
Duke Street	C2
Eastgate Street	B2
Edinburgh Way	C3
Egerton Street	A2
Elizabeth Crescent	C3
Foregate Street	B2
Forest Street	B2
Francis Street	A3
Frodsham Street	B2
Garden Lane	A1
George Street	A2
Gloucester Street	A2
Grey Friars	B1
Grosvenor Park Terrace	B3
Grosvenor Road	C1
Grosvenor Street	C1
Handbridge	C2
Hoole Road	A2
Hoole Way	A2
Hunter Street	B1
King Street	B1
Leadworks Lane	B3
Lightfoot Street	A3
Louise Street	A1
Love Street	B2
Lower Bridge Street	C2
Lower Park Road	C3
Mill Street	B3
Milton Street	A2
Newgate Street	B2
Nicholas Street	B1
Nicholas Street Mews	B1
Northern Pathway	C3
Northgate Avenue	A2
Northgate Street	B1
Nun's Road	C1
Old Dee Bridge	C2
Pepper Street	C2
Phillip Street	A3
Prince's Avenue	A3
Princess Street	B1
Queen's Avenue	A3
Queen's Drive	C3
Queen's Park Road	C2
Queen's Road	A3
Queen Street	B2
Raymond Street	A1
Russel Street	B3
St. Anne Street	A2
St. George's Crescent	C3
St. John's Road	C3
St. John Street	B2
St. Martins Way	A1
St. Oswalds Way	A2
St. Werburgh Street	B2
Seller Street	B3
Sibell Street	A3
Souter's Lane	C2
Stanley Street	B1
Station Road	A3
Steam Mill Street	B3
Talbot Street	A2
The Bars	B3
The Groves	C2
Trafford Street	A2
Union Street	B2
Upper Northgate Street	A1
Vicar's Lane	C2
Victoria Crescent	C3
Victoria Place	B2
Victoria Road	A1
Walker Street	A3
Walpole Street	A1
Walter Street	A2
Watergate Street	B1
Water Tower Street	B1
Weaver Street	B1
White Friars	C1
York Street	B2

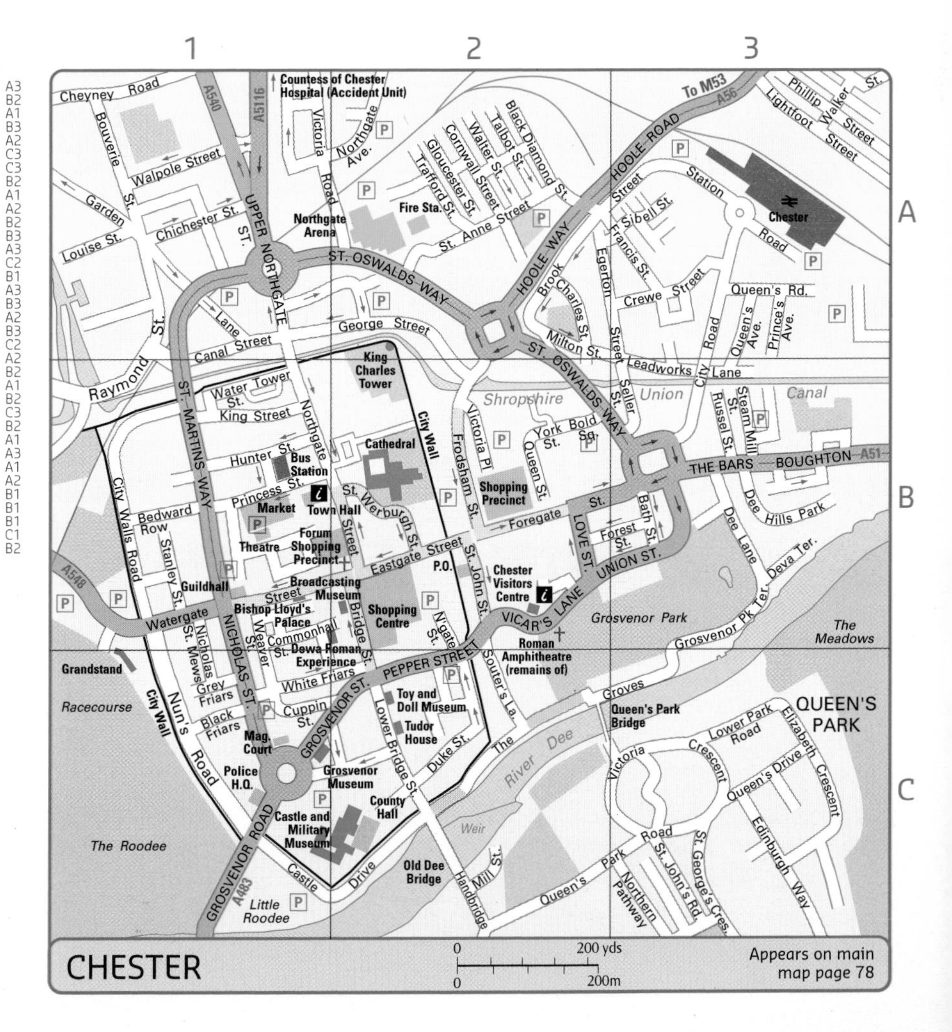

CHESTER

0   200 yds
0   200m

Appears on main
map page 78

Coventry

Tourist Information Centre: Bayley Lane
Tel: 024 7622 7264

Abbott's Lane	A1	Norfolk Street	B1
Acacia Avenue	C3	Oxford Street	B3
Albany Road	C1	Park Road	C2
Alma Street	B3	Parkside	C2
Asthill Grove	C2	Primrose Hill Street	A3
Barker's Butts Lane	A1	Priory Street	B2
Barras Lane	B1	Puma Way	C2
Berry Street	A3	Quarryfield Lane	C3
Bishop Street	A2	Queen's Road	C1
Blythe Road	A3	Queen Street	A3
Bond Street	B1	Queen Victoria Road	B1
Bramble Street	B3	Quinton Road	C2
Bretts Close	A3	Radford Road	A1
Broadway	C1	Raglan Street	B3
Burges	B2	Regent Street	C1
Butts Road	B1	Ringway Hill Cross	B1
Cambridge Street	A3	Ringway Queens	B1
Canterbury Street	A3	Ringway Rudge	B1
Clifton Street	A3	Ringway St. Johns	C2
Colchester Street	A3	Ringway St. Nicholas	A2
Cornwall Road	C3	Ringway St. Patricks	C2
Corporation Street	B2	Ringway Swanswell	B2
Coundon Road	A1	Ringway Whitefriars	B3
Coundon Street	A1	St. Nicholas Street	A2
Cox Street	B3	Sandy Lane	A2
Croft Road	B1	Seagrave Road	C3
Drapers Fields	A2	Silver Street	A2
Earl Street	B2	Sky Blue Way	B3
East Street	B3	South Street	B3
Eaton Road	C2	Spencer Avenue	C1
Fairfax Street	B2	Spon Street	B1
Far Gosford Street	B3	Srathmore Avenue	C3
Foleshill Road	A2	Stoney Road	C2
Fowler Road	C1	Stoney Stanton Road	A2
Gordon Street	C1	Swanswell Street	A2
Gosford Street	B3	The Precinct	B2
Greyfriars Road	B1	Tomson Avenue	A1
Gulson Road	B3	Trinity Street	B2
Hales Street	B2	Upper Hill Street	B1
Harnall Lane East	A3	Upper Well Street	B2
Harnall Lane West	B1	Vauxhall Street	B3
Harper Road	B3	Vecqueray Street	B3
Harper Street	B2	Victoria Street	A3
Hertford Street	B2	Vine Street	A3
Hewitt Avenue	A1	Warwick Road	C1
High Street	B2	Waveley Road	B1
Hill Street	B1	Westminster Road	C1
Holyhead Road	B1	White Street	A2
Hood Street	B3	Windsor Street	B1
Howard Street	A2	Wright Street	A3
Jordan Well	B2		
King William Street	A3		
Lamb Street	B2		
Leicester Row	A2		
Leigh Street	A3		
Little Park Street	C2		
London Road	C3		
Lower Ford Street	B3		
Market Way	B2		
Meadow Street	B1		
Michaelmas Road	C1		
Middleborough Road	A1		
Mile Lane	C2		
Mill Street	A1		
Minster Road	B1		
Much Park Street	B2		
New Union Street	B2		

COVENTRY

0   500 yds
0   500m

Appears on main map page 67

Derby

Tourist Information Centre: Assembly Rooms, Market Place
Tel: 01332 255802

Abbey Street	C1	Queen Street	A2
Agard Street	A1	Railway Terrace	C3
Albert Street	B2	Sacheverel Street	C1
Arthur Street	A1	Saddlergate	B2
Babington Lane	C1	St. Alkmunds Way	A2
Bath Street	A2	St. Helen's Street	A1
Becket Street	B1	St. James Street	B2
Bold Lane	B1	St. Mary's Gate	B1
Bradshaw Way	C2	St. Mary's Wharf Road	A3
Bridge Street	A1	St. Peter's Churchyard	C2
Brook Street	A1	St. Peter's Street	B2
Burton Road	C1	Siddals Road	C3
Calvert Street	C3	Sir Frank Whittle Road	A3
Canal Street	C3	Sitwell Street	C2
Cathedral Road	B1	Stafford Street	B1
City Road	A2	Station Approach	C3
Clarke Street	B3	Stockbrook Street	C1
Copeland Street	C2	Stores Road	A3
Cornmarket	B2	The Strand	B1
Corporation Street	B2	Traffic Street	C2
Cranmer Road	B3	Trinity Street	C2
Crompton Street	C1	Victoria Street	B1
Curzon Street	B1	Wardwick	B1
Darley Lane	A2	West Avenue	A1
Derwent Street	B2	Willow Row	B1
Drewry Lane	B1	Wilmot Street	C1
Duffield Road	A1	Wilson Street	C1
Duke Street	A2	Wolfa Street	C1
Dunton Close	B3	Woods Lane	C1
Eastgate	B3		
East Street	B2		
Edward Street	A1		
Exeter Street	B2		
Ford Street	B1		
Forester Street	C1		
Fox Street	A2		
Friar Gate	B1		
Friary Street	B1		
Full Street	B2		
Garden Street	A1		
Gerard Street	C1		
Gower Street	C2		
Green Lane	C1		
Grey Street	C1		
Handyside Street	A2		
Harcourt Street	C1		
Iron Gate	B2		
John Street	C2		
Kedleston Street	A1		
King Street	A1		
Leopold Street	C1		
Liversage Street	C2		
Lodge Lane	A1		
London Road	C2		
Macklin Street	B1		
Mansfield Road	A2		
Market Place	B2		
Meadow Road	B2		
Monk Street	C1		
Morledge	B2		
Normanton Road	C1		
North Parade	A2		
North Street	A1		
Nottingham Road	B3		
Osmaston Road	C2		
Parker Street	A1		
Pride Parkway	C3		

DERBY

0   300 yds
0   300m

Appears on main map page 81

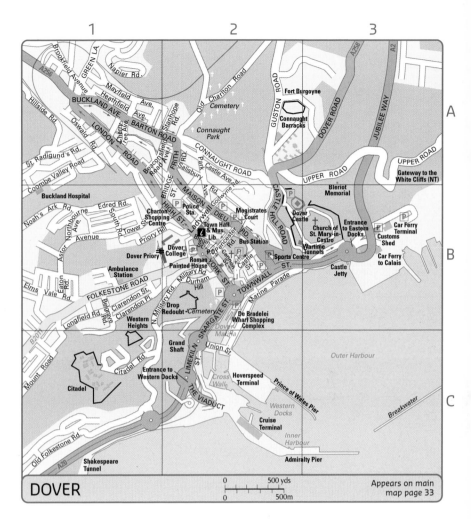

Tourist Information Centre: The Old Town Gaol, Biggin Street
Tel: 01304 205108

Astor Avenue	B1
Barton Road	A1
Beaconsfield Avenue	A1
Beaconsfield Road	A1
Belgrave Road	B1
Biggin Street	B2
Bridge Street	B2
Brookfield Avenue	A1
Buckland Avenue	A1
Cannon Street	B2
Canons Gate Road	B2
Castle Avenue	A2
Castle Hill Road	B2
Castle Street	B2
Cherry Tree Avenue	A1
Citadel Road	C1
Clarendon Place	B1
Clarendon Street	B1
Connaught Road	A2
Coombe Valley Road	B1
Dover Road	A3
Durham Hill	B2
Eaton Road	B1
Edred Road	B1
Elms Vale Road	B1
Folkestone Road	B1
Frith Road	A2
Godwyne Road	B2
Green Lane	A1
Guston Road	A2
Heathfield Avenue	A1
High Street	B2
Hillside Road	A1
Jubilee Way	A3
Ladywell	B2
Limekiln Street	C2
London Road	A1
Longfield Road	B1
Maison Dieu Road	B2
Marine Parade	B2
Mayfield Avenue	A1
Military Road	B2
Mount Road	C1
Napier Road	A1
Noah's Ark Road	B1
Northbourne Avenue	B1
North Military Road	B1
Old Charlton Road	A2
Old Folkestone Road	C1
Oswald Road	A1
Park Avenue	A2
Pencester Road	B2
Priory Hill	B1
St. Radigund's Road	A1
Salisbury Road	A2
Snargate Street	C2
South Road	B1
Stanhope Road	A2
The Viaduct	C2
Tower Street	B1
Townwall Street	B2
Union Street	C2
Upper Road	A3
York Street	B2

DOVER

0   500 yds
0   500m

Appears on main
map page 33

Tourist Information Centre: 21 Castle Street
Tel: 01382 527527

Adelaide Place	A1	Tannadice Street	A2	
Albany Terrace	A1	Tay Road Bridge	C2	
Albert Street	B3	Trades Lane	B2	
Alexander Street	A2	Upper Constitution Street	A1	
Ann Street	B2	Victoria Road	B2	
Arbroath Road	B3	Victoria Street	B3	
Arklay Street	A3	Ward Road	B1	
Arklay Terrace	A3	West Marketgait	B1	
Arthurstone Terrace	B3	West Port	B1	
Barrack Road	B1	William Street	B3	
Blackness Road	B1			
Blinshall Street	B1			
Brewery Lane	B1			
Brook Street	B1			
Broughty Ferry Road	B3			
Brown Street	B1			
Bruce Street	A1			
Byron Street	A1			
Canning Street	A2			
City Square	C2			
Clepington Road	A3			
Constitution Road	B2			
Constitution Street	A2			
Court Street	A3			
Cowgate Street	B2			
Dens Road	A2			
Douglas Street	B1			
Dudhope Street	A1			
Dudhope Terrace	A3			
Dundonald Street	A3			
Dura Street	B3			
East Dock Street	B3			
East Marketgait	B2			
Fairbairn Street	A2			
Guthrie Street	B1			
Hawkhill	B1			
High Street	C2			
Hill Street	A2			
Hilltown	A2			
Kenmore Terrace	A1			
Killin Avenue	A1			
Kinghorne Road	A1			
King Street	B2			
Larch Street	B1			
Law Crescent	A1			
Lawside Avenue	A1			
Law Street	A1			
Leng Street	A1			
Lochee Road	B1			
Lower Princes Street	B3			
Mains Road	A2			
Main Street	A2			
Meadowside	B2			
Morgan Street	B3			
Nelson Street	B2			
Nethergate	C1			
North Marketgait	B1			
Perth Road	C1			
Polepark Road	B1			
Princes Street	B3			
Riverside Drive	C1			
Roseangle	C1			
Rosebank Road	B2			
Seagate	B2			
South Marketgait	C2			
South Tay Street	C1			
Strathmartine Road	A2			

DUNDEE

0   400 yds
0   400m

Appears on main
map page 152

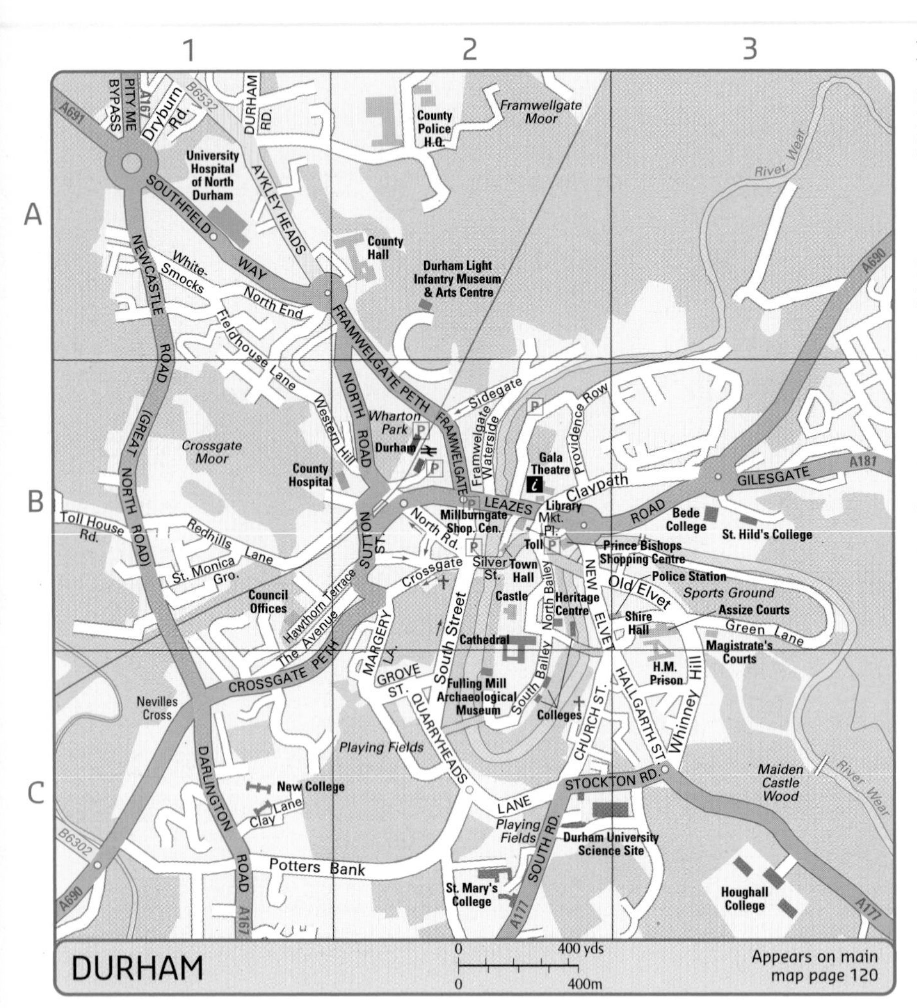

DURHAM

0 — 400 yds
0 — 400m

Appears on main map page 120

Tourist Information Centre: 2 Millennium Place
Tel: 0191 384 3720

Aykley Heads	A1
Church Street	C2
Clay Lane	C1
Claypath	B2
Crossgate	B2
Crossgate Peth	C1
Darlington Road	C1
Dryburn Road	A1
Durham Road	A1
Fieldhouse Lane	A1
Framwelgate	B2
Framwelgate Peth	A2
Framwelgate Waterside	B2
Gilesgate	B3
Great North Road	A1
Green Lane	B3
Grove Street	C2
Hallgarth Street	C3
Hawthorn Terrace	B1
Leazes Road	B2
Margery Lane	C2
Market Place	B2
Millburngate Bridge	B2
Newcastle Road	A1
New Elvet	B2
North Bailey	B2
North End	A1
North Road	B2
Old Elvet	B3
Pity Me Bypass	A1
Potters Bank	C1
Quarryheads Lane	C2
Providence Row	B2
Redhills Lane	B1
St. Monica Grove	B1
Sidegate	B2
Silver Street	B2
South Bailey	C2
South Road	C2
South Street	C2
Southfield Way	A1
Stockton Road	C2
Sutton Street	B2
The Avenue	C1
Toll House Road	B1
Western Hill	B1
Whinney Hill	C3
Whitesmocks	A1

EASTBOURNE

0 — 200 yds
0 — 200m

Appears on main map page 18

Tourist Information Centre: 3 Cornfield Road
Tel: 01323 411400

Arlington Road	B1	The Goffs	A1
Arundel Road	A2	Trinity Trees	B3
Ashford Road	B2/B3	Upper Avenue	A2
Avondale Road	A3	Upperton Lane	B2
Bedfordwell Road	A2	Upperton Road	A1
Belmore Road	A3	Watts Lane	A1
Blackwater Road	C2	Whitley Road	A1
Borough Lane	A1	Willingdon Road	A1
Bourne Street	B3	Winchcombe Road	A3
Carew Road	A1/A2		
Carlisle Road	C1		
Cavendish Avenue	A3		
Cavendish Place	B3		
College Road	C2		
Commercial Road	B2		
Compton Place Road	B1		
Compton Street	C2		
Cornfield Terrace	B2		
Denton Road	C1		
Devonshire Place	B2		
Dittons Road	B1		
Dursley Road	B3		
Enys Road	A2		
Eversfield Road	A2		
Fairfield Road	C1		
Firle Road	A3		
Furness Road	C2		
Gaudick Road	C1		
Gilbert Road	A3		
Gildredge Road	B2		
Gorringe Road	A2		
Grand Parade	C3		
Grange Road	C2		
Grassington Road	C2		
Grove Road	B2		
Hartfield Road	A2		
Hartington Place	B3		
High Street	A1		
Hyde Gardens	B2		
King Edward's Parade	C2		
Langney Road	B3		
Lewes Road	A2		
Marine Parade	B3		
Mark Lane	B2		
Meads Road	C1		
Melbourne Road	A3		
Mill Gap Road	A1		
Mill Road	A1		
Moat Croft Road	A1		
Moy Avenue	A3		
Ratton Road	A1		
Royal Parade	B3		
Saffrons Park	C1		
Saffrons Road	B1		
St. Anne's Road	A1		
St. Leonard's Road	B2		
Seaside	B3		
Seaside Road	B3		
Selwyn Road	A1		
Silverdale Road	C2		
South Street	B2		
Southfields Road	B1		
Station Parade	B2		
Susan's Road	B3		
Sydney Road	B2		
Terminus Road	B2		
The Avenue	B2		

Tourist Information Centre: Edinburgh & Scotland Information
Centre, 3 Princes Street Tel: 0131 473 3800

Abbey Hill	A3
Abercromby Place	A2
Albany Street	A2
Alva Street	B1
Ann Street	A1
Arden Street	C2
Atholl Crescent	B1
Bellevue	A2
Bread Street	B1
Brougham Street	C1
Broughton Street	A2
Brunswick Road	A3
Bruntsfield Place	C1
Buccleuch Place	C2
Buccleuch Street	C3
Calton Road	B3
Canongate	B3
Castle Street	A1
Castle Terrace	B1
Causewayside	C3
Chalmers Street	C2
Chambers Street	B2
Charlotte Square	B1
Clerk Street	C3
Coates Crescent	B1
Cowgate	B2
Cumberland Street	A1
Dalkeith Road	C3
Dean Terrace	A1
Doune Terrace	A1
Dumbiedykes Road	B3
Dundas Street	A1
Easter Road	A3
East London Street	A2
East Market Street	B2
East Preston Street	C3
Elgin Street	A3
Eyre Place	A2
Fettes Row	A1
Fountainbridge	C1
Frederick Street	A1
Gardners Crescent	B1
George IV Bridge	B2
George Square	C2
George Street	B1
Gilmore Place	C1
Gloucester Lane	A1
Grassmarket	B2
Great King Street	A1
Grove Street	B1
Hamilton Place	A1
Hanover Street	A2
Hatton Place	C2
Henderson Row	A1
Heriot Row	A1
High Riggs	B1
High Street	B2
Hill Street	A1
Hillside Crescent	A3
Holyrood Park Road	C3
Holyrood Road	B3
Home Street	C1
Howe Street	A1
India Street	A1
Jamaica Street	A1
Johnston Terrace	B1
Lauriston Gardens	C2
Lauriston Place	B2
Lawnmarket	B2
Leamington Terrace	C1
Leith Street	A2
Leith Walk	A3
Leven Street	C1
London Road	A3
London Street	A2
Lothian Road	B1
Marchmont Road	C2
Marchmont Crescent	C2
Market Street	B2
Melville Drive	C2
Melville Street	B1
Melville Terrace	C2
Montgomery Street	A3
Montpelier Park	C1
Moray Place	A1
Morrison Street	B1
Nicolson Street	B2
North Bridge	B2
Northumberland Street	A1
Pleasance	B3
Potterrow	B2
Princes Street	B1
Queen's Drive	B3
Queensferry Street	B1
Queen Street	A1
Raeburn Place	A1
Regent Road	A3
Regent Terrace	A3
Rose Street	B1
Royal Circus	A1
Royal Terrace	A3
St. Andrew's Square	A2
St. Leonards Street	C3
St. Stephen Street	A1
Salisbury Road	C3
Sciennes Road	C2
Scotland Street	A2
Shandwick Place	B1
South Bridge	B2
The Mound	B2
Thistle Street	A2
Union Street	A2
Viewforth	C1
Viewcraig Gardens	B3
Warrender Park Terrace	C1
Warrender Park Road	C1
Waterloo Place	A2
Waverley Bridge	B2
West Approach Road	C1
West Port	B1
Whitehouse Loan	C1
Young Street	A1
York Place	A2

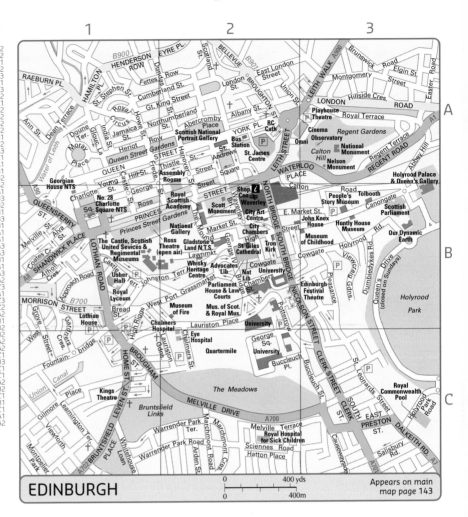

EDINBURGH

| 0 | 400 yds |
| 0 | 400m |

Appears on main
map page 143

Tourist Information Centre: Civic Centre, Paris Street
Tel: 01392 265700

Albion Street	C1
Alphington Street	C1
Barnfield Road	B2
Bartholomew Street West	B1
Bedford Street	B2
Belmont Road	A3
Blackboy Road	A3
Blackall Road	A2
Bonhay Road	B1
Buller Road	C1
Church Road	C1
Clifton Hill	A3
Clifton Road	B3
Clifton Street	B3
College Road	B3
Commercial Road	C1
Cowick Street	C1
Danes Road	A1
Denmark Road	A2
Devonshire Place	B3
East Grove Road	A3
Elmside	C3
Exe Street	A3
Fore Street	B1
Haldon Road	B2
Haven Road	B1
Heavitree Road	C2
Hele Road	B3
High Street	A1
Holloway Street	B2
Hoopern Street	C2
Howell Road	A2
Iddesleigh Road	A2
Iron Bridge	A3
Isca Road	B1
Jesmond Road	C2
Longbrook Street	A3
Looe Road	A2
Lyndhurst Road	A1
Magdalen Road	C3
Magdalen Street	B3
Marlborough Road	C2
Matford Avenue	C3
Matford Lane	C3
Mount Pleasant Road	C3
New Bridge Street	A3
New North Road	C1
Okehampton Road	A1/A2
Okehampton Street	C1
Old Tiverton Road	C1
Oxford Road	A3
Paris Street	B2
Paul Street	B2
Pennsylvania Road	B2
Portland Street	A2
Prince of Wales Road	B3
Prospect Park	A1
Queen's Road	A3
Queen Street	C1
Radford Road	B2
Richmond Road	C3
St. David's Hill	B1
St. James' Road	A1
St. Leonard's Road	A3
Sidwell Street	C3
Southernhay East	B2
South Street	B2
Spicer Road	B3
Station Road	B3
Streatham Drive	A1
Streatham Rise	A1
The Quay	C2
Thornton Hill	A2
Topsham Road	C2
Velwell Road	A1
Victoria Street	A3
Water Lane	C2
Well Street	A3
West Avenue	A2
Western Road	B1
Western Way	B2
Wonford Road	C3
York Road	A2

EXETER

| 0 | 400 yds |
| 0 | 400m |

Appears on main
map page 10

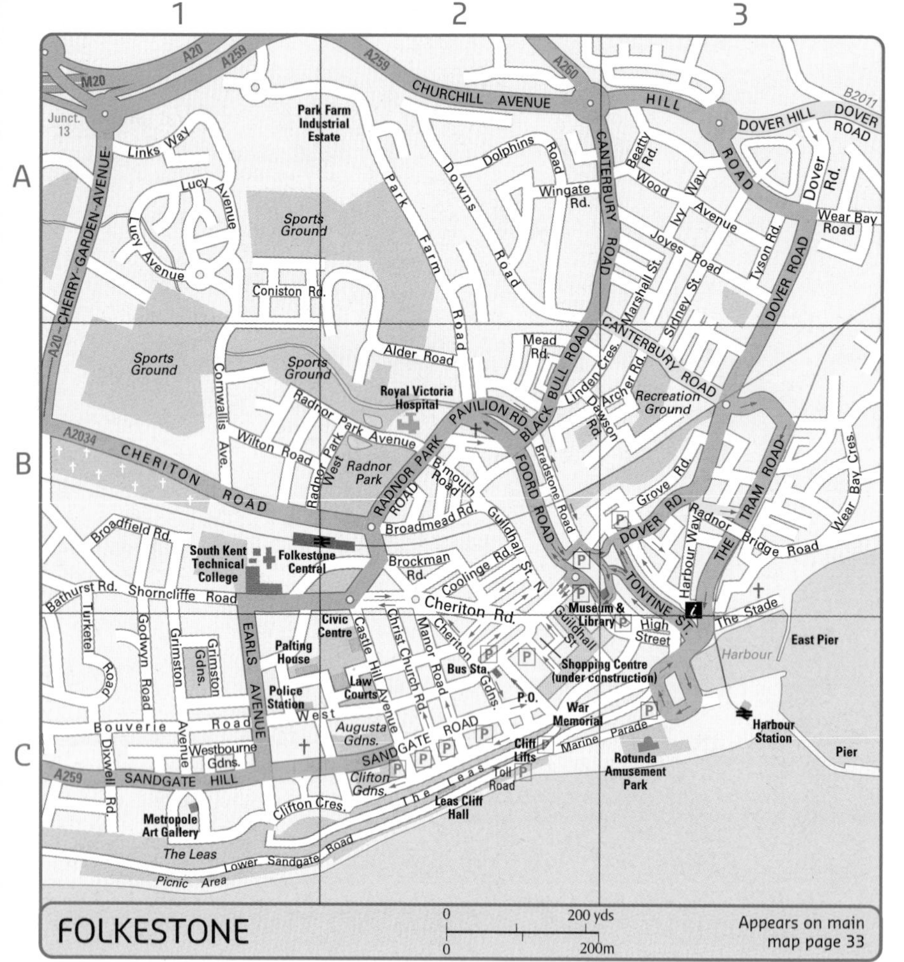

FOLKESTONE

0　200 yds
0　200m

Appears on main
map page 33

Tourist Information Centre: Harbour Street
Tel: 01303 258594

Alder Road	B2	Wingate Road	A2
Archer Road	B3	Wood Avenue	A3
Bathurst Road	B1	Wilton Road	B1
Beatty Road	A3		
Black Bull Road	B2		
Bournemouth Road	B2		
Bouverie Road West	C1		
Bradstone Road	B2		
Broadfield Road	B1		
Broadmead Road	B2		
Brockman Road	B2		
Canterbury Road	A3		
Castle Hill Avenue	C2		
Cheriton Gardens	C2		
Cheriton Road	B1/B2		
Cherry Garden Avenue	A1		
Christ Church Road	C2		
Churchill Avenue	A2		
Clifton Crescent	C1		
Coniston Road	A1		
Coolinge Road	B2		
Cornwallis Avenue	B1		
Dawson Road	B2		
Dixwell Road	C1		
Dolphins Road	A2		
Dover Hill	A3		
Dover Road	A3		
Downs Road	A2		
Earles Avenue	C1		
Foord Road	B2		
Godwyn Road	C1		
Grimston Avenue	C1		
Grimston Gardens	C1		
Guildhall Street	B2		
Guildhall Street North	B2		
Harbour Way	B3		
High Street	C3		
Hill Road	A3		
Ivy Way	A3		
Joyes Road	A3		
Linden Crescent	B2		
Links Way	A1		
Lower Sandgate Road	C1		
Lucy Avenue	A1		
Manor Road	C2		
Marine Parade	C2		
Marshall Street	A3		
Mead Road	B2		
Park Farm Road	A2		
Pavilion Road	B2		
Radnor Bridge Road	B3		
Radnor Park Avenue	B1		
Radnor Park Road	B1		
Radnor Park West	B1		
Sandgate Hill	C1		
Sandgate Road	C2		
Shorncliffe Road	B1		
Sidney Street	B3		
The Leas	C2		
The Stade	C3		
The Tram Road	B3		
Tontine Street	B3		
Turketel Road	C1		
Tyson Road	A3		
Wear Bay Crescent	B3		
Wear Bay Road	A3		
Westbourne Gardens	C1		

GLASGOW

0　200 yds
0　200m

Appears on main
map page 141

Tourist Information Centre: 11 George Square
Tel: 0141 204 4400

Argyle Street	B1	Pinkston Road	A3
Bain Street	C3	Pitt Street	B1
Baird Street	A3	Port Dundas Road	A2
Barrack Street	C3	Renfield Street	B2
Bath Street	A1/B1	Renfrew Street	A1
Bedford Street	C2	Robertson Street	B1
Bell Street	B3/C3	Rottenrow East	B3
Blythswood Street	B1	Saltmarket	C2
Bothwell Street	B1	Sauchiehall Street	A1
Bridge Street	C2	Scotland Street	C1
Broomielaw	B1	Scott Street	A1
Brown Street	B1	Springburn Road	A3
Buccleuch Street	A1	St. George's Road	A1
Buchanan Street	B2	St. James Road	B3
Cadogan Street	B1	St. Mungo Avenue	B3
Carlton Place	C2	St. Vincent Street	B1
Castle Street	B3	Stevenson Street	C3
Cathedral Street	B2	Stewart Street	A2
Clyde Place	C1	Stirling Road	B3
Clyde Street	C2	Stockwell Street	C2
Cochrane Street	B2	The Green	C3
Commerce Street	C1	Trongate	B2
Cook Street	C1	Union Street	B2
Cowcaddens Road	A2	Victoria Bridge	C2
Craighall Road	A2	Washington Street	B1
Dobbie's Loan	A2	Waterloo Street	B1
Duke Street	B3	Wellington Street	B1
Eglinton Street	C1	West Campbell Street	B1
Gallowgate	C3	West George Street	B1
Garnet Street	A1	West Graham Street	A1
Garscube Road	A1	West Nile Street	B2
George Square	B2	West Princes Street	A1
George Street	B3	West Regent Street	B1
George V Bridge	C1	West Street	C1
Glasgow Bridge	C2	Wilson Street	B2
Glassford Street	B2	Wishart Street	B3
Gloucester Street	C1	York Street	B1
Gordon Street	B2		
Great Western Road	A1		
Greendyke Street	C3		
High Street	B3		
Holland Street	B1		
Hope Street	B2		
Hunter Street	C3		
Ingram Street	B2		
Inner Ring Road	A3		
Jamaica Street	C2		
James Watt Street	B1		
Kennedy Street	A3		
Kingston Bridge	C1		
Kingston Street	C1		
Kyle Street	A2		
Lister Street	A3		
London Road	C3		
Maryhill Road	A1		
McAlpine Street	B1		
Mitchell Street	B2		
Molendinar Street	C3		
Montrose Street	B3		
Morrison Street	C1		
Nelson Street	C1		
New City Road	A1		
Norfolk Street	C2		
North Canal Bank Street	A2		
North Hanover Street	B2		
Oswald Street	C1		
Paisley Road	C1		

Gloucester   Guildford

239

Tourist Information Centre: 28 Southgate Street
Tel: 01452 421188

Adelaide Street	C2	Southgate Street	B1
Alexandra Road	A2	Spa Road	B1
Alfred Street	B3	Stanley Road	C2
Alma Place	C1	Station Road	B2
Alvin Street	A2	Stroud Road	C1
Archdeacon Street	A1	The Quay	B1
Argyll Road	A3	Tredworth Road	C2
Askwith Road	C3	Trier Way	C1
Barnwood Road	A3	Upton Street	C2
Barton Street	B2	Vicarage Road	C3
Black Dog Way	A2	Victoria Street	B2
Bristol Road	C1	Wellington Street	B2
Brunswick Road	B2	Westgate Street	A1
Bruton Way	B2	Weston Road	C1
Calton Road	C2	Wheatstone Road	C2
Cecil Road	C1	Willow Avenue	C3
Cheltenham Road	A3	Worcester Street	A2
Churchill Road	C1		
Conduit Street	C2		
Coney Hill Road	C3		
Dean's Way	A2		
Denmark Road	A2		
Derby Road	B2		
Estcourt Road	A2		
Eastern Avenue	C3		
Eastgate Street	B2		
Frampton Road	C1		
Gouda Way	A1		
Great Western Road	B2		
Greyfriars	B2		
Hatherley Road	C2		
Heathville Road	A2		
Henry Road	A2		
High Street	C2		
Hopewell Street	C2		
Horton Road	B3		
Howard Street	C2		
India Road	C2		
King Edward's Avenue	C2		
Kingsholm Road	A2		
Lansdown Road	A2		
Linden Road	C1		
Llanthony Road	B1		
London Road	A2		
Lower Westgate Street	A1		
Marlborough Road	C3		
Merevale Road	A3		
Metz Way	B2		
Midland Road	C2		
Millbrook Street	B2		
Myers Road	B3		
Northgate Street	B2		
Oxford Road	A2		
Oxstalls Lane	A3		
Painswick Road	C3		
Park Road	B2		
Parkend Road	C2		
Pitt Street	B1		
Quay Street	B1		
Regent Street	C2		
Robinson Road	C1		
Ryecroft Street	C2		
St. Ann Way	C1		
St. Oswald's Road	A1		
Secunda Way	B1		
Severn Road	B1		
Seymour Road	C1		

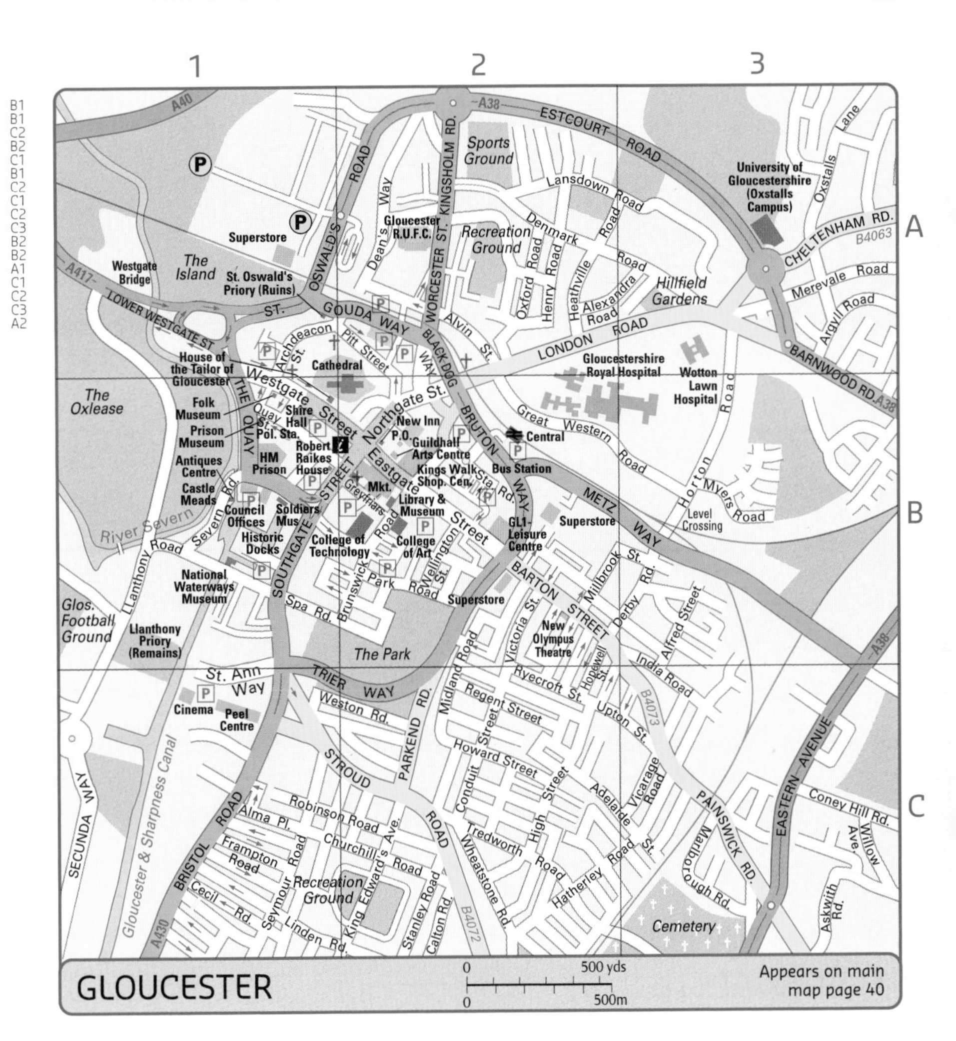

GLOUCESTER

0 — 500 yds
0 — 500m

Appears on main map page 40

Tourist Information Centre: 14 Tunsgate
Tel: 01483 444333

Abbot Road	C3	Victoria Road	A3
Artillery Road	A2	Walnut Tree Close	A1
Artillery Terrace	A2	Warwicks	C3
Bedford Road	A2	Wharf Road	A2
Bridge Street	B2	Wherwell Road	B1
Bright Hill	B3	Wodeland Avenue	C1
Bury Fields	C2	Woodbridge Road	A2
Bury Street	C2	York Road	A2
Castle Hill	C3		
Castle Square	B3		
Castle Street	B2		
Chertsey Street	A3		
Cheselden Road	B3		
Commercial Road	B2		
Dapdune Road	A2		
Dapdune Wharf	A2		
Dene Road	A3		
Denmark Road	A3		
Denzil Road	B1		
Drummond Road	A2		
Eagle Road	A3		
Eastgate Gardens	B1		
Farnham Road	C2		
Flower Walk	C3		
Fort Road	C3		
Friary Bridge	B2		
Friary Street	B2		
Genun Road	B1		
Guildford Park Avenue	A1		
Guildford Park Road	B1		
Harvey Road	B3		
Haydon Place	A2		
High Street	B2/B3		
Laundry Road	A2		
Lawn Road	C2		
Leap Lane	B2		
Leas Road	A2		
Ludlow Road	B1		
Market Street	B2		
Martyr Road	B2		
Mary Road	A2		
Millbrook	C2		
Millmead	B2		
Millmead Terrace	C2		
Mount Pleasant	C1		
Nightingale Road	A3		
North Street	B2		
Onslow Road	A3		
Onslow Street	B2		
Pannells Court	B3		
Park Road	A2		
Park Street	B2		
Pewley Hill	B3		
Portsmouth Road	C2		
Quarry Street	B2		
Rookwood Court	C1		
Sand Terrace	A2		
Semaphore Road	C3		
South Hill	B3		
Springfield Road	A3		
Station Approach	A3		
Station View	A1		
Stoke Road	A3		
Swan Lane	B2		
Sydenham Road	B3		
The Bars	B2		
The Mount	C1		

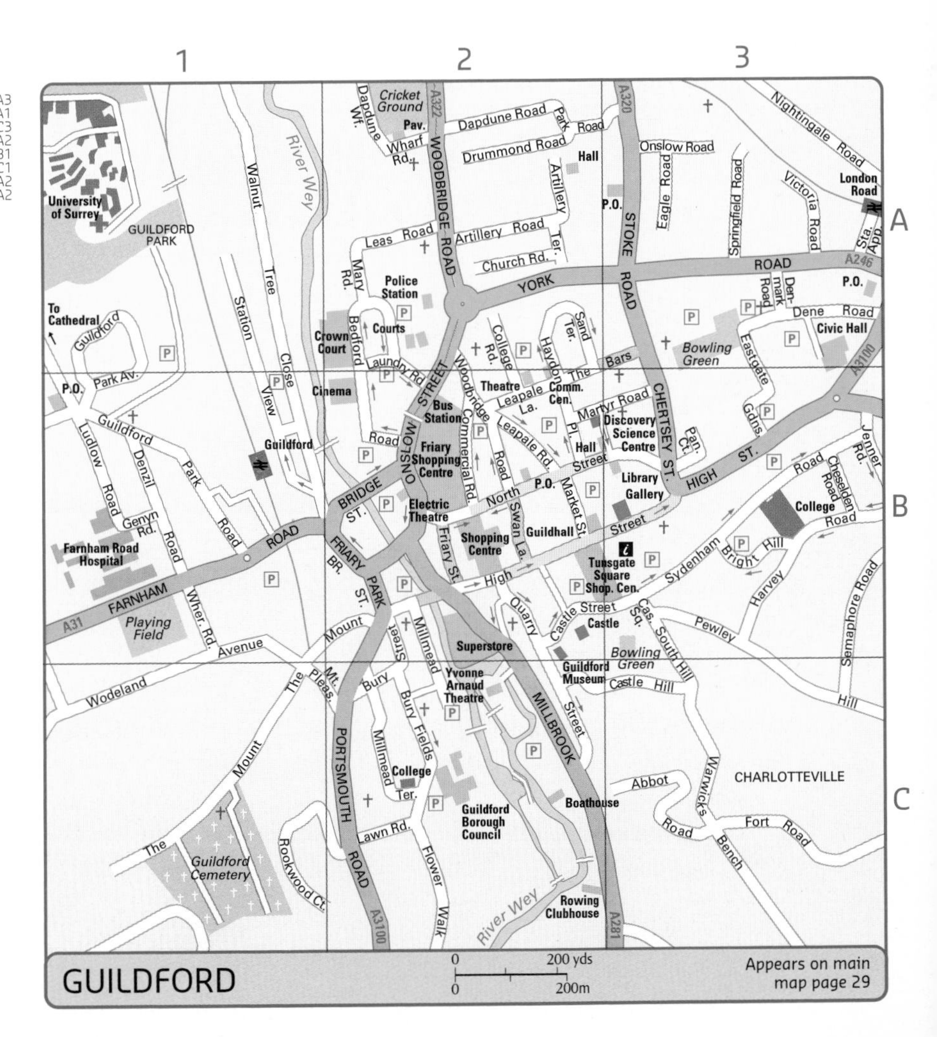

GUILDFORD

0 — 200 yds
0 — 200m

Appears on main map page 29

Harrogate

HARROGATE

| | | 1 | 2 | 3 |

0   150 yds
0   150m

Appears on main map page 102

Tourist Information Centre: Royal Baths Assembly Rooms, Crescent Road Tel: 01423 537300

Ainsty Road	A3	Regent Parade	A3
Albert Street	B2	Regent Street	A3
Alexandra Road	A2	Regent Terrace	A3
Arthington Avenue	B2	Ripon Road	A1
Beech Grove	C1	Robert Street	C2
Belford Road	B2	St. James Drive	C3
Bower Road	A2	St. Mary's Walk	C1
Bower Street	B2	Skipton Road	A3
Cambridge Street	B2	South Park Road	C2
Cavendish Avenue	C3	Springfield Avenue	A1
Chelmsford Road	B2	Spring Grove	A1
Cheltenham Mount	A2	Spring Mount	A1
Chudleigh Road	A3	Station Avenue	B2
Clarence Drive	B1	Station Parade	B2
Claro Road	A3	Stray Rein	C2
Cold Bath Road	C1	Stray Walk	C3
Commercial Street	A2	Studley Road	A2
Coppice Drive	A1	Swan Road	B1
Cornwall Road	B1	The Grove	A3
Crescent Gardens	B1	Tower Street	C2
Dragon Avenue	A2	Trinity Road	C2
Dragon Parade	A2	Valley Drive	B1
Dragon Road	A2	Victoria Avenue	B2
Duchy Road	A1	Victoria Road	C1
East Parade	B2	West End Avenue	C1
East Park Road	B2	West Park	B2
Franklin Mount	A2	Woodside	B2
Franklin Road	A2	York Place	C2
Gascoigne Crescent	A3	York Road	B1
Glebe Avenue	B1		
Glebe Road	C1		
Grove Park Terrace	A3		
Grove Road	A2		
Harcourt Drive	B3		
Harcourt Road	A3		
Heywood Road	C1		
Hollins Road	A1		
Homestead Road	B2		
James Street	B2		
Kent Road	A1		
King's Road	B1		
Knaresborough Road	B3		
Lancaster Road	C1		
Leeds Road	C2		
Lime Grove	A3		
Lime Street	A3		
Mayfield Grove	A2		
Montpellier Hill	B1		
Montpellier Street	B1		
Mowbray Square	A3		
North Park Road	B3		
Oatlands Drive	C3		
Otley Road	C1		
Oxford Street	B2		
Park Chase	A3		
Park Drive	C2		
Park Parade	B3		
Park Road	C1		
Park View	B2		
Parliament Street	B1		
Princes Villa Road	B2		
Providence Terrace	A2		
Queen Parade	B3		
Queen's Road	C1		
Raglan Street	B2		
Regent Avenue	A3		
Regent Grove	A3		

Hastings

HASTINGS

| | | 1 | 2 | 3 |

0   500 yds
0   500m

Appears on main map page 18

Tourist Information Centre: Queens Square, Priory Meadow Tel: 01424 781111

Albert Road	C2	St. Mary's Road	B2
All Saints Street	B3	St. Mary's Terrace	B2
Amherst Road	B3	St. Thomas's Road	B3
Ashburnham Road	B3	Thanet Way	A1
Ashford Road	A1	The Bourne	B3
Ashford Way	A1	Upper Park Road	B1
Baldslow Road	B2	Vicarage Road	B2
Beaconsfield Road	A2	Warrior Square	C1
Bembrook Road	B3	Wellington Road	B2
Bohemia Road	B1	White Rock	C1
Braybrooke Road	B2	Woodbrook Road	A2
Broomsgrove Road	A3	Wykeham Road	B1
Cambridge Road	C1		
Castle Hill Road	C2		
Castle Street	C2		
Chiltern Drive	A3		
Church Road	C1		
Collier Road	B3		
Cornwallis Terrace	C1		
Croft Road	B3		
De Cham Road	C1		
Denmark Place	C2		
Downs Road	A2		
East Parade	C3		
Elphinstone Road	A2		
Eversfield Place	C1		
Falaise Road	C1		
Farley Bank	A3		
Fearon Road	A2		
Fellows Road	A3		
Frederick Road	A3		
Freshwater Avenue	A1		
George Street	C3		
Harold Place	C2		
Harold Road	B3		
High Street	B3		
Hillside Road	A1		
Hoad's Wood Road	A2		
Hughenden Road	A2		
Laton Road	A2		
Linley Drive	A2		
Linton Road	B1		
Lower Park Road	B1		
Magdalen Road	C1		
Malvern Way	A3		
Marine Parade	C3		
Milward Road	B2		
Mount Pleasant Road	A2		
Old London Road	B3		
Park Avenue	A1		
Park Crescent	A1		
Park View	A1		
Park Way	A1		
Parker Road	A2		
Parkstone Road	A1		
Pelham Place	C2		
Priory Avenue	B2		
Priory Road	B3		
Queen's Road	B2		
Robertson Street	C2		
Rock-a-Nore Road	C3		
St. George's Road	B3		
St. Helen's Down	B2		
St. Helen's Park Road	B2		
St. Helen's Road	A1		
St. John's Road	C1		
St. Margaret's Road	C1		

Tourist Information Centre: 1 King Street
Tel: 01432 268430

Aubrey Street	B2
Barrs Court Road	A3
Barton Road	B1
Barton Yard	B1
Bath Street	B3
Belmont Avenue	C1
Berrington Street	B2
Bewell Street	B2
Blackfriars Street	A2
Blueschool Street	A2
Brewers Passage	B2
Bridge Street	B2
Broad Street	B2
Canonmoor Street	A1
Cantilupe Street	B3
Castle Street	B2
Catherine Street	A2
Central Avenue	B3
Church Street	B2
Commercial Road	A3
Commercial Street	B2
Coningsby Street	A2
East Street	B2
Edgar Street	A2
Eign Gate	B2
Eign Street	B1
Ferrers Street	B2
Friars Street	B1
Fryzer Court	B2
Gaol Street	B3
Green Street	C3
Grenfell Road	C3
Greyfriars Avenue	C1
Greyfriars Bridge	B2
Grove Road	C3
Harold Street	C3
High Street	B2
High Town	B2
King Street	B2
Kyrle Street	B3
Maylord Street	B2
Mill Street	C3
Monkmoor Street	A3
Moorfield Street	A1
Moor Street	A2
Mostyn Street	A1
Nelson Street	C3
Newmarket Street	A2
Park Street	C3
Penhaligon Way	A1
Plough Lane	A1
Portland Street	A1
Quay Street	B2
Ryeland Street	B1
St. Guthlac Street	B3
St. James Road	C3
St. Martin's Avenue	C2
St. Martin's Street	C2
St. Owen Street	B3
Station Approach	A3
Station Road	B1
Stonebow Road	A3
Symonds Street	B3
The Atrium	A2
Turner Street	C3
Union Street	B2
Union Walk	A3

Vaughan Street	B3
Victoria Street	B1
West Street	B2
Widemarsh Street	B2
Wye Street	C2

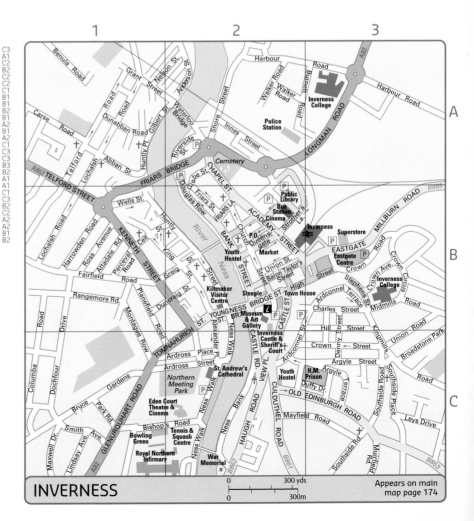

HEREFORD

0   250 yds
0   250m

Appears on main map page 53

Tourist Information Centre: Castle Wynd
Tel: 0845 2255121

Abban Street	A1
Academy Street	B2
Alexander Place	B2
Anderson Street	A2
Ardconnel Street	C2
Ardconnel Terrace	B3
Ardross Place	C2
Ardross Street	C2
Argyle Street	C3
Argyle Terrace	C3
Attadale Road	B1
Bank Street	B2
Baron Taylor's Street	B2
Benula Road	A1
Bishop's Road	C1
Bridge Street	B2
Broadstone Park	C3
Bruce Gardens	C1
Burnett Road	A3
Carse Road	A1
Castle Road	B2
Castle Street	B2
Celt Street	B1
Chapel Street	A2
Charles Street	B3
Church Street	B2
Columba Road	C1
Crown Avenue	B3
Crown Circus	B3
Crown Road	B3
Crown Street	C3
Culduthel Road	C2
Denny Street	C3
Dochfour Drive	C1
Douglas Row	A2
Duffy Drive	C2
Duncraig Street	B1
Eastgate	B3
Fairfield Road	B1
Friars Bridge	A1
Friars Lane	B2
Friars Street	B2
Gilbert Street	A1
Glebe Street	A2
Glen Urquhart Road	C1
Grant Street	A1
Greig Street	B1
Harbour Road	A2
Harrowden Road	A1
Haugh Road	C2
High Street	B2
Hill Street	B3
Hontly Place	A1
Huntly Street	B1
Innes Street	A2
Kenneth Street	B1
Kingsmills Road	B3
King Street	B1
Leys Drive	C3
Lindsay Avenue	C1
Lochalsh Road	A1
Longman Road	A2
Maxwell Drive	C1
Mayfield Road	C2
Midmills Road	B3
Millburn Road	B3
Montague Row	B1

Muirfield Road	C3
Nelson Street	A1
Ness Bank	C2
Ness Bridge	B2
Ness Walk	C2
Old Edinburgh Road	C2
Park Road	C1
Perceval Road	B1
Planefield Road	B1
Queensgate	B2
Rancemore Road	B1
Riverside Street	A2
Ross Avenue	B1
Shore Street	A2
Smith Avenue	C1
Southside Place	C3
Southside Road	C3
Stephens Street	B3
Strother's Lane	B2
Telford Road	A1
Telford Street	A1
Tomnahurich Street	C1
Union Road	C3
Union Street	B2
View Place	C2
Walker Road	A2
Waterloo Bridge	A2
Wells Street	B1
Young Street	B2

INVERNESS

0   300 yds
0   300m

Appears on main map page 174

KINGSTON UPON HULL

| 0 | 300 yds |
| 0 | 300m |

Appears on main map page 104

Tourist Information Centre: 1 Paragon Street
Tel: 01482 223559

Adelaide Street	C1	Worship Street	A2
Albion Street	B1	Wright Street	A1
Alfred Gelder Street	B2		
Anlaby Road	B1		
Anne Street	B1		
Beverley Road	A1		
Bond Street	B2		
Brunswick Avenue	A1		
Canning Street	B1		
Caroline Street	A2		
Carr Lane	B1		
Castle Street	A2		
Charles Street	A2		
Charterhouse Lane	A2		
Church Street	B3		
Citadel Way	B3		
Clarence Street	B3		
Cleveland Street	A3		
Dansom Lane	A3		
English Street	C1		
Ferensway	A1		
Francis Street	A2		
Freetown Way	A1		
Garrison Road	B3		
George Street	B2		
Great Union Street	A3		
Green Lane	A2		
Guildhall Road	B2		
Hessle Road	C1		
High Street	A3		
Hyperion Street	A3		
Jameson Street	B1		
Jarratt Street	A2		
Jenning Street	A2		
King Edward Street	B1		
Kingston Street	C1		
Liddell Street	A1		
Lime Street	A2		
Lister Street	C1		
Lowgate	B2		
Market Place	B2		
Myton Street	B1		
New Cleveland Street	A3		
New George Street	A2		
Norfolk Street	A1		
North Bridge	A2		
Osborne Street	B1		
Pilots Way	C3		
Porter Street	C1		
Princes Dock Street	B2		
Prospect Street	A1		
Queen Street	C2		
Reform Street	A2		
St. Lukes Street	B1		
St. Mark Street	A3		
Scale Lane	B2		
Scott Street	A2		
Scott Street Bridge	A2		
South Bridge Road	B3		
Spring Bank	A1		
Spring Street	B1		
Spyvee Street	A3		
Waterhouse Lane	C1		
Wellington Street West	C1		
William Street	C1		
Witham	A3		

LEEDS

| 0 | 300 yds |
| 0 | 300m |

Appears on main map page 102

Tourist Information Centre: Gateway Yorkshire, The Arcade,
City Station Tel: 0113 242 5242

Aire Street	C1	Skinner Lane	A3
Albion Place	B2	Swinegate	C2
Albion Street	B2	Templar Street	B3
Basinghall Street	B2	The Calls	C3
Bedford Street	B2	The Headrow	B2
Bishopgate Street	C2	Thoresby Place	B1
Blenheim Walk	A2	Trafalgar Street	B3
Boar Lane	C2	Vicar Lane	B3
Bridge End	C2	Victoria Square	B1
Bridge Street	B3	Wade Lane	B2
Briggate	C2	Wellington Street	C1
Byron Street	A3	Westgate	B1
Call Lane	C3	Whitehall Road	C1
Calverley Street	A1	Willow Terrace	A1
Carlton Gate	A2	Woodhouse Lane	A1/A2
City Square	C2	York Place	C1
Clarendon Way	A1		
Clay Pit Lane	A2		
Commercial Street	B2		
Concord Street	A3		
Concordia Street	C2		
Cookridge Street	B2		
Crown Point Road	C3		
Duke Street	C2		
Duncan Street	C2		
Dyer Street	B3		
East Parade	B1		
Eastgate	B2		
Elmwood Road	A2		
George Street	B3		
Gower Street	B3		
Grafton Street	A3		
Great George Street	B1		
Greek Street	B2		
High Court	C3		
Infirmary Street	B1		
Inner Ring Road	A1/A2		
King Edward Street	B2		
King Street	C1		
Kirkgate	C2/C3		
Lands Lane	B2		
Little Queen Street	C1		
Lovell Park Hill	A3		
Lovell Road	A3		
Melbourne Street	B3		
Merrion Street	B2		
Merrion Way	A2		
Neville Street	C2		
New Briggate	B2		
New Market Street	C3		
New Station Street	C2		
New York Road	B3		
New York Street	C3		
Northern Street	C1		
North Street	A3		
Park Place	B1		
Park Row	B2		
Park Square East	B1		
Park Square West	B1		
Park Street	B1		
Portland Crescent	A2		
Portland Way	A2		
Quebec Street	C1		
Queen Street	C1		
Sovereign Street	C2		
St. Paul's Street	B1		
St. Peter's Street	B3		

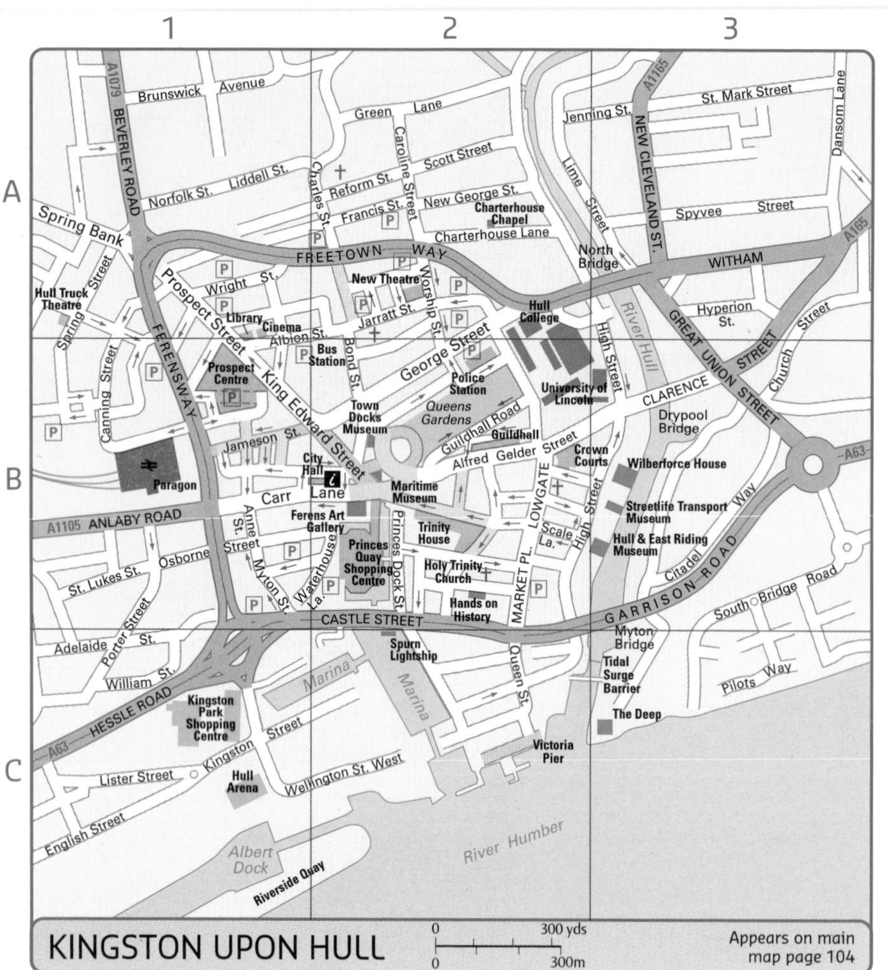

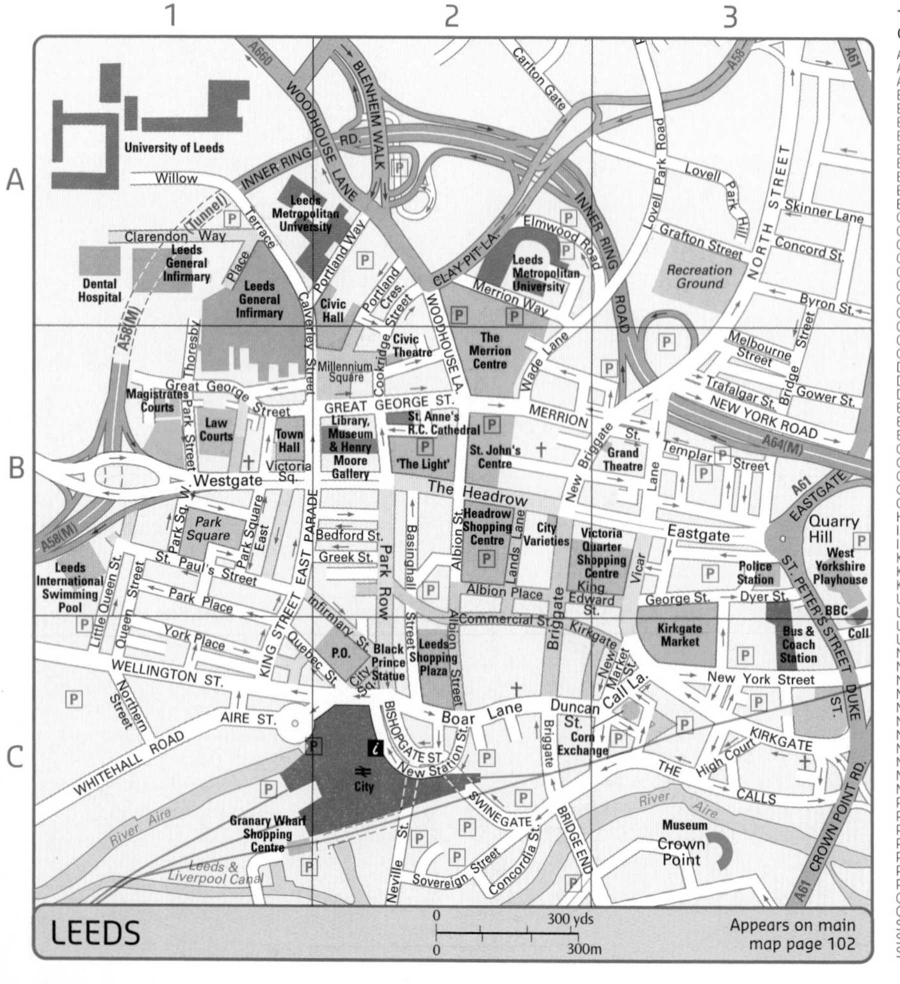

Leicester

Tourist Information Centre: 7-9 Every Street, Town Hall Square
Tel: 0906 294 1113 (Premium Rate)

Abbey Street	A2	Market Place South	B2
Albion Street	B2	Market Street	B2
All Saints Road	B1	Mill Lane	C1
Aylestone Road	C2	Millstone Lane	B2
Bassett Street	A1	Montreal Road	A3
Bath Lane	B1	Morledge Street	B3
Bedford Street North	A3	Narborough Road	C1
Belgrave Gate	A2	Narborough Road North	C1
Bell Lane	A3	Nelson Street	C1
Belvoir Street	B2	Newarke Close	B2
Braunstone Gate	B1	Northgate Street	A1
Burgess Street	A2	Ottawa Road	A3
Burleys Way	A2	Oxford Street	B2
Byron Street	A2	Pasture Lane	A1
Cank Street	B2	Peacock Lane	B2
Castle Street	B1	Pocklingtons Walk	B2
Charles Street	B3	Prebend Street	C3
Christow Street	A3	Princess Road East	C3
Church Gate	A2	Pringle Street	A1
Clarence Street	A2	Queen Street	B3
Clyde Street	A3	Regent Road	C2
College Street	B3	Regent Street	C2
Colton Street	B3	Repton Street	A1
Conduit Street	B3	Rutland Street	B3
Crafton Street East	A3	Samuel Street	B3
Cravan Street	A1	Sanvey Gare	A1
De Montfort Street	C3	Saxby Street	C3
Deacon Street	C2	Slater Street	A1
Dryden Street	A2	Soar Lane	A1
Duns Lane	B1	South Albion Street	B3
Dunton Street	A1	Southampton Street	B3
Eastern Boulevard	C1	Sparkenhoe Street	B3
Friar Lane	B2	St. George Street	B3
Friday Street	A2	St. George's Way	B3
Frog Island	A1	St. John's Street	A2
Gallowtree Gate	B2	St. Margaret's Way	A1
Gaul Street	C1	St. Matthew's Way	A3
Glebe Street	B3	St. Nicholas Circle	B1
Gotham Street	C3	St. Peter's Lane	A2
Granby Street	B2	Swain Street	B3
Grange Lane	C2	Swan Street	A1
Grasmere Street	C1	Taylor Road	A3
Great Central Street	A1	Thames Street	A2
Halford Street	B2	The Gateway	C1
Havelock Street	C2	The Newarke	B1
Haymarket	A2	Tower Street	C2
High Street	B2	Tudor Road	A1
Highcross Street	A1	Ullswater Street	C1
Hobart Street	B3	University Road	C3
Horsfair Street	B2	Upperton Road	C1
Humberstone Gate	B2	Vaughan Way	A1
Humberstone Road	A3	Vestry Street	B3
Infirmary Road	C2	Walnut Street	C1
Jarrom Street	C1	Waterloo Way	C3
Jarvis Street	B1	Welford Road	B2
Kamloops Crescent	A3	Wellington Street	B2
Kent Street	A3	West Street	C2
King Richard's Road	B1	Western Boulevard	C1
King Street	B2	Western Road	C1
Lancaster Road	C2	Wharf Street	A2
Lee Street	A2	Wharf Street North	A3
Lincoln Street	B3	Wilberforce Road	C1
London Road	C3	Windermere Street	C1
Loseby Lane	B2	Woodboy Street	A3
Lower Brown Street	B2	Yeoman Street	B2
Manitoba Road	A3	York Road	B2
Mansfield Street	A2		

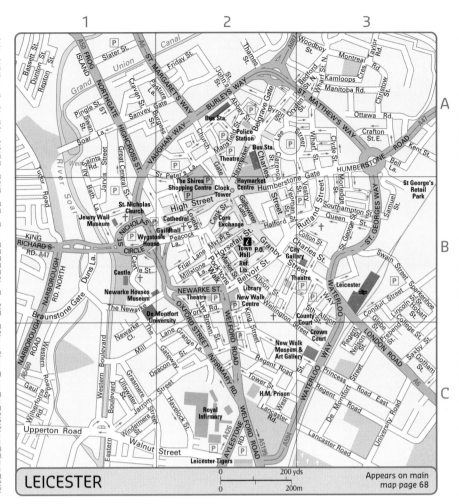

Lincoln

Tourist Information Centre: 9 Castle Hill
Tel: 01522 873213

Alexandra Terrace	B1	St. Anne's Road	B3
Baggholme Road	B3	St. Giles Avenue	A3
Ballgate	A2	St. Mark Street	C2
Beaumont Fee	B2	St. Mary's Street	C2
Beevor Street	C1	St. Rumbold Street	B2
Brayford Way	C1	Stamp End	C3
Brayford Wharf North	B1	Steep Hill	B2
Broadgate	B2	The Avenue	B1
Broadway	A2	Tritton Road	C1
Bruce Road	A3	Union Row	B2
Burton Road	A1	Upper Lindum Street	B3
Canwick Road	C2	Upper Long Leys Road	A1
Carholme Road	B1	Vere Street	A2
Carline Road	A1	Vine Street	B3
Carr Street	B1	Waterside North	C2
Cheviot Street	B3	Waterside South	C2
Church Lane	A2	West Parade	B1
Clasketgate	B2	Westgate	A2
Croft Street	B2	Wigford Way	B2
Cross Street	C2	Wilson Street	A1
Curle Avenue	A3	Winn Street	B3
Drury Lane	B2	Wragby Road	B3
East Gate	B2	Yarborough Road	A1
Firth Road	C1		
George Street	C3		
Great Northern Terrace	C2		
Greetwell Close	A3		
Greetwell Road	B3		
Gresham Street	B1		
Hampton Street	B1		
Harvey Street	C2		
High Street	C2		
John Street	B3		
Langworthgate	A2		
Lee Road	A3		
Lindum Road	B2		
Lindum Terrace	B3		
Long Leys Road	A1		
Mainwaring Road	A3		
Mill Road	A1		
Milman Road	B3		
Monks Road	B3		
Monson Street	C2		
Moor Street	B1		
Mount Street	A1		
Nettleham Road	A2		
Newland	B1		
Newland Street West	B1		
Newport	A2		
Northgate	A2		
Orchard Street	B1		
Pelham Bridge	C2		
Portland Street	C2		
Portland Street	C2		
Pottergate	B2		
Queensway	A3		
Rasen Lane	A2		
Richmond Road	B1		
Ripon Street	C2		
Rope Walk	C1		
Rosemary Lane	B2		
Ruskin Avenue	A3		
Saltergate	B2		
Sewell Road	B3		
Silver Street	B2		
Sincil Bank	C2		
Spa Road	C3		

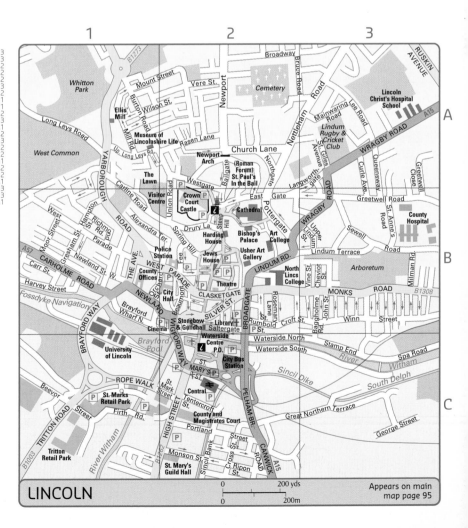

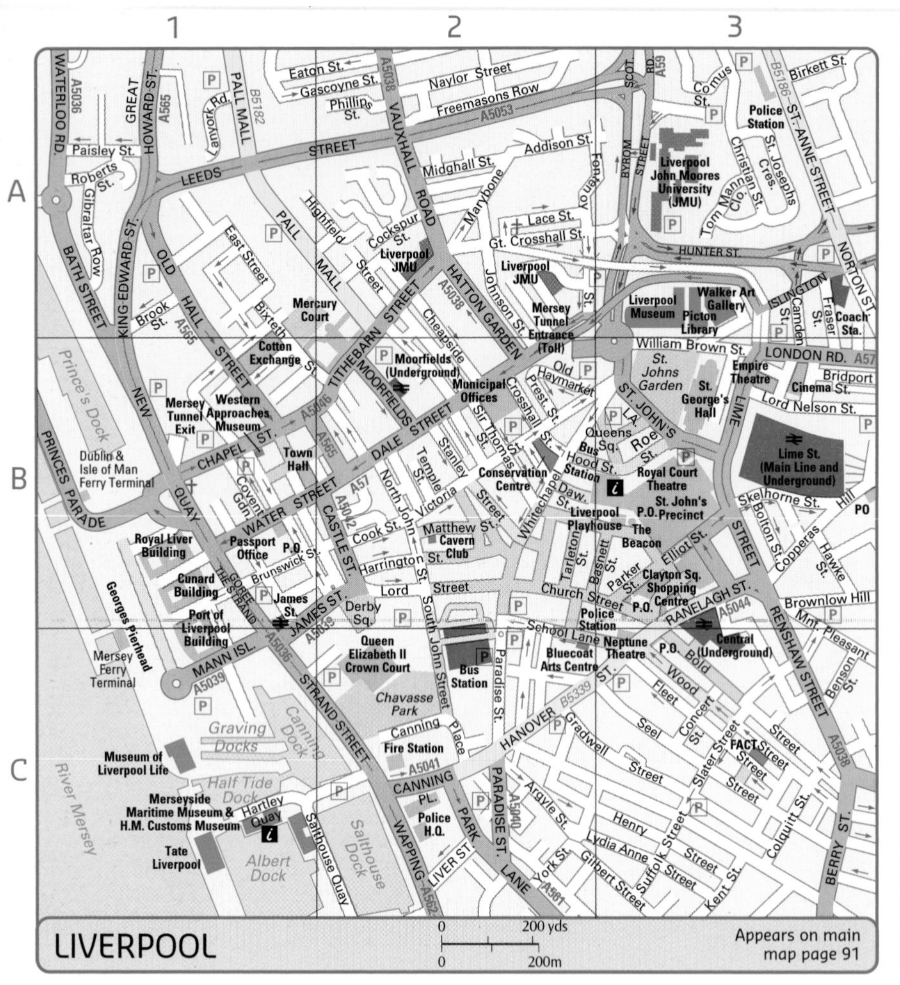

LIVERPOOL

0   200 yds
0   200m

Appears on main
map page 91

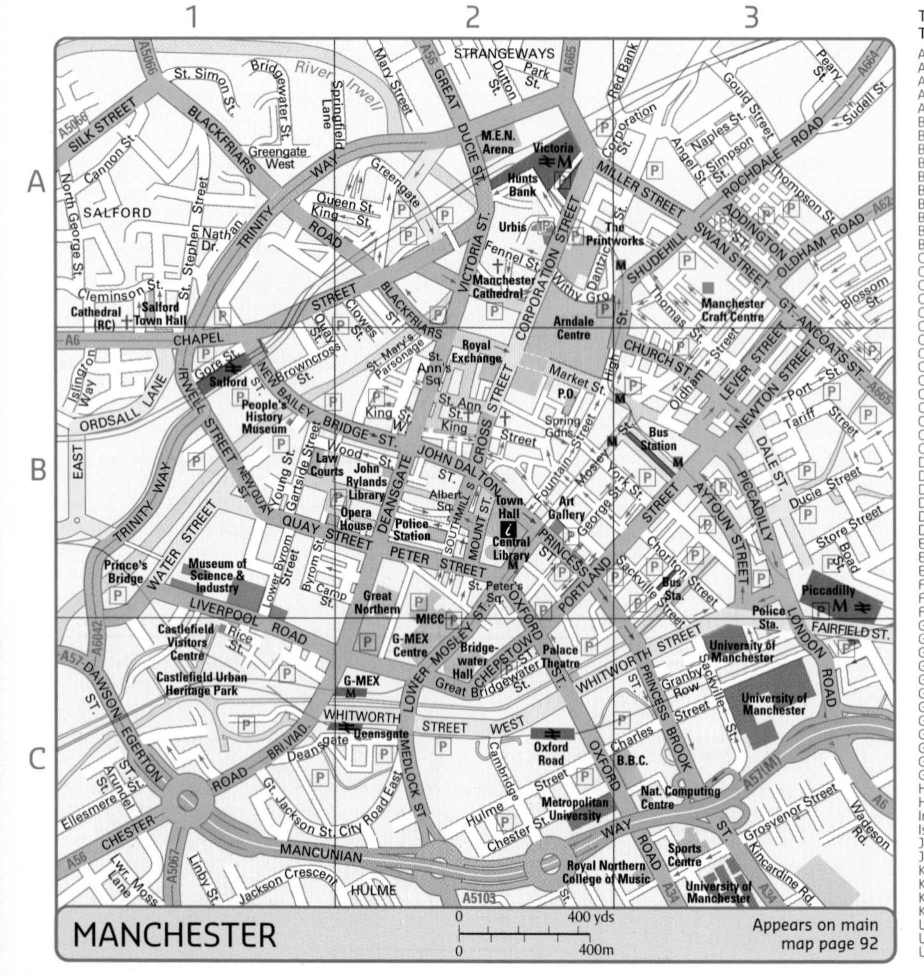

MANCHESTER

0   400 yds
0   400m

Appears on main
map page 92

Middlesbrough

Tourist Information Centre: 99-101 Albert Road
Tel: 01642 358086

Abingdon Road	B2
Aire Street	B1
Albert Road	A2
Ayresome Green Lane	B1
Ayresome Street	B1
Beech Grove Road	C2
Belle Vue Grove	C3
Bishopton Road	C2
Borough Road	A2/C3
Breckon Hill Road	B3
Bridge Street East	A2
Bridge Street West	A2
Burlam Road	C1
Cambridge Road	C1
Cannon Park Way	A1
Cannon Street	A1
Cargo Fleet Road	A3
Chipchase Road	C1
Clairville Road	B2
Clive Road	B1
Corporation Road	A2
Crescent Road	B1
Cumberland Road	C2
Deepdale Avenue	C2
Derwent Street	A1
Dockside Road	A2/A3
Douglas Street	B3
Eastbourne Road	C2
Emerson Avenue	C2
Forty Foot Road	A1
Grange Road	A2
Granville Road	B2
Gresham Road	B1
Harford Street	B1
Harrow Road	C1
Hartington Road	A1
Heywood Street	B1
Highfield Road	C3
Holwick Road	A1
Hutton Road	B3
Ingram Road	B3
Keith Road	C2
Lansdowne Road	B3
Linthorpe Road	C2
Longford Street	B1
Longlands Road	B3
Marsh Street	A1
Marton Burn Road	C2
Marton Road	B3/C3
Newport Road	A1/A2
North Ormesby Road	A3
Nut Lane	B3
Orchard Road	C1
Overdale Road	C3
Oxford Road	C1
Park Lane	B2
Park Road North	B2
Park Road South	B2
Park Vale Road	B2
Parliament Road	B1
Portman Street	B2
Princes Road	B1
Reeth Road	C1
Riverside Park Road	A1
Rockcliffe Road	C1
Roman Road	C1
Roseberry Road	B3
Saltwells Road	B3
Scotts Road	A3
Sheperdson Way	A3
Snowdon Road	A2
Southfield Road	B2
Southwell Road	C2
St. Barnabas Road	B1
Surrey Street	B1
Sycamore Road	C2
The Avenue	B3
The Crescent	C1
The Vale	C1
Thornfield Road	C1
Union Street	B1
Valley Road	B2
Victoria Road	B2
Victoria Street	A1
Westbourne Grove	B3
Westbourne Road	C1
Westminster Road	C2
Wilson Street	A2
Woodlands Road	B2

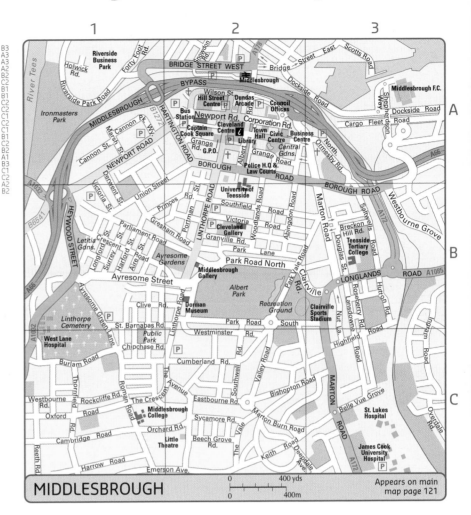

Milton Keynes

Tourist Information Centre: Margaret Powell Square,
890 Midsummer Boulevard Tel: 01908 558300

Avebury Boulevard	B2/A3
Boycott Avenue	C2
Bradwell Common Boulevard	A1
Bradwell Road	C1
Burnham Drive	A1
Chaffron Way	C3
Childs Way	C1/B3
Conniburrow Boulevard	A2
Dansteed Way	A1
Deltic Avenue	B1
Elder Gate	B1
Evans Gate	C2
Fennel Drive	A2
Fishermead Boulevard	B3
Fulwoods Drive	C3
Gibsons Green	A1
Glovers Lane	A1
Grafton Gate	B1
Grafton Street	A1/C2
Gurnards Avenue	B3
Hampstead Gate	A1
Harrier Drive	C3
Leys Road	C1
Lloyds	C3
Mallow Gate	A2
Marlborough Street	A3
Mayditch Place	B1
Midsummer Boulevard	B2/A3
Oldbrook Boulevard	C2
Patriot Drive	B1
Pentewan Gate	B3
Portway	B2/A3
Precedent Drive	B1
Quinton Drive	A1
Redland Drive	C1
Saxon Gate	B2
Saxon Street	A2/C3
Secklow Gate	A3
Silbury Boulevard	B2/A3
Skeldon Gate	A3
Snowdon Drive	C2
Stainton Drive	A1
Strudwick Drive	C3
Trueman Place	C3
Underwood Place	C2
Witan Gate	B2

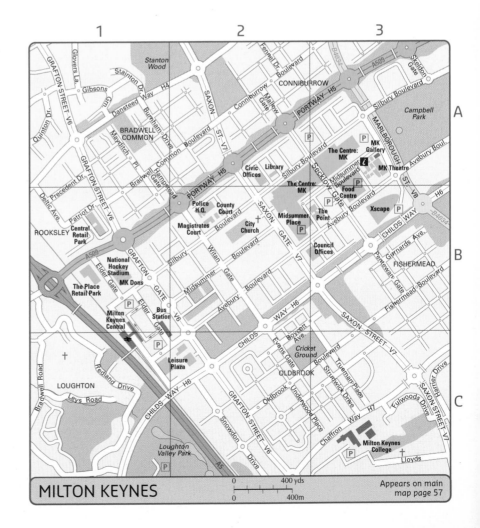

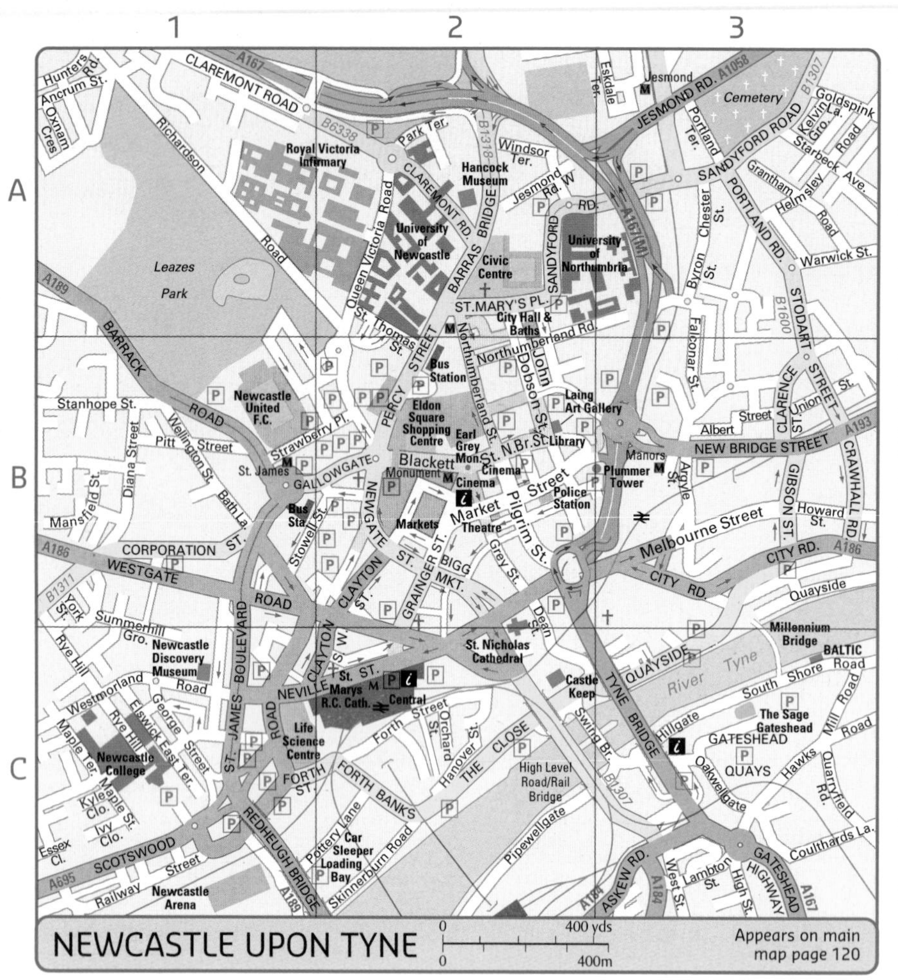

NEWCASTLE UPON TYNE

0 ___ 400 yds
0 ___ 400m

Appears on main map page 120

Tourist Information Centre: 132 Grainger Street
Tel: 0191 277 8000

Albert Street	B3	Portland Road	A3
Ancrum Street	A1	Portland Terrace	A3
Argyle Street	B3	Pottery Lane	C1
Askew Road	C3	Quarryfield Road	C3
Barrack Road	A1	Quayside	C3
Barras Bridge	A2	Queen Victoria Road	A2
Bath Lane	B1	Railway Street	C1
Bigg Market	B2	Redheugh Bridge	C1
Blackett Street	B2	Richardson Road	A1
Byron Street	A3	Rye Hill	C1
Chester Street	A3	St. James Boulevard	C1
City Road	B3	St. Mary's Place	A2
Claremont Road	A1	St. Thomas Street	A2
Clarence Street	B3	Sandyford Road	A2/A3
Clayton Street	B2	Scotswood Road	C1
Clayton Street West	C1	Skinnerburn Road	C2
Corporation Street	B1	South Shore Road	C3
Coulthards Lane	C3	Stanhope Street	B1
Crawhall Road	B3	Starbeck Avenue	A3
Dean Street	B2	Stodart Street	A3
Diana Street	B1	Stowell Street	B1
Elswick East Terrace	C1	Strawberry Place	B1
Eskdale Terrace	A3	Summerhill Grove	B1
Essex Close	C1	Swing Bridge	C2
Falconar Street	A3	The Close	C2
Forth Banks	C2	Tyne Bridge	C3
Forth Street	C1	Union Street	B3
Gallowgate	B1	Warwick Street	A3
Gateshead Highway	C3	Wellington Street	B1
George Street	C1	West Street	C3
Gibson Street	B3	Westgate Road	B1
Grainger Street	B2	Westmorland Road	C1
Grantham Road	A3	Windsor Terrace	A2
Grey Street	B2	York Street	B1
Hanover Street	C2		
Hawks Road	C3		
Helmsley Road	A3		
High Street	C3		
Hillgate	C3		
Howard Street	B3		
Hunters Road	A1		
Ivy Close	C1		
Jesmond Road	A3		
Jesmond Road West	A2		
John Dobson Street	B2		
Kelvin Grove	A3		
Kyle Close	C1		
Lambton Street	C3		
Mansfield Street	B1		
Maple Street	C1		
Maple Terrace	C1		
Market Street	B2		
Melbourne Street	B3		
Mill Road	C3		
Neville Street	C1		
New Bridge Street	B3		
Newgate Street	B2		
Northumberland Road	B2		
Northumberland Street	A2		
Oakwellgate	C3		
Orchard Street	C2		
Oxnam Crescent	A1		
Park Terrace	A2		
Percy Street	B2		
Pilgrim Street	B2		
Pipewellgate	C2		
Pitt Street	B1		

NORWICH

0 ___ 400 yds
0 ___ 400m

Appears on main map page 86

Tourist Information Centre: The Forum, Millennium Plain
Tel: 0870 225 4830

Albion Way	C3	Rampant Horse Street	B2
All Saints Green	C2	Recorder Road	B3
Ashby Street	C2	Red Lion Street	B2
Bakers Road	A1	Riverside	C3
Bank Plain	B2	Riverside Road	B3
Barker Street	A1	Rosary Road	B3
Barn Road	B1	Rose Lane	B2
Barrack Street	A2	Rouen Road	C2
Bedford Street	B2	Rupert Street	C1
Ber Street	C2	Russell Street	A1
Bethel Street	B1	St. Andrew's Street	B2
Bishopbridge Road	B3	St. Augustine's Street	A1
Bishopgate	B3	St. Benedict's Street	B1
Botolph Street	A2	St. Crispin's Road	A1
Brazen Gate	C2	St. Faiths Lane	B2
Britannia Road	A3	St. George's Street	A2
Brunswick Road	C1	St. Giles Street	B1
Bullclose Road	A2	St. James Close	A3
Canary Way	C3	St. Leonards Road	B3
Carrow Hill	C3	St. Martin's Road	A1
Carrow Road	C3	St. Stephen's Road	C1
Castle Meadow	B2	St. Stephen's Street	C2
Chapel Field Road	B1	Silver Road	A2
Chapelfield North	B1	Silver Street	A2
City Road	C2	Southwell Road	C2
Clarence Road	A3	Surrey Street	C2
Colegate	A2	Sussex Street	A1
Coslany Street	B1	Theatre Street	B1
Cowgate	A2	Thorn Lane	C2
Dereham Road	B1	Thorpe Road	B3
Duke Street	A2	Tombland	B2
Earlham Road	B1	Trinity Street	B1
Edward Street	A2	Trory Street	B1
Elm Hill	B2	Union Street	C1
Fishergate	A2	Unthank Road	C1
Gas Hill	A3	Vauxhall Street	C1
Grapes Hill	B1	Victoria Street	C1
Grove Avenue	C1	Wensum Street	A2
Grove Road	C1	Wessex Street	C2
Grove Walk	C1	Westwick Street	A1
Gurney Road	A3	Wherry Road	C3
Hall Road	C2	Whitefriars	A2
Hardy Road	C3	Wodehouse Street	A2
Heathgate	A3	York Street	C1
Heigham Street	A1		
Horns Lane	C2		
Ipswich Road	C1		
Ketts Hill	A3		
King Street	C2		
Koblenz Avenue	C3		
Lothian Street	B1		
Lower Clarence Road	B3		
Magdalen Street	A2		
Magpie Road	A2		
Market Avenue	B2		
Marlborough Road	A2		
Mountergate	B2		
Mousehold Street	A3		
Newmarket Road	C1		
Newmarket Street	C1		
Oak Street	A1		
Orchard Street	A1		
Palace Street	B2		
Pitt Street	A2		
Pottergate	B1		
Prince of Wales Road	B2		
Queens Road	C2		

Tourist Information Centre: 1-4 Smithy Row
Tel: 0115 915 5330

Abbotsford Drive	A2
Albert Street	B2
Angel Row	B1
Barker Gate	B3
Bath Street	A3
Beacon Hill Rise	A3
Bellar Gate	B3
Belward Street	B3
Bridlesmith Gate	B2
Broad Street	B2
Brook Street	A3
Burton Street	A1
Canal Street	C2
Carlton Street	B2
Carrington Street	C2
Castle Boulevard	C1
Castle Gate	B2
Castle Meadow Road	C1
Castle Road	C1
Chapel Bar	B1
Cheapside	B2
Chaucer Street	A1
City Link	C3
Clarendon Street	A1
Cliff Road	C2
Clumber Street	B2
College Street	B1
Collin Street	C2
Cranbrook Street	B3
Cromwell Street	A1
Curzon Street	A2
Derby Road	B1
Dryden Street	A1
Fisher Gate	B3
Fishpond Drive	C1
Fletcher Gate	B2
Forman Street	B2
Friar Lane	B1
Gedling Street	B3
George Street	B2
Gill Street	A1
Glasshouse Street	A2
Goldsmith Street	A1
Goose Gate	B3
Hamilton Drive	C1
Hampden Street	A1
Handel Street	B3
Heathcote Street	B3
High Pavement	B2
Hockley	B3
Hollowstone	B3
Hope Drive	C1
Huntingdon Drive	B1
Huntingdon Street	A2
Instow Rise	A3
Kent Street	A2
King Edward Street	B2
King Street	B2
Lamartine Street	A3
Lenton Road	C1
Lincoln Street	B2
Lister Gate	C2
London Road	C3
Low Pavement	B2
Lower Parliament Street	B2
Maid Marian Way	B1
Mansfield Road	A2

Manvers Street	B3
Market Street	B2
Middle Pavement	B2
Milton Street	A2
Mount Street	B1
North Church Street	A2
North Sherwood Street	A1
Park Row	B1
Park Terrace	B1
Park Valley	B1
Peel Street	A1
Pelham Street	B2
Pennyfoot Street	B3
Peveril Drive	C1
Pilcher Gate	B2
Plantagenet Street	A3
Popham Street	C2
Poplar Street	B3
Queens Road	C2
Queen Street	B2
Regent Street	B1
Robin Hood Street	A3
Roden Street	A3
St. Ann's Well Road	A3
St. James Street	B1
St. Mary's Gate	B2
St. Peter's Gate	B2
Shakespeare Street	A1
Shelton Street	A2
Smithy Row	B2
Sneinton Road	B3
South Parade	B2
South Sherwood Street	A2
Southwell Road	B3
Station Street	C2
Stoney Street	B3
Talbot Street	A1
The Great Northern Close	C3
The Rope Walk	B1
Union Road	B1
Upper Parliament Street	B1
Victoria Street	B2
Warser Gate	B2
Waverley Street	A1
Wheeler Gate	B2
Wilford Street	C1
Wollaton Street	B1
Woolpack Lane	B3

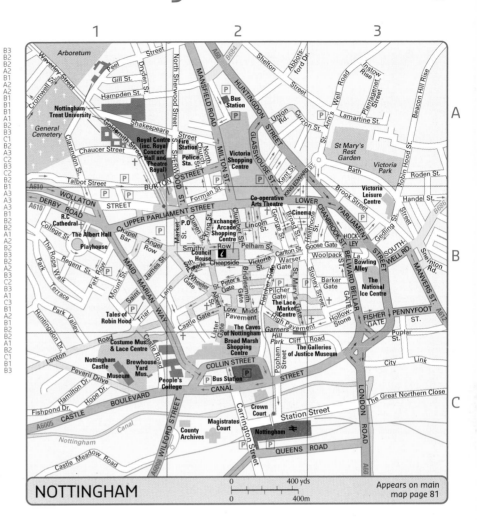

NOTTINGHAM

Appears on main map page 81

Tourist Information Centre: 15-16 Broad Street
Tel: 01865 726871

Albert Street	A1
Banbury Road	A2
Beaumont Street	B1
Becket Street	B1
Blackhall Road	A2
Botley Road	B1
Broad Street	B2
Canal Street	A1
Cattle Street	B2
Cornmarket	B2
Cowley Place	C3
Folly Bridge	C2
George Street	B1
Great Clarendon Street	A1
Hart Street	A1
High Street	B2
Hollybush Row	B1
Holywell Street	B2
Hythe Bridge Street	B1
Iffley Road	C3
Juxon Street	A1
Keble Road	A2
Kingston Road	A1
Littlegate Street	C2
Longwall Street	B3
Magdalen Bridge	B3
Manor Road	B3
Mansfield Road	A3
Marlborough Road	C2
Merton Street	C2
Mill Street	B1
Museum Road	A2
Nelson Street	B1
New Road	B1
Norham Gardens	A2
Observatory Street	A1
Oxpens Road	C1
Paradise Street	B1
Park End Street	B1
Parks Road	A2
Plantation Road	A1
Queen Street	B2
Rewley Road	B1
Richmond Road	B1
Rose Place	C2
St. Aldate's	C2
St. Bernards Road	A1
St. Cross Road	A3
St. Ebbe's Street	C2
St. Giles	A2
St. Thomas' Street	B1
South Parks Road	A2
Speedwell Street	C2
Thames Street	C2
Trinity Street	C1
Turl Street	B2
Walton Crescent	A1
Walton Street	A1
Walton Well Road	A1
Woodstock Road	A1

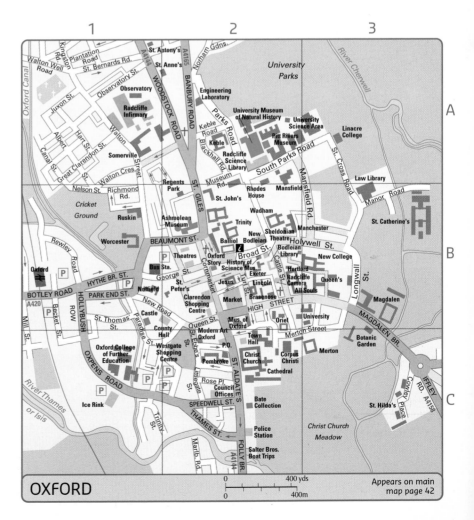

OXFORD

Appears on main map page 42

PLYMOUTH

Tourist Information Centre: Island House, 9 The Barbican
Tel: 01752 264849

Alexandra Road	A3	North Street	B2
Alma Road	A1	Notte Street	C2
Armada Street	B3	Oxford Street	B1
Armada Way	B2	Pentillie Road	A2
Ashford Road	A3	Ponsonby Road	A1
Barbican Approach	C3	Princess Street	C2
Beaumont Road	B3	Queen's Road	A3
Beechwood Avenue	A2	Royal Parade	B2
Belgrave Road	A3	Salisbury Road	B3
Bretonside	B2	Saltash Road	A1
Buckwell Street	C2	Seaton Avenue	A2
Camden Street	B3	Seymour Avenue	A3
Cattledown Road	C3	Southside Street	C2
Cecil Street	B1	Stoke Road	A1
Central Park Avenue	A1	Stuart Road	A1
Charles Street	B2	Sutton Road	B3
Citadel Road	C1	Sydney Street	B1
Clarence Place	B1	Teats Hill Road	C3
Cliff Road	C1	The Crescent	C1
Clifton Place	A2	Tothill Avenue	B3
Clovelly Road	C3	Tothill Road	B3
Cobourg Street	B2	Union Street	B1
Coleridge Road	A3	Vauxhall Street	C2
Connaught Avenue	A3	West Hoe Road	C1
Cornwall Street	B2	Western Approach	B1
Dale Road	A2	Whittington Street	A1
De-La-Hay Avenue	A1	Wilton Street	B1
Desborough Road	B3	Wyndham Street	B1
Drake Circus	B2		
East Street	C1		
Eastlake Street	B2		
Ebrington Street	B2		
Elliot Street	C1		
Embankment Road	B3		
Exeter Street	B2		
Ford Park Road	A2		
Furzehill Road	A3		
Gdynia Way	C3		
Glen Park Avenue	A2		
Grand Parade	C1		
Greenbank Avenue	B3		
Greenbank Road	A3		
Grenville Road	B3		
Harwell Street	B1		
Hill Park Crescent	A2		
Hoe Road	C2		
Houndiscombe Road	A2		
James Street	B2		
King Street	B1		
Knighton Road	B3		
Lipson Hill	A3		
Lipson Road	B3		
Lisson Grove	A3		
Lockyer Street	C2		
Looe Street	B2		
Madeira Road	C2		
Manor Road	B1		
Martin Street	C1		
Mayflower Street	B2		
Millbay Road	C1		
Mount Gould Road	A3		
Mutley Plain	A2		
New George Street	B1		
North Cross	B2		
North Hill	B2		
North Road East	B2		
North Road West	B1		

Scale: 0 400 yds / 0 400m
Appears on main map page 8

PORTSMOUTH

Tourist Information Centre: The Hard
Tel: 023 9282 6722

Albany Road	C3	Queen's Crescent	C3
Albert Grove	C3	Queen Street	B1
Alfred Road	B2	Raglan Street	B3
Anglesea Road	B2	Railway View	B3
Arundel Street	B3	St. Andrews Road	C3
Astley Street	C2	St. Edward's Road	C2
Bailey's Road	C3	St. George's Road	B1
Bellevue Terrace	C2	St. James Road	C2
Belmont Street	C3	St. James Street	B2
Bishop Street	A1	St. Paul's Road	B2
Blackfriars Road	B3	St. Thomas's Street	C1
Bradford Road	B3	Somers Road	B3
Britain Street	B1	Southsea Terrace	C2
Broad Street	C1	Station Street	B3
Burnaby Road	B2	Stone Street	C2
Cambridge Road	C2	Sultan Road	A3
Canal Walk	B3	Sussex Street	C2
Castle Road	C2	The Hard	B1
Church Road	A3	Turner Road	A3
Church Street	A3	Unicorn Road	A2
Clarendon Street	A3	Upper Arundel Street	B3
College Street	B1	Victoria Road North	C3
Commercial Road	B2	Warblington Street	C1
Cottage Grove	C3	Watts Road	A3
Crasswell Street	A3	White Hart Road	C1
Cross Street	A1	Wingfield Street	B2
Cumberland Street	A1	Winston Churchill Avenue	B2
Duke Crescent	A3	York Place	B2
Edinburgh Road	B2		
Eldon Street	C2		
Elm Grove	C3		
Flathouse Road	A3		
Fyning Street	C2		
Green Road	C2		
Greetham Street	B3		
Grosvenor Street	C3		
Grove Road South	C3		
Gunwharf Road	C1		
Hampshire Terrace	C2		
Havant Street	B1		
High Street	C1		
Holbrook Road	A3		
Hope Street	A2		
Hyde Park Road	B3		
Isambard Brunel Road	B2		
Kent Road	C2		
Kent Street	A1		
King Charles Street	C1		
King's Road	C2		
King's Terrace	C2		
King Street	C2		
Lake Road	A3		
Landport Terrace	C2		
Lombard Street	C1		
Margate Road	C3		
Market Way	A2		
Melbourne Place	C2		
Museum Road	C2		
Nelson Road	A3		
Norfolk Street	C2		
Northam Street	B3		
Outram Road	C3		
Pain's Road	C3		
Paradise Street	B3		
Park Road	C1		
Pembroke Road	C1		
Penny Street	C1		

Scale: 0 500 yds / 0 500m
Appears on main map page 15

Reading

Tourist Information Centre: Church House, Chain Street
Tel: 0118 956 6226

Addington Road	C3	London Road	B3
Addison Road	A1	London Street	B3
Alexandra Road	B3	Lower Henley Road	A3
Allcroft Road	C3	Mill Road	A3
Alpine Street	C2	Milford Road	A1
Amersham Road	A3	Milman Road	C2
Amity Road	B1	Minster Street	B2
Ardler Road	A2	Morgan Road	C3
Ashley Road	C1	Napier Road	B2
Audley Street	B1	Orts Road	B3
Baker Street	B1	Oxford Road	B1
Basingstoke Road	C2	Pell Street	C2
Bath Road	C1	Portman Road	A1
Bedford Road	B1	Priest Hill	A2
Berkeley Avenue	C1	Prospect Street *Caversham*	A2
Blagrave Street	B2	Prospect Street *Reading*	B1
Blenheim Road	B3	Queen's Road *Caversham*	A2
Briant's Avenue	A3	Queen's Road *Reading*	B2
Bridge Street	B2	Richfield Avenue	A1
Broad Street	B2	Rose Kiln Lane	C2
Cardiff Road	A1	Russell Street	B1
Castle Hill	B1	St. Anne's Road	A2
Castle Street	B2	St. John's Road	A3
Catherine Street	B1	St. Mary's Butts	B2
Caversham Road	B2	St. Peters Avenue	A1
Chatham Street	B1	St. Saviours Road	C1
Cheapside	B2	Silver Street	B2
Cholmeley Road	B3	South Street	B2
Christchurch Road	C2	Southampton Street	B2
Church Road	A1	South View Road	A3
Church Street	A2	Star Road	A3
Coley Avenue	C1	Station Hill	B2
Coley Place	B2	Station Road	B2
Cow Lane	B1	Swansea Road	A2
Craven Road	B3	Tessa Road	A1
Crown Place	B3	The Warren	A3
Crown Street	C2	Tilehurst Road	B1
Cumberland Road	B3	Upper Redlands Road	C3
Curzon Street	B1	Vastern Road	A2
De Beauvoir Road	B3	Waldelk Street	C2
Donnington Road	B3	Waterloo Road	C2
Duke Street	B2	Wensley Road	C1
East Street	B2	Western Elms Avenue	B1
Eldon Road	B3	Westfield Road	A2
Eldon Terrace	B3	West Street	A2
Elgar Road	C2	Whitley Road	C2
Elgar Road South	C2	Wolsey Road	C2
Elmhurst Road	C3	York Road	A2
Erleigh Road	B3		
Fobney Street	B2		
Forbury Road	B2		
Friar Street	B2		
Gas Work Road	B3		
George Street *Caversham*	A2		
George Street *Reading*	B1		
Gosbrook Road	A2		
Gower Street	B1		
Great Knollys Street	B1		
Greyfriars Road	B2		
Hemdean Road	A2		
Hill Street	C2		
Holybrook Road	C1		
Kenavon Drive	B3		
Kendrick Road	C2		
King's Road *Caversham*	A2		
King's Road *Reading*	B2		
Lesford Road	C1		

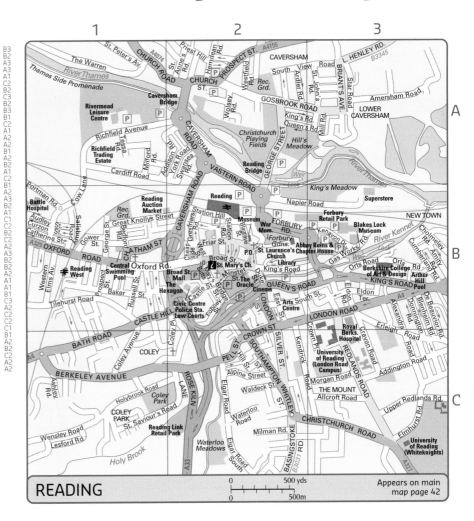

READING   0 500 yds / 0 500m   Appears on main map page 42

Salisbury

Tourist Information Centre: Fish Row
Tel: 01722 334956

Albany Road	A2	Silver Street	B2
Ashley Road	A1	Southampton Road	C3
Avon Terrace	A1	Swaynes Close	A2
Barnard Street	B3	Tollgate Road	B3
Bedwin Street	A2	Trinity Street	B3
Belle Vue Road	A2	Wain-a-long Road	A3
Bishops Walk	C2	West Walk	C2
Blackfriars Way	C3	Wilton Road	A1
Blue Boar Row	B2	Winchester Street	B2
Bourne Avenue	A3	Windsor Road	B1
Bourne Hill	A3	Wyndham Road	A2
Bridge Street	B2	York Road	A1
Brown Street	B2		
Butcher Row	B2		
Carmelite Way	C2		
Castle Street	A2		
Catherine Street	B2		
Chipper Lane	B2		
Churchfields Road	B1		
Churchill Way East	B3		
Churchill Way North	A2		
Churchill Way South	C2		
Churchill Way West	A1		
Clifton Road	A1		
College Street	A3		
Crane Bridge Road	B1		
Crane Street	B2		
De Vaux Place	C2		
Devizes Road	A1		
Elm Grove Road	B3		
Endless Street	A2		
Estcourt Road	A3		
Exeter Street	C2		
Fairview Road	A3		
Fisherton Street	B1		
Fowlers Hill	B3		
Fowlers Road	B3		
Friary Lane	C3		
Gas Lane	A1		
Gigant Street	B3		
Greencroft Street	A3		
Hamilton Road	A2		
High Street	B2		
Ivy Street	B2		
Kelsey Road	A3		
Laverstock Road	B3		
Manor Road	A3		
Marsh Lane	A1		
Meadow Road	A1		
Milford Hill	B3		
Milford Street	B2		
Mill Road	B1		
Millstream Approach	A2		
Minster Street	B2		
New Canal	B2		
New Street	B2		
North Walk	B2		
Park Street	A3		
Queens Road	A3		
Rampart Road	B3		
Rollestone Street	A2		
St. Ann Street	C3		
St. John's Street	B2		
St. Marks Road	A2		
St. Paul's Road	A1		
Salt Lane	B2		
Scots Lane	A2		

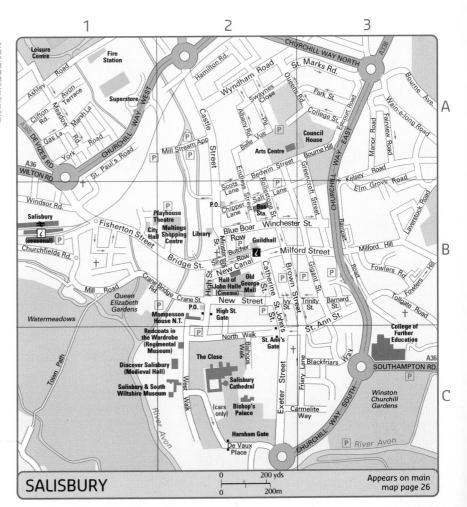

SALISBURY   0 200 yds / 0 200m   Appears on main map page 26

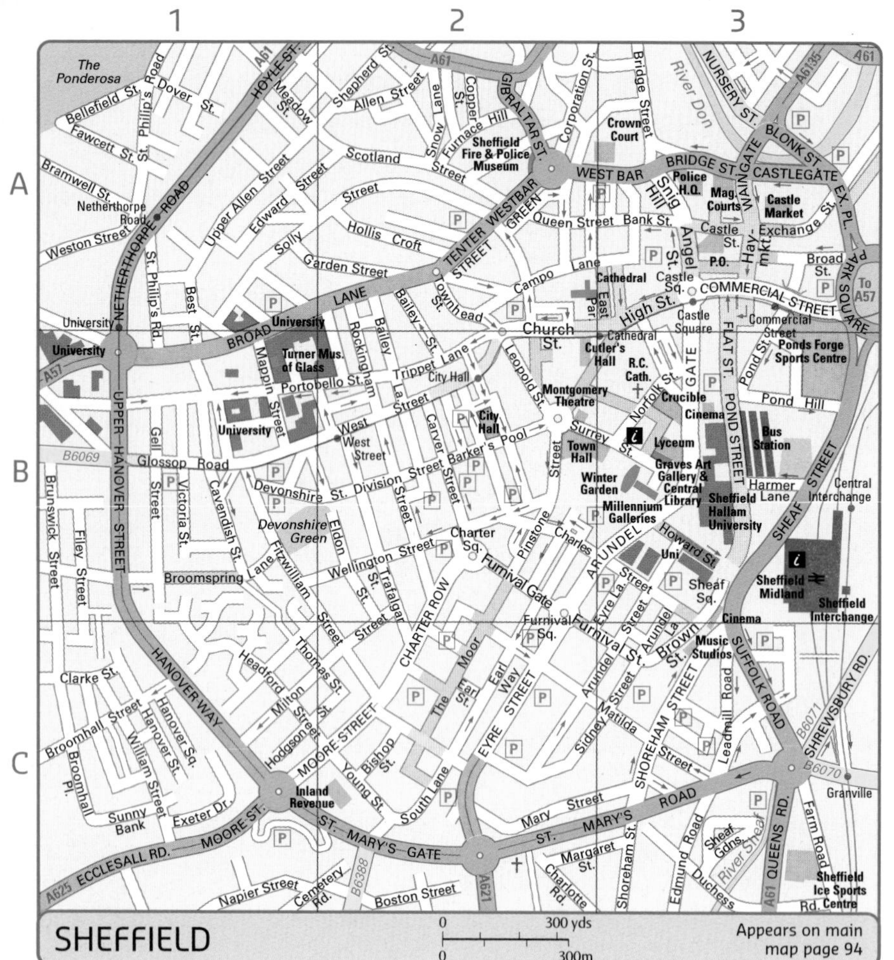

SHEFFIELD

0   300 yds
0   300m

Appears on main map page 94

Tourist Information Centre: 1 Tudor Square
Tel: 0114 221 1900

Allen Street	A2	Hanover Square	C1
Angel Street	A3	Hanover Street	C1
Arundel Gate	B2	Hanover Way	C1
Arundel Lane	C3	Harmer Lane	B3
Arundel Street	C2	Haymarket	A3
Bailey Lane	A2	Headford Street	C1
Bailey Street	A2	High Street	A3
Bank Street	A3	Hodgson Street	C1
Barker's Pool	B2	Hollis Croft	A2
Bellefield Street	A1	Howard Street	B3
Best Street	A1	Hoyle Street	A1
Bishop Street	C2	Leadmill Road	C3
Blonk Street	A3	Leopold Street	B2
Boston Street	C2	Mappin Street	B1
Bower Street	A1	Margaret Street	C2
Bramwell Street	A1	Mary Street	C2
Bridge Street	A3	Matilda Street	C3
Broad Lane	B1	Meadow Street	A1
Broad Street	A3	Milton Street	C1
Broomhall Street	C1	Moore Street	C1
Broomhall Place	C1	Napier Street	C1
Broomspring Lane	B1	Netherthorpe Road	A1
Brown Street	C3	Norfolk Street	B3
Brunswick Street	B1	Nursery Street	A3
Campo Lane	A2	Pinstone Street	B2
Carver Street	B2	Pond Hill	B3
Castle Square	A3	Pond Hill	B3
Castle Street	A3	Pond Street	B3
Castlegate	A3	Portobello Street	B1
Cavendish Street	B1	Queen Street	A2
Cemetery Road	C1	Queens Road	C3
Charles Street	B2/B3	Rockingham Street	B2
Charlotte Road	C3	St. Mary's Gate	C2
Charter Row	C2	St. Mary's Road	C2
Charter Square	B2	St. Philip's Road	A1
Church Street	A2	Scotland Street	A2
Clarke Street	C1	Sheaf Gardens	C3
Commercial Street	A3	Sheaf Square	B3
Copper Street	A2	Sheaf Street	B3
Corporation Street	A2	Shepherd Street	A2
Devonshire Street	B1	Shoreham Street	C2
Division Street	B2	Shrewsbury Road	C3
Dover Street	A1	Sidney Street	C2
Duchess Road	C3	Snig Hill	A3
Earl Street	C2	Snow Lane	A2
Earl Way	C2	Solly Street	A1
East Parade	A3	South Lane	C2
Ecclesall Road	C1	Spring Street	A2
Edmund Road	C3	Suffolk Road	C3
Edward Street	A1	Sunny Bank	C1
Eldon Street	B2	Surrey Street	B2
Exchange Street	A3	Tenter Street	A2
Exeter Drive	C1	The Moor	C2
Eyre Lane	B3	Thomas Street	C1
Eyre Street	C2	Townhead Street	A2
Farm Road	C3	Trafalgar Street	B2
Fawcett Street	A1	Trippet Lane	B2
Filey Street	B1	Upper Allen Street	A1
Fitzwilliam Street	B1	Upper Hanover Street	B1
Flat Street	A2	Victoria Street	B1
Furnace Hill	A2	Waingate	A3
Furnival Gate	B2	Wellington Street	B2
Furnival Square	B2	West Bar	A2
Furnival Street	B2	West Street	B1
Garden Street	A1	Westbar Green	A2
Gell Street	B1	Weston Street	A1
Gibraltar Street	A2	William Street	C1
Glossop Road	B1	Young Street	C2

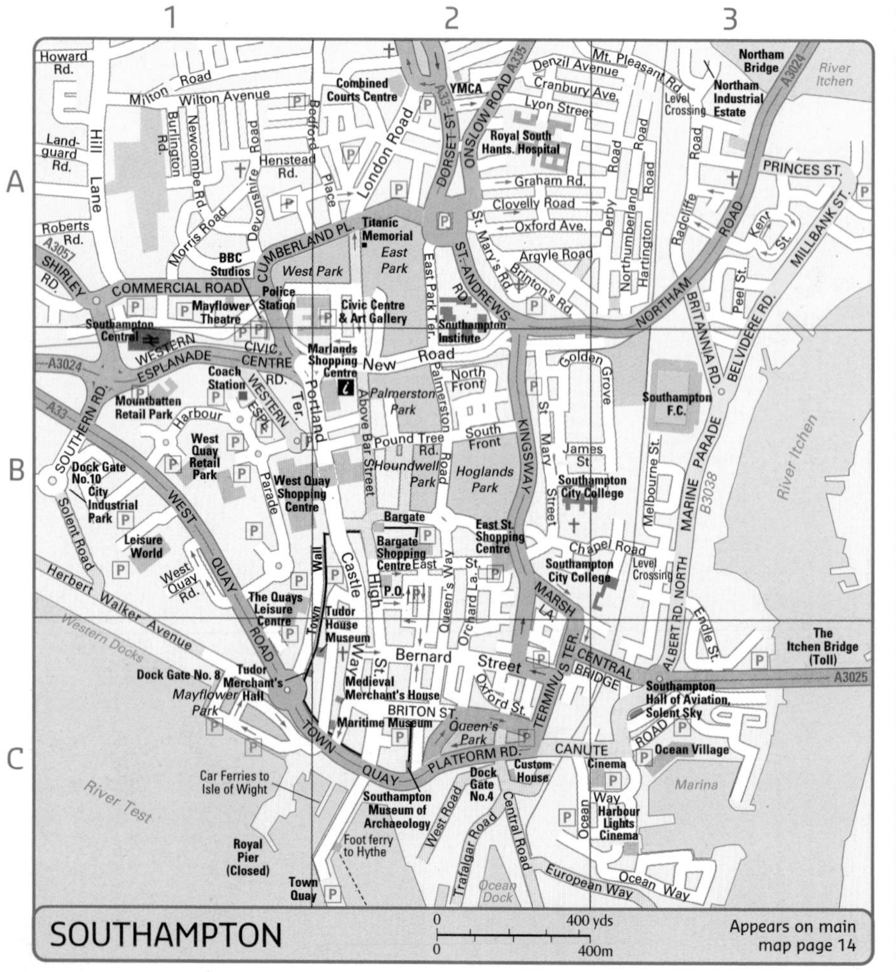

SOUTHAMPTON

0   400 yds
0   400m

Appears on main map page 14

Tourist Information Centre: 9 Civic Centre Road
Tel: 023 8083 3333

Above Bar Street	B2	Radcliffe Road	A3
Albert Road North	C3	Roberts Road	A1
Argyle Road	A2	St. Andrews Road	A2
Bedford Place	A1	St. Mary's Road	A2
Belvidere Road	B3	St. Mary Street	B2
Bernard Street	C2	Shirley Road	A1
Brintons Road	A2	Solent Road	B1
Britannia Road	A3	Southern Road	B1
Briton Street	C2	South Front	B2
Burlington Road	A1	Terminus Terrace	C2
Canute Road	C2	Town Quay	C1
Castle Way	B2	Trafalgar Road	C2
Central Bridge	C2	West Quay Road	B1
Central Road	C2	West Road	C2
Chapel Road	B2	Western Esplanade	B1
Civic Centre Road	B1	Wilton Avenue	A1
Clovelly Road	A2		
Commercial Road	A1		
Cranbury Avenue	A2		
Cumberland Place	A1		
Denzil Avenue	A2		
Derby Road	A3		
Devonshire Road	A1		
Dorset Street	A2		
East Park Terrace	A2		
East Street	B2		
Endle Street	B3		
European Way	C2		
Golden Grove	B2		
Graham Road	A2		
Harbour Parade	B1		
Hartington Road	A3		
Henstead Road	A1		
Herbert Walker Avenue	B1		
High Street	B2		
Hill Lane	A1		
Howard Road	A1		
James Street	B2		
Kent Street	A3		
Kingsway	B2		
Landguard Road	A1		
London Road	A2		
Lyon Street	A2		
Marine Parade	B3		
Marsh Lane	B3		
Melbourne Street	B3		
Millbank Street	A3		
Milton Road	A1		
Morris Road	A1		
Mount Pleasant Road	A2		
Newcombe Road	A1		
New Road	B2		
Northam Road	A3		
North Front	B2		
Northumberland Road	A3		
Ocean Way	C2		
Onslow Road	A2		
Orchard Lane	C2		
Oxford Avenue	A2		
Oxford Street	C2		
Palmerston Road	B2		
Peel Street	A3		
Platform Road	C2		
Portland Terrace	B1		
Pound Tree Road	B2		
Princes Street	A3		
Queen's Way	C2		

Tourist Information Centre: Potteries Shopping Cen, Quadrant Rd Tel: 01782 236000

Albion Street	A2
Ashford Street	B2
Avenue Road	B2
Aynsley Road	B2
Bedford Road	B2
Bedford Street	B1
Belmont Road	A1
Beresford Street	B2
Berry Hill Road	B3
Boon Avenue	C1
Botteslow Street	A3
Boughey Road	C2
Broad Street	A2
Bucknall New Road	A3
Bucknall Old Road	A3
Cauldon Road	B2
Cemetery Road	B1
Church Street	C2
Clough Street	A1
College Road	B2
Commercial Road	A3
Copeland Street	C2
Dewsbury Road	C3
Eagle Street	A3
Eastwood Road	A3
Elenora Street	A1
Etruria Road	A1
Etruria Vale Road	A1
Etruscan Street	B1
Festival Way	A1
Forge Lane	A1
Garner Street	B1
Glebe Street	C2
Greatbatch Avenue	C1
Hanley	A2
Hartshill Road	C1
Hill Street	C1
Honeywall	C1
Howard Place	B2
Ivy House Road	A3
Leek Road	C2
Lichfield Street	A3
Liverpool Road	C2
Lordship Lane	C2
Lytton Street	C2
Manor Street	C3
Marsh Street	A2
Newlands Street	B2
North Street	B1
Old Hall Street	A2
Oxford Street	C1
Parliament Row	A2
Potteries Way	A2
Potters Way	A3
Prince's Road	C1
Quarry Avenue	C1
Quarry Road	C1
Queen's Road	C1
Queensway	B1
Rectory Road	B2
Regent Road	B2
Richmond Street	B2
Ridgway Road	B2
Seaford Street	C2
Shelton New Road	B1
Shelton Old Road	C1
Snow Hill	B2
Stafford Street	A2
Station Road	C2
Stoke	C2
Stoke Road	C2
Stone Street	C1
Stuart Road	B3
Sun Street	A2
The Parkway	B2
Trentmill Road	B3
Victoria Road	B3
Warner Street	A2
Waterloo Street	B2
Wellesley Street	B2
Wellington Road	A3
West Avenue	C1
Westland Street	C1
Yoxall Avenue	C1

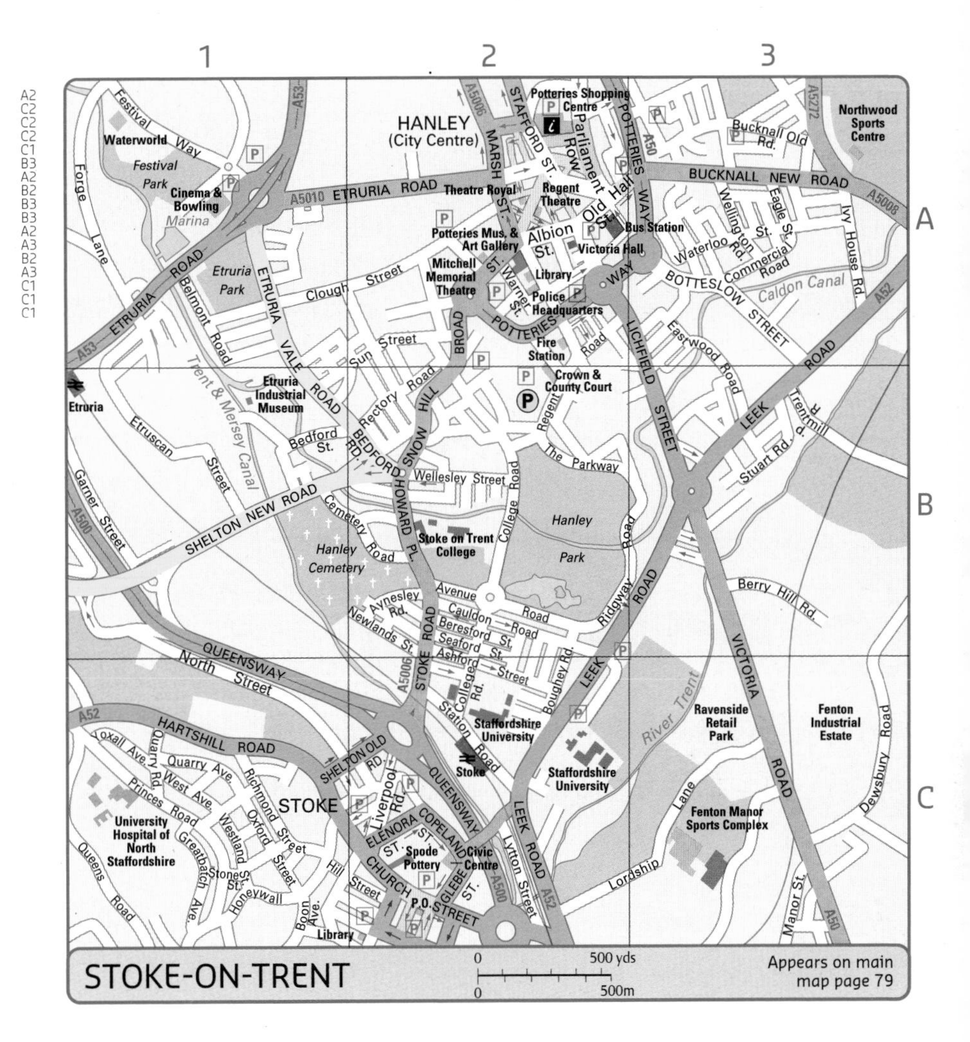

STOKE-ON-TRENT

0   500 yds
0   500m

Appears on main map page 79

Tourist Information Centre: Bridgefoot Tel: 0870 160 7930

Albany Road	B1
Alcester Road	A1
Arden Street	A1
Avonside	C2
Banbury Road	B3
Bancroft Place	B3
Birmingham Road	A1
Bridgefoot	B3
Bridge Street	B2
Bridgeway	B3
Bridgetown Road	C3
Broad Street	C1
Broad Walk	C1
Bull Street	C1
Chapel Lane	B2
Chapel Street	B2
Cherry Orchard	C1
Chestnut Walk	B1
Church Street	B3
Clopton Bridge	B3
Clopton Road	A2
College Lane	C2
College Street	C2
Ely Street	B2
Evesham Place	C1
Evesham Road	C1
Great William Street	A2
Greenhill Street	B1
Grove Road	B1
Guild Street	A2
Henley Street	A2
High Street	B2
Holtom Street	C1
John Street	A2
Kendall Avenue	A2
Maidenhead Road	A2
Mansell Street	A1
Meer Street	B2
Mill Lane	C2
Mulberry Street	A2
Narrow Lane	C1
New Street	C2
Old Town	C2
Old Tramway Walk	C3
Orchard Way	C1
Payton Street	A2
Rother Street	B1
Ryland Street	C1
St. Andrews Crescent	B1
St. Gregory's Road	A2
Sanctus Drive	C1
Sanctus Road	C1
Sanctus Street	C1
Sandfield Road	B1
Scholar's Lane	B2
Shakespeare Street	A2
Sheep Street	B2
Shipston Road	C3
Shottery Road	B1
Seven Meadow Road	C1
Southern Lane	C2
Station Road	A1
Swan's Nest Lane	B3
Tiddington Road	B3
Trinity Street	C2
Tyler Street	A2
Union Street	B2

Warwick Court	A2
Warwick Crescent	A3
Warwick Road	A3
Waterside	B2
Welcombe Road	A3
Westbourne Grove	B1
Western Road	A1
West Street	C1
Windsor Street	B2
Wood Street	B2

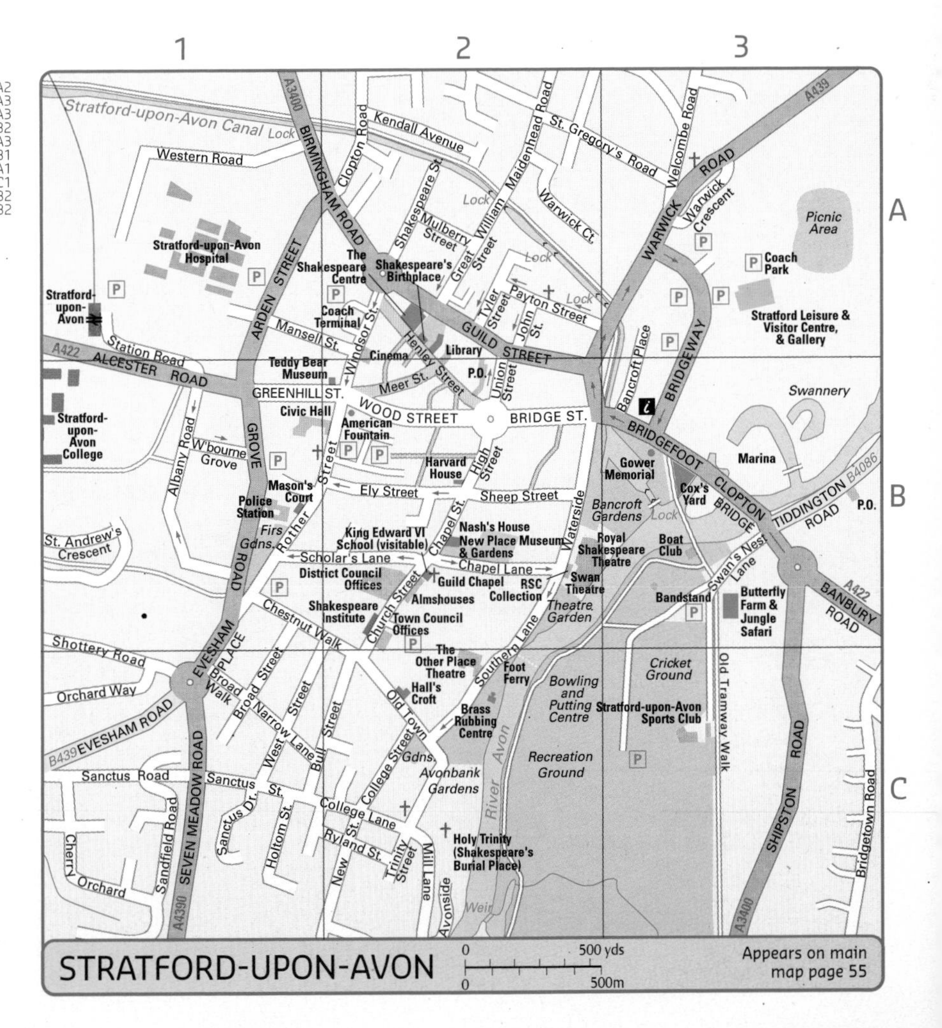

STRATFORD-UPON-AVON

0   500 yds
0   500m

Appears on main map page 55

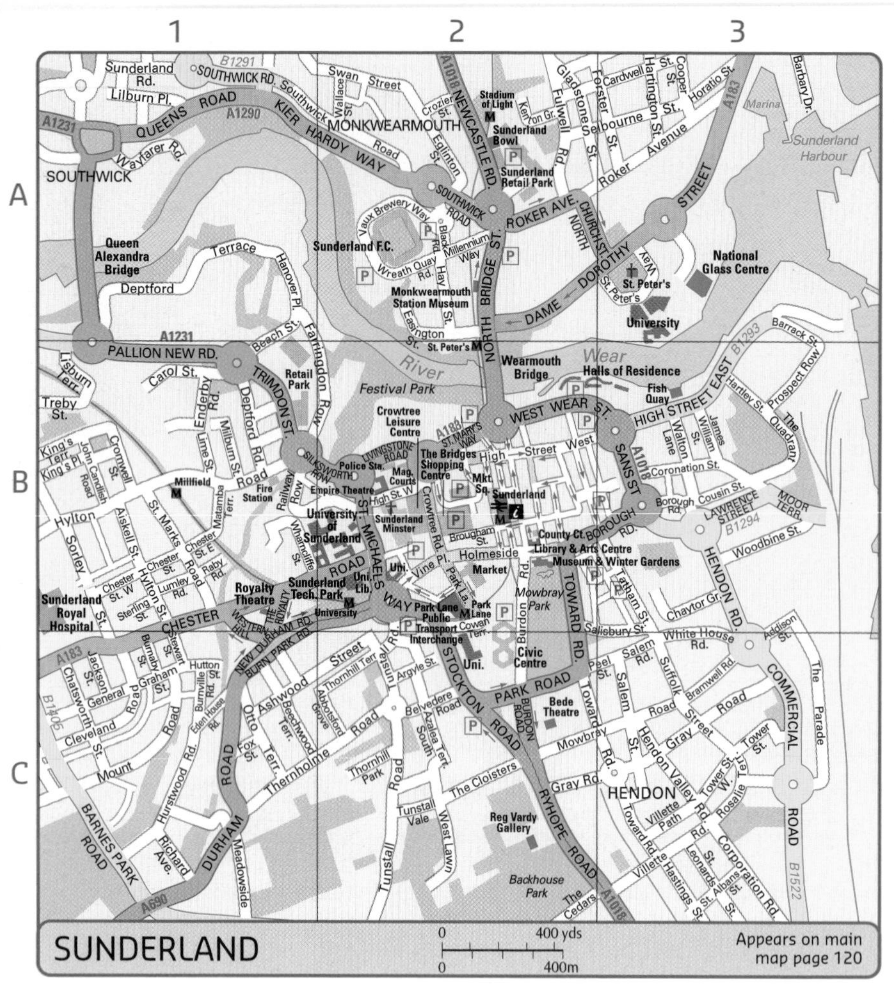

SUNDERLAND

0 400 yds
0 400m

Appears on main map page 120

Tourist Information Centre: 50 Fawcett Street
Tel: 0191 553 2000

Addison Street	C3	Lime Street	B1
Aiskell Street	B1	Livingstone Road	B2
Argyle Street	C2	Lumley Road	B1
Ashwood Street	C1	Matamba Terrace	B1
Azalea Terrace South	C2	Milburn Street	B1
Barnes Park Road	C1	Millennium Way	A2
Barrack Street	A3	Moor Terrace	B3
Beach Street	B1	Mount Road	C1
Beechwood Terrace	C1	Mowbray Road	C2
Belvedere Road	C2	New Durham Road	C1
Black Road	A2	Newcastle Road	A2
Borough Road	B2/B3	North Bridge Street	A2
Bramwell Road	C3	Otto Terrace	C1
Brougham Street	B2	Pallion New Road	B1
Burdon Road	C2	Park Lane	B2
Burn Park Road	C1	Park Road	C2
Burnaby Street	C1	Peel Street	C2
Burnville Road	C1	Prospect Row	B3
Carol Street	B1	Queens Road	A1
Chatsworth Street	C1	Raby Road	C2
Chaytor Grove	B3	Railway Row	B1
Chester Road	B1	Roker Avenue	A2/A3
Chester Street	B1	Rosalie Terrace	C3
Church Street North	A2	Ryhope Road	C3
Cleveland Road	C1	St. Albans Street	C3
Commercial Road	C3	St. Leonards Street	C3
Cooper Street	A3	St. Marks Road	B1
Coronation Street	B3	St. Mary's Way	B2
Corporation Road	C3	St. Michaels Way	B2
Cousin Street	B3	St. Peter's Way	A3
Cromwell Street	B1	Salem Road	C3
Crowtree Road	B2	Salem Street	C3
Crozier Street	A2	Salisbury Street	B2
Dame Dorothy Street	A2	Sans Street	B3
Deptford Road	B1	Selbourne Street	A2
Deptford Terrace	A1	Silksworth Row	B1
Durham Road	C1	Sorley Street	B1
Easington Street	A2	Southwick Road	A1
Eden House Road	C1	Southwick Road	A2
Eglinton Street	A2	Stockton Road	C2
Enderby Road	B1	Suffolk Street	C3
Farringdon Row	A1	Sunderland Road	A1
Forster Street	A3	Swan Street	A2
Fox Street	C1	Tatham Street	B3
Fulwell Road	A2	The Cedars	C2
General Graham Street	C1	The Cloisters	C2
Gladstone Street	A2	The Parade	C3
Gray Road	C2/C3	The Quadrant	B3
Hanover Place	A1	The Royalty	B1
Hartington Street	A3	Thernholme Road	C1
Hartley Street	B3	Thornhill Park	C2
Hastings Street	C3	Toward Road	B2/C3
Hay Street	A2	Tower Street	C3
Hendon Road	B3	Tower Street West	C3
Hendon Valley Road	C3	Trimdon Street	B1
High Street East	B3	Tunstall Road	C2
High Street West	B2	Tunstall Vale	C2
Holmeside	B2	Vaux Brewery Way	A2
Horatio Street	A3	Villette Road	C3
Hurstwood Road	C1	Vine Place	B2
Hutton Street	C1	Wallace Street	A2
Hylton Road	B1	West Lawn	C2
Hylton Road	B1	West Wear Street	B2
Jackson Street	C1	Western Hill	B1
James William Street	B3	Wharncliffe Street	B1
Kenton Grove	A2	White House Road	C3
Kier Hardy Way	A1	Woodbine Street	B3
King's Place	B1	Wreath Quay Road	A2
Lawrence Street	B3		

SWANSEA

0 500 yds
0 500m

Appears on main map page 36

Tourist Information Centre: Westway
Tel: 01792 468321

Aberdyberthi Street	A3	Neath Road	A3
Albert Row	C2	New Cut Road	B3
Alexandra Road	B2	New Orchard Street	A2
Argyle Street	C1	Nicander Parade	B1
Baptist Well Place	A2	Norfolk Street	B1
Baptist Well Street	A2	North Hill Road	A2
Beach Street	C1	Orchard Street	B2
Belgrave Lane	C1	Oystermouth Road	C1
Belle Vue Way	B2	Page Street	B2
Berw Road	A1	Pant-y-Celyn Road	B1
Berwick Terrace	A2	Park Terrace	A2
Bond Street	C1	Pedrog Terrace	A1
Brooklands Terrace	B1	Penlan Crescent	B1
Brunswick Street	C1	Pentre Guinea Road	A3
Brynmor Crescent	C1	Pen-y-Craig Road	A1
Brynmor Road	C1	Picton Terrace	B2
Burrows Place	C3	Powys Avenue	A1
Cambrian Place	C3	Princess Way	B2
Carig Crescent	A1	Quay Parade	B3
Carlton Terrace	B2	Rhondda Street	B1
Carmarthen Road	A2	Rose Hill	B1
Castle Street	B2	St. Elmo Avenue	A3
Clarence Terrace	C2	St. Helen's Avenue	C1
Colbourne Terrace	A2	St. Helen's Road	C1
Constitution Hill	B1	St. Mary Street	B2
Creidiol Road	A1	Singleton Street	C2
Cromwell Street	B1	Somerset Place	C3
Cwm Road	A3	South Guildhall Road	C1
De La Beche Street	B2	Strand	B3
Delhi Street	B3	Taliesyn Road	B1
Dyfatty Street	A2	Tan-y-Marian Road	B1
Dyfed Avenue	B1	Tegid Road	A1
Earl Street	A3	Teilo Crescent	A1
East Burrows Road	C3	Terrace Road	B1
Eigen Crescent	A1	The Kingsway	B2
Emlyn Road	B1	Townhill Road	A1
Fabian Way	B3	Trawler Road	C2
Ffynone Drive	B1	Villiers Street	A3
Ffynone Road	B1	Vincent Street	C1
Foxhole Road	A3	Walter Road	C1
Glamorgan Street	C2	Watkin Street	B2
Gors Avenue	A1	Waun-Wen Road	A2
Granogwen Road	A2	Wellington Street	C2
Grove Place	A2	West Way	C2
Gwent Road	A1	Westbury Street	C1
Gwili Terrace	A2	Western Street	C1
Hanover Street	B1	William Street	C2
Heathfield	B2	Windmill Terrace	A3
Hewson Street	B1	York Street	C3
High Street	B2		
High View	A2		
Islwyn Road	A1		
Kilvey Road	A3		
Kilvey Terrace	B3		
King Edward's Road	C1		
King's Road	B3		
Llangyfelach Road	A2		
Long Ridge	A2		
Lower Oxford Street	C1		
Mackworth Street	B3		
Maesteg Street	A3		
Mansel Street	B1		
Mayhill Road	A1		
Milton Terrace	B2		
Morris Lane	B2		
Mount Pleasant	B2		
Mumbles Road	C1		

Tourist Information Centre: 37 Regent Street
Tel: 01793 530328

Albion Street	C1	Westcott Place	C1
Bath Road	C2	Western Street	C3
Beatrice Street	A2	William Street	C1
Beckhampton Street	B3	York Road	B3
Birch Street	B1		
Bridge Street	B2		
Broad Street	A3		
Canal Walk	B2		
Caulfield Road	A3		
Church Place	B1		
Cirencester Way	A3		
Clifton Street	C2		
Commercial Road	B2		
County Road	A3		
Cricklade Street	C3		
Curtis Street	B2		
Dean Street	B1		
Drove Road	C3		
Eastcott Hill	C2		
Edmund Street	B2		
Elmina Road	A3		
Euclid Street	B3		
Faringdon Road	B1		
Farnby Street	B2		
Fleet Street	B2		
Fleming Way	B2		
Gladstone Street	A3		
Goddard Avenue	C2		
Great Western Way	A1		
Grosvenor Street	C1		
Groundwell Road	B3		
Hawksworth Way	A1		
High Street	C3		
Holbrook Way	B2		
Hythe Road	C2		
Jennings Street	B1		
Kemble Drive	A1		
Kent Road	C2		
Kingshill Street	C1		
Lansdown Road	C2		
Manchester Road	A2		
Market Street	B2		
Milford Street	B2		
Milton Road	B2		
Morris Street	A1		
Newburn Crescent	B1		
Newcombe Drive	A1		
North Star Avenue	A2		
Ocotal Way	A3		
Okus Road	C1		
Park Lane	B1		
Penzance Drive	B1		
Plymouth Street	B3		
Princes Street	B3		
Queen Street	B2		
Radnor Street	C1		
Redcliffe Street	B1		
Regent Street	B2		
Rodbourne Road	A1		
Rosebery Street	A3		
Spring Gardens	B3		
Stafford Street	C2		
Station Road	A2		
Swindon Road	C2		
The Parade	B2		
Upham Road	C3		
Victoria Road	B3		

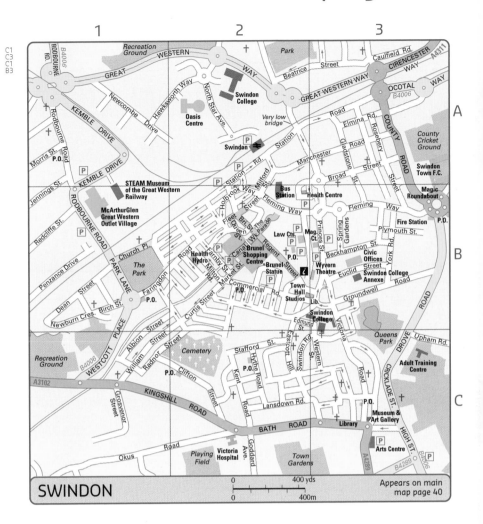

SWINDON

0   400 yds
0   400m

Appears on main map page 40

Tourist Information Centre: Vaughan Parade
Tel: 01803 297428

Abbey Road	B2	Thurlow Road	A2
Ash Hill Road	A2	Tor Hill Road	B2
Avenue Road	B1	Torbay Road	C1
Bampfylde Road	B1	Torwood Gardens Road	C3
Barton Road	A1	Torwood Street	C3
Belgrave Road	B1	Union Street	B2
Belmont Road	A3	Upton Hill	A2
Braddons Hill Road East	B3	Upton Road	A1
Bridge Road	B1	Vanehill Road	C3
Bronshill Road	A2	Victoria Parade	C3
Brunswick Square	B1	Walnut Road	C1
Carlton Road	A3	Warbro Road	A3
Cary Parade	C3	Warren Road	B2
Cedars Road	B3	Westhill Road	A2
Chestnut Avenue	B1	Windsor Road	A3
Cockington Lane	C1		
Croft Road	B2		
Crownhill Park	A1		
Dunmere Road	A3		
East Street	A1		
Ellacombe Church Road	A3		
Ellacombe Road	A2		
Falkland Road	B1		
Falkland Road	B1		
Fleet Street	B2		
Forest Road	A2		
Goshen Road	B1		
Hatfield Road	A2		
Hennapyn Road	C1		
Higher Warberry Road	B3		
Hillesdon Road	B3		
Kenwyn Road	A3		
Lower Warberry Road	B3		
Lucius Street	B1		
Lymington Road	A2		
Mallock Road	B1		
Market Street	B2		
Marnham Road	A3		
Meadfoot Lane	C3		
Meadfoot Road	C3		
Middle Warberry Road	B3		
Mill Lane	B1		
Newton Road	A1		
Old Mill Road	B1		
Old Mill Road	C1		
Parkfield Road	A2		
Parkhill Road	C3		
Prince's Road	B3		
Princes Road East	B3		
Quinta Road	A3		
Rathmore Road	C1		
Reddenhill Road	A3		
Rosehill Road	B3		
Sanford Road	B1		
Seaway Lane	C1		
Shedden Hill	B2		
Sherwell Lane	B1		
Shiphay Lane	A1		
Solsbro Road	C1		
South Street	B1		
St. Lukes Road	B2		
St. Marychurch Road	B2		
St. Michael's Road	A1		
Stitchill Road	B3		
Strand	C3		
Teignmouth Road	A1		
The King's Drive	B1		

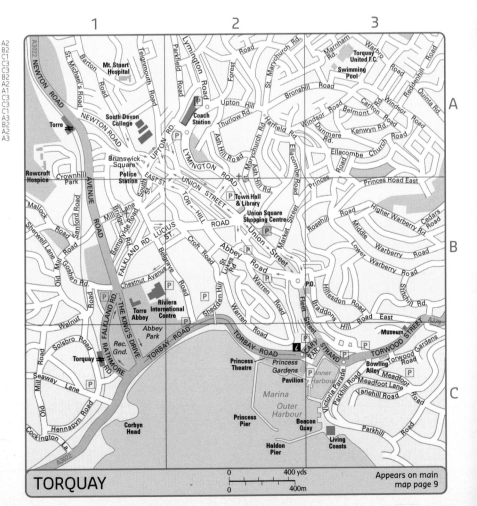

TORQUAY

0   400 yds
0   400m

Appears on main map page 9

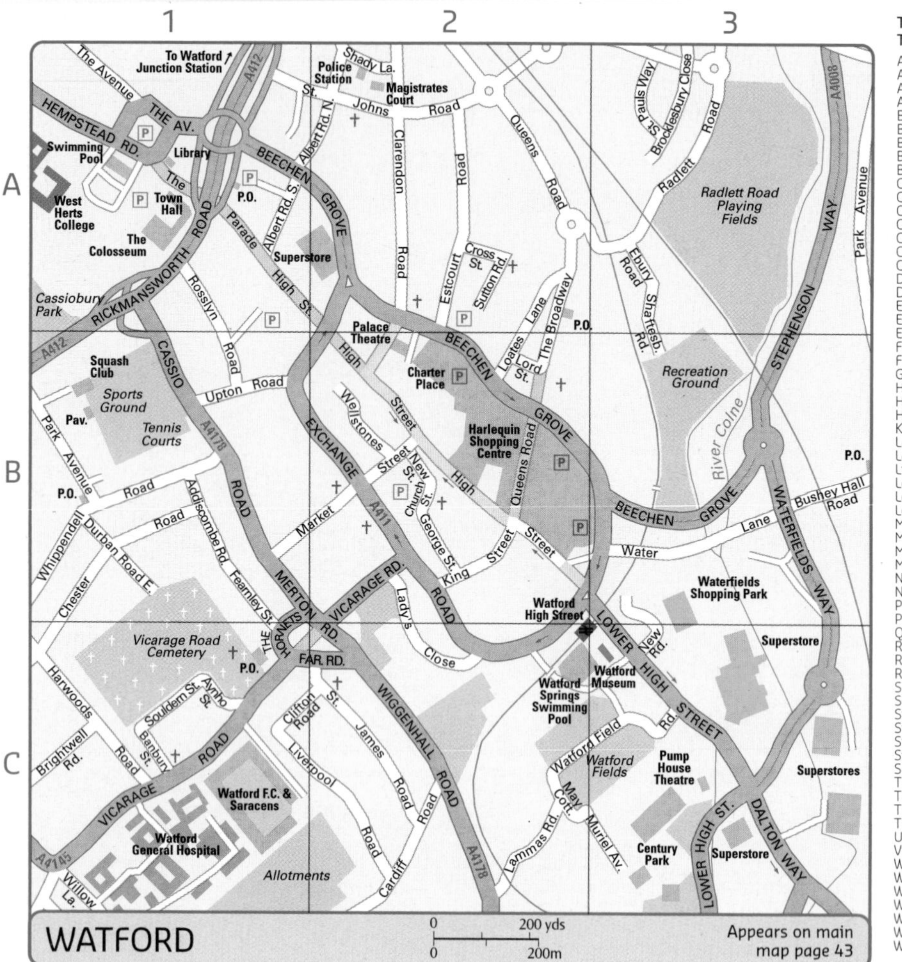

WATFORD

0   200 yds
0   200m

Appears on main map page 43

WESTON-SUPER-MARE

0   400 yds
0   400m

Appears on main map page 23

Winchester   Windsor

Tourist Information Centre: Guildhall, The Broadway
Tel: 01962 840500

Alison Way	A1
Andover Road	A1
Archery Lane	B1
Bar End Road	C3
Barfield Close	C3
Beaufort Road	C1
Beggar's Lane	B3
Blue Ball Hill	B3
Bridge Stret	B3
Broadway	B2
Canon Street	C2
Chesil Street	C3
Christchurch Road	C1
City Road	A1
Clifton Hill	B1
Clifton Road	A1
Clifton Terrace	B1
Colebrook Street	B2
College Street	C2
College Walk	C2
Compton Road	C1
Cranworth Road	A1
Culver Road	C2
Durnom Road	C3
Durngate	B3
East Hill	C3
Eastgate Street	B3
Easton Lane	A3
Ebden Road	A3
Edgar Road	C1
Elm Road	A1
Fairfield Road	A1
Friarsgate	B2
Gordon Road	A2
Great Minster Street	B2
Hatherley Road	A1
High Street	B2
Hyde Abbey Road	A2
Hyde Close	A2
Hyde Street	A2
Jewry Street	B2
King Alfred Place	A2
Kingsgate Street	C2
Little Minster Street	B2
Lower Brook Street	B2
Magdalen Hill	B3
Market Lane	B2
Middle Brook Street	B2
Middle Road	B1
Milland Road	C3
North Walls	A1
Parchment Street	B2
Park Avenue	A2
Peninsula Square	B1
Portal Road	C3
Quarry Road	C3
Romans' Road	C1
Romsey Road	B1
St. Catherine's Road	C3
St. Cross Road	C1
St. George's Street	B2
St. James Lane	B1
St. James Villas	C1
St. John's Street	B3
St. Michael's Road	C1
St. Paul's Hill	A1
St. Peter Street	B2
St. Swithun Street	C2
St. Thomas Street	C2
Saxon Road	A2
Silver Hill	B2
Southgate Street	C1
Staple Gardens	B2
Station Road	A1
Step Terrace	A1
Stockbridge Road	A1
Sussex Street	B1
Swan Lane	A2
Symond's Street	C2
Tanner Street	B2
The Square	B2
Tower Street	B1
Union Street	B3
Upper Brook Street	B2
Upper High Street	B1
Wales Street	B3
Water Lane	B3
Wharf Hill	C3
Worthy Lane	A1

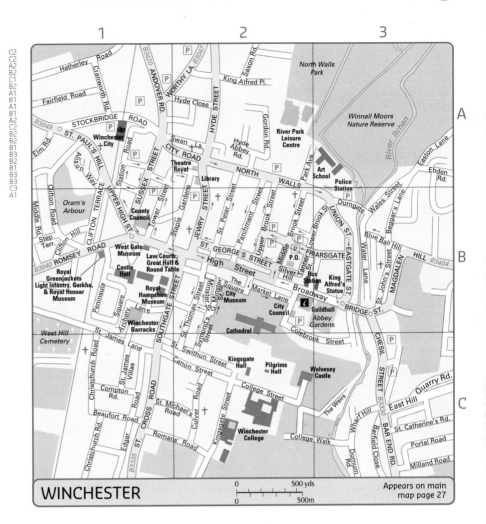

WINCHESTER — Appears on main map page 27

Tourist Information Centre: 24 High Street
Tel: 01753 743900

Adelaide Square	C3
Albert Street	B1
Alexandra Road	C2
Alma Road	B2/C2
Arthur Road	B2
Barry Avenue	A2
Bexley Street	B2
Bolton Avenue	C2
Bolton Crescent	C2
Bolton Road	C2
Bulkeley Avenue	C1
Castle Hill	B3
Charles Street	B2
Clarence Road	B1
Clarence Street	B2
College Crescent	C1
Dagmar Road	B2
Datchet Road	A3
Frances Road	C2
Goslar Way	B1
Goswell Road	B2
Green Lane	B1
Grove Road	B2
Helston Lane	B1
High Street (Eton)	A2
High Street (Windsor)	B3
Imperial Road	C1
King Edward VII Avenue	A3
Kings Road	C3
Meadow Lane	A2
Mill Lane	A1
Osborne Road	C2
Oxford Road	B2
Park Street	B3
Parsonage Lane	B1
Peascod Street	B2
Peel Close	C1
Princess Avenue	C1
Romney Lock Road	A3
St. Leonards Road	C2
St. Marks Road	B2
Sheet Street	B3
South Meadow Lane	A2
Springfield Road	C1
Stovell Road	A1
Thames Street	A3
The Long Walk	C3
Upcroft	C1
Vansittart Road	B2
Victoria Street	B2
Victor Road	C2
Westmead	C1
Windsor & Eton Relief Road	B1
York Avenue	C1
York Road	C1

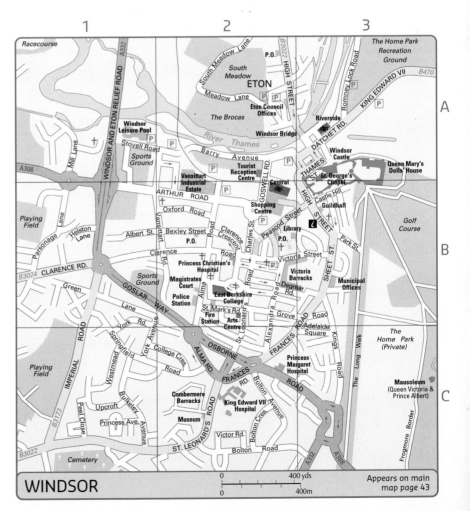

WINDSOR — Appears on main map page 43

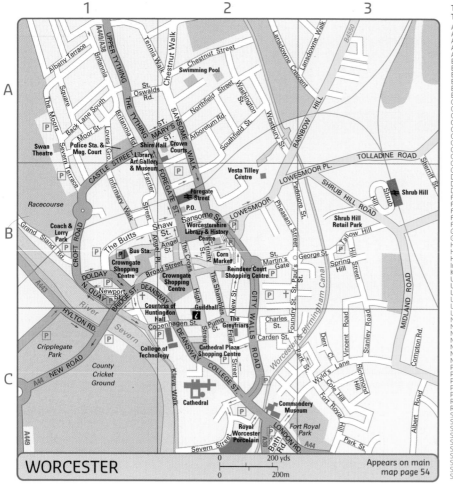

Worcester York

Tourist Information Centre: The Guildhall, High Street
Tel: 01905 726311

Albany Terrace A1
Albert Road C3
Angel Place B1
Angel Street B2
Arboretum Road A2
Back Lane South A1
Bath Road C2
Bridge Street B1
Britannia Road A1
Britannia Square A1
Broad Street B1
Carden Street C2
Castle Street B1
Charles Street C2
Chestnut Street A2
Chestnut Walk A2
City Walls Road B2
Cole Hill C3
College Street C2
Compton Road C3
Copenhagen Street C1
Croft Road B1
Deansway B1
Dent Close C3
Dolday B1
Farrier Street B1
Foregate Street B2
Fort Royal Hill C3
Foundry Street C2
Friar Street C2
George Street B3
Grand Stand Road B1
High Street B2
Hill Street B3
Hylton Road B1
Infirmary Walk B1
Kleve Walk C2
Lansdowne Crescent A2
Lansdowne Walk A3
London Road C2
Loves Grove A1
Lowesmoor B2
Lowesmoor Place B2
Midland Road C3
Moor Street A1
Newport Street B1
New Road C1
New Street B2
Northfield Street A2
North Quay B1
Padmore Street B2
Park Street C2
Park Street C3
Pheasant Street B2
Pump Street C2
Rainbow Hill A2
Richmond Hill C3
St. Martin's Gate B2
St. Mary's Street A1
St. Oswalds Road A1
St. Paul's Street B2
Sansome Street B2
Sansome Walk A2
Severn Street C2
Severn Terrace A1
Shaw Street B1
Sherriff Street A3
Shrub Hill B3
Shrub Hill Road B3
Sidbury C2
Southfield Street A2
Spring Hill B3
Stanley Road C3
Tallow Hill B3
Tennis Walk A1
The Butts B1
The Cross B2
The Moors A1
The Shambles B2
The Tything A1
Tolladine Road A3
Trinity Street B2
Upper Tything A1
Vincent Road C3
Washington Street A2
Westbury Street A2
Wyld's Lane C3

Tourist Information Centre: De Grey Rooms, Exhibition Square
Tel: 01904 621756

Abbey Street A1
Albemarle Road C1
Aldwark B2
Barbican Road C3
Bishopthorpe Road C2
Bishopgate Street C2
Blossom Street C1
Bootham A1
Bootham Crescent A1
Bridge Street B2
Bull Lane A3/B3
Burton Stone Lane A1
Cemetery Road C3
Charlotte Street B3
Church Street B2
Clarence Street A2
Clifford Street B2
Clifton A1
Coney Street B2
Dale Street C1
Dalton Terrace C1
Dodsworth Avenue A3
East Parade A3
Eldon Street A2
Fairfax Street C2
Fifth Avenue A3
Fishergate C2
Foss Bank B3
Fossgate B2
Foss Islands Road B3
Fourth Avenue B3
Gillygate A2
Goodramgate B2
Grange Garth C2
Grosvenor Road A1
Grosvenor Terrace A1
Hallfield Road B3
Haxby Road A2
Heslington Road C3
Heworth Green A3
Holgate Road C1
Hope Street C2
Huntington Road A3
Irwin Avenue A3
James Street B3
Kent Street C3
Lawrence Street C3
Layerthorpe B3
Leeman Road B1
Lendal B2
Longfield Terrace B1
Lord Mayor's Walk A2
Lowther Street A2
Malton Road A3
Marygate B1
Maurices Road B2
Micklegate B1
Monkgate A2
Moss Street C1
Mount Vale C1
Museum Street B2
Navigation Road B3
North Street B2
Nunnery Lane C1
Nunthorpe Road C1
Ousegate B2
Paragon Street C2
Park Grove A2
Park Street C1
Penley's Grove Street A2
Petergate B2
Piccadilly B2
Queen Street B1
Rougier Street B1
St. Andrewgate B2
St. John Street A2
St. Maurice's Road B2
St. Olave's Road A1
Scarcroft Hill C1
Scarcroft Road C1
Shambles B2
Sixth Avenue A3
Skeldergate B2
Southlands Road C1
Station Road B1
Terry Avenue C2
The Avenue A1
The Mount C1
The Stonebow B2
Thorpe Street C1
Tower Street B2
Vine Street C2
Walmgate B2
Water End A1
Watson Street C1
Wellington Street C3
Westminster Road A1
Wigginton Road A2

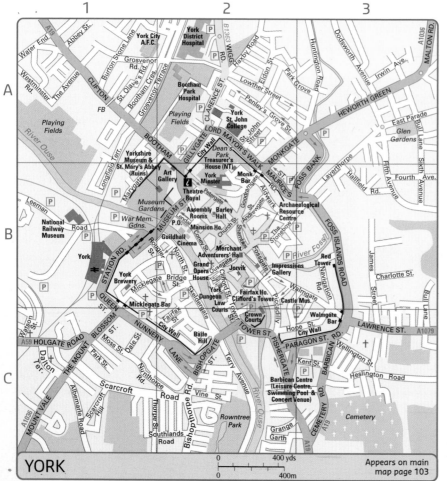

Index to place names in Britain

In this index places are followed by a page number and a grid reference. The place can be found by searching that grid square. Where more than one place has the same name, each can be distinguished by the abbreviated county or unitary authority name shown after the place name. A list of abbreviations used for these names is shown to the right.

Abbreviation	Name
Aber.	Aberdeenshire
Arg. & B.	Argyll & Bute
B'burn.	Blackburn with Darwen
B'pool	Blackpool
B. & H.	Brighton & Hove
B. & N.E.Som.	Bath & North East Somerset
B.Gwent	Blaenau Gwent
Beds.	Bedfordshire
Bourne.	Bournemouth
Brack.F.	Bracknell Forest
Bucks.	Buckinghamshire
Caerp.	Caerphilly
Cambs.	Cambridgeshire
Carmar.	Carmarthenshire
Cere.	Ceredigion
Chan.I.	Channel Islands
Ches.	Cheshire
Cornw.	Cornwall
Cumb.	Cumbria
D. & G.	Dumfries & Galloway
Darl.	Darlington
Denb.	Denbighshire
Derbys.	Derbyshire
Dur.	Durham
E.Ayr.	East Ayrshire
E.Dun.	East Dunbartonshire
E.Loth.	East Lothian
E.Renf.	East Renfrewshire
E.Riding	East Riding of Yorkshire
E.Suss.	East Sussex
Edin.	Edinburgh
Falk.	Falkirk
Flints.	Flintshire
Glas.	Glasgow
Glos.	Gloucestershire
Gt.Lon.	Greater London
Gt.Man.	Greater Manchester
Gwyn.	Gwynedd
Hants.	Hampshire
Hart.	Hartlepool
Here.	Herefordshire
Herts.	Hertfordshire
High.	Highland
Hull	Kingston upon Hull
I.o.A.	Isle of Anglesey
I.o.M.	Isle of Man
I.o.S.	Isles of Scilly
I.o.W.	Isle of Wight
Inclyde	Inverclyde
Lancs.	Lancashire
Leic.	Leicester
Leics.	Leicestershire
Lincs.	Lincolnshire
M.K.	Milton Keynes
M.Tyd.	Merthyr Tydfil
Med.	Medway
Mersey.	Merseyside
Middbro.	Middlesbrough
Midloth.	Midlothian
Mon.	Monmouthshire
N.Ayr.	North Ayrshire
N.E.Lincs.	North East Lincolnshire
N.Lan.	North Lanarkshire
N.Lincs.	North Lincolnshire
N.P.T.	Neath Port Talbot
N.Som.	North Somerset
N.Yorks.	North Yorkshire
Norf.	Norfolk
Northants.	Northamptonshire
Northumb.	Northumberland
Nott.	Nottingham
Notts.	Nottinghamshire
Ork.	Orkney
Oxon.	Oxfordshire
P. & K.	Perth & Kinross
Pembs.	Pembrokeshire
Peter.	Peterborough
Plym.	Plymouth
Ports.	Portsmouth
R. & C.	Redcar & Cleveland
R.C.T.	Rhondda Cynon Taff
Read.	Reading
Renf.	Renfrewshire
Rut.	Rutland
S'end	Southend
S'ham.	Southampton
S.Ayr.	South Ayrshire
S.Glos.	South Gloucestershire
S.Lan.	South Lanarkshire
S.Yorks.	South Yorkshire
Sc.Bord.	Scottish Borders
Shet.	Shetland
Shrop.	Shropshire
Slo.	Slough
Som.	Somerset
Staffs.	Staffordshire
Stir.	Stirling
Stock.	Stockton-on-Tees
Stoke	Stoke-on-Trent
Suff.	Suffolk
Surr.	Surrey
Swan.	Swansea
Swin.	Swindon
T. & W.	Tyne & Wear
Tel. & W.	Telford & Wrekin
Thur.	Thurrock
V. of Glam.	Vale of Glamorgan
W'ham	Wokingham
W. & M.	Windsor & Maidenhead
W.Berks.	West Berkshire
W.Dun.	West Dunbartonshire
W.Isles	Western Isles (Na h-Eileanan an Iar)
W.Loth.	West Lothian
W.Mid.	West Midlands
W.Suss.	West Sussex
W.Yorks.	West Yorkshire
Warks.	Warwickshire
Warr.	Warrington
Wilts.	Wiltshire
Worcs.	Worcestershire
Wrex.	Wrexham

A

Ab Kettleby 82 C5
Ab Lench 54 C2
Abbas Combe 25 E5
Abberley 53 G1
Abberley Common 53 G1
Abberton *Essex* 46 D1
Abberton *Worcs.* 54 B2
Abberwick 137 F5
Abbess Roding 45 E1
Abbey Dore 52 C4
Abbey Hulton 79 G3
Abbey St. Bathans 145 E3
Abbey Town 117 E1
Abbey Village 100 C5
Abbey Wood 45 D5
Abbeycwmhir 63 G5
Abbeydale 94 A4
Abbeystead 100 B2
Abbotrule 136 A5
Abbots Bickington 21 D4
Abbots Bromley 80 B5
Abbots Langley 43 F2
Abbots Leigh 39 E5
Abbots Morton 54 C2
Abbots Ripton 70 A5
Abbot's Salford 54 C2
Abbots Worthy 27 F4
Abbotsbury 12 B4
Abbotsfield Farm 91 G3
Abbotsham 21 E3
Abbotskerswell 9 E1
Abbotsley 58 A2
Abbotstone 27 G4
Abbotts Ann 27 E3
Abbott's Barton 27 F4
Abbottswood 27 E5
Abdon 65 E4
Abdy 94 B3
Abenhall 39 F1
Aber 50 A3
Aber Village 52 A5
Aberaeron 50 A1
Aberaman 37 G2
Aberangell 63 E2
Aber-Arad 49 G3
Aberarder 157 G1
Aberarder House 166 D2
Aberargie 151 G3
Aberarth 50 A1
Aberavon 36 D2
Aber-banc 49 G3
Aberbargoed 38 A2
Aberbeeg 38 B2
Aberbowlan 50 C4
Aberbran 51 F5
Abercanaid 37 G2
Abercarn 38 B3
Abercastle 48 B4
Abercegir 63 E2
Aberchalder 165 K4
Aberchirder 176 E5
Abercorn 143 E2
Abercraf 37 E1
Abercregan 37 E3
Abercrombie 152 D4
Abercrychan 51 D4
Abercwmboi 37 G2
Abercych 49 F3
Abercynafon 37 G1
Abercynon 37 G3
Abercywarch 63 E1
Aberdalgie 151 F2
Aberdare 37 F2
Aberdaron 74 A5
Aberdaugleddau (Milford Haven) 34 B2
Aberdeen 169 H4
Aberdeen Airport 169 G3
Aberdesach 74 D2
Aberdour 143 F1
Aberdovey (Aberdyfi) 62 C3
Aberduhonw 51 G2
Aberdulais 37 D3
Aberdyfi (Aberdovey) 62 C3
Aberedw 51 G3
Abereiddy 48 A4
Abererch 74 C4
Aberfan 37 G2
Aberfeldy 159 D5
Aberffraw 74 C1
Aberffrwd 62 C5
Aberford 102 D4
Aberfoyle 150 A4
Abergavenny (Y Fenni) 38 B1
Abergele 90 A5
Aber-Giâr 50 B3
Abergorlech 50 B4
Abergwaun (Fishguard) 48 C4
Abergwesyn 51 E2
Abergwili 50 A5
Abergwydol 63 D2
Abergwynant 62 C1
Abergwynfi 37 E3
Abergwyngregyn 89 E5
Abergynolwyn 62 C2
Aberhafesp 63 G3
Aberhonddu (Brecon) 51 G5
Aberhosan 63 E3
Aberkenfig 37 E4
Aberlady 144 B1
Aberlemno 160 D4
Aberllefenni 63 D2
Aber-llia 37 F1
Aberllynfi (Three Cocks) 52 A4
Aberlour (Charlestown of Aberlour) 175 K7
Abermad 62 B5
Abermaw (Barmouth) 62 C1
Abermeurig 50 B2
Abermule 64 A3
Abernaint 77 E5
Abernant *Carmar.* 49 G5
Aber-nant *R.C.T.* 37 G2
Abernethy 151 G3
Abernyte 152 A1
Aberpennar (Mountain Ash) 37 G3
Aberporth 49 F2
Aberriw (Berriew) 64 A2
Aberscross 174 E2
Abersky 166 C2
Abersoch 74 C5
Abersychan 38 B2
Abertawe (Swansea) 36 C3
Aberteifi (Cardigan) 49 E3
Aberthin 37 G5
Abertillery 38 B2
Abertridwr *Caerp.* 38 A4
Abertridwr *Powys* 63 G1
Abertysswg 38 A2
Aberuthven 151 E3
Aberyscir 51 F5
Aberystwyth 62 B4
Abhainnsuidhe 178 C7
Abingdon 41 G3
Abinger Common 29 G3
Abinger Hammer 29 F3
Abington 134 A3
Abington Pigotts 58 B3
Abingworth 16 D2
Ablington *Glos.* 40 D2
Ablington *Wilts.* 26 C3
Abney 93 F5
Above Church 80 B2
Aboyne 168 D5
Abram 92 A2
Abriachan 166 C1
Abridge 45 D3
Abronhill 142 B2
Abson 39 G5
Abthorpe 56 B3
Abune-the-Hill 184 B5
Aby 97 E5
Acaster Malbis 103 E3
Acaster Selby 103 E3
Accrington 101 D5
Accurrach 148 D2
Acha 154 A4
Achacha 156 B5
Achadacaie 139 G3
Achadh Mòr 179 F5
Achadh-chaorrunn 139 F4
Achadunan 149 E3
Achagavel 155 G4
Achaglass 139 F5
Achahoish 139 F2
Achalader 159 G5
Achallader 157 F5
Achamore 139 D2
Achandunie 174 D4
Achany 174 C1
Achaphubuil 156 C2
Acharacle 155 F3
Achargary 182 C3
Acharn *Arg. & B.* 148 D1
Acharn *P. & K.* 158 C5
Acharonich 147 D1
Acharosson 140 A2
Achateny 155 E2
Achath 169 F3
Achavanich 183 G4
Achddu 36 A2
Achduart 173 G1
Achentoul 182 D5
Achfary 180 E5
Achgarve 172 E2
Achiemore *High.* 181 F2
Achiemore *High.* 182 D3
Achies 183 G3
A'Chill 163 H4
Achiltibuie 173 G1
Achina 182 C2
Achindown 175 F7
Achinduich 174 C2
Achingills 183 G2
Achintee 173 F7
Achintee House 156 D2
Achintraid 164 E1
Achlean 167 F5
Achleanan 155 E4
Achleek 155 G4
Achlian 148 D2
Achlyness 180 E3
Achmelvich 180 C6
Achmony 166 C1
Achmore *High.* 164 E1
Achmore *High.* 173 G2
Achmore *Stir.* 150 A1
Achnaba 140 A1
Achnabat 166 C1
Achnabourin 182 C3
Achnacairn 148 B1
Achnacarnin 180 C5
Achnacarry 157 D1
Achnaclerach 174 B5
Achnacloich *Arg. & B.* 148 B1
Achnacloich *High.* 164 B4
Achnaclyth 183 F5
Achnacraig 155 D5
Achnacroish 156 A5
Achnadrish 155 D4
Achnafalnich 149 E2
Achnafauld 151 D1
Achnagairn 174 C7
Achnagarron 174 D4
Achnaha *High.* 155 F5
Achnaha *High.* 155 D3
Achnahanat 174 C2
Achnahannet 167 G2
Achnairn 181 H7
Achnalea 156 A3
Achnamara 139 F1
Achnanellan 155 G3
Achnasaul 157 D1
Achnasheen 173 H6
Achnashelloch 148 A5
Achnastank 167 K1
Achorn 183 G5
Achosnich *High.* 174 E2
Achosnich *High.* 154 D3
Achreamie 183 F2
Achriabhach 156 D3
Achriesgill 180 E3
Achtoty 181 J2
Achurch 69 F4
Achuvoldrach 181 H3
Achvaich 174 E2
Achvarasdal 182 E2
Achvlair 156 B4
Achvraie 173 G1
Ackenthwaite 107 G4
Ackergill 183 J3
Acklam *Middbro.* 111 D1
Acklam *N.Yorks.* 103 G1
Ackleton 65 G3
Acklington 129 E1
Ackton 102 D5
Ackworth Moor Top 94 B1
Acle 87 F4
Acock's Green 66 D4
Acol 33 F2
Acomb *Northumb.* 119 F1
Acomb *York* 103 E2
Aconbury 53 E4
Acre 101 D5
Acrefair 77 F3
Acrise Place 33 D4
Acton *Ches.* 78 D2
Acton *Dorset* 13 F5
Acton *Gt.Lon.* 44 A4
Acton *Shrop.* 64 C4
Acton *Staffs.* 79 F3
Acton *Suff.* 59 G3
Acton *Worcs.* 54 A1
Acton *Wrex.* 78 A2
Acton Beauchamp 53 F2
Acton Bridge 91 G5
Acton Burnell 65 E2
Acton Green 53 F2
Acton Pigott 65 E2
Acton Round 65 F3
Acton Scott 65 D4
Acton Trussell 66 B1
Acton Turville 40 A4
Adamhill 132 C2
Adbaston 79 E5
Adber 24 C5
Adderbury 55 G4
Adderley 79 D4
Adderstone 137 F3
Addiewell 143 D3
Addingham 101 G3
Addington *Bucks.* 56 C5
Addington *Gt.Lon.* 30 C2
Addington *Kent* 31 F3
Addiscombe 30 C2
Addlestone 29 F1
Addlethorpe 84 D1
Adel 102 B4
Adeney 65 G1
Adeyfield 43 F2
Adfa 63 G2
Adforton 64 D5
Adisham 33 E3
Adlestrop 55 E5
Adlingfleet 104 A5
Adlington *Ches.* 92 D4
Adlington *Lancs.* 91 G1
Admaston *Staffs.* 80 B5
Admaston *Tel. & W.* 65 F1
Admington 55 E3
Adsborough 23 F5
Adscombe 23 E4
Adstock 56 C4
Adstone 56 A2
Adversane 29 F5
Advie 167 J1
Adwalton 102 B5
Adwell 42 B3
Adwick le Street 94 C2
Adwick upon Dearne 94 B2
Adziel 177 H5
Ae Village 125 D2
Affetside 92 B1
Affleck 169 G2
Affpuddle 13 E3
Afon Wen 74 D4
Afon-wen 90 C5
Afton 14 C4
Afton Bridgend 133 E4
Agglethorpe 109 F4
Aigburth 91 E4
Aiginis 179 G4
Aike 104 C3
Aikerness 184 D2
Aikers 185 D8
Aiketgate 118 A3
Aikshaw 117 E2
Aikton 117 F1
Aikwood Tower 135 F3
Ailby 97 E5
Ailey 52 C3
Ailsworth 69 G3
Aimes Green 44 D2
Aimster 183 G2
Ainderby Quernhow 110 C4
Ainderby Steeple 110 C3
Aingers Green 60 C5
Ainsdale 91 E1
Ainsdale-on-Sea 91 E1
Ainstable 118 B3
Ainsworth 92 B1
Ainthorpe 111 G2
Aintree 91 E3
Aird *W.Isles* 170 C6
Aird *W.Isles* 179 H4
Aird a' Mhachair 170 C7
Aird a' Mhulaidh 178 D6
Aird Asaig 178 D7
Aird Dhail 179 G1
Aird Leimhe 171 G3
Aird Mhige 171 G2
Aird Mhighe 171 F3
Aird of Sleat 164 B4
Aird Thunga 179 G4
Aird Uig 178 C4
Airdrie *Fife* 153 D4
Airdrie *N.Lan.* 142 B3
Aire View 101 F3
Airidh a' Bhruaich 178 E6
Airieland 124 B5
Airies 122 A4
Airigh-drishaig 164 D1
Airmyn 103 G5
Airntully 151 F1
Airor 164 D4
Airth 142 C1
Airton 101 F2
Airyhassen 115 D2
Aisby *Lincs.* 95 F3
Aisby *Lincs.* 83 F4
Aisgernis (Askernish) 162 C2
Aisgill 108 C3
Aish *Devon* 8 C1
Aish *Devon* 9 E2
Aisholt 23 E4
Aiskew 110 B4
Aislaby *N.Yorks.* 112 B2
Aislaby *N.Yorks.* 111 G4
Aislaby *Stock.* 110 D1
Aisthorpe 95 G4
Aith *Ork.* 185 B6
Aith *Ork.* 184 F5
Aith *Shet.* 187 C7
Aith *Shet.* 186 F3
Aithsetter 187 D9
Aitnoch 167 G1
Akeld 137 D4
Akeley 56 C4
Akenham 60 C3
Albaston 7 E3
Albecq 9 E5
Alberbury 64 C1
Albert Town 34 C1
Albourne 17 E2
Albourne Green 17 E2
Albrighton *Shrop.* 66 A2
Albrighton *Shrop.* 65 D1
Alburgh 73 D3
Albury *Herts.* 58 C5
Albury *Oxon.* 42 B2
Albury *Surr.* 29 F3
Albury End 58 C5
Albury Heath 29 F3
Albyfield 118 B2
Alcaig 174 C6
Alcaston 65 D4
Alcester 54 C2
Alciston 18 A3
Alcombe 22 C3
Alconbury 69 G5
Alconbury Hill 69 G5
Alconbury Weston 69 G5
Aldborough *N.Yorks.* 102 D1
Aldborough *Norf.* 86 C2
Aldbourne 41 E5
Aldbrough 105 E4
Aldbrough St. John 110 B1
Aldbury 43 E1
Aldclune 159 E3
Aldeburgh 61 F2
Aldeby 73 F2
Aldenham 44 A3
Alderbury 26 C5
Alderford 86 C4
Alderholt 14 A1
Alderley 39 G3
Alderley Edge 92 C5
Aldermaston 27 G1
Aldermaston Wharf 28 B1
Alderminster 55 E3
Alderney 9 G4
Alderney Airport 9 F4
Alder's End 53 F4
Aldersey Green 78 B2
Aldershot 29 D2
Alderton *Glos.* 54 B4
Alderton *Northants.* 56 C3
Alderton *Suff.* 61 E3
Alderton *Wilts.* 40 A4
Alderwasley 81 E2
Aldfield 102 B1
Aldford 78 B2
Aldham *Essex* 60 A5
Aldham *Suff.* 60 B3
Aldie *Aber.* 177 J6
Aldie *High.* 174 E3
Aldingbourne 16 B3
Aldingham 107 D5
Aldington *Kent* 32 C5
Aldington *Worcs.* 54 C3
Aldivalloch 168 B2
Aldochlay 149 F5
Aldons 122 C2
Aldous's Corner 73 E3
Aldreth 70 C5
Aldridge 66 C2
Aldringham 61 F1
Aldsworth *Glos.* 41 D2
Aldsworth *W.Suss.* 15 G2
Aldunie 168 B2
Aldville 151 E1
Aldwark *Derbys.* 80 D2
Aldwark *N.Yorks.* 103 D1
Aldwick 16 B4
Aldwincle 69 F4
Aldworth 42 A5
Alexandria 141 E2
Aley 23 E4
Aley Green 43 F1
Alfardisworthy 20 C4
Alfington 11 E3
Alfold 29 F4
Alfold Crossways 29 F4
Alford *Aber.* 168 D3
Alford *Lincs.* 97 E5
Alford *Som.* 24 D4
Alfreton 81 F2
Alfrick 53 G2
Alfrick Pound 53 G2
Alfriston 18 A3
Algarkirk 84 A4
Alhampton 24 D4
Alkborough 104 A5
Alkerton 55 F3
Alkham 33 E4
Alkington 78 C4
Alkmonton 80 C4
All Cannings 26 B1
All Saints South Elmham 73 E3
All Stretton 65 D3
Allaleigh 9 E2
Allanaquoich 167 J5
Allancreich 168 D5
Allanfearn 174 E7
Allangillfoot 126 A2
Allanton *D. & G.* 124 D2
Allanton *E.Ayr.* 133 E2
Allanton *N.Lan.* 142 C4
Allanton *S.Lan.* 142 B4
Allanton *Sc.Bord.* 145 F4
Allardice 161 G2
Allathasdal 162 B4
Allbrook 27 F5
Allendale Town 119 E2
Allenheads 119 E3
Allen's Green 45 D1
Allensford 119 G2
Allensmore 53 D4
Allenton 81 E4
Aller 24 B5
Allerby 117 D3
Allercombe 10 D3
Allerford *Devon* 7 E2
Allerford *Som.* 22 C3
Allerston 112 B4
Allerthorpe 103 G3
Allerton *Mersey.* 91 F4
Allerton *W.Yorks.* 102 A4
Allerton Bywater 102 D5
Allerton Mauleverer 102 D2
Allesley 67 E4
Allestree 81 E4
Allet Common 4 B5
Allexton 68 D2
Allgreave 79 G1
Allhallows 32 A1
Allhallows-on-Sea 32 A1
Alligin Shuas 172 E6
Allimore Green 66 A1
Allington *Dorset* 12 A3
Allington *Lincs.* 83 D3
Allington *Wilts.* 26 D4
Allington *Wilts.* 26 B1
Allington *Wilts.* 40 A5
Allithwaite 107 E5
Allnabad 181 G4
Alloa 151 D5
Allonby 117 D2
Allostock 92 B5
Alloway 132 B4
Allowenshay 11 G1
Allscot 65 G3
Allscott 65 F1
Allt na h-Airbhe 173 H2
Alltachonaich 155 G4
Alltbeithe 165 G2
Alltforgan 76 C5
Alltmawr 51 G3
Alltnacaillich 181 G4
Allt-na-subh 165 F1
Alltsigh 166 B3
Alltwalis 50 A4
Alltwen 36 D2
Alltyblaca 50 B3
Allwood Green 72 B4
Almeley 52 C2
Almeley Wootton 52 C2
Almer 13 F3
Almington 79 E4
Almiston Cross 21 D3
Almondbank 151 F2
Almondbury 93 F1
Almondsbury 39 F4
Alne 103 D1
Alness 174 D5
Alnham 137 D5
Alnmouth 137 G5
Alnwick 137 F5
Alperton 44 A4
Alphamstone 59 G4
Alpheton 59 G2
Alphington 10 C3
Alport 80 D1
Alpraham 78 C2
Alresford 60 B5
Alrewas 67 D1
Alrick 159 G3
Alsager 79 E2
Alsagers Bank 79 F3
Alsop en le Dale 80 C2
Alston *Cumb.* 118 D3
Alston *Devon* 11 G2
Alston Sutton 24 B2
Alstone *Glos.* 54 B4
Alstone *Som.* 24 A3
Alstone *Staffs.* 66 A1
Alstonefield 80 C2
Alswear 22 A5
Alt 92 D2
Altandhu 180 B7
Altanduin 182 D6
Altarnun 5 G1
Altass 174 C1
Altens 169 H4
Alterwall 183 H2
Altham 101 D4
Althorne 46 C3
Althorpe 95 F2
Alticry 123 D5
Altnafeadh 157 E4
Altnaharra 181 H5
Altofts 102 C5
Alton *Derbys.* 81 E1
Alton *Hants.* 28 C4
Alton *Staffs.* 80 B3
Alton Barnes 26 C1
Alton Pancras 12 D2
Alton Priors 26 C1
Altonside 175 K6
Altrincham 92 B4
Altura 165 J5
Alva 151 D5
Alvanley 91 F5
Alvaston 81 E4
Alvechurch 66 C5
Alvecote 67 E2
Alvediston 26 A5
Alveley 65 G4
Alverdiscott 21 F3
Alverstoke 15 F3
Alverstone 15 E4
Alverthorpe 102 C5
Alverton 82 C3
Alves 175 J5
Alvescot 41 E2
Alveston *S.Glos.* 39 F4
Alveston *Warks.* 55 E2
Alvie 167 F4
Alvingham 97 D3
Alvington 39 F2
Alwalton 69 G3
Alweston 12 C1
Alwington 21 E3
Alwinton 128 B1
Alwoodley 102 C3
Alwoodley Gates 102 C3
Alyth 160 A5
Amalebra 2 B3
Ambaston 81 F4
Amber Hill 84 A3
Ambergate 81 E2
Amberley *Glos.* 40 A2
Amberley *W.Suss.* 16 C2
Amble 129 E1
Amblecote 66 A4
Ambleside 107 E2
Ambleston 48 D5
Ambrismore 140 B4
Ambrosden 42 B1
Amcotts 95 F1
Amersham 43 E3
Amerton 79 G5
Amesbury 26 C3
Ameysford 13 G2
Amington 67 E2
Amisfield Town 125 E2
Amlwch 88 C3
Amlwch Port 88 C3
Ammanford (Rhydaman) 36 C1
Amotherby 111 G5
Ampfield 27 E5
Ampleforth 111 E5
Ampleforth College 111 E5
Ampney Crucis 40 C2
Ampney St. Mary 40 C2
Ampney St. Peter 40 C2
Amport 27 E3
Ampthill 57 F4
Ampton 71 G5
Amroth 35 E2
Amulree 151 D1
An Tairbeart (Tarbert) 178 D7
An T-òb (Leverburgh) 171 F3
Anaboard 167 H1
Anaheilt 156 A3
Ancaster 83 E3
Anchor 64 A4
Anchor Corner 72 B2
Ancroft 145 G5
Ancrum 136 A4
Ancton 16 B3
Anderby 97 F5
Anderby Creek 97 F5
Andersea 24 A4
Andersfield 23 F4
Anderson 13 E3
Anderton 92 A5
Andover 27 E3
Andover Down 27 E3
Andoversford 40 C1
Andreas 98 C2
Anelog 74 A5
Anfield 91 E3
Angarrack 2 C3
Angarrick 3 E3
Angelbank 65 E5
Angerton 117 F1
Angle 34 B2
Angler's Retreat 62 D3
Anglesey (Ynys Môn) 88 B4
Angmering 16 C3
Angmering-on-Sea 16 C3
Angram *N.Yorks.* 103 E3
Angram *N.Yorks.* 109 D3
Anick 119 F1
Anie 150 A3

Ankerville 175 F4
Anlaby 104 C5
Anmer 85 F5
Anmore 15 F1
Anna Valley 27 E3
Annan 125 F4
Annaside 106 B4
Annat Arg. & B. 148 C2
Annat High. 172 E6
Annbank 132 C3
Annesley 81 G2
Annesley Woodhouse 81 F2
Annfield Plain 120 A2
Anniesland 141 G3
Annscroft 65 D2
Ansdell 99 G5
Ansford 24 D4
Ansley 67 E3
Anslow 80 D5
Anslow Gate 80 C5
Ansteadbrook 29 E4
Anstey Herts. 58 C4
Anstey Leics. 68 A2
Anstruther 153 D4
Ansty W.Suss. 17 E1
Ansty Warks. 67 F4
Ansty Wilts. 26 A5
Ansty Coombe 26 A5
Ansty Cross 13 D2
Anthill Common 15 F1
Anthorn 117 E1
Antingham 87 D2
Anton's Gowt 84 A3
Antony 7 D5
Antrobus 92 A5
Anvil Corner 21 D5
Anvil Green 32 D4
Anwick 83 G2
Anwoth 123 G5
Aoradh 138 A3
Apethorpe 69 F3
Apeton 66 A1
Apley 96 B5
Apperknowle 94 A5
Apperley 54 A5
Apperley Bridge 102 A4
Appersett 109 D3
Appin 156 B5
Appin House 156 B5
Appleby 95 G1
Appleby Magna 67 F1
Appleby Parva 67 F2
Appleby-in-Westmorland 118 C5
Applecross 172 D7
Appledore Devon 21 E2
Appledore Devon 11 D1
Appledore Kent 19 E1
Appledore Heath 32 B5
Appleford 42 A3
Appleshaw 27 E3
Applethwaite 117 F4
Appleton Halton 91 G4
Appleton Oxon. 41 G2
Appleton Roebuck 103 E3
Appleton Thorn 92 A4
Appleton Wiske 110 C2
Appleton-le-Moors 111 G4
Appleton-le-Street 111 G5
Appletreehall 135 G4
Appletreewick 101 G1
Appley 23 D5
Appley Bridge 91 G2
Apse Heath 15 E4
Apsey Green 61 D1
Apsley 43 F2
Apsley End 57 G4
Apuldram 16 A3
Arberth (Narberth) 35 E1
Arbirlot 161 D5
Arborfield 28 C1
Arborfield Cross 28 C1
Arborfield Garrison 28 C1
Arbourthorne 94 A4
Arbroath 161 E5
Arbuthnott 161 F2
Archdeacon Newton 110 B1
Archiestown 175 K7
Arclid 79 E1
Ard a' Chapuill 140 B1
Ardachearanbeg 140 B1
Ardacheranmor 140 B1
Ardachoil 147 G1
Ardachu 174 D1
Ardailly 139 E4
Ardalanish 146 C3
Ardallie 169 J1
Ardanaiseig 148 C2
Ardaneaskan 164 E1
Ardanstur 148 A3
Ardantiobairt 155 F4
Ardantrive 148 A2
Ardarroch 172 E7
Ardbeg Arg. & B. 140 B3
Ardbeg Arg. & B. 138 C5
Ardbeg Arg. & B. 140 C1
Ardblair 166 C1
Ardbrecknish 148 C2
Ardcharnich 173 H3
Ardchiavaig 146 C3
Ardchonnel 148 B1
Ardchonnell 148 B3
Ardchrishnish 146 D2
Ardchronie 174 D3
Ardchuilk 165 J1
Ardchullarie More 150 A3
Ardchyle 150 A2
Arddlin 64 B1
Ardechvie 165 H5
Ardeley 58 B5
Ardelve 164 E2
Arden 141 E1
Ardencaple House 147 G3
Ardens Grafton 54 D2
Ardentallan 148 A2
Ardentinny 140 C1
Ardeonaig 150 B1
Ardersier 174 E6
Ardery 155 G3
Ardessie 173 G3
Ardfad 147 G3
Ardfern 148 A4
Ardfin 138 C3
Ardgartan 149 E4
Ardgay 174 D2
Ardgenavan 149 D3
Ardgowan 140 D2
Ardgowse 168 E3
Ardgye 175 J5
Ardhallow 140 C2
Ardheslaig 172 D6
Ardiecow 176 D4
Ardinamar 147 G3
Ardindrean 173 H3
Ardingly 17 F1
Ardington 41 G4
Ardington Wick 41 G4
Ardintoul 164 E2
Ardkinglas House 149 D3
Ardlair 168 D2
Ardlamont 140 A3
Ardleigh 60 B5
Ardleigh Green 45 E4
Ardleigh Heath 60 B4
Ardleish 149 F3
Ardler 160 A5
Ardley 56 A5
Ardley End 45 E1
Ardlui 149 F3
Ardlussa 139 E1
Ardmaddy 148 C1
Ardmair 173 H2
Ardmaleish 140 B3
Ardmay 149 E4
Ardmenish 139 D2
Ardmhór 162 C4
Ardminish 139 E5
Ardmolich 155 G2
Ardmore Arg. & B. 138 C4
Ardmore Arg. & B. 147 G2
Ardmore Arg. & B. 141 E2
Ardmore High. 174 E3
Ardnackaig 147 G5
Ardnacross 155 E5
Ardnadam 140 C1
Ardnadrochit 147 G1
Ardnagoine 173 F1
Ardnagowan 148 D4
Ardnahein 149 D5
Ardnahoe 138 C2
Ardnarff 164 E1
Ardnastang 156 A3
Ardnave 138 A2
Ardno 149 D4
Ardo 169 G1
Ardoch D. & G. 133 G5
Ardoch Moray 175 J6
Ardoch P. & K. 151 F1
Ardochrig 142 A5
Ardoyne 168 E2
Ardpatrick 139 F3
Ardpeaton 140 D1
Ardradnaig 158 C5
Ardrishaig 139 G1
Ardroe 180 C6
Ardross 174 D4
Ardrossan 140 D5
Ardscalpsie 140 B4
Ardshave 174 E2
Ardshealach 155 F3
Ardshellach 147 G3
Ardsley 94 A2
Ardslignish 155 E3
Ardtalla 138 C4
Ardtalnaig 150 C1
Ardtaraig 140 B1
Ardteatle 148 D2
Ardtoe 155 F2
Ardtornish 155 G5
Ardtrostan 150 B2
Ardtur 156 B5
Arduaine 148 A3
Ardullie 174 C5
Ardura 147 F1
Ardvar 180 D5
Ardvasar 164 C4
Ardveenish 162 C4
Ardveich 150 B2
Ardverikie 158 A1
Ardvorlich Arg. & B. 149 F3
Ardvorlich P. & K. 150 B2
Ardwall 123 G5
Ardwell D. & G. 114 B2
Ardwell Moray 168 B1
Ardwell S.Ayr. 122 C1
Ardwick 92 C3
Areley Kings 66 A5
Arford 28 D4
Argaty 150 C4
Argoed 38 A3
Argoed Mill 51 F1
Argos Hill 18 A1
Argrennan House 124 B5
Arichamish 148 B4
Arichastlich 149 E1
Arichonan 147 G5
Aridhglas 146 C2
Arienskill 155 G1
Arileod 154 A4
Arinacrinachd 172 D6
Arinafad Beg 139 F1
Arinagour 154 B4
Arinambane 162 C2
Arisaig 155 F1
Arivegaig 155 F3
Arkendale 102 C1
Arkesden 58 C4
Arkholme 107 G5
Arkle Town 109 F2
Arkleby 117 E3
Arkleside 109 F4
Arkleton 126 B2
Arkley 44 B3
Arksey 94 C2
Arkwright Town 94 B5
Arlary 151 G4
Arle 54 B5
Arlecdon 116 D5
Arlesey 57 G4
Arleston 65 F1
Arley 92 A4
Arlingham 39 G1
Arlington Devon 21 G1
Arlington E.Suss. 18 A3
Arlington Glos. 40 D2
Arlington Beccott 21 G1
Armadale High. 182 C2
Armadale High. 164 C4
Armadale W.Loth. 142 D3
Armathwaite 118 B3
Arminghall 87 D5
Armitage 66 C1
Armitage Bridge 93 F1
Armley 102 B4
Armscote 55 E3
Armshead 79 G3
Armston 69 F4
Armthorpe 94 D2
Arnabost 154 B3
Arnaby 106 C4
Arncliffe 109 E5
Arncliffe Cote 109 E5
Arncroach 152 D4
Arne 13 F4
Arnesby 68 B3
Arngask 151 G3
Arngibbon 150 B5
Arngomery 150 B5
Arnhall 161 E3
Arnicle 130 C2
Arnipol 155 G1
Arnisdale 164 E3
Arnish 172 B7
Arniston Engine 144 A3
Arnol 179 F3
Arnold E.Riding 104 D3
Arnold Notts. 81 G3
Arnprior 150 B5
Arnside 107 F5
Arowry 78 B4
Arrad Foot 107 E4
Arradoul 176 C4
Arram 104 C3
Arran 131 E2
Arras 104 B3
Arrat 161 E4
Arrathorne 110 B3
Arreton 15 E4
Arrington 58 B2
Arrivain 149 E1
Arrochar 149 F4
Arrow 54 C2
Arscaig 181 H7
Arscott 64 D2
Arthington 102 B3
Arthingworth 68 C4
Arthog 62 C1
Arthrath 169 H1
Arthurstone 160 A5
Artrochie 169 J1
Aruadh 138 A3
Arundel 16 C3
Aryhoulan 156 C3
Asby 117 D4
Ascog 140 C3
Ascot 29 E1
Ascott 55 F4
Ascott d'Oyley 41 F1
Ascott Earl 41 E1
Ascott-under-Wychwood 41 F1
Ascreavie 160 B4
Asenby 110 D5
Asfordby 68 C1
Asfordby Hill 68 C1
Asgarby Lincs. 84 B1
Asgarby Lincs. 83 G3
Ash Dorset 13 E1
Ash Kent 33 E3
Ash Kent 31 F2
Ash Som. 24 B5
Ash Surr. 29 D2
Ash Barton 21 F5
Ash Bullayne 10 A2
Ash Green Surr. 29 E3
Ash Green Warks. 67 F4
Ash Magna 78 C4
Ash Mill 22 A5
Ash Parva 78 C4
Ash Priors 23 E5
Ash Street 60 B3
Ash Thomas 10 D1
Ash Vale 29 D2
Ashampstead 42 A5
Ashbocking 60 C2
Ashbourne 80 C3
Ashbrittle 23 D5
Ashburnham Place 18 B2
Ashburton 9 D1
Ashbury Devon 7 F1
Ashbury Oxon. 41 E4
Ashby 95 F2
Ashby by Partney 84 C1
Ashby cum Fenby 96 C2
Ashby de la Launde 83 F2
Ashby de la Zouch 67 F1
Ashby Dell 73 F2
Ashby Folville 68 C1
Ashby Hill 96 C2
Ashby Magna 68 A3
Ashby Parva 68 A4
Ashby Puerorum 96 D5
Ashby St. Ledgers 56 A1
Ashby St. Mary 87 E5
Ashchurch 54 B4
Ashcombe Devon 10 C5
Ashcombe N.Som. 24 A1
Ashcott 24 B4
Ashdon 59 D3
Ashe 27 G3
Asheldham 46 C2
Ashen 59 F3
Ashenden 32 A5
Ashendon 42 C1
Ashens 139 G2
Ashfield Arg. & B. 139 F1
Ashfield Here. 53 E5
Ashfield Stir. 150 C4
Ashfield Suff. 60 D1
Ashfield Green Suff. 73 D4
Ashfield Green Suff. 59 F2
Ashfold Crossways 17 E1
Ashford Devon 8 C3
Ashford Devon 21 F2
Ashford Hants. 14 A1
Ashford Kent 32 C4
Ashford Surr. 43 F5
Ashford Bowdler 65 E5
Ashford Carbonel 65 E5
Ashford Hill 27 G1
Ashford in the Water 93 F5
Ashgill 142 B4
Ashiestiel 135 F2
Ashill Devon 11 D1
Ashill Norf. 71 G2
Ashill Som. 11 G1
Ashingdon 46 B3
Ashington Northumb. 129 E3
Ashington Som. 24 C5
Ashington W.Suss. 16 D2
Ashkirk 135 F3
Ashlett 15 D2
Ashleworth 54 A5
Ashleworth Quay 54 A5
Ashley Cambs. 59 E1
Ashley Ches. 92 B4
Ashley Devon 21 G4
Ashley Glos. 40 B3
Ashley Hants. 27 E4
Ashley Hants. 14 B3
Ashley Kent 33 F4
Ashley Northants. 68 C3
Ashley Staffs. 79 E4
Ashley Wilts. 25 F1
Ashley Down 39 E5
Ashley Green 43 E2
Ashley Heath Dorset 14 A2
Ashley Heath Staffs. 79 E4
Ashmanhaugh 87 E3
Ashmansworth 27 F2
Ashmansworthy 20 D4
Ashmore Dorset 13 F1
Ashmore P. & K. 159 G4
Ashmore Green 27 G1
Ashorne 55 F2
Ashover 81 E1
Ashover Hay 81 E1
Ashow 67 F5
Ashperton 53 F3
Ashprington 9 E2
Ashreigney 21 G4
Ashtead 29 G2
Ashton Ches. 78 C1
Ashton Cornw. 2 D4
Ashton Cornw. 7 D4
Ashton Hants. 15 E1
Ashton Here. 53 E1
Ashton Inclyde 140 D2
Ashton Northants. 69 F4
Ashton Northants. 56 C3
Ashton Peter. 69 G2
Ashton Common 25 F2
Ashton Keynes 40 C3
Ashton under Hill 54 B4
Ashton upon Mersey 92 B3
Ashton-in-Makerfield 91 G3
Ashton-under-Lyne 92 D3
Ashurst Hants. 14 C1
Ashurst Kent 31 E5
Ashurst W.Suss. 17 D2
Ashurst Bridge 14 C1
Ashurstwood 30 D5
Ashwater 7 D1
Ashwell Herts. 58 A4
Ashwell Rut. 69 D1
Ashwell End 58 A3
Ashwellthorpe 72 C2
Ashwick 24 D3
Ashwicken 71 F1
Ashybank 135 G4
Askam in Furness 106 D5
Askern 94 C1
Askernish (Aisgernis) 162 C2
Askerswell 12 B3
Askett 42 D2
Askham Cumb. 118 B5
Askham Notts. 95 E5
Askham Bryan 103 E3
Askham Richard 103 E3
Asknish 148 B5
Askrigg 109 E3
Askwith 102 A3
Aslackby 83 F4
Aslacton 72 C2
Aslockton 82 C3
Asloun 168 D3
Aspall 60 C1
Aspatria 117 E2
Aspenden 58 B5
Asperton 84 A4
Aspley Guise 57 E4
Aspley Heath 57 E4
Aspull 92 A2
Asselby 103 G5
Asserby 97 E5
Assington 60 A4
Assington Green 59 F2
Astbury 79 F1
Astcote 56 B2
Asterby 96 C5
Asterley 64 C2
Asterton 64 D3
Asthall 41 E1
Asthall Leigh 41 F1
Astle 92 C5
Astley Gt.Man. 92 B2
Astley Shrop. 65 E1
Astley Warks. 67 F4
Astley Worcs. 53 G1
Astley Abbotts 65 G3
Astley Bridge 92 B1
Astley Cross 54 A1
Astley Green 92 B3
Astley Lodge 65 E1
Aston Ches. 78 D3
Aston Ches. 91 G5
Aston Derbys. 93 F4
Aston Derbys. 80 C4
Aston Flints. 78 A1
Aston Here. 65 D5
Aston Here. 53 D1
Aston Herts. 58 A5
Aston Oxon. 41 F2
Aston S.Yorks. 94 B4
Aston Shrop. 78 C5
Aston Shrop. 66 A3
Aston Staffs. 79 E3
Aston Tel. & W. 65 F2
Aston W'ham 42 C4
Aston W.Mid. 66 C4
Aston Abbotts 56 D5
Aston Botterell 65 F4
Aston Cantlow 54 D2
Aston Clinton 43 D1
Aston Crews 53 F5
Aston Cross 54 B4
Aston End 58 A5
Aston Eyre 65 F3
Aston Fields 54 B1
Aston Flamville 67 G3
Aston Heath 91 G5
Aston Ingham 53 F5
Aston juxta Mondrum 79 D2
Aston le Walls 55 G2
Aston Magna 55 D4
Aston Munslow 65 E4
Aston on Carrant 54 B4
Aston on Clun 64 C4
Aston Pigott 64 C2
Aston Rogers 64 C2
Aston Rowant 42 C3
Aston Sandford 42 C2
Aston Somerville 54 C4
Aston Subedge 54 D3
Aston Tirrold 42 A4
Aston Upthorpe 42 A4
Aston-by-Stone 79 G4
Aston-on-Trent 81 F5
Astwick 58 A4
Astwood 57 E3
Astwood Bank 54 C1
Aswarby 83 F3
Aswardby 97 D5
Aswick Grange 70 B1
Atch Lench 54 C2
Atcham 65 E2
Ath Linne 178 D6
Athelhampton 13 D3
Athelington 72 D4
Athelney 24 A5
Athelstaneford 144 C2
Atherington Devon 21 F3
Atherington W.Suss. 16 C3
Athersley North 94 A2
Atherstone 67 F3
Atherstone on Stour 55 E2
Atherton 92 A2
Atlow 80 D3
Attadale 165 F1
Attenborough 81 G4
Atterby 95 G3
Attercliffe 94 A4
Atterley 65 F3
Atterton 67 F3
Attleborough Norf. 72 B2
Attleborough Warks. 67 F3
Attlebridge 86 C4
Attleton Green 59 F2
Atwick 105 D2
Atworth 25 F1
Auberrow 53 D3
Aubourn 83 E1
Auch 149 F1
Auchairne 122 C2
Auchallater 159 G1
Auchameanach 139 G4
Auchamore 139 G5
Aucharnie 176 E6
Aucharrigill 174 B1
Auchattie 168 E5
Auchavan 159 G3
Auchbraad 139 G1
Auchbreck 167 K2
Auchenback 141 G4
Auchenblae 161 F2
Auchenbothie 141 E2
Auchenbrack 124 B1
Auchenbreck 140 B1
Auchencairn 124 B5
Auchencrow 145 F3
Auchendinny 143 G3
Auchendolly 124 B4
Auchenfoyle 141 E2
Auchengillan 141 G1
Auchengray 143 D4
Auchenhalrig 176 B4
Auchenheath 142 C5
Auchenhessnane 124 C1
Auchenlochan 140 A2
Auchenmalg 122 D5
Auchenrivock 126 B3
Auchentiber 141 E5
Auchenvennel 141 D1
Auchessan 149 G2
Auchgourish 167 G3
Auchinafaud 139 F4
Auchincruive 132 B3
Auchindarrach 139 G1
Auchindarroch 156 C4
Auchindrain 148 C4
Auchindrean 173 H3
Auchininna 176 E6
Auchinleck 132 D3
Auchinloch 142 A2
Auchinner 150 B3
Auchinroath 175 K6
Auchintoul Aber. 168 D3
Auchintoul Aber. 176 E5
Auchintoul High. 174 C2
Auchiries 169 J1
Auchleven 168 E2
Auchlochan 133 G2
Auchlunachan 173 H3
Auchlunies 169 G5
Auchlunkart 176 B6
Auchlyne 150 A2
Auchmacoy 169 H1
Auchmair 168 B2
Auchmantle 122 C4
Auchmithie 161 E5
Auchmuirbridge 152 A4
Auchmull 161 D2
Auchnabony 116 A2
Auchnabreac 148 C4
Auchnacloich 150 D1
Auchnacraig 147 G1
Auchnacree 160 C3
Auchnafree 150 D1
Auchnagallin 167 H1
Auchnagatt 177 H6
Auchnaha 140 A1
Auchnangoul 148 C4
Aucholzie 168 B5
Auchorrie 168 E4
Auchrannie 160 A4
Auchraw 150 A2
Auchreoch 149 F2
Auchronie 160 C1
Auchterarder 151 E3
Auchtercairn 172 E4
Auchterderran 152 A5
Auchterhouse 152 B1
Auchtermuchty 152 A3
Auchterneed 174 B6
Auchtertool 152 A5
Auchtertyre Angus 160 A5
Auchtertyre High. 164 E2
Auchtertyre Moray 175 J6
Auchtertyre Stir. 149 F2
Auchtubh 150 A2
Auckengill 183 J2
Auckley 94 D2
Audenshaw 92 D3
Audlem 79 D3
Audley 79 E2
Audley End Essex 58 D4
Audley End Essex 59 G4
Audley End Suff. 59 G2
Audmore 79 F5
Auds 176 E4
Aughton E.Riding 103 G4
Aughton Lancs. 91 E2
Aughton Lancs. 100 B1
Aughton S.Yorks. 94 B4
Aughton Wilts. 26 D2
Aughton Park 91 F2
Auldearn 175 G6
Aulden 53 D2
Auldgirth 124 D2
Auldhame 144 C1
Auldhouse 142 A4
Aulich 158 B4
Ault a' chruinn 165 F2
Ault Hucknall 81 F1
Aultanrynie 181 F5
Aultbea 172 E3
Aultgrishan 172 D3
Aultguish Inn 173 K4
Aultibea 183 F6
Aultiphurst 182 D2
Aultmore 176 C5
Ault-na-goire 166 C2
Aultnamain Inn 174 D3
Aultnapaddock 176 B6
Aulton 168 E2
Aultvaich 174 C7
Aultvoulin 164 D4
Aunby 69 F1
Aundorach 167 G3
Aunk 10 D2
Aunsby 83 F4
Auquhorthies 169 G2
Aust 39 E4
Austerfield 95 D3
Austrey 67 E2
Austwick 101 D1
Authorpe 97 E4
Authorpe Row 97 F5
Avebury 40 D5
Avebury Trusloe 26 B1
Aveley 45 E4
Avening 40 A3
Averham 82 C2
Avery Hill 44 D5
Aveton Gifford 8 C3
Avielochan 167 G3
Aviemore 167 F3
Avington Hants. 27 G4
Avington W.Berks. 27 E1
Avoch 174 D6
Avon 14 A3
Avon Dassett 55 G2
Avonbridge 142 D2
Avoncliff 25 F2
Avonmouth 39 E5
Avonwick 8 D2
Awbridge 27 E5
Awhirk 122 B5
Awkley 39 E4
Awliscombe 11 E2
Awre 39 G2
Awsworth 81 F3
Axbridge 24 B2
Axford Hants. 28 B3
Axford Wilts. 41 E5
Axminster 11 F3
Axmouth 11 F3
Axton 90 C4
Axtown 8 B1
Aycliffe 120 B5
Aydon 119 G1
Aylburton 39 F2
Ayle 118 D3
Aylesbeare 10 D3
Aylesbury 42 D1
Aylesby 96 C2
Aylesford 31 G3
Aylesham 33 E3
Aylestone 68 A2
Aylmerton 86 C2
Aylsham 86 C3
Aylton 53 F4
Aymestrey 52 D1
Aynho 56 A4
Ayot Green 44 B1
Ayot St. Lawrence 44 A1
Ayot St. Peter 44 B1
Ayr 132 B3
Aysgarth 109 F4
Ayshford 10 D1
Ayside 107 E4
Ayston 69 D2
Aythorpe Roding 45 E1
Ayton P. & K. 151 G3
Ayton Sc.Bord. 145 G3
Aywick 186 E4
Azerley 110 B5

▼ B

Babbacombe 9 F1
Babbinswood 78 A4
Babb's Green 44 C1
Babcary 24 C5
Babel 51 E4
Babell 90 C5
Babeny 7 G3
Bablock Hythe 41 G2
Babraham 58 D2
Babworth 95 D4
Baby's Hill 167 K1
Bac 179 G3
Bachau 88 C4
Back of Keppoch 155 F1
Back Street 59 F2
Backaland 184 E4
Backaskaill 184 D2
Backbarrow 107 E4
Backburn 168 D1
Backe 35 F1
Backfolds 177 J5
Backford 91 F5
Backhill 169 F1
Backhill of Clackriach 177 H6
Backhill of Trustach 168 E5
Backies High. 175 F1
Backies Moray 176 D5
Backlass 183 H3
Backside 168 C1
Backwell 24 B1
Backworth 129 E4
Bacon End 45 E1
Baconend Green 45 E1
Baconsthorpe 86 C2
Bacton Here. 52 C4
Bacton Norf. 87 E2
Bacton Suff. 60 B1
Bacton Green 60 B1
Bacup 101 E5
Badachro 172 D4
Badanloch Lodge 182 C5
Badavanich 173 H6
Badbea 183 F7
Badbury 41 D4
Badbury Wick 41 D4
Badby 56 A2
Badcall High. 180 D4
Badcall High. 180 E3
Badcaul 173 G2
Baddeley Green 79 G2
Badden 139 G1
Baddesley Clinton 67 D5
Baddesley Ensor 67 E3
Baddidarach 180 C6
Badenscoth 169 F1
Badenyon 168 B3
Badgall 5 G1
Badger 65 G3
Badgerbank 92 C5
Badgers Mount 31 D2
Badgeworth 40 B1
Badgworth 24 A2
Badicaul 164 D2
Badingham 61 E1
Badintagairt 181 G7
Badlesmere 32 C3
Badley 60 B2
Badlipster 183 H4
Badluarach 173 F2
Badminton 40 A4
Badnaban 180 C6
Badnabay 180 E4
Badnafrave 167 K3
Badnagie 183 G5
Badnambiast 158 C2
Badninish 174 E2
Badrallach 173 G2
Badsey 54 C3
Badshot Lea 29 D3
Badsworth 94 B1
Badwell Ash 60 A1
Badworthy 8 C1
Badyo 159 E3
Bae Cinmel (Kinmel Bay) 90 A4
Bae Colwyn (Colwyn Bay) 89 G5
Bae Penryhn (Penrhyn Bay) 89 G4
Bag Enderby 97 D5
Bagber 13 D1
Bagby 111 D4
Bagendon 40 C2
Bagginswood 65 F4
Baggrave Hall 68 B2
Baggrow 117 E2
Bàgh a' Chaisteil (Castlebay) 162 B5
Bàgh Mòr 170 D6
Baghasdal 162 C3
Bagillt 90 D5
Baginton 67 F5
Baglan 36 D3
Bagley Shrop. 78 B5
Bagley Som. 24 B3
Bagmore 28 B3
Bagnall 79 G2
Bagnor 27 F1
Bagpath 40 A3
Bagshot Surr. 29 E1
Bagshot Wilts. 27 E1
Bagstone 39 F4
Bagthorpe Norf. 85 F4
Bagthorpe Notts. 81 F2
Baguley 92 C4
Bagworth 67 G2
Bagwyllydiart 52 D5
Baildon 102 A4
Baile a' Mhanaich (Balivanich) 170 C6
Baile Ailein (Balallan) 178 E5
Baile an Truiseil 179 F2
Baile Boidheach 139 F2
Baile Gharbhaidh 170 C7
Baile Glas 170 D6
Baile Mhartainn 170 C4
Baile Mhic Phail 170 D4
Baile Mòr Arg. & B. 146 B2
Baile Mòr (Balemore) W.Isles 170 C5
Baile nan Cailleach 170 C6
Baile Raghaill 170 C5
Bailebeag 166 C3
Baileguish 167 F5
Baile-na-Cille 170 D3
Bailetonach 155 F2
Bailiesward 168 C1
Bailiff Bridge 102 A5
Baillieston 142 A3
Bainbridge 109 E3
Bainsford 142 C1
Bainshole 168 E1
Bainton E.Riding 104 B2
Bainton Oxon. 56 A5
Bainton Peter. 69 F2
Bairnkine 136 A5
Bakebare 168 B1
Baker Street 45 F4
Baker's End 44 C1
Bakewell 80 D1
Bala 76 C4
Balachuirn 172 B7
Balado 151 F4
Balafark 150 B5
Balaldie 175 F4
Balallan (Baile Ailein) 178 E5
Balavil 166 E4
Balbeg High. 166 B1
Balbeg High. 166 B2
Balbeggie 151 G2
Balbirnie 152 A4
Balbithan 169 F3
Balblair High. 174 E5
Balblair High. 174 C2
Balblair High. 174 E3
Balby 94 C2
Balcharn 174 C1
Balcherry 175 F3
Balchers 177 F5
Balchladich 180 C5
Balchraggan High. 174 C7
Balchraggan High. 166 C1
Balchrick 180 D3
Balcombe 30 C5
Balcurvie 152 B4
Baldernock 141 G2
Baldersby 110 C5
Baldersby St. James 110 C5
Balderstone Gt.Man. 92 D1
Balderstone Lancs. 100 C4
Balderton Ches. 78 A1
Balderton Notts. 82 D2
Baldhu 4 B5
Baldinnie 152 C3
Baldock 58 A4
Baldon Row 42 A2
Baldovan 152 B1

Baldovie *Angus* 160 B4
Baldovie *Dundee* 152 C1
Baldrine 98 C3
Baldslow 18 C2
Baldwin 98 B3
Baldwinholme 117 G1
Baldwin's Gate 79 E3
Baldwins Hill 30 C5
Bale 86 B2
Balelone 170 C4
Balemartine 154 A2
Balemore (Baile Mòr) 170 C5
Balendoch 160 A5
Balephuil 154 A2
Balerno 143 F3
Balernock 141 D1
Baleromindubh 146 C5
Balerominmore 146 C5
Baleshare (Bhaleshear) 170 C5
Balevulin 147 D2
Balfield 160 D3
Balfour *Aber.* 168 D5
Balfour *Ork.* 185 D6
Balfron 141 G1
Balfron Station 141 G1
Balgonar 151 F5
Balgove 169 G1
Balgowan *D. & G.* 114 B2
Balgowan *High.* 166 D5
Balgown 171 J5
Balgreen 177 F5
Balgreggan 122 B5
Balgy 172 E6
Balhaldie 150 D4
Balhalgardy 169 F2
Balham 44 B5
Balhary 160 A5
Balhelvie 152 B2
Balhousie 152 C4
Baliasta 186 F2
Baligill 182 D2
Baligrundle 156 A5
Balindore 148 B1
Balintore *Angus* 160 A4
Balintore *High.* 175 F4
Balintraid 174 E4
Balintyre 158 B5
Balivanich (Baile a' Mhanaich) 170 C6
Balkeerie 160 B5
Balkholme 103 G5
Balkissock 122 C2
Ball 78 A5
Ball Haye Green 79 G2
Ball Hill 27 F1
Balla 162 C3
Ballabeg 98 A4
Ballacannell 98 C3
Ballacarnane Beg 98 A3
Ballachulish 156 C4
Balladoole 98 A5
Ballafesson 98 A4
Ballagyr 98 A3
Ballajora 98 C2
Ballakilpheric 98 A4
Ballamodha 98 A4
Ballantrae 122 B2
Ballards Gore 46 C3
Ballasalla *I.o.M.* 98 A4
Ballasalla *I.o.M.* 98 B2
Ballater 168 B5
Ballaterach 168 C5
Ballaugh 98 B2
Ballaveare 98 B4
Ballchraggan 174 E4
Ballechin 159 E4
Balleich 150 A4
Ballencrieff 144 B2
Ballidon 80 D2
Balliekine 139 G5
Balliemeanoch 148 D4
Balliemore *Arg. & B.* 148 D5
Balliemore *Arg. & B.* 148 A2
Ballig 98 A3
Ballimeanoch 148 C3
Ballimore *Arg. & B.* 140 A1
Ballimore *Stir.* 150 A3
Ballinaby 138 A3
Ballindean 152 A2
Ballingdon 59 G3
Ballinger Common 43 E2
Ballingham 53 E4
Ballingry 151 G5
Ballinlick 159 E5
Ballinluig *P. & K.* 159 E4
Ballinluig *P. & K.* 159 F4
Ballintuim 159 G4
Balloch *Angus* 160 B4
Balloch *High.* 174 E7
Balloch *N.Lan.* 142 B2
Balloch *W.Dun.* 141 E1
Ballochan 168 D5
Ballochandrain 140 A1
Ballochford 168 B1
Ballochgair 130 C3
Ballochmartin 140 C4
Ballochmorrie 122 D2
Ballochmyle 132 D3
Ballochroy 139 F4
Ballogie 168 D5
Balls Cross 29 E5
Balls Green *Essex* 60 B5
Ball's Green *Glos.* 40 A3
Balls Hill 66 B3
Ballyaurgan 139 F2
Ballygown 154 D5
Ballygrant 138 B3
Ballyhaugh 154 A4
Ballymeanoch 148 A5
Ballymichael 131 E2
Balmacara 164 E2
Balmaclellan 124 A3
Balmacneil 159 E4
Balmadies 161 D5
Balmae 115 G2
Balmaha 149 G5
Balmalcolm 152 B4
Balmaqueen 171 K4
Balmeanach *Arg. & B.* 155 F5
Balmeanach *Arg. & B.* 146 D1
Balmedie 169 H3
Balmer Heath 78 B4
Balmerino 152 B2
Balmerlawn 14 C2
Balminnoch 123 D4
Balmore *E.Dun.* 142 A2
Balmore *High.* 175 F7
Balmore *High.* 165 K1
Balmore *High.* 171 H7
Balmore *P. & K.* 158 C4
Balmullo 152 C2
Balmungie 174 E6
Balmyle 159 F4
Balnaboth 160 B3
Balnabruaich 174 E4
Balnacra 173 F7
Balnafoich 166 D1
Balnagall 175 F3
Balnagown Castle 174 E4
Balnaguard 159 E4
Balnaguisich 174 D4
Balnahard *Arg. & B.* 146 D5
Balnahard *Arg. & B.* 147 D1
Balnain 166 B1
Balnakeil 181 F2
Balnaknock 171 K5
Balnamoon 160 D3
Balnapaling 174 E5
Balnespick 167 F4
Balquhidder 150 A2
Balsall 67 E5
Balsall Common 67 E5
Balsall Heath 66 C4
Balscote 55 F3
Balsham 59 D2
Baltasound 186 F2
Balterley 79 E2
Balterley Heath 79 E2
Baltersan 123 F4
Balthangie 177 G5
Balthayock 151 G2
Baltonsborough 24 C4
Baluachraig 148 A5
Balulive 138 C3
Balure *Arg. & B.* 148 C1
Balure *Arg. & B.* 148 A1
Balvaird 174 C6
Balvarran 159 F3
Balvicar 147 G3
Balvraid *High.* 164 E3
Balvraid *High.* 167 F1
Bamber Bridge 100 B5
Bamber's Green 59 D5
Bamburgh 137 F3
Bamff 160 A4
Bamford *Derbys.* 93 G4
Bamford *Gt.Man.* 92 C1
Bampton *Cumb.* 107 G1
Bampton *Devon* 22 C5
Bampton *Oxon.* 41 F2
Bampton Grange 107 G1
Banavie 156 D2
Banbury 55 G3
Bancffosfelen 36 A1
Banchor 175 G7
Banchory 169 F5
Banchory-Devenick 169 H4
Bancycapel 36 A1
Bancyfelin 35 G1
Bancyffordd 50 A4
Bandon 152 A4
Bandrake Head 107 E4
Banff 176 E4
Bangor 89 D5
Bangor-is-y-coed 78 A3
Bangor's Green 91 E2
Banham 72 B3
Bank 14 B2
Bank End 106 C4
Bank Newton 101 F2
Bank Street 53 F1
Bank Top *Lancs.* 91 G2
Bank Top *W.Yorks.* 102 A5
Bankend 125 E4
Bankfoot 151 F1
Bankglen 133 D4
Bankhead *Aber.* 168 E3
Bankhead *Aber.* 168 E4
Bankhead *Aberdeen* 169 G3
Bankhead *D. & G.* 116 A2
Bankland 24 A5
Banknock 142 B2
Banks *Cumb.* 118 B1
Banks *Lancs.* 99 G5
Bankshill 125 F2
Banningham 86 D3
Bannister Green 59 E5
Bannockburn 150 D5
Banstead 30 B3
Bantam Grove 102 B5
Bantham 8 C3
Banton 142 B2
Banwell 24 A2
Banwen Pyrddin 37 E2
Banyard's Green 73 E4
Bapchild 32 B2
Baptiston 141 G1
Bapton 26 A4
Bar End 27 F5
Bar Hill 58 B1
Barabhas (Barvas) 179 F3
Barachander 148 C2
Barassie 132 B2
Barbaraville 174 E4
Barber Booth 93 F4
Barber Green 107 E4
Barber's Moor 91 F1
Barbon 108 B4
Barbridge 78 D2
Barbrook 22 A3
Barby 68 A5
Barcaldine 156 B5
Barcaple 124 A5
Barcheston 55 E4
Barclose 118 A1
Barcombe 17 G2
Barcombe Cross 17 G2
Barden 110 A3
Barden Park 31 E4
Bardennoch 123 G1
Bardfield End Green 59 E4
Bardfield Saling 59 E5
Bardister 186 C5
Bardney 83 G1
Bardon *Leics.* 67 G1
Bardon *Moray* 175 K6
Bardon Mill 119 D1
Bardowie 141 G2
Bardsea 107 D5
Bardsey 102 C3
Bardsey Island (Ynys Enlli) 74 A5
Bardwell 72 A4
Bare 100 A1
Barewood 52 C2
Barfad 139 G3
Barford *Norf.* 86 C5
Barford *Warks.* 55 E1
Barford St. John 55 G4
Barford St. Martin 26 B4
Barford St. Michael 55 G4
Barfrestone 33 E3
Bargaly 123 F4
Bargany Mains 132 A5
Bargeddie 142 A3
Bargoed 38 A3
Bargrennan 123 E3
Barham *Cambs.* 69 G5
Barham *Kent* 33 E3
Barham *Suff.* 60 C2
Barharrow 124 A5
Barholm 69 F1
Barholm Mains 123 F5
Barkby 68 B2
Barkby Thorpe 68 B2
Barkers Green 78 C5
Barkestone-le-Vale 82 C4
Barkham 28 C1
Barking *Gt.Lon.* 44 D4
Barking *Suff.* 60 B2
Barking Tye 60 B2
Barkisland 101 G5
Barkston 83 E3
Barkston Ash 103 D4
Barkway 58 B4
Barlae 123 D4
Barland 52 B1
Barlaston 79 F4
Barlavington 16 B2
Barlborough 94 B5
Barlby 103 F4
Barlestone 67 G2
Barley *Herts.* 58 B4
Barley *Lancs.* 101 E3
Barley Green 72 D4
Barleycroft End 58 C5
Barleyhill 119 G2
Barleythorpe 68 D2
Barling 46 C4
Barlings 96 A5
Barlow *Derbys.* 94 A5
Barlow *N.Yorks.* 103 F5
Barlow *T. & W.* 120 A1
Barmby Moor 103 G3
Barmby on the Marsh 103 F5
Barmer 85 G4
Barmolloch 148 A5
Barmoor Lane End 137 E3
Barmouth (Abermaw) 62 C1
Barmpton 110 C1
Barmston 105 D2
Barnaby Green 73 F4
Barnacabber 140 C1
Barnacarry 148 B5
Barnack 69 F2
Barnacle 67 F4
Barnamuc 156 C5
Barnard Castle 109 F1
Barnard Gate 41 G1
Barnardiston 59 F3
Barnard's Green 53 G3
Barnbarroch *D. & G.* 123 E5
Barnbarroch *D. & G.* 124 C5
Barnburgh 94 B2
Barnby 73 F3
Barnby Dun 94 D2
Barnby in the Willows 83 D2
Barnby Moor 95 D4
Barndennoch 124 C2
Barne Barton 8 A2
Barnehurst 45 E5
Barnes 44 B5
Barnes Street 31 F4
Barnet 44 B3
Barnet Gate 44 B3
Barnetby le Wold 96 A2
Barney 86 A2
Barnham *Suff.* 71 G5
Barnham *W.Suss.* 16 B3
Barnham Broom 86 B5
Barnhead 161 E4
Barnhill *Ches.* 78 B2
Barnhill *Dundee* 152 C1
Barnhill *Moray* 175 J6
Barnhills 122 A3
Barningham *Dur.* 109 F1
Barningham *Suff.* 72 A4
Barningham Green 86 C2
Barnoldby le Beck 96 C2
Barnoldswick 101 E3
Barns Green 29 G5
Barnsdale Bar 94 C1
Barnsley *Glos.* 40 C2
Barnsley *S.Yorks.* 94 A2
Barnsole 33 E3
Barnstaple 21 F2
Barnston *Essex* 45 F1
Barnston *Mersey.* 91 D4
Barnstone 82 C4
Barnt Green 66 C5
Barnton *Ches.* 92 A5
Barnton *Edin.* 143 F2
Barnwell All Saints 69 F4
Barnwell St. Andrew 69 F4
Barnwood 40 A1
Barons' Cross 53 D2
Barr *Arg. & B.* 138 B3
Barr *High.* 155 F4
Barr *S.Ayr.* 123 D1
Barr *Som.* 23 E5
Barr Hall 59 F4
Barra (Barraigh) 162 B4
Barra (Tràigh Mhòr) Airport 162 B4
Barrachan 115 D2
Barrackan 147 G4
Barraer 123 E4
Barraglom 178 D4
Barrahormid 139 F1
Barraigh (Barra) 162 B4
Barran 149 D2
Barrapoll 154 A2
Barrasford 128 B4
Barravullin 148 A4
Barregarrow 98 B3
Barrets Green 78 C2
Barrhead 141 F4
Barrhill 122 D2
Barrington *Cambs.* 58 B3
Barrington *Som.* 11 G1
Barripper 2 D3
Barrisdale 164 E4
Barrmill 141 E4
Barrnacarry 148 A2
Barrock 183 H1
Barrow *Glos.* 54 A5
Barrow *Lancs.* 100 D4
Barrow *Rut.* 69 D1
Barrow *Shrop.* 65 F2
Barrow *Som.* 25 E4
Barrow *Som.* 24 C3
Barrow *Suff.* 59 F1
Barrow Gurney 24 C1
Barrow Hann 104 C5
Barrow Haven 104 C5
Barrow Hill 94 B5
Barrow Nook 91 F2
Barrow Street 25 F4
Barrow upon Humber 104 C5
Barrow upon Soar 68 A1
Barrow upon Trent 81 E5
Barroway Drove 71 D2
Barrowby 83 D4
Barrowcliff 112 D4
Barrowden 69 E2
Barrowford 101 E4
Barrow-in-Furness 99 F1
Barrows Green 107 G4
Barry *Angus* 152 D1
Barry *V. of Glam.* 23 E1
Barsby 68 B1
Barsham 73 E3
Barskimming 132 C3
Barsloisnoch 148 A5
Barston 67 E5
Bartestree 53 E3
Barthol Chapel 169 G1
Bartholomew Green 59 F5
Barthomley 79 E2
Bartley 14 C1
Bartley Green 66 C4
Bartlow 59 D3
Barton *Cambs.* 58 C2
Barton *Ches.* 78 B2
Barton *Cumb.* 118 A5
Barton *Glos.* 54 C5
Barton *Lancs.* 100 B4
Barton *Lancs.* 91 E2
Barton *N.Yorks.* 110 B2
Barton *Oxon.* 42 A2
Barton *Torbay* 9 F1
Barton *Warks.* 54 D2
Barton Bendish 71 F2
Barton End 40 A3
Barton Green 67 D1
Barton Hartshorn 56 B4
Barton Hill 103 G1
Barton in Fabis 81 G4
Barton in the Beans 67 F2
Barton Mills 71 F5
Barton on Sea 14 B3
Barton St. David 24 C4
Barton Seagrave 69 D5
Barton Stacey 27 F3
Barton Town 21 G1
Barton Turf 87 E3
Bartongate 55 G5
Barton-le-Clay 57 F4
Barton-le-Street 111 G5
Barton-le-Willows 103 G1
Barton-on-the-Heath 55 E4
Barton-under-Needwood 67 D1
Barton-upon-Humber 104 C5
Barvas (Barabhas) 179 F3
Barway 70 D5
Barwell 67 G3
Barwhinnock 124 A5
Barwick *Herts.* 44 C1
Barwick *Som.* 12 B1
Barwick in Elmet 102 C4
Barwinnock 115 D2
Baschurch 78 B5
Bascote 55 G1
Base Green 60 B1
Basford Green 79 G2
Bashall Eaves 100 C3
Bashall Town 100 D3
Bashley 14 B3
Basildon *Essex* 45 G4
Basildon *W.Berks.* 42 B5
Basingstoke 28 B2
Baslow 93 G5
Bason Bridge 24 A3
Bassaleg 38 B4
Bassenthwaite 117 F3
Basset's Cross 21 F5
Bassett 14 D1
Bassingbourn 58 B3
Bassingfield 82 B4
Bassingham 83 E2
Bassingthorpe 83 E5
Basta 186 E3
Baston 69 G1
Bastonford 54 A2
Bastwick 87 F4
Batavaime 149 G1
Batch 24 A2
Batchley 54 C1
Batchworth 43 F3
Batchworth Heath 43 F3
Batcombe *Dorset* 12 C2
Batcombe *Som.* 25 D4
Bate Heath 92 A5
Bath 25 E1
Bathampton 25 E1
Bathealton 23 D5
Batheaston 25 E1
Bathford 25 E1
Bathgate 143 D3
Bathley 82 C2
Bathpool *Cornw.* 5 G2
Bathpool *Som.* 23 F5
Bathway 24 C2
Batley 102 B5
Batsford 55 D4
Batson 8 D4
Battersby 111 E2
Battersea 44 B5
Battisborough Cross 8 C3
Battisford 60 B2
Battisford Tye 60 B2
Battle *E.Suss.* 18 C2
Battle *Powys* 51 G4
Battledown 54 B5
Battlefield 65 E1
Battlesbridge 45 G3
Battlesden 57 E5
Battlesea Green 72 D4
Battleton 22 C5
Battlies Green 60 A1
Battramsley 14 C3
Batt's Corner 28 D3
Bauds of Cullen 176 C4
Baugh 154 B2
Baughton 54 A3
Baughurst 27 G1
Baulds 168 E5
Baulking 41 F3
Baumber 96 C5
Baunton 40 C2
Baveney Wood 65 F5
Baverstock 26 B4
Bawburgh 86 C5
Bawdeswell 86 B3
Bawdrip 24 A4
Bawdsey 61 E3
Bawdsey Manor 61 E4
Bawsey 71 E1
Bawtry 95 D3
Baxenden 101 D5
Baxterley 67 E3
Baxter's Green 59 F2
Bay 25 F5
Baybridge 119 F3
Baycliff 107 D5
Baydon 41 E5
Bayford *Herts.* 44 C2
Bayford *Som.* 25 E5
Bayfordbury 44 C1
Bayham Abbey 31 F5
Bayles 118 D3
Baylham 60 C2
Baynards Green 56 A5
Baysham 53 E5
Bayston Hill 65 D2
Bayswater 44 B4
Baythorn End 59 F3
Bayton 65 F5
Bayworth 42 A2
Beach *High.* 155 G4
Beach *S.Glos.* 39 G5
Beachampton 56 C4
Beachamwell 71 F2
Beacharr 139 E5
Beachley 39 E3
Beacon *Devon* 11 E2
Beacon *Devon* 11 F2
Beacon Hill *Dorset* 13 F3
Beacon Hill *Essex* 46 B1
Beacon Hill *Surr.* 29 D4
Beacon's Bottom 42 C3
Beaconsfield 43 E3
Beacravik 171 G2
Beadlam 111 F4
Beadlow 57 G4
Beadnell 137 G4
Beaford 21 F4
Beal *N.Yorks.* 103 E5
Beal *Northumb.* 137 E2
Bealach 156 B4
Bealsmill 7 D3
Beambridge 78 D2
Beamhurst 80 B4
Beaminster 12 A2
Beamish 120 B2
Beamsley 101 G2
Bean 45 E5
Beanacre 26 A1
Beanley 137 E5
Beaquoy 184 C5
Beardon 7 F2
Beardwood 100 C5
Beare 10 C2
Beare Green 29 G3
Bearley 55 D1
Bearnie 169 H1
Bearnock 166 B1
Bearnus 154 C5
Bearpark 120 B3
Bearsbridge 119 D2
Bearsden 141 G2
Bearsted 31 G3
Bearstone 79 E4
Bearwood *Poole* 13 G3
Bearwood *W.Mid.* 66 C4
Beattock 134 B5
Beauchamp Roding 45 E1
Beauchief 94 A4
Beaudesert 55 D1
Beaufort 38 A1
Beaulieu 14 C2
Beauly 174 C7
Beaumaris (Biwmaris) 89 E5
Beaumont *Chan.I.* 8 C5
Beaumont *Cumb.* 117 G1
Beaumont *Essex* 60 C5
Beaumont Hill 110 B1
Beaumont Leys 68 A2
Beausale 67 E5
Beauvale 81 F3
Beauworth 27 G5
Beaver Green 32 B4
Beaworthy 7 E1
Beazley End 59 F5
Bebington 91 E4
Bebside 129 E3
Beccles 73 F2
Becconsall 100 A5
Beck Foot 108 B3
Beck Hole 112 B2
Beck Row 71 E5
Beck Side *Cumb.* 106 D4
Beck Side *Cumb.* 107 E4
Beckbury 65 G2
Beckenham 30 C2
Beckering 96 B4
Beckermet 106 B2
Beckermonds 109 D4
Beckett End 71 F3
Beckfoot *Cumb.* 106 C2
Beckfoot *Cumb.* 117 D2
Beckford 54 B4
Beckhampton 26 B1
Beckingham *Lincs.* 83 D2
Beckingham *Notts.* 95 E4
Beckington 25 F2
Beckley *E.Suss.* 19 D1
Beckley *Oxon.* 42 A1
Beck's Green 73 E3
Beckside 108 B4
Beckton 44 D4
Beckwithshaw 102 B2
Becontree 45 D4
Bedale 110 B4
Bedburn 119 G4
Bedchester 13 E1
Beddau 37 G4
Beddgelert 75 E3
Beddingham 17 G3
Beddington 30 B2
Beddington Corner 30 B2
Bedfield 60 D1
Bedfield Little Green 60 D1
Bedford 57 F3
Bedgebury Cross 31 G5
Bedgrove 42 D1
Bedham 29 F5
Bedhampton 15 G2
Bedingfield 60 C1
Bedingfield Green 60 C1
Bedingfield Street 60 C1
Bedingham Green 73 D2
Bedlam *Lancs.* 101 D5
Bedlam *N.Yorks.* 102 B1
Bedlar's Green 58 D5
Bedlington 129 E3
Bedlinog 37 G2
Bedminster 39 E5
Bedmond 43 F2
Bednall 66 B1
Bedol 90 D5
Bedrule 136 A5
Bedstone 64 C5
Bedwas 38 A4
Bedwell 58 A5
Bedwellty 38 A2
Bedworth 67 F4
Bedworth Woodlands 67 F4
Beeby 68 B2
Beech *Hants.* 28 B4
Beech *Staffs.* 79 F4
Beech Hill 28 B1
Beechingstoke 26 B2
Beechwood 91 G4
Beedon 41 G5
Beeford 104 D2
Beeley 81 D1
Beelsby 96 C2
Beenham 27 G1
Beeny 6 B1
Beer 11 F4
Beer Hackett 12 C1
Beercrocombe 24 A5
Beesands 9 E3
Beesby *Lincs.* 97 E4
Beesby *N.E.Lincs.* 96 C3
Beeson 9 E3
Beeston *Beds.* 57 G3
Beeston *Ches.* 78 C2
Beeston *Norf.* 86 A4
Beeston *Notts.* 81 G4
Beeston *W.Yorks.* 102 B4
Beeston Regis 86 C1
Beeston St. Lawrence 87 E3
Beeswing 124 C4
Beetham *Cumb.* 107 F5
Beetham *Som.* 11 F1
Beetley 86 A4
Beffcote 66 A1
Began 38 B4
Begbroke 41 G1
Begdale 70 C2
Begelly 35 E2
Beggar's Bush 52 B1
Beggearn Huish 22 D4
Beggshill 168 D1
Beguildy (Bugeildy) 64 A5
Beighton *Norf.* 87 E5
Beighton *S.Yorks.* 94 B4
Beili-glas 38 C2
Beinn na Faoghla (Benbecula) 170 D6
Beith 141 E4
Bekesbourne 33 D3
Belaugh 87 D4
Belbroughton 66 B5
Belchalwell 13 D2
Belchalwell Street 13 D2
Belchamp Otten 59 G3
Belchamp St. Paul 59 F3
Belchamp Walter 59 G3
Belchford 96 C5
Belfield 92 D1
Belford 137 F3
Belgrave 68 A2
Belhaven 145 D2
Belhelvie 169 H3
Belhinnie 168 C2
Bell Bar 44 B2
Bell Busk 101 F2
Bell End 66 B5
Bell Heath 66 B5
Bell Hill 28 C5
Bell o' th' Hill 78 C3
Bellabeg 168 B3
Belladrum 174 C7
Bellanoch 148 A5
Bellaty 160 A4
Belle Isle 102 C5
Belle Vue 117 G1
Belleau 97 E5
Belleheiglash 167 J1
Bellerby 110 A3
Bellever 7 G3
Bellfields 29 E2
Belliehill 161 D3
Bellingdon 43 E2
Bellingham *Gt.Lon.* 44 C5
Bellingham *Northumb.* 128 A3
Belloch 130 B2
Bellochantuy 130 B2
Bell's Cross 60 C2
Bells Yew Green 31 F5
Bellsbank 132 C5
Bellshill *N.Lan.* 142 B3
Bellshill *Northumb.* 137 F3
Bellside 142 C4
Bellsquarry 143 E3
Belluton 24 D1
Belmaduthy 174 D6
Belmesthorpe 69 F1
Belmont *B'burn.* 92 A1
Belmont *Gt.Lon.* 30 B2
Belmont *Gt.Lon.* 44 A3
Belmont *Shet.* 186 E2
Belnie 84 A4
Belowda 5 D3
Belper 81 E3
Belper Lane End 81 E3
Belsay 128 D4
Belsford 9 D2
Belsize 43 F2
Belstead 60 C3
Belston 132 B3
Belstone 7 G1
Belstone Corner 7 G1
Belsyde 143 D2
Belthorn 100 D5
Beltinge 33 D2
Beltingham 119 D1
Beltoft 95 F2
Belton *Leics.* 81 F5
Belton *Lincs.* 83 E4
Belton *N.Lincs.* 95 E2
Belton *Norf.* 87 F5
Belton *Rut.* 68 D2
Beltring 31 F4
Belvedere 45 D5
Belvoir 82 D4
Bembridge 15 F4
Bemersyde 135 G2
Bemerton 26 C4
Bempton 113 E5
Ben Alder Cottage 157 G3
Ben Alder Lodge 158 A2
Ben Rhydding 102 A3
Benacre 73 G3
Benbecula (Beinn na Faoghla) 170 D6
Benbecula (Balivanich) Airport 170 C6
Benbuie 124 B1
Benderloch 148 B1
Bendish 57 G5
Benenden 32 A5
Benfield 123 E4
Benfieldside 119 G2
Bengate 87 E3
Bengeo 44 C1
Bengeworth 54 C3
Benhall 54 B5
Benhall Green 61 E1
Benhall Street 61 E1
Benholm 161 G3
Beningbrough 103 E2
Benington *Herts.* 58 A5
Benington *Lincs.* 84 B3
Benington Sea End 84 C3
Benllech 88 D4
Benmore *Arg. & B.* 140 C1
Benmore *Stir.* 149 G2
Bennacott 6 C1
Bennan Cottage 124 A3
Bennett End 42 C3
Bennetts End 43 F2
Benniworth 96 C4
Benover 31 G4
Benson 42 B3
Benston 187 D7
Benthall *Northumb.* 137 G4
Benthall *Shrop.* 65 F2
Bentham 40 B1
Benthoul 169 G4
Bentlawnt 64 C2
Bentley *E.Riding* 104 C4
Bentley *Essex* 45 E3
Bentley *Hants.* 28 C3
Bentley *S.Yorks.* 94 C2
Bentley *Suff.* 60 C4
Bentley *W.Mid.* 66 B3
Bentley *W.Yorks.* 102 B4
Bentley *Warks.* 67 E3
Bentley Heath *Herts.* 44 B3
Bentley Heath *W.Mid.* 67 D5
Bentley Rise 94 C2
Benton 21 G2
Benton Square 129 E4
Bentpath 126 B2
Bentworth 28 B3
Benvie 152 B1
Benville Lane 12 B2
Benwell 120 B1
Benwick 70 B3
Beoley 54 C1
Beoraidbeg 164 C5
Bepton 16 A2
Berden 58 C5
Bere Alston 8 A1
Bere Ferrers 8 A1
Bere Regis 13 E3
Berea 48 A4
Berepper 3 D4
Bergh Apton 87 E5
Berinsfield 42 A3
Berkeley 39 F3
Berkhamsted 43 E2
Berkley 25 F3
Berkswell 67 E5
Bermondsey 44 C5
Bernera 164 E2
Berneray (Eilean Bhearnaraigh) 170 E3
Berners Roding 45 F2
Bernice 148 D5
Bernisdale 171 K6
Berrick Prior 42 B3
Berrick Salome 42 B3
Berriedale 183 G6
Berriew (Aberriw) 64 A2
Berrington *Northumb.* 137 E2
Berrington *Shrop.* 65 E2
Berrington *Worcs.* 53 E1
Berrington Green 53 E1
Berriowbridge 5 G2
Berrow *Som.* 23 F2
Berrow *Worcs.* 53 G4
Berrow Green 53 G2
Berry Cross 21 E4
Berry Down Cross 21 F1
Berry Hill *Glos.* 39 E1
Berry Hill *Pembs.* 49 D3
Berry Pomeroy 9 E1
Berryhillock 176 D4
Berrynarbor 21 F1
Berry's Green 30 D3
Bersham 78 A3
Berstane 185 D6
Berthlwyd 36 B3
Berwick 18 A3
Berwick Bassett 40 D5
Berwick Hill 129 D4
Berwick St. James 26 B4
Berwick St. John 26 A5
Berwick St. Leonard 26 A4
Berwick-upon-Tweed 145 G4
Bescar 91 E1
Bescot 66 C3
Besford *Shrop.* 78 C5
Besford *Worcs.* 54 B3
Bessacarr 94 D2
Bessels Leigh 41 G2
Besses o' th' Barn 92 C2
Bessingby 105 D1
Bessingham 86 C2
Best Beech Hill 31 F5
Besthorpe *Norf.* 72 B2
Besthorpe *Notts.* 82 D1
Bestwood Village 81 G3
Beswick *E.Riding* 104 C3
Beswick *Gt.Man.* 92 C3
Betchworth 30 B3
Bethania *Cere.* 50 B1
Bethania *Gwyn.* 76 A3
Bethel *Gwyn.* 75 E1
Bethel *Gwyn.* 76 C4

Bethel *I.o.A.* 88 B5
Bethersden 32 B5
Bethesda *Gwyn.* 75 F1
Bethesda *Pembs.* 35 D1
Bethlehem 50 C5
Bethnal Green 44 C4
Betley 79 E3
Betley Common 79 E3
Betsham 45 F5
Betteshanger 33 F3
Bettiscombe 11 G3
Bettisfield 78 B4
Betton *Shrop.* 64 C2
Betton *Shrop.* 79 D4
Betton Strange 65 E2
Bettws *Bridgend* 37 F4
Bettws *Newport* 38 B3
Bettws Bledrws 50 B2
Bettws Cedewain 64 A3
Bettws Gwerfil Goch
76 D3
Bettws Newydd 38 C2
Bettws-y-crwyn 64 B4
Bettyhill 182 C2
Betws 36 C1
Betws Disserth 52 A2
Betws Garmon 75 E2
Betws Ifan 49 G3
Betws-y-coed 76 A2
Betws-yn-Rhos 90 A5
Beulah *Cere.* 49 F3
Beulah *Powys* 51 F2
Bevendean 17 F3
Bevercotes 95 D5
Beverley 104 C4
Beverstone 40 A3
Bevington 39 F3
Bewaldeth 117 F3
Bewcastle 127 D4
Bewdley 65 G5
Bewerley 102 A1
Bewholme 105 D2
Bewley Common
26 A1
Bexhill 18 C3
Bexley 45 D5
Bexleyheath 45 D5
Bexwell 71 E2
Beyton 60 A1
Beyton Green 60 A1
Bhalamus 178 E7
Bhaleshear (Baleshare)
170 C5
Bhaltos 178 C4
Bhatarsaigh (Vatersay)
W.Isles 162 B5
Bhatarsaigh
(Vatersay) *W.Isles*
162 B5
Biallaid 166 E5
Bibury 40 D2
Bicester 56 A5
Bickenhall 11 F1
Bickenhill 67 D4
Bicker 84 A4
Bickershaw *Gt.Man.*
92 A2
Bickershaw *Gt.Man.*
92 A2
Bickerstaffe 91 F2
Bickerton *Ches.* 78 C2
Bickerton *Devon* 9 E4
Bickerton *N.Yorks.*
103 D2
Bickerton *Northumb.*
128 B1
Bickford 66 A1
Bickham 22 C3
Bickham Bridge 8 D2
Bickham House 10 C4
Bickington *Devon* 21 F2
Bickington *Devon* 10 A5
Bickleigh *Devon* 8 B1
Bickleigh *Devon* 10 C2
Bickleton 21 F2
Bickley 30 D2
Bickley Moss 78 C3
Bickley Town 78 C3
Bicknacre 45 G2
Bicknoller 23 E4
Bicknor 32 A3
Bickton 14 A1
Bicton *Here.* 53 D1
Bicton *Shrop.* 64 D1
Bicton *Shrop.* 64 B4
Bicton Heath 65 D1
Bidborough 31 E4
Biddenden 32 A5
Biddenden Green 32 A4
Biddenham 57 F3
Biddestone 40 A5
Biddick 120 C2
Biddisham 24 A2
Biddlesden 56 B3
Biddlestone 128 B1
Biddulph 79 F2
Biddulph Moor 79 G2
Bideford 21 E3
Bidford-on-Avon 54 D2
Bidlake 7 E2
Bidston 91 D3
Bidwell 57 F5
Bielby 103 G3
Bieldside 169 G4
Bierley *I.o.W.* 15 E5
Bierley *W.Yorks.* 102 A4
Bierton 42 D1
Big Sand 172 D4
Bigbury 8 C3
Bigbury-on-Sea 8 C3
Bigby 96 A2
Bigert Mire 106 C3
Biggar *Cumb.* 99 E1
Biggar *S.Lan.* 134 B2
Biggin *Derbys.* 81 D3
Biggin *Derbys.* 80 C2
Biggin *N.Yorks.* 103 E4
Biggin Hill 30 D3
Biggings 187 A6
Biggleswade 57 G3
Bigholms 126 B3
Bighouse 182 D2
Bighton 28 B4
Biglands 117 F1
Bignor 16 B2
Bigrigg 116 D5
Bigton 187 C10
Bilberry 5 E4
Bilborough 81 G3
Bilbrook *Som.* 22 D3
Bilbrook *Staffs.* 66 A2
Bilbrough 103 E3
Bilbster 183 H3
Bilby 94 D4
Bildershaw 120 A5
Bildeston 60 A3
Billericay 45 F3
Billesdon 68 C2
Billesley 54 D2
Billholm 126 A2
Billingborough 83 G4
Billinge 91 G3
Billingford *Norf.* 72 C4
Billingford *Norf.* 86 B3
Billingham 121 D5
Billinghay 83 G2
Billingley 94 B2
Billingshurst 29 F5
Billingsley 65 G4
Billington *Beds.* 57 E5
Billington *Lancs.* 100 D4
Billington *Staffs.* 79 F5
Billister 187 D6
Billockby 87 F4
Billy Row 120 A4
Bilsborrow 100 B4
Bilsby 97 E5
Bilsby Field 97 E5
Bilsdean 145 E2
Bilsham 16 B3
Bilsington 32 C5
Bilson Green 39 F1
Bilsthorpe 82 B1
Bilsthorpe Moor 82 B2
Bilston *Midloth.* 143 G3
Bilston *W.Mid.* 66 B3
Bilstone 67 F2
Bilting 32 C4
Bilton *E.Riding* 105 D4
Bilton *N.Yorks.* 102 C2
Bilton *Northumb.* 137 G5
Bilton *Warks.* 67 G5
Bilton-in-Ainsty 103 D3
Bimbister 185 C6
Binbrook 96 C3
Bincombe 12 C4
Bindal 175 G3
Bindon 23 E5
Binegar 24 D3
Bines Green 17 D2
Binfield 42 D5
Binfield Heath 42 C5
Bingfield 128 B4
Bingham 82 C4
Bingham's Melcombe
13 D2
Bingley 102 A4
Bings Heath 65 E1
Binham 86 A2
Binley *Hants.* 27 F2
Binley *W.Mid.* 67 F5
Binniehill 142 C2
Binsoe 110 B5
Binstead 15 E3
Binsted *Hants.* 28 C3
Binsted *W.Suss.* 16 B3
Binton 54 D2
Bintree 86 B3
Binweston 64 C2
Birch *Essex* 60 A5
Birch *Gt.Man.* 92 C2
Birch Cross 80 C4
Birch Green *Essex* 46 C1
Birch Green *Herts.* 44 B1
Birch Grove 17 G1
Birch Heath 78 C1
Birch Vale 93 E4
Birch Wood 11 F1
Bircham Newton 85 F4
Bircham Tofts 85 F4
Birchanger 58 D5
Bircher 53 D1
Bircher Common 53 D1
Birchfield 174 B2
Birchgrove *Cardiff* 38 A4
Birchgrove *Swan.* 36 D3
Birchington 33 F2
Birchmoor 67 E2
Birchover 80 D1
Birchwood *Lincs.* 83 E1
Birchwood *Warr.* 92 A3
Bircotes 94 D3
Bird Street 60 B2
Birdbrook 59 F3
Birdbush 26 A5
Birdfield 148 B5
Birdforth 111 D5
Birdham 16 A3
Birdingbury 55 G1
Birdlip 40 B1
Birdoswald 118 C1
Birds Green 45 E2
Birdsall 104 A1
Birdsgreen 65 G4
Birdsmoor Gate 11 G2
Birdston 142 A2
Birdwell 94 A2
Birdwood 39 G1
Birgham 136 B3
Birichen 174 E2
Birkby *Cumb.* 117 D3
Birkby *N.Yorks.* 110 C2
Birkdale *Mersey.* 91 E1
Birkdale *N.Yorks.* 109 D2
Birkenhead 91 E4
Birkenhills 177 F6
Birkenshaw 102 B5
Birkhall 168 B5
Birkhill *Angus* 152 B1
Birkhill *Sc.Bord.* 144 C5
Birkhill *Sc.Bord.* 134 D4
Birkholme 83 E5
Birkin 103 E5
Birks 102 B5
Birkwood 133 G2
Birley 53 D2
Birley Carr 94 A3
Birling *Kent* 31 F2
Birling *Northumb.* 129 E1
Birling Gap 18 A4
Birlingham 54 B3
Birmingham 66 C4
Birmingham International
Airport 67 D4
Birnam 159 F5
Birsay 184 B5
Birse 168 D5
Birsemore 168 D5
Birstall 68 A2
Birstall Smithies 102 B5
Birstwith 102 B2
Birthorpe 83 G4
Birtle 92 C1
Birtley *Here.* 52 C1
Birtley *Northumb.* 128 A4
Birtley *T.&W.* 120 B2
Birts Street 53 G4
Birtsmorton 54 A4
Bisbrooke 69 D3
Biscathorpe 96 C4
Bish Mill 22 A5
Bisham 43 D4
Bishampton 54 B2
Bishop Auckland 120 B5
Bishop Burton 104 B3
Bishop Middleham
120 C4
Bishop Monkton 102 C1
Bishop Norton 95 G3
Bishop Sutton 24 C2
Bishop Thornton 102 B1
Bishop Wilton 103 G2
Bishopbridge 96 A3
Bishopbriggs 142 A2
Bishopmill 175 K5
Bishops Cannings 26 B1
Bishop's Castle 64 C4
Bishop's Caundle 12 C1
Bishop's Cleeve 54 B5
Bishop's Frome 53 F3
Bishops Gate 43 E5
Bishop's Green *Essex*
45 F1
Bishop's Green *Hants.*
27 G1
Bishop's Hull 23 F5
Bishop's Itchington 55 F2
Bishop's Lydeard 23 E5
Bishop's Norton 54 A5
Bishops Nympton 22 A5
Bishop's Offley 79 E5
Bishop's Stortford 58 C5
Bishop's Sutton 28 B4
Bishop's Tachbrook 55 F1
Bishop's Tawton 21 F2
Bishop's Waltham 15 E1
Bishop's Wood 66 A2
Bishopsbourne 33 D3
Bishopsteignton 10 C5
Bishopstoke 15 D1
Bishopston *Bristol* 39 E5
Bishopston *Swan.* 36 B4
Bishopstone *Bucks.* 42 D1
Bishopstone *E.Suss.*
17 G3
Bishopstone *Here.* 52 D3
Bishopstone *Swin.* 41 E4
Bishopstone *Wilts.* 26 B5
Bishopstrow 25 F3
Bishopswood 11 F1
Bishopsworth 24 C1
Bishopthorpe 103 E3
Bishopton *Darl.* 120 C5
Bishopton *N.Yorks.*
110 B5
Bishopton *Renf.* 141 F2
Bishopton *Warks.* 55 D2
Bishton 38 C4
Bisley *Glos.* 40 B2
Bisley *Surr.* 29 E2
Bispham 99 G4
Bispham Green 91 F1
Bissoe 4 B5
Bisterne 14 A2
Bisterne Close 14 B2
Bitchet Green 31 E3
Bitchfield 83 E5
Bittadon 21 F1
Bittaford 8 C2
Bittering 86 A4
Bitterley 65 E5
Bitterne 15 D1
Bitteswell 68 A4
Bitton 25 D1
Biwmaris (Beaumaris)
89 E5
Bix 42 C4
Bixter 187 C7
Blaby 68 A3
Black Bourton 41 E2
Black Bridge 34 C2
Black Callerton 120 A1
Black Carr 72 B2
Black Clauchrie 123 D2
Black Corries Lodge
157 E4
Black Crofts 148 B1
Black Cross 4 D3
Black Dog 10 B2
Black Heddon 128 C4
Black Hill 55 E2
Black Marsh 64 C3
Black Moor 102 B3
Black Mount 157 E5
Black Notley 59 F5
Black Pill 36 C3
Black Street 73 G3
Black Torrington 21 E5
Blackaburn 127 F4
Blackacre 125 E1
Blackadder 145 F4
Blackawton 9 E2
Blackborough *Devon*
11 D2
Blackborough *Norf.* 71 E1
Blackborough End 71 E1
Blackboys 18 A1
Blackbraes *Aber.* 169 G3
Blackbraes *Falk.* 142 D2
Blackbrook *Derbys.* 81 E3
Blackbrook *Leics.* 67 G1
Blackbrook *Mersey.* 91 G3
Blackbrook *Staffs.* 79 E4
Blackburn *Aber.* 169 G3
Blackburn *B'burn.* 100 C5
Blackburn *W.Loth.*
143 D3
Blackbushe 28 C2
Blackcastle 175 F6
Blackchambers 169 F3
Blackcraig *D.&G.* 123 F4
Blackcraig *D.&G.* 124 B2
Blackden Heath 92 B5
Blackdog 169 H3
Blackdown *Devon* 7 F3
Blackdown *Dorset* 11 G2
Blackdown *Warks.* 55 F1
Blacker Hill 94 A2
Blackfen 45 D5
Blackfield 14 D2
Blackford *Aber.* 169 F1
Blackford *Cumb.* 126 B5
Blackford *P.&K.* 151 D4
Blackford *Som.* 25 D5
Blackford *Som.* 24 B3
Blackford Bridge 92 C2
Blackfordby 67 F1
Blackgang 15 D5
Blackhall *Edin.* 143 G2
Blackhall *Renf.* 141 F3
Blackhall Colliery 121 D4
Blackhall Mill 120 A2
Blackhall Rocks 121 D4
Blackham 31 E5
Blackhaugh 135 F2
Blackheath *Essex* 60 B5
Blackheath *Gt.Lon.* 44 C5
Blackheath *Suff.* 73 F4
Blackheath *Surr.* 29 F3
Blackheath *W.Mid.* 66 B4
Blackhill *Aber.* 177 J5
Blackhill *Aber.* 177 J6
Blackhillock 176 C6
Blackhills 175 K6
Blackland 26 B1
Blacklands 22 B4
Blackleach 100 A4
Blackley 92 C2
Blacklunans 159 G3
Blackmill 37 F4
Blackmoor *Hants.* 28 C4
Blackmoor *Som.* 11 E1
Blackmoor Gate 21 G1
Blackmoorfoot 93 E1
Blackmore 45 F2
Blackmore End *Essex*
59 F4
Blackmore End *Herts.*
44 A1
Blackness *Aber.* 168 E5
Blackness *Falk.* 143 E2
Blackness *High.* 183 H5
Blacknest 28 C3
Blackney 12 A3
Blacko 101 E3
Blackpole 54 A2
Blackpool *B'pool* 99 G4
Blackpool *Devon* 9 E3
Blackpool Airport 99 G4
Blackpool Bridge 35 D1
Blackpool Gate 126 D4
Blackridge 142 C3
Blackrock *Arg.&B.*
138 B3
Blackrock *Mon.* 38 B1
Blackrod 92 A1
Blackshaw 125 E4
Blackshaw Head 101 F5
Blacksmith's Green 60 C1
Blacksnape 100 D5
Blackstone 17 E2
Blackthorn 42 B1
Blackthorpe 60 A1
Blacktoft 104 A5
Blacktop 169 G4
Blacktown 38 B4
Blackwater *Cornw.* 4 B5
Blackwater *Hants.* 28 D2
Blackwater *I.o.W.* 15 E4
Blackwater *Norf.* 86 B3
Blackwater *Som.* 11 F1
Blackwaterfoot 131 E3
Blackwell *Darl.* 110 B1
Blackwell *Derbys.* 93 F5
Blackwell *Derbys.* 81 F2
Blackwell *W.Suss.* 30 C5
Blackwell *Warks.* 55 E3
Blackwell *Worcs.* 66 B5
Blackwells End 53 G5
Blackwood (Coed-duon)
Caerp. 38 A3
Blackwood *D.&G.*
124 D2
Blackwood *S.Lan.* 142 B5
Blackwood Hill 79 G2
Blacon 78 A1
Bladbean 33 D4
Bladnoch 123 F5
Bladon 41 G1
Blaen Clydach 37 F3
Blaenannerch 49 F3
Blaenau Dolwyddelan
75 F2
Blaenau Ffestiniog 75 F3
Blaenavon 38 B2
Blaenawey 38 B1
Blaencelyn 49 G2
Blaencwm 37 F2
Blaendyryn 51 F4
Blaenffos 49 E4
Blaengarw 37 F3
Blaengeuffordd 62 C4
Blaengweche 36 C1
Blaengwrach 37 E2
Blaengwynfi 37 E3
Blaenllechau 37 G3
Blaenos 51 D4
Blaenpennal 50 C1
Blaenplwyf 62 B5
Blaenporth 49 F3
Blaenrhondda 37 F2
Blaenwaun 49 F5
Blaen-y-coed 49 G5
Blagdon *N.Som.* 24 B2
Blagdon *Torbay* 9 E1
Blagdon Hill 11 F1
Blaguegate 91 F2
Blaich 156 C2
Blaina 38 A2
Blair 141 E5
Blair Atholl 159 D3
Blair Drummond 150 C5
Blairannaich 149 F4
Blairbuie 140 C2
Blairgowrie 159 G5
Blairhall 143 E1
Blairhoyle 150 B4
Blairhullichan 149 G4
Blairingone 151 E5
Blairkip 132 D2
Blairlogie 150 D5
Blairmore *Arg.&B.*
140 C1
Blairmore *High.* 174 E1
Blairmore *High.* 180 D3
Blairnairn 141 D1
Blairnamarrow 167 K3
Blairpark 140 D4
Blairquhan 132 B5
Blairquhosh 141 G1
Blair's Ferry 140 A3
Blairshinnoch 176 E4
Blairuskinmore 149 G4
Blairvadach 141 D1
Blairydryne 169 F5
Blairythan Cottage
169 H2
Blaisdon 39 G1
Blake End 59 F5
Blakebrook 66 A5
Blakedown 66 A5
Blakelaw *Sc.Bord.* 136 B3
Blakelaw *T.&W.* 120 B1
Blakeley 66 A3
Blakelow 79 D2
Blakemere 52 C3
Blakeney *Glos.* 39 F2
Blakeney *Norf.* 86 B1
Blakenhall *Ches.* 79 E3
Blakenhall *W.Mid.* 66 B3
Blakeshall 66 A4
Blakesley 56 B2
Blanchland 119 F2
Bland Hill 102 B2
Blandford Camp 13 F2
Blandford Forum 13 E2
Blandford St. Mary 13 E2
Blanefield 141 G2
Blanerne 145 F4
Blankney 83 F1
Blantyre 142 A4
Blar a' Chaorainn 156 D3
Blargie 166 D5
Blarglas 141 E1
Blarmachfoldach 156 C3
Blarnalearoch 173 H2
Blashford 14 A2
Blaston 68 D3
Blathaisbhal 170 D4
Blatherwycke 69 E3
Blawith 107 D4
Blaxhall 61 E2
Blaxton 95 D2
Blaydon 120 A1
Bleadney 24 B3
Bleadon 24 A2
Blean 32 D2
Bleasby *Lincs.* 96 B4
Bleasby *Notts.* 82 C3
Bleasby Moor 96 B4
Bleatarn 108 C1
Bleathwood Common
53 E1
Blebocraigs 152 C3
Bleddfa 52 B1
Bledington 55 E5
Bledlow 42 C2
Bledlow Ridge 42 C3
Blencarn 118 C4
Blencogo 117 E2
Blencow 118 A4
Blendworth 15 G1
Blennerhasset 117 E2
Blervie Castle 175 H6
Bletchingdon 42 A1
Bletchingley 30 C3
Bletchley *M.K.* 57 D4
Bletchley *Shrop.* 78 D4
Bletherston 49 D5
Bletsoe 57 F2
Blewbury 42 A4
Blickling 86 C3
Blidworth 81 G2
Blidworth Bottoms 81 G2
Blindburn *Aber.* 169 H1
Blindburn *Northumb.*
136 C5
Blindcrake 117 E3
Blindley Heath 30 C4
Blisland 5 E2
Bliss Gate 65 G5
Blissford 14 A1
Blisworth 56 C2
Blithbury 80 B5
Blitterlees 117 E1
Blo' Norton 72 B4
Blockley 55 D4
Blofield 87 E5
Blofield Heath 87 E4
Blore 80 C3
Blossomfield 66 D5
Blount's Green 80 B4
Blowick 91 E1
Bloxham 55 G4
Bloxholm 83 F2
Bloxwich 66 B2
Bloxworth 13 E3
Blubberhouses 102 A2
Blue Anchor *Cornw.* 4 D4
Blue Anchor *Som.* 22 D3
Blue Bell Hill 31 G2
Bluewater 45 E5
Blundellsands 91 E3
Blundeston 73 G2
Blunham 57 G2
Blunsdon St. Andrew
40 D4
Bluntington 66 A5
Bluntisham 70 B5
Blunts 6 D4
Blurton 79 F3
Blyborough 95 G3
Blyford 73 F4
Blymhill 66 A1
Blymhill Common 65 G1
Blymhill Lawn 66 A1
Blyth *Northumb.* 129 F3
Blyth *Notts.* 94 D4
Blyth Bridge 143 F5
Blyth End 67 E3
Blythburgh 73 F4
Blythe Bridge 79 G3
Blythe Marsh 79 G3
Blyton 95 F3
Boarhills 153 D3
Boarhunt 15 F2
Boars Hill 41 G2
Boarsgreave 101 E5
Boarshead 31 E5
Boarstall 42 B1
Boarzell 18 C1
Boasley Cross 7 F1
Boat o' Brig 176 B5
Boat of Garten 167 G3
Boath 174 C4
Bobbing 32 A2
Bobbington 66 A3
Bobbingworth 45 E2
Bocaddon 5 F4
Bochastle 150 B4
Bockhampton 41 F5
Bocking 59 F5
Bocking Churchstreet
59 F5
Bockleton 53 E1
Boconnoc 5 F3
Boddam *Aber.* 177 K6
Boddam *Shet.* 187 F9
Bodden 24 D3
Boddington 54 A5
Bodedern 88 B4
Bodelwyddan 90 B5
Bodenham *Here.* 53 E2
Bodenham *Wilts.* 26 C5
Bodenham Moor 53 E2
Bodesbeck 134 C5
Bodewryd 88 B3
Bodfari 90 B5
Bodffordd 88 C5
Bodfuan 74 C4
Bodham 86 C1
Bodiam 18 C1
Bodicote 55 G4
Bodieve 5 D2
Bodinnick 5 F4
Bodior 88 A5
Bodle Street Green 18 B2
Bodmin 5 E3
Bodney 71 G3
Bodorgan 74 C1
Bodrane 5 G3
Bodsham Green 32 D4
Bodwen 5 E3
Bodymoor Heath 67 D3
Bogallan 174 D6
Bogbain 174 E7
Bogbrae 169 J1
Bogbuie 174 C6
Bogend 132 B2
Bogfern 168 D4
Bogfields 168 D4
Bogfold 177 G5
Boghead *Aber.* 176 E5
Boghead *E.Ayr.* 133 E3
Boghead *S.Lan.* 142 B5
Boghole Farm 175 G6
Bogmoor 176 B4
Bogniebrae 176 D6
Bognor Regis 16 B4
Bograxie 169 F3
Bogroy 167 G2
Bogside 151 E5
Bogston 168 B4
Bogton 176 E5
Bogue 124 A2
Bohemia 14 B1
Bohenie 157 E1
Bohetherick 8 A1
Bohortha 3 F3
Bohuntine 157 E1
Boirseam 171 F3
Bojewyan 2 A3
Bokiddick 5 E3
Bolam *Dur.* 120 A5
Bolam *Northumb.* 128 C3
Bolberry 8 C4
Bold Heath 91 G4
Bolderwood 14 B2
Boldon 120 C1
Boldon Colliery 120 C1
Boldre 14 C3
Boldron 109 F1
Bole 95 E4
Bolehill 81 D2
Boleigh 2 B4
Bolenowe 3 D3
Boleside 135 F2
Bolfracks 158 D5
Bolgoed 36 C2
Bolham *Devon* 10 C1
Bolham *Notts.* 95 E4
Bolham Water 11 E1
Bolingey 4 B4
Bollington 92 D5
Bolney 17 E1
Bolnhurst 57 F2
Bolshan 161 E4
Bolsover 94 B5
Bolsterstone 93 G3
Bolstone 53 E4
Boltby 111 D4
Bolter End 42 C3
Bolton *Cumb.* 118 C5
Bolton *E.Loth.* 144 C2
Bolton *E.Riding* 103 G2
Bolton *Gt.Man.* 92 B2
Bolton *Northumb.* 137 F5
Bolton Abbey 101 G2
Bolton Bridge 101 G2
Bolton by Bowland
101 D3
Bolton Houses 100 A4
Bolton Low Houses
117 F2
Bolton Percy 103 E3
Bolton upon Dearne
94 B2
Bolton Wood Lane 117 F2
Boltonfellend 118 A1
Boltongate 117 F2
Bolton-le-Sands 100 A1
Bolton-on-Swale 110 B3
Bolventor 5 F2
Bombie 116 A2
Bomere Heath 65 D1
Bonar Bridge 174 D2
Bonawe 148 C1
Bonby 96 A1
Boncath 49 F4
Bonchester Bridge 135 G4
Bonchurch 15 E5
Bondleigh 21 G5
Bonds 100 A3
Bonehill 67 D2
Bo'ness 143 D1
Bonhill 141 E2
Boningale 66 A2
Bonjedward 136 A4
Bonkle 142 C4
Bonning Gate 107 F3
Bonnington *Edin.* 143 F3
Bonnington *Kent* 32 C5
Bonnybank 152 B4
Bonnybridge 142 C1
Bonnykelly 177 G5
Bonnyrigg 144 A3
Bonnyton *Aber.* 168 E1
Bonnyton *Angus* 153 D1
Bonnyton *Angus* 161 E4
Bonnyton *Angus* 152 B1
Bonsall 81 D2
Bont 38 C1
Bont Dolgadfan 63 E2
Bont Newydd 76 A5
Bontddu 62 C1
Bont-goch (Elerch) 62 C4
Bonthorpe 97 E5
Bont-newydd *Conwy*
90 B5
Bontnewydd *Gwyn.*
75 D1
Bontuchel 77 D2
Bonvilston 37 G5
Bon-y-maen 36 C3
Boode 21 F2
Boohay 9 F2
Booker 42 D3
Booley 78 C5
Boor 172 E3
Boosbeck 111 F1
Boose's Green 59 G4
Boot 106 C2
Boot Street 60 D3
Booth 101 G5
Booth Bank 93 E1
Booth Green 92 D4
Booth Wood 93 E1
Boothby Graffoe 83 E2
Boothby Pagnell 83 E4
Boothstown 92 B2
Boothville 56 C1
Bootle *Cumb.* 106 C4
Bootle *Mersey.* 91 E3
Booton 86 C3
Boots Green 92 B5
Booze 109 F2
Boquhan 141 G1
Boraston 65 F5
Bordeaux 9 F4
Borden *Kent* 32 A2
Borden *W.Suss.* 28 D5
Bordley 101 F1
Bordon 28 C4
Boreham *Essex* 45 G2
Boreham *Wilts.* 25 F3
Boreham Street 18 B2
Borehamwood 44 A3
Boreland *D.&G.* 125 F1
Boreland *D.&G.* 123 E4
Boreland *Stir.* 150 A1
Boreley 54 A1
Boreraig 171 G6
Borgh *W.Isles* 170 E3
Borgh *W.Isles* 162 B4
Borgh (Borve) *W.Isles*
179 G2
Borghastan 178 D3
Borgie 181 J3
Borgue *D.&G.* 115 G2
Borgue *High.* 183 G6
Borley 59 G3
Borley Green *Essex* 59 G3
Borley Green *Suff.* 60 A1
Bornais 162 C2
Borness 115 G2
Bornisketaig 171 J4
Borough Green 31 F3
Boroughbridge 102 C1
Borras Head 78 A2
Borrowash 81 F4
Borrowby *N.Yorks.*
111 G1
Borrowby *N.Yorks.*
110 D4
Borrowdale 117 F5
Borrowfield 169 G5
Borstal 31 G2
Borth 62 C4
Borthwick 144 A4
Borthwickbrae 135 F4
Borthwickshiels 135 F4
Borth-y-Gest 75 E4
Borve *High.* 171 K7
Borve (Borgh) *W.Isles*
179 G2
Borwick 107 G5
Borwick Rails 106 C5
Bosavern 2 A3
Bosbury 53 F3
Boscarne 5 E3
Boscastle 6 A1
Boscombe *Bourne.* 14 A3
Boscombe *Wilts.* 26 D4
Bosham 16 A3
Bosham Hoe 16 A3
Bosherston 34 C3
Bosley 79 G1
Bossall 103 G1
Bossiney 5 E1
Bossingham 33 D4
Bossington *Hants.* 27 E4
Bossington *Som.* 22 B3
Bostadh 178 D4
Bostock Green 79 D1
Boston 84 B3
Boston Spa 102 D3
Boswarthan 2 B3
Boswinger 5 D5
Botallack 2 A3
Botany Bay 44 C3
Botcheston 67 G2
Botesdale 72 B4
Bothal 129 E3
Bothamsall 95 D5
Bothel 117 E3
Bothenhampton 12 A3
Bothwell 142 B4
Botley *Bucks.* 43 E2
Botley *Hants.* 15 E1
Botley *Oxon.* 41 G2
Botloe's Green 53 G5
Botolph Claydon 56 C5
Botolphs 17 D3
Botolph's Bridge 32 D5
Bottacks 174 B5
Bottesford *Leics.* 82 D4
Bottesford *N.Lincs.* 95 F2
Bottisham 58 D1
Bottlesford 26 C2
Bottom Boat 102 C5
Bottom of Hutton 100 A5
Bottom o'th'Moor 92 A1
Bottomcraig 152 B2
Bottoms 101 F5
Botton Head 100 C1
Botusfleming 8 A1
Botwnnog 74 B4
Bough Beech 31 D4
Boughrood 52 A4
Boughspring 39 E3
Boughton *Norf.* 71 F2
Boughton *Northants.*
56 C1
Boughton *Notts.* 82 B1
Boughton Aluph 32 C4
Boughton Green 31 G3
Boughton Lees 32 C4
Boughton Malherbe
32 A4
Boughton Street 32 C3
Boulby 111 G1
Bouldnor 14 C4
Bouldon 65 E4
Boulge 61 D2
Boulmer 137 G5
Boulston 34 C1
Boultenstone Hotel
168 C3
Boultham 83 E1
Boundary *Derbys.* 67 F1
Boundary *Staffs.* 79 G3
Bourn 58 B2
Bourne 83 F5
Bourne End *Beds.* 57 E3
Bourne End *Bucks.* 43 D4
Bourne End *Herts.* 43 F2
Bournebridge 45 E3

Bournemouth 13 G3
Bournemouth Airport 14 A3
Bournheath 66 B5
Bournmoor 120 C2
Bournville 66 C4
Bourton *Bucks.* 56 C4
Bourton *Dorset* 25 E4
Bourton *N.Som.* 24 A1
Bourton *Oxon.* 41 E4
Bourton *Shrop.* 65 E3
Bourton *Wilts.* 26 B1
Bourton on Dunsmore 67 G5
Bourton-on-the-Hill 55 D4
Bourton-on-the-Water 55 D5
Bousd 154 B3
Boustead Hill 117 F1
Bouth 107 E4
Bouthwaite 110 A5
Bovain 150 A1
Boveney 43 E5
Boveridge 13 G1
Boverton 22 C1
Bovey Tracey 10 B5
Bovingdon 43 F2
Bovinger 45 E2
Bovington Camp 13 E4
Bow *Cumb.* 117 G1
Bow *Devon* 10 A2
Bow *Devon* 9 E2
Bow *Ork.* 185 C8
Bow Brickhill 57 E4
Bow of Fife 152 B3
Bow Street *Cere.* 62 C4
Bow Street *Norf.* 72 B2
Bowbank 119 F5
Bowburn 120 C4
Bowcombe 15 D4
Bowd 11 E3
Bowden *Devon* 9 E3
Bowden *Sc.Bord.* 135 G2
Bowden Hill 26 A1
Bowdon 92 B4
Bower 127 F3
Bower Hinton 12 A1
Bower House Tye 60 A3
Bowerchalke 26 B5
Bowerhill 26 A1
Bowermadden 183 H2
Bowers 79 F4
Bowers Gifford 45 G4
Bowershall 151 F5
Bowertower 183 H2
Bowes 109 E1
Bowgreave 100 A3
Bowhousebog 142 C4
Bowithick 5 F1
Bowker's Green 91 F2
Bowland Bridge 107 F4
Bowley 53 E2
Bowley Town 53 E2
Bowlhead Green 29 E4
Bowling *W.Dun.* 141 F2
Bowling *W.Yorks.* 102 A4
Bowling Bank 78 A3
Bowlish 24 D3
Bowmanstead 107 E3
Bowmore 138 B3
Bowness-on-Solway 126 A5
Bowness-on-Windermere 107 F3
Bowscale 117 G3
Bowsden 145 G5
Bowside Lodge 182 D2
Bowston 107 F3
Bowthorpe 86 C5
Bowtrees 142 D1
Box *Glos.* 40 A2
Box *Wilts.* 25 F1
Box End 57 F3
Boxbush *Glos.* 39 G1
Boxbush *Glos.* 53 F5
Boxford *Suff.* 60 A3
Boxford *W.Berks.* 41 G5
Boxgrove 16 B3
Boxley 31 G3
Boxmoor 43 F2
Box's Shop 20 C5
Boxted *Essex* 60 A4
Boxted *Suff.* 59 G2
Boxted Cross 60 A4
Boxwell 40 A3
Boxworth 58 B1
Boxworth End 58 B1
Boyden Gate 33 E2
Boydston 132 C2
Boylestone 80 C4
Boyndie 176 E4
Boynton 104 D1
Boys Hill 12 C2
Boysack 161 E5
Boyton *Cornw.* 6 D1
Boyton *Suff.* 61 E3
Boyton *Wilts.* 26 A4
Boyton Cross 45 F2
Boyton End 59 F3
Bozeat 57 E2
Braaid 98 B4
Braal Castle 183 G2
Brabling Green 61 D1
Brabourne 32 C4
Brabourne Lees 32 C4
Brabster 183 J2
Bracadale 163 J1
Braceborough 69 F1
Bracebridge Heath 83 E1
Braceby 83 F4
Bracewell 101 E3
Brachla 166 C1
Bracken Hill 102 A5
Brackenber 108 C1
Brackenbottom 108 D5
Brackenfield 81 E2
Brackens 177 F5
Bracklach 168 B2
Bracklamore 177 G5
Bracklesham 16 A4
Brackletter 157 D1
Brackley *Arg. & B.* 139 G1
Brackley *High.* 175 F6
Brackley *Northants.* 56 A4
Brackley Gate 81 E3
Brackley Hatch 56 B3
Bracknell 29 D1
Braco 150 D4
Bracobrae 176 D5
Bracon Ash 72 C2
Bracora 164 D5
Bracorina 164 D5
Bradbourne 80 D2
Bradbury 120 C5
Bradda 98 A4
Bradden 56 B3
Braddock 5 F3
Bradenham *Bucks.* 42 D3
Bradenham *Norf.* 86 A5
Bradenstoke 40 C5
Bradfield *Devon* 11 D2
Bradfield *Essex* 60 C4
Bradfield *Norf.* 87 D2
Bradfield *W.Berks.* 42 B5
Bradfield Combust 59 G2
Bradfield Green 79 D2
Bradfield Heath 60 C5
Bradfield St. Clare 60 A2
Bradfield St. George 60 A1
Bradford *Cornw.* 5 F2
Bradford *Derbys.* 80 D1
Bradford *Devon* 21 E5
Bradford *Northumb.* 137 F3
Bradford *Northumb.* 128 C4
Bradford *W.Yorks.* 102 A4
Bradford Abbas 12 B1
Bradford Leigh 25 F1
Bradford Peverell 12 C3
Bradford-on-Avon 25 F1
Bradford-on-Tone 23 E5
Bradiford 21 F2
Brading 15 F4
Bradley *Ches.* 91 G5
Bradley *Derbys.* 80 D3
Bradley *Hants.* 28 B3
Bradley *N.E.Lincs.* 96 C2
Bradley (Low Bradley) *N.Yorks.* 101 G3
Bradley *Staffs.* 66 A1
Bradley *W.Mid.* 66 B3
Bradley Fold 92 B2
Bradley Green *Warks.* 67 E2
Bradley Green *Worcs.* 54 B1
Bradley in the Moors 80 B3
Bradley Mills 93 F1
Bradley Stoke 39 F4
Bradmore *Notts.* 81 G4
Bradmore *W.Mid.* 66 A3
Bradney 24 A4
Bradninch 10 D2
Bradnop 80 B2
Bradnor Green 52 B2
Bradpole 12 A3
Bradshaw *Gt.Man.* 92 B1
Bradshaw *W.Yorks.* 101 G4
Bradstone 7 D2
Bradwall Green 79 E1
Bradwell *Derbys.* 93 F4
Bradwell *Devon* 21 E1
Bradwell *Essex* 59 G5
Bradwell *M.K.* 56 D4
Bradwell *Norf.* 87 G5
Bradwell Grove 41 E2
Bradwell Waterside 46 C2
Bradwell-on-Sea 46 D2
Bradworthy 20 D4
Brae *D. & G.* 124 C3
Brae *High.* 174 B1
Brae *Shet.* 187 C6
Brae of Achnahaird 180 C7
Braeantra 174 C4
Braedownie 160 A2
Braefoot 177 F6
Braegrum 151 F2
Braehead *D. & G.* 123 F5
Braehead *Glas.* 141 G3
Braehead *Moray* 176 B6
Braehead *Ork.* 185 E7
Braehead *Ork.* 184 D3
Braehead *S.Lan.* 133 G2
Braehead *S.Lan.* 143 D4
Braehead of Lunan 161 E4
Braehoulland 186 B5
Braeleny 150 B3
Braemar 167 J5
Braemore *High.* 174 C1
Braemore *High.* 183 F5
Braemore *High.* 173 H4
Braenaloin 167 K5
Braes of Enzie 176 B5
Braes of Foss 158 C4
Braes of Ullapool 173 H2
Braeswick 184 F4
Braeval 150 A4
Braewick 187 C7
Brafferton *Darl.* 120 B5
Brafferton *N.Yorks.* 110 D5
Brafield-on-the-Green 56 D2
Bragar 178 E3
Bragbury End 58 A5
Bragenham 57 E5
Bragleenbeg 148 B2
Braichmelyn 75 F1
Braides 100 A2
Braidley 109 F4
Braidwood 142 C5
Braigo 138 A3
Brailsford 81 D3
Brain's Green 39 F2
Braintree 59 F5
Braiseworth 72 C4
Braishfield 27 E5
Braithwaite *Cumb.* 117 F4
Braithwaite *S.Yorks.* 94 D1
Braithwaite *W.Yorks.* 101 G3
Braithwell 94 C3
Bramber 17 D2
Brambletye 30 D5
Brambridge 27 F5
Bramcote *Notts.* 81 G4
Bramcote *Warks.* 67 G4
Bramdean 28 B5
Bramerton 87 D5
Bramfield *Herts.* 44 B1
Bramfield *Suff.* 73 E4
Bramford 60 C3
Bramhall 92 C4
Bramham 102 D3
Bramhope 102 B3
Bramley *Hants.* 28 B2
Bramley *S.Yorks.* 94 B3
Bramley *Surr.* 29 F3
Bramley Corner 28 B2
Bramley Head 102 A2
Bramley Vale 81 F1
Bramling 33 E3
Brampford Speke 10 C3
Brampton *Cambs.* 70 A5
Brampton *Cumb.* 118 B1
Brampton *Cumb.* 118 C5
Brampton *Derbys.* 94 A5
Brampton *Lincs.* 95 F5
Brampton *Norf.* 86 D3
Brampton *S.Yorks.* 94 B2
Brampton *Suff.* 73 F3
Brampton Abbotts 53 F5
Brampton Ash 68 C4
Brampton Bryan 64 C5
Brampton en le Morthen 94 B4
Brampton Street 73 F3
Bramshall 80 B4
Bramshaw 14 B1
Bramshill 28 C1
Bramshott 28 D4
Bramwell 24 B5
Bran End 59 E5
Branault 155 E3
Brancaster 85 F3
Brancaster Staithe 85 F3
Brancepeth 120 B4
Branchill 175 H6
Brand Green 53 G5
Brandelhow 117 F4
Branderburgh 175 K4
Brandesburton 104 D3
Brandeston 60 D1
Brandis Corner 21 E5
Brandiston 86 C3
Brandon *Dur.* 120 B4
Brandon *Lincs.* 83 E3
Brandon *Northumb.* 137 E5
Brandon *Suff.* 71 F4
Brandon *Warks.* 67 G5
Brandon Bank 71 E4
Brandon Creek 71 E3
Brandon Parva 86 B5
Brandsby 111 E5
Brandy Wharf 96 A3
Brane 2 B4
Branksome 13 G3
Branksome Park 13 G3
Bransbury 27 F3
Bransby 95 F5
Branscombe 11 E4
Bransford 53 G2
Bransford Bridge 54 A2
Bransgore 14 A3
Bransholme 104 D4
Branson's Cross 66 C5
Branston *Leics.* 82 D5
Branston *Lincs.* 83 F1
Branston *Staffs.* 80 D5
Branston Booths 83 F1
Brant Broughton 83 E2
Brantham 60 C4
Branthwaite *Cumb.* 117 F3
Branthwaite *Cumb.* 117 D4
Brantingham 104 B5
Branton *Northumb.* 137 E5
Branton *S.Yorks.* 94 D2
Brantwood 107 E3
Branxholm Bridgend 135 F4
Branxholme 135 F4
Branxton 136 C3
Brassey Green 78 C1
Brassington 80 D2
Brasted 31 D3
Brasted Chart 31 D3
Brathens 168 E5
Bratoft 84 C1
Brattleby 95 G4
Bratton *Som.* 22 C3
Bratton *Tel. & W.* 65 F1
Bratton *Wilts.* 26 A2
Bratton Clovelly 7 E1
Bratton Fleming 21 G2
Bratton Seymour 25 D5
Braughing 58 B5
Brauncewell 83 F2
Braunston *Northants.* 56 A1
Braunston *Rut.* 68 D2
Braunstone 68 A2
Braunton 21 E2
Brawby 111 G5
Brawdy 48 B5
Brawith 111 E2
Brawl 182 D2
Brawlbin 183 F3
Bray 43 E5
Bray Shop 6 D3
Bray Wick 43 D5
Braybrooke 68 C4
Braydon Side 40 C4
Brayford 21 G2
Brayshaw 101 D2
Braythorn 102 B3
Brayton 103 F4
Braywoodside 43 D5
Brazacott 6 C1
Brea 4 A5
Breach *Kent* 33 D4
Breach *Kent* 32 A2
Breachwood Green 57 G5
Breacleit 178 D4
Breaden Heath 78 B4
Breadsall 81 E4
Breadstone 39 G2
Breage 2 D4
Breakon 186 E2
Bream 39 F2
Breamore 14 A1
Brean 23 F2
Breanais 178 B5
Brearton 102 C1
Breascleit 178 E4
Breaston 81 F4
Brechfa 50 B4
Brechin 161 E3
Brecklate 130 B4
Breckles 72 A2
Brecon (Aberhonddu) 51 G5
Breconside 133 G5
Bredbury 92 D3
Brede 18 D2
Bredenbury 53 F2
Bredfield 61 D2
Bredgar 32 A2
Bredhurst 31 G2
Bredon 54 B4
Bredon's Hardwick 54 B4
Bredon's Norton 54 B4
Bredwardine 52 C3
Breedon on the Hill 81 F5
Breibhig 179 G4
Breich 143 D3
Breightmet 92 B2
Breighton 103 G4
Breinton 53 D4
Breinton Common 53 D4
Bremhill 40 B5
Bremhill Wick 40 B5
Brenachoille 148 C4
Brenchley 31 F4
Brendon *Devon* 22 A3
Brendon *Devon* 21 D4
Brendon *Devon* 21 D5
Brenkley 129 E4
Brent Eleigh 60 A3
Brent Knoll 24 A2
Brent Pelham 58 C4
Brentford 44 A5
Brentingby 68 C1
Brentwood 45 E3
Brenzett 19 F1
Brenzett Green 19 F1
Breoch 124 B5
Brereton 66 C1
Brereton Green 79 E1
Brereton Heath 79 F1
Breretonhill 66 C1
Bressay 187 E8
Bressingham 72 B3
Bressingham Common 72 B3
Bretby 81 D5
Bretford 67 G5
Bretforton 54 C3
Bretherdale Head 107 G2
Bretherton 100 A5
Brettabister 187 D7
Brettenham *Norf.* 72 A3
Brettenham *Suff.* 60 A2
Bretton *Derbys.* 93 F5
Bretton *Flints.* 78 A1
Brevig 162 B5
Brewood 66 A2
Briach 175 H6
Briantspuddle 13 E3
Brick End 59 D5
Bricket Wood 44 A2
Brickkiln Green 59 F4
Bricklehampton 54 B3
Bride 98 C1
Bridekirk 117 E3
Bridell 49 E3
Bridestones 79 G1
Bridestowe 7 F2
Brideswell 168 D1
Bridford 10 B4
Bridge *Cornw.* 4 A5
Bridge *Kent* 33 D3
Bridge End *Bridgend* 106 D4
Bridge End *Devon* 8 C3
Bridge End *Essex* 59 E4
Bridge End *Lincs.* 83 G4
Bridge End *Shet.* 187 C9
Bridge Hewick 110 C5
Bridge o' Ess 168 D5
Bridge of Alford 168 D3
Bridge of Allan 150 C5
Bridge of Avon 167 J1
Bridge of Balgie 158 A5
Bridge of Bogendreip 168 E5
Bridge of Brewlands 159 G3
Bridge of Brown 167 J2
Bridge of Cally 159 G4
Bridge of Canny 168 E5
Bridge of Craigisla 160 A4
Bridge of Dee *Aber.* 167 J5
Bridge of Dee *Aber.* 168 E5
Bridge of Dee *D. & G.* 124 B4
Bridge of Don 169 H4
Bridge of Dun 161 E4
Bridge of Dye 161 E1
Bridge of Earn 151 G3
Bridge of Ericht 158 A4
Bridge of Feugh 168 E5
Bridge of Forss 183 F2
Bridge of Gairn 168 B5
Bridge of Gaur 158 A4
Bridge of Muchalls 169 G5
Bridge of Muick 168 B5
Bridge of Orchy 149 E1
Bridge of Tynet 176 B4
Bridge of Walls 187 B7
Bridge of Weir 141 E3
Bridge Reeve 21 G4
Bridge Sollers 52 D3
Bridge Street 59 G3
Bridge Trafford 91 F5
Bridgefoot *Angus* 152 B1
Bridgefoot *Cambs.* 58 C3
Bridgefoot *Cumb.* 117 D4
Bridgehampton 24 C5
Bridgehaugh 168 B1
Bridgehill 119 G2
Bridgemary 15 E2
Bridgemere 79 E3
Bridgend *Aber.* 168 D1
Bridgend *Aber.* 177 F6
Bridgend *Angus* 160 D3
Bridgend *Arg. & B.* 138 B3
Bridgend *Arg. & B.* 148 A5
Bridgend (Pen-y-bont ar Ogwr) *Bridgend* 37 F5
Bridgend *Cornw.* 5 F4
Bridgend *Cumb.* 107 F1
Bridgend *Fife* 152 B3
Bridgend *Moray* 168 B1
Bridgend *P. & K.* 151 G2
Bridgend *W.Loth.* 143 E2
Bridgend of Lintrathen 160 A4
Bridgerule 20 C5
Bridges 64 C3
Bridgeton *Aber.* 168 D3
Bridgeton *Glas.* 142 A3
Bridgetown *Cornw.* 6 D2
Bridgetown *Som.* 22 C4
Bridgeyate 39 F5
Bridgham 72 A3
Bridgnorth 65 G3
Bridgtown 66 B2
Bridgwater 23 F4
Bridlington 105 D1
Bridport 12 A3
Bridstow 53 E5
Brierfield 101 E4
Brierley *Glos.* 39 F1
Brierley *Here.* 53 D2
Brierley *S.Yorks.* 94 B1
Brierley Hill 66 B4
Brierton 121 D4
Briestfield 93 G1
Brig o'Turk 150 A4
Brigg 96 A2
Briggate 87 E3
Briggswath 112 B2
Brigham *Cumb.* 117 D3
Brigham *E.Riding* 104 C2
Brighouse 102 A5
Brighstone 14 D4
Brightgate 81 D2
Brighthampton 41 F2
Brightholmlee 93 G3
Brightling 18 C1
Brightlingsea 47 D1
Brighton *B. & H.* 17 F3
Brighton *Cornw.* 4 D4
Brightons 142 D2
Brightwalton 41 G5
Brightwalton Green 41 G5
Brightwell 60 D3
Brightwell Baldwin 42 B3
Brightwell Upperton 42 B3
Brightwell-cum-Sotwell 42 A3
Brignall 109 F1
Brigsley 96 C2
Brigsteer 107 F4
Brigstock 69 E4
Brill *Bucks.* 42 B1
Brill *Cornw.* 3 E4
Brilley 52 B3
Brilley Mountain 52 B2
Brimaston 48 C5
Brimfield 53 E1
Brimington 94 B5
Brimington Common 94 B5
Brimley 10 B5
Brimpsfield 40 B1
Brimpton 27 G1
Brims 185 B9
Brimscombe 40 A2
Brimstage 91 E4
Brinacory 164 D5
Brindham 24 C3
Brindister *Shet.* 187 D9
Brindister *Shet.* 187 B7
Brindle 100 B5
Brindley Ford 79 F2
Brineton 66 A1
Bringhurst 68 D3
Brington 69 F5
Brinian 184 D5
Briningham 86 B2
Brinkhill 97 D5
Brinkley *Cambs.* 59 E2
Brinkley *Notts.* 82 C2
Brinklow 67 G5
Brinkworth 40 C4
Brinmore 166 D2
Brinscall 100 C5
Brinsea 24 B1
Brinsley 81 F3
Brinsop 52 D3
Brinsworth 94 B3
Brinton 86 B2
Brisco 118 A2
Brisley 86 A3
Brislington 39 F5
Brissenden Green 32 B5
Bristol 39 E5
Bristol International Airport 24 C1
Briston 86 B2
Britannia 101 E5
Britford 26 C5
Brithdir *Caerp.* 38 A2
Brithdir *Gwyn.* 63 D1
Brithem Bottom 10 D1
Briton Ferry (Llansawel) 36 D3
Britwell 43 E4
Britwell Salome 42 B3
Brixham 9 F2
Brixton *Devon* 8 B2
Brixton *Gt.Lon.* 44 C5
Brixton Deverill 25 F4
Brixworth 68 C5
Brize Norton 41 E2
Broad Alley 54 A1
Broad Blunsdon 41 D3
Broad Campden 55 D4
Broad Carr 93 E1
Broad Chalke 26 B5
Broad Ford 31 G5
Broad Green *Beds.* 57 E3
Broad Green *Cambs.* 59 E2
Broad Green *Essex* 59 G5
Broad Green *Essex* 58 C4
Broad Green *Mersey.* 91 F3
Broad Green *Suff.* 60 B2
Broad Green *Worcs.* 53 G2
Broad Haven 34 B1
Broad Hill 71 D5
Broad Hinton 40 D5
Broad Laying 27 F1
Broad Marston 54 D3
Broad Oak *Carmar.* 50 B5
Broad Oak *Cumb.* 106 C3
Broad Oak *E.Suss.* 18 D2
Broad Oak *E.Suss.* 18 B1
Broad Oak *Here.* 53 D5
Broad Road 73 D4
Broad Street *E.Suss.* 19 D2
Broad Street *Kent* 32 A3
Broad Street *Kent* 32 D5
Broad Street *Wilts.* 26 C2
Broad Street Green 46 B2
Broad Town 40 C5
Broadbottom 93 D3
Broadbridge 16 A3
Broadbridge Heath 29 G4
Broadclyst 10 C3
Broadfield *Lancs.* 100 D5
Broadfield *Lancs.* 100 B5
Broadford 164 C2
Broadford Bridge 29 F5
Broadgate 106 C4
Broadhaugh 135 F5
Broadhaven 183 J3
Broadheath *Gt.Man.* 92 B4
Broadheath *Worcs.* 53 F1
Broadhembury 11 E2
Broadhempston 9 E1
Broadholme 95 F5
Broadland Row 18 D2
Broadlay 35 G2
Broadley *Lancs.* 92 C1
Broadley *Moray* 176 B4
Broadley Common 44 D2
Broadmayne 12 D4
Broadmeadows 135 F2
Broadmere 28 B3
Broadmoor 35 D2
Broadnymett 10 A2
Broadoak *Dorset* 12 A3
Broadoak *Glos.* 39 F1
Broadoak *Kent* 33 D2
Broadoak End 44 C1
Broadrashes 176 C5
Broad's Green 45 F1
Broadsea 177 H4
Broadstairs 33 F2
Broadstone *Poole* 13 G3
Broadstone *Shrop.* 65 E4
Broadstreet Common 38 C4
Broadwas 53 G2
Broadwater *Herts.* 58 A5
Broadwater *W.Suss.* 16 D3
Broadwater Down 31 E5
Broadwaters 66 A5
Broadway *Carmar.* 35 G2
Broadway *Carmar.* 35 F1
Broadway *Pembs.* 34 B1
Broadway *Som.* 11 G1
Broadway *Suff.* 73 E4
Broadway *Worcs.* 54 D4
Broadwell *Glos.* 55 E5
Broadwell *Oxon.* 41 E2
Broadwell *Warks.* 55 G1
Broadwell House 119 F2
Broadwey 12 C4
Broadwindsor 12 A2
Broadwood Kelly 21 G5
Broadwoodwidger 7 E2
Brobury 52 C3
Brocastle 37 F5
Brochel 172 B7
Brochloch 123 G1
Brock 154 B2
Brockamin 53 G2
Brockbridge 15 F1
Brockdish 72 D4
Brockenhurst 14 B2
Brockford Green 60 C1
Brockford Street 60 C1
Brockhall 56 B1
Brockham 29 G3
Brockhampton *Glos.* 54 C5
Brockhampton *Glos.* 54 B5
Brockhampton *Here.* 53 E4
Brockhampton *Here.* 53 F2
Brockhampton Green 12 D2
Brockholes 93 F1
Brockhurst *Hants.* 15 E2
Brockhurst *W.Suss.* 30 D5
Brocklebank 117 G2
Brocklesby 96 B1
Brockley *N.Som.* 24 B1
Brockley *Suff.* 59 G2
Brockley Green 59 F3
Brock's Green 27 F1
Brockton *Shrop.* 65 E3
Brockton *Shrop.* 65 G2
Brockton *Shrop.* 64 C2
Brockton *Shrop.* 64 C4
Brockton *Tel. & W.* 65 G1
Brockweir 39 E2
Brockwood Park 28 B5
Brockworth 40 A1
Brocton 66 B1
Brodick 131 F2
Brodsworth 94 C2
Brogborough 57 E4
Brogden 101 E3
Brogyntyn 77 F4
Broken Cross *Ches.* 92 C5
Broken Cross *Ches.* 92 A5
Brokenborough 40 B4
Brokes 110 A3
Bromborough 91 E4
Brome 72 C4
Brome Street 72 C4
Bromeswell 61 E2
Bromfield *Cumb.* 117 E2
Bromfield *Shrop.* 65 D5
Bromham *Beds.* 57 F2
Bromham *Wilts.* 26 A1
Bromley *Gt.Lon.* 30 D2
Bromley *S.Yorks.* 94 A3
Bromley Cross 92 B1
Bromley Green 32 B5
Brompton *Med.* 31 G2
Brompton *N.Yorks.* 110 C3
Brompton *N.Yorks.* 112 C4
Brompton *Shrop.* 65 E2
Brompton on Swale 110 B3
Brompton Ralph 23 D4
Brompton Regis 22 C4
Bromsash 53 F5
Bromsberrow 53 G4
Bromsberrow Heath 53 G4
Bromsgrove 66 B5
Bromstead Heath 66 A1
Bromyard 53 F2
Bromyard Downs 53 F2
Bronaber 76 A4
Brondesbury 44 B4
Brongest 49 G3
Bronington 78 B4
Bronllys 52 A4
Bronnant 50 C1
Bronwydd Arms 50 A5
Bronydd 52 B3
Bron-y-gaer 35 G1
Bronygarth 77 F4
Brook *Carmar.* 35 F2
Brook *Hants.* 14 B1
Brook *Hants.* 27 E5
Brook *I.o.W.* 14 C4
Brook *Kent* 32 C4
Brook *Surr.* 29 E4
Brook *Surr.* 29 F3
Brook Bottom 93 D2
Brook End *Beds.* 57 F1
Brook End *Herts.* 58 B5
Brook End *M.K.* 57 E3
Brook End *Worcs.* 54 A3
Brook Hill 14 B1
Brook Street *Essex* 45 E3
Brook Street *Kent* 32 B5
Brook Street *Suff.* 59 G3
Brook Street *W.Suss.* 17 F1
Brooke *Norf.* 73 D2
Brooke *Rut.* 68 D2
Brookend *Glos.* 39 E3
Brookend *Glos.* 39 F2
Brookfield 93 E3
Brookhampton 42 B3
Brookhouse *Ches.* 92 D5
Brookhouse *Denb.* 77 D1
Brookhouse *Lancs.* 100 B1
Brookhouse *S.Yorks.* 94 C4
Brookhouse Green 79 F1
Brookhouses 79 G3
Brookland 19 E1
Brooklands *D. & G.* 124 C3
Brooklands *Shrop.* 78 C3
Brookmans Park 44 B2
Brooks 64 A3
Brooks Green 29 G5
Brooksby 68 B1
Brookthorpe 40 A1
Brookwood 29 E2
Broom *Beds.* 57 G3
Broom *Fife* 152 B4
Broom *Warks.* 54 C2
Broom Green 86 A3
Broom Hill *Dorset* 13 G2
Broom Hill *Worcs.* 66 B5
Broom of Dalreach 151 F3
Broomcroft 65 E2
Broome *Norf.* 73 E2
Broome *Shrop.* 64 D4
Broome *Worcs.* 66 B5
Broome Wood 137 F5
Broomedge 92 B4
Broomer's Corner 29 G5
Broomfield *Aber.* 169 H1
Broomfield *Essex* 45 G1
Broomfield *Kent* 33 D2
Broomfield *Kent* 32 A3
Broomfield *Som.* 23 F4
Broomfleet 104 A5
Broomhall Green 78 D3
Broomhaugh 119 G1
Broomhead 177 H4
Broomhill *Bristol* 39 F5
Broomhill *Northumb.* 129 E1
Broomielaw 109 F1
Broomley 119 G1
Broompark 120 B3
Broom's Green 53 G4
Brora 175 G1
Broseley 65 F2
Brotherlee 119 F4
Brothertoft 84 A3
Brotherton 103 D5
Brotton 111 F1
Broubster 183 F2
Brough *Cumb.* 108 C1
Brough *Derbys.* 93 F4
Brough *E.Riding* 104 B5
Brough *High.* 183 H1
Brough *Notts.* 82 D2
Brough *Ork.* 185 C6
Brough *Shet.* 187 E8
Brough *Shet.* 186 D5
Brough *Shet.* 187 E6
Brough *Shet.* 186 E5
Brough Lodge 186 E3
Brough Sowerby 108 C1
Broughall 78 C3
Brougham 118 B5
Broughton *Bucks.* 42 D1
Broughton *Cambs.* 70 A5
Broughton *Flints.* 78 A1
Broughton *Hants.* 27 E4
Broughton *Lancs.* 100 B4
Broughton *M.K.* 57 D3
Broughton *N.Lincs.* 95 G2
Broughton *N.Yorks.* 111 G5
Broughton *N.Yorks.* 101 F2
Broughton *Northants.* 68 D5
Broughton *Ork.* 184 D3
Broughton *Oxon.* 55 G4
Broughton *Sc.Bord.* 134 C2
Broughton *V. of Glam.* 37 F5
Broughton Astley 68 A3
Broughton Beck 107 D4
Broughton Gifford 25 F1
Broughton Green 54 B1
Broughton Hackett 54 B2
Broughton in Furness 106 D4
Broughton Mills 106 D3
Broughton Moor 117 D3
Broughton Poggs 41 E2
Broughtown 184 F3
Broughty Ferry 152 C1
Browland 187 B7
Brown Candover 27 G4
Brown Edge *Lancs.* 91 E1
Brown Edge *Staffs.* 79 G2
Brown Heath 78 B1
Brown Lees 79 F2
Brown Street 60 B1
Brownber 108 C2
Browndown 15 E3
Brownheath 78 B5
Brownhill 177 G6
Brownhills *Fife* 152 D3
Brownhills *W.Mid.* 66 C2
Brownieside 137 F4
Brownlow 79 F1
Brownlow Heath 79 F1
Brown's Bank 78 D3
Brownsea Island 13 G4
Brownshill 40 A2
Brownshill Green 67 F4
Brownsover 68 A5
Brownston 8 C2
Browston Green 87 F5
Broxa 112 C3
Broxbourne 44 C2
Broxburn *E.Loth.* 145 D2
Broxburn *W.Loth.* 143 E2
Broxholme 95 G5
Broxted 59 D5

Broxton 78 B2
Broxwood 52 C2
Broyle Side 17 G2
Bru (Brue) 179 F3
Bruachmary 175 F7
Bruan 183 J5
Brue (Bru) 179 F3
Bruera 78 B1
Bruern 55 E5
Bruernish 162 C4
Bruichladdich 138 A3
Bruisyard 61 E1
Bruisyard Street 61 E1
Brumby 95 G1
Brund 80 C1
Brundall 87 E5
Brundish *Norf.* 73 E2
Brundish *Suff.* 61 D1
Brundish Street 73 D4
Brunstock 118 A2
Brunswick Village 129 E4
Bruntingthorpe 68 B3
Bruntland 168 C2
Brunton *Fife* 152 B2
Brunton *Northumb.* 137 G4
Brunton *Wilts.* 26 D2
Brushfield 93 F5
Brushford *Devon* 21 G5
Brushford *Som.* 22 C5
Bruton 25 D4
Bryanston 13 E2
Bryant's Bottom 43 D3
Brydekirk 125 F3
Brymbo 77 F2
Brympton 12 B1
Bryn *Caerp.* 38 A3
Bryn *Carmar.* 36 B2
Bryn *Ches.* 92 A5
Bryn *Gt.Man.* 91 G2
Bryn *N.P.T.* 37 E3
Bryn *Shrop.* 64 B4
Bryn Bwbach 75 F4
Bryn Gates 91 G2
Bryn Pen-y-lan 78 A3
Brynamman 36 D1
Brynberian 49 E4
Bryncae 37 F4
Bryncethin 37 F4
Bryncir 75 D3
Bryncoch *Bridgend* 37 F4
Bryn-côch *N.P.T.* 36 D3
Bryncroes 74 B4
Bryncrug 62 C2
Brynegiwys 77 E3
Brynford 90 C5
Bryngwran 88 B5
Bryngwyn *Mon.* 38 C2
Bryngwyn *Powys* 52 A3
Bryn-henllan 48 D4
Brynhoffnant 49 G2
Bryning 100 A4
Brynithel 38 B2
Brynmawr *B.Gwent* 38 A1
Bryn-mawr *Gwyn.* 74 B4
Brynmelyn 64 A5
Brynmenyn 37 F4
Brynna 37 F4
Brynnau Gwynion 37 F4
Brynog 50 B2
Bryn-penarth 64 A2
Brynrefail *Gwyn.* 75 E1
Brynrefail *I.o.A.* 88 C4
Brynsadler 37 G4
Brynsaithmarchog 77 D2
Brynsiencyn 75 D1
Bryn-teg *I.o.A.* 88 C4
Brynteg *Wrex.* 78 A2
Bryn-y-cochin 78 A4
Brynygwenin 38 C1
Bryn-y-maen 89 G5
Buaile nam Bodach 162 C4
Bualadubh 170 C7
Bualintur 163 K2
Bualnaluib 172 E2
Bubbenhall 67 F5
Bubnell 93 G5
Bubwith 103 G4
Buccleuch 135 E4
Buchan 124 B4
Buchanan Castle 141 F1
Buchanhaven 177 K6
Buchanty 151 E2
Buchlyvie 150 A5
Buckabank 117 G2
Buckby Wharf 56 B1
Buckden *Cambs.* 57 G1
Buckden *N.Yorks.* 109 E5
Buckenham 87 E5
Buckerell 11 E2
Buckfast 8 D1
Buckfastleigh 8 D1
Buckhaven 152 B5
Buckholm 135 F2
Buckholt 39 E1
Buckhorn Weston 25 E5
Buckhurst Hill 44 D3
Buckie 176 C4
Buckies 183 G2
Buckingham 56 B4
Buckland *Bucks.* 43 D1
Buckland *Devon* 8 C3
Buckland *Glos.* 54 C4
Buckland *Hants.* 14 C3
Buckland *Here.* 53 E2
Buckland *Herts.* 58 B4
Buckland *Kent* 33 F4
Buckland *Oxon.* 41 F3
Buckland *Surr.* 30 B3
Buckland Brewer 21 E3
Buckland Common 43 E2
Buckland Dinham 25 E2
Buckland Filleigh 21 E5
Buckland in the Moor 10 A5
Buckland Monachorum 8 A1
Buckland Newton 12 C2
Buckland Ripers 12 C4
Buckland St. Mary 11 F1
Buckland-tout-Saints 9 D3
Bucklebury 42 A5
Bucklerheads 152 C1
Bucklers Hard 14 D3
Bucklesham 60 D3
Buckley (Bwcle) 77 F1
Buckley Green 55 D1
Bucklow Hill 92 B4
Buckman Corner 29 G5
Buckminster 83 D5
Bucknall *Lincs.* 83 G1
Bucknall *Stoke* 79 G3
Bucknell *Oxon.* 56 A5
Bucknell *Shrop.* 64 C5
Buckridge 65 G5
Buck's Cross 20 D3
Bucks Green 29 F4
Bucks Hill 43 F2
Bucks Horn Oak 28 D3
Buck's Mills 21 D3
Bucksburn 169 G4
Buckspool 34 C3
Buckton *E.Riding* 113 E5
Buckton *Here.* 64 C5
Buckton *Northumb.* 137 E3
Buckton Vale 93 D2
Buckworth 69 G5
Budbrooke 55 E1
Budby 94 D5
Buddon 152 D1
Bude 20 C5
Budge's Shop 6 D5
Budlake 10 C2
Budle 137 F3
Budleigh Salterton 11 D4
Budock Water 3 E3
Budworth Heath 92 A5
Buerton 79 D3
Bugbrooke 56 B2
Bugeildy (Beguildy) 64 A5
Buglawton 79 F1
Bugle 5 E4
Bugthorpe 103 G2
Building End 58 C4
Buildwas 65 F2
Builth Road 51 G2
Builth Wells 51 G2
Bulby 83 F5
Bulcote 82 B3
Buldoo 182 E2
Bulford 26 C3
Bulford Camp 26 C3
Bulkeley 78 C2
Bulkington *Warks.* 67 F4
Bulkington *Wilts.* 26 A2
Bulkworthy 21 D4
Bull Bay 88 C3
Bull Green 32 B5
Bullbridge 81 E2
Bullbrook 29 D1
Bullen's Green 44 B2
Bulley 39 G1
Bullington 96 A5
Bullpot Farm 108 B4
Bulls Cross 44 C3
Bull's Green *Herts.* 44 B1
Bull's Green *Norf.* 73 F2
Bullwood 140 C2
Bulmer *Essex* 59 G3
Bulmer *N.Yorks.* 103 F1
Bulmer Tye 59 G4
Bulphan 45 F4
Bulstone 11 E4
Bulverhythe 18 C3
Bulwark 177 H6
Bulwell 81 G3
Bulwick 69 E3
Bumble's Green 44 D2
Bun Abhainn Eadarra 178 D7
Bun Loyne 165 J4
Bunarkaig 157 D1
Bunbury 78 C2
Bunbury Heath 78 C2
Bunchrew 174 D7
Bundalloch 164 E2
Buness 186 F2
Bunessan 146 C2
Bungay 73 E3
Bunker's Hill 84 A2
Bunlarie 130 C2
Bunloit 166 C2
Bunmhullin 162 C3
Bunnahabhain 138 C2
Bunny 81 G5
Buntait 165 K1
Buntingford 58 B5
Bunwell 72 C2
Bunwell Street 72 C2
Burbage *Derbys.* 93 E5
Burbage *Leics.* 67 G3
Burbage *Wilts.* 26 D1
Burchett's Green 42 D4
Burcombe 26 B4
Burcot *Oxon.* 42 A3
Burcot *Worcs.* 66 B5
Burcott 57 D5
Burdale 104 A1
Burdocks 29 F5
Burdon 120 C2
Burdrop 55 F4
Bures 60 A4
Bures Green 60 A4
Burfa 52 B1
Burford *Oxon.* 41 E1
Burford *Shrop.* 53 E1
Burg 154 C5
Burgate 72 B4
Burgates 28 C5
Burge End 57 G4
Burgess Hill 17 F2
Burgh 60 D2
Burgh by Sands 117 G1
Burgh Castle 87 F5
Burgh Heath 30 B3
Burgh le Marsh 84 C1
Burgh next Aylsham 86 D3
Burgh on Bain 96 C4
Burgh St. Margaret (Fleggburgh) 87 F4
Burgh St. Peter 73 F2
Burghclere 27 F1
Burghead 175 J5
Burghfield 28 B1
Burghfield Common 28 B1
Burghfield Hill 28 B1
Burghill 53 D3
Burghwallis 94 C1
Burham 31 G2
Buriton 28 C5
Burland 78 D2
Burlawn 5 D3
Burleigh 29 E1
Burlescombe 11 D1
Burleston 13 D3
Burley *Hants.* 14 B2
Burley *Rut.* 69 D1
Burley *W.Yorks.* 102 B4
Burley Gate 53 E3
Burley in Wharfedale 102 A3
Burley Street 14 B2
Burley Woodhead 102 A3
Burleydam 78 D3
Burlingjobb 52 B2
Burlow 18 A2
Burlton 78 B5
Burmarsh 32 D5
Burmington 55 E4
Burn 103 E5
Burn Farm 161 E2
Burn Naze 99 G3
Burn of Cambus 150 C4
Burnage 92 C3
Burnaston 81 D4
Burnby 104 A3
Burncross 94 A3
Burndell 16 B3
Burnden 92 B2
Burnedge 92 D1
Burnend 177 G6
Burneside 107 G3
Burness 184 F3
Burneston 110 C4
Burnett 25 D1
Burnfoot *High.* 182 D6
Burnfoot *P. & K.* 151 E4
Burnfoot *Sc.Bord.* 135 G4
Burnfoot *Sc.Bord.* 135 F4
Burnham *Bucks.* 43 E4
Burnham *N.Lincs.* 96 A1
Burnham Deepdale 85 G3
Burnham Green 44 B1
Burnham Market 85 G3
Burnham Norton 85 G3
Burnham Overy Staithe 85 G3
Burnham Overy Town 85 G3
Burnham Thorpe 85 G3
Burnham-on-Crouch 46 C3
Burnham-on-Sea 24 A3
Burnhaven 177 K6
Burnhead *D. & G.* 123 G2
Burnhead *D. & G.* 124 C1
Burnhervie 169 F3
Burnhill Green 65 G2
Burnhope 120 A3
Burnhouse 141 E4
Burniston 112 D3
Burnley 101 E4
Burnmouth 145 G3
Burnopfield 120 A2
Burn's Green 58 B5
Burnsall 101 G1
Burnside *Aber.* 169 F3
Burnside *Angus* 160 D4
Burnside *E.Ayr.* 133 D4
Burnside *Fife* 151 G4
Burnside *Shet.* 186 B5
Burnside *W.Loth.* 143 E2
Burnside of Duntrune 152 C1
Burnstones 118 C2
Burnswark 125 F3
Burnt Hill 42 A5
Burnt Houses 120 A5
Burnt Oak 44 B3
Burnt Yates 102 B1
Burntcliff Top 79 G1
Burntisland 143 G1
Burnton *E.Ayr.* 132 C4
Burnton *E.Ayr.* 132 C5
Burntwood 66 C2
Burntwood Green 66 C2
Burnworthy 11 E1
Burpham *Surr.* 29 F2
Burpham *W.Suss.* 16 C3
Burra 187 C9
Burradon *Northumb.* 128 B1
Burradon *T. & W.* 129 E4
Burrafirth 186 F1
Burraland 186 C5
Burras 3 D3
Burraton *Cornw.* 8 A1
Burraton *Cornw.* 8 A2
Burravoe *Shet.* 186 E5
Burravoe *Shet.* 187 C6
Burray 185 D8
Burrells 108 B1
Burrelton 152 A1
Burridge *Devon* 11 G2
Burridge *Hants.* 15 E1
Burrill 110 B4
Burringham 95 F2
Burrington *Devon* 21 G4
Burrington *Here.* 64 D5
Burrington *N.Som.* 24 B2
Burrough Green 59 E2
Burrough on the Hill 68 C1
Burrow *Som.* 22 C3
Burrow *Som.* 12 A1
Burrow Bridge 24 A4
Burrowhill 29 E1
Burrows Cross 29 F3
Burry 36 A3
Burry Green 36 A3
Burry Port 36 A2
Burscough 91 F1
Burscough Bridge 91 F1
Bursea 104 A4
Burshill 104 C3
Bursledon 15 D2
Burslem 79 F3
Burstall 60 C3
Burstock 12 A2
Burston *Norf.* 72 C3
Burston *Staffs.* 79 G4
Burstow 30 C4
Burstwick 105 E5
Burtersett 109 D4
Burthorpe 59 F1
Burthwaite 118 A3
Burtle 24 B3
Burtle Hill 24 A3
Burton *Ches.* 91 E5
Burton *Ches.* 78 C1
Burton *Dorset* 14 A3
Burton *Lincs.* 95 G5
Burton *Northumb.* 137 F3
Burton *Pembs.* 34 C2
Burton *Som.* 23 E3
Burton *Wilts.* 40 A5
Burton *Wilts.* 25 F4
Burton Agnes 104 D1
Burton Bradstock 12 A4
Burton Coggles 83 E5
Burton End 58 D5
Burton Ferry 34 C2
Burton Fleming 113 D5
Burton Green *Warks.* 67 E5
Burton Green *Wrex.* 78 A2
Burton Hastings 67 G4
Burton in Lonsdale 108 B5
Burton Joyce 82 B3
Burton Latimer 69 E5
Burton Lazars 68 C1
Burton Leonard 102 C1
Burton on the Wolds 81 G5
Burton Overy 68 B3
Burton Pedwardine 83 G3
Burton Pidsea 105 E4
Burton Salmon 103 D5
Burton Stather 95 F1
Burton upon Stather 95 F1
Burton upon Trent 80 D5
Burton-in-Kendal 107 G5
Burton's Green 59 G5
Burtonwood 91 G3
Burwardsley 78 C2
Burwarton 65 F4
Burwash 18 B1
Burwash Common 18 B1
Burwash Weald 18 B1
Burwell *Cambs.* 59 D1
Burwell *Lincs.* 97 D5
Burwen 88 C3
Burwick *Ork.* 185 D9
Burwick *Shet.* 187 C8
Bury *Cambs.* 70 A4
Bury *Gt.Man.* 92 C1
Bury *Som.* 22 C5
Bury *W.Suss.* 16 C2
Bury End 54 C4
Bury Green 58 C5
Bury St. Edmunds 59 G1
Buryas Bridge 2 B4
Burythorpe 103 G1
Busbridge 29 E3
Busby *E.Renf.* 141 G4
Busby *P. & K.* 151 F2
Buscot 41 E3
Bush 20 C5
Bush Bank 53 D2
Bush Crathie 167 K5
Bush Green 72 D3
Bushbury 66 B2
Bushby 68 B2
Bushey 44 A3
Bushey Heath 44 A3
Bushley 54 A4
Bushley Green 54 A4
Bushton 40 C5
Bushy Common 86 A4
Busk 118 C3
Buslingthorpe 96 A4
Bussage 40 A2
Busta 187 C6
Butcher's Common 87 E3
Butcher's Cross 18 A1
Butcher's Pasture 59 E5
Butcombe 24 C1
Bute 140 B3
Bute Town 38 A2
Buthill 175 J5
Butleigh 24 C4
Butleigh Wootton 24 C4
Butler's Cross 42 D2
Butler's Hill 81 G3
Butlers Marston 55 F3
Butlersbank 78 C5
Butley 61 E2
Butley Abbey 61 E3
Butley Low Corner 61 E3
Butley Mills 61 E2
Butley Town 92 D5
Butt Green 79 D2
Butt Lane 79 F2
Butterburn 127 E4
Buttercrambe 103 G2
Butterknowle 120 A5
Butterleigh 10 C2
Butterley 81 F2
Buttermere *Cumb.* 117 E5
Buttermere *Wilts.* 27 E1
Butters Green 79 F2
Buttershaw 102 A4
Butterstone 159 F5
Butterton *Staffs.* 80 B2
Butterton *Staffs.* 79 F3
Butterwick *Dur.* 120 C5
Butterwick *Lincs.* 84 B3
Butterwick *N.Yorks.* 112 C5
Butterwick *N.Yorks.* 111 G5
Buttington 64 B2
Buttonbridge 65 G5
Buttonoak 65 G5
Buttons' Green 60 A2
Butts 10 B4
Butt's Green *Essex* 45 G2
Butt's Green *Hants.* 27 D5
Buttsash 14 D2
Buxhall 60 B2
Buxted 17 G1
Buxton *Derbys.* 93 E5
Buxton *Norf.* 86 D3
Buxton Heath 86 C3
Buxworth 93 E4
Bwcle (Buckley) 77 F1
Bwlch 52 A5
Bwlch-clawdd 49 G4
Bwlch-derwin 75 D3
Bwlchgwyn 77 F2
Bwlch-llan 50 B2
Bwlchnewydd 49 G5
Bwlchtocyn 74 C5
Bwlch-y-cibau 64 A1
Bwlch-y-ddar 77 E5
Bwlchyfadfa 50 A3
Bwlch-y-ffridd 63 G3
Bwlch-y-groes 49 F4
Bwlchyllyn 75 E2
Bwlchymynydd 36 B3
Bwlch-y-sarnau 63 G5
Byers Green 120 B4
Byfield 56 A2
Byfleet 29 F1
Byford 52 C3
Bygrave 58 A4
Byker 120 B1
Byland Abbey 111 E5
Bylane End 5 G4
Bylchau 76 C1
Byley 79 E1
Bynea 36 B3
Byrness 127 F1
Bystock 10 D4
Bythorn 69 F5
Byton 52 C1
Bywell 119 G1
Byworth 29 E5

▼C

Cabharstadh 179 F5
Cabourne 96 B2
Cabourne Parva 96 B2
Cabrach *Arg. & B.* 138 C3
Cabrach *Moray* 168 B2
Cabus 100 A3
Cackle Street *E.Suss.* 18 D2
Cackle Street *E.Suss.* 17 G1
Cacrabank 135 E4
Cadboll 175 F4
Cadbury 10 C2
Cadbury Barton 21 G4
Cadbury Heath 39 F5
Cadder 142 A2
Cadderlie 148 C1
Caddington 43 F1
Caddleton 147 G3
Caddonfoot 135 F2
Cade Street 18 B1
Cadeby *Leics.* 67 G2
Cadeby *S.Yorks.* 94 C2
Cadeleigh 10 C2
Cader 76 D1
Cadgwith 3 E5
Cadham 152 A4
Cadishead 92 B3
Cadle 36 C3
Cadley *Lancs.* 100 B4
Cadley *Wilts.* 26 D1
Cadmore End 42 C3
Cadnam 14 B1
Cadney 96 A2
Cadole 77 F1
Cadover Bridge 8 B1
Cadoxton 23 E1
Cadoxton-Juxta-Neath 37 D3
Cadwell 57 G4
Cadwst 76 D4
Cadzow 142 B4
Cae Ddafydd 75 F3
Caeathro 75 E1
Caehopkin 37 E1
Caen 183 F7
Caenby 96 A4
Caenby Corner 95 G4
Caer Llan 39 D2
Caerau *Bridgend* 37 E3
Caerau *Cardiff* 38 A5
Caerdeon 62 C1
Caerdydd (Cardiff) 38 A5
Caerfarchell 48 A5
Caerfyrddin (Carmarthen) 50 A5
Caergeiliog 88 B5
Caergwrle 78 A2
Caergybi (Holyhead) 88 A4
Caerhun 89 F5
Caer-Lan 37 E1
Caerleon 38 C3
Caernarfon 75 D1
Caerphilly 38 A4
Caersws 63 G3
Caerwedros 49 G2
Caerwent 39 D3
Caerwys 90 C5
Caethle Farm 62 C3
Caggan 167 F3
Caggle Street 38 C1
Caim *High.* 155 E3
Caim *I.o.A.* 89 E4
Caio 50 C4
Cairinis (Carinish) 170 D5
Cairisiadar 178 C4
Cairminis 171 F3
Cairnargat 168 C1
Cairnbaan 148 A5
Cairnbeathie 168 D4
Cairnbrogie 169 G2
Cairnbulg 177 J4
Cairncross *Angus* 160 D2
Cairncross *Sc.Bord.* 145 F3
Cairncurran 141 E3
Cairndoon 115 D3
Cairndow 149 D3
Cairness 177 J4
Cairney Lodge 152 B3
Cairneyhill 143 E1
Cairnhill *Aber.* 169 H2
Cairnhill *Aber.* 168 E1
Cairnie *Aber.* 169 G4
Cairnie *Aber.* 176 C6
Cairnorrie 177 G6
Cairnryan 122 B4
Cairnsmore 123 F4
Caister-on-Sea 87 G4
Caistor 96 B2
Caistor St. Edmund 86 D5
Caistron 128 B1
Cake Street 72 B2
Cakebole 66 A5
Calanais (Callanish) 178 E4
Calbost 179 G6
Calbourne 14 D4
Calceby 97 D5
Calcoed 90 C5
Calcot 42 B5
Calcott *Kent* 33 D2
Calcott *Shrop.* 64 D1
Calcotts Green 39 G1
Calcutt 40 D3
Caldarvan 141 F1
Caldback 186 F2
Caldbeck 117 G3
Caldbergh 109 F4
Caldecote *Cambs.* 58 B2
Caldecote *Cambs.* 69 G4
Caldecote *Herts.* 58 A4
Caldecote *Northants.* 56 B2
Caldecote *Warks.* 67 F3
Caldecott *Northants.* 57 E1
Caldecott *Oxon.* 41 G3
Caldecott *Rut.* 69 D3
Calder Bridge 106 B2
Calder Grove 94 A1
Calder Mains 183 F3
Calder Vale 100 B3
Calderbank 142 B3
Calderbrook 92 D1
Caldercruix 142 C3
Calderglen 142 A4
Caldermill 142 A5
Caldey Island 35 E3
Caldhame 160 C5
Caldicot 39 D4
Caldwell *Derbys.* 67 E1
Caldwell *E.Renf.* 141 F4
Caldwell *N.Yorks.* 110 A1
Caldy 90 D4
Calebreck 117 G3
Caledrhydiau 50 A2
Calford Green 59 E3
Calfsound 184 E4
Calgary 154 C4
Califer 175 H6
California *Falk.* 142 D2
California *Norf.* 87 G4
California *Suff.* 60 D3
Calke 81 E5
Callakille 172 C6
Callaly 128 C1
Callander 150 B4
Callanish (Calanais) 178 E4
Callaughton 65 F3
Callerton Lane End 120 A1
Calliburn 130 C3
Calligarry 164 C4
Callington 7 D4
Callingwood 80 C5
Callisterhall 126 A3
Callow 53 D4
Callow End 54 A3
Callow Hill *Wilts.* 40 C4
Callow Hill *Worcs.* 65 G5
Callow Hill *Worcs.* 54 C1
Callows Grave 53 E1
Calmore 14 C1
Calmsden 40 C2
Calne 40 B5
Calow 94 B5
Calrossie 174 E4
Calshot 15 D2
Calstock 8 A1
Calstone Wellington 26 B1
Calthorpe 86 C2
Calthwaite 118 A3
Calton *N.Yorks.* 101 F2
Calton *Staffs.* 80 C2
Calveley 78 C2
Calver 93 G5
Calver Hill 52 C3
Calverhall 78 D4
Calverleigh 10 C1
Calverley 102 B4
Calvert 56 B5
Calverton *M.K.* 56 C4
Calverton *Notts.* 82 B3
Calvine 158 C3
Calvo 117 E1
Cam 39 G3
Camasnacroise 156 A4
Camastianavaig 164 B1
Camasunary 164 B3
Camault Muir 174 C7
Camb 186 E3
Camber 19 E2
Camberley 29 D1
Camberwell 44 C5
Camblesforth 103 F5
Cambo 128 C3
Cambois 129 F3
Camborne 3 D3
Cambridge *Cambs.* 58 C2
Cambridge *Glos.* 39 G2
Cambridge Airport 58 C2
Cambus 151 D5
Cambus o'May 168 C5
Cambusbarron 150 C5
Cambuskenneth 150 D5
Cambuslang 142 A3
Cambusnethan 142 C4
Camden Town 44 B4
Camel Hill 24 C5
Cameley 24 D2
Camelford 5 F1
Camelon 142 C1
Camelsdale 29 D4
Camer 31 F2
Cameron House 141 E1
Camerory 167 H1
Camer's Green 53 G4
Camerton *B. & N.E.Som.* 25 D2
Camerton *Cumb.* 116 D3
Camerton *E.Riding* 105 E5
Camghouran 158 A4
Camis Eskan 141 E1
Cammachmore 169 H5
Cammeringham 95 G4
Camore 174 E2
Camp Hill *Pembs.* 35 E1
Camp Hill *Warks.* 67 F3
Campbeltown 130 C3
Campbeltown (Machrihanish) Airport 130 B3
Camperdown 129 E4
Campmuir 152 A1
Camps 143 F3
Camps End 59 E3
Camps Heath 73 G2
Campsall 94 C1
Campsea Ashe 61 E2
Campton 57 G4
Camptown 136 A5
Camquhart 140 A1
Camrose 48 C5
Camserney 158 D5
Camstraddan House 149 F5
Camus Croise 164 C3
Camus-luinie 165 F2
Camusnagaul *High.* 156 C2
Camusnagaul *High.* 173 G3
Camusrory 164 E5
Camusteel 172 D7
Camusterrach 172 D7
Camusurich 150 B1
Camusvrachan 158 B5
Canada 14 B1
Canaston Bridge 35 D1
Candacraig 168 B5
Candlesby 84 C1
Candy Mill 143 E5
Cane End 42 B5
Canewdon 46 B3
Canfield End 59 D5
Canford Bottom 13 G2
Canford Cliffs 13 G4
Canford Magna 13 G3
Canham's Green 60 B1
Canisbay 183 J1
Canley 67 F5
Cann 25 F5
Cann Common 25 F5
Canna 163 H4
Cannard's Grave 24 D3
Cannich 165 K1
Canning Town 44 D4
Cannington 23 F4
Cannock 66 B2
Cannock Wood 66 C1
Cannop 39 F1
Canon Bridge 52 D3
Canon Frome 53 F3
Canon Pyon 53 D3
Canonbie 126 B4
Canons Ashby 56 A2
Canon's Town 2 C3
Canterbury *Aber.* 176 D5
Canterbury *Kent* 32 D3
Cantley *Norf.* 87 E5
Cantley *S.Yorks.* 94 D2
Cantlop 65 E2
Canton 38 A5
Cantray 174 E7
Cantraydoune 174 E7
Cantraywood 174 E7
Cantsfield 108 B5
Canvey Island 45 G4
Canwell Hall 66 D2
Canwick 83 E1
Canworthy Water 6 C1
Caol 156 D2
Caolas *Arg. & B.* 154 B2
Caolas *W.Isles* 162 B5
Caolas Scalpaigh (Kyles Scalpay) 171 H2
Caolasnacon 156 D3
Capel *Kent* 31 F4
Capel *Surr.* 29 G3
Capel Bangor 62 C4
Capel Betws Lleucu 50 C2
Capel Carmel 74 A5
Capel Celyn 76 B3
Capel Coch 88 C4
Capel Curig 76 A2
Capel Cynon 49 G3
Capel Dewi *Carmar.* 50 A5
Capel Dewi *Cere.* 62 C4
Capel Dewi *Cere.* 50 A3
Capel Garmon 76 B2
Capel Gwyn *Carmar.* 50 A5
Capel Gwyn *I.o.A.* 88 B5
Capel Gwynfe 50 D5
Capel Hendre 36 B1
Capel Isaac 50 B5
Capel Iwan 49 F4
Capel le Ferne 33 E5
Capel Llanilltern 37 G4
Capel Mawr 88 C5
Capel Parc 88 C4
Capel St. Andrew 61 E3
Capel St. Mary 60 B4
Capel St. Silin 50 B2
Capel Seion 62 C5
Capel Tygwydd 49 F3
Capeluchaf 74 D3
Capelulo 89 F5
Capel-y-ffin 52 B4
Capel-y-graig 75 E1
Capenhurst 91 E5
Capernwray 107 G5
Capheaton 128 C3
Caplaw 141 F4
Capon's Green 61 D1
Cappercleuch 134 D3
Capplegill 134 C5
Capstone 31 G2
Capton *Devon* 9 E2
Capton *Som.* 23 D4
Caputh 159 F5
Car Colston 82 C3
Caradon Town 5 G2
Carbellow 133 E3
Carbeth 141 G2
Carbis Bay 2 C3
Carbost *High.* 171 K7
Carbost *High.* 163 J1
Carbrain 142 B2
Carbrooke 86 A5
Carburton 94 D5
Carcary 161 E4
Carco 133 F4
Carcroft 94 C1
Cardenden 152 A5
Cardeston 64 C1
Cardew 117 G2
Cardiff (Caerdydd) 38 A5
Cardiff International Airport 23 D1
Cardigan (Aberteifi) 49 E3
Cardinal's Green 59 E3
Cardington *Beds.* 57 F3
Cardington *Shrop.* 65 E3
Cardinham 5 F3
Cardno 177 H4
Cardonald 141 G3
Cardoness 123 G5
Cardow 175 J7
Cardrona 135 D2
Cardross 141 E2
Cardurnock 117 E1
Careby 69 F1
Careston 160 D4
Carew 34 D2
Carew Cheriton 34 D2
Carew Newton 34 D2
Carey 53 E4
Carfin 142 B4
Carfrae 144 C3
Carfraemill 144 C4
Cargate Green 87 E4
Cargen 125 D3
Cargenbridge 125 D3
Cargill 151 G1
Cargo 117 G1
Cargreen 8 A1
Carham 136 B3
Carhampton 22 D3
Carharrack 4 B5
Carie *P. & K.* 158 B4
Carie *P. & K.* 150 B1
Carines 4 B4
Carinish (Cairinis) 170 D5
Carisbrooke 15 D4
Cark 107 E5
Carkeel 8 A1
Carlabhagh (Carloway) 178 E3
Carland Cross 4 C4

Carlatton 118 B2
Carlby 69 F1
Carlecotes 93 F2
Carleen 2 D4
Carleton *Cumb.* 118 A2
Carleton *Cumb.* 118 B5
Carleton *Lancs.* 99 G3
Carleton *N.Yorks.* 101 F3
Carleton *W.Yorks.* 103 D5
Carleton Fishery 122 C2
Carleton Forehoe 86 B5
Carleton Rode 72 C2
Carleton St. Peter 87 E5
Carlin How 111 G1
Carlisle 118 A2
Carloggas 4 C3
Carlops 143 F4
Carloway (Carlabhagh) 178 E3
Carlton *Beds.* 57 E2
Carlton *Cambs.* 59 E2
Carlton *Leics.* 67 F2
Carlton *N.Yorks.* 103 F5
Carlton *N.Yorks.* 109 F4
Carlton *N.Yorks.* 111 F4
Carlton *Notts.* 82 B3
Carlton *S.Yorks.* 94 A1
Carlton *Stock.* 120 C5
Carlton *Suff.* 61 E1
Carlton *W.Yorks.* 102 C5
Carlton Colville 73 G2
Carlton Curlieu 68 B3
Carlton Green 59 E2
Carlton Husthwaite 111 D5
Carlton in Lindrick 94 C4
Carlton Miniott 110 C4
Carlton Scroop 83 E3
Carlton-in-Cleveland 111 E2
Carlton-le-Moorland 83 E2
Carlton-on-Trent 82 D1
Carluke 142 C4
Carlyon Bay 5 E4
Carmacoup 133 F3
Carmarthen (Caerfyrddin) 50 A5
Carmel *Carmar.* 36 B1
Carmel *Flints.* 90 C5
Carmel *Gwyn.* 75 D2
Carmel *I.o.A.* 88 B4
Carmichael 134 A2
Carmont 161 G1
Carmunnock 141 G4
Carmyle 142 A3
Carmyllie 161 D5
Carn 138 A4
Carn Brea Village 4 A5
Carn Dearg 172 D4
Carnaby 104 D1
Carnach *High.* 165 G2
Carnach *High.* 173 G2
Carnach *W.Isles* 170 D5
Carnan 170 C7
Carnassarie 148 A4
Carnbee 152 D4
Carnbo 151 F4
Carndu 164 E2
Carnduncan 138 A3
Carnforth 107 F5
Carnhedryn 48 B5
Carnhell Green 2 D3
Carnichal 177 H5
Carnkie *Cornw.* 3 D3
Carnkie *Cornw.* 3 E3
Carnmore 138 B5
Carno 63 F3
Carnoch *High.* 165 K1
Carnoch *High.* 173 J6
Carnoch *High.* 175 F7
Carnock 143 E1
Carnon Downs 4 C5
Carnousie 176 E5
Carnoustie 153 D1
Carntyne 142 A3
Carnwath 143 D5
Carnyorth 2 A3
Carol Green 67 E5
Carperby 109 F4
Carr 94 C3
Carr Hill 95 D3
Carr Houses 91 E2
Carr Shield 119 E3
Carr Vale 94 B5
Carradale 130 C2
Carradale East 130 D2
Carragrich 171 G2
Carrbridge 167 G2
Carrefour Selous 8 C5
Carreg-lefn 88 B4
Carreg-wen 49 F3
Carrhouse 95 E2
Carrick 140 A1
Carrick Castle 149 D5
Carriden 143 E1
Carrine 130 B5
Carrington *Gt.Man.* 92 B3
Carrington *Lincs.* 84 B2
Carrington *Midloth.* 144 A3
Carroch 124 A1
Carrog *Conwy* 76 A3
Carrog *Denb.* 77 E3
Carroglen 150 C2
Carrol 175 F1
Carron *Arg. & B.* 148 B5
Carron *Falk.* 142 C1
Carron *Moray* 175 K7
Carron Bridge 142 B1
Carronbridge 124 C1
Carronshore 142 C1
Carrot 160 C5
Carrow Hill 38 D3
Carrutherstown 125 F3
Carruthmuir 141 E3
Carrville 120 C3
Carry 140 A3
Carsaig 147 E2
Carscreugh 122 D4
Carse 139 F3
Carse of Ardersier 175 F6
Carsegowan 123 F5
Carseriggan 123 E4
Carsethorn 125 D5
Carsgoe 183 G2
Carshalton 30 B2
Carshalton Beeches 30 B2
Carsington 81 D2
Carsluith 123 F5
Carsphairn 123 G1
Carstairs 142 D5
Carstairs Junction 143 D5
Carswell Marsh 41 F3
Carter's Clay 27 E5
Carterton 41 E2
Carterway Heads 119 G2
Carthew 5 E4
Carthorpe 110 C4
Cartington 128 C1
Cartland 142 C5
Cartmel 107 E5
Cartmel Fell 107 F4
Cartworth 93 F2
Carway 36 A2
Cascob 52 B1
Cas-gwent (Chepstow) 39 E3
Cashel Farm 149 G5
Cashes Green 40 A2
Cashlie 157 G5
Cashmoor 13 F1
Caskieberran 152 A4
Casnewydd (Newport) 38 C4
Cassencarie 123 F5
Cassington 41 G1
Cassop 120 C4
Castell 76 A1
Castell Gorfod 49 F5
Castell Howell 50 A3
Castell Newydd Emlyn (Newcastle Emlyn) 49 G3
Castellau 37 G4
Castell-Nedd (Neath) 37 D3
Castell-y-bwch 38 B3
Casterton 108 B5
Castle Acre 71 G1
Castle Ashby 57 D2
Castle Bolton 109 F3
Castle Bromwich 66 D4
Castle Bytham 69 E1
Castle Caereinion 64 A2
Castle Camps 59 E3
Castle Carrock 118 B2
Castle Cary 24 D4
Castle Combe 40 A5
Castle Donington 81 F5
Castle Douglas 124 B4
Castle Eaton 40 D3
Castle Eden 120 D4
Castle End 67 E5
Castle Frome 53 F3
Castle Gate 2 B3
Castle Goring 16 D3
Castle Green 29 E1
Castle Gresley 67 E1
Castle Heaton 145 G5
Castle Hedingham 59 F4
Castle Hill *Kent* 31 F4
Castle Hill *Suff.* 60 C3
Castle Kennedy 122 C5
Castle Leod 174 B6
Castle Levan 140 D2
Castle Madoc 51 G4
Castle Morris 48 C4
Castle O'er 126 A2
Castle Rising 85 E5
Castle Stuart 174 E7
Castlebay (Bàgh a' Chaisteil) 162 B5
Castlebythe 48 D5
Castlecary 142 B2
Castlecraig *High.* 175 F5
Castlecraig *Sc.Bord.* 143 F5
Castlefairn 124 B2
Castleford 102 D5
Castlemartin 34 C3
Castlemilk *D. & G.* 125 F3
Castlemilk *Glas.* 142 A4
Castlemorton 53 G4
Castlerigg 117 F4
Castleside 119 G3
Castlesteads 118 B1
Castlethorpe 56 D3
Castleton *Aber.* 177 F5
Castleton *Angus* 160 B5
Castleton *Arg. & B.* 139 G1
Castleton *Derbys.* 93 F4
Castleton *Gt.Man.* 92 C1
Castleton *N.Yorks.* 111 F2
Castleton *Newport* 38 B4
Castleton *Sc.Bord.* 126 D2
Castletown *Dorset* 12 C5
Castletown *High.* 183 G2
Castletown *High.* 174 E7
Castletown *I.o.M.* 98 A5
Castletown *T. & W.* 120 C2
Castleweary 135 F5
Castlewigg 115 E2
Castley 102 B3
Caston 72 A2
Castor 69 G3
Castramont 123 G4
Caswell 36 B4
Cat and Fiddle Inn 93 E5
Catacol 140 A5
Catbrain 39 E4
Catbrook 39 E2
Catchall 2 B4
Catcleugh 127 F1
Catcliffe 94 B4
Catcott 24 A4
Caterham 30 C3
Catfield 87 E3
Catfirth 187 D7
Catford 44 C5
Catforth 100 A4
Cathays 38 A5
Cathcart 141 G3
Cathedine 52 A5
Catherine-de-Barnes 67 D4
Catherington 15 F1
Catherston Leweston 11 G3
Catherton 65 F5
Cathkin 142 A4
Catisfield 15 E2
Catlodge 166 D5
Catlowdy 126 C4
Catmere End 58 C4
Catmore 41 G4
Caton *Devon* 10 A5
Caton *Lancs.* 100 B1
Caton Green 100 B1
Cator Court 7 G3
Catrine 132 D3
Catsfield 18 C2
Catsfield Stream 18 C2
Catshaw 93 G2
Catshill 66 B5
Cattadale 138 B3
Cattal 102 D2
Cattawade 60 B4
Catterall 100 B3
Catterick 110 B3
Catterick Bridge 110 B3
Catterick Garrison 110 A3
Catterlen 118 A4
Catterline 161 G2
Catterton 103 E3
Catteshall 29 E3
Catthorpe 68 A5
Cattishall 59 G1
Cattistock 12 B2
Catton *N.Yorks.* 110 C5
Catton *Norf.* 86 D4
Catton *Northumb.* 119 E2
Catton Hall 67 E1
Catwick 104 D3
Catworth 69 F5
Caudle Green 40 B1
Caulcott *Beds.* 57 F3
Caulcott *Oxon.* 56 A5
Cauldcots 161 E5
Cauldhame *Stir.* 150 B5
Cauldhame *Stir.* 150 D4
Cauldon 80 B3
Caulkerbush 124 D5
Caulside 126 C3
Caundle Marsh 12 C1
Caunsall 66 A4
Caunton 82 C1
Causeway End *D. & G.* 123 F4
Causeway End *Essex* 45 F1
Causeway End *Lancs.* 91 F1
Causewayhead *Cumb.* 117 E1
Causewayhead *Stir.* 150 D5
Causey 120 B2
Causey Park 129 D2
Causeyend 169 H3
Cautley 108 B3
Cavendish 59 G3
Cavendish Bridge 81 F5
Cavenham 59 F1
Cavens 125 D5
Cavers 135 G4
Caversfield 56 A5
Caversham 42 C5
Caverswall 79 G3
Cawdor 175 F6
Cawkeld 104 B2
Cawkwell 96 C4
Cawood 103 E4
Cawsand 8 A3
Cawston *Norf.* 86 C3
Cawston *Warks.* 67 G5
Cawthorn 111 G4
Cawthorne 93 G2
Cawthorpe 83 F5
Cawton 111 F5
Caxton 58 B2
Caxton Gibbet 58 A1
Caynham 65 E5
Caythorpe *Lincs.* 83 E3
Caythorpe *Notts.* 82 B3
Cayton 113 D4
Ceallan 170 D6
Ceann a' Bhàigh *W.Isles* 170 C5
Ceann a' Bhàigh *W.Isles* 171 F3
Ceann Loch Shiphoirt 178 E6
Ceann Lochroag (Kinlochroag) 178 D5
Ceannaridh 170 D6
Cearsiadar 179 F6
Ceathramh Meadhanach (Middlequarter) 170 D4
Cedig 76 C5
Cefn Berain 76 C1
Cefn Bycharn (Newbridge) 38 B3
Cefn Canol 77 F4
Cefn Cantref 51 G5
Cefn Coch 77 E2
Cefn Cribwr 37 E4
Cefn Cross 37 E4
Cefn Einion 64 B4
Cefn Hengoed 38 A3
Cefn Llwyd 62 C4
Cefn Rhigos 37 F2
Cefn-brith 76 C2
Cefn-caer-Ferch 74 D3
Cefn-coch 77 E5
Cefn-coed-y-cymmer 37 G2
Cefn-ddwysarn 76 C4
Cefndeuddwr 76 A5
Cefneithin 36 B1
Cefn-gorwydd 51 F3
Cefn-gwyn 64 A4
Cefn-mawr 77 F3
Cefnpennar 37 G2
Cefn-y-bedd 78 A2
Cefn-y-pant 49 E5
Cegidfa (Guilsfield) 64 B1
Ceidio 88 C4
Ceidio Fawr 74 B4
Ceinewydd (New Quay) 49 G1
Ceint 88 C5
Cellan 50 C3
Cellardyke 153 D4
Cellarhead 79 G3
Cemaes 88 B3
Cemmaes 63 E2
Cemmaes Road (Glantwymyn) 63 E2
Cenarth 49 F3
Cennin 75 D3
Ceos (Keose) 179 F5
Ceres 152 C3
Cerist 63 F4
Cerne Abbas 12 C2
Cerney Wick 40 C3
Cerrigceinwen 88 C5
Cerrigydrudion 76 C3
Cessford 136 B4
Ceunant 75 E1
Chaceley 54 A4
Chacewater 4 B5
Chackmore 56 B4
Chacombe 55 G3
Chad Valley 66 C4
Chadderton 92 D2
Chadderton Fold 92 C2
Chaddesden 81 E4
Chaddesley Corbett 66 A5
Chaddleworth 41 G5
Chadlington 55 F5
Chadshunt 55 F2
Chadstone 57 D2
Chadwell *Leics.* 82 C5
Chadwell *Shrop.* 65 G1
Chadwell St. Mary 45 F5
Chadwick End 67 E5
Chaffcombe 11 G1
Chafford Hundred 45 F5
Chagford 10 A4
Chailey 17 F2
Chainhurst 31 G4
Chalbury 13 G2
Chalbury Common 13 G2
Chaldon 30 C3
Chaldon Herring (East Chaldon) 13 D4
Chale 15 D5
Chale Green 15 D4
Chalfont Common 43 F3
Chalfont St. Giles 43 E3
Chalfont St. Peter 43 F3
Chalford *Glos.* 40 A2
Chalford *Wilts.* 25 F3
Chalgrove 42 B3
Chalk 45 F5
Chalk End 45 F1
Challacombe 21 G1
Challister 187 E6
Challoch 123 E4
Challock 32 C3
Chalmington 12 B2
Chalton *Beds.* 57 F5
Chalton *Hants.* 15 G1
Chalvey 43 E5
Chalvington 18 A3
Champany 143 E2
Chancery 62 B5
Chandler's Cross 43 F3
Chandler's Ford 27 F5
Channel Islands 8 A5
Channel's End 57 G2
Channerwick 187 D10
Chantry *Som.* 25 E3
Chantry *Suff.* 60 C3
Chapel 152 A5
Chapel Allerton *Som.* 24 B2
Chapel Allerton *W.Yorks.* 102 C4
Chapel Amble 5 D2
Chapel Brampton 56 C1
Chapel Chorlton 79 F4
Chapel Cleeve 22 D3
Chapel Cross 18 B1
Chapel End 57 F3
Chapel Green *Warks.* 67 E4
Chapel Green *Warks.* 55 G1
Chapel Haddlesey 103 E5
Chapel Hill *Aber.* 169 J1
Chapel Hill *Lincs.* 84 A2
Chapel Hill *Mon.* 39 E2
Chapel Hill *N.Yorks.* 102 C3
Chapel Knapp 25 F1
Chapel Lawn 64 C5
Chapel Leigh 23 E5
Chapel Milton 93 E4
Chapel of Garioch 169 F2
Chapel Rossan 114 B2
Chapel Row *Essex* 45 G2
Chapel Row *W.Berks.* 27 G1
Chapel St. Leonards 97 F5
Chapel Stile 107 E2
Chapel Town 4 C4
Chapelbank 151 F3
Chapeldonan 131 G5
Chapelend Way 59 F4
Chapel-en-le-Frith 93 E4
Chapelgate 84 C5
Chapelhall 142 B3
Chapelhill *High.* 175 F4
Chapelhill *P. & K.* 152 A2
Chapelhill *P. & K.* 151 F1
Chapelknowe 126 B4
Chapel-le-Dale 108 C5
Chapelthorpe 94 A1
Chapelton *Aber.* 161 G1
Chapelton *Angus* 161 E5
Chapelton *Devon* 21 F3
Chapelton *S.Lan.* 142 A5
Chapeltown *B'burn.* 92 B1
Chapeltown *Cumb.* 126 C4
Chapeltown *Moray* 167 K2
Chapeltown *S.Yorks.* 94 A3
Chapmans Well 7 D1
Chapmanslade 25 F3
Chapmore End 44 C1
Chappel 59 G5
Charaton 6 D4
Chard 11 G2
Chard Junction 11 G2
Chardleigh Green 11 G1
Chardstock 11 G2
Charfield 39 G3
Charing 32 B4
Charing Cross 14 A1
Charing Heath 32 B4
Charingworth 55 D4
Charlbury 41 F1
Charlcombe 25 E1
Charlecote 55 E2
Charles 21 G2
Charles Tye 60 B2
Charlesfield 135 G3
Charleshill 29 D3
Charleston 160 B5
Charlestown *Aber.* 177 J4
Charlestown *Aberdeen* 169 H4
Charlestown *Cornw.* 5 E4
Charlestown *Derbys.* 93 E3
Charlestown *Dorset* 12 C5
Charlestown *Fife* 143 E1
Charlestown *Gt.Man.* 92 C2
Charlestown *High.* 172 E4
Charlestown *High.* 174 D7
Charlestown *W.Yorks.* 102 A4
Charlestown *W.Yorks.* 101 F5
Charlestown of Aberlour (Aberlour) 175 K7
Charlesworth 93 E3
Charleton 152 C4
Charlinch 23 F4
Charlotteville 29 F3
Charlton *Gt.Lon.* 44 D5
Charlton *Hants.* 27 E3
Charlton *Herts.* 57 G5
Charlton *Northants.* 56 A4
Charlton *Northumb.* 128 A3
Charlton *Oxon.* 41 G4
Charlton *Som.* 25 D2
Charlton *Som.* 24 D3
Charlton *Som.* 23 F5
Charlton *Tel. & W.* 65 E1
Charlton *W.Suss.* 16 A2
Charlton *Wilts.* 26 A5
Charlton *Wilts.* 40 B4
Charlton *Wilts.* 26 C2
Charlton *Worcs.* 54 C3
Charlton Abbots 54 C5
Charlton Adam 24 C5
Charlton Horethorne 25 D5
Charlton Kings 54 B5
Charlton Mackrell 24 C5
Charlton Marshall 13 E2
Charlton Musgrove 25 E5
Charlton on the Hill 13 E2
Charlton-All-Saints 26 C5
Charlton-on-Otmoor 42 A1
Charltons 111 F1
Charlwood 30 B4
Charminster 12 C3
Charmouth 11 G3
Charndon 56 B5
Charney Bassett 41 F3
Charnock Richard 91 G1
Charsfield 61 D2
Chart Corner 31 G4
Chart Sutton 32 A4
Charter Alley 27 G2
Charterhouse 24 B2
Charterville Allotments 41 F2
Chartham 32 D3
Chartham Hatch 32 D3
Chartridge 43 E2
Charvil 42 C5
Charwelton 56 A2
Chase End Street 53 G4
Chase Terrace 66 C2
Chasetown 66 C2
Chastleton 55 E5
Chasty 20 D5
Chatburn 101 D3
Chatcull 79 E4
Chatham 31 G2
Chatham Green 45 G1
Chathill 137 F4
Chattenden 45 G5
Chatteris 70 B4
Chattisham 60 B3
Chatto 136 B5
Chatton 137 E4
Chaul End 57 F5
Chavey Down 29 D1
Chawleigh 10 A1
Chawley 41 G2
Chawston 57 G2
Chawton 28 C4
Chazey Heath 42 B5
Cheadle *Gt.Man.* 92 C4
Cheadle *Staffs.* 80 B3
Cheadle Heath 92 C4
Cheadle Hulme 92 C4
Cheam 30 B2
Cheapside 29 E1
Chearsley 42 C1
Chebsey 79 F5
Checkendon 42 B4
Checkley *Ches.* 79 E3
Checkley *Here.* 53 E4
Checkley *Staffs.* 80 B4
Checkley Green 79 E3
Chedburgh 59 F2
Cheddar 24 B2
Cheddington 43 E1
Cheddleton 79 G2
Cheddon Fitzpaine 23 F5
Chedglow 40 B3
Chedgrave 73 E2
Chedington 12 A2
Chediston 73 E4
Chediston Green 73 E4
Chedworth 40 C1
Chedzoy 24 A4
Cheesden 92 C1
Cheeseman's Green 32 C5
Cheetham Hill 92 C2
Cheglinch 21 F1
Cheldon 10 A1
Chelford 92 C5
Chellaston 81 E4
Chells 58 A5
Chelmarsh 65 G4
Chelmondiston 60 D4
Chelmorton 80 C1
Chelmsford 45 G2
Chelmsley Wood 67 D4
Chelsea 44 B5
Chelsfield 31 D2
Chelsham 30 C3
Chelston Heath 23 E5
Chelsworth 60 A3
Cheltenham 54 B5
Chelveston 57 E1
Chelvey 24 B1
Chelwood 24 D1
Chelwood Common 17 G1
Chelwood Gate 17 G1
Chelworth 40 B3
Cheney Longville 64 D4
Chenies 43 F3
Chepstow (Cas-gwent) 39 E3
Cherhill 40 C5
Cherington *Glos.* 40 B3
Cherington *Warks.* 55 E4
Cheriton *Devon* 22 A3
Cheriton *Hants.* 27 G5
Cheriton *Kent* 33 D5
Cheriton *Pembs.* 34 C3
Cheriton *Swan.* 36 A3
Cheriton Bishop 10 A3
Cheriton Cross 10 A3
Cheriton Fitzpaine 10 B2
Cherrington 79 D5
Cherry Burton 104 B3
Cherry Green 59 D5
Cherry Hinton 58 C2
Cherry Tree 100 C5
Cherry Willingham 96 A5
Chertsey 29 F1
Cheselbourne 13 D3
Chesham 43 E2
Chesham Bois 43 E2
Cheshunt 44 C2
Cheslyn Hay 66 B2
Chessington 29 G1
Chestall 66 C1
Chester 78 B1
Chester Moor 120 B3
Chesterblade 25 D3
Chesterfield *Derbys.* 94 A5
Chesterfield *Staffs.* 66 D2
Chester-le-Street 120 B2
Chesters *Sc.Bord.* 136 A5
Chesters *Sc.Bord.* 136 A4
Chesterton *Cambs.* 58 C1
Chesterton *Cambs.* 69 G3
Chesterton *Oxon.* 56 A5
Chesterton *Shrop.* 65 G3
Chesterton *Staffs.* 79 F3
Chesterton *Warks.* 55 F2
Chesterton Green 55 F2
Chestfield 32 D2
Cheston 8 C2
Cheswardine 79 E5
Cheswick 137 E2
Cheswick Buildings 137 E2
Cheswick Green 66 D5
Chetnole 12 C2
Chettiscombe 10 C1
Chettisham 71 D4
Chettle 13 F1
Chetton 65 F3
Chetwode 56 B5
Chetwynd Aston 65 G1
Chetwynd Park 79 E5
Cheveley 59 E1
Chevening 31 D3
Cheverell's Green 43 F1
Chevington 59 F2
Chevington Drift 129 E2
Chevithorne 10 C1
Chew Magna 24 C1
Chew Moor 92 A2
Chew Stoke 24 C1
Chewton Keynsham 24 D1
Chewton Mendip 24 C2
Chichacott 7 G1
Chicheley 57 E3
Chichester 16 A3
Chickerell 12 C4
Chickering 72 D4
Chicklade 26 A4
Chickney 59 D5
Chicksands 57 G4
Chidden 15 F1
Chidden Holt 15 F1
Chiddingfold 29 E4
Chiddingly 18 A2
Chiddingstone 31 D4
Chiddingstone Causeway 31 E4
Chiddingstone Hoath 31 D4
Chideock 12 A3
Chidham 15 G2
Chidswell 102 B5
Chieveley 41 G5
Chignall St. James 45 F2
Chignall Smealy 45 F1
Chigwell 44 D3
Chigwell Row 45 D3
Chilbolton 27 E3
Chilcomb 27 G5
Chilcombe 12 B3
Chilcompton 25 D2
Chilcote 67 E1
Child Okeford 13 E1
Childer Thornton 91 E5
Childerditch 45 F4
Childrey 41 F4
Child's Ercall 79 D5
Child's Hill 44 B4
Childswickham 54 C4
Childwall 91 F4
Childwick Green 44 A1
Chilfrome 12 B3
Chilgrove 16 A2
Chilham 32 C3
Chilhampton 26 B4
Chilla 21 E5
Chillaton 7 E2
Chillenden 33 E3
Chillerton 15 D4
Chillesford 61 E2
Chilley 9 D2
Chillingham 137 E4
Chillington *Devon* 9 D3
Chillington *Som.* 11 G1
Chilmark 26 A4
Chilson *Oxon.* 41 F1
Chilson *Som.* 11 G2
Chilsworthy *Cornw.* 7 E3
Chilsworthy *Devon* 20 D5
Chilthorne Domer 12 B1
Chilton *Bucks.* 42 B1
Chilton *Devon* 10 B2
Chilton *Dur.* 120 B5
Chilton *Oxon.* 41 G4
Chilton *Suff.* 59 G3
Chilton Candover 27 G4
Chilton Cantelo 24 C5
Chilton Foliat 41 F5
Chilton Polden 24 A4
Chilton Street 59 F3
Chilton Trinity 23 F4
Chilvers Coton 67 F3
Chilwell 81 G4
Chilworth *Hants.* 14 D1
Chilworth *Surr.* 29 F3
Chimney 41 F2
Chimney Street 59 F3
Chineham 28 B2
Chingford 44 C3
Chinley 93 E4
Chinley Head 93 E4
Chinnor 42 C2
Chipchase Castle 128 A4
Chipley 23 E5
Chipnall 79 E4
Chippenham *Cambs.* 59 E1
Chippenham *Wilts.* 40 B5
Chipperfield 43 F2
Chipping *Herts.* 58 B4
Chipping *Lancs.* 100 C3
Chipping Campden 55 D4
Chipping Hill 46 B1
Chipping Norton 55 F5
Chipping Ongar 45 E2
Chipping Sodbury 39 G4
Chipping Warden 55 G3
Chipstable 22 D5
Chipstead *Kent* 31 D3
Chipstead *Surr.* 30 B3
Chirbury 64 B3
Chirk (Y Waun) 77 F4
Chirk Green 77 F4
Chirmorrie 122 D3
Chirnside 145 F4
Chirnsidebridge 145 F4
Chirton *T. & W.* 120 C1
Chirton *Wilts.* 26 B2
Chisbury 27 D1
Chiscan 130 B4
Chiselborough 12 A1
Chiseldon 41 D5
Chiserley 101 G5
Chislehampton 42 A3
Chislehurst 44 D5
Chislet 33 E2
Chiswell Green 44 A2
Chiswick 44 B5
Chiswick End 58 B3
Chisworth 93 D3
Chithurst 28 D5
Chittering 70 C5
Chitterne 26 A3
Chittlehamholt 21 G3
Chittlehampton 21 G3
Chittoe 26 A1
Chivelstone 9 D4
Chivenor 21 F2
Chobham 29 E1
Choicelee 145 E4
Cholderton 26 D3
Cholesbury 43 E2
Chollerford 128 B4
Chollerton 128 B4
Cholsey 42 A4
Cholstrey 53 D2
Cholwell *B. & N.E.Som.* 24 D2
Cholwell *Devon* 7 E3
Chop Gate 111 E3
Choppington 129 E3
Chopwell 120 A2
Chorley *Ches.* 78 C2
Chorley *Lancs.* 91 G1
Chorley *Shrop.* 65 F4
Chorley *Staffs.* 66 C1
Chorleywood 43 F3
Chorlton 79 E2
Chorlton Lane 78 B3
Chorlton-cum-Hardy 92 C3
Chowley 78 B2
Chrishall 58 C4
Chrishall Grange 58 C3
Chrisswell 140 D2
Christchurch *Cambs.* 70 C3
Christchurch *Dorset* 14 A3
Christchurch *Glos.* 39 E1
Christchurch *Newport* 38 C4
Christian Malford 40 B5
Christleton 78 B1
Christmas Common 42 C3
Christon 24 A2
Christon Bank 137 G4
Christow 10 B4
Christskirk 168 E2
Chryston 142 A2
Chudleigh 10 B5
Chudleigh Knighton 10 B5
Chulmleigh 21 G4
Chunal 93 E3
Church 100 D5
Church Aston 65 G1
Church Brampton 56 C1
Church Brough 108 C1
Church Broughton 80 D4
Church Charwelton 56 A2
Church Common 61 E2
Church Crookham 28 D2
Church Eaton 66 A1
Church End *Beds.* 57 G4
Church End *Beds.* 57 E5
Church End *Beds.* 57 G2
Church End *Beds.* 57 E4
Church End *Beds.* 57 E4
Church End *Cambs.* 70 B2
Church End *Cambs.* 70 B5
Church End *Cambs.* 70 A4
Church End *E.Riding* 104 C2
Church End *Essex* 59 D3
Church End *Essex* 59 F5
Church End *Glos.* 54 A4
Church End *Hants.* 28 B2
Church End *Herts.* 44 A1
Church End *Herts.* 58 C5
Church End *Lincs.* 84 A4
Church End *Lincs.* 97 E3
Church End *Warks.* 67 E3
Church End *Wilts.* 40 C5
Church Enstone 55 F5
Church Fenton 103 E4
Church Green 11 E3
Church Gresley 67 E1
Church Hanborough 41 G1
Church Hill *Ches.* 78 D1
Church Hill *Derbys.* 81 F1
Church Houses 111 F3
Church Knowle 13 F4
Church Laneham 95 F5
Church Langley 45 D2
Church Langton 68 C3
Church Lawford 67 G5
Church Lawton 79 F2
Church Leigh 80 B4
Church Lench 54 C2
Church Mayfield 80 C3
Church Minshull 79 D1
Church Norton 16 A4
Church Preen 65 E3
Church Pulverbatch 64 D2
Church Stoke 64 B3
Church Stowe 56 B2
Church Street *Essex* 59 F3
Church Street *Kent* 45 G5
Church Stretton 65 D3
Church Town *Leics.* 67 F1
Church Town *Surr.* 30 C3
Church Village 37 G4

Church Warsop 81 G1
Church Westcote 55 E5
Church Wilne 81 F4
Churcham 39 G1
Churchdown 40 A1
Churchend *Essex* 46 D3
Churchend *Essex* 59 E5
Churchend *S.Glos.* 39 G3
Churchfield 66 C3
Churchgate 44 C2
Churchgate Street 45 D1
Churchill *Devon* 21 F1
Churchill *Devon* 11 F2
Churchill *N.Som.* 24 B2
Churchill *Oxon.* 55 E5
Churchill *Worcs.* 54 B2
Churchill *Worcs.* 66 A5
Churchingford 11 F1
Churchover 68 A4
Churchstanton 11 E1
Churchstow 8 D3
Churchtown *Devon* 21 G1
Churchtown *I.o.M.* 98 C2
Churchtown *Lancs.* 100 A3
Churchtown *Mersey.* 91 E1
Churnsike Lodge 127 E4
Churston Ferrers 9 F2
Churt 29 D4
Churton 78 B2
Churwell 102 B5
Chute Cadley 27 E2
Chute Standen 27 E2
Chwilog 74 D4
Chwitffordd (Whitford) 90 C5
Chyandour 2 B3
Chysauster 2 B3
Cilan Uchaf 74 B5
Cilcain 77 E1
Cilcennin 50 B1
Cilcewydd 64 B2
Cilfrew 37 D2
Cilfynydd 37 G3
Cilgerran 49 E3
Cilgwyn *Carmar.* 50 D4
Cilgwyn *Pembs.* 49 D4
Ciliau Aeron 50 B2
Cilldonnain (Kildonan) 162 C2
Cille Bhrighde 162 C3
Cille Pheadair 162 C3
Cilmaengwyn 36 D2
Cilmery 51 G2
Cilrhedyn 49 F4
Cilrhedyn Bridge 48 D4
Cilsan 50 B5
Ciltalgarth 76 B3
Cilwendeg 49 F4
Cilybebyll 36 D2
Cilycwm 51 D3
Cimla 37 D3
Cinderford 39 F1
Cippenham 43 E4
Cippyn 49 E3
Cirbhig 178 D3
Cirencester 40 C2
City *Gt.Lon.* 44 C4
City *V. of Glam.* 37 F5
City Airport 44 D4
City Dulas 88 C4
Clabhach 154 A4
Clachaig 140 C1
Clachan *Arg. & B.* 149 D3
Clachan *Arg. & B.* 156 A5
Clachan *Arg. & B.* 139 F4
Clachan *High.* 164 B1
Clachan *W.Isles* 170 C7
Clachan Mòr 154 A2
Clachan of Campsie 142 A2
Clachan of Glendaruel 140 A1
Clachan Strachur (Strachur) 148 C4
Clachan-a-Luib 170 D5
Clachandhu 147 D1
Clachaneasy 123 E3
Clachanmore 114 A2
Clachan-Seil 147 G3
Clachanturn 167 K5
Clachbreck 139 F2
Clachnabrain 160 B3
Clachnaharry 174 D7
Clachtoll 180 C6
Clackmannan 151 E5
Clackmarras 175 K6
Clacton-on-Sea 47 E1
Cladach a Bhale Shear 170 D5
Cladach a' Chaolais 170 C5
Cladach Chircebost 170 C5
Cladach Chnoc a Lin 170 C5
Cladich 148 C2
Cladswell 54 C2
Claggan *High.* 156 D2
Claggan *High.* 155 G5
Claigan 171 H6
Claines 54 A2
Clandown 25 D2
Clanfield *Hants.* 15 G1
Clanfield *Oxon.* 41 E2
Clannaborough Barton 10 A2
Clanville 27 E3
Claonaig 139 G4
Claonairigh 148 C4
Claonel 174 C1
Clapgate 58 C5
Clapham *Beds.* 57 F2
Clapham *Devon* 10 B4
Clapham *Gt.Lon.* 44 B5
Clapham *N.Yorks.* 100 D1
Clapham *W.Suss.* 16 C3
Clapham Green 57 F2
Clapham Hill 32 D2
Clappers 145 G4
Clappersgate 107 E2
Clapton *Som.* 12 A2
Clapton *Som.* 24 D2
Clapton-in-Gordano 39 D5
Clapton-on-the-Hill 41 D1
Clapworthy 21 G3
Clara Vale 120 A1
Clarach 62 C4
Clarbeston 49 D5
Clarbeston Road 48 D5
Clarborough 95 E4
Clardon 183 G2
Clare 59 F3
Clarebrand 124 B4
Clarencefield 125 E4
Clarilaw 135 G4
Clark's Green 29 G4
Clarkston 141 G4
Clashban 174 D2
Clashcoig 174 D2
Clashdorran 174 C7
Clashgour 157 E5
Clashindarroch 168 C1
Clashmore *High.* 174 E3
Clashmore *High.* 180 C5
Clashnessie 180 C5
Clashnoir 167 K2
Clatford 26 C1
Clathy 151 E2
Clatt 168 D2
Clatter 63 F3
Clattercote 55 G3
Clatterford 15 D4
Clatterford End 45 E2
Clatterin Brig 161 E2
Clatteringshaws 123 G3
Clatworthy 23 D4
Claughton *Lancs.* 100 B1
Claughton *Lancs.* 100 B3
Clavelshay 23 F4
Claverdon 55 D1
Claverham 24 B1
Clavering 58 C4
Claverley 65 G3
Claverton 25 E1
Claverton Down 25 E1
Clawdd-côch 37 G5
Clawdd-newydd 77 D2
Clawfin 132 D5
Clawthorpe 107 G5
Clawton 7 D1
Claxby 96 B3
Claxby Pluckacre 84 B1
Claxby St. Andrew 97 E5
Claxton *N.Yorks.* 103 F1
Claxton *Norf.* 87 E5
Claxton Grange 121 D5
Clay Common 73 F3
Clay Coton 68 A5
Clay Cross 81 E1
Clay End 58 B5
Clay Hill 39 F5
Clay of Allan 175 F4
Claybrooke Magna 67 G4
Claybrooke Parva 67 G4
Claydene 31 D4
Claydon *Oxon.* 55 G2
Claydon *Suff.* 60 C3
Claygate *Kent* 31 G4
Claygate *Surr.* 29 G1
Claygate Cross 31 F3
Clayhanger *Devon* 22 D5
Clayhanger *W.Mid.* 66 C2
Clayhidon 11 E1
Clayhill *E.Suss.* 18 D1
Clayhill *Hants.* 14 C2
Clayhithe 58 D1
Clayock 183 G3
Claypit Hill 58 B2
Claypits 39 G2
Claypole 82 D3
Claythorpe 97 E5
Clayton *S.Yorks.* 94 B2
Clayton *Staffs.* 79 F3
Clayton *W.Suss.* 17 E2
Clayton *W.Yorks.* 102 A4
Clayton Green 100 B5
Clayton West 93 G1
Clayton-le-Moors 100 D4
Clayton-le-Woods 100 B5
Clayworth 95 E4
Cleadale 155 D1
Cleadon 120 C1
Clearbrook 8 B1
Clearwell 39 E2
Cleasby 110 B1
Cleat *Ork.* 185 D9
Cleat *W.Isles* 162 B4
Cleatlam 110 A1
Cleatop 101 E1
Cleator 116 D5
Cleator Moor 116 D5
Cleckheaton 102 A5
Clee St. Margaret 65 E4
Cleedownton 65 E4
Cleehill 65 E5
Cleestanton 65 E5
Cleethorpes 96 D2
Cleeton St. Mary 65 F5
Cleeve *N.Som.* 24 B1
Cleeve *Oxon.* 42 B4
Cleeve Hill 54 B5
Cleeve Prior 54 C3
Cleghorn 142 C5
Clehonger 53 D4
Cleigh 148 A2
Cleish 151 F5
Cleland 142 B4
Clement's End 43 F1
Clench Common 26 C1
Clenchwarton 85 D5
Clennell 128 B1
Clent 66 B5
Cleobury Mortimer 65 F5
Cleobury North 65 F4
Clephanton 175 F6
Clerklands 135 G3
Clermiston 143 F2
Clestrain 185 C7
Cleuch Head 135 G4
Cleughbrae 125 E3
Clevancy 40 C5
Clevedon 38 D5
Cleveland Tontine Inn 110 D3
Cleveley 55 F5
Cleveleys 99 G3
Clevelode 54 A3
Cleverton 40 B4
Clewer 24 B2
Clewer Green 43 E5
Clewer Village 43 E5
Cley next the Sea 86 B1
Cliburn 118 B5
Cliddesden 28 B3
Cliff *Carmar.* 35 G2
Cliff *High.* 155 F3
Cliff End 19 D2
Cliff Grange 78 D4
Cliffe *Lancs.* 100 D4
Cliffe *Med.* 45 G5
Cliffe *N.Yorks.* 103 F4
Cliffe Woods 45 G5
Clifford *Here.* 52 B3
Clifford *W.Yorks.* 102 D3
Clifford Chambers 55 D2
Clifford's Mesne 53 F5
Cliffs End 33 F2
Clifton *Beds.* 57 G4
Clifton *Bristol* 39 E5
Clifton *Cumb.* 118 B5
Clifton *Derbys.* 80 C3
Clifton *Devon* 21 F1
Clifton *Lancs.* 100 A4
Clifton *N.Yorks.* 102 A3
Clifton *Northumb.* 129 E3
Clifton *Nott.* 81 G4
Clifton *Oxon.* 55 G4
Clifton *S.Yorks.* 94 C3
Clifton *Stir.* 149 F1
Clifton *W.Yorks.* 102 A5
Clifton *Worcs.* 54 A3
Clifton *York* 103 E2
Clifton Campville 67 E1
Clifton Hampden 42 A3
Clifton Maybank 12 B1
Clifton Reynes 57 E2
Clifton upon Dunsmore 68 A5
Clifton upon Teme 53 G1
Cliftonville 33 F1
Climping 16 C3
Climpy 142 D4
Clink 25 E3
Clint 102 B2
Clint Green 86 B4
Clinterty 169 G3
Clintmains 136 A3
Clippesby 87 F4
Clippings Green 86 B4
Clipsham 69 E1
Clipston *Northants.* 68 C4
Clipston *Notts.* 82 B4
Clipstone 81 G1
Clitheroe 100 D3
Clive 78 C5
Clivocast 186 F2
Clixby 96 B2
Clocaenog 77 D2
Clochan 176 C4
Clochtow 169 J1
Clock Face 91 G3
Clockhill 177 G6
Cloddach 175 J6
Cloddiau 64 A2
Clodock 52 C5
Cloford 25 E3
Cloichran 150 B1
Clola 177 J6
Clonrae 124 C1
Clophill 57 F4
Clopton 69 F4
Clopton Corner 60 D2
Clopton Green *Suff.* 59 F2
Clopton Green *Suff.* 60 D2
Close Clark 98 A4
Closeburn 124 C1
Closworth 12 B1
Clothall 58 A4
Clothan 186 D4
Clotton 78 C1
Clough *Cumb.* 108 C3
Clough *Gt.Man.* 92 D1
Clough *Gt.Man.* 92 D2
Clough *W.Yorks.* 93 E1
Clough Foot 101 F5
Clough Head 101 G5
Cloughfold 101 E5
Cloughton 112 D3
Cloughton Newlands 112 D3
Clounlaid 155 G4
Clousta 187 C7
Clouston 185 C6
Clova *Aber.* 168 C2
Clova *Angus* 160 B2
Clove Lodge 109 E1
Clovelly 20 D3
Clovelly Cross 20 D3
Clovenfords 135 F2
Clovenstone 169 F3
Cloverhill 169 H3
Cloves 175 J5
Clovullin 156 C3
Clow Bridge 101 E5
Clowne 94 B5
Clows Top 65 G5
Cloyntie 132 B5
Cluanach 138 B4
Clubworthy 6 C1
Cluddley 65 F1
Cluer 171 G2
Clun 64 B4
Clunas 175 F7
Clunbury 64 C4
Clune *High.* 166 E2
Clune *Moray* 176 D4
Clunes 157 E1
Clungunford 64 C5
Clunie *Aber.* 176 E5
Clunie *P. & K.* 159 G5
Clunton 64 C4
Cluny 152 A5
Clutton *B. & N.E.Som.* 24 D2
Clutton *Ches.* 78 B2
Clwt-y-bont 75 E1
Clwydyfagwyr 37 G2
Clydach *Mon.* 38 B1
Clydach *Swan.* 36 C2
Clydach Terrace 38 A1
Clydach Vale 37 F3
Clydebank 141 F2
Clydey 49 F4
Clyffe Pypard 40 C5
Clynder 140 D1
Clynderwen 35 E1
Clyne 37 E2
Clynelish 175 F1
Clynfyw 49 F4
Clynnog-fawr 74 D3
Clyro 52 B3
Clyst Honiton 10 C3
Clyst Hydon 10 D2
Clyst St. George 10 C4
Clyst St. Lawrence 10 D2
Clyst St. Mary 10 C3
Clyst William 11 D2
Cnewr 51 E5
Cnoc 179 G4
Cnoc an Torrain (Knockintorran) 170 C5
Cnwch Coch 62 C5
Coachford 176 C6
Coad's Green 5 G2
Coal Aston 94 A5
Coalbrookdale 65 F2
Coalbrookvale 38 A2
Coalburn 133 G2
Coalburns 120 A1
Coalcleugh 119 E3
Coaley 39 G2
Coalmoor 65 F2
Coalpit Heath 39 F4
Coalpit Hill 79 F2
Coalport 65 G2
Coalsnaughton 151 E5
Coaltown of Balgonie 152 B5
Coaltown of Wemyss 152 B5
Coalville 67 G1
Coalway 39 E1
Coanwood 118 C2
Coast 173 F2
Coat 24 B5
Coatbridge 142 B3
Coate *Swin.* 41 D4
Coate *Wilts.* 26 B1
Coates *Cambs.* 70 B3
Coates *Glos.* 40 B2
Coates *Lincs.* 95 G4
Coates *Notts.* 95 F4
Coates *W.Suss.* 16 B2
Coatham 121 E5
Coatham Mundeville 120 B5
Cobairdy 176 D6
Cobbaton 21 G3
Cobbler's Plain 39 D2
Cobby Syke 102 A2
Cobden 10 D3
Coberley 40 B1
Cobhall Common 53 D4
Cobham *Kent* 31 F2
Cobham *Surr.* 29 G1
Cobleland 150 A5
Cobley Hill 66 C5
Cobnash 53 D1
Coburty 177 H4
Cochno 141 F2
Cock Alley 81 F1
Cock Bank 78 A3
Cock Bevington 54 C2
Cock Bridge 167 K4
Cock Clarks 46 B2
Cock Green 45 G1
Cockayne 111 F3
Cockayne Hatley 58 A3
Cockburnspath 145 E2
Cockenzie and Port Seton 144 B2
Cocker Bar 100 B5
Cockerham 100 A2
Cockermouth 117 E3
Cockernhoe 57 G5
Cockerton 110 B1
Cockett 36 C3
Cockfield *Dur.* 120 A5
Cockfield *Suff.* 60 A2
Cockfosters 44 B3
Cocking 16 A2
Cockington 9 E1
Cocklake 24 B3
Cocklaw 128 B4
Cockle Park 129 E2
Cockleford 40 B1
Cockley Beck 106 D2
Cockley Cley 71 F2
Cockpen 144 A3
Cockpole Green 42 C4
Cockshutt 78 B5
Cockthorpe 86 A1
Cockwood *Devon* 10 C4
Cockwood *Som.* 23 F3
Cockyard 93 E4
Codda 5 F2
Coddenham 60 C2
Coddington *Ches.* 78 B2
Coddington *Here.* 53 G3
Coddington *Notts.* 82 D2
Codford St. Mary 26 A4
Codford St. Peter 26 A4
Codicote 44 B1
Codmore Hill 16 C2
Codnor 81 F3
Codnor Park 81 F2
Codrington 39 G5
Codsall 66 A2
Codsall Wood 66 A2
Coed Morgan 38 C1
Coed Ystumgwern 75 E5
Coedcae 38 B2
Coed-duon (Blackwood) 38 A3
Coedely 37 G4
Coedkernew 38 B4
Coedpoeth 77 F2
Coedway 64 C1
Coed-y-bryn 49 G3
Coed-y-caerau 38 C3
Coed-y-paen 38 C3
Coed-y-parc 75 F1
Coed-yr-ynys 52 A5
Coelbren 37 E1
Coffinswell 9 E1
Cofton 10 C4
Cofton Hackett 66 C5
Cogan 38 A5
Cogenhoe 56 D1
Cogges 41 F2
Coggeshall 59 G5
Coggeshall Hamlet 59 G5
Coggins Mill 18 A1
Cóig Peighinnean 179 H1
Coilantogle 150 A4
Coileitir 156 D5
Coilessan 148 D4
Coillaig 148 C2
Coille Mhorgil 165 G4
Coille-righ 165 F2
Coillore 163 J1
Coity 37 F4
Col 179 G4
Col Uarach 179 G4
Colaboll 181 H7
Colan 4 C3
Colaton Raleigh 11 D4
Colbost 171 H7
Colburn 110 A3
Colbury 14 C1
Colby *Cumb.* 118 C5
Colby *I.o.M.* 98 A4
Colby *Norf.* 86 D2
Colchester 60 A5
Colchester Green 60 A2
Colcot 23 E1
Cold Ash 27 G1
Cold Ashby 68 B5
Cold Ashton 39 G5
Cold Aston 40 D1
Cold Blow 35 E1
Cold Brayfield 57 E2
Cold Chapel 134 A3
Cold Cotes 108 C5
Cold Hanworth 96 A4
Cold Harbour 42 B4
Cold Hatton 78 D5
Cold Hatton Heath 78 D5
Cold Hesledon 120 D3
Cold Higham 56 B2
Cold Inn 35 E2
Cold Kirby 111 E4
Cold Newton 68 C2
Cold Northcott 5 G1
Cold Norton 46 B2
Cold Overton 68 D2
Cold Row 99 G3
Coldbackie 181 J2
Coldblow 45 E5
Coldean 17 F3
Coldeast 10 B5
Coldeaton 80 C2
Colden Common 27 F5
Coldfair Green 61 F1
Coldham 70 C2
Coldharbour *Glos.* 39 E2
Coldharbour *Surr.* 29 G3
Coldingham 145 G3
Coldrain 151 F4
Coldred 33 E4
Coldrey 28 C3
Coldridge 21 G5
Coldrife 128 C2
Coldstream 136 C3
Coldvreath 5 D4
Coldwaltham 16 C2
Coldwells 177 K6
Cole 25 D4
Cole End 67 D4
Cole Green 44 B1
Cole Henley 27 F2
Colebatch 64 C4
Colebrook 10 D2
Colebrooke 10 A2
Coleburn 175 K6
Coleby *Lincs.* 83 E1
Coleby *N.Lincs.* 95 F1
Coleford *Devon* 10 A2
Coleford *Glos.* 39 E1
Coleford *Som.* 25 D3
Colegate End 72 C3
Colehill 13 G2
Coleman Green 44 A1
Coleman's Hatch 31 D5
Colemere 78 B4
Colemore 28 C4
Colemore Green 65 G3
Colenden 151 G2
Coleorton 67 G1
Colerne 40 A5
Cole's Common 72 D3
Cole's Cross 9 D3
Cole's Green 61 D1
Colesbourne 40 C1
Colesden 57 G2
Coleshill *Bucks.* 43 E3
Coleshill *Oxon.* 41 E3
Coleshill *Warks.* 67 E4
Colestocks 11 D2
Coley *B. & N.E.Som.* 24 C2
Coley *Staffs.* 80 B5
Colfin 122 B5
Colgate 30 B5
Colgrain 141 E2
Colindale 44 B4
Colinsburgh 152 C4
Colinton 143 G3
Colintraive 140 B2
Colkirk 86 A3
Coll 154 A4
Collace 152 A1
Collafirth 187 D6
Collamoor Head 6 B1
Collaton St. Mary 9 E1
Collessie 152 A3
Colleton Mills 21 G4
Collett's Green 54 A2
Collier Row 45 E3
Collier Street 31 G4
Collier's End 58 B5
Collier's Wood 44 B5
Colliery Row 120 C3
Collieston 169 J2
Collin 125 E3
Collingbourne Ducis 26 D2
Collingbourne Kingston 26 D2
Collingham *Notts.* 82 D1
Collingham *W.Yorks.* 102 C3
Collington 53 F1
Collingtree 56 C2
Collins End 42 B5
Collins Green *Warr.* 91 G3
Collins Green *Worcs.* 53 G2
Colliston 161 E5
Colliton 11 D2
Collmuir 168 D4
Collycroft 67 F4
Collyhurst 92 C2
Collynie 169 G1
Collyweston 69 E2
Colmonell 122 C2
Colmworth 57 G2
Coln Rogers 40 C2
Coln St. Aldwyns 40 D2
Coln St. Dennis 40 C1
Colnabaichin 167 K4
Colnbrook 43 F5
Colne *Cambs.* 70 B5
Colne *Lancs.* 101 E4
Colne Engaine 59 G4
Colney 86 C5
Colney Heath 44 B2
Colney Street 44 A2
Colonsay 146 C5
Colonsay House 146 C5
Colpy 168 E1
Colquhar 144 A5
Colsterdale 110 A4
Colsterworth 83 E5
Colston Bassett 82 C4
Coltfield 175 J5
Colthouse 107 E3
Coltishall 87 D4
Coltness 142 C4
Colton *Cumb.* 107 E4
Colton *N.Yorks.* 103 E3
Colton *Norf.* 86 C5
Colton *Staffs.* 80 B5
Colton *W.Yorks.* 102 C4
Colva 52 B2
Colvend 124 C5
Colvister 186 E3
Colwall 53 G3
Colwall Green 53 G3
Colwall Stone 53 G3
Colwell 128 B4
Colwich 80 B5
Colwick 82 B4
Colwinston 37 F5
Colworth 16 B3
Colwyn Bay (Bae Colwyn) 89 G5
Colyford 11 F3
Colyton 11 F3
Combe *Here.* 52 C1
Combe *Oxon.* 41 G1
Combe *Som.* 24 B5
Combe *W.Berks.* 27 E1
Combe Common 29 E4
Combe Cross 10 A5
Combe Down 25 E1
Combe Florey 23 E4
Combe Hay 25 E2
Combe Martin 21 F1
Combe Pafford 9 F1
Combe Raleigh 11 E2
Combe St. Nicholas 11 G1
Combeinteignhead 10 B5
Comberbach 92 A5
Comberford 67 D2
Comberton *Cambs.* 58 B2
Comberton *Here.* 53 D1
Combpyne 11 F3
Combridge 80 B4
Combrook 55 F2
Combs *Derbys.* 93 E5
Combs *Suff.* 60 B2
Combs Ford 60 B2
Combwich 23 F3
Comer 149 F4
Comers 168 E4
Comhampton 54 A1
Comins Coch 62 C4
Commercial End 59 D1
Commins Coch 63 E2
Common Edge 99 G4
Common Moor 5 G2
Common Platt 40 D4
Common Side 94 A5
Common Square 96 A5
Commondale 111 F1
Commonside 80 D3
Compstall 93 D3
Compton *Devon* 9 E1
Compton *Hants.* 27 F5
Compton *Plym.* 8 A2
Compton *Staffs.* 66 A4
Compton *Surr.* 29 E3
Compton *W.Berks.* 42 A5
Compton *W.Suss.* 15 G1
Compton *W.Yorks.* 102 D3
Compton *Wilts.* 26 C2
Compton Abbas 13 E1
Compton Abdale 40 C1
Compton Bassett 40 C5
Compton Beauchamp 41 E4
Compton Bishop 24 A2
Compton Chamberlayne 26 B5
Compton Dando 24 D1
Compton Dundon 24 B4
Compton Martin 24 C2
Compton Pauncefoot 24 D5
Compton Valence 12 B3
Compton Verney 55 F2
Comra 166 C5
Comrie *Fife* 143 E1
Comrie *P. & K.* 150 C2
Conchra *Arg. & B.* 140 B1
Conchra *High.* 164 E2
Concraigie 159 G5
Conder Green 100 A2
Conderton 54 B4
Condicote 54 D5
Condorrat 142 B2
Condover 65 D2
Coney Weston 72 A4
Coneyhurst 29 G5
Coneysthorpe 111 G5
Coneythorpe 102 C2
Conford 28 D4
Congash 167 H2
Congdon's Shop 5 G2
Congerstone 67 F2
Congham 85 F5
Congleton 79 F1
Congresbury 24 B1
Congreve 66 B1
Conicavel 175 G6
Coningsby 84 A2
Conington *Cambs.* 69 G4
Conington *Cambs.* 58 B1
Conisbrough 94 C3
Conisby 138 A3
Conisholme 97 E3
Coniston *Cumb.* 107 E3
Coniston *E.Riding* 105 D4
Coniston Cold 101 F2
Conistone 101 F1
Conland 176 E6
Connah's Quay 77 F1
Connel 148 B1
Connel Park 133 E4
Connor Downs 2 C3
Conock 26 B2
Conon Bridge 174 C6
Cononish 149 F2
Cononley 101 F3
Cononsyth 161 D5
Consall 79 G3
Consett 120 A2
Constable Burton 110 A3
Constantine 3 E4
Constantine Bay 4 C2
Contin 174 B6
Contlaw 169 G4
Contullich 174 D4
Conwy 89 F5
Conyer 32 B2
Conyer's Green 59 G1
Cooden 18 C3
Coodham 132 C2
Cooil 98 B4
Cookbury 21 E5
Cookbury Wick 21 D5
Cookham 43 D4
Cookham Dean 43 D4
Cookham Rise 43 D4
Cookhill 54 C2
Cookley *Suff.* 73 E4
Cookley *Worcs.* 66 A4
Cookley Green *Oxon.* 42 B3
Cookley Green *Suff.* 73 E4
Cookney 169 G5
Cook's Green 60 A2
Cooksbridge 17 F2
Cooksey Green 54 B1
Cookshill 79 G3
Cooksmill Green 45 F2
Cookston 169 H1
Coolham 29 G5
Cooling 45 G5
Cooling Street 45 G5
Coombe *Cornw.* 5 D4
Coombe *Cornw.* 20 C4
Coombe *Cornw.* 4 A5
Coombe *Cornw.* 4 C5
Coombe *Devon* 9 D3
Coombe *Devon* 10 B4
Coombe *Devon* 11 E3
Coombe *Som.* 23 F5
Coombe *Som.* 12 A2
Coombe *Wilts.* 26 C2
Coombe Bissett 26 C5
Coombe End 22 D5
Coombe Hill 54 A5
Coombe Keynes 13 E4
Coombes 17 D3
Coombes Moor 52 C1
Cooper's Corner *E.Suss.* 18 C1
Cooper's Corner *Kent* 31 D4
Cooper's Green 44 A2
Coopersale Common 45 D2
Coopersale Street 45 D2
Cootham 16 C2
Cop Street 33 E3
Copdock 60 C3
Copford Green 60 A5
Copgrove 102 C1
Copister 186 D5
Cople 57 G3
Copley *Dur.* 119 G5
Copley *W.Yorks.* 101 G5
Coplow Dale 93 F5
Copmanthorpe 103 E3
Copmere End 79 F5
Copp 100 A4
Coppathorne 20 C5
Coppenhall 66 B1
Coppenhall Moss 79 E2
Copperhouse 2 C3
Coppicegate 65 G4
Coppingford 69 G4
Coppleridge 25 F5
Copplestone 10 A2
Coppull 91 G1
Coppull Moor 91 G1
Copsale 29 G5
Copse Hill 30 B2
Copster Green 100 C4
Copston Magna 67 G4
Copt Heath 67 D5
Copt Hewick 110 C5
Copt Oak 67 G1
Copthall Green 44 D2
Copthorne 30 C5
Copy Lake 21 G4
Copythorne 14 C1
Coralhill 177 J4
Corbets Tey 45 E4
Corbiegoe 183 J4
Corbridge 119 F1
Corby 69 D4
Corby Glen 83 F5
Cordach 168 E5
Coreley 65 F5
Corfcott Green 6 D1
Corfe 11 F1
Corfe Castle 13 F4
Corfe Mullen 13 F3
Corfton 65 D4
Corgarff 167 K4
Corhampton 28 B5
Corley 67 E4
Corley Ash 67 E4
Corley Moor 67 E4
Cornabus 138 B5
Cornard Tye 60 A3
Corndon 7 G2
Corney 106 C3
Cornforth 120 C4
Cornhill 176 D5
Cornhill on Tweed 136 C3
Cornholme 101 F5
Cornish Hall End 59 E4
Cornquoy 185 E7
Cornriggs 119 E3
Cornsay 120 A3
Cornsay Colliery 120 A3
Corntown *High.* 174 C6
Corntown *V. of Glam.* 37 F5
Cornwell 55 E5
Cornwood 8 C2
Cornworthy 9 E2
Corpach 156 D2
Corpusty 86 C3
Corrachree 168 C4
Corran *Arg. & B.* 149 E5
Corran *High.* 164 E4
Corran *High.* 156 C3
Corranbuie 139 G3
Corranmore 147 G4
Corrany 98 C3
Corribeg 156 B2
Corrie 140 B5
Corrie Common 126 A3
Corriechrevie 139 F4
Corriecravie 131 E3
Corriedoo 124 A2
Corriekinloch 181 F6
Corrielorne 148 A3
Corrievorrie 166 E2
Corrimony 165 K1
Corringham *Lincs.* 95 F3
Corringham *Thur.* 45 G4
Corris 63 D2
Corris Uchaf 62 D2
Corrlarach 156 B2
Corrour Shooting Lodge 157 G3
Corrow 149 D4
Corry 164 C2
Corrychurrachan 156 C3
Corrylach 130 C2
Corrymuckloch 151 D1
Corsback 183 H2
Corscombe 12 B2
Corse *Aber.* 176 E6
Corse *Glos.* 53 G5
Corse Lawn 54 A4

Corse of Kinnoir 176 D6
Corsebank 133 G4
Corsegight 177 G5
Corsehill 125 F2
Corsewall 122 B4
Corsham 40 A5
Corsindae 168 E4
Corsley 25 F3
Corsley Heath 25 F3
Corsock 124 B3
Corston B. & N.E.Som. 25 D1
Corston Wilts. 40 B4
Corstorphine 143 F2
Cortachy 160 B4
Corton Suff. 73 G2
Corton Wilts. 26 A3
Corton Denham 24 D5
Corwar House 123 D2
Corwen 77 D3
Coryton Devon 7 E2
Coryton Thur. 45 G4
Cosby 68 A3
Coscote 42 A4
Coseley 66 B3
Cosford Shrop. 65 G2
Cosford Warks. 68 A5
Cosgrove 56 C3
Cosham 15 F2
Cosheston 34 D2
Coshieville 158 C5
Coskills 96 A2
Cosmeston 23 E1
Cossall 81 F3
Cossington Leics. 68 B1
Cossington Som. 24 A3
Costa 184 C5
Costessey 86 C4
Costock 81 G5
Coston Leics. 82 D5
Coston Norf. 86 B5
Cote Oxon. 41 F2
Cote Som. 24 A3
Cotebrook 78 C1
Cotehill 118 A2
Cotes Cumb. 107 F4
Cotes Leics. 81 G5
Cotes Staffs. 79 F4
Cotesbach 68 A4
Cotgrave 82 B4
Cothall 169 G3
Cotham 82 C3
Cothelstone 23 E4
Cotheridge 53 G2
Cotherstone 109 F1
Cothill 41 G3
Cotleigh 11 F2
Cotmanhay 81 F3
Coton Cambs. 58 C2
Coton Northants. 68 B5
Coton Staffs. 79 G4
Coton Staffs. 67 D2
Coton Staffs. 79 F5
Coton Clanford 79 F5
Coton Hill 79 G4
Coton in the Clay 80 C5
Coton in the Elms 67 E1
Cotonwood Shrop. 78 C4
Cotonwood Staffs. 79 F5
Cott 9 D1
Cottam Lancs. 100 A4
Cottam Notts. 95 F4
Cottartown 167 H1
Cottenham 58 C1
Cotterdale 108 D3
Cottered 58 B5
Cotteridge 66 C5
Cotterstock 69 F3
Cottesbrooke 68 C5
Cottesmore 69 E1
Cottingham E.Riding 104 C4
Cottingham Northants. 68 D3
Cottingley 102 A4
Cottisford 56 A4
Cotton Staffs. 80 B3
Cotton Suff. 60 B1
Cotton End 57 F3
Cottonworth 27 E4
Cottown Aber. 168 D2
Cottown Aber. 177 G6
Cottown Aber. 169 F3
Cotts 8 A1
Cottwood 21 G4
Cotwall 65 F1
Cotwalton 79 G4
Couch's Mill 5 F4
Coughton Here. 53 E5
Coughton Warks. 54 C1
Cougie 165 J2
Coulaghailtro 139 F3
Coulags 173 F7
Coulby Newham 111 E1
Coulderton 106 A2
Coull 168 D4
Coulport 140 D1
Coulsdon 30 B3
Coulston 26 A2
Coulter 134 B2
Coultershaw Bridge 16 B2
Coultings 23 F3
Coulton 111 F5
Coultra 152 B2
Cound 65 E2
Coundlane 65 E2
Coundon Dur. 120 B5
Coundon W.Mid. 67 F4
Countersett 109 E4
Countess Wear 10 C3
Countesthorpe 68 A3
Countisbury 22 A3
Coup Green 100 B5
Coupar Angus 160 A5
Coupland Cumb. 108 C1
Coupland Northumb. 136 D3
Cour 139 G5
Court Colman 37 E4
Court Henry 50 B5
Court House Green 67 F4
Court-at-Street 32 C5
Courteenhall 56 C2
Courtsend 46 D3
Courtway 23 F4
Cousland 144 A3
Cousley Wood 31 F5
Coustonn 140 B2
Cove Arg. & B. 140 D1
Cove Devon 10 C1
Cove Hants. 28 D2
Cove High. 172 E2
Cove Sc.Bord. 145 E2
Cove Bay 169 H4
Cove Bottom 73 F3
Covehithe 73 G3
Coven 66 B2
Coveney 70 C4
Covenham St. Bartholomew 96 D3
Covenham St. Mary 96 D3
Coventry 67 F5
Coverack 3 E5
Coverham 110 A4
Covesea 175 J4
Covingham 41 D4
Covington Cambs. 69 F5
Covington S.Lan. 134 A2
Cowan Bridge 108 B5
Cowbeech 18 B2
Cowbit 70 A1
Cowbridge Som. 22 C3
Cowbridge V. of Glam. 37 F5
Cowden 31 D4
Cowden Pound 31 D4
Cowdenbeath 151 G5
Cowdenburn 143 G4
Cowers Lane 81 E3
Cowes 15 D3
Cowesby 111 D4
Cowesfield Green 27 D5
Cowey Green 60 B5
Cowfold 17 E1
Cowgill 108 C4
Cowie Aber. 161 G1
Cowie Stir. 142 C1
Cowlam Manor 104 B1
Cowley Devon 10 C3
Cowley Glos. 40 B1
Cowley Gt.Lon. 43 F4
Cowley Oxon. 42 A2
Cowling Lancs. 91 G1
Cowling N.Yorks. 101 F3
Cowling N.Yorks. 110 B4
Cowlinge 59 F2
Cowmes 93 F1
Cowpe 101 E5
Cowpen 129 E3
Cowpen Bewley 121 D5
Cowplain 15 F1
Cowsden 54 B2
Cowshill 119 E3
Cowthorpe 102 D2
Cox Common 73 E3
Coxbank 79 D3
Coxbench 81 E3
Coxbridge 24 C4
Coxford 85 G5
Coxheath 31 G3
Coxhoe 120 C4
Coxley 24 C3
Coxley Wick 24 C3
Coxpark 7 E3
Coxtie Green 45 E3
Coxwold 111 E5
Coychurch 37 F5
Coylet 140 C1
Coylton 132 C4
Coylumbridge 167 G3
Coynach 168 C4
Coynachie 168 C1
Coytrahen 37 E4
Crabbet Park 30 C5
Crabgate 86 B3
Crabtree Plym. 8 B2
Crabtree S.Yorks. 94 A4
Crabtree W.Suss. 17 E1
Crabtree Green 78 A3
Crackaig 138 D3
Crackenthorpe 118 C5
Crackington 6 B1
Crackington Haven 6 B1
Crackley 79 F3
Crackleybank 65 G1
Crackpot 109 E3
Crackthorn Corner 72 B4
Cracoe 101 F1
Craddock 11 D1
Cradhlastadh 178 C4
Cradley Here. 53 G3
Cradley W.Mid. 66 B4
Cradley Heath 66 B4
Crafthole 7 D5
Crafton 43 D1
Cragg 101 G5
Cragg Hill 102 B4
Craggan Moray 167 J1
Craggan P. & K. 150 D3
Cragganruar 158 B5
Craggie High. 166 E1
Craggie High. 182 D7
Craghead 120 B2
Craibstone Aberdeen 169 G3
Craibstone Moray 176 C5
Craichie 160 D5
Craig Arg. & B. 148 C1
Craig Arg. & B. 147 E1
Craig D. & G. 124 A4
Craig High. 172 D5
Craig High. 173 G7
Craig S.Ayr. 132 B5
Craig Berthlwyd 37 G3
Craigans 148 A5
Craigbeg 157 G1
Craig-cefn-parc 36 C2
Craigcleuch 126 B3
Craigculter 177 H5
Craigdallie 152 A2
Craigdam 169 G1
Craigdarroch D. & G. 124 B1
Craigdarroch E.Ayr. 133 E5
Craigdhu D. & G. 115 D2
Craigdhu High. 174 B7
Craigearn 169 F3
Craigellachie 175 K7
Craigellie 177 J4
Craigencallie 123 G3
Craigend Moray 175 J6
Craigend P. & K. 151 G2
Craigendive 140 B1
Craigendoran 141 E1
Craigengillan 132 C5
Craigenputtock 124 B2
Craigens 138 A3
Craigglas 148 A5
Craighall 152 C3
Craighat 141 F1
Craighead Fife 153 E3
Craighead High. 174 E5
Craighlaw 123 E4
Craighouse 138 D3
Craigie Aber. 169 H3
Craigie Dundee 152 C1
Craigie P. & K. 159 G5
Craigie S.Ayr. 132 C2
Craigie Brae 169 G1
Craigieburn 134 C5
Craigieholm 151 G1
Craigielaw 144 B2
Craiglockhart 143 G2
Craiglug 169 G5
Craigmaud 177 G5
Craigmillar 143 G2
Craigmore 140 C3
Craigmyle House 168 E4
Craignafeoch 140 A2
Craignant 77 F4
Craignavie 150 A1
Craigneil 122 C2
Craigneuk 142 B4
Craignure 147 G1
Craigo 161 E3
Craigoch 132 A5
Craigow 151 F4
Craigrothie 152 B3
Craigroy 175 J6
Craigroy Farm 167 J1
Craigruie 149 G2
Craigsanquhar 152 B3
Craigton Aberdeen 169 G4
Craigton Angus 152 D1
Craigton Angus 160 B4
Craigton High. 174 D7
Craigton Stir. 142 A1
Craigtown 182 D3
Craig-y-nos 37 E1
Craik Aber. 168 C2
Craik Sc.Bord. 135 E5
Crail 153 E4
Crailing 136 A4
Crailinghall 136 A4
Crakehill 110 D5
Crakemarsh 80 B4
Crambe 103 G1
Cramlington 129 E4
Cramond 143 F2
Cranage 79 E1
Cranberry 79 F4
Cranborne 13 G1
Cranbourne 43 E5
Cranbrook Gt.Lon. 44 D4
Cranbrook Kent 31 G5
Cranbrook Common 31 G5
Crane Moor 94 A2
Cranfield 57 E3
Cranford Devon 20 D3
Cranford Gt.Lon. 44 A5
Cranford St. Andrew 69 E5
Cranford St. John 69 E5
Cranham Glos. 40 A1
Cranham Gt.Lon. 45 E4
Crank 91 G3
Cranleigh 29 F4
Cranmer Green 72 B4
Cranmore I.o.W. 14 C4
Cranmore Som. 25 D3
Cranna 176 E5
Crannoch 176 C5
Cranoe 68 C3
Cransford 61 E1
Cranshaws 145 D3
Cranstal 98 C1
Crantock 4 B3
Cranwell 83 F3
Cranwich 71 F3
Cranworth 86 A5
Craobh Haven 147 G4
Crapstone 8 B1
Crarae 148 B5
Crask Inn 181 H6
Crask of Aigas 174 B7
Craskins 168 D4
Craster 137 G5
Craswall 52 B4
Crateford 66 B2
Cratfield 73 E4
Crathes 169 F5
Crathie Aber. 167 K5
Crathie High. 166 C5
Crathorne 110 D2
Craven Arms 64 D4
Craw 139 G5
Crawcrook 120 A1
Crawford Lancs. 91 F2
Crawford S.Lan. 134 A3
Crawfordjohn 133 G3
Crawfordton 124 B1
Crawick 133 F4
Crawley Devon 11 F2
Crawley Hants. 27 F4
Crawley Oxon. 41 F1
Crawley W.Suss. 30 B5
Crawley Down 30 C5
Crawleyside 119 F3
Crawshawbooth 101 E5
Crawton 161 G2
Crawyn 98 B2
Cray N.Yorks. 109 E5
Cray P. & K. 159 G3
Cray Powys 51 E5
Crayford 45 E5
Crayke 111 E5
Crays Hill 45 G3
Cray's Pond 42 B4
Crazies Hill 42 C4
Creacombe 10 B1
Creag Ghoraidh (Creagorry) 170 C7
Creagan 156 B5
Creagbheitheachain 156 B3
Creagorry (Creag Ghoraidh) 170 C7
Creamore Bank 78 C4
Creaton 68 C5
Creca 126 A4
Credenhill 53 D3
Crediton 10 B2
Creebridge 123 F4
Creech Heathfield 23 F5
Creech St. Michael 23 F5
Creed 4 D5
Creedy Park 10 B2
Creekmouth 45 D4
Creeting St. Mary 60 B2
Creeton 83 F5
Creetown 123 F5
Creggans 148 C4
Cregneash 98 A5
Cregrina 52 A2
Creich 152 B2
Creigau 39 D3
Creigiau 37 G4
Crelevan 165 K1
Crelly 3 D3
Cremyll 8 A2
Crendell 13 G1
Cressage 65 E2
Cressbrook 93 F5
Cresselly 35 D2
Cressing 59 F5
Cresswell Northumb. 129 E2
Cresswell Staffs. 79 G4
Cresswell Quay 35 D2
Creswell 94 C5
Cretingham 60 D2
Cretshengan 139 F3
Crewe Ches. 79 E2
Crewe Ches. 78 B2
Crewe Green 79 E2
Crewgreen 64 C1
Crewkerne 12 A2
Crew's Hole 39 F5
Crewton 81 E4
Crianlarich 149 F2
Cribbs Causeway 39 E4
Cribyn 50 B2
Criccieth 75 D4
Crich 81 E2
Crich Carr 81 E2
Crich Common 81 E2
Crichie 177 H6
Crichton 144 A3
Crick Mon. 39 D3
Crick Northants. 68 A5
Crickadarn 51 G3
Cricket Hill 28 D1
Cricket St. Thomas 11 G2
Crickham 24 B3
Crickheath 77 F5
Crickhowell 38 B1
Cricklade 40 D3
Cricklewood 44 B4
Crick's Green 53 F2
Criddlestyle 14 A1
Cridling Stubbs 103 E5
Crieff 151 D2
Criggan 5 E3
Criggion 64 B1
Crigglestone 94 A1
Crimble 92 C1
Crimchard 11 G2
Crimdon Park 121 D4
Crimond 177 J5
Crimonmogate 177 J5
Crimplesham 71 E2
Crinan 147 G5
Crinan Ferry 147 G5
Cringleford 86 C5
Cringletie 143 G5
Crinow 35 E1
Cripplestyle 13 G1
Cripp's Corner 18 C1
Crix 45 G1
Crizeley 52 D4
Croalchapel 124 D1
Croasdale 117 D5
Crock Street 11 G1
Crockenhill 31 E2
Crocker End 42 C4
Crockerhill 15 E2
Crockernwell 10 A3
Crockerton 25 F3
Crockerton Green 25 F3
Crocketford (Ninemile Bar) 124 C3
Crockey Hill 103 F3
Crockham Hill 30 D3
Crockhurst Street 31 F4
Crockleford Heath 60 B5
Croes Hywel 38 C1
Croes y pant 38 C2
Croesau Bach 77 F5
Croeserw 37 E3
Croesgoch 48 B4
Croes-lan 49 G3
Croesor 75 F3
Croespenmaen 38 A3
Croesyceiliog Carmar. 36 A1
Croesyceiliog Torfaen 38 C3
Croes-y-mwyalch 38 C3
Croesywaun 75 E2
Croford 23 E5
Croft Here. 53 D1
Croft Leics. 68 A3
Croft Lincs. 84 D1
Croft Warr. 92 A3
Croftamie 141 F1
Crofthead 126 B4
Croftmore 159 D3
Crofton W.Yorks. 94 A1
Crofton Wilts. 27 D1
Croft-on-Tees 110 B2
Crofts 124 B3
Crofts of Benachielt 183 G5
Crofts of Buinach 175 J6
Crofts of Haddo 169 G1
Crofty 36 B3
Crogen 76 D4
Croggan 147 G2
Croglin 118 B3
Croick High. 174 B2
Croick High. 182 D3
Croig 154 D4
Crois Dughaill 162 C3
Croit e Caley 98 A5
Cromarty 174 E5
Crombie 143 E1
Crombie Mill 152 D1
Cromblet 169 F1
Cromdale 167 H2
Cromer Herts. 58 A5
Cromer Norf. 86 D1
Cromford 81 D2
Cromhall 39 F3
Cromhall Common 39 F4
Cromore 179 G5
Crompton Fold 93 D1
Cromwell 82 C1
Cronberry 133 E3
Crondall 28 C3
Cronk-y-Voddy 98 B3
Cronton 91 F4
Crook Cumb. 107 F3
Crook Dur. 120 A4
Crook of Devon 151 F4
Crooked Soley 41 F5
Crookedholm 132 C2
Crookham Northumb. 136 D3
Crookham W.Berks. 27 G1
Crookham Eastfield 136 D3
Crookham Village 28 C2
Crooklands 107 G4
Cropredy 55 G3
Cropston 68 A1
Cropthorne 54 B3
Cropton 111 G4
Cropwell Bishop 82 B4
Cropwell Butler 82 B4
Cros (Cross) 179 H1
Crosbie 140 D5
Crosbost 179 F5
Crosby Cumb. 117 D3
Crosby I.o.M. 98 B4
Crosby Mersey. 91 E3
Crosby N.Lincs. 95 F1
Crosby Court 110 C3
Crosby Garrett 108 C2
Crosby Ravensworth 108 B1
Crosby Villa 117 D3
Crosby-on-Eden 118 A2
Croscombe 24 C3
Crosemere 78 B5
Crosland Hill 93 F1
Cross Som. 24 B2
Cross (Cros) W.Isles 179 H1
Cross Ash 38 D1
Cross Bank 65 G5
Cross End Beds. 57 F2
Cross End Essex 59 G4
Cross Foxes Inn 63 D1
Cross Gates 102 C4
Cross Green Devon 7 D2
Cross Green Staffs. 66 B2
Cross Green Suff. 60 A2
Cross Green Suff. 59 G2
Cross Green Suff. 59 G2
Cross Hands Carmar. 36 B1
Cross Hands Pembs. 35 D1
Cross Hill 81 F3
Cross Hills 101 G3
Cross Houses 65 E2
Cross in Hand 18 A1
Cross Inn Cere. 49 G2
Cross Inn Cere. 50 B1
Cross Inn R.C.T. 37 G4
Cross Keys 40 A5
Cross Lane 15 E4
Cross Lane Head 65 G3
Cross Lanes Cornw. 4 B5
Cross Lanes Cornw. 3 D4
Cross Lanes N.Yorks. 103 E1
Cross Lanes Wrex. 78 A3
Cross of Jackston 169 F1
Cross o'th'hands 81 D3
Cross Street 72 C4
Crossaig 139 G4
Crossapol 154 A4
Crossapoll 154 A2
Cross-at-Hand 31 G4
Crossbush 16 C3
Crosscanonby 117 D3
Crossdale Street 86 D2
Crossens 91 E1
Crossflatts 102 A3
Crossford D. & G. 124 C2
Crossford Fife 143 E1
Crossford S.Lan. 142 C5
Crossgate Lincs. 84 A5
Crossgate Staffs. 79 G4
Crossgatehall 144 A3
Crossgates Fife 143 F1
Crossgates N.Yorks. 112 D4
Crossgates P. & K. 151 F2
Crossgates Powys 51 G1
Crossgill 100 B1
Crosshands 132 C2
Crosshill Fife 151 G5
Crosshill S.Ayr. 132 B5
Crosshouse 132 B2
Crosskeys 38 B3
Crosskirk 183 F1
Crosslanes 64 C1
Crosslee Renf. 141 F3
Crosslee Sc.Bord. 135 E4
Crosslet 141 F2
Crossmichael 124 B4
Crossmoor 100 A4
Crossroads Aber. 169 F5
Crossroads E.Ayr. 132 C2
Crossway Mon. 38 D1
Crossway Powys 51 G2
Crossway Green Mon. 39 E3
Crossway Green Worcs. 54 A1
Crossways Dorset 13 D4
Crossways Glos. 39 E1
Crosswell 49 E4
Crosswood 62 C5
Crosthwaite 107 F3
Croston 91 F1
Crostwick 87 D4
Crostwight 87 E3
Crothair 178 D4
Crouch 31 F3
Crouch End 44 B4
Crouch Hill 12 D1
Croucheston 26 B5
Croughton 56 A4
Crovie 177 G4
Crow 14 A2
Crow Edge 93 F2
Crow Green 45 E3
Crow Hill 53 F5
Crowan 2 D3
Crowborough 31 E5
Crowborough Warren 31 E5
Crowcombe 23 E4
Crowdecote 80 C1
Crowden 93 E3
Crowdhill 27 F5
Crowell 42 C3
Crowfield Northants. 56 B3
Crowfield Suff. 60 C2
Crowhurst E.Suss. 18 C2
Crowhurst Surr. 30 C4
Crowhurst Lane End 30 C4
Crowland Lincs. 70 A1
Crowland Suff. 72 B4
Crowlas 2 C3
Crowle N.Lincs. 95 E1
Crowle Worcs. 54 B2
Crowle Green 54 B2
Crowmarsh Gifford 42 B4
Crown Corner 73 D4
Crownhill 8 A2
Crownthorpe 86 B5
Crowntown 2 D3
Crow's Nest 5 G3
Crows-an-wra 2 A4
Crowsnest 64 C2
Crowthorne 28 D1
Crowton 91 G5
Croxall 67 E1
Croxby 96 B3
Croxdale 120 B4
Croxden 80 B4
Croxley Green 43 F3
Croxton Cambs. 58 A2
Croxton N.Lincs. 96 A1
Croxton Norf. 71 G4
Croxton Staffs. 79 E4
Croxton Green 78 C2
Croxton Kerrial 82 D5
Croxtonbank 79 E4
Croy High. 174 E7
Croy N.Lan. 142 B2
Croyde 21 E2
Croyde Bay 21 E2
Croydon Cambs. 58 B3
Croydon Gt.Lon. 30 C2
Cruach 138 B4
Cruchie 176 D6
Cruckmeole 64 D2
Cruckton 64 D1
Cruden Bay 169 J1
Crudgington 65 F1
Crudwell 40 B3
Crug 64 A5
Crugmeer 4 D2
Crugybar 50 C4
Crùlabhig 178 D4
Crumlin 38 B3
Crumpsall 92 C2
Crumpsbrook 65 F5
Crundale Kent 32 C4
Crundale Pembs. 34 C1
Crunwere Farm 35 E1
Crutherland Farm 142 A4
Cruwys Morchard 10 B1
Crux Easton 27 F2
Crwbin 36 A1
Cryers Hill 43 D3
Crymlyn 89 E5
Crymych 49 E4
Crynant 37 D2
Crystal Palace 44 C5
Cuaig 172 D6
Cubbington 55 F1
Cubert 4 B4
Cubley 93 G2
Cublington Bucks. 56 D5
Cublington Here. 52 D4
Cuckfield 17 F1
Cucklington 25 E5
Cuckney 94 C5
Cuckold's Green 73 F3
Cuckoo Bridge 84 A5
Cuckoo's Corner 28 C3
Cuckoo's Nest 78 A1
Cuddesdon 42 A2
Cuddington Bucks. 42 C1
Cuddington Ches. 91 G5
Cuddington Heath 78 B3
Cuddy Hill 100 A4
Cudham 30 D3
Cudlipptown 7 F3
Cudworth S.Yorks. 94 A2
Cudworth Som. 11 G1
Cuerdley Cross 91 G4
Cuffley 44 C2
Cuidhaseadair 179 H2
Cuidhir 162 B4
Cuidhtinis (Quidinish) 171 F3
Cuidrach 171 J6
Cuilmuich 149 D5
Cuil-uaine 148 B1
Culag 149 F5
Culbo 174 D5
Culbokie 174 D6
Culbone 22 B3
Culburnie 174 B7
Culcabock 174 D7
Culcharan 148 B1
Culcharry 175 F6
Culcheth 92 A3
Culdrain 168 D1
Culduie 172 D7
Culford 59 G1
Culfordheath 71 G5
Culgaith 118 C5
Culgower 182 E7
Culham 42 A3
Culindrach 140 A4
Culkein 180 C5
Culkerton 40 B3
Cullachie 167 G2
Cullen 176 D4
Cullercoats 129 F4
Cullicudden 174 D5
Culligran 173 K7
Cullingworth 101 G4
Cullipool 147 G3
Cullivoe 186 E2
Culloch 150 C3
Culloden 174 E7
Cullompton 10 D2
Culmaily 175 F1
Culmalzie 123 E5
Culmington 65 D4
Culmstock 11 E1
Culnacraig 173 G1
Culnadalloch 148 B1
Culnaknock 172 B5
Culnamean 163 K2
Culpho 60 D3
Culquhirk 123 F5
Culrain 174 C2
Culross 143 D1
Culroy 132 B4
Culsh 168 B5
Culshabbin 123 E5
Culswick 187 B8
Culter Allers Farm 134 B2
Cultercullen 169 H2
Cults Aber. 168 D1
Cults Aberdeen 169 G4
Cults D. & G. 115 E2
Cultybraggan Camp 150 C3
Culverhouse Cross 38 A5
Culverstone Green 31 F2
Culverthorpe 83 F3
Culvie 176 D5
Culworth 56 A3
Cumberhead 133 F2
Cumberlow Green 58 B4
Cumbernauld 142 B2
Cumberworth 97 F5
Cuminestown 177 G6
Cumloden 123 F4
Cummersdale 117 G1
Cummertrees 125 F4
Cummingstown 175 J5
Cumnock 133 D3
Cumnor 41 G2
Cumrew 118 B2
Cumrue 125 E2
Cumstoun 124 A5
Cumwhinton 118 A2
Cumwhitton 118 B2
Cundall 110 D5
Cunninghamhead 141 E5
Cunningsburgh 187 D10
Cunnister 186 E3
Cunnoquhie 152 B3
Cupar 152 B3
Cupar Muir 152 B3
Curbar 93 G5
Curborough 66 D1
Curbridge Hants. 15 E1
Curbridge Oxon. 41 F2
Curdridge 15 E1
Curdworth 67 D3
Curland 11 F1
Curlew Green 61 E1
Curling Tye Green 46 B2
Curload 24 A5
Curridge 41 G5
Currie 143 F3
Curry Mallet 24 A5
Curry Rivel 24 A5
Curteis' Corner 32 A5
Curtisden Green 31 G4
Curtisknowle 8 D2
Cury 3 D4
Cusgarne 4 B5
Cushnie 177 F4
Cushuish 23 E4
Cusop 52 B3
Cusworth 94 C2
Cutcloy 115 E3
Cutcombe 22 C4
Cutgate 92 C1
Cuthill 174 E3
Cutiau 62 C1
Cutlers Green 59 D4
Cutnall Green 54 A1
Cutsdean 54 C4
Cutsyke 102 D5
Cutthorpe 94 A5
Cutts 187 D9
Cuttyhill 177 J5
Cuxham 42 B3
Cuxton 31 G2
Cuxwold 96 B2
Cwm B.Gwent 38 A2
Cwm Denb. 90 B5
Cwm Ffrwd-oer 38 B2
Cwm Gwaun 48 D4
Cwm Head 64 D4
Cwm Irfon 51 E3
Cwm Penmachno 76 A3
Cwm Plysgog 49 E3
Cwmafan 37 D3
Cwmaman 37 G3
Cwmann 50 B3
Cwmbach Carmar. 49 F5
Cwmbach Carmar. 36 A2
Cwmbach Powys 52 A4
Cwmbach Powys 51 G2
Cwmbach R.C.T. 37 G2
Cwmbelan 63 F4
Cwmbrân 38 B3
Cwmbrwyno 62 D4
Cwmcarn 38 B3
Cwmcarvan 39 D2
Cwm-Cewydd 63 E1
Cwm-cou 49 F3
Cwmcrawnon 38 A1
Cwmdare 37 F2
Cwmdu Carmar. 50 C4
Cwmdu Powys 52 A5
Cwmduad 49 G4
Cwmerfyn 62 D4
Cwmfelin 37 G2
Cwmfelin Boeth 35 E1
Cwmfelin Mynach 49 F5
Cwmfelinfach 38 A3
Cwmffrwd 36 A1
Cwmgiedd 37 D1
Cwmgors 36 D1
Cwmgwili 36 B1
Cwmgwrach 37 E2
Cwmgwyn 36 C3
Cwmhiraeth 49 G4
Cwmifor 50 C5
Cwmisfael 36 A1
Cwm-Llinau 63 E2
Cwmllyfri 35 G1
Cwmllynfell 36 D1
Cwm-mawr 36 B1
Cwm-miles 49 E5
Cwm-Morgan 49 F4
Cwm-parc 37 F3
Cwmpengraig 49 G4
Cwmpennar 37 G2
Cwmsychbant 50 A3
Cwmsymlog 62 C4
Cwmtillery 38 B2
Cwm-twrch Isaf 37 D1
Cwm-twrch Uchaf 37 D1
Cwm-y-glo 75 E1
Cwmyoy 52 C5
Cwm-yr-Eglwys 48 D3
Cwmyrhaiadr 63 D3
Cwmystwyth 63 D5
Cwrt 62 C2
Cwrt-newydd 50 A3
Cwrt-y-cadno 50 C3
Cwrt-y-gollen 38 B1
Cydwelli (Kidwelly) 36 A2
Cyffylliog 77 D2
Cyfronydd 64 A2
Cymau 77 F2
Cymmer N.P.T. 37 E3
Cymmer R.C.T. 37 G3
Cyncoed 38 A4
Cynghordy 51 E4
Cynheidre 36 A2
Cynwyd 77 D3
Cynwyl Elfed 49 G5

▼D

Dabton 124 C1
Daccombe 9 F1
Dacre Cumb. 118 A5
Dacre N.Yorks. 102 A1
Dacre Banks 102 A1
Daddry Shield 119 E4
Dadford 56 B4
Dadlington 67 G3

Dafen 36 B2
Daffy Green 86 A5
Dagdale 80 B4
Dagenham 45 D4
Daggons 14 A1
Daglingworth 40 B2
Dagnall 43 E1
Dail 148 C1
Dail Beag 178 E3
Dail Bho Dheas (South Dell) 179 G1
Dail Bho Thuath (North Dell) 179 G1
Dail Mòr 178 E3
Dailly 132 A5
Dailnamac 148 B1
Dainton 9 E1
Dairsie (Osnaburgh) 152 C3
Dairy House 105 E5
Daisy Bank 66 C3
Daisy Green 60 B1
Dalabrog 162 C2
Dalavich 148 B3
Dalballoch 166 D5
Dalbeattie 124 C4
Dalblair 133 E4
Dalbog 161 D2
Dalbreck 182 C7
Dalbury 81 D4
Dalby I.o.M. 98 A4
Dalby Lincs. 84 C1
Dalby N.Yorks. 111 F5
Dalcairnie 132 C5
Dalchalloch 158 C3
Dalchalm 175 G1
Dalchenna 148 C4
Dalchirach 167 J1
Dalchork 181 H7
Dalchreichart 165 J3
Dalchruin 150 C3
Dalcross 174 E7
Dalderby 84 A1
Dalditch 10 D4
Daldownie 167 K4
Dale Cumb. 118 B3
Dale Gt.Man. 93 D2
Dale Pembs. 34 B2
Dale Abbey 81 F4
Dale End Derbys. 80 D1
Dale End N.Yorks. 101 F3
Dale Head 107 F1
Dale of Walls 187 A7
Dale Park 16 B2
Dalehouse 111 G1
Dalelia 155 G3
Daless 167 F1
Dalestie 167 J3
Dalfad 168 B4
Dalganachan 183 F4
Dalgarven 141 D5
Dalgety Bay 143 F1
Dalgig 133 D4
Dalginross 150 C2
Dalgonar 133 F5
Dalguise 159 E5
Dalhalvaig 182 D3
Dalham 59 F1
Daligan 141 E1
Dalinlongart 140 C1
Dalivaddy 130 B3
Daljarrock 122 C2
Dalkeith 144 A3
Dallachulish 156 B5
Dallas 175 J6
Dallaschyle 175 F7
Dallash 123 F4
Dalleagles 133 D4
Dallinghoo 61 D2
Dallington E.Suss. 18 B2
Dallington Northants. 56 C1
Dallow 110 A5
Dalmadilly 169 F3
Dalmally 149 D2
Dalmarnock 159 F5
Dalmary 150 A5
Dalmellington 132 C5
Dalmeny 143 F2
Dalmichy 181 H7
Dalmigavie 166 E3
Dalmore 174 D5
Dalmuir 141 F2
Dalmunzie House Hotel 159 F2
Dalnabreck 155 G3
Dalnacarn 159 F3
Dalnaglar Castle 159 G3
Dalnaha 147 F2
Dalnahaitnach 167 F3
Dalnamain 174 E2
Dalnatrat 156 B4
Dalnavert 167 F4
Dalnavie 174 D4
Dalness 157 D4
Dalnessie 181 J7
Dalnigap 122 C3
Dalqueich 151 F4
Dalreoch 122 C2
Dalriech 150 C1
Dalroy 174 E7
Dalrulzian 159 G4
Dalry 141 D5
Dalrymple 132 B4
Dalscote 56 B2
Dalserf 142 B4
Dalsetter 186 E3
Dalshangan 123 G2
Dalskairth 124 D3
Dalston 117 G1
Dalswinton 124 D2
Daltomach 166 E2
Dalton Cumb. 107 G5
Dalton D. & G. 125 F3
Dalton Lancs. 91 F2
Dalton N.Yorks. 110 D5
Dalton N.Yorks. 110 A2
Dalton Northumb. 128 D4
Dalton Northumb. 119 F2
Dalton S.Yorks. 94 B3
Dalton Magna 94 B3
Dalton Piercy 121 D4
Dalton-in-Furness 106 D5
Dalton-le-Dale 120 D3
Dalton-on-Tees 110 B2
Daltote 139 F1
Daltra 175 G7
Dalveich 150 B2
Dalvennan 132 B4
Dalvourn 166 D1
Dalwhinnie 158 B1
Dalwood 11 F2
Dam Green 72 B3
Damask Green 58 A5
Damerham 14 A1
Damgate 87 F5
Damnaglaur 114 B3
Damside 151 E3
Danaway 32 A2
Danbury 45 G2
Danby 111 G2
Danby Wiske 110 C3
Dancers Hill 44 B3
Dandaleith 175 K7
Danderhall 144 A3
Dane Bank 92 D3
Dane End 58 B5
Dane Hills 68 A2
Danebridge 79 G1
Danehill 17 G1
Danesmoor 81 F1
Danestone 169 H3
Daniel's Water 32 B4
Danskine 144 C3
Danthorpe 105 E4
Danzey Green 54 D1
Darby End 66 B4
Darby Green 28 D1
Darenth 45 E5
Daresbury 91 G4
Darfield 94 B2
Dargate 32 C2
Dargues 128 A2
Darite 5 G3
Darland 31 G2
Darlaston 66 B3
Darley 102 B2
Darley Bridge 81 D1
Darley Dale 81 D1
Darley Head 102 A2
Darley Hillside 81 D1
Darlingscott 55 E3
Darlington 110 B1
Darliston 78 C4
Darlton 95 E5
Darnabo 177 F6
Darnall 94 A4
Darnconner 133 D3
Darnford 169 F5
Darngarroch 124 A4
Darnick 135 G2
Darowen 63 E2
Darra 177 F6
Darracott 20 C4
Darras Hall 129 D4
Darrington 94 B1
Darrow Green 73 D3
Darsham 61 F1
Dartfield 177 J5
Dartford 45 E5
Dartington 9 D1
Dartmeet 7 G3
Dartmouth 9 E2
Darton 94 A1
Darvel 133 D2
Darvell 18 C1
Darwell Hole 18 B2
Darwen 100 C5
Datchet 43 E5
Datchworth 44 B1
Datchworth Green 44 B1
Daubhill 92 A2
Daugh of Kinermony 175 K7
Dauntsey 40 B4
Dauntsey Green 40 B4
Dauntsey Lock 40 B4
Dava 167 H1
Davaar 130 C4
Davan 168 C4
Davenham 92 A5
Davenport Green 92 C4
Daventry 56 A1
Davidstow 5 F1
Davington 134 D5
Daviot Aber. 169 F2
Daviot High. 166 E1
Davoch of Grange 176 C5
Davyhulme 92 B3
Dawley 65 F2
Dawlish 10 C5
Dawn 89 G5
Daws Heath 46 B4
Daw's House 6 D2
Dawsmere 84 C4
Day Green 79 E2
Dayhills 79 G4
Dayhouse Bank 66 B5
Daylesford 55 E5
Ddôl 90 C5
Deadman's Cross 57 G3
Deadwaters 142 B5
Deal 33 F3
Deal Hall 46 D3
Dean Cumb. 117 D4
Dean Devon 8 D1
Dean Dorset 13 F1
Dean Hants. 15 E1
Dean Oxon. 55 F5
Dean Som. 25 D3
Dean Bank 120 B4
Dean Cross 21 F1
Dean Head 93 G2
Dean Prior 8 D1
Dean Row 92 C4
Dean Street 31 G3
Deanburnhaugh 135 E4
Deane Gt.Man. 92 A2
Deane Hants. 27 G2
Deanland 13 F1
Deanlane End 15 G1
Deans Bottom 32 A2
Deanscales 117 D4
Deansgreen 92 A4
Deanshanger 56 C4
Deanston 150 C4
Dearham 117 D3
Debach 60 D2
Debate 126 A3
Debden 59 D4
Debden Cross 59 D4
Debden Green Essex 59 D4
Debden Green Essex 44 D3
Debenham 60 C1
Deblin's Green 54 A3
Dechmont 143 E2
Decker Hill 65 G1
Deddington 55 G4
Dedham 60 B4
Dedham Heath 60 B4
Dedworth 43 E5
Deecastle 168 C5
Deene 69 E3
Deenethorpe 69 E3
Deepcar 93 G3
Deepcut 29 E2
Deepdale Cumb. 108 C4
Deepdale N.Yorks. 109 D5
Deeping Gate 69 G2
Deeping St. James 69 G2
Deeping St. Nicholas 70 A1
Deepweir 39 D4
Deerhill 176 C5
Deerhurst 54 A5
Deerhurst Walton 54 A5
Deerton Street 32 B2
Defford 54 B3
Defynnog 51 F5
Deganwy 89 F5
Degnish 147 G3
Deighton N.Yorks. 110 C2
Deighton W.Yorks. 93 F1
Deighton York 103 F3
Deiniolen 75 E1
Delabole 5 E1
Delamere 78 C1
Delavorar 167 J3
Delfrigs 169 H2
Dell Lodge 167 H3
Dell Quay 16 A3
Delliefure 167 H1
Delly End 41 F1
Delnabo 167 J3
Delny 174 E4
Delph 93 D2
Delphorrie 168 C3
Delves 120 A3
Delvine 159 G5
Dembleby 83 F4
Denaby 94 B3
Denaby Main 94 B3
Denbigh (Dinbych) 76 D1
Denbury 9 E1
Denby 81 E3
Denby Dale 93 G2
Denchworth 41 F3
Dendron 106 D5
Denend 168 E1
Denford 69 E5
Dengie 46 C2
Denham Bucks. 43 F4
Denham Suff. 72 C4
Denham Suff. 59 F1
Denham Green 43 F4
Denham Street 72 C4
Denhead Aber. 169 F3
Denhead Aber. 177 J5
Denhead Fife 152 C3
Denhead of Arbirlot 161 D5
Denhead of Gray 152 B1
Denholm 135 G4
Denholme 101 G4
Denholme Clough 101 G4
Denio 74 C4
Denmead 15 F1
Denmill 169 G3
Denmoss 176 E6
Dennington 61 D1
Denny 142 C1
Dennyloanhead 142 C1
Denshaw 93 D1
Denside 169 G5
Densole 33 E4
Denston 59 F2
Denstone 80 B3
Dent 108 C4
Denton Cambs. 69 G4
Denton Darl. 110 B1
Denton E.Suss. 17 G3
Denton Gt.Man. 92 D3
Denton Kent 33 E4
Denton Kent 45 F5
Denton Lincs. 83 D4
Denton N.Yorks. 102 A3
Denton Norf. 73 D3
Denton Northants. 56 D2
Denton Oxon. 42 A2
Denton's Green 91 F3
Denver 71 E2
Denvilles 15 G2
Denwick 137 G5
Deopham 86 B5
Deopham Green 72 B2
Depden 59 F2
Depden Green 59 F2
Deptford Gt.Lon. 44 C5
Deptford Wilts. 26 B4
Derby 81 E4
Derbyhaven 98 A5
Dereham (East Dereham) 86 A4
Dererach 147 E2
Deri 38 A2
Derril 20 D5
Derringstone 33 E4
Derrington 79 F5
Derriton 20 D5
Derry 150 B2
Derry Hill 40 B5
Derrythorpe 95 F2
Dersingham 85 E4
Dervaig 154 D4
Derwen 77 D2
Derwenlas 62 D3
Derwydd 36 C1
Derybruich 140 A2
Desborough 68 D4
Desford 67 G2
Detchant 137 E3
Dethick 81 E2
Detling 31 G3
Deuddwr 64 B1
Deunant 76 C1
Deuxhill 65 F4
Devauden 39 D3
Devil's Bridge (Pontarfynach) 62 D5
Devitts Green 67 E3
Devizes 26 B1
Devonport 8 A2
Devonside 151 E5
Devoran 3 E3
Dewar 144 A5
Dewlish 13 D3
Dewsall Court 53 D4
Dewsbury 102 B5
Dewsbury Moor 102 B5
Dhiseig 147 D1
Dhoon 98 C3
Dhoor 98 C2
Dhowin 98 C1
Dhuhallow 166 C2
Dial Green 29 E5
Dial Post 17 D2
Dibden 14 D2
Dibden Hill 43 E3
Dibden Purlieu 14 D2
Dickleburgh 72 C3
Dickleburgh Moor 72 C3
Didbrook 54 C4
Didcot 42 A3
Diddington 57 G1
Diddlebury 65 E4
Didley 53 D4
Didling 16 A2
Didmarton 40 A4
Didsbury 92 C3
Didworthy 8 C1
Digby 83 F2
Digg 171 K5
Diggle 93 E2
Digmoor 91 F2
Digswell 44 B1
Dihewyd 50 A2
Dildawn 124 B5
Dilham 87 E3
Dilhorne 79 G3
Dillington 57 G1
Dilston 119 F1
Dilton Marsh 25 F3
Dilwyn 52 D2
Dilwyn Common 52 D2
Dimple 92 B1
Dinas Carmar. 49 F4
Dinas Gwyn. 75 D2
Dinas Gwyn. 74 B4
Dinas Cross 48 D4
Dinas Dinlle 74 D2
Dinas Powys 38 A5
Dinas-Mawddwy 63 E1
Dinbych (Denbigh) 76 D1
Dinbych-y-Pysgod (Tenby) 35 E2
Dinckley 100 C4
Dinder 24 C3
Dinedor 53 E4
Dingestow 39 D1
Dingley 68 C4
Dingwall 174 C6
Dinlabyre 126 D2
Dinnet 168 C5
Dinnington S.Yorks. 94 C4
Dinnington Som. 12 A1
Dinnington T. & W. 129 E4
Dinorwig 75 E1
Dinton Bucks. 42 C1
Dinton Wilts. 26 B4
Dinvin 122 B5
Dinwoodie Mains 125 F1
Dinworthy 20 D4
Dipford 23 F5
Dippen Arg. & B. 130 C2
Dippen N.Ayr. 131 F3
Dippenhall 28 D3
Dipple Moray 176 B5
Dipple S.Ayr. 132 A5
Diptford 8 D2
Dipton 120 A2
Dirdhu 167 H2
Dirleton 144 C1
Discoed 52 B1
Diseworth 81 F5
Dishes 184 F5
Dishforth 110 C5
Dishley 81 G5
Disley 93 D4
Diss 72 C3
Disserth 51 G2
Distington 116 D4
Ditcheat 24 D4
Ditchingham 73 E2
Ditchley 55 F5
Ditchling 17 F2
Ditteridge 25 F1
Dittisham 9 E2
Ditton Halton 91 F4
Ditton Kent 31 G3
Ditton Green 59 E2
Ditton Priors 65 F4
Dixton Glos. 54 B4
Dixton Mon. 39 E1
Dobcross 93 D2
Dobwalls 5 G3
Doc Penfro (Pembroke Dock) 34 C2
Doccombe 10 A4
Dochgarroch 166 D1
Dockenfield 28 D3
Docker Cumb. 107 G3
Docker Lancs. 107 G5
Docking 85 F4
Docklow 53 E2
Dockray Cumb. 117 G4
Dockray Cumb. 117 F1
Dodbrooke 8 D3
Doddenham 53 G2
Doddinghurst 45 E3
Doddington Cambs. 70 C3
Doddington Kent 32 B3
Doddington Lincs. 95 G5
Doddington Northumb. 137 D3
Doddington Shrop. 65 F5
Doddiscombsleigh 10 B4
Doddycross 6 D4
Dodford Northants. 56 B1
Dodford Worcs. 66 B5
Dodington S.Glos. 39 G4
Dodington Som. 23 E3
Dodington Ash 39 G5
Dodleston 78 A1
Dods Leigh 80 B4
Dodscott 21 F4
Dodworth 94 A2
Doehole 81 E2
Doffcocker 92 A1
Dog Village 10 C3
Dogdyke 84 A2
Dogmersfield 28 C2
Dogsthorpe 70 A2
Dol Fawr 63 E2
Dolanog 63 G1
Dolau Powys 52 A1
Dolau R.C.T. 37 G4
Dolbenmaen 75 E3
Doley 79 E5
Dolfach 63 F5
Dolfor 64 A4
Dolgarreg 50 D4
Dolgarrog 76 A1
Dolgellau 62 D1
Dolgoch 62 C2
Dolgran 50 A4
Doll 175 F1
Dollar 151 E5
Dollarbeg 151 E5
Dolphin 90 C5
Dolphinholme 100 B2
Dolphinton 143 F5
Dolton 21 F4
Dolwen Conwy 89 G5
Dolwen Powys 63 F2
Dolwyddelan 76 A2
Dôl-y-bont 62 C4
Dol-y-cannau 52 A3
Dolyhir 52 B2
Dolywern 77 F4
Domgay 64 B1
Doncaster 94 C2
Donhead St. Andrew 26 A5
Donhead St. Mary 26 A5
Donibristle 143 F1
Doniford 23 D3
Donington Lincs. 84 A4
Donington Shrop. 66 A2
Donington le Heath 67 G1
Donington on Bain 96 C4
Donisthorpe 67 F1
Donna Nook 97 E3
Donnington Glos. 55 D5
Donnington Here. 53 G4
Donnington Shrop. 65 E2
Donnington Tel. & W. 65 G1
Donnington W.Berks. 27 F1
Donnington W.Suss. 16 A3
Donyatt 11 G1
Dorchester Dorset 12 C3
Dorchester Oxon. 42 A3
Dordon 67 E2
Dore 94 A4
Dores 166 C1
Dorket Head 81 G3
Dorking 29 G3
Dorley's Corner 61 E1
Dormans Park 30 C4
Dormansland 30 D4
Dormanstown 121 E5
Dormer's Wells 44 A4
Dormington 53 E3
Dormston 54 B2
Dorn 55 E4
Dorney 43 E5
Dorney Reach 43 E5
Dornie 164 E2
Dornoch 174 E3
Dornock 126 A5
Dorrery 183 F3
Dorridge 67 D5
Dorrington Lincs. 83 F2
Dorrington Shrop. 65 D2
Dorsell 168 D3
Dorsington 54 D3
Dorstone 52 C3
Dorton 42 B1
Dorusduain 165 F2
Dosthill 67 E3
Dotland 119 F2
Dottery 12 A3
Doublebois 5 F3
Dougalston 141 G2
Dougarie 131 D2
Doughton 40 A3
Douglas I.o.M. 98 B4
Douglas S.Lan. 133 G2
Douglas and Angus 152 C1
Douglas Water 133 G2
Douglastown 160 C5
Doulting 24 D3
Dounby 184 B5
Doune Arg. & B. 149 F5
Doune Arg. & B. 149 F3
Doune High. 167 F3
Doune High. 174 B1
Doune Stir. 150 C4
Dounepark 177 F4
Douneside 168 C4
Dounie High. 174 D3
Dounie High. 174 C2
Dounreay 182 E2
Dousland 8 B1
Dovaston 78 A5
Dove Holes 93 E5
Dovenby 117 D3
Dovendale 96 D4
Dover 33 F4
Dovercourt 60 D4
Doverdale 54 A1
Doveridge 80 C4
Doversgreen 30 B4
Dowally 159 F5
Dowdeswell 54 C5
Dowhill 132 A5
Dowlais 37 G2
Dowland 21 F4
Dowlands 11 F3
Dowlish Ford 11 G1
Dowlish Wake 11 G1
Down Ampney 40 D3
Down End 24 A3
Down Hatherley 54 A5
Down St. Mary 10 A2
Down Thomas 8 B3
Downderry 6 D5
Downe 30 D2
Downend I.o.W. 15 E4
Downend S.Glos. 39 F5
Downend W.Berks. 41 G5
Downfield 152 B1
Downfields 71 E5
Downgate 7 D3
Downham Essex 45 G3
Downham Lancs. 101 D3
Downham Northumb. 136 C3
Downham Market 71 E2
Downhead Cornw. 5 G1
Downhead Som. 25 D3
Downhead Som. 24 C5
Downholland Cross 91 E2
Downholme 110 A3
Downies 169 H5
Downley 43 D3
Downs 38 A5
Downside N.Som. 24 B1
Downside Som. 24 D3
Downside Som. 24 D2
Downside Surr. 29 G2
Downton Devon 7 F2
Downton Devon 9 E2
Downton Hants. 14 B3
Downton Wilts. 26 C5
Downton on the Rock 64 D5
Dowsby 83 G5
Dowthwaitehead 117 G4
Doxey 79 G5
Doynton 39 G5
Drabblegate 86 D3
Draethen 38 B4
Draffan 142 B5
Dragley Beck 107 D5
Drakeland Corner 8 B2
Drakelow 66 A4
Drakemyre 141 D4
Drakes Broughton 54 B3
Drakes Cross 66 C5
Draughton N.Yorks. 101 G2
Draughton Northants. 68 C5
Drax 103 F5
Draycot Foliat 41 D5
Draycote 55 G1
Draycott Derbys. 81 F4
Draycott Glos. 55 D4
Draycott Shrop. 66 A3
Draycott Som. 24 B2
Draycott Worcs. 54 A3
Draycott in the Clay 80 C5
Draycott in the Moors 79 G4
Drayford 10 A1
Draynes 5 G3
Drayton Leics. 68 D3
Drayton Lincs. 84 A4
Drayton Norf. 86 C4
Drayton Oxon. 55 G3
Drayton Oxon. 41 G3
Drayton Ports. 15 F2
Drayton Som. 24 B5
Drayton Warks. 55 D2
Drayton Worcs. 66 B5
Drayton Bassett 67 D2
Drayton Beauchamp 43 E1
Drayton Parslow 56 D5
Drayton St. Leonard 42 A3
Drebley 101 G2
Dreemskerry 98 C2
Dreenhill 34 C1
Drefach Carmar. 49 G4
Drefach Carmar. 36 B1
Dre-fach Cere. 50 B3
Drefelin 49 G4
Dreghorn 132 B2
Drem 144 C2
Dreumasdal (Drimsdale) 162 C1
Drewsteignton 10 A3
Driby 97 D5
Driffield E.Riding 104 C2
Driffield Glos. 40 C3
Drigg 106 B3
Drighlington 102 B5
Drimfern 148 C3
Drimlee 148 D3
Drimnin 155 E4
Drimore 170 C7
Drimpton 12 A2
Drimsdale (Dreumasdal) 162 C1
Drimsynie 149 D4
Drimvore 148 A5
Drinan 164 B3
Dringhouses 103 E2
Drinisiader 171 G2
Drinkstone 60 A1
Drinkstone Green 60 A1
Drishaig 149 D3
Drissaig 148 B3
Drointon 80 B5
Droitwich Spa 54 A1
Dron 151 G3
Dronfield 94 A5
Dronfield Woodhouse 94 A5
Drongan 132 C4
Dronley 152 B1
Droop 13 D2
Dropmore 43 E4
Droxford 15 F1
Droylsden 92 D3
Druid 76 D3
Druidston 34 B1
Druimarbin 156 C2
Druimavuic 156 C5
Druimdrishaig 139 F2
Druimindarroch 155 F1
Druimkinnerras 166 B1
Drum Arg. & B. 140 A2
Drum P. & K. 151 F4
Drumachloy 140 B3
Drumbeg 180 D5
Drumblade 176 D6
Drumblair 176 E6
Drumbuie D. & G. 133 F4
Drumbuie High. 164 D1
Drumburgh 117 F1
Drumchapel 141 G2
Drumchardine 174 C7
Drumchork 172 B3
Drumclog 133 E2
Drumdelgie 176 C6
Drumderfit 174 D6
Drumeldrie 152 C4
Drumelzier 134 C2
Drumfearn 164 C3
Drumfern 156 B2
Drumgarve 130 C3
Drumgley 160 C4
Drumguish 166 E5
Drumhead 168 E5
Drumin 167 J1
Drumine 174 E6
Drumjohn 123 G1
Drumlamford House 123 D3
Drumlasie 168 E4
Drumlemble 130 B4
Drumlithie 161 F1
Drummond High. 174 D5
Drummond Stir. 150 B4
Drummore 114 B3
Drummuir 176 B6
Drummuir Castle 176 B6
Drumnadrochit 166 C2
Drumnagorrach 176 D5
Drumnatorran 156 A3
Drumoak 169 F5
Drumore 130 C3
Drumour 151 E1
Drumrash 124 A3
Drumrunie 173 H1
Drums 169 H2
Drumsturdy 152 C1
Drumuie 171 K7
Drumuillie 167 G2
Drumvaich 150 B4
Drumwhindle 169 H1
Drumwhirn 124 B2
Drunkendub 161 E5
Druridge 129 E2
Drury 77 F1
Drws-y-nant 76 B5
Dry Doddington 82 D3
Dry Drayton 58 B1
Dry Harbour 172 C6
Dry Sandford 41 G2
Dry Street 45 F4
Drybeck 108 B1
Drybridge Moray 176 C4
Drybridge N.Ayr. 132 B2
Drybrook 39 F1
Dryburgh 135 G2
Drygrange 135 G2
Dryhope 135 D3
Drymen 141 F1
Drymuir 177 H6
Drynoch 163 K1
Dryslwyn 50 B5
Dryton 65 E2
Duachy 148 A2
Dubford 177 F4
Dubhchladach 139 G3
Dubheads 151 E2
Dublin 60 C1
Dubton 161 D4
Duchal 141 E3
Duchally 181 F7
Duchray 149 G4
Duck Bay 141 E1
Duck End Beds. 57 F3
Duck End Cambs. 58 A1
Duck End Essex 59 E5
Duck Street 102 A1
Duckington 78 B2
Ducklington 41 F2
Duckmanton 94 B5
Duck's Cross 57 G2
Ducks Island 44 B3
Duddenhoe End 58 C4
Duddingston 143 G2
Duddington 69 E2
Duddlestone 23 F5
Duddleswell 17 G1
Duddo 145 G5
Duddon 78 C1
Duddon Bridge 106 C4
Dudleston 78 A4
Dudleston Heath 78 A4
Dudley T. & W. 129 E4
Dudley W.Mid. 66 B3
Dudley Port 66 B3
Dudlow's Green 92 A4
Dudsbury 13 G3
Duffield 81 E3
Duffryn 37 E3
Dufftown 168 B1
Duffus 175 J5
Dufton 118 C5
Duggleby 104 A1
Duiar 167 J1
Duible 182 E6
Duiletter 149 D2
Duinish 158 B3
Duirinish 164 D1
Duisdealmor 164 D3
Duisky 156 C2
Duke End 67 E4
Dukestown 38 A1
Dukinfield 92 D3
Dulas 88 C4
Dulax 168 B3
Dulcote 24 C3
Dulford 11 D2
Dull 158 D5
Dullatur 142 B2
Dullingham 59 E2
Dullingham Ley 59 E2
Dulnain Bridge 167 G2
Duloe Beds. 57 G1
Duloe Cornw. 5 G4
Dulsie 175 G7
Dulverton 22 C5
Dulwich 44 C5
Dumbarton 141 E2
Dumbleton 54 C4
Dumcrieff 134 C5
Dumeath 168 C1
Dumfin 141 E1
Dumfries 125 D3
Dumgoyne 141 G1
Dummer 27 G3
Dun 161 E4
Dunach 148 A2
Dunalastair 158 C4
Dunan Arg. & B. 140 C2
Dunan High. 164 B2
Dunans 148 C5
Dunball 24 A3
Dunbar 145 D2
Dunbeath 183 G5
Dunbeg 148 A1
Dunblane 150 C4
Dunbog 152 A3
Dunbridge 27 E5
Duncanston Aber. 168 D2
Duncanston High. 174 C6
Dunchideock 10 B4
Dunchurch 67 G5
Duncote 56 B2
Duncow 125 D2
Duncraggan 150 A4
Duncrievie 151 G4
Duncroist 150 A1
Duncrub 151 F3
Duncryne 141 F1
Duncton 16 B2
Dundee 152 C1
Dundee Airport 152 B2
Dundon 24 B4
Dundon Hayes 24 B4
Dundonald 132 B2
Dundonnell 173 G3
Dundraw 117 F2
Dundreggan 165 K3
Dundrennan 116 A2
Dundridge 15 E1
Dundry 24 C1
Dunearn 143 G1
Dunecht 169 F4
Dunfermline 143 E1
Dunfield 40 D3
Dunford Bridge 93 F2
Dungate 32 B3
Dungavel 133 E2
Dungworth 93 G3
Dunham 95 F5
Dunham Town 92 B4
Dunham Woodhouses 92 B4
Dunham-on-the-Hill 91 F5
Dunhampton 54 A1
Dunholme 96 A5

Dunino 152 D3
Dunipace 142 C1
Dunira 150 C2
Dunkeld 159 F5
Dunkerton 25 E2
Dunkeswell 11 E2
Dunkeswick 102 C3
Dunkirk *Ches.* 91 E5
Dunkirk *Kent* 32 C3
Dunk's Green 31 F3
Dunlappie 161 D3
Dunley *Hants.* 27 F2
Dunley *Worcs.* 53 G1
Dunlop 141 F5
Dunloskin 140 C2
Dunmere 5 E3
Dunmore *Arg. & B.* 139 F3
Dunmore *Falk.* 142 C1
Dunn 183 G3
Dunn Street 31 G2
Dunnabie 126 A3
Dunnet 183 H1
Dunnichen 160 D5
Dunning 151 F3
Dunnington *E.Riding* 105 D2
Dunnington *Warks.* 54 C2
Dunnington *York* 103 F2
Dunnockshaw 101 E5
Dunoon 140 C2
Dunragit 122 C5
Dunrostan 139 F1
Duns 145 E4
Duns Tew 55 G5
Dunsa 93 G5
Dunsby 83 G5
Dunscore 124 C2
Dunscroft 95 D2
Dunsdale 111 F1
Dunsden Green 42 C5
Dunsfold 29 F4
Dunsford 10 B4
Dunshalt 152 A3
Dunshill 54 A4
Dunsinnan 151 G1
Dunsland Cross 21 E5
Dunsley *N.Yorks.* 112 B1
Dunsley *Staffs.* 66 A4
Dunsmore 43 D2
Dunsop Bridge 100 C2
Dunstable 57 F5
Dunstall 80 C5
Dunstall Green 59 F1
Dunstan 137 G5
Dunstan Steads 137 G4
Dunster 22 C3
Dunston *Lincs.* 83 F1
Dunston *Norf.* 86 D5
Dunston *Staffs.* 66 B1
Dunston Heath 66 B1
Dunston Hill 120 B1
Dunstone *Devon* 10 A5
Dunstone *Devon* 8 B2
Dunsville 95 D2
Dunswell 104 C4
Dunsyre 143 E5
Dunterton 7 D3
Duntisbourne Abbots 40 B2
Duntisbourne Leer 40 B2
Duntisbourne Rouse 40 B2
Duntish 12 C2
Duntocher 141 F2
Dunton *Beds.* 58 A3
Dunton *Bucks.* 56 D5
Dunton *Norf.* 85 G4
Dunton Bassett 68 A3
Dunton Green 31 E3
Dunton Wayletts 45 F3
Duntulm 171 K4
Dunure 132 A4
Dunure Mains 132 A4
Dunvant 36 B3
Dunvegan 171 H7
Dunwich 73 F4
Dura 152 C3
Durdar 118 A2
Durgan 3 E4
Durgates 31 F5
Durham 120 B3
Durham Tees Valley Airport 110 C1
Durinemast 155 F4
Durisdeer 133 G5
Durleigh 23 F4
Durley *Hants.* 15 E1
Durley *Wilts.* 26 D1
Durley Street 15 E1
Durlow Common 53 F4
Durnamuck 173 G2
Durness 181 G2
Durno 169 F2
Duror 156 B4
Durran *Arg. & B.* 148 B4
Durran *High.* 183 G2
Durrants 15 G2
Durrington *W.Suss.* 16 D3
Durrington *Wilts.* 26 C3
Dursley 39 G3
Dursley Cross 39 F1
Durston 23 F5
Durweston 13 E2
Dury 187 D6
Duston 56 C1
Duthil 167 G2
Dutlas 64 B5
Duton Hill 59 E5
Dutson 6 D2
Dutton 91 G5
Duxford 58 C3
Dwygyfylchi 89 F5
Dwyran 74 D1
Dyce 169 G3
Dyfatty 36 A2
Dyffryn *Bridgend* 37 E3
Dyffryn (Valley) *I.o.A.* 88 A5
Dyffryn *Pembs.* 48 C4
Dyffryn *V. of Glam.* 37 G5
Dyffryn Ardudwy 75 E5
Dyffryn Castell 63 D4
Dyffryn Ceidrych 50 D5
Dyffryn Cellwen 37 E1
Dyke *Devon* 20 D3
Dyke *Lincs.* 83 G5
Dyke *Moray* 175 G6
Dykehead *Angus* 160 B3
Dykehead *N.Lan.* 142 C4
Dykehead *Stir.* 150 A5
Dykelands 161 F3
Dykends 160 A4
Dykeside 177 F6
Dylife 63 E3
Dymchurch 19 G1
Dymock 53 G4
Dyrham 39 G5
Dysart 152 B5
Dyserth 90 B5

▼ E

Eachwick 128 D4
Eadar dha Fhadhail 178 C4
Eagland Hill 100 A3
Eagle 83 D1
Eagle Barnsdale 83 D1
Eagle Moor 83 D1
Eaglescliffe 110 D1
Eaglesfield *Cumb.* 117 D4
Eaglesfield *D. & G.* 126 A4
Eaglesham 141 G4
Eaglethorpe 69 F3
Eagley 92 B1
Eairy 98 A4
Eakley 56 D2
Eakring 82 B1
Ealand 95 E1
Ealing 44 A4
Eamont Bridge 118 B5
Earby 101 F3
Earcroft 100 C5
Eardington 65 G3
Eardisland 52 D2
Eardisley 52 C3
Eardiston *Shrop.* 78 A5
Eardiston *Worcs.* 53 F1
Earith 70 B5
Earl Shilton 67 G3
Earl Soham 60 D1
Earl Sterndale 80 B1
Earl Stonham 60 C2
Earle 137 D4
Earlestown 91 G3
Earley 42 C5
Earlham 86 C5
Earlish 171 J5
Earls Barton 57 D1
Earls Colne 59 G5
Earl's Common 54 B2
Earl's Court 44 B5
Earl's Croome 54 A3
Earl's Green 60 B1
Earlsdon 67 F5
Earlsferry 152 C4
Earlsford 169 G1
Earlsheaton 102 B5
Earlston 135 G2
Earlswood *Mon.* 39 D3
Earlswood *Surr.* 30 B4
Earlswood *Warks.* 66 D5
Earnley 16 A4
Earnshaw Bridge 100 B5
Earsairidh 162 C5
Earsdon 129 F4
Earsdon Moor 129 D2
Earsham 73 E3
Earsham Street 72 D4
Earswick 103 F2
Eartham 16 B3
Earthcott Green 39 F4
Easby 111 E2
Easdale *Arg. & B.* 147 G3
Easdale *Arg. & B.* 147 G3
Easebourne 29 D5
Easenhall 67 G5
Eashing 29 E3
Easington *Bucks.* 42 B1
Easington *Dur.* 120 D3
Easington *E.Riding* 97 D1
Easington *Northumb.* 137 F3
Easington *Oxon.* 42 B3
Easington *R. & C.* 111 G1
Easington Colliery 120 D3
Easington Lane 120 C3
Easingwold 103 E1
Easole Street 33 E3
Eassie 160 B5
East Aberthaw 22 D1
East Acton 44 B4
East Allington 9 D3
East Anstey 22 B5
East Anton 27 E3
East Appleton 110 B3
East Ardsley 102 C5
East Ashey 15 E4
East Ashling 16 A3
East Auchronie 169 G4
East Ayton 112 C4
East Barkwith 96 B4
East Barming 31 G3
East Barnby 112 B1
East Barnet 44 B3
East Barsham 86 A2
East Beckham 86 C2
East Bedfont 43 F5
East Bergholt 60 B4
East Bierley 102 A5
East Bilney 86 A4
East Blatchington 17 G4
East Boldon 120 C1
East Boldre 14 C2
East Bolton 137 F5
East Bower 24 A4
East Brent 24 A2
East Bridge 61 F1
East Bridgford 82 B3
East Brora 175 G1
East Buckland 21 G2
East Budleigh 11 D4
East Burnham 43 E4
East Burra 187 C9
East Burrafirth 187 C7
East Burton 13 E4
East Butsfield 120 A3
East Butterleigh 10 C2
East Butterwick 95 F2
East Cairnbeg 161 F2
East Calder 143 E3
East Carleton 86 C5
East Carlton *Northants.* 68 D4
East Carlton *W.Yorks.* 102 B3
East Chaldon (Chaldon Herring) 13 D4
East Challow 41 F4
East Charleton 9 D3
East Chelborough 12 B2
East Chiltington 17 F2
East Chinnock 12 A1
East Chisenbury 26 C2
East Clandon 29 F2
East Claydon 56 C5
East Clyne 175 G1
East Clyth 183 H5
East Coker 12 B1
East Compton *Dorset* 13 E1
East Compton *Som.* 24 D3
East Coombe 10 B2
East Cornworthy 9 E2
East Cottingwith 103 G3
East Cowes 15 E3
East Cowick 103 F5
East Cowton 110 C2
East Cramlington 129 E4
East Cranmore 25 D3
East Creech 13 F4
East Croachy 166 D2
East Darlochan 130 B3
East Davoch 168 C4
East Dean *E.Suss.* 18 A4
East Dean *Hants.* 27 D5
East Dean *W.Suss.* 16 B2
East Dereham (Dereham) 86 A4
East Down 21 F1
East Drayton 95 E5
East Dundry 24 C1
East Ella 104 C5
East End *E.Riding* 105 D4
East End *E.Riding* 105 E5
East End *Essex* 46 D2
East End *Hants.* 27 F1
East End *Hants.* 14 C3
East End *Herts.* 58 C5
East End *Kent* 32 A5
East End *Kent* 32 B1
East End *M.K.* 57 E3
East End *Oxon.* 41 F1
East End *N.Som.* 39 D5
East End *Poole* 13 F3
East End *Som.* 24 C2
East End *Suff.* 60 C4
East End *Suff.* 60 C2
East Farleigh 31 G3
East Farndon 68 C4
East Ferry 95 F3
East Firsby 96 A4
East Fleetham 137 G4
East Fortune 144 C2
East Garston 41 F5
East Ginge 41 G4
East Goscote 68 B1
East Grafton 27 D1
East Green *Suff.* 61 F1
East Green *Suff.* 59 E2
East Grimstead 26 D5
East Grinstead 30 C5
East Guldeford 19 E1
East Haddon 56 B1
East Hagbourne 42 A4
East Halton 96 B1
East Ham 44 D4
East Hanney 41 G3
East Hanningfield 45 G2
East Hardwick 94 B1
East Harling 72 A3
East Harlsey 110 D3
East Harnham 26 C5
East Harptree 24 C2
East Hartford 129 E4
East Harting 15 G1
East Hatch 26 A5
East Hatley 58 A2
East Hauxwell 110 A3
East Haven 153 D1
East Heckington 83 G3
East Hedleyhope 120 A3
East Helmsdale 183 F7
East Hendred 41 G4
East Herrington 120 C2
East Heslerton 112 C5
East Hewish 24 B1
East Hoathly 18 A2
East Holme 13 E4
East Horndon 45 F4
East Horrington 24 C3
East Horsley 29 F2
East Horton 137 E3
East Howe 13 G3
East Huntspill 24 A3
East Hyde 44 A1
East Ilsley 41 G4
East Keal 84 B1
East Kennett 26 C1
East Keswick 102 C3
East Kilbride 142 A4
East Kimber 7 E1
East Kirkby 84 B1
East Knapton 112 B5
East Knighton 13 E4
East Knowstone 22 B5
East Knoyle 25 F4
East Kyloe 137 E3
East Lambrook 12 A1
East Langdon 33 F4
East Langton 68 C3
East Langwell 174 E1
East Lavant 16 A3
East Lavington 16 B2
East Layton 110 A1
East Leake 81 G5
East Learmouth 136 C3
East Learney 168 E4
East Leigh *Devon* 10 A2
East Leigh *Devon* 10 A1
East Leigh *Devon* 9 D2
East Leigh *Devon* 8 C2
East Lexham 71 G1
East Lilburn 137 E4
East Linton 144 C2
East Liss 28 C5
East Lockinge 41 G4
East Looe 5 G4
East Lound 95 E2
East Lulworth 13 E4
East Lutton 104 B1
East Lydford 24 C4
East Lyn 22 A3
East Lyng 24 A5
East Mains 168 E5
East Malling 31 G3
East Malling Heath 31 F3
East March 152 C1
East Marden 16 A2
East Markham 95 E5
East Martin 13 G1
East Marton 101 F2
East Meon 28 B5
East Mere 10 C1
East Mersea 47 D1
East Mey 183 J1
East Molesey 29 G1
East Moor 102 C5
East Morden 13 F3
East Morriston 144 D5
East Morton 102 A3
East Ness 111 F5
East Newton 105 E4
East Norton 68 C2
East Oakley 27 G2
East Ogwell 10 B5
East Orchard 13 E1
East Ord 145 G4
East Panson 7 D1
East Parley 14 A3
East Peckham 31 F4
East Pennard 24 C4
East Portlemouth 8 D4
East Prawle 9 D4
East Preston 16 C3
East Pulham 12 D2
East Putford 21 D4
East Quantoxhead 23 E3
East Rainton 120 C3
East Ravendale 96 C3
East Raynham 85 G5
East Rigton 102 C3
East Rolstone 24 A1
East Rounton 110 D2
East Row 112 B1
East Rudham 85 G5
East Runton 86 D1
East Ruston 87 E3
East Saltoun 144 B3
East Shefford 41 F5
East Sleekburn 129 E3
East Somerton 87 F4
East Stockwith 95 E3
East Stoke *Dorset* 13 E4
East Stoke *Notts.* 82 C3
East Stour 25 F5
East Stourmouth 33 E2
East Stratton 27 G3
East Street 24 C4
East Studdal 33 F4
East Suisnish 164 B1
East Taphouse 5 F3
East Thirston 129 D2
East Tilbury 45 F5
East Tisted 28 C4
East Torrington 96 B4
East Town 24 D3
East Tuddenham 86 B4
East Tytherley 27 D5
East Tytherton 40 B5
East Village 10 B2
East Wall 65 E3
East Walton 71 F1
East Wellow 27 E5
East Wemyss 152 B5
East Whitburn 143 D3
East Wickham 45 D5
East Williamston 35 D2
East Winch 71 E1
East Winterslow 26 D4
East Wittering 15 G3
East Witton 110 A4
East Woodburn 128 B3
East Woodhay 27 F1
East Woodlands 25 E3
East Worldham 28 C4
East Worlington 10 A1
East Youlstone 20 C4
Eastacott 21 G3
Eastbourne 18 B4
Eastbrook 38 A5
Eastburn *E.Riding* 104 B2
Eastburn *W.Yorks.* 101 G3
Eastbury *Herts.* 44 A3
Eastbury *W.Berks.* 41 F5
Eastby 101 G2
Eastchurch 32 B1
Eastcombe *Glos.* 40 A2
Eastcombe *Som.* 23 E4
Eastcote *Gt.Lon.* 44 A4
Eastcote *Northants.* 56 B2
Eastcote *W.Mid.* 67 D5
Eastcott *Cornw.* 20 C4
Eastcott *Wilts.* 26 B2
Eastcourt 40 B3
Eastdown 9 E3
Eastend 55 F5
Easter Ardross 174 D4
Easter Balgedie 151 G4
Easter Balmoral 167 K5
Easter Boleskine 166 C2
Easter Borland 150 B4
Easter Brae 174 D5
Easter Buckieburn 142 B1
Easter Compton 39 E4
Easter Drummond 166 B3
Easter Dullater 150 A4
Easter Ellister 138 A4
Easter Fearn 174 D3
Easter Galcantray 175 F7
Easter Howlaws 145 E5
Easter Kinkell 174 C6
Easter Knox 161 D5
Easter Lednathie 160 B3
Easter Moniack 174 C7
Easter Ord 169 G4
Easter Poldar 150 B5
Easter Skeld (Skeld) 187 C8
Easter Suddie 174 D6
Easter Tulloch 161 F2
Easter Whyntie 176 E4
Eastergate 16 B3
Easterhouse 142 A3
Easterton 26 B2
Easterton Sands 26 B2
Eastertown 24 A2
Eastfield *Bristol* 39 E5
Eastfield *N.Lan.* 142 C3
Eastfield *N.Yorks.* 112 D4
Eastfield Hall 129 E1
Eastgate *Dur.* 119 F4
Eastgate *Lincs.* 69 G1
Eastgate *Norf.* 86 C3
Easthall 58 A5
Eastham *Mersey.* 91 E4
Eastham *Worcs.* 53 F1
Easthampstead 29 D1
Easthampton 52 D1
Easthaugh 86 B4
Eastheath 28 D1
Easthope 65 E3
Easthorpe *Essex* 60 A5
Easthorpe *Leics.* 82 D4
Easthorpe *Notts.* 82 C2
Easthouses 144 A3
Eastington *Devon* 10 A2
Eastington *Glos.* 40 D1
Eastington *Glos.* 39 G2
Eastleach Martin 41 E2
Eastleach Turville 41 E2
Eastleigh *Devon* 21 E3
Eastleigh *Hants.* 14 D1
Eastling 32 B3
Eastmoor *Derbys.* 94 A5
Eastmoor *Norf.* 71 F2
Eastnor 53 G4
Eastoft 95 F1
Eastoke 15 G3
Easton *Cambs.* 69 G5
Easton *Cumb.* 126 C4
Easton *Cumb.* 117 F1
Easton *Devon* 10 A4
Easton *Dorset* 12 C5
Easton *Hants.* 27 G4
Easton *I.o.W.* 14 C4
Easton *Lincs.* 83 E5
Easton *Norf.* 86 C4
Easton *Som.* 24 C3
Easton *Suff.* 61 D2
Easton *Wilts.* 40 A5
Easton Grey 40 A4
Easton Maudit 57 D2
Easton on the Hill 69 F2
Easton Royal 26 D1
Easton-in-Gordano 39 E5
Eastrea 70 A3
Eastriggs 126 A5
Eastrington 103 G4
Eastry 33 F3
Eastside 185 D8
East-the-Water 21 E3
Eastville 39 F5
Eastwell 82 C5
Eastwick 44 D1
Eastwood *Notts.* 81 F3
Eastwood *S'end* 46 B4
Eastwood *S.Yorks.* 94 B3
Eastwood *W.Yorks.* 101 F5
Eastwood End 70 C3
Eathorpe 55 F1
Eaton *Ches.* 79 F1
Eaton *Ches.* 78 C1
Eaton *Leics.* 82 C5
Eaton *Norf.* 86 D5
Eaton *Norf.* 85 E4
Eaton *Notts.* 95 E5
Eaton *Oxon.* 41 G2
Eaton *Shrop.* 65 E3
Eaton *Shrop.* 64 C4
Eaton Bishop 52 D4
Eaton Bray 57 E5
Eaton Constantine 65 F2
Eaton Ford 57 G2
Eaton Hall 78 B1
Eaton Hastings 41 E3
Eaton Socon 57 G2
Eaton upon Tern 79 D5
Eaves Green 67 E4
Eavestone 102 B1
Ebberston 112 B4
Ebbesborne Wake 26 A5
Ebbw Vale 38 A2
Ebchester 120 A2
Ebdon 24 A1
Ebford 10 C4
Ebley 40 A2
Ebnal 78 B3
Ebost 163 J1
Ebrington 55 D3
Ebsworthy Town 7 F1
Ecchinswell 27 F2
Ecclaw 145 E3
Ecclefechan 125 F3
Eccles *Gt.Man.* 92 B3
Eccles *Kent* 31 G2
Eccles *Sc.Bord.* 145 E5
Eccles Green 52 C3
Eccles Road 72 B2
Ecclesfield 94 A3
Ecclesgreig 161 F3
Eccleshall 79 F5
Eccleshill 102 A4
Ecclesmachan 143 E2
Eccles-on-Sea 87 F3
Eccleston *Ches.* 78 B1
Eccleston *Lancs.* 91 G1
Eccleston *Mersey.* 91 F3
Eccup 102 B3
Echt 169 F4
Eckford 136 B4
Eckington *Derbys.* 94 B5
Eckington *Worcs.* 54 B3
Ecton *Northants.* 56 D1
Ecton *Staffs.* 80 B2
Edale 93 F4
Eday 184 E4
Edburton 17 E2
Edderside 117 E2
Edderton 174 E3
Eddington 27 E1
Eddleston 143 G5
Eden Park 30 C2
Eden Vale 120 D4
Edenbridge 30 D4
Edendonich 149 D2
Edenfield 92 B1
Edenhall 118 B4
Edenham 83 F5
Edensor 93 G5
Edentaggart 149 F5
Edenthorpe 94 D2
Edern 74 B4
Edgarley 24 C4
Edgbaston 66 C4
Edgcote 56 A3
Edgcott *Bucks.* 56 B5
Edgcott *Som.* 22 B4
Edgcumbe 3 E3
Edge *Glos.* 40 A2
Edge *Shrop.* 64 C2
Edge End 39 E1
Edge Green *Ches.* 78 B2
Edge Green *Gt.Man.* 91 G3
Edge Green *Norf.* 72 B3
Edgebolton 78 C5
Edgefield 86 B2
Edgehead 144 A3
Edgeley 78 C3
Edgerley 64 C1
Edgerton 93 F1
Edgeworth 40 B2
Edginswell 9 E1
Edgmond 65 G1
Edgmond Marsh 79 E5
Edgton 64 C4
Edgware 44 B3
Edgworth 92 B1
Edinample 150 B2
Edinbanchory 168 C3
Edinbane 171 J6
Edinbarnet 141 G2
Edinburgh 143 G2
Edinburgh Airport 143 F2
Edinchip 150 A2
Edingale 67 E1
Edingley 82 B2
Edingthorpe 87 E2
Edingthorpe Green 87 E2
Edington *Som.* 24 A4
Edington *Wilts.* 26 A2
Edintore 176 C6
Edinvale 175 J6
Edistone 20 C3
Edith Weston 69 E2
Edithmead 24 A3
Edlaston 80 C3
Edlesborough 43 E1
Edlingham 128 D1
Edlington 96 C5
Edmondsham 13 G1
Edmondsley 120 B3
Edmondstown 37 G3
Edmondthorpe 69 D1
Edmonstone 184 E5
Edmonton *Cornw.* 5 D2
Edmonton *Gt.Lon.* 44 C3
Edmundbyers 119 G2
Ednam 136 B3
Ednaston 80 D3
Edney Common 45 F2
Edra 149 G3
Edradynate 159 D4
Edrom 145 F4
Edstaston 78 C4
Edstone 55 D1
Edvin Loach 53 F2
Edwalton 81 G4
Edwardstone 60 A3
Edwardsville 37 G3
Edwinsford 50 C4
Edwinstowe 82 B1
Edworth 58 A3
Edwyn Ralph 53 F2
Edzell 161 E3
Efail Isaf 37 G4
Efail-fâch 37 D3
Efailnewydd 74 C4
Efailwen 49 E5
Efenechtyd 77 E2
Effingham 29 G2
Effirth 187 C7
Efflinch 67 D1
Efford 10 B2
Egbury 27 F2
Egdean 29 E5
Egdon 54 B2
Egerton *Gt.Man.* 92 B1
Egerton *Kent* 32 B4
Egerton Forstal 32 A4
Egerton Green 78 C2
Egg Buckland 8 A2
Eggborough 103 E5
Eggerness 115 E2
Eggesford Barton 21 G4
Eggington 57 E5
Egginton 81 D5
Egglescliffe 110 D1
Eggleston 119 F5
Egham 43 F5
Egham Wick 43 E5
Egilsay 184 D5
Egleton 69 D2
Eglingham 137 F5
Eglinton 141 E5
Egloshayle 5 E2
Egloskerry 5 G1
Eglwys Cross 78 B3
Eglwys Fach 62 C3
Eglwys Nunydd 37 D4
Eglwysbach 89 G5
Eglwys-Brewis 22 D1
Eglwyswrw 49 E4
Egmanton 82 C1
Egmere 86 A2
Egremont 116 D5
Egton 112 B2
Egton Bridge 112 B2
Egypt 27 F3
Eigg 155 D1
Eight Ash Green 60 A5
Eignaig 155 G5
Eil 167 F3
Eilanreach 164 E3
Eildon 135 G2
Eilean Bhearnaraigh (Berneray) 170 E3
Eilean Darach 173 H3
Eilean Iarmain (Isleornsay) 164 C3
Eilean Leodhais (Isle of Lewis) 179 F3
Eilean Scalpaigh (Scalpay) 171 H2
Eilean Shona 155 F2
Einacleit 178 D5
Eiriosgaigh (Eriskay) 162 C3
Eisgean 179 F6
Eisingrug 75 F4
Eisteddfa Gurig 63 D4
Elan Village 51 F1
Elberton 39 F4
Elborough 24 A2
Elburton 8 B2
Elcho 151 G2
Elcombe 40 D4
Elder Street 59 D4
Eldernell 70 B3
Eldersfield 53 G4
Elderslie 141 F3
Eldon 120 B5
Eldrick 123 D2
Eldroth 101 D1
Eldwick 102 A3
Elemore Vale 120 C3
Elerch (Bont-goch) 62 C4
Elford *Northumb.* 137 F3
Elford *Staffs.* 67 D1
Elford Closes 70 D5
Elgin 175 K5
Elgol 164 B3
Elham 33 D4
Elie 152 C4
Elilaw 128 B1
Elim 88 B4
Eling *Hants.* 14 C1
Eling *W.Berks.* 42 A5
Eliock 133 G5
Elishader 171 K5
Elishaw 128 A2
Elkesley 95 D5
Elkington 68 B5
Elkstone 40 B1
Elland 102 A5
Elland Upper Edge 102 A5
Ellary 139 F2
Ellastone 80 C3
Ellbridge 8 A1
Ellel 100 A2
Ellemford 145 E3
Ellenborough 116 D3
Ellenhall 79 F5
Ellen's Green 29 F4
Ellerbeck 110 D3
Ellerby 111 G1
Ellerdine 78 D5
Ellerdine Heath 78 D5
Elleric 156 C5
Ellerker 104 B5
Ellerton *E.Riding* 103 G3
Ellerton *N.Yorks.* 110 B3
Ellerton *Shrop.* 79 E5
Ellerton Abbey 109 F3
Ellesborough 42 D2
Ellesmere 78 A4
Ellesmere Park 92 B3
Ellesmere Port 91 F5
Ellingham *Hants.* 14 A2
Ellingham *Norf.* 73 E2
Ellingham *Northumb.* 137 F4
Ellingstring 110 A4
Ellington *Cambs.* 69 G5
Ellington *Northumb.* 129 E2
Ellington Thorpe 69 G5
Elliot's Green 25 E3
Ellisfield 28 B3
Ellistown 67 G1
Ellon 169 H1
Ellonby 118 A4
Ellough 73 F3
Ellough Moor 73 F3
Elloughton 104 B5
Ellwood 39 E2
Elm 70 C2
Elm Park 45 E4
Elmbridge 54 B1
Elmdon *Essex* 58 C4
Elmdon *W.Mid.* 67 D4
Elmdon Heath 67 D4
Elmers End 30 C2
Elmer's Green 91 F2
Elmesthorpe 67 G3
Elmhurst 66 D1
Elmley Castle 54 B3
Elmley Lovett 54 A1
Elmore 39 G1
Elmore Back 39 G1
Elmscott 20 C3
Elmsett 60 B3
Elmstead *Essex* 60 B5
Elmstead *Gt.Lon.* 44 D5
Elmstead Market 60 B5
Elmstone 33 E2
Elmstone Hardwicke 54 B5
Elmswell *E.Riding* 104 B2
Elmswell *Suff.* 60 A1
Elmton 94 C5
Elphin 180 E7
Elphinstone 144 A2
Elrick *Aber.* 169 G4
Elrick *Moray* 168 C2
Elrig 114 D2
Elrigbeag 148 D3
Elsdon 128 B2
Elsecar 94 A2
Elsenham 58 D5
Elsfield 42 A1
Elsham 96 A1
Elsing 86 B4
Elslack 101 F3
Elson *Hants.* 15 F2
Elson *Shrop.* 78 A4
Elsrickle 143 E5
Elstead 29 E3
Elsted 16 A2
Elsthorpe 83 F5
Elstob 120 C5
Elston *Lancs.* 100 B4
Elston *Notts.* 82 C3
Elstone 21 G4
Elstow 57 F3
Elstree 44 A3
Elstronwick 105 E4
Elswick 100 A4
Elsworth 58 B1
Elterwater 107 E2
Eltham 44 D5
Eltisley 58 A2
Elton *Cambs.* 69 F3
Elton *Ches.* 91 F5
Elton *Derbys.* 80 D1
Elton *Glos.* 39 G1
Elton *Gt.Man.* 92 B1
Elton *Here.* 65 D5
Elton *Notts.* 82 C4
Elton *Stock.* 110 D1
Elton Green 91 F5
Elvanfoot 134 A4
Elvaston 81 F4
Elveden 71 G5
Elvingston 144 B2
Elvington *Kent* 33 E3
Elvington *York* 103 G3
Elwick *Hart.* 121 D4
Elwick *Northumb.* 137 F3
Elworth 79 E1
Elworthy 23 D4
Ely *Cambs.* 70 D5
Ely *Cardiff* 38 A5
Emberton 57 D3
Embleton *Cumb.* 117 E3
Embleton *Hart.* 120 D5
Embleton *Northumb.* 137 G4
Embo 175 F2
Embo Street 175 F2
Emborough 24 D2
Embsay 101 G2
Emerson Park 45 E4
Emery Down 14 B2
Emley 93 G1
Emmington 42 C2
Emneth 70 C2
Emneth Hungate 70 D2
Empingham 69 E2
Empshott 28 C4
Empshott Green 28 C4
Emsworth 15 G2
Enborne 27 F1
Enborne Row 27 F1
Enchmarsh 65 E3
Enderby 68 A3
Endmoor 107 G4
Endon 79 G2
Endon Bank 79 G2

Enfield 44 C3
Enfield Wash 44 C3
Enford 26 C2
Engine Common 39 F4
Englefield 42 B5
Englefield Green 43 E5
Englesea-brook 79 E2
English Bicknor 39 E1
English Frankton 78 B5
Englishcombe 25 E1
Enham Alamein 27 E3
Enmore 23 F4
Ennerdale Bridge 117 D5
Enniscaven 5 D4
Ennochdhu 159 F3
Ensay 154 C5
Ensdon 64 D1
Ensis 21 F3
Enson 79 G5
Enstone 55 F5
Enterkinfoot 133 G5
Enterpen 111 D2
Enton Green 29 E3
Enville 66 A4
Eolaigearraidh 162 C4
Eorabus 146 C2
Eorodal 179 H1
Eoropaidh 179 H1
Epney 39 G1
Epperstone 82 B3
Epping 45 D2
Epping Green *Essex* 44 D2
Epping Green *Herts.* 44 B2
Epping Upland 44 D2
Eppleby 110 A1
Eppleworth 104 C4
Epsom 30 B2
Epwell 55 F3
Epworth 95 E2
Epworth Turbary 95 E2
Erbistock 78 A3
Erbusaig 164 D2
Erchless Castle 174 B7
Erdington 66 D3
Eredine 148 B4
Eriboll 181 G3
Ericstane 134 B4
Eridge Green 31 E5
Eriff 132 D5
Erines 139 G2
Erisey Barton 3 E5
Eriskay (Eiriosgaigh) 162 C3
Eriswell 71 F5
Erith 45 E5
Erlestoke 26 A2
Ermington 8 C2
Ernesettle 8 A1
Erpingham 86 C2
Erringden Grange 101 F5
Errogie 166 C2
Errol 152 A2
Erroliston 169 J1
Erskine 141 F2
Ervie 122 A4
Erwarton 60 D4
Erwood 51 G3
Eryholme 110 C2
Eryrys 77 F2
Escart 139 G3
Escart Farm 139 G4
Escomb 120 A5
Escrick 103 F3
Esgair 49 G5
Esgairgeiliog 63 D2
Esgyryn 89 G5
Esh 120 A3
Esh Winning 120 A3
Esher 29 G1
Eshott 129 E2
Eshton 101 F2
Eskadale 166 B1
Eskbank 144 A3
Eskdale Green 106 C2
Eskdalemuir 126 A2
Eskham 97 D3
Esknish 138 B3
Esperley Lane Ends 120 A5
Espley Hall 129 D2
Esprick 100 A4
Essendine 69 F1
Essendon 44 B2
Essich 166 D1
Essington 66 B2
Esslemont 169 H2
Eston 111 E1
Eswick 187 D7
Etal 136 D3
Etchilhampton 26 B1
Etchingham 18 C1
Etchinghill *Kent* 33 D5
Etchinghill *Staffs.* 66 C1
Etherdwick Grange 105 E4
Etherley Dene 120 A5
Ethie Mains 161 E5
Eton 43 E5
Eton Wick 43 E5
Etteridge 166 D5
Ettiley Heath 79 E1
Ettington 55 E3
Etton *E.Riding* 104 B3
Etton *Peter.* 69 G2
Ettrick 135 D4
Ettrickbridge 135 E3
Ettrickhill 135 D4
Etwall 81 D4
Eudon George 65 F4
Eurach 148 A4
Euston 71 G5
Euxton 91 G1
Evanstown 37 F4
Evanton 174 D5
Evedon 83 F3
Evelix 174 E2
Evenjobb 52 B1
Evenley 56 A4
Evenlode 55 E5
Evenwood 120 A5
Evenwood Gate 120 A5
Everbay 184 F5
Evercreech 24 D4
Everdon 56 A2
Everingham 104 A3
Everleigh 26 D2
Everley *High.* 183 J2
Everley *N.Yorks.* 112 C4
Eversholt 57 E4
Evershot 12 B2
Eversley 28 C1
Eversley Cross 28 C1
Everthorpe 104 B4
Everton *Beds.* 58 A2
Everton *Hants.* 14 B3
Everton *Mersey.* 91 E3
Everton *Notts.* 95 D3
Evertown 126 B4
Eves Corner 46 C3
Evesbatch 53 F3
Evesham 54 C3
Evie 184 C5
Evington 68 B2
Ewart Newtown 137 D3
Ewden Village 93 G3
Ewell 30 B2
Ewell Minnis 33 E4
Ewelme 42 B3
Ewen 40 C3
Ewenny 37 F5
Ewerby 83 G3
Ewerby Thorpe 83 G3
Ewhurst *E.Suss.* 18 C1
Ewhurst *Surr.* 29 F3
Ewhurst Green 29 F4
Ewloe 78 A1
Ewloe Green 77 F1
Ewood 100 C5
Ewood Bridge 101 D5
Eworthy 7 E1
Ewshot 28 D3
Ewyas Harold 52 C5
Exbourne 21 G5
Exbury 14 D2
Exceat 18 A4
Exebridge 22 C5
Exelby 110 B4
Exeter 10 C3
Exeter Airport 10 C3
Exford 22 B4
Exfords Green 65 D2
Exhall *Warks.* 54 D2
Exhall *Warks.* 67 F4
Exlade Street 42 B4
Exminster 10 C4
Exmouth 10 D4
Exnaboe 187 F9
Exning 59 E1
Exton *Devon* 10 C4
Exton *Hants.* 28 B5
Exton *Rut.* 69 E1
Exton *Som.* 22 C4
Exwick 10 C3
Eyam 93 G5
Eydon 56 A3
Eye *Here.* 53 D1
Eye *Peter.* 70 A2
Eye *Suff.* 72 C4
Eye Green 70 A2
Eyemouth 145 G3
Eyeworth 58 A3
Eyhorne Street 32 A3
Eyke 61 E2
Eynesbury 57 G2
Eynort 163 J2
Eynsford 31 E2
Eynsham 41 G2
Eype 12 A3
Eyre 171 K6
Eythorne 33 E4
Eyton *Here.* 53 D1
Eyton *Shrop.* 64 C4
Eyton on Severn 65 E2
Eyton upon the Weald Moors 65 F1
Eywood 52 C2

▼F

Faccombe 27 E2
Faceby 111 D2
Fachwen 75 E1
Facit 92 C1
Faddiley 78 C2
Fadmoor 111 F4
Faebait 174 B6
Faifley 141 G2
Fail 132 C3
Failand 39 E5
Failford 132 C3
Failsworth 92 C2
Fain 173 H4
Fair Isle 186 A1
Fair Oak *Devon* 10 D1
Fair Oak *Hants.* 15 D1
Fair Oak *Hants.* 27 G1
Fair Oak Green 28 B1
Fairbourne 62 C1
Fairburn 103 D5
Fairfield *Derbys.* 93 E5
Fairfield *Gt.Man.* 92 D3
Fairfield *Kent* 19 E1
Fairfield *Mersey.* 91 D4
Fairfield *Stock.* 110 D1
Fairfield *Worcs.* 66 B5
Fairford 40 D2
Fairgirth 124 C5
Fairhaven 99 G5
Fairhill 142 B4
Fairholm 142 B4
Fairley 169 G4
Fairlie 140 D4
Fairlight 19 D2
Fairlight Cove 19 D2
Fairmile *Devon* 11 D3
Fairmile *Surr.* 29 G1
Fairmilehead 143 G3
Fairnington 136 A4
Fairoak 79 E4
Fairseat 31 F2
Fairstead 45 G1
Fairwarp 17 G1
Fairwater 38 A5
Fairy Cross 21 E3
Fairyhill 36 A3
Fakenham 86 A3
Fala 144 B3
Fala Dam 144 B3
Falahill 144 A4
Faldingworth 96 A4
Falfield *Fife* 152 C4
Falfield *S.Glos.* 39 F3
Falin-Wnda 49 G3
Falkenham 61 D4
Falkirk 142 C2
Falkland 152 A4
Falla 136 B5
Fallgate 81 E1
Fallin 150 D5
Falmer 17 F3
Falmouth 3 F3
Falsgrave 112 D4
Falstone 127 F3
Fanagmore 180 D4
Fanans 148 C2
Fancott 57 F5
Fangdale Beck 111 E3
Fangfoss 103 G2
Fankerton 142 B1
Fanmore 154 D5
Fanner's Green 45 F1
Fans 144 D5
Far Cotton 56 C2
Far Forest 65 G5
Far Gearstones 108 C4
Far Green 39 G2
Far Moor 91 G2
Far Oakridge 40 B2
Far Royds 102 B4
Far Sawrey 107 E3
Farcet 70 A3
Farden 65 E5
Fareham 15 E2
Farewell 66 C1
Farforth 96 D5
Faringdon 41 E3
Farington 100 B5
Farlam 118 B2
Farlary 174 E1
Farleigh *N.Som.* 24 C1
Farleigh *Surr.* 30 C2
Farleigh Hungerford 25 F2
Farleigh Wallop 28 B3
Farlesthorpe 97 E5
Farleton *Cumb.* 107 G4
Farleton *Lancs.* 100 B1
Farley *Derbys.* 81 D1
Farley *Shrop.* 64 C2
Farley *Staffs.* 80 B3
Farley *Wilts.* 26 D5
Farley Green *Suff.* 59 F2
Farley Green *Surr.* 29 F3
Farley Hill 28 C1
Farleys End 39 G1
Farlington 103 F1
Farlow 65 F4
Farm Town 67 F1
Farmborough 25 D1
Farmcote 54 C5
Farmington 40 D1
Farmoor 41 G2
Farmtown 176 D5
Farnborough *Gt.Lon.* 30 D2
Farnborough *Hants.* 29 D2
Farnborough *W.Berks.* 41 G4
Farnborough *Warks.* 55 G3
Farnborough Street 29 D2
Farncombe 29 E3
Farndish 57 E1
Farndon *Ches.* 78 B2
Farndon *Notts.* 82 C2
Farne Islands 137 G3
Farnell 161 E4
Farnham *Dorset* 13 F1
Farnham *Essex* 58 C5
Farnham *N.Yorks.* 102 C1
Farnham *Suff.* 61 E1
Farnham *Surr.* 28 D3
Farnham Common 43 E4
Farnham Green 58 C5
Farnham Royal 43 E4
Farningham 31 E2
Farnley *N.Yorks.* 102 B3
Farnley *W.Yorks.* 102 B4
Farnley Tyas 93 F1
Farnsfield 82 B2
Farnworth *Gt.Man.* 92 B2
Farnworth *Halton* 91 G4
Farr *High.* 182 C2
Farr *High.* 166 D1
Farr *High.* 167 F4
Farr House 166 D1
Farraline 166 C2
Farringdon 10 D3
Farrington Gurney 24 D2
Farsley 102 B4
Farthing Corner 32 A2
Farthing Green 32 A4
Farthinghoe 56 A4
Farthingstone 56 B2
Farthorpe 96 C5
Fartown 93 F1
Farway 11 E3
Fasag 172 E6
Fasagrianach 173 H3
Fascadale 155 E2
Faslane 140 D1
Fasnacloich 156 C5
Fasnakyle 165 K2
Fassfern 156 C2
Fatfield 120 C2
Fattahead 176 E5
Faugh 118 B2
Fauldhouse 142 D3
Faulkbourne 45 G1
Faulkland 25 E2
Fauls 78 C4
Faulston 26 B5
Faversham 32 C2
Favillar 167 K1
Fawdington 110 D5
Fawdon 120 B1
Fawfieldhead 80 B1
Fawkham Green 31 E2
Fawler 41 F1
Fawley *Bucks.* 42 C4
Fawley *Hants.* 15 D2
Fawley *W.Berks.* 41 F4
Fawley Chapel 53 E5
Fawsyde 161 G2
Faxfleet 104 A5
Faxton 68 C5
Faygate 30 B5
Fazakerley 91 E3
Fazeley 67 E2
Fearby 110 A4
Fearn 175 F4
Fearnan 158 C5
Fearnbeg 172 D6
Fearnhead 92 A3
Fearnmore 172 D5
Fearnoch *Arg. & B.* 140 B2
Fearnoch *Arg. & B.* 140 A1
Featherstone *Staffs.* 66 B2
Featherstone *W.Yorks.* 102 D5
Featherstone Castle 118 C1
Feckenham 54 C1
Feering 59 G5
Feetham 109 E3
Feith-hill 176 E6
Feizor 101 D1
Felbridge 30 C5
Felbrigg 86 D2
Felcourt 30 C4
Felden 43 F2
Felhampton 64 D4
Felindre *Carmar.* 50 D5
Felindre *Carmar.* 50 B5
Felindre *Carmar.* 49 G4
Felindre *Carmar.* 50 C4
Felindre *Cere.* 50 B2
Felindre *Powys* 64 A4
Felindre *Powys* 52 A5
Felindre *Swan.* 36 C2
Felinfach *Cere.* 50 B2
Felinfach *Powys* 51 G4
Felinfoel 36 B2
Felingwmisaf 50 B5
Felingwmuchaf 50 B5
Felixkirk 111 D4
Felixstowe 61 E4
Felixstowe Ferry 61 E4
Felkington 145 G5
Felldownhead 7 D2
Felling 120 B1
Fellonmore 147 F2
Felmersham 57 E2
Felmingham 87 D3
Felpham 16 B4
Felsham 60 A2
Felsted 59 E5
Feltham 44 A5
Felthamhill 44 A5
Felthorpe 86 C4
Felton *Here.* 53 E3
Felton *N.Som.* 24 C1
Felton *Northumb.* 129 D1
Felton Butler 64 C1
Feltwell 71 F3
Fen Ditton 58 C1
Fen Drayton 58 B1
Fen End 67 E5
Fen Street *Norf.* 72 A2
Fen Street *Norf.* 72 B4
Fen Street *Suff.* 72 A4
Fen Street *Suff.* 60 C1
Fenay Bridge 93 F1
Fence 101 E4
Fence Houses 120 C2
Fencott 42 A1
Fendike Corner 84 C1
Fenham 137 E2
Fenhouses 84 A3
Feniscowles 100 C5
Feniton 11 E3
Fenn Street 45 G5
Fenni-fach 51 G5
Fenny Bentley 80 C2
Fenny Bridges 11 E3
Fenny Compton 55 G2
Fenny Drayton 67 F3
Fenny Stratford 57 D4
Fenrother 129 D2
Fenstanton 58 B1
Fenton *Cambs.* 70 B5
Fenton *Lincs.* 95 F5
Fenton *Lincs.* 83 D2
Fenton *Northumb.* 137 D3
Fenton *Notts.* 95 E4
Fenton *Stoke* 79 F3
Fenton Barns 144 C1
Fenwick *E.Ayr.* 141 F5
Fenwick *Northumb.* 128 C4
Fenwick *Northumb.* 137 E2
Fenwick *S.Yorks.* 94 C1
Feochaig 130 C4
Feock 3 F3
Feolin 138 D3
Feolin Ferry 138 C3
Feorlan 130 B5
Feorlin 148 B5
Ferguslie Park 141 F3
Feriniquarrie 171 G6
Fern 160 C3
Ferndale 37 F3
Ferndown 13 G2
Ferness 175 G7
Fernham 41 E3
Fernhill Heath 54 A2
Fernhurst 29 D5
Fernie 152 B3
Fernilea 163 J1
Fernilee 93 E5
Fernybank 160 D2
Ferrensby 102 C1
Ferrindonald 164 C4
Ferring 16 C3
Ferry Hill 70 B4
Ferrybridge 103 D5
Ferryden 161 F4
Ferryhill 120 B4
Ferryside (Glanyferi) 35 G1
Fersfield 72 B3
Fersit 157 F2
Ferwig 49 E3
Feshiebridge 167 F4
Fetcham 29 G2
Fetlar 186 F3
Fetterangus 177 H5
Fettercairn 161 E2
Fetternear House 169 F3
Feus of Caldhame 161 E3
Fewcott 56 A5
Fewston 102 A2
Ffairfach 50 C5
Ffair-Rhos 50 D1
Ffaldybrenin 50 C3
Ffarmers 50 C3
Ffawyddog 38 B1
Ffestiniog (Llan Ffestiniog) 76 A3
Ffordd-las *Denb.* 77 E1
Fforddlas *Powys* 52 B4
Fforest 36 B2
Fforest-fach 36 C3
Ffostrasol 49 G3
Ffos-y-ffin 50 A1
Ffridd Uchaf 75 E2
Ffrith *Denb.* 90 B4
Ffrith *Flints.* 77 F2
Ffrwdgrech 51 G5
Ffynnon 35 G1
Ffynnon Taf (Taff's Well) 38 A4
Ffynnongroyw 90 C4
Fibhig 178 E3
Fichlie 168 C3
Fidden 146 C2
Fiddington *Glos.* 54 B4
Fiddington *Som.* 23 F3
Fiddleford 13 E1
Fiddler's Green *Glos.* 54 B5
Fiddler's Green *Here.* 53 E4
Fiddler's Green *Norf.* 71 G1
Fiddler's Green *Norf.* 72 B2
Fiddlers Hamlet 45 D2
Field 80 B4
Field Broughton 107 E4
Field Dalling 86 B2
Field Head 67 G2
Fife Keith 176 C5
Fifehead Magdalen 25 E5
Fifehead Neville 13 D1
Fifehead St. Quintin 13 D1
Fifield *Oxon.* 41 E1
Fifield *W. & M.* 43 E5
Fifield Bavant 26 B5
Figheldean 26 C3
Filby 87 F4
Filey 113 E4
Filgrave 57 D3
Filham 8 C2
Filkins 41 E2
Filleigh *Devon* 21 G3
Filleigh *Devon* 10 A1
Fillingham 95 G4
Fillongley 67 E4
Filmore Hill 28 B5
Filton 39 F5
Fimber 104 A1
Finavon 160 C4
Fincham 71 E2
Finchampstead 28 C1
Finchdean 15 G1
Finchingfield 59 E4
Finchley 44 B3
Findern 81 E4
Findhorn 175 H5
Findhorn Bridge 167 F2
Findhuglen 150 C3
Findo Gask 151 F2
Findochty 176 C4
Findon *Aber.* 169 H5
Findon *W.Suss.* 16 D3
Findon Mains 174 D5
Findon Valley 16 D3
Findrassie 175 J5
Findron 167 J3
Finedon 69 E5
Finegand 159 G3
Fingal Street 72 D4
Fingask 169 F2
Fingerpost 65 G5
Fingest 42 C3
Finghall 110 A4
Fingland *Cumb.* 117 F1
Fingland *D. & G.* 134 D5
Fingland *D. & G.* 133 F4
Finglesham 33 F3
Fingringhoe 60 B5
Finkle Street 94 A3
Finlarig 150 A1
Finmere 56 B4
Finnart *Arg. & B.* 149 E5
Finnart *P. & K.* 158 A4
Finney Hill 67 G1
Finningham 60 B1
Finningley 95 D3
Finnygaud 176 E5
Finsbay (Fionnsbhagh) 171 F3
Finsbury 44 C4
Finstall 66 B5
Finsthwaite 107 E4
Finstock 41 F1
Finstown 185 C6
Fintry *Aber.* 177 F5
Fintry *Stir.* 142 A1
Finwood 55 D1
Finzean 168 D5
Fionnphort 146 B2
Fionnsbhagh (Finsbay) 171 F3
Fir Tree 120 A4
Firbank 108 B3
Firbeck 94 C4
Firby *N.Yorks.* 110 B4
Firby *N.Yorks.* 103 G1
Firgrove 92 D1
Firs Lane 92 A2
Firsby 84 C1
Firsdown 26 D4
Firth 186 D5
Fishbourne *I.o.W.* 15 E3
Fishbourne *W.Suss.* 16 A3
Fishburn 120 C4
Fishcross 151 E5
Fisherford 168 E1
Fisher's Pond 27 F5
Fisher's Row 100 A3
Fishersgate 17 E3
Fisherstreet 29 E4
Fisherton *High.* 174 E6
Fisherton *S.Ayr.* 132 A4
Fisherton de la Mere 26 A4
Fishguard (Abergwaun) 48 C4
Fishlake 95 D1
Fishleigh Barton 21 F3
Fishley 87 F4
Fishnish 155 F5
Fishpond Bottom 11 G3
Fishponds 39 F5
Fishpool 92 C2
Fishtoft 84 B3
Fishtoft Drove 84 B3
Fishtown of Usan 161 F4
Fishwick *Lancs.* 100 B4
Fishwick *Sc.Bord.* 145 G4
Fiskerton *Lincs.* 96 A5
Fiskerton *Notts.* 82 C2
Fitling 105 E4
Fittleton 26 C3
Fittleworth 16 C2
Fitton End 70 C1
Fitz 64 D1
Fitzhead 23 E5
Fitzroy 23 E5
Fitzwilliam 94 B1
Fiunary 155 F5
Five Acres 39 E1
Five Ash Down 17 G1
Five Ashes 18 A1
Five Bridges 53 F3
Five Houses 14 D4
Five Lanes 38 D3
Five Oak Green 31 F4
Five Oaks *Chan.I.* 8 C5
Five Oaks *W.Suss.* 29 F5
Five Roads 36 A2
Five Turnings 64 B5
Five Wents 32 A3
Fivehead 24 A5
Fivelanes 5 G1
Flack's Green 45 G1
Flackwell Heath 43 D4
Fladbury 54 B3
Fladdabister 187 D9
Flagg 80 C1
Flamborough 113 F5
Flamstead 43 F1
Flamstead End 44 C2
Flansham 16 B3
Flanshaw 102 C5
Flasby 101 F2
Flash 80 B1
Flashader 171 J6
Flask Inn 112 C2
Flaunden 43 F2
Flawborough 82 C3
Flawith 103 D1
Flax Bourton 24 C1
Flax Moss 101 D5
Flaxby 102 C2
Flaxholme 81 E3
Flaxlands 72 C2
Flaxley 39 F1
Flaxpool 23 E4
Flaxton 103 F1
Fleckney 68 B3
Flecknoe 56 A1
Fledborough 95 F5
Fleet *Hants.* 28 D2
Fleet *Hants.* 15 G2
Fleet *Lincs.* 84 B5
Fleet Hargate 84 B5
Fleetville 44 A2
Fleetwood 99 G3
Fleggburgh (Burgh St. Margaret) 87 F4
Flemingston 37 G5
Flemington 142 A4
Flempton 59 G1
Fleoideabhagh 171 F3
Flesherin 179 H4
Fletchersbridge 5 F3
Fletchertown 117 F2
Fletching 17 G1
Flete 8 C2
Fleuchats 168 B4
Fleur-de-lis 38 A3
Flexbury 20 C5
Flexford 29 E3
Flimby 116 D3
Flimwell 31 G5
Flint (Y Fflint) 90 D5
Flint Cross 58 C3
Flint Mountain 90 D5
Flintham 82 C3
Flinton 105 E4
Flint's Green 67 E5
Flishinghurst 31 G5
Flitcham 85 F5
Flitholme 108 C1
Flitton 57 F4
Flitwick 57 F4
Flixborough 95 F1
Flixton *Gt.Man.* 92 B3
Flixton *N.Yorks.* 112 D5
Flixton *Suff.* 73 E3
Flockton 93 G1
Flockton Green 93 G1
Flodden 136 D3
Flodigarry 171 K4
Flood's Ferry 70 B3
Flookburgh 107 E5
Floors 176 C5
Flordon 72 C2
Flore 56 B1
Flotta 185 C8
Flotterton 128 C1
Flowton 60 B3
Flushdyke 102 B5
Flushing *Aber.* 177 J6
Flushing *Cornw.* 3 F3
Flushing *Cornw.* 3 E4
Fluxton 11 D3
Flyford Flavell 54 B2
Foals Green 73 D4
Fobbing 45 G4
Fochabers 176 B5
Fochriw 38 A2
Fockerby 95 F1
Fodderletter 167 J2
Fodderty 174 C6
Foddington 24 C5
Foel 63 F1
Foelgastell 36 B1
Foggathorpe 103 G4
Fogo 145 E5
Fogorig 145 E5
Fogwatt 175 K6
Foindle 180 D4
Folda 159 G3
Fole 80 B4
Foleshill 67 F4
Folke 12 C1
Folkestone 33 E5
Folkingham 83 F4
Folkington 18 A3
Folksworth 69 G4
Folkton 113 D5
Folla Rule 169 F1
Follifoot 102 C2
Folly *Dorset* 12 D2
Folly *Pembs.* 48 C5
Folly Gate 7 F1
Fonmon 23 D1
Fonthill Bishop 26 A4
Fonthill Gifford 26 A4
Fontmell Magna 13 E1
Fontmell Parva 13 E1
Fontwell 16 B3
Font-y-gary 23 D1
Foolow 93 F5
Footherley 66 D2
Foots Cray 45 D5
Forbestown 168 B3
Force Forge 107 E3
Force Green 30 D3
Forcett 110 A1
Forches Cross 10 A2
Ford *Arg. & B.* 148 A4
Ford *Bucks.* 42 C2
Ford *Devon* 8 C2
Ford *Devon* 21 E3
Ford *Devon* 9 D3
Ford *Glos.* 54 C5
Ford *Mersey.* 91 E3
Ford *Midloth.* 144 A3
Ford *Northumb.* 137 D3
Ford *Pembs.* 48 C5
Ford *Plym.* 8 A2
Ford *Shrop.* 64 D1
Ford *Som.* 23 D5
Ford *Staffs.* 80 B2
Ford *W.Suss.* 16 B3
Ford *Wilts.* 40 A5
Ford End 45 F1
Ford Green 100 A3
Ford Heath 64 D1
Ford Street 11 E1
Forda 7 F1
Fordbridge 67 D4
Fordcombe 31 E4
Fordell 143 F1
Forden 64 B2
Forder Green 9 D1
Fordgate 24 A4
Fordham *Cambs.* 71 E5
Fordham *Essex* 60 A5
Fordham *Norf.* 71 E3
Fordham Abbey 59 E1
Fordham Heath 60 A5
Fordhouses 66 B2
Fordingbridge 14 A1
Fordon 113 D5
Fordoun 161 F2
Ford's Green 60 B1
Fordstreet 60 A5
Fordwells 41 F1
Fordwich 33 D3
Fordyce 176 D4
Forebrae 151 E2
Forebridge 79 G5
Foredale 101 E1
Foreland 138 A3
Foremark 81 E5
Forest 110 B2
Forest Coal Pit 52 B5
Forest Gate 44 D4
Forest Green 29 G3
Forest Hall *Cumb.* 107 G2
Forest Hall *T. & W.* 120 B1
Forest Head 118 B2
Forest Hill *Gt.Lon.* 44 C5
Forest Hill *Oxon.* 42 A2
Forest Lane Head 102 C2
Forest Lodge *Arg. & B.* 157 E5
Forest Lodge *P. & K.* 159 E2
Forest Mill 151 E5
Forest Row 30 D5
Forest Side 15 D4
Forest Town 81 G1
Forestburn Gate 128 C2
Forest-in-Teesdale 119 E5
Forestside 15 G1
Forfar 160 C4
Forgandenny 151 F3
Forge 63 D3
Forgie 176 B5
Forhill 66 C5
Formby 91 D2
Forncett End 72 C2
Forncett St. Mary 72 C2
Forncett St. Peter 72 C2
Forneth 159 F5
Fornham All Saints 59 G1
Fornham St. Martin 59 G1
Fornighty 175 G6
Forres 175 H6
Forrest 142 C3
Forrest Lodge 123 G2
Forsbrook 79 G3
Forse 183 H5
Forsie 183 F2
Forsinain 182 E4
Forsinard 182 D4
Forston 12 C3
Fort Augustus 165 K4
Fort George 174 E6
Fort William 156 D2
Forter 159 G3
Forteviot 151 F3
Forth 142 D4
Forthampton 54 A4
Fortingall 158 C5
Fortis Green 44 B4
Forton *Hants.* 27 F3
Forton *Lancs.* 100 A2
Forton *Shrop.* 64 D1
Forton *Som.* 11 G2
Forton *Staffs.* 79 E5
Fortrie 176 E6
Fortrose 174 E6
Fortuneswell 12 C5
Forty Green 43 E3
Forty Hill 44 C3
Forward Green 60 B2
Fosbury 27 E2
Foscot 55 E5
Fosdyke 84 B4
Foss 158 C4
Foss Cross 40 C2
Fossdale 109 D3
Fossebridge 40 C1
Foster Street 45 D2
Fosterhouses 94 D1
Foster's Booth 56 B2
Foston *Derbys.* 80 C4
Foston *Leics.* 68 B3
Foston *Lincs.* 83 D3
Foston *N.Yorks.* 103 F1
Foston on the Wolds 104 D2
Fotherby 96 D3
Fotheringhay 69 F3
Foubister 185 E7
Foul Mile 18 B2
Foula 186 B3
Foulbog 134 D5
Foulden *Norf.* 71 F3
Foulden *Sc.Bord.* 145 G4
Foulness Island 46 D3
Foulridge 101 E3
Foulsham 86 B3
Foulstone 107 G4
Foulzie 177 F4
Fountainhall 144 B5
Four Ashes *Staffs.* 66 B2
Four Ashes *Staffs.* 66 A4
Four Ashes *Suff.* 72 A4
Four Crosses *Denb.* 76 D3
Four Crosses *Powys* 64 B1
Four Crosses *Powys* 63 G2
Four Crosses *Staffs.* 66 B2
Four Elms 31 D4
Four Forks 23 F4
Four Gotes 70 C1
Four Lane Ends *B'burn.* 100 C5
Four Lane Ends *Ches.* 78 C1

Four Lane Ends York 103 F2
Four Lanes 3 D3
Four Marks 28 B4
Four Mile Bridge 88 A5
Four Oaks E.Suss. 19 D1
Four Oaks Glos. 53 F5
Four Oaks W.Mid. 67 E4
Four Oaks W.Mid. 66 D3
Four Oaks Park 66 D3
Four Roads 36 A2
Four Throws 18 C1
Fourlane Ends 81 E2
Fourlanes End 79 F2
Fourpenny 175 F2
Fourstones 119 E1
Fovant 26 B5
Foveran House 169 H2
Fowey 5 F4
Fowlis 152 B1
Fowlis Wester 151 E2
Fowlmere 58 C3
Fownhope 53 E4
Fox Hatch 45 E3
Fox Lane 29 D2
Fox Street 60 B5
Foxbar 141 F3
Foxcombe Hill 41 G2
Foxcote Glos. 40 C1
Foxcote Som. 25 E2
Foxdale 98 A4
Foxearth 59 G3
Foxfield 106 D4
Foxham 40 B5
Foxhole Cornw. 5 D4
Foxhole High. 166 C1
Foxholes 112 D5
Foxhunt Green 18 A2
Foxley Here. 52 D3
Foxley Norf. 86 B3
Foxley Northants. 56 B2
Foxley Wilts. 40 A4
Foxt 80 B3
Foxton Cambs. 58 C3
Foxton Dur. 120 C5
Foxton Leics. 68 B3
Foxup 109 D5
Foxwist Green 78 D1
Foy 53 E5
Foyers 166 B2
Frachadil 154 C4
Fraddam 2 C3
Fraddon 4 D4
Fradley 67 D1
Fradswell 79 G4
Fraisthorpe 105 D1
Framfield 17 G1
Framingham Earl 87 D5
Framingham Pigot 87 D5
Framlingham 61 D1
Frampton Dorset 12 C3
Frampton Lincs. 84 B4
Frampton Cotterell 39 F4
Frampton Mansell 40 B2
Frampton on Severn 39 G2
Frampton West End 84 A3
Framsden 60 D2
Framwellgate Moor 120 B3
France Lynch 40 B2
Frances Green 100 C4
Franche 66 A5
Frandley 92 A5
Frankby 90 D4
Frankfort 87 E3
Frankley 66 C4
Franksbridge 52 A2
Frankton 67 G5
Frant 31 E5
Fraserburgh 177 H4
Frating 60 B5
Fratton 15 F2
Freasley 67 E3
Freathy 7 D5
Freckenham 71 E5
Freckleton 100 A5
Freeby 82 D5
Freefolk 27 F3
Freehay 80 B3
Freeland 41 G1
Freester 187 D7
Freethorpe 87 F5
Freethorpe Common 87 F5
Freiston 84 B3
Freiston Shore 84 B3
Fremington Devon 21 F2
Fremington N.Yorks. 109 F3
Frenchay 39 F5
Frenchbeer 7 G2
Frendraught 176 E6
Frenich 149 G4
Frensham 28 D3
Fresgoe 182 E2
Freshbrook 40 D4
Freshfield 91 D2
Freshford 25 E2
Freshwater 14 C4
Freshwater Bay 14 C4
Freshwater East 34 D3
Fressingfield 73 D4
Freston 60 C4
Freswick 183 J2
Fretherne 39 G2
Frettenham 86 D4
Freuchie 152 A4
Freystrop Cross 34 C1
Friars Carse 124 D2
Friar's Gate 31 D5
Friarton 151 G2
Friday Bridge 70 C2
Friday Street E.Suss. 18 B3
Friday Street Suff. 60 D2
Friday Street Suff. 61 E2
Friday Street Surr. 29 G3
Fridaythorpe 104 A2
Friern Barnet 44 B3
Friesthorpe 96 A4
Frieston 83 E3
Frieth 42 C3
Frilford 41 G3
Frilsham 42 A5
Frimley 29 D2
Frimley Green 29 D2
Frindsbury 31 G2
Fring 85 F4
Fringford 56 B5
Friningham 32 A3
Frinsted 32 A3
Frinton-on-Sea 47 F1
Friockheim 161 D4
Friog 62 C1
Frisby on the Wreake 68 B1
Friskney 84 C2
Friskney Eaudyke 84 C2
Friston E.Suss. 18 A4
Friston Suff. 61 F1
Fritchley 81 E2
Frith 32 B3
Frith Bank 84 B3
Frith Common 53 F1
Fritham 14 B1
Frithelstock 21 E4
Frithelstock Stone 21 E4
Frithville 84 B2
Frittenden 32 A4
Frittiscombe 9 E3
Fritton Norf. 72 D2
Fritton Norf. 87 F5
Fritwell 56 A5
Frizinghall 102 A4
Frizington 116 D5
Frocester 39 G2
Frochas 64 B2
Frodesley 65 E2
Frodesley Lane 65 E2
Frodingham 95 F1
Frodsham 91 G5
Frog End 58 C2
Frog Pool 53 G1
Frogden 136 B4
Froggatt 93 G5
Froghall 80 B3
Frogham 14 A1
Frogland Cross 39 F4
Frogmore Devon 9 D3
Frogmore Hants. 28 D2
Frogmore Herts. 44 A2
Frogwell 6 D4
Frolesworth 68 A3
Frome 25 E3
Frome Market 25 F2
Frome St. Quintin 12 B2
Frome Whitfield 12 C3
Fromes Hill 53 F3
Fron Gwyn. 74 C4
Fron Powys 64 B2
Fron Powys 51 G1
Fron Powys 64 A3
Fron Isaf 77 F4
Froncysyllte 77 F3
Fron-goch 76 C4
Frostenden 73 F3
Frosterley 119 G4
Froxfield 27 E1
Froxfield Green 28 C5
Fryerning 45 F2
Fugglestone St. Peter 26 C4
Fulbeck 83 E2
Fulbourn 58 D2
Fulbrook 41 E1
Fulflood 27 F5
Fulford Som. 23 F5
Fulford Staffs. 79 G4
Fulford York 103 F3
Fulham 44 B5
Fulking 17 E2
Full Sutton 103 G2
Fullaford 21 G2
Fuller Street 45 G1
Fuller's Moor 78 B2
Fullerton 27 E4
Fulletby 96 C5
Fullwood 141 F4
Fulmer 43 F4
Fulmodeston 86 A2
Fulnetby 96 B5
Fulready 55 E3
Fulstone 93 F2
Fulstow 96 D3
Fulwell Oxon. 55 F5
Fulwell T. & W. 120 C2
Fulwood Lancs. 100 B4
Fulwood S.Yorks. 94 A4
Fundenhall 72 C2
Fundenhall Street 72 C2
Funtington 16 A3
Funtley 15 E2
Funzie 186 F3
Furley 11 F2
Furnace Arg. & B. 148 C4
Furnace Carmar. 36 B2
Furnace Cere. 62 C3
Furnace High. 173 F4
Furnace End 67 E3
Furner's Green 17 G1
Furness Vale 93 E4
Furneux Pelham 58 C5
Furnham 11 G2
Further Quarter 32 A5
Furtho 56 C3
Furze Green 72 D3
Furze Platt 43 D4
Furzehill Devon 22 A3
Furzehill Dorset 13 G2
Furzeley Corner 15 F1
Furzey Lodge 14 C2
Furzley 14 B1
Fyfett 11 F1
Fyfield Essex 45 E2
Fyfield Glos. 41 E2
Fyfield Hants. 27 D3
Fyfield Oxon. 41 G3
Fyfield Wilts. 26 C1
Fyfield Wilts. 26 C1
Fylingthorpe 112 C2
Fyning 28 D5
Fyvie 169 F1

▼G

Gabalfa 38 A5
Gabhsunn Bho Dheas 179 G2
Gabhsunn Bho Thuath 179 G2
Gablon 174 E2
Gabroc Hill 141 F4
Gaddesby 68 B1
Gaddesden Row 43 F1
Gadebridge 43 F2
Gadshill 45 G5
Gaer Newport 38 B4
Gaer Powys 52 A5
Gaer-fawr 38 D3
Gaerllwyd 38 D3
Gaerwen 88 C5
Gagingwell 55 G5
Gaich High. 167 H2
Gaich High. 166 D1
Gaick Lodge 158 C1
Gailes 132 B2
Gailey 66 B1
Gainford 110 A1
Gainsborough 95 F3
Gainsford End 59 F4
Gairloch 172 D4
Gairlochy 157 D1
Gairney Bank 151 G5
Gairnshiel Lodge 167 K4
Gaitsgill 117 G2
Galabank 144 B5
Galashiels 135 F2
Galdenoch 122 C4
Gale 92 D1
Galgate 100 A2
Galhampton 24 D5
Gallanach 148 A2
Gallantry Bank 78 C2
Gallatown 152 A5
Gallchoille 147 G5
Gallery 161 E3
Galley Common 67 F3
Galleyend 45 G2
Galleywood 45 G2
Gallowfauld 160 C5
Gallowhill 141 F3
Gallows Green 80 B3
Gallowstree Common 42 B4
Gallowstree Elm 66 A4
Gallt Melyd (Meliden) 90 B4
Galltair 164 E2
Gallt-y-foel 75 E1
Gallypot Street 31 D5
Galmington 23 F5
Galmisdale 155 D1
Galmpton Devon 8 C3
Galmpton Torbay 9 E2
Galmpton Warborough 9 E2
Galphay 110 B5
Galston 132 C2
Galtrigill 171 G6
Gamble's Green 45 G1
Gamblesby 118 C4
Gamelsby 117 F1
Gamesley 93 E3
Gamlingay 58 A2
Gamlingay Cinques 58 A2
Gamlingay Great Heath 58 A2
Gammaton 21 E3
Gammaton Moor 21 E3
Gammersgill 109 F4
Gamrie 177 F4
Gamston Notts. 95 E5
Gamston Notts. 82 B4
Ganarew 39 E1
Gang 6 D4
Ganllwyd 76 A5
Gannochy 161 E2
Ganstead 105 D4
Ganthorpe 111 F5
Ganton 112 C5
Ganwick Corner 44 B3
Gaodhail 147 F1
Gappah 10 B5
Gara Bridge 8 D2
Garabal 149 F3
Garadheancal 173 F1
Garbat 174 B5
Garbhallt 148 C5
Garboldisham 72 B3
Garden 150 A5
Garden City 78 A1
Garden Village 93 G3
Gardeners Green 28 D1
Gardenstown 177 F4
Garderhouse 187 C8
Gardham 104 B3
Gare Hill 25 E3
Garelochhead 149 E5
Garford 41 G3
Garforth 102 D4
Gargrave 101 F2
Gargunnock 150 C5
Gariob 139 F1
Garlic Street 72 D3
Garlies Castle 123 F4
Garlieston 115 E2
Garlinge Green 32 D3
Garlogie 169 F4
Garmelow 79 F5
Garmond 177 G5
Garmony 155 F5
Garmouth 176 B4
Garmston 65 F2
Garnant 36 C1
Garndolbenmaen 75 D3
Garneddwen 63 D2
Garnett Bridge 107 G3
Garnfadryn 74 B4
Garnswllt 36 C2
Garrabost 179 H4
Garrachra 140 B1
Garralburn 176 C5
Garras 3 E4
Garreg 75 F3
Garreg Bank 64 B1
Garrett's Green 67 D4
Garrick 150 D3
Garrigill 118 D3
Garriston 110 A3
Garroch 123 G2
Garrochty 140 B4
Garros 171 K5
Garrow 150 D1
Garryhorn 123 G1
Garrynahine (Gearraidh na h-Aibhne) 178 E4
Garsdale 108 C4
Garsdale Head 108 C3
Garsdon 40 B4
Garshall Green 79 G4
Garsington 42 A2
Garstang 100 A3
Garston 91 F4
Garswood 91 G3
Gartachoil 150 A5
Gartally 166 B1
Gartavaich 139 G4
Gartbreck 138 A4
Gartcosh 142 A3
Garth Bridgend 37 E3
Garth Cere. 62 C4
Garth Gwyn. 89 D5
Garth I.o.M. 98 B4
Garth Powys 51 F3
Garth Shet. 187 B7
Garth Wrex. 77 F3
Garth Row 107 G3
Garthbrengy 51 G4
Garthdee 169 H4
Gartheli 50 B2
Garthmyl 64 A3
Garthorpe Leics. 82 D5
Garthorpe N.Lincs. 95 F1
Garths 107 G3
Garthynty 50 D3
Gartincaber 150 B4
Gartly 168 D1
Gartmore 150 A5
Gartnagrenach 139 F4
Gartnatra 138 B3
Gartness 141 G1
Gartocharn 141 F1
Garton 105 E4
Garton-on-the-Wolds 104 B1
Gartymore 183 F7
Garvald 144 C2
Garvamore 166 C5
Garvan 156 B2
Garvard 146 C5
Garve 173 K5
Garveld 130 B5
Garvestone 86 B5
Garvie 140 B1
Garvock Aber. 161 F2
Garvock Inclyde 141 D2
Garvock P. & K. 151 F3
Garwald 134 D5
Garwaldwaterfoot 134 D5
Garway 53 D5
Garway Hill 52 D5
Gask Aber. 177 J6
Gask Aber. 177 F6
Gask P. & K. 151 E3
Gaskan 156 A2
Gass 132 C5
Gastard 25 F1
Gasthorpe 72 A3
Gaston Green 45 E1
Gatcombe 15 D4
Gate Burton 95 F4
Gate Helmsley 103 F2
Gate House 139 D2
Gateacre 91 F4
Gateford 94 C4
Gateforth 103 E5
Gatehead 132 B2
Gatehouse 159 D5
Gatehouse of Fleet 124 A5
Gatelawbridge 124 D1
Gateley 86 A3
Gatenby 110 C4
Gatesgarth 117 E5
Gateshaw 136 B4
Gateshead 120 B1
Gatesheath 78 B1
Gateside Aber. 168 E3
Gateside Angus 160 C5
Gateside Fife 151 G4
Gateside N.Ayr. 141 E4
Gateslack 133 G5
Gathurst 91 G2
Gatley 92 C4
Gattonside 135 G2
Gatwick Airport (London Gatwick Airport) 30 B4
Gaufron 51 F1
Gaulby 68 B2
Gauldry 152 B2
Gauntons Bank 78 C3
Gaunt's Common 13 G2
Gaunt's Earthcott 39 F4
Gautby 96 B5
Gavinton 145 E4
Gawber 94 A2
Gawcott 56 B4
Gawsworth 92 C5
Gawthrop 108 B4
Gawthwaite 107 D4
Gay Bowers 45 G2
Gay Street 29 F5
Gaydon 55 F2
Gayhurst 56 D3
Gayle 109 D4
Gayles 110 A2
Gayton Mersey. 91 D4
Gayton Norf. 71 F1
Gayton Northants. 56 C2
Gayton Staffs. 79 G5
Gayton le Marsh 97 E4
Gayton le Wold 96 C4
Gayton Thorpe 71 F1
Gaywood 85 E5
Gazeley 59 F1
Geanies House 175 F4
Gearach 138 A4
Gearnsary 182 C5
Gearradh 156 B3
Gearradh Bhailteas 162 C2
Gearraidh Bhaird 179 F5
Gearraidh na h-Aibhne (Garrynahine) 178 E4
Gearraidh na Monadh 162 C3
Gearrannan 178 D3
Geary 171 H5
Gedding 60 A2
Geddington 69 D4
Gedgrave Hall 61 F3
Gedintailor 164 B1
Gedling 82 B3
Gedney 84 C5
Gedney Broadgate 84 C5
Gedney Drove End 84 C5
Gedney Dyke 84 C5
Gedney Hill 70 B1
Gee Cross 93 D3
Geilston 141 E2
Geirinis 170 C7
Geisiadar 178 D4
Geldeston 73 E2
Gell Conwy 76 B1
Gell Gwyn. 75 D4
Gelli 37 F3
Gelli Gynan 77 E2
Gellideg 37 G2
Gellifor 77 E1
Gelligaer 38 A3
Gellilydan 75 F4
Gellioedd 76 C3
Gelly 35 D1
Gellyburn 151 F1
Gellywen 49 F5
Gelston D. & G. 124 B5
Gelston Lincs. 83 E3
Gembling 104 D2
Gemmil 147 G4
Genoch 122 C5
Genoch Square 122 C5
Gentleshaw 66 C1
Geocrab 171 G2
George Green 43 F4
George Nympton 22 A5
Georgeham 21 E2
Georgetown 141 F3
Gerlan 75 F1
Germansweek 7 E1
Germoe 2 C4
Gerrans 3 F3
Gerrards Cross 43 F4
Gerston 183 G3
Gestingthorpe 59 G4
Geuffordd 64 B1
Geufron 63 E4
Gibbet Hill 25 E3
Gibbshill 124 B3
Gibraltar Lincs. 85 D2
Gibraltar Suff. 60 C2
Giddeahall 40 A5
Giddy Green 13 E4
Gidea Park 45 E4
Gidleigh 7 G2
Giffnock 141 G4
Gifford 144 C3
Giffordland 141 D5
Giffordtown 152 A3
Giggleswick 101 E1
Gigha 139 E5
Gilberdyke 104 A5
Gilbert's End 54 A3
Gilchriston 144 B3
Gilcrux 117 E3
Gildersome 102 B5
Gildingwells 94 C4
Gilesgate Moor 120 B3
Gileston 22 D1
Gilfach 38 A3
Gilfach Goch 37 F4
Gilfachrheda 50 A2
Gilgarran 116 D4
Gill 118 A5
Gillamoor 111 F4
Gillen 171 H5
Gillenbie 125 F2
Gillfoot 125 D3
Gilling East 111 F5
Gilling West 110 A2
Gillingham Dorset 25 F5
Gillingham Med. 31 G2
Gillingham Norf. 73 F2
Gillivoan 183 G5
Gillock 183 H3
Gillow Heath 79 F2
Gills 183 J1
Gill's Green 31 G5
Gilmanscleuch 135 E3
Gilmerton Edin. 143 G3
Gilmerton P. & K. 151 D2
Gilmilnscroft 133 D3
Gilmonby 109 E1
Gilmorton 68 A4
Gilsland 118 C1
Gilsland Spa 118 C1
Gilson 67 D4
Gilstead 102 A4
Gilston 144 B4
Gilston Park 44 D1
Giltbrook 81 F3
Gilwern 38 B1
Gimingham 87 D2
Gin Pit 92 A2
Ginclough 93 D5
Ginger's Green 18 B2
Giosla 178 D5
Gipping 60 B1
Gipsey Bridge 84 A3
Girlsta 187 D7
Girsby 110 C2
Girtford 57 G3
Girthon 124 A5
Girton Cambs. 58 C1
Girton Notts. 82 D1
Girvan 122 C1
Gisburn 101 E3
Gisburn Cotes 101 E3
Gisleham 73 G3
Gislingham 72 B4
Gissing 72 C3
Gittisham 11 E3
Givons Grove 29 G2
Glackour 173 H3
Gladestry 52 B2
Gladsmuir 144 B2
Glaic 140 B2
Glais 36 D2
Glaisdale 111 G2
Glaister 131 E2
Glame 172 B7
Glamis 160 B5
Glan Conwy 76 B2
Glanaber Terrace 76 A3
Glanaman 36 C1
Glanbran 51 E4
Glan-Denys 50 B2
Glanderston 168 D2
Glandford 86 B1
Glan-Duar 50 B3
Glandwr 49 E5
Glan-Dwyfach 75 D3
Glangrwyney 38 B1
Glanllynfi 37 E3
Glanmule 64 A3
Glan-rhyd N.P.T. 37 D2
Glanrhyd Pembs. 49 E3
Glanton 137 E5
Glanton Pyke 137 E5
Glantwymyn (Cemmaes Road) 63 E2
Glanvilles Wootton 12 C2
Glanwern 62 C4
Glanwydden 89 G4
Glan-y-don 90 C5
Glanyferi (Ferryside) 35 G1
Glan-y-llyn 38 A4
Glan-y-nant 63 F4
Glan-yr-afon Gwyn. 76 C3
Glan-yr-afon Gwyn. 76 D3
Glan-yr-afon I.o.A. 89 E4
Glan-y-Wern 75 F4
Glapthorn 69 F3
Glapwell 81 F1
Glasahoile 149 G4
Glasbury 52 A4
Glaschoil 167 H1
Glascoed Mon. 38 C2
Glascoed Wrex. 77 F2
Glascorrie 168 C5
Glascote 67 E2
Glascwm 52 A2
Glasdrum 156 C5
Glasfryn 76 C2
Glasgow 141 G3
Glasgow Airport 141 F3
Glasgow Prestwick International Airport (Prestwick International Airport) 132 B3
Glashmore 169 F4
Glasinfryn 75 E1
Glasnacardoch 164 C5
Glasnakille 164 B3
Glaspant 49 F4
Glaspwll 62 D3
Glassburn 165 K1
Glassel 168 E5
Glassenbury 31 G5
Glasserton 115 E3
Glassford 142 B5
Glasshouse 53 G5
Glasshouse Hill 53 G5
Glasshouses 102 A1
Glassingall 150 C4
Glasslie 152 A4
Glasson Cumb. 126 A5
Glasson Lancs. 100 A2
Glassonby 118 B4
Glasterlaw 161 D4
Glaston 69 D2
Glastonbury 24 B4
Glatton 69 G4
Glazebrook 92 A3
Glazebury 92 A3
Glazeley 65 G4
Gleadless 94 A4
Gleadsmoss 79 F1
Gleann Tholastaidh 179 H3
Gleaston 107 D5
Glecknabae 140 B3
Gledhow 102 C4
Gledrid 77 F4
Glemsford 59 G3
Glen D. & G. 124 C3
Glen D. & G. 123 G5
Glen Auldyn 98 C2
Glen Mona 98 C3
Glen Parva 68 A3
Glen Trool Lodge 123 F2
Glen Village 142 C2
Glen Vine 98 B4
Glenae 125 D2
Glenaladale 156 A2
Glenald 149 E5
Glenamachrie 148 B2
Glenapp Castle 122 B2
Glenarm 160 B3
Glenbarr 130 B2
Glenbatrick 138 D2
Glenbeg High. 173 K3
Glenbeg High. 167 H2
Glenbeg High. 155 E3
Glenbeich 150 B2
Glenbervie Aber. 161 F1
Glenbervie Falk. 142 C1
Glenboig 142 B3
Glenborrodale 155 F3
Glenbranter 148 D5
Glenbreck 134 B3
Glenbrittle 163 K2
Glenbuck 133 F3
Glenburn 141 F3
Glenbyre 147 E2
Glencaple 125 D4
Glencarse 151 G2
Glencat 168 D5
Glenceitlein 156 D5
Glencloy 131 F2
Glencoe 156 D4
Glenconglass 167 J2
Glencraig 151 G5
Glencripesdale 155 F4
Glencrosh 124 B2
Glencruittein 148 A2
Glencuie 168 C3
Glendearg D. & G. 134 D5
Glendearg Sc.Bord. 135 G2
Glendessary 165 F5
Glendevon 151 E4
Glendoebeg 166 B4
Glendoick 152 A2
Glendoll Lodge 160 A2
Glendoune 122 C1
Glendrissaig 122 C1
Glenduckie 152 A3
Glenduisk 122 D2
Glendye Lodge 161 E1
Gleneagles Hotel 151 E3
Gleneagles House 151 E4
Glenearn 151 G3
Glenegedale 138 B4
Glenelg 164 E3
Glenfarg 151 G3
Glenfeochan 148 A2
Glenfield 68 A2
Glenfinnan 156 B1
Glenfoot 151 G3
Glengalmadale 156 A4
Glengap 124 A5
Glengarnock 141 E4
Glengarrisdale 147 F5
Glengennet 123 D1
Glengolly 183 G2
Glengrasco 171 K7
Glengyle 149 F3
Glenhead 124 C2
Glenhead Farm 160 A3
Glenhurich 156 A3
Glenkerry 135 D4
Glenkiln 131 F2
Glenkin 140 C1
Glenkindie 168 C3
Glenlair 124 B3
Glenlatterach 175 K6
Glenlean 140 B1
Glenlee Angus 160 C2
Glenlee D. & G. 124 A2
Glenlichorn 150 C3
Glenlivet 167 J2
Glenlochar 124 B4
Glenluce 122 C5
Glenmallan 149 E5
Glenmanna 133 F5
Glenmavis 142 B3
Glenmaye 98 A4
Glenmeanie 173 J6
Glenmore Arg. & B. 140 B3
Glenmore High. 171 K7
Glenmore High. 167 G4
Glenmore Lodge 167 G4
Glenmoy 160 C3
Glenmuick 181 F7
Glennoe 148 C1
Glenochar 134 A4
Glenogil 160 C3
Glenprosen Village 160 B3
Glenquiech 160 C3
Glenramskill 130 C4
Glenrazie 123 E4
Glenridding 117 G5
Glenrisdell 139 G4
Glenrossal 174 B1
Glenrothes 152 A4
Glensanda 156 A5
Glensaugh 161 E2
Glensgaich 174 B5
Glenshalg 168 D4
Glenshellish 148 D5
Glensluain 148 C5
Glentaggart 133 G3
Glentham 96 A3
Glenton 168 E2
Glentress 135 D2
Glentrool 123 E3
Glentruan 98 C1
Glentworth 95 G4
Glenuachdarach 171 K6
Glenuig 155 F2
Glenure 156 C5
Glenurquhart 174 E5
Glenwhilly 122 C3
Glespin 133 G3
Gletness 187 D7
Glewstone 53 E5
Glinton 69 G2
Glooston 68 C3
Glororum 137 F3
Glossop 93 E3
Gloster Hill 129 E1
Gloucester 40 A1
Gloup 186 E2
Gloweth 4 B5
Glusburn 101 G3
Gluss 186 C5
Glympton 55 G5
Glyn 76 A2
Glyn Ceiriog 77 F4
Glynarthen 49 G3
Glyncoch 37 G3
Glyncorrwg 37 E3
Glyn-Cywarch 75 F4
Glynde 17 G3
Glyndebourne 17 G2
Glyndyfrdwy 77 E3
Glynneath 37 E2
Glynogwr 37 F4
Glyntaff 37 G4
Gnosall 79 F5
Gnosall Heath 79 F5
Goadby 68 C3
Goadby Marwood 82 C5
Goatacre 40 C5
Goatfield 148 C4
Goathill 12 C1
Goathland 112 B2
Goathurst 23 F4
Gobernuisgeach 182 E5
Gobhaig 178 C7
Gobowen 78 A4
Godalming 29 E3
Goddard's Corner 61 D1
Goddards Green 17 E1
Godden Green 31 E3
Goddington 31 D2
Godford Cross 11 E2
Godington 56 B5
Godleybrook 79 G3
Godmanchester 70 A5
Godmanstone 12 C3
Godmersham 32 C3
Godney 24 B3
Godolphin Cross 2 D3
Godor 64 B1
Godre'r-graig 37 D2
Godshill Hants. 14 A1
Godshill I.o.W. 15 E4
Godstone 30 C3
Godwick 86 A3
Goetre 38 C2
Goff's Oak 44 C2
Gogar 143 F2
Gogarth 89 F4
Goginan 62 C4
Goirtean a' Chladaich 156 C2
Goirtein 140 A1
Golan 75 E3
Golant 5 F4
Golberdon 6 D3
Golborne 92 A3
Golcar 93 F1
Gold Hill Cambs. 70 D3
Gold Hill Dorset 13 E1
Goldcliff 38 C4
Golden Cross 18 A2
Golden Green 31 F4
Golden Grove 36 B1
Golden Pot 28 C3
Golden Valley Derbys. 81 F2
Golden Valley Glos. 54 B5
Goldenhill 79 F2
Golders Green 44 B4
Goldhanger 46 C2
Goldielea 124 D3
Golding 65 E2
Goldington 57 F2
Goldsborough N.Yorks. 112 B1
Goldsborough N.Yorks. 102 C2
Goldsithney 2 C3
Goldstone 79 E5
Goldthorn Park 66 B3
Goldthorpe 94 B2
Goldworthy 21 D3
Golford 31 G5
Gollanfield 175 F6
Gollinglith Foot 110 A4
Golspie 175 F2
Golval 182 D2
Gomeldon 26 C4
Gomersal 102 B5
Gometra 154 C5
Gometra House 154 C5
Gomshall 29 F3
Gonachan Cottage 142 A1
Gonalston 82 B3
Gonerby Hill Foot 83 E4
Gonfirth 187 C6
Good Easter 45 F1
Gooderstone 71 F2
Goodleigh 21 G2
Goodmanham 104 A3
Goodmayes 45 D4
Goodnestone Kent 33 E3
Goodnestone Kent 32 C2
Goodrich 39 E1
Goodrington 9 E2
Goodshaw 101 E5

Goodshaw Fold 101 E5
Goodwick (Wdig) 48 C4
Goodworth Clatford 27 E3
Goodyers End 67 F4
Goole 103 G5
Goom's Hill 54 C2
Goonbell 4 B5
Goonhavern 4 B4
Goonvrea 4 B5
Goose Green *Essex* 60 C5
Goose Green *Essex* 60 C5
Goose Green *Gt.Man.* 91 G2
Goose Green *Kent* 31 F3
Goose Green *S.Glos.* 39 F5
Goose Pool 53 D4
Gooseham 20 C4
Goosehill Green 54 B1
Goosewell 8 B2
Goosey 41 F3
Goosnargh 100 B4
Goostrey 92 B5
Gorcott Hill 54 C1
Gorddinog 89 E5
Gordon 144 D5
Gordonbush 175 F1
Gordonstoun 175 J5
Gordonstown *Aber.* 176 D5
Gordonstown *Aber.* 169 F1
Gore Cross 26 B2
Gore End 27 F1
Gore Pit 46 B1
Gore Street 33 E2
Gorebridge 144 A3
Gorefield 70 C1
Gorey 8 D5
Gorgie 143 G2
Goring 42 B4
Goring Heath 42 B5
Goring-by-Sea 16 D3
Gorleston-on-Sea 87 G5
Gorllwyn 49 G4
Gornalwood 66 B3
Gorrachie 177 F5
Gorran Churchtown 5 D5
Gorran Haven 5 E5
Gors 62 C5
Gorsedd 90 C5
Gorseinon 36 B3
Gorseness 185 D6
Gorseybank 81 D2
Gorsgoch 50 A2
Gorslas 36 B1
Gorsley 53 F5
Gorsley Common 53 F5
Gorstage 92 A5
Gorstan 173 K5
Gorstanvorran 156 A2
Gorsty Hill 80 C5
Gorten 147 G1
Gortenbuie 147 E1
Gorteneorn 155 F3
Gorton *Arg. & B.* 154 A4
Gorton *Gt.Man.* 92 C3
Gosbeck 60 C2
Gosberton 84 A4
Gosberton Clough 83 G5
Goseley Dale 81 E5
Gosfield 59 F5
Gosford *Here.* 53 E1
Gosford *Oxon.* 42 A1
Gosforth *Cumb.* 106 B2
Gosforth *T. & W.* 120 B1
Gosland Green 78 C2
Gosmore 57 G5
Gospel End 66 B3
Gosport 15 F3
Gossabrough 186 E4
Gossington 39 G2
Gossops Green 30 B5
Goswick 137 E2
Gotham 81 G4
Gotherington 54 B5
Gothers 5 D4
Gott 187 D8
Gotton 23 F5
Goudhurst 31 G5
Goulceby 96 C5
Gourdas 177 F6
Gourdon 161 G2
Gourock 140 D2
Govan 141 G3
Goverton 82 C2
Goveton 9 D3
Govilon 38 B1
Gowanhill 177 J4
Gowdall 103 F5
Gowerton 36 B3
Gowkhall 143 E1
Gowkthrapple 142 B4
Gowthorpe 103 G2
Goxhill *E.Riding* 105 D3
Goxhill *N.Lincs.* 104 D5
Goytre 37 D4
Gozzard's Ford 41 G3
Grabhair 179 F6
Graby 83 F5
Gradbach 79 G1
Grade 3 E5
Gradeley Green 78 C2
Graffham 16 B2
Grafham *Cambs.* 57 G1
Grafham *Surr.* 29 F3
Grafton *Here.* 53 D4
Grafton *N.Yorks.* 102 D1
Grafton *Oxon.* 41 E2
Grafton *Shrop.* 64 D1
Grafton *Worcs.* 53 E1
Grafton *Worcs.* 54 B4
Grafton Flyford 54 B2
Grafton Regis 56 C3
Grafton Underwood 69 E4
Grafty Green 32 A4
Graianrhyd 77 F2
Graig *Carmar.* 36 A2
Graig *Conwy* 89 G5
Graig *Denb.* 90 B5
Graig-fechan 77 E2
Grain 32 A1
Grainel 138 A3
Grainhow 177 G6
Grains Bar 93 D2
Grainsby 96 C3
Grainthorpe 97 D3
Graiselound 95 E3
Gramisdale (Gramsdal) 170 D6
Grampound 4 D5
Grampound Road 4 D4
Gramsdal (Gramisdale) 170 D6
Granborough 56 C5
Granby 82 C4
Grandborough 55 G1
Grandes Rocques 9 F4
Grandtully 159 E4
Grange *Cumb.* 117 F5
Grange *E.Ayr.* 132 C2
Grange *High.* 165 K1
Grange *Med.* 31 G2
Grange *Mersey.* 90 D4
Grange *P. & K.* 152 A2
Grange Crossroads 176 C5
Grange de Lings 95 G5
Grange Hall 175 H5
Grange Hill 44 D3
Grange Moor 93 G1
Grange of Lindores 152 A3
Grange Villa 120 B2
Grangemill 80 D2
Grangemouth 142 D1
Grangemuir 152 D4
Grange-over-Sands 107 F5
Grangeston 122 D1
Grangetown *Cardiff* 38 A5
Grangetown *R. & C.* 121 E5
Granish 167 G3
Gransmoor 104 D2
Granston 48 B4
Grantchester 58 C2
Grantham 83 E4
Grantley 110 B5
Grantlodge 169 F3
Granton 143 G2
Granton House 134 B5
Grantown-on-Spey 167 H2
Grantsfield 53 E1
Grantshouse 145 F3
Grappenhall 92 A4
Grasby 96 A2
Grasmere 107 E2
Grass Green 59 F4
Grasscroft 93 D2
Grassendale 91 E4
Grassgarth 107 F3
Grassholme 119 F5
Grassington 101 G1
Grassmoor 81 F1
Grassthorpe 82 C1
Grateley 27 D3
Gratwich 80 B4
Gravel Hill 43 F3
Graveley *Cambs.* 58 A1
Graveley *Herts.* 58 A5
Gravelly Hill 66 D3
Gravels 64 C2
Graven 186 D5
Graveney 32 C2
Gravesend 45 F5
Grayingham 95 G3
Grayrigg 107 G3
Grays 45 F5
Grayshott 29 D4
Grayswood 29 E4
Grazeley 28 B1
Greasbrough 94 B3
Greasby 91 D4
Great Abington 58 D3
Great Addington 69 E5
Great Alne 54 D2
Great Altcar 91 E2
Great Amwell 44 C1
Great Asby 108 B1
Great Ashfield 60 A1
Great Ayton 111 E1
Great Baddow 45 G2
Great Bardfield 59 E4
Great Barford 57 G2
Great Barr 66 C3
Great Barrington 41 E1
Great Barrow 78 B1
Great Barton 59 G1
Great Barugh 111 G5
Great Bavington 128 B3
Great Bealings 60 D3
Great Bedwyn 27 D1
Great Bentley 60 C5
Great Bernera 178 D4
Great Billing 56 D1
Great Bircham 85 F4
Great Blakenham 60 C2
Great Bolas 78 D5
Great Bookham 29 G2
Great Bourton 55 G3
Great Bowden 68 C4
Great Bradley 59 E2
Great Braxted 46 B1
Great Bricett 60 B2
Great Brickhill 57 E4
Great Bridgeford 79 F5
Great Brington 56 B1
Great Bromley 60 B5
Great Broughton *Cumb.* 117 D3
Great Broughton *N.Yorks.* 111 E2
Great Buckland 31 F2
Great Budworth 92 A5
Great Burdon 110 C1
Great Burstead 45 F3
Great Busby 111 E2
Great Cambourne 58 B2
Great Canfield 45 E1
Great Canney 46 B2
Great Carlton 97 E4
Great Casterton 69 F2
Great Chalfield 25 F1
Great Chart 32 B4
Great Chatwell 65 G1
Great Chell 79 F2
Great Chesterford 58 D3
Great Cheverell 26 A2
Great Chishill 58 C4
Great Clacton 47 E1
Great Clifton 116 D4
Great Coates 96 C2
Great Comberton 54 B3
Great Corby 118 A2
Great Cornard 59 G3
Great Cowden 105 E3
Great Coxwell 41 E3
Great Crakehall 110 B4
Great Cransley 68 D5
Great Cressingham 71 G2
Great Crosby 91 E2
Great Crosthwaite 117 F4
Great Cubley 80 C4
Great Cumbrae 140 C4
Great Dalby 68 C1
Great Doddington 57 D1
Great Doward 39 E1
Great Dunham 71 G1
Great Dunmow 59 E5
Great Durnford 26 C4
Great Easton *Essex* 59 E5
Great Easton *Leics.* 68 D3
Great Eccleston 100 A3
Great Edstone 111 G4
Great Ellingham 72 B2
Great Elm 25 E3
Great Eversden 58 B2
Great Fencote 110 B3
Great Finborough 60 B2
Great Fransham 71 G1
Great Gaddesden 43 F1
Great Gidding 69 G4
Great Givendale 104 A2
Great Glemham 61 E1
Great Glen 68 B3
Great Gonerby 83 D4
Great Gransden 58 A2
Great Green *Cambs.* 58 A3
Great Green *Norf.* 73 D3
Great Green *Suff.* 60 A2
Great Green *Suff.* 72 C4
Great Green *Suff.* 72 B4
Great Habton 111 G5
Great Hale 83 G3
Great Hallingbury 45 E1
Great Hampden 42 D2
Great Harrowden 69 D5
Great Harwood 100 D4
Great Haseley 42 B2
Great Hatfield 105 D3
Great Haywood 80 B5
Great Heath 67 F4
Great Heck 103 E5
Great Henny 59 G4
Great Hinton 26 A2
Great Hockham 72 A2
Great Holland 47 F1
Great Horkesley 60 A4
Great Hormead 58 C4
Great Horton 102 A4
Great Horwood 56 C4
Great Houghton *Northants.* 56 C2
Great Houghton *S.Yorks.* 94 B2
Great Hucklow 93 F5
Great Kelk 104 D2
Great Kimble 42 D2
Great Kingshill 43 D3
Great Langton 110 B3
Great Leighs 45 G1
Great Limber 96 B2
Great Linford 56 D3
Great Livermere 71 G5
Great Longstone 93 G5
Great Lumley 120 B3
Great Lyth 65 D2
Great Malvern 53 G3
Great Maplestead 59 G4
Great Marton 99 G4
Great Massingham 85 F5
Great Melton 86 C5
Great Milton 42 B2
Great Missenden 43 D2
Great Mitton 100 D4
Great Mongeham 33 F3
Great Moulton 72 C2
Great Munden 58 B5
Great Musgrave 108 C1
Great Ness 64 D1
Great Notley 59 F5
Great Nurcot 22 C4
Great Oak 38 C2
Great Oakley *Essex* 60 C5
Great Oakley *Northants.* 69 D4
Great Offley 57 G5
Great Ormside 108 C1
Great Orton 117 G1
Great Ouseburn 102 D1
Great Oxendon 68 C4
Great Oxney Green 45 F2
Great Palgrave 71 G1
Great Parndon 44 D2
Great Paxton 58 A1
Great Plumpton 99 G4
Great Plumstead 87 E5
Great Ponton 83 E4
Great Potheridge 21 F4
Great Preston 102 C5
Great Purston 56 A4
Great Raveley 70 A4
Great Rissington 41 D1
Great Rollright 55 F4
Great Ryburgh 86 A3
Great Ryle 137 E5
Great Ryton 65 D2
Great Saling 59 F5
Great Salkeld 118 B4
Great Sampford 59 E4
Great Sankey 91 G4
Great Saredon 66 B2
Great Saxham 59 F1
Great Shefford 41 F5
Great Shelford 58 C2
Great Smeaton 110 C2
Great Snoring 86 A2
Great Somerford 40 B4
Great Stainton 120 C5
Great Stambridge 46 C3
Great Staughton 57 G1
Great Steeping 84 C1
Great Stonar 33 F3
Great Strickland 118 B5
Great Stukeley 70 A5
Great Sturton 96 C5
Great Sutton *Ches.* 91 E5
Great Sutton *Shrop.* 65 E4
Great Swinburne 128 B4
Great Tew 55 F5
Great Tey 59 G5
Great Thorness 15 D3
Great Thurlow 59 E3
Great Torr 8 C3
Great Torrington 21 E4
Great Tosson 128 C1
Great Totham *Essex* 46 B1
Great Totham *Essex* 46 B1
Great Tows 96 C3
Great Urswick 107 D5
Great Wakering 46 C4
Great Waldingfield 60 A3
Great Walsingham 86 A2
Great Waltham 45 F1
Great Warley 45 E3
Great Washbourne 54 B4
Great Weeke 10 A4
Great Welnetham 59 G2
Great Wenham 60 B4
Great Whittington 128 C4
Great Wigborough 46 C1
Great Wigsell 18 C1
Great Wilbraham 58 D2
Great Wilne 81 F4
Great Wishford 26 B4
Great Witcombe 40 B1
Great Witley 53 G1
Great Wolford 55 E4
Great Wratting 59 E3
Great Wymondley 58 A5
Great Wyrley 66 B2
Great Wytheford 65 E1
Great Yarmouth 87 G5
Great Yeldham 59 F4
Greatford 69 F1
Greatgate 80 B3
Greatham *Hants.* 28 C4
Greatham *Hart.* 121 D5
Greatham *W.Suss.* 16 C2
Greatness 31 E3
Greatstone-on-Sea 19 F1
Greatworth 56 A3
Green 77 D1
Green Cross 29 D4
Green End *Beds.* 57 G2
Green End *Bucks.* 57 E4
Green End *Cambs.* 70 A5
Green End *Cambs.* 70 B5
Green End *Herts.* 58 B5
Green End *Herts.* 58 B4
Green End *Warks.* 67 E4
Green Hammerton 103 D2
Green Hill 40 C4
Green Lane 54 C1
Green Moor 93 G3
Green Ore 24 C2
Green Quarter 107 F2
Green Street *E.Suss.* 18 C2
Green Street *Herts.* 44 A3
Green Street *Herts.* 58 C5
Green Street *W.Suss.* 29 G5
Green Street *Worcs.* 54 A3
Green Street Green *Gt.Lon.* 31 D2
Green Street Green *Kent* 45 E5
Green Tye 44 D1
Greenburn 160 C5
Greencroft 120 A3
Greendams 161 E1
Greendykes 137 E4
Greenend 55 F5
Greenfaulds 142 B2
Greenfield *Beds.* 57 F4
Greenfield (Maes-Glas) *Flints.* 90 C5
Greenfield *Gt.Man.* 93 E2
Greenfield *High.* 165 J4
Greenfield *Lincs.* 97 E5
Greenfield *Oxon.* 42 C3
Greenford 44 A4
Greengairs 142 B2
Greengates 102 A4
Greengill 117 E3
Greenhalgh 100 A4
Greenhall 168 E2
Greenham 27 F1
Greenhaugh 127 F3
Greenhead 118 C1
Greenheads 169 J1
Greenheys 92 B2
Greenhill *Gt.Lon.* 44 A4
Greenhill *High.* 175 G1
Greenhill *S.Yorks.* 94 A4
Greenhithe 45 E5
Greenholm 132 D2
Greenholme 107 G2
Greenhow Hill 102 A1
Greenigo 185 D7
Greenland 183 H2
Greenlands 42 C4
Greenlaw *Aber.* 176 E5
Greenlaw *Sc.Bord.* 145 E5
Greenloaning 150 D4
Greenmeadow 38 B3
Greenmoor Hill 42 B4
Greenmount 92 B1
Greenmyre 169 G1
Greenock 141 D2
Greenodd 107 E4
Greens Norton 56 B3
Greenscares 150 C3
Greenside *T. & W.* 120 A1
Greenside *W.Yorks.* 93 F1
Greenstead 60 B5
Greenstead Green 59 G5
Greensted 45 E2
Greensted Green 45 E2
Greenway *Pembs.* 49 D4
Greenway *Som.* 24 A5
Greenwell 118 B2
Greenwich 44 C5
Greet 54 C4
Greete 65 E5
Greetham *Lincs.* 96 D5
Greetham *Rut.* 69 E1
Greetland 101 G5
Gregson Lane 100 B5
Greinetobht (Grenitote) 170 D4
Greinton 24 B4
Grenaby 98 A4
Grendon *Northants.* 57 D1
Grendon *Warks.* 67 E3
Grendon Common 67 E3
Grendon Green 53 E2
Grendon Underwood 56 B5
Grenitote (Greinetobht) 170 D4
Grenofen 7 E3
Grenoside 94 A3
Greosabhagh 171 G2
Gresford 78 A2
Gresham 86 C2
Greshornish 171 J6
Gress (Griais) 179 G3
Gressenhall 86 A4
Gressingham 100 B1
Greta Bridge 109 F1
Gretna 126 B5
Gretna Green 126 B5
Gretton *Glos.* 54 C4
Gretton *Northants.* 69 E3
Gretton *Shrop.* 65 E3
Grewelthorpe 110 B5
Greygarth 110 A5
Greylake 24 A4
Greys Green 42 C4
Greysouthen 117 D4
Greystead 127 F3
Greystoke 118 A4
Greystone *Aber.* 167 K5
Greystone *Angus* 160 D5
Greystone *Lancs.* 101 E3
Greystones 94 A4
Greywell 28 C2
Griais (Gress) 179 G3
Gribthorpe 103 G4
Gribton 124 D2
Griff 67 F4
Griffithstown 38 B3
Grigadale 154 D3
Grigghall 107 F3
Grimeford Village 92 A1
Grimesthorpe 94 A3
Grimethorpe 94 B2
Griminis (Griminish) 170 C6
Griminish (Griminis) 170 C6
Grimister 186 D3
Grimley 54 A1
Grimmet 132 B4
Grimness 185 D8
Grimoldby 97 D4
Grimpo 78 A5
Grimsargh 100 B4
Grimsay (Griomsaigh) 170 D6
Grimsbury 55 G3
Grimsby 96 C2
Grimscote 56 B2
Grimscott 20 C5
Grimshader (Griomsiadar) 179 G5
Grimsthorpe 83 F5
Grimston *E.Riding* 105 E4
Grimston *Leics.* 82 B5
Grimston *Norf.* 85 F5
Grimstone 12 C3
Grimstone End 60 A1
Grindale 113 E5
Grindiscol 187 D9
Grindle 65 G2
Grindleford 93 G5
Grindleton 101 D3
Grindley 80 B5
Grindley Brook 78 C3
Grindlow 93 F5
Grindon *Northumb.* 145 G5
Grindon *Staffs.* 80 B2
Grindon *Stock.* 120 C5
Grindon *T. & W.* 120 C2
Gringley on the Hill 95 E3
Grinsdale 117 G1
Grinshill 78 C5
Grinton 109 F3
Griomarstaidh 178 E4
Griomsaigh (Grimsay) 170 D6
Griomsiadar (Grimshader) 179 G5
Grisdale 108 C3
Grishipoll 154 A4
Gristhorpe 113 D4
Griston 72 A2
Gritley 185 E7
Grittenham 40 C4
Grittleton 40 A5
Grizebeck 106 D4
Grizedale 107 E3
Grobister 184 F5
Groby 68 A2
Groes 76 D1
Groes-faen 37 G4
Groesffordd 74 B4
Groesffordd Marli 90 B5
Groeslon *Gwyn.* 75 D2
Groeslon *Gwyn.* 75 E1
Groes-lwyd 64 B1
Groes-wen 38 A4
Grogport 139 G5
Groigearraidh 162 C1
Gromford 61 E2
Gronant 90 B4
Groombridge 31 E5
Grosmont *Mon.* 52 D5
Grosmont *N.Yorks.* 112 B2
Grotaig 166 B2
Groton 60 A3
Groundistone Heights 135 F4
Grouville 8 C5
Grove *Bucks.* 57 E5
Grove *Dorset* 12 C5
Grove *Kent* 33 E2
Grove *Notts.* 95 E5
Grove *Oxon.* 41 G3
Grove End 32 A2
Grove Green 31 G3
Grove Park 44 D5
Grove Town 103 D5
Grovehill 43 F2
Grovesend *S.Glos.* 39 F4
Grovesend *Swan.* 36 B2
Gruids 174 C1
Grula 163 J2
Gruline 155 E5
Grumbla 2 B4
Grundcruie 151 F2
Grundisburgh 60 D2
Gruting 187 B8
Grutness 187 G10
Gualachulain 156 D5
Guardbridge 152 C3
Guarlford 54 A3
Guay 159 F5
Gubbergill 106 B3
Gubblecote 43 E1
Guernsey 9 F5
Guernsey Airport 9 E5
Guestling Green 19 D2
Guestling Thorn 19 D2
Guestwick 86 B3
Guestwick Green 86 B3
Guide 100 D5
Guide Post 129 E3
Guilden Down 64 C4
Guilden Morden 58 A3
Guilden Sutton 78 B1
Guildford 29 E3
Guildtown 151 G1
Guilsborough 68 B5
Guilsfield (Cegidfa) 64 B1
Guilthwaite 94 B4
Guisborough 111 F1
Guiseley 102 A3
Guist 86 B3
Guith 184 E4
Guiting Power 54 C5
Gulberwick 187 D9
Gullane 144 B1
Gulval 2 B3
Gulworthy 7 E3
Gumfreston 35 E2
Gumley 68 B3
Gunby *Lincs.* 83 E5
Gunby *Lincs.* 84 C1
Gundleton 28 B4
Gunn 21 G2
Gunnersbury 44 A5
Gunnerside 109 E3
Gunnerton 128 B4
Gunness 95 F1
Gunnislake 7 E3
Gunnista 187 E8
Gunnister 186 C5
Gunstone 66 A2
Gunter's Bridge 29 E5
Gunthorpe *Norf.* 86 B2
Gunthorpe *Notts.* 82 B3
Gunthorpe *Rut.* 69 D2
Gunville 15 D4
Gunwalloe 3 D4
Gupworthy 22 C4
Gurnard 15 D3
Gurnett 92 D5
Gurney Slade 24 D3
Gurnos *M.Tyd.* 37 G2
Gurnos *Powys* 37 D2
Gushmere 32 C3
Gussage All Saints 13 G1
Gussage St. Andrew 13 F1
Gussage St. Michael 13 F1
Guston 33 F4
Gutcher 186 E3
Guthram Gowt 83 G5
Guthrie 161 D4
Guyhirn 70 B2
Guynd 161 D5
Guy's Head 84 C5
Guy's Marsh 25 F5
Guyzance 129 E1
Gwaelod-y-garth 38 A4
Gwaenysgor 90 B4
Gwaithla 52 B2
Gwalchmai 88 B5
Gwastad 48 D5
Gwastadnant 75 F2
Gwaun-Cae-Gurwen 36 D1
Gwaynynog 76 D1
Gwbert 49 E3
Gweek 3 E4
Gwehelog 38 C2
Gwenddwr 51 G3
Gwendreath 3 E5
Gwennap 4 B5
Gwenter 3 E5
Gwernaffield 77 F1
Gwernesney 38 D2
Gwernogle 50 B4
Gwernymynydd 77 F1
Gwern-y-Steeple 37 G5
Gwersyllt 78 A2
Gwespyr 90 C4
Gwinear 2 C3
Gwithian 2 C2
Gwredog 88 C4
Gwrhay 38 A3
Gwyddelwern 77 D3
Gwyddgrug 50 A4
Gwynfryn 77 F2
Gwystre 51 G1
Gwytherin 76 B1
Gyfelia 78 A3
Gyre 185 C7
Gyrn Goch 74 C3

▼H

Habberley 64 C2
Habin 28 D5
Habrough 96 B1
Haccombe 10 B5
Hacconby 83 G5
Haceby 83 F4
Hacheston 61 E2
Hackbridge 30 B2
Hackenthorpe 94 B4
Hackford 86 B5
Hackforth 110 B3
Hackland 184 C5
Hacklet (Haclait) 170 D7
Hacklete (Tacleit) 178 D4
Hackleton 56 D2
Hacklinge 33 F3
Hackness *N.Yorks.* 112 C3
Hackness *Ork.* 185 C8
Hackney 44 C4
Hackthorn 95 G4
Hackthorpe 118 B5
Haclait (Hacklet) 170 D7
Hacton 45 E4
Hadden 136 B3
Haddenham *Bucks.* 42 C2
Haddenham *Cambs.* 70 C5
Haddington *E.Loth.* 144 C2
Haddington *Lincs.* 83 E1
Haddiscoe 73 F2
Haddon 69 G3
Hade Edge 93 F2
Hademore 67 D2
Hadfield 93 E3
Hadham Cross 44 D1
Hadham Ford 58 C5
Hadleigh *Essex* 46 B4
Hadleigh *Suff.* 60 B3
Hadleigh Heath 60 A3
Hadley *Tel. & W.* 65 F1
Hadley *Worcs.* 54 A1
Hadley End 80 C5
Hadley Wood 44 B3
Hadlow 31 F4
Hadlow Down 18 A1
Hadnall 78 C5
Hadspen 25 D4
Hadstock 59 D3
Hadston 129 E2
Hadzor 54 B1
Haffenden Quarter 32 A4
Hafod Bridge 50 C4
Hafod-Dinbych 76 B2
Hafodunos 76 B1
Hafodyrynys 38 B3
Haggate 101 E4
Haggbeck 126 C4
Haggersta 187 C8
Haggerston *Gt.Lon.* 44 C4
Haggerston *Northumb.* 137 E2
Haggrister 186 C5
Haggs 142 B2
Hagley *Here.* 53 E3
Hagley *Worcs.* 66 B4
Hagnaby *Lincs.* 84 B1
Hagnaby *Lincs.* 97 E5
Hague Bar 93 D4
Hagworthingham 84 B1
Haigh 92 A2
Haighton Green 100 B4
Hail Weston 57 G1
Haile 106 B2
Hailes 54 C4
Hailey *Herts.* 44 C1
Hailey *Oxon.* 42 B4
Hailey *Oxon.* 41 F1
Hailsham 18 A3
Haimer 183 G2
Hainault 45 D3
Haine 33 F2
Hainford 86 D4
Hainton 96 B4
Haisthorpe 104 D1
Hakin 34 B2
Halam 82 B2
Halbeath 143 F1
Halberton 10 D1
Halcro 183 H2
Hale *Cumb.* 107 G5
Hale *Gt.Man.* 92 B4
Hale *Halton* 91 F4
Hale *Hants.* 14 A1
Hale *Surr.* 28 D3
Hale Bank 91 F4
Hale Barns 92 B4
Hale Nook 99 G3
Hale Street 31 F4
Hales *Norf.* 73 E2
Hales *Staffs.* 79 E4
Hales Green 80 C3
Hales Place 32 D3
Halesgate 84 B5
Halesowen 66 B4
Halesworth 73 E4
Halewood 91 F4
Half Way Inn 10 D4
Halford *Devon* 10 B5
Halford *Shrop.* 64 D4
Halford *Warks.* 55 E3
Halfpenny 107 G4
Halfpenny Green 66 A3
Halfway *Carmar.* 50 C4
Halfway *Carmar.* 36 B2
Halfway *Powys* 51 E4
Halfway *S.Yorks.* 94 B4
Halfway *W.Berks.* 27 F1
Halfway Bridge 29 E5
Halfway House 64 C1
Halfway Houses *Kent* 32 B1
Halfway Houses *Lincs.* 83 D1
Halghton Mill 78 B3
Halifax 101 G5
Halistra 171 H6
Halket 141 F4
Halkirk 183 G3
Halkyn 90 D5
Hall 141 F4
Hall Cross 100 A5
Hall Dunnerdale 106 D3
Hall Green *Ches.* 79 F2
Hall Green *Lancs.* 100 A5
Hall Green *W.Mid.* 66 D4
Hall Grove 44 B1
Hall of the Forest 64 B4
Halland 18 A2
Hallaton 68 C3
Hallatrow 24 D2
Hallbankgate 118 B2
Hallen 39 E4
Hallfield Gate 81 E2
Hallglen 142 C2
Hallin 171 H6
Halling 31 G2
Hallington *Lincs.* 96 D4
Hallington *Northumb.* 128 B4
Halliwell 92 A1
Halloughton 82 B2
Hallow 54 A2
Hallow Heath 54 A2
Hallrule 135 G4
Halls 145 D2
Halls Green *Essex* 44 D2
Hall's Green *Herts.* 58 A5
Hallsands 9 E4
Hallthwaites 106 C4
Hallwood Green 53 F4
Hallworthy 5 F1
Hallyne 143 F5
Halmer End 79 E3
Halmond's Frome 53 F3
Halmore 39 F2
Halmyre Mains 143 F5
Halnaker 16 B3
Halsall 91 E1
Halse *Northants.* 56 A3
Halse *Som.* 23 E5
Halsetown 2 C3
Halsham 105 E5
Halsinger 21 F2
Halstead *Essex* 59 G4
Halstead *Kent* 31 D2
Halstead *Leics.* 68 C2
Halstock 12 B2
Halsway 23 E4
Haltemprice Farm 104 C4
Haltham 84 A1
Haltoft End 84 B3
Halton *Bucks.* 43 D1
Halton *Halton* 91 G4
Halton *Lancs.* 100 B1
Halton *Northumb.* 119 F1
Halton *Wrex.* 78 A4
Halton East 101 G2
Halton Gill 109 D5
Halton Green 100 B1
Halton Holegate 84 C1
Halton Lea Gate 118 C2
Halton Park 100 B1
Halton West 101 E2
Haltwhistle 118 D1
Halvergate 87 F5
Halwell 9 D2
Halwill 7 E1
Halwill Junction 7 E1
Ham *Devon* 11 F2
Ham *Glos.* 39 F3
Ham *Glos.* 54 B5
Ham *Gt.Lon.* 44 A5
Ham *High.* 183 H1

▶ Ham - Hig

Ham Kent 33 F3
Ham Plym. 8 A2
Ham Shet. 186 B1
Ham Som. 23 F5
Ham Som. 11 F1
Ham Wilts. 27 E1
Ham Common 25 F5
Ham Green Here. 53 G3
Ham Green Kent 32 A2
Ham Green Kent 19 D1
Ham Green N.Som. 39 E5
Ham Green Worcs. 54 C1
Ham Hill 31 F2
Ham Street 24 C4
Hambleden 42 C4
Hambledon Hants. 15 F1
Hambledon Surr. 29 E4
Hamble-le-Rice 15 D2
Hambleton Lancs. 99 G3
Hambleton N.Yorks. 103 E4
Hambridge 24 A5
Hambrook S.Glos. 39 F5
Hambrook W.Suss. 15 G2
Hameringham 84 B1
Hamerton 69 G5
Hamilton 142 B4
Hamlet Devon 11 E3
Hamlet Dorset 12 B2
Hammer 29 D4
Hammerpot 16 C3
Hammersmith 44 B5
Hammerwich 66 C2
Hammerwood 30 D5
Hammond Street 44 C2
Hammoon 13 E1
Hamnavoe Shet. 187 C9
Hamnavoe Shet. 186 D4
Hamnavoe Shet. 186 B4
Hamnavoe Shet. 186 D5
Hamnish Clifford 53 E2
Hamp 23 F4
Hampden Park 18 B3
Hamperden End 59 D4
Hampnett 40 D1
Hampole 94 C2
Hampreston 13 G3
Hampstead 44 B4
Hampstead Norreys 42 A5
Hampsthwaite 102 B2
Hampton Devon 11 F3
Hampton Gt.Lon. 29 G1
Hampton Kent 33 D2
Hampton Peter. 69 G3
Hampton Shrop. 65 G4
Hampton Swin. 41 D3
Hampton Worcs. 54 C3
Hampton Bishop 53 E4
Hampton Fields 40 A3
Hampton Heath 78 B3
Hampton in Arden 67 E4
Hampton Loade 65 G4
Hampton Lovett 54 A1
Hampton Lucy 55 E2
Hampton on the Hill 55 E1
Hampton Poyle 42 A1
Hampton Wick 29 G1
Hamptworth 14 B1
Hamsey 17 G2
Hamstall Ridware 66 D1
Hamstead 14 C3
Hamstead Marshall 27 F1
Hamsteels 120 A3
Hamsterley Dur. 120 A4
Hamsterley Dur. 120 A2
Hamstreet 32 C5
Hamworthy 13 F3
Hanbury Staffs. 80 C5
Hanbury Worcs. 54 B1
Hanbury Woodend 80 C5
Hanby 83 F4
Hanchurch 79 F3
Handa Island 180 D4
Handale 111 G1
Handbridge 78 B1
Handcross 30 B5
Handforth 92 C4
Handley Ches. 78 B2
Handley Derbys. 81 E1
Handley Green 45 F2
Handsacre 66 C1
Handside 44 B1
Handsworth S.Yorks. 94 B4
Handsworth W.Mid. 66 C3
Handwoodbank 64 D1
Handy Cross 43 D3
Hanford Dorset 13 E1
Hanford Stoke 79 F3
Hanging Bridge 80 C3
Hanging Houghton 68 C5
Hanging Langford 26 B4
Hangingshaw 125 F2
Hanham 39 F5
Hankelow 79 D3
Hankerton 40 B3
Hankham 18 B3
Hanley 79 F3
Hanley Castle 54 A3
Hanley Child 53 F1
Hanley Swan 54 A3
Hanley William 53 F1
Hanlith 101 F1
Hanmer 78 B4
Hannah 97 E5
Hannington Hants. 27 G2
Hannington Northants. 68 D5
Hannington Swin. 41 D3
Hannington Wick 41 D3
Hanslope 56 D3
Hanthorpe 83 F5
Hanwell Gt.Lon. 44 A4
Hanwell Oxon. 55 G3
Hanwood 64 D2
Hanworth Gt.Lon. 44 A5
Hanworth Norf. 86 C2
Happisburgh 87 E2
Happisburgh Common 87 E3
Hapsford 91 F5
Hapton Lancs. 101 D4
Hapton Norf. 72 C2
Harberton 9 D2
Harbertonford 9 D2
Harbledown 32 D3
Harborne 66 C4
Harborough Magna 67 G5
Harbost (Tarbost) 179 H1
Harbottle 128 B1
Harbourneford 8 D1
Harbridge 14 A1
Harbridge Green 14 A1
Harburn 143 E3
Harbury 55 F2
Harby Leics. 82 C4
Harby Notts. 95 F5
Harcombe 11 E3
Harcombe Bottom 11 G3
Harden W.Mid. 66 C2
Harden W.Yorks. 101 G4
Hardendale 107 G1
Hardenhuish 40 B5
Hardgate Aber. 169 F4
Hardgate N.Yorks. 102 B1
Hardham 16 C2
Hardhorn 99 G4
Hardingham 86 B5
Hardingstone 56 C2
Hardington 25 E2
Hardington Mandeville 12 B1
Hardington Marsh 12 B2
Hardington Moor 12 B1
Hardley 14 D2
Hardley Street 87 E5
Hardmead 57 E3
Hardraw 109 D3
Hardstoft 81 F1
Hardway Hants. 15 F2
Hardway Som. 25 E4
Hardwick Bucks. 42 D1
Hardwick Cambs. 58 B2
Hardwick Lincs. 95 F5
Hardwick Norf. 72 D2
Hardwick Northants. 57 D1
Hardwick Oxon. 41 F2
Hardwick Oxon. 56 A5
Hardwick S.Yorks. 94 B4
Hardwick W.Mid. 66 C3
Hardwick Village 94 D5
Hardwicke Glos. 54 B5
Hardwicke Glos. 39 G1
Hardwicke Here. 52 B3
Hardy's Green 60 A5
Hare Green 60 B5
Hare Hatch 42 D5
Hare Street Herts. 58 B5
Hare Street Herts. 58 B5
Hareby 84 B1
Harecroft 101 G4
Hareden 100 C2
Harefield 43 F3
Harehill 80 C4
Harehills 102 C4
Harehope 137 E4
Harelaw 142 D5
Hareplain 32 A5
Haresceugh 118 C3
Harescombe 40 A1
Haresfield 40 A1
Hareshaw N.Lan. 142 C3
Hareshaw S.Lan. 142 A5
Harestock 27 F4
Harewood 102 C3
Harewood End 53 E5
Harford Devon 8 C2
Harford Devon 10 B3
Hargate 72 C2
Hargatewall 93 F5
Hargrave Ches. 78 B1
Hargrave Northants. 69 F5
Hargrave Suff. 59 F2
Hargrave Green 59 F2
Harker 126 B5
Harkstead 60 C4
Harlaston 67 E1
Harlaxton 83 D4
Harle Syke 101 E4
Harlech 75 E4
Harlequin 82 B4
Harlescott 65 E1
Harlesden 44 B4
Harleston Devon 9 D3
Harleston Norf. 72 D3
Harleston Suff. 60 B1
Harlestone 56 C1
Harley S.Yorks. 94 A3
Harley Shrop. 65 E2
Harleyholm 134 A2
Harlington Beds. 57 F4
Harlington Gt.Lon. 43 F5
Harlosh 171 H7
Harlow 44 D1
Harlow Hill 119 G1
Harlthorpe 103 G4
Harlton 58 B2
Harlyn 4 C2
Harman's Cross 13 F4
Harmby 110 A4
Harmer Green 44 B1
Harmer Hill 78 B5
Harmondsworth 43 F5
Harmston 83 E1
Harnage 65 E2
Harnham 26 C5
Harnhill 40 C2
Harold Hill 45 E3
Harold Park 45 E3
Harold Wood 45 E3
Haroldston West 34 B1
Haroldswick 186 F1
Harome 111 F4
Harpenden 44 A1
Harpford 11 D3
Harpham 104 C1
Harpley Norf. 85 F5
Harpley Worcs. 53 F1
Harpole 56 B1
Harprigg 108 B4
Harpsdale 183 G3
Harpsden 42 C4
Harpswell 95 G4
Harpur Hill 93 E5
Harpurhey 92 C2
Harracott 21 F3
Harrapool 164 C2
Harrietfield 151 E1
Harrietsham 32 A3
Harringay 44 C4
Harrington Cumb. 116 C4
Harrington Lincs. 97 D5
Harrington Northants. 68 C5
Harringworth 69 E3
Harris 163 J5
Harris Green 72 D2
Harriseahead 79 F2
Harriston 117 E2
Harrogate 102 C2
Harrold 57 E2
Harrop Fold 100 D3
Harrow Gt.Lon. 44 A4
Harrow High. 183 H1
Harrow Green 59 G2
Harrow on the Hill 44 A4
Harrow Weald 44 A3
Harrowbarrow 7 E3
Harrowden 57 F3
Harrowgate Hill 110 B1
Harry Stoke 39 F5
Harston Cambs. 58 C2
Harston Leics. 82 D4
Harswell 104 A3
Hart 121 D4
Hartburn 128 C3
Hartest 59 G2
Hartfield E.Suss. 31 D5
Hartfield High. 172 D7
Hartford Cambs. 70 A5
Hartford Ches. 92 A5
Hartford Som. 22 C5
Hartford End 45 F1
Hartfordbridge 28 C2
Hartforth 110 A2
Hartgrove 13 E1
Harthill Ches. 78 C2
Harthill N.Lan. 142 D3
Harthill S.Yorks. 94 B4
Hartington 80 C1
Hartington Hall 128 C3
Hartland 20 C3
Hartland Quay 20 C3
Hartlebury 66 A5
Hartlepool 121 E4
Hartley Cumb. 108 C2
Hartley Kent 31 F2
Hartley Kent 31 G5
Hartley Northumb. 129 F4
Hartley Green 79 G5
Hartley Mauditt 28 C4
Hartley Wespall 28 B2
Hartley Wintney 28 C2
Hartlington 101 G1
Hartlip 32 A2
Hartoft End 111 G3
Harton N.Yorks. 103 G1
Harton Shrop. 65 D4
Harton T.&W. 120 C1
Hartpury 54 A5
Hartrigge 136 A4
Hartshead 102 A5
Hartshill 67 F3
Hartshorne 81 E5
Hartsop 107 F1
Hartwell Bucks. 42 C1
Hartwell E.Suss. 31 D5
Hartwell Northants. 56 C2
Hartwith 102 B1
Hartwood 142 C4
Harvel 31 F2
Harvington Worcs. 54 C3
Harvington Worcs. 66 A5
Harwell Notts. 95 D3
Harwell Oxon. 41 G4
Harwich 60 D4
Harwood Dur. 119 E4
Harwood Gt.Man. 92 B1
Harwood Northumb. 128 C2
Harwood Dale 112 C3
Harwood on Teviot 135 F5
Harworth 94 D3
Hasbury 66 B4
Hascombe 29 F3
Haselbech 68 C5
Haselbury Plucknett 12 A1
Haseley 55 E1
Haseley Knob 67 E5
Haselor 54 D2
Hasfield 54 A5
Hasguard 34 B2
Haskayne 91 E2
Hasketon 61 D2
Hasland 81 E1
Hasland Green 81 E1
Haslemere 29 E4
Haslingden 101 D5
Haslingden Grane 101 D5
Haslingfield 58 C2
Haslington 79 E2
Hassall 79 E2
Hassall Green 79 E2
Hassell Street 32 C4
Hassendean 135 G3
Hassingham 87 E5
Hassocks 17 F2
Hassop 93 G5
Haster 183 J3
Hasthorpe 84 C1
Hastigrow 183 H2
Hastingleigh 32 C4
Hastings E.Suss. 18 D3
Hastings Som. 11 G1
Hastingwood 45 D2
Hastoe 43 E2
Haswell 120 C3
Haswell Plough 120 C3
Hatch Beds. 57 G3
Hatch Hants. 28 B2
Hatch Beauchamp 24 A5
Hatch End 44 A3
Hatch Green 11 G1
Hatching Green 44 A1
Hatchmere 91 G5
Hatcliffe 96 C2
Hatfield Here. 53 E2
Hatfield Herts. 44 B2
Hatfield S.Yorks. 95 D2
Hatfield Broad Oak 45 E1
Hatfield Heath 45 E1
Hatfield Peverel 45 G1
Hatfield Woodhouse 95 D2
Hatford 41 F3
Hatherden 27 E2
Hatherleigh 21 F5
Hathern 81 F5
Hatherop 41 D2
Hathersage 93 G4
Hathersage Booths 93 G4
Hathershaw 92 D2
Hatherton Ches. 79 D3
Hatherton Staffs. 66 B1
Hatley St. George 58 A2
Hatt 7 D4
Hattingley 28 B4
Hatton Aber. 169 J1
Hatton Derbys. 80 D5
Hatton Gt.Lon. 44 A5
Hatton Lincs. 96 B5
Hatton Shrop. 65 D3
Hatton Warks. 55 E1
Hatton Warr. 91 G4
Hatton Castle 177 F6
Hatton Heath 78 B1
Hatton of Fintray 169 G3
Hattoncrook 169 G2
Haugh 97 E5
Haugh Head 137 E4
Haugh of Glass 168 C1
Haugh of Urr 124 C4
Haugham 96 D4
Haughhead 142 A2
Haughley 60 B1
Haughley Green 60 B1
Haughley New Street 60 B1
Haughs 176 D6
Haughton Ches. 78 C2
Haughton Notts. 95 D5
Haughton Powys 64 C1
Haughton Shrop. 65 F3
Haughton Shrop. 65 E1
Haughton Shrop. 78 A5
Haughton Staffs. 79 F5
Haughton Green 92 D3
Haughton Le Skerne 110 C1
Haultwick 58 B5
Haunn 162 C3
Haunton 67 E1
Hauxton 58 C2
Havannah 79 F1
Havant 15 G2
Haven 52 D2
Havenstreet 15 E3
Havercroft 94 A1
Haverfordwest (Hwlffordd) 34 C1
Haverhill 59 E3
Haverigg 106 C5
Havering Park 45 D3
Havering-atte-Bower 45 E3
Haversham 56 D3
Haverthwaite 107 E4
Haverton Hill 121 D5
Haviker Street 31 G4
Havyat 24 C4
Hawarden 78 A1
Hawbridge 54 B3
Hawbush Green 59 F5
Hawcoat 106 D5
Hawes 109 D4
Hawe's Green 72 D2
Hawick 135 G4
Hawkchurch 11 G2
Hawkedon 59 F2
Hawkenbury Kent 31 E5
Hawkenbury Kent 32 A4
Hawkeridge 25 F2
Hawkerland 11 D4
Hawkes End 67 E4
Hawkesbury 39 G4
Hawkesbury Upton 39 G4
Hawkhill 137 G5
Hawkhurst 31 G5
Hawkinge 33 E4
Hawkley 28 C5
Hawkridge 22 B4
Hawkshead 107 E3
Hawkshead Hill 107 E3
Hawksheads 100 A1
Hawksland 142 C5
Hawkswick 109 E5
Hawksworth Notts. 82 C3
Hawksworth W.Yorks. 102 A3
Hawksworth W.Yorks. 102 B4
Hawkwell Essex 46 B3
Hawkwell Northumb. 128 C4
Hawley Hants. 29 D2
Hawley Kent 45 E5
Hawley's Corner 30 D3
Hawling 54 C5
Hawnby 111 E4
Haworth 101 G4
Hawstead 59 G2
Hawstead Green 59 G2
Hawthorn Dur. 120 D3
Hawthorn Hants. 28 B4
Hawthorn R.C.T. 37 G4
Hawthorn Wilts. 25 F1
Hawthorn Hill Brack.F. 43 D5
Hawthorn Hill Lincs. 84 A2
Hawthorpe 83 F5
Hawton 82 C2
Haxby 103 F2
Haxey 95 E2
Haxted 30 D4
Haxton 26 C3
Hay Green 70 D1
Hay Mills 66 D4
Hay Street 58 B5
Haydock 91 G3
Haydon Dorset 12 C1
Haydon Swin. 40 D4
Haydon Bridge 119 E1
Haydon Wick 40 D4
Hayes Gt.Lon. 43 F4
Hayes Gt.Lon. 30 D2
Hayes End 43 F4
Hayfield Arg. & B. 148 C2
Hayfield Derbys. 93 E4
Hayfield Fife 152 A5
Hayfield High. 183 G2
Haygrove 23 F4
Hayhillock 160 D5
Hayle 2 C3
Hayling Island 15 G2
Haymoor Green 79 D2
Hayne 10 C1
Haynes 57 G3
Haynes Church End 57 F3
Haynes West End 57 F3
Hay-on-Wye 52 B3
Hayscastle 48 B5
Hayscastle Cross 48 C5
Hayton Cumb. 118 B2
Hayton Cumb. 117 E2
Hayton E.Riding 104 A3
Hayton Notts. 95 E4
Hayton's Bent 65 E4
Haytor Vale 10 A5
Haytown 21 D4
Haywards Heath 17 F1
Haywood Oaks 82 B2
Hazel End 58 C5
Hazel Grove 92 D4
Hazel Street 31 F5
Hazelbank Arg. & B. 148 C4
Hazelbank S.Lan. 142 C5
Hazelbury Bryan 12 D2
Hazeleigh 46 B2
Hazeley 28 C2
Hazelhurst 92 B1
Hazelside 133 G3
Hazelslack 107 F5
Hazelslade 66 C1
Hazelton Walls 152 B2
Hazelwood Derbys. 81 E3
Hazelwood Gt.Lon. 30 D2
Hazlefield 116 A2
Hazlehead Aberdeen 169 G4
Hazlehead S.Yorks. 93 F2
Hazlemere 43 D3
Hazlerigg 129 E4
Hazleton 40 C1
Hazon 129 D1
Heacham 85 E4
Head Bridge 21 G4
Headbourne Worthy 27 F4
Headcorn 32 A4
Headingley 102 B4
Headington 42 A2
Headlam 110 A1
Headless Cross 54 C1
Headley Hants. 28 D4
Headley Hants. 27 G1
Headley Surr. 30 B3
Headley Down 28 D4
Headley Heath 66 C5
Headon 95 E5
Heads Nook 118 A2
Heady Hill 92 C1
Heage 81 E2
Healaugh N.Yorks. 109 F3
Healaugh N.Yorks. 103 E3
Heald Green 92 C4
Heale Devon 21 G1
Heale Som. 24 A5
Healey Lancs. 92 C1
Healey N.Yorks. 110 A4
Healey Northumb. 119 G2
Healey W.Yorks. 102 B5
Healeyfield 119 G3
Healing 96 C1
Heamoor 2 B3
Heaning 107 F3
Heanish 154 B2
Heanor 81 F3
Heanton Punchardon 21 F2
Heanton Satchville 21 F4
Heap Bridge 92 C1
Heapey 100 C5
Heapham 95 F4
Hearn 28 D4
Hearthstane 134 C3
Heasley Mill 22 A4
Heast 164 C3
Heath Cardiff 38 A4
Heath Derbys. 81 F1
Heath W.Yorks. 94 A1
Heath and Reach 57 E5
Heath End Derbys. 81 E5
Heath End Hants. 27 G1
Heath End Hants. 27 F1
Heath End Surr. 28 D3
Heath Hayes 66 C1
Heath Hill 65 G1
Heath House 24 B3
Heath Town 66 B3
Heathbrook 78 D5
Heathcot 169 G4
Heathcote Derbys. 80 C1
Heathcote Shrop. 79 D5
Heathencote 56 C3
Heather 67 F1
Heathfield Devon 10 B5
Heathfield E.Suss. 18 A1
Heathfield N.Yorks. 102 A1
Heathfield Som. 23 E5
Heathrow Airport 43 F5
Heathton 66 A3
Heatley 92 B4
Heaton Lancs. 100 A1
Heaton Staffs. 79 G1
Heaton T.&W. 120 B1
Heaton W.Yorks. 102 A4
Heaton Moor 92 C3
Heaton's Bridge 91 F1
Heaverham 31 E3
Heaviley 92 D4
Heavitree 10 C3
Hebburn 120 C1
Hebden 101 G1
Hebden Bridge 101 F5
Hebden Green 78 D1
Hebing End 58 B5
Hebron Carmar. 49 E5
Hebron Northumb. 129 D3
Heck 125 E2
Heckfield 28 C1
Heckfield Green 72 C4
Heckfordbridge 60 A5
Heckingham 73 E2
Heckington 83 G3
Heckmondwike 102 B5
Heddington 26 A1
Heddle 185 C6
Heddon-on-the-Wall 120 A1
Hedenham 73 E2
Hedge End 15 D1
Hedgerley 43 E4
Hedging 24 A5
Hedley on the Hill 119 G2
Hednesford 66 C1
Hedon 105 D5
Hedsor 43 E4
Heeley 94 A4
Heglibister 187 C7
Heighington Darl. 120 B5
Heighington Lincs. 83 F1
Heightington 65 G5
Heights of Brae 174 C5
Heilam 181 G3
Heisker Islands (Monach Islands) 170 B5
Heithat 125 F2
Heiton 136 B3
Hele Devon 21 F1
Hele Devon 10 C2
Hele Devon 6 D1
Hele Devon 10 A5
Hele Som. 23 E5
Hele Torbay 9 F1
Hele Bridge 21 F5
Hele Lane 10 A1
Helebridge 20 C5
Helensburgh 141 D1
Helford 3 E4
Helhoughton 85 G5
Helions Bumpstead 59 E3
Hell Corner 27 E1
Hellaby 94 C3
Helland Cornw. 5 E2
Helland Som. 24 A5
Hellandbridge 5 E2
Hellesdon 86 D4
Hellidon 56 A2
Hellifield 101 E2
Hellingly 18 A2
Hellington 87 E5
Hellister 187 C8
Helmdon 56 A3
Helmingham 60 C2
Helmington Row 120 A4
Helmsdale 183 F7
Helmshore 101 D5
Helmsley 111 F4
Helperby 102 D1
Helperthorpe 112 C5
Helpringham 83 G3
Helpston 69 G2
Helsby 91 F5
Helsey 97 F5
Helston 3 D4
Helstone 5 E1
Helton 118 B5
Helwith 109 F2
Helwith Bridge 101 E1
Hem 64 B2
Hemborough Post 9 E2
Hemel Hempstead 43 F2
Hemerdon 8 B2
Hemingbrough 103 F4
Hemingby 96 C5
Hemingfield 94 A2
Hemingford Abbots 70 A5
Hemingford Grey 70 A5
Hemingstone 60 C2
Hemington Leics. 81 F5
Hemington Northants. 69 F4
Hemington Som. 25 E2
Hemley 61 D3
Hemlington 111 D1
Hemp Green 61 E1
Hempholme 104 C2
Hempnall 72 D2
Hempnall Green 72 D2
Hempriggs 175 J5
Hempriggs House 183 J4
Hempstead Essex 59 E4
Hempstead Med. 31 G2
Hempstead Norf. 87 F3
Hempstead Norf. 86 C2
Hempsted 40 A1
Hempton Norf. 86 A3
Hempton Oxon. 55 G4
Hemsby 87 F4
Hemswell 95 G3
Hemswell Cliff 95 G4
Hemsworth 94 B1
Hemyock 11 E1
Henbury Bristol 39 E5
Henbury Ches. 92 C5
Henderland 124 C3
Hendersyde Park 136 B3
Hendham 8 D2
Hendon Gt.Lon. 44 B4
Hendon T.&W. 120 C2
Hendraburnick 5 F1
Hendre Bridgend 37 F4
Hendre Gwyn. 74 C4
Hendreforgan 37 F4
Hendy 36 B2
Heneglwys 88 C5
Henfield S.Glos. 39 F5
Henfield W.Suss. 17 E2
Henford 7 D1
Henghurst 32 B5
Hengoed Caerp. 38 A3
Hengoed Powys 52 B2
Hengoed Shrop. 77 F4
Hengrave 59 G1
Henham 58 D5
Heniarth 64 A2
Henlade 23 F5
Henley Dorset 12 C2
Henley Shrop. 65 E5
Henley Som. 24 B4
Henley Som. 12 A2
Henley Suff. 60 C2
Henley W.Suss. 29 D5
Henley Corner 24 B4
Henley Park 29 E2
Henley-in-Arden 55 D1
Henley-on-Thames 42 C4
Henley's Down 18 C2
Henllan Carmar. 49 G3
Henllan Denb. 76 D1
Henllan Amgoed 49 E5
Henllys 38 B3
Henlow 57 G4
Hennock 10 B4
Henny Street 59 G4
Henryd 89 F5
Henry's Moat 48 D5
Hensall 103 E5
Henshaw 119 D1
Hensingham 116 C5
Henstead 73 F3
Hensting 27 F5
Henstridge 12 D1
Henstridge Ash 12 D1
Henstridge Bowden 25 D5
Henstridge Marsh 25 E5
Henton Oxon. 42 C2
Henton Som. 24 B3
Henwood 5 G2
Heogan 187 D8
Heol Senni 51 F5
Heolgerrig 37 G2
Heol-y-Cyw 37 F4
Hepburn 137 E4
Hepburn Bell 137 E4
Hepple 128 B1
Hepscott 129 E3
Hepthorne Lane 81 F1
Heptonstall 101 F5
Hepworth Suff. 72 A4
Hepworth W.Yorks. 93 F2
Hepworth South Common 72 A4
Herbrandston 34 B2
Hereford 53 E3
Heriot 144 A4
Herm 9 G5
Hermiston 143 F2
Hermitage D.& G. 124 B4
Hermitage Dorset 12 C2
Hermitage Sc.Bord. 126 D2
Hermitage W.Berks. 42 A5
Hermitage W.Suss. 15 G2
Hermitage Green 92 A3
Hermon Carmar. 49 G4
Hermon I.o.A. 74 C1
Hermon Pembs. 49 F4
Herne 33 D2
Herne Bay 33 D2
Herne Common 33 D2
Herne Pound 31 F3
Herner 21 F3
Hernhill 32 C2
Herodsfoot 5 G3
Herongate 45 F3
Heron's Ghyll 17 G1
Heronsgate 43 F3
Herriard 28 B3
Herringfleet 73 F2
Herring's Green 57 F3
Herringswell 59 F1
Herringthorpe 94 B3
Hersden 33 D2
Hersham Cornw. 20 C5
Hersham Surr. 29 G1
Herstmonceux 18 B2
Herston 185 D8
Hertford 44 C1
Hertford Heath 44 C1
Hertingfordbury 44 C1
Hesket Newmarket 117 G3
Hesketh Bank 100 A5
Hesketh Lane 100 C3
Heskin Green 91 G1
Hesleden 120 D4
Hesleyside 128 A3
Heslington 103 F2
Hessay 103 E2
Hessenford 6 D5
Hessett 60 A1
Hessle 104 C5
Hest Bank 100 A1
Hester's Way 54 B5
Hestley Green 60 C1
Heston 44 A5
Heswall 91 D4
Hethe 56 A5
Hethelpit Cross 53 G5
Hetherington 128 A4
Hethersett 86 C5
Hethersgill 118 A1
Hethpool 136 C4
Hett 120 B4
Hetton 101 F2
Hetton-le-Hole 120 C3
Heugh 128 C4
Heugh-head Aber. 168 B3
Heugh-head Aber. 168 D5
Heveningham 73 E4
Hever 31 D4
Heversham 107 F4
Hevingham 86 C3
Hewas Water 5 D5
Hewell Grange 54 C1
Hewell Lane 54 C1
Hewelsfield 39 E2
Hewelsfield Common 39 E2
Hewish N.Som. 24 B1
Hewish Som. 12 A2
Hewood 11 G2
Heworth 103 F2
Hewton 7 F1
Hexham 119 F1
Hextable 45 E5
Hexthorpe 94 C2
Hexton 57 G4
Hexworthy 7 G3
Hey 101 E3
Hey Houses 99 G5
Heybridge Essex 45 F3
Heybridge Essex 46 B2
Heybridge Basin 46 B2
Heybrook Bay 8 A3
Heydon Cambs. 58 C3
Heydon Norf. 86 C3
Heydour 83 F4
Heylipoll 154 A2
Heylor 186 B4
Heyop 64 B5
Heysham 100 A1
Heyshaw 102 A1
Heyshott 16 A2
Heyside 92 D2
Heytesbury 26 A3
Heythrop 55 F5
Heywood Gt.Man. 92 C1
Heywood Wilts. 25 F2
Hibaldstow 95 G2
Hibb's Green 59 G2
Hickleton 94 B2
Hickling Norf. 87 F3
Hickling Notts. 82 B5
Hickling Green 87 F3
Hickling Heath 87 F3
Hickstead 17 E1
Hidcote Bartrim 55 D3
Hidcote Boyce 55 D3
High Ackworth 94 B1
High Angerton 128 C3
High Balantyre 148 C3
High Bankhill 118 B3
High Beach 44 D3
High Bentham 100 C1
High Bickington 21 F3
High Birkwith 108 C5
High Blantyre 142 A4
High Bonnybridge 142 C2
High Borgue 124 A5
High Borve 179 G2
High Bradfield 93 G3
High Bradley 101 G3
High Bransholme 104 D4
High Bray 21 G2
High Bridge 117 G2
High Brooms 31 E4
High Bullen 21 F3
High Burton 110 B4
High Buston 129 E1
High Callerton 129 D4
High Casterton 108 B5
High Catton 103 G2
High Close 110 A1
High Cogges 41 F2
High Common 72 C3
High Coniscliffe 110 B1
High Crompton 92 D2
High Cross Hants. 28 C5
High Cross Herts. 44 C1
High Cross W.Suss. 17 E2
High Easter 45 F1
High Ellington 110 A4

High Entercommon 110 C2
High Ercall 65 E1
High Etherley 120 A5
High Ferry 84 B3
High Flatts 93 G2
High Garrett 59 F5
High Gate 101 F5
High Grange 120 A4
High Green Norf. 86 C5
High Green Norf. 86 A4
High Green Norf. 86 A5
High Green S.Yorks. 94 A3
High Green Suff. 59 G1
High Green Worcs. 54 A3
High Halden 32 A5
High Halstow 45 G5
High Ham 24 B4
High Harrington 116 D4
High Harrogate 102 C2
High Hatton 78 D5
High Hauxley 129 E1
High Hawsker 112 C2
High Heath Shrop. 79 D5
High Heath W.Mid. 66 C2
High Hesket 118 A3
High Hesleden 121 D4
High Hoyland 93 G1
High Hunsley 104 B4
High Hurstwood 17 G1
High Hutton 103 G1
High Ireby 117 F3
High Kelling 86 B2
High Kilburn 111 E5
High Kingthorpe 112 B4
High Knipe 107 G1
High Lane Derbys. 81 F3
High Lane Gt.Man. 93 D4
High Lane Worcs. 53 F1
High Laver 45 E2
High Legh 92 B4
High Leven 110 D1
High Littleton 24 D2
High Lorton 117 E4
High Marishes 112 B5
High Marnham 95 F5
High Melton 94 C2
High Moor 94 B4
High Newton 107 F4
High Newton-by-the-Sea 137 G4
High Nibthwaite 107 D3
High Offley 79 E5
High Ongar 45 E2
High Onn 66 A1
High Park Corner 60 B5
High Roding 45 F1
High Shaw 109 D3
High Spen 120 A1
High Stoop 120 A3
High Street Cornw. 5 D4
High Street Kent 31 G5
High Street Suff. 61 F2
High Street Suff. 73 E3
High Street Suff. 73 F4
High Street Suff. 59 G3
High Street Green 60 B2
High Throston 121 D4
High Town 66 B1
High Toynton 84 A1
High Trewhitt 128 C1
High Wham 120 A5
High Wigsell 18 C1
High Woolaston 39 E3
High Worsall 110 C2
High Wray 107 E3
High Wych 45 D1
High Wycombe 43 D3
Higham Derbys. 81 E2
Higham Kent 45 G5
Higham Lancs. 101 E4
Higham S.Yorks. 94 A2
Higham Suff. 59 F1
Higham Suff. 60 B4
Higham Dykes 128 D4
Higham Ferrers 57 E1
Higham Gobion 57 G4
Higham on the Hill 67 F3
Higham Wood 31 F4
Highampton 21 E5
Highams Park 44 C3
Highbridge Hants. 27 F5
Highbridge Som. 24 A3
Highbrook 30 C5
Highburton 93 F1
Highbury 25 D3
Highclere 27 F1
Highcliffe 14 B3
Higher Alham 25 D3
Higher Ansty 13 D2
Higher Ashton 10 B4
Higher Ballam 99 G4
Higher Blackley 92 C2
Higher Brixham 9 F2
Higher Cheriton 11 E2
Higher Combe 22 C4
Higher Folds 92 A2
Higher Gabwell 9 F1
Higher Green 92 B3
Higher Halstock Leigh 12 B2
Higher Kingcombe 12 B3
Higher Kinnerton 78 A1
Higher Muddiford 21 F2
Higher Nyland 25 E5
Higher Prestacott 7 D1
Higher Standen 101 D3
Higher Tale 11 D2
Higher Thrushgill 100 C1
Higher Town Cornw. 5 E3
Higher Town I.o.S. 4 B1
Higher Walreddon 7 E3
Higher Walton Lancs. 100 B5
Higher Walton Warr. 91 G4
Higher Wambrook 11 F2
Higher Whatcombe 13 E2
Higher Wheelton 100 C5
Higher Whiteleigh 6 C1
Higher Whitley 92 A4
Higher Wincham 92 A5
Higher Woodhill 92 B1
Higher Woodsford 13 D4
Higher Wraxall 12 B2
Higher Wych 78 B3
Highfield E.Riding 103 G4
Highfield N.Ayr. 141 E4
Highfield Oxon. 56 A5
Highfield S.Yorks. 94 A4
Highfield T.&W. 120 A2
Highfields Cambs. 58 B2
Highfields Northumb. 145 G4
Highgate E.Suss. 30 D5
Highgate Gt.Lon. 44 B4
Highgreen Manor 128 A2
Highlane Ches. 79 F1
Highlane Derbys. 94 B4
Highlaws 117 E2
Highleadon 53 G5
Highleigh Devon 22 C5
Highleigh W.Suss. 16 A4
Highley 65 G4
Highmead 50 B3
Highmoor Cross 42 B4
Highmoor Hill 39 D4
Highnam 39 G1
Highstead 33 E2
Highsted 32 B2
Highstreet 32 C2
Highstreet Green Essex 59 F4
Highstreet Green Surr. 29 E4
Hightae 125 E3
Highter's Heath 66 C5
Hightown Hants. 14 A2
Hightown Mersey. 91 D2
Hightown Green 60 A2
Highway 40 C5
Highweek 10 B5
Highwood 53 F1
Highwood Hill 44 B3
Highworth 41 E3
Hilborough 71 G2
Hilcote 81 F2
Hilcott 26 C2
Hilden Park 31 E4
Hildenborough 31 E4
Hildenley 111 G5
Hildersham 58 D3
Hilderstone 79 G4
Hilderthorpe 105 D1
Hilfield 12 C2
Hilgay 71 E3
Hill S.Glos. 39 F3
Hill Warks. 55 G1
Hill Worcs. 54 B3
Hill Brow 28 C5
Hill Chorlton 79 E4
Hill Common 87 F3
Hill Cottages 111 G3
Hill Croome 54 A3
Hill Deverill 25 F3
Hill Dyke 84 B3
Hill End Dur. 119 G4
Hill End Fife 151 F5
Hill End Glos. 54 A4
Hill End Gt.Lon. 43 F3
Hill End N.Yorks. 101 G2
Hill Green 58 C4
Hill Head 15 E2
Hill Houses 65 F5
Hill Mountain 34 C2
Hill of Beath 143 F1
Hill of Fearn 175 F4
Hill Ridware 66 C1
Hill Row 70 C5
Hill Side 93 F1
Hill Street 14 C1
Hill Top Hants. 14 D2
Hill Top S.Yorks. 94 B3
Hill Top S.Yorks. 93 G4
Hill View 13 F3
Hill Wootton 55 F1
Hillam 103 E5
Hillbeck 108 C1
Hillberry 98 B4
Hillborough 33 E2
Hillbrae Aber. 176 E6
Hillbrae Aber. 169 F2
Hillbrae Aber. 169 G1
Hillbutts 13 F2
Hillcliffane 81 D3
Hillend Aber. 176 C6
Hillend Fife 143 F1
Hillend Midloth. 143 G3
Hillend N.Lan. 142 C3
Hillend Swan. 36 A3
Hillend Green 53 G5
Hillersland 39 E1
Hillesden 56 B5
Hillesley 39 G4
Hillfarrance 23 E5
Hillfoot End 57 G4
Hillhead Devon 9 F2
Hillhead S.Ayr. 132 C3
Hillhead of Auchentumb 177 H5
Hillhead of Cocklaw 177 J6
Hilliard's Cross 67 D1
Hilliclay 183 G2
Hillingdon 43 F4
Hillington Glas. 141 G3
Hillington Norf. 85 F5
Hillmorton 68 A5
Hillockhead Aber. 168 B4
Hillockhead Aber. 168 C3
Hillowton 124 B4
Hillpound 15 E1
Hill's End 57 E4
Hills Town 81 F1
Hillsborough 94 A3
Hillsford Bridge 22 A3
Hillside Aber. 169 H5
Hillside Angus 161 F3
Hillside Moray 175 J5
Hillside Shet. 187 D6
Hillside Worcs. 53 G1
Hillswick 186 B5
Hillway 15 F4
Hillwell 187 F9
Hillyfields 14 C1
Hilmarton 40 C5
Hilperton 25 F2
Hilsea 15 F2
Hilston 105 E4
Hilton Cambs. 58 A1
Hilton Cumb. 118 D5
Hilton Derbys. 80 D4
Hilton Dorset 13 D2
Hilton Dur. 120 A5
Hilton High. 175 G3
Hilton Shrop. 65 G3
Hilton Staffs. 66 C2
Hilton Stock. 111 D1
Hilton Croft 169 H1
Hilton of Cadboll 175 F4
Hilton of Delnies 175 F6
Himbleton 54 B2
Himley 66 A3
Hincaster 107 G4
Hinchley Wood 29 G1
Hinckley 67 G3
Hinderclay 72 B4
Hinderton 91 E5
Hinderwell 111 G1
Hindford 78 A4
Hindhead 29 D4
Hindley Gt.Man. 92 A2
Hindley Northumb. 119 G2
Hindley Green 92 A2
Hindlip 54 A2
Hindolveston 86 B3
Hindon Som. 22 C3
Hindon Wilts. 26 A4
Hindringham 86 A2
Hingham 86 B5
Hinksford 66 A4
Hinstock 79 D5
Hintlesham 60 B3
Hinton Glos. 39 F2
Hinton Hants. 14 B3
Hinton Here. 52 C4
Hinton Northants. 56 A2
Hinton S.Glos. 39 G5
Hinton Shrop. 64 D2
Hinton Admiral 14 B3
Hinton Ampner 27 G5
Hinton Blewett 24 C2
Hinton Charterhouse 25 E2
Hinton Martell 13 G2
Hinton on the Green 54 C3
Hinton Parva Dorset 13 F2
Hinton Parva Swin. 41 E4
Hinton St. George 12 A1
Hinton St. Mary 13 D1
Hinton Waldrist 41 F3
Hinton-in-the-Hedges 56 A4
Hints Shrop. 65 F5
Hints Staffs. 67 D2
Hinwick 57 E1
Hinxhill 32 C4
Hinxton 58 C3
Hinxworth 58 A3
Hipperholme 102 A5
Hipsburn 137 G5
Hipswell 110 A3
Hirn 169 F4
Hirnant 77 D5
Hirst 129 E3
Hirst Courtney 103 F5
Hirwaen 77 E1
Hirwaun 37 F2
Hiscott 21 F3
Histon 58 C1
Hitcham Bucks. 43 E4
Hitcham Suff. 60 A2
Hitchin 57 G5
Hither Green 44 C5
Hittisleigh 10 A3
Hittisleigh Barton 10 A3
Hive 104 A4
Hixon 80 B5
Hoaden 33 E3
Hoaldalbert 52 C5
Hoar Cross 80 C5
Hoarwithy 53 E5
Hoath 33 E2
Hobarris 64 C5
Hobbister 185 C7
Hobbles Green 59 F2
Hobbs Cross 45 D3
Hobbs Lots Bridge 70 B2
Hobkirk 135 G4
Hobland Hall 87 G5
Hobson 120 A2
Hoby 68 B1
Hockerill 58 C5
Hockering 86 B4
Hockerton 82 C2
Hockley 46 B3
Hockley Heath 67 D5
Hockliffe 57 E5
Hockwold cum Wilton 71 F4
Hockworthy 10 D1
Hoddesdon 44 C2
Hoddlesden 100 D5
Hodgehill 79 F1
Hodgeston 34 D3
Hodnet 78 D5
Hodnetheath 78 D5
Hodsoll Street 31 F2
Hodson 41 D4
Hodthorpe 94 C5
Hoe 86 A4
Hoe Gate 15 F1
Hoff 108 B1
Hoffleet Stow 84 A4
Hoggard's Green 59 G2
Hoggeston 56 D5
Hoggie 176 D5
Hoggrill's End 67 E3
Hogha Gearraidh 170 C4
Hoghton 100 C5
Hognaston 80 D2
Hogsthorpe 97 F5
Holbeach 84 B5
Holbeach Bank 84 B5
Holbeach Clough 84 B5
Holbeach Drove 70 B1
Holbeach Hurn 84 B5
Holbeach St. Johns 70 B1
Holbeach St. Marks 84 B4
Holbeach St. Matthew 84 C4
Holbeck 94 C5
Holbeck Woodhouse 94 C5
Holberrow Green 54 C2
Holbeton 8 C2
Holborough 31 G2
Holbrook Derbys. 81 E3
Holbrook Suff. 60 C4
Holbrooks 67 F4
Holburn 137 E3
Holbury 14 D2
Holcombe Devon 10 C5
Holcombe Gt.Man. 92 B1
Holcombe Som. 25 D3
Holcombe Burnell Barton 10 B3
Holcombe Rogus 11 D1
Holcot 56 C1
Holden 101 D3
Holden Gate 101 E5
Holdenby 56 B1
Holdenhurst 14 A3
Holder's Green 59 E5
Holders Hill 44 B4
Holdgate 65 E4
Holdingham 83 F3
Holditch 11 G2
Hole 11 E1
Hole Park 32 A5
Hole Street 16 D2
Holehouse 93 E3
Hole-in-the-Wall 53 F5
Holford 23 E3
Holgate 103 E2
Holker 107 E5
Holkham 85 G3
Hollacombe Devon 21 D5
Hollacombe Devon 10 B2
Hollacombe Town 21 G4
Holland Ork. 184 D2
Holland Ork. 184 F5
Holland Surr. 30 D3
Holland Fen 84 A3
Holland-on-Sea 47 E1
Hollandstoun 184 G2
Hollee 126 A5
Hollesley 61 E3
Hollicombe 9 F1
Hollingbourne 32 A3
Hollingbury 17 F3
Hollingrove 18 B1
Hollington Derbys. 80 D4
Hollington E.Suss. 18 C2
Hollington Staffs. 80 B4
Hollingworth 93 E3
Hollins 94 A5
Hollins Green 92 A3
Hollins Lane 100 A2
Hollinsclough 80 B1
Hollinwood Gt.Man. 92 D2
Hollinwood Shrop. 78 C4
Hollocombe 21 G4
Hollow Meadows 93 G4
Holloway 81 E2
Hollowell 68 B5
Holly Bush 78 B3
Holly End 70 C2
Holly Green 42 C2
Hollybush Caerp. 38 A2
Hollybush E.Ayr. 132 B4
Hollybush Worcs. 53 G4
Hollyhurst 78 C3
Hollym 105 F5
Hollywater 28 D4
Hollywood 66 C5
Holm D.&G. 126 A2
Holm (Tolm) W.Isles 179 G4
Holm of Drumlanrig 124 C1
Holmbridge 93 F2
Holmbury St. Mary 29 G3
Holmbush 30 B5
Holme Cambs. 69 G4
Holme Cumb. 107 G5
Holme N.Lincs. 95 G2
Holme N.Yorks. 110 C4
Holme Notts. 82 D2
Holme W.Yorks. 93 F2
Holme Chapel 101 E5
Holme Hale 71 G2
Holme Lacy 53 E4
Holme Marsh 52 C2
Holme next the Sea 85 F3
Holme on the Wolds 104 B3
Holme Pierrepont 82 B4
Holme St. Cuthbert 117 E2
Holme-on-Spalding-Moor 104 A4
Holmer 53 E3
Holmer Green 43 E3
Holmes 91 F1
Holmes Chapel 79 E1
Holme's Hill 18 A2
Holmesfield 94 A5
Holmeswood 91 F1
Holmewood 81 F1
Holmfield 101 G5
Holmfirth 93 F2
Holmhead D.&G. 124 B2
Holmhead E.Ayr. 133 D3
Holmpton 105 F5
Holmrook 106 B2
Holmsgarth 187 D8
Holmside 120 B3
Holmsleigh Green 11 F2
Holmston 132 B3
Holmwrangle 118 B3
Holne 8 D1
Holnest 12 C2
Holnicote 22 C3
Holsworthy 20 D5
Holsworthy Beacon 21 D5
Holt Dorset 13 G2
Holt Norf. 86 B2
Holt Wilts. 25 F1
Holt Worcs. 54 A1
Holt Wrex. 78 B2
Holt End Hants. 28 B4
Holt End Worcs. 54 C1
Holt Fleet 54 A1
Holt Heath Dorset 13 G2
Holt Heath Worcs. 54 A1
Holt Wood 13 G2
Holtby 103 F2
Holton Oxon. 42 B2
Holton Som. 25 D5
Holton Suff. 73 F4
Holton cum Beckering 96 B4
Holton Heath 13 F3
Holton le Clay 96 C2
Holton le Moor 96 A3
Holton St. Mary 60 B4
Holtspur 43 E4
Holtye 31 D5
Holtye Common 31 D5
Holway 23 F5
Holwell Dorset 12 C1
Holwell Herts. 57 G4
Holwell Leics. 82 C5
Holwell Oxon. 41 E2
Holwell Som. 25 E3
Holwick 119 F5
Holworth 13 D4
Holy Cross 66 B5
Holy Island I.o.A. 88 A5
Holy Island Northumb. 137 F2
Holy Island (Lindisfarne) Northumb. 137 F2
Holybourne 28 C3
Holyfield 44 C2
Holyhead (Caergybi) 88 A4
Holymoorside 81 E1
Holyport 43 D5
Holystone 128 B1
Holytown 142 B3
Holywell Cambs. 70 B5
Holywell Cornw. 4 B4
Holywell Dorset 12 B2
Holywell E.Suss. 18 B4
Holywell (Treffynnon) Flints. 90 C5
Holywell Northumb. 129 F4
Holywell Green 93 E1
Holywell Lake 23 E5
Holywell Row 71 F5
Holywood 124 D2
Hom Green 53 E5
Homer 65 F2
Homersfield 73 D3
Homington 26 C5
Homore (Tobha Mòr) 162 C1
Honey Hill 32 D2
Honey Street 26 C1
Honey Tye 60 A4
Honeyborough 34 C2
Honeybourne 54 D3
Honeychurch 21 G5
Honicknowle 8 A2
Honiley 67 E5
Honing 87 E3
Honingham 86 C4
Honington Lincs. 83 E3
Honington Suff. 72 A4
Honington Warks. 55 E3
Honiton 11 E2
Honkley 78 A2
Honley 93 F1
Hoo Med. 45 G5
Hoo Suff. 61 D2
Hoo Green 92 B4
Hoo Meavy 8 B1
Hood Green 94 A2
Hood Hill 94 A3
Hooe E.Suss. 18 B3
Hooe Plym. 8 B2
Hooe Common 18 B2
Hook Cambs. 70 C3
Hook E.Riding 103 G5
Hook Gt.Lon. 29 G1
Hook Hants. 28 C2
Hook Hants. 15 E2
Hook Pembs. 34 C1
Hook Wilts. 40 C4
Hook Green Kent 31 F5
Hook Green Kent 31 F2
Hook Green Kent 45 F5
Hook Green Kent 45 E5
Hook Norton 55 F4
Hook-a-Gate 65 D2
Hooke 12 B2
Hookgate 79 E4
Hookway 10 B3
Hookwood 30 B4
Hoole 78 B1
Hooley 30 B3
Hoop 39 E2
Hooton 91 E5
Hooton Levitt 94 C3
Hooton Pagnell 94 B2
Hooton Roberts 94 B3
Hop Pole 69 G1
Hopcrofts Holt 55 G5
Hope Derbys. 93 F4
Hope Devon 8 C4
Hope Flints. 78 A2
Hope Powys 64 B2
Hope Shrop. 64 C2
Hope Staffs. 80 C2
Hope Bagot 65 E5
Hope Bowdler 65 D3
Hope End Green 59 D5
Hope Mansell 39 F1
Hope under Dinmore 53 E2
Hopehouse 135 D4
Hopeman 175 J5
Hope's Green 45 G4
Hopesay 64 C4
Hopkinstown 37 G3
Hopley's Green 52 C2
Hopperton 102 D2
Hopsford 67 G4
Hopstone 65 G3
Hopton Derbys. 81 D2
Hopton Norf. 73 G2
Hopton Shrop. 78 C5
Hopton Shrop. 78 A5
Hopton Staffs. 79 G5
Hopton Suff. 72 A4
Hopton Cangeford 65 E4
Hopton Castle 64 C5
Hopton Wafers 65 F5
Hoptonheath 64 C5
Hopwas 67 D2
Hopwood 66 C5
Horam 18 A2
Horbling 83 G4
Horbury 93 G1
Horden 120 D3
Horderley 64 D4
Hordle 14 B3
Hordley 78 A4
Horeb Carmar. 36 A2
Horeb Cere. 49 G3
Horeb Flints. 77 F2
Horfield 39 E5
Horham 72 D4
Horkesley Heath 60 A5
Horkstow 95 G1
Horley Oxon. 55 G3
Horley Surr. 30 B4
Horn Hill 43 F3
Hornblotton 24 C4
Hornblotton Green 24 C4
Hornby Lancs. 100 B1
Hornby N.Yorks. 110 B3
Hornby N.Yorks. 110 C2
Horncastle 84 A1
Hornchurch 45 E4
Horncliffe 145 G5
Horndean Hants. 15 G1
Horndean Sc.Bord. 145 G5
Horndon 7 F2
Horndon on the Hill 45 F4
Horne 30 C4
Horne Row 45 G2
Horner 22 B3
Horniehaugh 160 C3
Horning 87 E4
Horninghold 68 D3
Horninglow 80 D5
Horningsea 58 C1
Horningsham 25 F3
Horningtoft 86 A3
Horningtops 5 G3
Horns Cross Devon 21 D3
Horns Cross E.Suss. 18 D1
Horns Green 31 D3
Hornsbury 11 G1
Hornsby 118 B3
Hornsby Gate 118 B2
Hornsea 105 E3
Hornsey 44 C4
Hornton 55 F3
Horrabridge 8 B1
Horridge 10 A5
Horringer 59 G1
Horrocks Fold 92 B1
Horse Bridge 79 G2
Horsebridge Devon 7 E3
Horsebridge Hants. 27 E4
Horsebrook 66 A1
Horsecastle 24 B1
Horsehay 65 F2
Horseheath 59 E3
Horsehouse 109 F4
Horsell 29 E2
Horseman's Green 78 B3
Horsenden 42 C2
Horseshoe Green 31 D4
Horseway 70 C4
Horsey 87 F3
Horsey Corner 87 F3
Horsford 86 C4
Horsforth 102 B4
Horsham W.Suss. 29 G4
Horsham Worcs. 53 G2
Horsham St. Faith 86 D4
Horsington Lincs. 83 G1
Horsington Som. 25 E5
Horsington Marsh 25 E5
Horsley Derbys. 81 E3
Horsley Glos. 40 A3
Horsley Northumb. 119 G1
Horsley Northumb. 128 A2
Horsley Cross 60 C5
Horsley Woodhouse 81 E3
Horsleycross Street 60 C5
Horsleygate 94 A5
Horsleyhill 135 G4
Horsmonden 31 F4
Horspath 42 A2
Horstead 87 D4
Horsted Keynes 17 F1
Horton Bucks. 43 E1
Horton Dorset 13 G2
Horton Lancs. 101 E2
Horton Northants. 56 D2
Horton S.Glos. 39 G4
Horton Shrop. 78 B5
Horton Som. 11 G1
Horton Staffs. 79 G2
Horton Swan. 36 A4
Horton Tel.&W. 65 F1
Horton W.&M. 43 F5
Horton Wilts. 26 B1
Horton Cross 11 G1
Horton Grange 129 E4
Horton Green 78 B3
Horton Heath 15 D1
Horton in Ribblesdale 108 D5
Horton Inn 13 G2
Horton Kirby 31 E2
Horton-cum-Studley 42 B1
Horwich 92 A1
Horwich End 93 E4
Horwood 21 F3
Hoscar 91 F1
Hose 82 C5
Hoses 106 D3
Hosh 151 D2
Hosta 170 C4
Hoswick 187 D10
Hotham 104 A4
Hothfield 32 B4
Hoton 81 G5
Houbie 186 F3
Houdston 122 C1
Hough 79 E2
Hough Green 91 F4
Hougham 83 D3
Hough-on-the-Hill 83 E3
Houghton Cambs. 70 A5
Houghton Cumb. 118 A2
Houghton Devon 8 C3
Houghton Hants. 27 E4
Houghton Pembs. 34 C2
Houghton W.Suss. 16 C2
Houghton Bank 120 B5
Houghton Conquest 57 F3
Houghton le Spring 120 C3
Houghton on the Hill 68 B2
Houghton Regis 57 F5
Houghton St. Giles 86 A2
Houghton-le-Side 120 B5
Houlsyke 111 G2
Hound 15 D2
Hound Green 28 C2
Houndslow 144 D5
Houndsmoor 23 E5
Houndwood 145 F3
Hounsdown 14 C1
Hounslow 44 A5
Househay 184 F5
Househill 175 F6
Houses Hill 93 F1
Housetter 186 C4
Housham Tye 45 E1
Houss 187 C9
Houston 141 F3
Houstry 183 G5
Houstry of Dunn 183 H3
Houton 185 C7
Hove 17 E3
Hove Edge 102 A5
Hoveringham 82 B3
Hoveton 87 E4
Hovingham 111 F5
How 118 B2
How Caple 53 F4
How End 57 F3
How Green 31 D4
How Man 116 C5
Howbrook 94 A3
Howden 103 G5
Howden Clough 102 B5
Howden-le-Wear 120 A4
Howe Cumb. 107 F4
Howe High. 183 J2
Howe N.Yorks. 110 C4
Howe Norf. 73 D2
Howe Green 45 G2
Howe of Teuchar 177 F6
Howe Street Essex 45 F1
Howe Street Essex 59 E4
Howegreen 46 B2
Howell 83 G3
Howey 51 G2
Howgate Cumb. 116 C4
Howgate Midloth. 143 G4
Howgill Lancs. 101 E3
Howgill N.Yorks. 101 G2
Howick 137 G5
Howle 79 D5
Howle Hill 53 F5
Howlett End 59 D4
Howley 11 F2
Hownam 136 B5
Hownam Mains 136 B4
Howpasley 135 E5
Howsham N.Lincs. 96 A2
Howsham N.Yorks. 103 G1
Howt Green 32 A2
Howtel 136 C3
Howton 52 D5
Howwood 141 F3
Hoxa 185 D8
Hoxne 72 C4
Hoy High. 183 H2
Hoy Ork. 185 B8
Hoylake 90 D4
Hoyland 94 A2
Hoylandswaine 93 G2
Hoyle 16 B2
Hubberholme 109 E5
Hubberston 34 B2
Hubbert's Bridge 84 A3
Huby N.Yorks. 103 E1
Huby N.Yorks. 102 B3
Hucclecote 40 A1
Hucking 32 A3
Hucknall 81 G3
Huddersfield 93 F1
Huddington 54 B2
Huddlesford 66 D2
Hudnall 43 F1
Hudscott 21 G3
Hudswell 110 A3
Huggate 104 A2
Hugglescote 67 G1
Hugh Town 4 B1
Hughenden Valley 43 D3
Hughley 65 E3
Hugmore 78 A2
Hugus 4 B5
Huish Devon 21 F4
Huish Wilts. 26 C1
Huish Champflower 22 D5
Huish Episcopi 24 B5
Huisinis 178 B6
Hulcote 57 E4
Hulcott 43 D1
Hull 104 D5
Hulland 80 D3
Hulland Ward 81 D3
Hullavington 40 A4
Hullbridge 46 B3
Hulme 79 G3
Hulme End 80 C2
Hulme Walfield 79 F1
Hulver Street 73 F3
Hulverstone 14 C4
Humber Devon 10 B5
Humber Here. 53 E2
Humberside International Airport 96 A1
Humberston 96 D2
Humberstone 68 B2
Humberton 102 D1
Humbie 144 B3
Humbleton Dur. 109 F1
Humbleton E.Riding 105 E4
Humbleton Northumb. 137 D4
Humby 83 F4
Hume 145 E5
Humehall 145 E5
Hummer 12 B1
Humshaugh 128 B4
Huna 183 J1
Huncoat 101 D4
Huncote 68 A3
Hundalee 136 A5
Hundall 94 A5
Hunderthwaite 119 F5
Hundleby 84 B1
Hundleton 34 C2
Hundon 59 F3
Hundred Acres 15 E1
Hundred End 100 A5
Hundred House 52 A2
Hungarton 68 B2
Hungate End 56 C3
Hungerford Hants. 14 A1
Hungerford Shrop. 65 E4
Hungerford W.Berks. 27 E1
Hungerford Newtown 41 F5
Hungerton 83 D5
Hunglader 171 J4
Hunmanby 113 D5
Hunningham 55 F1
Hunningham Hill 55 F1
Hunny Hill 15 D4
Hunsdon 44 D1
Hunsingore 102 D2
Hunslet 102 C4
Hunsonby 118 B4
Hunspow 183 H1
Hunstanton 85 E3
Hunstanworth 119 F3
Hunston Suff. 60 A1
Hunston W.Suss. 16 A3
Hunsworth 102 A5
Hunt End 54 C1
Hunt House 112 B3
Huntercombe End 42 B4
Hunters Forstal 33 D2
Hunter's Inn 21 G1
Hunter's Quay 140 C2
Hunterston 140 C4
Huntford 127 E1
Huntham 24 A5
Huntingdon 70 A5
Huntingfield 73 E4
Huntingford 25 F4
Huntington Here. 52 B2
Huntington Here. 53 D3
Huntington Staffs. 66 B1

Huntington *Tel. & W.* 65 F2
Huntington *York* 103 F2
Huntingtower 151 F2
Huntley 39 G1
Huntly 168 D1
Huntlywood 144 D5
Hunton *Hants.* 27 F3
Hunton *Kent* 31 G4
Hunton *N.Yorks.* 110 A3
Hunton Bridge 43 F2
Hunt's Cross 91 F4
Huntscott 22 C3
Huntsham 22 D5
Huntshaw 21 F3
Huntshaw Cross 21 F3
Huntshaw Water 21 F3
Huntspill 24 A3
Huntworth 24 A4
Hunwick 120 A4
Hunworth 86 B2
Hurcott *Som.* 24 C5
Hurcott *Som.* 11 G1
Hurdley 64 B3
Hurdsfield 92 D5
Hurley *W. & M.* 42 D4
Hurley *Warks.* 67 E3
Hurley Bottom 42 D4
Hurlford 132 C2
Hurliness 185 B9
Hurlston Green 91 E1
Hurn 14 A3
Hursley 27 F5
Hurst *N.Yorks.* 109 F2
Hurst *W'ham* 42 C5
Hurst Green *E.Suss.* 18 C1
Hurst Green *Essex* 47 D1
Hurst Green *Lancs.* 100 C4
Hurst Green *Surr.* 30 C3
Hurst Wickham 17 E2
Hurstbourne Priors 27 F3
Hurstbourne Tarrant 27 E2
Hurstpierpoint 17 E2
Hurstwood 101 E4
Hurtmore 29 E3
Hurworth-on-Tees 110 C1
Hury 119 F5
Husabost 171 G6
Husbands Bosworth 68 B4
Husborne Crawley 57 E4
Husthwaite 111 E5
Hutcherleigh 9 D2
Huthwaite 81 F2
Huttoft 97 F5
Hutton *Cumb.* 118 A5
Hutton *Essex* 45 F3
Hutton *Lancs.* 100 A5
Hutton *N.Som.* 24 A2
Hutton *Sc.Bord.* 145 G4
Hutton Bonville 110 C2
Hutton Buscel 112 C4
Hutton Conyers 110 C5
Hutton Cranswick 104 C2
Hutton End 118 A4
Hutton Hang 110 A4
Hutton Henry 120 D4
Hutton Magna 110 A1
Hutton Mount 45 F3
Hutton Mulgrave 112 B2
Hutton Roof *Cumb.* 107 G5
Hutton Roof *Cumb.* 117 G3
Hutton Rudby 111 D2
Hutton Sessay 111 D5
Hutton Wandesley 103 E2
Hutton-le-Hole 111 G3
Huxham 10 C3
Huxham Green 24 C4
Huxley 78 C1
Huxter *Shet.* 187 C7
Huxter *Shet.* 187 E6
Huyton 91 F3
Hwlffordd (Haverfordwest) 34 C1
Hycemoor 106 B4
Hyde *Glos.* 40 A2
Hyde *Gt.Man.* 92 D3
Hyde End *W'ham* 28 C1
Hyde End *W.Berks.* 27 G1
Hyde Heath 43 E2
Hyde Lea 66 B1
Hydestile 29 E3
Hyndford Bridge 142 D5
Hyndlee 135 G5
Hynish 154 A3
Hyssington 64 C3
Hythe *Hants.* 14 D2
Hythe *Kent* 33 D5
Hythe End 43 F5
Hythie 177 J5
Hyton 106 B4

▼ I

Ianstown 176 C4
Iarsiadar 178 D4
Ibberton 13 D2
Ible 80 D2
Ibsley 14 A2
Ibstock 67 G1
Ibstone 42 C3
Ibthorpe 27 E2
Ibworth 27 G2
Icelton 24 A1
Ickburgh 71 G3
Ickenham 43 F4
Ickford 42 B2
Ickham 33 E3
Ickleford 57 G4
Icklesham 19 D2
Ickleton 58 C3
Icklingham 71 F5
Ickwell Green 57 G3
Icomb 55 E5
Idbury 55 E5
Iddesleigh 21 F5
Ide 10 C3
Ide Hill 31 D3
Ideford 10 B5
Iden 19 E1
Iden Green *Kent* 31 G5
Iden Green *Kent* 32 A5
Idle 102 A4
Idless 4 C5
Idlicote 55 E3
Idmiston 26 C4
Idridgehay 81 D3
Idridgehay Green 81 D3
Idrigil 171 J5
Idstone 41 E4
Idvies 160 D5
Iffley 42 A2
Ifield (Singlewell) *Kent* 45 F5
Ifield *W.Suss.* 30 B5
Ifieldwood 30 B5
Ifold 29 F4
Iford *Bourne.* 14 A3
Iford *E.Suss.* 17 G3
Ifton 39 D4
Ifton Heath 78 A4
Ightfield 78 C4
Ightham 31 E3
Iken 61 F2
Ilam 80 C2
Ilchester 24 C5
Ilderton 137 E4
Ilford 44 D4
Ilfracombe 21 F1
Ilkeston 81 F3
Ilketshall St. Andrew 73 E3
Ilketshall St. Lawrence 73 E3
Ilketshall St. Margaret 73 E3
Ilkley 102 A3
Illey 66 B4
Illidge Green 79 E1
Illington 72 A3
Illingworth 101 G5
Illogan 4 A5
Illston on the Hill 68 C3
Ilmer 42 C2
Ilmington 55 E3
Ilminster 11 G1
Ilsington *Devon* 10 A5
Ilsington *Dorset* 13 D3
Ilston 36 B3
Ilton *N.Yorks.* 110 A5
Ilton *Som.* 11 G1
Imachar 139 G5
Imber 26 A3
Immeroin 150 A3
Immingham 96 B1
Immingham Dock 96 C1
Impington 58 C1
Ince 91 F5
Ince Blundell 91 E2
Ince-in-Makerfield 91 G2
Inch Kenneth 146 D1
Inch of Arnhall 161 E2
Inchbae Lodge 174 B5
Inchbare 161 E3
Inchberry 176 B5
Inchbraoch 161 F4
Inchgrundle 160 C2
Inchindown 174 D4
Inchinnan 141 F3
Inchkinloch 181 J4
Inchlaggan 165 H4
Inchlumpie 174 C4
Inchmarlo 168 E5
Inchmarnock 140 B4
Inchnabobart 160 B1
Inchnacardoch Hotel 165 K3
Inchnadamph 180 E6
Inchock 161 E5
Inchrory 167 J4
Inchture 152 A2
Inchvuilt 165 J1
Inchyra 151 G2
Indian Queens 4 D4
Inerval 138 B5
Ingatestone 45 F3
Ingbirchworth 93 G2
Ingerthorpe 102 B1
Ingestre 79 G5
Ingham *Lincs.* 95 G4
Ingham *Norf.* 87 E3
Ingham *Suff.* 71 G5
Ingham Corner 87 E3
Ingleborough 70 C1
Ingleby *Derbys.* 81 E5
Ingleby *Lincs.* 95 F5
Ingleby Arncliffe 110 D2
Ingleby Barwick 110 D1
Ingleby Cross 110 D2
Ingleby Greenhow 111 E2
Ingleigh Green 21 G5
Inglesbatch 25 E1
Inglesham 41 E3
Ingleton *Dur.* 120 A5
Ingleton *N.Yorks.* 108 B5
Inglewhite 100 B4
Ingliston 143 F2
Ingmire Hall 108 B3
Ingoe 128 C4
Ingoldisthorpe 85 E4
Ingoldmells 85 D1
Ingoldsby 83 F4
Ingon 55 E2
Ingram 137 E5
Ingrave 45 F3
Ingrow 101 G4
Ings 107 F3
Ingst 39 E4
Ingworth 86 C3
Inhurst 27 G1
Inistrynich 148 D2
Injebreck 98 B3
Inkberrow 54 C2
Inkersall 94 B5
Inkersall Green 94 B5
Inkhorn 169 H1
Inkpen 27 E1
Inkstack 183 H1
Inmarsh 26 A1
Innellan 140 C3
Innergellie 153 D4
Innerleithen 135 E2
Innerleven 152 B4
Innermessan 122 B4
Innerwick *E.Loth.* 145 E2
Innerwick *P. & K.* 158 A5
Inninbeg 155 F5
Innsworth 54 A5
Insch 168 E2
Insh 167 F4
Inshore 181 F2
Inskip 100 A4
Instow 21 E2
Intake 94 C2
Intwood 86 C5
Inver *Aber.* 167 K5
Inver *Arg. & B.* 156 B5
Inver *High.* 175 F3
Inver *High.* 183 G5
Inver *P. & K.* 159 F5
Inver Mallie 156 D1
Inverailort 155 G1
Inveralligin 172 E6
Inverallochy 177 J4
Inveran 174 C2
Inveraray 148 C4
Inverardoch Mains 150 C4
Inverardran 149 F2
Inverarish 164 B1
Inverarity 160 C5
Inverarnan 149 F3
Inverasdale 172 E3
Inverbain 172 D6
Inverbeg 149 F5
Inverbervie 161 G2
Inverbroom 173 H3
Inverbrough 167 F2
Invercassley 174 B1
Inverchaolain 140 B2
Invercharnan 156 D5
Inverchorachan 149 E3
Inverchoran 173 J6
Invercreran 156 C5
Inverdruie 167 G3
Inverebrie 169 H1
Invereen 166 E1
Invererne 175 H5
Inveresk 144 A2
Inverey 159 F1
Inverfarigaig 166 C2
Invergarry 165 K4
Invergelder 167 K5
Invergeldie 150 C2
Invergloy 157 E1
Invergordon 174 E5
Invergowrie 152 B1
Inverguseran 164 D4
Inverhadden 158 B4
Inverharroch Farm 168 B1
Inverherive 149 F2
Inverhope 181 G2
Inverie 164 D4
Inverinan 148 B3
Inverinate 165 F2
Inverkeilor 161 E5
Inverkeithing 143 F1
Inverkeithny 176 E6
Inverkip 140 D2
Inverkirkaig 180 C7
Inverlael 173 H3
Inverlauren 141 E1
Inverliever 148 A4
Inverliver 148 C1
Inverlochlarig 149 G3
Inverlochy 149 D2
Inverlussa 139 E1
Invermay 151 F3
Invermoriston 166 B3
Invernaver 182 C2
Inverneil 139 G1
Inverness 174 D7
Inverness Airport 174 E6
Invernettie 177 K6
Invernoaden 148 D5
Inveroran Hotel 157 E5
Inverquharity 160 C4
Inverquhomery 177 J6
Inverroy 157 E1
Inversanda 156 B4
Invershiel 165 F3
Invershore 183 H5
Inversnaid Hotel 149 F4
Invertrossachs 150 A4
Inverugie 177 K6
Inveruglas 149 F4
Inveruglass 167 F4
Inverurie 169 F2
Invervar 158 B5
Invervegain 140 B2
Invery House 168 E5
Inverythan 177 F6
Inwardleigh 7 F1
Inworth 46 B1
Iochdar 170 C7
Iona 146 B2
Iping 29 D5
Ipplepen 9 E1
Ipsden 42 B4
Ipstones 80 B3
Ipswich 60 C3
Irby 91 D4
Irby Hill 91 D4
Irby in the Marsh 84 C1
Irby upon Humber 96 B2
Irchester 57 E1
Ireby *Cumb.* 117 F3
Ireby *Lancs.* 108 B5
Ireland *Ork.* 185 C7
Ireland *Shet.* 187 C10
Ireland's Cross 79 E3
Ireleth 106 D5
Ireshopeburn 119 E4
Irlam 92 B3
Irnham 83 F5
Iron Acton 39 F4
Iron Cross 54 C2
Ironbridge 65 F2
Irons Bottom 30 B4
Ironside 177 G5
Ironville 81 F2
Irstead 87 E3
Irthington 118 A1
Irthlingborough 69 E5
Irton 112 D4
Irvine 132 B2
Isauld 182 E2
Isbister *Ork.* 185 C6
Isbister *Ork.* 184 B5
Isbister *Shet.* 187 E6
Isbister *Shet.* 186 C3
Isfield 17 G2
Isham 69 D5
Ishriff 147 F1
Isington 28 C3
Island of Stroma 183 J1
Islawr-dref 62 C1
Islay 138 A3
Islay Airport 138 B4
Islay House 138 B3
Isle Abbotts 24 A5
Isle Brewers 24 A5
Isle of Lewis (Eilean Leodhais) 179 F3
Isle of Man 98 B3
Isle of Man Airport 98 A5
Isle of May 153 E5
Isle of Noss 187 E8
Isle of Sheppey 32 B1
Isle of Walney 99 E1
Isle of Whithorn 115 E3
Isle of Wight 15 D4
Isleham 71 E5
Isleornsay (Eilean Iarmain) 164 C3
Isles of Scilly (Scilly Isles) 4 B1
Islesburgh 187 C6
Isleworth 44 A5
Isley Walton 81 F5
Islibhig 178 B5
Islip *Northants.* 69 E5
Islip *Oxon.* 42 A1
Isombridge 65 F1
Istead Rise 31 F2
Itchen 14 D1
Itchen Abbas 27 G4
Itchen Stoke 27 G4
Itchingfield 29 G5
Itchington 39 F4
Itteringham 86 C2
Itton *Devon* 7 G1
Itton *Mon.* 39 D3
Itton Common 39 D3
Ivegill 118 A3
Ivelet 109 E3
Iver 43 F4
Iver Heath 43 F4
Iveston 120 A2
Ivetsey Bank 66 A1
Ivinghoe 43 E1
Ivinghoe Aston 43 E1
Ivington 53 D2
Ivington Green 53 D2
Ivy Hatch 31 E3
Ivy Todd 71 G2
Ivybridge 8 C2
Ivychurch 19 F1
Iwade 32 B2
Iwerne Courtney (Shroton) 13 E1
Iwerne Minster 13 E1
Ixworth 72 A4
Ixworth Thorpe 72 A4

▼ J

Jack Hill 102 A2
Jackfield 65 F2
Jacksdale 81 F2
Jackstown 169 F1
Jackton 141 G4
Jacobstow 6 B1
Jacobstowe 21 F5
Jacobswell 29 E2
Jameston 35 D3
Jamestown *D. & G.* 126 B2
Jamestown *High.* 174 B6
Jamestown *W.Dun.* 141 E1
Janefield 174 E6
Janetstown *High.* 183 F2
Janetstown *High.* 183 J3
Jarrow 120 C1
Jarvis Brook 31 E5
Jasper's Green 59 F5
Jawcraig 142 C2
Jayes Park 29 G3
Jaywick 47 E1
Jealott's Hill 43 D5
Jeater Houses 110 D3
Jedburgh 136 A4
Jeffreyston 35 D2
Jemimaville 174 E5
Jericho 92 C1
Jersay 142 C3
Jersey 8 C5
Jersey Airport 8 B5
Jersey Marine 36 D3
Jerviswood 142 C5
Jesmond 120 B1
Jevington 18 A3
Jockey End 43 F1
Jodrell Bank 92 B5
John o' Groats 183 J1
Johnby 118 A4
John's Cross 18 C1
Johnshaven 161 F3
Johnson Street 87 E4
Johnston 34 C1
Johnston Mains 161 F2
Johnstone 141 F3
Johnstone Castle 141 F3
Johnstonebridge 125 E1
Johnstown *Carmar.* 35 G1
Johnstown *Wrex.* 78 A3
Joppa 132 C4
Jordans 43 E3
Jordanston 48 C4
Jordanstone 160 A5
Joy's Green 39 F1
Jumpers Common 14 A3
Juniper Hill 56 A4
Jura 139 D1
Jura House 138 C3
Jurby East 98 B2
Jurby West 98 B2

▼ K

Kaber 108 C1
Kaimes 143 G3
Kames *Arg. & B.* 140 A2
Kames *Arg. & B.* 148 A3
Kames *E.Ayr.* 133 E3
Kea 4 C5
Keadby 95 F1
Keal Cotes 84 B1
Kearsley 92 B2
Kearstwick 108 B5
Kearton 109 F3
Kearvaig 180 E1
Keasden 100 D1
Kebholes 176 E5
Keckwick 91 G4
Keddington 96 D4
Keddington Corner 97 D4
Kedington 59 F3
Kedleston 81 D3
Keelby 96 B1
Keele 79 F3
Keeley Green 57 F3
Keelham 101 G4
Keeres Green 45 E1
Keeston 34 B1
Keevil 26 A2
Kegworth 81 F5
Kehelland 4 A5
Keig 168 E3
Keighley 101 G3
Keil *Arg. & B.* 130 B5
Keil *High.* 156 B4
Keilhill 177 F5
Keillmore 139 E1
Keillor 160 A5
Keillour 151 E2
Keills 138 C3
Keils 138 D3
Keinton Mandeville 24 C4
Keir House 150 C5
Keir Mill 124 C1
Keisby 83 F5
Keisley 118 D5
Keiss 183 J2
Keith 176 C5
Keithick 152 A1
Keithmore 168 B1
Keithock 161 E3
Kelbrook 101 F3
Kelby 83 F3
Keld *Cumb.* 107 G1
Keld *N.Yorks.* 109 D2
Keldholme 111 G4
Keldy Castle 111 G3
Kelfield *N.Lincs.* 95 F2
Kelfield *N.Yorks.* 103 E4
Kelham 82 C2
Kella 98 B2
Kellacott 7 E2
Kellan 155 E5
Kellas *Angus* 152 C1
Kellas *Moray* 175 J6
Kellaton 9 D4
Kellaways 40 B5
Kelleth 108 B2
Kelleythorpe 104 C2
Kelling 86 B1
Kellington 103 E5
Kelloe 120 C4
Kelloholm 133 F4
Kelly *Cornw.* 5 E2
Kelly *Devon* 7 D2
Kelly Bray 7 D3
Kelmarsh 68 C5
Kelmscott 41 E3
Kelsale 61 E1
Kelsall 78 C1
Kelsay 138 A4
Kelshall 58 B4
Kelsick 117 F1
Kelso 136 B3
Kelstedge 81 E1
Kelstern 96 C3
Kelston 25 E1
Keltneyburn 158 C5
Kelton 125 D3
Kelton Hill (Rhonehouse) 124 B5
Kelty 151 G5
Kelvedon 46 B1
Kelvedon Hatch 45 E3
Kelvinside 141 G3
Kelynack 2 A4
Kemacott 21 G1
Kemback 152 C3
Kemberton 65 G2
Kemble 40 B3
Kemerton 54 B4
Kemeys Commander 38 C2
Kemeys Inferior 38 C3
Kemnay 169 F3
Kemp Town 17 F3
Kempe's Corner 32 C4
Kempley 53 F5
Kempley Green 53 F5
Kemps Green 66 D5
Kempsey 54 A3
Kempsford 41 D3
Kempshott 27 G3
Kempston 57 F3
Kempston Hardwick 57 F3
Kempston West End 57 E3
Kempton 64 C4
Kemsing 31 E3
Kemsley 32 B2
Kenardington 32 B5
Kenchester 52 D3
Kencott 41 E2
Kendal 107 G3
Kenderchurch 52 D5
Kendleshire 39 F5
Kenfig 37 D4
Kenfig Hill 37 E4
Kenidjack 2 A3
Kenilworth 67 E5
Kenknock *P. & K.* 158 A5
Kenknock *Stir.* 149 G1
Kenley *Gt.Lon.* 30 C2
Kenley *Shrop.* 65 E2
Kenmore *Arg. & B.* 148 C4
Kenmore *High.* 172 D6
Kenmore *P. & K.* 158 C5
Kenmore *W.Isles* 178 E7
Kenn *Devon* 10 C4
Kenn *N.Som.* 24 B1
Kennacley 171 G2
Kennacraig 139 G3
Kennards House 5 G1
Kennavay 171 H2
Kenneggy Downs 2 C4
Kennerleigh 10 B2
Kennerty 168 E5
Kennet 151 E5
Kennethmont 168 D2
Kennett 59 E1
Kennford 10 C4
Kenninghall 72 B3
Kennington *Kent* 32 C4
Kennington *Oxon.* 42 A2
Kennoway 152 B4
Kenny 11 G1
Kennyhill 71 E5
Kennythorpe 103 G1
Kenovay 154 A2
Kensaleyre 171 K6
Kensington 44 B4
Kenstone 78 C5
Kensworth 43 F1
Kent Street *E.Suss.* 18 C2
Kent Street *Kent* 31 F3
Kentallen 156 C4
Kentchurch 52 D5
Kentford 59 F1
Kentisbeare 11 D2
Kentisbury 21 G1
Kentisbury Ford 21 G1
Kentish Town 44 B4
Kentmere 107 F2
Kenton *Devon* 10 C4
Kenton *Suff.* 60 C1
Kenton *T. & W.* 120 B1
Kenton Corner 60 D1
Kentra 155 F3
Kents Bank 107 E5
Kent's Green 53 G5
Kent's Oak 27 E5
Kenwick 78 B4
Kenwyn 4 C5
Kenyon 92 A3
Keoldale 181 F2
Keose (Ceos) 179 F5
Keppanach 156 C3
Keppoch *Arg. & B.* 141 E2
Keppoch *High.* 164 E2
Keprigan 130 B4
Kepwick 111 D3
Keresley 67 F4
Kernborough 9 D3
Kerrera 148 A2
Kerridge 92 D5
Kerris 2 B4
Kerry 64 A3
Kerrycroy 140 C3
Kerry's Gate 52 C4
Kerrysdale 172 E4
Kersall 82 C1
Kersey 60 B3
Kersey Vale 60 B3
Kershopefoot 126 C3
Kerswell 11 D2
Kerswell Green 54 A3
Kerthen Wood 2 C3
Kesgrave 60 D3
Kessingland 73 G3
Kessingland Beach 73 G3
Kestle 5 D5
Kestle Mill 4 C4
Keston 30 D2
Keswick *Cumb.* 117 F4
Keswick *Norf.* 86 D5
Keswick *Norf.* 87 E2
Ketley Bank 65 F1
Ketsby 97 D5
Kettering 69 D5
Ketteringham 86 C5
Kettins 152 A1
Kettle Corner 31 G3
Kettlebaston 60 A2
Kettlebridge 152 B4
Kettlebrook 67 E2
Kettleburgh 61 D1
Kettlehill 152 B4
Kettleholm 125 F3
Kettleness 112 B1
Kettleshulme 93 D5
Kettlesing 102 B2
Kettlesing Bottom 102 B2
Kettlesing Head 102 B2
Kettlestone 86 A2
Kettlethorpe 95 F5
Kettletoft 184 F4
Kettlewell 109 E5
Ketton 69 E2
Kevingtown 31 D2
Kew 44 A5
Kewstoke 24 A1
Kexbrough 94 A2
Kexby *Lincs.* 95 F4
Kexby *York* 103 G2
Key Green 79 F1
Keyham 68 B2
Keyhaven 14 C3
Keyingham 105 E5
Keymer 17 F2
Keynsham 25 D1
Key's Toft 84 C2
Keysoe 57 F1
Keysoe Row 57 F1
Keyston 69 F5
Keyworth 82 B4
Kibblesworth 120 B2
Kibworth Beauchamp 68 B3
Kibworth Harcourt 68 B3
Kidbrooke 44 D5
Kiddemore Green 66 A2
Kidderminster 66 A5
Kiddington 55 G5
Kidlington 41 G1
Kidmore End 42 B5
Kidnal 78 B3
Kidsdale 115 E3
Kidsgrove 79 F2
Kidstones 109 E4
Kidwelly (Cydweli) 36 A2
Kiel Crofts 148 A1
Kielder 127 E2
Kilbarchan 141 F3
Kilbeg 164 C4
Kilberry 139 F3
Kilbirnie 141 E4
Kilblaan 148 D3
Kilbraur 182 D7
Kilbrennan 154 D5
Kilbride *Arg. & B.* 148 A2
Kilbride *Arg. & B.* 140 B3
Kilbride *High.* 164 B2
Kilbride Farm 140 A3
Kilbridemore 148 C5
Kilburn *Derbys.* 81 E3
Kilburn *Gt.Lon.* 44 B4
Kilburn *N.Yorks.* 111 E5
Kilby 68 B3
Kilchattan Bay 140 C4
Kilchenzie 130 B3
Kilcheran 148 A1
Kilchiaran 138 A3
Kilchoan *Arg. & B.* 147 G3
Kilchoan *High.* 155 D3
Kilchoman 138 A3
Kilchrenan 148 C2
Kilchrist 130 B4
Kilconquhar 152 C4
Kilcot 53 F5
Kilcoy 174 C6
Kilcreggan 140 D1
Kildale 111 F2
Kildary 174 E4
Kildavie 130 C4
Kildermorie Lodge 174 C4
Kildonan *N.Ayr.* 131 F3
Kildonan (Cildonnain) *W.Isles* 162 C2
Kildonan Lodge 182 E6
Kildonnan 155 D1
Kildrochet House 122 B5
Kildrummy 168 C3
Kildwick 101 G3
Kilfinan 140 A2
Kilfinnan 165 J5
Kilgetty 35 E2
Kilgwrrwg Common 39 D3
Kilham *E.Riding* 104 C1
Kilham *Northumb.* 136 C3
Kilkenneth 154 A2
Kilkenny 40 C1
Kilkerran *Arg. & B.* 130 C4
Kilkerran *S.Ayr.* 132 B5
Kilkhampton 20 C4
Killamarsh 94 B4
Killay 36 C3
Killbeg 155 F5
Killean *Arg. & B.* 139 E5
Killean *Arg. & B.* 148 C4
Killearn 141 G1
Killellan 130 B4
Killen 174 D6
Killerby 120 A5
Killerton 10 C2
Killichonan 158 A4
Killiechonate 157 E1
Killiechronan 155 E5
Killiecrankie 159 E3
Killiehuntly 166 E5
Killiemor 147 D1
Killilan 165 F1
Killimster 183 J3
Killin *High.* 175 F1
Killin *Stir.* 150 A1
Killinallan 138 B2
Killinghall 102 B2
Killington *Cumb.* 108 B4
Killington *Devon* 21 G1
Killingworth 129 E4
Killochyett 144 B5
Killocraw 130 B2
Killunaig 147 D2
Killundine 155 E5
Kilmacolm 141 E3
Kilmaha 148 B4
Kilmahog 150 B4
Kilmalieu 156 A4
Kilmaluag 171 K4
Kilmany 152 B2
Kilmarie 164 B3
Kilmarnock 132 C2
Kilmartin 148 A5
Kilmaurs 141 F5
Kilmelford 148 A3
Kilmeny 138 B3
Kilmersdon 25 D2
Kilmeston 27 G5
Kilmichael 130 B3
Kilmichael Glassary 148 A5
Kilmichael of Inverlussa 139 F1
Kilmington *Devon* 11 F3
Kilmington *Wilts.* 25 E4
Kilmington Common 25 E4
Kilmorack 174 B7
Kilmore *Arg. & B.* 148 A2
Kilmore *High.* 164 C4
Kilmory *Arg. & B.* 139 F1
Kilmory *Arg. & B.* 139 F2
Kilmory *High.* 163 J4
Kilmory *High.* 155 E2
Kilmory *N.Ayr.* 131 E3
Kilmote 182 E7
Kilmuir *High.* 171 H7
Kilmuir *High.* 174 D7
Kilmuir *High.* 174 E4
Kilmuir *High.* 171 J4
Kilmun 140 C1
Kilmux 152 B4
Kiln Green *Here.* 39 F1
Kiln Green *W'ham* 42 D5
Kiln Pit Hill 119 G2
Kilnave 138 A2
Kilncadzow 142 C5
Kilndown 31 G5
Kilnhurst 94 B3
Kilninian 154 D5
Kilninver 148 A2
Kilnsea 97 E1
Kilnsey 101 F1
Kilnwick 104 B3
Kilnwick Percy 104 A2
Kiloran 146 C5
Kilpatrick 131 E3
Kilpeck 52 D4
Kilphedir 182 E7
Kilpin 103 G5
Kilpin Pike 103 G5
Kilrenny 153 D4
Kilsby 68 A5
Kilspindie 152 A2
Kilstay 114 B3
Kilsyth 142 B2
Kiltarlity 174 C7
Kilton *Notts.* 94 C5
Kilton *R. & C.* 111 F1
Kilton *Som.* 23 E3
Kilton Thorpe 111 F1
Kiltyrie 150 B1
Kilvaxter 171 J5
Kilve 23 E3
Kilverstone 71 G4
Kilvington 82 D3
Kilwinning 141 E5
Kimberley *Norf.* 86 B5
Kimberley *Notts.* 81 G3
Kimberworth 94 B3
Kimble Wick 42 D2
Kimblesworth 120 B3
Kimbolton *Cambs.* 57 F1
Kimbolton *Here.* 53 E1
Kimbridge 27 E5
Kimcote 68 A4
Kimmeridge 13 F5
Kimmerston 137 D3
Kimpton *Hants.* 27 D3
Kimpton *Herts.* 44 A1
Kinaldy 152 D3
Kinblethmont 161 E5
Kinbrace 182 D5
Kinbreack 165 G5
Kinbuck 150 C4
Kincaldrum 160 C5
Kincaple 152 C3
Kincardine *Fife* 142 D1
Kincardine *High.* 174 D3
Kincardine O'Neil 168 D5
Kinclaven 151 G1
Kincorth 169 H4
Kincraig *Aber.* 169 H2
Kincraig *High.* 167 F4
Kincraigie 159 E5
Kindallachan 159 E4
Kindrogan Field Centre 159 F3
Kinellar 169 G3
Kineton *Glos.* 54 C5
Kineton *Warks.* 55 F2
Kineton Green 66 D4
Kinfauns 151 G2
King Sterndale 93 E5
Kingarth 140 B4
Kingcoed 38 D2
Kingerby 96 A3
Kingham 55 E5
Kingholm Quay 125 D3

▶ Kin - Laz

Kinghorn 143 G1
Kinglassie 152 A5
Kingoodie 152 B2
King's Acre 53 D3
King's Bank 19 D1
Kings Bromley 66 D1
Kings Caple 53 E5
King's Cliffe 69 F3
King's Coughton 54 C2
King's Green 53 G4
King's Heath 66 C4
Kings Hill Kent 31 F3
King's Hill W.Mid. 66 B3
King's Hill Warks. 67 F5
Kings Langley 43 F2
King's Lynn 85 E5
Kings Meaburn 118 C5
Kings Mills 9 E5
King's Moss 91 G2
Kings Muir 135 D2
King's Newnham 67 G5
King's Newton 81 E5
King's Norton Leics. 68 B2
King's Norton W.Mid. 66 C5
Kings Nympton 21 G4
King's Pyon 52 D2
Kings Ripton 70 A5
King's Somborne 27 E4
King's Stag 12 D1
King's Stanley 40 A2
King's Sutton 55 G4
King's Tamerton 8 A2
King's Walden 57 G5
Kings Worthy 27 F4
Kingsand 8 A2
Kingsbarns 153 D3
Kingsbridge Devon 8 D3
Kingsbridge Som. 22 C4
Kingsburgh 171 J6
Kingsbury Gt.Lon. 44 A4
Kingsbury Warks. 67 E3
Kingsbury Episcopi 24 B5
Kingscavil 143 E2
Kingsclere 27 G2
Kingscote 40 A3
Kingscott 21 F4
Kingscross 131 F3
Kingsdale 152 B4
Kingsdon 24 C5
Kingsdown Kent 33 F4
Kingsdown Swin. 41 D4
Kingsdown Wilts. 25 F1
Kingseat 151 G5
Kingsey 42 C2
Kingsfold Pembs. 34 C3
Kingsfold W.Suss. 29 G4
Kingsford Aber. 177 F6
Kingsford Aber. 168 D3
Kingsford Aberdeen 169 G4
Kingsford E.Ayr. 141 F5
Kingsford Worcs. 66 A4
Kingsgate 33 F1
Kingshall Street 60 A1
Kingsheanton 21 F2
Kingshouse 150 A2
Kingshouse Hotel 157 E4
Kingshurst 67 D4
Kingskerswell 9 E1
Kingskettle 152 B4
Kingsland Here. 52 D1
Kingsland I.o.A. 88 A4
Kingsley Ches. 91 G5
Kingsley Hants. 28 C4
Kingsley Staffs. 80 B3
Kingsley Green 29 D4
Kingsley Holt 80 B3
Kingslow 65 G3
Kingsmoor 44 D2
Kingsmuir Angus 160 C5
Kingsmuir Fife 152 D4
Kingsnorth 32 C5
Kingsnorth Power Station 32 A1
Kingstanding 66 C3
Kingsteignton 10 B5
Kingsteps 175 G6
Kingsthorne 53 D4
Kingsthorpe 56 C1
Kingston Cambs. 58 B2
Kingston Cornw. 7 D3
Kingston Devon 8 C3
Kingston Devon 11 D4
Kingston Dorset 12 D2
Kingston Dorset 13 F5
Kingston E.Loth. 144 C1
Kingston Gt.Man. 92 D3
Kingston Hants. 14 A2
Kingston I.o.W. 15 D4
Kingston Kent 33 D3
Kingston Moray 176 B4
Kingston W.Suss. 16 C3
Kingston Bagpuize 41 F3
Kingston Blount 42 C3
Kingston by Sea 17 E3
Kingston Deverill 25 F4
Kingston Gorse 16 C3
Kingston Lisle 41 F4
Kingston Maurward 12 D3
Kingston near Lewes 17 F3
Kingston on Soar 81 G5
Kingston Russell 12 B3
Kingston St. Mary 23 F5
Kingston Seymour 24 B1
Kingston Stert 42 C2
Kingston Upon Hull 104 D5
Kingston upon Thames 29 G1
Kingston Warren 41 F4
Kingstone Here. 52 D4
Kingstone Here. 53 F5
Kingstone Som. 11 G1
Kingstone Staffs. 80 B5
Kingstone Winslow 41 E4
Kingstown 117 G1
Kingswear 9 E2
Kingswell 141 G5
Kingswells 169 G4
Kingswinford 66 A4
Kingswood Bucks. 42 B1
Kingswood Glos. 39 G3
Kingswood Here. 52 B2
Kingswood Kent 32 A3
Kingswood Powys 64 B2
Kingswood S.Glos. 39 F5
Kingswood Som. 23 E4
Kingswood Surr. 30 B3
Kingswood Warks. 67 D5
Kingthorpe 96 B5
Kington Here. 52 B2
Kington Worcs. 54 B2
Kington Langley 40 B5
Kington Magna 25 E5
Kington St. Michael 40 B5
Kingussie 166 A4
Kingweston 24 C4
Kinharrachie 169 H1
Kinharvie 124 D4
Kinkell 142 A2
Kinkell Bridge 151 E3
Kinknockie 177 J6
Kinlet 65 G4
Kinloch Fife 152 A3
Kinloch High. 181 F5
Kinloch High. 155 F4
Kinloch High. 163 K5
Kinloch High. 174 C4
Kinloch P. & K. 160 A5
Kinloch P. & K. 159 G5
Kinloch Hourn 165 F4
Kinloch Laggan 158 A1
Kinloch Rannoch 158 B4
Kinlochan 156 A3
Kinlochard 149 G4
Kinlocharkaig 165 F5
Kinlochbeoraid 156 A1
Kinlochbervie 180 E3
Kinlocheil 156 B2
Kinlochetive 156 D5
Kinlochewe 173 G5
Kinlochlaich 156 B5
Kinlochleven 157 D3
Kinlochmoidart 155 G2
Kinlochmorar 164 E5
Kinlochmore 157 D3
Kinlochroag (Ceann Lochroag) 178 D5
Kinlochspelve 147 F2
Kinloss 175 H5
Kinmel Bay (Bae Cinmel) 90 A4
Kinmuck 169 G3
Kinnaber 161 F3
Kinnadie 177 H6
Kinnaird 152 A2
Kinneff 161 G2
Kinnelhead 134 B5
Kinnell Angus 161 E4
Kinnell Stir. 150 A1
Kinnerley 78 A5
Kinnersley Here. 52 C3
Kinnersley Worcs. 54 A3
Kinnerton 52 B1
Kinnerton Green 78 A1
Kinnesswood 151 G4
Kinnettles 160 C5
Kinninvie 119 G5
Kinnordy 160 B4
Kinoulton 82 B4
Kinrara 167 F4
Kinross 151 G4
Kinrossie 151 G1
Kinsbourne Green 44 A1
Kinsham Here. 52 C1
Kinsham Worcs. 54 B4
Kinsley 94 B1
Kinson 13 G3
Kintarvie 178 E6
Kintbury 27 E1
Kintessack 175 G5
Kintillo 151 G3
Kintocher 168 D4
Kinton Here. 64 D5
Kinton Shrop. 64 C1
Kintore 169 F3
Kintour 138 C4
Kintra Arg. & B. 138 B5
Kintra Arg. & B. 146 C2
Kintradwell 175 G1
Kintraw 148 A4
Kinuachdrachd 147 G5
Kinveachy 167 G3
Kinver 66 A4
Kinwarton 54 D2
Kiplaw Croft 169 J1
Kipp 150 A3
Kippax 102 D4
Kippen P. & K. 151 F3
Kippen Stir. 150 B5
Kippenross House 150 C4
Kippford (Scaur) 124 C5
Kipping's Cross 31 F4
Kippington 31 E3
Kirbister Ork. 185 C7
Kirbister Ork. 184 F5
Kirbuster 184 B5
Kirby Bedon 87 D5
Kirby Bellars 68 C1
Kirby Cane 73 E2
Kirby Corner 67 E5
Kirby Cross 60 D5
Kirby Fields 68 A2
Kirby Green 73 E2
Kirby Grindalythe 104 B1
Kirby Hill N.Yorks. 110 A2
Kirby Hill N.Yorks. 102 C1
Kirby Knowle 111 D4
Kirby le Soken 60 D5
Kirby Misperton 111 G5
Kirby Muxloe 68 A2
Kirby Row 73 E2
Kirby Sigston 110 D3
Kirby Underdale 104 A2
Kirby Wiske 110 C4
Kirdford 29 F5
Kirk 183 H3
Kirk Bramwith 94 D1
Kirk Deighton 102 C2
Kirk Ella 104 C5
Kirk Hallam 81 F3
Kirk Hammerton 103 D2
Kirk Ireton 81 D2
Kirk Langley 81 D4
Kirk Merrington 120 B4
Kirk Michael 98 B2
Kirk of Shotts 142 C3
Kirk Sandall 94 D2
Kirk Smeaton 94 C1
Kirk Yetholm 136 C4
Kirkabister 187 D9
Kirkandrews 115 G2
Kirkandrews-upon-Eden 117 G1
Kirkbampton 117 G1
Kirkbean 125 D5
Kirkbride 117 F1
Kirkbuddo 160 D5
Kirkburn E.Riding 104 B2
Kirkburn Sc.Bord. 135 D2
Kirkburton 93 F1
Kirkby Lincs. 96 A3
Kirkby Mersey. 91 F3
Kirkby N.Yorks. 111 E2
Kirkby Fleetham 110 B3
Kirkby Green 83 F2
Kirkby in Ashfield 81 F2
Kirkby la Thorpe 83 F3
Kirkby Lonsdale 108 B5
Kirkby Malham 101 E1
Kirkby Mallory 67 G2
Kirkby Malzeard 110 B5
Kirkby on Bain 84 A1
Kirkby Overblow 102 C3
Kirkby Stephen 108 C2
Kirkby Thore 118 C5
Kirkby Underwood 83 F5
Kirkby Wharfe 103 E3
Kirkby Woodhouse 81 F2
Kirkby-in-Furness 106 D4
Kirkbymoorside 111 F4
Kirkcaldy 152 A5
Kirkcambeck 118 B1
Kirkcolm 122 B4
Kirkconnel 133 F4
Kirkconnell 125 D4
Kirkcowan 123 E4
Kirkcudbright 124 A5
Kirkdale House 123 G5
Kirkdean 143 F5
Kirkfieldbank 142 C5
Kirkgunzeon 124 C4
Kirkham Lancs. 100 A4
Kirkham N.Yorks. 103 G1
Kirkhamgate 102 C5
Kirkharle 128 C3
Kirkhaugh 118 C3
Kirkheaton Northumb. 128 C4
Kirkheaton W.Yorks. 93 F1
Kirkhill Angus 161 E3
Kirkhill High. 174 C7
Kirkhill Moray 176 B5
Kirkhope 135 E3
Kirkibost High. 164 B3
Kirkibost W.Isles 178 D4
Kirkinch 160 B5
Kirkinner 123 F5
Kirkintilloch 142 A2
Kirkland Cumb. 118 C4
Kirkland Cumb. 117 D5
Kirkland D. & G. 124 C1
Kirkland D. & G. 133 F4
Kirkland D. & G. 125 E2
Kirkland of Longcastle 115 D2
Kirkleatham 121 E5
Kirklevington 110 D1
Kirkley 73 G2
Kirklington N.Yorks. 110 C4
Kirklington Notts. 82 B2
Kirklinton 118 A1
Kirkliston 143 F2
Kirkmaiden 114 B3
Kirkmichael P. & K. 159 F3
Kirkmichael S.Ayr. 132 B5
Kirkmuirhill 142 B5
Kirknewton Northumb. 136 D3
Kirknewton W.Loth. 143 F3
Kirkney 168 D1
Kirkoswald Cumb. 118 B3
Kirkoswald S.Ayr. 132 A5
Kirkpatrick Durham 124 B3
Kirkpatrick-Fleming 126 A4
Kirksanton 106 C4
Kirkstall 102 B4
Kirkstead 83 G1
Kirkstile Aber. 168 D1
Kirkstile D. & G. 126 B2
Kirkstyle 183 J1
Kirkthorpe 102 C5
Kirkton Aber. 168 E2
Kirkton Aber. 176 E5
Kirkton Aber. 168 E3
Kirkton Angus 160 C5
Kirkton Arg. & B. 147 G4
Kirkton D. & G. 125 D2
Kirkton Fife 152 B2
Kirkton High. 166 D1
Kirkton High. 174 E2
Kirkton High. 174 E6
Kirkton High. 182 D2
Kirkton High. 164 E2
Kirkton P. & K. 151 E3
Kirkton Sc.Bord. 135 G4
Kirkton Manor 134 D2
Kirkton of Airlie 160 B4
Kirkton of Auchterhouse 152 B1
Kirkton of Barevan 175 F7
Kirkton of Bourtie 169 G2
Kirkton of Collace 151 G1
Kirkton of Craig 161 F4
Kirkton of Culsalmond 168 E1
Kirkton of Durris 169 F5
Kirkton of Glenbuchat 168 B3
Kirkton of Glenisla 160 A3
Kirkton of Kingoldrum 160 B4
Kirkton of Lethendy 159 G5
Kirkton of Logie Buchan 169 H2
Kirkton of Maryculter 169 G5
Kirkton of Menmuir 160 D3
Kirkton of Monikie 152 D1
Kirkton of Rayne 168 E1
Kirkton of Skene 169 G4
Kirkton of Tealing 152 C1
Kirktonhill Aber. 161 E3
Kirktonhill W.Dun. 141 E2
Kirktown 177 J5
Kirktown of Alvah 176 E4
Kirktown of Auchterless 177 F6
Kirktown of Deskford 176 D4
Kirktown of Fetteresso 161 G1
Kirktown of Slains 169 J2
Kirkwall 185 D6
Kirkwall Airport 185 D7
Kirkwhelpington 128 B3
Kirmington 96 B1
Kirmond le Mire 96 B3
Kirn 140 C2
Kirriemuir 160 B4
Kirstead Green 73 D2
Kirtlebridge 126 A4
Kirtleton 126 A3
Kirtling 59 E2
Kirtling Green 59 E2
Kirtlington 42 A1
Kirtomy 182 C2
Kirton Lincs. 84 B4
Kirton Notts. 82 B1
Kirton Suff. 61 D4
Kirton End 84 A3
Kirton Holme 84 A3
Kirton in Lindsey 95 G3
Kiscadale 131 F3
Kislingbury 56 B2
Kismeldon Bridge 21 D4
Kites Hardwick 55 G1
Kitley 8 B2
Kittisford 23 D5
Kittisford Barton 23 D5
Kittle 36 B4
Kitts End 44 B3
Kitt's Green 67 D4
Kitwood 28 B4
Kivernoll 53 D4
Kiveton Park 94 B4
Klibreck 181 H5
Knabbygates 176 D5
Knaith 95 F4
Knaith Park 95 F4
Knap Corner 25 F5
Knaphill 29 E2
Knaplock 22 B4
Knapp P. & K. 152 A1
Knapp Som. 24 A5
Knapthorpe 82 C2
Knaptoft 68 B4
Knapton Norf. 87 E2
Knapton York 103 E2
Knapton Green 52 D2
Knapwell 58 B1
Knaresborough 102 C2
Knarsdale 118 C2
Knarston 184 C5
Knaven 177 G6
Knayton 110 D4
Knebworth 58 A5
Knedlington 103 G5
Kneesall 82 C1
Kneesworth 58 B3
Kneeton 82 C3
Knelston 36 A4
Knenhall 79 G4
Knettishall 72 A3
Knightacott 21 G2
Knightcote 55 G2
Knightley 79 F5
Knightley Dale 79 F5
Knighton Devon 8 B3
Knighton Dorset 12 C1
Knighton Leic. 68 B2
Knighton Poole 13 G3
Knighton (Tref-y-clawdd) Powys 64 B5
Knighton Som. 23 E3
Knighton Staffs. 79 E5
Knighton Staffs. 79 E3
Knighton Wilts. 41 E5
Knighton on Teme 65 F5
Knightswood 141 G3
Knightwick 53 G2
Knill 52 B1
Knipoch 148 A2
Knipton 82 D4
Knitsley 120 A3
Kniveton 80 D2
Knock Arg. & B. 147 E1
Knock Cumb. 118 C5
Knock High. 164 C4
Knock Moray 176 D5
Knock of Auchnahannet 167 H1
Knockalava 148 B5
Knockally 183 G6
Knockaloe Moar 98 A3
Knockan 180 E7
Knockandhu 167 K2
Knockando 175 J7
Knockarthur 174 E1
Knockbain 174 D6
Knockban 173 J5
Knockbreck 174 E3
Knockbrex 115 F2
Knockdamph 173 J2
Knockdee 183 G2
Knockdow 140 C2
Knockdown 40 A4
Knockenkelly 131 F3
Knockentiber 132 B2
Knockfin 165 K2
Knockgray 123 G1
Knockholt 31 D3
Knockholt Pound 31 D3
Knockin 78 A5
Knockinlaw 132 C2
Knockintorran (Cnoc an Torrain) 170 C5
Knocklearn 124 B3
Knockmill 31 E2
Knocknaha 130 B4
Knocknain 122 A4
Knocknalling 123 G2
Knockrome 139 D2
Knocksharry 98 A3
Knockville 123 E3
Knockvologan 146 C3
Knodishall 61 F1
Knodishall Common 61 F1
Knodishall Green 61 F1
Knole 24 B5
Knolls Green 92 C5
Knolton 78 A4
Knook 26 A3
Knossington 68 D2
Knott End-on-Sea 99 G3
Knotting 57 F1
Knotting Green 57 F1
Knottingley 103 E5
Knotts 101 D2
Knotty Green 43 E3
Knowbury 65 E5
Knowe 123 E3
Knowes of Elrick 176 E5
Knowesgate 128 B3
Knoweside 132 A4
Knowetownhead 135 G4
Knowhead 177 H5
Knowl Green 59 F3
Knowl Hill 42 D5
Knowl Wall 79 F4
Knowle Bristol 39 F5
Knowle Devon 10 A2
Knowle Devon 21 E2
Knowle Devon 11 D4
Knowle Shrop. 65 E5
Knowle Som. 22 C3
Knowle W.Mid. 67 D5
Knowle Cross 10 D3
Knowle Green 100 C4
Knowle Hall 24 A3
Knowle St. Giles 11 G1
Knowlton Dorset 13 G1
Knowlton Kent 33 E3
Knowsley 91 F3
Knowstone 22 B5
Knox Bridge 31 G4
Knucklas 64 B5
Knutsford 92 B5
Knypersley 79 F2
Krumlin 93 E1
Kuggar 3 E5
Kyle of Lochalsh 164 D2
Kyleakin 164 D2
Kylerhea 164 D2
Kyles Scalpay (Caolas Scalpaigh) 171 H2
Kylesbeg 155 F2
Kylesknoydart 164 E5
Kylesku 180 E5
Kylesmorar 164 E5
Kylestrome 180 E5
Kyloag 174 D2
Kynaston 78 A5
Kynnersley 65 F1
Kyre Park 53 F1

▼L

Labost 178 E3
Lacasaigh 179 F5
Lacasdal (Laxdale) 179 G4
Laceby 96 C2
Lacey Green 42 D2
Lach Dennis 92 B5
Lacharn (Laugharne) 35 G1
Lackford 71 F5
Lacklee (Leac a' Li) 171 G2
Lacock 26 A1
Ladbroke 55 G2
Laddingford 31 F4
Lade Bank 84 B2
Ladies Hill 100 A3
Ladock 4 C4
Lady Hall 106 C4
Ladybank 152 B3
Ladycross 6 D2
Ladyfield 148 C3
Ladykirk 145 F5
Ladysford 177 H4
Ladywood 54 A1
Laga 155 F3
Lagalochan 148 A3
Lagavulin 138 C5
Lagg Arg. & B. 139 D2
Lagg N.Ayr. 131 E3
Lagg S.Ayr. 132 A4
Laggan Arg. & B. 138 A4
Laggan High. 165 J5
Laggan High. 166 D5
Laggan Moray 168 B1
Laggan Stir. 150 A3
Lagganulva 155 D5
Lagganvoulin 167 J3
Laglingarten 148 D4
Lagnalean 174 D7
Lagrae 133 F4
Laguna 151 G1
Laid 181 G3
Laide 173 F2
Laig 155 D1
Laight 133 E4
Lainchoil 167 H3
Laindon 45 F4
Lair 159 G3
Lairg 174 C1
Lairg Lodge 174 C1
Lairigmor 156 D3
Laisterdyke 102 A4
Laithers 176 E6
Laithes 118 A4
Lake Devon 21 F2
Lake Devon 8 B1
Lake I.o.W. 15 E4
Lake Wilts. 26 C4
Lakenham 86 D5
Lakenheath 71 F4
Lakesend 70 D3
Lakeside Cumb. 107 E4
Lakeside S.Yorks. 94 C2
Lakeside Thur. 45 E5
Laleham 29 F1
Laleston 37 E5
Lamancha 143 G4
Lamarsh 59 G4
Lamas 86 D3
Lamb Corner 60 B4
Lamb Roe 100 D4
Lambden 145 E5
Lamberhurst 31 F5
Lamberhurst Quarter 31 F5
Lamberton 145 G4
Lambfell Moar 98 A3
Lambley Northumb. 118 C2
Lambley Notts. 82 B3
Lambourn 41 F5
Lambourn Woodlands 41 F5
Lambourne End 45 D3
Lambs Green 30 B5
Lambston 34 C1
Lambton 120 B2
Lamellion 5 G3
Lamerton 7 E3
Lamesley 120 B2
Lamington High. 174 E4
Lamington S.Lan. 134 A2
Lamlash 131 F2
Lamloch 123 G1
Lamonby 118 A4
Lamorna 2 B4
Lamorran 4 C5
Lampert 127 E4
Lampeter 50 B3
Lampeter Velfrey 35 E1
Lamphey 34 D2
Lamplugh 117 D4
Lamport 68 C5
Lamyatt 25 D4
Lana Devon 6 D1
Lana Devon 20 D5
Lanark 142 C5
Lanarth 3 E4
Lancaster 100 A1
Lanchester 120 A3
Lancing 17 D3
Landbeach 58 C1
Landcross 21 E3
Landerberry 169 F4
Landewednack 3 E5
Landford 14 B1
Landhallow 183 G5
Landican 91 D4
Landimore 36 A3
Landkey 21 F2
Landmoth 110 D3
Landore 36 C3
Landrake 7 D4
Landscove 9 D1
Landshipping 34 D1
Landulph 8 A1
Landwade 59 E1
Landywood 66 B2
Lane Bottom 101 E4
Lane End Bucks. 42 D3
Lane End Cumb. 106 C3
Lane End Derbys. 81 F1
Lane End Dorset 13 E3
Lane End Hants. 27 G5
Lane End Here. 39 F1
Lane End Kent 45 E5
Lane End Wilts. 25 F3
Lane Ends Derbys. 80 D4
Lane Ends Gt.Man. 93 D3
Lane Ends Lancs. 101 D4
Lane Ends N.Yorks. 101 F3
Lane Green 66 A2
Lane Head Dur. 110 A1
Lane Head Dur. 119 G5
Lane Head Gt.Man. 92 A3
Lane Head W.Yorks. 93 F2
Lane Heads 100 A4
Lane Side 101 D5
Laneast 5 G1
Lane-end 5 E3
Laneham 95 F5
Lanehead Dur. 119 E3
Lanehead Northumb. 127 F3
Lanesend 35 D2
Lanesfield 66 B3
Laneshawbridge 101 F3
Langais 170 D5
Langamull 154 C4
Langar 82 C4
Langbank 141 E2
Langbar 101 G2
Langbaurgh 111 E1
Langcliffe 101 E1
Langdale End 112 C3
Langdon Cornw. 6 C1
Langdon Cornw. 6 D2
Langdon Beck 119 E4
Langdon Hills 45 F4
Langdon House 10 C5
Langdyke 152 B4
Langford Beds. 57 G3
Langford Essex 46 B2
Langford Notts. 82 D2
Langford Oxon. 41 E2
Langford Budville 23 E5
Langham Essex 60 B4
Langham Norf. 86 B1
Langham Rut. 68 D1
Langham Suff. 60 A1
Langham Moor 60 B4
Langho 100 C4
Langholm 126 B3
Langland 36 C4
Langlands 124 A5
Langlee 136 A5
Langleeford 136 D4
Langley Ches. 92 D5
Langley Derbys. 81 F3
Langley Essex 58 C4
Langley Glos. 54 C5
Langley Gt.Man. 92 C2
Langley Hants. 14 D2
Langley Herts. 58 A5
Langley Kent 31 G3
Langley Northumb. 119 E1
Langley Oxon. 41 F1
Langley Slo. 43 F5
Langley Som. 23 D5
Langley W.Suss. 28 D5
Langley Warks. 55 D1
Langley Burrell 40 B5
Langley Corner 43 F4
Langley Green Derbys. 81 D4
Langley Green W.Suss. 30 B5
Langley Green Warks. 55 E1
Langley Heath 32 A3
Langley Marsh 23 D5
Langley Mill 81 F3
Langley Moor 120 B3
Langley Park 120 B3
Langley Street 87 E5
Langney 18 B3
Langold 94 C4
Langore 5 G1
Langport 24 B5
Langrick 84 A3
Langrick Bridge 84 A3
Langridge B. & N.E.Som. 25 E1
Langridge Devon 21 F3
Langridgeford 21 F3
Langrigg 117 E2
Langrish 28 C5
Langsett 93 G2
Langshaw 135 G2
Langshawburn 135 D5
Langside Glas. 141 G3
Langside P. & K. 150 C3
Langskaill 184 D3
Langstone Hants. 15 G2
Langstone Newport 38 C3
Langthorne 110 B3
Langthorpe 102 C1
Langthwaite 109 F2
Langtoft E.Riding 104 C1
Langtoft Lincs. 69 G1
Langton Dur. 110 A1
Langton Lincs. 97 D5
Langton Lincs. 84 A1
Langton N.Yorks. 103 G1
Langton by Wragby 96 B5
Langton Green Kent 31 E5
Langton Green Suff. 72 C4
Langton Herring 12 C4
Langton Long Blandford 13 E2
Langton Matravers 13 F5
Langtree 21 E4
Langtree Week 21 E4
Langwathby 118 B4
Langwell 174 B1
Langwell House 183 G6
Langwith 94 C5
Langworth 96 A5
Lanivet 5 E3
Lank 5 E2
Lanlivery 5 E4
Lanner 4 B5
Lanoy 5 G2
Lanreath 5 F4
Lansallos 5 F4
Lansdown 25 E1
Lanteglos 5 E1
Lanteglos Highway 5 F4
Lanton Northumb. 136 D3
Lanton Sc.Bord. 136 A4
Lanvean 4 C3
Lapford 10 A2
Laphroaig 138 B5
Lapley 66 A1
Lapworth 67 D5
Larach na Gaibhre 139 F2
Larachbeg 155 F5
Larbert 142 C1
Larbreck 100 A3
Larden Green 78 C2
Larg 123 E3
Largie 168 E1
Largiemore 140 A1
Largoward 152 C4
Largs 140 D4
Largue 176 E6
Largybaan 130 B4
Largybeg 131 F3
Largymore 131 F3
Lark Hall 59 D2
Larkfield 140 D2
Larkhall 142 B4
Larkhill 26 C3
Larklands 81 F3
Larling 72 A3
Larriston 126 D2
Lartington 109 F1
Lary 168 B4
Lasborough 40 A3
Lasham 28 B3
Lashbrook 21 E5
Lashenden 32 A4
Lassington 53 G5
Lassintullich 158 C4
Lassodie 151 G5
Lasswade 144 A3
Lastingham 111 G3
Latchford 92 A4
Latchingdon 46 B2
Latchley 7 E3
Lately Common 92 A3
Lathallan Mill 152 C4
Lathbury 57 D3
Latheron 183 G5
Latheronwheel 183 G5
Lathockar 152 C3
Lathones 152 C4
Lathrisk 152 A4
Latimer 43 F3
Latteridge 39 F4
Lattiford 25 D5
Latton 40 C3
Lauchentyre 123 G5
Lauchintilly 169 F3
Lauder 144 C5
Laugharne (Lacharn) 35 G1
Laughterton 95 F5
Laughton E.Suss. 18 A2
Laughton Leics. 68 B4
Laughton Lincs. 83 F4
Laughton Lincs. 95 F3
Laughton en le Morthen 94 C4
Launcells 20 C5
Launcells Cross 20 C5
Launceston 6 D2
Launde Abbey 68 C2
Launton 56 B5
Laurencekirk 161 F2
Laurieston D. & G. 124 A4
Laurieston Falk. 142 D2
Lavendon 57 E2
Lavenham 60 A3
Laverhay 125 F1
Lavernock 23 E1
Laversdale 118 A1
Laverstock 26 C4
Laverstoke 27 F3
Laverton Glos. 54 C4
Laverton N.Yorks. 110 B5
Laverton Som. 25 E2
Lavister 78 A2
Law 142 C4
Lawers P. & K. 150 C2
Lawers P. & K. 150 B1
Lawford Essex 60 B4
Lawford Som. 23 E4
Lawhitton 7 D2
Lawkland 101 D1
Lawkland Green 101 D1
Lawley 65 F2
Lawnhead 79 F5
Lawrence Weston 39 E5
Lawrenny 34 D2
Laws 152 C1
Lawshall 59 G2
Lawshall Green 59 G2
Lawton 52 D2
Laxdale (Lacasdal) 179 G4
Laxey 98 C3
Laxfield 73 D4
Laxfirth Shet. 187 D7
Laxfirth Shet. 187 D8
Laxford Bridge 180 E4
Laxo 187 D6
Laxton E.Riding 103 G5
Laxton Northants. 69 E3
Laxton Notts. 82 C1
Laycock 101 G3
Layer Breton 46 C1
Layer de la Haye 46 C1
Layer Marney 46 C1
Layham 60 B3
Laymore 11 G2
Layter's Green 43 E3
Laytham 103 G4
Layton 99 G4
Lazenby 121 E5

Lazonby 118 B4
Lea *Derbys.* 81 E2
Lea *Here.* 53 F5
Lea *Lincs.* 95 F4
Lea *Shrop.* 64 C4
Lea *Shrop.* 64 D2
Lea *Wilts.* 40 B4
Lea Bridge 81 E2
Lea Green 53 F1
Lea Marston 67 E3
Lea Town 100 A4
Lea Yeat 108 C4
Leac a' Li (Lacklee) 171 G2
Leachd 148 C5
Leachkin 174 D7
Leadburn 143 G4
Leaden Roding 45 E1
Leadenham 83 E2
Leaderfoot 135 G2
Leadgate *Cumb.* 118 D3
Leadgate *Dur.* 120 A2
Leadgate *Northumb.* 120 A2
Leadhills 133 G4
Leadingcross Green 32 A3
Leafield 41 F1
Leagrave 57 F5
Leake Commonside 84 B2
Leake Hurn's End 84 C3
Lealands 18 A2
Lealholm 111 G2
Lealt *Arg. & B.* 147 F5
Lealt *High.* 172 B5
Leam 93 G5
Leamington Hastings 55 G1
Leamington Spa 55 F1
Leamoor Common 64 D4
Leanach *Arg. & B.* 148 C5
Leanach *High.* 174 E7
Leanaig 174 C6
Leanoch 175 J6
Leargybreck 138 D2
Leasgill 107 F4
Leasingham 83 F3
Leask 169 J1
Leason 36 A3
Leasowe 91 D3
Leat 6 D2
Leatherhead 29 G2
Leathley 102 B3
Leaton *Shrop.* 65 D1
Leaton *Tel. & W.* 65 F1
Leaveland 32 C3
Leavenheath 60 A4
Leavening 103 G1
Leaves Green 30 D2
Leavesden Green 44 A2
Lebberston 113 D4
Lechlade 41 E3
Leck 108 B5
Leckford 27 E4
Leckfurin 182 C3
Leckgruinart 138 A3
Leckhampstead *Bucks.* 56 C4
Leckhampstead *W.Berks.* 41 G5
Leckhampstead Thicket 41 G5
Leckhampton 40 B1
Leckie *High.* 173 G5
Leckie *Stir.* 150 B5
Leckmelm 173 H3
Leckroy 165 K5
Leckuary 148 A5
Leckwith 38 A5
Leconfield 104 C3
Ledaig 148 B1
Ledard 149 G4
Ledbeg 180 E7
Ledburn 57 D5
Ledbury 53 G4
Ledcharrie 150 A2
Ledgemoor 52 D2
Ledicot 52 D1
Ledmore *Arg. & B.* 155 E5
Ledmore *High.* 180 E7
Lednagullin 182 D2
Ledsham *Ches.* 91 E5
Ledsham *W.Yorks.* 103 D5
Ledston 102 D5
Ledstone 8 D3
Ledwell 55 G5
Lee *Arg. & B.* 146 D2
Lee *Devon* 21 E1
Lee *Hants.* 14 C1
Lee *Lancs.* 100 B2
Lee *Shrop.* 78 B4
Lee Brockhurst 78 C5
Lee Chapel 45 F4
Lee Clump 43 E2
Lee Mill Bridge 8 B2
Lee Moor 8 B1
Leebotten 187 D10
Leebotwood 65 D3
Leece 99 F1
Leeds *Kent* 32 A3
Leeds *W.Yorks.* 102 B4
Leeds Bradford International Airport 102 B3
Leedstown 2 D3
Leegomery 65 F1
Leek 79 G2
Leek Wootton 55 E1
Leekbrook 79 G2
Leeming *N.Yorks.* 110 B4
Leeming *W.Yorks.* 101 G4
Leeming Bar 110 B4
Lee-on-the-Solent 15 E2
Lees *Derbys.* 81 D4
Lees *Gt.Man.* 93 D2
Leeswood 77 F2
Leftwich 92 A5
Legars 145 E5
Legbourne 97 D4
Legerwood 144 C5
Legsby 96 B4
Leicester 68 A2
Leicester Forest East 68 A2
Leideag 162 B5
Leigh *Dorset* 12 C2
Leigh *Dorset* 13 G3
Leigh *Gt.Man.* 92 A2
Leigh *Kent* 31 E4
Leigh *Shrop.* 64 C2
Leigh *Surr.* 30 B4
Leigh *Wilts.* 40 C3
Leigh *Worcs.* 53 G2
Leigh Beck 46 B4
Leigh Common 25 E5
Leigh Delamere 40 A5
Leigh Green 32 B5
Leigh Park 15 G2
Leigh Sinton 53 G2
Leigh upon Mendip 25 D3
Leigh Woods 39 E5
Leigham 8 B2
Leighland Chapel 22 D4
Leigh-on-Sea 46 B4
Leighterton 40 A3
Leighton *N.Yorks.* 110 A5
Leighton *Powys* 64 B2
Leighton *Shrop.* 65 F2
Leighton *Som.* 25 E3
Leighton Bromswold 69 G5
Leighton Buzzard 57 E5
Leinthall Earls 52 D1
Leinthall Starkes 52 D1
Leintwardine 64 D5
Leire 68 A4
Leirinmore 181 G2
Leiston 61 F1
Leitfie 160 A5
Leith 143 G2
Leitholm 145 E5
Lelant 2 C3
Lelley 105 E4
Lemington 120 A1
Lemnas 177 G4
Lempitlaw 136 B3
Lemsford 44 B1
Lenchwick 54 C3
Lendalfoot 122 C1
Lendrick Lodge 150 A4
Lenham 32 A3
Lenham Heath 32 B4
Lenie 166 C2
Lenimore 139 G5
Lennel 145 F5
Lennox Plunton 124 A5
Lennoxtown 142 A2
Lent Rise 43 E4
Lenton *Lincs.* 83 F4
Lenton *Nott.* 81 G4
Lenton Abbey 81 G4
Lenwade 86 B4
Lenzie 142 A2
Leoch 152 B1
Leochel-Cushnie 168 D3
Leominster 53 D2
Leonard Stanley 40 A2
Leorin 138 B5
Lepe 14 D3
Lephin 171 G7
Lephinchapel 148 B5
Lephinmore 148 B5
Leppington 103 G1
Lepton 93 G1
Lerags 148 A2
Lerryn 5 F4
Lerwick 187 D8
Lesbury 137 G5
Leschangie 169 F3
Lescrow 5 F4
Leslie *Aber.* 168 D2
Leslie *Fife* 152 A4
Lesmahagow 133 G2
Lesnewth 6 B1
Lessendrum 176 D6
Lessingham 87 E3
Lessness Heath 45 D5
Lessonhall 117 F1
Leswalt 122 B4
Letchmore Heath 44 A3
Letchworth Garden City 58 A4
Letcombe Bassett 41 F4
Letcombe Regis 41 F4
Leth Meadhanach 162 C3
Letham *Angus* 160 D5
Letham *Falk.* 142 C1
Letham *Fife* 152 B3
Lethanhill 132 C4
Lethenty 177 G6
Letheringham 61 D2
Letheringsett 86 B2
Lettaford 10 A4
Letter Finlay 165 J5
Letterewe 173 F4
Letterfearn 164 E2
Lettermorar 155 G1
Lettermore *Arg. & B.* 155 D5
Lettermore *High.* 181 J4
Letters 173 H3
Lettershaws 133 G3
Letterston 48 C5
Lettoch *High.* 167 H3
Lettoch *High.* 167 J1
Letton *Here.* 64 C5
Letton *Here.* 52 C3
Letty Green 44 B1
Letwell 94 C4
Leuchars 152 C2
Leumrabhagh 179 F6
Leurbost (Liurbost) 179 F5
Leusdon 10 A5
Levedale 66 A1
Level's Green 58 C5
Leven *E.Riding* 104 D3
Leven *Fife* 152 B4
Levencorroch 131 F3
Levenhall 144 A2
Levens 107 F4
Levens Green 58 B5
Levenshulme 92 C3
Levenwick 187 D10
Leverburgh (An T-òb) 171 F3
Leverington 70 C1
Leverstock Green 43 F2
Leverton 84 B3
Leverton Lucasgate 84 C3
Leverton Outgate 84 C3
Levington 60 D4
Levisham 112 B3
Levishie 166 B3
Lew 41 F2
Lewannick 5 G1
Lewcombe 12 B2
Lewdown 7 E2
Lewes 17 G2
Leweston 48 C5
Lewisham 44 C5
Lewiston 166 C2
Lewistown 37 F4
Lewknor 42 C3
Leworthy 21 G2
Lewson Street 32 B2
Lewth 100 A4
Lewtrenchard 7 E2
Ley *Aber.* 168 D3
Ley *Cornw.* 5 F3
Ley Green 57 G5
Leybourne 31 F3
Leyburn 110 A3
Leyland 100 B5
Leylodge 169 F3
Leymoor 93 F1
Leys *Aber.* 177 J5
Leys *Aber.* 168 C4
Leys *P. & K.* 152 A1
Leys of Cossans 160 B5
Leysdown-on-Sea 32 C1
Leysmill 161 E5
Leysters 53 E1
Leyton 44 C4
Leytonstone 44 C4
Lezant 6 D3
Lezerea 3 D3
Lhanbryde 175 K5
Liatrie 165 J1
Libanus 51 F5
Libberton 143 D5
Libbery 54 B2
Liberton 143 G3
Liceasto 171 G2
Lichfield 66 D2
Lickey 66 B5
Lickey End 66 B5
Lickfold 29 E5
Liddaton Green 7 E2
Liddel 185 D9
Liddesdale 155 G4
Liddington 41 E4
Lidgate *Derbys.* 94 A5
Lidgate *Suff.* 59 F2
Lidgett 82 B1
Lidlington 57 E4
Lidsey 16 B3
Lidsing 31 G2
Lidstone 55 F5
Lienassie 165 F2
Lieurary 183 F2
Liff 152 B1
Lifton 7 D2
Liftondown 7 D2
Lightcliffe 102 A5
Lighthorne 55 F2
Lighthorne Heath 55 F2
Lightwater 29 E1
Lightwood 79 G3
Lightwood Green *Ches.* 78 D3
Lightwood Green *Wrex.* 78 A3
Lilbourne 68 A5
Lilburn Tower 137 E4
Lillesdon 24 A5
Lilleshall 65 G1
Lilley *Herts.* 57 G5
Lilley *W.Berks.* 41 G5
Lilliesleaf 135 G3
Lilling Green 103 F1
Lillingstone Dayrell 56 C4
Lillingstone Lovell 56 C3
Lillington *Dorset* 12 C1
Lillington *Warks.* 55 F1
Lilliput 13 G4
Lilly 21 F2
Lilstock 23 E3
Lilyhurst 65 G1
Limbury 57 F5
Lime Side 92 D2
Limefield 92 C1
Limehillock 176 D5
Limehurst 92 D2
Limekilnburn 142 B4
Limekilns 143 E1
Limerigg 142 C2
Limerstone 14 D4
Limington 24 C5
Limpenhoe 87 E5
Limpley Stoke 25 E1
Limpsfield 30 D3
Limpsfield Chart 30 D3
Linaclate (Lionacleit) 170 C7
Linbriggs 128 A1
Linby 81 G2
Linchmere 29 D4
Lincluden 125 D3
Lincoln 95 G5
Lincomb 54 A1
Lincombe *Devon* 8 D2
Lincombe *Devon* 8 D3
Lindal in Furness 107 D5
Lindale 107 F4
Lindean 135 F2
Lindertis 160 B4
Lindfield 17 F1
Lindford 28 D4
Lindifferon 152 B3
Lindisfarne (Holy Island) 137 F2
Lindley 102 B3
Lindores 152 A3
Lindow End 92 C5
Lindridge 53 F1
Lindsaig 140 A2
Lindsell 59 E5
Lindsey 60 A3
Lindsey Tye 60 A3
Linfitts 93 D2
Linford *Hants.* 14 A2
Linford *Thur.* 45 F5
Linford Wood 56 D3
Lingague 98 A4
Lingards Wood 93 E1
Lingdale 111 F1
Lingen 52 C1
Lingfield 30 C4
Lingley Green 91 G4
Lingwood 87 E5
Linhead 176 E5
Linhope 135 F5
Linicro 171 J5
Linkend 54 A4
Linkenholt 27 E2
Linkhill 18 D1
Linkinhorne 6 D3
Linklater 185 D9
Linksness *Ork.* 185 B7
Linksness *Ork.* 185 E6
Linktown 152 A5
Linley *Shrop.* 64 C3
Linley *Shrop.* 65 F3
Linley Green 53 F2
Linlithgow 143 E2
Linlithgow Bridge 143 D2
Linn of Muick Cottage 160 B1
Linnels 119 F1
Linney 34 B3
Linshiels 128 A1
Linsiadar 178 E4
Linsidemore 174 C2
Linslade 57 E5
Linstead Parva 73 E4
Linstock 118 A2
Linthwaite 93 F1
Lintlaw 145 F4
Lintmill 176 D4
Linton *Cambs.* 59 D3
Linton *Derbys.* 67 E1
Linton *Here.* 53 F5
Linton *Kent* 31 G3
Linton *N.Yorks.* 101 F1
Linton *Sc.Bord.* 136 B4
Linton *W.Yorks.* 102 C3
Linton-on-Ouse 103 D1
Lintzford 120 A2
Linwood *Hants.* 14 A2
Linwood *Lincs.* 96 B4
Linwood *Renf.* 141 F3
Lionacleit (Linaclate) 170 C7
Lional (Lionel) 179 H1
Lionel (Lional) 179 H1
Liphook 28 D4
Lipley 79 E4
Liscard 91 E3
Liscombe 22 B4
Liskeard 5 G3
L'Islet 9 F4
Lismore 148 A1
Liss 28 C5
Liss Forest 28 C5
Lissett 104 D2
Lissington 96 B4
Liston 59 G3
Lisvane 38 A4
Liswerry 38 C4
Litcham 71 G1
Litchborough 56 B2
Litchfield 27 F2
Litherland 91 E3
Litlington *Cambs.* 58 B3
Litlington *E.Suss.* 18 A3
Little Abington 58 D3
Little Addington 69 E5
Little Alne 54 D1
Little Altcar 91 E2
Little Amwell 44 C1
Little Ann 27 E3
Little Asby 108 B2
Little Assynt 180 D6
Little Aston 66 C3
Little Atherfield 15 D5
Little Ayton 111 E1
Little Baddow 45 G2
Little Badminton 40 A4
Little Ballinluig 159 E4
Little Bampton 117 F1
Little Bardfield 59 E4
Little Barford 57 G2
Little Barningham 86 C2
Little Barrington 41 E1
Little Barrow 78 B1
Little Barugh 111 G5
Little Bavington 128 B4
Little Bealings 60 D3
Little Bedwyn 27 D1
Little Beeby 68 B2
Little Bentley 60 C5
Little Berkhamsted 44 B2
Little Billing 56 D1
Little Birch 53 E4
Little Bispham 99 G3
Little Blakenham 60 C3
Little Bloxwich 66 C2
Little Bollington 92 B4
Little Bookham 29 G2
Little Bourton 55 G3
Little Bowden 68 C4
Little Bradley 59 E2
Little Brampton 64 C4
Little Braxted 46 B1
Little Brechin 161 D3
Little Brickhill 57 E4
Little Bridgeford 79 F5
Little Brington 56 B1
Little Bromley 60 B5
Little Broughton 117 D3
Little Budworth 78 C1
Little Burdon 110 C1
Little Burstead 45 F3
Little Burton 104 D3
Little Bytham 69 F1
Little Canford 13 G3
Little Carlton *Lincs.* 97 D4
Little Carlton *Notts.* 82 C2
Little Casterton 69 F1
Little Catwick 104 D3
Little Catworth 69 F5
Little Cawthorpe 97 D4
Little Chalfield 25 F1
Little Chalfont 43 E3
Little Chart 32 B4
Little Chesterford 58 D3
Little Chesterton 56 A5
Little Cheverell 26 A2
Little Clacton 47 E1
Little Clanfield 41 E2
Little Clifton 117 D4
Little Coates 96 C2
Little Comberton 54 B3
Little Common 18 C3
Little Compton 55 E4
Little Corby 118 A2
Little Cornard 59 G4
Little Cowarne 53 F2
Little Coxwell 41 E3
Little Crakehall 110 B3
Little Cransley 68 D5
Little Crawley 57 E3
Little Creaton 68 C5
Little Creich 174 D3
Little Cressingham 71 G3
Little Crosby 91 E2
Little Crosthwaite 117 F4
Little Cubley 80 C4
Little Dalby 68 C1
Little Dens 177 J6
Little Dewchurch 53 E4
Little Ditton 59 E2
Little Doward 39 E1
Little Down 27 E2
Little Downham 70 D4
Little Drayton 79 D4
Little Driffield 104 C2
Little Dunham 71 G1
Little Dunkeld 159 F5
Little Dunmow 59 E5
Little Durnford 26 C4
Little Easton 59 E5
Little Eaton 81 E3
Little Eccleston 100 A4
Little Ellingham 72 B2
Little End 45 E2
Little Everdon 56 A2
Little Eversden 58 B2
Little Fakenham 72 A4
Little Faringdon 41 E2
Little Fencote 110 B3
Little Fenton 103 E4
Little Finborough 60 B2
Little Fransham 86 A4
Little Gaddesden 43 E1
Little Garway 52 D5
Little Gidding 69 G4
Little Glemham 61 E2
Little Glenshee 151 E1
Little Gorsley 53 F5
Little Gransden 58 A2
Little Green *Cambs.* 58 A3
Little Green *Notts.* 82 C3
Little Green *Suff.* 72 B4
Little Green *Suff.* 72 B4
Little Green *Wrex.* 78 B3
Little Grimsby 96 D3
Little Gringley 95 E4
Little Gruinard 173 F3
Little Habton 111 G5
Little Hadham 58 C5
Little Hale 83 G3
Little Hallingbury 45 D1
Little Hampden 43 D2
Little Haresfield 40 A2
Little Harrowden 69 D5
Little Haseley 42 B2
Little Hatfield 105 D3
Little Hautbois 87 D3
Little Haven *Pembs.* 34 B1
Little Haven *W.Suss.* 29 G4
Little Hay 66 D2
Little Hayfield 93 E4
Little Haywood 80 B5
Little Heath 67 F4
Little Hereford 53 E1
Little Hockham 72 A2
Little Horkesley 60 A4
Little Hormead 58 C5
Little Horsted 17 G2
Little Horton 26 B1
Little Horwood 56 C4
Little Houghton 56 D2
Little Hucklow 93 F5
Little Hulton 92 B2
Little Hungerford 42 A5
Little Hutton 111 D5
Little Idoch 177 F6
Little Irchester 57 E1
Little Keyford 25 E3
Little Kimble 42 D2
Little Kineton 55 F2
Little Kingshill 43 D3
Little Langdale 107 E2
Little Langford 26 B4
Little Laver 45 E2
Little Lawford 67 G5
Little Leigh 92 A5
Little Leighs 45 G1
Little Lever 92 B2
Little Ley 168 E3
Little Linford 56 D3
Little Linton 59 D3
Little London *Bucks.* 42 B1
Little London *E.Suss.* 18 A2
Little London *Essex* 58 C5
Little London *Hants.* 27 E3
Little London *Hants.* 28 B2
Little London *I.o.M.* 98 B3
Little London *Lincs.* 84 C5
Little London *Lincs.* 84 A5
Little London *Lincs.* 96 D5
Little London *Lincs.* 96 B4
Little London *Norf.* 85 D5
Little London *Norf.* 71 F3
Little London *Oxon.* 42 A2
Little London *Powys* 63 G4
Little London *Suff.* 60 B2
Little London *W.Yorks.* 102 B4
Little Longstone 93 F5
Little Lyth 65 D2
Little Malvern 53 G3
Little Maplestead 59 G4
Little Marcle 53 F4
Little Marland 21 F4
Little Marlow 43 D4
Little Marsden 101 E4
Little Massingham 85 F5
Little Melton 86 C5
Little Milford 34 C1
Little Mill 38 C2
Little Milton 42 B2
Little Missenden 43 E3
Little Musgrave 108 C1
Little Ness 64 D1
Little Neston 91 D5
Little Newcastle 48 C5
Little Newsham 110 A1
Little Oakley *Essex* 60 D5
Little Oakley *Northants.* 69 D4
Little Odell 57 E2
Little Offley 57 G5
Little Onn 66 A1
Little Orton *Cumb.* 117 G1
Little Orton *Leics.* 67 F2
Little Ouse 71 E4
Little Ouseburn 102 D1
Little Overton 78 A3
Little Packington 67 E4
Little Parndon 44 D1
Little Paxton 57 G1
Little Petherick 4 D2
Little Plumpton 99 G4
Little Plumstead 87 E4
Little Ponton 83 E4
Little Posbrook 15 E2
Little Potheridge 21 F4
Little Preston 56 A2
Little Raveley 70 A4
Little Ribston 102 C2
Little Rissington 41 D1
Little Rogart 174 E1
Little Rollright 55 E4
Little Ryburgh 86 A3
Little Ryle 137 E5
Little Ryton 65 D2
Little Salkeld 118 B4
Little Sampford 59 E4
Little Saxham 59 G1
Little Scatwell 173 K6
Little Shelford 58 C2
Little Shrawardine 64 C1
Little Silver 10 C2
Little Singleton 99 G4
Little Smeaton *N.Yorks.* 94 C1
Little Smeaton *N.Yorks.* 110 C2
Little Snoring 86 A2
Little Sodbury 39 G4
Little Sodbury End 39 G4
Little Somborne 27 E4
Little Somerford 40 B4
Little Soudley 79 E5
Little Stainforth 101 E1
Little Stainton 110 C1
Little Stanney 91 F5
Little Staughton 57 G1
Little Steeping 84 C1
Little Stoke 79 G4
Little Stonham 60 C2
Little Street 70 D4
Little Stretton *Leics.* 68 B3
Little Stretton *Shrop.* 64 D3
Little Strickland 107 G1
Little Stukeley 70 A5
Little Sugnall 79 F4
Little Sutton 91 E5
Little Swinburne 128 B4
Little Tarrington 53 F3
Little Tew 55 F5
Little Tey 59 G5
Little Thetford 70 D5
Little Thornage 86 B2
Little Thornton 99 G3
Little Thorpe 120 D3
Little Thurlow 59 E2
Little Thurlow Green 59 E2
Little Thurrock 45 F5
Little Torboll 174 E2
Little Torrington 21 E4
Little Tosson 128 C1
Little Totham 46 B1
Little Town *Cumb.* 117 F5
Little Town *Lancs.* 100 C4
Little Town *Warr.* 92 A3
Little Twycross 67 F2
Little Urswick 107 D5
Little Wakering 46 C4
Little Walden 58 D3
Little Waldingfield 60 A3
Little Walsingham 86 A2
Little Waltham 45 G1
Little Warley 45 F3
Little Washbourne 54 B4
Little Weighton 104 B4
Little Welland 54 A4
Little Welnetham 59 G1
Little Wenham 60 B4
Little Wenlock 65 F2
Little Whittington 119 F1
Little Wilbraham 58 D2
Little Wishford 26 B4
Little Witcombe 40 B1
Little Witley 53 G1
Little Wittenham 42 A3
Little Wittingham Green 73 D4
Little Wolford 55 E4
Little Woodcote 30 B2
Little Wratting 59 E3
Little Wymington 57 E1
Little Wymondley 58 A5
Little Wyrley 66 C2
Little Wytheford 65 E1
Little Yeldham 59 F4
Littlebeck 112 B2
Littleborough *Devon* 10 B1
Littleborough *Gt.Man.* 92 D1
Littleborough *Notts.* 95 F4
Littlebourne 33 E3
Littlebredy 12 B4
Littlebury 58 D4
Littlebury Green 58 C4
Littledean 39 F1
Littleferry 175 F2
Littleham *Devon* 21 E3
Littleham *Devon* 10 D4
Littlehampton 16 C3
Littlehempston 9 E1
Littlehoughton 137 G5
Littlemill *E.Ayr.* 132 C4
Littlemill *High.* 175 G6
Littlemoor *Derbys.* 81 E1
Littlemoor *Dorset* 12 C4
Littlemore 42 A2
Littlemoss 92 D3
Littleover 81 E4
Littleport 71 D4
Littlestead Green 42 C5
Littlestone-on-Sea 19 F1
Littlethorpe 102 C1
Littleton *Ches.* 78 B1
Littleton *Hants.* 27 F4
Littleton *P. & K.* 152 A1
Littleton *Som.* 24 B4
Littleton *Surr.* 29 F1
Littleton Drew 40 A4
Littleton Panell 26 B2
Littleton-on-Severn 39 E3
Littletown *Dur.* 120 C3
Littletown *I.o.W.* 15 E3
Littlewick Green 42 D5
Littlewindsor 12 A2
Littleworth *Glos.* 54 D4
Littleworth *Oxon.* 41 F3
Littleworth *S.Yorks.* 94 D3
Littleworth *Staffs.* 66 C1
Littleworth *Worcs.* 54 A3
Littley Green 45 F1
Litton *Derbys.* 93 F5
Litton *N.Yorks.* 109 E5
Litton *Som.* 24 C2
Litton Cheney 12 B3
Liurbost (Leurbost) 179 F5
Liverpool 91 E3
Liverpool John Lennon Airport 91 F4
Liversedge 102 B5
Liverton *Devon* 10 B5
Liverton *R. & C.* 111 G1
Liverton Street 32 A4
Livingston 143 E3
Livingston Village 143 E3
Lixwm 90 C5
Lizard 3 E5
Llaingarreglwyd 50 A2
Llaingoch 88 A4
Llaithddu 63 G4
Llampha 37 F5
Llan 63 E2
Llan Ffestiniog (Ffestiniog) 76 A3
Llanaber 62 C1
Llanaelhaearn 74 C3
Llanaeron 50 A1
Llanafan 62 C5
Llanafan-fawr 51 F2
Llanafan-fechan 51 F2
Llanallgo 88 D4
Llanarmon 74 D4
Llanarmon Dyffryn Ceiriog 77 E4
Llanarmon-yn-Ial 77 E2
Llanarth *Cere.* 50 A2
Llanarth *Mon.* 38 C1
Llanarthney 50 B5
Llanasa 90 C4
Llanbabo 88 B4
Llanbadarn Fawr 62 B4
Llanbadarn Fynydd 63 G5
Llanbadarn-y-garreg 52 A3
Llanbadoc 38 C2
Llanbadrig 88 B3
Llanbeder 38 C3
Llanbedr *Gwyn.* 75 E5
Llanbedr *Powys* 52 B5
Llanbedr *Powys* 52 A3
Llanbedr-Dyffryn-Clwyd 77 E2
Llanbedrgoch 88 D4
Llanbedrog 74 C4
Llanbedr-y-cennin 76 A1
Llanberis 75 E2
Llanbethery 22 D1
Llanbister 64 A5
Llanblethian 37 F5
Llanboidy 49 F5
Llanbradach 38 A3
Llanbryn-mair 63 E2
Llancadle 22 D1
Llancarfan 37 G5
Llancayo 38 C2
Llancynfelyn 62 C3
Llandafal 38 A2
Llandaff 38 A5
Llandaff North 38 A5
Llandanwg 75 E5
Llandawke 35 F1
Llanddaniel Fab 88 C5
Llanddarog 36 A1
Llanddeiniol 62 B5
Llanddeiniolen 75 E1
Llandderfel 76 C4
Llanddeusant *Carmar.* 51 D5
Llanddeusant *I.o.A.* 88 B4
Llanddew 51 G4
Llanddewi 36 A4
Llanddewi Rhydderch 38 C1
Llanddewi Skirrid 38 C1
Llanddewi Velfrey 35 E1
Llanddewi Ystradenni 52 A1
Llanddewi-Brefi 50 C2
Llanddewi'r Cwm 51 G3
Llanddoged 76 B1
Llanddona 89 D5
Llanddowror 35 F1
Llanddulas 90 A5
Llanddwywe 75 E5
Llanddyfnan 88 D5
Llandefaelog Fach 51 G4
Llandefaelog-tre'r-graig 52 A5
Llandefalle 52 A4
Llandegfan 89 D5
Llandegla 77 E2
Llandegley 52 A1
Llandegveth 38 C3
Llandegwning 74 B4
Llandeilo 50 C5
Llandeilo Abercywyn 35 G1
Llandeilo Graban 51 G3
Llandeilo'r-Fan 51 E4
Llandeloy 48 B5
Llandenny 38 D2
Llandevaud 38 D3
Llandevenny 38 D4
Llandinabo 53 E5
Llandinam 63 G4
Llandissilio 49 E5
Llandogo 39 E2
Llandough *V. of Glam.* 38 A5
Llandough *V. of Glam.* 37 F5
Llandovery (Llanymddyfri) 51 D4
Llandow 37 F5
Llandre *Carmar.* 50 C3
Llandre *Carmar.* 49 E5
Llandre *Cere.* 62 C4
Llandrillo 76 D4
Llandrindod Wells 51 G1
Llandrinio 64 B1
Llandudno 89 F4
Llandudno Junction 89 F5
Llandudoch (St. Dogmaels) 49 E3
Llandwrog 75 D2
Llandybie 36 C1
Llandyfaelog 36 A1
Llandyfan 36 C1
Llandyfriog 49 G3
Llandyfrydog 88 C4
Llandygai 89 D5
Llandygwydd 49 F3
Llandyrnog 77 E1
Llandyry 36 A2
Llandysilio 64 B1
Llandyssil 64 A3
Llandysul 50 A3
Llanedeyrn 38 B4
Llanedy 36 B2
Llaneglwys 51 G4
Llanegryn 62 C2

Llanegwad 50 B5
Llaneilian 88 C3
Llanelian-yn-Rhos 89 G5
Llanelidan 77 E2
Llanelieu 52 A4
Llanellen 38 C1
Llanelli 36 B2
Llanelltyd 62 D1
Llanelly 38 B1
Llanelly Hill 38 B1
Llanelwedd 51 G2
Llanelwy (St. Asaph) 90 B5
Llanenddwyn 75 E5
Llanengan 74 B5
Llanerfyl 63 G2
Llaneuddog 88 C4
Llanfachraeth 88 B4
Llanfachreth 76 A5
Llanfaelog 88 B5
Llanfaelrhys 74 B5
Llanfaenor 38 D1
Llan-faes *I.o.A.* 89 E5
Llanfaes *Powys* 51 G5
Llanfaethlu 88 B4
Llanfaglan 75 D1
Llanfair 75 E5
Llanfair Caereinion 64 A2
Llanfair Clydogau 50 C2
Llanfair Dyffryn Clwyd 77 E2
Llanfair Talhaiarn 90 A5
Llanfair Waterdine 64 B5
Llanfairfechan 89 E5
Llanfair-Nant-Gwyn 49 E4
Llanfair-Orllwyn 49 G3
Llanfairpwllgwyngyll 88 D5
Llanfairynghornwy 88 B3
Llanfair-yn-neubwll 88 B5
Llanfallteg 35 E1
Llanfaredd 51 G2
Llanfarian 62 B5
Llanfechain 77 E5
Llanfechell 88 B3
Llanfendigaid 62 B2
Llanferres 77 E1
Llanfflewyn 88 B4
Llanfigael 88 B4
Llanfihangel Crucornau (Llanvihangel Crucorney) 52 C5
Llanfihangel Glyn Myfyr 76 C3
Llanfihangel Nant Bran 51 F4
Llanfihangel Rhydithon 52 A1
Llanfihangel Rogiet 38 D4
Llanfihangel Tal-y-llyn 52 A5
Llanfihangel-ar-arth 50 A3
Llanfihangel-nant-Melan 52 A2
Llanfihangel-uwch-Gwili 50 A5
Llanfihangel-y-Creuddyn 62 C5
Llanfihangel-yng-Ngwynfa 63 G1
Llanfihangel-yn-Nhywyn 88 B5
Llanfihangel-y-pennant *Gwyn.* 75 E3
Llanfihangel-y-pennant *Gwyn.* 62 C2
Llanfilo 52 A4
Llanfoist 38 B1
Llanfor 76 C4
Llanfrechfa 38 C3
Llanfrothen 75 F3
Llanfrynach 51 G5
Llanfwrog *Denb.* 77 E2
Llanfwrog *I.o.A.* 88 A4
Llanfyllin 64 A1
Llanfynydd *Carmar.* 50 B5
Llanfynydd *Flints.* 77 F2
Llanfyrnach 49 F4
Llangadfan 63 G1
Llangadog 50 D5
Llangadwaladr *I.o.A.* 74 C1
Llangadwaladr *Powys* 77 E4
Llangaffo 74 D1
Llangain 35 G1
Llangammarch Wells 51 F3
Llangan 37 F5
Llangarron 53 E5
Llangasty-Talyllyn 52 A5
Llangathen 50 B5
Llangattock 38 B1
Llangattock Lingoed 38 C1
Llangattock-Vibon-Avel 39 D1
Llangedwyn 77 E5
Llangefni 88 C5
Llangeinor 37 F4
Llangeitho 50 C2
Llangeler 49 G4
Llangelynin 62 B2
Llangendeirne 36 A1
Llangennech 36 B2
Llangennith 36 A3
Llangenny 38 B1
Llangernyw 76 B1
Llangian 74 B5
Llangiwg 36 D2
Llangloffan 48 C4
Llanglydwen 49 E5
Llangoed 89 E5
Llangoedmor 49 E3
Llangollen 77 F3
Llangolman 49 E5
Llangorse 52 A5
Llangorwen 62 C4
Llangovan 39 D2
Llangower 76 C4
Llangrannog 49 G2
Llangristiolus 88 C5
Llangrove 39 E1
Llangua 52 C5
Llangunllo 64 B5
Llangunnor 50 A5
Llangurig 63 F5
Llangwm *Conwy* 76 C3
Llangwm *Mon.* 38 D2
Llangwm *Pembs.* 34 C2
Llangwnnadl 74 B4
Llangwyfan 77 E1
Llangwyllog 88 C5
Llangwyryfon 62 C5
Llangybi *Cere.* 50 C2
Llangybi *Gwyn.* 74 D3
Llangybi *Mon.* 38 C3
Llangyfelach 36 C3
Llangynhafal 77 E1
Llangynidr 38 A1
Llangyniew 64 A2
Llangynin 35 F1
Llangynllo 49 G3
Llangynog *Carmar.* 35 G1
Llangynog *Powys* 77 D5
Llangynwyd 37 E4
Llanhamlach 51 G5
Llanharan 37 G4
Llanharry 37 G4
Llanhennock 38 C3
Llanhilleth 38 B2
Llanidloes 63 F4
Llaniestyn 74 B4
Llanigon 52 B4
Llanilar 62 C5
Llanilid 37 F4
Llanishen *Cardiff* 38 A4
Llanishen *Mon.* 39 D2
Llanllawddog 50 A5
Llanllechid 75 F1
Llanlleonfel 51 F2
Llanllugan 63 G2
Llanllwch 35 G1
Llanllwchaiarn 64 A3
Llanllwni 50 A3
Llanllyfni 75 D2
Llanllywel 38 C3
Llanmadoc 36 A3
Llanmaes 22 C1
Llanmartin 38 C4
Llanmerewig 64 A3
Llanmihangel 37 F5
Llan-mill 35 E1
Llanmiloe 35 F2
Llanmorlais 36 B3
Llannefydd 90 A5
Llannerch Hall 90 B5
Llannerch-y-medd 88 C4
Llannerch-y-Môr 90 C5
Llannon *Carmar.* 36 B2
Llan-non *Cere.* 50 B1
Llannor 74 C4
Llanover 38 C2
Llanpumsaint 50 A5
Llanreithan 48 B5
Llanrhaeadr 77 D1
Llanrhaeadr-ym-Mochnant 77 E5
Llanrhian 48 B4
Llanrhidian 36 A3
Llanrhyddlad 88 B4
Llanrhystud 50 B1
Llanrothal 39 D1
Llanrug 75 E1
Llanrumney 38 B4
Llanrwst 76 A1
Llansadurnen 35 F1
Llansadwrn *Carmar.* 50 C4
Llansadwrn *I.o.A.* 89 D5
Llansaint 35 G2
Llansamlet 36 C3
Llansanffraid 50 B1
Llansanffraid Glan Conwy 89 G5
Llansannan 76 C1
Llansannor 37 F5
Llansantffraed 52 A5
Llansantffraed-Cwmdeuddwr 51 F1
Llansantffraed-in-Elwel 51 G2
Llansantffraid-ym-Mechain 77 F5
Llansawel *Carmar.* 50 C4
Llansawel (Briton Ferry) *N.P.T.* 36 D3
Llansilin 77 F5
Llansoy 38 D2
Llanspyddid 51 G5
Llanstadwell 34 C2
Llansteffan 35 G1
Llanstephan 52 A3
Llantarnam 38 C3
Llanteg 35 E1
Llanthony 52 B5
Llantilio Crossenny 38 C1
Llantilio Pertholey 38 C1
Llantood 49 E3
Llantrisant *I.o.A.* 88 B4
Llantrisant *Mon.* 38 C3
Llantrisant *R.C.T.* 37 G4
Llantrithyd 37 G5
Llantwit Fardre 37 G4
Llantwit Major 22 C1
Llantysilio 77 E3
Llanuwchllyn 76 B5
Llanvaches 38 D3
Llanvair-Discoed 38 D3
Llanvapley 38 C1
Llanvetherine 38 C1
Llanveynoe 52 C4
Llanvihangel Crucorney (Llanfihangel Crucornau) 52 C5
Llanvihangel Gobion 38 C2
Llanvihangel-Ystern-Llewern 38 D1
Llanvithyn 37 G5
Llanwarne 53 E5
Llanwddyn 63 G1
Llanwenog 50 A3
Llanwern 38 C4
Llanwinio 49 F5
Llanwnda *Gwyn.* 75 D2
Llanwnda *Pembs.* 48 C4
Llanwnnen 50 B3
Llanwnog 63 G3
Llanwonno 37 G3
Llanwrda 50 D4
Llanwrin 63 D2
Llanwrthwl 51 F1
Llanwrtyd 51 E3
Llanwrtyd Wells 51 E3
Llanwyddelan 63 G2
Llanyblodwel 77 F5
Llanybri 35 G1
Llanybydder 50 B3
Llanycefn 49 E5
Llanychaer Bridge 48 C4
Llanycil 76 C4
Llanycrwys 50 C3
Llanymawddwy 63 E1
Llanymddyfri (Llandovery) 51 D4
Llanymynech 77 F5
Llanynghenedl 88 B4
Llanynys 77 E1
Llan-y-pwll 78 A2
Llanyre 51 G1
Llanystumdwy 75 D4
Llanywern 52 A5
Llawhaden 35 D1
Llawndy 90 C4
Llawnt 77 F4
Llawr-y-dref 74 B5
Llawryglyn 63 F3
Llay 78 A2
Llechcynfarwy 88 B4
Llecheiddior 75 D3
Llechfaen 51 G5
Llechryd *Caerp.* 38 A2
Llechryd *Cere.* 49 F3
Llechrydau 77 F4
Lledrod *Cere.* 62 C5
Lledrod *Powys* 77 F5
Llethrid 36 B3
Llidiad-Nenog 50 B4
Llidiardau 76 B4
Llithfaen 74 C3
Lloc 90 C5
Llong 77 F1
Llowes 52 A3
Lloyney 64 B5
Llundain-fach 50 B2
Llwydcoed 37 F2
Llwydiarth 63 G1
Llwyn *M.Tyd.* 37 G1
Llwyn *Shrop.* 64 B4
Llwyncelyn 50 A2
Llwyn-croes 50 A5
Llwyndafydd 49 G2
Llwynderw 64 B2
Llwyndyrys 74 C3
Llwyneinion 77 F3
Llwyngwril 62 B2
Llwynhendy 36 B3
Llwyn-Madoc 51 F2
Llwynmawr 77 F4
Llwyn-onn 50 A2
Llwyn-y-brain *Carmar.* 35 E1
Llwyn-y-brain *Carmar.* 50 D4
Llwyn-y-groes 50 B2
Llwynypia 37 F3
Llynclys 77 F5
Llynfaes 88 C5
Llysfaen 89 G5
Llyswen 52 A4
Llysworney 37 F5
Llys-y-frân 48 D5
Llywel 51 E4
Load Brook 93 G4
Loandhu 175 F4
Loanhead *Aber.* 169 H1
Loanhead *Midloth.* 143 G3
Loans 132 B2
Lobb 21 E2
Lobhillcross 7 E2
Loch a Charnain 170 D7
Loch Baghasdail (Lochboisdale) 162 C3
Loch Choire Lodge 181 J5
Loch Eil Outward Bound 156 C2
Loch Head *D. & G.* 114 D2
Loch Head *D. & G.* 123 F1
Loch na Madadh (Lochmaddy) 170 E5
Loch Sgioport 162 D1
Lochailort 155 G1
Lochaline 155 F5
Lochans 122 B5
Locharbriggs 125 D2
Lochawe 148 D2
Lochboisdale (Loch Baghasdail) 162 C3
Lochbuie 147 F2
Lochcarron 172 E7
Lochdhu Hotel 183 F4
Lochdon 147 G1
Lochdrum 173 J4
Lochearnhead 150 A2
Lochee 152 B1
Lochend *High.* 183 H2
Lochend *High.* 166 C1
Locheport (Locheuphort) 170 D5
Locheuphort (Locheport) 170 D5
Lochfoot 124 D3
Lochgair 148 B5
Lochgarthside 166 C3
Lochgelly 151 G5
Lochgilphead 139 G1
Lochgoilhead 149 E4
Lochgoyn 141 G5
Lochhill *E.Ayr.* 133 D4
Lochhill *Moray* 175 K5
Lochinch Castle 122 C4
Lochinver 180 C6
Lochlair 160 D5
Lochlane 150 D2
Lochlea 132 C2
Lochluichart 173 K5
Lochmaben 125 E2
Lochmaddy (Loch na Madadh) 170 E5
Lochore 151 G5
Lochportain 170 E4
Lochranza 140 A4
Lochside *Aber.* 161 F3
Lochside *High.* 181 G3
Lochside *High.* 182 D5
Lochside *High.* 183 H2
Lochslin 175 F3
Lochton 123 D2
Lochty 152 D4
Lochuisge 155 G4
Lochurr 124 B2
Lochussie 174 B6
Lochwinnoch 141 E4
Lockengate 5 E3
Lockerbie 125 F2
Lockeridge 26 C1
Lockerley 27 D5
Lockhills 118 B3
Locking 24 A2
Lockington *E.Riding* 104 B3
Lockington *Leics.* 81 F5
Lockleywood 79 D5
Locks Heath 15 E2
Locksbottom 30 D2
Locksgreen 14 D3
Lockton 112 B4
Loddington *Leics.* 68 C2
Loddington *Northants.* 68 D5
Loddiswell 8 D3
Loddon 73 E2
Lode 58 D1
Loders 12 A3
Lodsworth 29 E5
Lofthouse *N.Yorks.* 110 A5
Lofthouse *W.Yorks.* 102 C5
Loftus 111 G1
Logan *D. & G.* 114 A2
Logan *E.Ayr.* 133 D3
Loganlea 143 D3
Loggerheads 79 E4
Loggie 173 H2
Logie *Angus* 161 E3
Logie *Angus* 160 B4
Logie *Fife* 152 C2
Logie *Moray* 175 H6
Logie Coldstone 168 C4
Logie Hill 174 E4
Logie Newton 168 E1
Logie Pert 161 E3
Logierait 159 E4
Login 49 E5
Lolworth 58 B1
Lonbain 172 C6
Londesborough 104 A3
London 44 C4
London Apprentice 5 E5
London Beach 32 A5
London City Airport 44 D4
London Colney 44 A2
London Gatwick Airport (Gatwick Airport) 30 B4
London Heathrow Airport 43 F5
London Luton Airport (Luton Airport) 57 G5
London Minstead 14 B1
London Stansted Airport (Stansted Airport) 58 D5
Londonderry 110 B4
Londonthorpe 83 E4
Londubh 172 E3
Lonemore 174 E3
Long Ashton 39 E5
Long Bank 65 G5
Long Bennington 82 D3
Long Bredy 12 B3
Long Buckby 56 B1
Long Clawson 82 C5
Long Common 15 E1
Long Compton *Staffs.* 79 F5
Long Compton *Warks.* 55 E4
Long Crendon 42 B2
Long Crichel 13 F1
Long Dean 40 A5
Long Downs 3 E3
Long Drax 103 F5
Long Duckmanton 94 B5
Long Eaton 81 F4
Long Gill 101 D2
Long Green *Ches.* 91 F5
Long Green *Essex* 60 A5
Long Green *Worcs.* 54 A4
Long Hanborough 41 G1
Long Itchington 55 G1
Long Lane 65 F1
Long Lawford 67 G5
Long Load 24 B5
Long Marston *Herts.* 43 D1
Long Marston *N.Yorks.* 103 E2
Long Marston *Warks.* 55 D3
Long Marton 118 C5
Long Meadowend 64 D4
Long Melford 59 G3
Long Newnton 40 B3
Long Preston 101 E2
Long Riston 104 D3
Long Stratton 72 C2
Long Street 56 C3
Long Sutton *Hants.* 28 C3
Long Sutton *Lincs.* 84 C5
Long Sutton *Som.* 24 B5
Long Thurlow 60 B1
Long Whatton 81 F5
Long Wittenham 42 A3
Longbenton 120 B1
Longborough 55 D5
Longbridge *Plym.* 8 B2
Longbridge *W.Mid.* 66 C5
Longbridge *Warks.* 55 E1
Longbridge Deverill 25 F3
Longburgh 117 G1
Longburton 12 C1
Longcliffe 80 D2
Longcombe 9 E2
Longcot 41 E3
Longcroft 142 B2
Longcross *Devon* 7 E3
Longcross *Surr.* 29 E1
Longden 64 D2
Longdon *Staffs.* 66 C1
Longdon *Worcs.* 54 A4
Longdon Green 66 C1
Longdon upon Tern 65 F1
Longdown 10 B3
Longdrum 169 H3
Longfield 31 F2
Longfield Hill 31 F2
Longfleet 13 G3
Longford *Derbys.* 80 D4
Longford *Glos.* 54 A5
Longford *Gt.Lon.* 43 F5
Longford *Shrop.* 78 D4
Longford *Tel. & W.* 65 G1
Longford *W.Mid.* 67 F4
Longforgan 152 B2
Longformacus 145 D4
Longframlington 128 D1
Longham *Dorset* 13 G3
Longham *Norf.* 86 A4
Longhill 177 H5
Longhirst 129 E3
Longhope *Glos.* 39 F1
Longhope *Ork.* 185 C8
Longhorsley 128 D2
Longhoughton 137 G5
Longlands *Aber.* 168 C2
Longlands *Cumb.* 117 F3
Longlands *Gt.Lon.* 44 D5
Longlane *Derbys.* 81 D4
Longlane *W.Berks.* 41 G5
Longlevens 40 A1
Longley 93 F2
Longley Green 53 G2
Longmanhill 177 F4
Longmoor Camp 28 C4
Longmorn 175 K6
Longnewton *Sc.Bord.* 135 G3
Longnewton *Stock.* 110 C1
Longney 39 G1
Longniddry 144 B2
Longnor *Shrop.* 65 D2
Longnor *Staffs.* 80 B1
Longparish 27 F3
Longridge *Lancs.* 100 C4
Longridge *Staffs.* 66 B1
Longridge *W.Loth.* 143 D3
Longridge End 54 A5
Longridge Towers 145 G4
Longriggend 142 C2
Longrock 2 C3
Longsdon 79 G2
Longshaw 91 G2
Longside 177 J6
Longslow 79 D4
Longsowerby 117 G1
Longstanton 58 C1
Longstock 27 E4
Longstone 2 C3
Longstowe 58 B2
Longstreet 26 C2
Longthorpe 69 G3
Longton *Lancs.* 100 A5
Longton *Stoke* 79 G3
Longtown *Cumb.* 126 B5
Longtown *Here.* 52 C5
Longville in the Dale 65 E3
Longwell Green 39 F5
Longwick 42 C2
Longwitton 128 C3
Longworth 41 F3
Longyester 144 C3
Lonmay 177 J5
Lonmore 171 H7
Looe 5 G4
Loose 31 G3
Loosebeare 10 A2
Loosegate 84 B5
Loosley Row 42 D2
Lopcombe Corner 27 D4
Lopen 12 A1
Loppington 78 B5
Lorbottle 128 C1
Lorbottle Hall 128 C1
Lordington 15 G2
Lord's Hill 14 C1
Lorgill 171 G7
Lorn 141 E1
Lornty 159 G5
Loscoe 81 F3
Loscombe 12 A3
Losgaintir 171 F2
Lossiemouth 175 K4
Lossit 138 A4
Lostock Gralam 92 A5
Lostock Green 92 A5
Lostock Junction 92 A2
Lostwithiel 5 F4
Loth 184 F4
Lothbeg 182 E7
Lothersdale 101 F3
Lothmore 182 E7
Loudwater 43 E3
Loughborough 68 A1
Loughor 36 B3
Loughton *Essex* 44 D3
Loughton *M.K.* 56 D4
Loughton *Shrop.* 65 F4
Lound *Lincs.* 69 F1
Lound *Notts.* 95 D4
Lound *Suff.* 73 G2
Lount 67 F1
Lour 160 C5
Louth 96 D4
Love Clough 101 E5
Lovedean 15 F1
Lover 14 B1
Loversall 94 C3
Loves Green 45 F2
Lovesome Hill 110 C3
Loveston 35 D2
Lovington 24 C4
Low Ackworth 94 B1
Low Angerton 128 C3
Low Ballevain 130 B3
Low Barlay 123 G5
Low Barlings 96 A5
Low Bentham 100 C1
Low Bolton 109 F3
Low Bradfield 93 G3
Low Bradley (Bradley) 101 G3
Low Braithwaite 118 A3
Low Brunton 128 B4
Low Burnham 95 E2
Low Burton 110 B4
Low Buston 129 E1
Low Catton 103 G2
Low Coniscliffe 110 B1
Low Craighead 132 A5
Low Dinsdale 110 C1
Low Ellington 110 B4
Low Entercommon 110 C2
Low Etherley 120 A5
Low Fell 120 B2
Low Gate 119 F1
Low Grantley 110 B5
Low Green 59 G1
Low Habberley 66 A5
Low Ham 24 B5
Low Hawsker 112 C2
Low Haygarth 108 B3
Low Hesket 118 A3
Low Hesleyhurst 128 C2
Low Hutton 103 G1
Low Kingthorpe 112 B4
Low Laithe 102 A1
Low Langton 96 B5
Low Leighton 93 E4
Low Lorton 117 E4
Low Marishes 112 B5
Low Marnham 82 D1
Low Middleton 137 F3
Low Mill 111 G3
Low Moor *Lancs.* 100 D3
Low Moor *W.Yorks.* 102 A5
Low Moorsley 120 C3
Low Moresby 116 C4
Low Newton-by-the-Sea 137 G4
Low Row *Cumb.* 118 B1
Low Row *N.Yorks.* 109 E3
Low Stillaig 140 A3
Low Street 86 B5
Low Tharston 72 C2
Low Torry 143 E1
Low Town 128 D1
Low Toynton 96 C5
Low Wood 107 E4
Low Worsall 110 C2
Lowbands 53 G4
Lowdham 82 B3
Lowe 78 C4
Lowe Hill 79 G2
Lower Achachenna 148 C2
Lower Aisholt 23 F4
Lower Apperley 54 A5
Lower Arncott 42 B1
Lower Ashtead 29 G2
Lower Ashton 10 B4
Lower Assendon 42 C4
Lower Auchalick 140 A2
Lower Ballam 99 G4
Lower Barewood 52 C2
Lower Bartle 100 A4
Lower Bayble (Pabail Iarach) 179 H4
Lower Beeding 17 E1
Lower Benefield 69 E4
Lower Bentley 54 B1
Lower Berry Hill 39 E1
Lower Birchwood 81 F2
Lower Boddington 55 G2
Lower Boscaswell 2 A3
Lower Bourne 28 D3
Lower Brailes 55 F4
Lower Breakish 164 C2
Lower Bredbury 92 D3
Lower Broadheath 54 A2
Lower Brynamman 36 D1
Lower Bullingham 53 E4
Lower Bullington 27 F3
Lower Burgate 14 A1
Lower Burrow 24 B5
Lower Burton 52 D2
Lower Caldecote 57 G3
Lower Cam 39 G2
Lower Cambourne 58 B2
Lower Camster 183 H4
Lower Chapel 51 G4
Lower Cheriton 11 E2
Lower Chicksgrove 26 A4
Lower Chute 27 E2
Lower Clent 66 B4
Lower Creedy 10 B2
Lower Cumberworth 93 G2
Lower Darwen 100 C5
Lower Dean 57 F1
Lower Diabaig 172 D5
Lower Dicker 18 A2
Lower Dinchope 65 D4
Lower Down 64 C4
Lower Drift 2 B4
Lower Dunsforth 102 D1
Lower Earley 42 C5
Lower Edmonton 44 C3
Lower Elkstone 80 B2
Lower End *Bucks.* 42 B2
Lower End *M.K.* 57 E4
Lower End *Northants.* 57 D1
Lower Everleigh 26 C2
Lower Eythorne 33 E4
Lower Failand 39 E5
Lower Farringdon 28 C4
Lower Fittleworth 16 C2
Lower Foxdale 98 A4
Lower Freystrop 34 C1
Lower Froyle 28 C3
Lower Gabwell 9 F1
Lower Gledfield 174 C2
Lower Godney 24 B3
Lower Gravenhurst 57 G4
Lower Green *Essex* 58 C4
Lower Green *Herts.* 57 G4
Lower Green *Kent* 31 F4
Lower Green *Norf.* 86 A2
Lower Green *Staffs.* 66 B2
Lower Green Bank 100 B2
Lower Halstock Leigh 12 B2
Lower Halstow 32 A2
Lower Hardres 33 D3
Lower Harpton 52 B1
Lower Hartshay 81 E2
Lower Hartwell 42 C1
Lower Hawthwaite 106 D4
Lower Haysden 31 E4
Lower Hayton 65 E4
Lower Heath 79 F1
Lower Hergest 52 B2
Lower Heyford 55 G5
Lower Higham 45 G5
Lower Holbrook 60 C4
Lower Hopton 93 F1
Lower Hordley 78 A5
Lower Horncroft 16 C2
Lower Horsebridge 18 A2
Lower Houses 93 F1
Lower Howsell 53 G3
Lower Kersal 92 C2
Lower Kilchattan 146 C5
Lower Kilcott 39 G4
Lower Killeyan 138 A5
Lower Kingcombe 12 B3
Lower Kingswood 30 B3
Lower Kinnerton 78 A1
Lower Langford 24 B1
Lower Largo 152 C4
Lower Leigh 80 B4
Lower Lemington 55 E4
Lower Lovacott 21 F3
Lower Loxhore 21 G2
Lower Lydbrook 39 E1
Lower Lye 52 D1
Lower Machen 38 B4
Lower Maes-coed 52 C4
Lower Mannington 13 G2
Lower Middleton Cheney 56 A3
Lower Milton 24 C3
Lower Moor 54 B3
Lower Morton 39 F3
Lower Nash 34 D2
Lower Nazeing 44 C2
Lower Netchwood 65 F3
Lower Nyland 25 E5
Lower Oddington 55 E5
Lower Ollach 164 B1
Lower Penarth 38 A5
Lower Penn 66 A3
Lower Pennington 14 C3
Lower Peover 92 B5
Lower Pollicott 42 C1
Lower Quinton 55 D3
Lower Race 38 B2
Lower Rainham 32 A2
Lower Roadwater 22 D4
Lower Sapey 53 F1
Lower Seagry 40 B4
Lower Shelton 57 E3
Lower Shiplake 42 C5
Lower Shuckburgh 55 G1
Lower Slaughter 55 D5
Lower Soothill 102 B5
Lower Stanton St. Quintin 40 B4
Lower Stoke 32 A1
Lower Stondon 57 G4
Lower Stone 39 F3
Lower Stonnall 66 C2
Lower Stow Bedon 72 A2
Lower Street *Dorset* 13 E3
Lower Street *E.Suss.* 18 C2
Lower Street *Norf.* 87 D2
Lower Street *Norf.* 86 C2
Lower Street *Suff.* 60 C2
Lower Stretton 92 A4
Lower Sundon 57 F5
Lower Swanwick 15 D2
Lower Swell 55 D5
Lower Tadmarton 55 G4
Lower Tale 11 D2
Lower Tean 80 B4
Lower Thurlton 73 F2
Lower Thurnham 100 A2
Lower Town *Cornw.* 3 D4
Lower Town *Devon* 10 A5
Lower Town *I.o.S.* 4 B1
Lower Town *Pembs.* 48 C4
Lower Trebullett 6 D3
Lower Tysoe 55 F3
Lower Upcott 10 B4
Lower Upham 15 E1
Lower Upnor 45 G5
Lower Vexford 23 E4
Lower Wallop 64 C2
Lower Walton 92 A4
Lower Waterhay 40 C3
Lower Weald 56 C4
Lower Wear 10 C4
Lower Weare 24 B2
Lower Welson 52 B2
Lower Whatley 25 E3
Lower Whitley 92 A5
Lower Wick 54 A2
Lower Wield 28 B3
Lower Winchendon (Nether Winchendon) 42 C1
Lower Withington 79 F1
Lower Woodend 42 D4
Lower Woodford 26 C4
Lower Wyche 53 G3
Lowerhouse 101 E4
Lowertown 185 D8
Lowesby 68 C2
Lowestoft 73 G2
Loweswater 117 E4
Lowfield Heath 30 B4
Lowgill *Cumb.* 108 B3
Lowgill *Lancs.* 100 C1
Lowick *Cumb.* 107 D4
Lowick *Northants.* 69 E4
Lowick *Northumb.* 137 E3
Lowick Bridge 107 D4
Lowick Green 107 D4
Lownie Moor 160 C5
Lowsonford 55 D1
Lowther 118 B5
Lowther Castle 118 B5
Lowthorpe 104 C1
Lowton *Devon* 21 G5
Lowton *Gt.Man.* 92 A3
Lowton *Som.* 11 E1
Lowton Common 92 A3
Loxbeare 10 C1
Loxhill 29 F4
Loxhore 21 G2
Loxley 55 E2
Loxley Green 80 B4
Loxton 24 A2
Loxwood 29 F4
Lubachoinnich 174 B2
Lubcroy 173 K1
Lubenham 68 C4
Lubfearn 173 K4
Lubmore 173 G6
Lubreoch 157 G5
Luccombe 22 C3
Luccombe Village 15 E4
Lucker 137 F3
Luckett 7 D3
Luckington 40 A4
Lucklawhill 152 C2
Luckwell Bridge 22 C4
Lucton 52 D1
Lucy Cross 110 B1
Ludag 162 C3
Ludborough 96 C3
Ludbrook 8 C2
Ludchurch 35 E1
Ludden 101 G5
Luddenden Foot 101 G5
Luddenham Court 32 B2
Luddesdown 31 F2
Luddington *N.Lincs.* 95 F1
Luddington *Warks.* 55 D2
Luddington in the Brook 69 G4
Ludford *Lincs.* 96 B4
Ludford *Shrop.* 65 E5
Ludgershall *Bucks.* 42 B1
Ludgershall *Wilts.* 27 D2
Ludgvan 2 C3
Ludham 87 E4
Ludlow 65 E5
Ludney 97 D3
Ludstock 53 F4
Ludstone 66 A3
Ludwell 26 A5
Ludworth 120 C3
Luffincott 6 D1
Luffness 144 B1
Lufton 12 B1
Lugar 133 D3
Luggate 144 C2
Luggate Burn 144 D2
Luggiebank 142 B2
Lugton 141 F4
Lugwardine 53 E3
Luib 164 B2
Luibeilt 157 E3
Luing 147 G3
Lulham 52 D3

Lullington *Derbys.* 67 E1
Lullington *Som.* 25 E2
Lulsgate Bottom 24 C1
Lulsley 53 G2
Lulworth Camp 13 E4
Lumb *Lancs.* 101 E5
Lumb *W.Yorks.* 101 G5
Lumbutts 101 F5
Lumby 103 D4
Lumphanan 168 D4
Lumphinnans 151 G5
Lumsdaine 145 F3
Lumsdale 81 E1
Lumsden 168 C2
Lunan 161 E4
Lunanhead 160 C4
Luncarty 151 F2
Lund *E.Riding* 104 B3
Lund *N.Yorks.* 103 F4
Lund *Shet.* 186 E2
Lundale 178 D4
Lundavra 156 C3
Lunderton 177 K6
Lundie *Angus* 152 A1
Lundie *High.* 165 H3
Lundin Links 152 C4
Lundwood 94 A2
Lundy 20 B1
Lunga 148 A4
Lunna 187 D6
Lunning 187 E6
Lunnon 36 B4
Lunsford's Cross 18 C2
Lunt 91 E2
Luntley 52 C2
Luppitt 11 E2
Lupset 94 A1
Lupton 107 G4
Lurgashall 29 E5
Lurignich 156 B4
Lusby 84 B1
Luss 149 F5
Lussagiven 139 E1
Lusta 171 H6
Lustleigh 10 A4
Luston 53 D1
Luthermuir 161 E3
Luthrie 152 B3
Luton *Devon* 11 D2
Luton *Devon* 10 B5
Luton *Luton* 57 F5
Luton *Med.* 31 G2
Luton Airport (London Luton Airport) 57 G5
Lutterworth 68 A4
Lutton *Devon* 8 B2
Lutton *Dorset* 13 F4
Lutton *Lincs.* 84 C5
Lutton *Northants.* 69 G4
Luxborough 22 C4
Luxulyan 5 E4
Lybster *High.* 183 F2
Lybster *High.* 183 H5
Lydacott 21 E5
Lydbury North 64 C4
Lydcott 21 G2
Lydd 19 F1
Lydd Airport 19 F1
Lydden 33 E4
Lyddington 69 D3
Lydd-on-Sea 19 F1
Lyde Green 39 F5
Lydeard St. Lawrence 23 E4
Lydford 7 F2
Lydford-on-Fosse 24 C4
Lydgate *Gt.Man.* 93 D1
Lydgate *Gt.Man.* 93 D2
Lydgate *W.Yorks.* 101 F5
Lydham 64 C3
Lydiard Millicent 40 C4
Lydiard Tregoze 40 D4
Lydiate 91 E2
Lydlinch 12 D1
Lydney 39 F2
Lydstep 35 D3
Lye 66 B4
Lye Cross 24 B1
Lye Green *Bucks.* 43 E2
Lye Green *E.Suss.* 31 E5
Lye Green *Warks.* 55 D1
Lye's Green 25 F3
Lyford 41 F3
Lymbridge Green 32 D4
Lyme Regis 11 G3
Lymekilns 142 A4
Lyminge 33 D4
Lymington 14 C3
Lyminster 16 C3
Lymm 92 A4
Lymore 14 B3
Lympne 32 D5
Lympsham 24 A2
Lympstone 10 C4
Lynaberack 166 E5
Lynch 22 B3
Lynch Green 86 C5
Lynchat 166 E4
Lyndhurst 14 B2
Lyndon 69 E2
Lyne *Aber.* 169 F4
Lyne *Sc.Bord.* 143 G5
Lyne *Surr.* 29 F1
Lyne Down 53 F4
Lyne of Gorthleck 166 C2
Lyne of Skene 169 F3
Lyne Station 143 G5
Lyneal 78 B4
Lynedale House 171 J6
Lynegar 183 H3
Lyneham *Oxon.* 55 E5
Lyneham *Wilts.* 40 C5
Lyneholmeford 126 D4
Lynemore *High.* 167 H2
Lynemore *Moray* 167 J1
Lynemouth 129 E2
Lyness 185 C8
Lynford 71 G3
Lyng *Norf.* 86 B4
Lyng *Som.* 24 A5
Lyngate 87 E3
Lynmouth 22 A3
Lynn 65 G1
Lynsted 32 B2
Lynstone 20 C5
Lynton 22 A3
Lyon's Gate 12 C2
Lyonshall 52 C2
Lyrabus 138 A3
Lytchett Matravers 13 F3
Lytchett Minster 13 F3
Lyth 183 H2
Lytham 99 G5
Lytham St. Anne's 99 G5
Lythe 112 B1
Lythe Hill 29 E4
Lythes 185 D9
Lythmore 183 F2

▼M

Maaruig (Maraig) 178 E7
Mabe Burnthouse 3 E3
Mabie 125 D3
Mablethorpe 97 F4
Macclesfield 92 D5
Macclesfield Forest 93 D5
Macduff 177 F4
Macedonia 152 A4
Machan 142 B4
Machany 151 D3
Macharioch 130 C5
Machen 38 B4
Machrie *Arg. & B.* 138 A3
Machrie *Arg. & B.* 138 B5
Machrie *N.Ayr.* 131 D2
Machrihanish 130 B3
Machrins 146 C5
Machynlleth 62 D2
McInroy's Point 140 D2
Mackerye End 44 A1
Mackworth 81 E4
Macmerry 144 B2
Macterry 177 F6
Madderty 151 E2
Maddiston 142 D2
Madehurst 16 B2
Madeley *Staffs.* 79 E3
Madeley *Tel. & W.* 65 G2
Madeley Heath 79 E3
Maders 6 D3
Madford 11 E1
Madingley 58 B1
Madjeston 25 F5
Madley 52 D4
Madresfield 54 A3
Madron 2 B3
Maenaddwyn 88 C4
Maenclochog 49 D5
Maendy *Cardiff* 38 A5
Maendy *V. of Glam.* 37 G5
Maenporth 3 E4
Maentwrog 75 F3
Maen-y-groes 49 G2
Maer *Cornw.* 20 C5
Maer *Staffs.* 79 E4
Maerdy *Carmar.* 50 C5
Maerdy *Carmar.* 50 C5
Maerdy *Conwy* 76 D3
Maerdy *R.C.T.* 37 F3
Maesbrook 77 F5
Maesbury Marsh 78 A5
Maes-Glas (Greenfield) *Flints.* 90 C5
Maes-glas *Newport* 38 C4
Maesgwynne 49 F5
Maeshafn 77 F1
Maesllyn 49 G3
Maesmynis 51 G3
Maesteg 37 E3
Maes-Treylow 52 B1
Maesybont 36 B1
Maesycrugiau 50 A3
Maesycwmmer 38 A3
Maesyfed (New Radnor) 52 B1
Magdalen Laver 45 E2
Maggieknockater 176 B6
Maggots End 58 C5
Magham Down 18 B2
Maghull 91 E2
Magna Park 68 A4
Magor 38 D4
Magpie Green 72 B4
Maiden Bradley 25 E4
Maiden Head 24 C1
Maiden Law 120 A3
Maiden Newton 12 B3
Maiden Wells 34 C3
Maidencombe 9 F1
Maidenhayne 11 F3
Maidenhead 43 D4
Maidens 132 A5
Maiden's Green 43 D5
Maidensgrove 42 C4
Maidenwell *Cornw.* 5 F2
Maidenwell *Lincs.* 96 D5
Maidford 56 B2
Maids' Moreton 56 C4
Maidstone 31 G3
Maidwell 68 C5
Mail 187 D10
Maindee 38 C4
Mainland *Ork.* 185 B6
Mainland *Shet.* 187 C7
Mains of Ardestie 152 D1
Mains of Balgavies 160 D4
Mains of Balhall 160 D3
Mains of Ballindarg 160 C4
Mains of Burgie 175 H6
Mains of Culsh 177 G6
Mains of Dillavaird 161 F1
Mains of Drum 169 G4
Mains of Dudwick 169 H1
Mains of Faillie 166 E1
Mains of Fedderate 177 G6
Mains of Glack 169 F2
Mains of Glassaugh 176 D4
Mains of Glenbuchat 168 B3
Mains of Linton 169 F3
Mains of Melgund 160 D4
Mains of Pitfour 177 H6
Mains of Pittrichie 169 G2
Mains of Sluie 175 H6
Mains of Tannachy 176 B4
Mains of Thornton 161 E2
Mains of Tig 122 C2
Mains of Watten 183 H3
Mainsforth 120 C4
Mainsriddle 124 D5
Mainstone 64 B4
Maisemore 54 A5
Major's Green 66 D5
Makendon 128 A1
Makeney 81 E3
Makerstoun 136 A3
Malacleit 170 C4
Malborough 8 D4
Malden Rushett 29 G1
Maldon 46 B2
Malham 101 F1
Maligar 171 K5
Malinbridge 94 A4
Mallaig 164 C5
Mallaigmore 164 C5
Mallaigvaig 164 C5
Malleny Mills 143 F3
Malletsheugh 141 G4
Malling 150 A4
Mallows Green 58 C5
Malltraeth 74 D1
Mallwyd 63 E1
Malmesbury 40 B4
Malmsmead 22 A3
Malpas *Ches.* 78 B3
Malpas *Cornw.* 4 C5
Malpas *Newport* 38 C3
Maltby *Lincs.* 96 D4
Maltby *S.Yorks.* 94 C3
Maltby *Stock.* 111 D1
Maltby le Marsh 97 E4
Malting End 59 F2
Malting Green 46 C1
Maltman's Hill 32 A4
Malton 111 G5
Malvern Link 53 G3
Malvern Wells 53 G3
Mambeg 140 D1
Mamble 65 F5
Mamhead 10 C4
Mamhilad 38 C2
Manaccan 3 E4
Manadon 8 A2
Manafon 64 A2
Manais (Manish) 171 G3
Manaton 10 A4
Manby 97 D4
Mancetter 67 F3
Manchester 92 C3
Manchester Airport 92 C4
Mancot Royal 78 A1
Mandally 165 J4
Manea 70 C4
Maneight 132 D5
Manfield 110 B1
Mangaster 186 C5
Mangerton 12 A3
Mangotsfield 39 F5
Mangrove Green 57 G5
Mangurstadh 178 C4
Manish (Manais) 171 G3
Mankinholes 101 F5
Manley 91 G5
Manmoel 38 A2
Mannal 154 A2
Manningford Abbots 26 C2
Manningford Bohune 26 C2
Manningford Bruce 26 C2
Manningham 102 A4
Mannings Heath 17 E1
Mannington 13 G2
Manningtree 60 C4
Mannofield 169 H4
Manor Park 43 E4
Manorbier 35 D3
Manorbier Newton 34 D2
Manordeifi 49 F3
Manordeilo 50 C5
Manorowen 48 C4
Mansell Gamage 52 C3
Mansell Lacy 52 D3
Mansergh 108 B4
Mansfield 81 G1
Mansfield Woodhouse 81 G1
Manson Green 86 B5
Mansriggs 107 D4
Manston *Dorset* 13 E1
Manston *Kent* 33 F2
Manston *W.Yorks.* 102 C4
Manswood 13 F2
Manthorpe *Lincs.* 69 F1
Manthorpe *Lincs.* 83 E4
Manton *N.Lincs.* 95 G2
Manton *Notts.* 94 C5
Manton *Rut.* 69 D2
Manton *Wilts.* 26 C1
Manuden 58 C5
Manwood Green 45 E1
Maolachy 148 A3
Maperton 25 D5
Maple Cross 43 F3
Maplebeck 82 C1
Mapledurham 42 B5
Mapledurwell 28 B2
Maplehurst 29 G5
Maplescombe 31 E2
Mapleton 80 C3
Mapperley *Derbys.* 81 F3
Mapperley *Notts.* 81 G3
Mapperton *Dorset* 12 B3
Mapperton *Dorset* 13 F3
Mappleborough Green 54 C1
Mappleton 105 E3
Mapplewell 94 A2
Mappowder 12 D2
Mar Lodge 167 H5
Maraig (Maaruig) 178 E7
Marazion 2 C3
Marbhig 179 G6
Marbury 78 C3
March 70 C3
Marcham 41 G3
Marchamley 78 C5
Marchamley Wood 78 C4
Marchington 80 C4
Marchington Woodlands 80 C5
Marchwiel 78 A3
Marchwood 14 C1
Marcross 22 C1
Marcus 160 D4
Marden *Here.* 53 E3
Marden *Kent* 31 G4
Marden *T. & W.* 129 F4
Marden *Wilts.* 26 B2
Marden Ash 45 E2
Marden Beech 31 G4
Marden Thorn 31 G4
Marden's Hill 31 D5
Mardon 136 D3
Mardy 38 C1
Mare Green 24 A5
Marefield 68 C2
Mareham le Fen 84 A1
Mareham on the Hill 84 A1
Maresfield 17 G1
Marfleet 104 D4
Marford 78 A2
Margam 37 D4
Margaret Marsh 13 E1
Margaret Roding 45 E1
Margaretting 45 F2
Margaretting Tye 45 F2
Margate 33 F1
Margnaheglish 131 F2
Margreig 124 C3
Margrove Park 111 F1
Marham 71 F2
Marhamchurch 20 C5
Marholm 69 G2
Marian Cwm 90 B5
Mariandyrys 89 E4
Marian-Glas 88 D4
Mariansleigh 22 A5
Marine Town 32 B1
Marishader 171 K5
Maristow House 8 A1
Mark 24 A3
Mark Causeway 24 A3
Mark Cross 31 E5
Markbeech 31 D4
Markby 97 E5
Markdhu 122 C3
Markeaton 81 E4
Market Bosworth 67 G2
Market Deeping 69 G1
Market Drayton 79 D4
Market Harborough 68 C4
Market Lavington 26 B2
Market Overton 69 D1
Market Rasen 96 B4
Market Stainton 96 C5
Market Street 87 D3
Market Warsop 81 G1
Market Weighton 104 A3
Market Weston 72 A4
Markethill 152 A1
Markfield 67 G1
Markham 38 A2
Markham Moor 95 E5
Markinch 152 A4
Markington 102 B1
Marks Gate 45 D3
Marks Tey 60 A5
Marksbury 25 D1
Markwell 7 D5
Markyate 43 F1
Marl Bank 53 G3
Marland 92 C1
Marlborough 26 C1
Marlbrook 66 B5
Marlcliff 54 C2
Marldon 9 E1
Marle Green 18 A2
Marlesford 61 E2
Marley Green 78 C3
Marley Hill 120 B2
Marlingford 86 C5
Marloes 34 A2
Marlow *Bucks.* 43 D4
Marlow *Here.* 64 D5
Marlpit Hill 30 D4
Marlpool 81 F3
Marnhull 13 D1
Marnoch 176 D5
Marple 93 D4
Marple Bridge 93 D4
Marr 94 C2
Marrel 183 F7
Marrick 109 F3
Marrister 187 E6
Marros 35 F2
Marsden *T. & W.* 120 C1
Marsden *W.Yorks.* 93 E1
Marsett 109 E4
Marsh 11 F1
Marsh Baldon 42 A3
Marsh Benham 27 F1
Marsh Gibbon 56 B5
Marsh Green *Devon* 10 D3
Marsh Green *Gt.Man.* 91 G2
Marsh Green *Kent* 30 D4
Marsh Green *Tel. & W.* 65 F1
Marsh Lane 94 B5
Marsh Street 22 C3
Marshall Meadows 145 G4
Marshalsea 11 G2
Marshalswick 44 A2
Marsham 86 C3
Marshaw 100 B2
Marshborough 33 F3
Marshbrook 64 D4
Marshchapel 97 D3
Marshfield *Newport* 38 B4
Marshfield *S.Glos.* 39 G5
Marshgate 6 B1
Marshland St. James 70 D2
Marshside 91 E1
Marshwood 11 G3
Marske 110 A2
Marske-by-the-Sea 121 F5
Marsland Green 92 A3
Marston *Ches.* 92 A5
Marston *Here.* 52 C2
Marston *Lincs.* 83 D3
Marston *Oxon.* 42 A2
Marston *Staffs.* 79 G5
Marston *Staffs.* 66 A1
Marston *Warks.* 67 E3
Marston *Wilts.* 26 A2
Marston Doles 55 G2
Marston Green 67 D4
Marston Magna 24 C5
Marston Meysey 40 D3
Marston Montgomery 80 C4
Marston Moretaine 57 E3
Marston on Dove 80 D5
Marston St. Lawrence 56 A3
Marston Stannett 53 E2
Marston Trussell 68 B4
Marstow 39 E1
Marsworth 43 E1
Marten 27 D1
Marthall 92 B5
Martham 87 F4
Martin *Hants.* 13 G1
Martin *Lincs.* 83 G2
Martin *Lincs.* 84 A1
Martin Drove End 26 B5
Martin Hussingtree 54 A1
Martinhoe 21 G1
Martinscroft 92 A4
Martinstown 12 C4
Martlesham 60 D3
Martlesham Heath 60 D3
Martletwy 34 D1
Martley 53 G1
Martock 12 A1
Marton *Ches.* 79 F1
Marton *Cumb.* 106 D5
Marton *E.Riding* 105 D4
Marton *E.Riding* 105 E1
Marton *Lincs.* 95 F4
Marton *Middbro.* 111 E1
Marton *N.Yorks.* 102 D1
Marton *N.Yorks.* 111 G4
Marton *Shrop.* 64 B2
Marton *Shrop.* 78 B5
Marton *Warks.* 55 G1
Marton Abbey 103 E1
Marton-in-the-Forest 103 E1
Marton-le-Moor 110 C5
Martyr Worthy 27 G4
Martyr's Green 29 F2
Marwick 184 B5
Marwood 21 F2
Mary Tavy 7 F3
Marybank *High.* 174 B6
Marybank *W.Isles* 179 G4
Maryburgh 174 C6
Maryfield *Cornw.* 8 A2
Maryfield *Shet.* 187 D8
Marygold 145 F4
Maryhill *Aber.* 177 G6
Maryhill *Glas.* 141 G3
Marykirk 161 E3
Marylebone *Gt.Lon.* 44 B4
Marylebone *Gt.Man.* 91 G2
Marypark 167 J1
Maryport *Cumb.* 116 D3
Maryport *D. & G.* 114 B3
Marystow 7 E2
Maryton 161 E4
Marywell *Aber.* 169 H5
Marywell *Aber.* 168 D5
Marywell *Angus* 161 E5
Masham 110 B4
Mashbury 45 F1
Masongill 108 B5
Mastin Moor 94 B5
Mastrick 169 H4
Matchborough 54 C1
Matching 45 E1
Matching Green 45 E1
Matching Tye 45 E1
Matfen 128 C4
Matfield 31 F4
Mathern 39 E3
Mathon 53 G3
Mathry 48 B4
Matlaske 86 C2
Matlock 81 E1
Matlock Bank 81 E1
Matlock Bath 81 D2
Matson 40 A1
Matterdale End 117 G4
Mattersey 95 D4
Mattersey Thorpe 95 D4
Mattingley 28 C2
Mattishall 86 B4
Mattishall Burgh 86 B4
Mauchline 132 C3
Maud 177 H6
Maufant 8 C5
Maugersbury 55 D5
Maughold 98 C2
Mauld 165 K1
Maulden 57 F4
Maulds Meaburn 108 B1
Maunby 110 C4
Maund Bryan 53 E2
Maundown 23 D5
Mautby 87 F4
Mavesyn Ridware 66 C1
Mavis Enderby 84 B1
Maw Green 79 E2
Mawbray 117 D2
Mawdesley 91 F1
Mawdlam 37 E4
Mawgan 3 E4
Mawgan Porth 4 C3
Mawla 4 A5
Mawnan 3 E4
Mawnan Smith 3 E4
Mawsley 68 D5
Mawthorpe 97 E5
Maxey 69 G2
Maxstoke 67 E4
Maxted Street 32 D4
Maxton *Kent* 33 F4
Maxton *Sc.Bord.* 136 A3
Maxwellheugh 136 B3
Maxwelltown 125 D3
Maxworthy 6 C1
Mayals 36 C3
Maybole 132 B5
Maybury 29 F2
Mayen 176 D6
Mayfair 44 B4
Mayfield *E.Suss.* 18 A1
Mayfield *Midloth.* 144 A3
Mayfield *Staffs.* 80 C3
Mayford 29 E2
Mayland 46 C2
Maylandsea 46 C2
Maynard's Green 18 A2
Maypole *I.o.S.* 4 B1
Maypole *Kent* 33 D2
Maypole *Mon.* 39 D1
Maypole Green *Essex* 60 A5
Maypole Green *Norf.* 73 F2
Maypole Green *Suff.* 61 D1
Maypole Green *Suff.* 60 A2
May's Green *N.Som.* 24 A1
Mays Green *Oxon.* 42 C4
Maywick 187 C10
Mead 20 C4
Mead End 26 B5
Meadgate 25 D2
Meadle 42 D2
Meadow Green 53 G2
Meadowhall 94 A3
Meadowmill 144 B2
Meadowtown 64 C2
Meadwell 7 E2
Meaford 79 F4
Meal Bank 107 G3
Mealabost (Melbost Borve) 179 G2
Mealasta 178 B5
Meals 97 E3
Mealsgate 117 F2
Meanley 100 D3
Meanwood 102 B4
Mearbeck 101 E1
Meare 24 B3
Meare Green 23 F5
Mearns 141 G4
Mears Ashby 56 D1
Measham 67 F1
Meathop 107 F4
Meavy 8 B1
Medbourne 68 D3
Meddon 20 C4
Meden Vale 81 G1
Medlar 100 A4
Medmenham 42 D4
Medomsley 120 A2
Medstead 28 B4
Meer Common 52 C2
Meer End 67 E5
Meerbrook 79 G1
Meesden 58 C4
Meeson 79 D5
Meeth 21 F5
Meeting House Hill 87 E3
Meggethead 134 C3
Meidrim 49 F5
Meifod *Denb.* 76 D2
Meifod *Powys* 64 A1
Meigle 160 A5
Meikle Earnock 142 B4
Meikle Grenach 140 B3
Meikle Kilmory 140 B3
Meikle Rahane 140 D1
Meikle Strath 161 E2
Meikle Tarty 169 H2
Meikle Wartle 169 F1
Meikleour 151 G1
Meikleyard 132 D2
Meinciau 36 A1
Meir 79 G3
Meirheath 79 G4
Melbost 179 G4
Melbost Borve (Mealabost) 179 G2
Melbourn 58 B3
Melbourne *Derbys.* 81 E5
Melbourne *E.Riding* 103 G3
Melbury 21 D4
Melbury Abbas 13 E1
Melbury Bubb 12 B2
Melbury Osmond 12 B2
Melbury Sampford 12 B2
Melby 187 A7
Melchbourne 57 F1
Melcombe Bingham 13 D2
Melcombe Regis 12 C4
Meldon *Devon* 7 F1
Meldon *Northumb.* 128 D3
Meldreth 58 B3
Meledor 4 D4
Melfort 148 A3
Melgarve 166 B5
Melgum 168 C4
Meliden (Gallt Melyd) 90 B4
Melincourt 37 E2
Melin-y-coed 76 B1
Melin-y-ddol 63 G2
Melin-y-grug 63 G2
Melin-y-Wig 76 D3
Melkinthorpe 118 B5
Melkridge 118 D1
Melksham 26 A1
Melksham Forest 26 A1
Melldalloch 140 A2
Melling *Lancs.* 107 G5
Melling *Mersey.* 91 E2
Melling Mount 91 F2
Mellis 72 B4
Mellon Charles 172 E2
Mellon Udrigle 172 E2
Mellor *Gt.Man.* 93 D4
Mellor *Lancs.* 100 C4
Mellor Brook 100 C4
Mells 25 E3
Melmerby *Cumb.* 118 C4
Melmerby *N.Yorks.* 109 F4
Melmerby *N.Yorks.* 110 C5
Melplash 12 A3
Melrose *Aber.* 177 F4
Melrose *Sc.Bord.* 135 G2
Melsetter 185 B9
Melsonby 110 A2
Meltham 93 E1
Melton *E.Riding* 104 B5
Melton *Suff.* 61 D2
Melton Constable 86 B2
Melton Mowbray 68 C1
Melton Ross 96 A1
Meltonby 103 G2
Melvaig 172 D3
Melverley 64 C1
Melverley Green 64 C1
Melvich 182 D2
Membury 11 F2
Memsie 177 H4
Memus 160 C4
Menabilly 5 E4
Menai Bridge (Porthaethwy) 89 D5
Mendham 73 D3
Mendlesham 60 C1
Mendlesham Green 60 B1
Menethorpe 103 G1
Menheniot 5 G3
Menie House 169 H2
Menithwood 53 G1
Mennock 133 G5
Menston 102 A3
Menstrie 150 D5
Mentmore 43 E1
Meoble 155 G1
Meole Brace 65 D1
Meon 15 E2
Meonstoke 15 F1
Meopham 31 F2
Meopham Green 31 F2
Mepal 70 C4
Meppershall 57 G4
Merbach 52 C3
Mercaston 81 D3
Mere *Ches.* 92 B4
Mere *Wilts.* 25 F4
Mere Brow 91 F1
Mere Green 66 D3
Mere Heath 92 A5
Mereclough 101 E4
Mereside 99 G4
Meretown 79 E5
Mereworth 31 F3
Mergie 161 F1
Meriden 67 E4
Merkadale 163 J1
Merkinch 174 D7
Merkland 124 B3
Merley 13 G3
Merlin's Bridge 34 C1
Merridge 23 F4
Merrifield 9 E3
Merrington 78 B5
Merrion 34 C3
Merriott 12 A1
Merrivale 7 F3
Merrow 29 F2
Merry Hill *Herts.* 44 A3
Merry Hill *W.Mid.* 66 B4
Merry Hill *W.Mid.* 66 A3
Merrymeet 5 G3
Mersea Island 46 D1
Mersham 32 C5
Merstham 30 B3
Merston 16 A3
Merstone 15 E4
Merther 4 C5
Merthyr 49 G5
Merthyr Cynog 51 F4
Merthyr Dyfan 23 E1
Merthyr Mawr 37 E5
Merthyr Tydfil 37 G2
Merthyr Vale 37 G3
Merton *Devon* 21 F4
Merton *Norf.* 72 A2
Merton *Oxon.* 42 A1
Mervinslaw 136 A5
Meshaw 10 A1
Messing 46 C1
Messingham 95 F2
Metcombe 11 D3
Metfield 73 D3
Metheringham 83 F1
Metherwell 8 A1
Methil 152 B5
Methlem 74 A4
Methley 102 C5
Methley Junction 102 C5
Methlick 169 G1
Methven 151 F2
Methwold 71 F3
Methwold Hythe 71 F3
MetroCentre 120 B1
Mettingham 73 E3
Metton 86 C2
Mevagissey 5 E5
Mewith Head 100 D1
Mexborough 94 B3
Mey 183 H1
Meysey Hampton 40 D2
Miabhag *W.Isles* 171 G2
Miabhag *W.Isles* 178 C7
Miabhaig (Miavaig) 178 C4
Mial 172 D4
Miavaig (Miabhaig) 178 C4
Michaelchurch 53 E5
Michaelchurch Escley 52 C4
Michaelchurch-on-Arrow 52 B2
Michaelston-le-Pit 38 A5
Michaelston-super-Ely 38 A5
Michaelston-y-Fedw 38 B4
Michaelstow 5 E2
Michelcombe 8 C1
Micheldever 27 G4
Michelmersh 27 E5
Mickfield 60 C1
Mickle Trafford 78 B1
Micklebring 94 C3
Mickleby 112 B1
Micklefield 102 D4
Micklefield Green 43 F3
Mickleham 29 G2
Micklehurst 93 D2
Mickleover 81 E4
Micklethwaite *Cumb.* 117 F1
Micklethwaite *W.Yorks.* 101 G3
Mickleton *Dur.* 119 F5
Mickleton *Glos.* 55 D3
Mickletown 102 C5
Mickley *Derbys.* 94 A5
Mickley *N.Yorks.* 110 B5
Mickley Green 59 G2
Mickley Square 119 G1
Mid Ardlaw 177 H4
Mid Beltie 168 E4
Mid Calder 143 E3
Mid Clyth 183 H5
Mid Lambrook 12 A1
Mid Lavant 16 A3
Mid Letter 148 C4
Mid Lix 150 A1
Mid Mossdale 108 D3
Mid Yell 186 E3
Midbea 184 D3
Middle Assendon 42 C4
Middle Aston 55 G5
Middle Barton 55 G5
Middle Bickenhill 67 E4
Middle Bockhampton 14 A3
Middle Claydon 56 C5
Middle Drift 5 F3
Middle Drums 161 D4
Middle Duntisbourne 40 B2
Middle Handley 94 B5
Middle Harling 72 A3
Middle Kames 140 A1
Middle Littleton 54 C3
Middle Maes-coed 52 C4
Middle Marwood 21 F2
Middle Mill 48 B5
Middle Quarter 32 A5
Middle Rasen 96 A4
Middle Rigg 151 F4
Middle Salter 100 C1
Middle Sontley 78 A3
Middle Stoford 23 E5
Middle Taphouse 5 F3
Middle Town 4 B1
Middle Tysoe 55 F3
Middle Wallop 27 D4
Middle Winterslow 26 D4
Middle Woodford 26 C4
Middlebie 126 A4
Middlecliff 94 B2

Middlecott 21 E5
Middleham 110 A4
Middlehill *Aber.* 177 G6
Middlehill *Cornw.* 5 G3
Middlehope 65 E4
Middlemarsh 12 C2
Middlemoor 7 E3
Middlequarter (Ceathramh Meadhanach) 170 D4
Middlesbrough 121 D5
Middlesceugh 118 A3
Middleshaw 107 G4
Middlesmoor 109 F5
Middlestone 120 B4
Middlestone Moor 120 B4
Middlestown 93 G1
Middleton *Aber.* 169 G3
Middleton *Angus* 161 D5
Middleton *Cumb.* 108 B4
Middleton *Derbys.* 81 D2
Middleton *Derbys.* 80 C1
Middleton *Essex* 59 G3
Middleton *Gt.Man.* 92 C2
Middleton *Hants.* 27 F3
Middleton *Here.* 53 E1
Middleton *Lancs.* 100 A2
Middleton *Midloth.* 144 A4
Middleton *N.Yorks.* 111 G4
Middleton *Norf.* 71 E1
Middleton *Northants.* 68 D4
Middleton *Northumb.* 128 C3
Middleton *Northumb.* 137 E3
Middleton *P. & K.* 151 G4
Middleton *P. & K.* 159 G5
Middleton *Shrop.* 64 B3
Middleton *Shrop.* 65 E5
Middleton *Shrop.* 78 A5
Middleton *Suff.* 61 F1
Middleton *Swan.* 36 A4
Middleton *W.Yorks.* 102 A3
Middleton *W.Yorks.* 102 C5
Middleton *Warks.* 67 D3
Middleton Baggot 65 F3
Middleton Bank Top 128 C3
Middleton Cheney 55 G3
Middleton Green 79 G4
Middleton Hall 137 D4
Middleton Moor 61 F1
Middleton of Potterton 169 H3
Middleton on the Hill 53 E1
Middleton One Row 110 C1
Middleton Park 169 H3
Middleton Priors 65 F4
Middleton Quernhow 110 C5
Middleton St. George 110 C1
Middleton Scriven 65 F4
Middleton Stoney 56 A5
Middleton Tyas 110 B2
Middleton-in-Teesdale 119 F5
Middleton-on-Leven 111 D1
Middleton-on-Sea 16 B3
Middleton-on-the-Wolds 104 B3
Middletown *Cumb.* 106 A2
Middletown *Powys* 64 C1
Middlewich 79 E1
Middlewood *Ches.* 92 D4
Middlewood *S.Yorks.* 94 A3
Middlewood Green 60 B1
Middlezoy 24 A4
Middridge 120 B5
Midfield 181 H2
Midford 25 E1
Midge Hall 100 B5
Midgeholme 118 C2
Midgham 27 G1
Midgley *W.Yorks.* 93 G1
Midgley *W.Yorks.* 101 G5
Midhopestones 93 G3
Midhurst 29 D5
Midlem 135 G3
Midloe Grange 57 G1
Midpark 140 B4
Midsomer Norton 25 D2
Midthorpe 96 C5
Midtown *High.* 181 H2
Midtown *High.* 172 E3
Midtown of Barras 161 G1
Midville 84 B2
Midway 81 E5
Migdale 174 D2
Migvie 168 C4
Milarrochy 149 G5
Milber 10 B5
Milbethill 176 E5
Milborne Port 12 C1
Milborne St. Andrew 13 D3
Milborne Wick 25 D5
Milbourne *Northumb.* 128 D4
Milbourne *Wilts.* 40 B4
Milburn 118 C5
Milbury Heath 39 F3
Milcombe 55 G4
Milden 60 A3
Mildenhall *Suff.* 71 F5
Mildenhall *Wilts.* 26 D1
Mile Elm 26 A1
Mile End *Essex* 60 A5
Mile End *Glos.* 39 E1
Mile Oak 31 F4
Mile Town 32 B1
Milebrook 64 C5
Milebush 31 G4
Mileham 86 A4
Miles Green 79 F3
Miles Hope 53 E1
Milesmark 143 E1
Miles's Green 27 G1
Milfield 136 D3
Milford *Derbys.* 81 E3
Milford *Devon* 20 C3
Milford *Shrop.* 78 B5
Milford *Staffs.* 79 G5
Milford *Surr.* 29 E3
Milford Haven (Aberdaugleddau) 34 B2
Milford on Sea 14 B3
Milkwall 39 E2
Mill Bank 101 G5
Mill Brow 93 D4
Mill End *Bucks.* 42 C4
Mill End *Cambs.* 59 E2
Mill End *Herts.* 58 B4
Mill End Green 59 E5
Mill Green *Cambs.* 59 E3
Mill Green *Essex* 45 F2
Mill Green *Herts.* 44 B2
Mill Green *Norf.* 72 C3
Mill Green *Shrop.* 79 D5
Mill Green *Staffs.* 80 B5
Mill Green *Suff.* 61 E1
Mill Green *Suff.* 60 C2
Mill Green *Suff.* 60 A2
Mill Green *W.Mid.* 66 C2
Mill Hill *B'burn.* 100 C5
Mill Hill *Cambs.* 58 A2
Mill Hill *Gt.Lon.* 44 B3
Mill Houses 100 C1
Mill Lane 28 C2
Mill of Camsail 141 D1
Mill of Colp 177 F6
Mill of Elrick 177 H6
Mill of Fortune 150 C2
Mill of Kingoodie 169 G2
Mill of Monquich 169 G5
Mill of Uras 161 G1
Mill Side 107 F4
Mill Street *Kent* 31 F3
Mill Street *Norf.* 86 B4
Milland 28 D5
Millbank 177 J6
Millbeck 117 F4
Millbounds 184 E4
Millbreck 177 J6
Millbridge 28 D3
Millbrook *Beds.* 57 F4
Millbrook *Cornw.* 8 A2
Millbrook *S'ham.* 14 C1
Millburn *Aber.* 168 D2
Millburn *Aber.* 168 E1
Millcombe 9 E3
Millcorner 18 D1
Milldale 80 C2
Millden 169 H3
Milldens 160 D4
Millearne 151 E3
Millend 55 F5
Millenheath 78 C4
Millerhill 144 A3
Miller's Dale 93 F5
Millers Green *Derbys.* 81 D2
Miller's Green *Essex* 45 E2
Millgate 101 E5
Millhalf 52 B3
Millhayes *Devon* 11 E1
Millhayes *Devon* 11 F2
Millholme 107 G3
Millhouse *Arg. & B.* 140 A2
Millhouse *Cumb.* 117 G3
Millhouse Green 93 G2
Millhousebridge 125 F2
Millikenpark 141 F3
Millin Cross 34 C1
Millington 104 A2
Millington Green 81 D3
Millmeece 79 F4
Millness 165 K1
Millom 106 C4
Millow 58 A3
Millpool 5 F2
Millport 140 C4
Millthorpe 94 A5
Millthrop 108 B3
Milltimber 169 G4
Milltown *Aber.* 167 K4
Milltown *Cornw.* 5 F4
Milltown *D. & G.* 126 B4
Milltown *Derbys.* 81 E1
Milltown *Devon* 21 F2
Milltown *High.* 175 G7
Milltown of Aberdalgie 151 F2
Milltown of Auchindoun 168 B1
Milltown of Craigston 177 F5
Milltown of Edinvillie 175 K7
Milltown of Kildrummy 168 C3
Milltown of Rothiemay 176 D6
Milltown of Towie 168 C3
Milnathort 151 G4
Milners Heath 78 B1
Milngavie 141 G2
Milnrow 92 D1
Milnsbridge 93 F1
Milnthorpe 107 F4
Milovaig 171 G6
Milrig 132 D2
Milson 65 F5
Milstead 32 B3
Milston 26 C3
Milton *Angus* 160 B5
Milton *Cambs.* 58 C1
Milton *Cumb.* 118 B1
Milton *D. & G.* 124 C2
Milton *D. & G.* 124 C3
Milton *D. & G.* 122 D5
Milton *Derbys.* 81 E5
Milton *High.* 173 K6
Milton *High.* 174 E4
Milton *High.* 175 G6
Milton *High.* 172 D7
Milton *High.* 174 C7
Milton *High.* 183 J3
Milton *High.* 166 B1
Milton *Moray* 176 D4
Milton *N.Som.* 24 A1
Milton *Newport* 38 C4
Milton *Notts.* 95 E5
Milton *Oxon.* 55 G4
Milton *Oxon.* 41 G3
Milton *P. & K.* 151 E1
Milton *Pembs.* 34 D2
Milton *Ports.* 15 F3
Milton *Som.* 24 B5
Milton *Stir.* 150 A4
Milton *Stoke* 79 G2
Milton *W.Dun.* 141 F2
Milton Abbas 13 E2
Milton Abbot 7 E3
Milton Bridge 143 G3
Milton Bryan 57 E4
Milton Clevedon 25 D4
Milton Combe 8 A1
Milton Damerel 21 D4
Milton End 39 G1
Milton Ernest 57 F2
Milton Green 78 B2
Milton Hill 41 G3
Milton Keynes 57 D4
Milton Keynes Village 57 D4
Milton Lilbourne 26 C1
Milton Malsor 56 C2
Milton Morenish 150 B1
Milton of Auchinhove 168 D4
Milton of Balgonie 152 B4
Milton of Buchanan 149 G5
Milton of Cairnborrow 176 C6
Milton of Callander 150 A4
Milton of Campfield 168 E4
Milton of Campsie 142 A2
Milton of Coldwells 169 H1
Milton of Cullerlie 169 F4
Milton of Cushnie 168 D3
Milton of Dalcapon 159 E4
Milton of Inveramsay 169 F2
Milton of Noth 168 D2
Milton of Tullich 168 B5
Milton on Stour 25 E5
Milton Regis 32 A2
Milton Street 18 A3
Miltonduff 175 J5
Miltonhill 175 H5
Miltonise 122 C3
Milton-Lockhart 142 C5
Milton-under-Wychwood 41 E1
Milverton *Som.* 23 E5
Milverton *Warks.* 55 F1
Milwich 79 G4
Mimbridge 29 E1
Minard 148 B5
Minard Castle 148 B5
Minchington 13 F1
Minchinhampton 40 A2
Mindrum 136 C3
Mindrummill 136 C3
Minehead 22 C3
Minera 77 F2
Minety 40 C3
Minety Lower Moor 40 C3
Minffordd *Gwyn.* 62 D1
Minffordd *Gwyn.* 75 E4
Minffordd *Gwyn.* 89 D5
Miningsby 84 B1
Minions 5 G2
Minishant 132 B4
Minley Manor 28 D2
Minllyn 63 E1
Minnes 169 H2
Minngearraidh 162 C2
Minnigaff 123 F4
Minnonie 177 F4
Minskip 102 C1
Minstead 14 B1
Minsted 29 D5
Minster *Kent* 32 B1
Minster *Kent* 33 F2
Minster Lovell 41 F1
Minsteracres 119 G2
Minsterley 64 C2
Minsterworth 39 G1
Minterne Magna 12 C2
Minterne Parva 12 C2
Minting 96 B5
Mintlaw 177 J6
Minto 135 G3
Minton 64 D3
Minwear 34 D1
Minworth 67 D3
Miodar 154 B1
Mirbister 185 C6
Mirehouse 116 C5
Mireland 183 J2
Mirfield 102 B5
Miserden 40 B2
Miskin *R.C.T.* 37 G4
Miskin *R.C.T.* 37 G3
Misselfore 26 B5
Misson 95 D3
Misterton *Leics.* 68 A4
Misterton *Notts.* 95 E3
Misterton *Som.* 12 A2
Mistley 60 C4
Mitcham 30 B2
Mitchel Troy 39 D1
Mitcheldean 39 F1
Mitchell 4 C4
Mitchelland 107 F3
Mitcheltroy Common 39 D2
Mitford 129 D3
Mithian 4 B4
Mitton 66 A1
Mixbury 56 B4
Mixenden 101 G5
Moar 158 A5
Moat 126 C4
Moats Tye 60 B2
Mobberley *Ches.* 92 B5
Mobberley *Staffs.* 80 B3
Moccas 52 C3
Mochdre *Conwy* 89 G5
Mochdre *Powys* 63 G4
Mochrum 114 D2
Mockbeggar *Hants.* 14 A2
Mockbeggar *Kent* 31 G4
Mockerkin 117 D4
Modbury 8 C2
Moddershall 79 G4
Modsarie 181 J2
Moelfre *I.o.A.* 88 D4
Moelfre *Powys* 77 E5
Moffat 134 B5
Mogerhanger 57 G3
Moin'a'choire 138 B3
Moine House 181 H3
Moira 67 F1
Molash 32 C3
Mol-chlach 163 K3
Mold (Yr Wyddgrug) 77 F1
Molehill Green *Essex* 59 D5
Molehill Green *Essex* 59 F5
Molescroft 104 C3
Molesden 128 D3
Molesworth 69 F5
Mollance 124 B4
Molland 22 B5
Mollington *Ches.* 91 E5
Mollington *Oxon.* 55 G3
Mollinsburn 142 B2
Monach Islands (Heisker Islands) 170 B5
Monachty 50 B1
Monachyle 149 G3
Monevechadan 149 D4
Monewden 60 D2
Moneydie 151 F2
Moneyrow Green 43 D5
Moniaive 124 B1
Monifieth 152 D1
Monikie 152 D1
Monimail 152 A3
Monington 49 E3
Monk Bretton 94 A2
Monk Fryston 103 E5
Monk Hesleden 121 D4
Monk Sherborne 28 B2
Monk Soham 60 D1
Monk Soham Green 60 D1
Monk Street 59 E5
Monken Hadley 44 B3
Monkerton 10 C3
Monkhide 53 F3
Monkhill 117 G1
Monkhopton 65 F3
Monkland 53 D2
Monkleigh 21 E3
Monknash 37 F5
Monkokehampton 21 F5
Monks Eleigh 60 A3
Monks Eleigh Tye 60 A3
Monk's Gate 17 E1
Monks' Heath 92 C5
Monk's Hill 32 A4
Monks Kirby 67 G4
Monks Risborough 42 D2
Monkscross 7 D3
Monkseaton 129 F4
Monkshill 177 F6
Monksilver 23 D4
Monkstadt 171 J5
Monkswood 38 C2
Monkton *Devon* 11 E2
Monkton *Kent* 33 E2
Monkton *Pembs.* 34 C2
Monkton *S.Ayr.* 132 B3
Monkton *T. & W.* 120 C1
Monkton *V. of Glam.* 37 F5
Monkton Combe 25 E1
Monkton Deverill 25 F4
Monkton Farleigh 25 F1
Monkton Heathfield 23 F5
Monkton Up Wimborne 13 G1
Monkton Wyld 11 G3
Monkwearmouth 120 C2
Monkwood 28 B4
Monmouth (Trefynwy) 39 E1
Monnington Court 52 C4
Monnington on Wye 52 C3
Monreith 115 D2
Montacute 12 B1
Monteach 177 G6
Montford 64 D1
Montford Bridge 64 D1
Montgarrie 168 D3
Montgomery (Trefaldwyn) 64 B3
Montgreenan 141 E5
Montrave 152 B4
Montrose 161 F4
Monxton 27 E3
Monyash 80 C1
Monymusk 168 E3
Monzie 151 D2
Moodiesburn 142 A2
Moons Moat North 54 C1
Moonzie 152 B3
Moor Allerton 102 C4
Moor Cock 100 C1
Moor Crichel 13 F2
Moor End *Beds.* 57 F2
Moor End *Beds.* 57 E5
Moor End *Cumb.* 107 G5
Moor End *E.Riding* 104 A4
Moor End *Lancs.* 99 G3
Moor End *N.Yorks.* 103 E4
Moor End *W.Yorks.* 101 G5
Moor Green *W.Mid.* 66 C4
Moor Green *Wilts.* 25 F1
Moor Head 102 A4
Moor Monkton 103 E2
Moor Row 116 D5
Moor Side *Cumb.* 106 D5
Moor Side *Lancs.* 100 A4
Moor Side *Lancs.* 100 A4
Moor Side *Lincs.* 84 A2
Moor Street 32 A2
Moorby 84 A1
Moorcot 52 C2
Moordown 13 G3
Moore 91 G4
Moorend 117 G1
Moorends 95 D1
Moorfield 93 E3
Moorgreen *Hants.* 15 D1
Moorgreen *Notts.* 81 F3
Moorhall 94 A5
Moorhampton 52 C3
Moorhouse *Cumb.* 117 G1
Moorhouse *Notts.* 82 C1
Moorland (Northmoor Green) 24 A4
Moorlinch 24 A4
Moorsholm 111 F1
Moorside *Dorset* 13 D1
Moorside *Gt.Man.* 93 D2
Moorside *W.Yorks.* 102 B4
Moorthorpe 94 B1
Moortown *I.o.W.* 14 D4
Moortown *Lincs.* 96 A3
Moortown *Tel. & W.* 65 F1
Morangie 174 E3
Morar 164 C5
Morborne 69 G3
Morchard Bishop 10 A2
Morcombelake 12 A3
Morcott 69 E2
Morda 77 F5
Morden *Dorset* 13 F3
Morden *Gt.Lon.* 30 B2
Morden Park 30 B2
Mordiford 53 E4
Mordington Holdings 145 G4
Mordon 120 C5
More 64 C3
Morebath 22 C5
Morebattle 136 B4
Morecambe 100 A1
Morefield 173 H2
Moreleigh 9 D2
Morenish 150 B1
Moresby Parks 116 C5
Morestead 27 G5
Moreton *Dorset* 13 E4
Moreton *Essex* 45 E2
Moreton *Here.* 53 E1
Moreton *Mersey.* 91 D4
Moreton *Oxon.* 42 B2
Moreton *Staffs.* 80 C4
Moreton *Staffs.* 65 G1
Moreton Corbet 78 C5
Moreton Jeffries 53 F3
Moreton Mill 78 C5
Moreton Morrell 55 F2
Moreton on Lugg 53 E3
Moreton Paddox 55 F2
Moreton Pinkney 56 A3
Moreton Say 78 D4
Moreton Valence 39 G2
Moretonhampstead 10 A4
Moreton-in-Marsh 55 E4
Morfa *Carmar.* 36 B1
Morfa *Cere.* 49 G2
Morfa Bychan 75 E4
Morfa Glas 37 E2
Morfa Nefyn 74 B3
Morgan's Vale 26 C5
Morganstown 38 A4
Mork 39 E2
Morland 118 B5
Morley *Derbys.* 81 E3
Morley *Dur.* 120 A5
Morley *W.Yorks.* 102 B5
Morley Green 92 C4
Morley St. Botolph 72 B2
Mornick 6 D3
Morningside *Edin.* 143 G2
Morningside *N.Lan.* 142 C4
Morningthorpe 72 D2
Morpeth 129 E3
Morphie 161 F3
Morrey 66 D1
Morridge Side 80 B2
Morrilow Heath 79 G4
Morriston *S.Ayr.* 132 A5
Morriston *Swan.* 36 C3
Morristown 38 A5
Morroch 155 F1
Morston 86 B1
Mortehoe 21 E1
Morthen 94 B4
Mortimer 28 B1
Mortimer West End 28 B1
Mortimer's Cross 52 D1
Mortlake 44 B5
Morton *Derbys.* 81 F1
Morton *Lincs.* 83 F5
Morton *Lincs.* 95 F3
Morton *Lincs.* 83 D1
Morton *Notts.* 82 C2
Morton *S.Glos.* 39 F3
Morton *Shrop.* 77 F5
Morton Bagot 54 D1
Morton on the Hill 86 C4
Morton Tinmouth 120 A5
Morton-on-Swale 110 C3
Morvah 2 B3
Morval 5 G4
Morvich *High.* 165 F2
Morvich *High.* 174 E1
Morvil 48 D4
Morville 65 F3
Morwellham 8 A1
Morwenstow 20 C4
Morwick Hall 129 E1
Mosborough 94 B4
Moscow 141 F5
Mosedale 117 G3
Moselden Height 93 E1
Moseley *W.Mid.* 66 C4
Moseley *W.Mid.* 66 B3
Moseley *Worcs.* 54 A2
Moses Gate 92 B2
Moss *Arg. & B.* 154 A2
Moss *S.Yorks.* 94 C1
Moss *Wrex.* 78 A2
Moss Bank 91 G3
Moss Houses 92 C5
Moss Nook 92 C4
Moss of Barmuckity 175 K5
Moss Side *Gt.Man.* 92 C3
Moss Side *Lancs.* 99 G4
Moss Side *Mersey.* 91 E2
Mossat 168 C3
Mossbank 186 D5
Mossblown 132 C3
Mossburnford 136 A5
Mossdale 124 A3
Mossend 142 B3
Mossgiel 132 C3
Mosshead 168 D1
Mosside of Ballinshoe 160 C4
Mossley *Ches.* 79 F1
Mossley *Gt.Man.* 93 D2
Mossley Hill 91 E4
Mosspaul Hotel 126 B2
Moss-side *High.* 175 F6
Moss-side *Moray* 176 D5
Mosstodloch 176 B4
Mosston 160 D5
Mossy Lea 91 G1
Mosterton 12 A2
Moston *Gt.Man.* 92 C2
Moston *Shrop.* 78 C5
Moston Green 79 E1
Mostyn 90 C4
Motcombe 25 F5
Mothecombe 8 C3
Motherby 118 A5
Motherwell 142 B4
Mottingham 44 D5
Mottisfont 27 E5
Mottistone 14 D4
Mottram in Longdendale 93 D3
Mottram St. Andrew 92 C5
Mouldsworth 91 G5
Moulin 159 E4
Moulsecoomb 17 F3
Moulsford 42 A4
Moulsham 45 G2
Moulsoe 57 E3
Moulton *Ches.* 79 D1
Moulton *Lincs.* 84 B5
Moulton *N.Yorks.* 110 B2
Moulton *Northants.* 56 C1
Moulton *Suff.* 59 E1
Moulton *V. of Glam.* 37 G5
Moulton Chapel 70 A1
Moulton St. Mary 87 F5
Moulton Seas End 84 B5
Mounie Castle 169 F2
Mount *Cornw.* 4 B4
Mount *Cornw.* 5 F3
Mount *High.* 175 G7
Mount *Kent* 33 D4
Mount *W.Yorks.* 93 F1
Mount Ambrose 4 B5
Mount Bures 60 A4
Mount Charles 5 E4
Mount Hawke 4 B5
Mount Manisty 91 E5
Mount Oliphant 132 B4
Mount Pleasant *Ches.* 79 F2
Mount Pleasant *Derbys.* 81 E3
Mount Pleasant *Derbys.* 67 E1
Mount Pleasant *E.Suss.* 17 G2
Mount Pleasant *Flints.* 90 D5
Mount Pleasant *Gt.Lon.* 43 F3
Mount Pleasant *Hants.* 14 C3
Mount Pleasant *Norf.* 72 A2
Mount Pleasant *Suff.* 59 F3
Mount Sorrel 26 B5
Mount Tabor 101 G5
Mountain 101 G4
Mountain Ash (Aberpennar) 37 G3
Mountain Cross 143 F5
Mountain Water 48 C5
Mountbenger 135 E3
Mountblairy 176 E5
Mountblow 141 F2
Mountfield 18 C1
Mountgerald 174 C5
Mountjoy 4 C3
Mountnessing 45 F3
Mounton 39 E3
Mountsorrel 68 A1
Mousa 187 D10
Mousehole 2 B4
Mouswald 125 E3
Mow Cop 79 F2
Mowden 110 B1
Mowhaugh 136 C4
Mowsley 68 B4
Mowtie 161 G1
Moxley 66 B3
Moy *High.* 157 D1
Moy *High.* 157 G1
Moy *High.* 166 E1
Moy House 175 H6
Moylgrove 49 E3
Muasdale 139 E5
Much Birch 53 E4
Much Cowarne 53 F3
Much Dewchurch 53 D4
Much Hadham 44 D1
Much Hoole 100 A5
Much Hoole Town 100 A5
Much Marcle 53 F4
Much Wenlock 65 F2
Muchalls 169 H5
Muchelney 24 B5
Muchelney Ham 24 B5
Muchlarnick 5 G4
Muchra 134 D4
Muchrachd 165 J1
Muck 154 D2
Mucking 45 F4
Muckle Roe 187 C6
Muckleford 12 C3
Mucklestone 79 E4
Muckleton 78 C5
Muckletown 168 D2
Muckley 65 F3
Muckley Corner 66 C2
Muckton 97 D4
Mudale 181 H5
Muddiford 21 F2
Muddles Green 18 A2
Muddleswood 17 E2
Mudeford 14 A3
Mudford 12 B1
Mudgley 24 B3
Mugdock 141 G2
Mugeary 163 K1
Mugginton 81 D3
Muggintonlane End 81 D3
Muggleswick 119 G3
Mugswell 30 B3
Muie 174 D1
Muir 159 F1
Muir of Fowlis 168 D3
Muir of Lochs 176 B4
Muir of Ord 174 C6
Muirden 177 F5
Muirdrum 153 D1
Muiredge 152 B5
Muirhead *Aber.* 168 D3
Muirhead *Angus* 152 B1
Muirhead *Fife* 152 A4
Muirhead *Moray* 175 H5
Muirhead *N.Lan.* 142 A3
Muirhouses 143 E1
Muirkirk 133 E3
Muirmill 142 B1
Muirtack *Aber.* 169 H1
Muirtack *Aber.* 177 G6
Muirton *High.* 174 E5
Muirton *P. & K.* 151 E3
Muirton *P. & K.* 151 G2
Muirton of Ardblair 159 G5
Muirton of Ballochy 161 E3
Muirtown 175 G6
Muiryfold 177 F5
Muker 109 E3
Mulbarton 86 C5
Mulben 176 B5
Mulhagery 179 F7
Mull 147 E1
Mullach Charlabhaigh 178 E3
Mullacott Cross 21 F1
Mullion 3 D5
Mullion Cove 3 D5
Mumby 97 F5
Munderfield Row 53 F2
Munderfield Stocks 53 F2
Mundesley 87 E2
Mundford 71 G3
Mundham 73 E2
Mundon 46 B2
Mundurno 169 H3
Munerigie 165 J4
Mungasdale 173 F2
Mungoswells 144 B2
Mungrisdale 117 G3
Munlochy 174 D6
Munnoch 140 D5
Munsley 53 F3
Munslow 65 E4
Murchington 7 G2
Murcott *Oxon.* 42 A1
Murcott *Wilts.* 40 B3
Murdostoun 142 C4
Murieston 143 E3
Murkle 183 G2
Murlaganmore 150 A1
Murlaggan *High.* 165 G5
Murlaggan *High.* 157 F1
Murra 185 B7
Murrell Green 28 C2
Murroes 152 C1
Murrow 70 B2
Mursley 56 D5
Murston 32 B2
Murthill 160 C4
Murthly 151 F1
Murton *Cumb.* 118 D5
Murton *Dur.* 120 C3
Murton *Northumb.* 145 G5
Murton *Swan.* 36 B4
Murton *York* 103 F2
Musbury 11 F3
Muscliff 13 G3
Musdale 148 B2
Musselburgh 144 A2
Mustard Hyrn 87 F4
Muston *Leics.* 82 D4
Muston *N.Yorks.* 113 D5
Mustow Green 66 A5
Mutford 73 F3
Muthill 151 D3
Mutley 8 A2
Mutterton 10 D2
Muxton 65 G1
Mybster 183 G3
Myddfai 51 D4
Myddle 78 B5
Myddlewood 78 B5
Mydroilyn 50 A2
Myerscough College 100 A4
Myerscough Smithy 100 C4
Mylor 3 F3
Mylor Bridge 3 F3
Mynachdy 38 A5
Mynachlog-ddu 49 E4
Myndtown 64 C4
Mynydd Fechell 88 B3
Mynydd Llandygai 75 F1
Mynydd-bach *Mon.* 39 D3
Mynydd-bach *Swan.* 36 C3
Mynyddygarreg 36 A2
Mynytho 74 C4
Myrebird 169 F5
Mytchett 29 D2
Mytholm 101 F5
Mytholmroyd 101 G5
Mythop 99 G4
Myton-on-Swale 102 D1
Mytton 64 D1

▼ N

Naast 172 E3
Nab's Head 100 C5
Na-Buirgh 171 F2
Naburn 103 E3
Nackington 33 D3
Nacton 60 D3
Nadderwater 10 B3
Nafferton 104 C2
Nailbridge 39 F1
Nailsbourne 23 F5
Nailsea 39 D5
Nailstone 67 G2
Nailsworth 40 A3
Nairn 175 F6
Nancegollan 2 D3
Nancekuke 4 A5
Nancledra 2 B3
Nanhoron 74 B4
Nannau 76 A5
Nannerch 77 E1
Nanpantan 68 A1
Nanpean 5 D4
Nanstallon 5 E3
Nant Peris 75 F2
Nant-ddu 37 G1
Nanternis 49 G2
Nantgaredig 50 A5
Nantgarw 38 A4
Nant-glas 51 F1
Nantglyn 76 D1
Nantgwyn 63 F5
Nantlle 75 E2
Nantmawr 77 F5
Nantmel 51 G1
Nantmor 75 F3
Nantwich 79 E2
Nantycaws 36 A1
Nant-y-derry 38 C2
Nant-y-dugoed 63 F1
Nantyffyllon 37 E3
Nantyglo 38 A1
Nant-y-Gollen 77 F5
Nant-y-groes 51 G1
Nant-y-moel 37 F3
Nant-y-Pandy 89 E5

Naphill 43 D3
Napley Heath 79 E4
Nappa 101 E2
Napton on the Hill 55 G1
Narberth (Arberth) 35 E1
Narborough *Leics.* 68 A3
Narborough *Norf.* 71 F1
Narkurs 6 D5
Narrachan 148 B3
Nasareth 75 D3
Naseby 68 B5
Nash *Bucks.* 56 C4
Nash *Here.* 52 C1
Nash *Newport* 38 C4
Nash *Shrop.* 65 F5
Nash *V. of Glam.* 37 F5
Nash Street 31 F2
Nassington 69 F3
Nasty 58 B5
Nateby *Cumb.* 108 C2
Nateby *Lancs.* 100 A3
Nately Scures 28 C2
Natland 107 G4
Naughton 60 B3
Naunton *Glos.* 54 D5
Naunton *Worcs.* 54 A4
Naunton Beauchamp 54 B2
Navenby 83 E2
Navestock 45 E3
Navestock Side 45 E3
Navidale 183 F7
Navity 174 E5
Nawton 111 F4
Nayland 60 A4
Nazeing 44 D2
Neacroft 14 A3
Neal's Green 67 F4
Neap 187 E7
Neap House 95 F1
Near Sawrey 107 E3
Nearton End 56 D5
Neasden 44 B4
Neasham 110 C1
Neat Enstone 55 F5
Neath (Castell-Nedd) 37 D3
Neatham 28 C3
Neatishead 87 E3
Nebo *Cere.* 50 B1
Nebo *Conwy* 76 B2
Nebo *Gwyn.* 75 D2
Nebo *I.o.A.* 88 C3
Necton 71 G2
Nedd 180 D5
Nedderton 129 E3
Nedging 60 A3
Nedging Tye 60 B3
Needham 72 D3
Needham Market 60 B2
Needham Street 59 F1
Needingworth 70 B5
Needwood 80 C5
Neen Savage 65 F5
Neen Sollars 65 F5
Neenton 65 F4
Nefyn 74 C3
Neighbourne 24 D3
Neilston 141 F4
Neithrop 55 G3
Nelson *Caerp.* 38 A3
Nelson *Lancs.* 101 E4
Nelson Village 129 E4
Nemphlar 142 C5
Nempnett Thrubwell 24 C1
Nenthall 119 D3
Nenthead 119 D3
Nenthorn 136 A3
Neopardy 10 A3
Nerabus 138 A4
Nercwys 77 F1
Neriby 138 B3
Nerston 142 A4
Nesbit 137 D3
Nesfield 101 G3
Ness 91 E5
Ness of Tenston 185 B6
Nesscliffe 64 C1
Neston *Ches.* 91 D5
Neston *Wilts.* 25 F1
Nether Alderley 92 C5
Nether Auchendrane 132 B4
Nether Barr 123 F4
Nether Blainslie 144 C5
Nether Broughton 82 B5
Nether Burrow 108 B5
Nether Cerne 12 C3
Nether Compton 12 B1
Nether Crimond 169 G2
Nether Dalgliesh 135 D5
Nether Dallachy 176 B4
Nether Edge 94 A4
Nether End 93 G5
Nether Exe 10 C3
Nether Glasslaw 177 G5
Nether Handwick 160 B5
Nether Haugh 94 B3
Nether Heage 81 E2
Nether Heselden 109 D5
Nether Heyford 56 B2
Nether Kellet 100 B1
Nether Kinmundy 177 J6
Nether Langwith 94 C5
Nether Lenshie 176 E6
Nether Loads 81 E1
Nether Moor 81 E1
Nether Padley 93 G5
Nether Pitforthie 161 G2
Nether Poppleton 103 E2
Nether Silton 111 D3
Nether Skyborry 64 B5
Nether Stowey 23 E4
Nether Urquhart 151 G4
Nether Wallop 27 E4
Nether Wasdale 106 C2
Nether Wellwood 133 E3
Nether Welton 117 G2
Nether Westcote 55 E5
Nether Whitacre 67 E3
Nether Winchendon (Lower Winchendon) 42 C1
Nether Worton 55 G5
Netheravon 26 C3
Netherbrae 177 F5
Netherbrough 185 C6
Netherburn 142 C5
Netherbury 12 A3
Netherby *Cumb.* 126 B4
Netherby *N.Yorks.* 102 C3
Nethercott 55 G5
Netherend 39 E2
Netherfield *E.Suss.* 18 C2
Netherfield *Notts.* 82 B3
Netherfield *S.Lan.* 142 B5
Netherhall 140 D3
Netherhampton 26 C5
Netherhay 12 A2
Netherland Green 80 C4
Netherley 169 G5
Nethermill 125 E2
Nethermuir 177 H6
Netherseal 67 E1
Nethershield 133 D3
Netherstreet 26 A1
Netherthird *D. & G.* 124 B5
Netherthird *E.Ayr.* 133 D4
Netherthong 93 F2
Netherthorpe 94 C4
Netherton *Angus* 160 D4
Netherton *Ches.* 91 G5
Netherton *Devon* 10 B5
Netherton *Hants.* 27 E2
Netherton *Mersey.* 91 E2
Netherton *N.Lan.* 142 B4
Netherton *Northumb.* 128 B1
Netherton *Oxon.* 41 G2
Netherton *P. & K.* 159 G4
Netherton *S.Lan.* 142 D4
Netherton *W.Mid.* 66 B4
Netherton *W.Yorks.* 93 G1
Netherton *W.Yorks.* 93 F1
Netherton *Worcs.* 54 B3
Netherton Burnfoot 128 B1
Netherton Northside 128 B1
Nethertown *Cumb.* 106 A2
Nethertown *Ork.* 183 J1
Nethertown *Staffs.* 66 D1
Netherwitton 128 D2
Netherwood *D. & G.* 125 D3
Netherwood *E.Ayr.* 133 E3
Nethy Bridge 167 H2
Netley Abbey 15 D2
Netley Marsh 14 C1
Nettlebed 42 B4
Nettlebridge 24 D3
Nettlecombe *Dorset* 12 B3
Nettlecombe *I.o.W.* 15 E5
Nettlecombe *Som.* 23 D4
Nettleden 43 F1
Nettleham 96 A5
Nettlestead *Kent* 31 F3
Nettlestead *Suff.* 60 B3
Nettlestead Green 31 F3
Nettlestone 15 F3
Nettlesworth 120 B3
Nettleton *Lincs.* 96 B2
Nettleton *Wilts.* 40 A5
Nettleton Hill 93 E1
Netton *Devon* 8 B3
Netton *Wilts.* 26 C4
Neuadd *Cere.* 50 A2
Neuadd *I.o.A.* 88 B3
Neuadd *Powys* 51 F3
Nevendon 45 G3
Nevern 49 D4
Nevill Holt 68 D3
New Abbey 125 D4
New Aberdour 177 G4
New Addington 30 C2
New Alresford 27 G4
New Alyth 160 A5
New Arley 67 E3
New Arram 104 C3
New Ash Green 31 F2
New Balderton 82 D2
New Barn 31 F2
New Belses 135 G3
New Bewick 137 E4
New Bolingbroke 84 B2
New Boultham 95 G5
New Bradwell 56 D3
New Brancepeth 120 B3
New Bridge *D. & G.* 124 D3
New Bridge *Devon* 10 A5
New Brighton *Flints.* 77 F1
New Brighton *Hants.* 15 G2
New Brighton *Mersey.* 91 E3
New Brighton *W.Yorks.* 102 B5
New Brighton *Wrex.* 77 F2
New Brinsley 81 F2
New Broughton 78 A2
New Buckenham 72 B2
New Byth 177 G5
New Cheriton 27 G5
New Cross *Cere.* 62 C5
New Cross *Gt.Lon.* 44 C5
New Cumnock 133 E4
New Deer 177 G6
New Duston 56 C1
New Earswick 103 F2
New Edlington 94 C3
New Elgin 175 K5
New Ellerby 105 D4
New Eltham 44 D5
New End 54 C1
New England 69 G2
New Farnley 102 B4
New Ferry 91 E4
New Galloway 124 A3
New Gilston 152 C4
New Greens 44 A2
New Grimsby 4 A1
New Hartley 129 F4
New Haw 29 F1
New Heaton 136 C3
New Hedges 35 E2
New Herrington 120 C2
New Hinksey 42 A2
New Holland 104 C5
New Houghton *Derbys.* 81 G1
New Houghton *Norf.* 85 F5
New Houses 108 D5
New Hunwick 120 A4
New Hutton 107 G3
New Hythe 31 G3
New Inn *Carmar.* 50 A4
New Inn *Fife* 152 A4
New Inn *Mon.* 39 D2
New Inn *Torfaen* 38 B3
New Invention *Shrop.* 64 B5
New Invention *W.Mid.* 66 B2
New Kelso 173 F7
New Lanark 142 C5
New Lane 91 F1
New Lane End 92 A3
New Leake 84 C2
New Leeds 177 H5
New Leslie 168 D2
New Lodge 94 A2
New Longton 100 B5
New Luce 122 C4
New Mains 133 G2
New Mains of Ury 161 G1
New Malden 30 B2
New Marske 121 F5
New Marton 78 A4
New Mill *Cornw.* 2 B3
New Mill *Herts.* 43 E1
New Mill *W.Yorks.* 93 F2
New Mill End 44 A1
New Mills *Cornw.* 4 C4
New Mills *Derbys.* 93 E4
New Mills *Glos.* 39 F2
New Mills *Mon.* 39 E2
New Mills *Powys* 63 G2
New Milton 14 B3
New Mistley 60 C4
New Moat 49 D5
New Ollerton 82 B1
New Orleans 130 C4
New Oscott 66 C3
New Park *Cornw.* 5 F1
New Park *N.Yorks.* 102 B2
New Pitsligo 177 G5
New Polzeath 4 D2
New Quay (Ceinewydd) 49 G1
New Rackheath 87 D4
New Radnor (Maesyfed) 52 B1
New Rent 118 A4
New Ridley 119 G1
New Road Side 101 F3
New Romney 19 F1
New Rossington 94 D3
New Row *Cere.* 62 D5
New Row *Lancs.* 100 C4
New Sawley 81 F4
New Shoreston 137 F3
New Silksworth 120 C2
New Swannington 67 G1
New Totley 94 A5
New Town *Beds.* 57 G3
New Town *Cere.* 49 E3
New Town *Dorset* 13 F1
New Town *Dorset* 13 F2
New Town *E.Loth.* 144 B2
New Town *E.Suss.* 17 G1
New Town *Glos.* 54 C4
New Tredegar 38 A2
New Tupton 81 E1
New Ulva 139 F1
New Valley 179 G4
New Village 94 C2
New Walsoken 70 C2
New Waltham 96 C2
New Winton 144 B2
New World 70 B3
New Yatt 41 F1
New York *Lincs.* 84 A2
New York *T. & W.* 129 F4
Newall 102 B3
Newark *Ork.* 184 G3
Newark *Peter.* 70 A2
Newark-on-Trent 82 D2
Newarthill 142 B4
Newball 96 A5
Newbarn 33 D5
Newbarns 106 D5
Newbattle 144 A3
Newbiggin *Cumb.* 118 A5
Newbiggin *Cumb.* 118 C5
Newbiggin *Cumb.* 118 B3
Newbiggin *Cumb.* 99 F1
Newbiggin *Cumb.* 106 B3
Newbiggin *Dur.* 119 F5
Newbiggin *N.Yorks.* 109 F4
Newbiggin *N.Yorks.* 109 E3
Newbiggin *Northumb.* 119 F1
Newbiggin-by-the-Sea 129 F3
Newbigging *Aber.* 169 G5
Newbigging *Aber.* 159 G1
Newbigging *Angus* 152 C1
Newbigging *Angus* 152 C1
Newbigging *Angus* 160 A5
Newbigging *S.Lan.* 143 E5
Newbiggin-on-Lune 108 C2
Newbold *Derbys.* 94 A5
Newbold *Leics.* 67 G1
Newbold on Avon 67 G5
Newbold on Stour 55 E3
Newbold Pacey 55 E2
Newbold Verdon 67 G2
Newborough *I.o.A.* 74 D1
Newborough *Peter.* 70 A2
Newborough *Staffs.* 80 C5
Newbottle *Northants.* 56 A4
Newbottle *T. & W.* 120 C2
Newbourne 61 D3
Newbridge (Cefn Bychan) *Caerp.* 38 B3
Newbridge *Cornw.* 2 B3
Newbridge *Cornw.* 6 D4
Newbridge *E.Suss.* 31 D5
Newbridge *Edin.* 143 F2
Newbridge *Hants.* 14 B1
Newbridge *I.o.W.* 14 D4
Newbridge *N.Yorks.* 112 B4
Newbridge *Oxon.* 41 G2
Newbridge *Pembs.* 48 C4
Newbridge *Wrex.* 77 F3
Newbridge Green 54 A4
Newbridge on Wye 51 G2
Newbridge-on-Usk 38 C3
Newbrough 119 E1
Newbuildings 10 A2
Newburgh *Aber.* 177 H5
Newburgh *Aber.* 169 H2
Newburgh *Fife* 152 A3
Newburgh *Lancs.* 91 F1
Newburgh *Sc.Bord.* 135 E3
Newburn 120 A1
Newbury *Som.* 25 D2
Newbury *W.Berks.* 27 F1
Newbury *Wilts.* 25 F3
Newbury Park 44 D4
Newby *Cumb.* 118 B5
Newby *Lancs.* 101 E3
Newby *N.Yorks.* 111 E1
Newby *N.Yorks.* 100 D1
Newby *N.Yorks.* 112 D4
Newby Bridge 107 E4
Newby Cote 108 C5
Newby Cross 117 G1
Newby East 118 A2
Newby West 117 G1
Newby Wiske 110 C4
Newcastle *Bridgend* 37 E5
Newcastle *Mon.* 38 D1
Newcastle *Shrop.* 64 B4
Newcastle Emlyn (Castell Newydd Emlyn) 49 G3
Newcastle International Airport 129 D4
Newcastle upon Tyne 120 B1
Newcastleton 126 C3
Newcastle-under-Lyme 79 F3
Newchapel *Pembs.* 49 F4
Newchapel *Stoke* 79 F2
Newchapel *Surr.* 30 C4
Newchurch *Carmar.* 49 G5
Newchurch *I.o.W.* 15 E4
Newchurch *Kent* 32 C5
Newchurch *Lancs.* 101 E5
Newchurch *Lancs.* 101 E4
Newchurch *Mon.* 39 D3
Newchurch *Powys* 52 B2
Newchurch *Staffs.* 80 C5
Newcott 11 F2
Newcraighall 144 A2
Newdigate 29 G3
Newell Green 43 D5
Newenden 18 D1
Newent 53 G5
Newerne 39 F2
Newfield *Dur.* 120 B4
Newfield *Dur.* 120 B2
Newfield *High.* 174 E4
Newfound 27 G2
Newgale 48 B5
Newgate 86 B1
Newgate Street 44 C2
Newgord 186 E2
Newhall *Ches.* 78 D3
Newhall *Derbys.* 81 D5
Newham 137 F4
Newham Hall 137 F4
Newhaven 17 G3
Newhey 92 D1
Newholm 112 B1
Newhouse 142 B3
Newick 17 G1
Newingreen 32 D5
Newington *Edin.* 143 G2
Newington *Kent* 33 D5
Newington *Kent* 32 A2
Newington *Notts.* 95 D3
Newington *Oxon.* 42 B3
Newington Bagpath 40 A3
Newland *Cumb.* 107 E5
Newland *Glos.* 39 E2
Newland *Hull* 104 C4
Newland *N.Yorks.* 103 F5
Newland *Oxon.* 41 F1
Newland *Worcs.* 53 G3
Newlandrig 144 A3
Newlands *Cumb.* 117 G3
Newlands *Essex* 46 B4
Newlands *Northumb.* 119 G2
Newlands *Sc.Bord.* 126 D2
Newland's Corner 29 F3
Newlands of Geise 183 F2
Newlands of Tynet 176 B4
Newlyn 2 B4
Newmachar 169 G3
Newmains 142 C4
Newman's End 45 E1
Newman's Green 59 G3
Newmarket *Suff.* 59 E1
Newmarket *W.Isles* 179 G4
Newmill *Aber.* 161 F1
Newmill *Aber.* 177 G6
Newmill *Aber.* 169 G2
Newmill *Moray* 176 C5
Newmill *Sc.Bord.* 135 F4
Newmill of Inshewan 160 C3
Newmillerdam 94 A1
Newmills 174 D5
Newmiln *P. & K.* 151 G1
Newmiln *P. & K.* 151 F2
Newmilns 132 D2
Newney Green 45 F2
Newnham *Glos.* 39 F1
Newnham *Hants.* 28 C2
Newnham *Herts.* 58 A4
Newnham *Kent* 32 B3
Newnham *Northants.* 56 A2
Newnham Bridge 53 F1
Newnham Paddox 67 G4
Newnoth 168 D1
Newport *Cornw.* 6 D2
Newport *Devon* 21 F2
Newport *E.Riding* 104 A4
Newport *Essex* 58 D4
Newport *Glos.* 39 F3
Newport *High.* 183 G6
Newport *I.o.W.* 15 E4
Newport (Casnewydd) *Newport* 38 C4
Newport *Norf.* 87 G4
Newport (Trefdraeth) *Pembs.* 49 D4
Newport *Som.* 24 A5
Newport *Tel. & W.* 65 G1
Newport Pagnell 57 D3
Newport-on-Tay 152 C2
Newpound Common 29 F5
Newquay 4 C3
Newquay Cornwall Airport 4 C3
Newsbank 79 F1
Newseat 169 F1
Newsells 58 B4
Newsham *Lancs.* 100 B4
Newsham *N.Yorks.* 110 A1
Newsham *N.Yorks.* 110 C4
Newsham *Northumb.* 129 E4
Newsholme *E.Riding* 103 G5
Newsholme *Lancs.* 101 E2
Newsome 93 F1
Newstead *Northumb.* 137 F4
Newstead *Notts.* 81 G2
Newstead *Sc.Bord.* 135 G2
Newthorpe *N.Yorks.* 103 D4
Newthorpe *Notts.* 81 F3
Newtoft 96 A4
Newton *Aber.* 176 C6
Newton *Aber.* 177 J6
Newton *Arg. & B.* 148 C5
Newton *Bridgend* 37 E5
Newton *Cambs.* 70 C1
Newton *Cambs.* 58 C3
Newton *Cardiff* 38 B5
Newton *Ches.* 78 C2
Newton *Ches.* 91 G5
Newton *Cumb.* 106 D5
Newton *D. & G.* 125 F1
Newton *Derbys.* 81 F2
Newton *Gt.Man.* 93 D3
Newton *Here.* 52 C1
Newton *Here.* 53 E2
Newton *Here.* 52 C4
Newton *High.* 183 J3
Newton *High.* 174 E7
Newton *High.* 183 H3
Newton *High.* 180 E5
Newton *High.* 174 C6
Newton *High.* 174 E5
Newton *Lancs.* 100 C2
Newton *Lancs.* 107 G5
Newton *Lancs.* 99 G4
Newton *Lincs.* 83 F4
Newton *Moray* 176 B4
Newton *N.Ayr.* 140 A4
Newton *Norf.* 71 G1
Newton *Northants.* 69 D4
Newton *Northumb.* 119 G1
Newton *Northumb.* 128 B1
Newton *Notts.* 82 B3
Newton *P. & K.* 151 D1
Newton *Pembs.* 48 B5
Newton *Pembs.* 34 C2
Newton *S.Glos.* 39 F3
Newton *S.Lan.* 134 A2
Newton *Sc.Bord.* 136 A4
Newton *Shrop.* 78 B4
Newton *Som.* 23 E4
Newton *Staffs.* 80 B5
Newton *Suff.* 60 A3
Newton *Swan.* 36 C4
Newton *W.Loth.* 143 E2
Newton *W.Yorks.* 102 D5
Newton *Warks.* 68 A5
Newton *Wilts.* 26 D5
Newton Abbot 10 B5
Newton Arlosh 117 F1
Newton Aycliffe 120 B5
Newton Bewley 121 D5
Newton Blossomville 57 E2
Newton Bromswold 57 E1
Newton Burgoland 67 F2
Newton by Toft 96 A4
Newton Ferrers 8 B3
Newton Flotman 72 D2
Newton Green 39 E3
Newton Harcourt 68 B3
Newton Kyme 103 D3
Newton Longville 56 D4
Newton Mearns 141 G4
Newton Morrell *N.Yorks.* 110 B2
Newton Morrell *Oxon.* 56 B5
Newton Mountain 34 C2
Newton Mulgrave 111 G1
Newton of Affleck 152 C1
Newton of Ardtoe 155 F2
Newton of Balcanquhal 151 G3
Newton of Dalvey 175 H6
Newton of Falkland 152 A4
Newton of Leys 166 D1
Newton on the Hill 78 B5
Newton on Trent 95 F5
Newton Poppleford 11 D4
Newton Purcell 56 B4
Newton Regis 67 E2
Newton Reigny 118 A4
Newton St. Cyres 10 B3
Newton St. Faith 86 D4
Newton St. Loe 25 E1
Newton St. Petrock 21 E4
Newton Solney 81 D5
Newton Stacey 27 F3
Newton Stewart 123 F4
Newton Tony 26 D3
Newton Tracey 21 F3
Newton under Roseberry 111 E1
Newton Underwood 129 D3
Newton upon Derwent 103 G3
Newton Valence 28 C4
Newton with Scales 100 A4
Newtonairds 124 C2
Newtongrange 144 A3
Newtonhill 169 H5
Newton-le-Willows *Mersey.* 91 G3
Newton-le-Willows *N.Yorks.* 110 B4
Newtonmill 161 E3
Newtonmore 166 E5
Newton-on-Ouse 103 E2
Newton-on-Rawcliffe 112 B3
Newton-on-the-Moor 129 D1
Newtown *Bucks.* 43 E2
Newtown *Ches.* 78 C2
Newtown *Cornw.* 5 G2
Newtown *Cornw.* 2 C4
Newtown *Cumb.* 118 B1
Newtown *Derbys.* 93 D4
Newtown *Devon* 22 A5
Newtown *Devon* 11 D3
Newtown *Dorset* 12 A2
Newtown *Glos.* 39 F2
Newtown *Gt.Man.* 91 G2
Newtown *Gt.Man.* 92 B2
Newtown *Hants.* 15 F1
Newtown *Hants.* 27 F1
Newtown *Hants.* 14 B1
Newtown *Hants.* 27 E5
Newtown *Hants.* 15 E1
Newtown *Here.* 53 F3
Newtown *Here.* 53 D2
Newtown *High.* 165 K4
Newtown *I.o.M.* 98 B4
Newtown *I.o.W.* 14 D3
Newtown *Northumb.* 128 C1
Newtown *Northumb.* 137 E4
Newtown *Oxon.* 42 C4
Newtown (Y Drenewydd) *Powys* 64 A3
Newtown *R.C.T.* 37 G3
Newtown *Shrop.* 78 B4
Newtown *Som.* 23 F4
Newtown *Som.* 11 F1
Newtown *Staffs.* 79 G1
Newtown *Staffs.* 80 B1
Newtown *Staffs.* 66 B2
Newtown *Wilts.* 26 A5
Newtown *Wilts.* 27 E1
Newtown Linford 68 A2
Newtown St. Boswells 135 G2
Newtown Unthank 67 G2
Newtown-in-Saint-Martin 3 E4
Newtyle 160 A5
Newyears Green 43 F4
Neyland 34 C2
Nibley *Glos.* 39 F2
Nibley *S.Glos.* 39 F4
Nibley Green 39 G3
Nicholashayne 11 E1
Nicholaston 36 B4
Nidd 102 C1
Nigg *Aberdeen* 169 H4
Nigg *High.* 175 F4
Nightcott 22 B5
Nilig 76 D2
Nilston Rigg 119 E1
Nimlet 39 G5
Nine Ashes 45 E2
Nine Elms 40 D4
Nine Mile Burn 143 F4
Ninebanks 119 D2
Ninemile Bar (Crocketford) 124 C3
Nineveh 53 F1
Ninfield 18 C2
Ningwood 14 D4
Nisbet 136 A4
Niton 15 E5
Nitshill 141 G3
Nizels 31 E3
No Man's Heath *Ches.* 78 C3
No Man's Heath *Warks.* 67 E2
No Man's Land 5 G4
Noah's Ark 31 E3
Noak Hill 45 E3
Noblehill 125 D3
Noblethorpe 93 G2
Nobottle 56 B1
Nocton 83 F1
Noddsdale 140 D3
Nogdam End 87 E5
Noke 42 A1
Nolton 34 B1
Nolton Haven 34 B1
Nomansland *Devon* 10 B1
Nomansland *Wilts.* 14 B1
Noneley 78 B5
Nonington 33 E3
Nook *Cumb.* 126 C4
Nook *Cumb.* 107 G4
Noonsbrough 187 B7
Noranside 160 C3
Norbreck 99 G3
Norbury *Ches.* 78 C3
Norbury *Derbys.* 80 C3
Norbury *Gt.Lon.* 44 C5
Norbury *Shrop.* 64 C3
Norbury *Staffs.* 79 E5
Norbury Common 78 C3
Norbury Junction 79 E5
Norchard 35 D3
Norcott Brook 92 A4
Nordelph 71 D2
Norden *Dorset* 13 F4
Norden *Gt.Man.* 92 C1
Nordley 65 F3
Norham 145 G5
Norland Town 101 G5
Norley 91 G5
Norleywood 14 C3
Norlington 17 G2
Norman Cross 69 G3
Normanby *N.Lincs.* 95 F1
Normanby *N.Yorks.* 111 G4
Normanby *R. & C.* 111 E1
Normanby by Stow 95 F4
Normanby le Wold 96 B3
Normanby-by-Spital 96 A4
Normandy 29 E2
Normann's Ruh 154 D5
Norman's Bay 18 B3
Norman's Green 11 D2
Normanston 73 G2
Normanton *Derby* 81 E4
Normanton *Leics.* 82 D3
Normanton *Lincs.* 83 E3
Normanton *Notts.* 82 C2
Normanton *Rut.* 69 E2
Normanton *W.Yorks.* 102 C5
Normanton le Heath 67 F1
Normanton on Soar 81 G5
Normanton on Trent 82 C1
Normanton-on-the-Wolds 82 B4
Normoss 99 G4
Norrington Common 25 F1
Norris Green 8 A1
Norris Hill 67 F1
Norristhorpe 102 B5
North Acton 44 B4
North Anston 94 C4
North Ascot 29 E1
North Aston 55 G5
North Baddesley 14 C1
North Ballachulish 156 C3
North Balloch 123 E1
North Barrow 24 D5
North Barsham 86 A2
North Benfleet 45 G4
North Bersted 16 B3
North Berwick 144 C1
North Boarhunt 15 F1
North Bogbain 176 B5
North Bovey 10 A4
North Bradley 25 F2
North Brentor 7 E2
North Brewham 25 E4
North Bridge 29 E4
North Buckland 21 E1
North Burlingham 87 E4
North Cadbury 24 D5
North Cairn 122 A3
North Camp 29 D2
North Carlton *Lincs.* 95 G5
North Carlton *Notts.* 94 C4
North Cave 104 A4
North Cerney 40 C2
North Chailey 17 F1
North Charford 14 A1
North Charlton 137 F4
North Cheriton 25 D5
North Chideock 12 A3
North Cliffe 104 A4
North Clifton 95 F5
North Cockerington 97 D3
North Coker 12 B1
North Collafirth 186 C4
North Common *S.Glos.* 39 F5
North Common *Suff.* 72 A4
North Commonty 177 G6
North Connel 148 B1
North Coombe 10 B2
North Cornelly 37 E4
North Corner 39 F4
North Cotes 96 D2
North Cove 73 F3
North Cowton 110 B2
North Crawley 57 E3
North Cray 45 D5
North Creake 85 G4
North Curry 24 A5
North Dallens 156 B5
North Dalton 104 B2
North Dawn 185 D7
North Deighton 102 C2
North Dell (Dail Bho Thuath) 179 G1
North Duffield 103 F4
North Elkington 96 C3
North Elmham 86 A3
North Elmsall 94 B1
North End *Bucks.* 56 D5
North End *Dorset* 25 F5
North End *E.Riding* 105 D2
North End *E.Riding* 105 D3
North End *E.Riding* 105 E4
North End *Essex* 45 F1
North End *Hants.* 27 G5
North End *Hants.* 14 A1
North End *Leics.* 68 A1
North End *N.Som.* 24 B1
North End *Norf.* 72 B2
North End *Northumb.* 128 D1
North End *Ports.* 15 F2
North End *W.Suss.* 16 D2
North End *W.Suss.* 16 B3
North Erradale 172 D3
North Essie 177 J5
North Fambridge 46 B3
North Ferriby 104 B5
North Frodingham 104 D2
North Gorley 14 A1
North Green *Norf.* 72 D3
North Green *Suff.* 73 E4
North Green *Suff.* 61 E1
North Green *Suff.* 61 E1
North Grimston 104 A1
North Halling 31 G2
North Harby 95 F5
North Hayling 15 G2
North Hazelrigg 137 E3
North Heasley 22 A4
North Heath *W.Berks.* 41 G5
North Heath *W.Suss.* 29 F5
North Hill 5 G2
North Hillingdon 43 F4
North Hinksey 42 A2
North Holmwood 29 G3
North Houghton 27 E4
North Huish 8 D2
North Hykeham 83 E1
North Johnston 34 C1
North Kelsey 96 A2
North Kessock 174 D7
North Killingholme 96 B1
North Kilvington 110 D4
North Kilworth 68 B4
North Kingston 14 A2
North Kyme 83 G2
North Lancing 17 D3
North Lee 42 D2
North Lees 110 C5
North Leigh 41 F1
North Leverton with Habblesthorpe 95 E4
North Littleton 54 C3
North Lopham 72 B3

North Luffenham 69 E2
North Marden 16 A2
North Marston 56 C5
North Middleton *Midloth.* 144 A4
North Middleton *Northumb.* 137 E4
North Millbrex 177 G6
North Molton 22 A5
North Moreton 42 A4
North Mundham 16 A3
North Muskham 82 C2
North Newbald 104 B4
North Newington 55 G4
North Newnton 26 C2
North Newton 23 F4
North Nibley 39 G3
North Oakley 27 G2
North Ockendon 45 E4
North Ormesby 111 E1
North Ormsby 96 C3
North Otterington 110 C4
North Owersby 96 A3
North Perrott 12 A2
North Petherton 23 F4
North Petherwin 5 G1
North Pickenham 71 G2
North Piddle 54 B2
North Plain 125 F4
North Pool 9 D3
North Poorton 12 B3
North Quarme 22 C4
North Queensferry 143 F1
North Radworthy 22 A4
North Rauceby 83 F3
North Reston 97 D4
North Rigton 102 B3
North Rode 79 F1
North Roe 186 C4
North Ronaldsay 184 G2
North Runcton 71 E1
North Sandwick 186 E3
North Scale 99 E1
North Scarle 83 D1
North Seaton 129 E3
North Shian 156 B5
North Shields 120 C1
North Shoebury 46 C4
North Side 70 A3
North Skelton 111 F1
North Somercotes 97 E3
North Stainley 110 B5
North Stainmore 108 D1
North Stifford 45 F4
North Stoke *B. & N.E.Som.* 25 E1
North Stoke *Oxon.* 42 B4
North Stoke *W.Suss.* 16 C2
North Stoneham 14 D1
North Street *Hants.* 28 B4
North Street *Kent* 32 C3
North Street *Med.* 32 A1
North Street *W.Berks.* 42 B5
North Sunderland 137 G3
North Tamerton 6 D1
North Tarbothill 169 H3
North Tawton 21 G5
North Third 142 B1
North Thoresby 96 C3
North Tidworth 26 D3
North Togston 129 E1
North Town *Devon* 21 F5
North Town *Hants.* 29 D2
North Town *W. & M.* 43 D4
North Tuddenham 86 B4
North Uist (Uibhist a Tuath) 170 D4
North Walsham 87 D2
North Waltham 27 G3
North Warnborough 28 C2
North Water Bridge 161 E3
North Watten 183 H3
North Weald Bassett 45 D2
North Wembley 44 A4
North Wheatley 95 E4
North Whilborough 9 E1
North Wick 24 C1
North Widcombe 24 C2
North Willingham 96 B4
North Wingfield 81 F1
North Witham 83 E5
North Wootton *Dorset* 12 C1
North Wootton *Norf.* 85 E5
North Wootton *Som.* 24 C3
North Wraxall 40 A5
North Wroughton 40 D4
North Yardhope 128 B1
Northacre 72 A2
Northall 57 E5
Northall Green 86 A4
Northallerton 110 C3
Northam *Devon* 21 E3
Northam *S'ham.* 14 D1
Northampton 56 C1
Northaw 44 B2
Northay *Devon* 11 G2
Northay *Som.* 11 F1
Northbay 162 C4
Northbeck 83 F3
Northborough 69 G2
Northbourne *Kent* 33 F3
Northbourne *Oxon.* 42 A4
Northbridge Street 18 C1
Northbrook *Hants.* 27 G4
Northbrook *Oxon.* 55 G5
Northburnhill 177 G6
Northchapel 29 E5
Northchurch 43 E2
Northcote Manor 21 G4
Northcott 6 D1
Northcourt 42 A3
Northdyke 184 B5
Northedge 81 E1
Northend *B. & N.E.Som.* 25 E1
Northend *Bucks.* 42 C3
Northend *Warks.* 55 F2
Northfield *Aber.* 177 G4
Northfield *Aberdeen* 169 H4
Northfield *High.* 183 J4
Northfield *Hull* 104 C5
Northfield *Sc.Bord.* 145 G3
Northfield *Som.* 23 F4
Northfield *W.Mid.* 66 C5
Northfields 69 F2
Northfleet 45 F5
Northhouse 135 F5
Northiam 18 D1
Northill 57 G3
Northington *Glos.* 39 G2
Northington *Hants.* 27 G4
Northlands 84 B2
Northleach 40 D1
Northleigh *Devon* 11 E3
Northleigh *Devon* 21 G2
Northlew 7 F1
Northmoor 41 G2
Northmoor Green (Moorland) 24 A4
Northmuir 160 B4
Northney 15 G2
Northolt 44 A4
Northop 77 F1
Northop Hall 77 F1
Northorpe *Lincs.* 84 A4
Northorpe *Lincs.* 95 F3
Northorpe *Lincs.* 69 F1
Northover *Som.* 24 C5
Northover *Som.* 24 B4
Northowram 102 A5
Northport 13 F4
Northpunds 187 D10
Northrepps 86 D2
Northton (Taobh Tuath) 170 E3
Northtown 185 D8
Northway *Glos.* 54 B4
Northway *Som.* 23 E5
Northwich 92 A5
Northwick *S.Glos.* 39 E4
Northwick *Som.* 24 A3
Northwick *Worcs.* 54 A2
Northwold 71 F3
Northwood *Gt.Lon.* 43 F3
Northwood *I.o.W.* 15 D3
Northwood *Kent* 33 F2
Northwood *Mersey.* 91 F3
Northwood *Shrop.* 78 B4
Northwood Green 39 G1
Northwood Hills 44 A3
Norton *Glos.* 54 A5
Norton *Halton* 91 G4
Norton *Herts.* 58 A4
Norton *I.o.W.* 14 C4
Norton *Mon.* 52 D5
Norton *N.Som.* 24 A1
Norton *N.Yorks.* 111 G5
Norton *Northants.* 56 B1
Norton *Notts.* 94 C5
Norton *Powys* 52 C1
Norton *S.Yorks.* 94 C1
Norton *S.Yorks.* 94 A4
Norton *Shrop.* 65 E2
Norton *Shrop.* 65 G2
Norton *Shrop.* 65 D4
Norton *Stock.* 120 D5
Norton *Suff.* 60 A1
Norton *Swan.* 36 C4
Norton *V. of Glam.* 37 E5
Norton *W.Mid.* 66 A4
Norton *W.Suss.* 16 B3
Norton *W.Suss.* 16 A4
Norton *Wilts.* 40 A4
Norton *Worcs.* 54 A2
Norton *Worcs.* 54 C3
Norton Bavant 26 A3
Norton Bridge 79 F4
Norton Canes 66 C2
Norton Canon 52 C3
Norton Disney 83 D2
Norton Ferris 25 E4
Norton Fitzwarren 23 E5
Norton Green *Herts.* 58 A5
Norton Green *I.o.W.* 14 C4
Norton Green *Stoke* 79 G2
Norton Hawkfield 24 C1
Norton Heath 45 F2
Norton in Hales 79 E4
Norton in the Moors 79 F2
Norton Lindsey 55 E1
Norton Little Green 60 A1
Norton Malreward 24 D1
Norton Mandeville 45 E2
Norton St. Philip 25 E2
Norton Subcourse 73 F2
Norton Wood 52 C3
Norton Woodseats 94 A4
Norton-Juxta-Twycross 67 F2
Norton-le-Clay 110 D5
Norton-sub-Hamdon 12 A1
Norwell 82 C1
Norwell Woodhouse 82 C1
Norwich 86 D5
Norwich Airport 86 D4
Norwick 186 F1
Norwood End 45 E2
Norwood Green *Gt.Lon.* 44 A5
Norwood Green *W.Yorks.* 102 A5
Norwood Hill 30 B4
Norwood Park 24 C4
Noseley 68 C3
Noss Mayo 8 B3
Nosterfield 110 B4
Nosterfield End 59 E3
Nostie 164 E2
Notgrove 54 D5
Nottage 37 E5
Notting Hill 44 B4
Nottingham *High.* 183 H5
Nottingham *Nott.* 81 G3
Nottingham East Midlands Airport 81 F5
Nottington 12 C4
Notton *W.Yorks.* 94 A1
Notton *Wilts.* 26 A1
Nottswood Hill 39 G1
Nounsley 45 G1
Noutard's Green 53 G1
Nowton 59 G1
Nox 64 D1
Noyadd Trefawr 49 F3
Nuffield 42 B4
Nun Monkton 103 E2
Nunburnholme 104 A3
Nuneaton 67 F3
Nuneham Courtenay 42 A3
Nunney 25 E3
Nunnington *Here.* 53 E3
Nunnington *N.Yorks.* 111 F5
Nunnington Park 23 D5
Nunnykirk 128 C2
Nunsthorpe 96 C2
Nunthorpe *Middbro.* 111 E1
Nunthorpe *York* 103 E2
Nunton 26 C5
Nunwick *N.Yorks.* 110 C5
Nunwick *Northumb.* 128 A4
Nup End 44 B1
Nupend 39 G2
Nursling 14 C1
Nursted 28 C5
Nurton 66 A3
Nutbourne *W.Suss.* 16 C2
Nutbourne *W.Suss.* 15 G2
Nutfield 30 C3
Nuthall 81 G3
Nuthampstead 58 C4
Nuthurst *W.Suss.* 29 G5
Nuthurst *Warks.* 67 D5
Nutley *E.Suss.* 17 G1
Nutley *Hants.* 28 B3
Nutwell 94 D2
Nyadd 150 C5
Nybster 183 J2
Nyetimber 16 A4
Nyewood 28 C5
Nymet Rowland 10 A2
Nymet Tracey 10 A2
Nympsfield 40 A2
Nynehead 23 E5
Nythe 24 B4
Nyton 16 B3

▼O

Oad Street 32 A2
Oadby 68 B2
Oak Cross 7 F1
Oak Tree 110 C1
Oakamoor 80 B3
Oakbank *Arg. & B.* 147 G1
Oakbank *W.Loth.* 143 E3
Oakdale *Caerp.* 38 A3
Oakdale *Poole* 13 G3
Oake 23 E5
Oaken 66 A2
Oakenclough 100 B3
Oakengates 65 G1
Oakenhead 175 K5
Oakenholt 91 D5
Oakenshaw *Dur.* 120 B4
Oakenshaw *W.Yorks.* 102 A5
Oakerthorpe 81 E2
Oakes 93 F1
Oakfield *I.o.W.* 15 E3
Oakfield *Torfaen* 38 B3
Oakford *Cere.* 50 A2
Oakford *Devon* 22 C5
Oakfordbridge 22 C5
Oakgrove 79 G1
Oakham 69 D2
Oakhanger 28 C4
Oakhill 24 D3
Oakington 58 C1
Oaklands *Conwy* 76 B2
Oaklands *Herts.* 44 B1
Oakle Street 39 G1
Oakley *Beds.* 57 F2
Oakley *Bucks.* 42 B1
Oakley *Fife* 143 E1
Oakley *Hants.* 27 G2
Oakley *Oxon.* 42 C2
Oakley *Poole* 13 G3
Oakley *Suff.* 72 C4
Oakley Green 43 E5
Oakley Park 63 F4
Oakridge Lynch 40 B2
Oaks 64 D2
Oaks Green 80 C4
Oaksey 40 B3
Oakshaw Ford 126 D4
Oakshott 28 C5
Oakthorpe 67 F1
Oaktree Hill 110 C3
Oakwoodhill 29 G4
Oakworth 101 G4
Oare *Kent* 32 C2
Oare *Som.* 22 B3
Oare *Wilts.* 26 C1
Oasby 83 F4
Oatfield 130 B4
Oath 24 A5
Oathlaw 160 C4
Oatlands 102 C2
Oban 148 A2
Obley 64 C5
Oborne 12 C1
Obthorpe 69 F1
Occlestone Green 79 D1
Occold 72 C4
Occumster 183 H5
Ochiltree 132 D3
Ochr-y-foel 90 B5
Ochtermuthill 150 D3
Ochtertyre *P. & K.* 150 D2
Ochtertyre *Stir.* 150 C5
Ockbrook 81 F4
Ockeridge 53 G1
Ockham 29 F2
Ockle 155 E2
Ockley 29 G4
Ocle Pychard 53 E3
Octon 112 D5
Odcombe 12 B1
Odd Down 25 E1
Oddendale 108 B1
Oddingley 54 B2
Oddington 42 A1
Oddsta 186 E3
Odell 57 E2
Odham 21 E5
Odie 184 F5
Odiham 28 C2
Odsey 58 A4
Odstock 26 C5
Odstone 67 F2
Offchurch 55 F1
Offenham 54 C3
Offerton 92 D4
Offham *E.Suss.* 17 F2
Offham *Kent* 31 F3
Offham *W.Suss.* 16 C3
Offley Hoo 57 G5
Offleymarsh 79 E5
Offord Cluny 58 A1
Offord D'Arcy 58 A1
Offton 60 B3
Offwell 11 E3
Ogbourne Maizey 41 D5
Ogbourne St. Andrew 41 D5
Ogbourne St. George 41 D5
Ogil 160 C3
Ogle 128 D4
Oglet 91 F4
Ogmore 37 E5
Ogmore Vale 37 F3
Ogmore-by-Sea 37 E5
Oil Terminal 185 C8
Okeford Fitzpaine 13 E1
Okehampton 7 F1
Okehampton Camp 7 F1
Okraquoy 187 D9
Olchard 10 B5
Olchfa 36 C3
Old 68 C5
Old Aberdeen 169 H4
Old Alresford 27 G4
Old Arley 67 E3
Old Basford 81 G3
Old Basing 28 B2
Old Belses 135 G3
Old Bewick 137 E4
Old Blair 159 D3
Old Bolingbroke 84 B1
Old Bramhope 102 B3
Old Brampton 94 A5
Old Bridge of Urr 124 B4
Old Buckenham 72 B2
Old Burdon 120 C2
Old Burghclere 27 F2
Old Byland 111 E4
Old Cassop 120 C4
Old Church Stoke 64 B3
Old Cleeve 22 D3
Old Clipstone 82 B1
Old Colwyn 89 G5
Old Craig 169 H2
Old Craighall 144 A2
Old Crombie 176 D5
Old Dailly 122 D1
Old Dalby 82 B5
Old Dam 93 F5
Old Deer 177 H6
Old Dilton 25 F3
Old Down *S.Glos.* 39 F4
Old Down *Som.* 24 D2
Old Edlington 94 C3
Old Eldon 120 B5
Old Ellerby 105 D4
Old Felixstowe 61 E4
Old Fletton 69 G3
Old Ford 44 C4
Old Glossop 93 E3
Old Goginan 62 C4
Old Goole 103 G5
Old Gore 53 F5
Old Grimsby 4 A1
Old Hall 96 C1
Old Hall Green 58 B5
Old Hall Street 87 E2
Old Harlow 45 D1
Old Heath 60 B5
Old Heathfield 18 A1
Old Hill 66 B4
Old Hurst 70 B5
Old Hutton 107 G4
Old Kea 4 C5
Old Kilpatrick 141 F2
Old Kinnernie 169 F4
Old Knebworth 58 A5
Old Leake 84 C2
Old Leslie 168 D2
Old Malton 112 B5
Old Milton 14 B3
Old Milverton 55 E1
Old Montsale 46 D3
Old Netley 15 D1
Old Newton 60 B1
Old Philpstoun 143 E2
Old Poltalloch 148 A4
Old Radnor (Pencraig) 52 B2
Old Rattray 177 J5
Old Rayne 168 E2
Old Romney 19 F1
Old Scone 151 G2
Old Shields 142 C2
Old Sodbury 39 G4
Old Somerby 83 E4
Old Stratford 56 C3
Old Sunderlandwick 104 C2
Old Swarland 129 D1
Old Swinford 66 B4
Old Thirsk 110 D4
Old Town *Cumb.* 107 G4
Old Town *I.o.S.* 4 B1
Old Town Farm 128 A2
Old Tupton 81 E1
Old Warden 57 G3
Old Weston 69 F5
Old Windsor 43 E5
Old Wives Lees 32 C3
Old Woking 29 F2
Old Woodhall 84 A1
Old Woods 78 B5
Oldberrow 54 D1
Oldborough 10 A2
Oldbury *Kent* 31 E3
Oldbury *Shrop.* 65 G3
Oldbury *W.Mid.* 66 B4
Oldbury *Warks.* 67 F3
Oldbury Naite 39 F3
Oldbury on the Hill 40 A4
Oldbury-on-Severn 39 F3
Oldcastle *Bridgend* 37 F5
Oldcastle *Mon.* 52 C5
Oldcastle Heath 78 B3
Oldcotes 94 C4
Oldcroft 39 F2
Oldeamere 70 B3
Oldfield 54 A1
Oldford 25 E2
Oldhall *Aber.* 168 C5
Oldhall *High.* 183 H3
Oldham 92 D2
Oldham Edge 92 D2
Oldhamstocks 145 E2
Oldland 39 F5
Oldmeldrum 169 G2
Oldmill 168 D4
Oldpark 65 F2
Oldridge 10 B3
Oldshore Beg 180 D3
Oldshoremore 180 E3
Oldstead 111 E5
Oldtown 174 C3
Oldtown of Aigas 174 B7
Oldtown of Ord 176 E5
Oldwalls 36 A3
Oldways End 22 B5
Oldwhat 177 G5
Oldwich Lane 67 E5
Olgrinmore 183 G3
Oliver 134 C3
Oliver's Battery 27 F5
Ollaberry 186 C4
Ollerton *Ches.* 92 B5
Ollerton *Notts.* 82 B1
Ollerton *Shrop.* 79 D5
Olmstead Green 59 E3
Olney 57 D2
Olrig House 183 G2
Olton 66 D4
Olveston 39 F4
Ombersley 54 A1
Ompton 82 B1
Onchan 98 B4
Onecote 80 B2
Onehouse 60 B2
Ongar Hill 85 D5
Ongar Street 52 C1
Onibury 65 D5
Onich 156 C3
Onllwyn 37 E1
Onneley 79 E3
Onslow Green 45 F1
Onslow Village 29 E3
Opinan *High.* 172 E2
Opinan *High.* 172 D4
Orange Lane 145 E5
Orasaigh 179 F6
Orbliston 176 B5
Orbost 171 H7
Orby 84 C1
Orcadia 140 C3
Orchard 140 C1
Orchard Portman 23 F5
Orcheston 26 B3
Orcop 53 D5
Orcop Hill 53 D5
Ord 164 C3
Ordhead 168 E3
Ordie 168 C4
Ordiequish 176 B5
Ordsall 95 D5
Ore 18 D2
Oreham Common 17 E2
Oreston 8 B2
Oreton 65 F5
Orford *Suff.* 61 F3
Orford *Warr.* 92 A3
Organford 13 F3
Orgreave 66 D1
Orlestone 32 B5
Orleton *Here.* 53 D1
Orleton *Worcs.* 53 F1
Orleton Common 53 D1
Orlingbury 69 D5
Ormacleit 162 C1
Ormesby 111 E1
Ormesby St. Margaret 87 F4
Ormesby St. Michael 87 F4
Ormidale 140 B1
Ormiscaig 172 E2
Ormiston 144 B3
Ormlie 183 G2
Ormsaigmore 155 D3
Ormsary 139 F2
Ormskirk 91 F2
Oronsay 138 B1
Orphir 185 C7
Orpington 31 D2
Orrell *Gt.Man.* 91 G2
Orrell *Mersey.* 91 E3
Orrisdale 98 B2
Orrok House 169 H3
Orroland 116 A2
Orsett 45 F4
Orsett Heath 45 F4
Orslow 66 A1
Orston 82 C3
Orton *Cumb.* 108 B2
Orton *Northants.* 68 D5
Orton Longueville 69 G3
Orton Rigg 117 G1
Orton Waterville 69 G3
Orton-on-the-Hill 67 F2
Orwell 58 B2
Osbaldeston 100 C4
Osbaldwick 103 F2
Osbaston *Leics.* 67 G2
Osbaston *Shrop.* 78 A5
Osbaston *Tel. & W.* 65 E1
Osbaston Hollow 67 G2
Osborne 15 E3
Osbournby 83 F4
Oscroft 78 C1
Ose 171 J7
Osgathorpe 67 G1
Osgodby *Lincs.* 96 A3
Osgodby *N.Yorks.* 103 F4
Osgodby *N.Yorks.* 113 D4
Oskaig 164 B1
Osleston 80 D4
Osmaston *Derby* 81 E4
Osmaston *Derbys.* 80 C3
Osmington 12 D4
Osmington Mills 12 D4
Osmondthorpe 102 C4
Osmotherley 111 D3
Osnaburgh (Dairsie) 152 C3
Ospringe 32 C2
Ossett 102 B5
Ossett Street Side 102 B5
Ossington 82 C1
Ostend 46 C3
Osterley 44 A5
Oswaldkirk 111 F5
Oswaldtwistle 100 D5
Oswestry 77 F5
Oteley 78 B4
Otford 31 E3
Otham 31 G3
Otherton 66 B1
Othery 24 A4
Otley *Suff.* 60 D2
Otley *W.Yorks.* 102 B3
Otter 140 A2
Otter Ferry 140 A1
Otterbourne 27 F5
Otterburn *N.Yorks.* 101 E2
Otterburn *Northumb.* 128 A2
Otterburn Camp 128 A2
Otterden Place 32 B3
Otterham 6 B1
Otterham Quay 32 A2
Otterhampton 23 F3
Otternish 170 E4
Ottershaw 29 F1
Otterswick 186 E4
Otterton 11 D4
Otterwood 14 D2
Ottery St. Mary 11 D3
Ottinge 33 D4
Ottringham 105 E5
Oughterby 117 F1
Oughtershaw 109 D4
Oughterside 117 E2
Oughtibridge 94 A3
Oulston 111 E5
Oulton *Cumb.* 117 F1
Oulton *Norf.* 86 C3
Oulton *Staffs.* 79 G4
Oulton *Staffs.* 79 E5
Oulton *Suff.* 73 G2
Oulton *W.Yorks.* 102 C5
Oulton Broad 73 G2
Oulton Grange 79 G4
Oulton Street 86 C3
Oultoncross 79 G4
Oundle 69 F4
Ousby 118 C4
Ousdale 183 F6
Ousden 59 F2
Ousefleet 104 A5
Ouston *Dur.* 120 B2
Ouston *Northumb.* 128 C4
Out Newton 105 F5
Out Rawcliffe 100 A3
Outcast 107 E5
Outchester 137 F3
Outertown 185 B6
Outgate 107 E3
Outhgill 108 C2
Outlands 79 E5
Outlane 93 E1
Outwell 70 D2
Outwood *Surr.* 30 C4
Outwood *W.Yorks.* 102 C5
Outwoods 65 G1
Ouzlewell Green 102 C5
Ovenden 101 G5
Over *Cambs.* 70 B5
Over *Ches.* 78 D1
Over *Glos.* 40 A1
Over *S.Glos.* 39 E4
Over Burrows 81 D4
Over Compton 12 B1
Over Dinsdale 110 C1
Over End 93 G5
Over Green 67 D3
Over Haddon 80 D1
Over Hulton 92 A2
Over Kellet 100 B1
Over Kiddington 55 G5
Over Monnow 39 D1
Over Norton 55 F5
Over Peover 92 B5
Over Rankeilour 152 B3
Over Silton 111 D3
Over Stowey 23 E4
Over Stratton 12 A1
Over Tabley 92 B4
Over Wallop 27 D4
Over Whitacre 67 E3
Over Winchendon (Upper Winchendon) 42 C1
Over Worton 55 G5
Overbister 184 F3
Overbrae 177 G5
Overbury 54 B4
Overcombe 12 C4
Overgreen 94 A5
Overleigh 24 B4
Overpool 91 E5
Overscaig Hotel 181 G6
Overseal 67 E1
Overslade 67 G5
Oversland 32 C3
Oversley Green 54 C2
Overstone 56 D1
Overstrand 87 D1
Overthorpe 55 G3
Overton *Aber.* 169 F3
Overton *Aberdeen* 169 G3
Overton *Ches.* 91 G5
Overton *Hants.* 27 G3
Overton *Lancs.* 100 A2
Overton *N.Yorks.* 103 E2
Overton *Shrop.* 65 E5
Overton *Swan.* 36 A4
Overton *W.Yorks.* 93 G1
Overton *Wrex.* 78 A3
Overton Bridge 78 A3
Overtown *Lancs.* 108 B5
Overtown *N.Lan.* 142 C4
Overtown *Swin.* 41 D5
Overy 42 A3
Oving *Bucks.* 56 C5
Oving *W.Suss.* 16 B3
Ovingdean 17 F3
Ovingham 119 G1
Ovington *Dur.* 110 A1
Ovington *Essex* 59 F3
Ovington *Hants.* 27 G4
Ovington *Norf.* 86 A5
Ovington *Northumb.* 119 G1
Ower *Hants.* 14 C1
Ower *Hants.* 15 D2
Owermoigne 13 D4
Owler Bar 93 G5
Owlpen 39 G3
Owl's Green 61 D1
Owlswick 42 C2
Owmby 96 A2
Owmby-by-Spital 96 A4
Owslebury 27 G5
Owston 68 C2
Owston Ferry 95 F2
Owstwick 105 E4
Owthorpe 82 B4
Oxborough 71 F2
Oxcliffe Hill 100 A1
Oxcombe 96 D5
Oxen End 59 E5
Oxen Park 107 E4
Oxencombe 10 B4
Oxenhall 53 G5
Oxenholme 107 G3
Oxenhope 101 G4
Oxenpill 24 B3
Oxenton 54 B4
Oxenwood 27 E2
Oxford 42 A2
Oxhey 44 A3
Oxhill 55 F3
Oxley 66 B2
Oxley Green 46 C1
Oxley's Green 18 B1
Oxnam 136 B5
Oxnead 86 D3
Oxnop Ghyll 109 E3
Oxshott 29 G1
Oxspring 93 G2
Oxted 30 C3
Oxton *Mersey.* 91 E4
Oxton *Notts.* 82 B2
Oxton *Sc.Bord.* 144 B4
Oxwich 36 A4
Oxwich Green 36 A4
Oxwick 86 A3
Oykel Bridge 173 K1
Oyne 168 E2
Ozleworth 39 G3

▼P

Pabail Iarach (Lower Bayble) 179 H4
Pabail Uarach (Upper Bayble) 179 H4
Pabbay 170 E3
Packington 67 F1
Packwood 67 D5
Padanaram 160 C4
Padbury 56 C4
Paddington 44 B4
Paddlesworth 33 D4
Paddock 32 B3
Paddock Wood 31 F4
Paddockhaugh 175 K6
Paddockhole 126 A3
Paddolgreen 78 C4
Padeswood 77 F1
Padfield 93 E3
Padiham 101 D4
Padside 102 A2
Padstow 4 D2
Padworth 28 B1
Paganhill 40 A2
Pagham 16 A4
Paglesham Churchend 46 C3
Paglesham Eastend 46 C3
Paible 171 F2
Paignton 9 E1
Pailton 67 G4
Paine's Corner 18 B1
Painscastle 52 A3
Painshawfield 119 G1
Painswick 40 A2
Pairc 178 E3
Paisley 141 F3
Pakefield 73 G2
Pakenham 60 A1
Pale 76 C4
Palehouse Common 17 G2
Palestine 27 D3
Paley Street 43 D5
Palgowan 123 E2
Palgrave 72 C4
Pallinsburn House 136 C3
Palmarsh 32 D5
Palmers Cross 29 F3
Palmers Green 44 C3
Palmerscross 175 K5
Palmerstown 38 A5
Palnackie 124 C5
Palnure 123 F4
Palterton 81 F1
Pamber End 28 B2
Pamber Green 28 B2
Pamber Heath 28 B1
Pamington 54 B4
Pamphill 13 F3
Pampisford 58 C3
Pan 185 C8
Panborough 24 B3
Panbride 153 D1
Pancrasweek 20 C5
Pancross 22 D1
Pandy *Gwyn.* 62 C2
Pandy *Mon.* 52 C5
Pandy *Powys* 63 F2
Pandy *Wrex.* 77 E4
Pandy Tudur 76 B1
Pandy'r Capel 77 D2
Panfield 59 F5
Pangbourne 42 B5
Pannal 102 C2
Pannal Ash 102 B2
Panshanger 44 B1
Pant 77 F5
Pant Glas 75 D3
Pant Gwyn 76 B5
Pant Mawr 63 E4
Pantasaph 90 C5
Panteg 38 C3
Pantglas 63 D3
Pantgwyn *Carmar.* 50 B5
Pantgwyn *Cere.* 49 F3
Pant-lasau 36 C2
Panton 96 B5
Pant-pastynog 76 D1
Pantperthog 62 D2
Pant-y-dwr 63 F5
Pantyffordd 77 F2
Pant-y-ffridd 64 A2
Pantyffynnon 36 C1
Pantygasseg 38 B3
Pantygelli 38 C1
Pantymwyn 77 E1
Panxworth 87 E4
Papa Stour 187 A6
Papa Westray 184 D2
Papcastle 117 E3
Papil 187 C9
Papple 144 C2
Papplewick 81 G2
Papworth Everard 58 A1
Papworth St. Agnes 58 A1
Par 5 E4
Parbold 91 F1
Parbrook *Som.* 24 C4
Parbrook *W.Suss.* 29 F5
Parc 76 B4
Parcllyn 49 F2
Parcrhydderch 50 C2
Parc-Seymour 38 D3

Parc-y-rhôs 50 B3
Pardshaw 117 D4
Parham 61 E1
Parish Holm 133 F3
Park 176 D5
Park Close 101 E3
Park Corner *E.Suss.* 31 E5
Park Corner *Oxon.* 42 B4
Park End *Northumb.* 128 A4
Park End *Staffs.* 79 E2
Park End *Worcs.* 65 G5
Park Gate *Hants.* 15 E2
Park Gate *W.Yorks.* 102 A3
Park Gate *W.Yorks.* 93 G1
Park Gate *Worcs.* 66 B5
Park Green 60 C1
Park Hill 94 A4
Park Lane 78 B4
Park Langley 30 C2
Park Street 44 A2
Parkend *Cumb.* 117 G3
Parkend *Glos.* 39 F2
Parker's Green 31 F4
Parkeston 60 D4
Parkfield *Cornw.* 6 D4
Parkfield *S.Glos.* 39 F5
Parkfield *W.Mid.* 66 B3
Parkford 160 C4
Parkgate *Ches.* 91 D5
Parkgate *D. & G.* 125 E2
Parkgate *Kent* 32 A5
Parkgate *S.Yorks.* 94 B3
Parkgate *Surr.* 30 B4
Parkham 21 D3
Parkham Ash 21 D3
Parkhead 142 A3
Parkhill *Angus* 161 E5
Parkhill *P. & K.* 159 G5
Parkhouse 39 D2
Parkhurst 15 D3
Parkmill 36 B4
Parkmore 176 B6
Parkneuk 161 F2
Parkside 78 A2
Parkstone 13 G3
Parkway 24 C5
Parley Cross 13 G3
Parley Green 14 A3
Parlington 102 D4
Parracombe 21 G1
Parrog 48 D4
Parson Cross 94 A3
Parson Drove 70 B2
Parsonage Green 45 F1
Parsonby 117 E3
Partick 141 G3
Partington 92 B3
Partney 84 C1
Parton *Cumb.* 116 C4
Parton *D. & G.* 124 A3
Partridge Green 17 D2
Parwich 80 C2
Paslow Wood Common 45 E2
Passenham 56 C4
Passfield 28 D4
Passingford Bridge 45 E3
Paston 87 E2
Paston Street 87 E2
Pasturefields 79 G5
Patchacott 7 E1
Patcham 17 F3
Patchetts Green 44 A3
Patching 16 C3
Patchole 21 G1
Patchway 39 F4
Pateley Bridge 102 A1
Path of Condie 151 F3
Pathe 24 A4
Pathfinder Village 10 B3
Pathhead *Aber.* 161 F3
Pathhead *E.Ayr.* 133 E4
Pathhead *Fife* 152 A5
Pathhead *Midloth.* 144 A3
Pathlow 55 D2
Patmore Heath 58 C5
Patna 132 C4
Patney 26 B2
Patrick 98 A3
Patrick Brompton 110 B3
Patrington 105 F5
Patrington Haven 105 F5
Patrishow 52 B5
Patrixbourne 33 D3
Patterdale 117 G5
Pattingham 66 A3
Pattishall 56 B2
Pattiswick 59 G5
Paul 2 B4
Paulerspury 56 C3
Paull 105 D5
Paull Holme 105 D5
Paul's Green 2 D3
Paulton 25 D2
Pauperhaugh 128 C2
Pave Lane 65 G1
Pavenham 57 E2
Pawlett 24 A3
Pawston 136 C3
Paxford 55 D4
Paxhill Park 17 F1
Paxton 145 G4
Payden Street 32 B3
Payhembury 11 D2
Paythorne 101 E2
Peacehaven 17 G3
Peacemarsh 25 F5
Peachley 54 A2
Peak Dale 93 E5
Peak Forest 93 F5
Peakirk 69 G2
Pean Hill 32 D2
Pear Tree 81 E4
Pearsie 160 B4
Pearson's Green 31 F4
Peartree 44 B1
Peartree Green *Essex* 45 E3
Peartree Green *Here.* 53 F4
Pease Pottage 30 B5
Peasedown St. John 25 E2
Peasehill 81 F3
Peaseland Green 86 B4
Peasemore 41 G5
Peasenhall 61 E1
Peaslake 29 F3
Peasley Cross 91 G3
Peasmarsh *E.Suss.* 19 D1
Peasmarsh *Surr.* 29 E3
Peaston 144 B3
Peastonbank 144 B3
Peat Inn 152 C4
Peathill 177 H4
Peathrow 120 A5
Peatling Magna 68 A3
Peatling Parva 68 A4
Peaton 65 E4
Pebble Coombe 30 B3
Pebmarsh 59 G4
Pebworth 54 D3
Pecket Well 101 F5
Peckforton 78 C2
Peckham 44 C5
Peckleton 67 G2
Pedham 87 E4
Pedmore 66 B4
Pedwell 24 B4
Peebles 143 G5
Peel *I.o.M.* 98 A3
Peel *Lancs.* 99 G4
Peening Quarter 19 D1
Peggs Green 67 G1
Pegsdon 57 G4
Pegswood 129 E3
Pegwell 33 F2
Peighinn nan Aoireann 162 C1
Peinchorran 164 B1
Peinlich 171 K6
Pelaw 120 B1
Pelcomb 34 C1
Pelcomb Bridge 34 C1
Pelcomb Cross 34 C1
Peldon 46 C1
Pellon 101 G5
Pelsall 66 C2
Pelton 120 B2
Pelutho 117 E2
Pelynt 5 G4
Pemberton 91 G2
Pembrey (Pen-bre) 36 A2
Pembridge 52 C2
Pembroke (Penfro) 34 C2
Pembroke Dock (Doc Penfro) 34 C2
Pembury 31 F4
Penallt 39 E1
Penally 35 E3
Penalt 53 E5
Penare 5 D5
Penarran 64 A4
Penarth 38 A5
Pen-bont Rhydybeddau 62 C4
Penboyr 49 G4
Pen-bre (Pembrey) 36 A2
Penbryn 49 F2
Pencader 50 A4
Pen-cae 50 A2
Pen-cae-cwm 76 C1
Pencaenewydd 74 D3
Pencaitland 144 B3
Pencarnisiog 88 B5
Pencarreg 50 B3
Pencarrow 5 F1
Pencelli 51 G5
Pen-clawdd 36 B3
Pencoed 37 F4
Pencombe 53 E2
Pencoyd 53 E5
Pencraig *Here.* 53 E5
Pencraig *Powys* 76 D5
Pencraig (Old Radnor) *Powys* 52 B2
Pendeen 2 A3
Penderyn 37 F2
Pendine (Pentywyn) 35 F2
Pendlebury 92 B2
Pendleton 101 D4
Pendock 53 G4
Pendoggett 5 E2
Pendomer 12 B1
Pendoylan 37 G5
Penegoes 63 D2
Penelewey 4 C5
Pen-ffordd 49 D5
Penffordd-las (Staylittle) 63 E3
Penfro (Pembroke) 34 C2
Pengam 38 A3
Penge 44 C5
Pengenffordd 52 A5
Pengorffwysfa 88 C3
Pengover Green 5 G3
Pen-groes-oped 38 C2
Pengwern 90 B5
Penhale 3 D5
Penhallow 4 B4
Penhalvean 3 E3
Penhelig 62 C3
Penhill 41 D4
Penhow 38 D3
Penhurst 18 B2
Peniarth 62 C2
Penicuik 143 G3
Peniel 50 A5
Penifiler 171 K7
Peninver 130 C3
Penisa'r Waun 75 E1
Penisarcwn 63 G1
Penishawain 51 G4
Penistone 93 G2
Penjerrick 3 E3
Penketh 91 G4
Penkill 122 D1
Penkridge 66 B1
Penlean 6 C1
Penley 78 B4
Penllech 74 B4
Penllergaer 36 C3
Pen-llyn *I.o.A.* 88 B4
Penllyn *V. of Glam.* 37 F5
Pen-lôn 74 D1
Penmachno 76 A2
Penmaen 36 B4
Penmaenan 89 F5
Penmaenmawr 89 F5
Penmaenpool 62 C1
Penmaen-Rhôs 89 G5
Penmark 23 D1
Penmon 89 E4
Penmorfa 75 E3
Penmynydd 88 D5
Penn *Bucks.* 43 E3
Penn *W.Mid.* 66 A3
Penn Street 43 E3
Pennal 62 C2
Pennal-isaf 62 D2
Pennan 177 G4
Pennance 4 B5
Pennant *Cere.* 50 B1
Pennant *Powys* 63 E3
Pennant Melangell 76 D5
Pennar 34 C2
Pennard 36 B4
Pennerley 64 C3
Penninghame 123 E4
Pennington *Cumb.* 107 D5
Pennington *Hants.* 14 C3
Pennington Green 92 A2
Pennorth 52 A5
Pennsylvania 39 G5
Penny Bridge 107 E4
Pennycross 8 A2
Pennyfuir 148 A1
Pennygate 87 E3
Pennyghael 147 E2
Pennyglen 132 A4
Pennygown 155 F5
Pennymoor 10 B1
Penny's Green 72 C2
Pennyvenie 132 C5
Penparc *Cere.* 49 F3
Penparc *Pembs.* 48 B4
Penparcau 62 B4
Penpedairheol 38 C2
Penpethy 5 E1
Penpillick 5 E4
Penpol 3 F3
Penpoll 5 F4
Penponds 2 D3
Penpont *D. & G.* 124 C1
Penpont *Powys* 51 F5
Penprysg 37 F4
Penquit 8 C2
Penrherber 49 F4
Penrhiw 49 F3
Penrhiwceiber 37 G3
Penrhiwgoch 36 B1
Penrhiw-llan 49 G3
Penrhiw-pâl 49 G3
Penrhiwtyn 36 D3
Penrhos *Gwyn.* 74 C4
Penrhos *I.o.A.* 88 A4
Penrhos *Mon.* 38 D1
Penrhos *Powys* 37 E1
Penrhos-garnedd 89 D5
Penrhyn Bay (Bae Penrhyn) 89 G4
Penrhyn-coch 62 C4
Penrhyndeudraeth 75 F4
Penrhyn-side 89 G4
Penrhys 37 G3
Penrice 36 A4
Penrith 118 B5
Penrose *Cornw.* 4 C2
Penrose *Cornw.* 5 G1
Penruddock 118 A5
Penryn 3 E3
Pensarn *Carmar.* 36 A1
Pensarn *Conwy* 90 A5
Pen-sarn *Gwyn.* 75 E5
Pen-sarn *Gwyn.* 74 D3
Pensax 53 G1
Pensby 91 D4
Penselwood 25 E4
Pensford 24 D1
Pensham 54 B3
Penshaw 120 C2
Penshurst 31 E4
Pensilva 5 G3
Pensnett 66 B4
Penston 144 B2
Pentewan 5 E5
Pentir 75 E1
Pentire 4 B3
Pentireglaze 4 D2
Pentlepoir 35 E2
Pentlow 59 G3
Pentlow Street 59 G3
Pentney 71 F1
Penton Mewsey 27 E3
Pentonville 44 C4
Pentraeth 88 D5
Pentre *Powys* 77 D5
Pentre *Powys* 63 G4
Pentre *Powys* 52 B1
Pentre *Powys* 64 B3
Pentre *Powys* 64 A4
Pentre *R.C.T.* 37 F3
Pentre *Shrop.* 64 C1
Pentre *Shrop.* 64 C5
Pentre *Wrex.* 77 F3
Pentre *Wrex.* 78 A3
Pentre Berw 88 C5
Pentre Ffwrndan 91 D5
Pentre Galar 49 E4
Pentre Gwenlais 36 C1
Pentre Gwynfryn 75 E5
Pentre Halkyn 90 D5
Pentre Isaf 76 B1
Pentre Llanrhaeadr 77 D1
Pentre Maelor 78 A3
Pentre Meyrick 37 F5
Pentre Poeth 36 C3
Pentre Saron 76 D1
Pentre-bach *Cere.* 50 B3
Pentrebach *M.Tyd.* 37 G2
Pentre-bach *Powys* 51 F4
Pentrebach *R.C.T.* 37 G4
Pentrebach *Swan.* 36 B2
Pentre-bont 76 A2
Pentre-bwlch 77 E3
Pentrecagal 49 G3
Pentre-celyn *Denb.* 77 E2
Pentre-celyn *Powys* 63 E2
Pentre-chwyth 36 C3
Pentreclwydau 37 E2
Pentre-cwrt 49 G4
Pentre-Dolau-Honddu 51 F3
Pentredwr *Denb.* 77 E3
Pentre-dwr *Swan.* 36 C3
Pentrefelin *Carmar.* 50 C5
Pentrefelin *Cere.* 50 C3
Pentrefelin *Conwy* 89 G5
Pentrefelin *Gwyn.* 75 E4
Pentrefelin *Powys* 77 E5
Pentrefoelas 76 B2
Pentregat 49 G2
Pentreheyling 64 B3
Pentre-llwyn-llwyd 51 F2
Pentre-llyn 62 C5
Pentre-llyn-cymmer 76 C2
Pentre-piod 76 B4
Pentre-poeth 38 B4
Pentre'r beirdd 64 A1
Pentre'r Felin 76 B1
Pentre'r-felin 51 F4
Pentre-tafarn-y-fedw 76 B1
Pentre-ty-gwyn 51 E4
Pentrich 81 E2
Pentridge 13 G1
Pentwyn *Caerp.* 38 A2
Pen-twyn *Caerp.* 38 B2
Pentwyn *Cardiff* 38 B4
Pen-twyn *Mon.* 39 E2
Pentwyn-mawr 38 A3
Pentyrch 38 A4
Pentywyn (Pendine) 35 F2
Penuwch 50 B1
Penwithick 5 E4
Penwood 27 F1
Penwortham 100 B5
Penwortham Lane 100 B5
Penwyllt 37 E1
Pen-y-banc 50 C5
Pen-y-bont *Carmar.* 51 D4
Pen-y-bont *Carmar.* 49 G5
Pen-y-bont *Powys* 63 G1
Pen-y-bont *Powys* 77 F5
Penybont *Powys* 52 A1
Pen-y-bont ar Ogwr (Bridgend) 37 F5
Penybontfawr 77 D5
Penybryn *Caerp.* 38 A3
Pen-y-bryn *Gwyn.* 62 C1
Pen-y-bryn *Pembs.* 49 E3
Pen-y-bryn *Wrex.* 77 F3
Pen-y-cae *Powys* 37 E1
Penycae *Wrex.* 77 F3
Pen-y-cae-mawr 38 D3
Pen-y-cefn 90 C5
Pen-y-clawdd 39 D2
Pen-y-coedcae 37 G4
Penycwm 48 B5
Pen-y-Darren 37 G2
Pen-y-fai 37 E4
Penyffordd *Flints.* 78 A1
Pen-y-ffordd *Flints.* 90 C4
Penyffridd 75 E2
Pen-y-gaer 52 A5
Pen-y-garn *Carmar.* 50 B4
Pen-y-garn *Cere.* 62 C4
Penygarn *Torfaen* 38 B2
Penygarnedd 77 E5
Pen-y-garreg 51 G3
Pen-y-Graig *Gwyn.* 74 B4
Penygraig *R.C.T.* 37 G3
Penygroes *Carmar.* 36 B1
Penygroes *Gwyn.* 75 D2
Pen-y-Gwryd Hotel 75 F2
Pen-y-lan 38 A5
Penymynydd 78 A1
Pen-y-parc 77 F1
Pen-y-Park 52 B3
Pen-yr-englyn 37 F3
Pen-yr-heol *Mon.* 38 D1
Penyrheol *Swan.* 36 B3
Pen-y-sarn 88 C3
Pen-y-stryt 77 E2
Penywaun 37 F2
Penzance 2 B3
Penzance Heliport 2 B3
Peopleton 54 B2
Peover Heath 92 B5
Peper Harow 29 E3
Peplow 78 D5
Pepper Arden 110 B2
Pepper's Green 45 F1
Perceton 141 E5
Percie 168 D5
Percyhorner 177 H4
Perham Down 27 D3
Periton 22 C3
Perivale 44 A4
Perkhill 168 D4
Perkins Beach 64 C2
Perkin's Village 10 D3
Perlethorpe 94 D5
Perran Downs 2 C3
Perranarworthal 3 E3
Perranporth 4 B4
Perranuthnoe 2 C4
Perranzabuloe 4 B4
Perrott's Brook 40 C2
Perry Barr 66 C3
Perry Crofts 67 E2
Perry Green *Essex* 59 G5
Perry Green *Herts.* 44 D1
Perry Green *Wilts.* 40 B4
Perry Street 45 F5
Perrymead 25 E1
Pershall 79 F5
Pershore 54 B3
Persie House 159 G4
Pert 161 E3
Pertenhall 57 F1
Perth 151 G2
Perthcelyn 37 G3
Perthy 78 A4
Perton 66 A3
Pestalozzi Children's Village 18 C2
Peter Tavy 7 F3
Peterborough 69 G3
Peterburn 172 D3
Peterchurch 52 C4
Peterculter 169 G4
Peterhead 177 K6
Peterlee 120 D3
Peter's Green 44 A1
Peters Marland 21 E4
Peters Port (Port Pheadair) 170 D7
Petersfield 28 C5
Petersfinger 26 C5
Peterstone Wentlooge 38 B4
Peterston-super-Ely 37 G5
Peterstow 53 E5
Petham 32 D3
Petrockstowe 21 F5
Pett 19 D2
Pettaugh 60 C2
Petteril Green 118 A3
Pettinain 143 D5
Pettistree 61 D2
Petton *Devon* 22 D5
Petton *Shrop.* 78 B5
Petts Wood 30 D2
Petty 169 F1
Pettycur 143 G1
Pettymuick 169 H2
Petworth 29 E5
Pevensey 18 B3
Pevensey Bay 18 B3
Peverell 8 A2
Pewsey 26 C1
Pheasant's Hill 42 C4
Phesdo 161 E2
Philham 20 C3
Philiphaugh 135 F3
Phillack 2 C3
Philleigh 3 F3
Philpstoun 143 E2
Phocle Green 53 F5
Phoenix Green 28 C2
Phones 166 E5
Phorp 175 H6
Pibsbury 24 B5
Pica 116 D4
Piccadilly Corner 73 D3
Pickerells 45 E2
Pickering 111 G4
Pickering Nook 120 A2
Picket Piece 27 E3
Picket Post 14 A2
Pickford Green 67 E4
Pickhill 110 C4
Picklescott 64 D3
Pickletillem 152 C2
Pickmere 92 A5
Pickney 23 E5
Pickstock 79 E5
Pickston 151 E2
Pickup Bank 100 D5
Pickwell *Devon* 21 E1
Pickwell *Leics.* 68 C1
Pickworth *Lincs.* 83 F4
Pickworth *Rut.* 69 E1
Picton *Ches.* 91 F5
Picton *N.Yorks.* 110 D2
Piddinghoe 17 G3
Piddington *Bucks.* 42 D3
Piddington *Northants.* 56 D2
Piddington *Oxon.* 42 B1
Piddlehinton 12 D3
Piddletrenthide 12 D3
Pidley 70 B5
Piercebridge 110 B1
Pierowall 184 D3
Pigdon 129 D3
Pike Hill 101 E4
Pikehall 80 C2
Pikeshill 14 B2
Pilgrims Hatch 45 E3
Pilham 95 F3
Pill 39 E5
Pillaton *Cornw.* 7 D4
Pillaton *Staffs.* 66 B1
Pillerton Hersey 55 E3
Pillerton Priors 55 E3
Pilleth 52 B1
Pilley *Hants.* 14 C3
Pilley *S.Yorks.* 94 A2
Pilling 100 A3
Pilling Lane 99 G3
Pillowell 39 F2
Pilning 39 E4
Pilsbury 80 C1
Pilsdon 12 A3
Pilsgate 69 F2
Pilsley *Derbys.* 81 F1
Pilsley *Derbys.* 93 G5
Pilson Green 87 E4
Piltdown 17 G1
Pilton *Devon* 21 F2
Pilton *Northants.* 69 F4
Pilton *Rut.* 69 E2
Pilton *Som.* 24 C3
Pilton *Swan.* 36 A4
Pilton Green 36 A4
Pimhole 92 C1
Pimlico 43 F2
Pimperne 13 F2
Pin Mill 60 D4
Pinchbeck 84 A5
Pinchbeck Bars 84 A5
Pinchbeck West 84 A5
Pincheon Green 95 D1
Pinchinthorpe 111 E1
Pindon End 56 C3
Pinehurst 40 D4
Pinfold 91 E1
Pinged 36 A2
Pinhay 11 G3
Pinhoe 10 C3
Pinkneys Green 43 D4
Pinley Green 55 E1
Pinminnoch 122 C1
Pinmore 122 D1
Pinn 11 E4
Pinner 44 A4
Pinner Green 44 A3
Pinvin 54 B3
Pinwherry 122 C2
Pinxton 81 F2
Pipe and Lyde 53 E3
Pipe Gate 79 E3
Pipe Ridware 66 C1
Pipehill 66 C2
Piperhall 140 B4
Piperhill 175 F6
Pipers Pool 5 G1
Pipewell 68 D4
Pippacott 21 F2
Pipton 52 A4
Pirbright 29 E2
Pirnmill 139 G5
Pirton *Herts.* 57 G4
Pirton *Worcs.* 54 A3
Pisgah 150 C4
Pishill 42 C4
Pistyll 74 C3
Pitagowan 158 D3
Pitblae 177 H4
Pitcairngreen 151 F2
Pitcairns 151 F3
Pitcaple 169 F2
Pitch Green 42 C2
Pitch Place *Surr.* 29 E2
Pitch Place *Surr.* 29 D4
Pitchcombe 40 A2
Pitchcott 56 C5
Pitchford 65 E2
Pitcombe 25 D4
Pitcot 37 E5
Pitcox 144 D2
Pitcur 152 A1
Pitfichie 168 E3
Pitgrudy 174 E2
Pitinnan 169 F1
Pitkennedy 160 D4
Pitkevy 152 A4
Pitlessie 152 B4
Pitlochry 159 E4
Pitman's Corner 60 C1
Pitmedden 169 G2
Pitminster 11 F1
Pitmuies 161 D5
Pitmunie 168 E3
Pitnacree 159 E4
Pitney 24 B5
Pitroddie 152 A2
Pitscottie 152 C3
Pitsea 45 G4
Pitsford 56 C1
Pitsford Hill 23 D4
Pitstone 43 E1
Pitt *Devon* 10 D1
Pitt *Hants.* 27 F5
Pittendreich 175 J5
Pittentrail 174 E1
Pittenweem 152 D4
Pitteuchar 152 A5
Pittington 120 C3
Pittodrie House 168 E2
Pitton *Swan.* 36 A4
Pitton *Wilts.* 26 D4
Pittulie 177 H4
Pittville 54 B5
Pity Me 120 B3
Pityme 4 D2
Pixey Green 72 D4
Pixley 53 F4
Place Newton 112 B5
Plaidy 177 F5
Plain Dealings 35 D1
Plainfield 128 B1
Plains 142 B3
Plainsfield 23 E4
Plaish 65 E3
Plaistow *Gt.Lon.* 44 C4
Plaistow *W.Suss.* 29 F4
Plaitford 14 B1
Plaitford Green 27 D5
Plas 50 A5
Plas Gwynant 75 F2
Plas Isaf 77 D3
Plas Llwyd 90 A5
Plas Llwyngwern 63 D2
Plas Llysyn 63 F3
Plas Nantyr 77 E4
Plashett 35 F2
Plasisaf 76 C1
Plas-rhiw-Saeson 63 F2
Plastow Green 27 G1
Plas-yn-Cefn 90 B5
Platt 31 F3
Platt Bridge 92 A2
Platt Lane 78 C4
Platt's Heath 32 A3
Plawsworth 120 B3
Plaxtol 31 F3
Play Hatch 42 C5
Playden 19 E1
Playford 60 D3
Playing Place 4 C5
Playley Green 53 G4
Plealey 64 D2
Plean 142 C1
Pleasance 152 A3
Pleasant Valley 58 D4
Pleasington 100 C5
Pleasley 81 G1
Pleasleyhill 81 G1
Pleck *Dorset* 12 D1
Pleck *W.Mid.* 66 B3
Pledgdon Green 59 D5
Pledwick 94 A1
Plemstall 91 F5
Plenmeller 118 D1
Pleshey 45 F1
Plockton 164 E1
Plocropol 171 G2
Plomer's Hill 43 D3
Plot Gate 24 C4
Plough Hill 67 F3
Plowden 64 C4
Ploxgreen 64 C2
Pluckley 32 B4
Pluckley Thorne 32 B4
Plucks Gutter 33 E2
Plumbland 117 E3
Plumbley 94 B4
Plumley 92 B5
Plumpton *Cumb.* 118 A4
Plumpton *E.Suss.* 17 F2
Plumpton *Northants.* 56 B3
Plumpton Green 17 F2
Plumpton Head 118 B4
Plumstead *Gt.Lon.* 45 D5
Plumstead *Norf.* 86 C2
Plumtree 82 B4
Plungar 82 C4
Plush 12 D2
Plusha 5 G1
Plushabridge 6 D3
Plwmp 49 G2
Plym Bridge 8 B2
Plymouth 8 A2
Plymouth City Airport 8 B1
Plympton 8 B2
Plymstock 8 B2
Plymtree 11 D2
Pockley 111 F4
Pocklington 104 A3
Pockthorpe 86 B3
Pocombe Bridge 10 B3
Pode Hole 84 A5
Podimore 24 C5
Podington 57 E1
Podmore 79 E4
Podsmead 40 A1
Poffley End 41 F1
Point Clear 47 D1
Pointon 83 G4
Polanach 156 B4
Polapit Tamar 6 D2
Polbae 123 D3
Polbain 180 B7
Polbathic 6 D5
Polbeth 143 E3
Poldean 125 F1
Pole Moor 93 E1
Polebrook 69 F4
Polegate 18 A3
Poles 174 E2
Polesworth 67 E2
Polglass 173 G1
Polgooth 5 D4
Polgown 133 F5
Poling 16 C3
Poling Corner 16 C3
Polkerris 5 E4
Poll a' Charra 162 C3
Polla 181 F3
Pollardras 2 D3
Polldubh 156 D3
Pollie 182 C7
Pollington 94 D1
Polloch 155 G3
Pollok 141 G3
Pollokshaws 141 G3
Pollokshields 141 G3
Polmassick 5 D5
Polmont 142 D2
Polnoon 141 G4
Polperro 5 G4
Polruan 5 F4
Polsham 24 C3
Polstead 60 A4
Polstead Heath 60 A3
Poltalloch 148 A5
Poltimore 10 C3
Polton 143 G3
Polwarth 145 E4
Polyphant 5 G1
Polzeath 4 D2
Pomphlett 8 B2
Pond Street 58 C4
Ponders End 44 C3
Pondersbridge 70 A3
Ponsanooth 3 E3
Ponsonby 106 B2
Ponsongath 3 E5
Ponsworthy 10 A5
Pont Aber 50 D5
Pont Aberglaslyn 75 E3
Pont ar Hydfer 51 E5
Pont Crugnant 63 E3
Pont Cyfyng 76 A2
Pont Dolgarrog 76 A1
Pont Pen-y-benglog 75 F1
Pont Rhyd-sarn 76 B5
Pont Rhyd-y-cyff 37 E4
Pont Walby 37 E2
Pont yr Alwen 76 C2
Pontamman 36 C1
Pontantwn 36 A1
Pontardawe 36 D2
Pontarddulais 36 B2
Pontarfynach (Devil's Bridge) 62 D5
Pontargothi 50 B5
Pont-ar-llechau 50 D5
Pontarsais 50 A5
Pontblyddyn 77 F1
Pontbren Llwyd 37 F2
Pontefract 103 D5
Ponteland 129 D4
Ponterwyd 62 D4
Pontesbury 64 D2
Pontesbury Hill 64 C2
Pontesford 64 D2
Pontfadog 77 F4
Pontfaen *Pembs.* 48 D4
Pont-faen *Powys* 51 F4
Pontgarreg 49 G2
Pont-Henri 36 A2
Ponthir 38 C3
Ponthirwaun 49 F3
Pont-iets (Pontyates) 36 A2
Pontllanfraith 38 A3
Pontlliw 36 C2
Pontllyfni 74 D2
Pontlottyn 38 A2
Pontneddfechan 37 F2
Pontrhydfendigaid 50 D1
Pontrhydyfen 37 D3
Pont-rhyd-y-groes 62 D5
Pontrhydyrun 38 B3
Pontrilas 52 C5
Pontrobert 64 A1
Pont-rug 75 E1
Ponts Green 18 B2
Pontshill 53 F5
Pont-siân 50 A3
Pontsticill 37 G1
Pontwelly 50 A4
Pontyates (Pont-iets) 36 A2
Pontyberem 36 B1
Pont-y-blew 78 A4
Pontybodkin 77 F2
Pontyclun 37 G4
Pontycymer 37 F3
Pontygwaith 37 G3
Pontymister 38 B3
Pontymoel 38 B2
Pont-y-pant 76 A2
Pontypool 38 B2
Pontypridd 37 G3
Pont-y-rhyl 37 F4
Pontywaun 38 B3
Pooksgreen 14 C1
Pool *Cornw.* 4 A5
Pool *W.Yorks.* 102 B3
Pool Bank 107 F4
Pool Green 66 C2
Pool Head 53 E2
Pool of Muckhart 151 F4
Pool Quay 64 B1
Pool Street 59 F4
Poole 13 G3
Poole Keynes 40 B3
Poolend 79 G2
Poolewe 172 E3
Pooley Bridge 118 A5
Pooley Street 72 B3
Poolfold 79 F2
Poolhill 53 G5
Poolsbrook 94 B5
Poolthorne Farm 96 A2
Pope Hill 34 C1
Popeswood 29 D1
Popham 27 G3
Poplar 44 C4
Porchfield 14 D3
Porin 173 K6
Poringland 87 D5
Porkellis 3 D3
Porlock 22 B3
Porlock Weir 22 B3
Port Allen 152 A2
Port Appin 156 B5
Port Askaig 138 C3
Port Bannatyne 140 B3
Port Carlisle 126 A5
Port Charlotte 138 A4
Port Clarence 121 E5
Port Driseach 140 A2
Port e Vullen 98 C2
Port Ellen 138 B5
Port Elphinstone 169 F3
Port Erin 98 A5
Port Erroll 169 J1
Port Eynon 36 A4
Port Gaverne 5 E1
Port Glasgow 141 E2
Port Henderson 172 D4
Port Isaac 5 D1
Port Logan 114 A2
Port Mòr 154 D2
Port Mulgrave 111 G1
Port na Craig 159 E4
Port nan Giùran (Portnaguran) 179 H4
Port nan Long 170 D4
Port Nis (Port of Ness) 179 H1
Port o' Warren 124 C5
Port of Menteith 150 A4
Port of Ness (Port Nis) 179 H1

Port Penrhyn 89 D5
Port Pheadair (Peters Port) 170 D7
Port Quin 5 D1
Port Ramsay 156 A5
Port St. Mary 98 A5
Port Solent 15 F2
Port Sunlight 91 E4
Port Talbot 37 D3
Port Tennant 36 C3
Port Wemyss 138 A4
Port William 114 D2
Portachoillan 139 F4
Portavadie 140 A3
Portbury 39 E5
Portchester 15 F2
Portencross 140 C5
Portesham 12 C4
Portessie 176 C4
Portfield *Arg. & B.* 147 G2
Portfield *W.Suss.* 16 A3
Portfield Gate 34 C1
Portgate 7 E2
Portgordon 176 B4
Portgower 183 F7
Porth *Cornw.* 4 C3
Porth *R.C.T.* 37 G3
Porth Colmon 74 A4
Porth Navas 3 E4
Porthaethwy (Menai Bridge) 89 D5
Porthallow *Cornw.* 3 E4
Porthallow *Cornw.* 5 G4
Porthcawl 37 E5
Porthcothan 4 C2
Porthcurno 2 A4
Porthgain 48 B4
Porthill 79 F3
Porthkerry 23 D1
Porthleven 2 D4
Porthmadog 75 E4
Porthmeor 2 B3
Portholland 5 D5
Porthoustock 3 F4
Porthpean 5 E4
Porthtowan 4 A5
Porthyrhyd *Carmar.* 50 D4
Porthyrhyd *Carmar.* 36 B1
Porth-y-waen 77 F5
Portincaple 149 E5
Portington 103 G4
Portinnisherrich 148 B3
Portinscale 117 F4
Portishead 39 D5
Portknockie 176 C4
Portlethen 169 H5
Portlethen Village 169 H5
Portloe 3 G3
Portlooe 5 G4
Portmahomack 175 G3
Portmeirion 75 E4
Portmellon 5 E5
Portmore 14 C3
Port-na-Con 181 G2
Portnacroish 156 B5
Portnaguran (Port nan Giùran) 179 H4
Portnahaven 138 A4
Portnalong 163 J1
Portnaluchaig 155 F1
Portobello 144 A2
Porton 26 C4
Portpatrick 122 B5
Portreath 4 A5
Portree 171 K7
Portscatho 3 F3
Portsea 15 F2
Portskerra 182 D2
Portskewett 39 E4
Portslade 17 E3
Portslade-by-Sea 17 E3
Portslogan 122 A5
Portsmouth 15 F3
Portsonachan 148 C2
Portsoy 176 D4
Portuairk 154 D3
Portvoller 179 H4
Portway *Here.* 52 C3
Portway *Here.* 53 D3
Portway *Here.* 53 D4
Portway *Worcs.* 66 C5
Portwrinkle 7 D5
Portyerrock 115 E3
Posenhall 65 F2
Poslingford 59 F3
Postbridge 7 G3
Postcombe 42 C3
Postling 32 D5
Post-mawr (Synod Inn) 50 A2
Postwick 87 D5
Potarch 168 E5
Potsgrove 57 E5
Pott Row 85 F5
Pott Shrigley 92 D5
Potten End 43 F2
Potter Brompton 112 C5
Potter Heigham 87 F4
Potter Street 45 D2
Pottergate Street 72 C2
Potterhanworth 83 F1
Potterhanworth Booths 83 F1
Potterne 26 A2
Potterne Wick 26 B2
Potternewton 102 C4
Potters Bar 44 B2
Potters Crouch 44 A2
Potter's Green 67 F4
Potters Marston 67 G3
Potterspury 56 C3
Potterton *Aber.* 169 H3
Potterton *W.Yorks.* 102 D4
Pottle Street 25 F3
Potto 111 D2
Potton 58 A3
Pott's Green 60 A5
Poughill *Cornw.* 20 C5
Poughill *Devon* 10 B2
Poulshot 26 A2
Poulton 40 D2
Poulton-le-Fylde 99 G4
Pound Bank 53 G3
Pound Green *E.Suss.* 18 A1
Pound Green *Suff.* 59 F2
Pound Green *Worcs.* 65 G5
Pound Hill 30 B5
Pound Street 27 F1
Poundbury 12 C3
Poundffald 36 B3
Poundfield 31 E5
Poundgate 17 G1
Poundland 122 C2
Poundon 56 B5
Poundsbridge 31 E4
Poundsgate 10 A5
Poundstock 6 C1
Povey Cross 30 B4
Pow Green 53 G3
Powburn 137 E5
Powderham 10 C4
Powerstock 12 B3
Powfoot 125 F4
Powick 54 A2
Powler's Piece 21 D4
Powmill 151 F5
Poxwell 12 D4
Poyle 43 F5
Poynings 17 E2
Poyntington 25 D5
Poynton *Ches.* 92 D4
Poynton *Tel. & W.* 65 E1
Poynton Green 65 E1
Poyntzfield 174 E5
Poys Street 73 E4
Poyston 34 C1
Poyston Cross 34 C1
Poystreet Green 60 A2
Praa Sands 2 C4
Pratis 152 B4
Pratt's Bottom 31 D2
Praze-an-Beeble 2 D3
Predannack Wollas 3 D5
Prees 78 C4
Prees Green 78 C4
Prees Heath 78 C4
Prees Higher Heath 78 C4
Prees Lower Heath 78 C4
Preesall 99 G3
Preesgweene 77 F4
Prenbrigog 77 F1
Prendergast 34 C1
Prendwick 137 E5
Pren-gwyn 50 A3
Prenteg 75 E3
Prenton 91 E4
Prescot 91 F3
Prescott *Devon* 11 D1
Prescott *Shrop.* 78 B5
Presley 175 H6
Pressen 136 C3
Prestatyn 90 B4
Prestbury *Ches.* 92 D5
Prestbury *Glos.* 54 B5
Presteigne 52 C1
Presthope 65 E3
Prestleigh 24 D3
Prestolee 92 B2
Preston *B. & H.* 17 F3
Preston *Devon* 10 B5
Preston *Dorset* 12 D4
Preston *E.Loth.* 144 C2
Preston *E.Riding* 105 D4
Preston *Glos.* 53 F4
Preston *Glos.* 40 C2
Preston *Herts.* 57 G5
Preston *Kent* 32 C2
Preston *Kent* 33 E2
Preston *Lancs.* 100 B5
Preston *Northumb.* 137 F4
Preston *Rut.* 69 D2
Preston *Sc.Bord.* 145 E4
Preston *Shrop.* 65 E1
Preston *Som.* 23 D4
Preston *Suff.* 60 A2
Preston *Torbay* 9 E1
Preston *Wilts.* 40 C5
Preston Bagot 55 D1
Preston Bissett 56 B4
Preston Bowyer 23 E5
Preston Brockhurst 78 C5
Preston Brook 91 G4
Preston Candover 28 B3
Preston Capes 56 A2
Preston Deanery 56 C2
Preston Gubbals 65 D1
Preston on Stour 55 E3
Preston on the Hill 91 G4
Preston on Wye 52 C3
Preston Plucknett 12 B1
Preston upon the Weald Moors 65 F1
Preston Wynne 53 E3
Preston-le-Skerne 120 C5
Prestonpans 144 A2
Preston-under-Scar 109 F3
Prestwich 92 C2
Prestwick *Northumb.* 129 D4
Prestwick *S.Ayr.* 132 B3
Prestwick International Airport (Glasgow Prestwick International Airport) 132 B3
Prestwold 81 G5
Prestwood *Bucks.* 43 D2
Prestwood *Staffs.* 80 C3
Price Town 37 F3
Prickwillow 71 D4
Priddy 24 C2
Priest Hill 100 C4
Priest Hutton 107 G5
Priest Weston 64 B3
Priestcliffe 93 F5
Priestland 133 D2
Priestwood 31 F2
Primethorpe 68 A3
Primrose Green 86 B4
Primrose Hill 44 B4
Princes End 66 B3
Princes Gate 35 E1
Princes Risborough 42 D2
Princethorpe 67 G5
Princetown *Caerp.* 38 A1
Princetown *Devon* 7 F3
Prior Muir 152 D3
Prior's Frome 53 E4
Priors Halton 65 D5
Priors Hardwick 55 G2
Priors Marston 55 G2
Prior's Norton 54 A5
Priors Park 54 A4
Priorslee 65 G1
Priory Wood 52 B3
Priston 25 D1
Pristow Green 72 C3
Prittlewell 46 B4
Privett 28 B5
Prixford 21 F2
Proaig 138 C4
Probus 4 C5
Protstonhill 177 G4
Prudhoe 119 G1
Prussia Cove 2 C4
Pubil 157 G5
Publow 24 D1
Puckeridge 58 B5
Puckington 11 G1
Pucklechurch 39 F5
Pucknall 27 E5
Puckrup 54 A4
Puddinglake 79 E1
Puddington *Ches.* 91 E5
Puddington *Devon* 10 B1
Puddlebrook 39 F1
Puddledock 72 B2
Puddletown 13 D3
Pudleston 53 E2
Pudsey 102 B4
Pulborough 16 C2
Puldagon 183 J4
Puleston 79 E5
Pulford 78 A2
Pulham 12 D2
Pulham Market 72 C3
Pulham St. Mary 72 D3
Pulley 65 D2
Pulloxhill 57 F4
Pulrossie 174 E3
Pulverbatch 64 D2
Pumpherston 143 E3
Pumsaint 50 C3
Puncheston 48 D5
Puncknowle 12 B4
Punnett's Town 18 B1
Purbrook 15 F2
Purewell 14 A3
Purfleet 45 E5
Puriton 24 A3
Purleigh 46 B2
Purley 30 C2
Purley on Thames 42 B5
Purlogue 64 B5
Purlpit 25 F1
Purls Bridge 70 C4
Purse Caundle 12 C1
Purslow 64 C4
Purston Jaglin 94 B1
Purtington 11 G2
Purton *Glos.* 39 F2
Purton *Glos.* 39 F2
Purton *Wilts.* 40 C4
Purton Stoke 40 C3
Purves Hall 145 E5
Pury End 56 C3
Pusey 41 F3
Putley 53 F4
Putley Green 53 F4
Putney 44 B5
Putsborough 21 E1
Puttenham *Herts.* 43 D1
Puttenham *Surr.* 29 E3
Puttock End 59 G3
Putts Corner 11 E3
Puxton 24 B1
Pwll 36 A2
Pwllcrochan 34 C2
Pwlldefaid 74 A5
Pwll-glas 77 E2
Pwllgloyw 51 G4
Pwllheli 74 C4
Pwll-Mawr 38 B5
Pwllmeyric 39 E3
Pwll-trap 35 F1
Pwll-y-glaw 37 D3
Pye Corner *Herts.* 45 D1
Pye Corner *Kent* 32 A4
Pye Corner *Newport* 38 C4
Pye Green 66 B1
Pyecombe 17 E2
Pyle *Bridgend* 37 E4
Pyle *I.o.W.* 15 D5
Pyleigh 23 E4
Pylle 24 D4
Pymore *Cambs.* 70 C4
Pymore *Dorset* 12 A3
Pyrford 29 F2
Pyrford Green 29 F2
Pyrton 42 B3
Pytchley 69 D5
Pyworthy 20 D5

▼Q

Quabbs 64 B4
Quadring 84 A4
Quadring Eaudike 84 A4
Quainton 56 C5
Quarff 187 D9
Quarley 27 D3
Quarndon 81 E3
Quarr Hill 15 E3
Quarrier's Village 141 E3
Quarrington 83 F3
Quarrington Hill 120 C4
Quarry Bank 66 B4
Quarrybank 78 C1
Quarrywood 175 J5
Quarter 142 B4
Quatford 65 G3
Quatt 65 G4
Quebec 120 A3
Quedgeley 40 A1
Queen Adelaide 71 D4
Queen Camel 24 C5
Queen Charlton 24 D1
Queen Dart 10 B1
Queen Oak 25 E4
Queen Street 31 F4
Queenborough 32 B1
Queen's Bower 15 E4
Queen's Head 78 A5
Queensbury *Gt.Lon.* 44 A4
Queensbury *W.Yorks.* 102 A4
Queensferry (South Queensferry) *Edin.* 143 F2
Queensferry *Flints.* 78 A1
Queenzieburn 142 A2
Quemerford 26 B1
Quendale 187 F9
Quendon 58 D4
Queniborough 68 B1
Quenington 40 D2
Quernmore 100 B1
Queslett 66 C3
Quethiock 6 D4
Quholm 185 B6
Quick's Green 42 A5
Quidenham 72 B3
Quidhampton 27 G2
Quidinish (Cuidhtinis) 171 F3
Quilquox 169 H1
Quina Brook 78 C4
Quindry 185 D8
Quine's Hill 98 B4
Quinhill 139 F4
Quinton *Northants.* 56 C2
Quinton *W.Mid.* 66 B4
Quinton Green 56 C2
Quintrell Downs 4 C3
Quixhill 80 C3
Quoditch 7 E1
Quoig 150 D2
Quoiggs House 150 D4
Quoisley 78 C3
Quorn (Quorndon) 68 A1
Quorndon (Quorn) 68 A1
Quothquan 134 A2
Quoyloo 184 B5
Quoys 186 F1
Quoys of Reiss 183 J3

▼R

Raasay 172 B7
Raby 91 E5
Rachan 134 C2
Rachub 75 F1
Rackenford 10 B1
Rackham 16 C2
Rackheath 87 D4
Racks 125 E3
Rackwick *Ork.* 185 B8
Rackwick *Ork.* 184 D3
Radbourne 81 D4
Radcliffe *Gt.Man.* 92 B2
Radcliffe *Northumb.* 129 E1
Radcliffe on Trent 82 B4
Radclive 56 B4
Radcot 41 E3
Raddington 22 D5
Radernie 152 C4
Radford *B. & N.E.Som.* 25 D2
Radford *Nott.* 81 G3
Radford *Oxon.* 55 G5
Radford *W.Mid.* 67 F4
Radford Semele 55 F1
Radipole 12 C4
Radlett 44 A2
Radley 42 A3
Radley Green 45 F2
Radmore Green 78 C2
Radnage 42 C3
Radstock 25 D2
Radstone 56 A3
Radway 55 F3
Radway Green 79 E2
Radwell *Beds.* 57 F2
Radwell *Herts.* 58 A4
Radwinter 59 E4
Radyr 38 A4
Raechester 128 B3
Raemoir House 168 E5
Raffin 180 C5
Rafford 175 H6
Ragdale 82 B5
Ragged Appleshaw 27 E3
Raglan 38 D2
Ragnall 95 F5
Rahoy 155 F4
Rain Shore 92 C1
Rainford 91 F2
Rainham *Gt.Lon.* 45 E4
Rainham *Med.* 32 A2
Rainhill 91 F3
Rainhill Stoops 91 G3
Rainow 93 D5
Rainsough 92 B2
Rainton 110 C5
Rainworth 81 G2
Raisbeck 108 B2
Raise 118 D3
Rait 152 A2
Raithby *Lincs.* 84 B1
Raithby *Lincs.* 96 D4
Rake 28 D5
Raleigh's Cross 22 D4
Ram 50 B3
Ram Alley 26 D1
Ram Lane 32 B4
Ramasaig 171 G7
Rame *Cornw.* 3 E3
Rame *Cornw.* 8 A3
Rampisham 12 B2
Rampside 99 F1
Rampton *Cambs.* 58 C1
Rampton *Notts.* 95 F5
Ramsbottom 92 B1
Ramsbury 41 E5
Ramscraigs 183 G6
Ramsdean 28 C5
Ramsdell 27 G2
Ramsden 41 F1
Ramsden Bellhouse 45 G3
Ramsden Heath 45 G3
Ramsey *Cambs.* 70 A4
Ramsey *Essex* 60 D4
Ramsey *I.o.M.* 98 C2
Ramsey Forty Foot 70 B4
Ramsey Heights 70 A4
Ramsey Island *Essex* 46 C2
Ramsey Island *Pembs.* 48 A5
Ramsey Mereside 70 A4
Ramsey St. Mary's 70 A4
Ramsgate 33 F2
Ramsgate Street 86 B2
Ramsgill 110 A5
Ramsholt 61 E3
Ramshorn 80 B3
Ramsnest Common 29 E4
Ranachan 155 G3
Ranais (Ranish) 179 G5
Ranby *Lincs.* 96 C5
Ranby *Notts.* 95 D4
Rand 96 B5
Randwick 40 A2
Rangemore 80 C5
Rangeworthy 39 F4
Ranish (Ranais) 179 G5
Rankinston 132 C4
Rank's Green 45 G1
Ranmoor 94 A4
Rannoch School 158 A4
Ranochan 156 A1
Ranscombe 22 C3
Ranskill 95 D4
Ranton 79 F5
Ranton Green 79 F5
Ranworth 87 E4
Rapness 184 E3
Rapps 11 G1
Rascarrel 116 A2
Rash 108 B4
Rashwood 54 B1
Raskelf 110 D5
Rassau 38 A1
Rastrick 102 A5
Ratagan 165 F3
Ratby 68 A2
Ratcliffe Culey 67 F3
Ratcliffe on Soar 81 F5
Ratcliffe on the Wreake 68 B1
Ratford Bridge 34 B1
Ratfyn 26 C3
Rathen 177 H4
Rathillet 152 B2
Rathliesbeag 157 E1
Rathmell 101 E1
Ratho 143 F2
Ratho Station 143 F2
Rathven 176 C4
Ratley 55 F3
Ratling 33 E3
Ratlinghope 64 D3
Ratsloe 10 C3
Rattar 183 H1
Ratten Row *Cumb.* 117 G2
Ratten Row *Lancs.* 100 A3
Rattery 8 D1
Rattlesden 60 A2
Rattray 159 G5
Raughton Head 117 G2
Raunds 69 E5
Ravenfield 94 B3
Ravenglass 106 B3
Raveningham 73 E2
Raven's Green 60 C5
Ravenscar 112 C2
Ravensdale 98 B2
Ravensden 57 F2
Ravenshaw 101 F3
Ravenshayes 10 C2
Ravenshead 81 G2
Ravensmoor 78 D2
Ravensthorpe *Northants.* 68 B5
Ravensthorpe *W.Yorks.* 102 B5
Ravenstone *Leics.* 67 G1
Ravenstone *M.K.* 57 D2
Ravenstonedale 108 C2
Ravenstruther 142 D5
Ravensworth 110 A2
Raw 112 C2
Rawcliffe *E.Riding* 103 F5
Rawcliffe *York* 103 E2
Rawcliffe Bridge 103 F5
Rawdon 102 B4
Rawmarsh 94 B3
Rawnsley 66 C1
Rawreth 45 G3
Rawridge 11 F2
Rawson Green 81 E3
Rawtenstall 101 E5
Rawyards 142 B3
Raxton 169 G1
Raydon 60 B4
Raylees 128 B2
Rayleigh 46 B3
Raymond's Hill 11 G3
Rayne 59 F5
Rayners Lane 44 A4
Raynes Park 30 B2
Reach 59 D1
Read 101 D4
Reading 42 C5
Reading Green 72 C4
Reading Street 32 B5
Reagill 108 B1
Rearquhar 174 E2
Rearsby 68 B1
Rease Heath 78 D2
Reaster 183 H2
Reaveley 137 E5
Reawick 187 C8
Reay 182 E2
Reculver 33 E2
Red Ball 11 D1
Red Bull 79 F2
Red Dial 117 F2
Red Hill *Hants.* 15 G1
Red Hill *Warks.* 54 D2
Red Lodge 71 E5
Red Lumb 92 C1
Red Oaks Hill 59 D4
Red Point 172 D5
Red Post *Cornw.* 20 C5
Red Post *Devon* 9 E1
Red Rail 53 E5
Red Rock 91 G2
Red Roses 35 F1
Red Row 129 E2
Red Street 79 F2
Red Wharf Bay (Traeth Coch) 88 D4
Redberth 35 D2
Redbourn 44 A1
Redbourne 95 G3
Redbrook *Glos.* 39 E1
Redbrook *Wrex.* 78 C3
Redbrook Street 32 B5
Redburn *High.* 174 C5
Redburn *High.* 175 G7
Redburn *Northumb.* 119 D1
Redcar 121 F5
Redcastle *Angus* 161 E4
Redcastle *High.* 174 C7
Redcliff Bay 38 D5
Redcloak 161 G1
Reddingmuirhead 142 D2
Reddish 92 C3
Redditch 54 C1
Rede 59 G2
Redenhall 73 D3
Redesmouth 128 A3
Redford *Aber.* 161 F2
Redford *Angus* 161 D5
Redford *Dur.* 119 G4
Redford *W.Suss.* 29 D5
Redgrave 72 B4
Redheugh 160 C3
Redhill *Aber.* 168 E1
Redhill *Aber.* 169 F4
Redhill *Moray* 176 D6
Redhill *N.Som.* 24 B1
Redhill *Notts.* 81 G3
Redhill *Surr.* 30 B3
Redhill Aerodrome & Heliport 30 B4
Redhouse *Aber.* 168 D2
Redhouse *Arg. & B.* 139 G3
Redhouses 138 B3
Redisham 73 F3
Redland *Bristol* 39 E5
Redland *Ork.* 184 C5
Redlingfield 72 C4
Redlynch *Som.* 25 E4
Redlynch *Wilts.* 26 D5
Redmarley D'Abitot 53 G4
Redmarshall 120 C5
Redmile 82 C4
Redmire 109 F3
Redmoor 5 E3
Rednal 78 A5
Redpath 135 G2
Redruth 4 A5
Redscarhead 143 G5
Redshaw 133 G3
Redstone Bank 35 E1
Redwick *Newport* 38 D4
Redwick *S.Glos.* 39 E4
Redworth 120 B5
Reed 58 B4
Reed End 58 B4
Reedham 87 F5
Reedley 101 E4
Reedness 103 G5
Reef (Riof) 178 D4
Reepham *Lincs.* 96 A5
Reepham *Norf.* 86 B3
Reeth 109 F3
Regaby 98 C2
Regil 24 C1
Regoul 175 F6
Reiff 180 B7
Reigate 30 B3
Reighton 113 E5
Reinigeadal (Rhenigidale) 178 E7
Reisgill 183 H5
Reiss 183 J3
Rejerrah 4 B4
Releath 3 D3
Relubbus 2 C3
Relugas 175 G7
Remenham 42 C4
Remenham Hill 42 C4
Remony 158 C5
Rempstone 81 G5
Rendcomb 40 C1
Rendham 61 E1
Rendlesham 61 E2
Renfrew 141 G3
Renhold 57 F2
Renishaw 94 B5
Rennington 137 G5
Renton 141 E2
Renwick 118 B3
Repps 87 F4
Repton 81 E5
Rescobie 160 D4
Rescorla 5 E4
Resipole 155 G3
Resolis 174 D5
Resolven 37 E2
Resourie 156 A2
Respryn 5 F3
Reston 145 F3
Restormel 5 F3
Reswallie 160 D4
Reterth 4 D3
Retew 4 D4
Retford 95 E4
Rettendon 45 G3
Rettendon Place 45 G3
Retyn 4 C4
Revesby 84 A1
Revesby Bridge 84 B1
Rew 10 A5
Rew Street 15 D3
Rewe *Devon* 10 C3
Rewe *Devon* 10 B3
Reybridge 26 A1
Reydon 73 F4
Reydon Smear 73 G4
Reymerston 86 B5
Reynalton 35 D2
Reynoldston 36 A4
Rezare 7 D3
Rhadyr 38 C2
Rhandirmwyn 51 D3
Rhaoine 174 D1
Rhayader 51 F1
Rhedyn 74 B4
Rhegreanoch 180 C7
Rheindown 174 C7
Rhelonie 174 C2
Rhemore 155 E4
Rhenigidale (Reinigeadal) 178 E7
Rheola 37 E2
Rhes-y-cae 77 E1
Rhewl *Denb.* 77 E3
Rhewl *Denb.* 77 E1
Rhewl *Shrop.* 78 A4
Rhian 181 H7
Rhicarn 180 C6
Rhiconich 180 E3
Rhicullen 174 D4
Rhidorroch 173 H2
Rhifail 182 C4
Rhigos 37 F2
Rhilochan 174 E1
Rhinduie 174 C7
Rhireavach 173 G2
Rhiroy 173 H3
Rhiston 64 B3
Rhiw 74 B5
Rhiwargor 76 C5
Rhiwbina 38 A4
Rhiwbryfdir 75 F3
Rhiwderin 38 B4
Rhiwinder 37 G4
Rhiwlas *Gwyn.* 75 E1
Rhiwlas *Gwyn.* 76 C4
Rhiwlas *Powys* 77 F4
Rhode 23 F4
Rhodes Minnis 32 D4
Rhodesia 94 C5
Rhodiad-y-brenin 48 A5
Rhodmad 62 B5
Rhonadale 130 C2
Rhonehouse (Kelton Hill) 124 B5
Rhoose 23 D1
Rhos *Carmar.* 49 G4
Rhos *N.P.T.* 36 D2
Rhos Common 64 B1
Rhôs Lligwy 88 C4
Rhosaman 36 D1
Rhoscolyn 88 A5
Rhoscrowther 34 C2
Rhosesmor 77 F1
Rhos-fawr 74 C4
Rhosgadfan 75 E2
Rhos-goch *I.o.A.* 88 C4
Rhosgoch *Powys* 52 A3
Rhos-hill 49 E3
Rhoshirwaun 74 A5
Rhoslan 75 D3
Rhoslefain 62 B2
Rhosllanerchrugog 77 F3
Rhosmaen 50 C5
Rhosmeirch 88 C5
Rhosneigr 88 B5
Rhosnesni 78 A2
Rhôs-on-Sea 89 G4
Rhossili 36 A4
Rhosson 48 A5
Rhostrehwfa 88 C5
Rhostryfan 75 D2
Rhostyllen 78 A3
Rhos-y-bol 88 C4
Rhos-y-brithdir 77 E5
Rhosycaerau 48 C4
Rhos-y-garth 62 C5
Rhos-y-gwaliau 76 C4
Rhos-y-llan 74 B4
Rhos-y-mawn 76 B1
Rhos-y-Meirch 52 B1
Rhu 141 D1
Rhuallt 90 B5
Rhubodach 140 B2
Rhuddall Heath 78 C1
Rhuddlan 90 B5
Rhue 173 H2
Rhulen 52 A3
Rhumach 155 F1
Rhunahaorine 139 F5
Rhuthun (Ruthin) 77 E2
Rhyd *Gwyn.* 75 F3
Rhyd *Powys* 63 F2
Rhydaman (Ammanford) 36 C1
Rhydargaeau 50 A5
Rhydcymerau 50 B4
Rhyd-Ddu 75 E2
Rhydding 36 D3
Rhydgaled 76 C1
Rhydlanfair 76 B2
Rhydlewis 49 G3
Rhydlios 74 A4
Rhydlydan *Conwy* 76 B2
Rhydlydan *Powys* 63 G3
Rhydolion 74 B5
Rhydowen 50 A3
Rhyd-Rosser 50 B1
Rhydspence 52 B3
Rhydtalog 77 F2
Rhyd-uchaf 76 B4
Rhyd-wen 76 C5
Rhyd-wyn 88 B4
Rhyd-y-ceirw 77 F2
Rhyd-y-clafdy 74 C4
Rhydycroesau 77 F4
Rhydyfelin *Cere.* 62 B5
Rhydyfelin *R.C.T.* 37 G4
Rhyd-y-foel 90 A5
Rhyd-y-fro 36 D2
Rhyd-y-groes 75 E1
Rhydymain 76 B5
Rhydymwyn 77 F1
Rhyd-yr-onnen 62 C2
Rhyd-y-sarn 75 F3
Rhydywrach 35 E1
Rhyl 90 B4
Rhymney 38 A2
Rhyn 78 A4
Rhynd 151 G2
Rhynie *Aber.* 168 C2
Rhynie *High.* 175 F4
Ribbesford 65 G5
Ribchester 100 C4
Ribigill 181 H3
Riby 96 B2
Riccall 103 F4
Riccarton 132 C2
Richards Castle 53 D1
Richings Park 43 F5
Richmond *Gt.Lon.* 44 A5
Richmond *N.Yorks.* 110 A2
Richmond *S.Yorks.* 94 B4
Rich's Holford 23 E4
Rickarton 161 G1
Rickerscote 79 G5
Rickford 24 B2
Rickinghall 72 B4
Rickleton 120 B2
Rickling 58 C4
Rickling Green 58 D5
Rickmansworth 43 F3
Riddell 135 G3
Riddings 81 F2
Riddlecombe 21 G4
Riddlesden 101 G3
Ridge *Dorset* 13 F4
Ridge *Herts.* 44 B2
Ridge *Wilts.* 26 A4
Ridge Green 30 C4
Ridge Lane 67 E3
Ridgebourne 51 G1
Ridgeway 94 B4
Ridgeway Cross 53 G3
Ridgeway Moor 94 B4
Ridgewell 59 F3
Ridgewood 17 G1
Ridgmont 57 E4
Riding Gate 25 E5
Riding Mill 119 G1
Ridley 31 F2
Ridleywood 78 A2
Ridlington *Norf.* 87 E2
Ridlington *Rut.* 68 D2
Ridsdale 128 B3
Riechip 159 F5
Rievaulx 111 E4
Rift House 121 D4
Rigg *D. & G.* 126 A5
Rigg *High.* 172 B6
Riggend 142 B3
Rigifa 183 J1
Rigmaden Park 108 B4
Rigsby 97 E5
Rigside 133 G2
Riley Green 100 C5
Rileyhill 66 D1
Rilla Mill 5 G2
Rillaton 5 G2
Rillington 112 B5
Rimington 101 E3
Rimpton 24 D5

Rimswell 105 F5
Rinaston 48 C5
Ring o' Bells 91 F1
Ringford 124 A5
Ringinglow 93 G4
Ringland 86 C4
Ringles Cross 17 G1
Ringmer 17 G2
Ringmore Devon 8 C3
Ringmore Devon 10 C5
Ringorm 175 K7
Ring's End 70 C2
Ringsfield 73 F3
Ringsfield Corner 73 F3
Ringshall Herts. 43 E1
Ringshall Suff. 60 B2
Ringshall Stocks 60 B2
Ringstead Norf. 85 F3
Ringstead Northants. 69 E5
Ringwood 14 A2
Ringwould 33 F4
Rinloan 167 K4
Rinmore 168 C3
Rinnigill 185 C8
Rinsey 2 C4
Riof (Reef) 178 D4
Ripe 18 A3
Ripley Derbys. 81 E2
Ripley Hants. 14 A3
Ripley N.Yorks. 102 B1
Ripley Surr. 29 F2
Riplingham 104 B4
Ripon 110 C5
Rippingale 83 G5
Ripple Kent 33 F4
Ripple Worcs. 54 A4
Ripponden 93 E1
Risabus 138 B5
Risbury 53 E2
Risby E.Riding 104 C4
Risby Suff. 59 F1
Risca 38 B3
Rise 105 D3
Riseden 31 G5
Risegate 84 A5
Riseholme 95 G5
Riseley Beds. 57 F1
Riseley W'ham 28 C1
Rishangles 60 C1
Rishton 100 D4
Rishworth 93 E1
Risinghurst 42 A2
Risley Derbys. 81 F4
Risley Warr. 92 A3
Risplith 102 B1
Rispond 181 G2
Rivar 27 E1
Rivenhall 46 B1
Rivenhall End 46 B1
River Kent 33 E4
River W.Suss. 29 E5
River Bank 58 D1
River Bridge 24 A3
Riverford Bridge 9 D1
Riverhead 31 E3
Riverside 38 A5
Riverton 21 G2
Riverview Park 45 F5
Rivington 92 A1
Roa Island 99 F1
Roach Bridge 100 B5
Road Green 73 D2
Road Weedon 56 B2
Roade 56 C2
Roadhead 126 D4
Roadside High. 183 G2
Roadside Ork. 184 F3
Roadside of Kinneff 161 G2
Roadwater 22 D4
Roag 171 H7
Roast Green 58 C4
Roath 38 A5
Roberton S.Lan. 134 A3
Roberton Sc.Bord. 135 F4
Robertsbridge 18 C1
Robertstown Moray 175 K7
Robertstown R.C.T. 37 G2
Roberttown 102 A5
Robeston Cross 34 B2
Robeston Wathen 35 D1
Robeston West 34 B2
Robin Hood Derbys. 93 G5
Robin Hood Lancs. 91 G1
Robin Hood W.Yorks. 102 C5
Robin Hood Doncaster Sheffield Airport 95 D3
Robin Hood's Bay 112 C2
Robinhood End 59 F4
Robins 28 D5
Roborough Devon 21 F4
Roborough Plym. 8 B1
Roby 91 F3
Roby Mill 91 G2
Rocester 80 C4
Roch 48 B5
Roch Bridge 48 B5
Roch Gate 48 B5
Rochallie 159 G4
Rochdale 92 C1
Roche 5 D3
Rochester Med. 31 G2
Rochester Northumb. 128 A2
Rochford Essex 46 B3
Rochford Worcs. 53 F1
Rock Cornw. 4 D2
Rock Northumb. 137 G5
Rock Worcs. 65 G5
Rock Ferry 91 E4
Rockbeare 10 D3
Rockbourne 14 A1
Rockcliffe Cumb. 126 B5
Rockcliffe D. & G. 124 C5
Rockcliffe Cross 126 B5
Rockfield Arg. & B. 139 G4
Rockfield High. 175 G3
Rockfield Mon. 39 D1
Rockford 14 A2
Rockhampton 39 F3
Rockhead 5 E1
Rockingham 69 D3
Rockland All Saints 72 A2
Rockland St. Mary 87 E5
Rockland St. Peter 72 A2
Rockley 41 D5
Rockside 138 A3
Rockwell End 42 C4
Rockwell Green 11 E1
Rodborough 40 A2
Rodbourne 40 B4
Rodbridge Corner 59 G3
Rodd 52 C1
Roddam 137 E4
Rodden 12 C4
Rode 25 F2
Rode Heath 79 F2
Rodeheath 79 F1
Rodel (Roghadal) 171 F3
Roden 65 E1
Rodhuish 22 D4
Rodington 65 E1
Rodington Heath 65 E1
Rodley 39 G1
Rodmarton 40 B3
Rodmell 17 G3
Rodmersham 32 B2
Rodmersham Green 32 B2
Rodney Stoke 24 B2
Rodsley 80 D3
Rodway 23 F3
Roe Cross 93 D3
Roe Green 58 B4
Roecliffe 102 C1
Roehampton 44 B5
Roesound 187 C6
Roffey 29 G4
Rogart 174 E1
Rogate 28 D5
Rogerstone 38 B4
Roghadal (Rodel) 171 F3
Rogiet 39 D4
Rokemarsh 42 B3
Roker 120 D2
Rollesby 87 F4
Rolleston Leics. 68 C2
Rolleston Notts. 82 C2
Rollestone 26 B3
Rolleston-on-Dove 80 D5
Rolston 105 E3
Rolstone 24 A1
Rolvenden 32 A5
Rolvenden Layne 32 A5
Romaldkirk 119 F5
Romanby 110 C3
Romannobridge 143 F5
Romansleigh 22 A5
Romesdal 171 K6
Romford Dorset 13 G2
Romford Gt.Lon. 45 E4
Romiley 93 D3
Romney Street 31 E2
Romsey 27 E5
Romsley Shrop. 65 G4
Romsley Worcs. 66 B5
Rona 172 C6
Ronachan 139 F4
Ronague 98 A4
Ronnachmore 138 B4
Rood End 66 C4
Rookhope 119 F3
Rookley 15 E4
Rookley Green 15 E4
Rooks Bridge 24 A2
Rook's Nest 23 D4
Rookwith 110 B4
Roos 105 E4
Roose 99 F1
Roosebeck 99 F1
Roosecote 99 F1
Rootham's Green 57 F2
Rootpark 143 D4
Ropley 28 B4
Ropley Dean 28 B4
Ropley Soke 28 B4
Ropsley 83 E4
Rora 177 J5
Rorandle 168 E3
Rorrington 64 C2
Rosarie 176 B6
Rose 4 B4
Rose Ash 22 A5
Rose Green Essex 60 A5
Rose Green W.Suss. 16 B4
Rose Hill 17 G2
Roseacre Kent 31 G3
Roseacre Lancs. 100 A4
Rosebank 142 C5
Rosebrough 137 F4
Rosebush 49 D5
Rosecare 6 B1
Rosecliston 4 C4
Rosedale Abbey 111 G3
Roseden 137 E4
Rosehall 174 B1
Rosehearty 177 H4
Rosehill Aber. 168 D5
Rosehill Shrop. 65 D1
Roseisle 175 J5
Roselands 18 B3
Rosemarket 34 C2
Rosemarkie 174 E6
Rosemary Lane 11 E1
Rosemount P. & K. 159 G5
Rosemount S.Ayr. 132 B3
Rosenannon 5 D3
Rosenithon 3 F4
Rosepool 34 B1
Rosevean 5 E4
Roseville 66 B3
Rosewell 143 G3
Roseworth 120 D5
Rosgill 107 G1
Roshven 155 G2
Roskhill 171 H7
Roskorwell 3 E4
Rosley 117 G2
Roslin 143 G3
Rosliston 67 E1
Rosneath 141 D1
Ross D. & G. 115 G2
Ross Northumb. 137 F3
Ross P. & K. 150 C2
Ross Priory 141 F1
Rossdhu House 141 E1
Rossett 78 A2
Rossett Green 102 C2
Rosside 107 D5
Rossie Farm School 161 E4
Rossie Ochill 151 F3
Rossie Priory 152 A1
Rossington 94 D3
Rosskeen 174 D5
Rossmore 13 G3
Ross-on-Wye 53 F5
Roster 183 H5
Rostherne 92 B4
Rosthwaite Cumb. 117 F5
Rosthwaite Cumb. 106 D4
Roston 80 C3
Rosudgeon 2 C4
Rosyth 143 F1
Rothbury 128 C1
Rotherby 68 B1
Rotherfield 31 E5
Rotherfield Greys 42 C4
Rotherfield Peppard 42 C4
Rotherham 94 B3
Rothersthorpe 56 C2
Rotherwick 28 C2
Rothes 175 K7
Rothesay 140 B3
Rothiebrisbane 169 F1
Rothienorman 169 F1
Rothiesholm 184 F5
Rothley Leics. 68 A1
Rothley Northumb. 128 C3
Rothney 168 E2
Rothwell Lincs. 96 B3
Rothwell Northants. 68 D4
Rothwell W.Yorks. 102 C5
Rotsea 104 C2
Rottal 160 B3
Rotten Row Bucks. 42 C4
Rotten Row W.Mid. 67 D5
Rottingdean 17 F3
Rottington 116 C5
Roud 15 E4
Roudham 72 A3
Rough Close 79 G4
Rough Common 32 D3
Rougham Norf. 85 G5
Rougham Suff. 60 A1
Rougham Green 60 A1
Roughburn 157 F1
Roughlee 101 E3
Roughley 66 D3
Roughton Lincs. 84 A1
Roughton Norf. 86 D2
Roughton Shrop. 65 G3
Round Bush 44 A3
Roundbush Green 45 E1
Roundham 12 A2
Roundhay 102 C4
Roundstreet Common 29 F5
Roundway 26 B1
Rous Lench 54 C2
Rousay 184 C4
Rousdon 11 F3
Rousham 55 G5
Rousham Gap 55 G5
Routenburn 140 C3
Routh 104 C3
Rout's Green 42 C3
Row Cornw. 5 E2
Row Cumb. 107 F4
Row Cumb. 118 C4
Row Heath 47 E1
Row Town 29 F1
Rowanburn 126 C4
Rowardennan Lodge 149 F5
Rowarth 93 E4
Rowbarton 23 F5
Rowberrow 24 B2
Rowchoish 149 F4
Rowde 26 A1
Rowden 7 G1
Rowen 89 F5
Rowfields 80 C3
Rowfoot 118 C1
Rowhedge 60 B5
Rowhook 29 G4
Rowington 55 E1
Rowland 93 G5
Rowland's Castle 15 G1
Rowlands Gill 120 A2
Rowledge 28 D3
Rowlestone 52 C5
Rowley Devon 10 A1
Rowley Dur. 119 G3
Rowley Shrop. 64 C2
Rowley Park 79 G5
Rowley Regis 66 B4
Rowly 29 F3
Rowner 15 E2
Rowney Green 66 C5
Rownhams 14 C1
Rowrah 117 D5
Rowsham 43 D1
Rowsley 81 D1
Rowstock 41 G4
Rowston 83 F2
Rowthorne 81 F1
Rowton Ches. 78 B1
Rowton Shrop. 64 C1
Rowton Tel. & W. 65 F1
Roxburgh 136 B3
Roxby N.Lincs. 95 G1
Roxby N.Yorks. 111 G1
Roxton 57 G2
Roxwell 45 F2
Royal British Legion Village 31 G3
Royal Leamington Spa 55 F1
Royal Oak 91 F2
Royal Tunbridge Wells 31 E5
Roybridge 157 E1
Roydon Essex 44 D1
Roydon Norf. 72 B3
Roydon Norf. 85 F5
Roydon Hamlet 44 D2
Royston Herts. 58 B3
Royston S.Yorks. 94 A1
Royton 92 D2
Rozel 8 C5
Ruabon 78 A3
Ruaig 154 B2
Ruan Lanihorne 4 C5
Ruan Major 3 E5
Ruan Minor 3 E5
Ruanaich 146 B2
Ruardean 39 F1
Ruardean Hill 39 F1
Ruardean Woodside 39 F1
Rubery 66 B5
Ruckcroft 118 B3
Ruckinge 32 C5
Ruckland 96 D5
Rucklers Lane 43 F2
Ruckley 65 E2
Rudbaxton 48 C5
Rudby 111 D2
Rudchester 120 A1
Ruddington 81 G4
Ruddlemoor 5 E4
Rudford 53 G5
Rudge 25 F2
Rudgeway 39 F4
Rudgwick 29 F4
Rudhall 53 F5
Rudheath 92 A5
Rudley Green 46 B2
Rudloe 25 F1
Rudry 38 A4
Rudston 104 C1
Rudyard 79 G2
Rufford 91 F1
Rufforth 103 E2
Ruffside 119 F2
Rugby 68 A5
Rugeley 66 C1
Ruilick 174 C7
Ruishton 23 F5
Ruisigearraidh 170 E3
Ruislip 43 F4
Ruislip Gardens 43 F4
Ruislip Manor 44 A4
Rum 163 J5
Rumbling Bridge 151 F5
Rumburgh 73 E3
Rumford 4 C2
Rumleigh 8 A1
Rumney 38 B5
Rumwell 23 E5
Runacraig 150 A3
Runcorn 91 G4
Runcton 16 A3
Runcton Holme 71 E2
Rundlestone 7 F3
Runfold 29 D3
Runhall 86 B5
Runham Norf. 87 F4
Runham Norf. 87 G5
Runnington 23 E5
Runsell Green 45 G2
Runshaw Moor 91 G1
Runswick Bay 112 B1
Runtaleave 160 A3
Runwell 45 G3
Ruscombe Glos. 40 A2
Ruscombe W'ham 42 C5
Rush Green Gt.Lon. 45 E4
Rush Green Herts. 58 A5
Rushall Here. 53 F4
Rushall Norf. 72 C3
Rushall W.Mid. 66 C2
Rushall Wilts. 26 C2
Rushbrooke 59 G1
Rushbury 65 E3
Rushden Herts. 58 B4
Rushden Northants. 57 E1
Rushford Devon 7 E3
Rushford Norf. 72 A3
Rushgreen 92 A4
Rushlake Green 18 B2
Rushmere 73 F3
Rushmere St. Andrew 60 D3
Rushmoor 29 D3
Rushock 66 A5
Rusholme 92 C3
Rushton Ches. 78 C1
Rushton Northants. 68 D4
Rushton Shrop. 65 F2
Rushton Spencer 79 G1
Rushwick 54 A2
Rushy Green 17 G2
Rushyford 120 B5
Ruskie 150 B4
Ruskington 83 F2
Rusko 123 G5
Rusland 107 E4
Rusper 30 B5
Ruspidge 39 F1
Russ Hill 30 B4
Russel 172 E7
Russell Green 45 G1
Russell's Green 18 C2
Russell's Water 42 C3
Russel's Green 73 D4
Rusthall 31 E5
Rustington 16 C3
Ruston 112 C4
Ruston Parva 104 C1
Ruswarp 112 B2
Rutherend 142 A4
Rutherford 136 A3
Rutherglen 142 A3
Ruthernbridge 5 E3
Ruthers of Howe 183 J2
Ruthin (Rhuthun) Denb. 77 E2
Ruthin V. of Glam. 37 F5
Ruthrieston 169 H4
Ruthven Aber. 176 D6
Ruthven Angus 160 A5
Ruthven High. 167 F1
Ruthven High. 166 E5
Ruthvoes 4 D3
Ruthwaite 117 F3
Ruthwell 125 E4
Ruyton-XI-Towns 78 A5
Ryal 128 C4
Ryal Fold 100 C5
Ryall Dorset 12 A3
Ryall Worcs. 54 A3
Ryarsh 31 F3
Rydal 107 E2
Ryde 15 E3
Rydon 20 D5
Rye 19 E1
Rye Foreign 19 D1
Rye Harbour 19 E2
Rye Park 44 C2
Rye Street 53 G4
Ryebank 78 C4
Ryeford 53 F5
Ryehill Aber. 168 E2
Ryehill E.Riding 105 E5
Ryhall 69 F1
Ryhill 94 A1
Ryhope 120 D2
Rylands 81 G4
Rylstone 101 F2
Ryme Intrinseca 12 B1
Ryther 103 E4
Ryton Glos. 53 G4
Ryton N.Yorks. 111 G5
Ryton Shrop. 65 G2
Ryton T. & W. 120 A1
Ryton-on-Dunsmore 67 F5

▼S

Saasaig 164 C4
Sabden 101 D4
Sabden Fold 101 E4
Sackers Green 60 A4
Sacombe 44 C1
Sacombe Green 44 C1
Sacriston 120 B3
Sadberge 110 C1
Saddell 130 C2
Saddington 68 B3
Saddle Bow 71 E1
Sadgill 107 F2
Saffron Walden 58 D4
Sageston 35 D2
Saham Hills 86 A5
Saham Toney 71 G2
Saighdinis 170 D5
Saighton 78 B1
St. Abbs 145 G3
St. Agnes 4 B4
St. Albans 44 A2
St. Allen 4 C4
St. Andrews 152 D3
St. Andrews Major 38 A5
St. Anne 9 G4
St. Anne's 99 G5
St. Ann's 125 E1
St. Ann's Chapel Cornw. 7 E3
St. Ann's Chapel Devon 8 C3
St. Anthony 3 F3
St. Anthony-in-Meneage 3 E4
St. Anthony's Hill 18 B3
St. Arvans 39 E3
St. Asaph (Llanelwy) 90 B5
St. Athan 22 D1
St. Aubin 8 C5
St. Audries 23 E3
St. Austell 5 E4
St. Bees 116 C5
St. Blazey 5 E4
St. Blazey Gate 5 E4
St. Boswells 135 G2
St. Brelade 8 B5
St. Breock 5 D2
St. Breward 5 E2
St. Briavels 39 E2
St. Brides 34 B1
St. Brides Major 37 E5
St. Bride's Netherwent 38 D4
St. Brides Wentlooge 38 B4
St. Bride's-super-Ely 37 G5
St. Budeaux 8 A2
St. Buryan 2 B4
St. Catherine 25 E1
St. Catherines 148 D4
St. Clears 35 F1
St. Cleer 5 G3
St. Clement Chan.I. 8 C5
St. Clement Cornw. 4 C5
St. Clether 5 G1
St. Colmac 140 B3
St. Columb Major 4 D3
St. Columb Minor 4 C3
St. Columb Road 4 D4
St. Combs 177 J4
St. Cross South Elmham 73 D3
St. Cyrus 161 F3
St. Davids Fife 143 F1
St. David's P. & K. 151 E2
St. David's (Tyddewi) Pembs. 48 A5
St. Day 4 B5
St. Decumans 23 D3
St. Dennis 5 D4
St. Denys 14 D1
St. Dogmaels (Llandudoch) 49 E3
St. Dogwells 48 C5
St. Dominick 8 A1
St. Donats 22 C1
St. Edith's Marsh 26 A1
St. Endellion 5 D2
St. Enoder 4 C4
St. Erme 4 C5
St. Erney 7 D5
St. Erth 2 C3
St. Erth Praze 2 C3
St. Ervan 4 C2
St. Eval 4 C3
St. Ewe 5 D5
St. Fagans 38 A5
St. Fergus 177 J5
St. Fillans 150 B2
St. Florence 35 D2
St. Gennys 6 B1
St. George Bristol 39 F5
St. George Conwy 90 A5
St. Georges N.Som. 24 A1
St. George's Tel. & W. 65 G1
St. George's V. of Glam. 37 G5
St. Germans 7 D5
St. Giles in the Wood 21 F4
St. Giles on the Heath 7 D1
St. Harmon 63 F5
St. Helen Auckland 120 A5
St. Helena 86 C4
St. Helen's E.Suss. 18 D2
St. Helens I.o.W. 15 F4
St. Helens Mersey. 91 G3
St. Helier Chan.I. 8 C5
St. Helier Gt.Lon. 30 B2
St. Hilary Cornw. 2 C3
St. Hilary V. of Glam. 37 G5
St. Hill 30 C5
St. Ibbs 57 G5
St. Illtyd 38 B2
St. Ippollitts 57 G5
St. Ishmael 35 G2
St. Ishmael's 34 B2
St. Issey 4 D2
St. Ive 6 D4
St. Ives Cambs. 70 B5
St. Ives Cornw. 2 C2
St. Ives Dorset 14 A2
St. James South Elmham 73 E3
St. John Chan.I. 8 C4
St. John Cornw. 8 A2
St. John's Gt.Lon. 44 C5
St. John's I.o.M. 98 A3
St. John's Surr. 29 E2
St. John's Worcs. 54 A2
St. John's Chapel Devon 21 F3
St. John's Chapel Dur. 119 E4
St. John's Fen End 70 D1
St. John's Hall 119 G4
St. John's Highway 70 D1
St. John's Kirk 134 A2
St. John's Town of Dalry 124 A2
St. Judes 98 B2
St. Just 2 A3
St. Just in Roseland 3 F3
St. Katherines 169 F1
St. Keverne 3 E4
St. Kew 5 E2
St. Kew Highway 5 E2
St. Keyne 5 G3
St. Lawrence Cornw. 5 E3
St. Lawrence Essex 46 C2
St. Lawrence I.o.W. 15 E5
St. Leonards Bucks. 43 E2
St. Leonards Dorset 14 A2
St. Leonards E.Suss. 18 D3
St. Leonards Grange 14 D3
St. Leonard's Street 31 F3
St. Levan 2 A4
St. Lythans 38 A5
St. Mabyn 5 E2
St. Madoes 151 G2
St. Margaret South Elmham 73 E3
St. Margarets Here. 52 C4
St. Margarets Herts. 44 C1
St. Margarets Wilts. 26 D1
St. Margaret's at Cliffe 33 F4
St. Margaret's Hope 185 D8
St. Mark's 98 A4
St. Martin Chan.I. 9 F5
St. Martin Chan.I. 8 C5
St. Martin Cornw. 5 G4
St. Martin Cornw. 3 E4
St. Martin's I.o.S. 4 B1
St. Martins P. & K. 151 G1
St. Martin's Shrop. 78 A4
St. Mary 8 C5
St. Mary Bourne 27 F2
St. Mary Church 37 G5
St. Mary Cray 31 D2
St. Mary Hill 37 F5
St. Mary Hoo 45 G5
St. Mary in the Marsh 19 F1
St. Marychurch 9 F1
St. Mary's I.o.S. 4 B1
St. Mary's Ork. 185 D7
St. Mary's Airport 4 B1
St. Mary's Bay 19 F1
St. Mary's Croft 122 B4
St. Mary's Grove 24 B1
St. Maughans Green 39 D1
St. Mawes 3 F3
St. Mawgan 4 C3
St. Mellion 7 D4
St. Mellons 38 B4
St. Merryn 4 C2
St. Mewan 5 D4
St. Michael Caerhays 5 D5
St. Michael Church 24 A4
St. Michael Penkevil 4 C5
St. Michael South Elmham 73 E3
St. Michaels Fife 152 C2
St. Michaels Kent 32 A5
St. Michaels Worcs. 53 E1
St. Michael's on Wyre 100 A3
St. Minver 5 D2
St. Monans 152 D4
St. Neot 5 F3
St. Neots 57 G1
St. Newlyn East 4 C4
St. Nicholas Pembs. 48 C4
St. Nicholas V. of Glam. 37 G5
St. Nicholas at Wade 33 E2
St. Ninians 150 C5
St. Osyth 47 E1
St. Ouen 8 B5
St. Owen's Cross 53 E5
St. Paul's Cray 31 D2
St. Paul's Walden 57 G5
St. Peter 8 C5
St. Peter Port 9 F5
St. Peter's 33 F2
St. Petrox 34 C3
St. Pinnock 5 G3
St. Quivox 132 B3
St. Ruan 3 E5
St. Sampson 9 F4
St. Saviour Chan.I. 9 E5
St. Saviour Chan.I. 8 C5
St. Stephen 4 D4
St. Stephens Cornw. 8 A2
St. Stephens Cornw. 6 D2
St. Stephens Herts. 44 A2
St. Teath 5 E1
St. Thomas 10 C3
St. Tudy 5 E2
St. Twynnells 34 C3
St. Veep 5 F4
St. Vigeans 161 E5
St. Wenn 5 D3
St. Weonards 53 D5
St. Winnow 5 F4
St. y Nyll 37 G5
Saintbury 54 D4
Salachail 156 C4
Salcombe 8 D4
Salcombe Regis 11 E4
Salcott 46 C1
Sale 92 B3
Sale Green 54 B2
Saleby 97 E5
Salehurst 18 C1
Salem Carmar. 50 C5
Salem Cere. 62 C4
Salem Gwyn. 75 E2
Salen Arg. & B. 155 E5
Salen High. 155 F3
Salendine Nook 93 F1
Salesbury 100 C4
Saleway 54 B2
Salford Beds. 57 E4
Salford Gt.Man. 92 C3
Salford Oxon. 55 E5
Salford Priors 54 C2
Salfords 30 B4
Salhouse 87 E4
Saline 151 F5
Salisbury 26 C5
Salkeld Dykes 118 B4
Sallachan 156 B3
Sallachy 148 C3
Sallachy High. 174 C1
Sallachy High. 165 F1
Salle 86 C3
Salmonby 96 D5
Salmond's Muir 153 D1
Salperton 54 C5
Salph End 57 F2
Salsburgh 142 C3
Salt 79 G5
Salt Hill 43 E4
Salt Holme 121 D5
Saltaire 102 A4
Saltash 8 A2
Saltburn 174 E4
Saltburn-by-the-Sea 121 F5
Saltby 83 D5
Saltcoats Cumb. 106 B3
Saltcoats N.Ayr. 140 D5
Saltcotes 99 G5
Saltdean 17 F3
Salterbeck 116 C4
Salterforth 101 E3
Saltergate 112 B3
Salterhill 175 K5
Salterswall 78 D1
Saltfleet 97 E3
Saltfleetby All Saints 97 E3
Saltfleetby St. Clements 97 E3
Saltfleetby St. Peter 97 E4
Saltford 25 D1
Salthaugh Grange 105 E5
Salthouse 86 B1
Saltley 66 C4
Saltmarshe 103 G5
Saltness 185 B8
Saltney 78 A1
Salton 111 G4
Saltrens 21 E3
Saltwick 129 D4
Saltwood 33 D5
Salum 154 B2
Salvington 16 D3
Salwarpe 54 A1
Salwayash 12 A3
Sambourne 54 C1
Sambrook 79 E5
Samhla 170 C5
Samlesbury 100 C4
Sampford Arundel 11 E1
Sampford Brett 23 D3
Sampford Courtenay 21 G5
Sampford Moor 11 E1
Sampford Peverell 10 D1
Sampford Spiney 7 F3
Samuelston 144 B2
Sanaigmore 138 A2
Sancreed 2 B4
Sancton 104 B4
Sand Shet. 187 C8
Sand Som. 24 B3
Sand Hutton 103 F2
Sandaig Arg. & B. 154 A2
Sandaig High. 164 D4
Sandaig High. 164 D3
Sandal Magna 94 A1
Sanday 184 G3
Sandbach 79 E1
Sandbank 140 C1
Sandbanks 13 G4
Sandend 176 D4
Sanderstead 30 C2
Sandford Cumb. 108 C1
Sandford Devon 10 B2
Sandford Dorset 13 F4
Sandford I.o.W. 15 E4
Sandford N.Som. 24 B2
Sandford S.Lan. 142 B5
Sandford Shrop. 78 C4
Sandford Shrop. 78 A5
Sandford Orcas 24 D5
Sandford St. Martin 55 G5
Sandfordhill 177 K6
Sandford-on-Thames 42 A2
Sandgarth 185 E6
Sandgate 33 E5
Sandgreen 123 G5
Sandhaven 177 H4
Sandhead 122 B5
Sandhills Dorset 12 C1
Sandhills Dorset 12 B2
Sandhills Surr. 29 E4
Sandhills W.Yorks. 102 C4
Sandhoe 119 F1
Sandholme E.Riding 104 A4
Sandholme Lincs. 84 B4
Sandhurst Brack.F. 28 D1
Sandhurst Glos. 54 A5
Sandhurst Kent 18 C1
Sandhurst Cross 18 C1
Sandhutton 110 C4
Sandiacre 81 F4
Sandilands 97 F4
Sandiway 92 A5
Sandleheath 14 A1
Sandleigh 41 G2
Sandling 31 G3
Sandlow Green 79 E1
Sandness 187 A7
Sandon Essex 45 G2
Sandon Herts. 58 B4
Sandon Staffs. 79 G5
Sandown 15 F4
Sandplace 5 G4
Sandquoy 184 G3
Sandridge Devon 9 E2
Sandridge Herts. 44 A1
Sandridge Wilts. 26 A1
Sandringham 85 E5
Sandrocks 17 F1
Sandsend 112 B1
Sandside 107 F4
Sandside House 182 E2

Sandsound 187 C8
Sandtoft 95 E2
Sanduck 10 A4
Sandway 32 A3
Sandwell 66 C4
Sandwich 33 F3
Sandwick *Cumb.* 107 F1
Sandwick *Shet.* 187 D10
Sandwick (Sanndabhaig) *W.Isles* 179 G4
Sandwith 116 C5
Sandy *Beds.* 57 G3
Sandy *Carmar.* 36 A2
Sandy Bank 84 A2
Sandy Haven 34 B2
Sandy Lane *W.Yorks.* 102 A4
Sandy Lane *Wilts.* 26 A1
Sandy Lane *Wrex.* 78 B3
Sandy Way 15 D4
Sandycroft 78 A1
Sandygate *Devon* 10 B5
Sandygate *I.o.M.* 98 B2
Sandyhills 124 C5
Sandylands 100 A1
Sandypark 10 A4
Sandyway 53 D5
Sangobeg 181 G2
Sankyn's Green 53 G1
Sanna 155 D3
Sannaig 138 D3
Sanndabhaig (Sandwick) 179 G4
Sannox 140 B5
Sanquhar 133 F5
Santon Bridge 106 C2
Santon Downham 71 G4
Sapcote 67 G3
Sapey Common 53 G1
Sapiston 72 A4
Sapperton *Derbys.* 80 C4
Sapperton *Glos.* 40 B2
Sapperton *Lincs.* 83 F4
Saracen's Head 84 B5
Sarclet 183 J4
Sardis 34 C2
Sarisbury 15 E2
Sark 9 G5
Sarn *Bridgend* 37 F4
Sarn *Powys* 64 B3
Sarn Bach 74 C5
Sarn Meyllteyrn 74 B4
Sarnau *Carmar.* 35 G1
Sarnau *Cere.* 49 G2
Sarnau *Gwyn.* 76 C4
Sarnau *Powys* 64 B1
Sarnau *Powys* 51 G4
Sarnesfield 52 C2
Saron *Carmar.* 36 C1
Saron *Carmar.* 49 G4
Saron *Gwyn.* 75 E1
Saron *Gwyn.* 75 D2
Sarratt 43 F3
Sarre 33 E2
Sarsden 55 E5
Sarsgrum 181 F2
Sartfield 98 B2
Satley 120 A3
Satron 109 E3
Satterleigh 21 G3
Satterthwaite 107 E3
Sauchen 168 E3
Saucher 151 G1
Sauchie 151 D5
Sauchieburn 161 E3
Sauchrie 132 B4
Saughall 91 E5
Saughall Massie 91 D4
Saughtree 127 D2
Saul 39 G2
Saundby 95 E4
Saundersfoot 35 E2
Saunderton 42 C2
Saunton 21 E2
Sausthorpe 84 B1
Saval 174 C1
Savalbeg 174 C1
Saverley Green 79 G4
Savile Town 102 B5
Sawbridge 56 A1
Sawbridgeworth 45 D1
Sawdon 112 C4
Sawley *Derbys.* 81 F4
Sawley *Lancs.* 101 D3
Sawley *N.Yorks.* 102 B1
Sawston 58 C3
Sawtry 69 G4
Saxby *Leics.* 68 D1
Saxby *Lincs.* 96 A4
Saxby All Saints 95 G1
Saxelbye 82 B5
Saxham Street 60 B1
Saxilby 95 F5
Saxlingham 86 B2
Saxlingham Green 72 D2
Saxlingham Nethergate 72 D2
Saxlingham Thorpe 72 D2
Saxmundham 61 E1
Saxon Street 59 E2
Saxondale 82 B4
Saxtead 61 D1
Saxtead Green 61 D1
Saxtead Little Green 61 D1
Saxthorpe 86 C2
Saxton 103 D4
Sayers Common 17 E2
Scackleton 111 F5
Scadabhagh 171 G2
Scaftworth 95 D3
Scagglethorpe 112 B5
Scaitcliffe 101 D5
Scalasaig 146 C5
Scalby *E.Riding* 104 A5
Scalby *N.Yorks.* 112 D3
Scaldwell 68 C5
Scale Houses 118 B3
Scaleby 118 A1
Scalebyhill 118 A1
Scales *Cumb.* 117 G4
Scales *Cumb.* 107 D5
Scalford 82 C5
Scaling 111 G1
Scallasaig 164 E3
Scallastle 147 G1
Scalloway 187 C9
Scalpay *W.Isles* 171 H2
Scalpay (Eilean Scalpaigh) *W.Isles* 171 H2
Scamblesby 96 C5
Scammadale 148 A2
Scamodale 156 A2
Scampston 112 B5
Scampton 95 G5
Scaniport 166 D1
Scapa 185 D7
Scapegoat Hill 93 E1
Scar 184 F3
Scarborough 112 D4
Scarcewater 4 D4
Scarcliffe 81 F1
Scarcroft 102 C3
Scardroy 173 J6
Scarff 186 B4
Scarfskerry 183 H1
Scargill 109 F1
Scarinish 154 B2
Scarisbrick 91 E1
Scarning 86 A4
Scarrington 82 C3
Scarrowhill 118 B2
Scarth Hill 91 F2
Scarthingwell 103 D4
Scartho 96 C2
Scarwell 184 B5
Scatraig 166 E1
Scaur *D. & G.* 124 C3
Scaur (Kippford) *D. & G.* 124 C5
Scawby 95 G2
Scawby Brook 95 G2
Scawton 111 E4
Scayne's Hill 17 F1
Scealascro 178 D5
Scethrog 52 A5
Schaw 132 C3
Scholar Green 79 F2
Scholes *S.Yorks.* 94 A3
Scholes *W.Yorks.* 102 C4
Scholes *W.Yorks.* 93 F2
Scholes *W.Yorks.* 102 A5
School Green 78 D1
School House 11 G2
Schoose 116 D4
Sciberscross 174 E1
Scilly Isles (Isles of Scilly) 4 B1
Scissett 93 G1
Scleddau 48 C4
Sco Ruston 87 D3
Scofton 94 D4
Scole 72 C4
Scolpaig 170 C4
Scone 151 G2
Scones Lethendy 151 G2
Sconser 164 B1
Scoor 146 D3
Scopwick 83 F2
Scoraig 173 G2
Scorborough 104 C3
Scorrier 4 B5
Scorriton 8 D1
Scorton *Lancs.* 100 B3
Scorton *N.Yorks.* 110 B2
Scot Hay 79 F3
Scotby 118 A2
Scotch Corner 110 B2
Scotforth 100 A2
Scothern 96 A5
Scotland 83 F4
Scotland End 55 F4
Scotland Street 60 A4
Scotlandwell 151 G4
Scotnish 139 F1
Scots' Gap 128 C3
Scotsburn 174 E4
Scotston *Aber.* 161 F2
Scotston *P. & K.* 159 E5
Scotstoun 141 G3
Scotstown 156 A3
Scott Willoughby 83 F4
Scotter 95 F2
Scotterthorpe 95 F2
Scottlethorpe 83 F5
Scotton *Lincs.* 95 F3
Scotton *N.Yorks.* 110 A3
Scotton *N.Yorks.* 102 C2
Scottow 87 D3
Scoughall 144 D1
Scoulton 86 A5
Scounslow Green 80 B5
Scourie 180 D4
Scourie More 180 D4
Scousburgh 187 F9
Scouthead 93 D2
Scrabster 183 G1
Scrafield 84 B1
Scrainwood 128 B1
Scrane End 84 B3
Scraptoft 68 B2
Scratby 87 G4
Scrayingham 103 G2
Scredington 83 F3
Scremby 84 C1
Scremerston 137 E2
Screveton 82 C3
Scriven 102 C2
Scronkey 100 A3
Scrooby 95 D3
Scropton 80 C4
Scrub Hill 84 A2
Scruton 110 C3
Sculthorpe 85 G4
Scunthorpe 95 F1
Scurlage 36 A4
Sea 11 G1
Sea Mills 39 E5
Sea Palling 87 F3
Seabank 156 B5
Seaborough 12 A2
Seaburn 120 D1
Seacombe 91 D3
Seacroft *Lincs.* 85 D1
Seacroft *W.Yorks.* 102 C4
Seadyke 84 B4
Seafield *Arg. & B.* 139 F1
Seafield *S.Ayr.* 132 B3
Seafield *W.Loth.* 143 E3
Seaford 17 G4
Seaforth 91 E3
Seagrave 68 B1
Seagry Heath 40 B4
Seaham 120 D3
Seaham Grange 120 D2
Seahouses 137 G3
Seal 31 E3
Sealand 78 A1
Seale 29 D3
Sealyham 48 C5
Seamer *N.Yorks.* 111 D1
Seamer *N.Yorks.* 112 D4
Seamill 140 C5
Searby 96 A2
Seasalter 32 C2
Seascale 106 B2
Seathorne 85 D1
Seathwaite *Cumb.* 117 F5
Seathwaite *Cumb.* 106 D3
Seatle 107 E4
Seatoller 117 F5
Seaton *Cornw.* 6 D5
Seaton *Cumb.* 116 D3
Seaton *Devon* 11 F3
Seaton *Dur.* 120 C2
Seaton *E.Riding* 105 D3
Seaton *Northumb.* 129 F4
Seaton *Rut.* 69 E3
Seaton Burn 129 E4
Seaton Carew 121 E5
Seaton Delaval 129 F4
Seaton Junction 11 F3
Seaton Ross 103 G3
Seaton Sluice 129 F4
Seatown *Aber.* 177 J5
Seatown *Dorset* 12 A3
Seatown *Moray* 176 D4
Seave Green 111 E2
Seaview 15 F3
Seaville 117 E1
Seavington St. Mary 12 A1
Seavington St. Michael 12 A1
Seawick 47 E1
Sebastopol 38 B3
Sebergham 117 G2
Seckington 67 E2
Second Coast 173 F2
Sedbergh 108 B3
Sedbury 39 E3
Sedbusk 109 D3
Seddington 57 G3
Sedgeberrow 54 C4
Sedgebrook 83 D4
Sedgefield 120 C5
Sedgeford 85 F4
Sedgehill 25 F5
Sedgemere 67 E5
Sedgley 66 B3
Sedgwick 107 G4
Sedlescombe 18 C2
Sedlescombe Street 18 C2
Seend 26 A1
Seend Cleeve 26 A1
Seer Green 43 E3
Seething 73 E2
Sefton 91 E2
Seghill 129 E4
Seifton 65 D4
Seighford 79 F5
Seil 147 G3
Seilebost 171 F2
Seion 75 E1
Seisdon 66 A3
Seisiadar 179 H4
Selattyn 77 F4
Selborne 28 C4
Selby 103 F4
Selham 29 E5
Selhurst 30 C2
Selkirk 135 F3
Sellack 53 E5
Sellafield 106 B2
Sellafirth 186 E3
Sellindge 32 C5
Selling 32 C3
Sells Green 26 A1
Selly Oak 66 C4
Selmeston 18 A3
Selsdon 30 C2
Selsey 16 A4
Selsfield Common 30 C5
Selside *Cumb.* 107 G3
Selside *N.Yorks.* 108 C5
Selsley 40 A2
Selstead 33 E4
Selston 81 F2
Selworthy 22 C3
Semblister 187 C7
Semer 60 A3
Semington 25 F1
Semley 25 F5
Send 29 F2
Send Marsh 29 F2
Senghenydd 38 A3
Sennen 2 A4
Sennen Cove 2 A4
Sennybridge 51 F5
Senwick 115 G2
Sequer's Bridge 8 C2
Serlby 94 D4
Serrington 26 B4
Sessay 111 D5
Setchey 71 E1
Setley 14 C2
Setter *Shet.* 187 E8
Setter *Shet.* 187 C7
Settiscarth 185 C6
Settle 101 E1
Settrington 112 B5
Seven Ash 23 E4
Seven Bridges 40 D3
Seven Kings 45 D4
Seven Sisters 37 E2
Seven Springs 40 B1
Sevenhampton *Glos.* 54 C5
Sevenhampton *Swin.* 41 E3
Sevenoaks 31 E3
Sevenoaks Weald 31 E3
Severn Beach 39 E4
Severn Stoke 54 A3
Sevick End 57 F2
Sevington 32 C4
Sewards End 59 D4
Sewardstone 44 C3
Sewerby 105 D1
Seworgan 3 E3
Sewstern 83 D5
Seymour Villas 21 E1
Sezincote 55 D4
Sgarasta Mhòr 171 F2
Sgiogarstaigh 179 H1
Sgodachail 174 B2
Shabbington 42 B2
Shackerley 66 A2
Shackerstone 67 F2
Shackleford 29 E3
Shadfen 129 E3
Shadforth 120 C3
Shadingfield 73 F3
Shadoxhurst 32 B5
Shadsworth 100 D5
Shadwell *Norf.* 72 A3
Shadwell *W.Yorks.* 102 C3
Shaftenhoe End 58 C4
Shaftesbury 25 F5
Shafton 94 A1
Shalbourne 27 E1
Shalcombe 14 C4
Shalden 28 B3
Shalden Green 28 C3
Shaldon 10 C5
Shalfleet 14 D4
Shalford *Essex* 59 F5
Shalford *Surr.* 29 F3
Shalford Green 59 F5
Shallowford *Devon* 22 A3
Shallowford *Staffs.* 79 F5
Shalmsford Street 32 C3
Shalmstry 183 G2
Shalstone 56 B4
Shalunt 140 B2
Shambellie 125 D4
Shamley Green 29 F3
Shandon 141 D1
Shandwick 175 F4
Shangton 68 C3
Shankend 135 G5
Shankhouse 129 E4
Shanklin 15 E4
Shannochie 131 E3
Shantron 141 E1
Shantullich 174 D6
Shanzie 160 A4
Shap 107 G1
Shapinsay 185 E6
Shapwick *Dorset* 13 F2
Shapwick *Som.* 24 B4
Sharcott 26 C2
Shard End 67 D4
Shardlow 81 F4
Shareshill 66 B2
Sharlston 94 A1
Sharlston Common 94 A1
Sharnal Street 45 G5
Sharnbrook 57 E2
Sharneyford 101 E5
Sharnford 67 G3
Sharnhill Green 12 D2
Sharow 110 C5
Sharp Street 87 E3
Sharpenhoe 57 F4
Sharperton 128 B1
Sharpham House 9 E2
Sharpness 39 F2
Sharpthorne 30 C5
Sharrington 86 B2
Shatterford 65 G4
Shatterling 33 E3
Shaugh Prior 8 B1
Shave Cross 12 A3
Shavington 79 E2
Shaw *Gt.Man.* 92 D2
Shaw *Swin.* 40 D4
Shaw *W.Berks.* 27 F1
Shaw *Wilts.* 25 F1
Shaw Green *Herts.* 58 A4
Shaw Green *N.Yorks.* 102 B2
Shaw Mills 102 B1
Shaw Side 92 D2
Shawbost (Siabost) 178 E3
Shawbury 78 C5
Shawell 68 A4
Shawfield *Gt.Man.* 92 C1
Shawfield *Staffs.* 80 B1
Shawford 27 F5
Shawforth 101 E5
Shawhead 124 C3
Shawtonhill 142 A5
Sheanachie 130 C4
Sheandow 167 K1
Shearington 125 E4
Shearsby 68 B3
Shebbear 21 E5
Shebdon 79 E5
Shebster 183 F2
Shedfield 15 E1
Sheen 80 C1
Sheepridge 93 F1
Sheepscombe 40 A1
Sheepstor 8 B1
Sheepwash *Devon* 21 E5
Sheepwash *Northumb.* 129 E3
Sheepway 39 D5
Sheepy Magna 67 F2
Sheepy Parva 67 F2
Sheering 45 E1
Sheerness 32 B1
Sheet 28 C5
Sheffield 94 A4
Sheffield Bottom 28 B1
Sheffield Green 17 G1
Shefford 57 G4
Shefford Woodlands 41 F5
Sheigra 180 D2
Sheinton 65 F2
Shelderton 64 D5
Sheldon *Derbys.* 80 C1
Sheldon *Devon* 11 E2
Sheldon *W.Mid.* 66 D4
Sheldwich 32 C3
Sheldwich Lees 32 C3
Shelf *Bridgend* 37 F4
Shelf *W.Yorks.* 102 A5
Shelfanger 72 C3
Shelfield *W.Mid.* 66 C2
Shelfield *Warks.* 54 D1
Shelfield Green 54 D1
Shelford 82 B3
Shellachan *Arg. & B.* 148 A2
Shellachan *Arg. & B.* 148 C2
Shellbrook 67 F1
Shellbrook Hill 78 A3
Shelley *Essex* 45 E2
Shelley *Suff.* 60 B4
Shelley *W.Yorks.* 93 G1
Shellingford 41 F3
Shellow Bowells 45 F2
Shelsley Beauchamp 53 G1
Shelsley Walsh 53 G1
Shelswell 56 B4
Shelthorpe 68 A1
Shelton *Beds.* 57 F1
Shelton *Norf.* 72 D2
Shelton *Notts.* 82 C3
Shelton *Shrop.* 65 D1
Shelve 64 C3
Shelwick 53 E3
Shelwick Green 53 E3
Shenfield 45 F3
Shenington 55 F3
Shenley 44 A2
Shenley Brook End 56 D4
Shenley Church End 56 D4
Shenleybury 44 A2
Shenmore 52 C4
Shennanton 123 E4
Shenstone *Staffs.* 66 D2
Shenstone *Worcs.* 66 A5
Shenstone Woodend 66 D2
Shenton 67 F2
Shenval 167 K2
Shepeau Stow 70 B1
Shephall 58 A5
Shepherd's Bush 44 B5
Shepherd's Green 42 C4
Shepherd's Patch 39 G2
Shepherdswell (Sibertswold) 33 E4
Shepley 93 F2
Sheppardstown 183 H5
Shepperdine 39 F3
Shepperton 29 F1
Shepreth 58 B3
Shepshed 67 G1
Shepton Beauchamp 12 A1
Shepton Mallet 24 D3
Shepton Montague 25 D4
Shepway 31 G3
Sheraton 120 D4
Sherborne *Dorset* 12 C1
Sherborne *Glos.* 41 D1
Sherborne St. John 28 B2
Sherbourne 55 E1
Sherbourne Street 60 A3
Sherburn *Dur.* 120 C3
Sherburn *N.Yorks.* 112 C5
Sherburn Hill 120 C3
Sherburn in Elmet 103 D4
Shere 29 F3
Shereford 85 G5
Sherfield English 27 D5
Sherfield on Loddon 28 B2
Sherford *Devon* 9 D3
Sherford *Som.* 23 F5
Sheriff Hutton 103 F1
Sheriffhales 65 G1
Sheringham 86 C1
Sherington 57 D3
Shernal Green 54 B1
Shernborne 85 F4
Sherramore 166 C5
Sherrington 26 A4
Sherston 40 A4
Sherwood 81 G3
Sherwood Green 21 F3
Shettleston 142 A3
Shevington 91 G2
Shevington Moor 91 G1
Sheviock 7 D5
Shide 15 E4
Shiel Bridge 165 F3
Shieldaig *High.* 172 E6
Shieldaig *High.* 172 E4
Shieldhill 142 C2
Shielfoot 155 F2
Shielhill 160 C4
Shiels 168 E4
Shifford 41 F2
Shifnal 65 G2
Shilbottle 129 D1
Shildon 120 B5
Shillingford *Devon* 22 C5
Shillingford *Oxon.* 42 A3
Shillingford Abbot 10 C4
Shillingford St. George 10 C4
Shillingstone 13 E1
Shillington 57 G4
Shillmoor 128 A1
Shilstone 21 F5
Shilton *Oxon.* 41 E2
Shilton *Warks.* 67 G4
Shimpling *Norf.* 72 C3
Shimpling *Suff.* 59 G2
Shimpling Street 59 G2
Shincliffe 120 B3
Shiney Row 120 C2
Shinfield 28 C1
Shingay 58 B3
Shingham 71 F2
Shingle Street 61 E3
Shinness Lodge 181 H7
Shipbourne 31 E3
Shipbrookhill 92 A5
Shipdham 86 A5
Shipham 24 B2
Shiphay 9 E1
Shiplake 42 C5
Shiplake Row 42 C5
Shipley *Northumb.* 137 F5
Shipley *Shrop.* 66 A3
Shipley *W.Suss.* 29 G5
Shipley *W.Yorks.* 102 A4
Shipley Bridge *Devon* 8 C1
Shipley Bridge *Surr.* 30 C4
Shipley Common 81 F3
Shipmeadow 73 E2
Shippea Hill 71 E4
Shippon 41 G3
Shipston on Stour 55 E3
Shipton *Glos.* 40 C1
Shipton *N.Yorks.* 103 E2
Shipton *Shrop.* 65 E3
Shipton Bellinger 26 D3
Shipton Gorge 12 A3
Shipton Green 16 A3
Shipton Moyne 40 A4
Shipton Oliffe 40 C1
Shipton Solers 40 C1
Shipton-on-Cherwell 41 G1
Shiptonthorpe 104 A3
Shipton-under-Wychwood 41 E1
Shira 149 D3
Shirburn 42 B3
Shirdley Hill 91 E1
Shire Oak 66 C2
Shirebrook 81 G1
Shirecliffe 94 A3
Shiregreen 94 A3
Shirehampton 39 E5
Shiremoor 129 F4
Shirenewton 39 D3
Shireoaks 94 C4
Shirl Heath 52 D2
Shirland 81 E2
Shirley *Derbys.* 80 D3
Shirley *Gt.Lon.* 30 C2
Shirley *Hants.* 14 A3
Shirley *S'ham.* 14 D1
Shirley *W.Mid.* 66 D5
Shirley Heath 66 D5
Shirley Warren 14 C1
Shirleywich 79 G5
Shirrell Heath 15 E1
Shirwell 21 F2
Shirwell Cross 21 F2
Shiskine 131 E3
Shittlehope 119 G4
Shobdon 52 C1
Shobley 14 A2
Shobrooke 10 B2
Shocklach 78 B3
Shocklach Green 78 B3
Shoeburyness 46 C4
Sholden 33 F3
Sholing 15 D1
Shoot Hill 64 D1
Shooters Hill 44 D5
Shop *Cornw.* 4 C2
Shop *Cornw.* 20 C4
Shop Corner 60 D4
Shopnoller 23 E4
Shore 92 D1
Shoreditch 44 C4
Shoreham 31 E2
Shoreham-by-Sea 17 E3
Shoremill 174 E5
Shoresdean 145 G5
Shoreswood 145 G5
Shoreton 174 D5
Shorley 27 G5
Shorncote 40 C3
Shorne 45 F5
Shorne Ridgeway 45 F5
Short Cross 64 B2
Short Green 72 B3
Short Heath *Derbys.* 67 F1
Short Heath *W.Mid.* 66 C3
Shortacombe 7 F2
Shortbridge 17 G1
Shortfield Common 28 D3
Shortgate 17 G2
Shortgrove 58 D4
Shorthampton 55 F5
Shortlands 30 C2
Shortlanesend 4 C5
Shorton 9 E1
Shorwell 15 D4
Shoscombe 25 E2
Shotatton 78 A5
Shotesham 73 D2
Shotgate 45 G3
Shotley *Northants.* 69 E3
Shotley *Suff.* 60 D4
Shotley Bridge 119 G2
Shotley Gate 60 D4
Shotleyfield 119 G2
Shottenden 32 C3
Shottermill 29 D4
Shottery 55 D2
Shotteswell 55 G3
Shottisham 61 E3
Shottle 81 E3
Shottlegate 81 E3
Shotton *Dur.* 120 D4
Shotton *Dur.* 120 C5
Shotton *Flints.* 78 A1
Shotton *Northumb.* 129 E4
Shotton Colliery 120 C3
Shotts 142 C3
Shotwick 91 E5
Shouldham 71 E2
Shouldham Thorpe 71 E2
Shoulton 54 A2
Shover's Green 31 F5
Shrawardine 64 C1
Shrawley 54 A1
Shreding Green 43 F4
Shrewley 55 E1
Shrewsbury 65 D1
Shrewton 26 B3
Shripney 16 B3
Shrivenham 41 E4
Shropham 72 A2
Shroton (Iwerne Courtney) 13 E1
Shrub End 60 A5
Shucknall 53 E3
Shudy Camps 59 E3
Shurdington 40 B1
Shurlock Row 42 D5
Shurnock 54 C1
Shurrery 183 F3
Shurrery Lodge 183 F3
Shurton 23 F3
Shustoke 67 E3
Shut Heath 79 F5
Shute *Devon* 11 F3
Shute *Devon* 10 B2
Shutford 55 F3
Shuthonger 54 A4
Shutlanger 56 C3
Shutt Green 66 A2
Shuttington 67 E2
Shuttlewood 94 B5
Shuttleworth 92 B1
Siabost (Shawbost) 178 E3
Siabost Bho Dheas 178 E3
Siabost Bho Thuath 178 E3
Siadar Iarach 179 F2
Siadar Uarach 179 F2
Sibbaldbie 125 F2
Sibbertoft 68 B4
Sibdon Carwood 64 D4
Sibertswold (Shepherdswell) 33 E4
Sibford Ferris 55 F4
Sibford Gower 55 F4
Sible Hedingham 59 F4
Sibley's Green 59 E5
Sibsey 84 B2
Sibson *Cambs.* 69 F3
Sibson *Leics.* 67 F2
Sibster 183 J3
Sibthorpe 82 C3
Sibton 61 E1
Sibton Green 73 E4
Sicklesmere 59 G1
Sicklinghall 102 C3
Sidbury *Devon* 11 E3
Sidbury *Shrop.* 65 F4
Sidcot 24 B2
Sidcup 45 D5
Siddal 102 A5
Siddington *Ches.* 92 C5
Siddington *Glos.* 40 C3
Sidemoor 66 B5
Sidestrand 87 D2
Sidford 11 E3
Sidlesham 16 A4
Sidley 18 C3
Sidlow 30 B4
Sidmouth 11 E4
Sigford 10 A5
Sigglesthorne 105 D3
Sigingstone 37 F5
Signet 41 E1
Silchester 28 B1
Sildinis 178 E6
Sileby 68 B1
Silecroft 106 C4
Silfield 72 C2
Silian 50 B2
Silk Willoughby 83 F3
Silkstead 27 F5
Silkstone 93 G2
Silkstone Common 93 G2
Sill Field 107 G4
Silloth 117 E1
Sills 128 A1
Sillyearn 176 D5
Silpho 112 C3
Silsden 101 G3
Silsoe 57 F4
Silver End *Beds.* 57 G3
Silver End *Essex* 59 G5
Silver Green 73 D2
Silver Street *Kent* 32 A2
Silver Street *Som.* 24 C4
Silverburn 143 G3
Silvercraigs 139 G1
Silverdale *Lancs.* 107 F5
Silverdale *Staffs.* 79 F3
Silvergate 86 C3
Silverhill 18 C2
Silverlace Green 61 E2
Silverley's Green 73 D4
Silvermoss 169 G1
Silverstone 56 B3
Silverton 10 C2
Silvington 65 F5
Silwick 187 B8
Simister 92 C2
Simmondley 93 E3
Simonburn 128 A4
Simonsbath 22 A4
Simonside 120 C1
Simonstone *Bridgend* 37 F4
Simonstone *Lancs.* 101 D4
Simprim 145 F5
Simpson 57 D4
Sinclair's Hill 145 F4
Sinclairston 132 C4
Sinderby 110 C4
Sinderhope 119 E2
Sindlesham 28 C1
Sinfin 81 E4
Singdean 135 G5
Singleton *Lancs.* 99 G4
Singleton *W.Suss.* 16 A2
Singlewell (Ifield) 45 F5
Singret 78 A2
Sinkhurst Green 32 A4
Sinnahard 168 C3
Sinnington 111 G4
Sinton Green 54 A1
Siop y Fron (Upper Llandwrog) 75 E2
Sipson 43 F5
Sirhowy 38 A1
Sisland 73 E2
Sissinghurst 31 G5
Siston 39 F5
Sithney 2 D4
Sittingbourne 32 B2
Siulaisiadar 179 H4
Six Ashes 65 G4
Six Hills 82 B5
Six Mile Bottom 59 D2
Six Roads End 80 C5
Sixhills 96 B4
Sixmile 32 D4
Sixpenny Handley 13 G1
Sizewell 61 F1
Skail 182 C4
Skaill *Ork.* 185 B6
Skaill *Ork.* 185 E7
Skaill *Ork.* 184 D4
Skares *Aber.* 168 E1
Skares *E.Ayr.* 132 D4
Skarpigarth 187 A7
Skateraw 145 E2
Skaw 187 E6
Skeabost 171 K7
Skeabrae 184 B5
Skeeby 110 B2
Skeffington 68 C2
Skeffling 97 D1
Skegby 81 G1
Skegness 85 D1
Skelberry *Shet.* 187 F9
Skelberry *Shet.* 187 D6
Skelbo 174 E2
Skelbo Street 174 E2
Skelbrooke 94 C1
Skeld (Easter Skeld) 187 C8
Skeldon 132 B4
Skeldyke 84 B4
Skellingthorpe 95 G5
Skellister 187 D7
Skellow 94 C1
Skelmanthorpe 93 G1
Skelmersdale 91 F2
Skelmonae 169 G1
Skelmorlie 140 C3
Skelmuir 177 H6
Skelpick 182 C3
Skelton *Cumb.* 118 A4
Skelton *E.Riding* 103 G5
Skelton *N.Yorks.* 109 F2
Skelton *R. & C.* 111 F1
Skelton *York* 103 E2
Skelton-on-Ure 102 C1
Skelwick 184 D3
Skelwith Bridge 107 E2
Skendleby 84 C1
Skendleby Psalter 97 E5
Skenfrith 53 D5
Skerne 104 C2
Skeroblingarry 130 C3
Skerray 181 J2
Skerton 100 A1
Sketchley 67 G3
Sketty 36 C3
Skewen 36 D3
Skewsby 111 F5
Skeyton 86 D3
Skeyton Corner 87 D3
Skidbrooke 97 E3
Skidbrooke North End 97 E3

Skidby 104 C4
Skilgate 22 C5
Skillington 83 D5
Skinburness 117 E1
Skinflats 142 D1
Skinidin 171 H7
Skinnet 183 G2
Skinningrove 111 G1
Skipness 139 G4
Skippool 99 G3
Skipsea 105 D2
Skipsea Brough 105 D2
Skipton 101 F2
Skipton-on-Swale 110 C5
Skipwith 103 F4
Skirbeck 84 B3
Skirbeck Quarter 84 B3
Skirethorns 101 F1
Skirlaugh 104 D4
Skirling 134 B2
Skirmett 42 C4
Skirpenbeck 103 G2
Skirwith *Cumb.* 118 C4
Skirwith *N.Yorks.* 108 C5
Skirza 183 J2
Skittle Green 42 C2
Skomer Island 34 A2
Skulamus 164 C2
Skullomie 181 J2
Skyborry Green 64 B5
Skye 163 K1
Skye Green 59 G5
Skye of Curr 167 G2
Skyreholme 101 G1
Slack *Aber.* 168 D1
Slack *Derbys.* 81 E1
Slack *W.Yorks.* 101 F5
Slackhall 93 E4
Slackhead 176 C4
Slad 40 A2
Slade *Devon* 21 F1
Slade *Devon* 11 E2
Slade *Pembs.* 34 C1
Slade *Swan.* 36 A4
Slade Green 45 E5
Slade Hooton 94 C4
Sladesbridge 5 E2
Slaggyford 118 C2
Slaidburn 100 D2
Slains Park 161 G2
Slaithwaite 93 E1
Slaley 119 F2
Slamannan 142 C2
Slapton *Bucks.* 57 E5
Slapton *Devon* 9 E3
Slapton *Northants.* 56 B3
Slate Haugh 176 C4
Slatepit Dale 81 E1
Slattadale 172 E4
Slaugham 17 E1
Slaughden 61 F2
Slaughterford 40 A5
Slawston 68 C3
Sleaford *Hants.* 28 D4
Sleaford *Lincs.* 83 F3
Sleagill 107 G1
Sleap 78 B5
Sledge Green 54 A4
Sledmere 104 B1
Sleights 112 B2
Slepe 13 F3
Slerra 20 D3
Slickly 183 H2
Sliddery 131 E3
Sliemore 167 H2
Sligachan 163 K2
Slimbridge 39 G2
Slindon *Staffs.* 79 F4
Slindon *W.Suss.* 16 B3
Slinfold 29 G4
Sling 39 E2
Slingsby 111 F5
Slioch 168 D1
Slip End *Beds.* 43 F1
Slip End *Herts.* 58 A4
Slipton 69 E5
Slitting Mill 66 C1
Slochd 167 F2
Slockavullin 148 A5
Slogarie 124 A4
Sloley 87 D3
Slongaber 124 C3
Sloothby 97 E5
Slough 43 E4
Slough Green *Som.* 23 F5
Slough Green *W.Suss.* 17 E1
Sluggan 167 F2
Slyne 100 A1
Smailholm 136 A3
Small Dole 17 E2
Small Hythe 32 A5
Smallbridge 92 D1
Smallbrook 10 B3
Smallburgh 87 E3
Smallburn *Aber.* 177 J6
Smallburn *E.Ayr.* 133 E3
Smalldale 93 E5
Smalley 81 F3
Smallfield 30 C4
Smallford 44 A2
Smallridge 11 F2
Smallthorne 79 F2
Smallworth 72 B3
Smannell 27 E3
Smardale 108 C2
Smarden 32 A4
Smaull 138 A3
Smeatharpe 11 E1
Smeeth 32 C5
Smeeton Westerby 68 B3
Smerclet 162 C3
Smerral 183 G5
Smestow 66 A3
Smethwick 66 C4
Smethwick Green 79 F1
Smirisary 155 F2
Smisby 67 F1
Smith End Green 53 G2
Smithfield 118 A1
Smithies 94 A2
Smithincott 11 D1
Smith's End 58 B4
Smith's Green *Essex* 59 D5
Smith's Green *Essex* 59 E3
Smithstown 172 D4
Smithton 174 E7
Smithy Green 92 B5
Smockington 67 G4
Smyrton 122 C2
Smythe's Green 46 C1
Snailbeach 64 C2
Snailwell 59 E1
Snainton 112 C4
Snaith 103 F5
Snape *N.Yorks.* 110 B4
Snape *Suff.* 61 E2
Snape Green 91 E1
Snape Watering 61 E2
Snarestone 67 F2
Snarford 96 A4
Snargate 19 E1
Snave 19 F1
Sneachill 54 B2
Snead 64 C3
Snead's Green 54 A1
Sneath Common 72 C3
Sneaton 112 B2
Sneatonthorpe 112 C2
Snelland 96 A4
Snellings 106 A2
Snelston 80 C3
Snetterton 72 A2
Snettisham 85 E4
Snipeshill 32 B2
Snishival 162 C1
Snitter 128 C1
Snitterby 95 G3
Snitterfield 55 E2
Snitterton 81 D1
Snittlegarth 117 F3
Snitton 65 E5
Snodhill 52 C3
Snodland 31 G2
Snow End 58 C4
Snow Street 72 B3
Snowden Hill 93 G2
Snowshill 54 C4
Soar *Cardiff* 37 G4
Soar *Carmar.* 50 C5
Soar *Devon* 8 D4
Soay 163 K3
Soberton 15 F1
Soberton Heath 15 F1
Sockbridge 118 B5
Sockburn 110 C2
Sodom 90 B5
Sodylt Bank 78 A4
Softley 119 G5
Soham 71 D5
Soham Cotes 71 D5
Solas (Sollas) 170 D4
Soldon 20 D4
Soldon Cross 20 D4
Soldridge 28 B4
Sole Street *Kent* 32 C4
Sole Street *Kent* 31 F2
Soleburn 122 B4
Solihull 67 D5
Solihull Lodge 66 C5
Sollas (Solas) 170 D4
Sollers Dilwyn 52 D2
Sollers Hope 53 F4
Sollom 91 F1
Solomon's Tump 39 G1
Solsgirth 151 E5
Solva 48 A5
Solwaybank 126 B4
Somerby *Leics.* 68 C1
Somerby *Lincs.* 96 A2
Somercotes 81 F2
Somerford 66 B2
Somerford Keynes 40 C3
Somerley 16 A4
Somerleyton 73 F2
Somersal Herbert 80 C4
Somersby 96 D5
Somersham *Cambs.* 70 B5
Somersham *Suff.* 60 B3
Somerton *Newport* 38 C4
Somerton *Oxon.* 55 G5
Somerton *Som.* 24 B5
Somerton *Suff.* 59 G2
Sompting 17 D3
Sompting Abbotts 17 D3
Sonning 42 C5
Sonning Common 42 C4
Sonning Eye 42 C5
Sontley 78 A3
Sookholme 81 G1
Sopley 14 A3
Sopworth 40 A4
Sorbie 115 E2
Sordale 183 G2
Sorisdale 154 B3
Sorn 133 D3
Sornhill 132 D2
Soroba 148 A2
Sortat 183 H2
Sotby 96 C5
Sots Hole 83 G1
Sotterley 73 F3
Soudley 79 E5
Soughton 77 F1
Soulbury 57 D5
Soulby 108 C1
Souldern 56 A4
Souldrop 57 E1
Sound *Ches.* 78 D3
Sound *Shet.* 187 D8
Sound *Shet.* 187 C7
Sourhope 136 C4
Sourin 184 D4
Sourton 7 F1
Soutergate 106 D4
South Acre 71 G1
South Acton 44 A5
South Alkham 33 E4
South Allington 9 D4
South Alloa 151 D5
South Ambersham 29 E5
South Anston 94 C4
South Ascot 29 E1
South Baddesley 14 C3
South Ballachulish 156 C4
South Balloch 123 E1
South Bank 121 E5
South Barrow 24 D5
South Bellsdyke 142 D1
South Benfleet 45 G4
South Bersted 16 B3
South Blackbog 169 F1
South Bockhampton 14 A3
South Bowood 12 A3
South Brent 8 C1
South Brentor 7 E2
South Brewham 25 E4
South Broomhill 129 E2
South Burlingham 87 E5
South Cadbury 24 D5
South Cairn 122 A4
South Carlton 95 G5
South Cave 104 B4
South Cerney 40 C3
South Chard 11 G2
South Charlton 137 F4
South Cheriton 25 D5
South Church 120 B5
South Cliffe 104 A4
South Clifton 95 F5
South Cockerington 97 D4
South Collafirth 186 C4
South Common 17 F2
South Cornelly 37 E4
South Corriegills 131 F2
South Cove 73 F3
South Creagan 156 B5
South Creake 85 G4
South Crosland 93 F1
South Croxton 68 B1
South Dalton 104 B3
South Darenth 45 E5
South Dell (Dail Bho Dheas) 179 G1
South Duffield 103 F4
South Elkington 96 C4
South Elmsall 94 B1
South End *Bucks.* 57 D5
South End *Cumb.* 99 F1
South End *Hants.* 14 A1
South End *N.Lincs.* 104 D5
South Erradale 172 D4
South Fambridge 46 B3
South Fawley 41 F4
South Ferriby 104 B5
South Field 104 C5
South Flobbets 169 F1
South Garth 186 E3
South Godstone 30 C4
South Gorley 14 A1
South Green *Essex* 45 F3
South Green *Essex* 46 D1
South Green *Norf.* 86 B4
South Green *Suff.* 72 C4
South Gyle 143 F2
South Hall 140 B2
South Hanningfield 45 G3
South Harefield 43 F4
South Harting 15 G1
South Hayling 15 G3
South Hazelrigg 137 E3
South Heath 43 E2
South Heighton 17 G3
South Hetton 120 C3
South Hiendley 94 A1
South Hill 6 D3
South Hinksey 42 A2
South Hole 20 C4
South Holme 111 F5
South Holmwood 29 G3
South Hornchurch 45 E4
South Hourat 141 D4
South Huish 8 C3
South Hykeham 83 E1
South Hylton 120 C2
South Kelsey 96 A3
South Kessock 174 D7
South Killingholme 96 B1
South Kilvington 110 D4
South Kilworth 68 B4
South Kirkby 94 B1
South Kirkton 169 F4
South Knighton 10 B5
South Kyme 83 G3
South Lancing 17 D3
South Ledaig 148 B1
South Leigh 41 F2
South Leverton 95 E4
South Littleton 54 C3
South Lopham 72 B3
South Luffenham 69 E2
South Malling 17 G2
South Marston 41 D4
South Middleton 137 D4
South Milford 103 D4
South Milton 8 C3
South Mimms 44 B2
South Molton 22 A5
South Moor 120 A2
South Moreton 42 A4
South Mundham 16 A3
South Muskham 82 C2
South Newbald 104 B4
South Newington 55 G4
South Newton 26 B4
South Normanton 81 F2
South Norwood 30 C2
South Nutfield 30 C4
South Ockendon 45 E4
South Ormsby 97 D5
South Ossett 93 G1
South Otterington 110 C4
South Owersby 96 A3
South Oxhey 44 A3
South Park 30 B4
South Parks 152 A4
South Perrott 12 A2
South Petherton 12 A1
South Petherwin 6 D2
South Pickenham 71 G2
South Pool 9 D3
South Queensferry (Queensferry) 143 F2
South Radworthy 22 A4
South Rauceby 83 F3
South Raynham 85 G5
South Redbriggs 177 F6
South Reston 97 E4
South Ronaldsay 185 D9
South Ruislip 44 A4
South Runcton 71 E2
South Scarle 82 D1
South Shian 156 B5
South Shields 120 C1
South Somercotes 97 E3
South Somercotes Fen Houses 97 E3
South Stainley 102 C1
South Stoke *Oxon.* 42 B4
South Stoke *W.Suss.* 16 C3
South Street *E.Suss.* 17 F2
South Street *Gt.Lon.* 30 D3
South Street *Kent* 31 F2
South Street *Kent* 32 D2
South Street *Kent* 32 A2
South Tawton 7 G1
South Thoresby 97 E5
South Tidworth 26 D3
South Tottenham 44 C4
South Town *Devon* 10 C4
South Town *Hants.* 28 B4
South Uist (Uibhist a Deas) 162 C1
South Upper Barrack 177 H6
South View 28 B2
South Walsham 87 E4
South Warnborough 28 C3
South Weald 45 E3
South Weston 42 C3
South Wheatley *Cornw.* 6 C1
South Wheatley *Notts.* 95 E4
South Whiteness 187 C8
South Wigston 68 A3
South Willingham 96 B4
South Wingfield 81 E2
South Witham 69 E1
South Wonston 27 F4
South Woodham Ferrers 46 B3
South Wootton 85 E5
South Wraxall 25 F1
South Yardley 66 D4
South Zeal 7 G1
Southall 44 A4
Southam *Glos.* 54 B5
Southam *Warks.* 55 G1
Southampton 14 D1
Southampton Airport 15 D1
Southbar 141 F3
Southborough *Gt.Lon.* 30 D2
Southborough *Kent* 31 E4
Southbourne *Bourne.* 14 A3
Southbourne *W.Suss.* 15 G2
Southbrook 10 D3
Southburgh 86 B5
Southburn 104 B2
Southchurch 46 C4
Southcott *Devon* 7 F1
Southcott *Wilts.* 26 C2
Southcourt 42 D1
Southdean 127 E1
Southdene 91 F3
Southease 17 G3
Southend *Aber.* 177 F6
Southend *Arg. & B.* 130 B5
Southend *Bucks.* 42 C4
Southend *W.Berks.* 42 A5
Southend *Wilts.* 41 D5
Southend-on-Sea 46 B4
Southerfield 117 E2
Southerly 7 F2
Southern Green 58 B4
Southerndown 37 E5
Southerness 125 D5
Southery 71 E3
Southfield 152 A5
Southfields 44 B5
Southfleet 45 F5
Southgate *Cere.* 62 B4
Southgate *Gt.Lon.* 44 C3
Southgate *Norf.* 86 C3
Southgate *Norf.* 85 E4
Southgate *Swan.* 36 B4
Southill 57 G3
Southington 27 G3
Southleigh 11 F3
Southmarsh 25 E4
Southminster 46 C3
Southmuir 160 B4
Southoe 57 G1
Southolt 60 C1
Southorpe 69 F2
Southowram 102 A5
Southport 91 E1
Southrepps 87 D2
Southrey 83 G1
Southrop 41 D2
Southrope 28 B3
Southsea *Ports.* 15 F3
Southsea *Wrex.* 77 F2
Southstoke 25 E1
Southtown *Norf.* 87 G5
Southtown *Ork.* 185 D8
Southwaite *Cumb.* 108 C2
Southwaite *Cumb.* 118 A3
Southwater 29 G5
Southwater Street 29 G5
Southway 24 C3
Southwell *Dorset* 12 C5
Southwell *Notts.* 82 B2
Southwick *D. & G.* 124 D5
Southwick *Hants.* 15 F2
Southwick *Northants.* 69 F3
Southwick *Som.* 24 A3
Southwick *T. & W.* 120 C2
Southwick *W.Suss.* 17 E3
Southwick *Wilts.* 25 F2
Southwold 73 G4
Southwood 24 C4
Sowden 10 C4
Sower Carr 99 G3
Sowerby *N.Yorks.* 110 D4
Sowerby *W.Yorks.* 101 G5
Sowerby Bridge 101 G5
Sowerby Row 117 G2
Sowerhill 22 B5
Sowley Green 59 F2
Sowood 93 E1
Sowton 10 C3
Soyal 174 C2
Spa Common 87 D2
Spadeadam 127 D4
Spalding 84 A5
Spaldington 103 G4
Spaldwick 69 G5
Spalefield 153 D4
Spalford 82 D1
Spanby 83 F4
Sparham 86 B4
Spark Bridge 107 E4
Sparkford 24 D5
Sparkhill 66 C4
Sparkwell 8 B2
Sparrow Green 86 A4
Sparrowpit 93 E4
Sparrow's Green 31 F5
Sparsholt *Hants.* 27 F4
Sparsholt *Oxon.* 41 F4
Spartylea 119 E3
Spath 80 B4
Spaunton 111 G4
Spaxton 23 F4
Spean Bridge 157 E1
Spear Hill 16 D2
Speddoch 124 C2
Speedwell 39 F5
Speen *Bucks.* 42 D2
Speen *W.Berks.* 27 F1
Speeton 113 E5
Speke 91 F4
Speldhurst 31 E4
Spellbrook 45 D1
Spelsbury 55 F5
Spen Green 79 F1
Spencers Wood 28 C1
Spennithorne 110 A4
Spennymoor 120 B4
Spernall 54 C1
Spetchley 54 A2
Spetisbury 13 F2
Spexhall 73 E3
Spey Bay 176 B4
Speybridge 167 H2
Speyview 175 K7
Spilsby 84 B1
Spindlestone 137 F3
Spinkhill 94 B5
Spinningdale 174 D3
Spirthill 40 B5
Spital *High.* 183 G3
Spital *W. & M.* 43 E5
Spital in the Street 95 G3
Spitalbrook 44 C2
Spithurst 17 G2
Spittal *D. & G.* 123 F4
Spittal *D. & G.* 123 E5
Spittal *E.Loth.* 144 B2
Spittal *Northumb.* 137 E1
Spittal *Pembs.* 48 C5
Spittal of Glenmuick 160 B1
Spittal of Glenshee 159 G3
Spittalfield 159 G5
Spixworth 86 D4
Splayne's Green 17 G1
Splott 38 B5
Spofforth 102 C2
Spondon 81 F4
Spooner Row 72 B2
Spoonley 79 D4
Sporle 71 G1
Sportsman's Arms 76 C2
Spott 145 D2
Spratton 68 C5
Spreakley 28 D3
Spreyton 7 G1
Spriddlestone 8 B2
Spridlington 96 A4
Spring Grove 44 A5
Spring Vale 15 F3
Springburn 142 A3
Springfield *Arg. & B.* 140 B2
Springfield *D. & G.* 126 B5
Springfield *Fife* 152 B3
Springfield *Moray* 175 H6
Springfield *P. & K.* 151 G1
Springfield *W.Mid.* 66 C4
Springfields Outlet Village 84 A5
Springhill *Staffs.* 66 C2
Springhill *Staffs.* 66 B2
Springholm 124 C4
Springkell 126 A4
Springleys 169 F1
Springside 132 B2
Springthorpe 95 F4
Springwell 120 B2
Sproatley 105 D4
Sproston Green 79 E1
Sprotbrough 94 C2
Sproughton 60 C3
Sprouston 136 B3
Sprowston 86 D4
Sproxton *Leics.* 83 D5
Sproxton *N.Yorks.* 111 F4
Sprytown 7 E2
Spurlands End 43 D3
Spurstow 78 C2
Spyway 12 B3
Square Point 124 B3
Squires Gate 99 G4
Srondoire 139 G2
Sronphadruig Lodge 158 C2
Stableford *Shrop.* 65 G3
Stableford *Staffs.* 79 F4
Stacey Bank 93 G3
Stackhouse 101 E1
Stackpole 34 C3
Stacksteads 101 E5
Staddiscombe 8 B2
Staddlethorpe 104 A5
Staden 93 E5
Stadhampton 42 B3
Stadhlaigearraidh (Stilligarry) 162 C1
Staffield 118 B3
Staffin 171 K5
Stafford 79 G5
Stagden Cross 45 F1
Stagsden 57 E3
Stagshaw Bank 119 F1
Stain 183 J2
Stainburn *Cumb.* 116 D4
Stainburn *N.Yorks.* 102 B3
Stainby 83 E5
Staincross 94 A1
Staindrop 120 A5
Staines 43 F5
Stainfield *Lincs.* 83 F5
Stainfield *Lincs.* 96 B5
Stainforth *N.Yorks.* 101 E1
Stainforth *S.Yorks.* 94 D1
Staining 99 G4
Stainland 93 E1
Stainsacre 112 C2
Stainsby *Derbys.* 81 F1
Stainsby *Lincs.* 96 D5
Stainton *Cumb.* 107 G4
Stainton *Cumb.* 118 A5
Stainton *Dur.* 109 F1
Stainton *Middbro.* 111 D1
Stainton *N.Yorks.* 110 A3
Stainton *S.Yorks.* 94 C3
Stainton by Langworth 96 A5
Stainton le Vale 96 B3
Stainton with Adgarley 106 D5
Staintondale 112 C3
Stair *Cumb.* 117 F4
Stair *E.Ayr.* 132 C3
Stairfoot 94 A2
Staithes 111 G1
Stake Pool 100 A3
Stakeford 129 E3
Stakes 15 F2
Stalbridge 12 D1
Stalbridge Weston 12 D1
Stalham 87 E3
Stalham Green 87 E3
Stalisfield Green 32 B3
Stalling Busk 109 E4
Stallingborough 96 B1
Stallington 79 G4
Stalmine 99 G3
Stalybridge 93 D3
Stambourne 59 F4
Stamford *Lincs.* 69 F2
Stamford *Northumb.* 137 G5
Stamford Bridge *Ches.* 78 B1
Stamford Bridge *E.Riding* 103 G2
Stamfordham 128 C4
Stanah 99 G3
Stanborough 44 B1
Stanbridge *Beds.* 57 E5
Stanbridge *Dorset* 13 G2
Stanbridge Earls 27 E5
Stanbury 101 G4
Stand 142 B3
Standburn 142 D2
Standeford 66 B2
Standen 32 A5
Standen Street 32 A5
Standerwick 25 F2
Standford 28 D4
Standford Bridge 79 E5
Standish *Glos.* 40 A2
Standish *Gt.Man.* 91 G1
Standlake 41 F2
Standon *Hants.* 27 F5
Standon *Herts.* 58 B5
Standon *Staffs.* 79 F4
Standon Green End 44 C1
Stane 142 C4
Stanecastle 132 B2
Stanfield 86 A3
Stanford *Beds.* 57 G3
Stanford *Kent* 32 D5
Stanford *Shrop.* 64 C1
Stanford Bishop 53 F2
Stanford Bridge 53 G1
Stanford Dingley 42 A5
Stanford End 28 C1
Stanford in the Vale 41 F3
Stanford on Avon 68 A5
Stanford on Soar 81 G5
Stanford on Teme 53 G1
Stanford Rivers 45 E2
Stanford-le-Hope 45 F4
Stanfree 94 B5
Stanghow 111 F1
Stanground 70 A3
Stanhoe 85 G4
Stanhope *Dur.* 119 F4
Stanhope *Sc.Bord.* 134 C3
Stanion 69 E4
Stanklyn 66 A5
Stanley *Derbys.* 81 F3
Stanley *Dur.* 120 A2
Stanley *Notts.* 81 F1
Stanley *P. & K.* 151 G1
Stanley *Staffs.* 79 G2
Stanley *W.Yorks.* 102 C5
Stanley *Wilts.* 40 B5
Stanley Common 81 F3
Stanley Crook 120 A4
Stanley Gate 91 F2
Stanley Green 13 G3
Stanley Hill 53 F3
Stanleygreen 78 C4
Stanlow *Ches.* 91 F5
Stanlow *Shrop.* 65 G3
Stanmer 17 F2
Stanmore *Gt.Lon.* 44 A3
Stanmore *W.Berks.* 41 G5
Stannersburn 127 F3
Stanningfield 59 G2
Stanningley 102 B4
Stannington *Northumb.* 129 E4
Stannington *S.Yorks.* 94 A4
Stansbatch 52 C1
Stansfield 59 F2
Stanshope 80 C2
Stanstead 59 G3
Stanstead Abbotts 44 C1
Stansted 31 F2
Stansted Airport (London Stansted Airport) 58 D5
Stansted Mountfitchet 58 D5
Stanton *Derbys.* 67 E1
Stanton *Glos.* 54 C4
Stanton *Northumb.* 128 D2
Stanton *Staffs.* 80 C3
Stanton *Suff.* 72 A4
Stanton by Bridge 81 E5
Stanton by Dale 81 F4
Stanton Drew 24 C1
Stanton Fitzwarren 41 D3
Stanton Harcourt 41 G2
Stanton Hill 81 F1
Stanton in Peak 80 D1
Stanton Lacy 65 D5
Stanton Lees 81 D1
Stanton Long 65 E3
Stanton Prior 25 D1
Stanton St. Bernard 26 B1
Stanton St. John 42 A2
Stanton St. Quintin 40 B5
Stanton Street 60 A1
Stanton under Bardon 67 G1
Stanton upon Hine Heath 78 C5
Stanton Wick 24 D1
Stanton-on-the-Wolds 82 B4
Stanwardine in the Fields 78 B5
Stanwardine in the Wood 78 B5
Stanway *Essex* 60 A5
Stanway *Glos.* 54 C4
Stanway Green *Essex* 60 A5
Stanway Green *Suff.* 72 D4
Stanwell 43 F5
Stanwell Moor 43 F5
Stanwick 69 E5
Stanwix 118 A2
Stanydale 187 B7
Staoinebrig 162 C1
Stapeley 79 D3
Stapenhill 81 D5
Staple *Kent* 33 E3
Staple *Som.* 23 E3
Staple Cross 22 D5
Staple Fitzpaine 11 F1
Staplecross 18 C1
Staplefield 17 E1
Stapleford *Cambs.* 58 C2
Stapleford *Herts.* 44 C1
Stapleford *Leics.* 68 D1
Stapleford *Lincs.* 83 D2
Stapleford *Notts.* 81 F4
Stapleford *Wilts.* 26 B4
Stapleford Abbotts 45 D3
Stapleford Tawney 45 E3
Staplegrove 23 F5
Staplehay 23 F5
Staplehurst 31 G4
Staplers 15 E4
Staplestreet 32 C2
Stapleton *Cumb.* 126 D4
Stapleton *Here.* 52 C1
Stapleton *Leics.* 67 G3
Stapleton *N.Yorks.* 110 B1
Stapleton *Shrop.* 65 D2
Stapleton *Som.* 24 B5
Stapley 11 E1
Staploe 57 G1
Staplow 53 F3
Star *Fife* 152 B4
Star *Pembs.* 49 F4
Star *Som.* 24 B2
Starbotton 109 E5
Starcross 10 C4
Stareton 67 F5
Starkholmes 81 E2
Starling 92 B1
Starling's Green 58 C4
Starr 123 F1
Starston 72 D3
Startforth 109 F1
Startley 40 B4
Statham 92 A4
Stathe 24 A5
Stathern 82 C4
Station Town 120 D4
Staughton Green 57 G1
Staughton Highway 57 G1
Staunton *Glos.* 39 E1
Staunton *Glos.* 53 G5
Staunton Harold Hall 81 E5
Staunton in the Vale 82 D3
Staunton on Arrow 52 C1
Staunton on Wye 52 C3
Staveley *Cumb.* 107 F3
Staveley *Derbys.* 94 B5
Staveley *N.Yorks.* 102 C1
Staveley-in-Cartmel 107 E4
Staverton *Devon* 9 D1
Staverton *Glos.* 54 A5
Staverton *Northants.* 56 A1
Staverton *Wilts.* 25 F1
Staverton Bridge 54 A5
Stawell 24 A4
Stawley 23 D5
Staxigoe 183 J3
Staxton 112 D5
Staylittle (Penffordd-las) 63 E3
Staynall 99 G3
Staythorpe 82 C2
Stean 109 F5
Steane 56 A4
Stearsby 111 F5
Steart 23 F3
Stebbing 59 E5
Stebbing Green 59 E5
Stechford 66 D4
Stedham 29 D5
Steel Cross 31 E5
Steel Green 106 C5
Steele Road 126 D2
Steen's Bridge 53 E2
Steep 28 C5
Steep Marsh 28 C5
Steeple *Dorset* 13 F4
Steeple *Essex* 46 C2
Steeple Ashton 26 A2
Steeple Aston 55 G5
Steeple Barton 55 G5
Steeple Bumpstead 59 E3
Steeple Claydon 56 B5
Steeple Gidding 69 G4
Steeple Langford 26 B4
Steeple Morden 58 A3
Steeraway 65 F2
Steeton 101 G3
Stein 171 H6
Steinmanhill 177 F6
Stella 120 A1
Stelling Minnis 32 D4
Stembridge 24 B5
Stemster *High.* 183 G2
Stemster *High.* 183 G4
Stemster House 183 G2
Stenalees 5 E4
Stenhill 11 D1
Stenhousemuir 142 C1
Stenigot 96 C4
Stenis 179 G4
Stenness 186 B5
Stenscholl 171 K5
Stenson 81 E5
Stenton *E.Loth.* 144 D2
Stenton *P. & K.* 159 F5
Steornabhagh (Stornoway) 179 G4
Stepaside *Pembs.* 35 E2
Stepaside *Powys* 63 G4
Stepney 44 C4
Steppingley 57 F4
Stepps 142 A3
Sternfield 61 E1
Sterridge 21 F1
Stert 26 B2
Stetchworth 59 E2
Stevenage 58 A5
Stevenston 141 D5
Steventon *Hants.* 27 G3
Steventon *Oxon.* 41 G3
Steventon End 59 E3

Stevington 57 E2
Stewartby 57 F3
Stewarton *D. & G.* 115 E2
Stewarton *E.Ayr.* 141 F5
Stewkley 57 D5
Stewley 11 G1
Stewton 97 D4
Steyning 17 D2
Steynton 34 C2
Stibb 20 C4
Stibb Cross 21 E4
Stibb Green 26 D1
Stibbard 86 A3
Stibbington 69 F3
Stichill 136 B3
Sticker 5 D4
Stickford 84 B1
Sticklepath *Devon* 7 G1
Sticklepath *Som.* 11 G1
Stickling Green 58 C4
Stickney 84 B2
Stiff Street 32 A2
Stiffkey 86 A1
Stifford's Bridge 53 G3
Stileway 24 B3
Stilligarry (Stadhlaigearraidh) 162 C1
Stillingfleet 103 E3
Stillington *N.Yorks.* 103 E1
Stillington *Stock.* 120 C5
Stilton 69 G4
Stinchcombe 39 G3
Stinsford 12 D3
Stirchley *Tel. & W.* 65 G2
Stirchley *W.Mid.* 66 C4
Stirkoke House 183 J3
Stirling *Aber.* 177 K6
Stirling *Stir.* 150 C5
Stirton 101 F2
Stisted 59 G5
Stitchcombe 41 E5
Stithians 3 E3
Stittenham 174 D4
Stivichall 67 F5
Stix 158 C5
Stixwould 83 G1
Stoak 91 F5
Stobo 134 C2
Stoborough 13 F4
Stoborough Green 13 F4
Stobwood 143 D4
Stocinis (Stockinish) 171 G2
Stock 45 F3
Stock Green 54 B2
Stock Lane 41 E5
Stock Wood 54 C2
Stockbridge *Hants.* 27 E4
Stockbridge *Stir.* 150 C4
Stockbridge *W.Suss.* 16 A3
Stockbury 32 A2
Stockcross 27 F1
Stockdale 3 E3
Stockdalewath 117 G2
Stockerston 68 D3
Stocking Green *Essex* 59 D4
Stocking Green *M.K.* 56 D3
Stocking Pelham 58 C5
Stockingford 67 F3
Stockinish (Stocinis) 171 G2
Stockland *Cardiff* 38 A5
Stockland *Devon* 11 F2
Stockland Bristol 23 F3
Stockleigh English 10 B2
Stockleigh Pomeroy 10 B2
Stockley 26 B1
Stocklinch 11 G1
Stockport 92 C3
Stocksbridge 93 G3
Stocksfield 119 G1
Stockton *Here.* 53 E1
Stockton *Norf.* 73 E2
Stockton *Shrop.* 65 G3
Stockton *Shrop.* 64 B2
Stockton *Tel. & W.* 65 G1
Stockton *Warks.* 55 G1
Stockton *Wilts.* 26 A4
Stockton Heath 92 A4
Stockton on Teme 53 G1
Stockton on the Forest 103 F2
Stockton-on-Tees 110 D1
Stockwell 40 B1
Stockwell Heath 80 B5
Stockwood *Bristol* 24 D1
Stockwood *Dorset* 12 B2
Stodday 100 A2
Stodmarsh 33 E2
Stody 86 B2
Stoer 180 C6
Stoford *Som.* 12 B1
Stoford *Wilts.* 26 B4
Stogumber 23 D4
Stogursey 23 F3
Stoke *Devon* 20 C3
Stoke *Hants.* 27 F2
Stoke *Hants.* 15 G2
Stoke *Med.* 32 A1
Stoke *Plym.* 8 A2
Stoke *W.Mid.* 67 F5
Stoke Abbott 12 A2
Stoke Albany 68 D4
Stoke Ash 72 C4
Stoke Bardolph 82 B3
Stoke Bishop 39 E5
Stoke Bliss 53 F1
Stoke Bruerne 56 C2
Stoke by Clare 59 F3
Stoke Canon 10 C3
Stoke Charity 27 F4
Stoke Climsland 7 D3
Stoke D'Abernon 29 G2
Stoke Doyle 69 F4
Stoke Dry 69 D3
Stoke Edith 53 F3
Stoke Farthing 26 B5
Stoke Ferry 71 F3
Stoke Fleming 9 E3
Stoke Gabriel 9 E2
Stoke Gifford 39 F5
Stoke Golding 67 F3
Stoke Goldington 56 D3
Stoke Green 43 E4
Stoke Hammond 57 D5
Stoke Heath *Shrop.* 79 D5
Stoke Heath *Worcs.* 54 B1
Stoke Holy Cross 86 D5
Stoke Lacy 53 F3
Stoke Lyne 56 A5
Stoke Mandeville 42 D1
Stoke Newington 44 C4
Stoke on Tern 78 D5
Stoke Orchard 54 B5
Stoke Pero 22 B3
Stoke Poges 43 E4
Stoke Pound 54 B1
Stoke Prior *Here.* 53 E2
Stoke Prior *Worcs.* 54 B1
Stoke Rivers 21 G2
Stoke Rochford 83 E5
Stoke Row 42 B4
Stoke St. Gregory 24 A5
Stoke St. Mary 23 F5
Stoke St. Michael 25 D3
Stoke St. Milborough 65 E4
Stoke sub Hamdon 12 A1
Stoke Talmage 42 B3
Stoke Trister 25 E5
Stoke Villice 24 C1
Stoke Wake 13 D2
Stoke-by-Nayland 60 A4
Stokeford 13 E4
Stokeham 95 E5
Stokeinteignhead 10 C5
Stokenchurch 42 C3
Stokenham 9 E3
Stoke-on-Trent 79 F3
Stokesay 64 D4
Stokesby 87 F4
Stokesley 111 E2
Stolford 23 F3
Ston Easton 24 D2
Stonar Cut 33 F2
Stondon Massey 45 E2
Stone *Bucks.* 42 C1
Stone *Glos.* 39 F3
Stone *Kent* 45 E5
Stone *Kent* 19 E1
Stone *S.Yorks.* 94 C4
Stone *Som.* 24 C4
Stone *Staffs.* 79 G4
Stone *Worcs.* 66 A5
Stone Allerton 24 B2
Stone Cross *Dur.* 109 F1
Stone Cross *E.Suss.* 18 B3
Stone Cross *E.Suss.* 18 A1
Stone Cross *Kent* 32 C5
Stone Cross *Kent* 31 E5
Stone House 108 C4
Stone Street *Kent* 31 E3
Stone Street *Suff.* 73 E3
Stone Street *Suff.* 60 A4
Stonea 70 C3
Stonebridge *E.Suss.* 18 A1
Stonebridge *N.Som.* 24 A2
Stonebridge *Warks.* 67 E4
Stonebroom 81 F2
Stonecross Green 59 G2
Stonefield *Arg. & B.* 139 G2
Stonefield *Staffs.* 79 G4
Stonegate *E.Suss.* 18 B1
Stonegate *N.Yorks.* 111 G2
Stonegrave 111 F5
Stonehaugh 127 F4
Stonehaven 161 G1
Stonehill 29 E1
Stonehouse *Ches.* 91 G5
Stonehouse *D. & G.* 124 C4
Stonehouse *Glos.* 40 A2
Stonehouse *Northumb.* 118 C2
Stonehouse *Plym.* 8 A2
Stonehouse *S.Lan.* 142 B5
Stoneleigh *Surr.* 30 B2
Stoneleigh *Warks.* 67 F5
Stoneley Green 78 D2
Stonely 57 G1
Stoner Hill 28 C5
Stones 101 F5
Stones Green 60 C5
Stonesby 82 D5
Stonesfield 41 F1
Stonestreet Green 32 C5
Stonethwaite 117 F5
Stoney Cross 14 B1
Stoney Middleton 93 G5
Stoney Stanton 67 G3
Stoney Stoke 25 E4
Stoney Stratton 25 D4
Stoney Stretton 64 C2
Stoneyburn 143 D3
Stoneyford 11 D4
Stoneygate 68 B2
Stoneyhills 46 C3
Stoneykirk 122 B5
Stoneywood 169 G3
Stonganess 186 E2
Stonham Aspal 60 C2
Stonnall 66 C2
Stonor 42 C4
Stonton Wyville 68 C3
Stony Houghton 81 F1
Stony Stratford 56 C3
Stonybreck 186 A1
Stoodleigh *Devon* 10 C1
Stoodleigh *Devon* 21 G2
Stopham 16 C2
Stopsley 57 G5
Stoptide 4 D2
Storeton 91 E4
Stornoway (Steornabhagh) 179 G4
Stornoway Airport 179 G4
Storridge 53 G3
Storrington 16 C2
Storrs 93 G4
Storth 107 F4
Storwood 103 G3
Stotfield 175 K4
Stotfold 58 A4
Stottesdon 65 F4
Stoughton *Leics.* 68 B2
Stoughton *Surr.* 29 E2
Stoughton *W.Suss.* 15 G1
Stoughton Cross 24 B3
Stoul 164 D5
Stoulton 54 B3
Stour Provost 25 E5
Stour Row 25 F5
Stourbridge 66 A4
Stourpaine 13 E2
Stourport-on-Severn 66 A5
Stourton *Staffs.* 66 A4
Stourton *Warks.* 55 E4
Stourton *Wilts.* 25 E4
Stourton Caundle 12 D1
Stove 184 F4
Stoven 73 F3
Stow *Lincs.* 95 F4
Stow *Sc.Bord.* 144 B5
Stow Bardolph 71 E2
Stow Bedon 72 A2
Stow cum Quy 58 D1
Stow Longa 69 G5
Stow Maries 46 B3
Stow Pasture 95 F4
Stowbridge 71 D2
Stowe *Glos.* 39 E2
Stowe *Shrop.* 64 C5
Stowe *Staffs.* 66 D1
Stowe-by-Chartley 80 B5
Stowehill 56 B2
Stowell *Glos.* 40 C1
Stowell *Som.* 25 D5
Stowey 24 C2
Stowford *Devon* 7 E2
Stowford *Devon* 21 G3
Stowford *Devon* 11 E4
Stowlangtoft 60 A1
Stowmarket 60 B2
Stow-on-the-Wold 55 D5
Stowting 32 D4
Stowupland 60 B2
Straad 140 B3
Stracathro 161 E3
Strachan 168 E5
Strachur (Clachan Strachur) 148 C4
Stradbroke 72 D4
Stradishall 59 F2
Stradsett 71 E2
Stragglethorpe 83 E2
Straight Soley 41 F5
Straiton *Edin.* 143 G3
Straiton *S.Ayr.* 132 B5
Straloch *Aber.* 169 G2
Straloch *P. & K.* 159 F3
Stramshall 80 B4
Strands 106 C4
Strang 98 B4
Strangford 53 E5
Strannda 171 F3
Stranraer 122 B4
Strata Florida 50 D1
Stratfield Mortimer 28 B1
Stratfield Saye 28 B1
Stratfield Turgis 28 B2
Stratford *Beds.* 57 G3
Stratford *Glos.* 54 A4
Stratford *Gt.Lon.* 44 C4
Stratford St. Andrew 61 E2
Stratford St. Mary 60 B4
Stratford sub Castle 26 C4
Stratford Tony 26 B5
Stratford-upon-Avon 55 D2
Strath 183 H3
Strathan *High.* 180 C6
Strathan *High.* 165 F5
Strathaven 142 B5
Strathblane 141 G2
Strathcanaird 173 H1
Strathcarron 173 F7
Strathdon 168 B3
Strathgirnock 168 B5
Strathkinness 152 C3
Strathmiglo 152 A3
Strathpeffer 174 B6
Strathrannoch 173 K4
Strathtay 159 E4
Strathwhillan 131 F2
Strathy 182 D2
Strathyre 150 A3
Stratton *Cornw.* 20 C5
Stratton *Dorset* 12 C3
Stratton *Glos.* 40 C2
Stratton Audley 56 B5
Stratton Hall 60 D4
Stratton St. Margaret 41 D4
Stratton St. Michael 72 D2
Stratton Strawless 86 D3
Stratton-on-the-Fosse 25 D2
Stravanan 140 B4
Stravithie 152 D3
Strawberry Hill 44 A5
Stream 23 D4
Streat 17 F2
Streatham 44 B5
Streatham Vale 44 B5
Streatley *Beds.* 57 F5
Streatley *W.Berks.* 42 A4
Street *Devon* 11 E4
Street *Lancs.* 100 B2
Street *N.Yorks.* 111 G2
Street *Som.* 24 B4
Street *Som.* 11 G2
Street Ashton 67 G4
Street Dinas 78 A4
Street End 16 A4
Street Gate 120 B2
Street Houses 103 E3
Street Lane 81 E3
Street on the Fosse 24 D4
Streethay 66 D1
Streethouse 102 C5
Streetlam 110 C3
Streetly 66 C3
Streetly End 59 E3
Strefford 64 D4
Strelley 81 G3
Strensall 103 F1
Strensham 54 B3
Stretcholt 23 F3
Strete 9 E3
Stretford *Gt.Man.* 92 B3
Stretford *Here.* 52 D2
Stretford *Here.* 53 E2
Strethall 58 C4
Stretham 70 D5
Strettington 16 A3
Stretton *Ches.* 78 B2
Stretton *Derbys.* 81 E1
Stretton *Rut.* 69 E1
Stretton *Staffs.* 66 A1
Stretton *Staffs.* 81 D5
Stretton *Warr.* 92 A4
Stretton en le Field 67 F1
Stretton Grandison 53 F3
Stretton Heath 64 C1
Stretton Sugwas 53 D3
Stretton under Fosse 67 G4
Stretton Westwood 65 E3
Stretton-on-Dunsmore 67 G5
Stretton-on-Fosse 55 E4
Stribers 107 E4
Strichen 177 H5
Strines 93 D4
Stringston 23 E3
Strixton 57 E1
Stroat 39 E3
Stromeferry 164 E1
Stromemore 164 E1
Stromness 185 B7
Stronaba 157 E1
Stronachlachar 149 G3
Strone *Arg. & B.* 140 C1
Strone *High.* 166 C2
Strone *High.* 156 D1
Strone *Stir.* 149 G3
Stronechrubie 180 E7
Stronlonag 140 C1
Stronmilchan 149 D2
Stronsay 184 F5
Strontian 156 A3
Strontoiller 148 B2
Stronvar 150 A2
Strood 31 G2
Strood Green *Surr.* 30 B4
Strood Green *W.Suss.* 29 F5
Strood Green *W.Suss.* 29 G4
Stroquhan 124 C2
Stroud *Glos.* 40 A2
Stroud *Hants.* 28 C5
Stroud Common 29 F3
Stroud Green *Essex* 46 B3
Stroud Green *Glos.* 40 A2
Stroude 29 F1
Stroul 140 D1
Stroxton 83 E4
Struan *High.* 163 J1
Struan *P. & K.* 158 C3
Strubby *Lincs.* 97 E4
Strubby *Lincs.* 96 B5
Strumpshaw 87 E5
Struthers 152 B4
Strands 106 C4
Struy 166 B1
Stryd y Facsen 88 B4
Stryt-cae-rhedyn 77 F1
Stryt-issa 77 F3
Stuartfield 177 H6
Stub Place 106 B3
Stubber's Green 66 C2
Stubbington 15 E2
Stubbins 92 B1
Stubbs Green 73 E2
Stubhampton 13 F1
Stubley 94 A5
Stubshaw Cross 91 G2
Stubton 83 D3
Stuck *Arg. & B.* 140 B3
Stuck *Arg. & B.* 148 D5
Stuckbeg 149 E5
Stuckgowan 149 F4
Stuckindroin 149 F3
Stuckreoch 148 C5
Stuckton 14 A1
Stud Green 43 D5
Studdon 119 E2
Studfold 108 D5
Studham 43 F1
Studholme 117 F1
Studland 13 G4
Studley *Warks.* 54 C1
Studley *Wilts.* 40 B5
Studley Common 54 C1
Studley Green 42 C3
Studley Roger 110 B5
Stuggadhoo 98 B4
Stump Cross *Essex* 58 D3
Stump Cross *Lancs.* 100 B4
Stuntney 71 D5
Stunts Green 18 B2
Sturbridge 79 F4
Sturgate 95 F4
Sturmer 59 E3
Sturminster Common 13 D1
Sturminster Marshall 13 F2
Sturminster Newton 13 D1
Sturry 33 D2
Sturton by Stow 95 F4
Sturton le Steeple 95 E4
Stuston 72 C4
Stutton *N.Yorks.* 103 D3
Stutton *Suff.* 60 C4
Styal 92 C4
Styrrup 94 D3
Suainebost (Swainbost) 179 H1
Suardail 179 G4
Succoth *Aber.* 168 C1
Succoth *Arg. & B.* 149 E4
Succothmore 148 D4
Suckley 53 G2
Suckley Green 53 G2
Suckley Knowl 53 G2
Sudborough 69 E4
Sudbourne 61 F2
Sudbrook *Lincs.* 83 E3
Sudbrook *Mon.* 39 E4
Sudbrooke 96 A5
Sudbury *Derbys.* 80 C4
Sudbury *Gt.Lon.* 44 A4
Sudbury *Suff.* 59 G3
Sudden 92 C1
Sudgrove 40 B2
Suffield *N.Yorks.* 112 C3
Suffield *Norf.* 86 D2
Sugarloaf 32 B5
Sugnall 79 E4
Sugwas Pool 53 D3
Suie Lodge Hotel 149 G2
Suisnish 164 B3
Sulby *I.o.M.* 98 B2
Sulby *I.o.M.* 98 B3
Sulgrave 56 A3
Sulham 42 B5
Sulhamstead 28 B1
Sullington 16 C2
Sullom 186 C5
Sullom Voe Oil Terminal 186 C5
Sully 23 E1
Sumburgh 187 F10
Sumburgh Airport 187 F9
Summer Bridge 102 B1
Summer Isles 173 F1
Summer Lodge 109 E3
Summercourt 4 C4
Summerfield *Norf.* 85 F4
Summerfield *Worcs.* 66 A5
Summerhill 78 A2
Summerhouse 110 B1
Summerlands 107 G4
Summerleaze 38 D4
Summertown 42 A2
Summit 92 D1
Sun Green 93 D3
Sunadale 139 G5
Sunbiggin 108 B2
Sunbury 29 G1
Sundaywell 124 C2
Sunderland *Cumb.* 117 E3
Sunderland *Lancs.* 100 A2
Sunderland *T. & W.* 120 C2
Sunderland Bridge 120 B4
Sundhope 135 E3
Sundon Park 57 F5
Sundridge 31 D3
Sundrum Mains 132 C3
Sunhill 40 D2
Sunipol 154 C4
Sunk Island 96 C1
Sunningdale 29 E1
Sunninghill 29 E1
Sunningwell 41 G2
Sunniside *Dur.* 120 A4
Sunniside *T. & W.* 120 B2
Sunny Bank 107 D3
Sunny Brow 120 A4
Sunnylaw 150 C5
Sunnyside *Aber.* 169 G5
Sunnyside *Northumb.* 119 F1
Sunnyside *S.Yorks.* 94 B3
Sunnyside *W.Suss.* 30 C5
Sunton 26 D2
Sunwick 145 F4
Surbiton 29 G1
Surfleet 84 A5
Surfleet Seas End 84 A5
Surlingham 87 E5
Sustead 86 C2
Susworth 95 F2
Sutcombe 20 D4
Sutcombemill 20 D4
Suton 72 B2
Sutors of Cromarty 175 F5
Sutterby 97 D5
Sutterton 84 A4
Sutton *Beds.* 58 A3
Sutton *Cambs.* 70 C5
Sutton *Devon* 10 A2
Sutton *Devon* 8 D3
Sutton *Gt.Lon.* 30 B2
Sutton *Kent* 33 F4
Sutton *Lincs.* 83 D2
Sutton *Norf.* 87 E3
Sutton *Notts.* 82 C4
Sutton *Notts.* 95 D4
Sutton *Oxon.* 41 G2
Sutton *Pembs.* 34 C1
Sutton *Peter.* 69 F3
Sutton *S.Yorks.* 94 C1
Sutton *Shrop.* 65 G4
Sutton *Shrop.* 79 D4
Sutton *Shrop.* 65 E1
Sutton *Shrop.* 78 A5
Sutton *Staffs.* 79 E5
Sutton *Suff.* 61 E3
Sutton *W.Suss.* 16 B2
Sutton Abinger 29 G3
Sutton at Hone 45 E5
Sutton Bassett 68 C4
Sutton Benger 40 B5
Sutton Bingham 12 B1
Sutton Bonington 81 G5
Sutton Bridge 84 C5
Sutton Cheney 67 G2
Sutton Coldfield 66 D3
Sutton Courtenay 42 A3
Sutton Crosses 84 C5
Sutton Grange 110 B5
Sutton Green *Oxon.* 41 G2
Sutton Green *Surr.* 29 F2
Sutton Green *Wrex.* 78 B3
Sutton Holms 13 G2
Sutton Howgrave 110 C5
Sutton in Ashfield 81 F2
Sutton in the Elms 68 A3
Sutton Ings 104 D4
Sutton Lane Ends 92 D5
Sutton le Marsh 97 F4
Sutton Leach 91 G3
Sutton Maddock 65 G2
Sutton Mallet 24 A4
Sutton Mandeville 26 A5
Sutton Montis 24 D5
Sutton on Sea 97 F4
Sutton on the Hill 80 D4
Sutton on Trent 82 C1
Sutton Poyntz 12 D4
Sutton St. Edmund 70 B1
Sutton St. James 70 C1
Sutton St. Nicholas 53 E3
Sutton Scarsdale 81 F1
Sutton Scotney 27 F4
Sutton upon Derwent 103 G3
Sutton Valence 32 A4
Sutton Veny 25 F3
Sutton Waldron 13 E1
Sutton Weaver 91 G5
Sutton Wick *B. & N.E.Som.* 24 C2
Sutton Wick *Oxon.* 41 G3
Sutton-in-Craven 101 G3
Sutton-on-Hull 104 D4
Sutton-on-the-Forest 103 E1
Sutton-under-Brailes 55 F4
Sutton-under-Whitestonecliffe 111 D4
Swaby 97 D5
Swadlincote 67 F1
Swaffham 71 G2
Swaffham Bulbeck 59 D1
Swaffham Prior 59 D1
Swafield 87 D2
Swainbost (Suainebost) 179 H1
Swainby 111 D2
Swainsthorpe 86 D5
Swainswick 25 E1
Swalcliffe 55 F4
Swalecliffe 32 D2
Swallow 96 B2
Swallow Beck 83 E1
Swallowcliffe 26 A5
Swallowfield 28 C1
Swallows Cross 45 F3
Swampton 27 F2
Swan Green *Ches.* 92 B5
Swan Green *Suff.* 73 D4
Swan Street 59 G5
Swanage 13 G5
Swanbach 79 D3
Swanbourne 56 D5
Swanbridge 23 E1
Swancote 65 G3
Swanland 104 B5
Swanlaws 136 B5
Swanley 31 E2
Swanley Village 31 E2
Swanmore *Hants.* 15 E1
Swanmore *I.o.W.* 15 E3
Swannington *Leics.* 67 G1
Swannington *Norf.* 86 C4
Swanscombe 45 F5
Swansea (Abertawe) 36 C3
Swanston 143 G3
Swanton Abbot 87 D3
Swanton Morley 86 B4
Swanton Novers 86 B2
Swanton Street 32 A3
Swanwick *Derbys.* 81 F2
Swanwick *Hants.* 15 E2
Swanwick Green 78 C3
Swarby 83 F3
Swardeston 86 D5
Swarkestone 81 E5
Swarland 129 D1
Swarraton 27 G4
Swarthmoor 107 D5
Swaton 83 G4
Swavesey 58 B1
Sway 14 B3
Swayfield 83 E5
Swaythling 14 D1
Swaythorpe 104 C1
Sweetham 10 B3
Sweethay 23 F5
Sweetshouse 5 E3
Sweffling 61 E1
Swell 24 A5
Swepstone 67 F1
Swerford 55 F4
Swettenham 79 F1
Swffryd 38 B3
Swift's Green 32 A4
Swiftsden 18 C1
Swilland 60 C2
Swillington 102 C4
Swimbridge 21 G3
Swimbridge Newland 21 F2
Swinbrook 41 E1
Swincliffe 102 B2
Swincombe 21 G1
Swinden 101 E2
Swinderby 83 D1
Swindon *Staffs.* 66 A3
Swindon *Swin.* 41 D4
Swindon Village 54 B5
Swine 104 D4
Swinefleet 103 G5
Swineford 25 D1
Swineshead *Beds.* 57 F1
Swineshead *Lincs.* 84 A3
Swineshead Bridge 84 A3
Swineside 109 F4
Swiney 183 H5
Swinford *Leics.* 68 A5
Swinford *Oxon.* 41 G2
Swingate 81 G3
Swingfield Minnis 33 E4
Swingleton Green 60 A3
Swinhoe 137 G4
Swinhope 96 C3
Swining 187 D6
Swinithwaite 109 F4
Swinscoe 80 C3
Swinside Hall 136 B5
Swinstead 83 F5
Swinton *Gt.Man.* 92 B2
Swinton *N.Yorks.* 111 G5
Swinton *N.Yorks.* 110 B5
Swinton *S.Yorks.* 94 B3
Swinton *Sc.Bord.* 145 F5
Swinton Quarter 145 F5
Swintonmill 145 F5
Swithland 68 A1
Swordale 174 C5
Swordland 164 D5
Swordle 155 E2
Swordly 182 C2
Sworton Heath 92 A4
Swyddffynnon 50 C1
Swyncombe 42 B3
Swynnerton 79 F4
Swyre 12 B4
Sychnant 63 F5
Syde 40 B1
Sydenham *Gt.Lon.* 44 C5
Sydenham *Oxon.* 42 C2
Sydenham Damerel 7 E3
Syderstone 85 G4
Sydling St. Nicholas 12 C3
Sydmonton 27 F2
Sydney 79 E2
Syerston 82 C3
Sykehouse 94 D1
Sykes 100 C2
Sylen 36 B2
Symbister 187 E6
Symington *S.Ayr.* 132 B2
Symington *S.Lan.* 134 A2
Symonds Yat 39 E1
Symondsbury 12 A3
Synod Inn (Post-mawr) 50 A2
Syre 181 J4
Syreford 54 C5
Syresham 56 B3
Syston *Leics.* 68 B1
Syston *Lincs.* 83 E3
Sytchampton 54 A1
Sywell 56 D1

▼T

Taagan 173 G5
Tableyhill 92 B5
Tabost *W.Isles* 179 F6
Tabost (Harbost) *W.Isles* 179 H1
Tachbrook Mallory 55 F1
Tacher 183 G4
Tackley 55 G5
Tacleit (Hacklete) 178 D4
Tacolneston 72 C2
Tadcaster 103 D3
Tadden 13 F2
Taddington *Derbys.* 93 F5
Taddington *Glos.* 54 C4
Taddiport 21 E4
Tadley 28 B1
Tadlow 58 A3
Tadmarton 55 F4
Tadpole Bridge 41 F2
Tadworth 30 B3
Tafarnaubach 38 A1
Tafarn-y-bwlch 49 D4
Tafarn-y-Gelyn 77 E1
Taff Merthyr Garden Village 38 A3
Taff's Well (Ffynnon Taf) 38 A4
Tafolwern 63 E2
Taibach *N.P.T.* 37 D4
Tai-bach *Powys* 77 E5
Taicynhaeaf 62 C1
Tain *High.* 183 H2
Tain *High.* 174 E3
Tai'n Lôn 74 D2
Tai'r Bull 51 F5
Tairgwaith 36 D1
Tai'r-heol 38 A3
Tairlaw 132 C5
Tai'r-ysgol 36 C3
Takeley 59 D5
Takeley Street 58 D5
Talachddu 51 G4
Talacre 90 C4
Talardd 76 B5
Talaton 11 D3
Talbenny 34 B1
Talbot Green 37 G4
Talbot Village 13 G3
Talerddig 63 F2
Talgarreg 50 A2
Talgarth 52 A4
Taliesin 62 C3
Talisker 163 J1
Talke Pits 79 F2
Talkin 118 B2
Talla Linnfoots 134 C3
Talladale 173 F4
Talladh-a-Bheithe 158 A4
Talland 5 G4
Tallarn Green 78 B3
Tallentire 117 E3
Talley (Talyllychau) 50 C4
Tallington 69 F2
Talmine 181 H2
Talog 49 G5
Tal-sarn 50 B2
Talsarnau 75 F4
Talskiddy 4 D3
Talwrn *I.o.A.* 88 C5
Talwrn *Wrex.* 77 F3
Talwrn *Wrex.* 78 A3
Talybont *Cere.* 62 C4
Tal-y-bont *Conwy* 76 A1
Tal-y-bont *Gwyn.* 75 E5
Tal-y-bont *Gwyn.* 89 E5
Talybont-on-Usk 52 A5
Tal-y-Cae 75 F1
Tal-y-cafn 89 F5
Tal-y-coed 38 D1
Talygarn 37 G4
Talyllychau (Talley) 50 C4
Tal-y-llyn *Gwyn.* 62 D2
Talyllyn *Powys* 52 A5
Talysarn 75 D2
Tal-y-wern 63 E2
Tamavoid 150 A5
Tamerton Foliot 8 A1
Tamworth 67 E2
Tamworth Green 84 B3
Tan Office Green 59 F2
Tandem 93 F1
Tandridge 30 C3
Tanerdy 50 A5
Tanfield 120 A2
Tanfield Lea 120 A2
Tang 102 B2
Tang Hall 103 F2
Tangiers 34 C1
Tanglandford 169 G1
Tangley 27 E2
Tangmere 16 B3
Tangwick 186 B5
Tangy 130 B3
Tankerness 185 E7
Tankersley 94 A2
Tankerton 32 D2
Tan-lan 75 F3
Tannach 183 J4
Tannachie 161 F1
Tannachy 174 E1
Tannadice 160 C4
Tannington 60 D1
Tannochside 142 A3
Tansley 81 E2
Tansley Knoll 81 E2
Tansor 69 F3
Tantobie 120 A2
Tanton 111 E1
Tanworth in Arden 66 D5
Tan-y-fron 76 C1
Tan-y-graig 74 C4
Tanygrisiau 75 F3
Tan-y-groes 49 F3
Tan-y-pistyll 77 D5
Tan-yr-allt 90 B4
Taobh a' Deas Loch Baghasdail 162 C3
Taobh Siar 178 D7
Taobh Tuath (Northton) 170 E3
Tapeley 21 E3
Taplow 43 E4
Tapton Grove 94 B5
Taransay (Tarasaigh) 178 C7
Taraphocain 156 C5
Tarasaigh (Taransay) 178 C7
Tarbat House 174 E4
Tarbert *Arg. & B.* 139 G3
Tarbert *Arg. & B.* 139 E4
Tarbert *Arg. & B.* 139 E1
Tarbert *High.* 155 F3
Tarbert (An Tairbeart) *W.Isles* 178 D7
Tarbet *Arg. & B.* 149 F4
Tarbet *High.* 164 D5

Tarbet *High.* 180 D4
Tarbock Green 91 F4
Tarbolton 132 C3
Tarbrax 143 E4
Tardebigge 54 B1
Tardy Gate 100 B5
Tarfside 160 C2
Tarland 168 C4
Tarleton 100 A5
Tarlscough 91 F1
Tarlton 40 B3
Tarnbrook 100 B2
Tarnock 24 A2
Tarporley 78 C1
Tarr 23 E4
Tarrant Crawford 13 F2
Tarrant Gunville 13 F1
Tarrant Hinton 13 F1
Tarrant Keyneston 13 F2
Tarrant Launceston 13 F2
Tarrant Monkton 13 F2
Tarrant Rawston 13 F2
Tarrant Rushton 13 F2
Tarrel 175 F3
Tarring Neville 17 G3
Tarrington 53 F3
Tarrnacraig 131 E2
Tarsappie 151 G2
Tarskavaig 164 B4
Tarves 169 G1
Tarvie *High.* 174 B6
Tarvie *P. & K.* 159 F3
Tarvin 78 B1
Tarvin Sands 78 B1
Tasburgh 72 D2
Tasley 65 F3
Taston 55 F5
Tatenhill 80 D5
Tathall End 56 D3
Tatham 100 C1
Tathwell 96 D4
Tatsfield 30 D3
Tattenhall 78 B2
Tattenhoe 56 D4
Tatterford 85 G5
Tattersett 85 G4
Tattershall 84 A2
Tattershall Bridge 83 G2
Tattershall Thorpe 84 A2
Tattingstone 60 C4
Tatworth 11 G2
Tauchers 176 B6
Taunton 23 F5
Tavelty 169 F3
Taverham 86 C4
Tavernspite 35 E1
Tavistock 7 E3
Taw Bridge 21 G5
Taw Green 7 G1
Tawstock 21 F3
Taxal 93 E5
Tayburn 141 G5
Taychreggan 148 C2
Tayinloan 139 E5
Taylors Cross 20 C4
Taynafead 148 C3
Taynish 139 F1
Taynton *Glos.* 53 G5
Taynton *Oxon.* 41 E1
Taynuilt 148 C1
Tayock 161 E4
Tayovullin 138 A2
Tayport 152 C2
Tayvallich 139 F1
Tea Green 57 G5
Tealby 96 B3
Tealing 152 C1
Team Valley 120 B1
Teanamachar 170 C5
Teangue 164 C4
Teasses 152 C4
Tebay 108 B2
Tebworth 57 E5
Tedburn St. Mary 10 B3
Teddington *Glos.* 54 B4
Teddington *Gt.Lon.* 44 A5
Tedstone Delamere 53 F2
Tedstone Wafre 53 F2
Teeton 68 B5
Teffont Evias 26 A4
Teffont Magna 26 A4
Tegryn 49 F4
Teigh 69 D1
Teign Village 10 B4
Teigngrace 10 B5
Teignmouth 10 C5
Telford 65 F2
Telham 18 C2
Tellisford 25 F2
Telscombe 17 G3
Telscombe Cliffs 17 G3
Tempar 158 B4
Templand 125 E2
Temple *Cornw.* 5 F2
Temple *Midloth.* 144 A4
Temple Balsall 67 E5
Temple Bar 50 B2
Temple Cloud 24 D2
Temple End 59 E2
Temple Ewell 33 E4
Temple Grafton 54 D2
Temple Guiting 54 C5
Temple Herdewyke 55 F2
Temple Hirst 103 F5
Temple Normanton 81 F1
Temple Sowerby 118 C5
Templecombe 25 E5
Templeton *Devon* 10 B1
Templeton *Pembs.* 35 E1
Templeton Bridge 10 B1
Templewood 161 E3
Tempsford 57 G2
Ten Mile Bank 71 E3
Tenbury Wells 53 E1
Tenby (Dinbych-y-Pysgod) 35 E2
Tendring 60 C5
Tendring Green 60 C5
Tenga 155 E5
Tenterden 32 A5
Tepersie Castle 168 D2
Terally 114 B2
Terling 45 G1
Tern 65 F1
Ternhill 78 D4
Terregles 124 D3
Terriers 43 D3
Terrington 111 F5
Terrington St. Clement 85 D5
Terrington St. John 70 D1
Terry's Green 66 D5
Tervieside 167 K1
Teston 31 G3
Testwood 14 C1
Tetbury 40 A3
Tetbury Upton 40 A3
Tetchill 78 A4
Tetcott 6 D1
Tetford 96 D5
Tetney 96 D2
Tetney Lock 96 D2
Tetsworth 42 B2
Tettenhall 66 A2
Tettenhall Wood 66 A3
Tetworth 58 A2
Teuchan 169 J1
Teversal 81 F1
Teversham 58 C2
Teviothead 135 F5
Tewel 161 G1
Tewin 44 B1
Tewkesbury 54 A4
Teynham 32 B2
Thackley 102 A4
Thainston 161 E2
Thainstone 169 F3
Thakeham 16 D2
Thame 42 C2
Thames Ditton 29 G1
Thames Haven 45 G4
Thamesmead 45 D4
Thanington 32 D3
Thankerton 134 A2
Tharston 72 C2
Thatcham 27 G1
Thatto Heath 91 G3
Thaxted 59 E4
The Apes Hall 71 D3
The Bage 52 B3
The Balloch 150 D3
The Banking 169 F1
The Bar 29 G5
The Birks 169 F4
The Bog 64 C3
The Bourne 28 D3
The Bratch 66 A3
The Broad 53 D1
The Bryn 38 C2
The Burf 54 A1
The Burn 161 D2
The Butts 25 E3
The Camp 40 B2
The Chequer 78 B3
The City *Bucks.* 42 C3
The City *Suff.* 73 E3
The Common *Wilts.* 26 D4
The Common *Wilts.* 40 C4
The Craigs 174 B2
The Cronk 98 B2
The Delves 66 C3
The Den 141 E4
The Dicker 18 A3
The Down 65 F3
The Drums 160 B3
The Eaves 39 F2
The Flatt 127 D4
The Folly 44 A1
The Forge 52 C2
The Forstal *E.Suss.* 31 E5
The Forstal *Kent* 32 C5
The Grange *Lincs.* 97 F5
The Grange *Shrop.* 78 A4
The Grange *Surr.* 30 C4
The Green *Arg. & B.* 154 A2
The Green *Cumb.* 106 C4
The Green *Essex* 45 G1
The Green *Flints.* 77 F1
The Green *Wilts.* 25 F4
The Grove 54 A3
The Haven 29 F4
The Headland 121 E4
The Heath 80 B4
The Herberts 37 F5
The Hermitage 30 B3
The Hill 106 C4
The Holme 102 B2
The Howe 98 A5
The Isle 65 D1
The Laurels 73 E2
The Leacon 32 B5
The Lee 43 D2
The Leigh 54 A5
The Lhen 98 B1
The Lodge 149 D5
The Marsh 64 C3
The Moor *E.Suss.* 18 D2
The Moor *Kent* 18 C1
The Mumbles 36 C4
The Murray 142 A4
The Mythe 54 A4
The Narth 39 E2
The Neuk 169 F5
The Node 44 B1
The Oval 25 E1
The Polchar 167 G4
The Quarter 32 A4
The Reddings 54 B5
The Rhos 34 D1
The Rookery 79 F2
The Rowe 79 F4
The Sale 67 D1
The Sands 29 D3
The Shoe 40 A5
The Slade 42 A5
The Smithies 65 F3
The Stocks 19 E1
The Swillett 43 F3
The Thrift 58 B4
The Vauld 53 E3
The Wern 77 F2
The Wyke 65 G2
Theakston 110 C4
Thealby 95 F1
Theale *Som.* 24 B3
Theale *W.Berks.* 42 B5
Thearne 104 C4
Theberton 61 F1
Thedden Grange 28 B4
Theddingworth 68 B4
Theddlethorpe All Saints 97 E4
Theddlethorpe St. Helen 97 E4
Thelbridge Barton 10 A1
Thelbridge Cross 10 A1
Thelnetham 72 B4
Thelveton 72 C3
Thelwall 92 A4
Themelthorpe 86 B3
Thenford 56 A3
Therfield 58 B4
Thetford *Lincs.* 69 G1
Thetford *Norf.* 71 G4
Thethwaite 117 G2
Theydon Bois 44 D3
Theydon Garnon 45 D3
Theydon Mount 45 D3
Thickwood 40 A5
Thimbleby *Lincs.* 84 A1
Thimbleby *N.Yorks.* 110 D3
Thingley 25 F1
Thirkleby 111 D5
Thirlby 111 D4
Thirlestane 144 C5
Thirn 110 B4
Thirsk 110 D4
Thirston New Houses 129 D2
Thirtleby 105 D4
Thistleton *Lancs.* 100 A4
Thistleton *Rut.* 69 E1
Thistley Green 71 E5
Thixendale 104 A1
Thockrington 128 B4
Tholomas Drove 70 B2
Tholthorpe 103 D1
Thomas Chapel 35 E2
Thomas Close 118 A3
Thomastown 168 D1
Thompson 72 A2
Thomshill 175 K6
Thong 45 F5
Thongsbridge 93 F2
Thoralby 109 F4
Thoresby 94 D5
Thoresthorpe 97 E5
Thoresway 96 B3
Thorganby *Lincs.* 96 C3
Thorganby *N.Yorks.* 103 F3
Thorgill 111 G3
Thorington 73 F4
Thorington Street 60 B4
Thorlby 101 F2
Thorley 45 D1
Thorley Houses 58 C5
Thorley Street *Herts.* 45 D1
Thorley Street *I.o.W.* 14 C4
Thormanby 111 D5
Thornaby-on-Tees 111 D1
Thornage 86 B2
Thornborough *Bucks.* 56 C4
Thornborough *N.Yorks.* 110 B5
Thornbury *Devon* 21 D5
Thornbury *Here.* 53 F2
Thornbury *S.Glos.* 39 F3
Thornbury *W.Yorks.* 102 A4
Thornby 68 B5
Thorncliff 93 G1
Thorncliffe 80 B2
Thorncombe 11 G2
Thorncombe Street 29 F3
Thorncote Green 57 G3
Thorncross 14 D4
Thorndon 60 C1
Thorndon Cross 7 F1
Thorne 95 D1
Thorne St. Margaret 23 D5
Thorner 102 C4
Thorney *Bucks.* 43 F5
Thorney *Notts.* 95 F5
Thorney *Peter.* 70 A2
Thorney *Som.* 24 B5
Thorney Close 120 C2
Thorney Hill 14 B3
Thornfalcon 23 F5
Thornford 12 C1
Thorngrafton 119 D1
Thorngrove 24 A4
Thorngumbald 105 E5
Thornham 85 F3
Thornham Magna 72 C4
Thornham Parva 72 C4
Thornhaugh 69 F2
Thornhill *Cardiff* 38 A4
Thornhill *Cumb.* 106 B2
Thornhill *D. & G.* 124 C1
Thornhill *Derbys.* 93 F4
Thornhill *S'ham.* 15 D1
Thornhill *Stir.* 150 B4
Thornhill *W.Yorks.* 93 G1
Thornhill Lees 93 G1
Thornholme 104 D1
Thornicombe 13 E2
Thornley *Dur.* 120 C4
Thornley *Dur.* 120 A4
Thornley Gate 119 E2
Thornliebank 141 G4
Thornroan 169 G1
Thorns 59 F2
Thorns Green 92 B4
Thornsett 93 E4
Thornthwaite *Cumb.* 117 F4
Thornthwaite *N.Yorks.* 102 A2
Thornton *Angus* 160 B5
Thornton *Bucks.* 56 C4
Thornton *E.Riding* 103 G3
Thornton *Fife* 152 A5
Thornton *Lancs.* 99 G3
Thornton *Leics.* 67 G2
Thornton *Lincs.* 84 A1
Thornton *Mersey.* 91 E2
Thornton *Middbro.* 111 D1
Thornton *Northumb.* 145 G5
Thornton *P. & K.* 159 F5
Thornton *Pembs.* 34 C2
Thornton *W.Yorks.* 102 A4
Thornton Bridge 110 D5
Thornton Curtis 96 A1
Thornton Heath 30 C2
Thornton Hough 91 E4
Thornton in Lonsdale 108 B5
Thornton le Moor 96 A3
Thornton Park 145 G5
Thornton Rust 109 E4
Thornton Steward 110 A4
Thornton Watlass 110 B4
Thorntonhall 141 G4
Thornton-in-Craven 101 F3
Thornton-le-Beans 110 D3
Thornton-le-Clay 103 F1
Thornton-le-Dale 112 B4
Thornton-le-Moor 110 C4
Thornton-le-Moors 91 F5
Thornton-le-Street 110 D4
Thorntonloch 145 E2
Thornwood Common 45 D2
Thornyhill 161 E2
Thornylee 135 F2
Thoroton 82 C3
Thorp Arch 102 D3
Thorpe *Derbys.* 80 C2
Thorpe *E.Riding* 104 B3
Thorpe *Lincs.* 97 E4
Thorpe *N.Yorks.* 101 G1
Thorpe *Norf.* 73 F2
Thorpe *Notts.* 82 C2
Thorpe *Surr.* 29 F1
Thorpe Abbotts 72 C3
Thorpe Acre 68 A1
Thorpe Arnold 82 C5
Thorpe Audlin 94 B1
Thorpe Bassett 112 B5
Thorpe Bay 46 C4
Thorpe by Water 69 D3
Thorpe Constantine 67 E2
Thorpe Culvert 84 C1
Thorpe End 87 D4
Thorpe Green *Essex* 60 C5
Thorpe Green *Lancs.* 100 B5
Thorpe Green *Suff.* 60 A2
Thorpe Hall 111 E5
Thorpe Hesley 94 A3
Thorpe in Balne 94 C1
Thorpe in the Fallows 95 G4
Thorpe Langton 68 C3
Thorpe Larches 120 C5
Thorpe le Street 104 A3
Thorpe Malsor 68 D5
Thorpe Mandeville 56 A3
Thorpe Market 86 D2
Thorpe Morieux 60 A2
Thorpe on the Hill *Lincs.* 83 E1
Thorpe on the Hill *W.Yorks.* 102 C5
Thorpe Row 86 A5
Thorpe St. Andrew 87 D5
Thorpe St. Peter 84 C1
Thorpe Salvin 94 C4
Thorpe Satchville 68 C1
Thorpe Street 72 B4
Thorpe Thewles 120 D5
Thorpe Tilney Dales 83 G2
Thorpe Underwood *N.Yorks.* 103 D2
Thorpe Underwood *Northants.* 68 C4
Thorpe Waterville 69 F4
Thorpe Willoughby 103 E4
Thorpefield 110 D5
Thorpe-le-Soken 60 C5
Thorpeness 61 F1
Thorpland 71 E2
Thorrington 60 B5
Thorverton 10 C2
Thrandeston 72 C4
Thrapston 69 E5
Threapland 101 F1
Threapwood 78 B3
Threapwood Head 80 B3
Three Ashes 25 D3
Three Bridges 30 B5
Three Burrows 4 B5
Three Chimneys 32 A5
Three Cocks (Aberllynfi) 52 A4
Three Crosses 36 B3
Three Cups Corner 18 B1
Three Hammers 5 G1
Three Holes 70 D2
Three Leg Cross 31 F5
Three Legged Cross 13 G2
Three Mile Cross 28 C1
Three Oaks 18 D2
Threehammer Common 87 E4
Threekingham 83 F4
Threemilestone 4 B5
Threlkeld 117 G4
Threshfield 101 F1
Threxton Hill 71 G2
Thriepley 152 B1
Thrigby 87 F4
Thringarth 119 F5
Thringstone 67 G1
Thrintoft 110 C3
Thriplow 58 C3
Throapham 94 C4
Throckenholt 70 B2
Throcking 58 B4
Throckley 120 A1
Throckmorton 54 B3
Throop 13 E3
Throphill 128 D3
Thropton 128 C1
Througham 40 B2
Throwleigh 7 G1
Throwley 32 B3
Throws 59 E5
Thrumpton *Notts.* 81 G4
Thrumpton *Notts.* 95 E5
Thrumster 183 J4
Thrunton 137 E5
Thrupp *Glos.* 40 A2
Thrupp *Oxon.* 41 G1
Thrupp *Oxon.* 41 E3
Thruscross 102 A2
Thrushelton 7 E2
Thrussington 68 B1
Thruxton *Hants.* 27 D3
Thruxton *Here.* 52 D4
Thrybergh 94 B3
Thulston 81 F4
Thunder Bridge 93 F1
Thundergay 139 G5
Thundersley 46 B4
Thunderton 177 J6
Thundridge 44 C1
Thurcaston 68 A1
Thurcroft 94 B4
Thurdistoft 183 H2
Thurdon 20 C4
Thurgarton *Norf.* 86 C2
Thurgarton *Notts.* 82 B3
Thurgoland 93 G2
Thurlaston *Leics.* 68 A3
Thurlaston *Warks.* 67 G5
Thurlbear 23 F5
Thurlby *Lincs.* 69 G1
Thurlby *Lincs.* 83 E1
Thurlby *Lincs.* 97 E5
Thurleigh 57 F2
Thurlestone 8 C3
Thurloxton 23 F4
Thurlstone 93 G2
Thurlton 73 F2
Thurlwood 79 F2
Thurmaston 68 B2
Thurnby 68 B2
Thurne 87 F4
Thurnham 32 A3
Thurning *Norf.* 86 B3
Thurning *Northants.* 69 F4
Thurnscoe 94 B2
Thursby 117 G1
Thursden 101 F4
Thursford 86 A2
Thursley 29 E4
Thurso 183 G2
Thurstaston 90 D4
Thurston 60 A1
Thurston Clough 93 D2
Thurstonfield 117 G1
Thurstonland 93 F1
Thurton 87 E5
Thurvaston *Derbys.* 80 D4
Thurvaston *Derbys.* 80 C4
Thuster 183 H3
Thuxton 86 B5
Thwaite *N.Yorks.* 109 D3
Thwaite *Suff.* 60 C1
Thwaite Head 107 E3
Thwaite St. Mary 73 E2
Thwaites 101 G3
Thwaites Brow 101 G3
Thwing 113 D5
Tibbermore 151 F2
Tibberton *Glos.* 53 G5
Tibberton *Tel. & W.* 79 D5
Tibberton *Worcs.* 54 B2
Tibbie Shiels Inn 134 D3
Tibenham 72 C2
Tibertich 148 A4
Tibshelf 81 F1
Tibthorpe 104 B2
Ticehurst 31 F5
Tichborne 27 G4
Tickencote 69 E2
Tickenham 39 D5
Tickford End 57 D3
Tickhill 94 C3
Ticklerton 65 D3
Ticknall 81 E5
Tickton 104 C3
Tidbury Green 66 D5
Tidcombe 27 D2
Tiddington *Oxon.* 42 B2
Tiddington *Warks.* 55 E2
Tiddleywink 40 A5
Tidebrook 18 B1
Tideford 6 D5
Tideford Cross 6 D4
Tidenham 39 E3
Tidenham Chase 39 E3
Tideswell 93 F5
Tidmarsh 42 B5
Tidmington 55 E4
Tidpit 13 G1
Tidworth 26 D3
Tiers Cross 34 C1
Tiffield 56 B2
Tifty 177 F6
Tigerton 160 D3
Tigh a' Gearraidh 170 C4
Tighachnoic 155 F5
Tighnablair 150 C3
Tighnabruaich 140 A2
Tighnacomaire 156 B3
Tigley 9 D1
Tilbrook 57 F1
Tilbury 45 F5
Tilbury Green 59 F3
Tile Hill 67 E5
Tilehurst 42 B5
Tilford 29 D3
Tilgate 30 B5
Tilgate Forest Row 30 B5
Tillathrowie 168 C1
Tillers' Green 53 F4
Tillery 169 H2
Tilley 78 C5
Tillicoultry 151 E5
Tillingham 46 C2
Tillington *Here.* 53 D3
Tillington *W.Suss.* 29 E5
Tillington Common 53 D3
Tillyarblet 160 D3
Tillybirloch 168 E4
Tillycairn Castle 168 E3
Tillycorthie 169 H2
Tillydrine 168 E5
Tillyfar 177 G6
Tillyfour 168 D3
Tillyfourie 168 E3
Tillygreig 169 G2
Tillypronie 168 C4
Tilmanstone 33 F3
Tiln 95 E4
Tilney All Saints 71 D1
Tilney Fen End 70 D1
Tilney High End 71 D1
Tilney St. Lawrence 70 D1
Tilshead 26 B3
Tilstock 78 C4
Tilston 78 B2
Tilstone Fearnall 78 C1
Tilsworth 57 E5
Tilton on the Hill 68 C2
Tiltups End 40 A3
Timberland 83 G2
Timberland Dales 83 G1
Timbersbrook 79 F1
Timberscombe 22 C3
Timble 102 A2
Timewell 22 C5
Timperley 92 B4
Timsbury *B. & N.E.Som.* 25 D2
Timsbury *Hants.* 27 E5
Timsgearraidh 178 C4
Timworth 59 G1
Timworth Green 59 G1
Tincleton 13 D3
Tindale 118 C2
Tindon End 59 E4
Tingewick 56 B4
Tingley 102 B5
Tingrith 57 F4
Tingwall 184 D5
Tinhay 7 D2
Tinney 6 C1
Tinshill 102 B4
Tinsley 94 B3
Tinsley Green 30 B5
Tintagel 5 E1
Tintern Parva 39 E2
Tintinhull 12 A1
Tintwistle 93 E3
Tinwald 125 E2
Tinwell 69 F2
Tippacott 22 A3
Tipperty *Aber.* 161 F1
Tipperty *Aber.* 169 H2
Tips End 70 C3
Tiptoe 14 B3
Tipton 66 B3
Tipton St. John 11 D3
Tiptree 46 B1
Tiptree Heath 46 B1
Tirabad 51 E3
Tiree 154 A2
Tiree Airport 154 B2
Tirindrish 157 E1
Tirley 54 A5
Tirphil 38 A2
Tirril 118 B5
Tir-y-dail 36 C1
Tisbury 26 A5
Tisman's Common 29 F4
Tissington 80 C2
Tister 183 G2
Titchberry 20 C3
Titchfield 15 E2
Titchmarsh 69 F5
Titchwell 85 F3
Tithby 82 B4
Titley 52 C1
Titlington 137 F5
Titmore Green 58 A5
Titsey 30 D3
Titson 20 C5
Tittensor 79 F4
Tittleshall 85 G5
Tiverton *Ches.* 78 C1
Tiverton *Devon* 10 C1
Tivetshall St. Margaret 72 C3
Tivetshall St. Mary 72 C3
Tivington 22 C3
Tixall 79 G5
Tixover 69 E2
Toab *Ork.* 185 E7
Toab *Shet.* 187 F9
Tobermory 155 E4
Toberonochy 147 G4
Tobha Mòr (Homore) 162 C1
Tobson 178 D4
Tocher 168 E1
Tockenham 40 C5
Tockenham Wick 40 C4
Tockholes 100 C5
Tockington 39 F4
Tockwith 103 D2
Todber 25 E5
Toddington *Beds.* 57 F5
Toddington *Glos.* 54 C4
Todenham 55 E4
Todhills *Angus* 152 C1
Todhills *Cumb.* 126 B5
Todlachie 168 E3
Todmorden 101 F5
Todwick 94 B4
Toft *Cambs.* 58 B2
Toft *Lincs.* 69 F1
Toft *Shet.* 186 D5
Toft Hill 120 A5
Toft Monks 73 F2
Toft next Newton 96 A4
Toftcarl 183 J4
Toftrees 85 G5
Tofts 183 J2
Toftwood 86 A4
Togston 129 E1
Tokavaig 164 C3
Tokers Green 42 B5
Tolastadh 179 H3
Tolastadh a' Chaolais 178 D4
Tolastadh Úr 179 H3
Toll Bar 94 C2
Toll of Birness 169 J1
Tolland 23 E4
Tollard Farnham 13 F1
Tollard Royal 13 F1
Tollcross 142 A3
Toller Down Gate 12 B2
Toller Fratrum 12 B3
Toller Porcorum 12 B3
Toller Whelme 12 B2
Tollerton *N.Yorks.* 103 E1
Tollerton *Notts.* 82 B4
Tollesbury 46 C1
Tollesby 111 E1
Tolleshunt D'Arcy 46 C1
Tolleshunt Knights 46 C1
Tolleshunt Major 46 B1
Tolm (Holm) 179 G4
Tolmachan 178 C7
Tolpuddle 13 D3
Tolvah 167 F5
Tolworth 29 G1
Tom an Fhuadain 179 F6
Tomatin 167 F2
Tombreck 166 D1
Tomchrasky 165 J3
Tomdoun 165 H4
Tomdow 175 H7
Tomich *High.* 165 K2
Tomich *High.* 174 E4
Tomich *High.* 174 D1
Tomintoul 167 J3
Tomnacross 174 C7
Tomnamoon 175 H6
Tomnaven 168 C1
Tomnavoulin 167 K2
Tomvaich 167 H1
Ton Pentre 37 F3
Tonbridge 31 E4
Tondu 37 E4
Tonedale 23 E5
Tonfanau 62 B2
Tong *Kent* 32 A4
Tong *Shrop.* 65 G2
Tong *W.Yorks.* 102 B4
Tong Norton 65 G2
Tong Street 102 A4
Tonge 81 F5
Tongham 29 D3
Tongland 124 A5
Tongue 181 H3
Tongue House 181 H3
Tongwynlais 38 A4
Tonmawr 37 E3
Tonna 37 D3
Tonwell 44 C1
Tonypandy 37 F3
Tonyrefail 37 G4
Toot Baldon 42 A2
Toot Hill 45 E2
Toothill *Hants.* 14 C1
Toothill *Swin.* 40 D4
Tooting Graveney 44 B5
Top End 57 F1
Top of Hebers 92 C2
Topcliffe 110 D5
Topcroft 73 D2
Topcroft Street 73 D2
Toppesfield 59 F4
Toppings 92 B1
Toprow 72 C2
Topsham 10 C4
Topsham Bridge 8 D2
Torastan 154 B3
Torbain 167 J3
Torbeg *Aber.* 168 B5
Torbeg *N.Ayr.* 131 E3
Torbothie 142 C4
Torbryan 9 E1
Torcastle 156 D2
Torcross 9 E3
Tordarroch 166 D1
Tore 174 D6
Toreduff 175 J5
Toremore *High.* 167 J1
Toremore *High.* 183 G5
Torfrey 5 F4
Torgyle 165 K3
Torksey 95 F5
Torlum 170 C6
Torlundy 156 D2
Tormarton 39 G5
Tormisdale 138 A4
Tormore 131 D2
Tormsdale 183 G3
Tornagrain 174 E6
Tornahaish 167 K4
Tornaveen 168 E4
Torness 166 C2
Toronto 120 A4
Torpenhow 117 F3
Torphichen 143 D2
Torphins 168 E4
Torpoint 8 A2
Torquay 9 F1
Torquhan 144 B5
Torr 8 B2
Torran *Arg. & B.* 148 A4
Torran *High.* 174 E4
Torran *High.* 172 B7
Torrance 142 A2
Torrance House 142 A4
Torrancroy 168 B3
Torre *Som.* 22 D3
Torre *Torbay* 9 F1
Torrich 175 F6
Torridon 172 E6
Torrin 164 B2
Torrisdale *Arg. & B.* 130 C2
Torrisdale *High.* 181 J2
Torrish 182 E7
Torrisholme 100 A1
Torroble 174 C1
Torry *Aber.* 176 C6
Torry *Aberdeen* 169 H4
Torryburn 143 E1
Torsonce 144 B5
Torterston 177 J6
Torthorwald 125 E3
Tortington 16 B3
Torton 66 A5
Tortworth 39 G3
Torvaig 171 K7
Torver 107 D3
Torwood 142 C1
Torworth 95 D4
Tosberry 20 C3
Toscaig 164 D1
Toseland 58 A1
Tosside 101 D2
Tostarie 154 C5
Tostock 60 A1
Totaig 171 G6
Totamore 154 A4
Tote 171 K7
Tote Hill 29 D5
Totegan 182 D2
Totford 27 G4
Totham Hill 46 B1
Tothill 97 E4
Totland 14 C4
Totley 94 A5
Totnes 9 E1
Toton 81 G4
Totronald 154 A4
Totscore 171 J5
Tottenham 44 C3
Tottenhill 71 E1
Tottenhill Row 71 E1
Totteridge *Bucks.* 43 D3
Totteridge *Gt.Lon.* 44 B3
Totternhoe 57 E5
Tottington *Gt.Man.* 92 B1
Tottington *Norf.* 71 G3
Totton 14 C1
Toulton 23 E4
Tournaig 172 E3
Toux 177 H5
Tovil 31 G3
Tow Law 120 A4
Towan Cross 4 B5
Toward 140 C3
Towcester 56 B3
Towednack 2 B3
Tower End 71 E1
Towersey 42 C2
Towie *Aber.* 177 G4
Towie *Aber.* 168 D2
Towie *Aber.* 168 C3
Towiemore 176 B6
Town End *Cambs.* 70 C3
Town End *Cumb.* 107 F4
Town End *Mersey.* 91 F4
Town Green *Lancs.* 91 F2
Town Green *Norf.* 87 E4
Town of Lowton 92 A3
Town Row 31 E5
Town Street 71 F4
Town Yetholm 136 C4
Townend 141 F2
Townfield 119 F3
Townhead *D. & G.* 115 G2
Townhead *S.Yorks.* 93 F2
Townhead of Greenlaw 124 B4
Townhill *Fife* 143 F1

Townhill *Swan.* 36 C3
Towns End 27 G2
Towns Green 78 D1
Townshend 2 C3
Towthorpe *E.Riding* 104 B1
Towthorpe *York* 103 F2
Towton 103 D4
Towyn 90 A5
Toynton All Saints 84 B1
Toynton Fen Side 84 B1
Toynton St. Peter 84 C1
Toy's Hill 31 D3
Trabboch 132 C3
Traboe 3 E4
Tradespark *High.* 175 F6
Tradespark *Ork.* 185 D7
Traeth Coch (Red Wharf Bay) 88 D4
Trafford Centre 92 B3
Trafford Park 92 B3
Trallong 51 F5
Trallwn 36 C3
Tram Inn 53 D4
Tranent 144 B2
Tranmere 91 E4
Trantlebeg 182 D3
Trantlemore 182 D3
Tranwell 129 D3
Trap 36 C1
Trap Street 79 F1
Traprain 144 C2
Trap's Green 54 D1
Traquair 135 E2
Trawden 101 F4
Trawsfynydd 76 A4
Trealaw 37 G3
Treales 100 A4
Trearddur 88 A5
Treaslane 171 J6
Tre-Aubrey 37 G5
Trebanog 37 G3
Trebanos 36 D2
Trebarrow 6 C1
Trebartha 5 G2
Trebarvah 3 E3
Trebarwith 5 E1
Trebeath 5 G1
Trebetherick 4 D2
Trebister 187 D9
Tre-boeth 36 C3
Treborough 22 D4
Trebudannon 4 C3
Trebullett 6 D3
Treburley 6 D3
Treburrick 4 C2
Trebyan 5 E3
Trecastle 51 E5
Trecott 21 G5
Trecrogo 6 D2
Trecwn 48 C4
Trecynon 37 F2
Tredaule 5 G1
Tredavoe 2 B4
Treddiog 48 B5
Tredegar 38 A2
Tredington *Glos.* 54 B5
Tredington *Warks.* 55 E3
Tredinnick *Cornw.* 4 D3
Tredinnick *Cornw.* 5 G4
Tredogan 23 D1
Tredomen 52 A4
Tredrissi 49 D3
Tredunnock 38 C3
Tredustan 52 A4
Tredworth 40 A1
Treen *Cornw.* 2 A4
Treen *Cornw.* 2 B3
Treesmill 5 E4
Treeton 94 B4
Trefaldwyn (Montgomery) 64 B3
Trefasser 48 B4
Trefdraeth *I.o.A.* 88 C5
Trefdraeth (Newport) *Pembs.* 49 D4
Trefecca 52 A4
Trefechan 37 G2
Trefeglwys 63 F3
Trefenter 50 C1
Treffgarne 48 C5
Treffynnon (Holywell) *Flints.* 90 C5
Treffynnon *Pembs.* 48 B5
Trefgarn Owen 48 B5
Trefil 38 A1
Trefilan 50 B2
Treflach 77 F5
Trefnanney 64 B1
Trefnant 90 B5
Trefonen 77 F5
Trefor *Gwyn.* 74 C3
Trefor *I.o.A.* 88 B4
Treforest 37 G4
Treforest Industrial Estate 38 A4
Trefriw 76 A1
Tref-y-clawdd (Knighton) 64 B5
Trefynwy (Monmouth) 39 E1
Tregadillett 5 G1
Tregaian 88 C5
Tregare 38 D1
Tregarland 5 G4
Tregarne 3 E4
Tregaron 50 C2
Tregarth 75 F1
Tregaswith 4 C3
Tregavethan 4 B5
Tregear 4 C4
Tregeare 5 G1
Tregeiriog 77 E4
Tregele 88 B3
Tregidden 3 E4
Tregiskey 5 E5
Treglemais 48 B5
Tregolds 4 C2
Tregole 6 B1
Tregonetha 5 D3
Tregony 4 D5
Tregoodwell 5 F1
Tregoss 5 D3
Tregowris 3 E4
Tregoyd 52 A4
Tregrehan Mills 5 E4
Tre-groes 50 A3
Treguff 37 G5
Tregullon 5 E3
Tregunnon 5 G1
Tregurrian 4 C3
Tregynon 63 G3
Trehafod 37 G3
Trehan 8 A2
Treharris 37 G3
Treherbert 37 F3
Tre-hill 37 G5
Trekenner 6 D3
Treknow 5 E1
Trelan 3 E5
Trelash 6 B1
Trelassick 4 C4
Trelawnyd 90 B5
Trelech 49 F4
Treleddyd-fawr 48 A5
Trelewis 38 A3
Treligga 5 E1
Trelights 5 D2
Trelill 5 E2
Trelissick 3 F3
Trelleck 39 E2
Trelleck Grange 39 D2
Trelogan 90 C4
Trelowla 5 G4
Trelystan 64 B2
Tremadog 75 E3
Tremail 5 F1
Tremain 49 F3
Tremaine 5 G1
Tremar 5 G3
Trematon 7 D5
Tremeirchion 90 B5
Tremethick Cross 2 B3
Tremore 5 E3
Trenance *Cornw.* 4 C3
Trenance *Cornw.* 4 D2
Trenarren 5 E5
Trench *Tel. & W.* 65 F1
Trench *Wrex.* 78 A4
Trencreek 4 C3
Trenear 3 D3
Treneglos 5 G1
Trenewan 5 F4
Trengune 6 B1
Trent 12 B1
Trent Port 95 F4
Trent Vale 79 F3
Trentham 79 F3
Trentishoe 21 G1
Trenwheal 2 D3
Treoes 37 F5
Treorchy 37 F3
Treowen 38 B3
Trequite 5 E2
Tre'r-ddol 62 C3
Trerhyngyll 37 G5
Tre-Rhys 49 E3
Trerulefoot 6 D5
Tresaith 49 F2
Tresco 4 A1
Trescott 66 A3
Trescowe 2 C3
Tresean 4 B4
Tresham 39 G3
Treshnish 154 C5
Tresillian 4 C5
Tresinney 5 F1
Tresinwen 48 B3
Treskinnick Cross 6 C1
Treslea 5 F3
Tresmeer 5 G1
Tresowes Green 2 D4
Tresparrett 6 B1
Tresparrett Posts 6 B1
Tressait 158 D3
Tresta *Shet.* 186 F3
Tresta *Shet.* 187 C7
Treswell 95 E5
Trethewey 2 A4
Trethomas 38 A4
Trethurgy 5 E4
Tretio 48 A5
Tretire 53 E5
Tretower 52 A5
Treuddyn 77 F2
Trevadlock 5 G2
Trevalga 6 A1
Trevalyn 78 A2
Trevanson 5 D2
Trevarnon 2 C3
Trevarrack 2 B3
Trevarren 4 D3
Trevarrian 4 C3
Trevarrick 5 D5
Tre-vaughan *Carmar.* 49 G5
Trevaughan *Carmar.* 35 E1
Treveighan 5 E2
Trevellas 4 B4
Trevelmond 5 G3
Trevenen 3 D4
Treverva 3 E3
Trevescan 2 A4
Trevethin 38 B2
Trevigro 6 D4
Trevine *Arg. & B.* 148 C2
Trevine *Pembs.* 48 B4
Treviscoe 4 D4
Trevivian 5 F1
Trevone 4 C2
Trevor 77 F3
Trewalder 5 E1
Trewarmett 5 E1
Trewarthenick 4 D5
Trewassa 5 F1
Trewellard 2 A3
Trewen *Cornw.* 5 G1
Trewen *Here.* 39 E1
Trewennack 3 D4
Trewent 34 D3
Trewern 64 B1
Trewethern 5 E2
Trewidland 5 G4
Trewilym 49 E3
Trewint *Cornw.* 6 B1
Trewint *Cornw.* 5 G1
Trewithian 3 F3
Trewoon 5 D4
Treworga 4 C5
Treworlas 3 F3
Trewornan 5 D2
Treworthal 3 F3
Tre-wyn 52 C5
Treyarnon 4 C2
Treyford 16 A2
Trezaise 5 D4
Triangle 101 G5
Trickett's Cross 13 G2
Triermain 118 B1
Trimdon 120 C4
Trimdon Colliery 120 C4
Trimdon Grange 120 C4
Trimingham 87 D2
Trimley Lower Street 61 D4
Trimley St. Martin 61 D4
Trimley St. Mary 61 D4
Trimpley 65 G5
Trimsaran 36 A2
Trimstone 21 E1
Trinafour 158 C3
Trinant 38 B3
Tring 43 E1
Trinity *Angus* 161 E3
Trinity *Chan.I.* 8 C5
Trinity *Edin.* 143 G2
Trisant 62 D5
Triscombe *Som.* 22 C4
Triscombe *Som.* 23 E4
Trislaig 156 C2
Trispen 4 C4
Tritlington 129 E2
Trochry 151 E1
Troedyraur 49 G3
Troedyrhiw 37 G2
Trofarth 89 G5
Trondavoe 186 C5
Troon *Cornw.* 3 D3
Troon *S.Ayr.* 132 B2
Trosairidh 162 C3
Troston 71 G5
Troswell 6 C1
Trottick 152 C1
Trottiscliffe 31 F2
Trotton 28 D5
Trough Gate 101 E5
Troughend 128 A2
Troustan 140 B2
Troutbeck *Cumb.* 107 F2
Troutbeck *Cumb.* 117 G4
Troutbeck Bridge 107 F2
Trow Green 39 E2
Troway 94 A5
Trowbridge *Cardiff* 38 B4
Trowbridge *Wilts.* 25 F2
Trowell 81 F4
Trowle Common 25 F2
Trowley Bottom 43 F1
Trows 136 A3
Trowse Newton 86 D5
Troy 102 B4
Trudernish 138 C4
Trudoxhill 25 E3
Trull 23 F5
Trumaisgearraidh 170 D4
Trumpan 171 H5
Trumpet 53 F4
Trumpington 58 C2
Trumps Green 29 E1
Trunch 87 D2
Trunnah 99 G3
Truro 4 C5
Truscott 6 D2
Trusham 10 B4
Trusley 81 D4
Trusthorpe 97 F4
Truthan 4 C4
Trysull 66 A3
Tubney 41 G3
Tuckenhay 9 E2
Tuckhill 65 G4
Tuckingmill 4 A5
Tuddenham *Suff.* 60 C3
Tuddenham *Suff.* 71 F5
Tudeley 31 F4
Tudeley Hale 31 F4
Tudhoe 120 B4
Tudweiliog 74 B4
Tuesley 29 E3
Tuffley 40 A1
Tufton *Hants.* 27 F3
Tufton *Pembs.* 48 D5
Tugby 68 C2
Tugford 65 E4
Tughall 137 G4
Tulchan 151 E2
Tullibody 151 D5
Tullich *Arg. & B.* 148 C3
Tullich *Arg. & B.* 148 A3
Tullich *High.* 175 F4
Tullich *High.* 166 D2
Tullich *Moray* 176 B6
Tullich *Stir.* 150 A1
Tullich Muir 174 E4
Tulliemet 159 F4
Tulloch *Aber.* 169 G1
Tulloch *High.* 174 D2
Tulloch *Moray* 175 H6
Tullochgorm 148 B5
Tullochgribban High 167 G2
Tullochvenus 168 D4
Tulloes 160 D5
Tullybannocher 150 C2
Tullybelton 151 F1
Tullyfergus 160 A5
Tullymurdoch 159 G4
Tullynessle 168 D3
Tulse Hill 44 C5
Tumble (Y Tymbl) 36 B1
Tumby 84 A2
Tumby Woodside 84 A2
Tummel Bridge 158 C4
Tunbridge Wells 31 E5
Tundergarth Mains 125 F2
Tunga 179 G4
Tungate 87 D3
Tunley 25 D2
Tunstall *E.Riding* 105 F4
Tunstall *Kent* 32 A2
Tunstall *Lancs.* 108 B5
Tunstall *N.Yorks.* 110 B3
Tunstall *Norf.* 87 F5
Tunstall *Stoke* 79 F2
Tunstall *Suff.* 61 E2
Tunstall *T. & W.* 120 C2
Tunstead *Gt.Man.* 93 E2
Tunstead *Norf.* 87 E3
Tunstead Milton 93 E4
Tunworth 28 B3
Tupholme 83 G1
Tupsley 53 E4
Tupton 81 E1
Tur Langton 68 C3
Turbiskill 139 F1
Turclossie 177 G5
Turgis Green 28 B2
Turin 160 D4
Turkdean 40 D1
Turleigh 25 F1
Turn 92 C1
Turnastone 52 C4
Turnberry 132 A5
Turnchapel 8 A2
Turnditch 81 D3
Turner's Green 55 D1
Turners Hill 30 C5
Turners Puddle 13 E3
Turnford 44 C2
Turnworth 13 E2
Turret Bridge 165 K5
Turriff 177 F6
Turton Bottoms 92 B1
Turvey 57 E2
Turville 42 C3
Turville Heath 42 C3
Turweston 56 B4
Tutbury 80 D5
Tutnall 66 B5
Tutshill 39 E3
Tuttington 86 D3
Tutts Clump 42 A5
Tutwell 7 D3
Tuxford 95 E5
Twatt *Ork.* 184 B5
Twatt *Shet.* 187 C7
Twechar 142 B2
Tweedmouth 145 G4
Tweedsmuir 134 B3
Twelve Oaks 18 B1
Twelveheads 4 B5
Twemlow Green 79 E1
Twenty 83 G5
Twickenham 44 A5
Twigworth 54 A5
Twineham 17 E1
Twineham Green 17 E1
Twinhoe 25 E2
Twinstead 59 G4
Twiss Green 92 A3
Twiston 101 E3
Twitchen *Devon* 22 A4
Twitchen *Shrop.* 64 C5
Twitton 31 E3
Twizell House 137 F4
Two Bridges *Devon* 7 G3
Two Bridges *Glos.* 39 F2
Two Dales 81 D1
Two Gates 67 E2
Two Mills 91 E5
Twycross 67 F2
Twyford *Bucks.* 56 B5
Twyford *Derbys.* 81 E5
Twyford *Dorset* 13 E1
Twyford *Hants.* 27 F5
Twyford *Leics.* 68 C1
Twyford *Norf.* 86 B3
Twyford *Oxon.* 55 G4
Twyford *W'ham* 42 C5
Twyford Common 53 E4
Twyn Shôn-Ifan 38 A3
Twynholm 124 A5
Twyning 54 A4
Twynllanan 51 D5
Twyn-yr-odyn 38 A5
Twyn-y-Sheriff 38 D2
Twywell 69 E5
Tyberton 52 C4
Tycroes 36 C1
Tycrwyn 64 A1
Tydd Gote 70 C1
Tydd St. Giles 70 C1
Tydd St. Mary 70 C1
Tyddewi (St. David's) 48 A5
Tye Common 45 F3
Tye Green *Essex* 59 F5
Tye Green *Essex* 58 D5
Tye Green *Essex* 45 F1
Tye Green *Essex* 44 D2
Tyersal 102 A4
Ty-hen 74 A4
Tyldesley 92 A2
Tyle-garw 37 G4
Tyler Hill 32 D2
Tylers Green *Bucks.* 43 E3
Tyler's Green *Essex* 45 E2
Tylorstown 37 G3
Tylwch 63 F5
Ty-Mawr *Conwy* 76 C3
Ty-mawr *Denb.* 77 E3
Ty-nant *Conwy* 76 C3
Ty-nant *Gwyn.* 76 C5
Tyndrum 149 F1
Tyneham 13 E4
Tynehead 144 A4
Tynemouth 120 C1
Tynewydd 37 F3
Tyninghame 144 D2
Tynron 124 C1
Tyntesfield 39 E5
Tyn-y-cefn 77 D3
Ty'n-y-coedcae 38 A4
Tyn-y-cwm 63 E4
Tyn-y-ffridd 77 E4
Ty'n-y-garn 37 E4
Tyn-y-Gongl 88 D4
Tynygraig *Cere.* 50 C1
Tyn-y-graig *Powys* 51 G3
Ty'n-y-groes 89 F5
Tyrie 177 H4
Tyringham 57 D3
Tyseley 66 D4
Tythegston 37 E5
Tytherington *Ches.* 92 D5
Tytherington *S.Glos.* 39 F4
Tytherington *Som.* 25 E3
Tytherington *Wilts.* 26 A3
Tytherton Lucas 40 B5
Tyttenhanger 44 A2
Ty-uchaf 76 C5
Tywardreath 5 E4
Tywardreath Highway 5 E4
Tywyn 62 B2

▼U

Uachdar 170 D6
Uags 164 D1
Ubberley 79 G3
Ubbeston Green 73 E4
Ubley 24 C2
Uckerby 110 B2
Uckfield 17 G1
Uckinghall 54 A4
Uckington 54 B5
Uddingston 142 A3
Uddington 133 G2
Udimore 19 D2
Udley 24 B1
Udny Green 169 G2
Udny Station 169 H2
Udston 142 B4
Udstonhead 142 B5
Uffcott 40 D5
Uffculme 11 D1
Uffington *Lincs.* 69 F2
Uffington *Oxon.* 41 F4
Uffington *Shrop.* 65 E1
Ufford *Peter.* 69 F2
Ufford *Suff.* 61 D2
Ufton 55 F1
Ufton Green 28 B1
Ufton Nervet 28 B1
Ugborough 8 C2
Ugford 26 B4
Uggeshall 73 F3
Ugglebarnby 112 B2
Ugley 58 D5
Ugley Green 58 D5
Ugthorpe 111 G1
Uibhist a Deas (South Uist) 162 C1
Uibhist a Tuath (North Uist) 170 D4
Uidh 162 B5
Uig *Arg. & B.* 154 A4
Uig *Arg. & B.* 140 C1
Uig *High.* 171 J5
Uig *High.* 171 G6
Uigen 178 C4
Uiginish 171 H7
Uigshader 171 K7
Uisgebhagh (Uiskevagh) 170 D6
Uisken 146 C3
Uiskevagh (Uisgebhagh) 170 D6
Ulbster 183 J4
Ulcat Row 118 A5
Ulceby *Lincs.* 97 E5
Ulceby *N.Lincs.* 96 B1
Ulceby Cross 97 E5
Ulceby Skitter 96 B1
Ulcombe 32 A4
Uldale 117 F3
Uldale House 108 C3
Uley 39 G3
Ulgham 129 E2
Ullapool 173 H2
Ullenhall 54 D1
Ullenwood 40 B1
Ulleskelf 103 E4
Ullesthorpe 68 A4
Ulley 94 B4
Ullingswick 53 E3
Ullinish 163 J1
Ullock 117 D4
Ulpha *Cumb.* 106 C3
Ulpha *Cumb.* 107 F4
Ulrome 105 D2
Ulsta 186 D4
Ulting 46 B2
Uluvalt 147 E1
Ulva 146 D1
Ulverston 107 D5
Ulwell 13 G4
Ulzieside 133 F5
Umberleigh 21 G3
Unapool 180 E5
Underbarrow 107 F3
Undercliffe 102 A4
Underhill 44 B3
Underhoull 186 E2
Underling Green 31 G4
Underriver 31 E3
Underwood *Newport* 38 C4
Underwood *Notts.* 81 F2
Underwood *Plym.* 8 B2
Undley 71 E4
Undy 38 D4
Ungisiadar 178 D5
Unifirth 187 B7
Union Croft 169 G5
Union Mills 98 B4
Union Street 31 G5
Unst 186 F1
Unstone 94 A5
Unstone Green 94 A5
Unsworth 92 C2
Unthank *Cumb.* 118 A4
Unthank *Derbys.* 94 A5
Up Cerne 12 C2
Up Exe 10 C2
Up Hatherley 54 B5
Up Holland 91 G2
Up Marden 15 G1
Up Mudford 12 B1
Up Nately 28 B2
Up Somborne 27 E4
Up Sydling 12 C2
Upavon 26 C2
Upchurch 32 A2
Upcott *Devon* 7 E1
Upcott *Devon* 21 F2
Upcott *Here.* 52 C2
Upcott *Som.* 22 C5
Upend 59 E2
Upgate 86 C4
Upgate Street *Norf.* 72 B2
Upgate Street *Norf.* 73 D2
Uphall *Dorset* 12 B2
Uphall *W.Loth.* 143 E2
Uphall Station 143 E3
Upham *Devon* 10 B2
Upham *Hants.* 27 G5
Uphampton *Here.* 52 C1
Uphampton *Worcs.* 54 A1
Uphempston 9 E1
Uphill 24 A2
Uplands *Glos.* 40 A2
Uplands *Swan.* 36 C3
Uplawmoor 141 F4
Upleadon 53 G5
Upleatham 111 F1
Uplees 32 C2
Uploders 12 B3
Uplowman 10 D1
Uplyme 11 G3
Upminster 45 E4
Upottery 11 F2
Upper Affcot 64 D4
Upper Ardroscadale 140 B3
Upper Arley 65 G4
Upper Arncott 42 B1
Upper Astley 65 E1
Upper Aston 66 A3
Upper Astrop 56 A4
Upper Barvas 179 F2
Upper Basildon 42 B5
Upper Bayble (Pabail Uarach) 179 H4
Upper Beeding 17 D2
Upper Benefield 69 E4
Upper Bentley 54 B1
Upper Berwick 65 D1
Upper Bighouse 182 D3
Upper Boat 38 A4
Upper Boddam 168 E1
Upper Boddington 55 G2
Upper Borth 62 C4
Upper Boyndlie 177 H4
Upper Brailes 55 F4
Upper Breakish 164 C2
Upper Breinton 53 D3
Upper Broadheath 54 A2
Upper Broughton 82 B5
Upper Brynamman 36 D1
Upper Bucklebury 27 G1
Upper Burgate 14 A1
Upper Burnhaugh 169 G5
Upper Caldecote 57 G3
Upper Camster 183 H4
Upper Canada 24 A2
Upper Catesby 56 A2
Upper Catshill 66 B5
Upper Chapel 51 G3
Upper Cheddon 23 F5
Upper Chicksgrove 26 A4
Upper Chute 27 D2
Upper Clatford 27 E3
Upper Coberley 40 B1
Upper Colwall 53 G3
Upper Cotton 80 B3
Upper Cound 65 E2
Upper Cumberworth 93 G2
Upper Cwmbran 38 B3
Upper Dallachy 176 B4
Upper Dean 57 F1
Upper Denby 93 G2
Upper Denton 118 C1
Upper Derraid 167 H1
Upper Diabaig 172 E5
Upper Dicker 18 A2
Upper Dovercourt 60 D4
Upper Dunsforth 102 D1
Upper Dunsley 43 E1
Upper Eastern Green 67 E4
Upper Eathie 174 E5
Upper Egleton 53 F3
Upper Elkstone 80 B2
Upper End 93 E5
Upper Enham 27 E3
Upper Farringdon 28 C4
Upper Framilode 39 G1
Upper Froyle 28 C3
Upper Gills 183 J1
Upper Glendessarry 165 F5
Upper Godney 24 B3
Upper Gornal 66 B3
Upper Gravenhurst 57 G4
Upper Green *Essex* 58 C4
Upper Green *Essex* 59 D4
Upper Green *Mon.* 38 C1
Upper Green *W.Berks.* 27 E1
Upper Grove Common 53 E5
Upper Gylen 148 A2
Upper Hackney 81 D1
Upper Halliford 29 F1
Upper Halling 31 F2
Upper Hambleton 69 E2
Upper Harbledown 32 D3
Upper Hardres Court 33 D3
Upper Hartfield 31 D5
Upper Hatton 79 F4
Upper Hawkhillock 169 J1
Upper Hayesden 31 E4
Upper Hayton 65 E4
Upper Heath 65 E4
Upper Heaton 93 F1
Upper Hellesdon 86 D4
Upper Helmsley 103 F2
Upper Hengoed 77 F4
Upper Hergest 52 B2
Upper Heyford *Northants.* 56 B2
Upper Heyford *Oxon.* 55 G5
Upper Hill *Here.* 53 D2
Upper Hill *S.Glos.* 39 F3
Upper Horsebridge 18 A2
Upper Howsell 53 G3
Upper Hulme 80 B1
Upper Inglesham 41 E3
Upper Kilchattan 146 C5
Upper Killay 36 B3
Upper Knockando 175 J7
Upper Lambourn 41 F4
Upper Langford 24 B2
Upper Langwith 81 G1
Upper Largo 152 C4
Upper Leigh 80 B4
Upper Ley 39 G1
Upper Llandwrog (Siop y Fron) 75 E2
Upper Loads 81 E1
Upper Lochton 168 E5
Upper Longdon 66 C1
Upper Longwood 65 F2
Upper Ludstone 66 A3
Upper Lybster 183 H5
Upper Lydbrook 39 F1
Upper Lyde 53 D3
Upper Lye 52 C1
Upper Maes-coed 52 C4
Upper Midhope 93 G3
Upper Milovaig 171 G7
Upper Milton 41 E1
Upper Minety 40 C3
Upper Moor 54 B3
Upper Morton 39 F3
Upper Muirskie 169 G5
Upper Nash 34 D2
Upper Newbold 94 A5
Upper North Dean 43 D3
Upper Norwood 44 C5
Upper Obney 151 F1
Upper Oddington 55 E5
Upper Ollach 164 B1
Upper Padley 93 G5
Upper Pennington 14 B3
Upper Pollicott 42 C1
Upper Poppleton 103 E2
Upper Quinton 55 D3
Upper Ratley 27 E5
Upper Ridinghill 177 J5
Upper Rissington 55 E5
Upper Rochford 53 F1
Upper Sanday 185 E7
Upper Sapey 53 F1
Upper Scolton 48 C5
Upper Seagry 40 B4
Upper Shelton 57 E3
Upper Sheringham 86 C1
Upper Shuckburgh 55 G1
Upper Siddington 40 C3
Upper Skelmorlie 140 D3
Upper Slaughter 55 D5
Upper Sonachan 148 C2
Upper Soudley 39 F1
Upper Staploe 57 G2
Upper Stoke 87 D5
Upper Stondon 57 G4
Upper Stowe 56 B2
Upper Street *Hants.* 14 A1
Upper Street *Norf.* 87 E4
Upper Street *Norf.* 72 C4
Upper Street *Suff.* 60 C4
Upper Street *Suff.* 60 C2
Upper Strensham 54 B4
Upper Sundon 57 F5
Upper Swanmore 15 E1
Upper Swell 55 D5
Upper Tean 80 B4
Upper Thurnham 100 A2
Upper Tillyrie 151 G4
Upper Tooting 44 B5
Upper Town *Derbys.* 80 D1
Upper Town *Derbys.* 81 D2
Upper Town *Derbys.* 80 D2
Upper Town *Here.* 53 E3
Upper Town *N.Som.* 24 C1
Upper Tysoe 55 F3
Upper Upham 41 E5
Upper Upnor 45 G5
Upper Victoria 152 D1
Upper Vobster 25 E3
Upper Wardington 55 G3
Upper Waterhay 40 C3
Upper Weald 56 D4
Upper Weedon 56 B2
Upper Welson 52 B2
Upper Weston 25 E1
Upper Whiston 94 B4
Upper Wick 54 A2
Upper Wield 28 B4
Upper Winchendon (Over Winchendon) 42 C1
Upper Witton 66 C3
Upper Woodford 26 C4
Upper Woolhampton 27 G1
Upper Wootton 27 G2
Upper Wraxall 40 A5
Upper Wyche 53 G3
Upperby 118 A2
Uppermill 93 D2
Upperthong 93 F2
Upperton 29 E5
Uppertown *Derbys.* 81 E1
Uppertown *Ork.* 183 J1
Uppingham 69 D2
Uppington 65 E2
Upsall 111 D4
Upsettlington 145 F5
Upshire 44 D2
Upstreet 33 E2
Upthorpe 72 A4
Upton *Bucks.* 42 C1
Upton *Cambs.* 69 G5
Upton *Ches.* 78 B1
Upton *Cornw.* 5 G2
Upton *Cornw.* 20 C5
Upton *Devon* 11 D2
Upton *Devon* 8 D3
Upton *Dorset* 13 F3
Upton *Dorset* 12 D4
Upton *E.Riding* 104 D2
Upton *Hants.* 27 E2
Upton *Hants.* 14 C1
Upton *Leics.* 67 F3
Upton *Lincs.* 95 F4
Upton *Mersey.* 91 D4
Upton *Norf.* 87 E4
Upton *Northants.* 56 C1
Upton *Notts.* 95 E5
Upton *Notts.* 82 C2
Upton *Oxon.* 42 A4
Upton *Oxon.* 41 E1
Upton *Pembs.* 34 D2
Upton *Peter.* 69 G2
Upton *Slo.* 43 E5
Upton *Som.* 22 C5
Upton *Som.* 24 B5
Upton *W.Yorks.* 94 B1
Upton *Wilts.* 25 F4
Upton Bishop 53 F5
Upton Cheyney 25 D1
Upton Cressett 65 F3
Upton Crews 53 F5
Upton Cross 5 G2
Upton End 57 G4
Upton Grey 28 B3
Upton Hellions 10 B2
Upton Lovell 26 A3
Upton Magna 65 E1
Upton Noble 25 E4
Upton Park 44 D4
Upton Pyne 10 C3
Upton St. Leonards 40 A1
Upton Scudamore 25 F3
Upton Snodsbury 54 B2
Upton upon Severn 54 A3
Upton Warren 54 B1
Upwaltham 16 B2
Upware 70 D5
Upwell 70 D2
Upwey 12 C4
Upwick Green 58 C5
Upwood 70 A4
Uradale 187 D9
Urafirth 186 C5
Urchany 175 F7
Urchfont 26 B2
Urdimarsh 53 E3
Ure 186 B5
Urgha 171 G2
Urlay Nook 110 D1
Urmston 92 B3
Urpeth 120 B2
Urquhart *High.* 174 C6
Urquhart *Moray* 175 K5
Urra 111 E2
Urray 174 C6
Ushaw Moor 120 B3
Usk 38 C2
Usselby 96 A3
Usworth 120 C2
Utley 101 G3
Uton 10 B3
Utterby 96 D3
Uttoxeter 80 B4
Uwchmynydd 74 A5

Uxbridge 43 F4
Uyeasound 186 E2
Uzmaston 34 C1

▼V

Valley (Dyffryn) 88 A5
Valley Truckle 5 F1
Valleyfield D. & G. 124 A5
Valleyfield Fife 143 E1
Valsgarth 186 F1
Vange 45 G4
Vardre 36 C2
Varteg 38 B2
Vatersay (Bhatarsaigh) W.Isles 162 B5
Vatersay (Bhatarsaigh) W.Isles 162 B5
Vatsetter 186 E4
Vatten 171 H7
Vaul 154 B2
Vaynor 37 G1
Vaynor Park 64 A2
Veaullt 52 A2
Veensgarth 187 D8
Velindre Pembs. 49 D4
Velindre Powys 52 A4
Vellow 23 D4
Veness 184 E5
Venn 8 D3
Venn Ottery 11 D3
Venngreen 21 D4
Vennington 64 C2
Venny Tedburn 10 B3
Venterdon 7 D3
Ventnor 15 E5
Venton 8 B2
Vernham Dean 27 E2
Vernham Street 27 E2
Vernolds Common 65 D4
Verwood 13 G2
Veryan 3 G3
Veryan Green 4 D5
Vickerstown 99 E1
Victoria 5 D3
Vidlin 187 D6
Viewfield 183 F2
Viewpark 142 B3
Vigo 66 C2
Vigo Village 31 F2
Villavin 21 F4
Vinehall Street 18 C1
Vine's Cross 18 A2
Viney Hill 39 F2
Virginia Water 29 E1
Virginstow 7 D1
Virley 46 C1
Vobster 25 E3
Voe Shet. 187 D6
Voe Shet. 186 C4
Vowchurch 52 C4
Voy 185 B6
Vron Gate 64 C2

▼W

Waberthwaite 106 C3
Wackerfield 120 A5
Wacton 72 C2
Wadbister 187 D8
Wadborough 54 B3
Waddesdon 42 C1
Waddeton 9 E2
Waddicar 91 E3
Waddingham 95 G3
Waddington Lancs. 100 D3
Waddington Lincs. 83 E1
Waddingworth 96 B5
Waddon Devon 10 B5
Waddon Gt.Lon. 30 C2
Wadebridge 5 D2
Wadeford 11 G1
Wadenhoe 69 F4
Wadesmill 44 C1
Wadhurst 31 F5
Wadshelf 94 A5
Wadsley Bridge 94 A3
Wadworth 94 C3
Wadworth Hill 105 E5
Waen Denb. 77 E1
Waen Denb. 76 C1
Waen Aberwheeler 77 D1
Waen-fâch 64 B1
Waen-wen 75 E1
Wag 183 F6
Wainfleet All Saints 84 C2
Wainfleet Bank 84 C2
Wainford 73 E2
Waingroves 81 F3
Wainhouse Corner 6 B1
Wainscott 45 G5
Wainstalls 101 G5
Waitby 108 C2
Wakefield 102 C5
Wakerley 69 E3
Wakes Colne 59 G5
Walberswick 73 F4
Walberton 16 B3
Walbottle 120 A1
Walcot Lincs. 83 F4
Walcot Lincs. 83 G2
Walcot N.Lincs. 104 A5
Walcot Shrop. 64 C4
Walcot Tel. & W. 65 E1
Walcot Green 72 C3
Walcote Leics. 68 A4
Walcote Warks. 54 D2
Walcott 87 E2
Walcott Dales 83 G2
Walden 109 F4
Walden Head 109 E4
Walden Stubbs 94 C1
Walderslade 31 G2
Walderton 15 G1
Walditch 12 A3
Waldley 80 C4
Waldridge 120 B3
Waldringfield 61 D3
Waldron 18 A2
Wales 94 B4
Walesby Lincs. 96 B3
Walesby Notts. 95 D5
Waleswood 94 B4
Walford Here. 64 C5
Walford Here. 53 E5
Walford Shrop. 78 B5
Walford Staffs. 79 F4
Walford Heath 64 D1
Walgherton 79 D3
Walgrave 68 D5
Walhampton 14 C3
Walk Mill 101 E4
Walkden 92 B2
Walker 120 B1
Walker Fold 100 C3
Walkerburn 135 E2
Walkeringham 95 E3
Walkerith 95 E3
Walkern 58 A5
Walker's Green 53 E3
Walkford 14 B3
Walkhampton 8 B1
Walkingham Hill 102 C1
Walkington 104 B4
Walkwood 54 C1
Wall Cornw. 2 D3
Wall Northumb. 119 F1
Wall Staffs. 66 D2
Wall End 106 D4
Wall Heath 66 A4
Wall Houses 119 G1
Wall under Heywood 65 E3
Wallacehall 126 A4
Wallacetown 132 A5
Wallasey 91 D3
Wallaston Green 34 C2
Wallend 32 A1
Waller's Green 53 F4
Wallingford 42 B4
Wallington Gt.Lon. 30 B2
Wallington Hants. 15 E2
Wallington Herts. 58 A4
Wallington Wrex. 78 B3
Wallingwells 94 C4
Wallis 48 D5
Wallisdown 13 G3
Walliswood 29 G4
Walls 187 B8
Wallsend 120 C1
Wallyford 144 A2
Walmer 33 F3
Walmer Bridge 100 A5
Walmersley 92 C1
Walmley 66 D3
Walmsgate 97 D5
Walpole 73 E4
Walpole Cross Keys 70 D1
Walpole Highway 70 D1
Walpole Marsh 70 C1
Walpole St. Andrew 70 D1
Walpole St. Peter 70 D1
Walrond's Park 24 A5
Walrow 24 A3
Walsall 66 C3
Walsall Wood 66 C2
Walsden 101 F5
Walsgrave on Sowe 67 F4
Walsham le Willows 72 B4
Walshford 102 D2
Walsoken 70 C1
Walston 143 E5
Walsworth 57 G4
Walter's Ash 42 D3
Walterston 37 G5
Walterstone 52 C5
Waltham Kent 32 D4
Waltham N.E.Lincs. 96 C2
Waltham Abbey 44 C2
Waltham Chase 15 E1
Waltham Cross 44 C2
Waltham on the Wolds 82 C5
Waltham St. Lawrence 42 D5
Walthamstow 44 C4
Walton Bucks. 42 D1
Walton Cumb. 118 B1
Walton Derbys. 81 E1
Walton Leics. 68 A4
Walton M.K. 57 D4
Walton Mersey. 91 E3
Walton Peter. 69 G2
Walton Powys 52 B2
Walton Shrop. 65 D5
Walton Som. 24 B4
Walton Staffs. 79 F4
Walton Suff. 61 E4
Walton Tel. & W. 65 E1
Walton W.Yorks. 94 A1
Walton W.Yorks. 102 D3
Walton Warks. 55 E2
Walton Cardiff 54 B4
Walton East 48 D5
Walton Elm 13 D1
Walton Highway 70 C1
Walton Lower Street 61 D4
Walton on the Hill 30 B3
Walton on the Naze 61 D5
Walton on the Wolds 68 A1
Walton Park D. & G. 124 B3
Walton Park N.Som. 38 D5
Walton West 34 B1
Walton-in-Gordano 38 D5
Walton-le-Dale 100 B5
Walton-on-Thames 29 G1
Walton-on-the-Hill 79 G5
Walton-on-Trent 67 E1
Walwen Flints. 90 C5
Walwen Flints. 90 D5
Walwick 128 B4
Walworth 110 B1
Walworth Gate 120 B5
Walwyn's Castle 34 B1
Wambrook 11 F2
Wanborough Surr. 29 E3
Wanborough Swin. 41 E4
Wandel 134 A3
Wandon 137 E4
Wandon End 57 G5
Wandsworth 44 B5
Wandylaw 137 F4
Wangford Suff. 73 F4
Wangford Suff. 71 F4
Wanlip 68 B1
Wanlockhead 133 G4
Wannock 18 A3
Wansford E.Riding 104 C2
Wansford Peter. 69 F3
Wanshurst Green 31 G4
Wanstrow 25 E3
Wanswell 39 F2
Wantage 41 F4
Wapley 39 G5
Wappenbury 55 F1
Wappenham 56 B3
Warblebank 117 F2
Warbleton 18 B2
Warblington 15 G2
Warborough 42 A3
Warboys 70 B4
Warbreck 99 G4
Warbstow 6 C1
Warburton 92 A4
Warcop 108 C1
Ward End 66 D4
Ward Green 60 B1
Warden Kent 32 C1
Warden Northumb. 119 F1
Warden Hill 54 B5
Warden Street 57 G3
Wardhouse 168 D1
Wardington 55 G3
Wardle Ches. 78 D2
Wardle Gt.Man. 92 D1
Wardley Gt.Man. 92 B2
Wardley Rut. 68 D2
Wardley T. & W. 120 C1
Wardlow 93 F5
Wardsend 92 D4
Wardy Hill 70 C4
Ware Herts. 44 C1
Ware Kent 33 E2
Wareham 13 F4
Warehorne 32 B5
Waren Mill 137 F3
Warenford 137 F4
Warenton 137 F3
Wareside 44 C1
Waresley Cambs. 58 A2
Waresley Worcs. 66 A5
Warfield 43 D5
Wargrave Mersey. 91 G3
Wargrave W'ham 42 C5
Warham Here. 53 D4
Warham Norf. 86 A1
Wark Northumb. 128 A4
Wark Northumb. 136 C3
Warkleigh 21 G3
Warkton 69 D5
Warkworth Northants. 55 G3
Warkworth Northumb. 129 E1
Warland 101 F5
Warleggan 5 F3
Warley Essex 45 E3
Warley W.Mid. 66 C4
Warley Town 101 G5
Warlingham 30 C3
Warmfield 102 C5
Warmingham 79 E1
Warminghurst 16 D2
Warmington Northants. 69 F3
Warmington Warks. 55 G3
Warminster 25 F3
Warmlake 32 A4
Warmley 39 F5
Warmley Hill 39 F5
Warmsworth 94 C2
Warmwell 13 D4
Warndon 54 A2
Warners End 43 F2
Warnford 28 B5
Warnham 29 G4
Warningcamp 16 C3
Warninglid 17 E1
Warren Ches. 92 C5
Warren Pembs. 34 C3
Warren House 7 G2
Warren Row 42 D4
Warren Street 32 B3
Warrenby 121 E5
Warren's Green 58 A5
Warrington M.K. 57 D2
Warrington Warr. 92 A4
Warroch 151 F4
Warsash 15 D2
Warslow 80 B2
Warsop Vale 81 G1
Warter 104 A2
Warthill 103 F2
Wartle 168 D4
Wartling 18 B3
Wartnaby 82 C5
Warton Lancs. 107 G5
Warton Lancs. 100 A5
Warton Northumb. 128 C1
Warton Warks. 67 E2
Warton Bank 100 A5
Warwick 55 E1
Warwick Bridge 118 A2
Warwick Wold 30 C3
Warwick-on-Eden 118 A2
Wasbister 184 C4
Wasdale Head 106 C2
Wash 93 E4
Wash Common 27 F1
Washall Green 58 C4
Washaway 5 E3
Washbourne 9 D2
Washbrook 24 B3
Washfield 10 C1
Washfold 109 F2
Washford Som. 22 D3
Washford Warks. 54 C1
Washford Pyne 10 B1
Washingborough 96 A5
Washington T. & W. 120 C2
Washington W.Suss. 16 D2
Washmere Green 60 A3
Wasing 27 G1
Waskerley 119 G3
Wasperton 55 E2
Wasps Nest 83 F1
Wass 111 E5
Watchet 23 D3
Watchfield Oxon. 41 E3
Watchfield Som. 24 A3
Watchgate 107 G3
Watcombe 9 F1
Watendlath 117 F5
Water 101 E5
Water Eaton M.K. 57 D4
Water Eaton Oxon. 42 A1
Water End Beds. 57 G3
Water End Beds. 57 F4
Water End E.Riding 103 G4
Water End Essex 59 D3
Water End Herts. 44 B2
Water End Herts. 43 F1
Water Newton 69 G3
Water Orton 67 D3
Water Stratford 56 B4
Water Yeat 107 D4
Waterbeach 58 C1
Waterbeck 126 A4
Watercombe 13 D4
Waterend 42 C3
Waterfall 80 B2
Waterfoot E.Renf. 141 G4
Waterfoot Lancs. 101 E5
Waterford 44 C1
Watergate 5 F1
Waterhead Cumb. 107 E2
Waterhead D. & G. 124 B2
Waterheath 73 F2
Waterhill of Bruxie 177 H6
Waterhouses Dur. 120 A3
Waterhouses Staffs. 80 B2
Wateringbury 31 F3
Waterlane 40 B2
Waterloo Aber. 169 J1
Waterloo Derbys. 81 F1
Waterloo Gt.Man. 92 D2
Waterloo High. 164 C2
Waterloo Mersey. 91 E3
Waterloo N.Lan. 142 C4
Waterloo Norf. 86 D4
Waterloo P. & K. 151 F1
Waterloo Pembs. 34 C2
Waterloo Poole 13 G3
Waterloo Cross 11 D1
Waterloo Port 75 D1
Waterlooville 15 F1
Watermeetings 134 A4
Watermillock 118 A5
Waterperry 42 B2
Waterrow 23 D5
Waters Upton 65 F1
Watersfield 16 C2
Watersheddings 92 D2
Waterside Aber. 168 B3
Waterside Aber. 169 J2
Waterside B'burn. 100 D5
Waterside Bucks. 43 E2
Waterside E.Ayr. 132 C5
Waterside E.Ayr. 141 F5
Waterside E.Dun. 142 A2
Waterstock 42 B2
Waterston 34 C2
Waterthorpe 94 B4
Watford Herts. 44 A3
Watford Northants. 56 B1
Watford Park 38 A4
Wath N.Yorks. 110 C5
Wath N.Yorks. 102 A1
Wath Brow 116 D5
Wath upon Dearne 94 B2
Watley's End 39 F4
Watlington Norf. 71 E1
Watlington Oxon. 42 B3
Watnall 81 G3
Watten 183 H3
Wattisfield 72 B4
Wattisham 60 B2
Watton Dorset 12 A3
Watton E.Riding 104 C3
Watton Norf. 86 A5
Watton at Stone 44 C1
Watton Green 86 A5
Watton's Green 45 E3
Wattston 142 B3
Wattstown 37 G3
Wattsville 38 B3
Waughtonhill 177 H5
Waun Fawr 62 C4
Waun y Clyn 36 A2
Waunarlwydd 36 C3
Waunclunda 50 C4
Waunfawr 75 E2
Waun-Lwyd 38 A2
Wavendon 57 E4
Waverbridge 117 F2
Waverton Ches. 78 B1
Waverton Cumb. 117 F2
Wavertree 91 E4
Wawne 104 C4
Waxham 87 F3
Waxholme 105 F5
Way Gill 101 F1
Way Village 10 B1
Way Wick 24 A1
Wayford 12 A2
Waytown 12 A3
Wdig (Goodwick) 48 C4
Weachyburn 176 E5
Weacombe 23 E3
Weald 41 F2
Wealdstone 44 A3
Weardley 102 B3
Weare 24 B2
Weare Giffard 21 E3
Wearhead 119 E4
Wearne 24 B5
Weasenham All Saints 85 G5
Weasenham St. Peter 85 G5
Weathercote 108 C5
Weatheroak Hill 66 C5
Weaverham 92 A5
Weaverthorpe 112 C5
Webheath 54 C1
Webton 52 D4
Wedderlairs 169 G1
Weddington 67 F3
Wedhampton 26 B2
Wedmore 24 B3
Wednesbury 66 B3
Wednesfield 66 B3
Weedon 42 D1
Weedon Bec 56 B2
Weedon Lois 56 B3
Weeford 66 D2
Week Devon 10 A1
Week Devon 9 D1
Week Som. 22 C4
Week Orchard 20 C5
Week St. Mary 6 C1
Weeke 27 F4
Weekley 69 D4
Weel 104 C4
Weeley 60 C5
Weeley Heath 60 C5
Weem 158 D4
Weeping Cross 79 G5
Weethley 54 C2
Weeting 71 F4
Weeton E.Riding 105 F5
Weeton Lancs. 99 G4
Weeton N.Yorks. 102 B3
Weetwood 102 B4
Weir Essex 46 B4
Weir Lancs. 101 E5
Weir Quay 8 A1
Weirbrook 78 A5
Weisdale 187 C7
Welbeck Abbey 94 C5
Welborne 86 B5
Welbourn 83 E2
Welburn N.Yorks. 103 G1
Welburn N.Yorks. 111 F4
Welbury 110 C2
Welby 83 E4
Welches Dam 70 C4
Welcombe 20 C4
Weldon 69 E4
Welford Northants. 68 B4
Welford W.Berks. 41 G5
Welford-on-Avon 54 D2
Welham Leics. 68 C3
Welham Notts. 95 E4
Welham Green 44 B2
Well Hants. 28 C3
Well Lincs. 97 E5
Well N.Yorks. 110 B4
Well End Bucks. 43 D4
Well End Herts. 44 B3
Well Hill 31 D2
Well Street 31 F3
Well Town 10 C2
Welland 53 G3
Wellbank 152 C1
Wellesbourne 55 E2
Wellhill 175 G5
Wellhouse W.Berks. 42 A5
Wellhouse W.Yorks. 93 E1
Welling 45 D5
Wellingborough 57 D1
Wellingham 85 G5
Wellingore 83 E2
Wellington Cumb. 106 B2
Wellington Here. 53 D3
Wellington Som. 23 E5
Wellington Tel. & W. 65 F1
Wellington Heath 53 G3
Wellington Marsh 53 D3
Wellow B. & N.E.Som. 25 E2
Wellow I.o.W. 14 C4
Wellow Notts. 82 B1
Wells 24 C3
Wells Green 66 D4
Wellsborough 67 F2
Wells-next-the-Sea 86 A1
Wellstyle Green 45 F1
Wellwood 143 E1
Welney 70 D3
Welsh Bicknor 39 E1
Welsh End 78 C4
Welsh Frankton 78 A4
Welsh Hook 48 C5
Welsh Newton 39 D1
Welsh St. Donats 37 G5
Welshampton 78 B4
Welshpool (Y Trallwng) 64 B2
Welton B. & N.E.Som. 25 D2
Welton Cumb. 117 G2
Welton E.Riding 104 B5
Welton Lincs. 96 A4
Welton Northants. 56 A1
Welton le Marsh 84 C1
Welton le Wold 96 C4
Welwick 105 F5
Welwyn 44 B1
Welwyn Garden City 44 B1
Wem 78 C5
Wembdon 23 F4
Wembley 44 A4
Wembley Park 44 A4
Wembury 8 B3
Wembworthy 21 G4
Wemyss Bay 140 C3
Wenallt Cere. 62 C5
Wenallt Gwyn. 76 C3
Wendens Ambo 58 D4
Wendlebury 42 A1
Wendling 86 A4
Wendover 43 D2
Wendover Dean 43 D2
Wendron 3 D3
Wendy 58 B3
Wenfordbridge 5 E2
Wenhaston 73 F4
Wenlli 76 B1
Wennington Cambs. 70 A5
Wennington Gt.Lon. 45 E4
Wennington Lancs. 108 B5
Wensley Derbys. 81 D1
Wensley N.Yorks. 109 F4
Wentbridge 94 B1
Wentnor 64 C3
Wentworth Cambs. 70 C5
Wentworth S.Yorks. 94 A3
Wenvoe 38 A5
Weobley 52 C2
Weobley Marsh 52 D2
Weoley Castle 66 C4
Wepham 16 C3
Wepre 77 F1
Wereham 71 E2
Wergs 66 A2
Wern Gwyn. 75 E4
Wern Powys 64 B1
Wern Powys 38 A1
Wern Shrop. 77 F4
Wernffrwd 36 B3
Wern-olau 36 B3
Wernrheolydd 38 C1
Wern-y-cwrt 38 C2
Werrington Cornw. 6 D2
Werrington Peter. 69 G2
Werrington Staffs. 79 G3
Wervil Grange 49 G2
Wervin 91 F5
Wesham 100 A4
Wessington 81 E2
West Aberthaw 22 D1
West Acre 71 F1
West Acton 44 A4
West Allerdean 145 G5
West Alvington 8 D3
West Amesbury 26 C3
West Anstey 22 B5
West Ashby 96 C5
West Ashford 21 F2
West Ashling 16 A3
West Ashton 25 F2
West Auckland 120 A5
West Ayton 112 C4
West Bagborough 23 E4
West Barkwith 96 B4
West Barnby 112 B1
West Barns 145 D2
West Barsham 86 A2
West Bay 12 A3
West Beckham 86 C2
West Benhar 142 C3
West Bergholt 60 A5
West Bexington 12 B4
West Bilney 71 F1
West Blatchington 17 E3
West Boldon 120 C1
West Bourton 25 E5
West Bowling 102 A4
West Brabourne 32 C4
West Bradford 100 D3
West Bradley 24 C4
West Bretton 93 G1
West Bridgford 81 G4
West Bromwich 66 C3
West Buckland Devon 21 G2
West Buckland Som. 23 E5
West Burrafirth 187 B7
West Burton N.Yorks. 109 F4
West Burton W.Suss. 16 B2
West Butsfield 119 G3
West Butterwick 95 F2
West Byfleet 29 F1
West Cairncake 177 G6
West Caister 87 G4
West Calder 143 E3
West Camel 24 C5
West Carbeth 141 G2
West Carr Houses 95 E2
West Cauldcoats 142 A5
West Chaldon 13 D4
West Challow 41 F4
West Charleton 9 D3
West Chevington 129 E2
West Chiltington 16 C2
West Chiltington Common 16 C2
West Chinnock 12 A1
West Chisenbury 26 C2
West Clandon 29 F2
West Cliffe 33 F4
West Clyne 175 F1
West Coker 12 B1
West Compton Dorset 12 B3
West Compton Som. 24 C3
West Cowick 103 F5
West Cross 36 C4
West Crudwell 40 B3
West Curry 6 C1
West Curthwaite 117 G2
West Dean W.Suss. 16 A2
West Dean Wilts. 27 D5
West Deeping 69 G2
West Derby 91 E3
West Dereham 71 E2
West Ditchburn 137 F4
West Down 21 F1
West Drayton Gt.Lon. 43 F5
West Drayton Notts. 95 E5
West Dullater 150 A4
West Dunnet 183 H1
West Edington 129 D3
West Ella 104 C5
West End Beds. 57 E2
West End Brack.F. 43 D5
West End Caerp. 38 B3
West End Cambs. 70 C3
West End E.Riding 104 C1
West End Hants. 15 D1
West End Herts. 44 C2
West End Kent 33 D2
West End Lancs. 100 A1
West End Lincs. 97 D3
West End N.Som. 24 B1
West End N.Yorks. 102 A2
West End Norf. 87 F4
West End Norf. 86 A5
West End Oxon. 41 G2
West End Oxon. 42 A4
West End S.Lan. 143 D5
West End Suff. 73 F3
West End Surr. 29 G1
West End Surr. 29 E1
West End Wilts. 40 B5
West End Wilts. 26 A5
West End Wilts. 26 A5
West End Green 28 B1
West Farleigh 31 G3
West Farndon 56 A2
West Felton 78 A5
West Firle 17 G3
West Fleetham 137 F4
West Flotmanby 113 D5
West Garforth 102 C4
West Ginge 41 G4
West Glen 140 A2
West Grafton 26 D1
West Green Gt.Lon. 44 C4
West Green Hants. 28 C2
West Grimstead 26 D5
West Grinstead 29 G5
West Haddlesey 103 E5
West Haddon 68 B5
West Hagbourne 42 A4
West Hagley 66 B4
West Hall 118 B1
West Hallam 81 F3
West Halton 104 B5
West Ham 44 C4
West Handley 94 A5
West Hanney 41 G3
West Hanningfield 45 G3
West Hardwick 94 B1
West Harnham 26 C5
West Harptree 24 C2
West Harrow 44 A4
West Harting 28 C5
West Hatch Som. 23 F5
West Hatch Wilts. 26 A5
West Head 71 D2
West Heath Ches. 79 F1
West Heath Gt.Lon. 45 D5
West Heath Hants. 29 D2
West Heath Hants. 27 G2
West Heath W.Mid. 66 C5
West Helmsdale 183 F7
West Hendon 44 B4
West Hendred 41 G4
West Heslerton 112 C5
West Hewish 24 A1
West Hill Devon 11 D3
West Hill E.Riding 105 D1
West Hill N.Som. 39 D5
West Hoathly 30 C5
West Holme 13 E4
West Horndon 45 F4
West Horrington 24 C3
West Horsley 29 F2
West Horton 137 E3
West Hougham 33 E5
West Howe 13 G3
West Howetown 22 C4
West Huntspill 24 A3
West Hyde 43 F3
West Hythe 32 D5
West Ilsley 41 G4
West Itchenor 15 G2
West Keal 84 B1
West Kennett 26 C1
West Kilbride 140 D5
West Kingsdown 31 E2
West Kington 40 A5
West Kington Wick 40 A5
West Kirby 90 D4
West Knapton 112 B5
West Knighton 12 D4
West Knoyle 25 F4
West Kyloe 137 E2
West Lambrook 12 A1
West Langdon 33 F4
West Langwell 174 D1
West Lavington W.Suss. 29 D5
West Lavington Wilts. 26 B2
West Layton 110 A2
West Leake 81 G5
West Learmouth 136 C3
West Lees 111 D2
West Leigh Devon 21 G5
West Leigh Devon 9 D2
West Leigh Som. 23 E4
West Leith 43 E1
West Lexham 71 G1
West Lilling 103 F1
West Lingo 152 C4
West Linton 143 F4
West Liss 28 C5
West Littleton 39 G5
West Lockinge 41 G4
West Looe 5 G4
West Lulworth 13 E4
West Lutton 104 B1
West Lydford 24 C4
West Lyn 22 A3
West Lyng 24 A5
West Lynn 71 E1
West Mains 137 E2
West Malling 31 F3
West Malvern 53 G3
West Marden 15 G1
West Markham 95 E5
West Marsh 96 C2
West Marton 101 E2
West Melbury 25 F5
West Melton 94 B2
West Meon 28 B5
West Meon Hut 28 B5
West Mersea 46 D1
West Milton 12 A3
West Minster 32 B1
West Molesey 29 G1
West Monkton 23 F5
West Moors 13 G2
West Morden 13 F3
West Morriston 144 D5
West Morton 101 G3
West Mostard 108 C3
West Mudford 24 C5
West Muir 161 D3
West Ness 111 F5
West Newbiggin 110 C1
West Newton E.Riding 105 D4
West Newton Norf. 85 E5
West Norwood 44 C5
West Ogwell 9 E1
West Orchard 13 E1
West Overton 26 C1
West Panson 6 D1
West Park Aber. 169 F5
West Park Mersey. 91 G3
West Parley 13 G3
West Peckham 31 F3
West Pelton 120 B2
West Pennard 24 C4
West Pentire 4 B3
West Perry 57 G1
West Porlock 22 B3
West Prawle 9 D4
West Preston 16 C3
West Pulham 12 D2
West Putford 21 D4
West Quantoxhead 23 E3
West Raddon 10 B2
West Rainton 120 C3
West Rasen 96 A4
West Raynham 85 G5
West Retford 95 D4
West Rounton 110 D2
West Row 71 E5
West Rudham 85 G5
West Runton 86 C1
West Saltoun 144 B3
West Sandford 10 B2
West Sandwick 186 D4
West Scrafton 109 F4
West Shepton 24 D3
West Shinness Lodge 181 H7
West Somerton 87 F4
West Stafford 12 D4
West Stockwith 95 E3
West Stoke 16 A3
West Stonesdale 109 D2
West Stoughton 24 B3
West Stour 25 E5
West Stourmouth 33 E2
West Stow 71 G5
West Stowell 26 C1
West Stratton 27 G3
West Street Kent 32 B3
West Street Med. 45 G5
West Street Suff. 72 A4
West Tanfield 110 B5
West Taphouse 5 F3
West Tarbert 139 G3
West Tarring 16 D3
West Thirston 129 D1
West Thorney 15 G2
West Thurrock 45 E5
West Tilbury 45 F5

West Tisted 28 B5
West Tofts *Norf.* 71 G3
West Tofts *P. & K.* 151 G1
West Torrington 96 B4
West Town *B. & N.E.Som.* 24 C1
West Town *Hants.* 15 G3
West Town *N.Som.* 24 B1
West Town *Som.* 24 C4
West Tytherley 27 D5
West Walton 70 C1
West Wellow 14 B1
West Wembury 8 B3
West Wemyss 152 B5
West Wick 24 A1
West Wickham *Cambs.* 59 E3
West Wickham *Gt.Lon.* 30 C2
West Williamston 34 D2
West Winch 71 E1
West Winterslow 26 D4
West Wittering 15 G3
West Witton 109 F4
West Woodburn 128 A3
West Woodhay 27 E1
West Woodlands 25 E3
West Worldham 28 C4
West Worlington 10 A1
West Worthing 16 D3
West Wratting 59 E2
West Wycombe 42 D3
West Yatton 40 A5
West Yell 186 D4
West Youlstone 20 C4
Westbere 33 D2
Westborough 82 D3
Westbourne *Bourne.* 13 G3
Westbourne *W.Suss.* 15 G2
Westbourne Green 44 B4
Westbrook *Kent* 33 F1
Westbrook *W.Berks.* 41 G5
Westbrook *Wilts.* 26 A1
Westbury *Bucks.* 56 B4
Westbury *Shrop.* 64 C2
Westbury *Wilts.* 25 F2
Westbury Leigh 25 F2
Westbury on Trym 39 E5
Westbury-on-Severn 39 G1
Westbury-sub-Mendip 24 C3
Westby *Lancs.* 99 G4
Westby *Lincs.* 83 E5
Westcliff-on-Sea 46 B4
Westcombe 25 D4
Westcot 41 F4
Westcott *Bucks.* 42 C1
Westcott *Devon* 10 D2
Westcott *Surr.* 29 G3
Westcott Barton 55 G5
Westcourt 26 D1
Westdean 18 A4
Westdowns 5 E1
Westend Town 39 G5
Wester Aberchalder 166 C2
Wester Badentyre 177 F5
Wester Balgedie 151 G4
Wester Culbeuchly 176 E4
Wester Dechmont 143 E2
Wester Fintray 169 G3
Wester Foffarty 160 C5
Wester Greenskares 177 F4
Wester Gruinards 174 C2
Wester Hailes 143 G3
Wester Lealty 174 D4
Wester Lonvine 174 E4
Wester Newburn 152 C4
Wester Ord 169 G4
Wester Quarff 187 D9
Wester Skeld 187 B8
Westerdale *High.* 183 G3
Westerdale *N.Yorks.* 111 F2
Westerfield *Shet.* 187 C7
Westerfield *Suff.* 60 C3
Westergate 16 B3
Westerham 30 D3
Westerhope 120 A1
Westerleigh 39 F5
Westerloch 183 J3
Westerton *Aber.* 169 F5
Westerton *Angus* 161 E4
Westerton *Dur.* 120 B4
Westerton *P. & K.* 151 D3
Westerwick 187 B8
Westfield *Cumb.* 116 C4
Westfield *E.Suss.* 18 D2
Westfield *High.* 183 F2
Westfield *N.Lan.* 142 B2
Westfield *Norf.* 86 A5
Westfield *R. & C.* 121 E5
Westfield *W.Loth.* 142 D2
Westfield *W.Yorks.* 102 B5
Westfield Sole 31 G2
Westgate *Dur.* 119 F4
Westgate *N.Lincs.* 95 E2
Westgate *Norf.* 86 A1
Westgate *Northumb.* 128 D4
Westgate Hill 102 B5
Westgate on Sea 33 F1
Westhall *Aber.* 168 E2
Westhall *Suff.* 73 F3
Westham *Dorset* 12 C5
Westham *E.Suss.* 18 B3
Westham *Som.* 24 B3
Westhampnett 16 A3
Westhay *Devon* 11 G2
Westhay *Som.* 24 B3
Westhead 91 F2
Westhide 53 E3
Westhill *Aber.* 169 G4
Westhill *High.* 174 E7
Westhope *Here.* 53 D2
Westhope *Shrop.* 65 D4
Westhorp 56 A2
Westhorpe *Lincs.* 84 A4
Westhorpe *Notts.* 82 B2
Westhorpe *Suff.* 60 B1
Westhoughton 92 A2
Westhouse 108 B5
Westhouses 81 F2
Westhumble 29 G2
Westing 186 E2
Westlake 8 C2
Westlands 79 F3
Westlea 40 D4
Westleigh *Devon* 21 E3
Westleigh *Devon* 11 D1
Westleigh *Gt.Man.* 92 A2
Westleton 61 F1
Westley *Shrop.* 64 C2
Westley *Suff.* 59 G1
Westley Heights 45 F4
Westley Waterless 59 E2
Westlington 42 C1
Westlinton 126 B5
Westloch 143 G4
Westmancote 54 B4
Westmarsh 33 E2
Westmeston 17 F2
Westmill 58 B5
Westminster 44 B5
Westmuir 160 B4
Westness 184 C5
Westnewton *Cumb.* 117 E2
Westnewton *Northumb.* 136 D3
Westoe 120 C1
Weston *B. & N.E.Som.* 25 E1
Weston *Ches.* 79 E2
Weston *Devon* 11 E4
Weston *Devon* 11 E2
Weston *Dorset* 12 C5
Weston *Halton* 91 G4
Weston *Hants.* 28 C5
Weston *Here.* 52 C2
Weston *Herts.* 58 A4
Weston *Lincs.* 84 A5
Weston *Moray* 176 C4
Weston *N.Yorks.* 102 A3
Weston *Northants.* 56 A3
Weston *Notts.* 82 C1
Weston *S'ham.* 15 D1
Weston *Shrop.* 78 C5
Weston *Shrop.* 65 E3
Weston *Shrop.* 64 C5
Weston *Staffs.* 79 G5
Weston *W.Berks.* 41 G5
Weston Bampfylde 24 D5
Weston Beggard 53 E3
Weston by Welland 68 C3
Weston Colville 59 E2
Weston Corbett 28 B3
Weston Coyney 79 G3
Weston Favell 56 C1
Weston Green *Cambs.* 59 E2
Weston Green *Norf.* 86 C4
Weston Heath 65 G1
Weston Hills 84 A5
Weston in Arden 67 F4
Weston Jones 79 E5
Weston Longville 86 C4
Weston Lullingfields 78 B5
Weston Patrick 28 B3
Weston Point 91 F4
Weston Rhyn 77 F4
Weston Subedge 54 D3
Weston Town 25 E3
Weston Turville 43 D1
Weston under Penyard 53 F5
Weston under Wetherley 55 F1
Weston Underwood *Derbys.* 81 D3
Weston Underwood *M.K.* 57 D2
Westonbirt 40 A4
Westoning 57 F4
Weston-in-Gordano 39 D5
Weston-on-Avon 55 D2
Weston-on-the-Green 42 A1
Weston-on-Trent 81 F5
Weston-super-Mare 24 A1
Weston-under-Lizard 66 A1
Westonzoyland 24 A4
Westow 103 G1
Westport *Arg. & B.* 130 B3
Westport *Som.* 24 A5
Westra 38 A5
Westray 184 D3
Westridge Green 42 A5
Westrigg 142 D3
Westruther 144 D5
Westry 70 B3
Westside 169 G5
Westvale 91 F3
Westville 81 G3
Westward 117 F2
Westward Ho! 21 E3
Westwell *Kent* 32 B4
Westwell *Oxon.* 41 E2
Westwell Leacon 32 B4
Westwick *Cambs.* 58 C1
Westwick *Dur.* 109 F1
Westwick *N.Yorks.* 102 C1
Westwick *Norf.* 87 D3
Westwood *Devon* 10 D3
Westwood *Peter.* 69 G3
Westwood *S.Lan.* 142 A4
Westwood *Wilts.* 25 F2
Westwood Heath 67 E5
Westwoodside 95 E3
Wetham Green 32 A2
Wetheral 118 A2
Wetherby 102 D3
Wetherden 60 B1
Wetherden Upper Town 60 B1
Wetheringsett 60 C1
Wethersfield 59 F4
Wethersta 187 C6
Wetherup Street 60 C1
Wetley Abbey 79 G3
Wetley Rocks 79 G3
Wettenhall 78 D1
Wettenhall Green 78 D1
Wetton 80 C2
Wetwang 104 B2
Wetwood 79 E4
Wexcombe 27 D2
Wexham Street 43 E4
Weybourne *Norf.* 86 C1
Weybourne *Surr.* 29 D3
Weybread 73 D3
Weybread Street 73 D4
Weybridge 29 F1
Weycroft 11 G2
Weydale 183 G2
Weyhill 27 E3
Weymouth 12 C5
Whaddon *Bucks.* 56 D4
Whaddon *Cambs.* 58 B3
Whaddon *Glos.* 40 A1
Whaddon *Glos.* 54 B5
Whaddon *Wilts.* 26 C5
Whaddon *Wilts.* 25 F1
Whaddon Gap 58 B3
Whale 118 B5
Whaley 94 C5
Whaley Bridge 93 E4
Whaley Thorns 94 C5
Whaligoe 183 J4
Whalley 100 D4
Whalsay 187 E6
Whalton 128 D3
Wham 101 D1
Whaplode 84 B5
Whaplode Drove 70 B1
Whaplode St. Catherine 70 B1
Wharfe 101 D1
Wharles 100 A4
Wharley End 57 E3
Wharncliffe Side 93 G3
Wharram le Street 104 A1
Wharram Percy 104 A1
Wharton *Ches.* 79 D1
Wharton *Here.* 53 E2
Whashton 110 A2
Whatcote 55 F3
Whateley 67 E3
Whatfield 60 B3
Whatley 25 E3
Whatlington 18 C2
Whatsole Street 32 D4
Whatstandwell 81 E2
Whatton 82 C4
Whauphill 115 E2
Whaw 109 E2
Wheatacre 73 F2
Wheatcroft 81 E2
Wheatenhurst 39 G2
Wheatfield 42 B3
Wheathampstead 44 A1
Wheathill *Shrop.* 65 F4
Wheathill *Som.* 24 C4
Wheatley *Hants.* 28 C4
Wheatley *Oxon.* 42 B2
Wheatley *W.Yorks.* 101 G5
Wheatley Hill 120 C4
Wheatley Lane 101 E4
Wheatley Park 94 C2
Wheaton Aston 66 A1
Wheddon Cross 22 C4
Wheedlemont 168 C2
Wheelerstreet 29 E3
Wheelock 79 E2
Wheelock Heath 79 E2
Wheelton 100 C5
Wheen 160 B2
Wheldale 103 D5
Wheldrake 103 F3
Whelford 41 D3
Whelley 91 G2
Whelpley Hill 43 E2
Whelpo 117 G3
Whelston 90 D5
Whenby 103 F1
Whepstead 59 G2
Wherstead 60 C3
Wherwell 27 E3
Wheston 93 F5
Whetley Cross 12 A2
Whetsted 31 F4
Whetstone *Gt.Lon.* 44 B3
Whetstone *Leics.* 68 A3
Whicham 106 C4
Whichford 55 F4
Whickham 120 B1
Whiddon 21 E5
Whiddon Down 7 G1
Whifflet 142 B3
Whigstreet 160 C5
Whilton 56 B1
Whim 143 G4
Whimble 20 D5
Whimple 10 D3
Whimpwell Green 87 E3
Whin Lane End 99 G3
Whinburgh 86 B5
Whinny Hill 110 C1
Whinnyfold 169 J1
Whippingham 15 E3
Whipsnade 43 F1
Whipton 10 C3
Whirlow 94 A4
Whisby 83 E1
Whissendine 68 D1
Whissonsett 86 A3
Whisterfield 92 C5
Whistley Green 42 C5
Whiston *Mersey.* 91 F3
Whiston *Northants.* 57 D1
Whiston *S.Yorks.* 94 B3
Whiston *Staffs.* 80 B3
Whiston *Staffs.* 66 A1
Whiston Cross 65 G2
Whiston Eaves 80 B3
Whitacre Fields 67 E3
Whitacre Heath 67 E3
Whitbeck 106 C4
Whitbourne 53 G2
Whitburn *T. & W.* 120 D1
Whitburn *W.Loth.* 142 D3
Whitby *Ches.* 91 E5
Whitby *N.Yorks.* 112 B1
Whitbyheath 91 E5
Whitchurch *B. & N.E.Som.* 24 D1
Whitchurch *Bucks.* 56 D5
Whitchurch *Cardiff* 38 A4
Whitchurch *Devon* 7 E3
Whitchurch *Hants.* 27 F3
Whitchurch *Here.* 39 E1
Whitchurch *Pembs.* 48 A5
Whitchurch *Shrop.* 78 C3
Whitchurch *Warks.* 55 E3
Whitchurch Canonicorum 11 G3
Whitchurch Hill 42 B5
Whitchurch-on-Thames 42 B5
Whitcombe 12 D4
Whitcott Keysett 64 B4
White Ball 11 D1
White Colne 59 G5
White Coppice 92 A1
White Cross *Cornw.* 4 C4
White Cross *Devon* 10 D3
White Cross *Here.* 53 D3
White Cross *Wilts.* 25 E4
White End 54 A5
White Hill 25 F4
White Houses 95 E5
White Kirkley 119 G4
White Lackington 12 D3
White Ladies Aston 54 B2
White Lund 100 A1
White Mill 50 A5
White Moor 81 E3
White Notley 45 G1
White Ox Mead 25 E2
White Pit 97 D5
White Rocks 52 D5
White Roding 45 E1
White Waltham 42 D5
Whiteacen 175 K7
Whiteash Green 59 F4
Whitebirk 100 D5
Whitebog 177 H5
Whitebridge *High.* 183 H1
Whitebridge *High.* 166 B3
Whitebrook 39 E2
Whiteburn 144 C5
Whitecairn 122 D5
Whitecairns 169 H3
Whitecastle 143 E5
Whitechapel 100 B3
Whitechurch 49 E4
Whitecote 102 B4
Whitecraig 144 A2
Whitecroft 39 F2
Whitecrook 122 C5
Whitecross *Cornw.* 2 C3
Whitecross *Cornw.* 5 D2
Whitecross *Dorset* 12 A3
Whitecross *Falk.* 143 D2
Whiteface 174 E3
Whitefield *Aber.* 169 F2
Whitefield *Devon* 22 A4
Whitefield *Dorset* 13 F3
Whitefield *Gt.Man.* 92 C2
Whitefield *High.* 166 C2
Whitefield *High.* 183 H3
Whitefield *P. & K.* 151 G1
Whiteford 169 F2
Whitegate 78 D1
Whitehall *Devon* 11 E1
Whitehall *Hants.* 28 C2
Whitehall *Ork.* 184 F5
Whitehall *W.Suss.* 29 G5
Whitehaven 116 C5
Whitehill *Aber.* 177 H5
Whitehill *Hants.* 28 C4
Whitehill *Kent* 32 B3
Whitehill *Midloth.* 144 A3
Whitehill *N.Ayr.* 141 D4
Whitehills 176 E4
Whitehouse *Aber.* 168 E3
Whitehouse *Arg. & B.* 139 G3
Whitehouse Common 66 D3
Whitekirk 144 C1
Whitelackington 11 G1
Whitelaw 145 F4
Whiteleen 183 J4
Whitelees 132 B2
Whiteley 15 E2
Whiteley Bank 15 E4
Whiteley Green 92 D5
Whiteley Village 29 F1
Whiteleys 122 B5
Whitemans Green 17 F1
Whitemire 175 G6
Whitemoor 5 D4
Whiteness 187 C8
Whiteoak Green 41 F1
Whiteparish 26 D5
Whiterashes 169 G2
Whiterow 183 J4
Whiteshill 40 A2
Whiteside *Northumb.* 118 D1
Whiteside *W.Loth.* 143 D3
Whitesmith 18 A2
Whitestaunton 11 F1
Whitestone *Aber.* 168 E5
Whitestone *Arg. & B.* 130 C2
Whitestone *Devon* 10 B3
Whitestreet Green 60 A4
Whitestripe 177 H5
Whiteway 40 B1
Whitewell *Aber.* 177 H4
Whitewell *Lancs.* 100 C3
Whitewell *Wrex.* 78 B3
Whiteworks 7 G3
Whitewreath 175 K6
Whitfield *Here.* 52 D4
Whitfield *Kent* 33 F4
Whitfield *Northants.* 56 B4
Whitfield *Northumb.* 119 D2
Whitfield *S.Glos.* 39 F3
Whitford *Devon* 11 F3
Whitford (Chwitffordd) *Flints.* 90 C5
Whitgift 104 A5
Whitgreave 79 F5
Whithorn 115 E2
Whiting Bay 131 F3
Whitkirk 102 C4
Whitland 35 F1
Whitland Abbey 35 F1
Whitleigh 8 A1
Whitletts 132 B3
Whitley *N.Yorks.* 103 E5
Whitley *Read.* 28 C1
Whitley *W.Mid.* 67 F5
Whitley *Wilts.* 25 F1
Whitley Bay 129 F4
Whitley Chapel 119 F2
Whitley Heath 79 F5
Whitley Lower 93 G1
Whitley Row 31 D3
Whitlock's End 66 D5
Whitminster 39 G2
Whitmore *Dorset* 13 G2
Whitmore *Staffs.* 79 F3
Whitnage 10 D1
Whitnash 55 F1
Whitnell 23 F3
Whitney-on-Wye 52 B3
Whitrigg *Cumb.* 117 F1
Whitrigg *Cumb.* 117 F3
Whitsbury 14 A1
Whitsome 145 F4
Whitson 38 C4
Whitstable 32 D2
Whitstone 6 C1
Whittingham 137 E5
Whittingslow 64 D4
Whittington *Derbys.* 94 A5
Whittington *Glos.* 54 C5
Whittington *Lancs.* 108 B5
Whittington *Norf.* 71 F3
Whittington *Shrop.* 78 A4
Whittington *Staffs.* 67 D2
Whittington *Staffs.* 66 A4
Whittington *Worcs.* 54 A2
Whittlebury 56 B3
Whittle-le-Woods 100 B5
Whittlesey 70 A3
Whittlesford 58 C3
Whittlestone Head 92 B1
Whitton *Gt.Lon.* 44 A5
Whitton *N.Lincs.* 104 B5
Whitton *Northumb.* 128 C1
Whitton *Powys* 52 B1
Whitton *Shrop.* 65 E5
Whitton *Stock.* 120 C5
Whitton *Suff.* 60 C3
Whittonditch 41 E5
Whittonstall 119 G2
Whitway 27 F2
Whitwell *Derbys.* 94 C5
Whitwell *Herts.* 57 G5
Whitwell *I.o.W.* 15 E5
Whitwell *N.Yorks.* 110 B3
Whitwell *Rut.* 69 E2
Whitwell Street 86 C3
Whitwell-on-the-Hill 103 G1
Whitwick 67 G1
Whitwood 102 D5
Whitworth 92 C1
Whixall 78 C4
Whixley 102 D2
Whorlton *Dur.* 110 A1
Whorlton *N.Yorks.* 111 D2
Whygate 127 F4
Whyle 53 E1
Whyteleafe 30 C3
Wibdon 39 E3
Wibsey 102 A4
Wibtoft 67 G4
Wichenford 53 G1
Wichling 32 B3
Wick *Bourne.* 14 A3
Wick *Devon* 11 E2
Wick *High.* 183 J3
Wick *S.Glos.* 39 G5
Wick *Som.* 23 F3
Wick *Som.* 24 C4
Wick *V. of Glam.* 37 F5
Wick *W.Suss.* 16 C3
Wick *Wilts.* 26 C5
Wick *Worcs.* 54 B3
Wick Airport 183 J3
Wick Hill *Kent* 32 A4
Wick Hill *W'ham* 28 C1
Wick St. Lawrence 24 A1
Wicken *Cambs.* 71 D5
Wicken *Northants.* 56 C4
Wicken Bonhunt 58 C4
Wickenby 96 A4
Wicker Street Green 60 A3
Wickerslack 108 B1
Wickersley 94 B3
Wicketwood Hill 82 B3
Wickford 45 G3
Wickham *Hants.* 15 E1
Wickham *W.Berks.* 41 F5
Wickham Bishops 46 B1
Wickham Heath 27 F1
Wickham Market 61 E2
Wickham St. Paul 59 G4
Wickham Skeith 60 B1
Wickham Street *Suff.* 59 F2
Wickham Street *Suff.* 60 B1
Wickhambreaux 33 E3
Wickhambrook 59 F2
Wickhamford 54 C3
Wickhampton 87 F5
Wicklewood 86 B5
Wickmere 86 C2
Wickstreet 18 A3
Wickwar 39 G4
Widcombe 25 E1
Widdington 58 D4
Widdop 101 F4
Widdrington 129 E2
Widdrington Station 129 E2
Wide Open 129 E4
Widecombe in the Moor 10 A5
Widegates 5 G4
Widemouth Bay 20 C5
Widewall 185 D8
Widford *Essex* 45 F2
Widford *Herts.* 44 D1
Widford *Oxon.* 41 E1
Widgham Green 59 E2
Widmer End 43 D3
Widmerpool 82 B5
Widnes 91 G4
Widworthy 11 F3
Wigan 91 G2
Wiganthorpe 111 F5
Wigborough 12 A1
Wiggaton 11 E3
Wiggenhall St. Germans 71 D1
Wiggenhall St. Mary Magdalen 71 D1
Wiggenhall St. Mary the Virgin 71 D1
Wiggenhall St. Peter 71 E1
Wiggens Green 59 E3
Wigginton *Herts.* 43 E1
Wigginton *Oxon.* 55 F4
Wigginton *Shrop.* 78 A4
Wigginton *Staffs.* 67 E2
Wigginton *York* 103 F2
Wigglesworth 101 E2
Wiggonby 117 G1
Wiggonholt 16 C2
Wighill 103 D3
Wighton 86 A2
Wightwizzle 93 G3
Wigley 14 C1
Wigmore *Here.* 52 D1
Wigmore *Med.* 32 A2
Wigsley 95 F5
Wigsthorpe 69 F4
Wigston 68 B3
Wigston Parva 67 G4
Wigthorpe 94 C4
Wigtoft 84 A4
Wigton 117 F2
Wigtown 123 F5
Wike 102 C3
Wilbarston 68 D4
Wilberfoss 103 G2
Wilburton 70 C5
Wilby *Norf.* 72 B2
Wilby *Northants.* 57 D1
Wilby *Suff.* 72 D4
Wilcot 26 C1
Wilcott 64 C1
Wilcrick 38 D4
Wilday Green 94 A5
Wildboarclough 79 G1
Wilde Street 71 F5
Wilden *Beds.* 57 F2
Wilden *Worcs.* 66 A5
Wildhern 27 E2
Wildhill 44 B2
Wildmoor 66 B5
Wildsworth 95 F3
Wilford 81 G4
Wilkesley 78 D3
Wilkhaven 175 G3
Wilkieston 143 F3
Wilksby 84 A1
Willand *Devon* 10 D1
Willand *Som.* 11 E1
Willaston *Ches.* 91 E5
Willaston *Ches.* 79 D2
Willaston *Shrop.* 78 C4
Willen 57 D3
Willenhall *W.Mid.* 66 B3
Willenhall *W.Mid.* 67 F5
Willerby *E.Riding* 104 C4
Willerby *N.Yorks.* 112 D5
Willersey 54 D4
Willersley 52 C3
Willesborough 32 C4
Willesborough Lees 32 C4
Willesden 44 B4
Willesleigh 21 F2
Willesley 40 A4
Willett 23 E4
Willey *Shrop.* 65 F3
Willey *Warks.* 67 G4
Willey Green 29 E2
William's Green 60 A3
Williamscot 55 G3
Williamthorpe 81 F1
Willian 58 A4
Willimontswick 119 D1
Willingale 45 E2
Willingdon 18 A3
Willingham 70 C5
Willingham by Stow 95 F4
Willingham Green 59 E2
Willington *Beds.* 57 G2
Willington *Derbys.* 81 D5
Willington *Dur.* 120 A4
Willington *Kent* 31 G3
Willington *T. & W.* 120 C1
Willington *Warks.* 55 E4
Willington Corner 78 C1
Willisham 60 B2
Willitoft 103 G4
Williton 23 D3
Willoughbridge 79 E3
Willoughby *Lincs.* 97 E5
Willoughby *Warks.* 56 A1
Willoughby Waterleys 68 A3
Willoughby-on-the-Wolds 82 B5
Willoughton 95 G3
Willow Green 92 A5
Willows Green 45 G1
Willsbridge 39 F5
Willslock 80 B4
Willsworthy 7 F2
Willtown 24 A5
Wilmcote 55 D2
Wilmington *B. & N.E.Som.* 25 D1
Wilmington *Devon* 11 F2
Wilmington *E.Suss.* 18 A3
Wilmington *Kent* 45 E5
Wilmslow 92 C4
Wilnecote 67 E2
Wilney Green 72 B3
Wilpshire 100 C4
Wilsden 101 G4
Wilsford *Lincs.* 83 F3
Wilsford *Wilts.* 26 C4
Wilsford *Wilts.* 26 C2
Wilsham 22 A3
Wilshaw 93 F2
Wilsill 102 A1
Wilsley Green 31 G5
Wilsley Pound 31 G5
Wilson 81 F5
Wilstead 57 F3
Wilsthorpe *E.Riding* 105 D1
Wilsthorpe *Lincs.* 69 F1
Wilstone 43 E1
Wilton *Cumb.* 116 D5
Wilton *Here.* 53 E5
Wilton *N.Yorks.* 112 B4
Wilton *R. & C.* 121 E5
Wilton *Sc.Bord.* 135 F4
Wilton *Wilts.* 27 D1
Wilton *Wilts.* 26 B4
Wiltown 11 E1
Wimbish 59 D4
Wimbish Green 59 E4
Wimblebury 66 C1
Wimbledon 44 B5
Wimblington 70 C3
Wimborne Minster 13 G2
Wimborne St. Giles 13 G1
Wimbotsham 71 E2
Wimpole 58 B2
Wimpole Lodge 58 B3
Wimpstone 55 E3
Wincanton 25 E5
Winceby 84 B1
Wincham 92 A5
Winchburgh 143 E2
Winchcombe 54 C5
Winchelsea 19 E2
Winchelsea Beach 19 E2
Winchester 27 F5
Winchet Hill 31 G4
Winchfield 28 C2
Winchmore Hill *Bucks.* 43 E3
Winchmore Hill *Gt.Lon.* 44 C3
Wincle 79 G1
Wincobank 94 A3
Windermere 107 F3
Winderton 55 F3
Windhill 174 C7
Windle Hill 91 E5
Windlehurst 93 D4
Windlesham 29 E1
Windley 81 E3
Windmill Hill *E.Suss.* 18 B2
Windmill Hill *Som.* 11 G1
Windmill Hill *Worcs.* 54 B3
Windrush 41 D1
Windsor 43 E5
Windsor Green 59 G2
Windy Nook 120 B1
Windygates 152 B4
Windy-Yett 141 F4
Wineham 17 E1
Winestead 105 E5
Winewall 101 F4
Winfarthing 72 C3
Winford *I.o.W.* 15 E4
Winford *N.Som.* 24 C1
Winforton 52 B3
Winfrith Newburgh 13 E4
Wing *Bucks.* 57 D5
Wing *Rut.* 69 D2
Wingate 120 C4
Wingates *Gt.Man.* 92 A2
Wingates *Northumb.* 128 C2
Wingerworth 81 E1
Wingfield *Beds.* 57 F5
Wingfield *Suff.* 72 D4
Wingfield *Wilts.* 25 F2
Wingfield Green 72 D4
Wingham 33 E3
Wingham Well 33 E3
Wingmore 33 D4
Wingrave 43 D1
Winkburn 82 C2
Winkfield 43 E5
Winkfield Row 43 D5
Winkhill 80 B2
Winkleigh 21 G5
Winksley 110 B5
Winkton 14 A3
Winlaton 120 A1
Winlaton Mill 120 A1
Winless 183 J3
Winmarleigh 100 A3
Winnard's Perch 4 D3
Winnersh 42 C5
Winnington 92 A5
Winscombe 24 B2
Winsford *Ches.* 79 D1
Winsford *Som.* 22 C4
Winsham *Devon* 21 E2
Winsham *Som.* 11 G2
Winshill 81 D5
Winsh-wen 36 C3
Winskill 118 B4
Winslade 28 B3
Winsley 25 F1
Winslow 56 C5
Winson 40 C2
Winsor 14 C1
Winster *Cumb.* 107 F3
Winster *Derbys.* 80 D1
Winston *Dur.* 110 A1
Winston *Suff.* 60 C1
Winston Green 60 C1
Winstone 40 B2
Winswell 21 E4
Winterborne Came 12 D4
Winterborne Clenston 13 E2
Winterborne Herringston 12 C4
Winterborne Houghton 13 E2
Winterborne Kingston 13 E3
Winterborne Monkton 12 C4
Winterborne Stickland 13 E2
Winterborne Whitechurch 13 E2
Winterborne Zelston 13 E3
Winterbourne *S.Glos.* 39 F4
Winterbourne *W.Berks.* 41 G5
Winterbourne Abbas 12 C3
Winterbourne Bassett 40 D5
Winterbourne Dauntsey 26 C4
Winterbourne Earls 26 C4
Winterbourne Gunner 26 C4
Winterbourne Monkton 40 D5
Winterbourne Steepleton 12 C4
Winterbourne Stoke 26 B3
Winterbrook 42 B4
Winterburn 101 F2
Wintercleugh 134 A4
Winteringham 104 B5
Winterley 79 E2
Wintersett 94 A1
Wintershill 15 E1
Winterslow 26 D4
Winterton 95 G1
Winterton-on-Sea 87 F4
Winthorpe *Lincs.* 85 D1
Winthorpe *Notts.* 82 D2
Winton *Bourne.* 13 G3
Winton *Cumb.* 108 C1
Wintringham 112 B5
Winwick *Cambs.* 69 G4
Winwick *Northants.* 68 B5
Winwick *Warr.* 92 A3
Wirksworth 81 D2
Wirksworth Moor 81 E2
Wirswall 78 C3
Wisbech 70 C2
Wisbech St. Mary 70 C2
Wisborough Green 29 F5
Wiseton 95 E4
Wishaw *N.Lan.* 142 B4
Wishaw *Warks.* 67 D3
Wisley 29 F2

Wispington 96 C5
Wissett 73 E4
Wissington 60 A4
Wistanstow 64 D4
Wistanswick 79 D5
Wistaston 79 D2
Wiston Pembs. 34 D1
Wiston S.Lan. 134 A2
Wistow Cambs. 70 A4
Wistow N.Yorks. 103 E4
Wiswell 100 D4
Witcham 70 C5
Witchampton 13 F2
Witchburn 130 C3
Witchford 70 D5
Witcombe 24 B5
Witham 46 B1
Witham Friary 25 E3
Witham on the Hill 69 F1
Withcall 96 C4
Withcote 68 C2
Withdean 17 E3
Witherenden Hill 18 B1
Witherhurst 18 B1
Witheridge 10 B1
Witherley 67 F3
Withern 97 E4
Withernsea 105 F5
Withernwick 105 D3
Withersdale Street 73 D3
Withersfield 59 E3
Witherslack 107 F4
Witherslack Hall 107 F4
Withiel 5 D3
Withiel Florey 22 C4
Withielgoose 5 E3
Withington Glos. 40 C1
Withington Gt.Man. 92 C3
Withington Here. 53 E3
Withington Shrop. 65 E1
Withington Staffs. 80 B4
Withington Green 92 C5
Withington Marsh 53 E3
Withleigh 10 C1
Withnell 100 C5
Withnell Fold 100 C5
Withybrook Som. 25 D3
Withybrook Warks. 67 G4
Withycombe 22 D3
Withycombe Raleigh 10 D4
Withyham 31 D5
Withypool 22 B4
Witley 29 E4
Witnesham 60 C2
Witney 41 F2
Wittering 69 F2
Wittersham 19 D1
Witton Angus 161 D2
Witton Norf. 87 E5
Witton Worcs. 54 A1
Witton Bridge 87 E2
Witton Gilbert 120 B3
Witton Park 120 A4
Witton-le-Wear 120 A4
Wiveliscombe 23 D5
Wivelsfield 17 E1
Wivelsfield Green 17 F2
Wivenhoe 60 B5
Wiveton 86 B1
Wix 60 C5
Wixford 54 C2
Wixhill 78 C5
Wixoe 59 F3
Woburn 57 E4
Woburn Sands 57 E4
Wokefield Park 28 B1
Woking 29 F2
Wokingham 28 D1
Wolborough 10 B5
Wold Newton E.Riding 112 D5
Wold Newton N.E.Lincs. 96 C3
Woldingham 30 C3
Wolfelee 135 G5
Wolferlow 53 F1
Wolferton 85 E5
Wolfhampcote 56 A1
Wolfhill 151 G1
Wolfpits 52 B2
Wolf's Castle 48 C5
Wolfsdale 48 C5
Woll 135 F3
Wollaston Northants. 57 E1
Wollaston Shrop. 64 C1
Wollaston W.Mid. 66 A4
Wollaton 81 G4
Wollerton 78 D5
Wollescote 66 B4
Wolsingham 119 G4
Wolston 67 G5
Wolsty 117 E1
Wolvercote 42 A2
Wolverhampton 66 B3
Wolverley Shrop. 78 B4
Wolverley Worcs. 66 A5
Wolvers Hill 24 A1
Wolverton Hants. 27 G2
Wolverton M.K. 56 D3
Wolverton Warks. 55 E1
Wolverton Wilts. 25 E4

Wolverton Common 27 G2
Wolvesnewton 39 D3
Wolvey 67 G4
Wolvey Heath 67 G4
Wolviston 121 D5
Womaston 52 B1
Wombleton 111 F4
Wombourne 66 A3
Wombwell 94 A2
Womenswold 33 E3
Womersley 94 C1
Wonersh 29 F3
Wonford 10 C3
Wonson 7 G2
Wonston 27 F4
Wooburn 43 E4
Wooburn Green 43 E4
Wood Bevington 54 C2
Wood Burcote 56 B3
Wood Dalling 86 B3
Wood Eaton 66 A1
Wood End Beds. 57 F3
Wood End Beds. 57 F1
Wood End Bucks. 56 C4
Wood End Herts. 58 B5
Wood End W.Mid. 66 B2
Wood End Warks. 67 E5
Wood End Warks. 66 D5
Wood End Warks. 67 F3
Wood Enderby 84 A1
Wood Green Essex 44 D2
Wood Green Gt.Lon. 44 C3
Wood Green Norf. 72 D2
Wood Lane 78 B4
Wood Norton 86 B3
Wood Seats 94 A3
Wood Stanway 54 C4
Wood Street 87 E3
Wood Street Village 29 E2
Woodacott 21 D5
Woodale 109 F5
Woodall 94 B4
Woodbastwick 87 E4
Woodbeck 95 E5
Woodborough Notts. 82 B3
Woodborough Wilts. 26 C2
Woodbridge Devon 11 E3
Woodbridge Dorset 12 D1
Woodbridge Suff. 61 D3
Woodbury Devon 10 D4
Woodbury Som. 24 C3
Woodbury Salterton 10 D4
Woodchester 40 A2
Woodchurch Kent 32 B5
Woodchurch Mersey. 91 H4
Woodcombe 22 C1
Woodcote Oxon. 42 B4
Woodcote Tel. & W. 65 G1
Woodcote Green 66 B5
Woodcott 27 F2
Woodcroft 39 E3
Woodcutts 13 F1
Woodditton 59 E2
Woodeaton 42 A1
Woodend Aber. 168 E3
Woodend Cumb. 106 C3
Woodend High. 166 E2
Woodend High. 155 G3
Woodend Northants. 56 B3
Woodend P. & K. 158 C5
Woodend W.Suss. 16 A3
Woodend Green 59 D5
Woodfalls 26 C5
Woodfield Oxon. 56 A5
Woodfield S.Ayr. 132 B3
Woodfoot 108 B1
Woodford Cornw. 20 C4
Woodford Devon 9 D2
Woodford Glos. 39 F3
Woodford Gt.Lon. 44 D3
Woodford Gt.Man. 92 C4
Woodford Northants. 69 E5
Woodford Som. 23 D4
Woodford Bridge 44 D3
Woodford Green 44 D3
Woodford Halse 56 A2
Woodgate Devon 11 E1
Woodgate Norf. 86 B4
Woodgate W.Mid. 66 B4
Woodgate W.Suss. 16 B3
Woodgate Worcs. 54 B1
Woodgreen 14 A1
Woodhall Inclyde 141 E2
Woodhall N.Yorks. 109 E3
Woodhall Hills 102 A4
Woodhall Spa 83 G1
Woodham Bucks. 42 B1
Woodham Dur. 120 B5
Woodham Surr. 29 F1
Woodham Ferrers 45 G3
Woodham Mortimer 46 B2
Woodham Walter 46 B2
Woodhaven 152 C2
Woodhead Aber. 169 F1
Woodhead Staffs. 80 B3

Woodhey 91 E4
Woodhey Green 78 C2
Woodhill Shrop. 65 G4
Woodhill Som. 24 A5
Woodhorn 129 E3
Woodhouse Cumb. 107 G4
Woodhouse Leics. 68 A1
Woodhouse S.Yorks. 94 B4
Woodhouse W.Yorks. 102 B4
Woodhouse W.Yorks. 102 C5
Woodhouse W.Yorks. 102 A5
Woodhouse Down 39 F4
Woodhouse Eaves 68 A1
Woodhouse Green 79 G1
Woodhouses Gt.Man. 92 C2
Woodhouses Staffs. 67 G1
Woodhouses Staffs. 66 C2
Woodhuish 9 F2
Woodhurst 70 B5
Woodingdean 17 F3
Woodington 27 E5
Woodland Devon 9 D1
Woodland Dur. 119 G5
Woodland Kent 32 D4
Woodland Head 10 A3
Woodlands Dorset 13 G2
Woodlands Hants. 14 C1
Woodlands N.Yorks. 102 C5
Woodlands Shrop. 65 G4
Woodlands Som. 23 D5
Woodlands Park 43 D5
Woodlands St. Mary 41 F5
Woodlane 80 C5
Woodleigh 8 D3
Woodlesford 102 C5
Woodley Gt.Man. 92 D3
Woodley W'ham 42 C5
Woodmancote Glos. 40 C1
Woodmancote Glos. 54 B5
Woodmancote Glos. 39 G3
Woodmancote W.Suss. 17 D2
Woodmancote W.Suss. 15 G2
Woodmancott 27 G3
Woodmansey 104 C4
Woodmansterne 30 B3
Woodmanton 10 D4
Woodmill 80 C5
Woodminton 26 B5
Woodmoor 64 B2
Woodnesborough 33 F3
Woodnewton 69 F3
Woodperry 42 A1
Woodplumpton 100 B4
Woodrising 86 A5
Woodrow 13 D1
Wood's Corner 18 B2
Wood's Eaves 52 B3
Wood's Green 31 F5
Woodseaves Shrop. 79 D4
Woodseaves Staffs. 79 E5
Woodsend 41 E5
Woodsetts 94 C4
Woodsford 13 D5
Woodside Aberdeen 169 H4
Woodside Beds. 43 F1
Woodside Brack.F. 43 D5
Woodside Cumb. 116 D3
Woodside D. & G. 125 E3
Woodside Fife 152 A4
Woodside Fife 152 A4
Woodside Gt.Lon. 30 C2
Woodside Hants. 14 C3
Woodside Herts. 44 B3
Woodside N.Ayr. 141 G5
Woodside P. & K. 151 G1
Woodside Shrop. 64 C1
Woodside W.Mid. 66 B4
Woodside Green 32 B3
Woodstock Oxon. 41 G1
Woodstock Pembs. 48 D5
Woodthorpe Derbys. 94 B5
Woodthorpe Leics. 68 A1
Woodthorpe Lincs. 97 E4
Woodthorpe S.Yorks. 94 A4
Woodton 73 D2
Woodtown 21 E3
Woodvale 91 E1
Woodville 67 F1
Woodwall Green 79 E4
Woodwalton 70 A4
Woodwick 88 C5
Woodworth Green 78 C2
Woodyates 13 G1
Woofferton 53 E1
Wookey 24 A5
Wookey Hole 24 C5
Wool 13 E4

Woolacombe 21 E1
Woolage Green 33 E4
Woolage Village 33 E3
Woolaston 39 E2
Woolaston Slade 39 E2
Woolavington 24 A3
Woolbeding 29 D5
Woolcotts 22 C4
Wooldale 93 F2
Wooler 137 D4
Woolfardisworthy Devon 10 B2
Woolfardisworthy Devon 20 D3
Woolfold 92 B1
Woolfords Cottages 143 E3
Woolgarston 13 F4
Woolgreaves 94 A1
Woolhampton 27 G1
Woolhope 53 F2
Woolland 13 D2
Woollard 24 D1
Woollaton 21 E4
Woollensbrook 44 C2
Woolley B. & N.E.Som. 25 E1
Woolley Cambs. 69 G5
Woolley Cornw. 20 C4
Woolley Derbys. 81 E1
Woolley W.Yorks. 94 A1
Woolley Green W. & M. 43 D5
Woolley Green Wilts. 25 E1
Woolmer Green 44 B1
Woolmere Green 54 B1
Woolmersdon 23 E4
Woolpit 60 A1
Woolpit Green 60 A1
Woolscott 55 G1
Woolsgrove 10 A2
Woolstaston 65 D3
Woolsthorpe 82 D4
Woolstone by Colsterworth 83 E5
Woolston Devon 8 D3
Woolston S'ham. 14 D1
Woolston Shrop. 78 A5
Woolston Shrop. 64 D4
Woolston Warr. 92 A4
Woolston Green 9 D3
Woolstone 54 B4
Woolstone M.K. 57 D4
Woolstone Oxon. 41 E4
Woolton 91 F4
Woolton Hill 27 G1
Woolverstone 60 C4
Woolverton 25 E2
Woolwich 44 D5
Woonton 52 C2
Wooperton 137 E5
Woore 79 E3
Wootten Green 72 D4
Wootton Beds. 57 F3
Wootton Hants. 14 B3
Wootton I.o.W. 15 E3
Wootton Kent 33 E4
Wootton N.Lincs. 96 A1
Wootton Northants. 56 C2
Wootton Oxon. 41 G1
Wootton Oxon. 41 F1
Wootton Shrop. 65 D5
Wootton Shrop. 78 A5
Wootton Staffs. 79 F5
Wootton Staffs. 80 C3
Wootton Bassett 40 C4
Wootton Bridge 15 E3
Wootton Common 15 E3
Wootton Courtenay 22 C3
Wootton Fitzpaine 11 G3
Wootton Green 57 F3
Wootton Rivers 26 C1
Wootton St. Lawrence 27 G2
Wootton Wawen 55 D1
Worcester 54 A2
Worcester Park 30 B2
Wordsley 66 A4
Wordwell 71 G5
Worfield 66 A2
Worgret 13 F4
Work 185 D6
Workhouse End 57 G2
Workington 116 D4
Worksop 94 C5
Worlaby Lincs. 96 D5
Worlaby N.Lincs. 96 A1
World's End Bucks. 43 D2
Worlds End Hants. 15 F1
World's End W.Berks. 41 G5
Worlds End W.Mid. 66 D4
Worle 24 A1
Worleston 79 D2
Worlingham 73 F3
Worlington 71 E5
Worlingworth 60 D1
Wormald Green 102 C1
Wormbridge 52 D4
Wormegay 71 E1
Wormelow Tump 53 D4
Wormhill 93 E2
Wormiehills 153 E1

Wormingford 60 A4
Worminghall 42 B2
Wormington 54 C4
Worminster 24 C3
Wormiston 153 E4
Wormit 64 C2
Wormleighton 55 G2
Wormley Herts. 44 C2
Wormley Surr. 29 E4
Wormley Marsh 44 B2
Wormshill 32 A3
Wormsley 53 D3
Worplesdon 29 E2
Worrall 94 A3
Worsbrough 94 A2
Worsley 92 B2
Worstead 87 E3
Worsted Lodge 58 D2
Worsthorne 101 E4
Worston 101 D3
Worswell 8 B3
Worth Kent 33 F3
Worth W.Suss. 30 B5
Worth Matravers 13 F5
Wortham 72 B4
Worthen 64 C2
Worthenbury 78 B3
Worthing Norf. 86 A4
Worthing W.Suss. 16 D3
Worthington 81 F5
Worting 28 B2
Wortley Glos. 39 G3
Wortley S.Yorks. 94 A3
Wortley W.Yorks. 102 B4
Worton N.Yorks. 109 E4
Worton Wilts. 26 A2
Wortwell 73 D3
Wothersome 102 D3
Wotherton 64 B2
Wotter 8 B3
Wotton 29 G3
Wotton Underwood 42 B1
Wotton-under-Edge 39 G3
Woughton on the Green 57 D4
Wouldham 31 G2
Wrabness 60 C4
Wrae 177 E1
Wrafton 21 E2
Wragby 96 B5
Wragholme 97 D3
Wramplingham 86 C5
Wrangaton 8 C2
Wrangham 168 E1
Wrangle 84 C2
Wrangle Lowgate 84 C2
Wrangway 11 E1
Wrantage 24 A5
Wrawby 96 A2
Wraxall N.Som. 39 D5
Wraxall Som. 24 D4
Wray 100 D1
Wray Castle 107 E2
Wrays 30 B4
Wraysbury 43 F5
Wrayton 108 A5
Wrea Green 99 G4
Wreay Cumb. 118 A5
Wreay Cumb. 118 A3
Wrecclesham 28 D3
Wrecsam (Wrexham) 78 A3
Wrekenton 120 B2
Wrelton 111 G4
Wrenbury 78 C2
Wrench Green 112 C4
Wreningham 72 C2
Wrentham 73 F3
Wrenthorpe 102 C5
Wrentnall 64 D2
Wressle E.Riding 103 G4
Wressle N.Lincs. 95 G2
Wrestlingworth 58 A3
Wretham 72 A2
Wretton 71 E2
Wrexham (Wrecsam) 78 A3
Wrexham Industrial Estate 78 A3
Wribbenhall 65 G5
Wrightington Bar 91 G1
Wrightpark 150 B5
Wright's Green 45 E1
Wrinehill 79 E3
Wrington 24 B1
Writhlington 25 D2
Writtle 45 F2
Wrockwardine 65 F1
Wroot 95 E2
Wrose 102 A4
Wrotham 31 F3
Wrotham Heath 31 F3
Wrotham Hill Park 31 F2
Wrottesley 66 A2
Wroughton 40 D4
Wroxall I.o.W. 15 E5
Wroxall Warks. 67 G5
Wroxeter 65 E2
Wroxham 87 E4
Wroxton 55 G3
Wstrws 49 G3
Wyaston 80 C3
Wyberton 84 B3
Wyboston 57 F2
Wybunbury 79 D3

Wych Cross 30 D5
Wychbold 54 B1
Wychnor 67 D1
Wychnor Bridges 67 D1
Wyck 28 D2
Wyck Rissington 55 D5
Wycliffe 110 A1
Wycoller 101 F4
Wycomb 82 C5
Wycombe Marsh 43 D3
Wyddial 58 B2
Wye 32 C4
Wyesham 39 E1
Wyfordby 68 C1
Wyke Devon 10 B3
Wyke Dorset 25 E5
Wyke Shrop. 65 F2
Wyke Surr. 29 E2
Wyke W.Yorks. 102 A5
Wyke Champflower 25 D4
Wyke Regis 12 C5
Wykeham N.Yorks. 112 C4
Wykeham N.Yorks. 112 B5
Wyken Shrop. 65 G3
Wyken W.Mid. 67 G4
Wykey 78 A5
Wylam 120 A1
Wylde Green 66 D3
Wyllie 38 A3
Wylye 26 B4
Wymering 15 F2
Wymeswold 82 B5
Wymington 57 E1
Wymondham Leics. 69 D1
Wymondham Norf. 86 C5
Wyndham 37 F3
Wynford Eagle 12 B3
Wynnstay Park 78 A3
Wynyard 120 D5
Wyre Piddle 54 B3
Wyresdale Tower 100 C2
Wysall 82 B5
Wyson 53 E1
Wythall 66 C5
Wytham 41 G2
Wythburn 117 G5
Wythenshawe 92 C4
Wyton Cambs. 70 A5
Wyton E.Riding 105 D4
Wyverstone 60 B1
Wyverstone Street 60 B1
Wyville 82 D4
Wyvis Lodge 174 B4

▼ Y

Y Bryn 76 B5
Y Drenewydd (Newtown) 64 A3
Y Fan 63 F4
Y Felinheli 75 E1
Y Fenni (Abergavenny) 38 B1
Y Fflint (Flint) 90 D5
Y Ffôr 74 C4
Y Trallwng (Welshpool) 64 B2
Y Tymbl (Tumble) 36 B1
Y Waun (Chirk) 77 F4
Yaddlethorpe 95 F2
Yafford 14 D4
Yafforth 110 C3
Yalberton 9 F2
Yalding 31 F4
Yanley 24 C1
Yanwath 118 B5
Yanworth 40 C1
Yapham 103 G2
Yapton 16 B3
Yarburgh 96 D3
Yarcombe 11 F2
Yardley 66 D4
Yardley Gobion 56 C3
Yardley Hastings 57 D2
Yardro 52 B2
Yarford 23 F5
Yarkhill 53 F3
Yarlet 79 G5
Yarley 24 C3
Yarlington 25 D5
Yarm 120 D1
Yarmouth 14 C4
Yarnacott 21 G2
Yarnbrook 25 F2
Yarnfield 79 F4
Yarnscombe 21 F3
Yarnton 41 G1
Yarpole 53 D1
Yarrow Sc.Bord. 135 E3
Yarrow Som. 24 A3
Yarrow Feus 135 E3
Yarrowford 135 F3
Yarsop 52 D3
Yarwell 69 F3
Yate 39 G4
Yatehouse Green 79 D1
Yateley 28 D1
Yatesbury 40 C5
Yattendon 42 A5
Yatton Here. 52 D1

Yatton N.Som. 24 B1
Yatton Keynell 40 A5
Yaverland 15 F4
Yawl 11 G3
Yaxham 86 B4
Yaxley Cambs. 69 G3
Yaxley Suff. 72 C4
Yazor 52 D3
Yeabridge 12 A1
Yeading 44 A4
Yeadon 102 B3
Yealand Conyers 107 G5
Yealand Redmayne 107 G5
Yealand Storrs 107 G5
Yealmbridge 8 B2
Yealmpton 8 B2
Yearby 121 F5
Yearsley 111 E5
Yeaton 64 D1
Yeaveley 80 C3
Yeavering 136 D3
Yedingham 112 B5
Yelford 41 F2
Yell 186 D3
Yelland Devon 21 E2
Yelland Devon 7 F1
Yelling 58 A1
Yelvertoft 68 A5
Yelverton Devon 8 B1
Yelverton Norf. 87 D5
Yenston 25 E5
Yeo Mill 22 B5
Yeo Vale 21 E3
Yeoford 10 A3
Yeolmbridge 6 D2
Yeomadon 20 D5
Yeovil 12 B1
Yeovil Marsh 12 B1
Yeovilton 24 C5
Yerbeston 35 D2
Yesnaby 185 B6
Yetholm Mains 136 C4
Yetlington 137 E5
Yetminster 12 B1
Yettington 11 D4
Yetts o'Muckhart 151 F4
Yew Green 55 E1
Yielden 57 F1
Yieldshields 142 C4
Ynys 75 E4
Ynys Enlli (Bardsey Island) 74 A5
Ynys Môn (Anglesey) 88 B4
Ynys Tachwedd 62 C3
Ynysboeth 37 G3
Ynysddu 38 A3
Ynyshir 37 G3
Ynyslas 62 C3
Ynysmaerdy 37 G4
Ynysmeudwy 36 D2
Ynystawe 36 C2
Ynyswen 37 E3
Ynysybwl 37 G3
Yockenthwaite 109 E5
Yockleton 64 C1
Yokefleet 104 A5
Yoker 141 G3
Yonder Bognie 176 E6
York 103 F2
Yorkletts 32 C2
Yorkley 39 F2
Yorton 78 C5
Yorton Heath 78 C5
Youldon 20 D5
Youldonmoor Cross 20 D5
Youlgreave 80 D1
Youlthorpe 103 G2
Youlton 103 D1
Young's End 45 G1
Yoxall 66 D1
Yoxford 61 E1
Yr Wyddgrug (Mold) 77 F1
Ysbyty Cynfyn 63 D5
Ysbyty Ifan 76 B3
Ysbyty Ystwyth 62 D5
Ysceifiog 90 C5
Ysgubor-y-coed 62 C3
Ystalyfera 37 D2
Ystrad 37 F3
Ystrad Aeron 50 B2
Ystrad Meurig 50 D1
Ystrad Mynach 38 A3
Ystradfellte 37 F1
Ystradffin 51 D3
Ystradgynlais 37 D1
Ystradowen N.P.T. 36 D1
Ystradowen V. of Glam. 37 G5
Ystumtuen 62 D5
Ythanwells 168 E1
Ythsie 169 G1

▼ Z

Zeal Monachorum 10 A2
Zeals 25 E4
Zelah 4 C4
Zennor 2 B3
Zouch 81 G5

Index to place names in Ireland

In this index place names are followed by a page number and a grid reference. The place can be found by searching that grid square. Where more than one place has the same name, each can be distinguished by the abbreviated county name shown after the place name. A list of abbreviations used for these names is shown to the right.

Banbr.	Banbridge	N.Tipp.	North Tipperary	Wexf.	Wexford
Kilk.	Kilkenny	S.Dub.	South Dublin
N.Down	North Down	Water.	Waterford

Distance chart

Distances between two selected towns in this table are shown in miles and kilometres. In general, distances are based on the shortest routes by classified roads.

DISTANCE IN KILOMETRES

	Aberystwyth	Ayr	Birmingham	Bradford	Bristol	Cambridge	Cardiff	Carlisle	Coventry	Derby	Doncaster	Dover	Edinburgh	Exeter	Fishguard	Fort William	Glasgow	Gloucester	Harwich	Holyhead	Hull	Inverness	Kendal	Leeds	Leicester	Lincoln	Liverpool	London	Manchester	Newcastle upon Tyne	Norwich	Nottingham	Oxford	Penzance	Perth	Plymouth	Portsmouth	Salisbury	Sheffield	Shrewsbury	Southampton	Southend-on-Sea	Stoke-on-Trent	Stranraer	Thurso	Worcester	York
Aberdeen	748	282	657	509	788	719	796	342	688	613	535	903	192	904	776	246	224	735	826	694	554	165	422	505	643	597	535	793	535	362	758	603	768	1083	131	971	894	846	558	619	873	822	587	362	308	688	490
Aberystwyth		513	181	260	193	347	161	366	228	228	284	469	515	307	89	682	516	171	454	162	356	770	293	269	242	309	159	342	199	417	446	253	253	486	582	374	353	276	251	118	319	406	175	525	944	159	309
Ayr			457	318	588	556	595	147	488	428	372	740	119	704	577	217	58	534	663	428	391	322	222	332	480	435	334	638	335	235	594	439	568	882	156	770	694	645	378	418	672	659	394	79	504	488	332
Birmingham				177	136	156	160	310	32	67	146	309	458	252	271	626	460	83	264	238	206	714	237	172	70	135	143	182	129	319	255	81	107	431	525	319	232	181	119	70	211	234	73	472	888	42	196
Bradford					307	240	337	168	193	117	55	424	314	423	354	488	322	253	347	243	104	565	99	16	159	120	105	314	57	154	279	119	267	601	381	489	395	353	59	159	373	343	109	334	739	207	53
Bristol						234	65	441	147	203	287	313	590	119	225	758	591	55	316	329	340	845	369	318	184	266	256	190	260	467	342	218	111	298	657	185	144	76	279	163	113	254	205	603	1019	99	341
Cambridge							290	409	124	154	187	185	525	358	434	725	559	195	107	396	208	776	347	228	110	137	301	87	245	365	101	132	127	537	591	425	205	221	186	227	208	98	223	621	950	183	239
Cardiff								447	180	233	323	361	596	171	168	763	597	90	365	314	391	851	375	354	217	307	261	239	271	501	394	248	160	345	663	238	211	140	288	167	177	303	222	609	1025	118	378
Carlisle									341	282	225	593	148	557	460	316	150	387	516	349	244	400	75	180	333	289	188	491	188	93	448	292	420	736	213	624	547	499	225	271	526	512	240	160	573	341	185
Coventry										66	149	278	490	263	317	658	491	93	232	278	190	745	269	186	38	120	183	151	160	327	223	80	80	441	557	329	205	166	126	109	184	202	105	503	919	69	203
Derby											80	329	417	317	316	597	431	148	262	247	148	669	208	111	47	82	129	202	93	258	215	25	159	496	483	384	285	237	57	103	263	253	54	443	843	108	134
Doncaster												371	341	403	379	542	376	227	294	268	74	593	155	47	110	61	135	261	83	182	225	70	225	582	408	470	352	317	29	164	330	289	107	388	767	187	55
Dover													714	389	523	953	749	291	204	560	400	966	551	419	292	326	465	123	442	555	264	322	214	568	781	455	205	252	376	391	227	135	387	785	1139	306	429
Edinburgh														705	608	211	71	535	631	497	359	248	223	310	447	404	336	598	336	167	563	407	568	884	67	771	695	646	363	419	673	627	388	195	421	489	295
Exeter															334	873	707	170	403	445	457	961	484	440	299	383	371	273	376	587	454	334	227	176	772	69	200	142	374	275	170	338	320	719	1135	215	458
Fishguard																766	611	239	528	252	450	865	387	363	330	398	253	401	293	511	534	341	323	513	676	401	380	303	346	207	346	456	264	515	1038	238	403
Fort William																	165	704	833	618	561	105	392	502	650	605	504	808	504	378	764	609	737	1287	164	940	864	815	547	588	842	828	556	295	282	658	501
Glasgow																		537	666	462	394	270	225	336	483	439	338	642	338	228	598	453	571	1131	92	774	697	649	381	422	676	662	390	135	444	491	335
Gloucester																			282	285	286	791	315	255	129	212	209	165	206	402	296	164	77	349	603	237	171	111	201	123	140	228	151	549	965	45	278
Harwich																				504	301	884	454	337	217	230	409	120	352	473	102	240	208	581	699	469	244	265	294	335	252	95	331	729	1057	287	347
Holyhead																					339	722	275	252	283	318	149	428	189	399	467	273	357	624	565	512	452	397	245	167	421	479	192	367	900	245	292
Hull																						612	198	92	153	71	200	286	152	190	235	129	269	636	427	524	396	360	104	246	375	315	182	407	786	256	60
Inverness																							482	562	700	655	594	850	594	419	814	659	827	1151	180	1030	954	905	615	678	932	879	646	399	177	747	592
Kendal																								127	273	282	130	427	124	159	444	257	359	668	308	558	493	429	189	211	466	493	179	248	658	285	144
Leeds																									154	109	115	303	67	150	268	114	262	613	376	501	389	348	54	169	368	332	115	347	735	218	39
Leicester																										82	174	160	141	288	183	41	114	479	514	367	239	204	100	123	217	212	92	495	873	107	164
Lincoln																											188	211	136	245	164	58	196	562	471	450	321	286	71	192	302	239	137	458	829	176	114
Liverpool																												334	54	247	339	155	263	552	403	440	390	316	114	92	368	386	82	338	766	163	154
London																													310	439	179	203	92	452	665	340	114	136	256	259	123	65	255	653	1023	180	313
Manchester																														233	311	132	254	563	422	453	388	323	63	113	360	387	73	362	773	180	116
Newcastle upon Tyne																															409	257	411	768	249	658	545	523	209	343	517	471	312	262	604	384	143
Norwich																																203	233	651	680	541	327	335	249	327	322	158	323	620	1031	301	292
Nottingham																																	156	512	475	399	283	246	61	133	262	236	79	463	834	123	125
Oxford																																		405	637	293	125	101	208	166	104	155	185	583	999	92	274
Penzance																																			951	124	381	321	552	454	351	516	499	897	1313	393	637
Perth																																				839	762	714	429	486	741	693	455	228	354	556	361
Plymouth																																					268	209	440	342	239	405	387	785	1201	281	525
Portsmouth																																						68	337	286	30	179	311	710	1126	208	407
Salisbury																																							295	231	36	200	259	656	1077	153	372
Sheffield																																								134	314	281	76	392	787	164	83
Shrewsbury																																									252	311	59	440	850	77	207
Southampton																																										187	288	688	1103	176	384
Southend-on-Sea																																											308	706	1053	244	343
Stoke-on-Trent																																												401	817	105	153
Stranraer																																													582	503	346
Thurso																																														921	720
Worcester																																															238

DISTANCE IN MILES

	Aberdeen	Aberystwyth	Ayr	Birmingham	Bradford	Bristol	Cambridge	Cardiff	Carlisle	Coventry	Derby	Doncaster	Dover	Edinburgh	Exeter	Fishguard	Fort William	Glasgow	Gloucester	Harwich	Holyhead	Hull	Inverness	Kendal	Leeds	Leicester	Lincoln	Liverpool	London	Manchester	Newcastle upon Tyne	Norwich	Nottingham	Oxford	Penzance	Perth	Plymouth	Portsmouth	Salisbury	Sheffield	Shrewsbury	Southampton	Southend-on-Sea	Stoke-on-Trent	Stranraer	Thurso	Worcester
Aberystwyth	465																																														
Ayr	175	319																																													
Birmingham	408	112	284																																												
Bradford	316	161	198	110																																											
Bristol	490	120	365	85	191																																										
Cambridge	447	215	345	97	149	148																																									
Cardiff	494	100	370	99	209	40	180																																								
Carlisle	213	228	91	192	104	274	254	278																																							
Coventry	428	142	303	20	120	91	77	112	212																																						
Derby	381	142	266	42	73	126	96	145	175	41																																					
Doncaster	332	176	231	91	34	179	116	200	140	93	50																																				
Dover	561	291	460	192	264	194	115	225	369	173	204	230																																			
Edinburgh	119	320	74	285	195	367	325	370	92	304	259	212	444																																		
Exeter	561	191	437	157	263	74	223	106	346	163	197	250	242	438																																	
Fishguard	502	56	358	168	220	140	270	104	286	197	196	235	325	378	207																																
Fort William	153	424	135	389	303	471	451	474	196	409	371	337	592	131	543	476																															
Glasgow	139	321	36	286	200	368	347	371	93	305	268	234	465	44	439	380	102																														
Gloucester	456	106	332	51	157	34	121	56	241	58	92	141	181	333	106	148	437	334																													
Harwich	514	282	412	164	216	197	67	227	321	144	163	183	127	393	250	328	518	414	175																												
Holyhead	431	101	266	148	150	205	246	195	217	173	154	167	348	309	277	157	384	287	177	313																											
Hull	344	221	243	128	65	211	129	243	152	118	92	46	249	223	284	280	348	250	178	187	210																										
Inverness	103	479	200	444	351	525	482	529	248	463	416	369	600	154	597	537	65	168	492	549	449	380																									
Kendal	262	182	138	147	61	229	215	233	47	167	129	96	342	139	301	240	243	140	196	282	171	123	299																								
Leeds	314	167	207	107	10	197	142	220	112	116	69	29	260	193	273	226	312	209	158	209	156	57	349	79																							
Leicester	400	150	298	43	99	114	68	135	207	24	29	68	182	278	186	205	404	300	80	135	176	95	435	170	96																						
Lincoln	372	192	271	84	74	166	85	191	179	74	51	38	202	251	238	247	376	273	132	143	197	44	407	175	67	51																					
Liverpool	332	99	208	89	65	159	187	162	117	114	80	84	289	209	231	157	313	210	130	254	93	125	369	81	71	108	117																				
London	493	213	397	113	195	118	55	148	305	94	125	162	76	372	170	249	502	399	102	75	266	178	528	265	188	100	131	208																			
Manchester	332	124	208	80	35	162	152	169	117	99	58	51	275	209	234	182	313	210	128	219	117	95	369	77	41	88	84	33	193																		
Newcastle upon Tyne	225	259	146	199	96	290	227	311	58	203	160	113	345	104	365	317	235	142	250	294	248	118	260	99	93	179	152	153	273	145																	
Norwich	471	277	369	159	173	213	63	245	278	139	133	140	164	350	282	332	475	371	184	63	290	146	506	276	166	114	102	211	111	193	254																
Nottingham	374	157	273	50	74	316	82	154	182	50	16	44	200	253	208	212	378	281	102	150	170	80	410	160	71	26	36	96	126	82	160	126															
Oxford	477	157	353	67	166	69	79	100	261	49	99	140	133	353	141	201	458	355	48	129	222	167	514	223	163	71	123	164	57	158	255	145	97														
Penzance	673	302	548	288	374	185	334	214	457	274	308	362	353	549	109	319	800	703	217	361	388	395	715	415	381	298	349	343	281	350	477	405	318	252													
Perth	81	362	97	326	237	408	367	412	133	346	301	254	485	42	480	420	102	57	375	434	351	265	112	191	234	320	293	251	413	262	155	423	295	396	591												
Plymouth	603	232	479	198	304	115	264	148	387	205	239	292	283	479	43	249	584	481	147	291	318	326	640	347	311	228	280	273	211	281	409	336	248	182	77	521											
Portsmouth	556	219	431	144	245	90	128	131	340	127	177	219	128	432	124	236	537	433	106	152	281	246	593	307	242	149	199	242	71	241	339	203	176	78	237	474	167										
Salisbury	526	172	401	112	219	47	138	87	310	104	147	197	156	402	88	188	507	403	69	165	247	224	562	266	216	127	178	196	85	201	325	208	153	63	200	444	130	42									
Sheffield	347	156	235	74	37	173	116	179	140	78	36	18	234	226	232	215	340	237	125	183	152	64	382	117	34	62	44	71	159	39	130	155	38	129	343	267	274	210	184								
Shrewsbury	384	73	260	43	99	101	142	104	169	68	64	102	243	260	171	129	365	262	76	208	104	153	421	131	105	76	119	57	161	70	213	203	83	103	282	302	213	178	143	83							
Southampton	542	198	418	131	232	70	129	110	327	114	163	205	141	418	106	215	523	420	87	157	261	233	580	290	229	135	187	229	76	224	321	200	163	65	218	460	148	19	23	195	156						
Southend-on-Sea	511	252	409	145	213	158	61	188	318	126	157	180	84	389	210	289	515	411	142	59	298	196	546	306	206	132	148	239	40	241	293	98	147	96	321	431	252	111	124	180	193	116					
Stoke-on-Trent	365	109	245	46	68	127	139	138	149	65	34	66	240	241	199	164	346	242	94	206	119	113	402	111	72	57	85	51	158	45	194	201	49	115	310	283	241	193	161	47	37	179	191				
Stranraer	225	326	49	293	207	375	386	378	99	313	275	241	488	121	447	320	183	84	341	453	228	253	248	154	216	308	285	210	406	225	163	385	288	362	557	141	488	441	408	244	273	427	439	249			
Thurso	191	587	313	552	460	633	590	637	356	571	524	477	708	262	705	645	175	276	600	657	559	488	110	409	457	524	515	476	636	480	376	641	518	621	816	220	746	700	670	489	528	686	654	508	362		
Worcester	428	99	303	26	128	62	114	73	212	43	67	116	190	304	133	148	409	305	28	178	152	159	464	177	136	67	109	102	112	112	239	187	76	57	244	345	175	129	95	102	48	109	152	65	312	572	
York	304	192	206	122	33	212	149	235	115	126	83	34	267	183	285	250	311	208	173	216	181	38	368	89	24	102	71	96	194	72	89	182	78	173	396	224	326	253	231	52	129	239	213	95	215	447	148